CASSELL'S

CONCISE GERMAN-ENGLISH~~~~~~~~~~~~~~~~~~
  DICTIONARY

DEUTSCH-ENGLISCHES ENGLISCH-DEUTSCHES
  TASCHENWÖRTERBUCH

Cassell's Concise German-English English-German Dictionary

Compiled by

H.-C. Sasse, M.A. (Adel.), M.Litt. (Cantab.)
Lecturer in German in the
University of Newcastle upon Tyne

Dr. J. Horne
Formerly Lecturer in German in
the University of Birmingham

Dr. Charlotte Dixon

CASSELL

Cassell Publishers Limited
Artillery House, Artillery Row
London SW1P 1RT

CASSELL'S COMPACT GERMAN-ENGLISH
ENGLISH-GERMAN DICTIONARY
First edition 1966
Second edition, tenth impression (title changed to
CASSELL'S CONCISE GERMAN-
ENGLISH ENGLISH-GERMAN DICTIONARY) 1977
Second edition fifteenth impression 1987
This paperback edition published 1988

ISBN 0 304 31617 2

Printed in Great Britain by Anchor Brendon Ltd., Tiptree, Essex

Contents

Preface

Among the difficulties that arise in the compilation of a Concise Dictionary that of the selection of words is undoubtedly the most formidable one. The decision as to what to include and, much more difficult, what to exclude, must to a considerable extent depend on the type of student of a foreign language who is most likely to use it. Primarily a dictionary of this kind is intended for the student in the earlier stages of learning German, whether at school or university. As the study of German, even at an early stage, is likely to include the reading of literary texts from the eighteenth century onwards, it was felt that some attention at least must be paid to the inclusion of words no longer in common use today but frequently found in the prescribed texts, whether poetry, drama or prose. That in this respect severe limitations are imposed by the very concept of a 'Concise' Dictionary is of course obvious, but an attempt has been made to include at least some of the most common literary and poetical terms. However, the main emphasis throughout must of course be on straightforward contemporary German. In addition to the needs of the student, those of the traveller and the tourist, of the reader of contemporary literature and of newspapers and magazines, have been kept in mind. It is hoped that the student of science and technology too will find the dictionary useful, though in his case additional reference must of course be made to one of the growing number of specialized works dealing with the technical vocabulary of his particular discipline.

The aim of a Concise Dictionary must be to achieve some kind of viable compromise between conciseness on the one hand and completeness on the other. To make the dictionary as helpful as possible—given only a limited amount of space—certain economies were called for. Omissions were inevitable. What is similarly inevitable is that, except in the most obvious cases, no two experts are likely

Preface

to agree as to what may safely be omitted unless (as was attempted here) one makes frequency of usage and general usefulness the main criteria.

It should be remembered, lastly, that this is a concise dictionary which cannot remotely hope to do justice to all the finer meanings and nuances of two highly developed and complex languages. But it is hoped that the student and reader of German, especially in the earlier stages of learning the language, will find here all the help he needs.

For more detailed reference the user will find Cassell's New German Dictionary (ed. Dr. H. T. Betteridge) of considerable help, while the Duden works of reference on German are regarded as the authoritative last word on matters of controversy. In the final analysis there will always be areas of doubt and dispute. That is the prerogative of a living and developing language.

Finally, thanks are due on behalf of the publishers to Prof. W. E. Collinson, late of the University of Liverpool, who acted in a consultative capacity.

H.-C. Sasse

Advice to the User

As a guide to the nature of words which have inevitably been omitted from a dictionary of this size, it may be helpful to state that, when a German *Fremdwort* is identical with the corresponding English term and possesses no grammatical peculiarities, it appears only in the English–German section. For example, it was felt that the word *Atom* (and *a fortiori* derivative compounds such as *Atomphysik*) was unlikely to perplex any English reader and it has therefore been omitted from the German–English, but included in the English–German, section. For the same reason, a somewhat similar plan has been followed with regard to the names of countries. These have mostly been given in German–English only, whereas the corresponding nouns and adjectives of nationality or race are given in English–German only.

Arrangement of Entries

Strict alphabetical order seemed to be most helpful in a dictionary intended primarily for readers in the earlier stages of acquiring a knowledge of German. Within the entries themselves literal meanings and frequency of usage determine the sequence of definitions. Admittedly the second criterion is to a considerable extent a matter of personal linguistic judgment, indeed of *Sprachgefühl*, but it is hoped that in most cases the reader will thereby more readily discover the meaning of any particular word. It can generally be assumed that definitions separated by commas have much the same meaning, whereas differences in meaning or usage are marked by semicolons. Where it was thought desirable and feasible to include idiomatic phrases, relative frequency of usage appeared a more helpful criterion than strict alphabetic sequence.

Words which are spelt alike but are etymologically distinct

Zur Benutzung des Wörterbuches

Ein Hinweis auf die Art der Wörter, auf die in einem Taschenwörterbuch unweigerlich verzichtet werden muss, wird dem Leser die Anwendung dieses Nachschlagwerkes gewiss erleichtern: Ein deutsches Fremdwort, das mit dem entsprechenden englischen Ausdruck identisch ist und keine grammatikalischen Besonderheiten aufweist, erscheint als Stichwort nicht in beiden Sprachen, sondern wird nur im englisch–deutschen Teil aufgeführt. Man darf wohl annehmen, dass ein Wort wie z.B. *Atom* (und *a fortiori* abgeleitete Zusammensetzungen wie *Atomphysik*) einen englischen Leser kaum verwirren wird, weshalb es denn auch im deutsch–englischen Teil weggelassen, indessen im englisch–deutschen Teil berücksichtigt wurde. Aus dem gleichen Grunde wurde bei den Namen von Ländern ein ähnliches Prinzip beachtet. Diese wurden in der Regel nur im deutsch–englischen Teil aufgeführt, während die entsprechenden Substantive und Adjektive der Nationalität oder Rasse nur im englisch–deutschen Teil erscheinen.

Anordnung der Stichwörter

Die strikte alphabetische Reihenfolge schien vorteilhaft für ein Nachschlagwerk, das in erster Linie für Lernende gedacht ist, die die deutsche Sprache noch nicht völlig beherrschen. Bei den gegebenen Übersetzungen eines Stichwortes bestimmen die wörtliche Übertragung sowie die Häufigkeit des Gebrauches die Folge der Definitionen. Gewiss ist das zweite Kriterium weitgehend eine Angelegenheit der persönlichen linguistischen Beurteilung, in der Tat des Sprachgefühls. Doch ist zu hoffen, dass der Leser in den meisten Fällen gerade dadurch der Bedeutung eines Begriffes näher kommt. Allgemein gilt, dass durch ein Komma getrennte Wörter eine annähernd gleiche Bedeutung haben, während Unterschiede in Bedeutung oder Anwendung

Advice to the User

have been given separate, numbered entries for the sake of clarity.

A word should be added on the subject of compounds. Most students of German come to realize before long that the notoriously long German nouns, far from complicating the understanding of the language, are merely a matter of syntactical and grammatical convenience, a device for structural conciseness within a given sentence construction. In a 'Concise' Dictionary only such compounds can be given which have a meaning which can be arrived at only with difficulty or not at all. Where a compound is not given, the constituent parts of the word should be looked up. The meaning should then become self-evident.

Grammar

Parts of Speech. These are indicated by abbreviations in italics (*adj.*, *v.a.* etc.), the meaning of which will be found in the List of Abbreviations. It has not been felt necessary to indicate the nature of English proper names.

Genders. In the German-English section nouns are denoted by their gender (*m.*, *f.* or *n.*). In the English-German section gender is shown by the definite article preceding the noun; in a series of nouns the gender is sometimes omitted when it is the same as that of the preceding noun or nouns.

Declension. The Genitive singular and Nominative plural of German nouns are given in parentheses after the gender. The plurals of English nouns are not given, except for certain very irregular forms. The cases governed by prepositions have been included.

Verbs. In both German and English the indication *irr.* refers the user to the tables of Irregular Verbs. Where a compound irregular verb is not given, its forms are identical with those of the simple irregular verb in the table. "To" is omitted from English infinitives throughout. German inseparable verbs are described as such only when there is any possibility of doubt, *e.g.* in the case of prepositional prefixes. Where prefixes are axiomatically always part of an

durch ein Semikolon markiert sind. Wo es als notwendig und durchführbar erachtet wurde, idiomatische Redewendungen zu zitieren, schien die relative Häufigkeit der Anwendung ein nützlicheres Kriterium als die strenge alphabetische Folge. Orthographisch gleiche Wörter, die sich durch ihre etymologische Herkunft unterscheiden, wurden um der Klarheit willen als einzelne Stichwörter aufgeführt und mit Ziffern versehen. Noch ein Wort zum Thema der Wortzusammensetzungen: Die meisten Deutschlernenden werden bald erkennen, dass die berüchtigt langen deutschen Substantive das Verständnis der Sprache keineswegs erschweren. Sie sind lediglich eine Sache syntaktischer und grammatikalischer Vereinfachung, ein Hilfsmittel zu struktureller Kürze und Prägnanz innerhalb einer gegebenen Satzbildung. In einem Taschenwörterbuch können allein solche Wortverbindungen berücksichtigt werden, die nur mit Mühe oder überhaupt nicht abzuleiten sind. Ist eine Wortverbindung nicht angeführt, so sollten die einzelnen Bestandteile nachgesehen werden. Auf diese Weise wird sich der Sinn der Zusammensetzung von selbst ergeben.

Grammatik

Wortarten. Sie sind in abgekürzter Form durch Kursivschrift gekennzeichnet (*adj.*, *v.a.* etc.). Eine Erläuterung der Abkürzungen findet sich im Verzeichnis der Abkürzungen. Es wurde nicht für nötig befunden, die Zugehörigkeit von Eigennamen anzuzeigen.

Geschlecht. Im deutsch–englischen Teil sind die Substantive mit ihrem Geschlecht (*m.*, *f.* oder *n.*) gekennzeichnet. Im englisch–deutschen Teil ist das Geschlecht durch den bestimmten Artikel vor dem Substantiv angegeben. In einer Reihe aufeinanderfolgender Definitionen wurde der Artikel dort weggelassen, wo er mit dem vorhergehenden übereinstimmt.

Deklination. Die Endungen des Genitiv Singular und des Nominativ Plural deutscher Substantive sind in Klammern nach der Bezeichnung des Geschlechtes eingefügt. Der

inseparable verb (*be-*, *ent-*, *zer-* etc.) no such information is given, as it is assumed that the student will be familiar with the function of these prefixes long before he comes to use a dictionary.

Phonetics. Phonetic transcriptions, using the symbols of the International Phonetic Association, are given throughout for all entries in both sections of the dictionary as a help to correct pronunciation. The mark ' precedes the syllable which carries the stress. The glottal stop is not indicated.

Numbers. Only the most common numerals appear in the body of the dictionary. However, fuller coverage is given in the separate Numerical Tables.

Zur Benutzung des Wörterbuches

Plural englischer Substantive wurde nicht berücksichtigt ausser bei einigen stark unregelmässigen Formen. Fälle, die von Präpositionen regiert werden, wurden aufgenommen.

Verben. Im Deutschen wie im Englischen weist die Anmerkung *irr.* den Leser auf die Tabellen unregelmässiger Verben hin. Ist ein zusammengesetztes Verb nicht angeführt, so sind seine Formen mit denen des einfachen Verbs in der Tabelle identisch. "To" vor englischen Infinitivformen wurde durchgehend weggelassen. Deutsche untrennbare Verben werden nur dort als solche gekennzeichnet, wo Zweifel möglich sind, also bei Verben mit präpositionalen Vorsilben. Wo Vorsilben grundsätzlich Teile eines untrennbaren Verbes (*be-*, *ent-*, *zer-* etc.) bilden, ist kein solcher Hinweis angebracht, da angenommen werden darf, dass der Lernende die Funktion dieser Vorsilben kennt, lange bevor er dazu kommt, ein Wörterbuch zu konsultieren.

Phonetik. Jedes einzelne Stichwort ist auch in seiner phonetischen Transkription wiedergegeben. Dabei wurden die phonetischen Symbole der *International Phonetic Association* benutzt. Der Akzent ′ steht jeweils unmittelbar vor der betonten Silbe. Der Knacklaut ist indessen nicht markiert.

Zahlwörter. Nur die gebräuchlichsten Zahlen erscheinen im Hauptteil des Wörterbuches. Eine ausführliche Zusammenstellung findet sich in den besonderen Zahlentabellen.

Key to Pronunciation

Vowels

Phonetic Symbol	German Example	Phonetic Symbol	English Example
a	lassen ['lasən]	i:	seat [si:t]
a:	haben ['ha:bən], Haar ['ha:r]	i	finish ['fɪnɪʃ], physic ['fizik]
ɛ	häßlich ['hɛslɪç], Geld [gɛlt]	e	neck [nek]
ɛ:	Märchen ['mɛ:rçən], Zähne ['tsɛ:nə]	æ	man [mæn], malefactor ['mælifæktə]
e	Medizin [medi'tsi:n]	ɑ:	father ['fɑ:ðə], task [tɑ:sk]
e:	leben ['le:bən], See [ze:], lehnen ['le:nən]	ɔ	block [blɔk], waddle [wɔdl]
ə	rufen ['ru:fən]	ɔ:	shawl [ʃɔ:l], tortoise ['tɔ:təs]
ɪ	Fisch [fɪʃ], Mystik ['mɪstɪk]	o	domain [do'mein]
i	Militär [mili'tɛ:r]	u	good [gud], July [dʒu'lai]
i:	Berlin [bɛr'li:n], Liebe ['li:bə], ihm [i:m]	u:	moon [mu:n], tooth [tu:θ]
ɔ	Kopf [kɔpf]	ʌ	cut [kʌt], somewhere ['sʌmwɛə]
o	mobil [mo'bi:l]	ə:	search [sə:tʃ], surgeon ['sə:dʒən]
o:	Rose ['ro:zə], Boot [bo:t], ohne ['o:nə]	ə	cathedral [kə'θi:drəl], never ['nevə]
œ	Mörder ['mœrdər]		
ø	möblieren [mø'bli:rən]		
ø:	Löwe ['lø:və], Röhre ['rø:rə]		
u	Hund [hunt]		
u:	gut [gu:t], Uhr [u:r]		
y	fünf [fynf], Symbol [zym'bo:l]		
y:	Lübeck ['ly:bɛk], Mühe ['my:ə]		

Diphthongs

aɪ	Eis [aɪs], Waise ['vaɪzə]	ei	great [greit]
au	Haus [haus]	ou	show [ʃou]
ɔy	Beute ['bɔytə], Gebäude [gə'bɔydə]	ai	high [hai]
		au	crowd [kraud]
		ɔi	boy [bɔi]
		iə	steer [stiə]
		ɛə	hair [hɛə]
		uə	moor [muə]

Consonants

Phonetic Symbol	German Example	Phonetic Symbol	English Example
ç	Blech [blɛç], ich [ıç]	p	paper ['peipə]
f	Vater ['fa:tər]	b	ball [bɔ:l]
j	ja [ja:]	t	tea [ti:], train [trein]
ŋ	bringen ['brıŋən]	d	deed [di:d]
s	beißen ['baısən], wißen ['vısən], los [lo:s]	k	cake [keik], quest [kwest]
ʃ	schon [ʃo:n]	g	game [geim]
ts	Cäcilie [tsɛ'tsi:ljə], Zimmer ['tsımər]	m	mammoth ['mæməθ]
v	weiß [vaıs]	n	nose [nouz], nanny ['næni]
x	Bach [bax], kochen ['kɔxən], ruchbar ['ru:xba:r]	ŋ	bring [briŋ], finger ['fiŋgə]
z	lesen ['le:zən]	f	fair [fɛə], far [fa:]
b	Biene ['bi:nə]	v	vine [vain]
d	Dach [dax]	θ	thin [θin], bath [ba:θ]
g	geben ['ge:bən]	ð	thine [ðain], bathe [beið]
h	hier [hi:r]	s	since [sins]
k	Koch [kɔx], quartieren [kwar'ti:rən]	z	busy ['bizi]
l	Lied [li:t]	l	land [lænd], hill [hil]
m	Mirakel [mi'ra:kəl]	ʃ	shield [ʃi:ld], sugar ['ʃugə]
n	Nase ['na:zə]	ʒ	vision ['viʒən]
p	Probe ['pro:bə]	r	rat [ræt], train [trein]
r	rot [ro:t]	h	here [hiə], horse [hɔ:s]
t	Tisch [tıʃ]	x	coronach ['kɔrənæx], loch [lɔx]

Semi-Consonants

j	yellow ['jelou], yes [jes]
w	wall [wɔ:l]

List of Abbreviations

abbr.	abbreviation (of), abbreviated	*m.*	masculine
Acc.	Accusative	*Maths.*	Mathematics
adj.	adjective	*Meas.*	Measurement
adv.	adverb	*Mech.*	Mechanics
Agr.	agriculture	*Med.*	Medicine
Am.	American(ism)	*Met.*	Meteorology
Anat.	Anatomy	*Metall.*	Metallurgy
Archæol.	Archæology	*Mil.*	Military
Archit.	Architecture	*Min.*	Mining
Arith.	Arithmetic	*Motor.*	Motoring
art.	article	*Mount.*	Mountaineering
Astrol.	Astrology	*Mus.*	Music
Astron.	Astronomy	*Myth.*	Mythology
Austr.	Austrian	*n.*	neuter
aux.	auxiliary	*Naut.*	Nautical
Aviat.	Aviation	*Nav.*	Navigation
Bibl.	Biblical	*o.('s)*	one('s)
Bot.	Botany	*o.s.*	oneself
Br.	British	*obs.*	obsolete
Build.	Building	*Orn.*	Ornithology
Carp.	Carpentry	*p.*	person
Chem.	Chemistry	*Parl.*	Parliament
coll.	colloquial	*part.*	particle
collec.	collective	*pej.*	pejorative
Comm.	Commerce	*pers.*	person(al)
comp.	comparative	*Phil.*	Philosophy
conj.	conjunction	*Phonet.*	Phonetics
Cul.	Culinary	*Phot.*	Photography
Dat.	Dative	*Phys.*	Physics
def.	definite	*Physiol.*	Physiology
defect.	defective	*pl.*	plural
dem.	demonstrative	*Poet.*	Poetical
dial.	dialect	*Pol.*	Political
Eccl.	Ecclesiastical	*poss.*	possessive
Econ.	Economics	*p.p.*	past participle
Elec.	Electricity	*prec.*	preceded
emph.	emphatic	*pred.*	predicative
Engin.	Engineering	*prep.*	preposition
Ent.	Entomology	*pron.*	pronoun
excl.	exclamation	*Psych.*	Psychology
f.	feminine	*r.*	reflexive
fig.	figurative	*Rad.*	Radio
Fin.	Finance	*Railw.*	Railways
Footb.	Football	*reg.*	regular
Genit.	Genitive	*Rel.*	Religion
Geog.	Geography	*rel.*	relative
Geol.	Geology	*s.*	substantive
Geom.	Geometry	*Sch.*	School
Gram.	Grammar	*Scot.*	Scottish
Gymn.	Gymnastics	*sing.*	singular
Her.	Heraldry	*sl.*	slang
Hist.	History	*s.th.*	something
Hunt.	Hunting	*Tail.*	Tailoring
imper.	imperative	*Tech.*	Technical
impers.	impersonal	*Teleph.*	Telephone
Ind.	Industry	*temp.*	temporal
indecl.	indeclinable	*Text.*	Textiles
indef.	indefinite	*Theat.*	Theatre
infin.	infinitive	*Theol.*	Theology
insep.	inseparable	*Transp.*	Transport
int.	interjection	*Typ.*	Typography
interr.	interrogative	*Univ.*	University
intim.	intimate	*us.*	usually
iron.	ironical	*v.a.*	active *or* transitive verb
irr.	irregular	*v.n.*	neuter *or* intransitive verb
Ling.	Linguistics	*v.r.*	reflexive verb
Lit.	Literary	*Vet.*	Veterinary Science
Log.	Logic	*vulg.*	vulgar
		Zool.	Zoology

Cassell's German-English Dictionary

A

A, a [a:], *n. das A* (des —s, die —s) the letter A; (*Mus.*) the note A; *A Dur*, A major; *A Moll*, A minor.

Aal [a:l], *m.* (—s, *pl.* —e) eel.

Aas [a:s], *n.* (—es, *pl.* Äser *or* —e) carcass, carrion.

ab [ap], *adv.* off; down; away; (*Theat.*) exit *or* exeunt, — *und zu*, now and again, occasionally; *auf und* —, up and down, to and fro. — *prep.* from; — *Hamburg*, from Hamburg.

abändern ['apɛndərn], *v.a.* alter.

Abart ['apa:rt], *f.* (—, *pl.* —en) variety, species.

Abbau ['apbau], *m.* (—s, *no pl.*) demolition, dismantling; reduction (of staff).

abberufen ['apbəru:fən], *v.a. irr.* recall.

abbestellen ['apbəʃtɛlən], *v.a.* countermand, annul, cancel (an order).

Abbild ['apbɪlt], *n.* (—es, *pl.* —er) copy, image.

Abbildung ['apbɪlduŋ], *f.* (—, *pl.* —en) illustration.

Abbitte ['apbɪtə], *f.* (—, *pl.* —n) apology; — *leisten*, — *tun*, apologise.

abblenden ['apblɛndən], *v.a.* dim (lights).

Abbruch ['apbrux], *m.* (—s, *pl.* ‐e) breaking off; demolition; *einer Sache* — *tun*, damage s.th.

abdanken ['apdaŋkən], *v.n.* resign, abdicate, retire (from office).

abdecken ['apdɛkən], *v.a.* uncover, unroof; clear (the table).

Abdruck ['apdruk], *m.* (—s, *pl.* —e) impression, copy, reprint, cast.

Abend ['a:bənt], *m.* (—s, *pl.* —e) evening, eve.

Abendbrot ['a:bəntbro:t], *n.* (—s, *no pl.*) evening meal, (*Am.*) supper.

Abendland ['a:bəntlant], *n.* (—es, *no pl.*) occident, west.

Abendmahl ['a:bəntma:l], *n.* (—s, *no pl.*) supper; *das heilige* —, Holy Communion, the Lord's Supper.

abends ['a:bənts], *adv.* in the evening, of an evening.

Abenteuer ['a:bəntɔyər], *n.* (—s, *pl.* —) adventure.

aber ['a:bər], *conj.* but, however; (*emphatic*) — *ja!* yes, indeed! of course! —*prefix.* again, once more.

Aberglaube ['a:bərglaubə], *m.* (—ns, *no pl.*) superstition.

abermals ['a:bərma:ls], *adv.* again, once more.

Abessinien [abɛ'si:niən], *n.* Abyssinia.

abfahren ['apfa:rən], *v.n. irr.* (*aux.* sein) set out, depart, drive off.

Abfall ['apfal], *m.* (—s, *pl.* ‐e) scrap, remnant; secession; slope; (*pl.*) waste, refuse.

abfallen ['apfalən], *v.n. irr.* (*aux.* sein) fall off; desert; slope.

abfällig ['apfɛlɪç], *adj.* derogatory.

abfangen ['apfaŋən], *v.a. irr.* intercept, catch.

abfärben ['apfɛrbən], *v.n.* (*colours*) run; stain; lose colour.

abfassen ['apfasən], *v.a.* compose, draft.

abfertigen ['apfɛrtɪgən], *v.a.* despatch; deal with, serve (a customer *or* client).

abfeuern ['apfɔyərn], *v.a.* fire (off), launch (rocket, missile).

abfinden ['apfɪndən], *v.a. irr.* indemnify, compound with (o.'s creditors). —*v.r. sich* — *mit*, put up with, come to terms with.

Abflug ['apflu:k], *m.* (—s, *pl.* ‐e) take-off, departure (by air).

Abfluß ['apflus], *m.* (—sses, *pl.* ‐sse) flowing off; drain.

Abfuhr ['apfu:r], *f.* (—, *pl.* —en) removal, collection (of refuse); (*coll.*) rebuff.

abführen ['apfy:rən], *v.a.* arrest, lead away. —*v.n.* (*Med.*) act as a purgative.

Abführmittel ['apfy:rmɪtəl], *n.* (—s, *pl.* —) purgative, laxative.

Abgabe ['apga:bə], *f.* (—, *pl.* —n) delivery, tax, duty, levy.

abgabepflichtig ['apga:bəpflɪçtɪç], *adj.* taxable, subject to duty.

Abgang ['apgaŋ], *m.* (—(e)s, *pl.* ‐e) wastage, loss; departure; *Schul*—, school-leaving.

abgeben ['apge:bən], *v.a. irr.* deliver, cede; give (an opinion). — *v.r. sich mit etwas*, — concern o.s. with s.th.

abgedroschen ['apgədrɔʃən], *adj.* (*phrases etc.*) trite, hackneyed.

abgefeimt ['apgəfaimt], *adj.* cunning, crafty.

abgegriffen ['apgəgrɪfən], *adj.* well thumbed, worn.

abgehen ['apge:ən], *v.n. irr.* (*aux.* sein) leave, retire; branch off; (*Theat.*) make an exit.

abgelebt ['apgəle:pt], *adj.* (*of humans*) decrepit, worn out.

abgelegen ['apgəle:gən], *adj.* remote, distant.

abgemacht ['apgəmaxt], *adj., int.* agreed! done!

abgeneigt ['apgənaikt], *adj.* disinclined, averse.

Abgeordnete ['apgəɔrdnətə], *m., f.* (—n, *pl.* —n) political representative, deputy, Member of Parliament.

Abgesandte ['apgəzantə], *m., f.* (—n, *pl.* —n) delegate, ambassador.

1

abgeschieden [ˈapgəʃiːdən], *adj.* secluded, remote; deceased.

abgeschmackt [ˈapgəʃmakt], *adj.* insipid.

abgesehen [ˈapgəzeːən], *adv.* — *von*, apart from, except for.

abgespannt [ˈapgəʃpant], *adj.* worn out, run down, exhausted.

abgestorben [ˈapgəʃtɔrbən], *adj.* dead, numb.

abgetan [ˈapgətaːn], *adj.* finished, over, done with; *damit ist die Sache* —, that finishes the matter.

abgetragen [ˈapgətraːgən], *adj.* (*clothes*) shabby, threadbare.

abgewöhnen [ˈapgəvøːnən], *v.a. einem etwas* —, free (rid) s.o. from (of) a habit, wean from.

abgrasen [ˈapgraːzən], *v.a.* (*animals*) graze.

Abgrund [ˈapgrunt], *m.* (—es, *pl.* ⸚e) abyss, precipice.

Abguss [ˈapgus], *m.* (—es, *pl.* ⸚e) cast, plaster-cast, mould.

abhalten [ˈaphaltən], *v.a. irr.* restrain, hold back; hold (meeting etc.).

abhandeln [ˈaphandəln], *v.a. einem etwas* —, bargain for s.th.

abhanden [apˈhandən], *adv.* mislaid; — *kommen*, get lost.

Abhandlung [ˈaphandluŋ], *f.* (—, *pl.* —en) treatise, dissertation; (*pl.*) proceedings.

Abhang [ˈaphaŋ], *m.* (—es, *pl.* ⸚e) slope; declivity.

abhängen [ˈaphɛŋən], *v.a. irr.* take off, unhook; *von etwas oder jemandem* —, depend on s.th. *or* s.o.

abhärten [ˈaphɛrtən], *v.a.* inure against rigours, toughen.

abhold [ˈaphɔlt], *adj.* averse to (*Dat.*).

abholen [ˈaphoːlən], *v.a. etwas* —, fetch, collect s.th.; *einen* —, meet s.o. (at the station etc.).

Abitur [abiˈtuːr], *n.* (—s, *no pl.*) matriculation examination.

Abiturient [abituˈrjɛnt], *m.* (—en, *pl.* —en) matriculation candidate.

Abkehr [ˈapkeːr], *f.* (—, *no pl.*) turning away, renunciation.

abklären [ˈapklɛːrən], *v.a.* (*Chem.*) filter, clear.

Abkommen [ˈapkɔmən], *n.* (—s, *pl.* —) treaty, agreement, contract.

Abkömmling [ˈapkœmliŋ], *m.* (—s, *pl.* —e) descendant.

abkühlen [ˈapkyːlən], *v.a.* cool, chill.

Abkunft [ˈapkunft], *f.* (—, *no pl.*) descent, origin.

abkürzen [ˈapkyrtsən], *v.a.* shorten, abridge, curtail.

abladen [ˈaplaːdən], *v.a. irr.* unload, dump.

Ablaß [ˈaplas], *m.* (—sses, *pl.* ⸚sse) (*Eccl.*) indulgence.

ablassen [ˈaplasən], *v.n. irr. von etwas* —, desist from, refrain from s.th.— *v.a. einem etwas billig* —, reduce the price of s.th. for s.o.

Ablauf [ˈaplauf], *m.* (—es, *no pl.*) (*water*) drainage; (*ticket*) expiration; lapse (of time); (*bill*) maturity.

ablaufen [ˈaplaufən], *v.n. irr.* (*aux. sein*) (*water*) run off; (*ticket*) expire; *gut* —, turn out well.

Ableben [ˈapleːbən], *n.* (—s, *no pl.*) decease, death.

ablegen [ˈapleːgən], *v.a.* (*clothes*) take off; (*documents*) file; *Rechenschaft* —, account for; *eine Prüfung* —, take an examination.

Ableger [ˈapleːgər], *m.* (—s, *pl.* —) (*Hort.*) cutting.

Ablegung [ˈapleːguŋ], *f.* (—, *no pl.*) making (of a vow); taking (of an oath).

ablehnen [ˈapleːnən], *v.a.* refuse, decline.

ableiten [ˈaplaitən], *v.a.* divert, draw off; (*water*) drain; (*words*) derive from.

ablenken [ˈaplɛŋkən], *v.a.* (*aux. haben*) *einen von etwas* —, divert s.o.'s attention from s.th., distract.

ablesen [ˈapleːzən], *v.a. irr.* (*meter*) read off; (*field*) glean.

abliefern [ˈapliːfərn], *v.a.* deliver.

ablösen [ˈapløːzən], *v.a. einen* —, take the place of s.o., (*Mil.*) relieve; detach (a stamp from a letter etc.).

abmachen [ˈapmaxən], *v.a.* undo, detach; settle, arrange.

abmagern [ˈapmaːgərn], *v.n.* (*aux. sein*) get thinner, waste away.

Abmarsch [ˈapmarʃ], *m.* (—es, *no pl.*) (*Mil.*) marching off.

abmelden [ˈapmɛldən], *v.r. sich* —, give notice of departure.

abmessen [ˈapmɛsən], *v.a. irr.* measure (off), gauge.

abmühen [ˈapmyːən], *v.r. sich* —, exert o.s., strive.

Abnahme [ˈapnaːmə], *f.* (—, *pl.* —n) decline, loss of weight; (*moon*) waning; (*goods*) taking delivery.

abnehmen [ˈapneːmən], *v.n. irr.* lose weight; (*moon*) wane. — *v.a.* (*hat*) take off; *einem etwas* —, relieve s.o. (of trouble or work).

Abneigung [ˈapnaiguŋ], *f.* (—, *pl.* —en) antipathy, dislike.

abnutzen [ˈapnutsən], *v.a.* wear out by use.

Abonnement [abɔnəˈmaŋ], *n.* (—s, *pl.* —s) (*newspaper*) subscription; (*railway*) season-ticket.

Abonnent [abɔˈnɛnt], *m.* (—en, *pl.* —en) subscriber.

abonnieren [abɔˈniːrən], *v.a.* subscribe to (a paper).

Abordnung [ˈapɔrdnuŋ], *f.* (—, *pl.* —en) delegation, deputation.

Abort [aˈbɔrt], *m.* (—s, *pl.* —e) lavatory, toilet.

Abortus [aˈbɔrtus], *m.* (—us, *no pl.*) (*Med.*) abortion.

abplagen [ˈaplaːgən], *v.r. sich* —, slave, toil.

abprallen [ˈappralən], *v.n.* (*aux. sein*) *von etwas* —, bounce off, rebound.

abquälen [ˈapkvɛːlən], v.r. sich —, toil, make o.s. weary (mit, with).

abraten [ˈapraːtən], v.n. irr. einem von etwas —, dissuade s.o. from, advise or warn s.o. against.

abräumen [ˈaprɔymən], v.a. remove; den Tisch —, clear the table.

abrechnen [ˈaprɛçnən], v.a. reckon up. — v.n. mit einem —, settle accounts with s.o., (coll.) get even with s.o.

Abrede [ˈapreːdə], f. (—, pl. —n) agreement, arrangement; in — stellen, deny.

abreißen [ˈapraisən], v.a. irr. tear off.

abrichten [ˈapriçtən], v.a. (dogs) train, (horses) break in.

abriegeln [ˈapriːgəln], v.a. bolt, bar.

Abriß [ˈapris], m. (—sses, pl. —sse) sketch; summary, synopsis.

abrollen [ˈaprɔlən], v.a. uncoil. — v.n. (aux. sein) roll off.

abrunden [ˈaprundən], v.a. round off.

abrupfen [ˈaprupfən], v.a. (feathers) pluck; (flowers) pluck off.

abrüsten [ˈaprystən], v.n. disarm.

Abrüstung [ˈaprystun], f. (—, no pl.) disarmament.

abrutschen [ˈaprutʃən], v.n. (aux. sein) slide, slither down.

Absage [ˈapzaːgə], f. (—, pl. —n) cancellation, refusal.

absagen [ˈapzaːgən], v.n. refuse, beg to be excused, decline (an invitation).

Absatz [ˈapzats], m. (—es, pl. ːe) (shoe) heel; (letter) paragraph; (Comm.) guter —, ready sale.

abschaffen [ˈapʃafən], v.a. abolish, do away with.

abschälen [ˈapʃɛːlən], v.a. peel. — v.r. sich —, peel off.

abschätzen [ˈapʃɛtsən], v.a. estimate, appraise; (taxes) assess.

Abschaum [ˈapʃaum], m. (—es, no pl.) scum.

Abscheu [ˈapʃɔy], m. (—s, no pl.) abhorrence, detestation, loathing.

abscheulich [ˈapʃɔyliç], adj. abominable, repulsive.

abschieben [ˈapʃiːbən], v.a. irr. shove off, push off; schieb ab! scram!

Abschied [ˈapʃiːt], m. (—s, pl. —e) leave, departure, farewell; discharge; resignation.

abschießen [ˈapʃiːsən], v.a. irr. shoot off; discharge; (gun) fire; den Vogel —, win the prize.

abschinden [ˈapʃindən], v.r. irr. sich —, exhaust o.s. with hard work.

abschirren [ˈapʃirən], v.a. unharness.

abschlagen [ˈapʃlaːgən], v.a.irr. (attack) beat off; (branches) lop off; einem etwas —, deny s.o. s.th.; eine Bitte —, refuse a request.

abschlägig [ˈapʃlɛːgiç], adj. negative.

Abschlagszahlung [ˈapʃlaːkstsaːlun], f. (—, pl. —en) payment by instalments.

abschleifen [ˈapʃlaifən], v.a. irr. grind off.

abschleppen [ˈapʃlɛpən], v.a. (car) tow (away). — v.r. sich —, wear o.s. out by carrying heavy loads.

abschließen [ˈapʃliːsən], v.a. irr. lock up; (work) conclude; (accounts) balance; einen Vertrag —, conclude an agreement.

Abschluß [ˈapʃlus], m. (—sses, pl. ːsse) settlement, winding-up.

abschneiden [ˈapʃnaidən], v.a. irr. cut off. — v.n. gut —, come off well.

Abschnitt [ˈapʃnit], m. (—es, pl. —e) section; (book) paragraph.

abschnüren [ˈapʃnyːrən], v.a. lace up, tie up.

abschrecken [ˈapʃrɛkən], v.a. deter, frighten.

abschreiben [ˈapʃraibən], v.a. irr. copy, transcribe; crib; eine Schuld —, write off a debt.

Abschrift [ˈapʃrift], f. (—, pl. —en) copy, transcript, duplicate; beglaubigte —, certified copy.

Abschuß [ˈapʃus], m. (—sses, pl. ːsse) act of firing (a gun), shooting down (aircraft).

abschüssig [ˈapʃysiç], adj. steep.

abschütteln [ˈapʃytəln], v.a. shake off, cast off.

abschwächen [ˈapʃvɛçən], v.a. weaken, diminish.

abschweifen [ˈapʃvaifən], v.n. (aux. sein) digress (from), deviate.

abschwenken [ˈapʃvɛnkən], v.n. (aux. sein) wheel off (or aside).

abschwören [ˈapʃvøːrən], v.a. irr. abjure, renounce by oath.

absehbar [ˈapzeːbaːr], adj. imaginable, conceivable, foreseeable.

absehen [ˈapzeːən], v.a., v.n. irr. einem etwas —, copy s.th. from s.o.; auf etwas —, aim at s.th.; von etwas —, waive s.th.; refrain from s.th.

abseits [ˈapzaits], adv., prep. (Genit.) aside; — von, away from.

Absender [ˈapzɛndər], m. (—s, pl.—) sender; (Comm.) consigner.

absetzen [ˈapzɛtsən], v.a. set down; dismiss, deprive of office; depose; (Comm.) sell, dispose of.

Absicht [ˈapziçt], f. (—, pl. —en) intention, purpose, aim.

absondern [ˈapzɔndərn], v.a. separate, set apart; (Med.) secrete. — v.r. sich —, seclude o.s. from.

abspannen [ˈapʃpanən], v.a. unharness.

absparen [ˈapʃpaːrən], v.n. sich etwas vom Munde —, stint o.s. for s.th.

abspenstig [ˈapʃpɛnstiç], adj. — machen, alienate s.o.'s affections, entice s.o. away; — werden, desert.

absperren [ˈapʃpɛrən], v.a. (door) lock, shut up; (street) close, barricade; (gas, water) turn off.

absprechen [ˈapʃprɛçən], v.a. irr. einem das Recht —, deprive s.o. of the right to do s.th.

3

abspülen

abspülen ['apʃpy:lən], *v.a.* wash up, rinse.

abstammen ['apʃtamən], *v.n. (aux. sein)* descend from, originate from.

Abstand ['apʃtant], *m.* (—es, pl. ⁓e) distance; *von etwas — nehmen*, refrain from doing s.th.

abstatten ['apʃtatən], *v.a. einen Besuch —*, pay a visit; *einen Bericht —*, report on; *Dank —*, return thanks.

abstechen ['apʃtɛçən], *v.a. irr. Tiere —*, slaughter animals. — *v.n. von etwas —*, contrast with s.th.

Abstecher ['apʃtɛçər], *m.* (—s, pl. —) short trip, excursion; detour.

abstecken ['apʃtɛkən], *v.a.* mark off, peg out.

absteigen ['apʃtaɪɡən], *v.n. irr. (aux. sein)* descend, alight, dismount.

abstellen ['apʃtɛlən], *v.a.* put s.th. down; *(gas, water)* turn off.

absterben ['apʃtɛrbən], *v.n. irr. (aux. sein)* wither; die.

Abstieg ['apʃti:k], *m.* (—es, no pl.) descent.

Abstimmung ['apʃtɪmuŋ], *f.* (—, pl. —en) *(Parl.)* division; referendum, voting.

abstoßen ['apʃto:sən], *v.a. irr.* push off, kick off. —*v.n. (Naut.)* set sail.

abstoßend ['apʃto:sənt], *adj.* repulsive, repugnant.

abstreifen ['apʃtraɪfən], *v.a. irr.* strip off, pull off; cast, shed.

abstufen ['apʃtu:fən], *v.a.* grade.

abstumpfen ['apʃtumpfən], *v.a.* blunt, dull, take the edge off.

abstürzen ['apʃtyrtsən], *v.n. (aux. sein) (person)* fall; fall down; *(Aviat.)* crash.

Abt [apt], *m.* (—es, pl. ⁓e) abbot.

Abtei ['aptaɪ], *f.* (—, pl. —en) abbey.

Abteil ['aptaɪl], *n.* (—s, pl. —e) compartment.

abteilen ['aptaɪlən], *v.a.* divide, partition.

Abteilung [ap'taɪluŋ], *f.* (—, pl. —en) section, department.

Äbtissin [ɛp'tɪsɪn], *f.* (—, pl. —nen) abbess.

abtöten ['aptø:tən], *v.a.* mortify, deaden.

abtragen ['aptra:ɡən], *v.a. irr.* carry away; *(building)* demolish; *(dress, shoes)* wear out; *eine Schuld —*, pay a debt.

abtreiben ['aptraɪbən], *v.a. irr. (cattle)* drive off; procure an abortion. — *v.n. (aux. sein) (ship)* drift off.

Abtreibung ['aptraɪbuŋ], *f.* (—, pl. —en) abortion.

abtrennen ['aptrɛnən], *v.a. (s.th. sewn)* unpick; separate.

Abtretung ['aptre:tuŋ], *f.* (—, pl. —en) cession, conveyance.

Abtritt ['aptrɪt], *m.* (—es, pl. —e) W.C.; *(Theat.)* exit or exeunt.

abtrocknen ['aptrɔknən], *v.a.* dry.

abtrünnig ['aptrynɪç], *adj.* disloyal, faithless.

aburteilen ['apurtaɪlən], *v.a.* pass judgment on.

abwägen ['apvɛ:ɡən], *v.a. gegeneinander —*, weigh against each other.

abwälzen ['apvɛltsən], *v.a. etwas von sich —*, clear o.s. from s.th.

abwandeln ['apvandəln], *v.a.* change; *(verbs)* conjugate; *(nouns)* decline.

abwärts ['apvɛrts], *prep., adv.* downward.

abwaschen ['apvaʃən], *v.a. irr.* wash up.

abwechseln ['apvɛksəln], *v.a.* vary, alternate.

Abweg ['apve:k], *m.* (—es, pl. —e) wrong way; *auf —e geraten*, go astray.

abwehren ['apve:rən], *v.a.* ward off, parry.

abweichen ['apvaɪçən], *v.n. irr. (aux. sein) — von*, deviate from.

abweisen ['apvaɪzən], *v.a. irr.* refuse admittance to, rebuff.

abwenden ['apvɛndən], *v.a. irr.* avert, prevent. — *v.r. sich —*, turn away from.

abwesend ['apve:zənt], *adj.* absent.

Abwesenheit ['apve:zənhaɪt], *f.* (—, pl. —en) absence.

abwickeln ['apvɪkəln], *v.a.* uncoil; *(business)* wind up.

abwischen ['apvɪʃən], *v.a.* wipe clean; *sich die Stirn —*, mop o.'s brow.

abzahlen ['aptsa:lən], *v.a.* pay off; pay by instalments.

abzehren ['aptse:rən], *v.n. (aux. sein)* waste away.

Abzeichen ['aptsaɪçən], *n.* (—s, pl. —) badge, insignia.

abzeichnen ['aptsaɪçnən], *v.a.* sketch, draw from a model. — *v.r. sich —*, become clear.

abziehen ['aptsi:ən], *v.a. irr.* deduct, subtract; *(knife)* sharpen; strip *(a bed)*. — *v.n. (aux. sein)* depart; *(Mil.)* march off.

Abzug ['aptsu:k], *m.* (—es, pl. ⁓e) retreat, departure; photographic copy; *— der Kosten*, deduction of charges; *(steam, air)* outlet.

abzweigen ['aptsvaɪɡən], *v.n. (aux. sein)* fork off, branch off.

Achsel ['aksəl], *f.* (—, pl. —n) shoulder; *die —n zucken*, shrug o.'s shoulders.

Acht [axt], *f.* (—, no pl.) attention, care, caution, heed; *achtgeben*, pay attention; *sich in — acht nehmen*, be careful; ban, excommunication, outlawry; *in — und Bann tun*, outlaw, proscribe.

acht [axt], *num. adj.* eight; *in — Tagen*, in a week; *vor — Tagen*, a week ago.

achtbar ['axtba:r], *adj.* respectable.

achten ['axtən], *v.a.* hold in esteem, value; *— auf*, pay attention to, keep an eye on.

ächten ['ɛçtən], *v.a.* ban, outlaw, proscribe.

achtlos ['axtlo:s], *adj.* inattentive, negligent.

achtsam ['axtza:m], *adj.* attentive, careful.

Achtung ['axtuŋ], *f.* (—, no pl.) esteem, regard; *(Mil.)* attention!

Ächtung ['ɛçtuŋ], *f.* (—, no pl.) ban, proscription.

achtzehn ['axtse:n], *num. adj.* eighteen.

Alpdrücken

achtzig ['axtsɪç], *num. adj.* eighty.
ächzen ['ɛçtsən], *v.n.* groan.
Acker ['akər], *m.* (—s, *pl.* ⁻) field, arable land; *den — bestellen*, till the soil.
ackern ['akərn], *v.n.* till (the land).
addieren [a'di:rən], *v.a.* add, add up.
Adel ['a:dəl], *m.* (—s, *no pl.*) nobility, aristocracy.
ad(e)lig ['a:dlɪç], *adj.* of noble birth, aristocratic.
Ader ['a:dər], *f.* (—, *pl.* —n) vein; *zu — lassen*, bleed s.o.
Adler ['a:dlər], *m.* (—s, *pl.* —) eagle.
Adresse [a'drɛsə], *f.* (—, *pl.* —n) address.
adrett [a'drɛt], *adj.* neat, adroit, smart.
Affe ['afə], *m.* (—n, *pl.* —n) ape, monkey; (*fig.*) fool.
affektiert [afɛk'ti:rt], *adj.* affected, giving o.s. airs.
äffen ['ɛfən], *v.a.* ape, mimic.
Afghanistan [af'ganistan], *n.* Afghanistan.
Afrika ['a:frika], *n.* Africa.
After ['aftər], *m.* (—s, *pl.* —) anus.
Agentur [agɛn'tu:r], *f.* (—, *pl.* —en) agency.
Agraffe [a'grafə], *f.* (—, *pl.* —n) brooch, clasp.
Agrarier [a'gra:rjər], *m.* (—s, *pl.* —) landed proprietor.
Ägypten [ɛ'gyptən], *n.* Egypt.
Ahle ['a:lə], *f.* (—, *pl.* —n) awl, bodkin.
Ahn [a:n], *m.* (—en, *pl.* —en) ancestor, forefather.
ahnden ['a:ndən], *v.a.* avenge, punish.
Ahne ['a:nə] *see* **Ahn.**
ähneln ['ɛ:nəln], *v.a.* resemble, look like.
ahnen ['a:nən], *v.a., v.n.* have a presentiment, foresee, have a hunch.
ähnlich ['ɛ:nlɪç], *adj.* resembling, like, similar.
Ahnung ['a:nuŋ], *f.* (—, *pl.* —en) foreboding, presentiment, idea, (*Am.*) hunch.
Ahorn ['a:hɔrn], *m.* (—s, *pl.* —e) (*Bot.*) maple.
Ähre ['ɛ:rə], *f.* (—, *pl.* —n) ear of corn.
Akademiker [aka'de:mɪkər], *m.* (—s, *pl.* —) university graduate.
akademisch [aka'de:mɪʃ], *adj.* academic; — *gebildet*, with a university education.
Akazie [a'ka:tsjə], *f.* (—, *pl.* —n) (*Bot.*) acacia.
akklimatisieren [aklimati'zi:rən], *v.r. sich —*, become acclimatised.
Akkord [a'kɔrt], *m.* (—es, *pl.* —e) (*Mus.*) chord; *in — arbeiten*, work on piece-rates.
Akt [akt], *m.* (—es, *pl.* —e) deed, action; (*Theat.*) act; (*Art*) (depiction of) the nude.
Akte ['aktə], *f.* (—, *pl.* —n) document, deed; (*pl.*) records, files; *zu den —n legen*, pigeonhole, shelve.
Aktenstück ['aktənʃtyk], *n.* (—es, *pl.* —e) official document, file.
Aktie ['aktsjə], *f.* (—, *pl.* —n) (*Comm.*) share, (*Am.*) stock.

Aktiengesellschaft ['aktsjəngəzɛlʃaft], *f.* (—, *pl.* —en) joint stock company.
Aktionär [aktsjo'nɛ:r], *m.* (—s, *pl.* —e) shareholder, (*Am.*) stockholder.
Aktiv ['akti:f], *n.* (—s, *pl.* —e) (*Gram.*) active voice.
Aktiva [ak'ti:va], *n. pl.* (*Comm.*) assets.
aktuell [aktu'ɛl], *adj.* topical.
akzentuieren [aktsɛntu'i:rən], *v.a.* accentuate, stress, emphasize.
Albanien [al'ba:njən], *n.* Albania.
albern ['albərn], *adj.* silly, foolish.
Aliment [ali'mɛnt], *n.* (—es, *pl.* —e) (*usually pl.*—e) alimony, maintenance.
Alkali [al'ka:li], *n.* (—s, *pl.* —en) alkali.
Alkohol ['alkoho:l], *m.* (—s, *no pl.*) alcohol.
Alkoholiker [alko'ho:lɪkər], *m.* (—s, *pl.* —) drunkard, alcoholic.
All [al], *n.* (—s, *no pl.*) the universe, (outer) space.
all [al], *adj.* all, entire, whole; every, each, any.
alle ['alə], *adj.* all, everybody; — *beide*, both of them.
Allee [a'le:], *f.* (—, *pl.* —n) tree-lined walk, avenue.
allein [a'laɪn], *adj.* alone, sole. — *adv.* solely, only, merely. —*conj.* (*obs.*) only, but, however.
alleinig [a'laɪnɪç], *adj.* sole, only, exclusive.
allenfalls [alən'fals], *adv.* possibly, perhaps, if need be.
allenthalben [alənt'halbən], *adv.* everywhere, in all places.
allerdings [alər'dɪŋs], *adv.* of course, indeed, nevertheless.
allerhand [alər'hant], *adj.* of all sorts or kinds, various; *das ist ja —!* I say!
Allerheiligen [alər'haɪlɪgən], *pl.* All Saints' Day.
allerlei [alər'laɪ], *adj.* miscellaneous, various.
allerliebst [alər'li:pst], *adj.* (*Am.*) cute; charming.
allerseits ['alərzaɪts], *adv.* generally, on all sides, universally.
alles ['aləs], *adj.* everything, all.
allgemein [algə'maɪn], *adj.* universal, common, general.
alliieren [ali'i:rən], *v.a., v.n.* ally (o.s.).
allmächtig [al'mɛçtɪç], *adj.* omnipotent.
allmählich [al'mɛ:lɪç], *adj.* by degrees, gradual.
allseitig ['alzaɪtɪç], *adj.* universal, (*Am.*) all-round.
Alltag ['alta:k], *m.* (—s, *pl.* —e) working day, week-day.
allwissend [al'vɪsənt], *adj.* omniscient.
allzu ['altzu:], *adv.* too, much too.
Alm [alm], *f.* (—, *pl.* —en) Alpine meadow.
Almosen ['almo:zən], *n.* (—s, *pl.* —) alms, charity.
Alp [alp], *f.* (—, *pl.* —en) (*mostly pl.*) mountain(s), Alps.
Alpdrücken ['alpdrykən], *n.* (—s, *no pl.*) nightmare.

5

als

als [als], *conj.* than; (*after comparatives*) than; as, like; but; *er hat nichts — Schulden*, he has nothing but debts; (*temp.*) when, as.

alsbald [als'balt], *adv.* forthwith.

also ['alzo:], *adv.* thus, so, in this manner. — *conj.* consequently, therefore.

Alt [alt], *m.* (—**s**, *pl.* —**e**) (*Mus.*) alto.

alt [alt], *adj.* old, ancient; aged; antique.

Altan [al'ta:n], *m.* (—**s**, *pl.* —**e**) balcony, gallery.

Altar [al'ta:r], *m.* (—**s**, *pl.* —**e**) altar.

altbacken ['altbakən], *adj.* stale.

Alter ['altər], *n.* (—**s**, *no pl.*) age, old age; epoch.

altern ['altərn], *v.n.* (*aux.* sein) grow old.

Altertum ['altərtu:m], *n.* (—**s**, *pl.* —**er**) antiquity.

Altistin [al'tɪstɪn], *f.* (—, *pl.* —**nen**) (*Mus.*) contralto.

altklug ['altklu:k], *adj.* precocious.

ältlich ['eltlɪç], *adj.* elderly.

Altweibersommer [alt'vaɪbərzɔmər], *m.* (—**s**, *pl.* —) Indian summer.

Amboß ['ambɔs], *m.* (—**sses**, *pl.* —**sse**) anvil.

Ameise ['a:maɪzə], *f.* (—, *pl.* —**n**) (*Ent.*) ant.

Amerika [a'me:rika], *n.* America.

Amme ['amə], *f.* (—, *pl.* —**n**) wet nurse.

Ammoniak [amon'jak], *n.* (—**s**, *no pl.*) ammonia.

Ampel ['ampəl], *f.* (—, *pl.* —**n**) (hanging) light, lamp, lantern; traffic light.

Ampfer ['ampfər], *m.* (—**s**, *pl.* —) (*Bot.*) sorrel, dock.

Amsel ['amzəl], *f.* (—, *pl.* —**n**) (*Orn.*) blackbird.

Amt [amt], *n.* (—**es**, *pl.* —**er**) office, post, employment; administration, domain, jurisdiction; place of public business.

amtlich ['amtlɪç], *adj.* official.

Amtmann ['amtman], *m.* (—**s**, *pl.* —**er**) bailiff.

Amtsblatt ['amtsblat], *n.* (—**es**, *pl.* —**er**) official gazette.

Amtsgericht ['amtsgərɪçt], *n.* (—**s**, *pl.* —**e**) county court; (*Am.*) district court.

amüsieren [amy'zi:rən], *v.a.* amuse.— *v.r. sich* —, enjoy o.s.

an [an], *prep.* (*Dat. or Acc.*), at, to, on.

analog [ana'lo:k], *adj.* analogous.

Ananas ['ananas], *f.* (—, *pl.* —**n**) pineapple.

Anatom [ana'to:m], *m.* (—**en**, *pl.* —**en**) anatomist.

anbahnen ['anba:nən], *v.a.* initiate, open up, pave the way for.

anbändeln ['anbɛndəln], *v.n.* — *mit*, flirt with, make up to.

Anbau ['anbau], *m.* (—**s**, *pl.* —**ten**) (*grain*) cultivation; annex(e), wing (of building).

anbauen ['anbauən], *v.a.* cultivate; add to a building.

anbei [an'baɪ], *adv.* enclosed (in letter).

anbeißen ['anbaɪsən], *v.a. irr.* bite at,

take a bite of. — *v.n.* (*fish*) bite; (*coll.*) take the bait.

anbelangen ['anbəlaŋən], *v.a.* concern.

anberaumen ['anbəraumən], *v.a.* fix (a date).

anbeten ['anbe:tən], *v.a.* worship, adore, idolise.

anbiedern ['anbi:dərn], *v.r. sich mit einem* —, chum up with s.o.

anbieten ['anbi:tən], *v.a. irr.* offer.

anbinden ['anbɪndən], *v.a. irr.* tie on, bind to; *kurz angebunden sein*, be curt.

Anblick ['anblɪk], *m.* (—**s**, *no pl.*) view, sight, aspect, spectacle.

anbrechen ['anbreçən], *v.a. irr.* begin; break; start on. —*v.n.* dawn.

anbrennen ['anbrenən], *v.a. irr.* light, set fire to, burn. — *v.n.* (*aux.* sein) catch fire; burn.

anbringen ['anbrɪŋən], *v.a. irr.* fit to, place.

Anbruch ['anbrux], *m.* (—**s**, *no pl.*) beginning; — *der Nacht*, night-fall.

anbrüllen ['anbrylən], *v.a.* roar at.

Andacht ['andaxt], *f.* (—, *pl.* —**en**) (*Eccl.*) devotion(s).

andächtig ['andɛxtɪç], *adj.* devout.

andauern ['andauərn], *v.n.* last, continue.

Andenken ['andeŋkən], *n.* (—**s**, *pl.* —) memory; keepsake; souvenir.

anderer ['andərər], *adj.* other, different; *ein* —, another.

andermal ['andərma:l], *adv. ein* —, another time.

ändern ['endərn], *v.a.* alter, change.

andernfalls ['andərnfals], *adv.* otherwise, or else.

anders ['andərs], *adv.* differently, in another manner, otherwise.

anderthalb ['andərthalp], *adj.* one and a half.

anderweitig ['andərvaɪtɪç], *adj.* elsewhere.

andeuten ['andɔytən], *v.a.* hint at, intimate, indicate.

Andrang ['andraŋ], *m.* (—**es**, *no pl.*) throng, crowd.

aneignen ['anaɪgnən], *v.r. sich etwas* —, appropriate s.th.; (*an opinion*) adopt.

anekeln ['ane:kəln], *v.a.* disgust.

Anerbieten ['anɛrbi:tən], *n.* (—**s**, *pl.* —) offer.

anerkennen ['anɛrkenən], *v.a. irr.* acknowledge, appreciate, recognize, accept.

anfachen ['anfaxən], *v.a.* kindle (a flame).

Anfahrt ['anfa:rt], *f.* (—, *pl.* —**en**) drive; (*down a mine*) descent; (*Am.*) drive-way.

Anfall ['anfal], *m.* (—**s**, *pl.* —**e**) attack, assault; (*Med.*) seizure, fit; (*mood*) fit, burst.

anfallen ['anfalən], *v.a. irr. einen* —, attack s.o.

Anfang ['anfaŋ], *m.* (—**s**, *pl.* —**e**) beginning, start, commencement.

anfangen ['anfaŋən], *v.a. irr.* begin, start. — *v.n.* begin, originate.

Anfänger ['anfɛŋər], *m.* (**—s**, *pl.* **—**) beginner, novice.

anfänglich ['anfɛŋlɪç], *adv.* in the beginning, at first, initially.

anfassen ['anfasən], *v.a.* take hold of; touch; seize.

anfechtbar ['anfɛçtbaːr], *adj.* disputable, refutable, debatable.

anfechten ['anfɛçtən], *v.a.* (*a will, a verdict*) contest; (*jurors*) challenge.

anfeinden ['anfaɪndən], *v.a.* show enmity to.

anfertigen ['anfɛrtɪgən], *v.a.* make, manufacture, prepare; (*a list*) draw up.

anflehen ['anfleːən], *v.a.* implore, beseech.

Anflug ['anfluːk], *m.* (**—s**, *pl.* **—̈e**) (*Aviat.*) approach; (*beard*) down; touch.

anfordern ['anfordərn], *v.a.* demand, claim.

Anfrage ['anfraːgə], *f.* (**—**, *pl.* **—n**) enquiry.

anfügen ['anfyːgən], *v.a.* join to, annex.

anführen ['anfyːrən], *v.a.* lead; adduce, quote (examples), cite; *einen* **—**, dupe s.o., take s.o. in.

Anführungszeichen ['anfyːruŋstsaɪçən], *n.* (**—s**, *pl.* **—**) inverted commas, quotation marks.

anfüllen ['anfylən], *v.a.* *wieder* **—**, replenish.

Angabe ['angaːbə], *f.* (**—**, *pl.* **—n**) declaration, statement; data; instruction; bragging.

angeben ['angeːbən], *v.a. irr.* declare, state; *den Ton* **—**, lead the fashion; *den Wert* **—**, declare the value of.— *v.n. groß* **—**, brag, show off.

Angeber ['angeːbər], *m.* (**—s**, *pl.* **—**) informer; braggart.

Angebinde ['angəbɪndə], *n.* (**—s**, *pl.* **—**) (*obs.*) present, gift.

angeblich ['angeːplɪç], *adj.* ostensible, alleged, so-called.

angeboren ['angəboːrən], *adj.* innate, inborn.

Angebot ['angəboːt], *n.* (**—es**, *pl.* **—e**) offer, tender, bid; (*Comm.*) **—** *und Nachfrage*, supply and demand.

angebracht ['angəbraxt], *adj.* apt, appropriate, opportune.

angedeihen ['angədaɪən], *v.n. einem etwas* **—** *lassen*, bestow s.th. on s.o.

angegossen ['angəgɔsən], *adj. das sitzt wie* **—**, it fits like a glove.

angehen ['angeːən], *v.a. irr. einen um etwas* **—**, apply to s.o. for s.th.; *das geht Dich nichts an*, that is none of your business.

angehören ['angəhøːrən], *v.n.* belong to.

Angehörige ['angəhøːrɪgə], *m.*, *f.* (**—n**, *pl.* **—n**) near relative; next of kin.

Angeklagte ['angəklaːktə], *m.*, *f.* (**—n**, *pl.* **—n**) the accused, defendant, prisoner at the bar.

Angel ['aŋəl], *f.* (**—**, *pl.* **—n**) fishing-rod;

(*door*) hinge, pivot; *zwischen Tür und* **—**, in passing.

angelegen ['angəleːgən], *adj. sich etwas* **—** *sein lassen*, interest o.s. in s.th., concern o.s. in s.th.; *ich werde es mir* **—** *sein lassen*, I shall make it my business.

Angelegenheit ['angəleːgənhaɪt], *f.* (**—**, *pl.* **—en**) concern, matter, affair.

angeln ['aŋəln], *v.a.* fish, angle.

angemessen ['angəmɛsən], *adj.* proper, suitable, appropriate.

angenehm ['angəneːm], *adj.* acceptable, agreeable, pleasing, pleasant.

angenommen ['angənɔmən], *conj.* **—** *daß*, given that, supposing that, say.

Anger ['aŋər], *m.* (**—s**, *pl.* **—**) grassplot; green, common.

angesehen ['angəzeːən], *adj.* respected, esteemed, distinguished.

Angesicht ['angəzɪçt], *n.* (**—s**, *pl.* **—er**) face, countenance.

angestammt ['angəʃtamt], *adj.* ancestral, hereditary.

Angestellte ['angəʃtɛltə], *m.*, *f.* (**—n**, *pl.* **—n**) employee; (*pl.*) staff.

Angler ['aŋlər], *m.* (**—s**, *pl.* **—**) angler, fisherman.

angliedern ['angliːdərn], *v.a.* annex, attach.

Anglist [aŋ'glɪst], *m.* (**—en**, *pl.* **—en**) (*Univ.*) professor *or* student of English.

angreifen ['angraɪfən], *v.a. irr.* handle, touch; (*capital*) break into; attack, assail; *es greift mich an*, it taxes my strength.

angrenzen ['angrɛntsən], *v.n.* border upon, adjoin.

Angriff ['angrɪf], *m.* (**—s**, *pl.* **—e**) offensive, attack, assault.

Angst [aŋst], *f.* (**—**, *pl.* **—̈e**) anxiety; fear; anguish.

ängstigen ['ɛŋstɪgən], *v.a.* alarm, frighten. — *v.r. sich* **—**, feel uneasy, be afraid.

angucken ['anguːkən], *v.a.* look at.

anhaben ['anhaːbən], *v.a. irr.* have on, be dressed in, wear; *einem etwas* **—**, hold s.th. against s.o.

anhaften ['anhaftən], *v.n.* stick to, adhere to.

Anhalt ['anhalt], *m.* (**—es**, *no pl.*) support, basis.

anhalten ['anhaltən], *v.a. irr. einen* **—**, stop s.o. — *v.n.* stop, pull up, halt; *um ein Mädchen* **—**, ask for a girl's hand in marriage. — *v.r. sich an etwas halten*, cling to, hang on to s.th.

Anhaltspunkt ['anhaltspuŋkt], *m.* (**—es**, *pl.* **—e**) clue, (*Am.*) lead.

Anhang ['anhaŋ], *m.* (**—s**, *pl.* **—̈e**) appendix, supplement.

anhängen ['anhɛŋən], *v.a. irr.* hang on, fasten to, attach.

Anhänger ['anhɛŋər], *m.* (**—s**, *pl.* **—**) follower, adherent; (*Footb.*) supporter; pendant (on a necklace); label; (*Transp.*) trailer.

anhänglich ['anhɛŋlɪç], *adj.* attached, affectionate.

Anhängsel

Anhängsel ['anhɛŋsəl], *n.* (—s, *pl.* —) appendage.

anhauchen ['anhauxən], *v.a.* breathe upon.

anhäufen ['anhɔyfən], *v.a.* heap up, pile up, amass. —*v.r. sich* —, accumulate.

anheben ['anhe:bən], *v.a. irr.* lift. — *v.n.* (*obs.*) begin.

anheim [an'haim], *adv.* — *stellen,* leave to s.o.'s discretion.

anheimeln ['anhaiməln], *v.a.* remind one of home.

anheischig ['anhaiʃiç], *adj. sich* — *machen,* undertake, pledge o.s.

Anhieb ['anhi:p], *m.* (—s, *pl.* —e) (*fencing*) first stroke; *auf* —, at the first attempt.

Anhöhe ['anhø:ə], *f.* (—, *pl.* —n) hill, rising ground.

anhören ['anhø:rən], *v.a.* listen to; tell by s.o.'s voice *or* accent.

animieren [ani'mi:rən], *v.a.* instigate, egg on.

ankämpfen ['ankɛmpfən], *v.n. gegen etwas* —, struggle against s.th.

ankaufen ['ankaufən], *v.a.* purchase, buy. — *v.r. sich irgendwo* —, buy land somewhere.

Anker ['aŋkər], *m.* (—s, *pl.* —) (*Naut.*) anchor; *den* — *auswerfen,* cast anchor.

ankern ['aŋkərn], *v.a., v.n.* anchor, cast anchor.

Anklage ['ankla:gə], *f.* (—, *pl.* —n) accusation; *gegen einen* — *erheben,* bring a charge against s.o.

Ankläger ['anklɛ:gər], *m.* (—s, *pl.* —) accuser, prosecutor; plaintiff.

Anklang ['anklaŋ], *m.* (—s, *pl.* ⁻e) reminiscence; — *finden,* please, meet with approval.

ankleben ['ankle:bən], *v.a.* stick to, glue to, paste on.

ankleiden ['anklaidən], *v.a.* dress. — *v.r. sich* —, dress o.s., get dressed.

anklingeln ['anklɪŋəln], *v.a.* (*coll.*) *einen* —, ring s.o. up (on the telephone.)

anklopfen ['anklɔpfən], *v.n.* knock.

anknüpfen ['anknypfən], *v.a.* tie; join on to; *ein Gespräch* —, start a conversation; *wieder* —, resume.

ankommen ['ankɔmən], *v.n. irr.* (*aux.* sein) arrive; *es kommt darauf an,* it depends upon.

ankreiden ['ankraidən], *v.a.* chalk up.

ankündigen ['ankyndigən], *v.a.* announce, advertise, give notice of, proclaim.

Ankunft ['ankunft], *f.* (—, *no pl.*) arrival.

ankurbeln ['ankurbəln], *v.a.* (*Motor.*) crank up.

Anlage ['anla:gə], *f.* (—, *pl.* —n) (*capital*) investment; enclosure (*with a letter*); (*industrial*) plant; (*building*) lay-out; *öffentliche* —, pleasure grounds; talent.

anlangen ['anlaŋən], *v.n.* (*aux.* sein) arrive; concern; *was das anlangt,* as far as this is concerned.

Anlaß ['anlas], *m.* (—sses, *pl.* ⁻sse) cause, occasion, motive.

anlassen ['anlasən], *v.a. irr.* keep on; (*Motor.*) start. — *v.r. sich gut* —, promise well.

Anlasser ['anlasər], *m.* (—s, *pl.* —) (*Motor.*) starter.

anläßlich ['anlɛsliç], *prep.* (*Genit.*) à propos of, on the occasion of.

Anlauf ['anlauf], *m.* (—s, *pl.* ⁻e) start, run, (*Aviat.*) take-off run.

anlaufen ['anlaufən], *v.n. irr.* tarnish; call at (port).

anlegen ['anle:gən], *v.a. Geld* —, invest money; *Kleider* —, don clothes; *einen Garten* —, lay out a garden; *Hand* —, give a helping hand; *auf einen* —, take aim at s.o.; (*Naut.*) land, dock.

Anlegestelle '['anle:gəʃtelə], *f.* (—, *pl.* —n) landing place.

anlehnen ['anle:nən], *v.r. sich an etwas* —, lean against s.th.

Anleihe ['anlaiə], *f.* (—, *pl.* —n) loan, *öffentliche* —, government loan; *eine* — *machen,* raise a loan.

anleiten ['anlaitən], *v.a.* train, instruct.

anlernen ['anlernən], *v.a. einen* —, train, apprentice s.o. (in a craft).

Anliegen ['anli:gən], *n.* (—s, *pl.* —) request, petition, concern.

anmachen ['anmaxən], *v.a.* fix, fasten; light (a fire).

anmaßen ['anma:sən], *v.a. sich etwas* —, arrogate s.th.

anmaßend ['anma:sənt], *adj.* arrogant.

anmelden ['anmeldən], *v.a.* announce, (*claim*) give notice of. — *v.r. sich* —, notify o.'s arrival, make an appointment; *sich* — *lassen,* send in o.'s name.

Anmeldungsformular [an'meldunsformula:r], *n.* (—s, *pl.* —e) registration form.

Anmerkung ['anmerkuŋ], *f.* (—, *pl.* —en) remark, annotation, footnote.

anmessen ['anmesən], *v.a. irr.* measure (s.o. for a garment).

Anmut ['anmu:t], *f.* (—, *no pl.*) grace, charm.

annähen ['annɛ:ən], *v.a.* sew on (to).

annähern ['annɛ:ərn], *v.r. sich* —, approach, draw near; (*Maths.*) approximate.

Annäherung ['annɛ:əruŋ], *f.* (—, *pl.* —en) approach; (*Maths.*) approximation.

Annahme ['anna:mə], *f.* (—, *pl.* —n) acceptance; assumption, hypothesis.

annehmbar ['anne:mba:r], *adj.* acceptable; *ganz* —, passable.

annehmen ['anne:mən], *v.a. irr.* take, accept, take delivery of; suppose, assume, presume; *an Kindes Statt* —, adopt.

Annehmlichkeit ['anne:mliçkait], *f.* (—, *pl.* —en) amenity, comfort.

Annonce [an'nõ:sə], *f.* (—, *pl.* —n) (*classified*) advertisement (in newspaper).

anordnen ['anɔrdnən], *v.a.* arrange, regulate; order, direct.

8

ansspringen

anorganisch ['anɔrga:nɪʃ], *adj.* inorganic.

anpacken ['anpakən], *v.a.* get hold of, seize, grasp.

anpassen ['anpasən], *v.a.* fit, suit. — *v.r. sich* —, adapt o.s.

anpflanzen ['anpflantsən], *v.a.* plant, grow.

Anprall ['anpral], *m.* (—s, *no pl.*) impact, bounce, shock.

anpumpen ['anpumpən], *v.a.* (*coll.*) *einen* —, borrow money from s.o.

anrechnen ['anrɛçnən], *v.a. einem etwas* —, charge s.o. with s.th.; *einem etwas hoch* —, think highly of a person for s.th.

Anrecht ['anrɛçt], *n.* (—es, *no pl.*) — *auf*, title to, claim to.

Anrede ['anre:də], *f.* (—, *pl.* —n) (form of) address, title.

anreden ['anre:dən], *v.a.* address (s.o.).

anregen ['anre:gən], *v.a.* stimulate (s.o.); suggest (s.th.).

Anregung ['anre:guŋ], *f.* (—, *pl.* —en) suggestion, hint.

Anreiz ['anraits], *m.* (—es, *no pl.*) incentive; impulse.

Anrichte ['anrɪçtə], *f.* (—, *pl.* —n) dresser, sideboard.

anrichten ['anrɪçtən], *v.a.* (*meal*) prepare, serve (up); *Unheil* —, make mischief.

anrüchig ['anry:çɪç], *adj.* disreputable.

anrücken ['anrykən], *v.a.* bring near to. — *v.n.* (*aux.* sein) approach.

Anruf ['anru:f], *m.* (—s, *pl.* —e) (by *sentry*) challenge; telephone call.

anrufen ['anru:fən], *v.a. irr.* call to, challenge; implore; ring up; *Gott* —, invoke God.

anrühren ['anry:rən], *v.a.* handle, touch; (*Cul.*) mix.

Ansage ['anza:gə], *f.* (—, *pl.* —n) announcement.

ansagen ['anza:gən], *v.a.* announce, notify.

Ansager ['anza:gər], *m.* (—s, *pl.* —) announcer; compere.

ansammeln ['anzaməln], *v.a.* accumulate, gather. — *v.r. sich* —, gather, foregather, congregate, collect.

ansässig ['anzɛsɪç], *adj.* domiciled, resident; *sich* — *machen*, settle.

Ansatz ['anzats], *m.* (—es, *pl.* ˙e) start; (*Maths.*) construction; disposition (to), tendency (to).

anschaffen ['anʃafən], *v.a.* buy, purchase, get.

anschauen ['anʃauən], *v.a.* look at, view.

anschaulich ['anʃauliç], *adj.* clear; *einem etwas* — *machen*, give s.o. a clear idea of s.th.

Anschauung ['anʃauuŋ], *f.* (—, *pl.* —en) view, perception; *nach meiner* —, in my opinion.

Anschein ['anʃain], *m.* (—s, *no pl.*) appearance, semblance.

anscheinend ['anʃainənt], *adj.* apparent, ostensible, seeming.

anschicken ['anʃikən], *v.r. sich* — *zu*, prepare for, get ready for.

anschirren ['anʃirən], *v.a.* (*horses*) harness.

Anschlag ['anʃla:k], *m.* (—s, *pl.* ˙e) poster, placard; — *auf das Leben*, attempt at assassination.

Anschlagbrett ['anʃla:kbrɛt], *n.* (—es, *pl.* —er) notice-board.

anschlagen ['anʃla:gən], *v.a. irr.* (*keys of piano or typewriter*) strike, touch; (*knitting*) cast on; *zu hoch* —, over-estimate.

anschließen ['anʃli:sən], *v.a. irr.* fasten with a lock. — *v.a.* join, join in; (*club*) join.

Anschluß ['anʃlus], *m.* (—sses, *pl.* ˙sse) (*Railw., telephone*) connection; (*Pol.*) annexation.

Anschlußpunkt ['anʃluspuŋkt], *m.* (—es, *pl.* —e) junction; (*Elec.*) inlet point, power point.

anschmiegen ['anʃmi:gən], *v.r. sich* —, nestle closely to.

anschmieren ['anʃmi:rən], *v.a. einen* —, (*coll.*) deceive, cheat s.o.

anschnallen ['anʃnalən], *v.a.* buckle on.

anschnauzen ['anʃnautsən], *v.a.* snarl at, snap at.

anschneiden ['anʃnaidən], *v.a. irr.* cut into; *ein Thema* —, broach a subject.

Anschrift ['anʃrift], *f.* (—, *pl.* —en) address.

anschwellen ['anʃvɛlən], *v.n.* (*aux.* sein) swell.

Ansehen ['anze:ən], *n.* (—s, *no pl.*) respect; reputation; authority.

ansehen ['anze:ən], *v.a. irr.* look at *or* upon, consider, regard.

ansehnlich ['anze:nlɪç], *adj.* considerable, appreciable.

anseilen ['anzailən], *v.a.* (*Mount.*) rope together.

ansetzen ['anzɛtsən], *v.a.* join to; (*Maths.*) start, write out (an equation).

Ansicht ['anzɪçt], *f.* (—, *pl.* —en) opinion; view; (*Comm.*) approval.

ansichtig ['anzɪçtɪç], *adj.* — *werden*, get a glimpse of.

Ansichts(post)karte ['anzɪçts(pɔst)-kartə], *f.* (—, *pl.* —n) picture postcard.

ansiedeln ['anzi:dəln], *v.r. sich* —, settle (down), colonize.

Ansinnen ['anzinən], *n.* (—s, *pl.* —) demand, suggestion.

anspannen ['anʃpanən], *v.a.* tighten yoke, stretch; harness.

anspielen ['anʃpi:lən], *v.n.* (*Game, Sport*) lead off; *auf etwas* —, allude to s.th.

Ansporn ['anʃpɔrn], *m.* (—s, *no pl.*) spur, incentive.

Ansprache ['anʃpra:xə], *f.* (—, *pl.* —n) address, speech, talk.

ansprechen ['anʃprɛçən], *v.a. irr.* address, accost; please.

anspringen ['anʃpriŋən], *v.a. irr.* leap at. — *v.n.* (*Motor.*) start.

9

Anspruch ['anʃprux], *m.* (—s, *pl.* ⁓e) (*Law*) claim, title.

anspruchsvoll ['anʃpruxsfɔl], *adj.* demanding, hard to please.

anstacheln ['anʃtaxəln], *v.a.* goad, prod.

Anstalt ['anʃtalt], *f.* (—, *pl.* —en) institution, establishment; —*en treffen*, make arrangements (for).

Anstand ['anʃtant], *m.* (—es, *no pl.*) propriety; politeness, good manners, good grace; decency; (*Hunt.*) stand, butts.

anständig ['anʃtɛndɪç], *adj.* decent, proper, respectable.

Anstandsbesuch ['anʃtantsbəzu:x], *m.* (—es, *pl.* —e) formal visit.

anstandshalber ['anʃtantshalbər], *adv.* for decency's sake.

anstandslos ['anʃtantslo:s], *adv.* unhesitatingly.

anstarren ['anʃtarən], *v.a.* stare at.

anstatt [an'ʃtat], *prep.* (*Genit.*), *conj.* instead of, in lieu of, in the place of.

anstecken ['anʃtɛkən], *v.a.* pin on; set fire to; infect.

Ansteckung ['anʃtɛkuŋ], *f.* (—, *pl.* —en) infection, contagion.

anstehen ['anʃte:ən], *v.n. irr.* stand in a queue; — *lassen*, put off, delay.

ansteigen ['anʃtaɪgən], *v.n. irr.* (*aux.* sein) rise, increase.

anstellen ['anʃtɛlən], *v.a. einen* —, appoint s.o. to a post; employ; *Betrachtungen* —, speculate. — *v.r. sich* —, form a queue, line up.

anstellig ['anʃtɛlɪç], *adj.* able, skilful, adroit.

Anstellung ['anʃtɛluŋ], *f.* (—, *pl.* —en) appointment, employment.

anstiften ['anʃtɪftən], *v.a.* instigate.

anstimmen ['anʃtɪmən], *v.a.* intone.

Anstoß ['anʃto:s], *m.* (—es, *pl.* ⁓e) (*Footb.*) kick-off; — *erregen*, give offence; *den* — *geben zu*, initiate, give an impetus to; *Stein des* —*es*, stumbling block; — *nehmen*, take offence.

anstoßen ['anʃto:sən], *v.a. irr.* knock against, push against; give offence; clink (glasses); border on; *mit der Zunge* —, lisp.

anstößig ['anʃtø:sɪç], *adj.* shocking, offensive.

anstreichen ['anʃtraɪçən], *v.a. irr.* paint; *Fehler* —, mark wrong.

Anstreicher ['anʃtraɪçər], *m.* (—s, *pl.* —) house-painter.

anstrengen ['anʃtrɛŋən], *v.a.* strain exert; *eine Klage gegen einen* —, bring an action against s.o. — *v.r. sich* —, exert o.s.

Anstrengung ['anʃtrɛŋuŋ], *f.* (—, *pl.* —en) exertion, effort.

Anstrich ['anʃtrɪç], *m.* (—s, *pl.* —e) coat of paint.

Ansturm ['anʃturm], *m.* (—s, *no pl.*) attack, assault, charge.

Ansuchen ['anzu:xən], *n.* (—s, *pl.* —) application, request, petition.

ansuchen ['anzu:xən], *v.n. bei einem um etwas* —, apply to s.o. for s.th.

Anteil ['antaɪl], *m.* (—s, *pl.* —e) share, portion; sympathy.

Anteilnahme ['antaɪlna:mə], *f.* (—, *no pl.*) sympathy.

Antenne [an'tɛnə], *f.* (—, *pl.* —n) aerial; antenna.

antik [an'ti:k], *adj.* antique, ancient, classical.

Antike [an'ti:kə], *f.* (—, *pl.* —en) (classical) antiquity; ancient work of art (statue etc.).

Antiquar [anti'kva:r], *m.* (—s, *pl.* —e) second-hand dealer; antiquary.

Antiquariat [antikva'rja:t], *n.* (—s, *pl.* —e) second-hand bookshop.

antiquarisch [anti'kva:rɪʃ], *adj.* antiquarian, second-hand.

Antlitz ['antlɪts], *n.* (—es, *pl.* —e) countenance, (*Poet.*) face.

Antrag ['antra:k], *m.* (—s, *pl.* ⁓e) proposition, proposal, application; *einen* — *stellen*, bring in a motion; make application.

antragen ['antra:gən], *v.a. irr.* propose, make a proposal, offer to.

Antragsformular ['antra:ksfɔrmula:r], *n.* (—s, *pl.* —e) (*Insurance*) proposal form; application form.

Antragsteller ['antra:kʃtɛlər], *m.* (—s, *pl.* —) applicant, mover of a resolution.

antreten ['antre:tən], *v.a. irr. ein Amt* —, enter upon an office; *eine Reise* —, set out on a journey. — *v.n.* (*aux.* sein) (*Mil.*) fall in.

Antrieb ['antri:p], *m.* (—s, *pl.* —e) impulse, motive; incentive; *aus eigenem* —, voluntarily.

Antritt ['antrɪt], *m.* (—s, *no pl.*) start, commencement.

Antrittsvorlesung ['antrɪtsforle:zuŋ], *f.* (*Univ.*) inaugural lecture.

antun ['antu:n], *v.a. irr. einem etwas* —, do s.th. to s.o.

Antwort ['antvɔrt], *f.* (—, *pl.* —en) answer, reply; *abschlägige* —, refusal, rebuff.

antworten ['antvɔrtən], *v.a.* answer, reply to.

anvertrauen ['anfɛrtrauən], *v.a. einem etwas* —, entrust s.o. with s.th.; confide in s.o.

anverwandt ['anfɛrvant] *see* **verwandt**.

Anwalt ['anvalt], *m.* (—s, *pl.* ⁓e) lawyer, barrister, solicitor, attorney, advocate.

anwandeln ['anvandəln], *v.a.* befall.

Anwandlung ['anvandluŋ], *f.* (—, *pl.* —en) fit, turn.

Anwartschaft ['anvartʃaft], *f.* (—, *pl.* —en) (*Law*) reversion; candidacy.

anweisen ['anvaɪzən], *v.a. irr.* instruct, direct; *angewiesen sein auf*, depend upon.

Anweisung ['anvaɪzuŋ], *f.* (—, *pl.* —en) instruction, advice, method; (*Comm.*) voucher, credit voucher, cheque.

anwenden ['anvɛndən], *v.a. irr.* use, make use of, apply.

armselig

anwerben ['anvɛrbən], *v.a. irr.* (*Mil.*) recruit; *sich — lassen*, enlist.

anwesend ['anve:zənt], *adj.* at hand, present.

Anwesenheit ['anve:zənhaɪt], *f.* (—, *no pl.*) presence, attendance.

anwidern ['anvi:dərn], *v.a.* disgust.

Anzahl ['antsa:l], *f.* (—, *no pl.*) number, quantity.

anzahlen ['antsa:lən], *v.a.* pay a deposit.

Anzahlung ['antsa:luŋ], *f.* (—, *pl.* —en) deposit.

Anzeichen ['antsaɪçən], *n.* (—s, *pl.* —) indication, omen.

Anzeige ['antsaɪɡə], *f.* (—, *pl.* —n) notice, (classified) advertisement; denunciation; — *erstatten*, to lay information.

anzeigen ['antsaɪɡən], *v.a.* point out, indicate; announce; notify; advertise; denounce.

Anzeiger ['antsaɪɡər], *m.* (—s, *pl.* —) indicator; (*newspaper*) advertiser.

anzetteln ['antsɛtəln], *v.a.* plot, contrive.

anziehen ['antsi:ən], *v.a. irr.* pull, draw tight, give a tug; attract; stretch; dress; (*screws*) tighten. — *v.r. sich* —, dress, put on o.'s clothes.

anziehend ['antsi:ənt], *adj.* attractive.

Anziehung ['antsi:uŋ], *f.* (—, *no pl.*) attraction.

Anzug ['antsu:k], *m.* (—s, *pl.* ⸚e) (man's) suit; approach.

anzüglich ['antsy:klɪç],*adj.*allusive; suggestive; — *werden*, become offensive.

anzünden ['antsyndən], *v.a.* kindle, ignite.

apart [a'part], *adj.* charming, delightful; (*Am.*) cute.

Apfel ['apfəl], *m.* (—s, *pl.* ⸚) apple.

Apfelmost ['apfəlmɔst], *m.* (—s, *no pl.*) cider.

Apfelsine [apfəl'zi:nə], *f.* (—, *pl.* —n) orange.

Apostel [a'pɔstəl], *m.* (—s, *pl.* —) apostle.

Apotheke [apo'te:kə], *f.* (—, *pl.* —n) dispensary, pharmacy, chemist's shop; (*Am.*) drugstore.

Apparat [apa'ra:t], *m.* (—(e)s, *pl.* —e) apparatus; radio *or* television set; telephone.

appellieren [apɛ'li:rən], *v.n.* — *an*, appeal to.

appetitlich [ape'ti:tlɪç], *adj.* appetising, dainty.

Aprikose [aprɪ'ko:zə], *f.* (—, *pl.* —en) apricot.

Aquarell [akva'rɛl], *n.* (—s, *pl.* —e) water-colour (painting).

Ära ['ɛ:ra], *f.* (—, *no pl.*) era.

Arabien [a'ra:bjən], *n.* Arabia.

Arbeit ['arbaɪt], *f.* (—, *pl.* —en) work, labour; job; employment; workmanship; *an die — gehen*, set to work.

arbeiten ['arbaɪtən], *v.a., v.n.* work, labour, toil.

Arbeiter ['arbaɪtər], *m.* (—s, *pl.* —) worker, workman, labourer, hand.

Arbeiterschaft ['arbaɪtərʃaft], *f.* (—, *no pl.*) working men; workers.

arbeitsam ['arbaɪtza:m], *adj.* industrious, diligent.

Arbeitsamt ['arbaɪtsamt], *n.* (—s, *pl.* ⸚er) labour exchange.

arbeitsfähig ['arbaɪtsfɛ:ɪç], *adj.* capable of working, able-bodied.

arbeitslos ['arbaɪtslo:s], *adj.* unemployed, out of work.

Arbeitslosigkeit ['arbaɪtslo:zɪçkaɪt], *f.* (—, *no pl.*) unemployment.

Arbeitsnachweis ['arbaɪtsnaxvaɪs], *m.* (—es, *no pl.*) labour exchange; (*Am.*) labour registry-office.

Arbeitssperre ['arbaɪtsʃpɛrə], *f.* (—, *pl.* —n) (*Ind.*) lock-out.

Archäologe [arçɛo'lo:ɡə], *m.* (—n, *pl.* —n) archaeologist.

Arche ['arçə], *f.* (—, *pl.* —n) ark.

Archipel [arçi'pe:l], *m.* (—s, *pl.* —e) archipelago.

architektonisch [arçitɛk'to:nɪʃ], *adj.* architectural.

Archivar [arçi'va:r], *m.* (—s, *pl.* —e) keeper of archives.

arg [ark], *adj.* bad, wicked, mischievous.

Argentinien [arɡən'ti:njən], *n.* Argentina.

Ärger ['ɛrɡər], *m.* (—s, *no pl.*) anger, annoyance.

ärgerlich ['ɛrɡərlɪç], *adj.* annoying, aggravating, vexing; angry.

ärgern ['ɛrɡərn], *v.a.* annoy, vex, make angry. — *v.r. sich* —, get annoyed.

Ärgernis ['ɛrɡərnɪs], *n.* (—ses, *pl.* —se) scandal, nuisance.

arglistig ['arklɪstɪç], *adj.* crafty, sly.

arglos ['arklo:s], *adj.* unsuspecting, guileless, naive.

Argwohn ['arkvo:n], *m.* (—s, *no pl.*) mistrust, suspicion.

argwöhnisch ['arkvø:nɪʃ], *adj.* suspicious, distrustful.

Arie ['a:rjə], *f.* (—, *pl.* —n) (*Mus.*) aria.

Arm [arm], *m.* (—s, *pl.* —e) arm.

arm [arm], *adj.* poor, indigent, needy.

Armaturenbrett [arma'tu:rənbrɛt], *n.* (—s, *pl.* —e) dashboard.

Armband ['armbant], *n.* (—s, *pl.* ⸚er) bracelet.

Armbanduhr ['armbantu:r], *f.* (—, *pl.* —en) wrist-watch.

Armbrust ['armbrust], *f.* (—, *pl.* —e) cross-bow.

Ärmel ['ɛrməl], *m.* (—s, *pl.* —) sleeve.

Ärmelkanal ['ɛrməlkana:l], *m.* (—s, *no pl.*) English Channel.

Armenien [ar'me:njən], *n.* Armenia.

Armenhaus [ar'mənhaus], *n.* (—es, *pl.* ⸚er) poor-house, almshouse.

Armenpfleger ['armənpfle:ɡər], *m.* (—s, *pl.* —) almoner.

Armesündermiene [armə'zyndərmi:nə], *f.* (—, *pl.* —n) hangdog look.

ärmlich ['ɛrmlɪç], *adj.* poor, shabby, scanty.

armselig ['armze:lɪç], *adj.* poor, miserable, wretched; paltry.

11

Armut

Armut ['armu:t], *f.* (—, *no pl.*) poverty; *in — geraten*, be reduced to penury.

Arsch [arʃ], *m.* (—es, ¨e) (*vulg.*) arse.

Arsen(ik) [ar'ze:n(ɪk)], *n.* (—s, *no pl.*) arsenic.

Art [a:rt], *f.* (—, *pl.* —en) kind, species; race; sort; method, way, manner.

artig ['a:rtɪç], *adj.* well-behaved, civil.

Artigkeit ['a:rtɪçkaɪt], *f.* (—, *pl.* —en) politeness, courtesy.

Artikel [ar'ti:kəl], *m.* (—s, *pl.* —) article; commodity.

Artist [ar'tɪst], *m.* (—en, *pl.* —en) artiste (circus, variety).

Arznei [arts'naɪ], *f.* (—, *pl.* —en) medicine.

Arzneimittel [arts'naɪmɪtəl], *n.* (—s, *pl.*—) medicine, drug.

Arzt [artst], *m.* (—es, *pl.* ¨e) doctor, physician; *praktischer —*, general practitioner.

ärztlich ['ertstlɪç], *adj.* medical.

As (1) [as], *n.* (—ses, *pl.* —se) (*Mus.*) A flat; — *Dur*, A flat major, — *Moll*, A flat minor.

As (2) [as], *n.* (—sses, *pl.* —sse) (*Sport, cards*) ace.

Asbest [as'best], *m.* (—s, *no pl.*) asbestos.

Asche ['aʃə], *f.* (—, *no pl.*) ashes.

Aschenbecher ['aʃənbeçər], *m.* (—s, *pl.* —) ash-tray.

Aschenbrödel ['aʃənbrø:dəl]*or* **Aschenputtel** ['aʃənputəl], *n.* Cinderella.

Aschkraut ['aʃkraut], *n.* (—s, *pl.* ¨er) (*Bot.*) cineraria.

Askese [as'ke:zə], *f.* (—, *no pl.*) asceticism.

Asket [as'ke:t], *m.* (—en, *pl.* —en) ascetic.

Assessor [a'scsɔr], *m.* (—s, *pl.* —en) assistant; assistant judge.

Ast [ast], *m.* (—es, *pl.* ¨e) branch, bough.

Aster ['astər], *f.* (—, *pl.* —n) (*Bot.*) aster.

Astronaut [astro'naut], *m.* (—en, *pl.*—en) astronaut.

Astronom [astro'no:m], *m.* (—en, *pl.* —en) astronomer.

Asyl [a'zy:l], *n.* (—s, *pl.* —e) asylum, sanctuary.

Atem ['a:təm], *m.* (—s, *no pl.*) breath, breathing, respiration.

Atemzug ['a:təmtsu:k], *m.* (—s, *pl.* ¨e) breath.

Äthiopien [eti'o:pjən], *n.* Ethiopia.

Atlas (1) ['atlas], *m.* (—sses, *pl.* —sse *and* **Atlanten**) atlas, book of maps.

Atlas (2) ['atlas], *m.* (—sses, *pl.* —sse) satin.

atmen ['a:tmən], *v.n.* breathe.

atomar [ato'ma:r], *adj.* atomic.

Attentat [atɛn'ta:t], *n.* (—s, *pl.* —e) attempt on s.o.'s life.

Attest [a'test], *n.* (—s, *pl.* —e) (*Med.*) certificate.

ätzen ['ɛtsən], *v.a.* corrode; (*Art*) etch; (*Med.*) cauterise.

auch [aux], *conj.*, *adv.* also, too, likewise, as well.

Au(e) ['au(ə)], *f.* (—, *pl.* —en) green meadow, pasture.

auf [auf], *prep.* on, upon; — *der Straße*, in the road; — *deine Gefahr*, at your own risk; — *Befehl*, by order; — *einige Tage*, for a few days; — *dem Lande*, in the country; — *keinen Fall*, on no account.

aufatmen ['aufa:tmən], *v.n.* breathe a sigh of relief.

Aufbau ['aufbau], *m.* (—s, *no pl.*) building; (*Lit.*) composition, structure.

aufbauen ['aufbauən], *v.a.* erect, build, construct.

aufbäumen ['aufbɔymən], *v.r. sich —*, (horses) rear.

aufbewahren ['aufbəva:rən], *v.a.* keep, store; (*luggage*) take charge of.

Aufbewahrung ['aufbəva:ruŋ], *f.* (—, *pl.* —en) storage, safe keeping.

aufbieten ['aufbi:tən], *v.a. irr.* call up for service; exert (energies).

aufbinden ['aufbɪndən], *v.a. irr.* untie; *einem einen Bären —*, to hoax s.o.

aufblähen ['aufblɛ:ən], *v.a.* puff up, swell, inflate.

aufblühen ['aufbly:ən], *v.n.* (aux. sein) flourish, unfold.

aufbrausen ['aufbrauzən], *v.n.* (aux. sein) fly into a rage.

aufbringen ['aufbrɪŋən], *v.a. irr.* bring up; afford; annoy (s.o.).

Aufbruch ['aufbrux], *m.* (—s, *no pl.*) departure.

aufbürden ['aufbyrdən], *v.a. einem eine Last —*, burden s.o. with a thing.

aufdecken ['aufdɛkən], *v.a.* uncover, unveil.

aufdonnern ['aufdɔnərn], *v.r. sich —* dress up showily.

aufdrängen ['aufdrɛŋən], *v.a. einem etwas —*, press s.th. upon s.o. — *v.r. sich —*, force o.'s company on.

aufdrehen ['aufdre:ən], *v.a.* (tap) turn on.

aufdringlich ['aufdrɪŋlɪç], *adj.* importunate, officious, obtrusive.

Aufdruck ['aufdruk], *m.* (—s, *pl.* —e) imprint.

aufdrücken ['aufdrykən], *v.a.* press open; press on s.th.

Aufenthalt ['aufɛnthalt], *m.* (—s, *pl.* —e) stay, sojourn; delay; stop.

auferlegen ['auferle:gən], *v.a.* impose; enjoin.

auferstehen ['auferʃte:ən], *v.n. irr.* (aux. sein) (Rel.) rise from the dead.

auffahren ['auffa:rən], *v.n. irr.* (aux. sein) start (from o.'s sleep); mount; flare up (in anger).

Auffahrt ['auffa:rt], *f.* (—, *pl.* —en) ascent; approach to a house, drive.

auffallen ['auffalən], *v.n. irr.* (aux. sein) strike the ground; *einem —*, strike s.o., astonish.

auffangen ['auffaŋən], *v.a. irr.* (ball) catch; (blow) parry, ward off; (letter) intercept.

auffassen ['auffasən], *v.a.* take in, comprehend.

Auffassung ['auffasuŋ], *f.* (—, *pl.* —**en**) conception, interpretation; view.
aufflackern ['aufflakərn], *v.n.* (*aux.* sein) flare up, flicker.
auffordern ['auffɔrdərn], *v.a.* summon, request, ask, invite.
aufforsten ['auffɔrstən], *v.a.* afforest.
auffressen ['auffrɛsən], *v.a. irr.* devour; (*of animals*) eat up.
auffrischen ['auffrɪʃən], *v.a.* renew, redecorate; (*fig.*) brush up.
aufführen ['auffy:rən], *v.a.* (*Theat.*) perform; *einzeln* —, specify, particularise. — *v.r. sich* —, behave, conduct o.s.
Aufführung ['auffy:ruŋ], *f.* (—, *pl.* —**en**) (*Theat.*) performance.
Aufgabe ['aufga:bə], *f.* (—, *pl.* —**n**) giving up, abandonment; (*letters, telegrams*) posting, despatch; (*work*) task; (*Sch.*) exercise; (*Maths.*) problem.
aufgabeln ['aufga:bəln], *v.a.* (*sl.*) pick up.
Aufgang ['aufgaŋ], *m.* (—**s**, *pl.* ⸚**e**) ascent, stairs.
aufgeben ['aufge:bən], *v.a. irr.* give up, abandon, relinquish; (*Am.*) quit; (*luggage*) check.
aufgeblasen ['aufgəbla:zən], *adj.* conceited, stuck up.
Aufgebot ['aufgəbo:t], *n.* (—**s**, *pl.* —**e**) (*marriage*) banns; (*Mil.*) levy; *mit* — *aller Kräfte*, with the utmost exertion.
aufgebracht ['aufgəbraxt], *adj.* angry, annoyed.
aufgedunsen ['aufgədunzən], *adj.* bloated, sodden.
aufgehen ['aufge:ən], *v.n. irr.* (*aux.* sein) (*knot*) come undone; (*sun*) rise; (*dough*) swell, rise; (*Maths.*) leave no remainder, cancel out.
aufgehoben ['aufgəho:bən], *adj. gut* — *sein*, be in good hands.
aufgelegt ['aufgəle:kt], *adj.* disposed, inclined.
aufgeräumt ['aufgərɔymt], *adj.* merry, cheerful, in high spirits.
aufgeweckt ['aufgəvɛkt], *adj.* bright, clever, intelligent.
aufgießen ['aufgi:sən], *v.a. irr. Kaffee* —, make coffee.
aufgreifen ['aufgraɪfən], *v.a. irr.* seize.
Aufguß ['aufgus], *m.* (—**sses**, *pl.* ⸚**sse**) infusion.
aufhalsen ['aufhalzən], *v.a. einem etwas* —, (*coll.*) saddle s.o. with s.th.
aufhalten ['aufhaltən], *v.a. irr.* (*door*) hold open; *einen* —, delay s.o. — *v.r. sich an einem Ort* —, stay at a place; *sich über etwas* —, find fault with s.th.
aufhängen ['aufhɛŋən], *v.a. irr.* hang (up).
aufhäufen ['aufhɔyfən], *v.a.* pile up. — *v.r. sich* —, accumulate.
Aufheben ['aufhe:bən], *n.* (—**s**, *no pl.*) lifting up; ado; *viel* —*s machen*, make a great fuss.
aufheben ['aufhe:bən], *v.a. irr.* lift (up), pick up; keep, preserve; (*laws*) repeal, abolish; (*agreements*) rescind, annul.
Aufhebung ['aufhe:buŋ], *f.* (—, *pl.* —**en**) abolition, abrogation, annulment, repeal.
aufheitern ['aufhaɪtərn], *v.a.* cheer up; amuse. — *v.r. sich* —, (*weather*) brighten, clear up.
aufhelfen ['aufhɛlfən], *v.n. irr. einem* —, help s.o. up.
aufhellen ['aufhɛlən], *v.r. sich* —, (*weather*) clear up; (*face*) brighten up.
aufhetzen ['aufhɛtsən], *v.a.* rouse (s.o.); *einen* — *gegen*, incite s.o. against.
aufhorchen ['aufhɔrçən], *v.n.* prick up o.'s ears.
aufhören ['aufhø:rən], *v.n.* cease, stop; (*Am.*) quit; *ohne aufzuhören*, incessantly; *da hört sich doch alles auf!* that is the limit!
aufklären ['aufklɛ:rən], *v.a.* enlighten; clear up; *einen* —, enlighten s.o. — *v.r. sich* —, (*weather*) brighten.
Aufklärung ['aufklɛ:ruŋ], *f.* (—, *no pl.*) (age of) Enlightenment.
aufknacken ['aufknakən], *v.a.* crack (open).
aufknöpfen ['aufknœpfən], *v.a.* unbutton; *aufgeknöpft sein*, be in a talkative mood.
aufkommen ['aufkɔmən], *v.n. irr.* (*aux.* sein) come into use, spring up; *für etwas* —, pay for s.th.; *einen nicht* — *lassen*, give s.o. no chance.
aufkrempeln ['aufkrɛmpəln], *v.a.* (*coll.*) roll up (o.'s sleeves).
aufkündigen ['aufkyndɪgən], *v.a.* (*money*) recall; *einem die Freundschaft* —, break with s.o.
Auflage ['aufla:gə], *f.* (—, *pl.* —**n**) (*tax*) impost, duty, levy; (*book*) edition, impression; circulation.
auflassen ['auflasən], *v.a. irr.* leave open; (*Law*) cede.
auflauern ['auflauərn], *v.n. einem* —, lie in wait for s.o., waylay s.o.
Auflauf ['auflauf], *m.* (—**s**, *pl.* ⸚**e**) tumult, noisy street gathering; soufflé.
auflaufen ['auflaufən], *v.n. irr.* (*aux.* sein) swell, increase; (*ship*) run aground.
aufleben ['aufle:bən], *v.n.* (*aux.* sein) *wieder* —, revive.
auflegen ['aufle:gən], *v.a. irr.* lay upon, put on; (*book*) publish; (*tax, punishment*) impose, inflict.
auflehnen ['aufle:nən], *v.r. sich gegen einen* (or *etwas*) —, rebel against, mutiny, oppose.
auflesen ['aufle:zən], *v.a. irr.* pick up, gather.
aufleuchten ['auflɔyçtən], *v.n.* light up; (*eyes*) shine.
auflockern ['auflɔkərn], *v.a.* loosen.
auflodern ['auflo:dərn], *v.n.* (*aux.* sein) flare up, blaze up.

auflösen

auflösen [ˈauflø:zən], v.a. dissolve, loosen; (puzzle) solve, guess; (meeting) break up; (business) wind up; (partnership) dissolve; (army) disband. — v.r. sich —, melt, dissolve, be broken up.

aufmachen [ˈaufmaxən], v.a. (door, packet) open; (knot) undo; gut —, pack nicely. — v.r. sich —, get going, set out for.

Aufmachung [ˈaufmaxuŋ], f. (—, pl. —en) outward appearance, make-up, get-up.

Aufmarsch [ˈaufmarʃ], m. (—es, pl. ⁓e) (Mil.) parade.

aufmerksam [ˈaufmɛrkza:m], adj. attentive, observant; civil, kind; einen — machen auf, draw s.o.'s attention to.

aufmuntern [ˈaufmuntərn], v.a. encourage, cheer up.

Aufnahme [ˈaufna:mə], f. (—, pl. —n) reception; (Phot.) snap, photograph; (Geog.) mapping out, survey; (Mus.) recording.

aufnehmen [ˈaufne:mən], v.a. irr. take up; receive, give shelter to; (Phot.) photograph, film; (Mus.) record; (money) raise, borrow; (minutes) draw up; den Faden wieder —, take up the thread; die Arbeit wieder —, return to work, resume work; die Fährte —, (Hunt.) recover the scent; es mit einem —, be a match for s.o.; (Comm.) Inventar —, take stock, draw up an inventory.

aufnötigen [ˈaufnø:tɪgən], v.a. einem etwas —, force s.th. upon s.o.

aufpassen [ˈaufpasən], v.n. attend to, pay attention to, take notice of, take care of.

aufpeitschen [ˈaufpaɪtʃən], v.a. whip up.

aufpflanzen [ˈaufpflantsən], v.a. mount, erect. — v.r. sich vor einem —, plant o.s. in front of s.o.; mit aufgepflanztem Bajonett, with bayonets fixed.

Aufputz [ˈaufputs], m. (—es, no pl.) finery, trimmings.

aufraffen [ˈaufrafən], v.a. snatch up, rake up. — v.r. sich wieder —, pull o.s. together.

aufräumen [ˈaufrɔymən], v.a. put in order, clear away; (room) tidy up; mit etwas —, make a clean sweep of s.th.; aufgeräumt sein, be in a jolly mood.

aufrechnen [ˈaufrɛçnən], v.a. reckon up; set off against.

aufrecht [ˈaufrɛçt], adj. upright, erect; etwas — erhalten, maintain s.th.; (opinion) stick to, adhere to, uphold.

Aufrechterhaltung [ˈaufrɛçtərhaltuŋ], f. (—, no pl.) maintenance, preservation.

aufregen [ˈaufre:gən], v.a. excite, enrage.

aufreiben [ˈaufraɪbən], v.a. irr. rub sore; (Mil.) destroy, wipe out. — v.r. sich —, exhaust o.s. with worry (or work).

aufreizen [ˈaufraɪtsən], v.a. incite, provoke.

aufrichten [ˈaufrɪçtən], v.a. raise, erect, set upright; (fig.) comfort, console. — v.r. sich —, rise, sit up.

aufrichtig [ˈaufrɪçtɪç], adj. sincere, frank.

aufriegeln [ˈaufri:gəln], v.a. unbolt.

Aufriß [ˈaufrɪs], m. (—sses, pl. —sse) sketch, draft; (Archit.) elevation, section.

aufrücken [ˈaufrykən], v.n. (aux. sein) rise, be promoted (in rank), advance.

Aufruf [ˈaufru:f], m. (—s, pl. —e) summons, proclamation, appeal; (Law) citation.

aufrufen [ˈaufru:fən], v.a. irr. summons; (Sch.) call upon.

Aufruhr [ˈaufru:r], m. (—s, pl. —e) uproar, riot, tumult, rebellion, mutiny.

aufrühren [ˈaufry:rən], v.a. stir up, agitate, rouse to rebellion.

Aufrüstung [ˈaufrystuŋ], f. (—, no pl.) (Mil.) (re-)armament.

aufrütteln [ˈaufrytəln], v.a. rouse, shake s.o. out of his lethargy.

aufsagen [ˈaufza:gən], v.a. recite.

aufsässig [ˈaufzɛsɪç], adj. refractory, rebellious.

Aufsatz [ˈaufzats], m. (—es, pl. ⁓e) top, head-piece, table centre-piece; (Sch.) composition, essay; (newspaper) article.

aufscheuchen [ˈaufʃɔyçən], v.a. flush (game), startle.

aufschichten [ˈaufʃɪçtən], v.a. stack, pile up in layers.

aufschieben [ˈaufʃi:bən], v.a. irr. push open; delay, postpone, adjourn; (Parl.) prorogue.

Aufschlag [ˈaufʃla:k], m. (—s, pl. ⁓e) impact, striking; (sleeve) cuff; turn-up; (uniform) facings; (Comm.) increase in price; (Tennis) service.

aufschlagen [ˈaufʃla:gən], v.n. irr. (aux. sein) hit, strike (open); (Tennis) serve. — v.a. die Augen —, open o.s eyes; ein Lager —, pitch camp; ein Buch —, open a book.

aufschlitzen [ˈaufʃlɪtsən], v.a. rip open, slit open.

Aufschluß [ˈaufʃlus], m. (—sses, pl. ⁓sse) disclosure, information.

aufschneiden [ˈaufʃnaɪdən], v.a. irr. cut open. — v.n. brag, boast.

Aufschneider [ˈaufʃnaɪdər], m. (-s, pl. —) swaggerer, braggart.

Aufschnitt [ˈaufʃnɪt], m. (—s, no pl.) slice of cold meat or sausage.

aufschnüren [ˈaufʃny:rən], v.a. unlace, untie.

Aufschrei [ˈaufʃraɪ], m. (—s, pl. —e) outcry, screech, scream, shout, shriek.

Aufschrift [ˈaufʃrɪft], f. (—, pl. —en) inscription, address; heading.

Aufschub [ˈaufʃu:p], m. (—s, pl. ⁓e) delay, adjournment, postponement.

aufschütten [ˈaufʃytən], v.a. (liquid) pour upon; (dam) raise.

aufschwingen ['aufʃvɪŋən], v.r. irr. sich —, soar, rise; ich kann mich dazu nicht —, I cannot rise to that.

Aufschwung ['aufʃvʊŋ], m. (—s, no pl.) flight, rising; (Comm.) improvement, boom.

Aufsehen ['aufze:ən], n. (—s, no pl.) sensation, stir.

Aufseher ['aufze:ər], m. (—s, pl. —) overseer, inspector.

aufsein ['aufzaɪn], v.n. irr. (aux. sein) be out of bed, be up and about.

aufsetzen ['aufzɛtsən], v.a. (hat) put on; (letter, essay) draft.

Aufsicht ['aufzɪçt], f. (—, no pl.) inspection, supervision, control.

Aufsichtsrat ['aufzɪçtsra:t], m. (—s, pl. ⁓e) (Comm.) board of directors.

aufsitzen ['aufzɪtsən], v.n. irr. sit up, wait up at night; (horse) mount.

aufspannen ['aufʃpanən], v.a. (umbrella) put up; (tent) pitch.

aufspeichern ['aufʃpaɪçərn], v.a. store (up), warehouse.

aufsperren ['aufʃpɛrən], v.a. open wide, unlock.

aufspielen ['aufʃpi:lən], v.n. zum Tanz —, play music for dancing. — v.r. sich groß —, give o.s. airs.

aufspießen ['aufʃpi:sən], v.a. pierce on a spit; (joint) skewer.

aufspringen ['aufʃprɪŋən], v.n. irr. (aux. sein) leap up, jump up; (door) fly open; (hands in winter) chap.

aufspüren ['aufʃpy:rən], v.a. track, trace.

aufstacheln ['aufʃtaxəln], v.a. goad, incite.

Aufstand ['aufʃtant], m. (—s, pl. ⁓e) insurrection, revolt, sedition.

aufstapeln ['aufʃta:pəln], v.a. pile up, stack, store.

aufstechen ['aufʃtɛçən], v.a. irr. (Med.) lance.

aufstehen ['aufʃte:ən], v.n. irr. (aux. sein) (door) stand open; stand up; get up (from bed); rise (from a chair).

aufstellen ['aufʃtɛlən], v.a. set up, arrange; erect; (Pol.) put forward (candidate).

Aufstellung ['aufʃtɛlʊŋ], f. (—, pl. —en) arrangement; statement; inventory; (Pol.) nomination.

aufstemmen ['aufʃtɛmən], v.a. prise open.

Aufstieg ['aufʃti:k], m. (—s, pl. ⁓e) ascent, rise.

aufstöbern ['aufʃtø:bərn], v.a. stir (up); start; (fig.) discover, ferret out.

aufstoßen ['aufʃto:sən], v.a. irr. push open; bump against. — v.n. belch.

aufstreben ['aufʃtre:bən], v.n. soar; (fig.) aspire.

aufstreichen ['aufʃtraɪçən], v.a. irr. (paint) lay on; (butter) spread.

aufstülpen ['aufʃtylpən], v.a. turn up; (hat) clap on o.'s head.

auftakeln ['aufta:kəln], v.a. (Naut.) rig.

Auftakt ['auftakt], m. (—s, pl. ⁓e) (Mus.) arsis; (fig.) opening, prelude.

auftauchen ['auftauxən], v.n. (aux. sein) appear, emerge, surface.

auftauen ['auftauən], v.n. (aux. sein) thaw; (fig.) lose o.'s reserve.

auftischen ['auftɪʃən], v.a. dish up.

Auftrag ['auftra:k], m. (—s, pl. ⁓e) assignment, commission, errand; im — von, on behalf of.

auftragen ['auftra:gən], v.a. irr. (food) serve up; (paint) apply; einem etwas —, charge s.o. with a job; stark —, lay it on thick.

auftreiben ['auftraɪbən], v.a. irr. raise (money); procure, obtain. — v.n. (aux. sein) (ship) run aground.

auftrennen ['auftrɛnən], v.a. unstitch; (hem) unpick.

Auftreten ['auftre:tən], n. (—s, no pl.) (Theat.) appearance; behaviour.

auftreten ['auftre:tən], v.n. irr. (aux. sein) tread upon, step upon; (Theat.) appear, come on; energisch —, take strong measures, put o.'s foot down.

Auftritt ['auftrɪt], m. (—s, pl. ⁓e) (Theat.) scene; altercation, row.

auftun ['auftu:n], v.a. irr. open; den Mund —, speak. — v.r. sich —, (abyss) yawn.

auftürmen ['auftyrmən], v.a. pile up, heap up. — v.r. sich —, tower.

aufwachen ['aufvaxən], v.n. (aux. sein) awake, wake up.

aufwallen ['aufvalən], v.n. (aux. sein) boil up, bubble up, rage.

Aufwand ['aufvant], m. (—s, no pl.) expense, expenditure; sumptuousness.

aufwarten ['aufvartən], v.n. wait upon, attend on.

aufwärts ['aufvɛrts], adv. upward(s), aloft.

Aufwartung ['aufvartʊŋ], f. (—, pl. —en) attendance; seine — machen, pay a (formal) visit.

aufwaschen ['aufvaʃən], v.a. irr. wash the dishes.

aufweisen ['aufvaɪzən], v.a. irr. show, produce.

aufwenden ['aufvɛndən], v.a. irr. spend upon, expend upon.

aufwickeln ['aufvɪkəln], v.a. wind up; unwind.

aufwiegeln ['aufvi:gəln], v.a. stir up, incite to rebellion.

aufwiegen ['aufvi:gən], v.a. irr. outweigh, counter-balance, make up for.

aufwischen ['aufvɪʃən], v.a. wipe away, mop up.

aufwühlen ['aufvy:lən], v.a. dig, root up, (fig.) stir.

aufzählen ['auftse:lən], v.a. count up, enumerate, list.

aufzäumen ['auftsɔymən], v.a. bridle (horses).

aufzehren ['auftse:rən], v.a. eat up, consume.

aufzeichnen ['auftsaɪçnən], v.a. write down, take a note of, record.

15

aufziehen ['auftsi:ən], *v.a. irr.* draw up, pull up; pull open; (*pennant*) hoist; (*clock*) wind up; (*child*) bring up, rear; *einen* —, tease s.o.; *gelindere Saiten* —, be more lenient.

Aufzucht ['auftsuxt], *f.* (—, *no pl.*) breeding, rearing.

Aufzug ['auftsu:k], *m.* (—s, *pl.* ⸚e) lift; (*Am.*) elevator; (*Theat.*) act; dress, array, attire.

aufzwingen ['auftsvɪŋən], *v.a. irr. einem etwas* —, force s.th. on s.o.

Augapfel ['aukapfəl], *m.* (—s, *pl.* ⸚) eye-ball; (*fig.*) apple of o.'s eye.

Auge ['augə], *n.* (—s, *pl.* —n) eye; *aus den* —*n, aus dem Sinn,* out of sight, out of mind; *mit einem blauen* — *davonkommen,* escape by the skin of o.'s teeth, get off cheaply; *es wird mir schwarz vor den* —*n,* I feel faint.

Augenblick ['augənblɪk], *m.* (—s, *pl.* —e) moment, instant; *jeden* —, at any moment.

augenblicklich [augən'blɪklɪç], *adj.* momentary, instantaneous.— *adv.* at present, for the moment, immediately.

Augenbraue ['augənbrauə], *f.* (—, *pl.* —n) eye-brow.

augenfällig ['augənfɛlɪç], *adj.* visible, evident, conspicuous.

Augenglas ['augənglas], *n.* (—es, *pl.* ⸚er) eye-glass.

Augenhöhle ['augənhø:lə], *f.* (—, *pl.* —n) eye-socket.

Augenlicht ['augənlɪçt], *n.* (—s, *no pl.*) eye-sight.

Augenlid ['augənli:t], *n.* (—s, *pl.* —er) eye-lid.

Augenmaß ['augənma:s], *n.* (—es, *no pl.*) *gutes* —, good measuring ability with the eye, a sure eye.

Augenmerk ['augənmɛrk], *n.* (—s, *no pl.*) attention; *sein* — *auf etwas richten,* focus o.'s attention on s.th.

Augenschein ['augənʃain], *m.* (—s, *no pl.*) appearance; *in* — *nehmen,* view.

augenscheinlich ['augənʃainlɪç], *adj.* apparent, evident.

Augenweide ['augənvaidə], *f.* (—, *pl.* —n) delight to the eye, s.th. lovely to look at.

Augenwimper ['augənvimpər], *f.* (—, *pl.* —n) eye-lash.

Augenzeuge ['augəntsɔygə], *m.* (—n, *pl.* —n) eye-witness.

August [au'gust], *m.* (—s, *no pl.*) (*month*) August.

Augustiner [augus'ti:nər], *m.* (—s, *pl.* —) (*Eccl.*) Augustinian.

auktionieren [auktsjo'ni:rən], *v.a.* auction(eer), sell by auction.

Aula ['aula], *f.* (—, *pl.* —len) (*Sch., Univ.*) great hall; auditorium maximum.

Aurikel [au'ri:kəl], *f.* (—, *pl.* —n) (*Bot.*) auricula.

aus [aus], *prep.* (*Dat.*) from, out of, of, off. — *adv.* out, over, finished, done with, spent; *es ist alles* —, it is over and done with; *ich weiß weder ein noch* —, I am at my wits' end.

ausarten ['ausartən], *v.n.* (*aux.* sein) degenerate; (*fig.*) deteriorate.

Ausbau ['ausbau], *m.* (—s, *no pl.*) enlargement, extension.

ausbauen ['ausbauən], *v.a.* enlarge (a house); improve on.

ausbedingen ['ausbədɪŋən], *v.a. sich etwas* —, stipulate.

ausbessern ['ausbɛsərn], *v.a.* (*garment*) mend, repair.

Ausbeute ['ausbɔytə], *f.* (—, *no pl.*) gain, profit, produce.

Ausbeutung ['ausbɔytuŋ], *f.* (—, *no pl.*) exploitation, sweating; (*Min.*) working.

ausbezahlen ['ausbətsa:lən], *v.a.* pay in full.

ausbilden ['ausbɪldən], *v.a.* develop, train; (*Mil.*) drill.

Ausbildung ['ausbɪlduŋ], *f.* (—, *pl.* —en) training, education.

ausbleiben ['ausblaibən], *v.n. irr.* (*aux.* sein) fail to appear, be absent.

Ausblick ['ausblɪk], *m.* (—s, *pl.* —e) view (from window); (*fig.*) prospect, outlook.

ausborgen ['ausbɔrgən], *v.a.* (*sich*) *etwas* —, borrow s.th. from.

ausbreiten ['ausbraitən], *v.a.* spread (things); stretch out (o.'s arms). — *v.r. sich* —, spread, extend.

Ausbreitung ['ausbraituŋ], *f.* (—, *no pl.*) spreading, extension, distribution, expansion.

ausbringen ['ausbrɪŋən], *v.a. irr. einen Toast auf einen* —, drink s.o.'s health.

Ausbruch ['ausbrux], *m.* (—s, *pl.* ⸚e) breaking out, outbreak, eruption, burst (of laughter).

ausbrüten ['ausbry:tən], *v.a.* hatch; (*fig.*) plot.

Ausbund ['ausbunt], *m.* (—s, *pl.* ⸚e) paragon, embodiment.

Ausdauer ['ausdauər], *f.* (—, *no pl.*) perseverance, persistence, stamina.

ausdehnen ['ausde:nən], *v.a.* extend, stretch, distend; (*fig.*) prolong, protract. — *v.r. sich* —, expand, extend, stretch.

Ausdehnung ['ausde:nuŋ], *f.* (—, *pl.* —en) extension, expansion; dilation; (*Phys.*) dimension.

ausdenken ['ausdɛŋkən], *v.a. irr.* think out. — *v.r. sich etwas* —, devise s.th., invent s.th.; *das ist gar nicht auszudenken,* that is unimaginable, inconceivable.

Ausdeutung ['ausdɔytuŋ], *f.* (—, *pl.* —en) interpretation, explanation.

ausdörren ['ausdœrən], *v.a.* parch, dry (up).

ausdrehen ['ausdre:ən], *v.a.* (*gas, light, water*) turn off, switch off.

Ausdruck ['ausdruk], *m.* (—s, *pl.* ⸚e) expression, phrase.

ausdrücken ['ausdrykən], *v.a.* squeeze out, press out; (*fig.*) express.

ausdrücklich ['ausdryklɪç], *adj.* express, explicit.

Ausdrucksweise [ˈausdruksvaɪzə], *f.* (—, *pl.* **—n**) enunciation, manner of speech, (mode of) expression, style.

ausdünsten [ˈausdynstən], *v.a.* exhale, perspire.

auseinander [ausaɪnˈandər], *adv.* asunder, apart.

Auseinandersetzung [ausaɪnˈandərzetzuŋ], *f.* (—, *pl.* **—en**) altercation; discussion, explanation.

auserkoren [ˈausɛrkoːrən], *adj.* elect, chosen, selected.

auserlesen [ˈausɛrleːzən], *adj.* choice, picked, excellent, first class.

auserwählen [ˈausɛrvɛːlən], *v.a.* choose, select.

Ausfahrt [ˈausfaːrt], *f.* (—, *pl.* **—en**) drive; gateway; exit.

Ausfall [ˈausfal], *m.* (—s, *pl.* ⁻e) falling out; (*radioactivity*) fall-out; sortie, sally; deficiency, loss, cancellation; · result, outcome.

ausfallen [ˈausfalən], *v.n. irr.* (*aux.* sein) drop out, fall out; be cancelled, be omitted, fail to take place; turn out (well etc.).

ausfallend [ˈausfalənt], *adj.* offensive, abusive; — *werden,* become insulting.

ausfertigen [ˈausfɛrtɪgən], *v.a.* despatch, draw up, make out, issue.

ausfindig [ˈausfɪndɪç], *adj.* — *machen,* find out, locate, discover.

ausflicken [ˈausflɪkən], *v.a.* mend, patch.

Ausflucht [ˈausfluxt], *f.* (—, *pl.* ⁻e) evasion, excuse, subterfuge.

Ausflug [ˈausfluːk], *m.* (—s, *pl.* ⁻e) trip, excursion, outing.

Ausfluß [ˈausflus], *m.* (—sses, *pl.* ⁻sse) (*Engin.*) outflow, outlet; (*Med.*) discharge, suppuration.

ausfragen [ˈausfraːgən], *v.a. einen* —, question, quiz s.o.

Ausfuhr [ˈausfuːr], *f.* (—, *pl.* **—en**) export.

ausführbar [ˈausfyːrbaːr], *adj.* practicable, feasible; exportable.

ausführen [ˈausfyːrən], *v.a.* take out; lead out; export; carry out, perform, fulfil; point out.

ausführlich [ausˈfyːrlɪç], *adj.* detailed, full.

Ausführung [ˈausfyːruŋ], *f.* (—, *pl.* **—en**) execution, carrying out; finish; workmanship.

ausfüllen [ˈausfylən], *v.a.* (*forms*) fill up, fill in, complete.

ausfüttern [ˈausfytərn], *v.a.* line (a dress).

Ausgabe [ˈausgaːbə], *f.* (—, *pl.* **—en**) issue, distribution; (*goods*) dispatch, issuing counter; delivery; (*book*) edition; (*pl.*) expenses, expenditure.

Ausgang [ˈausgaŋ], *m.* (—s, *pl.* ⁻e) going out; exit; result, upshot; end, conclusion; time off (from duty).

Ausgangspunkt [ˈausgaŋspuŋkt], *m.* (—s, *pl.* **—e**) starting-point; point of departure.

ausgären [ˈausgɛːrən], *v.n. irr.* (*aux.* sein) ferment; *ausgegoren sein,* have fermented.

ausgeben [ˈausgeːbən], *v.a. irr.* (*work*) give out, distribute; (*money*) expend, spend; (*tickets*) issue. —*v.r. sich — für,* pass o.s. off as.

ausgebreitet [ˈausgəbraɪtət], *adj.* extensive, widespread.

Ausgeburt [ˈausgəburt], *f.* (—, *pl.* **—en**) monstrosity; — *des Hirns,* figment of the imagination.

ausgefahren [ˈausgəfaːrən], *adj.* (*street*) rutted, well-worn.

ausgehen [ˈausgeːən], *v.n. irr.* (*aux.* sein) go out; (*hair*) to fall out; (*colour*) come off, fade; (*breath, patience, money*) become exhausted; result, end in.

ausgelassen [ˈausgəlasən], *adj.* boisterous, exuberant, frolicsome, merry, jolly, unbridled.

ausgemacht [ˈausgəmaxt], *adj.* arranged, settled, decided; *eine —e Sache,* a matter of course, a foregone conclusion; *ein —er Schurke,* a downright scoundrel.

ausgeschlossen [ˈausgəflosən], *p.p. das ist —,* that is impossible, out of the question.

ausgewachsen [ˈausgəvaksən], *adj.* full-grown, fully grown.

ausgezeichnet [ˈausgətsaɪçnət], *adj.* excellent, first rate, distinguished.

ausgiebig [ˈausgiːbɪç], *adj.* abundant, plentiful; (*soil*) fertile, rich.

ausgießen [ˈausgiːsən], *v.a. irr.* pour out.

Ausgleich [ˈausglaɪç], *m.* (—s, *no pl.*) settlement, compromise, compensation, equalisation.

ausgleichen [ˈausglaɪçən], *v.a. irr.* make even, balance, equalise, compensate; (*sport*) equalise, draw.

ausgraben [ˈausgraːbən], *v.a. irr.* dig out, dig up, excavate, exhume.

Ausguck [ˈausguk], *m.* (—s, *pl.* **—e**) look-out; (*Naut.*) crow's nest.

Ausguß [ˈausgus], *m.* (—sses, *pl.* ⁻sse) sink, gutter.

aushalten [ˈaushaltən], *v.a. irr.* sustain, endure, bear, stand.

aushändigen [ˈaushɛndɪgən], *v.a.* deliver up, hand over.

Aushang [ˈaushaŋ], *m.* (—s, *pl.* ⁻e) sign, sign-board, placard.

ausharren [ˈausharən], *v.n.* persevere, hold out, wait patiently.

aushecken [ˈaushɛkən], *v.a.* hatch (a plot).

aushelfen [ˈaushɛlfən], *v.n. irr.* help out.

Aushilfe [ˈaushɪlfə], *f.* (—, *pl.* **—n**) help, aid, assistance.

aushilfsweise [ˈaushɪlfsvaɪzə], *adv.* temporarily, as a stop-gap.

aushöhlen [ˈaushøːlən], *v.a.* hollow out, excavate.

ausholen [ˈausho:lən], *v.a.* pump, sound s.o. — *v.n.* strike out; *weit —,* go far back (in a narration).

auskehren [ˈauskeːrən], v.a. sweep out.
auskennen [ˈauskɛnən], v.r. irr. sich in etwas —, know all about s.th.
auskleiden [ˈausklaɪdən], v.a. undress.
ausklingen [ˈausklɪŋən], v.n. irr. (aux. sein) (sound) die away.
ausklügeln [ˈausklyːgəln], v.a. puzzle out, contrive.
auskneifen [ˈausknaɪfən], v.n. irr. (aux. sein) (coll.) bolt, run away.
Auskommen [ˈauskɔmən], n. (—s, no pl.) sufficiency, subsistence, livelihood; mit dem ist kein —, there is no getting on with him.
auskommen [ˈauskɔmən], v.n. irr. (aux. sein) mit etwas —, have enough or sufficient of s.th., manage; mit einem gut —, be on good terms with s.o., get on well with s.o.
auskömmlich [ˈauskœmlɪç], adj. sufficient.
auskosten [ˈauskɔstən], v.a. taste or enjoy to the full.
auskramen [ˈauskraːmən], v.a. rummage out; (fig.) reminisce; talk freely.
auskundschaften [ˈauskuntʃaftən], v.a. spy out, reconnoitre, explore.
Auskunft [ˈauskunft], f. (—, pl. ˙e) information; (Tel.) enquiries; (Mil.) intelligence, enquiry.
auslachen [ˈauslaxən], v.a. laugh at, deride.
ausladen [ˈauslaːdən], v.a. irr. unload, discharge; cancel (invitation).
Auslage [ˈauslaːgə], f. (—, pl. —n) outlay, expenses, advance; shopwindow display.
Ausland [ˈauslant], n. (—s, no pl.) foreign country; ins — fahren, go abroad.
Ausländer [ˈauslendər], m. (—s, pl. —) foreigner, alien.
auslassen [ˈauslasən], v.a. irr. let off (steam); let out (a dress); melt (butter); leave off, omit. — v.r. sich über etwas —, speak o.'s mind about s.th.
Auslassung [ˈauslasuŋ], f. (—, pl. —en) utterance; omission.
auslaufen [ˈauslaufən], v.n. irr. (aux. sein) run out, leak out; (ship) put to sea; (result) turn out.
Ausläufer [ˈausloyfər], m. (—s, pl. —) errand boy; (mountain) spur.
Auslaut [ˈauslaut], m. (—s, pl. —e) (Phonet.) final sound.
auslegen [ˈausleːgən], v.a. lay out, spread out, display; interpret; (money) advance.
ausleihen [ˈauslaɪən], v.a. irr. lend, hire out. — v.r. sich etwas —, borrow s.th.
auslernen [ˈauslɛrnən], v.n. end o.'s apprenticeship.
ausliefern [ˈausliːfərn], v.a. hand over, deliver; surrender, give up, extradite.
auslöschen [ˈauslœʃən], v.a. extinguish, put out (fire).
auslosen [ˈausloːzən], v.a. raffle, draw lots for.

auslösen [ˈausløːzən], v.a. redeem, ransom, recover; (fig.) produce; arouse.
Auslosung [ˈausloːzuŋ], f. (—, pl. —en) raffle, draw.
Auslösung [ˈausløːzuŋ], f. (—, pl. —en) ransom.
auslüften [ˈauslyftən], v.a. air, ventilate.
ausmachen [ˈausmaxən], v.a. decide, settle; amount to; etwas mit einem —, arrange s.th. with s.o.; es macht nichts aus, it does not matter; wieviel macht das aus? how much is this? würde es Ihnen etwas —? would you mind?
Ausmaß [ˈausmaːs], n. (—es, pl. —e) dimension, amount, extent, scale.
ausmeißeln [ˈausmaɪsəln], v.a. chisel out, carve out.
ausmerzen [ˈausmɛrtsən], v.a. expunge, eradicate.
ausmisten [ˈausmɪstən], v.a. clean, clear up (mess).
ausmustern [ˈausmustərn], v.a. eliminate, reject; (Mil.) discharge.
Ausnahme [ˈausnaːmə], f. (—, pl. —n) exception.
ausnehmen [ˈausneːmən], v.a. irr. except, exclude; (poultry) draw; (fish) clean.
ausnutzen [ˈausnutsən], v.a. make the most of s.th.; take advantage of s.th.
ausnützen [ˈausnytsən], v.a. exploit.
auspacken [ˈauspakən], v.a. unpack. — v.n. talk freely; (coll.) open up.
auspfeifen [ˈauspfaɪfən], v.a. irr. (Theat.) hiss at, cat-call.
auspolstern [ˈauspɔlstərn], v.a. stuff.
ausprägen [ˈausprɛːgən], v.a. stamp, impress, coin.
ausprobieren [ˈausproːbiːrən], v.a. try out.
Auspuff [ˈauspuf], m. (—s, no pl.) (Motor.) exhaust.
auspusten [ˈauspuːstən], v.a. blow out.
ausputzen [ˈausputsən], v.a. clean out; adorn.
ausquartieren [ˈauskvartiːrən], v.a. (Mil.) billet out.
ausquetschen [ˈauskvɛtʃən], v.a. squeeze out.
ausradieren [ˈausradiːrən], v.a. erase.
ausrangieren [ˈausranʒiːrən], v.a. cast off, sort out.
ausräuchern [ˈausroyçərn], v.a. fumigate.
ausraufen [ˈausraufən], v.a. (obs.) tear or pull out (hair).
ausräumen [ˈausroymən], v.a. clear out, clear away.
ausrechnen [ˈausrɛçnən], v.a. reckon, compute, calculate; ausgerechnet du, (emph.) you of all people.
ausrecken [ˈausrɛkən], v.a. sich den Hals —, crane o.'s neck.
Ausrede [ˈausreːdə], f. (—, pl. —n) evasion, excuse, subterfuge.
ausreden [ˈausreːdən], v.a. einem etwas —, dissuade s.o. from s.th. — v.n. finish speaking; einen — lassen, allow s.o. to finish speaking.

ausreichen ['ausraɪçən], *v.n.* suffice.

ausreißen ['ausraɪsən], *v.a. irr.* pluck, pull out. — *v.n.* (*aux.* sein) run away, bolt.

ausrenken ['ausrɛŋkən], *v.a.* dislocate, sprain.

ausrichten ['ausrɪçtən], *v.a.* adjust, make straight; deliver (a message); accomplish; (*Mil.*) dress.

ausrotten ['ausrɔtən], *v.a.* root up; exterminate, extirpate.

ausrücken ['ausrykən], *v.n.* (*aux.* sein) (*Mil.*) march out; (*coll.*) decamp.

Ausruf ['ausruːf], *m.* (**—s**, *pl.* **—e**) exclamation, interjection, outcry; (*public*) proclamation.

Ausruf(ungs)zeichen ['ausruːf(uŋs)-tsaɪçən], *n.* (**—s**, *pl.* **—**) exclamation mark.

ausruhen ['ausruːən], *v.r.* sich **—**, rest, take a rest.

ausrüsten ['ausrystən], *v.a.* furnish, fit out, equip.

Ausrutscher ['ausrutʃən], *v.n.* (*aux.* sein) slip.

Aussage ['ausaːgə], *f.* (**—**, *pl.* **—n**) declaration, statement, evidence; (*Law*) deposition, affidavit; (*Gram.*) predicate.

aussagen ['ausaːgən], *v.a.* say, state, utter, declare; (*Law*) depose, give evidence.

Aussatz ['ausats], *m.* (**—es**, *no pl.*) leprosy.

Aussätzige ['ausɛtsɪgə], *m.* (**—n**, *pl.* **—n**) leper.

aussaugen ['ausaugən], *v.a.* suck dry.

ausschalten ['ausʃaltən], *v.a.* switch off.

Ausschank ['ausʃank], *m.* (**—s**, *no pl.*) pub, bar.

Ausschau ['ausʃau], *f.* (**—**, *no pl.*) watch; — *halten*, look out for.

ausscheiden ['ausʃaɪdən], *v.a. irr.* separate; (*Med.*) secrete. — *v.n.* (*aux.* sein) withdraw from, retire, secede.

Ausscheidung ['ausʃaɪduŋ], *f.* (**—**, *pl.* **—en**) retirement, withdrawal; (*Med.*) secretion.

Ausschlag ['ausʃlaːk], *m.* (**—s**, *pl.* **—e**) turn (of the scales); deflection (of the magnetic needle); (*Med.*) rash, eczema; *den — geben*, clinch the matter; give the casting vote.

ausschlagen ['ausʃlaːgən], *v.a. irr.* knock out; refuse, decline (an invitation); *das schlägt dem Faß den Boden aus*, that is the last straw. — *v.n.* (*aux.* sein) (*Hort.*) bud, shoot; *gut —*, turn out well.

auschlaggebend ['ausʃlaːkgebənt], *adj.* decisive; (*vote*) casting.

ausschließen ['ausʃliːsən], *v.a. irr.* lock out; exclude.

ausschließlich ['ausʃliːslɪç], *adj.* exclusive, sole.

ausschlüpfen ['ausʃlypfən], *v.n.* (*aux.* sein) hatch out.

Ausschluß ['ausʃlus], *m.* (**—sses**, *pl.* **-̈sse**) exclusion; *unter — der Öffentlichkeit*, in camera.

ausschmücken ['ausʃmykən], *v.a.* adorn, decorate, embellish.

Ausschnitt ['ausʃnɪt], *m.* (**—s**, *pl.* **—e**) cutting out; (*newspaper*) cutting; (*dress*) neck (line).

ausschreiben ['ausʃraɪbən], *v.a. irr.* write down in full; make out a bill; advertise (post) as vacant.

ausschreiten ['ausʃraɪtən], *v.n. irr.* (*aux.* sein) step out, stride along.

Ausschreitungen ['ausʃraɪtuŋən], *f. pl.* rioting; excesses.

Ausschuß ['ausʃus], *m.* (**—sses**, *pl.* **-̈sse**) dross, refuse, rejects, low quality goods; committee, commission, board.

ausschweifend ['ausʃvaɪfənt], *adj.* extravagant; licentious, dissolute.

aussehen ['ausˈzeːən], *v.n. irr.* look; look like, appear.

außen ['ausən], *adv.* outside, abroad, outward, without.

Außenhandel ['ausənhandəl], *m.* (**—s**, *no pl.*) export trade.

Außenministerium ['ausənmɪnɪsteːr-jum], *n.* (**—s**, *pl.* **—terien**) Ministry of Foreign Affairs; (*U.K.*) Foreign Office, (*U.S.*) State Department.

Außenstände ['ausənʃtɛndə], *m. pl.* outstanding claims, liabilities.

außer ['ausər], *prep.* (*Dat.*) in addition to, besides, apart from; out of, at the outside of, beside, without; — *Dienst*, retired. — *conj.* except, save, but.

außerdem ['ausərdeːm], *adv.* besides, moreover, furthermore.

Äußere ['ɔysərə], *n.* (**—n**, *no pl.*) exterior.

außerehelich ['ausərˈeːlɪç], *adj.* illegitimate.

außergewöhnlich ['ausərgəvøːnlɪç], *adj.* unusual, exceptional.

außerhalb ['ausərhalp], *prep.* outside.

äußerlich ['ɔysərlɪç], *adj.* external.

Äußerlichkeit ['ɔysərlɪçkaɪt], *f.* (**—**, *pl.* **—en**) formality.

äußern ['ɔysərn], *v.a.* utter, express. — *v.r.* sich *zu etwas —*, give o.'s opinion on some question; express o.s. on some subject.

außerordentlich [ausərˈɔrdəntlɪç], *adj.* extraordinary, unusual; (*Univ.*) — *er Professor*, senior lecturer *or* reader; (*Am.*) associate professor.

äußerst ['ɔysərst], *adj.* outermost, most remote; extreme, utmost.

außerstande ['ausərʃtandə], *adj.* unable.

Äußerung ['ɔysəruŋ], *f.* (**—**, *pl.* **—en**) utterance, remark, observation.

aussetzen ['auszɛtsən], *v.a.* set out, put out; offer (a reward); suspend; *etwas an einer Sache —*, find fault with s.th.; *sich einer Gefahr —*, expose o.s. to danger, run a risk. — *v.n.* pause, discontinue; (*Motor.*) stop, misfire.

Aussicht ['auszɪçt], *f.* (**—**, *pl.* **—en**) view, panorama; prospect, chance; *etwas in — stellen*, hold out the prospect of s.th.; *in — nehmen*, intend.

aussinnen

aussinnen ['auszɪnən],v. a. irr. imagine, invent, devise.

aussöhnen ['auszø:nən], v.r. sich mit einem —, become reconciled with s.o.

aussondern ['auszɔndərn], v.a. single out.

ausspannen ['ausʃpanən], v.a. (animals) unharness. — v.n. (coll.) relax.

ausspeien ['ausʃpaiən], v.a. spit out, vomit.

aussperren ['ausʃpɛrən], v.a. shut out; (industrial) lock out.

ausspielen ['ausʃpi:lən], v.n. finish playing (Sport, Game) lead (off).

Aussprache ['ausʃpra:xə], f. (—, no pl.) pronunciation; discussion; confidential talk.

aussprechen ['ausʃprɛçən], v.a. irr. have o.'s say; utter; pronounce. — v.r. sich —, speak o.'s mind.

Ausspruch ['ausʃprux], m. (—s, pl. ˙e) utterance, dictum.

ausspüren ['ausʃpy:rən], v.a. (Hunt.) track down.

ausstaffieren ['ausʃtafi:rən],v.a.furnish, equip.

Ausstand ['ausʃtant], m. (—s, pl. ˙e) (industry) strike; (pl.) outstanding debts, arrears.

ausständig ['ausʃtɛndɪç], adj. outstanding; on strike.

ausstatten ['ausʃtatən], v.a. endow with, provide with, equip.

Ausstattung ['ausʃtatuŋ], f. (—, pl. —en) outfit; (bridal) trousseau; (coll.) get-up.

ausstechen ['ausʃtɛçən], v.a. irr. pierce; einen —, (fig.) excel s.o.

ausstehen ['ausʃte:ən], v.n. irr. stand out; (money) be overdue. — v.a. endure, suffer, bear, undergo; ich kann ihn nicht —, I cannot stand him.

aussteigen ['ausʃtaigən], v.n. irr. (aux. sein) get out, alight; disembark.

ausstellen ['ausʃtɛlən], v.a. exhibit; display; make out (bill etc.).

Aussteller ['ausʃtɛlər], m. (—s, pl. —) drawer (of a cheque); exhibitor.

Ausstellung ['ausʃtɛluŋ], f. (—, pl. —en) exhibition; (Am.) exposition.

Aussteuer ['ausʃtɔyər], f. (—, pl. —n) trousseau.

ausstopfen ['ausʃtɔpfən], v.a. stuff.

ausstoßen ['ausʃtosən], v.a. irr. push out, expel; utter.

Ausstrahlung ['ausʃtra:luŋ], f. (—, pl. —en) radiation.

ausstrecken ['ausʃtrɛkən], v.a. stretch out, reach out, extend.

ausstreichen ['ausʃtraiçən], v.a. irr. strike out, erase, delete; smoothe.

ausstreuen ['ausʃtrɔyən], v.a. scatter, spread, sprinkle; Gerüchte —, circulate rumours.

ausstudieren ['ausʃtudi:rən], v.n. finish o.'s studies, graduate.

aussuchen ['auszu:xən], v.a. select.

Austausch ['austauʃ], m. (—es, pl. —e) barter, exchange; (thoughts, letters) interchange.

austauschen ['austauʃən], v.a. barter, exchange; (thoughts, letters) interchange.

austeilen ['austailən], v.a. distribute, allocate.

Auster ['austər], f. (—, pl. —n) oyster.

Austerbank ['austərbaŋk], f. (—, pl. ˙e) oyster-bed.

austilgen ['austɪlgən], v.a. exterminate, eradicate, extirpate.

Australien [au'stra:ljən], n. Australia.

austreiben ['austraibən], v.a. irr. drive out, expel; exorcise.

austreten ['austre:tən], v.a. irr. tread out; stretch (shoes) by walking; ausgetretene Stufen, worn steps. — v.n. (aux. sein) retire (from business); withdraw (from a club); (coll.) go to the lavatory.

Austritt ['austrɪt], m. (—s, pl. —e) withdrawal, retirement.

ausüben ['ausy:bən], v.a. exercise, practise; exert, commit.

Ausverkauf ['ausfɛrkauf], m. (—s, pl. ˙e) selling-off, clearance sale.

Auswahl ['ausva:l], f. (—, pl. —en) choice, selection.

Auswanderer ['ausvandərər], m. (—s, pl. —) emigrant.

auswärtig ['ausvɛrtɪç], adj. foreign, away.

auswärts ['ausvɛrts], adv. outward(s), away from home.

auswechseln ['ausvɛksəln], v.a. exchange; fit (spare parts).

Ausweg ['ausve:k], m. (—s, pl. —e) expedient; way out; ich weiß keinen —, I am at my wits' end.

ausweichen ['ausvaiçən], v.n. irr. (aux. sein) give way; evade, parry.

Ausweis ['ausvais], m. (—es, pl. —e) proof of identity, identity card.

ausweisen ['ausvaizən], v.a. irr. turn out, banish, exile, deport. — v.r. (aux. haben) sich —, show proof of o.'s identity.

auswendig ['ausvɛndɪç], adj. by heart.

auswirken ['ausvɪrkən], v.r. sich gut —, work out well, have a good effect.

Auswuchs ['ausvu:ks], m. (—es, pl. ˙e) sprouting, outgrowth, (fig.) excrescence.

Auswurf ['ausvurf], m. (—s, pl. ˙e) excretion; expectoration; der Menschheit, scum of the earth.

auszählen ['austsɛ:lən], v.n. count, number. — v.a. count out.

Auszahlung ['austsa:luŋ], f. (—, pl. —en) payment.

auszanken ['austsaŋkən], v.a. scold, chide.

auszehren ['austse:rən], v.n. (aux. sein) waste away, be consumed.

auszeichnen ['austsaiçnən], v.a. mark out, honour, decorate. — v.r. sich —, distinguish o.s.

Auszeichnung ['austsaiçnuŋ], f. (—, pl. —en) distinction, medal.

auszlehen ['austsi:ən], *v.a. irr.* undress, take off (clothes); (*Chem.*) extract; stretch. — *v.n.* (*aux.* sein) move out. — *v.r.* sich —, undress.

auszischen ['austsiʃən], *v.a.* (*Theat.*) hiss, cat-call.

Auszug ['austsu:k], *m.* (—s, *pl.* ⁀e) removal (from home); marching off; exodus; extract (from a book), abstract (from a deed).

Auto ['auto], *n.* (—s, *pl.* —s) motor-car, (*Am.*) automobile.

Autogramm [auto'gram], *n.* (—s, *pl.* —e) autograph.

Automat [auto'ma:t], *m.* (—en, *pl.* —en) slot machine.

Autor ['autor], *m.* (—s, *pl.* —en) author, writer.

Autorität [autori'tɛ:t], *f.* (—, *pl.* —en) authority.

avisieren [avi'zi:rən], *v.a.* notify, advise.

Axt [akst], *f.* (—, *pl.* ⁀e) axe.

Azur [a'tsu:r], *m.* (—s, *no pl.*) azure.

B

B [be:], *n.* (—s, *pl.*—s) the letter B; (*Mus.*) B flat; — *Dur*, B flat major; — *Moll*, B flat minor.

Bach [bax], *m.* (—es, *pl.* ⁀e) brook, rivulet.

Bachstelze ['baxʃtɛltsə], *f.* (—, *pl.* —n) wagtail.

Backe ['bakə], *f.* (—, *pl.* —n) cheek.

backen ['bakən], *v.a.* bake.

Backenstreich ['bakənʃtraiç], *m.* (—s, *pl.* —e) box on the ear.

Bäcker ['bɛkər], *m.* (—s, *pl.* —) baker.

Backfisch ['bakfiʃ], *m.* (—es, *pl.* —e) (*fig.*) teenage girl.

Backhuhn ['bakhu:n], *n.* (—s, *pl.* ⁀er) fried chicken.

Backobst ['bakopst], *n.* (—es, *no pl.*) dried fruit.

Backpfeife ['bakpfaifə], *f.* (—, *pl.* —n) box on the ear.

Backpflaume ['bakpflaumə], *f.* (—, *pl.* —n) prune.

Backstein ['bakʃtain], *m.* (—s, *pl.* —e) brick.

Backwerk ['bakvɛrk], *n.* (—s, *no pl.*) pastry.

Bad [ba:t], *n.* (—es, *pl.* ⁀er) bath: spa, watering-place.

Badeanstalt ['ba:dəanʃtalt], *f.* (—, *pl.* —en) public baths.

baden ['ba:dən], *v.n.* bathe, have a bath.

Badewanne ['ba:dəvanə], *f.* (—, *pl.* —n) bath-tub.

Bagage [ba'ga:ʒə], *f.* (—, *no pl.*) luggage; (*Am.*) baggage; (*sl.*) mob, rabble.

Bagger ['bagər], *m.* (—s, *pl.* —) dredger, dredging-machine.

baggern ['bagərn], *v.a.* dredge.

Bahn [ba:n], *f.* (—, *pl.* —en) road, path, course; (*Astr.*) orbit; railway(-line); — *brechen*, open a path.

bahnbrechend ['ba:nbrɛçənt], *adj.* pioneering, epoch-making.

bahnen ['ba:nən], *v.a.* make passable; pave (the way).

Bahngleis ['ba:nglais], *n.* (—es, *pl.* —e) railway-line, railway-track; (*Am.*) railroad-line, railroad-track.

Bahnhof ['ba:nho:f], *m.* (—s, *pl.* ⁀e) railway-station, (*Am.*) depot.

Bahnsteig ['ba:nʃtaik], *m.* (—s, *pl.* —e) platform.

Bahnwärter ['ba:nvɛrtər], *m.* (—s, *pl.* —) signal-man.

Bahre ['ba:rə], *f.* (—, *pl.* —n) litter, stretcher; bier.

Bahrtuch ['ba:rtu:x], *n.* (—s, *pl.* ⁀er) pall, shroud.

Bai [bai], *f.* (—, *pl.* —en) bay, cove.

Baisse ['bɛsə], *f.* (—, *pl.* —n) (*Comm.*) fall in share prices.

Bakkalaureat [bakalaure'a:t], *n.* (—s, *pl.* —e) bachelor's degree.

Bakterie [bak'te:rjə], *f.* (—, *pl.* —n) bacterium.

bald [balt], *adv.* soon, shortly, directly, presently.

Baldachin ['baldaxin], *m.* (—s, *pl.* —e) canopy.

baldig ['baldiç], *adj.* quick, speedy; *auf —es Wiedersehen*, see you again soon.

Baldrian ['baldria:n], *m.* (—s, *no pl.*) valerian.

Balearen, die [bale'a:rən, di:], *pl.* Balearic Islands.

Balg (1) [balk], *m.* (—s, *pl.* ⁀e) skin, slough, husk; bellows (of organ *or* forge).

Balg (2) [balk], *n.* (—s, *pl.* ⁀er) brat; naughty child.

balgen ['balgən], *v.r.* sich —, (*children*) fight, romp.

Balgerei [balgərai], *f.* (—, *pl.* —en) scuffle, scrimmage.

Balken ['balkən], *m.* (—s, *pl.* —) beam, joist, rafter.

Balkenwerk ['balkənvɛrk], *n.* (—s, *no pl.*) building-frame, timbers, wood-work.

Balkon [bal'kɔ̃], *m.* (—s, *pl.* —s, —e) balcony.

Ball [bal], *m.* (—s, *pl.* ⁀e) ball; globe; sphere; dance.

ballen ['balən], *v.a.* form into a ball; clench (o.'s fist).

Ballen ['balən], *m.* (—s, *pl.* —) bale, bundle, package; ball (of the hand *or* foot).

ballförmig ['balførmiç], *adj.* spherical.

Ballistik [ba'listik], *f.* (—, *no pl.*) ballistics.

Ballon [ba'lɔ̃], *m.* (—s, *pl.* —s, —e) balloon.

Balsam ['balza:m], *m.* (—s, *pl.* —e) balm, balsam.

Baltikum ['baltikum], *n.* (—s, *no pl.*) the Baltic countries.

Bambusrohr

Bambusrohr ['bambusro:r], n. (—s, pl. —e) bamboo (cane).

Banane [ba'na:nə], f. (—, pl. —n) banana.

Banause [ba'nauzə], m. (—n, pl. —n) narrow-minded person, philistine.

Band (1) [bant], n. (—s, pl. ̈er) ribbon, riband, tape; string; (Bot.) band; hoop (for a cask); (Anat.) ligament, tendon.

Band (2) [bant], n. (—s, pl. —e) (fig.) bond, fetter, chain, (pl.) bonds, ties (of friendship).

Band (3) [bant], m. (—es, pl. ̈e) volume.

Bändchen ['bɛntçən], n. (—s, pl. —) small ribbon, small piece of string; (book) small volume.

Bande ['bandə], f. (—, pl. —n) horde, gang, set.

bändigen ['bɛndɪgən], v.a. tame, subdue.

Bandmaß ['bantma:s], n. (—es, pl. —e) tape-measure.

Bandwurm ['bantvurm], m. (—s, pl. ̈er) (Zool.) tape-worm.

bange ['baŋə], adj. afraid, worried, alarmed.

Bangigkeit ['baŋɪçkaɪt], f. (—, no pl.) uneasiness, anxiety.

Bank (1) [bank], f. (—, pl. ̈e) bench, seat (in a park); auf die lange — schieben, delay, shelve; durch die —, without exception.

Bank (2) [bank], f. (—, pl. —en) bank; die — sprengen, break the bank.

Bänkelsänger ['bɛŋkəlzɛŋər], m. (—s, pl. —) ballad singer.

bank(e)rott [bank'rɔt], adj. bankrupt.

Bankett [baŋ'kɛt], n. (—s, pl. —e) banquet.

Bankkonto ['baŋkkɔnto], n. (—s, pl. —ten) bank-account.

Bann [ban], m. (—s, no pl.) ban, exile; (Eccl.) excommunication; in den — tun, outlaw, (Eccl.) excommunicate; (fig.) charm, spell.

bannen ['banən], v.a. banish, exile, cast out.

Banner ['banər], n. (—s, pl. —) banner, standard.

Bannmeile ['banmaɪlə], f. (—, pl. —n) boundary.

bar [ba:r], adv. in cash, ready money.

Bar [ba:r], f. (—, pl. —s) bar (for selling drinks etc.).

Bär [bɛ:r], m. (—en, pl. —en) (Zool.) bear; einem einen — aufbinden, to lead s.o. up the garden-path.

Barauslagen ['barausla:gən], f. pl. cash expenses.

Barbar [bar'ba:r], m. (—en, pl. —en) barbarian, vandal.

barbarisch [bar'ba:rɪʃ], adj. barbarous.

Barbestand ['ba:rbəʃtant], m. (—s, pl. ̈e) cash reserve, cash balance.

bärbeißig ['bɛ:rbaɪsɪç], adj. surly, morose.

Barchent ['barçənt], m. (—s, no pl.) fustian.

Barde ['bardə], m. (—n, pl. —n) bard, minstrel.

Bärenfell ['bɛ:rənfɛl], n. (—s, pl. —e) bear-skin.

Bärenmütze ['bɛ:rənmytsə], f. (—, pl. —n) (Mil.) busby.

Bärenzwinger ['bɛ:rəntsvɪŋər], m. (—s, pl. —) bear-garden.

Barett [ba'rɛt], n. (—s, pl. —e) cap, beret; (Eccl.) biretta.

barfuß ['barfu:s], adj. barefoot(ed).

Bargeld ['bargɛlt], n. (—(e)s, no pl.) cash.

barhäuptig ['barhɔyptɪç], adj. bareheaded.

Barkasse [bar'kasə], f. (—, pl. —n) launch.

Barke ['barkə], f. (—, pl. —n) barge, lighter.

barmherzig [barm'hɛrtsɪç], adj. merciful, charitable, compassionate.

Barock [ba'rɔk], n. (—s, no pl.) Baroque.

Baronin [ba'ro:nɪn], f. (—, pl. —nen) baroness.

Barren ['barən], m. (—s, pl. —) parallel bars.

Barsch [barʃ], m. (—es, pl. —e) (Zool.) perch.

barsch [barʃ], adj. rough, harsh, sharp, abrupt, unfriendly.

Barschaft ['ba:rʃaft], f. (—, pl. —en) ready money.

Bart [ba:rt], m. (—s, pl. ̈e) beard; (key) ward.

Bartflechte ['ba:rtflɛçtə], f. (—, pl. —n) barber's itch.

bärtig ['bɛ:rtɪç], adj. bearded.

Basalt [ba'zalt], m. (—s, pl. —e) (Min.) basalt.

Base ['ba:zə], f. (—, pl. —n) female cousin; (Chem.) base.

Basis ['ba:zɪs], f. (—, pl. **Basen**) base, foundation.

Baskenmütze ['baskənmytsə], f. (—, pl. —n) tam-o'-shanter, beret.

Baß [bas], m. (—sses, pl. ̈sse) (Mus.) bass.

Baßschlüssel ['basʃlysəl], m. (—s, pl. —) (Mus.) bass-clef.

Bassin [ba'sɛ̃], n. (—s, pl. —s) basin, reservoir.

Bast [bast], m. (—es, pl. —e) inner bark, fibre (of trees etc.); bast.

basta ['basta], int. and that's that!

Bastei [bas'taɪ], f. (—, pl. —en) bastion.

basteln ['bastəln], v.a. work on a hobby, tinker.

Batist [ba'tɪst], m. (—s, pl. —e) cambric.

Bau [bau], m. (—es, pl. —ten) building, structure, edifice; act of building; im — begriffen, in course of construction.

Bauart ['bauart], f. (—, pl. —en) (architectural) style, structure.

Bauch [baux], m. (—es, pl. ̈e) belly, stomach.

Bauchfell ['bauxfɛl], n. (—s, pl. —e) peritoneum.

bauchig ['bauçɪç], adj. bulgy.
Bauchredner ['bauxre:dnər], m. (—s, pl. —) ventriloquist.
bauen ['bauən], v.a. build, construct, erect. — v.n. auf etwas —, (fig.) rely on s.th., count on s.th.
Bauer (1) ['bauər], m. (—n, pl. —n) farmer, peasant; (chess) pawn.
Bauer (2) ['bauər], n. (—s, pl. —) (bird) cage.
Bauernfänger ['bauərnfɛŋər], m. (—s, pl. —) sharper, rook, confidence-trickster.
Bäuerin ['bɔyərɪn], f. (—, pl. —nen) farmer's wife.
Bauernstand ['bauərnʃtant], m. (—s, pl. ⁈e) peasantry.
baufällig ['baufɛlɪç], adj. dilapidated, ramshackle.
Baugerüst ['baugərʏst], n. (—s, pl. —e) scaffolding.
Baugewerbe ['baugəvɛrbə], n. (—s, no pl.) building trade.
Baukunst ['baukunst], f. (—, no pl.) architecture.
Baum [baum], m. (—(e)s, pl. ⁈e) tree.
Baumeister ['baumaɪstər], m. (—s, pl. —) architect, master-builder.
baumeln ['bauməln], v.n. dangle.
Baumkuchen ['baumku:xən], m. (—s, pl. —) pyramid-cake.
Baumschule ['baumʃu:lə], f. (—, pl. —n) plantation of trees, orchard, tree nursery.
Baumstamm ['baumʃtam], m. (—s, pl. ⁈e) stem, trunk.
Baumwolle ['baumvɔlə], f. (—, pl. —n) cotton.
Bauriß ['baurɪs], m. (—sses, pl. —sse) plan, architect's drawing.
Bausch [bauʃ], m. (—es, pl. ⁈e) pad, bolster; in — und Bogen, in the lump; all at once.
bauschig ['bauʃɪç], adj. baggy.
Bauwerk ['bauvɛrk] see **Gebäude.**
Bayern ['baɪərn], n. Bavaria.
Bazar [ba'za:r], m. (—s, pl. —e) bazaar, fair, emporium.
beabsichtigen [bə'apzɪçtɪgən], v.a. aim at, intend, have in view.
beachten [bə'axtən], v.a. observe, pay attention to.
Beamte [bə'amtə], m. (—n, pl. —n) official, officer, civil servant.
Beamtin [bə'amtɪn], f. (—, pl. —nen) female official, female civil servant.
beängstigen [bə'ɛŋstɪgən], v.a. alarm, make afraid.
beanspruchen [bə'anʃpruxən], v.a. demand, claim, lay claim to.
beanstanden [bə'anʃtandən], v.a. object to, raise objections to, query.
beantragen [bə'antra:gən], v.a. move, apply, lodge an application.
beantworten [bə'antvɔrtən], v.a. answer, reply to.
bearbeiten [bə'arbaɪtən], v.a. work (on); (book, play) adapt, arrange, revise; (Agr.) cultivate; (fig.) einen —, try to influence s.o., try to convince s.o.

Bearbeitung [bə'arbaɪtuŋ], f. (—, pl. —en) working, manipulation, operation; (Agr.) culture, cultivation; (book, play) adaptation, revision, arrangement.
beargwöhnen [bə'arkvø:nən], v.a. suspect, view with suspicion.
beaufsichtigen [bə'aufzɪçtɪgən], v.a. control, supervise, superintend.
beauftragen [bə'auftra:gən], v.a. commission, charge, authorize.
bebauen [bə'bauən], v.a. build upon; (Agr.) cultivate.
beben ['be:bən], v.n. shake, quake, tremble; vor Kälte —, shiver with cold.
Becher ['bɛçər], m. (—s, pl. —) beaker, cup, goblet, mug; (dice) box.
Becken ['bɛkən], n. (—s, pl. —) basin, bowl; (Anat.) pelvis; (Mus.) cymbal.
Bedacht [bə'daxt], m. (—s, no pl.) consideration; mit —, deliberately; ohne —, thoughtlessly.
bedächtig [bə'dɛçtɪç], adj. circumspect, deliberate, cautious, slow.
bedanken [bə'daŋkən], v.r. sich für etwas —, thank s.o. for s.th., decline with thanks (also iron.).
Bedarf [bə'darf], m. (—s, no pl.) need, requirement, demand.
bedauerlich [bə'dauərlɪç], adj. regrettable, deplorable.
bedauern [bə'dauərn], v.a. pity, commiserate, regret; ich bedaure, daß, I am sorry that . . .
bedecken [bə'dɛkən], v.a. cover (up); sich mit Ruhm —, cover o.s. with glory.
bedeckt [bə'dɛkt], adj. (sky) overcast.
bedenken [bə'dɛŋkən], v.a. irr. consider, bear in mind. — v.r. sich —, deliberate, hesitate; sich anders —, change o.'s mind.
bedenklich [bə'dɛŋklɪç], adj. (persons) doubtful, dubious; (things) risky, delicate, precarious; (illness) serious, grave.
Bedenkzeit [bə'dɛŋktsaɪt], f. (—, pl. —en) time to consider, respite.
bedeuten [bə'dɔytən], v.a. signify, mean, imply; direct, order.
bedeutend [bə'dɔytənt], adj. important, eminent, considerable, outstanding.
bedeutsam [bə'dɔytza:m], adj. significant.
Bedeutung [bə'dɔytuŋ], f. (—, pl. —en) significance, meaning; consequence, importance; nichts von —, nothing to speak of.
bedienen [bə'di:nən], v.a. serve, attend to, wait on; (machine) operate; (Cards) follow suit. — v.r. sich —, help o.s., make use of.
Bediente [bə'di:ntə], m. (—n, pl. —n) servant, attendant, footman, lackey.
Bedienung [bə'di:nuŋ], f. (—, pl. —en) service, attendance.
bedingen [bə'dɪŋən], v.a. stipulate, postulate, condition, cause.

23

bedingt [bə'dıŋkt], *adj.* conditional.

Bedingung [bə'dıŋuŋ], *f.* (—, *pl.* —en) stipulation, condition, term; *unter keiner* —, on no account.

bedingungsweise [bə'dıŋuŋsvaızə], *adv.* on condition, conditionally.

bedrängen [bə'drɛŋən], *v.a.* oppress; press hard, afflict.

Bedrängnis [bə'drɛŋnıs], *n.* (—ses, *pl.* —se) oppression, distress.

bedrohen [bə'dro:ən], *v.a.* threaten, menace.

bedrohlich [bə'dro:lıç], *adj.* threatening, menacing, ominous.

bedrücken [bə'drykən], *v.a.* oppress, harass, depress.

Beduine [bedu'i:nə], *m.* (—n, *pl.* —n) Bedouin.

bedünken [bə'dyŋkən], *v.a.* appear, seem; *es bedünkt mich*, methinks.

bedürfen [bə'dyrfən], *v.n. irr.* want, need, be in need of.

Bedürfnis [bə'dyrfnıs], *n.* (—ses, *pl.* —se) want, need, requirement, necessity; *es ist mir ein* —, I cannot but; *einem dringenden* — *abhelfen*, meet an urgent want *or* need; *ein* — *haben*, (*coll.*) need to relieve o.s.

Bedürfnisanstalt [bə'dyrfnısanʃtalt], *f.* (—, *pl.* —en) public lavatory, public convenience.

bedürftig [bə'dyrftıç], *adj.* needy, indigent, poor.

beeidigen [bə'aıdıgən], *v.a.* confirm by oath, swear in.

beeifern [bə'aıfərn], *v.r. sich* —, exert o.s., strive, be zealous.

beeilen [bə'aılən], *v.r. sich* —, hurry, hasten, make haste.

beeindrucken [bə'aındrukən], *v.a.* impress.

beeinflussen [bə'aınflusən], *v.a.* influence.

beeinträchtigen [bə'aıntrɛçtıgən], *v.a.* injure, lessen, diminish, detract from, curtail.

beenden [bə'ɛndən], *v.a.* end, finish, terminate, conclude.

beendigen [bə'ɛndıgən], *v.a.* end, finish, terminate, conclude.

beengen [bə'ɛŋən], *v.a.* cramp, narrow.

beerben [bə'ɛrbən], *v.a. einen* —, inherit from s.o.

beerdigen [bə'e:rdıgən], *v.a.* bury, inter.

Beere ['be:rə], *f.* (—, *pl.* —n) berry.

Beet [be:t], *n.* (—es, *pl.* —e) (flower) bed.

befähigen [bə'fɛ:ıgən], *v.a.* fit, enable, qualify.

Befähigung [bə'fɛ:ıguŋ], *f.* (—, *pl.* —en) qualification, capacity, aptitude.

befahren [bə'fa:rən], *v.a. irr.* pass over, travel over; (*Naut.*) navigate.

befallen [bə'falən], *v.a. irr.* befall, fall on; *von Traurigkeit* — *sein*, be overcome by sadness.

befangen [bə'faŋən], *adj.* biased, prejudiced; bashful, embarrassed.

befassen [bə'fasən], *v.a.* touch, handle. — *v.r. sich mit etwas* —, occupy o.s. with s.th.

befehden [bə'fe:dən], *v.a.* make war upon, show enmity towards.

Befehl [bə'fe:l], *m.* (—s, *pl.* —e) order, command; (*Mil.*) *zu* —, very good, sir; (*Mil.*) *den* — *führen über*, command.

befehlen [bə'fe:lən], *v.a. irr.* order, command.

befehligen [bə'fe:lıgən], *v.a.* (*Mil.*) command, head.

Befehlshaber [bə'fe:lsha:bər], *m.* (—s, *pl.* —) commander, commanding officer, chief.

befehlswidrig [bə'fe:lsvi:drıç], *adj.* contrary to orders.

befestigen [bə'fɛstıgən], *v.a.* fasten, fix, attach, affix; (*Mil.*) fortify; strengthen.

befeuchten [bə'fɔyçtən], *v.a.* wet, moisten, dampen.

Befinden [bə'fındən], *n.* (—s, *no pl.*) state of health.

befinden [bə'fındən], *v.a. irr.* think, deem, find. — *v.r. sich an einem Ort* —, be in some place; *sich wohl* —, feel well.

befindlich [bə'fıntlıç], *adj.* existing — *sein*, be contained in.

beflecken [bə'flɛkən], *v.a.* stain, spot, blot; defile, pollute.

befleißigen [bə'flaısıgən], *v.r. sich* —, devote o.s. to, take pains to.

beflissen [bə'flısən], *adj.* eager to serve, assiduous.

beflügeln [bə'fly:gəln], *v.a.* give wings; (*fig.*) accelerate, animate.

befolgen [bə'fɔlgən], *v.a.* follow, obey; *einen Befehl* —, comply with an order.

befördern [bə'fœrdərn], *v.a.* despatch, forward, send, post, mail, transmit; promote, advance.

Beförderung [bə'fœrdəruŋ], *f.* (—, *pl.* —en) forwarding, transmission; (*office*) promotion, advancement.

Beförderungsmittel [bə'fœrdəruŋsmıtəl], *n.* (—s, *pl.* —) conveyance, means of transport.

befragen [bə'fra:gən], *v.a.* question, interrogate, examine.

befreien [bə'fraıən], *v.a.* free, liberate.

befremden [bə'frɛmdən], *v.a.* appear strange, astonish, surprise.

befreunden [bə'frɔyndən], *v.a.* befriend. — *v.r. sich mit einem* —, make friends with s.o.

befriedigen [bə'fri:dıgən], *v.a.* content, satisfy; appease, calm.

befruchten [bə'fruxtən], *v.a.* fertilise; impregnate.

Befugnis [bə'fu:knıs], *f.* (—, *pl.* —se) authority, right, warrant.

Befund [bə'funt], *m.* (—s, *pl.* —e) (*Med.*) diagnosis, findings.

befürchten [bə'fyrçtən], *v.a.* fear, be afraid of.

befürworten [bə'fy:rvɔrtən], *v.a.* support, second.

begabt [bə'ga:pt], adj. gifted, talented, able.

Begabung [bə'ga:buŋ], f. (—, pl. —en) ability, talent, gift.

begaffen [bə'gafən], v.a. stare at, gape at.

begatten [bə'gatən], v.r. sich —, (Zool.) copulate.

begeben [bə'ge:bən], v.r. irr. sich an einen Ort —, go to a place, betake o.s. to a place; happen, occur.

Begebenheit [bə'ge:bənhaıt], f. (—, pl. —en) happening, event, occurrence.

begegnen [bə'ge:gnən], v.n. (aux. sein) meet, meet with, encounter, befall, happen.

begehen [bə'ge:ən], v.a. irr. (road) walk along, go over; (festival) celebrate; (crime) commit, perpetrate.

begehren [bə'ge:rən], v.a. desire, wish, covet, want.—v.n. nach etwas —, long for s.th.

begehrlich [bə'ge:rlıç], adj. covetous, greedy, desirous.

begeifern [bə'gaıfərn], v.a. spit at; (fig.) vilify, besmirch.

begeistern [bə'gaıstərn], v.a. inspire, fill with enthusiasm, enrapture.—v.r. sich für etwas —, become enthusiastic about s.th.

Begier(de) [bə'gi:r(də)], f. (—, pl. —den) desire, lust, appetite.

begierig [bə'gi:rıç], adj. desirous, lustful; anxious; curious (for news).

begießen [bə'gi:sən], v.a. irr. (plants) water; (meat etc.) baste; etwas festlich —, celebrate s.th. by drinking; sich die Nase —, (coll.) get tight.

Beginn [bə'gın], m. (—s, no pl.) beginning, commencement, start.

beginnen [bə'gınən], v.a., v.n. irr. begin, commence, start.

beglaubigen [bə'glaubıgən], v.a. attest; certify, verify; accredit (an ambassador).

Beglaubigungsschreiben [bə'glaubıguŋsʃraıbən], n. (—s, pl. —) credentials.

begleichen [bə'glaıçən], v.a. irr. (bill) pay, settle.

begleiten [bə'glaıtən], v.a. accompany, escort, see s.o. off, home etc.

Begleiter [bə'glaıtər], m. (—s, pl. —) companion, escort; (Mus.) accompanist.

Begleiterscheinung [bə'glaıtərʃaınuŋ], f. (—, pl. —en) concomitant; (Med.) complication, attendant symptom.

Begleitung [bə'glaıtuŋ], f. (—, pl. —en) company; (Mus.) accompaniment.

beglücken [bə'glykən], v.a. make happy.

beglückwünschen [bə'glykvynʃən], v.a. congratulate.

begnadet [bə'gna:dət], adj. highly talented.

begnadigen [bə'gna:dıgən], v.a. pardon, reprieve.

begnügen [bə'gny:gən], v.r. sich mit etwas —, content o.s. with s.th.

Begonie [bə'go:njə], f. (—, pl. —n) (Bot.) begonia.

begraben [bə'gra:bən], v.a. irr. bury, inter.

Begräbnis [bə'grɛ:pnıs], n. (—ses, pl. —se) burial, funeral, interment.

begreifen [bə'graıfən], v.a. irr. understand, comprehend, conceive.

begreiflich [bə'graıflıç], adj. comprehensible, conceivable, understandable.

begrenzen [bə'grɛntsən], v.a. bound, border, limit.

Begriff [bə'grıf], m. (—s, pl. —e) notion, concept, idea, conception; im — sein, be about to . . . .

begriffen [bə'grıfən], adj. — sein in, be engaged in.

begriffsstutzig [bə'grıfsʃtutsıç], adj. obtuse, dense, slow in the uptake.

begründen [bə'gryndən], v.a. base on, justify; found, establish.

begrüßen [bə'gry:sən], v.a. greet, salute, welcome.

begünstigen [bə'gynstıgən], v.a. favour, prefer.

Begutachter [bə'gu:taxtər], m. (—s, pl. —) expert; (Sch.) assessor, second examiner.

Begutachtung [bə'gu:taxtuŋ], f. (—, pl. —en) expert opinion, assessment, report.

begütert [bə'gy:tərt], adj. wealthy, rich, well-to-do.

behaart [bə'ha:rt], adj. covered with hair, hairy.

behäbig [bə'hɛ:bıç], adj. comfortable; corpulent, portly.

behaften [bə'haftən], v.a. charge, burden.

behagen [bə'ha:gən], v.n. please, be agreeable; es behagt mir nicht, I do not like it.

behaglich [bə'ha:klıç], adj. cosy, comfortable, snug.

behalten [bə'haltən], v.a. irr. retain, keep.

Behälter [bə'hɛltər], m. (—s, pl. —) container; box, bin; (water) reservoir; tank.

behandeln [bə'handəln], v.a. treat, use; (Med.) treat; (subject) treat; handle.

Behandlung [bə'handluŋ], f. (—, pl. —en) treatment, use; (Med.) treatment.

Behang [bə'haŋ], m. (—es, pl. ˙e) hanging(s); appendage.

behängen [bə'hɛŋən], v.a. irr. festoon with, drape.

beharren [bə'harən], v.n. persevere; persist, insist.

beharrlich [bə'harlıç], adj. persevering, persistent, constant, firm.

behauen [bə'hauən], v.a. (stones) hew, cut.

behaupten [bə'hauptən], v.a. claim, assert, affirm, maintain.

Behauptung

Behauptung [bə'hauptuŋ], *f.* (—, *pl.* —en) claim, assertion, affirmation.

Behausung [bə'hauzuŋ], *f.* (—, *pl.* —en) habitation, housing.

behelfen [bə'hɛlfən], *v.r. irr. sich — mit*, make do with.

behelfsmäßig [bə'hɛlfsmɛ:sɪç], *adj.* makeshift, temporary.

behelligen [bə'hɛlɪgən], *v.a.* trouble, molest, disturb.

behend(e) [bə'hɛndə], *adj.* quick, nimble, agile.

beherbergen [bə'hɛrbɛrgən], *v.a.* give shelter to, put up, harbour.

beherrschen [bə'hɛrʃən], *v.a.* rule, govern, dominate; *eine Sache —*, master a subject. — *v.r. sich —*, control o.s.

Beherrschung [bə'hɛrʃuŋ], *f.* (—, *pl.* (*rare*) —en) domination, sway; (*subject*) grasp; (*languages*) command.

beherzigen [bə'hɛrtsɪgən], *v.a.* take to heart, follow, heed.

Beherztheit [bə'hɛrtsthaɪt], *f.* (—, *no pl.*) courage, spirit.

behexen [bə'hɛksən], *v.a.* bewitch.

behilflich [bə'hɪlflɪç], *adj.* helpful, useful.

behindern [bə'hɪndərn], *v.a.* hinder, hamper.

Behörde [bə'hœrdə], *f.* (—, *pl.* —n) the authorities.

behufs [bə'hu:fs], *prep.* (*Genit.*) in order to, with a view to.

behüten [bə'hy:tən], *v.a.* guard, protect; *Gott behüte!* Heaven forbid!

behutsam [bə'hu:tza:m], *adj.* careful, cautious.

bei [baɪ], *prep.* (*Dat.*) (*locally*) near by, close by, next to, at.

beibehalten ['baɪbəhaltən], *v.a. irr.* keep, retain.

Beiblatt ['baɪblat], *n.* (—s, *pl.* ⸚er) supplement (to a newspaper).

beibringen ['baɪbrɪŋən], *v.a. irr.* adduce (proof); produce (witnesses); (*fig.*) teach; impart to.

Beichte ['baɪçtə], *f.* (—, *pl.* —n) confession.

Beichtstuhl ['baɪçtʃtu:l], *m.* (—s, *pl.* ⸚e) confessional.

beide ['baɪdə], *adj.* both, either, the two.

beiderlei ['baɪdərlaɪ], *adj.* of both kinds.

beidrehen ['baɪdre:ən], *v.n.* (*Naut.*) heave to.

Beifall ['baɪfal], *m.* (—s, *no pl.*) (*verbal*) approbation; (*shouting*) acclamation, acclaim; (*clapping*) applause.

beifällig ['baɪfɛlɪç], *adj.* favourable, approving, assenting.

beifügen ['baɪfy:gən], *v.a.* enclose, attach.

Beifuß ['baɪfu:s], *m.* (—es, *no pl.*) (*Bot.*) mugwort.

beigeben ['baɪge:bən], *v.a. irr.* add, join to. — *v.n. klein —*, give in.

Beigeschmack ['baɪgəʃmak], *m.* (—s, *no pl.*) aftertaste, tang.

beigesellen ['baɪgəzɛlən], *v.r. sich —*, associate with.

Beihilfe ['baɪhɪlfə], *f.* (—, *pl.* —n) aid, assistance, subsidy.

beikommen ['baɪkɔmən], *v.n. irr.* (*aux.* sein) *einer Sache —*, to grapple with s.th.; *ich kann ihm nicht —*, I cannot catch him out, get at him.

Beil [baɪl], *n.* (—s, *pl.* —e) hatchet, axe.

Beilage ['baɪla:gə], *f.* (—, *pl.* —n) enclosure (with a letter); supplement (to a newspaper); *Braten mit —*, joint with vegetables.

beiläufig ['baɪlɔyfɪç], *adv.* by the way, incidentally.

beilegen ['baɪle:gən], *v.a.* add, join; enclose (in letter).

beileibe [baɪ'laɪbə], *int.* — *nicht!* on no account!

Beileid ['baɪlaɪt], *n.* (—s, *no pl.*) condolence, sympathy.

beiliegen ['baɪli:gən], *v.n. irr.* be enclosed with.

beimengen ['baɪmɛŋən], *v.a.* (*Cul.*) mix with, add.

beimessen ['baɪmɛsən], *v.a. irr. einem etwas —*, impute s.th. to s.o.; *einem Glauben —*, credit s.o., give credence to.

Bein [baɪn], *n.* (—s, *pl.* —e) leg; *einem auf die —e helfen*, give a helping hand to s.o.

beinahe [baɪ'na:ə], *adv.* almost, nearly.

Beiname ['baɪna:mə], *m.* (—ns, *pl.* —n) surname; nickname.

Beinbruch ['baɪnbrux], *m.* (—s, *pl.* ⸚e) fracture of the leg; (*coll.*) *Hals- und Beinbruch!* good luck!

Beinkleider ['baɪnklaɪdər], *n. pl.* (*obs.*) pants, trousers.

beipflichten ['baɪpflɪçtən], *v.n. einem —*, agree with s.o.

beirren [bə'ɪrən], *v.a. sich nicht — lassen*, not let o.s. be dissuaded or put off.

beisammen [baɪ'zamən], *adv.* together.

Beischlaf ['baɪʃla:f], *m.* (—s, *no pl.*) cohabitation, coition.

Beisein ['baɪzaɪn], *n.* (—s, *no pl.*) *im — von*, in the presence of.

beiseite [baɪ'zaɪtə], *adv.* apart, aside; (*Theat.*) aside.

beisetzen ['baɪzɛtsən], *v.a.* bury, inter, entomb.

Beispiel ['baɪʃpi:l], *n.* (—s, *pl.* —e) example, instance; *zum —* (*abbr.* z.B.), for instance, for example.

beißen ['baɪsən], *v.a. irr.* bite; (*pepper, smoke*) burn, sting.

Beißzange ['baɪstsaŋə], *f.* (—, *pl.* —n) pair of pincers *or* nippers.

Beistand ['baɪʃtant], *m.* (—s, *pl.* ⸚e) assistance, help; (*Law*) counsel; *— leisten*, give assistance.

beistehen ['baɪʃte:ən], *v.n. irr. einem —*, stand by s.o., help s.o.

beisteuern ['baɪʃtɔyərn], *v.a. zu etwas —*, contribute to s.th.

beistimmen ['baɪʃtɪmən], *v.n.* agree with, assent.

26

belehren

Beistrich [ˈbaɪʃtrɪç], *m.* (—(e)s, *pl.* —e) comma.

beitragen [ˈbaɪtraːgən], *v.a. irr.* contribute; be conducive to.

beitreten [ˈbaɪtreːtən], *v.n. irr.* (*aux.* sein) join (a club); enter into partnership with (a firm).

Beitritt [ˈbaɪtrɪt], *m.* (—s, *no pl.*) accession, joining.

Beiwagen [ˈbaɪvaːgən], *m.* (—s, *pl.* —) trailer, sidecar (on motor cycle).

beiwohnen [ˈbaɪvoːnən], *v.n.* be present at, attend.

Beiwort [ˈbaɪvɔrt], *n.* (—s, *pl.* ˝er) adjective, epithet.

Beize [ˈbaɪtsə], *f.* (—, *pl.* —n) caustic fluid; (*wood*) stain.

beizeiten [baɪˈtsaɪtən], *adv.* betimes, early, in good time.

beizen [ˈbaɪtsən], *v.a.* cauterise; (*wood*) stain.

bejahen [bəˈjaːən], *v.a.* answer in the affirmative.

bejahrt [bəˈjaːrt], *adj.* aged, elderly, old.

bejammern [bəˈjamərn], *v.a.* bemoan, bewail.

bekannt [bəˈkant], *adj.* known, well-known; — *mit*, acquainted with.

Bekannte [bəˈkantə], *m.* (—n, *pl.* —n) acquaintance.

bekanntlich [bəˈkantlɪç], *adv.* as is well known.

Bekanntmachung [bəˈkantmaxuŋ], *f.* (—, *pl.* —en) publication, announcement.

Bekanntschaft [bəˈkantʃaft], *f.* (—, *pl.* —en) — *mit einem machen*, strike up an acquaintance with s.o.

bekehren [bəˈkeːrən], *v.a.* convert. — *v.r. sich* —, be converted *or* become a convert (to); reform.

bekennen [bəˈkɛnən], *v.a. irr.* confess, profess; admit, own up to.

Bekenner [bəˈkɛnər], *m.* (—s, *pl.* —) Confessor (as title).

Bekenntnis [bəˈkɛntnɪs], *n.* (—ses, *pl.* —se) confession (of faith), avowal, creed.

beklagen [bəˈklaːgən], *v.a.* lament, bewail, deplore. — *v.r. sich* — *über*, complain of.

Beklagte [bəˈklaːktə], *m.* (—n, *pl.* —n) (*Law*) defendant.

bekleiden [bəˈklaɪdən], *v.a.* clothe, dress, cover; (*office*) hold.

Bekleidung [bəˈklaɪduŋ], *f.* (—, *no pl.*) clothing, clothes; (*office*) administration, holding, exercise.

beklemmen [bəˈklɛmən], *v.a. irr.* oppress.

Beklemmung [bəˈklɛmuŋ], *f.* (—, *pl.* —en) oppression, anguish.

beklommen [bəˈklɔmən], *adj.* anxious, uneasy.

bekommen [bəˈkɔmən], *v.a. irr.* obtain, get, receive.

bekömmlich [bəˈkœmlɪç], *adj.* beneficial; digestible, wholesome.

beköstigen [bəˈkœstɪgən], *v.a.* board; feed.

bekräftigen [bəˈkrɛftɪgən], *v.a.* aver, corroborate, confirm.

bekränzen [bəˈkrɛntsən], *v.a.* wreathe, crown (with a garland).

bekreuzigen [bəˈkrɔytsɪgən], *v.r. sich* —, make the sign of the cross, cross o.s.

bekriegen [bəˈkriːgən], *v.a.* make war on.

bekritteln [bəˈkrɪtəln], *v.a.* criticise, carp at, find fault with.

bekritzeln [bəˈkrɪtsəln], *v.a.* scrawl on, doodle on.

bekümmern [bəˈkymərn], *v.a.* grieve, distress, trouble. — *v.r.* trouble o.s. about, grieve over.

bekunden [bəˈkundən], *v.a.* manifest, show; declare.

beladen [bəˈlaːdən], *v.a. irr.* load.

Belag [bəˈlaːk], *m.* (—s, *pl.* ˝e) covering, layer; spread (on sandwiches); fur (on the tongue).

belagern [bəˈlaːgərn], *v.a.* besiege.

Belang [bəˈlaŋ], *m.* (—s, *pl.* —e) importance; *von* —, of great moment *or* consequence; (*pl.*) concerns, interests.

belangen [bəˈlaŋən], *v.a.* (*Law*) sue, prosecute.

belanglos [bəˈlaŋloːs], *adj.* of small account; irrelevant, unimportant.

belassen [bəˈlasən], *v.a. irr. es dabei* —, leave things as they are.

belasten [bəˈlastən], *v.a.* load, burden; (*Comm.*) debit, charge; (*Law*) incriminate.

belästigen [bəˈlɛstɪgən], *v.a.* bother, pester, molest.

Belastung [bəˈlastuŋ], *f.* (—, *pl.* —en) load, burden; (*Comm.*) debiting; (*house*) mortgage; *erbliche* —, hereditary disposition.

Belastungszeuge [bəˈlastuŋstsɔygə], *m.* (—n, *pl.* —n) witness for the prosecution.

belaubt [bəˈlaupt], *adj.* covered with leaves, leafy.

belaufen [bəˈlaufən], *v.r. irr. sich* — *auf*, amount to, come to.

belauschen [bəˈlauʃən], *v.a.* eavesdrop, overhear.

beleben [bəˈleːbən], *v.a.* animate, enliven.

Belebtheit [bəˈleːpthaɪt], *f.* (—, *no pl.*) animation, liveliness.

Beleg [bəˈleːk], *m.* (—s, *pl.* —e) document, proof, receipt, voucher.

belegen [bəˈleːgən], *v.a.* cover, overlay; reserve, book (seat); support by documents, authenticate, prove.

Belegschaft [bəˈleːkʃaft], *f.* (—, *pl.* —en) workers, personnel, staff; (*Min.*) gang, shift.

belegt [bəˈleːkt], *adj.* (*tongue*) furred; —*es Brot*, sandwich.

belehnen [bəˈleːnən], *v.a.* enfeoff; invest (with a fief).

belehren [bəˈleːrən], *v.a.* instruct, advise, inform.

27

Belehrung

Belehrung [bə'le:ruŋ], *f.* (—, *pl.* —**en**) information, instruction, advice.

beleibt [bə'laɪpt], *adj.* stout, corpulent, obese.

beleidigen [bə'laɪdɪgən], *v.a.* insult, offend, give offence to.

belesen [bə'le:zən], *adj.* well-read.

beleuchten [bə'lɔʏçtən], *v.a.* illumine, illuminate; (*fig.*) throw light on, elucidate.

Beleuchtungskörper [bə'lɔʏçtuŋskœrpər], *m.* (—**s**, *pl.* —) lighting fixture, lamp.

Belgien ['bɛlgjən], *n.* Belgium.

belichten [bə'lɪçtən], *v.a.* (*Phot.*) expose.

belieben [bə'li:bən], *v.a., v.n.* please, like, choose.

beliebig [bə'li:bɪç], *adj.* optional; any, whatever.

beliebt [bə'li:pt], *adj.* popular, well-liked.

Beliebtheit [bə'li:pthaɪt], *f.* (—, *no pl.*) popularity.

bellen ['bɛlən], *v.n.* bark.

beloben [bə'lo:bən], *v.a.* praise, approve.

belohnen [bə'lo:nən], *v.a.* reward, recompense.

belügen [bə'ly:gən], *v.a. irr.* *einen* —, tell lies to s.o., deceive s.o. by lying.

belustigen [bə'lustɪgən], *v.a.* amuse, divert, entertain.

bemächtigen [bə'mɛçtɪgən], *v.r. sich einer Sache* —, take possession of s.th.

bemäkeln [bə'mɛːkəln], *v.a.* find fault with.

bemalen [bə'ma:lən], *v.a.* paint (over).

bemängeln [bə'mɛŋəln], *v.a.* find fault with.

bemannen [bə'manən], *v.a.* man.

bemänteln [bə'mɛntəln], *v.a.* cloak, hide.

bemeistern [bə'maɪstərn], *v.a.* master.

bemerkbar [bə'mɛrkba:r], *adj.* perceptible, noticeable.

bemerken [bə'mɛrkən], *v.a.* observe, perceive, notice.

Bemerkung [bə'mɛrkuŋ], *f.* (—, *pl.* —**en**) remark, observation, note.

bemessen [bə'mɛsən], *v.a. irr.* measure; curtail.

bemitleiden [bə'mɪtlaɪdən], *v.a.* pity, be sorry for.

bemittelt [bə'mɪtəlt], *adj.* well-off, well-to-do.

bemoost [bə'mo:st], *adj.* mossy.

bemühen [bə'my:ən], *v.a.* trouble, give trouble (to). — *v.r. sich* —, take pains, strive, endeavour.

bemüht [bə'my:t], *adj.* studious; — *sein*, endeavour, try to.

bemuttern [bə'mutərn], *v.a.* mother.

benachbart [bə'naxba:rt], *adj.* neighbouring, adjacent.

benachrichtigen [bə'naxrɪçtɪgən], *v.a.* inform, give notice of, notify.

benachteiligen [bə'naxtaɪlɪgən], *v.a.* prejudice, discriminate against, handicap.

benagen [bə'na:gən], *v.a.* gnaw at.

benebeln [bə'ne:bəln], *v.a.* befog, cloud; (*fig.*) dim, intoxicate.

benedeien [bene'daɪən], *v.a.* bless, glorify.

Benediktiner [benedɪk'ti:nər], *m.* (—**s**, *pl.* —) (monk) Benedictine; Benedictine liqueur.

Benefiz [bene'fi:ts], *n.* (—**es**, *pl.* —**e**) benefit; benefit performance.

Benehmen [bə'ne:mən], *n.* (—**s**, *no pl.*) conduct, behaviour.

benehmen [bə'ne:mən], *v.r. irr. sich* —, behave, conduct o.s.

beneiden [bə'naɪdən], *v.a.* *einen* — *um*, envy s.o. (s.th.).

benennen [bə'nɛnən], *v.a.* name.

benetzen [bə'nɛtsən], *v.a.* moisten.

Bengel ['bɛŋəl], *m.* (—**s**, *pl.* —) naughty boy, scamp; rascal, lout.

benommen [bə'nɔmən], *adj.* dazed, giddy.

benötigen [bə'nøːtɪgən], *v.a.* be in need of, require.

benutzen [bə'nutsən], *v.a.* make use of, utilise.

Benzin [bɛnt'si:n], *n.* (—**s**, *no pl.*) benzine; (*Motor.*) petrol; (*Am.*) gas, gasoline.

beobachten [bə'o:baxtən], *v.a.* watch, observe.

bequem [bə'kve:m], *adj.* comfortable, easy; convenient; indolent, lazy.

bequemen [bə'kve:mən], *v.r. sich* —, condescend (to), comply (with).

Bequemlichkeit [bə'kve:mlɪçkaɪt], *f.* (—, *pl.* —**en**) convenience, ease; indolence.

beraten [bə'ra:tən], *v.a. irr.* advise, assist with advice, counsel. — *v.r. sich* — *mit*, confer with, consult with.

beratschlagen [bə'ra:tʃla:gən], *v.n.* deliberate with.

Beratung [bə'ra:tuŋ], *f.* (—, *pl.* —**en**) council, deliberation, consultation.

berauben [bə'raubən], *v.a.* rob, deprive (s.o.) of (s.th.).

berauschen [bə'rauʃən], *v.a.* intoxicate.

berechnen [bə'rɛçnən], *v.a.* compute, charge, calculate, estimate.

berechtigen [bə'rɛçtɪgən], *v.a.* *einen zu etwas* —, entitle s.o. to s.th.; authorise s.o. to have *or* do s.th.

beredsam [bə're:tza:m], *adj.* eloquent.

beredt [bə're:t], *adj.* eloquent.

Bereich [bə'raɪç], *m. & n.* (—**s**, *pl.* —**e**) extent, realm, sphere, scope.

bereichern [bə'raɪçərn], *v.a.* enrich, enlarge.

bereisen [bə'raɪzən], *v.a.* travel over *or* through, tour (a country).

bereit [bə'raɪt], *adj.* ready, prepared.

bereiten [bə'raɪtən], *v.a.* prepare, get ready.

bereits [bə'raɪts], *adv.* already.

Bereitschaft [bə'raɪtʃaft], *f.* (—, *no pl.*) readiness, preparedness.

bereitwillig [bə'raɪtvɪlɪç], *adj.* willing, ready, obliging.

bereuen [bə'rɔyən], *v.a.* repent, be sorry for, regret.
Berg [bɛrk], *m.* (—es, *pl.* —e) mountain, hill.
bergab [bɛrk'ap], *adj.* downhill.
Bergamt ['bɛrkamt], *n.* (—s, *pl.* ⁝er) mining-office, mine authority.
bergan [bɛrk'an], *adj.* uphill.
Bergarbeiter ['bɛrkarbaɪtər], *m.* (—s, *pl.* —) miner, collier.
bergauf [bɛrk'auf], *adj.* uphill.
Bergbau ['bɛrkbau], *m.* (—s, *no pl.*) mining, mining industry.
bergen ['bɛrgən], *v.a. irr.* shelter, protect, save; (*flotsam*) save, recover, salvage.
bergig ['bɛrgɪç], *adj.* mountainous, hilly.
Bergkristall ['bɛrkkrɪstal], *m.* (—s, *pl.* —e) rock-crystal.
Bergleute ['bɛrklɔytə], *pl.* miners, colliers.
Bergmann ['bɛrkman], *m.* (—s, *pl.* **Bergleute**) miner, collier.
Bergpredigt ['bɛrkpre:dɪçt], *f.* (—, *no pl.*) Sermon on the Mount.
Bergschlucht ['bɛrkʃluxt], *f.* (—, *pl.* —en) ravine, gorge.
Bergsteiger ['bɛrkʃtaɪgər], *m.* (—s, *pl.* —) mountaineer.
Bergstock ['bɛrkʃtɔk], *m.* (—s, *pl.* ⁝e) alpenstock.
Bergsturz ['bɛrkʃturts], *m.* (—es, *pl.* ⁝e) landslip, landslide.
Bergung ['bɛrguŋ], *f.* (—, *pl.* —en) sheltering, salvaging; rescue operation.
Bergwerk ['bɛrkvɛrk], *n.* (—s, *pl.* —e) mine, pit.
Bericht [bə'rɪçt], *m.* (—s, *pl.* —e) report, account, statement; —*erstatten*, report, give an account of.
Berichterstatter [bə'rɪçtərʃtatər], *m.* (—s, *pl.* —) reporter.
berichtigen [bə'rɪçtɪgən], *v.a.* set right, correct, rectify, amend.
berieseln [bə'ri:zəln], *v.a.* irrigate.
beritten [bə'rɪtən], *adj.* mounted on horseback.
Berlin [bɛr'li:n], *n.* Berlin; —*er Blau*, Prussian blue.
Bern [bɛrn], *n.* Berne.
Bernhardiner [bɛrnhar'di:nər], *m.* (—s, *pl.* —) Cistercian monk; Newfoundland dog, St. Bernard dog.
Bernstein ['bɛrnʃtaɪn], *m.* (—s, *no pl.*) amber.
bersten ['bɛrstən], *v.n. irr.* (*aux.* sein) burst.
berüchtigt [bə'ryçtɪçt], *adj.* notorious, infamous.
berücken [bə'rykən], *v.a.* enchant, fascinate.
berücksichtigen [bə'rykzɪçtɪgən], *v.a.* have regard to, take into consideration, allow for.
Beruf [bə'ru:f], *m.* (—s, *pl.* —e) profession, occupation, calling, trade.
berufen [bə'ru:fən], *v.a. irr.* (*meeting*) call, convene; appoint (to an office). — *v.r. sich* — *auf*, appeal to, refer to. — *adj.* competent, qualified.

berufsmäßig [bə'ru:fsmɛ:sɪç], *adj.* professional.
Berufung [bə'ru:fuŋ], *f.* (—, *pl.* —en) call, vocation, appointment; (*Law*) appeal.
beruhen [bə'ru:ən], *v.n. auf etwas* —, be based on, be founded on.
beruhigen [bə'ru:ɪgən], *v.a.* calm, pacify; comfort, console, set at rest.
Beruhigung [bə'ru:ɪguŋ], *f.* (—, *pl.* —en) reassurance, quieting, calming.
berühmt [bə'ry:mt], *adj.* famous, celebrated, illustrious, renowned.
berühren [bə'ry:rən], *v.a.* touch, handle; (*subject*) mention, touch upon; *peinlich berührt*, unpleasantly affected.
berußt [bə'ru:st], *adj.* sooty.
Beryll [be'ryl], *m.* (—s, *pl.* —e) beryl.
besagen [bə'za:gən], *v.a.* mean, signify.
besagt [bə'za:kt], *adj.* aforesaid, above-mentioned.
besaiten [bə'zaɪtən], *v.a.* fit with strings.
Besan [bə'za:n], *m.* (—s, *pl.* —e) (*Naut.*) miz(z)en.
besänftigen [bə'zɛnftɪgən], *v.a.* calm, appease, pacify.
Besatz [bə'zats], *m.* (—es, *pl.* ⁝e) trimming, border.
Besatzung [bə'zatsuŋ], *f.* (—, *pl.* —en) crew; (*Mil.*) garrison, occupation.
besaufen [bə'zaufən], *v.r. irr.* (*vulg.*) *sich* —, get drunk.
beschädigen [bə'ʃɛ:dɪgən], *v.a.* damage.
beschaffen [bə'ʃafən], *v.a.* procure, get. — *adj.* conditioned, constituted.
Beschaffenheit [bə'ʃafənhaɪt], *f.* (—, *no pl.*) nature, kind, quality, condition.
beschäftigen [bə'ʃɛftɪgən], *v.a.* occupy, employ.
beschämen [bə'ʃɛ:mən], *v.a.* make ashamed, shame.
beschatten [bə'ʃatən], *v.a.* shade, shadow; follow (s.o.).
Beschau [bə'ʃau], *f.* (—, *no pl.*) examination; inspection.
beschauen [bə'ʃauən], *v.a.* view, look at.
beschaulich [bə'ʃaulɪç], *adj.* tranquil, contemplative.
Beschaulichkeit [bə'ʃaulɪçkaɪt], *f.* (—, *pl.* —en) tranquillity, contemplation.
Bescheid [bə'ʃaɪt], *m.* (—s, *pl.* —e) answer, information; (*Law*) decision; — *wissen*, know o.'s way about; know what's what.
bescheiden [bə'ʃaɪdən], *v.a. irr.* inform (s.o.); *einen zu sich* —, send for s.o. — *adj.* modest, unassuming.
Bescheidenheit [bə'ʃaɪdənhaɪt], *f.* (—, *no pl.*) modesty.
bescheinen [bə'ʃaɪnən], *v.a. irr.* shine upon.
bescheinigen [bə'ʃaɪnɪgən], *v.a. einem etwas* —, attest, certify.
beschenken [bə'ʃɛŋkən], *v.a.* give a present to.

bescheren

bescheren [bə'ʃeːrən], v.a. give (a present to), bestow (s.th. on s.o.).

Bescherung [bə'ʃeːruŋ], f. (—, pl. —en) giving (of present); *das ist eine schöne —*, (fig.) this is a nice mess!

beschicken [bə'ʃɪkən], v.a. *eine Ausstellung —*, contribute to an exhibition.

beschießen [bə'ʃiːsən], v.a. irr. shoot at, fire upon, bombard.

beschiffen [bə'ʃɪfən], v.a. navigate, sail.

beschimpfen [bə'ʃɪmpfən], v.a. insult, abuse, revile.

beschirmen [bə'ʃɪrmən], v.a. protect, shelter, defend.

Beschlag [bə'ʃlaːk], m. (—s, pl. ⁓e) mounting; metal fitting; (on stick) ferrule; *etwas mit — belegen*, or *in — nehmen*, sequestrate, confiscate, seize.

beschlagen [bə'ʃlaːgən], v.a. irr. shoe (a horse). — v.n. (window) mist over.

Beschlagnahme [bə'ʃlaːknaːmə], f. (—, pl. —n) confiscation, seizure.

beschleunigen [bə'ʃlɔynɪgən], v.a. hasten, speed up, accelerate.

beschließen [bə'ʃliːsən], v.a. irr. shut, lock up; close, conclude, finish; decide, resolve upon.

Beschluß [bə'ʃlus], m. (—sses, pl. ⁓sse) determination, resolution, decree.

beschmieren [bə'ʃmiːrən], v.a. soil, smear.

beschmutzen [bə'ʃmutsən], v.a. soil, dirty, foul.

beschneiden [bə'ʃnaɪdən], v.a. irr. cut, clip; (Hort.) lop, prune; (animals) crop; circumcise.

Beschneidung [bə'ʃnaɪduŋ], f. (—, pl. —en) lopping, pruning; circumcision.

beschönigen [bə'ʃøːnɪgən], v.a. palliate, excuse.

beschränken [bə'ʃrɛŋkən], v.a. limit, restrict.

beschränkt [bə'ʃrɛŋkt], adj. limited; *etwas —*, a little stupid; *Gesellschaft mit —er Haftung*, limited (liability) company.

Beschränkung [bə'ʃrɛŋkuŋ], f. (—, pl. —en) limitation, restriction.

beschreiben [bə'ʃraɪbən], v.a. irr. describe; write upon.

beschreiten [bə'ʃraɪtən], v.a. irr. tread on.

beschuldigen [bə'ʃuldɪgən], v.a. charge (s.o.), accuse.

beschützen [bə'ʃytsən], v.a. protect, shelter, guard.

Beschützer [bə'ʃytsər], m. (—s, pl. —) protector, defender.

Beschwerde [bə'ʃveːrdə], f. (—, pl. —en) trouble, hardship, difficulty; complaint, grievance.

beschweren [bə'ʃveːrən], v.a. make heavier, weight. — v.r. *sich über etwas —*, complain of s.th.

beschwerlich [bə'ʃveːrlɪç], adj. burdensome, hard, troublesome.

beschwichtigen [bə'ʃvɪçtɪgən], v.a. soothe, appease, still.

beschwindeln [bə'ʃvɪndəln], v.a. cheat, swindle (s.o.).

beschwingt [bə'ʃvɪŋkt], adj. winged, light-footed.

beschwipst [bə'ʃvɪpst], adj. (coll.) tipsy.

beschwören [bə'ʃvøːrən], v.a. irr. testify on oath; *einen —*, implore s.o.; conjure (up) (ghosts etc.); exorcize.

beseelen [bə'zeːlən], v.a. animate.

besehen [bə'zeːən], v.a. irr. look at, inspect.

beseitigen [bə'zaɪtɪgən], v.a. remove.

beseligt [bə'zeːlɪçt], adj. enraptured, beatified.

Besen ['beːzən], m. (—s, pl. —) broom, besom.

Besenstiel [bə'zənʃtiːl], m. (—s, pl. —e) broom-stick.

besessen [bə'zɛsən], adj. possessed, obsessed, mad.

besetzen [bə'zɛtsən], v.a. (dress) trim, lace; (Mil.) occupy, garrison; (office) fill; (Theat.) cast; (seat) occupy, take; *besetzt*, engaged.

Besetzung [bə'zɛtsuŋ], f. (—, pl. —en) lacing, trimming; appointment (to post); (Theat.) cast.

besichtigen [bə'zɪçtɪgən], v.a. view, go over, inspect, examine.

besiedeln [bə'ziːdəln], v.a. colonise.

besiegeln [bə'ziːgəln], v.a. seal, set o.'s seal to.

besiegen [bə'ziːgən], v.a. vanquish, conquer, overcome.

besinnen [bə'zɪnən], v.r. irr. reflect; *sich auf etwas —*, recollect, remember, think of.

besinnungslos [bə'zɪnuŋsloːs], adj. insensible, unconscious.

Besitz [bə'zɪts], m. (—es, no pl.) possession, property.

besitzanzeigend [bə'zɪtsantsaɪgənt], adj. (Gram.) possessive.

besitzen [bə'zɪtsən], v.a. irr. possess, own, have.

Besitzergreifung [bə'zɪtsergraɪfuŋ], f. (—, no pl.) occupation, taking possession (of).

besoffen [bə'zɔfən], adj. (vulg.) drunk.

besohlen [bə'zoːlən], v.a. sole (shoes).

besolden [bə'zɔldən], v.a. give a salary to, pay.

besonder [bə'zɔndər], adj. special, particular.

Besonderheit [bəː'zɔndərhaɪt], f. (—, pl. —en) particularity, peculiarity, strangeness.

besonders [bə'zɔndərs], adv. especially.

besonnen [bə'zɔnən], adj. prudent, cautious, collected, circumspect.

besorgen [bə'zɔrgən], v.a. take care of, provide, procure.

Besorgnis [bə'zɔrknɪs], f. (—, pl. —se) care, concern, anxiety, fear.

besorgt [bə'zɔrkt], adj. apprehensive, anxious, worried.

30

Besorgung [bə'zɔrguŋ], *f.* (—, *pl.* —en) care, management; purchase, commission; —en machen, go shopping.

bespannen [bə'ʃpanən], *v.a.* string (a musical instrument); put horses (to a carriage).

bespötteln [bə'ʃpœtəln], *v.a.* ridicule.

besprechen [bə'ʃprɛçən], *v.a. irr.* discuss, talk over; (book) review. — *v.r. sich* — mit, confer with.

bespritzen [bə'ʃpritsən], *v.a.* sprinkle, splash.

besser ['bɛsər], *adj.* better; um so —, so much the better; je mehr desto —, the more the better; — sein als, be better than, be preferable to; — werden, (weather) clear up; (health) improve.

bessern ['bɛsərn], *v.a.* better, improve. — *v.r. sich* —, reform, improve, mend o.'s ways.

Besserung ['bɛsəruŋ], *f.* (—pl. —en) improvement, amendment, reform; (Med.) recovery; gute —, get well soon.

Besserungsanstalt ['bɛsəruŋsanʃtalt], *f.* (—, *pl.* —en) reformatory.

best ['bɛst], *adj.* best.

bestallen [bə'ʃtalən], *v.a.* appoint.

Bestand [bə'ʃtant], *m.* (—s, *pl.* ⸚e) continuance, duration; stock; balance of cash; — haben, endure.

Bestandaufnahme [bə'ʃtantaufnaːmə], *f.* (—, *pl.* —n) (Comm.) stock-taking.

beständig [bə'ʃtɛndiç], *adj.* continual, perpetual; (persons) steady, steadfast, constant.

Bestandteil [bə'ʃtanttaɪl], *m.* (—s, *pl.* —e) constituent part, component, ingredient, essential part.

bestärken [bə'ʃtɛrkən], *v.a.* confirm, strengthen.

bestätigen [bə'ʃtɛːtɪgən], *v.a.* confirm, ratify, bear out, sanction; den Empfang eines Briefes —, acknowledge receipt of a letter.

bestatten [bə'ʃtatən], *v.a.* bury, inter.

bestäuben [bə'ʃtɔybən], *v.a.* cover with dust, spray; (Bot.) pollinate.

bestechen [bə'ʃtɛçən], *v.a. irr.* bribe, corrupt; (fig.) captivate.

bestechlich [bə'ʃtɛçliç], *adj.* corruptible.

Bestechung [bə'ʃtɛçuŋ], *f.* (—, *pl.* —en) corruption, bribery.

Besteck [bə'ʃtɛk], *n.* (—s, *pl.* —e) set of knife, fork and spoon; set or case (of instruments).

Bestehen [bə'ʃteːən], *n.* (—s, *no pl.*) existence.

bestehen [bə'ʃteːən], *v.a. irr.* undergo, endure, pass (an examination). — *v.n.* exist; aus etwas —, consist of s.th.; be composed of s.th.; auf (Dat.) —, insist upon s.th.

besteigen [bə'ʃtaɪgən], *v.a. irr.* ascend, mount, climb.

bestellen [bə'ʃtɛlən], *v.a.* order, book; appoint; put in order; (letter, message) deliver; (field) till.

Bestellung [bə'ʃtɛluŋ], *f.* (—, *pl.* —en) order, commission, delivery (of letter); tilling (of field); appointment; auf —, to order.

bestens ['bɛstəns], *adv.* in the best manner.

besteuern [bə'ʃtɔyərn], *v.a.* tax.

bestialisch [bɛsti'aːlɪʃ], *adj.* beastly, bestial.

Bestie ['bɛstjə], *f.* (—, *pl.* —n) beast, brute.

bestimmen [bə'ʃtɪmən], *v.a.* fix, settle; decide (s.th.); determine, define.

bestimmt [bə'ʃtɪmt], *adj.* decided, fixed, appointed; ganz —, positively, most decidedly.

Bestimmtheit [bə'ʃtɪmthaɪt], *f.* (—, *no pl.*) certainty.

Bestimmung [bə'ʃtɪmuŋ], *f.* (—, *pl.* —en) settlement, decision, determination; provision; destiny.

bestrafen [bə'ʃtraːfən], *v.a.* punish, chastise.

bestrahlen [bə'ʃtraːlən], *v.a.* irradiate; (Med.) treat by radiotherapy.

bestreben [bə'ʃtreːbən], *v.r. sich* —, exert o.s., strive (for), endeavour.

Bestrebung [bə'ʃtreːbuŋ], *f.* (—, *pl.* —en) effort, endeavour, exertion.

bestreichen [bə'ʃtraɪçən], *v.a. irr.* spread.

bestreiten [bə'ʃtraɪtən], *v.a. irr.* contest, deny, dispute; defray (costs).

bestreuen [bə'ʃtrɔyən], *v.a.* sprinkle, strew, powder.

bestricken [bə'ʃtrɪkən], *v.a.* ensnare, entangle.

bestürmen [bə'ʃtyrmən], *v.a.* storm, assail; (fig.) importune.

bestürzen [bə'ʃtyrtsən], *v.a.* dismay, confound, perplex.

Besuch [bə'zuːx], *m.* (—s, *pl.* —e) visit; (person) visitor.

besuchen [bə'zuːxən], *v.a.* visit, call on; attend; frequent.

besudeln [bə'zuːdəln], *v.a.* soil, foul.

betagt [bə'taːkt], *adj.* aged, elderly.

betätigen [bə'tɛːtɪgən], *v.a.* practise, operate. — *v.r. sich* —, take an active part, work, participate (in).

betäuben [bə'tɔybən], *v.a.* deafen; stun, benumb, anaesthetize.

Betäubung [bə'tɔybuŋ], *f.* (—, *pl.* —en) stupor, stupefaction; örtliche —, local anaesthetic.

beteiligen [bə'taɪlɪgən], *v.a.* einen an etwas —, give s.o. a share of s.th. — *v.r. sich an etwas* —, participate in s.th.; (Comm.) have shares in s.th.

Beteiligte [bə'taɪlɪçtə], *m.* (—n, *pl.*—n) person concerned.

Beteiligung [bə'taɪlɪguŋ], *f.* (—, *pl.* —en) participation, interest.

beten ['beːtən], *v.n.* pray, say o.'s prayers.

beteuern [bə'tɔyərn], *v.a.* aver, affirm solemnly.

betiteln [bə'tiːtəln], *v.a.* entitle, name.

Beton [be'tõ], *m.* (—s, *no pl.*) concrete.

betonen

betonen [bə'to:nən], *v.a.* accentuate, stress, emphasise.

Betonung [bə'to:nuŋ], *f.* (—, *pl.* —en) accentuation, emphasis, stress.

betören [bə'tø:rən], *v.a.* delude, infatuate.

Betracht [bə'traxt], *m.* (—s, *no pl.*) consideration, respect, regard.

betrachten [bə'traxtən], *v.a.* consider, look at, view; *etwas aufmerksam —*, contemplate s.th.

beträchtlich [bə'trɛçtlɪç], *adj.* considerable.

Betrachtung [bə'traxtuŋ], *f.* (—, *pl.* —en) contemplation, consideration.

Betrag [bə'tra:k], *m.* (—s, *pl.* ⁓e) amount, sum total.

betragen [bə'tra:gən], *v.a. irr.* amount to, come to. — *v.r. sich —*, behave, conduct o.s.

Betragen [bə'tra:gən], *n.* (—s, *no pl.*) behaviour, conduct, demeanour.

betrauen [bə'trauən], *v.a. einen mit etwas —*, entrust s.o. with s.th.

betrauern [bə'trauərn], *v.a.* mourn for, bemoan.

Betreff [bə'trɛf], *m.* (—s, *no pl.*) reference; *in —*, with regard to.

betreffen [bə'trɛfən], *v.a. irr.* concern, affect, relate to.

Betreiben [bə'traibən], *n.* (—s, *no pl.*) *auf — von*, at the instigation of.

betreiben [bə'traibən], *v.a. irr.* (*business*) carry on; (*factory*) run; (*trade*) follow, practise.

Betreten [bə'tre:tən], *n.* (—s, *no pl.*) entry, entering.

betreten [bə'tre:tən], *v.a. irr.* step upon, set foot on, enter. — *adj.* disconcerted, embarrassed.

betreuen [bə'trɔyən], *v.a.* care for, attend to.

Betrieb [bə'tri:p], *m.* (—s, *pl.* —e) management, business, factory, plant; *den — einstellen*, close down; *in — sein*, be in operation; *in — setzen*, start working.

betriebsam [bə'tri:pza:m], *adj.* active, busy, industrious, diligent.

Betriebsamkeit [bə'tri:pza:mkaɪt], *f.* (—, *pl.* —en) activity, industry, bustle.

betriebsfertig [bə'tri:psfɛrtɪç], *adj.* ready for service; operational.

Betriebsmaterial [bə'tri:psmaterja:l], *n.* (—s, *pl.* —ien) (*Railw.*) rolling-stock; (*factory*) working-stock.

Betriebspersonal [bə'tri:psperzona:l], *n.* (—s, *no pl.*) workmen, employees, staff.

betrinken [bə'trɪŋkən], *v.r. irr. sich —*, get drunk.

betroffen [bə'trɔfən], *adj.* perplexed, confounded.

betrüben [bə'try:bən], *v.a.* afflict, grieve.

Betrübnis [bə'try:pnɪs], *f.* (—ses, *pl.* —se) affliction, grief, distress, sorrow.

betrübt [bə'try:pt], *adj.* sad, grieved.

Betrug [bə'tru:k], *m.* (—s, *pl.* ⁓ereien) fraud, deceit, deception, imposture; *einen — begehen*, commit a fraud.

betrügen [bə'try:gən], *v.a. irr.* cheat, deceive.

Betrüger [bə'try:gər], *m.* (—s, —) swindler, cheat, deceiver, impostor.

betrunken [bə'truŋkən], *adj.* drunk, drunken, tipsy.

Bett [bɛt], *n.* —(e)s, *pl.* —en) bed; (*river*) bed, channel.

Bettdecke [bɛtdɛkə], *f.* (—, *pl.* —n) counterpane; (*Am.*) bedspread; *wollene —*, blanket; *gesteppte —*, quilt.

bettelarm [bɛtəlarm], *adj.* destitute.

Bettelei [bɛtə'laɪ], *f.* (—, *pl.* —en) begging, beggary, penury.

betteln [bɛtəln], *v.a.* beg, ask alms.

betten [bɛtən], *v.a.* bed, lay to rest. — *v.r.* (*fig.*) *sich —*, make o.'s bed.

bettlägerig [bɛtlɛgərɪç], *adj.* bedridden.

Bettlaken [bɛtla:kən], *n.* (—s, *pl.* —) sheet.

Bettler [bɛtlər], *m.* (—s, *pl.* —) beggar.

Bettstelle [bɛtʃtɛlə], *f.* (—, *pl.* —n) bedstead.

Bettvorleger [bɛtfo:rle:gər], *m.* (—s, *pl.* —) bedside-carpet *or* rug.

Bettwäsche [bɛtvɛʃə], *f.* (—, *no pl.*) bed linen, bed clothes.

Bettzeug [bɛttsɔyk], *n.* (—s, *no pl.*) bedding.

beugen [bɔygən], *v.a.* bend, bow. — *v.r. sich —*, bend down, stoop.

Beugung [bɔyguŋ], *f.* (—, *pl.* —en) (*Gram.*) inflection.

Beule [bɔylə], *f.* (—, *pl.* —n) bruise, bump, swelling, boil.

beunruhigen [bə'unru:ɪgən], *v.a.* alarm, trouble, disquiet.

beurkunden [bə'u:rkundən], *v.a.* authenticate, verify.

beurlauben [bə'u:rlaubən], *v.a.* grant leave of absence. — *v.r. sich —*, take leave.

beurteilen [bə'urtaɪlən], *v.a.* judge, criticise.

Beute [bɔytə], *f.* (—, *no pl.*) booty, loot; (*animals*) prey; (*Hunt.*) bag.

Beutel [bɔytəl], *m.* (—s, *pl.* —) bag; (*money*) purse; (*Zool.*) pouch.

Beuteltier [bɔytəlti:r], *n.* (—s, *pl.* —e) marsupial.

bevölkern [bə'fœlkərn], *v.a.* people, populate.

Bevölkerung [bə'fœlkəruŋ], *f.* (—, *pl.* —en) population.

bevollmächtigen [bə'fɔlmɛçtɪgən], *v.a.* empower, authorise.

bevor [bə'fo:r], *conj.* before, ere, beforehand.

bevormunden [bə'fo:rmundən], *v.a. insep.* act as guardian to; (*fig.*) browbeat.

bevorrechtigt [bə'fo:rrɛçtɪçt], *adj.* privileged.

bevorstehen [bə'fo:rʃteːən], *v.n. irr.* impend, lie ahead, be imminent; *einem —*, be in store for s.o.

bevorzugen [bə'fo:rtsuːgən], *v.a. insep.* prefer, favour.

bewachen [bə'vaxən], *v.a.* watch over, guard.

bewachsen [bə'vaksən], *adj.* overgrown.

bewaffnen [bə'vafnən], *v.a.* arm, supply with arms.

Bewahranstalt [bə'vaːranʃtalt], *f.* (—, *pl.* —en) kindergarten, nursery.

bewahren [bə'vaːrən], *v.a.* preserve, keep, take care of.

bewähren [bə'vɛːrən], *v.r. sich —*, prove o.s.

bewahrheiten [bə'vaːrhaɪtən], *v.r. sich —*, come true.

bewährt [bə'vɛːrt], *adj.* proved.

Bewährung [bə'vɛːruŋ], *f.* (—, *no pl.*) proof, verification.

Bewährungsfrist [bə'vɛːruŋsfrɪst], *f.* (—, *no pl.*) probation.

bewaldet [bə'valdət], *adj.* wooded, woody.

bewältigen [bə'vɛltɪgən], *v.a.* overcome; manage, master; cope *or* deal with.

bewandert [bə'vandərt], *adj.* versed, skilled, experienced, conversant.

bewandt [bə'vant], *adj.* such; *damit ist es so —*, it is like this.

Bewandtnis [bə'vantnɪs], *f.* (—, *pl.* —se) circumstance, condition, state; *es hat damit folgende —*, the circumstances are as follows.

bewässern [bə'vɛsərn], *v.a.* water, irrigate.

bewegen [bə've:gən], *v.a., v.r.* move, stir; take exercise. — *v.a. irr.* persuade, induce.

Beweggrund [bə've:kgrunt], *m.* (—es, *pl.* ⁻e) motive, reason, motivation.

beweglich [bə've:klɪç], *adj.* movable; agile, brisk, sprightly.

Bewegung [bə've:guŋ], *f.* (—, *pl.* —en) motion, movement; (*mind*) emotion, agitation.

beweinen [bə'vaɪnən], *v.a.* lament, bemoan, deplore.

Beweis [bə'vaɪs], *m.* (—es, *pl.* —e) proof, evidence; (*Maths.*) demonstration.

beweisen [bə'vaɪzən], *v.a. irr.* prove, show, demonstrate.

Beweiskraft [bə'vaɪskraft], *f.* (—, *no pl.*) probative force.

Beweismittel [bə'vaɪsmɪtəl], *n.* (—s, *pl.* —) evidence, proof.

Bewenden [bə'vɛndən], *n.* (—s, *no pl.*) *es hat damit sein —*, there the matter rests.

bewenden [bə'vɛndən], *v.n. irr. es dabei — lassen*, leave it at that.

bewerben [bə'vɛrbən], *v.r. irr. sich um etwas —*, apply for s.th.

Bewerber [bə'vɛrbər], *m.* (—s, *pl.* —) applicant, candidate; (*marriage*) suitor.

Bewerbung [bə'vɛrbuŋ], *f.* (—, *pl.* —en) application, candidature; (*marriage*) courtship.

bewerkstelligen [bə'vɛrkʃtɛlɪgən], *v.a.* perform, bring about.

bewerten [bə'vɛrtən], *v.a.* estimate, value.

bewilligen [bə'vɪlɪgən], *v.a.* grant, allow, permit.

bewillkommnen [bə'vɪlkɔmnən], *v.a.* welcome.

bewirken [bə'vɪrkən], *v.a.* effect, bring about.

bewirten [bə'vɪrtən], *v.a.* entertain, act as host (to).

bewirtschaften [bə'vɪrtʃaftən], *v.a.* manage.

bewohnen [bə'vo:nən], *v.a.* inhabit, occupy.

Bewohner [bə'vo:nər], *m.* (—s, *pl.* —) inhabitant, tenant, resident.

bewölken [bə'vœlkən], *v.r. sich —*, become overcast, become cloudy.

bewundern [bə'vundərn], *v.a.* admire.

bewundernswert [bə'vundərnsvert], *adj.* admirable.

bewußt [bə'vust], *adj.* conscious, aware; *es war mir nicht —*, I was not aware of.

bewußtlos [bə'vustlo:s], *adj.* unconscious; *— werden*, faint, lose consciousness.

Bewußtsein [bə'vustzaɪn], *n.* (—s, *no pl.*) consciousness; *einem etwas zum — bringen*, bring s.th. home to s.o.

bezahlbar [bə'tsaːlbaːr], *adj.* payable.

bezahlen [bə'tsaːlən], *v.a.* pay; (*bill*) settle.

bezähmen [bə'tsɛːmən], *v.a.* tame, restrain. — *v.r. sich —*, restrain o.s., control o.s.

bezaubern [bə'tsaubərn], *v.a.* bewitch, enchant, fascinate.

bezeichnen [bə'tsaɪçnən], *v.a.* mark, denote, indicate, designate.

bezeichnend [bə'tsaɪçnənt], *adj.* indicative, characteristic, significant.

bezeigen [bə'tsaɪgən], *v.a.* manifest, show.

bezeugen [bə'tsɔygən], *v.a.* attest, bear witness, testify.

bezichtigen [bə'tsɪçtɪgən], *v.a.* accuse (s.o.) of (s.th.).

beziehbar [bə'tsiːbaːr], *adj.* (*goods*) obtainable; (*house*) ready for occupation.

beziehen [bə'tsiːən], *v.a. irr.* cover; (*house etc.*) move into; (*instrument*) string; make up (a bed); *die Wache —*, mount guard. — *v.r. sich —*, (*sky*) cloud over; *sich auf etwas —*, refer to s.th.

Bezieher [bə'tsiːər], *m.* (—s, *pl.* —) customer; (*newspaper*) subscriber.

Beziehung [bə'tsiːuŋ], *f.* (—, *pl.* —en) relation, connection; reference, bearing; *in dieser —*, in this respect; (*Comm.*) *unter — auf*, with reference to.

beziehungsweise [bə'tsiːuŋsvaɪzə], *adv.* respectively, as the case may be, or.

beziffern [bəˈtsɪfərn], v.a. number.
Bezirk [bəˈtsɪrk], m. (—s, pl. —e) district; (Am.) precinct; (Parl.) constituency; (Law) circuit.
Bezirksgericht [bəˈtsɪrksɡərɪçt], n. (—s, pl. —e) county court.
Bezug [bəˈtsuːk], m. (—s, pl. ˙e) (pillow) case, cover; (goods) order, purchase; (fig.) relation; — haben auf, refer to; mit — auf, referring to; (pl.) emoluments, income.
bezüglich [bəˈtsyːklɪç], adj. with regard to, regarding.
Bezugnahme [bəˈtsuːknaːmə], f. (—, pl. —n) reference; unter — auf, with reference to.
Bezugsbedingung [bəˈtsuːksbədɪnʊn], f. (—, pl. —en) (usually pl.) (Comm.) conditions or terms of delivery.
Bezugsquelle [bəˈtsuːkskvɛlə], f. (—, pl. —n) source of supply.
bezwecken [bəˈtsvɛkən], v.a. aim at, intend.
bezweifeln [bəˈtsvaɪfəln], v.a. doubt, question.
bezwingen [bəˈtsvɪnən], v.a. irr. subdue, conquer. — v.r. sich —, restrain o.s.
Bibel [ˈbiːbəl], f. (—, pl. —n) Bible.
Bibelauslegung [ˈbiːbəlausleːɡun], f. (—, pl. —en) (Biblical) exegesis.
Biber [ˈbiːbər], m. (—s, pl. —) (Zool.) beaver.
Bibliothek [biblioˈteːk], f. (—, pl. —en) library.
Bibliothekar [biblioteˈkaːr], m. (—s, pl. —e) librarian.
biblisch [ˈbiːblɪʃ], adj. biblical, scriptural.
Bickbeere [ˈbɪkbeːrə], f. (—, pl. —n) bilberry.
bieder [ˈbiːdər], adj. upright, honest, decent.
Biederkeit [ˈbiːdərkaɪt], f. (—, no pl.) uprightness, probity.
Biedermann [ˈbiːdərman], m. (—s, pl. ˙er) honourable man; (iron.) Philistine.
biegen [ˈbiːɡən], v.a. irr. bend, bow. — v.n. (aux. sein) um die Ecke —, turn the corner. — v.r. sich —, curve; — oder brechen, by hook or by crook.
biegsam [ˈbiːkzaːm], adj. flexible, supple, pliant.
Biegung [ˈbiːɡun], f. (—, pl. —en) curve, bend; (Gram.) inflexion.
Biene [ˈbiːnə], f. (—, pl. —n) bee.
Bienenhaus [ˈbiːnənhaus], n. (—es, pl. ˙er) apiary.
Bienenkorb [ˈbiːnənkɔrp], m. (—s, pl. ˙e) beehive.
Bienenzüchter [ˈbiːnəntsyçtər], m. (—s, pl. —) apiarist, bee-keeper.
Bier [biːr], n. (—(e)s, pl. —) beer.
Bierkanne [ˈbiːrkanə], f. (—, pl. —n) tankard.
Biest [biːst], n. (—es, pl. —er) brute, beast.
bieten [ˈbiːtən], v.a. irr. offer; (auction) bid.

Bieter [ˈbiːtər], m. (—s, pl. —) (auction) bidder.
Bigotterie [biɡɔtəˈriː], f. (—, no pl.) bigotry.
Bijouterie [biʒutəˈriː], f. (—, pl. —n) trinkets, dress-jewellery.
Bilanz [biˈlants], f. (—, pl. —en) (Comm.) balance; (financial) statement.
Bild [bɪlt], n. (—es, pl. —er) picture, painting, portrait, image; idea; (coins) effigy; (Cards) court card; (books) illustration; (speech) figure of speech, metaphor.
bilden [ˈbɪldən], v.c. form, shape; (mind) cultivate. — v.r. sich —, improve o.'s mind, educate o.s.
bildend [ˈbɪldənt], adj. instructive, civilising; die —en Künste, the fine arts.
bilderreich [ˈbɪldəraɪç], adj. —e Sprache, flowery language, figurative style.
Bilderschrift [ˈbɪldərʃrɪft], f. (—, pl. —en) hieroglyphics.
Bilderstürmer [ˈbɪldərʃtyrmər], m. (—s, pl. —) iconoclast.
Bildhauer [ˈbɪlthauər], m. (—s, pl. —) sculptor.
bildhübsch [ˈbɪlthypʃ], adj. as pretty as a picture.
bildlich [ˈbɪltlɪç], adj. figurative.
Bildnis [ˈbɪltnɪs], n. (—ses, pl. —se) portrait, figure, image, effigy.
bildsam [ˈbɪltzaːm], adj. plastic, ductile.
bildschön [ˈbɪltʃøːn], adj. very beautiful.
Bildseite [ˈbɪltzaɪtə], f. (—, pl. —n) (coin) face, obverse.
Bildung [ˈbɪldun], f. (—, pl. (rare) —en) formation; (mind) education, culture; knowledge, learning, accomplishments, attainments.
Billard [ˈbɪljart], n. (—s, pl. —s) billiards.
Billett [bɪlˈjɛt], n. (—s, pl. —s) ticket.
billig [ˈbɪlɪç], adj. cheap, inexpensive; equitable, just, fair, reasonable.
billigen [ˈbɪlɪɡən], v.a. sanction, approve of, consent to.
Billigkeit [ˈbɪlɪçkaɪt], f. (—, no pl.) cheapness; fairness, equitableness, reasonableness.
Billigung [ˈbɪlɪɡun], f. (—, no pl.) approbation, approval, sanction.
Bilsenkraut [ˈbɪlzənkraut], n. (—s, pl. ˙er) henbane.
bimmeln [ˈbɪməln], v.n. (coll.) tinkle.
Bimsstein [ˈbɪmsʃtaɪn], m. (—s, pl. —e) pumice stone.
Binde [ˈbɪndə], f. (—, pl. —n) band, bandage; tie; ligature; sanitary towel.
Bindeglied [ˈbɪndegliːt], n. (—s, pl. —er) connecting link.
Bindehaut [ˈbɪndehaut], f. (—, pl. ˙e) (Anat.) conjunctiva.
Bindehautentzündung [ˈbɪndehautɛntsyndun], f. (—, pl. —en) conjunctivitis.

binden ['bɪndən], *v.a. irr.* bind, tie, fasten.

Bindestrich ['bɪndəʃtrɪç], *m.* (—(e)s, *pl.* —e) hyphen.

Bindewort ['bɪndəvɔrt], *n.* (—s, *pl.* ˙er) conjunction.

Bindfaden ['bɪntfɑːdən], *m.* (—s, *pl.* ˙) string, twine.

Bindung ['bɪnduŋ], *f.* (—, *pl.* —en) binding, bond; obligation; (*Mus.*) ligature.

binnen ['bɪnən], *prep.* (*Genit. & Dat.*), *adv.* within.

Binnenhafen ['bɪnənhɑːfən], *m.* (—s, *pl.* ˙) inland harbour.

Binnenhandel ['bɪnənhandəl], *m.* (—s, *no pl.*) inland trade.

Binse ['bɪnzə], *f.* (—, *pl.* —n) (*Bot.*) rush, reed.

Biographie [biogrɑˈfiː], *f.* (—, *pl.* —n) biography.

Birke ['bɪrkə], *f.* (—, *pl.* —n) (*Bot.*) birch, birch-tree.

Birma ['bɪrmɑː], *n.* Burma.

Birnbaum ['bɪrnbaum], *m.* (—s, *pl.* ˙e) pear-tree.

Birne ['bɪrnə], *f.* (—, *pl.* —n) pear; (*Elec.*) bulb.

birnförmig ['bɪrnfœrmɪç], *adj.* pear-shaped.

bis [bɪs], *prep.* (*time*) till, until; by; (*place*) to, up to; — *auf*, with the exception of — *conj.* till, until.

Bisam ['biːzam], *m.* (—s, *pl.* —e) musk.

Bischof ['bɪʃɔf], *m.* (—s, *pl.* ˙e) bishop.

bischöflich ['bɪʃœflɪç], *adj.* episcopal.

Bischofsstab ['bɪʃɔfsʃtɑːp], *m.* (—s, *pl.* ˙e) crosier.

bisher ['bɪsheːr], *adv.* hitherto, till now.

bisherig [bɪsˈheːrɪç], *adj.* up to this time, hitherto existing.

Biskayischer Meerbusen [bɪsˈkaːɪʃər ˈmeːrbuːzən]. Bay of Biscay.

Biß [bɪs], *m.* (—sses, *pl.* —sse) bite, sting.

Bißchen ['bɪsçən], *n.* (—s, *pl.* —) morsel; little bit.

Bissen ['bɪsən], *m.* (—s, *pl.* —) bite, morsel.

bissig ['bɪsɪç], *adj.* biting, cutting; sharp, vicious; sarcastic.

Bistum ['bɪstum], *n.* (—s, *pl.* ˙er) bishopric, diocese; see.

bisweilen [bɪsˈvailən], *adv.* sometimes, now and then, occasionally.

Bitte ['bɪtə], *f.* (—, *pl.* —n) request, entreaty.

bitte ['bɪtə], *int.* please.

bitten ['bɪtən], *v.a. irr.* ask; request.

bitter ['bɪtər], *adj.* bitter.

Bitterkeit ['bɪtərkait], *f.* (—, *no pl.*) bitterness.

bitterlich ['bɪtərlɪç], *adv.* (*fig.*) bitterly.

Bittersalz ['bɪtərzalts], *n.* (—es, *no pl.*) Epsom salts.

Bittgang ['bɪtgaŋ], *m.* (—(e)s, *pl.* ˙e) (*Eccl.*) procession.

Bittsteller ['bɪtʃtɛlər], *m.* (—s, *pl.* —) petitioner, suppli(c)ant.

Biwak ['biːvak], *m.* (—s, *pl.* —s) bivouac.

blähen ['blɛːən], *v.a.* inflate, puff up, swell.

Blähung ['blɛːuŋ], *f.* (—, *pl.* —en) (*Med.*) flatulence.

blaken ['blɑːkən], *v.n.* smoulder; smoke.

Blamage [blaˈmɑːʒə], *f.* (—, *pl.* —n) shame, disgrace.

blamieren [blaˈmiːrən], *v.a., v.r.* make (o.s.) ridiculous, make a fool of o.s.

blank [blaŋk], *adj.* shining, bright, smooth, polished.

Bläschen ['blɛːsçən], *n.* (—s, *pl.* —) little bubble, blister; (*Med.*) vesicle.

Blase ['blɑːzə], *f.* (—, *pl.* —n) (*soap*) bubble; (*skin*) blister; (*Anat.*) bladder.

Blasebalg ['blɑːzəbalk], *m.* (—s, *pl.* ˙e) pair of bellows.

blasen ['blɑːzən], *v.a. irr.* blow; (*Mus.*) sound.

Bläser ['blɛːzər], *m.* (—s, *pl.* —) (*glass*) blower; (*Mus.*) wind player.

blasiert [blaˈziːrt], *adj.* blasé, haughty.

Blasrohr ['blɑːsroːr], *n.* (—s, *pl.* —e) blow-pipe, pea-shooter.

blaß [blas], *adj.* pale, wan, pallid.

Blässe ['blɛsə], *f.* (—, *no pl.*) paleness, pallor.

Blatt [blat], *n.* (—s, *pl.* ˙er) leaf; (*paper*) sheet; blade.

Blatter ['blatər], *f.* (—, *pl.* —n) pustule; (*pl.*) smallpox.

blättern ['blɛtərn], *v.a.* turn the leaves (of a book).

Blätterteig ['blɛtərtaik], *m.* (—s, *no pl.*) puff pastry.

Blattgold ['blatgɔlt], *n.* (—es, *no pl.*) gold-leaf.

Blattlaus ['blatlaus], *f.* (—, *pl.* ˙e) (*Ent.*) plant-louse.

Blattpflanze ['blatpflantsə], *f.* (—, *pl.* —n) leaf-plant.

blau [blau], *adj.* blue; —*en Montag machen*, stay away from work; *sein* —*es Wunder erleben*, be amazed.

blauäugig ['blauɔygɪç], *adj.* blue-eyed.

Blaubeere ['blaubeːrə], *f.* (—, *pl.* —n) bilberry, blueberry.

blaublütig ['blaublyːtɪç], *adj.* aristocratic.

bläuen ['blɔyən], *v.a.* dye blue, rinse in blue.

bläulich ['blɔylɪç], *adj.* pale blue, bluish.

Blausäure ['blauzɔyrə], *f.* (—, *no pl.*) prussic acid.

Blaustrumpf ['blauʃtrumpf], *m.* (—s, *pl.* ˙e) blue-stocking.

Blech [blɛç], *n.* (—s, *pl.* —e) tinplate, sheet metal.

blechen ['blɛçən], *v.n.* (*coll.*) fork out money.

blechern ['blɛçərn], *adj.* made of tin, tinny.

Blechinstrument ['blɛçɪnstrumɛnt], *n.* (—s, *pl.* —e) (*Mus.*) brass instrument.

Blei [blaɪ], *n.* (—s, *no pl.*) lead.
bleiben ['blaɪbən], *v.n. irr.* (*aux.* sein) remain, stay.
bleich [blaɪç], *adj.* pale, wan, pallid.
Bleiche ['blaɪçə], *f.* (—, *pl.* —n) pallor; (*laundry*) bleaching-place.
bleichen ['blaɪçən], *v.a. irr.* bleach, whiten.
Bleichsucht ['blaɪçzuxt], *f.* (—, *no pl.*) chlorosis, anaemia.
bleiern ['blaɪərn], *adj.* leaden.
Bleiglanz ['blaɪglants], *m.* (—es, *no pl.*) (*Min.*) lead sulphide.
Bleisoldat ['blaɪzɔldaːt], *m.* (—en, *pl.* —en) tin soldier.
Bleistift ['blaɪʃtɪft], *m.* (—s, *pl.* —e) pencil.
Blende ['blɛndə], *f.* (—, *no pl.*) blind; (*Min.*) blende; (*Phot.*) shutter.
blenden ['blɛndən], *v.a.* dazzle, blind.
Blendlaterne ['blɛntlatɛrnə], *f.* (—, *pl.* —n) dark-lantern.
Blendung ['blɛnduŋ], *f.* (—, *pl.* —en) blinding, dazzling.
Blendwerk ['blɛntvɛrk], *n.* (—s, *no pl.*) (optical) illusion, false show.
Blick [blɪk], *m.* (—s, *pl.* —e) glance, look, glimpse.
blicken ['blɪkən], *v.n.* look, glance.
blind [blɪnt], *adj.* blind, sightless; —er *Passagier,* stowaway.
Blinddarm ['blɪntdarm], *m.* (—s, *pl.* ⸚e) appendix.
Blinddarmentzündung ['blɪntdarmɛntsynduŋ], *f.* (—, *pl.* —en) appendicitis.
Blindekuh [blɪndə'kuː], *f.* (—, *no pl.*) blind man's buff.
Blindgänger ['blɪntgɛŋər], *m.* (—s, *pl.* —) misfire, dud, blind.
Blindheit ['blɪnthaɪt], *f.* (—, *no pl.*) blindness.
blindlings ['blɪntlɪŋs], *adv.* blindly; at random.
Blindschleiche ['blɪntʃlaɪçə], *f.* (—, *pl.* —n) (*Zool.*) blind-worm.
blinken ['blɪŋkən], *v.n.* blink, flash, glitter, gleam.
blinzeln ['blɪntsəln], *v.n.* blink.
Blitz [blɪts], *m.* (—es, *pl.* —e) lightning, flash.
Blitzableiter ['blɪtsaplaɪtər], *m.* (—s, *pl.* —) lightning-conductor.
blitzblank ['blɪtsblaŋk], *adj.* as bright as a new pin; cleanly.
blitzen ['blɪtsən], *v.n.* flash; *es blitzt,* it is lightening; glitter, shine.
Blitzesschnelle ['blɪtsəsʃnɛlə], *f.* (—, *no pl.*) lightning-speed.
Blitzlicht ['blɪtslɪçt], *n.* (—s, *no pl.*) flashlight.
Blitzschlag ['blɪtsʃlaːk], *m.* (—s, *pl.* ⸚e) flash of lightning.
Blitzstrahl ['blɪtsʃtraːl], *m.* (—s, *pl.* —en) flash of lightning.
Block [blɔk], *m.* (—s, *pl.* ⸚e) block, log; pad.
Blockhaus ['blɔkhaus], *n.* (—es, *pl.* ⸚er) log-cabin.

blockieren [blɔ'kiːrən], *v.a.* block (up); (*Mil.*) blockade.
blöde ['bløːdə], *adj.* stupid, dull, thick-headed, dim.
Blödsinn ['bløːtsɪn], *m.* (—s, *no pl.*) nonsense, idiocy.
blöken ['bløːkən], *v.n.* bleat; (*cows*) low.
blond [blɔnt], *adj.* blond, fair, fair-headed.
bloß [bloːs], *adj.* naked, uncovered; bare, mere.
Blöße ['bløːsə], *f.* (—, *pl.* —n) naked-ness, bareness; (*fig.*) weak point.
bloßlegen ['bloːsleːgən], *v.a.* un-cover, lay bare; (*fig.*) reveal, expose.
bloßstellen ['bloːsʃtɛlən], *v.a.* com-promise, show up. — *v.r.* sich —, compromise o.s.
blühen ['blyːən], *v.n.* bloom, blossom, flower, flourish.
Blümchen ['blyːmçən], *n.* (—s, *pl.* —) small flower.
Blume ['bluːmə], *f.* (—, *pl.* —n) flower, bloom; (*wine*) bouquet; (*beer*) froth.
Blumenblatt ['bluːmənblat], *n.* (—s, *pl.* ⸚er) petal.
Blumenerde ['bluːməneːrdə], *f.* (—, *no pl.*) garden mould.
Blumenkelch ['bluːmənkɛlç], *m.* (—es, *pl.* —e) calyx.
Blumenkohl ['bluːmənkoːl], *m.* (—s, *pl.* —e) cauliflower.
Blumenstaub ['bluːmənʃtaup], *m.* (—s, *no pl.*) pollen.
Blumenstrauß ['bluːmənʃtraus], *m.* (—es, *pl.* ⸚e) bunch of flowers, posy, nosegay.
Blumenzucht ['bluːməntsuxt], *f.* (—, *no pl.*) floriculture.
Bluse ['bluːzə], *f.* (—, *pl.* —n) blouse.
Blut [bluːt], *n.* (—es, *no pl.*) blood.
blutarm ['bluːtarm], *adj.* anæmic; (*fig.*) very poor.
Blutbad ['bluːtbaːt], *n.* (—es, *pl.* ⸚er) massacre.
blutdürstig ['bluːtdyrstɪç], *adj.* blood-thirsty.
Blüte ['blyːtə], *f.* (—, *pl.* —n) blossom, flower, bloom.
Blutegel ['bluːteːgəl], *m.* (—s, *pl.* —) leech.
bluten ['bluːtən], *v.n.* bleed.
Bluterguß ['bluːtergus], *m.* (—es, *pl.* ⸚e) effusion of blood.
Blutgefäß ['bluːtgəfɛːs], *n.* (—es, *pl.* —e) blood-vessel.
blutig ['bluːtɪç], *adj.* bloody; cruel.
blutjung ['bluːtjuŋ], *adj.* very young.
Blutkörperchen ['bluːtkœrpərçən], *n.* (—s, *pl.* —) blood-corpuscle.
Blutlassen ['bluːtlasən], *n.* (—s, *no pl.*) (*Med.*) bloodletting.
Blutrache ['bluːtraxə], *f.* (—, *no pl.*) vendetta.
Blutsauger ['bluːtzaugər], *m.* (—s, *pl.* —) vampire.
Blutschande ['bluːtʃandə], *f.* (—, *no pl.*) incest.

blutstillend ['bluːʃtɪlənt], *adj.* styptic, blood-stanching.

Blutsturz ['bluːtʃturts], *m.* (**—es**, *no pl.*) haemorrhage; **einen — haben**, burst a blood-vessel.

Blutsverwandte ['bluːtsfɛrvantə], *m. or f.* (**—n**, *pl.* **—n**) blood-relation.

Blutvergießen ['bluːtfɛrgiːsən], *n.* (**—s**, *no pl.*) bloodshed.

Blutvergiftung ['bluːtfɛrgɪftuŋ], *f.* (**—**, *pl.* **—en**) blood poisoning.

Blutwurst ['bluːtvurst], *f.* (**—**, *pl.* ¨e) black-pudding.

Blutzeuge ['bluːttsɔygə], *m.* (**—n**, *pl.* **—n**) martyr.

Bö [bøː], *f.* (**—**, *pl.* **—en**) (*Naut.*) squall, sudden gust of wind.

Bock [bɔk], *m.* (**—s**, *pl.* ¨e) buck; he-goat; (*Gymn.*) horse; (*horse-drawn carriage*) box seat.

bockbeinig ['bɔkbaɪnɪç], *adj.* bow-legged; pigheaded, obstinate.

Bockbier ['bɔkbiːr], *n.* (**—s**, *no pl.*) bock beer.

bocken ['bɔkən], *v.n.* kick, be refractory; sulk.

Bockfell ['bɔkfɛl], *n.* (**—s**, *pl.* **—e**) buckskin.

bockig ['bɔkɪç], *adj.* pigheaded, obstinate.

Bocksbeutel ['bɔksbɔytəl], *m.* (**—s**, *pl.* **—**) leather bag; Franconian wine (bottle).

Bockshorn ['bɔkshɔrn], *n.* (**—s**, *pl.* ¨er) buck horn; **einen ins — jagen**, intimidate s.o.

Boden ['boːdən], *m.* (**—s**, *pl.* ¨) ground, bottom, soil, floor; garret, loft.

Bodenfenster ['boːdənfɛnstər], *n.* (**—s**, *pl.* **—**) attic window.

Bodenkammer ['boːdənkamər], *f.* (**—**, *pl.* **—n**) garret, attic.

bodenlos ['boːdənloːs], *adj.* bottomless; (*fig.*) unimaginable, enormous.

Bodensatz ['boːdənzats], *m.* (**—es**, *pl.* ¨e) sediment, dregs, deposit.

Bodensee ['boːdənzeː], *m.* Lake Constance.

Bogen ['boːgən], *m.* (**—s**, *pl.* ¨) arch, vault, curve; (*Maths.*) arc; (*violin*) bow; (*paper*) sheet; (*Mus.*) ligature.

bogenförmig ['boːgənfœrmɪç], *adj.* arch-shaped, arched.

Bogenführung ['boːgənfyːruŋ], *f.* (**—**, *no pl.*) (*Mus.*) bowing (technique).

Bogengang ['boːgəngaŋ], *m.* (**—es**, *pl.* ¨e) arcade.

Bogenlampe ['boːgənlampə], *f.* (**—**, *pl.* **—n**) arc-lamp.

Bogenschütze ['boːgənʃytsə], *m.* (**—n**, *pl.* **—n**) archer.

bogig ['boːgɪç], *adj.* bent, curved, arched.

Bohle ['boːlə], *f.* (**—**, *pl.* **—n**) board, plank.

Böhmen ['bøːmən], *n.* Bohemia.

Bohne ['boːnə], *f.* (**—**, *pl.* **—n**) bean; **grüne —n**, French (*Am.* string) beans; **dicke —n**, broad beans; **blaue —n**, (*fig.*) bullets.

Bohnenstange ['boːnənʃtaŋə], *f.* (**—**, *pl.* **—n**) bean-pole.

Bohnerbürste ['boːnərbyrstə], *f.* (**—**, *pl.* **—n**) polishing-brush.

bohnern ['boːnərn], *v.a.* polish, wax.

bohren ['boːrən], *v.a.* bore, pierce, drill.

Bohrer ['boːrər], *m.* (**—s**, *pl.* **—**) gimlet; drill.

Bohrturm ['boːrturm], *m.* (**—s**, *pl.* ¨e) derrick.

Boje ['boːjə], *f.* (**—**, *pl.* **—n**) (*Naut.*) buoy.

Bolivien [boˈliːvjən], *n.* Bolivia.

Böller ['bœlər], *m.* (**—s**, *pl.* **—**) (*Mil.*) small mortar.

Bollwerk ['bɔlvɛrk], *n.* (**—s**, *pl.* **—e**) bulwark.

Bolzen ['bɔltsən], *m.* (**—s**, *pl.* **—**) bolt, arrow, pin; (*smoothing iron*) heater.

Bombe ['bɔmbə], *f.* (**—**, *pl.* **—n**) bomb, bomb-shell.

Bombenerfolg ['bɔmbənɛrfɔlk], *m.* (**—(e)s**, *pl.* **—e**) (*Theat.*) smash hit.

Bonbon [bɔ̃ˈbɔ̃], *m.* (**—s**, *pl.* **—s**) sweet(s), bonbon; (*Am.*) candy.

Bonbonniere [bɔ̃bɔ̃ˈnjɛːrə], *f.* (**—**, *pl.* **—n**) box of sweets.

Bonze ['bɔntsə], *m.* (**—n**, *pl.* **—n**) (*coll.*) bigwig, (*Am.*) big shot.

Boot [boːt], *n.* (**—es**, *pl.* **—e**) boat.

Bootsanker ['boːtsaŋkər], *m.* (**—s**, *pl.* **—**) grapnel.

Bootsleine ['boːtslaɪnə], *f.* (**—**, *pl.* **—n**) tow-rope.

Bor [boːr], *n.* (**—s**, *no pl.*) (*Chem.*) boron.

Bord [bɔrt], *m.* (**—s**, *pl.* **—e**) rim; (*Naut.*) board.

Bordell [bɔrˈdɛl], *n.* (**—s**, *pl.* **—e**) brothel.

borgen ['bɔrgən], *v.a.*, *v.n.* borrow, borrow (*von*, from); lend (*Dat.*, to).

Borke ['bɔrkə], *f.* (**—**, *pl.* **—n**) bark, rind.

Born [bɔrn], *m.* (**—es**, **—e**) (*Poet.*) bourn, spring, well, source.

borniert [bɔrˈniːrt], *adj.* narrow-minded.

Borsäure ['boːrzɔyrə], *f.* (**—**, *no pl.*) boric acid.

Börse ['bœrzə], *f.* (**—**, *pl.* **—n**) purse; (*Comm.*) stock-exchange, bourse.

Börsenbericht ['bœrzənbərɪçt], *m.* (**—s**, *pl.* **—e**) stock-market report.

Borste ['bɔrstə], *f.* (**—**, *pl.* **—n**) bristle.

borstig ['bɔrstɪç], *adj.* bristly; (*fig.*) irritable.

Borte ['bɔrtə], *f.* (**—**, *pl.* **—n**) order, trimming.

bösartig ['bøːsartɪç], *adj.* malevolent, malicious, vicious; (*disease*) malignant.

Böschung ['bœʃuŋ], *f.* (**—**, *pl.* **—en**) slope, scarp.

böse ['bøːzə], *adj.* bad, wicked; evil; angry, cross (with, *Dat.*); **— auf** (*Acc.*), angry with s.o., (*Am.*) mad at s.o.

Bösewicht ['bøːzəvɪçt], *m.* (**—s**, *pl.* **—er**) villain, ruffian; wretch.

boshaft

boshaft ['bo:shaft], *adj.* spiteful, malicious.
Bosheit ['bo:shaɪt], *f.* (—, *pl.* —en) malice.
böswillig ['bø:svɪlɪç], *adj.* malevolent.
Botanik [bo'ta:nɪk], *f.* (—, *no pl.*) botany.
Botaniker [bo'ta:nɪkər], *m.* (—s, *pl.* —) botanist.
Botanisiertrommel [botani'zi:rtrɔməl], *f.* (—, *pl.* —n) specimen-box.
Bote ['bo:tə], *m.* (—n, *pl.* —n) messenger.
Botengang ['bo:təngaŋ], *m.* (—s, *pl.* ˙e) errand.
botmäßig [bo:tme:sɪç], *adj.* subject, subordinate.
Botschaft ['bo:tʃaft], *f.* (—, *pl.* —en) message; (*Pol.*) embassy; *gute* —, glad tidings.
Botschafter ['bo:tʃaftər], *m.* (—s, *pl.* —) ambassador.
Böttcher ['bœtçər], *m.* (—s, *pl.* —) cooper.
Bottich ['bɔtɪç], *m.* (—s, *pl.* —e) vat, tub.
Bouillon [bul'jõ], *f.* (—, *no pl.*) broth, meat soup.
Bowle ['bo:lə], *f.* (—, *no pl.*) bowl; spiced wine.
boxen ['bɔksən], *v.n.* box.
brach [bra:x], *adj.* fallow, unploughed, untilled.
Brand [brant], *m.* (—es, *pl.* ˙e) burning, fire, combustion, conflagration; (*Med.*) gangrene.
Brandblase ['brantbla:zə], *f.* (—, *pl.* —n) blister.
branden ['brandən], *v.n.* surge, break (waves).
brandig ['brandɪç], *adj.* blighted; (*Med.*) gangrenous.
Brandmal ['brantma:l], *n.* (—s, *pl.* —e) burn mark; brand (cattle); (*fig.*) stigma.
brandmarken ['brantmarkən], *v.a.* brand; (*fig.*) stigmatise.
Brandmauer ['brantmauər], *f.* (—, *pl.* —n) fire-proof wall.
brandschatzen ['brantʃatsən], *v.a.* levy contributions (from); pillage, plunder.
Brandsohle ['brantzo:lə], *f.* (—, *pl.* —n) inner sole, welt (of shoe).
Brandstifter ['brantʃtɪftər], *m.* (—s, *pl.* —) incendiary, fire-raiser.
Brandstiftung ['brantʃtɪftuŋ], *f.* (—, *pl.* —en) arson.
Brandung ['branduŋ], *f.* (—, *pl.* —en) breakers, surf, surge (of sea).
Branntwein ['brantvaɪn], *m.* (—s, *pl.* —e) brandy.
Brasilien [bra'zi:ljən], *n.* Brazil.
Braten ['bra:tən], *m.* (—s, *pl.* —) roast (meat), joint.
braten ['bra:tən], *v.a. reg. & irr.* roast, broil, bake, fry, grill. — *v.n.* (*coll.*) bask (in sun), roast.
Brathering ['bra:the:rɪŋ], *m.* (—s, *pl.* —e) grilled herring.

Brathuhn ['bra:thu:n], *n.* (—s, *pl.* ˙er) roast chicken.
Bratkartoffeln ['bra:tkartɔfəln], *f. pl.* roast *or* fried potatoes.
Bratpfanne ['bra:tpfanə], *f.* (—, *pl.* —n) frying pan.
Bratsche ['bratʃə], *f.* (—, *pl.* —n) (*Mus.*) viola.
Bratspieß ['bra:tʃpi:s], *m.* (—es, *pl.* —e) spit (roasting).
Bratwurst ['bra:tvurst], *f.* (—, *pl.* ˙e) sausage for frying; fried sausage.
Brau [brau], **Bräu,** [brɔy], *n. & m.* (—s, *no pl.*) brew.
Brauch [braux], *m.* (—es, *pl.* ˙e) usage, custom, habit.
brauchbar ['brauxba:r], *adj.* useful, serviceable.
brauchen ['brauxən], *v.a.* make use of, employ; need, require, want; (*time*) take.
Braue ['brauə], *f.* (—, *pl.* —n) brow, eye-brow.
brauen ['brauən], *v.a.* brew.
Brauer ['brauər], *m.* (—s, *pl.* —) brewer.
Brauerei ['brauəraɪ], *f.* (—, *pl.* —en) brewery.
Brauhaus ['brauhaus], *n.* (—es, *pl.* ˙er) brewery.
braun [braun], *adj.* brown.
bräunen ['brɔynən], *v.a.* make brown, tan.
Braunkohl ['braunko:l], *m.* (—s, *no pl.*) (*Bot.*) broccoli.
Braunschweig ['braunʃvaɪk], *n.* Brunswick.
Braus [braus], *m.* (—es, *no pl.*) bustle, tumult; *in Saus und — leben,* lead a riotous life.
Brause ['brauzə], *f.* (—, *pl.* —n) shower (bath); effervescence, (*coll.*) fizzy drink.
Brausekopf ['brauzəkɔpf], *m.* (—es, *pl.* ˙e) hothead.
Brauselimonade ['brauzəlimona:də], *f.* (—, *pl.* —n) effervescent *or* fizzy lemonade.
brausen ['brauzən], *v.n.* roar, bluster, rush; effervesce.
Brausepulver ['brauzəpulvər], *n.* (—s, *pl.* —) effervescent powder.
Braut [braut], *f.* (—, *pl.* ˙e) bride, betrothed, fiancée.
Brautführer ['brautfy:rər], *m.* (—s, *pl.* —) best man.
Bräutigam ['brɔytɪgam], *m.* (—s, *pl.* —e) bridegroom, betrothed, fiancé.
Brautjungfer ['brautjuŋfər], *f.* (—, *pl.* —n) bridesmaid.
bräutlich ['brɔytlɪç], *adj.* bridal.
Brautpaar ['brautpa:r], *n.* (—es, *pl.* —e) engaged couple.
Brautschau ['brautʃau], *f.* (—, *no pl.*) (*obs.*) search for a wife.
brav [bra:f], *adj.* honest, upright, worthy, honourable; well-behaved, good.
bravo! ['bra:vo], *int.* well done!

Bravourstück [bra'vu:rʃtyk], *n.* (—s, *pl.* —e) feat of valour.
Brechbohnen ['brɛçboːnən], *f. pl.* kidney-beans.
Brecheisen ['brɛçaɪzən], *n.* (—s, *pl.* —) jemmy.
brechen ['brɛçən], *v.a. irr.* break; (*flowers*) pluck, pick; vomit. — *v.n.* (*aux.* sein) break.
Brechmittel ['brɛçmɪtəl], *n.* (—s, *pl.* —) emetic.
Brechruhr ['brɛçruːr], *f.* (—, *no pl.*) cholera.
Brechstange ['brɛçʃtaŋə], *f.* (—, *pl.* —n) crow-bar.
Brechung ['brɛçuŋ], *f.* (—, *pl.* —en) breaking; (*Phys.*) refraction.
Brei [braɪ], *m.* (—s, *pl.* —e) pap, pulp, porridge.
breiartig ['braɪartɪç], *adj.* pulpy.
breiig ['braɪɪç], *adj.* pappy.
breit [braɪt], *adj.* broad, wide.
breitbeinig ['braɪtbaɪnɪç], *adj.* straddle-legged.
Breite ['braɪtə], *f.* (—, *pl.* —n) breadth, width; (*Geog.*) latitude.
Breitengrad ['braɪtəngraːt], *m.* (—es, *pl.* —e) (*Geog.*) degree of latitude.
Breitenkreis ['braɪtənkraɪs], *m.* (—es, *pl.* —e) (*Geog.*) parallel.
breitschultrig ['braɪtʃultrɪç], *adj.* broad-shouldered.
Bremse ['brɛmzə], *f.* (—, *pl.* —n) (*Ent.*) gad-fly; (*Motor.*) brake; (*horse*) barnacle.
bremsen ['brɛmzən], *v.a.* brake, pull up.
brennbar ['brɛnbaːr], *adj.* combustible.
Brenneisen ['brɛnaɪzən], *n.* (—s, *pl.* —) branding iron.
brennen ['brɛnən], *v.a. irr.* burn; (*Med.*) cauterise; (*alcohol*) distil; (*hair*) curl; (*coffee*) roast; (*coal*) char; (*bricks*) bake. — *v.n.* burn; (*fig.*) sting; (*eyes*) smart.
Brenner ['brɛnər], *m.* (—s, *pl.* —) (*person*) distiller; (*Tech.*) burner.
Brennerei [brɛnə'raɪ], *f.* (—, *pl.* —en) distillery.
Brennessel ['brɛnnɛsəl], *f.* (—, *pl.* —n) stinging nettle.
Brennholz ['brɛnhɔlts], *n.* (—es, *no pl.*) firewood.
Brennmaterial ['brɛnmaterjaːl], *n.* (—s, *pl.* —ien) fuel.
Brennofen ['brɛnoːfən], *m.* (—s, *pl.* ⁖n) kiln.
Brennpunkt ['brɛnpuŋkt], *m.* (—s, *pl.* —e) focus.
Brennschere ['brɛnʃeːrə], *f.* (—, *pl.* —n) curling-irons.
Brennstoff ['brɛnʃtɔf], *m.* (—(e)s, *pl.* —e) fuel.
brenzlich ['brɛntslɪç], *adj.* smelling (or tasting) of burning; (*fig.*) ticklish.
Bresche ['brɛʃə], *f.* (—, *pl.* —n) breach, gap.
Brett [brɛt], *n.* (—s, *pl.* —er) board, plank, shelf.
Brettspiel ['brɛtʃpiːl], *n.* (—s, *pl.* —e) table-game.

Brevier [bre'viːr], *n.* (—s, *pl.* (*rare*) —e) breviary.
Brezel ['breːtsəl], *f.* (—, *pl.* —n) cracknel, pretzel.
Brief [briːf], *m.* (—es, *pl.* —e) letter; epistle.
Briefanschrift ['briːfanʃrɪft], *f.* (—, *pl.* —en) address.
Briefbeschwerer ['briːfbəʃveːrər], *m.* (—s, *pl.* —) letter-weight, paperweight.
Briefbogen ['briːfboːgən], *m.* (—s, *pl.* —) sheet of notepaper.
Briefkasten ['briːfkastən], *m.* (—s, *pl.* ⁖) (*house*) letter-box; (*street*) pillar-box, (*Am.*) post-box.
brieflich ['briːflɪç], *adv.* by letter, in writing.
Briefmarke ['briːfmarkə], *f.* (—, *pl.* —n) postage stamp.
Briefpapier ['briːfpapiːr], *n.* (—s, *no pl.*) notepaper.
Briefporto ['briːfpɔrto], *n.* (—s, *pl.* —ti) postage.
Brieftasche ['briːftaʃə], *f.* (—, *pl.* —n) portfolio, wallet; (*Am.*) pocket-book.
Brieftaube ['briːftaubə], *f.* (—, *pl.* —n) carrier pigeon.
Briefträger ['briːftreːgər], *m.* (—s, *pl.* —) postman.
Briefumschlag ['briːfumʃlaːk], *m.* (—s, *pl.* ⁖e) envelope.
Briefwechsel ['briːfvɛksəl], *m.* (—s, *no pl.*) correspondence.
Brillant [bril'jant], *m.* (—en, *pl.* —en) brilliant, diamond. — *adj.* brilliant.
Brille ['brɪlə], *f.* (—, *pl.* —n) spectacles, glasses.
Brillenschlange ['brɪlənʃlaŋə], *f.* (—, *pl.* —n) (*Zool.*) hooded cobra.
bringen ['brɪŋən], *v.a. irr.* bring, fetch, carry to, take to, conduct to.
Brise ['briːzə], *f.* (—, *pl.* —n) breeze, light wind.
Britannien [bri'tanjən], *n.* Britain.
bröckeln ['brœkəln], *v.a., v.n.* crumble.
Brocken ['brɔkən], *m.* (—s, *pl.* —) bit, piece, fragment, scrap; (*bread*) crumb.
bröcklig ['brœklɪç], *adj.* crumbling.
brodeln ['broːdəln], *v.n.* bubble, simmer.
Brodem ['broːdəm], *m.* (—s, *no pl.*) (*Poet.*) steam, vapour, exhalation.
Brokat [bro'kaːt], *m.* (—s, *pl.* —e) brocade.
Brom [broːm], *n.* (—s, *no pl.*) (*Chem.*) bromine.
Brombeere ['brɔmbeːrə], *f.* (—, *pl.* —n) blackberry, bramble.
Bronze ['brɔ̃ːsə], *f.* (—, *pl.* —n) bronze.
Brosamen [bro'zaːmən], *pl.* crumbs.
Brosche ['brɔʃə], *f.* (—, *pl.* —n) brooch.
Broschüre [brɔ'ʃyːrə], *f.* (—, *pl.* —n) pamphlet, brochure, folder.
Brösel ['brøːzəl], *m.* (—s, *pl.* —) crumb.
Brot [broːt], *n.* (—es, *pl.* —e) bread, loaf; (*fig.*) livelihood.
Brötchen ['brøːtçən], *n.* (—s, *pl.* —) roll, bread-roll.

39

Broterwerb

Broterwerb ['bro:tərvɛrp], *m.* (—s, *no pl.*) livelihood.

Brotgeber ['bro:tge:bər], *m.* (—s, *pl.* —) employer, master.

Brotherr ['bro:thɛr], *m.* (—n, *pl.* —en) employer, master.

Brotkorb ['bro:tkɔrp], *m.* (—s, *pl.* ⁻e) bread-basket.

brotlos ['bro:tlo:s], *adj.* unemployed; (*fig.*) unprofitable.

Brotneid ['bro:tnait], *m.* (—s, *no pl.*) professional jealousy.

Bruch [brux], *m.* (—s, *pl.* ⁻e) breakage; rupture; (*Med.*) fracture, rupture, hernia; (*Maths.*) fraction.

Bruchband ['bruxbant], *f.* (—es, *pl.* ⁻er) abdominal belt, truss.

brüchig ['bryçiç], *adj.* brittle, full of flaws.

Bruchlandung ['bruxlanduŋ], *f.* (—, —en) (*Aviat.*) crash-landing.

Bruchrechnung ['bruxrɛçnuŋ], *f.* (—, *pl.* —en) (*Arith.*) fractions.

Bruchstück ['bruxʃtyk], *n.* (—s, *pl.* —e) fragment, scrap.

Bruchteil ['bruxtail], *m.* (—s, *pl.* —e) fraction.

Brücke ['brykə], *f.* (—, *pl.* —n) bridge.

Brückenpfeiler ['brykənpfailər], *m.* (—s, *pl.* —) pier.

Bruder ['bru:dər], *m.* (—s, *pl.* ⁻) brother; (*Eccl.*) friar.

brüderlich ['bry:dərliç], *adj.* fraternal, brotherly.

Bruderschaft ['bru:dərʃaft], *f.* (—, *pl.* —en) fraternity, brotherhood.

Brügge ['brygə], *n.* Bruges.

Brühe ['bry:ə], *f.* (—, *pl.* —n) broth, meat-soup.

brühen ['bry:ən], *v.a.* scald.

Brühkartoffeln ['bry:kartɔfəln], *f. pl.* potatoes cooked in broth.

brüllen ['brylən], *v.n.* roar, howl, yell; (*cows*) low, bellow.

Brummbaß ['brumbas], *m.* (—sses, *pl.* ⁻sse) (*Mus.*) double-bass.

Brummeisen ['brumaizən], *n.* (—s, *pl.* —) Jew's harp.

brummen ['brumən], *v.n.* growl, grumble, hum.

Brummer ['brumər], *m.* (—s, *pl.* —) (*Ent.*) blue-bottle.

Brunnen ['brunən], *m.* (—s, *pl.* —) well, fountain, spring.

Brunnenkur ['brunənku:r], *f.* (—, *pl.* —en) taking of mineral waters.

Brunst [brunst], *f.* (—, *pl.* ⁻e) (*Zool.*) rut, heat.

Brust [brust], *f.* (—, *pl.* ⁻e) breast; chest; bosom.

Brustbein ['brustbain], *n.* (—s, *pl.* —e) breastbone, sternum.

Brustbild ['brustbilt], *n.* (—s, *pl.* —er) half-length portrait.

brüsten ['brystən], *v.r. sich* —, boast, brag, plume o.s.

Brustfell ['brustfɛl], *n.* (—s, *pl.* —e) pleura.

Brustfellentzündung ['brustfɛlɛntsyn-duŋ], *f.* (—, *no pl.*) pleurisy.

Brusthöhle ['brusthø:lə], *f.* (—, *pl.* —n) thoracic cavity.

Brustkasten ['brustkastən], *m.* (—s, *pl.* ⁻n) chest.

Brusttee ['brustte:], *m.* (—s, *no pl.*) pectoral (herbal) tea.

Brüstung ['brystuŋ], *f.* (—, *pl.* —en) parapet.

Brustwarze ['brustvartsə], *f.* (—, *pl.* —n) nipple.

Brustwehr ['brustve:r], *f.* (—, *pl.* —en) breastwork, parapet.

Brut [bru:t], *f.* (—, *no pl.*) brood; (*fish*) fry.

brutal [bru'ta:l], *adj.* brutal.

brüten ['bry:tən], *v.a.* brood, hatch.

Brutofen ['bru:to:fən], *m.* (—s, *pl.* ⁻) incubator.

brutto ['bruto], *adv.* (*Comm.*) gross.

Bube ['bu:bə], *m.* (—n, *pl.* —n) boy, lad; (*cards*) knave, (*Am.*) jack; rogue, rascal.

Bubenstreich ['bu:bənʃtraiç], *m.* (—s, *pl.* —e) boyish prank; knavish trick.

Bubikopf ['bu:bikɔpf], *m.* (—(e)s, *pl.* ⁻e) bobbed hair.

Buch [bu:x], *n.* (—s, *pl.* ⁻er) book; quire (of paper).

Buchdruckerei ['bu:xdrukərai], *f.* (—, —en) printing works, printing office.

Buche ['bu:xə], *f.* (—, *pl.* —n) beech (tree).

buchen ['bu:xən], *v.a.* book, enter, reserve; (*fig.*) score.

Bücherei [by:çə'rai], *f.* (—, *pl.* —en) library.

Buchesche ['bu:xɛʃə], *f.* (—, *pl.* —n) hornbeam.

Buchfink ['bu:xfiŋk], *m.* (—en, *pl.* —en) (*Orn.*) chaffinch.

Buchhalter ['bu:xhaltər], *m.* (—s, *pl.* —) book-keeper.

Buchhändler ['bu:xhɛndlər], *m.* (—s, *pl.* —) bookseller.

Buchmarder ['bu:xmardər], *m.* (—s, *pl.* —) (*Zool.*) pine-marten.

Buchsbaum ['buksbaum], *m.* (—s, *pl.* ⁻e) (*Bot.*) box-tree.

Büchse ['byksə], *f.* (—, *pl.* —n) box, case; tin, can; rifle, gun.

Büchsenfleisch ['byksənflaiʃ], *n.* (—es, *no pl.*) tinned meat.

Büchsenlauf ['byksənlauf], *m.* (—s, *pl.* ⁻e) gun-barrel.

Büchsenöffner ['byksənœfnər], *m.* (—s, *pl.* —) tin-opener.

Buchstabe ['bu:xʃta:bə], *m.* (—n, —n) letter, character; *großer* —, capital (letter).

Buchstabenrätsel ['bu:xʃta:bənrɛtsəl], *n.* (—s, *pl.* —) anagram.

buchstabieren [bu:xʃta'bi:rən], *v.a.* spell (out).

buchstäblich ['bu:xʃtɛpliç], *adj.* literal.

Bucht [buxt], *f.* (—, *pl.* —en) inlet, bay, creek, bight.

Buchung ['bu:xuŋ], *f.* (—, *pl.* —en) (*Comm.*) entry (in a book); booking (of tickets).

Buchwissen ['bu:xvɪsən], *n.* (—s, *no pl.*) book-learning.
Buckel ['bukəl], *m.* (—s, *pl.* —) hump, humpback; boss, stud; (*coll.*) back.
bücken ['bykən], *v.r.* sich —, ·stoop, bow.
bucklig [bukliç], *adj.* humpbacked.
Bückling ['byklɪŋ], *m.* (—s, *pl.* —e) smoked herring; kipper.
buddeln ['budəln], *v.n.* (*coll.*) dig.
Bude ['bu:də], *f.* (—, *pl.* —n) shack, stall; (*coll.*) room; (*student's*) digs.
Büfett [by'fɛt], *n.* (—s, *pl.* —s) sideboard; buffet.
Büffel ['byfəl], *m.* (—s, *pl.* —) buffalo.
büffeln ['byfəln], *v.n.* (*coll.*) cram (for an examination), swot.
Bug [bu:k], *m.* (—s, *pl.* ˙e, —e) (*Naut.*) bow, (*Aviat.*) nose.
Buganker ['bu:kaŋkər], *m.* (—s, *pl.* —) bow-anchor.
Bügel ['by:gəl], *m.* (—s, *pl.* —) coathanger; (*trigger*) guard; (*horse*) stirrup.
bügeln ['by:gəln], *v.a.* iron, smoothe, press.
bugsieren [buk'si:rən], *v.a.* tow.
Bugspriet ['bu:kʃpri:t], *n.* (—s, *pl.* —e) bowsprit.
Buhle ['bu:lə], *m.* or *f.* (—n, *pl.* —n) (*Poet.*) paramour, lover.
buhlen ['bu:lən], *v.n.* (*Poet.*) woo, make love (to).
buhlerisch ['bu:lərɪʃ], *adj.* (*Poet.*) amorous, wanton, lewd.
Bühne ['by:nə], *f.* (—, *pl.* —n) (*Theat.*) stage; scaffold, platform.
Bühnenbild ['by:nənbɪlt], *n.* (—es, *pl.* —er) scenery.
Bukett [bu'kɛt], *n.* (—s, *pl.* —s) bunch of flowers, bouquet; bouquet (*wine*).
Bulgarien [bul'ga:rjən], *n.* Bulgaria.
Bulldogge ['buldɔgə], *f.* (—, *pl.* —n) bulldog.
Bulle (1) ['bulə], *m.* (—n, *pl.* —n) bull, bullock.
Bulle (2) ['bulə], *f.* (—, *pl.* —n) (*Eccl.*) (Papal) Bull.
bumm [bum], *int.* boom! bang!
Bummel ['buməl], *m.* (—s, *pl.* —) stroll.
Bummelei [bumə'lai], *f.* (—, *pl.* —en) idleness, negligence, casualness, carelessness.
bummeln ['buməln], *v.n.* lounge, waste o.'s time, dawdle; stroll.
Bummelzug ['buməltsu:k], *m.* (—s, *pl.* ˙e) slow train.
bums [bums], *int.* bang! crash!
Bund (1) [bunt], *m.* (—es, *pl.* ˙e) bond, tie, league, alliance, federation, confederacy; (*Eccl.*) covenant.
Bund (2) [bunt], *n.* (—es, *pl.* —e) bundle, bunch (of keys).
Bündel ['byndəl], *n.* (—s, *pl.* —) bundle, package.
Bundesgenosse ['bundəsgənɔsə], *m.* (—n, *pl.* —n) confederate, ally.
Bundesstaat ['bundəsʃta:t], *m.* (—es, *pl.* —en) federal state; federation.

Bundestag ['bundəsta:k], *m.* (—es, *pl.* —e) federal parliament.
Bundeswehr ['bundəsve:r], *f.* (—, *no pl.*) federal defence; armed forces.
bündig ['byndɪç], *adj.* binding: *kurz und* —, concise, terse, to the point.
Bündnis ['byntnɪs], *n.* (—ses, *pl.* —se) alliance.
Bundschuh ['buntʃu:], *m.* (—s, *pl.* —e) clog, sandal.
bunt [bunt], *adj.* many-coloured, chequered, variegated, motley; *das ist mir zu* —, this is going too far.
buntscheckig ['buntʃɛkɪç], *adj.* dappled, spotted.
Buntspecht ['buntʃpɛçt], *m.* (—s, *pl.* —e) (*Orn.*) (spotted) woodpecker.
Bürde ['byrdə], *f.* (—, *pl.* —n) load, burden.
Bure ['bu:rə], *m.* (—n, *pl.* —n) Boer.
Burg [burk], *f.* (—, *pl.* —en) castle, fortress, citadel, stronghold.
Bürge ['byrgə], *m.* (—n, *pl.* —n) surety, bail, guarantee; *einen* —n *stellen*, offer bail.
bürgen ['byrgən], *v.n.* give security, vouch (for), go bail (for).
Bürger ['byrgər], *m.* (—s, *pl.* —) citizen, townsman, bourgeois, commoner.
bürgerlich ['byrgərlɪç], *adj.* civic; middle-class, bourgeois; —*e Küche*, plain cooking.
Bürgermeister ['byrgərmaɪstər], *m.* (—s, *pl.* —) burgomaster, mayor.
Burggraf ['burkgra:f], *m.* (—en, *pl.* —en) burgrave.
Bürgschaft ['byrkʃaft], *f.* (—, *pl.* —en) bail, surety, guarantee; — *leisten*, provide security.
Burgund [bur'gunt], *n.* Burgundy.
Burgvogt ['burkfo:kt], *m.* (—s, *pl.* —e) (*obs.*) castellan, bailiff.
Burgwarte ['burkvartə], *f.* (—, *pl.* —n) watch-tower.
Büro [by'ro:], *n.* (—s, *pl.* —s) office, bureau, (professional) chambers.
Bursche ['burʃə], *m.* (—n, *pl.* —n) lad, boy, fellow; student; (*Mil.*) batman.
Burschenschaft ['burʃənʃaft], *f.* (—, *pl.* —en) students' association.
Bürste ['byrstə], *f.* (—, *pl.* —n) brush.
Burundi [bu'rundi], *n.* Burundi.
Busch [buʃ], *m.* (—es, *pl.* ˙e) bush, shrub, copse, thicket.
Büschel ['byʃəl], *n.* (—s, *pl.* —) bunch; (*hair*) tuft.
buschig ['buʃiç], *adj.* bushy, tufted.
Buschklepper ['buʃklɛpər], *m.* (—s, *pl.* —) bushranger.
Busen ['bu:zən], *m.* (—s, *pl.* —) bosom, breast; (*Geog.*) bay, gulf.
Bussard ['busart], *m.* (—s, *pl.* —e) (*Orn.*) buzzard.
Buße ['bu:sə], *f.* (—, *pl.* —n) penance; repentance; penalty.
büßen ['by:sən], *v.a., v.n.* repent, atone, expiate, make amends.
bußfertig ['bu:sfɛrtɪç], *adj.* penitent, repentant.

Büste

Büste ['bystə], *f.* (—, *pl.* —n) bust.
Büstenhalter ['bystənhaltər], *m.* (—s, *pl.* —) brassière.
Bütte ['bytə], *f.* (—, *pl.* —n) tub.
Büttel ['bytəl], *m.* (—s, *pl.* —) beadle; bailiff.
Büttenpapier ['bytənpapi:r], *n.* (—s, *no pl.*) hand-made paper.
Butter ['butər], *f.* (—, *no pl.*) butter.
Butterblume ['butərblu:mə], *f.* (—, *pl.* —n) buttercup.
Butterbrot ['butərbro:t], *n.* (—s, *pl.* —e) bread and butter.
buttern ['butərn], *v.a.,* *v.n.* smear with butter; churn.
Butterteig ['butərtaik], *m.* (—es, *pl.* —e) puff-pastry.
Butzenscheibe ['butsənʃaibə], *f.* (—, *pl.* —n) bull's-eyed pane.
Byzanz [by'tsants], *n.* Byzantium, Constantinople.

C

C [tse:], *n.* (—s, *pl.* —s) the letter C; (*Mus.*) *C dur,* C major; *C Moll,* C minor; *C-Schlüssel,* C clef.
Cäsar ['tsɛ:zar], *m.* Cæsar.
Ceylon ['tseilɔn], *n.* Ceylon.
Chaiselongue [ʃɛ:zə'lɔ:g], *f.* (—, *pl.* —s) couch, settee, sofa.
Champagner [ʃam'panjər], *m.* (—s, *pl.* —) champagne.
Champignon [ʃampin'jɔ̃], *m.* (—s, *pl.* —s) mushroom.
chaotisch [ka'o:tiʃ], *adj.* chaotic.
Charakter [ka'raktər], *m.* (—s, *pl.* —e) character; mental make-up, disposition.
Charakteristik [karaktər'istik], *f.* (—, *pl.* —en) characterisation.
charakteristisch [karaktər'istiʃ], *adj.* characteristic; typical.
Charge ['ʃarʒə], *f.* (—, *pl.* —n) office, appointment; (*pl.*) (*Mil.*) non-commissioned officers.
Chaussee [ʃo'se:], *f.* (—, *pl.* —n) main road, highway.
Chef [ʃef], *m.* (—s, *pl.* —s) chief, head, employer; (*coll.*) boss.
Chefredakteur ['ʃefredakto:r], *m.* (—s, *pl.* —e) editor-in-chief.
Chemie [çe'mi:], *f.* (—, *no pl.*) chemistry.
Chemikalien [çemi'ka:ljən], *f. pl.* chemicals.
Chemiker ['çe:mikər], *m.* (—s, *pl.* —) (analytical) chemist.
chemisch ['çe:miʃ], *adj.* chemical; *— gereinigt,* dry-cleaned.
Chiffre ['ʃifər], *f.* (—, *pl.* —n) cipher.
chiffrieren [ʃi'fri:rən], *v.a.* encipher.
Chile ['tʃi:lə, 'çi:lə], *n.* Chile.

China ['çi:na], *n.* China.
Chinarinde [çi:na'rində], *f.* (—, *no pl.*) Peruvian bark.
Chinin [çi'ni:n], *n.* (—s, *no pl.*) quinine.
Chirurg [çi'rurk], *m.* (—en, *pl.* —en) surgeon.
Chirurgie [çirur'gi:], *f.* (—, *no pl.*) surgery.
Chlor [klo:r], *n.* (—s, *no pl.*) chlorine.
Chlorkalk ['klo:rkalk], *m.* (—s, *no pl.*) chloride of lime.
Chlornatrium [klo:r'na:trjum], *n.* (—s, *no pl.*) sodium chloride.
Choleriker [ko'le:rikər], *m.* (—s, *pl.* —) irascible person.
Chor [ko:r], *m.* (—s, *pl.* ⁓e) chorus; choir; (*Archit.*) choir, chancel.
Choral [ko'ra:l], *m.* (—s, *pl.* ⁓e) hymn, chorale.
Choramt ['ko:ramt], *n.* (—s, *pl.* ⁓er) cathedral service.
Chorgesang ['ko:rgəsaŋ], *m.* (—s, *pl.* ⁓e) chorus, choral singing.
Chorhemd ['ko:rhɛmt], *n.* (—s, *pl.* —en) surplice.
Chorherr ['ko:rhɛr], *m.* (—n, *pl.* —en) canon, prebendary.
Christ [krist], *m.* (—en, *pl.* —en) Christian.
Christbaum ['kristbaum], *m.* (—s, *pl.* ⁓e) Christmas tree.
Christentum ['kristəntu:m], *n.* (—s, *no pl.*) Christendom, Christianity.
Christkind ['kristkint], *n.* (—s, *no pl.*) Infant Christ, Christ child.
christlich ['kristliç], *adj.* Christian.
Christmette ['kristmetə], *f.* (—, *pl.* —n) Christmas matins; midnight mass.
Christus ['kristus], *m.* (—i) Christ; *vor —,* B.C.; *nach —,* A.D.
Chrom [kro:m], *n.* (—s, *no pl.*) chrome.
chromatisch [kro'ma:tiʃ], *adj.* chromatic.
chromsauer ['kro:mzauər], *adj.* — chromate of; *—es Salz,* chromate.
Chronik ['kro:nik], *f.* (—, *pl.* —en) chronicle.
chronisch ['kro:niʃ], *adj.* chronic.
Chronist [kro'nist], *m.* (—en, *pl.* —en) chronicler.
Chrysantheme [kryzan'te:mə], *f.* (—, *pl.* —n) chrysanthemum.
Cis [tsis], (*Mus.*) C sharp.
Clique ['klikə], *f.* (—, *pl.* —n) clique, set.
Coeur [kø:r], *n.* (*Cards*) hearts.
coulant [ku'lant], *adj.* polite, friendly; (*Comm.*) fair, obliging.
Couleur [ku'lø:r], *f.* (—, *pl.* —en) colour; students' corporation.
Coupé [ku'pe:], *n.* (—s, *pl.* —s) (*train*) compartment.
Couplet [ku'ple:], *n.* (—s, *pl.* —s) comic song.
Coupon [ku'pɔ̃], *m.* (—s, *pl.* —s) coupon, check, dividend voucher.
Cour [ku:r], *f.* (—, *no pl.*) *einem Mädchen die — machen,* court a girl.

Courtage [kur'ta:ʒə], *f.* (—, *pl.* —n) brokerage.

Cousin [ku'zɛ̃], *m.* (—s, *pl.* —s) cousin.

Cousine [ku'zi:nə], *f.* (—, *pl.* —n) (female) cousin.

Cutaway ['katave:], *m.* (—s, *pl.* —s) morning coat.

Czar [tsa:r], *m.* (—en, *pl.* —en) Tsar, Czar.

D

D [de:], *n.* (—s, *pl.* —s) the letter D; (*Mus.*) *D dur*, D major; *D moll*, D minor; *D-Zug*, express train.

da [da:], *adv.* (*local*) there; here; (*temporal*) then, at that moment; (*Mil.*) *wer —?* who goes there? (*Poet. obs.*) where. — *conj.* (*temporal*) when, as; (*causal*) as, because, since.

dabei [da'baɪ], *adv.* nearby; besides, moreover; as well; —*sein*, be present, be about to (*infin.*); — *bleiben*, persist in.

Dach [dax], *n.* (—es, *pl.* ⁴er) roof.

Dachboden ['daxbo:dən], *m.* (—s, *pl.* ⁴) loft.

Dachdecker ['daxdɛkər], *m.* (—s, *pl.* —) slater, tiler.

Dachgiebel ['daxgi:bəl], *m.* (—s, *pl.* —) gable.

Dachluke ['daxlu:kə], *f.* (—, *pl.* —n) dormer window.

Dachpappe ['daxpapə], *f.* (—, *pl.* —n) roofing felt.

Dachrinne ['daxrɪnə], *f.* (—, *pl.* —n) gutter.

Dachs [daks], *m.* (—es, *pl.* —e) badger.

Dachstube ['daxʃtu:bə], *f.* (—, *pl.* —n) garret, attic (room).

Dachtraufe ['daxtraufə], *f.* (—, *pl.* —n) eaves.

dadurch [da'durç], *adv.* (*local*) through it; in that way; (*causal*) thereby.

dafür [da'fy:r], *adv.* for it; instead of it, in return for it; *ich kann nichts —*, it is not my fault, I can't help it.

Dafürhalten [da'fy:rhaltən], *n.* (—s, *no pl.*) opinion.

dagegen [da'ge:gən], *adv.* against it, compared to it. — *conj.* on the other hand.

daheim [da'haɪm], *adv.* at home.

daher [da'he:r], *adv.* thence, from that. — *conj.* therefore, for that reason.

dahin [da'hɪn], *adv.* thither, to that place; there; *bis —*, (*local*) thither; (*temporal*) till then; over, past, lost, gone.

dahinbringen [da'hɪnbrɪŋən], *v.a. irr.* *jemanden —*, induce s.o. to; *es —*, succeed in, manage to.

dahinsiechen [da'hɪnzi:çən], *v.n.* (*aux. sein*) pine away, be failing (in health).

dahinter [da'hɪntər], *adv.* behind that.

Dahlie ['da:ljə], *f.* (—, *pl.* —n) (*Bot.*) dahlia.

Dahome ['daome:], *n.* Dahomey.

damalig ['da:malɪç], *adj.* then; of that time; past.

damals ['da:mals], *adv.* then, at that time.

Damast [da'mast], *m.* (—s, *no pl.*) damask.

Damaszener [damas'tse:nər], *m.* (—s, *pl.* —) Damascene. — *adj.* — *Stahl*, Damascus steel, dagger.

Dame ['da:mə], *f.* (—, *pl.* —n) lady; (*cards, chess*) queen; draughts (*game*).

damit [da'mɪt], *adv.* therewith, with that, with it; *und — basta!* and that's all there is to it. — *conj.* in order that, so that; — *nicht*, lest.

dämlich ['dɛ:mlɪç], *adj.* (*coll.*) foolish, silly.

Damm [dam], *m.* (—es, *pl.* ⁴e) dam, dyke, mole; (*street*) roadway, causeway; (*rail*) embankment.

dämmen ['dɛmən], *v.a.* dam; (*fig.*) stop, restrain.

dämmerig ['dɛmərɪç], *adj.* dusky.

dämmern ['dɛmərn], *v.n.* grow dusky; dawn.

dämonisch [dɛ'mo:nɪʃ], *adj.* demoniac-(al), demonlike.

Dampf [dampf], *m.* (—es, *pl.* ⁴e) vapour, steam, mist, fume; smoke.

dampfen ['dampfən], *v.n.* smoke, fume, steam.

dämpfen ['dɛmpfən], *v.a.* damp, smother, steam; subdue, deaden, muffle, soften down.

Dampfer ['dampfər], *m.* (—s, *pl.* —) steamer.

Dämpfer ['dɛmpfər], *m.* (—s, *pl.* —) damper; (*Mus.*) mute.

Dampfkessel ['dampfkɛsəl], *m.* (—s, *pl.* —) boiler.

Dämpfung ['dɛmpfuŋ], *f.* (—, *pl.* —en) damping, smothering, suppression; (*Aviat.*) stabilization.

danach [da'na:x], *adv.* after that, thereafter; accordingly, according to that.

daneben [da'ne:bən], *adv.* near it, by it, close by; *es geht —*, it goes amiss. — *conj.* besides.

Dänemark ['dɛ:nəmark], *n.* Denmark.

Dank [daŋk], *m.* (—es, *no pl.*) thanks, gratitude; reward; *Gott sei —*, thank heaven!

dank [daŋk], *prep.* (*Dat.*) owing to, thanks to.

dankbar ['daŋkba:r], *adj.* grateful; thankful.

danken ['daŋkən], *v.n.* (*Dat.*) thank. — *v.a.* owe.

Dankgebet ['daŋkgəbe:t], *n.* (—s, *pl.* —e) (prayer of) thanksgiving.

dann [dan], *adv.* then, at that time, in that case; — *und wann*, now and then, occasionally.

Danzig ['dantsɪç], *n.* Dantzig.

43

daran, dran [da'ran, dran], *adv.* on it, at it, near that; thereon, thereby; *was liegt —?* what does it matter?

darauf, drauf [da'rauf, drauf], *adv.* (*local*) upon it, on it; (*temporal*) thereupon, thereon, thereafter.

daraufhin [darauf'hɪn], *adv.* thereupon; on the strength of that.

daraus, draus [da'raus, draus], *adv.* therefrom, hence, from that; *ich mache mir nichts —,* I do not care for it.

darben ['darbən], *v.n.* suffer want, go short; famish.

darbieten ['da:rbi:tən], *v.a. irr.* offer, tender, present.

Darbietung ['da:rbi:tuŋ], *f.* (—, *pl.* —en) offering, presentation, performance.

darbringen ['da:rbrɪŋən], *v.a. irr.* bring, present, offer.

darein, drein [da'raɪn, draɪn], *adv.* into it, therein.

darin, drin [da'rɪn, drɪn], *adv.* therein, in it, within.

darinnen, drinnen [da'rɪnən, 'drɪnən], *adv.* inside, in there.

darlegen ['da:rle:gən], *v.a.* demonstrate, explain; expound.

Darlehen ['da:rle:ən], *n.* (—s, *pl.* —) loan.

Darm [darm], *m.* (—s, *pl.* ꞉e) gut; (*pl.*) intestines, bowels.

Darmsaite ['darmzaɪtə], *f.* (—, *pl.* —n) catgut, gut-string.

darob [da'rɔp], *adv.* (*obs.*) on that account, on account of it.

darreichen ['da:raɪçən], *v.a.* offer, tender, present; (*Eccl.*) administer (sacraments).

darstellen ['da:rʃtɛlən], *v.a.* represent, delineate; (*Theat.*) perform.

Darstellung ['da:rʃtɛluŋ], *f.* (—, *pl.* —en) representation, exhibition, presentation; (*Theat.*) performance.

dartun ['da:rtu:n], *v.a. irr.* prove, demonstrate.

darüber, drüber [dar'y:bər, 'dry:bər], *adv.* over that, over it; concerning that.

darum, drum [da'rum, drum], *adv.* around it, around that, thereabout; therefore, for that reason.

darunter, drunter [da'runtər, 'druntər], *adv.* under that; thereunder; among; — *und drüber,* topsy-turvy.

das [das], *def. art. n.* the. — *dem. pron., dem. adj.* that, this. —*rel. pron.* which.

Dasein ['da:zaɪn], *n.* (—s, *no pl.*) presence, being, existence.

daselbst [da:'zɛlpst], *adv.* there, in that very place.

daß [das], *conj.* that; *es sei denn —,* unless; *—nicht,* lest.

dastehen ['da:ʃte:ən], *v.n. irr.* stand (there).

datieren [da'ti:rən], *v.a.* date, put a date to.

Dativ ['da:ti:f], *m.* (—s, *pl.* —e) dative.

dato [da'to], *adv. bis —,* till now, hitherto.

Dattel ['datəl], *f.* (—, *pl.* —n) (*Bot.*) date.

Datum ['da:tum], *n.* (—s, *pl.* Daten) date (*calendar*).

Dauer ['dauər], *f.* (—, *no pl.*) duration, length of time; continuance; permanence.

dauerhaft ['dauərhaft], *adj.* durable, lasting; (*colours*) fast.

Dauerkarte ['dauərkartə], *f.* (—, *pl.* —n) season ticket; (*Am.*) commutation ticket.

dauern ['dauərn], *v.n.* continue, last, endure.— *v.a.* move to pity; *er dauert mich,* I am sorry for him.

Dauerpflanze ['dauərpflantsə], *f.* (—, *pl.* —n) perennial plant.

Dauerwelle ['dauərvɛlə], *f.* (—, *pl.* —n) permanent wave, (*coll.*) perm.

Daumen ['daumən], *m.* (—s, *pl.* —) thumb; *einem den — halten,* wish s.o. well, keep o.'s fingers crossed for s.o.

Daune ['daunə], *f.* (—, *pl.* —n) down.

davon [da'fɔn], *adv.* thereof, therefrom, from that; off, away.

davonkommen [da'fɔnkɔmən], *v.n. irr.* (*aux.* sein) get off; *mit einem blauen Auge —,* get off lightly.

davor [da'fo:r], *adv.* before that, before it.

dawider [da'vi:dər], *adv.* against it.

dazu [da'tsu:], *adv.* thereto, to that, to it; in addition to that; for that purpose; *noch —,* besides.

dazumal ['da:tsuma:l], *adv.* then, at that time.

dazwischen [da'tsvɪʃən], *adv.* between, among; — *kommen,* intervene, interfere; — *treten,* intervene.

debattieren [deba'ti:rən], *v.a., v.n.* debate.

Debet ['de:bɛt], *n.* (—s, *pl.* —s) debit.

Debüt [de'by:], *n.* (—s, *pl.* —s) first appearance, début.

Dechant [de'çant], *m.* (—en, *pl.* —en) (*Eccl.*) dean.

dechiffrieren [deʃɪf'ri:rən], *v.a.* decode, decipher.

Deck [dɛk], *n.* (—s, *pl.* —e) (*Naut.*) deck.

Deckbett ['dɛkbɛt], *n.* (—s, *pl.* —en) coverlet.

Deckblatt ['dɛkblat], *n.* (—s, *pl.* ꞉er) (*Bot.*) bractea; (*cigar*) wrapper.

Decke ['dɛkə], *f.* (—, *pl.* —n) cover; blanket, rug; (*bed*) coverlet; (*room*) ceiling.

Deckel ['dɛkəl], *m.* (—s, *pl.* —) lid, top; (*book*) cover; (*coll.*) hat.

decken ['dɛkən], *v.a.* cover; (*Comm.*) secure, reimburse. — *v.r. sich —,* (*Maths.*) coincide; (*fig.*) square, tally.

Deckfarbe ['dɛkfarbə], *f.* (—, *pl.* —n) body colour.

Deckmantel ['dɛkmantəl], *m.* (—s, *pl.* ꞉) cloak, disguise.

Deckung ['dɛkuŋ], *f.* (—, *pl.* —en) covering, protection; (*Comm.*) reimbursement; security; (*Mil.*) cover.

dedizieren [dedɪ'tsi:rən], *v.a.* dedicate.

deduzieren [dedu'tsi:rən], v.a. deduce.

defekt [de'fɛkt], adj. defective, incomplete, imperfect.

defilieren [defi'li:rən], v.n. (Mil.) pass in review, march past.

definieren [defi'ni:rən], v.a. define.

Degen ['de:gən], m. (—s, pl. —) sword; (fig.) brave warrior.

degradieren [degra'di:rən], v.a. degrade, demote.

dehnbar ['de:nba:r], adj. extensible, ductile.

dehnen ['de:nən], v.a. extend, expand, stretch. — v.r. sich —, stretch o.s.

Deich [daɪç], m. (—es, pl. —e) dike, dam, embankment.

Deichsel ['daɪksəl], f. (—, pl. —n) thill, shaft, pole.

deichseln ['daɪksəln], v.a. (fig.) engineer; (coll.) manage; wangle.

dein [daɪn], poss. adj. your; (Poet.) thy. — poss. pron. yours; (Poet.) thine.

deinesgleichen [daɪnəs'glaɪçən], adj. pron. the like of you, such as you.

deinethalben ['daɪnəthalbən], adv. on your account, for your sake, on your behalf.

deinetwegen ['daɪnətve:gən], adv. because of you, on your account, for your sake, on your behalf.

deinetwillen ['daɪnətvɪlən], adv. um —, on your account, for your sake, on your behalf.

deinige ['daɪnɪgə], poss. adj. your; (Poet.) thy. — poss. pron. yours; (Poet.) thine.

Dekan [de'ka:n], m. (—s, pl. —e) (Eccl., Univ.) dean.

Dekanat [deka'na:t], n. (—s, pl. —e) (Eccl., Univ.) deanery, office of dean.

deklamieren [dekla'mi:rən], v.a., v.n. recite, declaim.

deklarieren [dekla'ri:rən], v.a. declare (for customs duty).

Deklination [deklina'tsjo:n], f. (—, pl. —en) (Gram.) declension; (Phys.) declination.

deklinieren [dekli'ni:rən], v.a. (Gram.) decline.

dekolletiert [dekɔle'ti:rt], adj. décolleté, low-necked.

Dekret [de'kre:t], n. (—s, pl. —e) decree, edict, official regulation.

dekretieren [dekre'ti:rən], v.a. decree, ordain.

delegieren [dele'gi:rən], v.a. delegate.

Delegierte [dele'gi:rtə], m. (—n, pl. —n) delegate.

delikat [deli'ka:t], adj. subtle, dainty, tasty; (coll.) tricky, difficult.

Delikatesse [delika'tɛsə], f. (—, pl. —n) delicacy, dainty; (pl.) (Am.) delicatessen.

Delikt [de'lɪkt], n. (—s, pl. —e) (Law) crime; misdemeanour.

Delle ['dɛlə], f. (—, pl. —n) dent.

Delphin [dɛl'fi:n], m. (—s, pl. —e) dolphin.

deltaförmig ['dɛltafœrmɪç], adj. deltoid.

dem [de:m], def. art. Dat. to the. —dem. adj. to this, to that: — dem. pron. to this, to that; wie — auch sei, however that may be. — rel. pron. to whom, to which.

demarkieren [demar'ki:rən], v.a. mark, demarcate.

Dementi [de'mɛnti], n. (—s, pl. —s) (official) denial.

dementieren [demɛn'ti:rən], v.a. (Pol.) deny, contradict.

demgemäß ['de:mgəmɛ:s], adv. accordingly.

demnach ['de:mnax], conj. therefore, consequently, in accordance with that.

demnächst ['de:mnɛ:çst], adv. shortly, soon, in the near future.

demokratisch [demo'kra:tiʃ], adj. democratic.

demolieren [demo'li:rən], v.a. demolish.

demonstrieren [demɔn'stri:rən], v.a., v.n. demonstrate.

Demut ['de:mu:t], f. (—, no pl.) humility, meekness.

demütig ['de:mytiç], adj. humble, meek, submissive.

demütigen ['de:mytigən], v.a. humble, humiliate, subdue.

Denkart ['dɛŋka:rt], f. (—, pl. —en) way of thinking.

denken ['dɛŋkən], v.a., v.n. irr. think, reflect (upon); imagine; (coll.) guess.

Denker ['dɛŋkər], m. (—s, pl. —) thinker, philosopher.

Denkmal ['dɛŋkma:l], n. (—s, pl. ˙er) monument.

Denkmünze ['dɛŋkmyntsə], f. (—, pl. —n) (commemorative) medal.

Denkschrift ['dɛŋkʃrɪft], f. (—, pl. —en) memorandum, memoir.

Denkspruch ['dɛŋkʃprux], m. (—s, pl. ˙e) aphorism, maxim, motto.

Denkungsart ['dɛŋkuŋsart], f. (pl. —en) see Denkart.

Denkweise ['dɛŋkvaɪzə], f. (—, pl. —n) see Denkart.

denkwürdig ['dɛŋkvyrdɪç], adj. memorable.

Denkzettel ['dɛŋktsɛtəl], m. (—s, pl. —) (fig.) reminder, punishment, lesson; einem einen — geben, give s.o. s.th. to think about or a sharp reminder.

denn [dɛn], conj. for. — adv. then; (after comparatives) than; es sei — dass, unless.

dennoch ['dɛnɔx], conj. yet, nevertheless, notwithstanding.

Denunziant [denun'tsjant], m. (—en, pl. —en) informer.

denunzieren [denun'tsi:rən], v.a. inform against, denounce.

Depesche [de'pɛʃə], f. (—, pl. —n) dispatch; telegram, wire.

deponieren [depo'ni:rən], v.a. deposit; (Law) depose.

Depositenbank [depo'zi:tənbaŋk], f. (—, pl. —en) deposit-bank.

45

deprimieren

deprimieren [depri'miːrən], v.a. depress.

Deputierte [depu'tiːrtə], m. (**—n**, pl. **—n**) deputy.

der [deːr], def. art. m. the. — dem. adj., dem. pron. this, that. — rel. pron. who, which, that.

derart ['deːraːrt], adv. so, in such a manner.

derartig ['deːraːrtɪç], adj. such.

derb [dɛrp], adj. firm, solid, coarse, blunt, uncouth; strong, robust.

dereinst [deːr'aɪnst], adv. one day (in future).

derenthalben ['deːrənthalbən], adv. for her (their) sake, on her (their) account, on whose account.

derentwegen ['deːrəntveːgən], adv. see **derenthalben**.

derentwillen ['deːrəntvɪlən], adv. see **derenthalben**.

dergestalt ['deːrgəʃtalt], adv. in such a manner; so.

dergleichen [deːr'glaɪçən], adv. such, such as, suchlike.

derjenige ['deːrjeːnɪgə], dem. adj., dem. pron. that, this; — welcher, he who.

derlei ['deːrlaɪ], adj. of that sort.

dermaßen ['deːrmaːsən], adv. to such an extent, to such a degree.

derselbe [deːr'zɛlbə], pron. the same.

derweilen [deːr'vaɪlən], adv. meanwhile.

Derwisch ['dɛrvɪʃ], m. (**—(e)s**, pl. **—e**) dervish.

derzeit ['deːrtsaɪt], adv. at present.

Des [dɛs], n. (**—**, pl. **—**) (Mus.) D flat; — Dur, D flat major; — Moll, D flat minor.

des [dɛs], def. art. m. & n. Genit. sing. of the.

desgleichen [dɛs'glaɪçən], adj. such, suchlike. — adv. likewise, ditto.

deshalb ['dɛshalp], adv., conj. therefore.

desinfizieren [dɛsɪnfɪt'siːrən], v.a. disinfect.

dessen ['dɛsən], dem. pron. m & n. Genit. sing. of it, of that. — rel. pron. m. & n. Genit. sing. whose, of whom, of which, whereof.

dessenungeachtet [dɛsənungə'axtət], conj. notwithstanding that, for all that, despite all that.

Destillateur [dɛstɪla'tøːr], m. (**—s**, pl. **—e**) distiller.

destillieren [dɛstɪ'liːrən], v.a. distil.

desto ['dɛsto], adv. the; — besser, so much the better; je . . . —, the . . . the.

deswegen ['dɛsveːgən], adv., conj. therefore.

Detaillist [deta'jɪst], m. (**—en**, pl. **—en**) retailer.

deucht [dɔyçt] see **dünken**; (obs.) mich deucht, methinks.

deuten ['dɔytən], v.a. point to, show; explain, interpret.

deutlich ['dɔytlɪç], adj. clear, distinct; evident, plain.

deutsch [dɔytʃ], adj. German.

Deutschland ['dɔytʃlant], n. Germany.

Deutschmeister ['dɔytʃmaɪstər], m. (**—s**, pl. **—**) Grand Master of the Teutonic Order.

Deutschtum ['dɔytʃtuːm], n. (**—s**, no pl.) German nationality, German customs, German manners.

Deutung ['dɔytuŋ], f. (**—**, pl. **—en**) explanation, interpretation.

Devise [de'viːzə], f. (**—**, pl. **—n**) device, motto; (pl.) foreign currency

devot [de'voːt], adj. submissive, respectful, humble.

Dezember [de'tsɛmbər], m. December

dezent [de'tsɛnt], adj. modest, decent unobtrusive.

Dezernent [detsɛr'nɛnt], m. (**—en**, pl. **—en**) head of section in ministry or city administration.

dezimieren [detsi'miːrən], v.a. decimate, reduce.

Diagramm [dia'gram], n. (**—s**, pl. **—e**) diagram, graph.

Diakon [dia'koːn], m. (**—s**, pl. **—e** (Eccl.) deacon.

Diakonisse, Diakonissin [diako'nɪsə diako'nɪsɪn], f. (**—**, pl. **—nen**) deaconess.

Dialektik [dia'lɛktɪk], f. (**—**, no pl.) dialectics.

Diamant [dia'mant], m. (**—en**, pl. **—en**) diamond.

diametral [diame'traːl], adj. diametrical.

Diapositiv [diapozi'tiːf], n. (**—s**, pl. **—e**) (lantern, Phot.) slide.

Diät [di'ɛːt], f. (**—**, pl. **—en**) diet; (pl.) daily allowance.

dich [dɪç], pers. pron. you. — refl. pron. yourself.

dicht [dɪçt], adj. tight; impervious (to water); dense, compact, solid, firm; — bei, hard by, close to.

Dichte ['dɪçtə], f. (**—**, no pl.) density.

dichten ['dɪçtən], v.a., v.n. write poetry, compose (verses etc.); (Tech.) tighten; (Naut.) caulk.

Dichter ['dɪçtər], m. (**—s**, pl. **—**) poet.

dichterisch ['dɪçtərɪʃ], adj. poetic(al).

Dichtigkeit ['dɪçtɪçkaɪt], f. (**—**, no pl.) closeness, compactness, thickness, density.

Dichtkunst ['dɪçtkunst], f. (**—**, no pl.) (art of) poetry.

Dichtung ['dɪçtuŋ], f. (**—**, pl. **—en**) poetry, poem; fiction; (Tech.) caulking; washer, gasket.

dick [dɪk], adj. thick; fat; (books) bulky; voluminous, stout, obese, corpulent.

Dicke ['dɪkə], f. (**—**, no pl.) thickness, stoutness.

dickfellig ['dɪkfɛlɪç], adj. thick-skinned.

Dickicht ['dɪkɪçt], n. (**—s**, pl. **—e**) thicket.

die [diː], def. art. f. & pl. the. — dem. adj., dem. pron. f. & pl. this, these. — rel. pron. f. & pl. who, that which.

Dieb [diːp], m. (**—s**, pl. **—e**) thief.

Diebstahl ['diːpʃtaːl], m. (**—s**, pl. **⁓e**) theft.

Diele ['di:lə], *f.* (—, *pl.* —n) floor; (entrance) hall; plank.

dielen ['di:lən], *v.a.* board, floor.

dienen ['di:nən], *v.n.* einem —, serve (s.o.); help (s.o.).

Diener ['di:nər], *m.* (—s, *pl.* —) servant, attendant; (*coll.*) bow.

dienlich ['di:nlɪç], *adj.* serviceable, useful; *für* — *halten*, think fit.

Dienst [di:nst], *m.* (—es, *pl.* —e) service, employment, duty; — *haben*, be on duty.

Dienstag ['di:nsta:k], *m.* (—s, *pl.* —e) Tuesday.

Dienstalter ['di:nstaltər], *n.* (—s, *pl.* —) seniority.

dienstbar ['di:nstba:r], *adj.* subject, subservient.

Dienstbarkeit ['di:nstba:rkaɪt], *f.* (—, *no pl.*) bondage, servitude.

dienstbeflissen ['di:nstbəflɪsən], *adj.* assiduous.

Dienstbote ['di:nstbo:tə], *m.* (—n, *pl.* —n) domestic servant.

dienstfertig ['di:nstfertɪç], *adj.* obliging, ready to serve.

Dienstleistung ['di:nstlaɪstuŋ], *f.* (—, *pl.* —en) service.

dienstlich ['di:nstlɪç], *adj.* official.

Dienstmädchen ['di:nstmɛ:tçən], *n.* (—s, *pl.* —) maidservant.

Dienstmann ['di:nstman], *m.* (—s, *pl.* :er) commissionaire, porter.

Dienstpflicht ['di:nstpflɪçt], *f.* (—, *no pl.*) official duty, liability to serve; (*Mil.*) (compulsory) military service.

Dienststunden ['di:nstʃtundən], *f. pl.* office hours.

diensttauglich ['di:nsttauklɪç], *adj.* (*Mil.*) fit for service.

Dienstverhältnis ['di:nstferheɪtnɪs], *n.* (—ses, *pl.* —se) (*pl.*) terms of service.

dies [di:s], *abbr.* dieses.

diesbezüglich ['di:sbətsy:klɪç], *adj.* concerning this, relating to this matter.

diese ['di:zə], *dem. adj., dem. pron. f. & pl.* this, these.

dieser ['di:zər], *dem. adj., dem. pron. m.* this.

dieses ['di:zəs], *dem. adj., dem. pron. n.* this.

diesjährig ['di:sjɛ:rɪç], *adj.* of this year, this year's.

diesmal ['di:sma:l], *adv.* this time, for this once.

Dietrich (1) ['di:trɪç], *m.* Derek.

Dietrich (2) ['di:trɪç], *m.* (—s, *pl.* —e) pick lock, master-key, skeleton key.

Differentialrechnung [dɪfərɛnts'ja:l-rɛçnuŋ], *f.* (—, *pl.* —en) differential calculus.

Differenz [dɪfə'rɛnts], *f.* (—, *pl.* —en) difference; quarrel.

Diktat [dɪk'ta:t], *n.* (—s, *pl.* —e) dictation.

diktatorisch [dɪkta'to:rɪʃ], *adj.* dictatorial.

Diktatur [dɪkta'tu:r], *f.* (—, *pl.* —en) dictatorship.

diktieren [dɪk'ti:rən], *v.a.* dictate.

Ding [dɪŋ], *n.* (—s, *pl.* —e) thing, object, matter.

dingen ['dɪŋən], *v.a.* hire, engage (a manual worker).

dingfest ['dɪŋfɛst], *adj.* — *machen*, arrest.

dinglich ['dɪŋlɪç], *adj.* real.

dinieren [di'ni:rən], *v.n.* dine.

Diözese [diø'tse:zə], *f.* (—, *pl.* —n) diocese.

Diphtherie [dɪftə'ri:], *f.* (—, *no pl.*) diphtheria.

Diplom [di'plo:m], *n.* (—s, *pl.* —e) diploma.

Diplomatie [dɪploma'ti:], *f.* (—, *no pl.*) diplomacy.

dir [di:r], *pers. pron. Dat.* to you.

direkt [di'rɛkt], *adj.* direct; —*er Wagen*, (*railway*) through carriage; — *danach*, immediately afterwards.

Direktion [dɪrɛk'sjo:n], *f.* (—, *pl.* —en) direction, management.

Direktor [di'rɛktɔr], *m.* (—s, *pl.* —en) (managing) director, manager; headmaster, principal.

Direktorium [dɪrɛk'to:rjum], *n.* (—s, *pl.* —rien) directorate, board of directors.

Direktrice [dɪrɛk'tri:sə], *f.* (—, *pl.* —n) manageress.

Dirigent [diri'gɛnt], *m.* (—en, *pl.* —en) (*Mus.*) conductor; (*Austr. Admin.*) head of section in Ministry.

dirigieren [diri'gi:rən], *v.a.* direct, manage; (*Mus.*) conduct.

Dirndl ['dɪrndl], *n.* (—s, *pl.* —) (*dial.*) young girl, country wench; (*fig.*) peasant dress, dirndl.

Dirne ['dɪrnə], *f.* (—, *pl.* —n) (*Poet.*) girl; prostitute.

Dis [dɪs], *n.* (—, *no pl.*) (*Mus.*) D sharp.

disharmonisch [dɪshar'mo:nɪʃ], *adj.* discordant.

Diskant [dɪs'kant], *m.* (—s, *pl.* —e) (*Mus.*) treble, soprano.

Diskont [dɪs'kɔnt], *m.* (—(e)s, *pl.* —e) discount, rebate.

diskret [dɪs'kre:t], *adj.* discreet.

Diskurs [dɪs'kurs], *m.* (—es, *pl.* —e) discourse.

diskutieren [dɪsku'ti:rən], *v.a.* discuss, debate.

Dispens [dɪs'pɛns], *m.* (—es, *pl.* —e) dispensation.

dispensieren [dɪspɛn'zi:rən], *v.a.* dispense (from); exempt (from).

disponieren [dɪspo'ni:rən], *v.n.* — *über*, dispose of; make plans about.

Dissident [dɪsi'dɛnt], *m.* (—en, *pl.* —en) dissenter, nonconformist.

distanzieren [dɪstan'tsi:rən], *v.r. sich* — *von*, keep o.'s distance from; dissociate o.s. from.

Distel ['dɪstəl], *f.* (—, *pl.* —n) thistle.

Distelfink ['dɪstəlfɪŋk], *m.* (—s, *pl.* —e) (*Orn.*) gold-finch.

disziplinarisch [dɪstsipli'na:rɪʃ], *adj.* diciplinary.

dito ['di:to], *adv.* ditto.

dividieren

dividieren [dɪvi'di:rən], *v.a.* divide.
Diwan ['di:van], *m.* (—**s**, *pl.* —**e**) divan, sofa, couch.
doch [dɔx], *adv., conj.* however, though, although, nevertheless, yet, but; after all, (*emphatic*) yes.
Docht [dɔxt], *m.* (—**es**, *pl.* —**e**) wick.
Dock [dɔk], *n.* (—**s**, *pl.* —**s**, —**e**) dock.
Dogge ['dɔgə], *f.* (—, *pl.* —**n**) bulldog, mastiff; Great Dane.
Dogmatiker [dɔg'ma:tɪkər], *m.* (—**s**, *pl.* —) dogmatist.
dogmatisch [dɔg'ma:tɪʃ], *adj.* dogmatic, doctrinal.
Dohle ['do:lə], *f.* (—, *pl.* —**n**) (*Orn.*) jackdaw.
Doktor ['dɔktɔr], *m.* (—**s**, *pl.* —**en**) doctor; physician, surgeon.
Dolch [dɔlç], *m.* (—**es**, *pl.* —**e**) dagger, dirk.
Dolde ['dɔldə], *f.* (—, *pl.* —**n**) (*Bot.*) umbel.
Dolmetscher ['dɔlmɛtʃər], *m.* (—**s**, *pl.* —) interpreter.
dolmetschen ['dɔlmɛtʃən], *v.a.* interpret.
Dolomiten [dolo'mi:tən], *pl.* Dolomites.
Dom [do:m], *m.* (—**s**, *pl.* —**e**) cathedral; dome, cupola.
Domherr ['do:mhɛr], *m.* (—**n**, *pl.* —**en**) canon, prebendary.
dominieren [domi'ni:rən], *v.a.* dominate, domineer.
Dominikaner [domini'ka:nər], *m.* (—**s**, *pl.* —) Dominican friar.
dominikanische Republik [domini'ka:nɪʃə rɛpu'bli:k], *f.* Dominican Republic.
Domizil [domi'tsi:l], *n.* (—**s**, *pl.* —**e**) domicile, residence, address.
Domkapitel ['do:mkapi:təl], *n.* (—**s**, *pl.* —) dean and chapter.
Dompfaff ['do:mpfaf], *m.* (—**s**, *pl.* —**en**) (*Orn.*) bullfinch.
Dompropst ['do:mpro:pst], *m.* (—**es**, *pl.* ⁓**e**) provost.
Donau ['do:nau], *f.* (—, *no pl.*) Danube.
Donner ['dɔnər], *m.* (—**s**, *no pl.*) thunder.
donnern ['dɔnərn], *v.n.* thunder; (*fig.*) storm, rage.
Donnerschlag ['dɔnərʃla:k], *m.* (—**s**, *pl.* ⁓**e**) thunderclap.
Donnerstag ['dɔnərsta:k], *m.* (—**s**, *pl.* —**e**) Thursday; *Grün* —, Maundy Thursday.
Donnerwetter ['dɔnərvɛtər], *n.* (—**s**, *pl.* —) thunderstorm; *zum* — (*nochmal*)! hang it all, confound it!
doppeldeutig ['dɔpəldɔytɪç], *adj.* ambiguous.
Doppelgänger ['dɔpəlgɛŋər], *m.* (—**s**, *pl.* —) double.
Doppellaut ['dɔpəllaut], *m.* (—**s**, *pl.* —**e**) diphthong.
doppeln ['dɔpəln] *see* **verdoppeln**.
doppelsinnig ['dɔpəlzɪnɪç] *see* **doppeldeutig**.
doppelt ['dɔpəlt], *adj.* double, twofold.

Doppelzwirn ['dɔpəltsvɪrn], *m.* (—**s**, *no pl.*) double-thread.
Dorf [dɔrf], *n.* (—**es**, *pl.* ⁓**er**) village.
dörflich ['dœrflɪç], *adj.* rural, rustic.
dorisch ['do:rɪʃ], *adj.* Doric.
Dorn [dɔrn], *m.* (—**s**, *pl.* —**en**) thorn, prickle; (*Bot.*) spine; (*buckle*) tongue.
dornig ['dɔrnɪç], *adj.* thorny.
Dornröschen ['dɔrnrø:sçən], *n.* (—**s**, *pl.* —) Sleeping Beauty.
Dorothea [doro'te:a], *f.* Dorothea, Dorothy.
dorren ['dɔrən] *see* **verdorren**.
dörren ['dœrən], *v.a.* dry, make dry, parch.
Dörrobst ['dœrrobst], *n.* (—**es**, *no pl.*) dried fruit.
Dorsch [dɔrʃ], *m.* (—**es**, *pl.* —**e**) cod, codfish.
dort [dɔrt], (*Austr.*) **dorten** ['dɔrtən], *adv.* there, yonder; *von* — *aus*, from that point, from there.
dorther ['dɔrthe:r], *adv.* from there, therefrom, thence.
dorthin ['dɔrthɪn], *adv.* to that place, thereto, thither.
dortig ['dɔrtɪç], *adj.* of that place, local.
Dose ['do:zə], *f.* (—, *pl.* —**n**) box, tin, can.
dösen ['dø:zən], *v.n.* doze, daydream.
Dosis ['do:zɪs], *f.* (—, *pl.* **Dosen**) dose.
Dotter ['dɔtər], *n.* (—**s**, *pl.* —) yolk (of egg).
Dozent [do'tsɛnt], *m.* (—**en**, *pl.* —**en**) university lecturer; (*Am.*) Assistant Professor.
dozieren [do'tsi:rən], *v.n.* lecture.
Drache ['draxə], *m.* (—**n**, *pl.* —**n**) dragon; kite; (*fig.*) termagant, shrew.
Dragoner [dra'go:nər], *m.* (—**s**, *pl.* —) dragoon.
Draht [dra:t], *m.* (—**es**, *pl.* ⁓**e**) wire.
drahten ['dra:tən], *v.a.* wire, telegraph.
Drahtgewebe ['dra:tgəve:bə], *n.* (—**s**, *pl.* —) wire-gauze.
Drahtgitter ['dra:tgɪtər], *m.* (—**s**, *pl.* —) wire grating.
drahtlos ['dra:tlo:s], *adj.* wireless.
Drahtseilbahn ['dra:tzailba:n], *f.* (—, *pl.* —**en**) cable (funicular) railway.
Drahtzange ['dra:ttsaŋə], *f.* (—, *pl.* —**n**) pliers.
drall [dral], *adj.* buxom, plump.
Drama ['dra:ma], *n.* (—**s**, *pl.* —**men**) drama.
Dramatiker [dra'ma:tɪkər], *m.* (—**s**, *pl.* —) dramatist.
dramatisch [dra'ma:tɪʃ], *adj.* dramatic.
dran [dran] *see* **daran**.
Drang [draŋ], *m.* (—**s**, *no pl.*) urge; rush; throng; pressure; impulse.
drängeln ['drɛŋəln], *v.a.* jostle.
drängen ['drɛŋən], *v.a.* press, urge; *die Zeit drängt*, time presses; *es drängt mich*, I feel called upon.
Drangsal ['dranza:l], *f. or n.* (—**s**, *pl.* —**e** *or* —**en**) distress, misery.
drapieren [dra'pi:rən], *v.a.* drape.

drastisch ['drastiʃ], adj. drastic.

drauf [drauf] see **darauf**.

Draufgänger ['draufgɛŋər], m. (—s, pl. —) daredevil.

draußen ['drausən], adv. outside, without, out of doors.

drechseln ['drɛksəln], v.a. turn (on a lathe); Phrasen —, turn phrases.

Drechsler ['drɛkslər], m. (—s, pl. —) turner.

Dreck [drɛk], m. (—s, no pl.) dirt, mire, dust, filth, dung.

dreckig ['drɛkiç], adj. dirty, filthy, muddy.

drehbar ['dre:ba:r], adj. revolving, swivelling.

Drehbuch ['dre:bu:x], n. (—s, pl. ̈er) (film) script.

drehen ['dre:ən], v.a. turn; (film) shoot. — v.n. turn round, veer.

Drehorgel ['dre:ɔrgəl], f. (—, pl. —n) barrel-organ.

Drehrad ['dre:ra:t], n. (—s, pl. ̈er) fly-wheel.

Drehung ['dre:uŋ], f. (—, pl. —en) rotation, turn, revolution.

drei [drai], num. adj. three.

dreiblätterig ['draiblɛtəriç], adj. trifoliate.

Dreieck ['draiɛk], n. (—s, pl. —e) triangle.

dreieckig ['draiɛkiç], adj. triangular, three-cornered.

dreieinig [drai'ainiç], adj. (Theol.) triune.

dreifach ['draifax], adj. threefold, triple.

Dreifaltigkeit [drai'faltiçkait], f. (—, no pl.) (Theol.) Trinity.

Dreifuß ['draifu:s], m. (—es, pl. ̈e) tripod.

dreijährlich ['draijɛrliç], adj. triennial.

Dreikönigsfest [drai'kø:niksfɛst], n. (—es, no pl.) Epiphany.

dreimonatlich ['draimo:natliç], adj. quarterly.

Dreirad ['draira:t], n. (—s, pl. ̈er) tricycle.

dreiseitig ['draizaitiç], adj. trilateral.

dreißig ['draisiç], num. adj. thirty.

dreist [draist], adj. bold, audacious; impudent.

dreistellig ['draiʃtɛliç], adj. —e Zahl, number of three figures.

dreistimmig ['draiʃtimiç], adj. for three voices.

Dreistufenrakete ['draiʃtu:fənra'ke:tə], f. (—, pl. —n) three-stage rocket.

dreistündig ['draiʃtyndiç], adj. lasting three hours.

dreitägig ['draitɛ:giç], adj. lasting three days.

dreiteilig ['draitailiç], adj. tripartite; three-piece.

dreizehn ['draitse:n], num. adj. thirteen.

Drell [drɛl], m. (—s, pl.) see **Drillich**.

Dresche ['drɛʃə], f. (—, no pl.) thrashing, beating.

dreschen ['drɛʃən], v.a. irr. (corn) thresh; (person) thrash.

Dreschflegel ['drɛʃfle:gəl], m. (—s, pl. —) flail.

dressieren [drɛ'si:rən], v.a. (animal) train; break in.

Dressur [drɛ'su:r], f. (—, pl. —en) training, breaking-in.

Drillbohrer ['drilbo:rər], m. (—s, pl. —) drill.

drillen ['drilən], v.a. (a hole) bore; (soldiers) drill.

Drillich ['driliç], m. (—s, pl. —e) drill, canvas.

Drilling ['driliŋ], m. (—s, pl. —e) three-barrelled gun; (pl.) triplets.

drin [drin] see **darin**.

dringen ['driŋən], v.n. irr. penetrate, force o.'s way through; auf etwas —, insist on s.th.

dringlich ['driŋliç], adj. urgent, pressing.

drinnen ['drinən], adv. inside, within.

drittens ['dritəns], adv. thirdly.

droben ['dro:bən], adv. up there, above, aloft, overhead.

Droge ['dro:gə], f. (—, pl. —n) drug.

Drogerie [dro:gə'ri:], f. (—, pl. —n) druggist's shop, chemist's; (Am.) drugstore.

drohen ['dro:ən], v.a., v.n. threaten, menace.

Drohne ['dro:nə], f. (—, pl. —n) drone.

dröhnen ['drø:nən], v.n. boom, roar.

Drohung ['dro:uŋ], f. (—, pl. —en) threat, menace.

drollig ['drɔliç], adj. droll, odd, quaint.

Dromedar [drɔmə'da:r], n. (—s, pl. —e) dromedary.

Droschke ['drɔʃkə], f. (—, pl. —n) cab, hansom, taxi.

Drossel ['drɔsəl], f. (—, pl. —n) thrush.

Drosselader ['drɔsala:dər], f. (—, pl. —n) jugular vein.

Drosselbein ['drɔsəlbain], n. (—s, pl. —e) collar-bone.

drosseln ['drɔsəln], v.a. throttle. See also **erdrosseln**.

drüben ['dry:bən], adv. over there, on the other side.

drüber ['dry:bər] see **darüber**.

Druck [druk], m. (—s, pl. ̈e, —e) pressure, squeeze; (Phys.) compression; (Typ.) impression, print; (fig.) hardship.

Druckbogen ['drukbo:gən], m. (—s, pl. —) proof-sheet, proof.

Druckbuchstabe ['drukbu:xʃta:bə], m. (—n, pl. —n) letter, type.

Drückeberger ['drykəbergər], m. (—s, pl. —) slacker, shirker.

drucken ['drukən], v.a. print.

drücken ['drykən], v.a. press, squeeze; trouble, oppress. — v.r. sich —, sneak away, shirk.

Drucker ['drukər], m. (—s, pl. —) printer.

Drücker ['drykər], m. (—s, pl. —) (door) handle, latch; (gun) trigger.

Druckerei ['drukərai], f. (—, pl. —en) printing shop.

Druckerschwärze ['drukərʃvɛrtsə], *f.* (—, *no pl.*) printing-ink.

Druckfehler ['drukfe:lər], *m.* (—s, *pl.* —) misprint, printer's error.

druckfertig ['drukfɛrtɪç], *adj.* ready for press.

Drucksache ['drukzaxə], *f.* (—, *pl.* —n) (*Postal*) printed matter.

drum [drum] *see* darum.

drunten ['druntən], *adv.* down there, below.

drunter ['druntər] *see* darunter.

Drüse ['dry:zə], *f.* (—, *pl.* —n) gland.

Dschungel ['dʒuŋəl], *m.* or *n.* (—s, *pl.* —) jungle.

du [du:], *pers. pron.* thou, you.

ducken ['dukən], *v.a.* bring down, humble. — *v.r. sich* —, duck, stoop, crouch.

dudeln ['du:dəln], *v.n.* play the bagpipes; tootle.

Dudelsack ['du:dəlzak], *m.* (—s, *pl.* ⸚e) bagpipe(s).

Duft [duft], *m.* (—s, *pl.* ⸚e) scent, odour, fragrance, aroma, perfume.

duften ['duftən], *v.n.* be fragrant.

duftig ['duftɪç], *adj.* fragrant, odoriferous, perfumed.

dulden ['duldən], *v.a.* suffer, endure, bear, tolerate.

duldsam ['dultza:m], *adj.* tolerant, indulgent, patient.

dumm [dum], *adj.* stupid, foolish, dull.

Dummheit ['dumhaɪt], *f.* (—, *pl.* —en) stupidity, folly.

dumpf [dumpf], *adj.* musty; (*air*) close; (*sound*) hollow; (*fig.*) gloomy.

dumpfig ['dumpfɪç], *adj.* damp, musty, stuffy.

Düne ['dy:nə], *f.* (—, *pl.* —n) dune, sand-hill.

Düngemittel ['dyŋəmɪtəl], *n.* (—s, *pl.* —) fertilizer.

düngen ['dyŋən], *v.a.* manure, fertilize.

Dünger ['dyŋər], *m.* (—s, *no pl.*) compost, artificial manure.

dunkel ['duŋkəl], *adj.* dark; (*fig.*) obscure, mysterious.

Dünkel ['dyŋkəl], *m.* (—s, *no pl.*) conceit, arrogance.

dünkelhaft ['dyŋkəlhaft], *adj.* conceited, arrogant.

Dunkelheit ['duŋkəlhaɪt], *f.* (—, *no pl.*) darkness, obscurity.

dunkeln ['duŋkəln], *v.n.* grow dark.

dünken ['dyŋkən], *v.n.* (*rare*) seem, appear. — *v.r. sich* —, fancy o.s., imagine o.s.

dünn [dyn], *adj.* thin, slim, weak.

Dunst [dunst], *m.* (—es, *pl.* ⸚e) vapour, fume; exhalation; haze; *einem blauen* — *vormachen*, humbug a p.

dünsten ['dynstən], *v.a.* stew.

dunstig ['dunstɪç], *adj.* misty, hazy.

Dunstkreis ['dunstkraɪs], *m.* (—es, *pl.* —e) atmosphere.

Dunstobst ['dunsto:pst], *n.* (—es, *no pl.*) stewed fruit.

duodez [duo'de:ts], *adj.* (*Typ.*) duodecimo (12mo).

Duodezfürst [duo'de:tsfyrst], *m.* (—s, *pl.* —en) petty prince, princeling.

Dur [du:r], *n.* (*Mus.*) major; sharp.

durch [durç], *prep.* (*Acc.*) (*local*) through, across; (*temporal*) during, throughout; (*manner*) by means of, by. — *adv.* thoroughly, through.

durchaus [durç'aus], *adv.* throughout, quite, by all means, absolutely.

Durchblick ['durçblɪk], *m.* (—s, *pl.* —e) vista, view.

durchbohren [durç'bo:rən], *v.a. insep.* perforate, pierce.

durchbrennen ['durçbrɛnən], *v.n. irr.* (*aux.* sein) abscond, bolt.

durchbringen ['durçbrɪŋən], *v.a. irr.* bring through, get through; squander (money); pull (a sick person) through. — *v.r. sich redlich* —, make an honest living.

Durchbruch ['durçbrux], *m.* (—s, *pl.* ⸚e) breach, break-through.

durchdrängen ['durçdrɛŋən], *v.r. sich* —, force o.'s way through.

durchdringen ['durçdrɪŋən], *v.n. irr. sep.* (*aux.* sein) get through. — [durç'drɪŋən], *v.a. irr.insep.* penetrate, pierce, permeate, pervade.

durchdrücken ['durçdrykən], *v.a.* press through; (*fig.*) carry through.

durcheilen [durç'aɪlən], *v.a. insep.* hurry through.

Durcheinander [durçaɪn'andər], *n.* (—s, *no pl.*) confusion, muddle.

durcheinander [durçaɪn'andər], *adv.* in confusion, pell-mell.

Durchfall ['durçfal], *m.* (—s, *no pl.*) diarrhoea; (*exams etc.*) failure.

durchfallen ['durçfalən], *v.n. irr.* (*aux.* sein) fall through, come to nought; (*exams etc.*) fail.

durchflechten [durç'flɛçtən], *v.a. irr.* interweave, intertwine.

durchfliegen [durç'fli:gən], *v.a. irr.* fly through; read superficially, skim through.

durchforschen [durç'fɔrʃən], *v.a. insep.* explore, scrutinise, examine thoroughly.

Durchfuhr ['durçfu:r], *f.* (—, *pl.* —en) passage, transit.

durchführbar ['durçfy:rba:r], *adj.* practicable, feasible.

durchführen ['durçfy:rən], *v.a.* escort through; (*fig.*) execute, bring about, carry through.

Durchgang ['durçgaŋ], *m.* (—s, *pl.* ⸚e) passage, thoroughfare; (*Comm.*) transit.

Durchgänger ['durçgɛŋər], *m.* (—s, *pl.* —) runaway horse, bolter; (*fig.*) hothead.

durchgängig ['durçgɛŋɪç], *adj.* general, universal.

durchgehen ['durçge:ən], *v.n. irr.* (*aux.* sein) go through; (*fig.*) abscond; (*horse*) bolt; (*proposal*) be carried. — *v.a. irr.* (*aux.* sein) peruse, review, go over.

durchgreifen ['durçgraɪfən], v.n. irr. act decisively, take strong action.

durchhauen ['durçhauən], v.a. cut through; einen —, flog s.o.

durchkommen ['durçkɔmən], v.n. irr. (aux. sein) get through; (exams etc.) pass.

durchkreuzen [durç'krɔytsən], v.a. insep. cross out; (fig.) thwart.

durchlassen ['durçlasən], v.a. irr. let pass.

Durchlaucht ['durçlauxt], f. (— pl. —en) Highness.

durchleuchten [durç'lɔyçtən], v.a. insep. (Med.) X-ray.

durchlöchern [durç'lœçərn], v.a. insep. perforate, riddle.

durchmachen ['durçmaxən], v.a. go through, suffer.

Durchmesser ['durçmɛsər], m. (—s, pl. —) diameter.

durchnässen [durç'nɛsən], v.a. insep. wet to the skin, soak.

durchnehmen [durç'ne:mən], v.a. irr. go over or cover (a subject).

durchpausen ['durçpauzən], v.a. trace, copy.

durchqueren [durç'kve:rən], v.a. insep. cross, traverse.

Durchsage ['durçza:gə], f. (—, pl. —n) (radio) announcement.

durchschauen [durç'ʃauən], v.a. insep. einen —, see through s.o.

durchscheinend ['durçʃaɪnənt], adj. transparent, translucent.

Durchschlag ['durçʃla:k], m. (—s, pl. ⁝e) strainer, sieve, colander, filter; carbon copy.

durchschlagen ['durçʃla:gən], v.a. irr. insep. strain, filter. — v.r. irr. sich —, fight o.'s way through.

durchschlagend ['durçʃla:gənt], adj. thorough, complete, effective.

Durchschnitt ['durçʃnɪt], m. (—s, pl. —e) average; (Med. etc.) cross section.

durchschnittlich ['durçʃnɪtlɪç], adj. average; ordinary.

durchschossen [durç'ʃɔsən], adj. interleaved; interwoven.

durchseihen ['durçzaɪən], v.a. see **durchsieben**.

durchsetzen [durç'zɛtsən], v.a. insep. intersperse; ['durçzɛtsən], v.a. sep. have o.'s way (with s.o.). — v.r. sep. sich —, make o.'s way successfully, succeed.

Durchsicht ['durçzɪçt], f. (—, no pl.) revision, inspection, perusal.

durchsichtig ['durçzɪçtɪç], adj. transparent.

durchsickern ['durçzɪkərn], v.n. (aux. sein) trickle through, ooze through.

durchsieben ['durçzi:bən], v.a. strain, filter, sift.

durchsprechen ['durçʃprɛxən], v.a. irr. talk over, discuss.

durchstöbern [durç'ʃtø:bərn], v.a. insep. rummage through.

durchstreichen ['durçʃtraɪçən], v.a. irr. cross out, delete.

durchstreifen [durç'ʃtraɪfən], v.a insep. roam (through).

durchströmen [durç'ʃtrø:mən], v.a. insep. flow through, permeate.

durchsuchen [durç'zu:xən], v.a. insep. search thoroughly, examine closely.

durchtrieben [durç'tri:bən], adj. artful, sly, cunning, crafty.

durchweben [durç've:bən], v.a. interweave.

durchweg(s) ['durçvɛk(s)], adv. without exception, every time, throughout.

durchwühlen [durç'vy:lən], v.a. insep. search; ransack.

durchziehen [durç'tsi:ən], v.a. irr. insep. wander through, traverse; ['durçtsi:ən], v.a. irr. sep. interlace (with threads); draw through.

durchzucken [durç'tsukən], v.a. insep. flash through, convulse.

Durchzug ['durçtsu:k], m. (—s, no pl.) passage, march through; (air) draught.

dürfen ['dyrfən], v.n. irr. be permitted; be allowed; dare; be likely.

dürftig ['dyrftɪç], adj. paltry, insufficient, poor.

dürr [dyr], adj. dry, arid, withered; (wood) dead; (persons) thin, gaunt.

Dürre ['dyrə], f. (—, pl. —n) aridity, dryness; drought; (persons) thinness.

Durst [durst], m. (—es, no pl.) thirst.

dürsten ['dyrstən], v.n. thirst.

durstig ['durstɪç], adj. thirsty.

Dusche ['du:ʃə], f. (—, pl. —n) shower (bath).

Düse ['dy:zə], f. (—, pl. —n) jet.

duselig ['du:zəlɪç], adj. drowsy; silly.

düster ['dy:stər], adj. dark, gloomy; sad, mournful; sombre.

Dutzend ['dutsənt], n. (—s, pl. —e) dozen.

Duzbruder ['du:tsbru:dər], m. (—s, pl. ⁝) crony, chum; close friend.

duzen ['du:tsen], v.a. be on close terms with.

dynamisch [dy'na:mɪʃ], adj. dynamic(al).

E

E [e:], n. (—s, pl. —s) the letter E; (Mus.) E Dur, E major; E Moll, E minor.

Ebbe ['ɛbə], f. (—, pl. —n) ebb, low tide; — und Flut, the tides.

ebben ['ɛbən], v.n. ebb.

eben ['e:bən], adj. even, level, plane; (fig.) plain. — adv. precisely, exactly.

Ebenbild ['e:bənbɪlt], n. (—es, pl. —er) likeness, image.

ebenbürtig ['e:bənbyrtɪç], adj. of equal birth or rank; equal.

ebenda

ebenda ['e:bəndɑ:], *adv.* in the same place.

ebendeswegen ['e:bəndɛsve:gən], *adv.* for that very reason.

Ebene ['e:bənə], *f.* (—, *pl.* —n) plain; level ground; (*Maths.*) plane; *schiefe* —, inclined plane.

ebenfalls ['e:bənfals], *adv.* likewise, also, too, as well.

Ebenholz ['e:bənhɔlts], *n.* (—es, *no pl.*) ebony.

Ebenmaß ['e:bənmɑ:s], *n.* (—es, *pl.* —e) symmetry.

ebenmäßig ['e:bənmɛ:sɪç], *adj.* symmetrical.

ebenso ['e:bənzo:], *adv.* in the same way; — *wie*, just as . . .

Eber ['e:bər], *m.* (—s, *pl.* —) (*Zool.*) boar.

Eberesche ['e:bərɛʃə], *f.* (—, *pl.* —n) (*Bot.*) mountain ash, rowan.

ebnen ['e:bnən], *v.a.* even out, level; smoothe.

echt [ɛçt], *adj.* genuine, real, true, authentic, pure.

Ecke ['ɛkə], *f.* (—, *pl.* —en) corner, nook.

eckig ['ɛkɪç], *adj.* angular.

Eckzahn ['ɛktsaːn], *m.* (—s, *pl.* —e) eye tooth; canine tooth.

Eckziegel ['ɛktsiːgəl], *m.* (—s, *pl.* —) (*Build.*) header.

edel ['e:dəl], *adj.* noble; well-born, aristocratic; (*metal*) precious.

Edelmann ['e:dəlman], *m.* (—s, *pl.* Edelleute) nobleman, aristocrat.

Edelmut ['e:dəlmuːt], *m.* (—s, *no pl.*) generosity, magnanimity.

Edelstein ['e:dəlʃtain], *m.* (—s, *pl.* —e) precious stone, jewel.

Edeltanne ['e:dəltanə], *f.* (—, *pl.* —n) (*Bot.*) silver fir.

Edelweiß ['e:dəlvais], *n.* (—sses, *no pl.*) (*Bot.*) edelweiss; lion's foot.

Eduard ['e:duart], *m.* Edward.

Efeu ['e:fɔy], *m.* (—s, *no pl.*) (*Bot.*) ivy.

Effekten [e'fɛktən], *m. pl.* goods and chattels; effects; stocks, securities.

Effektenbörse [e'fɛktənbœrzə], *f.* (—, *pl.* —n) Stock Exchange.

Effekthascherei [e'fɛkthaʃərai], *f.* (—, *pl.* —en) sensationalism, clap-trap.

effektuieren [efɛktu'iːrən], *v.a.* (*Comm.*) execute, effectuate.

egal [e'gaːl], *adj.* equal; all the same.

Egge ['ɛgə], *f.* (—, *pl.* —n) harrow.

Egoismus [ego'ismus], *m.* (—, *no pl.*) selfishness, egoism.

egoistisch [ego'istiʃ], *adj.* selfish, egoistic(al).

Ehe ['e:ə], *f.* (—, *pl.* —n) marriage.

ehe ['e:ə], *conj.* before; *adv.* formerly; *je —r, desto besser*, the sooner, the better.

Ehebrecher ['e:əbrɛçər], *m.* (—s, *pl.* —) adulterer.

Ehebruch ['e:əbrux], *m.* (—s, *pl.* Ʊe) adultery.

Ehefrau ['e:əfrau], *f.* (—, *pl.* —en) wife, spouse, consort.

Ehegatte ['e:əgatə], *m.* (—n, *pl.* —n) husband, spouse.

ehelich ['e:əlɪç], *adj.* matrimonial; (*children*) legitimate.

Ehelosigkeit ['e:əloːzɪçkait], *f.* (—, *no pl.*) celibacy.

ehemalig ['e:əmaːlɪç], *adj.* former, late.

ehemals ['e:əmaːls], *adv.* formerly, once, of old.

Ehemann ['e:əman], *m.* (—s, *pl.* Ʊer) husband.

ehern ['e:ərn], *adj.* brazen; of brass, of bronze.

Ehestand ['e:əʃtant], *m.* (—s, *no pl.*) matrimony.

ehestens ['e:əstəns], *adv.* as soon as possible.

Ehre ['e:rə], *f.* (—, *pl.* —n) honour, reputation, respect, distinction, glory.

ehren ['e:rən], *v.a.* honour, respect, esteem; *sehr geehrter Herr*, dear Sir.

Ehrenbezeigung ['e:rənbətsaigun], *f.* (—, *pl.* —en) mark of respect; (*Mil.*) salute.

Ehrenbürger ['e:rənbyrgər], *m.* (—s, *pl.* —) honorary citizen *or* freeman.

Ehrendame ['e:rəndaːmə], *f.* (—, *pl.* —n) maid of honour.

Ehrenerklärung ['e:rənɛrklɛːrun], *f.* (—, *pl.* —en) reparation, apology.

Ehrengericht ['e:rəngərɪçt], *n.* (—s, *pl.* —e) court of honour.

ehrenhaft ['e:rənhaft], *adj.* honourable, worthy.

Ehrenpreis ['e:rənprais], *m.* (—es, *pl.* —e) prize; (*no pl.*) (*Bot.*) speedwell.

Ehrenrettung ['e:rənrɛtun], *f.* (—, *pl.* —en) vindication.

ehrenrührig ['e:rənryːrɪç], *adj.* defamatory, calumnious.

ehrenvoll ['e:rənfɔl], *adj.* honourable.

ehrenwert ['e:rənvɛrt], *adj.* honourable, respectable.

ehrerbietig ['e:rərbiːtɪç], *adj.* reverential, respectful.

Ehrfurcht ['e:rfurçt], *f.* (—, *no pl.*) reverence, awe.

Ehrgefühl ['e:rgəfyːl], *n.* (—s, *no pl.*) sense of honour.

Ehrgeiz ['e:rgaits], *m.* (—es, *no pl.*) ambition.

ehrlich ['e:rlɪç], *adj.* honest; — *währt am längsten*, honesty is the best policy.

ehrlos ['e:rloːs], *adj.* dishonourable, infamous.

ehrsam ['e:rzaːm], *adj.* respectable, honourable.

Ehrwürden ['e:rvyrdən], *m. & f.* (*form of address*) *Euer* —, Reverend Sir, Your Reverence.

ehrwürdig ['e:rvyrdɪç], *adj.* venerable, reverend.

Ei [ai], *n.* (—s, *pl.* —er) egg, ovum.

ei [ai], *int.* ay, indeed.

Eibe ['aibə], *f.* (—, *pl.* —n) (*Bot.*) yew.

Eichamt ['aiçamt], *n.* (—s, *pl.* Ʊer) office of weights and measures; (*Am.*) bureau of standards.

Eichapfel ['aɪçapfəl], *m.* (—s, *pl.* ⸚) oak apple.

Eiche ['aɪçə], *f.* (—, *pl.* —n) (*Bot.*) oak.

Eichel ['aɪçəl], *f.* (—, *pl.* —n) acorn; (*Anat.*) glans; (*Cards*) clubs.

eichen ['aɪçən], *v.a.* gauge, calibrate. — *adj.* made of oak.

Eichhörnchen ['aɪçhœrnçən] or **Eichkätzchen** ['aɪçkɛtsçən], *n.* (—s, *pl.* —) squirrel.

Eid [aɪt], *m.* (—es, *pl.* —e) oath; *falscher* —, perjury.

Eidam ['aɪdam], *m.* (—s, *pl.* —e) (*obs.*) son-in-law.

eidbrüchig ['aɪtbryçɪç], *adj.* guilty of perjury.

Eidechse ['aɪdɛksə], *f.* (—, *pl.* —n) lizard.

Eidesleistung ['aɪdəslaɪstuŋ], *f.* (—, *pl.* —en) affidavit.

Eidgenosse ['aɪtgənɔsə], *m.* (—n, *pl.* —n) confederate.

Eidgenossenschaft ['aɪtgənɔsənʃaft], *f.* (—, *pl.* —en) confederacy.

eidlich ['aɪtlɪç], *adj.* by oath, sworn.

Eidotter ['aɪdɔtər], *m. & n.* (—s, *pl.* —) yolk of an egg.

Eierbecher ['aɪərbɛçər], *m.* (—s, *pl.* —) egg cup.

Eierkuchen ['aɪərku:xən], *m.* (—s, *pl.* —) omelet(te), pancake.

Eierschale ['aɪərʃa:lə], *f.* (—, *pl.* —n) egg shell.

Eierspeise ['aɪərʃpaɪzə], *f.* (—, *pl.* —n) dish prepared with eggs.

Eierstock ['aɪərʃtɔk], *m.* (—s, *pl.* ⸚e) ovary.

Eifer ['aɪfər], *m.* (—s, *no pl.*) zeal, eagerness, ardour, haste, passion, vehemence.

Eiferer ['aɪfərər], *m.* (—s, *pl.* —) zealot.

eifern ['aɪfərn], *v.n.* be zealous; *gegen einen* —, inveigh against s.o.

eiförmig ['aɪfœrmɪç], *adj.* oval, egg-shaped.

eifrig ['aɪfrɪç], *adj.* zealous, ardent, eager.

Eigelb ['aɪgɛlp], *n.* (—s, *no pl.*) yolk of (an) egg.

eigen ['aɪgən], *adj.* own; particular, peculiar.

Eigenart ['aɪgəna:rt], *f.* (—, *pl.* —en) peculiarity; idiosyncrasy.

eigenhändig ['aɪgənhɛndɪç], *adj.* with o.'s own hand.

Eigenheit ['aɪgənhaɪt], *f.* (—, *pl.* —en) peculiarity; idiosyncrasy.

eigenmächtig ['aɪgənmɛçtɪç], *adj.* arbitrary, autocratic, high-handed.

Eigenname ['aɪgənna:mə], *m.* (—ns, *pl.* —n) proper name.

Eigennutz ['aɪgənnuts], *m.* (—es, *no pl.*) self-interest, selfishness.

eigennützig ['aɪgənnytsɪç], *adj.* selfish, self-interested, self-seeking.

eigens ['aɪgəns], *adv.* particularly, specially.

Eigenschaft ['aɪgənʃaft], *f.* (—, *pl.* —en) quality, peculiarity; property.

Eigenschaftswort ['aɪgənʃaftsvɔrt], *n.* (—s, *pl.* ⸚er) (*Gram.*) adjective.

Eigensinn ['aɪgənzɪn], *m.* (—s, *no pl.*) obstinacy.

eigentlich ['aɪgəntlɪç], *adj.* true, real; exact, literal.

Eigentum ['aɪgəntu:m], *n.* (—s, *pl.* ⸚er) property, possession, estate.

Eigentümer ['aɪgənty:mər], *m.* (—s, *pl.* —) owner, proprietor.

eigenwillig ['aɪgənvɪlɪç], *adj.* self-willed.

eignen ['aɪgnən], *v.r. sich — für (zu)*, suit, fit, be suitable *or* fit for (to).

Eilbote ['aɪlbo:tə], *m.* (—n, *pl.* —n) special messenger.

Eile ['aɪlə], *f.* (—, *no pl.*) haste, hurry.

eilen ['aɪlən], *v.n.* (*aux.* sein), *v.r.* (*sich* —), hasten, hurry; be urgent.

eilends ['aɪlɛnts], *adv.* hastily.

eilfertig ['aɪlfɛrtɪç], *adj.* hasty.

Eilgut ['aɪlgu:t], *n.* (—s, *pl.* ⸚er) express goods.

eilig ['aɪlɪç], *adj.* hasty, speedy; pressing, urgent.

Eilzug ['aɪltsu:k], *m.* (—s, *pl.* ⸚e) fast train.

Eimer ['aɪmər], *m.* (—s, *pl.* —) pail, bucket.

ein(e) ['aɪn(ə)], *indef. art,* a, an; *was für* —; what kind of a(n). — *num. adj.* one; — *jeder*, each one.

einander [aɪn'andər], *adv.* each other, one another.

einarbeiten ['aɪnarbaɪtən], *v.a.* train, familiarise s.o. with, —*v.r.* (*aux.* haben) *sich* —, familiarize o.s.

einäschern ['aɪnɛʃərn], *v.a.* reduce to ashes, incinerate; cremate.

einatmen ['aɪna:tmən], *v.a.* breathe in, inhale.

einätzen ['aɪnɛtsən], *v.a.* etch in.

einäugig ['aɪnɔygɪç], *adj.* one-eyed.

Einbahnstraße ['aɪnba:nʃtra:sə], *f.* (—, *pl.* —n) one-way street.

Einband ['aɪnbant], *m.* (—s, *pl.* ⸚e) binding, cover of book.

einbändig ['aɪnbɛndɪç], *adj.* in one volume.

einbauen ['aɪnbauən], *v.a.* build in.

einbegreifen ['aɪnbəgraɪfən], *v.a. irr.* include, comprise.

einberufen ['aɪnbəru:fən], *v.a. irr.* convene, convoke; (*Mil.*) call up.

einbeziehen ['aɪnbətsi:ən], *v.a. irr.* include.

einbiegen ['aɪnbi:gən], *v.n. irr.* turn into (road).

einbilden ['aɪnbɪldən], *v.r. sich* —, imagine, fancy.

Einbildung ['aɪnbɪlduŋ], *f.* (—, *no pl.*) imagination, fancy, delusion; conceit.

einbinden ['aɪnbɪndən], *v.a. irr.* (*book*) bind.

Einblick ['aɪnblɪk], *m.* (—s, *no pl.*) insight.

Einbrecher ['aɪnbrɛçər], *m.* (—s, *pl.* —) burglar; intruder.

53

Einbrenne

Einbrenne ['aɪnbrɛnə], f. (—, pl. —n) thickening of soup.

einbringen ['aɪnbrɪŋən], v.a. irr. bring in, yield, fetch (a price); *wieder* —, retrieve.

einbrocken ['aɪnbrɔkən], v.a. crumble; *einem etwas* —, (*fig.*) get s.o. into trouble.

Einbruch ['aɪnbrux], m. (—s, pl. ⸚e) breaking-in; burglary, house-breaking.

Einbuchtung ['aɪnbuxtuŋ], f. (—, pl. —en) bight, bay.

einbürgern ['aɪnbyrgərn], v.a. naturalise.

Einbuße ['aɪnbu:sə], f. (—, pl. —n) loss.

einbüßen ['aɪnby:sən], v.a. suffer a loss from, lose, forfeit.

eindämmen ['aɪndɛmən], v.a. dam in (or up).

Eindecker ['aɪndɛkər], m. (—s, pl. —) (*Aviat.*) monoplane.

eindeutig ['aɪndɔytɪç], adj. unequivocal, unambiguous.

eindrängen ['aɪndrɛŋən], v.r. sich —, intrude (into), force o.'s way in(to), interfere.

eindrillen ['aɪndrɪlən], v.a. *einem etwas* —, drum s.th. into s.o.

eindringen ['aɪndrɪŋən], v.n. irr. (aux. sein) enter, intrude; invade; penetrate.

eindringlich ['aɪndrɪŋlɪç], adj. forceful, urgent; impressive.

Eindruck ['aɪndruk], m. (—s, pl. ⸚e) impression.

eindrücken ['aɪndrykən], v.a. press in, squeeze in.

eindrucksfähig ['aɪndruksfɛ:ɪç], adj. impressionable.

einengen ['aɪnɛŋən], v.a. compress, limit, confine, cramp.

Einer ['aɪnər], m. (—s, pl. —) (*Maths.*) digit, unit.

einerlei ['aɪnərlaɪ], adj. the same, all the same.

einerseits ['aɪnərzaɪts], adv. on the one hand.

einfach ['aɪnfax], adj. single; simple, plain, uncomplicated; modest, homely.

einfädeln ['aɪnfɛ:dəln], v.a. thread.

einfahren ['aɪnfa:rən], v.n. irr. (aux. sein) drive in, enter. — v.a. run in (new car).

Einfahrt ['aɪnfa:rt], f. (—, pl. —en) entrance, gateway, drive; (*Min.*) descent.

Einfall ['aɪnfal], m. (—s, pl. ⸚e) falling-in, downfall, fall; (*Mil.*) invasion; (*fig.*) idea, inspiration.

einfallen ['aɪnfalən], v.n. irr. (aux. sein) fall in, fall into; (*Mil.*) invade; (*fig.*) occur to s.o.

Einfalt ['aɪnfalt], f. (—, no pl.) simplicity; silliness.

Einfaltspinsel ['aɪnfaltspɪnzəl], m. (—s, pl. —) simpleton, dunce.

einfangen ['aɪnfaŋən], v.a. irr. catch, get hold of.

einfarbig ['aɪnfarbɪç], adj. of one colour; monochrome.

einfassen ['aɪnfasən], v.a. border, trim; (*diamonds*) set.

Einfassung ['aɪnfasuŋ], f. (—, pl. —en) bordering, trimming, edging, framing.

einfetten ['aɪnfɛtən], v.a. grease, lubricate.

einfinden ['aɪnfɪndən], v.r. irr. sich —, appear, be present.

einflechten ['aɪnflɛçtən], v.a. irr. plait; (*fig.*) insert.

einfließen ['aɪnfli:sən], v.n. irr. (aux. sein) flow in; — *lassen*, (*fig.*) mention casually, slip in (a word).

einflößen ['aɪnflø:sən], v.a. infuse; (*fig.*) instil, inspire with.

Einfluß ['aɪnflus], m. (—sses, pl. ⸚sse) influx; (*fig.*) influence.

einflußreich ['aɪnflusraɪç], adj. influential.

einflüstern ['aɪnflystərn], v.n. suggest, insinuate.

einförmig ['aɪnfœrmɪç], adj. uniform; monotonous.

einfriedigen ['aɪnfri:dɪgən], v.a. fence in, enclose.

einfügen ['aɪnfy:gən], v.a. insert, include, fit in. — v.r. sich —, adapt o.s., become a part of.

Einfühlungsvermögen ['aɪnfylungsfɛrmø:gən], n. (—s, no pl.) (*Phil.*) empathy, sympathetic understanding.

Einfuhr ['aɪnfu:r], f. (—, pl. —en) importation, import.

einführen ['aɪnfy:rən], v.a. introduce; (*goods*) import.

Einführung ['aɪnfy:ruŋ], f. (—, pl. —en) introduction; (*goods*) importation.

einfüllen ['aɪnfylən], v.a. fill in, pour into, bottle.

Eingabe ['aɪnga:bə], f. (—, pl. —n) petitition; application.

Eingang ['aɪngaŋ], m. (—s, pl. ⸚e) entry, entrance; arrival.

eingangs ['aɪngaŋs], adv. in or at the beginning.

eingeben ['aɪnge:bən], v.a. irr. inspire (with); (*petition*) present, deliver; (*claim*) file; (*complaint*) bring; (*medicine*) administer.

eingeboren ['aɪngəbo:rən], adj. native; (*Theol.*) only-begotten.

Eingeborene ['aɪngəbo:rənə], m. (—n, pl. —n) native.

Eingebrachte ['aɪngəbraxtə], n. (—n, no pl.) dowry.

Eingebung ['aɪngeːbuŋ], f. (—, pl. —en) inspiration.

eingedenk ['aɪngədɛŋk], prep. (*Genit.*) mindful of, remembering.

eingefleischt ['aɪngəflaɪʃt], adj. inveterate, confirmed.

eingehen ['aɪnge:ən], v.n. irr. (aux. sein) (*Comm.*) arrive; *auf etwas* —, enter into s.th., agree to s.th.; *auf etwas näher* —, enter into the details of s.th.; (*animals, plants*) die; (*cloth*) shrink.

eingehend ['aɪngeːənt], *adj.* thorough, exhaustive.

Eingemachte ['aɪngəmaxtə], *n.* (—n, *no pl.*) preserve.

eingenommen ['aɪngənɔmən], *adj.* enthusiastic for, infatuated with; — *von sich,* conceited.

Eingeschlossenheit ['aɪngəʃlɔsənhaɪt], *f.* (—, *no pl.*) isolation, seclusion.

eingeschrieben ['aɪngəʃriːbən], *adj.* registered (letter).

eingesessen ['aɪngəzɛsən], *adj.* old-established; resident.

Eingeständnis ['aɪngəʃtɛntnɪs], *n.* (—ses, *pl.* —se) confession.

eingestehen ['aɪngəʃteːən], *v.a. irr.* confess to, avow.

Eingeweide ['aɪngəvaɪdə], *n. pl.* bowels, intestines.

eingewöhnen ['aɪngəvøːnən], *v.r. sich* —, accustom o.s. to, get used to.

eingießen ['aɪngiːsən], *v.a. irr.* pour in; pour out.

eingleisig ['aɪnglaɪzɪç], *adj.* single-track.

eingliedern ['aɪngliːdərn], *v.r. sich* —, adapt o.s., fit in.

eingreifen ['aɪngraɪfən], *v.n. irr.* intervene in; interfere with, encroach on.

Eingriff ['aɪngrɪf], *m.* (—s, *pl.* —e) intervention, encroachment, infringement; *(Med.)* operation.

Einguß ['aɪngus], *m.* (—sses, *pl.* —sse) infusion; enema.

einhaken ['aɪnhaːkən], *v.a.* hook in. — *v.r. sich* —, (*fig.*) take a p.'s arm.

Einhalt ['aɪnhalt], *m.* (—s, *no pl.*) stop, check, prohibition, cessation; — *gebieten,* check, suppress.

einhalten ['aɪnhaltən], *v.a. irr.* observe, adhere to.

einhändigen ['aɪnhɛndɪgən], *v.a.* hand in, deliver.

einhauen ['aɪnhauən], *v.a.* hew in, break open.

Einhebung ['aɪnheːbuŋ], *f.* (—, *pl.* —en) *(taxes)* collection.

einheften ['aɪnhɛftən], *v.a.* sew in, stitch in; *(papers)* file.

einhegen ['aɪnheːgən], *v.a.* fence in, hedge in.

einheimisch ['aɪnhaɪmɪʃ], *adj.* native; *(Bot.)* indigenous.

einheimsen ['aɪnhaɪmzən], *v.a.* reap.

Einheit ['aɪnhaɪt], *f.* (—, *pl.* —en) unit, unity.

einheitlich ['aɪnhaɪtlɪç], *adj.* uniform, consistent.

einheizen ['aɪnhaɪtsən], *v.a., v.n.* heat the stove, light the fire.

einhellig ['aɪnhɛlɪç], *adj.* unanimous, harmonious.

einher [aɪn'heːr], *adv.* forth, along, on.

einholen ['aɪnhoːlən], *v.a.* obtain; catch up with. — *v.n.* go shopping.

Einhorn ['aɪnhɔrn], *n.* (—s, *pl.* —er) unicorn.

einhüllen ['aɪnhylən], *v.a.* wrap up, cover, envelop.

einig ['aɪnɪç], *adj.* at one. — *adv.* in agreement.

einige ['aɪnɪgə], *adj.* some, several.

einigemal ['aɪnɪgəmaːl], *adv.* several times.

einigen ['aɪnɪgən], *v.a.* unite. — *v.r. sich* — *mit,* come to an agreement with.

Einigkeit ['aɪnɪçkaɪt], *f.* (—, *no pl.*) union; unity, unanimity, harmony.

Einigung ['aɪnɪguŋ], *f.* (—, *no pl.*) agreement.

einimpfen ['aɪnɪmpfən], *v.a.* inoculate, vaccinate.

einjährig ['aɪnjɛːrɪg], *adj.* one-year-old, annual.

einkassieren ['aɪnkasiːrən], *v.a.* cash *(cheque),* collect *(money).*

Einkauf ['aɪnkauf], *m.* (—s, *pl.* —e) purchase, buy.

einkaufen ['aɪnkaufən], *v.a.* purchase, buy. — *v.n.* go shopping.

Einkäufer ['aɪnkɔyfər], *m.* (—s, *pl.* —) *(Comm.)* purchaser, buyer.

Einkehr ['aɪnkeːr], *f.* (—, *no pl.*) stopping (at an inn); (*fig.*) meditation.

einkehren ['aɪnkeːrən], *v.n.* stop *or* put up (at an inn).

einkerkern ['aɪnkɛrkərn], *v.a.* imprison.

einklagen ['aɪnklaːgən], *v.a. (Law)* sue for (money).

einklammern ['aɪnklamərn], *v.a.* bracket, enclose in brackets.

Einklang ['aɪnklaŋ], *m.* (—s, *no pl.*) accord, unison, harmony.

einkleben ['aɪnkleːbən], *v.a.* paste in.

einkleiden ['aɪnklaɪdən], *v.a.* clothe; (*fig.*) invest; *sich* — *lassen,* *(Eccl.)* take the veil.

einklemmen ['aɪnklɛmən], *v.a.* squeeze in, jam in.

einkochen ['aɪnkɔxən], *v.a.* preserve. — *v.n.* (*aux.* sein) boil down.

Einkommen ['aɪnkɔmən], *n.* (—s, *no pl.*) income, revenue.

einkommen ['aɪnkɔmən], *v.n. irr.* (*aux.* sein) *bei einem wegen etwas* —, apply to s.o. for s.th.

einkreisen ['aɪnkraɪzən], *v.a.* encircle, isolate.

Einkünfte ['aɪnkynftə], *pl.* income, revenue; emoluments.

einladen ['aɪnlaːdən], *v.a. irr.* load in; invite.

Einlage ['aɪnlaːgə], *f.* (—, *pl.* —en) *(letter)* enclosure; *(Theat.)* addition to programme; *(game)* stake; *(Comm.)* investment.

einlagern ['aɪnlaːgərn], *v.a. (goods)* store, warehouse; *(Mil.)* billet, quarter.

Einlaß ['aɪnlas], *m.* (—sses, *no pl.*) admission, admittance; *(water)* inlet.

einlassen ['aɪnlasən], *v.a. irr.* admit, allow in; let in. — *v.r. sich auf etwas* —, engage in s.th., enter into s.th.

Einlauf ['aɪnlauf], *m.* (—s, *no pl.*) entering; *(Med.)* enema.

einlaufen

einlaufen ['aɪnlaufən], *v.n. irr. (aux. sein) (Naut.)* enter harbour, put into port; *(materia!)* shrink.

einleben ['aɪnle:bən], *v.r. sich —,* grow accustomed to, settle down, acclimatise o.s.

einlegen ['aɪnle:gən], *v.a.* put in, lay in; enclose; *(money)* deposit; *(food)* pickle, preserve; *Fürbitte —,* intercede; *eingelegte Arbeit,* inlaid work.

einleiten ['aɪnlaɪtən], *v.a.* begin, introduce; institute.

Einleitung ['aɪnlaɪtuŋ], *f. (—, pl. —en)* introduction; *(book)* preface; *(Mus.)* prelude; *(Law)* institution.

einlenken ['aɪnlɛŋkən], *v.n.* turn in; give in, come round.

einleuchten ['aɪnlɔyçtən], *v.n.* become clear.

einlösen ['aɪnlø:zən], *v.a.* redeem; *(bill)* honour; *(cheque)* cash.

einmachen ['aɪnmaxən], *v.a.* preserve.

einmal ['aɪnma:l], *adv.* once; *es war —,* once upon a time; *auf —,* suddenly; *noch —,* once more; *nicht —,* not even.

Einmaleins ['aɪnma:laɪns], *n. (—es, no pl.)* multiplication table.

einmalig ['aɪnma:lɪç], *adv.* unique, unrepeatable.

Einmaster ['aɪnmastər], *m. (—s, pl. —) (Naut.)* brigantine, cutter.

einmauern ['aɪnmauərn], *v.a.* wall in, immure.

einmengen ['aɪnmɛŋən], *v.r. sich —,* meddle with, interfere.

einmieten ['aɪnmi:tən], *v.r. sich —,* take lodgings.

einmischen ['aɪnmɪʃən], *v.r. sich —,* meddle (with), interfere.

einmütig ['aɪnmy:tɪç], *adj.* unanimous, in harmony, united.

Einnahme ['aɪnna:mə], *f. (—, pl. —n)* income, revenue; receipts; *(Mil.)* occupation, capture.

einnehmen ['aɪnne:mən], *v.a. irr.* take in; *(money)* receive; *(medicine)* take; *(taxes)* collect; *(place)* take up, occupy; *(Mil.)* occupy, conquer; *(fig.)* captivate, fascinate.

einnehmend ['aɪnne:mənt], *adj.* fetching, engaging, charming.

einnicken ['aɪnnɪkən], *v.n. (aux. sein)* nod *or* doze off.

einnisten ['aɪnnɪstən], *v.r. sich —,* nestle down; *(fig.)* settle in a place.

Einöde ['aɪnø:də], *f. (—, pl. —n)* desert, solitude.

einordnen ['aɪnɔrdnən], *v.a.* place in order, file, classify.

einpauken ['aɪnpaukən], *v.a.* cram.

einpferchen ['aɪnpfɛrçən], *v.a.* pen in, coop up.

einpökeln ['aɪnpø:kəln], *v.a.* salt, pickle.

einprägen ['aɪnprɛ:gən], *v.a.* imprint; impress.

einquartieren ['aɪnkvarti:rən], *v.a. (Mil.)* quarter, billet.

einrahmen ['aɪnra:mən], *v.a.* frame.

einräumen ['aɪnrɔymən], *v.a.* stow (things) away; *einem etwas —,* concede s.th. to s.o.

Einrede ['aɪnre:də], *f. (—, pl. —n)* objection.

einreden ['aɪnre:dən], *v.a. einem etwas —,* persuade s.o. to; *v.r. sich etwas —,* get s.th. into o.'s head.

einreichen ['aɪnraɪçən], *v.a.* hand in, deliver; tender.

einreihen ['aɪnraɪən], *v.a.* place in line, arrange.

einreihig ['aɪnraɪɪç], *adj.* consisting of a single row; *(Tail.)* single-breasted (suit).

einreißen ['aɪnraɪsən], *v.a. irr.* make a tear in; *(houses)* pull down. *— v.n. (fig.)* gain ground.

einrenken ['aɪnrɛŋkən], *v.a. (Med.)* set; *(fig.)* settle.

einrichten ['aɪnrɪçtən], *v.a.* put in order, arrange; equip, set up; furnish.

Einrichtung ['aɪnrɪçtuŋ], *f. (—, pl. —en)* arrangement, management; furnishing; *(pl.)* facilities; equipment, amenities.

einrücken ['aɪnrykən], *v.n. (aux. sein)* march in. *— v.a.* insert (in the newspaper).

Eins [aɪns], *f. (—, pl. —en, —er)* one; *(Sch.)* top marks.

eins [aɪns], *num.* one; *es ist mir alles —,* it is all the same to me.

einsalzen ['aɪnzaltsən], *v.a.* salt, pickle, cure.

einsam ['aɪnza:m], *adj.* lonely, solitary, secluded.

Einsamkeit ['aɪnza:mkaɪt], *f. (—, no pl.)* loneliness, solitude, seclusion.

Einsatz ['aɪnzats], *m. (—es, pl. ⁔e) (game)* stake, pool; *(dress)* lace inset; *(Mus.)* entry (of a voice), starting intonation; *(Mil.)* sortie, mission.

einsaugen ['aɪnzaugən], *v.a.* suck in; *(fig.)* imbibe.

einsäumen ['aɪnzɔymən], *v.a.* hem (in).

einschalten ['aɪnʃaltən], *v.a.* insert, interpolate; switch on; put in gear.

einschärfen ['aɪnʃɛrfən], *v.a.* impress s.th. on s.o.

einschätzen ['aɪnʃɛtsən], *v.a.* assess.

einschenken ['aɪnʃɛŋkən], *v.a.* pour in *or* out, fill.

einschieben ['aɪnʃi:bən], *v.a.* push in; interpolate, insert.

Einschiebsel ['aɪnʃi:psəl], *n. (—s, pl. —)* interpolation; interpolated part.

einschiffen ['aɪnʃɪfən], *v.a.* embark; *(goods)* ship. *— v.r. sich —,* go aboard, embark.

einschlafen ['aɪnʃla:fən], *v.n. irr. (aux. sein)* fall asleep, go to sleep.

einschläfern ['aɪnʃlɛ:fərn], *v.a.* lull to sleep.

Einschlag ['aɪnʃla:k], *m. (—s, pl. ⁔e)* cover, envelope; *(weaving)* woof, weft; explosion; strike; *(fig.)* streak (of character); touch.

einschlagen ['aɪnʃlaːgən], v.a. irr.knock in; (nail) drive in; (parcel) wrap up; (road) take. — v.n. (lightning) strike; be a success.

einschlägig ['aɪnʃlɛːgɪç], adj. bearing on (the subject), pertinent.

einschleppen ['aɪnʃlɛpən], v.a. (disease) bring in, introduce.

einschließen ['aɪnʃliːsən], v.a. irr. lock in or up; (enemy) surround; (fig.) include.

einschlummern ['aɪnʃlumərn], v.n. (aux. sein) doze off, fall asleep.

Einschluß ['aɪnʃlus], m. (—sses, pl. ¨-sse) inclusion; mit — von, inclusive of.

einschmeicheln ['aɪnʃmaɪçəln], v.r. sich bei einem, ingratiate o.s. with s.o.

einschmelzen ['aɪnʃmɛltsən], v.a. irr. melt down.

einschmieren ['aɪnʃmiːrən], v.a. smear, grease, oil; (sore) put ointment on.

einschneidend ['aɪnʃnaɪdənt], adj. important, sweeping, incisive, trenchant.

einschneidig ['aɪnʃnaɪdɪç], adj. single-edged.

Einschnitt ['aɪnʃnɪt], m. (—s, pl. —e) incision, cut, notch; (verse) caesura.

einschnüren ['aɪnʃnyːrən], v.a. lace up; (parcel) tie up.

einschränken ['aɪnʃrɛŋkən], v.a. confine, limit, restrict. — v.r. sich —, curtail o.'s expenses, economize.

einschrauben ['aɪnʃraubən], v.a. screw in.

einschreiben ['aɪnʃraɪbən], v.a. irr. write in or down, inscribe; (letter) register. — v.r. sich —, enter o.'s name; enrol.

Einschreibesendung ['aɪnʃraɪbəzɛndʊŋ], f. (—, pl. —en) registered letter, registered parcel.

einschreiten ['aɪnʃraɪtən], v.n. irr. (aux. sein) step in, intervene.

einschrumpfen ['aɪnʃrumpfən], v.n. (aux. sein) shrink, shrivel.

einschüchtern ['aɪnʃyçtərn], v.a. intimidate, overawe.

Einschuß ['aɪnʃus], m. (—sses, pl. ¨-sse) share, advance of capital; (weaving) woof, weft.

einsegnen ['aɪnzeːgnən], v.a. consecrate, bless; (Eccl.) confirm.

Einsehen ['aɪnzeːən], n. (—s, no pl.) realisation; ein — haben, be reasonable.

einsehen ['aɪnzeːən], v.a. irr. look into, glance over; (fig.) comprehend, realise.

einseifen ['aɪnzaɪfən], v.a. soap, lather; (fig.) take s.o. in.

einseitig ['aɪnzaɪtɪç], adj. one-sided; (fig.) one-track (mind).

Einsenkung ['aɪnzɛŋkʊŋ], f. (—, pl. —en) depression (of the ground).

einsetzen ['aɪnzɛtsən], v.a. put in, set in; institute, establish; (money) stake; (Hort.) plant; (office) install s.o. — v.n. begin.

Einsetzung ['aɪnzɛtsʊŋ], f. (—, pl. —en) (office) investiture, installation; institution.

Einsicht ['aɪnzɪçt], f. (—, no pl.) inspection, examination; insight, understanding.

einsichtig ['aɪnzɪçtɪç], adj. intelligent, sensible, judicious.

Einsichtnahme ['aɪnzɪçtnaːmə], f. zur —, (Comm.) on approval, for inspection.

Einsiedler ['aɪnziːdlər], m. (—s, pl. —) hermit, recluse.

einsilbig ['aɪnzɪlbɪç], adj. monosyllabic; (fig.) taciturn, laconic.

einspannen ['aɪnʃpanən], v.a. stretch in a frame; harness; (coll.) put to work.

Einspänner ['aɪnʃpɛnər], m. (—s, pl. —) one-horse vehicle; one-horse cab, fiacre.

einsperren ['aɪnʃpɛrən], v.a. lock in, shut up, imprison.

einspinnen ['aɪnʃpɪnən], v.r. irr. sich —, spin a cocoon.

einsprengen ['aɪnʃprɛŋən], v.a. sprinkle.

einspringen ['aɪnʃprɪŋən], v.n. irr. (aux. sein) auf einen —, leap at; (lock) catch, snap; für einen —, deputize for s.o.

Einspruch ['aɪnʃprux], m. (—s, pl. ¨-e) objection, protest; — erheben, protest; (Law) appeal (against).

einspurig ['aɪnʃpuːrɪç], adj. (Railw.) single-track line.

einst [aɪnst], adv. (past) once, once upon a time; (future) some day.

Einstand ['aɪnʃtant], m. (—s, no pl.) (Tennis) deuce.

einstecken ['aɪnʃtɛkən], v.a. put in; pocket; post (a letter).

einstehen ['aɪnʃteːən], v.a. irr. zu etwas —, answer for s.th.; für einen —, stand security for s.o.

einsteigen ['aɪnʃtaɪgən], v.n. irr. (aux. sein) get in, climb on; board.

einstellen ['aɪnʃtɛlən], v.a. put in; (persons) engage, hire; adjust; (work) stop, strike; (payments) stop; (hostilities) suspend, cease fire. — v.r. sich —, turn up, appear.

einstellig ['aɪnʃtɛlɪç], adj. (Maths.) of one digit.

Einstellung ['aɪnʃtɛlʊŋ], f. (—, pl. —en) putting in; (persons) engagement, hiring; adjustment; (work) stoppage, strike; (payments) suspension; (hostilities) suspension, cessation; (fig.) opinion, attitude.

einstig ['aɪnstɪç], adj. (past) former, late, erstwhile; (future) future, to be, to come.

einstimmen ['aɪnʃtɪmən], v.n. join in, chime in.

einstimmig ['aɪnʃtɪmɪç], adj. (Mus.) (for) one voice, unison; (fig.) unanimous.

einstmals ['aɪnstmaːls], adv. once, formerly.

einstöckig

einstöckig [ˈaɪnʃtœkɪç], adj. one-storied.

einstreichen [ˈaɪnʃtraɪçən], v.a. irr. (money) take in, pocket.

einstreuen [ˈaɪnʃtrɔyən], v.a. strew; (fig.) intersperse.

einstudieren [ˈaɪnʃtudiːrən], v.a. study; (Theat., Mus.) rehearse.

einstürmen [ˈaɪnʃtyrmən], v.n. (aux. sein) auf einen —, rush at, fall upon.

Einsturz [ˈaɪnʃtʊrts], m. (—es, pl. ⁻e) fall, crash; subsidence, collapse.

einstürzen [ˈaɪnʃtʏrtsən], v.n. (aux. sein) fall in, fall into ruin, fall to pieces, collapse.

einstweilen [ˈaɪnstvaɪlən], adv. in the meantime, meanwhile, for the time being, provisionally.

einstweilig [ˈaɪnstvaɪlɪç], adj. temporary, provisional.

eintägig [ˈaɪntɛːgɪç], adj. one-day, ephemeral.

Eintagsfliege [ˈaɪntaːksfliːgə], f. (—, pl. —n) dayfly.

eintauschen [ˈaɪntaʊʃən], v.a. — gegen, exchange for, barter for.

einteilen [ˈaɪntaɪlən], v.a. divide; distribute; classify.

eintönig [ˈaɪntøːnɪç], adj. monotonous.

Eintracht [ˈaɪntraxt], f. (—, no pl.) concord, harmony.

einträchtig [ˈaɪntrɛçtɪç], adj. united, harmonious.

Eintrag [ˈaɪntraːk], m. (—s, pl. ⁻e) entry (in a book); prejudice, damage, detriment.

eintragen [ˈaɪntraːgən], v.a. irr. enter (in a book), register; bring in, yield.

einträglich [ˈaɪntrɛklɪç], adj. profitable, lucrative.

Eintragung [ˈaɪntraːgʊŋ], f. (—, pl. —en) entry (in a book); enrolment.

einträufeln [ˈaɪntrɔyfəln], v.a. instil.

eintreffen [ˈaɪntrɛfən], v.n. irr. (aux. sein) arrive; happen, come true.

eintreiben [ˈaɪntraɪbən], v.a. irr. drive home (cattle); collect (debts etc.).

eintreten [ˈaɪntreːtən], v.n. irr. (aux. sein) step in, enter; happen, take place; in einen Verein —, join a club; für einen —, speak up for s.o.

eintrichtern [ˈaɪntrɪçtərn], v.a. einem etwas —, cram s.th. into s.o.

Eintritt [ˈaɪntrɪt], m. (—s, no pl.) entry, entrance; beginning; kein —, no admission.

eintrocknen [ˈaɪntrɔknən], v.n. (aux. sein) shrivel, dry up.

einüben [ˈaɪnyːbən], v.a. practise, exercise.

einverleiben [ˈaɪnfɛrlaɪbən], v.a. incorporate in, embody in.

Einvernahme [ˈaɪnfɛrnaːmə], f. (—, pl. —n) (Austr.) see **Vernehmung**.

Einvernehmen [ˈaɪnfɛrneːmən], n. (—s, no pl.) understanding; im besten —, on the best of terms.

einvernehmen [ˈaɪnfɛrneːmən], v.a. (aux. haben) (Austr.) see **vernehmen**.

einverstanden [ˈaɪnfɛrʃtandən], (excl.)

agreed! — adj. — sein, agree.

Einverständnis [ˈaɪnfɛrʃtɛntnɪs], n. (—ses, no pl.) consent, agreement, accord.

Einwand [ˈaɪnvant], m. (—s, pl. ⁻e) objection, exception; — erheben, raise objections.

einwandern [ˈaɪnvandərn], v.n. (aux. sein) immigrate.

einwandfrei [ˈaɪnvantfraɪ], adj. irreproachable, unobjectionable.

einwärts [ˈaɪnvɛrts], adv. inward(s).

einwechseln [ˈaɪnvɛksəln], v.a. change, exchange.

einweichen [ˈaɪnvaɪçən], v.a. steep in water, soak.

einweihen [ˈaɪnvaɪən], v.a. dedicate; (Eccl.) consecrate; open (formally), inaugurate; initiate (into).

Einweihung [ˈaɪnvaɪʊŋ], f. (—, pl. —en) (Eccl.) consecration; inauguration, formal opening; initiation.

einwenden [ˈaɪnvɛndən], v.a. irr. object to, raise objections, urge against.

einwerfen [ˈaɪnvɛrfən], v.a. irr. throw in; smash in; interject.

einwickeln [ˈaɪnvɪkəln], v.a. wrap up, envelop.

einwilligen [ˈaɪnvɪlɪgən], v.n. consent, assent, agree, accede.

einwirken [ˈaɪnvɪrkən], v.n. auf einen —, influence s.o.

Einwohner [ˈaɪnvoːnər], m. (—s, pl. —) inhabitant.

Einwohnerschaft [ˈaɪnvoːnərʃaft], f. (—, no pl.) population, inhabitants.

Einwurf [ˈaɪnvurf], m. (—s, pl. ⁻e) (letter box) opening, slit; slot; objection.

einwurzeln [ˈaɪnvurtsəln], v.n. sich —, take root; eingewurzelt, deep-rooted.

Einzahl [ˈaɪntsaːl], f. (—, no pl.) singular.

einzahlen [ˈaɪntsaːlən], v.a. pay in, deposit.

einzäunen [ˈaɪntsɔynən], v.a. fence in.

einzeichnen [ˈaɪntsaɪçnən], v.a. draw in, sketch in. — v.r. sich —, enter o.'s name, sign.

Einzelhaft [ˈaɪntsəlhaft], f. (—, no pl.) solitary confinement.

Einzelheit [ˈaɪntsəlhaɪt], f. (—, pl. —en) detail, particular.

einzeln [ˈaɪntsəln], adj. single; isolated, detached, apart.

einziehen [ˈaɪntsiːən], v.a. irr. draw in, retract; (Law) confiscate, impound; (debts) collect, call in; (bill of sight) discount, cash; (money) withdraw (from circulation); (sails) furl; (Mil.) call up.

einzig [ˈaɪntsɪç], adj. sole, single; unique, only.

Einzug [ˈaɪntsuːk], m. (—s, pl. ⁻e) entry, entrance; move (into new house).

einzwängen [ˈaɪntsvɛŋən], v.a. force in, squeeze in.

Eis [aɪs], n. (—es, no pl.) ice; ice-cream.

E-is [ˈeːɪs], n. (—, pl. —) (Mus.) E sharp.

Eisbahn ['aɪsbaːn], *f.* (—, *pl.* —en) ice-rink, skating-rink.

Eisbär ['aɪsbɛːr], *m.* (—en, *pl.* —en) polar bear, white bear.

Eisbein ['aɪsbaɪn], *n.* (—s, *pl.* —e) pig's trotters.

Eisberg ['aɪsbɛrk], *m.* (—s, *pl.* —e) iceberg.

Eisblumen ['aɪsbluːmən], *f. pl.* frost patterns (*on glass*).

Eisen ['aɪzən], *n.* (—s, *pl.* —) iron; *altes* —, scrap iron.

Eisenbahn ['aɪzənbaːn], *f.* (—, *pl.* —en) railway.

Eisenfleck ['aɪzənflɛk], *m.* (—s, *pl.* —e) iron mould.

Eisengießerei ['aɪzəngiːsəraɪ], *f.* (—, *pl.* —en) iron foundry, iron forge.

Eisenguß ['aɪzəngus], *m.* (—sses, *pl.* ⁝sse) cast-iron.

Eisenhändler ['aɪzənhɛndlər], *m.* (—s, *pl.* —) ironmonger.

Eisenhütte ['aɪzənhytə], *f.* (—, *pl.* —n) *see* Eisengießerei.

Eisenschlacke ['aɪzənʃlakə], *f.* (—, *no pl.*) iron dross, iron slag.

eisern ['aɪzərn], *adj.* made of iron; (*coll. & fig.*) strong; strict.

Eisgang ['aɪsgaŋ], *m.* (—s, *pl.* ⁝e) drift of ice.

eisgrau ['aɪsgrau], *adj.* hoary.

eiskalt ['aɪskalt], *adj.* icy cold.

Eislauf ['aɪslauf], *m.* (—s, *no pl.*) ice-skating.

Eismeer ['aɪsmeːr], *n.* (—s, *pl.* —e) polar sea; *nördliches* —, Arctic Ocean; *südliches* —, Antarctic Ocean.

Eispickel ['aɪspɪkəl], *m.* (—s, *pl.* —) ice axe.

Eisvogel ['aɪsfoːgəl], *m.* (—s, *pl.* ⁝) (*Orn.*) kingfisher.

Eiszapfen ['aɪstsapfən], *m.* (—s, *pl.* —) icicle.

eitel ['aɪtəl], *adj.* vain, frivolous, conceited; (*obs.*) pure.

Eiter ['aɪtər], *m.* (—s, *no pl.*) (*Med.*) pus, matter.

Eitergeschwür ['aɪtərgəʃvyːr], *n.* (—s, *pl.* —e) abscess.

eitern ['aɪtərn], *v.n.* suppurate.

Eiterung ['aɪtəruŋ], *f.* (—, *pl.* —en) suppuration.

eitrig ['aɪtrɪç], *adj.* purulent.

Eiweis ['aɪvaɪs], *n.* (—es, *no pl.*) white of egg; albumen.

Ekel ['eːkəl], *m.* (—s, *no pl.*) nausea, disgust, distaste, aversion.

ekelhaft ['eːkəlhaft], *adj.* loathsome, disgusting, nauseous.

ekeln ['eːkəln], *v.r. sich — vor*, be disgusted (by), feel sick, loathe.

Ekuador [ɛkua'dɔr], *n.* Ecuador.

Elan [e'lã], *m.* (—s, *no pl.*) verve, vigour.

elastisch [e'lastɪʃ], *adj.* elastic, flexible, buoyant.

Elastizität [elastɪtsɪ'tɛːt], *f.* (—, *no pl.*) elasticity; (*mind*) buoyancy.

Elch [ɛlç], *m.* (—s, *pl.* —e) (*Zool.*) elk.

Elegie [ele'giː], *f.* (—, *pl.* —n) elegy.

elektrisieren [elɛktrɪ'ziːrən], *v.a.* electrify.

Elektrizität [elɛktritsɪ'tɛːt], *f.* (—, *no pl.*) electricity.

Elend ['eːlɛnt], *n.* (—s, *no pl.*) misery, distress, wretchedness.

elend ['eːlɛnt], *adj.* miserable, wretched, pitiful; weak; *sich — fühlen*, feel poorly.

elendiglich ['eːlɛndɪklɪç], *adv.* miserably, wretchedly.

Elentier ['eːlɛntiːr], *n.* (—s, *pl.* —e) (*Zool.*) elk.

elf [ɛlf], *num. adj.* eleven.

Elfe ['ɛlfə], *f.* (—, *pl.* —n) fairy.

Elfenbein ['ɛlfənbaɪn], *n.* (—s, *no pl.*) ivory.

Elisabeth [e'liːzabɛt], *f.* Elizabeth.

Ellbogen ['ɛlboːgən], *m.* (—s, *pl.* —) elbow.

Elle ['ɛlə], *f.* (—, *pl.* —n) yard, ell.

Elritze ['ɛlrɪtsə], *f.* (—, *pl.* —n) minnow.

Elsaß ['ɛlzas], *n.* Alsace.

Elster ['ɛlstər], *f.* (—, *pl.* —n) magpie.

Eltern ['ɛltərn], *pl.* parents.

Emaille [e'maːj], *n.* (—s, *no pl.*) enamel.

emailliert [ema(l)'jiːrt], *adj.* covered with vitreous enamel, enamelled.

Empfang [ɛm'pfaŋ], *m.* (—s, *pl.* ⁝e) receipt; reception.

empfangen [ɛm'pfaŋən], *v.a. irr.* receive, accept, take.

Empfänger [ɛm'pfɛŋər], *m.* (—s, *pl.* —) recipient, receiver.

empfänglich [ɛm'pfɛŋlɪç], *adj.* susceptible, impressionable.

Empfängnis [ɛm'pfɛŋnɪs], *f.* (—, *no pl.*) conception.

empfehlen [ɛm'pfeːlən], *v.a. irr.* commend, recommend; give compliments to. — *v.r. sich —*, take leave.

empfinden [ɛm'pfɪndən], *v.a. irr.* feel, perceive.

empfindlich [ɛm'pfɪntlɪç], *adj.* sensitive, susceptible; touchy, thin-skinned.

empfindsam [ɛm'pfɪntsaːm], *adj.* sentimental.

Empfindung [ɛm'pfɪnduŋ], *f.* (—, *pl.* —en) sensation, feeling, sentiment.

empor [ɛm'poːr], *adv.* upward(s), up.

Empore [ɛm'poːrə], *f.* (—, *pl.* —n) gallery (*in church*).

empören [ɛm'pøːrən], *v.a.* excite, enrage, shock. — *v.r. sich —*, revolt, rebel.

Emporkömmling [ɛm'poːrkœmlɪŋ], *m.* (—s, *pl.* —e) upstart.

empört [ɛm'pøːrt], *adj.* furious, shocked, disgusted.

Empörung [ɛm'pøːruŋ], *f.* (—, *pl.* —en) rebellion, revolt, mutiny, insurrection; indignation, disgust.

emsig ['ɛmzɪç], *adj.* assiduous, industrious, busy.

Emsigkeit ['ɛmzɪçkaɪt], *f.* (—, *no pl.*) assiduity, diligence.

Ende ['ɛndə], *n.* (—s, *pl.* —n) end, conclusion.

enden ['ɛndən], v.n. end, finish, conclude. — v.a. terminate, put an end to.

endgültig ['ɛntgyltɪç], adj. definitive, final.

Endivie [ɛn'di:vjə], f. (—, pl. —n) (Bot.) endive.

endlich ['ɛntlɪç], adj. finite, final, ultimate. — adv. at last, at length, finally.

endlos ['ɛntlo:s], adj. endless, never-ending, boundless.

Endung ['ɛnduŋ], f. (—, pl. —en) (Gram.) ending, termination.

Endziel ['ɛntsi:l], n. (—s, pl. —e) final aim.

Energie [enɛr'gi:], f. (—, pl. —n) energy.

energisch [e'nɛrgɪʃ], adj. energetic.

eng [ɛŋ], adj. narrow, tight; tight-fitting.

engagieren [ãga'ʒi:rən], v.a. engage, hire.

Enge ['ɛŋə], f. (—, pl. —n) narrowness, lack of space; einen in die — treiben drive s.o. into a corner.

Engel ['ɛŋəl], m. (—s, pl. —) angel.

engelhaft ['ɛŋəlhaft], adj. angelic.

Engelschar ['ɛŋəlʃaːr], f. (—, pl. —en) angelic host.

Engelwurzel ['ɛŋəlvurtsəl], f. (—, pl. —n) angelica.

engherzig ['ɛŋhɛrtsɪç], adj. narrow-minded.

England ['ɛŋlant], n. England.

englisch (1) ['ɛŋlɪʃ], adj. (obs.) angelic.

englisch (2) ['ɛŋlɪʃ], adj. English; —e Krankheit, rickets.

Engpaß ['ɛŋpas], m. (—sses, pl. ¨e) defile, narrow pass; (fig.) bottleneck.

engros [ã'gro:], adj. wholesale.

engstirnig ['ɛŋʃtɪrnɪç], adj. narrow-minded.

Enkel ['ɛŋkəl], m. (—s, pl. —) grandchild, grandson.

enorm [e'nɔrm], adj. enormous; (coll.) terrific.

entarten [ɛnt'artən], v.n. (aux. sein) degenerate.

entäußern [ɛnt'ɔysərn], v.r. sich einer Sache —, part with s.th.

entbehren [ɛnt'be:rən], v.a. lack, be in want of; spare.

entbehrlich [ɛnt'be:rlɪç], adj. dispensable, unnecessary, superfluous.

Entbehrung [ɛnt'be:ruŋ], f. (—, pl. —en) privation, want.

entbieten [ɛnt'bi:tən], v.a. irr. Grüße —, send o.'s respects.

entbinden [ɛnt'bɪndən], v.a. irr. einen von etwas —, release or dispense s.o. from s.th.; (Med.) deliver (a woman of a child).

Entbindung [ɛnt'bɪnduŋ], f. (—, pl. —en) (Med.) delivery, child-birth.

entblättern [ɛnt'blɛtərn], v.a. strip of leaves.

entblößen [ɛnt'blø:sən], v.a., v.r. (sich) —, uncover (o.s.), bare (o.s.).

entdecken [ɛnt'dɛkən], v.a. discover, detect.

Ente ['ɛntə], f. (—, pl. —n) duck; junge —, duckling; (fig.) hoax, fictitious newspaper report.

entehren [ɛnt'e:rən], v.a. dishonour, disgrace; deflower, ravish.

enterben [ɛnt'ɛrbən], v.a. disinherit.

Enterich ['ɛntərɪç], m. (—s, pl. —e) drake.

entfachen [ɛnt'faxən], v.a. set ablaze, kindle.

entfahren [ɛnt'fa:rən], v.n. irr. (aux. sein) slip off, escape.

entfallen [ɛnt'falən], v.n. irr. (aux. sein) escape o.'s memory; be left off.

entfalten [ɛnt'faltən], v.a. unfold; display. — v.r. sich —, develop, open up, expand.

entfärben [ɛnt'fɛrbən], v.r. sich —, lose colour, grow pale.

entfernen [ɛnt'fɛrnən], v.a. remove. — v.r. sich —, withdraw.

Entfernung [ɛnt'fɛrnuŋ], f. (—, pl. —en) removal; distance.

entfesseln [ɛnt'fɛsəln], v.a. unfetter; let loose.

Entfettungskur [ɛnt'fɛtuŋsku:r], f. (—, pl. —en) slimming-cure.

entflammen [ɛnt'flamən], v.a. inflame.

entfliegen [ɛnt'fli:gən], v.n. irr. (aux. sein) fly away.

entfliehen [ɛnt'fli:ən], v.n. irr. (aux. sein) run away, escape, flee.

entfremden [ɛnt'frɛmdən], v.a. estrange, alienate.

entführen [ɛnt'fy:rən], v.a. abduct, carry off; kidnap; elope with.

entgegen [ɛnt'ge:gən], prep. (Dat.), adv. against, contrary to; towards.

Entgegenkommen [ɛnt'ge:gənkɔmən], n. (—s, no pl.) obliging behaviour, courtesy.

entgegenkommen [ɛnt'ge:gənkɔmən], v.n. irr. (aux. sein) come towards s.o., come to meet s.o.; do a favour, oblige.

entgegennehmen [ɛnt'ge:gənne:mən], v.a. irr. receive, accept.

entgegensehen [ɛnt'ge:gənze:ən], v.n. irr. await, look forward to.

entgegnen [ɛnt'ge:gnən], v.a. reply, retort.

Entgegnung [ɛnt'ge:gnuŋ], f. (—, pl. —en) reply, retort, rejoinder.

entgehen [ɛnt'ge:ən], v.n. irr. (aux. sein) (Dat.) escape; — lassen, let slip.

Entgelt [ɛnt'gɛlt], n. (—s, no pl.) remuneration, recompense.

entgelten [ɛnt'gɛltən], v.a. irr. einen etwas — lassen, make s.o. pay for s.th. or suffer.

entgleisen [ɛnt'glaɪzən], v.n. (aux. sein) run off the rails, be derailed.

enthaaren [ɛnt'ha:rən], v.a. depilate.

enthalten [ɛnt'haltən], v.a. irr. hold, contain. — v.r. sich —, abstain from, refrain from.

enthaltsam [ɛnt'haltza:m], adj. abstinent, abstemious, temperate.

Enthaltung [ɛnt'haltuŋ], f. (—, no pl.) abstention.

enthaupten [ɛnt'hauptən], *v.a.* behead, decapitate.

entheben [ɛnt'he:bən], *v.a. irr. einen einer Sache* —, exempt *or* dispense from, suspend from, relieve of.

entheiligen [ɛnt'haɪlɪgən], *v.a.* profane, desecrate.

enthüllen [ɛnt'hylən], *v.a.* unveil; (*fig.*) reveal.

entkleiden [ɛnt'klaɪdən], *v.a.* unclothe, undress, strip.

entkommen [ɛnt'kɔmən], *v.n. irr.* (*aux.* sein) escape, get off.

entkräften [ɛnt'krɛftən], *v.a.* enfeeble, debilitate, weaken; (*fig.*) refute (an argument).

entladen [ɛnt'la:dən], *v.a. irr.* unload, discharge. — *v.r. sich* —, burst; (*gun*) go off.

Entladung [ɛnt'la:duŋ], *f.* (—, *pl.* —**en**) unloading, discharge, explosion.

entlang [ɛnt'laŋ], *prep.* along.

entlarven [ɛnt'larfən], *v.a.* unmask; expose.

Entlarvung [ɛnt'larfuŋ], *f.* (—, *pl.* —**en**) unmasking, exposure.

entlassen [ɛnt'lasən], *v.a. irr.* dismiss; (*Am.*) fire; discharge; pension off.

Entlastung [ɛnt'lastuŋ], *f.* (—, *no pl.*) exoneration; credit (to s.o.'s bank account).

entlaufen [ɛnt'laufən], *v.n. irr.* (*aux.* sein) run away.

entlausen [ɛnt'lauzən], *v.a.* delouse.

entledigen [ɛnt'le:dɪgən], *v.r. sich einer Sache* —, rid o.s. of *or* get rid of a thing; *sich einer Aufgabe* —, perform a task, discharge a commission.

entleeren [ɛnt'le:rən], *v.a.* empty.

entlegen [ɛnt'le:gən], *adj.* remote, distant, far off.

entlehnen [ɛnt'le:nən], *v.a.* borrow from.

entleihen [ɛnt'laɪən], *v.a. irr.* borrow.

entlocken [ɛnt'lɔkən], *v.a.* elicit from.

entmannen [ɛnt'manən], *v.a.* castrate, emasculate.

entmündigen [ɛnt'myndɪgən], *v.a.* place under care of a guardian *or* (*Law*) trustees.

Entmündigung [ɛnt'myndɪguŋ], *f.* (—, *no pl.*) placing under legal control.

entmutigen [ɛnt'mu:tɪgən], *v.a.* discourage, dishearten.

Entnahme [ɛnt'na:mə], *f.* (—, *pl.* —**n**) (*money*) withdrawal.

entnehmen [ɛnt'ne:mən], *v.a. irr.* (*money*) withdraw; understand, gather *or* infer from.

entnerven [ɛnt'nɛrfən], *v.a.* enervate.

entpuppen [ɛnt'pupən], *v.r. sich* —, burst from the cocoon; (*fig.*) turn out to be.

enträtseln [ɛnt'rɛ:tsəln], *v.a.* decipher, make out.

entreißen [ɛnt'raɪsən], *v.a. irr.* snatch away from; *einer Gefahr* —, save *or* rescue from danger.

entrichten [ɛnt'rɪçtən], *v.a.* pay (off).

entrinnen [ɛnt'rɪnən], *v.n. irr.* (*aux.* sein) escape from.

entrückt [ɛnt rykt], *adj.* enraptured.

entrüsten [ɛnt'rystən], *v.a.* make angry, exasperate. — *v.r. sich* —, become angry, fly into a passion.

entsagen [ɛnt'za:gən], *v.n.* renounce; waive; abdicate.

Entsatz [ɛnt'zats], *m.* (—**es**, *no pl.*) (*Mil.*) relief.

entschädigen [ɛnt'ʃɛ:dɪgən], *v.a.* indemnify, compensate.

entscheiden [ɛnt'ʃaɪdən], *v.a. irr.* decide. — *v.r. sich* — *für*, come to a decision for, decide in favour of.

Entscheidung [ɛnt'ʃaɪduŋ], *f.* (—, *pl.* —**en**) decision; verdict.

entschieden [ɛnt'ʃi:dən], *adj.* decided, determined, resolute, peremptory.

Entschiedenheit [ɛnt'ʃi:dənhaɪt], *f.* (—, *no pl.*) resolution, firmness, determination.

entschlafen [ɛnt'ʃla:fən], *v.n. irr.* (*aux.* sein) fall asleep; (*fig.*) die, depart this life.

entschleiern [ɛnt'ʃlaɪərn], *v.a.* unveil.

entschließen [ɛnt'ʃli:sən], *v.r. sich* —, decide (upon), resolve, make up o.'s mind.

Entschlossenheit [ɛnt'ʃlɔsənhaɪt], *f.* (—, *no pl.*) resoluteness, determination.

entschlummern [ɛnt'ʃlumərn], *v.n.* (*aux.* sein) fall asleep.

entschlüpfen [ɛnt'ʃlypfən], *v.n.* (*aux.* sein) slip away; escape.

Entschluß [ɛnt'ʃlus], *m.* (—**sses**, *pl.* ⸚**sse**) resolution; *einen — fassen*, resolve (to).

entschuldigen [ɛnt'ʃuldɪgən], *v.a.* excuse. — *v.r. sich* —, apologise.

entschwinden [ɛnt'ʃvɪndən], *v.n. irr.* (*aux.* sein) disappear, vanish.

entseelt [ɛnt'ze:lt], *adj.* inanimate, lifeless.

entsenden [ɛnt'zɛndən], *v.a. irr.* send off, despatch.

Entsetzen [ɛnt'zɛtsən], *n.* (—**s**, *no pl.*) horror, terror.

entsetzen [ɛnt'zɛtsən], *v.a.* (*Mil.*) relieve; frighten, shock, fill with horror. — *v.r. sich — über*, be horrified at.

entsetzlich [ɛnt'zɛtslɪç], *adj.* horrible, terrible, dreadful, awful.

entsiegeln [ɛnt'zi:gəln], *v.a.* unseal.

entsinnen [ɛnt'zɪnən], *v.r. sich einer Sache* —, recollect, remember, call s.th. to mind.

entspannen [ɛnt'ʃpanən], *v.a., v.r. (sich)* —, relax.

entspinnen [ɛnt'ʃpɪnən], *v.r. irr. sich* —, arise, begin.

entsprechen [ɛnt'ʃprɛçən], *v.n. irr.* respond to, correspond to, meet, suit.

entsprechend [ɛnt'ʃprɛçənt], *adj.* corresponding, suitable.

entsprießen [ɛnt'ʃpri:sən], *v.n. irr.* (*aux.* sein) spring up, sprout.

entspringen [ɛnt'ʃprɪŋən], *v.n. irr.* (*aux.* sein) escape, originate from; (*river*) have its source at, rise.

entstammen

entstammen [ɛnt'ʃtamən], v.n. (aux. sein) spring from, originate from.

entstehen [ɛnt'ʃteːən], v.n. irr. (aux. sein) arise, originate, begin, result, spring from.

Entstehung [ɛnt'ʃteːuŋ], f. (—, no pl.) origin, rise.

entstellen [ɛnt'ʃtɛlən], v.a. disfigure, deform, distort; (fig.) garble.

entsühnen [ɛnt'zyːnən], v.a. free from sin, purify, purge.

enttäuschen [ɛnt'tɔyʃən], v.a. disappoint.

entthronen [ɛnt'troːnən], v.a. dethrone.

entvölkern [ɛnt'fœlkərn], v.a. depopulate.

entwachsen [ɛnt'vaksən], v.n. irr. (aux. sein) grow out of, outgrow.

entwaffnen [ɛnt'vafnən], v.a. disarm.

entwässern [ɛnt'vɛsərn], v.a. drain.

entweder [ɛnt've:dər], conj. either; — ...oder, either ...... or.

entweichen [ɛnt'vaɪçən], v.n. irr. escape, run away.

entweihen [ɛnt'vaɪən], v.a. profane, desecrate.

entwenden [ɛnt'vɛndən], v.a. take away, steal, embezzle.

entwerfen [ɛnt'vɛrfən], v.a. irr. design, sketch, plan, draw up.

entwerten [ɛnt'vɛrtən], v.a. reduce in value, depreciate; (stamps) cancel.

entwickeln [ɛnt'vɪkəln], v.a. unfold, develop; (ideas) explain, explicate. — v.r. sich —, develop (into), evolve.

Entwicklung [ɛnt'vɪkluŋ], f. (—, pl. —en) unfolding, development, evolution.

entwinden [ɛnt'vɪndən], v.a. irr. wrench from, wrest from.

entwirren [ɛnt'vɪrən], v.a. unravel, disentangle.

entwischen [ɛnt'vɪʃən], v.n. (aux. sein) slip away, escape.

entwöhnen [ɛnt'vøːnən], v.a. disaccustom; break off a habit; (baby) wean.

entwürdigen [ɛnt'vyrdɪgən], v.a. disgrace, degrade.

Entwurf [ɛnt'vurf], m. (—s, pl. ⁻e) sketch, design, draft, plan, project.

entwurzeln [ɛnt'vurtsəln], v.a. uproot.

entziehen [ɛnt'tsiːən], v.a. irr. withdraw, take away, deprive of.

entziffern [ɛnt'tsɪfərn], v.a. decipher.

entzücken [ɛnt'tsykən], v.a. enchant, delight, charm.

entzündbar [ɛnt'tsyntbaːr], adj. inflammable.

entzünden [ɛnt'tsyndən], v.a. set on fire, light the fire; (fig.) inflame. — v.r. sich —, catch fire, ignite; (Med.) become inflamed.

Entzündung [ɛnt'tsynduŋ], f. (—, pl. —en) kindling, setting on fire; (Med.) inflammation.

entzwei [ɛnt'tsvaɪ], adv. in two, broken.

entzweien [ɛnt'tsvaɪən], v.a. disunite.

Enzian ['ɛntsjan], m. (—s, pl. —e) (Bot.) gentian.

Enzyklopädie [ɛntsyklopɛ'diː], f. (—, pl. —n) encyclopædia.

Epidemie [epɪde'miː], f. (—, pl. —en) epidemic.

epidemisch [epɪ'deːmɪʃ], adj. epidemic(al).

Epik ['eːpɪk], f. (—, no pl.) epic poetry.

episch ['eːpɪʃ], adj. epic.

Epos ['eːpɔs], n. (—, pl. **Epen**) epic poem.

Equipage [ekvi'paːʒə], f. (—, pl. —n) carriage.

er [eːr], pers. pron. he.

Erachten [ɛr'axtən], n. (—s, no pl.) opinion, judgment: meines —s, in my opinion.

erachten [ɛr'axtən], v.a. think, consider.

erarbeiten [ɛr'arbaɪtən], v.a. gain or achieve by working.

erb ['ɛrb], adj. (in compounds) hereditary.

erbarmen [ɛr'barmən], v.r. sich —, have mercy (on), take pity (on).

erbärmlich [ɛr'bɛrmlɪç], adj. miserable, pitiful; contemptible.

erbauen [ɛr'bauən], v.a. build, erect; (fig.) edify.

erbaulich [ɛr'baulɪç], adj. edifying.

Erbauung [ɛr'bauuŋ], f. (—, no pl.) building, erection; (fig.) edification.

Erbbesitz ['ɛrpbəzɪts], m. (—es, pl. —e) hereditary possession.

Erbe ['ɛrbə], m. (—n, pl. —n) heir. n. (—s, no pl.) inheritance; heritage.

erbeben [ɛr'beːbən], v.n. (aux. sein) shake, tremble, quake.

erbeigen ['ɛrpaɪgən], adj. inherited.

erben ['ɛrbən], v.a. inherit.

erbeten [ɛr'beːtən], v.a. sich etwas —, ask for s.th. by prayer; request.

erbetteln [ɛr'bɛtəln], v.a. obtain by begging.

erbeuten [ɛr'bɔytən], v.a. take as booty.

Erbfeind ['ɛrpfaɪnt], m. (—s, pl. —e) sworn enemy.

Erbfolge ['ɛrpfɔlgə], f. (—, no pl.) succession.

erbieten [ɛr'biːtən], v.r. irr. sich —, offer to do s.th.; volunteer; Ehre —, do homage.

Erbin ['ɛrbɪn], f. (—, pl. —nen) heiress.

erbitten [ɛr'bɪtən], v.a. irr. beg, request, ask for, gain by asking.

erbittern [ɛr'bɪtərn], v.a. embitter, anger, exasperate.

erblassen [ɛr'blasən], v.n. (aux. sein) turn pale.

Erblasser ['ɛrblasər], m. (—s, pl. —) testator.

erbleichen [ɛr'blaɪçən], v.n. irr. (aux. sein) turn pale, lose colour.

erblich ['ɛrplɪç], adj. hereditary, congenital.

erblicken [ɛr'blɪkən], v.a. perceive, behold, catch sight of.

erblinden [ɛr'blɪndən], v.n. (aux. sein) turn blind.

erblos ['ɛrploːs], adj. disinherited: without an heir.

erfreuen

erblühen [ɛrˈblyːən], *v.n.* (*aux.* sein) blossom (out).

Erbmasse [ˈɛrpmasə], *f.* (—, *no pl.*) estate.

erbosen [ɛrˈboːzən], *v.a.* make angry. — *v.r. sich* —, become angry.

erbötig [ɛrˈbøːtɪç], *adj.* — sein, be willing, be ready.

Erbpacht [ˈɛrppaxt], *f.* (—, *pl.* —en) hereditary tenure.

erbrechen [ɛrˈbrɛçən], *v.a. irr.* break open, open by force. — *v.r. sich* —, vomit.

Erbrecht [ˈɛrprɛçt], *n.* (—s, *no pl.*) law (*or* right) of succession.

Erbschaft [ˈɛrpʃaft], *f.* (—, *pl.* —en) inheritance, heritage, legacy.

Erbse [ˈɛrpsə], *f.* (—, *pl.* —n) pea.

Erbstück [ˈɛrpʃtyk], *n.* (—s, *pl.* —e) heirloom.

Erbsünde [ˈɛrpzyndə], *f.* (—, *no pl.*) original sin.

Erbteil [ˈɛrptaɪl], *n.* (—s, *pl.* —e) portion of inheritance.

Erdapfel [ˈeːrtapfəl], *m.* (—s, *pl.* ∷) (*Austr.*) potato.

Erdbahn [ˈeːrtbaːn], *f.* (—, *no pl.*) orbit of the earth.

Erdball [ˈeːrtbal], *m.* (—s, *pl.*) terrestrial globe.

Erdbeben [ˈeːrtbeːbən], *n.* (—s, *pl.*) earthquake.

Erdbeere [ˈeːrtbeːrə], *f.* (—, *pl.* —n) strawberry.

Erde [ˈeːrdə], *f.* (—, *pl.* —n) earth, soil ground.

erden [ˈeːrdən], *v.a.* (*Rad.*) earth.

erdenken [ɛrˈdɛŋkən], *v.a. irr.* think out; invent. — *v.r. sich etwas* —, invent s.th., devise s.th.

erdenklich [ɛrˈdɛŋklɪç], *adj.* imaginable, conceivable.

Erdenleben [ˈeːrdənleːbən], *n.* (—s, *no pl.*) life on this earth.

Erdfall [ˈeːrtfal], *m.* (—s, *pl.* ∷e) landslip.

Erdfläche [ˈeːrtflɛçə], *f.* (—, *no pl.*) surface of the earth.

Erdgeschoß [ˈeːrtgəʃɔs], *n.* (—sses, *pl.* —sse) ground floor.

Erdhügel [ˈeːrthyːgəl], *m.* (—s, *pl.* —) mound of earth.

erdichten [ɛrˈdɪçtən], *v.a.* think out, invent, feign.

Erdkunde [ˈeːrtkundə], *f.* (—, *no pl.*) geography.

Erdleitung [ˈeːrtlaɪtuŋ], *f.* (—, *pl.* —en) earth circuit, earth connexion.

Erdmaus [ˈeːrtmaus], *f.* (—, *pl.* ∷e) field mouse.

Erdmolch [ˈeːrtmɔlç], *m.* (—s, *pl.* —e) salamander.

Erdnuß [ˈeːrtnus], *f.* (—, *pl.* ∷sse) groundnut, peanut.

Erdöl [ˈeːrtøːl], *n.* (—s, *no pl.*) petroleum, mineral oil.

erdolchen [ɛrˈdɔlçən], *v.a.* stab (with a dagger).

Erdpech [ˈeːrtpɛç], *n.* (—s, *no pl.*) bitumen.

erdreisten [ɛrˈdraɪstən], *v.r. sich* —, dare, have the audacity.

erdrosseln [ɛrˈdrɔsəln], *v.a.* strangle, throttle.

erdrücken [ɛrˈdrykən], *v.a.* crush to death.

Erdrutsch [ˈeːrtrutʃ], *m.* (—es, *no pl.*) landslip, landslide.

Erdschicht [ˈeːrtʃɪçt], *f.* (—, *pl.* —en) (*Geol.*) layer, stratum.

Erdschnecke [ˈeːrtʃnɛkə], *f.* (—, *pl.* —n) slug, snail.

Erdscholle [ˈeːrtʃɔlə], *f.* (—, *pl.* —n) clod (of earth).

Erdsturz [ˈeːrtʃturts], *m.* (—es, *no pl.*) landslide.

erdulden [ɛrˈduldən], *v.a.* suffer, endure.

ereifern [ɛrˈaɪfərn], *v.r. sich* —, become heated, get excited.

ereignen [ɛrˈaɪgnən], *v.r. sich* —, happen, come to pass.

Ereignis [ɛrˈaɪknɪs], *n.* (—ses, *pl.* —se) event, occurrence, happening.

ereilen [ɛrˈaɪlən], *v.a.* overtake, befall.

Eremit [ereˈmiːt], *m.* (—en, *pl.* —en) hermit, recluse.

erfahren [ɛrˈfaːrən], *v.a. irr.* learn, hear; experience. — *adj.* experienced, practised; conversant with, versed in.

Erfahrenheit [ɛrˈfaːrənhaɪt], *f.* (—, *no pl.*) experience, skill.

Erfahrung [ɛrˈfaːruŋ], *f.* (—, *pl.* —en) experience, knowledge, expertness, skill; *in* — *bringen*, ascertain, come to know.

erfahrungsgemäß [ɛrˈfaːruŋsgəmɛːs], *adj.* based on *or* according to experience.

erfahrungsmäßig [ɛrˈfaːruŋsmɛːsɪç], *adj.* based on experience; empirical.

erfassen [ɛrˈfasən], *v.a.* get hold of, seize, comprehend, grasp.

erfinden [ɛrˈfɪndən], *v.a. irr.* invent, contrive.

erfinderisch [ɛrˈfɪndərɪʃ], *adj.* inventive, ingenious.

Erfindung [ɛrˈfɪnduŋ], *f.* (—, *pl.* —en) invention; contrivance.

Erfolg [ɛrˈfɔlk], *m.* (—s, *pl.* —e) success; result; effect; — *haben*, succeed, be successful; *keinen* — *haben*, fail.

erfolgen [ɛrˈfɔlgən], *v.n.* (*aux.* sein) ensue, follow, result.

erfolgreich [ɛrˈfɔlkraɪç], *adj.* successful.

erforderlich [ɛrˈfɔrdərlɪç], *adj.* necessary, required.

erfordern [ɛrˈfɔrdərn], *v.a.* demand, require.

Erfordernis [ɛrˈfɔrdərnɪs], *n.* (—ses, *pl.* —se) necessity, requirement, requisite.

erforschen [ɛrˈfɔrʃən], *v.a.* explore, investigate, conduct research into.

erfragen [ɛrˈfraːgən], *v.a.* find out by asking, ascertain.

erfreuen [ɛrˈfrɔyən], *v.a.* gladden, cheer, delight. — *v.r. sich* — *an*, enjoy, take pleasure in.

63

erfreulich [ɛr'frɔylıç], adj. pleasing, gratifying.

erfrieren [ɛr'fri:rən], v.n. irr. (aux. sein) freeze to death, die of exposure; become numb.

erfrischen [ɛr'frıʃən], v.a. refresh.

erfüllen [ɛr'fylən], v.a. fulfil, keep (promise); comply with; perform; seinen Zweck —, serve its purpose. — v.r. sich —, come true, be fulfilled.

Erfüllung [ɛr'fylun], f. (—, no pl.) fulfilment; granting; performance; in — gehen, come true, be realised.

ergänzen [ɛr'gɛntsən], v.a. complete, complement.

Ergänzung [ɛr'gɛntsuŋ], f. (—, pl. —en) completion; complement, supplement.

ergattern [ɛr'gatərn], v.a. pick up.

ergeben [ɛr'ge:bən], v.a. irr. give, yield, prove, show. — v.r. sich —, surrender (to), acquiesce (in); happen, result, follow. — adj. devoted, submissive, humble, obedient.

Ergebenheit [ɛr'ge:bənhaıt], f. (—, no pl.) devotion, obedience, humility, fidelity.

ergebenst [ɛr'ge:bənst], adj. Ihr —er (letter ending), yours very truly, your obedient servant. — adv. respectfully.

Ergebnis [ɛr'ge:pnıs], n. (—ses, pl. —se) outcome, result; (Agr.) yield.

Ergebung [ɛr'ge:buŋ], f. (—, no pl.) submission, resignation; surrender.

Ergehen [ɛr'ge:ən], n. (—s, no pl.) health, condition, well-being.

ergehen [ɛr'ge:ən], v.n. irr. (aux. sein) be promulgated or issued; — lassen, issue, publish; etwas über sich — lassen, submit to or suffer s.th. patiently. — v.r. sich —, (obs.) take a stroll.

ergiebig [ɛr'gi:bıç], adj. rich, productive, fertile, profitable.

ergießen [ɛr'gi:sən], v.r. irr. sich —, discharge, flow into.

erglänzen [ɛr'glɛntsən], v.n. (aux. sein) shine forth, sparkle.

erglühen [ɛr'gly:ən], v.n. (aux. sein) glow; blush.

ergötzen [ɛr'gœtsən], v.a. (obs.) amuse, delight. — v.r. sich — an, delight in.

ergrauen [ɛr'grauən], v.n. (aux. sein) become grey; grow old.

ergreifen [ɛr'graıfən], v.a. irr. seize, grasp, get hold of; move, touch, affect; Maßnahmen —, take measures.

Ergreifung [ɛr'graıfuŋ], f. (—, no pl.) seizure; (measure) adoption.

ergriffen [ɛr'grıfən], adj. moved, touched, impressed.

Ergriffenheit [ɛr'grıfənhaıt], f. (—, no pl.) emotion.

ergrimmen [ɛr'grımən], v.n. (aux. sein) grow angry, be enraged.

ergründen [ɛr'gryndən], v.a. get to the bottom of, investigate, fathom.

Erguß [ɛr'gus], m. (—sses, pl. ⸗sse) outpouring; (fig.) effusion.

erhaben [ɛr'ha:bən], adj. sublime, exalted; majestic, elevated.

Erhabenheit [ɛr'ha:bənhaıt], f. (—, no pl.) majesty, sublimity.

erhalten [ɛr'haltən], v.a. irr. receive, obtain, get, preserve; maintain, keep up. — v.r. sich — von, subsist on.

erhältlich [ɛr'hɛltlıç], adj. obtainable.

Erhaltung [ɛr'haltuŋ], f. (—, no pl.) preservation, conservation; (family) maintenance.

erhärten [ɛr'hɛrtən], v.a. make hard; (fig.) prove, confirm.

erhaschen [ɛr'haʃən], v.a. catch, snatch.

erheben [ɛr'he:bən], v.a. irr. lift up, raise; (fig.) elevate, exalt; Klage —, bring an action; Geld —, raise money; Steuern —, levy taxes. — v.r. sich —, rise, stand up.

erheblich [ɛr'he:plıç], adj. considerable, weighty, appreciable.

Erhebung [ɛr'he:buŋ], f. (—, pl. —en) elevation; (taxes) levying; revolt, rebellion, rising.

erheischen [ɛr'haıʃən], v.a. (rare) require, demand.

erheitern [ɛr'haıtərn], v.a. cheer, exhilarate.

erhellen [ɛr'hɛlən], v.a. light up, illuminate; (fig.) enlighten. — v.n. become evident.

erhitzen [ɛr'hıtsən], v.a. heat; (fig.) inflame, excite. — v.r. sich —, grow hot; grow angry.

erhöhen [ɛr'hø:ən], v.a. heighten, raise, intensify, increase; (value) enhance.

erholen [ɛr'ho:lən], v.r. sich —, recover, get better; relax (after work); take a rest.

erholungsbedürftig [ɛr'ho:luŋsbədyrftıç], adj. in need of a rest.

erhören [ɛr'hø:rən], v.a. hear, vouchsafe, grant.

Erich ['e:rıç], m. Eric.

erinnerlich [ɛr'ınərlıç], adj. remembered; soweit mir — ist, as far as I can remember.

erinnern [ɛr'ınərn], v.a. remind. — v.r. sich —, remember, recollect, recall, call to mind.

Erinnerung [ɛr'ınəruŋ], f. (—, pl. —en) remembrance; recollection; reminiscence.

erjagen [ɛr'ja:gən], v.a. hunt (down), chase.

erkalten [ɛr'kaltən], v.n. (aux. sein) grow cold.

erkälten [ɛr'kɛltən], v.r. sich —, catch cold.

Erkältung [ɛr'kɛltuŋ], f. (—, pl. —en) cold, chill.

erkämpfen [ɛr'kɛmpfən], v.a. obtain by fighting; obtain by great exertion.

erkaufen [ɛr'kaufən], v.a. purchase; bribe, corrupt.

erkennen [ɛr'kɛnən], v.a. irr. recognise; perceive, distinguish, discern; (Comm.) credit; zu — geben, give to understand; sich zu — geben, make o.s. known. — v.n. (Law) judge; — auf, (Law) announce verdict, pass sentence.

erkenntlich [ɛrˈkɛntlɪç], adj. grateful; (fig.) sich — zeigen, show o.s. grateful.
Erkenntlichkeit [ɛrˈkɛntlɪçkaɪt], f. (—, no pl.) gratitude.
Erkenntnis [ɛrˈkɛntnɪs], f. (—, pl. —e) perception, knowledge, comprehension, understanding; realisation, (Phil.) cognition.
Erkennung [ɛrˈkɛnuŋ], f. (—, no pl.) recognition.
Erker [ˈɛrkər], m. (—s, pl. —) alcove, bay, turret.
Erkerfenster [ˈɛrkərfɛnstər], n. (—s, pl. —) bay-window.
erklären [ɛrˈklɛːrən], v.a. explain, expound, account for; make a statement on, declare, state.
erklärlich [ɛrˈklɛːrlɪç], adj. explicable.
Erklärung [ɛrˈklɛːruŋ], f. (—, pl. —en) explanation; declaration, statement; (income tax) return.
erklecklich [ɛrˈklɛklɪç], adj. considerable.
erklettern [ɛrˈklɛtərn], v.a. climb.
erklimmen [ɛrˈklɪmən], v.a. irr. climb.
erklingen [ɛrˈklɪŋən], v.n. irr. (aux. sein) sound, resound.
erkoren [ɛrˈkoːrən], adj. select, chosen.
erkranken [ɛrˈkraŋkən], v.n. (aux. sein) fall ill.
erkühnen [ɛrˈkyːnən], v.r. sich —, dare, make bold, venture.
erkunden [ɛrˈkundən], v.a. explore, find out; (Mil.) reconnoitre.
erkundigen [ɛrˈkundɪgən], v.r. sich —, enquire (about), make enquiries.
erlaben [ɛrˈlaːbən], v.r. sich —, (obs.) refresh o.s.
erlahmen [ɛrˈlaːmən], v.n. (aux. sein) become lame; lose o.'s drive; grow tired.
erlangen [ɛrˈlaŋən], v.a. reach, gain, obtain; acquire; attain.
Erlaß [ɛrˈlas], m. (—sses, pl. ˙sse) remission, exemption, release, dispensation; (Comm.) deduction; (Law, Pol.) proclamation, edict, decree, writ; (Eccl.) indulgence; remission.
erlassen [ɛrˈlasən], v.a. irr. remit, release, let off; (Law, Pol.) enact, promulgate.
erläßlich [ɛrˈlɛslɪç], adj. remissible, dispensable, venial.
erlauben [ɛrˈlaubən], v.a. permit, allow; sich etwas —, take the liberty of, make bold to; have the impertinence to.
Erlaubnis [ɛrˈlaupnɪs], f. (—, no pl.) permission, leave, permit; die — haben, be permitted; um — bitten, beg leave; mit Ihrer —, by your leave.
erlaucht [ɛrˈlauxt], adj. illustrious, noble.
erlauschen [ɛrˈlauʃən], v.a. overhear.
erläutern [ɛrˈlɔytərn], v.a. explain, illustrate, elucidate.
Erle [ˈɛrlə], f. (—, pl. —n) (Bot.) alder.
erleben [ɛrˈleːbən], v.a. live to see; go through, experience.
Erlebnis [ɛrˈleːpnɪs], n. (—sses, pl. —sse) experience, adventure, occurrence.

erledigen [ɛrˈleːdɪgən], v.a. settle, finish off, clear up; dispatch; execute (commission etc.).
erledigt [ɛrˈleːdɪçt], adj. (coll.) worn-out; exhausted.
erlegen [ɛrˈleːgən], v.a. slay; pay down.
erleichtern [ɛrˈlaɪçtərn], v.a. lighten, ease, facilitate.
erleiden [ɛrˈlaɪdən], v.a. irr. suffer, endure, bear, undergo.
erlernen [ɛrˈlɛrnən], v.a. learn, acquire.
erlesen [ɛrˈleːzən], v.a. irr. select, choose. — adj. select, choice.
erleuchten [ɛrˈlɔyçtən], v.a. illumine, illuminate, floodlight; (fig.) enlighten, inspire.
erliegen [ɛrˈliːgən], v.n. irr. (aux. sein) succumb.
Erlkönig [ˈɛrlkøːnɪç], m. (—s, pl. —e) fairy-king, elf-king.
erlogen [ɛːrˈloːgən], adj. false, untrue; trumped-up.
Erlös [ɛrˈløːs], m. (—es, no pl.) proceeds.
erlöschen [ɛrˈlœʃən], v.n. irr. (aux. sein) be extinguished, die out; (fire) go out; (contract) expire.
erlösen [ɛrˈløːzən], v.a. redeem; release, save, deliver.
ermächtigen [ɛrˈmɛçtɪgən], v.a. empower; authorise.
ermahnen [ɛrˈmaːnən], v.a. admonish, exhort, remind.
ermäßigen [ɛrˈmɛːsɪgən], v.a. reduce.
ermatten [ɛrˈmatən], v.a. weaken, weary, tire. — v.n. (aux. sein) grow weak, become tired.
Ermessen [ɛrˈmɛsən], n. (—s, no pl.) judgment, opinion.
ermitteln [ɛrˈmɪtəln], v.a. ascertain, find out.
ermöglichen [ɛrˈmøːglɪçən], v.a. make possible.
ermorden [ɛrˈmɔrdən], v.a. murder.
ermüden [ɛrˈmyːdən], v.a. tire, fatigue. — v.n. (aux. sein) get tired, grow weary.
ermuntern [ɛrˈmuntərn], v.a. encourage, cheer up.
ermutigen [ɛrˈmuːtɪgən], v.a. encourage.
ernähren [ɛrˈnɛːrən], v.a. nourish, feed.
ernennen [ɛrˈnɛnən], v.a. irr. nominate, appoint.
erneuern [ɛrˈnɔyərn], v.a. renew, repair, renovate.
erniedrigen [ɛrˈniːdrɪgən], v.a. humble, humiliate, degrade. — v.r. sich —, humble o.s., abase o.s.
Ernst (1) [ɛrnst], m. Ernest.
Ernst (2) [ɛrnst], m. (—es, no pl.) earnestness, seriousness.
ernst [ɛrnst], adj. earnest, serious.
Ernte [ˈɛrntə], f. (—, pl. —n) harvest, crop.
ernüchtern [ɛrˈnyçtərn], v.a. sober; (fig.) disenchant, disillusion.
erobern [ɛrˈoːbərn], v.a. (Mil.) conquer; take, win.
eröffnen [ɛrˈœfnən], v.a. open, inaugurate; inform, reveal.
erörtern [ɛrˈœrtərn], v.a. discuss, debate, argue.

erpicht

erpicht [ɛrˈpɪçt], *adj.* eager for, bent on.
erpressen [ɛrˈprɛsən], *v.a.* extort, blackmail.
erquicken [ɛrˈkvɪkən], *v.a.* refresh.
erraten [ɛrˈraːtən], *v.a. irr.* guess.
erregen [ɛrˈreːgən], *v.a.* cause; stir up, excite, agitate; provoke.
erreichen [ɛrˈraɪçən], *v.a.* reach, arrive at; (*fig.*) attain, reach.
erretten [ɛrˈrɛtən], *v.a.* save, rescue.
errichten [ɛrˈrɪçtən], *v.a.* erect, raise, build.
erringen [ɛrˈrɪŋən], *v.a. irr.* obtain (by exertion), achieve.
erröten [ɛrˈrøːtən], *v.n.* (*aux.* sein) blush, redden.
Errungenschaft [ɛrˈruŋənʃaft], *f.* (—, *pl.* —en) achievement, acquisition.
Ersatz [ɛrˈzats], *m.* (**-es,** *no pl.*) substitute; compensation, amends; (*Mil. etc.*) replacement.
erschallen [ɛrˈʃalən], *v.n.* (*aux.* sein) resound, sound.
erschaudern [ɛrˈʃaudərn], *v.n.* (*aux.* sein) be seized with horror.
erscheinen [ɛrˈʃaɪnən], *v.n. irr.* (*aux.* sein) appear, make o.'s appearance; seem; be published.
erschießen [ɛrˈʃiːsən], *v.a. irr.* shoot dead.
erschlaffen [ɛrˈʃlafən], *v.n.* (*aux.* sein) flag, slacken.
erschlagen [ɛrˈʃlaːgən], *v.a. irr.* slay, kill.
erschließen [ɛrˈʃliːsən], *v.a. irr.* open up.
erschöpfen [ɛrˈʃœpfən], *v.a.* exhaust.
erschrecken [ɛrˈʃrɛkən], *v.a. irr.* startle, shock, terrify. — *v.n.* (*aux.* sein) be startled, be frightened, be terrified.
erschüttern [ɛrˈʃʏtərn], *v.a.* shake; (*fig.*) move, affect strongly.
erschweren [ɛrˈʃveːrən], *v.a.* (*fig.*) aggravate, make more difficult.
erschwingen [ɛrˈʃvɪŋən], *v.a. irr.* afford, be able to pay.
erschwinglich [ɛrˈʃvɪŋlɪç], *adj.* attainable, within o.'s means.
ersehen [ɛrˈzeːən], *v.a. irr.* — *aus,* gather (from).
ersehnen [ɛrˈzeːnən], *v.a.* long for, yearn for.
ersetzen [ɛrˈzɛtsən], *v.a.* replace, take the place of; restore, make good; repair; (*money*) refund.
ersichtlich [ɛrˈzɪçtlɪç], *adj.* evident.
ersinnen [ɛrˈzɪnən], *v.a. irr.* think out, imagine, devise, contrive.
ersparen [ɛrˈʃpaːrən], *v.a.* save.
ersprießlich [ɛrˈʃpriːslɪç], *adj.* useful, profitable, beneficial.
erst [eːrst], *num. adj.* first. — *adv.* first, at first, only, but; — *jetzt,* only now; *nun — recht,* now more than ever.
erstatten [ɛrˈʃtatən], *v.a.* reimburse, compensate, repay; *Bericht —,* report.
Erstattung [ɛrˈʃtatuŋ], *f.* (—, *pl.* —en) reimbursement, restitution.
Erstaufführung [ˈeːrstauffyːruŋ], *f.* (—, *pl.* —en) (*Theat.*) first night; première.

Erstaunen [ɛrˈʃtaunən], *n.* (**-s,** *no pl.*) amazement, astonishment, surprise.
erstechen [ɛrˈʃtɛçən], *v.a. irr.* stab.
erstehen [ɛrˈʃteːən], *v.n. irr.* (*aux.* sein) rise, arise. — *v.a.* buy, purchase.
ersteigen [ɛrˈʃtaɪgən], *v.a. irr.* climb, mount, ascend.
ersticken [ɛrˈʃtɪkən], *v.a. irr.* choke, stifle, suffocate. — *v.n.* (*aux.* sein) choke, suffocate.
erstmalig [ˈeːrstmaːlɪç], *adj.* first. — *adv.* for the first time.
erstreben [ɛrˈʃtreːbən], *v.a.* strive after.
erstrecken [ɛrˈʃtrɛkən], *v.r. sich —,* extend, reach to.
ersuchen [ɛrˈzuːxən], *v.a.* request, ask.
ertappen [ɛrˈtapən], *v.a.* catch, detect.
erteilen [ɛrˈtaɪlən], *v.a.* bestow, impart; *einen Auftrag —,* issue an order; *Unterricht —,* instruct; *die Erlaubnis —,* give permission.
ertönen [ɛrˈtøːnən], *v.n.* (*aux.* sein) sound, resound.
Ertrag [ɛrˈtraːk], *m.* (**-s,** *pl.* ˙e) produce; returns, yield; output; (*sale*) proceeds.
ertragen [ɛrˈtraːgən], *v.a. irr.* bear, suffer, endure.
ertränken [ɛrˈtrɛŋkən], *v.a.* drown.
ertrinken [ɛrˈtrɪŋkən], *v.n. irr.* (*aux.* sein) drown, be drowned.
erübrigen [ɛrˈyːbrɪgən], *v.a.* save, spare.
erwachen [ɛrˈvaxən], *v.n.* (*aux.* sein) awake, wake up.
erwachsen [ɛrˈvaksən], *adj.* grown-up, adult. — *v.n. irr.* grow up; ensue, follow, arise.
erwägen [ɛrˈveːgən], *v.a. irr.* weigh, ponder, consider.
erwähnen [ɛrˈvɛːnən], *v.a.* mention.
erwärmen [ɛrˈvɛrmən], *v.a.* warm (up), make warm.
erwarten [ɛrˈvartən], *v.a.* expect, await.
Erwartung [ɛrˈvartuŋ], *f.* (—, *pl.* —en) expectation.
erwecken [ɛrˈvɛkən], *v.a.* wake up, awaken, raise; rouse.
erwehren [ɛrˈveːrən], *v.r. sich —* (Genit.), defend o.s.; *ich kann mich des Lachens nicht —,* I cannot help laughing.
erweichen [ɛrˈvaɪçən], *v.a.* soften.
erweisen [ɛrˈvaɪzən], *v.a. irr.* prove, show; demonstrate.
erweitern [ɛrˈvaɪtərn], *v.a.* widen, enlarge, expand.
erwerben [ɛrˈvɛrbən], *v.a. irr.* acquire.
erwidern [ɛrˈviːdərn], *v.a.* reply, answer; return.
erwirken [ɛrˈvɪrkən], *v.a.* effect, secure.
erwischen [ɛrˈvɪʃən], *v.a. see* ertappen.
erwünschen [ɛrˈvynʃən], *v.a.* desire, wish for.
erwürgen [ɛrˈvyrgən], *v.a.* strangle, throttle.
Erz [eːrts], (**-es,** *pl.* —e) ore; brass, bronze.

66

erzählen [ɛrˈtsɛːlən], *v.a.* narrate, relate, tell.

Erzbischof [ˈɛrtsbiʃɔf], *m.* (—s, *pl.* ̈e) archbishop.

erzeugen [ɛrˈtsɔygən], *v.a.* engender; beget; produce; (*Elec.*) generate.

Erzherzog [ˈɛrtshɛrtsoːk], *m.* (—s, *pl.* ̈e) archduke.

erziehen [ɛrˈtsiːən], *v.a. irr.* educate, train, bring up, rear.

Erziehungsanstalt [ɛrˈtsiːuŋsanʃtalt], *f.* (—, *pl.* —en) approved school, reformatory.

erzielen [ɛrˈtsiːlən], *v.a.* obtain; fetch, realize (a price); *Gewinn* —, make a profit.

erzittern [ɛrˈtsɪtərn], *v.n.* (*aux.* sein) tremble, shake.

Erzofen [ɛrˈtsoːfən], *m.* (—s, *pl.* ̈n) furnace.

erzürnen [ɛrˈtsyrnən], *v.a.* make angry. — *v.r.* sich —, grow angry.

Erzvater [ˈɛrtsfaːtər], *m.* (—s, *pl.* ̈) patriarch.

erzwingen [ɛrˈtsvɪŋən], *v.a. irr.* enforce, force, compel.

es [ɛs], *pron.* it; — gibt, there is; — sind, there are; — lebe, long live!

Es [ɛs], *n.* (—, *pl.* —) (*Mus.*) E flat.

Esche [ˈɛʃə], *f.* (—, *pl.* —n) (*Bot.*) ash, ashtree.

Esel [ˈeːzəl], *m.* (—s, *pl.* —) ass, donkey.

Eselsohr [ˈeːzəlsoːr], *n.* (—s, *pl.* —en) (*fig.*) dog's ear.

Eskadron [ɛskaˈdroːn], *f.* (—, *pl.* —en) squadron.

Espe [ˈɛspə], *f.* (—, *pl.* —n) (*Bot.*) asp, aspen.

eßbar [ˈɛsbaːr], *adj.* edible.

Esse [ˈɛsə], *f.* (—, *pl.* —n) chimney, forge.

Essen [ˈɛsən], *n.* (—s, *no pl.*) meal; eating.

essen [ˈɛsən], *v.a. irr.* eat, have a meal.

Essenz [ɛˈsɛnts], *f.* (—, *pl.* —en) essence.

Essig [ˈɛsɪç], *m.* (—s, *no pl.*) vinegar.

Eßlöffel [ˈɛslœfəl], *m.* (—s, *pl.* —) table-spoon.

Estland [ˈɛstlant], *n.* Estonia.

Estrade [ɛˈstraːdə], *f.* (—, *pl.* —n) platform.

Estrich [ˈɛstrɪç], *m.* (—s, *no pl.*) floor, flooring, plaster-floor.

etablieren [etaˈbliːrən], *v.a.* establish, set up (business).

Etagenwohnung [eˈtaːʒənvoːnuŋ], *f.* (—, *pl.* —en) flat; (*Am.*) apartment.

Etappe [eˈtapə], *f.* (—, *pl.* —n) stage; (*Mil.*) lines of communication.

Etat [eˈtaː], *m.* (—s, *pl.* —s) (*Parl.*) estimates, budget; (*Comm.*) statement, balance sheet.

ethisch [ˈeːtɪʃ], *adj.* ethical.

Etikett [etiˈkɛt], *n.* (—s, *pl.* —s) label, ticket, tag.

Etikette [etiˈkɛtə], *f.* (—, *no pl.*) etiquette; ceremonial.

etikettieren [etikeˈtiːrən], *v.a.* label.

etliche [ˈɛtlɪçə], *pl. adj. & pron.* some, several, sundry.

Etui [eˈtviː], *n.* (—s, *pl.* —s) small case, small box.

etwa [ˈɛtva], *adv.* nearly, about; perhaps, perchance, in some way.

etwaig [ˈɛtvaɪç], *adj.* possible, any, eventual.

etwas [ˈɛtvas], *indef. pron.* some, something. — *adj.* some, any. — *adv.* a little, somewhat.

Etzel [ˈɛtsəl], *m.* Attila.

euch [ɔyç], *pers. pron. pl. Dat. & Acc.* you, yourselves.

euer [ˈɔyər], *poss. adj.* your. — *poss. pron.* yours.

Eule [ˈɔylə], *f.* (—, *pl.* —n) owl.

eurige [ˈɔyrɪgə], *poss. pron. der, die, das* —, yours.

Europa [ɔyˈroːpa], *n.* Europe.

Euter [ˈɔytər], *n.* (—s, *pl.* —) udder.

evangelisch [evanˈgeːlɪʃ], *adj.* Evangelical, Protestant.

Evangelium [evanˈgeːljum], *n.* (—s, *pl.* —lien) gospel.

eventuell [evɛntuˈɛl], *adj.* possible.

ewig [ˈeːvɪç], *adj.* eternal; perpetual.

Ewigkeit [ˈeːvɪçkaɪt], *f.* (—, *pl.* —en) eternity.

explodieren [ɛksploˈdiːrən], *v.n.* explode; detonate.

exponieren [ɛkspoˈniːrən], *v.a.* set forth, explain at length.

Extemporale [ɛkstɛmpoˈraːlə], *n.* (—s, *pl.* —lien) unprepared exercise.

extrahieren [ɛkstraˈhiːrən], *v.a.* extract.

Extremitäten [ɛkstremiˈtɛːtən], *f. pl.* extremities.

F

F [ɛf], *n.* (—s, *pl.* —s) the letter F; (*Mus.*) F *Dur*, F major; F *Moll*, F minor.

Fabel [ˈfaːbəl], *f.* (—, *pl.* —n) fable; (*fig.*) tale, fiction; (*drama*) plot, story.

fabelhaft [ˈfaːbəlhaft], *adj.* fabulous; phenomenal, gorgeous.

fabeln [ˈfaːbəln], *v.n.* tell fables; talk nonsense.

Fabrik [faˈbriːk], *f.* (—, *pl.* —en) factory; plant, works.

Fabrikant [fabriˈkant], *m.* (—en, *pl.* —en) manufacturer.

fabrizieren [fabriˈtsiːrən], *v.a.* manufacture, make.

fabulieren [fabuˈliːrən], *v.n.* tell fables; (*fig.*) tell tall stories.

Fach [fax], *n.* (—s, *pl.* ̈er) compartment; pigeon-hole, drawer; (*fig.*) subject of study, department, branch.

Fachausdruck [ˈfaxausdruk], *m.* (—s, *pl.* ̈e) technical term.

Fächer

Fächer ['fɛçər], *m.* (—s, *pl.* —) fan.
Fächertaube ['fɛçərtaubə], *f.* (—, *pl.* —n) fantail.
Fachmann ['faxman], *m.* (—s, *pl.* ̈er *or* **Fachleute**) expert, specialist.
Fachschule ['faxfu:lə], *f.* (—, *pl.* —n) technical school.
fachsimpeln ['faxzɪmpəln], *v.n.* talk shop.
Fachwerk ['faxvɛrk], *n.* (—s, *no pl.*) timbered framework.
Fackel ['fakəl], *f.* (—, *pl.* —n) torch.
fade ['fa:də], *adj.* tasteless; boring, insipid.
Faden ['fa:dən], *m.* (—s, *pl.* ̈) thread; (*measure*) fathom.
fadenscheinig ['fa:dənfainiç], *adj.* threadbare.
Fagott [fa'gɔt], *n.* (—s, *pl.* —̈e) (*Mus.*) bassoon.
fähig ['fɛ:iç], *adj.* able, capable; talented, gifted, competent.
fahl [fa:l], *adj.* pale, sallow.
Fähnchen ['fɛ:nçən], *n.* (—s, *pl.* —) small banner; pennon; (*Mil.*) (*obs.*) small troop.
fahnden ['fa:ndən], *v.a.* search for (officially).
Fahne ['fa:nə], *f.* (—, *pl.* —n) flag, banner, standard, colours; (*weather*) vane; (*Typ.*) galley proof.
Fahnenflucht ['fa:nənfluxt], *f.* (—, *no pl.*) (*Mil.*) desertion.
Fähnrich ['fɛ:nriç], *m.* (—s, *pl.* —e) ensign.
Fahrbahn ['fa:rba:n], *f.* (—, *pl.* —en) traffic lane, roadway.
fahrbar ['fa:rba:r], *adj.* passable, navigable, negotiable.
Fähre ['fɛ:rə], *f.* (—, *pl.* —n) ferry, ferry-boat.
fahren ['fa:rən], *v.a. irr.* drive. — *v.n.* (*aux.* sein) (*vehicle*) ride (in), be driven; (*vessel*) sail; go, travel.
Fahrer ['fa:rər], *m.* (—s, *pl.* —) driver, chauffeur.
Fahrgast ['fa:rgast], *m.* (—s, *pl.* —̈e) passenger.
fahrig ['fa:riç], *adj.* absent-minded, giddy, thoughtless.
Fahrkarte ['fa:rkartə], *f.* (—, *pl.* —n) ticket.
fahrlässig ['fa:rlɛsiç], *adj.* negligent, careless.
Fährmann ['fɛ:rman], *m.* (—s, *pl.* —̈er) ferry-man.
Fahrplan ['fa:rpla:n], *m.* (—s, *pl.* —̈e) timetable, railway-guide.
fahrplanmäßig ['fa:rplanmɛ:siç], *adj.* according to the timetable, scheduled.
Fahrpreis ['fa:rprais], *m.* (—es, *pl.* —e) cost of ticket, fare.
Fahrrad ['fa:rra:t], *n.* (—s, *pl.* —̈er) cycle, bicycle.
Fahrschein ['fa:rfain], *m.* (—s, *pl.* —e) ticket.
Fahrstraße ['fa:rftrasə], *f.* (—, *pl.* —n) roadway.
Fahrstuhl ['fa:rftu:l], *m.* (—s, *pl.* —̈e) lift; (*Am.*) elevator.

Fahrt [fa:rt], *f.* (—, *pl.* —en) drive, ride, journey; (*sea*) voyage, cruise.
Fährte ['fɛ:rtə], *f.* (—, *pl.* —n) track, trace, trail.
Fahrzeug ['fa:rtsɔyk], *n.* (—s, *pl.* —e) vehicle, conveyance; vessel, craft.
faktisch ['faktif], *adj.* real, actual.
Faktor ['faktɔr], *m.* (—s, *pl.* —en) foreman, overseer, factor; (*Maths.*) factor, component part.
Faktura [fak'tu:ra], *f.* (—, *pl.* —ren) (*Comm.*) invoice.
fakturieren [faktu'ri:rən], *v.a.* (*Comm.*) invoice.
Fakultät [fakul'tɛ:t], *f.* (—, *pl.* —en) (*Univ.*) faculty.
fakultativ [fakulta'ti:f], *adj.* optional.
Falbel ['falbəl], *f.* (—, *pl.* —n) flounce, furbelow.
Falke ['falkə], *m.* (—n, *pl.* —n) (*Orn.*) falcon, hawk.
Fall [fal], *m.* (—s, *pl.* —̈e) fall, falling; case; (*Geog.*) decline, incline, gradient; (*fig.*) fall, decline, downfall, failure.
Fallbaum ['falbaum], *m.* (—s, *pl.* —̈e) tollbar, turnpike.
Fallbeil ['falbail], *n.* (—s, *pl.* —e) guillotine.
Fallbrücke ['falbrykə], *f.* (—, *pl.* —n) draw-bridge.
Falle ['falə], *f.* (—, *pl.* —n) trap, snare.
fallen ['falən], *v.n. irr.* (*aux.* sein) fall, drop; (*Mil.*) be killed.
fällen ['fɛlən], *v.a.* fell, cut down, hew down; *ein Urteil* —, (*Law*) pronounce judgment.
Fallensteller ['falənftɛlər], *m.* (—s, *pl.* —) trapper.
fallieren [fa'li:rən], *v.n.* become bankrupt.
fällig ['fɛliç], *adj.* due, payable.
Fälligkeit ['fɛliçkait], *f.* (—, *pl.* —en) (*Comm.*) maturity.
Fallobst ['falo:pst], *n.* (—es, *no pl.*) windfall (of fruit).
falls [fals], *conj.* in case, if.
Fallschirm ['falfirm], *m.* (—s, *pl.* —e) parachute.
Fallstrick ['falftrik], *m.* (—s, *pl.* —e) snare, trap.
Fallsucht ['falzuxt], *f.* (—, *no pl.*) (*Med.*) epilepsy.
Falltür ['falty:r], *f.* (—, *pl.* —en) trap-door.
Fällung ['fɛluŋ], *f.* (—, *pl.* —en) cutting down.
falsch [falf], *adj.* false, incorrect, wrong; disloyal; counterfeit.
fälschen ['fɛlfən], *v.a.* falsify, forge, tamper with.
Falschheit ['falfhait], *f.* (—, *pl.* —en) falsehood, deceit, disloyalty.
fälschlich ['fɛlfliç], *adv.* wrongly, falsely.
Fälschung ['fɛlfuŋ], *f.* (—, *pl.* —en) falsification; forgery.
Falte ['faltə], *f.* (—, *pl.* —n) fold, pleat; (*face*) wrinkle.
falten ['faltən], *v.a.* fold, plait, pleat; wrinkle.

Falter ['faltər], *m.* (—s, *pl.* —) (*Ent.*) butterfly.

-fältig [fɛltɪç], *suffix* (*following numbers*). -fold (*e.g.* vierfältig, fourfold).

Falz [falts], *m.* (—es, *pl.* —e) groove, notch; joint.

Falzbein ['faltsbaɪn], *n.* (—s, *pl.* —e) paper-folder, paper-knife.

Falzmaschine ['faltsmaʃiːnə], *f.* (—, *pl.* —n) folding-machine.

familiär [famil'jɛːr], *adj.* familiar, intimate.

Familie [fa'miːljə], *f.* (—, *pl.* —n) family.

famos [fa'moːs], *adj.* (*coll.*) excellent, splendid.

fanatisch [fa'naːtɪʃ], *adj.* fanatic(al), bigoted.

Fanatismus [fana'tɪsmʊs], *m.* (—, *no pl.*) fanaticism.

Fang [faŋ], *m.* (—es, *pl.* ⸚e) catch, capture; (*bird*) talon, claw.

fangen ['faŋən], *v.a. irr.* catch, seize.

Fangzahn ['faŋtsaːn], *m.* (—s, *pl.* ⸚e) fang, tusk.

Fant [fant], *m.* (—s, *pl.* —e) fop, cockscomb.

Farbe ['farbə], *f.* (—, *pl.* —n) colour, hue, paint, dye.

färben ['fɛrbən], *v.a.* dye, stain.

Farbenbrett ['farbənbrɛt], *n.* (—s, *pl.* —er) palette.

Farb(en)druck ['farpdrʊk, farbəndrʊk], *m.* (—s, *pl.* —e) colour-printing.

Farbenspiel ['farbənʃpiːl], *n.* (—s, *no pl.*) iridescence.

Färber ['fɛrbər], *m.* (—s, *pl.* —) dyer.

farbig ['farbɪç], *adj.* coloured.

Farbstift ['farpʃtɪft], *m.* (—s, *pl.* —e) crayon.

Farbstoff ['farpʃtɔf], *m.* (—es, *pl.* —e) dye.

Farbton ['farptoːn], *m.* (—s, *pl.* ⸚e) hue, tone, tinge, shade.

Farn [farn], *m.* (—s, *pl.* —e) (*Bot.*) fern.

Färse ['fɛrzə], *f.* (—, *pl.* —n) (*Zool.*) heifer.

Fasan [fa'zaːn], *m.* (—s, *pl.* —e) (*Orn.*) pheasant.

Fasching ['faʃɪŋ], *m.* (—s, *no pl.*) (Shrovetide) carnival.

Faschismus [fa'ʃɪsmʊs], *m.* (—s, *no pl.*) fascism.

Faselei [fa:zə'laɪ], *f.* (—, *pl.* —en) silly talk, drivel.

faseln ['fa:zəln], *v.n.* drivel.

Faser ['fa:zər], *f.* (—, *pl.* —n) thread; string; fibre, filament.

fasern ['fa:zərn], *v.n.* fray.

Faß [fas], *n.* (—sses, *pl.* ⸚sser) barrel, vat, tun, tub, cask, keg; *Bier vom —*, draught beer; *Wein vom —*, wine from the wood.

Fassade [fa'sa:də], *f.* (—, *pl.* —n) façade.

faßbar ['fasba:r], *adj.* tangible.

Faßbinder ['fasbɪndər], *m.* (—s, *pl.* —) cooper.

fassen ['fasən], *v.a.* seize, take hold of, grasp; (*jewels*) set; contain, hold. — *v.r.* (*aux.* haben) *sich —*, compose o.s.; *sich kurz —*, be brief.

faßlich ['faslɪç], *adj.* comprehensible, understandable.

Fasson [fa's5], *f.* (—, *pl.* —s) fashion; (*fig.*) cut, style.

Fassung ['fasʊŋ], *f.* (—, *pl.* —en) (*jewels*) setting; (*speech*) wording, version; (*fig.*) composure.

fassungslos ['fasʊŋsloːs], *adj.* bewildered, disconcerted; distraught, speechless.

fast [fast], *adv.* almost, nearly.

fasten ['fastən], *v.n.* fast.

Fastenzeit ['fastəntsaɪt], *f.* (—, *pl.* —en) time of fasting; Lent.

Fastnacht ['fastnaxt], *f.* (—, *no pl.*) Shrove Tuesday; Shrovetide.

fauchen ['fauxən], *v.n.* spit, hiss.

faul [faul], *adj.* (*food*) rotten, putrid, decayed; (*persons*) lazy, idle.

Fäule ['fɔylə], *f.* (—, *no pl.*) rot.

faulen ['faulən], *v.n.* (*aux.* sein) rot.

faulenzen ['faulɛntsən], *v.n.* laze, idle.

Faulenzer ['faulɛntsər], *m.* (—s, *pl.* —) idler, sluggard, lazybones.

Faulenzerei ['faulɛntsərai], *f.* (—, *pl.* —en) idleness, laziness.

Faulheit ['faulhait], *f.* (—, *no pl.*) idleness, laziness, sluggishness.

faulig ['faulɪç], *adj.* putrid, rotten.

Fäulnis ['fɔylnɪs], *f.* (—, *no pl.*) rottenness, putridity.

Faust [faust], *f.* (—, *pl.* ⸚e) fist.

Fäustchen ['fɔystçən], *n.* (—s, *pl.* —) small fist; *sich ins — lachen*, laugh in o.'s sleeve.

Faustkampf ['faustkampf], *m.* (—es, *pl.* ⸚e) boxing (match).

Faxen ['faksən], *f. pl.* foolery; — *machen*, play the buffoon.

Fazit ['fatsɪt], *n.* (—s, *no pl.*) sum, amount.

Februar ['fe:brua:r], *m.* (—s, *no pl.*) February.

fechten ['fɛçtən], *v.n. irr.* fight; fence; (*fig.*) beg.

Feder ['fe:dər], *f.* (—, *pl.* —n) (*bird*) feather; (*hat*) plume; (*writing*) pen; (*antique*) quill; (*Tech.*) spring.

Federball ['fe:dərbal], *m.* (—s, *pl.* ⸚e) shuttle-cock.

federig ['fe:dərɪç], *adj.* feathery; (*Tech.*) springy, resilient.

Federlesen(s) ['fe:dərle:zən(s)], *n.* (—s, *no pl.*) *nicht viel — machen*, make short work of.

Fee [fe:], *f.* (—, *pl.* —n) fairy.

feenhaft ['fe:ənhaft], *adj.* fairy-like, magical.

Fegefeuer ['fe:gəfɔyər], *n.* (—s, *no pl.*) purgatory.

fegen ['fe:gən], *v.a.* clean, sweep. — *v.n.* (*aux.* sein) tear along.

Fehde ['fe:də], *f.* (—, *pl.* —n) feud, quarrel.

Fehdehandschuh ['fe:dəhantʃu:], *m.* (—s, *pl.* —e) gauntlet.

fehlbar ['fe:lbar], *adj.* fallible.
Fehlbetrag ['fe:lbətra:k], *m.* (—s, *pl.* ⸚e) deficit.
fehlen ['fe:lən], *v.a.* miss. — *v.n.* err, do wrong; be absent; be wanting; *er fehlt mir*, I miss him.
Fehler ['fe:lər], *m.* (—s, *pl.* —) fault, defect; mistake, error.
Fehlgeburt ['fe:lgəburt], *f.* (—, *pl.* —en) miscarriage.
Fehlschlag ['fe:lʃla:k], *m.* (—s, *pl.* ⸚e) failure, disappointment.
feien ['faɪən], *v.a. einen — gegen*, charm s.o. against; *gefeit*, proof.
Feier ['faɪər], *f.* (—, *pl.* —n) celebration, festival, holiday, festive day.
Feierabend ['faɪəra:bənt], *m.* (—s, *pl.* —e) time for leaving off work; — *machen*, knock off (work).
feierlich ['faɪərlɪç], *adj.* festive, solemn, stately.
feiern ['faɪərn], *v.a.* celebrate; honour, praise. — *v.n.* rest from work.
Feiertag ['faɪərta:k], *m.* (—s, *pl.* —e) holiday, festive day.
feig [faɪk], *adj.* cowardly.
Feige ['faɪgə], *f.* (—, *pl.* —n) (*Bot.*) fig.
Feigheit ['faɪkhaɪt], *f.* (—, *pl.* —en) cowardice, cowardliness.
Feigling ['faɪklɪŋ], *m.* (—s, *pl.* —e) coward.
Feigwurz ['faɪkvurts], *m.* (—es, *no pl.*) (*Bot.*) fennel.
feil [faɪl], *adj.* (*obs.*) for sale; venal.
feilbieten ['faɪlbi:tən], *v.a.* offer for sale.
Feile ['faɪlə], *f.* (—, *pl.* —n) file.
feilen ['faɪlən], *v.a.* file.
feilhalten ['faɪlhaltən], *v.a.* have for sale, be ready to sell.
feilschen ['faɪlʃən], *v.n.* bargain, haggle.
Feilspäne ['faɪlʃpɛ:nə], *m. pl.* filings.
fein [faɪn], *adj.* fine; neat, pretty, nice; delicate; (*clothes*) elegant; (*behaviour*) refined, polished.
Feinbäckerei ['faɪnbɛkəraɪ], *f.* (—, *pl.* —en) confectioner's shop.
Feind [faɪnt], *m.* (—es, *pl.* —e) enemy, foe, adversary.
Feindschaft ['faɪntʃaft], *f.* (—, *pl.* —en) enmity, hostility.
feindselig ['faɪntze:lɪç], *adj.* hostile, malignant.
feinfühlend ['faɪnfy:lənt], *adj.* delicate, sensitive.
Feinheit ['faɪnhaɪt], *f.* (—, *pl.* —en) fineness, elegance, politeness, delicacy.
Feinschmecker ['faɪnʃmɛkər], *m.* (—s, *pl.* —), gourmet.
Feinsliebchen ['faɪnsˈli:pçən], *n.* (—s, *pl.* —) (*Poet. obs.*) sweetheart.
feist [faɪst], *adj.* fat, obese.
Feld [fɛlt], *n.* (—es, *pl.* —er) field, plain; (*chess*) square; (*fig.*) sphere, province.
Feldbett ['fɛltbɛt], *n.* (—s, *pl.* —en) camp-bed.
Feldherr ['fɛlthɛr], *m.* (—n, *pl.* —en) commander, general.

Feldmesser ['fɛltmɛsər], *m.* (—s, *pl.* —) land-surveyor.
Feldscher ['fɛltʃe:r], *m.* (—s, *pl.* —e) army-surgeon.
Feldstecher ['fɛltʃtɛçər], *m.* (—s, *pl.* —) field-glass(es).
Feldwebel ['fɛltve:bəl], *m.* (—s, *pl.* —) sergeant-major.
Feldzug ['fɛlttsu:k], *m.* (—es, *pl.* ⸚e) campaign, expedition.
Felge ['fɛlgə], *f.* (—, *pl.* —n) (*wheel*) felloe, felly, rim.
Fell [fɛl], *n.* (—s, *pl.* —e) hide, skin, pelt.
Felsabhang ['fɛlsaphaŋ], *m.* (—s, *pl.* ⸚e) rocky slope.
Felsen ['fɛlzən], *m.* (—s, *pl.* —) rock, cliff.
Felsengebirge ['fɛlzəngəbɪrgə], *n.* Rocky Mountains.
Felsenriff ['fɛlzənrɪf], *n.* (—s, *pl.* —e) reef.
felsig ['fɛlzɪç], *adj.* rocky.
Feme ['fe:mə], *f.* (—, *pl.* —n) secret tribunal.
Fenchel ['fɛnçəl], *m.* (—s, *no pl.*) (*Bot.*) fennel.
Fenster ['fɛnstər], *n.* (—s, *pl.* —) window.
Fensterbrett ['fɛnstərbrɛt], *n.* (—s, *pl.* —er) window-sill.
Fensterflügel ['fɛnstərfly:gəl], *m.* (—s, *pl.* —) (window) casement.
Fensterladen ['fɛnstərla:dən], *m.* (—s, *pl.* ⸚) shutter.
Fensterscheibe ['fɛnstərʃaɪbə], *f.* (—, *pl.* —n) pane.
Ferien ['fe:rjən], *pl.* holidays.
Ferkel ['fɛrkəl], *n.* (—s, *pl.* —) young pig, piglet.
Fermate [fɛrˈma:tə], *f.* (—, *pl.* —n) (*Mus.*) pause, fermata.
fern [fɛrn], *adj.* far, distant, remote.
Fernbleiben ['fɛrnblaɪbən], *n.* (—s, *no pl.*) absence.
Ferne ['fɛrnə], *f.* (—, *pl.* —n) distance, remoteness.
ferner ['fɛrnər], *adv.* further, furthermore, moreover.
fernerhin ['fɛrnərhɪn], *adv.* henceforth.
Ferngespräch ['fɛrngəʃprɛx], *n.* (—s, *pl.* —e) long-distance telephone call, trunk call.
Fernglas ['fɛrngla:s], *n.* (—es, *pl.* ⸚er) binoculars.
fernhalten ['fɛrnhaltən], *v.a. irr.* keep away.
fernher ['fɛrnhe:r], *adv. von —*, from afar.
fernliegen ['fɛrnli:gən], *v.n. irr.* be far from.
Fernrohr ['fɛrnro:r], *n.* (—s, *pl.* —e) telescope.
Fernschreiber ['fɛrnʃraɪbər], *m.* (—s, *pl.* —) teleprinter.
Fernsehen ['fɛrnze:ən], *n.* (—s, *no pl.*) television.
fernsehen ['fɛrnze:ən], *v.n. irr.* watch television.

Fernsehgerät ['fɛrnze:gərɛ:t], n. (—s, —e) television set.

Fernsprechamt ['fɛrnʃprɛçamt], n. (—s, pl. ⸚er) telephone exchange.

Fernsprecher ['fɛrnʃprɛçər], m. (—s, pl. —) telephone.

Fernstehende ['fɛrnʃte:əndə], m. (—n, pl. —n) outsider.

Fernverkehr ['fɛrnfɛrke:r], m. (—s, no pl.) long-distance traffic.

Ferse ['fɛrzə], f. (—, pl. —n) heel.

Fersengeld ['fɛrzəngɛlt], n. (—s, no pl.) — geben, take to o.'s heels.

fertig ['fɛrtiç], adj. ready, finished; (coll.) worn-out, ruined, done for.

Fertigkeit ['fɛrtiçkait], f. (—, pl. —en) dexterity, skill.

Fes [fɛs], n. (—, pl. —) (Mus.) F flat.

fesch [fɛʃ], adj. smart, stylish; (dial.) good-looking.

Fessel ['fɛsəl], f. (—, pl. —n) fetter, shackle.

Fesselballon ['fɛsəlbal3], m. (—s, pl. —s) captive balloon.

Fesselbein ['fɛsəlbain], n. (—s, pl. —e) pastern-joint.

fesseln ['fɛsəln], v.a. fetter, shackle, chain; (fig.) captivate.

Fest [fɛst], n. (—es, pl. —e) feast, festival.

fest [fɛst], adj. fast, firm; solid, hard; sound; fixed; constant, steadfast.

Feste ['fɛstə], f. (—, pl. —n) fortress, stronghold.

festigen ['fɛstigən], v.a. make firm; strengthen.

Festland ['fɛstlant], n. (—es, pl. ⸚er) continent.

festlich ['fɛstliç], adj. festive, solemn.

festmachen ['fɛstmaxən], v.a. fasten.

Festnahme ['fɛstna:mə], f. (—, no pl.) apprehension, arrest.

festnehmen ['fɛstne:mən], v.a. irr. seize, arrest.

Festrede ['fɛstre:də], f. (—, pl. —n) formal address.

festschnallen ['fɛstʃnalən], v.a. buckle on, fasten.

Festschrift ['fɛstʃrift], f. (—, pl. —en) commemorative volume (in honour of a person or an occasion).

festsetzen ['fɛstzɛtsən], v.a. fix, decree.

Festspiel ['fɛstʃpi:l], n. (—s, pl. —e) festival (play).

feststehen ['fɛstʃte:ən], v.n. irr. stand firm; es steht fest, it is certain.

feststellen ['fɛstʃtɛlən], v.a. ascertain; state; find; determine; diagnose; establish.

Festtag ['fɛstta:k], m. (—s, pl. —e) feast-day, holiday.

Festung ['fɛstuŋ], f. (—, pl. —en) fortress, stronghold, citadel.

festziehen ['fɛsttsi:ən], v.a. irr. tighten.

Festzug ['fɛsttsu:k], m. (—s, pl. ⸚e) procession.

Fett [fɛt], n. (—s, pl. —e) fat, grease, lard.

fett [fɛt], adj. fat, greasy.

fettartig ['fɛtartiç], adj. fatty.

fetten ['fɛtən], v.a. oil, grease.

Fettfleck ['fɛtflɛk], m. (—s, pl. —e) spot of grease.

fettgedruckt ['fɛtgədrukt], adj. in heavy type.

fetthaltig ['fɛthaltiç], adj. greasy; adipose.

fettig ['fɛtiç], adj. greasy.

fettleibig ['fɛtlaibiç], adj. corpulent, obese.

Fetzen ['fɛtsən], m. (—s, pl. —) piece, rag, tatter, shred.

feucht [fɔyçt], adj. moist; (weather) muggy, wet; (room) damp.

Feuchtigkeit ['fɔyçtiçkait], f. (—, no pl.) moisture, humidity, dampness, wetness.

feudal [fɔy'da:l], adj. feudal; (coll.) distinguished, magnificent.

Feuer ['fɔyər], n. (—s, pl. —) fire; (jewels) brilliancy; (fig.) ardour, passion.

feuerbeständig ['fɔyərbəʃtɛndiç], adj. fire-proof.

Feuerbestattung ['fɔyərbəʃtatuŋ], f. (—, pl. —en) cremation.

Feuereifer ['fɔyəraifər], m. (—s, no pl.) ardour.

feuerfest ['fɔyərfɛst], adj. fire-proof, incombustible.

feuergefährlich ['fɔyərgəfɛ:rliç], adj. inflammable.

Feuerlilie ['fɔyərli:ljə], f. (—, pl. —n) tiger lily.

Feuermal ['fɔyərma:l], n. (—s, pl. —e) burn, birth-mark.

Feuermauer ['fɔyərmauər], f. (—, pl. —n) fire-proof wall, party-wall.

Feuermelder ['fɔyərmɛldər], m. (—s, pl. —) fire-alarm.

feuern ['fɔyərn], v.a. (Mil.) fire, discharge; (coll.) fire, sack.

Feuerprobe ['fɔyərpro:bə], f. (—, pl. —n) ordeal by fire.

Feuerrad ['fɔyərra:t], n. (—s, pl. ⸚er) Catherine wheel.

Feuerrohr ['fɔyərro:r], n. (—s, pl. —e) gun, matchlock.

Feuersbrunst ['fɔyərsbrunst], f. (—, pl. ⸚e) (rare) fire, conflagration.

Feuerspritze ['fɔyərʃpritsə], f. (—, pl. —n) fire-engine.

Feuerstein ['fɔyərʃtain], m. (—s, no pl.) flint.

Feuertaufe ['fɔyərtaufə], f. (—, pl. —n) baptism of fire.

Feuerwarte ['fɔyərvartə], f. (—, pl. —en) beacon; lighthouse.

Feuerwehr ['fɔyərve:r], f. (—, no pl.) fire-brigade.

Feuerwerk ['fɔyərvɛrk], n. (—, no pl.) fireworks.

Feuerwerkskunst ['fɔyərvɛrkskunst], f. (—, no pl.) pyrotechnics.

Feuerzange ['fɔyərtsaŋə], f. (—, pl. —n) fire-tongs.

Feuerzeug ['fɔyərtsɔyk], n. (—s, pl. —e) match-box; cigarette-lighter.

feurig ['fɔyriç], adj. fiery, burning; (fig.) ardent, impassioned, fervent; (wine) heady.

Fiaker

Fiaker [fi'akər], *m.* (**—s,** *pl.* **—)** (*Austr.*) cab, hansom; (*Am.*) coach.

Fiasko [fi'asko:], *n.* (**—s,** *pl.* **—s**) failure.

Fibel ['fi:bəl], *f.* (**—,** *pl.* **—n**) primer, spelling-book.

Fiber ['fi:bər], *f.* (**—,** *pl.* **—n**) fibre.

Fichte ['fiçtə], *f.* (**—,** *pl.* **—n**) (*Bot.*) pine, pine-tree.

fidel [fi'de:l], *adj.* merry, jolly.

Fidibus ['fi:dibus], *m.* (**—ses,** *pl.* **—se**) spill, fidibus.

Fidschi ['fidʒi:], Fiji.

Fieber ['fi:bər], *n.* (**—s,** *no pl.*) fever.

fieberhaft ['fi:bərhaft], *adj.* feverish, vehement.

fieberig ['fi:bəriç], *adj.* feverish, racked by fever.

Fieberkälte ['fi:bərkɛltə], *f.* (**—,** *no pl.*) chill, shivering (fit).

fiebern ['fi:bərn], *v.n.* have a fever; (*fig.*) rave.

fiebrig ['fi:briç], *see* **fieberig**.

Fiedel ['fi:dəl], *f.* (**—,** *pl.* **—n**) (*Mus.*) fiddle, violin.

Figur [fi'gu:r], *f.* (**—,** *pl.* **—en**) figure, statue, sculpture; chessman.

figürlich [fi'gy:rliç], *adj.* figurative.

Filet [fi'le:], *n.* (**—s,** *pl.* **—s**) netting, net-work; (*meat*) fillet.

Filiale [fi'ja:lə], *f.* (**—,** *pl.* **—n**) branch, branch-establishment, branch-office.

Filigran [fili'gra:n], *n.* (**—s,** *no pl.*) filigree.

Film [film], *m.* (**—s,** *pl.* **—e**) film; (*motion*) picture.

Filter ['filtər], *m.* (**—s,** *pl.* **—**) filter.

filtrieren [fil'tri:rən], *v.a.* filter.

Filz [filts], *m.* (**—es,** *pl.* **—e**) felt; (*fig.*) niggard, miser, skinflint.

Filzlaus ['filtslaus], *f.* (**—,** *pl.* **⁝e**) crab-louse.

Finanzamt [fi'nantsamt], *n.* (**—s,** *pl.* **⁝er**) income-tax office; revenue-office.

Finanzen [fi'nantsən], *f. pl.* finances, revenue.

Findelkind ['findəlkint], *n.* (**—s,** *pl.* **—er**) foundling.

finden ['findən], *v.a. irr.* find. — *v.r. sich —, das wird sich —,* we shall see.

Finder ['findər], *m.* (**—s,** *pl.* **—**) finder.

findig ['findiç], *adj.* resourceful, ingenious.

Findling ['fintliŋ], *m.* (**—s,** *pl.* **—e**) foundling.

Finger ['fiŋər], *m.* (**—s,** *pl.* **—**) finger.

Fingerabdruck ['fiŋərapdruk], *m.* (**—s,** *pl.* **⁝e**) finger-print.

fingerfertig ['fiŋərfɛrtiç], *adj.* nimble-fingered.

Fingerhut ['fiŋərhu:t], *m.* (**—s,** *pl.* **⁝e**) thimble; (*Bot.*) foxglove.

fingern ['fiŋərn], *v.a.* touch with the fingers, finger.

Fingersatz ['fiŋərzats], *m.* (**—es,** *pl.* **⁝e**) (*Mus.*) fingering.

Fingerspitze ['fiŋərʃpitsə], *f.* (**—,** *pl.* **—n**) finger-tip.

Fingerzeig ['fiŋərtsaik], *m.* (**—s,** *pl.* **—e**) hint.

fingieren [fiŋ'gi:rən], *v.a.* sham.

fingiert [fiŋ'gi:rt], *adj.* fictitious.

Fink [fiŋk], *m.* (**—en,** *pl.* **—en**) (*Orn.*) finch.

Finne (1) ['finə], *m.* (**—n,** *pl.* **—n**) Finn.

Finne (2) ['finə], *f.* (**—,** *pl.* **—n**) pimple; (*fish*) fin.

finnig ['finiç], *adj.* pimpled; (*fish*) finny.

Finnland ['finlant], *n.* Finland.

finster ['finstər], *adj.* dark, obscure; (*fig.*) gloomy, sinister.

Finsternis ['finstərnis], *f.* (**—,** *no pl.*) darkness, gloom.

Finte ['fintə], *f.* (**—,** *pl.* **—n**) feint; (*fig.*) pretence, trick.

Firlefanz ['firləfants], *m.* (**—es,** *no pl.*) foolery.

Firma ['firma], *f.* (**—,** *pl.* **—men**) (*business*) firm, company.

Firmung ['firmuŋ], *f.* (**—,** *pl.* **—en**) (*Eccl.*) confirmation.

Firnis ['firnis], *m.* (**—ses,** *pl.* **—se**) varnish.

firnissen ['firnisən], *v.a.* varnish.

First [first], *m.* (**—s,** *pl.* **—e**) (*house*) roof-ridge; (*mountain*) top.

Fis [fis], *n.* (**—,** *pl.* **—**) (*Mus.*) F sharp.

Fisch [fiʃ], *m.* (**—es,** *pl.* **—e**) fish.

Fischadler ['fiʃa:dlər], *m.* (**—s,** *pl.* **—**) osprey, sea-eagle.

Fischbein ['fiʃbain], *n.* (**—s,** *no pl.*) whalebone.

fischen ['fiʃən], *v.a., v.n.* fish, angle.

Fischer ['fiʃər], *m.* (**—s,** *pl.* **—**) fisherman, fisher.

Fischerei [fiʃə'rai], *f.* (**—,** *no pl.*) fishing; fishery.

Fischergerät ['fiʃərgərɛ:t], *n.* (**—s,** *pl.* **—e**) fishing-tackle.

Fischgräte ['fiʃgrɛːtə], *f.* (**—,** *pl.* **—n**) fish-bone.

Fischkelle ['fiʃkɛlə], *f.* (**—,** *pl.* **—n**) fish-slice.

Fischlaich ['fiʃlaiç], *m.* (**—s,** *no pl.*) spawn.

Fischmilch ['fiʃmilç], *f.* (**—,** *no pl.*) soft roe, milt.

Fischotter ['fiʃɔtər], *m.* (**—s,** *pl.* **—n**) common otter.

Fischreiher ['fiʃraiər], *m.* (**—s,** *pl.* **—**) (*Orn.*) heron.

Fischreuse ['fiʃrɔyzə], *f.* (**—,** *pl.* **—n**) bow-net; weir.

Fischrogen ['fiʃro:gən], *m.* (**—s,** *no pl.*) roe.

Fischschuppe ['fiʃʃupə], *f.* (**—,** *pl.* **—n**) scale.

Fischtran ['fiʃtra:n], *m.* (**—s,** *no pl.*) train-oil.

Fischzucht ['fiʃtsuxt], *f.* (**—,** *no pl.*) fish-breeding, pisciculture.

Fiskus ['fiskus], *m.* (**—,** *pl.* **—ken**) Treasury, Exchequer.

Fisole [fi'zo:lə], *f.* (**—,** *pl.* **—n**) (*Austr.*) French bean.

flink

Fistelstimme ['fɪstəlʃtɪmə], *f.* (—, *no pl.*) (*Mus.*) falsetto.

Fittich ['fɪtɪç], *m.* (—es, *pl.* —e) (*Poet.*) wing, pinion.

fix [fɪks], *adj.* quick, sharp; — *und fertig,* quite ready.

Fixum ['fɪksum], *n.* (—s, *pl.* —xa) fixed amount; regular salary.

flach [flax], *adj.* flat, plain, smooth, level; (*water*) shallow.

Fläche ['flɛçə], *f.* (—, *pl.* —n) plain; (*Maths.*) plane; (*crystal*) face.

Flächeninhalt ['flɛçənɪnhalt], *m.* (—s, *no pl.*) area.

Flächenmaß ['flɛçənmaːs], *n.* (—es, *pl.* —e) square-measure.

Flächenraum ['flɛçənraum], *m.* (—es, *no pl.*) surface area.

Flachheit ['flaxhaɪt], *f.* (—, *no pl.*) flatness; (*fig.*) shallowness.

Flachs [flaks], *m.* (—es, *no pl.*) flax.

flackern ['flakərn], *v.n.* flare, flicker.

Fladen ['flaːdən], *m.* (—s, *pl.* —) flat cake; cow-dung.

Flagge ['flagə], *f.* (—, *pl.* —n) flag.

Flame ['flaːmə], *m.* (—n, *pl.* —n) Fleming.

flämisch ['flɛːmɪʃ], *adj.* Flemish.

Flamme ['flamə], *f.* (—, *pl.* —n) flame; blaze.

flammen ['flamən], *v.n.* flame, blaze, sparkle.

Flammeri ['flaməːri], *m.* (—s, *pl.* —s) blanc-mange.

Flandern ['flandərn], *n.* Flanders.

Flanell [fla'nɛl], *m.* (—s, *pl.* —e) flannel.

Flaneur [fla'nøːr], *m.* (—s, *pl.* —e) lounger, stroller.

flanieren [fla'niːrən], *v.n.* lounge, stroll.

Flanke ['flaŋkə], *f.* (—, *pl.* —n) flank; *in die — fallen,* (*Mil.*) attack in the flank.

Flasche ['flaʃə], *f.* (—, *pl.* —en) bottle, flask.

Flaschenzug ['flaʃəntsuːk], *m.* (—es, *pl.* —e) pulley.

flatterhaft ['flatərhaft], *adj.* fickle, inconstant, flighty.

flattern ['flatərn], *v.n.* flutter.

flau [flau], *adj.* insipid, stale; (*fig.*) dull.

Flaum [flaum], *m.* (—s, *no pl.*) down.

Flausch [flauʃ], *m.* (—es, *no pl.*) pilot-cloth.

Flaute ['flautə], *f.* (—, *pl.* —n) (*Nav.*) calm; (*fig.*) (*Comm.*) depression.

Flechte ['flɛçtə], *f.* (—, *pl.* —n) twist, plait, braid; (*Med.*) eruption, ringworm; (*Bot.*) lichen.

flechten ['flɛçtən], *v.a. irr.* plait; wreathe.

Flechtwerk ['flɛçtvɛrk], *n.* (—s, *no pl.*) wicker-work, basketry.

Fleck [flɛk], *m.* (—s, *pl.* —e) spot; place, piece (of ground); (*fig.*) stain, blemish.

Flecken ['flɛkən], *m.* (—s, *pl.* —) market town, small town.

fleckenlos ['flɛkənloːs], *adj.* spotless.

fleckig ['flɛkɪç], *adj.* spotted, speckled.

Fledermaus ['fleːdərmaus], *f.* (—, *pl.* —e) (*Zool.*) bat.

Flederwisch ['fleːdərvɪʃ], *m.* (—es, *pl.* —e) feather-duster.

Flegel ['fleːgəl], *m.* (—s, *pl.* —) flail; (*fig.*) boor.

flegelhaft ['fleːgəlhaft], *adj.* boorish, churlish, rude.

Flegeljahre ['fleːgəljaːrə], *n. pl.* years of indiscretion; teens, adolescence.

flehen ['fleːən], *v.a., v.n.* implore, supplicate, entreat.

Fleisch [flaɪʃ], *n.* (—es, *no pl.*) (raw) flesh; (*for cooking*) meat; (*fruit*) pulp.

Fleischbrühe ['flaɪʃbryːə], *f.* (—, *pl.* —n) broth, beef-tea.

Fleischer ['flaɪʃər], *m.* (—s, *pl.* —) butcher.

fleischfressend ['flaɪʃfrɛsənt], *adj.* carnivorous.

Fleischhacker ['flaɪʃhakər], **Fleischhauer** ['flaɪʃhauər], *m.* (—s, *pl.* —) butcher.

fleischlich ['flaɪʃlɪç], *adj.* fleshly, carnal.

fleischlos ['flaɪʃloːs], *adj.* vegetarian.

Fleischpastete ['flaɪʃpasteːtə], *f.* (—, *pl.* —n) meat-pie.

Fleiß [flaɪs], *m.* (—es, *no pl.*) diligence, assiduity, industry.

fleißig ['flaɪsɪç], *adj.* diligent, assiduous, industrious, hard-working.

fletschen ['flɛtʃən], *v.a. die Zähne —,* show o.'s teeth.

Flicken ['flɪkən], *m.* (—s, *pl.* —) patch.

flicken ['flɪkən], *v.a.* patch, repair, mend; (*shoes*) cobble; (*stockings*) darn.

Flieder ['fliːdər], *m.* (—s, *pl.* —) (*Bot.*) elder, lilac.

Fliege ['fliːgə], *f.* (—, *pl.* —n) (*Ent.*) fly; (*beard*) imperial.

fliegen ['fliːgən], *v.n. irr.* (*aux.* sein) fly; (*coll.*) get the sack, be fired. — *v.a.* fly, pilot (an aircraft).

Flieger ['fliːgər], *m.* (—s, *pl.* —) airman, aviator; pilot.

fliehen ['fliːən], *v.n. irr.* (*aux.* sein) flee, run away; *zu einem —,* take refuge with s.o. — *v.a. irr.* avoid, shun (s.o.).

Fliehkraft ['fliːkraft], *f.* (—, *no pl.*) centrifugal force.

Fliese ['fliːzə], *f.* (—, *pl.* —n) floor-tile, flagstone.

Fließband ['fliːsbant], *n.* (—(e)s, *pl.* —er) (*Ind.*) assembly line.

fließen ['fliːsən], *v.n. irr.* (*aux.* sein) flow.

Fließpapier ['fliːspapiːr], *n.* (—s, *no pl.*) blotting-paper.

Flimmer ['flɪmər], *m.* (—s, *no pl.*) glittering, sparkling, glimmer.

flimmern ['flɪmərn], *v.n.* glisten, glitter.

flink [flɪŋk], *adj.* brisk, agile, quick, sharp, nimble.

73

Flinte ['flɪntə], f. (—, pl. —n) gun, musket, rifle.

Flitter ['flɪtər], m. (—s, no pl.) tinsel, spangle, frippery.

Flitterwochen ['flɪtərvɔxən], f. pl. honeymoon.

flitzen ['flɪtsən], v.n. (aux. sein) vorbei —, flit or rush past, dash along.

Flocke ['flɔkə], f. (—, pl. —n) (snow) flake; (wool) flock.

Floh [flo:], m. (—s, pl. ⸚e) (Ent.) flea.

Flor [flo:r], m. (—s, pl. —e) bloom; gauze, crape; in —, blossoming, blooming.

Florenz [flo'rɛnts], n. Florence.

Florett [flo'rɛt], n. (—s, pl. —e) (fencing) foil.

florieren [flo'ri:rən], v.n. flourish.

Florstrumpf ['flo:rʃtrumpf], m. (—s, pl. ⸚e) lisle stocking.

Floskel ['flɔskəl], f. (—, pl. —n) rhetorical ornament; oratorical flourish; phrase.

Floß [flo:s], n. (—es, pl. ⸚e) raft.

Flosse ['flɔsə], f. (—, pl. —n) fin.

flößen ['flo:sən], v.a. float.

Flößer ['flo:sər], m. (—s, pl. —) raftsman.

Flöte ['flo:tə], f. (—, pl. —n) (Mus.) flute.

Flötenzug ['flo:təntsu:k], m. (—es, pl. ⸚e) (organ) flute-stop.

flott [flɔt], adj. (Naut.) afloat, floating; (fig.) gay, jolly, lively, smart; — leben, lead a fast life.

Flotte ['flɔtə], f. (—, pl. —n) fleet, navy.

Flottille [flɔ'tiljə], f. (—, pl. —n) flotilla, squadron.

Flöz [flo:ts], n. (—es, pl. —e) layer, stratum; (coal) seam.

Fluch [flu:x], m. (—es, pl. ⸚e) curse, spell; (verbal) curse, oath, swearword.

fluchen ['flu:xən], v.n. curse, swear.

Flucht [fluxt], f. (—, pl. —en) flight, fleeing; suite (of rooms).

flüchten ['flʏçtən], v.n. (aux. sein), v.r. flee, run away, escape.

flüchtig ['flʏçtɪç], adj. fugitive; (Chem.) volatile; (fig.) superficial; evanescent; hasty; slight.

Flüchtling ['flʏçtlɪŋ], m. (—s, pl. —e) fugitive, refugee.

Flug [flu:k], m. (—s, pl. ⸚e) (Aviat.) flight.

Flugblatt ['flu:kblat], n. (—s, pl. ⸚er) broadsheet, leaflet.

Flügel ['fly:gəl], m. (—s, pl. —) wing; (Mus.) grand piano; (door) leaf.

Flügelschlag ['fly:gəlʃla:k], m. (—s, pl. ⸚e) wing-stroke.

Flügeltür ['fly:gəlty:r], f. (—, pl. —en) folding-door.

flügge ['flʏgə], adj. fledged.

Flughafen ['flu:kha:fən], m. (—s, pl. ⸚) airport; aerodrome.

Flugpost ['flu:kpɔst], f. (—, no pl.) air mail.

flugs [fluks], adv. quickly, instantly; (Lit., obs.) anon.

Flugsand ['flu:kzant], m. (—s, no pl.) quicksand, drifting sand.

Flugzeug ['flu:ktsɔyk], m. (—s, pl. —e) aeroplane; (Am.) airplane.

Flugzeugführer ['flu:ktsɔykfy:rər], m. (—s, pl. —) (Aviat.) pilot.

Fluidum ['flu:idum], n. (—s, pl. —da) fluid; (fig.) atmosphere.

Flunder ['flundər], f. (—, pl. —n) (fish) flounder.

Flunkerer ['fluŋkərər], m. (—s, pl. —) (coll.) fibber, story-teller.

Flur (1) [flu:r], f. (—, pl. —en) field, plain; auf weiter —, in the open.

Flur (2) [flu:r], m. (—s, pl. —e) (house) hall, vestibule; corridor.

Flurschaden ['flu:rʃa:dən], m. (—s, pl. ⸚) damage to crops.

Fluß [flus], m. (—sses, pl. ⸚sse) river, stream; flow, flowing; flux.

Flußbett ['flusbet], n. (—s, pl. —en) channel, riverbed.

flüssig ['flʏsɪç], adj. fluid, liquid; —e Gelder, ready cash; liquid assets.

flüstern ['flʏstərn], v.a. whisper.

Flut [flu:t], f. (—, pl. —en) flood; high-tide, high water; torrent; deluge.

fluten ['flu:tən], v.n. flow.

Focksegel ['fɔkse:gəl], n. (—s, pl. —) foresail.

Fockmast ['fɔkmast], m. (—s, pl. —en) foremast.

Föderalismus [fo:dəra'lismus], m. (—, no pl.) federalism.

Fohlen ['fo:lən], n. (—s, pl. —) foal.

fohlen ['fo:lən], v.n. foal.

Föhn [fo:n], m. (—s, pl. —e) (warm) Alpine wind.

Föhre ['fo:rə], f. (—, pl. —n) (Bot.) fir, fir-tree.

Folge ['fɔlgə], f. (—, pl. —n) succession; series, sequence; continuation; consequence.

folgen ['fɔlgən], v.n. (aux. sein) follow; succeed; result from, be the consequence of; obey.

folgendermaßen ['fɔlgəndərma:sən], adv. as follows.

folgenschwer ['fɔlgənʃve:r], adj. momentous, portentous.

folgerichtig ['fɔlgərɪçtɪç], adj. consistent, logical.

folgern ['fɔlgərn], v.a. draw a conclusion, infer, conclude, deduce.

Folgerung ['fɔlgərʊŋ], f. (—, pl. —en) induction, deduction, inference.

folglich ['fɔlklɪç], conj. consequently, therefore.

folgsam ['fɔlkza:m], adj. obedient.

Foliant [fo:l'jant], m. (—en, pl. —en) folio-volume, tome.

Folie ['fo:ljə], f. (—, pl. —n) foil.

Folter ['fɔltər], f. (—, pl. —n) rack, torture.

Folterbank ['fɔltərbaŋk], f. (—, pl. ⸚e) rack.

Fond [fɔ:], m. (—s, pl. —s) back seat.

Fontäne [fɔ'tɛːnə], *f.* (—, *pl.* —n) fountain.

foppen ['fɔpən], *v.a.* chaff, banter, tease.

Fopperei [fɔpə'raɪ], *f.* (—, *pl.* —en) chaff, banter, teasing.

forcieren [fɔr'siːrən], *v.a.* strain, overdo.

Förderer ['fœrdərər], *m.* (—s, *pl.* —) promoter, backer.

Förderkarren ['fœrdərkarən], *m.* (—s, *pl.* —) (*Min.*) truck, trolley.

förderlich ['fœrdərlɪç], *adj.* useful, conducive (to).

Fördermaschine ['fœrdərmaʃiːnə], *f.* (—, *pl.* —n) hauling-machine.

fordern ['fɔrdərn], *v.a.* demand, claim, ask for; (*duel*) challenge.

fördern ['fœrdərn], *v.a.* further, advance, promote, back; hasten; (*Min.*) haul.

Förderschacht ['fœrdərʃaxt], *m.* (—s, *pl.* ⁀e) (*Min.*) winding shaft.

Forderung ['fɔrdəruŋ], *f.* (—, *pl.* —en) demand, claim; (*duel*) challenge.

Förderung ['fœrdəruŋ], *f.* (—, *no pl.*) furtherance, promotion, advancement; (*Min.*) hauling.

Forelle [fo'rɛlə], *f.* (—, *pl.* —n) trout.

Forke ['fɔrkə], *f.* (—, *pl.* —n) pitchfork, garden-fork.

Form [fɔrm], *f.* (—, *pl.* —en) form, shape, figure; manner; condition; (*casting*) mould; (*grammar*) form, voice.

Formalien [fɔr'maːljən], *pl.* formalities.

Formalität [fɔrmalɪ'tɛːt], *f.* (—, *pl.* —en) formality, form.

Format [fɔr'maːt], *n.* (—s, *pl.* —e) (*book, paper*) size; format; (*fig.*) stature.

Formel ['fɔrməl], *f.* (—, *pl.* —n) formula.

formell [fɔr'mɛl], *adj.* formal.

Formfehler ['fɔrmfeːlər], *m.* (—s, *pl.* —) faux pas, breach of etiquette.

formieren [fɔr'miːrən], *v.a.* form. — *v.r. sich* —, fall into line.

förmlich ['fœrmlɪç], *adj.* formal: downright.

formlos ['fɔrmloːs], *adj.* shapeless; (*fig.*) unconventional, informal, unceremonious.

Formular [fɔrmu'laːr], *n.* (—s, *pl.* —e) (printed) form, schedule.

formulieren [fɔrmu'liːrən], *v.a.* formulate, word.

formvollendet ['fɔrmfɔlɛndət], *adj.* well-rounded, well-finished.

forsch [fɔrʃ], *adj.* dashing.

forschen ['fɔrʃən], *v.n.* search, enquire (after), do research.

Forschung ['fɔrʃuŋ], *f.* (—, *pl.* —en) research, investigation; search, exploration.

Forst [fɔrst], *m.* (—es, *pl.* —e) forest.

Förster ['fœrstər], *m.* (—s, *pl.* —) forester, forest-keeper; (*Am.*) ranger.

Forstfrevel ['fɔrstfreːfəl], *m.* (—s, *no pl.*) infringement of forest-laws.

Forstrevier ['fɔrstreviːr], *n.* (—s, *pl.* —e) section of forest.

Forstwesen ['fɔrstveːzən], *n.* (—s, *no pl.*) forestry.

Forstwirtschaft ['fɔrstvɪrtʃaft], *f.* (—, *no pl.*) forestry.

fort [fɔrt], *adv.* away; lost, gone, forth, forward.

Fort [fɔːrt], *n.* (—s, *pl.* —s) fort.

fortan [fɔrt'an], *adv.* henceforth.

fortbilden ['fɔrtbɪldən], *v.r. sich* —, improve o.s., receive further education.

fortbleiben ['fɔrtblaɪbən], *v.n. irr.* (*aux.* sein) stay away.

Fortdauer ['fɔrtdauər], *f.* (—, *no pl.*) continuance, duration.

fortfahren ['fɔrtfaːrən], *v.n. irr.* (*aux.* sein) drive off; (*Naut.*) set sail; (*fig.*) continue, go on.

Fortgang ['fɔrtgaŋ], *m.* (—s, *no pl.*) going away, departure; (*fig.*) continuation, progress.

Fortkommen ['fɔrtkɔmən], *n.* (—s, *no pl.*) advancement, progress; (*fig.*) livelihood.

fortkommen ['fɔrtkɔmən], *v.n. irr.* (*aux.* sein) *gut* —, prosper, succeed.

fortlassen ['fɔrtlasən], *v.a. irr.* allow to go; leave out, omit; *nicht* —, detain.

fortlaufen ['fɔrtlaufən], *v.n. irr.* (*aux.* sein) run away.

fortpflanzen ['fɔrtpflantsən], *v.r. sich* —, propagate, multiply; (*sickness*) spread.

forträumen ['fɔrtrɔymən], *v.a.* clear away, remove.

fortschaffen ['fɔrtʃafən], *v.a.* carry away, get rid of.

fortscheren ['fɔrtʃeːrən], *v.r. sich* — (*coll.*) beat it, go away.

fortscheuchen ['fɔrtʃɔyçən], *v.a.* scare away.

fortschreiten ['fɔrtʃraɪtən], *v.n. irr.* (*aux.* sein) progress, advance.

Fortschritt ['fɔrtʃrɪt], *m.* (—s, *pl.* —e) progress, advancement, proficiency.

fortsetzen ['fɔrtzɛtsən], *v.a.* continue, carry on.

fortwährend ['fɔrtvɛːrənt], *adv.* continual, perpetual, unceasing.

Fracht [fraxt], *f.* (—, *pl.* —en) freight, cargo, load.

Frack [frak], *m.* (—s, *pl.* —s, ⁀e) dress-suit, evening dress.

Frage ['fraːgə], *f.* (—, *pl.* —n) question, query.

Fragebogen ['fraːgəboːgən], *m.* (—s, *pl.* —) questionnaire.

fragen ['fraːgən], *v.a.* ask, enquire, question.

Fragesteller ['fraːgəʃtɛlər], *m.* (—s, *pl.* —) interrogator, questioner.

fraglich ['fraːklɪç], *adj.* questionable, problematic(al).

fragwürdig ['fraːkvyrdɪç], *adj.* doubtful, questionable.

Fraktion [frak'tsjoːn], *f.* (—, *pl.* —en) (*Pol.*) party group.

Frakturschrift

Frakturschrift [frak'tu:rʃrɪft], *f.* (—, *no pl.*) (*lettering*) Gothic type, Old English type, Black Letter type.

Frank [fraŋk], *m.* (—en, *pl.* —en) (*money*) franc.

Franke ['fraŋkə], *m.* (—n, *pl.* —n) Frank, Franconian.

frankieren [fraŋ'ki:rən], *v.a.* (*post*) prepay, frank.

franko ['fraŋko], *adj.* post-paid; *gratis und* —, gratuitously.

Frankreich ['fraŋkraɪx], *n.* France.

Franse ['franzə], *f.* (—, *pl.* —n) fringe.

Franzose [fran'tso:zə], *m.* (—n, *pl.* —n) Frenchman.

französisch [fran'tsö:zɪʃ], *adj.* French.

frappant [fra'pant], *adj.* striking.

frappieren [fra'pi:rən], *v.a.* strike, astonish.

Fraß [fra:s], *m.* (—es, *no pl.*) (*animals*) feed, fodder; (*sl.*) grub.

Fratz [frats], *m.* (—es, *pl.* —en) brat, little monkey.

Fratze ['fratsə], *f.* (—, *pl.* —en) grimace, caricature.

Frau [frau], *f.* (—, *pl.* —en) woman, wife, lady; (*title*) Mrs.; *gnädige* —, Madam.

Frauenkirche ['frauənkɪrçə], *f.* (—, *no pl.*) Church of Our Lady.

Frauenzimmer ['frauəntsɪmər], *n.* (—s, *pl.* —) (*pej.*) woman, female.

Fräulein ['frɔylaɪn], *n.* (—s, *pl.* —) young lady; (*title*) Miss.

frech [frɛç], *adj.* insolent, impudent, cheeky, pert, saucy.

Frechheit ['frɛçhaɪt], *f.* (—, *pl.* —en) insolence, impudence.

Fregatte [fre'gatə], *f.* (—, *pl.* —n) frigate.

frei [fraɪ], *adj.* free, exempt, unhampered, independent, disengaged; vacant; candid, frank.

Freibeuter ['fraɪbɔytər], *m.* (—s, *pl.* —) freebooter, pirate.

Freibrief ['fraɪbri:f], *m.* (—s, *pl.* —e) patent, licence; permit.

freien ['fraɪən], *v.a.* woo, court.

Freier ['fraɪər], *m.* (—s, *pl.* —) (*obs.*) suitor.

Freigabe ['fraɪga:bə], *f.* (—, *no pl.*) release.

freigeben ['fraɪge:bən], *v.a. irr.* release.

freigebig ['fraɪge:bɪç], *adj.* liberal, generous.

Freigebigkeit ['fraɪgə:bɪçkaɪt], *f.* (—, *no pl.*) liberality, munificence, generosity.

Freigut ['fraɪgu:t], *n.* (—s, *pl.* —er) freehold.

Freiheit ['fraɪhaɪt], *f.* (—, *pl.* —en) freedom, liberty, immunity, privilege.

Freiherr ['fraɪhɛr], *m.* (—n, *pl.* —en) baron.

Freikorps ['fraɪko:r], *n.* (—, *no pl.*) volunteer-corps.

Freilauf ['fraɪlauf], *m.* (—s, *no pl.*) (*bicycle*) free-wheel.

freilich ['fraɪlɪç], *adv.* to be sure, it is true, indeed, of course.

Freilicht- ['fraɪlɪxt], *adj.* (*in compounds*) open-air.

Freimarke ['fraɪmarkə], *f.* (—, *pl.* —n) postage stamp.

freimütig ['fraɪmy:tɪç], *adj.* frank, open, candid.

Freisprechung ['fraɪʃprɛçuŋ], *f.* (—, *no pl.*) acquittal; absolution.

Freistätte ['fraɪʃtɛtə], *f.* (—, *pl.* —n) refuge, asylum.

Freistoß ['fraɪʃto:s], *m.* (—es, *pl.* ̈e) (*Footb.*) free-kick.

Freitag ['fraɪta:k], *m.* (—s, *pl.* —e) Friday.

Freitreppe ['fraɪtrɛpə], *f.* (—, *pl.* —n) outside staircase.

Freiübung ['fraɪy:buŋ], *f.* (—. *pl.* —en) (*mostly pl.*) physical exercises, gymnastics.

freiwillig ['fraɪvɪlɪç], *adj.* voluntary, of o.'s own accord; spontaneous.

Freiwillige ['fraɪvɪlɪgə], *m.* (—n, *pl.* —n) (*Mil.*) volunteer.

fremd [frɛmt], *adj.* strange, foreign, outlandish; odd.

fremdartig ['frɛmtartɪç], *adj.* strange, odd.

Fremde (1) ['frɛmdə], *f.* (—, *no pl.*) foreign country; *in die* — *gehen*, go abroad.

Fremde (2) ['frɛmdə], *m.* (—n, *pl.* —n) stranger, foreigner.

Fremdheit ['frɛmthaɪt], *f.* (—, *no pl.*) strangeness.

Freßbeutel ['frɛsbɔytəl], *m.* (—s, *pl.* —) nose-bag.

Fresse ['frɛsə], *f.* (—, *pl.* —n) (*vulg.*) mouth, snout.

fressen ['frɛsən], *v.a. irr.* (*animals*) eat; (*also fig.*) devour.

Fresserei ['frɛsəraɪ], *f.* (—, *no pl.*) gluttony.

Frettchen ['frɛtçən], *n.* (—s, *pl.* —) (*Zool.*) ferret.

Freude ['frɔydə], *f.* (—, *pl.* —n) joy, joyfulness, gladness, enjoyment, delight, pleasure.

Freudenfest ['frɔydənfɛst], *n.* (—s, *pl.* —e) feast, jubilee.

Freudenhaus ['frɔydənhaus], *n.* (—es, *pl.* ̈er) brothel.

Freudenmädchen ['frɔydənmɛ:tçən], *n.* (—s, *pl.* —) prostitute.

freudig ['frɔydɪç], *adj.* joyful, cheerful, glad.

freudlos ['frɔytlo:s], *adj.* joyless.

freuen ['frɔyən], *v.r. sich* —, rejoice (at); be glad (of); *sich auf etwas* —, look forward to s.th.

Freund [frɔynt], *m.* (—es, *pl.* —e) friend.

freundlich ['frɔyntlɪç], *adj.* friendly, kind, affable, pleasing, cheerful, pleasant, genial.

Freundschaft ['frɔyntʃaft], *f.* (—, *pl.* —en) friendship.

Frevel ['fre:fəl], *m.* (—s, *pl.* —) crime, misdeed, offence.

freveln ['fre:fəln], *v.n.* do wrong, trespass, commit an outrage.

Friede(n) ['fri:də(n)], *m.* (**—ns**, *no pl.*) peace.

friedfertig ['fri:fɛrtɪç], *adj.* peaceable.

Friedhof ['fri:tho:f], *m.* (**—s**, *pl.* ⁻e) churchyard, cemetery.

friedlich ['fri:tlɪç], *adj.* peaceful.

friedliebend ['fri:tli:bənt], *adj.* peaceable, peace-loving.

Friedrich ['fri:drɪç], *m.* Frederic(k).

friedselig ['fri:tze:lɪç], *adj.* peaceable.

frieren ['fri:rən], *v.n. irr.* feel cold, freeze.

Fries [fri:s], *m.* (**—es**, *pl.* **—e**) frieze.

Friese ['fri:zə], *m.* (**—n**, *pl.* **—n**) Frisian.

frisch [frɪʃ], *adj.* fresh; new; (*weather*) crisp; (*fig.*) lively, brisk, gay.

Frische ['frɪʃə], *f.* (**—**, *no pl.*) freshness, liveliness, gaiety.

Friseur [fri'zo:r], *m.* (**—s**, *pl.* **—e**) hairdresser, barber.

Friseuse [fri'zo:zə], *f.* (**—**, *pl.* **—n**) female hairdresser.

frisieren [fri'zi:rən], *v.a.* dress (s.o.'s) hair.

Frist [frɪst], *f.* (**—**, *pl.* **—en**) time, term, period; (fixed) term; delay, respite.

fristen ['frɪstən], *v.a. das Leben* **—**, gain a bare living.

Frisur [fri'zu:r], *f.* (**—**, *pl.* **—en**) coiffure, hair-style.

frivol [fri'vo:l], *adj.* frivolous.

Frivolität [frivo·li'tɛ:t], *f.* (**—**, *pl.* **—en**) frivolity.

froh [fro:], *adj.* glad, joyful, joyous.

frohgelaunt ['fro:gəlaunt], *adj.* good-humoured, cheerful.

fröhlich ['frø:lɪç], *adj.* gay, merry.

frohlocken [fro:'lɔkən], *v.n.* (*rare*) exult.

Frohsinn ['fro:zɪn], *m.* (**—s**, *no pl.*) good humour, gaiety.

fromm [frɔm], *adj.* pious, religious, devout.

frommen ['frɔmən], *v.n.* (*obs.*) be of advantage (to s.o.).

Frömmigkeit ['frœmɪçkaɪt], *f.* (**—**, *no pl.*) piety, devoutness.

Fron [fro:n], *f.* (**—**, *no pl.*) (feudal) service; statute labour.

frönen ['frø:nən], *v.n.* (*fig.*) be a slave to; indulge in (*Dat.*).

Fronleichnam [fro:n'laıxna:m], *m.* (*Eccl.*) (feast of) Corpus Christi.

Front [frɔnt], *f.* (**—**, *pl.* **—en**) front, forepart; (*building*) elevation; (*Mil.*) front line.

Frosch [frɔʃ], *m.* (**—es**, *pl.* ⁻e) (*Zool.*) frog.

Frost [frɔst], *m.* (**—es**, *pl.* ⁻e) frost; coldness, chill.

Frostbeule ['frɔstbɔylə], *f.* (**—**, *pl.* **—n**) chilblain.

frösteln ['frœstəln], *v.n.* feel a chill, shiver.

frostig ['frɔstɪç], *adj.* frosty; cold, chilly.

frottieren [frɔ'ti:rən], *v.a.* rub (down).

Frottiertuch [frɔ'ti:rtu:x], *n.* (**—s**, *pl.* ⁻er) Turkish towel, bath towel.

Frucht [fruxt], *f.* (**—**, *pl.* ⁻e) fruit; (*fig.*) result, effect; (*Med.*) foetus.

fruchtbar ['fruxtba:r], *adj.* fruitful, productive, fertile.

fruchten ['fruxtən], *v.n.* produce fruit; (*fig.*) be effectual.

Fruchtknoten ['fruxtkno:tən], *m.* (**—s**, *pl.* **—**) (*Bot.*) seed-vessel.

früh(e) [fry:(ə)], *adj.* early.

Frühe ['fry:ə], *f.* (**—**, *no pl.*) early morning, dawn.

früher ['fry:ər], *adv.* earlier (on), formerly.

frühestens ['fry:əstəns], *adv.* at the earliest (possible moment).

Frühjahr ['fry:ja:r], *n.*, **Frühling** ['fry:lɪŋ], *m.* (**—s**, *pl.* **—e**) spring.

frühreif ['fry:raɪf], *adj.* precocious.

Frühschoppen ['fry:ʃɔpən], *m.* (**—s**, *pl.* **—**) morning pint (beer *or* wine).

Frühstück ['fry:ʃtyk], *n.* (**—s**, *pl.* **—e**) breakfast; *zweites* **—**, lunch.

Fuchs [fuks], *m.* (**—es**, *pl.* ⁻e) fox; chestnut (horse); (*fig.*) cunning chap; (*student*) freshman.

Fuchsbau ['fuksbau], *m.* (**—s**, *pl.* **—e**) fox-hole.

Fuchseisen ['fuksaɪzən], *n.* (**—s**, *pl.* **—**) fox-trap.

fuchsen ['fuksən], *v.r. sich* **—** *über*, be annoyed about.

Fuchsie ['fuksjə], *f.* (**—**, *pl.* **—n**) (*Bot.*) fuchsia.

fuchsig ['fuksɪç], *adj.* (*coll.*) very angry.

Füchsin ['fyksɪn], *f.* (**—**, *pl.* **—innen**) vixen.

fuchsrot ['fuksro:t], *adj.* fox-coloured, sorrel.

Fuchsschwanz ['fukʃʃvants], *m.* (**—es**, *pl.* ⁻e) fox-brush; pad saw.

Fuchtel ['fuxtəl], *f.* (**—**, *pl.* **—n**) sword blade; rod, whip.

Fuder ['fu:dər], *n.* (**—s**, *pl.* **—**) load, cart-load; wine measure (c. 270 gallons).

Fug ['fu:k], *m.* (**—s**, *no pl.*) (*rare*) right, justice; *mit* **—** *und Recht*, with every right.

Fuge (1) ['fu:gə], *f.* (**—**, *pl.* **—n**) joint, groove.

Fuge (2) ['fu:gə], *f.* (**—**, *pl.* **—n**) (*Mus.*) fugue.

fügen ['fy:gən], *v.a.* fit together, join, dovetail. **—** *v.r. sich* **—**, submit (to), accommodate o.s. (to).

fügsam ['fy:kza:m], *adj.* pliant, submissive, yielding.

Fügung ['fy:guŋ], *f.* (**—**, *pl.* **—en**) coincidence; dispensation (of Providence); Providence.

fühlbar ['fy:lba:r], *adj.* perceptible; tangible; *sich* **—** *machen*, make o.s. felt.

fühlen ['fy:lən], *v.a.* feel, touch, sense, be aware of.

Fühler ['fy:lər], *m.* (**—s**, *pl.* **—**) tentacle, feeler.

Fühlhorn

Fühlhorn ['fy:lhɔrn], *n.* (—s, *pl.* ¨er) feeler, antenna, tentacle.

Fühlung ['fy:luŋ], *f.* (—, *no pl.*) — *haben mit,* be in touch with.

Fuhre ['fu:rə], *f.* (—, *pl.* —n) conveyance, vehicle, cart-load.

führen ['fy:rən], *v.a.* lead, guide, conduct, command; (*pen*) wield; (*law-suit*) carry on; (*conversation*) have, keep up; (*name, title*) bear; (*goods*) stock, deal in; *Krieg* —, wage war; *etwas im Schilde* —, have a plan; *das Wort* —, be spokesman; *einen hinters Licht* —, cheat s.o.

Führer ['fy:rər], *m.* (—s, *pl.* —) leader, guide; head, manager; conductor; driver, pilot.

Führerschaft ['fy:rərʃaft], *f.* (—, *no pl.*) leadership.

Führerschein ['fy:rərʃain], *m.* (—s, *pl.* —e) driving-licence.

Führersitz ['fy:rərzɪts], *m.* (—es, *pl.* —e) driver's seat; pilot's cockpit.

Fuhrlohn ['fu:rlo:n], *m.* (—s, *no pl.*) cartage, carriage.

Fuhrmann ['fu:rman], *m.* (—s, *pl.* ¨er) carter, carrier.

Führung ['fy:ruŋ], *f.* (—, *no pl.*) guidance; leadership; conducted tour; management, direction; behaviour, conduct.

Führungszeugnis ['fy:ruŋstsɔyknɪs], *n.* (—sses, *pl.* —sse) certificate of good conduct.

Fuhrwerk ['fu:rvɛrk], *n.* (—s, *pl.* —e) carriage, vehicle, waggon.

Fuhrwesen ['fu:rve:zən], *n.* (—s, *no pl.*) transport services, transportation.

Fülle ['fylə], *f.* (—, *no pl.*) fullness; abundance, plenty.

Füllen ['fylən], *n.* (—s, *pl.* —) foal.

füllen ['fylən], *v.a.* fill, fill up; stuff.

Füllfederhalter ['fylfe:dərhaltər], *m.* (—s, *pl.* —) fountain-pen.

Füllung ['fyluŋ], *f.* (—, *pl.* —en) filling; stuffing; (*door*) panel.

fummeln ['fuməln], *v.n.* fumble.

Fund [funt], *m.* (—es, *pl.* —e) find; discovery.

Fundbüro ['funtbyro], *n.* (—s, *pl.* —s) lost property office.

Fundgrube ['funtgru:bə], *f.* (—, *pl.* —n) gold-mine, source, treasure-house.

fundieren [fun'di:rən], *v.a.* found; establish.

fünf [fynf], *num. adj.* five.

Fünfeck ['fynfek], *n.* (—s, *pl.* —e) pentagon.

Fünffüßler ['fynffy:slər], *m.* (—s, *pl.* —) (*Poet.*) pentameter.

fünfjährig ['fynfjɛ:rɪç], *num. adj.* five-year-old.

fünfjährlich ['fynfjɛ:rlɪç], *num. adj.* quinquennial, five-yearly.

fünfzehn ['fynftse:n], *num. adj.* fifteen.

fünfzig ['fynftsɪç], *num. adj.* fifty.

fungieren [fuŋ'gi:rən], *v.n.* — *als,* act as, officiate as.

Funk [funk], *m.* (—s, *no pl.*) radio; wireless; telegraphy.

Funke ['funkə], *m.* (—n, *pl.* —n) spark, sparkle.

funkeln ['funkəln], *v.n.* sparkle, glitter; (*stars*) twinkle.

funkelnagelneu ['funkəlna:gəlnɔy], *adj.* (*coll.*) brand-new.

funken ['funkən], *v.a.* flash (messages); telegraph, broadcast.

Funker ['funkər], *m.* (—s, *pl.* —) wireless operator.

Funksender ['funkzɛndər], *m.* (—s, *pl.* —) radio-transmitter.

Funkspruch ['funkʃprux], *m.* (—s, *pl.* ¨e) wireless-message.

Funktelegramm ['funktelegram], *n.* (—s, *pl.* —e) radio telegram.

für [fy:r], *prep.* (*Acc.*) for, instead of; *ein — allemal,* once and for all; *und — sich,* in itself.

Fürbitte ['fy:rbɪtə], *f.* (—, *pl.* —n) intercession.

Furche ['furçə], *f.* (—, *pl.* —n) furrow; (*face*) wrinkle.

furchen ['furçən], *v.a.* furrow; (*face*) wrinkle.

Furcht [furçt], *f.* (—, *no pl.*) fear, worry, anxiety; dread, fright, terror, apprehension.

furchtbar ['furçtba:r], *adj.* dreadful, terrible, frightful.

fürchten ['fyrçtən], *v.a.* fear, be afraid of. — *v.r. sich* — *vor,* be afraid of.

fürchterlich ['fyrçtərlɪç], *adj.* terrible, horrible, awful.

furchtsam ['furçtza:m], *adj.* timid, fearful, apprehensive.

Furie ['fu:rjə], *f.* (—, *pl.* —n) fury, virago.

fürlieb [fyr'li:p], *adv. mit etwas — nehmen,* put up with, be content with s.th.

Furnier [fur'ni:r], *n.* (—s, *pl.* —e) veneer, inlay.

Furore [fu'ro:rə], *n.* (—s, *no pl.*) — *machen,* cause a sensation, create an uproar.

Fürsorge ['fy:rzɔrgə], *f.* (—, *no pl.*) solicitude; provision; welfare.

fürsorglich ['fy:rzɔrglɪç], *adj.* thoughtful, with loving care.

Fürsprache ['fy:rʃpra:xə], *f.* (—, *no pl.*) advocacy, intercession.

Fürst [fyrst], *m.* (—en, *pl.* —en) prince, sovereign.

Furt [furt], *f.* (—, *pl.* —en) ford.

Furunkel [fu'runkəl], *m.* (—s, *pl.* —) furuncle, boil.

Fürwort ['fy:rvɔrt], *n.* (—s, *pl.* ¨er) pronoun.

Fusel ['fu:zəl], *m.* (—s, *no pl.*) bad liquor, (*Am.*) hooch (*sl.*).

Fuß [fu:s], *m.* (—es, *pl.* ¨e) (*human*) foot; (*object*) base.

Fußangel ['fu:saŋəl], *f.* (—, *pl.* —n) man-trap.

Fußball ['fu:sbal], *m.* (—s, *pl.* ¨e) football.

78

Fußboden ['fu:sbo:dən], *m.* (**—s,** *pl.* ∷) floor.

fußen ['fu:sən], *v.n.* — *auf*, be based upon.

fußfrei ['fu:sfraɪ], *adj.* ankle-length.

Fußgänger ['fu:sgɛŋər], *m.* (**—s,** *pl.* —) pedestrian.

Fußgestell ['fu:sgəʃtɛl], *n.* (**—s,** *pl.* **—e**) pedestal.

Fußpflege ['fu:spfle:gə], *f.* (**—,** *no pl.*) chiropody.

Fußpunkt ['fu:spuŋkt], *m.* (**—s,** *no pl.*) nadir.

Fußtritt ['fu:strɪt], *m.* (**—s,** *pl.* **—e**) kick.

futsch [futʃ], *excl.* (*coll.*) gone, lost.

Futter ['futər], *n.* (**—s,** *no pl.*) (*dress*) lining; (*animals*) fodder, feed.

Futteral [futə'ra:l], *n.* (**—s,** *pl.* **—e**) case; sheath.

Futterkräuter ['futərkrɔytər], *n. pl.* herbage.

futtern ['futərn], *v,n.* (*coll.*) feed, stuff o.s.

füttern ['fytərn], *v.a.* feed ; (*garment*) line.

G

G [ge:], *n.* (**—s,** *pl.* **—s**) the letter G; (*Mus.*) G *Dur*, G major; (*Mus.*) G *Moll*, G minor; (*Mus.*) — -*Saite*, G string.

Gabe ['ga:bə], *f.* (**—,** *pl.* **—n**) gift, present; donation; *barmherzige* —, alms; (*fig.*) gift, talent.

Gabel ['ga:bəl], *f.* (**—,** *pl.* **—n**) fork; (*deer*) antler; (*cart*) shafts.

gabelig ['ga:bəlɪç], *adj.* forked.

Gabelung ['ga:bəluŋ], *f.* (**—,** *pl.* **—en**) bifurcation, branching (of road).

Gabelzinke ['ga:bəltsɪŋkə], *f.* (**—,** *pl.* **—n**) prong, tine.

Gabun [ga'bu:n], *n.* Gaboon.

gackern ['gakərn], *v.n.* cackle; (*fig.*) chatter.

gaffen ['gafən], *v.n.* gape at, stare.

Gage ['ga:ʒə], *f.* (**—,** *pl.* **—n**) salary, pay, fee.

gähnen ['gɛ:nən], *v.n.* yawn, gape.

Galan [ga'la:n], *m.* (**—s,** *pl.* **—e**) lover, gallant.

galant [ga'lant], *adj.* polite, courteous; *—es Abenteuer*, love affair.

Galanterie [galantə'ri:], *f.* (**—,** *pl.* **—n**) courtesy.

Galanteriewaren [galantə'ri:va:rən], *f. pl.* fancy goods.

Galeere [ga'le:rə], *f.* (**—,** *pl.* **—n**) galley.

Galerie [galə'ri:], *f.* (**—,** *pl.* **—n**) gallery.

Galgen ['galgən], *m.* (**—s,** *pl.* —) gallows, gibbet; scaffold.

Galgenfrist ['galgənfrɪst], *f.* (**—,** *no pl.*) short delay, respite.

Galgenhumor ['galgənhumo:r], *m.* (**—s,** *no pl.*) wry *or* grim humour.

Galgenvogel ['galgənfo:gəl], *m.* (**—s,** *pl.* ∷) gallows-bird.

Galizien [ga'li:tsjən], *n.* Galicia.

Gallapfel ['galapfəl], *m.* (**—s,** *pl.* ∷) gall-nut.

Galle ['galə], *f.* (**—,** *pl.* **—n**) gall, bile.

Gallenblase ['galənbla:zə], *f.* (**—,** *pl.* **—n**) gall-bladder.

Gallert ['galərt], *n.* (**—s,** *no pl.*) jelly.

Gallien ['galjən], *n.* Gaul.

gallig ['galɪç], *adj.* bilious.

galvanisieren [galvanɪ'zi:rən], *v.a.* galvanize.

Gamaschen [ga'maʃən], *f. pl.* spats, gaiters.

Gang [gaŋ], *m.* (**—es,** *pl.* ∵e) walk, gait; (*horse*) pace; (*house*) passage, corridor; (*meal*) course, dish; (*action*) progress, course; (*sport*) round, bout; (*machine*) motion; stroke; (*Motor.*) gear.

gang [gaŋ], *adj.* — *und gäbe*, customary, usual, common.

Gangart ['gaŋa:rt], *f.* (**—,** *pl.* **—en**) gait; (*horse*) pace.

gangbar ['gaŋba:r], *adj.* marketable, saleable; (*road*) passable, practicable.

Gans [gans], *f.* (**—,** *pl.* ∵e) (*Orn.*) goose.

Gänseblümchen ['gɛnzəbly:mçən], *n.* (**—s,** *pl.*—) daisy.

Gänsefüßchen ['gɛnzəfy:sçən], *n. pl.* (*coll.*) inverted commas, quotation marks.

Gänsehaut ['gɛnzəhaut], *f.* (**—,** *no pl.*) goose-flesh, goose-pimples.

Gänserich ['gɛnzərɪç], *m.* (**—s,** *pl.* **—e**) (*Orn.*) gander.

ganz [gants], *adj.* whole, entire, all; complete, total.

gänzlich ['gɛntslɪç], *adj.* whole, total, entire, full, complete.

gar [ga:r], *adj.* sufficiently cooked, done. — *adv.* very, quite.

garantieren [garan'ti:rən], *v.a.* guarantee, warrant.

Garaus ['ga:raus], *m.* (**—,** *no pl.*) *einem den* — *machen*, finish s.o., kill s.o.

Garbe ['garbə], *f.* (**—,** *pl.* **—n**) sheaf.

Garde ['gardə], *f.* (**—,** *pl.* **—n**) guard, guards.

Garderobe [gardə'ro:bə], *f.* (**—,** *pl.* **—n**) wardrobe; cloak-room; (*Theat.*) dressing-room.

Gardine [gar'di:nə], *f.* (**—,** *pl.* **—n**) curtain.

Gardist [gar'dɪst], *m.* (**—en,** *pl.* **—en**) guardsman.

gären ['gɛ:rən], *v.n.* ferment; effervesce.

Garn [garn], *n.* (**—s,** *pl.* **—e**) yarn, thread.

Garnele [gar'ne:lə], *f.* (**—,** *pl.* **—n**) (*Zool.*) shrimp; *große* —, prawn.

garnieren [gar'ni:rən], *v.a.* trim, garnish.

Garnison [garni'zo:n], *f.* (**—,** *pl.* **—en**) garrison.

Garnitur

Garnitur [garni'tu:r], *f.* (—, *pl.* —en) trimming; set.

Garnröllchen ['garnrœlçən], *n.* (—s, *pl.* —) reel of thread.

garstig ['garstɪç], *adj.* nasty, loathsome, ugly.

Garten ['gartən], *m.* (—s, *pl.* ∺) garden.

Gartenlaube ['gartənlaubə], *f.* (—, *pl.* —n) bower, arbour.

Gärtner ['gɛrtnər], *m.* (—s, *pl.* —) gardener.

Gärtnerei [gɛrtnə'raɪ], *f.* (—, *pl.* —en) horticulture; market-garden; (plant) nursery.

Gärung ['gɛ:ruŋ], *f.* (—, *pl.* —en) fermentation, effervescence.

Gas [ga:s], *n.* (—es, —e) gas; — geben, (*Motor.*) accelerate.

gasartig ['ga:sartɪç], *adj.* gaseous.

Gäßchen ['gɛsçən], *n.* (—s, *pl.* —) narrow alley; lane.

Gasse ['gasə], *f.* (—, *pl.* —n) alleyway, lane; (*rare*) street.

Gassenbube ['gasənbu:bə] *see* **Gassenjunge**.

Gassenhauer ['gasənhauər], *m.* (—s, *pl.* —), street-song, vulgar ballad; pop song.

Gassenjunge ['gasənjuŋə], *m.* (—n, *pl.* —n) street-urchin.

Gast [gast], *m.* (—s, *pl.* ∺e) guest, visitor.

gastfrei ['gastfraɪ], *adj.* hospitable.

Gastfreund ['gastfrɔynt], *m.* (—s, *pl.* —e) guest; host.

Gastfreundschaft ['gastfrɔyntʃaft], *f.* (—, *no pl.*) hospitality.

Gastgeber ['gastge:bər], *m.* (—s, *pl.* —) host.

Gasthaus ['gasthaus], *n.* (—es, *pl.* ∺er), **Gasthof** ['gastho:f], *m.* (—es, *pl.* ∺e) inn, hotel, public house.

gastieren [gas'ti:rən], *v.n.* (*Theat.*) appear as a guest artist; star.

gastlich ['gastlɪç], *adj.* hospitable.

Gastmahl ['gastma:l], *n.* (—s, *pl.* —e) banquet, feast.

Gastrecht ['gastrɛçt], *n.* (—s, *no pl.*) right of hospitality.

Gastspiel ['gastʃpi:l], *n.* (—s, *pl.* —e) (*Theat.*) performance by visiting company.

Gaststätte ['gastʃtɛtə], *f.* (—, *pl.* —n) restaurant.

Gaststube ['gastʃtu:bə], *f.* (—, *pl.* —n) hotel lounge; guest room.

Gastwirt ['gastvɪrt], *m.* (—s, *pl.* —e) landlord.

Gastwirtin ['gastvɪrtɪn], *f.* (—, *pl.* —nen) landlady.

Gastzimmer ['gasttsɪmər], *n.* (—s, *pl.* —) *see* **Gaststube**; spare bedroom.

Gatte ['gatə], *m.* (—n, *pl.* —n) husband, spouse, consort.

Gatter ['gatər], *n.* (—s, *pl.* —) grate, lattice, grating.

Gattin ['gatɪn], *f.* (—, *pl.* —nen) wife, spouse, consort.

Gattung ['gatuŋ], *f.* (—, *pl.* —en) kind, species, sort, class; breed, genus; (*Lit.*) genre.

Gau [gau], *m.* (—s, *pl.* —e) district, province.

gaukeln ['gaukəln], *v.n.* juggle. — *v.a.* dazzle.

Gaul [gaul], *m.* (—s, *pl.* ∺e) (old) horse, nag; *einem geschenkten — sieht man nicht ins Maul*, never look a gift horse in the mouth.

Gaumen ['gaumən], *m.* (—s, *pl.* —) palate.

Gauner ['gaunər], *m.* (—s, *pl.* —) rogue, sharper, swindler, cheat.

gaunern ['gaunərn], *v.n.* cheat, trick, swindle.

Gaunersprache ['gaunərʃpra:xə], *f.* (—, *no pl.*) thieves' slang.

Gaze ['ga:zə], *f.* (—, *pl.* —n) gauze.

Gazelle [ga'tsɛlə], *f.* (—, *pl.* —n) (*Zool.*) gazelle, antelope.

Geächtete [gə'ɛçtətə], *m.* (—n, *pl.* —n) outlaw.

Geächze [gə'ɛçtsə], *n.* (—s, *no pl.*) moaning, groaning.

Geäder [gə'ɛ:dər], *n.* (—s, *no pl.*) veins, arteries; veining.

geädert [gə'ɛdart], *adj.* veined, streaked; grained.

-geartet [gə'a:rtət], *adj.* (*suffix in compounds*) -natured.

Gebäck [gə'bɛk], *n.* (—s, *no pl.*) pastry, rolls, cakes.

Gebälk [gə'bɛlk], *n.* (—s, *no pl.*) timberwork, timber-frame.

Gebärde [gə'bɛ:rdə], *f.* (—, *pl.* —n) gesture.

gebärden [gə'bɛ:rdən], *v.r. sich* —, behave.

Gebaren [gə'ba:rən], *n.* (—s, *no pl.*) demeanour.

gebären [gə'bɛ:rən], *v.a. irr.* bear, bring forth, give birth to, be delivered of.

Gebärmutter [gə'bɛ:rmutər], *f.* (—, *no pl.*) womb, uterus.

Gebäude [gə'bɔydə], *n.* (—s, *pl.* —) building, edifice.

Gebein [gə'baɪn], *n.* (—s, *pl.* —e) bones, skeleton; (*fig.*) remains.

Gebell [gə'bɛl], *n.* (—s, *no pl.*) barking.

geben ['ge:bən], *v.a. irr.* give, present; confer, bestow; yield; (*cards*) deal. — *v.r. sich* —, show o.s., behave; abate; *das gibt sich*, that won't last long; *es gibt . . .*, there is . . .; *was gibt's?* what's the matter?

Geber ['ge:bər], *m.* (—s, *pl.* —) giver, donor.

Gebet [gə'be:t], *n.* (—s, *pl.* —e) prayer; *sein — verrichten*, say o.'s prayers; *ins — nehmen*, question s.o. thoroughly.

Gebiet [gə'bi:t], *n.* (—s, *pl.* —e) district, territory; (*Am.*) precinct; jurisdiction; (*fig.*) province, field, sphere, domain.

gebieten [gə'bi:tən], *v.a. irr.* command, order.

Gebieter [gə'bi:tər], *m.* (—s, *pl.* —) lord, master, ruler.

Gebilde [gə'bɪldə], n. (—s, pl. —) form, thing; formation, structure; figment.

gebildet [gə'bɪldət], adj. educated, cultured, refined.

Gebirge [gə'bɪrgə], n. (—s, pl. —) mountains.

Gebirgskamm [gə'bɪrkskam], m. (—s, pl. ·-e) mountain-ridge.

Gebiß [gə'bɪs], n. (—sses, pl. —sse) set of (false) teeth, denture; (horse) bit.

Gebläse [gə'blɛːzə], n. (—s, pl. —) bellows; blower.

Gebläsemaschine [gə'blɛːzəmaʃiːnə], f. (—, pl. —n) blower.

Gebläseofen [gə'blɛːzəːfən], m. (—s, pl. ·-) blast-furnace.

geblümt [gə'blyːmt], adj. flowered.

Geblüt [gə'blyːt], n. (—s, no pl.) blood; race, line, lineage, stock.

geboren [gə'boːrən], adj. born.

geborgen [gə'bɔrgən], adj. saved, hidden, sheltered, rescued.

Gebot [gə'boːt], n. (—s, pl. —e) order, decree, command; (Bibl.) Commandment.

geboten [gə'boːtən], adj. necessary, advisable.

Gebräu [gə'brɔy], n. (—s, no pl.) brew, concoction, mixture.

Gebrauch [gə'braux], m. (—s, pl. ·-e) use; employment; custom, usage, habit, practice; (rare) rite.

gebrauchen [gə'brauxən], v.a. use, make use of, employ.

gebräuchlich [gə'brɔyçlɪç], adj. usual, customary, common.

Gebrauchsanweisung [gə'brauxsanvaɪzuŋ], f. (—, pl. —en) directions for use.

gebraucht [gə'brauxt], adj. used, second-hand.

Gebrechen [gə'brɛçən], n. (—s, pl. —) infirmity.

gebrechen [gə'brɛçən], v.n. irr. es gebricht mir an, I am in want of, I lack.

gebrechlich [gə'brɛçlɪç], adj. infirm, frail, weak.

gebrochen [gə'brɔxən], adj. broken; —es Deutsch, broken German.

Gebrüder [gə'bryːdər], m. pl. (Comm.) brothers.

Gebrüll [gə'bryl], n. (—s, no pl.) roaring; (cows) lowing.

Gebühr [gə'byːr], f. (—, pl. —en) charge, due; fee; tax, duty.

gebühren [gə'byːrən], v.n. be due to s.o. —v.r. sich —, wie es sich gebührt, as it ought to be, as is right and proper.

gebunden [gə'bundən], adj. (fig.) bound, committed; (Poet.) metrical.

Geburt [gə'burt], f. (—, pl. —en) birth.

gebürtig [gə'byrtɪç], adj. a native of.

Geburtsfehler [gə'burtsfeːlər], m. (—s, pl. —) congenital defect.

Geburtshelfer [gə'burtshɛlfər], m. (—s, pl. —) obstetrician.

Geburtshelferin [gə'burtshɛlfərin], f. (—, pl. —nen) midwife.

Geburtsort [gə'burtsɔrt], m. (—s, pl. —e) birthplace.

Geburtsschein [gə'burtsʃain], m. (—(e)s, pl. —e) birth certificate.

Geburtswehen [gə'burtsveːən], f. pl. birthpangs; labour pains.

Gebüsch [gə'byʃ], n. (—es, pl. —e) bushes, thicket; underwood.

Geck [gɛk], m. (—en, pl. —en) fop, dandy; (carnival) fool.

geckenhaft ['gɛkənhaft], adj. foppish, dandyish.

Gedächtnis [gə'dɛçtnɪs], n. (—ses, no pl.) memory; remembrance, recollection; im — behalten, keep in mind.

Gedanke [gə'daŋkə], m. (—ns, pl. —n) thought, idea.

Gedankenfolge [gə'daŋkənfɔlgə], f. (—, no pl.), **Gedankengang** [gə'daŋkəngaŋ], m. (—s, pl. ·-e) sequence of thought, train of thought.

Gedankenstrich [gə'daŋkənʃtrɪç], m. (—s, pl. —e) dash; hyphen.

Gedärm [gə'dɛrm], n. (—s, pl. —e) bowels, intestines, entrails.

Gedeck [gə'dɛk], n. (—s, pl. —e) cover; menu; place laid at a table.

gedeihen [gə'daiən], v.n. irr. (aux. sein) thrive, prosper; progress.

gedeihlich [gə'dailɪç], adj. thriving, salutary.

gedenken [gə'dɛŋkən], v.n. irr. (Genit.) think of, remember; — etwas zu tun, intend to do s.th.

Gedenken [gə'dɛŋkən], n. (—s, no pl.) remembrance.

Gedenkfeier [gə'dɛŋkfaiər], f. (—, pl. —n) commemoration.

Gedicht [gə'dɪçt], n. (—s, pl. —e) poem.

gediegen [gə'diːgən], adj. solid, sound, genuine, true, honourable, sterling.

Gedränge [gə'drɛŋə], n. (—s, no pl.) crowd, throng; crush.

Gedrängtheit [gə'drɛŋkthait], f. (—, no pl.) conciseness.

gedrungen [gə'druŋən], adj. thick-set, stocky; compact; concise (style).

Geduld [gə'dult], f. (—, no pl.) patience, forbearance.

gedulden [gə'duldən], v.r. sich —, be patient.

geduldig [gə'duldɪç], adj. patient, forbearing, indulgent.

Geduld(s)spiel [gə'dult(s)ʃpiːl], n. (—s, pl. —e) puzzle; (Cards) patience.

gedunsen [gə'dunzən], adj. bloated.

geeignet [gə'aignet], adj. suitable, fit, appropriate, apt.

Gefahr [gə'faːr], f. (—, pl. —en) danger, peril, hazard, risk; — laufen, run the risk.

gefährden [gə'fɛːrdən], v.a. endanger, imperil, jeopardize.

gefährlich [gə'fɛːrlɪç], adj. dangerous, perilous.

Gefährt [gə'fɛːrt], n. (—s, pl. —e) (obs.) vehicle, conveyance.

Gefährte [gə'fɛːrtə], m. (—en, pl. —en) comrade, companion, fellow.

Gefälle

Gefälle [gəˈfɛlə], n. (—s, pl. —e) fall, descent, incline, gradient.

Gefallen (1) [gəˈfalən], m. (—s, no pl.) pleasure, liking; favour, kindness.

gefallen (1) [gəˈfalən], v.n. irr. please; es gefällt mir, I like it; wie gefällt Ihnen . . .; how do you like . . . .

gefallen (2) [gəˈfalən], adj. (Mil.) fallen, killed in action.

gefällig [gəˈfɛlɪç], adj. pleasing, accommodating, obliging, anxious to please; was ist —? what can I do for you?

Gefälligkeit [gəˈfɛlɪçkaɪt], f. (—, pl. —en) courtesy; favour, service, good turn.

gefälligst [gəˈfɛlɪçst], adv. if you please.

Gefallsucht [gəˈfalzuxt], f. (—, no pl.) coquetry.

gefallsüchtig [gəˈfalzyçtɪç], adj. coquettish.

gefangen [gəˈfaŋən], adj. in prison, imprisoned, captive.

Gefangene [gəˈfaŋənə], m. (—n, pl. —n) prisoner, captive.

Gefangennahme [gəˈfaŋənnaːmə], f. (—, no pl.) arrest, capture.

Gefangenschaft [gəˈfaŋənʃaft], f. (—, no pl.) captivity, imprisonment, detention; in — geraten, be taken prisoner.

Gefängis [gəˈfɛŋnɪs], n. (—sses, pl. —sse) prison, gaol.

Gefäß [gəˈfɛːs], n. (—es, pl. —e) vessel.

gefaßt [gəˈfast], adj. collected, composed, ready; calm; sich auf etwas — machen, prepare o.s. for s.th.

Gefecht [gəˈfɛçt], n. (—s, pl. —e) fight, battle, combat; action, engagement.

gefeit [gəˈfaɪt], adj. proof against.

Gefieder [gəˈfiːdər], n. (—s, no pl.) plumage, feathers.

Gefilde [gəˈfɪldə], n. (—s, pl. —s) (Poet.) fields, plain.

Geflecht [gəˈflɛçt], n. (—s, no pl.) wicker-work, texture.

geflissentlich [gəˈflɪsəntlɪç], adj. intentional, wilful, with a purpose.

Geflügel [gəˈflyːgəl], n. (—s, no pl.) fowls, poultry.

geflügelt [gəˈflyːgəlt], adj. winged; —e Worte, household word, familiar quotation.

Geflüster [gəˈflystər], n. (—s, no pl.) whispering, whisper.

Gefolge [gəˈfɔlgə], n. (—s, no pl.) retinue, following.

gefräßig [gəˈfrɛːsɪç], adj. voracious, gluttonous.

Gefreite [gəˈfraɪtə], m. (—n, pl. —n) (Mil.) lance-corporal.

gefrieren [gəˈfriːrən], v.n. irr. (aux. sein) freeze; congeal.

Gefrierpunkt [gəˈfriːrpuŋkt], m. (—s, no pl.) freezing point, zero.

Gefrorene [gəˈfroːrənə], n. (—n, no pl.) ice-cream.

Gefüge [gəˈfyːgə], n. (—s, no pl.) joints, structure, construction; frame.

gefügig [gəˈfyːgɪç], adj. pliant; docile; einen — machen, make s.o. amenable, persuade s.o.

Gefühl [gəˈfyːl], n. (—s, pl. —e) feeling, sense, sensation.

gegen [ˈgeːgən], prep. (Acc.) against; towards; about, near; in comparison with; in the direction of; opposed to; in exchange for; — Quittung, against receipt. — adv., prefix. counter, opposing, contrary.

Gegend [ˈgeːgənt], f. (—, pl. —en) region, country, part.

Gegengewicht [ˈgeːgəngəvɪçt], n. (—s, pl. —e) counterweight, counterpoise.

Gegengift [ˈgeːgəngɪft], n. (—s, pl. —e) antidote.

Gegenleistung [ˈgeːgənlaɪstuŋ], f. (—, pl. —en) return; service in return; Leistung und —, give and take.

Gegenrede [ˈgeːgənreːdə], f. (—, pl. —n) contradiction; objection.

Gegensatz [ˈgeːgənzats], m. (—es, pl. ˙e) contrast, opposition, antithesis.

gegensätzlich [ˈgeːgənzɛtslɪç], adj. contrary, adverse.

Gegenseite [ˈgeːgənzaɪtə], f. (—, pl. —n) opposite side; (coin) reverse.

gegenseitig [ˈgeːgənzaɪtɪç], adj. reciprocal, mutual.

Gegenstand [ˈgeːgənʃtant], m. (—s, pl. ˙e) object; subject, matter.

gegenstandslos [ˈgeːgənʃtantsloːs], adj. superfluous, irrelevant.

Gegenstück [ˈgeːgənʃtyk], n. (—s, pl. —e) counterpart.

Gegenteil [ˈgeːgəntaɪl], n. (—s, no pl.) contrary; im —, on the contrary.

gegenüber [geːgənˈyːbər], prep. (Dat.) opposite to, facing. — adv. opposite.

Gegenüberstellung [geːgənˈyːbərʃteluŋ], f. (—, pl. —en) confrontation.

Gegenwart [ˈgeːgənvart], f. (—, no pl.) presence; (Gram.) present tense.

Gegenwehr [ˈgeːgənveːr], f. (—, no pl.) defence, resistance.

Gegenwirkung [ˈgeːgənvɪrkuŋ], f. (—, pl. —en) reaction, counter-effect.

gegenzeichnen [ˈgeːgəntsaɪçnən], v.a. countersign.

Gegner [ˈgeːgnər], m. (—s, pl. —) opponent, adversary, antagonist.

gegnerisch [ˈgeːgnərɪʃ], adj. adverse, antagonistic.

Gegnerschaft [ˈgeːgnərʃaft], f. (—, no pl.) antagonism; opposition.

Gehalt (1) [gəˈhalt], m. (—s, no pl.) contents; (fig.) value, standard.

Gehalt (2) [gəˈhalt], n. (—s, pl. ˙er) salary, stipend; pay.

Gehaltszulage [gəˈhaltstsuːlaːgə], f. (—, pl. —n) rise (in salary); increment; (Am.) raise.

gehaltvoll [gəˈhaltfɔl], adj. substantial.

Gehänge [gəˈhɛŋə], n. (—s, pl. —) slope; festoon, garland.

geharnischt [gəˈharnɪʃt], adj. armoured, steel-clad; (fig.) severe.

gehässig [gəˈhɛsɪç], adj. malicious, spiteful.

Gehäuse [gə'hɔyzə], *n.* (—s, *pl.* —) casing, case; (*snail*) shell.

Gehege [gə'he:gə], *n.* (—s, *pl.* —) enclosure; *einem ins — kommen*, trespass on s.o.'s preserves.

geheim [gə'haɪm], *adj.* secret, clandestine.

Geheimnis [gə'haɪmnɪs], *n.* (—ses, *pl.* —se) secret, mystery.

geheimnisvoll [gə'haɪmnɪsfɔl], *adj.* mysterious.

Geheimrat [gə'haɪmra:t], *m.* (—s, *pl.* ·:e) Privy Councillor.

Geheimschrift [gə'haɪmʃrɪft], *f.* (—, *pl.* —en) cryptography.

Geheimsprache [gə'haɪmʃpra:xə], *f.* (—, *pl.* —en) cipher.

Geheiß [gə'haɪs], *n.* (—es, *no pl.*) command, order, bidding.

gehen ['ge:ən], *v.n. irr.* (*aux.* sein) go, walk; (*Mach.*) work, function; (*goods*) sell; (*dough*) rise; *er lässt sich —*, he lets himself go; *er lässt es sich gut —*, he enjoys himself; *einem an die Hand —*, lend s.o. a hand, assist s.o.; *in Erfüllung —*, come true; *in sich —*, reflect; *wie geht es dir?* how are you? *es geht mir gut*, I am well.

geheuer [gə'hɔyər], *adj.* (*only in neg.*) *nicht geheuer —*, creepy, eerie, uncanny; (*coll.*) fishy.

Gehilfe [gə'hɪlfə], *m.* (—n, *pl.* —n) assistant, helper.

Gehirn [gə'hɪrn], *n.* (—s, *pl.* —e) brain, brains.

Gehirnhautentzündung [gə'hɪrnhautɛntsynduŋ], *f.* (—, *pl.* —en) meningitis, cerebral inflammation.

Gehirnschlag [gə'hɪrnʃla:k], *m.* (—s, *pl.* ·:e) apoplexy.

Gehöft [gə'hœft], *n.* (—es, *pl.* —e) farmstead.

Gehör [gə'hø:r], (—s, *no pl.*) hearing; *gutes —*, musical ear.

gehorchen [gə'hɔrçən], *v.n.* obey; *nicht —*, disobey.

gehören [gə'hø:rən], *v.n.* belong. — *v.r. sich —*, be the proper thing to do.

gehörig [gə'hø:rɪç], *adj. dazu —*, belonging to, referring to; due, fit, proper, thorough; (*fig.*) sound.

Gehörn [gə'hœrn], *n.* (—s, *pl.* —e) horns, antlers.

gehörnt [gə'hœrnt], *adj.* horned; (*fig.*) duped (husband).

Gehorsam [gə'ho:rza:m], *m.* (—s, *no pl.*) obedience; *— leisten*, show obedience; *den — verweigern*, refuse to obey.

gehorsam [gə'ho:rza:m], *adj.* obedient, dutiful, submissive.

Gehrock ['ge:rɔk], *m.* (—s, *pl.* ·:e) frock-coat.

Geier ['gaɪər], *m.* (—s, *pl.* —) (*Orn.*) vulture.

Geifer ['gaɪfər], *m.* (—s, *no pl.*) saliva, drivel; (*animals*) foam; (*fig.*) venom, rancour.

geifern ['gaɪfərn], *v.n.* slaver, drivel; (*fig.*) foam at the mouth; give vent to o.'s anger.

Geige ['gaɪgə], *f.* (—, *pl.* —n) violin, fiddle.

Geigenharz ['gaɪgənha:rts], *n.* (—es, *no pl.*) colophony; rosin.

Geigensteg ['gaɪgənʃte:k], *m.* (—s, *pl.* —e) bridge of a violin.

Geiger ['gaɪgər], *m.* (—s, *pl.* —) violin-player, violinist.

geil [gaɪl], *adj.* rank; lecherous, lascivious.

Geisel ['gaɪzəl], *f.* (—, *pl.* —n) hostage.

Geiß [gaɪs], *f.* (—, *pl.* —en) goat, she-goat.

Geißblatt ['gaɪsblat], *n.* (—s, *no pl.*) (*Bot.*) honeysuckle.

Geißbock ['gaɪsbɔk], *m.* (—s, *pl.* ·:e) billy-goat.

Geißel ['gaɪsəl], *f.* (—, *pl.* —n) scourge.

geißeln ['gaɪsəln], *v.a.* scourge, whip, flagellate.

Geist [gaɪst], *m.* (—es, *pl.* —er) spirit, mind; brains, intellect; wit; apparition, ghost.

Geisterbeschwörung ['gaɪstərbəʃvø:ruŋ], *f.* (—, *pl.* —en) evocation (of spirits); necromancy; exorcism.

geisterhaft ['gaɪstərhaft], *adj.* ghostly, spectral, weird.

Geisterwelt ['gaɪstərvɛlt], *f.* (—, *no pl.*) world of spirits.

geistesabwesend ['gaɪstəsapve:zənt], *adj.* absent-minded.

Geistesfreiheit ['gaɪstəsfraɪhaɪt], *f.* (—, *no pl.*) freedom of thought.

Geistesgegenwart ['gaɪstəsge:gənvart], *f.* (—, *no pl.*) presence of mind.

Geisteskraft ['gaɪstəskraft], *f.* (—, *pl.* ·:e) faculty of the mind.

Geistesstörung ['gaɪstəsʃtø:ruŋ], *f.* (—, *pl.* —en) mental aberration.

Geistesverfassung ['gaɪstəsfɛrfasuŋ], *f.* (—, *no pl.*) state of mind.

geistesverwandt ['gaɪstəsfɛrvant], *adj.* congenial.

Geistesverwirrung ['gaɪstəsfɛrvɪruŋ], *f.* (—, *no pl.*) bewilderment.

Geisteswissenschaften ['gaɪstəsvɪsənʃaftən], *f.pl.* (*Univ.*) Arts, Humanities.

Geisteszerrüttung ['gaɪstəstsɛrytuŋ], *f.* (—, *no pl.*) mental derangement, insanity.

geistig ['gaɪstɪç], *adj.* intellectual, mental; spiritual; *—e Getränke*, alcoholic liquors.

geistlich ['gaɪstlɪç], *adj.* spiritual; religious; ecclesiastical, clerical; *—er Orden*, religious order; *—er Stand*, holy orders, the Clergy.

Geistliche ['gaɪstlɪçə], *m.* (—n, *pl.* —n) priest, clergyman, cleric; minister of religion.

Geistlichkeit ['gaɪstlɪçkaɪt], *f.* (—, *no pl.*) clergy.

geistlos ['gaɪstlo:s], *adj.* dull, stupid.

geistreich ['gaɪstraɪç], *adj.* clever, witty.

Geiz [gaɪts], *m.* (—es, *no pl.*) avarice, covetousness.

geizen ['gaɪtsən], *v.n.* be miserly.

Geizhals

Geizhals ['gaɪtshals], *m.* (**—es**, *pl.* ˙˙e) miser, niggard.

Geizkragen ['gaɪtskra:gən], *m.* (**—s**, *pl.* **—**) *see* **Geizhals**.

Gekreisch [gə'kraɪʃ], *n.* (**—es**, *no pl.*) screaming, shrieks.

Gekritzel [gə'krɪtsəl], *n.* (**—s**, *no pl.*) scrawling, scribbling.

Gekröse [gə'krø:zə], *n.* (**—s**, *no pl.*) tripe; (*Anat.*) mesentery.

gekünstelt [gə'kynstəlt], *adj.* artificial, affected.

Gelächter [gə'lɛçtər], *n.* (**—s**, *no pl.*) laughter.

Gelage [gə'la:gə], *n.* (**—s**, *pl.* **—**) (*obs.*) feast, banquet.

Gelände [gə'lɛndə], *n.* (**—s**, *pl.* **—**) terrain, region; landscape.

Geländer [gə'lɛndər], *n.* (**—s**, *pl.* **—**) railing, balustrade, banister.

gelangen [gə'laŋən], *v.n.* (*aux.* sein) arrive, come (to).

Gelaß [gə'las], *n.* (**—sses**, *pl.* **—sse**) (*obs.*) room, chamber.

gelassen [gə'lasən], *adj.* calm, composed, collected.

geläufig [gə'lɔyfɪç], *adj.* fluent.

gelaunt [gə'launt], *adj.* disposed.

Geläute [gə'lɔytə], *n.* (**—s**, *no pl.*) ringing, chiming; bells.

geläutert [gə'lɔytərt], *adj.* purified, cleansed.

gelb [gɛlp], *adj.* yellow, amber.

Gelbschnabel ['gɛlpʃna:bəl], *m.* (**—s**, *pl.* ˙˙) (*Orn.*) fledg(e)ling; greenhorn.

Gelbsucht ['gɛlpzuxt], *f.* (**—**, *no pl.*) jaundice.

Geld [gɛlt], *n.* (**—es**, *pl.* **—er**) money, currency, coin; *bares* **—**, ready money, hard cash; *kleines* **—**, small change.

Geldanweisung ['gɛltanvaɪzuŋ], *f.* (**—** *pl.* **—en**) money-order.

Geldbuße ['gɛltbu:sə], *f.* (**—**, *pl.* **—n**) fine.

Geldkurs ['gɛltkurs], *m.* (**—es**, *pl.* **—e**) rate of exchange.

Geldmittel ['gɛltmɪtəl], *n. pl.* pecuniary resources, financial resources.

Geldschrank ['gɛltʃraŋk], *m.* (**—s**, *pl.* ˙˙e) safe.

Geldstrafe ['gɛltʃtra:fə], *f.* (**—**, *pl.* **—n**) fine.

Geldverlegenheit ['gɛltfɛrle:gənhaɪt], *f.* (**—**, *pl.* **—en**) pecuniary embarrassment, financial straits.

Geldwährung ['gɛltvɛ:ruŋ], *f.* (**—**, *pl.* **—en**) currency.

Geldwechsel ['gɛltvɛksəl], *m.* (**—s**, *no pl.*) exchange.

Gelee [ʒə'le:], *n.* (**—s**, *pl.* **—s**) jelly.

gelegen [gə'le:gən], *adj.* situated, situate; *das kommt mir gerade* **—**, that suits me; *mir ist daran* **—**, *dass*, I am anxious that.

Gelegenheit [gə'le:gənhaɪt], *f.* (**—**, *pl.* **—en**) occasion, chance, opportunity; facility; *bei* **—**, one of these days.

Gelegenheitskauf [gə'le:gənhaɪtskauf], *m.* (**—s**, *pl.* ˙˙e) bargain.

gelegentlich [gə'le:gəntlɪç], *adj.* occasional.

gelehrig [gə'le:rɪç], *adj.* docile, tractable.

Gelehrsamkeit [gə'le:rzamkaɪt], *f.* (**—**, *no pl.*) learning, erudition.

gelehrt [gə'le:rt], *adj.* learned, erudite.

Gelehrte [gə'le:rtə], *m.* (**—n**, *pl.* **—n**) scholar, man of learning, savant.

Geleise [gə'laɪzə], *n.* (**—s**, *pl.* **—**) *see* **Gleis**.

Geleit [gə'laɪt], *n.* (**—s**, *no pl.*) escort, accompaniment; (*Naut.*) convoy; *sicheres* **—**, safe conduct.

geleiten [gə'laɪtən], *v.a.* accompany, conduct, escort.

Gelenk [gə'lɛŋk], *n.* (**—s**, *pl.* **—e**) (*human*) joint; (*chain*) link.

Gelenkentzündung [gə'lɛŋkɛnttsyn-duŋ], *f.* (**—**, *pl.* **—en**) (*Med.*) arthritis.

gelenkig [gə'lɛŋkɪç], *adj.* flexible, pliant, nimble, supple.

Gelenkrheumatismus [gə'lɛŋkrɔyma-tismus], *m.* (**—**, *no pl.*) (*Med.*) rheumatoid arthritis, rheumatic gout.

Gelichter [gə'lɪçtər], *n.* (**—s**, *no pl.*) riff-raff.

Geliebte [gə'li:ptə], *m.* (**—n**, *pl.* **—n**) lover, sweetheart, beloved. — *f.* (**—n**, *pl.* **—n**) mistress; beloved.

gelinde [gə'lɪndə], *adj.* soft, smooth, gentle, mild; — *gesagt*, to say the least.

Gelingen [gə'lɪŋən], *n.* (**—s**, *no pl.*) success.

gelingen [gə'lɪŋən], *v.n. irr.* (*aux.* sein) succeed; *es gelingt mir*, I succeed.

gellen ['gɛlən], *v.n.* yell; shrill.

geloben [gə'lo:bən], *v.a.* (*aux.* haben) promise solemnly, vow; *das Gelobte Land*, the Promised Land.

Gelöbnis [gə'lø:pnɪs], *n.* (**—ses**, *pl.* **—se**) vow, promise.

gelt [gɛlt], *inter.* (*coll.*) isn't it? don't you think so?

gelten ['gɛltən], *v.a. irr.* be worth, cost. — *v.n.* count (as), be valid.

Geltung ['gɛltuŋ], *f.* (**—**, *no pl.*) value, importance.

Gelübde [gə'lypdə], *n.* (**—s**, *pl.* **—**) vow, solemn promise *or* undertaking.

gelungen [gə'luŋən], *adj.* (*coll.*) funny, capital.

Gelüst [gə'lyst], *n.* (**—s**, *pl.* **—e**) appetite, desire.

gelüsten [gə'lystən], *v.a.* — *nach*, long for, covet.

Gemach [gə'ma:x], *n.* (**—es**, *pl.* ˙˙er) (*Poet.*) chamber, room; apartment.

gemach [gə'ma:x], *adv.* slowly, softly, by degrees.

gemächlich [gə'mɛçlɪç], *adj.* slow, soft, easy, unhurried, leisurely.

Gemahl [gə'ma:l], *m.* (**—s**, *pl.* **—e**) spouse, husband, consort.

Gemahlin [gə'ma:lɪn], *f.* (**—**, *pl.* **—nen**) spouse, wife, consort.

Gemälde [gə'mɛ:ldə], *n.* (**—s**, *pl.* **—**) picture, painting, portrait.

gemäß [gə'mɛ:s], *prep.* (*Dat.*) in accordance with, according to.

gemäßigt [gə'mɛ:sıçt], *adj.* temperate, moderate; *—es Klima,* temperate climate.

Gemäuer [gə'mɔyər], *n.* (—s, *no pl.*) ancient walls, ruins.

gemein [gə'maın], *adj.* common, mean, low, vulgar, base.

Gemeinde [gə'maındə], *f.* (—, *pl.* —n) community, parish, municipality; *(Eccl.)* congregation.

Gemeindevorstand [gə'maındefor-ʃtant], *m.* (—es, *no pl.*) town or borough council.

gemeingefährlich [gə'maıngəfɛ:rlıç], *adj.* dangerous to the public.

Gemeinheit [gə'maınhaıt], *f.* (—, *pl.* —en) meanness; baseness; dirty trick.

gemeinhin [gə'maınhın], *adv.* commonly.

Gemeinplatz [gə'maınplats], *m.* (—es, *pl.* ˙e) commonplace, truism.

gemeinsam [gə'maınza:m], *adj.* common, joint; *der — Markt,* (*Pol.*) Common Market; *—e Sache machen,* make common cause. — *adv.* together.

Gemeinschaft [gə'maınʃaft], *f.* (—, *pl.* —en) community; association; *in — mit,* jointly; *in — haben,* hold in common.

gemeinschaftlich [gə'maınʃaftlıç], *adj.* common. — *adv.* in common, together.

Gemeinsinn [gə'maınzın], *m.* (—s, *no pl.*) public spirit.

Gemeinwesen [gə'maınve:zən], *n.* (—s, *no pl.*) community.

Gemeinwohl [gə'maınvo:l], *n.* (—s, *no pl.*) common weal; common good.

Gemenge [gə'mɛŋə], *n.* (—s, *no pl.*) mixture; (*fig.*) scuffle.

Gemengsel [gə'mɛŋsəl], *n.* (—s, *no pl.*) medley, hotchpotch.

gemessen [gə'mɛsən], *adj.* deliberate.

Gemessenheit [gə'mɛsənhaıt], *f.* (—, *no pl.*) precision, deliberation.

Gemetzel [gə'mɛtsəl], *n.* (—s, *no pl.*) slaughter, massacre.

Gemisch [gə'mıʃ], *n.* (—es, *pl.* —e) mixture, motley.

Gemme ['gɛmə], *f.* (—, *pl.* —n) gem, cameo.

Gemse ['gɛmzə], *f.* (—, *pl.* —n) chamois.

Gemüse [gə'my:zə], *n.* (—s, *pl.* —) vegetables, greens.

Gemüsehändler [gə'my:zəhɛndlər], *m.* (—s, *pl.* —) greengrocer.

gemustert [gə'mustərt], *adj.* patterned, figured; (*Comm.*) *—e Sendung,* delivery as per sample.

Gemüt [gə'my:t], *n.* (—s, *pl.* —er) mind, soul, heart; disposition, nature, spirit, temper; feeling.

gemütlich [gə'my:tlıç], *adj.* cosy, snug, comfortable; genial, friendly, pleasant.

Gemütlichkeit [gə'my:tlıçkaıt], *f.* (—, *no pl.*) cosiness, snugness; *da hört die — auf,* that is more than I will stand for.

gemütlos [gə'my:tlo:s], *adj.* unfeeling.

Gemütsart [gə'my:tsa:rt], *f.* (—, *no pl.*) disposition; character.

Gemütsbewegung [gə'my:tsbəve:guŋ], *f.* (—, *pl.* —en) emotion.

gemütskrank [gə'my:tskraŋk], *adj.* sick in mind; melancholy.

Gemütsleben [gə'my:tsle:bən], *n.* (—s, *no pl.*) emotional life.

Gemütsmensch [gə'my:tsmɛnʃ], *m.* (—en, *pl.* —en) man of feeling or sentiment; (*pej.*) sentimentalist.

gemütvoll [gə'my:tfɔl], *adj.* full of feeling, sympathetic.

gen [gen], *prep. contraction* of **gegen**, (*Poet.*) towards, to (*Acc.*).

Genannte [gə'nantə], *m.* (—n, *pl.* —n) named person, aforesaid.

genäschig [gə'nɛʃıç], *adj.* fond of sweets, sweet-toothed.

genau [gə'nau], *adj.* precise, exact, accurate; strict, parsimonious.

Genauigkeit [gə'nauıçkaıt], *f.* (—, *no pl.*) accuracy, exactitude, precision.

Gendarm [ʒã'darm], *m.* (—en, *pl.* —en) policeman, constable.

genehm [gə'ne:m], *adj.* agreeable, acceptable, convenient.

genehmigen [gə'ne:mıgən], *v.a.* approve of, agree to, permit; (*contract*) ratify.

geneigt [gə'naıkt], *adj.* inclined (to), disposed (to), prone (to); *einem — sein,* be well disposed towards s.o.; (*Lit.*) *der —e Leser,* gentle reader.

Geneigtheit [gə'naıkthaıt], *f.* (—, *no pl.*) inclination, proneness, propensity; favour, kindness.

General [gena'ra:l], *m.* (—s, *pl.* —e, ˙e) general.

Generalfeldmarschall [gena'ra:lfɛlt-marʃal], *m.* (—s, *pl.* ˙e) field marshal.

Generalkommando [gena'ra:lkɔmando], *n.* (—s, *pl.* —s) general's headquarters; (corps) headquarters.

Generalkonsul [gena'ra:lkɔnzul], *m.* (—s, *pl.* —e) consul-general.

Generalnenner [gena'ra:lnɛnər], *m.* (—s, *pl.* —) (*Maths.*) common denominator.

Generalprobe [gena'ra:lpro:bə], *f.* (—, *pl.* —n) dress-rehearsal.

Generalvollmacht [gena'ra:lfɔlmaxt], *f.* (—, *pl.* —en) (*Law*) general power of attorney.

generell [gena'rɛl], *adj.* general, common.

generös [gena'rø:s], *adj.* generous, magnanimous.

genesen [gə'ne:zən], *v.n. irr.* (*aux.* sein) recover, be restored to health; convalesce.

Genf [genf], *n.* Geneva.

genial [gen'ja:l], *adj.* ingenious; extremely gifted.

Genick [gə'nık], *n.* (—s, *pl.* —e) nape, neck.

Genickstarre [gə'nıkʃtarə], *f.* (—, *no pl.*) (*Med.*) (cerebrospinal) meningitis.

Genie [ʒe'ni:], *n.* (—s, *pl.* —s) genius.

genieren

genieren [ʒeˈniːrən], *v.a.* trouble, embarrass, disturb. — *v.r. sich* —, feel embarrassed; *sich nicht* —, make o.s. at home.

genießbar [gəˈniːsbaːr], *adj.* eatable, edible, palatable; drinkable; (*fig.*) pleasant, agreeable.

genießen [gəˈniːsən], *v.a. irr.* enjoy; have the use of; (*food*) eat, partake of; *Ansehen* —, enjoy respect.

Geniestreich [ʒeˈniːˌʃtraɪç], *m.* (—s, *pl.* —e) stroke of genius.

Genitiv [ˈɡeːnitiːf], *m.* (—s, *pl.* —e) (*Gram.*) genitive.

Genosse [gəˈnɔsə], *m.* (—n, *pl.* —n) comrade, mate, colleague; (*crime*) accomplice.

Genossenschaft [gəˈnɔsənʃaft], *f.* (—, *pl.* —en) association, company, confederacy, co-operative, union.

Genre [ˈʒãrə], *n.* (—s, *pl.* —s) genre; style, kind.

Gent [gɛnt], *n.* Ghent.

Genua [ˈgeːnua], *n.* Genoa.

genug [gəˈnuːk], *indecl. adj.* enough, sufficient; —! that will do!

Genüge [gəˈnyːgə], *f.* (—, *no pl.*) *zur* —, sufficiently; *einem* — *leisten*, give satisfaction to s.o.

genügen [gəˈnyːgən], *v.n.* be enough, suffice; *sich etwas* — *lassen*, be content with s.th.

genügsam [gəˈnyːkzaːm], *adj.* easily satisfied; temperate, sober.

Genügsamkeit [gəˈnyːkzaːmkaɪt], *f.* (—, *no pl.*) contentedness, moderation; temperateness, sobriety.

Genugtuung [gəˈnuːktuːuŋ], *f.* (—, *no pl.*) satisfaction; reparation; atonement.

Genuß [gəˈnus], *m.* (—sses, *pl.* ⸚sse) enjoyment; use; (*food*) consumption.

Genußmittel [gəˈnusmɪtəl], *n.* (—s, *pl.* —) (*mostly pl.*) luxuries; (*Am.*) delicatessen.

genußreich [gəˈnusraɪç], *adj.* enjoyable, delightful.

Genußsucht [gəˈnuszuxt], *f.* (—, *no pl.*) thirst for pleasure.

Geograph [geoˈgraːf], *m.* (—en, *pl.* —en) geographer.

Geographie [geograˈfiː], *f.* (—, *no pl.*) geography.

Geologe [geoˈloːgə], *m.* (—n, *pl.* —n) geologist.

Geologie [geoloˈgiː], *f.* (—, *no pl.*) geology.

Geometer [geoˈmeːtər], *m.* (—s, *pl.* —) geometrician; land-surveyor.

Geometrie [geomeˈtriː], *f.* (—, *no pl.*) geometry.

Georg [geˈɔrk], *m.* George.

Georgine [geɔrˈgiːnə], *f.* (—, *pl.* —n) (*Bot.*) dahlia.

Gepäck [gəˈpɛk], *n.* (—s, *no pl.*) luggage; (*Am.*) baggage.

Gepäckaufbewahrung [gəˈpɛkaufbəvaːruŋ], *f.* (—, *pl.* —en) left luggage office.

86

Gepäckträger [gəˈpɛktrɛːgər], *m.* (—s, *pl.* —) porter.

Gepflogenheit [gəˈpfloːgənhaɪt], *f.* (—, *pl.* —en) habit, custom, wont.

Geplänkel [gəˈplɛnkəl], *n.* (—s, *pl.* —) (*rare*) skirmish.

Geplärr [gəˈplɛr], *n.* (—s, *no pl.*) bawling.

Geplauder [gəˈplaudər], *n.* (—s, *no pl.*) chatting; small talk.

Gepräge [gəˈprɛːgə], *n.* (—s, *no pl.*) impression, stamp.

Gepränge [gəˈprɛŋə], *n.* (—s, *no pl.*) pomp, ceremony, splendour.

Ger [geːr], *m.* (—s, *pl.* —e) (*rare*) spear, javelin.

Gerade [gəˈraːdə], *f.* (—n, *pl.* —n) (*Maths.*) straight line.

gerade [gəˈraːdə], *adj.* straight, direct, erect, even; (*fig.*) upright, honest. — *adv.* quite, just; *jetzt* —, now more than ever; *fünf* — *sein lassen*, stretch a point; — *heraus*, in plain terms.

geradeaus [gəˈraːdəaus], *adv.* straight on.

gerädert [gəˈrɛːdərt], *adj.* (*fig.*) fatigued, exhausted, worn out.

geradeswegs [gəˈraːdəsveːks], *adv.* straightaway, immediately.

geradezu [gəˈraːdətsuː], *adv.* frankly, downright; *das ist* — *scheußlich*, this is downright nasty.

Geradheit [gəˈraːthaɪt], *f.* (—, *no pl.*) straightness; (*fig.*) straightforwardness.

geradlinig [gəˈraːtliːnɪç], *adj.* rectilinear.

geradsinnig [gəˈraːtzinɪç], *adj.* honest, upright.

gerändert [gəˈrɛndərt], *adj.* with a milled edge.

Geranie [gəˈraːnjə], *f.* (—, *pl.* —n) (*Bot.*) geranium.

Gerät [gəˈrɛːt], *n.* (—s, *pl.* —e) tool, implement, device; appliance; (radio, television) set; apparatus.

geraten [gəˈraːtən], *v.n. irr.* (*aux.* sein) turn out; *gut* —, turn out well; — *auf*, come upon.

Geräteturnen [gəˈrɛːtəturnən], *n.* (—s, *no pl.*) gymnastics with apparatus.

Geratewohl [gəˈraːtəvoːl], *n.* (—s, *no pl.*) *aufs* —, at random.

geraum [gəˈraum], *adj.* —*e Zeit*, a long time.

geräumig [gəˈrɔymɪç], *adj.* spacious, large, wide, roomy.

Geräusch [gəˈrɔyʃ], *n.* (—es, *pl.* —e) noise; sound.

gerben [ˈgɛrbən], *v.a.* tan, taw; *einem die Haut* —, give s.o. a hiding.

Gerber [ˈgɛrbər], *m.* (—s, *pl.* —) tanner.

Gerbsäure [ˈgɛrpsɔyrə], *f.* (—, *no pl.*) tannin.

gerecht [gəˈrɛçt], *adj.* just, fair; (*Bibl.*) righteous; *einem* — *werden*, do justice to s.o.

Gerechtigkeit [gəˈrɛçtɪçkaɪt], *f.* (—, *no pl.*) justice, fairness; (*Bibl.*) righteousness.

Geschick

Gerede [gəˈreːdə], *n.* (**—s**, *no pl.*) talk, rumour, gossip.

gereichen [gəˈraɪçən], *v.n.* turn out to be; *einem zur Ehre —*, redound to s.o.'s honour.

gereizt [gəˈraɪtst], *adj.* irritated, annoyed.

gereuen [gəˈrɔyən] *see* reuen.

Gerhard [ˈgeːrhart], *m.* Gerard, Gerald.

Gericht [gəˈrɪçt], *n.* (**—s**, *pl.* **—e**) court of justice, tribunal; (*food*) course, dish; *das Jüngste —*, Last Judgment.

gerichtlich [gəˈrɪçtlɪç], *adj.* judicial, legal; *einen — belangen*, sue s.o.

Gerichtsbarkeit [gəˈrɪçtsbarkaɪt], *f.* (**—**, *no pl.*) jurisdiction.

Gerichtsdiener [gəˈrɪçtsdiːnər], *m.* (**—s**, *pl.* **—**) (*law court*) usher.

Gerichtshof [gəˈrɪçtshoːf], *m.* (**—es**, *pl.* ˙̈e) court of justice.

Gerichtskanzlei [gəˈrɪçtskantslaɪ], *f.* (**—**, *pl.* **—en**) record office.

Gerichtskosten [gəˈrɪçtskɔstən], *f. pl.* (*Law*) costs.

Gerichtsordnung [gəˈrɪçtsɔrdnuŋ], *f.* (**—**, *pl* **—en**) legal procedure.

Gerichtstermin [gəˈrɪçtstermiːn], *m.* (**—s**, *pl.* **—e**) day fixed for a hearing.

Gerichtsverhandlung [gəˈrɪçtsfer-handluŋ], *f.* (**—**, *pl.* **—en**) hearing; trial.

Gerichtsvollzieher [gəˈrɪçtsfɔltsiːər], *m.* (**—s**, *pl.* **—**) bailiff.

gerieben [gəˈriːbən], *adj.* ground; crafty, cunning.

gering [gəˈrɪŋ], *adj.* small, little, mean, petty, unimportant, of little value, trifling; low, base.

geringfügig [gəˈrɪŋfyːgɪç], *adj.* small, petty, insignificant.

geringschätzig [gəˈrɪŋʃetsɪç], *adj.* contemptuous, disdainful, supercilious; derogatory.

gerinnen [gəˈrɪnən], *v.n. irr.* (*aux.* sein) coagulate, clot; curdle.

Gerinnsel [gəˈrɪnzəl], *n.* (**—s**, *pl.* **—**) embolism (of the blood); clot.

Gerippe [gəˈrɪpə], *n.* (**—s**, *pl.* **—**) skeleton; frame; (*Aviat.*) air-frame.

gerippt [gəˈrɪpt], *adj.* ribbed, fluted.

gerissen [gəˈrɪsən], *adj.* (*coll.*) sharp, cunning.

Germane [gɛrˈmaːnə], *m.* (**—n**, *pl.* **—n**) Teuton.

Germanist [ˈgɛrmanɪst], *m.* (**—en**, *pl.* **—en**) (*Univ.*) student of *or* expert in German language and/or literature.

gern [gɛrn], *adv.* gladly, willingly, readily, with pleasure; *— haben*, like.

Geröll [gəˈrœl], *n.* (**—s**, *no pl.*) boulders, rubble.

Gerste [ˈgɛrstə], *f.* (**—**, *no pl.*) (*Bot.*) barley.

Gerstenschleim [ˈgɛrstənʃlaɪm], *m.* (**—s**, *no pl.*) barley water.

Gerte [ˈgɛrtə], *f.* (**—**, *pl.* **—n**) whip, switch, rod.

Geruch [gəˈruːx], *m.* (**—s**, *pl.* ˙̈e) smell, odour, scent; *guter —*, fragrance, aroma.

geruchlos [gəˈruːxloːs], *adj.* scentless, odourless, without smell.

Geruchsinn [gəˈruːxzɪn], *m.* (**—es**, *no pl.*) sense of smell.

Gerücht [gəˈryçt], *n.* (**—s**, *pl.* **—e**) rumour, report.

Gerümpel [gəˈrympəl], *n.* (**—s**, *no pl.*) lumber, trash.

Gerundium [gəˈrundjum], *n.* (**—s**, *pl.* **—dien**) (*Gram.*) gerund.

Gerüst [gəˈryst], *n.* (**—es**, *pl.* **—e**) scaffolding.

Ges [gɛs], *n.* (**—**, *pl.* **—**) (*Mus.*) G flat.

gesamt [gəˈzamt], *adj.* entire, all, complete.

Gesamtheit [gəˈzamthaɪt], *f.* (**—**, *no pl.*) totality.

Gesandte [gəˈzantə], *m.* (**—n**, *pl.* **—n**) messenger; ambassador, envoy; *päpstlicher —*, papal nuncio.

Gesandtschaft [gəˈzantʃaft], *f.* (**—**, *pl.* **—en**) embassy, legation.

Gesang [gəˈzaŋ], *m.* (**—s**, *pl.* ˙̈e) song, air; hymn; (*Lit.*) canto.

Gesangbuch [gəˈzaŋbuːx], *n.* (**—s**, *pl.* ˙̈er) hymnal, hymn-book.

Gesäß [gəˈzɛːs], *n.* (**—es**, *pl.* **—e**) seat, buttocks.

Geschäft [gəˈʃeft], *n.* (**—s**, *pl.* **—e**) business; trade, commerce; affairs; occupation; shop; (*Am.*) store.

geschäftig [gəˈʃeftɪç], *adj.* active, bustling, busy.

geschäftlich [gəˈʃeftlɪç], *adj.* concerning business. — *adv.* on business.

Geschäftsführer [gəˈʃeftsfyːrər], *m.* (**—s**, *pl.* **—**) manager.

Geschäftshaus [gəˈʃeftshaus], *n.* (**—es**, *pl.* ˙̈er) firm; business premises.

geschäftskundig [gəˈʃeftskundɪç], *adj.* experienced in business.

Geschäftslokal [gəˈʃeftsloka:l], *n.* (**—s**, *pl.* **—e**) business premises, shop.

Geschäftsordnung [gəˈʃeftsɔrdnuŋ], *f.* (**—**, *pl.* **—en**) standing orders; agenda.

Geschäftsträger [gəˈʃeftstre:gər], *m.* (**—s**, *pl.* **—**) (*Comm.*) agent; (*Pol.*) chargé d'affaires.

Geschäftsverkehr [gəˈʃeftsferke:r], *m.* (**—s**, *no pl.*) business dealings.

Geschehen [gəˈʃe:ən], *n.* (**—s**, *no pl.*) happening.

geschehen [gəˈʃe:ən], *v.n. irr.* (*aux.* sein) happen, occur; take place; be done; *das geschieht dir recht*, it serves you right.

gescheit [gəˈʃaɪt], *adj.* clever, intelligent.

Geschenk [gəˈʃeŋk], *n.* (**—s**, *pl.* **—e**) gift, present, donation.

Geschichte [gəˈʃɪçtə], *f.* (**—**, *pl.* **—n**) tale; story; history.

Geschichtenbuch [gəˈʃɪçtənbuːx], *n.* (**—es**, *pl.* ˙̈er) story-book.

geschichtlich [gəˈʃɪçtlɪç], *adj.* historical.

Geschichtsschreiber [gəˈʃɪçtsʃraɪbər], *m.* (**—s**, *pl.* **—**) historian.

Geschick [gəˈʃɪk], *n.* (**—es**, *no pl.*) fate, destiny; dexterity, skill, knack, aptitude.

Geschicklichkeit

Geschicklichkeit [gə'ʃɪklɪçkaɪt], *f.* (—, *pl.* —en) dexterity, adroitness, skill.

geschickt [gə'ʃɪkt], *adj.* skilled, skilful, clever, able.

Geschirr [gə'ʃɪr], *n.* (—s, *no pl.*) crockery, plates and dishes; (*horses*) harness.

Geschlecht [gə'ʃlɛçt], *n.* (—s, *pl.* —er) sex; kind, race, species, extraction, family; (*Gram.*) gender.

geschlechtlich [gə'ʃlɛçtlɪç], *adj.* sexual; generic.

Geschlechtsart [gə'ʃlɛçtsa:rt], *f.* (—, *pl.* —en) generic character.

Geschlechtskrankheit [gə'ʃlɛçtskraŋk-haɪt], *f.* (—, *pl.* —en) venereal disease.

Geschlechtskunde [gə'ʃlɛçtskundə], *f.* (—, *no pl.*) genealogy.

Geschlechtsreife [gə'ʃlɛçtsraɪfə], *f.* (—, *no pl.*) puberty.

Geschlechtsteile [gə'ʃlɛçtstaɪlə], *m. pl.* genitals.

Geschlechtstrieb [gə'ʃlɛçtstri:p], *m.* (—s, *no pl.*) sexual instinct.

Geschlechtswort [gə'ʃlɛçtsvɔrt], *n.* (—s, *pl.* ⁻er) (*Gram.*) article.

geschliffen [gə'ʃlɪfən], *adj.* polished; (*glass*) cut.

Geschmack [gə'ʃmak], *m.* (—s, *pl.* ⁻er) taste, flavour.

geschmacklos [gə'ʃmaklo:s], *adj.* tasteless, insipid; in bad taste.

Geschmacksrichtung [gə'ʃmaksrɪç-tuŋ], *f.* (—, *pl.* —en) prevailing taste; vogue; tendency.

Geschmeide [gə'ʃmaɪdə], *n.* (—s, *pl.* —) jewels, jewellery; trinkets.

geschmeidig [gə'ʃmaɪdɪç], *adj.* flexible, pliant, supple; (*Tech.*) malleable.

Geschmeiß [gə'ʃmaɪs], *n.* (—es, *no pl.*) dung; vermin; (*fig.*) rabble.

Geschnatter [gə'ʃnatər], *n.* (—s, *no pl.*) cackling.

geschniegelt [gə'ʃni:gəlt], *adj.* spruce, dressed up.

Geschöpf [gə'ʃœpf], *n.* (—es, *pl.* —e) creature.

Geschoß [gə'ʃɔs], *n.* (—sses, *pl.* —sse) shot, shell, projectile, missile; (*house*) storey.

geschraubt [gə'ʃraupt], *adj.* (*style*) stilted, affected.

Geschrei [gə'ʃraɪ], *n.* (—s, *no pl.*) shrieking, shouting, screaming; (*fig.*) stir, great noise.

Geschreibsel [gə'ʃraɪpsəl], *n.* (—s, *no pl.*) scrawl, scribbling.

Geschütz [gə'ʃyts], *n.* (—es, *pl.* —e) artillery, guns; *schweres — auffahren*, bring o.'s. guns into play.

Geschützweite [gə'ʃytsvaɪtə], *f.* (—, *no pl.*) calibre.

Geschwader [gə'ʃva:dər], *n.* (—s, *pl.*—) squadron.

Geschwätz [gə'ʃvɛts], *n.* (—es, *no pl.*) chatter, gossip, prattle, tittle-tattle.

geschweige [gə'ʃvaɪgə], *adv.* let alone, to say nothing of.

geschwind [gə'ʃvɪnt], *adj.* quick, nimble, fast, swift, fleet.

Geschwindigkeitsmesser [gə'ʃvɪndɪç-kaɪtsmɛsər], *m.* (—s, *pl.* —) (*Motor.*) speedometer.

Geschwister [gə'ʃvɪstər], *pl.* brothers and sisters.

geschwollen [gə'ʃvɔlən], *adj.* stilted, turgid, pompous.

Geschworene [gə'ʃvo:rənə], *m.* (—n, *pl.* —n) juror, juryman; (*pl.*) jury.

Geschwulst [gə'ʃvulst], *f.* (—, *pl.* ⁻e) swelling, tumour.

Geschwür [gə'ʃvy:r], *n.* (—s, *pl.* —e) sore, ulcer, abscess.

Geselle [gə'zɛlə], *m.* (—n, *pl.* —n) journeyman; companion, comrade, mate.

gesellen [gə'zɛlən], *v.a., v.r.* join, associate with, keep company with.

gesellig [gə'zɛlɪç], *adj.* sociable, companionable; gregarious.

Gesellschaft [gə'zɛlʃaft], *f.* (—, *pl.* —en) society; community; (formal) party; company, club; *geschlossene —*, private party; *einem — leisten*, keep s.o. company; (*Comm.*) *mit beschränkter Haftung*, (abbr.) *GmbH*, limited company, (*abbr.*) Ltd.

gesellschaftlich [gə'zɛlʃaftlɪç], *adj.* social.

Gesellschaftsanzug [gə'zɛlʃaftsan-tsu:k], *m.* (—s, *pl.* ⁻e) evening dress.

Gesellschaftsspiel [gə'zɛlʃaftsʃpi:l], *n.* (—s, *pl.* —e) round game, party game.

Gesellschaftsvertrag [gə'zɛlʃaftsfer-tra:k], *m.* (—es, *pl.* ⁻e) (*Law*) partnership agreement; deed of partnership.

Gesellschaftszimmer [gə'zɛlʃaftstsɪ-mər], *n.* (—s, *pl.* —) drawing-room, reception room.

Gesetz [gə'zɛts], *n.* (—es, *pl.* —e) law, statute, regulation.

Gesetzbuch [gə'zɛtsbu:x], *n.* (—es, *pl.* ⁻er) code of laws; statute book.

Gesetzentwurf [gə'zɛtsentvurf], *m.* (—es, *pl.* ⁻er) (*Parl.*) draft bill.

gesetzgebend [gə'zɛtsge:bənt], *adj.* legislative.

gesetzlich [gə'zɛtslɪç], *adj.* lawful, legal.

Gesetzlichkeit [gə'zɛtslɪçkaɪt], *f.* (—, *no pl.*) lawfulness, legality.

gesetzlos [gə'zɛtslo:s], *adj.* lawless, anarchical.

gesetzmäßig [gə'zɛtsmɛsɪç], *adj.* conforming to law, lawful, legitimate.

gesetzt [gə'zɛtst], *adj.* steady, sedate, staid; *von —em Alter*, of mature age; *— daß*, supposing that.

Gesetztheit [gə'zɛtsthaɪt], *f.* (—, *no pl.*) sedateness, steadiness.

gesetzwidrig [gə'zɛtsvi:drɪç], *adj.* illegal, unlawful.

Gesicht (1) [gə'zɪçt], *n.* (—s, *pl.* —er) face, physiognomy, look.

Gesicht (2) [gə'zɪçt], *n.* (—s, *pl.* —e) sight; vision, apparition.

Gesichtsausdruck [gə'zɪçtsausdruk], *m.* (—s, *no pl.*) face, mien; expression.

Gesichtsfeld [gə'zɪçtsfɛlt], *n.* (—es, *pl.* —er) field of vision.

Gesichtskreis [gə'zɪçtskraɪs], *m.* (—es, *pl.* —e) horizon.

Gesichtspunkt [gə'zɪçtspuŋkt], *m.* (—es, *pl.* —e) point of view.

Gesichtszug [gə'zɪçtstsu:k], *m.* (—s, *pl.* ⁀e) feature.

Gesims [gə'zɪms], *n.* (—es, *pl.* —e) cornice, moulding, ledge.

Gesinde [gə'zɪndə], *n.* (—s, *no pl.*) (domestic) servants.

Gesindel [gə'zɪndəl], *n.* (—s, *no pl.*) mob, rabble.

gesinnt [gə'zɪnt], *adj.* disposed.

Gesinnung [gə'zɪnuŋ], *f.* (—, *pl.* —en) disposition, sentiment; conviction.

gesinnungslos [gə'zɪnuŋslo:s], *adj.* unprincipled.

gesinnungstreu [gə'zɪnuŋstrɔy], *adj.* loyal, staunch.

Gesinnungswechsel [gə'zɪnuŋsvɛksəl], *m.* (—s, *no pl.*) change of opinion, volte-face.

gesittet [gə'zɪtət], *adj.* civilised, well-mannered.

Gesittung [gə'zɪtuŋ], *f.* (—, *no pl.*) (*rare*) civilisation, good manners.

gesonnen [gə'zɔnən] *see* **gesinnt**.

Gespann [gə'ʃpan], *n.* (—s, *pl.* —e) team, yoke (oxen etc.).

gespannt [gə'ʃpant], *adj.* stretched; intense, thrilled; tense; filled with suspense.

Gespanntheit [gə'ʃpanthaɪt], *f.* (—, *no pl.*) tension, strain, suspense.

Gespenst [gə'ʃpɛnst], *n.* (—es, *pl.* —er) ghost, spectre, apparition.

gespenstisch [gə'ʃpɛnstɪʃ], *adj.* ghostly, spectral.

Gespiele [gə'ʃpi:lə], *m.* (—n, *pl.* —n) playmate.

Gespielin [gə'ʃpi:lɪn], *f.* (—, *pl.* —innen) (girl) playmate.

Gespinst [gə'ʃpɪnst], *n.* (—es, *pl.* —e) web.

Gespött [gə'ʃpœt], *n.* (—s, *no pl.*) mocking, mockery, jeering, derision; (*fig.*) laughing stock.

Gespräch [gə'ʃprɛːç], *n.* (—s, *pl.* —e) conversation, discourse, talk; (*phone*) call; *ein — anknüpfen*, start a conversation.

gesprächig [gə'ʃprɛ:çɪç], *adj.* talkative, communicative.

gespreizt [gə'ʃpraɪtst], *adj.* wide apart; (*fig.*) affected, pompous.

gesprenkelt [gə'ʃprɛŋkəlt], *adj.* speckled.

gesprungen [gə'ʃpruŋən], *adj.* cracked (glass etc.).

Gestade [gə'ʃta:də], *n.* (—s, *pl.* —) shore, coast, bank.

Gestalt [gə'ʃtalt], *f.* (—, *pl.* —en) form, figure, shape; configuration; stature; fashion; manner, way.

gestalten [gə'ʃtaltən], *v.a.* form, shape, fashion, make. — *v.r. sich*, turn out.

Gestaltung [gə'ʃtaltuŋ], *f.* (—, *pl.* —en) formation; arrangement; planning.

geständig [gə'ʃtɛndɪç], *adj.* confessing; — *sein*, confess.

Geständnis [gə'ʃtɛntnɪs], *n.* (—ses, *pl.* —se) confession, admission.

Gestank [gə'ʃtaŋk], *m.* (—s, *no pl.*) stink, stench.

gestatten [gə'ʃtatən], *v.a.* permit, allow, grant; *wir — uns*, we beg leave to; — *Sie !* pardon me, excuse me.

Geste ['gɛstə], *f.* (—, *pl.* —n) gesture, gesticulation.

gestehen [gə'ʃte:ən], *v.a. irr.* confess, admit, own; *offen gstanden*, quite frankly.

Gestein [gə'ʃtaɪn], *n.* (—s, *pl.* —e) (*Poet.*) rock; (*Geol.*) rocks, minerals.

Gestell [gə'ʃtɛl], *n.* (—s, *pl.* —e) rack, frame; (*table*) trestle; (*books*) stand.

Gestellung [gə'ʃtɛluŋ], *f.* (—, *no pl.*) (*Mil.*) reporting for service.

gestern ['gɛstərn], *adv.* yesterday; —*abend*, last night.

gestiefelt [gə'ʃti:fəlt], *adj.* booted; *der —e Kater*, Puss in Boots.

gestielt [gə'ʃti:lt], *adj.* (*axe*) helved; (*Bot.*) stalked, stemmed.

gestikulieren [gɛstiku'li:rən], *v.n.* gesticulate.

Gestirn [gə'ʃtɪrn], *n.* (—s, *pl.* —e) star, constellation.

gestirnt [gə'ʃtɪrnt], *adj.* starred, starry.

Gestöber [gə'ʃtø:bər], *n.* (—s, *pl.* —) (*snow, dust*) drift, storm, blizzard.

Gesträuch [gə'ʃtrɔyç], *n.* (—es, *no pl.*) bushes, shrubs; thicket.

gestreift [gə'ʃtraɪft], *adj.* striped.

gestreng [gə'ʃtrɛŋ], *adj.* (*obs.*) strict, severe.

gestrig ['gɛstrɪç], *adj.* of yesterday.

Gestrüpp [gə'ʃtryp], *n.* (—s, *no pl.*) bushes, underwood, shrubs, shrubbery.

Gestüt [gə'ʃty:t], *n.* (—s, *pl.* —e) stud (-farm).

Gestüthengst [gə'ʃty:thɛŋst], *m.* (—es, *pl.* —e) stallion.

Gesuch [gə'zu:x], *n.* (—s, *pl.* —e) petition, request, application.

gesucht [gə'zu:xt], *adj.* in demand; (*style*) far-fetched; affected; studied.

gesund [gə'zunt], *adj.* healthy, wholesome; *der —e Menschenverstand*, common sense.

Gesundbrunnen [gə'zuntbrunən], *m.* (—s, *pl.* —) mineral waters; spa.

gesunden [gə'zundən], *v.n.* (*aux.* sein) recover o.'s health.

Gesundheit [gə'zunthaɪt], *f.* (—, *no pl.*) health.

Gesundheitslehre [gə'zunthaɪtsle:rə], *f.* (—, *no pl.*) hygiene.

Getäfel [gə'tɛ:fəl], *n.* (—s, *no pl.*) wainscot, wainscoting, panelling.

Getändel [gə'tɛndəl], *n.* (—s, *no pl.*) (*rare*) flirting, dallying.

Getier [gə'ti:r], *n.* (—s, *no pl.*) (*collective term*) animals.

Getöse [gə'tø:zə], *n.* (—s, *no pl.*) loud noise, din.

Getränk

Getränk [gə'trɛŋk], *n.* (—s, *pl.* —e) drink, beverage.

getrauen [gə'trauən], *v.r. sich* —, dare, venture.

Getreide [gə'traɪdə], *n.* (—s, *pl.* —) corn, grain.

getreu [gə'trɔy], *adj.* faithful, true, loyal.

getreulich [gə'trɔylɪç], *adv.* faithfully, truly, loyally.

Getriebe [gə'tri:bə], *n.* (—s, *pl.* —) machinery; (*Motor.*) gear; drive; *das — der Welt*, the bustle of life.

getrieben [gə'tri:bən], *adj.* (*Tech.*) chased (work.)

Getrödel [gə'trø:dəl], *n.* (—s, *no pl.*) dawdling.

getrost [gə'tro:st], *adj.* confident, cheerful; *— sein*, be of good cheer.

Getto ['gɛto], *n.* (—s, *pl.* —s) ghetto.

Getue [gə'tu:ə], *n.* (—s, *no pl.*) pretence, fuss.

Getümmel [gə'tyməl], *n.* (—s, *no pl.*) bustle, turmoil.

geübt [gə'y:pt], *adj.* skilled, versed.

Geübtheit [gə'y:pthaɪt], *f.* (—, *no pl.*) skill, experience, dexterity.

Gevatter [gə'fatər], *m.* (—s, *pl.* —) (*obs.*) godfather.

gevierteilt [gə'fi:rtaɪlt], *adj.* quartered.

Gewächs [gə'vɛks], *n.* (—es, *pl.* —e) plant, growth; (*Med.*) excrescence.

gewachsen [gə'vaksən], *adj. einem (einer Sache) — sein*, be equal to s.o. (s.th.).

Gewächshaus [gə'vɛkshaus], *n.* (—es, *pl.* ⁻er) green-house, hot-house, conservatory.

gewagt [gə'va:kt], *adj.* risky, hazardous; daring.

gewählt [gə'vɛ:lt], *adj.* choice, select.

gewahr [gə'va:r], *adj. einer Sache — werden*, become aware of s.th., perceive s.th.

Gewähr [gə'vɛ:r], *f.* (—, *no pl.*) surety; guarantee; warranty; *— leisten*, guarantee.

gewahren [gə'va:rən], *v.a.* perceive, see, become aware of.

gewähren [gə'vɛ:rən], *v.a.* allow, grant; *einen — lassen*, let s.o. do as he pleases, let be.

Gewährleistung [gə'vɛ:rlaɪstuŋ], *f.* (—, *pl.* —en) grant of security (or bail); guarantee.

Gewahrsam [gə'va:rza:m], *m.* (—s, *no pl.*) safe-keeping, custody.

Gewährsmann [gə'vɛ:rsman], *m.* (—es, *pl.* ⁻er) authority; informant.

Gewährung [gə'vɛ:ruŋ,] *f.* (—, *no pl.*) granting of request).

Gewalt [gə'valt], *f.* (—, *pl.* —en) power, force, might; authority; violence; *höhere —*, (*Law*) act of God, force majeure; *sich in der — haben*, have control over o.s.

Gewalthaber [gə'valtha:bər], *m.* (—s, *pl.* —) tyrant; despot, autocrat; person in authority.

gewaltig [gə'valtɪç], *adj.* powerful, mighty, enormous, stupendous.

gewaltsam [gə'valtza:m], *adj.* forcible, violent.

Gewaltstreich [gə'valtʃtraɪç], *m.* (—s, *pl.* —e) bold stroke; coup d'état.

Gewalttat [gə'valtta:t], *f.* (—, *pl.* —en) violent action, violence, outrage.

gewalttätig [gə'valttɛ:tɪç], *adj.* violent, fierce, outrageous.

Gewand [gə'vant], *n.* (—es, *pl.* ⁻er) (*Lit.*) garment, dress; (*Eccl.*) vestment.

gewandt [gə'vant], *adj.* nimble, deft, clever; (*mind*) versatile.

gewärtig [gə'vɛrtɪç], *adj. einer Sache — sein*, expect s.th. to happen.

Gewäsch [gə'vɛʃ], *n.* (—es, *no pl.*) stuff and nonsense; rubbish.

Gewässer [gə'vɛsər], *n.* (—s, *pl.* —) waters.

Gewebe [gə've:bə], *n.* (—s, *pl.* —) (*Physiol.*, *Text.*) tissue; web, weft, texture.

geweckt [gə'vɛkt], *adj.* smart, wide-awake.

Gewehr [gə've:r], *n.* (—s, *pl.* —e) gun, fire-arm, rifle.

Gewehrlauf [gə've:rlauf], *m.* (—s, *pl.* ⁻e) barrel.

Geweih [gə'vaɪ], *n.* (—s, *pl.* —e) horns, antlers.

geweiht [gə'vaɪt], *adj.* consecrated; holy.

gewellt [gə'vɛlt], *adj.* corrugated, wavy.

Gewerbe [gə'vɛrbə], *n.* (—s, *pl.* —) trade, profession, business; calling; industry.

Gewerbekunde [gə'vɛrbəkundə], *f.* (—, *no pl.*) technology.

Gewerbeschein [gə'vɛrbəʃaɪn], *m.* (—s, *pl.* —e) trade-licence.

gewerblich [gə'vɛrplɪç], *adj.* industrial.

gewerbsmäßig [gə'vɛrpsmɛ:sɪç], *adj.* professional.

Gewerkschaft [gə'vɛrkʃaft], *f.* (—, *pl.* —en) trade union.

Gewicht [gə'vɪçt], *n.* (—s, *pl.* —e) weight; *schwer ins — fallen*, carry great weight, weigh heavily.

gewichtig [gə'vɪçtɪç], *adj.* weighty, ponderous; (*fig.*) momentous, important, strong.

gewiegt [gə'vi:kt], *adj.* experienced, clever.

gewillt [gə'vɪlt], *adj.* willing.

Gewimmel [gə'vɪməl], *n.* (—s, *no pl.*) milling crowd, swarm, throng.

Gewinde [gə'vɪndə], *n.* (—s, *pl.* —) (*screw*) thread; (*flowers*) garland.

Gewinn [gə'vɪn], *m.* (—s, *pl.* —e) gain, profit; (*lottery*) prize; (*gambling*) winnings.

gewinnen [gə'vɪnən], *v.a. irr.* win, gain, obtain, get, earn.

gewinnend [gə'vɪnənt], *adj.* prepossessing; engaging.

Gewinnung [gə'vɪnuŋ], *f.* (—, *no pl.*) (*Ind.*, *Chem.*) extraction; output, production.

Gewinsel [gə'vɪnzəl], *n.* (—s, *no pl.*) whimpering.

Gewinst [gə'vɪnst], *m.* (—es, *pl.* —e) (*obs.*) gain, profit.

Gewirr [gə'vɪr], *n.* (—s, *no pl.*) entanglement, confusion.

gewiß [gə'vɪs], *adj.* (*Genit.*) certain, sure. — *adv.* indeed.

Gewissen [gə'vɪsən], *n.* (—s, *no pl.*) conscience.

gewissenhaft [gə'vɪsənhaft], *adj.* conscientious, scrupulous.

gewissenlos [gə'vɪsənlo:s], *adj.* unscrupulous.

Gewissensbiß [gə'vɪsənsbɪs], *m.* (—sses, *pl.* —sse) (*mostly pl.*) pangs of conscience.

gewissermaßen [gə'vɪsərma:sən], *adv.* to a certain extent, so to speak.

Gewißheit [gə'vɪshaɪt], *f.* (—, *no pl.*) certainty.

gewißlich [gə'vɪslɪç], *adv.* surely.

Gewitter [gə'vɪtər], *n.* (—s, *pl.* —) thunderstorm.

gewittern [gə'vɪtərn], *v.n.* thunder.

gewitzigt, gewitzt [gə'vɪtsɪçt, gə'vɪtst], *adj.* knowing, clever; shrewd.

gewogen [gə'vo:gən], *adj.* kindly disposed, favourable; *einem — sein,* be favourably inclined towards s.o.

Gewogenheit [gə'vo:gənhaɪt], *f.* (—, *no pl.*) kindness, favour.

gewöhnen [gə'vø:nən], *v.a.* accustom to. — *v.r. sich — an,* get used to, accustom o.s. to.

Gewohnheit [gə'vo:nhaɪt], *f.* (—, *pl.* —en) (*general*) custom, usage; (*personal*) habit.

gewohnheitsmäßig [gə'vo:nhaɪtsmɛːsɪç], *adj.* habitual. — *adv.* by force of habit.

Gewohnheitsrecht [gə'vo:nhaɪtsreçt], *n.* (—s, *no pl.*) common law.

gewöhnlich [gə'vø:nlɪç], *adj.* customary, usual; (*fig.*) common, mean, vulgar.

gewohnt [gə'vo:nt], *adj.* accustomed to, used to.

Gewöhnung [gə'vø:nuŋ], *f.* (—, *no pl.*) habit, use, habituation.

Gewölbe [gə'vœlbə], *n.* (—s, *pl.* —) vault, arch.

Gewölk [gə'vœlk], *n.* (—s, *no pl.*) clouds, cloud formation.

Gewühl [gə'vy:l], *n.* (—s, *no pl.*) crowd, throng, bustle.

gewunden [gə'vundən], *adj.* tortuous.

Gewürm [gə'vyrm], *n.* (—s, *no pl.*) reptiles, worms; vermin.

Gewürz [gə'vyrts], *n.* (—es, *pl.* —e) spice.

Gewürznelke [gə'vyrtsnɛlkə], *f.* (—, *pl.* —n) clove.

Gezänk [gə'tsɛŋk], *n.* (—s, *no pl.*) quarrelling, bickering.

Gezeiten [gə'tsaɪtən], *f. pl.* tides.

Gezeter [gə'tse:tər], *n.* (—s, *no pl.*) screaming, yelling; (*fig.*) outcry.

geziemen [gə'tsi:mən], *v.r. sich für einen —,* befit or become s.o.

geziert [gə'tsi:rt], *adj.* affected.

Gezischel [gə'tsɪʃəl], *n.* (—s, *no pl.*) whispering.

Gezücht [gə'tsyçt], *n.* (—s, *no pl.*) brood, breed.

Gezweig [gə'tsvaɪk], *n.* (—s, *no pl.*) branches, boughs.

Gezwitscher [gə'tsvɪtʃər], *n.* (—s, *no pl.*) chirping.

Gezwungenheit [gə'tsvuŋənhaɪt], *f.* (—, *no pl.*) constraint.

Gicht [gɪçt], *f.* (—, *no pl.*) (*Med.*) gout.

gichtbrüchig [gɪçtbryçɪç], *adj.* (*obs.*) paralytic; gouty.

gichtig ['gɪçtɪç], *adj.* gouty.

Giebel ['gi:bəl], *m.* (—s, *pl.* —) gable.

Giebelfenster ['gi:bəlfɛnstər], *n.* (—s, *pl.* —) gable-window, dormer-window.

gieb(e)lig ['gi:b(ə)lɪç], *adj.* gabled.

Gier [gi:r], *f.* (—, *no pl.*) greediness, eagerness.

gieren ['gi:rən], *v.n.* (*rare*) — *nach,* thirst for, yearn for.

gierig ['gi:rɪç], *adj.* eager, greedy.

Gießbach ['gi:sbax], *m.* (—s, *pl.* –̈e) mountain-torrent.

gießen ['gi:sən], *v.a. irr.* (*liquids*) pour, shed; (*metal*) cast, found.

Gießer ['gi:sər], *m.* (—s, *pl.* —) founder.

Gießerei [gi:sə'raɪ], *f.* (—, *pl.* —en) foundry.

Gießform ['gi:sfɔrm], *f.* (—, *pl.* —en) casting-mould.

Gießkanne ['gi:skanə], *f.* (—, *pl.* —n) watering-can.

Gift [gɪft], *n.* (—es, *pl.* —e) poison, venom; (*fig.*) virulence; (*coll.*) *darauf kannst du — nehmen,* you can bet your life on it.

Giftbaum ['gɪftbaum], *m.* (—s, *pl.* –̈e) upas-tree.

Giftdrüse ['gɪftdry:zə], *f.* (—, *pl.* —n) poison-gland.

giftig ['gɪftɪç], *adj.* poisonous; (*fig.*) venomous; (*Med.*) toxic.

Giftlehre ['gɪftle:rə], *f.* (—, *no pl.*) toxicology.

Giftpilz ['gɪftpɪlts], *m.* (—es, *pl.* —e) poisonous toadstool.

Giftschlange ['gɪftʃlaŋə], *f.* (—, *pl.* —n) poisonous snake.

Giftstoff ['gɪftʃtɔf], *m.* (—es, *pl.* —e) poison, virus.

Gigant [gɪ'gant], *m.* (—en, *pl.* —en) giant.

Gigerl ['gi:gərl], *m.* (—s, *pl.* —) (*Austr. dial.*) fop, coxcomb.

Gilde ['gɪldə], *f.* (—, *pl.* —n) guild, corporation.

Gimpel ['gɪmpəl], *m.* (—s, *pl.* —) (*Orn.*) bullfinch, chaffinch; (*fig.*) simpleton.

Ginster ['gɪnstər], *m.* (—s, *no pl.*) (*Bot.*) gorse, furze, broom.

Gipfel ['gɪpfəl], *m.* (—s, *pl.* —) summit, peak; (*fig.*) acme, culmination, height.

gipfeln ['gɪpfəln], *v.n.* culminate.

Gips [gɪps], *m.* (—, *no pl.*) gypsum, stucco, plaster of Paris.

Gipsabdruck ['gɪpsapdruk], *m.* (—s, *pl.* –̈e) plaster-cast.

Gipsbild ['gɪpsbɪlt], n. (—s, pl. —er) plaster-figure.

Gipsverband ['gɪpsfɛrbant], m. (—es, pl. ˙e) (Med.) plaster of Paris dressing.

girieren [ʒɪ'riːrən], v.a. (Comm.) endorse (a bill).

Girlande [gɪr'landə], f. (—, pl. —n) garland.

Girobank ['ʒiːrobaŋk], f. (—, pl. —en) transfer or clearing bank.

Gis [gɪs], n. (—, pl. —) (Mus.) G sharp; — Moll, G sharp minor.

gischen ['gɪʃən], v.n. foam, froth.

Gischt [gɪʃt], f. (—, pl. —e) foam, froth; spray.

Gitarre [gi'tarə], f. (—, pl. —n) guitar.

Gitter ['gɪtər], n. (—s, pl. —) trellis, grate, fence; railing; lattice; (colour-printing) screen.

Gitterwerk ['gɪtərvɛrk], n. (—s, no pl.) trellis-work.

Glacéhandschuh [gla'se:hantʃuː], m. (—s, pl. —e) kid-glove.

Glanz [glants], m. (—es, no pl.) brightness, lustre, gloss; polish, sheen; (fig.) splendour.

glänzen ['glɛntsən], v.n. shine, glitter, glisten; (fig.) sparkle.

glänzend ['glɛntsənt], adj. glossy; (fig.) splendid, magnificent.

Glanzfirnis ['glantsfɪrnɪs], m. (—ses, pl. —se) glazing varnish.

Glanzleder ['glantsle:dər], n. (—s, no pl.) patent leather.

Glanzleinwand ['glantslaɪnvant], f. (—, no pl.) glazed linen.

glanzlos ['glantslo:s], adj. lustreless, dull.

glanzvoll ['glantsfɔl], adj. splendid, brilliant.

Glanzzeit ['glantstsaɪt], f. (—, pl. —en) golden age.

Glas [gla:s], n. (—es, pl. ˙er) glass, tumbler.

glasartig ['gla:sa:rtɪç], adj. vitreous, glassy.

Glaser ['gla:zər], m. (—s, pl. —) glazier.

Glaserkitt ['gla:zərkɪt], m. (—s, no pl.) putty.

gläsern ['glɛ:zərn], adj. vitreous, glassy, made of glass.

Glashütte ['gla:shytə], f. (—, pl. —n) glass-works.

glasieren [gla'zi:rən], v.a. glaze; (cake etc.) ice.

glasiert [gla'zi:rt], adj. glazed; (Cul.) frosted, iced; (Art.) varnished.

Glasröhre ['gla:srø:rə], f. (—, pl. —n) glass-tube.

Glasscheibe ['gla:sʃaɪbə], f. (—, pl. —n) glass-pane, sheet of glass.

Glassplitter ['gla:sʃplɪtər], m. (—s, pl. —) splinter of glass.

Glasur [gla'zu:r], f. (—, pl. —en) (potter's) glaze, glazing; enamel, varnish; (cake) icing.

glatt [glat], adj. smooth, sleek; even, plain, glossy; glib; downright. — adv. entirely; — rasiert, close-shaven.

Glätte ['glɛtə], f. (—, no pl.) smoothness, evenness, slipperiness; polish.

Glatteis ['glataɪs], n. (—es, no pl.) slippery ice; sheet ice; (Am.) glaze; einen aufs — führen, lead s.o. up the garden path.

glätten ['glɛtən], v.a. smooth; (dial.) iron.

Glatze ['glatsə], f. (—, pl. —n) bald head.

glatzköpfig ['glatskœpfɪç], adj. bald, bald-pated.

Glaube(n) ['glaubə(n)], m. (—ns, no pl.) faith, belief; creed, religion.

glauben ['glaubən], v.a. believe; think, suppose. — v.n. an etwas (Acc.) —, believe in s.th.

Glaubensbekenntnis ['glaubənsbə-kɛntnɪs], n. (—ses, pl. —se) confession of faith; creed.

Glaubensgericht ['glaubənsgərɪçt], n. (—es, no pl.) inquisition.

Glaubersalz ['glaubərzalts], n. (—es, no pl.) phosphate of soda, Glauber's salts.

glaubhaft ['glauphaft], adj. credible, authentic.

gläubig ['glɔybɪç], adj. believing, faithful; (Eccl.) die Gläubigen, the faithful.

Gläubiger ['glɔybɪgər], m. (—s, pl. —) creditor.

glaublich ['glauplɪç], adj. credible, believable.

glaubwürdig ['glaupvyrdɪç], adj. authentic, worthy of belief; plausible.

gleich [glaɪç], adj. same, like, equal, even; auf —e Weise, likewise; es ist mir ganz —, it is all the same to me. — adv. alike, at once; almost; just as; ich komme —, I shall be there in a moment; — und — gesellt sich gern, birds of a feather flock together.

gleichaltrig ['glaɪçaltrɪç], adj. of the same age.

gleichartig ['glaɪça:rtɪç], adj. of the same kind, homogeneous.

gleichberechtigt ['glaɪçbərɛçtɪçt], adj. entitled to equal rights.

Gleiche ['glaɪçə], n. (—n, pl. —n) the like; the same; etwas ins — bringen, straighten s.th. out.

gleichen ['glaɪçən], v.n. irr. be like, resemble, be equal to.

gleichermaßen ['glaɪçərma:sən], adv. in a like manner, likewise.

gleichfalls ['glaɪçfals], adv. likewise, equally, as well; danke —, thanks, the same to you.

gleichförmig ['glaɪçfœrmɪç], adj. uniform; monotonous.

gleichgesinnt ['glaɪçgəzɪnt], adj. congenial, of the same mind.

Gleichgewicht ['glaɪçgəvɪçt], n. (—s, no pl.) balance, equilibrium.

gleichgültig ['glaɪçgyltɪç], adj. indifferent; es ist mir —, it's all the same to me.

Gleichheit ['glaɪçhaɪt], f. (—, pl. —en) equality, likeness.

Gleichklang ['glaɪçklaŋ], m. (—s, pl. ⁝e) consonance.

gleichmachen ['glaɪçmaxən], v.a. level, equate; dem Erdboden —, raze to the ground.

Gleichmaß ['glaɪçma:s], n. (—es, no pl.) proportion, symmetry.

gleichmäßig ['glaɪçmɛ:sɪç], adj. proportionate, symmetrical.

Gleichmut ['glaɪçmu:t], m. (—s, no pl.) equanimity, calm.

gleichmütig ['glaɪçmy:tɪç], adj. even-tempered, calm.

gleichnamig ['glaɪçna:mɪç], adj. homonymous.

Gleichnis ['glaɪçnɪs], n. (—ses, pl. ⁝se) simile; (Bibl.) parable.

gleichsam ['glaɪçza:m], adv. as it were, as if.

gleichschenklig ['glaɪçʃeŋklɪç], adj. (Maths.) isosceles.

gleichseitig ['glaɪçzaɪtɪç], adj. (Maths.) equilateral.

Gleichsetzung ['glaɪçzetsuŋ], f. (—, no pl.), **Gleichstellung** ['glaɪçʃtɛluŋ], f. (—, pl. —en) equalisation.

Gleichstrom ['glaɪçʃtro:m], m. (—s, no pl.) (Elec.) direct current.

gleichtun ['glaɪçtu:n], v.a. irr. es einem —, emulate s.o.

Gleichung ['glaɪçuŋ], f. (—, pl. —en) (Maths.) equation.

gleichwohl ['glaɪçvo:l], adv., conj. nevertheless, however, yet.

gleichzeitig ['glaɪçtsaɪtɪç], adj. simultaneous, contemporary.

Gleis [glaɪs], n. (—es, pl. —e) (Railw.) track; rails; (Am.) track.

gleiten ['glaɪtən], v.n. irr. (aux. sein) glide, slide, slip.

Gleitflug ['glaɪtflu:k], m. (—es, pl. ⁝e) (Aviat.) gliding.

Gletscher ['glɛtʃər], m. (—s, pl. —) glacier.

Gletscherspalte ['glɛtʃərʃpaltə], f. (—, pl. —n) crevasse.

Glied [gli:t], n. (—es, pl. —er) limb, joint; member; link; rank, file.

Gliederlähmung ['gli:dərlɛ:muŋ], f. (—, no pl.) paralysis.

gliedern ['gli:dərn], v.a. articulate, arrange, form.

Gliederreißen ['gli:dərraɪsən], n. (—s, no pl.) pain in the limbs, rheumatism, arthritis etc.

Gliederung ['gli:dəruŋ], f. (—, pl. —en) articulation, disposition, structure, arrangement, organisation.

Gliedmaßen ['gli:tma:sən], f. pl. limbs.

glimmen ['glɪmən], v.n. irr. glimmer, glow, burn faintly; —de Asche, embers.

Glimmer ['glɪmər], m. (—s, no pl.) (Min.) mica.

glimpflich ['glɪmpflɪç], adj. gentle.

glitschen ['glɪtʃən], v.n. (aux. sein) (coll.) slide.

glitschig ['glɪtʃɪç], adj. (coll.) slippery.

glitzern ['glɪtsərn], v.n. glisten, glitter.

Globus ['glo:bus], m. (—ses, pl. —se) globe.

Glöckchen ['glœkçən], n. (—s, pl. —) small bell; hand-bell.

Glocke ['glɔkə], f. (—, pl. —n) bell; etwas an die große — hängen, make a great fuss about s.th.

Glockenblume ['glɔkənblu:mə], f. (—, pl. —n) (Bot.) bluebell.

Glockengießer ['glɔkəngi:sər], m. (—s, pl. —) bell-founder.

glockenklar ['glɔkənkla:r], adj. as clear as a bell.

Glockenläuter ['glɔkənlɔytər], m. (—s, pl. —) bell-ringer.

Glockenspiel ['glɔkənʃpi:l], n. (—s, pl. —e) chime; (Mus.) glockenspiel, carillon.

Glockenstuhl ['glɔkənʃtu:l], m. (—s, pl. ⁝e) belfry.

Glockenzug ['glɔkəntsu:k], m. (—s, pl. ⁝e) bell-rope; (Mus.) bell-stop.

Glöckner ['glœknər], m. (—s, pl. —) bellringer, sexton.

glorreich ['glo:raɪç], adj. glorious.

Glosse ['glɔsə], f. (—, pl. —n) gloss, comment, annotation; —n machen über, comment upon; find fault with; scoff at.

glotzen ['glɔtsən], v.n. stare wide-eyed; gape.

Glück [glyk], n. (—s, no pl.) luck, good luck, fortune, happiness; — haben, be in luck; auf gut —, at random; zum —, fortunately, luckily; viel —, good luck.

Glucke ['glukə], f. (—, pl. —n) (sitting) hen.

glücken ['glykən], v.n. succeed; es ist mir geglückt, I have succeeded in.

glücklich ['glyklɪç], adj. fortunate, lucky, happy.

glückselig [glyk'ze:lɪç], adj. blissful, happy.

glucksen ['gluksən], v.n. gurgle.

Glücksfall ['glyksfal], m. (—es, pl. ⁝e) lucky chance, windfall, stroke of good fortune.

Glückspilz ['glykspɪlts], m. (—es, pl. —e) (coll.) lucky dog.

glückverheißend ['glykfɛrhaɪsənt], adj. auspicious, propitious.

Glückwunsch ['glykvunʃ], m. (—es, pl. ⁝e) congratulation; felicitation.

glühen ['gly:ən], v.a. make red-hot; (wine) mull. — v.n. glow, be red-hot.

glühend ['gly:ənt], adj. glowing, burning; red-hot; (coal) live; (fig.) ardent, fervent.

Glühstrumpf ['gly:ʃtrumpf], m. (—es, pl. ⁝e) incandescent mantle.

Glühwein ['gly:vaɪn], m. (—s, no pl.) mulled wine.

Glut [glu:t], f. (—, no pl.) glowing fire; heat; (fig.) ardour.

glutrot ['glu:tro:t], adj. fiery red.

Glyzerin ['glytsəri:n], n. (—s, no pl.) glycerine.

93

Gnade

Gnade ['gna:də], *f.* (—, *pl.* —n) grace; favour; pardon, clemency, mercy; kindness; *Euer* —*n*, Your Grace.

Gnadenakt ['gna:dənakt], *m.* (—s, *pl.* —e) act of grace.

Gnadenbrot ['gna:dənbro:t], *n.* (—s, *no pl.*) *das* — *essen*, live on charity.

Gnadenfrist ['gna:dənfrɪst], *f.* (—, *pl.* —en) respite.

Gnadenort ['gna:dənɔrt], *m.* (—(e)s, *pl.* —e) place of pilgrimage.

Gnadenstoß ['gna:dənʃto:s], *m.* (—es, *pl.* ⁻e) finishing stroke, coup de grâce, death-blow.

gnadenvoll ['gna:dənfɔl], *adj.* merciful, gracious.

Gnadenweg ['gna:dənve:k], *m.* (—es, *no pl.*) act of grace; *auf dem* —, by reprieve (as an act of grace).

gnädig ['gnɛ:dɪç], *adj.* gracious, merciful, kind; —*e Frau*, Madam; —*er Herr*, Sir.

Gnostiker ['gnɔstikər], *m.* (—s, *pl.* —) gnostic.

Gnu [gnu:], *n.* (—s, *pl.* —s) (*Zool.*) gnu.

Gold [gɔlt], *n.* (—(e)s, *no pl.*) gold.

Goldammer ['gɔltamər], *f.* (—, *pl.* —n) (*Orn.*) yellow-hammer.

Goldamsel ['gɔltamzəl], *f.* (—, *pl.* —n) (*Orn.*) yellow-thrush.

Goldarbeiter ['gɔltarbaɪtər], *m.* (—s, *pl.* —) goldsmith.

Goldbarren ['gɔltbarən], *m.* (—s, *pl.* —) ingot of gold.

Goldbergwerk ['gɔltberkverk], *n.* (—s, *pl.* —e) gold-mine.

Goldfisch ['gɔltfɪʃ], *m.* (—es, *pl.* —e) goldfish.

Goldgewicht ['gɔltgəvɪçt], *n.* (—s, *no pl.*) gold-weight, troy-weight.

Goldgrube ['gɔltgru:bə], *f.* (—, *pl.* —n) gold-mine.

goldig ['gɔldɪç], *adj.* golden; (*fig.*) sweet, cute, charming.

Goldklumpen ['gɔltklumpən], *m.* (—s, *pl.* —) nugget (of gold).

Goldlack ['gɔltlak], *m.* (—s, *no pl.*) gold-coloured varnish; (*Bot.*) wall-flower.

Goldmacher ['gɔltmaxər], *m.* (—s, *pl.* —) alchemist.

Goldregen ['gɔltre:gən], *m.* (—s, *pl.* —) (*Bot.*) laburnum.

Goldscheider ['gɔltʃaɪdər], *m.* (—s, *pl.* —) gold-refiner.

Goldschmied ['gɔltʃmi:t], *m.* (—s, *pl.* —e) goldsmith.

Goldschnitt ['gɔltʃnɪt], *m.* (—s, *no pl.*) gilt edge.

Golf (1) [gɔlf], *m.* (—s, *pl.* —e) gulf.

Golf (2) [gɔlf], *n.* (—s, *no pl.*) golf.

Gondel ['gɔndəl], *f.* (—, *pl.* —n) gondola.

gondeln ['gɔndəln], *v.n.* (*aux.* sein) ride in a gondola; (*coll.*) travel, get about.

gönnen ['gœnən], *v.a. einem etwas* —, not grudge s.o. s.th.; *wir* — *es ihm*, we are happy for him.

Gönner ['gœnər], *m.* (—s, *pl.* —) patron, protector.

gönnerhaft ['gœnərhaft], *adj.* patronising.

Gönnerschaft ['gœnərʃaft], *f.* (—, *no pl.*) patronage.

gordisch ['gɔrdɪʃ], *adj.* Gordian; *der* —*e Knoten*, the Gordian knot.

Göre ['gø:rə], *f.* (—, *pl.* —n) (*coll.*) brat; (*Am.*) kid.

Gosse ['gɔsə], *f.* (—, *pl.* —n) gutter.

Gote ['go:tə], *m.* (—n, *pl.* —n) Goth.

Gotik ['go:tik], *f.* (—, *no pl.*) Gothic style (architecture etc.).

gotisch ['go:tɪʃ], *adj.* Gothic.

Gott [gɔt], *m.* (—es, *pl.* ⁻er) God, god; — *befohlen*, goodbye; *grüß* —! (*Austr.*) good day; — *sei Dank*, thank God, thank heaven.

gottbegnadet ['gɔtbegna:dət], *adj.* favoured by God, inspired.

Götterbild ['gœtərbɪlt], *n.* (—es, *pl.* —er) image of a god.

gottergeben ['gɔterge:bən], *adj.* submissive to God's will, devout.

Götterlehre ['gœtərle:rə], *f.* (—, *pl.* —n) mythology.

Götterspeise ['gœtərʃpaɪzə], *f.* (—, *pl.* —n) ambrosia.

Götterspruch ['gœtərʃprux], *m.* (—es, *no pl.*) oracle.

Göttertrank ['gœtərtraŋk], *m.* (—s, *pl.* ⁻e) nectar.

Gottesacker ['gɔtəsakər], *m.* (—s, *pl.* —) God's acre, churchyard.

Gottesdienst ['gɔtəsdi:nst], *m.* (—es, *pl.* —e) divine service, public worship.

gottesfürchtig ['gɔtəsfyrçtɪç], *adj.* God-fearing, pious.

Gottesgelehrsamkeit ['gɔtəsgəle:rza:mkaɪt], *f.* (—, *no pl.*) (*rare*) theology, divinity.

Gottesgericht ['gɔtəsgərɪçt], *n.* (—s, *pl.* —e) ordeal.

Gotteshaus ['gɔtəshaus], *n.* (—es, *pl.* ⁻er) house of God; (*rare*) church.

Gotteslästerer ['gɔtəslɛstərər], *m.* (—s, *pl.* —) blasphemer.

Gottesleugner ['gɔtəslɔygnər], *m.* (—s, *pl.* —) atheist.

Gottfried ['gɔtfri:t], *m.* Godfrey, Geoffrey.

gottgefällig ['gɔtgəfɛlɪç], *adj.* pleasing to God.

Gottheit ['gɔthaɪt], *f.* (—, *pl.* —en) deity, divinity.

Göttin ['gœtɪn], *f.* (—, *pl.* —nen) goddess.

göttlich ['gœtlɪç], *adj.* divine, godlike; (*fig.*) heavenly.

gottlob! [gɔt'lo:p], *excl.* thank God!

gottlos ['gɔtlo:s], *adj.* godless, ungodly, impious; (*fig.*) wicked.

gottvergessen ['gɔtfergesən], *adj.* reprobate, impious.

gottverlassen ['gɔtferlasən], *adj.* God-forsaken.

Götze ['gœtsə], *m.* (—n, *pl.* —n) idol, false deity.

94

Götzenbild ['gœtsənbɪlt], n. (—es, pl. —er) idol.
Götzendienst ['gœtsəndi:nst], m. (—es, no pl.) idolatry.
Gouvernante [guvɛr'nantə], f. (—, pl. —n) governess.
Gouverneur [guvɛr'nø:r], m. (—s, pl. —e) governor.
Grab [gra:p], n. (—s, pl. "er) grave, tomb; sepulchre.
Graben ['gra:bən], m. (—s, pl. ") ditch, trench.
graben ['gra:bən], v.a. irr. dig.
Grabgeläute ['gra:pgəlɔytə], n. (—s, no pl.) death-knell.
Grabhügel ['gra:phy:gəl], m. (—s, pl. —) tumulus, mound.
Grablegung ['gra:ple:guŋ], f. (—, no pl.) (rare) burial, interment.
Grabmal ['gra:pma:l], n. (—s, pl. —e, "er) tomb, sepulchre, monument.
Grabschrift ['gra:pʃrɪft], f. (—, pl. —n) epitaph.
Grabstichel ['gra:pʃtɪçəl], m. (—s, pl. —) graving-tool.
Grad [gra:t], m. (—s, pl. —e) degree; rank; grade; extent; point; *in gewissem —e*, to a certain degree; *im höchsten —e*, in the highest degree, extremely.
Gradeinteilung ['gra:taɪntaɪluŋ], f. (—, pl —en) gradation, graduation.
Gradmesser ['gra:tmɛsər], m. (—s, pl. —) graduator; (fig.) index.
gradweise ['gra:tvaɪzə], adv. gradually, by degrees.
Graf [gra:f], m. (—en, pl. —en) count, earl.
Gräfin ['grɛfɪn], f. (—, pl. —en) countess.
gräflich ['grɛflɪç], adj. belonging to a count or earl.
Grafschaft ['gra:fʃaft], f. (—, pl. —en) county, shire.
Gral [gra:l], m. (—s, no pl.) Holy Grail.
Gram [gra:m], m. (—s, no pl.) grief, sorrow.
grämen ['grɛ:mən], v.a. grieve. — v.r. sich —, grieve, fret, worry.
gramgebeugt ['gra:mgəbɔykt], adj. prostrate with grief.
grämlich ['grɛ:mlɪç], adj. sullen, morose, ill-humoured.
Gramm [gram], n. (—s, pl. —e) gramme (15.438 grains); (Am.) gram.
Grammatik [gra'matɪk], f. (—, pl. —en) grammar.
grammatikalisch, **grammatisch** [gramatɪ'ka:lɪʃ, gra'matɪʃ], adj. grammatical.
Gran [gra:n], n. (—s, pl. —e) (weight) grain.
Granat [gra'na:t], m. (—s, pl. —e) garnet.
Granatapfel [gra'na:tapfəl], m. (—s, pl. ") (Bot.) pomegranate.
Granate [gra'na:tə], f. (—, pl. —n) shell, grenade.
Grande ['grandə], m. (—n, pl. —n) grandee.

Grandezza [gran'dɛtsa], f. (—, no pl.) grandeur; sententiousness; pomposity.
grandios [grandɪ'o:s], adj. grand.
Granit [gra'ni:t], m. (—s, pl. —e) granite.
Granne ['granə], f. (—, pl. —n) (corn) awn, beard.
graphisch ['gra:fɪʃ], adj. graphic.
Graphit [gra'fi:t], m. (—s, no pl.) blacklead.
Gras [gra:s], n. (—es, pl. "er) grass; *ins — beißen*, bite the dust.
grasartig ['gra:sa:rtɪç], adj. gramineous.
grasen ['gra:zən], v.n. graze.
Grasfleck ['gra:sflɛk], m. (—s, pl. —e) grass-stain.
Grashalm ['gra:shalm], m. (—s, pl. —e) grass-blade.
Grashüpfer ['gra:shypfər], m. (—s, pl. —) (Ent.) grass-hopper.
grasig ['gra:zɪç], adj. grassy.
Grasmäher ['gra:smɛ:ər], m. (—s, pl. —) lawn-mower.
Grasmücke ['gra:smykə], f. (—, pl. —n) (Orn.) hedge-sparrow.
grassieren [gra'si:rən], v.n. (epidemics etc.) spread, rage.
gräßlich ['grɛslɪç], adj. hideous, horrible, ghastly.
Grasweide ['gra:svaɪdə], f. (—, pl. —n) pasture.
Grat [gra:t], m. (—s, pl. —e) edge, ridge.
Gräte ['grɛ:tə], f. (—, pl. —n) fish-bone.
Grätenstich ['grɛ:tənʃtɪç], m. (—s, pl. —e) (embroidery) herring-bone stitch.
grätig ['grɛ:tɪç], adj. full of fishbones; (fig.) grumpy.
gratis ['gra:tɪs], adj. gratis, — und franko, for nothing.
Gratulation [gratula'tsjo:n], f. (—, pl. —en) congratulation.
gratulieren [gratu'li:rən], v.n. einem zu etwas —, congratulate s.o. on s.th.
grau [grau], adj. grey; (Am.) gray; *vor —en Zeiten*, in times of yore.
Grauen ['grauən], n. (—s, no pl.) horror, aversion.
grauen ['grauən], v.n. (morning) dawn; *es graut mir vor*, I shudder at.
grauenhaft ['grauənhaft], adj. horrible, awful, ghastly.
graulen ['graulən], v.r. sich —, shudder, be afraid (of ghosts etc.).
graulich ['graulɪç], adj. mir ist ganz —, I shudder.
Graupe ['graupə], f. (—, pl. —n) groats, peeled barley.
graupeln ['graupəln], v.n. imp. (coll.) drizzle, sleet.
Graus [graus], m. (—es, no pl.) horror, dread.
grausam ['grauza:m], adj. cruel.
Grauschimmel ['grauʃɪməl], m. (—s, pl. —) grey (horse).
grausen ['grauzən], v.n. es graut mir vor, I shudder at.
grausig ['grauzɪç], adj. dread, gruesome, horrible.

Graveur

Graveur [gra'vø:r], *m.* (—s, *pl.* —e) engraver.

gravieren [gra'vi:rən], *v.a.* engrave.

Gravität [gravi'tɛːt], *f.* (—, *no pl.*) gravity.

gravitätisch [gravi'tɛːtɪʃ], *adj.* grave, solemn.

Grazie ['gra:tsjə], *f.* (—, *pl.* —n) grace, charm; (*goddess*) Grace.

graziös [gra'tsjø:s], *adj.* graceful.

Greif [graɪf], *m.* (—(e)s, *pl.* —e) griffin.

greifbar ['graɪfba:r], *adj.* to hand; (*fig.*) tangible, palpable.

greifen ['graɪfən], *v.a. irr.* grasp, seize, touch, handle; *etwas aus der Luft* —, invent s.th.; *um sich* —, gain ground.

greinen ['graɪnən], *v.n.* (*dial. & coll.*) cry, blubber.

Greis [graɪs], *m.* (—es, *pl.* —e) old man.

greisenhaft ['graɪzənhaft], *adj.* senile.

grell [grɛl], *adj.* (*colour*) glaring; (*light*) dazzling; (*tone*) shrill, sharp.

Grenadier [grena'di:r], *m.* (—s, *pl.* —e) grenadier.

Grenadiermütze [grena'di:rmytsə], *f.* (—, *pl.* —n) busby, bearskin.

Grenze ['grɛntsə], *f.* (—, *pl.* —n) boundary; frontier; borders; (*fig.*) limit.

grenzen ['grɛntsən], *v.n.* — *an*, border on; (*fig.*) verge on.

Grenzlinie ['grɛntsli:njə], *f.* (—, *pl.* —n) boundary-line, line of demarcation.

Greuel ['grɔyəl], *m.* (—s, *pl.* —) horror, abomination; *das ist mir ein* —, I abominate it.

Greueltat ['grɔyəlta:t], *f.* (—, *pl.* —en) atrocity.

greulich ['grɔylɪç], *adj.* horrible, dreadful, shocking, heinous.

Griebe ['gri:bə], *f.* (—, *pl.* —n) (*mostly pl.*) greaves.

Griebs [gri:ps], *m.* (—es, *pl.* —e) (*dial.*) (*apple*) core.

Grieche ['gri:çə], *m.* (—n, *pl.* —n) Greek.

Griechenland ['gri:çənlant], *n.* Greece.

Griesgram ['gri:sgra:m], *m.* (—s, *pl.* —e) grumbler.

griesgrämig ['gri:sgrɛːmɪç], *adj.* morose, grumbling.

Grieß ['gri:s], *m.* (—es, *no pl.*) groats, semolina.

Grießbrei ['gri:sbraɪ], *m.* (—s, *pl.* —e) gruel.

Griff [grɪf], *m.* (—s, *pl.* —e) grip, hold, handle.

griffbereit ['grɪfbəraɪt], *adj.* handy.

Grille ['grɪlə], *f.* (—, *pl.* —n) (*Ent.*) cricket; (*fig.*) whim; —*n haben*, be capricious; —*n fangen*, be crotchety, be depressed.

grillenhaft ['grɪlənhaft], *adj.* whimsical; capricious.

Grimasse [gri'masə], *f.* (—, *pl.* —n) grimace.

Grimm [grɪm], *m.* (—s, *no pl.*) fury, rage, wrath.

Grimmen ['grɪmən], *n.* (—s, *no pl.*) gripes; (*Med.*) colic.

grimmig ['grɪmɪç], *adj.* fierce, furious, grim.

Grind [grɪnt], *m.* (—s, *pl.* —e) scab, scurf.

grinsen ['grɪnzən], *v.n.* grin.

Grippe ['grɪpə], *f.* (—, *pl.* —n) influenza, grippe.

Grips [grɪps], *m.* (—es, *no pl.*) (*coll.*) sense, brains; *einen beim* — *nehmen*, take s.o. by the scruff of his neck.

grob [grɔp], *adj.* coarse; rough; gross; rude, crude, uncouth, impolite; (*jewels*) rough, unpolished.

Grobheit ['grɔphaɪt], *f.* (—, *pl.* —en) rudeness; abusive language.

Grobian ['gro:bja:n], *m.* (—s, *pl.* —e) boor, rude fellow.

Grobschmied ['grɔpʃmi:t], *m.* (—s, *pl.* —e) blacksmith.

Grog [grɔk], *m.* (—s, *pl.* —s) grog, toddy.

grölen ['grø:lən], *v.n.* (*coll.*) scream, squall, bawl.

Groll [grɔl], *m.* (—s, *no pl.*) resentment, anger, rancour; *einen* — *gegen einen haben*, bear s.o. a grudge.

grollen ['grɔlən], *v.n.* (*thunder*) rumble; *einem* —, bear s.o. ill-will; (*Poet.*) be angry (with).

Grönland ['grø:nlant], *n.* Greenland.

Gros (1) [grɔs], *n.* (—ses, *pl.* —se) gross; twelve dozen.

Gros (2) [gro:], *n.* (—s, *no pl.*) bulk, majority; *en* —, wholesale.

Groschen ['grɔʃən], *m.* (—s, *pl.* —) small coin, penny; one 100th of an Austrian shilling; ten-pfennig piece; *einen schönen* — *verdienen*, make good money.

groß [gro:s], *adj.* great, big, large; tall; vast; eminent, famous; intense; —*e Augen machen*, stare; *Grosser Ozean*, Pacific (Ocean).

großartig ['gro:sa:rtɪç], *adj.* grand, sublime, magnificent, splendid.

Großbetrieb ['gro:sbətri:p], *m.* (—s, *pl.* —e) large business; large (industrial) concern.

Großbritannien [gro:sbri'tanjən], *n.* Great Britain.

Größe ['grø:sə], *f.* (—, *pl.* —n) size, largeness, greatness; height; quantity; power; celebrity, star; importance.

Großeltern ['gro:sɛltərn], *pl.* grandparents.

Großenkel ['gro:sɛŋkəl], *m.* (—s, *pl.* —) great-grandson.

Größenverhältnis ['grø:sənferhɛltnɪs], *n.* (—ses, *pl.* —se) proportion, ratio.

Größenwahn ['grø:sənva:n], *m.* (—s, *no pl.*) megalomania; delusion of grandeur.

Großfürst ['gro:sfyrst], *m.* (—en, *pl.* —en) grand-duke.

Großfürstin ['gro:sfyrstɪn], f. (—, pl. —nen) grand-duchess.

Großgrundbesitz ['gro:sgruntbəzɪts], m. (—es, pl. —e) large landed property, estates.

Großhandel ['gro:shandəl], m. (—s, no pl.) wholesale business.

großherzig ['gro:shertsɪç], adj. magnanimous.

Grossist [grɔ'sɪst], m. (—en, pl. —en) wholesale merchant.

großjährig ['gro:sjɛːrɪç], adj. of age; — werden, come of age.

großmächtig ['gro:smɛçtɪç], adj. (fig.) high and mighty.

großmäulig ['gro:smɔylɪç], adj. bragging, swaggering.

Großmut ['gro:smu:t], f. (—, no pl.) magnanimity, generosity.

Großmutter ['gro:smutər], f. (—, pl. ⁖) grandmother.

Großsiegelbewahrer [gro:s'zi:gəlbəva:rər], m. (—s, pl. —) Lord Chancellor; Keeper of the Great Seal.

Großstadt ['gro:sʃtat], f. (—, pl. ⁖e) large town, city, metropolis.

Großtat ['gro:sta:t], f. (—, pl. —en) achievement, exploit, feat.

Großtuer ['gro:stu:ər], m. (—s, pl. —) boaster, braggart.

großtun ['gro:stu:n], v.r. irr. sich — mit, brag of; show off, parade.

Großvater ['gro:sfa:tər], m. (—s, pl. ⁖) grandfather.

großziehen ['gro:stsi:ən], v.a. irr. bring up, rear.

großzügig ['gro:stsy:gɪç], adj. boldly conceived; grand, generous.

Grotte ['grɔtə], f. (—, pl. —n) grotto.

Grübchen ['gry:pçən], n. (—s, pl. —) dimple.

Grube ['gru:bə], f. (—, pl. —n) hole, pit; (Min.) mine; in die — fahren, (Bibl.) go down to the grave.

Grübelei [gry:bəlaɪ], f. (—, pl. —en) brooding, musing.

grübeln ['gry:bəln], v.n. brood (over s.th.)

Grubenarbeiter ['gru:bənarbaɪtər], m. (—s, pl. —) miner.

Grubengas ['gru:bənga:s], n. (—es, pl. —e) fire-damp.

Grubenlampe ['gru:bənlampə], f. (—, pl. —n) miner's lamp.

Gruft [gruft], f. (—, pl. ⁖e) tomb, sepulchre; vault, mausoleum.

grün [gry:n], adj. green; grüne Bohnen, French beans, runner beans; (fig.) unripe, immature, inexperienced; am —en Tisch, at the conference table; (fig.) in theory; auf einen —en Zweig kommen, thrive, get on in the world; einem nicht — sein, dislike s.o.

Grund [grunt], m. (—s, pl. ⁖e) ground, soil; earth; land; bottom; foundation, basis; valley; reason, cause, argument; motive.

Grundbedeutung ['gruntbədɔytuŋ], f. (—, pl. —en) primary meaning, basic meaning.

Grundbesitz ['gruntbəzɪts], m. (—es, no pl.) landed property.

Grundbuch ['gruntbu:x], n. (—s, pl. ⁖er) land register.

grundehrlich ['grunte:rlɪç], adj. thoroughly honest.

Grundeigentum ['gruntaɪgəntu:m], n. (—s, pl. ⁖er) landed property.

Grundeis ['gruntaɪs], n. (—es, no pl.) ground-ice.

gründen ['gryndən], v.a. found, establish, float (a company). — v.r. sich — auf, be based on.

grundfalsch ['gruntfalʃ], adj. radically false.

Grundfarbe ['gruntfarbə], f. (—, pl. —n) primary colour.

Grundfläche ['gruntflɛçə], f. (—, pl. —n) basis, base.

Grundherr ['grunther], m. (—n, pl. —en) lord of the manor, freeholder.

grundieren [grun'di:rən], v.a. prime, size, paint the undercoat.

Grundkapital ['gruntkapita:l], n. (—s, no pl.) original stock.

Grundlage ['gruntla:gə], f. (—, pl. —n) foundation, basis.

Grundlegung ['gruntle:guŋ], f. (—, no pl.) laying the foundation.

gründlich ['gryntlɪç], adj. thorough, solid.

grundlos ['gruntlo:s], adj. bottomless; groundless, unfounded, without foundation.

Grundmauer ['gruntmauər], f. (—, pl. —n) foundation wall.

Gründonnerstag [gry:n'dɔnərsta:k], m. (—s, pl. —e) Maundy Thursday.

Grundpfeiler ['gruntpfaɪlər], m. (—s, pl. —) (main) pillar.

Grundriß ['gruntrɪs], m. (—sses, pl. —sse) design, groundplan; compendium, elements; blueprint.

Grundsatz ['gruntzats], m. (—es, pl. ⁖e) principle, maxim; axiom.

grundschlecht ['gruntʃlɛçt], adj. thoroughly bad.

Grundschuld ['gruntʃult], f. (—, pl. —en) mortgage (on land).

Grundstein ['gruntʃtaɪn], m. (—s, pl. —e) foundation-stone.

Grundsteuer ['gruntʃtɔyər], f. (—, pl. —n) land-tax.

Grundstoff ['gruntʃtɔf], m. (—es, pl. —e) raw material.

Grundstück ['gruntʃtyk], n. (—s, pl. —e) real estate; plot of land; lot.

Grundtugend ['grunttu:gənt], f. (—, pl. —en) cardinal virtue.

Gründung ['grynduŋ], f. (—, pl. —en) foundation, establishment.

grundverschieden ['gruntfərʃi:dən], adj. radically different.

Grundwasser ['gruntvasər], n. (—s, no pl.) underground water.

Grundzahl ['grunttsa:l], f. (—, pl. —en) cardinal number.

Grundzug ['grunttsu:k], m. (—s, pl. ⁖e) characteristic; distinctive feature.

Grüne ['gry:nə], *n.* (**—n**, *no pl.*) greenness, verdure; *ins — gehen*, take a walk in the open country.

grünen ['gry:nən], *v.n.* become green; (*fig.*) flourish.

Grünfutter ['gry:nfutər], *n.* (**—s**, *no pl.*) green food.

Grünkohl ['gry:nko:l], *m.* (**—s**, *no pl.*) green kale.

Grünkramhändler ['gry:nkra:mhɛndlər], *m.* (**—s**, *pl.* **—**) greengrocer.

Grünschnabel ['gry:nʃna:bəl], *m.* (**—s**, *pl.* ⸚) greenhorn.

Grünspan ['gry:nʃpa:n], *m.* (**—s**, *no pl.*) verdigris.

Grünspecht ['gry:nʃpɛçt], *m.* (**—s**, *pl.* **—e**) (*Orn.*) green woodpecker.

grunzen ['gruntsən], *v.n.* grunt.

Grünzeug ['gry:ntsɔyk], *n.* (**—s**, *no pl.*) greens, herbs.

Gruppe ['grupə], *f.* (**—**, *pl.* **—n**) group.

gruppieren [gru'pi:rən], *v.a.* group.

gruselig ['gru:zəlɪç], *adj.* creepy, uncanny.

gruseln ['gru:zəln], *v.a. es gruselt mir* I shudder, it gives me the creeps.

Gruß [gru:s], *m.* (**—es**, *pl.* ⸚e) salutation, greeting; (*pl.*) regards; *mit herzlichem —*, with kind regards; *einen — ausrichten*, convey s.o.'s regards.

grüßen ['gry:sən], *v.a.* greet; *einen — lassen*, send o.'s regards to s.o.; *Sie ihn von mir*, remember me to him.

Grütze ['grytsə], *f.* (**—**, *pl.* **—n**) peeled grain, groats; (*fig.*) (*coll.*) gumption, brains.

Guatemala [guatə'ma:la], *n.* Guatemala.

gucken ['gukən], *v.n.* look, peep.

Guinea [gɪ'ne:a], *n.* Guinea.

Gulasch ['gulaʃ], *n.* (**—s**, *no pl.*) goulash.

Gulden ['guldən], *m.* (**—s**, *no pl.*) florin, guilder.

gülden ['gyldən], *adj.* (*Poet.*) golden.

gültig ['gyltɪç], *adj.* valid; (*money*) current, legal (tender).

Gummi ['gumi:], *m.* (**—s**, *no pl.*) gum, rubber.

Gummiarabikum [gumia'ra:bɪkum], *n.* gum arabic.

gummiartig ['gumia:rtɪç], *adj.* gummy; like rubber.

Gummiball ['gumibal], *m.* (**—s**, *pl.* ⸚e) rubber-ball.

Gummiband ['gumibant], *n.* (**—s**, *pl.* ⸚er) rubber-band, elastic.

Gummielastikum [gumie'lastıkum], *n.* indiarubber.

gummieren [gu'mi:rən], *v.a.* gum.

Gummireifen ['gumiraıfən], *m.* (**—s**, *pl.* **—**) tyre; (*Am.*) tire.

Gummischuhe ['gumiʃu:ə], *m. pl.* galoshes; (*Am.*) rubbers.

Gunst [gunst], *f.* (**—**, *no pl.*) favour; *zu seinen —en*, in his favour.

Gunstbezeigung ['gunstbətsaɪgun], *f.* (**—**, *pl.* **—en**) favour, kindness, goodwill.

günstig ['gynstɪç], *adj.* favourable, propitious.

Günstling ['gynstlɪŋ], *m.* (**—s**, *pl.* **—e**) favourite.

Gurgel ['gurgəl], *f.* (**—**, *pl.* **—n**) gullet, throat.

gurgeln ['gurgəln], *v.n.* gargle; gurgle.

Gurke ['gurkə], *f.* (**—**, *pl.* **—n**) (*Bot.*) cucumber; (*pickled*) gherkin.

Gurt [gurt], *m.* (**—es**, *pl.* **—e**) belt; strap; harness.

Gürtel ['gyrtəl], *m.* (**—s**, *pl.* **—**) girdle, belt; (*Geog.*) zone.

Guß [gus], *m.* (**—sses**, *pl.* ⸚sse) gush, downpour; founding, cast; (*Cul.*) icing.

Gut [gu:t], *n.* (**—(e)s**, *pl.* ⸚er) good thing, blessing; property, possession; country seat; estate; (*pl.*) goods.

gut [gu:t], *adj.* good; beneficial; kind; virtuous. — *adv.* well; *es — haben*, be well off; *—er Dinge sein*, be of good cheer; *kurz und —*, in short.

Gutachten ['gu:taxtən], *n.* (**—s**, *pl.* **—**) expert opinion, expert evidence.

gutartig ['gu:ta:rtɪç], *adj.* good-natured; benign.

Güte ['gy:tə], *f.* (**—**, *no pl.*) goodness, kindness, quality.

Güterabfertigung ['gy:tərapfɛrtɪguŋ], *f.* (**—**, *pl.* **—en**) (*Railw.*) goods-depot, goods-office.

Güterabtretung ['gy:təraptre:tuŋ], *f.* (**—**, *pl.* **—en**) cession of goods; (*Law*) surrender of an estate.

gutgelaunt ['gu:tgəlaunt], *adj.* in good spirits, good-humoured.

gutgemeint ['gu:tgəmaɪnt], *adj.* well-meant, well-intentioned.

gutgesinnt ['gu:tgəzɪnt], *adj.* well-intentioned.

Guthaben ['gu:tha:bən], *n.* (**—s**, *pl.* **—**) credit-balance, assets.

gutheißen ['gu:thaɪsən], *v.a. irr.* approve.

gütig ['gy:tɪç], *adj.* kind, benevolent.

gütlich ['gy:tlıç], *adj.* amicable, friendly; *—er Vergleich*, amicable settlement; *sich — tun*, indulge o.s.

gutmachen ['gu:tmaxən], *v.a. etwas wieder —*, make amends for s.th., compensate.

gutmütig ['gu:tmy:tɪç], *adj.* good-natured, good-tempered.

Gutsbesitzer ['gu:tsbəzɪtsər], *m.* (**—s**, *pl.* **—**) landowner; proprietor of an estate.

gutschreiben ['gu:tʃraɪbən], *v.a. irr. einem etwas —*, enter a sum to s.o.'s credit.

Gutsverwalter ['gu:tsfɛrvaltər], *m.* (**—s**, *pl.* **—**) land-steward, agent, bailiff.

gutwillig ['gu:tvɪlɪç], *adj.* willing, of o.'s own free will.

Gymnasialbildung [gymnaz'ja:lbɪlduŋ], *f.* (**—**, *no pl.*) classical *or* grammar school education.

Gymnasiast [gymnaz'jast], *m.* (**—en**, *pl.* **—en**) grammar-school pupil.

Gymnasium [gym'na:zjum], *n.* (—s, *pl.* —sien) high school.
Gymnastik [gym'nastık], *f.* (—, *no pl.*) gymnastics.
gymnastisch [gym'nastıʃ], *adj.* gymnastic(al); —e Übungen, physical exercises.

H

H [ha:], *n.* (—s, *pl.* —s) the letter H; (*Mus.*) H Dur, B major; H Moll, B minor.
ha! [ha:], *excl.* ha!
Haag, Den [ha:k, de:n], *m.* The Hague.
Haar [ha:r], *n.* (—s, *pl.* —e) hair; wool; nap; aufs —, exactly, to a hair; um ein —, very nearly, within a hair's breadth.
haaren ['ha:rən], *v.r.* sich —, shed o.'s hair.
haargenau ['ha:rgənau], *adj.* (very) exactly; to a nicety.
haarig ['ha:rıç], *adj.* hairy.
Haarlocke ['ha:rlɔkə], *f.* (—, *pl.* —n) curl, ringlet.
Haarnadel ['ha:rna:dəl], *f.* (—, *pl.* —n) hairpin.
Haaröl ['ha:røːl], *n.* (—s, *no pl.*) hair-oil.
Haarpinsel ['ha:rpınzəl], *m.* (—s, *pl.* —) camel-hair brush.
Haarröhrchen ['ha:rrøːrçən], *n.* (—s, *pl.* —) capillary tube.
Haarschleife ['ha:rʃlaifə], *f.* (—, *pl.* —en) bow in the hair.
Haarschnitt ['ha:rʃnıt], *m.* (—s, *pl.* —e) hair-cut.
Haarschuppen ['ha:rʃupən], *f. pl.* dandruff.
Haarspalterei ['ha:rʃpaltərai], *f.* (—, *pl.* —en) hair-splitting.
haarsträubend ['ha:rʃtrɔybənt], *adj.* hair-raising, monstrous.
Haarwäsche ['ha:rvɛʃə], *f.* (—, *no pl.*) shampooing.
Haarwickel ['ha:rvıkəl], *m.* (—s, *pl.* —) curler.
Haarzange ['ha:rtsaŋə], *f.* (—, *pl.* —n) tweezers.
Habe ['ha:bə], *f.* (—, *no pl.*) property, belongings, effects; Hab und Gut, all o.'s belongings, goods and chattels.
Haben ['ha:bən], *n.* (—s, *no pl.*) credit: Soll und —, debit and credit.
haben ['ha:bən], *v.a. irr.* have, possess; da hast du's, there you are; es ist nicht zu —, it is not available.
Habenichts ['ha:bənıçts], *m.* (—es, *no pl.*) have-not.
Habgier ['ha:pgi:r], *f.* (—, *no pl.*) greediness, avarice, covetousness.

habhaft ['ha:phaft], *adj.* einer Sache — werden, get possession of a thing.
Habicht ['ha:bıçt], *m.* (—s, *pl.* —e) (*Orn.*) hawk.
Habichtsinseln ['ha:bıçtsınzəln], *f. pl.* the Azores.
Habichtsnase ['ha:bıçtsna:zə], *f.* (—, *pl.* —n) hooked nose, aquiline nose.
Habilitation [habilita'tsjo:n], *f.* (—, *pl.* —en) admission or inauguration as a university lecturer.
habilitieren [habili'ti:rən], *v.r.* sich —, qualify as a university lecturer.
Habseligkeiten ['ha:pzelıçkaitən], *f. pl.* property, effects, chattels.
Habsucht ['ha:pzuxt], *f.* (—, *no pl.*) avarice, greediness.
Hackbeil ['hakbail], *n.* (—s, *pl.* —e) cleaver, chopping-knife.
Hackbrett ['hakbrɛt], *n.* (—s, *pl.* —er) chopping-board.
Hacke ['hakə], *f.* (—, *pl.* —n) hoe, mattock; heel.
Hacken ['hakən], *m.* (—s, *pl.* —) heel; sich auf die — machen, be off, take to o.'s heels.
hacken ['hakən], *v.a.* hack, chop, hoe; mince; (*birds*) peck.
Hacker ['hakər], *m.* (—s, *pl.* —) chopper.
Häckerling ['hɛkərlıŋ], *m.* (—s, *no pl.*) chopped straw.
Hackfleisch ['hakflaiʃ], *n.* (—es, *no pl.*) minced meat.
Häcksel ['hɛksəl], *n.* (—s, *no pl.*) chopped straw.
Hader ['ha:dər], *m.* (—s, *no pl.*) quarrel, dispute.
hadern ['ha:dərn], *v.n.* quarrel, have a dispute.
Hafen ['ha:fən], *m.* (—s, *pl.* ⁓) harbour, port; refuge, haven.
Hafendamm ['ha:fəndam], *m.* (—s, *pl.* ⁓e) jetty, mole, pier.
Hafensperre ['ha:fɛnʃpɛrə], *f.* (—, *pl.* —n) embargo, blockade.
Hafenzoll ['ha:fəntsɔl], *m.* (—s, *no pl.*) anchorage, harbour due.
Hafer ['ha:fər], *m.* (—s, *no pl.*) oats; es sticht ihn der —, he is getting cheeky, insolent.
Haferbrei ['ha:fərbrai], *m.* (—s, *no pl.*) porridge.
Hafergrütze ['ha:fərgrytsə], *f.* (—, *no pl.*) ground-oats, oatmeal.
Haferschleim ['ha:fərʃlaim], *m.* (—s, *no pl.*) oat-gruel, porridge.
Haff [haf], *n.* (—s, *pl.* —e) bay, lagoon.
Haft [haft], *f.* (—, *no pl.*) custody, imprisonment, arrest.
haftbar ['haftba:r], *adj.* answerable; (*Law*) liable.
Haftbefehl ['haftbəfeːl], *m.* (—s, *pl.* —e) warrant for arrest.
haften ['haftən], *v.n.* stick, cling, adhere; für einen —, go bail for s.o.; für etwas —, answer for, be liable for s.th.

99

Häftling

Häftling ['hɛftlɪŋ], *m.* (—s, *pl.* —e) prisoner.

Haftpflicht ['haftpflɪçt], *f.* (—, *no pl.*) liability.

Haftung ['haftuŋ], *f.* (—, *no pl.*) liability, security; (*Comm.*) *Gesellschaft mit beschränkter* —, limited liability company, (*abbr.*) Ltd.

Hag [ha:k], *m.* (—es, *pl.* —e) hedge, enclosure.

Hagebuche ['ha:gəbu:xə], *f.* (—, *pl.* —n) hornbeam.

Hagebutte ['ha:gəbutə], *f.* (—, *pl.* —n) (*Bot.*) hip, haw.

Hagedorn ['ha:gədɔrn], *m.* (—s, *no pl.*) (*Bot.*) hawthorn.

Hagel ['ha:gəl], *m.* (—s, *no pl.*) hail.

hageln ['ha:gəln], *v.n.* hail.

Hagelschauer ['ha:gəlʃauər], *m.* (—s, *pl.* —) hailstorm.

hager ['ha:gər], *adj.* thin, lean, lank, gaunt.

Häher ['hɛ:ər], *m.* (—s, *pl.* —) (*Orn.*) jay.

Hahn [ha:n], *m.* (—s, *pl.* ̈e) (*Orn.*) cockerel, cock; (*water, gas*) cock, tap, faucet; — *im Korbe sein*, rule the roost; *da kräht kein* — *danach*, nobody cares two hoots about it.

Hahnenbalken ['ha:nənbalkən], *m.* (—s, *pl.* —) cock-loft; hen-roost.

Hahnenfuß ['ha:nənfu:s], *m.* (—es, *no pl.*) (*Bot.*) crow-foot.

Hahnensporn ['ha:nənʃpɔrn], *m.* (—s, *no pl.*) cockspur.

Hahnentritt ['ha:nəntrɪt], *m.* (—s, *no pl.*) cock's tread.

Hahnrei ['ha:nraɪ], *m.* (—s, *pl.* —e) cuckold; *einen zum* — *machen*, cuckold s.o.

Hai [haɪ], *m.* (—s, *pl.* —e) (*Zool.*) shark.

Haifisch ['haɪfɪʃ], *m.* (—es, *pl.* —e) (*Zool.*) shark.

Hain [haɪn], *m.* (—s, *pl.* —e) (*Poet.*) grove, thicket.

Haiti [ha'iti], *n.* Haiti.

Häkchen ['hɛ:kçən], *n.* (—s, *pl.* —) small hook, crotchet; apostrophe.

häkeln ['hɛ:kəln], *v.a. v.n.* crochet; (*fig.*) tease; (*Am.*) needle (*coll.*).

Haken ['ha:kən], *m.* (—s, *pl.* —) hook, clasp; (*fig.*) hitch, snag.

Hakenkreuz ['ha:kənkrɔyts], *n.* (—es, *pl.* —e) swastika.

halb [halp], *adj.* half; *halb neun*, half past eight.

halbieren [hal'bi:rən], *v.a.* halve, divide into halves; (*Maths.*) bisect.

Halbinsel ['halpɪnzəl], *f.* (—, *pl.* —n) peninsula.

Halbmesser ['halpmɛsər], *m.* (—s, *pl.* —) radius.

halbpart ['halppart], *adj.* — *mit einem machen*, go halves with s.o.

halbstündig ['halpʃtyndɪç], *adj.* lasting half an hour.

halbstündlich ['halpʃtyntlɪç], *adj.* half-hourly, every half-hour.

halbwegs ['halpve:ks], *adv.* (*coll.*) reasonably, tolerably.

Halbwelt ['halpvɛlt], *f.* (—, *no pl.*) demi-monde.

halbwüchsig ['halpvy:ksɪç], *adj.* teenage.

Halde ['haldə], *f.* (—, *pl.* —n) declivity, hill; (*Min.*) waste-heap, slag-heap.

Hälfte ['hɛlftə], *f.* (—, *pl.* —n) half; (*obs.*) moiety.

Halfter ['halftər], *f.* (—, *pl.* —n) halter.

Hall [hal], *m.* (—s, *no pl.*) sound, echo.

Halle ['halə], *f.* (—, *pl.* —n) hall, vestibule; portico; porch.

hallen ['halən], *v.n.* sound, resound; clang.

Halm [halm], *m.* (—es, *pl.* —e) stalk; (*grass*) blade.

Hals [hals], *m.* (—es, *pl.* ̈e) neck, throat; — *über Kopf*, head over heels, hastily, hurriedly.

Halsader ['halsa:dər], *f.* (—, *pl.* —n) jugular vein.

Halsbinde ['halsbɪndə], *f.* (—, *pl.* —n) scarf, tie.

Halsentzündung ['halsɛntsynduŋ], *f.* (—, *pl.* —en) inflammation of the throat.

Halskrause ['halskrauzə], *f.* (—, *pl.* —n) frill, ruff.

halsstarrig ['halsʃtarɪç], *adj.* stubborn, obstinate.

Halsweh ['halsve:], *n.* (—s, *no pl.*) sore throat.

Halt [halt], *m.* (—es, *no pl.*) halt; stop; hold; (*also fig.*) support.

haltbar ['haltba:r], *adj.* durable, strong; tenable, valid.

halten ['haltən], *v.a. irr.* hold; keep; detain; deliver (speech, lecture); observe, celebrate. — *v.n.* stop; stand firm; insist; *halt!* stop! stop it! — *v.r. sich* —, hold out, keep, behave.

haltlos ['haltlo:s], *adj.* unprincipled; floundering, unsteady.

Haltung ['haltuŋ], *f.* (—, *pl.* —en) carriage, posture, attitude; (*fig.*) behaviour, demeanour; attitude.

Halunke [ha'luŋkə], *m.* (—n, *pl.* —n) scoundrel, rascal, scamp.

hämisch ['hɛ:mɪʃ], *adj.* malicious, spiteful.

Hammel ['haməl], *m.* (—s, *pl.* —) (*meat*) mutton.

Hammelkeule ['haməlkɔylə], *f.* (—, *pl.* —n) leg of mutton.

Hammer ['hamər], *m.* (—s, *pl.* ̈) hammer; *unter den* — *kommen*, be sold by auction.

Hämorrhoiden [hɛmo'ri:dən], *f. pl.* (*Med.*) piles, haemorrhoids.

Hand [hant], *f.* (—, *pl.* ̈e) hand.

Handarbeit ['hantarbaɪt], *f.* (—, *pl.* —en) manual labour; needlework.

Handel ['handəl], *m.* (—s, *no pl.*) trade, commerce; — *treiben*, carry on trade, do business.

Händel ['hɛndəl], *m. pl.* quarrel, difference, dispute.

handeln ['handəln], *v.n.* act; — *in*, deal in; *es handelt sich um* ... it is a question of ... ; *es handelt von* ..., it deals with ... .
handelseinig ['handəlsaınıç], *adj.* — *werden*, come to terms.
Handelsgenossenschaft ['handəls-gənɔsənʃaft], *f.* (—, *pl.* —en) trading company.
Handelsgeschäft ['handəlsgəʃeft], *n.* (—es, *pl.* —e) commercial transaction.
Handelsgesellschaft ['handəlsgəzel-ʃaft], *f.* (—, *pl.* —en) trading company; joint-stock company.
Handelskammer ['handəlskamər], *f.* (—, *pl.* —n) chamber of commerce.
Handelsmarke ['handəlsmarkə], *f.* (—, *pl.* —n) trade-mark.
Handelsreisende ['handəlsraızəndə], *m.* (—n, *pl.* —n) commercial traveller.
händelsüchtig ['hendəlzyçtıç], *adj.* quarrelsome; litigious.
Handelsvertrag ['handəlsfertra:k], *m.* (—es, *pl.* ꞌꞌe) commercial treaty; contract.
Handelszweig ['handəlstsvaık], *m.* (—es, *pl.* —e) branch of trade.
Handfeger ['hantfe:gər], *m.* (—s, *pl.* —) hand-broom, handbrush.
Handfertigkeit ['hantfertıçkaıt], *f.* (—, *no pl.*) dexterity, manual skill; handicrafts.
handfest ['hantfest], *adj.* robust, strong.
Handgeld ['hantgelt], *n.* (—es, *no pl.*) earnest; (*money*) advance.
Handgelenk ['hantgəlenk], *n.* (—s, *pl.* —e) wrist.
handgemein ['hangəmaın], *adj.* — *werden*, come to blows.
Handgemenge ['hantgəmeŋə], *n.* (—s, *no pl.*) fray, scuffle.
handgreiflich ['hantgraıflıç], *adj.* palpable; evident, plain.
Handgriff ['hantgrıf], *m.* (—es, *pl.* —e) handle; (*fig.*) knack.
Handhabe ['hantha:bə], *f.* (—, *pl.* —n) (*fig.*) hold, handle.
handhaben ['hantha:bən], *v.a.* handle, manage; operate.
Handlanger ['hantlaŋər], *m.* (—s, *pl.* —) helper, carrier.
Händler ['hendlər], *m.* (—s, *pl.* —) dealer, merchant.
handlich ['hantlıç], *adj.* handy, manageable.
Handlung ['hantluŋ], *f.* (—, *pl.* —en) shop; (*Am.*) store; commercial house, mercantile business; action, act, deed; (*Lit.*) plot.
Handrücken ['hantrykən], *m.* (—s, *pl.* —) back of the hand.
Handschelle ['hantʃelə], *f.* (—, *pl.* —n) manacle, handcuff.
Handschlag ['hantʃla:k], *m.* (—s, *pl.* ꞌꞌe) handshake.

Handschuh ['hantʃu:], *m.* (—s, *pl.* —e) glove; (*of iron*) gauntlet.
Handstreich ['hantʃtraıç], *m.* (—es, *pl.* —e) (*Mil.*) surprise attack, coup de main.
Handtuch ['hanttu:x], *n.* (—es, *pl.* ꞌꞌer) towel.
Handumdrehen ['hantumdre:ən], *n.* (—s, *no pl.*) *im* —, in no time, in a jiffy.
Handwerk ['hantverk], *n.* (—s, *pl.* —e) handicraft, trade, craft.
Handwörterbuch ['hantvœrtərbu:x], *n.* (—es, *pl.* ꞌꞌer) compact dictionary.
Handwurzel ['hantvurtsəl], *f.* (—, *pl.* —n) wrist.
Hanf [hanf], *m.* (—es, *no pl.*) hemp.
Hänfling ['henflıŋ], *m.* (—s, *pl.* —e) (*Orn.*) linnet.
Hang [haŋ], *m.* (—es, *pl.* ꞌꞌe) slope, declivity; (*fig.*) (*no pl.*) inclination, propensity.
Hängematte ['heŋəmatə], *f.* (—, *pl.* —n) hammock.
hängen ['heŋən], *v.a. irr.* hang, suspend. — *v.r. sich* —, hang o.s. — *v.n.* hang, be suspended; be hanged (*execution*).
Hannover [ha'no:fər], *n.* Hanover.
Hänselei ['henzəlaı], *f.* (—, *pl.* —en) chaffing, leg-pulling, teasing.
hänseln ['henzəln], *v.a.* tease, chaff.
Hantel ['hantəl], *f.* (—, *pl.* —n) dumb-bell.
hantieren [han'ti:rən], *v.n.* busy o.s., work, occupy o.s. (with).
hapern ['ha:pərn], *v.n.* lack, be deficient; *da hapert es*, that's the snag.
Häppchen ['hepçən], *n.* (—s, *pl.* —) morsel.
Happen ['hapən], *m.* (—s, *pl.* —) mouthful.
happig ['hapıç], *adj.* greedy; excessive.
Härchen ['he:rçən], *n.* (—s, *pl.* —) short hair.
Harfe ['harfə], *f.* (—, *pl.* —n) (*Mus.*) harp.
Harke ['harkə], *f.* (—, *pl.* —n) rake.
Harm [harm], *m.* (—es, *no pl.*) grief, sorrow; injury, wrong.
härmen ['hermən], *v.r. sich* — *um*, grieve over.
harmlos ['harmlo:s], *adj.* harmless, innocuous.
Harmonielehre [harmo'ni:le:rə], *f.* (—, *pl.* —n) (*Mus.*) harmonics; harmony.
harmonieren [harmo'ni:rən], *v.n. mit einem* —, be in concord with s.o., agree with s.o.
Harmonika [har'mo:nıka], *f.* (—, *pl.* —ken) (*Mus.*) accordion, concertina; mouth-organ.
Harn [harn], *m.* (—s, *no pl.*) urine.
Harnisch ['harnıʃ], *m.* (—es, *pl.* —e) harness, armour; *in* — *bringen*, enrage.
Harpune [har'pu:nə], *f.* (—, *pl.* —n) harpoon.
harren ['harən], *v.n.* wait for, hope for.

harsch

harsch [harʃ], *adj.* harsh; rough; unfriendly.

hart [hart], *adj.* hard, severe, cruel, austere.

Härte [ˈhɛrtə], *f.* (—, *pl.* —n) hardness, severity.

härten [ˈhɛrtən], *v.a.* harden.

hartleibig [ˈhartlaɪbɪç], *adj.* constipated.

hartnäckig [ˈhartnɛkɪç], *adj.* stubborn, obstinate; undaunted.

Harz (1) [harts], *m.* (*Geog.*) (—es, *no pl.*) the Hartz mountains.

Harz (2) [harts], *n.* (—es, *pl.* —e) resin, rosin.

harzig [ˈhartsɪç], *adj.* resinous.

Hasardspiel [haˈzartʃpiːl], *n.* (—es, *pl.* —e) game of chance, gamble.

Haschee [haˈʃeː], *n.* (—s, *pl.* —s) puree, hash, mash.

haschen [ˈhaʃən], *v.a.* catch, snatch, seize. — *v.n.* — *nach*, strain after, snatch at.

Häschen [ˈhɛːsçən], *n.* (—s, *pl.* —) (*Zool.*) small hare, leveret.

Häscher [ˈhɛʃər], *m.* (—s, *pl.* —) bailiff.

Hase [ˈhaːzə], *m.* (—n, *pl.* —n) (*Zool.*) hare.

Haselrute [ˈhaːzəlruːtə], *f.* (—, *pl.* —n) hazel-switch.

Hasenfuß [ˈhaːzənfuːs], *m.* (—es, *no pl.*) coward.

Hasenklein [ˈhaːzənklaɪn], *n.* (—s, *no pl.*) jugged hare.

Hasenscharte [ˈhaːzənʃartə], *f.* (—, *pl.* —n) hare-lip.

Haspe [ˈhaspə], *f.* (—, *pl.* —n) hasp, hinge.

Haspel [ˈhaspəl], *f.* (—, *pl.* —n) reel.

haspeln [ˈhaspəln], *v.a.* wind on a reel; (*fig.*) rattle off.

Haß [has], *m.* (—sses *no pl.*) hatred, hate, detestation.

hassen [ˈhasən], *v.a.* hate, detest.

haßerfüllt [ˈhasərfylt], *adj.* full of spite, full of hatred.

häßlich [ˈhɛslɪç], *adj.* ugly, repulsive; (*fig.*) unpleasant, unkind; unseemly.

Hast [hast], *f.* (—, *no pl.*) haste, hurry, hastiness, rashness.

hastig [ˈhastɪç], *adj.* hasty, hurried.

hätscheln [ˈhɛtʃəln], *v.a.* pamper, caress, fondle.

Hatz [hats], *f.* (—, *pl.* —en) baiting; hunt; revelry.

Haube [ˈhaubə], *f.* (—, *pl.* —n) bonnet, cap; (*Motor.*) bonnet, (*Am.*) hood.

Haubenlerche [ˈhaubənlɛrçə], *f.* (—, *pl.* —n) (*Orn.*) crested lark.

Haubitze [hauˈbɪtsə], *f.* (—, *pl.* —n) howitzer.

Hauch [haux], *m.* (—es, *no pl.*) breath, whiff; (*fig.*) touch, tinge.

hauchdünn [ˈhaux dyn], *adj.* extremely thin.

hauchen [ˈhauxən], *v.n.* breathe.

Hauchlaut [ˈhauxlaut], *m.* (—es, *pl.* —e) (*Phonet.*) aspirate.

Haudegen [ˈhaudeːgən], *m.* (—s, *pl.* —) broad-sword; *ein alter* —, an old bully.

Haue [ˈhauə], *f.* (—, *no pl.*) (*coll.*) thrashing.

hauen [ˈhauən], *v.a.* hew; cut; strike; hit; give a hiding to. — *v.n. über die Schnur* —, kick over the traces.

Hauer [ˈhauər], *m.* (—s, *pl.* —) hewer, cutter; (*animal*) fang, tusk.

Häuer [ˈhɔyər], *m.* (—s, *pl.* —) miner.

Haufen [ˈhaufən], *m.* (—s, *pl.* —) heap, pile.

häufen [ˈhɔyfən], *v.a.* heap, pile. — *v.r. sich* —, accumulate, multiply, increase.

häufig [ˈhɔyfɪç], *adj.* frequent, abundant. — *adv.* frequently, often.

Häufung [ˈhɔyfuŋ], *f.* (—, *pl.* —en) accumulation.

Haupt [haupt], *n.* (—es, *pl.* ¨er) head; leader; chief, principal; (*compounds*) main—; *aufs* — *schlagen*, inflict a total defeat on; *ein bemoostes* —, an old student.

Hauptaltar [ˈhauptaltaːr], *m.* (—s, *pl.* ¨e) (*Eccl.*) high altar.

Hauptbuch [ˈhauptbuːx], *n.* (—es, *pl.* ¨er) ledger.

Häuptling [ˈhɔyptlɪŋ], *m.* (—s, *pl.* —e) chieftain.

Hauptmann [ˈhauptman], *m.* (—s, *pl.* ¨er, **Hauptleute**) (*Mil.*) captain.

Hauptnenner [ˈhauptnɛnər], *m.* (—s, *pl.* —) (*Maths.*) common denominator.

Hauptquartier [ˈhauptkvartiːr], *n.* (—es, *pl.* —e) headquarters.

Hauptsache [ˈhauptzaxə], *f.* (—, *pl.* —n) main thing, substance, main point; *in der* —, in the main.

hauptsächlich [ˈhauptzɛçlɪç], *adj.* chief, main, principal, essential.

Hauptsatz [ˈhauptzats], *m.* (—es, *pl.* ¨e) (*Gram.*) principal sentence.

Hauptschriftleiter [ˈhauptʃriftlaɪtər], *m.* (—s, *pl.* —) editor-in-chief.

Hauptschule [ˈhauptʃuːlə], *f.* (—, *pl.* —n) intermediate school.

Hauptstadt [ˈhauptʃtat], *f.* (—, *pl.* ¨e) capital, metropolis.

Hauptton [ˈhauptoːn], *m.* (—s, *pl.* ¨e) (*Mus.*) key-note; (*Phonet.*) primary accent.

Haupttreffer [ˈhaupttrɛfər], *m.* (—s, *pl.* —) first prize; jackpot.

Hauptverkehrsstunden [ˈhauptfɛrkeːrsʃtundən], *f. pl.* (*traffic etc.*) rush-hour.

Hauptwache [ˈhauptvaxə], *f.* (—, *pl.* —n) central guardroom.

Hauptwort [ˈhauptvɔrt], *n.* (—es, *pl.* ¨er) noun, substantive.

Hauptzahl [ˈhaupttsaːl], *f.* (—, *pl.* —en) cardinal number.

Haus [haus], *n.* (—es, *pl.* ¨er) house; home; household; firm; *zu* —*e*, at home; *nach* —*e*, home.

Hausarbeit [ˈhausarbaɪt], *f.* (—, *pl.* —en) housework, domestic work; homework.

Hausarrest ['hausarɛst], *m.* (—es, no *pl.*) house arrest.

Hausarzt ['hausartst], *m.* (—es, *pl.* ⁚e) family doctor.

hausbacken ['hausbakən], *adj.* home-made; homely; humdrum.

Häuschen ['hɔysçən], *n.* (—s, *pl.* —) small house, cottage; *ganz aus dem — sein*, be beside o.s.

Hausen ['hauzən], *m.* (—s, *pl.* —) sturgeon.

hausen ['hauzən], *v.n.* reside, be domiciled; *übel —*, play havoc among.

Hausflur ['hausflu:r], *m.* (—s, *pl.* —e) entrance hall (of a house), vestibule.

Hausfrau ['hausfrau], *f.* (—, *pl.* —en) housewife, mistress of the house.

Hausfriedensbruch ['hausfri:dənsbrux], *m.* (—s, *pl.* ⁚e) (*Law*) intrusion, trespass.

Hausgenosse ['hausgənɔsə], *m.* (—n, *pl.* —n) fellow-lodger.

Haushalt ['haushalt], *m.* (—es, no *pl.*) household.

Haushaltung ['haushaltuŋ], *f.* (—, no *pl.*) housekeeping.

Hausherr ['hausher], *m.* (—n, *pl.* —en) master of the house, householder.

Haushofmeister ['haushofmaistər], *m.* (—s, *pl.* —) steward; butler.

hausieren [hau'zi:rən], *v.n.* peddle, hawk.

Hauslehrer ['hausle:rər], *m.* (—s, *pl.* —) private tutor.

Häusler ['hɔyslər], *m.* (—s, *pl.* —) cottager.

häuslich ['hɔysliç], *adj.* domestic, domesticated.

Hausmädchen ['hausmɛdçən], *n.* (—s, *pl.* —) housemaid.

Hausmannskost ['hausmanskɔst], *f.* (—, no *pl.*) plain fare.

Hausmeister ['hausmaistər], *m.* (—s, *pl.* —) house-porter, caretaker.

Hausmittel ['hausmitəl], *n.* (—s, *pl.* —) household remedy.

Hausrat ['hausra:t], *m.* (—s, no *pl.*) household furnishings, household effects.

Hausschlüssel ['hausʃlysəl], *m.* (—s, *pl.* —) latch-key.

Hausschuh ['hausʃu:], *m.* (—s, *pl.* —e) slipper.

Hausstand ['hausʃtant], *m.* (—es, *pl.* ⁚e) household.

Haustier ['hausti:r], *n.* (—es, *pl.* —e) domestic animal.

Hausvater ['hausfa:tər], *m.* (—s, *pl.* ⁚) paterfamilias.

Hausverwalter ['hausfervaltər], *m.* (—s, *pl.* —) steward, caretaker; (*Am.*) janitor.

Hauswesen ['hausve:zən], *n.* (—s, no *pl.*) household management or affairs.

Hauswirt ['hausvirt], *m.* (—es, *pl.* —e) landlord.

Hauswirtin ['hausvirtin], *f.* (—, *pl.* —nen) landlady.

Hauswirtschaft ['hausvirtʃaft], *f.* (—, no *pl.*) housekeeping, domestic economy.

Haut [haut], *f.* (—, *pl.* ⁚e) (*human*) skin; (*animal*) hide; (*fruit*) peel; (*on liquid*) skin; membrane; film; *aus der — fahren*, flare up.

Hautausschlag ['hautausʃla:k], *m.* (—s, *pl.* ⁚e) rash, eczema.

Häutchen ['hɔytçən], *n.* (—s, *pl.* —) cuticle, pellicle, membrane.

häuten ['hɔytən], *v.a.* skin, flay, strip off the skin. — *v.r. sich —*, cast off (skin) or slough.

Hebamme ['he:pamə], *f.* (—, *pl.* —n) midwife.

Hebel ['he:bəl], *m.* (—s, *pl.* —) lever.

heben ['he:bən], *v.a. irr.* raise, lift, hoist, heave; elevate; improve; *aus der Taufe —*, be godfather (godmother) to (s.o.).

Heber ['he:bər], *m.* (—s, *pl.* —) siphon.

Hebräer [he'brɛ:ər], *m.* (—s, *pl.* —) Hebrew.

Hechel ['hɛçəl], *f.* (—, *pl.* —n) hackle, flax-comb.

hecheln ['hɛçəln], *v.a.* dress flax; hackle; (*fig.*) taunt, heckle.

Hecht [hɛçt], *m.* (—es, *pl.* —e) (*Zool.*) pike; (*swimming*) dive.

Hechtsprung ['hɛçtʃpruŋ], *m.* header.

Heck [hɛk], *n.* (—s, *pl.* —e) (*Naut.*) stern; (*Motor.*) rear; (*Aviat.*) tail.

Heckbord ['hɛkbɔrt], *m.* (—s, *pl.* —e) (*Naut.*) taffrail.

Hecke ['hɛkə], *f.* (—, *pl.* —n) hedge.

hecken ['hɛkən], *v.n.* breed, bring forth.

Heckpfennig ['hɛkpfeniç], *m.* (—s, *pl.* —e) lucky sixpence.

heda! ['he:da:], *excl.* hey, you!

Heer [he:r], *n.* (—es, *pl.* —e) army; multitude; *stehendes —*, regular army.

Heeresmacht ['he:rəsmaxt], *f.* (—, *pl.* ⁚e) armed forces, troops.

Heerschar ['he:rʃa:r], *f.* (—, *pl.* —en) host; corps, legion; (*Bibl.*) *der Herr der —en*, the Lord of Hosts.

Heerschau ['he:rʃau], *f.* (—, *pl.* —en) review, muster, parade.

Heerstraße ['he:rʃtra:sə], *f.* (—, *pl.* —en) military road; highway; (*Am.*) highroad.

Heerwesen ['he:rve:zən], *n.* (—s, no *pl.*) military affairs.

Hefe ['he:fə], *f.* (—, no *pl.*) yeast; dregs, sediment.

Hefeteig ['he:fətaik], *m.* (—s, *pl.* —e) leavened dough.

Heft [hɛft], *n.* (—es, *pl.* —e) exercise-book, copy-book; haft, handle, hilt.

heften ['hɛftən], *v.a.* fasten; baste, stitch, fix, pin.

heftig ['hɛftiç], *adj.* vehement, violent.

Heftnadel ['hɛftna:dəl], *f.* (—, *pl.* —n) stitching-needle.

hegen ['he:gən], *v.a.* enclose, protect, preserve; (*fig.*) cherish; entertain; hold; *— und pflegen*, nurse carefully.

Hehl

Hehl [he:l], *n.* (—es, *no pl.*) conceal-ment, secret.

hehlen ['he:lən], *v.n.* receive stolen goods.

Hehler ['hə:lər], *m.* (—s, *pl.* —) receiver of stolen goods, (*sl.*) fence.

hehr [he:r], *adj.* (*Lit.*) exalted, august, sublime.

Heide (1) ['haɪdə], *m.* (—n, *pl.* —n) heathen, pagan.

Heide (2) ['haɪdə], *f.* (—, *pl.* —n) heath.

Heidekraut ['haɪdəkraut], *n.* (—es, *no pl.*) heath, heather.

Heidelbeere ['haɪdəlbe:rə], *f.* (—, *pl.* —n) (*Bot.*) bilberry; (*Am.*) blueberry.

Heidenangst ['haɪdənaŋst], *f.* (—, *no pl.*) (*coll.*) mortal fear.

Heidenlärm ['haɪdənlɛrm], *m.* (—es, *no pl.*) hullabaloo.

Heidenröschen ['haɪdənrø:sçən], *n.* (—s, *pl.* —) (*Bot.*) sweet-briar.

Heidentum ['haɪdəntu:m], *n.* (—s, *no pl.*) paganism.

heidnisch ['haɪdnɪʃ], *adj.* pagan, heathen.

Heidschnuke ['haɪtʃnu:kə], *f.* (—, *pl.* —n) moorland sheep.

heikel ['haɪkəl], *adj.* delicate, sensitive, critical.

Heil [haɪl], *n.* (—(e)s, *no pl.*) safety, welfare; (*Theol.*) salvation; *sein — versuchen*, have a try, try o.'s luck. — *int.* hail! — *der Königin*, God save the Queen.

heil [haɪl], *adj.* unhurt, intact.

Heiland ['haɪlant], *m.* (—s, *no pl.*) Saviour, Redeemer.

Heilanstalt ['haɪlanʃtalt], *f.* (—, *pl.* —en) sanatorium, convalescent home; (*Am.*) sanitarium.

heilbar ['haɪlba:r], *adj.* curable.

heilbringend ['haɪlbrɪŋənt], *adj.* salutary.

heilen ['haɪlən], *v.a.* cure, heal. — *v.n.* (*aux.* sein) heal.

heilig ['haɪlɪç], *adj.* holy, sacred; *der Heilige Abend*, Christmas Eve; *— sprechen*, canonise; (*before name*) *der*, *die —e*, Saint.

Heiligenschein ['haɪlɪgənʃaɪn], *m.* (—s, *pl.* —e) halo; (*clouds*) nimbus.

Heiligkeit ['haɪlɪçkaɪt], *f.* (—, *no pl.*) holiness, sanctity, sacredness.

Heiligtum ['haɪlɪçtu:m], *n.* (—s, *pl.* ˙er) sanctuary, shrine; holy relic.

Heiligung ['haɪlɪguŋ], *f.* (—, *pl.* —en) sanctification, consecration.

heilkräftig ['haɪlkrɛftɪç], *adj.* curative, salubrious.

Heilkunde ['haɪlkundə], *f.* (—, *no pl.*) therapeutics.

heillos ['haɪllo:s], *adj.* wicked, mis-chievous; (*fig.*) awful.

Heilmittel ['haɪlmɪtəl], *n.* (—s, *pl.* —) remedy.

heilsam ['haɪlza:m], *adj.* salubrious, salutary.

Heilsamkeit ['haɪlza:mkaɪt], *f.* (—, *no pl.*) salubrity, salubriousness.

Heilsarmee ['haɪlsarme:], *f.* (—, *no pl.*) Salvation Army.

Heilslehre ['haɪlsle:rə], *f.* (—, *pl.* —n) doctrine of salvation.

Heiltrank ['haɪltraŋk], *m.* (—es, *no pl.*) (medicinal) potion.

Heim [haɪm], *n.* (—es, *pl.* —e) home.

heim [haɪm], *adv. prefix (to verbs)* home.

Heimat ['haɪmat], *f.* (—, *no pl.*) native place, home, homeland.

Heimatschein ['haɪmatʃaɪn], *m.* (—es, *pl.* —e) certificate of origin *or* domicile.

Heimchen ['haɪmçən], *n.* (—s, *pl.* —) (*Ent.*) cricket.

heimführen ['haɪmfy:rən], *v.a.* bring home (a bride); (*fig.*) marry.

Heimgang ['haɪmgaŋ], *m.* (—es, *no pl.*) going home; (*fig.*) decease, death.

heimisch ['haɪmɪʃ], *adj.* native, in-digenous; *sich — fühlen*, feel at home.

heimkehren ['haɪmke:rən], *v.n.* return (home).

heimleuchten ['haɪmlɔyçtən], *v.n. einem —*, tell s.o. the plain truth, give s.o. a piece of o.'s mind.

heimlich ['haɪmlɪç], *adj.* secret, clan-destine, furtive.

heimsuchen ['haɪmzu:xən], *v.a.* visit; afflict, punish.

Heimtücke ['haɪmtykə], *f.* (—, *no pl.*) malice.

heimwärts ['haɪmvɛrts], *adv.* home-ward.

Heimweh ['haɪmve:], *n.* (—s, *no pl.*) homesickness; nostalgia.

heimzahlen ['haɪmtsa:lən], *v.a.* pay back, retaliate.

Hein [haɪn], *m.* (*coll.*) *Freund —*, Death.

Heinzelmännchen ['haɪntsəlmɛnçən], *n.* (—s, *pl.* —) goblin, brownie, imp.

Heirat ['haɪra:t], *f.* (—, *pl.* —en) marriage, wedding.

heiraten ['haɪra:tən], *v.a.* marry, wed.

Heiratsgut ['haɪra:tsgu:t], *n.* (—es, *pl.* ˙er) dowry.

heischen ['haɪʃən], *v.a.* (*Poet.*) ask, demand.

heiser ['haɪzər], *adj.* hoarse.

heiß [haɪs], *adj.* hot; (*fig.*) ardent; (*climate*) torrid.

heißen ['haɪsən], *v.a. irr.* bid, com-mand. — *v.n.* be called; be said; signify, mean; *es heißt*, it is said; *das heißt (d.h.)*, that is to say; *wie — Sie?* what is your name?

heißgeliebt ['haɪsgəli:pt], *adj.* dearly beloved.

heiter ['haɪtər], *adj.* clear; serene; cheerful.

Heiterkeit ['haɪtərkaɪt], *f.* (—, *no pl.*) serenity; cheerfulness.

heizen ['haɪtsən], *v.a. v.n.* heat.

Heizkissen ['haɪtskɪsən], *n.* (—s, *pl.* —) electric pad *or* blanket.

Heizkörper ['haɪtskœrpər], *m.* (—s, *pl.* —) radiator; heater.

Heizung ['haɪtsuŋ], *f.* (—, *pl.* —en) heating.

hektisch ['hɛktɪʃ], *adj.* hectic.

104

hektographieren [hɛktogra'fiːrən], *v.a.* stencil, duplicate.

Hektoliter ['hɛktoliːtər], *m.* (—s, *pl.* —) hectolitre (22 gallons).

Held [hɛlt], *m.* (—en, *pl.* —en) hero.

Heldengedicht ['hɛldəngədiçt], *n.* (—es, *pl.* —e) heroic poem, epic.

heldenhaft ['hɛldənhaft], *adj.* heroic. — *adv.* heroically.

Heldenmut ['hɛldənmuːt], *m.* (—es, *no pl.*) heroism.

helfen ['hɛlfən], *v.n. irr.* (*Dat.*) help, aid, assist.

Helfershelfer ['hɛlfərshɛlfər], *m.* (—s, *pl.* —) accomplice, accessory.

Helgoland ['hɛlgolant], *n.* Heligoland.

hell [hɛl], *adj.* clear, bright, light; (*coll.*) clever, wide awake.

Helldunkel ['hɛldunkəl], *n.* (—s, *no pl.*) twilight; (*Art*) chiaroscuro.

Helle ['hɛlə], *f.* (—, *no pl.*) clearness; brightness; daylight.

Heller ['hɛlər], *m.* (—s, *pl.* —) small coin, farthing.

hellhörig ['hɛlhøːrɪç], *adj.* keen of hearing.

Helligkeit ['hɛlɪçkaɪt], *f.* (—, *no pl.*) clearness; daylight.

Hellseher ['hɛlzeːər], *m.* (—s, *pl.* —) clairvoyant.

hellsichtig ['hɛlzɪxtɪç], *adj.* clairvoyant; clear-sighted.

Helm [hɛlm], *m.* (—es, *pl.* —e) helmet.

Helmbusch ['hɛlmbuʃ], *m.* (—es, *pl.* ⸚e) crest (of helmet).

Helmgitter ['hɛlmgɪtər], *n.* (—s, *pl.* —) eye-slit (in helmet).

Helsingfors ['hɛlzɪnfɔrs], *n.* Helsinki.

Helsingör [hɛlzɪn'øːr], *n.* Elsinore.

Hemd [hɛmt], *n.* (—es, *pl.* —en) shirt; vest.

Hemdenstoff ['hɛmdənʃtɔf], *m.* (—es, *pl.* —e) shirting.

hemmen ['hɛmən], *v.a.* stop, hamper, hinder, restrain; (*fig.*) inhibit.

Hemmschuh ['hɛmʃuː], *m.* (—s, *pl.* —e) brake; (*fig.*) drag, obstruction.

Hemmung ['hɛmuŋ], *f.* (—, *pl.* —en) stoppage, hindrance, restraint; (*watch*) escapement; (*fig.*) inhibition, reluctance.

Hengst [hɛŋkst], *m.* (—es, *pl.* —e) stallion.

Henkel ['hɛŋkəl], *m.* (—s, *pl.* —) handle.

henken ['hɛŋkən], *v.a* hang (s.o.).

Henker ['hɛŋkər], *m.* (—s, *pl.* —) hangman, executioner.

Henne ['hɛnə], *f.* (—, *pl.* —n) (*Zool.*) hen; *junge* —, pullet.

her [heːr], *adv.* hither, here, to me; (*temp.*) since, ago; *von alters* —, from olden times; *von je* —, from time immemorial; *wo kommst du* —? where do you come from? *wie lange ist es* —? how long ago was it?

herab [hɛ'rap], *adv.* downwards, down to; *die Treppe* —, downstairs.

herablassen [hɛ'raplasən], *v.r. irr. sich* — *etwas zu tun*, condescend to do s.th.

herabsehen [hɛ'rapzeːən], *v.n. irr.* look down; (*fig.*) look down upon s.o.

herabsetzen [hɛ'rapzɛtsən], *v.a.* put down; degrade; (*value*) depreciate; (*price*) reduce, lower; (*fig.*) disparage.

herabwürdigen [hɛ'rapvyrdɪgən], *v.a.* degrade, abase.

herabziehen [hɛ'raptsiːən], *v.a. irr.* pull down.

Heraldik [he'raldɪk], *f.* (—, *no pl.*) heraldry.

heran [hɛ'ran], *adv.* up to, on, near.

heranbilden [hɛ'ranbɪldən], *v.a.* train. — *v.r. sich* —, train, qualify.

herangehen [hɛ'rangeːən], *v.n. irr.* (*aux. sein*) approach, sidle up (to); *an etwas* —, set to work on s.th.

heranmachen [hɛ'ranmaxən], *v.r. sich an etwas* —, set to work on s.th., set about s.th.

herannahen [hɛ'rannaːən], *v.n.* (*aux. sein*) approach, draw near.

heranrücken [hɛ'ranrykən], *v.a.* move near. — *v.n.* (*aux. sein*) advance, draw near.

heranschleichen [hɛ'ranʃlaɪçən], *v.r. irr. sich* — *an*, sneak up to.

heranwachsen [hɛ'ranvaksən], *v.n. irr.* (*aux. sein*) grow up.

heranwagen [hɛ'ranvaːgən], *v.r. sich* —, venture near.

heranziehen [hɛ'rantsiːən], *v.a. irr.* draw near; *als Beispiel* —, cite as an example; (*fig.*) enlist (s.o.'s aid). — *v.n.* (*aux. sein*) draw near, approach.

herauf [hɛ'rauf], *adv.* up, upwards.

heraufbeschwören [hɛ'raufbeʃvøːrən], *v.a.* conjure up.

heraus [hɛ'raus], *adv.* out, out of.

herausfordern [hɛ'rausfordərn], *v.a.* challenge.

Herausgabe [hɛ'rausgaːbə], *f.* (—, *pl.* —n) delivery; (*book*) publication; editing.

herausgeben [hɛ'rausgeːbən], *v.a. irr.* give out, deliver; (*money*) give change; (*book*) publish, edit.

Herausgeber [hɛ'rausgeːbər], *m.* (—s, *pl.* —) publisher; editor.

heraushaben [hɛ'raushaːbən], *v.a. irr. etwas* —, have the knack of s.th.

herausputzen [hɛ'rausputsən], *v.r. sich* —, dress up.

herausrücken [hɛ'rausrykən], *v.n. mit Geld* —, fork out money; *mit der Sprache* —, speak out, come out with.

herausschlagen [hɛ'rausʃlaːgən], *v.a. irr. die Kosten* —, recover expenses; *viel* —, make the most of; profit by.

herausstellen [hɛ'rausʃtɛlən], *v.a.* put out, expose. — *v.r. sich* — *als*, turn out to be.

herausstreichen [hɛ'rausʃtraɪçən], *v.a. irr.* extol, praise.

heraussuchen [hɛ'rauszuːxən], *v.a.* pick out.

herauswollen

herauswollen [hɛˈrausvɔlən], v.n. *nicht mit der Sprache —,* hesitate to speak out.

herb [hɛrp], adj. sour, sharp, tart, acrid; (fig.) austere, harsh, bitter; (*wine*) dry.

herbei [hɛrˈbaɪ], adv. hither, near.

herbeischaffen [hɛrˈbaɪʃafən], v.a. procure.

herbeiströmen [hɛrˈbaɪʃtrøːmən], v.n. (*aux.* sein) crowd, flock.

Herberge [ˈhɛrbɛrgə], f. (—, pl. —n) shelter, lodging, inn.

Herbst [hɛrpst], m. (—es, pl. —e) autumn; (*Am.*) fall.

Herbstrose [ˈhɛrpstroːzə], f. (—, pl. —n) (*Bot.*) hollyhock.

Herbstzeitlose [ˈhɛrpsttsaɪtloːzə], f. (—, pl. —n) (*Bot.*) meadow-saffron.

Herd [heːrt], m. (—es, pl. —e) hearth, fireplace; cooking-stove; (*fig.*) focus.

Herde [ˈheːrdə], f. (—, pl. —n) flock, herd; (*fig.*) troop.

herein [heˈraɪn], adv. in, inside. — int. —! come in!

hereinbrechen [heˈraɪnbrɛçən], v.n. irr. (*aux.* sein) *über einen —,* befall s.o., overtake s.o.; (*night*) close in.

hereinfallen [heˈraɪnfalən], v.n. irr. (*aux.* sein) (*fig.*) be taken in, fall for s.th.

herfallen [ˈheːrfalən], v.n. irr. (*aux.* sein) *über einen —,* go for s.o., set upon s.o.

Hergang [ˈheːrgaŋ], m. (—es, no pl.) proceedings, course of events; circumstances; story, plot.

hergeben [ˈheːrgeːbən], v.a. irr. give up, surrender.

hergebracht [ˈheːrgəbraxt], adj. traditional, time-honoured.

hergehen [ˈheːrgeːən], v.n. irr. (*aux.* sein) proceed; *es geht lustig her,* they are having a gay time.

hergelaufen [ˈheːrgəlaufən], adj. *ein —er Kerl,* an adventurer, an upstart.

herhalten [ˈheːrhaltən], v.n. irr. suffer, serve (as a butt).

Hering [ˈheːrɪŋ], m. (—s, pl. —e) (*Zool.*) herring; *geräucherter —,* smoked herring, bloater; *gesalzener —,* pickled herring.

herkommen [ˈheːrkɔmən], v.n. irr. (*aux.* sein) come here; be derived from, descend from.

herkömmlich [ˈheːrkœmlɪç], adj. traditional, customary, usual.

Herkunft [ˈheːrkunft], f. (—, no pl.) descent, extraction; origin.

herleiern [ˈheːrlaɪərn], v.a. recite monotonously; reel off.

herleiten [ˈheːrlaɪtən], v.a. derive from.

Hermelin [hɛrməˈliːn], m. (—s, no pl.) ermine (*fur*).

hermetisch [hɛrˈmeːtɪʃ], adj. hermetical.

hernach [hɛrˈnaːx], adv. after, afterwards; hereafter.

hernehmen [ˈheːrneːmən], v.a. irr. take, get (from); take (s.o.) to task.

hernieder [hɛrˈniːdər], adv. down.

Herr [hɛr], m. (—n, pl. —en) master; lord; nobleman; gentleman; (*Theol.*) Lord; principal, governor; *mein —,* Sir; *meine Herren,* gentlemen; *— Schmidt,* Mr. Smith; *einer Sache — werden,* master s.th.

Herrenhaus [ˈhɛrənhaus], n. (—es, pl. ⸚er) mansion, manor house; (*Parl.*) House of Lords.

Herrenhof [ˈhɛrənhoːf], m. (—es, pl. ⸚e) manor, country-seat.

Herrenstand [ˈhɛrənʃtant], m. (—es, no pl.) nobility, gentry.

Herrenzimmer [ˈhɛrəntsimər], n. (—s, pl. —) study.

Herrgott [ˈhɛrgɔt], the Lord God.

herrichten [ˈheːrrɪçtən], v.a. prepare, fix up.

Herrin [ˈhɛrɪn], f. (—, pl. —innen) mistress, lady.

herrisch [ˈhɛrɪʃ], adj. imperious, lordly.

herrlich [ˈhɛrlɪç], adj. magnificent, splendid, glorious, excellent.

Herrnhuter [ˈhɛrnhuːtər], m. (—s, pl. —) Moravian; (*pl.*) Moravian brethren.

Herrschaft [ˈhɛrʃaft], f. (—, pl. —en) mastery, rule, dominion; master, mistress; *meine —en!* ladies and gentlemen!

herrschaftlich [ˈhɛrʃaftlɪç], adj. belonging to a lord; (*fig.*) elegant, fashionable, distinguished.

herrschen [ˈhɛrʃən], v.n. rule, govern, reign.

Herrscher [ˈhɛrʃər], m. (—s, pl. —) ruler.

herrühren [ˈheːrryːrən], v.n. come from, originate in.

hersagen [ˈheːrzaːgən], v.a. recite, reel off.

herschaffen [ˈheːrʃafən], v.a. procure.

herstammen [ˈheːrʃtamən], v.n. come from, stem from, originate from; be derived from.

herstellen [ˈheːrʃtɛlən], v.a. place here; manufacture; *wieder —,* restore; (*sick person*) restore to health.

Herstellung [ˈheːrʃtɛluŋ], f. (—, no pl.) manufacture, production.

herstürzen [ˈheːrʃtyrtsən], v.n. (*aux.* sein) *über einen —,* rush at s.o.

herüber [heˈryːbər], adv. over, across; *— und hinüber,* there and back.

herum [heˈrum], adv. round, about; around.

herumbalgen [heˈrumbalgən], v.r. *sich —,* scrap; scuffle.

herumbekommen [heˈrumbəkɔmən], v.a. irr. (*coll.*) talk s.o. over, win s.o. over.

herumbummeln [heˈrumbuməln], v.n. loaf about.

herumstreichen [heˈrumʃtraɪçən], v.n. irr. (*aux.* sein) gad about.

herumtreiben [heˈrumtraɪbən], v.r. irr. *sich —,* loaf about, gad about.

herumzanken [heˈrumtsaŋkən], v.r. *sich —,* squabble, quarrel; live like cat and dog.

Hexenschuß

herumziehen [hɛˈrumtsiːən], v.a. irr.
drag about. — v.n. (aux. sein)
wander about, move from place to
place.

herunter [hɛˈruntər], adj. down, downward; ich bin ganz —, I feel
poorly.

heruntergekommen [hɛˈruntərgəkɔ-
mən], adj. decayed, broken down; in
straitened circumstances; depraved.

herunterhandeln [hɛˈruntərhandəln],
v.a. einem etwas —, beat s.o. down (in
price).

herunterwürgen [hɛˈruntərvyrgən],
v.a. swallow s.th. with dislike.

hervor [hɛrˈfoːr], adv. forth, forward,
out.

hervorheben [hɛrˈfoːrheːbən], v.a. irr.
emphasize, stress.

hervorragen [hɛrˈfoːrraːgən], v.n.
stand out, project; (fig.) be distinguished, excel.

hervorragend [hɛrˈfoːrraːgənt], adj.
prominent; (fig.) outstanding, excellent.

hervorrufen [hɛrˈfoːrruːfən], v.a. irr.
call forth; (fig.) evoke, bring about,
create, cause.

hervorstechen [hɛrˈfoːrʃtɛçən], v.n.
irr. be predominant, stand out.

hervortun [hɛrˈfoːrtuːn], v.r. irr. sich
—, distinguish o.s.

Herz [hɛrts], n. (—ens, pl. —en)
heart; courage; mind; spirit; feeling;
core; (Cards) hearts; (coll.) darling;
einem etwas ans — legen, impress
s.th. upon s.o.; von —en gern, with
all my heart; sich etwas zu —en
nehmen, take s.th. to heart.

herzählen [ˈhɛːrtsɛːlən], v.a. enumerate.

Herzanfall [ˈhɛrtsanfal], m. (—s, pl.
ˀe) (Med.) heart attack.

Herzbube [ˈhɛrtsbuːbə], m. (—n, pl.
—n) (Cards) knave or jack of hearts.

Herzdame [ˈhɛrtsdaːmə], f. (—, pl.
—n) (Cards) queen of hearts.

Herzeleid [ˈhɛrtsəlaɪt], n. (—es, no pl.)
heartbreak, sorrow, anguish, grief.

herzen [ˈhɛrtsən], v.a. hug.

Herzenseinfalt [ˈhɛrtsənsaɪnfalt], f.
(—, no pl.) simple-mindedness.

Herzensgrund [ˈhɛrtsənsgrunt], m.
(—es, no pl.) aus —, with all my
heart.

Herzenslust [ˈhɛrtsənslust], f. (—, no
pl.) heart's delight; nach —, to o.'s
heart's content.

Herzfehler [ˈhɛrtsfeːlər], m. (—s, pl.
—) (Med.) cardiac defect; organic
heart disease.

Herzfell [ˈhɛrtsfɛl], n. (—s, pl. —e)
pericardium.

herzförmig [ˈhɛrtsfœrmɪç], adj. heart-
shaped.

herzhaft [ˈhɛrtshaft], adj. stout-
hearted; courageous, bold; resolute;
hearty.

herzig [ˈhɛrtsɪç], adj. lovely, charming,
sweet; (Am.) cute.

Herzkammer [ˈhɛrtskamər], f. (—, pl.
—n) ventricle (of the heart).

Herzklappe [ˈhɛrtsklapə], f. (—, pl.
—n) valve of the heart.

Herzklopfen [ˈhɛrtsklɔpfən], n. (—s, no
pl.) palpitations.

herzlich [ˈhɛrtslɪç], adj. hearty, cordial,
affectionate; —e, warm, with pleasure;
—e Grüße, kind regards.

Herzog [ˈhɛrtsoːk], m. (—s, pl. ˀe)
duke.

Herzogtum [ˈhɛrtsoːktuːm], n. (—s, pl.
ˀer) duchy, dukedom.

Herzschlag [ˈhɛrtsʃlaːk], m. (—es, pl.
ˀe) heartbeat; (Med.) heart attack,
cardiac failure.

Hetäre [heˈtɛːrə], f. (—, pl. —n)
courtesan.

Hetzblatt [ˈhɛtsblat], n. (—s, pl. ˀer)
gutter press.

Hetze [ˈhɛtsə], f. (—, pl. —n) chase,
hunt, hurry, rush; agitation.

hetzen [ˈhɛtsən], v.a. bait, fluster,
chase, hunt, incite. — v.n. herum —,
rush around.

Hetzer [ˈhɛtsər], m. (—s, pl. —)
instigator, rabble-rouser.

Heu [hɔy], n. (—s, no pl.) hay.

Heuboden [ˈhɔyboːdən], m. (—s, pl. ˀ)
hayloft.

Heuchelei [hɔyçəˈlaɪ], f. (—, pl. —en)
hypocrisy.

heucheln [ˈhɔyçəln], v.n. play the
hypocrite, dissemble. — v.a. simulate,
affect, feign.

Heuchler [ˈhɔyçlər], m. (—s, pl. —)
hypocrite.

Heuer [ˈhɔyər], f. (—, pl. —n) (Naut.)
engagement; hire, wages.

heuer [ˈhɔyər], adv. (dial.) this year,
this season.

heuern [ˈhɔyərn], v.a. (Naut.) engage,
hire.

Heugabel [ˈhɔygaːbəl], f. (—, pl. —n)
pitchfork.

heulen [ˈhɔylən], v.n. howl; roar; cry,
yell, scream.

Heupferd [ˈhɔypfɛrt], n. (—es, pl. —e)
(Ent.) grasshopper.

heurig [ˈhɔyrɪç], adj. of this year, this
year's (wine etc.).

Heuschnupfen [ˈhɔyʃnupfən], m. (—s,
no pl.) hay-fever.

Heuschober [ˈhɔyʃoːbər], m. (—s, pl.
—) hayrick.

Heuschrecke [ˈhɔyʃrɛkə], f. (—, pl.
—n) (Ent.) locust.

heute [ˈhɔytə], adv. today, this day;
— in acht Tagen, today week, a
week today; — abend, tonight.

heutig [ˈhɔytɪç], adj. today's, this
day's; modern.

heutzutage [ˈhɔytsutaːgə], adv. nowadays.

Hexe [ˈhɛksə], f. (—, pl. —n) witch,
sorceress, hag.

hexen [ˈhɛksən], v.n. use witchcraft;
practise sorcery.

Hexenschuß [ˈhɛksənʃus], m. (—sses,
no pl.) (Med.) lumbago.

107

Hexerei

Hexerei [hɛksəˈraɪ], *f.* (—, *pl.* —en) witchcraft, sorcery, juggling.

hie [hiː], *adv.* (*dial.*) here.

Hieb [hiːp], *m.* (—es, *pl.* —e) cut, stroke; hit, blow; (*pl.*) a thrashing.

hienieden [hiːˈniːdən], *adv.* here below, down here.

hier [hiːr], *adv.* here, in this place.

Hiersein [ˈhiːrzaɪn], *n.* (—s, *no pl.*) presence, attendance.

hiesig [ˈhiːzɪç], *adj.* of this place, of this country, local.

Hifthorn [ˈhɪfthɔrn], *n.* (—s, *pl.* ⁝er) hunting-horn.

Hilfe [ˈhɪlfə], *f.* (—, *pl.* —n) help, aid, assistance, succour, relief.

hilflos [ˈhɪlfloːs], *adj.* helpless.

hilfreich [ˈhɪlfraɪç], *adj.* helpful.

Hilfsmittel [ˈhɪlfsmɪtəl], *n.* (—s, *pl.* —) expedient, remedy.

Hilfsschule [ˈhɪlfsʃuːlə], *f.* (—, *pl.* —n) school for backward children.

Hilfszeitwort [ˈhɪlfstsaɪtvɔrt], *n.* (—s, *pl.* ⁝er) (*Gram.*) auxiliary verb.

Himbeere [ˈhɪmbeːrə], *f.* (—, *pl.* —n) raspberry.

Himmel [ˈhɪməl], *m.* (—s, *pl.* —) heaven, heavens; sky; firmament.

himmelan [hɪməlˈan], *adv.* heavenward.

himmelangst [ˈhɪməlaŋkst], *adv.* *ihm war —*, he was panic-stricken.

Himmelbett [ˈhɪməlbɛt], *n.* (—s, *pl.* —en) fourposter.

himmelblau [ˈhɪməlblau], *adj.* sky-blue.

Himmelfahrt [ˈhɪməlfaːrt], *f.* (—, *no pl.*) Ascension.

Himmelschlüssel [ˈhɪməlʃlysəl], *m.* (—s, *pl.* —) (*Bot.*) primrose.

himmelschreiend [ˈhɪməlʃraɪənt], *adj.* atrocious, revolting.

Himmelsgewölbe [ˈhɪməlsgəvœlbə], *n.* (—s, *pl.* —) firmament.

Himmelsstrich [ˈhɪməlsʃtrɪç], *m.* (—s, *pl.* —e) climate, zone.

Himmelszeichen [ˈhɪməlstsaɪçən], *n.* (—s, *pl.* —) sign of the zodiac.

himmelweit [ˈhɪməlvaɪt], *adj.* enormous; — *entfernt*, poles apart.

himmlisch [ˈhɪmlɪʃ], *adj.* celestial, heavenly.

hin [hɪn], *adv.* there, towards that place; finished, gone; ruined; — *und her*, to and fro.

hinab [hɪnˈap], *adv.* down.

hinan [hɪnˈan], *adv.* up.

hinarbeiten [ˈhɪnarbaɪtən], *v.n. auf etwas* —, work towards s.th.

hinauf [hɪnˈauf], *adv.* up, up to.

hinaus [hɪnˈaus], *adv.* out, out of; *es kommt auf dasselbe* —, it comes to the same thing.

hinauswollen [hɪnˈausvɔlən], *v.n.* wish to go out; (*fig.*) *hoch* —, aim high.

hinausziehen [hɪnˈaustsiːən], *v.a. irr.* draw out; drag on; (*fig.*) protract.

Hinblick [ˈhɪnblɪk], *m.* (—es, *no pl.*) *im* — *auf*, in consideration of, with regard to.

hinbringen [ˈhɪnbrɪŋən], *v.a. irr.* bring to; escort; *Zeit* —, while away time.

hinderlich [ˈhɪndərlɪç], *adj.* obstructive, cumbersome.

hindern [ˈhɪndərn], *v.a.* hinder, obstruct, hamper, impede.

hindeuten [ˈhɪndɔytən], *v.n. auf etwas* —, point to s.th., hint at s.th.

Hindin [ˈhɪndɪn], *f.* (—, *pl.* —innen) (*Poet.*) hind.

hindurch [hɪnˈdurç], *adv.* through; throughout; *die ganze Zeit* —, all the time.

hinein [hɪnˈaɪn], *adv.* in, into; *in den Tag* — *leben*, live for the present, lead a life of carefree enjoyment.

hineinfinden [hɪnˈaɪnfɪndən], *v.r. irr. sich in etwas* —, reconcile *or* accustom o.s. to s.th.

hinfällig [ˈhɪnfɛlɪç], *adj.* frail, feeble, weak; shaky, void, invalid.

Hingabe [ˈhɪngaːbə], *f.* (—, *no pl.*) surrender; (*fig.*) devotion.

hingeben [ˈhɪngeːbən], *v.a. irr.* give up, surrender. — *v.r. sich einer Sache* —, devote o.s. to a task.

hingegen [hɪnˈgeːgən], *adv.* on the other hand.

hinhalten [ˈhɪnhaltən], *v.a. irr.* (*thing*) hold out; (*person*) keep in suspense, put off.

hinken [ˈhɪŋkən], *v.n.* limp.

hinlänglich [ˈhɪnlɛŋlɪç], *adj.* sufficient.

hinlegen [ˈhɪnleːgən], *v.a.* lay down, put away. — *v.r. sich* —, lie down, go to bed.

hinnehmen [ˈhɪnneːmən], *v.a. irr.* take, submit to, accept.

hinreichen [ˈhɪnraɪçən], *v.a.* pass to. — *v.n.* suffice, be sufficient.

Hinreise [ˈhɪnraɪzə], *f.* (—, *pl.* —n) outward journey.

hinreißen [ˈhɪnraɪsən], *v.r. irr. sich* — *lassen*, allow o.s. to be carried away.

hinreißend [ˈhɪnraɪsənt], *adj.* charming, ravishing, enchanting.

hinrichten [ˈhɪnrɪçtən], *v.a.* execute, put to death.

hinscheiden [ˈhɪnʃaɪdən], *v.n. irr.* die, pass away.

hinschlängeln [ˈhɪnʃlɛŋəln], *v.r. sich* —, meander, wind along.

Hinsicht [ˈhɪnzɪçt], *f.* (—, *no pl.*) view, consideration, regard.

hinsichtlich [ˈhɪnzɪçtlɪç], *prep.* (*Genit.*) with regard to.

hinstellen [ˈhɪnʃtɛlən], *v.a.* put down; make out to be.

hinten [ˈhɪntən], *adv.* behind; *von* —, from behind.

hinter [ˈhɪntər], *prep.* (*Dat.*) behind, after.

Hinterachse [ˈhɪntəraksə], *f.* (—, *pl.* —n) (*Motor.*) rear-axle.

Hinterbein [ˈhɪntərbaɪn], *n.* (—s, *pl.* —e) hind-leg; (*fig.*) *sich auf die* — *stellen*, get up on o.'s hind-legs.

108

Hinterbliebene [hıntər'bli:bənə], *m.*
(—n, *pl.* —n) survivor; mourner;
(*pl.*) the bereaved.

hinterbringen [hıntər'brıŋən], *v.a.*
irr. give information about, (*coll.*)
tell on.

Hinterdeck ['hıntərdɛk], *n.* (—s, *no pl.*)
(*Naut.*) quarter deck.

hinterdrein ['hıntərdraın], *adv.* afterwards, after; behind.

hintereinander [hıntəraın'andər], *adv.*
in succession, one after another.

Hintergedanke ['hıntərgədaŋkə], *m.*
(—n, *pl.* —n) mental reservation,
ulterior motive.

hintergehen [hıntər'ge:ən], *v.a. irr.*
deceive, circumvent.

Hintergrund ['hıntərgrunt], *m.* (—es,
pl. ⁻e) background; (*Theat.*) back-
cloth, back-drop.

Hinterhalt ['hıntərhalt], *m.* (—s, *pl.*
—e) ambush; (*fig.*) reserve.

hinterhältig ['hıntərhɛltıç], *adj.* furtive, secretive; insidious.

hinterher [hıntər'he:r], *adv.* behind;
in the rear; afterwards.

Hinterindien [hıntərındjən], *n.* Indo-
China.

Hinterkopf ['hıntərkɔpf], *m.* (—es, *pl.*
⁻e) occiput, back of the head.

Hinterlader ['hıntərla:dər], *m.* (—s,
pl. —) breech-loader.

hinterlassen [hıntər'lasən], *v.a. irr.*
leave (a legacy), bequeath; leave
(word).

Hinterlassenschaft [hıntər'lasənʃaft],
f. (—, *pl.* —en) inheritance, bequest.

Hinterlegung [hıntər'le:guŋ], *f.* (—,
pl. —en) deposition.

Hinterlist ['hıntərlıst], *f.* (—, *no pl.*)
fraud, deceit; cunning.

hinterrücks [hıntər'ryks], *adv.* from
behind; (*fig.*) treacherously, behind
s.o.'s back.

Hintertreffen ['hıntərtrɛfən], *n.* (—s,
no pl.) ins — geraten, be left out in the
cold, fall behind.

hintertreiben [hıntər'traıbən], *v.a. irr.*
prevent, frustrate.

Hintertreppe ['hıntərtrɛpə], *f.* (—, *pl.*
—n) back-stairs.

Hintertreppenroman ['hıntərtrɛpən-
roma:n], *m.* (—s, *pl.* —e) (*Lit.*) cheap
thriller.

hinterziehen ['hıntərtsi:ən], *v.a. irr.*
insep. defraud.

hinträumen ['hıntrɔymən], *v.n. vor
sich* —, daydream.

hinüber [hın'y:bər], *adv.* over, across.

hinunter [hın'untər], *adv.* down;
den Berg —, downhill.

hinweg [hın'vɛk], *adv.* away, off.

hinwegsetzen [hın'vɛkzɛtsən], *v.r. sich
über etwas* —, make light of s.th.

Hinweis ['hınvaıs], *m.* (—es, *pl.* —e)
hint, indication, reference; *unter* —
auf, with reference to.

hinweisen ['hınvaızən], *v.a. irr. auf
etwas* —, refer to, point to s.th.

hinwerfen ['hınvɛrfən], *v.a. irr.* throw
down; *hingeworfene Bemerkung*, casual
remark.

hinziehen ['hıntsi:ən], *v.a. irr.* draw
along; attract. — *v.n.* (*aux. sein*)
march along. — *v.r. sich* —, drag on.

hinzielen ['hıntsi:lən], *v.n. auf etwas* —,
aim at s.th., have s.th. in mind.

hinzu [hın'tsu:], *adv.* to, near; besides,
in addition.

hinzufügen [hın'tsu:fy:gən], *v.a.* add.

hinzukommen [hın'tsu:kɔmən], *v.n.
irr.* (*aux. sein*) be added.

hinzuziehen [hın'tsutsi:ən], *v.a. irr.*
include, add; call in (expert).

Hiobsbotschaft ['hi:ɔpsbo:tʃaft], *f.* (—,
no pl.) bad news.

Hirn [hırn], *n.* (—es, *pl.* —e) brain,
brains. *See also Gehirn.*

Hirngespinst ['hırngəʃpınst], *n.* (—es,
pl. —e) fancy, chimera, illusion,
figment of the imagination.

hirnverbrannt ['hırnfɛrbrant], *adj.*
crazy, insane, mad; (*coll.*) crack-
brained.

Hirsch [hırʃ], *m.* (—es, *pl.* —e) (*Zool.*)
stag, hart.

Hirschbock ['hırʃbɔk], *m.* (—s, *pl.* ⁻e)
(*Zool.*) stag.

Hirschfänger ['hırʃfɛŋər], *m.* (—s, *pl.*
—) hunting-knife.

Hirschgeweih ['hırʃgəvaı], *n.* (—s, *pl.*
—e) horns, antlers.

Hirschhorn ['hırʃhɔrn], *n.* (—s, *no pl.*)
(*Chem.*) hartshorn.

Hirschkäfer ['hırʃkɛ:fər], *m.* (—s, *pl.*
—) (*Ent.*) stag beetle.

Hirschkeule ['hırʃkɔylə], *f.* (—, *pl.* —n)
haunch of venison.

Hirschkuh ['hırʃku:], *f.* (—, *pl.* ⁻e)
(*Zool.*) hind, doe.

Hirse ['hırzə], *f.* (—, *no pl.*) (*Bot.*)
millet.

Hirt [hırt], *m.* (—en, *pl.* —en) shepherd, herdsman.

Hirtenbrief ['hırtənbri:f], *m.* (—s,
pl. —e) (*Eccl.*) pastoral letter.

His [hıs], *n.* (—, *pl.* —) (*Mus.*) B sharp.

hissen ['hısən], *v.a.* hoist (the flag).

Historiker [hı'sto:rıkər], *m.* (—s, *pl.*
—) historian.

historisch [hı'sto:rıʃ], *adj.* historical.

Hitzblase ['hıtsbla:zə], *f.* (—, *pl.* —n)
blister, heat-rash.

Hitze ['hıtsə], *f.* (—, *no pl.*) heat, hot
weather.

hitzig ['hıtsıç], *adj.* hot-headed, hasty,
passionate.

Hitzschlag ['hıtsʃla:k], *m.* (—es, *pl.* ⁻e)
sunstroke, heat-stroke.

Hobel ['ho:bəl], *m.* (—s, *pl.* —) (*tool*)
plane.

Hoch [ho:x], *n.* (—s, *no pl.*) toast
(*drink*); (*Met.*) high.

hoch, hoh [ho:x, ho:], *adj.* high; (*fig.*)
eminent, sublime.

Hochachtung ['ho:xaxtuŋ], *f.* (—, *no
pl.*) esteem, regard, respect.

hochachtungsvoll ['ho:xaxtuŋsfɔl],
adj., adv. (*letters*) yours faithfully.

109

Hochamt

Hochamt ['hoːxamt], n. (—es, pl. ⁺er) (Eccl.) High Mass.

Hochbau ['hoːxbau], m. (—s, pl. —ten) superstructure.

hochbetagt ['hoːxbətaːkt], adj. advanced in years.

Hochburg ['hoːxburk], f. (—, pl. —en) (fig.) stronghold, citadel.

Hochebene ['hoːxeːbənə], f. (—, pl. —n) table-land, plateau.

hochfahrend ['hoːxfaːrənt], adj. haughty, high-flown; (coll.) stuck-up.

Hochgefühl ['hoːxgəfyːl], n. (—s, no pl.) exaltation.

Hochgenuß ['hoːxgənus], m. (—sses, pl. ⁺sse) exquisite enjoyment; treat.

Hochgericht ['hoːxgəriçt], n. (—s, pl. —e) place of execution, scaffold.

hochherzig ['hoːxhɛrtsiç], adj. magnanimous.

Hochmeister ['hoːxmaɪstər], m. (—s, pl. —) Grand Master.

Hochmut ['hoːxmuːt], m. (—s, no pl.) haughtiness, pride.

hochnäsig ['hoːxnɛːziç], adj. supercilious, stuck-up.

hochnotpeinlich ['hoːxnoːtpaɪnliç], adj. (obs.) penal, criminal; —es Verhör, criminal investigation.

Hochofen ['hoːxoːfən], m. (—s, pl. ⁺) blast-furnace.

Hochschule ['hoːxʃuːlə], f. (—, pl. —n) academy; university.

Hochschüler ['hoːxʃyːlər], m. (—s, pl. —) student, undergraduate.

höchst [høːçst], adj. highest, most. — adv. most, extremely.

Hochstapler ['hoːxʃtaːplər], m. (—s, pl. —) confidence trickster, swindler.

höchstens ['høːçstəns], adv. at most, at best.

hochtrabend ['hoːxtraːbənt], adj. (horse) high-stepping; (fig.) high-sounding, bombastic.

hochverdient ['hoːxfɛrdiːnt], adj. highly meritorious.

Hochverrat ['hoːxfɛraːt], m. (—s, no pl.) high treason.

Hochwild ['hoːxvɪlt], n. (—es, no pl.) deer; big game.

hochwohlgeboren ['hoːxvoːlgəboːrən], adj. (obs.) noble; Euer Hochwohlgeboren, Right Honourable Sir.

hochwürden ['hoːxvyrdən], adj. Euer Hochwürden, Reverend Sir.

Hochzeit ['hɔxtsaɪt], f. (—, pl. —en) wedding; nuptials.

hochzeitlich ['hɔxtsaɪtliç], adj. nuptial, bridal.

Hochzeitsreise ['hɔxtsaɪtsraɪzə], f. (—, pl. —n) honeymoon.

Hocke ['hɔkə], f. (—, pl. —n) squatting posture; shock, stook.

hocken ['hɔkən], v.n. crouch, squat; zu Hause —, be a stay-at-home.

Hocker ['hɔkər], m. (—s, pl. —) stool.

Höcker ['hœkər], m. (—s, pl. —) hump.

höckerig ['hœkəriç], adj. hump-backed, hunch-backed.

Hode ['hoːdə], f. (—, pl. —n) testicle.

Hof [hoːf], m. (—es, pl. ⁺e) yard, courtyard; farm(stead); (royal) court; (moon) halo; einem den — machen, court s.o.

Hofarzt ['hoːfartst], m. (—es, pl. ⁺e) court physician.

hoffähig ['hoːffɛːiç], adj. presentable at court.

Hoffart ['hɔfart], f. (—, no pl.) pride, arrogance.

hoffärtig ['hɔfɛrtiç], adj. proud, arrogant.

hoffen ['hɔfən], v.n. hope; fest auf etwas —, trust.

hoffentlich ['hɔfəntliç], adv. as I hope, I trust that.

Hoffnung ['hɔfnuŋ], f. (—, pl. —en) hope, expectation, anticipation, expectancy; guter — sein, be full of hope; be expecting a baby; sich — machen auf, cherish hopes of.

hoffnungslos ['hɔfnuŋsloːs], adj. hopeless, past hope.

hofieren [ho'fiːrən], v.a. court.

höfisch ['høːfiʃ], adj. courtlike, courtly.

höflich ['høːfliç], adj. courteous, civil, polite.

Hoflieferant ['hoːfliːfərant], m. (—en, pl. —en) purveyor to His or Her Majesty.

Höfling ['høːfliŋ], m. (—s, pl. —e) courtier.

Hofmarschall ['hoːfmarʃal], m. (—s, pl. —e) Lord Chamberlain.

Hofmeister ['hoːfmaɪstər], m. (—s, pl. —) (obs.) steward; tutor.

Hofnarr ['hoːfnar], m. (—en, pl. —en) court jester, court fool.

Hofrat ['hoːfraːt], m. (—s, pl. ⁺e) Privy Councillor.

Hofschranze ['hoːfʃrantsə], m. (—n, pl. —n) courtier; flunkey.

Hofsitte ['hoːfzɪtə], f. (—, pl. —n) court etiquette.

Höhe ['høːə], f. (—, pl. —n) height, altitude; bis zur — von, up to the level of; in die —, upwards; in die — fahren, give a start, get excited.

Hoheit ['hoːhaɪt], f. (—, pl. —en) grandeur; sovereignty; (title) Highness.

Hohelied [hoːə'liːt], n. (—s, no pl.) Song of Solomon.

Höhenmesser ['høːənmɛsər], m. (—s, pl. —) (Aviat.) altimeter.

Höhensonne ['høːənzɔnə], f. (—, pl. —n) Alpine sun; (Med.) ultra-violet lamp.

Höhenzug ['høːəntsuːk], m. (—s, pl. ⁺e) mountain range.

Höhepunkt ['høːəpuŋkt], m. (—s, pl. —e) climax, culmination, acme; peak.

höher ['høːər], comp. adj. higher.

hohl [hoːl], adj. hollow; (tooth) decayed, hollow.

Höhle ['høːlə], f. (—, pl. —n) cave, cavern, den.

hohlgeschliffen [ˈhoːlgəʃlɪfən], *adj.* concave, hollow-ground.
Hohlheit [ˈhoːlhaɪt], *f.* (—, *no pl.*) hollowness.
Hohlleiste [ˈhoːllaɪstə], *f.* (—, *pl.* —n) groove, channel.
Hohlmaß [ˈhoːlmaːs], *n.* (—es, *pl.* —e) dry measure.
Hohlmeißel [ˈhoːlmaɪsəl], *m.* (—s, *pl.* —) gouge.
Hohlsaum [ˈhoːlzaum], *m.* (—s, *pl.* ⁝e) hemstitch.
Hohlspiegel [ˈhoːlʃpiːgəl], *m.* (—s, *pl.* —) concave mirror.
Höhlung [ˈhøːluŋ], *f.* (—, *pl.* —en) hollow, cavity.
Hohlziegel [ˈhoːltsiːgəl], *m.* (—s, *pl.* —) hollow brick.
Hohn [hoːn], *m.* (—s, *no pl.*) scorn, derision, mockery; sneer.
höhnen [ˈhøːnən], *v.a.* deride, sneer at; *see* **verhöhnen.**
Höker [ˈhøːkər], *m.* (—s, *pl.* —) hawker, huckster.
hold [hɔlt], *adj.* kind, friendly; gracious; graceful; sweet.
Holder [ˈhɔldər] *see* **Holunder.**
holdselig [ˈhɔltzeːlɪç], *adj.* sweet, charming, gracious.
holen [ˈhoːlən], *v.a.* fetch, collect, get.
Holland [ˈhɔlant], *n.* Holland.
Hölle [ˈhœlə], *f.* (—, *no pl.*) hell.
Holm [hɔlm], *m.* (—es, *pl.* —e) islet, holm; (*Gymn.*) bar.
holperig [ˈhɔlpərɪç], *adj.* rough, bumpy.
holpern [ˈhɔlpərn], *v.n.* jolt, stumble; (*fig.*) falter.
Holunder [hoˈlundər], *m.* (—s, *pl.* —) (*Bot.*) elder; *spanischer* —, lilac.
Holz [hɔlts], *n.* (—es, *pl.* ⁝er) wood, timber; (*Am.*) lumber; (*no pl.*) forest; bush.
Holzapfel [ˈhɔltsapfəl], *m.* (—s, *pl.* ⁝) (*Bot.*) crab-apple.
holzartig [ˈhɔltsartɪç], *adj.* woody, ligneous.
holzen [ˈhɔltsən], *v.a.* cut *or* gather wood.
hölzern [ˈhœltsərn], *adj.* wooden; (*fig.*) stiff.
Holzhändler [ˈhɔltshɛndlər], *m.* (—s, *pl.* —) timber-merchant; (*Am.*) lumber merchant.
Holzhauer [ˈhɔltshauər], *m.* (—s, *pl.* —) wood-cutter.
holzig [ˈhɔltsɪç], *adj.* woody, wooded; (*asparagus*) woody, hard; (*beans*) stringy.
Holzkohle [ˈhɔltskoːlə], *f.* (—, *no pl.*) charcoal.
Holzscheit [ˈhɔltsʃaɪt], *n.* (—s, *pl.* —e) log of wood.
Holzschlag [ˈhɔltsʃlaːk], *m.* (—es, *pl.* ⁝e) clearing; felling area.
Holzschnitt [ˈhɔltsʃnɪt], *m.* (—es, *pl.* —e) wood-cut.
Holzschuh [ˈhɔltsʃuː], *m.* (—s, *pl.* —e) clog.

Holzweg [ˈhɔltsveːk], *m.* (—s, *pl.* —e) timbertrack; (*fig.*) *auf dem — sein,* be on the wrong tack.
Holzwolle [ˈhɔltsvɔlə], *f.* (—, *no pl.*) wood shavings.
homogen [homoˈgeːn], *adj.* homogeneous.
homolog [homoˈloːg], *adj.* homologous.
honett [hɔˈnɛt], *adj.* (*obs.*) respectable, genteel.
Honig [ˈhoːnɪç], *m.* (—s, *no pl.*) honey.
Honigkuchen [ˈhoːnɪçkuːxən], *m.* (—s, *pl.* —) ginger-bread.
Honigwabe [ˈhoːnɪçvaːbə], *f.* (—, *pl.* —n) honeycomb.
Honorar [honoˈraːr], *n.* (—s, *pl.* —e) remuneration; (*professional*) fee; honorarium.
Honoratioren [honoraˈtsjoːrən], *m. pl.* people of rank; dignitaries.
honorieren [honoˈriːrən], *v.a.* pay a fee to, remunerate.
Hopfen [ˈhɔpfən], *m.* (—s, *no pl.*) (*Bot.*) hop, hops; *an dem ist — und Malz verloren,* he is beyond help.
Hopfenstange [ˈhɔpfənʃtaŋə], *f.* (—, *pl.* —n) hop-pole; (*fig.*) tall thin person.
hopsen [ˈhɔpsən], *v.n.* (*aux.* sein) (*coll.*) hop, jump.
hörbar [ˈhøːrbaːr], *adj.* audible.
horchen [ˈhɔrçən], *v.n.* listen, eavesdrop.
Horde [ˈhɔrdə], *f.* (—, *pl.* —n) horde.
hören [ˈhøːrən], *v.a.*, *v.n.* hear.
Hörer [ˈhøːrər], *m.* (—s, *pl.*⁝—) listener; (*Univ.*) student; (*telephone*) receiver.
Hörerin [ˈhøːrərɪn], *f.* (—, *pl.* —innen) female listener; (*Univ.*) woman student.
Hörerschaft [ˈhøːrərʃaft], *f.* (—, *no pl.*) audience.
Hörgerät [ˈhøːrgərɛːt], *n.* (—es, *pl.* —e) hearing aid.
hörig [ˈhøːrɪç], *adj.* in bondage, a slave to.
Horizont [horiˈtsɔnt], *m.* (—es, *pl.* —e) horizon.
Horizontale [horitsɔnˈtaːlə], *f.* (—, *pl.* —n) horizontal line.
Horn [hɔrn], *n.* (—s, *pl.* ⁝er) horn; (*Mus.*) French horn.
Hörnchen [ˈhœrnçən], *n.* (—s, *pl.* —) French roll, croissant.
hörnern [ˈhœrnərn], *adj.* horny, made of horn.
Hornhaut [ˈhɔrnhaut], *f.* (—, *pl.* ⁝te) horny skin; (*eye*) cornea.
Hornhautverpflanzung [ˈhɔrnhautfɛrpflantsuŋ], *f.* (—, *no pl.*) corneal graft.
hornig [ˈhɔrnɪç], *adj.* hard, horny.
Hornisse [hɔrˈnɪsə], *f.* (—, *pl.* —n) (*Ent.*) hornet.
horrend [hɔˈrɛnt], *adj.* exorbitant; stupendous.
Hörrohr [ˈhøːrroːr], *n.* (—s, *pl.* —e) ear trumpet.
Hörsaal [ˈhøːrzaːl], *m.* (—s, *pl.* —säle) auditorium, lecture room.

111

Hörspiel

Hörspiel [ˈhøːrʃpiːl], *n.* (—s, *pl.* —e) radio play.

Horst [hɔrst], *m.* (—es, *pl.* —e) eyrie.

Hort [hɔrt], *m.* (—es, *pl.* —e) (*Poet.*) treasure; stronghold.

Hortensie [hɔrˈtɛnzjə], *f.* (—, *pl.* —n) (*Bot.*) hydrangea.

Hose [ˈhoːzə], *f.* (—, *pl.* —n) trousers, pants, breeches; (*women*) slacks.

Hosenband [ˈhoːzənbant], *n.* (—es, *pl.* ⸚er) garter.

Hosenträger [ˈhoːzəntrɛgər], *m. pl.* braces, suspenders.

Hospitant [hɔspiˈtant], *m.* (—en, *pl.* —en) (*Univ.*) temporary student, non-registered student.

hospitieren [hɔspiˈtiːrən], *v.n.* attend lectures as a visitor.

Hostie [ˈhɔstjə], *f.* (—, *pl.* —n) (*Eccl.*) the Host.

hüben [ˈhyːbən], *adv.* on this side; — *und drüben*, on either side.

hübsch [hypʃ], *adj.* pretty, attractive; handsome; good-looking.

Hubschrauber [ˈhuːpʃraubər], *m.* (—s, *pl.* —) (*Aviat.*) helicopter.

huckepack [ˈhukəpak], *adv.* — *tragen*, carry pick-a-back.

Huf [huːf], *m.* (—es, *pl.* —e) hoof.

Hufe [ˈhuːfə], *f.* (—, *pl.* —n) hide (of land).

Hufeisen [ˈhuːfaizən], *n.* (—s, *pl.* —) horseshoe.

Huflattich [ˈhuːflatiç], *m.* (—s, *pl.* —e) (*Bot.*) colt's foot.

Hufschlag [ˈhuːfʃlaːk], *m.* (—s, *pl.* ⸚e) (*of a horse*) hoof-beat.

Hüfte [ˈhyftə], *f.* (—, *pl.* —n) (*Anat.*) hip; (*animals*) haunch.

Hügel [ˈhyːgəl], *m.* (—s, *pl.* —) hill, hillock.

hügelig [ˈhyːgəliç], *adj.* hilly.

Huhn [huːn], *n.* (—s, *pl.* ⸚er) fowl; hen.

Hühnchen [ˈhyːnçən], *n.* (—s, *pl.* —) pullet, chicken.

Hühnerauge [ˈhyːnəraugə], *n.* (—s, *pl.* —n) corn (*on the foot*).

Huld [hult], *f.* (—, *no pl.*) grace, favour.

huldigen [ˈhuldigən], *v.n.* pay homage.

huldvoll [ˈhultfɔl], *adj.* gracious.

Hülle [ˈhylə], *f.* (—, *pl.* —n) cover, covering; veil; *in — und Fülle*, in abundance, in profusion.

hüllen [ˈhylən], *v.a.* cover, veil, wrap.

Hülse [ˈhylzə], *f.* (—, *pl.* —n) hull, husk, shell; cartridge-case.

Hülsenfrucht [ˈhylzənfruxt], *f.* (—, *pl.* ⸚e) (*Bot.*) leguminous plant.

human [huˈmaːn], *adj.* humane.

humanistisch [humaˈnistiʃ], *adj.* classical; humanistic.

Hummel [ˈhuməl], *f.* (—, *pl.* —n) (*Ent.*) bumble-bee.

Hummer [ˈhumər], *m.* (—s, *pl.* —) (*Zool.*) lobster.

Humor [huˈmoːr], *m.* (—s, *no pl.*) humour.

humoristisch [humoˈristiʃ], *adj.* humorous, witty.

humpeln [ˈhumpəln], *v.n.* hobble, limp.

Humpen [ˈhumpən], *m.* (—s, *pl.* —) deep drinking-cup, bowl, tankard.

Humus [ˈhuːmus], *m.* (—, *no pl.*) garden-mould, humus.

Hund [hunt], *m.* (—es, *pl.* —e) dog; (*hunting*) hound; (*fig.*) rascal, scoundrel.

Hundehaus [ˈhundəhaus], *n.* (—es, *pl.* ⸚er) dog-kennel.

hundert [ˈhundərt], *num. adj.* a hundred, one hundred.

Hündin [ˈhyndin], *f.* (—, *pl.* —innen) bitch.

Hundstage [ˈhuntstaːgə], *m. pl.* dog days (July to August).

Hundszahn [ˈhuntstsaːn], *m.* (—es, *pl.* ⸚e) (*Bot.*) dandelion.

Hüne [ˈhyːnə], *m.* (—n, *pl.* —n) giant, colossus; (*fig.*) tall man.

Hünengrab [ˈhyːnəngraːp], *n.* (—es, *pl.* ⸚er) tumulus, burial mound, barrow, cairn.

Hunger [ˈhuŋər], *m.* (—s, *no pl.*) hunger; starvation.

hungern [ˈhuŋərn], *v.n.* hunger, be hungry.

Hungertuch [ˈhuŋərtuːx], *n.* (—es, *no pl.*) *am — nagen*, go without food; live in poverty.

hungrig [ˈhuŋriç], *adj.* hungry; (*fig.*) desirous (of).

Hupe [ˈhuːpə], *f.* (—, *pl.* —n) motor-horn, hooter (of a car).

hüpfen [ˈhypfən], *v.n.* (*aux.* sein) hop, skip.

Hürde [ˈhyrdə], *f.* (—, *pl.* —n) hurdle.

Hure [ˈhuːrə], *f.* (—, *pl.* —n) whore, prostitute, harlot; (*coll.*) tart.

hurtig [ˈhurtiç], *adj.* nimble, agile; quick, speedy, swift.

Husar [huˈzaːr], *m.* (—en, *pl.* —en) hussar.

husch! [huʃ], *excl.* quick!

huschen [ˈhuʃən], *v.n.* (*aux.* sein) scurry, slip away.

hüsteln [ˈhyːstəln], *v.n.* cough slightly; clear o.'s throat.

husten [ˈhuːstən], *v.n.* cough.

Hut (1) [huːt], *m.* (—es, *pl.* ⸚e) hat; *steifer —*, bowler.

Hut (2) [huːt], *f.* (—, *no pl.*) guard, keeping, care.

hüten [ˈhyːtən], *v.a.* guard, tend, care for; *Kinder —*, baby-sit; *das Bett —*, be confined to o.'s bed, be ill in bed. — *v.r. sich — vor*, be on o.'s guard against, beware of.

Hüter [ˈhyːtər], *m.* (—s, *pl.* —) guardian, keeper; (*cattle*) herdsman.

Hutkrempe [ˈhuːtkrempə], *f.* (—, *pl.* —n) hat-brim.

Hütte [ˈhytə], *f.* (—, *pl.* —n) hut, cottage; (*Tech.*) furnace, forge, foundry.

Hüttenarbeiter [ˈhytənarbaitər], *m.* (—s, *pl.* —) smelter, foundry worker.

Hyäne [hyˈɛːnə], *f.* (—, *pl.* —n) (*Zool.*) hyena.

Individuum

Hyazinthe [hyat'sıntə], f. (—, pl. —n) (Bot.) hyacinth.

Hyperbel [hy'pɛrbəl], f. (—, pl. —n) hyperbola.

hypnotisch [hyp'no:tıʃ], adj. hypnotic.

hypnotisieren [hypnoti'zi:rən], v.a. hypnotise.

Hypochonder [hypo'xɔndər], m. (—s, pl. —) hypochondriac.

Hypothek [hypo'te:k], f. (—, pl. —en) mortgage.

Hysterie [hystε'ri:], f. (—, no pl.) hysterics, hysteria.

hysterisch [hys'te:rıʃ], adj. hysterical.

I

I [i:], n. (—, no pl.) the letter I. — excl. i wo! (dial.) certainly not, of course not.

ich [ıç], pers. pron. I, myself.

ideal [ide'a:l], adj. ideal.

idealisieren [ideali'zi:rən], v.a. idealise.

Idealismus [idea'lısmus], m. (—, no pl.) idealism.

Idee [i'de:], f. (—, pl. —n) idea, notion, conception.

identifizieren [ıdɛntifi'tsi:rən], v.a. identify.

identisch [i'dɛntıʃ], adj. identical.

Identität [ıdɛnti'tε:t], f. (—, no pl.) identity.

idiomatisch [idio'ma:tıʃ], adj. idiomatic.

Idyll [i'dyl], n. (—s, pl. —e) idyll.

Idylle [i'dylə], f. (—, pl. —n) idyll.

idyllisch [i'dylıʃ], adj. idyllic.

Igel [ˈiːɡəl], m. (—s, pl. —) (Zool.) hedgehog.

ignorieren [ıgno'ri:rən], v.a. ignore, take no notice of.

ihm [i:m], pers. pron. Dat. to him, it.

ihn [i:n], pers. pron. Acc., him, it.

Ihnen [ˈiːnən], pers. pron. Dat. you, to you.

ihnen [ˈiːnən], pers. pron. pl. Dat. them, to them.

Ihr [i:r], poss. adj. your; of your. — poss. pron. yours.

ihr [i:r], pers. pron. to her; (pl.) (intim.) you. — poss. adj. her, their. — poss. pron. hers, theirs.

Ihrer [ˈiːrər], pers. pron. of you. — poss. adj. of your.

ihrer [ˈiːrər], pers. pron. of her, of it; (pl.) of them. — poss. adj of her; to her; (pl.) of them.

ihresgleichen [ˈiːrəsɡlaıçən], adv. of her, its or their kind.

ihrethalben [ˈiːrəthalbən], adv. for her sake, for their sake, on her account, on their account.

ihretwegen [ˈiːrətveːɡən] see ihrethalben.

ihretwillen [ˈiːrətvılən] see ihrethalben.

Ihrige [i:rıgə], poss. pron. yours.

ihrige [ˈiːrıgə], poss. pron. hers, its, theirs.

illegitim [ılegi'ti:m], adj. illegitimate.

illuminieren [ılumi'ni:rən], v.a. illuminate, floodlight.

illustrieren [ılu'stri:rən], v.a. illustrate.

Iltis [ˈıltıs], m. (—ses, pl. —se) (Zool.) polecat, fitchet.

im [ım], contraction of in dem, in the.

Imbiß [ˈımbıs], m. (—sses, pl. —sse) snack, refreshment, light meal.

Imker [ˈımkər], m. (—s, pl. —) beekeeper.

immatrikulieren [ımmatriku'li:rən], v.a. (Univ.) matriculate, enrol.

Imme [ˈımə], f. (—, pl. —n) (dial., Poet.) bee.

immer [ˈımər], adv. always, ever; — mehr, more and more; — noch, still; — wieder, time and again: — größer, larger and larger; auf —, for ever.

immerdar [ˈımərda:r], adv. for ever.

immerhin [ˈımərhın], adv. nevertheless, still, after all.

immerzu [ˈımərtsu:], adv. always, constantly.

Immobilien [ımo'bi:ljən], pl. real estate.

Immortelle [ımɔr'tɛlə], f. (—, pl. —n) (Bot.) everlasting flower.

immun [ı'mu:n], adj. immune.

impfen [ˈımpfən], v.a. vaccinate, inoculate; (Hort.) graft.

imponieren [ımpo'ni:rən], v.n. impress.

Import [ım'pɔrt], m. (—s, pl. —e) import, importation.

imposant [ımpo'zant], adj. imposing, impressive.

imstande [ım'ʃtandə], adv. capable, able; — sein, be able.

in [ın], prep. (Dat., Acc.) in, into; at; within.

Inangriffnahme [ın'angrıfna:mə], f. (—, no pl.) start, beginning, inception.

Inbegriff [ˈınbəgrıf], m. (—es, no pl.) essence, epitome.

inbegriffen [ˈınbəgrıfən], adv. inclusive.

Inbrunst [ˈınbrunst], f. (—, no pl.) ardour, fervour.

indem [ın'de:m], adv. meanwhile. — conj. while, whilst; as, because, in that.

indessen [ın'dɛsən], adv. meanwhile, in the meantime. — conj. however, nevertheless, yet.

Indien [ˈındjən], n. India.

Individualität [ındividuali'tε:t], f. (—, pl. —en) individuality, personality.

individuell [ındividu'εl], adj. individual.

Individuum [ındi'vi:duum], n. (—s, pl. —duen) individual.

113

Indizienbeweis [ɪnˈdiːtsjənbəvaɪs], *m.* (—es, *pl.* —e) (*Law*) circumstantial evidence *or* proof.

indossieren [ɪndɔˈsiːrən], *v.a.* endorse.

Industrie [ɪndusˈtriː], *f.* (—, *pl.* —n) industry; manufacture.

industriell [ɪndustriˈɛl], *adj.* industrial.

Industrielle [ɪndustriˈɛlə], *m.* (—n, *pl.* —n) manufacturer, industrialist.

ineinander [ɪnaɪˈnandər], *adv.* into each other, into one another.

infam [ɪnˈfaːm], *adj.* infamous.

Infantin [ɪnˈfantɪn], *f.* (—, *pl.* —en) Infanta.

infizieren [ɪnfiˈtsiːrən], *v.a.* infect.

infolge [ɪnˈfɔlgə], *prep.* (*Genit.*) in consequence of, owing to.

informieren [ɪnfɔrˈmiːrən], *v.a.* inform, advise.

Ingenieur [ɪnʒenˈjøːr], *m.* (—s, *pl.* —e) engineer.

Ingrimm [ˈɪngrɪm], *m.* (—s, *no pl.*) anger, rage, wrath.

Ingwer [ˈɪŋvər], *m.* (—s, *no pl.*) ginger.

Inhaber [ˈɪnhaːbər], *m.* (—s, *pl.* —) possessor, owner; proprietor; occupant.

inhaftieren [ɪnhafˈtiːrən], *v.a.* imprison; arrest.

inhalieren [ɪnhaˈliːrən], *v.a.* inhale.

Inhalt [ˈɪnhalt], *m.* (—(e)s, *no pl.*) content; contents; tenor.

Inhaltsverzeichnis [ˈɪnhaltsfɛrtsaɪçnɪs], *n.* (—ses, *pl.* —se) (table of) contents; index.

inhibieren [ɪnhiˈbiːrən], *v.a.* inhibit, prevent.

Inkasso [ɪnˈkaso], *n.* (—s, *pl.* —s) encashment.

inklinieren [ɪnkliˈniːrən], *v.n.* be inclined to.

inklusive [ɪnkluˈziːvə], *adv.* inclusive of, including.

inkonsequent [ˈɪnkɔnzəkvɛnt], *adj.* inconsistent.

Inkrafttreten [ɪnˈkrafttreːtən], *m.* (—s, *no pl.*) enactment; coming into force.

Inland [ˈɪnlant], *n.* (—s, *no pl.*) inland, interior.

Inländer [ˈɪnlɛndər], *m.* (—s, *pl.* —) native.

Inlett [ˈɪnlɛt], *n.* (—s, *pl.* —e) bed-tick, ticking.

inliegend [ˈɪnliːgənt], *adj.* enclosed.

inmitten [ɪnˈmɪtən], *prep.* (*Genit.*) in the midst of.

innehaben [ˈɪnəhaːbən], *v.a.* irr. possess; occupy; hold.

innehalten [ˈɪnəhaltən], *v.a.* irr. (*conditions*) keep to, observe; (*time*) come promptly at. — *v.n.* stop, pause.

innen [ˈɪnən], *adv.* within; nach —, inwards; von —, from within.

Innenminister [ˈɪnənmɪnɪstər], *m.* (—s, *pl.* —) Minister for Internal Affairs; Home Secretary; (*Am.*) Secretary of the Interior.

inner [ˈɪnər], *adj.* inner, interior, internal; intrinsic.

innerhalb [ˈɪnərhalp], *prep.* (*Genit.*) within.

innerlich [ˈɪnərlɪç], *adj.* internal; inside o.s.; inward.

innerste [ˈɪnərstə], *adj.* inmost, innermost.

innewerden [ˈɪnəveːrdən], *v.a.* irr. (*aux.* sein) perceive, become aware of.

innewohnen [ˈɪnəvoːnən], *v.n.* be inherent in.

innig [ˈɪnɪç], *adj.* heartfelt, cordial.

Innung [ˈɪnuŋ], *f.* (—, *pl.* —en) guild, corporation.

Insasse [ˈɪnzasə], *m.* (—n, *pl.* —n) inmate; occupant.

insbesondere [ɪnsbəˈzɔndərə], *adv.* especially, particularly, in particular.

Inschrift [ˈɪnʃrɪft], *f.* (—, *pl.* —en) inscription.

Insel [ˈɪnzəl], *f.* (—, *pl.* —n) island.

Inserat [ɪnzəˈraːt], *n.* (—es, *pl.* —e) classified advertisement; (*coll.*) (small) ad.

inserieren [ɪnzəˈriːrən], *v.a.* advertise; insert.

insgeheim [ɪnsɡəˈhaɪm], *adv.* privately, secretly.

insgesamt [ɪnsɡəˈzamt], *adv.* altogether, in a body.

insofern [ɪnzoˈfɛrn], *conj.* — als, in so far as, inasmuch as, so far as.

inspirieren [ɪnspiˈriːrən], *v.a.* inspire.

installieren [ɪnstaˈliːrən], *v.a.* install, fit.

instandhalten [ɪnˈʃtanthaltən], *v.a.* irr. maintain, preserve, keep in repair.

inständig [ˈɪnʃtɛndɪç], *adj.* urgent; fervent.

instandsetzen [ɪnˈʃtantzɛtsən], *v.a.* restore, repair; einen — etwas zu tun, enable s.o. to do s.th.

Instanz [ɪnˈstants], *f.* (—, *pl.* —en) (*Law*) instance; letzte —, highest court of appeal, last resort.

Institut [ɪnstiˈtuːt], *n.* (—es, *pl.* —e) institute, institution, establishment; (*Univ.*) department.

instruieren [ɪnstruˈiːrən], *v.a.* instruct.

Insulaner [ɪnzuˈlaːnər], *m.* (—s, *pl.* —) islander.

inszenieren [ɪnstseˈniːrən], *v.a.* put on the stage, produce.

Inszenierung [ɪnstseˈniːruŋ], *f.* (—, *pl.* —en) (*Theat.*) production, staging.

intellektuell [ɪntɛlɛktuˈɛl], *adj.* intellectual.

Intendant [ɪntɛnˈdant], *m.* (—en, *pl.* —en) (*Theat.*) director.

interessant [ɪntərɛˈsant], *adj.* interesting.

Interesse [ɪntəˈrɛsə], *n.* (—s, *pl.* —n) interest.

Interessent [ɪntərɛˈsɛnt], *m.* (—en, *pl.* —en) interested party.

interessieren [ɪntərɛˈsiːrən], *v.a.* interest. — *v.r.* sich —, be interested (in).

intern [ɪnˈtɛrn], *adj.* internal.

Internat [ɪntɛrˈnaːt], *n.* (—es, *pl.* —e) boarding-school.

Interne [In'tɛrnə], *m.* (—n, *pl.* —n) resident (pupil *or* doctor), boarder.
Internist [Intɛr'nɪst], *m.* (—en, *pl.* —en) specialist in internal diseases.
interpunktieren [Intərpunk'ti:rən], *v.a.* punctuate.
Interpunktion [Intərpunkts'jo:n], *f.* (—, *pl.* —en) punctuation.
intim [In'ti:m], *adj.* intimate; *mit einem — sein,* b : on close terms with s.o.
intonieren [Into'ni:rən], *v.n.* intone.
Intrigant [Intri'gant], *m.* (—en, *pl.* —en) intriguer, schemer.
intrigieren [Intri'gi:rən], *v.n.* intrigue, scheme.
Inventar [Invɛn'ta:r], *n.* (—s, *pl.* —e) inventory; *ein — aufnehmen,* draw up an inventory.
Inventur [Invɛn'tu:r], *f.* (—, *pl.* —en) stock-taking.
inwärts ['Invɛrts], *adv.* inwards.
inwendig ['Invɛndɪç], *adj.* inward, internal, inner.
inwiefern [Invi:'fɛrn], *adv.* to what extent.
inwieweit [Invi:'vaɪt], *adv.* how far.
Inzucht ['Intsuxt], *f.* (—, *no pl.*) inbreeding.
inzwischen [In'tsvIʃən], *adv.* meanwhile, in the meantime.
Irak [i'ra:k], *n.* Iraq.
Iran [i'ra:n], *n.* Iran.
irden ['Irdən], *adj.* earthen.
irdisch ['Irdɪʃ], *adj.* earthly, worldly; terrestrial, temporal.
irgend ['Irgənt], *adv.* any, some; *wenn es — geht,* if it can possibly be done.
irgendein [Irgənt'aɪn], *pron.* any, some.
Irland ['Irlant], *n.* Ireland.
ironisch [I'ro:nIʃ], *adj.* ironic, ironical.
Irre (1) ['Irə], *f.* (—, *no pl.*) *in die — gehen,* go astray.
Irre (2) ['Irə], *m.* (—n, *pl.* —n) madman, lunatic.
irre ['Irə], *adj.* astray; wrong, confused; crazy, demented.
irren ['Irən], *v.n.* err, go astray, be wrong. — *v.r. sich —,* be mistaken.
Irrenarzt ['Irənartst], *m.* (—es, *pl.* ⁖e) psychiatrist.
Irrenhaus ['Irənhaus], *n.* (—es, *pl.* ⁖er) lunatic asylum, mental hospital.
Irrfahrt ['Irfa:rt], *f.* (—, *pl.* —en) wandering.
Irrglaube ['Irglaubə], *m.* (—ns, *no pl.*) heresy.
irrig ['IrIç], *adj.* erroneous.
irritieren [Iri'ti:rən], *v.a.* irritate.
Irrlicht ['IrlIçt], *n.* (—s, *pl.* —er) will-o'-the-wisp.
Irrsinn ['IrzIn], *m.* (—s, *no pl.*) madness, insanity, lunacy.
irrsinnig ['IrzInIç], *adj.* insane, deranged.
Irrtum ['Irtu:m], *m.* (—s, *pl.* ⁖er) error, mistake, fault, oversight.
Irrweg ['Irve:k], *m.* (—s, *pl.* —e) wrong track.
Irrwisch ['IrvIʃ], *m.* (—es, *pl.* —e) will-o'-the-wisp.

Ischias ['IsçIas], *f., m.* (*Med.*) sciatica.
Isegrim ['i:zəgrIm], *m.* (—s, *pl.* —e) (*fable*) the wolf; a bear (with a sore head) (*also fig.*).
Island ['i:slant], *n.* Iceland.
isolieren [izo'li:rən], *v.a.* (*Electr.*) insulate; (*fig.*) isolate.
Isolierung [izo'li:ruŋ], *f.* (—, *pl.* —en) (*Electr.*) insulation; (*fig.*) isolation.
Italien [i'ta:ljən], *n.* Italy.

J

J [jɔt], *n.* (—, *no pl.*) the letter J.
ja [ja:], *adv., part.* yes; indeed, certainly; even; — *doch,* to be sure; — *freilich,* certainly.
Jacht [jaxt], *f.* (—, *pl.* —en) yacht.
Jacke ['jakə], *f.* (—, *pl.* —n) jacket, tunic.
Jackett [ja'kɛt], *n.* (—s, *pl.* —s) jacket, short coat.
Jagd [ja:kt], *f.* (—, *pl.* —en) hunt, hunting; shooting; chase.
Jagdhund ['ja:kthunt], *m.* (—es, *pl.* —e) retriever, setter; hound.
Jagdrevier ['ja:ktrevi:r], *n.* (—s, *pl.* —e) hunting-ground.
jagen ['ja:gən], *v.a.* hunt; chase; (*fig.*) tear along.
Jäger ['jɛ:gər], *m.* (—s, *pl.* —) hunter, huntsman; game-keeper.
Jägerei [jɛ:gə'raɪ], *f.* (—, *no pl.*) huntsmanship.
jäh [jɛ:], *adj.* abrupt; steep, precipitous; (*fig.*) hasty, rash, sudden.
jählings ['jɛ:lIŋs], *adv.* abruptly, suddenly, hastily.
Jahr [ja:r], *n.* (—es, *pl.* —e) year.
jähren ['jɛ:rən], *v.r. sich —,* (*anniversary*) come round.
Jahresfeier ['ja:rəsfaɪər], *f.* (—, *pl.* —n) anniversary.
Jahresrente ['ja:rəsrɛntə], *f.* (—, *pl.* —n) annuity.
Jahreszeit ['ja:rəstsaɪt], *f.* (—, *pl.* —en) season.
Jahrgang ['ja:rgaŋ], *m.* (—s, *pl.* ⁖e) age group; class; year of publication; vintage.
Jahrhundert [ja:r'hundərt], *n.* (—s, *pl.* —e) century.
jährig ['jɛ:rIç], *adj.* year-old.
jährlich ['jɛ:rlIç], *adj.* yearly, annual. — *adv.* every year.
Jahrmarkt ['ja:rmarkt], *m.* (—s, *pl.* ⁖e) annual fair.
Jahrtausend [ja:r'tauzənt], *n.* (—s, *pl.* —e) millennium.
Jahrzehnt [ja:r'tse:nt], *n.* (—s, *pl.* —e) decade.
Jähzorn ['jɛ:tsɔrn], *m.* (—s, *no pl.*) irascibility.

Jalousie

Jalousie [ʒalu'zi:], *f.* (—, *pl.* —n) Venetian blind.

Jamaika [ja'maika], *n.* Jamaica.

Jambus ['jambus], *m.* (—, *pl.* —ben) (*Poet.*) iambic foot.

Jammer ['jamər], *m.* (—s, *no pl.*) lamentation; misery; (*fig.*) pity.

jämmerlich ['jɛmərliç], *adj.* lamentable, miserable, wretched, piteous.

jammerschade ['jamərʃa:də], *adv.* a thousand pities.

Jänner ['jɛnər] (*Austr.*) *see* **Januar**.

Januar ['janua:r], *m.* (—s, *pl.* —e) January.

Japan ['ja:pan], *n.* Japan.

Jaspis ['jaspɪs], *m.* (—ses, *pl.* —se) jasper.

jäten ['jɛ:tən], *v.a.* weed.

Jauche ['jauxə], *f.* (—, *pl.* —n) liquid manure.

jauchzen ['jauxtsən], *v.n.* exult, shout with joy.

Jauchzer ['jauxtsər], *m.* (—s, *pl.* —) shout of joy.

jawohl [ja'vo:l], *int.* yes, indeed! certainly, of course.

je [je:], *adv.* ever; at any time; at a time; each; *von — her*, always; *— nachdem*, it depends; *— zwei*, in twos; *— eher — besser*, the sooner the better.

jedenfalls ['je:dənfals], *adv.* at all events, in any case, at any rate, anyway.

jeder, -e, -es ['je:dər], *adj.* every, each; *— beliebige*, any. *— pron.* each, each one; everybody.

jederlei ['je:dərlai], *adj.* of every kind.

jedoch [je'dɔx], *adv.*, however, nevertheless, yet, notwithstanding.

jeglicher, -e, -es ['je:klɪçər], *adj.* every, each. *— pron.* every man, each.

jemals ['je:mals], *adv.* ever, at any time.

jemand ['je:mant], *pron.* somebody, someone; anybody, anyone.

Jemen ['je:mən], *n.* Yemen.

jener, e, -es ['je:nər], *dem. adj.* that, (*Poet.*) yonder. *— dem. pron.* that one, the former.

Jenseits ['jɛnzaɪts], *n.* (—, *no pl.*) the next world, the hereafter, the life to come.

jenseits ['jɛnzaɪts], *prep.* (*Genit.*) on the other side, beyond.

jetzig ['jɛtsɪç], *adj.* present, now existing, current, extant.

jetzt [jɛtst], *adv.* now, at this time, at present.

jeweilig ['je:vaɪlɪç], *adj.* momentary; actual, for the time being.

Joch [jɔx], *n.* (—es, *pl.* —e) yoke.

Jochbein ['jɔxbaɪn], *n.* (—s, *pl.* —e) cheek-bone.

Jockei ['jɔkaɪ], *m.* (—s, *pl.* —s) jockey.

Jod [jo:t], *n.* (—s, *no pl.*) iodine.

jodeln ['jo:dəln], *v.n.* yodel.

Jodler ['jo:dlər], *m.* (—s, *pl.* —) (*person*) yodeler; (*sound*) yodelling.

Johannisbeere [jo'hanɪsbe:rə], *f.* (—, *pl.* —n) (*Bot.*) red currant.

Johannisfest [jo'hanɪsfɛst], *n.* (—s, *pl.* —e) Midsummer Day, St. John the Baptist's Day (June 24th).

Johanniskäfer [jo'hanɪske:fər], *m.* (—s, *pl.* —) (*Ent.*) glow-worm.

Johannisnacht [jo'hanɪsnaxt], *f.* (—, *pl.* ˙e) Midsummer Eve.

johlen ['jo:lən], *v.n.* bawl.

Joppe ['jɔpə], *f.* (—, *pl.* —n) shooting jacket.

Jota ['jo:ta], *n.* (—s, *pl.* —s) iota, jot.

Journalismus [ʒurna'lɪsmus], *m. see* **Journalistik**.

Journalistik [ʒurna'lɪstɪk], *f.* (—, *no pl.*) journalism.

jubeln ['ju:bəln], *v.n.* rejoice, exult.

Jubilar [ju:bi'la:r], *m.* (—s, *pl.* —e) person celebrating a jubilee.

Jubiläum [ju:bi'lɛ:um], *n.* (—s, *pl.* —läen) jubilee.

jubilieren [ju:bi'li:rən], *v.n.* exult, shout with glee.

juchhe [jux'he:], *excl.* hurrah!

Juchten ['juxtən], *m.* (—, *no pl.*) Russian leather.

jucken ['jukən], *v.a.* scratch. *— v.n.* itch.

Jude ['ju:də], *m.* (—n, *pl.* —n) Jew; Israelite.

Judentum ['ju:dəntu:m], *n.* (—s, *no pl.*) Judaism.

Judenviertel ['ju:dənfi:rtəl], *n.* (—s, *pl.* —) Jewish quarter, ghetto.

Jüdin ['jy:dɪn], *f.* (—, *pl.* —innen) Jewess.

jüdisch ['jy:dɪʃ], *adj.* Jewish.

Jugend ['ju:gənt], *f.* (—, *no pl.*) youth.

jugendlich ['ju:gəntlɪç], *adj.* youthful, juvenile.

Jugoslawien [ju:go'sla:vjən], *n.* Jugoslavia.

Julfest ['ju:lfɛst], *n.* (—es, *pl.* —e) Yule.

Juli ['ju:li], *m.* (—s, *pl.* —s) July.

jung [juŋ], *adj.* young.

Junge (1) ['juŋə], *m.* (—n, *pl.* —n) boy, lad.

Junge (2) ['juŋə], *n.* (—n, *pl.* —n) young animal.

jungenhaft ['juŋənhaft], *adj.* boyish.

Jünger ['jyŋər], *m.* (—s, *pl.* —) disciple, devotee, follower.

Jungfer ['juŋfər], *f.* (—, *pl.* —n) (*obs.*) virgin, maid, maiden; lady's maid.

jüngferlich ['jyŋfərlɪç], *adj.* maidenly, coy, prim.

Jungfrau ['juŋfrau], *f.* (—, *pl.* —en) virgin.

Junggeselle ['juŋgəzɛlə], *m.* (—n, *pl.* —n) bachelor; *eingefleischter —*, confirmed bachelor.

Jüngling ['jyŋlɪŋ], *m.* (—s, *pl.* —e) young man.

jüngst [jyŋst], *adv.* lately, recently.

Juni ['ju:ni], *m.* (—s, *pl.* —s) June.

Junker ['juŋkər], *m.* (—s, *pl.* —) country squire; titled landowner.

Jura ['ju:ra], *n. pl.* jurisprudence, law; (*Univ.*) *— studieren*, read law.

Jurisprudenz [ju:rɪspru'dɛnts], *f.* (—, *no pl.*) jurisprudence.

Jurist [ju:'rɪst], *m.* (—en, *pl.* —en) lawyer, jurist.

juristisch [ju:'rɪstɪʃ], *adj.* juridical; legal.

just [just], *adv.* just now.

Justiz [jus'ti:ts], *f.* (—, *no pl.*) administration of the law or of justice.

Justizrat [jus'ti:tsra:t], *m.* (—s, *pl.* —e) (*Law*) Counsellor; King's (Queen's) Counsel.

Jute ['ju:tə], *f.* (—, *no pl.*) jute.

Juwel [ju've:l], *n.* (—s, *pl.* —en) jewel; (*pl.*) jewellery; (*Am.*) jewelry.

Juwelier [juvə'li:r], *m.* (—s, *pl.* —e) jeweller, goldsmith.

K

K [ka:], *n.* (—, *no pl.*) the letter K.

Kabel ['ka:bəl], *n.* (—s, *pl.* —) cable.

Kabeljau [kabəl'jau], *m.* (—s, *pl.* —e) (*Zool.*) cod, codfish.

kabeln ['ka:bəln], *v.n.* cable, send a cablegram.

Kabine [ka'bi:nə], *f.* (—, *pl.* —n) cabin, cubicle.

Kabinett [kabi'nɛt], *n.* (—s, *pl.* —e) closet; cabinet.

Kabinettsrat [kabi'nɛtsra:t], *m.* (—s, *pl.* —e) cabinet or ministerial committee; political adviser.

Kabüse [ka'by:zə], *f.* (—, *pl.* —n) ship's galley.

Kachel ['kaxəl], *f.* (—, *pl.* —n) glazed tile.

Kadaver [ka'da:vər], *m.* (—s, *pl.* —) carrion, carcass; corpse.

Kadenz [ka'dɛnts], *f.* (—, *pl.* —en) (*Mus.*) cadenza.

Kadett [ka'dɛt], *m.* (—en, *pl.* —en) cadet.

Käfer ['kɛ:fər], *m.* (—s, *pl.* —) (*Ent.*) beetle, (*Am.*) bug.

Kaffee ['kafe], *m.* (—s, *no pl.*) coffee.

Käfig ['kɛ:fɪç], *m.* (—s, *pl.* —e) cage.

kahl [ka:l], *adj.* bald; (*trees*) leafless; (*landscape*) barren; — *geschoren*, close-cropped.

Kahn ['ka:n], *m.* (—s, *pl.* —e) boat; punt.

Kai [kai], *m.* (—s, *pl.* —s) quay, wharf, landing-place.

Kaimeister ['kaimaistər], *m.* (—s, *pl.* —) wharfinger.

Kaiser ['kaizər], *m.* (—s, *pl.* —) emperor; *um des —s Bart streiten*, quarrel about nothing.

kaiserlich ['kaizərlɪç], *adj.* imperial.

Kaiserschnitt ['kaizərʃnɪt], *m.* (—es, *pl.* —e) (*Med.*) Caesarean operation.

Kajüte [ka'jy:tə], *f.* (—, *pl.* —n) cabin.

Kakadu ['kakadu:], *m.* (—s, *pl.* —s) (*Orn.*) cockatoo.

Kakao [ka'ka:o], *m.* (—s, *no pl.*) cocoa.

Kalauer ['ka:lauər], *m.* (—s, *no pl.*) pun; stale joke.

Kalb [kalp], *n.* (—es, *pl.* —er) calf; (*roe*) fawn; (*fig.*) colt, calf.

Kalbfleisch ['kalpflaiʃ], *n.* (—es, *no pl.*) veal.

Kälberei [kɛlbə'rai], *f.* (—, *pl.* —en) friskiness.

kälbern ['kɛlbərn], *v.n.* frisk, frolic.

Kalbsbraten ['kalpsbra:tən], *m.* (—s, *pl.* —) roast veal.

Kalbshaxe ['kalpshaksə], *f.* (—, *pl.* —n) knuckle of veal.

Kalbskeule ['kalpskɔylə], *f.* (—, *pl.* —n) leg of veal.

Kalbsmilch ['kalpsmɪlç], *f.* (—, *no pl.*) sweetbread.

Kaldaunen [kal'daunən], *f. pl.* (*dial.*) tripe.

Kalesche [ka'lɛʃə], *f.* (—, *pl.* —n) chaise, light carriage.

Kali ['ka:li], *n.* (—s, *no pl.*) potash.

Kaliber [ka'li:bər], *n.* (—s, *pl.* —) calibre; (*fig.*) sort, quality.

kalibrieren [kali'bri:rən], *v.a.* (*Tech.*) calibrate, graduate, gauge.

Kalifornien [kali'fɔrnjən], *n.* California.

Kalium ['ka:ljum], *n.* (—s, *no pl.*) (*Chem.*) potassium.

Kalk [kalk], *m.* (—s, *pl.* —e) lime; *gebrannter* —, quicklime; *mit* — *bewerfen*, rough-cast.

kalkartig ['kalka:rtɪç], *adj.* calcareous.

Kalkbewurf ['kalkbəvurf], *m.* (—es, *pl.* —e) coat of plaster.

kalken ['kalkən], *v.a.* whitewash; (*Agr.*) lime.

kalkig ['kalkɪç], *adj.* limy, calcareous.

kalkulieren [kalku'li:rən], *v.n.* calculate, reckon.

kalt [kalt], *adj.* cold, frigid; *mir ist* —, I am cold.

kaltblütig ['kaltbly:tɪç], *adj.* cold-blooded, cool.

Kälte ['kɛltə], *f.* (—, *no pl.*) cold, coldness.

Kaltschale ['kaltʃa:lə], *f.* (—, *pl.* —n) cold beer (or wine) soup.

Kambodscha [kam'bɔtʃa], *f.* Cambodia.

Kamee [ka'me:], *f.* (—, *pl.* —n) cameo.

Kamel [ka'me:l], *n.* (—s, *pl.* —e) (*Zool.*) camel.

Kamelziege [ka'me:ltsi:gə], *f.* (—, *pl.* —n) (*Zool.*) Angora-goat, llama.

Kamerad [kamə'ra:t], *m.* (—en, *pl.* —en) comrade, companion, mate.

Kameradschaft [kamə'ra:tʃaft], *f.* (—, *pl.* —en) comradeship, fellowship.

Kamerun [kamə'ru:n], *n.* the Cameroons.

Kamille [ka'mɪlə], *f.* (—, *pl.* —n) camomile.

Kamin [ka'mi:n], *m.* (—s, *pl.* —e) chimney; funnel; fireplace, fireside.

Kaminaufsatz [ka'mi:naufzats], *m.* (—es, *pl.* —e) mantel-piece, over-mantel.

Kaminfeger [ka'mi:nfe:gər], *m.* (—s, *pl.* —) chimney-sweep.

117

Kaminsims

Kaminsims [ka'mi:nzīms], *m.* or *n.* (—es, *pl.* —e) mantel-piece.

Kamm [kam], *m.* (—es, *pl.* ˙e) comb; (*cock*) crest; (*mountains*) ridge.

kämmen ['kɛmən], *v.a.* comb; (*wool*) card.

Kammer ['kamər], *f.* (—, *pl.* —n) chamber, small room; (*Am.*) closet; (*authority*) board; (*Parl. etc.*) chamber.

Kammerdiener ['kamərdi:nər], *m.* (—s, *pl.* —) valet.

Kämmerer ['kɛmərər], *m.* (—s, *pl.* —) Chamberlain, Treasurer.

Kammergericht ['kamərgərɪçt], *n.* (—s, *pl.* —e) Supreme Court of Justice.

Kammergut ['kamərgu:t], *n.* (—s, *pl.* ˙er) domain, demesne; crown land.

Kammerherr ['kamərhɛr], *m.* (—n, *pl.* —en) chamberlain.

Kammersänger ['kamərzɛŋər], *m.* (—s, *pl.* —) court singer; title given to prominent singers.

Kammgarn ['kamgarn], *n.* (—s, no *pl.*) worsted.

Kammwolle ['kamvɔlə], *f.* (—, no *pl.*) carded wool.

Kampagne [kam'panjə], *f.* (—, *pl.* —n) (*Mil.*) campaign.

Kämpe ['kɛmpə], *m.* (—n, *pl.* —n) (*Poet.*) champion, warrior; *alter* —, old campaigner.

Kampf [kampf], *m.* (—es, *pl.* ˙e) combat, fight, struggle; (*fig.*) conflict.

kämpfen ['kɛmpfən], *v.n.* fight, combat, struggle.

Kampfer ['kampfər], *m.* (—s, no *pl.*) camphor.

Kämpfer ['kɛmpfər], *m.* (—s, *pl.* —) fighter, combatant.

kampfunfähig ['kampfunfɛ:ɪç], *adj.* (*Mil.*) disabled; — *machen*, disable, put out of action.

kampieren [kam'pi:rən], *v.n.* be encamped, camp.

Kanada ['kanada], *n.* Canada.

Kanal [ka'na:l], *m.* (—s, *pl.* ˙e) (*natural*) channel; (*artificial*) canal; sewer; *der Ärmelkanal*, the English Channel.

kanalisieren [kanali'zi:rən], *v.a.* canalise; (*streets*) drain by means of sewers.

Kanapee ['kanape:], *n.* (—s, *pl.* —s) sofa, divan.

Kanarienvogel [ka'na:rjənfo:gəl], *m.* (—s, *pl.* ˙) (*Orn.*) canary.

Kanarische Inseln [ka'na:rɪʃə 'ɪnzəln], *f.pl.* Canary Islands.

Kandare [kan'da:rə], *f.* (—, *pl.* —n) bridle, bit.

Kandelaber [kandə'la:bər], *m.* (—s, *pl.* —) candelabrum, chandelier.

kandidieren [kandi'di:rən], *v.n.* be a candidate (for), apply (for) (*post*); (*Parl.*) stand (for), (*Am.*) run (for election).

kandieren [kan'di:rən], *v.a.* candy.

Kandiszucker ['kandɪstsukər], *m.* (—, no *pl.*) sugar-candy.

Kanevas ['kanəvas], *m.* (—ses, *pl.* —se) canvas.

Känguruh ['kɛŋguru:], *n.* (—s, *pl.* —s) (*Zool.*) kangaroo.

Kaninchen [ka'ni:nçən], *n.* (—s, *pl.* —) (*Zool.*) rabbit.

Kaninchenbau [ka'ni:nçənbau], *m.* (—s, *pl.* —e) rabbit-warren, burrow.

Kanne ['kanə], *f.* (—, *pl.* —n) can, tankard, mug; jug; pot; quart.

Kannegießer ['kanəgi:sər], *m.* (—s, *pl.* —) pot-house politician.

kannelieren [kanə'li:rən], *v.a.* flute; channel.

Kannibale [kani'ba:lə], *m.* (—n, *pl.* —n) cannibal.

Kanoe [ka'nu:], *n. see* **Kanu**.

Kanone [ka'no:nə], *f.* (—, *pl.* —n) cannon, gun; *unter aller* —, beneath contempt; beneath criticism.

Kanonier [kano'ni:r], *m.* (—s, *pl.* —e) gunner.

Kanonikus [ka'no:nikus], *m.* (—, *pl.* —ker) canon, prebendary.

kanonisieren [kanoni'zi:rən], *v.a.* canonise.

Kante ['kantə], *f.* (—, *pl.* —n) edge, rim, brim, brink, ledge; (*cloth*) list, selvedge.

Kanten ['kantən], *m.* (—s, *pl.* —) (*bread*) crust.

kanten ['kantən], *v.a.* edge, tilt.

Kanthaken ['kantha:kən], *m.* (—s, *pl.* —) cant-hook; grapple; grappling hook.

kantig ['kantɪç], *adj.* angular.

Kantine [kan'ti:nə], *f.* (—, *pl.* —n), canteen, mess.

Kanton [kan'to:n], *m.* (—s, *pl.* —e) (*Swiss*) canton; district, region.

Kantonist [kanto'nɪst], *m.* (—en, *pl.* —en) *unsicherer* —, shifty fellow.

Kantor ['kantɔr], *m.* (—s, *pl.* —en) precentor, organist; cantor.

Kanu [ka'nu:], *n.* (—s, *pl.* —s) canoe.

Kanzel ['kantsəl], *f.* (—, *pl.* —n) pulpit; (*Aviat.*) cockpit.

Kanzlei [kants'lai], *f.* (—, *pl.* —en) office, secretariat; chancellery, chancery office; lawyer's office.

Kanzleipapier [kants'laipapi:r], *n.* (—s, no *pl.*) foolscap (paper).

Kanzleistil [kants'laiʃti:l], *m.* (—s, no *pl.*) legal jargon.

Kanzler ['kantslər], *m.* (—s, *pl.* —) Chancellor.

Kanzlist [kants'lɪst], *m.* (—en, *pl.* —en) chancery clerk; copying clerk.

Kap [kap], *n.* (—s, *pl.* —s) (*Geog.*) cape, promontory.

Kapaun [ka'paun], *m.* (—s, *pl.* —e) capon.

Kapazität [kapatsi'tɛ:t], *f.* (—, *pl.* —en) capacity; (*fig.*) (*person*) authority.

Kapelle [ka'pɛlə], *f.* (—, *pl.* —n) chapel; (*Mus.*) band.

Kapellmeister [ka'pɛlmaistər], *m.* (—s, *pl.* —) (*Mus.*) band leader, conductor.

Kaper ['ka:pər], *f.* (—, *pl.* —n) (*Bot.*) caper.

kapern ['ka:pərn], v.a. capture, catch.

kapieren [ka'pi:rən], v.a. (coll.) understand, grasp.

Kapital [kapi'ta:l], n. (—s, pl. —ien) (money) capital, stock.

Kapitäl, Kapitell [kapɪ'tɛ:l, kapɪ'tɛl], n. (—s, pl. —e) (Archit.) capital.

Kapitalanlage [kapi'talanla:gə], f. (— pl. —n) investment.

kapitalisieren [kapitali'zi:rən], v.a. capitalise.

kapitalkräftig [kapi'ta:lkrɛftɪç], adj. wealthy, moneyed, affluent; (business, firm) sound.

Kapitalverbrechen [kapi'ta:lfɛrbreçən], n. (—s, pl. —) capital offence.

Kapitän [kapi'tɛ:n], m. (—s, pl. —e) captain (of a ship), master.

Kapitel [ka'pɪtəl], n. (—s, pl. —) chapter.

Kapitulation [kapitulats'jo:n], f. (—, pl. —en) surrender.

kapitulieren [kapitu'li:rən], v.n. surrender; capitulate.

Kaplan [kap'la:n], m. (—s, pl. ⸗e) chaplain; assistant priest.

Kapotte [ka'pɔtə], f. (—, pl. —n) hood.

Kappe ['kapə], f. (—, pl. —n) cap, bonnet; (shoe) toe-cap.

Käppi ['kɛpi], n. (—s, pl. —s) military cap.

Kapriole [kapri'o:lə], f. (—, pl. —n) caper.

kaprizieren [kapri'tsi:rən], v.r. sich auf etwas —, set o.'s heart on s.th., be obstinate about s.th.

kapriziös [kapri'tsjø:s], adj. whimsical, capricious.

Kapsel ['kapzəl], f. (—, pl. —n) capsule.

kaputt [ka'put], adj. broken, ruined, done for; — machen, break, ruin.

Kapuze [ka'pu:tsə], f. (—, pl. —n) hood; monk's cowl.

Kapuziner [kaput'si:nər], m. (—s, pl. —) Capuchin (friar); (coffee) cappuccino.

Kapuzinerkresse [kaput'si:nərkresə], f. (—, no pl.) (Bot.) nasturtium.

Karabiner [kara'bi:nər], m. (—s, pl. —) (rifle) carbine.

Karaffe [ka'rafə], f. (—, pl. —n) carafe, decanter.

Karambolage [karambo'la:ʒə], f. (—, pl. —n) collision; (billiards) cannon.

Karawane [kara'va:nə], f. (—, pl. —n) convoy; caravan.

Karbol [kar'bo:l], n. (—s, no pl.) carbolic acid.

Karbunkel [kar'buŋkəl], m. (—s, pl. —) (Med.) carbuncle.

Karfreitag [kar'fraɪta:k], m. Good Friday.

Karfunkel [kar'fuŋkəl], m. (—s, pl. —) (Min.) carbuncle.

karg [kark], adj. scant; meagre; parsimonious.

kargen ['kargən], v.n. be stingy, be niggardly.

kärglich ['kɛrklɪç], adj. sparing, scanty, poor, paltry.

karieren [ka'ri:rən], v.a. checker.

kariert [ka'ri:rt], adj. checked, checkered.

Karikatur [karika'tu:r], f. (—, pl. —en) caricature, cartoon.

karikieren [kari'ki:rən], v.a. caricature, distort.

Karl [karl], m. Charles; — der Grosse, Charlemagne.

Karmeliter [karme'li:tər], m. (—s, pl. —) Carmelite (friar).

karminrot [kar'mi:nrɔ:t], adj. carmine.

karmoisin [karmoa'zi:n], adj. crimson.

Karneol [karne'o:l], m. (—s, pl. —e) (Min.) cornelian, carnelian.

Karneval ['karnəval], m. (—s, pl. —s) carnival; Shrovetide festivities.

Karnickel [kar'nɪkəl], m. (—s, pl. —) rabbit; er war das —, he was to blame.

Kärnten ['kɛrntən], n. Carinthia.

Karo ['ka:ro], n. (—s, pl. —s) check, square; (cards) diamonds.

Karosse [ka'rɔsə], f. (—, pl. —n) statecoach.

Karosserie [karɔsə'ri:], f. (—, pl. —n) (Motor.) body(-work).

Karotte [ka'rɔtə], f. (—, pl. —n) (Bot.) carrot.

Karpfen ['karpfən], m. (—s, pl. —) (fish) carp.

Karre ['karə], f. (—, pl. —n) cart, wheelbarrow.

Karren ['karən], m. (—s, pl. —) cart, wheelbarrow, dray.

Karrete [ka're:tə], f. (—, pl. —n) (Austr.) rattletrap, rickety coach.

Karriere [ka'rjɛ:rə], f. (—, pl. —n) career; — machen, get on well.

Kärrner ['kɛrnər], m. (—s, pl. —) (obs.) carter.

Karst [karst], m. (—s, pl. —e) mattock.

Karthago [kar'ta:go], n. Carthage.

Kartätsche [kar'tɛ:tʃə], f. (—, pl. —n) grape-shot, shrapnel.

Kartäuser [kar'tɔyzər], m. (—s, pl. —) Carthusian (monk).

Karte ['kartə], f. (—, pl. —n) card; ticket; map; chart; (pl.) pack ((Am.) deck) of cards.

Kartei [kar'taɪ], f. (—, pl. —en) card index.

Kartell [kar'tɛl], n. (—s, pl. —e) cartel; ring; syndicate.

Kartoffel [kar'tɔfəl], f. (—, pl. —n) (Bot.) potato.

Kartoffelpuffer [kar'tɔfəlpufər], m. (—s, pl. —) potato-pancake.

Karton [kar'tɔŋ], m. (—s, pl. —s) carton, cardboard-box; (material) cardboard, paste-board; cartoon.

Kartusche [kar'tuʃə], f. (—, pl. —n) cartridge.

Karussell [karu'sɛl], n. (—s, pl. —e) merry-go-round.

Karwoche ['ka:rvɔxə], f. Holy Week.

Karzer ['kartsər], m. (—s, pl. —) lock-up, prison.

Kaschmir ['kaʃmi:r], m. (—s, no pl.) cashmere.

Käse

Käse ['kɛːzə], *m.* (—s, *pl.* —) cheese.
käseartig ['kɛːzəa:rtɪç], *adj.* like cheese; caseous.
Kaserne [ka'zɛrnə], *f.* (—, *pl.* —n) barracks.
kasernieren [kazɛr'ni:rən], *v.a.* put into barracks.
Käsestoff ['kɛːzəʃtɔf], *m.* (—s, *pl.* —e) casein.
käseweiß ['kɛːzəvaɪs], *adj.* deathly pale.
käsig ['kɛːzɪç], *adj.* cheese-like, cheesy, caseous; (*fig.*) sallow.
Kasperle ['kaspɛrlə], *n.* (—s, *pl.* —) Punch.
Kasperl(e)theater ['kaspɛrl(ə)tea:tər], *n.* (—s, *pl.* —) Punch-and-Judy show.
Kaspisches Meer ['kaspɪʃəsme:r], *n.* Caspian Sea.
Kasse ['kasə], *f.* (—, *pl.* —n) money-box, till; cash-desk; box-office; cash, ready money.
Kassenanweisung ['kasənanvaɪzuŋ], *f.* (—, *pl.* —en) treasury-bill; cash voucher.
Kassenbuch ['kasənbu:x], *n.* (—es, *pl.* ⸚er) cash-book.
Kassenschrank ['kasənʃraŋk], *m.* (—s, *pl.* ⸚e) strong-box, safe.
Kasserolle [kasə'rɔlə], *f.* (—, *pl.* —n) stew-pot, casserole.
Kassette [ka'sɛtə], *f.* (—, *pl.* —n) deed-box; casket; (*Phot.*) plate-holder.
kassieren [ka'si:rən], *v.a.* cash, collect (money); cashier, annul, discharge.
Kastagnette [kastan'jɛtə], *f.* (—, *pl.* —n) castanet.
Kassierer [ka'si:rər], *m.* (—s, *pl.* —) cashier; teller.
Kastanie [kas'tanjə], *f.* (—, *pl.* —n) (*Bot.*) chestnut, (*coll.*) conker; chestnut-tree.
Kästchen ['kɛstçən], *n.* (—s, *pl.* —) casket, little box.
Kaste ['kastə], *f.* (—, *pl.* —n) caste.
kasteien [ka'staɪən], *v.r. sich* —, castigate *or* mortify o.s.
Kastell [ka'stɛl], *n.* (—s, *pl.* —e) citadel, small fort; castle.
Kastellan [kastɛ'la:n], *m.* (—s, *pl.* —e) castellan; caretaker.
Kasten ['kastən], *m.* (—s, *pl.* ⸚) box, chest, case, crate.
Kastengeist ['kastəngaɪst], *m.* (—es, *no pl.*) exclusiveness; class consciousness.
Kastilien [ka'sti:ljən], *n.* Castile.
Kastrat [ka'stra:t], *m.* (—en, *pl.* —en) eunuch.
kastrieren [ka'stri:rən], *v.a.* castrate.
Katafalk [kata'falk], *m.* (—s, *pl.* —e) catafalque.
katalogisieren [katalogi'zi:rən], *v.a.* catalogue.
Katarakt [kata'rakt], *m.* (—es, *pl.* —e) cataract; waterfall.
Katasteramt [ka'tastəramt], *n.* (—es, *pl.* ⸚er) land-registry office.
katechisieren [kateçi'zi:rən], *v.a.* catechise, instruct.

kategorisch [kate'go:rɪʃ], *adj.* categorical, definite.
Kater ['ka:tər], *m.* (—s, *pl.* —) tom-cat; (*fig.*) hangover; *der gestiefelte* —, Puss-in-Boots.
Katheder [ka'te:dər], *n.* (—s, *pl.* —) desk; rostrum; lecturing-desk; (*fig.*) professorial chair.
Kathedrale [kate'dra:lə], *f.* (—, *pl.* —n) cathedral.
Katholik [kato'li:k], *m.* (—en, *pl.* —en) (Roman) Catholic.
katholisch [ka'to:lɪʃ], *adj.* (Roman) Catholic.
Kattun [ka'tu:n], *m.* (—s, *pl.* —e) calico, cotton.
Kätzchen ['kɛtsçən], *n.* (—s, *pl.* —) kitten; (*Bot.*) catkin.
Katze ['katsə], *f.* (—, *pl.* —n) cat; *die* — *im Sack kaufen,* buy a pig in a poke; *für die* —, no good at all, useless.
katzenartig ['katsəna:rtɪç], *adj.* cat-like, feline.
Katzenauge ['katsənaugə], *n.* (—s, *pl.* —n) cat's-eye.
Katzenbuckel ['katsənbukəl], *m.* (—s, *pl.* —) arched back of a cat.
Katzenjammer ['katsənjamər], *m.* (—s, *pl.* —) hangover.
Katzenmusik ['katsənmuzi:k], *f.* (—, *no pl.*) caterwauling; cacophony, discordant music.
Katzensprung ['katsənʃpruŋ], *m.* (—es, *no pl.*) (*fig.*) stone's throw.
Kauderwelsch ['kaudərvɛlʃ], *n.* (—es, *no pl.*) gibberish, double-Dutch.
kauen ['kauən], *v.a., v.n.* chew.
kauern ['kauərn], *v.n.* cower, squat, crouch.
Kauf [kauf], *m.* (—es, *pl.* ⸚e) purchase, buy; bargain.
Kaufbummel ['kaufbuməl], *m.* (—s, *no pl.*) shopping-spree.
kaufen ['kaufən], *v.a.* (*things*) buy, purchase; (*persons*) bribe.
Käufer ['kɔyfər], *m.* (—s, *pl.* —) buyer, purchaser.
Kaufhaus ['kaufhaus], *n.* (—es, *pl.* ⸚er) department store, emporium.
Kaufladen ['kaufla:dən], *m.* (—s, *pl.* ⸚) shop.
käuflich ['kɔyflɪç], *adj.* (*things*) purchasable, marketable; (*persons*) open to bribery, venal.
Kaufmann ['kaufman], *m.* (—s, *pl.* **Kaufleute**) merchant; shopkeeper; (*Am.*) store-keeper.
kaufmännisch ['kaufmɛnɪʃ], *adj.* commercial, mercantile.
Kaugummi ['kaugumi], *m.* (—s, *no pl.*) chewing gum.
Kaukasus ['kaukazus], *m.* Caucasus (Mountains).
Kaulquappe ['kaulkvapə], *f.* (—, *pl.* —n) (*Zool.*) tadpole.
kaum [kaum], *adv.* scarcely, hardly; no sooner.
Kaurimuschel ['kaurimuʃəl], *f.* (—, *pl.* —n) (*Zool.*) cowrie shell.

120

Kautabak ['kautabak], *m.* (—s, *no pl.*) chewing-tobacco.

Kaution [kau'tsjo:n], *f.* (—, *pl.* —en) security, bail, surety; *eine — stellen*, go, give *or* stand bail.

Kautschuk ['kautʃuk], *m.* (—s, *no pl.*) caoutchouc, India-rubber.

Kauz [kauts], *m.* (—es, *pl.* ⁻e) (*Orn.*) screech-owl; (*fig.*) *komischer —*, queer customer.

Käuzchen ['koytsçan], *n.* (—s, *pl.* —) little owl; (*fig.*) imp.

Kavalier [kava'li:r], *m.* (—s, *pl.* —e) gentleman; lady's man.

keck [kɛk], *adj.* bold, daring; pert, saucy.

Kegel ['ke:gəl], *m.* (—s, *pl.* —) ninepin, skittle; (*Geom.*) cone; *mit Kind und —*, bag and baggage.

Kegelbahn ['ke:gəlba:n], *f.* (—, *pl.* —en) skittle-alley, bowling-alley.

kegelförmig ['ke:gəlfœrmɪç], *adj.* conical.

kegeln ['ke:gəln], *v.n.* bowl, play at ninepins.

Kehle ['ke:lə], *f.* (—, *pl.* —n) throat, windpipe.

Kehlkopf ['ke:lkɔpf], *m.* (—es, *pl.* ⁻e) larynx.

Kehllaut ['ke:llaut], *m.* (—es, *pl.* —e) (*Phonet.*) guttural sound.

Kehlung ['ke:luŋ], *f.* (—, *pl.* —en) channel, flute, groove.

Kehraus ['ke:raus], *m.* (—, *no pl.*) last dance; (*fig.*) break-up, end.

kehren ['ke:rən], *v.a.* sweep; turn; *den Rücken —*, turn o.'s back. — *v.r. sich — an*, pay attention to, regard.

Kehricht ['ke:rɪçt], *m.* (—s, *no pl.*) sweepings; rubbish.

Kehrreim ['ke:rraim], *m.* (—s, *pl.* —e) refrain.

Kehrseite ['ke:rzaitə], *f.* (—, *pl.* —n) reverse.

kehrtmachen ['ke:rtmaxən], *v.n.* turn around; (*Mil.*) face about; turn back.

keifen ['kaifən], *v.n.* scold, nag.

Keil [kail], *m.* (—s, *pl.* —e) wedge.

Keile ['kailə], *f.* (—, *no pl.*) blows; (*coll.*) hiding; — *kriegen*, get a thrashing.

keilen ['kailən], *v.a.* wedge; (*coll.*) thrash.

Keilerei [kailə'rai], *f.* (—, *pl.* —en) brawl, fight.

keilförmig ['kailfœrmɪç], *adj.* wedge-shaped.

Keilschrift ['kailʃrɪft], *f.* (—, *pl.* —en) cuneiform writing.

Keim [kaim], *m.* (—es, *pl.* —e) germ, seed.

keimen ['kaimən], *v.n.* germinate.

keimfrei ['kaimfrai], *adj.* sterile, germ-free.

keiner, -e, -es [kainər], *adj.* no, not a, not any. — *pron.* no one, none.

keinerlei ['kainərlai], *adj.* no, of no sort, no ... whatever.

keineswegs ['kainəsve:ks], *adv.* by no means, on no account.

Keks [ke:ks], *m.* (—es, *pl.* —e) biscuit.

Kelch [kɛlç], *m.* (—es, *pl.* —e) cup; (*Eccl.*) chalice; (*Bot.*) calyx.

Kelchblatt ['kɛlçblat], *n.* (—es, *pl.* ⁻er) sepal.

kelchförmig ['kɛlçfœrmɪç], *adj.* cup-shaped.

Kelle ['kɛlə], *f.* (—, *pl.* —n) ladle; (*mason*) trowel.

Keller ['kɛlər], *m.* (—s, *pl.* —) cellar, basement.

Kellergewölbe ['kɛlərgəvœlbə], *n.* (—s, *pl.* —) vault.

Kellner ['kɛlnər], *m.* (—s, *pl.* —) waiter.

keltern ['kɛltərn], *v.a.* press (*grapes*).

Kenia ['ke:nja], *n.* Kenya.

kennbar ['kɛnba:r], *adj.* recognisable, conspicuous.

kennen ['kɛnən], *v.a. irr.* know, be acquainted with.

Kenner ['kɛnər], *m.* (—s, *pl.* —) connoisseur, expert.

Kennkarte ['kɛnkartə], *f.* (—, *pl.* —n) identity card.

kenntlich ['kɛntlɪç], *adj.* distinguishable.

Kenntnis ['kɛntnɪs], *f.* (—, *pl.* —se) knowledge; (*language*) command.

Kennzeichen ['kɛntsaixən], *n.* (—s, *pl.* —) characteristic, distinguishing mark; sign; symptom; criterion.

Kenterhaken ['kɛntərha:kən], *m.* (—s, *pl.* —) grappling-iron.

kentern ['kɛntərn], *v.n.* (*aux.* sein) capsize.

keramisch [ke'ra:mɪʃ], *adj.* ceramic.

Kerbe ['kɛrbə], *f.* (—, *pl.* —n) notch, indentation.

kerben ['kɛrbən], *v.a.* notch.

Kerbholz ['kɛrphɔlts], *n.* (—es, *no pl.*) tally; *auf dem —*, on o.'s conscience, charged against o.

Kerbtier ['kɛrpti:r], *n.* (—es, *pl.* —e) insect.

Kerker ['kɛrkər], *m.* (—s, *pl.* —) prison, jail, gaol; dungeon.

Kerl [kɛrl], *m.* (—s, *pl.* —e) fellow, chap; (*Am.*) guy (*coll.*).

Kern [kɛrn], *m.* (—es, *pl.* —e) (*nut*) kernel; (*fruit*) stone; (*fig.*) heart, crux; pith; (*Phys.*) nucleus.

kerngesund ['kɛrngəzunt], *adj.* hale and hearty, fit as a fiddle.

kernig ['kɛrnɪç], *adj.* solid, pithy.

Kernphysik ['kɛrnfyzi:k], *f.* (—, *no pl.*) nuclear physics.

Kernpunkt ['kɛrnpuŋkt], *m.* (—es, *pl.* —e) gist, essential point.

Kernwaffe ['kɛrnvafə], *f.* (—, *pl.* —n) nuclear weapon.

Kerze ['kɛrtsə], *f.* (—, *pl.* —n) candle.

Kessel ['kɛsəl], *m.* (—s, *pl.* —) kettle, cauldron; (*steam*) boiler.

Kesselschmied ['kɛsəlʃmi:t], *m.* (—s, *pl.* —e) boiler maker.

Kesselstein ['kɛsəlʃtain], *m.* (—s, *no pl.*) fur, deposit, scale (on boiler).

Kette ['kɛtə], *f.* (—, *pl.* —n) chain.

ketten ['kɛtən], *v.a.* chain, fetter.

Kettenstich ['kɛtənʃtɪç], *m.* (—es, *pl.* —e) chain stitch; (*Naut.*) chain knot.

Ketzer ['kɛtsər], *m.* (—s, *pl.* —) heretic.
Ketzerei [kɛtsə'raı], *f.* (—, *pl.* —en) heresy.
ketzerisch ['kɛtsərɪʃ], *adj.* heretical.
keuchen ['kɔyçən], *v.n.* pant, puff, gasp.
Keuchhusten ['kɔyçhu:stən], *m.* (—s, *no pl.*) whooping-cough.
Keule ['kɔylə], *f.* (—, *pl.* —n) club; (*meat*) leg.
keusch [kɔyʃ], *adj.* chaste, pure.
kichern ['kɪçərn], *v.n.* titter, giggle.
Kiebitz ['ki:bɪts], *m.* (—es, *pl.* —e) (*Orn.*) lapwing, peewit; (*fig.*) onlooker; (*coll.*) rubber-neck (at chess or cards).
Kiefer (1) ['ki:fər], *m.* (—s, *pl.* —) jaw, jaw-bone.
Kiefer (2) ['ki:fər], *f.* (—, *pl.* —n) (*Bot.*) pine.
Kiel [ki:l], *m.* (—es, *pl.* —e) keel; (*pen*) quill.
Kielwasser ['ki:lvasər], *n.* (—s, *no pl.*) wake.
Kieme ['ki:mə], *f.* (—, *pl.* —n) (*fish*) gill.
Kien [ki:n], *m.* (—s, *no pl.*) pine-resin, resinous pinewood.
Kienspan ['ki:nʃpa:n], *m.* (—s, *pl.* ⸚e) pine-splinter.
Kiepe ['ki:pə], *f.* (—, *pl.* —n) (*dial.*) creel, wicker basket.
Kies [ki:s], *m.* (—es, *no pl.*) gravel.
Kiesel ['ki:zəl], *m.* (—s, *pl.* —) pebble; flint.
Kieselsäure ['ki:zəlzɔyrə], *f.* (—, *no pl.*) silicic acid.
Kieselstein ['ki:zəlʃtaın], *m.* (—s, *pl.* —e) pebble.
Kilogramm ['ki:logram], *n.* (—s, *pl.* —e) kilogram (1000 grammes).
Kilometer ['ki:lome:tər], *m.* (—s, *pl.* —) kilometre; (*Am.*) kilometer (1000 metres).
Kimme ['kımə], *f.* (—, *pl.* —n) notch.
Kind [kınt], *n.* (—es, *pl.* —er) child; (*law*) infant; — und *Kegel*, bag and baggage.
Kind(e)l ['kınd(ə)l], *n.* (—s, *pl.* —) (*dial.*) small child, baby; *Münchner* —, Munich beer.
Kinderei [kındə'raı], *f.* (—, *pl.* —en) childishness; childish prank.
Kinderfräulein ['kındərfrɔylaın], *n.* (—s, *pl.* —) nurse, (*coll.*) nannie.
Kindergarten ['kındərgartən], *m.* (—s, *pl.* ⸚) kindergarten, infant-school.
Kinderhort ['kındərhɔrt], *m.* (—s, *pl.* —e) crèche.
kinderleicht ['kındərlaıçt], *adj.* extremely easy, child's play.
Kindermärchen ['kındərmɛːrçən], *n.* (—s, *pl.* —) fairy-tale.
Kinderstube ['kındərʃtu:bə], *f.* (—, *pl.* —n) nursery; *eine gute* —, a good upbringing.
Kinderwagen ['kındərva:gən], *m.* (—s, *pl.* —) perambulator, pram.
Kindesbeine ['kındəsbaınə], *n. pl. von* —n *an*, from infancy.

Kindeskind ['kındəskınt], *n.* (—es, *pl.* —er) (*obs.*) grandchild.
Kindheit ['kınthaıt], *f.* (—, *no pl.*) childhood, infancy.
kindisch ['kındıʃ], *adj.* childish.
kindlich ['kıntlıç], *adj.* childlike; naïve.
Kinn [kın], *n.* (—s, *pl.* —e) chin.
Kinnbacken ['kınbakən], *m.* (—s, *Anat.*) jaw-bone.
Kinnbackenkrampf ['kınbakənkrampf], *m.* (—s, *pl.* ⸚e) (*Med.*) lock-jaw.
Kinnlade ['kınla:də], *f.* (—, *pl.* —n) (*Anat.*) jaw-bone.
Kino ['ki:no], *n.* (—s, *pl.* —s) cinema; (*coll.*) pictures; (*Am.*) motion picture theatre; motion pictures, (*coll.*) movies.
Kipfel ['kıpfəl], *n.* (—s, *pl.* —) (*dial.*) roll, croissant.
kippen ['kıpən], *v.a.* tilt, tip over.
Kirche ['kırçə], *f.* (—, *pl.* —n) church.
Kirchenbann ['kırçənban], *m.* (—s, *no. pl.*) excommunication.
Kirchenbuch ['kırçənbu:x], *n.* (—es, *pl.* ⸚er) parish-register.
Kirchengut ['kırçəngu:t], *n.* (—es, *pl.* ⸚er) church-property.
Kirchenlicht ['kırçənlıçt], *n.* (—es, *pl.* —er) (*fig.*) shining light, bright spark.
Kirchenrecht ['kırçənrɛçt], *n.* (—es, *no pl.*) canon law.
Kirchenschiff ['kırçənʃıf], *n.* (—es, *pl.* —e) nave.
Kirchenstuhl ['kırçənʃtu:l], *m.* (—s, *pl.* ⸚e) pew.
Kirchenversammlung ['kırçənfɛrzamluŋ], *f.* (—, *pl.* —en) synod; convocation.
Kirchenvorsteher ['kırçənforʃte:ər], *m.* (—s, *pl.* —) churchwarden.
kirchlich ['kırçlıç], *adj.* ecclesiastic(al), religious.
Kirchspiel ['kırçʃpi:l], *n.* (—es, *pl.* —e) parish.
Kirchsprengel ['kırçʃprɛŋəl], *m.* (—s, *pl.* —) diocese.
Kirchturm ['kırçturm], *m.* (—s, *pl.* ⸚e) steeple.
Kirchweih ['kırçvaı], *f.* (—, *pl.* —en) consecration (of a church); church fair.
Kirmes ['kırmes], *f.* (—, *pl.* —sen) *see* **Kirchweih**.
kirre ['kırə], *adj.* tame; (*fig.*) amenable.
kirren ['kırən], *v.a.* tame, allure. — *v.n.* coo.
Kirsch(branntwein) [kırʃ(brantvaın)], *m.* (—s, *no pl.*) cherry-brandy.
Kirsche ['kırʃə], *f.* (—, *pl.* —n) (*Bot.*) cherry; *mit ihr ist nicht gut* —n *essen*, she is hard to get on with *or* not pleasant to deal with.
Kirschsaft ['kırʃzaft], *m.* (—es, *no pl.*) cherry-juice.
Kirschwasser ['kırʃvasər], *n.* (—s, *no pl.*) cherry-brandy.
Kissen ['kısən], *n.* (—s, *pl.* —) cushion, pillow.

kleiden

Kiste ['kɪstə], *f.* (—, *pl.* —n) box, case, chest; crate; coffer.
Kitsch [kɪtʃ], *m.* (—es, *no pl.*) trash; rubbish.
Kitt [kɪt], *m.* (—s, *pl.* —e) cement; (*Glazing*) putty.
Kittel ['kɪtəl], *m.* (—s, *pl.* —) smock; overall, tunic; frock.
kitten ['kɪtən], *v.a.* cement, glue.
Kitzchen ['kɪtsçən], *n.* (—s, *pl.* —) kid; fawn; kitten.
Kitzel ['kɪtsəl], *m.* (—s, *no pl.*) tickling, titillation; itch; (*fig.*) desire, appetite.
kitzeln ['kɪtsəln], *v.a.* tickle, titillate.
kitzlich ['kɪtslɪç], *adj.* ticklish; (*fig.*) delicate.
Kladderadatsch ['kladəradatʃ], *m.* (—es, *no pl.*) bang; mess, muddle.
klaffen ['klafən], *v.n.* gape, yawn.
kläffen ['klɛfən], *v.n.* bark, yelp.
Klafter ['klaftər], *f.* (—, *pl.* —n) fathom; (*wood*) cord.
klagbar ['kla:kba:r], *adj.* (*Law*) actionable.
Klage ['kla:gə], *f.* (—, *pl.* —n) complaint; (*Law*) suit, action.
Klagelied ['kla:gəli:t], *n.* (—es, *pl.* —er) dirge, lamentation.
klagen ['kla:gən], *v.n.* complain, lament; (*Law*) sue.
Kläger ['klɛ:gər], *m.* (—s, *pl.* —) complainant; (*Law*) plaintiff.
Klageschrift ['kla:gəʃrɪft], *f.* (—, *pl.* —en) bill of indictment; written complaint.
kläglich ['klɛ:klɪç], *adj.* woeful, pitiful, deplorable.
klaglos ['kla:klo:s], *adj.* uncomplaining.
Klamm [klam], *f.* (—, *pl.* —en) gorge, ravine.
klamm [klam], *adj.* tight, narrow; numb; clammy.
Klammer ['klamər], *f.* (—, *pl.* —n) clamp, clasp, hook; peg; clip; bracket, parenthesis.
klammern ['klamərn], *v.a.* fasten, peg. — *v.r. sich — an*, cling to.
Klang [klaŋ], *m.* (—es, *pl.* ⁻e) sound, tone; *ohne Sang und —,* unheralded and unsung.
klanglos ['klaŋlo:s], *adj.* soundless.
klangnachahmend ['klaŋnaxa:mənt], *adj.* onomatopoeic.
klangvoll ['klaŋfɔl], *adj.* sonorous.
Klappe ['klapə], *f.* (—, *pl.* —en) flap; (*Tech.*) valve; (*vulg.*) *halt die — !* shut up!
klappen ['klapən], *v.n.* flap; (*fig.*) tally, square; *es hat geklappt,* it worked.
Klapper ['klapər], *f.* (—, *pl.* —n) rattle.
klappern ['klapərn], *v.n.* rattle; (*teeth*) chatter.
Klapperschlange ['klapərʃlaŋə], *f.* (—, *pl.* —n) (*Zool.*) rattle-snake.
Klapphut ['klaphu:t], *m.* (—es, *pl.* ⁻e) opera-hat; chapeau-claque.
Klapps [klaps], *m.* (—es, *pl.* ⁻e) slap, smack; (*fig.*) touch of madness, kink.
Klappstuhl ['klapʃtu:l], *m.* (—s, *pl.* ⁻e) camp-stool, folding-chair.

Klapptisch ['klaptɪʃ], *m.* (—es, *pl.* —e) folding-table.
klar [kla:r], *adj.* clear; bright; (*fig.*) evident; plain, distinct.
Kläranlage ['klɛ:ranla:gə], *f.* (—, *pl.* —n) sewage-farm; filter plant.
klären ['klɛ:rən], *v.a.* clear.
Klarheit ['kla:rhaɪt], *f.* (—, *no pl.*) clearness, plainness.
Klarinette [klari'nɛtə], *f.* (—, *pl.* —n) (*Mus.*) clarinet.
Klärmittel ['klɛ:rmɪtəl], *n.* (—s, *pl.* —) clarifier.
Klärung ['klɛ:ruŋ], *f.* (—, *pl.* —en) clarification; (*fig.*) elucidation.
Klasse ['klasə], *f.* (—, *pl.* —n) class, order; (*Sch.*) form.
klassifizieren [klasifi'tsi:rən], *v.a.* classify.
Klassiker ['klasɪkər], *m.* (—s, *pl.* —) classic.
klassisch ['klasɪʃ], *adj.* classic(al), standard.
Klatsch [klatʃ], *m.* (—es, *no pl.*) gossip, scandal.
klatschen ['klatʃən], *v.n.* clap; gossip; (*rain*) patter; *Beifall —,* applaud.
Klatscherei [klatʃə'raɪ], *f.* (—, *pl.* —en) gossip, scandalmongering.
klauben ['klaubən], *v.a.* pick.
Klaue ['klauə], *f.* (—, *pl.* —n) claw, talon; paw.
klauen ['klauən], *v.a.* steal, (*coll.*) pinch.
Klauenseuche ['klauənzɔyçə], *f.* (—, *pl.* —n) *Maul und —,* foot and mouth disease.
Klause ['klauzə], *f.* (—, *pl.* —n) cell, hermitage; (*coll.*) den.
Klausel ['klauzəl], *f.* (—, *pl.* —n) clause, paragraph.
Klausner ['klausnər], *m.* (—s, *pl.* —) hermit, recluse, anchorite.
Klausur [klau'zu:r], *f.* (—, *pl.* —en) seclusion; written examination.
Klaviatur [klavja'tu:r], *f.* (—, *pl.* —en) keyboard.
Klavier [kla'vi:r], *n.* (—s, *pl.* —e) piano, pianoforte.
Klavierstück [kla'vi:rʃtyk], *n.* (—s, *pl.* —e) piece of piano music.
Klebemittel ['kle:bəmɪtəl], *n.* (—s, *pl.* —) adhesive, glue.
kleben ['kle:bən], *v.a.* paste, stick, glue. — *v.n.* stick, adhere.
klebrig ['kle:brɪç], *adj.* sticky; clammy.
Klebstoff ['kle:pʃtɔf], *m.* (—es, *no pl.*) gum; glue.
Klecks [klɛks], *m.* (—es, *pl.* —e) blot, blotch.
Kleckser ['klɛksər], *m.* (—s, *pl.* —) scrawler; (*painter*) dauber.
Klee [kle:], *m.* (—s, *no pl.*) (*Bot.*) clover, trefoil.
Kleid [klaɪt], *n.* (—es, *pl.* —er) frock, garment, dress. gown; (*Poet.*) garb; (*pl.*) clothes; *—er machen Leute,* clothes make the man.
Kleidchen ['klaɪtçən], *n.* (—s, *pl.* —) child's dress.
kleiden ['klaɪdən], *v.a.* dress, clothe.

Kleiderbügel

Kleiderbügel ['klaɪdərbyːgəl], *m.* (—s, *pl.* —) coat-hanger.

Kleiderpuppe ['klaɪdərpupə], *f.* (—, *pl.* —n) tailor's dummy.

Kleiderschrank ['klaɪdərʃraŋk], *m.* (—s, *pl.* ˙e) wardrobe.

kleidsam ['klaɪtza:m], *adj.* becoming; well-fitting, a good fit.

Kleidung ['klaɪduŋ], *f.* (—, *no pl.*) clothing, clothes, dress.

Kleie ['klaɪə], *f.* (—, *no pl.*) bran.

klein [klaɪn], *adj.* little, small; minute; petty; *ein — wenig*, a little bit.

Kleinasien [klaɪnˈaːzjən], *n.* Asia Minor.

Kleinbahn ['klaɪnbaːn], *f.* (—, *pl.* —en) narrow-gauge railway.

kleinbürgerlich ['klaɪnbyrgərlɪç], *adj.* (petit) bourgeois.

Kleingeld ['klaɪngɛlt], *n.* (—(e)s, *no pl.*) small change.

kleingläubig ['klaɪnglɔybɪç], *adj.* faint-hearted.

Kleinhandel ['klaɪnhandəl], *m.* (—s, *no pl.*) retail-trade.

Kleinigkeit ['klaɪnɪçkaɪt], *f.* (—, *pl.* —en) trifle, small matter.

Kleinkram ['klaɪnkraːm], *m.* (—s, *no pl.*) trifles.

kleinlaut ['klaɪnlaut], *adj.* subdued, dejected, low-spirited.

kleinlich ['klaɪnlɪç], *adj.* petty; mean; narrow-minded; pedantic.

Kleinmut ['klaɪnmuːt], *m.* (—es, *no pl.*) faint-heartedness; dejection.

Kleinod ['klaɪnoːt], *n.* (—s, *pl.* —ien) jewel; trinket.

Kleinstadt ['klaɪnʃtat], *f.* (—, *pl.* ˙e) small town.

Kleister ['klaɪstər], *m.* (—s, *no pl.*) paste.

Klemme ['klɛmə], *f.* (—, *pl.* —n) (*Tech.*) vice; clamp; (*fig.*) difficulty, straits; (*coll.*) fix, jam.

klemmen ['klɛmən], *v.a.* pinch, squeeze, jam.

Klemmer ['klɛmər], *m.* (—s, *pl.*—) (*eye*) glasses, pince-nez.

Klempner ['klɛmpnər], *m.* (—s, *pl.*—) tin-smith; plumber.

Klerus ['kleːrus], *m.* (—, *no pl.*) clergy.

Klette ['klɛtə], *f.* (—, *pl.* —n) burdock, bur(r); (*fig.*) hanger-on.

klettern ['klɛtərn], *v.n.* (*aux.* sein) climb, clamber.

Klima ['kliːma], *n.* (—s, *pl.* —s) climate.

Klimaanlage ['kliːmaanlaːgə], *f.* (—, *pl.* —n) air conditioning plant.

Klimbim ['klɪmˈbɪm], *m.* (—s, *no pl.*) goings-on; festivity; fuss; *der ganze —*, the whole caboodle.

klimpern ['klɪmpərn], *v.n.* (*piano*) strum; (*money*) jingle.

Klinge ['klɪŋə], *f.* (—, *pl.* —n) blade.

Klingel ['klɪŋəl], *f.* (—, *pl.* —n) (*door, telephone*) bell.

Klingelbeutel ['klɪŋəlbɔytəl], *m.* (—s, *pl.*—) collecting-bag.

klingeln ['klɪŋəln], *v.n.* ring, tinkle.

Klingelzug ['klɪŋəltsuːk], *m.* . (—es, *pl.* ˙e) bell-rope, bell-pull.

klingen ['klɪŋən], *v.n.* *irr.* sound; (*metals*) clang; (*ears*) tingle; *—de Münze*, hard cash, ready money.

Klinke ['klɪŋkə], *f.* (—, *pl.* —en) (*door*) handle, latch.

klipp [klɪp], *adv.* *— und klar*, as clear as daylight.

Klippe ['klɪpə], *f.* (—, *pl.* —n) cliff, crag, rock.

klirren ['klɪrən], *v.n.* clatter, rattle.

Klischee [kliˈʃeː], *n.* (—s, *pl.* —s) (*Typ.*) plate, printing-block; (*fig.*) cliché, hackneyed expression, tag.

Klistier [klɪˈstiːr], *n.* (—s, *pl.* —e) (*Med.*) enema.

Kloake [kloˈaːkə], *f.* (—, *pl.* —n) sewer, drain.

Kloben ['kloːbən], *m.* (—s, *pl.* —) log, block (of wood); pulley.

klopfen ['klɔpfən], *v.a., v.n.* knock, beat.

Klöppel ['klœpəl], *m.* (—s, *pl.* —) mallet; (*bell*) tongue, clapper; (*drum*) stick; (*lace*) bobbin.

klöppeln ['klœpəln], *v.a* make (bone) lace.

Klöppelspitze ['klœpəlʃpɪtsə], *f.* (—, *no pl.*) bone-lace.

Klops [klɔps], *m.* (—es, *pl.* —e) meat-dumpling.

Klosett [kloˈzɛt], *n.* (—s, *pl.* —e) lavatory, water-closet, toilet.

Kloß [kloːs], *m.* (—es, *pl.* ˙e) dumpling.

Kloster ['kloːstər], *n.* (—s, *pl.* ˙) cloister; monastery; convent.

Klostergang ['kloːstərgaŋ], *m.* (—es, *pl.* ˙e) cloisters.

Klotz [klɔts], *m.* (—es, *pl.* ˙e) block, trunk, stump; (*fig.*) *ein grober —*, a great lout.

klotzig ['klɔtsɪç], *adj.* cloddy; lumpish; (*sl.*) enormous.

Klub [klup], *m.* (—s, *pl.* —s) club.

Kluft [kluft], *f.* (—, *pl.* ˙e) gap; gulf, chasm; (*fig.*) cleavage.

klug [kluːk], *adj.* clever, wise, prudent, judicious, sagacious; *ich kann daraus nicht — werden*, I cannot make head nor tail of it.

klügeln ['klyːgəln], *v.n.* ponder; quibble.

Klugheit ['kluːkhaɪt], *f.* (—, *no pl.*) cleverness, wisdom, prudence, judiciousness.

Klumpfuß ['klumpfuːs], *m.* (—es, *pl.* ˙e) club-foot.

Klumpen ['klumpən], *m.* (—s, *pl.* —) lump, mass, clod; (*blood*) clot; (*metal*) ingot; (*gold*) nugget.

Klüngel ['klyŋəl], *m.* (—s, *pl.* —) clique, set.

knabbern ['knabərn], *v.n.* nibble.

Knabe ['knaːbə], *m.* (—n, *pl.* —n) boy.

Knäblein ['knɛːblaɪn], *n.* (—s, *pl.* —) (*Poet.*) baby boy, small boy.

knack [knak], *int.* crack! snap!

Knäckebrot ['knɛkəbroːt], *n.* (—es, *no pl.*) crispbread.

knacken ['knakən], *v.a.* crack.

Kobaltblau

Knackmandel [ˈknakmandəl], *f.* (—, *pl.* —n) shell-almond.
Knackwurst [ˈknakvurst], *f.* (—, *pl.* ⁻e) saveloy.
Knacks [knaks], *m.* (—es, *pl.* —e) crack.
knacksen [ˈknaksən], *v.n.* (*coll.*) crack.
Knall [knal], *m.* (—es, *pl.* —e) report, bang, detonation; — *und Fall,* quite suddenly, then and there.
Knallbüchse [ˈknalbyksə], *f.* (—, *pl.* —n) pop-gun.
Knalleffekt [ˈknalɛfɛkt], *m.* (—s, *pl.* —e) coup de théâtre; sensation.
knallen [ˈknalən], *v.n.* pop, explode, crack.
Knallgas [ˈknalga:s], *n.* (—es, *no pl.*) oxyhydrogen gas.
knallrot [ˈknalro:t], *adj.* scarlet; glaring red.
knapp [knap], *adj.* tight; scarce, insufficient; (*style*) concise; (*majority*) narrow, bare.
Knappe [ˈknapə], *m.* (—n, *pl.* —n) esquire, shield-bearer; miner.
Knappheit [ˈknaphaɪt], *f.* (—, *no pl.*) scarcity, shortage.
Knappschaft [ˈknapʃaft], *f.* (—, *pl.* —en) miners' association.
Knarre [ˈknarə], *f.* (—, *pl.* —n) rattle.
knarren [ˈknarən], *v.n.* rattle, creak.
Knaster [ˈknastər], *m.* (—s, *pl.* —) tobacco.
knattern [ˈknatərn], *v.n.* crackle.
Knäuel [ˈknɔyəl], *m.*, *n.* (—s, *pl.* —) skein, clew, ball.
Knauf [knauf], *m.* (—es, *pl.* ⁻e) (*stick*) knob, head; (*Archit.*) capital.
Knauser [ˈknauzər], *m.* (—s, *pl.* —) niggard, skinflint.
knausern [ˈknauzərn], *v.n.* be stingy, scrimp.
Knebel [ˈkne:bəl], *m.* (—s, *pl.* —) cudgel; gag.
knebeln [ˈkne:bəln], *v.a.* tie, bind; gag; (*fig.*) muzzle.
Knecht [knɛçt], *m.* (—es, *pl.* —e) servant, farm hand, menial; vassal, slave.
Knechtschaft [ˈknɛçtʃaft], *f.* (—, *no pl.*) servitude, slavery.
kneifen [ˈknaɪfən], *v.a.* irr. pinch.— *v.n.* (*fig. coll.*) back out (of), shirk.
Kneifer [ˈknaɪfər], *m.* (—s, *pl.* —) pince-nez.
Kneifzange [ˈknaɪftsaŋə], *f.* (—, *pl.* —n) pincers.
Kneipe [ˈknaɪpə], *f.* (—, *pl.* —n) pub, saloon.
kneten [ˈkne:tən], *v.a.* knead; massage.
knick(e)beinig [ˈknɪk(ə)baɪnɪç], *adj.* knock-kneed.
knicken [ˈknɪkən], *v.a.* crack, break.
Knicks [knɪks], *m.* (—es, *pl.* —e) curtsy.
knicksen [ˈknɪksən], *v.n.* curtsy.
Knie [kni:], *n.* (—s, *pl.* —) knee; *etwas übers* — *brechen,* make short work of.
Kniekehle [ˈkni:ke:lə], *f.* (—, *pl.* —n) hollow of the knee.

knien [ˈkni:ən], *v.n.* kneel.
Kniescheibe [ˈkni:ʃaɪbə], *f.* (—, *pl.* —n) knee-cap.
Kniff [knɪf], *m.* (—es, *pl.* —e) fold; (*fig.*) trick, knack, dodge.
knipsen [ˈknɪpsən], *v.a.* (*tickets*) clip, punch; (*Phot.*) take a snap of.
Knirps [knɪrps], *m.* (—es, *pl.* —e) pigmy; (*fig.*) urchin.
knirschen [ˈknɪrʃən], *v.n.* crunch, grate, gnash (teeth).
knistern [ˈknɪstərn], *v.n.* crackle.
knittern [ˈknɪtərn], *v.a.* rumple, wrinkle, crinkle, crease.
Knobel [ˈkno:bəl], *m.pl.* dice.
Knoblauch [ˈkno:blaux], *m.* (—s, *no pl.*) (*Bot.*) garlic.
Knöchel [ˈknœçəl], *m.* (—s, *pl.* —) knuckle, joint; ankle.
Knochen [ˈknɔxən], *m.* (—s, *pl.* —) bone.
Knochengerüst [ˈknɔxəngəryst], *n.* (—es, *pl.* —e) skeleton.
knöchern [ˈknœçərn], *adj.* made of bone.
knochig [ˈknɔxɪç], *adj.* bony.
Knödel [ˈknø:dəl], *m.* (—s, *pl.* —) dumpling.
Knollen [ˈknɔlən], *m.* (—s, *pl.* —) lump, clod; (*Bot.*) tuber, bulb.
knollig [ˈknɔlɪç], *adj.* knobby, bulbous.
Knopf [knɔpf], *m.* (—es, *pl.* ⁻e) button; stud; (*stick*) head, knob.
knöpfen [ˈknœpfən], *v.a.* button.
Knorpel [ˈknɔrpəl], *m.* (—s, *pl.* —) gristle, cartilage.
knorplig [ˈknɔrplɪç], *adj.* gristly.
knorrig [ˈknɔrɪç], *adj.* knotty, gnarled.
Knospe [ˈknɔspə], *f.* (—, *pl.* —n) bud.
Knote [ˈkno:tə], *m.* (—n, *pl.* —n) (*fig.*) bounder; lout.
Knoten [ˈkno:tən], *m.* (—s, *pl.* —) knot; (*fig.*) difficulty; (*Theat.*) plot.
Knotenpunkt [ˈkno:tənpuŋkt], *m.* (—es, *pl.* —e) (*Railw.*) junction.
Knotenstock [ˈkno:tənʃtɔk], *m.* (—es, *pl.* ⁻e) knotty stick.
knotig [ˈkno:tɪç], *adj.* knotty, nodular.
knüllen [ˈknylən], *v.a.* crumple.
knüpfen [ˈknypfən], *v.a.* tie; knot; form (a friendship etc.).
Knüppel [ˈknypəl], *m.* (—s, *pl.* —) cudgel.
knurren [ˈknurən], *v.n.* grunt, snarl; (*fig.*) growl, grumble.
knurrig [ˈknurɪç], *adj.* surly, grumpy.
knusprig [ˈknusprɪç], *adj.* crisp, crunchy.
Knute [ˈknu:tə], *f.* (—, *pl.* —n) knout.
knutschen [ˈknu:tʃən], *v.r. sich —,* (*coll.*) cuddle; (*Am.*) neck.
Knüttel [ˈknytəl], *m.* (—s, *pl.* —) cudgel, bludgeon.
Knüttelvers [ˈknytəlfɛrs], *m.* (—es, *pl.* —e) doggerel, rhyme.
Kobalt [ˈko:balt], *m.* (—s, *no pl.*) cobalt.
Kobaltblau [ˈko:baltblau], *n.* (—s, *no pl.*) smalt.

125

Koben

Koben ['ko:bən], m. (—s, pl. —) pig-sty.

Kober ['ko:bər], m. (—s, pl. —) (dial.) basket, hamper.

Kobold ['ko:bolt], m. (—(e)s, pl. —e) goblin, hobgoblin.

Koch [kɔx], m. (—es, pl. ⁻e) cook, chef.

kochen ['kɔxən], v.a. cook, boil. — v.n. boil; (fig.) seethe.

Kocher ['kɔxər], m. (—s, pl. —) boiler.

Köcher ['kœçər], m. (—s, pl. —) quiver.

Köchin ['kœçɪn], f. (—, pl. —innen) (female) cook.

Kochsalz ['kɔxzalts], n. (—es, no pl.) common salt.

Köder ['kø:dər], m. (—s, no pl.) bait, lure; (fig.) decoy.

ködern ['kø:dərn], v.a. bait; (fig.) decoy.

Kodex ['ko:dɛks], m. (—es, pl. —e) codex; old MS.; (Law) code.

kodifizieren [ko:difi'tsi:rən], v.a. codify.

Koffein [kɔfɛ'i:n], n. (—s, no pl.) caffeine.

Koffer ['kɔfər], m. (—s, pl. —) box, trunk, suitcase, portmanteau.

Kofferradio ['kɔfarra:djo], n. (—s, pl. —s) portable radio.

Kofferraum ['kɔfarraum], m. (—s, no pl.) (Motor.) boot, (Am.) trunk.

Kohl [ko:l], m. (—s, no pl.) (Bot.) cabbage; (fig.) nonsense, rot.

Kohle ['ko:lə], f. (—, pl. —n) coal.

Kohlenflöz ['ko:lənflø:ts], n. (—es, pl. —e) coal-seam.

Kohlenoxyd ['ko:lənɔksy:t], n. (—s, no pl.) carbon monoxide.

Kohlensäure ['ko:lənzɔyrə], f. (—, no pl.) carbonic acid.

Kohlenstift ['ko:lənʃtɪft], m. (—es, pl. —e) charcoal-crayon.

Köhler ['kø:lər], m. (—s, pl. —) charcoal-burner.

Koje ['ko:jə], f. (—, pl. —n) (Naut.) berth, bunk.

Kokarde [ko'kardə], f. (—, pl. —n) cockade.

kokett [ko'kɛt], adj. coquettish.

Kokette [ko'kɛtə], f. (—, pl. —n) coquette, flirt.

kokettieren [kokɛ'ti:rən], v.n. flirt.

Kokon [ko'kõ], m. (—s, pl. —s) cocoon.

Kokosnuß ['ko:kɔsnus], f. (—, pl. ⁻sse) (Bot.) coconut.

Koks [ko:ks], m. (—es, no pl.) coke.

Kolben ['kɔlbən], m. (—s, pl. —) club; (rifle) butt-end; (engine) piston; (Chem.) retort.

Kolbenstange ['kɔlbənʃtaŋə], f. (—, pl. —n) piston-rod.

Kolibri ['ko:libri:], m. (—s, pl. —s) (Orn.) humming-bird.

Kolkrabe ['kɔlkra:bə], m. (—n, pl. —n) (Orn.) raven.

Kolleg [kɔ'le:k], n. (—s, pl. —ien) course of lectures; lecture.

Kollege [kɔ'le:gə], m. (—n, pl. —n) colleague.

Kollekte [kɔ'lɛktə], f. (—, pl. —n) collection; (Eccl.) collect.

Koller ['kɔlər], m. (—s, no pl.) frenzy, rage.

kollidieren [kɔli'di:rən], v.n. collide.

Köln [kœln], n. Cologne.

kölnisch ['kœlnɪʃ], adj. of Cologne; —Wasser, eau de Cologne.

kolonisieren [koloni'zi:rən], v.a. colonise.

Kolonnade [kolo'na:də], f. (— pl. —n) colonnade.

Koloratur [kolora'tu:r], f. (—, pl. —n) coloratura.

kolorieren [kolo'ri:rən], v.a. colour.

Koloß [ko'lɔs], m. (—sses, pl. —sse) colossus.

Kolportage [kɔlpɔr'ta:ʒə], f. (—, pl. —n) colportage, door-to-door sale of books; sensationalism.

Kolportageroman [kɔlpɔr'ta:ʒəroma:n], m. (—s, pl. —e) penny dreadful, shocker.

kolportieren [kɔlpɔr'ti:rən], v.a. hawk; spread, disseminate.

Kombinationsgabe [kɔmbina'tsjo:nsga:bə], f. (—, pl. —en) power of deduction.

kombinieren [kɔmbi'ni:rən], v.a. combine; deduce.

Kombüse [kɔm'by:zə], f. (— pl. —n) galley, caboose.

Komik ['ko:mɪk], f. (—, no pl.) comicality; humour; funny side.

Komiker ['ko:mɪkər], m. (—s, pl. —) comedian.

komisch ['ko:mɪʃ], adj. comical, funny; peculiar, strange, odd.

Kommandantur [kɔmandan'tu:r], f. (—, pl. —en) commander's office; garrison headquarters.

kommandieren [kɔman'di:rən], v.a. command.

Kommanditgesellschaft [kɔman'di:tgəzɛlʃaft], f. (—, pl. —en) limited partnership.

Kommando [kɔ'mando], n. (—s, pl. —s) command.

kommen ['kɔmən], v.n. irr. (aux. sein) come, arrive; come about; um etwas —, lose s.th.; zu etwas —, come by s.th.; zu sich —, come to, regain consciousness.

Kommentar [kɔmɛn'ta:r], m. (—s, pl. —e) comment, commentary.

Kommers [kɔ'mɛrs], m. (—es, pl. —e) students' festivity; drinking party.

Kommersbuch [kɔ'mɛrsbu:x], n. (—es, pl. ⁻er) students' song-book.

kommerziell [kɔmɛrts'jɛl], adj. commercial.

Kommerzienrat [kɔ'mɛrtsjənra:t], m. (—s, pl. ⁻e) Councillor to the Chamber of Commerce.

Kommilitone [kɔmili'to:nə], m. (—n, pl. —n) fellow-student.

Kommis [kɔ'mi:], m. (—, pl. —) clerk.

Kommiß [kɔ'mɪs], m. (—sses, pl. —) military fatigue-dress; (fig.) military service.

126

können

Kommißbrot [kɔ'mɪsbro:t], *n.* (—es, *no pl.*) (coarse) army bread.
Kommissar [kɔmɪ'sa:r], *m.* (—s, *pl.* —e) commissioner.
Kommissariat [kɔmɪsar'ja:t], *n.* (—s, *pl.* —e) commissioner's office.
Kommission [kɔmɪs'jo:n], *f.* (—, *pl.* —en) commission, mission, committee.
kommod [kɔ'mo:d], *adj.* (*coll.*) snug, comfortable.
Kommode [kɔ'mo:də], *f.* (—, *pl.* —n) chest of drawers.
Kommune [kɔ'mu:nə], *f.* (—, *pl.* —n) (*coll.*) Communist Party; Reds.
Kommunismus [kɔmu'nɪsmus], *m.* (—, *no pl.*) Communism.
kommunistisch [kɔmu'nɪstɪʃ], *adj.* Communist.
Komödiant [kɔmød'jant], *m.* (—en, *pl.* —en) comedian, player; humbug.
Komödie [kɔ'mø:djə], *f.* (—, *pl.* —n) comedy, play; make-believe; — **spielen,** (*fig.*) sham, pretend, play-act.
Kompagnon ['kɔmpanjɔ̃], *m.* (—s, *pl.* —s) partner, associate.
Kompanie [kɔmpa'ni:], *f.* (—, *pl.* —n) (*Mil.*) company; (*Comm.*) partnership, company.
Kompaß ['kɔmpas], *m.* (—sses, *pl.* —sse) compass.
Kompaßrose ['kɔmpasro:zə], *f.* (—, *pl.* —n) compass-card.
kompensieren [kɔmpɛn'zi:rən], *v.a.* compensate.
komplementär [kɔmpləmɛn'tɛ:r], *adj.* complementary.
komplett [kɔm'plɛt], *adj.* complete.
komplimentieren [kɔmplimɛn'ti:rən], *v.a.* compliment, flatter.
Komplize [kɔm'pli:tsə], *m.* (—n, *pl.* —n) accomplice.
kompliziert [kɔmpli'tsi:rt], *adj.* complicated.
Komplott [kɔm'plɔt], *n.* (—s, *pl.* —e) plot, conspiracy.
Komponente [kɔmpo'nɛntə], *f.* (—, *pl.* —n) component part; constituent.
komponieren [kɔmpo'ni:rən], *v.a.* compose, set to music.
Komponist [kɔmpo'nɪst], *m.* (—en, *pl.* —en) composer.
Kompositum [kɔm'po:zitum], *n.* (—s, *pl.* —ta) (*Gram.*) compound word.
Kompott [kɔm'pɔt], *n.* (—s, *pl.* —e) stewed fruit, compote; sweet, dessert.
Kompresse [kɔm'prɛsə], *f.* (—, *pl.* —n) compress.
komprimieren [kɔmpri'mi:rən], *v.a.* compress.
Kompromiß [kɔmpro'mɪs], *m.* (—sses, *pl.* —sse) compromise, settlement.
kompromittieren [kɔmprɔmɪ'ti:rən], *v.a.* compromise. — *v.r.* **sich** —, compromise o.s.
kondensieren [kɔndɛn'zi:rən], *v.a.* condense.
Konditor [kɔn'di:tɔr], *m.* (—s, *pl.* —en) confectioner, pastry-cook.

Konditorei [kɔndito'raɪ], *f.* (—, *pl.* —en) confectioner's shop, pastry-shop; café.
kondolieren [kɔndo'li:rən], *v.n.* condole with s.o.
Kondukteur [kɔnduk'tø:r], *m.* (—s, *pl.* —e) (*Swiss & Austr. dial.*) guard (on train), conductor (on tram or bus).
Konfekt [kɔn'fɛkt], *n.* (—s, *pl.* —e) chocolates; (*Am.*) candy.
Konfektion [kɔnfɛk'tsjo:n], *f.* (—, *no pl.*) ready-made clothes; outfitting.
Konfektionär [kɔnfɛktsjo'nɛ:r], *m.* (—s, *pl.* —e) outfitter.
Konferenz [kɔnfe'rɛnts], *f.* (—, *pl.* —en) conference.
konfessionell [kɔnfɛsjo'nɛl], *adj.* denominational, confessional.
Konfirmand [kɔnfɪr'mant], *m.* (—en, *pl.* —en) confirmation candidate.
konfirmieren [kɔnfɪr'mi:rən], *v.a.* (*Eccl.*) confirm.
konfiszieren [kɔnfɪs'tsi:rən], *v.a.* confiscate.
Konfitüren [kɔnfi'ty:rən], *f. pl.* confectionery, candied fruit, preserves.
konform [kɔn'fɔrm], *adj.* in conformity (with).
konfus [kɔn'fu:s], *adj.* confused, puzzled, disconcerted.
Kongo ['kɔŋgo], *m.* Congo.
Kongruenz [kɔŋgru'ɛnts], *f.* (—, *no pl.*) congruity.
König ['kø:nɪç], *m.* (—s, *pl.* —e) king.
Königin ['kø:nɪgɪn], *f.* (—, *pl.* —nen) queen.
königlich ['kø:nɪglɪç], *adj.* royal, regal, kingly, king-like.
Königreich ['kø:nɪçraɪç], *n.* (—(e)s, *pl.* —e) kingdom.
Königsadler ['kø:nɪçsa:dlər], *m.* (—s, *pl.* —) golden eagle.
Königsschlange ['kø:nɪçsʃlaŋə], *f.* (—, *pl.* —n) (*Zool.*) boa constrictor.
Königstiger ['kø:nɪçsti:gər], *m.* (—s, *pl.* —) (*Zool.*) Bengal tiger.
Königtum ['kø:nɪçtu:m], *n.* (—s, *no pl.*) kingship.
Konjunktur [kɔnjuŋk'tu:r], *f.* (—, *pl.* —en) state of the market, (*coll.*) boom.
Konkordat [kɔnkɔr'da:t], *n.* (—s, *pl.* —e) concordat.
konkret [kɔn'kre:t], *adj.* concrete.
Konkurrent [kɔnku'rɛnt], *m.* (—en, *pl.* —en) competitor, (business) rival.
Konkurrenz [kɔnku'rɛnts], *f.* (—, *no pl.*) competition.
konkurrieren [kɔnku'ri:rən], *v.n.* compete.
Konkurs [kɔn'kurs], *m.* (—es, *pl.* —e) bankruptcy.
Konkursmasse [kɔn'kursmasə], *f.* (—, *pl.* —n) bankrupt's estate, bankrupt's stock.
Können ['kœnən], *n.* (—s, *no pl.*) ability; knowledge.
können ['kœnən], *v.a., v.n. irr.* be able to, be capable of; understand; *ich kann,* I can; *er kann Englisch,* he speaks English.

127

konsequent [kɔnze'kvɛnt], *adj.* consistent.

Konsequenz [kɔnze'kvɛnts], *f.* (—, *pl.* —en) (*characteristic*) consistency; (*result*) consequence.

Konservatorium [kɔnzɛrva'to:rjum], *n.* (—s, *pl.* —rien) (*Mus.*) conservatoire, conservatorium.

Konserve [kɔn'zɛrvə], *f.* (—, *pl.* —n) preserve; tinned, *or* (*Am.*) canned food.

konservieren [kɔnzɛr'vi:rən], *v.a.* preserve.

Konsistorium [kɔnzɪs'to:rjum], *n.* (—s, *pl.* —rien) (*Eccl.*) consistory.

Konsole [kɔn'zo:lə], *f.* (—, *pl.* —n) bracket.

konsolidieren [kɔnzoli'di:rən], *v.a.* consolidate.

Konsonant [kɔnzo'nant], *m.* (—en, *pl.* —en) (*Phonet.*) consonant.

Konsorte [kɔn'zɔrtə], *m.* (—n, *pl.* —n) associate, accomplice.

Konsortium [kɔn'zɔrtsjum], *n.* (—s, *pl.* —tien) syndicate.

konstatieren [kɔnsta'ti:rən], *v.a.* state, note, assert.

konsternieren [kɔnstɛr'ni:rən], *v.a.* dismay, disconcert.

konstituieren [kɔnstitu'i:rən], *v.a.* constitute.

konstitutionell [kɔnstitutsjo'nɛl], *adj.* constitutional.

konstruieren [kɔnstru'i:rən], *v.a.* construct; (*Gram.*) construe.

konsularisch [kɔnzu'la:rɪʃ], *adj.* consular.

Konsulat [kɔnzu'la:t], *n.* (—s, *pl.* —e) consulate.

Konsulent [kɔnzu'lɛnt], *m.* (—en, *pl.* —en) (*Law*) counsel; consultant.

konsultieren [kɔnzul'ti:rən], *v.a.* consult.

Konsum [kɔn'zu:m], *m.* (—s, *no pl.*) (*Econ.*) consumption.

Konsumverein [kɔn'zu:mfɛraɪn], *m.* (—s, *pl.* —e) cooperative society.

konsumieren [kɔnzu'mi:rən], *v.a.* consume.

Konterbande [kɔntər'bandə], *f.* (—, *no pl.*) contraband.

Konterfei [kɔntər'faɪ], *n.* (—s, *pl.* —e) (*obs.*) portrait, likeness.

Kontertanz ['kɔntərtants], *m.* (—es, *pl.* ˝e) square dance, quadrille.

kontinuierlich [kɔntinu'i:rlɪç], *adj.* continuous.

Kontinuität [kɔntinui'tɛːt], *f.* (—, *no pl.*) continuity.

Konto ['kɔnto], *n.* (—s, *pl.* —ten) (*bank*) account; à —, on account.

Kontokorrent [kɔntoko'rɛnt], *n.* (—s, *pl.* —e) current account.

Kontor [kɔn'to:r], *n.* (—s, *pl.* —e) (*obs.*) office.

Kontorist [kɔnto'rɪst], *m.* (—en, *pl.* —en) clerk.

Kontrabaß ['kɔntrabas], *m.* (—sses, *pl.* ˝sse) double-bass.

Kontrapunkt ['kɔntrapuŋkt], *m.* (—es, *pl.* —e) (*Mus.*) counterpoint.

kontrastieren [kɔntras'ti:rən], *v.a., v.n.* contrast.

kontrollieren [kɔntrɔ'li:rən], *v.a.* check, verify.

Kontroverse [kɔntro'vɛrzə], *f.* (—, *pl.* —n) controversy.

Kontur [kɔn'tu:r], *f.* (—, *pl.* —en) outline, (*pl.*) contours.

Konvent [kɔn'vɛnt], *m.* (—s, *pl.* —e) convention, assembly, congress.

konventionell [kɔnvɛntsjo'nɛl], *adj.* conventional, formal.

Konversationslexikon [kɔnvɛrza-'tsjo:nslɛksɪkɔn], *n.* (—s, *pl.* —) encyclopaedia.

konvertieren [kɔnvɛr'ti:rən], *v.a., v.n.* convert.

Konvertit [kɔnvɛr'tɪt], *m.* (—en, *pl.* —en) convert.

Konvolut [kɔnvo'lu:t], *n.* (—s, *pl.* —e) bundle; scroll.

konvulsivisch [kɔnvul'zi:vɪʃ], *adj.* convulsive.

konzentrieren [kɔntsɛn'tri:rən], *v.a., v.r.* concentrate; *auf etwas* —, centre upon.

konzentrisch [kɔn'tsɛntrɪʃ], *adj.* concentric.

Konzept [kɔn'tsɛpt], *n.* (—es, *pl.* —e) rough draft, sketch; *aus dem — bringen*, unsettle, disconcert.

Konzeptpapier [kɔn'tsɛptpapi:r], *n.* (—s, *no pl.*) scribbling paper.

Konzern [kɔn'tsɛrn], *m.* (—s, *pl.* —e) (*Comm.*) combine.

Konzert [kɔn'tsɛrt], *n.* (—es, *pl.* —e) concert, (*musical*) recital.

Konzertflügel [kɔn'tsɛrtfly:gəl], *m.* (—s, *pl.* —) grand piano.

konzertieren [kɔntsɛr'ti:rən], *v.n.* give recitals; play in a concert.

Konzertmeister [kɔn'tsɛrtmaɪstər], *m.* (—s, *pl.* —) impresario.

Konzession [kɔntsɛ'sjo:n], *f.* (—, *pl.* —en) concession, licence.

konzessionieren [kɔntsesjo'ni:rən], *v.a.* license.

Konzil [kɔn'tsi:l], *n.* (—s, *pl.* —ien) (*Eccl.*) council.

konzipieren [kɔntsi'pi:rən], *v.a.* draft, plan.

Koordinierung [ko:ɔrdi'ni:ruŋ], *f.* (—, *pl.* —en) co-ordination.

Kopf [kɔpf], *m.* (—es, *pl.* ˝e) head; top; heading; (*fig.*) mind, brains, judgment; *aus dem* —, by heart.

köpfen ['kœpfən], *v.a.* behead, decapitate; (*Bot.*) lop.

Kopfhaut ['kɔpfhaut], *f.* (—, *no pl.*) scalp.

Kopfhörer ['kɔpfhø:rər], *m.* (—s, *pl.* —) headphone, receiver.

Kopfkissen ['kɔpfkɪsən], *n.* (—s, *pl.* —) pillow.

Kopfsalat ['kɔpfzala:t], *m.* (—s, *pl.* —e) (garden) lettuce.

kopfscheu ['kɔpfʃɔy], *adj.* afraid; alarmed, timid; — *machen*, scare; — *werden*, take fright, jib.

Kopfschmerz ['kɔpfʃmɛrts], *m.* (**—es**, *pl.* **—en**) (*mostly pl.*) headache.

Kopfsprung ['kɔpfʃpruŋ], *m.* (**—s**, *pl.* ⁓e) (*diving*) header.

kopfüber [kɔpf'y:bər], *adv.* head over heels; headlong.

Kopfweh ['kɔpfve:], *n.* (**—s**, *no pl.*) headache.

Kopfzerbrechen ['kɔpftsɛrbrɛçən], *n.* (**—s**, *no pl.*) racking o.'s brains.

Kopie [ko'pi:] *f.* (**—**, *pl.* **—n**) copy, duplicate.

kopieren [ko'pi:rən], *v.a.* copy, ape, mimic, take off.

Koppe ['kɔpə], *f. see* **Kuppe**.

Koppel ['kɔpəl], *f.* (**—**, *pl.* **—n**) (*dogs*) couple, leash; (*ground*) enclosure, paddock.

koppeln ['kɔpəln], *v.a.* couple, leash.

kopulieren [kopu'li:rən], *v.a.* (*obs.*) marry; pair; (*Hort.*) graft.

Koralle [ko'ralə], *f.* (**—**, *pl.* **—n**) coral.

Korallenriff [ko'ralənrif], *n.* (**—es**, *pl.* **—e**) coral-reef.

Korb [kɔrp], *m.* (**—s**, *pl.* ⁓e) basket, hamper; *einen — geben*, turn s.o. down, refuse an offer of marriage.

Korbweide ['kɔrpvaɪdə], *f.* (**—**, *pl.* **—n**) (*Bot.*) osier.

Kord [kɔrt], *m.* (**—s**, *no pl.*) corduroy.

Kordel ['kɔrdəl], *f.* (**—**, *pl.* **—n**) cord, twine, thread.

Korea [ko're:a], *n.* Korea.

Korinthe [ko'rintə], *f.* (**—**, *pl.* **—n**) (*Bot.*) currant.

Korken ['kɔrkən], *m.* (**—s**, *pl.* **—**) cork, stopper.

Korkenzieher ['kɔrkəntsi:ər], *m.* (**—s**, *pl.* **—**) cork-screw.

Korn [kɔrn], *n.* (**—s**, *pl.* **—e**, ⁓er) (*Bot.*) corn, grain, cereal, rye; (*gun*) sight, *aufs — nehmen*, take aim at.

Kornblume ['kɔrnblu:mə], *f.* (**—**, *pl.* **—n**) (*Bot.*) corn-flower.

Kornbranntwein ['kɔrnbrantvaɪn], *m.* (**—s**, *no pl.*) corn-brandy, whisky.

Kornett [kɔr'nɛt], *m.* (**—s**, *pl.* **—e**) (*Mil.*, *Mus.*) cornet.

körnig ['kœrnɪç], *adj.* granular, granulous; grained.

Kornrade ['kɔrnra:də], *f.* (**—**, *pl.* **—n**) (*Bot.*) corn-cockle.

Kornspeicher ['kɔrnʃpaɪçər], *m.* (**—s**, *pl.* **—**) granary, corn-loft.

Körper ['kœrpər], *m.* (**—s**, *pl.* **—**) body; (*Phys.*) solid.

Körperbau ['kœrpərbau], *m.* (**—s**, *no pl.*) build, frame.

Köpergeruch ['kœrpərgəru:x], *m.* (**—s**, *no pl.*) body odour.

körperlich ['kœrpərlɪç], *adj.* bodily, physical; *—e Züchtigung*, corporal punishment.

Körpermaß ['kœrpərma:s], *n.* (**—es**, *pl.* **—e**) cubic measure.

Körperschaft ['kœrpərʃaft], *f.* (**—**, *pl.* **—en**) corporation.

Korps [ko:r], *n.* (**—**, *pl.* **—**) (*Mil.*) corps; students' corporation.

Korrektheit [kɔ'rɛkthaɪt], *f.* (**—**, *no pl.*) correctness.

Korrektionsanstalt [kɔrek'tsjo:nsanʃtalt], *f.* (**—**, *pl.* **—en**) penitentiary, Borstal institution.

Korrektor [kɔ'rɛktɔr], *m.* (**—s**, *pl.* **—en**) proof-reader.

Korrektur [kɔrek'tu:r], *f.* (**—**, *pl.* **—en**) correction; proof-correction; revision.

Korrekturbogen [kɔrek'tu:rbo:gən], *m.* (**—s**, *pl.* **—**) (*Typ.*) proof-sheet, galley.

Korrespondenzkarte [kɔrɛspɔn'dɛntskartə], *f.* (**—**, *pl.* **—n**) post-card.

korrigieren [kɔri'gi:rən], *v.a.* correct, revise; read (proofs).

Korsett [kɔr'zɛt], *n.* (**—s**, *pl.* **—s**) corset, bodice, stays.

Koryphäe [kori'fɛ:ə], *m.* (**—n**, *pl.* **—n**) celebrity, authority, master mind.

Koseform ['ko:zəfɔrm], *f.* (**—**, *pl.* **—en**) term of endearment, pet-name, diminutive.

kosen ['ko:zən], *v.a.*, *v.n.* caress, fondle; make love (to).

Kosinus ['ko:zinus], *m.* (**—**, *pl.* **—**) (*Maths.*) cosine.

Kosmetik [kɔs'me:tɪk], *f.* (**—**, *no pl.*) cosmetics.

kosmetisch [kɔs'me:tɪʃ], *adj.* cosmetic.

kosmisch ['kɔzmiʃ], *adj.* cosmic.

Kosmopolit [kɔsmopo'li:t], *m.* (**—en**, *pl.* **—en**) cosmopolitan.

kosmopolitisch [kɔsmopo'li:tɪʃ], *adj.* cosmopolitan.

Kost [kɔst], *f.* (**—**, *no pl.*) food, fare; board.

Kostarika [kɔsta'rika], *n.* Costa Rica.

kostbar ['kɔstba:r], *adj.* valuable, precious, costly.

Kostbarkeit ['kɔstba:rkaɪt], *f.* (**—**, *pl.* **—en**) costliness, preciousness; (*pl.*) (*goods*) valuables.

Kosten ['kɔstən], *pl.* cost(s), expenses, charges; (*Law*) costs.

kosten ['kɔstən], *v.a.* taste; (*money*) cost; take, require; *was kostet das?* how much is this?

Kosten(vor)anschlag ['kɔstən(for)anʃla:k], *m.* (**—s**, *pl.* ⁓e) estimate.

Kostenaufwand ['kɔstənaufvant], *m.* (**—s**, *pl.* ⁓e) expenditure.

Kostenersatz ['kɔstənerzats], *m.* (**—es**, *no pl.*) refund of expenses, compensation.

kostenfrei ['kɔstənfraɪ], *adj.* free (of charge), gratis.

kostenlos ['kɔstənlo:s], *see* **kostenfrei**.

Kostgänger ['kɔstgɛŋər], *m.* (**—s**, *pl.* **—**) boarder.

Kostgeld ['kɔstgɛlt], *n.* (**—es**, *no pl.*) maintenance *or* board allowance.

köstlich ['kœstlɪç], *adj.* excellent, precious; delicious; *ein —er Witz*, a capital joke.

kostspielig ['kɔstʃpi:lɪç], *adj.* expensive, costly.

Kostüm [kɔ'sty:m], *n.* (**—s**, *pl.* **—e**) costume; fancy dress.

Kostümfest [kɔ'sty:mfɛst], *n.* (**—s**, *pl.* **—e**) fancy-dress ball.

kostümieren

kostümieren [kɔsty'miːrən], *v.a.* dress up.

Kot [koːt], *m.* (—es, *no pl.*) mud, dirt; filth, mire; excrement.

Kotelett [kɔt'lɛt], *n.* (—s, *pl.* —s) cutlet.

Köter [ˈkøːtər], *m.* (—s, *pl.* —) cur, mongrel.

Koterie [koːtəˈriː], *f.* (—, *pl.* —n) clique, set, coterie.

Kotflügel [ˈkoːtflyːgəl], *m.* (—s, *pl.* —) (*Motor.*) mudguard.

kotig [ˈkoːtɪç], *adj.* dirty, miry.

kotzen [ˈkɔtsən], *v.n.* (*vulg.*) vomit.

Koweit [ˈkoːvaɪt], *n.* Kuwait.

Krabbe [ˈkrabə], *f.* (—, *pl.* —n) (*Zool.*) crab; shrimp; (*fig.*) brat, imp.

krabbeln [ˈkrabəln], *v.n.* crawl.

Krach [krax], *m.* (—es, *pl.* —e) crack, crash; din, noise; (*Comm.*) slump; quarrel, row.

krachen [ˈkraxən], *v.n.* crack, crash.

krächzen [ˈkrɛçtsən], *v.n.* croak.

Kraft [kraft], *f.* (—, *pl.* —e) strength, vigour; force; power, energy; intensity; *in — treten*, come into force.

kraft [kraft], *prep.* (*Genit.*) by virtue of, by authority of, on the strength of.

Kraftausdruck [ˈkraftausdruk], *m.* (—s, *pl.* —e) forcible expression; expletive.

Kraftbrühe [ˈkraftbryːə], *f.* (—, *pl.* —n) meat-soup, beef-tea.

Kraftfahrer [ˈkraftfaːrər], *m.* (—s, *pl.* —) motorist.

kräftig [ˈkrɛftɪç], *adj.* strong, powerful, vigorous, energetic; (*food*) nourishing.

Kraftlehre [ˈkraftleːrə], *f.* (—, *no pl.*) dynamics.

kraftlos [ˈkraftloːs], *adj.* weak, feeble.

Kraftwagen [ˈkraftvaːgən], *m.* (—s, *pl.* —) motor car, automobile, car; lorry, truck.

Kragen [ˈkraːgən], *m.* (—s, *pl.* —) collar; *es geht mir an den —*, it will cost me dearly.

Krähe [ˈkrɛːə], *f.* (—, *pl.* —n) (*Orn.*) crow.

krähen [ˈkrɛːən], *v.n.* crow.

Krähenfüße [ˈkrɛːənfyːsə], *m. pl.* crow's feet (wrinkles).

Krakau [ˈkraːkau], *n.* Cracow.

krakeelen [kraˈkeːlən], *v.n.* (*coll.*) kick up a row.

Kralle [ˈkralə], *f.* (—, *pl.* —n) claw, talon.

Kram [kraːm], *m.* (—s, *no pl.*) small wares (trade); stuff, rubbish, litter; *es paßt mir nicht in den —*, it does not suit my purpose.

kramen [ˈkraːmən], *v.n.* rummage.

Krämer [ˈkrɛːmər], *m.* (—s, *pl.* —) retailer, general dealer, shopkeeper.

Kramladen [ˈkraːmlaːdən], *m.* (—s, *pl.* —) small retail-shop, general shop or store.

Krampe [ˈkrampə], *f.* (—, *pl.* —n) staple.

Krampf [krampf], *m.* (—es, *pl.* —e) cramp, spasm, convulsion.

Krampfader [ˈkrampfaːdər], *f.* (—, *pl.* —n) varicose vein.

krampfartig [ˈkrampfaːrtɪç], *adj.* spasmodic.

krampfhaft [ˈkrampfhaft], *adj.* convulsive.

Kran [kraːn], *m.* (—s, *pl.* —e) (*Engin.*) crane.

Kranich [ˈkraːnɪç], *m.* (—s, *pl.* —e) (*Orn.*) crane.

krank [krank], *adj.* sick, ill.

kränkeln [ˈkrɛŋkəln], *v.n.* be ailing, be in poor health.

kranken [ˈkraŋkən], *v.n. an etwas —*, suffer from s.th., be afflicted with s.th.

kränken [ˈkrɛŋkən], *v.a.* vex, grieve, offend, insult.

Krankenbahre [ˈkraŋkənbaːrə], *f.* (—, *pl.* —n) stretcher.

Krankenhaus [ˈkraŋkənhaus], *n.* (—es, *pl.* —er) hospital.

Krankenkasse [ˈkraŋkənkasə], *f.* (—, *pl.* —n) sick-fund; health insurance.

Krankenkost [ˈkraŋkənkɔst], *f.* (—, *no pl.*) invalid diet.

Krankenschwester [ˈkraŋkənʃvɛstər], *f.* (—, *pl.* —n) nurse.

Krankenstuhl [ˈkraŋkənʃtuːl], *m.* (—s, *pl.* —e) invalid chair.

Krankenversicherung [ˈkraŋkənfɛrzɪçəruŋ], *f.* (—, *pl.* —en) health insurance.

Krankenwärter [ˈkraŋkənvɛrtər], *m.* (—s, *pl.* —) attendant, male nurse.

krankhaft [ˈkraŋkhaft], *adj.* morbid.

Krankheit [ˈkraŋkhaɪt], *f.* (—, *pl.* —en) illness, sickness, disease, malady; complaint; *englische —*, rickets.

Krankheitserscheinung [ˈkraŋkhaɪtsɛrʃaɪnuŋ], *f.* (—, *pl.* —en) symptom.

kränklich [ˈkrɛŋklɪç], *adj.* sickly, infirm, in poor health.

Kränkung [ˈkrɛŋkuŋ], *f.* (—, *pl.* —en) grievance, annoyance; offence, insult.

Kranz [krants], *m.* (—es, *pl.* —e) wreath, garland.

Kränzchen [ˈkrɛntsçən], *n.* (—s, *pl.* —) little garland; (*fig.*) (ladies') weekly tea party; circle, club.

kränzen [ˈkrɛntsən], *v.a.* garland, wreathe.

Krapfen [ˈkrapfən], *m.* (—s, *pl.* —) doughnut.

kraß [kras], *adj.* crass, crude.

Krater [ˈkraːtər], *m.* (—s, *pl.* —) crater.

Kratzbürste [ˈkratsbyrstə], *f.* (—, *pl.* —n) scraper; (*fig.*) cross-patch, irritable person.

Krätze [ˈkrɛtsə], *f.* (—, *no pl.*) (*Med.*) scabies, itch, mange.

kratzen [ˈkratsən], *v.a., v.n.* scratch, scrape, itch.

krauen [ˈkrauən], *v.a.* scratch softly.

kraus [kraus], *adj.* frizzy, curly; crisp, fuzzy; creased; (*fig.*) abstruse; *die Stirn — ziehen*, frown, knit o.'s brow.

Krause [ˈkrauzə], *f.* (—, *pl.* —n) ruff.

kräuseln [ˈkrɔyzəln], *v.a., v.r.* crisp, curl; ripple.

Krauskohl [ˈkrauskoːl], *m.* (—s, *no pl.*) Savoy cabbage.

Kriminalbeamte

Kraut [kraut], n. (—es, pl. ⁻er) herb; plant; (dial.) cabbage; wie — und Rüben, higgledy-piggledy.
krautartig ['krauta:rtıç], adj. herbaceous.
Kräuterkäse ['krɔytərke:zə], m. (—s, pl. —) green cheese.
Kräutertee ['krɔytərte:], m. (—s, no pl.) herb-tea, infusion of herbs.
Krawall [kra'val], m. (—s, pl. —e) (coll.) row, uproar; shindy.
Krawatte [kra'vatə], f. (—, pl. —n) cravat, tie.
kraxeln ['kraksəln], v.n. (coll.) climb, clamber.
Krebs [kre:ps], m. (—es, pl. —e) (Zool.) crayfish, crab; (Med.) cancer, carcinoma; (Geog.) Tropic of Cancer.
krebsartig ['kre:psa:rtıç], adj. cancerous.
Krebsbutter ['kre:psbutər], f. (—, no pl.) crab-cheese.
Krebsgang ['kre:psgaŋ], m. (—es, no pl.) crab's walk, sidling; den — gehen, retrograde, decline.
Krebsschaden ['kre:psʃa:dən], m. (—s, pl. ⁻) cancerous sore or affection; (fig.) canker, inveterate evil.
Kredenz [kre'dents], f. (—, pl. —en) buffet, serving table, sideboard.
kredenzen [kre'dentsən], v.a. taste (wine); (obs.) present, offer.
kreditieren [kredi'ti:rən], v.a. einem etwas —, credit s.o. with s.th.
Kreide ['kraidə], f. (—, pl. —n) chalk; (Art) crayon.
kreieren [kre'i:rən], v.a. create.
Kreis [krais], m. (—es, pl. —e) circle; (Astron.) orbit; district; range; sphere.
Kreisabschnitt ['kraisapʃnit], m. (—s, pl. —e) segment.
Kreisausschnitt ['kraisausʃnit], m. (—s, pl. —e) sector.
Kreisbogen ['kraisbo:gən], m. (—s, pl. ⁻) arc.
kreischen ['kraiʃən], v.n. scream, shriek.
Kreisel ['kraizəl], m. (—s, pl. —) (toy) (spinning) top; gyroscope.
kreisen ['kraizən], v.n. circle, revolve; circulate.
Kreislauf ['kraislauf], m. (—es, pl. ⁻e) circular course; (Astron.) orbit; (blood) circulation.
kreißen ['kraisən], v.n. (Med.) be in labour.
Kreisstadt ['kraisʃtat], f. (—, pl. ⁻e) county town.
Kreisumfang ['kraisumfaŋ], m. (—s, pl. ⁻e) circumference.
Kreml [kreml], m. (—s, no pl.) the Kremlin.
Krempe ['krempə], f. (—, pl. —n) (hat) brim.
Krempel ['krempəl], m. (—s, no pl.) (coll.) refuse, rubbish; stuff.
Kren [kre:n], m. (—s, no pl.) (Austr.) horse-radish.
krepieren [kre'pi:rən], v.n. (aux. sein) (animals) die; (humans) (coll.) perish miserably; explode.

Krepp [krep], m. (—s, no pl.) crape, crêpe.
Kresse ['kresə], f. (—, pl. —n) cress.
Kreta ['kre:ta], n. Crete.
Kreuz [krɔyts], n. (—es, pl. —e) cross, crucifix; (Anat.) small of the back; (fig.) calamity; affliction; kreuz und quer, in all directions.
Kreuzband ['krɔytsbant], n. (—es, pl. ⁻er) wrapper (for printed matter).
kreuzbrav ['krɔytsbra:f], adj. as good as gold.
kreuzen ['krɔytsən], v.a. cross. — v.r. sich —, make the sign of the cross.
Kreuzfahrer ['krɔytsfa:rər], m. (—s, pl. —) crusader.
kreuzfidel ['krɔytsfide:l], adj. jolly, merry, as merry as a cricket.
Kreuzgang ['krɔytsgaŋ], m. (—es, pl. ⁻e) cloisters.
kreuzigen ['krɔytsıgən], v.a. crucify.
Kreuzritter ['krɔitsrıtər], m. (—s, pl. —) Knight of the Cross; crusader.
Kreuzschmerzen ['krɔytsʃmertsən], m. pl. lumbago.
Kreuzstich ['krɔytsʃtıç], m. (—es, no pl.) (Embroidery) cross-stitch.
Kreuzung ['krɔytsuŋ], f. (—, pl. —en) (road) crossing; (animals) cross-breeding.
Kreuzverhör ['krɔytsferhø:r], n. (—s, pl. —e) cross-examination.
Kreuzweg ['krɔytsve:k], m. (—s, pl. —e) crossroads; (Eccl.) Stations of the Cross.
Kreuzworträtsel ['krɔytsvɔrtre:tsəl], n. (—s, pl. —) crossword-puzzle.
Kreuzzug ['krɔytstsu:k], m. (—es, pl. ⁻e) crusade.
kriechen ['kri:çən], v.n. irr. (aux. sein) creep, crawl; (fig.) cringe, fawn.
kriecherisch ['kri:çərıʃ], adj. fawning, cringing.
Kriechtier ['kri:çti:r], n. (—s, pl. —e) reptile.
Krieg [kri:k], m. (—es, pl. —e) war.
kriegen ['kri:gən], v.a. get, obtain.
Krieger ['kri:gər], m. (—s, pl. —) warrior.
kriegerisch ['kri:gərıʃ], adj. warlike, martial.
kriegführend ['kri:kfy:rənt], adj. belligerent.
Kriegsfuß ['kri:ksfu:s], m. (—s, no pl.) auf —, at loggerheads.
Kriegsgewinnler ['kri:ksgəvınlər], m. (—s, pl. —) war-profiteer.
Kriegslist ['kri:kslıst], f. (—, pl. —en) stratagem.
Kriegsschauplatz ['kri:ksʃauplats], m. (—es, pl. ⁻e) theatre of war.
Kriegsschiff ['kri:ksʃıf], n. (—es, pl. —e) man-of-war, warship.
Kriegswesen ['kri:ksve:zən], n. (—s, no pl.) military affairs.
Kriegszug ['kri:kstsu:k], m. (—es, pl. ⁻e) campaign.
Krim [kri:m], f. the Crimea.
Kriminalbeamte [krimi'na:lbəamtə], m. (—n, pl. —n) crime investigator.

131

Kriminalprozeß

Kriminalprozeß [krɪmi'naːlprotsɛs], *m.* (**—sses,** *pl.* **—sse**) criminal procedure *or* trial.

Krimskrams ['krɪmskrams], *m.* (**—,** *no pl.*) whatnots, knick-knacks, medley.

Krippe ['krɪpə], *f.* (**—,** *pl.* **—n**) crib, manger; crèche.

Krise ['kriːzə], *f.* (**—,** *pl.* **—n**) crisis.

Kristall [krɪ'stal], *m.* (**—s,** *pl.* **—e**) crystal; cut glass.

kristallartig [krɪ'stalaːrtɪç], *adj.* crystalline.

kristallisieren [krɪstali'ziːrən], *v.a., v.n.* (*aux.* sein), crystallise.

Kristallkunde [krɪ'stalkundə], *f.* (**—,** *no pl.*) crystallography.

Kriterium [kri'teːrjum], *n.* (**—s,** *pl.* **—rien**) criterion, test.

Kritik [kri'tiːk], *f.* (**—,** *pl.* **—en**) criticism, review; *unter aller —*, extremely bad.

Kritiker ['kriːtɪkər], *m.* (**—s,** *pl.* **—**) critic.

kritisch ['kriːtɪʃ], *adj.* critical; precarious, crucial.

kritisieren [kriti'ziːrən], *v.a.* criticise; review; censure.

kritteln ['krɪtəln], *v.n.* cavil (at), find fault.

Krittler ['krɪtlər], *m.* (**—s,** *pl.* **—**) caviller, fault-finder.

Kritzelei [krɪtsə'lai], *f.* (**—,** *pl.* **—en**) scrawling, scribbling.

kritzeln ['krɪtsəln], *v.a.* scrawl, scribble.

Kroatien [kro'aːtsjən], *n.* Croatia.

Krokodil [kroko'diːl], *n.* (**—s,** *pl.* **—e**) (*Zool.*) crocodile.

Kronbewerber ['kroːnbeverbər], *m.* (**—s,** *pl.* **—**) aspirant to the crown, pretender.

Krone ['kroːnə], *f.* (**—,** *pl.* **—n**) crown; (*Papal*) tiara; (*fig.*) head, top, flower.

krönen ['krøːnən], *v.a.* crown.

Kronerbe ['kroːnɛrbə], *m.* (**—n,** *pl.* **—n**) heir apparent.

Kronleuchter ['kroːnlɔyçtər], *m.* (**—s,** *pl.* **—**) chandelier.

Kronsbeere ['kroːnsbeːrə], *f.* (**—,** *pl.* **—n**) (*Bot.*) cranberry.

Krönung ['krøːnuŋ], *f.* (**—,** *pl.* **—en**) coronation.

Kropf [krɔpf], *m.* (**—es,** *pl.* **ⁱⁱe**) (*human*) goitre, wen; (*birds*) crop, craw.

kropfartig ['krɔpfaːrtɪç], *adj.* goitrous.

kröpfen ['krœpfən], *v.a.* (*birds*) cram.

Kropftaube ['krɔpftaubə], *f.* (**—,** *pl.* **—n**) (*Orn.*) pouter-pigeon.

Kröte ['krøːtə], *f.* (**—,** *pl.* **—n**) toad.

Krücke ['krykə], *f.* (**—,** *pl.* **—n**) crutch; (*fig.*) rake.

Krückstock ['krykʃtɔk], *m.* (**—s,** *pl.* **ⁱⁱe**) crutch.

Krug [kruːk], *m.* (**—es,** *pl.* **ⁱⁱe**) jug, pitcher, mug; (*fig.*) pub, inn.

Krüger ['kryːgər], *m.* (**—s,** *pl.* **—**) pub-keeper, tapster.

Krume ['kruːmə], *f.* (**—,** *pl.* **—n**) crumb.

krüm(e)lig ['kryːm(ə)lɪç], *adj.* crumbly, crumby.

krümeln ['kryːmeln], *v.n.* crumble.

krumm [krum], *adj.* crooked, curved; *etwas — nehmen*, take s.th. amiss.

krummbeinig ['krumbainɪç], *adj.* bandy-legged.

krümmen ['krymən], *v.a.* crook, bend, curve. *— v.r. sich —*, (*fig.*) writhe, cringe.

Krummholz ['krumhɔlts], *n.* (**—es,** *no pl.*) (*Bot.*) dwarf-pine.

Krummschnabel ['krumʃnaːbəl], *m.* (**—s,** *pl.* **ⁱⁱ**) (*Orn.*) curlew, crook-bill.

Krümmung ['krymuŋ], *f.* (**—,** *pl.* **—en**) curve; turning, winding.

Krüppel ['krypəl], *m.* (**—s,** *pl.* **—**) cripple.

krüppelhaft ['krypəlhaft], *adj.* crippled, lame.

krüpp(e)lig ['kryp(ə)lɪç], *adj.* crippled, lame.

Kruste ['krustə], *f.* (**—,** *pl.* **—n**) crust.

Kübel ['kyːbəl], *m.* (**—s,** *pl.* **—**) tub, bucket.

Kubikfuß [ku'biːkfuːs], *m.* (**—es,** *pl.* **—**) cubic foot.

Kubikinhalt [ku'biːkɪnhalt], *m.* (**—s,** *no pl.*) cubic content.

Kubismus [ku'bɪsmus], *m.* (**—,** *no pl.*) cubism.

Küche ['kyçə], *f.* (**—,** *pl.* **—n**) (*room*) kitchen; (*food*) cooking, cookery, cuisine.

Kuchen ['kuːxən], *m.* (**—s,** *pl.* **—**) cake.

Küchengeschirr ['kyçəngəʃɪr], *n.* (**—s,** *no pl.*) kitchen utensils.

Küchenherd ['kyçənheːrt], *m.* (**—es,** *pl.* **—e**) kitchen-range.

Küchenlatein ['kyçənlatain], *n.* (**—s,** *no pl.*) dog-Latin.

Küchenmeister ['kyçənmaistər], *m.* (**—s,** *pl.* **—**) chef, head cook.

Küchenschrank ['kyçənʃraŋk], *m.* (**—s,** *pl.* **ⁱⁱe**) dresser.

Kuchenteig ['kuːxəntaik], *m.* (**—s,** *pl.* **—e**) dough (for cake).

Küchenzettel ['kyçəntsetəl], *m.* (**—s,** *pl.* **—**) bill of fare.

Küchlein ['kyːçlain], *n.* (**—s,** *pl.* **—**) young chicken, pullet.

Kücken ['kykən], *n.* (**—s,** *pl.* **—**) young chicken, pullet.

Kuckuck ['kukuk], *m.* (**—s,** *pl.* **—e**) (*Orn.*) cuckoo; *scher Dich zum —!* go to blazes!

Kufe ['kuːfə], *f.* (**—,** *pl.* **—n**) tub, vat; (*sleigh*) runner; (*cradle*) rocker.

Küfer ['kyːfər], *m.* (**—s,** *pl.* **—**) cooper.

Kugel ['kuːgəl], *f.* (**—s,** *pl.* **—n**) ball, bullet, sphere, globe.

kugelfest ['kuːgəlfest], *adj.* bulletproof.

kugelförmig ['kuːgəlfœrmɪç], *adj.* spherical, globular.

Kugelgelenk ['kuːgəlgəleŋk], *n.* (**—s,** *pl.* **—e**) ball and socket joint.

Kugellager ['kuːgəlaːgər], *n.* (**—s,** *pl.* **—**) ball-bearing.

Kugelmaß ['kuːgəlmaːs], *n.* (**—es,** *pl.* **—e**) ball-calibre.

kugeln ['kuːgəln], *v.a.* roll; bowl.

Kugelregen ['ku:gəlre:gən], *m.* (—s, *no pl.*) hail of bullets.

kugelrund ['ku:gəlrunt], *adj.* round as a ball, well-fed.

Kugelschreiber ['ku:gəlʃraɪbər], *m.* (—s, *pl.* —) ball-point pen.

Kuh [ku:] *f.* (—, *pl.* ˙e) cow; *junge* —, heifer.

Kuhblattern ['ku:blatərn], *f. pl.* cow-pox.

Kuhblume ['ku:blu:mə], *f.* (—, *pl.* —n) (*Bot.*) marigold.

Kuhfladen ['ku:fla:dən], *m.* (—s, *pl.* —) cow-dung.

Kuhhaut ['ku:haut], *f.* (—, *pl.* ˙e) cow-hide; *das geht auf keine* —, that defies description.

kühl [ky:l], *adj.* cool, fresh; (*behaviour*) reserved.

Kühle ['ky:lə], *f.* (—, *no pl.*) coolness, freshness; (*behaviour*) reserve.

kühlen ['ky:lən], *v.a.* cool, freshen.

Kühlraum ['ky:lraum], *m.* (—es, *pl.* ˙e) refrigerating-chamber.

Kühlschrank ['ky:lʃraŋk], *m.* (—s, *pl.* ˙e) refrigerator, (*coll.*) fridge.

Kühltruhe ['ky:ltru:ə], *f.* (—, *pl.* —n) deep freeze.

Kühlung ['ky:luŋ], *f.* (—, *pl.* —en) refrigeration.

Kuhmist ['ku:mɪst], *m.* (—s, *no pl.*) cow-dung.

kühn [ky:n], *adj.* bold, daring, audacious.

Kühnheit ['ky:nhaɪt], *f.* (—, *no pl.*) boldness, daring, audacity.

Kujon [ku'jo:n], *m.* (—s, *pl.* —e) bully, scoundrel.

kujonieren [kujo'ni:rən], *v.a.* bully, exploit.

Kukuruz ['kukuruts], *m.* (—es, *no pl.*) (*Austr.*) maize.

kulant [ku'lant], *adj.* obliging; (*terms*) easy.

Kulanz [ku'lants], *f.* (—, *no pl.*) accommodating manner.

Kuli ['ku:li:], *m.* (—s, *pl.* —s) coolie.

kulinarisch [kuli'na:rɪʃ], *adj.* culinary.

Kulisse [ku'lɪsə], *f.* (—, *pl.* —n) (*Theat.*) back-drop, side-scene, wings.

Kulissenfieber [ku'lɪsənfi:bər], *n.* (—s, *no pl.*) stage-fright.

kulminieren [kulmi'ni:rən], *v.n.* culminate.

kultivieren [kulti'vi:rən], *v.a.* cultivate.

Kultur [kul'tu:r], *f.* (—, *pl.* —en) (*Agr.*) cultivation; (*fig.*) culture, civilization.

Kultus ['kultus], *m.* (—, *pl.* Kulte) cult, worship.

Kultusministerium ['kultusmɪnɪste:rjum], *n.* (—s, *pl.* —rien) Ministry of Education.

Kümmel ['kymǝl], *m.* (—s, *no pl.*) caraway-seed; (*drink*) kümmel.

Kummer ['kumǝr], *m.* (—s, *no pl.*) grief, sorrow, trouble.

kümmerlich ['kymǝrlɪç], *adj.* miserable, pitiful.

kummerlos ['kumǝrlo:s], *adj.* untroubled.

kümmern ['kymǝrn], *v.r. sich — um,* mind, look after, be worried about, care for.

Kümmernis ['kymǝrnɪs], *f.* (—, *pl.* —se) grief, sorrow.

kummervoll ['kumǝrfɔl], *adj.* sorrowful, painful, grievous.

Kumpan [kum'pa:n], *m.* (—s, *pl.* —e) companion; mate; *lustiger* —, jolly fellow, good companion.

kund [kunt], *adj.* known, public; *etwas — tun,* make s.th. public; — *und zu wissen sei hiermit,* (*obs.*) we hereby give notice.

kundbar ['kuntba:r], *adj.* known; *etwas — machen,* announce s.th., make s.th. known.

kündbar ['kyntba:r], *adj.* (*loan, capital etc.*) redeemable; capable of being called in, terminable.

Kunde (1) ['kundə], *m.* (—n, *pl.* —n) customer; *ein schlauer* —, an artful dodger.

Kunde (2) ['kundə], *f.* (—, *pl.* —n) news; information, notification; (*compounds*) science.

Kundgebung ['kuntge:buŋ], *f.* (—, *pl.* —en) publication; rally; demonstration.

kundig ['kundɪç], *adj.* versed in, conversant with.

Kundige ['kundɪgə], *m.* (—n, *pl.* —n) expert, initiate.

kündigen ['kyndɪgən], *v.n.* give notice (*Dat.*).

Kundmachung ['kuntmaxuŋ], *f.* (—, *pl.* —en) publication.

Kundschaft ['kuntʃaft], *f.* (—, *no pl.*) clientele, customers; information, reconnaissance.

kundschaften ['kuntʃaftən], *v.n.* reconnoitre, scout.

künftig ['kynftɪç], *adj.* future, prospective, to come.

Kunst [kunst], *f.* (—, *pl.* ˙e) art; skill.

Kunstbutter ['kunstbutər], *f.* (—, *no pl.*) margarine.

Künstelei [kynstə'laɪ], *f.* (—, *pl.* —en) affectation, mannerism.

kunstfertig ['kunstfɛrtɪç], *adj.* skilled, skilful.

Kunstfreund ['kunstfrɔynt], *m.* (—es, *pl.* —e) art-lover.

kunstgerecht ['kunstgərɛçt], *adj.* workmanlike.

Kunstgewerbe ['kunstgəvɛrbə], *n.* (—s, *no pl.*) arts and crafts.

Kunstgriff ['kunstgrɪf], *m.* (—s, *pl.* —e) trick, dodge, artifice, knack.

Kunsthändler ['kunsthɛndlər], *m.* (—s, *pl.* —) art-dealer.

Kunstkenner ['kunstkɛnər], *m.* (—s, *pl.* —) connoisseur.

Künstler ['kynstlər], *m.* (—s, *pl.* —) artist, performer.

künstlerisch ['kynstlərɪʃ], *adj.* artistic, elaborate, ingenious.

künstlich ['kynstlɪç], *adj.* artificial.

kunstlos ['kunstlo:s], *adj.* artless, unaffected.

kunstreich

kunstreich ['kunstraɪç], *adj.* ingenious.
Kunstseide ['kunstzaɪdə], *f.* (—, *no pl.*) artificial silk.
Kunststickerei ['kunstʃtɪkəraɪ], *f.* (—, *no pl.*) art needlework.
Kunststoff ['kunstʃtɔf], *m.* (—es, *pl.* —e) plastics.
Kunststopfen ['kunstʃtɔpfən], *n.* (—s, *no pl.*) invisible mending.
Kunststück ['kunstʃtyk], *n.* (—es, *pl.* —e) trick, feat.
Kunstverständige ['kunstfɛrʃtɛndɪgə], *m.* (—n, *pl.* —n) art expert.
Küpe ['ky:pə], *f.* (—, *pl.* —n) large tub; (dyeing) copper.
Kupfer ['kupfər], *n.* (—s, *no pl.*) copper.
Kupferblech ['kupfərblɛç], *n.* (—es, *no pl.*) copper-sheet.
Kupferdraht ['kupfərdra:t], *m.* (—es, *pl.* ‍e) copper-wire.
kupferhaltig ['kupfərhaltɪç], *adj.* containing copper.
Kupferrost ['kupfərrɔst], *m.* (—es, *no pl.*) verdigris.
Kupferstecher ['kupfərʃteçər], *m.* (—s, *pl.* —) (copperplate) engraver.
kupieren [ku'pi:rən], *v.a.* (*rare*) (*ticket*) punch; (*Austr.*) (*horse*) dock.
Kuppe ['kupə], *f.* (—, *pl.* —n) (*hill*) top, summit.
Kuppel ['kupəl], *f.* (—, *pl.* —n) cupola, dome.
kuppeln ['kupəln], *v.n.* procure, pimp; make a match.
Kuppler ['kuplər], *m.* (—s, *pl.* —) procurer, pimp; matchmaker.
Kupplung ['kuplun], *f.* (—, *pl.* —en) (*Railw.*) coupling, joint; (*Motor.*) clutch.
Kur [ku:r], *f.* (—, *pl.* —en) cure; *eine — machen*, undergo medical treatment.
Kuranstalt ['ku:ranʃtalt], *f.* (—, *pl.* —en) sanatorium; (*Am.*) sanatorium.
Küraß ['ky:ras], *m.* (—sses, *pl.* —sse) cuirass.
Kuratel [kura'tel], *f.* (—, *pl.* —en) guardianship, trusteeship.
Kuratorium [kura'to:rjum], *n.* (—s, *pl.* —rien) board of guardians *or* trustees; council, governing body.
Kurbel ['kurbəl], *f.* (—, *pl.* —n) crank, winch.
Kurbelstange ['kurbəlʃtaŋə], *f.* (—, *pl.* —n) connecting rod.
Kurbelwelle ['kurbəlvɛlə], *f.* (—, *pl.* —n) crankshaft.
Kürbis ['kyrbɪs], *m.* (—ses, *pl.* —se) (*Bot.*) pumpkin, gourd.
küren ['ky:rən], *v.a.* irr. (*Poet.*) choose, elect.
Kurfürst ['ku:rfyrst], *m.* (—en, *pl.* —en) Elector (of the Holy Roman Empire).
Kurhaus ['ku:rhaus], *n.* (—es, *pl.* ‍er) spa; hotel; pump room.
Kurie ['ku:rjə], *f.* (—, *pl.* —n) (*Eccl.*) Curia; Papal Court.

Kurier [ku'ri:r], *m.* (—s, *pl.* —e) courier.
kurieren [ku'ri:rən], *v.a.* cure.
kurios [kur'jo:s], *adj.* curious, queer, strange.
Kuriosität [kurjozi'tɛ:t], *f.* (—, *pl.* —en) curio, curiosity.
Kurort ['ku:rɔrt], *m.* (—es, *pl.* —e) spa, watering-place, health-resort.
Kurrentschrift ['ku'rɛntʃrɪft], *f.* (—, *no pl.*) running hand, cursive writing.
Kurs [kurs], *m.* (—es, *pl.* —e) rate of exchange; quotation; circulation; course.
Kursaal ['ku:rza:l], *m.* (—s, *pl.* —säle) hall, (*Am.*) pump-room, casino.
Kursbericht ['kursbərɪçt], *m.* (—es, *pl.* —e) market report.
Kursbuch ['kursbu:x], *n.* (—es, *pl.* ‍er) railway-guide, time-table.
Kürschner ['kyrʃnər], *m.* (—s, *pl.* —) furrier, skinner.
kursieren [kur'zi:rən], *v.n.* be current, circulate.
Kursivschrift [kur'zi:rʃrɪft], *f.* (—, *no pl.*) italics.
Kursstand ['kursʃtant], *m.* (—es, *no pl.*) rate of exchange.
Kursus ['kurzus], *m.* (—, *pl.* **Kurse**) course (of lectures).
Kurszettel ['kursʃtetəl], *m.* (—s, *pl.* —) quotation-list.
Kurve ['kurvə], *f.* (—, *pl.* —n) curve.
kurz [kurts], *adj.* short, brief, concise; curt, abrupt.
kurzangebunden [kurts'aŋgəbundən], *adj.* terse, abrupt, curt.
kurzatmig ['kurtsa:tmɪç], *adj.* short-winded, short of breath.
Kürze ['kyrtsə], *f.* (—, *no pl.*) shortness, brevity.
kürzen ['kyrtsən], *v.a.* shorten, abbreviate, condense; (*Maths.*) reduce.
kürzlich ['kyrtslɪç], *adv.* lately, recently, the other day.
Kurzschluß ['kurtsʃlus], *m.* (—sses, *pl.* —sse) short circuit.
Kurzschrift ['kurtsʃrɪft], *f.* (—, *no pl.*) shorthand.
kurzsichtig ['kurtszɪçtɪç], *adj.* short-sighted.
kurzum [kurts'um], *adv.* in short.
Kürzung ['kyrtsuŋ], *f.* (—, *pl.* —en) abbreviation, abridgment.
Kurzwaren ['kurtsva:rən], *f. pl.* haberdashery.
kurzweg [kurts've:k], *adv.* simply, offhand, briefly.
Kurzweil ['kurtsvaɪl], *f.* (—, *no pl.*) pastime.
kurzweilig ['kurtsvaɪlɪç], *adj.* amusing, diverting, entertaining.
kusch! [kuʃ], *excl.* (*to dogs*) lie down!
kuschen ['kuʃən], *v.n., v.r.* crouch, lie down.
Kuß [kus], *m.* (—sses, *pl.* ‍sse) kiss.
küssen ['kysən], *v.a., v.n., v.r.* kiss.
Küste ['kystə], *f.* (—, *pl.* —n) coast, shore.

134

Küstenstadt ['kystənʃtat], f. (—, pl. ̈e) seaside town.
Küster ['kystər], m. (—s, pl. —) sacristan, sexton, verger.
Kustos ['kustɔs], m. (—, pl. —oden) custodian; director of museum.
Kutschbock ['kutʃbɔk], m. (—s, pl. ̈e) box(-seat).
Kutsche ['kutʃə], f. (—, pl. —n) coach, carriage.
kutschieren [kut'ʃiːrən], v.n. drive a coach.
Kutte ['kutə], f. (—, pl. —n) cowl.
Kutter ['kutər], m. (—s, pl. —) (Naut.) cutter.
Kuvert [ku'vɛːr], n. (—s, pl. —s) envelope; (dinner) place laid.
kuvertieren [kuver'tiːrən], v.a. envelop, wrap.
Kux [kuks], m. (—es, pl. —e) share in a mining concern.
Kybernetik [kyːbɛr'neːtɪk], f. (—, no pl.) cybernetics.

L

L [ɛl], n. (—, pl. —) the letter L.
Lab [laːp], n. (—es, pl. —e) rennet.
labbern ['labərn], v.a., v.n. dribble, slobber; blab.
Labe ['laːbə], f. (—, no pl.) (Poet.) refreshment; comfort.
laben ['laːbən], v.a. refresh, restore, revive.
labil [la'biːl], adj. unstable.
Laborant [labo'rant], m. (—en, pl. —en) laboratory assistant.
Laboratorium [labora'toːrjum], n. (—s, pl. —rien) laboratory.
laborieren [labo'riːrən], v.n. experiment; suffer (from).
Labsal ['laːpzaːl], n. (—s, pl. —e) restorative, refreshment.
Labung ['laːbuŋ], f. (—, pl. —en) refreshment, comfort.
Lache ['laxə], f. (—, pl. —n) pool, puddle.
Lächeln ['lɛçəln], n. (—s, no pl.) smile; albernes —, smirk; höhnisches —, sneer.
lächeln ['lɛçəln], v.n. smile.
Lachen ['laxən], n. (—s, no pl.) laugh, laughter.
lachen ['laxən], v.n. laugh.
lächerlich ['lɛçərlɪç], adj. laughable, ridiculous; preposterous; ludicrous; sich — machen, make a fool of o.s.; etwas — machen, ridicule s.th.
Lachgas ['laxgaːs], n. (—es, no pl.) nitrous oxide, laughing-gas.
lachhaft ['laxhaft], adj. laughable, ridiculous.

Lachkrampf ['laxkrampf], m. (—es, pl. ̈e) hysterical laughter, a fit of laughter.
Lachs [laks], m. (—es, pl. —e) salmon.
Lachsalve ['laxzalvə], f. (—, pl. —n) peal of laughter.
Lack [lak], m. (—s, pl. —e) lac, lacquer, varnish.
lackieren [la'kiːrən], v.a. lacquer, varnish.
Lackmus ['lakmus], n. (—, no pl.) litmus.
Lackschuh ['lakʃuː], m. (—s, pl. —e) patent-leather shoe.
Lackwaren ['lakvaːrən], f. pl. japanned goods.
Lade ['laːdə], f. (—, pl. —n) box, chest, case, drawer.
Ladebaum ['laːdəbaum], m. derrick.
Ladefähigkeit ['laːdəfɛːɪçkaɪt], f. (—, pl. —en), carrying capacity, loading capacity; tonnage.
Ladegeld ['laːdəgɛlt], n. (—es, pl. —er) loading charges.
Laden ['laːdən], m. (—s, pl. ̈) (window) shutter; shop, store.
laden ['laːdən], v.a. irr. load; (Elec.) charge; (Law) summon; (fig.) incur.
Ladenhüter ['laːdənhyːtər], m. (—s, pl. —) unsaleable article.
Ladenpreis ['laːdənpraɪs], m. (—es, pl. —e) retail-price.
Ladentisch ['laːdəntɪʃ], m. (—es, pl. —e) counter.
Ladeschein ['laːdəʃaɪn], m. (—s, pl. —e) bill of lading.
Ladestock ['laːdəʃtɔk], m. (—es, pl. ̈e) ramrod.
Ladung ['laːduŋ], f. (—, pl. —en) loading, lading, freight; shipment, cargo; (gun) charge; (Law) summons.
Laffe ['lafə], m. (—n, pl. —n) fop.
Lage ['laːgə], f. (—, pl. —n) site, position, situation; state, condition; stratum, layer.
Lager ['laːgər], n. (—s, pl. —) couch, bed, divan; (Geol.) seam, vein; (Tech.) bearing; (Comm.) warehouse, store; camp.
Lageraufnahme ['laːgəraufnaːmə], f. (—, pl. —n) stock-taking, inventory.
Lager(bier) ['laːgər(biːr)], n. (—s, pl. —e) lager.
Lagergeld ['laːgərgɛlt], n. (—es, pl. —er) storage charge.
Lagerist [laːgə'rɪst], m. (—en, pl. —en) warehouse-clerk.
lagern ['laːgərn], v.a. store, warehouse.
Lagerstätte ['laːgərʃtɛtə], f. (—, pl. —n) couch, resting-place; camp site.
Lagerung ['laːgəruŋ], f. (—, pl. —en) encampment; storage; stratification.
Lagune [la'guːnə], f. (—, pl. —n) lagoon.
lahm [laːm], adj. lame, paralysed, crippled.
lahmen ['laːmən], v.n. be lame, limp.
lähmen ['lɛːmən], v.a. paralyse.
lahmlegen ['laːmleːgən], v.a. paralyse.

Lähmung

Lähmung ['lɛ:muŋ], *f.* (—, *pl.* —en) paralysis.

Laib [laip], *m.* (—es, *pl.* —e) (*bread*) loaf.

Laich [laiç], *m.* (—es, *pl.* —e) spawn.

laichen ['laiçən], *v.n.* spawn.

Laie ['laiə], *m.* (—n, *pl.* —n) layman, (*pl.*) laity.

Lakai [la'kai], *m.* (—en, *pl.* —en) lackey, flunkey, footman.

Lake ['la:kə], *f.* (—, *pl.* —n) brine, pickle.

Laken ['la:kən], *n.* (—s, *pl.* —) (*bed*) sheet.

lakonisch [la'ko:nɪʃ], *adj.* laconic.

Lakritze [la'krɪtsə], *f.* (—, *pl.* —n) liquorice.

lallen ['lalən], *v.a.*, *v.n.* stammer; babble.

Lama (1) ['la:ma:], *n.* (—s, *pl.* —s) (*animal*) llama.

Lama (2) ['la:ma:], *m.* (—s, *pl.* —s) (*priest*) lama.

lamentieren [lamɛn'ti:rən], *v.n.* lament, wail.

Lamm [lam], *n.* (—es, *pl.* ⸚er) (*Zool.*) lamb.

Lämmchen ['lɛmçən], *n.* (—s, *pl.* —) (*Zool.*) lambkin.

Lämmergeier ['lɛmərgaiər], *m.* (—s, *pl.* —) (*Orn.*) great bearded vulture.

Lampe ['lampə], *f.* (—, *pl.* —n) lamp.

Lampenfieber ['lampənfi:bər], *n.* (—s, *no pl.*) stage-fright.

Lampenputzer ['lampənputsər], *m.* (—s, *pl.* —) lamplighter.

Lampenschirm ['lampənʃɪrm], *m.* (—s, *pl.* —e) lampshade.

Lampion [lam'pjɔ̃], *m. & n.* (—s, *pl.* —s) Chinese lantern.

lancieren [lãˈsiːrən], *v.a.* thrust; launch.

Land [lant], *n.* (—es, *pl.* —e (*Poet.*) and ⸚er) land, country; state; ground, soil; *das Gelobte* —, the Promised Land; *an — gehen*, go ashore; *aufs — gehen*, go into the country.

Landadel ['lanta:dəl], *m.* (—s, *no pl.*) landed gentry.

Landarbeiter ['lantarbaitər], *m.* (—s, *pl.* —) farm-worker.

Landauer ['landauər], *m.* (—s, *pl.* —) landau.

Landebahn ['landəba:n], *f.* (—, *pl.* —en) (*Aviat.*) runway.

landen ['landən], *v.n.* (*aux. sein*) land, disembark; (*aircraft*) land, touch down.

Landenge ['lantɛŋə], *f.* (—, *pl.* —n) isthmus.

Ländereien ['lɛndəraiən], *f. pl.* landed property, estate.

Landeserzeugnis ['landəsɛrtsɔyknɪs], *n.* (—sses, *pl.* —sse) home produce.

Landesfürst ['landəsfyrst], *m.* (—en, *pl.* —en) sovereign.

Landesherr ['landəshɛr], *m.* (—n, *pl.* —en) (reigning) prince; sovereign.

Landeshoheit ['landəshohait], *f.* (—, *no pl.*) sovereignty.

Landeskirche ['landəskɪrçə], *f.* (—, *pl.* —n) established church; national church.

Landesschuld ['landəsʃult], *f.* (—, *no pl.*) national debt.

Landessprache ['landəsʃpra:xə], *f.* (—, *pl.* —n) vernacular.

Landestracht ['landəstraxt], *f.* (—, *pl.* —en) national costume.

landesüblich ['landəsy:plɪç], *adj.* conventional, usual, customary.

Landesverweisung ['landəsfɛrvaizuŋ], *f.* (—, *pl.* —en) exile, banishment.

landflüchtig ['lantflyçtɪç], *adj.* fugitive.

Landfrieden ['lantfri:dən], *m.* (—s, *no pl.*) King's (*or* Queen's) peace; (*medieval*) public peace.

Landgericht ['lantgərɪçt], *n.* (—es, *pl.* —e) district court; county court.

Landgraf ['lantgra:f], *m.* (—en, *pl.* —en) landgrave, count.

Landhaus ['lanthaus], *n.* (—es, *pl.* ⸚er) country house.

Landjunker ['lantjuŋkər], *m.* (—s, *pl.* —) country squire.

Landkarte ['lantkartə], *f.* (—, *pl.* —n) map.

landläufig ['lantlɔyfɪç], *adj.* customary, conventional.

ländlich ['lɛntlɪç], *adj.* rural, rustic.

Landmann ['lantman], *m.* (—es, *pl.* **Landleute**) rustic, peasant.

Landmesser ['lantmɛsər], *m.* (—s, *pl.* —) surveyor.

Landpartie ['lantparti:], *f.* (—, *pl.* —n) country excursion, picnic.

Landplage ['lantpla:gə], *f.* (—, *pl.* —n) scourge, calamity; *eine richtige* —, a public nuisance.

Landrat ['lantra:t], *m.* (—s, *pl.* ⸚e) district president *or* magistrate.

Landratte ['lantratə], *f.* (—, *pl.* —n) landlubber.

Landrecht ['lantrɛçt], *n.* (—es, *no pl.*) common law.

Landregen ['lantre:gən], *m.* (—s, *no pl.*) steady downpour; persistent rain.

Landschaft ['lantʃaft], *f.* (—, *pl.* —en) landscape.

landschaftlich ['lantʃaftlɪç], *adj.* scenic.

Landsknecht ['lantsknɛçt], *m.* (—es, *pl.* —e) mercenary; hired soldier.

Landsmann ['lantsman], *m.* (—es, *pl.* **Landsleute**) fellow-countryman, compatriot.

Landspitze ['lantʃpɪtsə], *f.* (—, *pl.* —n) cape, headland, promontory.

Landstraße ['lantʃtra:sə], *f.* (—, *pl.* —n) open road, main road, highway.

Landstreicher ['lantʃtraiçər], *m.* (—s, *pl.* —) vagabond, tramp, (*Am.*) hobo.

Landstrich ['lantʃtrɪç], *m.* (—es, *pl.* —e) tract of land.

Landsturm ['lantʃturm], *m.* (—s, *no pl.*) (*Milit.*) militia; Home Guard.

Landtag ['lantta:k], *m.* (—s, *pl.* —e) (*Parl.*) diet.

Landung ['landuŋ], *f.* (—, *pl.* —en) landing.

Landvermesser *see* **Landmesser**.

Landvogt ['lantfoːkt], *m.* (—es, *pl.* ⸚e) (provincial) governor.

Landweg ['lantveːk], *m.* (—s, *pl.* —e) overland route.

Landwehr ['lantveːr], *f.* (—, *pl.* —en) militia.

Landwirt ['lantvɪrt], *m.* (—s, *pl.* —e) farmer, husbandman.

Landwirtschaft ['lantvɪrtʃaft], *f.* (—, *no pl.*) agriculture.

Landzunge ['lanttsuŋə], *f.* (—, *pl.* —n) spit of land.

lang [laŋ], *adj.* long, tall. — *adv.*, *prep.* (*prec. by Acc.*) for, during, long.

langatmig ['laŋaːtmɪç], *adj.* long-winded.

lange ['laŋə], *adv.* a long time; *wie* —? how long? *so* — *wie*, as long as.

Länge ['lɛŋə], *f.* (—, *pl.* —n) length; (*Geog.*) longitude.

langen ['laŋən], *v.a.* reach, hand, give s.o. s.th. — *v.n.* suffice, be enough.

Längengrad ['lɛŋəngraːt], *m.* (—s, *pl.* —e) degree of longitude.

Längenkreis ['lɛŋənkraɪs], *m.* (—es, *pl.* —e) meridian.

Längenmaß ['lɛŋənmaːs], *n.* (—es, *pl.* —e) linear measure.

Langeweile ['laŋəvaɪlə], *f.* (—, *no pl.*) boredom, ennui.

Langfinger ['laŋfɪŋər], *m.* (—s, *pl.* —) pickpocket.

langjährig ['laŋjɛːrɪç], *adj.* of long standing.

Langlebigkeit ['laŋleːbɪçkaɪt], *f.* (—, *no pl.*) longevity.

länglich ['lɛŋlɪç], *adj.* oblong.

Langmut ['laŋmuːt], *f.* (—, *no pl.*) forbearance, patience.

längs [lɛŋs], *prep.* (*Genit.*, *Dat.*) along.

langsam ['laŋzaːm], *adj.* slow; deliberate.

längst [lɛŋst], *adv.* long ago, long since.

längstens ['lɛŋstəns], *adv.* at the longest; at the latest.

Languste [laŋˈgustə], *f.* (—, *pl.* —n) (*Zool.*) spiny lobster.

langweilen ['laŋvaɪlən], *v.a.*(*insep.*) bore, tire. — *v.r. sich* —, feel bored, be bored.

langwierig ['laŋviːrɪç], *adj.* lengthy, protracted, wearisome.

Lanze ['lantsə], *f.* (—, *pl.* —n) lance, spear; *eine* — *brechen*, take up the cudgels, stand up for (s.th. *or* s.o.).

Lanzenstechen ['lantsənʃtɛçən], *n.* (—s, *no pl.*) tournament.

Lanzette [lanˈtsɛtə], *f.* (—, *pl.* —n) lancet.

Lanzknecht ['lantsknɛçt], *m.* (—es, *pl.* —e) see **Landsknecht**.

Laos ['laːɔs], *n.* Laos.

Lappalie [laˈpaːljə], *f.* (—, *pl.* —n) trifle.

Lappen ['lapən], *m.* (—s, *pl.* —) rag, duster, patch; (*ear*) lobe.

Läpperschulden ['lɛpərʃuldən], *f. pl.* petty debts.

läppisch ['lɛpɪʃ], *adj.* silly, foolish, trifling.

Lappland ['lapland], *n.* Lapland.

Lärche ['lɛrçə], *f.* (—, *pl.* —n) (*Bot.*) larch.

Lärm [lɛrm], *m.* (—s, *no pl.*) noise, din.

lärmen ['lɛrmən], *v.n.* make a noise, brawl.

Larve ['larfə], *f.* (—, *pl.* —n) mask; (*Ent.*) grub, larva.

lasch [laʃ], *adj.* limp; insipid.

Lasche ['laʃə], *f.* (—, *pl.* —n) flap; (*shoe*) gusset, strip.

lassen ['lasən], *v.a.*, *v.n. irr.* let, allow, suffer, permit; leave; make, cause; order, command; desist.

läßlich ['lɛslɪç], *adj.* (*Eccl.*) venial (*sin*).

lässig ['lɛsɪç], *adj.* indolent, sluggish, inactive.

Lässigkeit ['lɛsɪçkaɪt], *f.* (—, *no pl.*) lassitude, inaction, indolence; negligence.

Last [last], *f.* (—, *pl.* —en) load, burden, weight, charge.

lasten ['lastən], *v.n.* be heavy; weigh (on).

lastenfrei ['lastənfraɪ], *adj.* unencumbered.

Laster ['lastər], *n.* (—s, *pl.* —) vice.

Lästerer ['lɛstərər], *m.* (—s, *pl.* —) slanderer, calumniator; blasphemer.

lasterhaft ['lastərhaft], *adj.* vicious, wicked; corrupt.

Lasterhöhle ['lastərhøːlə], *f.* (—, *pl.* —n) den of vice.

lästerlich ['lɛstərlɪç], *adj.* blasphemous.

lästern ['lɛstərn], *v.a.* slander, defame; blaspheme.

lästig ['lɛstɪç], *adj.* tiresome, troublesome.

Lasttier ['lasttiːr], *n.* (—es, *pl.* —e) beast of burden.

Lastwagen ['lastvaːgən], *m.* (—s, *pl.* —) lorry, (*Am.*) truck.

Lasur [laˈzuːr], *m.* (—s, *pl.* —e) lapis-lazuli; ultramarine.

Latein [laˈtaɪn], *n.* (—s, *no pl.*) Latin.

lateinisch [laˈtaɪnɪʃ], *adj.* Latin.

Laterne [laˈtɛrnə], *f.* (—, *pl.* —n) lantern; (*street*) lamp.

latschen ['laːtʃən], *v.n.* shuffle along.

Latte ['latə], *f.* (—, *pl.* —n) lath, batten; *eine lange* —, lanky person.

Lattich ['latɪç], *m.* (—s, *pl.* —e) lettuce.

Latz [lats], *m.* (—es, *pl.* ⸚e) flap, bib; pinafore.

lau [lau], *adj.* tepid, lukewarm, insipid; (*fig.*) half-hearted.

Laub [laup], *n.* (—es, *no pl.*) foliage, leaves.

Laube ['laubə], *f.* (—, *pl.* —n) arbour, summer-house.

Laubengang ['laubəngaŋ], *m.* (—es, *pl.* ⸚e) arcade, covered walk.

Laubfrosch ['laupfrɔʃ], *m.* (—es, *pl.* ⸚e) (*Zool.*) tree-frog.

Laubsäge ['laupzɛːgə], *f.* (—, *pl.* —n) fret-saw.

Lauch [laux], *m.* (—es, *no pl.*) (*Bot.*) leek.

Lauer ['lauər], *f.* (—, *no pl.*) ambush, hiding-place; *auf der* — *sein*, lie in wait.

lauern

lauern ['lauərn], v.n. lurk, lie in wait (for), watch (for).

Lauf [lauf], m. (—es, pl. ⁝e) course, run; running; operation; (*river*) current; (*gun*) barrel; (*fig.*) rein.

Laufbahn ['laufba:n], f. (—, pl. —en) career, *die medizinische — einschlagen*, enter upon a medical career.

Laufband ['laufbant], n. (—s, pl. ⁝er) (*baby*) rein, leading-string; (*Tech.*) conveyor-belt.

Laufbrücke ['laufbrykə], f. (—, pl. —n) gangway.

Laufbursche ['laufburʃə], m. (—n, pl. —n) errand-boy.

laufen ['laufən], v.n. irr. (*aux.* sein) run; walk; (*wheel*) turn; flow, trickle down.

laufend ['laufənt], adj. current.

Läufer ['lɔyfər], m. (—s, pl. —) runner; (*carpet*) rug; (*Chess*) bishop; (*Footb.*) half-back.

Lauffeuer ['lauffɔyər], n. (—s, no pl.) wildfire.

Laufgraben ['laufgra:bən], m. (—s, pl. ⁝) trench.

läufig ['lɔyfɪç], adj. (*animals*) ruttish.

Laufpaß ['laufpas], m. (—sses, no pl.) *den — geben*, give (s.o.) the sack.

Laufschritt ['laufʃrɪt], m. (—es, pl. —e) march; *im —*, at the double.

Laufzeit ['lauftsaɪt], f. (—, pl. —en) running-time; currency; (*animals*) rutting time.

Lauge ['laugə], f. (—, pl. —en) (*Chem.*) lye, alkali.

Lauheit ['lauhaɪt], f. (—, no pl.) tepidity, lukewarmness; (*fig.*) half-heartedness.

Laune ['launə], f. (—, pl. —n) humour, temper, mood, whim.

launenhaft ['launənhaft], adj. moody.

launig ['launɪç], adj. humorous.

launisch ['launɪʃ], adj. moody, fitful, bad-tempered.

Laus [laus], f. (—, pl. ⁝e) (*Zool.*) louse.

Lausbub ['lausbu:p], m. (—en, pl. —en) young scamp, rascal.

lauschen ['lauʃən], v.n. listen, eavesdrop.

Lausejunge ['lauzəjuŋə], m. (—n, pl. —n) rascal, lout.

lausig ['lauzɪç], adj. (*vulg.*) sordid, lousy.

laut [laut], adj. loud, noisy, audible, clamorous. — prep. (*Genit.*) as per, according to, in virtue of.

Laut [laut], m. (—es, pl. —e) sound.

lautbar ['lautba:r], adj. — *machen*, make known.

Laute ['lautə], f. (—, pl. —n) (*Mus.*) lute.

lauten ['lautən], v.n. purport, run, read.

läuten ['lɔytən], v.a., v.n. ring; toll; *es läutet*, the bell is ringing.

lauter ['lautər], adj. clear, pure; (*fig.*) single-minded; genuine; nothing but. — adv. merely.

Lauterkeit ['lautərkaɪt], f. (—, no pl.) clearness, purity; (*fig.*) single-mindedness, integrity.

läutern ['lɔytərn], v.a. clear, purify; refine.

Läuterung ['lɔytəruŋ], f. (—, pl. —en) clearing, purification; refinement.

lautieren [lau'ti:rən], v.a. read phonetically.

Lautlehre ['lautle:rə], f. (—, no pl.) phonetics.

lautlich ['lautlɪç], adj. phonetic.

lautlos ['lautlo:s], adj. mute, silent; noiseless.

Lautmalerei ['lautma:lərai], f. (—, no pl.) onomatopoeia.

Lautsprecher ['lautʃprɛçər], m. (—s, pl. —) loudspeaker.

Lautverschiebung ['lautfɛrʃi:buŋ], f. (—, pl. —en) sound shift.

lauwarm ['lauvarm], adj. lukewarm, tepid; (*fig.*) half-hearted.

Lava ['la:va], f. (—, no pl.) lava.

Lavendel [la'vɛndəl], m. (—s, no pl.) (*Bot.*) lavender.

lavieren [la'vi:rən], v.n. tack; (*fig.*) wangle.

Lawine [la'vi:nə], f. (—, pl. —n) avalanche.

lax [laks], adj. lax, loose.

Laxheit ['lakshait], f. (—, pl. —en) laxity.

Laxiermittel [lak'si:rmɪtəl], n. (—s, pl. —) laxative, aperient.

Lazarett [latsa'rɛt], n. (—s, pl. —e) infirmary, military hospital.

Lebemann ['le:bəman], m. (—es, pl. ⁝er) man about town.

Leben ['le:bən], n. (—s, pl. —) life; (*fig.*) existence; activity; animation, bustle, stir.

leben ['le:bən], v.n. live, be alive.

lebend ['le:bənt], adj. alive, living; (*language*) modern.

lebendig [le'bɛndɪç], adj. living, alive, quick.

Lebensanschauung ['le:bənsanʃauuŋ], f. (—, pl. —en) conception of life, philosophy of life.

Lebensart ['le:bənsa:rt], f. (—, no pl.) way of living; (*fig.*) behaviour; *gute —*, good manners.

lebensfähig ['le:bənsfɛ:ɪç], adj. capable of living, viable.

lebensgefährlich ['le:bənsgəfɛ:rlɪç], adj. perilous, extremely dangerous.

Lebensgeister ['le:bənsgaistər], m. pl. spirits.

lebensgroß ['le:bənsgro:s], adj. life-size.

lebenslänglich ['le:bənslɛŋlɪç], adj. lifelong, for life; *—e Rente*, life annuity.

Lebenslauf ['le:bənslauf], m. (—es, pl. ⁝e) curriculum vitae.

Lebensmittel ['le:bənsmɪtəl], n. pl. food, provisions, victuals.

lebensmüde ['le:bənsmy:də], adj. weary of life.

Lebensunterhalt ['le:bənsuntərhalt], m. (—s, no pl.) livelihood.

Lebenswandel ['le:bənsvandəl], m. (—s, no pl.) conduct, mode of life.

Lebensweise ['le:bənsvaɪzə], *f.* (—, *no pl.*) habits, way of life.

Leber ['le:bər], *f.* (—, *pl.* —n) liver; *frisch von der — weg*, frankly, without mincing matters.

Leberblümchen ['le:bərbly:mçən], *n.* (—s, *pl.* —) (*Bot.*) liverwort.

Leberfleck ['le:bərflɛk], *m.* (—s, *pl.* —e) mole.

Lebertran ['le:bərtra:n], *m.* (—s, *no pl.*) cod-liver oil.

Leberwurst ['le:bərvurst], *f.* (—, *pl.* ̈e) liver sausage.

Lebewesen ['le:bəve:zən], *n.* (—s, *pl.* —) living creature.

Lebewohl ['le:bəvo:l], *n.*, *excl.* farewell, good-bye; *— sagen*, bid farewell.

lebhaft ['le:phaft], *adj.* lively, vivacious, brisk, animated.

Lebkuchen ['le:pku:xən], *m.* (—s, *pl.* —) gingerbread.

Lebzeiten ['le:ptsaɪtən], *f. pl. zu — von* (*Genit.*), in the lifetime of.

lechzen ['lɛçtsən], *v.n.* be parched with thirst; *nach etwas —*, (*fig.*) long for s.th., pine for s.th.

Leck [lɛk], *n.* (—s, *pl.* —e) leak; *ein — bekommen*, spring a leak.

leck [lɛk], *adj.* leaky.

lecken ['lɛkən], *v.a.* lick, lap.

lecker ['lɛkər], *adj.* delicate, delicious, dainty.

Leckerbissen ['lɛkərbɪsən], *m.* (—s, *pl.* —) delicacy; dainty, tit-bit.

Leckerei [lɛkə'raɪ], *f.* (—, *pl.* —en) delicacy.

Leder ['le:dər], *n.* (—s, *no pl.*) leather.

ledern ['le:dərn], *adj.* (of) leather, leathery; (*fig.*) dull, boring.

ledig ['le:dɪç], *adj.* unmarried, single; (*fig.*) rid of, free from.

lediglich ['le:dɪklɪç], *adv.* merely, only, solely.

leer [le:r], *adj.* empty, void; blank; (*fig.*) hollow, futile, empty, vain, inane.

Leere ['le:rə], *f.* (—, *no pl.*) emptiness, void, vacuum.

leeren ['le:rən], *v.a.* empty, evacuate.

Leerlauf ['le:rlauf], *m.* (—s, *no pl.*) (*Motor.*) idling; (*gear*) neutral.

legalisieren [legali'zi:rən], *v.a.* legalise, authenticate.

Legat (1) [le'ga:t], *m.* (—en, *pl.* —en) legate.

Legat (2) [le'ga:t], *n.* (—s, *pl.* —e) legacy, bequest.

Legationsrat [lega'tsjo:nsra:t], *m.* (—s, *pl.* ̈e) counsellor in a legation.

legen ['le:gən], *v.a.* lay, put, place. *— v.r. sich —*, lie down; cease, subside.

Legende [le'gɛndə], *f.* (—, *pl.* —n) legend.

Legierung [lə'gi:ruŋ], *f.* (—, *pl.* —en) alloy.

Legion [le'gjo:n], *f.* (—, *pl.* —en) legion.

Legionär [le:gjo'nɛ:r], *m.* (—s, *pl.* —e) legionary.

legitim [legi'ti:m], *adj.* legitimate.

Legitimation [legitima'tsjo:n], *f.* (—, *pl.* —en) proof of identity.

legitimieren [legiti'mi:rən], *v.a.* legitimise. *— v.r. sich —*, prove o.'s identity.

Lehen ['le:ən], *n.* (—s, *pl.* —) fief; *zu — geben*, invest with, enfeoff; *zu — tragen*, hold in fee.

Lehensdienst *see* **Lehnsdienst**.

Lehenseid *see* **Lehnseid**.

Lehensmann *see* **Lehnsmann**.

Lehm [le:m], *m.* (—s, *no pl.*) loam, clay, mud.

lehmig ['le:mɪç], *adj.* clayey, loamy.

Lehne ['le:nə], *f.* (—, *pl.* —n) support, prop; (*chair*) back, arm-rest.

lehnen ['le:nən], *v.a.*, *v.n.* lean. *— v.r. sich — an*, lean against.

Lehnsdienst ['le:nsdi:nst], *m.* (—es, *pl.* —e) feudal service.

Lehnseid ['le:nsaɪt], *m.* (—es, *pl.* —e) oath of allegiance.

Lehnsmann ['le:nsman], *m.* (—es, *pl.* ̈er) feudal tenant, vassal.

Lehnstuhl ['le:nʃtu:l], *m.* (—s, *pl.* ̈e) armchair, easy chair.

Lehramt ['le:ramt], *n.* (—es, *pl.* ̈er) professorship; teaching post *or* profession.

Lehrbrief ['le:rbri:f], *m.* (—es, *pl.* —e) apprentice's indentures; certificate of apprenticeship.

Lehrbuch ['le:rbu:x], *n.* (—es, *pl.* ̈er) textbook, manual.

Lehre ['le:rə], *f.* (—, *pl.* —n) teaching, advice, rule, doctrine, dogma, moral; (*craft*) apprenticeship.

lehren ['le:rən], *v.a.* teach, inform, instruct; profess.

Lehrer ['le:rər], *m.* (—s, *pl.* —) teacher, instructor, schoolmaster.

Lehrgang ['le:rgaŋ], *m.* (—es, *pl.* ̈e) course (of instruction).

Lehrgegenstand ['le:rge:gənʃtant], *m.* (—es, *pl.* ̈e) subject of instruction; branch of study.

Lehrgeld ['le:rgɛlt], *n.* (—es, *pl.* —er) premium for apprenticeship; *— zahlen*, (*fig.*) pay for o.'s experience.

Lehrkörper ['le:rkœrpər], *m.* (—s, *no pl.*) teaching staff; (*Univ.*) faculty.

Lehrling ['le:rlɪŋ], *m.* (—s, *pl.* —e) apprentice.

Lehrmädchen ['le:rmɛ:tçən], *n.* (—s, *pl.* —) girl apprentice.

Lehrmeister ['le:rmaɪstər], *m.* (—s, *pl.* —) teacher, instructor, master.

Lehrmittel ['le:rmɪtəl], *n.* (—s, *pl.* —) teaching appliance *or* aid.

lehrreich ['le:rraɪç], *adj.* instructive.

Lehrsatz ['le:rzats], *m.* (—es, *pl.* ̈e) tenet, dogma, rule; (*Maths.*) theorem.

Lehrstuhl ['le:rʃtu:l], *m.* (—s, *pl.* ̈e) (*Univ.*) chair; professorship.

Lehrzeit ['le:rtsaɪt], *f.* (—, *pl.* —en) apprenticeship.

Leib [laɪp], *m.* (—es, *pl.* —er) body; abdomen; womb.

Leibarzt ['laɪpa:rtst], *m.* (—es, *pl.* ̈e) court surgeon.

139

Leibbinde

Leibbinde ['laɪpbɪndə], *f.* (—, *pl.* —n) abdominal belt.

Leibchen ['laɪpçən], *n.* (—s, *pl.* —) bodice, corset; vest.

leibeigen [laɪp'aɪgən], *adj.* in bondage, in thraldom, in serfdom.

Leibeserbe ['laɪbəsɛrbə], *m.* (—n, *pl.* —n) heir, descendant, offspring; (*pl.*) issue.

Leibesfrucht ['laɪbəsfruxt], *f.* (—, *pl.* ⸚e) embryo, foetus.

Leibeskraft ['laɪbəskraft], *f.* (—, *pl.* ⸚e) bodily strength; *aus* —en, with might and main.

Leibesübung ['laɪbəsyːbuŋ], *f.* (—, *pl.* —en) physical exercise; (*pl.*) gymnastic exercises.

Leibgericht ['laɪpgərɪçt], *n.* (—s, *pl.* —e) favourite dish.

leibhaftig [laɪp'haftɪç], *adj.* real, incarnate, in person.

leiblich ['laɪplɪç], *adj.* bodily, corporeal.

Leibrente ['laɪprɛntə], *f.* (—, *pl.* —n) life-annuity.

Leibschmerzen ['laɪpʃmɛrtsən], *m. pl.* stomach-ache.

Leibspeise ['laɪpʃpaɪzə], *f.* (—, *pl.* —n) favourite dish.

Leibwache ['laɪpvaxə], *f.* (—, *no pl.*) body-guard.

Leibwäsche ['laɪpvɛʃə], *f.* (—, *no pl.*) underwear.

Leiche ['laɪçə], *f.* (—, *pl.* —n) (dead) body, corpse; (*dial.*) funeral.

Leichenbegängnis ['laɪçənbəgɛŋnɪs], *n.* (—ses, *pl.* —se) funeral, burial, interment.

Leichenbeschauer ['laɪçənbəʃauər], *m.* (—s, *pl.* —) coroner.

Leichenbestatter ['laɪçənbəʃtater], *m.* (—s, *pl.* —) undertaker; (*Am.*) mortician.

leichenhaft ['laɪçənhaft], *adj.* corpselike, cadaverous.

Leichenschau ['laɪçənʃau], *f.* (—, *no pl.*) post mortem (examination), (coroner's) inquest.

Leichentuch ['laɪçəntuːx], *n.* (—es, *pl.* ⸚er) shroud, pall.

Leichenverbrennung ['laɪçənfɛrbrɛnuŋ], *f.* (—, *pl.* —en) cremation.

Leichenwagen ['laɪçənvaːgən], *m.* (—s, *pl.* —) hearse.

Leichenzug ['laɪçəntsuːk], *m.* (—es, *pl.* ⸚e) funeral procession.

Leichnam ['laɪçnaːm], *m.* (—s, *pl.* —e) (dead) body, corpse.

leicht [laɪçt], *adj.* light; slight; weak; easy.

leichtfertig ['laɪçtfɛrtɪç], *adj.* frivolous, irresponsible.

leichtgläubig ['laɪçtglɔybɪç], *adj.* credulous, gullible.

leichthin ['laɪçthɪn], *adv.* lightly.

Leichtigkeit ['laɪçtɪçkaɪt], *f.* (—, *no pl.*) ease, facility.

Leichtsinn ['laɪçtzɪn], *m.* (—s, *no pl.*) thoughtlessness; carelessness; frivolity.

Leid [laɪt], *n.* (—es, *no pl.*) sorrow, grief; harm, hurt; *einem etwas zu* —*e tun*, harm s.o.

leid [laɪt], *adj.* *es tut mir* —, I am sorry; *du tust mir* —, I am sorry for you.

Leiden ['laɪdən], *n.* (—s, *pl.* —) suffering, misfortune; (*illness*) affliction, complaint; *das* — *Christi*, the Passion.

leiden ['laɪdən], *v.a., v.n. irr.* suffer, bear, endure, undergo.

Leidenschaft ['laɪdənʃaft], *f.* (—, *pl.* —en) passion.

leider ['laɪdər], *adv.* unfortunately.

leidig ['laɪdɪç], *adj.* tiresome, unpleasant.

leidlich ['laɪtlɪç], *adj.* tolerable, moderate.

leidtragend ['laɪttraːgənt], *adj.* in mourning.

Leidtragende ['laɪttraːgəndə], *m. or f.* (—n, *pl.* —n) mourner.

Leidwesen ['laɪtveːzən], *n.* (—s, *no pl.*) *zu meinem* —, to my regret.

Leier ['laɪər], *f.* (—, *pl.* —n) lyre.

Leierkasten ['laɪərkastən], *m.* (—s, *pl.* ⸚) barrel organ.

leiern ['laɪərn], *v.n.* drone, drawl on.

leihen ['laɪən], *v.a. irr. einem etwas* —, lend s.o. s.th.; *von einem etwas* —, borrow s.th. from s.o.

Leim [laɪm], *m.* (—s, *no pl.*) glue; *einem auf den* — *gehen*, be taken in by s.o., fall for s.th.

Leimfarbe ['laɪmfarbə], *f.* (—, *pl.* —en) water-colour, distemper.

Lein [laɪn], *m.* (—s, *pl.* —e) linseed, flax.

Leine ['laɪnə], *f.* (—, *pl.* —n) line, cord.

Leinen ['laɪnən], *n.* (—s, *no pl.*) linen.

Leinöl ['laɪnøːl], *n.* (—s, *no pl.*) linseed oil.

Leintuch ['laɪntuːx], *n.* (—es, *pl.* ⸚er) linen sheet, sheeting.

Leinwand ['laɪnvant], *f.* (—, *no pl.*) linen, sheeting; (*Art*) canvas; (*film*) screen.

leise ['laɪzə], *adj.* low, soft, gentle, faint, slight; delicate.

Leiste ['laɪstə], *f.* (—, *pl.* —n) ledge, border; groin.

Leisten ['laɪstən], *m.* (—s, *pl.* —) (*shoe*) last, form.

leisten ['laɪstən], *v.a.* do, perform; accomplish; *ich kann es mir nicht* —, I cannot afford it.

Leistenbruch ['laɪstənbrux], *m.* (—es, *pl.* ⸚e) hernia, rupture.

Leistung ['laɪstuŋ], *f.* (—, *pl.* —en) performance, accomplishment, achievement.

leistungsfähig ['laɪstuŋsfɛːɪç], *adj.* efficient.

leiten ['laɪtən], *v.a.* lead, guide, manage; preside over.

Leiter (1) ['laɪtər], *m.* (—s, *pl.* —) leader, manager; conductor; head.

Leiter (2) ['laɪtər], *f.* (—, *pl.* —n) ladder.

Leiterwagen ['laɪtərvaːgən], *m.* (—s, *pl.* —) rack-wagon; (*Austr.*) small hand-cart.

Liebhaberin

Leitfaden ['laItfa:dən], *m.* (—s, *pl.* ∶) (*book*) manual, textbook, guide.

Leitstern ['laItʃtern], *m.* (—s, *pl.* —e) pole-star; (*fig.*) lodestar, guiding star.

Leitung ['laItuŋ], *f.* (—, *pl.* —en) management, direction; (*Elec.*) lead, connection; line; . (water- *or* gas-) main(s); pipeline; *eine lange — haben*, be slow in the uptake.

Leitungsvermögen ['laItuŋsfɛrmø:-gən], *n.* (—s, *no pl.*) conductivity.

Leitwerk ['laItverk], *n.* (—s, *no pl.*) (*Aviat.*) tail unit.

Lektion [lɛkts'jo:n], *f.* (—, *pl.* —en) lesson; *einem eine — geben*, lecture s.o.

Lektor ['lɛktɔr], *m.* (—s, *pl.* —en) publisher's reader; teacher, lector.

Lektüre [lɛk'ty:rə], *f.* (—, *pl.* —n) reading matter, books.

Lende ['lɛndə], *f.* (—, *pl.* —n) (*Anat.*) loin.

lendenlahm ['lɛndənla:m], *adj.* weak-kneed, lame.

lenkbar ['lɛŋkba:r], *adj.* dirigible, manageable, tractable, governable.

lenken ['lɛŋkən], *v.a.* drive, steer; (*fig.*) direct, rule, manage.

Lenkstange ['lɛŋkʃtaŋə], *f.* (—, *pl.* —n) connecting-rod; (*bicycle*) handle-bar.

Lenz [lɛnts], *m.* (—es, *pl.* —e) (*Poet.*) spring.

Lepra ['le:pra], *f.* (—, *no pl.*) leprosy.

Lerche ['lɛrçə], *f.* (—, *pl.* —n) (*Orn.*) lark, skylark.

lernbegierig ['lɛrnbəgi:riç], *adj.* studious, eager to learn.

lernen ['lɛrnən], *v.a.* learn; study; *einen kennen —*, make s.o.'s acquaintance; *auswendig —*, learn by heart.

Lesart ['le:sa:rt], *f.* (—, *pl.* —en) reading, version.

lesbar ['le:sba:r], *adj.* legible; readable.

Lese ['le:zə], *f.* (—, *pl.* —n) gathering (of fruit); vintage.

lesen ['le:zən], *v.a. irr.* gather; glean; read; *die Messe —*, celebrate *or* say mass; *über etwas —*, (*Univ.*) lecture on s.th.

lesenswert ['le:zənsvert], *adj.* worth reading.

Leser ['le:zər], *m.* (—s, *pl.* —) gatherer, gleaner; reader.

leserlich ['le:zərliç], *adj.* legible.

Lettland ['lɛtlant], *n.* Latvia.

letzen ['lɛtsən], *v.a.* (*Poet.*) comfort, cheer, refresh.

letzt [lɛtst], *adj.* last, extreme, ultimate, final.

letztens ['lɛtstəns], *adv.* lastly, in the end.

letztere ['lɛtstərə], *adj.* latter.

letzthin ['lɛtsthIn], *adv.* (*rare*) lately, the other day, recently.

Leu [lɔy], *m.* (—en, *pl.* —en) (*Poet.*) lion.

Leuchte ['lɔyçtə], *f.* (—, *pl.* —n) light, lamp, lantern; (*fig.*) luminary, star.

leuchten ['lɔyçtən], *v.n.* light, shine.

leuchtend ['lɔyçtənt], *adj.* shining, bright; luminous.

Leuchter ['lɔyçtər], *m.* (—s, *pl.* —) candlestick, candelabrum.

Leuchtrakete ['lɔyçtrake:tə], *f.* (—, *pl.* —n) Roman candle; flare.

Leuchtturm ['lɔyçtturm], *m.* (—s, *pl.* ∶e) lighthouse.

leugnen ['lɔygnən], *v.a.* deny, disclaim; *nicht zu —*, undeniable.

Leumund ['lɔymunt], *m.* (—es, *no pl.*) renown, reputation.

Leute ['lɔytə], *pl.* persons, people, men; servants, domestic staff.

Leutnant ['lɔytnant], *m.* (—s, *pl.* —s) lieutenant.

leutselig ['lɔytze:liç], *adj.* affable, friendly; condescending.

Levkoje [lɛf'ko:jə], *f.* (—, *pl.* —n) (*Bot.*) stock.

Lexikon ['lɛksikɔn], *n.* (—s, *pl.* —s, —ka) dictionary, lexicon, encyclopaedia.

Libanon ['li:banɔn], *m.* Lebanon.

Libelle [li'bɛlə], *f.* (—, *pl.* —n) (*Ent.*) dragonfly.

Liberia [li'be:rja], *n.* Liberia.

Libyen ['li:b'jən], *n.* Libya.

Licht [lIçt], *n.* (—es, *pl.* —er) light, candle; luminary.

licht [lIçt], *adj.* light, clear, open.

Lichtbild ['lIçtbIlt], *n.* (—es, *pl.* —er) photograph.

Lichtbrechung ['lIçtbrɛçuŋ], *f.* (—, *pl.* —en) refraction of light.

lichten ['lIçtən], *v.a.* clear, thin; *den Anker —*, weigh anchor.

lichterloh ['lIçtərlo:], *adv.* blazing, ablaze.

Lichthof ['lIçtho:f], *m.* (—s, *pl.* ∶e) well of a court, quadrangle.

Lichtmeß ['lIçtmes], *f.* (—, *no pl.*) (*Eccl.*) Candlemas.

Lichtschirm ['lIçtʃIrm], *m.* (—s, *pl.* —e) screen, lamp-shade.

Lichtspieltheater ['lIçtʃpi:ltea:tər], *n.* (—s, *pl.* —) cinema.

Lichtung ['lIçtuŋ], *f.* (—, *pl.* —en) glade, clearing.

Lid [li:t], *n.* (—s, *pl.* —er) eye-lid.

lieb [li:p], *adj.* dear; beloved; good; *das ist mir —*, I am glad of it; *der —e Gott*, God; *unsere —e Frau*, Our Lady; *bei einem — Kind sein*, be a favourite with s.o., curry favour with s.o.

liebäugeln ['li:pɔygəln], *v.n. insep.* ogle.

Liebchen ['li:pçən], *n.* (—s, *pl.* —) sweetheart, love, darling.

Liebe ['li:bə], *f.* (—, *no pl.*) love.

Liebelei [li:bə'laI], *f.* (—, *pl.* —en) flirtation.

lieben ['li:bən], *v.a.* love, like, be fond of.

liebenswürdig ['li:bənsvyrdIç], *adj.* amiable, kind, charming.

lieber ['li:bər], *adv.* rather, better, sooner; *etwas — tun*, prefer to do s.th.

Liebhaber ['li:pha:bər], *m.* (—s, *pl.* —) lover; (*fig.*) amateur, dilettante; (*Theat.*) leading man.

Liebhaberin ['li:phabərIn], *f.* leading lady.

141

liebkosen ['li:pko:zən], *v.a. insep.* fondle, caress.

lieblich ['li:pliç], *adj.* lovely, charming, sweet.

Liebling ['li:pliŋ], *m.* (—s, *pl.* —e) darling, favourite.

lieblos ['li:plo:s], *adj.* hard-hearted; unkind.

Liebreiz ['li:praits], *m.* (—es, *no pl.*) charm, attractiveness.

liebreizend ['li:praitsənt], *adj.* charming.

Liebschaft ['li:pʃaft], *f.* (—, *pl.* —en) love affair.

Lied [li:t], *n.* (—es, *pl.* —er) song, air, tune; *geistliches* —, hymn.

liederlich ['li:dərliç], *adj.* careless, slovenly; dissolute, debauched; —*es Leben*, profligacy.

Lieferant [li:fə'rant], *m.* (—en, *pl.* —en) supplier, purveyor, contractor; *Eingang für* —*en*, tradesmen's entrance.

liefern ['li:fərn], *v.a.* deliver, furnish, supply.

Lieferschein ['li:fərʃain], *m.* (—s, *pl.* —e) delivery note.

liegen ['li:gən], *v.n. irr.* lie; be situated; *es liegt mir daran*, it is of importance to me, I have it at heart; *es liegt mir nichts daran*, it is of no consequence to me.

Liegenschaft ['li:gənʃaft], *f.* (—, *pl.* —en) landed property, real estate.

Liga ['li:ga:], *f.* (—, *pl.* —gen) league.

Liguster [li'gustər], *m.* (—s, *no pl.*) privet.

liieren [li'i:rən], *v.r.* (*aux.* haben) *sich* — *mit*, unite with, combine with.

Likör [li'kø:r], *m.* (—s, *pl.* —e) liqueur.

lila ['li:la:] *adj.* (*colour*) lilac.

Lilie ['li:ljə], *f.* (—, *pl.* —n) (*Bot.*) lily.

Limonade [limo'na:də], *f.* (—, *pl.* —n) lemonade.

lind [lint], *adj.* soft, gentle, mild.

Linde ['lində], *f.* (—, *pl.* —n) (*Bot.*) lime-tree, linden.

lindern ['lindərn], *v.a.* soften, assuage, mitigate, soothe, allay.

Lindwurm ['lintvurm], *m.* (—s, *pl.* ·er) (*Poet.*) dragon.

Lineal [line'a:l], *n.* (—s, *pl.* —e) ruler, rule.

Linie ['li:njə], *f.* (—, *pl.* —n) line; lineage, descent; *in erster* —, in the first place.

Linienschiff ['li:njənʃif], *n.* (—es, *pl.* —e) (*Naut.*) liner.

lin(i)ieren [lin'(j)i:rən], *v.a.* rule.

linkisch ['linkiʃ], *adj.* awkward, clumsy.

links [liŋks], *adv.* to the left, on the left-hand side; —*um!* left about turn!

Linnen ['linən], *n.* (—s, *no pl.*) (*Poet.*) linen.

Linse ['linzə], *f.* (—, *pl.* —n) (*vegetable*) lentil; (*optical*) lens.

linsenförmig ['linzənfœrmiç], *adj.* lens-shaped.

Linsengericht ['linzəngəriçt], *n.* (—s, *pl.* —e) (*Bibl.*) mess of pottage.

Lippe ['lipə], *f.* (—, *pl.* —n) lip; (*coll.*) *eine* — *riskieren*, be cheeky.

Lippenlaut ['lipənlaut], *m.* (—s, *pl.* —e) (*Phonet.*) labial.

Lippenstift ['lipənʃtift], *m.* (—s, *pl.* —e) lipstick.

liquidieren [likvi'di:rən], *v.a.* liquidate, wind up, settle; charge.

lispeln ['lispəln], *v.n.* lisp.

Lissabon [lisa'bon], *n.* Lisbon.

List [list], *f.* (—, *pl.* —en) cunning, craft; trick, stratagem, ruse.

Liste ['listə], *f.* (—, *pl.* —n) list, roll, catalogue.

listig ['listiç], *adj.* cunning, crafty, sly.

Listigkeit ['listiçkait], *f.* (—, *no pl.*) slyness, craftiness.

Litanei [lita'nai], *f.* (—, *pl.* —en) litany.

Litauen ['litauən], *n.* Lithuania.

Liter ['li:tər], *m. & n.* (—s, *pl.* —) litre.

literarisch [litə'ra:riʃ], *adj.* literary.

Literatur [litəra'tu:r], *f.* (—, *pl.* —en) literature, letters.

Litfaßsäule ['litfaszoylə], *f.* (—, *pl.* —n) advertisement pillar.

Liturgie [litur'gi:], *f.* (—, *pl.* —n) liturgy.

Litze ['litsa], *f.* (—, *pl.* —n) lace, braid, cord; (*Elec.*) flex.

Livland ['li:flant], *n.* Livonia.

Livree [li'vre:], *f.* (—, *pl.* —n) livery.

Lizenz [li'tsents], *f.* (—, *pl.* —en) licence.

Lob [lo:p], *n.* (—es, *no pl.*) praise, commendation.

loben ['lo:bən], *v.a.* praise, commend.

lobesam ['lo:bəza:m], *adj.* (*Poet.*) worthy, honourable.

Lobgesang ['lo:pgəzaŋ], *m.* (—s, *pl.* ·e) hymn of praise.

Lobhudelei [lo:phu:də'lai], *f.* (—, *pl.* —en) adulation, flattery, toadying.

löblich ['lø:pliç], *adj.* laudable, commendable, meritorious.

lobpreisen ['lo:ppraizən], *v.a. insep.* eulogise, extol.

Lobrede ['lo:pre:də], *f.* (—, *pl.* —n) panegyric, eulogy.

Loch [lɔx], *n.* (—es, *pl.* ·er) hole.

Lochbohrer ['lɔxbo:rər], *m.* (—s, *pl.*—) auger.

lochen ['lɔxən], *v.a.* perforate, punch.

Locher ['lɔxər], *m.* (—s, *pl.* —) perforator, punch.

löcherig ['lœçəriç], *adj.* full of holes.

Lochmeißel ['lɔxmaisəl], *m.* (—s, *pl.* —) mortice-chisel.

Locke ['lɔkə], *f.* (—, *pl.* —n) curl, lock, ringlet, tress.

locken ['lɔkən], *v.a.* allure, decoy, entice.

locker ['lɔkər], *adj.* loose; slack; spongy; dissolute; *nicht* — *lassen*, stick to o.'s guns.

lockern ['lɔkərn], *v.a.* loosen.

lockig ['lɔkiç], *adj.* curled, curly.

Lockmittel ['lɔkmitəl], *n.* (—s, *pl.* —) inducement, lure, bait.

Lockspeise ['lɔkʃpaizə], *f.* (—, *pl.* —n) lure, bait.

Lotrechtstarter

Lockung ['lɔkʊŋ], f. (—, pl. —en) allurement, enticement.

Lockvogel ['lɔkfo:gəl], m. (—s, pl. ⁖) decoy-bird.

Loden ['lo:dən], m. (—s, pl. —) coarse cloth, frieze.

lodern ['lo:dərn], v.n. blaze, flame.

Löffel ['lœfəl], m. (—s, pl. —) spoon; (animal) ear; einen über den — barbieren, take s.o. in.

Logarithmus [loga'rɪtmʊs], m. (—, pl. —men) logarithm.

Logbuch ['lɔkbu:x], n. (—es, pl. ⁖er) logbook.

Loge ['lo:ʒə], f. (—, pl. —n) (Theat.) box; (Freemasonry) lodge.

Logenschließer ['lo:ʒənʃli:sər], m. (—s, pl. —) (Theat.) attendant.

logieren [lo'ʒi:rən], v.n. board (with).

Logis [lo'ʒi:], n. (—, pl. —) lodgings.

logisch ['lo:gɪʃ], adj. logical.

Lohe ['lo:hə], f. (—, pl. —n) tanning bark; flame.

Lohgerber ['lo:gɛrbər], m. (—s, pl. —) tanner.

Lohn [lo:n], m. (—s, pl. ⁖e) wages, pay; reward; recompense.

lohnen ['lo:nən], v.a. reward, recompense, remunerate; pay wages to; es lohnt sich nicht, it is not worth while.

Lohnstopp ['lo:nʃtɔp], m. (—s, pl. —s) pay pause, wage freeze.

Löhnung ['lø:nʊŋ], f. (—, pl. —en) pay, payment.

Lokal [lo'ka:l], n. (—s, pl —e) locality, premises; inn, pub, café.

lokalisieren [lokali'zi:rən], v.a. localise.

Lokalität [lokali'tɛ:t], f. (—, pl. —en) see Lokal.

Lokomotive [lokomo'ti:və], f. (—, pl. —n) (Railw.) locomotive, engine.

Lokomotivführer [lokomo'ti:ffy:rər], m. (—s, pl. —) (Railw.) engine-driver.

Lombard [lɔm'bart], m. (—s, pl. —e) deposit-bank, loan bank.

Lombardei [lɔmbar'dai], f. Lombardy.

Lorbeer ['lɔrbe:r], m. (—s, pl. —en) laurel.

Lorbeerbaum ['lɔrbe:rbaum], m. (—s, pl. ⁖e) laurel-tree, bay-tree.

Lorbeerspiritus ['lɔrbe:rʃpi:ritus], m. (—, no pl.) bay rum.

Lorgnon [lɔrn'jɔ̃], n. (—s, pl. —s) monocle, eye-glass.

Los [lo:s], n. (—es, pl. —e) share, ticket; lot, fate; das große —, first prize.

los [lo:s], adj. loose, untied; free from, released from, rid of; (Am.) quit of; was ist los? what is going on? what's the matter? etwas — werden, get rid of s.th.; schieß los! fire away!

lösbar ['lø:sba:r], adj. (question, riddle) soluble.

losbinden ['lo:sbɪndən], v.a. irr. untie, unbind, loosen.

losbrechen ['lo:sbrɛçən], v.a. irr. break off. — v.n. (aux. sein) break loose.

Löschblatt ['lœʃblat], n. (—es, pl. ⁖er) blotting-paper.

Löscheimer ['lœʃaimər], m. (—s, pl. —) fire-bucket.

löschen ['lœʃən], v.a. put out; extinguish; (debt) cancel; (writing) efface, blot; (freight) (Naut.) unload; (thirst) quench.

Löschpapier ['lœʃpapi:r], n. (—s, no pl.) blotting-paper.

Löschung ['lœʃʊŋ], f. (—, pl. —en) (freight) (Naut.) discharging, landing, unloading.

losdrücken ['lo:sdrykən], v.n. discharge, fire.

lose ['lo:zə], adj. loose, slack; (fig.) dissolute; —s Maul, malicious tongue.

Lösegeld ['lø:zəgɛlt], n. (—es, pl. —er) ransom.

losen ['lo:zən], v.n. draw lots.

lösen ['lø:zən], v.a. loosen, untie; absolve, free, deliver; dissolve; solve; (relations) break off; (tickets) take, buy.

losgehen ['lo:sge:ən], v.n. irr. (aux. sein) begin; (gun) go off; auf einen —, go for s.o.; jetzt kann's —, now for it.

loskaufen ['lo:skaufən], v.a. redeem, ransom.

loskommen ['lo:skɔmən], v.n. irr. (aux. sein) come loose; von etwas —, get rid of s.th.

löslich ['lø:slɪç], adj. (Chem.) soluble.

loslösen ['lo:slø:zən], v.a. detach.

losmachen ['lo:smaxən], v.a. free from. — v.r. sich — von, disengage o.s. from.

losreißen ['lo:sraisən], v.a. irr. pull away, separate. — v.n. (aux. sein), break loose. — v.r. sich — von, tear o.s. away from.

lossagen ['lo:sza:gən], v.r. sich — von, renounce s.th., dissociate o.s. from s.th.

losschlagen ['lo:sʃla:gən], v.a. knock loose; let fly; (fig.) sell, dispose of.

lossprechen ['lo:sʃprɛçən], v.a. irr. (Eccl.) absolve; (Law) acquit.

lossteuern ['lo:sʃtɔyərn], v.n. — auf, make for.

Losung ['lo:zuŋ], f. (—, pl. —en) watchword, motto, password, slogan.

Lösung ['lø:zuŋ], f. (—, pl. —en) loosening; solution.

losziehen ['lo:stsi:ən], v.n. irr. (Mil.) set out; gegen einen —, inveigh against s.o.; (fig., coll.) run s.o. down.

Lot [lo:t], n. (—es, pl. —e) lead, plummet; (weight) half an ounce; (Maths.) perpendicular (line).

Löteisen ['lø:taizən], n. (—s, pl. —) soldering iron.

loten ['lo:tən], v.a., v.n. (Naut.) take soundings, plumb.

löten ['lø:tən], v.a. solder.

Lothringen ['lo:trɪŋən], n. Lorraine.

Lötkolben ['lø:tkɔlbən], m. (—s, pl. —) soldering iron.

Lotleine ['lo:tlainə], f. (—, pl. —n) sounding-line.

Lotrechtstarter ['lo:trɛçtʃtartər], m. (—s, pl. —) (Aviat.) vertical take-off plane (V.T.O.L.).

143

Lötrohr

Lötrohr ['lø:tro:r], *n.* (—s, *pl.* —e) soldering-pipe.

Lotse ['lo:tsə], *m.* (—n, *pl.* —n) (*Naut.*) pilot.

Lotterbett ['lɔtərbɛt], *n.* (—es, *pl.* —en) bed of idleness; (*obs.*) couch.

Lotterie [lɔtə'ri:], *f.* (—, *pl.* —n) lottery, sweep-stake.

Lotterleben ['lɔtərle:bən], *n.* (—s, *no pl.*) dissolute life.

Löwe ['lø:və], *m.* (—n, *pl.* —n) (*Zool.*) lion.

Löwenbändiger ['lø:vənbɛndigər], *m.* (—s, *pl.* —) lion tamer.

Löwengrube ['lø:vəngru:bə], *f.* (—, *pl.* —n) lion's den.

Löwenmaul ['lø:vənmaul], *n.* (—s, *no pl.*) (*Bot.*) snapdragon.

Löwenzahn ['lø:vəntsa:n], *m.* (—s, *no pl.*) (*Bot.*) dandelion.

Löwin ['lø:vɪn], *f.* (—, *pl.* —nen) (*Zool.*) lioness.

Luchs [luks], *m.* (—es, *pl.* —e) lynx.

Lücke ['lykə], *f.* (—, *pl.* —n) gap, breach; (*fig.*) omission, defect, blank.

Lückenbüßer ['lykənby:sər], *m.* (—s, *pl.* —) stop-gap, stand-in.

lückenhaft ['lykənhaft], *adj.* fragmentary, incomplete, imperfect.

Luder ['lu:dər], *n.* (—s, *pl.* —) (*rare*) carrion; (*vulg.*) beast, trollop; *dummes* —, silly ass, fathead.

Luderleben ['lu:dərle:bən], *n.* (—s, *no pl.*) dissolute life.

ludern ['lu:dərn], *v.n.* lead a dissolute life.

Luft [luft], *f.* (—, *pl.* ̈e) air.

Luftbrücke ['luftbrykə], *f.* (—, *no pl.*) air-lift.

Lüftchen ['lyftçən], *n.* (—s, *pl.* —) gentle breeze.

luftdicht ['luftdɪçt], *adj.* airtight.

Luftdruck ['luftdruk], *m.* (—s, *no pl.*) air pressure, atmospheric pressure; blast.

Luftdruckmesser ['luftdrukmɛsər], *m.* (—s, *pl.* —) barometer, pressure-gauge.

lüften ['lyftən], *v.a.* air, ventilate.

luftförmig ['luftfœrmɪç], *adj.* gaseous.

luftig ['luftɪç], *adj.* airy, windy.

Luftklappe ['luftklapə], *f.* (—, *pl.* —n) air-valve.

Luftkurort ['luftku:rɔrt], *m.* (—s, *pl.* —e) health resort.

Luftlinie ['luftli:njə], *f.* (—, *pl.* —n) bee-line; *in der* —, as the crow flies; (*Aviat.*) airline.

Luftloch ['luftlɔx], *n.* (—s, *pl.* ̈er) air-pocket.

Luftraum ['luftraum], *m.* (—s, *no pl.*) atmosphere; air space.

Luftröhre ['luftrø:rə], *f.* (—, *pl.* —n) windpipe.

Luftschiff ['luftʃɪf], *n.* (—es, *pl.* —e) air-ship.

Luftschiffahrt ['luftʃifa:rt], *f.* (—, *no pl.*) aeronautics.

Luftspiegelung ['luftʃpi:gəluŋ], *f.* (—, *pl.* —en) mirage.

Luftsprung ['luftʃpruŋ], *m.* (—s, *pl.* ̈e) caper, gambol; *̈e machen*, caper, gambol.

Lüftung ['lyftuŋ], *f.* (—, *no pl.*) airing, ventilation.

Lug [lu:k], *m.* (—s, *no pl.*) (*obs.*) lie; — *und Trug*, a pack of lies.

Lüge ['ly:gə], *f.* (—, *pl.* —n) lie, falsehood, fib; *einen* — *strafen*, give s.o. the lie.

lügen ['ly:gən], *v.n. irr.* lie, tell a lie.

lügenhaft ['ly:gənhaft], *adj.* lying, false, untrue.

Lügner ['ly:gnər], *m.* (—s, *pl.* —) liar.

Luke ['lu:kə], *f.* (—, *pl.* —n) dormer-window; (*ship*) hatch.

Lümmel ['lymǝl], *m.* (—s, *pl.* —) lout; hooligan.

Lump [lump], *m.* (—s, —en, *pl.* —e, —en) scoundrel, blackguard.

Lumpen ['lumpən], *m.* (—s, *pl.* —) rag, tatter.

Lumpengesindel ['lumpəngəzɪndəl], *n.* (—s, *no pl.*) rabble, riffraff.

Lumpenpack ['lumpənpak], *n.* (—s, *no pl.*) rabble, riffraff.

Lumpensammler ['lumpənzamlər], *m.* (—s, *pl.* —) rag-and-bone-man.

Lumperei [lumpə'rai], *f.* (—, *pl.* —en) shabby trick; meanness; trifle.

lumpig ['lumpɪç], *adj.* ragged; (*fig.*) shabby, mean.

Lunge ['luŋə], *f.* (—, *pl.* —n) (*human*) lung; (*animals*) lights.

Lungenentzündung ['luŋənɛntsyn-duŋ], *f.* (—, *pl.* —en) pneumonia.

Lungenkrankheit ['luŋənkraŋkhait], *f.* (—, *pl.* —en) pulmonary disease.

Lungenkraut ['luŋənkraut], *n.* (—s, *pl.* ̈er) lungwort.

Lungenschwindsucht ['luŋənʃvint-zuxt], *f.* (—, *no pl.*) pulmonary consumption, tuberculosis.

lungern ['luŋərn], *v.n.* idle, loiter.

Lunte ['luntə], *f.* (—, *pl.* —n) fuse, slow-match; — *riechen*, smell a rat.

Lupe ['lu:pə], *f.* (—, *pl.* —n) magnifying glass, lens; *etwas durch die* — *besehen*, examine s.th. closely, scrutinise s.th.; *unter die* — *nehmen*, examine closely.

lüpfen ['lypfən], *v.a.* lift.

Lupine [lu'pi:nə], *f.* (—, *pl.* —n) (*Bot.*) lupin.

Lust [lust], *f.* (—, *pl.* ̈e) enjoyment, pleasure, delight; desire, wish, inclination, liking; — *bekommen zu*, feel inclined to; — *haben auf*, have a mind to, feel like; *nicht übel* — *haben*, have half a mind to.

Lustbarkeit ['lustba:rkait], *f.* (—, *pl.* —en) amusement, diversion, entertainment, pleasure.

Lustdirne ['lustdɪrnə], *f.* (—, *pl.* —n) prostitute.

lüstern ['lystərn], *adj.* lustful, lascivious.

lustig ['lustɪç], *adj.* gay, merry, cheerful, amusing, funny; — *sein*, make merry; *sich über einen* — *machen*, poke fun at s.o.

Lüstling ['lystlıŋ], m. (—s, pl. —e) libertine, lecher.

Lustmord ['lustmort], m. (—es, pl. —e) sex murder.

Lustreise ['lustraızə], f. (—, pl. —n) pleasure trip.

Lustschloß ['lustʃlɔs], n. (—sses, pl. ²sser) country house, country seat.

Lustspiel ['lustʃpi:l], n. (—s, pl. —e) comedy.

lustwandeln ['lustvandəln], v.n. insep. (aux. sein) stroll, promenade.

Lutherisch ['lutərıʃ], adj. Lutheran.

lutschen ['lutʃən], v.a. suck.

Lüttich ['lytıç], n. Liège.

Luxus ['luksus], m. (—, no pl.) luxury.

Luzern [lu'tsɛrn], n. Lucerne.

Luzerne [lut'sɛrnə], f. (—, pl. —n) (Bot.) lucerne.

Lymphe ['lymfə], f. (—, pl. —n) lymph.

lynchen ['lynçən], v.a. lynch.

Lyrik ['ly:rık], f. (—, no pl.) lyric poetry.

lyrisch ['ly:rıʃ], adj. lyric(al).

Lyzeum [ly'tse:um], n. (—s, pl. Lyzeen) lyceum, grammar school or high school for girls.

M

M [ɛm], n. (—s, pl. —s) the letter M.

Maas [ma:s], f. River Meuse.

Maat [ma:t], m. (—s, pl. —s, —en) (Naut.) mate.

Mache ['maxə], f. (—, no pl.) put-up job, humbug, sham, eyewash.

machen ['maxən], v.a. make, do, produce, manufacture; cause; amount to; mach schon, be quick; das macht nichts, it does not matter; mach's kurz, cut it short; etwas — lassen, have s.th. made; sich auf den Weg —, set off; sich viel (wenig) aus etwas —, care much (little) for s.th.; mach, daß du fortkommst! get out! scram!

Macherlohn ['maxərlo:n], m. (—es, pl. ²e) charge for making s.th.

Macht [maxt], f. (—, pl. ²e) might, power; force, strength; authority; mit aller —, with might and main.

Machtbefugnis ['maxtbəfu:knıs], f. (—, pl. —se) competence.

Machtgebot ['maxtgəbo:t], n. (—s, pl. —e) authoritative order.

Machthaber ['maxtha:bər], m. (—s, pl. —) potentate, ruler.

mächtig ['mɛçtıç], adj. mighty, powerful; einer Sache — sein, to have mastered s.th.

machtlos ['maxtlo:s], adj. powerless.

Machtspruch ['maxtʃprux], m. (—s, pl. ²e) authoritative dictum; command; decree.

Machtvollkommenheit ['maxtfɔlkəmənhaıt], f. (—, pl. —en) absolute power; sovereignty; aus eigner —, of o.'s own authority.

Machtwort ['maxtvort], n. (—es, pl. —e) word of command, fiat; ein — sprechen, bring o.'s authority to bear, speak with authority.

Machwerk ['maxvɛrk], n. (—s, pl. —e) shoddy product; bad job; concoction; (story) pot-boiler.

Madagaskar [mada'gaskar], n. Madagascar.

Mädchen ['mɛ:tçən], n. (—s, pl. —) girl; (servant) maid; — für alles, maid-of-all-work.

mädchenhaft ['mɛ:tçənhaft], adj. girlish, maidenly.

Mädchenhandel ['mɛ:tçənhandəl], m. (—s, no pl.) white slave trade.

Made ['ma:də], f. (—, pl. —n) maggot, mite.

Mädel ['mɛ:dəl], n. (—s, pl. —) (coll.) see **Mädchen**.

madig ['ma:dıç], adj. maggoty.

Magazin [maga'tsi:n], n. (—s, pl. —e) warehouse, storehouse; journal.

Magd [ma:kt], f. (—, pl. ²e) maid, maidservant; (Poet.) maiden.

Magen ['ma:gən], m. (—s, pl. —) (human) stomach; (animals) maw.

Magengrube ['ma:gəngru:bə], f. (—, pl. —n) pit of the stomach.

Magensaft ['ma:gənzaft], m. (—es, pl. ²e) gastric juice.

mager ['ma:gər], adj. lean, thin, slender, slim; (fig.) meagre.

Magerkeit ['ma:gərkaıt], f. (—, no pl.) leanness, thinness, slenderness.

Magie [ma'gi:], f. (—, no pl.) magic.

Magier ['ma:gjər], m. (—s, pl. —) magician.

Magister [ma'gıstər], m. (—s, pl. —) schoolmaster; (Univ.) Master; — der freien Künste, Master of Arts.

Magistrat [magıs'tra:t], m. (—s, pl. —e) municipal board, local authority.

magnetisch [mag'ne:tıʃ], adj. magnetic.

magnetisieren [magneti'zi:rən], v.a. magnetise.

Magnetismus [magne'tısmus], m. (—, pl. —men) magnetism; (person) mesmerism; Lehre vom —, magnetics.

Magnifizenz [magnifi'tsɛnts], f. (—, pl. —en) magnificence; seine —, (Univ.) title of Vice-Chancellor.

Mahagoni [maha'go:ni], n. (—s, no pl.) mahogany.

Mahd [ma:t], f. (—, pl. —en) mowing.

mähen ['mɛ:ən], v.a. mow.

Mäher ['mɛ:ər], m. (—s, pl. —) mower.

Mahl [ma:l], n. (—s, pl. —e, ²er) meal, repast.

mahlen ['ma:lən], v.a. grind.

Mahlstrom ['ma:lʃtro:m], m. (—s, no pl.) maelstrom, whirlpool, eddy.

Mahlzahn ['ma:ltsa:n], m. (—s, pl. ²e) molar, grinder.

145

Mahlzeit

Mahlzeit ['ma:ltsaɪt], f. (—, pl. —en) meal, repast.

Mähmaschine ['mɛ:maʃi:nə], f. (—, pl. —n) reaping-machine; lawn-mower.

Mähne ['mɛ:nə], f. (—, pl. —n) mane.

mahnen ['ma:nən], v.a. remind, admonish, warn; (debtor) demand payment, dun.

Mähre ['mɛ:rə], f. (—, pl. —n) mare.

Mähren ['mɛ:rən], n. Moravia.

Mai [maɪ], m. (—s, pl. —e) May.

Maid [maɪt], f. (—, no pl.) (Poet.) maiden.

Maiglöckchen ['maɪɡlœkçən], n. (—s, pl. —) (Bot.) lily of the valley.

Maikäfer ['maɪkɛ:fər], m. (—s, pl. —) (Ent.) cockchafer.

Mailand ['maɪlant], n. Milan.

Mais [maɪs], m. (—es, no pl.) (Bot.) maize, Indian corn.

Majestät [majɛs'tɛ:t], f. (—, pl. —en) majesty.

majestätisch [majɛs'tɛ:tiʃ], adj. majestic.

Major [ma'jo:r], m. (—s, pl. —e) (Mil.) major.

Majoran [majo'ra:n], m. (—s, no pl.) (Bot.) marjoram.

Majorat [majo'ra:t], n. (—s, pl. —e) primogeniture; entail.

majorenn [majo'rɛn], adj. (obs.) of age, over twenty-one.

Majorität [majori'tɛ:t], f. (—, pl. —en) majority.

Makel ['ma:kəl], m. (—s, pl. —) spot, blot; (fig.) blemish, flaw, defect.

Mäkelei [mɛ:kə'laɪ], f. (—, pl. —en) fault-finding, carping; fastidiousness.

makellos ['ma:kəllo:s], adj. spotless, immaculate.

mäkeln ['mɛ:kəln], v.n. find fault (with), cavil (at).

Makkabäer [maka'bɛ:ər], m. Maccabee.

Makler ['ma:klər], m. (—s, pl. —) broker.

Mäkler ['mɛ:klər], m. (—s, pl. —) fault-finder, caviller.

Maklergebühr ['ma:klərɡəby:r], f. (—, pl. —en) brokerage.

Makrele [ma'kre:lə], f. (—, pl. —n) (Zool.) mackerel.

Makrone [ma'kro:nə], f. (—, pl. —n) macaroon.

Makulatur [makula'tu:r], f. (—, no pl.) waste paper.

Mal [ma:l], n. (—s, pl. —e) mark, sign, token; monument; mole, birthmark; stain; time; dieses —, this time, this once; manches —, sometimes; mehrere —e, several times; mit einem —, all of a sudden.

mal [ma:l], adv. & part. once; noch—, once more; (coll.) hör —, I say.

Malaya [ma'laɪa], n. Malaya.

malen ['ma:lən], v.a. paint.

Maler ['ma:lər], m. (—s, pl. —) painter.

Malerei [ma:lə'raɪ], f. (—, pl. —en) painting; picture.

malerisch ['ma:lərɪʃ], adj. picturesque.

Malerleinwand ['ma:lərlaɪnvant], f. (—, no pl.) canvas.

Malheur [ma'lø:r], n. (—s, pl. —e) misfortune, mishap.

Mali [ma:li] n. Mali.

maliziös [mali'tsjø:s], adj. malicious.

Malkasten ['ma:lkastən], m. (—s, pl. ⁝) paint-box.

Malstein ['ma:lʃtaɪn], m. (—s, pl. —e) monument; boundary stone.

Malstock ['ma:lʃtɔk], m. (—s, pl. ⁝e) maulstick, mahlstick.

Malteserorden [mal'te:zərɔrdən], m. (—s, no pl.) Order of the Knights of Malta.

malträtieren [maltrɛ'ti:rən], v.a. illtreat.

Malve ['malvə], f. (—, pl. —n) (Bot.) mallow.

Malz [malts], n. (—es, no pl.) malt; an ihm ist Hopfen und — verloren, he is hopeless.

Malzbonbon ['maltsbɔbõ], m. (—s, pl. —s) cough-lozenge, malt drop.

Mälzer ['mɛltsər], m. (—s, pl. —) maltster.

Mama [ma'ma:], f. (—, pl. —s) (fam.) mummy, mum, (Am.) ma.

Mammon ['mamɔn], m. (—s, no pl.) mammon; schnöder —, filthy lucre.

Mammut ['mamut], n. (—s, pl. —e) mammoth.

Mamsell [mam'zɛl], f. (—, pl. —en) housekeeper.

man [man], indef. pron. one, they, people, men; — sagt, they say.

manch [manç], pron. (—er, —e, —es) many a, some, several.

mancherlei [mançər'laɪ], adj. several; of several kinds.

Manchester [man'çɛstər], m. (—s, no pl.) corduroy.

manchmal ['mançma:l], adv. sometimes.

Mandant [man'dant], m. (—en, pl. —en) client.

Mandantin [man'dantin], f. (—, pl. —innen) female client.

Mandarine [manda'ri:nə], f. (—, pl. —n) mandarin (orange), tangerine.

Mandat [man'da:t], n. (—s, pl. —e) mandate.

Mandel ['mandəl], f. (—, pl. —n) almond; (Anat.) tonsil; (quantity) fifteen; eine — Eier, fifteen eggs.

Mandoline [mando'li:nə], f. (—, pl. —n) mandolin.

Mangan [maŋ'ga:n], n. (—s, no pl.) (Chem.) manganese.

Mangel (1) ['maŋəl], f. (—, pl. —n) mangle, wringer.

Mangel (2) ['maŋəl], m. (—s, pl. ⁝) deficiency, defect; blemish; lack, shortage, want; aus —, for want of; — haben an, be short of, lack (s.th.).

mangelhaft ['maŋəlhaft], adj. defective, imperfect.

mangeln (1) ['maŋəln], v.a. (laundry) mangle.

146

mangeln (2) ['maŋəln], *v.n.* be in want of, be short of; *es —t uns an . . .,* we lack . . . .

mangels ['maŋəls], *prep.* (*Genit.*) for lack of, for want of.

Mangold ['maŋɔlt], *m.* (—s, *no pl.*) (*Bot.*) beet, mangel-wurzel.

Manie [ma'ni:], *f.* (—, *pl.* —n) mania, craze.

Manier [ma'ni:r], *f.* (—, *pl.* —en) manner, habit; *gute —en haben,* have good manners.

manieriert [mani'ri:rt], *adj.* affected; (*Art*) mannered.

manierlich [ma'ni:rlɪç], *adj.* well behaved, civil, polite.

manipulieren [manipu'li:rən], *v.a.* manipulate.

Manko ['maŋko:], *n.* (—s, *pl.* —s) deficit, deficiency.

Mann [man], *m.* (—(e)s, *pl.* ⁻er, (*Poet.*) —en) man; husband; *etwas an den — bringen,* get s.th. off o.'s hands, dispose of s.th.; *seinen — stellen,* hold o.'s own; *bis auf den letzten —,* to a man.

Mannbarkeit ['manba:rkaɪt], *f.* (—, *no pl.*) puberty; marriageable age.

Männchen ['mɛnçən], *n.* (—s, *pl.* —) little man, manikin; (*Zool.*) male; *mein —,* (*coll.*) my hubby; *— machen,* (*dogs*) sit on the hindlegs, beg.

mannhaft ['manhaft], *adj.* manly, stout, valiant.

mannigfaltig ['manɪçfaltɪç], *adj.* manifold, multifarious.

männlich ['mɛnlɪç], *adj.* male; (*fig.*) manly; (*Gram.*) masculine.

Mannsbild ['mansbɪlt], *n.* (—es, *pl.* —er) (*coll.*) man, male person.

Mannschaft ['manʃaft], *f.* (—, *pl.* —en) men; crew, team.

mannstoll ['manstɔl], *adj.* man-mad.

Mannszucht ['manstsuxt], *f.* (—, *no pl.*) discipline.

Manöver [ma'nø:vər], *n.* (—s, *pl.* —) manoeuvre.

manövrieren [manø'vri:rən], *v.a.* manoeuvre.

Mansarde [man'zardə], *f.* (—, *pl.* —n) garret, attic.

manschen ['manʃən], *v.a., v.n.* dabble; splash (about).

Manschette [man'ʃɛtə], *f.* (—, *pl.* —n) cuff.

Mantel ['mantəl], *m.* (—s, *pl.* ⁻) cloak, overcoat, coat, mantle, wrap; *den — nach dem Winde hängen,* be a timeserver.

Manufaktur [manufak'tu:r], *f.* (—, *pl.* —en) manufacture.

Mappe ['mapə], *f.* (—, *pl.* —n) portfolio, case, file.

Mär [mɛ:r], *f.* (—, *pl.* —en) (*Poet.*) tale, tidings, legend.

Märchen ['mɛ:rçən], *n.* (—s, *pl.* —) fairy-tale, fable; fib.

märchenhaft ['mɛ:rçənhaft], *adj.* fabulous, legendary; (*coll.*) marvellous.

Marder ['mardər], *m.* (—s, *pl.* —) (*Zool.*) marten.

Maria [ma'ri:a], *f.* Mary; *die Jungfrau —,* the Virgin Mary.

Marienbild [ma'ri:ənbɪlt], *n.* (—es, *pl.* —er) image of the Virgin Mary.

Marienblume [ma'ri:ənblu:mə], *f.* (—, *pl.* —n) (*Bot.*) daisy.

Marienglas [ma'ri:ənglas], *n.* (—es, *no pl.*) mica.

Marienkäfer [ma'ri:ɔnkɛ:fər], *m.* (—s, *pl.* —) (*Ent.*) lady-bird.

Marine [ma'ri:nə], *f.* (—, *pl.* —n) navy.

marinieren [mari'ni:rən], *v.a.* pickle.

Marionette [mario'nɛtə], *f.* (—, *pl.* —n) puppet, marionette.

Mark (1) [mark], *n.* (—s, *no pl.*) (*bone*) marrow; (*fruit*) pith, pulp.

Mark (2) [mark], *f.* (—, *pl.* —en) boundary, frontier province.

Mark (3) [mark], *f.* (—, *pl.* —) (*coin*) mark.

markant [mar'kant], *adj.* striking, prominent; (*remark*) pithy.

Marke ['markə], *f.* (—, *pl.* —n) (*trade*) mark, brand; (*postage*) stamp; (*game*) counter.

markieren [mar'ki:rən], *v.a.* mark.

markig ['markɪç], *adj.* marrowlike; (*fig.*) pithy, strong.

Markise [mar'ki:zə], *f.* (—, *pl.* —n) (sun)blind, awning.

Markt [markt], *m.* (—es, *pl.* ⁻e) market, market-square, fair.

Marktflecken ['marktflɛkən], *m.* (—s, *pl.* —) borough; (*small*) market town.

Marktschreier ['marktʃraɪər], *m.* (—s, *pl.* —) cheap-jack, quack, charlatan.

Markus ['markus], *m.* Mark.

Marmel ['marməl], *f.* (—, *pl.* —n) (*obs.*) marble.

Marmelade [marmə'la:də], *f.* (—, *pl.* —n) marmalade, jam.

Marmor ['marmor], *m.* (—s, *no pl.*) marble.

Marokko [ma'rɔko], *n.* Morocco.

Marone [ma'ro:nə], *f.* (—, *pl.* —n) sweet chestnut.

Maroquin [maro'kɛ̃], *n.* (—s, *no pl.*) Morocco leather.

Marotte [ma'rɔtə], *f.* (—, *pl.* —n) whim; fad.

Marquise [mar'ki:zə], *f.* (—, *pl.* —n) marchioness.

Marsch (1) [marʃ], *m.* (—es, *pl.* ⁻e) march; *sich in — setzen,* set out; march off.

Marsch (2) [marʃ], *f.* (—, *pl.* —en) fen, marsh.

marsch! [marʃ], *int.* march! be off! get out!

Marschboden ['marʃbo:dən], *m.* (—s, *no pl.*) marshy soil, marshland.

marschieren [mar'ʃi:rən], *v.n.* (*aux.* sein) march.

Marstall ['marʃtal], *m.* (—s, *pl.* ⁻e) royal stud.

Marter ['martər], *f.* (—, *pl.* —n) torture, torment.

martern

martern ['martərn], *v.a.* torture, torment.

Märtyrer ['mertyrər], *m.* (—s, *pl.* —) martyr.

Martyrium [mar'ty:rjum], *n.* (—s, *pl.* —rien) martyrdom.

März [merts], *m.* (—es, *pl.* —e) (*month*) March.

Masche ['maʃə], *f.* (—, *pl.* —n) mesh; (*knitting*) stitch; (*dial.*) bow tie; (*coll.*) racket.

Maschine [ma'ʃi:nə], *f.* (—, *pl.* —n) machine; engine; *mit der — geschrieben,* typewritten.

Maschinengarn [ma'ʃi:nəngarn], *n.* (—s, *no pl.*) twist.

Maschinerie [maʃinə'ri:], *f.* (—, *pl.* —en) machinery.

Maser ['ma:zər], *f.* (—, *pl.* —n) (*wood*) vein, streak.

Masern ['ma:zərn], *f. pl.* measles.

Maske ['maskə], *f.* (—, *pl.* —n) mask, visor.

Maskerade [maskə'ra:də], *f.* (—, *pl.* —n) masquerade.

maskieren [mas'ki:rən], *v.a.* mask. — *v.r. sich —,* put on a mask.

Maß (1) [ma:s], *n.* (—es, *pl.* —e) measure, size, moderation, propriety; degree, extent; proportion; — *halten,* be moderate; *einem — nehmen,* measure s.o. (for); *in starkem —,* to a high degree; *mit —,* in moderation; *nach —,* to measure; *ohne — und Ziel,* immoderately, with no holds barred; *über alle —en,* exceedingly.

Maß (2) [ma:s], *m. & f.* (—, *pl.* —e) (*drink*) quart.

massakrieren [masa'kri:rən], *v.a.* massacre, slaughter.

Maßarbeit ['ma:sarbaɪt], *f.* (—, *pl.* —en) (*work*) made to measure; bespoke tailoring.

Masse ['masə], *f.* (—, *pl.* —n) mass, bulk; multitude; *eine —,* a lot.

Maßeinheit ['ma:saɪnhaɪt], *f.* (—, *pl.* —n) measuring-unit.

massenhaft ['masənhaft], *adj.* abundant.

Maßgabe ['ma:sga:bə], *f.* (—, *pl.* —n) *nach —,* according to, in proportion to.

maßgebend ['ma:sge:bənt], *adj.* standard; (*fig.*) authoritative.

massieren [ma'si:rən], *v.a.* massage.

mäßig ['mɛ:sɪç], *adj.* moderate, temperate, frugal.

Mäßigkeit ['mɛ:sɪçkaɪt], *f.* (—, *no pl.*) moderation, temperance, frugality.

Mäßigung ['mɛ:sɪguŋ], *f.* (—, *no pl.*) moderation.

Massiv [ma'si:f], *n.* (—s, *pl.* —e) (*mountains*) massif, range.

Maßliebchen ['ma:sli:pçən], *n.* (—s, *pl.* —) (*Bot.*) daisy.

maßlos ['ma:slo:s], *adj.* immoderate; (*fig.*) extravagant.

Maßnahme ['ma:sna:mə], *f.* (—, *pl.* —n) measure; —*n ergreifen,* take steps.

Maßregel ['ma:sre:gəl], *f.* (—, *pl.* —n) measure.

maßregeln ['ma:sre:gəln], *v.a.* reprove, reprimand.

Maßstab ['ma:sʃta:p], *m.* (—es, *pl.* ⁻e) standard; (*maps*) scale; *in kleinem (großem) —,* on a small (large) scale.

maßvoll ['ma:sfɔl], *adj.* moderate.

Mast (1) [mast], *m.* (—es, *pl.* —e) mast; pylon.

Mast (2) [mast], *f.* (—, *no pl.*) fattening.

Mastbaum ['mastbaum], *m.* (—s, *pl.* ⁻e) mast.

Mastdarm ['mastdarm], *m.* (—s, *pl.* ⁻e) rectum.

mästen ['mɛstən], *v.a.* feed, fatten.

Mastkorb ['mastkɔrp], *m.* (—s, *pl.* ⁻e) masthead.

Mästung ['mɛstuŋ], *f.* (—, *no pl.*) fattening, cramming.

Materialwaren [mate'rjalva:rən], *f. pl.* groceries; household goods.

materiell [mate'rjel], *adj.* material, real; materialistic.

Mathematik [matema'ti:k], *f.* (—, *no pl.*) mathematics.

mathematisch [mate'ma:tɪʃ], *adj.* mathematical.

Matratze [ma'tratsə], *f.* (—, *pl.* —n) mattress.

Matrikel [ma'tri:kəl], *f.* (—, *pl.* —n) register, roll.

Matrize [ma'tri:tsə], *f.* (—, *pl.* —n) matrix, die, stencil.

Matrose [ma'tro:zə], *m.* (—n, *pl.* —n) sailor, seaman.

Matsch [matʃ], *m.* (—es, *no pl.*) slush; mud.

matt [mat], *adj.* tired, exhausted, spent; languid; weak, feeble; (*light*) dim; (*gold*) dull; (*silver*) tarnished; (*Chess*) (check-)mate; — *setzen,* (*Chess*) to (check-)mate.

Matte ['matə], *f.* (—, *pl.* —n) mat, matting.

Matthäus [ma'tɛ:us], *m.* Matthew.

Mattheit ['mathaɪt], *f.* (—, *no pl.*) tiredness, exhaustion, languor, feebleness; (*light*) dimness; (*gold*) dullness.

mattherzig ['mathɛrtsɪç], *adj.* poor-spirited, faint-hearted.

Matura [ma'tu:ra], *f.* (—, *pl.* —en) (*Austr.*) school-leaving *or* matriculation examination.

Mätzchen ['mɛtsçən], *n.* (—s, *pl.* —) nonsense; trick; *mach keine —,* don't be silly.

Mauer ['mauər], *f.* (—, *pl.* —n) wall.

Mauerkelle ['mauərkɛlə], *f.* (—, *pl.* —n) trowel.

mauern ['mauərn], *v.a.* build. — *v.n.* lay bricks, construct a wall.

Mauerwerk ['mauərverk], *n.* (—s, *no pl.*) brick-work.

Maul [maul], *n.* (—es, *pl.* ⁻er) (*animals*) mouth, muzzle; (*vulg.*) mouth; *das — halten,* shut up, hold o.'s tongue; *ein loses — haben,* have a loose tongue; *nicht aufs — gefallen sein,* have a quick tongue; (*vulg.*) *halt's —,* shut up.

Meinung

Maulaffe ['maulafə], *m.* (—n, *pl.* —n) booby; —*n feilhalten*, stand gaping.
Maulbeere ['maulbe:rə], *f.* (—, *pl.* —n) (*Bot.*) mulberry.
maulen ['maulən], *v.n.* pout, sulk.
Maulesel ['maule:zəl], *m.* (—s, *pl.* —) (*Zool.*) mule.
maulfaul ['maulfaul], *adj.* tongue-tied; taciturn.
Maulheld ['maulhɛlt], *m.* (—en *pl.* —en) braggart.
Maulkorb ['maulkɔrp], *m.* (—s, *pl.* ⸚e) muzzle.
Maulschelle ['maulʃɛlə], *f.* (—, *pl.* —n) box on the ear.
Maultier ['maulti:r], *n.* (—s, *pl.* —e) (*Zool.*) mule.
Maulwerk ['maulvɛrk], *n.* (—s, *no pl.*) *ein großes — haben*, (*coll.*) have the gift of the gab.
Maulwurf ['maulvurf], *m.* (—s, *pl.* ⸚e) (*Zool.*) mole.
Maurer ['maurər], *m.* (—s, *pl.* —) mason, bricklayer.
Maus [maus], *f.* (—, *pl.* ⸚e) mouse.
Mausefalle ['mauzəfalə], *f.* (—, *pl.* —n) mouse-trap.
mausen ['mauzən], *v.n.* catch mice. — *v.a.* (*fig.*) pilfer, pinch.
Mauser ['mauzər], *f.* (—, *no pl.*) moulting.
mausern ['mauzərn], *v.r. sich —,* moult.
mausetot ['mauzəto:t], *adj.* dead as a door-nail.
mausig ['mauzɪç], *adj. sich — machen,* put on airs.
Maxime [mak'si:mə], *f.* (—, *pl.* —n) maxim, motto, device.
Mazedonien [matsə'do:njən], *n.* Macedonia.
Mäzen [mɛ'tse:n], *m.* (—s, *pl.* —e) patron of the arts, Maecenas.
Mechanik [me'ça:nɪk], *f.* (—, *no pl.*) mechanics.
Mechaniker [me'ça:nɪkər], *m.* (—s, *pl.* —) mechanic.
mechanisch [me'ça:nɪʃ], *adj.* mechanical.
meckern ['mɛkərn], *v.n.* bleat; (*fig.*) grumble, complain.
Medaille [me'daljə], *f.* (—, *pl.* —n) medal.
Medaillon [medal'jõ], *n.* (—s, *pl.* —s) locket.
meditieren [medi'ti:rən], *v.n.* meditate.
Medizin [medi'tsi:n], *f.* (—, *pl.* —en) medicine, physic.
Mediziner [medi'tsi:nər], *m.* (—s, *pl.* —) physician, medical practitioner, student of medicine.
medizinisch [medi'tsi:nɪʃ], *adj.* medical, medicinal.
Meer [me:r], *n.* (—es, *pl.* —e) sea, ocean; *offnes —,* high seas; *am —,* at the seaside; *auf dem —,* at sea; *übers —,* overseas.
Meerbusen ['me:rbu:zən], *m.* (—s, *pl.* —) bay, gulf, bight.

Meerenge ['me:rɛŋə], *f.* (—, *pl.* —n) straits.
Meeresspiegel ['me:rəsʃpi:gəl], *m.* (—s, *no pl.*) sea-level.
Meerkatze ['me:rkatsə], *f.* (—, *pl.* —n) long-tailed monkey.
Meerrettich ['me:rrɛtɪç], *m.* (—s, *pl.* —e) (*Bot.*) horse-radish.
Meerschaum ['me:rʃaum], *m.* (—s, *no pl.*) sea-foam; (*pipe*) meerschaum.
Meerschwein ['me:rʃvain], *n.* (—s, *pl.* —e) (*Zool.*) porpoise.
Meerschweinchen ['me:rʃvainçən], *n.* (—s, *pl.* —) (*Zool.*) guinea-pig.
Mehl [me:l], *n.* (—es, *no pl.*) flour; meal; dust, powder.
Mehlkleister ['me:lklaistər], *m.* (—s, *no pl.*) flour paste.
Mehlspeise ['me:lʃpaizə], *f.* (—, *pl.* —n) (*dial.*) pudding, sweet.
mehr [me:r], *indecl. adj., adv.* more; *umso —,* all the more; *immer —,* more and more; *— als genug,* enough and to spare.
Mehrbetrag ['me:rbətra:k], *m.* (—s, *pl.* ⸚e) surplus.
mehrdeutig ['me:rdɔytɪç], *adj.* ambiguous.
mehren ['me:rən], *v.r. sich —,* multiply, increase in numbers.
mehrere ['me:rərə], *pl. adj.* several.
mehrfach ['me:rfax], *adj.* repeated.
Mehrheit ['me:rhait], *f.* (—, *pl.* —en) majority.
mehrmals ['me:rma:ls], *adv.* several times.
Mehrzahl ['me:rtsa:l], *f.* (—, *no pl.*) (*Gram.*) plural; majority, bulk.
meiden ['maidən], *v.a. irr.* shun, avoid.
Meierei [maiə'rai], *f.* (—, *pl.* —en) (*dairy*) farm.
Meile ['mailə], *f.* (—, *pl.* —n) mile; league.
Meiler ['mailər], *m.* (—s, *pl.* —) charcoal-kiln, charcoal-pile.
mein(e) ['main(ə)], *poss. adj.* my. — *poss. pron.* mine.
Meineid ['mainait], *m.* (—s, *pl.* —e) perjury; *einen — schwören,* perjure o.s.
meineidig ['mainaidɪç], *adj.* perjured, forsworn.
meinen ['mainən], *v.a.* mean, intend, think.
meinerseits ['mainərzaits], *adv.* I, for my part.
meinethalben ['mainəthalbən], *adv.* on my account, speaking for myself, for my sake; I don't care, I don't mind.
meinetwegen ['mainətve:gən], *adv. see* meinethalben.
meinetwillen ['mainətvilən], *adv. um —,* for my sake, on my behalf.
meinige ['mainigə], *poss. pron.* mine.
Meinung ['mainuŋ], *f.* (—, *pl.* —en) opinion; meaning; notion; *öffentliche —,* public opinion; *der — sein,* be of the opinion, hold the opinion; *einem die — sagen,* give s.o. a piece of o.'s mind; *meiner — nach,* in my opinion.

149

Meinungsverschiedenheit

Meinungsverschiedenheit ['maınuŋs-ferʃi:dənhaıt], *f.* (—, *pl.* —en) difference of opinion, disagreement.
Meise ['maızə], *f.* (—, *pl.* —n) (*Orn.*) titmouse.
Meißel ['maısəl], *m.* (—s, *pl.* —) chisel.
meißeln ['maısəln], *v.a.* chisel, sculpt.
meist [maıst], *adj.* most. — *adv.* usually, generally.
meistens ['maıstəns]; *adv.* mostly.
Meister ['maıstər], *m.* (—s, *pl.* —) (*craft*) master; (*sport*) champion; *seinen — finden,* meet o.'s match.
meisterhaft ['maıstərhaft], *adj.* masterly.
meisterlich ['maıstərlıç], *adj.* masterly.
meistern ['maıstərn], *v.a.* master.
Meisterschaft ['maıstərʃaft], *f.* (—, *pl.* —en) mastery; (*sport*) championship.
Mekka ['mɛka], *n.* Mecca.
Meldeamt ['mɛldəamt], *n.* (—s, *pl.* ꞋꞋer) registration office.
melden ['mɛldən], *v.a.* announce, inform, notify; (*Mil.*) report. — *v.r. sich —,* answer the phone; *sich lassen,* send in o.'s name, have o.s. announced; *sich zu etwas —,* apply for s.th.
Meldezettel ['mɛldətsetəl], *m.* (—s, *pl.* —) registration form.
meliert [me'li:rt], *adj.* mixed; (*hair*) iron grey, streaked with grey.
melken ['mɛlkən], *v.a.* irr. milk.
Melodie [melo'di:], *f.* (—, *pl.* —n) melody, tune.
Melone [me'lo:nə], *f.* (—, *pl.* —n) (*Bot.*) melon; (*coll.*) bowler hat.
Meltau ['me:ltau], *m.* (—s, *no pl.*) mildew.
Membrane [mɛm'bra:nə], *f.* (—, *pl.* —n) membrane, diaphragm.
Memme ['mɛmə], *f.* (—, *pl.* —n) coward, poltroon.
memorieren [memo'ri:rən], *v.a.* memorise, learn by heart.
Menage [me'na:ʒə], *f.* (—, *pl.* —n) household.
Menge ['mɛŋə], *f.* (—, *pl.* —n) quantity, amount; multitude, crowd; *eine —,* a lot.
mengen ['mɛŋən], *v.a.* mix. — *v.r. sich — in,* interfere in.
Mensch (1) [mɛnʃ], *m.* (—en, *pl.* —en) human being; man; person; *kein —,* nobody.
Mensch (2) [mɛnʃ], *n.* (—es, *pl.* —er) (*vulg.*) wench.
Menschenfeind ['mɛnʃənfaınt], *m.* (—es, *pl.* —e) misanthropist.
Menschenfreund ['mɛnʃənfrɔynt], *m.* (—es, *pl.* —e) philanthropist.
Menschengedenken ['mɛnʃəngədɛŋkən], *n.* (—s, *no pl.*) *seit —,* from time immemorial.
Menschenhandel ['mɛnʃənhandəl], *m.* (—s, *no pl.*) slave-trade.
Menschenkenner ['mɛnʃənkɛnər], *m.* (—s, *pl.* —) judge of character.

Menschenmenge ['mɛnʃənmɛŋə], *f.* (—, *no pl.*) crowd.
Menschenraub ['mɛnʃənraup], *m.* (—s, *no pl.*) kidnapping.
Menschenverstand ['mɛnʃənferʃtant], *m.* (—es, *no pl.*) human understanding; *gesunder —,* commonsense.
Menschheit ['mɛnʃhaıt], *f.* (—, *no pl.*) mankind, human race.
menschlich ['mɛnʃlıç], *adj.* human.
Menschwerdung ['mɛnʃverduŋ], *f.* (—, *no pl.*) incarnation.
Mensur [mɛn'zu:r], *f.* (—, *pl.* —en) students' duel.
Mergel ['mɛrgəl], *m.* (—s, *no pl.*) marl.
merkbar ['mɛrkba:r], *adj.* perceptible, noticeable.
merken ['mɛrkən], *v.a.* note, perceive, observe, notice; *sich etwas —,* bear in mind; *sich nichts — lassen,* show no sign.
merklich ['mɛrklıç], *adj.* perceptible, appreciable.
Merkmal ['mɛrkma:l], *n.* (—s, *pl.* —e) mark, characteristic, feature.
merkwürdig ['mɛrkvyrdıç], *adj.* remarkable, curious, strange.
Merle ['mɛrlə], *f.* (—, *pl.* —n) (*dial.*) blackbird.
Mesner ['mɛsnər], *m.* (—s, *pl.* —) sexton, sacristan.
meßbar ['mɛsba:r], *adj.* measurable.
Meßbuch ['mɛsbu:x], *n.* (—es, *pl.* ꞋꞋer) missal.
Messe ['mɛsə], *f.* (—, *pl.* —n) (*Eccl.*) Mass; *stille —,* Low Mass; (*Comm.*) fair; (*Mil.*) mess.
messen ['mɛsən], *v.a. irr.* measure, gauge. — *v.r. sich mit einem —,* pit oneself against s.o.
Messer (1) ['mɛsər], *m.* (—s, *pl.* —) gauge, meter.
Messer (2) ['mɛsər], *n.* (—s, *pl.* —) knife.
Messerheld ['mɛsərhelt], *m.* (—en, *pl.* —en) cut-throat, hooligan, rowdy.
Messias [mɛ'si:as], *m.* Messiah.
Meßgewand ['mɛsgəvant], *n.* (—es, *pl.* ꞋꞋer) chasuble, vestment.
Meßkunst ['mɛskunst], *f.* (—, *no pl.*) surveying.
Messing ['mɛsıŋ], *n.* (—s, *no pl.*) brass; *aus —,* brazen.
Metall [me'tal], *n.* (—s, *pl.* —e) metal; *unedle —e,* base metals.
Metallkunde [me'talkundə], *f.* (—, *no pl.*) metallurgy.
meteorologisch [meteoro'lo:gıʃ], *adj.* meteorological.
Meter ['me:tər], *n. & m.* (—s, *pl.* —) (*linear measure*) metre; (*Am.*) meter; (*Poet.*) metre.
methodisch [me'to:dıʃ], *adj.* methodical.
Metrik ['me:trık], *f.* (—, *no pl.*) prosody, versification.
Mette ['mɛtə], *f.* (—, *pl.* —n) (*Eccl.*) matins.

150

Mischling

Metze ['mɛtsə], *f.* (—, *pl.* —n) (*obs.*) prostitute.

Metzelei [mɛtsə'laɪ], *f.* (—, *pl.* —en) slaughter, massacre.

metzeln ['mɛtsəln], *v.a.* massacre, butcher.

Metzger ['mɛtsgər], *m.* (—s, *pl.* —) butcher.

Meuchelmörder ['mɔyçəlmœrdər], *m.* (—s, *pl.* —) assassin.

meucheln ['mɔyçəln], *v.a.* assassinate.

meuchlings ['mɔyçlɪŋs], *adv.* treacherously, insidiously.

Meute ['mɔytə], *f.* (—, *pl.* —n) pack of hounds; (*fig.*) gang.

Meuterei [mɔytə'raɪ], *f.* (—, *pl.* —en) mutiny, sedition.

meutern ['mɔytərn], *v.n.* mutiny.

Mezzanin ['mɛtsanɪn], *n.* (—s, *pl.* —e) half-storey, mezzanine.

miauen [mi'auən], *v.n.* mew.

mich [mɪç], *pers. pron.* me, myself.

Michaeli(s) [mɪça'e:li(s)], *n.* Michaelmas.

Michel ['mɪçəl], *m.* Michael; *deutscher* —, plain honest German.

Mieder ['mi:dər], *n.* (—s, *pl.* —) bodice.

Miene ['mi:nə], *f.* (—, *pl.* —n) mien, air; (facial) expression.

Miete ['mi:tə], *f.* (—, *pl.* —n) rent; hire; (*corn*) rick, stack.

mieten ['mi:tən], *v.a.* rent, hire.

Mieter ['mi:tər], *m.* (—s, *pl.* —) tenant, lodger.

Mietskaserne [mi:tskazɛrnə], *f.* (—, *pl.* —en) tenement house.

Mietzins ['mi:tstsɪns], *m.* (—es, *pl.* —e) rent.

Milbe ['mɪlbə], *f.* (—, *pl.* —n) mite.

Milch [mɪlç], *f.* (—, *no pl.*) milk; (*fish*) soft roe; *abgerahmte* —, skim(med) milk; *geronnene* —, curdled milk.

Milchbart ['mɪlçba:rt], *m.* (—s, *pl.* ꞏe) milksop.

Milchbruder ['mɪlçbru:dər], *m.* (—s, *pl.* ꞏ) foster-brother.

milchen ['mɪlçən], *v.n.* yield milk.

Milcher ['mɪlçer], *m.* (—s, *pl.* —) (*fish*) milter.

Milchgesicht ['mɪlçgəzɪçt], *n.* (—s, *pl.* —er) baby face; smooth complexion.

Milchglas ['mɪlçglas], *n.* (—es, *no pl.*) opalescent glass, frosted glass.

Milchstraße ['mɪlçʃtra:sə], *f.* (—, *no pl.*) Milky Way.

Milde ['mɪldə], *f.* (—, *no pl.*) mildness, softness; (*fig.*) gentleness, (*rare*) charity, generosity.

mildern ['mɪldərn], *v.a.* soften, alleviate, mitigate, soothe, allay; —*de Umstände*, extenuating circumstances.

Milderung ['mɪldərʊŋ], *f.* (—, *pl.* —en) mitigation, moderation; soothing.

mildtätig ['mɪlttɛ:tɪç], *adj.* charitable, benevolent, munificent.

Militär [mili'tɛ:r], *n.* (—s, *no pl.* military, army; *beim* — *sein*, serve in the army.

Miliz [mi'li:ts], *f.* (—, *no pl.*) militia.

Milliarde [mɪl'jardə], *f.* (—, *pl.* —n) a thousand millions; (*Am.*) billion.

Million [mɪl'jo:n], *f.* (—, *pl.* —en) million.

Millionär [mɪljo'nɛ:r], *m.* (—s, *pl.* —e) millionaire.

Milz [mɪlts], *f.* (—, *pl.* —en) spleen.

Mime ['mi:mə], *m.* (—n, *pl.* —n) mime, actor.

Mimik ['mi:mɪk], *f.* (—, *no pl.*) mime, miming.

Mimiker ['mi:mɪkər], *m.* (—s, *pl.* —) mimic.

Mimose [mi'mo:zə], *f.* (—, *pl.* —n) (*Bot.*) mimosa.

minder ['mɪndər], *adj.* lesser, smaller, minor, inferior.

Minderheit ['mɪndərhaɪt], *f.* (—, *pl.* —en) minority.

minderjährig ['mɪndərjɛ:rɪç], *adj.* (*Law*) under age.

mindern ['mɪndərn], *v.a.* diminish, lessen.

minderwertig ['mɪndərvɛrtɪç], *adj.* inferior, of poor quality.

Minderwertigkeitskomplex ['mɪndərvɛrtɪçkaɪtskɔmplɛks], *m.* (—es, *pl.* —e) inferiority complex.

mindest ['mɪndəst], *adj.* least, smallest, minimum, lowest; *nicht im* —*en*, not in the least, not at all.

mindestens ['mɪndəstəns], *adv.* at least.

Mine ['mi:nə], *f.* (—, *pl.* —n) mine; (*ball point pen*) refill; (*pencil*) lead.

minimal [mini'ma:l], *adj.* infinitesimal, minimum.

Ministerialrat [minister'ja:lra:t], *m.* (—s, *pl.* ꞏe) senior civil servant.

ministeriell [mɪnɪster'jɛl], *adj.* ministerial.

Ministerium [mini'ste:rjum], *n.* (—s, *pl.* —rien) ministry.

Ministerpräsident [mi'nɪstərprɛ:zident], *m.* (—en, *pl.* —en) prime minister; premier.

Ministerrat [mi'nɪstərra:t], *m.* (—s, *pl.* ꞏe) cabinet, council of ministers.

Ministrant [mini'strant], *m.* (—en, *pl.* —en) acolyte; sacristan.

Minne ['mɪnə], *f.* (—, *no pl.*) (*obs., Poet.*) love.

Minnesänger [mɪnə'zɛŋər], *m.* (—s, *pl.* —) minnesinger; troubadour, minstrel.

Minus ['mi:nus], *n.* (—, *no pl.*) deficit.

Minze ['mɪntsə], *f.* (—, *pl.* —n) (*Bot.*) mint.

mir [mi:r], *pers. pron.* to me.

Mirakel [mi'ra:kəl], *n.* (—s, *pl.* —) miracle, marvel, wonder.

mischen ['mɪʃən], *v.a.* mix; (*Cards*) shuffle; (*coffee, tea*) blend.

Mischling ['mɪʃlɪŋ], *m.* (—s, *pl.* —e) mongrel, hybrid.

151

Mischrasse

Mischrasse ['mɪʃrasə], f. (—, pl. —n) cross-breed.

Mischung ['mɪʃuŋ], f. (—, pl. —en) mixture, blend.

Misere [mi'ze:rə], f. (—, no pl.) unhappiness, misery.

Mispel ['mɪspəl], f. (—, pl. —n) (Bot.) medlar (tree).

mißachten [mɪs'axtən], v.a. disregard, despise.

mißarten [mɪs'a:rtən], v.n. (aux. sein) degenerate.

Mißbehagen ['mɪsbəha:gən], n. (—s, no pl.) displeasure, uneasiness.

mißbilligen [mɪs'bilɪgən], v.a. object (to), disapprove (of).

Mißbrauch ['mɪsbraux], m. (—s, pl. ⸚e) abuse, misuse.

missen ['mɪsən], v.a. lack, be without, feel the lack of.

Missetat ['mɪsəta:t], f. (—, pl. —en) misdeed, felony.

mißfallen [mɪs'falən], v.n. irr. displease.

mißförmig ['mɪsfœrmɪç], adj. deformed, misshapen.

Mißgeburt ['mɪsgəburt], f. (—, pl. —en) abortion; monster.

mißgelaunt ['mɪsgəlaunt], adj. ill-humoured.

Mißgeschick ['mɪsgəʃɪk], n. (—s, no pl.) mishap, misfortune.

mißgestimmt ['mɪsgəʃtɪmt], adj. grumpy, out of sorts.

mißglücken [mɪs'glykən], v.n. (aux. sein) fail, be unsuccessful.

Mißgriff ['mɪsgrɪf], m. (—s, pl. ⸚e) blunder, mistake.

Mißgunst ['mɪsgunst], f. (—, no pl.) jealousy, envy.

mißhandeln [mɪs'handəln], v.a. ill-treat.

Missionar [mɪsjo'na:r], m. (—s, pl. —e) missionary.

mißlich ['mɪslɪç], adj. awkward; difficult, unpleasant.

mißliebig ['mɪsli:bɪç], adj. unpopular, odious.

mißlingen [mɪs'lɪŋən], v.n. irr. (aux. sein) miscarry, go wrong, misfire, prove a failure, turn out badly.

mißraten [mɪs'ra:tən], v.n. irr. (aux. sein) miscarry, turn out badly.

Mißstand ['mɪsʃtant], m. (—es, pl. ⸚e) grievance, abuse.

Mißton ['mɪsto:n], m. (—s, pl. ⸚e) dissonance.

mißtrauen [mɪs'trauən], v.n. distrust, mistrust.

Mißverhältnis ['mɪsfərhɛltnɪs], n. (—ses, no pl.) disproportion.

Mißverständnis ['mɪsfərʃtɛntnɪs], n. (—ses, pl. —se) misunderstanding.

Mist [mɪst], m. (—es, no pl.) dung, manure, muck; (fig.) rubbish.

Mistel ['mɪstəl], f. (—, pl. —n) (Bot.) mistletoe.

Mistfink ['mɪstfɪŋk], m. (—s, pl. —e) (fig.) dirty child; mudlark.

mit [mɪt], prep. (Dat.) with. — adv. also, along with.

mitarbeiten ['mɪtarbaɪtən], v.n. collaborate, cooperate; (lit. work) contribute.

mitbringen ['mɪtbrɪŋən], v.a. irr. bring along.

Mitbürger ['mɪtbyrgər], m. (—s, pl. —) fellow-citizen.

mitempfinden ['mɪtɛmpfɪndən], v.a. irr. sympathise with.

Mitesser ['mɪtɛsər], m. (—s, pl. —) (Med.) blackhead.

mitfahren ['mɪtfa:rən], v.n. irr. (aux. sein) ride with s.o.; einen — lassen, give s.o. a lift.

mitfühlen ['mɪtfy:lən], v.n. sympathise.

mitgehen ['mɪtge:ən], v.n. irr. (aux. sein) go along (with), accompany (s.o.); etwas — heißen or lassen, pilfer, pocket, pinch.

Mitgift ['mɪtgɪft], f. (—, no pl.) dowry.

Mitglied ['mɪtgli:t], n. (—s, pl. —er) member, fellow, associate.

mithin [mɪt'hɪn], adv., conj. consequently, therefore.

Mitläufer ['mɪtlɔyfər], m. (—s, pl. —) (Polit.) fellow-traveller.

Mitlaut ['mɪtlaut], m. (—s, pl. —e) (Phonet.) consonant.

Mitleid ['mɪtlaɪt], n. (—s, no pl.) compassion, sympathy, pity; mit einem — haben, take pity on s.o.

Mitleidenschaft ['mɪtlaɪdənʃaft], f. (—, no pl.) einen in — ziehen, involve s.o., implicate s.o.

mitmachen ['mɪtmaxən], v.a., v.n. join in, participate in; do as others do; go through, suffer.

Mitmensch ['mɪtmɛnʃ], m. (—en, pl. —en) fellow-man, fellow-creature.

mitnehmen ['mɪtne:mən], v.a. irr. take along, take with o.; strain, take it out of o., weaken.

mitnichten [mɪt'nɪçtən], adv. by no means.

mitreden ['mɪtre:dən], v.n. join in a conversation; contribute.

mitsamt [mɪt'zamt], prep. (Dat.) together with.

Mitschuld ['mɪtʃult], f. (—, no pl.) complicity.

Mitschüler ['mɪtʃy:lər], m. (—s, pl. —) schoolfellow, fellow-pupil, fellow-student, classmate.

Mittag ['mɪta:k], m. (—s, pl. —e) midday, noon, noontide; zu — essen, have dinner or lunch.

Mittagessen ['mɪta:kɛsən], n. (—s, pl. —) lunch, luncheon.

Mittagsseite ['mɪta:kszaɪtə], f. (—, no pl.) south side.

Mittäter ['mɪttɛːtər], m. (—s, pl. —) accomplice.

Mitte ['mɪtə], f. (—, no pl.) middle, midst.

mitteilen ['mɪttaɪlən], v.a. (Dat.) communicate, inform, impart.

mitteilsam ['mɪttaɪlza:m], *adj.* communicative.

Mitteilung ['mɪttaɪluŋ], *f.* (—, *pl.* —en) communication.

Mittel ['mɪtəl], *n.* (—s, *pl.*) means, expedient, way, resource; remedy; (*pl.*) money, funds; *als*— *zum Zweck,* as a means to an end; *sich ins* — *legen,* mediate, intercede.

Mittelalter ['mɪtəlaltər], *n.* (—s, *no pl.*) Middle Ages.

mittelbar ['mɪtəlba:r], *adj.* indirect.

Mitteldidng ['mɪtəldɪŋ], *n.* (—s, *pl.* —e) medium; something in between.

Mittelgebirge ['mɪtəlgəbɪrgə], *n.* (—s, *pl.* —) hills; (subalpine) mountains.

mittelländisch ['mɪtəllendɪʃ], *adj.* Mediterranean.

mittellos ['mɪtəllo:s], *adj.* penniless, impecunious.

Mittelmaß ['mɪtəlma:s], *n.* (—es, *pl.* —e) average.

mittelmäßig ['mɪtəlmɛ:sɪç], *adj.* mediocre.

Mittelmeer ['mɪtəlme:r], *n.* (—s, *no pl.*) Mediterranean.

Mittelpunkt ['mɪtəlpuŋkt], *m.* (—s, *pl.* —e) centre; focus.

mittels ['mɪtəls], *prep.* (*Genit.*) by means of.

Mittelschule ['mɪtəlʃu:lə], *f.* (—, *pl.* —n) secondary (intermediate) school; (*Austr.*) grammar school; (*Am.*) high school.

Mittelstand ['mɪtəlʃtant], *m.* (—es, *no pl.*) middle class.

mittelste ['mɪtəlstə], *adj.* middlemost, central.

Mittelstürmer ['mɪtəlʃtyrmər], *m.* (—s, *pl.* —) (*Footb.*) centre-forward.

Mittelwort ['mɪtəlvɔrt], *n.* (—es, *pl.* ·er) (*Gram.*) participle.

mitten ['mɪtən], *adv.* in the midst; — *am Tage,* in broad daylight.

Mitternacht ['mɪtərnaxt], *f.* (—, *no pl.*) midnight.

Mittler ['mɪtlər], *m.* (—s, *pl.* —) mediator.

mittlere ['mɪtlərə], *adj.* middle; average; mean.

Mittwoch ['mɪtvɔx], *m.* (—s, *pl.* —e) Wednesday.

mitunter [mɪt'untər], *adv.* now and then, occasionally, sometimes.

mitunterzeichnen ['mɪtuntərtsaɪçnən], *v.a., v.n.* countersign; add o.'s signature (to).

Miturheber ['mɪtu:rhe:bər], *m.* (—s, *pl.* —) co-author.

Mitwelt ['mɪtvɛlt], *f.* (—, *no pl.*) the present generation, contemporaries, our own times; the world outside.

mitwirken ['mɪtvɪrkən], *v.n.* cooperate.

Mnemotechnik [mne:mo'tɛçnɪk], *f.* (—, *no pl.*) mnemonics.

Möbel ['mø:bəl], *n.* (—s, *pl.* —) piece of furniture; (*pl.*) furniture.

mobil [mo'bi:l], *adj.* mobile, active, quick; — *machen,* mobilise, put in motion.

Mobiliar [mobil'ja:r], *n.* (—s, *pl.* Mobilien) furniture, movables.

mobilisieren [mobili'zi:rən], *v.a.* mobilise.

möblieren [mø'bli:rən], *v.a.* furnish; *neu* —, refurnish.

Mode ['mo:də], *f.* (—, *pl.* —n) mode, fashion; custom, use; *in der* —, in fashion, in vogue.

Modell [mo'dɛl], *n.* (—s, *pl.* —e) model; — *stehen,* model; (*fig.*) be the prototype.

modellieren [modɛ'li:rən], *v.a.* (*dresses*) model; (*Art*) mould.

Moder ['mo:dər], *m.* (—s, *no pl.*) mould.

moderig ['mo:drɪç] *see* **modrig**.

modern(1)['mo:dərn],*v.n.* moulder,rot.

modern(2) [mo'dɛrn], *adj.* modern, fashionable, up-to-date.

modernisieren [modɛrni'zi:rən], *v.a.* modernise.

modifizieren [modifi'tsi:rən], *v.a.* modify.

modisch ['mo:dɪʃ], *adj.* stylish, fashionable.

Modistin [mo'dɪstɪn], *f.* (—, *pl.* —nen) milliner.

modrig ['mo:drɪç], *adj.* mouldy.

modulieren [modu'li:rən], *v.a.* modulate.

Modus ['mo:dus], *m.* (—, *pl.* **Modi**) (*Gram.*) mood; mode, manner.

mogeln ['mo:gəln], *v.n.* cheat.

mögen ['mø:gən], *v.n. irr.* like, desire, want, be allowed, have a mind to; (*modal auxiliary*) may, might; *ich möchte gern,* I should like to.

möglich ['mø:klɪç], *adj.* possible, practicable; feasible; *sein —stes tun,* do o.'s utmost; *nicht —!* you don't say (so)!

Möglichkeit ['mø:klɪçkaɪt], *f.* (—, *pl.* —en) possibility, feasibility, practicability; (*pl.*) potentialities; contingencies, prospects (of career).

Mohn [mo:n], *m.* (—es, *no pl.*) poppy(seed).

Mohr [mo:r], *m.* (—en, *pl.* —en) Moor; negro.

Möhre ['mø:rə], *f.* (—, *pl.* —n) carrot.

Mohrenkopf ['mo:rənkɔpf], *m.* (—es, *pl.* ·e) chocolate éclair.

Mohrrübe ['mo:rry:bə], *f.* (—, *pl.* —n) carrot.

mokieren [mɔ'ki:rən], *v.r. sich* — *über,* sneer at, mock at, be amused by.

Mokka ['mɔka], *m.* (—s, *no pl.*) Mocha coffee.

Molch [mɔlç], *m.* (—es, *pl.* —e) (*Zool.*) salamander.

Moldau ['mɔldau], *f.* Moldavia.

Mole ['mo:lə], *f.* (—, *pl.* —n) breakwater, jetty, pier.

Molekül [mole'ky:l], *n.* (—s, *pl.* —e) molecule.

Molke ['mɔlkə], *f.* (—, *pl.* —n) whey.

Molkerei [mɔlke'raɪ], *f.* (—, *pl.* —en dairy.

moll [mɔl], *adj.* (*Mus.*) minor.

Molluske

Molluske [mɔ'luskə], *f.* (—, *pl.* —n) (*Zool.*) mollusc.

Moment (1) [mo'mɛnt], *m.* (—s, *pl.* —e) moment, instant.

Moment (2) [mo'mɛnt], *n.* motive, factor; (*Phys.*) momentum.

Momentaufnahme [mo'mɛntaufna:-mə], *f.* (—, *pl.* —n) snapshot.

momentan [momɛn'ta:n], *adv.* at the moment, for the present, just now.

Monarch [mo'narç], *m.* (—en, *pl.* —en) monarch.

Monarchie [monar'çi:], *f.* (—, *pl.* —n) monarchy.

Monat ['mo:nat], *m.* (—s, *pl.* —e) month.

monatlich ['mo:natlıç], *adj.* monthly.

Monatsfluß ['mo:natsflus], *m.* (—sses, *pl.* ˙sse) menses.

Monatsschrift ['mo:natsʃrıft], *f.* (—, *pl.* —en) monthly (*journal*).

Mönch [mœnç], *m.* (—es, *pl.* —e) monk, friar.

Mönchskappe ['mœnçskapə], *f.* (—, *pl.* —n) cowl, monk's hood.

Mönchskutte ['mœnçskutə], *f.* (—, *pl.* —n) cowl.

Mond [mo:nt], *m.* (—es, *pl.* —e) moon; *zunehmender* —, waxing moon; *abnehmender* —, waning moon.

Mondfinsternis ['mo:ntfınstɐnıs], *f.* (—, *pl.* —se) eclipse of the moon.

mondsüchtig ['mo:ntzyçtıç], *adj.* given to sleep-walking; (*fig.*) moonstruck.

Mondwandlung ['mo:ntvandluŋ], *f.* (—, *pl.* —en) phase of the moon.

Moneten [mo'ne:tən], *pl.* (*sl.*) money, cash, funds.

Mongolei [mɔŋɡo'laı], *f.* Mongolia.

monieren [mo'ni:rən], *v.a.* remind (a debtor); censure.

monogam [mono'ga:m], *adj.* monogamous.

Monopol [mono'po:l], *n.* (—s, *pl.* —e) monopoly.

monoton [mono'to:n], *adj.* monotonous.

Monstrum ['mɔnstrum], *n.* (—s, *pl.* Monstra) monster, monstrosity.

Monsun [mɔn'zu:n], *m.* (—s, *pl.* —e) monsoon.

Montag ['mo:nta:k], *m.* (—s, *pl.* —e) Monday; *blauer* —, Bank Holiday Monday.

Montage [mɔn'ta:ʒə], *f.* (—, *pl.* —n) fitting (up), setting up, installation, assembling.

Montanindustrie [mɔn'ta:nındustri:], *f.* (—, *no pl.*) mining industry.

Montanunion [mɔn'ta:nunjo:n], *f.* (—, *no pl.*) (*Pol.*) European Coal and Steel Community.

Monteur [mɔn'tø:r], *m.* (—s, *pl.* —e) fitter.

montieren [mɔn'ti:rən], *v.a.* fit (up), set up, mount, install.

Montur [mɔn'tuːr], *f.* (—, *pl.* —en) uniform, livery.

Moor [mo:r], *n.* (—es, *pl.* —e) swamp, fen, bog.

Moos [mo:s], *n.* (—es, *pl.* —e) moss; (*sl.*) cash.

Moped ['mo:pɛt], *n.* (—s, *pl.* —s) moped, motorised pedal cycle.

Mops [mɔps], *m.* (—es, *pl.* ˙e) pug (dog).

mopsen ['mɔpsən], *v.r. sich* —, feel bored.

Moral [mo'ra:l], *f.* (—, *no pl.*) moral, morals.

moralisch [mo'ra:lıʃ], *adj.* moral.

Morast [mo'rast], *m.* (—es, *pl.* ˙e) morass, bog, fen, mire.

Moratorium [mora'to:rjum], *n.* (—s, *pl.* —rien) (*payments etc.*) respite.

Morchel ['mɔrçəl], *f.* (—, *pl.* —n) (*Bot.*) morel (edible fungus).

Mord [mɔrt], *m.* (—es, *pl.* —e) murder.

morden ['mɔrdən], *v.a., v.n.* murder.

Mörder ['mœrdər], *m.* (—s, *pl.* —) murderer.

Mordsgeschichte ['mɔrtsɡəʃıçtə], *f.* (—, *pl.* —n) (*coll.*) cock-and-bull story.

Mordskerl ['mɔrtskɛrl], *m.* (—s, *pl.* —e) devil of a fellow; (*Am.*) great guy.

Mordtat ['mɔrtta:t], *f.* (—, *pl.* —en) murder.

Morelle [mo'rɛlə], *f.* (—, *pl.* —n) (*Bot.*) morello cherry.

Morgen ['mɔrɡən], *m.* (—s, *pl.* —) morning, daybreak; (*Poet.*) east; measure of land; *eines* —s, one morning.

morgen ['mɔrɡən], *adv.* tomorrow; — *früh*, tomorrow morning; *heute* —, this morning.

Morgenblatt ['mɔrɡənblat], *n.* (—s, *pl.* ˙er) morning paper.

morgendlich ['mɔrɡəntlıç], *adj.* of or in the morning; matutinal.

Morgenland ['mɔrɡənlant], *n.* (—es, *pl.* —) orient, east.

Morgenrot ['mɔrɡənro:t], *n.* (—s, *no pl.*) dawn, sunrise.

morgens ['mɔrɡəns], *adv.* in the morning.

morgig ['mɔrɡıç], *adj.* tomorrow's.

Morphium ['mɔrfjum], *n.* (—s, *no pl.*) morphia, morphine.

morsch [mɔrʃ], *adj.* brittle, rotten, decayed.

Mörser ['mœrzər], *m.* (—s, *pl.* —) mortar.

Mörserkeule ['mœrzərkɔylə], *f.* (—, *pl.* —n) pestle.

Mörtel ['mœrtəl], *m.* (—s, *no pl.*) mortar, plaster.

Mörtelkelle ['mœrtəlkɛlə], *f.* (—, *pl.* —n) trowel.

Mosaik [moza'i:k], *n.* (—s, *pl.* —e) mosaic (work); inlaid work.

mosaisch [mo'za:ıʃ], *adj.* Mosaic.

Moschee [mo'ʃe:], *f.* (—, *pl.* —n) mosque.

Moschus ['mɔʃus], *m.* (—, *no pl.*) musk.

Mosel ['mo:zəl], *f.* Moselle.

Moskau ['mɔskau], *n.* Moscow.

Moskito [mɔs'ki:to], *m.* (—s, *pl.* —s) (*Ent.*) mosquito.

Most [mɔst], *m.* (—es, *no pl.*) new wine, cider.

Mostrich ['mɔstrɪç], *m.* (—s, *no pl.*) mustard.

Motiv [mo'ti:f], *n.* (—es, *pl.* —e) motive; (*Mus., Lit.*) motif, theme.

motivieren [moti'vi:rən], *v.a.* motivate.

Motorrad ['mo:tɔrra:t], *n.* (—es, *pl.* ⸚er) motor-cycle.

Motte ['mɔtə], *f.* (—, *pl.* —n) (*Ent.*) moth.

moussieren [mu'si:rən], *v.n.* effervesce, sparkle.

Möwe ['mø:və], *f.* (—, *pl.* —n) (*Orn.*) seagull.

Mucke ['mukə], *f.* (—, *pl.* —n) whim, caprice; obstinacy.

Mücke ['mykə], *f.* (—, *pl.* —n) (*Ent.*) gnat, fly, mosquito.

Muckerei [mukə'raɪ], *f.* (—, *pl.* —en) cant.

mucksen ['muksən], *v.n.* stir, move, budge.

müde ['my:də], *adj.* tired, weary; — *machen*, tire.

Muff [muf], *m.* (—es, *pl.* —e) muff.

muffig ['mufɪç], *adj.* musty, fusty, stuffy.

Mühe ['my:ə], *f.* (—, *pl.* —n) trouble, pains; effort, labour, toil; *sich* — *geben*, take pains.

mühelos ['my:əlo:s], *adj.* effortless, easy.

mühen ['my:ən], *v.r. sich* —, exert o.s., take pains.

Mühewaltung ['my:əvaltuŋ], *f.* (—, *pl.* —en) exertion, effort.

Mühle ['my:lə], *f.* (—, *pl.* —n) (*flour*) mill; (*coffee*) grinder; game.

Muhme ['mu:mə], *f.* (—, *pl.* —n) (*obs.*) aunt.

Mühsal ['my:za:l], *f.* (—, *pl.* —e) hardship, misery, toil.

mühsam ['my:za:m], *adj.* troublesome, laborious.

mühselig ['my:ze:lɪç], *adj.* painful, laborious; miserable.

Mulatte [mu'latə], *m.* (—n, *pl.* —n) mulatto.

Mulde ['muldə], *f.* (—, *pl.* —n) trough.

muldenförmig ['muldənfœrmɪç], *adj.* trough-shaped.

Mull [mul], *m.* (—s, *no pl.*) Indian muslin.

Müll [myl], *m.* (—s, *no pl.*) dust, rubbish; (*Am.*) garbage.

Müller ['mylər], *m.* (—s, *pl.* —) miller.

mulmig ['mulmɪç], *adj.* dusty, mouldy, decayed.

multiplizieren [multipli'tsi:rən], *v.a.* multiply.

Mumie ['mu:mjə], *f.* (—, *pl.* —n) (*Archaeol.*) mummy.

Mummenschanz ['mumənʃants], *m.* (—es, *no pl.*) mummery, masquerade.

München ['mynçən], *n.* Munich.

Mund [munt], *m.* (—es, *pl.* ⸚er) mouth; *den* — *halten*, keep quiet; *einen großen* — *haben*, talk big; *sich den* — *verbrennen*, put o.'s foot in it.

Mundart ['munta:rt], *f.* (—, *pl.* —en) (local) dialect.

Mündel ['myndəl], *m., f. & n.* (—s, *pl.* —) ward, minor, child under guardianship.

mündelsicher ['myndəlzɪçər], *adj.* gilt-edged.

munden ['mundən], *v.n. es mundet mir*, I like the taste, I relish it.

münden ['myndən], *v.n.* discharge (into), flow (into).

mundfaul ['muntfaul], *adj.* tongue-tied; taciturn.

mundgerecht ['muntgəreçt], *adj.* palatable; (*fig.*) suitable.

Mundharmonika ['muntharmo:nika], *f.* (—, *pl.* —kas, —ken) mouth organ.

mündig ['myndɪç], *adj.* of age; — *werden*, come of age.

mündlich ['myntlɪç], *adj.* verbal, oral, by word of mouth; (*examination*) viva voce.

Mundschenk ['muntʃɛŋk], *m.* (—s, *pl.* —e) cupbearer.

mundtot ['muntto:t], *adj.* — *machen*, silence, gag.

Mündung ['myndun], *f.* (—, *pl.* —en) (*river*) estuary, mouth; (*gun*) muzzle.

Mundvorrat ['muntfɔrra:t], *m.* (—s, *pl.* ⸚e) provisions, victuals.

Mundwerk ['muntverk], *n.* (—s, *no pl.*) mouth; (*fig.*) gift of the gab.

Munition [muni'tsjo:n], *f.* (—, *no pl.*) ammunition.

munkeln ['munkəln], *v.n.* whisper; *man munkelt*, it is rumoured.

Münster ['mynstər], *n.* (—s, *pl.* —) minster, cathedral.

munter ['muntər], *adj.* awake; lively, active, sprightly, vivacious, cheerful, gay.

Münze ['myntsə], *f.* (—, *pl.* —n) coin.

Münzeinheit ['myntsainhait], *f.* (—, *no pl.*) monetary unit.

Münzfälscher ['myntsfɛlʃər], *m.* (—s, *pl.* —) (counterfeit) coiner.

Münzkunde ['myntskundə], *f.* (—, *no pl.*) numismatics.

Münzprobe ['myntspro:bə], *f.* (—, *pl.* —n) assay of a coin.

mürbe ['myrbə], *adj.* mellow; (*meat*) tender; (*cake*) crisp; brittle; *einen* — *machen*, soften s.o. up, force s.o. to yield.

Murmel ['murməl], *f.* (—, *pl.* —n) (*toy*) marble.

murmeln ['murməln], *v.n.* murmur, mutter.

Murmeltier ['murməlti:r], *n.* (—s, *pl.* —e) (*Zool.*) marmot; *wie ein* — *schlafen*, sleep like a log.

murren ['murən], *v.n.* grumble, growl.

mürrisch ['myrɪʃ], *adj.* morose, surly, sulky, peevish, sullen.

Mus

Mus [mu:s], *n.* (**—es**, *no pl.*) purée, (apple) sauce; pulp.
Muschel ['muʃəl], *f.* (**—**, *pl.* **—n**) mussel, shell; (*telephone*) ear-piece.
Muse ['mu:zə], *f.* (**—**, *pl.* **—n**) muse.
Muselman ['mu:zəlman], *m.* (**—en**, *pl.* **—en**) Muslim, Moslem.
Musik [mu'zi:k], *f.* (**—**, *no pl.*) music.
musikalisch [muzi'ka:lɪʃ], *adj.* musical.
Musikant [muzi'kant], *m.* (**—en**, *pl.* **—en**) musician; performer.
Musiker ['mu:zɪkər], *m.* (**—s**, *pl.* **—**) musician.
musizieren [muzi'tsi:rən], *v.n.* play music.
Muskateller [muska'tɛlər], *m.* (**—s**, *no pl.*) muscatel (wine).
Muskatnuß [mus'ka:tnus], *f.* (**—**, *pl.* **-̈sse**) nutmeg.
Muskel ['muskəl], *m.* (**—s**, *pl.* **—n**) muscle.
muskelig ['musklɪç] *see* **musklig**.
Muskete [mus'ke:tə], *f.* (**—**, *pl.* **—n**) musket.
Musketier [muske'ti:r], *m.* (**—s**, *pl.* **—e**) musketeer.
musklig ['musklɪç], *adj.* muscular.
muskulös [musku'lø:s], *adj.* muscular.
Muße ['mu:sə], *f.* (**—**, *no pl.*) leisure; *mit —*, leisurely, at leisure.
Musselin [musə'li:n], *m.* (**—s**, *pl.* **—e**) muslin.
müssen ['mysən], *v.n. irr.* have to, be forced, be compelled, be obliged; *ich muß*, I must, I have to.
müßig ['my:sɪç], *adj.* idle, lazy, unemployed.
Müßiggang ['my:sɪçgaŋ], *m.* (**—s**, *no pl.*) idleness, laziness, sloth.
Muster ['mustər], *n.* (**—s**, *pl.* **—**) sample; pattern; (proto-)type; (*fig.*) example.
Musterbild ['mustərbɪlt], *n.* (**—s**, *pl.* **—er**) paragon.
mustergültig ['mustərgyltɪç], *adj.* exemplary; standard; excellent.
musterhaft ['mustərhaft], *adj.* exemplary.
mustern ['mustərn], *v.a.* examine, muster, scan; (*troops*) review, inspect.
Musterung ['mustəruŋ], *f.* (**—**, *pl.* **—en**) review; examination, inspection.
Mut ['mu:t], *m.* (**—es**, *no pl.*) courage, spirit; *— fassen*, take heart, muster up courage.
Mutation [muta'tsjo:n], *f.* (**—**, *pl.* **—en**) change.
mutieren [mu'ti:rən], *v.n.* change; (*voice*) break.
mutig ['mu:tɪç], *adj.* courageous, brave.
mutlos ['mu:tlo:s], *adj.* discouraged, dejected, despondent.
mutmaßen ['mu:tma:sən], *v.a. insep.* surmise, suppose, conjecture.
Mutter ['mutər], *f.* (**—**, *pl.* **-̈**) mother; (*screw*) nut.
Mutterkorn ['mutərkorn], *n.* (**—s**, *no pl.*) ergot.

Mutterkuchen ['mutərku:xən], *m.* (**—s**, *pl.* **—**) placenta, after-birth.
Mutterleib ['mutərlaip], *m.* (**—s**, *no pl.*) womb, uterus.
Muttermal ['mutərma:l], *n.* (**—s**, *pl.* **—e**) birth-mark.
Mutterschaft ['mutərʃaft], *f.* (**—**, *no pl.*) motherhood, maternity.
mutterseelenallein ['mutərze:lənalain], *adj.* quite alone; (*coll.*) all on o.'s own.
Muttersöhnchen ['mutərzø:nçən], *n.* (**—s**, *pl.* **—**) mother's darling, spoilt child.
Mutterwitz ['mutərvɪts], *m.* (**—es**, *no pl.*) mother-wit, native wit, common sense.
Mutwille ['mu:tvɪlə], *m.* (**—ns**, *no pl.*) mischievousness, wantonness.
Mütze ['mytsə], *f.* (**—**, *pl.* **—n**) cap; bonnet; beret.
Myrrhe ['mɪrə], *f.* (**—**, *pl.* **—n**) myrrh.
Myrte ['mɪrtə], *f.* (**—**, *pl.* **—n**) (*Bot.*) myrtle.
Mysterium [mɪs'te:rjum], *n.* (**—s**, *pl.* **—rien**) mystery.
Mystik ['mɪstɪk], *f.* (**—**, *no pl.*) mysticism.
Mythologie [mytolo'gi:], *f.* (**—**, *pl.* **—n**) mythology.
Mythus ['mytus], *m.* (**—**, *pl.* **Mythen**) myth.

N

N [ɛn], *n.* (**—s**, *pl.* **—s**) the letter N.
na [na], *int.* well, now; *—nu!* well, I never! *— und?* so what?
Nabe ['na:bə], *f.* (**—**, *pl.* **—n**) hub.
Nabel ['na:bəl], *m.* (**—s**, *pl.* **—**) navel.
Nabelschnur ['na:bəlʃnu:r], *f.* (**—**, *pl.* **-̈e**) umbilical cord.
nach [na:x], *prep.* (*Dat.*) after, behind, following; to, towards; according to, in conformity *or* accordance with; in imitation of. — *adv.*, *prefix*. after, behind; afterwards, later; *— und —*, little by little, by degrees, gradually.
nachäffen ['na:xɛfən], *v.a.* ape, mimic, imitate; (*coll.*) take off.
nachahmen ['na:xa:mən], *v.a.* imitate, copy; counterfeit.
nacharbeiten ['na:xarbaitən], *v.n.* work after hours *or* overtime. — *v.a.* copy (*Dat.*).
nacharten ['na:xa:rtən], *v.n.* (*aux. sein*) resemble, (*coll.*) take after.
Nachbar ['naxba:r], *m.* (**—s**, **—n**, *pl.* **—n**) neighbour.
Nachbarschaft ['naxba:rʃaft], *f.* (**—**, *no pl.*) neighbourhood, vicinity; (*people*) neighbours.
nachbestellen ['na:xbəʃtɛlən], *v.a.* order more, re-order.

nachbilden ['na:xbɪldən], *v.a.* copy, reproduce.

nachdem [na:x'de:m], *adv.* afterwards, after that. — *conj.* after, when; *je* —, according to circumstances, that depends.

nachdenken ['na:xdɛŋkən], *v.n. irr.* think (over), meditate, muse, ponder.

nachdenklich ['na:xdɛŋklɪç], *adj.* reflective, pensive, wistful; — *stimmen*, set thinking.

Nachdruck ['na:xdruk], *m.* (—s, *pl.* —e) reprint; stress, emphasis.

nachdrucken ['na:xdrukən], *v.a.* reprint.

nachdrücklich ['na:xdryklɪç], *adj.* emphatic; — *betonen*, emphasise.

nacheifern ['na:xaɪfərn], *v.n. einem* —, emulate s.o.

nacheinander ['na:xaɪnandər], *adv.* one after another.

nachempfinden ['na:xɛmpfɪndən], *v.a. irr.* sympathize with, feel for.

Nachen ['naxən], *m.* (—s, *pl.* —) (*Poet.*) boat, skiff.

Nachfolge ['na:xfɔlgə], *f.* (—, *pl.* —n) succession.

nachfolgend ['na:xfɔlgənt], *adj.* following, subsequent.

Nachfolger ['na:xfɔlgər], *m.* (—s, *pl.* —) successor.

nachforschen ['na:xfɔrʃən], *v.a.* search after; enquire into, investigate.

Nachfrage ['na:xfra:gə], *f.* (—, *no pl.*) enquiry; (*Comm.*) demand; *Angebot und* —, supply and demand.

nachfühlen ['na:xfy:lən], *v.a. einem etwas* —, enter into s.o.'s feelings, sympathize with s.o.

nachfüllen ['na:xfylən], *v.a.* replenish, fill up.

nachgeben ['na:xge:bən], *v.n. irr.* relax, slacken, yield; give in, relent, give way.

nachgehen ['na:xge:ən], *v.n. irr.* (*aux. sein*) *einem* —, follow s.o., go after s.o.; (*clock*) be slow; follow up, investigate.

nachgerade ['na:xgəra:də], *adv.* by this time, by now; gradually.

nachgiebig ['na:xgi:bɪç], *adj.* yielding, compliant.

nachgrübeln ['na:xgry:bəln], *v.n.* speculate.

Nachhall ['na:xhal], *m.* (—s, *no pl.*) echo, resonance.

nachhaltig ['na:xhaltɪç], *adj.* lasting, enduring.

nachhängen ['na:xhɛŋən], *v.n. irr. seinen Gedanken* —, muse.

nachher ['na:xhe:r], *adv.* afterwards, later on.

nachherig ['na:xhe:rɪç], *adj.* subsequent, later.

Nachhilfestunde ['na:xhɪlfəʃtundə], *f.* (—, *pl.* —n) private coaching.

nachholen ['na:xho:lən], *v.a.* make good; make up for.

Nachhut ['na:xhu:t], *f.* (—, *no pl.*) (*Mil.*) rearguard.

nachjagen ['na:xja:gən], *v.n.* (*aux sein*) pursue.

Nachklang ['na:xklaŋ], *m.* (—s, *pl.* ⁓e) echo; (*fig.*) after-effect, reminiscence.

Nachkomme ['na:xkɔmə], *m.* (—n, *pl.* —n) descendant, offspring.

nachkommen ['na:xkɔmən], *v.n. irr.* (*aux. sein*) come after, follow; *seiner Pflicht* —, do o.'s duty; comply with; *einem Versprechen* —, keep a promise; *seinen Verpflichtungen nicht — können*, be unable to meet o.'s commitments.

Nachkommenschaft ['na:xkɔmənʃaft], *f.* (—, *no pl.*) descendants, offspring, issue, progeny.

Nachlaß ['na:xlas], *m.* (—sses, *pl.* ⁓sse) inheritance, estate, bequest; remission, discount, allowance.

nachlassen ['na:xlasən], *v.a. irr.* leave behind, bequeath; (*trade*) give a discount of. — *v.n.* abate, subside, slacken.

nachlässig ['na:xlɛsɪç], *adj.* negligent, remiss, careless.

nachlaufen ['na:xlaufən], *v.n. irr.* (*aux. sein*) *einem* —, run after s.o.

Nachlese ['na:xle:zə], *f.* (—, *pl.* —n) gleaning.

nachliefern ['na:xli:fərn], *v.a.* supply subsequently, complete delivery of.

nachmachen ['na:xmaxən], *v.a.* copy, imitate; counterfeit, forge.

nachmals ['na:xma:ls], *adv.* afterwards, subsequently.

Nachmittag ['na:xmɪta:k], *m.* (—s, *pl.* —e) afternoon.

Nachnahme ['na:xna:mə], *f.* (—, *no pl.*) *per* —, cash *or* (*Am.*) collect (payment) on delivery (*abbr.* C.O.D.).

nachplappern ['na:xplapərn], *v.a.* repeat mechanically.

Nachrede ['na:xre:də], *f.* (—, *pl.* —n) epilogue; *üble* —, slander.

Nachricht ['na:xrɪçt], *f.* (—, *pl.* —en) news, information; (*Mil.*) intelligence; — *geben*, send word.

nachrücken ['na:xrykən], *v.n.* (*aux. sein*) move up.

Nachruf ['na:xru:f], *m.* (—s, *pl.* —e) obituary.

nachrühmen ['na:xry:mən], *v.a. einem etwas* —, speak well of s.o.

Nachsatz ['na:xzats], *m.* (—es, *pl.* ⁓e) concluding clause; postscript.

nachschauen ['na:xʃauən], *v.n. jemandem* —, gaze after s.o.

nachschlagen ['na:xʃla:gən], *v.a. irr.* look up, consult (a book).

Nachschlagewerk ['na:xʃla:gəvɛrk], *n.* (—s, *pl.* —e) work of reference, reference book.

Nachschlüssel ['na:xʃlysəl], *m.* (—s, *pl.* —) master-key, skeleton-key.

Nachschrift ['na:xʃrɪft], *f.* (—, *pl.* —en) postscript, (*abbr.* P.S.).

Nachschub ['na:xʃu:p], *m.* (—s, *pl.* ⁓e) (fresh) supply; (*Mil.*) reinforcements.

Nachsehen ['na:xze:ən], *n.* (—s, *no pl.*) *das — haben*, be left out in the cold.

157

nachsehen

nachsehen ['na:xze:ən], *v.a.*, *v.n. irr.* look for, look s.th. up, refer to s.th.; *einem etwas —*, be indulgent with s.o.

Nachsicht ['na:xzɪçt], *f.* (—, *no pl.*) forbearance, indulgence.

Nachsilbe ['na:xzɪlbə], *f.* (—, *pl.* —n) suffix.

nachsinnen ['na:xzɪnən], *v.n.* muse, reflect.

nachsitzen ['na:xzɪtsən], *v.n.* be kept in after school.

Nachsommer ['na:xzɔmər], *m.* (—s, *pl.* —) Indian summer.

Nachspeise ['na:xʃpaɪzə], *f.* (—, *pl.* —n) dessert.

nachspüren ['na:xʃpy:rən], *v.n. einem* —, trace, track.

nächst [nɛːçst], *prep.* (*Dat.*) next to, nearest to. — *adj.* next.

Nächste ['nɛːçstə], *m.* (—n, *pl.* —n) fellow-man, neighbour.

nachstehen ['na:xʃte:ən], *v.n. irr. einem* —, be inferior to s.o.; *keinem* —, be second to none.

nachstehend ['na:xʃte:ənt], *adv.* below, hereinafter. — *adj.* following.

nachstellen ['na:xʃtelən], *v.n. einem* —, lie in wait for s.o.

Nachstellung ['na:xʃtelʊŋ], *f.* (—, *pl.* —en) persecution, ambush; (*Gram.*) postposition.

nächstens ['nɛːçstəns], *adv.* soon, shortly.

nachstöbern ['na:xʃtø:bərn], *v.n.* rummage.

nachströmen ['na:xʃtrø:mən], *v.n.* (*aux. sein*) crowd after.

Nacht [naxt], *f.* (—, *pl.* ⁓e) night; *die ganze — hindurch*, all night; *bei —*, at night; *gute — wünschen*, bid goodnight; *über —*, overnight; *in der —*, during the night; *bei — und Nebel*, in the dead of night.

Nachteil ['na:xtaɪl], *m.* (—s, *pl.* —e) disadvantage, damage.

Nachtessen ['naxtesən], *n.* (—s, *pl.* —) supper; evening meal.

Nachtfalter ['naxtfaltər], *m.* (—s, *pl.* —) (*Ent.*) moth.

Nachtgeschirr ['naxtgəʃɪr], *n.* (—s, *pl.* —e) chamber-pot.

Nachtgleiche ['naxtglaɪçə], *f.* (—, *pl.* —n) equinox.

Nachthemd ['naxthemt], *n.* (—es, *pl.* —en) night-dress, night-gown.

Nachtigall ['naxtɪgal], *f.* (—, *pl.* —en) (*Orn.*) nightingale.

nächtigen ['nɛçtɪgən], *v.n.* spend the night.

Nachtisch ['naxtɪʃ], *m.* (—es, *pl.* —e) dessert.

Nachtlager ['naxtla:gər], *n.* (—s, *pl.* —) lodgings for the night; (*Mil.*) bivouac.

Nachtmahl ['naxtma:l], *n.* (—s, *pl.* —e) (*Austr.*) supper.

nachtönen ['na:xtø:nən], *v.n.* resound.

Nachtrag ['na:xtra:k], *m.* (—s, *pl.* ⁓e) supplement, postscript, addition; (*pl.*) addenda.

nachtragen ['na:xtra:gən], *v.a. irr.* carry after; add; (*fig.*) *einem etwas —*, bear s.o. a grudge.

nachträglich ['na:xtrɛːklɪç], *adj.* subsequent; supplementary; additional; further; later.

Nachtrupp ['na:xtrup], *m.* (—s, *no pl.*) rearguard.

Nachtschwärmer ['naxtʃvermər], *m.* (—s, *pl.* —) night-reveller.

Nachttisch ['naxttɪʃ], *m.* (—es, *pl.* —e) bedside-table.

nachtun ['na:xtu:n], *v.a. irr. einem etwas —*, imitate s.o., emulate s.o.

Nachtwächter ['naxtveçtər], *m.* (—s, *pl.* —) night-watchman.

Nachtwandler ['naxtvandlər], *m.* (—s, *pl.* —) sleep-walker, somnambulist.

Nachwahl ['na:xva:l], *f.* (—, *pl.* —en) by(e)-election.

Nachwehen ['na:xve:ən], *f. pl.* aftermath; unpleasant consequences.

Nachweis ['na:xvaɪs], *m.* (—es, *pl.* —e) proof; (*Lit.*) reference; agency.

nachweisen ['na:xvaɪzən], *v.a. irr.* prove, establish; (*Lit.*) refer.

Nachwelt ['na:xvelt], *f.* (—, *no pl.*) posterity.

Nachwort ['na:xvɔrt], *n.* (—es, *pl.* —e) epilogue.

Nachwuchs ['na:xvu:ks], *m.* (—es, *no pl.*) coming generation; recruits.

Nachzahlung ['na:xtsa:lʊŋ], *f.* (—, *pl.* —en) additional payment, supplementary payment.

Nachzählung ['na:xtsɛːlʊŋ], *f.* (—, *pl.* —en) recount.

nachziehen ['na:xtsi:ən], *v.a. irr.* drag, tow; tighten; trace, pencil. — *v.n.* follow.

Nachzügler ['na:xtsy:glər], *m.* (—s, *pl.* —) straggler.

Nacken ['nakən], *m.* (—s, *pl.* —) nape, scruff of the neck.

nackend ['nakənt], *adj.* naked.

nackt [nakt], *adj.* nude, naked; (*bird*) callow; (*fig.*) bare; *sich — ausziehen*, strip.

Nadel ['na:dəl], *f.* (—, *pl.* —n) needle, pin; *wie auf —n sitzen*, be on tenterhooks.

Nadelöhr ['na:dəlø:r], *n.* (—s, *pl.* —e) eye of a needle.

Nagel ['na:gəl], *m.* (—s, *pl.* ⁓) nail; (*wooden*) peg; (*ornament*) stud; *etwas an den — hängen*, lay s.th. aside, give s.th. up.

nagelneu ['na:gəlnɔy], *adj.* brand new.

nagen ['na:gən], *v.a.*, *v.n.* gnaw; (*fig.*) rankle.

Näharbeit ['nɛːarbaɪt], *f.* (—, *pl.* —en) sewing, needlework.

nahe ['na:ə], *adj.*, *adv.* near, close, nigh; *— bei*, close to; *— daran sein*, be on the point of; *es geht mir —*, it grieves me, it touches me; *einem zu — treten*, hurt s.o.'s feelings; *es liegt —*, it is obvious, it suggests itself.

Nähe ['nɛːə], *f.* (—, *no pl.*) nearness, proximity; *in der —*, at hand, close by.

nahen ['na:ən], *v.n.* (*aux.* sein) draw near, approach.

nähen ['nɛ:ən], *v.a.* sew, stitch.

Nähere ['nɛ:ərə], *n.* (—n, *no pl.*) details, particulars.

Näherin ['nɛ:ərɪn], *f.* (—, *pl.* — innen) seamstress, needlewoman.

nähern ['nɛ:ərn], *v.r. sich* —, draw near, approach.

nahestehen ['na:əʃte:ən], *v.n.* be closely connected *or* friendly (with s.o.).

Nährboden ['nɛ:rbo:dən], *m.* (—s, *pl.* ∵) rich soil; (*Med., Biol.*) culture-medium.

nähren ['nɛ:rən], *v.a.* nourish, feed. — *v.r. sich* — *von*, feed on; (*fig.*) gain a livelihood.

nahrhaft ['na:rhaft], *adj.* nourishing, nutritive, nutritious.

Nährstand ['nɛ:rʃtant], *m.* (—es, *no pl.*) peasants, producers.

Nahrung ['na:ruŋ], *f.* (—, *no pl.*) nourishment.

Nahrungsmittel ['na:ruŋsmɪtəl], *n.* (—s, *pl.* —) food, provisions, victuals.

Naht [na:t], *f.* (—, *pl.* ∵e) seam.

Nähzeug ['nɛ:tsɔyk], *n.* (—s, *no pl.*) sewing kit, work box.

naiv [na'i:f], *adj.* naïve, artless, guileless.

Naivität [naivi'tɛ:t], *f.* (—, *no pl.*) artlessness, guilelessness, naïveté.

Name ['na:mə], *m.* (—ns, *pl.* —n) name; *guter* —, good name, renown, reputation; *dem* — *nach*, by name; *etwas beim rechten* —*n nennen*, call a spade a spade.

namens ['na:məns], *adv.* called; by the name of.

Namensvetter ['na:mənsfɛtər], *m.* (—s, *pl.* —n) namesake.

namentlich ['na:məntlɪç], *adj.* by name; particularly.

Namenverzeichnis ['na:mənfɛrtsaɪç-nɪs], *n.* (—ses, *pl.* —se) list of names; (*scientific*) nomenclature.

namhaft ['na:mhaft], *adj.* distinguished, renowned; considerable; — *machen*, name.

nämlich ['nɛ:mlɪç], *adv.* namely, to wit.

Napf [napf], *m.* (—es, *pl.* ∵e) bowl, basin.

Napfkuchen ['napfku:xən], *m.* (—s, *pl.* —) pound-cake, large cake.

Narbe ['narbə], *f.* (—, *pl.* —n) scar; (*leather*) grain.

Narkose [nar'ko:zə], *f.* (—, *pl.* —n) anaesthesia; narcosis.

Narr [nar], *m.* (—en, *pl.* —en) fool; jester, buffoon; *einen zum* —*en haben*, make a fool of s.o.; *an einem einen* —*en gefressen haben*, dote on, be infatuated with s.o.

Narrheit ['narhaɪt], *f.* (—, *pl.* —en) foolishness, folly.

närrisch ['nɛrɪʃ], *adj.* foolish, comical; odd; merry; eccentric, mad; — *werden*, go mad.

Narzisse [nar'tsɪsə], *f.* (—, *pl.* —n) (*Bot.*) narcissus; *gelbe* —, daffodil.

naschen ['naʃən], *v.a., v.n.* pilfer titbits; nibble at, eat sweets.

Näscherei [nɛʃər'aɪ], *f.* (—, *pl.* —en) sweets, dainties, sweetmeats.

naschhaft ['naʃhaft], *adj.* sweet-toothed.

Naschkatze ['naʃkatsə], *f.* (—, *pl.* —n) sweet tooth.

Nase ['na:zə], *f.* (—, *pl.* —n) nose; (*animal*) snout; scent; *stumpfe* —, snub nose; *gebogene* —, Roman nose; *immer der* — *nach*, follow your nose; *die* — *hoch tragen*, be stuck-up; *eine feine* (*gute*) — *haben*, be good at; *nicht miss much*; *die* — *rümpfen*, turn up o.'s nose; *seine* — *in alles stecken*, poke o.'s nose into everything; *einem etwas unter die* — *reiben*, bring s.th. home to s.o.

näseln ['nɛ:zəln], *v.n.* speak with a twang.

Nasenbein ['na:zənbaɪn], *n.* (—s, *pl.* —e) nasal bone.

Nasenbluten ['na:zənblu:tən], *n.* (—s, *no pl.*) nose-bleed.

Nasenflügel ['na:zənfly:gəl], *m.* (—s, *pl.* —) side of the nose; nostril.

naseweis ['na:zəvaɪs], *adj.* pert, saucy.

Nashorn ['na:shɔrn], *n.* (—s, *pl.* ∵er) (*Zool.*) rhinoceros.

Naß [nas], *n.* (—sses, *no pl.*) (*Poet.*) fluid.

naß [nas], *adj.* wet, moist, damp.

Nässe ['nɛsə], *f.* (—, *no pl.*) wetness, dampness, moisture, humidity.

nationalisieren [natsjonali'zi:rən], *v.a.* nationalise.

Nationalität [natsjonali'tɛ:t], *f.* (—, *pl.* —en) nationality.

Natrium ['na:trjum], *n.* (—s, *no pl.*) sodium.

Natron ['na:trɔn], *n.* (—s, *no pl.*) sodium carbonate; *doppeltkohlensaures* —, sodium bicarbonate; bicarbonate of soda.

Natter ['natər], *f.* (—, *pl.* —n) (*Zool.*) adder, viper.

Natur [na'tu:r], *f.* (—, *pl.* —en) nature; (*body*) constitution; (*mind*) disposition; *von* —, by nature, constitutionally; *nach der* — *zeichnen*, draw from nature.

naturalisieren [naturali'zi:rən], *v.a.* naturalise.

Naturalleistung [natu'ra:llaɪstuŋ], *f.* (—, *pl.* —en) payment in kind.

Naturell [natu'rɛl], *n.* (—s, *pl.* —e) natural disposition, temper.

Naturforscher [na'tu:rfɔrʃər], *m.* (—s, *pl.* —) naturalist.

naturgemäß [na'tu:rgəmɛ:s], *adj.* natural.

Naturgeschichte [na'tu:rgəʃɪçtə], *f.* (—, *no pl.*) natural history.

naturgetreu [na'tu:rgətrɔy], *adj.* true to nature, lifelike.

Naturkunde [na'tu:rkundə], *f.* (—, *no pl.*) natural history.

Naturlehre [na'tu:rle:rə], *f.* (—, *no pl.*) natural philosophy; physics.

natürlich [na'ty:rlıç], *adj.* natural; innate, inherent; unaffected, artless. — *adv.* of course, naturally.

Naturspiel [na'tu:rʃpi:l], *n.* (—s, *pl.* —e) freak of nature.

Naturtrieb [na'tu:rtri:p], *m.* (—s, *no pl.*) natural impulse, instinct.

naturwidrig [na'tu:rvi:drıç], *adj.* contrary to nature, unnatural.

Naturwissenschaft [na'tu:rvɪsənʃaft], *f.* (—, *pl.* —en) (natural) science.

naturwüchsig [na'tu:rvy:ksıç], *adj.* original; unsophisticated.

Nautik ['nautık], *f.* (—, *no pl.*) nautical science.

nautisch ['nautıʃ], *adj.* nautical.

Nazi ['na:tsi], *abbr.* National Socialist.

Neapel [ne'a:pəl], *n.* Naples.

Nebel ['ne:bəl], *m.* (—s, *pl.* —) fog; *leichter* —, haze, mist; *dichter* —, (*London*) pea-souper; (*with soot*) smog.

Nebelschicht ['ne:bəlʃıçt], *f.* (—, *pl.* —n) fog-bank.

neben ['ne:bən], *prep.* (*Dat., Acc.*) near, by, beside, besides, close to, next to; (*in compounds*) secondary, subsidiary, side-. — *adv.* beside, besides.

nebenan [ne:bən'an], *adv.* next door, nearby.

nebenbei [ne:bən'baı], *adv.* besides, by the way, incidentally.

Nebenbuhler [ne:bənbu:lər], *m.* (—s, *pl.* —) rival.

nebeneinander [ne:bənaın'andər], *adv.* side by side, abreast.

Nebenfluß ['ne:bənflus], *m.* (—sses, *pl.* ⁚sse) tributary, affluent.

nebenher [ne:bən'he:r], *adv.* by the side of, along with.

Nebenmensch ['ne:bənmenʃ], *m.* (—en, *pl.* —en) fellow creature.

Nebensatz ['ne:bənzats], *m.* (—es, *pl.* ⁚e) (*Gram.*) subordinate clause.

Nebenzimmer ['ne:bəntsımər], *n.* (—s, *pl.* —) adjoining room.

neblig ['ne:blıç], *adj.* foggy, misty, hazy.

nebst [ne:pst], *prep.* (*Dat.*) together with, including.

necken ['nɛkən], *v.a.* tease, chaff, banter.

neckisch ['nɛkıʃ], *adj.*, droll, playful, arch.

Neffe ['nɛfə], *m.* (—n, *pl.* —n) nephew.

Neger ['ne:gər], *m.* (—s, *pl.* —) Negro.

negerartig ['ne:gəra:rtıç], *adj.* Negroid.

negieren [ne'gi:rən], *v.a.* deny, negate, negative.

nehmen ['ne:mən], *v.a. irr.* take, seize; receive, accept; *einem etwas* —, take s.th. from s.o.; *das lasse ich mir nicht* —, I insist on that, I am not to be done out of that; *ein Ende* —, come to an end; *etwas in die Hand* —, take s.th. in hand; *Schaden* —, suffer damage; *einen beim Wort* —, take s.o. at his word; *sich in acht* —, take care.

Nehrung ['ne:ruŋ], *f.* (—, *pl.* —en) narrow tongue of land, spit.

Neid [naıt], *m.* (—es, *no pl.*) envy, grudge.

Neidhammel ['naıthaməl], *m.* (—s, *pl.* —) dog in the manger.

neidisch ['naıdıʃ], *adj.* envious, grudging, jealous.

Neige ['naıgə], *f.* (—, *pl.* —n) remnant, sediment; *zur* — *gehen*, be on the decline, run short, dwindle.

neigen ['naıgən], *v.a., v.n.* incline, bow, bend; *zu etwas* —, be inclined to, be prone to. — *v.r. sich* —, bow.

Neigung ['naıguŋ], *f.* (—, *pl.* —en) inclination, proneness; affection; (*ground*) dip, slope, gradient; (*ship*) list.

Neigungsfläche ['naıguŋsflɛçə], *f.* (—, *pl.* —n) inclined plane.

nein [naın], *adv.* no.

Nekrolog [nekro'lo:k], *m.* (—(e)s, *pl.* —e) obituary.

Nelke ['nɛlkə], *f.* (—, *pl.* —n) (*Bot.*) pink, carnation; (*condiment*) clove.

nennen ['nɛnən], *v.a. irr.* name, call by name, term, style.

Nenner ['nɛnər], *m.* (—s, *pl.* —) denominator.

Nennung ['nɛnuŋ], *f.* (—, *pl.* —en) naming, mentioning.

Nennwert ['nɛnve:rt], *m.* (—s, *pl.* —e) nominal value.

Nepal ['ne:pal], *n.* Nepal.

Nerv [nɛrf], *m.* (—s, *pl.* —en) nerve, sinew; *einem auf die* —*en gehen*, get on s.o.'s nerves.

Nervenlehre ['nɛrfənle:rə], *f.* (—, *no pl.*) neurology.

nervig ['nɛrvıç], *adj.* strong; (*fig.*) pithy.

nervös [nɛr'vø:s], *adj.* nervous, irritable, fidgety.

Nerz [nɛrts], *m.* (—es, *pl.* —e) mink.

Nessel ['nɛsəl], *f.* (—, *pl.* —n) nettle.

Nesseltuch ['nɛsəltu:x], *n.* (—es, *no pl.*) muslin.

Nest [nɛst], *n.* (—es, *pl.* —er) nest; (*eagle*) eyrie; *kleines* —, small town.

Nesthäkchen ['nɛsthɛːkçən], *n.* (—s, *pl.* —) youngest child.

nett [nɛt], *adj.* nice, kind, friendly; neat, trim.

netto ['nɛto], *adv.* (*Comm.*) net, clear.

Netz [nɛts], *n.* (—es, *pl.* —e) net; (*Electr.*) grid; *Eisenbahn* —, railway network *or* system.

netzen ['nɛtsən], *v.a.* (*obs., Poet.*) wet, moisten.

Netzhaut ['nɛtshaut], *f.* (—, *pl.* ⁚e) retina.

neu [nɔy], *adj.* new, fresh; modern; recent; *aufs* —*e*, *von* —*em*, anew, afresh; —*e*, —*ere Sprachen*, modern languages.

Neuenburg ['nɔyənburk], *n.* Neuchâtel.

neuerdings ['nɔyərdıŋs], *adv.* newly, lately.

Neuerer ['nɔyərər], *m.* (—s, *pl.* —) innovator.

neuerlich ['nɔyərlɪç], *adj.* late, repeated.

Neufundland [nɔy'funtlant], *n.* Newfoundland.

Neugier(de) ['nɔygi:r(də)], *f.* (—, *no pl.*) inquisitiveness, curiosity.

neugierig ['nɔygi:rɪç], *adj.* curious, inquisitive.

Neuheit ['nɔyhaɪt], *f.* (—, *pl.* —en) novelty.

Neuigkeit ['nɔyɪçkaɪt], *f.* (—, *pl.* —en) piece of news.

neulich ['nɔylɪç], *adv.* lately, recently.

Neuling ['nɔylɪŋ], *m.* (—s, *pl.* —e) novice, beginner, tyro, newcomer; (*Am.*) greenhorn.

neumodisch ['nɔymo:dɪʃ], *adj.* newfangled, in vogue.

Neumond ['nɔymo:nt], *m.* (—s, *pl.* —e) new moon.

neun [nɔyn], *num. adj.* nine.

Neunauge ['nɔynaugə], *n.* (—s, *pl.* —n) river lamprey.

neunzehn ['nɔyntse:n], *num. adj.* nineteen.

neunzig ['nɔyntsɪç], *num. adj.* ninety.

Neuregelung ['nɔyre:gəluŋ], *f.* (—, *pl.* —en) rearrangement.

Neuseeland [nɔy'ze:lant], *n.* New Zealand.

neutralisieren [nɔytrali'zi:rən], *v.a.* neutralise.

Neutralität [nɔytrali'tɛ:t], *f.* (—, *no pl.*) neutrality.

Neutrum ['nɔytrum], *n.* (—s, *pl.* —ren) (*Gram.*) neuter.

Neuzeit ['nɔytsaɪt], *f.* (—, *no pl.*) modern times.

nicht [nɪçt], *adv.* not; *auch* —, nor; — *doch*, don't; — *einmal*, not even; *durchaus* —, not at all, by no means; — *mehr*, no more, no longer; not any more; *noch* —, not yet; — *wahr?* isn't it? aren't you? (*in compounds*) non-, dis-, a- (*negativing*).

Nichte ['nɪçtə], *f.* (—, *pl.* —n) niece.

nichten ['nɪçtən], *adv.* (*obs.*) *mit*—, by no means, not at all.

nichtig ['nɪçtɪç], *adj.* null, void, invalid.

Nichtigkeit ['nɪçtɪçkaɪt], *f.* (—, *no pl.*) invalidity, nullity.

nichts [nɪçts], *pron.* nothing, nought; — *als*, nothing but.

nichtsdestoweniger [nɪçtsdesto've:nɪgər], *adv.* nevertheless.

Nichtsnutz ['nɪçtsnuts], *m.* (—es, *pl.* —e) good for nothing.

Nickel ['nɪkəl], *n.* (—s, *no pl.*) (*metal*) nickel.

nicken ['nɪkən], *v.n.* nod.

nie [ni:], *adv.* never, at no time.

nieder ['ni:dər], *adj.* low, lower, nether; mean, inferior. — *adv.* down.

niedergeschlagen ['ni:dərgəʃla:gən], *adj.* dejected, low-spirited, depressed.

niederkommen ['ni:dərkɔmən], *v.n. irr.* (*aux. sein*) (*rare*) be confined.

Niederkunft ['ni:dərkunft], *f.* (—, *no pl.*) confinement, childbirth.

Niederlage ['ni:dərla:gə], *f.* (—, *pl.* —n) (*enemy*) defeat, overthrow; (*goods*) depot, warehouse; agency.

Niederlande ['ni:dərlandə], *n. pl.* the Netherlands.

niederlassen ['ni:dərlasən], *v.a. irr.* let down. — *v.r. sich* —, sit down, take a seat; settle; establish o.s. in business.

Niederlassung ['ni:dərlasuŋ], *f.* (—, *pl.* —en) establishment; settlement, colony; branch, branch establishment.

niederlegen ['ni:dərle:gən], *v.a.* lay down, put down; (*office*) resign, abdicate. — *v.r. sich* —, lie down.

Niederschlag ['ni:dərʃla:k], *m.* (—s, *pl.* ẹe) precipitation, sediment, deposit; rain.

niederschlagen ['ni:dərʃla:gən], *v.a. irr.* strike down; (*fig.*) depress, discourage; (*Law*) quash, cancel; (*eyes*) cast down; (*Chem.*) precipitate; (*Boxing*) knock out.

Niedertracht ['ni:dərtraxt], *f.* (—, *no pl.*) baseness, meanness, villainy, beastliness.

Niederung ['ni:dəruŋ], *f.* (—, *pl.* —en) low ground, marsh.

niedlich ['ni:tlɪç], *adj.* pretty, dainty; (*Am.*) cute.

niedrig ['ni:drɪç], *adj.* low; (*fig.*) base, vile.

niemals ['ni:ma:ls], *adv.* never, at no time.

niemand ['ni:mant], *pron.* nobody, no one.

Niere ['ni:rə], *f.* (—, *pl,* —n) kidney.

Nierenbraten ['ni:rənbra:tən], *m.* (—s, *no pl.*) roast loin.

Nierenfett ['ni:rənfɛt], *n.* (—s, *no pl.*) suet.

nieseln ['ni:zəln], *v.n. imp.* drizzle.

niesen ['ni:zən], *v.n.* sneeze.

Nießbrauch ['ni:sbraux], *m.* (—s, *no pl.*) usufruct, benefit.

Niete ['ni:tə], *f.* (—, *pl.* —n) blank; (*Engin.*) rivet; failure.

Niger ['ni:gər], *n.* Niger.

Nigeria [ni'ge:rja], *n.* Nigeria.

Nikaragua [nika'ra:gua], *n.* Nicaragua.

Nikolaus ['nɪkolaus], *m.* Nicholas; *Sankt* —, Santa Claus.

Nil [ni:l], *m.* (—s, *no pl.*) Nile.

Nilpferd ['ni:lpfe:rt], *n.* (—s, *pl.* —e) (*Zool.*) hippopotamus.

nimmer (mehr) ['nɪmər (me:r)], *adv.* never, never again.

nippen ['nɪpən], *v.a., v.n.* sip, (take a) nip (of).

Nippsachen ['nɪpzaxən], *f. pl.* knick-knacks.

nirgends ['nɪrgənts], *adv.* nowhere.

Nische ['ni:ʃə], *f.* (—, *pl.* —n) niche.

Nisse ['nɪsə], *f.* (—, *pl.* —n) nit.

nisten ['nɪstən], *v.n.* nest.

Niveau [ni'vo:], *n.* (—s, *pl.* —s) level, standard.

nivellieren [nivɛ'li:rən], *v.a.* level.

Nixe ['nɪksə], *f.* (—, *pl.* —n) water-nymph, mermaid, water-sprite.

Nizza ['nıtsa], *n.* Nice.
nobel ['no:bǝl], *adj.* noble, smart; (*Am.*) swell; munificent, open-handed, magnanimous.
noch [nɔx], *adv.* still, yet; — *einmal*, — *mals*, once more; *weder* ... — ..., neither ... nor ...; — *nicht*, not yet; — *nie*, never yet, never before.
nochmalig ['nɔxma:lıç], *adj.* repeated.
Nomade [no'ma:dǝ], *m.* (—**n**, *pl.* —**n**) nomad.
nominell [nomi'nɛl], *adj.* nominal.
nominieren [nomi'ni:rǝn], *v.a.* nominate.
Nonne ['nɔnǝ], *f.* (—, *pl.* —**n**) nun.
Noppe ['nɔpǝ], *f.* (—, *pl.* —**n**) nap.
Norden ['nɔrdǝn], *m.* (—**s**, *no pl.*) north.
nördlich ['nœrtlıç], *adj.* northern, northerly.
Nordsee ['nɔrtze:], *f.* North Sea.
nörgeln ['nœrgǝln], *v.n.* find fault, cavil, carp, nag.
Norm ['nɔrm], *f.* (—, *pl.* —**en**) standard, rule, norm.
normal [nɔr'ma:l], *adj.* normal, standard.
Norwegen ['nɔrve:gǝn], *n.* Norway.
Not [no:t], *f.* (—, *pl.* ⁻e) need, necessity; misery, want, trouble, distress; (*in compounds*) emergency.
not [no:t], *pred. adj.* — *tun*, be necessary.
Nota ['no:ta], *f.* (—, *pl.* —**s**) bill, statement.
Notar [no'ta:r], *m.* (—**s**, *pl.* —**e**) notary.
Notdurft ['no:tdurft], *f.* (—, *pl.* ⁻e) want, necessaries, necessity; *seine* — *verrichten*, ease o.s.
notdürftig ['no:tdyrftıç], *adj.* scanty, makeshift.
Note ['no:tǝ], *f.* (—, *pl.* —**n**) note; (*Mus.*) note; (*School*) mark(s); *nach* —*n*, (*fig.*) with a vengeance.
Notenbank ['no:tǝnbaŋk], *f.* (—, *pl.* —**en**) bank of issue.
Notenblatt ['no:tǝnblat], *n.* (—**s**, *pl.* ⁻er) sheet of music.
notgedrungen ['no:tgǝdruŋǝn], *adj.* compulsory, forced; perforce.
Nothelfer ['no:thɛlfǝr], *m.* (—**s**, *pl.* —) helper in time of need.
notieren [no'ti:rǝn], *v.a.* note, book; (*Comm.*) quote.
notifizieren [notifi'tsi:rǝn], *v.a.* notify.
nötig ['nø:tıç], *adj.* necessary; — *haben*, want, need.
nötigen ['nø:tıgǝn], *v.a.* compel, press, force, urge; necessitate; *sich* — *lassen*, stand upon ceremony.
Notiz [no'ti:ts], *f.* (—, *pl.* —**en**) note, notice; — *nehmen von*, take notice of; (*pl.*) notes, jottings.
notleidend ['no:tlaıdǝnt], *adj.* financially distressed, indigent, needy.
notorisch [no'to:rıʃ], *adj.* notorious.
Notstand ['no:tʃtant], *m.* (—**s**, *no pl.*) state of distress; emergency.

Notverband ['no:tfɛrbant], *m.* (—**es**, *pl.* ⁻e) first-aid dressing.
Notwehr ['no:tve:r], *f.* (—, *no pl.*) self-defence.
notwendig ['no:tvɛndıç], *adj.* necessary, essential, needful.
Notzucht ['no:ttsuxt], *f.* (—, *no pl.*) rape, violation.
Novelle [no'vɛlǝ], *f.* (—, *pl.* —**n**) (*Lit.*) novella, short story, short novel.
Novize [no'vi:tsǝ], *m.* (—**n**, *pl.* —**n**) or *f.* (—, *pl.* —**n**) novice.
Nu [nu:], *m. & n.* (—, *no pl.*) moment; *im* —, in no time, in an instant.
Nubien ['nu:bjǝn], *n.* Nubia.
nüchtern ['nyçtǝrn], *adj.* fasting; sober; jejune; (*fig.*) dry, matter-of-fact, realistic.
Nüchternheit ['nyçtǝrnhaıt], *f.* (—, *no pl.*) sobriety; (*fig.*) dryness.
Nudel ['nu:dǝl], *f.* (—, *pl.* —**n**) noodles, macaroni, vermicelli; *eine komische* —, a funny person.
Null [nul], *f.* (—, *pl.* —**en**) nought, zero; (*fig.*) nonentity.
null [nul], *adj.* null; nil; — *und nichtig*, null and void; *etwas für* — *und nichtig erklären*, annul.
numerieren [nume'ri:rǝn], *v.a.* number.
Nummer ['numǝr], *f.* (—, *pl.* —**n**) number, size, issue.
nun [nu:n], *adv., conj.* now, at present; since; —*!* now! well! *von* — *an*, henceforth; — *und nimmermehr*, nevermore; *was* —*?* what next?
nunmehr ['nu:nme:r], *adv.* now, by this time.
Nunzius ['nuntsjus], *m.* (—, *pl.* —**zien**) (Papal) nuncio.
nur [nu:r], *adv.* only, solely, merely, but; *wenn* —, if only, provided that; — *das nicht*, anything but that; — *zu*, go to it!
Nürnberg ['nyrnbɛrk], *n.* Nuremberg.
Nuß [nus], *f.* (—, *pl.* ⁻sse) nut.
Nußhäher ['nushɛ:ǝr], *m.* (—**s**, *pl.* —) (*Orn.*) jay.
Nüster ['nystǝr], *f.* (—, *pl.* —**n**) (*horse*) nostril.
Nutzanwendung ['nutsanvɛnduŋ], *f.* (—, *pl.* —**en**) practical application.
nutzbar ['nutsba:r], *adj.* useful, usable, productive.
nütze ['nytsǝ], *adj.* useful, of use.
Nutzen ['nutsǝn], *m.* (—**s**, *pl.* —) use, utility; profit, gain, advantage, benefit; — *bringen*, yield profit; — *ziehen aus*, derive profit from.
nützen ['nytsǝn], *v.a.* make use of, use. — *v.n.* be of use, serve, be effective, work.
nützlich ['nytslıç], *adj.* useful.
nutzlos ['nutslo:s], *adj.* useless.
Nutznießer ['nutsni:sǝr], *m.* (—**s**, *pl.* —) beneficiary, usufructuary.
Nymphe ['nymfǝ], *f.* (—, *pl.* —**en**) nymph.

O

O [o:], *n*, (**—s**, *pl.* **—s**) the letter O.
o! [o:], *excl.* oh!
Oase [o'a:zə], *f.* (**—**, *pl.* **—n**) oasis.
ob [ɔp], *conj.* whether; if; *als* **—**, as if; *und* **—!** rather! yes, indeed! — *prep.* (*Genit.*, *Dat.*) on account of; upon, on.
Obacht ['o:baxt], *f.* (**—**, *no pl.*) heed, care; — *geben*, pay attention, look out.
Obdach ['ɔpdax], *n.* (**—es**, *no pl.*) shelter, lodging.
Obduktion ['ɔpdukts'jo:n], *f.* (**—**, *pl.* **—en**) post-mortem examination.
oben [o:bən], *adv.* above, aloft, on top; (*house*) upstairs; (*water*) on the surface; *von* **—** *bis unten*, from top to bottom; *von* **—** *herab*, from above; (*fig.*) haughtily, superciliously.
obendrein [o:bən'drain], *adv.* besides, into the bargain.
obengenannt ['o:bəngənant], *adj.* above-mentioned.
Ober ['o:bər], *m.* (**—s**, *pl.* **—**) head waiter; *Herr* **—!**, waiter!; (*in compounds*) upper, chief.
ober ['o:bər], *adj.* upper, higher; chief; superior.
Oberfläche ['o:bərflɛçə], *f.* (**—**, *pl.* **—n**) surface.
oberflächlich ['o:bərflɛçlɪç], *adj.* superficial, casual.
oberhalb ['o:bərhalp], *adv.*, *prep.* (*Genit.*) above.
Oberin ['o:bərɪn], *f.* (**—**, *pl.* **—innen**) (*Eccl.*) Mother Superior; hospital matron.
Oberschule ['o:bərʃu:lə], *f.* (**—**, *pl.* **—n**) high school, secondary school.
Oberst ['o:bərst], *m.* (**—en**, *pl.* **—en**) colonel.
Oberstaatsanwalt ['o:bərʃta:tsanvalt], *m.* (**—s**, *pl.* **⸚e**) Attorney-General.
oberste ['o:bərstə], *adj.* uppermost, highest, supreme.
Oberstimme ['o:bərʃtɪmə], *f.* (**—**, *pl.* **—n**) (*Mus.*) treble, soprano.
Oberstübchen ['o:bərʃty:pçən], *n.* (**—s**, *pl.* **—**) (*fig.*) *nicht richtig im* **—** *sein*, have bats in the belfry.
Obervolta ['o:bərvɔltə], *n.* Upper Volta.
obgleich [ɔp'glaiç], *conj.* though, although.
Obhut ['ɔphu:t], *f.* (**—**, *no pl.*) keeping, care, protection.
obig ['o:bɪç], *adj.* foregoing, above-mentioned, aforementioned, aforesaid.
objektiv [ɔpjɛk'ti:f], *adj.* objective, impartial, unprejudiced.
Oblate [o'bla:tə], *f.* (**—**, *pl.* **—n**) wafer; (*Eccl.*) Host.

obliegen ['ɔpli:gən], *v.n. irr.* be incumbent upon s.o.; be o.'s duty; apply o.s. to.
Obmann ['ɔpman], *m.* (**—es**, *pl.* **⸚er**) chairman; (*jury*) foreman.
Obrigkeit ['o:brɪçkait], *f.* (**—**, *pl.* **—en**) authorities.
obschon [ɔp'ʃo:n] *see under* **obwohl**.
Observatorium ['ɔpzɛrva'to:rjum], *n.* (**—s**, *pl.* **—rien**) observatory.
obsiegen ['ɔpzi:gən], *v.n.* (*rare*) be victorious.
Obst [o:pst], *n.* (**—es**, *no pl.*) fruit.
obszön [ɔps'tsø:n], *adj.* obscene.
obwalten ['ɔpvaltən], *v.n.* (*rare*) exist, prevail, obtain; *unter den* **—den** *Umständen*, in the circumstances, as matters stand.
obwohl [ɔp'vo:l] (*also* **obschon** [ɔp'ʃo:n], **obzwar** [ɔp'tsva:r]), *conj.* though, although.
Ochse ['ɔksə], *m.* (**—n**, *pl.* **—n**) (*Zool.*) ox; bullock; (*fig.*) blockhead.
ochsen ['ɔksən], *v.n.* (*sl.*) swot, cram.
Ochsenauge ['ɔksənaugə], *n.* (**—s**, *pl.* **—n**) ox-eye, bull's eye; (*Archit.*) oval dormer window; porthole light.
Ochsenziemer ['ɔksəntsi:mər], *m.* (**—s**, *pl.* **—**) (*obs.*) horse-whip.
Ocker ['ɔkər], *m.* (**—n**, *no pl.*) ochre.
Öde ['ø:də], *f.* (**—**, *pl.* **—n**) wilderness.
öde ['ø:də], *adj.* desolate, bleak, dreary.
Odem ['o:dəm], *m.* (**—s**, *no pl.*) (*Poet.*) breath.
oder ['o:dər], *conj.* or; — *aber*, or else; — *auch*, or rather.
Ofen ['o:fən], *m.* (**—s**, *pl.* **⸚**) stove; oven, furnace.
Ofenpest [o:fən'pɛst], *n.* Budapest.
offen ['ɔfən], *adj.* open; (*fig.*) candid, sincere, frank; — *gestanden*, frankly speaking.
offenbar [ɔfən'ba:r], *adj.* obvious, manifest, evident.
offenbaren [ɔfən'ba:rən], *v.a. insep.* make known, reveal, disclose. — *v.r. sich einem* **—**, open o.'s heart to s.o.; unbosom o.s.
Offenheit ['ɔfənhait], *f.* (**—**, *pl.* **—en**) frankness, candour.
offenkundig ['ɔfənkundɪç], *adj.* obvious, manifest.
offensichtlich ['ɔfənzɪçtlɪç], *adj.* obvious; apparent.
öffentlich ['œfəntlɪç], *adj.* public.
offerieren [ɔfe'ri:rən], *v.a.* offer.
Offerte [ɔ'fɛrtə], *f.* (**—**, *pl.* **—n**) offer, tender.
offiziell [ɔfi'tsjɛl], *adj.* official.
Offizier [ɔfi'tsi:r], *m.* (**—s**, *pl.* **—e**) officer, lieutenant.
Offizierspatent [ɔfi'tsi:rspatɛnt], *n.* (**—s**, *pl.* **—e**) (*Mil.*) commission.
offiziös [ɔfi'tsjø:s], *adj.* semi-official.
öffnen ['œfnən], *v.a.* open.
oft [ɔft], **oftmals** ['ɔftma:ls], *adv.* often, frequently.
öfters ['œftərs], *adv.* often, frequently.

Oheim

Oheim ['o:haɪm], *m.* (—s, *pl.* —e) (*Poet.*) uncle.

ohne ['o:nə], *prep.* (*Acc.*) without, but for, except.

ohnehin ['o:nəhɪn], *adv.* as it is.

Ohnmacht ['o:nmaxt], *f.* (—, *pl.* —en) fainting-fit, swoon; impotence; *in — fallen*, faint.

Ohr [o:r], *n.* (—es, *pl.* —en) ear; *bis über beide —en*, head over heels; *die —en spitzen*, prick up o.'s ears.

Ohrenbläser ['o:rənble:zər], *m.* (—s, *pl.* —) tale-bearer.

Ohrensausen ['o:rənzauzən], *n.* (—s, *no pl.*) humming in the ears.

Ohrenschmaus ['o:rənʃmaus], *m.* (—es, *no pl.*) musical treat.

Ohrfeige ['o:rfaɪgə], *f.* (—, *pl.* —n) box on the ear.

Ohrläppchen ['o:rlɛpçən], *n.* (—s, *pl.* —) lobe of the ear.

Ohrmuschel ['o:rmuʃəl], *f.* (—, *pl.* —n) auricle.

oktav [ɔk'ta:f], *adj.* octavo.

Oktober [ɔk'to:bər], *m.* (—s, *pl.* —) October.

oktroyieren [ɔktroa'ji:rən], *v.a.* dictate, force s.th. upon s.o.

okulieren [oku'li:rən], *v.a.* (*trees*) graft.

Öl [ø:l], *n.* (—s, *pl.* —e) oil; (*rare*) olive-oil.

Ölanstrich ['ø:lanʃtrɪç], *m.* (—s, *pl.* —e) coat of oil-paint.

ölen ['ø:lən], *v.a.* oil, lubricate; (*rare*) anoint.

Ölgemälde ['ø:lgəmɛ:ldə], *n.* (—s, *pl.* —) oil painting.

Ölung ['ø:luŋ], *f.* (—, *pl.* —en) oiling; anointing; (*Eccl.*) *die letzte —*, Extreme Unction.

Olymp [o'lymp], *m.* Mount Olympus.

olympisch [o'lympɪʃ], *adj.* Olympian.

Omelett [ɔmə'lɛt], *n.* (—s, *pl.* —s) omelette.

Onkel ['ɔŋkəl], *m.* (—s, *pl.* —) uncle.

Oper ['o:pər], *f.* (—, *pl.* —n) opera.

operieren [opə'ri:rən], *v.a., v.n.* operate (on); *sich — lassen*, be operated on; undergo an operation.

Opfer ['ɔpfər], *n.* (—s, *pl.* —) sacrifice; victim.

opfern ['ɔpfərn], *v.a., v.n.* offer (up), sacrifice, immolate.

opponieren [ɔpo'ni:rən], *v.n.* oppose.

Optiker ['ɔptɪkər], *m.* (—s, *pl.* —) optician.

oratorisch [ora'to:rɪʃ], *adj.* oratorical.

Orchester [ɔr'kɛstər], *n.* (—s, *pl.* —) orchestra, band.

orchestrieren [ɔrkɛs'tri:rən], *v.a.* orchestrate, score for orchestra.

Orchidee [ɔrçi'de:], *f.* (—, *pl.* —n) (*Bot.*) orchid.

Orden ['ɔrdən], *m.* (—s, *pl.* —) medal; (*Eccl.*) (religious) order.

ordentlich ['ɔrdəntlɪç], *adj.* orderly, tidy, methodical, neat; regular; respectable, steady; sound; *—er Professor*, (full) professor.

Order ['ɔrdər], *f.* (—, *pl.* —s) (*Comm.*) order.

Ordinarius [ɔrdi'na:rjus], *m.* (—, *pl.* —ien) (*Univ.*) professor; (*Eccl.*) ordinary.

ordinär [ɔrdi'nɛ:r], *adj.* common, vulgar.

ordnen ['ɔrdnən], *v.a.* put in order, tidy, arrange, dispose.

Ordnung ['ɔrdnuŋ], *f.* (—, *pl.* —en) order, arrangement, disposition, routine; tidiness; class, rank; *in —*, all right, in good trim; *nicht in —*, out of order, wrong.

ordnungsgemäß ['ɔrdnuŋsgəmɛ:s], *adv.* duly.

ordnungsmäßig ['ɔrdnuŋsmɛsɪç], *adj.* regular.

ordnungswidrig ['ɔrdnuŋsvi:drɪç], *adj.* irregular.

Ordnungszahl ['ɔrdnuŋstsa:l], *f.* (—, *pl.* —en) ordinal number.

Ordonnanz [ɔrdo'nants], *f.* (—, *pl.* —en) (*Mil.*) orderly.

Organ [ɔr'ga:n], *n.* (—s, *pl.* —e) organ.

organisieren [ɔrgani'zi:rən], *v.a.* organise.

Orgel ['ɔrgəl], *f.* (—, *pl.* —n) (*Mus.*) organ.

Orgelzug ['ɔrgəltsu:k], *m.* (—s, *pl.* —e) organ-stop.

Orgie ['ɔrgjə], *f.* (—, *pl.* —n) orgy.

orientalisch [orjen'ta:lɪʃ], *adj.* oriental, eastern.

orientieren [orjen'ti:rən], *v.a.* inform, orientate; set s.o. right. — *v.r. sich — über*, orientate o.s., find out about; get o.'s bearings.

Orkan [ɔr'ka:n], *m.* (—s, *pl.* —e) hurricane, gale, typhoon.

Ornat [ɔr'na:t], *m.* (—es, *pl.* —e) official robes; vestments.

Ort [ɔrt], *m.* (—es, *pl.* —e, —er) place, spot; region; (*in compounds*) local.

örtlich ['œrtlɪç], *adj.* local.

Ortschaft ['ɔrtʃaft], *f.* (—, *pl.* —en) place, township, village.

Öse ['ø:zə], *f.* (—, *pl.* —n) loop; *Haken und —n*, hooks and eyes.

Ostasien ['ɔsta:zjən], *n.* Eastern Asia, the Far East.

Ost(en) ['ɔst(ən)], *m.* (—s, *no pl.*) east.

ostentativ [ɔstɛnta'ti:f], *adj.* ostentatious.

Osterei ['o:stəraɪ], *n.* (—s, *pl.* —er) Easter egg.

Ostern ['o:stərn], *f. pl.* (used as *n. sing.*) Easter.

Österreich ['ø:stərraɪç], *n.* Austria.

Ostindien ['ɔstɪndjən], *n.* the East Indies.

östlich ['œstlɪç], *adj.* eastern, easterly.

Oxyd [ɔk'sy:t], *n.* (—es, *pl.* —e) oxide.

oxydieren [ɔksy'di:rən], *v.a., v.n.* oxidise.

Ozean ['o:tsea:n], *m.* (—s, *pl.* —e) ocean, sea; *Grosser —*, Pacific (Ocean).

Ozon [o'tso:n], *n.* (—s, *no pl.*) ozone.

P

P [pe:], *n.* (—s, *pl.* —s) the letter P.
Paar [pa:r], *n.* (—es, *pl.* —e) pair, couple.
paar [pa:r], *adj. ein* —, a few, some.
Pacht [paxt], *f.* (—, *pl.* —en) lease; *in* — *nehmen*, take on lease.
Pachthof ['paxtho:f], *m.* (—s, *pl.* ⁻e) leasehold estate, farm.
Pack (1) [pak], *m.* (—s, *pl.* ⁻e) pack, bale, packet; *mit Sack und* —, (with) bag and baggage.
Pack (2) [pak], *n.* (—s, *no pl.*) rabble, mob.
Päckchen ['pɛkçən], *n.* (—s, *pl.* —) pack, packet; (small) parcel.
packen ['pakən], *v.a.* pack; seize; (*fig.*) —*d*, thrilling; *pack dich!* be off! scram!
pädagogisch [pɛ:da'go:gɪʃ], *adj.* educational, pedagogic(al).
paddeln ['padəln], *v.n.* paddle.
paff [paf], *excl.* bang! *ich bin ganz* —, I am astounded.
paffen ['pafən], *v.n.* puff; draw (at a pipe).
Page ['pa:ʒə], *m.* (—n, *pl.* —n) page-boy.
Paket [pa'ke:t], *n.* (—s, *pl.* —e) packet, package, parcel.
paktieren [pak'ti:rən], *v.n.* come to terms.
Palast [pa'last], *m.* (—es, *pl.* ⁻e) palace.
Palästina [palɛ'sti:na], *n.* Palestine.
Paletot ['paləto:], *m.* (—s, *pl.* —s) overcoat.
Palisanderholz [pali'zandərhɔlts], *n.* (—es, *no pl.*) rosewood.
Palme ['palmə], *f.* (—, *pl.* —n) (*Bot.*) palm-tree.
Palmkätzchen ['palmkɛtsçən], *n.* (—s, *pl.* —) (*Bot.*) catkin.
Palmwoche ['palmvɔxə], *f.* Holy Week.
Pampelmuse ['pampəlmu:zə], *f.* (—, *pl.* —n) (*Bot.*) grapefruit.
Panama ['pa:nama], *n.* Panama.
Panier [pa'ni:r], *n.* (—s, *pl.* —e) standard, banner.
panieren [pa'ni:rən], *v.a.* dress (*meat etc.*), roll in bread-crumbs.
Panne ['panə], *f.* (—, *pl.* —n) puncture; (*Motor.*) break-down; mishap.
panschen ['panʃən], *v.n.* splash about in water. — *v.a.* adulterate.
Pantoffel [pan'tɔfəl], *m.* (—s, *pl.* —n) slipper; *unter dem* — *stehen*, be henpecked.
Pantoffelheld [pan'tɔfəlhɛlt], *m.* (—en, *pl.* —en) henpecked husband.

Panzer ['pantsər], *m.* (—s, *pl.* —) armour, breast-plate, coat of mail; (*Mil.*) tank.
Papagei [papa'gaɪ], *m.* (—s, *pl.* —en) (*Orn.*) parrot.
Papier [pa'pi:r], *n.* (—s, *pl.* —e) paper; (*Comm.*) stocks; (*pl.*) papers, documents; *ein Bogen* —, a sheet of paper.
Papierkrieg [pa'pi:rkri:k], *m.* (—s, *no / pl.*) (*coll.*) red tape.
Papierwaren [pa'pi:rva:rən], *f. pl.* stationery.
Pappdeckel ['papdɛkəl], *m.* (—s, *pl.* —) pasteboard.
Pappe ['papə], *f.* (—, *no pl.*) paste, cardboard, pasteboard.
Pappel ['papəl], *f.* (—, *pl.* —n) poplar.
pappen ['papən], *v.a.* stick; glue, paste.
Pappenstiel ['papənʃti:l], *m.* (—s, *pl.* —e) trifle.
papperlapapp ['papərlapap], *excl.* fiddlesticks! nonsense!
Papst [pa:pst], *m.* (—es, *pl.* ⁻e) Pope.
päpstlich ['pɛ:pstlɪç], *adj.* papal; —*er als der Papst*, fanatically loyal, outheroding Herod; over-zealous.
Parabel [pa'ra:bəl], *f.* (—, *pl.* —n) parable; (*Maths.*) parabola.
paradieren [para'di:rən], *v.n.* parade, make a show.
Paradies [para'di:s], *n.* (—es, *pl.* —e) paradise.
paradox [para'dɔks], *adj.* paradoxical.
Paragraph [para'gra:f], *m.* (—en, *pl.* —en) paragraph, article, clause, section.
Paraguay ['paragvaɪ, para'gua:ɪ], *n.* Paraguay.
Paralyse [para'ly:zə], *f.* (—, *pl.* —n) paralysis.
parat [pa'ra:t], *adj.* prepared, ready.
Pardon [par'dɔ̃], *m.* (—s, *no pl.*) pardon, forgiveness.
Parfüm [par'fy:m], *n.* (—s, *pl.* —e) perfume, scent.
pari ['pa:ri:], *adv.* at par.
parieren [pa'ri:rən], *v.a.* parry, keep off. — *v.n.* obey; *aufs Wort* —. obey implicitly *or* to the letter.
Parität [pari'tɛ:t], *f.* (—, *no pl.*) parity; (*religious*) equality.
Parkanlagen [park'anla:gən], *f. pl.* parks; public gardens.
parken ['parkən], *v.a.* park.
Parkett [par'kɛt], *m.* (—s, *pl.* —e) parquet flooring; (*Theat.*) stalls.
Parkuhr [park'u:r], *f.* (—, *pl.* —en) parking-meter.
Parlament [parla'mɛnt], *n.* (—s, *pl.* —e) parliament.
Parlamentär [parlamen'tɛ:r], *m.* (—s, *pl.* —e) officer negotiating a truce.
Parlamentarier [parlamen'ta:rjər], *m.* (—s, *pl.* —) parliamentarian, member of a parliament.
Parole [pa'ro:lə], *f.* (—, *pl.* —n) watchword, cue, motto, slogan, pass-word.

Partei

Partei [par'taɪ], *f.* (—, *pl.* —en) party, faction; — *nehmen für*, side with.

Parteigänger [par'taɪgɛnər], *m.* (—s, *pl.* —) partisan.

Parteigenosse [par'taɪgənɔsə], *m.* (—n, *pl.* —n) party member (especially National Socialist); comrade.

parteiisch [par'taɪɪʃ], *adj.* partial, biased, prejudiced.

Parteinahme [par'taɪna:mə], *f.* (—, *no pl.*) partisanship.

Parteitag [par'taɪta:k], *m.* (—s, *pl.* —e) party conference; congress.

Parterre [par'tɛrə], *n.* (—s, *pl.* —s) ground floor; (*Theat.*) pit; stalls.

Partie [par'ti:], *f.* (—, *pl.* —n) (*Comm.*) parcel; (*marriage*) match; (*chess etc.*) game; (*bridge*) rubber; outing, excursion, trip.

Partitur [parti'tu:r], *f.* (—, *pl.* —en) (*Mus.*) score.

Partizip [parti'tsi:p], *n.* (—s, *pl.* —e, —ien) (*Gram.*) participle.

Parzelle [par'tsɛlə], *f.* (—, *pl.* —n) allotment, lot, parcel.

paschen ['paʃən], *v.a.* smuggle.

Paß [pas], *m.* (—sses, *pl.* ˙sse) (*mountain*) pass; (*travelling*) passport; (*horse*) amble.

Passagier [pasa'ʒi:r], *m.* (—s, *pl.* —e) passenger; *blinder* —, stowaway.

Passant [pa'sant], *m.* (—en, *pl.* —en) passer-by.

Passatwind [pa'sa:tvɪnt], *m.* (—s, *pl.* —e) trade-wind.

passen ['pasən], *v.n.* fit, suit, be suitable, be convenient; (*Cards*) pass.

passieren [pa'si:rən], *v.a.* sieve; (*road*) pass, cross, negotiate. — *v.n.* (*aux. sein*) pass; happen, take place, come about.

Passif, Passivum [pa'si:f *or* 'pasi:f, pa'si:vum], *n.* (—s, *pl.* —e; —, *pl.* —va) (*Gram.*) passive voice; (*Comm.*) (*pl.*) debts, liabilities.

Passus ['pasus], *m.* (—, *pl.* —) passage (in book).

Pasta, Paste ['pasta, 'pastə], *f.* (—, *pl.* —ten) paste.

Pastell [pa'stɛl], *m.* (—s, *pl.* —e) pastel, crayon; — *malen*, draw in pastel.

Pastete [pa'ste:tə], *f.* (—, *pl.* —n) pie, pastry.

Pastille [pa'stɪlə], *f.* (—, *pl.* —n) lozenge, pastille.

Pastor ['pastɔr], *m.* (—s, *pl.* —en) minister, pastor; parson; vicar, rector.

Pate ['pa:tə], *m.* (—n, *pl.* —n) godparent; — *stehen*, be godfather to.

patent [pa'tɛnt], *adj.* fine, grand, (*sl.*) smashing.

Patent [pa'tɛnt], *n.* (—(e)s, *pl.* —e) patent; charter, licence.

patentieren [patɛn'ti:rən], *v.a.* patent, license.

pathetisch [pa'te:tɪʃ], *adj.* elevated, solemn, moving.

Patin ['pa:tɪn], *f.* (—, *pl.* —innen) godmother.

patriotisch [patri'o:tɪʃ], *adj.* patriotic.

Patrone [pa'tro:nə], *f.* (—, *pl.* —n) cartridge; stencil, pattern.

Patrouille [pa'truljə], *f.* (—, *pl.* —n) (*Mil.*) patrol.

Patsche ['patʃə], *f.* (—, *pl.* —n) (*dial.*) hand; (*fig.*) mess, pickle; *in eine — geraten*, get into a jam.

patschen ['patʃən], *v.n.* (*aux. sein*) splash.

Patt [pat], *n.* (—s, *pl.* —s) (*Chess*) stalemate.

patzig ['patsɪç], *adj.* rude; cheeky, saucy.

Pauke ['paukə], *f.* (—, *pl.* —n) kettledrum; *mit* —*n und Trompeten*, with drums beating and colours flying.

pauken ['paukən], *v.n.* beat the kettledrum; (*coll.*) swot, plod, grind; fight a duel.

pausbackig ['pausbakɪç], *adj.* chubby-faced, bonny.

Pauschale [pau'ʃa:lə], *f.* (—, *pl.* —n) lump sum.

Pause ['pauzə], *f.* (—, *pl.* —n) pause, stop; (*Theat.*) interval; (*Sch.*) playtime, break; (*Tech.*) tracing.

pausen ['pauzən], *v.a.* trace.

pausieren [pau'zi:rən], *v.n.* pause.

Pavian ['pa:vja:n], *m.* (—s, *pl.* —e) (*Zool.*) baboon.

Pech [pɛç], *n.* (—es, *no pl.*) pitch; (*shoemaker's*) wax; (*fig.*) bad luck, rotten luck.

pechschwarz ['pɛçʃvarts], *adj.* black as pitch.

Pechvogel ['pɛçfo:gəl], *m.* (—s, *pl.* ˙) unlucky fellow.

Pedell [pe'dɛl], *m.* (—s, *pl.* —e) beadle; porter, caretaker; (*Univ. sl.*) bulldog.

Pegel ['pe:gəl], *m.* (—s, *pl.* —) watergauge.

peilen ['paɪlən], *v.a., v.n.* sound, measure, take bearings (of).

Pein [paɪn], *f.* (—, *no pl.*) pain, torment.

peinigen ['paɪnɪgən], *v.a.* torment; harass, distress.

peinlich ['paɪnlɪç], *adj.* painful, disagreeable; embarrassing; delicate; strict, punctilious; (*Law*) capital, penal.

Peitsche ['paɪtʃə], *f.* (—, *pl.* —n) whip.

pekuniär [pekun'jɛ:r], *adj.* financial.

Pelerine [pelə'ri:nə], *f.* (—, *pl.* —n) cape.

Pelle ['pɛlə], *f.* (—, *pl.* —n) peel, husk.

Pellkartoffeln ['pɛlkartɔfəln], *f. pl.* potatoes in their jackets.

Pelz [pɛlts], *m.* (—es, *pl.* —e) pelt, fur; fur coat.

pelzig ['pɛltsɪç], *adj.* furry.

Pendel ['pɛndəl], *n.* (—s, *pl.* —) pendulum.

pendeln ['pɛndəln], *v.n.* swing, oscillate; commute.

pennen ['pɛnən], *v.n.* (*sl.*) sleep.

Pension [pā'sjo:n], *f.* (—, *pl.* —en) pension; boarding-house; board and lodging.
Pensionat [pāsjo'na:t], *n.* (—s, *pl.* —e) boarding-school.
pensionieren [pāsjo'ni:rən], *v.a.* pension off; *sich — lassen*, retire.
Pensum ['pɛnzum], *n.* (—s, *pl.* —sen) task; curriculum, syllabus.
per [pɛr], *prep. — Adresse*, care of.
Perfekt [pɛr'fɛkt], *n.* (—s, *pl.* —e) (*Gram.*) perfect (tense).
perforieren [pɛrfo'ri:rən], *v.a.* perforate, punch.
Pergament [pɛrga'mɛnt], *n.* (—s, *pl.* —e) parchment, vellum.
Perle ['pɛrlə], *f.* (—, *pl.* —n) pearl; (*glass*) bead; (*fig.*) gem, treasure.
perlen ['pɛrlən], *v.n.* sparkle.
Perlgraupe ['pɛrlgraupə], *f.* (—, *no pl.*) (*Bot.*) pearl-barley.
Perlhuhn ['pɛrlhu:n], *n.* (—s, *pl.* ̈er) (*Zool.*) guinea-fowl.
Perlmutter ['pɛrlmutər], *f.* (—, *no pl.*) mother-of-pearl.
Perpendikel [pɛrpən'di:kəl], *m. & n.* (—s, *pl.* —) pendulum.
Perser ['pɛrzər], *m.* (—s, *pl.* —) Persian; *echter —*, genuine Persian carpet.
Persien ['pɛrzjən], *n.* Persia.
Personal [pɛrzo'na:l], *n.* (—s, *no pl.*) personnel, staff.
Personalien [pɛrzo'na:ljən], *n. pl.* particulars (of a person).
Personenverkehr [pɛr'zo:nənfɛrkeːr], *m.* (—s, *no pl.*) passenger-traffic.
Personenzug [pɛr'zo:nəntsu:k], *m.* (—s, *pl.* ̈e) (slow) passenger train.
personifizieren [pɛrzonifi'tsi:rən], *v.a.* personify, embody, impersonate.
Persönlichkeit [pɛr'zø:nlɪçkait], *f.* (—, *pl.* —en) personality, person.
perspektivisch [pɛrspɛk'ti:vɪʃ], *adj.* perspective.
Peru [pe'ru:], *n.* Peru.
Perücke [pe'rykə], *f.* (—, *pl.* —n) wig.
Pest [pɛst], *f.* (—, *no pl.*) plague, pestilence.
pestartig ['pɛsta:rtiç], *adj.* pestilential.
Petersilie [pe:tər'zi:ljə], *f.* (—, *no pl.*) (*Bot.*) parsley.
petitionieren [petitsjo'ni:rən], *v.a.* petition.
Petschaft ['pɛtʃaft], *n.* (—s, *pl.* —e) seal, signet.
Petz [pɛts], *m.* (—es, *pl.* —e) *Meister —*, Bruin (the bear).
petzen ['pɛtsən], *v.n.* tell tales (about), sneak.
Pfad [pfa:t], *m.* (—es, *pl.* —e) path.
Pfadfinder ['pfa:tfɪndər], *m.* (—s, *pl.* —) Boy Scout.
Pfaffe ['pfafə], *m.* (—n, *pl.* —n) (*pej.*) cleric, priest.
Pfahl [pfa:l], *m.* (—s, *pl.* ̈e) post, stake.
Pfahlbauten ['pfa:lbautən], *m. pl.* lake dwellings.

pfählen ['pfɛ:lən], *v.a.* fasten with stakes; impale.
Pfand [pfant], *n.* (—s, *pl.* ̈er) pawn, pledge; security; (*game*) forfeit; *ein — einlösen*, redeem a pledge.
pfänden ['pfɛndən], *v.a.* take in pledge; seize.
Pfänderspiel ['pfɛndərʃpi:l], *n.* (—s, *pl.* —e) game of forfeits.
Pfandgeber ['pfantge:bər], *m.* (—s, *pl.* —) pawner.
Pfandleiher ['pfantlaiər], *m.* (—s, *pl.* —) pawnbroker.
Pfandrecht ['pfantrɛçt], *n.* (—s, *no pl.*) lien.
Pfändung ['pfɛnduŋ], *f.* (—, *pl.* —en) seizure, attachment, distraint.
Pfanne ['pfanə], *f.* (—, *pl.* —n) pan, frying-pan.
Pfannkuchen ['pfanku:xən], *m.* (—s, *pl.* —) pancake; *Berliner —*, doughnut.
Pfarre ['pfarə], *f.* (—, *pl.* —n) living, parish; (*house*) vicarage, parsonage, manse.
Pfarrer ['pfarər], *m.* (—s, *pl.* —) parson; vicar, (parish) priest.
Pfau [pfau], *m.* (—en, *pl.* —en) (*Orn.*) peacock.
Pfauenauge ['pfauənaugə], *n.* (—s, *pl.* —n) (*Ent.*) peacock butterfly.
Pfeffer ['pfɛfər], *m.* (—s, *no pl.*) pepper; *spanischer —*, red pepper, cayenne.
Pfefferkuchen ['pfɛfərku:xən], *m.* (—s, *pl.* —) gingerbread, spiced cake.
Pfefferminz ['pfɛfərmɪnts], *n.* (—, *no pl.*) peppermint.
Pfeife ['pfaifə], *f.* (—, *pl.* —n) whistle, fife; pipe.
pfeifen ['pfaifən], *v.a., v.n. irr.* whistle, play the fife; (*Theat.*) boo, hiss; (*bullets*) whiz(z).
Pfeifenrohr ['pfaifənro:r], *n.* (—s, *pl.* —e) pipe-stem.
Pfeil [pfail], *m.* (—es, *pl.* —e) arrow, dart, bolt.
Pfeiler ['pfailər], *m.* (—s, *pl.* —) pillar.
Pfeilwurz ['pfailvurts], *f.* (—, *no pl.*) (*Bot.*) arrow root.
Pfennig ['pfɛniç], *m.* (—s, *pl.* —e) one hundredth of a mark; (*loosely*) penny.
Pferch [pfɛrç], *m.* (—es, *pl.* —e) fold, pen.
Pferd [pfe:rt], *n.* (—es, *pl.* —e) horse; *zu —*, on horseback; *vom — steigen*, dismount.
Pferdeknecht ['pfe:rdəknɛçt], *m.* (—es, *pl.* —e) groom.
Pferdestärke ['pfe:rdəʃtɛrkə], *f.* (—, *no pl.*) horse-power (*abbr.* PS).
Pfiff [pfɪf], *m.* (—es, *pl.* —e) whistle.
Pfifferling ['pfɪfərliŋ], *m.* (—s, *pl.* —e) (*Bot.*) mushroom; chanterelle; *einen — wert*, worthless.
pfiffig ['pfɪfɪç], *adj.* cunning, sly, crafty.
Pfiffikus ['pfɪfikus], *m.* (—, *pl.* —se) (*coll.*) sly dog.

Pfingsten

Pfingsten ['pfɪŋkstən], *n.* Whitsun (-tide), Pentecost.
Pfingstrose ['pfɪŋkstroːzə], *f.* (—, *pl.* (*Bot.*) peony.
Pfirsich ['pfɪrzɪç], *m.* (—s, *pl.* —e) (*Bot.*) peach.
Pflanze ['pflantsə], *f.* (—, *pl.* —n) plant.
pflanzen ['pflantsən], *v.a.* plant.
Pflanzer ['pflantsər], *m.* (—s, *pl.* —) planter.
pflanzlich ['pflantslɪç], *adj.* vegetable, botanical.
Pflänzling ['pflɛntslɪŋ], *m.* (—s, *pl.* —e) seedling, young plant.
Pflanzung ['pflantsuŋ], *f.* (—, *pl.* —en) plantation.
Pflaster ['pflastər], *n.* (—s, *pl.* —) (*Med.*) plaster; (*street*) pavement; *ein teures* —, an expensive place to live in.
Pflaume ['pflaumə], *f.* (—, *pl.* —n) plum; *getrocknete* —, prune.
Pflege ['pfleːgə], *f.* (—, *no pl.*) care, attention, nursing, fostering.
Pflegeeltern ['pfleːgəɛltərn], *pl.* foster-parents.
pflegen ['pfleːgən], *v.a.* nurse, look after, take care of; *Umgang* — *mit,* associate with. — *v.n.* be used to, be in the habit of.
Pflegling ['pfleːklɪŋ], *m.* (—s, *pl.* —e) foster-child, ward.
Pflicht [pflɪçt], *f.* (—, *pl.* —en) duty, obligation.
Pflichtgefühl ['pflɪçtgəfyːl], *n.* (—s, *no pl.*) sense of duty.
pflichtgemäß ['pflɪçtgəmɛːs], *adj.* dutiful.
pflichtschuldig ['pflɪçtʃuldɪç], *adj.* in duty bound.
Pflock [pflɔk], *m.* (—s, *pl.* ⁓e) plug, peg.
pflücken ['pflykən], *v.a.* pluck, pick, gather.
Pflug [pfluːk], *m.* (—es, *pl.* ⁓e) plough.
Pflugschar ['pfluːkʃaːr], *f.* (—, *pl.* —en) ploughshare.
Pforte ['pfɔrtə], *f.* (—, *pl.* —n) gate, door, porch.
Pförtner ['pfœrtnər], *m.* (—s, *pl.* —) door-keeper, porter.
Pfosten ['pfɔstən], *m.* (—s, *pl.* —) post, stake; (*door*) jamb.
Pfote ['pfoːtə], *f.* (—, *pl.* —n) paw.
Pfriem [pfriːm], *m.* (—es, *pl.* —e) awl.
Pfropf(en) ['pfrɔpf(ən)], *m.* (—s, *pl.* —en) cork, stopper; (*gun*) wad.
pfropfen ['pfrɔpfən], *v.a.* graft; cork.
Pfründe ['pfryndə], *f.* (—, *pl.* —n) living, benefice.
Pfuhl [pfuːl], *m.* (—es, *pl.* —e) pool, puddle.
Pfühl [pfyːl], *m.* (—es, *pl.* —e) (*Poet.*) bolster, pillow, cushion.
pfui! [pfui], *excl.* shame! ugh! — *Teufel!* shame! a damned shame!
Pfund [pfunt], *n.* (—es, *pl.* —e) pound.
pfuschen ['pfuʃən], *v.n.* botch; *einem ins Handwerk* —, poach on s.o. else's preserve.

Pfütze ['pfytsə], *f.* (—, *pl.* —n) puddle.
Phänomen [fɛnoˈmeːn], *n.* (—s, *pl.* —e) phenomenon.
Phantasie [fantaˈziː], *f.* (—, *pl.* —n) fancy, imagination; (*Mus.*) fantasia.
phantasieren [fantaˈziːrən], *v.n.* indulge in fancies; (*sick person*) rave, wander, be delirious; (*Mus.*) improvise.
Phantast [fanˈtast], *m.* (—en, *pl.* —en) dreamer, visionary.
Pharisäer [fariˈzɛːər], *m.* (—s, *pl.* —) Pharisee.
Phase ['faːzə], *f.* (—, *pl.* —n) phase, stage (of process *or* development).
Philippinen [filiˈpiːnən], *f. pl.* Philippines.
Philister [fiˈlɪstər], *m.* (—s, *pl.* —) Philistine.
philisterhaft [fiˈlɪstərhaft], *adj.* philistine, narrow-minded, conventional.
Philologie [filoloˈgiː], *f.* (—, *no pl.*) philology; study of languages.
Philosoph [filoˈzoːf], *m.* (—en, *pl.* —en) philosopher.
Philosophie [filozoˈfiː], *f.* (—, *pl.* —n) philosophy.
Phiole [fiˈoːlə], *f.* (—, *pl.* —n) phial, vial.
Phlegma ['flɛgma], *n.* (—s, *no pl.*) phlegm.
Phonetik [foˈneːtɪk], *f.* (—, *no pl.*) phonetics.
photogen [fotoˈgeːn], *adj.* photogenic.
Photograph [fotoˈgraːf], *m.* (—en, *pl.* —en) photographer.
Photographie [fotograˈfiː], *f.* (—, *pl.* —n) photograph, photo; (*Art*) photography.
photographieren [fotograˈfiːrən], *v.a.* photograph.
Physik [fyˈziːk], *f.* (—, *no pl.*) physics.
physikalisch [fyziˈkaːlɪʃ], *adj.* physical (of physics).
Physiker ['fyːzɪkər], *m.* (—s, *pl.* —) physicist.
Physiologe [fyːzjoˈloːgə], *m.* (—en, *pl.* —en) physiologist.
physiologisch [fyːzjoˈloːgɪʃ], *adj.* physiological.
physisch ['fyːzɪʃ], *adj.* physical.
Pickel ['pɪka], *f.* (—, *pl.* —n) pickaxe, axe.
Pickel ['pɪkəl], *m.* (—s, *pl.* —) pimple.
Piedestal [pjeˈdɛstaːl], *n.* (—s, *pl.* —e) pedestal.
piepen ['piːpən], *v.n.* squeak, chirp.
piepsen ['piːpsən], *v.n.* squeak, chirp.
Pietät [pieˈtɛːt], *f.* (—, *no pl.*) piety, reverence.
Pik [piːk], *n.* (—s, *pl.* —s) (*cards*) spades.
pikant [piˈkant], *adj.* piquant, spicy; (*fig.*) risqué.
Pikee [piˈkeː], *m.* (—s, *pl.* —s) piqué.
pikiert [piˈkiːrt], *adj.* irritated, annoyed, piqued.
Pikkolo ['pɪkolo], *m.* (—s, *pl.* —s) apprentice waiter, boy (waiter); (*Mus.*) piccolo, flute.

pochen

Pilger ['pɪlgər], *m.* (—s, *pl.* —) pilgrim.
Pille ['pɪlə], *f.* (—, *pl.* —n) pill.
Pilz [pɪlts], *m.* (—es, *pl.* —e) fungus, mushroom.
Piment [pi'mɛnt], *n.* (—s, *pl.* —e) pimento, Jamaican pepper, all-spice.
pimplig ['pɪmplɪç], *adj.* effeminate.
Pinguin [pɪŋɡu'i:n], *m.* (—s, *pl.* —e) (*Orn.*) penguin.
Pinie ['pi:njə], *f.* (—, *pl.* —n) (*Bot.*) stone-pine.
Pinne ['pɪnə], *f.* (—, *pl.* —n) drawing-pin; peg.
Pinscher ['pɪnʃər], *m.* (—s, *pl.* —) terrier.
Pinsel ['pɪnzəl], *m.* (—s, *pl.* —) (*Painting*) brush, pencil; (*fig.*) simpleton.
Pinzette [pɪn'tsɛtə], *f.* (—, *pl.* —n) pincers, tweezers.
Pirsch [pɪrʃ], *f.* (—, *no pl.*) (deer-) stalking.
Piste ['pɪstə], *f.* (—, *pl.* —n) track; (*Aviat.*) runway.
pittoresk [pɪto'rɛsk], *adj.* picturesque.
placken ['plakən], *v.r. sich* —, toil, drudge.
plädieren [plɛ'di:rən], *v.n.* plead.
Plädoyer [plɛ:doa'je:], *n.* (—s, *pl.* —s) speech for the prosecution *or* the defence (in a court of law), plea, pleading.
Plage ['pla:ɡə], *f.* (—, *pl.* —n) torment, trouble; calamity; plague.
plagen ['pla:ɡən], *v.a.* plague, trouble, torment, vex. — *v.r. sich* —, toil.
Plagiat [plaɡ'ja:t], *n.* (—es, *pl.* —e) plagiarism.
Plaid [plɛ:t], *n.* (—s, *pl.* —s) travelling-rug.
Plakat [pla'ka:t], *n.* (—(e)s, *pl.* —e) poster, placard, bill.
Plan [pla:n], *m.* (—es, *pl.* ⁓e) plan, scheme, plot; map, ground-plan.
Plane ['pla:nə], *f.* (—, *pl.* —n) awning, cover.
planieren [pla'ni:rən], *v.a.* level, plane down; bulldoze, flatten.
Planke ['plaŋkə], *f.* (—, *pl.* —n) plank, board.
Plänkelei [plɛnkə'laɪ], *f.* (—, *pl.* —en) skirmish.
planmäßig ['pla:nmɛːsɪç], *adj.* according to plan.
planschen ['planʃən], *v.n.* splash; paddle.
Plantage [plan'ta:ʒə], *f.* (—, *pl.* —n) plantation.
planvoll ['pla:nfɔl], *adj.* systematic, well-planned.
Planwagen ['pla:nva:ɡən], *m.* (—s, *pl.* —) tilt-cart.
plappern ['plapərn], *v.n.* prattle, chatter.
plärren ['plɛrən], *v.n.* blubber, bawl.
Plastik ['plastɪk], *f.* (—, *pl.* —en) plastic art; plastic (material).
Platane [pla'ta:nə], *f.* (—, *pl.* —n) plane-tree.

Platin ['pla:ti:n], *n.* (—s, *no pl.*) platinum.
platonisch [pla'to:nɪʃ], *adj.* platonic.
plätschern ['plɛtʃərn], *v.n.* splash about.
platt [plat], *adj.* flat, level, even; insipid; downright; —*e Redensart*, commonplace, platitude; (*coll.*) *ich bin ganz* —, I am astonished *or* dumbfounded.
Plättbrett ['plɛtbrɛt], *n.* (—es, *pl.* —er) ironing board.
plattdeutsch ['platdɔytʃ], *adj.* Low German.
Platte ['platə], *f.* (—, *pl.* —n) plate; dish; board; slab; sheet; ledge; (*fig.*) bald head; (*Mus.*) (gramophone) record.
plätten ['plɛtən], *v.a.* iron (clothes).
Plattfisch ['platfɪʃ], *m.* (—es, *pl.* —e) (*Zool.*) plaice.
Plattfuß ['platfu:s], *n.* (—es, *pl.* ⁓e) flat foot.
Plattheit ['plathaɪt], *f.* (—, *pl.* —en) flatness; (*fig.*) platitude.
Platz [plats], *m.* (—es, *pl.* ⁓e) place, town, spot, site; space, room; (*town*) square; seat; — *nehmen*, take a seat, be seated.
Platzanweiserin ['platsanvaɪzərɪn], *f.* (—, *pl.* —nen) usherette.
Plätzchen ['plɛtsçən], *n.* (—s, *pl.* —) small place; drop; biscuit.
platzen ['platsən], *v.n.* (*aux.* sein) burst, explode.
Platzregen ['platsre:ɡən], *m.* (—s, *no pl.*) downpour, heavy shower.
Plauderei [plaudə'raɪ], *f.* (—, *pl.* —en) chat.
Plaudertasche ['plaudərtaʃə], *f.* (—, *pl.* —n) chatterbox.
Pleite ['plaɪtə], *f.* (—, *pl.* —n) (*coll.*) bankruptcy; — *machen*, go bankrupt.
Plenum ['ple:num], *n.* (—s, *no pl.*) plenary session.
Pleuelstange ['plɔyəlʃtaŋə], *f.* (—, *pl.* —n) connecting-rod.
Plinsen ['plɪnzən], *f. pl.* (*Austr.*) fritters.
Plissee [plɪ'se:], *n.* (—s, *pl.* —s) pleating.
Plombe ['plɔmbə], *f.* (—, *pl.* —n) lead, seal; (*teeth*) filling.
plombieren [plɔm'bi:rən], *v.a.* seal with lead; (*teeth*) fill.
plötzlich ['plœtslɪç], *adj.* sudden.
plump [plump], *adj.* clumsy, ungainly, awkward; crude, coarse.
plumps [plumps], *excl.* bump! oops!
Plunder ['plundər], *m.* (—s, *no pl.*) lumber, trash.
plündern ['plyndərn], *v.a.* plunder, pillage.
Plüsch [ply:ʃ], *m.* (—es, *no pl.*) plush.
pneumatisch [pnɔy'ma:tɪʃ], *adj.* pneumatic.
Pöbel ['pø:bəl], *m.* (—s, *no pl.*) mob, rabble.
pochen ['pɔxən], *v.a., v.n.* knock, beat, throb.

169

Pocke

Pocke ['pɔkə], *f.* (—, *pl.* —n) pockmark; (*pl.*) smallpox.

pockennarbig ['pɔkənnarbɪç], *adj.* pockmarked.

Podagra ['po:dagra:], *n.* (—s, *no pl.*) (*Med.*) gout.

Pointe [po'ɛ̃tə], *f.* (—, *pl.* —n) (of a *story*) point.

Pokal [po'ka:l], *m.* (—s, *pl.* —e) goblet, cup; trophy.

Pökelfleisch ['pø:kəlflaɪʃ], *n.* (—es, *no pl.*) salted meat.

Pol [po:l], *m.* (—s, *pl.* —e) pole.

polemisch [po'le:mɪʃ], *adj.* polemic(al), controversial.

Polen ['po:lən], *n.* Poland.

Police [po'li:sə], *f.* (—, *pl.* —n) insurance policy.

polieren [po'li:rən], *v.a.* polish, furbish, burnish.

Poliklinik ['po:likli:nɪk], *f.* (—, *pl.* —en) (*Med.*) out-patients' department.

Politik [poli'ti:k], *f.* (—, *no pl.*) politics; policy.

politisieren [politi'zi:rən], *v.n.* talk politics.

Politur [poli'tu:r], *f.* (—, *no pl.*) polish, gloss.

Polizei [poli'tsaɪ], *f.* (—, *no pl.*) police.

polizeilich [poli'tsaɪlɪç], *adj.* of the police.

Polizeistunde [poli'tsaɪʃtundə], *f.* (—, *no pl.*) closing time.

Polizeiwache [poli'tsaɪvaxə], *f.* (—, *pl.* —n) police station.

Polizist [poli'tsɪst], *m.* (—en, *pl.* —en) policeman, constable.

Polizze [po'lɪtsə], *f.* (—, *pl.* —n) (*Austr. dial.*) insurance policy.

polnisch ['pɔlnɪʃ], *adj.* Polish.

Polster ['pɔlstər], *n.* (—s, *pl.* —) cushion, bolster.

Polterabend ['pɔltəra:bənt], *m.* (—s, *pl.* —e) wedding-eve party.

Poltergeist ['pɔltərgaɪst], *m.* (—es, *pl.* —er) poltergeist, hobgoblin.

poltern ['pɔltərn], *v.n.* rumble; make a noise; bluster.

Polyp [po'ly:p], *m.* (—en, *pl.* —en) (*Zool.*) polyp; (*Med.*) polypus.

Pomeranze [poma'rantsə], *f.* (—, *pl.* —n) (*Bot.*) orange.

Pommern ['pɔmərn], *n.* Pomerania.

Pope ['po:pə], *m.* (—n, *pl.* —n) Greek Orthodox priest.

Popo [po'po:], *m.* (—s, *pl.* —s) (*coll.*) backside, bottom.

populär [popu'lɛ:r], *adj.* popular.

porös [po'rø:s], *adj.* porous.

Porree ['pɔre:], *m.* (—s, *no pl.*) leek.

Portefeuille [pɔrt'fœj], *n.* (—s, *pl.* —s) portfolio.

Portier [pɔr'tje:], *m.* (—s, *pl.* —s) doorkeeper, caretaker; porter.

Porto ['pɔrto:], *n.* (—s, *pl.* **Porti**) postage.

Porzellan [pɔrtsɛ'la:n], *n.* (—s, *pl.* —e) china, porcelain; *Meißner* —, Dresden china.

Posamenten [poza'mɛntən], *n. pl.* trimmings.

Posaune [po'zaunə], *f.* (—, *pl.* —n) (*Mus.*) trombone.

Positur [pozi'tu:r], *f.* (—, *pl.* —en) posture; *sich in — setzen*, strike an attitude.

Posse ['pɔsə], *f.* (—, *pl.* —n) (*Theat.*) farce, skit.

Possen ['pɔsən], *m.* (—s, *pl.* —) trick; *einem einen — spielen*, play a trick on s.o.

possierlich [pɔ'si:rlɪç], *adj.* droll, funny, comic(al).

Post [pɔst], *f.* (—, *pl.* —en) post, mail; (*building*) post-office.

Postament [pɔsta'mɛnt], *n.* (—s, *pl.* —e) plinth, pedestal.

Postanweisung ['pɔstanvaɪzuŋ], *f.* (—, *pl.* —en) postal order, money order.

Posten ['pɔstən], *m.* (—s, *pl.* —) post, station; place; (*goods*) parcel, lot, job lot; (*Comm.*) item; (*Mil.*) outpost; *— stehen*, stand sentry; *nicht auf dem — sein*, be unwell.

Postfach ['pɔstfax], *n.* (—es, *pl.* ⁻er) post-office box.

postieren [pɔs'ti:rən], *v.a.* post, place, station.

postlagernd ['pɔstla:gərnt], *adj.* poste restante, to be called for.

Postschalter ['pɔstʃaltər], *m.* (—s, *pl.* —) post-office counter.

postulieren [pɔstu'li:rən], *v.a.* postulate.

postwendend ['pɔstvɛndənt], *adj.* by return of post.

Postwertzeichen ['pɔstve:rttsaɪçən], *n.* (—s, *pl.* —) stamp.

Potenz [po'tɛnts], *f.* (—, *pl.* —en) (*Maths.*) power; *zur dritten —*, cubed, to the power of three.

potenzieren [poten'tsi:rən], *v.a.* (*Math.*) raise; intensify.

Pottasche ['pɔtaʃə], *f.* (—, *no pl.*) potash.

potzblitz ['pɔtsblɪts], *excl.* good Heavens! good gracious!

potztausend ['pɔtstauzənt], *excl.* great Scott! good Heavens!

Pracht [praxt], *f.* (—, *no pl.*) splendour, magnificence; (*in compounds*) de luxe.

prächtig ['prɛ:çtɪç], *adj.* splendid, magnificent, sumptuous.

prachtvoll ['praxtfɔl], *adj.* gorgeous, magnificent.

Prädikat [prɛ:di'ka:t], *n.* (—s, *pl.* —e) mark; (*Gram.*) predicate.

Prag [pra:k], *n.* Prague.

prägen ['prɛ:gən], *v.a.* coin, mint, stamp.

prägnant [prɛg'nant], *adj.* meaningful, precise.

prahlen ['pra:lən], *v.n.* boast, brag, talk big, show off.

Praktikant [prakti'kant], *m.* (—en, *pl.* —en) probationer; apprentice.

Praktiken ['praktɪkən], *f. pl.* machinations.

praktisch ['praktɪʃ], *adj.* practical; —*er Arzt*, general practitioner.
praktizieren [praktɪ'tsi:rən], *v.a.* practise.
Prall [pral], *m.* (—**es**, *pl.* —**e**) impact.
prall [pral], *adj.* tense, tight; (*cheeks*) chubby.
prallen ['pralən], *v.n.* (*aux.* sein) *auf etwas* —, bounce against s.th.
Prämie ['prɛ:mjə], *f.* (—, *pl.* —**n**) prize; (*insurance*) premium; (*dividend*) bonus.
prangen ['praŋən], *v.n.* shine, glitter, make a show.
Pranger ['praŋər], *m.* (—**s**, *pl.* —) pillory; *etwas an den* — *stellen*, expose s.th., pillory.
präparieren [prɛpa'ri:rən], *v.a.*, *v.r.* prepare.
Präsens ['prɛ:zɛns], *n.* (—, *pl.* —**ntia**) (*Gram.*) present tense.
präsentieren [prɛzɛn'ti:rən], *v.a.* present; *präsentiert das Gewehr!* present arms!
prasseln ['prasəln], *v.n.* (*fire*) crackle; rattle.
prassen ['prasən], *v.n.* revel, gorge (o.s.), guzzle, feast.
Prätendent [prɛtɛn'dɛnt], *m.* (—**en**, *pl.* —**en**) pretender, claimant.
Präteritum [prɛ'te:ritum], *n.* (—**s**, *pl.* —**ta**) (*Gram.*) preterite, past tense.
Praxis ['praksɪs], *f.* (—, *no pl.*) practice.
präzis [prɛ'tsi:s], *adj.* precise, exact.
präzisieren [prɛtsi'zi:rən], *v.a.* define exactly.
predigen ['pre:dɪgən], *v.a.*, *v.n.* preach.
Predigt ['pre:dɪçt], *f.* (—, *pl.* —**en**) sermon; (*fig.*) homily, lecture.
Preis [prats], *m.* (—**es**, *pl.* —**e**) price, rate, value; (*reward*) prize; praise; *um jeden* —, at any price, at all costs; *um keinen* —, not for all the world; *feste* —*e*, fixed prices; no rebate, no discount.
Preisausschreiben ['praɪsausʃraɪbən], *n.* (—**s**, *pl.* —) prize competition.
Preiselbeere ['praɪzəlbe:rə], *f.* (—, *pl.* —**n**) (*Bot.*) bilberry, cranberry.
preisen ['praɪzən], *v.a. irr.* praise, laud; glorify.
preisgeben ['praɪsge:bən], *v.a. irr.* give up, abandon, part with; *dem Spott preisgegeben sein*, become a laughing-stock.
Preisunterbietung ['praɪsuntərbi:- tuŋ], *f.* (—, *pl.* —**en**) under-cutting.
Prellbock ['prɛlbɔk], *m.* (—**s**, *pl.* ⸚**e**) buffer (-block).
prellen ['prɛlən], *v.a.* cheat, defraud.
Prellstein ['prɛlʃtaɪn], *m.* (—**s**, *pl.* —**e**) kerbstone.
pressant [prɛ'sant], *adj.* (*Austr.*) urgent.
Presse ['prɛsə], *f.* (—, *pl.* —**n**) press; newspapers; (*coll.*) coaching establishment, crammer.
pressieren [prɛ'si:rən], *v.n.* be urgent.
Preßkohle ['prɛsko:lə], *f.* (—, *no pl.*) briquette(s).

Preßkolben ['prɛskɔlbən], *m.* (—**s**, *pl.* —) piston.
Preßluft ['prɛsluft], *f.* (—, *no pl.*) compressed air.
Preußen ['prɔysən], *n.* Prussia.
prickeln ['prɪkəln], *v.n.* prick, prickle, sting, tickle.
Prieme ['pri:mə], *f.* (—, *pl.* —**n**) chew, quid.
Priester ['pri:stər], *m.* (—**s**, *pl.* —) priest; *zum* — *weihen*, ordain to the priesthood.
Prima ['pri:ma:], *f.* (—, *pl.* **Primen**) highest form at a grammar school (sixth form).
prima ['pri:ma:], *adj.* excellent, splendid, first-rate.
Primaner [pri'ma:nər], *m.* (—**s**, *pl.* —) pupil in the highest form at a grammar school, sixth form boy.
Primel ['pri:məl], *f.* (—, *pl.* —**n**) (*Bot.*) primrose, primula.
Primus ['pri:mus], *m.* (—, *no pl.*) (*School*) head boy, captain of the school.
Prinzip [prɪn'tsi:p], *n.* (—**s**, *pl.* —**ien**) principle.
Priorität [priori'tɛ:t], *f.* (—, *no pl.*) priority, precedence.
Prise ['pri:zə], *f.* (—, *pl.* —**n**) pinch of snuff.
Prisma ['prɪsma:], *n.* (—**s**, *pl.* —**men**) prism.
Pritsche ['prɪtʃə], *f.* (—, *pl.* —**n**) plank-bed.
Privatdozent [pri'va:tdotsɛnt], *m.* (—**en**, *pl.* —**en**) (*Univ.*) (unsalaried) lecturer.
privatisieren [privati'zi:rən], *v.n.* have private means.
Probe ['pro:bə], *f.* (—, *pl.* —**n**) experiment, trial, probation, test; (*Theat.*, *Mus.*) rehearsal; sample, pattern; *auf* —, on trial; *auf die* — *stellen*, put to the test or on probation.
Probeabzug ['pro:baaptsu:k], *m.* (—**s**, *pl.* ⸚*e*) (*Printing*) proof.
proben ['pro:bən], *v.a.* rehearse.
probieren [pro'bi:rən], *v.a.* try, attempt; taste.
Probst [pro:pst], *m.* (—**es**, *pl.* ⸚**e**) provost.
Produzent [produ'tsɛnt], *m.* (—**en**, *pl.* —**en**) producer (of goods), manufacturer.
produzieren [produ'tsi:rən], *v.a.* produce (goods). — *v.r. sich* —, perform, show off.
profanieren [profa'ni:rən], *v.a.* desecrate, profane.
Professur [profɛ'su:r], *f.* (—, *pl.* —**en**) (*Univ.*) professorship, Chair.
profitieren [profi'ti:rən], *v.a.*, *v.n.* profit (by), take advantage (of).
projizieren [proji'tsi:rən], *v.a.* project.
Prokura [pro'ku:ra:], *f.* (—, *no pl.*) (*Law*) power of attorney.
Prokurist [proku'rɪst], *m.* (—**en**, *pl.* —**en**) confidential clerk; company secretary.

prolongieren

prolongieren [prolɔŋˈgiːrən], *v.a.* prolong, extend.

promenieren [proməˈniːrən], *v.n.* take a stroll.

Promotion [promoˈtsjoːn], *f.* (—, *pl.* —en) graduation, degree ceremony.

promovieren [promoˈviːrən], *v.n.* graduate, take a degree.

promulgieren [promulˈgiːrən], *v.a.* promulgate.

Pronomen [proˈnoːmən], *n.* (—s, *pl.* —mina) (*Gram.*) pronoun.

prophezeien [profeˈtsaɪən], *v.a.* prophesy, predict, forecast.

prophylaktisch [profyˈlaktɪʃ], *adj.* preventive, prophylactic.

Propst [proːpst], *m.* (—es, *pl.* ⸚e) provost.

Prosa [ˈproːzaː], *f.* (—, *no pl.*) prose.

prosit [ˈproːzɪt], *excl.* cheers! here's to you! your health!

Prospekt [proˈspɛkt], *m.* (—es, *pl.* —e) prospect; (*booklet*) prospectus.

Prostituierte [prostituˈiːrtə], *f.* (—n, *pl.* —n) prostitute; (*coll.*) tart.

protegieren [proteˈʒiːrən], *v.a.* favour, patronize.

Protektion [protɛkˈtsjoːn], *f.* (—, *no pl.*) patronage, favouritism.

protestieren [protɛsˈtiːrən], *v.n.* make a protest, protest (against s.th.).

Protokoll [protoˈkɔl], *n.* (—s, *pl.* —e) minutes, record; protocol; regulations.

Protokollführer [protoˈkɔlfyːrər], *m.* (—s, *pl.* —) recorder, clerk of the minutes.

Protz [prɔts], *m.* (—en, *pl.* —en) snob, upstart; show-off.

Proviant [proˈvjant], *m.* (—s, *no pl.*) provisions, stores.

provinziell [provɪnˈtsjɛl], *adj.* provincial.

Provinzler [proˈvɪntslər], *m.* (—s, *pl.* —) provincial.

Provision [proviˈzjoːn], *f.* (—, *pl.* —en) (*Comm.*) commission, brokerage.

Provisor [proˈviːzɔr], *m.* (—s, *pl.* —en) dispenser.

provisorisch [proviˈzoːrɪʃ], *adj.* provisional, temporary.

provozieren [provoˈtsiːrən], *v.a.* provoke.

Prozedur [protseˈduːr], *f.* (—, *pl.* —en) proceedings, procedure.

Prozent [proˈtsɛnt], *m. & n.* (—s, *pl.* —e) per cent.

Prozentsatz [proˈtsɛntzats], *m.* (—es, *pl.* ⸚e) percentage, rate of interest.

Prozeß [proˈtsɛs], *m.* (—es, *pl.* —e) process; lawsuit, litigation; trial; *mit etwas kurzen — machen*, deal summarily with.

Prozeßwesen [proˈtsɛsveːzən], *n.* (—s, *no pl.*) legal procedure.

prüde [ˈpryːdə], *adj.* prudish, prim.

prüfen [ˈpryːfən], *v.a.* test, examine.

Prüfung [ˈpryːfuŋ], *f.* (—, *pl.* —en) trial, test; examination; (*fig.*) temptation, affliction.

Prügel [ˈpryːgəl], *m.* (—s, *pl.* —) cudgel; (*pl.*) thrashing; *eine Tracht —*, a good hiding.

prügeln [ˈpryːgəln], *v.a.* beat, give a hiding to.

Prunk [pruŋk], *m.* (—(e)s, *no pl.*) splendour, ostentation, pomp.

prusten [ˈpruːstən], *v.n.* snort.

Psalm [psalm], *m.* (—es, *pl.* —e) psalm.

Psalter [ˈpsaltər], *m.* (—s, *pl.* —) (*book*) psalter; (*instrument*) psaltery.

Psychiater [psyçiˈaːtər], *m.* (—s, *pl.* —) psychiatrist.

Psychologe [psyçoˈloːgə], *m.* (—n, *pl.* —n) psychologist.

Pubertät [puberˈtɛːt], *f.* (—, *no pl.*) puberty.

Publikum [ˈpuːblikum], *n.* (—s, *no pl.*) public; (*Theat.*) audience.

publizieren [publiˈtsiːrən], *v.a.* publish; promulgate.

Pudel [ˈpuːdəl], *m.* (—s, *pl.* —) poodle; *des —s Kern*, the gist of the matter.

Puder [ˈpuːdər], *m.* (—s, *no pl.*) powder, face-powder.

pudern [ˈpuːdərn], *v.a.* powder.

Puff [puf], *m.* (—es, *pl.* ⸚e) cuff, thump.

puffen [ˈpufən], *v.a.* cuff, thump.

Puffer [ˈpufər], *m.* (—s, *pl.* —) buffer.

Puffspiel [ˈpufʃpiːl], *n.* (—s, *pl.* —e) backgammon.

pullen [ˈpuːlən], *v.n.* rein in (a horse); (*coll.*) piddle.

Pulsader [ˈpulsaːdər], *f.* (—, *pl.* —n) artery; aorta.

pulsieren [pulˈziːrən], *v.n.* pulsate; pulse, throb.

Pulsschlag [ˈpulsʃlaːk], *m.* (—s, *pl.* ⸚e) pulse-beat; pulsation.

Pult [pult], *n.* (—es, *pl.* —e) desk, writing-table; lectern.

Pulver [ˈpulvər], *n.* (—s, *pl.* —) powder.

Pump [pump], *m.* (—s, *no pl.*) (*sl.*) credit; *auf —*, on tick.

pumpen [ˈpumpən], *v.a., v.n.* pump; (*fig.*) (*sl.*) *sich etwas —*, borrow s.th., touch s.o. for s.th.; lend.

Pumpenschwengel [ˈpumpənʃvɛŋəl], *m.* (—s, *pl.* —) pump-handle.

Pumpernickel [ˈpumpərnɪkəl], *m.* (—s, *pl.* —) black bread, Westphalian rye-bread.

Pumphosen [ˈpumphoːzən], *f. pl.* plus-fours.

Punkt [puŋkt], *m.* (—es, *pl.* —e) point, dot, spot; (*Gram.*) full stop.

punktieren [puŋkˈtiːrən], *v.a.* dot; punctuate.

pünktlich [ˈpyŋktlɪç], *adj.* punctual.

punktum [ˈpuŋktum], *excl. und damit —*, that's the end of it; that's it.

Puppe [ˈpupə], *f.* (—, *pl.* —n) doll; (*Ent.*) pupa, chrysalis.

pur [puːr], *adj.* pure, sheer; (*drink*) neat.

Quitte

Puritaner [puri'ta:nər], *m.* (—s, *pl.* —) puritan.
Purpur ['purpur], *m.* (—s, *no pl.*) purple.
Purzelbaum ['purtsəlbaum], *m.* (—s, *pl.* ‑̈e) somersault.
purzeln ['purtsəln], *v.n.* tumble.
Pustel ['pustəl], *f.* (—, *pl.* —n) pustule.
pusten ['pu:stən], *v.n.* puff, blow.
Pute ['pu:tə], *f.* (—, *pl.* —n) (*Orn.*) turkey-hen; *dumme* —, silly goose.
Puter ['pu:tər], *m.* (—s, *pl.* —) turkey-cock.
puterrot ['pu:tərro:t], *adj.* as red as a turkey-cock.
Putsch [putʃ], *m.* (—es, *pl.* —e) coup de main, insurrection, riot.
Putz [puts], *m.* (—es, *no pl.*) finery; cleaning; rough-cast.
putzen ['putsən], *v.a.* polish, shine; clean. — *v.r. sich* —, dress up.
Putzfrau ['putsfrau], *f.* (—, *pl.* —en) charwoman.
Putzmacherin ['putsmaxərin], *f.* (—, *pl.* —nen) milliner.
Pyramide [pyra'mi:də], *f.* (—, *pl.* —n) pyramid.
Pyrenäen [pyrə'nɛ:ən], *pl.* Pyrenees; —halbinsel, Iberian Peninsula.

Q

Q [ku:], *n.* (—s, *pl.* —s) the letter Q.
quabbeln ['kvabəln], *v.n.* shake, wobble.
Quacksalber ['kvakzalbər], *m.* (—s, *pl.* —) quack, mountebank.
Quacksalberei [kvakzalbə'rai], *f.* (—, *pl.* —en) quackery.
Quaderstein ['kva:dərʃtain], *m.* (—s, *pl.* —e) ashlar, hewn stone.
Quadrat [kva'dra:t], *n.* (—es, *pl.* —e) square; *zum* (or *ins*) — *erheben*, square (a number).
Quadratur [kvadra'tu:r], *f.* (—, *pl.* —en) quadrature; *die* — *des Kreises finden*, square the circle.
quadrieren [kva'dri:rən], *v.a.* square.
quaken ['kva:kən], *v.n.* (*frog*) croak; (*duck*) quack.
quäken ['kvɛ:kən], *v.n.* squeak.
Quäker ['kvɛ:kər], *m.* (—s, *pl.* —) Quaker.
Qual [kva:l], *f.* (—, *pl.* —en) anguish, agony, torment.
quälen ['kvɛ:lən], *v.a.* torment, torture, vex. — *v.r. sich* —, toil.
qualifizieren [kvalifi'tsi:rən], *v.a.* qualify.
Qualität [kvali'tɛ:t], *f.* (—, *pl.* —en) quality.

Qualle ['kvalə], *f.* (—, *pl.* —n) (*Zool.*) jelly-fish.
Qualm [kvalm], *m.* (—es, *no pl.*) dense smoke.
Quantität [kvanti'tɛ:t], *f.* (—, *pl.* —en) quantity.
Quantum ['kvantum], *n.* (—s, *pl.* —ten) portion, quantity.
Quappe ['kvapə], *f.* (—, *pl.* —n) (*Zool.*) tadpole.
Quarantäne [kvaran'tɛ:nə], *f.* (—, *no pl.*) quarantine.
Quark [kvark], *m.* (—s, *no pl.*) curds; cream-cheese; (*fig.*) trash, rubbish, nonsense, bilge.
Quarta ['kvarta:], *f.* (—, *no pl.*) fourth form.
Quartal [kvar'ta:l], *n.* (—s, *pl.* —e) quarter of a year; term.
Quartier [kvar'ti:r], *n.* (—s, *pl.* —e) quarters, lodging; (*Mil.*) billet.
Quarz [kvarts], *m.* (—es, *no pl.*) quartz.
Quaste ['kvastə], *f.* (—, *pl.* —n) tassel.
Quatember [kva'tɛmbər], *m.* (—s, *pl.* —) quarter day; (*Eccl.*) Ember Day.
Quatsch [kvatʃ], *m.* (—es, *no pl.*) nonsense, drivel.
Quecke ['kvɛkə], *f.* (—, *pl.* —n) couch-grass, quick-grass.
Quecksilber ['kvɛkzilbər], *n.* (—s, *no pl.*) quicksilver, mercury.
Quelle ['kvɛlə], *f.* (—, *pl.* —n) well, spring, fountain; (*fig.*) source; *aus sicherer* —, on good authority.
Quentchen ['kvɛntçən], *n.* (—s, *pl.* —) small amount, dram.
quer [kve:r], *adj.* cross, transverse, oblique, diagonal. — *adv.* across; *kreuz und* —, in all directions.
Querbalken ['kve:rbalkən], *m.* (—s, *pl.* —) cross-beam.
querdurch ['kve:rdurç], *adv.* across.
querfeldein ['kve:rfɛltain], *adv.* cross-country.
Querkopf ['kve:rkopf], *m.* (—es, *pl.* ‑̈e) crank.
Quersattel ['kve:rzatəl], *m.* (—s, *pl.* ‑̈) side-saddle.
Querschiff ['kve:rʃif], *n.* (—es, *pl.* —e) (*church*) transept.
Querschnitt ['kve:rʃnit], *m.* (—es, *pl.* —e) cross-section; (*fig.*) average.
Querulant [kveru'lant], *m.* (—en, *pl.* —en) grumbler.
quetschen ['kvetʃən], *v.a.* squeeze, crush, mash; bruise.
Queue [kø:], *n.* (—s, *pl.* —s) (*Billiards*) cue.
quieken ['kvi:kən], *v.n.* squeak.
Quinta ['kvinta:], *f.* (—, *no pl.*) fifth form.
Quinte ['kvintə], *f.* (—, *pl.* —n) (*Mus.*) fifth.
Quirl [kvirl], *m.* (—s, *pl.* —e) whisk; (*Bot.*) whorl.
quitt [kvit], *adj.* — *sein*, be quits.
Quitte ['kvitə], *f.* (—, *pl.* —n) (*Bot.*) quince.

173

quittegelb ['kvɪtəgɛlp], *adj.* bright yellow.
quittieren [kvɪ'tiːrən], *v.a.* receipt; give a receipt; *den Dienst* —, leave the service.
Quittung ['kvɪtuŋ], *f.* (—, *pl.* —en) receipt.
Quodlibet ['kvɔdlɪbɛt], *n.* (—s, *pl.* —s) medley.
Quote ['kvoːtə], *f.* (—, *pl.* —n) quota, share.
quotieren [kvo'tiːrən], *v.a.* (*stock exchange*) quote (prices).

R

R [ɛr], *n.* (—s, *pl.* —s) the letter R.
Rabatt [ra'bat], *m.* (—s, *pl.* —e) rebate, discount.
Rabatte [ra'batə], *f.* (—, *pl.* —n) flower-border.
Rabbiner [ra'biːnər], *m.* (—s, *pl.* —) rabbi.
Rabe ['raːbə], *m.* (—n, *pl.* —n) (*Orn.*) raven; *ein weißer* —, a rare bird.
Rabenaas ['raːbənaːs], *n.* (—es, *pl.* —e) carrion.
rabiat [ra'bjaːt], *adj.* furious, rabid.
Rache ['raxə], *f.* (—, *no pl.*) revenge, vengeance.
Rachen ['raxən], *m.* (—s, *pl.* —) jaws, throat.
rächen ['rɛçən], *v.a.* avenge. — *v.r. sich* —, avenge o.s., take vengeance.
Rachenbräune ['raxənbrɔynə], *f.* (—, *no pl.*) croup, quinsy.
Rachitis [ra'xiːtɪs], *f.* (—, *no pl.*) (*Med.*) rickets.
rachsüchtig ['raxzyçtɪç], *adj.* vindictive, vengeful.
rackern ['rakərn], *v.r. sich* —, (*coll.*) toil, work hard.
Rad [raːt], *n.* (—es, *pl.* —er) wheel; bicycle; *ein* — *schlagen*, turn a cart-wheel; (*peacock*) spread the tail.
Radau [ra'dau], *m.* (—s, *no pl.*) noise, din, shindy.
Rade ['raːdə], *f.* (—, *pl.* —n) corn-cockle.
radebrechen ['raːdəbrɛçən], *v.a. insep.* murder a language.
radeln ['raːdəln], *v.n.* (*aux.* sein) (*coll.*) cycle.
Rädelsführer ['rɛːdəlsfyːrər], *m.* (—s, *pl.* —) ringleader.
rädern ['rɛːdərn], *v.a.* break on the wheel; *gerädert sein*, (*fig.*) ache in all o.'s bones, be exhausted.
Radfahrer ['raːtfaːrər], *m.* (—s, *pl.* —) cyclist.
radieren [ra'diːrən], *v.n.* erase; etch.
Radierung [ra'diːruŋ], *f.* (—, *pl.* —en) etching.

Radieschen [ra'diːsçən], *n.* (—s, *pl.* —) (*Bot.*) radish.
Radio ['raːdjo], *n.* (—s, *pl.* —s) wireless, radio.
raffen ['rafən], *v.a.* snatch up, gather up.
Raffinade [rafi'naːdə], *f.* (—, *no pl.*) refined sugar.
Raffinement [rafinə'mãː], *n.* (—s, *no pl.*) elaborateness.
raffinieren [rafi'niːrən], *v.a.* refine.
raffiniert [rafi'niːrt], *adj.* refined; elaborate, crafty, wily, cunning.
ragen ['raːgən], *v.n.* tower, soar.
Rahm [raːm], *m.* (—es, *no pl.*) cream; *den* — *abschöpfen*, skim; (*fig.*) skim the cream off.
Rahmen ['raːmən], *m.* (—s, *pl.* —) frame; milieu, limit, scope, compass; *im* — *von*, within the framework of.
rahmig ['raːmɪç], *adj.* creamy.
raisonnieren [rɛzɔ'niːrən], *v.n.* reason, argue; (*fig.*) grumble, answer back.
Rakete [ra'keːtə], *f.* (—, *pl.* —n) rocket, sky-rocket.
Rakett [ra'kɛt], *n.* (—s, *pl.* —s) (*tennis*) racket.
rammen ['ramən], *v.a.* ram.
Rampe ['rampə], *f.* (—, *pl.* —n) ramp, slope; platform; (*Theat.*) apron.
ramponiert [rampo'niːrt], *adj.* battered, damaged.
Ramsch [ramʃ], *m.* (—es, *pl.* —e) odds and ends; (*Comm.*) job lot.
Rand [rant], *m.* (—es, *pl.* —er) edge, border, verge, rim; (*book*) margin; (*hat*) brim; *am* — *des Grabes*, with one foot in the grave; *außer* — *und Band geraten*, get completely out of hand.
randalieren [randa'liːrən], *v.n.* kick up a row.
Randbemerkung ['rantbəmɛrkuŋ], *f.* (—, *pl.* —en) marginal note, gloss.
rändern [rɛndərn], *v.a.* border, edge, mill.
Ränftchen ['rɛnftçən], *n.* (—s, *pl.* —) crust (of bread).
Rang [raŋ], *m.* (—es, *pl.* —e) rank, grade, rate; order, class; standing (in society); (*Theat.*) circle, tier, gallery.
Range ['raŋə], *m.* (—n, *pl.* —n) scamp, rascal. — *f.* (—, *pl.* —n) tomboy, hoyden.
rangieren [rãʒiːrən], *v.a.* (*Railw.*) shunt. — *v.n.* rank.
Ranke ['raŋkə], *f.* (—, *pl.* —n) tendril, shoot.
Ränke ['rɛŋkə], *m. pl.* intrigues, tricks.
ranken ['raŋkən], *v.r.* (*aux.* haben) *sich* —, (*plant*) climb (with tendrils).
Ränkeschmied ['rɛŋkəʃmiːt], *m.* (—es, *pl.* —e) plotter, intriguer.
Ranzen ['rantsən], *m.* (—s, *pl.* —) satchel, knapsack, rucksack.
ranzig ['rantsɪç], *adj.* rancid, rank.
Rappe ['rapə], *m.* (—n, *pl.* —n) black horse.

Raute

Rappel ['rapəl], *m.* (—s, *no pl.*) *(coll.)* slight madness; rage, fit.

Rappen ['rapən], *m.* (—s, *pl.* —) small Swiss coin; centime.

rapportieren [rapɔr'tiːrən], *v.a.* report.

Raps [raps], *m.* (—es, *no pl.*) rapeseed.

rar [raːr], *adj.* rare, scarce; exquisite.

rasch [raʃ], *adj.* quick, swift.

rascheln ['raʃəln], *v.n.* rustle.

Rasen ['raːzən], *m.* (—s, *pl.* —) lawn, turf, sod.

rasen ['raːzən], *v.n.* rave, rage, be delirious; rush, speed; *in —der Eile*, in a tearing hurry.

Raserei [raːzə'raɪ], *f.* (—, *pl.* —en) madness; *(fig.)* fury.

Rasierapparat [ra'ziːrapaːt], *m.* (—s, *pl.* —e) (safety-)razor; shaver.

rasieren [ra'ziːrən], *v.a.* shave; *sich — lassen*, be shaved, get a shave.

Rasierzeug [ra'ziːrtsɔyk], *n.* (—s, *no pl.*) shaving-tackle.

Raspel ['raspəl], *f.* (—, *pl.* —n) rasp.

Rasse ['rasə], *f.* (—, *pl.* —n) race; breed; *reine —*, thoroughbred; *gekreuzte —*, cross-breed.

Rassel ['rasəl], *f.* (—, *pl.* —n) rattle.

rasseln ['rasəln], *v.n.* rattle, clank.

Rassendiskriminierung ['rasəndɪskriminiːruŋ], *f.* (—, *no pl.*) racial discrimination.

Rast [rast], *f.* (—, *no pl.*) rest, repose.

rasten ['rastən], *v.n.* rest, take a rest; halt.

Raster ['rastər], *m.* (—s, *pl.* —) *(Phot.)* screen.

rastlos ['rastloːs], *adj.* restless.

Rat (1) [raːt], *m.* (—es, *pl.* —schläge) advice, counsel; deliberation.

Rat (2) [raːt], *m.* (—es, *pl.* —e) council, councillor; *mit — und Tat*, with advice and assistance; *einem einen — geben*, give s.o. advice, counsel s.o.; *einen um — fragen*, consult s.o.; *— schaffen*, find ways and means.

Rate ['raːtə], *f.* (—, *pl.* —n) instalment, rate.

raten ['raːtən], *v.a., v.n. irr.* advise; guess, conjecture.

Ratgeber ['raːtgeːbər], *m.* (—s, *pl.* —) adviser, counsellor.

Rathaus ['raːthaus], *n.* (—es, *pl.* —er) town-hall.

Ratifizierung [ratifi'tsiːruŋ], *f.* (—, *pl.* —en) ratification.

Ration [ra'tsjoːn], *f.* (—, *pl.* —en) ration, share, portion.

rationell [ratsjo'nɛl], *adj.* rational.

ratlos ['raːtloːs], *adj.* helpless, perplexed.

ratsam ['raːtzaːm], *adj.* advisable.

Ratschlag ['raːtʃlaːk], *m.* (—s, *pl.* —e) advice, counsel.

Ratschluß ['raːtʃlus], *m.* (—sses, *pl.* —sse) decision, decree.

Ratsdiener ['raːtsdiːnər], *m.* (—s, *pl.* —) beadle, tipstaff, summoner.

Rätsel ['rɛːtsəl], *n.* (—s, *pl.* —) riddle, puzzle, mystery, enigma, conundrum.

Ratsherr ['raːtshɛr], *m.* (—n, *pl.* —en) alderman, (town-)councillor, senator.

Ratte ['ratə], *f.* (—, *pl.* —n) *(Zool.)* rat.

Raub [raup], *m.* (—es, *no pl.*) robbery; booty, prey.

rauben ['raubən], *v.a.* rob, plunder; *es raubt mir den Atem*, it takes my breath away.

Räuber ['rɔybər], *m.* (—s, *pl.* —) robber, thief; highwayman; *— und Gendarm*, cops and robbers.

Raubgier ['raupgiːr], *f.* (—, *no pl.*) rapacity.

Rauch [raux], *m.* (—s, *no pl.*) smoke, vapour.

Rauchen ['rauxən], *n.* (—s, *no pl.*) smoking; *— verboten*, no smoking.

rauchen ['rauxən], *v.a., v.n.* smoke.

räuchern ['rɔyçərn], *v.a.* (*meat, fish*) smoke-dry, cure; *(disinfect)* fumigate. *— v.n. (Eccl.)* burn incense.

Rauchfang ['rauxfaŋ], *m.* (—s, *pl.* —e) chimney-flue.

Räude ['rɔydə], *f.* (—, *no pl.*) mange.

Raufbold ['raufbɔlt], *m.* (—s, *pl.* —e) brawler, bully.

raufen ['raufən], *v.a.* (*hair*) tear out, pluck. *— v.n.* fight, brawl. *— v.r. sich — mit*, scuffle with, fight, have a scrap with.

rauh [rau], *adj.* rough; *(fig.)* harsh, rude; hoarse; *(weather)* raw, inclement.

Rauheit ['rauhaɪt], *f.* (—, *no pl.*) roughness; hoarseness; *(fig.)* harshness, rudeness; *(weather)* inclemency; *(landscape)* ruggedness.

rauhen ['rauən], *v.a.* (*cloth*) nap.

Raum [raum], *m.* (—es, *pl.* —e) space, room; outer space; *(fig.)* scope; *dem Gedanken — geben*, entertain an idea.

räumen ['rɔymən], *v.a.* clear, empty; quit, leave; *das Feld —*, abandon the field, clear out.

Rauminhalt ['raumɪnhalt], *m.* (—s, *no pl.*) volume.

räumlich ['rɔymlɪç], *adj.* spatial; *(in compounds)* space-.

Räumlichkeiten ['rɔymlɪçkaɪtən], *f. pl.* premises.

Raumschiff ['raumʃɪf], *n.* (—es, *pl.* —e) spaceship, spacecraft.

Räumung ['rɔymuŋ], *f.* (—, *pl.* —en) evacuation.

raunen ['raunən], *v.a., v.n.* whisper.

Raupe ['raupə], *f.* (—, *pl.* —n) *(Ent.)* caterpillar.

Rausch [rauʃ], *m.* (—es, *pl.* —e) intoxication; delirium, frenzy; *einen — haben*, be drunk, intoxicated; *seinen — ausschlafen*, sleep it off.

rauschen ['rauʃən], *v.n.* rustle, rush, roar.

Rauschgift ['rauʃgɪft], *n.* (—s, *pl.* —e) drug; narcotic.

Rauschgold ['rauʃgɔlt], *n.* (—es, *no pl.*) tinsel.

räuspern ['rɔyspərn], *v.r. sich —*, clear o.'s throat.

Raute ['rautə], *f.* (—, *pl.* —n) *(Maths.)* rhombus; lozenge; *(Bot.)* rue.

175

Razzia

Razzia ['ratsja], *f.* (—, *pl.* —zzien) (police-)raid, swoop.

reagieren [rea'giːrən], *v.n.* react (on).

realisieren [reali'ziːrən], *v.a.* convert into money, realise.

Realschule [re'aːlʃuːlə], *f.* (—, *pl.* —n) technical grammar school; secondary modern school.

Rebe ['reːbə], *f.* (—, *pl.* —n) vine.

Rebell [re'bɛl], *m.* (—en, *pl.* —en) rebel, mutineer, insurgent.

Rebensaft ['reːbənzaft], *m.* (—s, *pl.* ⁼e) grape-juice, wine.

Rebhuhn ['reːphuːn], *n.* (—s, *pl.* ⁼er) (*Orn.*) partridge.

Reblaus ['reːplaus], *f.* (—, *pl.* ⁼e) (*Ent.*) phylloxera.

Rechen ['rɛçən], *m.* (—s, *pl.* —) (*garden*) rake; (*clothes*) rack.

Rechenaufgabe ['rɛçənaufgaːbə], *f.* (—, *pl.* —n) sum; mathematical *or* arithmetical problem.

Rechenmaschine ['rɛçənmaʃiːnə], *f.* (—, *pl.* —n) calculating machine, adding-machine.

Rechenschaft ['rɛçənʃaft], *f.* (—, *no pl.*) account; — *ablegen*, account for; *zur* — *ziehen*, call to account.

Rechenschieber ['rɛçənʃiːbər], *m.* (—s, *pl.* —) slide-rule.

Rechentabelle ['rɛçəntabɛlə], *f.* (—, *pl.* —n) ready reckoner.

rechnen ['rɛçnən], *v.a.*, *v.n.* reckon, calculate, do sums, compute; *auf etwas* —, count on s.th.; *auf einen* —, rely on s.o.

Rechnung ['rɛçnuŋ], *f.* (—, *pl.* —en) reckoning, account, computation; (*document*) invoice, bill, statement, account; *einer Sache* — *tragen*, make allowances for s.th.; take s.th. into account; *einem einen Strich durch die* — *machen*, put a spoke in s.o.'s wheel; *eine* — *begleichen*, settle an account.

Rechnungsabschluß ['rɛçnuŋsapʃlus], *m.* (—sses, *pl.* ⁼sse) balancing of accounts, balance-sheet.

Rechnungsprüfer ['rɛçnuŋspryːfər], *m.* (—s, *pl.* —) auditor.

Rechnungsrat ['rɛçnuŋsraːt], *m.* (—s, *pl.* ⁼e) member of the board of accountants, (senior government) auditor.

Recht [rɛçt], *n.* (—es, *pl.* —e) right, justice; claim on, title to; law, jurisprudence; *von* —s *wegen*, by right; — *sprechen*, administer justice; *die* —*e studieren*, study law.

recht [rɛçt], *adj.* right; just; real, true; suitable; proper; *zur* —*en Zeit*, in time; *es geht nicht mit* —*en Dingen zu*, there is s.th. queer about it; *was dem einen* —, *ist dem andern billig*, what is sauce for the goose is sauce for the gander; *einem* — *geben*, agree with s.o.; — *haben*, be (in the) right.

Rechteck ['rɛçtɛk], *n.* (—s, *pl.* —e) rectangle.

rechten ['rɛçtən], *v.n.* *mit einem* —, dispute, remonstrate with s.o.

rechtfertigen ['rɛçtfɛrtɪgən], *v.a.* justify. — *v.r. sich* —, exculpate o.s.

rechtgläubig ['rɛçtglɔybɪç], *adj.* orthodox.

rechthaberisch ['rɛçthaːbərɪʃ], *adj.* stubborn, obstinate.

rechtlich ['rɛçtlɪç], *adj.* legal, lawful, legitimate; (*Law*) judicial, juridical.

rechtmäßig ['rɛçtmɛːsɪç], *adj.* lawful, legitimate, legal.

rechts [rɛçts], *adv.* to the right, on the right.

Rechtsabtretung ['rɛçtsaptreːtuŋ], *f.* (—, *pl.* —en) cession, assignment.

Rechtsanwalt ['rɛçtsanvalt], *m.* (—s, *pl.* ⁼e) lawyer, solicitor, attorney.

Rechtsbeistand ['rɛçtsbaɪʃtant], *m.* (—s, *pl.* ⁼e) (legal) counsel.

rechtschaffen ['rɛçtʃafən], *adj.* upright, honest, righteous.

Rechtschreibung ['rɛçtʃraɪbuŋ], *f.* (—, *no pl.*) orthography, spelling.

Rechtshandel ['rɛçtshandəl], *m.* (—s, *pl.* ⁼) action, case, lawsuit.

rechtskräftig ['rɛçtskrɛftɪç], *adj.* legal, valid.

Rechtslehre ['rɛçtsleːrə], *f.* (—, *pl.* —n) jurisprudence.

Rechtsspruch ['rɛçtsʃprux], *m.* (—(e)s, *pl.* ⁼e) verdict.

Rechtsverhandlung ['rɛçtsfɛrhandluŋ], *f.* (—, *pl.* —en) legal proceedings.

Rechtsweg ['rɛçtsveːk], *m.* (—(e)s, *pl.* —e) course of law.

rechtswidrig ['rɛçtsviːdrɪç], *adj.* against the law, illegal.

Rechtszuständigkeit ['rɛçtstsuːʃtɛndɪçkaɪt], *f.* (—, *pl.* —en) (legal) competence.

rechtwinklig ['rɛçtvɪŋklɪç], *adj.* rectangular.

rechtzeitig ['rɛçttsaɪtɪç], *adj.* opportune. — *adv.* in time, at the right time.

Reck [rɛk], *n.* (—s, *pl.* —e) horizontal bar.

Recke ['rɛkə], *m.* (—n, *pl.* —n) (*Poet.*) hero.

recken ['rɛkən], *v.a.* stretch, extend.

Redakteur [redak'tøːr], *m.* (—s, *pl.* —e) editor (newspaper, magazine).

Redaktion [redak'tsjoːn], *f.* (—, *pl.* —en) editorship, editorial staff; (*room*) editorial office.

Rede ['reːdə], *f.* (—, *pl.* —n) speech, oration; address; *es geht die* —, people say; *es ist nicht der* — *wert*, it is not worth mentioning; *eine* — *halten*, deliver a speech; *zur* — *stellen*, call to account.

reden ['reːdən], *v.a.* speak, talk, discourse; *einem nach dem Munde* —, humour s.o.; *in den Wind* —, speak in vain, preach to the winds; *mit sich* — *lassen*, be amenable to reason.

Redensart ['re:dənsa:rt], *f.* (—, *pl.* —en) phrase, idiom; cliché; *einen mit leeren —en abspeisen*, put s.o. off with fine words.

Redewendung ['re:dəvenduŋ], *f.* (—, *pl.* —en) turn of phrase.

redigieren [redi'gi:rən], *v.a.* edit.

redlich ['re:tliç], *adj.* honest, upright.

Redner ['re:dnər], *m.* (—s, *pl.* —) speaker, orator.

Reede ['re:də], *f.* (—, *pl.* —n) (*Naut.*) roadstead.

Reederei [re:də'rai], *f.* (—, *pl.* —en) shipping-business.

reell [re'ɛl], *adj.* honest, fair, sound, bona fide.

Reep [re:p], *n.* (—s, *pl.* —e) (*Naut.*) rope.

Referat [refe'ra:t], *n.* (—s, *pl.* —e) report; paper (to a learned society), lecture.

Referendar [referɛn'da:r], *m.* (—s, *pl.* —e) junior barrister *or* teacher.

Referent [refe'rɛnt], *m.* (—en, *pl.* —en) reporter, reviewer; lecturer; expert (adviser).

Referenz [refe'rɛnts], *f.* (—, *pl.* —en) reference (to s.o. *or* s.th.).

referieren [refe'ri:rən], *v.a.*, *v.n.* report (on), give a paper (on).

reflektieren [reflɛk'ti:rən], *v.a.* reflect. — *v.n. auf etwas* —, be a prospective buyer of s.th., have o.'s eye on s.th.

Reformator [refɔr'ma:tɔr], *m.* (—s, *pl.* —en) reformer.

reformieren [refɔr'mi:rən], *v.a.* reform.

Regal [re'ga:l], *n.* (—s, *pl.* —e) shelf.

rege ['re:gə], *adj.* brisk, lively, animated.

Regel ['re:gəl], *f.* (—, *pl.* —n) rule, precept, principle; *in der* —, as a rule, generally.

regelmäßig ['re:gəlmɛ:siç], *adj.* regular.

regeln ['re:gəln], *v.a.* regulate, arrange, order.

Regelung ['re:gəluŋ], *f.* (—, *pl.* —en) regulation.

regelwidrig ['re:gəlvi:driç], *adj.* contrary to rule, irregular, foul.

Regen ['re:gən], *m.* (—s, *no pl.*) rain.

regen ['re:gən], *v.r. sich* —, move, stir.

Regenbogen ['re:gənbo:gən], *m.* (—s, *pl.* —) rainbow.

Regenbogenhaut ['re:gənbo:gənhaut], *f.* (—, *pl.* ⸚e) (*eye*) iris.

Regenguß ['re:gəngus], *m.* (—sses, *pl.* ⸚sse) downpour, violent shower.

Regenmantel ['re:gənmantəl], *m.* (—s, *pl.* ⸚) waterproof, raincoat, mac.

Regenpfeifer ['re:gənpfaifər], *m.* (—s, *pl.* ⸚) (*Orn.*) plover.

Regenrinne ['re:gənrinə], *f.* (—, *pl.* —n) eaves.

Regenschirm ['re:gənʃirm], *m.* (—s, *pl.* —e) umbrella.

Regentschaft [re'gɛntʃaft], *f.* (—, *pl.* —en) regency.

Regie [re'ʒi:], *f.* (—, *pl.* —n) stage management, production, direction.

regieren [re'gi:rən], *v.a.* rule, reign over, govern. — *v.n.* reign; (*fig.*) prevail, predominate.

Regierung [re'gi:ruŋ], *f.* (—, *pl.* —en) government; reign.

Regierungsrat [re'gi:ruŋsra:t], *m.* (—s, *pl.* ⸚e) government adviser.

Regiment (1) [regi'mɛnt], *n.* (—s, *pl.* —e) rule, government.

Regiment (2) [regi'mɛnt], *n.* (—s, *pl.* —er) (*Mil.*) regiment.

Regisseur [reʒi'sø:r], *m.* (—s, *pl.* —e) stage-manager, producer, director.

Registrator [regis'tra:tɔr], *m.* (—s, *pl.* —en) registrar, recorder; registering machine.

Registratur [registra'tu:r], *f.* (—, *pl.* —en) record office, registry; filing-cabinet.

registrieren [regis'tri:rən], *v.a.* register, record, file.

reglos ['re:klo:s], *adj.* motionless.

regnen ['re:gnən], *v.n.* rain; *es regnet in Strömen*, it is raining cats and dogs.

Regreß [re'grɛs], *m.* (—sses, *pl.* —sse) recourse, remedy.

regsam ['re:kza:m], *adj.* quick, alert, lively.

regulieren [regu'li:rən], *v.a.* regulate.

Regung ['re:guŋ], *f.* (—, *pl.* —en) movement; impulse.

Reh [re:], *n.* (—(e)s, *pl.* —e) doe, roe.

rehabilitieren [rehabili'ti:rən], *v.a.* rehabilitate.

Rehbock ['re:bɔk], *m.* (—s, *pl.* ⸚e) (*Zool.*) roe-buck.

Rehkeule ['re:kɔylə], *f.* (—, *pl.* —n) haunch of venison.

reiben ['raibən], *v.a. irr.* rub, grate, grind; *einem etwas unter die Nase* —, throw s.th. in s.o.'s teeth, bring s.th. home to o.

Reibung ['raibuŋ], *f.* (—, *pl.* —en) friction.

Reich [raiç], *n.* (—(e)s, *pl.* —e) kingdom, realm, empire, state.

reich [raiç], *adj.* rich, wealthy, opulent.

reichen ['raiçən], *v.a.* reach, pass, hand; *einem die Hand* —, shake hands with s.o. — *v.n.* reach, extend; be sufficient.

reichhaltig ['raiçhaltiç], *adj.* abundant, copious.

reichlich ['raiçliç], *adj.* ample, plentiful.

Reichskammergericht ['raiçs'kamərgəriçt], *n.* (—s, *no pl.*) Imperial High Court of Justice (*Holy Roman Empire*).

Reichskanzlei ['raiçskantslai], *f.* (—, *pl.* —en) (Imperial) Chancery.

Reichskanzler ['raiçskantslər], *m.* (—s, *pl.* —) (Imperial) Chancellor.

Reichsstände ['raiçsʃtɛndə], *m. pl.* Estates (of the Holy Roman Empire).

Reichstag ['raiçsta:k], *m.* (—s, *pl.* —e) Imperial Parliament, Reichstag, Diet.

Reichtum

Reichtum ['raɪçtu:m], *m.* (**—s,** *pl.* ̈er) riches, wealth, opulence.

Reif (1) [raɪf], *m.* (**—s,** *no pl.*) hoar-frost.

Reif (2) [raɪf], *m.* (**—s,** *pl.* **—e**) ring.

reif [raɪf], *adj.* ripe, mature.

Reifen ['raɪfən], *m.* (**—s,** *pl.* **—**) hoop; tyre; — *schlagen,* trundle a hoop.

reifen ['raɪfən], *v.n.* (*aux.* sein) ripen, mature, grow ripe.

Reifeprüfung ['raɪfəpry:fuŋ], *f.* (**—,** *pl.* **—en**) matriculation examination.

reiflich ['raɪflɪç], *adj.* sich etwas — *überlegen,* give careful consideration to s.th.

Reigen ['raɪgən], *m.* (**—s,** *pl.* **—**) round-dance, roundelay.

Reihe ['raɪə], *f.* (**—,** *pl.* **—n**) series; file; row; progression, sequence; (*Theat.*) tier; in — und Glied, in closed ranks; nach der —, in turns; ich bin an der —, it is my turn.

Reihenfolge ['raɪənfɔlgə], *f.* (**—,** *no pl.*) succession.

Reiher ['raɪər], *m.* (**—s,** *pl.* **—**) (*Orn.*) heron.

Reim [raɪm], *m.* (**—(e)s,** *pl.* **—e**) rhyme.

rein [raɪn], *adj.* clean, pure, clear, neat; —e Wahrheit, plain truth; ins —e bringen, settle, clear up; ins —e schreiben, make a fair copy of; einem —en Wein einschenken, have a straight talk with s.o.

Reineke ['raɪnəkə], *m.* (**—,** *no pl.*) — Fuchs, Reynard the Fox.

Reinertrag ['raɪnɛrtra:k], *m.* (**—(e)s,** *pl.* ̈e) net proceeds.

Reinfall ['raɪnfal], *m.* (**—s,** *pl.* ̈e) sell, wild-goose chase; disappointment.

reinfallen ['raɪnfalən], *v.n. irr.* (*aux.* sein) be unsuccessful.

Reingewinn ['raɪngəvɪn], *m.* (**—s,** *pl.* **—e**) net proceeds.

Reinheit ['raɪnhaɪt], *f.* (**—,** *no pl.*) purity.

reinigen ['raɪnɪgən], *v.a.* clean, cleanse; dry-clean; purge.

Reinigung ['raɪnɪguŋ], *f.* (**—,** *pl.* **—en**) cleaning; (*fig.*) purification, cleansing; chemische —, dry-cleaning.

reinlich ['raɪnlɪç], *adj.* clean, neat.

Reis (1) [raɪs], *m.* (**—es,** *no pl.*) rice.

Reis (2) [raɪs], *n.* (**—es,** *pl.* **—er**) twig, sprig; scion; cutting.

Reisbesen ['raɪsbe:zən], *m.* (**—s,** *pl.* **—**) birch-broom, besom.

Reise ['raɪzə], *f.* (**—,** *pl.* **—n**) tour, trip, journey, travels; voyage; gute —! bon voyage!

reisefertig ['raɪzəfɛrtɪç], *adj.* ready to start.

Reisegeld ['raɪzəgɛlt], *n.* (**—es,** *pl.* **—er**) travel allowance.

reisen ['raɪzən], *v.n.* (*aux.* sein) travel, tour, journey, take a trip.

Reisende ['raɪzəndə], *m.* (**—n,** *pl.* **—n**) traveller; commercial traveller.

Reisig ['raɪzɪç], *n.* (**—s,** *no pl.*) brush-wood.

Reisige ['raɪzɪgə], *m.* (**—n,** *pl.* **—n**) (*obs.*) trooper, horseman.

Reißaus [raɪs'aus], *n.* (**—,** *no pl.*) — nehmen, take to o.'s heels.

Reißbrett ['raɪsbrɛt], *n.* (**—es,** *pl.* **—er**) drawing-board.

reißen ['raɪsən], *v.a. irr.* tear; rend; pull; snatch; etwas an sich —, seize s.th., usurp.

reißend ['raɪsənt], *adj.* rapid; ravening; carnivorous; (*Comm.*) brisk, rapid (sales).

Reißnagel ['raɪsna:gəl], *m. see* Reißzwecke.

Reißschiene ['raɪsʃi:nə], *f.* (**—,** *pl.* **—n**) T-square.

Reißverschluß ['raɪsfɛrʃlus], *m.* (**—sses,** *pl.* ̈sse) zip-fastener.

Reißzwecke ['raɪstsvɛkə], *f.* (**—,** *pl.* **—n**) drawing-pin.

reiten ['raɪtən], *v.a. irr.* ride (a horse). — *v.n.* (*aux.* sein) ride, go on horse-back.

Reiterei [raɪtə'raɪ], *f.* (**—,** *pl.* **—en**) cavalry.

Reitknecht ['raɪtknɛçt], *m.* (**—es,** *pl.* **—e**) groom.

Reiz [raɪts], *m.* (**—es,** *pl.* **—e**) charm, attraction, fascination, allure; stimulus; irritation; (*Phys.*) impulse.

reizbar ['raɪtsba:r], *adj.* susceptible, irritable.

reizen ['raɪtsən], *v.a.* irritate; stimulate, charm, entice.

reizend ['raɪtsənt], *adj.* charming.

Reizmittel ['raɪtsmɪtəl], *n.* (**—s,** *pl.* **—**) stimulant; irritant.

rekeln ['re:kəln], *v.r.* (*dial.*) sich —, loll about.

Reklame [re'kla:mə], *f.* (**—,** *pl.* **—n**) propaganda, advertisement, advertising, publicity.

reklamieren [rekla'mi:rən], *v.a.* claim, reclaim. — *v.n.* complain.

rekognoszieren [rekɔgnɔs'tsi:rən], *v.a.* reconnoitre.

rekommandieren [rekɔman'di:rən], *v.a.* (*Austr.*) register (a letter).

Rekonvaleszent [rekɔnvalɛs'tsɛnt], *m.* (**—en,** *pl.* **—en**) convalescent.

Rekrut [re'kru:t], *m.* (**—en,** *pl.* **—en**) recruit.

rekrutieren [rekru'ti:rən], *v.a.* recruit. — *v.r. sich — aus,* be recruited from.

rektifizieren [rɛktifi'tsi:rən], *v.a.* rectify.

Rektor ['rɛktɔr], *m.* (**—s,** *pl.* **—en**) (school) principal; (*Univ.*) president.

Rektorat [rɛkto'ra:t], *n.* (**—es,** *pl.* **—e**) rectorship, presidency.

relativ [rela'ti:f], *adj.* relative, comparative.

relegieren [rele'gi:rən], *v.a.* expel; (*Univ.*) send down, rusticate.

Relief [rɛl'jef], *n.* (**—s,** *pl.* **—s**) (*Art*) relief.

religiös [reli'gjø:s], *adj.* religious.

Reliquie [re'li:kvjə], *f.* (**—,** *pl.* **—n**) (*Rel.*) relic.

Remise [re'mi:zə], f. (—, pl. —n) coach-house.
Remittent [remɪ'tɛnt], m. (—en, pl. —en) remitter.
Renegat [rene'ga:t], m. (—en, pl. —en) renegade.
Renette [rɛ'nɛtə], f. (—, pl. —n) rennet(-apple).
renken ['rɛŋkən], v.a. wrench, bend, twist.
Rennbahn ['rɛnba:n], f. (—, pl. —en) race-course; (cinder)-track; (Motor.) racing-circuit.
rennen ['rɛnən], v.n. irr. (aux. sein) run, race, rush.
Renommé [renɔ'me:], n. (—s, no pl.) renown, repute, reputation.
renommieren [renɔ'mi:rən], v.n. brag, boast.
renovieren [reno'vi:rən], v.a. renovate, restore, redecorate, renew.
rentabel [rɛn'ta:bəl], adj. profitable, lucrative.
Rente ['rɛntə], f. (—, pl. —n) pension, annuity.
Rentier [rɛn'tje:], m. (—s, pl. —s) rentier, person of independent means.
rentieren [rɛn'ti:rən], v.r. sich —, be profitable, be worthwhile, pay.
Rentner ['rɛntnər], m. (—s, pl. —) pensioner.
Reparatur [repara'tu:r], f. (—, pl. —en) repair.
reparieren [repa'ri:rən], v.a. repair.
Repräsentant [reprɛzɛn'tant], m. (—en, pl. —en) representative.
Repräsentantenkammer [reprɛzɛn'tantənkamər], f. (—, pl. —n) (Am.) House of Representatives.
Repressalien [reprɛ'sa:ljən], f. pl. reprisals, retaliation.
reproduzieren [reprodu'tsi:rən], v.a. reproduce.
Republikaner [republi'ka:nər], m. (—s, pl. —) republican.
requirieren [rekvi'ri:rən], v.a. requisition.
Reseda [re'ze:da], f. (—, pl. —s) (Bot.) mignonette.
Reservat [rezɛr'va:t], n. (—es, pl. —e) reservation, reserve.
Residenz [rezi'dɛnts], f. (—, pl. —en) residence, seat of the Court.
residieren [rezi'di:rən], v.n. reside.
Residuum [re'zi:duum], n. (—s, pl. —duen) residue, dregs.
resignieren [rezɪg'ni:rən], v.n., v.r. resign; be resigned (to s.th.); give up.
Respekt [re'spɛkt], m. (—es, no pl.) respect, regard; mit — zu sagen, with all due respect.
respektieren [rɛspɛk'ti:rən], v.a. respect, honour.
Ressort [rɛ'so:r], n. (—s, pl. —s) department, domain.
Rest [rɛst], m. (—es, pl. —e) rest, residue, remainder; remnant; (money) balance.
restaurieren [rɛstɔ'ri:rən], v.a. restore, renovate.

Resultat [rezul'ta:t], n. (—es, pl. —e) result, outcome.
Resümee [rezy'me:], n. (—s, pl. —s) résumé, précis, digest, summary, synopsis, abstract.
retten ['rɛtən], v.a. save, preserve; rescue, deliver; die Ehre —, vindicate o.'s honour.
Rettich ['rɛtɪç], m. (—s, pl. —e) radish.
Rettung ['rɛtuŋ], f. (—, pl. —en) saving, rescue, deliverance.
retuschieren [retu'ʃi:rən], v.a. retouch.
Reue ['rɔyə], f. (—, no pl.) repentance, remorse, contrition.
reuen ['rɔyən], v.a., v.n. repent, regret; es reut mich, I am sorry.
Reugeld ['rɔygɛlt], n. (—es, pl. —er) forfeit-money, penalty.
reüssieren [rey'si:rən], v.n. succeed.
Revanche [re'vã:ʃə], f. (—, pl. —n) revenge; (fig.) return.
revanchieren [revã'ʃi:rən], v.r. sich —, repay a service, have or take o.'s revenge.
Reverenz [reve'rɛnts], f. (—, pl. —en) bow, curtsy.
revidieren [revi'di:rən], v.a. revise, check.
Revier [re'vi:r], n. (—s, pl. —e) district, precinct, quarter; preserve.
Revisor [re'vi:zɔr], m. (—s, pl. —en) accountant, auditor.
revoltieren [revɔl'ti:rən], v.n. rise, revolt.
revolutionieren [revolutsjo'ni:rən], v.a. revolutionise.
Revolverblatt [re'vɔlvərblat], n. (—s, pl. ̈er) gutter press.
Revue [re'vy:], f. (—, pl. —n) revue; review; — passieren lassen, pass in review.
Rezensent [retsɛn'zɛnt], m. (—en, pl. —en) reviewer, critic.
rezensieren [retsɛn'zi:rən], v.a. review.
Rezept [re'tsɛpt], n. (—es, pl. —e) (Med.) prescription; (Cul.) recipe.
rezitieren [retsi'ti:rən], v.a. recite.
Rhabarber [ra'barbər], m. (—s, no pl.) (Bot.) rhubarb.
Rhein [raɪn], m. (—s, no pl.) (River) Rhine.
Rhodesien [ro'de:zjən], n. Rhodesia.
Rhodus ['ro:dus], n. Rhodes.
Rhythmus ['rytmus], m. (—, pl. —men) rhythm.
Richtbeil ['rɪçtbaɪl], n. (—s, pl. —e) executioner's axe.
richten ['rɪçtən], v.a., v.n. direct, point at; prepare; die Augen — auf, fix o.'s eyes upon; einen zugrunde —, ruin s.o.; judge, try, pass sentence on, condemn; —v.r. sich nach (Dat.) —, be guided by.
Richter ['rɪçtər], m. (—s, pl. —) judge; justice.
richtig ['rɪçtɪç], adj. right, correct, exact, true; nicht ganz — sein, be not quite right in the head.

179

Richtlot ['rıçtlo:t], *n.* (—s, *pl.* —e) plumb-line.

Richtschnur ['rıçtʃnu:r], *f.* (—, *pl.* —en) plumb-line; (*fig.*) rule, precept.

Richtung ['rıçtuŋ], *f.* (—, *pl.* —en) direction.

riechen ['ri:çən], *v.a., v.n. irr.* smell, scent, reek; *Lunte* —, smell a rat.

Riege ['ri:gə], *f.* (—, *pl.* —n) row, section.

Riegel ['ri:gəl], *m.* (—s, *pl.* —) bar, bolt; *ein* — *Schokolade*, a bar of chocolate.

Riemen ['ri:mən], *m.* (—s, *pl.* —) strap, thong; oar.

Ries [ri:s], *n.* (—es, *pl.* —e) (*paper*) ream.

Riese ['ri:zə], *m.* (—n, *pl.* —n) giant.

rieseln ['ri:zəln], *v.n.* murmur, babble, ripple, trickle; drizzle.

Riesenschlange ['ri:zənʃlaŋə], *f.* (—, *pl.* —n) anaconda.

Riff [rıf], *n.* (—es, *pl.* —e) reef.

rigoros [rigo'ro:s], *adj.* strict, rigorous.

Rille ['rılə], *f.* (—, *pl.* —n) groove, small furrow; (*Archit.*) flute, chamfer.

Rind [rınt], *n.* (—es, *pl.* —er) ox, cow; (*pl.*) cattle, horned cattle, head of cattle.

Rinde ['rındə], *f.* (—, *pl.* —n) rind, bark, peel; (*bread*) crust.

Rinderbraten ['rındərbra:tən], *m.* (—s, *pl.* —) roast beef.

Rindfleisch ['rıntflaıʃ], *n.* (—es, *no pl.*) beef.

Rindvieh ['rıntfi:], *n.* (—s, *no pl.*) cattle; (*fig.*) blockhead, ass.

Ring [rıŋ], *m.* (—(e)s, *pl.* —e) ring; (*chain*) link; (*under the eye*) dark circle; (*Comm.*) syndicate, trust.

Ringelblume ['rıŋəlblu:mə], *f.* (—, *pl.* —n) (*Bot.*) marigold.

ringeln ['rıŋəln], *v.r., sich* —, curl.

ringen ['rıŋən], *v.a. irr.* wring. — *v.n.* wrestle.

Ringer ['rıŋər], *m.* (—s, *pl.* —) wrestler.

Ringmauer ['rıŋmauər], *f.* (—, *pl.* —n) city or town wall.

rings [rıŋs], *adv.* around.

ringsum(her) [rıŋ'sum(he:r)], *adv.* round about.

Rinne ['rınə], *f.* (—, *pl.* —n) furrow, gutter; groove.

rinnen ['rınən], *v.n. irr.* (*aux,* sein) run, leak, drip.

Rinnsal ['rınza:l], *n.* (—s, *pl.* —e) channel, water-course.

Rinnstein ['rınʃtaın], *m.* (—s, *pl.* —e) gutter.

Rippe ['rıpə], *f.* (—, *pl.* —n) rib.

Rippenfellentzündung ['rıpənfɛlɛnt-tsynduŋ], *f.* (—, *pl.* —en) pleurisy.

Rippenspeer ['rıpənʃpe:r], *m.* (—s, *pl.* —e) (*Casseler*) —, spare-rib, ribs of pork.

Rippenstoß ['rıpənʃto:s], *m.* (—es, *pl.* ⁚e) dig in the ribs, nudge.

Rips [rıps], *m.* (—es, *no pl.*) rep.

Risiko ['ri:ziko], *n.* (—s, *pl.* —ken) risk.

riskant [rıs'kant], *adj.* risky.

riskieren [rıs'ki:rən], *v.a.* risk.

Riß [rıs], *m.* (—sses, *pl.* —sse) rent, tear; sketch, design, plan.

rissig ['rısıç], *adj.* cracked, torn.

Ritt [rıt], *m.* (—(e)s, *pl.* —e) ride.

Ritter ['rıtər], *m.* (—s, *pl.* —) knight; *einen zum* — *schlagen*, dub s.o. a knight.

ritterlich ['rıtərlıç], *adj.* knightly; (*fig.*) chivalrous, valiant, gallant.

Ritterschlag ['rıtərʃla:k], *m.* (—(e)s, *pl.* ⁚e) accolade.

Rittersporn ['rıtərʃpɔrn], *m.* (—s, *pl.* —e) (*Bot.*) larkspur.

rittlings ['rıtlıŋs], *adv.* astride.

Rittmeister ['rıtmaıstər], *m.* (—s, *pl.* —) captain (of cavalry).

Ritus ['ri:tus], *m.* (—, *pl.* Riten) rite.

Ritz [rıts], *m.* (—es, *pl.* —e) chink, fissure, cleft, crevice; (*glacier*) crevasse.

ritzen ['rıtsən], *v.a.* scratch.

Rivale [ri'va:lə], *m.* (—n, *pl.* —n) rival.

Rivalität [rivali'tɛ:t], *f.* (—, *pl.* —en) rivalry.

Rizinusöl ['ri:tsinusø:l], *n.* (—s, *no pl.*) castor oil.

Robbe ['rɔbə], *f.* (—, *pl.* —n) (*Zool.*) seal.

Robe ['ro:bə], *f.* (—, *pl.* —n) dress, robe; gown.

röcheln ['rœçəln], *v.n.* rattle in o.'s throat.

rochieren [rɔ'xi:rən], *v.n.* (*Chess*) castle.

Rock [rɔk], *m.* (—(e)s, *pl.* ⁚e) (*woman*) skirt; (*man*) coat.

rodeln ['ro:dəln], *v.n.* (*aux.* haben & sein) toboggan.

roden ['ro:dən], *v.a.* clear, weed, thin out (plants).

Rogen ['ro:gən], *m.* (—s, *no pl.*) (*fish*) roe, spawn.

Roggen ['rɔgən], *m.* (—s, *no pl.*) rye.

roh [ro:], *adj.* raw; rough, rude, coarse, crude; *ein —er Mensch*, a brute; (*in compounds*) rough-; preliminary, unrefined.

Rohbilanz ['ro:bilants], *f.* (—, *pl.* —en) trial balance.

Roheisen ['ro:aızən], *n.* (—s, *no pl.*) pig-iron.

Roheit ['ro:haıt], *f.* (—, *pl.* —en) coarseness, rudeness, crudity.

Rohr [ro:r], *n.* (—es, *pl.* —e, ⁚en) tube, pipe; reed, cane; (*gun*) barrel.

Rohrdommel ['ro:rdɔməl], *f.* (—, *pl.* —n) (*Orn.*) bittern.

Röhre ['rø:rə], *f.* (—, *pl.* —n) tube, pipe; (*Radio*) valve.

Röhricht ['rø:rıçt], *n.* (—s, *pl.* —e) reeds.

Rohrpfeife ['ro:rpfaıfə], *f.* (—, *pl.* —n) reed-pipe.

Rohrpost ['ro:rpɔst], *f.* (—, *no pl.*) pneumatic post.

Rohrzucker ['ro:rtsukər], *m.* (—s, *no pl.*) cane-sugar.

Rolladen ['rɔladən], *m.* (—s, *pl.* ⁓) sliding shutter, roller blind.

Rollbahn ['rɔlba:n], *f.* (—, *pl.* —en) (*Aviat.*) runway.

Rolle ['rɔlə], *f.* (—, *pl.* —n) reel, roll; pulley; (*Theat.*) part; rôle; (*laundry*) mangle.

rollen ['rɔlən], *v.a.* roll, reel; (*laundry*) mangle. — *v.n.* (*aux.* sein) roll (along); (*thunder*) roar, roll.

Roller ['rɔlər], *m.* (—s, *pl.* —) scooter.

Rollmops ['rɔlmɔps], *m.* (—es, *pl.* ⁓e) soused herring.

Rollschuh ['rɔlʃu:], *m.* (—s, *pl.* —e) roller-skate.

Rollstuhl ['rɔlʃtu:l], *m.* (—s, *pl.* ⁓e) wheel-chair, bath-chair.

Rolltreppe ['rɔltrɛpə], *f.* (—, *pl.* —n) escalator, moving staircase.

Rom [ro:m], *n.* Rome.

Roman [ro'ma:n], *m.* (—s, *pl.* —e) novel.

romanisch [ro'ma:nɪʃ], *adj.* Romanesque.

Romanliteratur [ro'ma:nlitəratu:r], *f.* (—, *no pl.*) fiction.

Romanschriftsteller [ro'ma:nʃrɪftʃtɛlər], *m.* (—s, *pl.* —) novelist.

Römer ['rø:mər], *m.* (—s, *pl.* —) Roman; (*glass*) rummer.

Rondell [rɔn'dɛl], *n.* (—s, *pl.* —e) circular flower-bed.

Röntgenstrahlen ['rœntgənʃtra:lən], *m. pl.* X-rays.

rosa ['ro:za:], *adj.* pink, rose-coloured.

Rose ['ro:zə], *f.* (—, *pl.* —n) rose.

Rosenkranz ['ro:zənkrants], *m.* (—es, *pl.* ⁓e) garland of roses; (*Eccl.*) rosary.

Rosenkreuzer ['ro:zənkrɔytsər], *m.* (—s, *pl.* —) Rosicrucian.

Rosine [ro'zi:nə], *f.* (—, *pl.* —n) sultana, raisin.

Rosmarin ['rɔsmari:n], *m.* (—s, *no pl.*) (*Bot.*) rosemary.

Roß [rɔs], *n.* (—sses, *pl.* —sse) horse, steed.

Roßbremse ['rɔsbrɛmzə], *f.* (—, *pl.* —n) (*Ent.*) horsefly, gadfly.

Rössel ['rœsəl], *n.* (—s, *pl.* —) (*Chess*) knight.

Roßhaarmatratze ['rɔsha:rmatratsə], *f.* (—, *pl.* —n) hair-mattress.

Roßkastanie ['rɔskasta:njə], *f.* (—, *pl.* —n) (*Bot.*) horse-chestnut.

Rost (1) [rɔst], *m.* (—es, *no pl.*) rust.

Rost (2) [rɔst], *m.* (—s, *pl.* —e) grate; gridiron.

Rostbraten ['rɔstbra:tən], *m.* (—s, *pl.* —) roast meat.

rosten ['rɔstən], *v.n.* go rusty; rust; *alte Liebe rostet nicht*, love that's old rusts not away.

rösten ['rø:stən], *v.a.* toast, roast, grill.

rot [ro:t], *adj.* red; — *werden*, redden, blush.

Rotauge ['ro:taugə], *n.* (—s, *pl.* —n) (*Zool.*) roach.

Röte ['rø:tə], *f.* (—, *no pl.*) redness, red colour.

Röteln ['rø:təln], *m. pl.* (*Med.*) German measles, rubella.

Rotfink ['ro:tfɪŋk], *m.* (—en, *pl.* —en) (*Orn.*) bullfinch.

Rotfuchs ['ro:tfuks], *m.* (—es, *pl.* ⁓e) (*Zool.*) sorrel horse.

rotieren [ro'ti:rən], *v.n.* rotate.

Rotkäppchen ['ro:tkɛpçən], *n.* Little Red Riding Hood.

Rotkehlchen ['ro:tke:lçən], *n.* (—s, *pl.* —) robin.

Rotlauf ['ro:tlauf], *m.* (—s, *no pl.*) (*Med.*) erysipelas.

Rotschimmel ['ro:tʃɪməl], *m.* (—s, *pl.* —) roan-horse.

Rotspon ['ro:tʃpo:n], *m.* (—s, *no pl.*) (*dial.*) claret.

Rotte ['rɔtə], *f.* (—, *pl.* —n) band, gang, rabble; (*Mil.*) file, squad.

Rotwild ['ro:tvɪlt], *n.* (—s, *no pl.*) red deer.

Rotz [rɔts], *m.* (—es, *no pl.*) (*vulg.*) mucus; snot.

Rouleau [ru'lo:], *n.* (—s, *pl.* —s) sun-blind, roller-blind.

routiniert [ruti'ni:rt], *adj.* smart; experienced.

Rübe ['ry:bə], *f.* (—, *pl.* —n) (*Bot.*) turnip; *rote* —, beetroot; *gelbe* —, carrot.

Rubel ['ru:bəl], *m.* (—s, *pl.* —) rouble.

Rübenzucker ['ry:bəntsukər], *m.* (—s, *no pl.*) beet-sugar.

Rubin [ru'bi:n], *m.* (—s, *pl.* —e) ruby.

Rubrik [ru'bri:k], *f.* (—, *pl.* —en) rubric; title, heading, category, column.

Rübsamen ['ry:pza:mən], *m.* (—s, *no pl.*) rape-seed.

ruchbar ['ru:xba:r], *adj.* manifest, known, notorious.

ruchlos ['ru:xlo:s], *adj.* wicked, profligate, vicious.

Ruck [ruk], *m.* (—(e)s, *pl.* —e) pull, jolt, jerk.

Rückblick ['rykblɪk], *m.* (—s, *pl.* —e) retrospect, retrospective view.

Rücken ['rykən], *m.* (—s, *pl.* —) back; (*mountains*) ridge; *einem den* — *kehren*, turn o.'s back upon s.o.

rücken ['rykən], *v.a.* move, push. — *v.n.* move along.

Rückenmark ['rykənmark], *n.* (—s, *no pl.*) spinal marrow.

Rückenwirbel ['rykənvɪrbəl], *m.* (—s, *pl.* —) dorsal vertebra.

rückerstatten ['rykərʃtatən], *v.a.* refund.

Rückfahrkarte ['rykfa:rkartə], *f.* (—, *pl.* —n) return ticket.

Rückfall ['rykfal], *m.* (—s, *pl.* ⁓e) relapse.

rückgängig ['rykgɛŋɪç], *adj.* — *machen*, cancel, annul, reverse (a decision).

Rückgrat ['rykgra:t], *n.* (—s, *pl.* —e) backbone, spine.

Rückhalt ['rykhalt], *m.* (—s, *no pl.*) reserve; support, backing.

Rückkehr

Rückkehr ['rykke:r], *f.* (—, *no pl.*) return.

Rücklicht ['ryklıçt], *n.* (—s, *pl.* —er) (*Motor. etc.*) tail-light.

rücklings ['ryklıŋks], *adv.* from behind.

Rucksack ['rukzak], *m.* (—s, *pl.* ⸚e) rucksack; knapsack.

Rückschritt ['rykʃrıt], *m.* (—es, *pl.* —e) step backward, retrograde step, regression.

Rücksicht ['rykzıçt], *f.* (—, *pl.* —en) consideration, regard.

Rücksprache ['rykʃpra:xə], *f.* (—, *pl.* —n) conference, consultation; — *nehmen mit,* consult, confer with.

rückständig ['rykʃtɛndıç], *adj.* outstanding; old-fashioned; backward.

Rücktritt ['ryktrıt], *m.* (—s, *no pl.*) resignation.

ruckweise ['rukvaızə], *adv.* by fits and starts; jerkily.

Rückwirkung ['rykvırkuŋ], *f.* (—, *pl.* —en) reaction, retroaction.

Rüde ['ry:də], *m.* (—n, *pl.* —n) male (dog, fox etc.).

Rudel ['ru:dəl], *n.* (—s, *pl.* —) flock, herd, pack.

Ruder ['ru:dər], *n.* (—s, *pl.* —) oar, rudder, paddle; *am — sein,* be at the helm; (*Pol.*) be in power.

rudern ['ru:dərn], *v.a., v.n.* row.

Ruf [ru:f], *m.* (—(e)s, *pl.* —e) call; shout; reputation, renown; *einen guten (schlechten) — haben,* be well (ill) spoken of (bad) reputation, be well (ill) spoken of s.o.

rufen ['ru:fən], *v.a., v.n.* irr. call, shout; *einen — lassen,* send for s.o.

Rüffel ['ryfəl], *m.* (—s, *pl.* —) (*coll.*) reprimand; (*sl.*) rocket.

Rüge ['ry:gə], *f.* (—, *pl.* —n) censure, blame, reprimand.

Ruhe ['ru:ə], *f.* (—, *no pl.*) rest, repose; quiet, tranquillity; *sich zur — setzen,* retire (from business etc.).

Ruhegehalt ['ru:əgəhalt], *n.* (—es, *pl.* ⸚er) retirement pension, superannuation.

ruhen ['ru:ən], *v.n.* rest, repose, take a rest.

Ruhestand ['ru:əʃtant], *m.* (—es, *no pl.*) retirement.

ruhig ['ru:ıç], *adj.* quiet, tranquil, peaceful, calm; *sich — verhalten,* keep quiet.

Ruhm [ru:m], *m.* (—(e)s, *no pl.*) glory, fame, renown; *einem zum — gereichen,* be or redound to s.o.'s credit.

rühmen ['ry:mən], *v.a.* praise, extol, glorify; — *v.r. sich —,* boast.

Ruhr (1) [ru:r], *f.* (River) Ruhr.

Ruhr (2) [ru:r], *f.* (—, *no pl.*) dysentery.

Rührei ['ry:raı], *n.* (—s, *pl.* —er) scrambled egg.

rühren ['ry:rən], *v.a.* stir, move, touch; — *v.r. sich —,* move, stir; get a move on.

rührig ['ry:rıç], *adj.* active, alert.

rührselig ['ry:rze:lıç], *adj.* oversentimental; lachrymose.

Rührung ['ry:ruŋ], *f.* (—, *no pl.*) emotion.

Ruin [ru'i:n], *m.* (—s, *no pl.*) (*fig.*) ruin; decay; bankruptcy.

Ruine [ru'i:nə], *f.* (—, *pl.* —n) ruin(s).

rülpsen ['rylpsən], *v.n.* belch.

Rum [rum], *m.* (—s, *no pl.*) rum.

Rumänien [ru'mɛ:njən], *n.* Rumania.

Rummel ['ruməl], *m.* (—s, *no pl.*) tumult, row, hubbub.

Rumor [ru'mo:r], *m.* (—s, *no pl.*) noise; rumour.

rumoren [ru'mo:rən], *v.n.* make a noise.

Rumpelkammer ['rumpəlkamər], *f.* (—, *pl.* —n) lumber-room, junk-room.

rumpeln ['rumpəln], *v.n.* rumble.

Rumpf [rumpf], *m.* (—(e)s, *pl.* ⸚e) (*Anat.*) trunk; (*ship*) hull; (*Aviat.*) fuselage.

rümpfen ['rympfən], *v.a. die Nase —,* turn up o.'s nose.

rund [runt], *adj.* round, rotund; — *heraus,* flatly; *etwas — abschlagen,* refuse s.th. flatly; — *herum,* round about.

Runde ['rundə], *f.* (—, *pl.* —n) round; (*Sport*) round, bout; *die — machen,* (*watchman*) patrol.

Rundfunk ['runtfuŋk], *m.* (—s, *no pl.*) broadcasting, wireless; radio.

Rundgang ['runtgaŋ], *m.* (—s, *pl.* ⸚e) round, tour (of inspection).

rundlich ['runtlıç], *adj.* plump.

Rundschau ['runtʃau], *f.* (—, *no pl.*) panorama; review, survey.

Rundschreiben ['runtʃraıbən], *n.* (—s, *pl.* —) circular letter.

rundweg ['runtve:k], *adv.* flatly, plainly.

Rune ['ru:nə], *f.* (—, *pl.* —n) rune; runic writing.

Runkelrübe ['ruŋkəlry:bə], *f.* (—, *pl.* —n) beetroot.

Runzel ['runtsəl], *f.* (—, *pl.* —n) wrinkle, pucker.

Rüpel ['ry:pəl], *m.* (—s, *pl.* —) bounder, lout.

rupfen ['rupfən], *v.a.* pluck; *einen —,* (*fig.*) fleece s.o.

Rupie ['ru:pjə], *f.* (—, *pl.* —n) rupee.

ruppig ['rupıç], *adj.* unfriendly, rude; scruffy.

Ruprecht ['ru:preçt], *m. Knecht —,* Santa Claus.

Rüsche ['ry:ʃə], *f.* (—, *pl.* —n) ruche.

Ruß [ru:s], *m.* (—es, *no pl.*) soot.

Rüssel ['rysəl], *m.* (—s, *pl.* —) snout; (*elephant*) trunk.

Rußland ['ruslant], *n.* Russia.

rüsten ['rystən], *v.a.* prepare, fit (out); equip; (*Mil.*) arm, mobilise.

Rüster ['rystər], *f.* (—, *pl.* —n) elm.

rüstig ['rystıç], *adj.* vigorous, robust.

Rüstung ['rystuŋ], *f.* (—, *pl.* —en) armour; preparation; (*Mil.*) armament.

Sambia

Rüstzeug ['rystts>yk], *n.* (—s, *no pl.*) equipment.
Rute ['ru:tə], *f.* (—, *pl.* —n) rod, twig; (*fox*) brush.
Rutengänger ['ru:təngɛnər], *m.* (—s, *pl.* —) water-diviner.
rutschen ['rutʃən], *v.n.* (*aux.* sein) slip, slide, skid, slither.
rütteln ['rytəln], *v.a., v.n.* shake, jolt.

S

S [ɛs], *n.* (—s, *pl.* —s) the letter S.
Saal [za:l], *m.* (—(e)s, *pl.* **Säle**) hall, large room.
Saat [za:t], *f.* (—, *pl.* —en) seed; sowing; standing corn.
Sabbat ['zabat], *m.* (—s, *pl.* —e) sabbath.
sabbern ['zabərn], *v.n.* (*sl.*) slaver, drivel.
Säbel ['zɛ:bəl], *m.* (—s, *pl.* —) sabre; *krummer* —, falchion, scimitar.
säbeln ['zɛ:bəln], *v.a.* sabre, hack at.
sachdienlich ['zaxdi:nlɪç], *adj.* relevant, pertinent.
Sache ['zaxə], *f.* (—, *pl.* —n) thing, matter, affair; (*Law*) action, case; *die — ist (die) daß*, the fact is that; *das gehört nicht zur* —, that is beside the point; *bei der — sein*, pay attention to the matter in hand; *das ist meine* —, that is my business; *die — der Unterdrückten verteidigen*, take up the cause of the oppressed.
Sachlage ['zaxla:gə], *f.* (—, *no pl.*) state of affairs.
sachlich ['zaxlɪç], *adj.* pertinent; objective.
sächlich ['zɛçlɪç], *adj.* (*Gram.*) neuter.
Sachse ['zaksə], *m.* (—n, *pl.* —n) Saxon.
Sachsen ['zaksən], *n.* Saxony.
sachte ['zaxtə], *adj.* soft, slow, quiet, careful, gentle.
Sachverhalt ['zaxfɛrhalt], *m.* (—s, *no pl.*) facts (of a case), state of things, circumstances.
sachverständig ['zaxfɛrʃtɛndɪç], *adj.* expert, competent, experienced.
Sachwalter ['zaxvaltər], *m.* (—s, *pl.* —) manager, counsel, attorney.
Sack [zak], *m.* (—(e)s, *pl.* —e) sack, bag; *mit — und Pack*, (with) bag and baggage.
Säckel ['zɛkəl], *m.* (—s, *pl.* —) purse.
Sackgasse ['zakgasə], *f.* (—, *pl.* —n) cul-de-sac, blind alley; *einen in eine — treiben*, corner s.o.
Sackpfeife ['zakpfaɪfə], *f.* (—, *pl.* —n) bagpipe.
Sacktuch ['zaktu:x], *n.* (—es, *pl.* —er) sacking; (*dial.*) pocket-handkerchief.

säen ['zɛ:ən], *v.a.* sow.
Saffian ['zafja:n], *m.* (—s, *no pl.*) morocco-leather.
Saft [zaft], *m.* (—(e)s, *pl.* —e) juice; (*tree*) sap; (*meat*) gravy; *ohne — und Kraft*, insipid; *im eigenen — schmoren*, stew in o.'s own juice.
Sage ['za:gə], *f.* (—, *pl.* —n) legend, fable, myth; *es geht die* —, it is rumoured.
Säge ['zɛ:gə], *f.* (—, *pl.* —n) saw.
sagen ['za:gən], *v.a.* say, tell; *einem etwas — lassen*, send word to s.o.; *es hat nichts zu* —, it does not matter; *was Du nicht sagst!* you don't say (so)!
sägen ['zɛ:gən], *v.a., v.n.* saw; (*fig.*) snore.
sagenhaft ['za:gənhaft], *adj.* legendary, mythical; (*fig.*) fabulous.
Sahne ['za:nə], *f.* (—, *no pl.*) cream.
Saite ['zaɪtə], *f.* (—, *pl.* —n) string; *strengere —n aufziehen*, (*fig.*) take a stricter line.
Sakko ['zako], *m.* (—s, *pl.* —s) lounge jacket.
Sakristei [zakrɪ'staɪ], *f.* (—, *pl.* —en) vestry.
Salat [za'la:t], *m.* (—(e)s, *pl.* —e) salad; (*plant*) lettuce; (*sl.*) mess.
salbadern ['zalba:dərn], *v.n.* prate, talk nonsense.
Salbe ['zalbə], *f.* (—, *pl.* —n) ointment, salve.
Salbei ['zalbaɪ], *m.* (—s, *no pl.*) (*Bot.*) sage.
salben ['zalbən], *v.a.* anoint.
salbungsvoll ['zalbuŋsfɔl], *adj.* unctuous.
Saldo ['zaldo], *m.* (—s, *pl.* —s) balance.
Saline [za'li:nə], *f.* (—, *pl.* —n) salt-mine, salt-works.
Salkante ['za:lkantə], *f.* (—, *pl.* —n) selvedge, border.
Salm [zalm], *m.* (—s, *pl.* —e) (*Zool.*) salmon.
Salmiakgeist ['zalmjakgaɪst], *m.* (—s, *no pl.*) ammonia.
Salon [za'lɔ̃], *m.* (—s, *pl.* —s) salon; saloon; drawing-room.
salonfähig [za'lɔ̃fɛ:ɪç], *adj.* presentable, socially acceptable.
salopp [za'lɔp], *adj.* careless, slovenly, shabby, sloppy.
Salpeter [zal'pe:tər], *m.* (—s, *no pl.*) nitre, saltpetre.
salutieren [zalu'ti:rən], *v.a., v.n.*, salute.
Salve ['zalvə], *f.* (—, *pl.* —n) volley, discharge, salute.
Salz [zalts], *n.* (—es, *pl.* —e) salt.
Salzfaß ['zaltsfas], *n.* (—sses, *pl.* —sser) salt-cellar.
Salzlake ['zaltsla:kə], *f.* (—, *pl.* —n) brine.
Salzsäure ['zaltsz>yrə], *f.* (—, *no pl.*) hydrochloric acid.
Sämann ['zɛ:man], *m.* (—s, *pl.* —ner) sower.
Sambia ['zambia], *n.* Zambia.

183

Same(n) ['za:mə(n)], *m.* (—ns, *pl.* —n) seed; sperm; spawn.

Samenstaub ['za:mənʃtaup], *m.* (—s, *no pl.*) pollen.

Sämereien [zɛːməˈraɪən], *f. pl.* seeds, grain.

sämisch ['zɛːmɪʃ], *adj.* chamois.

Sammelband ['zaməlbant], *m.* (—es, *pl.* ˙e) miscellany, anthology.

sammeln ['zaməln], *v.a.* collect, gather. — *v.r.* sich —, meet; collect o.'s thoughts, compose o.s.

Sammler ['zamlər], *m.* (—s, *pl.* —) collector; accumulator.

Samstag ['zamsta:k], *m.* (—s, *pl.* —e) Saturday.

Samt [zamt], *m.* (—(e)s, *pl.* —e) velvet.

samt [zamt], *adv.* together, all together; — und sonders, jointly and severally.— *prep.* (*Dat.*) together with.

sämtlich ['zɛmtlɪç], *adj.* each and every.

Sand [zant], *m.* (—es, *no pl.*) sand; feiner —, grit; grober —, gravel.

Sandtorte ['zanttɔrtə], *f.* (—, *pl.* —n) sponge-cake, madeira-cake.

Sanduhr ['zantuːr], (—, *pl.* —en) hour-glass.

sanft [zanft], *adj.* soft, gentle.

Sänfte ['zɛnftə], *f.* (—, *pl.* —n) sedan-chair.

Sang [zaŋ], *m.* (—es, *pl.* **Gesänge**) song; ohne — und Klang, (*fig.*) unostentatiously, without fuss, without ceremony.

sanieren [zaˈniːrən], *v.a.* cure; (*company*) reconstruct, put on a sound financial basis.

sanitär [zaniˈtɛːr], *adj.* sanitary.

Sanitäter [zaniˈtɛːtər], *m.* (—s, *pl.*—) medical orderly; ambulance man.

Sankt [zaŋkt], *indecl. adj.* Saint; (*abbr.*) St.

sanktionieren [zaŋktsjoˈniːrən], *v.a.* sanction.

Sansibar ['zanziba:r], *n.* Zanzibar.

Sardelle [zarˈdɛlə], *f.* (—, *pl.* —n) (*Zool.*) anchovy.

Sardinien [zarˈdiːnjən], *n.* Sardinia.

Sarg [zark], *m.* (—es, *pl.* ˙e) coffin.

sarkastisch [zarˈkastɪʃ], *adj.* sarcastic.

Satellit [zatəˈliːt], *m.* (—en, *pl.* —en) satellite.

Satiriker [zaˈtiːrɪkər], *m.* (—s, *pl.*—) satirist.

satt [zat], *adj.* sated, satiated, satisfied; (*colours*) deep, rich; sich — essen, eat o.'s fill; einer Sache — sein, be sick of s.th., have had enough of s.th.

Sattel [zatəl], *m.* (—s, *pl.* ˙) saddle; einen aus dem — heben, (*fig.*) oust s.o.; fest im — sitzen, (*fig.*) be master of a situation; in allen ˙n gerecht, versatile.

satteln ['zatəln], *v.a.* saddle.

Sattheit ['zathaɪt], *f.* (—, *no pl.*) satiety.

sättigen ['zɛtɪɡən], *v.a.* satisfy, sate, satiate; (*Chem.*) saturate.

sattsam ['zatza:m], *adv.* enough, sufficiently.

saturieren [zatuˈriːrən], *v.a.* (*Chem.*) saturate.

Satz [zats], *m.* (—es, *pl.* ˙e) sentence; proposition; thesis; (*Mus.*) movement; (*Typ.*) composition; (*dregs*) sediment; (*gambling*) stake; mit einem —, with one leap (or jump or bound).

Satzbildung ['zatsbɪlduŋ], *f.* (—, *pl.* —en) (*Gram.*) construction; (*Chem.*) sedimentation.

Satzlehre ['zatsle:rə], *f.* (—, *no pl.*) syntax.

Satzung ['zatsuŋ], *f.* (—, *pl.* —en) statute.

Satzzeichen ['zatstsaɪçən], *n.* (—s, *pl.* —) punctuation-mark.

Sau [zau], *f.* (—, *pl.* ˙e) sow; (*vulg.*) dirty person, slut.

sauber ['zaubər], *adj.* clean, neat, tidy.

säubern ['zɔybərn], *v.a.* clean, cleanse; (*fig.*) purge.

Saubohne ['zaubo:nə], *f.* (—, *pl.* —n) broad bean.

Saudiarabien ['zaudiara:bjən], *n.* Saudi Arabia.

sauer ['zauər], *adj.* sour, acid; (*fig.*) troublesome; morose.

Sauerbrunnen ['zauərbrunən], *m.* (—s, *pl.* —) mineral water.

Sauerei [zauəˈraɪ], *f.* (—, *pl.* —en) (*sl.*) filthiness; mess.

Sauerkraut ['zauərkraut], *n.* (—s, *no pl.*) pickled cabbage.

säuerlich ['zɔyərlɪç], *adj.* acidulous.

Sauerstoff ['zauərʃtɔf], *m.* (—(e)s, *no pl.*) oxygen.

Sauerteig ['zauərtaɪk], *m.* (—(e)s, *pl.* —e) leaven.

sauertöpfisch ['zauərtœpfɪʃ], *adj.* morose, peevish.

saufen ['zaufən], *v.a., v.n. irr.* (*animals*) drink; (*humans*) drink to excess.

Säufer ['zɔyfər], *m.* (—s, *pl.* —) drunkard, drinker, alcoholic.

saugen ['zauɡən], *v.a., v.n.* suck.

säugen ['zɔyɡən], *v.a.* suckle.

Säugetier ['zɔyɡəti:r], *n.* (—s, *pl.* —e) mammal.

Saugheber ['zaukhe:bər], *m.* (—s, *pl.* —) suction-pump; siphon.

Säugling ['zɔyklɪŋ], *m.* (—s, *pl.* —e) suckling, baby.

Saugwarze ['zaukvartsə], *f.* (—, *pl.* —n) nipple.

Säule ['zɔylə], *f.* (—, *pl.* —n) pillar, column.

Säulenbündel ['zɔylənbyndəl], *n.* (—s, *pl.* —) (*Archit.*) clustered column.

Säulenfuß ['zɔylənfu:s], *m.* (—es, *pl.* ˙e) (*Archit.*) base, plinth.

Säulengang ['zɔylənɡaŋ], *m.* (—s, *pl.* ˙e) colonnade.

Saum [zaum], *m.* (—(e)s, *pl.* ˙e) seam, hem, border, edge; selvedge.

saumäßig ['zaumɛːsɪç], *adj.* (*sl.*) beastly, filthy, piggish; enormous.

säumen (1) ['zɔymən], *v.a.* hem.

säumen (2) ['zɔymən], *v.n.* delay, tarry.

säumig ['zɔymɪç], *adj.* tardy, slow, dilatory.

schamrot

Saumpferd ['zaumpfe:rt], *n.* (**—s,** *pl.* **—e**) pack-horse.
saumselig ['zaumze:liç], *adj.* tardy, dilatory.
Säure ['zɔyrə], *f.* (**—,** *pl.* **—n**) acid; (*Med.*) acidity.
Saurier ['zaurjər], *m.* (**—s,** *pl.* **—**) saurian.
Saus [zaus], *m.* (**—es,** *no pl.*) rush; revel, riot; *in — und Braus leben,* live a wild life, live riotously.
säuseln ['zɔyzəln], *v.n.* rustle, murmur.
sausen ['zauzən], *v.n.* bluster, blow, howl, whistle; (*coll.*) rush, dash.
Saustall ['zauftal], *m.* (**—s,** *pl.* **-̈e**) pigsty.
Schabe ['ʃa:bə], *f.* (**—,** *pl.* **—n**) (*Ent.*) cockroach.
schaben ['ʃa:bən], *v.a.* scrape, shave, rub.
Schabernack ['ʃa:bərnak], *m.* (**—s,** *pl.* **—e**) practical joke, trick.
schäbig ['ʃɛ:bɪç], *adj.* shabby.
Schablone [ʃa'blo:nə], *f.* (**—,** *pl.* **—n**) model, mould, pattern, stencil; (*fig.*) routine.
Schach [ʃax], *n.* (**—(e)s,** *no pl.*) chess; *— bieten,* check; *— spielen,* play chess; *in — halten,* keep in check.
Schacher ['ʃaxər], *m.* (**—s,** *no pl.*) haggling, bargaining, barter.
Schächer ['ʃɛçər], *m.* (**—s,** *pl.* **—**) wretch, felon, robber.
Schacht [ʃaxt], *m.* (**—(e)s,** *pl.* **-̈e**) shaft.
Schachtel ['ʃaxtəl], *f.* (**—,** *pl.* **—n**) box, (cardboard) box, (small) case.
Schachtelhalm ['ʃaxtəlhalm], *m.* (**—s,** *pl.* **—e**) (*grass*) horse-tail.
Schächter ['ʃɛçtər], *m.* (**—s,** *pl.* **—**) (kosher) butcher.
schade ['ʃa:də], *int.* a pity, a shame, unfortunate; *wie —,* what a pity! *sehr —,* a great pity.
Schädel ['ʃɛ:dəl], *m.* (**—s,** *pl.* **—**) skull.
Schaden ['ʃa:dən], *m.* (**—s,** *pl.* **-̈**) damage, injury, detriment; *zu — kommen,* come to grief.
schaden ['ʃa:dən], *v.n.* do harm, do damage, do injury; *es schadet nichts,* it does not matter.
Schadenersatz ['ʃa:dənɛrzats], *m.* (**—es,** *no pl.*) indemnity, compensation, indemnification; (*money*) damages.
Schadenfreude ['ʃa:dənfrɔydə], *f.* (**—,** *no pl.*) malicious pleasure.
Schadensforderung ['ʃa:dənsfordə-ruŋ], *f.* (**—,** *pl.* **—en**) claim (for damages).
schadhaft ['ʃa:thaft], *adj.* defective, faulty.
schädlich ['ʃɛ:tlɪç], *adj.* injurious, noxious, pernicious, noisome.
schadlos ['ʃa:tlo:s], *adj.* indemnified; *einen — halten,* indemnify s.o., compensate s.o.; *sich an einem — halten,* recoup o.s. from s.o.
Schadlosigkeit ['ʃa:tlo:zɪçkaɪt], *f.* (**—,** *no pl.*) harmlessness.
Schaf [ʃa:f], *n.* (**—(e)s,** *pl.* **—e**) sheep.

Schafblattern ['ʃa:fblatərn], *f. pl.* (*Med.*) chicken-pox.
Schafdarm ['ʃa:fdarm], *m.* (**—s,** *pl.* **-̈e**) sheep-gut.
Schäfer ['ʃɛ:fər], *m.* (**—s,** *pl.* **—**) shepherd.
Schäferstündchen ['ʃɛ:fərʃtyntçən], *n.* (**—s,** *pl.* **—**) tryst; rendezvous.
schaffen ['ʃafən], *v.a., v.n. irr.* make, produce, create. — *v.a. reg.* provide; manage; *aus dem Wege —,* remove. — *v.n. reg.* work; *einem zu — machen,* give s.o. trouble.
Schaffner ['ʃafnər], *m.* (**—s,** *pl.* **—**) (*Railw. etc.*) guard, conductor.
Schafgarbe ['ʃa:fgarbə], *f.* (**—,** *pl.* **—n**) (*Bot.*) common yarrow.
Schafhürde ['ʃa:fhyrdə], *f.* (**—,** *pl.* **—n**) sheep-fold.
Schafott [ʃa'fɔt], *n.* (**—(e)s,** *pl.* **—e**) scaffold.
Schafschur ['ʃa:fʃu:r], *f.* (**—,** *pl.* **—en**) sheep-shearing.
Schaft [ʃaft], *m.* (**—(e)s,** *pl.* **-̈e**) shaft; (*gun*) stock.
Schafwolle ['ʃa:fvɔlə], *f.* (**—,** *no pl.*) sheep's wool, fleece.
Schakal [ʃa'ka:l], *m.* (**—s,** *pl.* **—e**) (*Zool.*) jackal.
Schäkerei [ʃɛ:kə'raɪ], *f.* (**—,** *pl.* **—en**) playfulness, teasing, dalliance, flirtation.
Schal [ʃa:l], *m.* (**—s,** *pl.* **—e**) scarf, shawl.
schal [ʃa:l], *adj.* stale, flat, insipid.
Schale ['ʃa:lə], *f.* (**—,** *pl.* **—n**) (*nut, egg*) shell; (*fruit*) peel, rind; dish, bowl; (*Austr.*) cup; (*fig.*) outside.
schälen ['ʃɛ:lən], *v.a.* shell; peel.
Schalk [ʃalk], *m.* (**—(e)s,** *pl.* **—e**) knave, rogue; wag, joker.
Schall [ʃal], *m.* (**—(e)s,** *no pl.*) sound.
Schallbecken ['ʃalbɛkən], *n.* (**—s,** *pl.* **—**) cymbal.
Schallehre ['ʃalle:rə], *f.* (**—,** *no pl.*) acoustics.
schallen ['ʃalən], *v.n.* sound, reverberate.
Schalmei [ʃal'maɪ], *f.* (**—,** *pl.* **—en**) (*Poet., Mus.*) shawm.
Schallplatte ['ʃalplatə], *f.* (**—,** *pl.* **—n**) (gramophone) record.
schalten ['ʃaltən], *v.n.* rule; switch; (*Motor.*) change gear; *— und walten,* manage.
Schalter ['ʃaltər], *m.* (**—s,** *pl.* **—**) (*Elec.*) switch; booking-office; counter.
Schalthebel ['ʃalthe:bəl], *m.* (**—s,** *pl.* **—**) (*Motor.*) gear lever.
Schaltier [ʃa'lti:r], *n.* (**—s,** *pl.* **—e**) (*Zool.*) crustacean.
Schaltjahr ['ʃaltja:r], *n.* (**—s,** *pl.* **—e**) leap year.
Schalttafel ['ʃaltta:fəl], *f.* (**—,** *pl.* **—n**) switch-board.
Scham [ʃa:m], *f.* (**—,** *no pl.*) shame, modesty; private parts.
schämen ['ʃɛ:mən], *v.r. sich —,* be ashamed (of).
schamlos ['ʃa:mlo:s], *adj.* shameless.
schamrot ['ʃa:mro:t], *adj.* blushing; *— werden,* blush.

185

schandbar

schandbar ['ʃantba:r], *adj.* ignominious, infamous.
Schande ['ʃandə], *f.* (—, *no pl.*) shame, disgrace; dishonour, ignominy.
schänden ['ʃɛndən], *v.a.* dishonour, disgrace; violate, ravish.
Schandfleck ['ʃantflɛk], *m.* (—s, *pl.* —e) stain, blemish.
schändlich ['ʃɛntlɪç], *adj.* shameful, disgraceful, infamous.
Schändung ['ʃɛnduŋ], *f.* (—, *pl.* —en) violation.
Schank ['ʃaŋk], *m.* (—s, *no pl.*) sale of liquor.
Schanzarbeiter ['ʃantsarbaɪtər], *m.* (—s, *pl.* —) sapper.
Schanze ['ʃantsə], *f.* (—, *pl.* —n) redoubt, bulwark; *in die — schlagen*, risk, venture.
Schar [ʃa:r], *f.* (—, *pl.* —en) troop, band; host.
Scharade [ʃa'ra:də], *f.* (—, *pl.* —n) charade.
scharen ['ʃa:rən], *v.r. sich — um*, assemble, congregate, gather round.
Schären ['ʃɛ:rən], *f. pl.* reefs, skerries.
scharf [ʃarf], *adj.* sharp, keen, acute, acrid, pungent; piercing; (*fig.*) severe, rigorous.
Schärfe ['ʃɛrfə], *f.* (—, *no pl.*) sharpness, keenness, acuteness; pungency, acridness; severity, rigour.
schärfen ['ʃɛrfən], *v.a.* sharpen, whet; (*fig.*) strengthen, intensify.
Scharfrichter ['ʃarfrɪçtər], *m.* (—s, *pl.* —) executioner.
scharfsichtig ['ʃarfzɪçtɪç], *adj.* sharp-eyed, (*fig.*) penetrating, astute.
scharfsinnig ['ʃarfzɪnɪç], *adj.* clear-sighted, sagacious, ingenious.
Scharlach ['ʃarlax], *m.* (—s, *no pl.*) scarlet; (*Med.*) scarlet-fever.
Scharlatan ['ʃarlata:n], *m.* (—s, *pl.* —e) charlatan, humbug.
scharmant [ʃar'mant], *adj.* charming.
Scharmützel [ʃar'mytsəl], *n.* (—s, *pl.* —) skirmish.
Scharnier [ʃar'ni:r], *m.* (—s, *pl.* —e) hinge, joint.
Schärpe ['ʃɛrpə], *f.* (—, *pl.* —n) sash.
Scharpie [ʃar'pi:], *f.* (—, *no pl.*) lint.
scharren ['ʃarən], *v.a., v.n.* scrape, rake.
Scharte ['ʃartə], *f.* (—, *pl.* —n) notch, crack; *eine — auswetzen*, repair a mistake, make up for s.th.
Scharteke [ʃar'te:kə], *f.* (—, *pl.* —n) worthless book, trash; *eine alte —*, an old fuddy-duddy, frump.
scharwenzeln [ʃar'vɛntsəln], *v.n.* dance attendance, be obsequious.
Schatten ['ʃatən], *m.* (—s, *pl.* —) shade, shadow.
Schattenbild ['ʃatənbɪlt], *n.* (—s, *pl.* —er) silhouette.
Schattenriß ['ʃatənrɪs], *m.* (—sses, *pl.* —sse) silhouette.
schattieren [ʃa'ti:rən], *v.a.* shade (drawing).
schattig ['ʃatɪç], *adj.* shady.

Schatulle [ʃa'tulə], *f.* (—, *pl.* —n) cash-box; privy purse.
Schatz [ʃats], *m.* (—es, *pl.* ⸚e) treasure; (*fig.*) sweetheart, darling.
Schatzamt ['ʃatsamt], *n.* (—s, *pl.* ⸚er) Treasury, Exchequer.
schätzbar ['ʃɛtsba:r], *adj.* estimable.
Schätzchen ['ʃɛtsçən], *n.* (—s, *pl.* —) (*coll.*) sweetheart.
schätzen ['ʃɛtsən], *v.a.* value, estimate; esteem; reckon at.
Schatzkammer ['ʃatskamər], *f.* (—, *pl.* —n) treasury.
Schatzmeister ['ʃatsmaɪstər], *m.* (—s, *pl.* —) treasurer.
Schätzung ['ʃɛtsuŋ], *f.* (—, *pl.* —en) valuation, estimate; (*fig.*) esteem.
Schau [ʃau], *f.* (—, *pl.* —en) show, view, spectacle; *zur — stellen*, display, parade.
Schauder ['ʃaudər], *m.* (—s, *pl.* —) shudder, shiver; horror.
schaudern ['ʃaudərn], *v.n.* shudder, shiver.
schauen ['ʃauən], *v.a.* see, view. — *v.n.* look, gaze (*auf*, at), *schau mal*, look here.
Schauer ['ʃauər], *m.* (—s, *pl.* —) shiver, paroxysm; (*fig.*) thrill, awe; (*rain*) shower.
schauern ['ʃauərn], *v.n.* shudder, shiver; (*rain*) shower.
Schauerroman ['ʃauərroma:n], *m.* (—s, *pl.* —e) (*novel*) penny dreadful, thriller.
Schaufel ['ʃaufəl], *f.* (—, *pl.* —n) shovel.
Schaufenster ['ʃaufɛnstər], *n.* (—s, *pl.* —) shop-window.
Schaukel ['ʃaukəl], *f.* (—, *pl.* —n) swing.
schaulustig ['ʃaulustɪç], *adj.* curious.
Schaum [ʃaum], *m.* (—es, *pl.* ⸚e) foam, froth; bubbles; scum; *— schlagen*, whip cream.
schäumen ['ʃɔymən], *v.n.* foam, froth, sparkle.
Schauplatz ['ʃauplats], *m.* (—es, *pl.* ⸚e) scene, stage.
schaurig ['ʃaurɪç], *adj.* grisly, horrid, horrible.
Schauspiel ['ʃauʃpi:l], *n.* (—s, *pl.* —e) spectacle; drama, play.
Schauspieler ['ʃauʃpi:lər], *m.* (—s, *pl.* —) actor, player.
Schaustellung ['ʃauʃtɛluŋ], *f.* (—, *pl.* —en) exhibition.
Scheck [ʃɛk], *m.* (—s, *pl.* —s) cheque.
scheckig ['ʃɛkɪç], *adj.* piebald, spotted, dappled.
scheel [ʃe:l], *adj.* squint-eyed; envious; *einen — ansehen*, look askance at s.o.
Scheffel ['ʃɛfəl], *m.* (—s, *pl.* —) bushel.
scheffeln ['ʃɛfəln], *v.a.* rake in; accumulate.
Scheibe ['ʃaɪbə], *f.* (—, *pl.* —n) disc; (*window*) pane; (*shooting*) target; (*bread*) slice.
Scheibenhonig ['ʃaɪbənho:nɪç], *m.* (—s, *no pl.*) honey in the comb.

Scheibenschießen ['ʃaɪbənʃiːsən], *n.* (—s, *no pl.*) target-practice.

Scheich [ʃaɪç], *m.* (—s, *pl.* —e) sheikh.

Scheide ['ʃaɪdə], *f.* (—, *pl.* —n) sheath, scabbard; (*Anat.*) vagina.

Scheidemünze ['ʃaɪdəmyntsə], *f.* (—, *pl.* —n) small coin, change.

scheiden ['ʃaɪdən], *v.a. irr.* divide; separate, divorce; *sich — lassen,* obtain a divorce. — *v.n.* (*aux.* sein) part, depart; *aus dem Amte —,* resign office.

Scheidewand ['ʃaɪdəvant], *f.* (—, *pl.* ⁻e) partition-wall.

Scheideweg ['ʃaɪdəveːk], *m.* (—s, *pl.* —e) cross-roads; *am — stehen,* be at the parting of the ways.

Scheidung ['ʃaɪdʊŋ], *f.* (—, *pl.* —en) divorce.

Schein [ʃaɪn], *m.* (—(e)s, *no pl.*) shine, sheen, lustre, splendour; semblance, pretence; *den — wahren,* keep up appearances; *der — trügt,* appearances are deceptive; (*in compounds*) mock, would-be, apparent; (*pl.* —e) (piece of) paper, chit, note; (*fig.*) attestation, certificate.

scheinbar ['ʃaɪnbaːr], *adj.* apparent; ostensible, specious. — *adv.* seemingly.

scheinen ['ʃaɪnən], *v.n. irr.* shine, sparkle; seem, appear.

scheinheilig ['ʃaɪnhaɪlɪç], *adj.* hypocritical.

Scheinheiligkeit ['ʃaɪnhaɪlɪçkaɪt], *f.* (—, *no pl.*) hypocrisy.

scheintot ['ʃaɪntoːt], *adj.* in a cataleptic trance; seemingly dead.

Scheinwerfer ['ʃaɪnvɛrfər], *m.* (—s, *pl.* —) headlight; searchlight; floodlight.

Scheit [ʃaɪt], *n.* (—(e)s, *pl.* —e) piece of wood, billet.

Scheitel ['ʃaɪtəl], *m.* (—s, *pl.* —) (*hair*) parting; top, vertex.

Scheiterhaufen ['ʃaɪtərhaufən], *m.* (—s, *pl.* —) stake; funeral pyre.

scheitern ['ʃaɪtərn], *v.n.* (*aux.* sein) (*ship*) founder, be wrecked; (*fig.*) miscarry, fail.

Schelle ['ʃɛlə], *f.* (—, *pl.* —n) bell.

Schellen ['ʃɛlən], *f. pl.* (*Cards*) diamonds.

schellen ['ʃɛlən], *v.n.* ring the bell.

Schellfisch ['ʃɛlfɪʃ], *m.* (—es, *pl.* —e) (*Zool.*) haddock.

Schelm [ʃɛlm], *m.* (—(e)s, *pl.* —e) rogue, knave, villain.

schelten ['ʃɛltən], *v.a. irr.* scold, chide, rebuke, reprimand.

Schema ['ʃeːma], *n.* (—s, *pl.* —s) schedule, model, plan, scheme.

Schemel ['ʃeːməl], *m.* (—s, *pl.* —) foot-stool.

Schenk ['ʃɛŋk], *m.* (—en, *pl.* —en) cupbearer; publican.

Schenke ['ʃɛŋkə], *f.* (—, *pl.* —n) alehouse, tavern, pub.

Schenkel ['ʃɛŋkəl], *m.* (—s, *pl.* —) thigh; (*Geom.*) side of triangle.

schenken ['ʃɛŋkən], *v.a.* present s.o. with, donate, give.

Schenkstube ['ʃɛŋkʃtuːbə], *f.* (—, *pl.* —n) tap-room.

Scherbe ['ʃɛrbə], *f.* (—, *pl.* —n) potsherd; fragment of glass etc.

Schere ['ʃeːrə], *f.* (—, *pl.* —n) scissors; (*garden*) shears; (*crab*) claw.

scheren ['ʃeːrən], *v.a.* shave; clip, shear; bother, concern. — *v.r. sich —,* clear off; *scher dich zum Teufel!* go to blazes!

Scherereien [ʃerəˈraɪən], *f. pl.* vexation, bother, trouble.

Scherflein ['ʃɛrflaɪn], *n.* (—s, *pl.* —) mite; *sein — beitragen,* contribute o.'s share.

Scherge ['ʃɛrgə], *m.* (—n, *pl.* —n) (*obs.*) beadle.

Scherz [ʃɛrts], *m.* (—es, *pl.* —e) jest, joke; *— beiseite,* joking apart.

scheu [ʃɔy], *adj.* shy, bashful, timid; skittish.

scheuchen ['ʃɔyçən], *v.a.* scare away.

scheuen ['ʃɔyən], *v.a.* shun, avoid, fight shy of, fear. — *v.n.* take fright.

Scheuer ['ʃɔyər], *f.* (—, *pl.* —n) barn.

scheuern ['ʃɔyərn], *v.a.* scour, scrub.

Scheuklappe ['ʃɔyklapə], *f.* (—, *pl.* —n) blinker.

Scheune ['ʃɔynə], *f.* (—, *pl.* —n) barn.

Scheusal ['ʃɔyzaːl], *n.* (—s, *pl.* —e) monster.

scheußlich ['ʃɔyslɪç], *adj.* frightful, dreadful, abominable, hideous.

Schicht [ʃɪçt], *f.* (—, *pl.* —en) layer, stratum, seam; (*society*) class; (*work*) shift.

schicken ['ʃɪkən], *v.a.* send, despatch, convey. — *v.r. sich —,* be proper; *sich in etwas —,* put up with s.th., resign o.s. to s.th.

schicklich ['ʃɪklɪç], *adj.* proper, becoming, suitable, seemly.

Schicksal ['ʃɪkzaːl], *n.* (—s, *pl.* —e) fate, destiny, lot.

Schickung ['ʃɪkʊŋ], *f.* (—, *pl.* —en) Divine Will, Providence.

schieben ['ʃiːbən], *v.a. irr.* shove, push; *die Schuld auf einen —,* put the blame on s.o.

Schieber ['ʃiːbər], *m.* (—s, *pl.* —) bolt, slide; (*fig.*) profiteer, spiv.

Schiedsgericht ['ʃiːtsgərɪçt], *n.* (—es, *pl.* —e) arbitration tribunal.

Schiedsrichter ['ʃiːtsrɪçtər], *m.* (—s, *pl.* —) referee, umpire, arbiter.

schief [ʃiːf], *adj.* slanting, oblique, bent, crooked; wry; *—e Ebene,* inclined plane; *— gehen,* go wrong.

Schiefe ['ʃiːfə], *f.* (—, *no pl.*) obliquity.

Schiefer ['ʃiːfər], *m.* (—s, *no pl.*) slate.

schiefrig ['ʃiːfrɪç], *adj.* slaty.

schielen ['ʃiːlən], *v.n.* squint, be cross-eyed.

Schienbein ['ʃiːnbaɪn], *n.* (—s, *pl.* —e) shin-bone, shin.

Schiene

Schiene [ˈʃiːnə], *f.* (—, *pl.* —n) rail; (*Med.*) splint.

schier [ʃiːr], *adj.* (*rare*) sheer, pure. — *adv.* almost, very nearly.

Schierling [ˈʃiːrlɪŋ], *m.* (—s, *pl.* —e) (*Bot.*) hemlock.

schießen [ˈʃiːsən], *v.a., v.n. irr.* shoot, fire, discharge; (*fig.*) rush; *etwas — lassen,* let go of s.th.; *die Zügel — lassen,* loosen o.'s hold on the reins; *ein Kabel — lassen,* pay out a cable; *das ist zum —,* that's very funny.

Schiff [ʃɪf], *n.* (—(e)s, *pl.* —e) ship, vessel, boat; (*church*) nave.

schiffbar [ˈʃɪfbaːr], *adj.* navigable.

Schiffbruch [ˈʃɪfbrux], *m.* (—s, *pl* ¨e) shipwreck.

Schiffbrücke [ˈʃɪfbrykə], *f.* (—, *pl.* —n) pontoon-bridge.

schiffen [ˈʃɪfən], *v.n.* sail; navigate.

Schiffsboden [ˈʃɪfsboːdən], *m.* (—s, *pl.* ¨) (ship's) hold.

Schiffsmaat [ˈʃɪfsmaːt], *m.* (—s, *pl.* —e) shipmate.

Schiffsrumpf [ˈʃɪfsrumpf], *m.* (—es, *pl.* ¨e) hull.

Schiffsschnabel [ˈʃɪfsʃnaːbəl], *m.* (—s, *pl.* ¨) prow, bows.

Schiffsvorderteil [ˈʃɪfsfɔrdərtaɪl], *n.* (—s, *pl.* —e) forecastle, prow.

Schiffszwieback [ˈʃɪfstsviːbak], *m.* (—s, *no pl.*) ship's biscuit.

Schikane [ʃiˈkaːnə], *f.* (—, *pl.* —n) chicanery.

Schild (1) [ʃɪlt], *m.* (—(e)s, *pl.* —e) shield, buckler, escutcheon; *etwas im — führen,* have designs on s.th., plan s.th.

Schild (2) [ʃɪlt], *n.* (—s, *pl.* —er) signboard, plate.

Schilderhaus [ˈʃɪldərhaus], *n.* (—es, *pl.* ¨er) sentry-box.

Schildermaler [ˈʃɪldərmaːlər], *m.* (—s, *pl.* —) sign-painter.

schildern [ˈʃɪldərn], *v.a.* describe, depict.

Schildknappe [ˈʃɪltknapə], *m.* (—n, *pl.* —n) shield-bearer, squire.

Schildkrot [ˈʃɪltkroːt], *n.* (—s, *no pl.*) tortoise-shell.

Schildkröte [ˈʃɪltkrøːtə], *f.* (—, *pl.* —n) (*Zool.*) turtle, tortoise.

Schildpatt [ˈʃɪltpat], *n.* (—s, *no pl.*) tortoise-shell.

Schildwache [ˈʃɪltvaxə], *f.* (—, *pl.* —n) sentinel, sentry; — *stehen,* be on sentry duty, stand guard.

Schilf(rohr) [ˈʃɪlf(roːr)], *n.* (—(e)s, *no pl.*) (*Bot.*) reed, rush, sedge.

schillern [ˈʃɪlərn], *v.n.* opalesce, glitter, change colour, be iridescent.

Schilling [ˈʃɪlɪŋ], *m.* (—s, *pl.* —e) Austrian coin; shilling.

Schimmel (1) [ˈʃɪməl], *m.* (—s, *pl.* —) white horse.

Schimmel (2) [ˈʃɪməl], *m.* (—s, *no pl.*) mould, mustiness.

schimmeln [ˈʃɪməln], *v.n.* (*aux.* sein) go mouldy, moulder.

Schimmer [ˈʃɪmər], *m.* (—s, *pl.* —) glitter, gleam; *ich habe keinen —,* I haven't a clue.

schimmlig [ˈʃɪmlɪç], *adj.* mouldy, musty, mildewed.

Schimpanse [ʃɪmˈpanzə], *m.* (—n, *pl.* —n) (*Zool.*) chimpanzee.

Schimpf [ʃɪmpf], *m.* (—es, *no pl.*) abuse, affront, insult; *mit — und Schande,* in disgrace.

schimpfen [ˈʃɪmpfən], *v.n.* curse, swear; — *auf,* (*fig.*) run (s.o.) down. — *v.a.* insult (s.o.), call (s.o.) names; scold.

Schindel [ˈʃɪndəl], *f.* (—, *pl.* —n) shingle.

schinden [ˈʃɪndən], *v.a. irr.* flay; (*fig.*) grind, oppress, sweat. — *v.r. sich —,* slave, drudge.

Schindluder [ˈʃɪntluːdər], *n.* (—s, *pl.* —) worn-out animal; *mit einem — treiben,* exploit s.o.

Schinken [ˈʃɪŋkən], *m.* (—s, *pl.* —) ham.

Schinkenspeck [ˈʃɪŋkənʃpɛk], *m.* (—s, *no pl.*) bacon.

Schippe [ˈʃɪpə], *f.* (—, *pl.* —n) shovel, spade.

Schirm [ʃɪrm], *m.* (—(e)s, *pl.* —e) screen; umbrella; parasol, sunshade; lampshade; (*fig.*) shield, shelter, cover.

schirmen [ˈʃɪrmən], *v.a.* protect (from), shelter.

Schirmherr [ˈʃɪrmhɛr], *m.* (—n, *pl.* —en) protector, patron.

Schlacht [ʃlaxt], *f.* (—, *pl.* —en) battle; fight; *eine — liefern,* give battle; *die — gewinnen,* carry the day, win the battle.

Schlachtbank [ˈʃlaxtbaŋk], *f.* (—, *pl.* ¨e) shambles; *zur — führen,* lead to the slaughter.

schlachten [ˈʃlaxtən], *v.a.* kill, butcher, slaughter.

Schlachtenbummler [ˈʃlaxtənbumlər], *m.* (—s, *pl.* —) camp follower.

Schlachtfeld [ˈʃlaxtfɛlt], *n.* (—s, *pl.* —er) battlefield.

Schlachtruf [ˈʃlaxtruːf], *m.* (—s, *pl.* —e) battle-cry.

Schlacke [ˈʃlakə], *f.* (—, *pl.* —n) slag, clinker, dross.

Schlackwurst [ˈʃlakvurst], *f.* (—, *pl.* ¨e) (*North German*) sausage.

Schlaf [ʃlaːf], *m.* (—(e)s, *no pl.*) sleep; slumber, rest; *in tiefem —,* fast asleep; *in den — wiegen,* rock to sleep.

Schläfchen [ˈʃleːfçən], *n.* (—s, *pl.* —) nap; *ein — machen,* have forty winks.

Schläfe [ˈʃleːfə], *f.* (—, *pl.* —n) temple.

schlafen [ˈʃlaːfən], *v.n. irr.* sleep; *schlaf wohl,* sleep well; — *gehen,* go to bed.

schlaff [ʃlaf], *adj.* slack, loose, lax, flabby; weak; remiss.

schlaflos [ˈʃlaːfloːs], *adj.* sleepless.

Schlafmittel [ˈʃlaːfmɪtəl], *n.* (—s, *pl.* —) soporific, sleeping tablet, sleeping draught.

schläfrig [ˈʃleːfrɪç], *adj.* drowsy, sleepy.

188

Schlafrock ['ʃla:frɔk], s. (—s, pl. ˙-e) dressing-gown; *Äpfel im —*, apple fritters.

schlafwandeln ['ʃla:fvandəln], v.n. (*aux.* sein) walk in o.'s sleep, sleep-walk.

Schlag [ʃla:k], m. (—(e)s, pl. ˙-e) blow, stroke; beat; (*Elec.*) shock; *ein Mann von gutem —*, a good type of man; *vom — gerührt*, struck by apoplexy; *— fünf*, at five o'clock sharp.

Schlagader ['ʃla:ka:dər], f. (—, pl. —n) artery.

Schlaganfall ['ʃla:kanfal], m. (—s, pl. ˙-e) stroke, apoplexy.

Schlagballspiel ['ʃla:kbalʃpi:l], n. (—s, pl. —e) rounders.

Schlagbaum ['ʃla:kbaum], m. (—s, pl. ˙-e) turnpike.

schlagen ['ʃla:gən], v.a. irr. beat, strike, hit; (*tree*) fell; (*money*) coin; *Alarm —*, sound the alarm; *ans Kreuz —*, crucify; *ein Kreuz —*, make the sign of the cross. — v.n. (*clock*) strike; (*birds*) warble; *aus der Art —*, degenerate. — v.r. *sich —*, fight; *sich auf Säbel —*, fight with sabres; *sich an die Brust —*, beat o.'s breast.

Schlager ['ʃla:gər], m. (—s, pl. —) hit, pop song; (*fig.*) success.

Schläger ['ʃlɛ:gər], m. (—s, pl. —) rapier; bat; (tennis-)racket; (golf-) club.

Schlägerei [ʃlɛ:gə'raɪ], f. (—, pl. —en) fray, scuffle.

schlagfertig ['ʃla:kfɛrtɪç], adj. quick-witted.

Schlagkraft ['ʃla:kkraft], f. (—, no pl.) striking power.

Schlaglicht ['ʃla:klɪçt], n. (—s, pl. —er) strong direct light.

Schlagsahne ['ʃla:kza:nə], f. (—, no pl.) double cream, raw cream; whipped cream.

Schlagschatten ['ʃla:kʃatən], m. (—s, pl. —) deep shadow.

Schlagseite ['ʃla:kzaɪtə], f. (—, no pl.) *— bekommen*, (*Naut.*) list.

Schlagwort ['ʃla:kvɔrt], n. (—s, pl. ˙-er) catchword, slogan; trite saying.

Schlagzeile ['ʃla:ktsaɪlə], f. (—, pl. —n) headline.

Schlamm [ʃlam], m. (—(e)s, no pl.) mud, mire.

Schlampe ['ʃlampə], f. (—, pl. —n) slut.

Schlange ['ʃlaŋə], f. (—, pl. —n) snake, serpent; (*fig.*) queue.

schlängeln ['ʃlɛŋəln], v.r. sich —, wind, meander.

schlangenartig ['ʃlaŋəna:rtɪç], adj. snaky, serpentine.

schlank [ʃlaŋk], adj. slim, slender.

schlapp [ʃlap], adj. limp, tired, weak, slack; *— machen*, break down, collapse.

Schlappe ['ʃlapə], f. (—, pl. —n) reverse, defeat; *eine — erleiden*, suffer a set-back.

Schlappschwanz ['ʃlapʃvants], m. (—es, pl. ˙-e) weakling; milksop.

Schlaraffenland [ʃla'rafənlant], n. (—(e)s, pl. ˙-er) land of milk and honey.

schlau [ʃlau], adj. cunning, crafty, sly, shrewd.

Schlauch [ʃlaux], m. (—(e)s, pl. ˙-e) hose; tube.

Schlaukopf ['ʃlaukɔpf], m. (—(e)s, pl. ˙-e) slyboots; (*Am.*) wiseacre.

schlecht [ʃlɛçt], adj. bad, evil, wicked; poor; *mir ist —*, I feel ill; *—e Zeiten*, hard times; *—es Geld*, base money.

schlechterdings ['ʃlɛçtərdɪŋs], adv. simply, positively, absolutely.

schlechthin ['ʃlɛçthɪn], adv. simply, plainly.

Schlechtigkeit ['ʃlɛçtɪçkaɪt], f. (—, pl. —en) wickedness, baseness.

Schlegel ['ʃle:gəl], m. (—s, pl. —) mallet; drumstick; (*bell*) clapper.

Schlehdorn ['ʃle:dɔrn], m. (—s, pl. —e) blackthorn, sloe-tree.

schleichen ['ʃlaɪçən], v.n. irr. (*aux.* sein) sneak, prowl, slink; *—de Krankheit*, lingering illness.

Schleichhandel ['ʃlaɪçhandəl], m. (—s, pl. ˙:) smuggling, black marketeering.

Schleie ['ʃlaɪə], f. (—, pl. —n) tench.

Schleier ['ʃlaɪər], m. (—s, pl. —) veil.

Schleife ['ʃlaɪfə], f. (—, pl. —n) bow, loop, noose.

schleifen ['ʃlaɪfən], v.a. irr. drag along, trail; grind, polish, sharpen, whet, hone; cut.

Schleim [ʃlaɪm], m. (—(e)s, no pl.) slime, mucus, phlegm.

Schleimhaut ['ʃlaɪmhaut], f. (—, pl. ˙-e) mucous membrane.

Schleimsuppe ['ʃlaɪmzupə], f. (—, pl. —n) gruel.

schleißen ['ʃlaɪsən], v.a. irr. split, slit; (*feathers*) strip.

schlemmen ['ʃlɛmən], v.n. carouse, gormandise.

schlendern ['ʃlɛndərn], v.n. (*aux.* sein) saunter along, stroll.

Schlendrian ['ʃlɛndria:n], m. (—s, no pl.) old jog-trot, routine.

schlenkern ['ʃlɛŋkərn], v.a. dangle, swing.

Schleppdampfer ['ʃlɛpdampfər], m. (—s, pl. —) steam-tug, tug-boat, tow-boat.

Schleppe ['ʃlɛpə], f. (—, pl. —n) train (of a dress).

schleppen ['ʃlɛpən], v.a. carry (s.th. heavy), drag, tow.

Schleppenträger ['ʃlɛpəntrɛ:gər], (—s, pl. —) train-bearer.

Schleppnetz ['ʃlɛpnɛts], n. (—es, pl. —e) dragnet.

Schlesien ['ʃle:zjən], n. Silesia.

Schleuder ['ʃlɔydər], f. (—, pl. —n) sling; catapult.

schleudern ['ʃlɔydərn], v.a. sling, throw, fling away. — v.n. (*Motor.*) skid; (*Comm.*) sell cheaply, under-sell.

schleunigst ['ʃlɔynɪçst], *adv.* very quickly, with the utmost expedition, promptly.

Schleuse ['ʃlɔyzə], *f.* (—, *pl.* —n) sluice, flood-gate, lock.

Schlich [ʃlɪç], *m.* (—es, *pl.* —e) trick, dodge; *einem hinter seine —e kommen,* be up to s.o.'s tricks.

schlicht [ʃlɪçt], *adj.* plain, simple, homely; *—er Abschied,* curt dismissal.

schlichten ['ʃlɪçtən], *v.a.* level; (*argument*) settle; adjust, compose.

Schlichtheit ['ʃlɪçthaɪt], *f.* (—, *no pl.*) plainness, simplicity, homeliness.

schließen ['ʃliːsən], *v.a. irr.* shut, close; contract; *etwas — aus,* conclude s.th. from; (*meeting*) close; *Frieden —,* make peace; *einen in die Arme —,* embrace s.o.; *etwas in sich —,* imply, entail.

Schließer ['ʃliːsər], *m.* (—s, *pl.* —) doorkeeper; (*prison*) jailer, turnkey.

schließlich ['ʃliːslɪç], *adv.* lastly, finally, in conclusion.

Schliff [ʃlɪf], *m.* (—(e)s, *no pl.*) polish, refinement.

schlimm [ʃlɪm], *adj.* bad, evil, ill; sad; serious, sore; disagreeable; naughty; *um so —er,* so much the worse, worse luck.

Schlinge ['ʃlɪŋə], *f.* (—, *pl.* —n) loop, knot; noose, snare.

Schlingel ['ʃlɪŋəl], *m.* (—s, *pl.* —) little rascal.

schlingen ['ʃlɪŋən], *v.a. irr.* sling, wind; swallow, devour.

Schlips [ʃlɪps], *m.* (—es, *pl.* —e) (neck-)tie, cravat.

Schlitten ['ʃlɪtən], *m.* (—s, *pl.* —) sledge, sled, sleigh.

Schlittschuh ['ʃlɪtʃuː], *m.* (—s, *pl.* —e) skate; *— laufen,* skate.

Schlitz [ʃlɪts], *m.* (—es, *pl.* —e) slit.

schlohweiß ['ʃloːvaɪs], *adj.* white as sloe-blossom, snow-white.

Schloß [ʃlɔs], *n.* (—sses, *pl.* ·sser) (*door*) lock, padlock; (*gun*) lock; palace, castle; *unter — und Riegel,* under lock and key.

Schloße ['ʃloːsə], *f.* (—, *pl.* —n) hail-stone.

Schlosser ['ʃlɔsər], *m.* (—s, *pl.* —) locksmith.

Schlot [ʃloːt], *m.* (—(e)s, *pl.* —e) chimney, funnel.

schlottern ['ʃlɔtərn], *v.n.* wobble, dodder; tremble.

Schlucht [ʃluxt], *f.* (—, *pl.* —en) deep valley, defile, cleft, glen, ravine, gorge.

schluchzen ['ʃluxtsən], *v.n.* sob.

schlucken ['ʃlukən], *v.a.* gulp down, swallow. — *v.n.* hiccup.

Schlucker ['ʃlukər], *m.* (—s, *pl.* —) *armer —,* poor wretch.

Schlummer ['ʃlumər], *m.* (—s, *no pl.*) slumber.

Schlumpe ['ʃlumpə], *f.* (—, *pl.* —n) slut, slattern.

Schlund [ʃlunt], *m.* (—(e)s, *pl.* ·e) throat, gorge, gullet; gulf, abyss.

schlüpfen ['ʃlypfən], *v.n.* (*aux.* sein) slip, slide, glide.

Schlüpfer ['ʃlypfər], *m. pl.* knickers.

schlüpfrig ['ʃlypfrɪç], *adj.* slippery; (*fig.*) obscene, indecent.

schlürfen ['ʃlyrfən], *v.a.* drink noisily, lap up. — *v.n.* (*aux.* sein) (*dial.*) shuffle along.

Schluß [ʃlus], *m.* (—sses, *pl.* ·sse) end, termination; conclusion.

Schlüssel ['ʃlysəl], *m.* (—s, *pl.* —) key; (*Mus.*) clef.

Schlüsselbein ['ʃlysəlbaɪn], *n.* (—s, *pl.* —e) collar-bone.

Schlüsselblume ['ʃlysəlbluːmə], *f.* (—, *pl.* —n) (*Bot.*) cowslip, primrose.

Schlußfolgerung ['ʃlusfɔlgərʊŋ], *f.* (—, *pl.* —en) conclusion, inference, deduction.

schlüssig ['ʃlysɪç], *adj.* resolved, determined; sure; (*Law*) well-grounded; *sich — werden über,* resolve on.

Schmach [ʃmaːx], *f.* (—, *no pl.*) disgrace, ignomy.

schmachten ['ʃmaxtən], *v.n.* languish, pine.

schmächtig ['ʃmeçtɪç], *adj.* slender, slim, spare.

schmackhaft ['ʃmakhaft], *adj.* tasty, savoury.

schmähen ['ʃmeːən], *v.a.* revile, abuse, calumniate.

Schmähschrift ['ʃmeːʃrɪft], *f.* (—, *pl.* —en) lampoon.

schmal [ʃmaːl], *adj.* narrow.

schmälen ['ʃmeːlən], *v.a.* chide, scold.

schmälern ['ʃmeːlərn], *v.a.* lessen, diminish, curtail; detract from, belittle.

Schmalz [ʃmalts], *n.* (—es, *no pl.*) grease, lard, fat.

schmarotzen [ʃmaˈrɔtsən], *v.n.* sponge on others.

Schmarren ['ʃmarən], *m.* (—s, *pl.* —) trash; (*dial.*) omelette.

Schmatz [ʃmats], *m.* (—es, *pl.* ·e) (*dial.*) smacking kiss.

schmauchen ['ʃmauxən], *v.a., v.n.* smoke.

Schmaus [ʃmaus], *m.* (—es, *pl.* —e) feast, banquet.

schmecken ['ʃmekən], *v.a.* taste. — *v.n.* taste; *es schmeckt mir,* I like it.

Schmeichelei [ʃmaɪçəˈlaɪ], *f.* (—, *pl.* —en) flattery, adulation.

schmeicheln ['ʃmaɪçəln], *v.n.* flatter; fondle, pet.

schmeißen ['ʃmaɪsən], *v.a. irr.* throw, hurl, fling; (*sl.*) *ich werde die Sache schon —,* I shall pull it off.

Schmeißfliege ['ʃmaɪsfliːgə], *f.* (—, *pl.* —n) (*Ent.*) bluebottle.

Schmelz [ʃmelts], *m.* (—es, *no pl.*) enamel; melting; (*voice*) mellowness.

schmelzbar ['ʃmeltsbaːr], *adj.* fusible.

schmelzen ['ʃmeltsən], *v.a. irr.* smelt, melt. — *v.n.* (*aux.* sein) (*ice*) melt; (*fig.*) decrease, diminish.

Schmelztiegel ['ʃmɛltsti:gəl], m. (—s, pl. —) crucible; melting pot.

Schmelztopf ['ʃmɛltstɔpf], m. see Schmelztiegel.

Schmerbauch ['ʃmeːrbaux], m. (—(e)s, pl. ‥e) (coll.) paunch, belly.

Schmerz [ʃmɛrts], m. (—es, pl. —en) ache, pain; grief, sorrow; einem —en verursachen, give or cause s.o. pain.

schmerzlich ['ʃmɛrtslɪç], adj. painful, distressing.

Schmetterling ['ʃmɛtərlɪŋ], m. (—s, pl. —e) (Ent.) butterfly, moth.

schmettern ['ʃmɛtərn], v.n. resound; (trumpets) blare; (bird) warble.

Schmied [ʃmiːt], m. (—s, pl. —e) (black)smith.

Schmiede ['ʃmiːdə], f. (—, pl. —n) forge, smithy.

schmiegen ['ʃmiːgən], v.r. sich —, bend, yield; sich an einen —, cling to s.o., nestle against s.o.

Schmiere ['ʃmiːrə], f. (—, pl. —n) grease, salve; (Theat.) troop of strolling players.

schmieren ['ʃmiːrən], v.a. smear, grease, spread; (fig.) bribe; (bread) butter. — v.n. scrawl, scribble.

Schmierfink ['ʃmiːrfɪŋk], m. (—en, pl. —en) dirty person; muckraker.

Schmiermittel ['ʃmiːrmɪtəl], n. (—s, pl. —) lubricant.

Schmierseife ['ʃmiːrzaɪfə], f. (—, no pl.) soft soap.

Schminke ['ʃmɪŋkə], f. (—, pl. —n) greasepaint; rouge; make-up, cosmetics.

Schmirgel ['ʃmɪrgəl], m. (—s, no pl.) emery.

Schmiß [ʃmɪs], m. (—sses, pl. —sse) cut in the face, (duelling) scar; (fig.) smartness, verve.

Schmöker ['ʃmøːkər], m. (—s, pl. —) trashy book.

schmollen ['ʃmɔlən], v.n. sulk, pout.

Schmorbraten ['ʃmoːrbraːtən], m. (—s, pl. —) stewed meat.

Schmuck [ʃmuk], m. (—(e)s, pl. —stücke) ornament, jewels, jewellery; (Am.) jewelry.

schmuck [ʃmuk], adj. neat, spruce, dapper, smart.

schmücken ['ʃmykən], v.a. adorn, embellish.

Schmucksachen ['ʃmukzaxən], f. pl. jewels, finery, jewellery, articles of adornment; (Am.) jewelry.

schmuggeln ['ʃmugəln], v.a. smuggle.

schmunzeln ['ʃmuntsəln], v.n. smirk, grin.

Schmutz [ʃmuts], m. (—es, no pl.) dirt, filth.

schmutzen ['ʃmutsən], v.n. get soiled, get dirty.

Schmutzkonkurrenz ['ʃmutskɔnkurɛnts], f. (—, no pl.) unfair competition.

Schnabel ['ʃnaːbəl], m. (—s, pl. ‥) bill, beak; (ship) prow; halt den —, keep your mouth shut; er spricht, wie ihm

der — gewachsen ist, he calls a spade a spade.

Schnabeltier ['ʃnaːbəltiːr], n. (—s, pl. —e) duck-bill, duck-billed platypus.

Schnaderhüpfel ['ʃnaːdərhypfəl], n. (—s, pl. —) (dial.) Alpine folk-song.

Schnalle ['ʃnalə], f. (—, pl. —n) buckle.

schnalzen ['ʃnaltsən], v.n. click; snap.

schnappen ['ʃnapən], v.n. snap; snatch at s.th.; nach Luft —, gasp for breath.

Schnaps [ʃnaps], m. (—es, pl. ‥e) spirits, brandy, gin.

schnarchen ['ʃnarçən], v.n. snore.

Schnarre ['ʃnarə], f. (—, pl. —n) rattle.

schnattern ['ʃnatərn], v.n. cackle; gabble; chatter.

schnauben ['ʃnaubən], v.n. puff and blow; snort; vor Zorn —, fret and fume.

schnaufen ['ʃnaufən], v.n. breathe heavily, pant.

Schnauze ['ʃnautsə], f. (—, pl. —n) (animals) snout; (vulg.) mouth, trap; nozzle.

schnauzen ['ʃnautsən], v.n. snarl, shout (at).

Schnecke ['ʃnɛkə], f. (—, pl. —n), (Zool.) snail, slug.

Schnee [ʃneː], m. (—s, no pl.) snow.

Schneegestöber ['ʃneːgəʃtøːbər], n. (—s, pl. —) snow-storm.

Schneeglöckchen ['ʃneːglœkçən], n. (—s, pl. —) (Bot.) snowdrop.

Schneeschläger ['ʃneːʃleːgər], m. (—s, pl. —) whisk.

Schneetreiben ['ʃneːtraɪbən], n. (—s, no pl.) snow-storm, blizzard.

Schneewittchen [ʃneː'vɪtçən], n. (—s, no pl.) Snow White.

Schneid [ʃnaɪt], m. (—s, no pl.) go, push, dash, courage.

Schneide ['ʃnaɪdə], f. (—, pl. —n) edge.

Schneidebohne ['ʃnaɪdəbɔːnə], f. (—, pl. —n) French bean, string-bean.

Schneidemühle ['ʃnaɪdəmyːlə], f. (—, pl. —n) saw mill.

schneiden ['ʃnaɪdən], v.a. irr. cut, trim, carve; (fig.) ignore, cut; Gesichter —, make faces. — v.r. sich —, cut o.s.; (Maths.) intersect; sich die Haare — lassen, have o.'s hair cut.

Schneider ['ʃnaɪdər], m. (—s, pl. —) tailor.

Schneiderei [ʃnaɪdə'raɪ], f. (—, no pl.) tailoring; dressmaking.

Schneidezahn ['ʃnaɪdətsaːn], m. (—s, pl. ‥e) incisor.

schneidig ['ʃnaɪdɪç], adj. dashing.

schneien ['ʃnaɪən], v.n. snow.

Schneise ['ʃnaɪzə], f. (—, pl. —n) (forest) glade, cutting.

schnell [ʃnɛl], adj. quick, swift, speedy, fast, rapid; mach —, hurry up.

Schnelle ['ʃnɛlə], f. (—, pl. —n) (river) rapids.

schnellen ['ʃnɛlən], v.n. spring, jump.

Schnelligkeit

Schnelligkeit [ˈʃnɛlɪçkaɪt], *f.* (—, *no pl.*) quickness, speed, swiftness, rapidity; (*Tech.*) velocity.

Schnepfe [ˈʃnɛpfə], *f.* (—, *pl.* **—n**) (*Orn.*) snipe, woodcock.

schneuzen [ˈʃnɔytsən], *v.r.* sich (*die Nase*) —, blow o.'s nose.

schniegeln [ˈʃniːgəln], *v.r.* sich —, (*coll.*) dress up, deck out; *geschniegelt und gebügelt*, spick and span.

Schnippchen [ˈʃnɪpçən], *n.* (—s, *pl.* —) *einem ein — schlagen*, play a trick on s.o.

schnippisch [ˈʃnɪpɪʃ], *adj.* pert, perky.

Schnitt [ʃnɪt], *m.* (—(e)s, *pl.* —e) cut, incision; section; (*beer*) small glass; (*dress*) cut-out pattern; (*book*) edge.

Schnittbohne [ˈʃnɪtboːnə], *f.* (—, *pl.* —n) (*Bot.*) French bean.

Schnitte [ˈʃnɪtə], *f.* (—, *pl.* —n) slice (of bread).

Schnitter [ˈʃnɪtər], *m.* (—s, *pl.* —) reaper.

Schnittlauch [ˈʃnɪtlaux], *m.* (—s, *no pl.*) (*Bot.*) chives.

Schnittmuster [ˈʃnɪtmustər], *n.* (—s, *pl.* —) cut-out pattern.

Schnittwaren [ˈʃnɪtvaːrən], *f. pl.* dry goods, drapery.

Schnitzel [ˈʃnɪtsəl], *n.* (—s, *pl.* —) (*Cul.*) cutlet; *Wiener* —, veal cutlet; snip; (*pl.*) shavings.

schnitzen [ˈʃnɪtsən], *v.a.* carve (in wood).

schnodd(e)rig [ˈʃnɔd(ə)rɪç], *adj.* (*coll.*) cheeky, insolent.

schnöde [ˈʃnøːdə], *adj.* base, heinous, mean, vile; —*r Mammon*, filthy lucre; —*r Undank*, rank ingratitude.

Schnörkel [ˈʃnœrkəl], *m.* (—s, *pl.* —) (*writing*) flourish.

schnorren [ˈʃnɔrən], *v.n.* (*rare*) cadge, beg.

schnüffeln [ˈʃnyfəln], *v.n.* sniff; (*fig.*) pry, snoop.

Schnuller [ˈʃnulər], *m.* (—s, *pl.* —) baby's dummy; (*Am.*) pacifier.

Schnupfen [ˈʃnupfən], *m.* (—s, *pl.* —) cold (in the head); *den — haben*, have a (running) cold; *den — bekommen*, catch cold.

schnupfen [ˈʃnupfən], *v.a., v.n.* take snuff.

Schnupftuch [ˈʃnupftuːx], *n.* (—(e)s, *pl.* ˝er) (*dial.*) (pocket-) handkerchief.

schnuppe [ˈʃnupə], *adj.* (*sl.*) *mir ist alles —*, it is all the same to me, I don't care.

schnuppern [ˈʃnupərn], *v.n.* smell, snuffle.

Schnur [ʃnuːr], *f.* (—, *pl.* —en, ˝e) twine, cord, string; (*Elec.*) lead, extension cord.

Schnurrbart [ˈʃnurbaːrt], *m.* (—s, *pl.* ˝e) moustache; *sich einen — wachsen lassen*, grow a moustache.

Schnürchen [ˈʃnyːrçən], *n.* (—s, *pl.* —) *wie am —*, like clockwork.

schnüren [ˈʃnyːrən], *v.a.* lace, tie up; *sein Ränzel —*, pack o.'s bag.

Schnurre [ˈʃnurə], *f.* (—, *pl.* —n) funny story, yarn.

schnurren [ˈʃnurən], *v.n.* purr.

Schnürsenkel [ˈʃnyːrzɛŋkəl], *m.* (—s, *pl.* —) (*shoe*) lace.

schnurstracks [ˈʃnuːrʃtraks], *adv.* directly, immediately, on the spot.

Schober [ˈʃoːbər], *m.* (—s, *pl.* —) stack, rick.

Schock (1) [ʃɔk], *n.* (—(e)s, *pl.* —e) sixty, three score.

Schock (2) [ʃɔk], *m.* (—(e)s, *pl.* —s) shock; blow; stroke.

Schöffe [ˈʃœfə], *m.* (—n, *pl.* —n) (*Law*) juror; member of jury.

Schokolade [ʃokoˈlaːdə], *f.* (—, *pl.* —n) chocolate; *eine Tafel —*, a bar of chocolate.

Scholle [ˈʃɔlə], *f.* (—, *pl.* —n) plaice; (*ice*) floe; clod; soil.

schon [ʃoːn], *adv.* already; indeed; yet; *na wenn —*, so what; — *gut*, that'll do; — *gestern*, as early as yesterday.

schön [ʃøːn], *adj.* beautiful, fair, handsome, lovely; —*e Literatur*, belles-lettres, good books.

schonen [ˈʃoːnən], *v.a.* spare, save; treat considerately.

Schoner [ˈʃoːnər], *m.* (—s, *pl.* —) antimacassar; (*Naut.*) schooner.

Schönheit [ˈʃøːnhaɪt], *f.* (—, *no pl.*) beauty.

Schonung [ˈʃoːnuŋ], *f.* (—, *pl.* —en) forbearance, considerate treatment; (*forest*) plantation of young trees.

Schonzeit [ˈʃoːntsaɪt], *f.* (—, *pl.* —en) close season.

Schopf [ʃɔpf], *m.* (—es, *pl.* ˝e) tuft, head of hair; (*bird*) crest; *das Glück beim —e fassen*, take time by the forelock, make hay while the sun shines.

Schöpfbrunnen [ˈʃœpfbrunən], *m.* (—s, *pl.* —) (draw-)well.

schöpfen [ˈʃœpfən], *v.a.* (*water*) draw; derive; *Verdacht —*, become suspicious; *frische Luft —*, get a breath of fresh air; *Mut —*, take heart.

Schöpfer [ˈʃœpfər], *m.* (—s, *pl.* —) creator.

Schöpfkelle [ˈʃœpfkɛlə], *f.* (—, *pl.* —n) scoop.

Schopflerche [ˈʃɔpflɛrçə], *f.* (—, *pl.* —n) (*Orn.*) crested lark.

Schöpfung [ˈʃœpfuŋ], *f.* (—, *pl.* —en) creation.

Schoppen [ˈʃɔpən], *m.* (—s, *pl.* —) (*approx.*) half a pint.

Schöps [ʃœps], *m.* (—es, *pl.* —e) (*Zool.*) wether; (*fig.*) simpleton.

Schorf [ʃɔrf], *m.* (—(e)s, *pl.* —e) scab, scurf.

Schornstein [ˈʃɔrnʃtaɪn], *m.* (—s, *pl.* —e) chimney; (*ship*) funnel.

Schoß [ʃoːs], *m.* (—es, *pl.* ˝e) lap; (*Poet.*) womb; skirt, tail; *die Hände in den — legen*, be idle, fold o.'s arms, twiddle o.'s thumbs.

Schößling ['ʃœslɪŋ], m. (—s, pl. —e) shoot, sprig.

Schote ['ʃo:tə], f. (—, pl. —n) pod, husk, shell; (pl.) green peas.

Schotter ['ʃɔtər], m. (—s, no pl.) road-metal, broken stones, gravel.

Schottland ['ʃɔtlant], n. Scotland.

schraffieren [ʃra'fi:rən], v.a. (Art) hatch.

schräg ['ʃrɛ:k], adj. oblique, sloping, slanting, diagonal.

Schramme ['ʃramə], f. (—, pl. —n) scratch, scar.

Schrank [ʃraŋk], m. (—(e)s, pl. ˉe) cupboard, wardrobe.

Schranken ['ʃraŋkən], f. pl. barriers, (level crossing) gates, limits, bounds; in — halten, limit, keep within bounds.

schränken ['ʃrɛŋkən], v.a. cross; fold.

Schranze ['ʃrantsə], m. (—n, pl. —n) sycophant, toady.

Schraube ['ʃraubə], f. (—, pl. —n) screw; bolt; propeller.

Schraubengewinde ['ʃraubəngəvɪndə], n. (—s, pl. —) thread of a screw.

Schraubenmutter ['ʃraubənmutər], f. (—, pl. —n) female screw, nut.

Schraubenzieher ['ʃraubəntsi:ər], m. (—s, pl. —) screw-driver.

Schraubstock ['ʃraupʃtɔk], m. (—s, pl. ˉe) (tool) vise.

Schreck(en) ['ʃrɛk(ən)], m. (—s, pl. —) fright, terror, alarm, horror; shock.

Schrecknis ['ʃrɛknɪs], n. (—ses, pl. —se) terror, horror.

Schrei [ʃrai], m. (—s, pl. —e) cry; scream.

Schreiben ['ʃraibən], n. (—s, pl. —) letter, missive.

schreiben ['ʃraibən], v.a. irr. write; ins Reine —, make a fair copy.

Schreibfehler ['ʃraipfe:lər], m. (—s, pl. —) slip of the pen.

Schreibkrampf ['ʃraipkrampf], m. (—(e)s, pl. ˉe) writer's cramp.

Schreibmaschine ['ʃraipmaʃi:nə], f. (—, pl. —n) typewriter.

Schreibwaren ['ʃraipva:rən], f. pl. stationery.

Schreibweise ['ʃraipvaizə], f. (—, pl. —n) style; spelling.

schreien ['ʃraiən], v.a., v.n. irr. cry, shout, scream, yell.

Schreihals ['ʃraihals], m. (—es, pl. ˉe) cry-baby, noisy child.

Schrein [ʃrain], m. (—(e)s, pl. —e) box, chest; shrine.

schreiten ['ʃraitən], v.n. irr. (aux. sein) stride, step, pace.

Schrift [ʃrɪft], f. (—, pl. —en) writing; handwriting, calligraphy; publication; type; Heilige —, Holy Writ, Holy Scripture.

Schriftführer ['ʃrɪftfy:rər], m. (—s, pl. —) secretary.

Schriftgießerei ['ʃrɪftgi:sərai], f. (—, pl. —en) type-foundry.

Schriftleiter ['ʃrɪftlaitər], m. (—s, pl. —) editor.

schriftlich ['ʃrɪftlɪç], adj. written. — adv. in writing, by letter.

Schriftsetzer ['ʃrɪftzɛtsər], m. (—s, pl. —) compositor.

Schriftsteller ['ʃrɪftʃtɛlər], m. (—s, pl. —) writer, author.

Schriftstück ['ʃrɪftʃtyk], n. (—s, pl. —e) document, deed.

Schriftwechsel ['ʃrɪftvɛksəl], m. (—s, no pl.) exchange of notes, correspondence.

Schriftzeichen ['ʃrɪftsaiçən], n. (—s, pl. —) character, letter (of alphabet).

schrill [ʃrɪl], adj. shrill.

Schritt [ʃrɪt], m. (—(e)s, pl. —e) step, pace, move; lange —e machen, stride; — halten, keep pace; — fahren, drive slowly, drive at walking pace; aus dem —, out of step; in einer Sache —e tun, make a move or take steps about s.th.

schrittweise ['ʃrɪtvaizə], adv. step by step, gradually.

schroff ['ʃrɔf], adj. steep, precipitous; (fig.) gruff, blunt, rough, harsh.

schröpfen ['ʃrœpfən], v.a. (Med.) cup; (fig.) fleece.

Schrot [ʃro:t], m. & n. (—(e)s, pl. —e) grape-shot, small shot; ein Mann vom alten —, a man of the utmost probity.

Schrotbrot ['ʃro:tbro:t], n. (—es, no pl.) wholemeal bread.

Schrott [ʃrɔt], m. (—(e)s, pl. —e), old iron, scrap metal.

Schrulle ['ʃrulə], f. (—, pl. —n) fad, whim.

schrumpfen ['ʃrumpfən], v.n. (aux. sein) shrink, shrivel.

Schub [ʃup], m. (—s, pl. ˉe) shove, push; batch.

Schubkarren ['ʃupkarən], m. (—s, pl. —) wheelbarrow.

Schublade ['ʃupla:də], f. (—, pl. —n) drawer.

schüchtern ['ʃyçtərn], adj. shy, bashful, timid.

Schuft [ʃuft], m. (—(e)s, pl. —e) blackguard, scoundrel.

schuften ['ʃuftən], v.n. work hard, toil.

Schufterei [ʃufta'rai], f. (—, no pl.) drudgery.

schuftig ['ʃuftɪç], adj. rascally, mean.

Schuh [ʃu:], m. (—s, pl. —e) shoe; einem etwas in die — e schieben, lay the blame at s.o.'s door.

Schuhwerk ['ʃu:vɛrk], n. (—s, no pl.) footwear.

Schuhwichse ['ʃu:vɪksə], f. (—, no pl.) shoe-polish.

Schuld [ʃult], f. (—, pl. —en) guilt, offence, sin; fault; blame; cause; (money) debt; in —en geraten, run into debt.

schuld [ʃult], adj. ich bin —, it is my fault, I am to blame.

schulden ['ʃuldən], v.a. owe, be indebted to.

schuldig ['ʃuldɪç], adj. guilty, culpable; sich — bekennen, plead guilty; einen — sprechen, pronounce s.o. guilty;

Schuldigkeit

ihm ist Anerkennung —, appreciation is due to him.

Schuldigkeit [ˈʃuldɪçkaɪt], *f.* (—, *no pl.*) obligation, duty.

schuldlos [ˈʃultloːs], *adj.* innocent, guiltless.

Schuldner [ˈʃuldnər], *m.* (—s, *pl.* —) debtor.

Schule [ˈʃuːlə], *f.* (—, *pl.* —n) school; *in die* — *gehen*, go to school, attend school; *die* — *schwänzen*, play truant; *hohe* —, (*Riding*) advanced horsemanship.

schulen [ˈʃuːlən], *v.a.* train, instruct.

Schüler [ˈʃyːlər], *m.* (—s, *pl.* —) schoolboy, pupil, student, scholar.

Schulklasse [ˈʃuːlklasə], *f.* (—, *pl.* —n) class, form.

Schulleiter [ˈʃuːllaɪtər], *m.* (—s, *pl.* —) headmaster.

Schulrat [ˈʃuːlraːt], *m.* (—s, *pl.* ⁚e) school-inspector.

Schulter [ˈʃultər], *f.* (—, *pl.* —n) shoulder.

Schulterblatt [ˈʃultərblat], *n.* (—s, *pl.* ⁚er) shoulder-blade.

Schultheiß [ˈʃulthaɪs], *m.* (—en, *pl.* —en) village magistrate, mayor.

Schulunterricht [ˈʃuːluntərrɪçt], *m.* (—s, *no pl.*) school teaching, lessons.

schummeln [ˈʃuməln], *v.n.* (*coll.*) cheat.

Schund [ʃunt], *m.* (—(e)s, *no pl.*) trash.

Schuppe [ˈʃupə], *f.* (—, *pl.* —n) scale; (*pl.*) dandruff.

Schuppen [ˈʃupən], *m.* (—s, *pl.* —) shed.

Schuppentier [ˈʃupəntiːr], *n.* (—s, *pl.* —e) (*Zool.*) armadillo.

Schur [ʃuːr], *f.* (—, *pl.* —en) shearing.

schüren [ˈʃyːrən], *v.a.* (*fire*) poke, rake; (*fig.*) stir up, fan, incite.

schürfen [ˈʃyrfən], *v.a.* scratch. — *v.n.* (*Min.*) prospect.

schurigeln [ˈʃuːrɪɡəln], *v.a.* bully, pester.

Schurke [ˈʃurkə], *m.* (—n, *pl.* —n) scoundrel, villain, blackguard.

Schurz [ʃurts], *m.* (—es, *pl.* —e) apron, overall.

Schürze [ˈʃyrtsə], *f.* (—, *pl.* —n) apron, pinafore.

schürzen [ˈʃyrtsən], *v.a.* tuck up, pin up.

Schürzenjäger [ˈʃyrtsənjɛːɡər], *m.* (—s, *pl.* —) ladies' man.

Schurzfell [ˈʃurtsfɛl], *n.* (—s, *pl.* —e) leather apron.

Schuß [ʃus], *m.* (—sses, *pl.* ⁚sse) shot, report; dash; *weit vom* —, out of harm's way; wide of the mark.

Schüssel [ˈʃysəl], *f.* (—, *pl.* —n) dish.

Schußwaffe [ˈʃusvafə], *f.* (—, *pl.* —n) fire-arm.

Schuster [ˈʃuːstər], *m.* (—s, *pl.* —) shoemaker, cobbler; *auf* —*s Rappen*, on Shanks's pony.

schustern [ˈʃuːstərn], *v.n.* cobble, make or mend shoes.

Schutt [ʃut], *m.* (—(e)s, *no pl.*) rubbish, refuse; rubble; — *abladen*,

dump refuse.

Schütte [ˈʃytə], *f.* (—, *pl.* —n) (*dial.*) bundle, truss.

schütteln [ˈʃytəln], *v.a.* shake, jolt.

schütten [ˈʃytən], *v.a.* shoot; pour; pour out.

schütter [ˈʃytər], *adj.* (*dial.*) (*hair*) thin; scarce.

Schutz [ʃuts], *m.* (—es, *no pl.*) protection, shelter, cover; *einen in* — *nehmen gegen*, defend s.o. against.

Schutzbefohlene [ˈʃutsbəfoːlənə], *m.* (—n, *pl.* —n) charge, person in o.'s care, ward.

Schutzbündnis [ˈʃutsbyntnɪs], *n.* (—ses, *pl.* —se) defensive alliance.

Schütze [ˈʃytsə], *m.* (—n, *pl.* —n) rifleman, sharpshooter, marksman; (*Astrol.*) Sagittarius.

schützen [ˈʃytsən], *v.a.* protect, shelter, defend. — *v.r. sich* — *vor*, guard o.s. against.

Schützengraben [ˈʃytsəngraːbən], *m.* (—s, *pl.* —) trench.

Schutzgebiet [ˈʃutsɡəbiːt], *n.* (—s, *pl.* —e) protectorate.

Schutzgitter [ˈʃutsɡɪtər], *n.* (—s, *pl.* —) grid, guard.

Schutzheilige [ˈʃutshaɪlɪɡə], *m.* (—n, *pl.* —n) patron saint.

Schützling [ˈʃytslɪŋ], *m.* (—s, *pl.* —e) protégé, charge.

Schutzmann [ˈʃutsman], *m.* (—s, *pl.* ⁚er, **Schutzleute**) policeman, constable.

Schutzmarke [ˈʃutsmarkə], *f.* (—, *pl.* —n) trade-mark.

Schutzzoll [ˈʃutstsɔl], *m.* (—s, *pl.* ⁚e) protective duty, tariff.

Schwaben [ˈʃvaːbən], *n.* Swabia.

Schwabenstreich [ˈʃvaːbənʃtraɪç], *m.* (—s, *pl.* —e) tomfoolery.

schwach [ʃvax], *adj.* weak, frail, feeble; (*noise*) faint; (*pulse*) low; —*e Seite*, foible; —*e Stunde*, unguarded moment.

Schwäche [ˈʃvɛçə], *f.* (—, *pl.* —n) weakness, faintness; infirmity.

schwächen [ˈʃvɛçən], *v.a.* weaken, debilitate.

Schwächling [ˈʃvɛçlɪŋ], *m.* (—s, *pl.* —e) weakling.

Schwachsinn [ˈʃvaxzɪn], *m.* (—s, *no pl.*) feeble-mindedness.

Schwächung [ˈʃvɛçuŋ], *f.* (—, *pl.* —en) weakening, lessening.

Schwadron [ʃvaˈdroːn], *f.* (—, *pl.* —en) squadron.

Schwadroneur [ʃvadroˈnøːr], *m.* (—s, *pl.* —e) swaggerer.

schwadronieren [ʃvadroˈniːrən], *v.n.* talk big, swagger.

schwafeln [ˈʃvaːfəln], *v.n.* (*sl.*) talk nonsense, waffle.

Schwager [ˈʃvaːɡər], *m.* (—s, *pl.* ⁚) brother-in-law.

Schwägerin [ˈʃvɛːɡərɪn], *f.* (—, *pl.* —nen) sister-in-law.

Schwalbe [ˈʃvalbə], *f.* (—, *pl.* —n) (*Orn.*) swallow.

Schwellung

Schwalbenschwanz ['ʃvalbənʃvants], *m.* (—es, *pl.* ⁝e) (*butterfly*) swallow's tail; (*joinery*) dovetail.

Schwall [ʃval], *m.* (—(e)s, *no pl.*) flood; (*fig.*) deluge, torrent.

Schwamm [ʃvam], *m.* (—(e)s, *pl.* ⁝e) sponge; fungus, mushroom; dry rot.

schwammig ['ʃvamɪç], *adj.* spongy, fungous.

Schwan [ʃvaːn], *m.* (—(e)s, *pl.* ⁝e) swan; *junger* —, cygnet.

schwanen ['ʃvaːnən], *v.n. imp. es schwant mir,* I have a foreboding.

Schwang [ʃvaŋ], *m. im —e sein,* be in fashion, be the rage.

schwanger ['ʃvaŋər], *adj.* pregnant.

schwängern ['ʃvɛŋərn], *v.a.* make pregnant, get with child; (*fig.*) impregnate.

Schwangerschaft ['ʃvaŋərʃaft], *f.* (—, *pl.* —en) pregnancy.

Schwank [ʃvaŋk], *m.* (—(e)s, *pl.* ⁝e) funny story, joke; (*Theat.*) farce.

schwank [ʃvaŋk], *adj.* flexible, supple; *ein —es Rohr,* a reed shaken by the wind.

schwanken ['ʃvaŋkən], *v.n.* totter, stagger; (*fig.*) waver, vacillate; (*prices*) fluctuate.

Schwanz [ʃvants], *m.* (—es, *pl.* ⁝e) tail.

schwänzeln ['ʃvɛntsəln], *v.n.* (*animal*) wag the tail; (*fig.*) fawn, cringe.

schwänzen ['ʃvɛntsən], *v.a. die Schule* —, play truant.

Schwären ['ʃvɛːrən], *m.* (—s, *pl.* —) ulcer, abscess.

schwären ['ʃvɛːrən], *v.n.* fester, suppurate.

Schwarm [ʃvarm], *m.* (—(e)s, *pl.* ⁝e) (*insects*) swarm; (*humans*) crowd; (*birds*) flight.

Schwärmerei [ʃvɛrmə'raɪ], *f.* (—, *pl.* —en) enthusiasm, passion, craze.

Schwarte ['ʃvartə], *f.* (—, *pl.* —n) rind; crust; *alte* —, (*fig.*) old volume; tome.

schwarz [ʃvarts], *adj.* black.

Schwarzamsel ['ʃvartsamzəl], *f.* (—, *pl.* —n) (*Orn.*) blackbird.

Schwarzdorn ['ʃvartsdɔrn], *m.* (—s, *no pl.*) (*Bot.*) blackthorn, sloe.

Schwärze ['ʃvɛrtsə], *f.* (—, *no pl.*) blackness; printer's ink.

schwärzen ['ʃvɛrtsən], *v.a.* blacken.

Schwarzkünstler ['ʃvartskynstlər], *m.* (—s, *pl.* —) magician, necromancer.

Schwarzwald ['ʃvartsvalt], *m.* Black Forest.

Schwarzwild ['ʃvartsvɪlt], *n.* (—(e)s, *no pl.*) wild boar.

schwatzen ['ʃvatsən], *v.n.* chat, chatter, prattle.

Schwätzer ['ʃvɛtsər], *m.* (—s, *pl.* —) chatterbox.

Schwatzhaftigkeit ['ʃvatshaftɪçkaɪt], *f.* (—, *no pl.*) loquacity, talkativeness.

Schwebe ['ʃveːbə], *f.* (—, *pl.* —n) suspense; suspension.

Schwebebaum ['ʃveːbəbaum], *m.* (—s, *pl.* ⁝e) horizontal bar.

schweben ['ʃveːbən], *v.n.* be suspended, hover; (*fig.*) be pending; *in Gefahr* —, be in danger; *es schwebt mir auf der Zunge,* it is on the tip of my tongue.

Schwede ['ʃveːdə], *m.* (—n, *pl.* —n) Swede; *alter* —, (*fig.*) old boy.

Schweden ['ʃveːdən], *n.* Sweden.

Schwedenhölzer ['ʃveːdənhœltsər], *n. pl.* (*rare*) matches.

Schwefel ['ʃveːfəl], *m.* (—s, *no pl.*) sulphur, brimstone.

Schwefelhölzchen ['ʃveːfəlhœltsçən], *n.* (—s, *pl.* —) (*obs.*) match.

schwefeln ['ʃveːfəln], *v.a.* impregnate with sulphur, fumigate.

Schwefelsäure ['ʃveːfəlzɔyrə], *f.* (—, *no pl.*) sulphuric acid.

Schweif [ʃvaɪf], *m.* (—(e)s, *pl.* —e) tail.

schweifen ['ʃvaɪfən], *v.n.* (*aux. sein*) ramble, stray, wander.

schweifwedeln ['ʃvaɪfveːdəln], *v.n.* fawn.

Schweigegeld ['ʃvaɪgəgelt], *n.* (—(e)s, *pl.* —er) (*coll.*) hush-money.

Schweigen ['ʃvaɪgən], *n.* (—s, *no pl.*) silence.

schweigen ['ʃvaɪgən], *v.n. irr.* be silent; be quiet; *ganz zu — von,* to say nothing of.

schweigsam ['ʃvaɪkzaːm], *adj.* taciturn.

Schwein [ʃvaɪn], *n.* (—(e)s, *pl.* —e) pig, hog; swine; *wildes* —, boar; (*fig.*) luck, fluke; — *haben,* be lucky.

Schweinekoben ['ʃvaɪnəkoːbən], *m.* (—s, *pl.* —) pigsty.

Schweinerei [ʃvaɪnə'raɪ], *f.* (—, *pl.* —en) filth; (*fig.*) smut, filthiness, obscenity; mess.

Schweineschmalz ['ʃvaɪnəʃmalts], *n.* (—es, *no pl.*) lard.

Schweinigel ['ʃvaɪnɪgəl], *m.* (—s, *pl.* —) (*Zool.*) hedgehog, porcupine; (*fig.*) dirty pig, filthy wretch.

Schweinskeule ['ʃvaɪnskɔylə], *f.* (—, *pl.* —n) leg of pork.

Schweiß [ʃvaɪs], *m.* (—es, *no pl.*) sweat, perspiration.

schweißen ['ʃvaɪsən], *v.a.* weld, solder.

Schweiz [ʃvaɪts], *f.* Switzerland.

Schweizer ['ʃvaɪtsər], *m.* (—s, *pl.* —) Swiss; (*fig.*) dairyman.

Schweizerei [ʃvaɪtsə'raɪ], *f.* (—, *pl.* —en) dairy.

schwelen ['ʃveːlən], *v.n.* burn slowly, smoulder.

schwelgen ['ʃvɛlgən], *v.n.* carouse, revel.

Schwelgerei [ʃvɛlgə'raɪ], *f.* (—, *pl.* —en) revelry.

schwelgerisch ['ʃvɛlgərɪʃ], *adj.* luxurious, voluptuous.

Schwelle ['ʃvɛlə], *f.* (—, *pl.* —n) threshold; (*Railw.*) sleeper, tie.

schwellen ['ʃvɛlən], *v.n. irr.* (*aux. sein*) swell; (*water*) rise.

Schwellung ['ʃvɛluŋ], *f.* (—, *pl.* —en) swelling.

195

schwemmen

schwemmen ['ʃvɛmən], *v.a.* wash, soak, carry off.
Schwengel ['ʃvɛŋəl], *m.* (—s, *pl.* —) (*bell*) clapper; (*pump*) handle.
schwenken ['ʃvɛŋkən], *v.a.* swing; shake, brandish; (*glasses*) rinse.
Schwenkung ['ʃvɛŋkuŋ], *f.* (—, *pl.* —en) change; (*Mil.*) wheeling.
schwer [ʃveːr], *adj.* heavy; difficult, hard; ponderous; severe; — *von Begriff*, obtuse, slow in the uptake; —*e Speise*, indigestible food; *einem das Herz — machen*, grieve s.o.
schwerblütig ['ʃveːrblyːtɪç], *adj.* phlegmatic.
Schwere ['ʃveːrə], *f.* (—, *no pl.*) weight, heaviness; gravity.
Schwerenöter ['ʃveːrənøːtər], *m.* (—s, *pl.* —) gay dog, ladies' man.
schwerfällig ['ʃveːrfɛlɪç], *adj.* ungainly, cumbrous, unwieldy; (*fig.*) thickheaded, dense.
Schwergewicht ['ʃveːrgəvɪçt], *n.* (—s, *no pl.*) (*Sport*) heavyweight; (*fig.*) emphasis.
schwerhörig ['ʃveːrhøːrɪç], *adj.* hard of hearing, deaf.
Schwerkraft ['ʃveːrkraft], *f.* (—, *no pl.*) gravity.
schwerlich ['ʃveːrlɪç], *adv.* hardly, scarcely.
schwermütig ['ʃveːrmyːtɪç], *adj.* melancholy.
Schwerpunkt ['ʃveːrpuŋkt], *m.* (—s, *pl.* —e) centre of gravity.
Schwert [ʃveːrt], *n.* (—(e)s, *pl.* —er) sword.
Schwertgriff ['ʃveːrtgrɪf], *m.* (—s, *pl.* —e) hilt.
Schwertlilie ['ʃveːrtliːljə], *f.* (—, *pl.* —n) (*Bot.*) iris; fleur-de-lys.
Schwertstreich ['ʃveːrtʃtraɪç], *m.* (—(e)s, *pl.* —e) sword-blow, swordstroke.
schwerwiegend ['ʃveːrviːgənt], *adj.* weighty.
Schwester ['ʃvɛstər], *f.* (—, *pl.* —n) sister; *barmherzige* —, sister of mercy.
Schwesternschaft ['ʃvɛstərnʃaft], *f.* (—, *pl.* —en) sisterhood; (*Am.*) sorority.
Schwibbogen ['ʃvɪpboːgən], *m.* (—s, *pl.* —) (*Archit.*) flying buttress.
Schwiegersohn ['ʃviːgərzoːn], *m.* (—s, *pl.* ⸚e) son-in-law.
Schwiegertochter ['ʃviːgərtɔxtər], *f.* (—, *pl.* ⸚) daughter-in-law.
Schwiele ['ʃviːlə], *f.* (—, *pl.* —n) hard skin, callus, weal.
schwielig ['ʃviːlɪç], *adj.* callous, horny.
schwierig ['ʃviːrɪç], *adj.* difficult, hard.
Schwierigkeit ['ʃviːrɪçkaɪt], *f.* (—, *pl.* —en) difficulty; *auf —en stoßen*, meet with difficulties.
schwimmen ['ʃvɪmən], *v.n. irr.* (*aux.* sein) swim, float.
Schwimmer ['ʃvɪmər], *m.* (—s, *pl.* —) swimmer.

Schwimmgürtel ['ʃvɪmgyrtəl], *m.* (—s, *pl.* —) life-belt.
Schwindel ['ʃvɪndəl], *m.* (—s, *pl.* —) giddiness, dizziness, vertigo; swindle, fraud.
Schwindelanfall ['ʃvɪndəlanfal], *m.* (—s, *pl.* ⸚e) attack of giddiness, vertigo.
Schwindelei [ʃvɪndə'laɪ], *f.* (—, *pl.* —en) swindle, fraud, deceit.
schwindelhaft ['ʃvɪndəlhaft], *adj.* fraudulent.
schwinden ['ʃvɪndən], *v.n. irr.* (*aux.* sein) dwindle; disappear, vanish.
Schwindler ['ʃvɪndlər], *m.* (—s, *pl.* —) swindler, humbug, cheat.
schwindlig ['ʃvɪndlɪç], *adj.* dizzy, giddy.
Schwindsucht ['ʃvɪntzuxt], *f.* (—, *no pl.*) (*Med.*) tuberculosis, consumption.
schwindsüchtig ['ʃvɪntzyçtɪç], *adj.* (*Med.*) tubercular.
Schwinge ['ʃvɪŋə], *f.* (—, *pl.* —n) wing.
schwingen ['ʃvɪŋən], *v.a. irr.* brandish. — *v.n.* swing, vibrate. — *v.r. sich* —, vault; *sich auf den Thron* —, usurp *or* take possession of the throne.
Schwingung ['ʃvɪŋuŋ], *f.* (—, *pl.* —en) vibration, oscillation.
Schwips [ʃvɪps], *m.* (—es, *pl.* —e) (*coll.*) tipsiness; *einen* — *haben*, be tipsy.
schwirren ['ʃvɪrən], *v.n.* whir, buzz.
Schwitzbad ['ʃvɪtsbaːt], *n.* (—es, *pl.* ⸚er) Turkish bath, steam-bath.
schwitzen ['ʃvɪtsən], *v.n.* sweat, perspire.
schwören ['ʃvøːrən], *v.a., v.n. irr.* swear, take an oath; *darauf kannst du* —, you can be quite sure of that, you bet; *falsch* —, forswear o.s., perjure o.s.
schwül [ʃvyːl], *adj.* sultry, close.
Schwüle ['ʃvyːlə], *f.* (—, *no pl.*) sultriness.
Schwulst [ʃvulst], *m.* (—es, *no pl.*) bombast.
schwülstig ['ʃvylstɪç], *adj.* bombastic, turgid.
Schwülstigkeit ['ʃvylstɪçkaɪt], *f.* (—, *pl.* —en) bombastic style, turgidity.
Schwund [ʃvunt], *m.* (—(e)s, *no pl.*) dwindling, decline; shrinkage.
Schwung [ʃvuŋ], *m.* (—(e)s, *pl.* ⸚e) swing, leap, bound; (*fig.*) verve, élan; (*Poet.*) flight, soaring.
schwunghaft ['ʃvuŋhaft], *adj.* flourishing, soaring.
Schwungkraft ['ʃvuŋkraft], *f.* (—, *no pl.*) centrifugal force; (*mental*) resilience.
Schwungrad ['ʃvuŋraːt], *n.* (—s, *pl.* ⸚er) fly-wheel.
schwungvoll ['ʃvunfɔl], *adj.* spirited.
Schwur [ʃvuːr], *m.* (—(e)s, *pl.* ⸚e) oath.
Schwurgericht ['ʃvuːrgərɪçt], *n.* (—s, *pl.* —e) (*Law*) assizes.
sechs [zɛks], *num. adj.* six.
Sechseck ['zɛksɛk], *n.* (—s, *pl.* —e) hexagon.
sechseckig ['zɛksɛkɪç], *adj.* hexagonal.

Segen

Sechser ['zɛksər], *m.* (—s, *pl.* —) coin of small value.
sechsspännig ['zɛksʃpɛnɪç], *adj.* drawn by six horses.
sechzehn ['zɛçtseːn], *num. adj.* sixteen.
sechzig ['zɛçtsɪç], *num. adj.* sixty.
Sediment [zedi'mɛnt], *n.* (—s, *pl.* —e) sediment.
See (1) [zeː], *m.* (—s, *pl.* —n) lake, pool.
See (2) [zeː], *f.* (—, *no pl.*) sea, ocean; *hohe* —, high seas; *zur* — *gehen*, go to sea, become a sailor.
Seeadler ['zeːadlər], *m.* (—s, *pl.* —) (*Orn.*) osprey.
Seebad ['zeːbaːt], *n.* (—s, *pl.* ⁓er) seaside resort; bathe in the sea.
Seebär ['zeːbɛːr], *m.* (—en, *pl.* —en) (*fig.*) old salt.
Seefahrer ['zeːfaːrər], *m.* (—s, *pl.* —) mariner, navigator.
Seefahrt ['zeːfaːrt], *f.* (—, *pl.* —en) seafaring; voyage, cruise.
seefest ['zeːfɛst], *adj.* (*ship*) seaworthy; (*person*) a good sailor.
Seefischerei ['zeːfɪʃərai], *f.* (—, *no pl.*) deep-sea fishing.
Seeflotte ['zeːflɔtə], *f.* (—, *pl.* —n) navy, fleet.
Seegang ['zeːgaŋ], *m.* (—s, *no pl.*) swell.
Seegras ['zeːgraːs], *n.* (—es, *no pl.*) seaweed.
Seehandel ['zeːhandəl], *m.* (—s, *no pl.*) maritime trade.
Seehund ['zeːhunt], *m.* (—s, *pl.* —e) (*Zool.*) seal.
Seeigel ['zeːiːgəl], *m.* (—s, *pl.* —) (*Zool.*) sea-urchin.
Seejungfrau ['zeːjuŋfrau], *f.* (—, *pl.* —en) mermaid.
Seekadett ['zeːkadɛt], *m.* (—en, *pl.* —en) midshipman; (naval) cadet.
Seekarte ['zeːkartə], *f.* (—, *pl.* —n) chart.
seekrank ['zeːkraŋk], *adj.* seasick.
Seekrieg ['zeːkriːk], *m.* (—s, *pl.* —e) naval war.
Seeküste ['zeːkystə], *f.* (—, *pl.* —n) sea-coast, shore, beach.
Seele [zeːlə], *f.* (—, *pl.* —n) soul; *mit ganzer* —, with all my heart.
Seelenamt ['zeːlənamt], *n.* (—s, *pl.* ⁓er) (*Eccl.*) office for the dead, requiem.
Seelenangst ['zeːlənaŋkst], *f.* (—, *pl.* ⁓e) anguish, agony.
Seelenheil ['zeːlənhail], *n.* (—s, *no pl.*) (*Theol.*) salvation.
Seelenhirt ['zeːlənhirt], *m.* (—en, *pl.* —en) pastor.
seelenlos ['zeːlənloːs], *adj.* inanimate.
Seelenmesse ['zeːlənmɛsə], *f.* (—, *pl.* —n) requiem; Mass for the dead.
Seelenruhe ['zeːlənruːə], *f.* (—, *no pl.*) tranquillity of mind.
seelenruhig ['zeːlənruːiç], *adj.* cool, calm, collected, unperturbed.
Seelenstärke ['zeːlənʃtɛrkə], *f.* (—, *no pl.*) fortitude; composure.

seelenvergnügt ['zeːlənfɛrgnyːkt], *adj.* blissfully happy.
Seelenverwandtschaft ['zeːlənfɛrvantʃaft], *f.* (—, *pl.* —en) mental affinity, (mutual) understanding.
seelenvoll ['zeːlənfɔl], *adj.* wistful, soulful.
Seelenwanderung ['zeːlənvandəruŋ], *f.* (—, *no pl.*) transmigration of souls, metempsychosis.
Seeleute ['zeːlɔytə] *see under* **Seemann.**
seelisch ['zeːlɪʃ], *adj.* mental, psychological, psychic(al).
Seelsorge ['zeːlzɔrgə], *f.* (—, *no pl.*) (*Eccl.*) cure of souls; pastoral duties or work.
Seemann ['zeːman], *m.* (—s, *pl.* ⁓er, **Seeleute**) seaman, sailor, mariner.
Seemeile ['zeːmailə], *f.* (—, *pl.* —n) knot, nautical mile.
Seemöwe ['zeːmøːvə], *f.* (—, *pl.* —n) (*Orn.*) seagull.
Seemuschel ['zeːmuʃəl], *f.* (—, *pl.* —n) sea-shell.
Seepflanze ['zeːpflantsə], *f.* (—, *pl.* —n) marine plant.
Seerabe ['zeːraːbə], *m.* (—n, *pl.* —n) (*Orn.*) cormorant.
Seeräuber ['zeːrɔybər], *m.* (—s, *pl.* —) pirate.
Seerose ['zeːroːzə], *f.* (—, *pl.* —n) (*Bot.*) water-lily.
Seesalz ['zeːzalts], *n.* (—es, *no pl.*) bay salt, sea salt.
Seeschlacht ['zeːʃlaxt], *f.* (—, *pl.* —en) naval engagement, naval battle.
Seestern ['zeːʃtɛrn], *m.* (—s, *pl.* —e) (*Zool.*) starfish.
Seestille ['zeːʃtɪlə], *f.* (—, *no pl.*) calm (at sea).
Seetang ['zeːtaŋ], *m.* (—s, *no pl.*) (*Bot.*) seaweed.
seetüchtig ['zeːtyçtɪç], *adj.* seaworthy.
Seeuhr ['zeːuːr], *f.* (—, *pl.* —en) marine chronometer.
Seeuntüchtigkeit ['zeːuntyçtɪçkait], *f.* (—, *no pl.*) unseaworthiness.
Seewasser ['zeːvasər], *n.* (—s, *no pl.*) sea-water, brine.
Seewesen ['zeːvezən], *n.* (—s, *no pl.*) naval affairs.
Seezunge ['zeːtsuŋə], *f.* (—, *pl.* —n) sole (*fish*).
Segel ['zeːgəl], *n.* (—s, *pl.* —) sail; *großes* —, mainsail; *unter* — *gehen*, set sail, put to sea; *die* — *streichen*, strike sail.
segelfertig ['zeːgəlfɛrtɪç], *adj.* ready to sail; *sich* — *machen*, get under sail.
Segelflugzeug ['zeːgəlfluːktsɔyk], *n.* (—s, *pl.* —e) glider(-plane).
Segelschiff ['zeːgəlʃif], *n.* (—s, *pl.* —e) sailing-vessel.
Segelstange ['zeːgəlʃtaŋə], *f.* (—, *pl.* —n) sail-yard.
Segen ['zeːgən], *m.* (—s, *no pl.*) blessing, benediction; (*fig.*) abundance; — *sprechen*, give the blessing, say grace.

197

segensreich ['ze:gənsraɪç], *adj.* blessed, full of blessings; prosperous.

Segenswunsch ['ze:gənsvunʃ], *m.* (—es, *pl.* ⁻e) good wish.

segnen ['ze:gnən], *v.a.* bless.

sehen ['ze:ən], *v.a. irr.* see, behold, perceive; *etwas gern* —, like s.th., approve of s.th. — *v.n.* look, see; *sich* — *lassen*, parade, show o.s., *wir werden* —, that remains to be seen, we shall see.

sehenswert ['ze:ənsve:rt], *adj.* worth seeing.

Sehenswürdigkeit ['ze:ənsvyrdɪçkaɪt], *f.* (—, *pl.* —en) curiosity, object of interest, tourist attraction; (*pl.*) sights.

Seher ['ze:ər], *m.* (—s, *pl.* —) seer, prophet.

Sehne ['ze:nə], *f.* (—, *pl.* —n) sinew, tendon; string.

sehnig ['ze:nɪç], *adj.* sinewy, muscular; (*meat*) tough.

sehnlich ['ze:nlɪç], *adj.* earnest, passionate, eager.

Sehnsucht ['ze:nzuxt], *f.* (—, *no pl.*) longing, yearning, desire.

sehr [ze:r], *adv.* very, much, greatly, very much; *zu* —, too much; — *gut*, very good; — *wohl*, very well.

Sehweite ['ze:vaɪtə], *f.* (—, *no pl.*) range of vision.

seicht [zaɪçt], *adj.* shallow, superficial.

Seide ['zaɪdə], *f.* (—, *pl.* —n) silk.

Seidel ['zaɪdəl], *n.* (—s, *pl.* —) (*dial.*) mug, tankard; pint.

seiden ['zaɪdən], *adj.* silk, silken, silky.

Seidenpapier ['zaɪdənpapi:r], *n.* (—s, *no pl.*) tissue-paper.

Seidenraupe ['zaɪdənraupə], *f.* (—, *pl.* —n) (*Ent.*) silkworm.

Seidenstoff ['zaɪdənʃtɔf], *m.* (—es, *pl.* —e) spun silk.

Seife ['zaɪfə], *f.* (—, *pl.* —n) soap; *ein Stück* —, a cake of soap.

seifen ['zaɪfən], *v.a.* soap.

Seifenschaum ['zaɪfənʃaum], *m.* (—s, *no pl.*) lather.

Seifenwasser ['zaɪfənvasər], *n.* (—s, *no pl.*) soap-suds.

seifig ['zaɪfɪç], *adj.* soapy, saponaceous.

seihen ['zaɪən], *v.a.* strain, filter.

Seil [zaɪl], *n.* (—(e)s, *pl.* —e) rope; *straffes* —, taut rope, tight rope; *schlaffes* —, slack rope.

Seilbahn ['zaɪlba:n], *f.* (—, *pl.* —en) funicular railway; cable car.

Seilbrücke ['zaɪlbrykə], *f.* (—, *pl.* —n) rope bridge.

Seiltänzer ['zaɪltɛntsər], *m.* (—s, *pl.* —) tight-rope walker.

Seilziehen ['zaɪltsi:ən], *n.* (—s, *no pl.*) tug of war.

Seim [zaɪm], *m.* (—(e)s, *pl.* —e) strained honey.

Sein [zaɪn], *n.* (—s, *no pl.*) being, existence.

sein (1) [zaɪn], *v.n. irr.* (*aux.* sein) be, exist.

sein (2) [zaɪn], *poss. adj.* his, her, its; one's. — *pers. pron.* his.

seinerseits ['zaɪnərzaɪts], *adv.* for his part.

seinerzeit ['zaɪnərtsaɪt], *adv.* at that time, at the time, formerly.

seinesgleichen ['zaɪnəsglaɪçən], *indecl. adj. & pron.* of his sort, such as he.

seinethalben ['zaɪnəthalbən], *adv.* on his account, for his sake, on his behalf.

seinetwegen ['zaɪnətve:gən], *adv.* on his account, for his sake, on his behalf.

Seinige ['zaɪnɪgə], *n.* (—n, *pl.* —n) his, his property; (*pl.*) his family, his people; *das* — *tun*, do o.'s share.

seit [zaɪt], *prep.* (*Dat.*) since, for; — *gestern*, since yesterday, from yesterday onwards; — *einiger Zeit*, for some time past. — *conj. see* seitdem.

seitdem [zaɪt'de:m], *adv.* since then, since that time. — *conj.* since.

Seite ['zaɪtə], *f.* (—, *pl.* —n) side, flank; (*book*) page; *etwas auf die* — *bringen*, put s.th. aside; *ich bin auf seiner* —, I side with him, I am on his side; *er hat seine guten* —n, he has his good points.

Seitenansicht ['zaɪtənanzɪçt], *f.* (—, *pl.* —en) profile.

Seitengleis ['zaɪtənglaɪs], *n.* (—es, *pl.* —e) (*railway*) siding.

Seitenhieb ['zaɪtənhi:p], *m.* (—s, *pl.* —e) innuendo, sly hit, dig.

seitens ['zaɪtəns], *prep.* (*Genit.*) on the part of.

Seitensprung ['zaɪtənʃpruŋ], *m.* (—s, *pl.* ⁻e) side-leap, caper; (*fig.*) (amorous) escapade.

Seitenstraße ['zaɪtənʃtra:sə], *f.* (—, *pl.* —n) side-street.

Seitenstück ['zaɪtənʃtyk], *n.* (—s, *pl.* —e) companion-piece.

Seitenzahl ['zaɪtəntsa:l], *f.* (—, *pl.* —en) page-number; number of pages.

seither [zaɪt'he:r], *adv.* since that time, since then.

seitlich ['zaɪtlɪç], *adj.* lateral.

Sekretär [zekre'tɛ:r], *m.* (—s, *pl.* —e) secretary.

Sekretariat [zekreta'rja:t], *n.* (—s, *pl.* —e) secretariat, secretary's office.

Sekt [zɛkt], *m.* (—s, *pl.* —e) champagne.

Sekte ['zɛktə], *f.* (—, *pl.* —n) sect.

Sektierer [zɛk'ti:rər], *m.* (—s, *pl.* —) sectarian.

Sektion [zɛk'tsjo:n] *f.* (—, *pl.* —en) section; (*Med.*) dissection.

Sekundaner [zekun'da:nər], *m.* (—s, *pl.* —) pupil in the second (highest) form.

Sekundant [zekun'dant], *m.* (—en, *pl.* —en) (*Duelling*) second.

sekundär [zekun'dɛ:r], *adj.* secondary.

Sekunde [ze'kundə], *f.* (—, *pl.* —n) (*time*) second.

Sekundenzeiger [ze'kundəntsaɪgər], *m.* (—s, *pl.* —) (*clock*) second-hand.

sekundieren [zekun'di:rən], *v.n. einem* —, second s.o.

selber ['zɛlbər], *indecl. adj. & pron.* self.

selb(ig) ['zɛlb(ɪg)], *adj.* the same.

selbst [zɛlpst], *indecl. adj. & pron.* self; — *ist der Mann*, depend on yourself; *von* —, of its own accord, spontaneously. — *adv.* even; — *wenn*, even if, even though; — *dann nicht*, not even then.

selbständig ['zɛlpʃtɛndɪç], *adj.* independent.

Selbstbestimmung ['zɛlpstbəʃtɪmuŋ], *f.* (—, *no pl.*) self-determination, autonomy.

selbstbewußt ['zɛlpstbəvust], *adj.* self-assertive, self-confident, conceited.

selbstherrlich ['zɛlpstherlɪç], *adj.* autocratic, tyrannical.

Selbstlaut ['zɛlpstlaut], *m.* (—s, *pl.* —e) vowel.

selbstlos ['zɛlpstlo:s], *adj.* unselfish, selfless, altruistic.

Selbstlosigkeit [zɛlpst'lo:zɪçkaɪt], *f.* (—, *no pl.*) unselfishness, altruism.

Selbstmord ['zɛlpstmɔrt], *m.* (—s, *pl.* —e) suicide.

selbstredend ['zɛlpstre:dənt], *adj.* self-evident, obvious.

Selbstsucht ['zɛlpstzuxt], *f.* (—, *no pl.*) selfishness, ego(t)ism.

selbstsüchtig ['zɛlpstzyçtɪç], *adj.* selfish, ego(t)istic(al).

selbstverständlich ['zɛlpstferʃtɛntlɪç], *adj.* self-evident. — *adv.* of course, obviously.

Selbstzweck ['zɛlpsttsvɛk], *m.* (—s, *no pl.*) end in itself.

selig ['ze:lɪç], *adj.* blessed, blissful; (*fig.*) delighted; deceased, late; — *sprechen*, beatify.

Seligkeit ['ze:lɪçkaɪt], *f.* (—, *pl.* —en) bliss, blissfulness; (*Eccl.*) salvation, beatitude.

Seligsprechung ['ze:lɪçʃpreçuŋ], *f.* (—, *pl.* —en) beatification.

Sellerie ['zɛləri:], *m.* (—s, *pl.* —s) (*Bot.*) celery.

selten ['zɛltən], *adj.* rare, scarce; (*fig.*) remarkable. — *adv.* seldom, rarely, infrequently.

Seltenheit ['zɛltənhaɪt], *f.* (—, *pl.* —en) rarity, curiosity, scarcity; (*fig.*) remarkableness.

Selterwasser ['zɛltərvasər], *n.* (—s, *no pl.*) soda-water.

seltsam ['zɛltza:m], *adj.* strange, unusual, odd, curious.

Semester [ze'mɛstər], *n.* (—s, *pl.* —) university term, semester.

Semit [ze'mi:t], *m.* (—en, *pl.* —en) Semite, Jew.

semmelblond ['zɛməlblɔnt], *adj.* flaxen-haired.

Semmelkloß ['zɛməlklo:s], *m.* (—es, *pl.* ̈e) bread dumpling.

Senator [ze'na:tɔr], *m.* (—s, *pl.* —en) senator.

senden ['zɛndən], *v.a. irr.* send, despatch; (*money*) remit. — *v.a. reg.* (*Rad.*) broadcast.

Sender ['zɛndər], *m.* (—s, *pl.* —) sender; (*Rad.*) (broadcasting) station, transmitter.

Sendling ['zɛntlɪŋ], *m.* (—s, *pl.* —e) (*Poet.*) emissary.

Sendschreiben ['zɛntʃraɪbən], *n.* (—s, *pl.* —) epistle, missive.

Sendung ['zɛnduŋ], *f.* (—, *pl.* —en) (*Comm.*) shipment, consignment; (*fig.*) mission; (*Rad.*) broadcast, transmission.

Senegal ['ze:nəgal], *n.* Senegal.

Senf [zɛnf], *m.* (—s, *no pl.*) mustard.

sengen ['zɛŋən], *v.a.* singe, scorch; — *und brennen*, lay waste.

Senkblei ['zɛŋkblaɪ], *n.* (—s, *pl.* —e) plummet.

Senkel ['zɛŋkəl], *m.* (—s, *pl.* —) shoe-lace.

senken ['zɛŋkən], *v.a.* lower, sink. — *v.r. sich* —, sink, go down; dip, slope, subside.

senkrecht ['zɛŋkrɛçt], *adj.* perpendicular.

Senkung ['zɛŋkuŋ], *f.* (—, *pl.* —en) depression, dip, subsidence.

Senn(e) ['zɛn(ə)], *m.* (—n, *pl.* —(e)n) Alpine herdsman.

Sennerin ['zɛnərɪn], *f.* (—, *pl.* —nen) Alpine dairy-woman.

Senneschoten ['zɛnəʃo:tən], *f. pl.* senna pods.

Sennhütte ['zɛnhytə], *f.* (—, *pl.* —n) Alpine dairy; chalet.

sensationell [zɛnzatsjo'nɛl], *adj.* sensational.

Sense ['zɛnzə], *f.* (—, *pl.* —n) scythe.

sensibel [zɛn'zi:bəl], *adj.* sensitive.

Sentenz [zɛn'tɛnts], *f.* (—, *pl.* —en) aphorism.

sentimental [zɛntimɛn'ta:l], *adj.* sentimental.

separat [zepa'ra:t], *adj.* separate, special.

September [zɛp'tɛmbər], *m.* (—s, *pl.* —) September.

Serbien ['zɛrbjən], *n.* Serbia.

Serie ['ze:rjə], *f.* (—, *pl.* —n) series.

Service [zɛr'vi:s], *n.* (—s, *pl.* —) dinner-set, dinner-service.

servieren [zɛr'vi:rən], *v.a., v.n.* serve, wait at table.

Serviertisch [zɛr'vi:rtɪʃ], *m.* (—es, *pl.* —e) sideboard.

Sessel ['zɛsəl], *m.* (—s, *pl.* —) armchair, easy-chair; (*Austr. dial.*) chair.

seßhaft ['zɛshaft], *adj.* settled, domiciled.

setzen ['zɛtsən], *v.a.* set, put, place; (*monument*) erect; (*bet*) stake; (*Typ.*) compose. — *v.r. sich* —, sit down; (*coffee*) settle; *sich bei einem in Gunst* —, ingratiate o.s. with s.o.

Setzer ['zɛtsər], *m.* (—s, *pl.* —) compositor.

Setzling ['zɛtslɪŋ], *m.* (—s, *pl.* —e) young tree, young plant.

Seuche ['zɔyçə], *f.* (—, *pl.* —n) pestilence; epidemic.

seufzen ['zɔyftsən], *v.n.* sigh.

Seufzer ['zɔyftsər], *m.* (—s, *pl.* —) sigh.

Sexta ['zɛksta:], *f.* (—, *pl.* —s) (*Sch.*) sixth form, lowest form.

Sextant

Sextant [zɛks'tant], *m.* (—en, *pl.* —en) sextant.

sexuell [zɛksu'ɛl], *adj.* sexual.

sezieren [ze'tsi:rən], *v.a.* dissect.

Seziersaal [ze'tsi:rza:l], *m.* (—s, *pl.* —säle) dissecting-room.

Sibirien [zi'bi:rjən], *n.* Siberia.

sich [zɪç], *pron.* oneself, himself, herself, itself, themselves; each other.

Sichel ['zɪçəl], *f.* (—, *pl.* —n) sickle.

sicher ['zɪçər], *adj.* certain, sure, secure, safe; confident, positive; *seiner Sache — sein*, be sure of o.'s ground; — *stellen*, secure.

Sicherheit ['zɪçərhaɪt], *f.* (—, *pl.* —en) certainty; security, safety; confidence, positiveness; *in — bringen*, secure.

sichern ['zɪçərn], *v.a.* secure, make secure; assure, ensure.

Sicherung ['zɪçəruŋ], *f.* (—, *pl.* —en) securing; (*Elec.*) fuse; (*gun*) safety-catch.

Sicht [zɪçt], *f.* (—, *no pl.*) sight.

sichtbar ['zɪçtba:r], *adj.* visible; conspicuous.

sichten ['zɪçtən], *v.a.* sift, sort out; sight.

sichtlich ['zɪçtlɪç], *adv.* visibly.

Sichtwechsel ['zɪçtvɛksəl], *m.* (—s, *pl.* —) (*Banking*) sight-bill, bill payable on sight.

Sichtweite ['zɪçtvaɪtə], *f.* (—, *no pl.*) range of vision.

sickern ['zɪkərn], *v.n.* (*aux.* sein) leak, ooze, seep.

Sie [zi:], *pron.* (*formal*) you.

sie [zi:], *pers. pron.* she, her; they, them.

Sieb [zi:p], *n.* (—(e)s, *pl.* —e) sieve; riddle; colander.

sieben (1) ['zi:bən], *v.a.* (*Cul.*) sift, strain.

sieben (2) ['zi:bən], *num. adj.* seven; *meine — Sachen*, my belongings.

Siebeneck ['zi:bənɛk], *n.* (—s, *pl.* —e) heptagon.

Siebengestirn ['zi:bəngəʃtɪrn], *n.* (—s, *no pl.*) Pleiades.

siebenmal ['zi:bənma:l], *adv.* seven times.

Siebenmeilenstiefel [zi:bən'maɪlənʃti:fəl], *m. pl.* seven-league boots.

Siebenschläfer ['zi:bənʃlɛːfər], *m.* (—s, *pl.* —) lazy-bones.

siebzehn ['zi:ptse:n], *num. adj.* seventeen.

siebzig ['zi:ptsɪç], *num. adj.* seventy.

siech [zi:ç], *adj.* (*rare*) sick, infirm.

siechen ['zi:çən], *v.n.* be in bad health.

sieden ['zi:dən], *v.a., v.n.* boil, seethe.

siedeln ['zi:dəln], *v.n.* settle.

Siedlung ['zi:dluŋ], *f.* (—, *pl.* —en) settlement; housing estate.

Sieg [zi:k], *m.* (—(e)s, *pl.* —e) victory; *den — davontragen*, win the day.

Siegel ['zi:gəl], *n.* (—s, *pl.* —) seal; *Brief und —*, sign and seal.

Siegelbewahrer ['zi:gəlbəva:rər], *m.* (—s, *pl.* —) Lord Privy Seal; keeper of the seal.

Siegellack ['zi:gəllak], *n.* (—s, *no pl.*) sealing wax.

siegeln ['zi:gəln], *v.a.* seal.

siegen ['zi:gən], *v.n.* conquer, win, be victorious, triumph (over).

Sieger ['zi:gər], *m.* (—s, *pl.* —) victor, conqueror.

Siegesbogen ['zi:gəsbo:gən], *m.* (—s, *pl.* ˙) triumphal arch.

Siegeszeichen ['zi:gəstsaɪçən], *n.* (—s, *pl.* —) sign of victory, trophy.

sieghaft ['zi:khaft], *adj.* victorious, triumphant.

siegreich ['zi:kraɪç], *adj.* victorious, triumphant.

siehe! ['zi:ə], *excl.* see! look! lo and behold!

Sierra Leone ['siɛra le'o:nə], *f.* Sierra Leone.

Signal [zɪg'na:l], *n.* (—s, *pl.* —e) signal.

Signalement [zɪgnalə'mã], *n.* (—s, *pl.* —s) personal description.

Signalglocke [zɪg'na:lglɔkə], *f.* (—, *pl.* —n) warning-bell.

signalisieren [zɪgnali'zi:rən], *v.a.* signal.

Signatarmacht [zɪgna'ta:rmaxt], *f.* (—, *pl.* ˙e) signatory power.

signieren [zɪg'ni:rən], *v.a.* sign.

Silbe ['zɪlbə], *f.* (—, *pl.* —n) syllable.

Silbenmaß ['zɪlbənma:s], *n.* (—es, *pl.* —e) (*Poet.*) metre.

Silbenrätsel ['zɪlbənrɛːtsəl], *n.* (—s, *pl.* —) charade.

Silber ['zɪlbər], *n.* (—s, *no pl.*) silver; plate.

Silberbuche ['zɪlbərbu:xə], *f.* (—, *pl.* —n) white beech(-tree).

Silberfuchs ['zɪlbərfuks], *m.* (—es, *pl.* ˙e) (*Zool.*) silver fox.

silbern ['zɪlbərn], *adj.* made of silver, silvery.

Silberpappel ['zɪlbərpapəl], *f.* (—, *pl.* —n) (*Bot.*) white poplar(-tree).

Silberschimmel ['zɪlbərʃɪməl], *m.* (—s, *pl.* —) grey-white horse.

Silberzeug ['zɪlbərtsɔyk], *n.* (—(e)s, *pl.* —) (silver) plate.

Silvester [zɪl'vɛstər], *m.* (—s, *pl.* —) New Year's Eve.

Similistein ['zi:milɪʃtaɪn], *m.* (—s, *pl.* —e) imitation *or* paste jewellery.

Sims [zɪms], *m.* (—es, *pl.* —e) cornice, moulding, shelf, ledge.

Simulant [zimu'lant], *m.* (—en, *pl.* —en) malingerer.

simulieren [zimu'li:rən], *v.a.* simulate.

simultan [zimul'ta:n], *adj.* simultaneous.

Singapur [zɪŋga'pu:r], *n.* Singapore.

Singdrossel ['zɪŋdrɔsəl], *f.* (—, *pl.* —n) (*Orn.*) common thrush.

singen ['zɪŋən], *v.a., v.n. irr.* sing.

Singspiel ['zɪŋʃpi:l], *n.* (—s, *pl.* —e) musical comedy, light opera, opera buffa.

Singular ['zɪŋgula:r], *m.* (—s, *pl.* —e) singular.

skrupulös

sinken ['zıŋkən], *v.n. irr.* (*aux.* sein) sink; (*price*) decline, drop, fall; *den Mut — lassen*, lose heart.

Sinn [zın], *m.* (—(e)s, *pl.* —e) sense; intellect, mind; consciousness, memory; taste, meaning, purport; wish; *etwas im — haben*, have s.th. in mind, intend s.th.; *leichter —*, lightheartedness; *andern —es werden*, change o's mind; *das hat keinen —*, there is no sense in that; *von —en sein*, be out of o.'s senses; *seine fünf —e beisammen haben*, be in o.'s right mind; *sich etwas aus dem — schlagen*, dismiss s.th. from o.'s mind; *es kommt mir in den —*, it occurs to me.

Sinnbild ['zınbılt], *n.* (—s, *pl.* —er) symbol, emblem.

sinnen ['zınən], *v.n. irr.* meditate, reflect.

Sinnesänderung ['zınəsɛndəruŋ], *f.* (—, *pl.* —en) change of mind.

Sinnesart ['zınəsa:rt], *f.* (—, *no pl.*) disposition, character.

Sinnesorgan ['zınəsɔrga:n], *n.* (—s, *pl.* —e) sense-organ.

Sinnestäuschung ['zınəstɔyʃuŋ], *f.* (—, *pl.* —en) illusion, hallucination.

sinnfällig ['zınfɛlıç], *adj.* obvious, striking.

Sinngedicht ['zıngədıçt], *n.* (—es, *pl.* —e) epigram.

sinnig ['zınıç], *adj.* thoughtful, meaningful; judicious, fitting.

sinnlich ['zınlıç], *adj.* sensual, sensuous.

Sinnlichkeit ['zınlıçkaıt], *f.* (—, *no pl.*) sensuality, sensuousness.

sinnlos ['zınlo:s], *adj.* senseless, meaningless, pointless.

sinnreich ['zınraıç], *adj.* ingenious.

Sinnspruch ['zınʃprux], *m.* (—es, *pl.* ˙e) sentence, maxim, device, motto.

sinnverwandt ['zınfɛrvant], *adj.* synonymous.

sinnvoll ['zınfɔl], *adj.* meaningful, significant.

sinnwidrig ['zınvi:drıç], *adj.* nonsensical, absurd.

Sintflut ['zıntflu:t], *f.* (—, *no pl.*) (*Bibl.*) the Flood.

Sinus ['zi:nus], *m.* (—, *pl.* —se) (*Maths.*) sine.

Sippe ['zıpə], *f.* (—, *pl.* —n) kin, tribe, family, clan.

Sippschaft ['zıpʃaft], *f.* (—, *pl.* —en) kindred; *die ganze —*, the whole caboodle.

Sirene [zi're:nə], *f.* (—, *pl.* —n) siren.

Sirup ['zi:rup], *m.* (—s, *no pl.*) syrup, treacle.

Sitte ['zıtə], *f.* (—, *pl.* —n) custom, mode, fashion; (*pl.*) manners, morals; *—n und Gebräuche*, manners and customs.

Sittengesetz ['zıtəngəzɛts], *n.* (—es, *pl.* —e) moral law.

Sittenlehre ['zıtənle:rə], *f.* (—, *no pl.*) moral philosophy, ethics.

sittenlos ['zıtənlo:s], *adj.* immoral, profligate, licentious.

Sittenprediger ['zıtənpre:dıgər], *m.* (—s, *pl.* —) moraliser.

Sittich ['zıtıç], *m.* (—s, *pl.* —e) (*Orn.*) budgerigar; parakeet.

sittig ['zıtıç], *adj.* well-behaved.

sittlich ['zıtlıç], *adj.* moral.

Sittlichkeit ['zıtlıçkaıt], *f.* (—, *no pl.*) morality, morals.

sittsam ['zıtza:m], *adj.* modest, demure.

situiert [zitu'i:rt], *adj. gut* (*schlecht*) —, well (badly) off.

Sitz [zıts], *m.* (—es, *pl.* —e) seat, chair; residence, location, place; (*Eccl.*) see.

Sitzarbeit ['zıtsarbaıt], *f.* (—, *pl.* —en) sedentary work.

Sitzbad ['zıtsba:t], *n.* (—(e)s, *pl.* ˙er) hip bath.

sitzen ['zıtsən], *v.n. irr.* sit, be seated; (*fig.*) be in prison; (*dress*) fit; *— lassen*, throw over, jilt; *— bleiben*, remain seated; (*school*) stay in the same class, not be moved up; be a wallflower; remain unmarried.

Sitzfleisch ['zıtsflaıʃ], *n.* (—es, *no pl.*) (*coll.*) *kein — haben*, be restless, lack application.

Sitzplatz ['zıtsplats], *m.* (—es, *pl.* ˙e) seat.

Sitzung ['zıtsuŋ], *f.* (—, *pl.* —en) meeting, sitting, session.

Sitzungsprotokoll ['zıtsuŋsprotokɔl], *n.* (—s, *pl.* —e) minutes (of a meeting).

Sitzungssaal ['zıtsuŋsza:l], *m.* (—s, *pl.* —säle) board-room, conference room.

Sizilien [zi'tsi:ljən], *n.* Sicily.

Skala ['ska:la], *f.* (—, *pl.* —len) scale; (*Mus.*) gamut.

Skandal [skan'da:l], *m.* (—s, *pl.* —e) scandal; row, riot; *— machen*, kick up a row.

skandalös [skanda'lø:s], *adj.* scandalous.

skandieren [skan'di:rən], *v.a.* (*Poet.*) scan.

Skandinavien [skandı'na:vjən], *n.* Scandinavia.

Skelett [ske'lɛt], *n.* (—s, *pl.* —e) skeleton.

Skepsis ['skɛpsıs], *f.* (—, *no pl.*) scepticism, doubt.

skeptisch ['skɛptıʃ], *adj.* sceptical, doubtful.

Skizze ['skıtsə], *f.* (—, *pl.* —n) sketch.

skizzieren [skı'tsi:rən], *v.a.* sketch.

Sklave ['skla:və], *m.* (—n, *pl.* —n) slave; *zum —n machen*, enslave.

Sklavendienst ['skla:vəndi:nst], *m.* (—es, *no pl.*) slavery.

Sklaverei [skla:və'raı], *f.* (—, *no pl.*) slavery, thraldom.

Skonto ['skɔnto], *m. & n.* (—s, *pl.* —s) discount.

Skrupel ['skru:pəl], *m.* (—s, *pl.* —) scruple; *sich — machen*, have scruples.

skrupulös [skrupu'lø:s], *adj.* scrupulous, meticulous.

201

Skulptur

Skulptur [skulp'tu:r], *f.* (—, *pl.* —en) sculpture.

skurril [sku'ri:l], *adj.* ludicrous.

Slawe ['sla:və], *m.* (—n, *pl.* —n) Slav.

slawisch ['sla:vɪʃ], *adj.* Slav, Slavonic.

Slowake [slo'va:kə], *m.* (—n, *pl.* —n) Slovakian.

Slowene [slo've:nə], *m.* (—n, *pl.* —n) Slovenian.

Smaragd [sma'rakt], *m.* (—(e)s, *pl.* —e) emerald.

smaragden [sma'raktən], *adj.* emerald.

Smoking ['smo:kɪŋ], *m.* (—s, *pl.* —s) dinner-jacket.

so [zo:], *adv.* so, thus, in this way, like this; —? really? — *ist es*, that is how it is; — *daß*, so that; — ... *wie*, as ... as; *na — was!* well, I never! — *conj.* then, therefore.

sobald [zo'balt], *conj.* as soon as, directly.

Socke ['zɔkə], *f.* (—, *pl.* —n) sock.

Sockel ['zɔkəl], *m.* (—s, *pl.* —) pedestal, plinth, stand, base.

Soda ['zo:da], *n.* (—s, *no pl.*) (carbonate of) soda.

sodann [zo'dan], *adv. conj.* then.

Sodbrennen ['zo:tbrɛnən], *n.* (—s, *no pl.*) heartburn.

soeben [zo'e:bən], *adv.* just now.

sofern [zo'fɛrn], *conj.* if, in case, so far as.

sofort [zo'fɔrt], *adv.* at once, immediately.

Sog [zo:k], *m.* (—(e)s, *pl.* —e) undertow, suction.

sogar [zo'ga:r], *adv.* even.

sogenannt [zogə'nant], *adj.* so-called, would-be.

sogleich [zo'glaɪç], *adv.* at once, immediately.

Sohle ['zo:lə], *f.* (—, *pl.* —n) sole; (*mine*) floor.

Sohn [zo:n], *m.* (—(e)s, *pl.* ⸚e) son; *der verlorene* —, the prodigal son.

solange [zo'laŋə], *conj.* as long as.

Solbad ['zo:lba:t], *n.* (—s, *pl.* ⸚er) saline bath.

solch [zɔlç], *adj., dem. pron.* such.

solcherlei ['zɔlçərlaɪ], *adj.* of such a kind, suchlike.

Sold [zɔlt], *m.* (—(e)s, *no pl.*) army pay.

Soldat [zɔl'da:t], *m.* (—en, *pl.* —en) soldier.

Soldateska [zɔlda'tɛska], *f.* (—, *pl.* —s) soldiery.

Söldner ['zœldnər], *m.* (—s, *pl.* —) mercenary, hireling.

Sole ['zo:lə], *f.* (—, *pl.* —n) salt-water, brine.

Solei ['zo:laɪ], *n.* (—s, *pl.* —er) pickled egg.

solidarisch [zoli'da:rɪʃ], *adj.* joint, jointly responsible; unanimous.

Solidarität [zolidari'tɛ:t], *f.* (—, *no pl.*) solidarity.

Solist [zo'lɪst], *m.* (—en, *pl.* —en) soloist.

Soll [zɔl], *n.* (—s, *no pl.*) debit; — *und Haben*, debit and credit.

sollen ['zɔlən], *v.n. irr.* be obliged, be compelled; have to; be supposed to; (*aux.*) shall, should etc.; *ich soll*, I must, I am to; *er soll krank sein*, he is said to be ill; *ich sollte eigentlich*, I really ought to.

Söller ['zœlər], *m.* (—s, *pl.* —) loft, garret, balcony.

Somali [zɔ'ma:li], *n.* Somalia.

somit [zo'mɪt], *adv.* consequently, therefore, accordingly.

Sommer ['zɔmər], *m.* (—s, *pl.* —) summer.

Sommerfäden ['zɔmərfɛ:dən], *m. pl.* gossamer.

Sommerfrische ['zɔmərfrɪʃə], *f.* (—, *pl.* —n) holiday resort.

Sommergetreide ['zɔmərgətraɪdə], *n.* (—s, *no pl.*) spring corn.

Sommersonnenwende ['zɔmərzɔnənvɛndə], *f.* (—, *pl.* —n) summer solstice.

Sommersprosse ['zɔmərʃprɔsə], *f.* (—, *pl.* —n) freckle.

sonach [zo'na:x], *adv.* therefore, consequently.

Sonate [zo'na:tə], *f.* (—, *pl.* —n) sonata.

Sonde ['zɔndə], *f.* (—, *pl.* —n) sounding-lead, plummet; probe.

sonder ['zɔndər], (*obs.*) *prep.* (*Acc.*) without.

Sonderausgabe ['zɔndərausga:bə], *f.* (—, *pl.* —n) separate edition; special edition.

Sonderausschuß ['zɔndərausʃus], *m.* (—sses, *pl.* ⸚sse) select committee.

sonderbar ['zɔndərba:r], *adj.* strange, odd, queer, singular, peculiar.

sonderlich ['zɔndərliç], *adj.* special, especial, particular. — *adv. nicht* —, not much.

Sonderling ['zɔndərlɪŋ], *m.* (—s, *pl.* —e) freak, odd character, crank.

sondern ['zɔndərn], *v.a.* separate, distinguish, differentiate. — *conj.* but; *nicht nur*, ... — *auch*, not only ... but also.

Sonderrecht ['zɔndərrɛçt], *n.* (—s, *pl.* —e) special privilege.

sonders ['zɔndərs], *adv.* samt und —, all and each, all and sundry.

Sonderstellung ['zɔndərʃtɛluŋ], *f.* (—, *no pl.*) exceptional position.

Sonderung ['zɔndəruŋ], *f.* (—, *pl.* —en) separation.

Sonderzug ['zɔndərtsu:k], *m.* (—s, *pl.* ⸚e) special train.

sondieren [zɔn'di:rən], *v.a.* (*wound*) probe; (*ocean*) plumb; (*fig.*) sound.

Sonett [zo'nɛt], *n.* (—(e)s, *pl.* —e) sonnet.

Sonnabend ['zɔna:bənt], *m.* (—s, *pl.* —e) Saturday.

Sonne ['zɔnə], *f.* (—, *pl.* —n) sun.

sonnen ['zɔnən], *v.r. sich* —, bask in the sun, sunbathe.

Sonnenaufgang ['zɔnənaufgaŋ], *m.* (—s, *pl.* ⸚e) sunrise.

Sonnenbrand ['zɔnənbrant], *m.* (—s, *pl.* ⸚e) sunburn.

Sonnendeck ['zɔnəndɛk], n. (—s, pl. —e) awning.

Sonnenfinsternis ['zɔnənfɪnstərnɪs], f. (—, pl. —se) eclipse of the sun.

sonnenklar ['zɔnənklaːr], adj. very clear, as clear as daylight.

Sonnenschirm ['zɔnənʃɪrm], m. (—s, pl. —e) parasol, sunshade.

Sonnenstich ['zɔnənʃtɪç], n. (—(e)s, no pl.) sunstroke.

Sonnenuhr ['zɔnənuːr], f. (—, pl. —en) sundial.

Sonnenuntergang ['zɔnənuntərgaŋ], m. (—s, pl. ⁝e) sunset.

Sonnenwende ['zɔnənvɛndə], f. (—, no pl.) solstice.

Sonntag ['zɔntaːk], m. (—s, pl. —e) Sunday.

sonntags ['zɔntaːks], adv. on Sundays, of a Sunday.

Sonntagsjäger ['zɔntaːksjɛːgər], m. (—s, pl. —) amateur sportsman.

sonor [zo'noːr], adj. sonorous.

sonst [zɔnst], adv. else, otherwise, besides, at other times; — noch etwas? anything else?

sonstig ['zɔnstɪç], adj. other, existing besides.

sonstwo ['zɔnstvo], adv. elsewhere, somewhere else.

Sopran [zo'praːn], m. (—s, pl. —e) soprano.

Sorbett ['zɔrbɛt], n. (—s, pl. —s) sherbet.

Sorge ['zɔrgə], f. (—, pl. —n) care; grief, worry; sorrow; anxiety; concern; (pl.) troubles, worries; — tragen dass . . . , see to it that . . . ; — tragen zu, take care of; — um, concern for.

sorgen ['zɔrgən], v.n. — für, care for, provide for, look after. — v.r. sich — um, worry about.

sorgenvoll ['zɔrgənfɔl], adj. uneasy, troubled, anxious.

Sorgfalt ['zɔrkfalt], f. (—, no pl.) care, attention.

sorgfältig ['zɔrkfɛltɪç], adj. careful, painstaking; elaborate.

sorglos ['zɔrkloːs], adj. careless, irresponsible, unconcerned, indifferent; carefree.

sorgsam ['zɔrkzaːm], adj. careful, heedful.

Sorte ['zɔrtə], f. (—, pl. —n) sort, kind, species, brand.

sortieren [zɔr'tiːrən], v.a. sort (out).

Sortiment [zɔrti'mɛnt], n. (—s, pl. —e) assortment; bookshop.

Sortimentsbuchhändler [zɔrti'mɛntsbuːxhɛndlər], m. (—s, pl. —) retail bookseller.

Soße ['zoːsə], f. (—, pl. —n) sauce, gravy.

Souffleur [su'løːr], m. (—s, pl. —e) prompter.

Soutane [su'taːnə], f. (—, pl. —n) cassock, soutane.

Souterrain [sutɛ'rɛ̃], n. (—s, pl. —s) basement.

souverän [suːvə'rɛːn], adj. sovereign; (fig.) supremely good.

Souveränität [suːvɛrɛːni'tɛːt], f. (—, no pl.) sovereignty.

soviel [zo'fiːl], adv. so much; — wie, as much as. — conj. so far as; — ich weiß, as far as I know.

sowie [zo'viː], conj. as, as well as, as soon as.

Sowjet [sɔv'jɛt], m. (—s, pl. —s) Soviet.

sowohl [zo'voːl], conj. — wie, as well as.

sozial [zo'tsjaːl], adj. social.

sozialisieren [zotsjali'ziːrən], v.a. nationalise.

Sozialwissenschaft [zo'tsjaːlvɪsənʃaft], f. (—, pl. —en) sociology; social science.

Sozietät [zotsje'tɛːt], f. (—, pl. —en) partnership.

Sozius ['zoːtsjus], m. (—, pl. —se, Socii) partner; pillion-rider; —sitz, (motor cycle) pillion (seat).

sozusagen ['zoːtsuzaːgən], adv. as it were, so to speak.

Spagat [ʃpa'gaːt], m. (—(e)s, pl. —e) (dial.) string, twine; (Dancing) the splits.

spähen ['ʃpɛːən], v.n. look out, watch; (Mil.) scout; spy.

Späher ['ʃpɛːər], m. (—s, pl. —) scout; spy.

Spalier [ʃpa'liːr], n. (—s, pl. —e) trellis; — bilden, form a lane (of people).

Spalierobst [ʃpa'liːroːpst], n. (—(e)s, no pl.) wall-fruit.

Spalt [ʃpalt], m. (—(e)s, pl. —e) crack, rift, cleft, rent; (glacier) crevasse.

Spalte ['ʃpaltə], f. (—, pl. —n) (newspaper) column.

spalten ['ʃpaltən], v.a. split, cleave, slit. — v.r. sich —, divide, break up, split up; (in two) bifurcate.

Spaltholz ['ʃpalthɔlts], n. (—es, no pl.) fire-wood.

Spaltpilz ['ʃpaltpɪlts], m. (—es, pl. —e) fission-fungus.

Spaltung ['ʃpaltuŋ], f. (—, pl. —en) cleavage; (atomic) fission; (fig.) dissension, rupture; (Eccl.) schism.

Span [ʃpaːn], m. (—(e)s, pl. ⁝e) chip, chippings, shavings.

Spange ['ʃpaŋə], f. (—, pl. —n) clasp, buckle.

Spanien ['ʃpaːnjən], n. Spain.

spanisch ['ʃpaːnɪʃ], adj. Spanish; —e Wand, folding screen; es kommt mir — vor, it is Greek to me.

Spann [ʃpan], m. (—(e)s, pl. —e) instep.

Spanne ['ʃpanə], f. (—, pl. —n) span; eine — Zeit, a short space of time.

spannen ['ʃpanən], v.a. stretch, strain, span.

spannend ['ʃpanənt], adj. thrilling, tense.

Spannkraft ['ʃpankraft], f. (—, no pl.) elasticity.

Spannung ['ʃpanuŋ], f. (—, pl. —en) tension, suspense, strain; (fig.) eager expectation, curiosity, suspense, close attention; (Elec.) voltage.

Sparbüchse

Sparbüchse [ˈʃpaːrbyksə], *f.* (—, *pl.* —n) money-box.

sparen [ˈʃpaːrən], *v.a., v.n.* save, economise, put by, lay by.

Spargel [ˈʃpargəl], *m.* (—s, *pl.* —) asparagus.

Spargelder [ˈʃpaːrgɛldər], *n. pl.* savings.

Sparkasse [ˈʃpaːrkasə], *f.* (—, *pl.* —n) savings bank.

spärlich [ˈʃpɛːrliç], *adj.* scant, scanty, sparse.

Sparpfennig [ˈʃpaːrpfɛniç], *m.* (—s, *pl.* —e) nest-egg.

Sparren [ˈʃparən], *m.* (—s, *pl.* —) spar, rafter; *er hat einen —,* he has a screw loose.

sparsam [ˈʃpaːrzaːm], *adj.* economical, thrifty, frugal.

Spaß [ʃpaːs], *m.* (—es, *pl.* ⁝e) jest, fun, joke; *aus —, im —, zum —,* in fun; *— verstehen,* take a joke; *es macht mir —,* it amuses me, it is fun for me.

spaßen [ˈʃpaːsən], *v.n.* jest, joke.

spaßhaft [ˈʃpaːshaft], *adj.* funny, facetious, jocular.

Spaßverderber [ˈʃpaːsfɛrdɛrbər], *m.* (—s, *pl.* —) spoil-sport.

Spaßvogel [ˈʃpaːsfoːgəl], *m.* (—s, *pl.* ⁝) wag.

Spat [ʃpaːt], *m.* (—(e)s, *pl.* —e) (*Min.*) spar.

spät [ʃpɛːt], *adj.* late; *wie — ist es?* what is the time? *zu — kommen,* be late.

Spätabend [ˈʃpɛːtaːbənt], *m.* (—s, *pl.* —e) latter part of the evening, late evening.

Spatel [ˈʃpaːtəl], *m.* (—s, *pl.* —) spatula.

Spaten [ˈʃpaːtən], *m.* (—s, *pl.* —) spade.

Spatenstich [ˈʃpaːtənʃtiç], *m.* (—(e)s, *pl.* —e) *den ersten — tun,* turn the first sod.

später [ˈʃpɛːtər], *adv.* later (on), afterwards.

spätestens [ˈʃpɛːtəstəns], *adv.* at the latest.

Spätling [ˈʃpɛːtliŋ], *m.* (—s, *pl.* —e) late arrival; late fruit.

Spätsommer [ˈʃpɛːtzɔmər], *m.* (—s, *pl.* —) Indian summer.

Spatz [ʃpats], *m.* (—en *pl.* —en) (*Orn.*) sparrow.

spazieren [ʃpaˈtsiːrən], *v.n.* (*aux.* sein) walk leisurely, stroll; *— gehen,* go for a walk, take a stroll; *— führen,* take for a walk.

Spazierfahrt [ʃpaˈtsiːrfaːrt], *f.* (—, *pl.* —en) (pleasure-)drive.

Spazierstock [ʃpaˈtsiːrʃtɔk], *m.* (—s, *pl.* ⁝e) walking-stick.

Spazierweg [ʃpaˈtsiːrveːk], *m.* (—s, *pl.* —e) walk, promenade.

Specht [ʃpɛçt], *m.* (—(e)s, *pl.* —e) (*Orn.*) woodpecker.

Speck [ʃpɛk], *m.* (—(e)s, *no pl.*) bacon; *eine Scheibe —,* a rasher of bacon.

speckig [ˈʃpɛkiç], *adj.* fat.

Speckschwarte [ˈʃpɛkʃvartə], *f.* (—, *pl.* —n) bacon-rind.

Speckseite [ˈʃpɛkzaɪtə], *f.* (—, *pl.* —n) flitch of bacon.

spedieren [ʃpeˈdiːrən], *v.a.* forward; despatch.

Spediteur [ʃpediˈtøːr], *m.* (—s, *pl.* —e) forwarding agent, furniture-remover, carrier.

Spedition [ʃpediˈtsjoːn], *f.* (—, *pl.* —en) conveyance; forwarding agency.

Speer [ʃpeːr], *m.* (—(e)s, *pl.* —e) spear, lance.

Speiche [ˈʃpaɪçə], *f.* (—, *pl.* —n) spoke.

Speichel [ˈʃpaɪçəl], *m.* (—s, *no pl.*) spittle, saliva.

Speicher [ˈʃpaɪçər], *m.* (—s, *pl.* —) granary; warehouse, storehouse; loft.

speien [ˈʃpaɪən], *v.a., v.n. irr.* spit; vomit, be sick.

Speise [ˈʃpaɪzə], *f.* (—, *pl.* —n) food, nourishment, dish.

Speisekammer [ˈʃpaɪzəkamər], *f.* (—, *pl.* —n) larder, pantry.

Speisekarte [ˈʃpaɪzəkartə], *f.* (—, *pl.* —n) bill of fare, menu.

speisen [ˈʃpaɪzən], *v.a.* feed, give to eat. — *v.n.* eat, dine, sup, lunch.

Speiseröhre [ˈʃpaɪzərøːrə], *f.* (—, *pl.* —n) gullet.

Speisewagen [ˈʃpaɪzəvaːgən], *m.* (—s, *pl.* —) (*Railw.*) dining-car.

Spektakel [ʃpɛkˈtaːkəl], *m.* (—s, *no pl.*) uproar, hubbub; shindy, rumpus; noise, row.

Spektrum [ˈʃpɛktrum], *n.* (—s, *pl.* Spektren) spectrum.

Spekulant [ʃpekuˈlant], *m.* (—en, *pl.* —en) speculator.

spekulieren [ʃpekuˈliːrən], *v.n.* speculate; theorise.

Spende [ˈʃpɛndə], *f.* (—, *pl.* —n) gift, donation; bounty.

spenden [ˈʃpɛndən], *v.a.* bestow, donate, contribute.

Spender [ˈʃpɛndər], *m.* (—s, *pl.* —) donor, giver, benefactor.

spendieren [ʃpɛnˈdiːrən], *v.a.* (give a) treat, pay for, stand.

Sperber [ˈʃpɛrbər], *m.* (—s, *pl.* —) (*Orn.*) sparrow-hawk.

Sperling [ˈʃpɛrliŋ], *m.* (—s, *pl.* —e) (*Orn.*) sparrow.

sperrangelweit [ˈʃpɛraŋəlvaɪt], *adv.* wide open.

Sperre [ˈʃpɛrə], *f.* (—, *pl.* —n) shutting, closing, blockade, blocking; closure; ban; (*Railw.*) barrier.

sperren [ˈʃpɛrən], *v.a.* spread out; (*Typ.*) space; shut, close, block; cut off; *ins Gefängnis —,* put in prison. — *v.r. sich — gegen,* offer resistance to.

Sperrhaken [ˈʃpɛrhaːkən], *m.* (—s, *pl.* —) catch, ratchet.

Sperrsitz [ˈʃpɛrzits], *m.* (—es, *pl.* —e) (*Theat.*) stall.

Sperrung [ˈʃpɛruŋ], *f.* (—, *pl.* —en) barring, obstruction, block, blockade; (*Comm.*) embargo.

Sperrzeit [ˈʃpɛrtsaɪt], *f.* (—, *pl.* —en) closing-time.

Spesen [ˈʃpeːzən], *f. pl.* charges, expenses.

spesenfrei [ˈʃpeːzənfraɪ], *adj.* free of charge; expenses paid.

Spezereien [ʃpeːtsəˈraɪən], *f. pl.* spices.

spezial [ʃpeˈtsjaːl], *adj.* special, particular.

spezialisieren [ʃpetsjaliˈziːrən], *v.a.* specify. — *v.r. sich* —, specialise.

Spezialist [ʃpetsjaˈlɪst], *m.* (—en, *pl.* —en) specialist, expert.

Spezialität [ʃpetsjaliˈtɛːt], *f.* (—, *pl.* —en) speciality, (*Am.*) specialty.

Spezies [ˈʃpeːtsjes], *f.* (—, *pl.* —) species; (*Maths.*) rule.

Spezifikation [ʃpetsifikaˈtsjoːn], *f.* (—, *pl.* —en) specification.

spezifisch [ʃpeˈtsiːfɪʃ], *adj.* specific.

spezifizieren [ʃpetsifiˈtsiːrən], *v.a.* specify.

Spezifizierung [ʃpetsifiˈtsiːruŋ], *f.* (— *pl.* —en) specification.

Spezimen [ˈʃpeːtsimən], *n.* (—s, *pl.* —mina) specimen.

Sphäre [ˈsfɛːrə], *f.* (—, *pl.* —n) sphere.

sphärisch [ˈsfɛːrɪʃ], *adj.* spherical.

Spickaal [ˈʃpɪkaːl], *m.* (—s, *pl.* —e) smoked eel.

spicken [ˈʃpɪkən], *v.a.* lard; *den Beutel* —, fill o.'s purse.

Spiegel [ˈʃpiːɡəl], *m.* (—s, *pl.* —) mirror, looking-glass.

spiegelblank [ˈʃpiːɡəlblaŋk], *adj.* sparkling, shiny, polished.

Spiegelei [ˈʃpiːɡəlaɪ], *n.* (—s, *pl.* —er) fried egg.

Spiegelfechterei [ˈʃpiːɡəlfɛçtəraɪ], *f.* (—, *pl.* —en) shadow-boxing, make-believe.

Spiegelfenster [ˈʃpiːɡəlfɛnstər], *n.* (—s, *pl.* —) plate-glass window.

spiegeln [ˈʃpiːɡəln], *v.n.* glitter, shine. — *v.a.* reflect. — *v.r. sich* —, be reflected.

Spiegelscheibe [ˈʃpiːɡəlʃaɪbə], *f.* (—, *pl.* —n) plate-glass pane.

Spiegelung [ˈʃpiːɡəluŋ], *f.* (—, *pl.* —en) reflection; mirage.

Spiel [ʃpiːl], *n.* (—(e)s, *pl.* —e) play; game; sport; (*Theat.*) acting, performance; (*Mus.*) playing; *ehrliches* (*unehrliches*) —, fair (foul) play; *leichtes* —, walk-over; *auf dem* — *stehen*, be at stake; *aufs* — *setzen*, stake, risk; *die Hand im* — *haben*, have a finger in the pie; *gewonnenes* — *haben*, gain o.'s point; *ein gewagtes* — *treiben*, play a bold game; *sein* — *mit einem treiben*, trifle with s.o.

Spielart [ˈʃpiːlaːrt], *f.* (—, *pl.* —en) manner of playing; variety.

Spielbank [ˈʃpiːlbaŋk], *f.* (—, *pl.* —en) casino; gambling-table.

Spieldose [ˈʃpiːldoːzə], *f.* (—, *pl.* —n) musical box.

spielen [ˈʃpiːlən], *v.a.*, *v.n.* play; gamble; (*Mus.*) play; (*Theat.*) act; *eine Rolle* —, play a part; *mit dem Gedanken* —, toy with the idea.

spielend [ˈʃpiːlənt], *adv.* easily.

Spieler [ˈʃpiːlər], *m.* (—s, *pl.* —) player; gambler; gamester.

Spielerei [ʃpiːləˈraɪ], *f.* (—, *pl.* —en) child's play; trivialities.

Spielhölle [ˈʃpiːlhœlə], *f.* (—, *pl.* —n) gambling-den.

Spielmann [ˈʃpiːlman], *m.* (—s, *pl.* **Spielleute**) musician, fiddler; (*Middle Ages*) minstrel.

Spielmarke [ˈʃpiːlmarkə], *f.* (—, *pl.* —n) counter, chip.

Spielplan [ˈʃpiːlplaːn], *m.* (—s, *pl.* —e) (*Theat.*) repertory.

Spielplatz [ˈʃpiːlplats], *m.* (—es, *pl.* —e) playground.

Spielraum [ˈʃpiːlraum], *m.* (—s, *no pl.*) elbow-room; (*fig.*) scope; margin; clearance.

Spielsache [ˈʃpiːlzaxə], *f.* (—, *pl.* —n) toy, plaything.

Spielschule [ˈʃpiːlʃuːlə], *f.* (—, *pl.* —n) infant-school, kindergarten.

Spieltisch [ˈʃpiːltɪʃ], *m.* (—es, *pl.* —e) card-table.

Spieluhr [ˈʃpiːluːr], *f.* (—, *pl.* —en) musical clock.

Spielverderber [ˈʃpiːlfɛrdɛrbər], *m.* (—s, *pl.* —) spoilsport.

Spielwaren [ˈʃpiːlvaːrən], *f. pl.* toys.

Spielzeit [ˈʃpiːltsaɪt], *f.* (—, *pl.* —en) playtime; (*Theat.*) season.

Spielzeug [ˈʃpiːltsɔyk], *n.* (—s, *pl.* —e) plaything, toy.

Spieß [ʃpiːs], *m.* (—es, *pl.* —e) spear, pike; (*Cul.*) spit.

Spießbürger [ˈʃpiːsbyrɡər], *m.* (—s, *pl.* —) Philistine.

spießen [ˈʃpiːsən], *v.a.* spear, pierce.

Spießer [ˈʃpiːsər], *m.* (—s, *pl.* —) Philistine.

Spießgeselle [ˈʃpiːsɡəzelə], *m.* (—n, *pl.* —n) accomplice, companion *or* partner in crime.

spießig [ˈʃpiːsɪç], *adj.* (*coll.*) Philistine, uncultured, narrow-minded.

Spießruten [ˈʃpiːsruːtən], *f. pl.* — *laufen*, run the gauntlet.

Spinat [ʃpiˈnaːt], *m.* (—s, *no pl.*) spinach.

Spind [ʃpɪnt], *n.* (—(e)s, *pl.* —e) cupboard.

Spindel [ˈʃpɪndəl], *f.* (—, *pl.* —n) spindle; distaff; (*staircase*) newel.

spindeldürr [ˈʃpɪndəldyr], *adj.* as thin as a lath.

Spindelholz [ˈʃpɪndəlhɔlts], *n.* (—es, *no pl.*) spindle-tree wood.

Spinett [ʃpiˈnet], *n.* (—s, *pl.* —e) spinet.

Spinne [ˈʃpɪnə], *f.* (—, *pl.* —n) spider.

spinnefeind [ˈʃpɪnəfaɪnt], *adj. einander* — *sein*, hate each other like poison.

spinnen [ˈʃpɪnən], *v.a. irr.* spin. — *v.n.* (*coll.*) be off o.'s head, be crazy.

Spinnerei [ʃpɪnəˈraɪ], *f.* (—, *pl.* —en) spinning-mill.

Spinngewebe [ˈʃpɪnɡəveːbə], *n.* (—s, *pl.* —) cobweb.

Spinnrocken [ˈʃpɪnrɔkən], *m.* (—s, *pl.* —) distaff.

spintisieren [ʃpɪntiˈziːrən], *v.n.* muse, meditate.

Spion

Spion [ʃpi'o:n], *m.* (—s, *pl.* —e) spy.

spionieren [ʃpio'ni:rən], *v.n.* spy, pry.

Spirale [ʃpi'ra:lə], *f.* (—, *pl.* —n) spiral.

Spirituosen [ʃpiritu'o:zən], *pl.* spirits, liquors.

Spiritus ['ʃpi:ritus], *m.* (—, *pl.* —se) alcohol, spirits of wine; *denaturierter* —, methylated spirits.

Spiritusbrennerei ['ʃpi:ritusbrɛnərai], *f.* (—, *pl.* —en) distillery.

Spiritusgehalt ['ʃpi:ritusgəhalt], *m.* (—s, *pl.* —e) *(alcoholic)* strength, proof.

Spital [ʃpi'ta:l], *n.* (—s, *pl.* ⁻er) infirmary; hospital.

Spitz [ʃpits], *m.* (—es, *pl.* —e) Pomeranian dog; *einen — haben*, *(coll.)* be slightly tipsy.

spitz [ʃpits], *adj.* pointed; *(fig.)* snappy, biting.

Spitzbart ['ʃpitsba:rt], *m.* (—s, *pl.* ⁻e) imperial (beard), pointed beard.

Spitzbogen ['ʃpitsbo:gən], *m.* (—s, *pl.* —) pointed arch, Gothic arch.

Spitzbogenfenster ['ʃpitsbo:gənfɛnstər], *n.* (—s, *pl.* —) lancet window.

Spitzbube ['ʃpitsbu:bə], *m.* (—n, *pl.* —n) rogue; rascal; scamp.

Spitzbubenstreich ['ʃpitsbu:bənʃtraiç], *m.* (—(e)s, *pl.* —e) act of roguery, knavery.

spitzbübisch ['ʃpitsby:biʃ], *adj.* roguish.

Spitze ['ʃpitsə], *f.* (—, *pl.* —n) point; tip; top, peak; extremity; *(pipe)* mouthpiece; *(cigarette)* holder; *(pen)* nib; lace; *etwas auf die — treiben*, carry s.th. to extremes; *an der — stehen*, be at the head of.

Spitzel ['ʃpitsəl], *m.* (—s, *pl.* —) police-agent; informer.

spitzen ['ʃpitsən], *v.a.* sharpen; *die Ohren —*, prick up o.'s ears; *sich auf etwas —*, await s.th. eagerly, be all agog for s.th.

Spitzenbelastung ['ʃpitsənbəlastuŋ], *f.* (—, *pl.* —en) peak load.

Spitzenleistung ['ʃpitsənlaistuŋ], *f.* (—, *pl.* —en) maximum output; peak performance.

Spitzentuch ['ʃpitsəntu:x], *n.* (—(e)s, *pl.* ⁻er) lace scarf.

spitzfindig ['ʃpitsfindiç], *adj.* subtle, crafty; hair-splitting.

Spitzhacke ['ʃpitshakə], *f.* (—, *pl.* —n) pickaxe.

spitzig ['ʃpitsiç], *adj.* pointed, sharp; *(fig.)* biting, poignant.

Spitzmaus ['ʃpitsmaus], *f.* (—, *pl.* ⁻e) *(Zool.)* shrew.

Spitzname ['ʃpitsna:mə], *m.* (—ns, *pl.* —n) nickname.

spitzwinklig ['ʃpitsviŋkliç], *adj.* acute-angled.

spleißen ['ʃplaisən], *v.a. irr.* split, cleave.

Splitter ['ʃplitər], *m.* (—s, *pl.* —) splinter, chip.

splitternackt ['ʃplitərnakt], *adj.* stark naked.

splittern ['ʃplitərn], *v.n.* *(aux.* sein) splinter.

spontan [ʃpɔn'ta:n], *adj.* spontaneous.

sporadisch [ʃpo'ra:diʃ], *adj.* sporadic.

Spore ['ʃpo:rə], *f.* (—, *pl.* —n) spore.

Sporn [ʃpɔrn], *m.* (—s, *pl.* **Sporen**) spur.

spornstreichs ['ʃpɔrnʃtraiçs], *adv.* post-haste, at once.

Sportler ['ʃpɔrtlər], *m.* (—s, *pl.* —) athlete, sportsman.

sportlich ['ʃpɔrtliç], *adj.* athletic; sporting.

sportsmäßig ['ʃpɔrtsmɛ:siç], *adj.* sportsmanlike.

Spott [ʃpɔt], *m.* (—(e)s, *no pl.*) mockery; scorn; *Gegenstand des —s*, laughing-stock; *— treiben mit*, mock, deride; *zum Schaden den — hinzufügen*, add insult to injury.

spottbillig ['ʃpɔtbiliç], *adj.* ridiculously cheap, dirt-cheap.

Spöttelei [ʃpœtə'lai], *f.* (—, *pl.* —en) sarcasm.

spötteln ['ʃpœtəln], *v.n.* mock, jeer.

spotten ['ʃpɔtən], *v.a., v.n.* deride, scoff (at); *es spottet jeder Beschreibung*, it defies description.

Spötter ['ʃpœtər], *m.* (—s, *pl.* —) mocker, scoffer.

Spötterei [ʃpœtə'rai], *f.* (—, *pl.* —en) mockery, derision.

Spottgedicht ['ʃpɔtgədiçt], *n.* (—(e)s, *pl.* —e) satirical poem.

spöttisch ['ʃpœtiʃ], *adj.* mocking, satirical, ironical, scoffing.

spottlustig ['ʃpɔtlustiç], *adj.* flippant, satirical.

Spottschrift ['ʃpɔtʃrift], *f.* (—, *pl.* —en) satire, lampoon.

Sprache ['ʃpra:xə], *f.* (—, *pl.* —n) speech, language; tongue; expression; diction; discussion; *etwas zur — bringen*, bring a subject up; *zur — kommen*, come up for discussion; *heraus mit der —!* speak out!

Sprachfehler ['ʃpra:xfe:lər], *m.* (—s, *pl.* —) impediment in o.'s speech.

sprachfertig ['ʃpra:xfɛrtiç], *adj.* having a ready tongue; a good linguist, fluent.

Sprachgebrauch ['ʃpra:xgəbraux], *m.* (—(e)s, *no pl.*) (linguistic) usage.

Sprachkenner ['ʃpra:xkɛnər], *m.* (—s, *pl.* —) linguist.

sprachkundig ['ʃpra:xkundiç], *adj.* proficient in languages.

Sprachlehre ['ʃpra:xle:rə], *f.* (—, *no pl.*) grammar.

sprachlich ['ʃpra:xliç], *adj.* linguistic.

sprachlos ['ʃpra:xlo:s], *adj.* speechless, tongue-tied; *— dastehen*, be dumb-founded.

Sprachrohr ['ʃpra:xro:r], *n.* (—s, *pl.* —e) megaphone, speaking-tube; *(fig.)* mouthpiece.

Sprachschatz ['ʃpra:xʃats], *m.* (—es, *no pl.*) vocabulary.

Sprachvergleichung ['ʃpra:xfɛrglaiçuŋ], *f.* (—, *no pl.*) comparative philology.

Sprachwerkzeug ['ʃpraːxvərktsɔyk], n. (—s, pl. —e) organ of speech.

Sprachwissenschaft ['ʃpraːxvisənʃaft], f. (—, pl. —en) linguistics, philology.

sprechen ['ʃpreçən], v.a.,v.n. irr. speak, declare, say; talk; *für einen* —, put in a good word for s.o., speak up for s.o.; *er ist nicht zu* —, he is not available; *auf einen gut zu* — *sein*, feel well disposed towards s.o.; *schuldig* —, pronounce guilty; *das Urteil* —, pass sentence.

sprechend ['ʃpreçənt], adj. expressive; — *ähnlich*, strikingly alike.

Sprecher ['ʃpreçər], m. (—s, pl. —) speaker, orator, spokesman; (*Rad.*) announcer.

Sprechstunde ['ʃpreçʃtundə], f. (—, pl. —n) consulting hours, surgery hours; office hours.

Sprechzimmer ['ʃpreçtsimər], n. (—s, pl.—) consulting-room.

spreizen ['ʃpraitsən], v.a. spread open; *die Beine* —, plant o.'s legs wide apart, straddle. — v.r. *sich* —, give o.s. airs.

Sprengbombe ['ʃprɛŋbɔmbə], f. (—, pl. —n) (high explosive) bomb.

Sprengel ['ʃprɛŋəl], m. (—s, pl. —) diocese.

sprengen ['ʃprɛŋən], v.a. sprinkle; water; burst, explode; burst open, blow up; *eine Versammlung* —, break up a meeting. — v.n. (aux. sein) ride at full speed, gallop.

Sprengpulver ['ʃprɛŋpulvər], n. (—s, no pl.) blasting-powder.

Sprengstoff ['ʃprɛŋʃtɔf], m. (—es, pl. —e) explosive.

Sprengwagen ['ʃprɛŋvaːgən], m. (—s, pl. —) sprinkler; water-cart.

sprenkeln ['ʃprɛŋkəln], v.a. speckle.

Spreu [ʃprɔy], f. (—, no pl.) chaff.

Sprichwort ['ʃpriçvɔrt], n. (—s, pl. ꞏꞏer) proverb, adage, saying.

sprießen ['ʃpriːsən], v.n. irr. sprout, shoot, germinate.

Springbrunnen ['ʃpriŋbrunən], m. (—s, pl. —) fountain.

springen ['ʃpriŋən], v.n. irr. (aux. sein) spring, leap, jump; (*glass*) burst; *etwas* — *lassen*, (coll.) treat s.o. to s.th.

Springer ['ʃpriŋər], m. (—s, pl. —) jumper, acrobat; (*Chess*) knight.

Springflut ['ʃpriŋfluːt], f. (—, pl. —en) spring-tide.

Springtau ['ʃpriŋtau], n. (—s, pl. —e) skipping-rope; (*Naut.*) slip-rope.

Sprit [ʃprit], m. (—s, pl. —e) spirit alcohol; (*sl.*) fuel, petrol.

Spritze ['ʃpritsə], f. (—, pl. —n) squirt, syringe; fire-engine; (coll.) injection.

spritzen ['ʃpritsən], v.a. squirt, spout, spray, sprinkle; (coll.) inject. — v.n. gush forth.

Spritzkuchen ['ʃpritskuːxən], m. (—s, pl. —) fritter.

Spritztour ['ʃpritstuːr], f. (—, pl. —en) (coll.) pleasure trip, outing; (coll.) spin.

spröde ['ʃprøːdə], adj. (*material*) brittle; (*person*) stubborn; coy, prim, prudish.

Sprödigkeit ['ʃprøːdiçkait], f. (—, no pl.) (*material*) brittleness; (*person*) stubbornness; coyness, primness, prudery.

Sproß [ʃprɔs], m. (—sses, pl. —sse) sprout, shoot, germ; (*fig.*) scion, offspring.

Sprosse ['ʃprɔsə], f. (—, pl. —n) (*ladder*) step, rung.

Sprößling ['ʃprœsliŋ], m. (—s, pl. —e) scion, offspring.

Sprotte ['ʃprɔtə], f. (—, pl. —n) sprat.

Spruch [ʃprux], m. (—(e)s, pl. ꞏꞏe) saying, aphorism; proverb; (*obs.*) saw; (*judge*) sentence, verdict.

spruchreif ['ʃpruxraif], adj. ripe for judgment; ready for a decision.

Sprudel ['ʃpruːdəl], m. (—s, pl. —) bubbling spring; (coll.) soda water.

sprudeln ['ʃpruːdəln], v.n. bubble, gush.

sprühen ['ʃpryːən], v.a. sprinkle, scatter, spray. — v.n. sparkle, emit sparks; (*rain*) drizzle.

sprühend ['ʃpryːənt], adj. (*fig.*) sparkling, scintillating, brilliant.

Sprühregen ['ʃpryːreːgən], m. (—s, no pl.) drizzling rain, drizzle.

Sprung [ʃpruŋ], m. (—(e)s, pl. ꞏꞏe) leap, bound, jump; chink, crack; *nur auf einen* — *zu Besuch kommen*, pay a flying visit; *auf dem* — *sein zu*, be on the point of; *sich auf den* — *machen*, cut and run, (coll.) fly; *große* ꞏꞏe *machen*, (coll.) live it up, cut a dash.

Sprungfeder ['ʃpruŋfeːdər], f. (—, pl. —n) spring.

Sprungkraft ['ʃpruŋkraft], f. (—, no pl.) springiness, elasticity, buoyancy.

Spucke ['ʃpukə], f. (—, no pl.) spittle, saliva.

spucken ['ʃpukən], v.a.,v.n. spit.

Spuk [ʃpuːk], m. (—s, pl. —e) haunting; ghost, spectre, apparition; (coll.) spook.

spuken ['ʃpuːkən], v.n. haunt; be haunted.

spukhaft ['ʃpuːkhaft], adj. uncanny, phantom-like, ghost-like, spooky.

Spule ['ʃpuːlə], f. (—, pl. —n) spool; (*Elec.*) coil.

Spüleimer ['ʃpyːlaimər], m. (—s, pl. —) slop-pail.

spülen ['ʃpyːlən], v.a. rinse, wash.

Spülicht ['ʃpyːliçt], n. (—s, no pl.) dish-water.

Spund [ʃpunt], m. (—(e)s, pl. ꞏꞏe) bung.

Spundloch ['ʃpuntlɔx], n. (—s, pl. ꞏꞏer) bung-hole.

Spur [ʃpuːr], f. (—, pl. —en) footprint, track, trail; spoor; (*fig.*) trace, vestige; *frische* —, hot scent; *einer Sache auf die* — *kommen*, be on the track of s.th.; *keine* — *von*, not a trace of, not an inkling of.

spüren ['ʃpyːrən], v.a. trace, track (down); feel, sense, notice.

Spürhund ['ʃpyːrhunt], m. (—s, pl. —e) tracker dog, setter, beagle; (*fig.*) spy, sleuth.

spurlos

spurlos ['ʃpuːrloːs], *adj.* trackless, without a trace; *es ging — an ihm vorüber*, it left no mark on him; *— verschwinden*, vanish into thin air.

Spürsinn ['ʃpyːrzɪn], *m.* (—s, *no pl.*) scent; flair; sagacity, shrewdness.

Spurweite ['ʃpuːrvaɪtə], *f.* (—, *pl.* —n) gauge, width of track.

sputen ['ʃpuːtən], *v.r. sich —*, make haste, hurry.

Staat [ʃtaːt], *m.* (—(e)s, *pl.* —en) state; government; pomp, show, parade; *— machen*, make a show of.

Staatenbund ['ʃtaːtənbunt], *m.* (—(e)s, *pl.* ·e) confederacy, federation.

staatlich ['ʃtaːtlɪç], *adj.* belonging to the state, public, national.

Staatsangehörige ['ʃtaːtsangəhøːrɪgə], *m.* (—n, *pl.* —n) citizen (of a country), subject, national.

Staatsangehörigkeit ['ʃtaːtsangəhøːrɪçkaɪt], *f.* (—, *pl.* —en) nationality.

Staatsanwalt ['ʃtaːtsanvalt], *m.* (—s, *pl.* ·e) public prosecutor, Attorney-General.

Staatsbeamte ['ʃtaːtsbəamtə], *m.* (—n, *pl.* —n) civil servant, employee of the state.

Staatsbürger ['ʃtaːtsbyrgər], *m.* (—s, *pl.* —) citizen, national.

Staatsdienst ['ʃtaːtsdiːnst], *m.* (—(e)s, *pl.* —e) civil service, government service.

Staatseinkünfte ['ʃtaːtsaɪnkynftə], *f. pl.* public revenue.

Staatsgesetz ['ʃtaːtsgəzɛts], *n.* (—es, *pl.* —e) statute law.

Staatsgewalt ['ʃtaːtsgəvalt], *f.* (—, *no pl.*) executive power.

Staatshaushalt ['ʃtaːtshaushalt], *m.* (—s, *no pl.*) state finances, budget.

Staatshaushaltsanschlag ['ʃtaːtshaushaltsanʃlaːk], *m.* (—s, *pl.* ·e) budget estimates.

Staatskanzler ['ʃtaːtskantslər], *m.* (—s, *pl.* —) Chancellor.

Staatskasse ['ʃtaːtskasə], *f.* (—, *no pl.*) public exchequer, treasury.

Staatskörper ['ʃtaːtskœrpər], *m.* (—s, *pl.* —) body politic.

Staatskosten ['ʃtaːtskɔstən], *f. pl. auf —*, at (the) public expense.

Staatskunst ['ʃtaːtskunst], *f.* (—, *no pl.*) statesmanship; statecraft.

Staatsminister ['ʃtaːtsmɪnɪstər], *m.* (—s, *pl.* —) cabinet minister; minister of state.

Staatsrat ['ʃtaːtsraːt], *m.* (—s, *no pl.*) council of state; (*pl.* ·e) councillor of state.

Staatsrecht ['ʃtaːtsrɛçt], *n.* (—(e)s, *no pl.*) constitutional law.

Staatssiegel ['ʃtaːtsziːgəl], *n.* (—s, *pl.* —) Great Seal, official seal.

Staatsstreich ['ʃtaːtsʃtraɪç], *m.* (—(e)s, *pl.* —e) coup d'état.

Staatswirtschaft ['ʃtaːtsvɪrtʃaft], *f.* (—, *no pl.*) political economy.

Staatszimmer ['ʃtaːtstsɪmər], *n.* (—s, *pl.* —) state apartment.

Stab [ʃtaːp], *m.* (—(e)s, *pl.* ·e) staff; stick, rod, pole; crosier; mace; (*Mil.*) field-officers, staff; *den — über einen brechen*, condemn s.o. (to death).

stabil [ʃtaˈbiːl], *adj.* steady, stable, firm.

stabilisieren [ʃtabiliˈziːrən], *v.a.* stabilise.

Stabreim ['ʃtaːpraɪm], *m.* (—s, *no pl.*) alliteration.

Stabsarzt ['ʃtaːpsartst], *m.* (—es, *pl.* ·e) (*Mil.*) medical officer.

Stabsquartier ['ʃtaːpskvartiːr], *n.* (—s, *pl.* —e) (*Mil.*) headquarters.

Stachel ['ʃtaxəl], *m.* (—s, *pl.* —n) (*animal*) sting; (*plant*) prickle, thorn; (*fig.*) keen edge, sting; stimulus; *wider den — löcken*, kick against the pricks.

Stachelbeere ['ʃtaxəlbeːrə], *f.* (—, *pl.* —n) (*Bot.*) gooseberry.

Stachelschwein ['ʃtaxəlʃvaɪn], *n.* (—s, *pl.* —e) (*Zool.*) hedgehog, porcupine.

stachlig ['ʃtaxlɪç], *adj.* prickly, thorny; (*fig.*) disagreeable.

Stadion ['ʃtaːdjɔn], *n.* (—s, *pl.* —dien) sports-arena, stadium.

Stadium ['ʃtaːdjum], *n.* (—s, *pl.* —dien) stage (of development), phase.

Stadt [ʃtat], *f.* (—, *pl.* ·e) town; city.

Stadtbahn ['ʃtatbaːn], *f.* (—, *pl.* —en) metropolitan railway.

Städtchen ['ʃtɛtçən], *n.* (—s, *pl.* —) small town, township.

Städter ['ʃtɛtər], *m.* (—s, *pl.* —) townsman.

Stadtgemeinde ['ʃtatgəmaɪndə], *f.* (—, *pl.* —n) municipality.

städtisch ['ʃtɛtɪʃ], *adj.* municipal.

Stadtmauer ['ʃtatmauər], *f.* (—, *pl.* —n) town wall, city wall.

Stadtrat ['ʃtatraːt], *m.* (—s, *no pl.*) town council; (*pl.* ·e) town councillor; alderman.

Stadtteil ['ʃtattaɪl], *m.* (—s, *pl.* —e) ward, district, part of a town.

Stadttor ['ʃtattoːr], *n.* (—s, *pl.* —e) city-gate.

Stadtverordnete ['ʃtatfɛrɔrdnətə], *m.* (—n, *pl.* —n) town councillor.

Stafette [ʃtaˈfɛtə], *f.* (—, *pl.* —n) courier; relay.

Staffel ['ʃtafəl], *f.* (—, *pl.* —n) step, rundle, rung, round; relay; (*fig.*) degree; (*Aviat.*) squadron.

Staffelei [ʃtafəˈlaɪ], *f.* (—, *pl.* —en) easel.

staffeln ['ʃtafəln], *v.a.* grade; differentiate; stagger.

Staffelung ['ʃtafəluŋ], *f.* (—, *pl.* —en) gradation.

stagnieren [ʃtagˈniːrən], *v.n.* stagnate.

Stahl [ʃtaːl], *m.* (—(e)s, *pl.* ·e) steel.

stählen ['ʃtɛːlən], *v.a.* steel, harden, temper; brace.

stählern ['ʃtɛːlərn], *adj.* made of steel, steely.

Stahlquelle ['ʃtaːlkvɛlə], *f.* (—, *pl.* —n) chalybeate spring; mineral spring.

Stahlstich ['ʃtaːlʃtɪç], *m.* (—(e)s, *pl.* —e) steel-engraving.

stark

Stählung ['ʃtɛːluŋ], f. (—, no pl.) steeling; (fig.) bracing.

Stahlwaren ['ʃtaːlvaːrən], f. pl. hardware, cutlery.

Stall [ʃtal], m. (—(e)s, pl. ∺e) stable; (pig) sty; (dog) kennel.

Stallbursche ['ʃtalburʃə], m. (—n, pl. —n) stable-boy, groom.

Stallungen ['ʃtaluŋən], f. pl. stabling, stables.

Stambul ['ʃtambul], n. Istanbul.

Stamm [ʃtam], m. (—(e)s, pl. ∺e) (tree) trunk; (people) tribe, family, race; (words) stem; root.

Stammaktie ['ʃtamaktsjə], f. (—, pl. —n) (Comm.) original share.

Stammbaum ['ʃtambaum], m. (—s, pl. ∺e) pedigree; family tree.

Stammbuch ['ʃtambuːx], n. (—(e)s, pl. ∺er) album.

stammeln ['ʃtaməln], v.a., v.n. stammer, stutter; falter.

stammen ['ʃtamən], v.n. (aux. sein) be descended from, spring from, originate from, stem from; be derived from.

Stammesgenosse ['ʃtaməsgənɔsə], m. (—n, pl. —n) kinsman, clansman.

Stammgast ['ʃtamgast], m. (—es, pl. ∺e) regular customer.

Stammgut ['ʃtamguːt], n. (—s, pl. ∺er) family estate.

Stammhalter ['ʃtamhaltər], m. (—s, pl. —) son and heir; eldest son.

Stammhaus ['ʃtamhaus], n. (—es, pl. ∺er) ancestral mansion; (royalty) dynasty; (Comm.) business headquarters, head office.

stämmig ['ʃtɛmɪç], adj. sturdy, strong.

Stammler ['ʃtamlər], m. (—s, pl. —) stammerer, stutterer.

Stammsilbe ['ʃtamzilbə], f. (—, pl. —n) (Ling.) radical syllable.

Stammtafel ['ʃtamtaːfəl], f. (—, pl. —n) genealogical table.

Stammvater ['ʃtamfaːtər], m. (—s, pl. ∺) ancestor, progenitor.

stammverwandt ['ʃtamfɛrvant], adj. cognate, kindred.

stampfen ['ʃtampfən], v.a. stamp, pound, ram down. — v.n. stamp, trample.

Stand [ʃtant], m. (—(e)s, pl. ∺e) stand; (market) stall; situation, state (of affairs), condition; reading, position; rank, station (in life); (pl.) the classes, the estates.

Standarte [ʃtan'dartə], f. (—, pl. —n) standard, banner.

Standbild ['ʃtantbilt], n. (—(e)s, pl. ∺er) statue.

Ständchen ['ʃtɛntçən], n. (—s, pl. —) serenade; einem ein — bringen, serenade s.o.

Ständehaus ['ʃtɛndəhaus], n. (—es, pl. ∺er) state assembly-hall.

Ständer ['ʃtɛndər], m. (—s, pl. —) stand, pedestal; post; (upright) desk.

Standesamt ['ʃtandəsamt], n. (—s, pl. ∺er) registry office.

Standesbeamte ['ʃtandəsbəamtə], m. (—n, pl. —n) registrar (of births, marriages and deaths).

Standesbewußtsein ['ʃtandəsbəvustzain], n. (—s, no pl.) class-feeling, class-consciousness.

Standesperson ['ʃtandəspɛrzoːn], f. (—, pl. —en) person of rank.

Standgericht ['ʃtantgəriçt], n. (—es, pl. —e) court-martial; summary court of justice.

standhaft ['ʃtanthaft], adj. constant, firm, steadfast.

standhalten ['ʃtanthaltən], v.n. irr. bear up, stand o.'s ground, withstand, resist.

ständig ['ʃtɛndiç], adj. permanent.

ständisch ['ʃtɛndiʃ], adj. relating to the estates (of the realm).

Standort ['ʃtantɔrt], m. (—s, pl. —e) location; station.

Standpauke ['ʃtantpaukə], f. (—, pl. —n) (coll.) harangue; severe reprimand.

Standpunkt ['ʃtantpuŋkt], m. (—(e)s, pl. —e) standpoint; point of view; den — vertreten, take the line; einen den — klar machen, give s.o. a piece of o.'s mind.

Standrecht ['ʃtantreçt], n. (—(e)s, no pl.) martial law.

Standuhr ['ʃtantuːr], f. (—, pl. —en) grandfather-clock.

Stange ['ʃtaŋə], f. (—, pl. —n) stick, pole; bei der — bleiben, stick to the point, persevere.

Stank [ʃtaŋk], m. (—s, no pl.) (dial.) stench; discord, trouble.

Stänker ['ʃtɛŋkər], m. (—s, pl. —) (coll.) mischief-maker, quarrelsome person.

stänkern ['ʃtɛŋkərn], v.n. pick quarrels; ferret about, make trouble.

Stanniol [ʃta'njoːl], n. (—s, no pl.) tinfoil.

stanzen ['ʃtantsən], v.a. punch, stamp.

Stapel ['ʃtaːpəl], m. (—s, pl. —) pile, heap; (Naut.) slipway; ein Schiff vom — lassen, launch a ship.

Stapellauf ['ʃtaːpəllauf], m. (—s, pl. ∺e) (Naut.) launch, launching.

stapeln ['ʃtaːpəln], v.a. pile up.

Stapelnahrung ['ʃtaːpəlnaːruŋ], f. (—, no pl.) staple diet.

Stapelplatz ['ʃtaːpəlplats], m. (—es, pl. ∺e) mart, emporium.

Stapelware ['ʃtaːpəlvaːrə], f. (—, pl. —n) staple goods.

Stapfen ['ʃtapfən], m. or f. pl. footsteps.

Star (1) [ʃtaːr], m. (—(e)s, pl. —e) (Med.) cataract; einem den — stechen, operate for cataract; (fig.) open s.o.'s eyes.

Star (2) [ʃtaːr], m. (—(e)s, pl. —en) (Orn.) starling.

stark [ʃtark], adj. strong, stout; robust; vigorous; heavy; considerable; —er Esser, hearty eater. — adv. very much.

209

Stärke

Stärke [ˈʃtɛrkə], *f.* (—, *no pl.*) strength, vigour, robustness; strong point; starch.

Stärkekleister [ˈʃtɛrkəklaɪstər], *m.* (—s, *no pl.*) starch-paste.

Stärkemehl [ˈʃtɛrkəme:l], *n.* (—s, *no pl.*) starch-flour.

stärken [ˈʃtɛrkən], *v.a.* strengthen; corroborate; starch. — *v.r. sich* —, take some refreshment.

stärkend [ˈʃtɛrkənt], *adj.* strengthening, restorative; —*es Mittel,* tonic.

starkleibig [ˈʃtarklaɪbɪç], *adj.* corpulent, stout, obese.

Stärkung [ˈʃtɛrkuŋ], *f.* (—, *pl.* —en) strengthening, invigoration; refreshment.

starr [ʃtar], *adj.* stiff, rigid; fixed; inflexible; stubborn; *einen — ansehen,* stare at s.o.

starren [ˈʃtarən], *v.n.* stare.

Starrheit [ˈʃtarhaɪt], *f.* (—, *no pl.*) stiffness, rigidity; fixedness; inflexibility; stubbornness.

starrköpfig [ˈʃtarkœpfɪç], *adj.* headstrong, stubborn, obstinate, pigheaded.

Starrkrampf [ˈʃtarkrampf], *m.* (—(e)s, *no pl.*) (*Med.*) tetanus.

Starrsinn [ˈʃtarzɪn], *m.* (—s, *no pl.*) stubbornness, obstinacy.

Station [ʃtaˈtsjo:n], *f.* (—, *pl.* —en) (*Railw.*) station; (*main*) terminus; stop, stopping-place; (*hospital*) ward; *freie* —, board and lodging found.

stationär [ʃtatsjoˈnɛ:r], *adj.* stationary.

stationieren [ʃtatsjoˈni:rən], *v.a.* station.

Stationsvorsteher [ʃtatˈsjo:nsfɔrʃte:-ər], *m.* (—s, *pl.* —) station-master.

statisch [ˈʃta:tiʃ], *adj.* static.

Statist [ʃtaˈtɪst], *m.* (—en, *pl.* —en) (*Theat.*) extra, walking-on part; (*pl.*) supers.

Statistik [ʃtaˈtɪstɪk], *f.* (—, *pl.* —en) statistics.

Statistiker [ʃtaˈtɪstɪkər], *m.* (—s, *pl.* —) statistician.

Stativ [ʃtaˈti:f], *n.* (—s, *pl.* —e) stand, tripod.

Statt [ʃtat], *f.* (—, *no pl.*) place, stead; *an seiner* —, in his place.

statt [ʃtat], *prep.* (*Genit.*) instead of, in lieu of.

Stätte [ˈʃtɛtə], *f.* (—, *pl.* —n) place, abode.

stattfinden [ˈʃtatfɪndən], *v.n. irr.* take place.

stattgeben [ˈʃtatge:bən], *v.n. irr. einer Bitte* —, grant a request.

statthaft [ˈʃtathaft], *adj.* admissible, allowable, lawful.

Statthalter [ˈʃtathaltər], *m.* (—s, *pl.* —) governor.

stattlich [ˈʃtatlɪç], *adj.* stately, handsome, distinguished, comely; portly; considerable; *eine* —*e Summe,* a tidy sum.

statuieren [ʃtatuˈi:rən], *v.a.* decree; *ein Exempel* —, make an example of.

Statut [ʃtaˈtu:t], *n.* (—s, *pl.* —en) statute, regulation.

Staub [ʃtaup], *m.* (—(e)s, *no pl.*) dust, powder; *sich aus dem — machen,* take French leave; abscond.

Stäubchen [ˈʃtɔypçən], *n.* (—s, *pl.* —) mote, particle of dust.

stauben [ˈʃtaubən], *v.n. es staubt,* it is dusty.

Staubgefäß [ˈʃtaupgəfɛ:s], *n.* (—es, *pl.* —e) stamen.

staubig [ˈʃtaubɪç], *adj.* dusty.

Staubkamm [ˈʃtaupkam], *m.* (—s, *pl.* ⸚e) fine-tooth comb.

Staublappen [ˈʃtauplapən], *m.* (—s, *pl.* —) duster.

Staubmantel [ˈʃtaupmantəl], *m.* (—s, *pl.* ⸚) overall, smock; dust(er)coat, (*Am.*) duster.

Staubsauger [ˈʃtaupzaugər], *m.* (—s, *pl.* —) vacuum cleaner.

Staubtuch [ˈʃtauptu:x], *n.* (—es, *pl.* ⸚er) duster.

Staubwedel [ˈʃtaupve:dəl], *m.* (—s, *pl.* —) feather duster.

Staubwolke [ˈʃtaupvɔlkə], *f.* (—, *pl.* —n) cloud of dust.

Staubzucker [ˈʃtauptsukər], *m.* (—s, *no pl.*) castor-sugar, icing-sugar.

Staudamm [ˈʃtaudam], *m.* (—s, *pl.* ⸚e) dam, dyke.

Staude [ˈʃtaudə], *f.* (—, *pl.* —n) shrub, bush.

stauen [ˈʃtauən], *v.a.* stow; (*water*) dam. — *v.r. sich* —, be congested.

staunen [ˈʃtaunən], *v.n.* be astonished, be surprised, wonder (at).

Staupe [ˈʃtaupə], *f.* (—, *pl.* —n) (*animals*) distemper.

stäupen [ˈʃtɔypən], *v.a.* (*obs.*) scourge, flog.

Stauung [ˈʃtauuŋ], *f.* (—, *pl.* —en) stowage; (*water*) damming-up, swell, rising; (*blood*) congestion; (*traffic*) jam, build-up.

stechen [ˈʃteçən], *v.a. irr.* prick, sting; stab; (*cards*) trump.

stechend [ˈʃteçənt], *adj.* pungent, biting.

Stechmücke [ˈʃteçmykə], *f.* (—, *pl.* —n) (*Ent.*) gnat, mosquito.

Stechpalme [ˈʃteçpalmə], *f.* (—, *pl.* —n) (*Bot.*) holly.

Steckbrief [ˈʃtɛkbri:f], *m.* (—s, *pl.* —e) warrant (for arrest).

stecken [ˈʃtɛkən], *v.a.* stick into, put, place, fix; (*plants*) set, plant; *in Brand* —, set on fire, set fire to. — *v.n. irgendwo* —, be about somewhere; — *bleiben,* get stuck, break down; *er steckt dahinter,* he is at the bottom of it. — *v.r. sich hinter einen* —, shelter behind s.o.

Stecken [ˈʃtɛkən], *m.* (—s, *pl.* —) stick, staff.

Stecker [ˈʃtɛkər], *m.* (—s, *pl.* —) (*Elec.*) plug.

Steckkontakt [ˈʃtɛkkɔntakt], *m.* (—(e)s, *pl.* —e) (*Elec.*) plug, point.

Stecknadel [ˈʃtɛkna:dəl], *f.* (—, *pl.* —n) pin.

Steg [ʃte:k], *m.* (—(e)s, *pl.* —e) plank, foot-bridge; jetty; (*violin*) bridge.

Stegreif ['ʃteːkraɪf], *m.* (—s, *pl.* —e) (*obs.*) stirrup; *aus dem — sprechen*, extemporise, improvise.

stehen ['ʃteːən], *v.n. irr.* stand; be; stand still; *einem gut —*, fit *or* suit s.o. well; *mit einem gut —*, be on good terms with s.o.; *gut —*, be in a fair way, look promising; *was steht zu Diensten?* what can I do for you? — *bleiben*, stand still, stop, pull up.

stehlen ['ʃteːlən], *v.a. irr.* steal.

Steiermark ['ʃtaɪərmark], *f.* Styria.

steif [ʃtaɪf], *adj.* stiff; (*grog*) strong; awkward; ceremonious, punctilious, formal. — *adv. etwas — und fest behaupten*, swear by all that's holy.

steifen ['ʃtaɪfən], *v.a.* stiffen, starch.

Steifheit ['ʃtaɪfhaɪt], *f.* (—, *no pl.*) stiffness; (*fig.*) formality.

Steifleinen ['ʃtaɪflaɪnən], *n.* (—s, *no pl.*) buckram.

Steig [ʃtaɪk], *m.* (—(e)s, *pl.* —e) path, (mountain) track.

Steigbügel ['ʃtaɪkbyːgəl], *m.* (—s, *pl.* —) stirrup.

Steigen ['ʃtaɪgən], *n.* (—s, *no pl.*) rising, increase; (*price*) advance, rise; *im —*, on the increase.

steigen ['ʃtaɪgən], *v.n. irr.* (*aux.* sein) climb, mount, ascend; (*barometer*) rise; (*population*) increase; (*horse*) rear; (*price*) advance, rise.

Steiger ['ʃtaɪgər], *m.* (—s, *pl.* —) climber, mountaineer; mining-surveyor, overseer.

steigern ['ʃtaɪgərn], *v.a.* (*price*) raise; (*fig.*) enhance, increase. — *v.r. sich —*, increase.

Steigerung ['ʃtaɪgəruŋ], *f.* (—, *pl.* —en) raising; (*fig.*) enhancement; increase; (*Gram.*) comparison.

Steigung ['ʃtaɪguŋ], *f.* (—, *pl.* —en) gradient.

steil [ʃtaɪl], *adj.* steep.

Stein [ʃtaɪn], *m.* (—(e)s, *pl.* —e) stone, rock; flint; jewel, gem; monument; (*Chess*) piece, chessman; (*Draughts*) man; (*fruit*) stone, kernel; — *des Anstoßes*, stumbling block; *mir fällt ein — vom Herzen*, it is a load off my mind; *bei einem einen — im Brett haben*, be in s.o.'s good books; *einem —e in den Weg legen*, put obstacles in s.o.'s way; *der — des Weisen*, the philosopher's stone.

Steinadler ['ʃtaɪnaːdlər], *m.* (—s, *pl.* —) (*Orn.*) golden eagle.

steinalt ['ʃtaɪnalt], *adj.* very old.

Steinbock ['ʃtaɪnbɔk], *m.* (—s, *pl.* ⁀e) ibex; (*Astrol.*) Capricorn.

Steinbruch ['ʃtaɪnbrux], *m.* (—s, *pl.* ⁀e) stone-pit, quarry.

Steinbutt ['ʃtaɪnbut], *m.* (—s, *pl.* —e) (*Zool.*) turbot.

Steindruck ['ʃtaɪndruk], *m.* (—s, *no pl.*) lithography.

steinern ['ʃtaɪnərn], *adj.* stony; built of stone.

Steingut ['ʃtaɪnguːt], *n.* (—s, *no pl.*) earthenware, stoneware, pottery.

Steinhagel ['ʃtaɪnhaːgəl], *m.* (—s, *no pl.*) shower of stones.

Steinhaue ['ʃtaɪnhauə], *f.* (—, *pl.* —n) pickaxe.

Steinhügel ['ʃtaɪnhyːgəl], *m.* (—s, *pl.* —) cairn.

steinig ['ʃtaɪnɪç], *adj.* stony, rocky.

steinigen ['ʃtaɪnɪgən], *v.a.* stone.

Steinkalk ['ʃtaɪnkalk], *m.* (—s, *no pl.*) quicklime.

Steinkohle ['ʃtaɪnkoːlə], *f.* (—, *no pl.*) pit-coal.

Steinkrug ['ʃtaɪnkruːk], *m.* (—s, *pl.* ⁀e) stone jar.

Steinmarder ['ʃtaɪnmardər], *m.* (—s, *pl.* —) (*Zool.*) stone-marten.

Steinmetz ['ʃtaɪnmɛts], *m.* (—es, *pl.* —e) stone-cutter, stone-mason.

Steinobst ['ʃtaɪnoːpst], *n.* (—es, *no pl.*) stone-fruit.

Steinplatte ['ʃtaɪnplatə], *f.* (—, *pl.* —n) slab, flagstone.

steinreich ['ʃtaɪnraɪç], *adj.* as rich as Croesus.

Steinsalz ['ʃtaɪnzalts], *n.* (—es, *no pl.*) rock-salt, mineral-salt.

Steinwurf ['ʃtaɪnvurf], *m.* (—s, *pl.* ⁀e) *einen — entfernt*, within a stone's throw.

Steiß [ʃtaɪs], *m.* (—es, *pl.* —e) rump; (*coll.*) buttocks, posterior.

Stellage [ʃtɛˈlaːʒə], *f.* (—, *pl.* —n) stand, frame.

Stelldichein ['ʃtɛldɪçaɪn], *n.* (—s, *no pl.*) assignation, rendezvous, tryst; (*coll.*) date.

Stelle ['ʃtɛlə], *f.* (—, *pl.* —n) place, spot; job, position; situation; (*book*) passage; figure, digit; department; *offene —*, vacancy; *auf der —*, at once, immediately; *an deiner —*, if I were you; *nicht von der — kommen*, remain stationary; *zur — sein*, be at hand.

stellen ['ʃtɛlən], *v.a.* put, place, set; *richtig —*, regulate, correct, amend; (*clock*) set right; *seinen Mann —*, play o.'s part, pull o.'s weight. — *v.r. sich —*, come forward; pretend; *sich krank —*, feign illness, malinger, pretend to be ill.

Stellenbewerber ['ʃtɛlənbəvɛrbər], *m.* (—s, *pl.* —) applicant (for a job).

Stellengesuch ['ʃtɛləngəzuːx], *n.* (—s, *pl.* —e) application (for a job).

Stellenvermittlung ['ʃtɛlənfɛrmɪtluŋ], *f.* (—, *pl.* —en) employment office, employment exchange.

stellenweise ['ʃtɛlənvaɪzə], *adv.* in parts, here and there.

Stellmacher ['ʃtɛlmaxər], *m.* (—s, *pl.* —) wheelwright.

Stellung ['ʃtɛluŋ], *f.* (—, *pl.* —en) position, posture; attitude; situation; job; (*Mil.*) trenches; — *nehmen zu*, express o.'s views on.

Stellvertreter ['ʃtɛlfɛrtreːtər], *m.* (—s, *pl.* —) representative, deputy; substitute, supply, proxy, relief; (*doctor*) locum.

Stelzbein ['ʃtɛltsbaɪn], *n.* (—s, *pl.* —e) wooden leg.

Stemmeisen

Stemmeisen ['ʃtɛmaɪzən], n. (—s, pl. —) crowbar.

stemmen ['ʃtɛmən], v.a. (water) stem, dam; (weight) lift. — v.r. sich — gegen, resist fiercely.

Stempel ['ʃtɛmpəl], m. (—s, pl. —) stamp, rubber-stamp, die; pounder; (Bot.) pistil.

Stempelgebühr ['ʃtɛmpəlgəby:r], f. (—, pl. —en) stamp-duty.

stempeln ['ʃtɛmpəln], v.a. stamp, hallmark; brand; cancel (postage stamp). — v.n. (coll.) — gehen, be on the dole.

Stengel ['ʃtɛŋəl], m. (—s, pl. —) stalk.

Stenografie [ʃtenogra'fi:], f. (—, no pl.) stenography, shorthand.

stenografisch [ʃteno'gra:fiʃ], adj. in shorthand.

Stenogramm [ʃteno'gram], n. (—s, pl. —e) shorthand-note.

Stenotypistin [ʃtenoty'pɪstɪn], f. (—, pl. —nen) shorthand-typist.

Stephan ['ʃtefan], m. Stephen.

Steppdecke ['ʃtɛpdɛkə], f. (—, pl. —n) quilt.

Steppe ['ʃtɛpə], f. (—, pl. —n) steppe.

steppen ['ʃtɛpən], v.a. stitch, quilt.

Sterbeglocke ['ʃtɛrbəglɔkə], f. (—, pl. —n) passing bell, death bell.

Sterbehemd ['ʃtɛrbəhɛmt], n. (—(e)s, pl. —en) shroud, winding-sheet.

sterben ['ʃtɛrbən], v.n. irr. (aux. sein) die.

Sterbenswörtchen ['ʃtɛrbənsvœrtçən], n. (—s, pl. —) nicht ein —, not a syllable.

Sterbesakramente ['ʃtɛrbəzakramɛntə], n. pl. (Eccl.) last sacraments, last rites.

sterblich ['ʃtɛrplɪç], adj. mortal; — verliebt, desperately in love.

Sterblichkeit ['ʃtɛrplɪçkaɪt], f. (—, no pl.) mortality.

stereotyp [stereo'ty:p], adj. stereotyped.

sterilisieren [sterili'zi:rən], v.a. sterilise.

Sterilität [sterili'tɛ:t], f. (—, no pl.) sterility.

Stern [ʃtɛrn], m. (—(e)s, pl. —e) star; (Typ.) asterisk.

Sternbild ['ʃtɛrnbɪlt], n. (—s, pl. —er) constellation.

Sterndeuter ['ʃtɛrndɔytər], m. (—s, pl. —e) astrologer.

Sterndeutung ['ʃtɛrndɔytuŋ], f. (—, no pl.) astrology.

Sternenschimmer ['ʃtɛrnənʃɪmər], m. (—s, no pl.) starlight.

sternförmig ['ʃtɛrnfœrmɪç], adj. star-like, star-shaped.

Sterngucker ['ʃtɛrngukər], m. (—s, pl. —e) stargazer.

sternhagelvoll ['ʃtɛrnha:gəlfɔl], adj. (coll.) as drunk as a lord.

Sternkunde ['ʃtɛrnkundə], f. (—, no pl.) astronomy.

Sternkundige ['ʃtɛrnkundɪgə], m. (—n, pl. —n) astronomer.

Sternschnuppe ['ʃtɛrnʃnupə], f. (—, pl. —n) falling star, shooting star, meteorite.

Sternwarte ['ʃtɛrnvartə], f. (—, pl. —n) observatory.

stetig ['ʃte:tɪç], adj. continual, continuous, constant.

stets [ʃte:ts], adv. always, ever, continually.

Steuer (1) ['ʃtɔyər], n. (—s, pl. —) rudder, helm, steering wheel.

Steuer (2) ['ʃtɔyər], f. (—, pl. —n) tax; (local) rate; (import) customs duty.

Steueramt ['ʃtɔyəramt], n. (—s, pl. ̈er) inland revenue office, tax office.

Steuerbeamte ['ʃtɔyərbəamtə], m. (—n, pl. —n) revenue officer, tax collector.

Steuerbord ['ʃtɔyərbɔrt], n. (—s, no pl.) starboard.

Steuereinnehmer ['ʃtɔyəraɪnne:mər], m. (—s, pl. —) tax collector.

steuerfrei ['ʃtɔyərfraɪ], adj. duty-free, exempt from taxes.

Steuerhinterziehung ['ʃtɔyərhɪntərtsi:uŋ], f. (—, pl. —en) tax evasion.

steuerlos ['ʃtɔyərlo:s], adj. rudderless, adrift.

Steuermann ['ʃtɔyərman], m. (—s, pl. ̈er) mate; helmsman.

steuern ['ʃtɔyərn], v.a. steer; einem Unheil —, avoid or steer clear of an evil.

steuerpflichtig ['ʃtɔyərpflɪçtɪç], adj. taxable, liable to tax, dutiable.

Steuerrad ['ʃtɔyərra:t], n. (—s, pl. ̈er) steering-wheel.

Steuerung ['ʃtɔyəruŋ], f. (—, no pl.) steering, controls.

Steuerveranlagung ['ʃtɔyərfɛranla:guŋ], f. (—, pl. —en) tax-assessment.

stibitzen [ʃti'bɪtsən], v.a. (coll.) pilfer, filch.

Stich [ʃtɪç], m. (—(e)s, pl. —e) sting; prick; stitch; stab; (Cards) trick; (Art) engraving; einen im — lassen, leave s.o. in the lurch.

Stichel [ʃtɪçəl], m. (—s, pl. —) (Art) graver.

Stichelei [ʃtɪçə'laɪ], f. (—, pl. —en) taunt, sneer, gibe.

sticheln [ʃtɪçəln], v.a. taunt, nag.

stichhaltig ['ʃtɪçhaltɪç], adj. valid, sound.

Stichhaltigkeit ['ʃtɪçhaltɪçkaɪt], f. (—, no pl.) validity, cogency.

Stichprobe ['ʃtɪçpro:bə], f. (—, pl. —n) sample taken at random, sampling.

Stichwahl ['ʃtɪçva:l], f. (—, pl. —en) second ballot.

Stichwort ['ʃtɪçvɔrt], n. (—s, pl. —e) key-word; (Theat.) cue.

sticken ['ʃtɪkən], v.a., v.n. embroider.

Stickerei [ʃtɪkə'raɪ], f. (—, pl. —en) embroidery.

Stickgarn ['ʃtɪkgarn], n. (—s, pl. —e) embroidery cotton or silk.

Stickhusten ['ʃtɪkhu:stən], m. (—s, no pl.) choking cough.

stickig ['ʃtɪkɪç], *adj.* stuffy.

Stickmuster ['ʃtɪkmʊstər], *n.* (—s, *pl.* —) embroidery-pattern.

Stickstoff ['ʃtɪkʃtɔf], *m.* (—(e)s, *no pl.*) nitrogen.

stieben ['ʃtiːbən], *v.n.* (*aux.* sein) scatter, spray; *auseinander* —, disperse.

Stiefbruder ['ʃtiːfbruːdər], *m.* (—s, *pl.* ∵) step-brother.

Stiefel ['ʃtiːfəl], *m.* (—s, *pl.* —) boot.

Stiefelknecht ['ʃtiːfəlknɛçt], *m.* (—(e)s, *pl.* —e) boot-jack.

Stiefelputzer ['ʃtiːfəlpʊtsər], *m.* (—s, *pl.* —) shoe-black; (*Am.*) shoe-shine; (*hotel*) boots.

Stiefeltern ['ʃtiːfɛltərn], *pl.* step-parents.

Stiefmütterchen ['ʃtiːfmʏtərçən], *n.* (—s, *pl.* —) (*Bot.*) pansy.

stiefmütterlich ['ʃtiːfmʏtərlɪç], *adj.* like a stepmother; niggardly.

Stiefsohn ['ʃtiːfzoːn], *m.* (—s, *pl.* ∵e) stepson.

Stiege ['ʃtiːgə], *f.* (—, *pl.* —n) staircase.

Stieglitz ['ʃtiːglɪts], *m.* (—es, *pl.* —e) goldfinch.

Stiel [ʃtiːl], *m.* (—(e)s, *pl.* —e) handle; (*plant*) stalk.

Stier [ʃtiːr], *m.* (—(e)s, *pl.* —e) bull; *junger* —, bullock; (*Astrol.*) Taurus.

stieren ['ʃtiːrən], *v.n.* stare (at), goggle.

Stift (1) [ʃtɪft], *m.* (—(e)s, *pl.* —e) tack, pin, peg; pencil; (*coll.*) apprentice; young chap.

Stift (2) [ʃtɪft], *n.* (—(e)s, *pl.* —e) charitable *or* religious foundation.

stiften ['ʃtɪftən], *v.a.* establish, give, donate; found, set on foot, originate; *Frieden* —, bring about peace.

Stifter ['ʃtɪftər], *m.* (—s, *pl.* —) founder, originator, donor.

Stiftung ['ʃtɪftʊŋ], *f.* (—, *pl.* —en) establishment, foundation; institution; charitable foundation; endowment, donation.

Stil [ʃtiːl], *m.* (—(e)s, *pl.* —e) style; (*fig.*) manner.

stilisieren [ʃtiliˈziːrən], *v.a.* word, draft.

Stilistik [ʃtiˈlɪstɪk], *f.* (—, *no pl.*) art of composition.

stilistisch [ʃtiˈlɪstɪʃ], *adj.* stylistic.

still [ʃtɪl], *adj.* quiet, still, silent; calm; —*er Teilhaber*, sleeping partner; *im* —*en*, secretly, on the sly.

Stille ['ʃtɪlə], *f.* (—, *no pl.*) silence, quietness, tranquillity; calm, calmness; *in der* —, silently; *in der* — *der Nacht*, at dead of night.

stillen ['ʃtɪlən], *v.a.* allay; (*blood*) staunch; (*baby*) suckle, feed, nurse; (*thirst*) quench; (*hunger*) appease.

stillos ['ʃtiːloːs], *adj.* incongruous; in bad taste.

Stillung ['ʃtɪlʊŋ], *f.* (—, *no pl.*) allaying; (*blood*) staunching; (*baby*) suckling, feeding, nursing; (*thirst*) quenching; (*hunger*) appeasing.

stilvoll ['ʃtiːlfɔl], *adj.* harmonious; stylish; in good taste.

Stimmband ['ʃtɪmbant], *n.* (—s, *pl.* ∵er) vocal chord.

stimmberechtigt ['ʃtɪmbərɛçtɪçt], *adj.* entitled to vote, enfranchised.

Stimmbruch ['ʃtɪmbrux], *m.* (—s, *no pl.*) breaking of the voice.

Stimme ['ʃtɪmə], *f.* (—, *pl.* —n) voice; (*election*) vote, suffrage; *die* — *abgeben*, vote.

stimmen ['ʃtɪmən], *v.a.* (*piano*) tune; *einen günstig* —, dispose s.o. favourably towards s.th. — *v.n.* agree, tally (with), square (with), accord (with); vote.

Stimmeneinheit ['ʃtɪmənainhait], *f.* (—, *no pl.*) unanimity.

Stimmengleichheit ['ʃtɪmənglaɪçhait], *f.* (—, *no pl.*) equality of votes, tie.

Stimmer ['ʃtɪmər], *m.* (—s, *pl.* —) (*piano*) tuner.

Stimmführer ['ʃtɪmfyːrər], *m.* (—s, *pl.* —) leader, spokesman.

Stimmgabel ['ʃtɪmgaːbəl], *f.* (—, *pl.* —n) tuning fork.

stimmhaft ['ʃtɪmhaft], *adj.* (*Phonet.*) voiced.

Stimmlage ['ʃtɪmlaːgə], *f.* (—, *pl.* —n) (*Mus.*) register.

stimmlos ['ʃtɪmloːs], *adj.* voiceless; (*Phonet.*) unvoiced.

Stimmrecht ['ʃtɪmrɛçt], *n.* (—s, *no pl.*) suffrage, right to vote; *allgemeines* —, universal suffrage.

Stimmung ['ʃtɪmʊŋ], *f.* (—, *no pl.*) tuning; (*fig.*) disposition, humour, mood; atmosphere; *in guter* —, in high spirits, *in gedrückter* —, in low spirits.

stimmungsvoll ['ʃtɪmʊŋsfɔl], *adj.* impressive, full of atmosphere.

Stimmwechsel ['ʃtɪmvɛksəl], *m.* (—s, *no pl.*) breaking of the voice.

Stimmzettel ['ʃtɪmtsɛtəl], *m.* (—s, *pl.* —) ballot-paper.

stinken ['ʃtɪŋkən], *v.n. irr.* stink, reek, smell.

Stinktier ['ʃtɪŋktiːr], *n.* (—s, *pl.* —e) (*Zool.*) skunk.

Stipendium [ʃtiˈpɛndjum], *n.* (—s, *pl.* —dien) scholarship.

Stirn [ʃtɪrn], *f.* (—, *pl.* —en) forehead, brow; *die* — *runzeln*, frown, knit o.'s brow; *die* — *haben zu*, have the cheek to; *einem die* — *bieten*, face s.o., defy s.o.

Stirnhöhle ['ʃtɪrnhøːlə], *f.* (—, *pl.* —en) frontal cavity.

Stirnseite ['ʃtɪrnzaɪtə], *f.* (—, *pl.* —n) front.

stöbern ['ʃtøːbərn], *v.n.* rummage about; (*snow*) drift.

stochern ['ʃtɔxərn], *v.a., v.n.* (*food*) pick (at); (*teeth*) pick.

Stock (1) [ʃtɔk], *m.* (—(e)s, *pl.* ∵e) stick, cane, walking-stick; *über* — *und Stein*, over hedges and ditches.

Stock (2) [ʃtɔk], *m.* (—es, *pl.* —werke) storey, floor.

stocken

stocken ['ʃtɔkən], *v.n.* stop; (*blood*) run cold; (*linen*) go mildewed; hesitate, falter; (*conversation*) flag.

stockfinster ['ʃtɔkfınstər], *adj.* pitch dark.

Stockfisch ['ʃtɔkfıʃ], *m.* (—es, *pl.* —e) dried cod; dried fish.

stöckisch ['ʃtœkıʃ], *adj.* obstinate, stubborn.

Stockrose ['ʃtɔkro:zə], *f.* (—, *pl.* —n) (*Bot.*) hollyhock.

Stockschnupfen ['ʃtɔkʃnupfən], *m.* (—s, *no pl.*) heavy or chronic cold.

stocksteif ['ʃtɔkʃtaıf], *adj.* stiff as a poker.

stockstill ['ʃtɔkʃtıl], *adj.* quite still, stock-still.

stocktaub ['ʃtɔktaup], *adj.* deaf as a post.

Stockung ['ʃtɔkuŋ], *f.* (—, *pl.* —en) stagnation; hesitation; block, blockage; stopping, standstill.

Stockwerk ['ʃtɔkvɛrk], *n.* (—s, *pl.* —e) storey, floor.

Stoff [ʃtɔf], *m.* (—(e)s, *pl.* —e) fabric, material; substance; subject matter.

Stoffwechsel ['ʃtɔfvɛksəl], *m.* (—s, *no pl.*) metabolism.

stöhnen ['ʃtø:nən], *v.n.* groan, moan.

Stoiker ['ʃto:ıkər], *m.* (—s, *pl.* —) stoic.

Stola ['ʃto:la:], *f.* (—, *pl.* —len) (*Eccl.*) stole.

Stollen ['ʃtɔlən], *m.* (—s, *pl.* —) fruit-cake; (*Min.*) gallery, adit.

stolpern ['ʃtɔlpərn], *v.n.* (*aux.* sein) stumble, trip.

Stolz [ʃtɔlts], *m.* (—es, *no pl.*) haughtiness, pride.

stolz [ʃtɔlts], *adj.* haughty, proud; stuck-up, conceited; (*fig.*) majestic.

stolzieren [ʃtɔl'tsi:rən], *v.n.* (*aux.* sein) strut; prance.

stopfen ['ʃtɔpfən], *v.a.* stuff; fill; darn, mend; *einem den Mund* —, cut s.o. short.

Stopfgarn ['ʃtɔpfgarn], *n.* (—s, *pl.* —e) darning-thread.

Stoppel ['ʃtɔpəl], *f.* (—, *pl.* —n) stubble.

stoppeln ['ʃtɔpəln], *v.a.* glean; *etwas zusammen* —, compile s.th. badly.

Stöpsel ['ʃtœpsəl], *m.* (—s, *pl.* —) stopper, cork; *kleiner* —, little mite.

stöpseln ['ʃtœpsəln], *v.a.* cork.

Stör [ʃtø:r], *m.* (—(e)s, *pl.* —e) (*Zool.*) sturgeon.

Storch [ʃtɔrç], *m.* (—(e)s, *pl.* ⸚e) (*Orn.*) stork.

Storchschnabel ['ʃtɔrçʃna:bəl], *m.* (—s, *pl.* ⸚) stork's bill; (*Tech.*) pantograph.

stören ['ʃtø:rən], *v.a.* disturb, trouble; (*Rad.*) jam. — *v.n.* intrude, be in the way.

Störenfried ['ʃtø:rənfri:d], *m.* (—s, *pl.* —e) intruder, mischief-maker, nuisance.

Störer ['ʃtø:rər], *m.* (—s, *pl.* —) disturber.

stornieren [ʃtɔr'ni:rən], *v.a.* cancel, annul.

störrisch ['ʃtœrıʃ], *adj.* stubborn obstinate.

Störung ['ʃtø:ruŋ], *f.* (—, *pl.* —en) disturbance, intrusion; (*Rad.*) jamming.

Stoß [ʃto:s], *m.* (—es, *pl.* ⸚e) push, thrust; impact; blow, stroke, jolt; (*papers*) heap, pile; (*documents*) bundle.

Stoßdegen ['ʃto:sde:gən], *m.* (—s, *pl.* —) rapier.

Stößel ['ʃtø:səl], *m.* (—s, *pl.* —) pestle; (*Motor.*) tappet.

stoßen ['ʃto:sən], *v.a. irr.* thrust, push; pound; *vor den Kopf* —, offend. — *v.n.* bump, jolt; — *an*, border upon; *auf etwas* —, come across s.th., stumble on s.th.; *ins Horn* —, blow a horn. — *v.r. sich* —, hurt o.s.; *sich an etwas* —, take offence at s.th., take exception to s.th.

Stoßseufzer ['ʃto:szɔyftsər], *m.* (—s, *pl.* —) deep sigh.

Stoßwaffe ['ʃto:svafə], *f.* (—, *pl.* —n) thrusting or stabbing weapon.

stoßweise ['ʃto:svaızə], *adv.* by fits and starts.

Stotterer ['ʃtɔtərər], *m.* (—s, *pl.* —) stutterer, stammerer.

stottern ['ʃtɔtərn], *v.n.* stutter, stammer.

stracks [ʃtraks], *adv.* straight away, directly.

Strafanstalt ['ʃtra:fanʃtalt], *f.* (—, *pl.* —en) penitentiary, prison.

Strafarbeit ['ʃtra:farbaıt], *f.* (—, *pl.* —en) (*Sch.*) imposition.

strafbar ['ʃtra:fba:r], *adj.* punishable, criminal, culpable.

Strafbarkeit ['ʃtra:fba:rkaıt], *f.* (—, *no pl.*) culpability.

Strafe ['ʃtra:fə], *f.* (—, *pl.* —n) punishment; (*money*) fine, penalty; *bei* — *von*, on pain of.

strafen ['ʃtra:fən], *v.a.* punish, rebuke; (*money*) fine.

Straferlaß ['ʃtra:fərlas], *m.* (—sses, *pl.* —sse) remission of penalty, amnesty.

straff [ʃtraf], *adj.* tight, tense, taut.

Strafgericht ['ʃtra:fgərıçt], *n.* (—es, *no pl.*) punishment; judgment; (*Law*) Criminal Court.

Strafgesetzbuch ['ʃtra:fgəzɛtsbu:x], *n.* (—(e)s, *pl.* ⸚er) penal code.

sträflich ['ʃtrɛ:flıç], *adj.* punishable; culpable; reprehensible, blameworthy.

Sträfling ['ʃtrɛ:flıŋ], *m.* (—s, *pl.* —e) convict.

Strafporto ['ʃtra:fpɔrto], *n.* (—s, *pl.* —ti) excess postage.

Strafpredigt ['ʃtra:fpredıçt], *f.* (—, *pl.* —en) severe admonition, stern reprimand.

Strafprozess ['ʃtra:fprotsɛs], *m.* (—es, *pl.* —e) criminal proceedings.

Strafrecht ['ʃtra:frɛçt], *n.* (—(e)s, *no pl.*) criminal law.

Strafverfahren ['ʃtra:ffɛrfa:rən], *n.* (—s, *pl.* —) criminal procedure.

Strahl [ʃtra:l], *m.* (—(e)s, *pl.* —en) beam, ray; (*water etc.*) jet, spout; (*lightning*) flash; —en werfen, emit rays.

Strahlantrieb ['ʃtra:lantri:p], *m.* (—s, *no pl.*) (*Aviat.*) jet propulsion.

strahlen ['ʃtra:lən], *v.n.* radiate, shine, beam, emit rays; (*fig.*) beam (with joy).

strählen ['ʃtrɛ:lən], *v.a.* (*rare*) comb.

Strahlenbrechung ['ʃtra:lənbrɛçuŋ], *f.* (—, *pl.* —en) refraction.

strahlenförmig ['ʃtra:lənfœrmɪç], *adj.* radiate.

Strahlenkrone ['ʃtra:lənkro:nə], *f.* (—, *pl.* —n) aureole, halo.

Strahlung ['ʃtra:luŋ], *f.* (—, *pl.* —en) radiation; (*fig.*) radiance.

Strähne ['ʃtrɛ:nə], *f.* (—, *pl.* —n) skein, hank; *eine — Pech*, a spell of bad luck.

Stramin [ʃtra'mi:n], *m.* (—s, *pl.* —e) embroidery canvas.

stramm [ʃtram], *adj.* tight; rigid; sturdy, strapping.

strampeln ['ʃtrampəln], *v.n.* struggle; (*baby*) kick.

Strand [ʃtrant], *m.* (—(e)s, *pl.* —e) shore, beach, strand.

stranden ['ʃtrandən], *v.n.* be stranded, founder.

Strandkorb ['ʃtrantkɔrp], *m.* (—s, *pl.* ⸚e) beach-chair.

Strandwache ['ʃtrantvaxə], *f.* (—, *no pl.*) coast-guard.

Strang [ʃtraŋ], *m.* (—(e)s, *pl.* ⸚e) rope, cord; *über die ⸚e schlagen*, kick over the traces; *zum — verurteilen*, condemn to be hanged.

strangulieren [ʃtraŋgu'li:rən], *v.a.* strangle.

Strapaze [ʃtra'patsə], *f.* (—, *pl.* —n) over-exertion, fatigue, hardship.

strapazieren [ʃtrapa'tsi:rən], *v.a.* over-exert, fatigue.

strapaziös [ʃtrapa'tsjø:s], *adj.* fatiguing, exacting.

Straße ['ʃtra:sə], *f.* (—, *pl.* —n) (*city*) street; (*country*) road, highway; (*sea*) strait; *auf der —*, in the street; *über die — gehen*, cross the street.

Straßenbahn ['ʃtra:sənba:n], *f.* (—, *pl.* —en) tram; tramcar, (*Am.*) street-car.

Straßendamm ['ʃtra:səndam], *m.* (—s, *pl.* ⸚e) roadway.

Straßendirne ['ʃtra:səndɪrnə], *f.* (—, *pl.* —n) prostitute, street-walker.

Straßenfeger ['ʃtra:sənfe:gər], *m.* (—s, *pl.* —) roadman, road-sweeper, scavenger, crossing-sweeper.

Straßenpflaster ['ʃtra:sənpflastər], *n.* (—s, *no pl.*) pavement.

Straßenraub ['ʃtra:sənraup], *m.* (—s, *no pl.*) highway-robbery.

Stratege [ʃtra'te:gə], *m.* (—n, *pl.* —n) strategist.

sträuben ['ʃtrɔybən], *v.r. sich —*, bristle; (*fig.*) struggle (against), oppose.

Strauch [ʃtraux], *m.* (—(e)s, *pl.* ⸚er) bush, shrub.

straucheln ['ʃtrauxəln], *v.n.* (*aux.* sein) stumble.

Strauchritter ['ʃtrauxrɪtər], *m.* (—s, *pl.* —) footpad, vagabond, highwayman.

Strauß (1) [ʃtraus], *m.* (—es, *pl.* ⸚e) (*Poet.*) fight, tussle; (*flowers*) bunch, bouquet, nosegay.

Strauß (2) [ʃtraus], *m.* (—es, *pl.* —e) (*Orn.*) ostrich.

Sträußchen ['ʃtrɔysçən], *n.* (—s, *pl.* —) small bunch of flowers, nosegay.

Straußfeder ['ʃtrausfe:dər], *f.* (—, *pl.* —n) ostrich-feather.

Strazze ['ʃtratsə], *f.* (—, *pl.* —n) scrapbook.

Strebe ['ʃtre:bə], *f.* (—, *pl.* —n) buttress, prop, stay.

Strebebogen ['ʃtre:bəbo:gən], *m.* (—s, *pl.* —) (*Archit.*) arch, buttress; flying buttress.

Streben ['ʃtre:bən], *n.* (—s, *no pl.*) ambition, aspiration; effort, endeavour, striving.

streben ['ʃtre:bən], *v.n.* strive, aspire, endeavour.

Streber ['ʃtre:bər], *m.* (—s, *pl.* —) pushing person, (social) climber. (*Am. coll.*) go-getter.

strebsam ['ʃtre:pza:m], *adj.* ambitious, assiduous, industrious.

streckbar ['ʃtrɛkba:r], *adj.* ductile, extensible.

Streckbett ['ʃtrɛkbɛt], *n.* (—s, *pl.* —en) orthopaedic bed.

Strecke ['ʃtrɛkə], *f.* (—, *pl.* —n) stretch, reach, extent; distance; tract; line; *zur — bringen*, (*Hunt.*) bag, run to earth.

strecken ['ʃtrɛkən], *v.a.* stretch, extend; (*metal*) hammer out, roll; make (s.th.) last; *die Waffen —*, lay down arms.

Streich [ʃtraɪç], *m.* (—(e)s, *pl.* —e) stroke, blow; (*fig.*) prank; trick; *dummer —*, piece of folly, lark.

streicheln ['ʃtraɪçəln], *v.a.* stroke, caress.

streichen ['ʃtraɪçən], *v.a. irr.* stroke, touch; paint, spread; cancel; strike; (*sail*) lower. — *v.n.* move past, fly past; wander.

Streichholz ['ʃtraɪçhɔlts], *n.* (—s, *pl.* ⸚er) match.

Streichinstrument ['ʃtraɪçɪnstrumɛnt], *n.* (—s, *pl.* —e) stringed instrument.

Streif [ʃtraɪf], *m.* (—(e)s, *pl.* —e) stripe, strip, streak.

Streifband ['ʃtraɪfbant], *n.* (—s, *pl.* ⸚er) wrapper.

Streifblick ['ʃtraɪfblɪk], *m.* (—s, *pl.* —e) glance.

Streife ['ʃtraɪfə], *f.* (—, *pl.* —n) raid; patrol (*police etc.*).

Streifen ['ʃtraɪfən], *m.* (—s, *pl.* —) stripe, streak; (*Mil.*) bar.

streifen

streifen ['ʃtraɪfən], *v.a.* graze, touch in passing; take off (*remove*). — *v.n.* (*aux.* sein) ramble, roam, rove.

streifig ['ʃtraɪfɪç], *adj.* striped, streaky.

Streik [ʃtraɪk], *m.* (—(e)s, *pl.* —s) strike; *in den* — *treten*, go on strike.

Streikbrecher ['ʃtraɪkbrɛçər], *m.* (—s, *pl.* —) blackleg.

streiken ['ʃtraɪkən], *v.n.* (*workers*) strike, be on strike.

Streit [ʃtraɪt], *m.* (—(e)s, *pl.* —e) dispute, quarrel, conflict; (*words*) argument; *einen* — *anfangen*, pick a quarrel.

Streitaxt ['ʃtraɪtakst], *f.* (—, *pl.* ⁻e) battle-axe.

streitbar ['ʃtraɪtbaːr], *adj.* warlike, martial.

streiten ['ʃtraɪtən], *v.n. irr.* quarrel, fight; —*de Kirche*, Church Militant.

Streitfrage ['ʃtraɪtfraːgə], *f.* (—, *pl.* —n) moot point, point at issue; controversy.

Streithammel ['ʃtraɪthaməl], *m.* (—s, *pl.* —) squabbler.

Streithandel ['ʃtraɪthandəl], *m.* (—s, *pl.* ⁻) law-suit.

streitig ['ʃtraɪtɪç], *adj.* disputable, doubtful, at issue; *einem etwas* — *machen*, contest s.o.'s right to s.th.

Streitkräfte ['ʃtraɪtkrɛftə], *f. pl.* (*Mil.*) forces.

streitlustig ['ʃtraɪtlustɪç], *adj.* argumentative.

Streitschrift ['ʃtraɪtʃrɪft], *f.* (—, *pl.* —en) pamphlet, polemical treatise.

Streitsucht ['ʃtraɪtzuxt], *f.* (—, *no pl.*) quarrelsomeness; (*Law*) litigiousness.

streitsüchtig ['ʃtraɪtzyçtɪç], *adj.* quarrelsome, litigious.

streng [ʃtrɛŋ], *adj.* severe, strict, rigorous; —*e Kälte*, biting cold; *im* —*sten Winter*, in the depth of winter. — *adv.* —*genommen*, strictly speaking.

Strenge ['ʃtrɛŋə], *f.* (—, *no pl.*) severity, rigour.

strenggläubig ['ʃtrɛŋgləybɪç], *adj.* strictly orthodox.

Streu [ʃtrɔy], *f.* (—, *pl.* —en) litter, bed of straw.

Streubüchse ['ʃtrɔybyksə], *f.* (—, *pl.* —n) castor.

streuen ['ʃtrɔyən], *v.a.* strew, scatter, sprinkle.

streunen ['ʃtrɔynən], *v.n.* roam (about).

Streuung ['ʃtrɔyuŋ], *f.* (—, *pl.* —en) strewing; (*shot*) dispersion.

Streuzucker ['ʃtrɔytsukər], *m.* (—s, *no pl.*) castor-sugar.

Strich [ʃtrɪç], *m.* (—(e)s, *pl.* —e) stroke, line, dash; (*land*) tract; (*Art*) touch; region; *gegen den* —, against the grain; *einem einen* — *durch die Rechnung machen*, put a spoke in s.o.'s wheel, frustrate s.o.

Strichpunkt ['ʃtrɪçpuŋkt], *m.* (—s, *pl.* —e) semicolon.

Strichregen ['ʃtrɪçreːgən], *m.* (—s, *pl.* —) passing shower.

Strick [ʃtrɪk], *m.* (—(e)s, *pl.* —e) cord, line, rope; *du* —, (*fig.*) you scamp! *einem einen* — *drehen*, give s.o. enough rope to hang himself, lay a trap for s.o.

stricken ['ʃtrɪkən], *v.a., v.n.* knit.

Strickerei [ʃtrɪkəˈraɪ], *f.* (—, *pl.* —en) knitting; knitting business, workshop.

Strickleiter ['ʃtrɪklaɪtər], *f.* (—, *pl.* —n) rope-ladder.

Strickzeug ['ʃtrɪktsɔyk], *n.* (—s, *pl.* —e) knitting.

Striegel ['ʃtriːgəl], *m.* (—s, *pl.* —) curry-comb.

striegeln ['ʃtriːgəln], *v.a.* curry.

Strieme ['ʃtriːmə], *f.* (—, *pl.* —n) weal, stripe.

Strippe ['ʃtrɪpə], *f.* (—, *pl.* —n) strap, band, string; cord.

strittig ['ʃtrɪtɪç], *adj.* contentious, debatable.

Stroh [ʃtroː], *n.* (—s, *no pl.*) straw; (*roof*) thatch; *mit* — *decken*, thatch; *leeres* — *dreschen*, beat the air.

Strohfeuer ['ʃtroːfɔyər], *n.* (—s, *no pl.*) (*fig.*) flash in the pan; short-lived enthusiasm.

Strohhalm ['ʃtroːhalm], *m.* (—s, *pl.* —e) straw.

Strohhut ['ʃtroːhuːt], *m.* (—s, *pl.* ⁻e) straw-hat.

Strohkopf ['ʃtroːkɔpf], *m.* (—(e)s, *pl.* ⁻e) (*coll.*) stupid person.

Strohmann ['ʃtroːman], *m.* (—s, *pl.* ⁻er) (*coll.*) man of straw; (*Cards*) dummy.

Strohmatte ['ʃtroːmatə], *f.* (—, *pl.* —n) straw-mat.

Strohwitwe ['ʃtroːvɪtvə], *f.* (—, *pl.* —n) grass-widow.

Strolch [ʃtrɔlç], *m.* (—(e)s, *pl.* —e) vagabond; (*fig.*) scamp.

Strom [ʃtroːm], *m.* (—(e)s, *pl.* ⁻e) river, torrent; (*also fig.*) flood; stream; (*also Elec.*) current; (*coll.*) electricity; *gegen den* — *schwimmen*, swim against the current, be an individualist.

stromab ['ʃtroːmap], *adv.* downstream.

stromauf ['ʃtroːmauf], *adv.* upstream.

strömen ['ʃtrøːmən], *v.n.* (*aux.* sein) flow, stream; (*rain*) pour; (*people*) flock.

Stromer ['ʃtroːmər], *m.* (—s, *pl.* —) vagabond, tramp, vagrant.

Stromkreis ['ʃtroːmkraɪs], *m.* (—es, *pl.* —e) (*Elec.*) circuit.

Stromschnelle ['ʃtroːmʃnɛlə], *f.* (—, *pl.* —n) rapids.

Strömung ['ʃtrøːmuŋ], *f.* (—, *pl.* —en) current; (*fig.*) tendency.

Strophe ['ʃtroːfə], *f.* (—, *pl.* —n) verse, stanza.

strotzen ['ʃtrɔtsən], *v.n.* be puffed up; overflow, burst, teem.

strotzend ['ʃtrɔtsənt], *adj. vor Gesundheit* —, bursting with health.

Strudel ['ʃtruːdəl], *m.* (—s, *pl.* —) whirl, whirlpool, vortex, eddy; pastry.

Struktur [ʃtrukˈtuːr], *f.* (—, *pl.* —en) structure.

Strumpf [ʃtrumpf], m. (—(e)s, pl. ꞈe) stocking; (short) sock.

Strumpfband [ʃtrumpfbant], n. (—(e)s, pl. ꞈer) garter.

Strumpfwaren [ʃtrumpfva:rən], f. pl. hosiery.

Strumpfwirker [ʃtrumpfvɪrkər], m. (—s, pl. —) stocking-weaver.

Strunk [ʃtruŋk], m. (—(e)s, pl. ꞈe) (tree) stump, trunk; (plant) stalk.

struppig [ʃtrupɪç], adj. rough, unkempt, frowsy.

Stube [ʃtu:bə], f. (—, pl. —n) room, chamber; gute —, sitting-room.

Stubenarrest [ʃtu:bənarɛst], m. (—s, pl. —e) confinement to quarters.

Stubenhocker [ʃtu:bənhɔkər], m. (—s, pl. —) stay-at-home.

Stubenmädchen [ʃtu:bənmɛːtçən], n. (—s, pl. —) housemaid.

Stuck [ʃtuk], m. (—(e)s, no pl.) stucco, plaster.

Stück [ʃtyk], n. (—(e)s, pl. —e) piece; part; lump; (Theat.) play; aus freien —en, of o.'s own accord; große —e auf einen halten, think highly of s.o.

Stückarbeit [ʃtykarbaɪt], f. (—, pl. —en) piece-work.

Stückchen [ʃtykçən], n. (—s, pl. —) small piece, morsel, bit.

stückeln [ʃtykəln], v.a. cut in(to) pieces; patch, mend.

stückweise [ʃtykvaɪzə], adv. piecemeal.

Stückwerk [ʃtykvɛrk], n. (—s, no pl.) (fig.) patchy or imperfect work, a bungled job.

Stückzucker [ʃtyktsukər], m. (—s, no pl.) lump sugar.

Student [ʃtu'dɛnt], m. (—en, pl. —en) (Univ.) student, undergraduate.

studentenhaft [ʃtu'dɛntənhaft], adj. student-like.

Studentenverbindung [ʃtu'dɛntənferbɪnduŋ], f. (—, pl. —en) students' association or union.

Studie [ʃtu:djə], f. (—, pl. —n) study, (Art) sketch; (Lit.) essay; (pl.) studies.

Studienplan [ʃtu:djənpla:n], m. (—s, pl. ꞈe) curriculum.

Studienrat [ʃtu:djənra:t], m. (—s, pl. ꞈe) grammar school teacher, assistant master.

studieren [ʃtu'di:rən], v.a., v.n. study, read (a subject); be at (the) university.

studiert [ʃtu'di:rt], adj. educated; (fig.) affected, deliberate, studied.

Studierte [ʃtu'di:rtə], m. (coll.) egghead.

Studium [ʃtu:djum], n. (—s, pl. —dien) study, pursuit; university education.

Stufe [ʃtu:fə], f. (—, pl. —n) step; (fig.) degree; auf gleicher — mit, on a level with.

stufenweise [ʃtu:fənvaɪzə], adv. gradually, by degrees.

Stuhl [ʃtu:l], m. (—s, pl. ꞈe) chair, seat; der Heilige —, the Holy See.

Stuhlgang [ʃtu:lgaŋ], m. (—s, no pl.) (Med.) stool, evacuation (of the bowels), movement, motion.

Stukkatur [ʃtuka'tu:r], f. (—, no pl.) stucco-work.

Stulle [ʃtulə], f. (—, pl. —n) (dial.) slice of bread and butter.

Stulpe [ʃtulpə], f. (—, pl. —n) cuff.

stülpen [ʃtylpən], v.a. turn up, invert.

Stulpnase [ʃtulpna:zə], f. (—, pl. —n) turned-up nose, pug-nose.

Stulpstiefel [ʃtulpʃti:fəl], m. (—s, pl. —) top-boot.

stumm [ʃtum], adj. mute, dumb, silent.

Stumme [ʃtumə], m. & f. (—n, pl. —n) dumb person, mute.

Stummel [ʃtuməl], m. (—s, pl. —) stump; (cigarette) end, butt.

Stummheit [ʃtumhaɪt], f. (—, no pl.) dumbness.

Stümper [ʃtympər], m. (—s, pl. —) bungler, botcher.

stümperhaft [ʃtympərhaft], adj. bungling, botchy.

stümpern [ʃtympərn], v.a., v.n. bungle, botch.

Stumpf [ʃtumpf], m. (—(e)s, pl. ꞈe) stump, trunk; mit — und Stiel ausrotten, destroy root and branch.

stumpf [ʃtumpf], adj. blunt; (angle) obtuse; (fig.) dull; — machen, blunt, dull.

Stumpfsinn [ʃtumpfzɪn], m. (—s, no pl.) stupidity, dullness.

stumpfwinklig [ʃtumpfvɪŋklɪç], adj. obtuse-angled.

Stunde [ʃtundə], f. (—, pl. —n) hour; lesson.

stunden [ʃtundən], v.a. give a respite, allow time (to pay up).

Stundenglas [ʃtundənglas], n. (—es, pl. ꞈer) hour-glass.

Stundenplan [ʃtundənpla:n], m. (—s, pl. ꞈe) (Sch.) schedule.

Stundenzeiger [ʃtundəntsaɪgər], m. (—s, pl. —) hour-hand.

Stündlein [ʃtyntlaɪn], n. (—s, pl. —) sein — hat geschlagen, his last hour has come.

Stundung [ʃtunduŋ], f. (—, pl. —en) respite, grace.

stupend [ʃtu'pɛnt], adj. stupendous.

stur [ʃtu:r], adj. obdurate, unwavering, stolid, dour, stubborn.

Sturm [ʃturm], m. (—(e)s, pl. ꞈe) storm, gale, tempest, hurricane; (Mil.) attack, assault; — und Drang, (Lit.) Storm and Stress; — im Wasserglas, storm in a teacup; — laufen gegen, storm against.

Sturmband [ʃturmbant], n. (—s, pl. ꞈer) chinstrap.

Sturmbock [ʃturmbɔk], m. (—s, pl. ꞈe) battering-ram.

stürmen [ʃtyrmən], v.a. storm, take by assault. — v.n. be violent, be stormy; (Mil.) advance.

Stürmer [ʃtyrmər], m. (—s, pl. —) assailant; (football) centre-forward.

Sturmglocke [ʃturmglɔkə], f. (—, pl. —n) tocsin, alarm-bell.

Sturmhaube [ˈʃturmhaubə], f. (—, pl. —en) (Mil.) morion, helmet.

stürmisch [ˈʃtyrmiʃ], adj. stormy, tempestuous; (fig.) boisterous, turbulent, tumultuous, impetuous; —er Beifall, frantic applause; —e Überfahrt, rough crossing.

Sturmschritt [ˈʃturmʃrit], m. (—s, no pl.) double march.

Sturmvogel [ˈʃturmfoːgəl], m. (—s, pl. ⸚) (Orn.) stormy petrel.

Sturz [ʃturts], m. (—es, pl. ⸚e) fall, tumble; crash; collapse; (Comm.) failure, smash; (government) overthrow.

Sturzacker [ˈʃturtsakər], m. (—s, pl. ⸚) freshly ploughed field.

Sturzbach [ˈʃturtsbax], m. (—(e)s, pl. ⸚e) torrent.

Stürze [ˈʃtyrtsə], f. (—, pl. —n) pot-lid, cover.

stürzen [ˈʃtyrtsən], v.a. hurl, overthrow; ruin. — v.n. (aux. sein) (person) have a fall; (object) tumble down; (business) fail; crash; plunge; (water) rush. — v.r. throw oneself; sich — auf, rush at, plunge into.

Sturzhelm [ˈʃturtshelm], m. (—s, pl. —e) crash-helmet.

Sturzsee [ˈʃturtszeː], f. (—, no pl.) heavy sea.

Sturzwelle [ˈʃturtsvɛlə], f. (—, pl. —n) breaker, roller.

Stute [ˈʃtuːtə], f. (—, pl. —n) mare.

Stutzbart [ˈʃtutsbaːrt], m. (—s, pl. ⸚e) short beard.

Stütze [ˈʃtytsə], f. (—, pl. —n) prop, support, stay.

Stutzen [ˈʃtutsən], m. (—s, pl. —) short rifle, carbine.

stutzen [ˈʃtutsən], v.a. (hair) clip, trim; (horse) dock, crop; (tree) prune, lop. — v.n. be taken aback, hesitate.

stützen [ˈʃtytsən], v.a. prop, support; base or found (on). — v.r. sich — auf, lean upon; (fig.) rely upon.

Stutzer [ˈʃtutsər], m. (—s, pl. —) dandy, fop, beau.

stutzerhaft [ˈʃtutsərhaft], adj. dandified.

stutzig [ˈʃtutsiç], adj. startled, puzzled; — werden, be non-plussed, be taken aback or puzzled.

Stützmauer [ˈʃtytsmauər], f. (—, pl. —n) buttress, retaining wall.

Stützpunkt [ˈʃtytspuŋkt], m. (—s, pl. —e) point of support; foothold; (Mil.) base; (Tech.) fulcrum.

Subjekt [zupˈjɛkt], n. (—s, pl. —e) subject; (fig.) creature.

subjektiv [zupjɛkˈtiːf], adj. subjective, personal, prejudiced.

sublimieren [zubliˈmiːrən], v.a. sublimate.

Substantiv [zupstanˈtiːf], n. (—(e)s, pl. —e) (Gram.) substantive, noun.

subtil [zupˈtiːl], adj. subtle.

subtrahieren [zuptraˈhiːrən], v.a. subtract.

Subvention [zupvɛnˈtsjoːn], f. (—, pl. —en) subsidy, grant-in-aid.

Suche [ˈzuːxə], f. (—, no pl.) search, quest; auf der — nach, in quest of.

suchen [ˈzuːxən], v.a., v.n. seek, look for; attempt, endeavour.

Sucht [zuxt], f. (—, pl. ⸚e) mania, addiction, passion.

süchtig [ˈzyxtiç], adj. addicted (to).

Sud [zuːd], m. (—(e)s, pl. —e) boiling, brewing; suds.

Sudan [ˈzuːdan], m. the Sudan.

sudeln [ˈzuːdəln], v.a., v.n. smear, daub, make a mess (of).

Süden [ˈzyːdən], m. (—s, no pl.) south.

Südfrüchte [ˈzyːdfryçtə], f. pl. Mediterranean or tropical fruit.

südlich [ˈzyːtliç], adj. southern, southerly; in —er Richtung, southward.

Südosten [zyːtˈʔɔstən], m. (—s, no pl.) south-east.

Suff [zuf], m. (—(e)s, no pl.) (sl.) boozing, tippling.

suggerieren [zugeˈriːrən], v.a. suggest.

Sühne [ˈzyːnə], f. (—, no pl.) expiation, atonement.

sühnen [ˈzyːnən], v.a. expiate, atone for.

Sühneopfer [ˈzyːnəɔpfər], n. (—s, pl. —) expiatory sacrifice; atonement.

Suite [ˈsviːtə], f. (—, pl. —n) retinue, train.

sukzessiv [zuktsɛˈsiːf], adj. gradual, successive.

Sülze [ˈzyltsə], f. (—, pl. —n) brawn, aspic, jelly.

Summa [ˈzuˈmaː], f. (—, pl. Summen) — summarum, sum total.

summarisch [zuˈmaːriʃ], adj. summary.

Summe [ˈzumə], f. (—, pl. —n) sum, amount.

summen [ˈzumən], v.a. hum. — v.n. buzz, hum.

summieren [zuˈmiːrən], v.a. sum up, add up. — v.r. sich —, mount up.

Sumpf [zumpf], m. (—(e)s, pl. ⸚e) bog, morass, marsh, moor, swamp.

sumpfig [ˈzumpfiç], adj. boggy, marshy.

Sund [zunt], m. (—(e)s, pl. —e) straits, sound.

Sünde [ˈzyndə], f. (—, pl. —n) sin.

Sündenbock [ˈzyndənbɔk], m. (—s, pl. ⸚e) scapegoat.

Sündenfall [ˈzyndənfal], m. (—s, no pl.) (Theol.) the Fall (of man).

Sündengeld [ˈzyndəngɛlt], n. (—(e)s, no pl.) ill-gotten gains; (coll.) vast sum of money.

sündenlos [ˈzyndənloːs], adj. sinless, impeccable.

Sündenpfuhl [ˈzyndənpfuːl], m. (—s, pl. —e) sink of iniquity.

Sünder [ˈzyndər], m. (—s, pl. —) sinner; armer —, poor devil; du alter —, you old scoundrel.

sündhaft [ˈzynthaft], adj. sinful, iniquitous.

sündig [ˈzyndiç], adj. sinful.

sündigen [ˈzyndigən], v.n. sin, err.

Sündigkeit [ˈzyndiçkait], f. (—, no pl.) sinfulness.

Superlativ [ˈzuːpərlatiːf], m. (—s, pl. —e) superlative (degree).

Suppe ['zupə], f. (—, pl. —n) soup; *eingebrannte* —, thick soup; *einem edi — versalzen*, spoil s.o.'s little game.
Suppenfleisch ['zupənflaiʃ], n. (—es, no pl.) stock-meat.
Suppenkelle ['zupənkɛlə], f. (—, pl. —n) soup ladle.
Suppenterrine ['zupəntɛri:nə], f. (—, pl. —n) tureen.
Surrogat [zuro'ga:t], n. (—s, pl. —e) substitute.
süß [zy:s], adj. sweet.
Süße ['zy:sə], f. (—, no pl.) sweetness.
süßen ['zy:sən], v.a. sweeten.
Süßholz ['zy:sholts], n. (—es, no pl.) liquorice; — *raspeln*, talk sweet nothings, pay compliments.
Süßigkeit ['zy:sıçkaıt], f. (—, pl. —en) sweetness; (pl.) sweets.
süßlich ['zy:slıç], adj. sweetish; (fig.) fulsome, mawkish, cloying.
Süßspeise ['zy:sʃpaizə], f. (—, pl. —n) dessert.
Süßwasser ['zy:svasər], n. (—s, no pl.) fresh water.
Symbolik [zym'bo:lık], f. (—, no pl.) symbolism.
symbolisch [zym'bo:lıʃ], adj. symbolic(al).
symbolisieren [zymboli'zi:rən], v.a. symbolize.
symmetrisch [zy'me:trıʃ], adj. symmetrical.
Sympathie [zympa'ti:], f. (—, no pl.) sympathy.
sympathisch [zym'pa:tıʃ], adj. congenial, likeable.
Synagoge [zyna'go:gə], f. (—, pl. —n) synagogue.
synchronisieren [zynkroni'zi:rən], v.a. synchronise.
Syndikus ['zyndikus], m. (—, pl. **Syndizi**) syndic.
Synode [zy'no:də], f. (—, pl. —n) synod.
synthetisch [zyn'te:tıʃ], adj. synthetic.
Syrien [zy:rjən] n. Syria.
systematisch [zyste'ma:tıʃ], adj. systematic(al).
Szenarium [stse'na:rjum], n. (—s, pl. —rien) scenario, stage, scene.
Szene ['stse:nə], f. (—, pl. —n) scene; *in — setzen*, stage, produce; (coll.) get up; *sich in — setzen*, show off.
Szenerie [stsenə'ri:], f. (—, pl. —n) scenery.
szenisch ['stse:nıʃ], adj. scenic.
Szepter ['stsɛptər], n. (—s, pl. —) sceptre, mace.

T

T [te:], n. (—, pl. —) the letter T.
Tabak ['ta:bak], m. (—s, pl. —e) tobacco.

Tabaksbeutel ['ta:baksbɔytəl], m. (—s, pl. —) tobacco-pouch.
Tabatiere [ta:ba'tjɛ:rə], f. (—, pl. —n) snuff-box.
tabellarisch [tabɛ'la:rıʃ], adj. in tables, tabular.
Tabelle [ta'bɛlə], f. (—, pl. —n) table, index, schedule.
Tablett [ta'blɛt], n. (—s, pl. —s) tray.
Tablette [ta'blɛtə], f. (—, pl. —n) tablet, pill.
Tabulatur [tabula'tu:r], f. (—, pl. —en) tablature, tabling, index.
Tadel ['ta:dəl], m. (—s, pl. —) blame, censure, reproach; (Sch.) bad mark; *ohne* —, blameless.
tadellos ['ta:dəllo:s], adj. blameless, faultless, impeccable.
tadeln ['ta:dəln], v.a. blame, censure, find fault with; reprimand.
tadelnswert ['ta:dəlnsve:rt], adj. blameworthy, culpable.
Tafel ['ta:fəl], f. (—, pl. —n) board; (Sch.) blackboard; slate; (fig.) (obs.) dinner, banquet; festive fare; (chocolate) slab, bar.
Täfelchen ['tɛ:fəlçən], n. (—s, pl. —) tablet.
tafelförmig ['ta:fəlfœrmıç], adj. tabular.
tafeln ['ta:fəln], v.n. dine, feast.
täfeln ['tɛ:fəln], v.a. wainscot, panel.
Täfelung ['tɛ:fəluŋ], f. (—, pl. —en) wainscoting, panelling.
Taft, Taffet [taft, 'ta:fət], m. (—(e)s, pl. —e) taffeta.
Tag [ta:k], m. (—(e)s, pl. —e) day; (fig.) light; *der jüngste* —, Doomsday; *bei* —, in the daytime, by daylight; *sich etwas bei — besehen*, examine s.th. in the light of day; — *für* —, day by day; *von — zu —*, from day to day; *dieser —e*, one of these days, shortly; *etwas an den — bringen*, bring s.th. to light; *in den — hinein leben*, live improvidently; —- *und Nachtgleiche*, equinox.
tagen ['ta:gən], v.n. dawn; (gathering) meet; (Law) sit.
Tagesanbruch ['ta:gəsanbrux], m. (—s, pl. —e) daybreak, dawn.
Tagesbericht ['ta:gəsbərıçt], m. (—(e)s, pl. —e) daily report.
Tagesgespräch ['ta:gəsgəʃprɛ:ç], n. (—(e)s, pl. —e) topic of the day.
Tagesordnung ['ta:gəsɔrdnuŋ], f. (—, pl. —en) agenda.
Tagewerk ['ta:gəverk], n. (—s, no pl.) day's work, daily round.
täglich ['tɛ:klıç], adj. daily.

Tagbau ['ta:kbau], m. (—s, no pl.) opencast mining.
Tageblatt ['ta:gəblat], n. (—s, pl. ⸚er) daily paper.
Tagebuch ['ta:gəbu:x], n. (—(e)s, pl. ⸚er) diary, journal.
Tagedieb ['ta:gədi:p], m. (—(e)s, pl. —e) idler, wastrel.
Tagelöhner ['ta:gəlø:nər], m. (—s, pl. —) day-labourer.

219

tagsüber ['ta:ksy:bər], *adv.* in the daytime, during the day.

Taille ['taljə], *f.* (—, *pl.* —n) waist.

takeln ['ta:kəln], *v.a.* tackle, rig.

Takelwerk ['ta:kəlvɛrk], *n.* (—s, *no pl.*) rigging.

Takt (1) [takt], *m.* (—es, *pl.* —e) (*Mus.*) time, measure, bar; — *schlagen*, beat time.

Takt (2) [takt], *m.* (—, *no pl.*) tact, discretion.

taktfest ['taktfɛst], *adj.* (*Mus.*) good at keeping time; (*fig.*) firm.

taktieren [tak'ti:rən], *v.n.* (*Mus.*) beat time.

Taktik ['taktɪk], *f.* (—, *pl.* —en) tactics.

Taktiker ['taktɪkər], *m.* (—s, *pl.* —) tactician.

taktisch ['taktɪʃ], *adj.* tactical.

taktlos ['taktlo:s], *adj.* tactless.

Taktmesser ['taktmɛsər], *m.* (—s, *pl.* —) metronome.

Taktstock ['taktʃtɔk], *m.* (—s, *pl.* ⸚e) baton.

Tal [ta:l], *n.* (—(e)s, *pl.* ⸚er) valley, dale, glen.

talab [ta'lap], *adv.* downhill.

Talar [ta'la:r], *m.* (—s, *pl.* —e) gown.

Talent [ta'lɛnt], *n.* (—(e)s, *pl.* —e) talent, accomplishment, gift.

talentiert [talən'ti:rt], *adj.* talented, gifted, accomplished.

talentvoll [ta'lɛntfɔl], *adj.* talented, gifted, accomplished.

Taler ['ta:lər], *m.* (—s, *pl.* —) old German coin; thaler.

Talfahrt ['ta:lfa:rt], *f.* (—, *pl.* —en) descent.

Talg [talk], *m.* (—(e)s, *no pl.*) tallow.

Talk [talk], *m.* (—(e)s, *no pl.*) talc.

Talkerde ['talke:rdə], *f.* (—, *no pl.*) magnesia.

Talkessel ['ta:lkɛsəl], *m.* (—s, *pl.* —) (*Geog.*) hollow, narrow valley.

Talmulde ['ta:lmuldə], *f.* (—, *pl.* —n) narrow valley, trough.

Talschlucht ['ta:lʃluxt], *f.* (—, *pl.* —en) glen.

Talsohle ['ta:lzo:lə], *f.* (—, *pl.* —n) floor of a valley.

Talsperre ['ta:lʃpɛrə], *f.* (—, *pl.* —n) dam (across valley); barrage.

Tambour ['tambu:r], *m.* (—s, *pl.* —e) drummer.

Tamtam ['tamtam], *n.* (—s, *no pl.*) tom-tom; (*fig.*) palaver.

Tand [tant], *m.* (—(e)s, *no pl.*) knick-knack, trifle; rubbish.

Tändelei [tɛndə'laɪ], *f.* (—, *pl.* —en) trifling, toying; (*fig.*) flirting.

Tändelmarkt ['tɛndəlmarkt], *m.* (—s, *pl.* ⸚e) rag-fair.

tändeln ['tɛndəln], *v.n.* trifle, dally, toy; (*fig.*) flirt.

Tang [taŋ], *m.* (—s, *pl.* —e) (*Bot.*) seaweed.

Tanganjika [taŋga'nji:ka], *n.* Tanganyika.

Tangente [taŋ'gɛntə], *f.* (—, *pl.* —n) tangent.

Tanger ['taŋər], *n.* Tangier.

Tank [taŋk], *m.* (—(e)s, *pl.* —e) tank.

tanken ['taŋkən], *v.n.* refuel; fill up (with petrol).

Tankstelle ['taŋkʃtɛlə], *f.* (—, *pl.* —n) filling-station.

Tanne ['tanə], *f.* (—, *pl.* —n) (*Bot.*) fir.

Tannenbaum ['tanənbaum], *m.* (—s, *pl.* ⸚e) (*Bot.*) fir-tree.

Tannenholz ['tanənhɔlts], *n.* (—es, *no pl.*) (*timber*) deal.

Tannenzapfen ['tanəntsapfən], *m.* (—s, *pl.* —) (*Bot.*) fir-cone.

Tansania [tanza'ni:a], *n.* Tanzania.

Tante ['tantə], *f.* (—, *pl.* —n) aunt.

Tantieme [tã'tjɛ:ma], *f.* (—, *pl.* —n) royalty, share (in profits), percentage.

Tanz [tants], *m.* (—es, *pl.* ⸚e) dance.

Tanzboden ['tantsbo:dən], *m.* (—s, *pl.* ⸚) ballroom, dance-hall.

tänzeln ['tɛntsəln], *v.n.* skip about, frisk; (*horses*) amble.

tanzen ['tantsən], *v.a., v.n.* dance.

tanzlustig ['tantslustɪç], *adj.* fond of dancing.

Tapet [ta'pe:t], *n.* (—s, *no pl.*) *aufs — bringen*, broach, bring up for discussion.

Tapete [ta'pe:tə], *f.* (—, *pl.* —n) wall-paper.

tapezieren [tapə'tsi:rən], *v.a.* paper.

Tapezierer [tapə'tsi:rər], *m.* (—s, *pl.* —) paperhanger; upholsterer.

tapfer ['tapfər], *adj.* brave, valiant, gallant, courageous.

Tapferkeit ['tapfərkaɪt], *f.* (—, *no pl.*) valour, bravery, gallantry.

Tapisserie [tapɪsə'ri:], *f.* (—, *no pl.*) needlework; tapestry.

tappen ['tapən], *v.n.* grope about.

täppisch ['tɛpɪʃ], *adj.* clumsy, awkward, unwieldy.

tarnen ['tarnən], *v.a.* camouflage.

Tasche ['taʃə], *f.* (—, *pl.* —n) pocket; bag, pouch; *in die — stecken*, pocket; *in die — greifen*, pay, fork out; put o.'s hand in o.'s pocket.

Taschendieb ['taʃəndi:p], *m.* (—(e)s, *pl.* —e) pickpocket; *vor —en wird gewarnt*, beware of pickpockets.

Taschenformat ['taʃənfɔrma:t], *n.* (—s, *no pl.*) pocket-size.

Taschenspieler ['taʃənʃpi:lər], *m.* (—s, *pl.* —) juggler, conjurer.

Taschentuch ['taʃəntu:x], *n.* (—s, *pl.* ⸚er) (pocket-)handkerchief.

Taschenuhr ['taʃənu:r], *f.* (—, *pl.* —en) pocket-watch.

Tasse ['tasə], *f.* (—, *pl.* —n) cup.

Tastatur [tasta'tu:r], *f.* (—, *pl.* —en) keyboard.

Taste ['tastə], *f.* (—, *pl.* —n) (*Mus.*) key.

tasten ['tastən], *v.n.* grope about, feel o.'s way.

Tastsinn ['tastzɪn], *m.* (—s, *no pl.*) sense of touch.

Tat [ta:t], *f.* (—, *pl.* —en) deed, act, action; feat, exploit; *in der* —, in fact, indeed; *auf frischer* —, in the very act; *einem mit Rat und* — *beistehen*, give s.o. advice and guidance, help by word and deed.

Tatbestand ['ta:tbəʃtant], *m.* (—es, *pl.* ꞏe) (*Law*) facts of the case.

Tatendrang ['ta:tandraŋ], *m.* (—(e)s, *no pl.*) urge for action; impetuosity.

tatenlos ['ta:tənlo:s], *adj.* inactive.

Täter ['tɛ:tər], *m.* (—s, *pl.* —) perpetrator, doer; culprit.

tätig ['tɛ:tɪç], *adj.* active, busy.

Tätigkeit ['tɛ:tɪçkaɪt], *f.* (—, *pl.* —en) activity.

Tätigkeitswort ['tɛ:tɪçkaɪtsvɔrt], *n.* (—(e)s, *pl.* ꞏer) (*Gram.*) verb.

Tatkraft ['ta:tkraft], *f.* (—, *no pl.*) energy.

tätlich ['tɛ:tlɪç], *adj.* — *werden*, become violent.

tätowieren [tɛ:to'vi:rən], *v.a.* tattoo.

Tatsache ['ta:tzaxə], *f.* (—, *pl.* —en) fact, matter of fact.

tatsächlich ['ta:tzɛçlɪç], *adj.* actual. — *excl.* really!

tätscheln ['tɛ:tʃəln], *v.a.* fondle.

Tatterich ['tatərɪç], *m.* (—s, *no pl.*) (*coll.*) trembling, shakiness.

Tatze ['tatsə], *f.* (—, *pl.* —n) paw.

Tau (1) [tau], *m.* (—s, *no pl.*) thaw; dew.

Tau (2) [tau], *n.* (—s, *pl.* —e) rope, cable.

taub [taup], *adj.* deaf; (*nut*) hollow, empty; — *machen*, deafen; — *sein gegen*, turn a deaf ear to.

Täubchen ['tɔypçən], *n.* (—s, *pl.* —) little dove; (*fig.*) sweetheart.

Taube ['taubə], *f.* (—, *pl.* —n) (*Orn.*) pigeon, dove.

Taubenschlag ['taubənʃla:k], *m.* (—s, *pl.* ꞏe) dovecote.

Taubenschwanz ['taubənʃvants], *m.* (—es, *pl.* ꞏe) (*Ent.*) hawkmoth.

Tauber ['taubər], *m.* (—s, *pl.* —) (*Orn.*) cock-pigeon.

Taubheit ['tauphait], *f.* (—, *no pl.*) deafness.

Taubnessel ['taupnesəl], *f.* (—, *pl.* —n) (*Bot.*) deadnettle.

taubstumm ['taupʃtum], *adj.* deaf and dumb, deaf-mute.

tauchen ['tauçən], *v.n.* (*aux.* haben & sein) dive, plunge. — *v.a.* immerse, dip.

Tauchsieder ['tauçzi:dər], *m.* (—s, *pl.* —) (*Elec.*) immersion heater.

tauen ['tauən], *v.a.*, *v.n.* thaw, melt.

Taufbecken ['taufbɛkən], *n.* (—s, *pl.* —) (baptismal) font.

Taufe ['taufə], *f.* (—, *pl.* —n) baptism, christening; *aus der* — *heben*, stand godparent.

taufen ['taufən], *v.a.* baptise, christen.

Taufkleid ['taufklaɪt], *n.* (—s, *pl.* —er) christening robe.

Täufling ['tɔyflɪŋ], *m.* (—s, *pl.* —e) infant presented for baptism; neophyte.

Taufname ['taufna:mə], *m.* (—ns, *pl.* —n) Christian name.

Taufpate ['taufpa:tə], *m.* (—n, *pl.* —n) godfather, godmother.

Taufstein ['taufʃtaɪn], *n.* (—s, *pl.* —e) (baptismal) font.

taugen ['taugən], *v.n.* be good for, be fit for; *nichts* —, be good for nothing.

Taugenichts ['taugənɪçts], *m.* (—, *pl.* —e) ne'er-do-well, scapegrace, good-for-nothing.

tauglich ['tauklɪç], *adj.* able; useful, fit, suitable.

Taumel ['tauməl], *m.* (—s, *no pl.*) giddiness, dizziness, staggering; (*fig.*) whirl; ecstasy, frenzy, delirium, intoxication.

taumeln ['tauməln], *v.n.* (*aux.* sein) reel, stagger.

Tausch [tauʃ], *m.* (—es, *no pl.*) exchange, barter.

tauschen ['tauʃən], *v.a.* exchange for, barter against, swop; *die Rollen* —, change places.

täuschen ['tɔyʃən], *v.a.* deceive, delude. — *v.r. sich* —, be mistaken.

Tauschhandel ['tauʃhandəl], *m.* (—s, *no pl.*) barter.

Tauschmittel ['tauʃmɪtəl], *n.* (—s, *pl.* —) medium of exchange.

Täuschung ['tɔyʃuŋ], *f.* (—, *pl.* —en) deceit, deception; illusion.

Täuschungsversuch ['tɔyʃuŋsferzu:ç], *m.* (—es, *pl.* —e) attempt at deception; (*Mil.*) diversion.

tausend ['tauzənt], *num. adj.* a thousand.

tausendjährig ['tauzəntje:rɪç], *adj.* millennial, of a thousand years; *das —e Reich*, the millennium.

Tausendsasa ['tauzəntzasa], *m.* (—s, *pl.* —) devil of a fellow.

Tautropfen ['tautrɔpfən], *m.* (—s, *pl.* —) dew-drop.

Tauwetter ['tauvetər], *n.* (—s, *no pl.*) thaw.

Taxameter [taksa'me:tər], *m.* (—s, *pl.* —) taximeter.

Taxe ['taksə], *f.* (—, *pl.* —n) set rate, tariff; (taxi)cab; *nach der* — *verkauft werden*, be sold *ad valorem*.

taxieren [tak'si:rən], *v.a.* appraise, value.

Taxus ['taksus,] *m.* (—, *pl.* —) (*Bot.*) yew(-tree).

Technik ['tɛçnɪk], *f.* (—, *pl.* —en) technology, engineering; technique; skill, execution.

Techniker ['tɛçnɪkər], *m.* (—s, *pl.* —) technician, technical engineer.

Technikum ['tɛçnɪkum], *n.* (—s, *pl.* —s) technical school, college.

technisch ['tɛçnɪʃ], *adj.* technical; *—er Ausdruck*, technical term; *—e Störung*, technical hitch *or* breakdown.

technologisch [tɛçno'lo:gɪʃ], *adj.* technological.

Techtelmechtel

Techtelmechtel ['tɛçtəlmɛçtəl], *n.* (—s, *pl.* —) (*coll.*) love affair, flirtation.
Tee [te:], *m.* (—s, *no pl.*) tea.
Teedose ['te:do:zə], *f.* (—, *pl.* —n) tea-caddy.
Teekanne ['te:kanə], *f.* (—, *pl.* —n) tea-pot.
Teelöffel ['te:lœfəl], *m.* (—s, *pl.* —) tea-spoon.
Teemaschine ['te:maʃi:nə], *f.* (—, *pl.* —n) tea-urn.
Teer [te:r], *m.* (—(e)s, *no pl.*) tar.
Teerleinwand ['te:rlaɪnvant], *f.* (—, *no pl.*) tarpaulin.
Teerose ['te:ro:zə], *f.* (—, *pl.* —n) (*Bot.*) tea rose.
Teerpappe ['te:rpapə], *f.* (—, *no pl.*) roofing-felt.
teeren ['te:rən], *v.a.* tar.
Teesieb ['te:zi:p], *n.* (—(e)s, *pl.* —e) tea-strainer.
Teich [taɪç], *m.* (—(e)s, *pl.* —e) pond.
Teig [taɪk], *m.* (—(e)s, *pl.* —e) dough, paste.
teigig ['taɪgɪç], *adj.* doughy.
Teigrolle ['taɪkrɔlə], *f.* (—, *pl.* —n) rolling-pin.
Teil [taɪl], *m. & n.* (—(e)s, *pl.* —e) part; portion; piece, component; share; *edler* —, vital part; *zum* —, partly; *zu gleichen* —*en*, share and share alike.
teilbar ['taɪlba:r], *adj.* divisible.
Teilchen ['taɪlçən], *n.* (—s, *pl.* —) particle.
teilen ['taɪlən], *v.a.* divide; share; partition off. — *v.r. sich* —, share in; (*road*) fork.
Teiler ['taɪlər], *m.* (—s, *pl.* —) divider; (*Maths.*) divisor.
teilhaben ['taɪlha:bən], *v.n. irr.* (have a) share in, participate in.
Teilhaber ['taɪlha:bər], *m.* (—s, *pl.* —) partner.
teilhaftig ['taɪlhaftɪç], *adj.* sharing, participating; *einer Sache* — *werden*, partake of s.th., come in for s.th.
Teilnahme ['taɪlna:mə], *f.* (—, *no pl.*) participation; (*fig.*) sympathy, interest.
teilnahmslos ['taɪlna:mslo:s], *adj.* unconcerned, indifferent.
Teilnahmslosigkeit ['taɪlna:mslo:zɪçkaɪt], *f.* (—, *no pl.*) unconcern; listlessness, indifference.
teilnahmsvoll ['taɪlna:msfəl], *adj.* solicitous.
teilnehmen ['taɪlne:mən], *v.n. irr.* take part (in), participate, partake; (*fig.*) sympathise.
Teilnehmer ['taɪlne:mər], *m.* (—s, *pl.* —) member, participant; (*telephone*) subscriber.
teils [taɪls], *adv.* partly.
Teilstrecke ['taɪlʃtrekə], *f.* (—, *pl.* —n) section (of a railway).
Teilung ['taɪluŋ], *f.* (—, *pl.* —en) division, partition; distribution.
Teilungszahl ['taɪluŋstsa:l], *f.* (—, *pl.* —en) (*Maths.*) dividend; quotient.

teilweise ['taɪlvaɪzə], *adv.* partly, in part.
Teilzahlung ['taɪltsa:luŋ], *f.* (—, *pl.* —en) part-payment, instalment.
Teint [tɛ̃], *m.* (—s, *no pl.*) complexion.
telephonieren [telefo'ni:rən], *v.a., v.n.* telephone.
Telegraphie [telegra'fi:], *f.* (—, *no pl.*) telegraphy.
telegraphisch [tele'gra:fɪʃ], *adj.* telegraphic, by telegram.
Telegramm [tele'gram], *n.* (—s, *pl.* —e) telegram, wire, cable.
Telegrammadresse [tele'gramadrɛsə], *f.* (—, *pl.* —n) telegraphic address.
Telegrammformular [tele'gramfɔrmula:r], *n.* (—s, *pl.* —e) telegram-form.
Teleskop [teles'ko:p], *n.* (—s, *pl.* —e) telescope.
Teller ['tɛlər], *m.* (—s, *pl.* —) plate.
Tempel ['tɛmpəl], *m.* (—s, *pl.* —) temple.
Temperament [tɛmpəra'mɛnt], *n.* (—s, *pl.* —e) temperament, disposition; (*fig.*) spirits.
temperamentvoll [tɛmpəra'mɛntfɔl], *adj.* full of spirits, vivacious; lively.
Temperatur [tɛmpəra'tu:r], *f.* (—, *pl.* —en) temperature.
Temperenzler [tɛmpə'rɛntslər], *m.* (—s, *pl.* —) total abstainer, teetotaller.
temperieren [tɛmpə'ri:rən], *v.a.* temper.
Tempo ['tɛmpo:], *n.* (—s, *pl.* —s, **Tempi**) time, measure, speed.
temporisieren [tɛmpori'zi:rən], *v.n.* temporise.
Tendenz [tɛn'dɛnts], *f.* (—, *pl.* —en) tendency.
tendenziös [tɛndɛn'tsjø:s], *adj.* biased, coloured, tendentious.
Tender ['tɛndər], *m.* (—s, *pl.* —) (*Railw.*) tender.
Tenne ['tɛnə], *f.* (—, *pl.* —n) threshing floor.
Tenor [te'no:r], *m.* (—s, *pl.* ·e) (*Mus.*) tenor.
Teppich ['tɛpɪç], *m.* (—s, *pl.* —e) carpet.
Termin [tɛr'mi:n], *m.* (—s, *pl.* —e) time, date, appointed day; *einen* — *ansetzen*, fix a day (for a hearing, examination etc.).
Termingeschäft [tɛr'mi:ngəʃɛft], *n.* (—s, *pl.* —e) (business in) futures.
Terminologie [tɛrminolo'gi:], *f.* (—, *pl.* —n) terminology.
Terpentin [tɛrpɛn'ti:n], *n.* (—s, *no pl.*) turpentine.
Terrain [tɛ'rɛ̃], *n.* (—s, *pl.* —s) ground, terrain.
Terrasse [tɛ'rasə], *f.* (—, *pl.* —n) terrace.
Terrine [tɛ'ri:nə], *f.* (—, *pl.* —n) tureen.
territorial [tɛrito'rja:l], *adj.* territorial.
Territorium [tɛrɪ'to:rjum], *n.* (—s, *pl.* —torien) territory.

tertiär [tɛrˈtsjɛːr], *adj.* tertiary.

Terzett [tɛrˈtsɛt], *n.* (—s, *pl.* —e) trio.

Testament [tɛstaˈmɛnt], *n.* (—s, *pl.* —e) testament, will; (*Bibl.*) Testament; *ohne* —, intestate.

testamentarisch [tɛstamɛnˈtaːrɪʃ], *adj.* testamentary.

Testamentseröffnung [tɛstaˈmɛntsɛrœfnuŋ], *f.* (—, *pl.* —en) reading of the will.

Testamentsvollstrecker [tɛstaˈmɛntsfɔlʃtrɛkər], *m.* (—s, *pl.* —) executor.

teuer [ˈtɔyər], *adj.* dear; costly, expensive; *einem — zu stehen kommen*, cost s.o. dear.

Teuerung [ˈtɔyəruŋ], *f.* (—, *pl.* —en) scarcity, dearth.

Teufel [ˈtɔyfəl], *m.* (—s, *pl.* —) devil, fiend; *armer —*, poor devil; *scher dich zum —*, go to blazes; *den — an die Wand malen*, talk of the devil.

Teufelei [tɔyfəˈlaɪ], *f.* (—, *pl.* —en) devilry, devilish trick.

teuflisch [ˈtɔyflɪʃ], *adj.* devilish, diabolical.

Thailand [ˈtaɪlant], *n.* Thailand.

Theater [teˈaːtər], *n.* (—s, *pl.* —) theatre, stage.

Theaterkarte [teˈaːtərkartə], *f.* (—, *pl.* —n) theatre-ticket.

Theaterkasse [teˈaːtərkasə], *f.* (—, *pl.* —n) box-office.

Theaterstück [teˈaːtərʃtyk], *n.* (—(e)s, *pl.* —e) play, drama.

Theatervorstellung [teˈaːtərfoːrʃtɛluŋ], *f.* (—, *pl.* —en) theatre performance.

Theaterzettel [teˈaːtərtsɛtəl], *m.* (—s, *pl.* —) play-bill.

theatralisch [teaˈtraːlɪʃ], *adj.* theatrical; dramatic; histrionic.

Thema [ˈteːmaː], *n.* (—s, *pl.* —men, **Themata**) theme, subject, topic.

Themse [ˈtɛmzə], *f.* Thames.

Theologe [teoˈloːgə], *m.* (—n, *pl.* —n) theologian.

Theologie [teoloˈgiː], *f.* (—, *no pl.*) theology, divinity.

theoretisch [teoˈreːtɪʃ], *adj.* theoretical.

theoretisieren [teoretiˈziːrən], *v.n.* theorise.

Theorie [teoˈriː], *f.* (—, *pl.* —n) theory.

Therapie [teraˈpiː], *f.* (—, *no pl.*) therapy.

Therme [ˈtɛrmə], *f.* (—, *pl.* —n) hot spring.

Thermometer [tɛrmoˈmeːtər], *n.* (—s, *pl.* —) thermometer.

Thermosflasche [ˈtɛrmɔsflaʃə], *f.* (—, *pl.* —n) thermos-flask.

These [ˈteːzə], *f.* (—, *pl.* —n) thesis.

Thron [troːn], *m.* (—(e)s, *pl.* —e) throne; *auf den — setzen*, place on the throne, enthrone; *vom — stoßen*, dethrone, depose.

Thronbesteigung [ˈtroːnbəʃtaɪguŋ], *f.* (—, *pl.* —en) accession (to the throne).

Thronbewerber [ˈtroːnbəvɛrbər], *m.* (—s, *pl.* —) claimant to the throne, pretender.

thronen [ˈtroːnən], *v.n.* sit enthroned.

Thronerbe [ˈtroːnɛrbə], *m.* (—n, *pl.* —n) heir apparent, crown prince.

Thronfolge [ˈtroːnfɔlgə], *f.* (—, *no pl.*) line *or* order of succession.

Thronfolger [ˈtroːnfɔlgər], *m.* (—s, *pl.* —) heir to the throne, heir apparent.

Thronhimmel [ˈtroːnhɪməl], *m.* (—s, *pl.* —) canopy.

Thronrede [ˈtroːnreːdə], *f.* (—, *pl.* —n) speech from the throne.

Thunfisch [ˈtuːnfɪʃ], *m.* (—es, *pl.* —e) (*Zool.*) tunny, (*Am.*) tuna.

Thüringen [ˈtyːrɪŋən], *n.* Thuringia.

Thymian [ˈtyːmjaːn], *m.* (—s, *no pl.*) (*Bot.*) thyme.

ticken [ˈtɪkən], *v.n.* tick.

tief [tiːf], *adj.* deep, profound, low; far; extreme; (*voice*) bass; (*fig.*) profound; *in —ster Nacht*, in the dead of night; *aus —stem Herzen*, from the bottom of o.'s heart. — *adv.* — *atmen*, take a deep breath; — *in Schulden*, head over ears in debt; — *verletzt*, cut to the quick.

Tiefbau [ˈtiːfbau], *m.* (—s, *no pl.*) underground workings.

tiefbedrückt [ˈtiːfbədrykt], *adj.* deeply distressed; very depressed.

tiefbewegt [ˈtiːfbəveːkt], *adj.* deeply moved.

Tiefe [ˈtiːfə], *f.* (—, *pl.* —en) depth; (*fig.*) profundity.

tiefgebeugt [ˈtiːfgəbɔykt], *adj.* bowed down.

tiefgreifend [ˈtiːfgraɪfənt], *adj.* radical, sweeping.

tiefschürfend [ˈtiːfʃyrfənt], *adj.* profound; thoroughgoing.

Tiefsee [ˈtiːfzeː], *f.* (—, *no pl.*) deep sea.

Tiefsinn [ˈtiːfzɪn], *m.* (—s, *no pl.*) pensiveness, melancholy.

tiefsinnig [ˈtiːfzɪnɪç], *adj.* pensive, melancholy, melancholic(al).

Tiegel [ˈtiːgəl], *m.* (—s, *pl.* —) crucible; saucepan.

Tier [tiːr], *n.* (—(e)s, *pl.* —e) animal, beast; *ein großes —*, (*coll.*) a V.I.P., a bigwig; (*Am.*) a swell, a big shot.

Tierart [ˈtiːraːrt], *f.* (—, *pl.* —en) (*Zool.*) species.

Tierarzt [ˈtiːraːrtst], *m.* (—es, *pl.* ⸚e) veterinary surgeon.

Tierbändiger [ˈtiːrbɛndɪgər], *m.* (—s, *pl.* —) animal-tamer.

Tiergarten [ˈtiːrgartən], *m.* (—s, *pl.* ⸚) zoological gardens, zoo.

tierisch [ˈtiːrɪʃ], *adj.* animal, brute, brutal, bestial.

Tierkreis [ˈtiːrkraɪs], *m.* (—es, *no pl.*) zodiac.

Tierkunde [ˈtiːrkundə], *f.* (—, *no pl.*) zoology.

Tierquälerei [ˈtiːrkvɛːləraɪ], *f.* (—, *pl.* —en) cruelty to animals.

Tierreich [ˈtiːrraɪç], *n.* (—(e)s, *no pl.*) animal kingdom.

Tierschutzverein [ˈtiːrʃutsfəraɪn], *m.* (—s, *pl.* —e) society for the prevention of cruelty to animals.

Tierwärter

Tierwärter ['tiːrvɛrtər], *m.* (—s, *pl.* —) keeper (at a zoo).
Tiger ['tiːgər], *m.* (—s, *pl.* —) (*Zool.*) tiger.
Tigerin ['tiːgərɪn], *f.* (—, *pl.* —nen) (*Zool.*) tigress.
tilgbar ['tɪlkbaːr], *adj.* extinguishable; (*debt*) redeemable.
tilgen ['tɪlgən], *v.a.* strike out, efface, annul; (*debt*) discharge; (*sin*) expiate, atone for.
Tilgung ['tɪlguŋ], *f.* (—, *pl.* —en) striking out, obliteration; annulment, payment; redemption.
Tilgungsfonds ['tɪlguŋsfɔ̃], *m.* (—, *pl.* —) sinking fund.
Tingeltangel ['tɪŋəltaŋəl], *m. & n.* (—s, *pl.* —) (*coll.*) music-hall.
Tinktur [tɪŋkˈtuːr], *f.* (—, *pl.* —en) tincture.
Tinte ['tɪntə], *f.* (—, *pl.* —n) ink; *in der — sein,* be in a jam, be in the soup.
Tintenfaß ['tɪntənfas], *n.* (—sses, *pl.* ·sser) ink-pot, ink-stand.
Tintenfisch ['tɪntənfɪʃ], *m.* (—es, *pl.* —e) (*Zool.*) cuttle-fish.
Tintenfleck ['tɪntənflɛk], *m.* (—s, *pl.* —e) blot, ink-spot.
Tintenklecks ['tɪntənklɛks], *m.* (—es, *pl.* —e) blot.
Tintenstift ['tɪntənʃtɪft], *m.* (—s, *pl.* —e) indelible pencil.
Tintenwischer ['tɪntənvɪʃər], *m.* (—s, *pl.* —) pen-wiper.
tippen ['tɪpən], *v.a.* tap; (*coll.*) type.
Tirol [tiˈroːl], *n.* Tyrol.
Tisch [tɪʃ], *m.* (—es, *pl.* —e) table, board; *den — decken,* lay the table; *zu — gehen,* sit down to dinner.
Tischdecke ['tɪʃdɛkə], *f.* (—, *pl.* —n) tablecloth.
Tischgebet ['tɪʃgəbeːt], *n.* (—s, *pl.* —e) grace.
Tischler ['tɪʃlər], *m.* (—s, *pl.* —) joiner, cabinet-maker, carpenter.
Tischlerei [tɪʃləˈraɪ], *f.* (—, *no pl.*) joinery, cabinet-making, carpentry.
Tischrede ['tɪʃreːdə], *f.* (—, *pl.* —n) after-dinner speech.
Tischrücken ['tɪʃrʏkən], *n.* (—s, *no pl.*) table-turning.
Tischtennis ['tɪʃtɛnɪs], *n.* (—, *no pl.*) table-tennis, ping-pong.
Tischtuch ['tɪʃtuːx], *n.* (—(e)s, *pl.* ·er) tablecloth.
Tischzeit ['tɪʃtsaɪt], *f.* (—, *pl.* —en) mealtime.
Titane [tiˈtaːnə], *m.* (—n, *pl.* —n) Titan.
titanenhaft [tiˈtaːnənhaft], *adj.* titanic.
Titel ['tiːtəl], *m.* (—s, *pl.* —) title; claim; heading, headline.
Titelbild ['tiːtəlbɪlt], *n.* (—(e)s, *pl.* —er) frontispiece.
Titelblatt ['tiːtəlblat], *n.* (—(e)s, *pl.* ·er) title page.
Titelrolle ['tiːtəlrɔlə], *f.* (—, *pl.* —n) title role.
titulieren [tituˈliːrən], *v.a.* style, address.

toben ['toːbən], *v.n.* rave; rage, roar; be furious; be wild.
tobsüchtig ['toːpzyçtɪç], *adj.* raving, mad.
Tochter ['tɔxtər], *f.* (—, *pl.* ·) daughter.
töchterlich ['tœçtərlɪç], *adj.* filial, daughterly.
Tod [toːt], *m.* (—es, *pl.* —esfälle *or* (*rare*) —e) death, decease, demise; *dem — geweiht,* doomed; *Kampf auf — und Leben,* fight to the death; *zum — verurteilen,* condemn to death.
Todesangst ['toːdəsaŋst], *f.* (—, *pl.* ·e) agony, mortal terror.
Todesanzeige ['toːdəsantsaɪgə], *f.* (—, *pl.* —n) announcement of death; obituary notice.
Todesfall ['toːdəsfal], *m.* (—(e)s, *pl.* ·e) death, decease; fatality.
Todesgefahr ['toːdəsgəfaːr], *f.* (—, *pl.* —en) mortal danger.
Todeskampf ['toːdəskampf], *m.* (—(e)s, *pl.* ·e) death agony.
todesmutig ['toːdəsmuːtɪç], *adj.* death-defying.
Todesstoß ['toːdəsʃtoːs], *m.* (—es, *pl.* ·e) death-blow.
Todesstrafe ['toːdəsʃtraːfə], *f.* (—, *no pl.*) capital punishment.
Todfeind ['toːtfaɪnt], *m.* (—es, *pl.* —e) mortal enemy.
todkrank ['toːtkraŋk], *adj.* sick unto death, dangerously *or* mortally ill.
tödlich ['tœːtlɪç], *adj.* mortal, deadly, fatal.
todmüde ['toːtmyːdə], *adj.* tired to death.
Todsünde ['toːtzyndə], *f.* (—, *pl.* —n) mortal sin.
Togo ['toːgo], *n.* Togo.
Toilette [toaˈlɛtə], *f.* (—, *pl.* —n) lavatory, toilet; (*fig.*) dress.
tolerant [toleˈrant], *adj.* tolerant.
Toleranz [toleˈrants], *f.* (—, *no pl.*) toleration; tolerance.
tolerieren [toleˈriːrən], *v.a.* tolerate.
toll [tɔl], *adj.* mad, frantic; wild; *—er Streich,* mad prank; *zum — werden,* enough to drive o. mad.
Tolle ['tɔlə], *f.* (—, *pl.* —n) (*dial.*) forelock, tuft of hair, top-knot.
Tollhaus ['tɔlhaus], *n.* (—es, *pl.* ·er) madhouse, lunatic asylum.
Tollheit ['tɔlhaɪt], *f.* (—, *pl.* —en) foolhardiness, mad prank.
Tollkirsche ['tɔlkɪrʃə], *f.* (—, *pl.* —n) belladonna, deadly nightshade.
Tollwut ['tɔlvuːt], *f.* (—, *no pl.*) frenzy; rabies.
Tolpatsch ['tɔlpatʃ], *m.* (—es, *pl.* —e) clumsy person.
Tölpel ['tœlpəl], *m.* (—s, *pl.* —) blockhead, lout, hobbledehoy.
Tölpelei [tœlpəˈlaɪ], *f.* (—, *pl.* —en) clumsiness, awkwardness.
tölpelhaft ['tœlpəlhaft], *adj.* clumsy, doltish, loutish.
Tomate [toˈmaːtə], *f.* (—, *pl.* —n) tomato.

Ton (1) [to:n], *m.* (—(e)s, *pl.* ˙e)
sound, tone, accent, note; shade;
manners; *guter (schlechter)* —, good
(bad) form, etiquette; *den — angeben,*
set the fashion.

Ton (2) [to:n], *m.* (—s, *no pl.*) clay,
potter's earth.

Tonabnehmer [ˈto:nabne:mər], *m.*
(—s, *pl.* —) *(gramophone)* pick-up.

tonangebend [ˈto:nange:bənt], *adj.*
leading in fashion, setting the pace;
leading, fashionable.

Tonart [ˈto:na:rt], *f.* (—, *pl.* —en)
(Mus.) key.

Tonbandgerät [ˈto:nbantgɛrɛ:t], *n.*
(—s, *pl.* —e) tape-recorder.

tönen [ˈtø:nən], *v.n.* sound.

Tonerde [ˈto:ne:rdə], *f.* (—, *no pl.*)
clay.

tönern [ˈtø:nərn], *adj.* earthen.

Tonfall [ˈto:nfal], *m.* (—s, *no pl.*)
cadence, intonation (of voice).

Tonfolge [ˈto:nfɔlgə], *f.* (—, *pl.* —n)
(Mus.) succession of notes.

Tonführung [ˈto:nfy:ruŋ], *f.* (—, *no pl.*)
modulation.

Tonkunst [ˈto:nkunst], *f.* (—, *no pl.*)
music.

Tonkünstler [ˈto:nkynstlər], *m.* (—s,
pl. —) musician.

Tonleiter [ˈto:nlaɪtər], *f.* (—, *pl.* —n)
scale, gamut.

Tonne [ˈtɔnə], *f.* (—, *pl.* —n) tun, cask,
barrel; ton.

Tonnengewölbe [ˈtɔnəngəvœlbə], *n.*
(—s, *pl.* —) cylindrical vault.

Tonpfeife [ˈto:npfaɪfə], *f.* (—, *pl.* —n)
clay-pipe.

Tonsatz [ˈto:nzats], *m.* (—es, *pl.* ˙e)
(Mus.) composition.

Tonsur [tɔnˈzu:r], *f.* (—, *pl.* —en)
tonsure.

Tonwelle [ˈto:nvɛlə], *f.* (—, *pl.* —n)
sound-wave.

Topas [toˈpa:s], *m.* (—es, *pl.* —e) topaz.

Topf [tɔpf], *m.* (—(e)s, *pl.* ˙e) pot;
alles in einen — werfen, lump everything together.

Topfblume [ˈtɔpfblu:mə], *f.* (—, *pl.*
—n) pot-plant.

Topfdeckel [ˈtɔpfdɛkəl], *m.* (—s, *pl.* —)
lid of a pot.

Töpfer [ˈtœpfər], *m.* (—s, *pl.* —)
potter.

Töpferarbeit [ˈtœpfərarbaɪt], *f.* (—, *pl.*
—en) pottery.

Töpferscheibe [ˈtœpfərʃaɪbə], *f.* (—,
pl. —n) potter's wheel.

Töpferware [ˈtœpfərva:rə], *f.* (—, *pl.*
—n) pottery, earthenware.

Topfgucker [ˈtɔpfgukər], *m.* (—s, *pl.*
—) busybody; inquisitive person.

Topographie [topograˈfi:], *f.* (—, *no
pl.*) topography.

Tor (1) [to:r], *m.* (—en, *pl.* —en)
(obs.) fool, simpleton.

Tor (2) [to:r], *n.* (—(e)s, *pl.* —e) gate;
(Footb.) goal.

Torangel [ˈto:raŋəl], *f.* (—, *pl.* —n)
hinge.

Tor(es)schluß [ˈto:r(əs)ʃlus], *m.* (—es,
no pl.) shutting of the gate; *noch
gerade vor* —, at the eleventh hour.

Torf [tɔrf], *m.* (—(e)s, *no pl.*) peat,
turf.

Torfgrube [ˈtɔrfgru:bə], *f.* (—, *pl.*
—n) turf-pit.

Torfmoor [ˈtɔrfmo:r], *n.* (—s, *pl.* —e)
peat-bog.

Torfstecher [ˈtɔrfʃtɛçər], *m.* (—s, *pl.*
—) peat-cutter.

Torheit [ˈto:rhaɪt], *f.* (—, *pl.* —en)
foolishness, folly.

Torhüter [ˈto:rhy:tər], *m.* (—s, *pl.* —)
gate-keeper.

töricht [ˈtø:rɪçt], *adj.* foolish, silly.

Törin [ˈtø:rɪn], *f.* (—, *pl.* —nen) *(rare)*
foolish woman.

torkeln [ˈtɔrkəln], *v.n.* *(aux.* sein)
(coll.) stagger, reel.

Tornister [tɔrˈnɪstər], *m.* (—s, *pl.* —)
knapsack, satchel.

Torpedo [tɔrˈpe:do], *m.* (—s, *pl.* —s)
torpedo.

Torso [ˈtɔrzo], *m.* (—s, *pl.* —s) trunk,
torso.

Tort [tɔrt], *m.* (—s, *no pl.*) injury,
wrong; *einem einen — antun,* wrong
s.o.; play a trick on s.o.

Torte [ˈtɔrtə], *f.* (—, *pl.* —n) cake,
pastry, tart.

Tortur [tɔrˈtu:r], *f.* (—, *pl.* —en)
torture.

Torwächter [ˈto:rvɛçtər], *m.* (—s, *pl.*
—) gate-keeper; porter.

tosen [ˈto:zən], *v.n.* roar.

tot [to:t], *adj.* dead, deceased.

total [toˈta:l], *adj.* total, complete.

Totalisator [totaliˈza:tɔr], *m.* (—s, *pl.*
—en) totalisator; *(coll.)* tote.

Totalleistung [toˈta:llaɪstuŋ], *f.* (—,
pl. —en) full effect; total output.

Tote [ˈto:tə], *m.,f.* (—n, *pl.* —n) dead
person, the deceased.

töten [ˈtø:tən], *v.a.* kill, put to death.

Totenacker [ˈto:tənakər], *m.* (—s, *pl.*
˙) churchyard, cemetery.

Totenamt [ˈto:tənamt], *n.* (—s, *no pl.*)
office for the dead, requiem, Mass for
the dead.

Totenbahre [ˈto:tənba:rə], *f.* (—, *pl.*
—n) bier.

Totengräber [ˈto:təngrɛ:bər], *m.* (—s,
pl. —) grave-digger.

Totenhemd [ˈto:tənhɛmt], *n.* (—(e)s,
pl. —en) shroud, winding-sheet.

Totenklage [ˈto:tənkla:gə], *f.* (—, *no
pl.*) lament.

Totenschein [ˈto:tənʃaɪn], *m.* (—(e)s,
pl. —e) death-certificate.

Totenstille [ˈto:tənʃtɪlə], *f.* (—, *no pl.*)
dead calm.

Totenwache [ˈto:tənvaxə], *f.* (—, *no
pl.*) wake.

totgeboren [ˈto:tgəbo:rən], *adj.* still-
born, born dead.

Totschlag [ˈto:tʃla:k], *m.* (—s, *no pl.*)
manslaughter.

totschlagen [ˈto:tʃla:gən], *v.a.* *irr.*
kill, strike dead.

Totschläger ['to:tʃlɛ:gər], *m.* (—s, *pl.* —) loaded cane, cudgel.
totschweigen ['to:tʃvaɪgən], *v.a. irr.* hush up.
Tötung ['tø:tuŋ], *f.* (—, *pl.* —en) killing.
Tour [tu:r], *f.* (—, *pl.* —en) tour, excursion; *in einer* —, ceaselessly; *auf* —*en bringen,*(coll.) (*Motor.*) rev up.
Tournee [tur'ne:], *f.* (—, *pl.* —n) (*Theat.*) tour.
Trab [tra:p], *m.* (—(e)s, *no pl.*) trot.
Trabant [tra'bant], *m.* (—en, *pl.* —en) satellite.
traben ['tra:bən], *v.n.* (aux. sein) trot.
Trabrennen ['tra:prɛnən], *n.* (—s, *pl.* —) trotting-race.
Tracht [traxt], *f.* (—, *pl.* —en) dress, costume; national costume; native dress; *eine* — *Prügel*, a good hiding.
trachten ['traxtən], *v.n.* strive, aspire, endeavour; *einem nach dem Leben* —, seek to kill s.o.
trächtig ['trɛçtɪç], *adj.* (*animal*) pregnant, with young.
Trafik [tra'fik], *m.* (—s, *pl.* —s) (*Austr.*) tobacco-kiosk.
Tragbahre ['tra:kba:rə], *f.* (—, *pl.* —n) stretcher.
Tragbalken ['tra:kbalkən], *m.* (—s *pl.*, —) girder.
tragbar ['tra:kba:r], *adj.* portable; tolerable.
träge ['trɛ:gə], *adj.* lazy, indolent, inert, sluggish.
tragen ['tra:gən], *v.a. irr.* bear, carry; (*dress*) wear; (*fig.*) bear, endure; *Bedenken* —, hesitate, have doubts; *Zinsen* —, yield interest; *einen auf Händen* —, care lovingly for s.o.
Träger ['trɛ:gər], *m.* (—s, *pl.* —) porter, carrier; girder.
Trägheit ['trɛ:khaɪt], *f.* (—, *no pl.*) indolence, laziness, inertia.
tragisch ['tra:gɪʃ], *adj.* tragic(al).
Tragkraft ['tra:kkraft], *f.* (—, *no pl.*) carrying *or* load capacity; lifting power.
Tragödie [tra'gø:djə], *f.* (—, *pl.* —n) tragedy.
Tragsessel ['tra:kzɛsəl], *m.* (—s, *pl.* —) sedan-chair.
Tragweite ['tra:kvaɪtə], *f.* (—, *no pl.*) significance, importance, range.
trainieren [trɛ'ni:rən], *v.a.* train.
Traktat [trak'ta:t], *n.* (—s, *pl.* —e) treatise, tract.
Traktätchen [trak'tɛ:tçən], *n.* (—s, *pl.* —) (short) tract.
traktieren [trak'ti:rən], *v.a.* treat; treat badly.
trällern ['trɛlərn], *v.n.* trill, hum.
Trambahn ['tramba:n], *f.* (—, *pl.* —en) tram; (*Am.*) streetcar.
Trampel ['trampəl], *n.* (—s, *pl.* —) clumsy person, bumpkin; (*Am.*) hick.
trampeln ['trampəln], *v.n.* trample.
Trampeltier ['trampəlti:r], *n.* (—s, *pl.* —e) camel; (*fig.*) clumsy person.
Tran [tra:n], *m.* (—(e)s, *no pl.*) whale-oil.

tranchieren [trã'ʃi:rən], *v.a.* carve.
Tranchiermesser [trã'ʃi:rmɛsər], *n.* (—s, *pl.* —) carving-knife.
Träne ['trɛ:nə], *f.* (—, *pl.* —n) tear, teardrop; *zu* —*n gerührt*, moved to tears.
tränen ['trɛ:nən], *v.n.* (*eyes*) water.
Tränendrüse ['trɛ:nəndry:zə], *f.* (—, *pl.* —n) lachrymal gland.
tränenleer ['trɛ:nənle:r], *adj.* tearless.
Tränenstrom ['trɛ:nənʃtro:m], *m.* (—s, *pl.* ⸚e) flood of tears.
tränenvoll ['trɛ:nənfɔl], *adj.* tearful.
tranig ['tra:nɪç], *adj.* dull, slow.
Trank [traŋk], *m.* (—(e)s, *pl.* ⸚e) drink, beverage, potion.
Tränke ['trɛŋkə], *f.* (—, *pl.* —n) (*horse*) watering-place.
tränken ['trɛŋkən], *v.a.* give to drink, water; impregnate, saturate.
transitiv ['tranziti:f], *adj.* transitive.
Transitlager ['tranzɪtla:gər], *n.* (—s, *pl.* —) bonded warehouse; transit camp.
transitorisch [tranzi'to:rɪʃ], *adj.* transitory.
transpirieren [transpi'ri:rən], *v.n.* perspire.
transponieren [transpo'ni:rən], *v.a.* transpose.
Transportkosten [trans'pɔrtkɔstən], *f. pl.* shipping charges.
Transportmittel [trans'pɔrtmɪtəl], *n.* (—s, *pl.* —) means of carriage, conveyance, transport.
Trapez [tra'pe:ts], *n.* (—es, *pl.* —e) trapeze; (*Maths.*) trapezoid.
Tratsch [tra:tʃ], *m.* (—es, *no pl.*) (coll.) gossip, tittle-tattle.
tratschen ['tra:tʃən], *v.n.* (coll.) gossip.
Tratte ['tratə], *f.* (—, *pl.* —n) (*Comm.*) draft, bill of exchange.
Traube ['traubə], *f.* (—, *pl.* —n) (*Bot.*) grape, bunch of grapes.
Traubensaft ['traubənzaft], *m.* (—s, *pl.* ⸚e) grape-juice; (*Poet.*) wine.
traubig ['traubɪç], *adj.* clustered, grape-like.
trauen ['trauən], *v.a.* marry; join in marriage; *sich* — *lassen*, get married. — *v.n. einem* —, trust s.o., confide in s.o. — *v.r. sich* —, dare, venture.
Trauer ['trauər], *f.* (—, *no pl.*) mourning; sorrow, grief.
Trauermarsch ['trauərmarʃ], *m.* (—es, *pl.* ⸚e) funeral march.
trauern ['trauərn], *v.n.* mourn, be in mourning.
Trauerspiel ['trauərʃpi:l], *n.* (—s, *pl.* —e) tragedy.
Trauerweide ['trauərvaɪdə], *f.* (—, *pl.* —n) (*Bot.*) weeping willow.
Traufe ['traufə], *f.* (—, *pl.* —n) eaves; *vom Regen in die* —, out of the frying pan into the fire.
träufeln ['trɔyfəln], *v.a.* drip, drop.
Traufröhre ['traufrø:rə], *f.* (—, *pl.* —n) gutter-pipe.

treulos

traulich ['traulıç], *adj.* familiar, homely, cosy.

Traum [traum], *m.* (—(e)s, *pl.* ⁓e) dream; *das fällt mir nicht im —e ein*, I should not dream of it.

Traumbild ['traumbılt], *n.* (—s, *pl.* —er) vision.

Traumdeutung ['traumdɔytuŋ], *f.* (—, *no pl.*) interpretation of dreams.

träumen ['trɔymən], *v.n.* dream; *sich etwas nicht — lassen*, have no inkling of, not dream of s.th.; not believe s.th.

Träumer ['trɔymər], *m.* (—s, *pl.* —) dreamer; (*fig.*) visionary.

Träumerei [trɔymə'raɪ], *f.* (—, *pl.* —en) dreaming, reverie.

traumhaft ['traumhaft], *adj.* dream-like.

traurig ['traurıç], *adj.* sad, mournful, sorrowful.

Traurigkeit ['traurıçkaɪt], *f.* (—, *no pl.*) sadness, melancholy.

Trauring ['traurıŋ], *m.* (—s, *pl.* —e) wedding-ring.

Trauschein ['trauʃaɪn], *m.* (—s, *pl.* —e) marriage certificate.

traut [traut], *adj.* dear, beloved; cosy; *—es Heim Glück allein*, east, west, home's best; there's no place like home.

Trauung ['trauuŋ], *f.* (—, *pl.* —en) marriage ceremony.

Trauzeuge ['trautsɔygə], *m.* (—n, *pl.* —n) witness to a marriage.

trecken ['trɛkən], *v.a.* (*dial.*) draw, drag, tug.

Trecker ['trɛkər], *m.* (—s, *pl.* —) tractor.

Treff [trɛf], *n.* (—s, *no pl.*) (*Cards*) clubs.

Treffen ['trɛfən], *n.* (—s, *pl.* —) action, battle, fight; meeting, gathering; *etwas ins — führen*, put s.th. forward, urge s.th.

treffen ['trɛfən], *v.a. irr.* hit, meet; *nicht —*, miss; *wie vom Donner getroffen*, thunderstruck; *ins Schwarze —*, hit the mark, score a bull's eye. — *v.r. sich —*, happen.

treffend ['trɛfənt], *adj.* appropriate, pertinent.

Treffer ['trɛfər], *m.* (—s, *pl.* —) (*lottery*) win, prize; (*Mil.*) hit.

trefflich ['trɛflıç], *adj.* excellent.

Treffpunkt ['trɛfpuŋkt], *m.* (—s, *pl.* —e) meeting-place.

Treffsicherheit ['trɛfzıçərhaɪt], *f.* (—, *no pl.*) accurate aim.

Treibeis ['traɪpaɪs], *n.* (—es, *no pl.*) floating-ice, ice floe.

treiben ['traɪbən], *v.a. irr.* drive, urge; incite; (*trade*) carry on, ply; *Studien —*, study; *was treibst du?* what are you doing? *etwas zu weit —*, carry s.th. too far; *einen in die Enge —*, drive s.o. into a corner. — *v.n.* be adrift, drift.

Treiben ['traɪbən], *n.* (—s, *no pl.*) driving; doings; bustle.

Treiber ['traɪbər], *m.* (—s, *pl.* —) (*Hunt.*) driver; beater.

Treibhaus ['traɪphaus], *n.* (—es, *pl.* ⁓er) hothouse, greenhouse.

Treibkraft ['traɪpkraft], *f.* (—, *no pl.*) impulse, driving power.

Treibriemen ['traɪpri:mən], *m.* (—s, *pl.* —) driving-belt.

Treibsand ['traɪpzant], *m.* (—s, *no pl.*) quicksand, shifting sand.

Treibstange ['traɪpʃtaŋə], *f.* (—, *pl.* —en) main rod, connecting-rod.

Treibstoff ['traɪpʃtɔf], *m.* (—(e)s, *pl.* —e) fuel.

treideln ['traɪdəln], *v.a.* (*Naut.*) tow.

Treidelsteig ['traɪdəlʃtaɪk], *m.* (—s, *pl.* —e) towpath.

trennbar ['trɛnba:r], *adj.* separable.

trennen ['trɛnən], *v.a.* separate, sever. — *v.r. sich —*, part.

Trennung ['trɛnuŋ], *f.* (—, *pl.* —en) separation, segregation; parting; division.

Trennungsstrich ['trɛnuŋsʃtrıç], *m.* (—es, *pl.* —e) hyphen, dash.

treppab [trɛp'ap], *adv.* downstairs.

treppauf [trɛp'auf], *adv.* upstairs.

Treppe ['trɛpə], *f.* (—, *pl.* —n) stairs, staircase, flight of stairs.

Treppenabsatz ['trɛpənapzats], *m.* (—es, *pl.* ⁓e) (*staircase*) landing.

Treppengeländer ['trɛpəngɛlɛndər], *n.* (—s, *pl.* —) balustrade, banisters.

Treppenhaus ['trɛpənhaus], *n.* (—es, *pl.* ⁓er) stair-well, staircase.

Treppenläufer ['trɛpənlɔyfər], *m.* (—s, *pl.* —) stair-carpet.

Treppenstufe ['trɛpənʃtu:fə], *f.* (—, *pl.* —n) step, stair.

Treppenwitz ['trɛpənvıts], *m.* (—es, *no pl.*) afterthought, esprit de l'escalier.

Tresor [tre'zo:r], *m.* (—s, *pl.* —e) safe, strongroom.

Tresse ['trɛsə], *f.* (—, *pl.* —n) braid, lace, galloon.

treten ['tre:tən], *v.a., v.n. irr.* tread, step, trample upon; go; — *Sie näher*, step this way; *in Verbindung — mit*, make contact with; *in den Ehestand —*, get married; *einem zu nahe —*, offend s.o., tread on s.o.'s toes.

treu [trɔy], *adj.* faithful, loyal, true; conscientious.

Treubruch ['trɔybrux], *m.* (—(e)s, *pl.* ⁓e) breach of faith, disloyalty.

Treue ['trɔyə], *f.* (—, *no pl.*) faithfulness, loyalty, fidelity; *meiner Treu!* upon my soul! *auf Treu und Glauben*, on trust.

Treueid ['trɔyaɪt], *m.* (—s, *pl.* —e) oath of allegiance.

Treuhänder ['trɔyhɛndər], *m.* (—s, *pl.* —) trustee.

treuherzig ['trɔyhɛrtsıç], *adj.* guileless, trusting.

treulich ['trɔylıç], *adv.* faithfully.

treulos ['trɔylo:s], *adj.* faithless, perfidious; unfaithful.

227

Treulosigkeit ['trɔylo:zɪçkaɪt], *f.* (—, *no pl.*) faithlessness, perfidy, disloyalty.

Tribüne [tri'by:nə], *f.* (—, *pl.* —n) tribune, platform; (*racing*) grandstand.

Tribut [tri'bu:t], *m.* (—s, *pl.* —e) tribute.

tributpflichtig [tri'bu:tpflɪçtɪç], *adj.* tributary.

Trichter ['trɪçtər], *m.* (—s, *pl.* —) funnel.

trichterförmig ['trɪçtərfœrmɪç], *adj.* funnel-shaped.

Trieb [tri:p], *m.* (—(e)s, *pl.* —e) (*plant*) shoot, growth; instinct, bent, propensity, inclination; (*Psych.*) drive.

Triebfeder ['tri:pfe:dər], *f.* (—, *pl.* —n) mainspring; (*fig.*) motive, guiding principle.

Triebkraft ['tri:pkraft], *f.* (—, *pl.* ⁴e) motive power.

Triebwagen ['tri:pva:gən], *m.* (—s, *pl.* —) rail-car.

Triebwerk ['tri:pvɛrk], *n.* (—s, *pl.* —e) power unit, drive.

triefen ['tri:fən], *v.n. irr. & reg.* trickle, drip; be wet through, be soaking wet.

Trient [tri'ɛnt], *n.* Trent.

Trier [tri:r], *n.* Treves.

Triest [tri'ɛst], *n.* Trieste.

Trift [trɪft], *f.* (—, *pl.* —en) pasture, pasturage, common, meadow.

triftig ['trɪftɪç], *adj.* weighty, valid, conclusive, cogent.

Trikot [tri'ko:], *m. & n.* (—s, *pl.* —s) stockinet; (*circus, ballet*) tights.

Triller ['trɪlər], *m.* (—s, *pl.* —) (*Mus.*) trill, shake.

trillern ['trɪlərn], *v.n.* trill, quaver, shake; warble.

Trinität [trini'tɛ:t], *f.* (—, *no pl.*) Trinity.

trinkbar ['trɪŋkba:r], *adj.* drinkable.

Trinkbecher ['trɪŋkbɛçər], *m.* (—s, *pl.* —) drinking-cup.

trinken ['trɪŋkən], *v.a., v.n. irr.* drink.

Trinker ['trɪŋkər], *m.* (—s, *pl.* —) drinker, drunkard.

Trinkgelage ['trɪŋkgəla:gə], *n.* (—s, *pl.* —) drinking-bout.

Trinkgeld ['trɪŋkgɛlt], *n.* (—s, *pl.* —er) tip, gratuity.

Trinkhalle ['trɪŋkhalə], *f.* (—, *pl.* —n) (*spa*) pump-room.

Trinkspruch ['trɪŋkʃprux], *m.* (—(e)s, *pl.* ⁴e) toast.

Trinkstube ['trɪŋkʃtu:bə], *f.* (—, *pl.* —n) tap-room.

Tripolis ['tri:polɪs], *n.* Tripoli.

trippeln ['trɪpəln], *v.n.* trip (daintily), patter.

Tripper ['trɪpər], *m.* (—s, *no pl.*) (*Med.*) gonorrhoea.

Tritt [trɪt], *m.* (—(e)s, *pl.* —e) step, pace; kick.

Trittbrett ['trɪtbrɛt], *n.* (—s, *pl.* —er) foot-board; carriage-step; (*organ*) pedal.

Triumph [tri'umf], *m.* (—(e)s, *pl.* —e) triumph.

Triumphzug [tri'umftsu:k], *m.* (—(e)s, *pl.* ⁴e) triumphal procession.

Trivialität [trivjali'tɛ:t], *f.* (—, *pl.* —en) triviality, platitude.

trocken ['trɔkən], *adj.* dry, arid; (*fig.*) dull, dry as dust; (*wine*) dry.

Trockenfäule ['trɔkənfɔylə], *f.,* **Trockenfäulnis** ['trɔkənfɔylnɪs], *f.* (—, *no pl.*) dry rot.

Trockenboden ['trɔkənbo:dən], *m.* (—s, *pl.* ⁴) loft.

Trockenfutter ['trɔkənfutər], *n.* (—s, *no pl.*) fodder.

Trockenfütterung ['trɔkənfytəruŋ], *f.* (—, *pl.* —en) dry feeding.

Trockenhaube ['trɔkənhaubə], *f.* (—, *pl.* —n) hair drier.

Trockenheit ['trɔkənhaɪt], *f.* (—, *no pl.*) dryness; drought.

Trockenschleuder ['trɔkənʃlɔydər], *f.* (—, *pl.* —n) spin-drier.

trocknen ['trɔknən], *v.a., v.n.* dry, air.

Troddel ['trɔdəl], *f.* (—, *pl.* —n) tassel.

Trödel ['trø:dəl], *m.* (—s, *no pl.*) junk, lumber, rubbish.

Trödelladen ['trø:dəlla:dən], *m.* (—s, *pl.* ⁴) junk-shop.

Trödelmarkt ['trø:dəlmarkt], *m.* (—s, *no pl.*) kettle market, jumble sale.

trödeln ['trø:dəln], *v.n.* dawdle, loiter.

Trödler ['trø:dlər], *m.* (—s, *pl.* —) second-hand dealer; (*coll.*) dawdler, loiterer.

Trog [tro:k], *m.* (—(e)s, *pl.* ⁴e) trough.

Troja ['tro:ja], *n.* Troy.

trollen ['trɔlən], *v.r. sich* —, decamp, toddle off, make o.s. scarce.

Trommel ['trɔmǝl], *f.* (—, *pl.* —n) drum; cylinder, barrel; tin box; *die* — *rühren*, beat the big drum.

Trommelfell ['trɔmǝlfɛl], *n.* (—s, *pl.* —e) drum-skin; ear-drum.

trommeln ['trɔmǝln], *v.n.* drum, beat the drum.

Trommelschlegel ['trɔmǝlʃle:gǝl], *m.* (—s, *pl.* —) drumstick.

Trommelwirbel ['trɔmǝlvɪrbǝl], *m.* (—s, *pl.* —) roll of drums.

Trommler ['trɔmlǝr], *m.* (—s, *pl.* —) drummer.

Trompete [trɔm'pe:tǝ], *f.* (—, *pl.* —n) trumpet; *die* … *blasen*, blow the trumpet.

trompeten [trɔm'pe:tǝn], *v.n.* trumpet, sound the trumpet.

Trompetengeschmetter [trɔm'pe:tǝngǝʃmɛtǝr], *n.* (—s, *no pl.*) flourish of trumpets.

Tropen ['tro:pǝn], *f. pl.* the tropics.

Tropenfieber ['tro:pǝnfi:bǝr], *n.* (—s, *no pl.*) tropical fever.

tröpfeln ['trœpfǝln], *v.a., v.n.* trickle, sprinkle.

Tropfen ['trɔpfǝn], *m.* (—s, *pl.* —) drop; *steter* — *höhlt den Stein*, constant dripping wears away a stone.

tropfen ['trɔpfǝn], *v.n.* drop, drip.

Tücke

Trophäe [tro'fɛə], *f.* (—, *pl.* —n) trophy.
tropisch ['tro:pɪʃ], *adj.* tropical, tropic.
Troß [trɔs], *m.* (—sses, *pl.* -sse) (*Mil.*) baggage-train; (*fig.*) hangers-on, camp-followers.
Troßpferd ['trɔspfe:rt], *n.* (—s, *pl.* —e) pack-horse.
Trost [tro:st], *m.* (—es, *no pl.*) consolation, comfort; *geringer* —, cold comfort; *du bist wohl nicht bei* —? have you taken leave of your senses?
trösten ['trø:stən], *v.a.* comfort, console; *tröste dich,* cheer up.
Tröster ['trø:stər], *m.* (—s, *pl.* —) comforter, consoler; (*Theol.*) Holy Ghost, Comforter.
tröstlich ['trø:stlɪç], *adj.* consoling, comforting.
trostlos ['tro:stlo:s], *adj.* disconsolate, inconsolable; desolate, bleak.
Trostlosigkeit ['tro:stlo:zɪçkaɪt], *f.* (—, *no pl.*) disconsolateness; (*fig.*) wretchedness; dreariness.
Trott [trɔt], *m.* (—s, *no pl.*) trot.
Trottel ['trɔtəl], *m.* (—s, *pl.* —) (*coll.*) idiot.
Trottoir [trɔto'a:r], *n.* (—s, *pl.* —e) pavement, footpath; (*Am.*) sidewalk.
trotz [trɔts], *prep.* (*Genit.*, *Dat.*) in spite of, despite; — *alledem,* all the same.
Trotz [trɔts], *m.* (—es, *no pl.*) defiance, obstinacy, refractoriness; *einem* — *bieten,* defy s.o.; *einem etwas zum* — *machen,* do s.th. in defiance of s.o.
trotzdem [trɔts'de:m], *conj.* notwithstanding that, albeit, although. — *adv.* nevertheless.
trotzen ['trɔtsən], *v.n.* defy; sulk, be obstinate; *Gefahren* —, brave dangers.
trotzig ['trɔtsɪç], *adj.* defiant; sulky, refractory; headstrong, stubborn, obstinate.
Trotzkopf ['trɔtskɔpf], *m.* (—(e)s, *pl.* —e) obstinate child; pig-headed person.
trübe ['try:bə], *adj.* dim, gloomy; (*weather*) dull, cloudy, overcast; (*water*) troubled; (*glass*) misted; —*s Lächeln,* wan smile.
Trubel ['tru:bəl], *m.* (—s, *no pl.*) tumult, turmoil, disturbance.
trüben ['try:bən], *v.a.* darken, sadden, trouble; (*glass*) mist; (*metal*) tarnish; (*fig.*) obscure.
Trübsal ['try:pza:l], *f.* (—, *pl.* —e), *n.* (—s, *pl.* —e) misery, trouble, distress; — *blasen,* mope.
trübselig ['try:pze:lɪç], *adj.* woeful, lamentable; woebegone, forlorn.
Trübsinn ['try:pzɪn], *m.* (—s, *no pl.*) sadness, dejection.
trübsinnig ['try:pzɪnɪç], *adj.* sad, dejected.
Trüffel ['tryfəl], *f.* (—, *pl.* —n) truffle.
Trug [tru:k], *m.* (—(e)s, *no pl.*) deceit, fraud; *Lug und* —, a pack of lies.

Trugbild ['tru:kbɪlt], *n.* (—es, *pl.* —er) phantom.
trügen ['try:gən], *v.a. irr.* deceive.
trügerisch ['try:gərɪs], *adj.* deceptive, illusory, fallacious.
Truggewebe ['tru:kgəve:bə], *n.* (—s, *pl.* —) tissue of lies.
Trugschluß ['tru:kʃlus], *m.* (—sses, *pl.* ⸚sse) fallacy, false deduction.
Truhe ['tru:ə], *f.* (—, *pl.* —n) chest, trunk, coffer.
Trumm [trum], *m.* (—s, *pl.* ⸚er) lump, broken piece.
Trümmer ['trymər], *m. pl.* fragments, debris, ruins; *in* — *gehen,* go to wrack and ruin; *in* — *schlagen,* wreck.
Trümmerhaufen ['trymərhaufən], *m.* (—s, *pl.* —) heap of ruins, heap of rubble.
Trumpf [trumpf], *m.* (—(e)s, *pl.* ⸚e) trump, trump-card.
trumpfen ['trumpfən], *v.a.* trump.
Trumpffarbe ['trumpffarbə], *f.* (—, *pl.* —n) trump-suit.
Trunk [truŋk], *m.* (—(e)s, *pl.* ⸚e) draught, potion, drinking; *sich dem* — *ergeben,* take to drink.
trunken ['truŋkən], *adj.* drunk, intoxicated; (*fig.*) elated.
Trunkenbold ['truŋkənbɔlt], *m.* (—s, *pl.* —e) drunkard.
Trunkenheit ['truŋkənhaɪt], *f.* (—, *no pl.*) drunkenness, intoxication.
Trunksucht ['truŋkzuxt], *f.* (—, *no pl.*) dipsomania, alcoholism.
trunksüchtig ['truŋkzyçtɪç], *adj.* dipsomaniac, addicted to drinking.
Trupp [trup], *m.* (—s, *pl.* —s) troop, band.
Truppe ['trupə], *f.* (—, *pl.* —n) (*Mil.*) company, troops, forces; (*actors*) troupe.
Truppengattung ['trupəngatuŋ], *f.* (—, *pl.* —en) branch of the armed forces.
Truthahn ['tru:tha:n], *m.* (—s, *pl.* ⸚e) (*Orn.*) turkey cock.
Truthenne ['tru:thɛnə], *f.* (—, *pl.* —n) (*Orn.*) turkey hen.
Truthühner ['tru:thy:nər], *n. pl.* (*Orn.*) turkey-fowl.
Trutz [truts], *m.* (—es, *no pl.*) (*Poet.*) defiance; *zum Schutz und* —, offensively and defensively.
Tschad [tʃat], *n.* Chad.
Tschechoslowakei [tʃɛçoslova'kaɪ], *f.* Czechoslovakia.
Tuch (1) [tu:x], *n.* (—(e)s, *pl.* ⸚er) shawl, wrap.
Tuch (2) [tu:x], *n.* (—s, *pl.* —e) cloth, fabric.
Tuchhändler ['tu:xhɛndlər], *m.* (—s, *pl.* —) draper, clothier.
tüchtig ['tyçtɪç], *adj.* able, competent, efficient. — *adv.* largely, much, heartily.
Tüchtigkeit ['tyçtɪçkaɪt], *f.* (—, *no pl.*) ability, competence, efficiency.
Tücke ['tykə], *f.* (—, *pl.* —n) malice, spite.

229

tückisch

tückisch ['tykɪʃ], adj. malicious, insidious.

Tugend ['tu:gənt], f. (—, pl. —en) virtue.

Tugendbold ['tu:gəntbɔlt], m. (—s, pl. —e) paragon.

tugendhaft ['tu:gənthaft], adj. virtuous.

Tugendlehre ['tu:gəntle:rə], f. (—, no pl.) ethics, morals.

Tüll [tyl], m. (—s, pl. —e) tulle.

Tulpe ['tulpə], f. (—, pl. —n) (Bot.) tulip.

Tulpenzwiebel ['tulpəntsvi:bəl], f. (—, pl. —n) tulip-bulb.

tummeln ['tuməln], v.r. sich —, romp about; make haste.

Tummelplatz ['tuməlplats], m. (—es, pl. ⸚e) playground, fairground.

Tümpel ['tympəl], m. (—s, pl. —) pond, pool, puddle.

Tun [tu:n], n. (—s, no pl.) doing; sein — und Lassen, his conduct.

tun [tu:n], v.a. irr. do, make; put; tut nichts, it does not matter; viel zu — haben, have a lot to do, be busy; Not —, be necessary; Buße —, repent.

Tünche ['tynçə], f. (—, pl. —n) whitewash.

tünchen ['tynçən], v.a. whitewash.

Tunichtgut ['tu:nɪçtgu:t], m. (—s, no pl.) ne'er-do-well, scamp.

Tunke ['tuŋkə], f. (—, pl. —n) sauce, gravy.

tunken ['tuŋkən], v.a. dip, steep; (Am.) dunk.

tunlich ['tu:nlɪç], adj. feasible, practicable, expedient.

tunlichst ['tu:nlɪçst], adv. if possible, possibly.

Tunnel ['tunəl], m. (—s, pl. —) tunnel.

Tunnelbau ['tunəlbau], m. (—s, no pl.) tunnelling.

tüpfeln ['typfəln], v.a. dot, spot.

Tupfen ['tupfən], m. (—s, pl. —) dot, polka-dot.

Tür [ty:r], f. (—, pl. —en) door; einem die — weisen, show s.o. the door; vor der — stehen, be imminent; kehr vor deiner eigenen —, mind your own business; put your own house in order; offene —en einrennen, flog a willing horse; zwischen — und Angel stecken, be undecided.

Türangel ['ty:raŋəl], f. (—, pl. —n) door-hinge.

Türhüter ['ty:rhy:tər], m. (—s, pl. —) doorkeeper.

Türkei [tyr'kai], f. Turkey.

Türkensäbel ['tyrkənze:bəl], m. (—s, pl. —) scimitar.

Türkis [tyr'ki:s], m. (—es, pl. —e) turquoise.

Türklinke ['ty:rklɪŋkə], f. (—, pl. —n) door-handle.

Turm [turm], m. (—(e)s, pl. ⸚e) tower; spire, steeple; belfry; (Chess) castle.

Turmalin [turma'li:n], m. (—s, pl. —e) tourmaline.

Türmchen ['tyrmçən], n. (—s, pl. —) turret.

türmen ['tyrmən], v.a. pile up. — v.n. (coll.) bolt, run away. — v.r. sich —, rise high, be piled high.

Turmspitze ['turmʃpɪtsə], f. (—, pl. —n) spire.

turnen ['turnən], v.n. do exercises or gymnastics.

Turnen ['turnən], n. (—s, no pl.) gymnastics, physical training.

Turner ['turnər], m. (—s, pl. —) gymnast.

Turngerät ['turngərɛ:t], n. (—es, pl. —e) gymnastic apparatus.

Turnhalle ['turnhalə], f. (—, pl. —n) gymnasium.

Turnier [tur'ni:r], n. (—s, pl. —e) tournament.

Turnübung ['turny:buŋ], f. (—, pl. —en) gymnastic exercise.

Turnverein ['turnfərain], m. (—s, pl. —e) athletics club, gymnastics club.

Türpfosten ['ty:rpfostən], m. (—s, pl. —) door-post.

Türriegel ['ty:rri:gəl], m. (—s, pl. —) bolt.

Türschild ['ty:rʃɪlt], n. (—(e)s, pl. —e) (door)plate.

Türschloß ['ty:rʃlɔs], n. (—sses, pl. ⸚sser) lock.

Türschlüssel ['ty:rʃlysəl], m. (—s, pl. —) door-key, latch-key.

Türschwelle ['ty:rʃvɛlə], f. (—, pl. —n) threshold.

Tusch [tuʃ], m. (—es, pl. —e) (Mus.) flourish.

Tusche ['tuʃə], f. (—, pl. —n) watercolour; Indian ink.

tuscheln ['tuʃəln], v.n. whisper.

tuschen ['tuʃən], v.a. draw in Indian ink.

Tuschkasten ['tuʃkastən], m. (—s, pl. ⸚) paint-box.

Tüte ['ty:tə], f. (—, pl. —n) paper bag.

Tutel [tu'te:l], f. (—, no pl.) guardianship.

tuten ['tu:tən], v.n. hoot, honk, blow a horn.

Tütendreher ['ty:təndre:ər], m. (—s, pl. —) (sl.) small shopkeeper.

Typ [ty:p], m. (—s, pl. —en) type.

Type ['ty:pə], f. (—, pl. —n) (Typ.) type; (fig.) queer fish.

Typhus ['ty:fus], m. (—, no pl.) (Med.) typhoid (fever).

typisch ['ty:pɪʃ], adj. typical.

Typus ['ty:pus], m. (—, pl. Typen) type.

Tyrann [ty'ran], m. (—en, pl. —en) tyrant.

Tyrannei [tyra'nai], f. (—, pl. —en) tyranny, despotism.

tyrannisch [ty'ranɪʃ], adj. tyrannical, despotic.

tyrannisieren [tyrani'zi:rən], v.a. tyrannize over, oppress, bully.

U

U [u:], *n.* (—s, *pl.* —s) the letter U.

U-Bahn ['u:ba:n], *f.* (—, *no pl.*) underground (railway);(*Am.*)subway.

Übel ['y:bəl], *n.* (—s, *pl.* —) evil, trouble; misfortune; disease.

übel ['y:bəl], *adj.* evil, ill, bad; *mir ist —*, I feel sick; *nicht —*, not too bad; *— daran sein*, be in a bad way, be in a mess.

übelgesinnt ['y:bəlgəzɪnt], *adj.* evil-minded; ill-disposed; *einem — sein*, bear s.o. a grudge.

Übelkeit ['y:bəlkaɪt], *f.* (—, *pl.* —en) nausea, sickness.

übellaunig ['y:bəllaunɪç], *adj.* ill-humoured, bad-tempered.

übelnehmen ['y:bəlne:mən], *v.a. irr.* take amiss, resent, be offended at.

übelnehmerisch ['y:bəlne:mərɪʃ], *adj.* touchy, easily offended.

Übelstand ['y:bəlʃtant], *m.* (—(e)s, *pl.* ⁀e) inconvenience, drawback; (*pl.*) abuses.

Übeltat ['y:bəlta:t], *f.* (—, *pl.* —en) misdeed.

Übeltäter ['y:bəlte:tər], *m.* (—s, *pl.* —) evildoer, malefactor.

übelwollend ['y:bəlvɔlənt], *adj.* malevolent.

üben ['y:bən], *v.a.* practise, exercise; *Rache —*, wreak vengeance.

über ['y:bər], *prep.* (*Dat., Acc.*) over, above; across; about; more than, exceeding; via, by way of; concerning, on. — *adv.* over, above; *— und —*, all over; *— kurz oder lang*, sooner or later; *heute —s Jahr*, a year from today.

überall ['y:bəral], *adv.* everywhere, anywhere.

überanstrengen [y:bər'anʃtrɛŋən], *v.a. insep.* overtax s.o.'s strength, strain. *— v.r. sich —*, overtax o.'s strength, overexert o.s.

Überanstrengung [y:bər'anʃtrɛŋuŋ], *f.* (—, *pl.* —en) over-exertion, strain.

überantworten [y:bər'antvɔrtən], *v.a. insep.* deliver up, surrender.

überarbeiten [y:bər'arbaɪtən], *v.a. insep.* revise, do again. — *v.r. sich —*, overwork o.s.

überarbeitet [y:bər'arbaɪtət], *adj.* overwrought, overworked.

überaus ['y:bəraus], *adv.* exceedingly, extremely.

überbauen [y:bər'bauən], *v.a. insep.* build over.

überbieten [y:bər'bi:tən], *v.a. irr. insep.* outbid (s.o.); (*fig.*) surpass.

Überbleibsel ['y:bərblaɪpsəl], *n.* (—s, *pl.* —) remainder, remnant, residue, rest.

Überblick ['y:bərblɪk], *m.* (—(e)s, *pl.* —e) survey, general view.

überblicken [y:bər'blɪkən], *v.a. insep.* survey, look over.

überbringen [y:bər'brɪŋən], *v.a. irr. insep.* bear, deliver, hand in.

Überbringung [y:bər'brɪŋuŋ], *f.* (—, *no pl.*) delivery.

überbrücken [y:bər'brykən], *v.a. insep.* bridge, span.

überdachen [y:bər'daxən], *v.a. insep.* roof (over).

überdauern [y:bər'dauərn], *v.a. insep.* outlast; tide over.

überdenken [y:bər'dɛŋkən], *v.a. irr. insep.* think over, consider.

überdies [y:bər'di:s], *adv.* besides, moreover.

überdrucken [y:bər'drukən], *v.a. insep.* overprint.

Überdruß ['y:bərdrus], *m.* (—sses, *no pl.*) weariness; disgust; *zum —*, ad nauseam.

überdrüssig ['y:bərdrysɪç],*adj.* weary of.

Übereifer ['y:bəraɪfər], *m.* (—s, *no pl.*) excessive zeal.

übereifrig ['y:bəraɪfrɪç], *adj.* excessively zealous, officious.

übereilen [y:bər'aɪlən], *v.r. insep. sich —*, hurry too much, overshoot the mark.

übereilt [y:bər'aɪlt], *adj.* overhasty, rash.

übereinkommen [y:bər'aɪnkɔmən], *v.n. irr.* (*aux. sein*) agree.

Übereinkunft [y:bər'aɪnkunft], *f.* (—, *pl.* ⁀e) agreement, convention.

übereinstimmen [y:bər'aɪnʃtɪmən], *v.n.* agree, concur, harmonize, be of one mind, be of the same opinion; (*things*) tally, be square.

Übereinstimmung [y:bər'aɪnʃtɪmuŋ], *f.* (—, *no pl.*) accord, agreement, conformity, harmony.

überfahren (1) [y:bər'fa:rən], *v.a. irr. insep.* traverse, pass over; run over (s.o.).

überfahren (2) ['y:bərfa:rən], *v.a. irr. insep.* ferry across. — *v.n.* (*aux. sein*) cross.

überfahren (3) ['y:bərfa:rən], *v.n.* (*aux. sein*) cross.

Überfahrt ['y:bərfa:rt], *f.* (—, *pl.* —en) passage, crossing.

Überfall ['y:bərfal], *m.* (—s, *pl.* ⁀e) sudden attack, raid.

überfallen (1) ['y:bərfalən], *v.n. irr.* (*aux. sein*) (*p.p.* übergefallen) fall over.

überfallen (2) [y:bər'falən], *v.a. irr. insep.* (*p.p.* überfallen) attack suddenly, raid.

überfliegen [y:bər'fli:gən], *v.a. irr. insep.* fly over; (*fig.*) glance over, skim.

überfließen ['y:bərfli:sən], *v.n. irr.* (*aux. sein*) overflow.

231

überflügeln [y:bər'fly:gəln], *v.a. insep.* surpass, outstrip.

Überfluß ['y:bərflus], *m.* (—**sses**, *no pl.*) abundance, plenty, profusion; surplus; — **haben an**, abound in, have too much of.

überflüssig ['y:bərflysıç], *adj.* superfluous, unnecessary.

überfluten [y:bər'flu:tən], *v.a. insep.* overflow, flood.

überführen (1) ['y:bərfy:rən], *v.a.* convey, conduct (across).

überführen (2) [y:bər'fy:rən], *v.a. insep.* convict; transport a coffin.

Überführung [y:bər'fy:ruŋ], *f.* (—, *pl.* —**en**) conviction (for a crime); transport (of a coffin).

Überfüllung [y:bər'fyluŋ], *f.* (—, *no pl.*) overcrowding.

Übergabe ['y:bərga:bə], *f.* (—, *no pl.*) surrender, yielding up; delivery, handing over.

Übergang ['y:bərgaŋ], *m.* (—**s**, *pl.* —**e**) passage, (*Railw.*) crossing; (*fig.*) change-over, transition.

übergeben [y:bər'ge:bən], *v.a. irr. insep.* deliver up, hand over. — *v.r. sich* —, vomit.

übergehen (1) ['y:bərge:ən], *v.n. irr.* (*aux.* sein) (*p.p.* übergegangen) go over, change over, turn (into); *zum Feinde* —, go over to the enemy; *in andre Hände* —, change hands.

übergehen (2) [y:bər'ge:ən], *v.a. irr. insep.* (*p.p.* übergangen) pass over, pass by.

Übergehung [y:bər'ge:uŋ], *f.* (—, *no pl.*) omission; passing over.

übergeordnet [y:bərgəərdnət], *adj.* superior.

Übergewicht ['y:bərgəvıçt], *n.* (—(e)s, *no pl.*) overweight; (*fig.*) preponderance, superiority.

übergießen [y:bər'gi:sən], *v.a. irr. insep.* pour over, douse with.

überglücklich ['y:bərglyklıç], *adj.* overjoyed.

übergreifen ['y:bərgraıfən], *v.n. irr.* overlap; encroach (upon); spread.

Übergriff ['y:bərgrıf], *m.* (—(e)s, *pl.* —e) encroachment.

übergroß ['y:bərgro:s], *adj.* excessively large, overlarge.

überhaben ['y:bərha:bən], *v.a. irr.* have enough of, be sick of.

überhandnehmen [y:bər'hantne:mən], *v.n. irr.* gain the upper hand; run riot.

überhangen ['y:bərhaŋən], *v.n. irr.* hang over.

überhängen ['y:bərhɛŋən], *v.a. irr.* cover, hang upon.

überhäufen [y:bər'hɔyfən], *v.a. insep.* overwhelm.

überhaupt [y:bər'haupt], *adv.* in general, altogether, at all.

überheben [y:bər'he:bən], *v.r. insep. sich* —, strain o.s. by lifting; (*fig.*) be overbearing.

überheblich [y:bər'he:plıç], *adj.* overbearing, arrogant.

überheizen [y:bər'haıtsən], *v.a. insep.* overheat.

überhitzt [y:bər'hıtst], *adj.* overheated; impassioned.

überholen [y:bər'ho:lən], *v.a. insep.* overtake, out-distance; (*fig.*) overhaul.

überhören [y:bər'hø:rən], *v.a. insep.* hear s.o.'s lessons; ignore, miss (s.th.).

überirdisch ['y:bərırdıʃ], *adj.* celestial, superterrestrial.

Überkleid ['y:bərklaıt], *n.* (—(e)s, *pl.* —er) outer garment; overall.

überklug ['y:bərklu:k], *adj.* too clever by half, conceited.

überkochen ['y:bərkɔxən], *v.n.* (*aux.* sein) boil over.

überkommen [y:bər'kɔmən], *adj.* — *sein von*, be seized with.

überladen [y:bər'la:dən], *v.a. irr. insep.* overload. — *adj.* overdone, too elaborate; bombastic.

überlassen [y:bər'lasən], *v.a. irr. insep.* leave, relinquish, give up, yield.

überlasten [y:bər'lastən], *v.a. insep.* overburden.

überlaufen (1) ['y:bərlaufən], *v.a. irr.* run over; (*to the enemy*) desert.

überlaufen (2) [y:bər'laufən], *v.a. insep.* (*p.p.* überlaufen) overrun.

Überläufer ['y:bərlɔyfər], *m.* (—**s**, *pl.* —) deserter, runaway.

überleben [y:bər'le:bən], *v.a. insep.* survive, outlive; (*fig.*) live (s.th.) down; *sich überlebt haben*, be out of date, be dated.

Überlebende [y:bər'le:bəndə], *m.* (—**n**, *pl.* —**n**) survivor.

überlegen (1) ['y:bərle:gən], *v.a.* lay over, cover.

überlegen (2) [y:bər'le:gən], *v.a. insep.* (*p.p.* überlegt) think over, consider, turn over in o.'s mind. — *adj.* superior; — *sein*, outdo, be superior to.

Überlegenheit [y:bər'le:gənhaıt], *f.* (—, *no pl.*) superiority.

Überlegung [y:bər'le:guŋ], *f.* (—, *pl.* —**en**) consideration, deliberation; *bei näherer* —, on second thoughts, on thinking it over.

überliefern [y:bər'li:fərn], *v.a. insep.* hand down (to posterity), hand on, pass on.

Überlieferung [y:bər'li:fəruŋ], *f.* (—, *pl.* —**en**) tradition.

überlisten [y:bər'lıstən], *v.a. insep.* outwit.

Übermacht ['y:bərmaxt], *f.* (—, *no pl.*) superiority, superior force.

übermalen [y:bər'ma:lən], *v.a. insep.* paint over.

übermangansauer [y:bərmaŋ'ga:nzauər], *adj.* permanganate of; —*saueres Kali*, permanganate of potash.

übermannen [y:bər'manən], *v.a. insep.* overpower.

Übermaß ['y:bərma:s], *n.* (—es, *no pl.*) excess; *im* —, to excess.

überspannt

übermäßig ['y:bərmɛ:sɪç], *adj.* excessive, immoderate.

Übermensch ['y:bərmɛnʃ], *m.* (**—en**, *pl.* **—en**) superman.

übermenschlich ['y:bərmɛnʃlɪç], *adj.* superhuman.

übermitteln [y:bər'mɪtəln], *v.a. insep.* convey.

übermorgen ['y:bərmɔrgən], *adv.* the day after tomorrow.

Übermut ['y:bərmu:t], *m.* (**—s**, *no pl.*) wantonness; high spirits.

übermütig ['y:bərmy:tɪç], *adj.* wanton; full of high spirits.

übernachten [y:bər'naxtən], *v.n. insep.* pass *or* spend the night.

übernächtig [y:bər'nɛçtɪç], *adj.* haggard, tired by a sleepless night.

Übernahme ['y:bərna:mə], *f.* (**—**, *no pl.*) taking possession, taking charge.

übernatürlich ['y:bərnaty:rlɪç], *adj.* supernatural.

übernehmen [y:bər'ne:mən], *v.a. irr. insep.* take possession of, take upon o.s., take over. — *v.r. sich* **—**, overtax o.'s strength.

überordnen ['y:bərɔrdnən], *v.a.* place above.

überprüfen [y:bər'pry:fən], *v.a. insep.* examine, overhaul.

überquellen ['y:bərkvɛlən], *v.n. irr. insep.* (*aux. sein*) bubble over.

überqueren [y:bər'kve:rən], *v.a. insep.* cross.

überragen [y:bər'ra:gən], *v.a. insep.* tower above, overtop; (*fig.*) surpass, outstrip.

überraschen [y:bər'raʃən], *v.a. insep.* surprise, take by surprise.

Überraschung [y:bər'raʃuŋ], *f.* (**—**, *pl.* **—en**) surprise.

überreden [y:bər're:dən], *v.a. insep.* persuade, talk s.o. into (s.th.).

Überredung [y:bər're:duŋ], *f.* (**—**, *no pl.*) persuasion.

überreichen [y:bər'raɪçən], *v.a. insep.* hand over, present formally.

überreichlich ['y:bərraɪçlɪç], *adj.* superabundant.

Überreichung [y:bər'raɪçuŋ], *f.* (**—**, *no pl.*) formal presentation.

überreizen [y:bər'raɪtsən], *v.a. insep.* over-excite, over-stimulate.

überrennen [y:bər'rɛnən], *v.a. irr. insep.* take by storm, overrun.

Überrest ['y:bərrɛst], *m.* (**—es**, *pl.* **—e**) remainder, remnant, residue.

überrumpeln [y:bər'rumpəln], *v.a. insep.* catch unawares, surprise.

übersättigen [y:bər'zɛtɪgən], *v.a. insep.* saturate; surfeit, cloy.

Übersättigung [y:bər'zɛtɪguŋ], *f.* (**—**, *no pl.*) saturation; surfeit.

Überschallgeschwindigkeit ['y:bərʃalgəʃvɪndɪçkaɪt], *f.* (**—**, *no pl.*) supersonic speed.

überschatten [y:bər'ʃatən], *v.a. insep.* overshadow.

überschätzen [y:bər'ʃɛtsən], *v.a. insep.* overrate, over-estimate.

überschauen [y:bər'ʃauən], *v.a. insep.* survey.

überschäumen ['y:bərʃɔymən], *v.n.* (*aux. sein*) bubble over.

überschäumend ['y:bərʃɔymənt], *adj.* ebullient, exuberant.

Überschlag ['y:bərʃla:k], *m.* (**—s**, *pl.* **—e**) somersault; estimate.

überschlagen [y:bər'ʃla:gən], *v.a. irr. insep.* (*pages*) miss, skip; estimate, compute. — *v.r. sich* **—**, turn a somersault, overturn. — *adj.* tepid, lukewarm.

überschnappen ['y:bərʃnapən], *v.n.* (*aux. sein*) snap; (*fig., coll.*) go out of o.'s mind.

überschreiben [y:bər'ʃraɪbən], *v.a. irr. insep.* superscribe, entitle.

überschreiten [y:bər'ʃraɪtən], *v.a. irr. insep.* cross; go beyond, exceed.

Überschrift ['y:bərʃrɪft], *f.* (**—**, *pl.* **—en**) heading, headline.

Überschuß ['y:bərʃus], *m.* (**—sses**, *pl.* **—sse**) surplus.

überschüssig [y:bər'ʃysɪç], *adj.* surplus, remaining.

überschütten [y:bər'ʃytən], *v.a. insep.* shower with, overwhelm with.

Überschwang ['y:bərʃvaŋ], *m.* (**—s**, *no pl.*) exaltation, rapture.

überschwemmen [y:bər'ʃvemən], *v.a. insep.* flood, inundate.

Überschwemmung [y:bər'ʃvemuŋ], *f.* (**—**, *pl.* **—en**) inundation, flood, deluge.

überschwenglich [y:bər'ʃvɛŋlɪç], *adj.* exuberant, exalted.

Übersee ['y:bərze:], *f.* (**—**, *no pl.*) overseas.

übersehen [y:bər'ze:ən], *v.a. irr. insep.* survey, look over; overlook, disregard.

übersenden [y:bər'zɛndən], *v.a. irr. insep.* send, forward, transmit; (*money*) remit.

Übersendung [y:bər'zɛnduŋ], *f.* (**—**, *pl.* **—en**) sending, forwarding, transmission; remittance.

übersetzen (1) ['y:bərzɛtsən], *v.a.* (*p.p.* übergesetzt) ferry across, cross (a river).

übersetzen (2) [y:bər'zɛtsən], *v.a. insep.* (*p.p.* übersetzt) translate.

Übersetzer [y:bər'zɛtsər], *m.* (**—s**, *pl.* **—**) translator.

Übersetzung [y:bər'zɛtsuŋ], *f.* (**—**, *pl.* **—en**) translation.

Übersicht ['y:bərzɪçt], *f.* (**—**, *pl.* **—en**) survey, summary; epitome.

übersichtlich ['y:bərzɪçtlɪç], *adj.* clearly arranged, readable at a glance, lucid.

übersiedeln [y:bər'zi:dəln], *v.n.* (*aux. sein*) remove, move, settle in a different place.

Übersiedlung [y:bər'zi:dluŋ], *f.* (**—**, *pl.* **—en**) removal.

überspannen [y:bər'ʃpanən], *v.a. insep.* overstretch.

überspannt [y:bər'ʃpant], *adj.* eccentric, extravagant.

233

Überspanntheit [y:bər'ʃpanthaɪt], *f.* (—, *pl.* —en) eccentricity.

überspringen [y:bər'ʃprɪŋən], *v.a. irr. insep.* jump over; (*fig.*) skip.

übersprudeln [y:bər'ʃpru:dəln], *v.n.* (*aux.* sein) bubble over.

überstechen [y:bər'ʃteçən], *v.a. irr.* (*cards*) trump higher.

überstehen [y:bər'ʃte:ən], *v.a. irr. insep.* overcome, endure, get over, weather.

übersteigen [y:bər'ʃtaɪgən], *v.a. irr. insep.* exceed, surpass.

überstrahlen [y:bər'ʃtra:lən], *v.a. insep.* outshine, surpass in splendour.

überstreichen [y:bər'ʃtraɪçən], *v.a. irr. insep.* paint over.

überströmen [y:bər'ʃtrø:mən], *v.a. insep.* flood, overflow.

Überstunde ['y:bərʃtundə], *f.* (—, *pl.* —n) extra working time, overtime.

überstürzen [y:bər'ʃtyrtsən], *v.r. insep. sich* —, act in haste.

übertäuben [y:bər'tɔybən], *v.a. insep.* deafen.

überteuern [y:bər'tɔyərn], *v.a. insep.* overcharge.

übertölpeln [y:bər'tœlpəln], *v.a. insep.* cheat.

übertönen [y:bər'tø:nən], *v.a. insep.* (*sound*) drown.

übertragen [y:bər'tra:gən], *v.a. irr. insep.* transfer, hand over; convey; broadcast; translate; (*Comm.*) carry over; *einem ein Amt* —, confer an office on s.o.

Übertragung [y:bər'tra:guŋ], *f.* (—, *pl.* —en) cession; transference; handing over; (*Comm.*) carrying over; (*Rad.*) transmission; (*Med.*) transfusion.

übertreffen [y:bər'trɛfən], *v.a. irr. insep.* surpass, excel, outdo.

übertreiben [y:bər'traɪbən], *v.a. irr. insep.* exaggerate.

Übertreibung [y:bər'traɪbuŋ], *f.* (—, *pl.* —en) exaggeration.

übertreten (1) ['y:bərtre:tən], *v.n. irr.* (*aux.* sein) go over to; (*river*) overflow; (*religion*) change to, join (*church, party*).

übertreten (2) [y:bər'tre:tən], *v.a. irr. insep.* transgress, trespass against, infringe, violate.

Übertretung [y:bər'tre:tuŋ], *f.* (—, *pl.* —en) transgression, trespass, violation, infringement.

übertrieben [y:bər'tri:bən], *adj.* excessive, immoderate, exaggerated.

Übertritt ['y:bərtrɪt], *m.* (—s, *no pl.*) defection, going over; (*Rel.*) change, conversion.

übertünchen [y:bər'tynçən], *v.a. insep.* whitewash, rough-cast; (*fig.*) gloss over.

Übervölkerung [y:bər'fœlkəruŋ], *f.* (—, *no pl.*) overpopulation.

übervoll [y:bər'fɔl], *adj.* overful, brimful, chock-full.

übervorteilen [y:bər'fo:rtaɪlən], *v.a. insep.* cheat, defraud.

überwachen [y:bər'vaxən], *v.a. insep.* watch over, superintend, supervise.

Überwachung [y:bər'vaxuŋ], *f.* (—, *no pl.*) superintendence, supervision.

überwachsen [y:bər'vaksən], *v.a. insep.* overgrow.

überwältigen [y:bər'vɛltɪgən], *v.a. insep.* overcome, overpower, subdue.

überwältigend [y:bər'vɛltɪgənt], *adj.* overwhelming.

Überwältigung [y:bər'vɛltɪguŋ], *f.* (—, *no pl.*) overpowering.

überweisen [y:bər'vaɪzən], *v.a. irr. insep.* assign; (*money*) remit.

Überweisung [y:bər'vaɪzuŋ], *f.* (—, *pl.* —en) assignment; (*money*) remittance.

überwerfen (1) ['y:bərvɛrfən], *v.a.* throw over; (*clothes*) slip on.

überwerfen (2) [y:bər'vɛrfən], *v.r. irr. insep. sich* — mit, fall out with s.o.

überwiegen [y:bər'vi:gən], *v.n. irr. insep.* prevail.

überwiegend [y:bər'vi:gənt], *adj.* paramount, overwhelming, predominant.

überwinden [y:bər'vɪndən], *v.a. irr. insep.* overcome, conquer. — *v.r sich* —, prevail upon o.s., bring o.s. (to).

Überwindung [y:bər'vɪnduŋ], *f.* (—, *no pl.*) conquest; reluctance.

überwintern [y:bər'vɪntərn], *v.n. insep.* winter, hibernate.

Überwinterung [y:bər'vɪntəruŋ], *f.* (—, *no pl.*) hibernation.

überwölkt [y:bər'vœlkt], *adj.* overcast.

Überwurf ['y:bərvurf], *m.* (—s, *pl.* ⁓e) wrap, shawl, cloak.

Überzahl ['y:bərtsa:l], *f.* (—, *no pl.*) *in der* —, in the majority.

überzählig ['y:bərtsɛ:lɪç], *adj.* supernumerary, surplus.

überzeichnen ['y:bərtsaɪçnən], *v.a. insep.* (*Comm.*) over-subscribe.

überzeugen [y:bər'tsɔygən], *v.a. insep.* convince. — *v.r. sich*—, satisfy o.s.

Überzeugung [y:bər'tsɔyguŋ], *f.* (—, *no pl.*) conviction.

überziehen (1) ['y:bərtsi:ən], *v.a. irr.* put on (a garment).

überziehen (2) [y:bər'tsi:ən], *v.a. irr. insep.* cover; (*bed*) put fresh linen on; (*Bank*) overdraw.

Überzieher ['y:bərtsi:ər], *m.* (—s, *pl.* —) overcoat.

Überzug ['y:bərtsu:k], *m.* (—s, *pl.* ⁓e) case, cover; bed-tick; coating.

üblich ['y:plɪç], *adj.* usual, customary; *nicht mehr* —, out of use, obsolete.

übrig ['y:brɪç], *adj.* remaining, left over; *die* —en, the others; — *bleiben*, be left, remain; — *haben*, have left; — *sein*, be left; *im* —en, for the rest; *ein* —es *tun*, stretch a point; *für einen etwas* — *haben*, like s.o.

übrigens ['y:brɪgəns], *adv.* besides, moreover; by the way.

Übung ['y:buŋ], *f.* (—, *pl.* —en) exercise, practice.

Ufer ['u:fər], *n.* (—s, *pl.* —) (*river*) bank; (*sea*) shore, beach.

Uganda [u'ganda], *n.* Uganda.

Uhr [u:r], *f.* (—, *pl.* —en) clock; watch; *elf* —, eleven o'clock; *wieviel* — *ist es?* what is the time?

Uhrmacher ['u:rmaxər], *m.* (—s, *pl.* —) watchmaker, clockmaker.

Uhrwerk ['u:rvɛrk], *n.* (—s, *pl.* —e) clockwork.

Uhrzeiger ['u:rtsaɪgər], *m.* (—s, *pl.* —) hand (of clock *or* watch).

Uhu ['u:hu:], *m.* (—s, *pl.* —s) (*Orn.*) eagle-owl.

ulkig ['ulkɪç], *adj.* funny.

Ulme ['ulmə], *f.* (—, *pl.* —en) (*Bot.*) elm, elm-tree.

Ultrakurzwelle ['ultrakurtsvɛlə], *f.* (—, *pl.* —n) ultra-short wave.

ultrarot ['ultraro:t], *adj.* infra-red.

Ultrastrahlung ['ultraʃtra:luŋ], *f.* (—, *pl.* —en) cosmic radiation.

ultraviolett ['ultraviolet], *adj.* ultra-violet.

um [um], *prep.* (*Acc.*) about; around; approximately, near; for, because of; by; — *Geld bitten,* ask for money; — *5 Uhr,* at five o'clock. — *conj.* to, in order to. — *adv.* up, past, upside down; round about; around.

umarbeiten ['umarbaɪtən], *v.a.* do again, remodel, revise; recast.

umarmen [um'armən], *v.a. insep.* embrace.

Umarmung [um'armuŋ], *f.* (—, *pl.* —en) embrace.

umbauen (1) ['umbauən], *v.a.* rebuild.

umbauen (2) [um'bauən], *v.a. insep.* surround with buildings.

umbiegen ['umbi:gən], *v.a. irr.* bend.

umbilden ['umbɪldən], *v.a.* transform, reform, recast, remould.

umbinden ['umbɪndən], *v.a. irr. sich etwas* —, tie s.th. around o.s.

umblicken ['umblɪkən], *v.r. sich* —, look round.

umbringen ['umbrɪŋən], *v.a. irr.* kill, slay, murder.

umdrehen ['umdre:ən], *v.a.* turn over, turn round, revolve. — *v.r. sich* —, turn round.

Umdrehung .[um'dre:uŋ], *f.* '(—, *pl.* —en) revolution, rotation.

umfahren (1) [um'fa:rən], *v.a. irr. insep.* drive round, circumnavigate.

umfahren (2) ['umfa:ren], *v.a. irr.* run down.

umfallen ['umfalən], *v.n. irr.* (*aux.* sein) fall down, fall over.

Umfang ['umfaŋ], *m.* (—s, *pl.* ⁓e) circumference; (*fig.*) extent.

umfangen [um'faŋən], *v.a. irr. insep.* encircle, embrace.

umfangreich ['umfaŋraɪç], *adj.* extensive, voluminous.

umfassen [um'fasən], *v.a. insep.* comprise, contain.

umfassend [um'fasənt], *adj.* comprehensive.

umfließen [um'fli:sən], *v.a. irr. insep.* surround by water.

umformen ['umfɔrmən], *v.a.* transform, remodel.

Umformung ['umfɔrmuŋ], *f.* (—, *pl.* —en) transformation, remodelling.

Umfrage ['umfra:gə], *f.* (—, *pl.* —n) enquiry, poll, quiz.

umfrieden [um'fri:dən], *v.a. irr. insep.* enclose.

Umfriedung [um'fri:duŋ], *f.* (—, *pl.* —en) enclosure.

Umgang ['umgaŋ], *m.* (—s, *pl.* ⁓e) circuit, procession; (*fig.*) acquaintance, association; relations, connection; — *haben mit,* associate with.

umgänglich ['umgɛŋlɪç], *adj.* sociable, companionable.

Umgangsformen ['umgaŋsfɔrmən], *f. pl.* manners.

Umgangssprache ['umgaŋsʃpra:xə], *f.* (— *pl.* —en) colloquial speech.

umgeben [um'ge:bən], *v.a. irr. insep.* surround.

Umgebung [um'gə:buŋ], *f.* (—, *pl.* —en) environment, surroundings.

umgehen (1) ['umge:ən], *v.n. irr.* (*aux.* sein) associate with s.o.; handle s.th.; — *in,* haunt.

umgehen (2) [um'ge:ən], *v.a. irr. insep.* go round; (*flank*) turn; (*fig.*) evade, shirk.

umgehend ['umge:ənt], *adv.* immediately; (*letter*) by return mail.

Umgehung [um'ge:uŋ], *f.* (—, *pl.* —en) shirking, evasion: detour; (*Mil.*) flank movement, turning.

umgekehrt ['umgəke:rt], *adj.* reverse. — *adv.* conversely.

umgestalten ['umgəʃtaltən], *v.a.* transform, recast.

Umgestaltung ['umgəʃtaltuŋ], *f.* (—, *pl.* —en) transformation; recasting.

umgraben ['umgra:bən], *v.a. irr.* dig up.

umgrenzen [um'grɛntsən], *v.a. insep.* limit, set bounds to.

Umgrenzung [um'grɛntsuŋ], *f.* (—, *pl.* —en) boundary; limitation.

umgucken ['umgukən], *v.r. sich* —, look about o.

umhalsen [um'halzən], *v.a. insep.* hug, embrace.

Umhang ['umhaŋ], *m.* (—s, *pl.* ⁓e) shawl, cloak.

umher [um'he:r], *adv.* around, round, about.

umherblicken [um'he:rblɪkən], *v.n.* look round.

umherflattern [um'he:rflatərn], *v.n.* (*aux.* sein) flutter about.

umherlaufen [um'he:rlaufən], *v.n. irr.* (*aux.* sein) run about; roam about, ramble, wander.

umherziehend [um'he:rtsi:ənt], *adj.* itinerant.

umhüllen [um'hylən], *v.a. insep.* envelop, wrap up.

Umkehr ['umke:r], *f.* (—, *no pl.*) return; change; (*fig.*) conversion.

umkehren [ˈumkeːrən], v.a. turn (back), upset, overturn. — v.n. (aux. sein) turn back, return.

Umkehrung [ˈumkeːruŋ], f. (—, pl. —en) inversion.

umkippen [ˈumkɪpən], v.a. upset, overturn. — v.n. (aux. sein) capsize, tilt over.

umklammern [umˈklamərn], v.a. insep. clasp; clutch; (fig.) cling to.

umkleiden (1) [ˈumklaɪdən], v.r. sich —, change o.'s clothes.

umkleiden (2) [umˈklaɪdən], v.a. insep. cover.

umkommen [ˈumkɔmən], v.n. irr. (aux. sein) perish.

Umkreis [ˈumkraɪs], m. (—es, pl. —e) circumference, compass.

Umlauf [ˈumlauf], m. (—s, no pl.) circulation; in — bringen, put into circulation.

Umlaut [ˈumlaut], m. (—s, pl. —e) (Phonet.) modification of vowels.

umlegen [ˈumleːgən], v.a. lay down, move, shift, put about; (sl.) kill.

umleiten [ˈumlaɪtən], v.a. (traffic) divert.

umlernen [ˈumlɛrnən], v.a., v.n. relearn; retrain (for new job).

umliegend [ˈumliːgənt], adj. surrounding.

ummodeln [ˈummoːdəln], v.a. remodel, recast, change, fashion differently.

Umnachtung [umˈnaxtuŋ], f. (—, no pl.) mental derangement.

umpacken [ˈumpakən], v.a. repack.

umpflanzen [ˈumpflantsən], v.a. transplant.

Umpflanzung [ˈumpflantsuŋ], f. (—, pl. —en) transplantation.

umrahmen [ˈumraːmən], v.a. insep. frame, surround.

umrändern [umˈrɛndərn], v.a. insep. border, edge.

umrechnen [ˈumrɛçnən], v.a. (figures) reduce, convert.

umreißen (1) [ˈumraɪsən], v.a. irr. pull down, break up.

umreißen (2) [umˈraɪsən], v.a. irr. insep. sketch, outline.

umrennen [ˈumrɛnən], v.a. irr. run down, knock over.

umringen [umˈrɪŋən], v.a. insep. encircle, surround.

Umriß [ˈumrɪs], m. (—sses, pl. —sse) outline, contour.

umrühren [ˈumryːrən], v.a. (Cul.) stir.

umsatteln [ˈumzatəln], v.n. (fig.) change o.'s profession.

Umsatz [ˈumzats], m. (—es, pl. —e) turnover.

umschalten [ˈumʃaltən], v.a. (Elec.) switch (over); reverse (current).

Umschau [ˈumʃau], f. (—, no pl.) review, survey; — halten, look round, muster, review.

umschauen [ˈumʃauən], v.r. sich —, look round.

umschichtig [ˈumʃɪçtɪç], adv. turn and turn about, in turns.

umschiffen (1) [ˈumʃɪfən], v.a. tranship, transfer (cargo, passengers).

umschiffen (2) [umˈʃɪfən], v.a. insep. sail round, circumnavigate.

Umschlag [ˈumʃlaːk], m. (—(e)s, pl. —e) (weather) break, sudden change; (letter) envelope; (Med.) poultice, compress.

umschlagen [ˈumʃlaːgən], v.n. irr. (aux. sein) (weather) change suddenly; capsize; turn sour.

umschließen [umˈʃliːsən], v.a. irr. insep. enclose, surround; comprise.

umschlingen [umˈʃlɪŋən], v.a. irr. insep. embrace.

umschnallen [ˈumʃnalən], v.a. buckle on.

umschreiben (1) [ˈumʃraɪbən], v.a. irr. insep. rewrite, write differently.

umschreiben (2) [umˈʃraɪbən], v.a. irr. insep. circumscribe, paraphrase.

Umschreibung [umˈʃraɪbuŋ], f. (—, pl. —en) paraphrase.

Umschweife [ˈumʃvaɪfə], m.pl. fuss, talk; circumlocution; ohne —, point-blank.

Umschwung [ˈumʃvuŋ], m. (—s, no pl.) sudden change, revolution.

umsegeln [umˈzeːgəln], v.a. insep. sail round.

umsehen [ˈumzeːən], v.r. irr. sich —, look round; look out (for), cast about (for).

Umsicht [ˈumzɪçt], f. (—, no pl.) circumspection.

umsichtig [ˈumzɪçtɪç], adj. cautious, circumspect.

umsinken [ˈumzɪŋkən], v.n. irr. (aux. sein) sink down.

umsonst [umˈzɔnst], adv. without payment, gratis, for nothing; in vain, vainly, to no purpose.

umspannen (1) [ˈumʃpanən], v.a. change horses.

umspannen (2) [umˈʃpanən], v.a. insep. encompass, span.

umspringen [ˈumʃprɪŋən], v.n. irr. (aux. sein) (wind) change suddenly; mit einem —, (fig.) deal with s.o.

Umstand [ˈumʃtant], m. (—s, pl. —e) circumstance; fact; factor; (pl.) fuss; in anderen —en sein, be expecting a baby; unter keinen —en, on no account.

umständlich [ˈumʃtɛntlɪç], adj. circumstantial, ceremonious; complicated, fussy.

Umstandswort [ˈumʃtantsvɔrt], n. (—es, pl. —er) (Gram.) adverb.

umstehend [ˈumʃteːənt], adv. on the next page.

Umstehenden [ˈumʃteːəndən], pl. bystanders.

umsteigen [ˈumʃtaɪgən], v.n. irr. (aux. sein) change (trains etc.).

umstellen (1) [ˈumʃtɛlən], v.a. place differently, transpose, change over.

umstellen (2) [umˈʃtɛlən], v.a. insep. surround, beset.

Umstellung ['umʃtɛluŋ], *f.* (—, *pl.* —en) transposition; (*Gram.*) inversion; change of position in team.

umstimmen ['umʃtɪmən], *v.a.* turn s.o. from his opinion, bring s.o. round to (s.th.).

umstoßen ['umʃtoːsən], *v.a. irr.* knock down, upset, overthrow; (*judgment*) reverse.

umstricken [um'ʃtrɪkən], *v.a. insep.* ensnare.

umstritten [um'ʃtrɪtən], *adj.* controversial, disputed.

umstülpen ['umʃtylpən], *v.a.* turn up, turn upside down.

Umsturz ['umʃturts], *m.* (—es, *no pl.*) downfall; subversion; revolution.

umstürzen ['umʃtyrtsən], *v.a.* upset, overturn; overthrow.

umtaufen ['umtaufən], *v.a.* rename, rechristen.

Umtausch ['umtauʃ], *m.* (—s, *no pl.*) exchange.

umtauschen ['umtauʃən], *v.a.* exchange, change.

Umtriebe ['umtriːbə], *m. pl.* plots, goings-on, intrigues.

umtun ['umtuːn], *v.r. irr. sich — nach*, look for, cast about for.

Umwälzung ['umvɛltsuŋ], *f.* (—, *pl.* —en) turning-about; (*fig.*) revolution.

umwandeln ['umvandəln], *v.a.* change, transform; (*Gram.*) inflect.

umwechseln ['umvɛksəln], *v.a.* exchange.

Umweg ['umveːk], *m.* (—s, *pl.* —e) roundabout way, detour.

Umwelt ['umvɛlt], *f.* (—, *no pl.*) environment, milieu.

umwenden ['umvɛndən], *v.a. irr.* turn round; turn over. — *v.r. sich* —, turn round.

umwerben [um'vɛrbən], *v.a. irr. insep.* court.

umwerfen ['umvɛrfən], *v.a. irr.* overturn, knock over, upset.

umwickeln [um'vɪkəln], *v.a. insep.* wrap round, wind round.

umwölken [um'vœlkən], *v.r. insep. sich* —, (*sky*) darken, become overcast.

umzäunen [um'tsɔynən], *v.a. insep.* hedge in, fence in, enclose.

umziehen (1) ['umtsiːən], *v.a. irr.* change (clothes). — *v.n.* (*aux.* sein) move (abode).— *v.r. sich* —, change o.'s clothes.

umziehen (2) [um'tsiːən], *v.r. irr. insep. sich* —, get overcast, cloud over.

umzingeln [um'tsɪŋəln], *v.a. insep.* surround.

Umzug ['umtsuːk], *m.* (—s, *pl.* ⸚e) procession; removal; move.

unabänderlich [unap'ɛndərlɪç], *adj.* unalterable, irrevocable.

Unabänderlichkeit ['unapɛndərlɪçkaɪt], *f.* (—, *no pl.*) unchangeableness, irrevocability.

unabhängig ['unaphɛŋɪç], *adj.* independent, autonomous; unrelated.

Unabhängigkeit ['unaphɛŋɪçkaɪt], *f.* (—, *no pl.*) independence, self-sufficiency.

unabkömmlich ['unapkœmlɪç], *adj.* indispensable.

unablässig ['unaplɛsɪç], *adj.* unceasing, continual, unremitting.

unabsehbar ['unapzeːbaːr], *adj.* immeasurable, immense; unfathomable.

unabsichtlich ['unapzɪçtlɪç], *adj.* unintentional, accidental.

unabwendbar [unap'vɛntbaːr], *adj.* irremediable; unavoidable.

unachtsam ['unaxtzaːm], *adj.* inattentive, inadvertent, negligent, careless.

Unachtsamkeit ['unaxtzaːmkaɪt], *f.* (—, *pl.* —en) inadvertence, inattention, negligence, carelessness.

unähnlich ['unɛːnlɪç], *adj.* unlike, dissimilar.

unanfechtbar ['unanfɛçtbaːr], *adj.* indisputable, incontestable.

unangebracht ['unangəbraxt], *adj.* out of place, inapposite.

unangefochten ['unangəfɔxtən], *adj.* undisputed, uncontested.

unangemeldet ['unangəmɛldət], *adj.* unannounced, unheralded.

unangemessen ['unangəmɛsən], *adj.* unsuitable, inappropriate, inadequate.

unangenehm ['unangəneːm], *adj.* disagreeable, unpleasant; *einen — berühren*, jar, grate on s.o.

unangetastet ['unangətastət], *adj.* untouched.

unangreifbar ['unangraɪfbaːr], *adj.* unassailable, secure.

unannehmbar ['unanneːmbaːr], *adj.* unacceptable.

Unannehmlichkeit ['unanneːmlɪçkaɪt], *f.* (—, *pl.* —en) unpleasantness, annoyance.

unansehnlich ['unanzeːnlɪç], *adj.* insignificant; unattractive.

unanständig ['unanʃtɛndɪç], *adj.* improper, indecent.

Unanständigkeit ['unanʃtɛndɪçkaɪt], *f.* (—, *pl.* —en) indecency, immodesty, impropriety.

unantastbar ['unantastbaːr], *adj.* unimpeachable.

unappetitlich ['unapetiːtlɪç], *adj.* distasteful, unsavoury, unappetising.

Unart ['unaːrt], *f.* (—, *pl.* —en) bad habit, naughtiness.

unartig ['unaːrtɪç], *adj.* ill-behaved, naughty.

unästhetisch ['unɛsteːtɪʃ], *adj.* offensive, coarse; inartistic.

unauffällig ['unauffɛlɪç], *adj.* unobtrusive.

unaufgefordert ['unaufgəfɔrdərt], *adj.* unbidden.

unaufgeklärt ['unaufgəklɛːrt], *adj.* unexplained, unsolved.

unaufgeschnitten ['unaufgəʃnɪtən], *adj.* uncut.

unaufhaltsam ['unaufhaltzaːm], *adj.* incessant, irresistible.

unaufhörlich ['unaufhøːrliç], *adj.* incessant, continual.

unauflöslich ['unauflø:sliç], *adj.* indissoluble.

unaufmerksam ['unaufmɛrkzaːm], *adj.* inattentive.

unaufrichtig ['unaufriçtiç], *adj.* insincere.

unaufschiebbar ['unaufʃiːpbaːr], *adj.* urgent, pressing, brooking no delay.

unausbleiblich ['unausblaipliç], *adj.* inevitable, unfailing.

unausführbar ['unausfyːrbaːr], *adj.* impracticable.

unausgebildet ['unausgəbildət], *adj.* untrained, unskilled.

unausgefüllt ['unausgəfylt], *adj.* not filled up; (*form*) blank.

unausgegoren ['unausgəgoːrən], *adj.* crude; (*wine*) unfermented.

unausgesetzt ['unausgəzɛtst], *adj.* continual, continuous.

unausgesprochen ['unausgəʃprɔxən], *adj.* unsaid; (*fig.*) implied.

unauslöschlich [ˈunauslø:ʃliç], *adj.* indelible, inextinguishable.

unaussprechlich ['unausʃprɛçliç], *adj.* inexpressible, unspeakable.

unausstehlich ['unausʃteːliç], *adj.* insufferable.

unausweichlich ['unausvaiçliç], *adj.* inevitable.

unbändig ['unbɛndiç], *adj.* intractable, unmanageable; (*fig.*) extreme.

unbarmherzig ['unbarmhɛrtsiç], *adj.* merciless.

unbeabsichtigt ['unbəapziçtiçt], *adj.* unintentional.

unbeanstandet ['unbəanʃtandət], *adj.* unexceptionable; unopposed; with impunity.

unbeantwortlich ['unbəantvɔrtliç], *adj.* unanswerable.

unbeaufsichtigt ['unbəaufziçtiçt], *adj.* unattended to, not looked after; without supervision.

unbebaut ['unbəbaut], *adj.* (*Agr.*) uncultivated; undeveloped (by building).

unbedacht ['unbədaxt], *adj.* thoughtless.

unbedenklich ['unbədɛŋkliç], *adj.* harmless, innocuous. — *adv.* without hesitation.

unbedeutend ['unbədɔytənt], *adj.* insignificant.

unbedingt ['unbədiŋkt], *adj.* unconditional, unlimited, absolute. — *adv.* quite definitely; without fail.

unbeeinflußt ['unbəainflust], *adj.* uninfluenced.

unbefahrbar ['unbəfaːrbaːr], *adj.* impassable, impracticable.

unbefangen ['unbəfaŋən], *adj.* unbiased, unprejudiced; easy, unselfconscious, unembarrassed, uninhibited; natural.

Unbefangenheit ['unbəfaŋənhait], *f.*

(—, *no pl.*) impartiality; ease of manner, unselfconsciousness, openness, naturalness.

unbefestigt ['unbəfɛstiçt], *adj.* unfortified.

unbefleckt ['unbəflɛkt], *adj.* immaculate; —*e Empfängnis*, Immaculate Conception.

unbefriedigend ['unbəfriːdigənt], *adj.* unsatisfactory.

unbefriedigt ['unbəfriːdiçt], *adj.* not satisfied, unsatisfied.

unbefugt ['unbəfuːkt], *adj.* unauthorised.

unbegreiflich ['unbəgraifliç], *adj.* incomprehensible, inconceivable.

unbegrenzt ['unbəgrɛntst], *adj.* unlimited, unbounded.

unbegründet ['unbəgryndət], *adj.* unfounded, groundless.

Unbehagen ['unbəhaːgən], *n.* (—*s*, *no pl.*) uneasiness, discomfort.

unbehaglich ['unbəhaːkliç], *adj.* uncomfortable; *sich — fühlen*, feel ill at ease.

unbehelligt ['unbəhɛliçt], *adj.* unmolested.

unbeholfen ['unbəhɔlfən], *adj.* awkward, clumsy.

unbeirrt ['unbəirt], *adj.* unswerving, uninfluenced, unperturbed.

unbekannt ['unbəkant], *adj.* unknown, unacquainted; *ich bin hier —*, I am a stranger here.

unbekümmert ['unbəkymərt], *adj.* unconcerned, careless, indifferent.

unbelehrt ['unbəleːrt], *adj.* uninstructed.

unbeliebt ['unbəliːpt], *adj.* unpopular.

unbemannt ['unbəmant], *adj.* without crew, unmanned.

unbemerkbar ['unbəmɛrkbaːr], *adj.* unnoticeable, imperceptible.

unbemerkt ['unbəmɛrkt], *adj.* unnoticed.

unbemittelt ['unbəmitəlt], *adj.* impecunious, poor.

unbenommen ['unbənɔmən], *adj. es bleibt dir —*, you are free to.

unbenutzt ['unbənutst], *adj.* unused.

unbequem ['unbəkveːm], *adj.* uncomfortable, inconvenient, troublesome.

Unbequemlichkeit ['unbəkveːmliçkait], *f.* (—, *pl.* —**en**) inconvenience.

unberechenbar ['unbərɛçənbaːr], *adj.* incalculable; (*fig.*) erratic.

unberechtigt ['unbərɛçtiçt], *adj.* unwarranted, unjustified.

unberücksichtigt ['unbərykziçtiçt], *adj.* disregarded; — *lassen*, ignore.

unberufen ['unbəruːfən], *adj.* unauthorized. — *excl.* touch wood!

unbeschadet ['unbəʃaːdət], *prep.* (*Genit.*) without prejudice to.

unbeschädigt ['unbəʃeːdiçt], *adj.* undamaged.

unbeschäftigt ['unbəʃɛftiçt], *adj.* unemployed, disengaged.

unbescheiden ['unbəʃaɪdən], *adj.* presumptuous, greedy, immodest; unblushing; exorbitant; arrogant.

Unbescheidenheit ['unbəʃaɪdənhaɪt], *f.* (—, *no pl.*) presumptuousness, greed.

unbescholten ['unbəʃɔltən], *adj.* irreproachable, of unblemished character.

Unbescholtenheit ['unbəʃɔltənhaɪt], *f.* (—, *no pl.*) blamelessness, good character, unsullied reputation.

unbeschränkt ['unbəʃrɛŋkt], *adj.* unlimited, unbounded; —e *Monarchie*, absolute monarchy.

unbeschreiblich ['unbəʃraɪplɪç], *adj.* indescribable.

unbeschrieben ['unbəʃriːbən], *adj.* unwritten; *ein —es Papier*, a blank sheet of paper.

unbeschwert ['unbəʃvɛrt], *adj.* unburdened; easy.

unbeseelt ['unbəzeːlt], *adj.* inanimate.

unbesiegbar [unbə'ziːkbaːr], *adj.* invincible.

unbesoldet ['unbəzɔldət], *adj.* unpaid, unsalaried.

unbesonnen ['unbəzɔnən], *adj.* thoughtless, rash.

Unbesonnenheit ['unbəzɔnənhaɪt], *f.* (—, *pl.* —en) thoughtlessness.

unbesorgt ['unbəzɔrkt], *adj.* unconcerned; *sei* —, never fear.

unbeständig ['unbəʃtendɪç], *adj.* fickle, inconstant; (*weather*) unsettled.

unbestechlich ['unbəʃtɛçlɪç], *adj.* incorruptible.

unbestellbar ['unbəʃtɛlbaːr], *adj.* not deliverable; (*letters etc.*) address(ee) unknown.

unbestellt ['unbəʃtɛlt], *adj.* not ordered; (*Agr.*) uncultivated, untilled.

unbestimmt ['unbəʃtɪmt], *adj.* uncertain, not settled; indefinite; irresolute; vague.

unbestraft ['unbəʃtraːft], *adj.* unpunished; without previous conviction.

unbestreitbar ['unbəʃtraɪtbaːr], *adj.* indisputable, incontestable.

unbestritten ['unbəʃtrɪtən], *adj.* uncontested, undoubted, undisputed.

unbeteiligt ['unbətaɪlɪçt], *adj.* unconcerned, indifferent.

unbeträchtlich ['unbətrɛçtlɪç], *adj.* inconsiderable, trivial.

unbetreten ['unbətreːtən], *adj.* untrodden, untouched.

unbeugsam ['unbɔykzaːm], *adj.* inflexible, unyielding.

unbewacht ['unbəvaxt], *adj.* unguarded.

unbewaffnet ['unbəvafnət], *adj.* unarmed; *mit —em Auge*, with the naked eye.

unbewandert ['unbəvandərt], *adj.* unversed in, unfamiliar with.

unbezahlt ['unbətsaːlt], *adj.* unpaid.

unbezähmbar ['unbətsɛːmbaːr], *adj.* uncontrollable; indomitable.

unbezwinglich ['unbətsvɪŋlɪç], *adj.* invincible, unconquerable.

Unbildung ['unbɪldʊŋ], *f.* (—, *no pl.*) lack of education *or* knowledge *or* culture.

Unbill ['unbɪl], *f.* (—, *pl.* **Unbilden**) injustice, wrong, injury; (*weather*) inclemency.

unbillig ['unbɪlɪç], *adj.* unreasonable, unfair.

Unbilligkeit ['unbɪlɪçkaɪt], *f.* (—, *no pl.*) unreasonableness, injustice, unfairness.

unbotmäßig ['unboːtmɛːsɪç], *adj.* unruly, insubordinate.

unbußfertig ['unbuːsfɛrtɪç], *adj.* impenitent, unrepentant.

und [unt], *conj.* and; — *nicht*, nor; — *so weiter* (abbr. *u.s.w.*), etc., and so on, and so forth; — *wenn*, even if.

Undank ['undaŋk], *m.* (—s, *no pl.*) ingratitude.

undankbar ['undaŋkbaːr], *adj.* ungrateful; *eine —e Aufgabe*, a thankless task.

Undankbarkeit ['undaŋkbaːrkaɪt], *f.* (—, *no pl.*) ingratitude.

undenkbar ['undɛŋkbaːr], *adj.* unthinkable, unimaginable, inconceivable.

undenklich ['undɛŋklɪç], *adj. seit —en Zeiten*, from time immemorial.

undeutlich ['undɔytlɪç], *adj.* indistinct; inarticulate; (*fig.*) unintelligible.

Unding ['undɪŋ], *n.* (—s, *no pl.*) absurdity.

unduldsam ['undultzaːm], *adj.* intolerant.

undurchdringlich ['undurçdrɪŋlɪç], *adj.* impenetrable.

undurchführbar ['undurçfyːrbaːr], *adj.* impracticable, unworkable.

undurchsichtig ['undurçzɪçtɪç], *adj.* opaque, not transparent.

uneben ['uneːbən], *adj.* uneven, rugged; (*coll.*) *nicht* —, not bad.

unecht ['unɛçt], *adj.* false, not genuine, spurious, counterfeit.

unedel ['uneːdəl], *adj.* (*metal*) base.

unehelich ['uneːəlɪç], *adj.* illegitimate.

Unehre ['uneːrə], *f.* (—, *no pl.*) dishonour, disgrace, discredit.

unehrlich ['uneːrlɪç], *adj.* dishonest.

Unehrlichkeit ['uneːrlɪçkaɪt], *f.* (—, *pl.* —en) dishonesty.

uneigennützig ['unaɪgənnytsɪç], *adj.* unselfish, disinterested, public-spirited.

uneingedenk ['unaɪngədɛŋk], *adj.* (*Genit.*) unmindful, forgetful.

uneingeschränkt ['unaɪngəʃrɛŋkt], *adj.* unrestrained, unlimited.

uneinig ['unaɪnɪç], **uneins** ['unaɪns], *adj.* disunited, divided; — *werden*, fall out; — *sein*, disagree.

Uneinigkeit ['unaɪnɪçkaɪt], *f.* (—, *pl.* —en) disharmony, discord.

uneinnehmbar ['unaɪnneːmbaːr], *adj.* unconquerable, impregnable.

uneins *see under* **uneinig.**

unempfänglich ['unɛmpfɛŋlıç], *adj.* insusceptible; unreceptive.

unempfindlich ['unɛmpfɪntlıç], *adj.* insensitive, indifferent; unfeeling.

unendlich [un'ɛntlıç], *adj.* endless, infinite.

unentbehrlich ['unɛntbe:rlıç], *adj.* indispensable, (absolutely) essential.

unentgeltlich [unɛnt'gɛltlıç], *adj.* free (of charge).

unentschieden ['unɛntʃi:dən], *adj.* undecided, undetermined; irresolute; (*game*) drawn, tied.

unentschlossen ['unɛntʃlɔsən], *adj.* irresolute.

Unentschlossenheit ['unɛntʃlɔsən-haıt], *f.* (—, *no pl.*) irresolution, indecision.

unentschuldbar ['unɛntʃultba:r], *adj.* inexcusable.

unentstellt ['unɛntʃtɛlt], *adj.* undistorted.

unentwegt ['unɛntve:kt], *adj.* steadfast, unflinching, unswerving.

unentwickelt ['unɛntvɪkəlt], *adj.* undeveloped; —*e Länder,* underdeveloped countries.

unentwirrbar ['unɛntvɪrba:r], *adj.* inextricable.

unentzifferbar ['unɛnttsɪfərba:r], *adj.* indecipherable.

unentzündbar ['unɛnttsyntba:r], *adj.* non-inflammable.

unerachtet ['unɛraxtət], *prep.* (*Genit.*) (*obs.*) notwithstanding.

unerbeten ['unɛrbe:tən], *adj.* unsolicited.

unerbittlich ['unɛrbɪtlıç], *adj.* inexorable.

unerfahren ['unɛrfa:rən], *adj.* inexperienced.

unerforschlich ['unɛrfɔrʃlıç], *adj.* inscrutable.

unerfreulich ['unɛrfrɔylıç], *adj.* unpleasant, displeasing, disagreeable.

unerfüllbar ['unɛrfylba:r], *adj.* unrealisable.

unerfüllt ['unɛrfylt], *adj.* unfulfilled.

unergründlich ['unɛrgryntlıç], *adj.* unfathomable, impenetrable.

unerheblich ['unɛrhe:plıç], *adj.* trifling, unimportant.

unerhört ['unɛrhø:rt], *adj.* unprecedented, unheard of, shocking, outrageous; not granted; turned down.

unerkannt ['unɛrkant], *adj.* unrecognised.

unerkennbar ['unɛrkɛnba:r], *adj.* unrecognisable.

unerklärlich ['unɛrklɛ:rlıç], *adj.* inexplicable.

unerläßlich ['unɛrlɛslıç], *adj.* indispensable.

unerlaubt ['unɛrlaupt], *adj.* unlawful, illicit.

unermeßlich ['unɛrmɛslıç], *adj.* immense, vast.

unermüdlich ['unɛrmy:tlıç], *adj.* untiring, indefatigable.

unerquicklich ['unɛrkvɪklıç], *adj.* unedifying, disagreeable.

unerreichbar ['unɛrraıçba:r], *adj.* unattainable, inaccessible.

unerreicht ['unɛrraıçt], *adj.* unequalled.

unersättlich ['unɛrzɛtlıç], *adj.* insatiable, greedy.

unerschöpflich ['unɛrʃœpflıç], *adj.* inexhaustible.

unerschöpft ['unɛrʃœpft], *adj.* unexhausted.

unerschrocken ['unɛrʃrɔkən], *adj.* intrepid, undaunted.

unerschütterlich ['unɛrʃytərlıç], *adj.* imperturbable.

unerschüttert ['unɛrʃytərt], *adj.* unshaken, unperturbed.

unerschwinglich ['unɛrʃvɪŋlıç], *adj.* prohibitive, exorbitant, unattainable.

unersetzlich ['unɛrzɛtslıç], *adj.* irreplaceable.

unersprießlich ['unɛrʃpri:slıç], *adj.* unprofitable.

unerträglich ['unɛrtrɛ:klıç], *adj.* intolerable, insufferable.

unerwartet ['unɛrvartət], *adj.* unexpected.

unerwidert ['unɛrvɪ:dərt], *adj.* (*love*) unrequited; (*letter*) answered.

unerwünscht ['unɛrvynʃt], *adj.* undesirable, unwelcome.

unerzogen ['unɛrtso:gən], *adj.* uneducated; ill-bred, unmannerly.

unfähig ['unfɛ:ıç], *adj.* incapable, unable, unfit.

Unfähigkeit ['unfɛ:ıçkaıt], *f.* (—, *no pl.*) incapability, inability, unfitness.

Unfall ['unfal], *m.* (—s, *pl.* ¨e) accident.

unfaßbar ['unfasba:r], *adj.* incomprehensible, inconceivable.

unfehlbar ['unfe:lba:r], *adj.* inevitable; infallible.

Unfehlbarkeit ['unfe:lba:rkaıt], *f.* (—, *no pl.*) infallibility.

unfein ['unfaın], *adj.* indelicate, coarse, impolite.

unfern ['unfɛrn], *prep.* (*Genit., Dat.*) not far from.

unfertig ['unfɛrtıç], *adj.* unfinished, unready.

unflätig ['unflɛ:tıç], *adj.* obscene, nasty, filthy.

unfolgsam ['unfɔlkza:m], *adj.* disobedient, recalcitrant.

unförmig ['unfœrmıç], *adj.* deformed, ill-shaped, misshapen.

unförmlich ['unfœrmlıç], *adj.* shapeless; free and easy, unceremonious.

unfrankiert ['unfraŋki:rt], *adj.* (*letter*) not prepaid, unstamped, unfranked.

unfrei ['unfraı], *adj.* not free; subjugated; constrained.

unfreiwillig ['unfraıvɪlıç], *adj.* involuntary.

ungern

unfreundlich [ˈunfrɔyntlɪç], *adj.* unfriendly, unkind; (*weather*) inclement.
Unfreundlichkeit [ˈunfrɔyntlɪçkaɪt], *f.* (—, *pl.* —en) unfriendliness, unkindness; (*weather*) inclemency.
Unfrieden [ˈunfriːdən], *m.* (—s, *no pl.*) discord, dissension.
unfruchtbar [ˈunfruxtbaːr], *adj.* barren, sterile; (*fig.*) fruitless.
Unfug [ˈunfuːk], *m.* (—s, *no pl.*) disturbance, misconduct; mischief; *grober* —, public nuisance.
unfühlbar [ˈunfyːlbaːr], *adj.* imperceptible.
ungangbar [ˈunɡaŋbaːr], *adj.* impassable.
Ungarn [ˈuŋɡarn], *n.* Hungary.
ungastlich [ˈunɡastlɪç], *adj.* inhospitable.
ungeachtet [ˈunɡəaxtət], *prep.* (*Genit.*) notwithstanding.
ungeahndet [ˈunɡəaːndət], *adj.* unpunished, with impunity.
ungeahnt [ˈunɡəaːnt], *adj.* unexpected, unsuspected, undreamt of.
ungebändigt [ˈunɡəbɛndɪçt], *adj.* untamed.
ungebärdig [ˈunɡəbɛːrdɪç], *adj.* unmannerly, refractory.
ungebeten [ˈunɡəbeːtən], *adj.* uninvited, unbidden.
ungebleicht [ˈunɡəblaɪçt], *adj.* unbleached.
ungebraucht [ˈunɡəbrauxt], *adj.* unused.
Ungebühr [ˈunɡəbyːr], *f.* (—, *no pl.*) unseemliness, impropriety, excess.
ungebührlich [ˈunɡəbyːrlɪç], *adj.* unseemly.
ungebunden [ˈunɡəbundən], *adj.* unbound, in sheets; unrestrained, loose; unlinked; —*e Rede*, prose.
Ungeduld [ˈunɡədult], *f.* (—, *no pl.*) impatience.
ungeduldig [ˈunɡəduldɪç], *adj.* impatient.
ungeeignet [ˈunɡəaɪɡnət], *adj.* unfit, unsuitable.
ungefähr [ˈunɡəfɛːr], *adj.* approximate, rough. — *adv.* approximately, roughly, about, round.
ungefährlich [ˈunɡəfɛːrlɪç], *adj.* not dangerous, harmless, safe.
ungefällig [ˈunɡəfɛlɪç], *adj.* ungracious, disobliging.
ungefärbt [ˈunɡəfɛrpt], *adj.* uncoloured; (*fig.*) unvarnished.
ungefüge [ˈunɡəfyːɡə], *adj.* clumsy.
ungehalten [ˈunɡəhaltən], *adj.* indignant, angry.
ungeheißen [ˈunɡəhaɪsən], *adj.* unbidden. — *adv.* of o.'s own accord.
ungehemmt [ˈunɡəhɛmt], *adj.* unchecked, uninhibited.
ungeheuchelt [ˈunɡəhɔyçəlt], *adj.* unfeigned.
Ungeheuer [ˈunɡəhɔyər], *n.* (—s, *pl.* —) monster, monstrosity.

ungeheuer [ˈunɡəhɔyər], *adj.* huge, immense; atrocious, frightful.
ungehobelt [ˈunɡəhoːbəlt], *adj.* unplaned; (*fig.*) boorish, uncultured, unpolished.
ungehörig [ˈunɡəhøːrɪç], *adj.* unseemly, improper.
Ungehorsam [ˈunɡəhoːrzaːm], *m.* (—s, *no pl.*) disobedience.
ungehorsam [ˈunɡəhoːrzaːm], *adj.* disobedient; — *sein*, disobey.
Ungehorsamkeit [ˈunɡəhoːrzaːmkaɪt], *f.* (—, *pl.* —en) disobedience, insubordination.
ungekämmt [ˈunɡəkɛmt], *adj.* unkempt.
ungekünstelt [ˈunɡəkynstəlt], *adj.* artless, unstudied.
ungeladen [ˈunɡəlaːdən], *adj.* (*gun*) unloaded, not charged; uninvited.
ungeläutert [ˈunɡəlɔytərt], *adj.* unrefined; unpurified.
ungelegen [ˈunɡəleːɡən], *adj.* inconvenient, inopportune.
Ungelegenheit [ˈunɡəleːɡənhaɪt], *f.* (—, *pl.* —en) inconvenience, trouble.
ungelehrig [ˈunɡəleːrɪç], *adj.* intractable, unintelligent.
ungelenk [ˈunɡəlɛŋk], *adj.* clumsy, awkward; ungainly.
ungelöscht [ˈunɡəlœʃt], *adj.* unquenched; (*lime*) unslaked; (*mortgage*) unredeemed.
Ungemach [ˈunɡəmaːx], *n.* (—(e)s, *no pl.*) adversity, toil, privation.
ungemein [ˈunɡəmaɪn], *adj.* uncommon, extraordinary. — *adv.* very much, exceedingly.
ungemütlich [ˈunɡəmyːtlɪç], *adj.* uncomfortable, cheerless, unpleasant.
ungeniert [ˈunʒeniːrt], *adj.* free and easy, unceremonious, unabashed.
ungenießbar [ˈunɡəniːsbaːr], *adj.* unpalatable, uneatable, inedible.
ungenügend [ˈunɡənyːɡənt], *adj.* insufficient, unsatisfactory.
ungenügsam [ˈunɡənyːkzaːm], *adj.* insatiable, greedy.
ungeordnet [ˈunɡəɔrdnət], *adj.* illassorted, confused.
ungepflegt [ˈunɡəpfleːkt], *adj.* uncared for, neglected.
ungerade [ˈunɡəraːdə], *adj.* uneven; — *Zahl*, odd number.
ungeraten [ˈunɡəraːtən], *adj.* abortive, unsuccessful, spoiled; undutiful; illbred.
ungerecht [ˈunɡərɛçt], *adj.* unjust, unfair.
ungerechtfertigt [ˈunɡərɛçtfertɪçt], *adj.* unwarranted, unjustified.
Ungerechtigkeit [ˈunɡərɛçtɪçkaɪt], *f.* (—, *pl.* —en) injustice.
ungeregelt [ˈunɡərəɡəlt], *adj.* not regulated, irregular.
ungereimt [ˈunɡəraɪmt], *adj.* rhymeless; —*es Zeug*, nonsense, absurdity.
ungern [ˈunɡɛrn], *adv.* unwillingly, reluctantly.

241

ungerufen

ungerufen ['ungəru:fən], *adj.* unbidden.

ungerührt ['ungəry:rt], *adj.* unmoved.

ungesäumt ['ungəzɔymt], *adj.* unseamed, unhemmed; (*fig.*) immediate. — *adv.* immediately, without delay.

ungeschehen ['ungəʃe:ən], *adj.* undone; — *machen*, undo.

Ungeschick ['ungəʃik], *n.* (**—s**, *no pl.*) awkwardness, clumsiness.

Ungeschicklichkeit ['ungəʃikliçkait], *f.* (**—**, *pl.* **—en**) awkwardness, clumsiness.

ungeschickt ['ungəʃikt], *adj.* awkward, clumsy, unskilful.

ungeschlacht ['ungəʃlaxt], *adj.* uncouth, unwieldy; coarse, rude.

ungeschliffen ['ungəʃlifən], *adj.* unpolished; (*fig.*) coarse.

Ungeschliffenheit ['ungəʃlifənhait], *f.* (**—**, *no pl.*) coarseness, uncouthness.

ungeschmälert ['ungəʃmɛ:lərt], *adj.* undiminished, unimpaired.

ungeschminkt ['ungəʃmiŋkt], *adj.* without cosmetics *or* make-up, not made up; (*truth*) plain, unvarnished.

ungeschoren ['ungəʃo:rən], *adj.* unshorn; *laß mich —*, leave me alone.

ungeschult ['ungəʃu:lt], *adj.* untrained.

ungeschwächt ['ungəʃvɛçt], *adj.* unimpaired.

ungesellig ['ungəzɛliç], *adj.* unsociable.

ungesetzlich ['ungəzɛtsliç], *adj.* illegal, unlawful, illicit.

ungesetzmäßig ['ungəzɛtsmɛ:siç], *adj.* illegitimate, lawless; exceptional; not regular.

ungesiegelt ['ungəzi:gəlt], *adj.* unsealed.

Ungestalt ['ungəʃtalt], *f.* (**—**, *no pl.*) deformity.

ungestalt ['ungəʃtalt], *adj.* misshapen, deformed.

ungestempelt ['ungəʃtempəlt], *adj.* unstamped, uncancelled, not postmarked.

ungestillt ['ungəʃtilt], *adj.* unquenched, unslaked; not fed, unsatisfied.

ungestört ['ungəʃtø:rt], *adj.* undisturbed.

ungestraft ['ungəʃtra:ft], *adj.* unpunished. — *adv.* with impunity.

ungestüm ['ungəʃty:m], *adj.* impetuous.

Ungestüm ['ungəʃty:m], *m. & n.* (**—s**, *no pl.*) impetuosity.

ungesund ['ungəzunt], *adj.* unwholesome, unhealthy, sickly; (*fig.*) unnatural, morbid.

ungetan ['ungəta:n], *adj.* not done, left undone.

ungetreu ['ungətrɔy], *adj.* disloyal, faithless.

ungetrübt ['ungətry:pt], *adj.* untroubled.

ungewandt ['ungəvant], *adj.* unskilful.

ungewaschen ['ungəvaʃən], *adj.* unwashed; (*sl.*) *—es Mundwerk*, malicious tongue.

ungeweiht ['ungəvait], *adj.* unconsecrated.

ungewiß ['ungəvis], *adj.* uncertain, doubtful.

Ungewißheit ['ungəvishait], *f.* (**—**, *no pl.*) uncertainty, suspense.

Ungewitter ['ungəvitər], *n.* (**—s**, *pl.* **—**) storm, thunderstorm.

ungewöhnlich ['ungəvø:nliç], *adj.* unusual, uncommon.

Ungewohnheit ['ungəvo:nthait], *f.* (**—**, *no pl.*) strangeness; want of practice.

ungezähmt ['ungətsɛ:mt], *adj.* untamed; (*fig.*) uncurbed.

Ungeziefer ['ungətsi:fər], *n.* (**—s**, *pl.* **—**) vermin.

ungeziert ['ungətsi:rt], *adj.* unaffected, natural.

ungezogen ['ungətso:gən], *adj.* illmannered, naughty.

ungezügelt ['ungətsy:gəlt], *adj.* unbridled; (*fig.*) unruly.

ungezwungen ['ungətsvuŋən], *adj.* unforced; (*fig.*) unaffected.

Ungezwungenheit ['ungətsvuŋənhait], *f.* (**—**, *no pl.*) naturalness, ease.

Unglaube ['unglaubə], *m.* (**—ns**, *no pl.*) disbelief.

unglaubhaft ['unglauphaft], *adj.* unauthenticated, incredible.

ungläubig ['unglɔybiç], *adj.* incredulous, disbelieving.

Ungläubige ['unglɔybigə], *m.* (**—n**, *pl.* **—n**) unbeliever.

unglaublich ['unglaupliç], *adj.* incredible, unbelievable.

unglaubwürdig ['unglaupvyrdiç], *adj.* unauthenticated, incredible.

ungleichartig ['unglaiça:rtiç], *adj.* dissimilar, heterogeneous.

ungleichförmig ['unglaiçfœrmiç], *adj.* not uniform; dissimilar.

Ungleichheit ['unglaiçhait], *f.* (**—**, *pl.* **—en**) inequality; unlikeness, dissimilarity; unevenness.

ungleichmäßig ['unglaiçmɛ:siç], *adj.* unequal, irregular; changeable, fitful.

Unglimpf ['unglimpf], *m.* (**—(e)s**, *no pl.*) harshness; insult.

Unglück ['unglyk], *n.* (**—s**, *pl.* **—sfälle**) misfortune, adversity, ill-luck; accident, disaster; distress, sorrow, affliction.

unglückbringend ['unglykbriŋənt], *adj.* disastrous, unpropitious.

unglücklich ['unglykliç], *adj.* unfortunate, unhappy, unlucky; *—e Liebe*, unrequited love.

unglücklicherweise ['unglykliçərvaizə], *adv.* unfortunately, unluckily.

Unglücksbotschaft ['unglyksbo:tʃaft], *f.* (**—**, *pl.* **—en**) bad news.

unglückselig ['unglykze:liç], *adj.* luckless, wretched, unfortunate, calamitous.

Unglücksfall ['unglyksfal], *m.* (**—(e)s**, *pl.* **-e**) accident.

Unordnung

Unglücksgefährte ['unglyksgɛfɛ:rtə], *m.* (—**n**, *pl.* —**n**) companion in misfortune.
Ungnade ['ungna:də], *f.* (—, *no pl.*) disgrace.
ungültig ['ungyltıç], *adj.* invalid, void; — *machen*, invalidate, annul.
Ungunst ['ungunst], *f.* (—, *no pl.*) disfavour; unpropitiousness; *(weather)* inclemency.
ungünstig ['ungynstıç], *adj.* unfavourable, adverse.
ungut ['ungu:t], *adv. etwas für — nehmen*, take s.th. amiss.
unhaltbar ['unhaltba:r], *adj.* untenable.
Unheil ['unhaıl], *n.* (—**s**, *no pl.*) mischief, harm; disaster.
unheilbar ['unhaılba:r], *adj.* incurable.
unheilbringend ['unhaılbrıŋənt], *adj.* ominous, unlucky; disastrous.
Unheilstifter ['unhaılʃtıftər], *m.* (—**s**, *pl.* —) mischief-maker.
unheilvoll ['unhaılfɔl], *adj.* calamitous, disastrous.
unheimlich ['unhaımlıç], *adj.* weird, eerie, uncanny.
unhöflich ['unhø:flıç], *adj.* impolite, uncivil, discourteous.
Unhold ['unhɔlt], *m.* (—**s**, *pl.* —**e**) fiend, monster.
Unhörbarkeit ['unhø:rba:rkaıt], *f.* (—, *no pl.*) inaudibility.
Uniformität [uniformi'tɛ:t], *f.* (—, *no pl.*) uniformity.
Unikum ['u:nikum], *n.* (—**s**, *pl.* —**s**) unique thing *or* person; eccentric.
Universalmittel [univer'za:lmıtəl], *n.* (—**s**, *pl.* —) panacea, universal remedy.
Universität [univerzi'tɛ:t], *f.* (—, *pl.* —**en**) university.
Universitätsdozent [univerzi'tɛ:tsdotsent], *m.* (—**en**, *pl.* —**en**) university lecturer.
Universum [uni'vɛrzum], *n.* (—**s**, *no pl.*) universe.
unkaufmännisch ['unkaufmɛnıʃ], *adj.* unbusinesslike.
Unke ['uŋkə], *f.* (—, *pl.* —**n**) *(Zool.)* toad; *(fig.)* grumbler, pessimist.
unken ['uŋkən], *v.n.* grumble, grouse.
unkenntlich ['unkɛntlıç], *adj.* indiscernible, unrecognisable.
Unkenntlichkeit ['unkɛntlıçkaıt], *f.* (—, *no pl.*) *bis zur* —, past recognition.
Unkenntnis ['unkɛntnıs], *f.* (—, *no pl.*) ignorance.
unklug ['unklu:k], *adj.* imprudent.
Unkosten ['unkɔstən], *f. pl.* expenses, costs, charges; overheads.
Unkraut ['unkraut], *n.* (—**s**, *no pl.*) weed(s).
unkündbar ['unkyntba:r], *adj.* irredeemable; irrevocable, permanent.
unkundig ['unkundıç], *adj.* ignorant (of), unacquainted (with).
unlängst ['unlɛŋst], *adv.* recently, lately, not long ago.

unlauter ['unlautər], *adj.* sordid, squalid; unfair.
unleidlich ['unlaıtlıç], *adj.* intolerable.
unleserlich ['unle:zərlıç], *adj.* illegible.
unleugbar ['unlɔykba:r], *adj.* undeniable, indisputable.
unlieb ['unli:p], *adj.* disagreeable.
unliebenswürdig ['unli:bənsvyrdıç], *adj.* sullen, surly.
unlösbar ['unlø:sba:r], *adj.* insoluble.
unlöslich ['unlø:slıç], *adj. (substance)* indissoluble, insoluble.
Unlust ['unlust], *f.* (—, *no pl.*) aversion, disinclination; slackness.
unlustig ['unlustıç], *adj.* averse, disinclined.
unmanierlich ['unmani:rlıç], *adj.* ill-mannered.
unmännlich ['unmɛnlıç], *adj.* unmanly, effeminate.
Unmaß ['unma:s], *n.* (—**es**, *no pl.*) excess.
Unmasse ['unmasə], *f.* (—, *pl.* —**n**) vast quantity.
unmaßgeblich ['unma:sge:plıç], *adj.* unauthoritative, open to correction; *(fig.)* humble.
unmäßig ['unmɛ:sıç], *adj.* intemperate, excessive.
Unmenge ['unmɛŋə], *f.* (—, *pl.* —**n**) vast quantity.
Unmensch ['unmɛnʃ], *m.* (—**en**, *pl.* —**en**) brute.
unmenschlich ['unmɛnʃlıç], *adj.* inhuman, brutal; *(coll.)* vast.
unmerklich ['unmɛrklıç], *adj.* imperceptible.
unmeßbar ['unmɛsba:r], *adj.* immeasurable.
unmittelbar ['unmıtəlba:r], *adj.* immediate, direct.
unmöglich ['unmø:klıç], *adj.* impossible.
unmündig ['unmyndıç], *adj.* under age, minor.
Unmündige ['unmyndıgə], *m.* (—**n**, *pl.* —**n**) *(Law)* minor.
Unmündigkeit ['unmyndıçkaıt], *f.* (—, *no pl.*) minority.
Unmut ['unmu:t], *m.* (—**s**, *no pl.*) ill-humour; displeasure, indignation, petulance.
unmutig ['unmu:tıç], *adj.* ill-humoured, petulant, indignant.
unnachahmlich ['unnaxa:mlıç], *adj.* inimitable.
unnachgiebig ['unnaxgi:bıç], *adj.* relentless, unyielding.
unnachsichtig ['unnaxzıçtıç], *adj.* unrelenting, relentless.
unnahbar ['unna:ba:r], *adj.* unapproachable, stand-offish.
unnennbar ['unnɛnba:r], *adj.* unutterable.
unnütz ['unnyts], *adj.* useless.
unordentlich ['unɔrdəntlıç], *adj.* untidy, slovenly.
Unordnung ['unɔrdnuŋ], *f.* (—, *no pl.*) disorder, untidiness, muddle, confusion.

243

unparteiisch ['unpartaııʃ], *adj.* impartial, unbiased, objective.

unpassend ['unpasənt], *adj.* unsuitable, inappropriate; improper.

unpassierbar ['unpasi:rba:r], *adj.* impassable.

unpäßlich ['unpɛslıç], *adj.* indisposed, unwell, out of sorts.

Unpäßlichkeit ['unpɛslıçkaıt], *f.* (—, *pl.* —en) indisposition.

unproportioniert ['unpropɔrtsjoni:rt], *adj.* disproportionate; unshapely.

unqualifizierbar ['unkvalifitsi:rba:r], *adj.* unspeakable, nameless.

Unrat ['unra:t], *m.* (—(e)s, *no pl.*) dirt, rubbish.

unratsam ['unra:tza:m], *adj.* inadvisable.

Unrecht ['unrɛçt], *n.* (—(e)s, *no pl.*) wrong, injustice; — *haben,* be in the wrong.

unrecht ['unrɛçt], *adj.* wrong, unjust.

unrechtmäßig ['unrɛçtmɛ:sıç], *adj.* unlawful, illegal.

unredlich ['unre:tlıç], *adj.* dishonest.

unregelmäßig ['unre:gəlmɛ:sıç], *adj.* irregular.

unreif ['unraıf], *adj.* unripe, immature; (*fig.*) crude, raw.

Unreife ['unraıfə], *f.* (—, *no pl.*) immaturity.

unrein ['unraın], *adj.* unclean; (*fig.*) impure.

Unreinheit ['unraınhaıt], *f.* (—, *pl.* —en) impurity.

Unreinlichkeit ['unraınlıçkaıt], *f.* (—, *no pl.*) uncleanliness.

unrentabel ['unrɛnta:bəl], *adj.* unprofitable.

unrettbar ['unrɛtba:r], *adj.* irretrievable, hopelessly lost.

unrichtig ['unrıçtıç], *adj.* incorrect, erroneous, wrong.

Unrichtigkeit ['unrıçtıçkaıt], *f.* (—, *no pl.*) error, falsity, incorrectness.

Unruhe ['unru:ə], *f.* (—, *pl.* —en) unrest, restlessness; disquiet, uneasiness; riot, disturbance; (*clock*) balance.

Unruhestifter ['unru:əʃtıftər], *m.* (—s, *pl.* —) disturber (of the peace); troublemaker.

unruhig ['unru:ıç], *adj.* restless; troublesome, turbulent, uneasy (about), fidgety.

unrühmlich ['unry:mlıç], *adj.* inglorious.

uns [uns], *pers. pron.* us, ourselves; to us.

unsachlich ['unzaxlıç], *adj.* subjective; irrelevant.

unsagbar ['unza:kba:r], *adj.* unutterable, unspeakable.

unsanft ['unzanft], *adj.* harsh, violent.

unsauber ['unzaubər], *adj.* unclean, dirty; (*fig.*) squalid.

unschädlich ['unʃe:tlıç], *adj.* harmless, innocuous.

unschätzbar ['unʃɛtsba:r], *adj.* invaluable.

unscheinbar ['unʃaınba:r], *adj.* plain, homely, insignificant.

unschicklich ['unʃıklıç], *adj.* unbecoming, indecent, improper, unseemly.

unschlüssig ['unʃlysıç], *adj.* irresolute, undecided.

Unschuld ['unʃult], *f.* (—, *no pl.*) innocence; *verfolgte* —, injured innocence.

unschuldig ['unʃuldıç], *adj.* innocent, guiltless; chaste; *—es Vergnügen,* harmless pleasure.

unschwer ['unʃve:r], *adv.* easily.

Unsegen ['unze:gən], *m.* (—s, *no pl.*) misfortune; curse.

unselbständig ['unzɛlpʃtendıç], *adj.* dependent.

unselig ['unze:lıç], *adj.* unfortunate, luckless, fatal.

unser ['unzər], *poss. adj.* our. — *pers. pron.* of us.

unsereiner ['unzəraınər], *pron.* s.o. in our position; one of us, people in our position.

unserthalben, unsertwegen ['unzərthalbən, unzərtve:gən], *adv.* for our sake, on our account.

unsertwillen ['unzərtvılən], *adv. um* —, for our sake, on our account.

unsicher ['unzıçər], *adj.* unsafe; uncertain, doubtful; (*route*) precarious; (*hand*) unsteady; (*legs*) shaky.

unsichtbar ['unzıçtba:r], *adj.* invisible.

Unsinn ['unzın], *m.* (—s, *no pl.*) nonsense.

unsinnig ['unzınıç], *adj.* nonsensical; mad, insane.

Unsitte ['unzıtə], *f.* (—, *pl.* —n) abuse, nuisance; bad habit.

unsittlich ['unzıtlıç], *adj.* immoral.

unstät, unstet ['unʃte:t, 'unʃte:t], *adj.* unsteady, inconstant; restless.

unstatthaft ['unʃtathaft], *adj.* illicit.

unsterblich ['unʃtɛrplıç], *adj.* immortal.

Unsterblichkeit ['unʃtɛrplıçkaıt], *f.* (—, *no pl.*) immortality.

unstillbar ['unʃtılba:r], *adj.* unappeasable, unquenchable.

unstreitig ['unʃtraıtıç], *adj.* indisputable, unquestionable.

Unsumme ['unzumə], *f.* (—, *pl.* —n) vast amount (of money).

unsympathisch ['unzympa:tıʃ], *adj.* uncongenial, disagreeable; *er ist mir* —, I dislike him.

untadelhaft, untadelig ['unta:dəlhaft, 'unta:dəlıç], *adj.* blameless, irreproachable, unimpeachable.

Untat ['unta:t], *f.* (—, *pl.* —en) misdeed, crime.

untätig ['unte:tıç], *adj.* inactive, idle, supine.

untauglich ['untauklıç], *adj.* unfit, useless; incompetent; (*Mil.*) disabled.

unteilbar [un'taılba:r], *adj.* indivisible.

unten ['untən], *adv.* below, beneath; (*house*) downstairs.

unter ['untər], *prep.* (*Dat., Acc.*) under, beneath, below, among, between.

Unterbau ['untərbau], *m.* (—s, *pl.* —ten) substructure, foundation.

Unterbewußtsein ['untərbəvustzaIn], *n.* (—s, *no pl.*) subconscious mind, subconsciousness.

unterbieten [untər'bi:tən], *v.a. irr. insep.* underbid, undersell.

Unterbilanz ['untərbilants], *f.* (—, *pl.* —en) deficit.

unterbinden [untər'bIndən], *v.a. irr. insep.* tie up, bind up; (*fig.*) prevent, check.

unterbleiben [untər'blaIbən], *v.n. irr. insep.* (*aux. sein*) remain undone, be left undone, cease.

unterbrechen [untər'brɛçən], *v.a. irr. insep.* interrupt; (*journey*) break; (*speech*) cut short.

Unterbrechung [untər'brɛçuŋ], *f.* (—, *pl.* —en) interruption.

unterbreiten (1) ['untərbraItən], *v.a.* spread under.

unterbreiten (2) [untər'braItən], *v.a. insep.* submit, lay before.

unterbringen ['untərbrIŋən], *v.a. irr.* provide (*a place*) for; (*goods*) dispose of; (*money*) invest; (*people*) accommodate, put up.

Unterbringung ['untərbrIŋuŋ], *f.* (—, *no pl.*) provision for; (*goods*) disposal of; (*money*) investment; (*people*) accommodation.

unterdessen [untər'dɛsən], *adv., conj.* in the meantime, meanwhile.

unterdrücken [untər'drykən], *v.a. insep.* suppress, curb, check; oppress.

Unterdrückung [untər'drykuŋ], *f.* (—, *no pl.*) oppression, suppression.

untereinander [untəraIn'andər], *adv.* with each other, mutually, among themselves.

unterfangen [untər'faŋən], *v.r. irr. insep. sich —*, dare, venture, presume.

Untergang ['untərgaŋ], *m.* (—s, *pl.* ⁻e) (*sun*) setting; (*ship*) sinking; (*fig.*) decline.

untergeben [untər'ge:bən], *adj.* subject, subordinate.

Untergebene [untər'ge:bənə], *m.* (—n, *pl.* —n) subordinate.

untergehen ['untərge:ən], *v.n. irr.* (*aux. sein*) (*sun*) go down, set; (*ship*) sink; (*fig.*) perish, decline.

Untergeschoß ['untərgəʃɔs], *n.* (—sses, *pl.* —sse) ground floor; basement.

Untergestell ['untərgəʃtɛl], *n.* (—s, *pl.* —e) undercarriage, chassis.

untergraben [untər'gra:bən], *v.a. irr. insep.* undermine.

unterhalb ['untərhalp], *prep.* (*Genit.*) below, under.

Unterhalt ['untərhalt], *m.* (—s, *no pl.*) maintenance, support, livelihood.

unterhalten (1) ['untərhaltən], *v.a. irr.* hold under.

unterhalten (2) [untər'haltən], *v.a. irr. insep.* maintain, keep, support; entertain. — *v.r. sich —*, converse, make conversation; *sich gut —*, enjoy o.s.

unterhaltend [untər'haltənt], *adj.* entertaining, amusing, lively.

Unterhaltskosten ['untərhaltskɔstən], *f. pl.* maintenance; (*house*) cost of repairs.

Unterhaltung [untər'haltuŋ], *f.* (—, *pl.* —en) maintenance; conversation; amusement, entertainment.

Unterhaltungslektüre [untər'haltuŋslɛkty:rə], *f.* (—, *no pl.*) light reading, fiction.

unterhandeln [untər'handəln], *v.n. insep.* negotiate.

Unterhändler ['untərhɛndlər], *m.* (—s, *pl.* —) negotiator, mediator.

Unterhandlung [untər'handluŋ], *f.* (—, *pl.* —en) negotiation.

Unterhaus ['untərhaus], *n.* (—es, *pl.* ⁻er) ground floor; (*Parl.*) lower house; House of Commons.

Unterhemd ['untərhɛmt], *n.* (—(e)s, *pl.* —en) vest.

unterhöhlen [untər'hø:lən], *v.a. insep.* undermine.

Unterholz ['untərhɔlts], *n.* (—es, *no pl.*) undergrowth, underwood.

Unterhosen ['untərho:zən], *f. pl.* (*women*) briefs; (*men*) underpants.

unterirdisch ['untərIrdIʃ], *adj.* subterranean, underground.

unterjochen [untər'jɔxən], *v.a. insep.* subjugate, subdue.

Unterkiefer ['untərki:fər], *m.* (—s, *pl.* —) lower jaw.

Unterkleid ['untərklaIt], *n.* (—s, *pl.* ⁻er) under-garment.

unterkommen ['untərkɔmən], *v.n. irr.* (*aux. sein*) find accommodation *or* shelter; (*fig.*) find employment.

Unterkommen ['untərkɔmən], *n.* (—s, *no pl.*) shelter, accommodation; (*fig.*) employment, place.

Unterkörper ['untərkœrpər], *m.* (—s, *pl.* —) lower part of the body.

unterkriegen ['untərkri:gən], *v.a.* get the better of; *lass dich nicht —*, stand firm.

Unterkunft ['untərkunft], *f.* (—, *pl.* ⁻e) shelter, accommodation; employment.

Unterlage ['untərla:gə], *f.* (—, *pl.* —n) foundation, base; blotting pad; (*pl.*) documents, files.

unterlassen [untər'lasən], *v.a. irr. insep.* omit (to do), fail (to do), neglect; forbear.

Unterlassung [untər'lasuŋ], *f.* (—, *pl.* —en) omission, neglect.

Unterlassungssünde [untər'lasuŋszyndə], *f.* (—, *pl.* —n) sin of omission.

Unterlauf ['untərlauf], *m.* (—(e)s, *pl.* ⁻e) (*river*) lower course.

Unterlaufen

unterlaufen [untər'laufən], *v.n. irr. insep.* (*aux.* sein) run under; (*mistake*) creep in. — *adj.* suffused, blood-shot.

unterlegen (1) ['untərle:gən], *v.a.* lay under; *einen anderen Sinn* —, put a different construction upon.

unterlegen (2) [untər'le:gən], *adj.* inferior.

Unterleib ['untərlaip], *m.* (—s, *no pl.*) abdomen.

unterliegen [untər'li:gən], *v.n. irr. insep.* (*aux.* sein) succumb, be overcome; be subject (to).

Untermieter ['untərmi:tər], *m.* (—s, *pl.* —) subtenant.

unterminieren [untərmi'ni:rən], *v.a. insep.* undermine.

unternehmen [untər'ne:mən], *v.a. irr. insep.* undertake, take upon o.s., attempt.

Unternehmen [untər'ne:mən], *n.* (—s, *pl.* —) enterprise, undertaking.

unternehmend [untər'ne:mənt], *adj.* bold, enterprising.

Unternehmer [untər'ne:mər], *m.* (—s, *pl.* —) contractor, entrepreneur.

Unteroffizier ['untərɔfitsi:r], *m.* (—s, *pl.* —e) (*army*) non-commissioned officer; (*navy*) petty officer.

unterordnen ['untərɔrdnən], *v.a.* subordinate. — *v.r. sich* —, submit (to).

Unterordnung ['untərɔrdnuŋ], *f.* (—, *no pl.*) subordination, submission; (*Biol.*) sub-order.

Unterpacht ['untərpaxt], *f.* (—, *no pl.*) sublease.

Unterpfand ['untərpfant], *n.* (—(e)s, *no pl.*) (*obs.*) pawn, pledge.

Unterredung [untər're:duŋ], *f.* (—, *pl.* —en) conference, interview, talk.

Unterricht ['untərrɪçt], *m.* (—(e)s, *no pl.*) instruction, tuition, teaching.

unterrichten [untər'rɪçtən], *v.a. insep.* instruct, teach.

Unterrichtsanstalt ['untərrɪçtsanʃtalt], *f.* (—, *pl.* —en) educational establishment *or* institution.

Unterrichtsgegenstand ['untərrɪçtsge:gənʃtant], *m.* (—s, *pl.* ⁝e) subject of instruction.

Unterrock ['untərrɔk], *m.* (—s, *pl.* ⁝e) petticoat, slip; underskirt.

untersagen [untər'za:gən], *v.a. insep.* forbid; *Rauchen untersagt*, smoking prohibited.

Untersatz ['untərzats], *m.* (—es, *pl.* ⁝e) basis, holder, stand, trestle; saucer.

unterschätzen [untər'ʃɛtsən], *v.a. insep.* underrate, underestimate.

unterscheiden [untər'ʃaidən], *v.a. irr. insep.* distinguish, discriminate, discern, differentiate. — *v.r. sich* —, differ; *ich kann sie nicht* —, I cannot tell them apart.

Unterscheidung [untər'ʃaiduŋ], *f.* (—, *pl.* —en) distinction, differentiation.

Unterscheidungsmerkmal [untər-ʃaiduŋsmɛrkma:l], *n.* (—s, *pl.* —e) distinctive mark, characteristic.

Unterscheidungsvermögen [untər-ʃaiduŋsfɛrmø:gən], *n.* (—s, *no pl.*) power of discrimination.

Unterscheidungszeichen [untər'ʃaiduŋstsaiçən], *n.* (—s, *pl.* —) criterion.

Unterschenkel ['untərʃɛŋkəl], *m.* (—s, *pl.* —) shank, lower part of the thigh.

Unterschicht ['untərʃɪçt], *f.* (—, *pl.* —en) substratum, subsoil.

unterschieben (1) ['untərʃi:bən], *v.a. irr.* substitute; interpolate; forge; foist upon.

unterschieben (2) [untər'ʃi:bən], *v.a. irr. insep.* (*fig.*) attribute falsely, pass s.o. off as.

Unterschiebung [untər'ʃi:buŋ], *f.* (—, *pl.* —en) substitution; forgery.

Unterschied ['untərʃi:t], *m.* (—(e)s, *pl.* —e) difference.

unterschiedlich ['untərʃi:tlɪç], *adj.* different, diverse.

unterschiedslos ['untərʃi:tslo:s], *adv.* indiscriminately.

unterschlagen [untər'ʃla:gən], *v.a. irr. insep.* embezzle, intercept.

Unterschlagung [untər'ʃla:guŋ], *f.* (—, *pl.* —en) embezzlement.

Unterschlupf [untər'ʃlupf], *m.* (—es, *pl.* ⁝e) shelter, refuge.

unterschlüpfen [untər'ʃlypfən], *v.n.* (*aux.* sein) find shelter, slip away; (*fig.*) hide.

unterschreiben [untər'ʃraibən], *v.a. irr. insep.* sign, subscribe to.

Unterschrift ['untərʃrɪft], *f.* (—, *pl.* —en) signature.

Unterseeboot ['untərze:bo:t], *n.* (—s, *pl.* —e) submarine.

untersetzt [untər'zɛtst], *adj.* thickset, dumpy.

untersinken ['untərzɪŋkən], *v.n. irr.* (*aux.* sein) go down.

unterst ['untərst], *adj.* lowest, undermost, bottom.

Unterstaatssekretär [untər'ʃta:tssekretɛ:r], *m.* (—s, *pl.* —e) undersecretary of state.

unterstehen (1) ['untərʃte:ən], *v.n. irr.* (*aux.* sein) find shelter (under).

unterstehen (2) [untər'ʃte:ən], *v.n. irr. insep.* be subordinate. — *v.r. sich* —, dare, venture.

unterstellen (1) ['untərʃtɛlən], *v.a.* place under. — *v.r. sich* —, take shelter (under).

unterstellen (2) [untər'ʃtɛlən], *v.a. insep.* put under the authority of; impute (s.th. to s.o.).

Unterstellung [untər'ʃtɛluŋ], *f.* (—, *pl.* —en) imputation, insinuation.

unterstreichen [untər'ʃtraiçən], *v.a. irr. insep.* underline.

Unterstreichung [untər'ʃtraiçuŋ], *f.* (—, *pl.* —en) underlining.

Unterströmung ['untərʃtrø:muŋ], *f.* (—, *pl.* —en) undercurrent.

unterstützen [untər'ʃtytsən], *v.a. insep.* support, assist, aid; (*fig.*) countenance.

unvereinbar

Unterstützung [untər'ʃtytsuŋ], *f.* (—, *pl.* —en) support, aid, assistance, relief.

Unterstützungsanstalt [untər'ʃtytsuŋsanʃtalt], *f.* (—, *pl.* —en) charitable institution.

unterstützungsbedürftig [untər'ʃtytsuŋsbədyrftɪç], *adj.* indigent.

untersuchen [untər'zu:xən], *v.a. insep.* investigate, examine, look over.

Untersuchung [untər'zu:xuŋ], *f.* (—, *pl.* —en) investigation, inquiry; (*medical*) examination.

Untersuchungshaft [untər'zu:xuŋshaft], *f.* (—, *no pl.*) imprisonment pending investigation.

Untersuchungsrichter [untər'zu:xuŋsrɪçtər], *m.* (—s, *pl.* —) examining magistrate.

Untertan [untərta:n], *m.* (—s, *pl.* —en) subject, vassal.

untertan [untərta:n], *adj.* subject.

untertänig [untərtɛ:nɪç], *adj.* humble, obsequious, submissive, servile.

Untertasse [untərtasə], *f.* (—, *pl.* —n) saucer.

untertauchen [untərtauxən], *v.a.* dip, duck, submerge. — *v.n.* (*aux.* sein) dive.

unterwegs [untər've:ks], *adv.* on the way.

unterweisen [untər'vaɪzən], *v.a. irr. insep.* teach, instruct.

Unterweisung [untər'vaɪzuŋ], *f.* (—, *pl.* —en) instruction, teaching.

Unterwelt [untərvɛlt], *f.* (—, *no pl.*) Hades, the underworld.

unterwerfen [untər'vɛrfən], *v.a. irr. insep.* subject, subdue. — *v.r. sich* —, submit (to), resign o.s. (to).

Unterwerfung [untər'vɛrfuŋ], *f.* (—, *no pl.*) subjection, submission.

unterwühlen [untər'vy:lən], *v.a. insep.* root up; (*fig.*) undermine.

unterwürfig [untər'vyrfɪç], *adj.* submissive, subject; obsequious.

Unterwürfigkeit [untər'vyrfɪçkaɪt], *f.* (—, *no pl.*) submissiveness; obsequiousness.

unterzeichnen [untər'tsaɪçnən], *v.a. insep.* sign.

Unterzeichner [untər'tsaɪçnər], *m.* (—s, *pl.* —) signatory; (*insurance*) underwriter.

Unterzeichnete [untər'tsaɪçnətə], *m.* (—n, *pl.* —n) undersigned.

Unterzeichnung [untər'tsaɪçnuŋ], *f.* (—, *pl.* —en) signature.

unterziehen [untər'tsi:ən], *v.r. irr. insep. sich* —, submit to, undertake; (*operation*) undergo.

Untiefe [unti:fə], *f.* (—, *pl.* —n) shallow water, flat, shoal, sands.

Untier [unti:r], *n.* (—s, *pl.* —e) monster.

untilgbar [untɪlkba:r], *adj.* indelible; (*debt*) irredeemable.

untrennbar [untrɛnba:r], *adj.* inseparable.

untreu [untrɔy], *adj.* faithless, unfaithful, disloyal, perfidious.

Untreue [untrɔyə], *f.* (—, *no pl.*) faithlessness, unfaithfulness, disloyalty, perfidy.

untröstlich [untrø:stlɪç], *adj.* inconsolable, disconsolate.

untrüglich [untry:klɪç], *adj.* unmistakable, infallible.

untüchtig [untyçtɪç], *adj.* inefficient; incompetent.

unüberlegt [uny:bərle:kt], *adj.* inconsiderate, thoughtless; rash.

unübersehbar [uny:bərze:ba:r], *adj.* immense, vast.

unübersteiglich [uny:bərʃtaɪklɪç], *adj.* insurmountable.

unübertrefflich [uny:bərtrɛflɪç], *adj.* unsurpassable, unequalled, unrivalled.

unübertroffen [uny:bərtrɔfən], *adj.* unsurpassed.

unüberwindlich [uny:bərvɪntlɪç], *adj.* invincible, unconquerable.

unumgänglich [unumgɛŋlɪç], *adj.* indispensable, unavoidable, inevitable.

unumschränkt [unumʃrɛŋkt], *adj.* unlimited, absolute.

unumstößlich [unumʃtø:slɪç], *adj.* irrefutable.

unumwunden [unumvundən], *adj.* frank, plain.

ununterbrochen [ununtərbrɔxən], *adj.* uninterrupted, unremitting.

unveränderlich [unfɛrɛndərlɪç], *adj.* unchangeable, unalterable.

unverändert [unfɛrɛndərt], *adj.* unchanged, unaltered.

unverantwortlich [unfɛrantvortlɪç], *adj.* irresponsible, inexcusable, unjustifiable.

unveräußerlich [unfɛrɔysərlɪç], *adj.* not for sale; inalienable.

unverbesserlich [unfɛrbɛsərlɪç], *adj.* incorrigible.

unverbindlich [unfɛrbɪntlɪç], *adj.* not binding, without prejudice, without obligation.

unverblümt [unfɛrblymt], *adj.* blunt, point-blank.

unverbrennlich [unfɛrbrɛnlɪç], *adj.* incombustible.

unverbrüchlich [unfɛrbryçlɪç], *adj.* inviolable.

unverbürgt [unfɛrbyrkt], *adj.* unwarranted, unofficial; unconfirmed.

unverdaulich [unfɛrdaulɪç], *adj.* indigestible.

unverdaut [unfɛrdaut], *adj.* undigested.

unverdient [unfɛrdi:nt], *adj.* unmerited, undeserved.

unverdientermaßen [unfɛrdi:ntərma:sən], *adv.* undeservedly.

unverdorben [unfɛrdɔrbən], *adj.* unspoiled, uncorrupted, innocent.

unverdrossen [unfɛrdrɔsən], *adj.* indefatigable.

unvereidigt [unfɛraɪdɪçt], *adj.* unsworn.

unvereinbar [unfɛraɪnba:r], *adj.* incompatible, inconsistent.

Unvereinbarkeit [ˈunfɛraɪnbaːrkaɪt], f. (—, no pl.) incompatibility, inconsistency.

unverfälscht [ˈunfɛrfɛlʃt], adj. unadulterated, genuine, pure.

unverfänglich [ˈunfɛrfɛŋlɪç], adj. harmless.

unverfroren [ˈunfɛrfroːrən], adj. cheeky, impudent.

unvergeßlich [ˈunfɛrgɛslɪç], adj. memorable, not to be forgotten, unforgettable.

unvergleichlich [ˈunfɛrglaɪçlɪç], adj. incomparable.

unverhältnismäßig [ˈunfɛrhɛltnɪsmɛːsɪç], adj. disproportionate.

unverheiratet [ˈunfɛrhaɪraːtət], adj. unmarried.

unverhofft [ˈunfɛrhɔft], adj. unexpected.

unverhohlen [ˈunfɛrhoːlən], adj. unconcealed, undisguised, candid.

unverkennbar [ˈunfɛrkɛnbaːr], adj. unmistakable.

unverlangt [ˈunfɛrlaŋkt], adj. unsolicited, not ordered.

unverletzlich [ˈunfɛrlɛtslɪç], adj. invulnerable; (fig.) inviolable.

unverletzt [ˈunfɛrlɛtst], adj. (persons) unhurt; (things) undamaged, intact.

unvermeidlich [ˈunfɛrmaɪtlɪç], adj. inevitable, unavoidable.

unvermindert [ˈunfɛrmɪndərt], adj. undiminished.

unvermittelt [ˈunfɛrmɪtəlt], adj. sudden, abrupt.

Unvermögen [ˈunfɛrmøːgən], n. (—s, no pl.) inability, incapacity.

unvermögend [ˈunfɛrmøːgənt], adj. incapable; impecunious.

unvermutet [ˈunfɛrmuːtət], adj. unexpected, unforeseen.

unverrichtet [ˈunfɛrrɪçtət], adj. —er Sache, empty-handed; unsuccessfully.

unverschämt [ˈunfɛrʃɛːmt], adj. impudent, brazen.

unverschuldet [ˈunfɛrʃuldət], adj. not in debt, unencumbered; (fig.) undeserved.

unversehens [ˈunfɛrzeːəns], adv. unexpectedly, unawares.

unversehrt [ˈunfɛrzeːrt], adv. (persons) unhurt, safe; (things) undamaged.

unversiegbar [ˈunfɛrziːkbaːr], adj. inexhaustible.

unversiegt [ˈunfɛrziːkt], adj. unexhausted.

unversöhnlich [ˈunfɛrzøːnlɪç], adj. implacable, irreconcilable.

unversöhnt [ˈunfɛrzøːnt], adj. unreconciled.

unversorgt [ˈunfɛrzɔrkt], adj. unprovided for.

Unverstand [ˈunfɛrʃtant], m. (—(e)s, no pl.) want of judgment, indiscretion.

unverständig [ˈunfɛrʃtɛndɪç], adj. foolish, unwise, imprudent.

unverständlich [ˈunfɛrʃtɛntlɪç], adj. unintelligible, incomprehensible.

unversteuert [ˈunfɛrʃtɔyərt], adj. with duty or tax unpaid.

unversucht [ˈunfɛrzuːxt], adj. untried; nichts — lassen, leave no stone unturned.

unverträglich [ˈunfɛrtrɛːklɪç], adj. quarrelsome.

unverwandt [ˈunfɛrvant], adj. unrelated; fixed, constant; immovable.

unverwundbar [ˈunfɛrvuntbaːr], adj. invulnerable.

unverwüstlich [ˈunfɛrvyːstlɪç], adj. indestructible.

unverzagt [ˈunfɛrtsaːkt], adj. undaunted, intrepid.

unverzeihlich [ˈunfɛrtsaɪlɪç], adj. unpardonable.

unverzinslich [ˈunfɛrtsɪnslɪç], adj. (money) gaining no interest.

unverzollt [ˈunfɛrtsɔlt], adj. duty unpaid.

unverzüglich [ˈunfɛrtsyːklɪç], adj. immediate.

unvollendet [ˈunfɔlɛndət], adj. unfinished.

unvollständig [ˈunfɔlʃtɛndɪç], adj. incomplete.

unvorbereitet [ˈunfoːrbəraɪtət], adj. unprepared.

unvordenklich [ˈunfoːrdɛŋklɪç], adj. seit —en Zeiten, from time immemorial.

unvorhergesehen [ˈunfoːrheːrgəzeːən], adj. unforeseen, unlooked for.

unvorsichtig [ˈunfoːrzɪçtɪç], adj. imprudent, incautious, careless.

unvorteilhaft [ˈunfɔrtaɪlhaft], adj. unprofitable, disadvantageous; — aussehen, not look o.'s best.

unwägbar [ˈunvɛːkbaːr], adj. imponderable.

unwahr [ˈunvaːr], adj. untrue, false.

Unwahrhaftigkeit [ˈunvaːrhaftɪçkaɪt], f. (—, no pl.) want of truthfulness, unreliability, dishonesty.

Unwahrheit [ˈunvaːrhaɪt], f. (—, pl. —en) lie, untruth, falsehood.

unwegsam [ˈunveːkzaːm], adj. impassable, impracticable.

unweigerlich [ˈunvaɪgərlɪç], adj. unhesitating, unquestioning. — adv. without fail.

unweit [ˈunvaɪt], prep. (Genit.) not far from, near.

Unwesen [ˈunveːzən], n. (—s, no pl.) nuisance; sein — treiben, be up to o.'s tricks.

Unwetter [ˈunvɛtər], n. (—s, pl. —) bad weather, thunderstorm.

unwichtig [ˈunvɪçtɪç], adj. unimportant; insignificant, of no consequence.

unwiderleglich [ˈunviːdərleːklɪç], adj. irrefutable.

unwiderruflich [ˈunviːdərruːflɪç], adj. irrevocable.

unwidersprechlich [ˈunviːdərʃpreçlɪç], adj. incontestable.

unwidersprochen [ˈunviːdərʃprɔxən], adj. uncontradicted.

Ursprung

unwiderstehlich ['unvi:dərʃteːlɪç], *adj.* irresistible.

unwiederbringlich ['unvi:dərbrɪŋlɪç], *adj.* irrecoverable, irretrievable.

Unwille ['unvɪlə], *m.* (**—ns**, *no pl.*) displeasure, indignation.

unwillkürlich ['unvɪlkyːrlɪç], *adj.* involuntary; instinctive.

unwirsch ['unvɪrʃ], *adj.* petulant, testy; curt, uncivil.

unwirtlich ['unvɪrtlɪç], *adj.* inhospitable.

unwirtschaftlich ['unvɪrtʃaftlɪç], *adj.* not economic, uneconomic.

unwissend ['unvɪsənt], *adj.* illiterate, ignorant.

Unwissenheit ['unvɪsənhaɪt], *f.* (**—**, *no pl.*) ignorance.

unwissenschaftlich ['unvɪsənʃaftlɪç], *adj.* unscholarly; unscientific.

unwissentlich ['unvɪsəntlɪç], *adv.* unknowingly, unconsciously.

unwohl ['unvoːl], *adj.* unwell, indisposed.

Unwohlsein ['unvoːlzaɪn], *n.* (**—s**, *no pl.*) indisposition.

unwürdig ['unvyrdɪç], *adj.* unworthy, undeserving.

Unzahl ['untsaːl], *f.* (**—**, *no pl.*) vast number.

unzählbar [un'tsɛːlbaːr], *adj.* innumerable, numberless.

unzählig [un'tsɛːlɪç], *adj.* innumerable; **—e Male**, over and over again.

unzart ['untsaːrt], *adj.* indelicate, rude, rough; unceremonious.

Unzeit ['untsaɪt], *f.* (**—**, *no pl.*) **zur —**, out of season, inopportunely.

unzeitgemäß ['untsaɪtɡəmɛːs], *adj.* out of date, behind the times; unfashionable.

unzeitig ['untsaɪtɪç], *adj.* unseasonable; untimely, inopportune.

unziemlich ['untsiːmlɪç], *adj.* unseemly, unbecoming.

Unzier ['untsiːr], *f.* (**—**, *no pl.*) disfigurement; flaw.

Unzucht ['untsuxt], *f.* (**—**, *no pl.*) unchastity; lewdness; fornication.

unzüchtig ['untsyçtɪç], *adj.* unchaste, lascivious, lewd.

unzufrieden ['untsufriːdən], *adj.* discontented, dissatisfied.

unzugänglich ['untsuɡɛnlɪç], *adj.* inaccessible.

unzulänglich ['untsulɛnlɪç], *adj.* inadequate, insufficient.

Unzulänglichkeit ['untsulɛnlɪçkaɪt], *f.* (**—**, *no pl.*) inadequacy.

unzulässig ['untsulɛsɪç], *adj.* inadmissible.

unzurechnungsfähig ['untsurɛçnuŋsfɛːɪç], *adj.* not accountable (for o.'s actions), non compos mentis, insane.

Unzurechnungsfähigkeit ['untsurɛçnuŋsfɛːɪçkaɪt], *f.* (**—**, *no pl.*) irresponsibility; feeblemindedness.

unzusammenhängend ['untsuzamənhɛŋənt], *adj.* incoherent.

unzuständig ['untsuʃtɛndɪç], *adj.* incompetent, not competent (*Law etc.*).

unzuträglich ['untsutrɛːklɪç], *adj.* unwholesome.

unzutreffend ['untsutrɛfənt], *adj.* inapposite; unfounded; inapplicable.

unzuverlässig ['untsufɛrlɛsɪç], *adj.* unreliable.

unzweckmäßig ['untsvɛkmɛːsɪç], *adj.* inexpedient.

unzweideutig ['untsvaɪdɔytɪç], *adj.* unequivocal, explicit, unambiguous.

üppig ['ypɪç], *adj.* abundant; opulent, luxurious, luxuriant, voluptuous.

uralt ['uːralt], *adj.* very old, old as the hills; ancient.

uranfänglich ['uːranfɛŋlɪç], *adj.* primordial, primeval.

Uraufführung ['uːrauffyːruŋ], *f.* (**—**, *pl.* **—en**) (*Theat.*) first night, première.

urbar ['uːrbaːr], *adj.* arable, under cultivation; **— machen**, cultivate.

Urbarmachung ['uːrbaːrmaxuŋ], *f.* (**—**, *no pl.*) cultivation.

Urbild ['uːrbɪlt], *n.* (**—(e)s**, *pl.* **—er**) prototype; (*fig.*) ideal.

ureigen ['uːraɪɡən], *adj.* quite original; idiosyncratic.

Ureltern ['uːrɛltərn], *pl.* ancestors.

Urenkel ['uːrɛŋkəl], *m.* (**—s**, *pl.* **—**) great-grandson, great-grandchild.

Urenkelin ['uːrɛŋkəlɪn], *f.* (**—**, *pl.* **—nen**) great-granddaughter.

Urfehde ['uːrfeːdə], *f.* (**—**, *no pl.*) oath to keep the peace.

Urform ['uːrfɔrm], *f.* (**—**, *pl.* **—en**) primitive form; original form; archetype.

Urgroßmutter ['uːrɡroːsmutər], *f.* (**—**, *pl.* ⸚) great-grandmother.

Urgroßvater ['uːrɡroːsfaːtər], *m.* (**—s**, *pl.* ⸚) great-grandfather.

Urheber ['uːrheːbər], *m.* (**—s**, *pl.* **—**) author, originator.

Urheberrecht ['uːrheːbərrɛçt], *n.* (**—s**, *pl.* **—e**) copyright.

Urheberschaft ['uːrheːbərʃaft], *f.* (**—**, *no pl.*) authorship.

Urin [u'riːn], *m.* (**—s**, *no pl.*) urine.

Urkunde ['uːrkundə], *f.* (**—**, *pl.* **—n**) document, deed, charter; **zur — dessen**, (*obs.*) in witness whereof.

Urkundenbeweis ['uːrkundənbəvaɪs], *m.* (**—es**, *pl.* **—e**) documentary evidence.

urkundlich ['uːrkuntlɪç], *adj.* documentary.

Urlaub ['uːrlaup], *m.* (**—s**, *pl.* **—e**) leave of absence; vacation; (*Mil.*) furlough.

urplötzlich ['uːrplœtslɪç], *adj.* sudden. **— adv.** all at once, suddenly.

Urquell ['uːrkvɛl], *m.* (**—s**, *pl.* **—en**) fountain-head, original source.

Ursache ['uːrzaxə], *f.* (**—**, *pl.* **—n**) cause; **keine —**, don't mention it.

Urschrift ['uːrʃrɪft], *f.* (**—**, *pl.* **—en**) original text.

Ursprache ['uːrʃpraːxə], *f.* (**—**, *pl.* **—n**) original language.

Ursprung ['uːrʃpruŋ], *m.* (**—s**, *pl.* ⸚e) origin; extraction.

ursprünglich

ursprünglich ['u:rʃpryŋlɪç], *adj.* original.

Urteil ['urtaɪl], *n.* (—s, *pl.* —e) opinion; (*Law*) judgment, verdict, sentence; *ein — fällen,* pass judgment on; *nach meinem —,* in my opinion.

urteilen ['urtaɪlən], *v.n.* judge.

Urteilsspruch ['urtaɪlsʃprux], *m.* (—s, *pl.* ˙e) judgment, sentence.

Uruguay [uru'gwaɪ], *n.* Uruguay.

Urureltern ['u:ru:rɛltərn], *pl.* ancestors.

Urvater ['u:rfa:tər], *m.* (—s, *pl.* ˙) forefather.

Urvolk ['u:rfɔlk], *n.* (—(e)s, *pl.* ˙er) primitive people, aborigines.

Urwald ['u:rvalt], *m.* (—(e)s, *pl.* ˙er) primæval forest, virgin forest.

Urwelt ['u:rvɛlt], *f.* (—, *no pl.*) primæval world.

Urzeit ['u:rtsaɪt], *f.* (—, *pl.* —en) prehistoric times.

V

V [fau], *n.* (—s, *pl.* —s) the letter V.

Vagabund [vaga'bunt], *m.* (—en, *pl.* —en) vagabond, tramp; (*Am.*) hobo.

vag ['va:k], *adj.* vague.

Vakuumbremse ['va:kuumbrɛmzə], *f.* (—, *pl.* —n) air-brake, vacuum-brake.

Vase ['va:zə], *f.* (—, *pl.* —n) vase.

Vater ['fa:tər], *m.* (—s, *pl.* ˙) father.

Vaterland ['fa:tərlant], *n.* (—(e)s, *pl.* ˙er) mother-country, native country; —*sliebe,* patriotism.

vaterländisch ['fa:tərlɛndɪʃ], *adj.* patriotic.

vaterlandslos ['fa:tərlantslo:s], *adj.* having no mother country; unpatriotic.

väterlich ['fɛ:tərlɪç], *adj.* fatherly, paternal. — *adv.* like a father.

vaterlos ['fa:tərlo:s], *adj.* fatherless.

Vatermord ['fa:tərmɔrt], *m.* (—(e)s, *pl.* —e) parricide; patricide.

Vatermörder ['fa:tərmœrdər], *m.* (—s, *pl.* —) parricide; (*fig.*) high *or* standup collar.

Vaterschaft ['fa:tərʃaft], *f.* (—, *no pl.*) paternity.

Vatersname ['fa:tərsna:mə], *m.* (—ns, *pl.* —n) surname, family name.

Vaterstadt ['fa:tərʃtat], *f.* (—, *pl.* ˙e) native town.

Vaterstelle ['fa:tərʃtɛlə], *f.* (—, *pl.* —n) — *vertreten,* act as a father, be a father (to).

Vaterunser ['fa:tər'unzər], *n.* (—s, *pl.* —) Lord's Prayer.

Vatikan [vati'ka:n], *m.* (—s, *no pl.*) Vatican.

vegetieren [vege'ti:rən], *v.n.* vegetate.

Veilchen ['faɪlçən], *n.* (—s, *pl.* —) (*Bot.*) violet.

Vene ['ve:nə], *f.* (—, *pl.* —n) vein.

Venezuela [vɛnətsu'e:la], *n.* Venezuela.

Ventil [vɛn'ti:l], *n.* (—s, *pl.* —e) valve.

ventilieren [vɛnti'li:rən], *v.a.* ventilate, air; (*fig.*) discuss, ventilate.

verabfolgen [fɛr'apfɔlgən], *v.a.* deliver, hand over, remit; serve.

Verabfolgung [fɛr'apfɔlgun], *f.* (—, *no pl.*) delivery.

verabreden [fɛr'apre:dən], *v.a.* agree (upon); stipulate; *etwas mit einem —,* agree on s.th. with s.o. — *v.r. sich mit einem —,* make an appointment with s.o.; (*coll.*) have a date.

Verabredung [fɛr'apre:dun], *f.* (—, *pl.* —en) agreement, arrangement, appointment; (*coll.*) date.

verabreichen [fɛr'apraɪçən], *v.a.* deliver, dispense.

verabsäumen [fɛr'apzɔymən], *v.a.* neglect, omit.

verabscheuen [fɛr'apʃɔyən], *v.a.* detest, loathe, abhor.

Verabscheuung [fɛr'apʃɔyun], *f.* (—, *no pl.*) abhorrence, detestation, loathing.

verabscheuungswürdig [fɛr'apʃɔyuns-vyrdɪç], *adj.* abominable, detestable.

verabschieden [fɛr'apʃi:dən], *v.a.* dismiss, discharge. — *v.r. sich —,* take leave, say good-bye; (*Pol.*) pass (of an Act).

Verabschiedung [fɛr'apʃi:dun], *f.* (—, *no pl.*) dismissal; discharge; (*Pol.*) passing (of an Act).

verachten [fɛr'axtən], *v.a.* despise, scorn.

verächtlich [fɛr'ɛçtlɪç], *adj.* despicable, contemptible; contemptuous, scornful.

Verachtung [fɛr'axtun], *f.* (—, *no pl.*) contempt, disdain, scorn.

verallgemeinern [fɛralgə'maɪnərn], *v.a., v.n.* generalise.

veralten [fɛr'altən], *v.n.* (*aux.* sein) become obsolete, date.

veraltet [fɛr'altət], *adj.* obsolete.

Veranda [ve'randa], *f.* (—, *pl.* —den) verandah, porch.

veränderlich [fɛr'ɛndərlɪç], *adj.* changeable, variable; (*fig.*) inconstant, fickle.

verändern [fɛr'ɛndərn], *v.a.* change, alter. — *v.r. sich —,* change, vary; change o.'s job.

verankern [fɛr'aŋkərn], *v.a.* anchor.

veranlagt [fɛr'anla:kt], *adj.* inclined; gifted; having a propensity (to); *gut —,* talented; (*tax*) assessed.

Veranlagung [fɛr'anla:gun], *f.* (—, *pl.* —en) bent; talent; predisposition; (*tax*) assessment.

veranlassen [fɛr'anlasən], *v.a.* bring about, cause, motivate; *einen —,* induce s.o., cause s.o.; *etwas —,* bring s.th. about, cause s.th.

250

verbrämen

Veranlassung [fɛr'anlasuŋ], f. (—, no pl.) cause, motive; occasion; inducement; auf seine —, at his suggestion; ohne irgend eine —, without the slightest provocation.

veranschaulichen [fɛr'anʃauliçən], v.a. illustrate, make clear.

veranschlagen [fɛr'anʃla:gən], v.a. estimate, assess.

Veranschlagung [fɛr'anʃla:guŋ], f. (—, pl. —en) estimate.

veranstalten [fɛr'anʃtaltən], v.a. organise, arrange.

Veranstalter [fɛr'anʃtaltər], m. (—s, pl. —) organiser.

Veranstaltung [fɛr'anʃtaltuŋ], f. (—, pl. —en) arrangement; entertainment; show; event; (sporting) fixture.

verantworten [fɛr'antvɔrtən], v.a. account for. — v.r. sich —, answer (for), justify o.s.

verantwortlich [fɛr'antvɔrtliç], adj. responsible, answerable, accountable.

Verantwortlichkeit [fɛr'antvɔrtliçkait], f. (—, no pl.) liability, obligation.

Verantwortung [fɛr'antvɔrtuŋ], f. (—, no pl.) responsibility, justification, excuse; defence; auf deine —, at your own risk; einen zur — ziehen, call s.o. to account.

verantwortungsvoll [fɛr'antvɔrtuŋsfɔl], adj. responsible.

verarbeiten [fɛr'arbaitən], v.a. manufacture, process; (fig.) digest.

Verarbeitung [fɛr'arbaituŋ], f. (—, no pl.) manufacture; process; finish; (fig.) digestion.

verargen [fɛr'argən], v.a. einem etwas —, blame or reproach s.o. for s.th.

verärgern [fɛr'ɛrgərn], v.a. annoy, make angry.

Verarmung [fɛr'armuŋ], f. (—, no pl.) impoverishment.

verausgaben [fɛr'ausga:bən], v.r. sich —, overspend, run short of money; spend o.s., wear o.s. out.

veräußern [fɛr'ɔysərn], v.a. dispose of, sell.

Veräußerung [fɛr'ɔysəruŋ], f. (—, no pl.) sale; alienation.

Verband [fɛr'bant], m. (—s, pl. ⁻e) bandage, dressing; association, union; unit.

verbannen [fɛr'banən], v.a. banish, exile, outlaw.

Verbannte [fɛr'bantə], m. (—n, pl. —n) exile, outlaw.

Verbannung [fɛr'banuŋ], f. (—, pl. —en) banishment, exile.

verbauen [fɛr'bauən], v.n. obstruct; build up; use up or spend in building.

verbeißen [fɛr'baisən], v.a. irr. sich etwas —, suppress s.th.; sich das Lachen —, stifle a laugh. — v.r. sich in etwas —, stick doggedly to s.th.

verbergen [fɛr'bɛrgən], v.a. irr. conceal, hide.

verbessern [fɛr'bɛsərn], v.a. improve, correct, mend.

Verbesserung [fɛr'bɛsəruŋ], f. (—, pl. —en) improvement; correction.

verbeugen [fɛr'bɔygən], v.r. sich —, bow.

Verbeugung [fɛr'bɔyguŋ], f. (—, pl. —en) bow, obeisance.

verbiegen [fɛr'bi:gən], v.a. irr. twist, distort, bend the wrong way.

verbieten [fɛr'bi:tən], v.a. irr. forbid, prohibit.

verbilligen [fɛr'biligən], v.a. cheapen, reduce the price of.

verbinden [fɛr'bindən], v.a. irr. tie up, bind up, connect; (Med.) dress, bandage; unite, join; die Augen —, blindfold. — v.r. sich —, unite, join; (Chem.) combine.

verbindlich [fɛr'bintliç], adj. binding, obligatory; obliging; —en Dank, my best thanks.

Verbindlichkeit [fɛr'bintliçkait], f. (—, pl. —en) liability, obligation; compliment.

Verbindung [fɛr'binduŋ], f. (—, pl. —en) connexion, connection, junction; association; alliance; (Railw.) connection; (Chem.) compound.

Verbindungsglied [fɛr'binduŋsgli:t], n. (—(e)s, pl. —er) connecting link.

Verbindungslinie [fɛr'binduŋsli:njə], f. (—, pl. —n) line of communication.

verbissen [fɛr'bisən], adj. obstinate, grim; soured. — adv. doggedly.

verbitten [fɛr'bitən], v.a. irr. sich etwas —, forbid s.th. determinedly; insist on s.th. not being done, object to.

verbittern [fɛr'bitərn], v.a. embitter.

Verbitterung [fɛr'bitəruŋ], f. (—, no pl.) exasperation.

verblassen [fɛr'blasən], v.n. turn pale.

Verbleib [fɛr'blaip], m. (—(e)s, no pl.) whereabouts.

verbleiben [fɛr'blaibən], v.n. irr. (aux. sein) remain.

verblenden [fɛr'blɛndən], v.a. dazzle, delude, blind.

Verblendung [fɛr'blɛnduŋ], f. (—, no pl.) infatuation; delusion.

verblüffen [fɛr'blyfən], v.n. amaze, stagger, dumbfound.

Verblüffung [fɛr'blyfuŋ], f. (—, no pl.) bewilderment.

verblühen [fɛr'bly:ən], v.n. (aux. sein) wither, fade.

verblümt [fɛr'bly:mt], adj. veiled.

verbluten [fɛr'blu:tən], v.n. (aux. sein) bleed to death.

verborgen (1) [fɛr'bɔrgən], v.a. lend out.

verborgen (2) [fɛr'bɔrgən], adj. concealed, hidden; im —en, secretly.

Verborgenheit [fɛr'bɔrgənhait], f. (—, no pl.) concealment, seclusion.

Verbot [fɛr'bo:t], n. (—(e)s, pl. —e) prohibition.

verboten [fɛr'bo:tən], adj. forbidden, prohibited.

verbrämen [fɛr'brɛ:mən], v.a. (garment) edge, border.

251

verbrauchen

verbrauchen [fɛr'brauxən], *v.a.* consume, use up; spend.
Verbraucher [fɛr'brauxər], *m.* (—s, *pl.* —) consumer.
Verbrechen [fɛr'brɛçən], *n.* (—s, *pl.* —) crime.
verbrechen [fɛr'brɛçən], *v.a. irr.* commit, perpetrate.
Verbrecher [fɛr'brɛçər], *m.* (—s, *pl.* —) criminal.
Verbrecheralbum [fɛr'brɛçəralbum], *n.* (—s, *no pl.*) rogues' gallery.
verbreiten [fɛr'braItən], *v.a.* spread, diffuse.
verbreitern [fɛr'braItərn], *v.a.* widen.
Verbreitung [fɛr'braItuŋ], *f.* (—, *no pl.*) spread(ing), propaganda, extension.
verbrennbar [fɛr'brɛnba:r], *adj.* combustible.
verbrennen [fɛr'brɛnən], *v.a. irr.* burn; cremate; *von der Sonne verbrannt,* sunburnt. — *v.n.* (*aux.* sein) get burnt. — *v.r. sich* —, scald o.s., burn o.s.
Verbrennung [fɛr'brɛnuŋ], *f.* (—, *pl.* —en) burning, combustion; cremation.
verbrieft [fɛr'bri:ft], *adj.* vested; documented.
verbringen [fɛr'brIŋən], *v.a. irr.* (*time*) spend, pass.
verbrüdern [fɛr'bry:dərn], *v.r. sich* —, fraternise.
verbrühen [fɛr'bry:ən], *v.r.* scald.
verbummeln [fɛr'buməln], *v.a. die Zeit* —, fritter the time away.
verbunden [fɛr'bundən], *adj. einem* — *sein,* be obliged to s.o.
verbünden [fɛr'byndən], *v.r. sich* — *mit,* ally o.s. with.
Verbündete [fɛr'byndətə], *m.* (—n, *pl.* —n) ally, confederate.
verbürgen [fɛr'byrgən], *v.a.* warrant, guarantee. — *v.r. sich für etwas* —, vouch for s.th.; guarantee s.th.
Verdacht [fɛr'daxt], *m.* (—(e)s, *no pl.*) suspicion.
verdächtig [fɛr'dɛçtIç], *adj.* suspicious, doubtful, questionable.
verdächtigen [fɛr'dɛçtIgən], *v.a.* throw suspicion on, suspect.
verdammen [fɛr'damən], *v.a.* condemn, damn.
verdammenswert [fɛr'damənsve:rt], *adj.* damnable.
Verdammung [fɛr'damuŋ], *f.* (—, *no pl.*) condemnation.
verdampfen [fɛr'dampfən], *v.n.* (*aux.* sein) evaporate.
verdanken [fɛr'daŋkən], *v.a. einem etwas* —, be indebted to s.o. for s.th.; owe s.th. to s.o.
verdauen [fɛr'dauən], *v.a.* digest.
verdaulich [fɛr'daulIç], *adj.* digestible.
Verdauung [fɛr'dauuŋ], *f.* (—, *no pl.*) digestion.
Verdauungsstörung [fɛr'dauuŋsʃtø:ruŋ], *f.* (—, *pl.* —en) indigestion.
Verdeck [fɛr'dɛk], *n.* (—s, *pl.* —e) awning; (*Naut.*) deck.

verdecken [fɛr'dɛkən], *v.a.* cover, hide.
verdenken [fɛr'dɛŋkən], *v.a. irr. einem etwas* —, blame s.o. for s.th.
Verderb [fɛr'dɛrp], *m.* (—s, *no pl.*) ruin, decay.
verderben [fɛr'dɛrbən], *v.a. irr.* spoil, corrupt, pervert. — *v.n.* (*aux.* sein) decay, go bad.
Verderben [fɛr'dɛrbən], *n.* (—s, *no pl.*) corruption, ruin.
Verderber [fɛr'dɛrbər], *m.* (—s, *pl.*—) corrupter, perverter.
verderblich [fɛr'dɛrplIç], *adj.* ruinous, pernicious, destructive; (*goods*) perishable.
Verderbnis [fɛr'dɛrpnIs], *f.* (—, *no pl.*) corruption, depravity; perversion; perdition.
Verderbtheit [fɛr'dɛrpthaIt], *f.* (—, *no pl.*) corruption, perversion, depravity.
verdeutlichen [fɛr'dɔytlIçən], *v.a.* illustrate, clarify.
verdichten [fɛr'dIçtən], *v.a.*, *v.r.* thicken, condense, liquefy.
Verdichtung [fɛr'dIçtuŋ], *f.* (—, *no pl.*) condensation; solidification.
verdicken [fɛr'dIkən], *v.a.* thicken; solidify.
verdienen [fɛr'di:nən], *v.a.* earn; deserve.
Verdienst (1) [fɛr'di:nst], *m.* (—es, *pl.* —e) profit, gain, earnings.
Verdienst (2) [fɛr'di:nst], *n.* (—es, *pl.* —e) merit, deserts.
verdienstvoll [fɛr'di:nstfɔl], *adj.* meritorious, deserving; distinguished.
verdient [fɛr'di:nt], *adj. sich* — *machen um,* deserve well of, serve well (a cause etc.).
verdientermaßen [fɛr'di:ntərmasən], *adv.* deservedly.
verdingen [fɛr'dIŋən], *v.r. irr. sich* —, enter service (with), take a situation (with).
verdolmetschen [fɛr'dɔlmɛtʃən], *v.a.* interpret, translate.
verdoppeln [fɛr'dɔpəln], *v.a.* double.
verdorben [fɛr'dɔrbən], *adj.* spoilt; corrupted, depraved, debauched.
verdrängen [fɛr'drɛŋən], *v.a.* crowd out; (*Phys.*) displace; (*fig.*) supplant, supersede; (*Psych.*) inhibit, repress.
Verdrängung [fɛr'drɛŋuŋ], *f.* (—, *no pl.*) supplanting; (*Phys.*) displacement; (*Psych.*) inhibition, repression.
verdrehen [fɛr'dre:ən], *v.a.* twist (the wrong way); (*fig.*) misrepresent, distort.
verdreht [fɛr'dre:t], *adj.* cracked, cranky, crazy, queer.
Verdrehtheit [fɛr'dre:thaIt], *f.* (—, *no pl.*) crankiness.
Verdrehung [fɛr'dre:uŋ], *f.* (—, *pl.* —en) distortion; (*fig.*) misrepresentation.
verdrießen [fɛr'dri:sən], *v.a. irr.* vex, annoy.
verdrießlich [fɛr'dri:slIç], *adj.* (*thing*) vexatious, tiresome; (*person*) morose, peevish.

Verfälschung

verdrossen [fɛr'drɔsən], *adj.* annoyed; fretful, sulky.

Verdrossenheit [fɛr'drɔsənhaɪt], *f.* (—, *no pl.*) annoyance; fretfulness, sulkiness.

verdrücken [fɛr'drykən], *v.a.* (*sl.*) eat o.'s fill of. — *v.r.* (*coll.*) sich —, slink away; sneak away.

Verdruß [fɛr'drus], *m.* (—sses, *no pl.*) vexation, annoyance; — *bereiten*, give trouble, cause annoyance.

verduften [fɛr'duftən], *v.n.* (*aux.* sein) evaporate; (*fig.*) (*coll.*) take French leave, clear out.

verdummen [fɛr'dumən], *v.n.* (*aux.* sein) become stupid.

verdunkeln [fɛr'duŋkəln], *v.a.* blackout, obscure; (*fig.*) eclipse.

Verdunk(e)lung [fɛr'duŋk(ə)luŋ], *f.* (—, *no pl.*) darkening, eclipse; blackout.

Verdunk(e)lungsgefahr [vɛr'duŋk(ə)-luŋsgəfaːr], *f.* (—, *no pl.*) (*Law*) danger of prejudicing the course *or* administration of justice.

verdünnen [fɛr'dynən], *v.a.* thin out, dilute.

Verdünnung [fɛr'dynuŋ], *f.* (—, *no pl.*) attenuation; dilution.

verdunsten [fɛr'dunstən], *v.n.* (*aux.* sein) evaporate.

verdursten [fɛr'durstən], *v.n.* (*aux.* sein) die of thirst, perish with thirst.

verdüstern [fɛr'dyːstərn], *v.a.* darken, make gloomy.

verdutzen [fɛr'dutsən], *v.a.* disconcert, bewilder, nonplus.

Veredlung [fɛr'eːdluŋ], *f.* (—, *no pl.*) improvement, refinement.

verehelichen [fɛr'eːəlɪçən], *v.r.* (*obs.*) sich —, get married.

verehren [fɛr'eːrən], *v.a.* respect, revere, esteem; worship, adore.

Verehrer [fɛr'eːrər], *m.* (—s, *pl.* —) admirer; lover.

verehrlich [fɛr'eːrlɪç], *adj.* venerable.

verehrt [fɛr'eːrt], *adj.* honoured; *sehr —er Herr*, dear Sir.

Verehrung [fɛr'eːruŋ], *f.* (—, *no pl.*) reverence, veneration; worship, adoration.

verehrungswürdig [fɛr'eːruŋsvyrdɪç], *adj.* venerable.

vereidigt [fɛr'aɪdɪçt], *adj.* sworn in, bound by oath, under oath; —*er Bücherrevisor*, chartered accountant.

Vereidigung [fɛr'aɪdɪguŋ], *f.* (—, *no pl.*) swearing in; oathtaking.

Verein [fɛr'aɪn], *m.* (—s, *pl.* —e) union, association, society; club.

vereinbar [fɛr'aɪnbaːr], *adj.* compatible.

vereinbaren [fɛr'aɪnbaːrən], *v.a.* agree upon, arrange.

Vereinbarung [fɛr'aɪnbaːruŋ], *f.* (—, *pl.* —en) arrangement, agreement.

vereinen [fɛr'aɪnən], *v.a.* unite.

vereinfachen [fɛr'aɪnfaxən], *v.a.* simplify.

vereinigen [fɛr'aɪnɪgən], *v.a.* unite. — *v.r.* sich — *mit*, associate o.s. with, join with.

Vereinigung [fɛr'aɪnɪguŋ], *f.* (—, *pl.* —en) union; association.

vereinnahmen [fɛr'aɪnnaːmən], *v.a.* receive, take (*money*).

vereinsamen [fɛr'aɪnzaːmən], *v.n.* (*aux.* sein) become isolated, become lonely.

vereint [fɛr'aɪnt], *adj.* united, joined. — *adv.* in concert, (all) together.

vereinzelt [fɛr'aɪntsəlt], *adj.* sporadic, isolated. — *adv.* here and there, now and then.

Vereinzelung [fɛr'aɪntsəluŋ], *f.* (—, *pl.* —en) isolation; individualization.

vereisen [fɛr'aɪzən], *v.n.* become frozen, freeze; congeal.

Vereisung [fɛr'aɪzuŋ], *f.* (—, *pl.* —en) freezing, icing (up).

vereiteln [fɛr'aɪtəln], *v.a.* frustrate, thwart.

Vereitelung [fɛr'aɪtəluŋ], *f.* (—, *pl.* —en) frustration, thwarting.

vereitern [fɛr'aɪtərn], *v.n.* suppurate.

Vereiterung [fɛr'aɪtəruŋ], *f.* (—, *pl.* —en) suppuration.

verenden [fɛr'ɛndən], *v.n.* (*aux.* sein) (*animal*) die.

verengen [fɛr'ɛŋən], *v.a.* narrow, straighten, constrict.

Verengung [fɛr'ɛŋuŋ], *f.* (—, *pl.* —en) narrowing, straightening, contraction.

vererben [fɛr'ɛrbən], *v.a.* leave (by will), bequeath. — *v.r.* sich — *auf*, devolve upon, be hereditary.

vererblich [fɛr'ɛrplɪç], *adj.* (in)heritable, hereditary.

Vererbung [fɛr'ɛrbuŋ], *f.* (—, *no pl.*) heredity.

verewigen [fɛr'eːvɪgən], *v.a.* immortalise.

Verewigte [fɛr'eːvɪçtə], *m.* (—n, *pl.* —n) (*Poet.*) deceased.

Verfahren [fɛr'faːrən], *n.* (—s, *pl.* —) process; (*Law*) procedure; proceedings; *das — einstellen*, quash proceedings.

verfahren [fɛr'faːrən], *v.n.* *irr.* (*aux.* sein) proceed, act, operate. — *v.a.* spend (*money etc.*) on travelling. — *v.r.* sich —, (*Motor.*) lose o.'s way.

Verfall [fɛr'fal], *m.* (—s, *no pl.*) decay, decline; downfall, ruin; (*Comm.*) expiration, maturity; *in — geraten*, fall into ruin, decay.

verfallen [fɛr'falən], *v.n.* *irr.* (*aux.* sein) decay; go to ruin; lapse; (*Comm.*) fall due, expire; (*pledge*) become forfeit; *einem —*, become the property of, accrue to, devolve upon s.o.; (*fig.*) become the slave of s.o.; (*health*) decline, fail; *auf etwas —*, hit upon an idea. — *adj.* decayed, ruined.

Verfalltag [fɛr'falta:k], *m.* (—s, *pl.* —e) day of payment; maturity.

verfälschen [fɛr'fɛlʃən], *v.a.* falsify; adulterate.

Verfälschung [fɛr'fɛlʃuŋ], *f.* (—, *pl.* —en) falsification; adulteration.

verfangen

verfangen [fɛr'faŋən], *v.r. irr. sich* —, get entangled; *sich in ein Lügennetz* —, entangle o.s. in a tissue of lies.

verfänglich [fɛr'fɛŋlɪç], *adj.* risky; insidious.

verfärben [fɛr'fɛrbən], *v.r. sich* —, change colour.

verfassen [fɛr'fasən], *v.a.* compose, write, be the author of.

Verfasser [fɛr'fasər], *m.* (—s, *pl.* —) author, writer.

Verfassung [fɛr'fasuŋ], *f.* (—, *pl.* —en) composition; (*state*) constitution; state, condition, disposition.

verfassungsgemäß [fɛr'fasuŋsgəmɛːs], *adj.* constitutional.

verfassungswidrig [fɛr'fasuŋsviːdrɪç], *adj.* unconstitutional.

verfaulen [fɛr'faulən], *v.n.* (*aux.* sein) rot, putrefy.

verfechten [fɛr'fɛçtən], *v.a. irr.* defend, advocate; maintain.

verfehlen [fɛr'feːlən], *v.a.* fail, miss; fail to meet; fail to do; *den Weg* —, lose o.'s way.

verfehlt [fɛr'feːlt], *adj.* unsuccessful, false, abortive; *eine* —*e Sache*, a failure.

Verfehlung [fɛr'feːluŋ], *f.* (—, *pl.* —en) lapse.

verfeinern [fɛr'fainərn], *v.a.* refine, improve.

Verfeinerung [fɛr'fainəruŋ], *f.* (—, *pl.* —en) refinement, polish.

verfertigen [fɛr'fɛrtɪgən], *v.a.* make, manufacture.

verfilmen [fɛr'fɪlmən], *v.a.* make a film of, film.

verfinstern [fɛr'fɪnstərn], *v.r. sich* —, get dark; be eclipsed.

verflechten [fɛr'flɛçtən], *v.a. irr.* interweave, interlace. — *v.r. sich* —, (*fig.*) become entangled, become involved.

verfließen [fɛr'fliːsən], *v.n. irr.* (*aux.* sein) flow away; (*time*) elapse.

verflossen [fɛr'flɔsən], *adj.* past, bygone.

verfluchen [fɛr'fluːxən], *v.a.* curse, execrate.

verflucht [fɛr'fluːxt], *excl.* damn!

verflüchtigen [fɛr'flyçtɪgən], *v.r. sich* —, become volatile; evaporate; (*coll.*) make off, make o.s. scarce.

Verfluchung [fɛr'fluːxuŋ], *f.* (—, *pl.* —en) malediction, curse.

Verfolg [fɛr'fɔlk], *m.* (—(e)s, *no pl.*) progress, course.

verfolgen [fɛr'fɔlgən], *v.a.* pursue; persecute; prosecute.

Verfolger [fɛr'fɔlgər], *m.* (—s, *pl.* —) pursuer, persecutor.

Verfolgung [fɛr'fɔlguŋ], *f.* (—, *pl.* —en) pursuit; persecution; prosecution.

Verfolgungswahn [fɛr'fɔlguŋsvaːn], *m.* (—s, *no pl.*) persecution mania.

verfrüht [fɛr'fryːt], *adj.* premature.

verfügbar [fɛr'fyːkbaːr], *adj.* available.

verfügen [fɛr'fyːgən], *v.a.* decree, order. — *v.n.* — *über etwas*, have

control of s.th, have s.th. at o.'s disposal.

Verfügung [fɛr'fyːguŋ], *f.* (—, *pl.* —en) decree, ordinance; disposition, disposal; *einem zur* — *stehen*, be at s.o.'s service *or* disposal.

verführen [fɛr'fyːrən], *v.a.* seduce.

verführerisch [fɛr'fyːrərɪʃ], *adj.* seductive, alluring; (*coll.*) fetching.

Verführung [fɛr'fyːruŋ], *f.* (—, *no pl.*) seduction.

vergällen [fɛr'gɛlən], *v.a.* spoil, mar.

vergallopieren [fɛrgalo'piːrən], *v.r.* (*coll.*) *sich* —, blunder, overshoot the mark.

vergangen [fɛr'gaŋən], *adj.* past, gone, last.

Vergangenheit [fɛr'gaŋənhait], *f.* (—, *no pl.*) past, time past; (*Gram.*) past tense.

vergänglich [fɛr'gɛŋlɪç], *adj.* transient, transitory.

Vergaser [fɛr'gaːzər], *m.* (—s, *pl.* —) (*Motor.*) carburettor.

vergeben [fɛr'geːbən], *v.a. irr.* give away; forgive, pardon; confer, bestow.

vergebens [fɛr'geːbəns], *adv.* in vain, vainly.

vergeblich [fɛr'geːplɪç], *adj.* vain, futile, fruitless. — *adv.* in vain.

Vergebung [fɛr'geːbuŋ], *f.* (—, *no pl.*) forgiveness, pardon; (*office*) bestowal.

vergegenwärtigen [fɛrgeːgən'vɛrtɪgən], *v.a.* bring to mind, imagine.

Vergehen [fɛr'geːən], *n.* (—s, *pl.* —) offence lapse.

vergehen [fɛr'geːən], *v.n. irr.* (*aux.* sein) go away, pass (away); elapse; perish; (*time*) pass. — *v.r. sich* —, go wrong; offend; violate (*Law*, person).

vergelten [fɛr'gɛltən], *v.a. irr.* repay, reward, recompense.

Vergeltung [fɛr'gɛltuŋ], *f.* (—, *no pl.*) requital, retribution; reward, recompense.

vergessen [fɛr'gɛsən], *v.a. irr.* forget; *bei einem* —, leave behind.

Vergessenheit [fɛr'gɛsənhait], *f.* (— *no pl.*) oblivion.

vergeßlich [fɛr'gɛslɪç], *adj.* forgetful.

vergeuden [fɛr'gɔydən], *v.a.* waste, squander.

vergewaltigen [fɛrgə'valtɪgən], *v.a.* assault criminally, rape, violate; (*fig.*) coerce, force.

Vergewaltigung [fɛrgə'valtɪguŋ], *f.* (—, *no pl.*) criminal assault, rape; (*fig.*) coercion.

vergewissern [fɛrgə'vɪsərn], *v.r. sich* —, ascertain, make sure.

vergießen [fɛr'giːsən], *v.a. irr.* spill; shed.

vergiften [fɛr'gɪftən], *v.a.* poison.

Vergiftung [fɛr'gɪftuŋ], *f.* (—, *pl.* —en) poisoning.

vergilbt [fɛr'gɪlpt], *adj.* yellow with age.

Vergißmeinnicht [fɛr'gɪsmainnɪçt], *n.* (—s, *pl.* —e) (*Bot.*) forget-me-not.

Vergleich [fɛr'glaɪç], *m.* (—(e)s, *pl.* —e) comparison; agreement; (*Law*) compromise.

vergleichbar [fɛr'glaɪçba:r], *adj.* comparable.

vergleichen [fɛr'glaɪçən], *v.a. irr.* compare.

vergleichsweise [fɛr'glaɪçsvaɪzə], *adv.* by way of comparison; comparatively; (*Law*) by way of agreement.

Vergnügen [fɛr'gny:gən], *n.* (—s, *no pl.*) pleasure, enjoyment, fun.

vergnügen [fɛr'gny:gən], *v.a.* amuse, delight.

Vergnügung [fɛr'gny:guŋ], *f.* (—, *pl.* —en) entertainment, amusement.

vergönnen [fɛr'gœnən], *v.a.* grant, allow; not (be)grudge.

vergöttern [fɛr'gœtərn], *v.a.* idolise, worship.

vergraben [fɛr'gra:bən], *v.a. irr.* hide in the ground, bury.

vergrämt [fɛr'grɛ:mt], *adj.* careworn.

vergreifen [fɛr'graɪfən], *v.r. irr. sich — an,* lay violent hands on, violate.

vergriffen [fɛr'grɪfən], *adj.* out of stock, out of print.

vergrößern [fɛr'grø:sərn], *v.a.* enlarge, expand; increase; magnify; (*fig.*) exaggerate.

Vergrößerung [fɛr'grø:səruŋ], *f.* (—, *pl.* —en) magnification, enlargement, increase.

Vergrößerungsglas [fɛr'grø:səruŋsglas], *n.* (—es, *pl.* ⁻er) magnifying glass.

Vergünstigung [fɛr'gynstɪguŋ], *f.* (—, *pl.* —en) privilege, favour, special facility, concession.

vergüten [fɛr'gy:tən], *v.a. einem etwas —,* compensate s.o. for s.th.; reimburse s.o. for s.th.

Vergütung [fɛr'gy:tuŋ], *f.* (—, *pl.* —en) indemnification, compensation, reimbursement.

verhaften [fɛr'haftən], *v.a.* arrest.

Verhaftung [fɛr'haftuŋ], *f.* (—, *pl.* —en) arrest.

verhallen [fɛr'halən], *v.n.* (*aux.* sein) (*sound*) fade, die away.

verhalten [fɛr'haltən], *v.r. irr. sich —,* act, behave.

Verhalten [fɛr'haltən], *n.* (—s, *no pl.*) behaviour, conduct, demeanour.

Verhältnis [fɛr'hɛltnɪs], *n.* (—ses, *pl.* —se) (*Maths.*) proportion, ratio; relation; footing; love-affair, liaison; (*coll.*) mistress.

verhältnismäßig [fɛr'hɛltnɪsmɛsɪç], *adj.* proportionate, comparative.

Verhältniswort [fɛr'hɛltnɪsvɔrt], *n.* (—es, *pl.* ⁻er) preposition.

Verhältniszahl [fɛr'hɛltnɪstsa:l], *f.* (—, *pl.* —en) proportional number.

Verhaltungsmaßregel [fɛr'haltuŋsma:sre:gəl], *f.* (—, *pl.* —n) rule of conduct; instruction.

verhandeln [fɛr'handəln], *v.a.* discuss, transact. — *v.n.* negotiate.

Verhandlung [fɛr'handluŋ], *f.* (—, *pl.* —en) discussion, negotiation, transaction; (*Law*) proceedings.

verhängen [fɛr'hɛŋən], *v.a.* cover with; decree; inflict (a penalty) on s.o.

Verhängnis [fɛr'hɛŋnɪs], *n.* (—ses, *pl.* —se) fate, destiny; misfortune.

Verhängnisglaube [fɛr'hɛŋnɪsglaubə], *m.* (—ns, *no pl.*) fatalism.

verhängnisvoll [fɛr'hɛŋnɪsfɔl], *adj.* fateful, portentous; fatal.

verhärmt [fɛr'hɛrmt], *adj.* careworn.

verharren [fɛr'harən], *v.n.* remain; persist.

Verhärtung [fɛr'hɛrtuŋ], *f.* (—, *pl.* —en) hardening, hardened state; (*skin*) callosity; (*fig.*) obduracy.

verhaßt [fɛr'hast], *adj.* hated, odious.

verhätscheln [fɛr'hɛtʃəln], *v.a.* pamper, coddle.

verhauen [fɛr'hauən], *v.a.* beat, thrash.

Verheerung [fɛr'he:ruŋ], *f.* (—, *pl.* —en) devastation.

verhehlen [fɛr'he:lən], *v.a.* conceal, hide.

verheilen [fɛr'haɪlən], *v.n.* (*aux.* sein) heal.

verheimlichen [fɛr'haɪmlɪçən], *v.a.* keep secret, hush up.

verheiraten [fɛr'haɪra:tən], *v.a.* give in marriage, marry off. — *v.r. sich —,* marry, get married.

verheißen [fɛr'haɪsən], *v.a. irr.* promise.

Verheißung [fɛr'haɪsuŋ], *f.* (—, *pl.* —en) promise.

verhelfen [fɛr'hɛlfən], *v.n. irr. einem zu etwas —,* help s.o. to s.th.

Verherrlichung [fɛr'hɛrlɪçuŋ], *f.* (—, *no pl.*) glorification.

Verhetzung [fɛr'hɛtsuŋ], *f.* (—, *pl.* —en) incitement, instigation.

verhexen [fɛr'hɛksən], *v.a.* bewitch.

verhindern [fɛr'hɪndərn], *v.a.* hinder, prevent.

Verhinderung [fɛr'hɪndəruŋ], *f.* (—, *pl.* —en) prevention, obstacle.

verhöhnen [fɛr'hø:nən], *v.a.* deride, scoff at, jeer at.

Verhöhnung [fɛr'hø:nuŋ], *f.* (—, *pl.* —en) derision.

Verhör [fɛr'hø:r], *n.* (—s, *pl.* —e) hearing; (judicial) examination; *ins — nehmen,* question, interrogate, cross-examine.

verhören [fɛr'hø:rən], *v.a.* examine judicially, interrogate. — *v.r. sich —,* misunderstand.

verhüllen [fɛr'hylən], *v.a.* cover, wrap up, veil.

verhungern [fɛr'huŋərn], *v.n.* (*aux.* sein) starve.

verhungert [fɛr'huŋərt], *adj.* famished.

verhunzen [fɛr'huntsən], *v.a.* spoil, bungle.

verhüten [fɛr'hy:tən], *v.a.* prevent, avert.

Verhütung [fɛr'hy:tuŋ], *f.* (—, *no pl.*) prevention, warding off.

verirren [fɛr'ɪrən], *v.r. sich —,* go astray, lose o.'s way.

verirrt [fɛr'ɪrt], *adj.* stray, straying, lost.
verjagen [fɛr'ja:gən], *v.a.* drive away, chase away.
verjährt [fɛr'jɛ:rt], *adj.* statute-barred; prescriptive; obsolete; old.
verjubeln [fɛr'ju:bəln], *v.a.* play ducks and drakes with; squander.
verjüngen [fɛr'jyŋən], *v.a.* make younger; (*Archit.*) taper. — *v.r.* sich —, grow younger.
Verjüngung [fɛr'jyŋuŋ], *f.* (—, *pl.* —en) rejuvenation.
verkannt [fɛr'kant], *adj.* misunderstood.
verkappt [fɛr'kapt], *adj.* disguised, secret, in disguise.
Verkauf [fɛr'kauf], *m.* (—(e)s, *pl.* ‐e) sale.
verkaufen [fɛr'kaufən], *v.a.* sell.
Verkäufer [fɛr'kɔyfər], *m.* (—s, *pl.* —) seller; shop assistant, salesman.
verkäuflich [fɛr'kɔyflɪç], *adj.* for sale, saleable; mercenary.
Verkaufspreis [fɛr'kaufsprais], *m.* (—es, *pl.* —e) selling-price.
Verkehr [fɛr'ke:r], *m.* (—s, *no pl.*) traffic; commerce; intercourse; communication; — *mit,* association with; service (*trains, buses etc.*), transport.
verkehren [fɛr'ke:rən], *v.a.* turn upside down; transform; pervert. — *v.n.* frequent (a place), visit, associate (with); run, operate.
Verkehrsstraße [fɛr'ke:rsʃtra:sə], *f.* (—, *pl.* —n) thoroughfare.
Verkehrsstockung [fɛr'ke:rsʃtokuŋ], *f.* (—, *pl.* —en) traffic jam.
verkehrt [fɛr'ke:rt], *adj.* upside down; (*fig.*) wrong.
Verkehrtheit [fɛr'ke:rthait], *f.* (—, *pl.* —en) absurdity, piece of folly.
Verkehrung [fɛr'ke:ruŋ], *f.* (—, *pl.* —en) turning; inversion; perversion; misrepresentation; (*Gram.*) inversion.
verkennen [fɛr'kɛnən], *v.a.* *irr.* mistake, fail to recognize; misjudge (s.o.'s intentions).
verklagen [fɛr'kla:gən], *v.a.* sue; accuse.
verklären [fɛr'klɛ:rən], *v.a.* transfigure, illumine.
verklärt [fɛr'klɛ:rt], *adj.* transfigured; radiant.
verkleben [fɛr'kle:bən], *v.a.* paste over.
verkleiden [fɛr'klaidən], *v.a., v.r.* disguise (o.s.).
Verkleidung [fɛr'klaiduŋ]. *f.* (— *pl.* —en) disguise.
verkleinern [fɛr'klainərn], *v.a.* make smaller, diminish, reduce; belittle, disparage.
Verkleinerung [fɛr'klainəruŋ], *f.* (—, *pl.* —en) diminution, reduction; belittling, detraction.
Verkleinerungswort [fɛr'klainəruŋs-vort], *n.* (—s, *pl.* ‐er) (*Gram.*) diminutive.
verkneifen [fɛr'knaifən], *v.r.* *irr.* (*coll.*) sich etwas —, deny o.s. s.th.

verkniffen [fɛr'knifən], *adj.* pinched; shrewd; hard-bitten.
verknöchern [fɛr'knœçərn], *v.n.* (*aux.* sein) ossify; (*fig.*) become fossilised or inflexible.
Verknöcherung [fɛr'knœçəruŋ], *f.* (—, *pl.* —en) ossification; (*fig.*) fossilisation.
verknüpfen [fɛr'knypfən], *v.a.* tie, connect, link.
verkochen [fɛr'kɔxən], *v.n.* (*aux.* sein) boil away.
verkommen [fɛr'kɔmən], *v.n.* *irr.* (*aux.* sein) go from bad to worse, go to seed, decay, become depraved. — *adj.* demoralised, down and out, depraved.
Verkommenheit [fɛr'kɔmənhait], *f.* (—, *no pl.*) demoralisation; depravity.
verkörpern [fɛr'kœrpərn], *v.a.* embody.
verkrachen [fɛr'kraxən], *v.r.* sich —, quarrel, (*coll.*) have a row.
verkriechen [fɛr'kri:çən], *v.r.* *irr.* sich —, creep or crawl away; slink away, lie low.
verkümmern [fɛr'kymərn], *v.n.* (*aux.* sein) wear away, waste away; pine away.
verkünden [fɛr'kyndən], *v.a.* proclaim, announce, publish, prophesy.
Verkündigung [fɛr'kyndiguŋ], *f.* (—, *pl.* —en) announcement, proclamation; prediction.
Verkündung [fɛr'kynduŋ], *f.* (—, *pl.* —en) publication, proclamation.
Verkürzung [fɛr'kyrtsuŋ], *f.* (—, *pl.* —en) shortening, curtailment.
verlachen [fɛr'laxən], *v.a.* laugh at, deride.
verladen [fɛr'la:dən], *v.a.* *irr.* load, ship, freight.
Verladung [fɛr'la:duŋ], *f.* (—, *pl.* —en) loading, shipping.
Verlag [fɛr'la:k], *m.* (—(e)s, *pl.* —e) publication; publishing-house, (firm of) publishers.
Verlagsrecht [fɛr'la:ksrɛçt], *n.* (—s, *pl.* —e) copyright.
Verlangen [fɛr'laŋən], *n.* (—s, *no pl.*) demand, request; longing, desire.
verlangen [fɛr'laŋən], *v.a.* ask, demand, request.
verlängern [fɛr'lɛŋərn], *v.a.* lengthen, prolong, extend.
Verlängerung [fɛr'lɛŋəruŋ], *f.* (—, *pl.* —en) lengthening; (*period*) prolongation, extension.
verlangsamen [fɛr'laŋza:mən], *v.a.* slow down, slacken, decelerate.
Verlaß [fɛr'las], *m.* (—sses, *no pl.*) *es ist kein* — *auf dich,* you cannot be relied on.
verlassen [fɛr'lasən], *v.a.* *irr.* leave, abandon. — *v.r.* sich — *auf,* rely on, depend upon. — *adj.* forlorn, forsaken, deserted, desolate, lonely.
Verlassenheit [fɛr'lasənhait], *f.* (—, *no pl.*) desolation, loneliness, solitude.
verläßlich [fɛr'lɛslɪç], *adj.* reliable, trustworthy.

Verlauf [fɛr'lauf], *m.* (—(e)s, *no pl.*) lapse, expiration; course.

verlaufen [fɛr'laufən], *v.n. irr.* (*aux.* sein) (*time*) pass; (*period*) expire, elapse; develop(e), turn out. — *v.r. sich* —, lose o.'s way; (*colour*) run.

verlauten [fɛr'lautən], *v.n.* transpire.

verleben [fɛr'le:bən], *v.a.* pass, spend.

verlebt [fɛr'le:pt], *adj.* worn out; spent; (*Am.*) played out.

verlegen [fɛr'le:gən], *v.a.* (*domicile*) move, remove; (*things*) mislay; (*books*) publish; obstruct; adjourn; change to another date or place. — *v.r. sich auf etwas* —, devote o.s. to s.th. — *adj.* embarrassed, ill at ease.

Verlegenheit [fɛr'le:gənhait], *f.* (—, *pl.* —en) embarrassment, perplexity; predicament, difficulty.

Verleger [fɛr'le:gər], *m.* (—s, *pl.* —) publisher.

verleiden [fɛr'laidən], *v.a. einem etwas* —, spoil s.th. for s.o.

verleihen [fɛr'laiən], *v.a. irr.* lend; (*honour, title*) confer; bestow, award.

Verleiher [fɛr'laiər], *m.* (—s, *pl.* —) lender.

Verleihung [fɛr'laiuŋ], *f.* (—, *pl.* —en) lending, loan; (*medal, prize*) investiture; grant, conferring.

verleiten [fɛr'laitən], *v.a.* mislead, entice, induce; seduce.

Verleitung [fɛr'laituŋ], *f.* (—, *no pl.*) misleading, enticement, inducement; seduction.

verlernen [fɛr'lɛrnən], *v.a.* unlearn; forget.

verlesen [fɛr'le:zən], *v.a. irr.* read aloud, read out, recite. — *v.r. sich* —, misread.

verletzen [fɛr'lɛtsən], *v.a.* injure, hurt, wound, violate.

verletzend [fɛr'lɛtsənt], *adj.* offensive, insulting; cutting.

verletzlich [fɛr'lɛtslɪç], *adj.* vulnerable.

Verletzlichkeit [fɛr'lɛtslɪçkait], *f.* (—, *no pl.*) vulnerability.

Verletzung [fɛr'lɛtsuŋ], *f.* (—, *pl.* —en) hurt, wound; (*Law*) violation.

verleugnen [fɛr'lɔygnən], *v.a.* deny, renounce, disown.

Verleugnung [fɛr'lɔygnuŋ], *f.* (—, *pl.* —en) denial, abnegation.

verleumden [fɛr'lɔymdən], *v.a.* slander, calumniate, traduce.

Verleumdung [fɛr'lɔymduŋ], *f.* (—, *pl.* —en) slander, libel, calumny.

verlieben [fɛr'li:bən], *v.r. sich* — *in*, fall in love with.

Verliebte [fɛr'li:ptə], *m. or f.* (—n, *pl.* —n) person in love, lover.

Verliebtheit [fɛr'li:pthait], *f.* (—, *no pl.*) infatuation, amorousness.

verlieren [fɛr'li:rən], *v.a. irr.* lose.

Verlierer [fɛr'li:rər], *m.* (—s, *pl.* —) loser.

Verlies [fɛr'li:s], *n.* (—(s)es, *pl.* —(s)e) dungeon.

verloben [fɛr'lo:bən], *v.r. sich* — *mit*, become engaged to.

Verlöbnis [fɛr'lø:pnɪs], *n.* (—ses, *pl.* —se) (*rare*) engagement.

Verlobte [fɛr'lo:ptə], *m.* (—n, *pl.* —n) and *f.* (—n, *pl.* —n) fiancé(e), betrothed.

Verlobung [fɛr'lo:buŋ], *f.* (—, *pl.* —en) engagement, betrothal.

verlocken [fɛr'lɔkən], *v.a.* tempt, entice.

verlogen [fɛr'lo:gən], *adj.* lying, mendacious.

Verlogenheit [fɛr'lo:gənhait], *f.* (—, *no pl.*) mendacity.

verlohnen [fɛr'lo:nən], *v. impers.* be worth while.

verlöschen [fɛr'lœʃən], *v.a.* extinguish.

verlosen [fɛr'lo:zən], *v.a.* raffle; draw *or* cast lots for.

Verlosung [fɛr'lo:zuŋ], *f.* (—, *pl.* —en) raffle, lottery.

verlöten [fɛr'lø:tən], *v.a.* solder.

verlottern [fɛr'lɔtərn], *v.n.* (*aux.* sein) go to the dogs.

Verlust [fɛr'lust], *m.* (—es, *pl.* —e) loss; (*death*) bereavement; (*Mil.*) casualty.

verlustig [fɛr'lustɪç], *adj.* — *gehen*, lose s.th., forfeit s.th.

vermachen [fɛr'maxən], *v.a. einem etwas* —, bequeath s.th. to s.o.

Vermächtnis [fɛr'mɛçtnɪs], *n.* (—ses, *pl.* —sse) will; legacy, bequest; (*fig.*) *heiliges* —, sacred trust.

vermahlen [fɛr'ma:lən], *v.a.* grind (down).

Vermählung [fɛr'mɛ:luŋ], *f.* (—, *pl.* —en) marriage, wedding.

Vermahnung [fɛr'ma:nuŋ], *f.* (—, *pl.* —en) admonition, exhortation.

vermauern [fɛr'mauərn], *v.a.* wall up.

vermehren [fɛr'me:rən], *v.a.* augment, multiply, increase. — *v.r. sich* —, multiply.

Vermehrung [fɛr'me:ruŋ], *f.* (—, *pl.* —en) increase, multiplication.

vermeiden [fɛr'maidən], *v.a. irr.* avoid, shun, shirk.

vermeidlich [fɛr'maitlɪç], *adj.* avoidable.

Vermeidung [fɛr'maiduŋ], *f.* (—, *no pl.*) avoidance.

vermeintlich [fɛr'maintlɪç], *adj.* supposed, alleged, pretended; (*heir*) presumptive.

vermelden [fɛr'mɛldən], *v.a.* announce, notify.

vermengen [fɛr'mɛŋən], *v.a.* mingle, mix.

Vermerk [fɛr'mɛrk], *m.* (—s, *pl.* —e) entry, notice, note.

vermerken [fɛr'mɛrkən], *v.a.* observe, jot down.

vermessen [fɛr'mɛsən], *v.a. irr.* measure; (*land*) survey. — *adj.* bold, daring, audacious; arrogant.

Vermessenheit [fɛr'mɛsənhait], *f.* (—, *no pl.*) boldness, audacity; arrogance.

Vermesser [fɛr'mɛsər], *m.* (—s, *pl.* —) (*land*) surveyor.

Vermessung

Vermessung [fɛr'mɛsuŋ], *f.* (—, *pl.* —en) (*land*) survey; measuring.

vermieten [fɛr'mi:tən], *v.a.* let, lease, hire out.

Vermieter [fɛr'mi:tər], *m.* (—s, *pl.* —) landlord; hirer.

vermindern [fɛr'mɪndərn], *v.a.* diminish, lessen.

Verminderung [fɛr'mɪndəruŋ], *f.* (—, *pl.* —en) diminution, reduction, decrease, lessening.

vermischen [fɛr'mɪʃən], *v.a.* mix, mingle, blend.

vermissen [fɛr'mɪsən], *v.a.* miss; *vermißt sein*, be missing; *vermißt werden*, be missed.

vermitteln [fɛr'mɪtəln], *v.n.* mediate. — *v.a.* adjust; negotiate, secure.

Vermittler [fɛr'mɪtlər], *m.* (—s, *pl.* —) mediator; agent, middleman.

Vermittlung [fɛr'mɪtluŋ], *f.* (—, *pl.* —en) mediation, intervention.

vermöbeln [fɛr'mø:bəln], *v.a.* (*sl.*) *einen* —, thrash s.o.

vermodern [fɛr'mo:dərn], *v.n.* (*aux.* sein) moulder, rot.

vermöge [fɛr'mø:gə], *prep.* (*Genit.*) by virtue of, by dint of, on the strength of.

Vermögen [fɛr'mø:gən], *n.* (—s, *pl.* —) faculty, power; means, assets; fortune, wealth, riches; *er hat* —, he is a man of property; *nach bestem* —, to the best of o.'s ability.

vermögen [fɛr'mø:gən], *v.a. irr.* be able to, have the power to, be capable of.

vermögend [fɛr'mø:gənt], *adj.* wealthy.

Vermögensbestand [fɛr'mø:gənsbəʃtant], *m.* (—s, *pl.* ⁻e) assets.

Vermögenssteuer [fɛr'mø:gənsʃtɔyər], *f.* (—, *pl.* —n) property tax.

vermorscht [fɛr'mɔrʃt], *adj.* mouldering, rotten.

vermuten [fɛr'mu:tən], *v.a.* suppose, conjecture, surmise, presume; guess.

vermutlich [fɛr'mu:tlɪç], *adj.* likely, probable.

Vermutung [fɛr'mu:tuŋ], *f.* (—, *pl.* —en) guess, supposition, conjecture.

vernachlässigen [fɛr'naxlɛsɪgən], *v.a.* neglect.

Vernachlässigung [fɛr'naxlɛsɪguŋ], *f.* (—, *pl.* —en) neglect, negligence.

vernarren [fɛr'narən], *v.r. sich* — (*in*, *Acc.*), become infatuated (with).

vernarrt [fɛr'nart], *adj.* madly in love.

vernaschen [fɛr'naʃən], *v.a.* squander (money) on sweets.

vernehmbar [fɛr'ne:mba:r], *adj.* audible; *sich* — *machen*, make o.s. heard.

Vernehmen [fɛr'ne:mən], *n.* (—s, *no pl.*) *dem* — *nach*, from what o. hears.

vernehmen [fɛr'ne:mən], *v.a. irr.* hear, learn; (*Law*) examine, interrogate.

vernehmlich [fɛr'ne:mlɪç], *adj.* audible, distinct, clear.

Vernehmlichkeit [fɛr'ne:mlɪçkaɪt], *f.* (—, *no pl.*) audibility.

Vernehmung [fɛr'ne:muŋ], *f.* (—, *pl.* —en) (*Law*) interrogation, examination.

verneigen [fɛr'naɪgən], *v.r. sich* —, curts(e)y, bow.

Verneigung [fɛr'naɪguŋ], *f.* (—, *pl.* —en) curts(e)y, bow.

verneinen [fɛr'naɪnən], *v.a.* deny, answer in the negative.

Verneinung [fɛr'naɪnuŋ], *f.* (—, *pl.* —en) negation, denial; (*Gram.*) negation, negative.

vernichten [fɛr'nɪçtən], *v.a.* annihilate, destroy utterly, exterminate.

Vernichtung [fɛr'nɪçtuŋ], *f.* (—, *no pl.*) annihilation, extinction, destruction.

vernieten [fɛr'ni:tən], *v.a.* rivet.

Vernunft [fɛr'nunft], *f.* (—, *no pl.*) reason, sense, intelligence, judgment; *gesunde* —, common sense; — *annehmen*, listen to reason; *einen zur* — *bringen*, bring s.o. to his senses.

vernünftig [fɛr'nynftɪç], *adj.* sensible, reasonable, rational.

veröden [fɛr'ø:dən], *v.n.* (*aux.* sein) become desolate, become devastated.

Verödung [fɛr'ø:duŋ], *f.* (—, *no pl.*) devastation, desolation.

veröffentlichen [fɛr'œfəntlɪçən], *v.a.* publish.

Veröffentlichung [fɛr'œfəntlɪçuŋ], *f.* (—, *pl.* —en) publication.

verordnen [fɛr'ɔrdnən], *v.a.* order, command, ordain; (*Med.*) prescribe.

Verordnung [fɛr'ɔrdnuŋ], *f.* (—, *pl.* —en) order; (*Law*) decree, edict, statute; (*Med.*) prescription.

verpassen [fɛr'pasən], *v.a.* lose by delay, let slip; (*train etc.*) miss.

verpfänden [fɛr'pfɛndən], *v.a.* pawn, pledge.

Verpfänder [fɛr'pfɛndər], *m.* (—s, *pl.* —) mortgager.

Verpfändung [fɛr'pfɛnduŋ], *f.* (—, *pl.* —en) pawning, pledging.

verpflanzen [fɛr'pflantsən], *v.a.* transplant.

Verpflanzung [fɛr'pflantsuŋ], *f.* (—, *pl.* —en) transplantation.

verpflegen [fɛr'pfle:gən], *v.a.* board, provide food for, feed; nurse.

Verpflegung [fɛr'pfle:guŋ], *f.* (—, *no pl.*) board, catering; food.

Verpflegungskosten [fɛr'pfle:guŋskɔstən], *f. pl.* (cost of) board and lodging.

verpflichten [fɛr'pflɪçtən], *v.a.* bind, oblige, engage.

verpflichtend [fɛr'pflɪçtənt], *adj.* obligatory.

Verpflichtung [fɛr'pflɪçtuŋ], *f.* (—, *pl.* —en) obligation, duty; liability, engagement.

verplaudern [fɛr'plaudərn], *v.a.* spend (time) chatting.

verplempern [fɛr'plɛmpərn], *v.a.* (*coll.*) spend foolishly, fritter away.

verpönt [fɛr'pø:nt], *adj.* frowned upon; taboo.

verprassen [fɛr'prasən], *v.a.* squander (money) in riotous living.

verpuffen [fɛr'pufən], v.n. (aux. sein) (coll.) fizzle out.

verpulvern [fɛr'pulvərn], v.a. fritter away.

Verputz [fɛr'puts], m. (—es, no pl.) plaster.

verquicken [fɛr'kvɪkən], v.a. amalgamate; mix up.

Verrat [fɛr'raːt], m. (—(e)s, no pl.) treachery, treason.

verraten [fɛr'raːtən], v.a. irr. betray; disclose; das verrät die Hand des Künstlers, this proclaims the hand of the artist.

Verräter [fɛr'rɛːtər], m. (—s, pl. —) traitor.

verräterisch [fɛr'rɛːtərɪʃ], adj. treacherous, treasonable, perfidious; (fig.) tell-tale.

verrauchen [fɛr'rauxən], v.n. (aux. sein) evaporate; (fig.) blow over; cool down.

verräuchern [fɛr'rɔyçərn], v.a. smoke, fill with smoke.

verräumen [fɛr'rɔymən], v.a. misplace, mislay.

verrauschen [fɛr'rauʃən], v.n. (aux. sein) (sound) die away; pass away.

verrechnen [fɛr'rɛçnən], v.a. reckon up. — v.r. sich —, miscalculate.

Verrechnung [fɛr'rɛçnuŋ], f. (—, pl. — en) reckoning-up.

Verrechnungsscheck [fɛr'rɛçnuŋsʃɛk], m. (—s, pl. —e, —s) crossed cheque, non-negotiable cheque.

verregnen [fɛr'reːgnən], v.a. spoil by rain.

verreiben [fɛr'raibən], v.a. irr. rub away; rub hard.

verreisen [fɛr'raizən], v.n. (aux. sein) go on a journey.

verrenken [fɛr'rɛŋkən], v.a. sprain, dislocate.

Verrenkung [fɛr'rɛŋkuŋ], f. (—, pl. —en) sprain, dislocation.

verrichten [fɛr'rɪçtən], v.a. do, perform, acquit o.s. of; (prayer) say.

verriegeln [fɛr'riːgəln], v.a. bolt.

verringern [fɛr'rɪŋərn], v.a. reduce, diminish.

Verringerung [fɛr'rɪŋəruŋ], f. (—, no pl.) diminution, reduction.

verrinnen [fɛr'rɪnən], v.n. irr. (aux. sein) run off; (fig.) elapse.

verrosten [fɛr'rɔstən], v.n. (aux. sein) rust.

verrottet [fɛr'rɔtət], adj. rotten.

verrucht [fɛr'ruːxt], adj. villainous, atrocious, heinous, infamous.

Verruchtheit [fɛr'ruːxthait], f. (—, no pl.) villainy.

verrücken [fɛr'rykən], v.a. shift, displace.

verrückt [fɛr'rykt], adj. crazy, mad.

Verrückte [fɛr'ryktə], m. (—n, pl. —n) madman. — f. (—n, pl. —n) madwoman.

Verrücktheit [fɛr'rykthait], f. (—, pl. —en) craziness; mad act.

Verruf [fɛr'ruːf], m. (—s, no pl.) discredit, ill repute.

verrufen [fɛr'ruːfən], adj. notorious, of ill repute.

Vers [fɛrs], m. (—es, pl. —e) verse.

versagen [fɛr'zaːgən], v.a. einem etwas —, deny s.o. s.th., refuse s.o. s.th. — v.n. fail, break down; (voice) falter; sich etwas —, abstain from s.th., deny o.s. s.th.

Versager [fɛr'zaːgər], m. (—s, pl. —) misfire; failure, unsuccessful person, flop.

versammeln [fɛr'zaməln], v.a. gather around, convene. — v.r. sich —, assemble, meet.

Versammlung [fɛr'zamluŋ], f. (—, pl. —en) assembly, meeting, gathering, convention.

Versand [fɛr'zant], m. (—s, no pl.) dispatch, forwarding, shipping, shipment.

versanden [fɛr'zandən], v.n. (aux. sein) silt up.

Versandgeschäft [fɛr'zantgəʃɛft], n. (—s, pl. —e) export business; mail order business.

Versatzamt [fɛr'zatsamt], n. (—s, pl. ⸚er) pawn-shop.

versauen [fɛr'zauən], v.a. (sl.) make a mess of.

versauern [fɛr'zauərn], v.n. (aux. sein) turn sour; (fig.) become morose.

versaufen [fɛr'zaufən], v.a. irr. (sl.) squander (money) on drink, drink away.

versäumen [fɛr'zɔymən], v.a. miss, omit, lose by delay; leave undone; neglect.

Versäumnis [fɛr'zɔymnɪs], n. (—ses, pl. —se) neglect, omission; (time) loss.

Versbau ['fɛrsbau], m. (—s, no pl.) versification; verse structure.

verschachern [fɛr'ʃaxərn], v.a. barter away.

verschaffen [fɛr'ʃafən], v.a. provide, procure, obtain, get.

verschämt [fɛr'ʃɛːmt], adj. shamefaced, bashful.

verschanzen [fɛr'ʃantsən], v.a. fortify.

Verschanzung [fɛr'ʃantsuŋ], f. (—, pl. —en) fortification, entrenchment.

verschärfen [fɛr'ʃɛrfən], v.a. heighten, intensify, sharpen.

verscharren [fɛr'ʃarən], v.a. cover with earth; bury hurriedly.

verscheiden [fɛr'ʃaidən], v.n. irr. (aux. sein) die, pass away.

verschenken [fɛr'ʃɛŋkən], v.a. make a present of, give away.

verscherzen [fɛr'ʃɛrtsən], v.a. sich etwas —, forfeit s.th.

verscheuchen [fɛr'ʃɔyçən], v.a. scare away, frighten away; Sorgen —, banish care.

verschicken [fɛr'ʃɪkən], v.a. send on, send out, forward, transmit; evacuate.

Verschickung [fɛr'ʃɪkuŋ], f. (—, no pl.) forwarding, transmission; evacuation; banishment, exile.

verschieben [fɛrˈʃiːbən], *v.a. irr.* shift, move; delay, put off, defer, postpone.

Verschiebung [fɛrˈʃiːbuŋ], *f.* (—, *pl.* —en) removal; postponement; (*fig.*) black marketeering.

verschieden [fɛrˈʃiːdən], *adj.* different, diverse; deceased, departed; (*pl.*) some, several, sundry.

verschiedenartig [fɛrˈʃiːdənaːrtɪç], *adj.* varied, various, heterogeneous.

verschiedenerlei [fɛrˈʃiːdənərlaɪ], *indecl. adj.* diverse, of various kinds.

Verschiedenheit [fɛrˈʃiːdənhaɪt], *f.* (—, *pl.* —en) difference; diversity, variety.

verschiedentlich [fɛrˈʃiːdəntlɪç], *adv.* variously, severally; repeatedly.

verschiffen [fɛrˈʃɪfən], *v.a.* export, ship.

verschimmeln [fɛrˈʃɪməln], *v.n. (aux. sein)* go mouldy.

verschlafen [fɛrˈʃlaːfən], *v.a. irr.* sleep through, sleep away. — *v.r. sich —,* oversleep. — *adj.* sleepy, drowsy.

Verschlag [fɛrˈʃlaːk], *m.* (—s, *pl.* ⸚e) partition, box, cubicle.

verschlagen [fɛrˈʃlaːgən], *v.a. irr. es verschlägt mir den Atem,* it takes my breath away. — *adj.* cunning, crafty, sly.

verschlechtern [fɛrˈʃlɛçtərn], *v.a.* worsen, make worse. — *v.r. sich —,* deteriorate.

Verschlechterung [fɛrˈʃlɛçtəruŋ], *f.* (—, *no pl.*) deterioration.

verschleiern [fɛrˈʃlaɪərn], *v.a.* veil.

Verschleierung [fɛrˈʃlaɪəruŋ], *f.* (—, *pl.* —en) veiling, concealment; camouflage.

verschleißen [fɛrˈʃlaɪsən], *v.a. irr.* wear out, waste.

verschlemmen [fɛrˈʃlɛmən], *v.a.* squander on eating and drinking.

verschleppen [fɛrˈʃlɛpən], *v.a.* carry off, deport; kidnap; protract, spread; put off, procrastinate.

verschleudern [fɛrˈʃlɔydərn], *v.a.* waste; sell at cut prices.

verschließen [fɛrˈʃliːsən], *v.a. irr.* lock, lock up.

verschlimmern [fɛrˈʃlɪmərn], *v.a.* make worse. — *v.r. sich —,* get worse, worsen, deteriorate.

Verschlimmerung [fɛrˈʃlɪməruŋ], *f.* (—, *no pl.*) worsening, deterioration.

verschlingen [fɛrˈʃlɪŋən], *v.a. irr.* swallow up, devour.

verschlossen [fɛrˈʃlɔsən], *adj.* reserved, uncommunicative, withdrawn.

Verschlossenheit [fɛrˈʃlɔsənhaɪt], *f.* (—, *no pl.*) reserve.

verschlucken [fɛrˈʃlukən], *v.a.* swallow, gulp down; (*fig.*) suppress. — *v.r. sich —,* swallow the wrong way.

verschlungen [fɛrˈʃluŋən], *adj.* intricate, complicated.

Verschluß [fɛrˈʃlus], *m.* (—sses. *pl.* ⸚sse) lock; clasp; fastening; *unter — haben,* keep under lock and key.

Verschlußlaut [fɛrˈʃluslaut], *m.* (—s, *pl.* —e) (*Phon.*) explosive, plosive, stop.

verschmachten [fɛrˈʃmaxtən], *v.n. (aux. sein)* languish, pine; be parched.

Verschmähung [fɛrˈʃmɛːuŋ], *f.* (—, *no pl.*) disdain, scorn, rejection.

Verschmelzung [fɛrˈʃmɛltsuŋ], *f.* (—, *no pl.*) coalescence, fusion, blending.

verschmerzen [fɛrˈʃmɛrtsən], *v.a.* get over; bear stoically, make the best of.

verschmitzt [fɛrˈʃmɪtst], *adj.* cunning, crafty, mischievous.

verschmutzen [fɛrˈʃmutsən], *v.n. (aux. sein)* get dirty.

verschnappen [fɛrˈʃnapən], *v.r. sich —,* blurt out a secret, give o.s. away, let the cat out of the bag.

verschneiden [fɛrˈʃnaɪdən], *v.a. irr.* (*wings*) clip; (*trees*) prune; (*animals*) castrate; (*wine*) blend.

verschneien [fɛrˈʃnaɪən], *v.n. (aux. sein)* be snowed up, be covered with snow, be snowbound.

Verschnitt [fɛrˈʃnɪt], *m.* (—s, *no pl.*) blended wine, blend.

Verschnittene [fɛrˈʃnɪtənə], *m.* (—n, *pl.* —n) eunuch.

verschnörkelt [fɛrˈʃnœrkəlt], *adj.* adorned with flourishes.

verschnupft [fɛrˈʃnupft], *adj.* — *sein,* have a cold in the head; (*fig.*) be vexed.

verschnüren [fɛrˈʃnyːrən], *v.a.* (*shoes*) lace up; (*parcel*) tie up.

verschonen [fɛrˈʃoːnən], *v.a.* spare, exempt from.

verschönern [fɛrˈʃøːnərn], *v.a.* embellish, beautify.

Verschönerung [fɛrˈʃøːnəruŋ], *f.* (—, *pl.* —en) embellishment, adornment.

Verschonung [fɛrˈʃoːnuŋ], *f.* (—, *no pl.*) exemption; forbearance.

verschossen [fɛrˈʃɔsən], *adj.* faded, discoloured; (*fig.*) madly in love.

verschreiben [fɛrˈʃraɪbən], *v.a. irr.* prescribe. — *v.r. sich —,* make a mistake in writing.

verschrien [fɛrˈʃriːən], *adj.* notorious.

verschroben [fɛrˈʃroːbən], *adj.* cranky, eccentric.

Verschrobenheit [fɛrˈʃroːbənhaɪt], *f.* (—, *pl.* —en) crankiness, eccentricity.

verschrumpfen [fɛrˈʃrumpfən], *v.n.* (*aux. sein*) shrivel up.

verschüchtern [fɛrˈʃyçtərn], *v.a.* intimidate.

verschulden [fɛrˈʃuldən], *v.a.* bring on, be the cause of; be guilty of.

verschuldet [fɛrˈʃuldət], *adj.* in debt.

Verschuldung [fɛrˈʃulduŋ], *f.* (—, *no pl.*) indebtedness.

verschütten [fɛrˈʃytən], *v.a.* spill; bury alive.

verschwägern [fɛrˈʃvɛːgərn], *v.r. sich —,* become related by marriage.

Verschwägerung [fɛrˈʃvɛːgəruŋ], *f.* (—, *no pl.*) relationship by marriage.

verschwatzen [fɛrˈʃvatsən], *v.a.* gossip (the time) away, spend o.'s time gossiping.

verschweigen [fɛrˈʃvaɪgən], *v.a. irr.* keep secret, keep (news) from, hush up.

Verständnis

verschwenden [fɛrˈʃvɛndən], *v.a.* squander, waste.

verschwenderisch [fɛrˈʃvɛndərɪʃ], *adj.* prodigal, profuse, lavish; wasteful.

Verschwendung [fɛrˈʃvɛnduŋ], *f.* (—, *no pl.*) waste, extravagance.

Verschwendungssucht [fɛrˈʃvɛnduŋs- zuxt], *f.* (—, *no pl.*) prodigality; extravagance.

verschwiegen [fɛrˈʃviːgən], *adj.* discreet, close, secretive.

Verschwiegenheit [fɛrˈʃviːgənhait], *f.* (—, *no pl.*) discretion, secrecy.

verschwimmen [fɛrˈʃvɪmən], *v.n. irr.* (*aux.* sein) become blurred.

verschwinden [fɛrˈʃvɪndən], *v.n. irr.* (*aux.* sein) disappear, vanish.

verschwommen [fɛrˈʃvɔmən], *adj.* vague, blurred.

verschwören [fɛrˈʃvøːrən], *v.r. irr. sich —*, plot, conspire.

Verschwörer [fɛrˈʃvøːrer], *m.* (—s, *pl.* —) conspirator.

Verschwörung [fɛrˈʃvøːruŋ], *f.* (—, *pl.* —en) conspiracy.

Versehen [fɛrˈzeːən], *n.* (—s, *pl.* —) error, mistake, oversight.

versehen [fɛrˈzeːən], *v.a. irr.* provide; perform; fill (an office); *einen — mit*, furnish s.o. with. *— v.r. sich —*, make a mistake.

versehren [fɛrˈzeːrən], *v.a.* wound; disable.

versenden [fɛrˈzɛndən], *v.a. irr.* forward, consign, send off.

Versender [fɛrˈzɛndər], *m.* (—s, *pl.*—) consigner, exporter.

Versendung [fɛrˈzɛnduŋ], *f.* (—, *no pl.*) transmission, shipping.

Versendungskosten [fɛrˈzɛnduŋskɔs- tən], *f. pl.* forwarding charges.

versengen [fɛrˈzɛŋən], *v.a.* singe, scorch.

versenken [fɛrˈzɛŋkən], *v.a.* sink; (*ship*) scuttle.

Versenkung [fɛrˈzɛŋkuŋ], *f.* (—, *no pl.*) sinking; hollow; (*ship*) scuttling; (*Theat.*) trap-door.

versessen [fɛrˈzɛsən], *adj. — sein auf*, be bent upon, be mad on.

versetzen [fɛrˈzɛtsən], *v.a.* transplant, remove; give; pawn, pledge; transfer; (*pupil*) promote to a higher form. *— v.r. sich in die Lage eines anderen —*, put o.s. in s.o. else's position.

versichern [fɛrˈzɪçərn], *v.a.* assert, declare, aver, assure (s.o. of s.th); insure (s.th.).

Versicherung [fɛrˈzɪçəruŋ], *f.* (—, *pl.* —en) assurance, assertion; insurance.

Versicherungsgesellschaft [fɛrˈzɪçə- ruŋsgəzɛlʃaft], *f.* (—, *pl.* —en) insurance company.

Versicherungsprämie [fɛrˈzɪçəruŋs- prɛːmjə], *f.* (—, *pl.* —n) insurance premium.

versiegbar [fɛrˈziːkbaːr], *adj.* exhaustible.

versiegeln [fɛrˈziːgəln], *v.a.* seal (up).

versiegen [fɛrˈziːgən], *v.n.* (*aux.* sein) dry up, be exhausted.

versilbern [fɛrˈzɪlbərn], *v.a.* plate with silver; (*fig.*) convert into money.

versinken [fɛrˈzɪŋkən], *v.n. irr.* sink; (*ship*) founder; sink; *versunken sein*, be absorbed (in s.th.).

Versmaß [ˈfɛrsmaːs], *n.* (—es, *pl.* —e) metre.

versoffen [fɛrˈzɔfən], *adj.* (*vulg.*) drunken.

versohlen [fɛrˈzoːlən], *v.a.* (*coll.*) thrash (s.o.).

versöhnen [fɛrˈzøːnən], *v.r. sich mit einem —*, become reconciled with s.o.

versöhnlich [fɛrˈzøːnlɪç], *adj.* propitiatory, conciliatory.

Versöhnung [fɛrˈzøːnuŋ], *f.* (—, *no pl.*) reconciliation.

versorgen [fɛrˈzɔrgən], *v.a.* provide with; take care of; support, maintain.

Versorger [fɛrˈzɔrgər], *m.* (—s, *pl.* —) provider.

Versorgung [fɛrˈzɔrguŋ], *f.* (—, *no pl.*) provision, maintenance.

verspäten [fɛrˈʃpɛːtən], *v.r. sich —*, be late, be behind time; (*train*) be overdue.

Verspätung [fɛrˈʃpɛːtuŋ], *f.* (—, *no pl.*) delay; lateness.

verspeisen [fɛrˈʃpaizən], *v.a.* eat up.

versperren [fɛrˈʃpɛrən], *v.a.* block up, barricade, close.

verspielen [fɛrˈʃpiːlən], *v.a.* lose (at play); gamble away. *— v.r. sich —*, play wrong.

verspielt [fɛrˈʃpiːlt], *adj.* playful.

verspotten [fɛrˈʃpɔtən], *v.a.* deride, scoff at.

versprechen [fɛrˈʃprɛçən], *v.a. irr.* promise. *— v.r. sich —*, make a slip of the tongue.

Versprechen [fɛrˈʃprɛçən], *n.* (—s, *pl.* —) promise.

versprengen [fɛrˈʃprɛŋən], *v.a.* disperse.

verspüren [fɛrˈʃpyːrən], *v.a.* feel, perceive.

verstaatlichen [fɛrˈʃtaːtlɪçən], *v.a.* nationalise.

Verstand [fɛrˈʃtant], *m.* (—(e)s, *no pl.*) intellect, intelligence, sense; understanding, reason, mind.

verstandesmäßig [fɛrˈʃtandəsmɛːsɪç], *adj.* rational, reasonable.

Verstandesschärfe [fɛrˈʃtandəsʃɛrfə], *f.* (—, *no pl.*) penetration, acumen.

verständig [fɛrˈʃtɛndɪç], *adj.* judicious, sensible, reasonable.

verständigen [fɛrˈʃtɛndɪgən], *v.a.* inform, notify. *— v.r. sich mit einem —*, come to an agreement with s.o.

Verständigung [fɛrˈʃtɛndɪguŋ], *f.* (—, *pl.* —en) understanding, agreement; information; arrangement.

verständlich [fɛrˈʃtɛntlɪç], *adj.* intelligible, clear, understandable.

Verständnis [fɛrˈʃtɛntnɪs], (—ses, *no pl.*) comprehension, understanding, perception, insight.

verständnisinnig

verständnisinnig [fɛrˈʃtɛntnɪsɪnɪç], *adj.* sympathetic; having profound insight.

verstärken [fɛrˈʃtɛrkən], *v.a.* strengthen, reinforce, intensify.

Verstärker [fɛrˈʃtɛrkər], *m.* (—s, *pl.* —) amplifier; magnifier.

Verstärkung [fɛrˈʃtɛrkuŋ], *f.* (—, *pl.* —en) strengthening, intensification, amplification; (*Mil.*) reinforcements.

verstauben [fɛrˈʃtaubən], *v.n.* (*aux.* sein) get dusty.

verstauchen [fɛrˈʃtauxən], *v.a.* wrench, sprain, dislocate.

verstauen [fɛrˈʃtauən], *v.a.* stow away.

Versteck [fɛrˈʃtɛk], *n.* (—s, *pl.* —e) hiding-place; place of concealment; —(en) *spielen*, play hide-and-seek.

verstecken [fɛrˈʃtɛkən], *v.a.* hide, conceal.

versteckt [fɛrˈʃtɛkt], *adj.* indirect, veiled.

verstehen [fɛrˈʃteːən], *v.a. irr.* understand, comprehend.

versteigen [fɛrˈʃtaigən], *v.r. irr. sich* —, climb too high; (*fig.*) go too far.

versteigern [fɛrˈʃtaigərn], *v.a.* sell by auction.

Versteigerung [fɛrˈʃtaigəruŋ], *f.* (—, *pl.* —en) auction, public sale.

versteinern [fɛrˈʃtainərn], *v.n.* (*aux.* sein) turn into stone, petrify.

verstellbar [fɛrˈʃtɛlbaːr], *adj.* adjustable.

verstellen [fɛrˈʃtɛlən], *v.a.* adjust; (*voice*) disguise. — *v.r. sich* —, sham, pretend.

versterben [fɛrˈʃtɛrbən], *v.n. irr.* (*aux.* sein) (*Poet.*) die.

versteuern [fɛrˈʃtɔyərn], *v.a.* pay tax on.

verstiegen [fɛrˈʃtiːgən], *adj.* eccentric, extravagant.

verstimmen [fɛrˈʃtɪmən], *v.a.* (*Mus.*) put out of tune; (*fig.*) put out of humour, annoy.

Verstimmtheit [fɛrˈʃtɪmthait], *f.* (—, *no pl.*) ill-humour, ill-temper, pique.

Verstimmung [fɛrˈʃtɪmuŋ], *f.* (—, *pl.* —en) bad temper, ill-feeling.

verstockt [fɛrˈʃtɔkt], *adj.* stubborn, obdurate.

Verstocktheit [fɛrˈʃtɔkthait], *f.* (—, *no pl.*) stubbornness, obduracy.

verstohlen [fɛrˈʃtoːlən], *adj.* surreptitious, clandestine, furtive.

verstopfen [fɛrˈʃtɔpfən], *v.a.* stop up; block (up); *verstopft sein*, be constipated.

Verstopfung [fɛrˈʃtɔpfuŋ], *f.* (—, *pl.* —en) obstruction; constipation.

verstorben [fɛrˈʃtɔrbən], *adj.* deceased, late.

verstört [fɛrˈʃtøːrt], *adj.* troubled, worried; distracted.

Verstörtheit [fɛrˈʃtøːrthait], *f.* (—, *no pl.*) consternation, agitation; distraction; haggardness.

Verstoß [fɛrˈʃtoːs], *m.* (—es, *pl.* —e) blunder, mistake; offence.

verstoßen [fɛrˈʃtoːsən], *v.a. irr.* cast off, disown, repudiate. — *v.n.* —

gegen, offend against, act in a manner contrary to.

verstreichen [fɛrˈʃtraiçən], *v.n. irr.* (*aux.* sein) (*time*) elapse, pass away.

verstricken [fɛrˈʃtrɪkən], *v.a.* entangle, ensnare.

Verstrickung [fɛrˈʃtrɪkuŋ], *f.* (—, *pl.* —en) entanglement.

verstümmeln [fɛrˈʃtyməln], *v.a.* mutilate, mangle.

verstummen [fɛrˈʃtumən], *v.n.* (*aux.* sein) grow silent; become speechless.

Verstümmlung [fɛrˈʃtymluŋ], *f.* (—, *pl.* —en) mutilation.

Versuch [fɛrˈzuːx], *m.* (—s, *pl.* —e) attempt, trial, endeavour; (*science*) experiment; (*Lit.*) essay.

versuchen [fɛrˈzuːxən], *v.a.* try, attempt, endeavour; (*food*) taste; *einen* —, tempt s.o.

Versucher [fɛrˈzuːxər], *m.* (—s, *pl.* —) tempter.

Versuchskaninchen [fɛrˈzuːxskaniːnçən], *n.* (—s, *pl.* —) (*fig.*) guinea-pig.

Versuchung [fɛrˈzuːxuŋ], *f.* (—, *pl.* —en) temptation.

versündigen [fɛrˈzyndɪgən], *v.r. sich* —, sin (against).

Versunkenheit [fɛrˈzuŋkənhait], *f.* (—, *no pl.*) absorption, preoccupation.

vertagen [fɛrˈtaːgən], *v.a.* adjourn, prorogue.

Vertagung [fɛrˈtaːguŋ], *f.* (—, *pl.* —en) adjournment, prorogation.

vertauschen [fɛrˈtauʃən], *v.a.* exchange, barter, mistake, confuse.

verteidigen [fɛrˈtaidɪgən], *v.a.* defend, uphold, vindicate; (*fig.*) maintain.

Verteidiger [fɛrˈtaidɪgər], *m.* (—s, *pl.* —) defender; (*Law*) counsel for the defence.

Verteidigung [fɛrˈtaidɪguŋ], *f.* (—, *no pl.*) defence; justification.

Verteidigungskrieg [fɛrˈtaidɪguŋskriːk], *m.* (—(e)s, *pl.* —e) defensive war.

verteilen [fɛrˈtailən], *v.a.* distribute, allot, allocate.

Verteilung [fɛrˈtailuŋ], *f.* (—, *pl.* —en) distribution, apportionment.

verteuern [fɛrˈtɔyərn], *v.a.* make dearer, raise the price of.

verteufelt [fɛrˈtɔyfəlt], *adj.* devilish. — *adv.* (*coll.*) awfully, infernally.

vertiefen [fɛrˈtiːfən], *v.a.* deepen.

vertieft [fɛrˈtiːft], *adj.* absorbed, deep in thought.

Vertiefung [fɛrˈtiːfuŋ], *f.* (—, *pl.* —en) cavity, recess, hollow; (*knowledge*) deepening; (*fig.*) absorption.

vertilgen [fɛrˈtɪlgən], *v.a.* wipe out, exterminate; (*food*) (*coll.*) polish off.

Vertilgung [fɛrˈtɪlguŋ], *f.* (—, *no pl.*) extermination, extirpation.

Vertrag [fɛrˈtraːk], *m.* (—(e)s, *pl.* ⁀e) contract, agreement; (*Pol.*) treaty, pact, convention.

vertragen [fɛrˈtraːgən], *v.a. irr.* suffer, endure; (*food*) digest. — *v.r. sich* — *mit*, get on well with.

262

Verwandlung

vertraglich [fɛr'traːklɪç], *adj.* as per contract, according to agreement.

verträglich [fɛr'trɛːklɪç], *adj.* accommodating, peaceable.

vertragsmäßig [fɛr'traːksmɛːsɪç], *adj.* according to contract.

vertragswidrig [fɛr'traːksvɪːdrɪç], *adj.* contrary to contract.

vertrauen [fɛr'trauən], *v.n.* rely (upon), trust (in).

Vertrauen [fɛr'trauən], *n.* (—s, *no pl.*) confidence, trust, reliance.

vertrauenerweckend [fɛr'trauənɛrvɛkənt], *adj.* inspiring confidence.

Vertrauensbruch [fɛr'trauənsbrux], *m.* (—es, *pl.* ⁻e) breach of faith.

Vertrauensmann [fɛr'trauənsman], *m.* (—s, *pl.* ⁻er) confidant; delegate; person entrusted with s.th.; (*Ind.*) shop steward.

vertrauensselig [fɛr'trauənszeːlɪç], *adj.* confiding, trusting.

Vertrauensvotum [fɛr'trauənsvoːtum], *n.* (—s, *pl.* —ten) vote of confidence.

vertrauenswürdig [fɛr'trauənsvyrdɪç], *adj.* trustworthy.

vertraulich [fɛr'traulɪç], *adj.* confidential; familiar.

Vertraulichkeit [fɛr'traulɪçkaɪt], *f.* (—, *pl.* —en) familiarity.

verträumt [fɛr'trɔymt], *adj.* dreamy.

vertraut [fɛr'traut], *adj.* intimate, familiar; conversant.

Vertraute [fɛr'trautə], *m.* (—n, *pl.* —n) close friend, confidant.

Vertrautheit [fɛr'trauthaɪt], *f.* (—, *no pl.*) familiarity.

vertreiben [fɛr'traɪbən], *v.a. irr.* drive away, expel; eject; (*person*) banish; (*time*) pass, kill; (*goods*) sell.

Vertreibung [fɛr'traɪbuŋ], *f.* (—, *no pl.*) expulsion; banishment.

vertreten [fɛr'treːtən], *v.a. irr.* represent (s.o.), deputise for (s.o.).

Vertreter [fɛr'treːtər], *m.* (—s, *pl.* —) representative, deputy; (*Comm.*) agent.

Vertretung [fɛr'treːtuŋ], *f.* (—, *pl.* —en) representation, agency.

Vertrieb [fɛr'triːp], *m.* (—s, *pl.* —e) sale; distribution.

vertrinken [fɛr'trɪŋkən], *v.a. irr.* spend *or* waste money on drink.

vertrocknen [fɛr'trɔknən], *v.n.* (*aux.* sein) dry up, wither.

vertrödeln [fɛr'trøːdəln], *v.a.* fritter (o.'s time) away.

vertrösten [fɛr:trøːstən], *v.a.* console; put off; put (s.o.) off with fine words; fob (s.o.) off with vain hopes.

Vertröstung [fɛr'trøːstuŋ], *f.* (—, *pl.* —en) comfort; empty promises.

vertun [fɛr'tuːn], *v.a. irr.* squander, waste.

vertuschen [fɛr'tuʃən], *v.a.* hush up.

verübeln [fɛr'yːbəln], *v.a.* take amiss.

verüben [fɛr'yːbən], *v.a.* commit, perpetrate.

verunehren [fɛr'uneːrən], *v.a.* dishonour, disgrace.

verunglimpfen [fɛr'unglɪmpfən], *v.a.* bring into disrepute; defame, calumniate.

Verunglimpfung [fɛr'unglɪmpfuŋ], *f.* (—, *pl.* —en) defamation, detraction, calumny.

verunglücken [fɛr'unglykən], *v.n.* (*aux.* sein) (*person*) meet with an accident; be killed; (*thing*) misfire, fail.

verunreinigen [fɛr'unraɪnɪgən], *v.a.* contaminate.

Verunreinigung [fɛr'unraɪnɪguŋ], *f.* (—, *pl.* —en) contamination.

verunstalten [fɛr'unʃtaltən], *v.a.* disfigure, deface.

Verunstaltung [fɛr'unʃtaltuŋ], *f.* (—, *pl.* —en) disfigurement.

Veruntreuung [fɛr'untrɔyuŋ], *f.* (—, *pl.* —en) embezzlement, misappropriation.

verunzieren [fɛr'untsiːrən], *v.a.* disfigure, spoil.

verursachen [fɛr'uːrzaxən], *v.a.* cause, occasion.

verurteilen [fɛr'urtaɪlən], *v.a.* condemn; (*Law*) sentence.

Verurteilung [fɛr'urtaɪluŋ], *f.* (—, *no pl.*) condemnation; (*Law*) sentence.

vervielfältigen [fɛr'fiːlfɛltɪgən], *v.a.* multiply; duplicate, make copies of.

Vervielfältigung [fɛr'fiːlfɛltɪguŋ], *f.* (—, *pl.* —en) multiplication; duplication, copying.

vervollkommnen [fɛr'fɔlkɔmnən], *v.a.* improve, perfect.

Vervollkommnung [fɛr'fɔlkɔmnuŋ], *f.* (—, *no pl.*) improvement, perfection.

vervollständigen [fɛr'fɔlʃtɛndɪgən], *v.a.* complete.

Vervollständigung [fɛr'fɔlʃtɛndɪguŋ], *f.* (—, *no pl.*) completion.

verwachsen [fɛr'vaksən], *v.n. irr.* (*aux.* sein) grow together; be overgrown. — *adj.* deformed.

verwahren [fɛr'vaːrən], *v.a.* take care of, preserve, secure. — *v.r.* sich — gegen, protest against.

verwahrlosen [fɛr'vaːrloːzən], *v.a.* neglect. — *v.n.* (*aux.* sein) be in need of care and protection, be neglected.

Verwahrlosung [fɛr'vaːrloːzuŋ], *f.* (—, *no pl.*) neglect.

Verwahrung [fɛr'vaːruŋ], *f.* (—, *no pl.*) keeping; charge; *in* — *geben*, deposit, give into s.o.'s charge; — *einlegen gegen*, enter a protest against.

verwalten [fɛr'valtən], *v.a.* manage, administer.

Verwalter [fɛr'valtər], *m.* (—s, *pl.* —) administrator, manager; steward, bailiff.

Verwaltung [fɛr'valtuŋ], *f.* (—, *pl.* —en) administration, management; Civil Service.

Verwaltungsbezirk [fɛr'valtuŋsbətsɪrk], *m.* (—s, *pl.* —e) administrative district.

Verwandlung [fɛr'vandluŋ], *f.* (—, *pl.* —en) alteration, transformation.

Verwandlungskünstler

Verwandlungskünstler [fɛr'vandluŋs-kynstlər], *m.* (—s, *pl.* —) quick-change artist.

verwandt [fɛr'vant], *adj.* related; cognate; congenial.

Verwandte [fɛr'vantə], *m.* (—n, *pl.* —n) relative, relation; kinsman; *der nächste* —, next of kin.

Verwandtschaft [fɛr'vantʃaft], *f.* (—, *pl.* —en) relationship; relations, family; congeniality, sympathy.

verwarnen [fɛr'varnən], *v.a.* admonish, forewarn.

Verwarnung [fɛr'varnuŋ], *f.* (—, *pl.* —en) admonition.

Verwässerung [fɛr'vɛsərun], *f.* (—, *pl.* —en) dilution.

verwechseln [fɛr'vɛksəln], *v.a.* confuse; mistake for.

Verwechslung [fɛr'vɛksluŋ], *f.* (—, *pl.* —en) confusion, mistake.

verwegen [fɛr've:gən], *adj.* bold, audacious.

Verwegenheit [fɛr've:gənhaɪt], *f.* (—, *pl.* —en) boldness, audacity.

verweichlichen [fɛr'vaɪçliçən], *v.a.* coddle. — *v.n.* (*aux.* sein) become effeminate.

verweigern [fɛr'vaɪgərn], *v.a.* refuse, deny; reject.

Verweigerung [fɛr'vaɪgəruŋ], *f.* (—, *pl.* —en) refusal, denial; rejection.

verweilen [fɛr'vaɪlən], *v.n.* remain; tarry; stay (with), dwell (on).

verweint [fɛr'vaɪnt], *adj.* (*eyes*) red with weeping.

Verweis [fɛr'vaɪs], *m.* (—es, *pl.* —e) reproof, reprimand, rebuke.

verweisen [fɛr'vaɪzən], *v.a.* irr. reprimand; banish, exile; — *auf etwas*, refer to s.th., hint at s.th.

Verweisung [fɛr'vaɪzuŋ], *f.* (—, *pl.* —en) banishment, exile; reference.

verweltlichen [fɛr'vɛltliçən], *v.a.* secularise, profane.

verwenden [fɛr'vɛndən], *v.a.* use, make use of; apply to, employ in, utilize.

Verwendung [fɛr'vɛnduŋ], *f.* (—, *pl.* —en) application, use, expenditure, employment.

verwerfen [fɛr'vɛrfən], *v.a.* irr. reject, disapprove of.

verwerflich [fɛr'vɛrfliç], *adj.* objectionable.

Verwertung [fɛr've:rtuŋ], *f.* (—, *no pl.*) utilisation.

verwesen [fɛr've:zən], *v.a.* administer. — *v.n.* (*aux.* sein) rot, decompose, putrefy.

Verweser [fɛr've:zər], *m.* (—s, *pl.* —) administrator.

Verwesung [fɛr've:zuŋ], *f.* (—, *no pl.*) (*office*) administration; putrefaction, rotting.

verwickeln [fɛr'vɪkəln], *v.a.* entangle, involve.

verwickelt [fɛr'vɪkəlt], *adj.* intricate, complicated, involved.

Verwicklung [fɛr'vɪkluŋ], *f.* (—, *pl.* —en) entanglement, involvement, complication.

verwildern [fɛr'vɪldərn], *v.n.* (*aux.* sein) run wild.

verwildert [fɛr'vɪldərt], *adj.* wild, uncultivated, overgrown; (*fig.*) intractable.

Verwilderung [fɛr'vɪldəruŋ], *f.* (—, *no pl.*) running wild, growing wild.

verwirken [fɛr'vɪrkən], *v.a.* forfeit.

verwirklichen [fɛr'vɪrkliçən], *v.a.* realise. — *v.r. sich* —, materialise, come true.

Verwirklichung [fɛr'vɪrkliçuŋ], *f.* (—, *no pl.*) realisation, materialisation.

Verwirkung [fɛr'vɪrkuŋ], *f.* (—, *no pl.*) forfeiture.

verwirren [fɛr'vɪrən], *v.a.* disarrange, throw into disorder, entangle; puzzle, bewilder, confuse, disconcert.

Verwirrung [fɛr'vɪruŋ], *f.* (—, *pl.* —en) bewilderment, confusion.

verwischen [fɛr'vɪʃən], *v.a.* blot out, smudge, obliterate.

verwittern [fɛr'vɪtərn], *v.n.* (*aux.* sein) be weather-beaten.

verwöhnen [fɛr'vø:nən], *v.a.* spoil, pamper, coddle.

verworfen [fɛr'vɔrfən], *adj.* profligate; rejected, reprobate.

verworren [fɛr'vɔrən], *adj.* confused, perplexed; intricate; (*speech*) rambling.

verwundbar [fɛr'vuntba:r], *adj.* vulnerable.

verwunden [fɛr'vundən], *v.a.* wound, hurt, injure.

verwundern [fɛr'vundərn], *v.r. sich* —, be surprised, wonder, be amazed.

Verwunderung [fɛr'vundəruŋ], *f.* (—, *no pl.*) surprise, astonishment, amazement.

Verwundung [fɛr'vunduŋ], *f.* (—, *pl.* —en) wounding, wound, injury.

verwunschen [fɛr'vunʃən], *adj.* enchanted, spellbound, bewitched.

verwünschen [fɛr'vynʃən], *v.a.* curse; cast a spell on, bewitch.

verwünscht [fɛr'vynʃt], *excl.* confound it!

Verwünschung [fɛr'vynʃuŋ], *f.* (—, *pl.* —en) curse, malediction.

verwüsten [fɛr'vy:stən], *v.a.* devastate, ravage, lay waste.

Verwüstung [fɛr'vy:stuŋ], *f.* (—, *pl.* —en) devastation.

verzagen [fɛr'tsa:gən], *v.n.* (*aux.* sein) lose heart, lose courage.

verzagt [fɛr'tsa:kt], *adj.* fainthearted, discouraged.

Verzagtheit [fɛr'tsa:kthaɪt], *f.* (—, *no pl.*) faintheartedness.

verzählen [fɛr'tsɛ:lən], *v.r. sich* —, miscount.

verzapfen [fɛr'tsapfən], *v.a.* sell (liquor) on draught; (*fig.*) tell (a story), talk (nonsense).

verzärteln [fɛr'tsɛ:rtəln], *v.a.* pamper, coddle; spoil.

verzaubern [fɛr'tsaubərn], *v.a.* bewitch, charm, put a spell on.

Vision

verzehren [fɛr'tseːrən], *v.a.* consume, eat. — *v.r. sich* — *in*, pine away with, be consumed with.

Verzehrung [fɛr'tseːruŋ], *f.* (—, *no pl.*) (*obs.*) consumption, tuberculosis.

verzeichnen [fɛr'tsaɪçnən], *v.a.* draw badly; note down, register, record.

Verzeichnis [fɛr'tsaɪçnɪs], *n.* (—ses, *pl.* —se) catalogue, list, register.

verzeihen [fɛr'tsaɪən], *v.a. irr.* forgive, pardon.

verzeihlich [fɛr'tsaɪlɪç], *adj.* pardonable, forgivable, excusable, venial.

Verzeihung [fɛr'tsaɪuŋ], *f.* (—, *no pl.*) pardon, forgiveness; *ich bitte um* —, I beg your pardon.

verzerren [fɛr'tsɛrən], *v.a.* distort.

Verzerrung [fɛr'tsɛruŋ], *f.* (—, *pl.* —en) distortion; (*face*) grimace.

verzetteln [fɛr'tsɛtəln], *v.a.* disperse, scatter.

Verzicht [fɛr'tsɪçt], *m.* (—(e)s, *no pl.*) renunciation, resignation.

verzichten [fɛr'tsɪçtən], *v.n.* forgo, renounce.

verziehen [fɛr'tsiːən], *v.a. irr.* distort; spoil (*child*). — *v.n.* (*aux.* sein) go away, move away.

Verzierung [fɛr'tsiːruŋ], *f.* (—, *pl.* —en) decoration, ornament.

verzögern [fɛr'tsøːgərn], *v.a.* delay, defer, retard, protract, procrastinate. — *v.r. sich* —, be delayed.

Verzögerung [fɛr'tsøːgəruŋ], *f.* (—, *pl.* —en) delay, retardation, procrastination; time-lag.

verzollen [fɛr'tsɔlən], *v.a.* pay duty on.

Verzücktheit [fɛr'tsʏkthaɪt], *f.* (—, *no pl.*) ecstasy, rapture.

Verzug [fɛr'tsuːk], *m.* (—s, *no pl.*) delay.

verzweifeln [fɛr'tsvaɪfəln], *v.n.* despair, be desperate.

Verzweiflung [fɛr'tsvaɪfluŋ], *f.* (—, *no pl.*) despair.

verzwickt [fɛr'tsvɪkt], *adj.* complicated, intricate, tricky.

Vesuv [ve'zuːf], *m.* Mount Vesuvius.

Vetter ['vɛtər], *m.* (—s, *pl.* —n) cousin.

Vetternwirtschaft ['vɛtərnvɪrtʃaft], *f.* (—, *no pl.*) nepotism.

Vexierbild [vɛ'ksiːrbɪlt], *n.* (—s, *pl.* —er) picture-puzzle.

Vexierspiegel [vɛ'ksiːrʃpiːgəl], *m.* (—s, *pl.* —) distorting mirror.

vibrieren [vi'briːrən], *v.n.* vibrate.

Vieh [fiː], *n.* (—s, *no pl.*) cattle, livestock.

Viehfutter ['fiːfutər], *n.* (—s, *no pl.*) forage, fodder, feeding-stuff.

viehisch ['fiːɪʃ], *adj.* beastly, brutal.

Viehwagen ['fiːvaːgən], *m.* (—s, *pl.* —) cattle-truck.

Viehweide ['fiːvaɪdə], *f.* (—, *pl.* —n) pasture, pasturage.

Viehzüchter ['fiːtsʏçtər], *m.* (—s, *pl.* —) cattle-breeder.

viel [fiːl], *adj.* much, a great deal, a lot; (*pl.*) many.

vielartig ['fiːlartɪç], *adj.* multifarious.

vieldeutig ['fiːldɔytɪç], *adj.* ambiguous, equivocal.

Vieleck ['fiːlɛk], *n.* (—s, *pl.* —e) polygon.

vielerlei ['fiːlərlaɪ], *adj.* of many kinds, various.

vielfältig ['fiːlfɛltɪç], *adj.* manifold.

vielfarbig ['fiːlfarbɪç], *adj.* multicoloured, variegated.

Vielfraß ['fiːlfraːs], *m.* (—es, *pl.* —e) glutton.

vielgeliebt ['fiːlgəliːpt], *adj.* much loved.

vielgereist ['fiːlgəraɪst], *adj.* much travelled.

vielleicht [fi'laɪçt], *adv.* perhaps, maybe.

vielmals ['fiːlmaːls], *adv.* many times, frequently, much.

Vielmännerei ['fiːlmɛnəˌraɪ], *f.* (—, *no pl.*) polyandry.

vielmehr [fiːl'meːr], *adv.* rather, much more. — *conj.* rather, on the other hand.

vielsagend ['fiːlzaːgənt], *adj.* expressive, full of meaning.

vielseitig ['fiːlzaɪtɪç], *adj.* multilateral; (*fig.*) versatile.

Vielseitigkeit ['fiːlzaɪtɪçkaɪt], *f.* (—, *no pl.*) versatility.

vielverheißend ['fiːlfɛrhaɪsənt], *adj.* promising, auspicious.

Vielweiberei ['fiːlvaɪbəˌraɪ], *f.* (—, *no pl.*) polygamy.

vier [fiːr], *num. adj.* four.

Viereck ['fiːrɛk], *n.* (—s, *pl.* —e) square, quadrangle.

viereckig ['fiːrɛkɪç], *adj.* square.

vierfüßig ['fiːrfyːsɪç], *adj.* four-footed.

vierhändig ['fiːrhɛndɪç], *adj.* four-handed; — *spielen*, (*piano*) play duets.

vierschrötig ['fiːrʃrøːtɪç], *adj.* robust, thick-set, stocky.

vierseitig ['fiːrzaɪtɪç], *adj.* quadrilateral.

vierstimmig ['fiːrʃtɪmɪç], *adj.* (*Mus.*) four-part; for four voices.

vierteilen ['fiːrtaɪlən], *v.a.* quarter, divide into four parts.

Viertel ['fɪrtəl], *n.* (—s, *pl.* —) quarter, fourth part.

Viertelstunde [fɪrtəl'ʃtundə], *f.* (—, *pl.* —n) quarter of an hour.

viertens ['fiːrtəns], *num. adv.* fourthly, in the fourth place.

Vierwaldstättersee [fiːr'valtʃtɛtərzeː], *m.* Lake Lucerne.

vierzehn ['fɪrtseːn], *num. adj.* fourteen; — *Tage*, a fortnight.

vierzig ['fɪrtsɪç], *num. adj.* forty.

Vietnam [vjet'naːm], *n.* Vietnam.

Vikar [vi'kaːr], *m.* (—s, *pl.* —e) curate.

Violinschlüssel [vio'liːnʃlʏsəl], *m.* (—s, *pl.* —) (*Mus.*) treble clef.

Virtuosität [vɪrtuozi'tɛːt], *f.* (—, *no pl.*) mastery, virtuosity.

Visage [vi'zaːʒə], *f.* (—, *pl.* —n) (*coll.*) face.

Visier [vi'ziːr], *n.* (—, *pl.* —e) visor; (*gun*) sight.

Vision [vi'zjoːn], *f.* (—, *pl.* —en) vision.

Visionär

Visionär [vizjo'nɛ:r], *m.* (**—s,** *pl.* **—e**) visionary.

Visitenkarte [vi'zi:tənkartə], *f.* (**—,** *pl.* **—n**) card, visiting card.

Visum ['vi:zum], *n.* (**—s,** *pl.* **Visa**) visa.

Vizekönig ['vi:tsəkø:nɪç], *m.* (**—s,** *pl.* **—e**) viceroy.

Vlies [fli:s], *n.* (**—es,** *pl.* **—e**) fleece.

Vogel ['fo:gəl], *m.* (**—s,** *pl.* **⸚**) bird; (*coll.*) fellow; *einen — haben,* be off o.'s head.

Vogelbauer ['fo:gəlbauər], *n.* (**—s,** *pl.* **—**) bird-cage.

Vogelfänger ['fo:gəlfɛŋər], *m.* (**—s,** *pl.* **—**) fowler, bird-catcher.

vogelfrei ['fo:gəlfraɪ], *adj.* outlawed, proscribed.

Vogelfutter ['fo:gəlfutər], *n.* (**—s,** *no pl.*) bird-seed.

Vogelhändler ['fo:gəlhɛndlər], *m.* (**—s,** *pl.* **—**) bird-dealer.

Vogelhaus ['fo:gəlhaus], *n.* (**—es,** *pl.* **⸚er**) aviary.

Vogelkenner ['fo:gəlkɛnər], *m.* (**—s,** *pl.* **—**) ornithologist.

Vogelkunde ['fo:gəlkundə], *f.* (**—,** *no pl.*) ornithology.

Vogelperspektive ['fo:gəlpɛrspɛkti:və], *f.* (**—,** *no pl.*) bird's-eye view.

Vogelschau ['fo:gəlʃau], *f.* (**—,** *no pl.*) bird's-eye view.

Vogelsteller ['fo:gəlʃtɛlər], *m.* (**—s,** *pl.* **—**) fowler, bird-catcher.

Vogesen [vo'ge:zən], *pl.* Vosges Mountains.

Vogler ['fo:glər], *m.* (**—s,** *pl.* **—**) fowler.

Vogt [fo:kt], *m.* (**—(e)s,** *pl.* **⸚e**) prefect, bailiff, steward, provost.

Vogtei [fo:k'taɪ], *f.* (**—,** *pl.* **—en**) prefecture, bailiwick.

Vokabel [vo'ka:bəl], *f.* (**—,** *pl.* **—n**) word, vocable.

Vokabelbuch [vo'ka:bəlbu:x], *n.* (**—(e)s,** *pl.* **⸚er**) vocabulary (book).

Vokal [vo'ka:l], *m.* (**—s,** *pl.* **—e**) vowel.

Vokativ [voka'ti:f], *m.* (**—s,** *pl.* **—e**) (*Gram.*) vocative.

Volk [fɔlk], *n.* (**—(e)s,** *pl.* **⸚er**) people, nation; *das gemeine —,* mob, the common people.

Völkerkunde ['fœlkərkundə], *f.* (**—,** *no pl.*) ethnology.

Völkerrecht ['fœlkərrɛçt], *n.* (**—s,** *no pl.*) international law.

Völkerschaft ['fœlkərʃaft], *f.* (**—,** *pl.* **—en**) tribe, people.

Völkerwanderung ['fœlkərvandəruŋ], *f.* (**—,** *pl.* **—en**) mass migration.

Volksabstimmung ['fɔlksapʃtimuŋ], *f.* (**—,** *pl.* **—en**) referendum.

Volksausgabe ['fɔlksausga:bə], *f.* (**—,** *pl.* **—n**) popular edition.

Volksbeschluß ['fɔlksbəʃlus], *m.* (**—sses,** *pl.* **⸚sse**) plebiscite.

Volksbibliothek ['fɔlksbibliote:k], *f.* (**—,** *pl.* **—en**) public library.

Volkscharakter ['fɔlkskaraktər], *m.* (**—s,** *no pl.*) national character.

Volksentscheid ['fɔlksɛntʃaɪt], *m.* (**—s,** *pl.* **—e**) plebiscite.

Volksführer ['fɔlksfy:rər], *m.* (**—s,** *pl.* **—**) demagogue.

Volksheer ['fɔlkshe:r], *n.* (**—s,** *pl.* **—e**) national army.

Volksherrschaft ['fɔlkshɛrʃaft], *f.* (**—,** *no pl.*) democracy.

Volkshochschule ['fɔlkshoxʃu:lə], *f.* (**—,** *no pl.*) adult education (classes).

Volksjustiz ['fɔlksjusti:ts], *f.* (**—,** *no pl.*) lynch-law.

Volkskunde ['fɔlkskundə], *f.* (**—,** *no pl.*) folklore.

Volkslied ['fɔlksli:t], *n.* (**—s,** *pl.* **—er**) folk-song.

Volksschicht ['fɔlksʃɪçt], *f.* (**—,** *pl.* **—en**) class.

Volksschule ['fɔlksʃu:lə], *f.* (**—,** *pl.* **—n**) primary school; elementary school.

Volkssitte ['fɔlkszɪtə], *f.* (**—,** *pl.* **—n**) national custom.

Volkssprache ['fɔlksʃpra:xə], *f.* (**—,** *pl.* **—n**) vernacular.

Volksstamm ['fɔlksʃtam], *m.* (**—s,** *pl.* **⸚e**) tribe.

Volkstracht ['fɔlkstraxt], *f.* (**—,** *pl.* **—en**) national costume.

volkstümlich ['fɔlksty:mlɪç], *adj.* national, popular.

Volksvertretung ['fɔlksfɛrtre:tuŋ], *f.* (**—,** *no pl.*) representation of the people, parliamentary representation.

Volkswirt ['fɔlksvɪrt], *m.* (**—s,** *pl.* **—e**) political economist.

Volkswirtschaft ['fɔlksvɪrtʃaft], *f.* (**—,** *no pl.*) political economy.

Volkszählung ['fɔlkstse:luŋ], *f.* (**—,** *pl.* **—en**) census.

voll [fɔl], *adj.* full, filled; whole, complete, entire.

vollauf ['fɔlauf], *adv.* abundantly.

Vollbart ['fɔlba:rt], *m.* (**—s,** *pl.* **⸚e**) beard.

vollberechtigt ['fɔlbərɛçtɪçt], *adj.* fully entitled.

Vollbild ['fɔlbɪlt], *n.* (**—s,** *pl.* **—er**) full-length portrait, full-page illustration.

Vollblut ['fɔlblu:t], *n.* (**—s,** *pl.* **⸚er**) thoroughbred.

vollblütig ['fɔlbly:tɪç], *adj.* full-blooded, thoroughbred.

vollbringen [fɔl'brɪŋən], *v.a.* irr. accomplish, achieve, complete.

Vollbringung [fɔl'brɪŋuŋ], *f.* (**—,** *no pl.*) achievement.

Volldampf ['fɔldampf], *m.* (**—es,** *no pl.*) full steam.

vollenden [fɔl'ɛndən], *v.a.* finish, complete.

vollendet [fɔl'ɛndət], *adj.* finished; accomplished.

vollends ['fɔlɛnts], *adv.* quite, altogether, wholly, entirely, moreover.

Vollendung [fɔl'ɛnduŋ], *f.* (**—,** *no pl.*) completion; perfection.

Völlerei [fœlə'raɪ], *f.* (**—,** *pl.* **—en**) gluttony.

266

vollführen [fɔl'fy:rən], *v.a.* execute, carry out.
Vollgefühl ['fɔlgəfy:l], *n.* (—s, *no pl.*) consciousness, full awareness.
Vollgenuß ['fɔlgənus], *m.* (—sses, *no pl.*) full enjoyment.
vollgültig ['fɔlgyltɪç], *adj.* fully valid; unexceptionable.
Vollheit ['fɔlhaɪt], *f.* (—, *no pl.*) fullness, plenitude.
völlig ['fœlɪç], *adj.* entire, whole, complete.
vollinhaltlich ['fɔlɪnhaltlɪç], *adv.* to its full extent.
volljährig ['fɔljɛ:rɪç], *adj.* of age.
Volljährigkeit ['fɔljɛ:rɪçkaɪt], *f.* (—, *no pl.*) adult years, majority.
vollkommen ['fɔlkɔmən], *adj.* perfect. — *adv.* entirely.
Vollkommenheit [fɔl'kɔmənhaɪt], *f.* (—, *no pl.*) perfection.
Vollmacht ['fɔlmaxt], *f.* (—, *pl.* —en) authority; fullness of power; power of attorney.
vollsaftig ['fɔlzaftɪç], *adj.* juicy, succulent.
vollständig ['fɔlʃtɛndɪç], *adj.* complete, full. — *adv.* entirely.
vollstrecken [fɔl'ʃtrɛkən], *v.a.* execute, carry out.
Vollstrecker [fɔl'ʃtrɛkər], *m.* (—s, *pl.* —) executor.
volltönig ['fɔltø:nɪç], *adj.* sonorous.
vollwertig ['fɔlvɛrtɪç], *adj.* standard, sterling.
vollzählig ['fɔltsɛ:lɪç], *adj.* complete.
vollziehen [fɔl'tsi:ən], *v.a. irr.* execute, carry out, ratify.
vollziehend [fɔl'tsi:ənt], *adj.* executive.
Vollziehungsgewalt [fɔl'tsi:uŋsgəvalt], *f.* (—, *no pl.*) executive power.
Vollzug [fɔl'tsu:k], *m.* (—s, *no pl.*) execution; fulfilment.
Volontär [volɔ'tɛ:r], *m.* (—s, *pl.* —e) volunteer.
von [fɔn] (*von dem* becomes **vom**), *prep.* (*Dat.*) by, from; of; concerning, about; — *Shakespeare*, by Shakespeare; — *Beruf*, by profession; *er kommt — London*, he comes from London; — *fern*, from afar; — *jetzt an*, from now on; — *einem sprechen*, speak of s.o.; *dein Brief vom 15.*, your letter of the 15th.
vonnöten [fɔn'nø:tən], *adv.* — *sein*, be necessary.
vonstatten [fɔn'ʃtatən], *adv.* — *gehen*, progress; go off.
vor [fo:r], *prep.* (*Dat., Acc.*) (*place*) before, ahead of, in front of; (*time*) before, prior to, earlier than; from; of; with; above; in presence of, because of; more than; — *dem Hause*, in front of the house; — *Sonnenaufgang*, before sunrise; —*zwei Tagen*, two days ago; *sich — einem verstecken*, hide from s.o.; *sich hüten* —, beware of; *starr — Kälte*, stiff with cold; — *allem*, above all. — *adv.* before; *nach wie* —, now as before.

Vorabend ['fo:ra:bənt], *m.* (—s, *pl.* —e) eve.
Vorahnung ['fo:ra:nuŋ], *f.* (—, *pl.* —en) presentiment, foreboding.
voran [fo'ran], *adv.* before, in front, forward, on.
vorangehen [fo'range:ən], *v.n. irr.* (*aux.* sein) take the lead, go ahead.
Voranzeige ['fo:rantsaɪgə], *f.* (—, *pl.* —n) advance notice; (*film*) trailer.
Vorarbeiter ['fo:rarbaɪtər], *m.* (—s, *pl.* —) foreman.
voraus [fo'raus], *adv.* before, in front, foremost; in advance; *im* or *zum* —, beforehand; (*thanks*) in anticipation.
vorauseilen [fo'rausaɪlən], *v.n.* (*aux.* sein) run ahead.
vorausgehen [fo'rausge:ən], *v.n. irr.* (*aux.* sein) walk ahead; *einem* —, go before; precede s.o.
voraushaben [fo'rausha:bən], *v.n. irr. etwas vor einem* —, have the advantage over s.o.
Voraussage [fo'rausza:gə], *f.* (—, *pl.* —n) prediction, prophecy; (*weather*) forecast.
voraussagen [fo'rausza:gən], *v.a.* predict, foretell; (*weather*) forecast.
voraussehen [fo'rausze:ən], *v.a. irr.* foresee.
voraussetzen [fo'rausztsən], *v.a.* presuppose, take for granted.
Voraussetzung [fo'rausztsuŋ], *f.* (—, *pl.* —en) supposition, presupposition; *unter der* —, on the understanding.
Voraussicht [fo'rauszɪçt], *f.* (—, *no pl.*) foresight, forethought; *aller* — *nach*, in all probability.
voraussichtlich [fo'rauszɪçtlɪç], *adj.* prospective, presumptive, probable, expected. — *adv.* probably, presumably.
Vorbau ['fo:rbau], *m.* (—s, *pl.* —ten) frontage.
Vorbedacht ['fo:rbədaxt], *m.* (—s, *no pl.*) premeditation; *mit* —, on purpose, deliberately.
vorbedacht ['fo:rbədaxt], *adj.* premeditated.
Vorbedeutung ['fo:rbədɔytuŋ], *f.* (—, *pl.* —en) omen.
Vorbehalt ['fo:rbəhalt], *m.* (—s, *pl.* —e) reservation, proviso.
vorbehalten ['fo:rbəhaltən], *v.a. irr.* reserve; make reservation that.
vorbehaltlich ['fo:rbəhaltlɪç], *prep.* (*Genit.*) with the proviso that.
vorbei [fo:r'baɪ], *adv.* by; along; past, over, finished, gone.
vorbeigehen [fo:r'baɪge:ən], *v.n. irr.* (*aux.* sein) pass by; go past; march past.
vorbeilassen [fo:r'baɪlasən], *v.a.* let pass.
Vorbemerkung ['fo:rbəmɛrkuŋ], *f.* (—, *pl.* —en) preface, prefatory note.
vorbereiten ['fo:rbəraɪtən], *v.a.* prepare.
Vorbereitung ['fo:rbəraɪtuŋ], *f.* (—, *pl.* —en) preparation.

Vorbesitzer

Vorbesitzer ['fo:rbəzıtsər], *m.* (—s, *pl.* —) previous owner.

Vorbesprechung ['fo:rbəʃprɛçuŋ], *f.* (—, *pl.* —en) preliminary discussion.

vorbestimmen ['fo:rbəʃtımən], *v.a.* predestine, predetermine.

Vorbestimmung ['fo:rbəʃtımuŋ], *f.* (—, *no pl.*) predestination.

vorbestraft ['fo:rbəʃtra:ft], *adj.* previously convicted.

vorbeten ['fo:rbe:tən], *v.n.* lead in prayer.

vorbeugen ['fo:rbɔygən], *v.n.* prevent, preclude, obviate. — *v.r.* sich —, bend forward.

Vorbeugung ['fo:rbɔyguŋ], *f.* (—, *no pl.*) prevention; prophylaxis.

Vorbeugungsmaßnahme ['fo:rbɔyguŋsma:sna:mə], *f.* (—, *pl.* —n) preventive measure.

Vorbild ['fo:rbılt], *n.* (—s, *pl.* —er) model, example, pattern, ideal.

vorbildlich ['fo:rbıltlıç], *adj.* exemplary; typical; — *sein*, be a model.

Vorbildung ['fo:rbılduŋ], *f.* (—, *no pl.*) preparatory training.

Vorbote ['fo:rbo:tə], *m.* (—n, *pl.* —n) herald, precursor, forerunner.

vorbringen ['fo:rbrıŋən], *v.a. irr.* produce, proffer; advance, utter, allege, assert, claim.

vordatieren ['fo:rdati:rən], *v.a.* antedate.

vordem [for'de:m], *adv.* (*obs.*) formerly, once.

Vorderachse ['fordəraksə], *f.* (—, *pl.* —n) front axle.

Vorderansicht ['fordəranzıçt], *f.* (—, *pl.* —en) front view.

Vorderarm ['fordərarm], *m.* (—s, *pl.* —e) forearm.

Vordergrund ['fordərg·unt], *m.* (—s, *pl.* ˙e) foreground.

vorderhand ['fordərhant], *adv.* for the present.

Vorderseite ['fordərzaıtə], *f.* (—, *pl.* —n) front.

vorderst ['fordərst], *adj.* foremost, first.

Vordertür ['fordərty:r], *f.* (—, *pl.* —en) front door.

Vordertreffen ['fordərtrefən], *n.* (—s, *no pl.*) *ins* — *kommen*, be in the vanguard, come to the fore.

vordrängen ['fo:rdreŋən], *v.r.* sich —, press forward, jump the queue.

vordringen ['fo:rdrıŋən], *v.n. irr.* (*aux.* sein) advance, push forward.

vordringlich ['fo:rdrıŋlıç], *adj.* urgent; forward, importunate.

Vordruck ['fo:rdruk], *m.* (—s, *pl.* —e) (*printed*) form.

voreilen ['fo:raılən], *v.n.* (*aux.* sein) rush forward.

voreilig ['fo:raılıç], *adj.* over-hasty, rash.

Voreiligkeit ['fo:raılıçkaıt], *f.* (—, *no pl.*) hastiness, rashness.

voreingenommen ['fo:raıŋənɔmən], *adj.* biased, prejudiced.

Voreingenommenheit ['fo:raıŋənɔmənhaıt], *f.* (—, *no pl.*) bias, prejudice.

Voreltern ['fo:rɛltərn], *pl.* forefathers, ancestors.

vorenthalten ['fo:rɛnthaltən], *v.a. irr. sep. & insep.* withhold.

Vorentscheidung ['fo:rɛntʃaıduŋ], *f.* (—, *pl.* —en) preliminary decision.

vorerst [fo:r'e·rst], *adv.* first of all, firstly; for the time being.

vorerwähnt ['fo:rɛrvɛ·nt], *adj.* aforementioned.

Vorfahr ['fo:rfa:r], *m.* (—en, *pl.* —en) ancestor.

vorfahren ['fo:rfa:rən], *v.n. irr.* (*aux.* sein) drive up (to a house *etc.*).

Vorfall ['fo:rfal], *m.* (—s, *pl.* ˙e) occurrence, incident.

vorfinden ['fo:rfındən], *v.a. irr.* find, find present, meet with.

Vorfrage ['fo:rfra:gə], *f.* (—, *pl.* —n) preliminary question.

vorführen ['fo:rfy:rən], *v.a.* bring forward, produce.

Vorführung ['fo:rfy:ruŋ], *f.* (—, *pl.* —en) production, presentation; performance.

Vorgang ['fo:rgaŋ], *m.* (—s, *pl.* ˙e) occurrence, event, happening; proceeding, precedent; procedure.

Vorgänger ['fo:rgeŋər], *m.* (—s, *pl.* —) predecessor.

Vorgarten ['fo:rgartən], *m.* (—s, *pl.* ˙) front garden.

vorgeben ['fo:rge:bən], *v.a. irr.* pretend; allow (in advance).

Vorgebirge ['fo:rgəbırgə], *n.* (—s, *no pl.*) cape, promontory.

vorgeblich ['fo:rge:plıç], *adj.* pretended; ostensible.

vorgefaßt ['fo:rgəfast], *adj.* preconceived.

Vorgefühl ['fo:rgəfy:l], *n.* (—s, *pl.* —e) presentiment.

vorgehen ['fo:rge:ən], *v.n. irr.* (*aux.* sein) advance, walk ahead; proceed; (*clock*) be fast, gain; (*fig.*) take precedence; occur, happen; *was geht hier vor?* what's going on here?

Vorgehen ['fo:rge:ən], *n.* (—s, *no pl.*) (course of) action, (manner of) procedure.

vorgenannt ['fo:rgənant], *adj.* aforenamed.

Vorgericht ['fo:rgərıçt], *n.* (—s, *pl.* —e) hors d'œuvre, entrée.

Vorgeschichte ['fo:rgəʃıçtə], *f.* (—, *no pl.*) prehistory; early history; antecedents.

vorgeschichtlich ['fo:rgəʃıçtlıç], *adj.* prehistoric.

Vorgeschmack ['fo:rgəʃmak], *m.* (—s, *no pl.*) foretaste.

Vorgesetzte ['fo:rgəzɛtstə], *m.* (—n, *pl.* —n) superior, senior; boss.

vorgestern ['fo:rgɛstərn], *adv.* the day before yesterday.

vorgreifen ['fo:rgraıfən], *v.n. irr.* anticipate, forestall.

Vorhaben ['fo:rha:bən], *m.* (**—s**, *no pl.*) intention, purpose, design.

vorhaben ['fo:rha:bən], *v.a. irr.* intend; be busy with; *etwas mit einem —*, have designs on s.o.; have plans for s.o.

Vorhalle ['fo:rhalə], *f.* (—, *pl.* —n) vestibule, hall, porch.

vorhalten ['fo:rhaltən], *v.a. irr.* hold s.th. before s.o.; (*fig.*) remonstrate (with s.o. about s.th.); reproach. — *v.n.* last.

Vorhaltungen ['fo:rhaltuŋən], *f. pl.* remonstrances, expostulations.

vorhanden [for'handən], *adj.* at hand, present, in stock, on hand.

Vorhandensein [for'handənzain], *n.* (**—s**, *no pl.*) existence; availability.

Vorhang ['fo:rhaŋ], *m.* (**—s**, *pl.* **-e**) curtain.

Vorhängeschloß ['fo:rhɛŋəʃlɔs], *n.* (**—sses**, *pl.* **-sser**) padlock.

vorher ['fo:rhe:r], *adv.* before, beforehand, in advance.

vorhergehen [fo:r'he:rge:ən], *v.n. irr.* (*aux.* sein) go before, precede.

vorhergehend [fo:r'he:rge:ənt], *adj.* foregoing, aforesaid, preceding.

vorherig [fo:r'he:rɪç], *adj.* preceding, previous, former.

vorherrschen ['fo:rhɛrʃən], *v.n.* prevail, predominate.

vorhersagen [fo:r'he:rza:gən], *v.a.* predict, foretell.

vorhersehen [fo:r'he:rze:ən], *v.a. irr.* foresee.

vorheucheln ['fo:rhɔyçəln], *v.a. einem etwas —*, pretend s.th. to s.o.

vorhin [fo:r'hɪn], *adv.* just before, a short while ago.

Vorhof ['fo:rho:f], *m.* (**—s**, *pl.* **-e**) forecourt.

Vorhölle ['fo:rhœlə], *f.* (—, *no pl.*) limbo.

Vorhut ['fo:rhu:t], *f.* (—, *no pl.*) vanguard.

vorig ['fo:rɪç], *adj.* former, preceding.

Vorjahr ['fo:rja:r], *n.* (**—s**, *pl.* **-e**) preceding year.

vorjammern ['fo:rjamərn], *v.n. einem etwas —*, moan to s.o. about s.th.

Vorkämpfer ['fo:rkɛmpfər], *m.* (**—s**, *pl.* —) champion; pioneer.

vorkauen ['fo:rkauən], *v.a.* (*fig.*) predigest; spoon-feed.

Vorkaufsrecht ['fo:rkaufsrɛçt], *n.* (**—s**, *no pl.*) right of first refusal, right of pre-emption.

Vorkehrung ['fo:rke:ruŋ], *f.* (—, *pl.* —en) preparation; precaution; (*pl.*) arrangements.

Vorkenntnisse ['fo:rkɛntnɪsə], *f. pl.* rudiments, elements, grounding; previous knowledge.

vorkommen ['fo:rkɔmən], *v.n. irr.* (*aux.* sein) occur, happen; be found.

Vorkommnis ['fo:rkɔmnɪs], *n.* (**—ses**, *pl.* **—se**) occurrence, event, happening.

Vorkriegs- ['fo:rkri:ks], *prefix.* prewar.

Vorladung ['fo:rla:duŋ], *f.* (—, *pl.* —en) summons, writ, subpœna.

Vorlage ['fo:rla:gə], *f.* (—, *pl.* —n) pattern, master-copy.

vorlagern ['fo:rla:gərn], *v.n.* (*aux.* sein) extend (in front of).

Vorland ['fo:rlant], *n.* (**—s**, *pl.* **-er**) cape, foreland, foreshore.

vorlassen ['fo:rlasən], *v.a. irr.* give precedence to; admit, show in.

Vorläufer ['fo:rlɔyfər], *m.* (**—s**, *pl.* —) forerunner, precursor.

vorläufig [fo:r'lɔyfɪç], *adj.* provisional, preliminary, temporary. — *adv.* for the time being.

vorlaut ['fo:rlaut], *adj.* pert, forward.

Vorleben ['fo:rle:bən], *n.* (**—s**, *no pl.*) antecedents, past life.

vorlegen ['fo:rle:gən], *v.a.* put before s.o.; submit, propose; (*food*) serve.

Vorleger ['fo:rle:gər], *m.* (**—s**, *pl.* —) rug, mat.

Vorlegeschloß ['fo:rle:gəʃlɔs], *n.* (**—sses**, *pl.* **-sser**) padlock.

vorlesen ['fo:rle:zən], *v.a. irr.* read aloud, read out.

Vorlesung ['fo:rle:zuŋ], *f.* (—, *pl.* —en) lecture.

vorletzte ['fo:rlɛtstə], *adj.* last but one, penultimate.

Vorliebe ['fo:rli:bə], *f.* (—, *no pl.*) predilection, partiality.

vorliebnehmen [for'li:pne:mən], *v.n. — mit etwas*, be content with s.th., take pot luck.

vorliegen ['fo:rli:gən], *v.n. irr.* (*aux.* sein) be under consideration.

vorlügen [fo:r'ly:gən], *v.a. irr. einem etwas —*, tell lies to s.o.

vormachen ['fo:rmaxən], *v.a. einem etwas —*, show s.o. how a thing is done; (*fig.*) play tricks on s.o., deceive s.o.

vormalig ['fo:rma:lɪç], *adj.* former, erstwhile, late.

vormals ['fo:rma:ls], *adv.* formerly.

Vormarsch ['fo:rmarʃ], *m.* (**—es**, *pl.* **-e**) (*Mil.*) advance.

vormerken ['fo:rmɛrkən], *v.a.* make a note of, take down; book.

Vormittag ['fo:rmɪta:k], *m.* (**—s**, *pl.* —e) morning, forenoon.

vormittags ['fo:rmɪta:ks], *adv.* in the morning; before noon.

Vormund ['fo:rmunt], *m.* (**—s**, *pl.* **-er**) guardian.

Vormundschaft ['fo:rmuntʃaft], *f.* (—, *pl.* —en) guardianship.

Vormundschaftsgericht ['fo:rmuntʃaftsgərɪçt], *n.* (**—s**, *pl.* —e) Court of Chancery.

vorn [fɔrn], *adv.* before, in front of; in front; (*Naut.*) fore.

Vorname ['fo:rna:mə], *m.* (**—ns**, *pl.*—n) first name, Christian name.

vornehm ['fo:rne:m], *adj.* of noble birth, refined; distinguished, elegant.

vornehmen ['fo:rne:mən], *v.a. irr.* take in hand; *sich etwas —*, undertake s.th.; plan *or* intend to do s.th.

Vornehmheit

Vornehmheit ['fo:rne:mhaɪt], *f.* (—, *no pl.*) refinement, distinction.
vornehmlich ['fo:rne:mlɪç], *adv.* chiefly, principally, especially.
vornherein ['fɔrnhɛraɪn], *adv. von* —, from the first; from the beginning.
Vorort ('fo:rɔrt], *m.* (—s, *pl.* —e) suburb.
Vorortsbahn ['fo:rɔrtsba:n], *f.* (—, *pl.* —en) suburban (railway) line.
Vorplatz ['fo:rplats], *m.* (—es, *pl.* ˙e) forecourt.
Vorposten ['fo:rpɔstən], *m.* (—s, *pl.* —) (*Mil.*) outpost, pickets.
Vorpostengefecht ['fo:rpɔstəngəfɛçt], *n.* (—s, *pl.* —e) outpost skirmish.
Vorprüfung ['fo:rpry:fuŋ], *f.* (—, *pl.* —en) preliminary examination.
Vorrang ['fo:raŋ], *m.* (—s, *no pl.*) precedence, first place, priority.
Vorrat ['fo:rra:t], *m.* (—s, *pl.* ˙e) store, stock, provision.
Vorratskammer ['fo:rra:tskamər], *f.* (—, *pl.* —n) store-room; larder.
Vorrecht ['fo:rrɛçt], *n.* (—s, *pl.* —e) privilege, prerogative.
Vorrede ['fo:rre:də], *f.* (—, *pl.* —n) preface; introduction.
Vorredner ['fo:rre:dnər], *m.* (—s, *pl.* —) previous speaker.
vorrichten ['fo:rrɪçtən], *v.a.* prepare, fix up, get ready.
Vorrichtung ['fo:rrɪçtuŋ], *f.* (—, *pl.* —en) appliance, device, contrivance.
vorrücken ['fo:rrykən], *v.a.* move forward, advance; (*clock*) put on. — *v.n.* (*aux.* sein) (*Mil.*) advance.
Vorsaal ['fo:rza:l], *m.* (—s, *pl.* —säle) hall, entrance hall.
Vorsatz ['fo:rzats], *m.* (—es, *pl.* ˙e) purpose, design, intention.
vorsätzlich ['fo:rzɛtslɪç], *adj.* intentional, deliberate.
Vorschein ['fo:rʃaɪn], *m. zum* — *kommen,* turn up; appear.
vorschießen ['fo:rʃi:sən], *v.a.* irr. (*money*) advance, lend.
Vorschlag ['fo:rʃla:k], *m.* (—s, *pl.* ˙e) proposal, offer, proposition.
vorschlagen ['fo:rʃla:gən], *v.a.* irr. put forward, propose, suggest; recommend.
vorschnell ['fo:rʃnɛl], *adj.* hasty, rash, precipitate.
vorschreiben ['fo:rʃraɪbən], *v.a.* irr. write out (for s.o.); (*fig.*) prescribe, order.
Vorschrift ['fo:rʃrɪft], *f.* (—, *pl.* —en) prescription, direction, order, command, regulation.
vorschriftsmäßig ['fo:rʃrɪftsmɛ:sɪç], *adj.* according to regulations.
vorschriftswidrig ['fo:rʃrɪftsvi:drɪç], *adj.* contrary to regulations.
Vorschub ['fo:rʃup], *m.* (—s, *no pl.*) aid, assistance; — *leisten,* countenance, encourage, abet.
Vorschule ['fo:rʃu:lə], *f.* (—, *pl.* —n) preparatory school.
Vorschuß ['fo:rʃus], *m.* (—sses, *pl.* ˙sse) advance (of cash).

vorschützen ['fo:rʃytsən], *v.a.* use as a pretext, pretend, plead.
vorschweben ['fo:rʃve:bən], *v.n.* be present in o.'s mind.
vorsehen ['fo:rze:ən], *v.r.* irr. *sich* —, take heed, be careful, look out, beware.
Vorsehung ['fo:rze:uŋ], *f.* (—, *no pl.*) Providence.
vorsetzen ['fo:rzɛtsən], *v.a.* set before; serve; (*word*) prefix.
Vorsicht ['fo:rzɪçt], *f.* (—, *no pl.*) care, precaution, caution, circumspection.
vorsichtig ['fo:rzɪçtɪç], *adj.* cautious, careful, circumspect.
vorsichtshalber ['fo:rzɪçtshalbər], *adv.* as a precautionary measure.
Vorsichtsmaßnahme ['fo:rzɪçtsma:sna:mə], *f.* (—, *pl.* —n) precautionary measure, precaution.
Vorsilbe ['fo:rzɪlbə], *f.* (—, *pl.* —n) prefix.
vorsintflutlich ['fo:rzɪntflu:tlɪç], *adj.* antediluvian; (*fig.*) out-of-date.
Vorsitzende ['fo:rzɪtsəndə], *m.* (—n, *pl.* —n) chairman, president.
Vorsorge ['fo:rzɔrgə], *f.* (—, *no pl.*) care, precaution.
vorsorglich ['fo:rzɔrklɪç], *adj.* provident, careful.
vorspiegeln ['fo:rʃpi:gəln], *v.a. einem etwas* —, deceive s.o.; pretend.
Vorspiegelung ['fo:rʃpi:gəluŋ], *f.* (—, *pl.* —en) pretence; — *falscher Tatsachen,* false pretences.
Vorspiel ['fo:rʃpi:l], *n.* (—s, *pl.* —e) prelude; overture.
vorsprechen ['fo:rʃprɛçən], *v.n.* irr. *bei einem* —, call on s.o. — *v.a. einem etwas* —, say s.th. for s.o.; repeat.
vorspringen ['fo:rʃprɪŋən], *v.n.* irr. (*aux.* sein) leap forward; jut out, project.
Vorsprung ['fo:rʃpruŋ], *m.* (—s, *pl.* ˙e) projection, prominence; (*fig.*) advantage (over), start, lead.
Vorstadt ['fo:rʃtat], *f.* (—, *pl.* ˙e) suburb.
vorstädtisch ['fo:rʃtɛtɪʃ], *adj.* suburban.
Vorstand ['fo:rʃtant], *m.* (—s, *pl.* ˙e) board of directors; director, principal.
Vorstandssitzung ['fo:rʃtantszɪtuŋ], *f.* (—, *pl.* —en) board meeting.
vorstehen ['fo:rʃte:ən], *v.n.* irr. project, protrude; (*office*) administer, govern, direct, manage.
vorstehend ['fo:rʃte:ənt], *adj.* projecting, protruding; above-mentioned, foregoing.
Vorsteher ['fo:rʃte:ər], *m.* (—s, *pl.* —) director, manager; supervisor.
Vorsteherdrüse ['fo:rʃte:ərdry:zə], *f.* (—, *pl.* —n) prostate gland.
vorstellbar ['fo:rʃtɛlba:r], *adj.* imaginable.
vorstellen ['fo:rʃtɛlən], *v.a.* (*thing*) put forward; (*person*) present, introduce; (*Theat.*) impersonate; represent; (*clock*) put on; *sich etwas* —, visualise s.th., imagine s.th.

270

vorstellig ['fo:rʃtɛlıç], *adj.* — *werden*, petition; lodge a complaint.

Vorstellung ['fo:rʃtɛluŋ], *f.* (—, *pl.* —en) (*person*) presentation, introduction; (*Theat.*) performance; idea, notion, image; representation.

Vorstellungsvermögen ['fo:rʃtɛluŋs-fɛr'mø:gǝn], *n.* (—s, *no pl.*) imagination, imaginative faculty.

Vorstoß ['fo:rʃto:s], *m.* (—es, *pl.* ¨e) (*Mil.*) sudden advance, thrust.

vorstoßen ['fo:rʃto:sǝn], *v.a. irr.* push forward. — *v.n.* (*aux.* sein) (*Mil.*) advance suddenly.

Vorstrafe ['fo:rʃtra:fǝ], *f.* (—, *pl.* —n) previous conviction.

vorstrecken ['fo:rʃtrɛkǝn], *v.a.* stretch forward, protrude; (*money*) advance.

Vorstufe ['fo:rʃtu:fǝ], *f.* (—, *pl.* —n) first step.

Vortänzerin ['fo:rtɛntsǝrın], *f.* (—, *pl.* —nen) prima ballerina.

Vorteil ['fɔrtaıl], *m.* (—s, *pl.* —e) advantage, profit.

vorteilhaft ['fɔrtaılhaft], *adj.* advantageous, profitable, lucrative.

Vortrag ['fo:rtra:k], *m.* (—s, *pl.* ¨e) recitation, delivery, rendering; statement, report; talk, speech, lecture.

vortragen ['fo:rtra:gǝn], *v.a. irr.* make a report; (*poem*) recite, declaim; make a request; (*Comm.*) carry forward; lecture on.

Vortragskunst ['fo:rtra:kskunst], *f.* (—, *no pl.*) elocution; (art of) public speaking.

vortrefflich [for'trɛflıç], *adj.* excellent, splendid.

Vortrefflichkeit [for'trɛflıçkaıt], *f.* (—, *no pl.*) excellence.

vortreten ['fo:rtre:tǝn], *v.n. irr.* (*aux.* sein) step forward.

Vortritt ['fo:rtrıt], *m.* (—s, *no pl.*) precedence.

vorüber [for'y:bǝr], *adv.* past, gone, over, finished, done with.

vorübergehen [for'y:bǝrge:ǝn], *v.n. irr.* (*aux.* sein) pass by, pass, go past.

vorübergehend [for'y:bǝrge:ǝnt], *adj.* passing, temporary, transitory.

Vorübung ['fo:ry:buŋ], *f.* (—, *pl.* —en) preliminary exercise.

Voruntersuchung ['fo:runtǝrzu:xuŋ], *f.* (—, *pl.* —en) preliminary inquiry; trial in magistrate's court.

Vorurteil ['fo:rurtaıl], *n.* (—s, *pl.* —e) bias, prejudice.

vorurteilslos ['fo:rurtaılslo:s], *adj.* impartial, unprejudiced, unbiased.

Vorvater ['fo:rfa:tǝr], *m.* (—s, *pl.* ¨) progenitor, ancestor.

Vorverkauf ['fo:rfɛrkauf], *m.* (—s, *pl.* ¨e) booking in advance, advance booking.

vorwagen ['fo:rva:gǝn], *v.r. sich* —, dare to go (*or* come) forward.

vorwaltend ['fo:rvaltǝnt], *adj.* prevailing, predominating.

Vorwand ['fo:rvant], *m.* (—s, *pl.* ¨e) pretence, pretext; *unter dem* —, under pretence of.

vorwärts ['fɔrvɛrts], *adv.* forward.

vorwärtskommen ['fɔrvɛrtskɔmǝn], *v.n. irr.* (*aux.* sein) make headway, get on.

vorweg [for'vɛk], *adv.* before.

vorwegnehmen [for'vɛkne:mǝn], *v.a. irr.* anticipate.

vorweisen ['fo:rvaızǝn], *v.a. irr.* show, produce, exhibit.

Vorwelt ['fo:rvɛlt], *f.* (—, *no pl.*) primitive world; former ages.

vorweltlich ['fo:rvɛltlıç], *adj.* primæval, prehistoric.

vorwerfen ['fo:rvɛrfǝn], *v.a. irr. einem etwas* —, blame s.o. for s.th.; charge s.o. with s.th., tax s.o. with s.th.

vorwiegen ['fo:rvi:gǝn], *v.n. irr.* prevail.

vorwiegend ['fo:rvi:gǝnt], *adv.* mostly, for the most part.

Vorwissen ['fo:rvısǝn], *n.* (—s, *no pl.*) foreknowledge, prescience.

Vorwitz ['fo:rvıts], *m.* (—es, *no pl.*) pertness.

vorwitzig ['fo:rvıtsıç], *adj.* forward, pert, meddlesome.

Vorwort (1) ['fo:rvɔrt], *n.* (—s, *pl.* —e) preface.

Vorwort (2) ['fo:rvɔrt], *n.* (—s, *pl.* ¨er) (*Gram.*) preposition.

Vorwurf ['fo:rvurf], *m.* (—s, *pl.* ¨e) reproach; theme, subject.

vorwurfsfrei ['fo:rvurfsfraı], *adj.* free from blame, irreproachable.

vorwurfsvoll ['fo:rvurfsfɔl], *adj.* reproachful.

Vorzeichen ['fo:rtsaıxǝn], *n.* (—s, *pl.* —) omen, token; (*Maths.*) sign.

vorzeigen ['fo:rtsaıgǝn], *v.a.* show, produce, exhibit, display.

Vorzeit ['fo:rtsaıt], *f.* (—, *no pl.*) antiquity, olden times.

vorzeiten [for'tsaıtǝn], *adv.* (*Poet.*) in olden times, formerly.

vorzeitig ['fo:rtsaıtıç], *adj.* premature.

vorziehen ['fo:rtsi:ǝn], *v.a. irr.* prefer.

Vorzimmer ['fo:rtsımǝr], *n.* (—s, *pl.* —) anteroom, antechamber.

Vorzug ['fo:rtsu:k], *m.* (—s, *pl.* ¨e) preference, advantage; excellence, superiority.

vorzüglich [for'tsy:klıç], *adj.* superior, excellent, exquisite.

Vorzüglichkeit [for'tsy:klıçkaıt], *f.* (—, *no pl.*) excellence, superiority.

Vorzugsaktie ['fo:rtsu:ksaktsjǝ], *f.* (—, *pl.* —n) preference share.

vorzugsweise ['fo:rtsu:ksvaızǝ], *adv.* for choice, preferably.

vulgär [vul'gɛ:r], *adj.* vulgar.

Vulkan [vul'ka:n], *m.* (—s, *pl.* —e) volcano.

vulkanisch [vul'ka:nıʃ], *adj.* volcanic. ◦

W

W [ve:] *n.* (—s, *pl.* —s) the letter W.

Waage ['va:gə], *f.* (—, *pl.* —n) balance, pair of scales.

waag(e)recht ['va:g(ə)rɛçt], *adj.* horizontal.

Waagschale ['va:kʃa:lə], *f.* (—, *pl.* —n) pan of a balance.

Wabe ['va:bə], *f.* (—, *pl.* —n) honeycomb.

Waberlohe ['va:bərlo:ə], *f.* (—, *no pl.*) (*Poet.*) flickering flames, magic fire.

wach [vax], *adj.* awake; alert; *völlig* —, wide awake.

Wachdienst ['vaxdi:nst], *m.* (—es, *no pl.*) guard, sentry duty.

Wache ['vaxə], *f.* (—, *pl.* —n) guard, watch; (*person*) sentry, sentinel.

wachen ['vaxən], *v.n.* be awake; guard; — *über*, watch, keep an eye on.

Wacholder [va'xɔldər], *m.* (—s, *pl.* —) (*Bot.*) juniper.

wachrufen ['vax'ru:fən], *v.a. irr.* (*fig.*) call to mind.

Wachs [vaks], *n.* (—es, *no pl.*) wax.

wachsam ['vaxza:m], *adj.* watchful, vigilant.

Wachsamkeit ['vaxza:mkaɪt], *f.* (—, *no pl.*) watchfulness, vigilance.

Wachsbild ['vaksbɪlt], *n.* (—s, *pl.* —er) waxen image.

wachsen ['vaksən], *v.n. irr.* (*aux.* sein) grow, increase.

wächsern ['vɛksərn], *adj.* waxen, made of wax.

Wachsfigur ['vaksfigu:r], *f.* (—, *pl.* —en) wax figure.

Wachsfigurenkabinett ['vaksfigu:rənkabinet], *n.* (—s, *pl.* —e) waxworks.

Wachsleinwand ['vakslaɪnvant], *f.* (—, *no pl.*) oil-cloth.

Wachstuch ['vakstu:x], *n.* (—(e)s, *no pl.*) oil-cloth; American cloth.

Wachstum ['vakstu:m], *n.* (—s, *no pl.*) growth, increase.

Wacht [vaxt], *f.* (—, *pl.* —en) watch, guard.

Wachtdienst ['vaxtdi:nst] *see* **Wachdienst.**

Wachtel ['vaxtəl], *f.* (—, *pl.* —n) (*Orn.*) quail.

Wachtelhund ['vaxtəlhunt], *m.* (—(e)s, *pl.* —e) (*Zool.*) spaniel.

Wächter ['vɛçtər], *m.* (—s, *pl.* —) watchman, warder, guard.

wachthabend ['vaxtha:bənt], *adj.* on duty.

Wachtmeister ['vaxtmaɪstər], *m.* (—s, *pl.* —) sergeant.

Wachtparade [vaxtpara:də], *f.* (—, *pl.* —n) mounting of the guard.

Wachtposten ['vaxtpɔstən], *m.* (—s, *pl.* —) guard, picket.

Wachtraum ['vaxtraum], *m.* (—s, *pl.* ːe) day-dream, waking dream.

Wachtturm ['vaxtturm], *m.* (—s, *pl.* ːe) watch-tower.

wackeln ['vakəln], *v.n.* totter, shake, wobble.

wacker ['vakər], *adj.* gallant, brave, valiant; upright.

wacklig ['vaklɪç], *adj.* tottering, shaky; (*furniture*) rickety; (*tooth*) loose.

Wade ['va:də], *f.* (—, *pl.* —n) calf (of the leg).

Wadenbein ['va:dənbaɪn], *n.* (—s, *pl.* —e) shin-bone.

Waffe ['vafə], *f.* (—, *pl.* —n) weapon, arm; *die* —n *strecken*, surrender.

Waffel ['vafəl], *f.* (—, *pl.* —n) wafer; waffle.

Waffeleisen ['vafəlaɪzən], *n.* (—s, *pl.* —) waffle-iron.

Waffenbruder ['vafənbru:dər], *m.* (—s, *pl.* ː) brother-in-arms, comrade.

waffenfähig ['vafənfɛ:ɪç], *adj.* able to bear arms.

Waffengewalt ['vafəngəvalt], *f.* (—, *no pl.*) *mit* —, by force of arms.

Waffenglück ['vafənglyk], *n.* (—s, *no pl.*) fortunes of war.

Waffenrock ['vafənrɔk], *m.* (—s, *pl.* ːe) tunic.

Waffenruf ['vafənru:f], *m.* (—s, *no pl.*) call to arms.

Waffenschmied [vafənʃmi:t], *m.* (—s, *pl.* —e) armourer.

Waffenstillstand ['vafənʃtɪlʃtant], *m.* (—s, *no pl.*) armistice, truce.

waffnen ['vafnən], *v.a.* arm.

Wage *see* **Waage.**

Wagebalken ['va:gəbalkən], *m.* (—s, *pl.* —) scale-beam.

Wagen ['va:gən], *m.* (—s, *pl.* —) vehicle, conveyance, carriage, coach, car, cab, wagon, cart, truck, van, dray.

wagen ['va:gən], *v.a., v.n.* dare, venture, risk.

wägen ['vɛ:gən], *v.a., irr.* weigh, balance; (*words*) consider.

Wagenverkehr ['va:gənferke:r], *m.* (—s, *no pl.*) vehicular traffic.

wagerecht *see* **waagerecht.**

Waggon [va'gõ], *m.* (—s, *pl.* —s) railway car, goods van, freight car.

waghalsig ['va:khalzɪç], *adj.* foolhardy, rash, daring.

Wagnis ['va:knɪs], *n.* (—ses, *pl.* —se) venture, risky undertaking; risk.

Wagschale *see* **Waagschale.**

Wahl [va:l], *f.* (—, *pl.* —en) choice; election; selection; alternative.

Wahlakt ['va:lakt], *m.* (—s, *pl.* —e) poll, election.

Wahlaufruf ['va:laufru:f], *m.* (—s, *pl.* —e) manifesto, election address.

wählbar ['vɛ:lba:r], *adj.* eligible.

Wählbarkeit ['vɛ:lba:rkaɪt], *f.* (—, *no pl.*) eligibility.

Walze

wahlberechtigt [ˈvaːlbərɛçtɪçt], *adj.*
entitled to vote.

wählen [ˈvɛːlən], *v.a.* choose; *(Parl.)*
elect; *(Telephone)* dial.

Wähler [ˈvɛːlər], *m.* (—s, *pl.* —)
elector; constituent.

wählerisch [ˈvɛːlərɪʃ], *adj.* fastidious,
particular.

Wählerschaft [ˈvɛːlərʃaft], *f.* (—,
pl. —en) constituency.

wahlfähig [ˈvaːlfɛːɪç], *adj.* eligible.

Wahlliste [ˈvaːllɪstə], *f.* (—, *pl.* —n)
electoral list, register (of electors).

wahllos [ˈvaːlloːs], *adj.* indiscriminate.

Wahlrecht [ˈvaːlrɛçt], *n.* (—s, *no pl.*)
franchise.

Wahlspruch [ˈvaːlʃprux], *m.* (—s,
pl. ⸚e) device, motto.

wahlunfähig [ˈvaːlunfɛːɪç], *adj.* ineligible.

Wahlurne [ˈvaːlurnə], *f.* (—, *pl.* —n)
ballot-box.

Wahlverwandtschaft [ˈvaːlfɛrvantʃaft],
f. (—, *no pl.*) elective affinity, congeniality.

Wahlzettel [ˈvaːltsɛtəl], *m.* (—s, *pl.* —)
ballot-paper.

Wahn [vaːn], *m.* (—(e)s, *no pl.*) delusion.

Wahnbild [ˈvaːnbɪlt], *n.* (—s, *pl.* —er)
hallucination, delusion; phantasm.

wähnen [ˈvɛːnən], *v.a.* fancy, believe.

Wahnsinn [ˈvaːnzɪn], *m.* (—s, *no pl.*)
madness, lunacy.

wahnsinnig [ˈvaːnzɪnɪç], *adj.* insane,
mad, lunatic; *(coll.)* terrific.

Wahnsinnige [ˈvaːnzɪnɪgə], *m.* (—n,
pl. —n) madman, lunatic.

Wahnwitz [ˈvaːnvɪts], *m.* (—es, *no pl.*)
madness.

wahnwitzig [ˈvaːnvɪtsɪç], *adj.* mad.

wahr [vaːr], *adj.* true, real, genuine.

wahren [ˈvaːrən], *v.a.* guard, watch
over.

währen [ˈvɛːrən], *v.n.* last.

während [ˈvɛːrənt], *prep. (Genit.)*
during. — *conj.* while, whilst; whereas.

wahrhaft [ˈvaːrhaft], *adj.* truthful,
veracious.

wahrhaftig [vaːrˈhaftɪç], *adv.* truly,
really, in truth.

Wahrhaftigkeit [vaːrˈhaftɪçkaɪt], *f.*
(—, *no pl.*) truthfulness, veracity.

Wahrheit [ˈvaːrhaɪt], *f.* (—, *pl.* —en)
truth; reality; *die — sagen*, tell the
truth.

Wahrheitsliebe [ˈvaːrhaɪtsliːbə], *f.* (—,
no pl.) love of truth, truthfulness.

wahrlich [ˈvaːrlɪç], *adv.* truly, in truth.

wahrnehmbar [ˈvaːrneːmbaːr], *adj.*
perceptible.

wahrnehmen [ˈvaːrneːmən], *v.a. irr.*
perceive, observe.

Wahrnehmung [ˈvaːrneːmuŋ], *f.* (—,
pl. —en) perception, observation.

wahrsagen [ˈvaːrzaːgən], *v.n.* prophesy;
tell fortunes.

Wahrsager [ˈvaːrzaːgər], *m.* (—s,
pl. —) fortune-teller, soothsayer.

wahrscheinlich [vaːrˈʃaɪnlɪç], *adj.*
likely, probable; *es wird — regnen*, it
will probably rain.

Wahrscheinlichkeit [vaːrˈʃaɪnlɪçkaɪt],
f. (—, *pl.* —en) likelihood, probability.

Wahrung [ˈvaːruŋ], *f.* (—, *no pl.*)
protection, preservation, maintenance.

Währung [ˈvɛːruŋ], *f.* (—, *pl.* —en)
currency, standard.

Wahrzeichen [ˈvaːrtsaɪçən], *n.* (—s,
pl. —) landmark; *(fig.)* sign, token.

Waibling(er) [ˈvaɪblɪŋ(ər)], *m.* Ghibelline.

Waidmann [ˈvaɪtman], *m.* (—s, *pl.*
⸚er) huntsman, hunter.

waidmännisch [ˈvaɪtmɛnɪʃ], *adj.* sportsmanlike.

Waise [ˈvaɪzə], *f.* (—, *pl.* —n) orphan.

Waisenhaus [ˈvaɪzənhaus], *n.* (—es,
pl. ⸚er) orphanage.

Waisenmutter [ˈvaɪzənmutər], *f.* (—,
pl. ⸚) foster-mother.

Waisenvater [ˈvaɪzənfaːtər], *m.* (—s,
pl. ⸚) foster-father.

Wald [valt], *m.* (—es, *pl.* ⸚er) wood,
forest; woodland.

Waldbrand [ˈvaltbrant], *m.* (—s, *pl.*
⸚e) forest-fire.

Waldlichtung [ˈvaltlɪçtuŋ], *f.* (—,
pl. —en) forest glade, clearing.

Waldmeister [ˈvaltmaɪstər], *m.* (—s,
no pl.) *(Bot.)* woodruff.

Waldung [ˈvalduŋ], *f.* (—, *pl.* —en)
woods, woodland.

Waldwiese [ˈvaltviːzə], *f.* (—, *pl.* —en)
forest-glade.

Walfisch [ˈvaːlfɪʃ], *m.* (—es, *pl.* —e)
whale.

Walfischfang [ˈvaːlfɪʃfaŋ], *m.* (—s, *no
pl.*) whaling.

Walfischfänger [ˈvaːlfɪʃfɛŋər], *m.* (—s,
pl. —) whaler, whale fisher.

Walfischtran [ˈvaːlfɪʃtraːn], *m.* (—s,
no pl.) train-oil.

Walküre [valˈkyːrə], *f.* (—, *pl.* —n)
Valkyrie.

Wall [val], *m.* (—(e)s, *pl.* ⸚e) rampart,
dam, vallum; mound.

Wallach [ˈvalax], *m.* (—s, *pl.* —e)
castrated horse, gelding.

wallen [ˈvalən], *v.n.* bubble, boil up;
wave, undulate.

Wallfahrer [ˈvalfaːrər], *m.* (—s, *pl.* —)
pilgrim.

Wallfahrt [ˈvalfaːrt], *f.* (—, *pl.* —en)
pilgrimage.

wallfahrten [ˈvalfaːrtən], *v.n. (aux.
sein)* go on a pilgrimage.

Walnuß [ˈvalnus], *f.* (—, *pl.* ⸚sse)
(Bot.) walnut.

Walpurgisnacht [valˈpurgɪsnaxt], *f.*
witches' sabbath.

Walroß [ˈvalrɔs], *n.* (—sses, *pl.* —sse)
sea-horse, walrus.

Walstatt [ˈvalʃtat], *f.* (—, *pl.* ⸚en)
(Poet.) battlefield.

walten [ˈvaltən], *v.n.* rule; *seines Amtes
—*, do o.'s duty, carry out o.'s duties.

Walze [ˈvaltsə], *f.* (—, *pl.* —n) roller,
cylinder.

walzen

walzen ['valtsən], *v.a.* roll. — *v.n.* waltz.

wälzen ['vɛltsən], *v.a.* roll, turn about.

walzenförmig ['valtsənfœrmɪç], *adj.* cylindrical.

Walzer ['valtsər], *m.* (—s, *pl.* —) waltz.

Wälzer ['vɛltsər], *m.* (—s, *pl.* —) tome; thick volume.

Walzwerk ['valtsvɛrk], *n.* (—s, *pl.* —e) rolling-mill.

Wams [vams], *n.* (—es, *pl.* ˝e) (*obs.*) doublet, jerkin.

Wand [vant], *f.* (—, *pl.* ˝e) wall; side.

Wandbekleidung ['vantbəklaɪduŋ], *f.* (—, *pl.* —en) wainscot, panelling.

Wandel ['vandəl], *m.* (—s, *no pl.*) mutation, change; behaviour, conduct; *Handel und* —, trade and traffic.

wandelbar ['vandəlba:r], *adj.* changeable, inconstant.

Wandelgang ['vandəlgaŋ], *m.* (—s, *pl.* ˝e) lobby; lounge, foyer; (*in the open*) covered way, covered walk.

wandeln ['vandəln], *v.a.* (*aux.* haben) change. — *v.n.* (*aux.* sein) walk, wander. — *v.r. sich* —, change.

Wanderbursche ['vandərburʃə], *m.* (—n, *pl.* —n) travelling journeyman.

Wanderer ['vandərər], *m.* (—s, *pl.* —) wanderer, traveller; hiker.

Wanderleben ['vandərle:bən], *n.* (—s, *no pl.*) nomadic life.

Wanderlehrer ['vandərle:rər], *m.* (—s, *pl.* —) itinerant teacher.

Wanderlust ['vandərlust], *f.* (—, *no pl.*) urge to travel; call of the open.

wandern ['vandərn], *v.n.* (*aux.* sein) wander, travel; migrate.

Wanderschaft ['vandərʃaft], *f.* (—, *no pl.*) wanderings.

Wandersmann ['vandərsman], *m.* (—s, *pl.* ˝er) wayfarer.

Wandertruppe ['vandərtrupə], *f.* (—, *pl.* —n) (*Theat.*) strolling players.

Wanderung ['vandəruŋ], *f.* (—, *pl.* —en) walking tour; hike.

Wandervolk ['vandərfɔlk], *n.* (— (e)s, *pl.* ˝er) nomadic tribe.

Wandgemälde ['vantgəmɛːldə], *n.* (—s, *pl.* —) mural painting, mural.

Wandlung ['vandluŋ], *f.* (—, *pl.* —en) transformation; (*Theol.*) transubstantiation.

Wandspiegel ['vantʃpi:gəl], *m.* (—s, *pl.* —) pier-glass.

Wandtafel ['vantta:fəl], *f.* (—, *pl.* —n) blackboard.

Wange ['vaŋə], *f.* (—, *pl.* —n) cheek.

Wankelmut ['vaŋkəlmu:t], *m.* (—s, *no pl.*) fickleness, inconstancy.

wankelmütig ['vaŋkəlmy:tɪç], *adj.* inconstant, fickle.

wanken ['vaŋkən], *v.n.* totter, stagger; (*fig.*) waver, be irresolute.

wann [van], *adv.* when; *dann und* —, now and then, sometimes.

Wanne ['vanə], *f.* (—, *pl.* —n) tub, bath.

wannen ['vanən], *adv.* (*obs.*) von —, whence.

Wannenbad ['vanənba:t], *n.* (—s, *pl.* ˝er) bath.

Wanst [vanst], *m.* (—es, *pl.* ˝e) belly, paunch.

Wanze ['vantsə], *f.* (—, *pl.* —n) (*Ent.*) bug.

Wappen ['vapən], *n.* (—s, *pl.* —) crest, coat-of-arms.

Wappenbild ['vapənbɪlt], *n.* (—s, *pl.* —er) heraldic figure.

Wappenkunde ['vapənkundə], *f.* (—, *no pl.*) heraldry.

Wappenschild ['vapənʃɪlt], *m.* (—s, *pl.* —e) escutcheon.

Wappenspruch ['vapənʃprux], *m.* (—(e)s, *pl.* ˝e) motto, device.

wappnen ['vapnən], *v.a.* arm.

Ware ['va:rə], *f.* (—, *pl.* —n) article, commodity; (*pl.*) merchandise, goods, wares.

Warenausfuhr ['va:rənausfu:r], *f.* (—, *no pl.*) exportation, export.

Warenbörse ['va:rənbœrzə], *f.* (—, *pl.* —n) commodity exchange.

Wareneinfuhr ['va:rənaɪnfu:r], *f.* (—, *no pl.*) importation, import.

Warenhaus ['va:rənhaus], *n.* (—es, *pl.* ˝er) department store, emporium; (*Am.*) store.

Warenlager ['va:rənla:gər], *n.* (—s, *pl.* —) magazine; stock; warehouse.

Warensendung ['va:rənzɛnduŋ], *f.* (—, *pl.* —en) consignment of goods.

Warentausch ['va:rəntauʃ], *m.* (—es, *no pl.*) barter.

warm [varm], *adj.* warm, hot.

warmblütig ['varmbly:tɪç], *adj.* warm-blooded.

Wärme ['vɛrmə], *f.* (—, *no pl.*) warmth; heat.

Wärmeeinheit ['vɛrməaɪnhaɪt], *f.* (—, *pl.* —en) thermal unit; calorie.

Wärmegrad ['vɛrməgra:t], *m.* (—s, *pl.* —e) degree of heat; temperature.

Wärmeleiter ['vɛrməlaɪtər], *m.* (—s, *pl.* —) conductor of heat.

Wärmemesser ['vɛrməmɛsər], *m.* (—s, *pl.* —) thermometer.

wärmen ['vɛrmən], *v.a.* warm, heat.

Wärmflasche ['vɛrmflaʃə], *f.* (—, *pl.* —n) hot-water bottle.

warnen ['varnən], *v.a.* warn; caution.

Warnung ['varnuŋ], *f.* (—, *pl.* —en) warning, caution, admonition; notice.

Warschau ['varʃau], *n.* Warsaw.

Warte ['vartə], *f.* (—, *pl.* —n) watch-tower, belfry, look-out.

Wartegeld ['vartəgɛlt], *n.* (—s, *pl.* —er) half pay; (*ship*) demurrage charges.

warten ['vartən], *v.n.* wait; — *auf* (*Acc.*), wait for, await. — *v.a.* tend, nurse.

Wärter ['vɛrtər], *m.* (—s, *pl.* —) keeper, attendant; warder; male nurse.

Wartesaal ['vartəza:l], *m.* (—s, *pl.* —säle) (*Railw.*) waiting-room.

Wartung ['vartuŋ], *f.* (—, *no pl.*) nursing, attendance; servicing; maintenance.

warum [va'rum], *adv.*, *conj.* why, for what reason.

Warze ['vartsə], *f.* (—, *pl.* —**n**) wart.

was [vas], *interr. pron.* what? — *rel. pron.* what, that which.

Waschanstalt ['vaʃanʃtalt], *f.* (—, *pl.* —**en**) laundry.

waschbar ['vaʃbaːr], ·*adj.* washable.

Waschbär ['vaʃbɛːr], *m.* (—**en**, *pl.* —**en**) (*Zool.*) raccoon.

Waschbecken ['vaʃbɛkən], *n.* (—**s**, *pl.* —) wash-basin.

Wäsche ['vɛʃə], *f.* (—, *no pl.*) washing, wash, laundry; linen.

waschecht ['vaʃɛçt], *adj.* washable; (*fig.*) genuine.

waschen ['vaʃən], *v.a. irr.* wash.

Wäscherin ['vɛʃərin], *f.* (—, *pl.* —**nen**) washerwoman, laundress.

Waschhaus ['vaʃhaus], *n.* (—**es**, *pl.* ⁚er) wash-house, laundry; (*reg. trade name*) launderette.

Waschkorb ['vaʃkɔrp], *m.* (—**s**, *pl.* ⁚e) clothes-basket.

Waschküche ['vaʃkʏçə], *f.* (—, *pl.* —**en**) wash-house.

Waschlappen ['vaʃlapən], *m.* (—**s**, *pl.* —) face-flannel, face-cloth, face-washer; (*fig.*) milksop.

Waschleder ['vaʃleːdər], *n.* (—**s**, *no pl.*) chamois leather, wash-leather.

Waschmaschine ['vaʃmaʃiːnə], *f.* (—, *pl.* —**n**) washing-machine.

Waschtisch ['vaʃtiʃ], *m.* (—**es**, *pl.* —**e**) wash-stand.

Waschwanne ['vaʃvanə], *f.* (—, *pl.* —**n**) wash-tub.

Wasser ['vasər], *n.* (—**s**, *pl.* —) water; *stille — sind tief*, still waters run deep.

wasserarm ['vasərarm], *adj.* waterless, dry, arid.

Wasserbehälter ['vasərbəhɛltər], *m.* (—**s**, *pl.* —) reservoir, cistern, tank.

Wasserblase ['vasərblaːzə], *f.* (—, *pl.* —**n**) bubble.

Wässerchen ['vɛsərçən], *n.* (—**s**, *pl.* —) brook, streamlet; *er sieht aus, als ob er kein — trüben könnte*, he looks as if butter would not melt in his mouth.

Wasserdampf ['vasərdampf], *m.* (—**e**)**s**, *no pl.*) steam.

wasserdicht ['vasərdiçt], *adj.* water-proof.

Wasserdruck ['vasərdruk], *m.* (—**s**, *no pl.*) hydrostatic pressure, hydraulic pressure.

Wassereimer ['vasəraimər], *m.* (—**s**, *pl.* —) pail, water-bucket.

Wasserfall ['vasərfal], *m.* (—**s**, *pl.* ⁚e) waterfall, cataract, cascade.

Wasserfarbe ['vasərfarbə], *f.* (—, *pl.* —**n**) water-colour.

Wasserheilanstalt ['vasərhailanʃtalt], *f.* (—, *pl.* —**en**) spa.

wässerig ['vɛsəriç], *adj.* watery; (*fig.*) insipid, flat, diluted.

Wasserkanne ['vasərkanə], *f.* (—, *pl.* —**n**) pitcher, ewer.

Wasserkessel ['vasərkɛsəl], *m.* (—**s**, *pl.* —**en**) boiler; kettle.

Wasserkopf ['vasərkɔpf], *m.* (—(**e**)**s**, *pl.* ⁚e) (*Med.*) hydrocephalus.

Wasserkur ['vasərkuːr], *f.* (—, *pl.* —**en**) hydropathic treatment.

Wasserleitung ['vasərlaituŋ], *f.* (—, *pl.* —**en**) aqueduct; water main.

Wasserlinsen ['vasərlinzən], *f. pl.* (*Bot.*) duck-weed.

Wassermann ['vasərman], *m.* (—**s**, *no pl.*) (*Astron.*) Aquarius.

wässern ['vɛsərn], *v.a.* water, irrigate, soak.

Wassernixe ['vasərniksə], *f.* (—, *pl.* —**n**) water nymph.

Wassernot ['vasərnoːt], *f.* (—, *no pl.*) drought, scarcity of water.

Wasserrabe ['vasərraːbə], *m.* (—**n**, *pl.* —**n**) (*Orn.*) cormorant.

Wasserrinne ['vasərrinə], *f.* (—, *pl.* —**n**) gutter.

Wasserröhre ['vasərrøːrə], *f.* (—, *pl.* —**n**) water-pipe.

Wasserscheide ['vasərʃaidə], *f.* (—, *pl.* —**n**) watershed.

Wasserscheu ['vasərʃɔy], *f.* (—, *no pl.*) hydrophobia.

Wasserspiegel ['vasərʃpiːgəl], *m.* (—**s**, *pl.* —) water-level.

Wasserspritze ['vasərʃpritsə], *f.* (— *pl.* —**n**) squirt; sprinkler.

Wasserstand ['vasərʃtant], *m.* (—**s**, *no pl.*) water-level.

Wasserstiefel ['vasərʃtiːfəl], *m.* (—**s**, *pl.* —) wader, gumboot.

Wasserstoff ['vasərʃtɔf], *m.* (—(**e**)**s**, *no pl.*) hydrogen.

Wassersucht ['vasərzuxt], *f.* (—, *no pl.*) dropsy.

Wassersuppe ['vasərzupə], *f.* (—, *pl.* —**n**) water-gruel.

Wässerung ['vɛsəruŋ], *f.* (—, *pl.* —**en**) watering, irrigation.

Wasserverdrängung ['vasərfɛrdrɛŋuŋ], *f.* (—, *no pl.*) displacement (of water).

Wasserwaage ['vasərvaːgə], *f.* (—, *pl.* —**n**) water-balance, water-level; hydrometer.

Wasserweg ['vasərveːk], *m.* (—**s**, *pl.* —**e**) waterway; *auf dem —*, by water, by sea.

Wasserzeichen ['vasərtsaiçən], *n.* (—**s**, *pl.* —) watermark.

waten ['vaːtən], *v.n.* (*aux.* sein) wade.

watscheln ['vaːtʃəln], *v.n.* (*aux.* sein) waddle.

Watt (1) [vat], *n.* (—**s**, *pl.* —**e**) sand-bank; (*pl.*) shallows.

Watt (2) [vat], *n.* (—**s**, *pl.* —) (*Elec.*) watt.

Watte ['vatə], *f.* (—, *no pl.*) wadding, cotton-wool.

wattieren [va'tiːrən], *v.a.* pad.

Webe ['veːbə], *f.* (—, *pl.* —**n**) web, weft.

weben ['veːbən], *v.a.* weave.

Weber ['veːbər], *m.* (—**s**, *pl.* —) weaver.

Weberei [veːbə'rai], *f.* (—, *pl.* —**en**) weaving-mill.

Weberschiffchen ['ve:bərʃɪfçən], *n.* (—s, *pl.* —) shuttle.

Wechsel ['vɛksəl], *m.* (—s, *pl.* —) change; turn, variation; vicissitude; (*Comm.*) bill of exchange.

Wechselbalg ['vɛksəlbalk], *m.* (—s, *pl.* ⁻e) changeling.

Wechselbank ['vɛksəlbaŋk], *f.* (—, *pl.* ⁻e) discount-bank.

Wechselbeziehung ['vɛksəlbətsi:uŋ], *f.* (—, *pl.* —en) reciprocal relation, correlation.

Wechselfälle ['vɛksəlfɛlə], *m. pl.* vicissitudes.

Wechselfieber ['vɛksəlfi:bər], *n.* (—s, *pl.* —) intermittent fever.

Wechselfolge ['vɛksəlfɔlgə], *f.* (—, *no pl.*) rotation, alternation.

Wechselgeld ['vɛksəlgɛlt], *n.* (—(e)s, *no pl.*) change.

wechseln ['vɛksəln], *v.a.* change, exchange. — *v.n.* change, alternate, change places.

wechselseitig ['vɛksəlzaItIç], *adj.* reciprocal, mutual.

Wechselstrom ['vɛksəlʃtro:m], *m.* (—s, *no pl.*) alternating current.

Wechselstube ['vɛksəlʃtu:bə], *f.* (—, *pl.* —n) exchange office.

wechselvoll ['vɛksəlfɔl], *adj.* eventful, chequered; changeable.

wechselweise ['vɛksəlvaIzə], *adv.* reciprocally, mutually; by turns, alternately.

Wechselwinkel ['vɛksəlvIŋkəl], *m.* (—s, *pl.* —) alternate angle.

Wechselwirkung ['vɛksəlvIrkuŋ], *f.* (—, *pl.* —en) reciprocal effect.

Wechselwirtschaft ['vɛksəlvIrtʃaft], *f.* (—, *no pl.*) rotation of crops.

Wecken ['vɛkən], *m.* (—s, *pl.* —) (*dial.*) bread-roll.

wecken ['vɛkən], *v.a.* wake, rouse, awaken.

Wecker ['vɛkər], *m.* (—s, *pl.* —) alarm-clock.

Weckuhr ['vɛku:r], *f.* (—, *pl.* —en) alarm-clock.

Wedel ['ve:dəl], *m.* (—s, *pl.* —) feather-duster, fan; tail.

wedeln ['ve:dəln], *v.n. mit dem Schwanz* —, wag its tail.

weder ['ve:dər], *conj.* neither; — . . . *noch*, neither . . . nor.

Weg [ve:k], *m.* (—(e)s, *pl.* —e) way, path, route, road; walk, errand; *am* —, by the wayside.

weg [vɛk], *adv.* away, gone, off, lost.

wegbegeben ['vɛkbəge:bən], *v.r. irr. sich* —, go away, leave.

wegbekommen ['vɛkbəkɔmən], *v.a. irr. etwas* —, get the hang of s.th.; get s.th. off *or* away.

Wegbereiter ['ve:kbəraItər], *m.* (—s, *pl.* —en) forerunner, pathfinder, pioneer.

wegblasen ['vɛkbla:zən], *v.a. irr.* blow away; *wie weggeblasen*, without leaving a trace.

wegbleiben ['vɛkblaIbən], *v.n. irr.* (*aux.* sein) stay away.

wegblicken ['vɛkblIkən], *v.n.* look the other way.

wegbringen ['vɛkbrIŋən], *v.a. irr. einen* —, get s.o. away.

wegdrängen ['vɛkdrɛŋən], *v.a.* push away.

Wegebau ['ve:gəbau], *m.* (—s, *no pl.*) road-making.

wegeilen ['vɛkaIlən], *v.n.* (*aux.* sein) hasten away, hurry off.

wegelagern ['ve:gəla:gərn], *v.a.* waylay.

wegen ['ve:gən], *prep.* (*Genit., Dat.*) because of, on account of, owing to, by reason of.

Wegfall ['vɛkfal], *m.* (—s, *no pl.*) omission.

wegfallen ['vɛkfalən], *v.n. irr.* (*aux.* sein) fall off; be omitted; cease.

Weggang ['vɛkgaŋ], *m.* (—s, *no pl.*) departure, going away.

weggießen ['vɛkgi:sən], *v.a. irr.* pour away.

weghaben ['vɛkha:bən], *v.a. irr. etwas* —, understand how to do s.th, have the knack of doing s.th.

wegkommen ['vɛkkɔmən], *v.n. irr.* (*aux.* sein) get away; be lost.

wegkönnen ['vɛkkœnən], *v.n. irr. nicht* —, not be able to get away.

Weglassung ['vɛklasuŋ], *f.* (—, *pl.* —en) omission.

wegmachen ['vɛkmaxən], *v.r. sich* —, decamp, make off.

wegmüssen ['vɛkmysən], *v.n. irr.* be obliged to go; have to go.

Wegnahme ['vɛkna:mə], *f.* (—, *no pl.*) taking, seizure, capture.

Wegreise ['vɛkraIzə], *f.* (—, *no pl.*) departure.

Wegscheide ['ve:kʃaIdə], *f.* (—, *pl.* —n) crossroads, crossways.

wegscheren ['vɛkʃe:rən], *v.a.* clip; shave off. — *v.r. sich* —, be off.

wegschnappen ['vɛkʃnapən], *v.a.* snatch away.

wegsehnen ['vɛkze:nən], *v.r. sich* —, wish o.s. far away; long to get away.

wegsein ['vɛkzaIn], *v.n. irr.* (*aux.* sein) (*person*) be gone, be away; have gone off; (*things*) be lost; *ganz* —, (*coll.*) be beside o.s. *or* amazed.

wegsetzen ['vɛkzɛtsən], *v.a.* put away.

wegspülen ['vɛkʃpy:lən], *v.a.* wash away.

Wegstunde ['ve:kʃtundə], *f.* (—, *pl.* —n) an hour's walk.

Wegweiser ['ve:kvaIzər], *m.* (—s, *pl.* —) signpost, road-sign.

wegwenden ['vɛkvɛndən], *v.r. irr. sich* —, turn away.

wegwerfen ['vɛkvɛrfən], *v.a. irr.* throw away.

wegwerfend ['vɛkvɛrfənt], *adj.* disparaging, disdainful.

Wegzehrung ['ve:ktse:ruŋ], *f.* (—, *no pl.*) food for the journey; (*Eccl.*) viaticum.

wegziehen ['vɛktsiːən], *v.a. irr.* draw away, pull away. — *v.n.* (*aux.* sein) march away; (*fig.*) move, remove.

Wegzug ['vɛktsuːk], *m.* (—s, *no pl.*) removal; moving away.

Weh [veː], *n.* (—s, *no pl.*) pain; grief, pang; misfortune.

weh [veː], *adj.* painful, sore; *mir ist — ums Herz,* I am sick at heart; my heart aches. — *adv.* — *tun,* ache; pain, hurt, offend, distress, grieve. — *int.* — *mir!* woe is me!

Wehen ['veːən], *n. pl.* birth-pangs, labour-pains.

wehen ['veːən], *v.n.* (*wind*) blow.

Wehgeschrei ['veːgəʃraɪ], *n.* (—s, *no pl.*) wailings.

Wehklage ['veːklaːgə], *f.* (—, *pl.* —n) lamentation.

wehklagen ['veːklaːgən], *v.n. insep.* lament, wail.

wehleidig ['veːlaɪdɪç], *adj.* tearful; easily hurt; self-pitying.

wehmütig ['veːmyːtɪç], *adj.* sad, melancholy, wistful.

Wehr (1) [veːr], *n.* (—s, *pl.* —e) weir.

Wehr (2) [veːr], *f.* (—, *pl.* —en) defence, bulwark.

wehren ['veːrən], *v.r. sich —,* defend o.s., offer resistance.

wehrhaft ['veːrhaft], *adj.* capable of bearing arms, able-bodied.

wehrlos ['veːrloːs], *adj.* defenceless, unarmed; (*fig.*) weak, unprotected.

Wehrpflicht ['veːrpflɪçt], *f.* (—, *no pl.*) compulsory military service, conscription.

Wehrstand ['veːrʃtant], *m.* (—s, *no pl.*) the military.

Weib [vaɪp], *n.* (—(e)s, *pl.* —er) woman; (*Poet.*) wife.

Weibchen ['vaɪpçən], *n.* (—s, *pl.* —) (*animal*) female.

Weiberfeind ['vaɪbərfaɪnt], *m.* (—s, *pl.* —e) woman-hater, misogynist.

Weiberherrschaft ['vaɪbərhɛrʃaft], *f.* (—, *no pl.*) petticoat rule.

weibisch ['vaɪbɪʃ], *adj.* womanish, effeminate.

weiblich ['vaɪplɪç], *adj.* female, feminine; womanly.

Weiblichkeit ['vaɪplɪçkaɪt], *f.* (—, *no pl.*) womanliness, femininity.

Weibsbild ['vaɪpsbɪlt], *n.* (—s, *pl.* —er) (*sl.*) female; wench.

weich [vaɪç], *adj.* weak; soft; tender, gentle; effeminate; sensitive; — *machen,* soften; — *werden,* relent.

Weichbild ['vaɪçbɪlt], *n.* (—s, *no pl.*) precincts; city boundaries.

Weiche ['vaɪçə], *f.*·(—, *pl.* —n) (*Railw.*) switch, points.

weichen (1) ['vaɪçən], *v.a.* steep, soak, soften.

weichen (2) ['vaɪçən], *v.n. irr.* (*aux.* sein) yield, make way, give ground.

Weichensteller ['vaɪçənʃtɛlər], *m.* (—s, *pl.* —) (*Railw.*) pointsman, signalman.

Weichheit ['vaɪçhaɪt], *f.* (—, *no pl.*) softness; (*fig.*) weakness, tenderness.

weichherzig ['vaɪçhɛrtsɪç], *adj.* soft-hearted, tender-hearted.

weichlich ['vaɪçlɪç], *adj.* soft; (*fig.*) weak, effeminate.

Weichling ['vaɪçlɪŋ], *m.* (—s, *pl.* —e) weakling.

Weichsel ['vaɪksəl], *f.* Vistula.

Weichselkirsche ['vaɪksəlkɪrʃə], *f.* (—, *pl.* —n) sour cherry; morello.

Weide ['vaɪdə], *f.* (—, *pl.* —n) pasture, pasturage; (*Bot.*) willow.

Weideland ['vaɪdəlant], *n.* (—s, *pl.* ːer) pasture-ground.

weiden ['vaɪdən], *v.a.,v.n.* pasture, feed.

Weidenbaum ['vaɪdənbaum], *m.* (—s, *pl.* ːe) willow-tree.

Weiderich ['vaɪdərɪç], *m.* (—s, *pl.* —e) willow-herb, loose-strife, rose bay.

Weidgenosse ['vaɪtgənɔsə], *m.* (—en, *pl.* —en) fellow huntsman.

weidlich ['vaɪtlɪç], *adv.* (*rare*) greatly, thoroughly.

Weidmann ['vaɪtman], *m.* (—s, *pl.* ːer) sportsman, huntsman.

Weidmannsheil! ['vaɪtmanshaɪl], *excl.* tally-ho!

weigern ['vaɪgərn], *v.r. sich —,* refuse, decline.

Weigerung ['vaɪgəruŋ], *f.* (—, *pl.* —en) refusal, denial.

Weih [vaɪ], *m.* (—en, *pl.* —en) (*Orn.*) kite.

Weihbischof ['vaɪbɪʃɔf], *m.* (—s, *pl.* ːe) suffragan bishop.

Weihe ['vaɪə], *f.* (—, *pl.* —en) consecration; (*priest*) ordination; initiation; (*fig.*) solemnity.

weihen ['vaɪən], *v.a.* bless, consecrate; ordain. — *v.r. sich —,* devote o.s. (to).

Weiher ['vaɪər], *m.* (—s, *pl.* —) pond, fishpond.

weihevoll ['vaɪəfɔl], *adj.* solemn.

Weihnachten ['vaɪnaxtən], *n. or f.* Christmas.

Weihnachtsabend ['vaɪnaxtsaːbənt], *m.* (—s, *pl.* —e) Christmas Eve.

Weihnachtsfeiertag ['vaɪnaxtsfaɪərtaːk], *m.* (—s, *pl.* —e) Christmas Day; *zweiter —,* Boxing Day.

Weihnachtsgeschenk ['vaɪnaxtsgəʃɛŋk], *n.* (—s, *pl.* —e) Christmas box, Christmas present.

Weihnachtslied ['vaɪnaxtsliːt], *n.* (—(e)s, *pl.* —er) Christmas carol.

Weihnachtsmann ['vaɪnaxtsman], *m.* (—(e)s, *pl.* ːer) Santa Claus, Father Christmas.

Weihrauch ['vaɪraux], *m.* (—s, *no pl.*) incense.

Weihwasser ['vaɪvasər], *n.* (—s, *no pl.*) holy water.

weil [vaɪl], *conj.* because, as, since.

weiland ['vaɪlant], *adv.* (*obs.*) formerly, once.

Weile ['vaɪlə], *f.* (—, *no pl.*) while, short time; leisure.

weilen ['vaɪlən], *v.n.* tarry, stay, abide.

Wein [vaɪn], *m.* (—(e)s, *pl.* —e) wine; (*plant*) vine; *einem reinen — einschenken,* tell s.o. the truth.

Weinbau

Weinbau ['vaɪnbau], *m.* (—s, *no pl.*) vine growing, viticulture.

Weinbeere ['vaɪnbeːrə], *f.* (—, *pl.* —n) grape.

Weinberg ['vaɪnberk], *m.* (—s, *pl.* —e) vineyard.

Weinbrand ['vaɪnbrant], *m.* (—s, *no pl.*) brandy.

weinen ['vaɪnən], *v.n.* weep, cry.

Weinernte ['vaɪnɛrntə], *f.* (—, *pl.* —n) vintage.

Weinessig ['vaɪnɛsɪç], *m.* (—s, *no pl.*) (wine) vinegar.

Weinfaß ['vaɪnfas], *n.* (—sses, *pl.* ˸sser) wine-cask.

Weingeist ['vaɪngaɪst], *m.* (—es, *no pl.*) spirits of wine, alcohol.

Weinhändler ['vaɪnhɛndlər], *m.* (—s, *pl.* —) wine merchant.

Weinkarte ['vaɪnkartə], *f.* (—, *pl.* —n) wine-list.

Weinkeller ['vaɪnkɛlər], *m.* (—s, *pl.* —) wine-cellar; wine-tavern.

Weinkellerei ['vaɪnkɛləraɪ], *f.* (—, *pl.* —en) wine-store.

Weinkelter ['vaɪnkɛltər], *f.* (—, *pl.* —n) wine-press.

Weinkneipe ['vaɪnknaɪpə], *f.* (—, *pl.* —n) wine-tavern.

Weinkoster ['vaɪnkɔstər], *m.* (—s, *pl.* —) wine-taster.

Weinlaub ['vaɪnlaup], *n.* (—s, *no pl.*) vine-leaves.

Weinlese ['vaɪnleːzə], *f.* (—, *pl.* —n) vintage, grape harvest.

Weinranke ['vaɪnraŋkə], *f.* (—, *pl.* —n) vine-branch, tendril.

Weinschenke ['vaɪnʃɛŋkə], *f.* (—, *pl.* —n) wine-house, tavern.

weinselig ['vaɪnzeːlɪç], *adj.* tipsy.

Weinstein ['vaɪnʃtaɪn], *m.* (—s, *no pl.*) tartar.

Weinsteinsäure ['vaɪnʃtaɪnzɔyrə], *f.* (—, *no pl.*) tartaric acid.

Weinstock ['vaɪnʃtɔk], *m.* (—s, *pl.* ˸e) vine.

Weintraube ['vaɪntraubə], *f.* (—, *pl.* —n) grape, bunch of grapes.

weinumrankt ['vaɪnumraŋkt], *adj.* vine-clad.

weise ['vaɪzə], *adj.* wise, prudent.

Weise (1) ['vaɪzə], *m.* (—n, *pl.* —n) wise man, sage.

Weise (2) ['vaɪzə], *f.* (—, *pl.* —n) manner, fashion; method, way; tune, melody.

weisen ['vaɪzən], *v.a. irr.* point to, point out, show.

Weiser ['vaɪzər], *m.* (—s, *pl.* —) signpost; indicator; (*clock*) hand.

Weisheit ['vaɪshaɪt], *f.* (—, *pl.* —en) wisdom, prudence.

Weisheitszahn ['vaɪshaɪtstsaːn], *m.* (—s, *pl.* ˸e) wisdom tooth.

weislich ['vaɪslɪç], *adv.* wisely, prudently, advisedly.

weismachen ['vaɪsmaxən], *v.a.* *einem etwas* —, (*coll.*) spin a yarn to s.o.; *laß dir nichts* —, don't be taken in.

weissagen ['vaɪsaːgən], *v.a. insep.* prophesy, foretell.

Weissager ['vaɪsaːgər], *m.* (—s, *pl.* —) prophet, soothsayer.

Weissagung ['vaɪsaːguŋ], *f.* (—, *pl.* —en) prophecy.

weiß [vaɪs], *adj.* white, clean, blank.

Weißbuche ['vaɪsbuːxə], *f.* (—, *pl.* —n) (*Bot.*) hornbeam.

Weiße ['vaɪsə], *f.* (—, *no pl.*) whiteness; (*fig.*) (*dial.*) pale ale.

weißglühend ['vaɪsglyːənt], *adj.* at white heat, incandescent, white hot.

Weißnäherin ['vaɪsnɛːərɪn], *f.* (—, *pl.* —nen) seamstress.

Weißwaren ['vaɪsvaːrən], *f. pl.* linen.

Weisung ['vaɪzuŋ], *f.* (—, *pl.* —en) order, direction, instruction; directive.

weit [vaɪt], *adj.* distant, far, far off; wide, broad, vast, extensive; (*clothing*) loose, too big.

weitab [vaɪt'ap], *adv.* far away.

weitaus [vaɪt'aus], *adv.* by far.

weitblickend ['vaɪtblɪkənt], *adj.* far-sighted.

Weite ['vaɪtə], *f.* (—, *pl.* —n) width, breadth; distance.

weiten ['vaɪtən], *v.a.* widen, expand.

weiter ['vaɪtər], *adj.* further, farther, wider.

weiterbefördern ['vaɪtərbəfœrdərn], *v.a.* send, forward, send on.

weiterbilden ['vaɪtərbɪldən], *v.a.* improve, develop(e), extend.

Weitere ['vaɪtərə], *n.* (—n, *no pl.*) rest, remainder.

weiterführen ['vaɪtərfyːrən], *v.a.* continue, carry on.

weitergeben ['vaɪtərgeːbən], *v.a. irr.* pass on.

weitergehen ['vaɪtərgeːən], *v.n. irr.* (*aux.* sein) walk on.

weiterhin ['vaɪtərhɪn], *adv.* furthermore; in time to come; in future.

weiterkommen ['vaɪtərkɔmən], *v.n. irr.* (*aux.* sein) get on, advance.

Weiterung ['vaɪtəruŋ], *f.* (—, *pl.* —en) widening, enlargement.

weitgehend ['vaɪtgeːənt], *adj.* far-reaching, sweeping.

weitläufig ['vaɪtlɔyfɪç], *adj.* ample, large; detailed, elaborate; distant, widespread; diffuse, long-winded.

weitschweifig ['vaɪtʃvaɪfɪç], *adj.* prolix, diffuse, rambling.

weitsichtig ['vaɪtzɪçtɪç], *adj.* long-sighted.

weittragend ['vaɪttraːgənt], *adj.* portentous, far-reaching.

weitverbreitet ['vaɪtfɛrbraɪtət], *adj.* widespread.

Weizen ['vaɪtsən], *m.* (—s, *no pl.*) wheat.

Weizengrieß ['vaɪtsəngriːs], *m.* (—es, *no pl.*) semolina; grits.

welch [vɛlç], *pron.* what (a).

welcher, -e, -es ['vɛlçər], *interr. pron.* which? what? — *rel. pron.* who which, that; (*indef.*) (*coll.*) some.

welcherlei ['vɛlçərlaɪ], *indecl. adj.* of what kind.

Welfe ['vɛlfə], *m.*(—n, *pl.* —n) Guelph.

welk [vɛlk], *adj.* faded, withered; — *werden*, fade, wither.

welken ['vɛlkən], *v.n.* (*aux.* sein) wither, fade, decay.

Wellblech ['vɛlblɛç], *n.* (—s, *no pl.*) corrugated iron.

Welle ['vɛlə], *f.* (—, *pl.* —n) wave, billow.

wellen ['vɛlən], *v.a.* wave.

Wellenbewegung ['vɛlənbəve:guŋ], *f.* (—, *pl.* —en) undulation.

Wellenlinie ['vɛlənli:njə], *f.* (—, *pl.* —n) wavy line.

wellig ['vɛlɪç], *adj.* wavy, undulating.

welsch [vɛlʃ], *adj.* foreign; Italian; French.

Welschkohl ['vɛlʃko:l], *m.* (—s, *no pl.*) (*Bot.*) savoy cabbage.

Welschkorn ['vɛlʃkɔrn], *n.* (—s, *no pl.*) (*Bot.*) Indian corn.

Welt [vɛlt], *f.* (—, *pl.* —en) world, earth; universe; society.

Weltall ['vɛltal], *n.* (—s, *no pl.*) universe, cosmos; (outer) space.

Weltanschauung ['vɛltanʃauuŋ], *f.* (—, *pl.* —en) view of life, philosophy of life, ideology.

Weltbeschreibung ['vɛltbəʃraɪbuŋ], *f.* (—, *no pl.*) cosmography.

Weltbürger ['vɛltbyrgər], *m.* (—s, *pl.* —) cosmopolitan.

welterschütternd ['vɛltərʃytərnt], *adj.* world-shaking.

weltfremd ['vɛltfrɛmt], *adj.* unwordly, unsophisticated.

Weltgeschichte ['vɛltgəʃɪçtə], *f.* (—, *no pl.*) world history.

Weltherrschaft ['vɛltherʃaft], *f.* (—, *no pl.*) world dominion.

Weltkenntnis ['vɛltkɛntnɪs], *f.* (—, *no pl.*) worldly wisdom.

weltklug ['vɛltklu:k], *adj.* astute, worldly-wise.

Weltkrieg ['vɛltkri:k], *m.* (—es, *pl.* —e) world war.

weltlich ['vɛltlɪç], *adj.* worldly; (*Eccl.*) temporal, secular.

Weltmacht ['vɛltmaxt], *f.* (—, *pl.* ⁻e) world power, great power.

Weltmeer ['vɛltme:r], *n.* (—s, *pl.* —e) ocean.

Weltmeisterschaft ['vɛltmaɪstərʃaft], *f.* (—, *pl.* —en) world championship.

Weltordnung ['vɛltɔrdnuŋ], *f.* (—, *pl.* —en) cosmic order.

Weltraum ['vɛltraum], *m.* (—s, *no pl.*) space.

Weltraumflug ['vɛltraumflu:k], *m.* (—(e)s, *pl.* ⁻e) space flight.

Weltraumforschung ['vɛltraumfɔrʃuŋ], *f.* (—, *no pl.*) space exploration.

Weltraumgeschoss ['vɛltraumgəʃɔs], *n.* (—es, *pl.* —e) space rocket.

Weltruf ['vɛltru:f], *m.* (—s, *no pl.*) world-wide renown.

Weltschmerz ['vɛltʃmɛrts], *m.* (—es, *no pl.*) world-weariness, Wertherism; melancholy.

Weltsprache ['vɛltʃpra:xə], *f.* (—, *pl.* —en) universal language; world language.

Weltstadt ['vɛltʃtat], *f.* (—, *pl.* ⁻e) metropolis.

Weltumseglung ['vɛltumze:gluŋ], *f.* (—, *pl.* —en) circumnavigation (of the globe).

Weltuntergang ['vɛltuntərgaŋ], *m.* —s, *no pl.*) end of the world.

Weltwirtschaft ['vɛltvirtʃaft], *f.* (—, *no pl.*) world trade.

wem [ve:m], *pers. pron.* (*Dat. of* wer) to whom — *interr. pron.* to whom?

wen [ve:n], *pers. pron.* (*Acc. of* wer) whom — *interr. pron.* whom?

Wende ['vɛndə], *f.* (—, *pl.* —n) turn, turning(point).

Wendekreis ['vɛndəkraɪs], *m.* (—es, *pl.* —e) tropic.

Wendeltreppe ['vɛndəltrɛpə], *f.* (—, *pl.* —n) spiral staircase.

wenden ['vɛndən], *v.a. reg. & irr.* turn.

Wendepunkt ['vɛndəpuŋkt], *m.* (—es, *pl.* —e) turning point; crisis.

Wendung ['vɛnduŋ], *f.* (—, *pl.* —en) turn, turning; crisis; (*speech*) phrase.

wenig ['ve:nɪç], *adj.* little, few; *ein —*, a little.

weniger ['ve:nɪgər], *adj.* less, fewer.

wenigstens ['ve:nɪçstəns], *adv.* at least.

wenn [vɛn], *conj.* if; when; whenever, in case; — *nicht*, unless.

wenngleich [vɛn'glaɪç], *conj.* though, although.

wer [ve:r], *rel. pron.* who, he who; — *auch*, whoever. — *interr. pron.* who? which? — *da?* who goes there?

Werbekraft ['vɛrbəkraft], *f.* (—, *no pl.*) (*Advertising*) attraction; appeal; publicity value.

werben ['vɛrbən], *v.n. irr.* advertise, canvass; court, woo. — *v.a.* (*soldiers*) recruit.

Werbung ['vɛrbuŋ], *f.* (—, *pl.* —en) advertising, publicity, propaganda; recruiting; courtship.

Werdegang ['ve:rdəgaŋ], *m.* (—s, *no pl.*) evolution, development.

werden ['ve:rdən], *v.n. irr.* (*aux.* sein) become, get; grow; turn; *Arzt —*, become a doctor; *alt —*, grow old; *bleich —*, turn pale.

werdend ['ve:rdənt], *adj.* becoming; nascent, incipient, budding.

werfen ['vɛrfən], *v.a. irr.* throw, cast.

Werft (1) [vɛrft], *m.* (—(e)s, *pl.* —e) warp.

Werft (2) [vɛrft], *f.* (—, *pl.* —en) dockyard, shipyard, wharf.

Werk [vɛrk], *n.* (—(e)s, *pl.* —e) work, action, deed; undertaking; (*Ind.*) works, plant, mill, factory.

Werkführer ['vɛrkfy:rər], *m.* (—s, *pl.* —) foreman.

Werkleute ['vɛrklɔytə], *pl.* workmen.

Werkmeister ['vɛrkmaɪstər], *m.* (—s, *pl.* —) overseer.

werktätig ['vɛrktɛ:tɪç], *adj.* active, practical; hard-working.

Werkzeug

Werkzeug ['vɛrktsɔyk], *n.* (—s, *pl.* —e) implement, tool, jig, instrument.

Wermut ['vɛːrmuːt], *m.* (—s, *no pl.*) absinthe, vermouth.

Wert [veːrt], *m.* (—(e)s, *pl.* —e) value, worth, price; use; merit; importance.

wert [veːrt], *adj.* valuable; worth; dear, esteemed.

Wertangabe ['veːrtangaːbə], *f.* (—, *pl.* —n) declared value.

Wertbestimmung ['veːrtbəʃtimuŋ], *f.* (—, *no pl.*) appraisal, assessment, valuation.

Wertbrief ['veːrtbriːf], *m.* (—s, *pl.* —e) registered letter.

werten ['veːrtən], *v.a.* value.

Wertgegenstand ['veːrtgeːgənʃtant], *m.* (—s, *pl.* ⸚e) article of value.

Wertmesser ['veːrtmɛsər], *m.* (—s, *pl.* —) standard.

Wertpapiere ['veːrtpapiːrə], *n. pl.* securities.

Wertsachen ['veːrtzaxən], *f. pl.* valuables.

wertschätzen ['veːrtʃɛtsən], *v.a.* esteem (highly).

wertvoll ['veːrtfɔl], *adj.* of great value, valuable.

Wertzeichen ['veːrttsaiçən], *n.* (—s, *pl.* —) stamp; coupon.

wes [vɛs], *pers. pron.* (*obs.*) whose.

Wesen ['veːzən], *n.* (—s, *pl.* —) being, creature; reality; essence, nature, substance; character, demeanour; (*in compounds*) organisation, affairs.

wesenlos ['veːzənloːs], *adj.* disembodied, unsubstantial, shadowy: trivial.

wesensgleich ['veːzənsglaiç], *adj.* identical, substantially the same.

wesentlich ['veːzəntliç], *adj.* essential, material.

weshalb [vɛs'halp], *conj., adv.* wherefore, why; therefore.

Wespe ['vɛspə], *f.* (—, *pl.* —n) (*Ent.*) wasp.

Wespennest ['vɛspənnɛst], *n.* (—s, *pl.* —er,) wasp's nest; *in ein — stechen*, stir up a hornet's nest.

wessen ['vɛsən], *pers .pron.* (*Genit. of* **wer**) whose. — *interr. pron.* whose?

Weste ['vɛstə], *f.* (—, *pl.* —n) waistcoat.

Westen ['vɛstən], *m.* (—s, *no pl.*) west; *nach —*, westward.

Westfalen [vɛst'faːlən], *n.* Westphalia.

Westindien [vɛst'indjən], *n.* the West Indies.

weswegen [vɛs've:gən] *see* **weshalb**.

Wettbewerb ['vɛtbəvɛrp], *m.* (—s, *pl.* —e) competition, rivalry; *unlauterer —*, unfair competition.

Wettbewerber ['vɛtbəvɛrbər], *m.* (—s, *pl.* —) rival, competitor.

Wette ['vɛtə], *f.* (—, *pl.* —n) bet, wager; *um die — laufen*, race one another.

Wetteifer ['vɛtaifər], *m.* (—s, *no pl.*) rivalry.

wetteifern ['vɛtaifərn], *v.n. insep.* vie (with), compete.

wetten ['vɛtən], *v.a., v.n.* bet, lay a wager, wager.

Wetter ['vɛtər], *n.* (—s, *pl.* —) weather; bad weather, storm; *schlagende —*, (*Min.*) fire-damp.

Wetterbeobachtung ['vɛtərbəobaxtuŋ], *f.* (—, *pl.* —en) meteorological observation.

Wetterbericht ['vɛtərbəriçt], *m.* (—s, *pl.* —e) weather report *or* forecast.

Wetterfahne ['vɛtərfaːnə], *f.* (—, *pl.* —en) weather-cock, vane; (*fig.*) turncoat.

wetterfest ['vɛtərfɛst], *adj.* weatherproof.

Wetterglas ['vɛtərglaːs], *n.* (—es, *pl.* ⸚er) barometer.

Wetterhahn ['vɛtərhaːn], *m.* (—s, *pl.* ⸚e) weather-cock.

Wetterkunde ['vɛtərkundə], *f.* (—, *no pl.*) meteorology.

Wetterleuchten ['vɛtərlɔyçtən], *n.* (—s, *no pl.*) summer lightning; sheet lightning.

wettern ['vɛtərn], *v.n.* be stormy; (*fig.*) curse, swear, thunder (against), storm.

Wettervorhersage ['vɛtərfoːrheːrzaːgə], *f.* (—, *pl.* —n) weather forecast.

wetterwendisch ['vɛtərvɛndiʃ], *adj.* changeable; irritable, peevish.

Wettkampf ['vɛtkampf], *m.* (—(e)s, *pl.* ⸚e) contest, tournament.

Wettlauf ['vɛtlauf], *m.* (—s, *pl.* ⸚e) race.

wettmachen ['vɛtmaxən], *v.a.* make up for.

Wettrennen ['vɛtrenən], *n.* (—s, *pl.* —) racing, race.

Wettstreit ['vɛtʃtrait], *m.* (—s, *pl.* —e) contest, contention.

wetzen ['vɛtsən], *v.a.* whet, hone, sharpen.

Wichse ['viksə], *f.* (—, *pl.* —n) blacking, shoe-polish; (*fig.*) thrashing.

wichsen ['viksən], *v.a.* black, shine; (*fig.*) thrash.

Wicht [viçt], *m.* (—(e)s, *pl.* —e) creature; (*coll.*) chap.

Wichtelmännchen ['viçtəlmɛnçən], *n.* (—s, *pl.* —) pixie, goblin.

wichtig ['viçtiç], *adj.* important; weighty; significant; *sich — machen*, put on airs.

Wichtigkeit ['viçtiçkait], *f.* (—, *no pl.*) importance; significance.

Wicke ['vikə], *f.* (—, *pl.* —n) (*Bot.*) vetch.

Wickel ['vikəl], *m.* (—s, *pl.* —) roller; (*hair*) curler; (*Med.*) compress.

Wickelkind ['vikəlkint], *n.* (—s, *pl.* —er) babe in arms.

wickeln ['vikəln], *v.a.* roll, coil; wind; wrap (up); (*babies*) swaddle; (*hair*) curl.

Widder ['vidər], *m.* (—s, *pl.* —) ram; (*Astrol.*) Aries.

wider ['viːdər], *prep.* (*Acc.*) against, in opposition to, contrary to.

widerfahren [vi:dər'fa:rən], *v.n. irr. insep. (aux. sein)* happen to s.o., befall s.o.; *einem Gerechtigkeit — lassen*, give s.o. his due.

Widerhaken ['vi:dərha:kən], *m.* (—s, *pl.* —) barb.

Widerhall ['vi:dərhal], *m.* (—s, *pl.* —e) echo, resonance; (*fig.*) response.

widerlegen [vi:dər'le:gən], *v.a. insep.* refute, disprove, prove (s.o.) wrong.

Widerlegung [vi:dər'le:guŋ], *f.* (—, *pl.* —en) refutation, rebuttal.

widerlich ['vi:dərlɪç], *adj.* disgusting, nauseating, repulsive.

widernatürlich ['vi:dərnaty:rlɪç], *adj.* unnatural; perverse.

widerraten [vi:dər'ra:tən], *v.a. irr. insep.* advise against; dissuade from.

widerrechtlich ['vi:dərrɛçtlɪç], *adj.* illegal, unlawful.

Widerrede ['vi:dərre:də], *f.* (—, *pl.* —n) contradiction.

Widerruf ['vi:dəru:f], *m.* (—s, *pl.* —e) revocation, recantation.

widerrufen [vi:dər'ru:fən], *v.a. irr. insep.* recant, retract, revoke.

Widersacher ['vi:dərzaxər], *m.* (—s, *pl.* —) adversary, antagonist.

Widerschein ['vi:dərʃaɪn], *m.* (—s, *no pl.*) reflection.

widersetzen [vi:dər'zɛtsən], *v.r. insep. sich —*, resist, (*Dat.*) oppose.

widersetzlich ['vi:dər'zɛtslɪç], *adj.* refractory, insubordinate.

Widersinn ['vi:dərzɪn], *m.* (—s, *no pl.*) nonsense, absurdity; paradox.

widersinnig ['vi:dərzɪnɪç], *adj.* nonsensical, absurd; paradoxical.

widerspenstig ['vi:dərʃpɛnstɪç], *adj.* refractory, rebellious, obstinate, stubborn.

widerspiegeln [vi:dər'ʃpi:gəln], *v.a.* reflect, mirror.

widersprechen [vi:dər'ʃprɛçən], *v.n. irr. insep.* (*Dat.*) contradict, gainsay.

Widerspruch ['vi:dərʃprux], *m.* (—(e)s, *pl.* -̈e) contradiction.

widerspruchsvoll ['vi:dərʃpruxsfɔl], *adj.* contradictory.

Widerstand ['vi:dərʃtant], *m.* (—s, *pl.* -̈e) resistance, opposition.

widerstandsfähig ['vi:dərʃtantsfɛ:ɪç], *adj.* resistant, hardy.

widerstehen [vi:dər'ʃte:ən], *v.n. irr. insep.* (*Dat.*) resist, withstand; be distasteful (to).

Widerstreben [vi:dər'ʃtre:bən], *n.* (—s, *no pl.*) reluctance.

widerstreben [vi:dər'ʃtre:bən], *v.n. insep.* (*Dat.*) strive against, oppose; be distasteful to a p.

Widerstreit ['vi:dərʃtraɪt], *m.* (—s, *no pl.*) contradiction, opposition; conflict.

widerwärtig ['vi:dərvɛrtɪç], *adj.* unpleasant, disagreeable, repugnant, repulsive; hateful, odious.

Widerwille ['vi:dərvɪlə], *m.* (—ns, *no pl.*) aversion (to).

widmen ['vɪdmən], *v.a.* dedicate.

Widmung ['vɪdmuŋ], *f.* (—, *pl.* —en) dedication.

widrig ['vi:drɪç], *adj.* contrary, adverse, inimical, unfavourable.

widrigenfalls ['vi:drɪgənfals], *adv.* failing this, otherwise, else.

wie [vi:], *adv.* how. — *conj.* as, just as, like; — *geht's?* how are you?

wieder ['vi:dər], *adv.* again, anew, afresh; back, in return.

Wiederabdruck ['vi:dərapdruk], *m.* (—s, *pl.* —e) reprint.

Wiederaufbau [vi:dər'aufbau], *m.* (—s, *no pl.*) rebuilding.

Wiederaufnahme [vi:dər'aufna:mə], *f.* (—, *no pl.*) resumption.

Wiederbelebungsversuch ['vi:dərbə-le:buŋsfɛrzu:x], *m.* (—es, *pl.* —e) attempt at resuscitation.

Wiederbezahlung ['vi:dərbətsa:luŋ], *f.* (—, *pl.* —en) reimbursement.

wiederbringen ['vi:dərbrɪŋən], *v.a. irr. insep.* bring back, restore.

Wiedereinrichtung ['vi:dəraɪnrɪçtuŋ], *f.* (—, *no pl.*) reorganisation, re-establishment.

Wiedereinsetzung ['vi:dəraɪnzɛtsuŋ], *f.* (—, *pl.* —en) restoration, reinstatement, rehabilitation.

wiedererkennen ['vi:dərɛrkɛnən], *v.a. irr.* recognise.

Wiedererstattung ['vi:dərɛrʃtatuŋ], *f.* (—, *no pl.*) restitution.

Wiedergabe ['vi:dərga:bə], *f.* (—, *no pl.*) restitution, return; (*fig.*) rendering, reproduction.

wiedergeben ['vi:dərge:bən], *v.a. irr.* return, give back; (*fig.*) render.

Wiedergeburt ['vi:dərgəbu:rt], *f.* (—, *no pl.*) rebirth, regeneration, renascence.

Wiedergutmachung [vi:dər'gu:t-maxuŋ], *f.* (—, *no pl.*) reparation.

Wiederherstellung [vi:dər'he:rʃtɛluŋ], *f.* (—, *no pl.*) restoration; recovery.

Wiederherstellungsmittel [vi:dər-'he:rʃtɛluŋsmɪtəl], *n.* (—s, *pl.* —) restorative, tonic.

wiederholen [vi:dər'ho:lən], *v.a. insep.* repeat, reiterate.

Wiederholung [vi:dər'ho:luŋ], *f.* (—, *pl.* —en) repetition.

Wiederkäuer ['vi:dərkɔyər], *m.* (—s, *pl.* —) ruminant.

Wiederkehr ['vi:dərke:r], *f.* (—, *no pl.*) return; recurrence.

wiederkehren ['vi:dərke:rən], *v.n.* (*aux.* sein) return.

wiederklingen ['vi:dərklɪŋən], *v.n. irr.* reverberate.

wiederkommen ['vi:dərkɔmən], *v.n. irr.* (*aux.* sein) return, come back.

Wiedersehen ['vi:dərze:ən], *n.* (—s, *no pl.*) reunion, meeting after separation; *auf —*, good-bye! so long! see you again!

wiedersehen ['vi:dərze:ən], *v.a. irr.* see again, meet again.

wiederum

wiederum ['vi:dərum], *adv.* again, anew, afresh.

Wiedervereinigung ['vi:dərfɛraɪnɪguŋ], *f.* (—, *pl.* —en) reunion, reunification.

Wiedervergeltung ['vi:dərfɛrgɛltuŋ], *f.* (—, *no pl.*) requital, retaliation, reprisal.

Wiederverkauf ['vi:dərfɛrkauf], *m.* (—s, *no pl.*) resale.

Wiederverkäufer ['vi:dərfɛrkɔyfər], *m.* (—s, *pl.* —) retailer.

Wiederversöhnung ['vi:dərfɛrzø:nuŋ], *f.* (—, *no pl.*) reconciliation.

Wiederwahl ['vi:dərva:l], *f.* (—, *no pl.*) re-election.

Wiege ['vi:gə], *f.* (—, *pl.* —n) cradle.

wiegen ['vi:gən], *v.a.* rock (the cradle). — *v.r. sich* —, delude o.s. with. — *v.a., v.n. irr.* weigh.

Wiegenfest ['vi:gənfɛst], *n.* (—es, *pl.* —e) (*Poet., Lit.*) birthday.

Wiegenlied ['vi:gənli:t], *n.* (—s, *pl.* —er) cradle-song, lullaby.

wiehern ['vi:ərn], *v.n.* neigh.

Wien [vi:n], *n.* Vienna.

Wiese ['vi:zə], *f.* (—, *pl.* —n) meadow.

Wiesel ['vi:zəl], *n.* (—s, *pl.* —) (*Zool.*) weasel.

wieso [vi'zo:] *adv.* why? how do you mean? in what way?

wieviel [vi'fi:l], *adv.* how much, how many; *den* —*ten haben wir heute?* what is the date today?

wiewohl [vi'vo:l], *conj.* although, though.

Wild [vɪlt], *n.* (—(e)s, *no pl.*) game; venison.

wild [vɪlt], *adj.* wild, savage, fierce; furious.

Wildbach ['vɪltbax], *m.* (—s, *pl.* ⸚e) (mountain) torrent.

Wilddieb ['vɪltdi:p], *m.* (—(e)s, *pl.* —e) poacher.

Wilde ['vɪldə], *m.* (—n, *pl.* —n) savage.

wildern ['vɪldərn], *v.n.* poach.

Wildfang ['vɪltfaŋ], *m.* (—s, *pl.* ⸚e) scamp, tomboy.

wildfremd ['vɪltfrɛmt], *adj.* completely strange.

Wildhüter ['vɪlthy:tər], *m.* (—s, *pl.* —) gamekeeper.

Wildleder ['vɪltle:dər], *n.* (—s, *no pl.*) suède, doeskin, buckskin.

Wildnis ['vɪltnɪs], *f.* (—, *pl.* —se) wilderness, desert.

Wildpark ['vɪltpark], *m.* (—s, *pl.* —s) game-reserve.

Wildpret ['vɪltprɛt], *n.* (—s, *no pl.*) game; venison.

Wildschwein ['vɪltʃvaɪn], *n.* (—s, *pl.* —e) wild boar.

Wille ['vɪlə], *m.* (—ns, *no pl.*) will, wish, design, purpose.

willenlos ['vɪlənlo:s], *adj.* weak-minded.

willens ['vɪləns], *adv.* — *sein*, be willing, have a mind to.

Willenserklärung ['vɪlənsɛrklɛ:ruŋ], *f.* (—, *pl.* —en) (*Law*) declaratory act.

Willensfreiheit ['vɪlənsfraɪhaɪt], *f.* (—, *no pl.*) free will.

Willenskraft ['vɪlənskraft], *f.* (—, *no pl.*) strength of will, will-power.

willentlich ['vɪləntlɪç], *adv.* purposely, on purpose, intentionally, wilfully.

willfahren [vɪl'fa:rən], *v.n. insep.* (*Dat.*) comply with, gratify.

willfährig ['vɪlfɛ:rɪç], *adj.* compliant, complaisant.

willig ['vɪlɪç], *adj.* willing, ready, docile.

willkommen [vɪl'kɔmən], *adj.* welcome; — *heißen*, welcome.

Willkür ['vɪlky:r], *f.* (—, *no pl.*) free will; discretion; caprice, arbitrariness.

willkürlich ['vɪlky:rlɪç], *adj.* arbitrary.

wimmeln ['vɪməln], *v.n.* swarm, teem (with).

wimmern ['vɪmərn], *v.n.* whimper.

Wimpel ['vɪmpəl], *m.* (—s, *pl.* —) pennon, pennant, streamer.

Wimper ['vɪmpər], *f.* (—, *pl.* —n) eyelash; *ohne mit der* — *zu zucken*, without turning a hair, without batting an eyelid.

Wind [vɪnt], *m.* (—(e)s, *pl.* —e) wind, breeze; *von etwas* — *bekommen*, get wind of.

Windbeutel ['vɪntbɔytəl], *m.* (—s, *pl.* —) cream puff; (*fig.*) windbag.

Windbüchse ['vɪntbyksə], *f.* (—, *pl.* —n) air-gun.

Winde ['vɪndə], *f.* (—, *pl.* —n) (*Tech.*) windlass; (*Bot.*) bindweed.

Windel ['vɪndəl], *f.* (—, *pl.* —n) (baby's) napkin; (*Am.*) diaper.

windelweich ['vɪndəlvaɪç], *adj.* very soft, limp; *einen* — *schlagen*, beat s.o. to a jelly.

winden ['vɪndən], *v.a. irr.* wind, reel; wring; (*flowers*) make a wreath of. — *v.r. sich* —, writhe.

Windeseile ['vɪndəsaɪlə], *f.* (—, *no pl.*) lightning speed.

Windfahne ['vɪntfa:nə], *f.* (—, *pl.* —n) weather-cock, vane.

windfrei ['vɪntfraɪ], *adj.* sheltered.

Windhund ['vɪnthunt], *m.* (—s, *pl.* —e) greyhound; (*fig.*) windbag.

windig ['vɪndɪç], *adj.* windy.

Windklappe ['vɪntklapə], *f.* (—, *pl.* —n) air-valve.

Windlicht ['vɪntlɪçt], *n.* (—s, *pl.* —er) torch; storm lantern.

Windmühle ['vɪntmy:lə], *f.* (—, *pl.* —n) windmill.

Windpocken ['vɪntpɔkən], *f. pl.* (*Med.*) chicken-pox.

Windrichtung ['vɪntrɪçtuŋ], *f.* (—, *pl.* —en) direction of the wind.

Windrose ['vɪntro:zə], *f.* (—, *pl.* —n) compass card; windrose.

Windsbraut ['vɪntsbraut], *f.* (—, *no pl.*) gust of wind, squall; gale.

windschief ['vɪntʃi:f], *adj.* warped, bent.

Windschutzscheibe ['vɪntʃutsʃaɪbə], *f.* (—, *pl.* —n) (*Motor.*) windscreen.

Windseite ['vɪntzaɪtə], *f.* (—, *pl.* —n) windward side.

Witterungsverhältnisse

Windspiel ['vɪntʃpiːl], *n.* (—s, *pl.* —e) greyhound.

windstill ['vɪntʃtɪl], *adj.* calm.

Windung ['vɪnduŋ], *f.* (—, *pl.* —en) winding; convolution; twist, loop; coil; meandering.

Wink [vɪŋk], *m.* (—(e)s, *pl.* —e) sign, nod; (*fig.*) hint, suggestion.

Winkel ['vɪŋkəl], *m.* (—s, *pl.* —) corner; (*Maths.*) angle.

Winkeladvokat ['vɪŋkəlatvokaːt], *m.* (—en, *pl.* —en) quack lawyer.

Winkelmaß ['vɪŋkəlmaːs], *n.* (—es, *pl.* —e) set-square.

Winkelmesser ['vɪŋkəlmɛsər], *m.* (—s, *pl.* —) protractor.

Winkelzug ['vɪŋkəltsuːk], *m.* (—s, *pl.* ⁓e) evasion, trick, shift.

winken ['vɪŋkən], *v.n.* signal, nod, beckon, wave.

winklig ['vɪŋklɪç], *adj.* angular.

winseln ['vɪnzəln], *v.n.* whimper, whine, wail.

Winter ['vɪntər], *m.* (—s, *pl.* —) winter.

Wintergarten ['vɪntərgartən], *m.* (—s, *pl.* ⁓) conservatory.

Wintergewächs ['vɪntərgəvɛks], *n.* (—es, *pl.* —e) perennial plant.

Wintergrün ['vɪntərgryːn], *n.* (—s, *no pl.*) evergreen; wintergreen.

wintern ['vɪntərn], *v.n.* become wintry.

Winterschlaf ['vɪntərʃlaːf], *m.* (—s, *no pl.*) hibernation; den — halten, hibernate.

Winzer ['vɪntsər], *m.* (—s, *pl.* —) vine-grower.

winzig ['vɪntsɪç], *adj.* tiny, diminutive.

Wipfel ['vɪpfəl], *m.* (—s, *pl.* —) top (of a tree), tree-top.

Wippe ['vɪpə], *f.* (—, *pl.* —n) seesaw.

wippen ['vɪpən], *v.n.* balance, see-saw.

wir [viːr], *pers. pron.* we.

Wirbel ['vɪrbəl], *m.* (—s, *pl.* —) (*water*) whirlpool, eddy; whirlwind; (*drum*) roll; (*head*) crown; (*back*) vertebra.

wirbeln ['vɪrbəln], *v.a., v.n.* whirl.

Wirbelsäule ['vɪrbəlzɔylə], *f.* (—, *pl.* —n) spine, vertebral column.

Wirbelwind ['vɪrbəlvɪnt], *m.* (—s, *pl.* —e) whirlwind.

Wirken ['vɪrkən], *n.* (—s, *no pl.*) activity.

wirken ['vɪrkən], *v.a.* effect, work; bring to pass; (*materials*) weave; (*dough*) knead. — *v.n.* work.

Wirker ['vɪrkər], *m.* (—s, *pl.* —) weaver.

wirklich ['vɪrklɪç], *adj.* real, actual; true, genuine.

Wirklichkeit ['vɪrklɪçkaɪt], *f.* (—, *no pl.*) reality.

wirksam ['vɪrkzaːm], *adj.* effective, efficacious.

Wirksamkeit ['vɪrkzaːmkaɪt], *f.* (—, *no pl.*) efficacy, efficiency.

Wirkung ['vɪrkuŋ], *f.* (—, *pl.* —en) working, operation; reaction; efficacy; effect, result, consequence; force, in-

fluence; *eine — ausüben auf*, have an effect on; influence s.o. *or* s.th.

Wirkungskreis ['vɪrkuŋskraɪs], *m.* (—es, *pl.* —e) sphere of activity.

wirkungslos ['vɪrkuŋsloːs], *adj.* ineffectual.

wirkungsvoll ['vɪrkuŋsfɔl], *adj.* effective, efficacious; (*fig.*) impressive.

wirr [vɪr], *adj.* tangled, confused; — *durcheinander*, higgledy-piggledy; *mir ist ganz — im Kopf*, my head is going round.

Wirren ['vɪrən], *f. pl.* troubles, disorders, disturbances.

wirrköpfig ['vɪrkœpfɪç], *adj.* muddleheaded.

Wirrsal ['vɪrzaːl], *n.* (—s, *pl.* —e) confusion, disorder.

Wirrwarr ['vɪrvar], *m.* (—s, *no pl.*) jumble, hurly-burly, hubbub.

Wirt [vɪrt], *m.* (—(e)s, *pl.* —e) host; innkeeper; landlord.

Wirtin ['vɪrtɪn], *f.* (—, *pl.* —innen) hostess, landlady, innkeeper's wife.

wirtlich ['vɪrtlɪç], *adj.* hospitable.

Wirtschaft ['vɪrtʃaft], *f.* (—, *pl.* —en) housekeeping; administration; economy; household; housekeeping; inn, ale-house; (*coll.*) mess.

wirtschaften ['vɪrtʃaftən], *v.n.* keep house, housekeep; administer, run; (*coll.*) rummage.

Wirtschafterin ['vɪrtʃaftərɪn], *f.* (—, *pl.* —innen) housekeeper.

wirtschaftlich ['vɪrtʃaftlɪç], *adj.* economical, thrifty.

Wirtschaftlichkeit ['vɪrtʃaftlɪçkaɪt], *f.* (—, *no pl.*) economy; profitability.

Wirtschaftsgeld ['vɪrtʃaftsgɛlt], *n.* (—s, *pl.* —er) housekeeping-money.

Wirtshaus ['vɪrtshaus], *n.* (—es, *pl.* ⁓er) inn.

Wisch [vɪʃ], *m.* (—es, *pl.* —e) scrap of paper, rag.

wischen ['vɪʃən], *v.a.* wipe.

wispern ['vɪspərn], *v.a., v.n.* whisper.

Wißbegier(de) ['vɪsbəgiːr(də)], *f.* (—, *no pl.*) craving for knowledge; curiosity.

Wissen ['vɪsən], *n.* (—s, *no pl.*) knowledge, learning, erudition.

wissen ['vɪsən], *v.a. irr.* know, be aware of (a fact); be able to.

Wissenschaft ['vɪsənʃaft], *f.* (—, *pl.* —en) learning, scholarship; science.

wissenschaftlich ['vɪsənʃaftlɪç], *adj.* learned, scholarly; scientific.

wissenswert ['vɪsənsveːrt], *adj.* worth knowing.

Wissenszweig ['vɪsənstsvaɪk], *m.* (—s, *pl.* —e) branch of knowledge.

wissentlich ['vɪsəntlɪç], *adj.* deliberate, wilful. — *adv.* knowingly.

wittern ['vɪtərn], *v.a.* scent, smell; (*fig.*) suspect.

Witterung ['vɪtəruŋ], *f.* (—, *no pl.*) weather; trail; scent.

Witterungsverhältnisse ['vɪtəruŋsferhɛltnɪsə], *n. pl.* atmospheric conditions.

283

Witterungswechsel

Witterungswechsel [ˈvɪtəruŋsvɛksəl], *m.* (**—s**, *no pl.*) change in the weather.

Witwe [ˈvɪtvə], *f.* (**—**, *pl.* **—n**) widow.

Witwer [ˈvɪtvər], *m.* (**—s**, *pl.* **—**) widower.

Witz [vɪts], *m.* (**—es**, *pl.* **—e**) wit, brains; joke, jest, witticism; funny story.

Witzblatt [ˈvɪtsblat], *n.* (**—s**, *pl.* **ᵉer**) satirical *or* humorous journal.

Witzbold [ˈvɪtsbɔlt], *m.* (**—es**, *pl.* **—e**) wag; wit.

witzeln [ˈvɪtsəln], *v.n.* poke fun (at).

witzig [ˈvɪtsɪç], *adj.* witty; funny, comical; bright.

wo [voː], *interr. adv.* where? — *conj.* when.

wobei [voːˈbaɪ], *adv.* by which, at which, in connection with which; whereby; in doing so.

Woche [ˈvɔxə], *f.* (**—**, *pl.* **—n**) week.

Wochenbericht [ˈvɔxənbərɪçt], *m.* (**—s**, *pl.* **—e**) weekly report.

Wochenbett [ˈvɔxənbɛt], *n.* (**—s**, *no pl.*) confinement.

Wochenblatt [ˈvɔxənblat], *n.* (**—s**, *pl.* **ᵉer**) weekly (paper).

Wochenlohn [ˈvɔxənloːn], *m.* (**—s**, *pl.* **ᵉe**) weekly wage(s).

Wochenschau [ˈvɔxənʃau], *f.* (**—**, *no pl.*) newsreel.

Wochentag [ˈvɔxəntaːk], *m.* (**—s**, *pl.* **—e**) week-day.

wöchentlich [ˈvœçəntlɪç], *adj.* weekly, every week.

wodurch [voːˈdurç], *adv.* whereby, by which, through which; (*interr.*) by what?

wofern [voːˈfɛrn], *conj.* if, provided that.

wofür [voːˈfyːr], *adv.* for what, for which, wherefore.

Woge [ˈvoːgə], *f.* (**—**, *pl.* **—n**) wave, billow.

wogegen [voːˈgeːgən], *adv.* against what, against which, in return for which.

wogen [ˈvoːgən], *v.n.* heave, sway; (*fig.*) fluctuate.

woher [voːˈheːr], *adv.* whence, from what place, how.

wohin [voːˈhɪn], *adv.* whither, where.

wohingegen [voːhɪnˈgeːgən], *conj.* (*obs.*) whereas.

Wohl [voːl], *n.* (**—(e)s**, *no pl.*) welfare, health; *auf dein —*, your health! cheers!

wohl [voːl], *adv.* well, fit; indeed, doubtless, certainly; *ja —*, to be sure.

wohlan! [voːlˈan], *excl.* well! now then!

wohlauf! [voːlˈauf], *excl.* cheer up! — *sein*, be in good health.

wohlbedacht [ˈvoːlbədaxt], *adj.* well considered.

Wohlbefinden [ˈvoːlbəfɪndən], *n.* (**—s**, *no pl.*) good health.

Wohlbehagen [ˈvoːlbəhaːgən], *n.* (**—s**, *no pl.*) comfort, ease, wellbeing.

wohlbehalten [ˈvoːlbəhaltən], *adj.* safe.

wohlbekannt [ˈvoːlbəkant], *adj.* well known.

wohlbeleibt [ˈvoːlbəlaɪpt], *adj.* corpulent, stout.

wohlbestallt [ˈvoːlbəʃtalt], *adj.* duly installed.

Wohlergehen [ˈvoːlɛrgeːən], *n.* (**—s**, *no pl.*) welfare, wellbeing.

wohlerhalten [ˈvoːlɛrhaltən], *adj.* well preserved.

wohlerzogen [ˈvoːlɛrtsoːgən], *adj.* well bred, well brought up.

Wohlfahrt [ˈvoːlfaːrt], *f.* (**—**, *no pl.*) welfare, prosperity.

wohlfeil [ˈvoːlfaɪl], *adj.* cheap, inexpensive.

Wohlgefallen [ˈvoːlgəfalən], *n.* (**—s**, *no pl.*) pleasure, delight, approval.

wohlgefällig [ˈvoːlgəfɛlɪç], *adj.* pleasant, agreeable.

Wohlgefühl [ˈvoːlgəfyːl], *n.* (**—s**, *no pl.*) comfort, ease.

wohlgelitten [ˈvoːlgəlɪtən], *adj.* popular.

wohlgemeint [ˈvoːlgəmaɪnt], *adj.* well meant.

wohlgemerkt [ˈvoːlgəmɛrkt], *adv.* mind you! mark my words!

wohlgemut [ˈvoːlgəmuːt], *adj.* cheerful, merry.

wohlgeneigt [ˈvoːlgənaɪkt], *adj.* well disposed (towards).

wohlgepflegt [ˈvoːlgəpfleːkt], *adj.* well kept.

wohlgeraten [ˈvoːlgəraːtən], *adj.* successful; well turned out; good, well behaved.

Wohlgeruch [ˈvoːlgəruːx], *m.* (**—es**, *pl.* **ᵉe**) sweet scent, perfume, fragrance.

Wohlgeschmack [ˈvoːlgəʃmak], *m.* (**—s**, *no pl.*) pleasant flavour, agreeable taste.

wohlgesinnt [ˈvoːlgəzɪnt], *adj.* well disposed.

wohlgestaltet [ˈvoːlgəʃtaltət], *adj.* well shaped.

wohlgezielt [ˈvoːlgətsiːlt], *adj.* well aimed.

wohlhabend [ˈvoːlhaːbənt], *adj.* well-to-do, wealthy, well off.

wohlig [ˈvoːlɪç], *adj.* comfortable, cosy.

Wohlklang [ˈvoːlklaŋ], *m.* (**—s**, *pl.* **ᵉe**) harmony, euphony.

wohlklingend [ˈvoːlklɪŋənt], *adj.* harmonious, euphonious, sweet-sounding.

Wohlleben [ˈvoːlleːbən], *n.* (**—s**, *no pl.*) luxurious living.

wohllöblich [ˈvoːllœːplɪç], *adj.* worshipful.

wohlmeinend [ˈvoːlmaɪnənt], *adj.* well-meaning.

wohlschmeckend [ˈvoːlʃmɛkənt], *adj.* savoury, tasty, delicious.

Wohlsein [ˈvoːlzaɪn], *n.* (**—s**, *no pl.*) good health, wellbeing.

Wohlstand [ˈvoːlʃtant], *m.* (**—s**, *no pl.*) prosperity.

Wohltat [ˈvoːltaːt], *f.* (**—**, *pl.* **—en**) benefit; kindness; (*pl.*) benefaction, charity; (*fig.*) treat.

worüber

Wohltäter ['vo:ltɛ:tər], *m.* (—s, *pl.* —) benefactor.

Wohltätigkeit ['vo:ltɛ:tɪçkaɪt], *f.* (—, *no pl.*) charity.

wohltuend ['vo:ltu:ənt], *adj.* soothing.

wohltun ['vo:ltu:n], *v.n. irr.* do good; be comforting.

wohlweislich ['vo:lvaɪslɪç], *adj.* wisely.

Wohlwollen ['vo:lvɔlən], *n.* (—s, *no pl.*) benevolence; favour, patronage.

wohnen ['vo:nən], *v.n.* reside, dwell, live.

wohnhaft ['vo:nhaft], *adj.* domiciled, resident; — *sein*, reside, be domiciled.

Wohnhaus ['vo:nhaus], *n.* (—es, *pl.* ꞊er) dwelling-house.

wohnlich ['vo:nlɪç], *adj.* comfortable, cosy.

Wohnort ['vo:nɔrt], *m.* (—s, *pl.* —e) place of residence.

Wohnsitz ['vo:nzɪts], *m.* (—es, *pl.* —e) domicile, abode, residence.

Wohnstätte ['vo:nʃtɛtə], *f.* (—, *pl.* —n) abode, home.

Wohnung ['vo:nuŋ], *f.* (—, *pl.* —en) residence, dwelling; house, flat, lodging; apartment.

Wohnungsmangel ['vo:nuŋsmaŋəl], *m.* (—s, *no pl.*) housing shortage.

Wohnwagen ['vo:nva:gən], *m.* (—s, *pl.* —) caravan.

Wohnzimmer ['vo:ntsɪmər], *n.* (—s, *pl.* —) sitting-room, living-room.

wölben ['vœlbən], *v.r. sich* —, vault, arch.

Wölbung ['vœlbuŋ], *f.* (—, *pl.* —en) vault, vaulting.

Wolf [vɔlf], *m.* (—(e)s, *pl.* ꞊e) wolf.

Wolke ['vɔlkə], *f.* (—, *pl.* —n) cloud.

Wolkenbruch ['vɔlkənbrux], *m.* (—s, *pl.* ꞊e) cloudburst, violent downpour.

Wolkenkratzer ['vɔlkənkratsər], *m.* (—s, *pl.* —) sky-scraper.

Wolkenkuckucksheim [vɔlkən'kukukshaɪm], *n.* (—s, *no pl.*) Utopia, cloud cuckoo land.

Wolldecke ['vɔldɛkə], *f.* (—, *pl.* —n) blanket.

Wolle ['vɔlə], *f.* (—, *pl.* —n) wool.

wollen (1) ['vɔlən], *v.a., v.n. irr.* wish, want to, be willing, intend; *was — Sie*, what do you want?

wollen (2) ['vɔlən], *ad.* woollen, made of wool.

Wollgarn ['vɔlgarn], *n.* (—s, *pl.* —e) woollen yarn.

Wollhandel ['vɔlhandəl], *m.* (—s, *no pl.*)-wool-trade.

wollig ['vɔlɪç], *adj.* woolly.

Wollsamt ['vɔlzamt], *m.* (—s, *no pl.*) plush, velveteen.

Wollust ['vɔlust], *f.* (—, *pl.* ꞊e) voluptuousness; lust.

wollüstig ['vɔlystɪç], *adj.* voluptuous.

Wollwaren ['vɔlva:rən], *f. pl.* woollen goods.

Wollzupfen ['vɔltsupfən], *n.* (—s, *no pl.*) wool-picking.

womit [vo:'mɪt], *adv.* wherewith, with which; (*interr.*) with what?

womöglich [vo:'mø:klɪç], *adv.* if possible, perhaps.

wonach [vo:'na:x], *adv.* whereafter, after which; according to which.

Wonne ['vɔnə], *f.* (—, *pl.* —n) delight, bliss, rapture.

wonnetrunken ['vɔnətruŋkən], *adj.* enraptured.

wonnig ['vɔnɪç], *adj.* delightful.

woran [vo:'ran], *adv.* whereat, whereby; (*interr.*) by what? at what?

worauf [vo:'rauf], *adv.* upon which, at which; whereupon; (*interr.*) on what?

woraufhin [vo:rauf'hɪn], *conj.* whereupon.

woraus [vo:'raus], *adv.* (*rel. & interr.*) whence, from which; by or out of which.

worein [vo:'raɪn], *adv.* (*rel. & interr.*) into which; into what.

worin [vo:'rɪn], *adv.* (*rel.*) wherein; (*interr.*) in what?

Wort [vɔrt], *n.* (—(e)s, *pl.* ꞊er, —e) word, term; expression, saying.

wortarm ['vɔrtarm], *adj.* poor in words, deficient in vocabulary.

Wortarmut ['vɔrtarmu:t], *f.* (—, *no pl.*) paucity of words, poverty of language.

Wortbildung ['vɔrtbɪlduŋ], *f.* (—, *pl.* —en) word-formation.

wortbrüchig ['vɔrtbryçɪç], *adj.* faithless, disloyal.

Wörterbuch ['vœrtərbu:x], *n.* (—(e)s, *pl.* ꞊er) dictionary.

Worterklärung ['vɔrtɛrklɛ:ruŋ], *f.* (—, *pl.* —en) definition.

Wortforschung ['vɔrtfɔrʃuŋ], *f.* (—, *no pl.*) etymology.

Wortfügung ['vɔrtfy:guŋ], *f.* (—, *no pl.*) syntax.

Wortführer ['vɔrtfy:rər], *m.* (—s, *pl.* —) spokesman.

Wortgefecht ['vɔrtgəfɛçt], *n.* (—es, *pl.* —e) verbal battle.

wortgetreu ['vɔrtgətrɔy], *adj.* literal, verbatim.

wortkarg ['vɔrtkark], *adj.* laconic, sparing of words, taciturn.

Wortlaut ['vɔrtlaut], *m.* (—s, *pl.* —e) wording, text.

wörtlich ['vœrtlɪç], *adj.* verbal; literal, word for word.

wortlos ['vɔrtlo:s], *adj.* speechless. — *adv.* without uttering a word.

wortreich ['vɔrtraɪç], *adj.* (*language*) rich in words; (*fig.*) verbose, wordy.

Wortreichtum ['vɔrtraɪçtum], *m.* (—s, *no pl.*) (*language*) wealth of words; (*fig.*) verbosity, wordiness.

Wortschwall ['vɔrtʃval], *m.* (—s, *no pl.*) bombast; torrent of words.

Wortspiel ['vɔrtʃpi:l], *n.* (—s, *pl.* —e) pun.

Wortversetzung ['vɔrtfɛrzetsuŋ], *f.* (—, *pl.* —en) inversion (of words).

Wortwechsel ['vɔrtvɛksəl], *m.* (—s, *pl.* —) dispute, altercation.

worüber [vo'ry:bər], *adv.* (*rel.*) about which, whereof; (*interr.*) about what?

285

worunter [vo'runtər], *adv.* (*rel.*) whereunder; (*interr.*) under what?

woselbst [vo'zɛlpst], *adv.* where.

wovon [vo:'fɔn], *adv.* (*rel.*) whereof; (*interr.*) of what?

wovor [vo:'fo:r], *adv.* (*rel.*) before which; (*interr.*) before what?

wozu [vo:'tsu:], *adv.* (*rel.*) whereto; (*interr.*) why? for what purpose? to what end?

Wrack [vrak], *n.* (—s, *pl.* —s) wreck.

wringen ['vriŋən], *v.a.* wring.

Wringmaschine ['vriŋmaʃi:nə], *f.* (—, *pl.* —n) wringer, mangle.

Wucher ['vu:xər], *m.* (—s, *no pl.*) usury.

wucherisch ['vu:xəriʃ], *adj.* usurious, extortionate.

wuchern ['vu:xərn], *v.n.* practise usury; (*plants*) luxuriate, grow profusely.

Wucherungen ['vu:xəruŋən], *f. pl.* (*Med.*) excrescence, growth.

Wuchs [vu:ks], *m.* (—es, *no pl.*) growth; shape, build.

Wucht [vuxt], *f.* (—, *no pl.*) power, force; weight; impetus.

wuchten ['vuxtən], *v.n.* (*Poet.*) press heavily. — *v.a.* prise up.

wuchtig ['vuxtiç], *adj.* weighty, forceful.

Wühlarbeit ['vy:larbaIt], *f.* (—, *pl.* —en) subversive activity.

wühlen ['vy:lən], *v.a., v.n.* dig, burrow; (*fig.*) agitate.

Wühler ['vy:lər], *m.* (—s, *pl.* —) agitator, demagogue.

Wühlmaus ['vy:lmaus], *f.* (—, *pl.* —e) (*Zool.*) vole.

Wulst [vulst], *m.* (—es, *pl.* —e) roll, pad; swelling.

wülstig ['vylstiç], *adj.* padded, stuffed; swollen.

wund [vunt], *adj.* sore, wounded.

Wundarzt ['vuntartst], *m.* (—es, *pl.* —e) (*obs.*) surgeon.

Wundbalsam ['vuntbalzam], *m.* (—s, *pl.* —e) balm.

Wunde ['vundə], *f.* (—, *pl.* —n) wound, hurt.

Wunder ['vundər], *n.* (—s, *pl.* —) marvel, wonder, miracle.

wunderbar ['vundərba:r], *adj.* wonderful, marvellous.

Wunderding ['vundərdiŋ], *n.* (—s, *pl.* —e) marvel.

Wunderdoktor ['vundərdɔktɔr], *m.* (—s, *pl.* —en) quack doctor.

Wunderglaube ['vundərglaubə], *m.* (—ns, *no pl.*) belief in miracles.

wunderhübsch [vundər'hypʃ], *adj.* exceedingly pretty.

Wunderkind ['vundərkint], *n.* (—s, *pl.* —er) infant prodigy.

Wunderlampe ['vundərlampə], *f.* (—, *pl.* —n) magic lantern.

wunderlich ['vundərliç], *adj.* strange, odd, queer.

wundern ['vundərn], *v.r. sich — über*, be surprised at, be astonished at.

wundersam ['vundərza:m], *adj.* wonderful, strange.

wunderschön ['vundərʃø:n], *adj.* lovely, gorgeous; exquisite.

Wundertat ['vundərta:t], *f.* (—, *pl.* —en) miraculous deed.

wundertätig ['vundərtɛ:tiç], *adj.* miraculous.

Wundertier ['vundərti:r], *n.* (—s, *pl.* —e) monster; (*fig.*) prodigy.

Wunderwerk ['vundərverk], *n.* (—s, *pl.* —e) miracle.

Wundmal ['vuntma:l], *n.* (—s, *pl.* —e) scar.

Wunsch [vunʃ], *m.* (—es, *pl.* ⸚e) wish, desire, aspiration.

Wünschelrute ['vynʃəlru:tə], *f.* (—, *pl.* —n) divining-rod.

wünschen ['vynʃən], *v.a.* wish, desire, long for.

wünschenswert ['vynʃənsve:rt], *adj.* desirable.

Wunschform ['vunʃfɔrm], *f.* (—, *no pl.*) (*Gram.*) optative form.

wuppdich! ['vupdiç], *excl.* here goes!

Würde ['vyrdə], *f.* (—, *pl.* —n) dignity, honour.

Würdenträger ['vyrdəntrɛ:gər], *m.* (—s, *pl.* —) dignitary.

würdevoll ['vyrdəfɔl], *adj.* dignified.

würdig ['vyrdiç], *adj.* worthy (of), deserving, meritorious.

würdigen ['vyrdigən], *v.a.* honour; *ich weiss es zu —*, I appreciate it.

Würdigung ['vyrdigun], *f.* (—, *pl.* —en) appreciation.

Wurf [vurf], *m.* (—(e)s, *pl.* ⸚e) cast, throw.

Würfel ['vyrfəl], *m.* (—s, *pl.* —) die; (*Geom.*) cube; — *spielen*, play at dice.

würfelförmig ['vyrfəlfœrmiç], *adj.* cubic, cubiform.

würfeln ['vyrfəln], *v.n.* play at dice.

Wurfgeschoß ['vurfgəʃo:s], *n.* (—sses, *pl.* —sse) missile, projectile.

Wurfmaschine ['vurfmaʃi:nə], *f.* (—, *pl.* —n) catapult.

Wurfscheibe ['vurfʃaIbə], *f.* (—, *pl.* —n) discus, quoit.

Wurfspieß ['vurfʃpi:s], *m.* (—es, *pl.* —e) javelin.

würgen ['vyrgən], *v.a.* strangle, throttle. — *v.n.* choke.

Würgengel ['vyrgɛŋəl], *m.* (—s, *no pl.*) avenging angel.

Würger ['vyrgər], *m.* (—s, *pl.* —) strangler, murderer; (*Poet.*) slayer; (*Orn.*) shrike, butcher-bird.

Wurm [vurm], *m.* (—(e)s, *pl.* ⸚er) worm; (*apple*) maggot.

wurmen ['vurmən], *v.a.* vex.

wurmstichig ['vurmʃtiçiç], *adj.* worm-eaten.

Wurst [vurst], *f.* (—, *pl.* ⸚e) sausage.

wurstig ['vurstiç], *adj.* (*sl.*) quite indifferent.

Wurstigkeit ['vurstiçkaIt], *f.* (—, *no pl.*) callousness, indifference.

Würze ['vyrtsə], *f.* (—, *pl.* —n) seasoning, spice, condiment.

Wurzel ['vurtsəl], *f.* (—, *pl.* —n) root.

wurzeln ['vurtsəln], *v.n.* be rooted.

würzen ['vyrtsən], *v.a.* season, spice.

würzig ['vyrtsiç], *adj.* spicy, fragrant.

Wust [vust], *m.* (**—es**, *no pl.*) chaos, trash.

wüst [vy:st], *adj.* waste, desert; desolate; dissolute.

Wüste ['vy:stə], *f.* (**—**, *pl.* **—n**) desert, wilderness.

Wüstling ['vy:stlɪŋ], *m.* (**—s**, *pl.* **—e**) profligate, libertine.

Wut [vu:t], *f.* (**—**, *no pl.*) rage, fury, passion.

wüten ['vy:tən], *v.n.* rage, storm, fume.

wutentbrannt ['vu:təntbrant], *adj.* enraged, infuriated.

Wüterich ['vy:tərɪç], *m.* (**—s**, *pl.* **—e**) tyrant; ruthless fellow.

Wutgeschrei ['vu:tgəʃraɪ], *n.* (**—s**, *no pl.*) yell of rage.

wutschnaubend ['vu:tʃnaubənt], *adj.* foaming with rage.

X

X [ɪks], *n.* (**—s**, *pl.* **—s**) the letter X.

X-Beine ['ɪksbaɪnə], *n. pl.* knock-knees.

x-beliebig ['ɪksbəli:bɪç], *adj.* any, whatever (one likes).

Xenie ['kse:njə], *f.* (**—**, *pl.* **—n**) epigram.

Xereswein ['kse:rəsvaɪn], *m.* (**—s**, *pl.* **—e**) sherry.

x-mal ['ɪksma:l], *adv.* (*coll.*) so many times, umpteen times.

X-Strahlen ['ɪksʃtra:lən], *m. pl.* X-rays.

Xylographie [ksylogra'fi:], *f.* (**—**, *no pl.*) wood-engraving.

Xylophon [ksylo'fo:n], *n.* (**—s**, *pl.* **—e**) (*Mus.*) xylophone.

Y

Y ['ypsilɔn], *n.* (**—s**, *pl.* **—s**) the letter Y.

Yak [jak], *m.* (**—s**, *pl.* **—s**) (*Zool.*) yak.

Yamswurzel ['jamsvurtsəl], *f.* (**—**, *pl.* **—n**) yam.

Ysop [y'zo:p], *m.* (**—s**, *no pl.*) hyssop.

Z

Z [tsɛt], *n.* (**—s**, *pl.* **—s**) the letter Z.

Zabel ['tsa:bəl], *m.* (**—s**, *pl.* **—**) (*obs.*) chess-board.

Zacke ['tsakə], *f.* (**—**, *pl.* **—n**) tooth, spike; (*fork*) prong.

zackig ['tsakɪç], *adj.* pronged, toothed, indented; (*rock*) jagged; (*sl.*) smart.

zagen ['tsa:gən], *v.n.* quail, blench, be disheartened, be fainthearted.

zaghaft ['tsa:khaft], *adj.* faint-hearted.

Zaghaftigkeit ['tsa:khaftɪçkaɪt], *f.* (**—**, *no pl.*) faintheartedness, timidity.

zäh [tsɛ:], *adj.* tough.

Zähigkeit ['tsɛ:ɪçkaɪt], *f.* (**—**, *no pl.*) toughness.

Zahl [tsa:l], *f.* (**—**, *pl.* **—en**) number, figure.

zahlbar ['tsa:lba:r], *adj.* payable, due.

zählbar ['tsɛ:lba:r], *adj.* calculable.

zahlen ['tsa:lən], *v.a.* pay; *Ober!* **—**, waiter! the bill, please.

zählen ['tsɛ:lən], *v.a., v.n.* count, number.

Zahlenfolge ['tsa:lənfɔlgə], *f.* (**—**, *no pl.*) numerical order.

Zahlenlehre ['tsa:lənle:rə], *f.* (**—**, *no pl.*) arithmetic.

Zahlenreihe ['tsa:lənraɪə], *f.* (**—**, *pl.* **—n**) numerical progression.

Zahlensinn ['tsa:lənzɪn], *m.* (**—s**, *no pl.*) head for figures.

Zahler ['tsa:lər], *m.* (**—s**, *pl.* **—**) payer.

Zähler ['tsɛ:lər], *m.* (**—s**, *pl.* **—**) counter, teller; meter; (*Maths.*) numerator.

Zahlkellner ['tsa:lkɛlnər], *m.* (**—s**, *pl.* **—**) head waiter.

Zahlmeister ['tsa:lmaɪstər], *m.* (**—s**, *pl.* **—**) paymaster, treasurer, bursar.

zahlreich ['tsa:lraɪç], *adj.* numerous.

Zahltag ['tsa:lta:k], *m.* (**—s**, *pl.* **—e**) pay-day.

Zahlung ['tsa:luŋ], *f.* (**—**, *pl.* **—en**) payment; **—** *leisten*, make payment; *die —en einstellen*, stop payment.

Zählung ['tsɛ:luŋ], *f.* (**—**, *pl.* **—en**) counting, computation; census.

Zahlungseinstellung ['tsa:luŋsaɪnʃte-luŋ], *f.* (**—**, *pl.* **—en**) suspension of payment.

zahlungsfähig ['tsa:luŋsfɛ:ɪç], *adj.* solvent.

Zahlungsmittel ['tsa:luŋsmɪtəl], *n.* (**—s**, *pl.* **—**) means of payment; *gesetzliches —*, legal tender.

Zahlungstermin ['tsa:luŋstɛrmi:n], *m.* (**—s**, *pl.* **—e**) time of payment.

zahlungsunfähig ['tsa:luŋsunfɛ:ɪç], *adj.* insolvent.

Zahlwort ['tsa:lvɔrt], *n.* (**—s**, *pl.* ⁻er) (*Gram.*) numeral.

zahm [tsa:m], *adj.* tame; domestic(ated); **—** *machen*, tame.

zähmen ['tsɛ:mən], *v.a.* tame, domesticate.

Zähmer ['tsɛ:mər], *m.* (**—s**, *pl.* **—**) tamer.

Zahmheit ['tsa:mhaɪt], *f.* (**—**, *no pl.*) tameness.

Zähmung ['tsɛ:muŋ], *f.* (**—**, *no pl.*) taming, domestication.

Zahn [tsa:n], *m.* (**—(e)s**, *pl.* ⁻e) tooth; (*wheel*) cog.

Zahnarzt

Zahnarzt ['tsa:nartst], *m.* (—es, *pl.* ⁓e) dentist, dental surgeon.

Zahnbürste ['tsa:nbyrstə], *f.* (—, *pl.* —n) tooth-brush.

Zähneklappern ['tsɛ:nəklapərn], *n.* (—s, *no pl.*) chattering of teeth.

Zähneknirschen ['tsɛ:nəknɪrʃən], *n.* (—s, *no pl.*) gnashing of teeth.

zahnen ['tsa:nən], *v.n.* teethe, cut o.'s teeth.

zähnen ['tsɛ:nən], *v.a.* indent, notch.

Zahnfleisch ['tsa:nflaɪʃ], *n.* (—es, *no pl.*) gums.

Zahnfüllung ['tsa:nfylun], *f.* (—, *pl.* —en) filling, stopping (of tooth).

Zahnheilkunde ['tsa:nhaɪlkundə], *f.* (—, *no pl.*) dentistry, dental surgery.

Zahnlücke ['tsa:nlykə], *f.* (—, *pl.* —n) gap in the teeth.

Zahnpaste ['tsa:npastə], *f.* (—, *no pl.*) tooth-paste.

Zahnpulver ['tsa:npulvər], *n.* (—s, *no pl.*) tooth-powder.

Zahnrad ['tsa:nra:t], *n.* (—s, *pl.* ⁓er) cog-wheel.

Zahnradbahn ['tsa:nra:tba:n], *f.* (—, *pl.* —en) rack-railway.

Zahnschmerzen ['tsa:nʃmɛrtsən], *m. pl.* toothache.

Zahnstocher ['tsa:nʃtɔxər], *m.* (—s, *pl.* —) tooth-pick.

Zähre ['tsɛ:rə], *f.* (—, *pl.* —n) (*Poet.*) tear.

Zander ['tsandər], *m.* (—s, *pl.* —) (*fish*) pike.

Zange ['tsaŋə], *f.* (—, *pl.* —n) tongs; pincers, tweezers, nippers; (*Med.*) forceps.

Zank [tsaŋk], *m.* (—es, *pl.* ⁓ereien) quarrel, altercation, tiff.

Zankapfel ['tsaŋkapfəl], *m.* (—s, *pl.* ⁓) bone of contention.

zanken ['tsaŋkən], *v.r. sich* —, quarrel, dispute.

zänkisch ['tsɛnkɪʃ], *adj.* quarrelsome.

Zanksucht ['tsaŋkzuxt], *f.* (—, *no pl.*) quarrelsomeness.

zanksüchtig ['tsaŋkzyçtɪç], *adj.* quarrelsome, cantankerous.

Zapfen ['tsapfən], *m.* (—s, *pl.* —) pin, peg; (*cask*) bung, spigot; (*fir*) cone.

zapfen ['tsapfən], *v.a.* tap, draw.

Zapfenstreich ['tsapfənʃtraɪç], *m.* (—s, *no pl.*) (*Mil.*) tattoo, retreat.

zapp(e)lig ['tsap(ə)lɪç], *adj.* fidgety.

zappeln ['tsapəln], *v.n.* kick, struggle, wriggle.

Zar [tsa:r], *m.* (—en, *pl.* —en) Czar, Tsar.

zart [tsart], *adj.* tender, sensitive, delicate, gentle; — *besaitet*, (*iron.*) sensitive, highly strung.

Zartgefühl ['tsartɡəfy:l], *n.* (—s, *no pl.*) delicacy, sensitivity.

Zartheit ['tsarthaɪt], *f.* (—, *no pl.*) tenderness, gentleness.

zärtlich ['tsɛ:rtlɪç], *adj.* loving, amorous, tender.

Zärtlichkeit ['tsɛ:rtlɪçkaɪt], *f.* (—, *pl.* —en) tenderness; caresses.

Zartsinn ['tsartzɪn], *m.* (—s, *no pl.*) delicacy.

Zauber ['tsaubər], *m.* (—s, *no pl.*) charm, spell, enchantment; magic; fascination.

Zauberei [tsaubə'raɪ], *f.* (—, *pl.* —en) magic, witchcraft, sorcery.

Zauberer ['tsaubərər], *m.* (—s, *pl.* —) magician, sorcerer, wizard.

zauberisch ['tsaubərɪʃ], *adj.* magical; (*fig.*) enchanting.

Zauberkraft ['tsaubərkraft], *f.* (—, *pl.*) magic power, witchcraft.

Zaubermittel ['tsaubərmɪtəl], *n.* (—s, *pl.* —) charm.

zaubern ['tsaubərn], *v.n.* practise magic; conjure.

Zauberspruch ['tsaubərʃprux], *m.* (—s, *pl.* ⁓e) spell, charm.

Zauberstab ['tsaubərʃta:p], *m.* (—s, *pl.* ⁓e) magic wand.

Zauderer ['tsaudərər], *m.* (—s, *pl.* —) loiterer, temporizer, procrastinator.

zaudern ['tsaudərn], *v.n.* delay; hesitate, procrastinate.

Zaum [tsaum], *m.* (—(e)s, *pl.* ⁓e) bridle; *im* — *halten*, check, restrain.

zäumen ['tsɔymən], *v.a.* bridle.

Zaun [tsaun], *m.* (—(e)s, *pl.* ⁓e) hedge, fence; *einen Streit vom* — *brechen*, pick a quarrel.

Zaungast ['tsaungast], *m.* (—s, *pl.* ⁓e) onlooker, outsider; intruder.

Zaunkönig ['tsaunkø:nɪç], *m.* (—s, *pl.* —e) (*Orn.*) wren.

Zaunpfahl ['tsaunpfa:l], *m.* (—s, *pl.* ⁓e) pale, hedge-pole; *mit dem* — *winken*, give s.o. a broad hint.

Zaunrebe ['tsaunre:bə], *f.* (—, *pl.* —n) (*Bot.*) Virginia creeper.

zausen ['tsauzən], *v.a.* tousle; (*hair*) disarrange, ruffle.

Zechbruder ['tsɛçbru:dər], *m.* (—s, *pl.* ⁓) tippler, toper.

Zeche ['tsɛçə], *f.* (—, *pl.* —n) bill (in a restaurant); mine; *die* — *bezahlen*, foot the bill, pay the piper.

Zeder ['tse:dər], *f.* (—, *pl.* —n) (*Bot.*) cedar.

zedieren [tse'di:rən], *v.a.* cede.

Zehe ['tse:ə], *f.* (—, *pl.* —n) toe.

Zehenspitze ['tse:ənʃpɪtsə], *f.* (—, *pl.* —n) tip of the toe, tiptoe.

zehn [tse:n], *num. adj.* ten.

Zehneck ['tse:nɛk], *n.* (—s, *pl.* —e) decagon.

Zehnte ['tse:ntə], *m.* (—n, *pl.* —n) tithe.

zehren ['tse:rən], *v.n. von etwas* —, live on s.th., prey upon s.th.

Zehrfieber ['tse:rfi:bər], *n.* (—s, *no pl.*) hectic fever.

Zehrgeld ['tse:rɡɛlt], *n.* (—s, *pl.* —er) subsistence, allowance.

Zehrvorrat ['tse:rfo:rra:t], *m.* (—s, *pl.* ⁓e) provisions.

Zehrung ['tse:ruŋ], *f.* (—, *pl.* —en) consumption; victuals; (*Eccl.*) *letzte* —, viaticum.

Zeichen ['tsaɪçən], *n.* (—s, *pl.* —) sign, token, symptom, omen; indication; badge; signal.

Zeichenbrett ['tsaɪçənbrɛt], *n.* (—s, *pl.* —er) drawing-board.

Zeichendeuter ['tsaɪçəndɔytər], *m.* (—s, *pl.* —) astrologer.

Zeichendeuterei [tsaɪçəndɔytə'raɪ], *f.* (—, *no pl.*) astrology.

Zeichenerklärung ['tsaɪçənɛrklɛːruŋ], *f.* (— *pl.* —en) legend, key.

Zeichensprache ['tsaɪçənʃpraːxə], *f.* (—, *no pl.*) sign-language.

Zeichentinte ['tsaɪçəntɪntə], *f.* (—, *no pl.*) marking ink.

zeichnen ['tsaɪçnən], *v.a.* draw; mark; (*money*) subscribe; (*letter*) sign.

Zeichner ['tsaɪçnər], *m.* (—s, *pl.* —) draughtsman, designer.

Zeichnung ['tsaɪçnuŋ], *f.* (—, *pl.* —en) drawing.

Zeigefinger ['tsaɪgəfɪŋər], *m.* (—s, *pl.* —) forefinger, index finger.

zeigen ['tsaɪgən], *v.a.* show, point to, prove.

Zeiger ['tsaɪgər], *m.* (—s, *pl.* —) indicator; hand (of watch, clock).

zeihen ['tsaɪən], *v.a. irr. einen einer Sache —,* tax s.o. with s.th.

Zeile ['tsaɪlə], *f.* (—, *pl.* —n) line; furrow; (*pl.*) letter.

Zeisig ['tsaɪzɪç], *m.* (—s, *pl.* —e) (*Orn.*) siskin.

Zeit [tsaɪt], *f.* (—, *pl.* —en) time; *zur —,* at present; *auf —,* on credit.

Zeitabschnitt ['tsaɪtapʃnɪt], *m.* (—s, *pl.* —e) period; epoch.

Zeitalter ['tsaɪtaltər], *n.* (—s, *pl.* —) age, era.

Zeitdauer ['tsaɪtdauər], *f.* (—, *no pl.*) space of time.

Zeitfrage ['tsaɪtfraːgə], *f.* (—, *pl.* —n) topical question; question of time.

Zeitgeist ['tsaɪtgaɪst], *m.* (—s, *no pl.*) spirit of the age.

zeitgemäß ['tsaɪtgəmɛːs], *adj.* timely, seasonable, opportune, modern.

Zeitgenosse ['tsaɪtgənɔsə], *m.* (—n, *pl.* —n) contemporary.

zeitig ['tsaɪtɪç], *adj.* early, timely.

zeitigen ['tsaɪtɪgən], *v.a.* engender, generate. — *v.n.* mature, ripen.

Zeitkarte ['tsaɪtkartə], *f.* (—; *pl.* —n) season ticket.

Zeitlauf ['tsaɪtlauf], *m.* (—s, *pl.* ⸚e) course of time, conjuncture.

zeitlebens ['tsaɪtleːbəns], *adv.* for life, (for) all his (*or* her) life.

zeitlich ['tsaɪtlɪç], *adj.* temporal, earthly; secular; temporary, transient.

zeitlos ['tsaɪtloːs], *adj.* lasting, permanent.

Zeitmangel ['tsaɪtmaŋəl], *m.* (—s, *no pl.*) lack of time.

Zeitmesser ['tsaɪtmɛsər], *m.* (—s, *pl.* —) chronometer, timepiece; metronome.

Zeitpunkt ['tsaɪtpuŋkt], *m.* (—s, *pl.* —e) moment, date; point of time.

zeitraubend ['tsaɪtraubənt], *adj.* time-consuming.

Zeitraum ['tsaɪtraum], *m.* (—s, *pl.* ⸚e) space of time, period.

Zeitschrift ['tsaɪtʃrɪft], *f.* (—, *pl.* —en) periodical, journal, magazine.

Zeitung ['tsaɪtuŋ], *f.* (—, *pl.* —en) newspaper.

Zeitungsente ['tsaɪtuŋsɛntə], *f.* (—, *pl.* —n) canard, newspaper hoax.

Zeitungskiosk ['tsaɪtuŋskiɔsk], *m.* (—s, *pl.* —e) newspaper-stall.

Zeitungsnachricht ['tsaɪtuŋsnaːxrɪçt], *f.* (—, *pl.* —en) newspaper report.

Zeitungswesen ['tsaɪtuŋsveːzən], *n.* (—s, *no pl.*) journalism.

Zeitverlust ['tsaɪtfɛrlust], *m.* (—s, *no pl.*) loss of time; *ohne —,* without delay.

Zeitvertreib ['tsaɪtfɛrtraɪp], *m.* (—s, *no pl.*) pastime, amusement; *zum —,* to pass the time.

zeitweilig ['tsaɪtvaɪlɪç], *adj.* temporary.

zeitweise ['tsaɪtvaɪzə], *adv.* from time to time.

Zeitwort ['tsaɪtvɔrt], *n.* (—s, *pl.* ⸚er) (*Gram.*) verb.

Zelle ['tsɛlə], *f.* (—, *pl.* —n) cell; booth.

Zelt [tsɛlt], *n.* (—(e)s, *pl.* —e) tent.

Zeltdecke ['tsɛltdɛkə], *f.* (—, *pl.* —n) awning, marquee.

Zement [tse'mɛnt], *m.* (—s, *no pl.*) cement.

Zenit [tse'niːt], *m.* (—s, *no pl.*) zenith.

zensieren [tsɛn'ziːrən], *v.a.* review, censure; (*Sch.*) mark.

Zensor ['tsɛnzor], *m.* (—s, *pl.* —en) censor.

Zensur [tsɛn'zuːr], *f.* (—, *pl.* —en) censure; (*Sch.*) report, mark; censorship.

Zentimeter ['tsɛntimeːtər], *m.* (—s, *pl.* —) centimetre.

Zentner ['tsɛntnər], *m.* (—s, *pl.* —) hundredweight.

zentral [tsɛn'traːl], *adj.* central.

Zentrale [tsɛn'traːlə], *f.* (—, *pl.* —n) control room; head office.

zentralisieren [tsɛntrali'ziːrən], *v.a.* centralise.

Zentrum ['tsɛntrum], *n.* (—s, *pl.* —tren) (*Am.*) center.

Zephir ['tseːfiːr], *m.* (—s, *pl.* —e) zephyr.

Zepter ['tsɛptər], *m. & n.* (—s, *pl.* —) sceptre, mace.

zerbrechen [tser'brɛçən], *v.a., v.n. irr.* (*aux.* sein) break to pieces; shatter; *sich den Kopf —,* rack o.'s brains.

zerbrechlich [tser'brɛçlɪç], *adj.* brittle, fragile.

zerbröckeln [tser'brœkəln], *v.a., v.n.* (*aux.* sein) crumble.

zerdrücken [tser'drykən], *v.a.* crush, bruise.

Zeremonie [tseremo'niː], *f.* (—, *pl.* —n) ceremony.

zeremoniell [tseremo'njɛl], *adj.* ceremonial, formal.

Zerfahrenheit [tser'faːrənhaɪt], *f.* (—, *no pl.*) absent-mindedness.

Zerfall [tser'fal], *m.* (—s, *no pl.*) disintegration; decay.

zerfallen [tser'falən], *v.n. irr.* (*aux.* sein) fall to pieces. — *adj.* in ruins.

289

zerfleischen

zerfleischen [tsɛrˈflaɪʃən], v.a. lacerate, tear to pieces.

zerfließen [tsɛrˈfliːsən], v.n. irr. (aux. sein) dissolve, melt.

zerfressen [tsɛrˈfrɛsən], v.a. irr. gnaw, corrode.

zergehen [tsɛrˈgeːən], v.n. irr. (aux. sein) dissolve, melt.

zergliedern [tsɛrˈgliːdərn], v.a. dissect; (fig.) analyse.

zerhauen [tsɛrˈhauən], v.a. hew in pieces, chop up.

zerkauen [tsɛrˈkauən], v.a. chew.

zerkleinern [tsɛrˈklaɪnərn], v.a. cut into small pieces; (firewood) chop.

zerklüftet [tsɛrˈklyftət], adj. rugged.

zerknirscht [tsɛrˈknɪrʃt], adj. contrite.

Zerknirschung [tsɛrˈknɪrʃuŋ], f. (—, no pl.) contrition.

zerknittern [tsɛrˈknɪtərn], v.a. crumple.

zerknüllen [tsɛrˈknylən], v.a. rumple.

zerlassen [tsɛrˈlasən], v.a. irr. melt, liquefy.

zerlegen [tsɛrˈleːgən], v.a. resolve; take to pieces; cut up, carve; (fig.) analyse.

zerlumpt [tsɛrˈlumpt], adj. ragged, tattered.

zermahlen [tsɛrˈmaːlən], v.a. grind to powder.

zermalmen [tsɛrˈmalmən], v.a. crush.

zermartern [tsɛrˈmartərn], v.a. torment; sich das Hirn —, rack o.'s brains.

zernagen [tsɛrˈnaːgən], v.a. gnaw (away).

zerquetschen [tsɛrˈkvɛtʃən], v.a. squash, crush.

zerraufen [tsɛrˈraufən], v.a. dishevel.

Zerrbild [ˈtsɛrbɪlt], n. (—s, pl. —er) caricature.

zerreiben [tsɛrˈraɪbən], v.a. irr. grind to powder, pulverise.

zerreißen [tsɛrˈraɪsən], v.a. irr. tear, rend, tear up; break; rupture. — v.n. (aux. sein) be torn; (clothes) wear out.

zerren [ˈtsɛrən], v.a. pull, tug, drag; strain.

zerrinnen [tsɛrˈrɪnən], v.n. irr. (aux. sein) dissolve, melt; (fig.) vanish.

zerrütten [tsɛrˈrytən], v.a. unsettle, disorder, unhinge; ruin, destroy.

zerschellen [tsɛrˈʃɛlən], v.n. (aux. sein) be dashed to pieces, be wrecked.

zerschlagen [tsɛrˈʃlaːgən], v.a. irr. break, smash to pieces, batter.

zerschmettern [tsɛrˈʃmɛtərn], v.a. dash to pieces, break, crush; shatter, overwhelm.

zersetzen [tsɛrˈzɛtsən], v.a., v.r. break up; disintegrate.

zerspalten [tsɛrˈʃpaltən], v.a. cleave, split, slit.

zersprengen [tsɛrˈʃprɛŋən], v.a. explode, burst; (crowd) disperse; (Mil.) rout.

zerspringen [tsɛrˈʃprɪŋən], v.n. irr. (aux. sein) crack; fly to pieces, split.

zerstampfen [tsɛrˈʃtampfən], v.a. crush, pound.

zerstäuben [tsɛrˈʃtɔybən], v.a. spray, atomize.

zerstörbar [tsɛrˈʃtøːrbaːr], adj. destructible.

zerstören [tsɛrˈʃtøːrən], v.a. destroy, devastate.

Zerstörer [tsɛrˈʃtøːrər], m. (—s, pl. —) destroyer.

Zerstörung [tsɛrˈʃtøːruŋ], f. (—, pl. —en) destruction.

Zerstörungswut [tsɛrˈʃtøːruŋsvuːt], f. (—, no pl.) vandalism.

zerstoßen [tsɛrˈʃtoːsən], v.a. irr. bruise, pound.

zerstreuen [tsɛrˈʃtrɔyən], v.a. scatter, disperse; divert.

zerstreut [tsɛrˈʃtrɔyt], adj. absent-minded.

Zerstreuung [tsɛrˈʃtrɔyuŋ], f. (—, pl. —en) dispersion; amusement, diversion, distraction.

zerstückeln [tsɛrˈʃtykəln], v.a. dismember.

Zerstückelung [tsɛrˈʃtykəluŋ], f. (—, no pl.) dismemberment.

zerteilen [tsɛrˈtaɪlən], v.a. divide, separate; disperse, dissipate. — v.r. sich —, dissolve.

Zertifikat [tsɛrtifiˈkaːt], n. (—s, pl. —e) certificate, attestation.

zertrennen [tsɛrˈtrɛnən], v.a. rip up, unstitch.

zertrümmern [tsɛrˈtrymərn], v.a. destroy, break up, demolish.

Zerwürfnis [tsɛrˈvyrfnis], n. (—ses, pl. —se) discord, dissension.

zerzausen [tsɛrˈtsauzən], v.a. dishevel, tousle.

zerzupfen [tsɛrˈtsupfən], v.a. pick to pieces, pluck.

Zession [tsɛsˈjoːn], f. (—, pl. —en) cession, assignment, transfer.

Zetergeschrei [ˈtseːtərgəʃraɪ], n. (—s, no pl.) outcry, hullabaloo.

zetern [ˈtseːtərn], v.n. yell; (coll.) kick up a row.

Zettel [ˈtsɛtəl], m. (—s, pl. —) slip of paper; label, chit.

Zettelkasten [ˈtsɛtəlkastən], m. (—s, pl. ᵘ) card-index, filing cabinet.

Zeug [tsɔyk], n. (—(e)s, no pl.) stuff, material; implements, kit, utensils; (coll.) things.

Zeuge [ˈtsɔygə], m. (—n, pl. —n) witness; zum —n aufrufen, call to witness.

zeugen [ˈtsɔygən], v.a. beget, generate, engender. — v.n. give evidence.

Zeugenaussage [ˈtsɔygənausaːgə], f. (—, pl. —n) evidence, deposition.

Zeugenbeweis [ˈtsɔygənbəvaɪs], m. (—es, pl. —e) evidence, proof.

Zeugeneid [ˈtsɔygənaɪt], m. (—s, pl. —e) oath of a witness.

Zeughaus [ˈtsɔykhaus], n. (—es, pl. ᵘer) (obs.) arsenal.

Zeugin [ˈtsɔygɪn], f. (—, pl. —innen) female witness.

290

Zeugnis ['tsɔyknɪs], n. (—ses, pl. —se) (Law.) deposition; testimonial; certificate, reference; character; school report; — ablegen, give evidence, bear witness; einem ein gutes — ausstellen, give s.o. a good reference.

Zeugung ['tsɔygun], f. (—, pl. —en) procreation, generation.

Zeugungskraft ['tsɔygunskraft], f. (—, no pl.) generative power.

Zeugungstrieb ['tsɔygunstri:p], m. (—s, no pl.) procreative instinct.

Zichorie [tsɪ'ço:rjə], f. (—, pl. —n) chicory.

Zicke ['tsɪkə], f. (—, pl. —n) dial. for Ziege.

Ziege ['tsi:gə], f. (—, pl. —n) goat.

Ziegel ['tsi:gəl], m. (—s, pl. —) (roof) tile; (wall) brick.

Ziegelbrenner ['tsi:gəlbrenər], m. (—s, pl. —s) tile-maker, tiler; brickmaker.

Ziegelbrennerei [tsi:gəlbrenə'raɪ], f. (—, pl. —en) tile-kiln; brickyard.

Ziegeldach ['tsi:gəldax], n. (—s, pl. —er) tiled roof.

Ziegeldecker ['tsi:gəldɛkər], m. (—s, pl. —) tiler.

Ziegelei [tsi:gə'laɪ], f. (—, pl. —en) brickyard, brickworks.

Ziegelerde ['tsi:gələrdə], f. (—, no pl.) brick-clay.

Ziegenbart ['tsi:gənba:rt], m. (—s, pl. —e) goat's beard; (human) goatee.

Ziegenleder ['tsi:gənle:dər], n. (—s, no pl.) kid (leather).

Ziegenpeter ['tsi:gənpe:tər], m. (—s, no pl.) (Med.) mumps.

ziehen ['tsi:ən], v.a. irr. draw, pull, drag; pull out; cultivate; breed; (game) move. — v.n. draw, be an attraction; (aux. sein) go, move. — v.r. sich —, extend.

Ziehkind ['tsi:kɪnt], n. (—s, pl. —er) foster-child.

Ziehmutter ['tsi:mutər], f. (—, pl. —) foster-mother.

Ziehung ['tsi:un], f. (—, pl. —en) draw (in a lottery).

Ziehvater ['tsi:fa:tər], m. (—s, pl. —) foster-father.

Ziel [tsi:l], n. (—s, pl. —e) goal, aim, purpose, intention, end; butt, target; (Mil.) objective; (sports) winning-post.

zielbewußt ['tsi:lbəvust], adj. purposeful; systematic.

zielen ['tsi:lən], v.n. aim (at), take aim (at).

Ziellosigkeit ['tsi:llo:zɪçkaɪt], f. (—, no pl.) aimlessness.

Zielscheibe ['tsi:lʃaɪbə], f. (—, pl. —en) target, butt.

ziemen ['tsi:mən], v.r. sich —, become s.o., behove s.o., be proper for, befit.

Ziemer ['tsi:mər], n. & m. (—s, pl. —) whip.

ziemlich ['tsi:mlɪç], adj. moderate, tolerable, middling, fairly considerable, fair. — adv. rather, fairly.

Zier [tsi:r], f. (—, pl. —den) ornament.

Zieraffe ['tsi:rafə], m. (—n, pl. —n) fop, affected person.

Zierat ['tsi:ra:t], m. (—s, no pl.) ornament, finery.

Zierde ['tsi:rdə], f. (—, pl. —n) decoration, embellishment; (fig.) credit, pride.

Ziererei [tsi:rə'raɪ], f. (—, pl. —en) affectation.

Ziergarten ['tsi:rgartən], m. (—s, pl. —) flower-garden, ornamental garden.

zierlich ['tsi:rlɪç], adj. dainty, graceful, pretty.

Zierpflanze ['tsi:rpflantsə], f. (—, pl. —n) ornamental plant.

Zierpuppe ['tsi:rpupə], f. (—, pl. —n) overdressed woman.

Ziffer ['tsɪfər], f. (—, pl. —n) figure, numeral.

Zifferblatt ['tsɪfərblat], n. (—s, pl. —er) dial, face.

ziffernmäßig ['tsɪfərnmɛ:sɪç], adj. statistical.

Ziffernschrift ['tsɪfərnʃrɪft], f. (—, pl. —en) code.

Zigarette [tsiga'rɛtə], f. (—, pl. —n) cigarette.

Zigarettenetui [tsiga'rɛtənetvi:], n. (—s, pl. —s) cigarette-case.

Zigarettenspitze [tsiga'rɛtənʃpɪtsə], f. (—, pl. —n) cigarette-holder.

Zigarettenstummel [tsiga'rɛtənʃtumməl], m. (—s, pl. —) cigarette-end.

Zigarre [tsi'garə], f. (—, pl. —n) cigar.

Zigarrenkiste [tsi'garənkɪstə], f. (—, pl. —n) cigar-box.

Zigarrenstummel [tsi'garənʃtumməl], m. (—s, pl. —) cigar-end.

Zigeuner [tsi'gɔynər], m. (—s, pl. —) gipsy.

Zikade [tsi'ka:də], f. (—, pl. —n) (Ent.) grasshopper.

Zimmer ['tsɪmər], n. (—s, pl. —) room.

Zimmermädchen ['tsɪmərmɛ:tçən], n. (—s, pl. —) chambermaid.

Zimmermann ['tsɪmərman], m. (—s, pl. Zimmerleute) carpenter, joiner.

zimmern ['tsɪmərn], v.a. carpenter, construct, build.

Zimmernachweis ['tsɪmərna:xvaɪs], m. (—es, pl. —e) accommodation bureau.

Zimmerreihe ['tsɪmərraɪə], f. (—, pl. —n) suite of rooms.

Zimmervermieter ['tsɪmərfermi:tər], m. (—s, pl. —) landlord.

zimperlich ['tsɪmpərlɪç], adj. simpering; prim; finicky, hypersensitive.

Zimt [tsɪmt], m. (—(e)s, no pl.) cinnamon.

Zink [tsɪŋk], n. (—s, no pl.) zinc.

Zinke ['tsɪŋkə], f. (—, pl. —n) prong, tine.

Zinn [tsɪn], n. (—s, no pl.) tin; pewter.

Zinnblech ['tsɪnblɛç], n. (—s, no pl.) tin-plate.

Zinne ['tsɪnə], f. (—, pl. —n) battlement, pinnacle.

zinnern ['tsɪnern], *adj.* made of pewter, of tin.

Zinnober [tsɪn'oːbər], *m.* (—s, *no pl.*) cinnabar; (*coll.*) fuss.

Zinnsäure ['tsɪnzɔyrə], *f.* (—, *no pl.*) stannic acid.

Zins [tsɪns], *m.* (—es, *pl.* —en) duty, tax; rent; (*pl.*) interest.

zinsbar ['tsɪnsbaːr], *adj.* tributary; — *anlegen*, invest at interest; — *machen*, force to pay a tribute.

Zinsen ['tsɪnzən], *m. pl.* interest.

zinsentragend ['tsɪnzəntraːgənt], *adj.* interest-bearing.

Zinseszins ['tsɪnzəstsɪns], *m.* (—, *no pl.*) compound interest.

Zinsfuß ['tsɪnsfuːs], *m.* (—es, *pl.* ⸚e) rate of interest.

zinspflichtig ['tsɪnspflɪçtɪç], *adj.* subject to tax.

Zinsrechnung ['tsɪnsrɛçnuŋ], *f.* (—, *pl.* —en) interest account, calculation of interest.

Zinsschein ['tsɪnsʃaɪn], *m.* (—s, *pl.* —e) coupon, dividend warrant.

Zipfel ['tsɪpfəl], *m.* (—s, *pl.* —) tassel, edge, point, tip.

Zipperlein ['tsɪpərlaɪn], *n.* (—s, *no pl.*) (*coll.*) gout.

zirka ['tsɪrka], *adv.* circa, about, approximately.

Zirkel ['tsɪrkəl], *m.* (—s, *pl.* —) circle; (*Maths.*) pair of compasses; gathering.

zirkulieren [tsɪrku'liːrən], *v.n.* circulate; — *lassen*, put in circulation.

Zirkus ['tsɪrkus], *m.* (—, *pl.* —se) circus.

zirpen ['tsɪrpən], *v.n.* chirp.

zischeln ['tsɪʃəln], *v.n.* whisper.

zischen ['tsɪʃən], *v.n.* hiss; sizzle.

Zischlaut ['tsɪʃlaʊt], *m.* (—s, *pl.* —e) (*Phon.*) sibilant.

Zisterne [tsɪs'tɛrnə], *f.* (—, *pl.* —n) cistern.

Zisterzienser [tsɪstɛr'tsjɛnzər], *m.* (—s, *pl.* —) Cistercian (monk).

Zitadelle [tsɪta'dɛlə], *f.* (—, *pl.* —n) citadel.

Zitat [tsi'taːt], *n.* (—(e)s, *pl.* —e) quotation, reference; *falsches* —, misquotation.

Zither ['tsɪtər], *f.* (—, *pl.* —n) zither.

zitieren [tsi'tiːrən], *v.a.* cite, quote; *falsch* —, misquote.

Zitronat [tsitro'naːt], *n.* (—s, *no pl.*) candied lemon peel.

Zitrone [tsi'troːnə], *f.* (—, *pl.* —n) lemon.

Zitronenlimonade [tsi'troːnənlimonaːdə], *f.* (—, *pl.* —n) lemonade, lemon drink.

Zitronensaft [tsi'troːnənzaft], *m.* (—s, *pl.* ⸚e) lemon-juice.

Zitronensäure [tsi'troːnənzɔyrə], *f.* (—, *no pl.*) citric acid.

Zitronenschale [tsi'troːnənʃaːlə], *f.* (—, *pl.* —n) lemon-peel.

zitterig ['tsɪtərɪç], *adj.* shaky, shivery.

zittern ['tsɪtərn], *v.n.* tremble, shiver, quake.

Zitterpappel ['tsɪtərpapəl], *f.* (—, *pl.* —n) (*Bot.*) aspen-tree.

Zivil [tsi'viːl], *n.* (—s, *no pl.*) civilians, *in* —, in plain clothes; (*coll.*) in civvies *or* mufti.

Zivilbeamte [tsi'viːlbəamtə], *m.* (—n, *pl.* —n) civil servant.

Zivildienst [tsi'viːldiːnst], *m.* (—es, *no pl.*) civil service.

Zivilehe [tsi'viːleːə], *f.* (—, *pl.* —n) civil marriage.

Zivilgesetzbuch [tsi'viːlgəzɛtsbuːx], *n.* (—s, *pl.* ⸚er) code of civil law.

Zivilingenieur [tsi'viːlɪnʒenjøːr], *m.* (—s, *pl.* —e) civil engineer.

Zivilisation [tsiviliza'tsjoːn], *f.* (—, *pl.* —en) civilisation.

zivilisatorisch [tsiviliza'toːrɪʃ], *adj.* civilising.

zivilisieren [tsivili'ziːrən], *v.a.* civilise.

Zivilist [tsivi'lɪst], *m.* (—en, *pl.* —en) civilian.

Zivilkleidung [tsi'viːlklaɪduŋ], *f.* (—, *no pl.*) civilian dress, plain clothes.

Zobel ['tsoːbəl], *m.* (—s, *pl.* —) sable.

Zobelpelz ['tsoːbəlpɛlts], *m.* (—es, *pl.* —e) sable fur; sable-coat.

Zofe ['tsoːfə], *f.* (—, *pl.* —n) lady's maid.

zögern ['tsøːgərn], *v.n.* hesitate, tarry, delay.

Zögerung ['tsøːgəruŋ], *f.* (—, *pl.* —en) hesitation, delay.

Zögling ['tsøːklɪŋ], *m.* (—s, *pl.* —e) pupil, charge.

Zölibat [tsøli'baːt], *m. & n.* (—s, *no pl.*) celibacy.

Zoll (1) [tsɔl], *m.* (—s, *no pl.*) inch.

Zoll (2) [tsɔl], *m.* (—s, *pl.* ⸚e) customs duty; (*bridge*) toll.

Zollabfertigung ['tsɔlapfɛrtiguŋ], *f.* (—, *no pl.*) customs clearance.

Zollamt ['tsɔlamt], *n.* (—s, *pl.* ⸚er) custom house.

Zollaufschlag ['tsɔlaʊfʃlaːk], *m.* (—s, *pl.* ⸚e) additional duty.

Zollbeamte ['tsɔlbəamtə], *m.* (—n, *pl.* —n) customs officer.

zollbreit ['tsɔlbraɪt], *adj.* one inch wide.

zollen ['tsɔlən], *v.a. Ehrfurcht* —, pay o.'s respects; *Beifall* —, applaud; *Dank* —, show gratitude.

zollfrei ['tsɔlfraɪ], *adj.* duty-free, exempt from duty.

Zöllner ['tsœlnər], *m.* (—s, *pl.* —) tax-gatherer.

zollpflichtig ['tsɔlpflɪçtɪç], *adj.* liable to duty, dutiable.

Zollsatz ['tsɔlzats], *m.* (—es, *pl.* ⸚e) customs tariff.

Zollverein ['tsɔlfəraɪn], *m.* (—s, *no pl.*) customs union.

Zollverschluß ['tsɔlfɛrʃlus], *m.* (—sses, *pl.* ⸚sse) bond.

Zone ['tsoːnə], *f.* (—, *pl.* —n) zone.

Zoologe [tsoːo'loːgə], *m.* (—n, *pl.* —n) zoologist.

Zoologie [tsoːolo'giː], *f.* (—, *no pl.*) zoology.

zoologisch [tso:o'lo:gɪʃ], *adj.* zoological; *—er Garten,* zoological gardens, zoo.

Zopf [tsɔpf], *m.* (—(e)s, *pl.* ⁓e) plait, pigtail; (*coll.*) (old-fashioned) pedantry.

Zorn [tsɔrn], *m.* (—(e)s, *no pl.*) wrath, anger, indignation; *seinen — auslassen,* vent o.'s anger; *in — geraten,* get angry.

zornglühend ['tsɔrnglyːənt], *adj.* boiling with rage.

zornig ['tsɔrnɪç], *adj.* angry, wrathful, irate; *— werden,* get angry.

Zote ['tsoːtə], *f.* (—, *pl.* —n) smutty story, ribaldry, bawdiness.

zotig ['tsoːtɪç], *adj.* loose, ribald, smutty.

zottig ['tsɔtɪç], *adj.* shaggy.

zu [tsuː], *prep.* (*Dat.*) to, towards; in addition to; at, in, on; for; — *Anfang.* in the beginning; — *Fuß,* on foot; — *Hause,* at home; — *Wasser,* at sea, by sea; — *deinem Nutzen,* for your benefit. — *adv. & prefix,* to, towards; closed; too; — *sehr,* too; — *viel,* too much.

Zubehör ['tsuːbəhøːr], *n.* (—s, *no pl.*) accessory, appurtenance.

zubekommen ['tsuːbəkɔmən], *v.a. irr.* get in addition.

Zuber ['tsuːbər], *m.* (—s, *pl.* —) tub.

zubereiten ['tsuːbəraɪtən], *v.a.* prepare.

Zubereitung ['tsuːbəraɪtuŋ], *f.* (—, *no pl.*) preparation.

zubilligen ['tsuːbɪlɪɡən], *v.a.* allow, grant.

zubleiben ['tsuːblaɪbən], *v.n. irr.* (*aux. sein*) remain shut.

zubringen ['tsuːbrɪŋən], *v.a. irr. die Zeit —,* spend the time.

Zubringerdienst ['tsuːbrɪŋərdiːnst], *m.* (—es, *pl.* —) shuttle-service, tender-service.

Zubuße ['tsuːbuːsə], *f.* (—, *pl.* —n) (additional) contribution.

Zucht [tsuxt], *f.* (—, *no pl.*) race, breed; discipline; breeding, rearing; education, discipline; (good) manners; *in — halten,* keep in hand.

züchten ['tsyçtən], *v.a.* cultivate; rear, breed; grow.

Züchter ['tsyçtər], *m.* (—s, *pl.* —) (*plants*) nurseryman; (*animals*) breeder.

Zuchthaus ['tsuxthaus], *n.* (—es, *pl.* ⁓er) penitentiary, convict prison.

Zuchthäusler ['tsuxthɔyslər], *m.* (—s, *pl.* —) convict.

Zuchthengst ['tsuxthɛŋst], *m.* (—es, *pl.* ⁓e) stallion.

züchtig ['tsyçtɪç], *adj.* modest, chaste.

züchtigen ['tsyçtɪɡən], *v.a.* chastise, lash.

Züchtigkeit ['tsyçtɪçkaɪt], *f.* (—, *no pl.*) modesty, chastity.

Züchtigung ['tsyçtɪɡuŋ], *f.* (—, *pl.* —en) chastisement; *körperliche —,* corporal punishment.

Zuchtlosigkeit ['tsuxtloːzɪçkaɪt], *f.* (—, *no pl.*) want of discipline.

Zuchtmeister ['tsuxtmaɪstər], *m.* (—s, *pl.* —) disciplinarian, taskmaster.

Zuchtochse ['tsuxtɔksə], *m.* (—n, *pl.* —n) bull.

Zuchtstute ['tsuxtʃtuːtə], *f.* (—, *pl.* —n) brood-mare.

Züchtung ['tsyçtuŋ], *f.* (—, *pl.* —en) (*plants*) cultivation; (*animals*) rearing, breeding.

Zuchtvieh ['tsuxtfiː], *n.* (—s, *no pl.*) breeding stock.

Zuchtwahl ['tsuxtvaːl], *f.* (—, *no pl.*) (*breeding*) selection.

zucken ['tsukən], *v.n.* quiver, twitch; wince; start, jerk.

Zucken ['tsukən], *n.* (—s, *no pl.*) palpitation, convulsion, twitch, tic.

Zucker ['tsukər], *m.* (—s, *no pl.*) sugar.

Zuckerbäcker ['tsukərbɛkər], *m.* (—s, *pl.* —) confectioner.

Zuckerguß ['tsukərɡus], *m.* (—es, *no pl.*) (sugar-)icing.

Zuckerkandis ['tsukərkandɪs], *m.* (—, *no pl.*) sugar-candy.

zuckerkrank ['tsukərkraŋk], *adj.* (*Med.*) diabetic.

Zuckerkrankheit ['tsukərkraŋkhaɪt], *f.* (—, *no pl.*) (*Med.*) diabetes.

zuckern ['tsukərn], *v.a.* sugar.

Zuckerpflanzung ['tsukərpflantsuŋ], *f.* (—, *pl.* —en) sugar-plantation.

Zuckerraffinerie ['tsukərrafinəriː], *f.* (—, *pl.* —en) sugar-refinery.

Zuckerrohr ['tsukərroːr], *n.* (—s, *no pl.*) sugar-cane.

Zuckerrübe ['tsukərryːbə], *f.* (—, *pl.* —n) sugar-beet.

Zuckerwerk ['tsukərvɛrk], *n.* (—s, *no pl.*) confectionery.

Zuckerzange ['tsukərtsaŋə], *f.* (—, *pl.* —n) sugar-tongs.

Zuckung ['tsukuŋ], *f.* (—, *pl.* —en) convulsion, spasm.

zudecken ['tsuːdɛkən], *v.a.* cover up.

zudem [tsuːˈdeːm], *adv.* besides, moreover.

Zudrang ['tsuːdraŋ], *m.* (—s, *no pl.*) crowd(ing); rush (on), run (on).

zudrehen ['tsuːdreːən], *v.a.* turn off.

zudringlich ['tsuːdrɪŋlɪç], *adj.* importunate; intruding.

zudrücken ['tsuːdrykən], *v.a.* close (by pressing), shut.

zueignen ['tsuːaɪɡnən], *v.a.* dedicate.

zuerkennen ['tsuːɛrkɛnən], *v.a. irr.* award, adjudicate.

zuerst [tsuːˈeːrst], *adv.* at first, first, in the first instance.

Zufahrt ['tsuːfaːrt], *f.* (—, *no pl.*) approach, drive.

Zufall ['tsuːfal], *m.* (—s, *pl.* ⁓e) chance, coincidence; *durch —,* by chance.

zufallen ['tsuːfalən], *v.n. irr.* (*aux. sein*) close, fall shut; come —, devolve upon s.o., fall to s.o.'s lot.

zufällig ['tsuːfɛlɪç], *adj.* accidental, casual, fortuitous. — *adv.* by chance.

Zuflucht ['tsuːfluxt], *f.* (—, *no pl.*) refuge, shelter, haven, recourse.

Zufluchtsort

Zufluchtsort ['tsu:fluxtsɔrt], *m.* (—(e)s, *pl.* —e) asylum, shelter, place of refuge.

Zufluß ['tsu:flus], *m.* (—sses, *pl.* ⸚sse) supply; influx.

zuflüstern ['tsu:flystərn], *v.a.* *einem etwas —*, whisper s.th. to s.o.

zufolge [tsu'fɔlgə], *prep.* (*Genit.*, *Dat.*) in consequence of, owing to, due to, on account of.

zufrieden [tsu'fri:dən], *adj.* content, contented, satisfied; *— lassen*, leave alone.

zufriedenstellen [tsu'fri:dənʃtɛlən], *v.a.* satisfy.

zufügen ['tsu:fy:gən], *v.a.* add (to); inflict.

Zufuhr ['tsu:fu:r], *f.* (—, *pl.* —en) (*goods*) supplies.

Zug [tsu:k], *m.* (—(e)s, *pl.* ⸚e) drawing, pull, tug; draught; march, procession; (*Railw.*) train; (*face*) feature; (*chess*) move; (*character*) trait; (*pen*) stroke; (*birds*) flight; migration; (*mountains*) range.

Zugabe ['tsu:ga:bə], *f.* (—, *pl.* —n) addition, make-weight, extra; (*concert*) encore; *als —*, into the bargain.

Zugang ['tsu:gan], *m.* (—s, *pl.* ⸚e) approach, entry, entrance, admittance, access.

zugänglich ['tsu:gɛŋlɪç], *adj.* accessible, available; (*person*) affable.

Zugbrücke ['tsu:kbrykə], *f.* (—, *pl.* —n) drawbridge.

zugeben ['tsu:ge:bən], *v.a. irr.* give in addition; concede, admit.

zugegen [tsu'ge:gən], *adv.* present.

zugehen ['tsu:ge:ən], *v.n. irr.* (*aux.* sein) (*door*) shut (of itself), close; happen; *auf einen —*, walk towards s.o.; *so geht es im Leben zu*, such is life; *das geht nicht mit rechten Dingen zu*, there is something wrong about it.

zugehörig ['tsu:gəhø:rɪç], *adj.* belonging, appertaining.

zugeknöpft ['tsu:gəknœpft], *adj.* reserved, taciturn.

Zügel ['tsy:gəl], *m.* (—s, *pl.* —) rein, bridle.

zügeln ['tsy:gəln], *v.a.* bridle, curb, check.

zugesellen ['tsu:gəzɛlən], *v.r. sich —*, associate with, join.

Zugeständnis ['tsu:gəʃtɛntnɪs], *n.* (—sses, *pl.* —sse) admission; concession.

zugestehen ['tsu:gəʃte:ən], *v.a. irr.* admit; concede; *einem etwas —*, allow s.o. s.th.

zugetan ['tsu:gəta:n], *adj.* attached, devoted.

Zugführer ['tsu:kfy:rər], *m.* (—s, *pl.* —) (*Railw.*) guard; (*Mil.*) platoon commander.

zugießen ['tsu:gi:sən], *v.a. irr.* fill up, pour on.

zugig ['tsu:gɪç], *adj.* windy, draughty.

Zugkraft ['tsu:kkraft], *f.* (—, *no pl.*) tractive power, magnetic attraction;

(*fig.*) pull, attraction; publicity value.

zugleich [tsu'glaɪç], *adv.* at the same time; *— mit*, together with.

Zugluft ['tsu:kluft], *f.* (—, *no pl.*) draught (of air).

zugreifen ['tsu:graɪfən], *v.n. irr.* grab; lend a hand; (*at table*) help o.s.

Zugrolle ['tsu:krɔlə], *f.* (—, *pl.* —n) pulley.

zugrunde [tsu'grundə], *adv. — gehen*, perish, go to ruin, go to the dogs; *— legen*, base upon.

Zugstück ['tsu:kʃtyk], *n.* (—s, *pl.* —e) (*Theat.*) popular show; (*coll.*) success, hit.

zugucken ['tsu:gukən], *v.n.* look on, watch.

zugunsten [tsu'gunstən], *prep.* (*Genit.*) for the benefit of.

zugute [tsu'gu:tə], *adv. — halten*, make allowances.

Zugvogel ['tsu:kfo:gəl], *m.* (—s, *pl.* ⸚) bird of passage.

zuhalten ['tsu:haltən], *v.a. irr.* keep closed.

Zuhälter ['tsu:hɛltər], *m.* (—s, *pl.* —) souteneur; pimp.

Zuhilfenahme [tsu'hɪlfəna:mə], *f.* (—, *no pl.*) *unter —*, with the help of, by means of.

zuhören ['tsu:hø:rən], *v.n.* listen to, attend to.

Zuhörerschaft ['tsu:hø:rərʃaft], *f.* (—, *pl.* —en) audience.

zujubeln ['tsu:ju:bəln], *v.n. einem —*, acclaim s.o., cheer s.o.

zukehren ['tsu:ke:rən], *v.a. einem den Rücken —*, turn o.'s back on s.o.

zuknöpfen ['tsu:knœpfən], *v.a.* button (up).

zukommen ['tsu:kɔmən], *v.n. irr.* (*aux.* sein) *auf einen —*, advance towards s.o.; *einem —*, be due to s.o.; become s.o.; reach s.o.

Zukost ['tsu:kɔst], *f.* (—, *no pl.*) (*food*) trimmings, extras.

Zukunft ['tsu:kunft], *f.* (—, *no pl.*) future; prospects.

zukünftig ['tsu:kynftɪç], *adj.* future, prospective.

Zukunftsmusik ['tsu:kunftsmuzi:k], *f.* (—, *no pl.*) daydreams, pipedreams.

zulächeln ['tsu:lɛçəln], *v.a. einem —*, smile at s.o.

Zulage ['tsu:la:gə], *f.* (—, *pl.* —n) addition; increase of salary, rise; (*Am.*) raise.

zulangen ['tsu:laŋən], *v.n.* be sufficient; (*at table*) help o.s.

zulänglich ['tsu:lɛŋlɪç], *adj.* sufficient, adequate.

zulassen ['tsu:lasən], *v.a. irr.* leave unopened; allow; admit; permit.

zulässig ['tsu:lɛsɪç], *adj.* admissible; *das ist nicht —*, that is not allowed.

Zulassung ['tsu:lasuŋ], *f.* (—, *pl.* —en) admission.

Zulauf ['tsu:lauf], *m.* (—s, *no pl.*) run (of customers); crowd, throng.

zurücklassen

zulaufen ['tsu:laufən], *v.n. irr.* (*aux.* sein) *auf einen —*, run towards s.o.; *spitz —*, taper, come to a point.

zulegen ['tsu:le:gən], *v.a.* add; increase; *sich etwas —*, make o.s. a present of s.th.; get s.th.

zuletzt [tsu'lɛtst], *adv.* last, at last, lastly, finally, eventually, in the end.

zuliebe [tsu'li:bə], *adv. einem etwas — tun*, oblige s.o.; do s.th. for s.o.'s sake.

zum = zu dem.

zumachen ['tsu:maxən], *v.a.* shut, close.

zumal [tsu'ma:l], *adv.* especially, particularly. *— conj.* especially since.

zumeist [tsu'maɪst], *adv.* mostly, for the most part.

zumute [tsu'mu:tə], *adv. mir ist nicht gut —*, I don't feel well.

zumuten ['tsu:mu:tən], *v.a. einem etwas —*, expect or demand s.th. of s.o.

Zumutung ['tsu:mu:tuŋ], *f.* (—, *pl.* —en) unreasonable demand.

zunächst [tsu'nɛ:çst], *adv.* first, above all.

Zunahme ['tsu:na:mə], *f.* (—, *pl.* —n) increase.

Zuname ['tsu:na:mə], *m.* (—ns, *pl.* —n) surname, family name.

zünden ['tsyndən], *v.n.* catch fire, ignite.

Zunder ['tsundər], *m.* (—s, *no pl.*) tinder.

Zünder ['tsyndər], *m.* (—s, *pl.* —) lighter, detonator, fuse.

Zündholz ['tsynthɔlts], *n.* (—es, *pl.* ⁓er) match.

Zündkerze ['tsyntkɛrtsə], *f.* (—, *pl.* —n) (*Motor.*) sparking-plug.

Zündstoff ['tsyntʃtɔf], *m.* (—s, *pl.* —e) fuel.

Zündung ['tsynduŋ], *f.* (—, *pl.* —en) ignition; detonation.

zunehmen ['tsu:ne:mən], *v.n. irr.* increase, put on weight; (*moon*) wax.

zuneigen ['tsu:naɪgən], *v.r. sich —*, incline towards.

Zuneigung ['tsu:naɪguŋ], *f.* (—, *pl.* —en) affection, inclination.

Zunft [tsunft], *f.* (—, *pl.* ⁓e) company, guild, corporation; (*fig.*) brotherhood.

Zunftgenosse ['tsunftgənɔsə], *m.* (—n, *pl.* —n) member of a guild.

zünftig ['tsynftɪç], *adj.* professional; proper.

zunftmäßig ['tsunftmɛ:sɪç], *adj.* professional; competent.

Zunge ['tsuŋə], *f.* (—, *pl.* —n) tongue; (*buckle*) catch; (*fig.*) language; (*fish*) sole.

züngeln ['tsyŋəln], *v.n.* (*flame*) shoot out, lick.

Zungenband ['tsuŋənbant], *n.* (—s, *pl.* ⁓er) ligament of the tongue.

zungenfertig ['tsuŋənfɛrtɪç], *adj.* voluble, glib.

Zungenlaut ['tsuŋənlaut], *m.* (—s, *pl.* —e) (*Phon.*) lingual sound.

Zungenspitze ['tsuŋənʃpɪtsə], *f.* (—, *pl.* —n) tip of the tongue.

zunichte [tsu'nɪçtə], *adv. — machen*, ruin, undo, destroy; *— werden*, come to nothing.

zupfen ['tsupfən], *v.a.* pick, pluck.

zurechnungsfähig ['tsu:rɛçnuŋsfɛ:ɪç], *adj.* accountable, of sane mind, compos mentis.

zurecht [tsu'rɛçt], *adv.* aright, right(ly), in order.

zurechtfinden [tsu'rɛçtfɪndən], *v.r. irr. sich —*, find o.'s way about.

zurechtkommen [tsu'rɛçtkɔmən], *v.n. irr.* (*aux.* sein) arrive in (good) time; *mit einem gut —*, get on well with s.o.

zurechtlegen [tsu'rɛçtle:gən], *v.a.* put in order, get ready.

zurechtmachen [tsu'rɛçtmaxən], *v.a.* get s.th. ready, prepare s.th. — *v.r. sich —*, prepare o.s.; (*women*) make up; (*coll.*) put on o.'s face.

zurechtweisen [tsu'rɛçtvaɪzən], *v.a. irr.* reprove (s.o.), set (s.o.) right; direct.

Zurechtweisung [tsu'rɛçtvaɪzuŋ], *f.* (—, *pl.* —en) reprimand.

Zureden ['tsu:re:dən], *n.* (—s, *no pl.*) encouragement; entreaties.

zureden ['tsu:re:dən], *v.n.* encourage (s.o.), persuade (s.o.)

zureichen ['tsu:raɪçən], *v.a.* reach, hand. — *v.n.* be sufficient, be enough, suffice.

zurichten ['tsu:rɪçtən], *v.a. etwas (einen) übel —*, maltreat s.th. (s.o.).

zürnen ['tsyrnən], *v.n.* be angry (with).

zurück [tsu'ryk], *adv.* back; behind; backwards; — *excl.* stand back!

zurückbegeben [tsu'rykbəge:bən], *v.r. irr. sich —*, go back, return.

zurückbehalten [tsu'rykbəhaltən], *v.a. irr.* retain, keep back.

zurückbekommen [tsu'rykbəkɔmən], *v.a. irr.* get back, recover (s.th.).

zurückberufen [tsu'rykbəru:fən], *v.a. irr.* recall.

zurückfordern [tsu'rykfɔrdərn], *v.a.* demand back, demand the return of.

zurückführen [tsu'rykfy:rən], *v.a.* lead back; *auf etwas —*, attribute to; trace back to.

zurückgeblieben [tsu'rykgəbli:bən], *adj.* retarded, mentally deficient, backward.

zurückgezogen [tsu'rykgətso:gən], *adj.* secluded, retired.

zurückhalten [tsu'rykhaltən], *v.a. irr.* keep back, retain.

zurückhaltend [tsu'rykhaltənt], *adj.* reserved.

zurückkehren [tsu'rykke:rən], *v.n.* (*aux.* sein) return.

zurückkommen [tsu'rykkɔmən], *v.n. irr.* (*aux.* sein) come back.

zurücklassen [tsu'ryklasən], *v.a. irr.* leave behind, abandon.

295

zurücklegen

zurücklegen [tsu'rykle:gǝn], *v.a.* lay aside, put by; *eine Strecke —,* cover a distance. — *v.r. sich —,* lean back; *zurückgelegter Gewinn,* undistributed profits.

zurückmüssen [tsu'rykmysǝn], *v.n. irr.* be obliged to return.

zurücknehmen [tsu'rykne:mǝn], *v.a. irr.* take back.

zurückschrecken [tsu'rykʃrɛkǝn], *v.a.* frighten away. — *v.n. irr. (aux.* sein) recoil (from).

zurücksehnen [tsu'rykze:nǝn], *v.r. sich —,* long to return, wish o.s. back.

zurücksetzen [tsu'rykzɛtsǝn], *v.a.* put back; slight; discriminate against; neglect.

Zurücksetzung [tsu'rykzɛtsuŋ], *f.* (—, *pl.* —en) slight, rebuff.

zurückstrahlen [tsu'rykʃtra:lǝn], *v.a.* reflect.

zurücktreten [tsu'ryktre:tǝn], *v.n. irr. (aux.* sein) stand back, withdraw; resign.

zurückverlangen [tsu'rykfɛrlaŋǝn], *v.a.* demand back, request the return of.

zurückversetzen [tsu'rykfɛrzɛtsǝn], *v.a. (Sch.)* put in a lower form. — *v.r. sich —,* turn o.'s thoughts back (to), hark back.

zurückweichen [tsu'rykvaɪçǝn], *v.n. irr. (aux.* sein) withdraw, retreat.

zurückweisen [tsu'rykvaɪzǝn], *v.a. irr.* refuse, reject, repulse.

zurückwollen [tsu'rykvɔlǝn], *v.n.* wish to return.

zurückziehen [tsu'ryktsi:ǝn], *v.a.* draw back; *(fig.)* withdraw, retract, countermand. — *v.r. sich —,* retire, withdraw.

Zuruf ['tsu:ru:f], *m.* (—s, *pl.* —e) call, acclaim, acclamation.

Zusage ['tsu:za:gǝ], *f.* (—, *pl.* —n) promise; acceptance.

zusagen ['tsu:za:gǝn], *v.a.* promise; *es sagt mir zu,* I like it. — *v.n.* accept.

zusagend ['tsu:za:gǝnt], *adj.* affirmative, agreeable.

zusammen [tsu'zamǝn], *adv.* together, jointly.

zusammenbeißen [tsu'zamǝnbaɪsǝn], *v.a. irr. die Zähne —,* set o.'s teeth.

zusammenbetteln [tsu'zamǝnbɛtǝln], *v.a. sich etwas —,* collect (by begging).

zusammenbrechen [tsu'zamǝnbrɛ-çǝn], *v.n. irr. (aux.* sein) break down, collapse.

Zusammenbruch [tsu'zamǝnbrux], *m.* (—s, *pl.* —e) breakdown, collapse, débâcle.

zusammendrängen [tsu'zamǝndrɛŋ-ǝn], *v.a.* press together; *(fig.)* abridge, condense.

zusammendrücken [tsu'zamǝndry-kǝn], *v.a.* compress.

zusammenfahren [tsu'zamǝnfa:rǝn], *v.n. irr. (aux.* sein) collide; give a start.

zusammenfallen [tsu'zamǝnfalǝn], *v.n. irr. (aux.* sein) collapse.

zusammenfassen [tsu'zamǝnfasǝn], *v.a.* sum up, summarize.

Zusammenfassung [tsu'zamǝnfasuŋ], *f.* (—, *no pl.*) summing-up, summary.

zusammenfinden [tsu'zamǝnfindǝn], *v.r. irr. sich —,* discover a mutual affinity, come together.

Zusammenfluß [tsu'zamǝnflus], *m.* (—sses, *pl.* ¨sse) confluence.

zusammengeben [tsu'zamǝnge:bǝn], *v.a. irr.* join in marriage.

Zusammengehörigkeit [tsu'zamǝngǝ-høː'rɪçkaɪt], *f.* (—, *no pl.*) solidarity; *(Am.)* togetherness.

zusammengesetzt [tsu'zamǝngǝzɛtst], *adj.* composed (of), consisting (of); complicated; *(Maths.)* composite.

zusammengewürfelt [tsu'zamǝngǝ-vyrfalt], *adj.* motley, mixed.

Zusammenhalt [tsu'zamǝnhalt], *m.* (—s, *no pl.*) holding together; unity.

Zusammenhang [tsu'zamǝnhaŋ], *m.* (—s, *pl.* ¨e) coherence; connection, context.

zusammenhängen [tsu'zamǝnhɛŋǝn], *v.n. irr.* hang together, cohere; *(fig.)* be connected (with).

Zusammenklang [tsu'zamǝnklaŋ], *m.* (—s, *pl.* ¨e) unison, harmony.

Zusammenkunft [tsu'zamǝnkunft], *f.* (—, *pl.* ¨e) meeting, convention, conference; reunion.

zusammenlaufen [tsu'zamǝnlaufǝn], *v.n. irr. (aux.* sein) crowd together, converge; flock together; *(milk)* curdle; *(material)* shrink.

zusammenlegen [tsu'zamǝnle:gǝn], *v.a.* put together; *(money)* collect; *(letter)* fold up.

zusammennehmen [tsu'zamǝnne:-mǝn], *v.a. irr.* gather up. — *v.r. sich —,* get a firm grip on o.s., pull o.s. together.

zusammenpassen [tsu'zamǝnpasǝn], *v.n.* fit together, match; agree; be compatible.

zusammenpferchen [tsu'zamǝnpfɛr-çǝn], *v.a.* pen up, crowd together in a small space.

zusammenpressen [tsu'zamǝnprɛsǝn], *v.a.* squeeze together.

zusammenraffen [tsu'zamǝnrafǝn], *v.a.* gather up hurriedly, collect. — *v.r. sich —,* pluck up courage; pull o.s. together.

zusammenrechnen [tsu'zamǝnrɛç-nǝn], *v.a.* add up.

zusammenreimen [tsu'zamǝnraɪmǝn], *v.a. sich etwas —,* figure s.th. out.

zusammenrücken [tsu'zamǝnrykǝn], *v.a.* move together, draw closer. — *v.n.* move closer together, move up.

zusammenschießen [tsu'zamǝnʃi:sǝn], *v.a. irr.* shoot to pieces, shoot down; *Geld —,* club together, raise a subscription.

zusammenschlagen [tsu'zamǝnʃla-gǝn], *v.a. irr.* beat up; strike together; clap, fold.

Zustimmung

zusammenschließen [tsu'zamənʃli:-sən], *v.r. irr. sich —,* join, unite, ally o.s. (with).

zusammenschweißen [tsu'zamənʃvai-sən], *v.a.* weld together.

Zusammensein [tsu'zamənzain], *n.* (**—s,** *no pl.*) meeting, social gathering.

Zusammensetzung [tsu'zamənzɛtsuŋ], *f.* (**—,** *no pl.*) construction; composition.

Zusammenspiel [tsu'zamənʃpi:l], *n.* (**—s,** *no pl.*) (*Theat., Mus.*) ensemble.

zusammenstellen [tsu'zamənʃtɛlən], *v.a.* compose, concoct; put together, compile.

Zusammenstellung [tsu'zamənʃtɛluŋ], *f.* (**—,** *pl.* **—en**) combination, compilation; juxtaposition.

zusammenstoppeln [tsu'zamənʃtɔp-əln], *v.a.* string together, patch up.

Zusammenstoß [tsu'zamənʃto:s], *m.* (**—es,** *pl.* **⁻e**) clash, conflict; collision.

zusammenstoßen [tsu'zamənʃto:sən], *v.n. irr.* (*aux.* sein) clash; crash, come into collision, collide.

zusammentragen [tsu'zaməntra:gən], *v.a. irr.* collect, compile.

zusammentreffen [tsu'zaməntrɛfən], *v.n. irr.* meet; coincide.

zusammentreten [tsu'zaməntre:tən], *v.n. irr.* (*aux.* sein) meet.

zusammentun [tsu'zaməntu:n], *v.r. irr. sich — mit,* associate with, join.

zusammenwirken [tsu'zamənvɪrkən], *v.n.* cooperate, collaborate.

zusammenwürfeln [tsu'zamənvyr-fəln], *v.a.* jumble up.

zusammenzählen [tsu'zamənstɛ:lən], *v.a.* add up.

zusammenziehen [tsu'zaməntsi:ən], *v.n. irr.* (*aux.* sein) move in together. — *v.a.* draw together, contract. — *v.r. sich —,* shrink; (*storm*) gather; *Zahlen —,* add up.

Zusammenziehung [tsu'zaməntsi:uŋ], *f.* (**—,** *no pl.*) contraction.

Zusatz [tsu'zats], *m.* (**—es,** *pl.* **⁻e**) addition, supplement, admixture; (*will*) codicil.

zuschanzen [tsu:ʃantsən], *v.a. einem etwas —,* obtain s.th. for s.o.

zuschauen [tsu:ʃauən], *v.n.* look on, watch.

Zuschauer [tsu:ʃauər], *m.* (**—s,** *pl.* **—**) onlooker, spectator.

Zuschauerraum [tsu:ʃauərraum], *m.* (**—s,** *pl.* **⁻e**) (*Theat.*) auditorium.

zuschaufeln [tsu:ʃaufəln], *v.a.* shovel in, fill up.

zuschieben [tsu:ʃi:bən], *v.a. irr.* push towards; shut; *einem etwas —,* shove (blame) on to s.o.

zuschießen [tsu:ʃi:sən], *v.a. irr. Geld —,* put money into (an undertaking).

Zuschlag [tsu:ʃla:k], *m.* (**—s,** *pl.* **⁻e**) addition; (*Railw.*) excess fare.

zuschlagen [tsu:ʃla:gən], *v.a. irr.* add; (*door*) bang; (*auction*) knock down to (s.o.). — *v.n.* strike hard.

zuschlag(s)pflichtig [tsu:ʃla:k(s)pflɪç-tɪç], *adj.* liable to a supplementary charge.

zuschmeißen [tsu:ʃmaisən], *v.a. irr.* (*door*) slam to, bang.

zuschneiden [tsu:ʃnaidən], *v.a. irr.* (*pattern*) cut out; cut up.

Zuschneider [tsu:ʃnaidər], *m.* (**—s,** *pl.*—) (*Tail.*) cutter.

Zuschnitt [tsu:ʃnit], *m.* (**—s,** *no pl.*) (*clothing*) cut.

zuschreiben [tsu:ʃraibən], *v.a. irr. einem etwas —,* impute s.th. to s.o.; attribute *or* ascribe s.th. to s.o.

Zuschrift [tsu:ʃrift], *f.* (**—,** *pl.* **—en**) communication, letter.

Zuschuß [tsu:ʃus], *m.* (**—sses,** *pl.* **⁻sse**) additional money, supplementary allowance, subsidy.

zuschütten [tsu:ʃytən], *v.a.* fill up.

Zusehen [tsu:ze:ən], *n.* (**—s,** *no pl.*) *das — haben,* be left out in the cold.

zusehen [tsu:ze:ən], *v.n. irr.* look on, watch; be a spectator; see to it.

zusehends [tsu:ze:ənts], *adv.* visibly.

zusetzen [tsu:zɛtsən], *v.a.* add to, admix; lose. — *v.n. einem —,* pester s.o.; attack s.o.

zusichern [tsu:zɪçərn], *v.a.* promise, assure.

Zusicherung [tsu:zɪçəruŋ], *f.* (**—,** *pl.* **—en**) promise, assurance.

Zuspeise [tsu:ʃpaizə], *f.* (**—,** *no pl.*) (*dial.*) (*food*) trimmings; vegetables.

zusperren [tsu:ʃpɛrən], *v.a.* shut, close, lock up.

zuspitzen [tsu:ʃpitsən], *v.a.* sharpen to a point. — *v.r. sich —,* come to a climax.

zusprechen [tsu:ʃprɛçən], *v.n. irr. dem Wein —,* drink heavily. — *v.a. Mut —,* comfort.

Zuspruch [tsu:ʃprux], *m.* (**—s,** *pl.* **⁻e**) exhortation; consolation.

Zustand [tsu:ʃtant], *m.* (**—s,** *pl.* **⁻e**) condition, state of affairs, situation.

zustande [tsu:ʃtandə], *adv. — kommen,* come off, be accomplished; *— bringen,* accomplish.

zuständig [tsu:ʃtɛndɪç], *adj.* competent; appropriate.

Zuständigkeit [tsu:ʃtɛndɪçkait], *f.* (**—,** *no pl.*) competence.

zustecken [tsu:ʃtɛkən], *v.a.* pin up; *einem etwas —,* slip s.th. into s.o.'s hand.

zustehen [tsu:ʃte:ən], *v.n. irr.* be due to, belong to; be s.o.'s business to.

zustellen [tsu:ʃtɛlən], *v.a.* deliver, hand over; (*Law*) serve (a writ).

Zustellung [tsu:ʃtɛluŋ], *f.* (**—,** *pl.* **—en**) delivery; (*Law*) service.

zusteuern [tsu:ʃtɔyərn], *v.a.* contribute. — *v.n.* (*aux.* sein) steer for; (*fig.*) aim at.

zustimmen [tsu:ʃtimən], *v.n.* agree to.

Zustimmung [tsu:ʃtimuŋ], *f.* (**—,** *pl.* **—en**) assent, consent, agreement.

297

zustopfen ['tsu:ʃtɔpfən], v.a. fill up, stop up, plug; darn, mend.

zustoßen ['tsu:ʃto:sən], v.a. irr. push to, shut.

zustürzen ['tsu:ʃtyrtsən], v.n. (aux. sein) auf einen —, rush at or towards s.o.

Zutaten ['tsu:ta:tən], f. pl. ingredients, garnishings.

zuteil [tsu'taɪl], adv. — werden, fall to s.o.'s share.

zutragen ['tsu:tra:gən], v.a. irr. report, tell. — v.r. sich —, happen.

Zuträger ['tsu:trɛ:gər], m. (—s, pl. —) informer, tale-bearer.

zuträglich ['tsu:trɛ:klɪç], adj. advantageous, wholesome.

Zutrauen ['tsu:trauən], n. (—s, no pl.) confidence.

zutrauen ['tsu:trauən], v.a. einem etwas —, credit s.o. with s.th.

zutraulich ['tsu:traulɪç], adj. trusting, familiar, intimate; tame.

zutreffen ['tsu:trɛfən], v.n. irr. prove correct, take place.

zutreffend ['tsu:trɛfənt], adj. apposite, pertinent.

Zutritt ['tsu:trɪt], m. (—s, no pl.) entry; access, admittance; — verboten, no admittance.

zutunlich ['tsu:tu:nlɪç], adj. confiding; obliging.

zuverlässig ['tsu:fɛrlɛsɪç], adj. reliable; authentic.

Zuversicht ['tsu:fɛrzɪçt], f. (—, no pl.) trust, confidence.

zuversichtlich ['tsu:fɛrzɪçtlɪç], adj. confident.

zuvor [tsu'fo:r], adv. before, first, formerly.

zuvorkommend [tsu'fo:rkɔmənt], adj. obliging, polite.

Zuwachs ['tsu:vaks], m. (—es, no pl.) increase, accretion, growth.

zuwachsen ['tsu:vaksən], v.n. irr. (aux. sein) become overgrown.

zuwandern ['tsu:vandərn], v.n. (aux. sein) immigrate.

zuwegebringen [tsu've:gəbrɪŋən], v.a. irr. bring about, effect.

zuweilen [tsu'vaɪlən], adv. sometimes, at times.

zuweisen ['tsu:vaɪzən], v.a. irr. assign, apportion.

zuwenden ['tsu:vɛndən], v.a. turn towards; give.

zuwerfen ['tsu:vɛrfən], v.a. irr. throw towards, cast; (door) slam.

zuwider ['tsu:vi:dər], prep. (Dat.) against, contrary to. — adv. repugnant.

Zuwiderhandlung [tsu'vi:dərhandluŋ], f. (—, pl. —en) contravention.

zuwiderlaufen [tsu'vi:dərlaufən], v.n. irr. (aux. sein) be contrary to, fly in the face of.

zuzählen ['tsu:tsɛ:lən], v.a. add to.

zuziehen ['tsu:tsi:ən], v.a. irr. draw together; tighten; consult; (curtain) draw. — v.r. sich eine Krankheit —, catch a disease.

Zuzug ['tsu:tsu:k], m. (—s, no pl.) immigration; population increase.

zuzüglich ['tsu:tsy:klɪç], prep. (Genit.) in addition to, including, plus.

Zwang [tsvaŋ], m. (—s, no pl.) coercion, force; compulsion; (fig.) constraint; sich — auferlegen, restrain o.s.; tu deinen Gefühlen keinen — an, let yourself go.

zwanglos ['tsvaŋlo:s], adj. informal, free and easy.

Zwangsarbeit ['tsvaŋsarbaɪt], f. (—, pl. —en) forced labour.

Zwangsjacke ['tsvaŋsjakə], f. (—, pl. —en) strait-jacket.

Zwangsmaßnahme ['tsvaŋsma:sna:mə], f. (—, pl. —en) compulsory measure, compulsion.

Zwangsversteigerung ['tsvaŋsfɛrʃtaɪgəruŋ], f. (—, pl. —en) enforced sale.

Zwangsvollstreckung ['tsvaŋsfɔlʃtrekuŋ], f. (—, pl. —en) distraint.

zwangsweise ['tsvaŋsvaɪzə], adv. by force, compulsorily.

Zwangswirtschaft ['tsvaŋsvɪrtʃaft], f. (—, no pl.) price control, controlled economy.

zwanzig ['tsvantsɪç], num. adj. twenty.

zwar [tsva:r], adv. to be sure, indeed, it is true, true; (Am.) sure.

Zweck [tsvɛk], m. (—(e)s, pl. —e) end, object, purpose.

zweckdienlich ['tsvɛkdi:nlɪç], adj. useful, expedient.

Zwecke ['tsvɛkə], f. (—, pl. —n) tack, drawing-pin.

zwecksprechend ['tsvɛkɛntʃprɛçənt], adj. suitable, appropriate.

zweckmäßig ['tsvɛkmɛ:sɪç], adj. expedient, suitable, proper.

zwecks [tsvɛks], prep. (Genit.) for the purpose of.

zwei [tsvaɪ], num. adj. two.

zweibändig ['tsvaɪbɛndɪç], adj. in two volumes.

zweideutig ['tsvaɪdɔytɪç], adj. ambiguous, equivocal; (fig.) suggestive.

Zweideutigkeit ['tsvaɪdɔytɪçkaɪt], f. (—, pl. —en) ambiguity.

Zweifel ['tsvaɪfəl], m. (—s, pl. —) doubt, scruple; ohne —, no doubt.

zweifelhaft ['tsvaɪfəlhaft], adj. doubtful, dubious.

zweifellos ['tsvaɪfəllo:s], adv. doubtless.

zweifeln ['tsvaɪfəln], v.n. doubt, question; ich zweifle nicht daran, I have no doubt about it.

Zweifelsfall ['tsvaɪfəlsfal], m. (—s, pl. ⁀e) doubtful matter; im —, in case of doubt.

Zweifler ['tsvaɪflər], m. (—s, pl. —) doubter, sceptic.

Zweig [tsvaɪk], m. (—(e)s, pl. —e) twig, bough, branch.

zweigen ['tsvaɪgən], v.r. sich —, bifurcate, fork, branch.

Zweigniederlassung ['tsvaɪkni:dərlasuŋ], f. (—, pl. —en) branch establishment.

zwitschern

zweihändig ['tsvaɪhɛndɪç], *adj.* two-handed; (*keyboard music*) solo.

Zweihufer ['tsvaɪhuːfər], *m.* (—s, *pl.* —) cloven-footed animal.

zweijährig ['tsvaɪjɛːrɪç], *adj.* two-year-old; of two years' duration.

zweijährlich ['tsvaɪjɛːrlɪç], *adj.* biennial. — *adv.* every two years.

Zweikampf ['tsvaɪkampf], *m.* (— (e)s, *pl.* ⁼e) duel.

zweimal ['tsvaɪmaːl], *adv.* twice; — *soviel*, twice as much.

zweimotorig ['tsvaɪmotoːrɪç], *adj.* twin- (*or* two-) engined.

Zweirad ['tsvaɪraːt], *n.* (—s, *pl.* ⁼er) bicycle.

zweireihig ['tsvaɪraɪɪç], *adj.* (*suit*) double-breasted.

zweischneidig ['tsvaɪʃnaɪdɪç], *adj.* two-edged.

zweiseitig ['tsvaɪzaɪtɪç], *adj.* two-sided, bilateral.

zweisprachig ['tsvaɪʃpraːxɪç], *adj.* bilingual, in two languages.

zweitälteste ['tsvaɪtɛltəstə], *adj.* second (eldest).

zweitbeste ['tsvaɪtbɛstə], *adj.* second best.

zweite ['tsvaɪtə], *num. adj.* second; *aus —r Hand*, secondhand; *zu zweit*, in twos, two of (us, them).

Zweiteilung ['tsvaɪtaɪluŋ], *f.* (—, *pl.* —en) bisection.

zweitens ['tsvaɪtəns], *adv.* secondly, in the second place.

zweitletzte ['tsvaɪtlɛtstə], *adj.* last but one, penultimate.

zweitnächste ['tsvaɪtnɛçstə], *adj.* next but one.

Zwerchfell ['tsvɛrçfɛl], *n.* (—s, *pl.* —e) diaphragm, midriff.

zwerchfellerschütternd ['tsvɛrçfɛlərʃytərnt], *adj.* side-splitting.

Zwerg [tsvɛrk], *m.* (—s, *pl.* —e) dwarf, pigmy.

zwerghaft ['tsvɛrkhaft], *adj.* dwarfish.

Zwetsche ['tsvɛtʃə], *f.* (—, *pl.* —n) (*Bot.*) damson.

Zwickel ['tsvɪkəl], *m.* (—s, *pl.* —) gusset; *komischer* —, (*coll.*) queer fish.

zwicken ['tsvɪkən], *v.a.* pinch, nip.

Zwicker ['tsvɪkər], *m.* (—s, *pl.* —) pince-nez.

Zwickmühle ['tsvɪkmyːlə], *f.* (—, *pl.* —n) *in der — sein*, be on the horns of a dilemma, be in a jam.

Zwickzange ['tsvɪktsaŋə], *f.* (—, *pl.* —n) pincers.

Zwieback ['tsviːbak], *m.* (—s, *pl.* —e) rusk.

Zwiebel ['tsviːbəl], *f.* (—, *pl.* —n) onion; bulb.

zwiebelartig ['tsviːbəlaːrtɪç], *adj.* bulbous.

zwiebeln ['tsviːbəln], *v.a. einen* —, bully, torment s.o.

Zwielicht ['tsviːlɪçt], *n.* (—s, *no pl.*) twilight.

Zwiespalt ['tsviːʃpalt], *m.* (—s, *pl.* —e) difference, dissension; schism.

Zwiesprache ['tsviːʃpraːxə], *f.* (—, *pl.* —n) dialogue; discussion.

Zwietracht ['tsviːtraxt], *f.* (—, *no pl.*) discord, disharmony.

zwieträchtig ['tsviːtrɛçtɪç], *adj.* discordant, at variance.

Zwillich ['tsvɪlɪç], *m.* (—s, *pl.* —e) ticking.

Zwilling ['tsvɪlɪŋ], *m.* (—s, *pl.* —e) twin; (*pl.*) (*Astron.*) Gemini.

Zwingburg ['tsvɪŋburk], *f.* (—, *pl.* —en) stronghold.

Zwinge ['tsvɪŋə], *f.* (—, *pl.* —n) ferrule.

zwingen ['tsvɪŋən], *v.a. irr.* force, compel; master, overcome, get the better of. — *v.r. sich* —, force o.s. (to), make a great effort (to).

zwingend ['tsvɪŋənt], *adj.* cogent, imperative, convincing.

Zwinger ['tsvɪŋər], *m.* (—s, *pl.* —) keep, donjon, fort; bear-pit.

Zwingherrschaft ['tsvɪŋhɛrʃaft], *f.* (—, *pl.* —en) despotism, tyranny.

zwinkern ['tsvɪŋkərn], *v.n.* wink; (*stars*) twinkle.

Zwirn [tsvɪrn], *m.* (—(e)s, *pl.* —e) thread, sewing cotton.

Zwirnrolle ['tsvɪrnrɔlə], *f.* (—, *pl.* —n) ball of thread, reel of cotton.

zwischen ['tsvɪʃən], *prep.* (*Dat., Acc.*) between; among, amongst.

Zwischenakt ['tsvɪʃənakt], *m.* (—s, *pl.* —e) (*Theat.*) interval.

Zwischenbemerkung ['tsvɪʃənbəmɛrkuŋ], *f.* (—, *pl.* —en) interruption, digression.

Zwischendeck ['tsvɪʃəndɛk], *n.* (—s, *pl.* —e) (*ship*) steerage, between decks.

zwischendurch ['tsvɪʃəndurç], *adv.* in between, at intervals.

Zwischenfall ['tsvɪʃənfal], *m.* (—s, *pl.* ⁼e) incident; episode.

Zwischengericht ['tsvɪʃəngərɪçt], *n.* (—s, *pl.* —e) (*food*) entrée, entremets.

Zwischenglied ['tsvɪʃənɡliːt], *n.* (—s, *pl.* —er) link.

Zwischenhändler ['tsvɪʃənhɛndlər], *m.* (—s, *pl.* —) middleman.

Zwischenpause ['tsvɪʃənpauzə], *f.* (—, *pl.* —n) interval; pause.

Zwischenraum ['tsvɪʃənraum], *m.* (—s, *pl.* ⁼e) intermediate space, gap.

Zwischenrede ['tsvɪʃənreːdə], *f.* (—, *pl.* —n) interruption.

Zwischenruf ['tsvɪʃənruːf], *m.* (—s, *pl.* —e) interruption, interjection.

Zwischensatz ['tsvɪʃənzats], *m.* (—es, *pl.* ⁼e) parenthesis; interpolation.

Zwischenspiel ['tsvɪʃənʃpiːl], *n.* (—s, *pl.* —e) interlude, intermezzo.

Zwischenzeit ['tsvɪʃəntsaɪt], *f.* (—, *no pl.*) interval, interim, meantime; *in der* —, meanwhile.

Zwist [tsvɪst], *m.* (—es, *pl.* —e) discord, quarrel, dispute.

Zwistigkeiten ['tsvɪstɪçkaɪtən], *f. pl.* hostilities.

zwitschern ['tsvɪtʃərn], *v.n.* chirp, twitter.

Zwitter ['tsvɪtər], *m.* (—s, *pl.* —) hybrid, cross-breed, mongrel; hermaphrodite.

zwitterhaft ['tsvɪtərhaft], *adj.* hybrid; bisexual.

zwölf [svœlf], *num. adj.* twelve.

Zwölffingerdarm ['tsvœlffɪŋərdarm], *m.* (—s, *pl.* ⁻e) duodenum.

Zyankali [tsy:an'ka:li], *n.* (—s, *no pl.*) potassium cyanide.

Zyklon [tsy'klo:n], *m.* (—s, *pl.* —e) cyclone.

Zyklus ['tsyklus], *m.* (—, *pl.* **Zyklen**) cycle; course, series.

zylinderförmig [tsy'lɪndərfœrmɪç], *adj.* cylindric(al).

Zylinderhut [tsy'lɪndərhu:t], *m.* (—s, *pl.* ⁻e) top-hat, silk-hat.

zylindrisch [tsy'lɪndrɪʃ], *adj.* cylindric(al).

Zyniker ['tsy:nɪkər], *m.* (—s, *pl.* —) cynic.

zynisch ['tsy:nɪʃ], *adj.* cynical.

Zynismus [tsy'nɪsmus], *m.* (—, *no pl.*) cynicism.

Zypern ['tsy:pərn], *n.* Cyprus.

Zypresse [tsy'prɛsə], *f.* (—, *pl.* —n) (*Bot.*) cypress.

Cassell's English-German Dictionary

A

A [ei]. das A (*also Mus.*).

a [ə, ei] (**an** [ən, æn] *before vowel or silent h*), *indef. art.* ein, eine, ein; *two at a time*, zwei auf einmal; *many a*, mancher; *two shillings a pound*, zwei Schilling das Pfund.

abacus ['æbəkəs], *s.* das Rechenbrett.

abandon [ə'bændən], *v.a.* (*give up*) aufgeben; (*forsake*) verlassen; (*surrender*) preisgeben.

abandonment [ə'bændənmənt], *s.* das Verlassen (*active*); das Verlassensein (*passive*); die Wildheit, das Sichgehenlassen.

abasement [ə'beismənt], *s.* die Demütigung, Erniedrigung.

abash [ə'bæʃ], *v.a.* beschämen.

abate [ə'beit], *v.n.* nachlassen.

abbess ['æbes], *s.* die Äbtissin.

abbey ['æbi], *s.* die Abtei.

abbot ['æbət], *s.* der Abt.

abbreviate [ə'bri:vieit], *v.a.* abkürzen.

abbreviation [əbri:vi'eifən], *s.* die Abkürzung.

abdicate ['æbdikeit], *v.a., v.n.* entsagen (*Dat.*), abdanken.

abdomen [æb'doumən, 'æbdəmən], *s.* (*Anat.*) der Unterleib, Bauch.

abdominal [æb'dɔminəl], *adj.* (*Anat.*) Bauch-, Unterleibs-.

abduct [æb'dʌkt], *v.a.* entführen.

abed [ə'bed], *adv.* zu Bett, im Bett.

aberration [æbə'reifən], *s.* die Abirrung; die Verirrung; (*Phys.*) die Strahlenbrechung.

abet [ə'bet], *v.a.* helfen (*Dat.*), unterstützen.

abeyance [ə'beiəns], *s.* die Unentschiedenheit, (der Zustand der) Ungewißheit; *in* —, unentschieden.

abhor [əb'hɔː], *v.a.* verabscheuen.

abhorrence [əb'hɔrəns], *s.* die Abscheu (*of*, vor, *Dat.*).

abhorrent [əb'hɔrənt], *adj.* widerlich, ekelhaft.

abide [ə'baid], *v.n. irr.* bleiben, verweilen; (*last*) dauern. — *v.a.* aushalten.

ability [ə'biliti], *s.* die Fähigkeit, Tüchtigkeit; (*pl.*) die Geisteskräfte, *f. pl.*

abject ['æbdʒekt], *adj.* elend; (*submissive*) unterwürfig, verächtlich.

ablaze [ə'bleiz], *adj., adv.* in Flammen.

able [eibl], *adj.* fähig; (*clever*) geschickt; (*efficient*) tüchtig.

ablution [ə'blu:ʃən], *s.* die Abwaschung, Waschung.

abnormal [æb'nɔːməl], *adj.* abnorm, ungewöhnlich.

abnormality [æbnɔː'mæliti], *s.* die Ungewöhnlichkeit.

aboard [ə'bɔːd], *adv.* an Bord.

abode [ə'boud], *s.* der Wohnsitz, Wohnort.

abolish [ə'bɔliʃ], *v.a.* aufheben, abschaffen.

abolition [æbo'liʃən], *s.* die Abschaffung, Aufhebung.

abominable [ə'bɔminəbl], *adj.* abscheulich, scheußlich.

abominate [ə'bɔmineit], *v.a.* verabscheuen.

abomination [əbɔmi'neifən], *s.* der Abscheu, Greuel.

aboriginal [æbə'ridʒinəl], *adj.* eingeboren, einheimisch. — *s.* der Eingeborene.

aborigines [æbə'ridʒiniːz], *s. pl.* die Eingeborenen, Ureinwohner.

abortion [ə'bɔːʃən], *s.* die Fehlgeburt; die Abtreibung.

abortive [ə'bɔːtiv], *adj.* mißlungen.

abound [ə'baund], *v.n.* wimmeln von (*Dat.*).

about [ə'baut], *prep.* um; (*toward*) gegen; *about 3 o'clock*, gegen drei; (*concerning*) über, betreffend. — *adv.* umher, herum; (*round*) rund herum; (*nearly*) etwa, ungefähr; (*everywhere*) überall; *to be* — *to*, im Begriffe sein *or* stehen zu . . .

above [ə'bʌv], *prep.* über; — *all things*, vor allen Dingen; *this is* — *me*, das ist mir zu hoch; — *board*, offen, ehrlich. — *adv.* oben, darüber, *over and* —, obendrein; — *mentioned*, obenerwähnt.

abrade [ə'breid], *v.a.* abschaben, abschürfen.

abrasion [ə'breiʒən], *s.* die Abschürfung; Abnutzung.

abreast [ə'brest], *adj., adv.* nebeneinander, Seite an Seite; *keep* —, (sich) auf dem Laufenden halten; Schritt halten (mit).

abridge [ə'bridʒ], *v.a.* (ab)kürzen.

abridgement [ə'bridʒmənt], *s.* die (Ab)kürzung; (*book etc.*) der Auszug.

abroad [ə'brɔːd], *adv.* im Ausland, auswärts; *to go* —, ins Ausland reisen.

abrogate ['æbrogeit], *v.a.* abschaffen.

abrogation [æbro'geifən], *s.* (*Pol.*) die Abschaffung.

abrupt [ə'brʌpt], *adj.* plötzlich; (*curt*) schroff; kurz; jäh.

abruptness [ə'brʌptnis], *s.* (*speech*) die Schroffheit; (*suddenness*) die Plötzlichkeit; (*drop*) die Steilheit.

abscess ['æbses], *s.* das Geschwür, die Schwellung, der Abszeß.

abscond

abscond [əb'skɔnd], *v.n.* sich davonmachen.

absence ['æbsəns], *s.* die Abwesenheit;
leave of —, der Urlaub.

absent (1) ['æbsənt], *adj.* abwesend; —
minded, zerstreut.

absent (2) [æb'sent], *v.r.* — *oneself,*
fehlen, fernbleiben; (*go away*) sich entfernen.

absentee [æbsən'ti:], *s.* der Abwesende.

absolute ['æbsəlu:t], *adj.* absolut, unumschränkt.

absolve [əb'zɔlv], *v.a.* freisprechen
(*from,* von), lossprechen, entbinden.

absorb [əb'sɔ:b], *v.a.* absorbieren,
aufsaugen; (*attention*) in Anspruch
nehmen.

absorbed [əb'sɔ:bd], *adj.* versunken.

absorbent [əb'sɔ:bənt], *adj.* absorbie-
rend.

absorption [əb'sɔ:pʃən], *s.* (*Chem.*) die
Absorption; (*attention*) das Versun-
kensein.

abstain [əb'stein], *v.n.* sich enthalten;
— *from voting,* sich der Stimme
enthalten.

abstainer [əb'steinə], *s.* der Abstinenz-
ler, Antialkoholiker.

abstemious [əb'sti:miəs], *adj.* enthaltsam.

abstention [əb'stenʃən], *s.* die Enthaltung.

abstinence ['æbstinəns], *s.* die Enthaltsamkeit, das Fasten (*food*).

abstract [æb'strækt], *v.a.* abstrahieren,
abziehen; (*summarize*) kürzen, ausziehen. —['æbstrækt] *adj.* abstrakt;
(*Maths.*) rein. — *s.* der Auszug, Abriß
(*of article, book, etc.*).

abstracted [æb'stræktid], *adj.* zerstreut,
geistesabwesend.

abstraction [æb'strækʃən], *s.* die Ab-
straktion; der abstrakte Begriff.

abstruse [æb'stru:s], *adj.* schwerver-
ständlich, tiefsinnig.

absurd [əb'sɔ:d], *adj.* absurd, töricht;
(*unreasonable*) unvernünftig, gegen
alle Vernunft; (*laughable*) lächerlich.

absurdity [əb'sɔ:diti], *s.* die Torheit,
Unvernünftigkeit.

abundance [ə'bʌndəns], *s.* die Fülle, der
Überfluß.

abundant [ə'bʌndənt], *adj.* reichlich.

abuse [ə'bju:z], *v.a.* mißbrauchen;
(*insult*) beschimpfen; (*violate*) schänden. —[ə'bju:s], *s.* der Mißbrauch;
(*language*) die Beschimpfung; (*violation*) die Schändung.

abusive [ə'bju:siv], *adj.* (*language*)
grob; schimpfend, schmähend.

abut [ə'bʌt], *v.n.* anstoßen, angrenzen.

abysmal [ə'bizməl], *adj.* bodenlos.

abyss [ə'bis], *s.* der Abgrund, Schlund.

Abyssinian [æbi'sinjən], *adj.* abes-
sinisch. — *s.* der Abessinier.

acacia [ə'keiʃə], *s.* (*Bot.*) die Akazie.

academic [ækə'demik], *adj.* akademisch.
— *s.* der Akademiker.

academy [ə'kædəmi], *s.* die Akademie.

acajou ['ækəʒu:], *s.* (*Bot.*) der Nieren-
baum.

accede [æk'si:d], *v.n.* beistimmen; einwilligen; — *to the throne,* den Thron
besteigen.

accelerate [æk'seləreit], *v.a.* beschleunigen. — *v.n.* schneller fahren.

acceleration [æksələ'reiʃən], *s.* die
Beschleunigung.

accelerator [æk'seləreitə], *s.* (*Motor.*)
der Gashebel, das Gaspedal.

accent (1), **accentuate** [æk'sent, æk-
'sentjueit], *v.a.* akzentuieren, betonen.

accent (2) ['æksənt], *s.* (*Phon.*) der
Ton, Wortton, die Betonung; der
Akzent (*dialect*), die Aussprache.

accentuation [æksentju'eiʃən], *s.* die
Aussprache, Akzentuierung, Betonung.

accept [æk'sept], *v.a.* annehmen.

acceptable [æk'septəbl], *adj.* angenehm,
annehmbar, annehmlich.

acceptance [æk'septəns], *s.* die Annahme; (*Comm.*) das Akzept.

access ['ækses], *s.* der Zugang, Zutritt.

accessible [æk'sesibl], *adj.* erreichbar,
zugänglich.

accession [æk'seʃən], *s.* der Zuwachs;
— *to the throne,* die Thronbesteigung.

accessory [æk'sesəri], *adj.* zugehörig;
hinzukommend; (*Law*) mitschuldig;
(*subsidiary*) nebensächlich. — *s.* (*Law*)
der Mitschuldige; (*pl.*) das Zubehör.

accidence [æk'sidəns], *s.* (*Gram.*) die
Flexionslehre.

accident ['æksidənt], *s.* (*chance*) der
Zufall; (*mishap*) der Unfall, Unglücksfall.

accidental [æksi'dentəl], *adj.* zufällig;
(*inessential*) unwesentlich; durch Unfall.

acclaim [ə'kleim], *v.a.* akklamieren, mit
Beifall aufnehmen. — *v.n.* zujubeln.
— *s.* der Beifall.

acclamation [æklə'meiʃən], *s.* der
Beifall, Zuruf.

acclimatize [ə'klaimətaiz], *v.a., v.r.*
akklimatisieren; sich anpassen, eingewöhnen.

accommodate [ə'kɔmədeit], *v.a.*
(*adapt*) anpassen; (*lodge*) unterbringen, beherbergen, aufnehmen;
einem aushelfen; (*with money*) jemandem Geld leihen. — *v.r.* — *oneself to,*
sich an etwas anpassen, sich in etwas
fügen.

accommodating [ə'kɔmədeitiŋ], *adj.*
gefällig, entgegenkommend.

accommodation [əkɔmə'deiʃən], *s.*
(*adaptation*) die Anpassung; (*dispute*)
die Beilegung; (*room*) die Unterkunft.

accompaniment [ə'kʌmpənimənt], *s.*
die Begleitung.

accompany [ə'kʌmpəni], *v.a.* begleiten.

accomplice [ə'kʌmplis *or* ə'kɔmplis], *s.*
der Komplize, Mitschuldige, Mit-
täter.

accomplish [ə'kʌmpliʃ *or* ə'kɔmpliʃ],
v.a. vollenden, zustandebringen, vollbringen; (*objective*) erreichen.

accomplished [ə'kʌmpliʃd *or* ə'kɔm-
pliʃd], *adj.* vollendet.

actual

accomplishment [ə'kʌmpliʃmənt *or* ə'kɔmpliʃmənt], *s. (of project)* die Ausführung; *(of task)* die Vollendung; *(of prophecy)* die Erfüllung; *(pl.)* die Talente, *n. pl.*, Gaben, Kenntnisse, *f. pl.*

accord [ə'kɔ:d], *s. (agreement)* die Übereinstimmung; *(unison)* die Eintracht. — *v.n.* übereinstimmen *(with, mit)* — *v.a.* bewilligen.

accordance [ə'kɔ:dəns], *s.* die Übereinstimmung.

according [ə'kɔ:diŋ], *prep.* — *to,* gemäß, nach, laut.

accordingly [ə'kɔ:diŋli], *adv.* demgemäß, demnach, folglich.

accordion [ə'kɔ:diən], *s. (Mus.)* die Ziehharmonika, das Akkordeon.

accost [ə'kɔst], *v.a.* ansprechen, anreden.

account [ə'kaunt], *s.* die Rechnung; *(report)* der Bericht; *(narrative)* die Erzählung; *(importance)* die Bedeutung; *(Fin.)* das Konto, Guthaben; *cash* —, die Kassenrechnung; *on no* —, auf keinen Fall; *on his* —, seinetwegen, um seinetwillen; *on* — *of,* wegen *(Genit.); on that* —, darum; *of no* —, unbedeutend. — *v.n.* — *for,* Rechenschaft ablegen über *(Acc.); (explain)* erklären.

accountable [ə'kauntəbl], *adj.* verrechenbar *(item);* verantwortlich *(person).*

accountant [ə'kauntənt], *s.* der Bücherrevisor, Rechnungsführer; *junior* —, der Buchhalter.

accredit [ə'kredit], *v.a.* akkreditieren, beglaubigen; *(authorize)* ermächtigen, bevollmächtigen.

accretion [ə'kri:ʃən], *s.* der Zuwachs.

accrue [ə'kru:], *v.n. (Comm.)* zuwachsen, erwachsen, zufallen.

accumulate [ə'kju:mjuleit], *v.a., v.n.* anhäufen; sich anhäufen, zunehmen, sich ansammeln.

accumulation [əkju:mju'leiʃən], *s.* die Ansammlung, Anhäufung.

accuracy [ə'kjurəsi], *s.* die Genauigkeit.

accurate [ə'kjurit], *adj.* genau, richtig.

accursed [ə'kə:sid], *adj.* verflucht, verwünscht.

accusation [ækju'zeiʃən], *s.* die Anklage.

accusative [ə'kju:zətiv], *s. (Gram.)* der Akkusativ.

accuse [ə'kju:z], *v.a.* anklagen, beschuldigen *(of, Genit.).*

accustom [ə'kʌstəm], *v.a.* gewöhnen *(to,* an, *Acc.).*

ace [eis], *s. (Cards)* das As, die Eins.

acerbity [ə'sə:biti], *s.* die Rauheit, Herbheit; *(manner)* die Grobheit.

acetate [ə'æsiteit], *s.* das Azetat; essigsaures Salz.

acetic [ə'si:tik, ə'setik], *adj.* essigsauer.

acetylene [ə'setili:n], *s.* das Azetylen.

ache [eik], *s.* der Schmerz. — *v.n.* schmerzen, weh(e)tun.

achieve [ə'tʃi:v], *v.a.* erreichen, erlangen; *(accomplish)* vollenden; *(perform)* ausführen; *(gain)* erlangen, erwerben.

achievement [ə'tʃi:vmənt], *s. (accomplishment)* die Leistung, der Erfolg; die Errungenschaft; *(gain)* die Erwerbung.

achromatic [ækro'mætik], *adj.* achromatisch, farblos.

acid [ə'æsid], *adj.* sauer, scharf. — *s. (Chem.)* die Säure.

acidulated [ə'sidjuleitid], *adj. (Chem.)* angesäuert.

acknowledge [æk'nɔlidʒ], *v.a.* anerkennen; *(admit)* zugeben; *(confess)* bekennen; *(letter)* den Empfang bestätigen.

acknowledgement [æk'nɔlidʒmənt], *s.* die Anerkennung, *(receipt)* Bestätigung, Quittung; *(pl.)* die Dankesbezeigung; die Erkenntlichkeit.

acme [ə'ækmi], *s.* der Gipfel, Höhepunkt.

acorn [ə'eikɔ:n], *s. (Bot.)* die Eichel.

acoustics [ə'ku:stiks], *s. pl.* die Akustik; *(subject, study)* die Schallehre.

acquaint [ə'kweint], *v.a.* bekanntmachen; *(inform)* mitteilen *(Dat.),* informieren, unterrichten.

acquaintance [ə'kweintəns], *s.* die Bekanntschaft; der Bekannte, die Bekannte *(person);* die Kenntnis *(with,* von).

acquiesce [ækwi'es], *v.n.* einwilligen, sich fügen.

acquiescence [ækwi'esəns], *s.* die Einwilligung *(in,* in, *Acc.),* Zustimmung *(in,* zu, *Dat.)*

acquiescent [ækwi'esənt], *adj.* fügsam.

acquire [ə'kwaiə], *v.a.* erlangen, erwerben; *(language)* erlernen.

acquisition [ækwi'ziʃən], *s.* die Erlangung, Erwerbung.

acquit [ə'kwit], *v.a.* freisprechen.

acre [ə'eikə], *s.* der Acker *(appr.* 0.4 *Hektar).*

acrid [ə'ækrid], *adj.* scharf, beißend.

acrimonious [ækri'mouniəs], *adj.* scharf, bitter.

across [ə'krɔs, ə'krɔ:s], *adv.* kreuzweise, (quer) hinüber. — *prep.* quer durch, über; *come* —, (zufällig) treffen, *come* — *a problem,* auf ein Problem stoßen.

act [ækt], *s. (deed)* die Tat; *(Theat.)* der Akt; *(Parl. etc.)* die Akte. — *v.a. (Theat.)* spielen. — *v.n.* handeln *(do something);* sich benehmen *or* tun, als ob *(act as if, pretend); (Theat.)* spielen; *(Chem.)* wirken *(react).*

action [ə'ækʃən], *s.* die Handlung *(play, deed);* Wirkung *(effect); (Law)* der Prozeß; der Gang.

active [ə'æktiv], *adj. (person, Gram.)* aktiv; tätig; rührig *(industrious);* wirksam *(effective).*

activity [æk'tiviti], *s.* die Tätigkeit; *(Chem.)* Wirksamkeit.

actor [ə'æktə], *s.* der Schauspieler.

actress [ə'æktrəs], die Schauspielerin.

actual [ə'æktjuəl], *adj.* tatsächlich, wirklich.

actuality

actuality [æktju'æliti], *s.* die Wirklich-keit.

actuary ['æktjuəri], *s.* der Aktuar, Versicherungsbeamte.

actuate ['æktjueit], *v.a.* betreiben, in Bewegung setzen.

acuity [ə'kju:iti], *s.* der Scharfsinn (*mind*), die Schärfe (*vision etc.*).

acute [ə'kju:t], *adj.* scharf, scharfsinnig (*mind*); spitz (*angle*); fein (*sense*); — *accent*, der Akut.

adage ['ædidʒ], *s.* das Sprichwort.

adamant ['ædəmənt], *adj.* sehr hart, unerbittlich (*inexorable*).

adapt [ə'dæpt], *v.a.* anpassen, anglei-chen; bearbeiten.

adaptable [ə'dæptəbl], *adj.* anpassungs-fähig.

adaptation [ædæp'teiʃən], *s.* die Anpas-sung, die Bearbeitung (*of book*).

adaptive [ə'dæptiv], *adj.* anpassungs-fähig.

add [æd], *v.a.* hinzufügen, (*Maths.*) addieren.

adder ['ædə], *s.* (*Zool.*) die Natter.

addict ['ædikt], *s.* der Süchtige.

addiction [ə'dikʃən], *s.* die Sucht.

addicted [ə'diktid], *adj.* verfallen.

addition [ə'diʃən], *s.* die Hinzufügung, Zugabe, (*Maths.*) Addition.

additional [ə'diʃənəl], *adj.* zusätzlich, nachträglich.

address [ə'dres], *s.* die Anschrift, Adresse (*letter*); die Ansprache (*speech*). — *v.a.* (*letter*) adressieren, richten an (*Acc.*).

addressee [ædre'si:], *s.* der Adressat, der Empfänger.

adduce [ə'dju:s], *v.a.* anführen (*proof, beweis*).

adenoid ['ædinɔid], *s.* (*usually pl.*) (*Med.*) die Wucherung.

adept ['ædept], *adj.* geschickt, erfahren.

adequacy ['ædikwəsi], *s.* die Angemes-senheit, das Gewachsensein, die Zulänglichkeit.

adequate ['ædikwət], *adj.* gewachsen (*Dat.*); angemessen, hinreichend (*suf-ficient*).

adhere [əd'hiə], *v.n.* haften, anhängen; — *to one's opinion*, bei seiner Meinung bleiben.

adherence [əd'hiərəns], *s.* das Festhal-ten (an, *Dat.*).

adhesion [əd'hi:ʒən], *s.* (*Phys.*) die Adhäsion; das Anhaften.

adhesive [əd'hi:ziv], *adj.* haftend, klebrig; — *plaster*, das Heftpflaster.

adipose ['ædipous], *adj.* fett, feist.

adjacent [ə'dʒeisənt], *adj.* naheliegend, benachbart, angrenzend.

adjective ['ædʒektiv], *s.* (*Gram.*) das Adjektiv; Eigenschaftswort.

adjoin [ə'dʒɔin], *v.a.* anstoßen, angren-zen.

adjourn [ə'dʒə:n], *v.a.* vertagen, auf-schieben.

adjudicate [ə'dʒu:dikeit], *v.a.* beurtei-len, richten.

adjunct ['ædʒʌŋkt], *s.* der Zusatz.

adjust [ə'dʒʌst], *v.a.* ordnen; (*adapt*) anpassen; regulieren, einstellen.

adjustable [ə'dʒʌstəbl], *adj.* verstellbar, einstellbar.

adjustment [ə'dʒʌstmənt], *s.* die Ein-stellung, Anpassung; (*Law*) Schlich-tung; Berichtigung.

administer [əd'ministə], *v.a.* verwalten (*an enterprise*); verabreichen (*me-dicine*); abnehmen (*an oath*, einen Eid).

administration [ədminis'treiʃən], *s.* die Verwaltung, Regierung; die Darrei-chung (*sacraments*).

administrative [əd'ministrətiv], *adj.* Verwaltungs-; verwaltend.

admirable ['ædmirəbl], *adj.* bewun-dernswert.

admiral ['ædmirəl], *s.* der Admiral.

Admiralty ['ædmirəlti], *s.* die Admirali-tät.

admiration [ædmi'reiʃən], *s.* die Be-wunderung.

admire [əd'maiə], *v.a.* bewundern, verehren.

admirer [əd'maiərə], *s.* der Bewunde-rer, Verehrer.

admissible [əd'misibl], *adj.* zulässig.

admission [əd'miʃən], *s.* die Zulassung; (*entry*) der Eintritt; Zutritt; (*confes-sion*) das Eingeständnis, Zugeständnis.

admit [əd'mit], *v.a.* zulassen; aufneh-men; zugeben (*deed*); gelten lassen (*argument*).

admittance [əd'mitəns], *s.* der Zugang, Eintritt, Zutritt.

admixture [əd'mikstʃə], *s.* die Beimi-schung, Beigabe.

admonish [əd'mɔniʃ], *v.a.* ermahnen, mahnen, warnen.

admonition [ædmə'niʃən], *s.* die Er-mahnung, Warnung.

ado [ə'du:], *s.* der Lärm, das Tun, das Treiben; *without further* —, ohne weiteres.

adolescence [ædo'lesəns], *s.* die Adoles-zenz, Jugend, Jugendzeit.

adolescent [ædo'lesənt], *s.* der Jugend-liche. — *adj.* jugendlich.

adopt [ə'dɔpt], *v.a.* (*Law*) annehmen, adoptieren.

adoption [ə'dɔpʃən], *s.* (*Law*) die An-nahme, Adoption.

adoptive [ə'dɔptiv], *adj.* Adoptiv-, angenommen.

adorable [ə'dɔ:rəbl], *adj.* anbetungs-würdig; (*coll.*) wunderbar, schön.

adoration [ædo'reiʃən], *s.* die Anbe-tung.

adore [ə'dɔ:], *v.a.* anbeten; verehren.

adorn [ə'dɔ:n], *v.a.* (aus)schmücken, zieren.

Adriatic (**Sea**) [eidri'ætik (si:)]. das adriatische Meer.

adrift [ə'drift], *adv.* treibend; *cut o.s.* —, sich absondern.

adroit [ə'drɔit], *adj.* gewandt, ge-schickt.

adroitness [ə'drɔitnis], *s.* die Gewandt-heit, die Geschicklichkeit.

adulation [ædju'leiʃən], s. die Schmei-chelei.

adulator ['ædjuleitə], s. der Schmeich-ler.

adulatory ['ædjuleitəri], adj. schmeich-lerisch.

adult [ə'dʌlt or 'ædʌlt], adj. erwachsen. — s. der Erwachsene.

adulterate [ə'dʌltəreit], v.a. verfäl-schen; verwässern.

adulterer [ə'dʌltərə], s. der Ehebrecher.

adultery [ə'dʌltəri], s. der Ehebruch.

adumbrate [ə'dʌmbreit or 'æd-], v.a. skizzieren, entwerfen, andeuten.

advance [əd'va:ns], v.a. fördern (a cause); vorschießen (money); geltend machen (claim). — v.n. vorrücken, vorstoßen; (make progress, gain pro-motion) aufsteigen. — s. der Fort-schritt (progress); der Vorschuß (money); in —, im voraus.

advancement [əd'va:nsmənt], s. der Fortschritt (progress), der Aufstieg, die Beförderung (promotion); die Förderung (of a cause).

advantage [əd'va:ntidʒ], s. der Vorteil, Nutzen; (superiority) die Überlegen-heit.

Advent ['ædvent]. (Eccl.) der Advent.

advent ['ædvənt], s. die Ankunft.

adventitious [ædven'tiʃəs], adj. zufällig.

adventure [əd'ventʃə], s. das Aben-teuer. — v.n. auf Abenteuer ausgehen, wagen.

adventurer [əd'ventʃərə], s. der Aben-teurer.

adventurous [əd'ventʃərəs], adj. aben-teuerlich, unternehmungslustig.

adverb ['ædvə:b], s. (Gram.) das Adverb(ium), Umstandswort.

adverbial [əd'və:biəl], adj. adverbial.

adversary ['ædvəsəri], s. der Gegner, Widersacher.

adverse ['ædvə:s], adj. widrig, feind-lich, ungünstig.

adversity [əd'və:siti], s. das Unglück, Mißgeschick; in —, im Unglück.

advert [əd'və:t], v.n. hinweisen.

advertise ['ædvətaiz], v.a. anzeigen; annoncieren (in press), Reklame machen.

advertisement [əd'və:tizmənt], s. die Anzeige, Annonce; Reklame.

advertiser ['ædvətaizə], s. der An-zeiger.

advice [əd'vais], s. der Rat, Ratschlag; die Nachricht (information).

advise [əd'vaiz], v.a. raten (Dat.), beraten; benachrichtigen (inform); verständigen.

advisable [əd'vaizəbl], adj. ratsam.

advisedly [əd'vaizidli], adv. absicht-lich, mit Bedacht.

adviser [əd'vaizə], s. der Berater.

advisory [əd'vaizəri], adj. beratend, ratgebend, Rats-.

advocacy ['ædvəkəsi], s. (Law) die Verteidigung; die Fürsprache (cham-pioning of, für, Acc.); die Vertretung (of view).

Aegean (**Sea**) [i:'dʒi:ən (si:)]. das ägäische Meer.

aerated ['ɛəreitid], adj. kohlensauer.

aerial ['ɛəriəl], s. (Rad.) die Antenne. — adj. luftig, Luft-.

aerie ['ɛəri, 'iəri], s. see eyrie.

aerodrome ['ɛərodroum], s. der Flug-platz, Flughafen.

aeronautical [ɛəro'nɔːtikəl], adj. aero-nautisch.

aeronautics [ɛəro'nɔːtiks], s. pl. die Aeronautik, Luftfahrt.

aeroplane, (Am.) **airplane** ['ɛəroplein, 'ɛərplein], s. das Flugzeug.

aesthetic(al) [i:s'θetik(əl)], adj. ästhe-tisch.

aesthetics [i:s'θetiks], s. die Ästhetik.

afar [ə'fa:], adv. fern, weit entfernt; from —, von weitem, (von) weit her.

affability [æfə'biliti], s. die Leutselig-keit, Freundlichkeit.

affable ['æfəbl], adj. freundlich, leut-selig.

affair [ə'fɛə], s. die Affäre; die Angele-genheit (matter); das Anliegen (concern).

affect [ə'fekt], v.a. beeinflußen; rühren; wirken auf; vortäuschen (pretend); zur Schau tragen (exhibit).

affectation [æfek'teiʃən], s. die Ziererei, das Affektieren, die Affektiertheit.

affected [ə'fektid], adj. affektiert, ge-künstelt, geziert; befallen, angegriffen (illness).

affection [ə'fekʃən], s. die Zuneigung, Zärtlichkeit.

affectionate [ə'fekʃənit], adj. zärtlich, liebevoll; (in letters) yours —ly, herz-lichst.

affinity [ə'finiti], s. (Chem.) die Affinität; die Verwandtschaft (relationship).

affirm [ə'fə:m], v.a. behaupten, bestäti-gen, versichern; bekräftigen (confirm).

affirmation [æfə'meiʃən], s. die Be-hauptung, Bekräftigung.

affirmative [ə'fə:mətiv], adj. bejahend, positiv; in the —, bejahend.

affix [ə'fiks], v.a. anheften, aufkleben (stick); anbringen (join to an, Acc.).

afflict [ə'flikt], v.a. quälen, plagen.

affliction [ə'flikʃən], s. die Plage, Qual; das Mißgeschick; die Not; das Leiden.

affluence ['æfluəns], s. der Überfluß (abundance); der Reichtum.

affluent ['æfluənt], adj. reich, wohlha-bend. — s. der Nebenfluß (tributary).

afford [ə'fɔ:d], v.a. geben, bieten; (sich) leisten (have money for); gewäh-ren (give); hervorbringen (yield).

afforest [ə'fɔrist], v.a. aufforsten.

affray [ə'frei], s. die Schlägerei.

African ['æfrikən], adj. afrikanisch. — s. der Afrikaner.

affront [ə'frʌnt], s. die Beleidigung. — v.a. beleidigen.

Afghan ['æfgæn], adj. afghanisch. — s. der Afghane.

afield [ə'fi:ld], adj., adv. im Felde; weit umher; weit weg.

afire [ə'faiə], adv., adv. in Flammen.

aflame

aflame [ə'fleim], *adj., adv.* in Flammen.

afloat [ə'flout], *adj., adv.* schwimmend, dahintreibend.

afoot [ə'fut], *adj., adv.* im Gange.

afore [ə'fɔ:], *adv.* vorher.

aforesaid [ə'fɔ:sed], *adj. the* —, das Obengesagte, der Vorhergenannte.

afraid [ə'freid], *adj.* ängstlich, furchtsam; *be* —, fürchten (*of s.th.*, etwas, *Acc.*); sich fürchten.

afresh [ə'freʃ], *adv.* von neuem.

aft [ɑ:ft], *adv.* (*Naut.*) achtern.

after ['ɑ:ftə], *prep.* nach (*time*); nach, hinter (*place*); *the day — tomorrow*, übermorgen. — *adj.* hinter, später. — *adv.* hinterher, nachher (*time*); darauf, dahinter (*place*). — *conj.* nachdem.

afternoon [ɑ:ftə'nu:n], *s.* der Nachmittag.

afterwards ['ɑ:ftəwədz], *adv.* nachher, daraufhin, später.

again [ə'gein], *adv.* wieder, abermals, noch einmal; zurück (*back*); dagegen (*however*); *as much* —, noch einmal soviel; — *and* —, immer wieder.

against [ə'geinst], *prep.* gegen, wider; nahe bei (*near, Dat.*); bis an (*up to, Acc.*); — *the grain*, wider *or* gegen den Strich.

agate ['ægeit], *s.* der Achat.

agave [ə'geivi], *s.* (*Bot.*) die Agave.

age [eidʒ], *s.* das Alter (*person*); das Zeitalter (*period*); die Reife; *come of* —, volljährig werden; mündig werden; *old* —, das Greisenalter; *for* —s, seit einer Ewigkeit. — *v.n.* altern, alt werden.

aged ['eidʒid], *adj.* bejahrt.

agency ['eidʒənsi], *s.* die Agentur (*firm*); die Mitwirkung (*participation*); die Hilfe (*assistance*); die Vermittlung (*mediation*).

agenda [ə'dʒendə], *s.* das Sitzungsprogramm; die Tagesordnung.

agent ['eidʒənt], *s.* der Agent, Vertreter.

agglomerate [ə'glɔməreit], *v.a.* zusammenhäufen. — *v.n.* sich zusammenhäufen, sich ballen.

aggrandisement [ə'grændizmənt], *s.* die Überhebung, Übertreibung, Erweiterung.

aggravate ['ægrəveit], *v.a.* verschlimmern; ärgern.

aggravation [ægrə'veiʃən], *s.* die Verschlimmerung (*of condition*); der Ärger (*annoyance*).

aggregate ['ægrigit], *adj.* gesamt, vereinigt, vereint. — *s.* das Aggregat.

aggregation [ægri'geiʃən], *s.* (*Geol., Chem.*) die Vereinigung, Anhäufung, Ansammlung.

aggression [ə'greʃən], *s.* der Angriff, Überfall.

aggressive [ə'gresiv], *adj.* aggressiv, angreifend.

aggressor [ə'gresə], *s.* der Angreifer.

aggrieve [ə'gri:v], *v.a.* kränken.

aghast [ə'gɑ:st], *adj.* bestürzt; sprachlos; entsetzt.

agile ['ædʒail], *adj.* behend, flink, beweglich.

agitate ['ædʒiteit], *v.a.* bewegen; beunruhigen; aufrühren; stören.

agitation [ædʒi'teiʃən], *s.* (*Pol.*) die Agitation; die Unruhe (*unrest*); der Aufruhr (*revolt*).

agitator ['ædʒiteitə], *s.* (*Pol.*) der Agitator; der Aufwiegler (*inciter*).

aglow [ə'glou], *adj.* glühend.

agnostic [æg'nɔstik], *s.* der Agnostiker.

ago [ə'gou], *adv.* vor; *long* —, vor langer Zeit; *not long* —, kürzlich; *a month* —, vor einem Monat.

agog [ə'gɔg], *adv.* erregt, gespannt, neugierig (*for, auf, Acc.*).

agonize ['ægənaiz], *v.a.* quälen, martern. — *v.n.* Qual erleiden; mit dem Tode ringen *or* kämpfen.

agonising ['ægənaiziŋ], *adj.* schmerzhaft, qualvoll.

agony ['ægəni], *s.* die Pein, Qual; der Todeskampf; — *column*, die Seufzerspalte.

agrarian [ə'grɛəriən], *adj.* landwirtschaftlich; — *party*, die Bauernpartei.

agree [ə'gri:], *v.n.* übereinstimmen (*be in agreement*); übereinkommen (*come to an agreement*), sich einigen.

agreeable [ə'gri:əbl], *adj.* angenehm, gefällig.

agreement [ə'gri:mənt], *s.* die Übereinstimmung, das Übereinkommen; der Vertrag, die Verständigung (*understanding*).

agricultural [ægri'kʌltʃərəl], *adj.* landwirtschaftlich.

agriculture ['ægrikʌltʃə], *s.* die Landwirtschaft.

aground [ə'graund], *adj., adv.* (*Naut.*) gestrandet; *to run* —, stranden.

ague ['eigju:], *s.* (*Med.*) der Schüttelfrost.

ah! [ɑ:], *interj.* ach!; aha! (*surprise*).

aha! [ɑ'hɑ:], *interj.* ach so!

ahead [ə'hed], *adv.* vorwärts, voran (*movement*), voraus (*position*), *go* — (*carry on*), fortfahren; *go* — (*make progress*), vorwärtskommen.

ahoy! [ə'hɔi], *interj.* (*Naut.*) ahoi!

aid [eid], *v.a.* helfen (*Dat.*), unterstützen (*Acc.*), beistehen (*Dat.*). — *s.* die Hilfe, der Beistand.

aide-de-camp ['eiddə'kɑ̃], *s.* der Adjutant (eines Generals).

ail [eil], *v.n.* schmerzen; krank sein.

ailing ['eiliŋ], *adj.* kränklich, leidend.

ailment ['eilmənt], *s.* das Leiden.

aim [eim], *v.a.* (*weapon, blow etc.*) richten (*at*, auf). — *v.n.* zielen (auf, *Acc.*); trachten (nach, *strive for*). — *s*, das Ziel, der Zweck (*purpose*); die Absicht (*intention*).

aimless ['eimlis], *adj.* ziellos, zwecklos.

allow

air [ɛə], *s.* die Luft; die Melodie (*tune*);
die Miene (*mien*); *air force,* die Luftwaffe; *air pocket,* das Luftloch; *air
raid,* der Luftangriff; *in the open* —,
im Freien; *on the* —, im Rundfunk; *to
give oneself* —s, vornehm tun. — *v.a.*
lüften (*room*); trocknen (*washing*);
aussprechen (*views*).

airbase ['ɛəbeis], *s.* der Fliegerstützpunkt.

airconditioning ['ɛəkəndiʃəniŋ], *s.* die
Klimaanlage.

aircraft ['ɛəkrɑːft], *s.* das Luftfahrzeug,
Flugzeug.

airgun ['ɛəgʌn], *s.* die Windbüchse,
das Luftgewehr.

airiness ['ɛərinis], *s.* die Luftigkeit,
Leichtigkeit.

airletter ['ɛəletə], *s.* der Luftpostbrief.

airliner ['ɛəlainə], *s.* das Verkehrsflugzeug.

airmail ['ɛəmeil], *s.* die Luftpost.

airman ['ɛəmæn], *s.* der Flieger.

airplane *see* **aeroplane**.

airport ['ɛəpɔːt], *s.* der Flughafen.

airtight ['ɛətait], *adj.* luftdicht.

airy ['ɛəri], *adj.* luftig.

aisle [ail], *s.* das Seitenschiff (*church*);
der Gang.

Aix-la-Chapelle ['eikslaʃæ'pel], Aachen,
n.

ajar [ə'dʒɑː], *adv.* angelehnt, halb
offen.

akimbo [ə'kimbou], *adv.* Hände an den
Hüften, Arme in die Seiten gestemmt.

akin [ə'kin], *adj.* verwandt (*to,* mit,
Dat.)

alack [ə'læk], *interj.* ach! oh, weh! *alas
and* —, ach und wehe!

alacrity [ə'lækriti], *s.* die Bereitwilligkeit; Munterkeit.

alarm [ə'lɑːm], *s.* der Alarm; Lärm
(*noise*); die Warnung; Angst, Bestürzung; — *clock,* der Wecker. — *v.a.*
erschrecken.

alas! [ə'læs], *interj.* ach, wehe!

Albanian [æl'beiniən], *adj.* albanisch.
— *s.* der Albanier.

album ['ælbəm], *s.* das Album.

albumen [æl'bjuːmən], *s.* das Eiweiß,
(*Chem.*) der Eiweißstoff.

albuminous [æl'bjuːminəs], *adj.* eiweißhaltig, Eiweiß-.

alchemist ['ælkimist], *s.* der Alchimist.

alchemy ['ælkimi], *s.* die Alchimie.

alcohol ['ælkəhɔl], *s.* der Alkohol.

alcoholic [ælkə'hɔlik], *adj.* alkoholisch.
— *s.* der Trinker, Alkoholiker.

alcove ['ælkouv], *s.* der Alkoven.

alder ['ɔːldə], *s.* (*Bot.*) die Erle.

alderman ['ɔːldəmən], *s.* der Ratsherr,
der Stadtrat.

ale [eil], *s.* englisches Bier.

alert [ə'ləːt], *adj.* wachsam, aufmerksam; *on the* —, auf der Hut.

algebra ['ældʒibrə], *s.* die Algebra.

Algerian [æl'dʒiəriən], *adj.* algerisch.
— *s.* der Algerier.

Algiers [æl'dʒiəz], Algier, *n.*

alias ['eiliəs], *adv.* sonst genannt.

alien ['eiliən], *adj.* fremd, ausländisch.
— *s.* der Fremde, Ausländer.

alienate ['eiliəneit], *v.a.* entfremden.

alienation [eiliə'neiʃən], *s.* die Entfremdung; — *of mind,* die Geisteserkrankung, Geistesgestörtheit.

alienist ['eiliənist], *s.* der Irrenarzt.

alight (1) [ə'lait], *v.n.* absteigen (*from
horse*); aussteigen (*from carriage etc.*).

alight (2) [ə'lait], *adj.* brennend, in
Flammen.

alike [ə'laik], *adj.* gleich, ähnlich. —
adv. great and small —, sowohl große
wie kleine.

alimentary [æli'mentəri], *adj.* Nahrungs-, Verdauungs-; — *canal,* (*Anat.*)
der Darmkanal.

alimentation [ælimen'teiʃən], *s.* die
Beköstigung; (*Law*) der Unterhalt.

alimony ['æliməni], *s.* der Unterhaltsbeitrag; (*pl.*) Alimente. *s, n.pl.*

alive [ə'laiv], *adj.* lebendig; — *and
kicking,* wohlauf, munter; — *to,*
empfänglich für.

alkali ['ælkəlai], *s.* (*Chem.*) das Laugensalz, Alkali.

alkaline ['ælkəlain], *adj.* (*Chem.*) alkalisch, laugensalzig.

all [ɔːl], *adj., pron.* all, ganz (*whole*);
sämtliche, alle; *above* —, vor allem;
once and for —, ein für allemal; *not
at* —, keineswegs; *All Saints,* Allerheiligen; *All Souls,* Allerseelen. —
adv. ganz, gänzlich, völlig; — *the
same,* trotzdem; — *the better,* umso
besser.

allay [ə'lei], *v.a.* lindern, beruhigen,
unterdrücken.

allegation [æli'geiʃən], *s.* die Behauptung.

allege [ə'ledʒ], *v.a.* behaupten, aussagen.

allegiance [ə'liːdʒəns], *s.* die Treue,
Ergebenheit; Untertanenpflicht.

allegorical [æli'gɔrikəl], *adj.* allegorisch, sinnbildlich.

alleviate [ə'liːvieit], *v.a.* erleichtern,
mildern.

alleviation [əliːvi'eiʃən], *s.* die Erleichterung, Milderung.

alley ['æli], *s.* die Gasse; Seitenstraße;
bowling —, die Kegelbahn.

alliance [ə'laiəns], *s.* (*Pol.*) die Allianz,
das Bündnis (*treaty*); der Bund
(*league*).

allied [ə'laid, 'ælaid], *adj.* verbündet,
vereinigt; alliiert; verwandt.

alliteration [əlitə'reiʃən], *s.* die Alliteration, der Stabreim.

allocate ['æləkeit], *v.a.* zuweisen,
zuteilen.

allot [ə'lɔt], *v.a.* zuteilen (*assign*);
verteilen (*distribute*).

allotment [ə'lɔtmənt], *s.* der Anteil;
die Zuteilung; die Landparzelle, die
Laubenkolonie, der Schrebergarten
(*garden*).

allow [ə'lau], *v.a.* gewähren (*grant*);
erlauben (*permit*); zulassen (*admit*). —
v.n. — *for,* Rücksicht nehmen auf
(*Acc.*); in Betracht ziehen.

allowance

allowance [ə'lauəns], *s.* die Rente; das Taschengeld (*money*); die Erlaubnis (*permission*); die Genehmigung (*approval*); die Nachsicht (*indulgence*).

alloy [ə'lɔi, 'æbɔi], *s.* die Legierung. — *v.a.* (*Metall.*) legieren.

allude [ə'lu:d], *v.a.* anspielen (*to*, auf).

allure [ə'ljuə], *v.a.* locken, anlocken.

allurement [ə'ljuəmənt], *s.* der Reiz, die Lockung.

allusion [ə'lu:ʒən], *s.* die Anspielung.

alluvial [ə'lu:viəl], *adj.* angeschwemmt.

alluvium [ə'lu:viəm], *s.* das Schwemmgebiet, Schwemmland.

ally ['ælai], *s.* der Verbündete, Bundesgenosse, Alliierte. — [ə'lai], *v.a., v.r.* (sich) vereinigen, (sich) verbünden.

almanac ['ɔ:lmənæk], *s.* der Almanach.

almighty [ɔ:l'maiti], *adj.* allmächtig; *God Almighty!* allmächtiger Gott!

almond ['ɑ:mənd], *s.* (*Bot.*) die Mandel.

almoner ['ælmənə], *s.* der Wohlfahrtsbeamte, die Fürsorgerin.

almost [ɔ:lmoust], *adv.* fast, beinahe.

alms [ɑ:mz], *s.* das Almosen.

aloe ['ælou], *s.* (*Bot.*) die Aloe.

aloft [ə'lɔft], *adv.* droben, (hoch) oben; empor.

alone [ə'loun], *adj., adv.* allein; *all* —, ganz allein; *leave* —, in Ruhe lassen; *let* —, geschweige (denn).

along [ə'lɔŋ], *adv.* längs, der Länge nach; entlang, weiter; *come* —! komm mit!; *get* — (*with*), auskommen. — *prep.* längs; entlang.

alongside [əlɔŋ'said], *adv.* nebenan. — [ə'lɔŋsaid], *prep.* neben.

aloof [ə'lu:f], *adj., adv.* fern, weitab; *keep* —, sich fernhalten.

aloofness [ə'lu:fnis], *s.* das Sichfernhalten; das Vornehmtun.

aloud [ə'laud], *adj., adv.* laut; hörbar.

alphabet ['ælfəbet], *s.* das Alphabet, Abc.

Alpine ['ælpain], *adj.* alpinisch, Alpen-.

Alps, The [ælps, ði] die Alpen, *pl.*

already [ɔ:l'redi], *adv.* schon, bereits.

Alsatian [æl'seiʃən], *adj.* elsässisch. — *s.* der Elsässer; (*dog*) der Wolfshund, deutscher Schäferhund.

also [ɔ:lsou], *adv.* (*likewise*) auch, ebenfalls; (*moreover*) ferner.

altar ['ɔ:ltə], *s.* der Altar.

alter ['ɔ:ltə], *v.a.* ändern, verändern. — *v.n.* sich (ver)ändern.

alterable ['ɔ:ltərəbl], *adj.* veränderlich.

alteration [ɔ:ltə'reiʃən], *s.* die Änderung, Veränderung.

altercation [ɔ:ltə'keiʃən], *s.* der Zank, Streit; Wortwechsel.

alternate ['ɔ:ltəneit], *v.a., v.n.* abwechseln lassen, abwechseln.

alternative [ɔ:l'tə:nativ], *adj.* abwechselnd, alternativ, zur Wahl gestellt. — *s.* die Alternative, die Wahl.

although [ɔ:l'ðou], *conj.* obgleich, obwohl, obschon.

altimeter ['æltimi:tə], *s.* der Höhenmesser.

altitude ['æltitju:d], *s.* die Höhe.

alto ['æltou], *s.* (*Mus.*) die Altstimme, der Alt.

altogether [ɔ:ltu'geðə], *adv.* zusammen, zusammengenommen, allesamt; (*wholly*) ganz und gar, durchaus.

alum ['æləm], *s.* (*Chem.*) der Alaun.

aluminium [ælju'minjəm], (*Am.*) **aluminum** [ə'lu:minəm], *s.* das Aluminium.

always ['ɔ:lweiz], *adv.* immer, stets.

am [æm] *see* **be**.

amalgamate [ə'mælgəmeit], *v.a.* amalgamieren. — *v.n.* sich vereinigen, vermischen.

amalgamation [əmælgə'meiʃən], *s.* die Verbindung, Vereinigung.

amass [ə'mæs], *v.a.* anhäufen, zusammentragen.

amateur [æmə'tə: *or* 'æmətjuə], *s.* der Amateur, Liebhaber.

amatory ['æmətəri], *adj.* Liebes-, verliebt, sinnlich.

amaze [ə'meiz], *v.a.* erstaunen, in Erstaunen versetzen; verblüffen (*baffle*).

amazement [ə'meizmənt], *s.* das Erstaunen, Staunen, die Verwunderung.

amazing [ə'meiziŋ], *adj.* erstaunlich, wunderbar.

Amazon (1) ['æməzən], *s.* (*Myth.*) die Amazone.

Amazon (2) ['æməzən], *s.* (*river*) der Amazonas.

ambassador [æm'bæsədə], *s.* der Botschafter.

ambassadorial [æmbæsə'dɔ:riəl], *adj.* Botschafts-, gesandtschaftlich.

amber ['æmbə], *s.* der Bernstein.

ambidextrous [æmbi'dekstrəs], *adj.* (mit beiden Händen gleich) geschickt.

ambiguity [æmbi'gju:iti], *s.* die Zweideutigkeit, der Doppelsinn.

ambiguous [æm'bigjuəs], *adj.* zweideutig; dunkel (*sense*).

ambit ['æmbit], *s.* der Umkreis, die Umgebung.

ambition [æm'biʃən], *s.* die Ambition, der Ehrgeiz.

ambitious [æm'biʃəs], *adj.* ehrgeizig.

amble ['æmbl], *v.n.* schlendern, (gemächlich) spazieren.

ambulance ['æmbjuləns], *s.* der Krankenwagen.

ambush ['æmbuʃ], *v.a.* überfallen (*Acc.*), auflauern (*Dat.*). — *s.* die Falle, der Hinterhalt.

ameliorate [ə'mi:liəreit], *v.a.* verbessern.

amenable [ə'mi:nəbl], *adj.* zugänglich; unterworfen.

amend [ə'mend], *v.a.* verbessern, berichtigen; ändern.

amendment [ə'mendmənt], *s.* die Verbesserung; der Zusatz, die zusätzliche Änderung (*proposal*).

amends [ə'mendz], *s. pl.* der Schadenersatz; *make* —, Schadenersatz leisten; wiedergutmachen.

amenity [ə'mi:niti *or* ə'meniti], *s.* die Behaglichkeit, Annehmlichkeit; (*pl.*) die Vorzüge, *m pl.*; die Einrichtungen, *f. pl.*

American [ə'merikən], *adj.* amerikanisch; — *cloth*, das Wachstuch. — *s.* der Amerikaner.

amiability [eimjə'biliti], *s.* die Liebenswürdigkeit.

amiable ['eimjəbl], *adj.* liebenswürdig.

amicable ['æmikəbl], *adj.* freundschaftlich.

amidst [ə'midst], *prep.* mitten in, mitten unter (*Dat.*), inmitten (*Gen.*).

amiss [ə'mis], *adj., adv.* übel; verkehrt; *take* —, übelnehmen.

amity ['æmiti], *s.* die Freundschaft.

ammonia [ə'mouniə], *s.* das Ammoniak; *liquid* —, der Salmiakgeist.

ammunition [æmju'niʃən], *s.* die Munition.

amnesty ['æmnisti], *s.* die Amnestie, Begnadigung.

among(st) [ə'mʌŋ(st)], *prep.* (mitten) unter, zwischen, bei.

amorous ['æmərəs], *adj.* verliebt.

amorphous [ə'mɔ:fəs], *adj.* amorph, gestaltlos, formlos.

amortization [əmɔ:ti'zeiʃən], *s.* die Amortisierung (*debt*); (*Comm.*) Tilgung, Abtragung.

amount [ə'maunt], *s.* der Betrag (*sum of money*); die Menge (*quantity*). — *v.n.* betragen; — *to*, sich belaufen auf (*Acc.*).

amphibian [æm'fibiən], *adj.* amphibisch. — *s.* (*Zool.*) die Amphibie.

amphibious [æm'fibiəs], *adj.* amphibienhaft.

ample [æmpl], *adj.* weit, breit (*scope*); voll, reichlich; ausgebreitet; genügend.

amplification [æmplifi'keiʃən], *s.* die Ausbreitung; Verbreiterung, Erklärung, Erweiterung; (*Elec.*) die Verstärkung (*sound*).

amplifier ['æmplifaiə], *s.* der Verstärker; der Lautsprecher.

amplify ['æmplifai], *v.a.* erweitern, ausführen, vergrößern; verstärken (*sound*).

amputate ['æmpjuteit], *v.a.* amputieren.

amputation [æmpju'teiʃən], *s.* die Amputation.

amuck [ə'mʌk], *adv.* amok.

amulet ['æmjulit], *s.* das Amulett.

amuse [ə'mju:z], *v.a.* unterhalten, amüsieren.

amusement [ə'mju:zmənt], *s.* die Unterhaltung, das Vergnügen.

an *see under* a.

Anabaptist [ænə'bæptist], *s.* der Wiedertäufer.

anachronism [ə'nækrənizm], *s.* der Anachronismus.

anaemia [ə'ni:miə], *s.* (*Med.*) die Blutarmut.

anaemic [ə'ni:mik], *adj.* (*Med.*) blutarm.

anaesthetic [ænəs'θetik], *adj.* schmerzbetäubend. — *s.* die Narkose.

analogous [ə'næləgəs], *adj.* analog.

analogy [ə'nælədʒi], *s.* die Analogie.

analyse ['ænəlaiz], *v.a.* analysieren.

analysis [ə'nælisis], *s.* die Analyse.

anarchic(al) [ə'na:kik(əl)], *adj.* anarchisch.

anarchy ['ænəki], *s.* die Anarchie.

anathema [ə'næθimə], *s.* (*Eccl.*) der Kirchenbann.

anatomical [ænə'tɔmikəl], *adj.* anatomisch.

anatomist [ə'nætəmist], *s.* der Anatom.

anatomize [ə'nætəmaiz], *v.a.* zergliedern, zerlegen.

anatomy [ə'nætəmi], *s.* die Anatomie.

ancestor ['ænsəstə], *s.* der Vorfahre, Ahnherr.

ancestry ['ænsəstri], *s.* die Ahnenreihe, Herkunft, der Stammbaum (*family tree*).

anchor ['æŋkə], *s.* der Anker. — *v.a.* verankern. — *v.n.* ankern.

anchorage ['æŋkəridʒ], *s.* die Verankerung; der Ankerplatz.

anchovy [æn'tʃouvi *or* 'æntʃəvi], *s.* (*Zool.*) die Sardelle.

ancient ['einʃənt], *adj.* alt, uralt, antik; althergebracht (*traditional*). — *s.* (*pl.*) die Alten (Griechen und Römer).

and [ænd], *conj.* und.

Andes, the ['ændi:z, ði]. die Anden, *pl.*

anecdote ['ænekdout], *s.* die Anekdote.

anemone [ə'neməni], *s.* (*Bot.*) die Anemone, das Windröschen; (*Zool.*) *sea* —, die Seeanemone.

anew [ə'nju:], *adv.* von neuem.

angel ['eindʒəl], *s.* der Engel.

angelic [æn'dʒelik], *adj.* engelhaft, engelgleich.

anger ['æŋgə], *s.* der Zorn, Unwille, Ärger. — *v.a.* erzürnen, verärgern, ärgerlich machen.

angle [æŋgl], *s.* (*Geom.*) der Winkel; die Angel (*fishing*). — *v.n.* angeln (*for*, nach).

Angles [æŋglz], *s. pl.* die Angeln, *m. pl.*

Anglo-Saxon [æŋglou'sæksən], *adj.* angelsächsisch. — *s.* der Angelsachse.

anglicism ['æŋglisizm], *s.* der Anglizismus (*style*).

anguish ['æŋgwiʃ], *s.* die Qual, Pein.

angular ['æŋgjulə], *adj.* winklig, eckig.

anhydrous [æn'haidrəs], *adj.* wasserfrei, (*Chem.*) wasserlos.

aniline ['ænilain], *s.* das Anilin. — *adj.* — *dye*, die Anilinfarbe.

animal ['æniməl], *s.* das Tier, Lebewesen.

animate ['ænimeit], *v.a.* beleben, beseelen; (*fig.*) anregen.

animated ['ænimeitid], *adj.* belebt; munter.

animation [æni'meiʃən], *s.* die Belebung.

animosity [æni'mɔsiti], *s.* die Feindseligkeit, Abneigung, Erbitterung.

anise ['ænis], *s.* (*Bot.*) der Anis.

ankle

ankle [æŋkl], s. (*Anat.*) der Fußknöchel; — socks, kurze Socken.

anklet [ˈæŋklit], s. der Fußring.

annalist [ˈænəlist], s. der Chronist, Geschichtsschreiber.

annals [ˈænəlz], s. pl. die Annalen (s. pl.); die Chronik (sing.).

anneal [əˈniːl], v.a. ausglühen.

annex [əˈneks], v.a. annektieren, angliedern, sich aneignen.

annex(e) [ˈæneks], s. der Anhang, der Anbau.

annexation [ænekˈseiʃən], s. die Angliederung, Aneignung.

annihilate [əˈnaiileit], v.a. vernichten, zerstören.

annihilation [ənaiiˈleiʃən], s. die Vernichtung, Zerstörung.

anniversary [æniˈvəːsəri], s. der Jahrestag, die Jahresfeier.

annotate [ˈænoteit], v.a. anmerken, mit Anmerkungen versehen.

annotation [ænoˈteiʃən], s. die Anmerkung, Notiz.

announce [əˈnauns], v.a. melden, ankündigen; anzeigen; (*Rad.*) ansagen.

announcement [əˈnaunsmənt], s. die Ankündigung, Bekanntmachung; (*Rad.*) die Ansage.

announcer [əˈnaunsə], s. (*Rad.*) der Ansager.

annoy [əˈnoi], v.a. ärgern; belästigen.

annoyance [əˈnoiəns], s. das Ärgernis; die Belästigung.

annual [ˈænjuəl], adj. jährlich, Jahres-. — s. der Jahresband (*serial publication*); das Jahrbuch; (*Bot.*) die einjährige Pflanze.

annuity [əˈnjuːiti], s. die Jahresrente, Lebensrente.

annul [əˈnʌl], v.a. annullieren, ungültig machen, für ungültig erklären.

annulment [əˈnʌlmənt], s. die Annullierung, Ungültigkeitserklärung.

Annunciation [ənʌnsiˈeiʃən], s. (*Eccl.*) die Verkündigung.

anode [ˈænoud], s. die Anode.

anodyne [ˈænodain], adj. schmerzstillend.

anoint [əˈnoint], v.a. salben.

anomalous [əˈnomələs], adj. abweichend, unregelmäßig, anomal.

anomaly [əˈnoməli], s. die Anomalie, Abweichung, Unregelmäßigkeit.

anon [əˈnon], adv. sogleich, sofort.

anonymous [əˈnoniməs], adj. (*abbr.* **anon.**) anonym; namenlos; unbekannt.

anonymity [ænoˈnimiti], s. die Anonymität.

another [əˈnʌðə], adj. & pron. ein anderer; ein zweiter; noch einer; one —, einander.

answer [ˈɑːnsə], v.a. beantworten. — v.n. antworten. — s. die Antwort, Erwiderung.

answerable [ˈɑːnsərəbl], adj. verantwortlich (*responsible*); beantwortbar (*capable of being answered*).

ant [ænt], s. (*Ent.*) die Ameise.

antagonise [ænˈtægənaiz], v.a. sich (*Dat.*) jemanden zum Gegner machen.

antagonism [ænˈtægənizm], s. der Widerstreit, Konflikt; der Antagonismus.

Antarctic [æntˈɑːktik], adj. Südpol-, antarktisch. — s. der südliche Polarkreis.

antecedence [æntiˈsiːdəns], s. der Vortritt (*rank*).

antecedent [æntiˈsiːdənt], s. (pl.) das Vorhergehende, die Vorgeschichte.

antedate [ˈæntideit], v.a. vordatieren.

antediluvian [æntidiˈluːviən], adj. vorsintflutlich; (*fig.*) überholt; altmodisch.

antelope [ˈæntiloup], s. (*Zool.*) die Antilope.

antenna [ænˈtenə], s. (*Ent.*) der Fühler; (*Rad.*) die Antenne.

anterior [ænˈtiəriə], adj. vorder (*in space*), älter, vorherig, vorhergehend, (*in time*).

anteroom [ˈæntiruːm], s. das Vorzimmer.

anthem [ˈænθəm], s. die Hymne, der Hymnus.

anther [ˈænθə], s. (*Bot.*) der Staubbeutel.

antic [ˈæntik], s. die Posse; (pl.) komisches Benehmen.

anticipate [ænˈtisipeit], v.a. vorwegnehmen; zuvorkommen; ahnen (*guess*); erwarten (*await*); vorgreifen.

anticipation [æntisiˈpeiʃən], s. die Vorwegnahme; die Erwartung.

antidote [ˈæntidout], s. das Gegengift.

antipathy [ænˈtipəθi], s. die Antipathie, der Widerwille.

antipodal [ænˈtipədəl], adj. antipodisch; entgegengesetzt.

antiquarian [æntiˈkwɛəriən], adj. altertümlich; antiquarisch.

antiquary [ˈæntikwəri], s. der Altertumsforscher, Antiquar.

antiquated [ˈæntikweitid], adj. überholt, unmodern, veraltet.

antique [ænˈtiːk], s. die Antike; das alte Kunstwerk. — adj. alt, antik; altmodisch.

antiquity [ænˈtikwiti], s. die Antike, das Altertum; die Vorzeit (*period of history*).

antiseptic [æntiˈseptik], adj. antiseptisch — s. das antiseptische Mittel.

antler [ˈæntlə], s. die Geweihsprosse; (pl.) das Geweih.

anvil [ˈænvil], s. der Amboß.

anxiety [æŋˈzaiəti], s. die Angst (*fear*); Besorgnis (*uneasiness*); Unruhe.

anxious [ˈæŋkʃəs], adj. ängstlich (*afraid*); besorgt (*worried*); eifrig bemüht (*keen*, um, on, Acc.).

any [ˈeni], adj. & pron. jeder; irgendein; etwas; (pl.) einige; (*neg.*) not —, kein.

anybody, anyone [ˈenibodi, ˈeniwən], pron. irgendeiner, jemand; jeder.

anyhow, anyway [ˈenihau, ˈeniwei], adv. irgendwie, auf irgendeine Weise; auf alle Fälle.

anyone see under **anybody**.

apprentice

anything [′eniθiŋ], s. irgend etwas; alles.

anyway see under **anyhow**.

anywhere [′enihwɛə], adv. irgendwo; überall; not —, nirgends.

apace [ə′peis], adv. geschwind, hurtig, flink.

apart [ə′pɑːt], adv. für sich, abgesondert; einzeln; poles —, weit entfernt; take —, zerlegen; — from, abgesehen von.

apartment [ə′pɑːtmənt], s. das Zimmer; (Am.) die Wohnung (flat).

apathy [′æpəθi], s. die Apathie, Interesselosigkeit, Gleichgültigkeit.

apathetic [æpə′θetik], adj. apathisch, uninteressiert; teilnahmslos.

ape [eip], s. (Zool.) der Affe. — v.a. nachäffen, nachahmen.

aperient [ə′piəriənt], adj. (Med.) abführend. — s. (Med.) das Abführmittel.

aperture [′æpətʃə], s. die Öffnung.

apex [′eipeks], s. die Spitze, der Gipfel.

aphorism [′æfərizm], s. der Aphorismus.

apiary [′eipiəri], s. das Bienenhaus.

apiece [ə′piːs], adv. pro Stück, pro Person.

apologetic [əpɔlə′dʒetik], adj. entschuldigend, reumütig; verteidigend.

apologize [ə′pɔlədʒaiz], v.n. sich entschuldigen (for, wegen; to, bei).

apology [ə′pɔlədʒi], s. die Entschuldigung; Abbitte; Rechtfertigung.

apoplectic [æpə′plektik], adj. (Med.) apoplektisch.

apoplexy [′æpəpleksi], s. (Med.) der Schlagfluß, Schlaganfall (fit).

apostle [ə′pɔsl], s. der Apostel.

apostolic [æpəs′tɔlik], adj. apostolisch.

apostrophe [ə′pɔstrəfi], s. der Apostroph (punctuation); die Anrede (speech).

apostrophize [ə′pɔstrəfaiz], v.a. apostrophieren; anreden (speak to).

apotheosis [əpɔθi′ousis], s. die Apotheose.

appal [ə′pɔːl], v.a. erschrecken.

appalling [ə′pɔːliŋ], adj. schrecklich.

apparatus [æpə′reitəs], s. das Gerät, die Apparatur; (coll.) der Apparat.

apparel [ə′pærəl], s. die Kleidung.

apparent [ə′pærənt], adj. scheinbar; offensichtlich; augenscheinlich; heir —, der rechtmäßige Erbe.

apparition [æpə′riʃən], s. die Erscheinung; der Geist, das Gespenst (ghost).

appeal [ə′piːl], v.n. appellieren (make an appeal); (Law) Berufung einlegen; gefallen (please). — s. (public, Mil.) der Appell; die Bitte (request).

appear [ə′piə], v.n. erscheinen; scheinen; auftreten.

appearance [ə′piərəns], s. die Erscheinung; das Auftreten (stage, etc.); der Schein (semblance); keep up —s, den Schein wahren; to all —s, allem Anschein nach.

appease [ə′piːz], v.a. besänftigen.

appeasement [ə′piːzmənt], s. die Besänftigung, (Pol.) die Befriedung.

appellation [æpe′leiʃən], s. die Benennung.

append [ə′pend], v.a. anhängen, beifügen.

appendicitis [əpendi′saitis], s. (Med.) die Blinddarmentzündung.

appendix [ə′pendiks], s. der Anhang; (Med.) der Blinddarm.

appertain [æpə′tein], v.n. gehören (to, zu).

appetite [′æpitait], s. der Appetit.

appetizing [′æpitaiziŋ], adj. appetitlich, appetitanregend.

applaud [ə′plɔːd], v.a., v.n. applaudieren, Beifall klatschen (Dat.).

applause [ə′plɔːz], s. der Applaus, Beifall.

apple [æpl], s. der Apfel.

appliance [ə′plaiəns], s. das Gerät, die Vorrichtung.

applicable [′æplikəbl], adj. anwendbar, passend (to, auf).

applicant [′æplikənt], s. der Bewerber (for, um).

application [æpli′keiʃən], s. die Bewerbung (for, um); das Gesuch; die Anwendung (to, auf); letter of —, der Bewerbungsbrief; — form, das Bewerbungsformular.

apply [ə′plai], v.a. anwenden (auf, to, Acc.); gebrauchen. — v.n. sich bewerben (um, for, Acc.); (Dat.) this does not —, das trifft nicht zu; — within, drinnen nachfragen.

appoint [ə′pɔint], v.a. bestimmen; ernennen; ausrüsten.

appointment [ə′pɔintmənt], s. die Festsetzung; die Ernennung; die Bestellung, die Stellung (position); make an —, jemanden ernennen (fill a post); then verabreden (arrange to meet); by —, Hoflieferant (to, Genit.).

apportion [ə′pɔːʃən], v.a. zuteilen, zuweisen, zumessen.

apposite [′æpəzit], adj. passend, angemessen.

appositeness [′æpəzitnis], s. die Angemessenheit.

appraise [ə′preiz], v.a. beurteilen.

appraisal [ə′preizəl], s. die Beurteilung, Abschätzung.

appreciable [ə′priːʃəbl], adj. merklich; nennenswert.

appreciate [ə′priːʃieit], v.a. würdigen, schätzen.

appreciation [əpriːʃi′eiʃən], s. die Schätzung, Würdigung.

apprehend [æpri′hend], v.a. verhaften, ergreifen (arrest); befürchten (fear).

apprehension [æpri′henʃən], s. die Verhaftung (arrest); die Befürchtung (fear).

apprehensive [æpri′hensiv], adj. besorgt, in Furcht (for, um), furchtsam.

apprentice [ə′prentis], s. der Lehrling; Praktikant. — v.a. in die Lehre geben (with, bei, Dat.).

apprenticeship

apprenticeship [ə'prentiʃip], *s.* die Lehre, Lehrzeit, Praktikantenzeit; *student* —, die Studentenpraxis.

apprise [ə'praiz], *v.a.* benachrichtigen, informieren.

approach [ə'proutʃ], *v.a., v.n.* sich nähern (*Dat.*). — *s.* die Annäherung, das Herankommen, Näherrücken.

approachable [ə'proutʃəbl], *adj.* zugänglich, freundlich.

approbation [æpro'beiʃən], *s.* die (offizielle) Billigung, Zustimmung.

appropriate [ə'proupriit], *adj.* angemessen, gebührend, geeignet (*suitable*). — [ə'prouprieit], *v.a.* requirieren, sich aneignen.

appropriation [əproupri'eiʃən], *s.* die Requisition, Aneignung, Übernahme, Besitznahme.

approval [ə'pru:vəl], *s.* die Billigung, der Beifall, die Zustimmung.

approve [ə'pru:v], *v.a.* loben, billigen; genehmigen; annehmen (*work*).

approved [ə'pru:vd], *adj.* anerkannt.

approximate [ə'prɔksimit], *adj.* ungefähr, annähernd. —*v.n. & a.*[ə'prɔksimeit], sich nähern.

approximation [əprɔksi'meiʃən], *s.* die Annäherung.

approximative [ə'prɔksimətiv], *adj.* annähernd.

appurtenance [ə'pə:tənəns], *s.* das (*or der*) Zubehör.

appurtenant [ə'pə:tənənt], *adj.* zugehörig.

apricot ['eiprikɔt], *s.* (*Bot.*) die Aprikose.

April ['eipril]. der April.

apron ['eiprən], *s.* die Schürze; der Schurz; — *stage,* die Vorbühne, das Proszenium.

apropos [ɑ:prɔ'pou], *adv.* beiläufig; mit Bezug auf, diesbezüglich.

apse [æps], *s.* (*Archit.*) die Apsis.

apt [æpt], *adj.* geeignet, passend; fähig.

aptitude ['æptitju:d], *s.* die Eignung, Fähigkeit.

aptness ['æptnis], *s.* die Angemessenheit, Eignung.

aquatic [ə'kwɔtik *or* ə'kwætik], *adj.* Wasser-, wasser-; — *display,* Wasserkünste. — *s.* (*pl.*) der Wassersport.

aqueduct ['ækwidʌkt], *s.* die Wasserleitung; der Aquädukt.

aqueous ['eikwiəs], *adj.* (*Chem.*) wässerig.

aquiline ['ækwilain], *adj.* adlerartig, Adler-.

Arab ['ærəb], *s.* der Araber.

Arabian [ə'reibiən], *adj.* arabisch; — *Nights,* Tausend-und-eine-Nacht.

Arabic ['ærəbik], *adj.* arabisch (*language, literature*).

arable ['ærəbl], *adj.* pflügbar, bestellbar.

arbiter [ɑ:'bitə], *s.* der Schiedsrichter.

arbitrary ['ɑ:bitrəri], *adj.* willkürlich.

arbitrate ['ɑ:bitreit], *v.n.* vermitteln.

arbitration [ɑ:bi'treiʃən], *s.* die Vermittlung; Entscheidung; (*Ccmm.*) Arbitrage.

arboriculture ['ɑ:bɔrikʌltʃə], *s.* die Baumzucht.

arbour ['ɑ:bə], *s.* die Laube, Gartenlaube.

arc [ɑ:k], *s.* (*Geom.*) der Bogen; — *lamp,* die Bogenlampe; — *welding,* das Lichtschweißen.

arcade [ɑ:'keid], *s.* die Arkade.

Arcadian [ɑ:'keidiən], *adj.* arkadisch. — *s.* der Arkadier.

arch [ɑ:tʃ], *s.* der Bogen, die Wölbung; —*way,* der Bogengang. — *v.a., v.n.* wölben, sich wölben. — *adj.* schelmisch, listig. — *prefix* oberst; erst Haupt-; — *-enemy,* der Erzfeind.

archaeological [ɑ:kiə'lɔdʒikəl], *adj.* archäologisch.

archaeologist [ɑ:ki'ɔlədʒist], *s.* der Archäologe.

archaeology [ɑ:ki'ɔlədʒi], *s.* die Archäologie.

archaic [ɑ:'keiik], *adj.* altertümlich.

archaism ['ɑ:keiizm], *s.* der Archaismus (*style*).

archbishop [ɑ:tʃ'biʃəp], *s.* der Erzbischof.

archduke [ɑ:tʃ'dju:k], *s.* der Erzherzog.

archer ['ɑ:tʃə], *s.* der Bogenschütze.

archery ['ɑ:tʃəri], *s.* das Bogenschießen.

architect ['ɑ:kitekt], *s.* der Architekt, Baumeister.

architecture ['ɑ:kitektʃə], *s.* die Architektur, Baukunst.

archives ['ɑ:kaivz], *s. pl.* das Archiv.

Arctic ['ɑ:ktik], *adj.* arktisch. — *s.* die Nordpolarländer, *n. pl.*

ardent ['ɑ:dənt], *adj.* heiß, glühend, brennend.

ardour ['ɑ:də], *s.* die Hitze, die Inbrunst, der Eifer.

arduous ['ɑ:djuəs], *adj.* schwierig, mühsam.

area ['ɛəriə], *s.* das Areal (*measurement*); das Gebiet, die Zone; die Fläche (*region*).

arena [ə'ri:nə], *s.* die Arena, der Kampfplatz.

Argentine ['ɑ:dʒəntain], *adj.* argentinisch. — (*Republic*), Argentinien, *n.*

Argentinian [ɑ:dʒən'tiniən], *adj.* argentinisch. — *s.* der Argentin(i)er.

argue ['ɑ:gju:], *v.n.* disputieren, streiten; folgern, schließen.

argument ['ɑ:gjumənt], *s.* das Argument; (*Log.*) der Beweis; der Streit (*dispute*).

argumentative [ɑ:gju'mentətiv], *adj.* streitsüchtig.

arid ['ærid], *adj.* trocken, dürr.

aright [ə'rait], *adv.* richtig, zurecht.

arise [ə'raiz], *v.n. irr.* aufstehen; sich erheben; entstehen (*originate*); *arising from the minutes,* es ergibt sich aus dem Protokoll.

aristocracy [æris'tɔkrəsi], *s.* die Aristokratie, der Adel.

aristocratic [æris'ɔ'krætik], *adj.* aristokratisch, adlig.

arithmetic [ə'riθmətik], *s.* die Arithmetik.

Asiatic

arithmetical [æriθ′metikəl], *adj.* arithmetisch.

ark [ɑːk], *s.* die Arche; — *of the Covenant*, die Bundeslade.

arm (1) [ɑːm], *s.* (*Anat.*) der Arm.

arm (2) [ɑːm], *s.* die Waffe; *up in —s*, in Aufruhr. — *v.a.*, *v.n.* bewaffnen, sich bewaffnen, rüsten, sich rüsten.

armament [′ɑːməmənt], *s.* die Rüstung, Bewaffnung.

armature [′ɑːmətiuə], *s.* die Armatur.

armchair [′ɑːmtʃɛə], *s.* der Lehnstuhl; der Sessel.

Armenian [ɑː′miːniən], *adj.* armenisch. — *s.* der Armenier.

armistice [′ɑːmistis], *s.* der Waffenstillstand.

armour [′ɑːmə], *s.* die Rüstung, der Harnisch; —*-plated*, gepanzert; —*ed car*, der Panzerwagen.

armourer [′ɑːmərə], *s.* der Waffenschmied.

armoury [′ɑːməri], *s.* die Rüstkammer, Waffenschmiede.

army [′ɑːmi], *s.* die Armee, das Heer.

aroma [ə′roumə], *s.* das Aroma, der Duft.

aromatic [ærə′mætik], *adj.* aromatisch. —*s.* (*Chem.*) das Aromat.

around [ə′raund], *adv.* herum, rundringsherum, umher, im Kreise; *stand —*, herumstehen; *be —*, sich in der Nähe halten. — *prep.* um; bei, um ... herum.

arouse [ə′rauz], *v.a.* aufwecken, aufrütteln.

arraignment [ə′reinmənt], *s.* die Anklage.

arrange [ə′reindʒ], *v.a.* anordnen, arrangieren, einrichten, vereinbaren.

arrangement [ə′reindʒmənt], *s.* die Anordnung; die Einrichtung; die Vereinbarung (*agreement*); (*Law*) die Vergleichung, der Vergleich.

arrant [′ærənt], *adj.* durchtrieben.

array [ə′rei], *v.a.* schmücken, aufstellen. — *s.* die Ordnung; Aufstellung.

arrears [ə′riəz], *s. pl.* der Rückstand, die Schulden.

arrest [ə′rest], *v.a.* (*Law*) festnehmen, verhaften; festhalten; aufhalten (*hinder*). — *s.* die Festnahme; die Festhaltung.

arrival [ə′raivəl], *s.* die Ankunft.

arrive [ə′raiv], *v.n.* ankommen.

arrogance [′ærəgəns], *s.* die Anmaßung, Überheblichkeit.

arrogant [′ærəgənt], *adj.* anmaßend, hochfahrend, überheblich.

arrow [′ærou], *s.* der Pfeil.

arrowroot [′ærouruːt], *s.* (*Bot.*) die Pfeilwurz.

arsenal [′ɑːsinəl], *s.* das Arsenal, Zeughaus.

arsenic [′ɑːsənik], *s.* das Arsen.

arson [′ɑːsən], *s.* die Brandstiftung.

art [ɑːt], *s.* die Kunst; *fine —*, schöne Kunst; (*Univ.*) —*s faculty*, die philosophische Fakultät; —*s* (*subject*), das humanistische Fach, die Geisteswissenschaften.

arterial [ɑː′tiəriəl], *adj.* Pulsader-, Schlagader-; — *road*, die Hauptverkehrsader, die Hauptstraße.

artery [′ɑːtəri], *s.* die Pulsader, Schlagader; der Hauptverkehrsweg.

artesian [ɑː′tiːʒən], *adj.* artesisch.

artful [′ɑːtful], *adj.* listig, schlau.

article [′ɑːtikl], *s.* (*Gram.*, *Law*, *Press*) der Artikel; der Posten (*item in list*). — *v.a.* *be —d to a solicitor*, bei einem Advokaten assistieren.

articulate [ɑː′tikjuleit], *v.a.* artikulieren (*pronounce clearly*). — [—lit], *adj.* deutlich (*speech*).

articulation [ɑːtikju′leiʃən], *s.* die Artikulation, deutliche Aussprache.

artifice [′ɑːtifis], *s.* der Kunstgriff, die List.

artificer [ɑː′tifisə], *s.* der Handwerker.

artificial [ɑːti′fiʃəl], *adj.* künstlich, Kunst-; — *silk*, die Kunstseide.

artillery [ɑː′tiləri], *s.* die Artillerie.

artisan [ɑːti′zæn], *s.* der Handwerker.

artist [′ɑːtist], *s.* der Künstler, die Künstlerin.

artistic [ɑː′tistik], *adj.* künstlerisch.

artless [′ɑːtlis], *adj.* arglos, natürlich, naiv.

Aryan [′ɛəriən], *adj.* arisch. — *s.* der Arier.

as [æz], *adv.*, *conj.* so, als, wie, ebenso; als, während, weil; — *big —*, so groß wie; — *well —*, sowohl als auch; *such —*, wie; — *it were*, gleichsam.

asbestos [æz′bestɔs], *s.* der Asbest.

ascend [ə′send], *v.a.*, *v.n.* ersteigen, besteigen; emporsteigen.

ascendancy, -ency [ə′sendənsi], *s.* der Aufstieg; der Einfluß; das Übergewicht.

ascendant, -ent [ə′sendənt], *s. in the —*, aufsteigend.

ascent [ə′sent], *s.* der Aufstieg, die Besteigung.

ascension [ə′senʃən], *s.* (*Astron.*) das Aufsteigen; *Ascension Day*, Himmelfahrt(stag).

ascertain [æsə′tein], *v.a.* in Erfahrung bringen, erkunden, feststellen.

ascertainable [æsə′teinəbl], *adj.* erkundbar, feststellbar.

ascetic [ə′setik], *adj.* asketisch.

asceticism [ə′setisizm], *s.* die Askese.

ascribe [ə′skraib], *v.a.* zuschreiben.

ascribable [ə′skraibəbl], *adj.* zuzuschreiben, zuschreibbar.

ash (1) [æʃ], *s.* (*Bot.*) die Esche.

ash (2) [æʃ], *s.* die Asche.

ashamed [ə′ʃeimd], *adj.* beschämt; *be —*, sich schämen.

ashcan [′æʃkæn], (*Am.*) *see* **dustbin**.

ashen [′æʃən], *adj.* aschgrau, aschfarben.

ashore [ə′ʃɔː], *adv.* am Land; am Ufer, ans Ufer *or* Land.

ashtray [′æʃtrei], *s.* der Aschenbecher.

Ash Wednesday [æʃ′wenzdei], *s.* der Aschermittwoch.

Asiatic [eiʃi′ætik], *adj.* asiatisch. — *s.* der Asiat.

313

aside

aside [əˈsaid], *adv.* seitwärts, zur Seite; abseits.

ask [ɑːsk], *v.a.*, *v.n.* fragen *(question)*; bitten *(request)*; fordern *(demand)*; einladen *(invite)*.

asleep [əˈsliːp], *pred. adj.*, *adv.* schlafend, im Schlaf; eingeschlafen.

asp [æsp], *s.* *(Zool.)* die Natter.

asparagus [æsˈpærəgəs], *s.* *(Bot.)* der Spargel.

aspect [ˈæspekt], *s.* der Anblick, die Ansicht *(view, angle)*; der Gesichtspunkt.

aspen [ˈæspən], *s.* *(Bot.)* die Espe.

asperity [æsˈperiti], *s.* die Härte; Rauheit.

aspersion [æsˈpəːʃən], *s.* die Verleumdung; Schmähung.

asphalt [ˈæsfælt], *s.* der Asphalt.

asphyxia [æsˈfiksiə], *s.* *(Med.)* die Erstickung.

aspirant [əˈspaiərənt, ˈæsp-], *s.* der Bewerber, Anwärter.

aspirate [ˈæspireit], *v.a.* *(Phon.)* aspirieren. — [—rit] *adj.* aspiriert. — *s.* der Hauchlaut.

aspiration [æspiˈreiʃən], *s.* der Atemzug; das Streben *(striving)* ; *(Phon.)* die Aspiration.

aspire [əˈspaiə], *v.n.* streben, verlangen.

ass [æs], *s.* der Esel.

assail [əˈseil], *v.a.* angreifen, anfallen.

assailable [əˈseiləbl], *adj.* angreifbar.

assassin [əˈsæsin], *s.* der Meuchelmörder.

assassinate [əˈsæsineit], *v.a.* meuchlings ermorden.

assassination [əsæsiˈneiʃən], *s.* der Meuchelmord, die Ermordung.

assault [əˈsɔːlt], *v.a.* angreifen, überfallen. — *s.* der Überfall, Angriff.

assay [əˈsei], *s.* die Metallprobe. — *v.a.* (auf Edelmetall hin) prüfen.

assemble [əˈsembl], *v.a.*, *v.n.* versammeln, sich versammeln.

assembly [əˈsembli], *s.* die Versammlung *(assemblage)*; — line, das laufende Band, das Fließband.

assent [əˈsent], *v.n.* beistimmen *(Dat.)*, billigen *(Acc.)*. — *s.* die Zustimmung (zu, *Dat.*), Billigung *(Genit.)*.

assert [əˈsəːt], *v.a.* behaupten.

assertion [əˈsəːʃən], *s.* die Behauptung.

assess [əˈses], *v.a.* schätzen, beurteilen.

assessment [əˈsesmənt], *s.* die Beurteilung, Schätzung, Wertung.

assessor [əˈsesə], *s.* der Beurteiler, Einschätzer, Bewerter, Assessor; der Beisitzer *(second examiner)*.

assets [ˈæsets], *s. pl.* *(Comm.)* die Aktiva; Vorzüge *(personal)*.

assiduity [æsiˈdjuːiti], *s.* der Fleiß, die Emsigkeit.

assiduous [əˈsidjuəs], *adj.* fleißig, unablässig, emsig.

assign [əˈsain], *v.a.* zuteilen, anweisen, zuweisen *(apportion)*, festsetzen *(fix)*.

assignable [əˈsainəbl], *adj.* zuteilbar; bestimmbar.

assignation [æsigˈneiʃən], *s.* die Zuweisung; *(Law)* die Übertragung; die Verabredung.

assignment [əˈsainmənt], *s.* die Zuweisung, Übertragung; die Aufgabe.

assimilate [əˈsimileit], *v.a.*, *v.n.* assimilieren, angleichen; sich assimilieren, sich angleichen, ähnlich werden.

assist [əˈsist], *v.a.*, *v.n.* beistehen *(Dat.)*, helfen *(Dat.)*, unterstützen *(Acc.)*.

assistance [əˈsistəns], *s.* der Beistand, die Hilfe; die Aushilfe; *(financial)* der Zuschuß.

assistant [əˈsistənt], *s.* der Assistent, Helfer.

assize [əˈsaiz], *s.* die Gerichtssitzung; *(pl.)* das Schwurgericht.

associate [əˈsouʃieit], *v.a.* verbinden *(link)*. — *v.n.* verkehren *(company)*; sich verbinden; *(Comm.)* sich vereinigen. — [—iit], *s.* *(Comm.)* der Partner.

association [əsousiˈeiʃən], *s.* die Vereinigung, der Bund, Verein; die Gesellschaft; der Verkehr.

assonance [ˈæsənəns], *s.* *(Phon.)* die Assonanz, der Gleichlaut.

assort [əˈsɔːt], *v.a.* ordnen, aussuchen, sortieren; —ed sweets, gemischte Bonbons.

assortment [əˈsɔːtmənt], *s.* die Sammlung, Mischung, Auswahl.

assuage [əˈsweidʒ], *v.a.* mildern, besänftigen, stillen.

assume [əˈsjuːm], *v.a.* annehmen; übernehmen, ergreifen.

assuming [əˈsjuːmiŋ], *adj.* anmaßend; — that, angenommen daß . . ., gesetzt den Fall.

assumption [əˈsʌmpʃən], *s.* die Annahme *(opinion)*; Übernahme *(taking up)*; Aneignung *(appropriation)*; Assumption of the Blessed Virgin, Mariä Himmelfahrt.

assurance [əˈʃuərəns], *s.* die Versicherung; Sicherheit *(manner)*.

assure [əˈʃuə], *v.a.* versichern, sicher stellen, ermutigen.

assuredly [əˈʃuəridli], *adv.* sicherlich, gewiß.

aster [ˈæstə], *s.* *(Bot.)* die Aster.

asterisk [ˈæstərisk], *s.* *(Typ.)* das Sternchen.

astern [əˈstəːn], *adv.* *(Naut.)* achteraus.

asthma [ˈæsθmə], *s.* das Asthma.

asthmatic [æsθˈmætik], *adj.* asthmatisch.

astir [əˈstəː], *adv.* wach, in Bewegung.

astonish [əˈstɔniʃ], *v.a.* in Erstaunen versetzen, verblüffen.

astonishment [əˈstɔniʃmənt], *s.* das Erstaunen, die Verwunderung; die Bestürzung.

astound [əˈstaund], *v.a.* in Erstaunen versetzen, bestürzen.

astounding [əˈstaundiŋ], *adj.* erstaunlich, verblüffend.

astral [ˈæstrəl], *adj.* Stern(en)-, gestirnt.

314

astray [ə'strei], *pred. adj.*, *adv.* irre; *go* —, sich verirren; (*fig.*) abschweifen.

astride [ə'straid], *pred.adj.*, *adv.* rittlings.

astringent [ə'strindʒənt], *adj.* zusammenziehend.

astrologer [ə'strɔlədʒə], *s.* der Sterndeuter, Astrolog(e).

astrological [æstrə'lɔdʒikəl], *adj.* astrologisch.

astrology [æ'strɔlədʒi], *s.* die Astrologie, Sterndeuterei.

astronaut ['æstrənɔːt], *s.* der Astronaut.

astronomer [ə'strɔnəmə], *s.* der Astronom.

astronomical [æstrə'nɔmikəl], *adj.* astronomisch.

astronomy [ə'strɔnəmi], *s.* die Astronomie, Sternkunde.

astute [ə'stjuːt], *adj.* listig, schlau.

astuteness [ə'stjuːtnis], *s.* die Schlauheit, Listigkeit, der Scharfsinn.

asunder [ə'sʌndə], *adv.* auseinander, entzwei.

asylum [ə'sailəm], *s.* das Asyl, der Zufluchtsort (*refuge*); *lunatic* —, das Irrenhaus.

at [æt], *prep.* an; auf; bei, für; in, nach; mit, gegen; um, über; von, aus, zu; — *my expense*, auf meine Kosten; — *all*, überhaupt; — *first*, zuerst; — *last*, zuletzt, endlich; — *peace*, in Frieden; *what are you driving* — *?* worauf wollen sie hinaus?

atheism ['eiθiizm], *s.* der Atheismus.

atheist ['eiθiist], *s.* der Atheist.

atheistic [eiθi'istik], *adj.* atheistisch, gottlos.

Athens ['æθənz]. Athen, *n.*

Athenian [ə'θiːnjən], *s.* der Athener. — *adj.* athenisch.

athlete ['æθliːt], *s.* der Athlet.

athletic [æθ'letik], *adj.* athletisch.

athletics [æθ'letiks], *s. pl.* die Leichtathletik, Athletik.

Atlantic (Ocean) [ət'læntik ('ouʃən)]. der Atlantik.

atlas ['ætləs], *s.* der Atlas.

atmosphere ['ætməsfiə], *s.* die Atmosphäre.

atmospheric(al) [ætməs'ferik(əl)], *adj.* atmosphärisch. — *s.* (*pl.*) atmosphärische Störungen, *f. pl.*

atoll [ə'tɔl], *s.* die Koralleninsel, das Atoll.

atom ['ætəm], *s.* das Atom.

atomic [ə'tɔmik], *adj.* (*Phys.*) Atom-, atomisch, atomar; (*theory*) atomistisch; — *bomb*, die Atombombe; — *pile*, der Atomreaktor; — *armament*, die atomare Aufrüstung.

atone [ə'toun], *v.n.* sühnen, büßen.

atonement [ə'tounmənt], *s.* die Buße, Sühne, Versöhnung.

atonic [ei'tɔnik], *adj.* tonlos, unbetont.

atrocious [ə'trouʃəs], *adj.* gräßlich, schrecklich, entsetzlich.

atrocity [ə'trɔsiti], *s.* die Gräßlichkeit, Grausamkeit, Greueltat.

atrophy ['ætrəfi], *s.* (*Med.*) die Abmagerung, Atrophie. — ['ætrəfai], *v.n.* absterben, auszehren.

attach [ə'tætʃ], *v.a.* anheften, beilegen, anhängen; (*fig.*) beimessen (*attribute*).

attachment [ə'tætʃmənt], *s.* das Anhaften (*sticking to*, an, *Acc.*); das Anhängsel (*appendage*); die Freundschaft (*to*, für, *Acc.*); die Anhänglichkeit (*loyalty*, an, *Acc.*).

attack [ə'tæk], *v.a.* angreifen. — *s.* die Attacke, der Angriff; (*Med.*) der Anfall.

attain [ə'tein], *v.a.* erreichen, erlangen.

attainable [ə'teinəbl], *adj.* erreichbar.

attainment [ə'teinmənt], *s.* die Erlangung, Erreichung; Errungenschaft; (*pl.*) Kenntnisse, *f. pl.*

attempt [ə'tempt], *s.* der Versuch. — *v.a.* versuchen.

attend [ə'tend], *v.a.*, *v.n.* begleiten, anwesend sein (*be present, at*, bei, *Dat.*); beiwohnen (*be present as guest*); zuhören (*listen to*); bedienen (*customer*); behandeln (*patient*).

attendance [ə'tendəns], *s.* die Begleitung (*accompaniment*); die Anwesenheit (*presence*); die Zuhörerschaft (*audience*); *to be in* —, Dienst tun (*at*, bei); anwesend sein (*be present*).

attendant [ə'tendənt], *s.* der Diener, Wärter.

attention [ə'tenʃən], *s.* die Aufmerksamkeit, Achtung.

attentive [ə'tentiv], *adj.* aufmerksam.

attenuate [ə'tenjueit], *v.a.* verdünnen (*dilute*). — *v.n.* abmagern.

attest [ə'test], *v.a.* attestieren, bezeugen, bescheinigen.

attestation [ætes'teiʃən], *s.* die Bescheinigung; das Zeugnis.

Attic ['ætik], *adj.* attisch, klassisch.

attic ['ætik], *s.* die Dachkammer, die Dachstube.

attire [ə'taiə], *v.a.* ankleiden, kleiden. — *s.* die Kleidung.

attitude ['ætitjuːd], *s.* die Haltung, Stellung (*toward*, zu), Einstellung.

attorney [ə'təːni], *s.* der Anwalt; *Attorney–General*, der Kronanwalt; (*Am.*) der Staatsanwalt; — *at law*, Rechtsanwalt.

attract [ə'trækt], *v.a.* anziehen.

attraction [ə'trækʃən], *s.* die Anziehung; der Reiz (*appeal*); die Anziehungskraft.

attractive [ə'træktiv], *adj.* anziehend, reizvoll.

attribute [ə'tribjuːt], *v.a.* zuschreiben, beimessen. — *s.* ['ætribjuːt], (*Gram.*) das Attribut, die Eigenschaft.

attributive [ə'tribjutiv], *adj.* (*Gram.*) attributiv; beilegend.

attrition [ə'triʃən], *s.* die Zermürbung, Aufreibung, Reue.

attune [ə'tjuːn], *v.a.* (*Mus.*) stimmen, anpassen (*adapt to*, an, *Acc.*).

auburn ['ɔːbəːn], *adj.* rotbraun.

auction ['ɔːkʃən], *s.* die Auktion, die Versteigerung.

auctioneer [ɔːkʃə'niə], *s.* der Auktionator, Versteigerer.

315

audacious

audacious [ɔ:'deiʃəs], *adj.* waghalsig, kühn, dreist.

audacity [ɔ:'dæsiti], *s.* die Kühnheit (*valour*); Frechheit (*impudence*).

audible ['ɔ:dibl], *adj.* hörbar.

audibility [ɔ:di'biliti], *s.* die Hörbarkeit, Vernehmbarkeit.

audience ['ɔ:djəns], *s.* die Audienz (*of the Pope*, beim Papst); (*Theat.*) das Publikum; (*listeners*) die Zuhörer.

audit ['ɔ:dit], *s.* die Rechnungsprüfung, Revision. — *v.a.* revidieren, prüfen.

auditor ['ɔ:ditə], *s.* der Rechnungsrevisor, Buchprüfer.

auditory ['ɔ:ditəri], *adj.* Gehör–, Hör–.

auditorium [ɔ:di'tɔ:riəm], *s.* der Hörsaal, Vortragssaal.

auger ['ɔ:gə], *s.* der (große) Bohrer.

aught [ɔ:t], *pron.* (*obs.*) irgend etwas (*opp. to* naught).

augment [ɔ:g'ment], *v.a., v.n.* vermehren, vergrößern; zunehmen.

augmentation [ɔ:gmen'teiʃən], *s.* die Vergrößerung, Erhöhung, Zunahme.

augur ['ɔ:gə], *v.a.* weissagen, prophezeien.

August ['ɔ:gəst]. der August.

august [ɔ:'gʌst], *adj.* erhaben.

aunt [ɑ:nt], *s.* die Tante.

aurora [ɔ:'rɔ:rə], *s.* die Morgenröte.

auscultation [ɔ:skəl'teiʃən], *s.*(*Med.*) die Auskultation, Untersuchung.

auspices ['ɔ:spisiz], *s.* die Auspizien.

auspicious [ɔ:'spiʃəs], *adj.* unter glücklichem Vorzeichen, verheißungsvoll, günstig.

austere [ɔ:s'tiə], *adj.* streng, ernst, schmucklos.

austerity [ɔ:s'teriti], *s.* die Strenge.

Australian [ɔ:s'treiljən], *adj.* australisch. — *s.* der Australier.

Austrian [ɔ:s'striən], *adj.* österreichisch. — *s.* der Österreicher.

authentic [ɔ:'θentik], *adj.* authentisch, echt.

authenticity [ɔ:θen'tisiti], *s.* die Authentizität, Echtheit.

author, authoress ['ɔ:θə, ɔ:θər'es], *s.* der Autor, die Autorin; der Verfasser, die Verfasserin.

authoritative [ɔ:'θɔritətiv], *adj.* autoritativ, maßgebend.

authority [ɔ:'θɔriti], *s.* die Autorität, Vollmacht (*power of attorney*); das Ansehen; *the authorities*, die Behörden.

authorization [ɔ:θərai'zeiʃən], *s.* die Bevollmächtigung, Befugnis.

authorize [ɔ:θəraiz], *v.a.* autorisieren, bevollmächtigen, berechtigen.

authorship ['ɔ:θəʃip], *s.* die Autorschaft.

autobiographical [ɔ:tobaiə'græfikl], *adj.* autobiographisch.

autobiography [ɔ:tobai'ɔgrəfi], *s.* die Autobiographie.

autocracy [ɔ:'tɔkrəsi], *s.* die Selbstherrschaft.

autocrat ['ɔ:tokræt], *s.* der Autokrat, Selbstherrscher.

autograph ['ɔ:togræf, -grɑ:f], *s.* die eigene Handschrift, Unterschrift; das Autogramm.

automatic [ɔ:to'mætik], *adj.* automatisch.

automatize [ɔ:'tɔmətaiz], *v.a.* automatisieren, auf Automation umstellen.

automation [ɔ:to'meiʃən], *s.* (*Engin.*) die Automation; Automatisierung.

automaton [ɔ:'tɔmətən], *s.* der Automat.

automobile ['ɔ:tomobi:l], *s.* der Kraftwagen, das Auto.

autonomous [ɔ:'tɔnəməs], *adj.* autonom, unabhängig.

autonomy [ɔ:'tɔnəmi], *s.* die Autonomie, Unabhängigkeit.

autopsy ['ɔ:tɔpsi], *s.* die Autopsie; Obduktion, Leichenschau.

autumn ['ɔ:təm], *s.* der Herbst.

autumnal [ɔ:'tʌmnəl], *adj.* herbstlich.

auxiliary [ɔ:g'ziljəri], *adj.* Hilfs–.

avail [ə'veil], *v.n.* nützen, helfen, von Vorteil sein. — *v.r.* - *o.s of a th.*, sich einer Sache bedienen. — *s.* der Nutzen; *of no* —, nutzlos.

available [ə'veiləbl], *adj.* vorrätig, verfügbar, zur Verfügung (stehend).

avalanche ['ævəlɑ:nʃ], *s.* die Lawine.

avarice ['ævəris], *s.* der Geiz, die Habsucht, Gier.

avaricious [ævə'riʃəs], *adj.* geizig, habsüchtig, begierig.

avenge [ə'vendʒ], *v.a.* rächen.

avenue ['ævənju:], *s.* die Allee; der Zugang.

average ['ævəridʒ], *adj.* durchschnittlich; *not more than* —, mäßig. — *s.* der Durchschnitt; *on an* —, durchschnittlich, im Durchschnitt. — *v.a.* den Durchschnitt nehmen.

averse [ə'və:s], *adj.* abgeneigt (*to, Dat.*).

aversion [ə'və:ʃən], *s.* die Abneigung, der Widerwille.

avert [ə'və:t], *v.a.* abwenden.

aviary ['eiviəri], *s.* das Vogelhaus.

aviation [əivi'eiʃən], *s.* das Flugwesen.

aviator ['eivieitə], *s.* der Flieger.

avid ['ævid], *adj.* begierig (*of* or *for*, nach).

avidity [æ'viditi], *s.* die Begierde, Gier (*for*, nach).

avoid [ə'vɔid], *v.a.* vermeiden.

avoidable [ə'vɔidəbl], *adj.* vermeidlich, vermeidbar.

avoidance [ə'vɔidəns], *s.* die Vermeidung, das Meiden.

avow [ə'vau], *v.a.* eingestehen, anerkennen (*acknowledge*).

avowal [ə'vauəl], *s.* das Geständnis; die Erklärung.

await [ə'weit], *v.a.* erwarten, warten auf (*Acc.*).

awake(n) [ə'weik(ən)], *v.a., v.n. irr.* aufwecken, wecken; aufwachen (*wake up*). — *adj. wide awake*, schlau, auf der Hut.

award [ə'wɔ:d], *s.* die Zuerkennung, Auszeichnung; Belohnung (money); (Law) das Urteil. — *v.a.* zuerkennen; — *damages*, Schadenersatz zusprechen; verleihen (grant).

aware [ə'wɛə], *adj.* gewahr, bewußt (Genit.).

away [ə'wei], *adv.* weg; hinweg, fort.

awe [ɔ:], *s.* die Ehrfurcht; Furcht.

awful ['ɔ:ful], *adj.* furchtbar, schrecklich.

awhile [ə'wail], *adv.* eine Weile, eine kurze Zeit.

awkward ['ɔ:kwəd], *adv.* ungeschickt, unbeholfen, ungelenk; unangenehm (difficult); — *situation*, peinliche Situation, Lage.

awkwardness ['ɔkwədnis], *s.* die Ungeschicklichkeit, Unbeholfenheit.

awl [ɔ:l], *s.* die Ahle, der Pfriem.

awning ['ɔ:niŋ], *s.* die Plane; das Sonnendach.

awry [ə'rai], *adj.* schief, verkehrt.

axe [æks], *s.* die Axt, das Beil.

axiom ['æksiəm], *s.* das Axiom, der Satz, Lehrsatz, Grundsatz.

axiomatic [æksiə'mætik], *adj.* axiomatisch, grundsätzlich; gewiß.

axis ['æksis], *s.* die Achse.

axle [æksl], *s.* die Achse.

ay(e) (1) [ai], *adv.* ja, gewiß.

ay(e) (2) [ei], *adv.* ständig, ewig.

azalea [ə'zeiliə], *s.* (Bot.) die Azalie.

azure ['æʒə, 'eiʒə], *adj.* himmelblau, azurblau.

B

B [bi:]. das B; (Mus.) das H.

baa [ba:], *v.n.* blöken.

babble [bæbl], *v.n.* schwatzen, schwätzen. — *s.* das Geschwätz; das Murmeln (water).

babe, **baby** [beib, 'beibi], *s.* der Säugling, das Baby, das kleine Kind, das Kindlein.

baboon [bə'bu:n], *s.* (Zool.) der Pavian.

bachelor ['bætʃələ], *s.* der Junggeselle; (Univ.) Bakkalaureus.

back [bæk], *s.* der Rücken, die Rückseite. — *adj.* Hinter-, Rück-; — *door*, die Hintertür; — *stairs*, die Hintertreppe. — *adv.* rückwärts, zurück. — *v.a.* unterstützen; (Comm.) indossieren; gegenzeichnen; wetten auf (Acc.) (bet on).

backbone ['bækboun], *s.* (Anat.) das Rückgrat.

backfire ['bækfaiə], *s.* (Motor.) die Frühzündung; (gun) die Fehlzündung. — [bæk'faiə], *v.n.* (Motor.) frühzünden; (gun) fehlzünden.

backgammon [bæk'gæmən], *s.* das Bordspiel, das Puffspiel.

background ['bækgraund], *s.* der Hintergrund.

backhand ['bækhænd], *s.* (Sport) die Rückhand; a —ed compliment, eine verblümte Grobheit.

backside [bæk'said], *s.* (vulg.) der Hintere.

backslide [bæk'slaid], *v.n.* abfallen, abtrünnig werden.

backward ['bækwəd], *adj.* zurückgeblieben. **backward(s)** *adv.* rückwärts, zurück.

backwater ['bækwɔ:tə], *s.* das Stauwasser.

backwoods ['bækwudz], *s. pl.* der Hinterwald.

bacon ['beikən], *s.* der Speck.

bad [bæd], *adj.* schlecht, schlimm; böse (immoral); (coll.) unwohl (unwell); not too —, ganz gut; from — to worse, immer schlimmer; — language, unanständige Worte, das Fluchen; — luck, Unglück, Pech; want —ly, nötig brauchen.

badge [bædʒ], *s.* das Abzeichen; Kennzeichen (mark).

badger (1) ['bædʒə], *s.* (Zool.) der Dachs.

badger (2) ['bædʒə], *v.a.* ärgern, stören, belästigen.

badness ['bædnis], *s.* die Schlechtigkeit, Bosheit, das schlechte Wesen, die Bösartigkeit.

baffle [bæfl], *v.a.* täuschen, verblüffen. — *s.* (obs.) die Täuschung; (Build.) Verkleidung; (Elec.) Verteilerplatte.

bag [bæg], *s.* der Sack, Beutel; die Tasche; shopping —, Einkaufstasche; travelling —, Reisehandtasche. — *v.a.* einstecken, als Beute behalten (hunt).

bagatelle [bægə'tel], *s.* die Bagatelle, Lappalie, Kleinigkeit; das Kugelspiel (pin-table ball-game).

baggage ['bægidʒ], *s.* das Gepäck.

bagging ['bægiŋ], *s.* die Sackleinwand.

baggy ['bægi], *adj.* ungebügelt; bauschig.

bagpipe ['bægpaip], *s.* der Dudelsack.

bagpiper ['bægpaipə], *s.* der Dudelsackpfeifer.

bail [beil], *s.* der Bürge; die Bürgschaft; stand —, für einen bürgen; allow —, Bürgschaft zulassen. — *v.a.* Bürgschaft leisten; — *out*, (durch Kaution) in Freiheit setzen.

bailiff ['beilif], *s.* der Amtmann; Gerichtsvollzieher.

bait [beit], *s.* der Köder. — *v.a.* ködern, locken (attract).

baiter ['beitə], *s.* der Hetzer, Verfolger.

baiting ['beitiŋ], *s.* die Hetze.

bake [beik], *v.a., v.n.* backen.

baker ['beikə], *s.* der Bäcker; —'s dozen, 13 Stück.

bakery ['beikəri], *s.* die Bäckerei.

baking ['beikiŋ], *s.* das Backen.

balance ['bæləns], *s.* die Waage (*scales*); die Bilanz (*audit*); das Gleichgewicht (*equilibrium*); (*Comm.*) der Saldo, der Überschuß (*profit*); die Unruhe (*watch*). — *v.a., v.n.* wägen, abwägen (*scales*); ausgleichen (— *up*), einen Saldo ziehen (— *an account*); ins Gleichgewicht bringen (*bring into equilibrium*).

balcony ['bælkəni], *s.* der Balkon, der Söller (*castle*); Altan (*villa*).

bald [bɔːld], *adj.* kahl, haarlos; (*fig.*) armselig, schmucklos.

baldness ['bɔːldnis], *s.* die Kahlheit (*hairlessness*); Nacktheit (*bareness*).

bale (1) [beil], *s.* der Ballen.

bale (2) [beil], *v.n.* — *out*, abspringen; aussteigen.

Balearic Islands [bæli'ærik ailəndz], *s. pl.* die Balearen, Baleärischen Inseln. — *adj.* balearisch.

baleful ['beilful], *adj.* unheilvoll.

balk [bɔːk], *v.a.* aufhalten, hemmen. — *v.n.* scheuen, zurückscheuen (*at*, *vor*).

ball (1) [bɔːl], *s.* der Ball; die Kugel; — *cock*, der Absperrhahn; —*point pen*, der Kugelschreiber.

ball (2) [bɔːl], *s.* der Ball (*dance*).

ballad ['bæləd], *s.* die Ballade.

ballast ['bæləst], *s.* der Ballast.

ballet ['bælei], *s.* das Ballett.

balloon [bə'luːn], *s.* der Ballon.

ballot ['bælət], *s.* die geheime Wahl, Abstimmung; — *box*, die Wahlurne; — *paper*, der Stimmzettel. —*v. n.* wählen, abstimmen.

balm [baːm], *s.* der Balsam.

balsam ['bɔlsəm], *s.* der Balsam.

Baltic ['bɔːltik], *adj.* baltisch. — (*Sea*), die Ostsee; — *Provinces*, das Baltikum.

balustrade ['bæləstreid], *s.* die Balustrade, das Geländer.

bamboo [bæm'buː], *s.* (*Bot.*) der Bambus.

bamboozle [bæm'buːzl], *v.a.* verblüffen; beschwindeln (*cheat*).

ban [bæn], *v.a.* bannen, verbannen; verbieten. — *s.* der Bann, das Verbot.

banal [bæ'næl, 'beinəl], *adj.* banal.

banality [bæ'næliti], *s.* die Banalität, Trivialität.

banana [bə'naːnə], *s.* die Banane.

band [bænd], *s.* das Band (*ribbon etc.*); (*Mus.*) die Kapelle; die Bande (*robbers*). — *v.n.* — *together*, sich verbinden; sich zusammentun.

bandage ['bændidʒ], *s.* der Verband, die Bandage.

bandit ['bændit], *s.* der Bandit.

bandmaster ['bændmaːstə], *s.* der Kapellmeister.

bandstand ['bændstænd], *s.* der Musikpavillon.

bandy ['bændi], *adj.* — *legged*, krummbeinig. — *v.a.* — *words*, Worte wechseln; streiten.

bane [bein], *s.* das Gift; (*fig.*) Verderben.

baneful ['beinful], *adj.* verderblich.

bang [bæŋ], *s.* der Knall (*explosion*), das Krachen (*clap*). — *v.n.* knallen, krachen lassen. — *v.a.* — *a door*, eine Türe zuwerfen.

banish ['bæniʃ], *v.a.* verbannen, bannen.

banisters ['bænistəz], *s. pl.* das Treppengeländer.

bank [bæŋk], *s.* (*Fin.*) die Bank; das Ufer (*river*); der Damm (*dam*). — *v.a.* einlegen, einzahlen, auf die Bank bringen (*sum of money*); eindämmen (*dam up*). — *v.n.* ein Konto haben (*have an account, with*, bei).

banker ['bæŋkə], *s.* der Bankier.

bankrupt ['bæŋkrʌpt], *adj.* bankrott; zahlungsunfähig; (*coll.*) pleite.

bankruptcy ['bæŋkrʌptsi], *s.* der Bankrott.

banns [bænz], *s. pl.* das Heiratsaufgebot.

banquet ['bæŋkwit], *s.* das Bankett, Festessen.

bantam ['bæntəm], *s.* das Bantamhuhn, Zwerghuhn; (*Boxing*) —*weight*, das Bantamgewicht.

banter ['bæntə], *v.n.* scherzen, necken. — *s.* das Scherzen, der Scherz.

baptism ['bæptizm], *s.* die Taufe.

Baptist ['bæptist], *s.* der Täufer; Baptist.

baptize [bæp'taiz], *v.a.* taufen.

bar [baː], *s.* die Barre, Stange (*pole*); der Riegel; Balken; Schlagbaum (*barrier*); (*fig.*) das Hindernis; der Schanktisch (*in public house*); *prisoner at the* —, Gefangener vor (dem) Gericht; *call to the* —, zur Gerichtsadvokatur (*or* als Anwalt) zulassen; (*Mus.*) der Takt. — *v.a.* verriegeln (*door*); (*fig.*) hindern (*from action*); verbieten (*prohibit*); ausschließen (*exclude*).

barb [baːb], *s.* die Spitze (*of wire*); der Widerhaken (*hook*).

barbed [baːbd], *adj.* spitzig; — *remark*, die spitze Bemerkung; — *wire*, der Stacheldraht.

barbarian [baː'bɛəriən], *s.* der Barbar. — *adj.* barbarisch.

barbarism [baː'bɑːrizm], *s.* die Roheit; der Barbarismus.

barber ['baːbə], *s.* der Barbier, Friseur.

barberry ['baːbəri], *s.* (*Bot.*) der Berberitze.

bard [baːd], *s.* der Barde, Sänger.

bare [bɛə], *adj.* nackt, bloß; — *headed*, barhäuptig. — *v.a.* entblößen.

barefaced ['bɛəfeisd], *adj.* schamlos.

barely ['bɛəli], *adv.* kaum.

bargain ['baːgin], *s.* der Kauf, Gelegenheitskauf; der Handel (*trading*); das Geschäft; *into the* —, noch dazu, obendrein. — *v.n.* feilschen, handeln (*haggle*) (*for*, um).

barge [baːdʒ], *s.* der Lastkahn, die Barke. — *v.n.* (*coll.*) — *in*, stören.

bargee [baː'dʒiː], *s.* der Flußschiffer, Bootsmann.

baritone ['bæritoun], *s.* (*Mus.*) der Bariton.

beam

bark (1) [bɑːk], *s.* die Rinde (*of tree*).
bark (2) [bɑːk], *v.n.* bellen (*dog*); — *up the wrong tree*, auf falscher Fährte sein. — *s.* das Gebell (*dog*).
barley ['bɑːli], *s.* (*Bot.*) die Gerste.
barmaid ['bɑːmeid], *s.* die Kellnerin.
barman ['bɑːmən], *s.* der Kellner.
barn [bɑːn], *s.* die Scheune; — *owl*, die Schleiereule.
barnacle ['bɑːnəkl], *s.* die Entenmuschel; die Klette.
barnstormer [bɑːnstɔːmə], *s.* der Schmierenkomödiant.
barometer [bəˈrɔmitə], *s.* das Barometer.
baron ['bærən], *s.* der Baron, Freiherr.
barony ['bærəni], *s.* die Baronswürde.
baroque [bəˈrɔk], *adj.* barock. — *s.* das Barock.
barque [bɑːk], *s.* die Bark.
barracks ['bærəks], *s. pl.* die Kaserne.
barrage ['bærɑːʒ, 'bæridʒ], *s.* das Sperrfeuer (*firing*); das Wehr, der Damm.
barrel ['bærəl], *s.* das Faß (*vat*), die Tonne (*tun*); der Gewehrlauf (*rifle*); die Trommel (*cylinder*); — *organ*, die Drehorgel.
barren ['bærən], *adj.* unfruchtbar, dürr.
barrenness ['bærinnis], *s.* die Unfruchtbarkeit.
barricade ['bæriˈkeid], *s.* die Barrikade. — *v.a.* verrammeln, verschanzen.
barrier ['bæriə], *s.* die Barriere, der Schlagbaum; das Hindernis; (*Railw.*) die Schranke.
barrister ['bæristə], *s.* der Rechtsanwalt, Advokat.
barrow (1) ['bærou], *s.* der Schubkarren, Handkarren; — *-boy*, der Höker, Schnellverkäufer.
barrow (2) ['bærou], *s.* (*Archaeol.*) das Hünengrab, Heldengrab.
barter ['bɑːtə], *v.a.* tauschen, austauschen. — *s.* der Tauschhandel.
Bartholomew [bɑːˈθɔləmjuː]. Bartholomäus, *m.*; *Massacre of St. Bartholomew's Eve*, Bartholomäusnacht, Pariser Bluthochzeit.
basalt [bæsɔːlt, bæˈsɔːlt], *s.* der Basalt.
base [beis], *s.* die Basis, Grundlage; der Sockel; (*Chem.*) die Base. — *adj.* niedrig, gemein; (*Metall.*) unedel. — *v.a.* basieren, beruhen, fundieren (*upon*, auf).
baseless ['beislis], *adj.* grundlos.
basement ['beismənt], *s.* das Kellergeschoß.
baseness ['beisnis], *s.* die Gemeinheit, Niedrigkeit.
bashful ['bæʃful], *adj.* verschämt, schamhaft, schüchtern.
basic ['beisik], *adj.* grundlegend.
basin ['beisn], *s.* das Becken.
basis ['beisis], *s.* die Basis, Grundlage.
bask [bɑːsk], *v.n.* sich sonnen.
basket ['bɑːskit], *s.* der Korb.
bass (1) [beis], *s.* (*Mus.*) der Baß, die Baßstimme.

bass (2) [bæs], *s.* (*Zool.*) der Barsch.
bassoon [bəˈsuːn], *s.* (*Mus.*) das Fagott.
bastard ['bæstəd], *s.* der Bastard.
baste [beist], *v.a.* mit Fett begießen (*roast meat*); (*coll.*) prügeln.
bastion ['bæstiən], *s.* die Bastion, Festung, das Bollwerk.
bat (1) [bæt], *s.* die Fledermaus.
bat (2) [bæt], *s.* der Schläger. — *v.n.* (den Ball) schlagen; (*cricket*) am Schlagen sein (*be batting*).
batch [bætʃ], *s.* der Stoß (*pile*); die Menge (*people*); (*Mil.*) der Trupp.
bath [bɑːθ], *s.* das Bad; (*Am.*) —*robe*, der Schlafrock, Bademantel; — *tub*, die Badewanne.
bathe [beið], *v.n.* baden; *bathing pool*, das Schwimmbad; *bathing suit*, der Badeanzug.
batman ['bætmən], *s.* der Offiziersbursche.
baton ['bætən], *s.* der Stab.
batsman ['bætsmən], *s.* der Schläger (*cricket*).
batten [bætn], *s.* die Holzlatte. — *v.a.* mästen, füttern. — *v.n.* fett werden.
batter ['bætə], *s.* der Schlagteig. — *v.a.* schlagen, zertrümmern; —*ing ram*, (*Mil.*) der Sturmbock.
battery ['bætəri], *s.* die Batterie.
battle [bætl], *s.* die Schlacht; — *cruiser*, der Schlachtkreuzer; —*ship*, das Schlachtschiff. — *v.n.* kämpfen (*for*, um).
Bavarian [bəˈvɛəriən], *adj.* bayrisch. — *s.* der Bayer.
bawl [bɔːl], *v.n.* plärren, schreien.
bay (1) [bei], *adj.* rötlich braun.
bay (2) [bei], *s.* die Bucht, Bai; — *window*, das Erkerfenster.
bay (3) [bei], *s. keep at —*, in Schach halten, *stand at —*, sich zur Wehr setzen.
bay (4) [bei], *s.* (*Bot.*) der Lorbeer.
bay (5) [bei], *v.n.* bellen, heulen; — *for the moon*, das Unmögliche wollen.
bayonet ['beiənet], *s.* das Bajonett.
bazaar [bəˈzɑː], *s.* der Basar.
be [biː], *v.n. irr.* sein, existieren; sich befinden; vorhanden sein; — *off*, sich fortmachen (*move*); ungenießbar sein (*meat, food*); nicht mehr da sein (— *off the menu*).
beach [biːtʃ], *s.* der Strand, das Gestade.
beacon ['biːkən], *s.* das Leuchtfeuer; der Leuchtturm; das Lichtsignal.
bead [biːd], *s.* das Tröpfchen (*drop*); die Perle (*pearl*); (*pl.*) die Perlschnur; der Rosenkranz.
beadle [biːdl], *s.* (*Univ.*) der Pedell; (*Eccl.*) Kirchendiener.
beagle [biːgl], *s.* der Jagdhund, Spürhund.
beak [biːk], *s.* der Schnabel.
beaker ['biːkə], *s.* der Becher.
beam [biːm], *s.* der Balken (*wood*); der Strahl (*ray*), Glanz. — *v.n.* strahlen.

319

bean

bean [bi:n], *s.* (*Bot.*) die Bohne; *not a —,* keinen Heller *or* Pfennig.

bear (1) [bɛə], *s.* (*Zool.*) der Bär.

bear (2) [bɛə], *v.a. irr.* tragen, ertragen; gebären (*a child*); hegen (*sorrow etc.*). — *v.n. — upon,* drücken auf (*pressure*), Einfluß haben (*effect*); — *up,* geduldig sein.

bearable ['bɛərəbl], *adj.* tragbar, erträglich.

beard [biəd], *s.* der Bart. — *v.a.* trotzen (*Dat.*).

bearded ['biədid], *adj.* bärtig.

bearer ['bɛərə], *s.* der Träger, Überbringer.

bearing ['bɛəriŋ], *s.* das Benehmen, die Haltung (*manner*); (*pl.*) (*Geog.*) die Richtung; *lose o.'s —s,* sich verlaufen; *ball —s,* (*Engin.*) das Kugellager.

bearpit ['bɛəpit], *s.* der Bärenzwinger.

beast [bi:st], *s.* das Tier; die Bestie.

beastliness ['bi:stlinis], *s.* das tierische Benehmen; die Grausamkeit (*cruelty*); die Gemeinheit.

beastly ['bi:stli], *adj.* grausam, (*coll.*) schrecklich.

beat [bi:t], *s.* der Schlag, das Schlagen; (*Mus.*) der Takt; die Runde, das Revier (*patrol district*). — *v.a. irr.* schlagen; — *time,* den Takt schlagen; — *carpets,* Teppich klopfen. — *v.n. — it,* sich davonmachen.

beater ['bi:tə], *s.* (*Hunt.*) der Treiber.

beatify [bi:'ætifai], *v.a.* seligsprechen.

beau [bou], *s.* der Stutzer, Geck.

beautiful ['bju:tiful], *adj.* schön.

beautify ['bju:tifai], *v.a.* schön machen, verschönern.

beauty ['bju:ti], *s.* die Schönheit; — *salon,* der Schönheitssalon; *Sleeping Beauty,* das Dornröschen.

beaver ['bi:və], *s.* (*Zool.*) der Biber.

becalm [bi'ka:m], *v.a.* besänftigen.

because [bi'kɔz], *conj.* weil, da; — *of,* wegen, um … willen.

beck [bek], *s.* der Wink; *be at s.o.'s — and call,* jemandem zu Gebote stehen.

beckon ['bekən], *v.a., v.n.* winken, heranwinken, zuwinken (*Dat.*).

become [bi'kʌm], *v.n. irr.* werden. — *v.a.* anstehen, sich schicken, passen (*Dat.*).

becoming [bi'kʌmiŋ], *adj.* passend, kleidsam.

bed [bed], *s.* das Bett; Beet (*flowers*); (*Geol.*) das Lager, die Schicht. — *v.a.* betten, einbetten.

bedaub [bi'dɔ:b], *v.a.* beflecken, beschmieren.

bedding ['bediŋ], *s.* das Bettzeug.

bedevil [bi'devəl], *v.a.* behexen, verhexen.

bedew [bi'dju:], *v.a.* betauen.

bedlam ['bedləm], *s.* (*coll.*) das Irrenhaus; *this is —,* die Hölle ist los.

Bedouin [beduin], *s.* der Beduine.

bedpost ['bedpoust], *s.* der Bettpfosten.

bedraggle [bi'drægl], *v.a.* beschmutzen.

bedridden ['bedridn], *adj.* bettlägerig, ans Bett gefesselt.

bedroom ['bedru:m], *s.* das Schlafzimmer.

bedtime ['bedtaim], *s.* die Schlafenszeit.

bee [bi:], *s.* (*Ent.*) die Biene; *have a — in o.'s bonnet,* einen Vogel haben.

beech [bi:tʃ], *s.* (*Bot.*) die Buche.

beef [bi:f], *s.* das Rindfleisch; — *tea,* die Fleischbrühe.

beehive ['bi:haiv], *s.* der Bienenkorb.

beeline ['bi:lain], *s.* die Luftlinie, gerade Linie; *make a — for s.th.,* schnurstracks auf etwas losgehen.

beer [biə], *s.* das Bier; *small —,* Dünnbier, (*fig.*) unbedeutend.

beet [bi:t], *s.* (*Bot.*) die Runkelrübe; *sugar —,* die Zuckerrübe.

beetle [bi:tl], *s.* (*Ent.*) der Käfer; — *brows,* buschige Augenbrauen.

beetroot [bi:'tru:t], *s.* (*Bot.*) die rote Rübe.

befall [bi'fɔ:l], *v.a. irr.* widerfahren (*Dat.*). — *v.n.* zustoßen (*happen, Dat.*).

befit [bi'fit], *v.a.* sich geziemen, sich gebühren.

befog [bi'fɔg], *v.a.* in Nebel hüllen; umnebeln.

before [bi'fɔ:], *adv.* vorn; voraus, voran; (*previously*) vorher, früher; (*already*) bereits, schon. — *prep.* vor. — *conj.* bevor, ehe.

beforehand [bi'fɔ:hænd], *adv.* im voraus, vorher.

befoul [bi'faul], *v.a.* beschmutzen.

befriend [bi'frend], *v.a.* befreunden, unterstützen (*support*).

beg [beg], *v.a., v.n.* betteln (um, *for*); ersuchen, bitten (*request*).

beget [bi'get], *v.a. irr.* zeugen.

beggar ['begə], *s.* der Bettler.

begin [bi'gin], *v.a., v.n. irr.* beginnen, anfangen.

beginner [bi'ginə], *s.* der Anfänger.

beginning [bi'giniŋ], *s.* der Anfang.

begone [bi'gɔn], *interj.* hinweg! fort! mach dich fort!

begrudge [bi'grʌdʒ], *v.a.* nicht gönnen, mißgönnen.

beguile [bi'gail], *v.a.* bestricken, betrügen; — *the time,* die Zeit vertreiben.

behalf [bi'ha:f], *s. on — of,* um … (*Genit.*) willen; im Interesse von, im Namen von.

behave [bi'heiv], *v.n.* sich benehmen, sich betragen.

behaviour [bi'heivjə], *s.* das Benehmen, Gebaren.

behead [bi'hed], *v.a.* enthaupten.

behind [bi'haind], *adv.* hinten, zurück; hinterher. — *prep.* hinter.

behindhand [bi'haindhænd], *adj., adv.* im Rückstand (*in arrears*); zurück (*backward*).

behold [bi'hould], *v.a. irr.* ansehen; er blicken; *lo and — !* siehe da!

beholden [bi'houldən], *adj.* verpflichtet (*to, Dat.*).

beholder [bi'houldə], *s.* der Zuschauer.

better

behove [bi'houv], *v.a.* sich geziemen, ziemen, gebühren.

being ['bi:iŋ], *pres. part for the time* —, vorläufig, für jetzt. — *s.* das Sein, die Existenz; das Wesen (*creature*).

belated [bi'leitid], *adj.* verspätet.

belch [beltʃ], *v.n.* rülpsen, aufstoßen.

belfry ['belfri], *s.* der Glockenturm.

Belgian ['beldʒən], *adj.* belgisch. — *s.* der Belgier.

belie [bi'lai], *v.a.* täuschen, Lügen strafen.

belief [bi'li:f], *s.* der Glaube, die Meinung.

believable [bi'li:vəbl], *adj.* glaubhaft, glaublich.

believe [bi'li:v], *v.a., v.n.* glauben (*an*, *Acc.*), vertrauen (*Dat.*).

believer [bi'li:və], *s.* der Gläubige.

belittle [bi'litl], *v.a.* schmälern, verkleinern, verächtlich machen.

bell [bel], *s.* die Glocke; Schelle, Klingel; — -*founder*, der Glockengießer; — -*boy*, (*Am.*) —*hop*, der Hotelpage.

belligerent [bi'lidʒərənt], *adj.* kriegführend. — *s.* der Kriegführende.

bellow ['belou], *v.n.* brüllen. — *s.* das Gebrüll.

bellows ['belouz], *s.* der Blasebalg.

belly ['beli], *s.* der Bauch.

belong [bi'lɔŋ], *v.n.* gehören (*Dat.*), angehören (*Dat.*).

belongings [bi'lɔŋiŋz], *s. pl.* die Habe, das Hab und Gut, der Besitz.

beloved [bi'lʌvd, -vid], *adj.* geliebt, lieb.

below [bi'lou], *adv.* unten. — *prep.* unterhalb (*Genit.*), unter (*Dat.*).

Belshazzar [bel'ʃæzə], Belsazar, *m.*

belt [belt], *s.* der Gürtel, Gurt; der Riemen; (*Tech.*) Treibriemen; *below the* —, unfair. — *v.a.* umgürten; (*coll.*) prügeln.

bemoan [bi'moun], *v.a.* beklagen.

bench [bentʃ], *s.* die Bank; der Gerichtshof (*court of law*); *Queen's Bench*, der oberste Gerichtshof.

bend [bend], *v.a., v.n. irr.* biegen; beugen; sich krümmen. — *s.* die Biegung, Krümmung, Kurve.

bendable ['bendəbl], *adj.* biegsam.

beneath [bi'ni:θ] *see below*.

Benedictine [beni'dikti:n], *s.* der Benediktiner.

benediction [beni'dikʃən], *s.* der Segensspruch, der Segen; die Segnung.

benefaction [beni'fækʃən], *s.* die Wohltat.

benefactor ['benifæktə], *s.* der Wohltäter.

benefactress ['benifæktris], *s.* die Wohltäterin.

beneficent [be'nefisənt], *adj.* wohltätig.

beneficial [beni'fiʃəl], *adj.* vorteilhaft, gut (*for*, für), wohltuend.

benefit ['benifit], *s.* der Vorteil, Nutzen. — *v.n.* Nutzen ziehen. — *v.a.* nützen.

benevolence [be'nevələns], *s.* das Wohlwollen.

benevolent [be'nevələnt], *adj.* wohlwollend; — *society*, der Unterstützungsverein; — *fund*, der Unterstützungsfond.

Bengali [ben'gɔ:li], *adj.* bengalisch. — *s.* der Bengale.

benign [bi'nain], *adj.* gütig, mild.

bent [bent], *adj.* gebogen, krumm; — *on something*, versessen auf etwas. — *s.* die Neigung, der Hang; — *for*, Vorliebe für.

benzene [benzi:n], *s.* das Benzol, Kohlenbenzin.

benzine ['benzi:n], *s.* das Benzin.

bequeath [bi'kwi:θ], *v.a.* vermachen, hinterlassen.

bequest [bi'kwest], *s.* das Vermächtnis.

bereave [bi'ri:v], *v.a. irr.* berauben (durch Tod).

bereavement [bi'ri:vmənt], *s.* der Verlust (durch Tod).

beret ['berei], *s.* die Baskenmütze.

Bernard ['bə:nəd], Bernhard, *m.*; *St.* — *dog*, der Bernhardiner.

berry ['beri], *s.* die Beere.

berth [bə:θ], *s.* (*Naut.*) der Ankerplatz; die Koje. — *v.a., v.n.* anlegen; vor Anker gehen (*boat*).

beseech [bi'si:tʃ], *v.a. irr.* bitten, anflehen.

beset [bi'set], *v.a. irr.* bedrängen, bedrücken, umringen.

beside [bi'said], *prep.* außer, neben, nahe bei; — *the point*, unwesentlich; *quite* — *the mark*, weit vom Schuß.

besides [bi'saidz], *adv.* überdies, außerdem.

besiege [bi'si:dʒ], *v.a.* belagern.

besmirch [bi'smə:tʃ], *v.a.* besudeln.

besom ['bi:zəm], *s.* der Besen.

bespatter [bi'spætə], *v.a.* bespritzen.

bespeak [bi'spi:k], *v.a. irr.* bestellen; (*Tail.*) *bespoke*, nach Maß gemacht or angefertigt.

best [best], *adj.* (*superl. of good*) best; — *adv.* am besten. — *s. want the* — *of both worlds*, alles haben wollen; *to the* — *of my ability*, nach besten Kräften; *to the* — *of my knowledge*, soviel ich weiß.

bestial ['bestjəl], *adj.* bestialisch, tierisch.

bestow [bi'stou], *v.a.* verleihen, erteilen.

bet [bet], *s.* die Wette. — *v.a., v.n. irr.* wetten.

betray [bi'trei], *v.a.* verraten.

betrayal [bi'treiəl], *s.* der Verrat.

betrayer [bi'treiə], *s.* der Verräter.

betroth [bi'trouð], *v.a.* verloben.

betrothal [bi'trouðəl], *s.* die Verlobung.

better ['betə], *adj.* (*comp. of good*) besser. — *adv. you had* — *go*, es wäre besser, Sie gingen; *think* — *of it*, sich eines Besseren besinnen, sich's überlegen. — *s. get the* — *of*, überwinden; *so much the* —, desto *or* umso besser. — *v.a.* verbessern; — *oneself*, seine Lage verbessern.

321

betterment

betterment ['betəmənt], *s.* die Verbesserung.

between [bi'twi:n], *adv.* dazwischen. — *prep.* zwischen; unter (*among*).

bevel ['bevəl], *s.* der Winkelpasser; die Schräge. — *v.a.* abkanten.

beverage ['bevəridʒ], *s.* das Getränk.

bevy ['bevi], *s.* die Schar (*of beauties*, von Schönen).

bewail [bi'weil], *v.a.*, *v.n.* betrauern, beweinen; trauern um.

beware [bi'wɛə], *v.n.* sich hüten (*of*, vor).

bewilder [bi'wildə], *v.a.* verwirren.

bewitch [bi'witʃ], *v.a.* bezaubern.

beyond [bi'jɔnd], *adv.* jenseits, drüben. — *prep.* über … hinaus; jenseits; außer.

biannual [bai'ænjuəl], *adj.* halbjährlich.

bias ['baiəs], *s.* die Neigung; das Vorurteil (*prejudice*). — *v.a.* beeinflussen.

bias(s)ed ['baiəsd], *adj.* voreingenommen.

bib [bib], *s.* der Schürzenlatz; das Lätzchen.

Bible [baibl], *s.* die Bibel.

Biblical ['biblikəl], *adj.* biblisch.

bibliography [bibli'ɔgrəfi], *s.* die Bibliographie.

bibliophile ['bibliəfail], *s.* der Bücherfreund.

biceps ['baiseps], *s.* der Bizeps, Armmuskel.

bicker ['bikə], *v.n.* zanken, hadern.

bickering ['bikəriŋ], *s.* das Gezänk, Hadern, der Hader.

bicycle ['baisikl], (*coll.*) **bike** [baik], *s.* das Fahrrad.

bicyclist ['baisiklist], *s.* der Radfahrer.

bid [bid], *v.a.*, *v.n.* irr. gebieten, befehlen (*Dat.*) (*order*); bieten (*at auction*); — *farewell*, Lebewohl sagen. — *s.* das Gebot, Angebot (*at auction*).

bidding ['bidiŋ], *s.* der Befehl (*order*); das Bieten (*at auction*); die Einladung (*invitation*).

bide [baid], *v.n.* irr. verbleiben, verharren (*in*, *by*, bei).

biennial [bai'eniəl], *adj.* zweijährig, alle zwei Jahre.

bier [biə], *s.* die Bahre, Totenbahre.

big [big], *adj.* groß, dick (*fat*); *talking* —, großsprecherisch; *talk* —, prahlen.

bigamy ['bigəmi], *s.* die Bigamie, die Doppelehe.

bigness ['bignis], *s.* die Größe, Dicke.

bigoted ['bigətid], *adj.* bigott, fanatisch.

bigotry ['bigətri], *s.* die Bigotterie.

bigwig ['bigwig], *s.* (*coll.*) die vornehme Person, der Würdenträger.

bike *see* bicycle.

bilberry ['bilbəri], *s.* (*Bot.*) die Heidelbeere.

bile [bail], *s.* die Galle.

bilge [bildʒ], *s.* die Bilge, der Schiffsboden; (*coll.*) Unsinn (*nonsense*).

bilious ['biljəs], *adj.* gallig.

bill (1) [bil], *s.* der Schnabel (*bird*).

bill (2) [bil], die Rechnung (*account*); — *of exchange*, der Wechsel; — *of entry*, die Zolldeklaration; — *of fare*, die Speisekarte; (*Parl.*) der Gesetzentwurf; das Plakat (*poster*). — *v.a.* anzeigen.

billboard ['bilbɔːd], *s.* (*Am.*) das Anschlagbrett.

billet ['bilit], *s.* das Billett (*card*); das Quartier, die Unterkunft (*army*).

billfold ['bilfould], *s.* (*Am.*) die Brieftasche.

billhook ['bilhuk], *s.* die Hippe.

billiards ['biljədz], *s.* das Billardspiel.

billow ['bilou], *s.* die Woge. — *v.n.* wogen.

bin [bin], *s.* der Behälter.

bind [baind], *v.a.* irr. binden, verpflichten; (*Law*) — *over*, zu gutem Benehmen verpflichten.

binder ['baində], *s.* der Binder, Buchbinder.

bindery ['baindəri], *s.* die Buchbinderei, Binderwerkstatt.

binding ['baindiŋ], *s.* der Einband.

binnacle ['binəkl], *s.* das Kompaßhäuschen.

binocular [bi'nɔkjulə], *adj.* für beide Augen. — *s.* (*pl.*) das Fernglas, der Feldstecher.

binomial [bai'noumiəl], *adj.* binomisch. — *s.* (*pl.*) (*Maths.*) das Binom, der zweigliedrige Ausdruck.

biochemical [baio'kemikəl], *adj.* biochemisch.

biochemistry [baio'kemistri], *s.* die Biochemie.

biographer [bai'ɔgrəfə], *s.* der Biograph.

biographical [baio'græfikəl], *adj.* biographisch.

biography [bai'ɔgrəfi], *s.* die Biographie, die Lebensbeschreibung.

biological [baio'lɔdʒikəl], *adj.* biologisch.

biology [bai'ɔlədʒi], *s.* die Biologie.

biometric(al) [baio'metrik(əl)], *adj.* biometrisch.

biometry [bai'ɔmitri], *s.* die Biometrie.

biophysical [baio'fizikəl], *adj.* biophysisch.

biophysics [baio'fiziks], *s.* die Biophysik.

biped ['baiped], *s.* der Zweifüßler.

biplane ['baiplein], *s.* (*Aviat.*) der Doppeldecker.

birch [bəːtʃ], *s.* (*Bot.*) die Birke; die Birkenrute, Rute (*cane*). — *v.a.* (mit der Rute) züchtigen.

bird [bəːd], *s.* der Vogel; — *of passage*, der Wandervogel, Zugvogel; —*cage*, der Vogelkäfig, das Vogelbauer; —*fancier*, der Vogelzüchter; —*'s-eye view*, die Vogelperspektive.

birth [bəːθ], *s.* die Geburt; — *certificate*, der Geburtsschein.

birthday ['bəːθdei], *s.* der Geburtstag.

biscuit ['biskit], *s.* der *or* das Keks; der Zwieback.

bisect [bai'sekt], *v.a.* entzweischneiden, halbieren.

bisection [bai'sekʃən], *s.* die Zweiteilung, Halbierung.

bishop ['biʃəp], *s.* der Bischof; (*Chess*) der Läufer.

bishopric ['biʃəprik], *s.* das Bistum.

bismuth ['bizməθ], *s.* der *or* das Wismut.

bison ['baisən], *s.* (*Zool.*) der Bison.

bit [bit], *s.* der Bissen (*bite*), das Bißchen (*little* —); das Gebiß (*bridle*); der Bart (*of* key).

bitch [bitʃ], *s.* die Hündin.

bite [bait], *v.a. irr.* beißen. — *s.* das Beißen (*mastication*); der Biß (*morsel*).

biting ['baitiŋ], *adj.* (*also fig.*) beißend, scharf. — *adv.* — *cold*, bitterkalt.

bitter ['bitə], *adj.* bitter.

bitterness ['bitənis], *s.* die Bitterkeit.

bittern ['bitə:n], *s.* (*Orn.*) die Rohrdommel.

bitumen [bi'tju:mən], *s.* der Bergteer, Asphalt.

bivouac ['bivuæk], *s.* (*Mil.*) das Biwak, Lager.

bizarre [bi'za:], *adj.* bizarr, wunderlich.

blab [blæb], *v.a., v.n.* schwatzen, ausplaudern (*give away*).

blabber ['blæbə], *s.* (*coll.*) der Schwätzer.

black [blæk], *adj.* schwarz; — *sheep*, der Taugenichts; — *pudding*, die Blutwurst; *Black Forest*, der Schwarzwald; *Black Maria*, der Polizeiwagen; (*coll.*) die grüne Minna; *Black Sea*, das schwarze Meer.

blackberry ['blækbəri], *s.* (*Bot.*) die Brombeere.

blackbird ['blækbə:d], *s.* (*Orn.*) die Amsel.

blackguard ['blæga:d], *s.* der Spitzbube, Schurke.

blackmail ['blækmeil], *v.a.* erpressen. — *s.* die Erpressung.

bladder ['blædə], *s.* (*Anat.*) die Blase.

blacksmith ['blæksmiθ], *s.* der Grobschmied.

blade [bleid], *s.* die Klinge (*razor*); der Halm (*grass*); *shoulder* —, das Schulterblatt.

blamable ['bleiməbl], *adj.* tadelnswert, tadelhaft.

blame [bleim], *s.* der Tadel, die Schuld. — *v.a.* tadeln, beschuldigen, die Schuld zuschreiben (*Dat.*).

blameless ['bleimlis], *adj.* tadellos, schuldlos.

blanch [bla:ntʃ], *v.n.* erbleichen, weiß werden. — *v.a.* weiß machen.

bland [blænd], *adj.* mild, sanft.

blandish ['blændiʃ], *v.a.* schmeicheln (*Dat.*).

blandishment ['blændiʃmənt], *s.* (*mostly in pl.*) die Schmeichelei.

blandness ['blændnis], *s.* die Milde, Sanftheit.

blank [blæŋk], *adj.* blank, leer; reimlos (*verse*); *leave a* —, einen Raum freilassen; — *cartridge*, die Platzpatrone.

blanket ['blæŋkit], *s.* die Decke; (*coll.*) *a wet* —, ein langweiliger Kerl, der Spielverderber.

blare [bleə], *v.n.* schmettern.

blaspheme [blæs'fi:m], *v.a., v.n.* lästern, fluchen.

blasphemous ['blæsfiməs], *adj.* lästerlich.

blasphemy ['blæsfəmi], *s.* die Gotteslästerung.

blast [bla:st], *v.a.* sprengen, zerstören. — *s.* der Windstoß (*gust*); der Stoß (*trumpets*); die Explosion (*bomb*); — *furnace*, der Hochofen. — *excl.* (*sl.*) —! zum Teufel!

blasting ['bla:stiŋ], *s.* das Sprengen.

blatant ['bleitənt], *adj.* laut, lärmend, dreist.

blaze [bleiz], *s.* die Flamme (*flame*); das Feuer; der Glanz (*colour etc.*). — *v.n.* flammen; leuchten (*shine*). — *v.a.* ausposaunen, bekannt machen (*make known*).

blazer ['bleizə], *s.* die Sportjacke, Klubjacke.

blazon ['bleizən], *v.a.* verkünden.

bleach [bli:tʃ], *v.a.* bleichen. — *s.* das Bleichmittel.

bleak [bli:k], *adj.* öde, rauh; trübe, freudlos.

bleakness ['bli:knis], *s.* die Öde (*scenery*), Traurigkeit, Trübheit.

bleary ['bliəri], *adj.* trübe; — *eyed*, triefäugig.

bleat [bli:t], *v.n.* blöken.

bleed [bli:d], *v.n. irr.* bluten. — *v.a.* bluten lassen; erpressen (*blackmail*).

blemish ['blemiʃ], *s.* der Makel, der Fehler. — *v.a.* schänden, entstellen.

blench [blentʃ], *v.n.* zurückweichen, stutzen.

blend [blend], *v.a., v.n.* mischen, vermengen; sich mischen. — *s.* die Mischung, Vermischung.

bless [bles], *v.a.* segnen; beglücken; loben.

blessed [blest, 'blesid], *adj.* gesegnet, selig.

blessing ['blesiŋ], *s.* der Segen.

blight [blait], *s.* der Meltau. — *v.a.* verderben.

blind [blaind], *adj.* blind; — *man's buff*, Blinde Kuh; — *spot*, der schwache Punkt. — *s.* die Blende, das Rouleau; *Venetian* —, die Jalousie. — *v.a.* blind machen, täuschen.

blindfold ['blaindfould], *adj.* mit verbundenen Augen.

blindness ['blaindnis], *s.* die Blindheit.

blindworm ['blaindwə:m], *s.* (*Zool.*) die Blindschleiche.

blink [bliŋk], *s.* das Blinzeln. — *v.n.* blinzeln, blinken. — *v.a.* nicht sehen wollen.

blinkers ['bliŋkəz], *s. pl.* die Scheuklappen.

bliss [blis], *s.* die Wonne, Seligkeit.

blissful ['blisful], *adj.* wonnig, selig.

blister ['blistə], *s.* die Blase. — *v.n.* Blasen ziehen, Blasen bekommen.

blithe [blaið], *adj.* munter, lustig, fröhlich.

blitheness ['blaiðnis], *s.* die Munterkeit, Fröhlichkeit.

blizzard ['blizəd], *s.* der Schneesturm.

bloated ['bloutid], *adj.* aufgeblasen, aufgedunsen.

bloater ['bloutə], *s.* (*Zool.*) der Bückling.

blob [blɔb], *s.* der Kleks.

block [blɔk], *s.* der Block, Klotz (*wood*); Häuserblock (*houses*); — *letters*, große Druckschrift. — *v.a.* blockieren, hemmen (*hinder*); sperren (*road*).

blockade [blɔ'keid], *s.* die Blockade.

blockhead ['blɔkhed], *s.* der Dummkopf.

blonde [blɔnd], *adj.* blond. — *s.* die Blondine.

blood [blʌd], *s.* das Blut; — *vessel*, das Blutgefäß.

bloodcurdling ['blʌdkə:dliŋ], *adj.* haarsträubend.

bloodless ['blʌdlis], *adj.* blutlos, unblutig.

bloodthirsty ['blʌdθə:sti], *adj.* blutdürstig.

bloody ['blʌdi], *adj.* blutig; (*vulg.*) verflucht.

bloom [blu:m], *s.* die Blüte; die Blume. — *v.n.* blühen.

bloomers ['blu:məz], *s. pl.* altmodische Unterhosen für Damen.

blooming ['blu:miŋ], *adj.* blühend.

blossom ['blɔsəm], *s.* die Blüte. — *v.n.* blühen, Blüten treiben.

blot [blɔt], *s.* der Kleks; Fleck; (*fig.*) der Schandfleck. — *v.a.* beflecken; löschen (*ink*); — *out*, ausmerzen, austilgen; *blotting paper*, das Löschpapier.

blotch [blɔtʃ], *s.* der Hautfleck; die Pustel; der Kleks (*blot*).

blotter ['blɔtə], *s.* der Löscher.

blouse [blauz], *s.* die Bluse.

blow (1) [blou], *s.* der Schlag.

blow (2) [blou], *v.a. irr.* blasen, wehen; — *o.'s own trumpet*, prahlen; anfachen (*fire*); — *o.'s nose*, sich schneuzen. — *v.n.* schnaufen, keuchen; — *up*, in die Luft sprengen.

blower ['blouə], *s.* das Gebläse; der Bläser.

blowpipe ['bloupaip], *s.* das Lötrohr.

blubber ['blʌbə], *s.* der Walfischspeck, der Tran. — *v.n.* schluchzen, heulen, flennen.

bludgeon ['blʌdʒən], *s.* der Knüppel; die Keule (*club*). — *v.a.* niederschlagen.

blue [blu:], *adj.* blau; schwermütig (*sad*); — *blooded*, aus edlem Geblüte.

bluebell ['blu:bel], *s.* (*Bot.*) die Glockenblume.

bluebottle ['blu:bɔtl], *s.* (*Ent.*) die Schmeißfliege.

bluestocking ['blu:stɔkiŋ], *s.* der Blaustrumpf.

bluff [blʌf], *adj.* grob, schroff. — *s.* der Bluff, die Täuschung, der Trick. — *v.a., v.n.* vortäuschen (*pretend*), bluffen; verblüffen (*deceive*).

blunder ['blʌndə], *s.* der Fehler, Schnitzer. — *v.n.* einen Fehler machen.

blunderer ['blʌndərə], *s.* der Tölpel.

blunderbuss ['blʌndəbʌs], *s.* die Donnerbüchse.

blunt [blʌnt], *adj.* stumpf (*edge*); derb, offen (*speech*). — *v.a.* abstumpfen; verderben (*appetite*).

bluntness ['blʌntnis], *s.* die Stumpfheit (*edge*); die Derbheit (*speech*).

blur [blə:], *s.* der Fleck. — *v.a.* verwischen.

blurt [blə:t], *v.a.* — *out*, herausplatzen.

blush [blʌʃ], *v.n.* erröten. — *s.* die Schamröte, das Erröten.

bluster ['blʌstə], *s.* das Toben, Brausen. — *v.n.* toben, brausen.

blustering ['blʌstəriŋ], *adj.* lärmend, tobend.

boa ['bouə], *s.* (*Zool.*) die Boa.

boar [bɔ:], *s.* (*Zool.*) der Eber.

board [bɔ:d], *s.* das Brett (*wood*); die Tafel (*notice* —); die Verpflegung (*food*); — *and lodging*, die Vollpension; die Behörde, der Ausschuß (*officials*). — *v.a.* — *up*, vernageln, zumachen; — *someone*, verpflegen; — *a steamer*, an Bord gehen; — *ing school*, das Internat, das Pensionat.

boarder ['bɔ:də], *s.* der Internatsschüler; der Pensionär.

boast [boust], *v.n.* prahlen, sich rühmen. — *s.* der Stolz (*pride*).

boastful ['boustful], *adj.* prahlerisch.

boat [bout], *s.* das Boot; *rowing* —, das Ruderboot; der Kahn.

bob [bɔb], *s.* der Knicks; (*coll.*) der Schilling. — *v.n.* baumeln; springen; *bobbed hair*, der Bubikopf.

bobbin ['bɔbin], *s.* die Spule, der Klöppel.

bobsleigh ['bɔbslei], *s.* der Bob(sleigh), Rennschlitten.

bodice ['bɔdis], *s.* das Mieder, Leibchen.

bodied ['bɔdid], *adj. suffix; able-* —, gesund, stark.

body ['bɔdi], *s.* der Körper; die Körperschaft (*organisation*).

bodyguard ['bɔdiga:d], *s.* die Leibwache.

Boer ['bouə], *s.* der Bure.

bog [bɔg], *s.* der Sumpf. — *v.a.* (*coll.*) — *down*, einsinken.

Bohemian [bo'hi:miən], *s.* der Böhme. — *adj.* böhmisch; künstlerhaft.

boil (1) [bɔil], *v.a., v.n.* kochen, sieden. — *s.* das Kochen; — *ing point*, der Siedepunkt.

boil (2) [bɔil], *s.* (*Med.*) die Beule, der Furunkel.

boisterous ['bɔistərəs], *adj.* ungestüm; laut (*noisy*).

boisterousness ['bɔistərəsnis], *s.* die Heftigkeit, Lautheit.

bound

bold [bould], *adj.* kühn, dreist; *make —*, sich erkühnen.

boldness ['bouldnis], *s.* die Kühnheit, Dreistigkeit.

Bolivian [bə'liviən], *adj.* bolivianisch. *—s.* der Bolivianer.

bolster ['boulstə], *s.* das Polster, Kissen.

bolt [boult], *s.* der Bolzen, Riegel (*on door*); der Pfeil (*arrow*). — *v.a.* verriegeln (*bar*); verschlingen (*devour*). — *v.n.* davonlaufen (*run away*), durchgehen (*abscond*).

bomb [bɔm], *s.* die Bombe. — *v.a.* bombardieren.

bombard [bɔm'ba:d], *v.a.* bombardieren.

bombardment [bɔm'ba:dmənt], *s.* die Beschießung.

bombastic [bɔm'bæstik], *adj.* schwülstig, bombastisch (*style*).

bombproof ['bɔmpru:f], *adj.* bombensicher.

bond [bɔnd], *s.* das Band (*link*); die Schuldverschreibung (*debt*); *in —*, unter Zollverschluß; (*pl.*) die Fesseln (*fetters*). — *v.a.* (*Chem.*) binden; (*Comm.*) zollpflichtig erklären (*declare dutiable*).

bondage ['bɔndidʒ], *s.* die Knechtschaft.

bone [boun], *s.* der Knochen; die Gräte (*fish*); *— china*, feines Geschirr, das Porzellan; *— of contention*, der Zankapfel; *— dry*, staubtrocken; *— idle*, stinkfaul; *— lace*, die Klöppelspitze. — *v.a.* Knochen oder Gräten entfernen.

bonfire ['bɔnfaiə], *s.* das Freudenfeuer.

bonnet ['bɔnit], *s.* die Haube, das Häubchen.

bonny ['bɔni], *adj.* hübsch, nett.

bony ['bouni], *adj.* beinern, knöchern.

book [buk], *s.* das Buch. — *v.a.* belegen (*seat*); eine Karte lösen (*ticket*); engagieren (*engage*).

bookbinder ['bukbaində], *s.* der Buchbinder.

bookcase ['bukkeis], *s.* der Bücherschrank.

bookie *see* **bookmaker**.

booking-office ['bukiŋɔfis], *s.* der Fahrkartenschalter; die Kasse (*Theat. etc.*)

book-keeper ['bukki:pə], *s.* der Buchhalter.

book-keeping ['bukki:piŋ], *s.* die Buchhaltung; *double entry —*, doppelte Buchführung, *single entry —*, einfache Buchführung.

bookmaker ['bukmeikə] (*abbr.* **bookie** ['buki]), *s.* (*Racing*) der Buchmacher.

bookmark(er) ['bukma:k(ə)], *s.* das Lesezeichen.

bookseller ['buksɛlə], *s.* der Buchhändler.

bookshop ['bukʃɔp], *s.* die Buchhandlung.

bookstall ['bukstɔ:l], *s.* der Bücherstand.

bookworm ['bukwə:m], *s.* der Bücherwurm.

boom (1) [bu:m], *s.* der Aufschwung; Boom; (*Comm.*) die Konjunktur; Hausse.

boom (2) [bu:m], *v.n.* dröhnen, (dumpf) schallen.

boon [bu:n], *s.* die Wohltat.

boor [buə], *s.* der Lümmel.

boorish ['buəriʃ], *adj.* lümmelhaft.

boot [bu:t], *s.* der Stiefel, hohe Schuh. — *v.a.* mit dem Stiefel stoßen, kicken.

booth [bu:ð], *s.* die Bude, Zelle (*Teleph.*).

bootlace ['bu:tleis], *s.* der Schnürsenkel, der Schnürriemen.

booty ['bu:ti], *s.* die Beute.

booze [bu:z], *v.n.* (*coll.*) saufen.

boozy ['bu:zi], *adj.* (*coll.*) angeheitert, leicht betrunken.

border ['bɔ:də], *s.* der Rand; die Grenze. — *v.a., v.n.* angrenzen (*on*); einsäumen (*surround*).

borderer ['bɔ:dərə], *s.* der Grenzbewohner.

bore [bɔ:], *v.a.* bohren; langweilen (*be boring*). — *s.* das Bohrloch (*drill-hole*), die Bohrung (*drilling*); der langweilige Kerl (*person*).

boredom ['bɔ:dəm], *s.* die Langeweile.

borer ['bɔ:rə], *s.* der Bohrer (*drill*).

born [bɔ:n], *adj.* geboren.

borrow ['bɔrou], *v.a.* borgen, entlehnen.

borrowing ['bɔrouiŋ], *s.* das Borgen, Entlehnen.

bosom ['buzəm], *s.* der Busen.

boss [bɔs], *s.* der Beschlag, der Buckel; (*coll.*) der Chef.

botanical [bo'tænikəl], *adj.* botanisch.

botanist ['bɔtənist], *s.* der Botaniker.

botany ['bɔtəni], *s.* die Botanik.

botch [bɔtʃ], *s.* das Flickwerk. — *v.a.* verderben, verhunzen.

both [bouθ], *adj., pron.* beide, beides; *— of them*, beide. — *conj.* ... *and*, sowohl ... als auch.

bother ['bɔðə], *v.a.* plagen, stören, belästigen; *— it!* zum Henker damit! — *v.n.* sich bemühen. — *s.* die Belästigung, das Ärgernis.

bottle [bɔtl], *s.* die Flasche. — *v.a.* in Flaschen abfüllen.

bottom ['bɔtəm], *s.* der Boden, Grund (*ground*); die Ursache (*cause*); (*Naut.*) der Schiffsboden.

bottomless ['bɔtəmlis], *adj.* grundlos, bodenlos.

bough [bau], *s.* der Zweig, Ast.

boulder ['bouldə], *s.* der Felsblock.

bounce [bauns], *v.a.* aufprallen lassen (*ball*). — *v.n.* aufprallen. — *s.* der Rückprall, Aufprall.

bound (1) [baund], *s.* der Sprung; *by leaps and —s*, sehr schnell, sprunghaft. — *v.n.* springen, prallen.

bound (2) [baund], *v.a.* begrenzen, einschränken. — *adj.* verpflichtet; *— to* (*inf.*), wird sicherlich ...

325

bound

bound (3) [baund], *adj.* — *for*, auf
dem Wege nach.

boundary ['baundəri], *s.* die Grenzlinie,
Grenze.

bounder ['baundə], *s.* der ungezogene
Bursche.

boundless ['baundlis], *adj.* grenzenlos,
unbegrenzt.

bounteous ['bauntiəs], *adj.* freigebig;
reichlich (*plenty*).

bounty ['baunti], *s.* die Freigebigkeit
(*generosity*); (*Comm.*) Prämie.

bouquet [bu'kei], *s.* das Bukett, der
Blumenstrauß; die Blume (*wine*).

bourgeois ['buəʒwa:], *s.* der Bürger;
Philister. — *adj.* kleinbürgerlich,
philisterhaft.

bow (1) [bau], *s.* (*Naut.*) der Bug;
—*sprit*, das Bugspriet.

bow (2) [bau], *s.* die Verbeugung,
Verneigung. — *v.n.* sich verneigen,
sich verbeugen. — *v.a.* neigen.

bow (3) [bou], *s.* (*Mus.*) der Bogen;
die Schleife (*ribbon*). — *v.a.* streichen
(*violin*).

bowel ['bauəl], *s.* der Darm; (*pl.*) die
Eingeweide.

bowl (1) [boul], *s.* die Schale, der
Napf, die Schüssel.

bowl (2) [boul], *s.* die Holzkugel; (*pl.*)
das Rasenkugelspiel, Bowlingspiel.
— *v.n.* (*Cricket*) den Ball werfen.

bowler (1) ['boulə], *s.* (*hat*) der steife
Hut, die Melone.

bowler (2) ['boulə], *s.* (*Sport*) der
Ballmann.

box (1) [bɔks], *s.* (*Bot.*) der Buchsbaum.

box (2) [bɔks], *s.* die Büchse, Dose,
Schachtel, der Kasten; (*Theat.*) die
Loge; — *office*, die Theaterkasse.

box (3) [bɔks], *s.* der Schlag; — *on the
ear*, die Ohrfeige. *v.n.* boxen.

boxer ['bɔksə], *s.* der Boxer; Box-
kämpfer.

Boxing Day ['bɔksiŋ'dei], der zweite
Weihnachtstag.

boy [bɔi], *s.* der Junge, Knabe; Diener
(*servant*).

boyish ['bɔiiʃ], *adj.* knabenhaft.

boyhood ['bɔihud], *s.* das Knaben-
alter.

brace [breis], *s.* das Band; die Klammer (*clamp*); — *of partridges*, das Paar
Rebhühner; die Spange (*denture*).
— *v.a.* spannen, straffen. — *v.r.* —
yourself! stähle dich!

bracelet ['breislit], *s.* das Armband.

braces ['breisiz], *s. pl.* die Hosenträger.

bracken ['brækən], *s.* (*Bot.*) das Farnkraut.

bracket ['brækit], *s.* die Klammer;
income —, die Einkommensgruppe.
— *v.a.* (ein-)klammern; (*Maths.*) in
Klammern setzen.

brackish ['brækiʃ], *adj.* salzig.

brad [bræd], *s.* der kopflose Nagel; —
awl, der Vorstechbohrer.

brag [bræg], *v.n.* prahlen.

braggart ['brægət], *s.* der Prahlhans.

Brahmin ['bra:min], *s.* der Brah-
mane.

braid [breid], *s.* die Borte; der Saum-
besatz. — *v.a.* (mit Borten) besetzen.

Braille [breil], *s.* die Blindenschrift.

brain [brein], *s.* das Gehirn, Hirn;
scatter- —*ed*, zerstreut.

brainwave ['breinweiv], *s.* der Geistes-
blitz.

brake [breik], *s.* die Bremse. — *v.a.*
bremsen.

bramble [bræmbl], *s.* der (*Bot.*) Brom-
beerstrauch.

bran [bræn], *s.* die Kleie.

branch [bra:ntʃ], *s.* der Ast, Zweig;
(*Comm.*) die Zweigstelle, Filiale. —
v.n. — *out*, sich verzweigen. — *out
into*, sich ausbreiten, etwas Neues
anfangen; — *off*, abzweigen.

brand [brænd], *s.* der (Feuer) Brand;
das Brandmal (*on skin*); die Sorte,
Marke (*make*); — *new*, funkelnagelneu. — *v.a.* brandmarken, kennzeichnen.

brandish ['brændiʃ], *v.a.* schwingen,
herumschwenken.

brandy ['brændi], *s.* der Branntwein,
Kognac, Weinbrand.

brass [bra:s], *s.* das Messing; — *band*,
die Blechmusik, Militärmusikkapelle;
— *founder*, Erzgießer, Gelbgießer;
(*sl.*) die Frechheit (*impudence*).

brassiere ['bræsiə], *s.* der Büstenhalter.

brat [bræt], *s.* (*coll.*) das Kind, der
Balg.

brave [breiv], *adj.* tapfer, kühn. —
v.a. trotzen, standhalten (*Dat.*). — *s.*
der Held, Krieger; der Indianer
(*redskin*).

bravery ['breivəri], *s.* die Tapferkeit.

brawl [brɔ:l], *s.* der Krawall, die
Rauferei. — *v.n.* zanken, lärmen.

brawn [brɔ:n], *s.* die Sülze; (*fig.*) die
Körperkraft, Stärke.

brawny ['brɔ:ni], *adj.* stark, sehnig.

bray [brei], *v.n.* sagen, Eselslaute
von sich geben (*donkey*). — *s.* das
Iah des Esels, das Eselsgeschrei.

brazen [breizn], *adj.* (*Metall.*) aus
Erz; unverschämt (*shameless*).

brazenfaced ['breiznfeisd], *adj.* unverschämt.

brazier ['breiziə], *s.* der Kupfer-
schmied; die Kohlenpfanne.

Brazil [brə'zil], Brasilien, *n.*; — *nut*, die
Paranuß.

Brazilian [brə'ziliən], *adj.* brasilianisch.
— *s.* der Brasilianer.

breach [bri:tʃ], *s.* die Bresche; der
Bruch (*break*); die Verletzung; der
Vertragsbruch (*of contract*); der
Verstoß (*of*, gegen, *etiquette etc.*).

bread [bred], *s.* das Brot; *brown* —,
das Schwarzbrot; — *and butter*, das
Butterbrot.

breadth [bretθ], *s.* die Breite,
Weite.

326

break [breik], *s.* der Bruch (*breach*); die Lücke (*gap*); die Chance (*chance*); *a lucky* —, ein glücklicher Zufall, ein Glücksfall; die Pause (*from work*). — *v.a.*, *v.n. irr.* brechen; — *off,* Pause machen; — *in,* unterbrechen (*interrupt*); — *in,* (*horse*) einschulen, zureiten; — *up,* abbrechen (*school, work*); — *away,* sich trennen, absondern; — *down,* zusammenbrechen (*health*); (*Am.*) analysieren; auflösen.

breakage ['breikidʒ], *s.* der Bruch, der Schaden (*damage*).

breakdown ['breikdoun], *s.* der Zusammenbruch (*health*); die Panne (*car*); (*Am.*) die Analyse (*analysis*).

breaker ['breikə], *s.* die Brandungswelle, Brandung.

breakfast ['brekfəst], *s.* das Frühstück. *v.n.* frühstücken.

breast [brest], *s.* die Brust.

breath [breθ], *s.* der Atem; der Hauch (*exhalation*); *with bated* —, mit verhaltenem Atem.

breathe [briːð], *v.n.* atmen.

breathing ['briːðiŋ], *s.* die Atmung.

breathless ['breθlis], *adj.* atemlos.

breech [briːtʃ], *s.* der Boden; (*pl.*) die Reithosen, *f. pl.*

breed [briːd], *v.a. irr.* zeugen, züchten (*cattle, etc.*). — *v.n.* sich vermehren. — *s.* die Zucht, die Art (*type*); die Rasse (*race*).

breeder ['briːdə], *s.* der Züchter.

breeding ['briːdiŋ], *s.* die Zucht; die Kinderstube (*manners*); die Erziehung; das Züchten (*of plants, cattle etc.*).

breeze [briːz], *s.* die Brise.

breezy ['briːzi], *adj.* windig; lebhaft (*manner*), beschwingt (*tone*).

brethren ['breðrən], *s. pl.* (*obs.*) die Brüder.

Breton [bretn], *adj.* bretonisch. — *s.* der Bretagner, Bretone.

brevet ['brevit], *s.* das Patent.

breviary ['briːviəri], *s.* das Brevier.

brevity ['breviti], *s.* die Kürze.

brew [bruː], *v.a.* brauen. — *s.* das Gebräu, Bräu (*beer*).

brewer ['bruːə], *s.* der Brauer, Bierbrauer.

brewery ['bruːəri], *s.* die Brauerei, das Brauhaus.

briar, brier ['braiə], *s.* (*Bot.*) der Dornstrauch, die wilde Rose.

bribe [braib], *v.a.* bestechen. — *s.* das Bestechungsgeld.

bribery ['braibəri], *s.* die Bestechung.

brick [brik], *s.* der Ziegel, Backstein; *drop a* —, eine Taktlosigkeit begehen, einen Schnitzer machen.

bricklayer ['brikleiə], *s.* der Maurer.

bridal [braidl], *adj.* bräutlich.

bride [braid], *s.* die Braut.

bridegroom ['braidgruːm], *s.* der Bräutigam.

bridesmaid ['braidzmeid], *s.* die Brautjungfer.

bridge [bridʒ], *s.* die Brücke. — *v.a.* überbrücken; — *the gap,* die Lücke füllen.

bridle [braidl], *s.* der Zaum, Zügel. — *v.a.* aufzäumen. — *v.n.* sich brüsten.

brief [briːf], *adj.* kurz, bündig, knapp. — *s.* der Schriftsatz, der Rechtsauftrag, die Instruktionen, *f. pl.* (*instructions*). — *v.a.* instruieren, beauftragen; informieren (*inform*).

brigade [bri'geid], *s.* die Brigade.

brigand ['brigənd], *s.* der Brigant, Straßenräuber.

bright [brait], *adj.* hell, glänzend (*shiny*); klug, intelligent (*clever*).

brighten [braitn], *v.a.* glänzend machen (*polish etc.*); erhellen, aufheitern (*cheer*).

brightness ['braitnis], *s.* der Glanz; die Helligkeit; die Klugheit (*cleverness*).

brill [bril], *s.* (*Zool.*) der Glattbutt.

brilliance, brilliancy ['briljəns, -jənsi], *s.* der Glanz, die Pracht.

brim [brim], *s.* der Rand (*glass*); die Krempe (*hat*). — *v.n.* — (*over*) *with,* überfließen von.

brimful ['brimful], *adj.* übervoll.

brimstone ['brimstoun], *s.* der Schwefel; — *butterfly,* der Zitronenfalter.

brindled ['brindld], *adj.* scheckig, gefleckt.

brine [brain], *s.* die Salzsole, das Salzwasser.

bring [briŋ], *v.a. irr.* bringen; — *about,* zustande bringen; — *forth,* hervorbringen; gebären; — *forward,* fördern; anführen; — *on,* herbeiführen; — *up,* erziehen, aufziehen.

brink [briŋk], *s.* (*fig.*) der Rand, — *of a precipice,* Rand eines Abgrundes.

briny ['braini], *adj.* salzig.

brisk [brisk], *adj.* frisch, munter, feurig (*horse*).

brisket ['briskit], *s.* die Brust (eines Tieres).

briskness ['brisknis], *s.* die Lebhaftigkeit.

bristle [brisl], *s.* die Borste. — *v.n.* sich sträuben.

British ['britiʃ], *adj.* britisch.

Britisher, Briton ['britiʃə, 'britən], *s.* der Brite.

brittle [britl], *adj.* zerbrechlich, spröde.

brittleness ['britlnis], *s.* die Sprödigkeit, Zerbrechlichkeit.

broach [broutʃ], *v.a.* anzapfen, anschneiden; — *a subject,* ein Thema berühren.

broad [brɔːd], *adj.* breit, weit; ordinär, derb (*joke*); — -*minded,* duldsam, weitherzig.

broadcast ['brɔːdkɑːst], *v.a.* senden, übertragen (*radio*). — *s.* die Sendung, das Programm.

broadcaster ['brɔːdkɑːstə], *s.* der im Radio Vortragende *or* Künstler (*artist*); Ansager.

broadcasting ['brɔːdkɑːstiŋ], *s.* das Senden, der Rundfunk; — *station,* der Sender, die Rundfunkstation.

broadcloth

broadcloth ['brɔ:dclθ], s. das feine Tuch.

broaden [brɔ:dn], v.a. erweitern, verbreitern.

brocade [bro'keid], s. der Brokat.

brogue [broug], s. der grobe Schuh; der irische Akzent.

broil ['brɔil], v.a. braten, rösten.

broke [brouk], adj. (coll.) pleite.

broken ['broukən], adj. gebrochen; zerbrochen; unterbrochen (interrupted).

broker ['broukə], s. der Makler.

bronchial ['brɔŋkjəl], adj. (Anat.) bronchial, in or von der Luftröhre, Luftröhren-.

bronchitis [brɔŋ'kaitis], s. (Med.) die Luftröhrenentzündung, Bronchitis.

bronze [brɔnz], s. (Metall.) die Bronze, Bronzefarbe.

brooch [broutʃ], s. die Brosche.

brood [bru:d], s. die Brut. — v.n. brüten; grübeln (meditate).

brook (1) [bruk], s. der Bach.

brook (2) [bruk], v.a. ertragen, leiden.

brooklet ['bruklit], s. das Bächlein.

broom [bru:m], s. der Besen; (Bot.) der Ginster.

broth [brɔθ], s. die Brühe; meat —, Fleischbrühe.

brothel ['brɔθəl], s. das Bordell.

brother ['brʌðə], s. der Bruder; — -in-law, der Schwager.

brotherhood ['brʌðəhud], s. die Bruderschaft.

brotherly ['brʌðəli], adj. brüderlich.

brow [brau], s. die Braue, Augenbraue; der Kamm (hill); die Stirn(e) (forehead).

browbeat ['braubi:t], v.a. einschüchtern.

brown [braun], adj. braun; in a — study, in tiefem Nachsinnen.

browse [brauz], v.n. weiden (cattle); stöbern, (durch-)blättern (in books etc.).

Bruin ['bru:in]. Braun, Meister Petz, der Bär.

bruise [bru:z], v.a. quetschen, stoßen; (wund) schlagen. — s. die Quetschung.

Brunswick ['brʌnzwik]. Braunschweig, n.

brunt [brʌnt], s. der Anprall; bear the —, der Wucht ausgesetzt sein, den Stoß auffangen.

brush [brʌʃ], s. die Bürste (clothes); der Pinsel (paint, painting); — stroke, der Pinselstrich. — v.a., v.n. bürsten, abbürsten; — against s.o., mit jemandem zusammenstoßen, streifen (an, Acc.); — up one's English, das Englisch auffrischen; — off, abschütteln.

brushwood ['brʌʃwud], s. das Gestrüpp.

brusque [brusk], adj. brüsk, barsch.

Brussels ['brʌsəlz]. Brüssel. n.; — sprouts, (Bot.) der Rosenkohl.

brutal [bru:tl], adj. brutal, grausam.

brutality [bru:'tæliti], s. die Brutalität.

brute [bru:t], s. der Unmensch.

bubble [bʌbl], s. die Blase; (fig.) der Schwindel (swindle). — v.n. sprudeln, wallen, schäumen.

buccaneer [bʌkə'niə], s. der Seeräuber.

buck [bʌk], s. (Zool.) der Bock; (Am. sl.) der Dollar. — v.a. — up, aufmuntern. — v.n. — up, sich zusammenraffen.

bucket ['bʌkit], s. der Eimer, Kübel.

buckle [bʌkl], s. die Schnalle. — v.a. zuschnallen; biegen. — v.n. sich krümmen.

buckler ['bʌklə], s. der Schild.

buckram ['bʌkrəm], s. die Steifleinwand.

buckskin ['bʌkskin], s. das Wildleder.

buckwheat ['bʌkwi:t], s. (Bot.) der Buchweizen.

bucolic [bju:'kɔlik], adj. bukolisch, ländlich, Schäfer-.

bud [bʌd], s. (Bot.) die Knospe. — v.n. knospen.

buddy ['bʌdi], s.(coll.Am.) der Freund, Kamerad.

budge [bʌdʒ], v.n. sich rühren, sich regen.

budget ['bʌdʒit], s. das Budget; der Haushaltsplan; der Etat; present the —, den Staatsetat vorlegen. — v.n. voranschlagen (for), planen.

buff [bʌf], adj. ledergelb.

buffalo ['bʌfəlou], s. (Zool.) der Büffel.

buffer ['bʌfə], s. der Puffer.

buffet (1) ['bʌfit], s. der Puff, Faustschlag (blow). — v.a. schlagen, stoßen.

buffet (2) ['bufei], s. das Buffet, der Anrichtetisch.

buffoon [bʌ'fu:n], s. der Possenreißer.

buffoonery [bʌ'fu:nəri], s. die Possen, f. pl.; das Possenreißen.

bug [bʌg], s. (Ent.) die Wanze; (Am.) der Käfer; (coll.) das Insekt.

buggy ['bʌgi], s. der Einspänner.

bugle [bju:gl], s. (Mus.) das Signalhorn, die Signaltrompete.

bugler ['bju:glə], s. (Mus.) der Trompeter.

build [bild], v.a., v.n. irr. bauen; errichten; — on, sich verlassen auf (rely on). — s. die Statur, Figur (figure).

builder ['bildə], s. der Bauherr, Baumeister (employer); Bauarbeiter (worker).

building ['bildin], s. das Gebäude, der Bau; — site, der Bauplatz.

bulb [bʌlb], s. (Bot.) der Knollen, die Zwiebel; Dutch —, die Tulpe; (Elec.) die Birne.

bulbous ['bʌlbəs], adj. zwiebelartig; dickbäuchig.

Bulgarian [bʌl'gɛəriən], adj. bulgarisch. — s. der Bulgare.

bulge [bʌldʒ], s. die Ausbauchung; die Ausbuchtung (in fighting line). — v.n. herausragen, anschwellen.

bulk [bʌlk], s. die Masse, Menge; buy in —, im Großen einkaufen.

buttery

bulky ['bʌlki], *adj.* schwer (*heavy*); massig (*stodgy*); unhandlich.
bull (1) [bul], *s.* (*Zool.*) der Bulle, Stier; —'s eye, das Schwarze (*target*).
bull (2) [bul], *s.* (*Papal*) die Bulle, der Erlass.
bulldog ['buldɔg], *s.* der Bullenbeißer.
bullet ['bulit], *s.* die Kugel, das Geschoß.
bulletin ['bulitin], *s.* das Bulletin, der Tagesbericht.
bullfight ['bulfait], *s.* der Stierkampf.
bullfinch ['bulfintʃ], *s.* (*Orn.*) der Dompfaff.
bullfrog ['bulfrɔg], *s.* (*Zool.*) der Ochsenfrosch.
bullion ['buljən], *s.* die Goldbarren, Silberbarren.
bullock ['bulɔk], *s.* (*Zool.*) der Ochse.
bully ['buli], *s.* der Raufbold, Angeber, Großtuer (*braggart*); der Tyrann. — *v. a.* tyrannisieren, einschüchtern.
bulrush ['bulrʌʃ], *s.* (*Bot.*) die Binse.
bulwark ['bulwək], *s.* das Bollwerk, die Verteidigung.
bump [bʌmp], *s.* der Schlag, der Stoß. — *v.a.* stoßen.
bun [bʌn], *s.* das Rosinenbrötchen; das süße Brötchen; (*hair*) der Knoten.
bunch [bʌntʃ], *s.* der Bund (*keys*); der Strauß (*flowers*); die Traube (*grapes*). — *v a.* zusammenfassen, zusammenbinden, zusammenraffen.
bundle ['bʌndl], *s.* das Bündel.
bung [bʌŋ], *s.* der Spund (*in barrel*).
bungle ['bʌŋgl], *v.a.* verpfuschen, verderben.
bungler ['bʌŋglə], *s.* der Stümper.
bunion ['bʌnjən], *s.* die Fußschwiele.
bunk (1) [bʌŋk], *s.* die (Schlaf-)Koje.
bunk (2) [bʌŋk], *s.* (*coll.*) der Unsinn.
bunker ['bʌŋkə], *s.* der Kohlenraum, Bunker.
bunting ['bʌntiŋ], *s.* das Flaggentuch.
buoy [bɔi], *s.* die Boje.
buoyant ['bɔiənt], *adj.* schwimmend; lebhaft, heiter.
buoyancy ['bɔiənsi], *s.* die Schwimmkraft; die Schwungkraft.
burden (1) [bə:dn], *s.* die Bürde, Last. — *v.a.* belasten, beladen.
burden (2) [bə:dn], *s.* der Refrain; der Hauptinhalt.
burdensome ['bə:dnsəm], *adj.* beschwerlich.
bureau [bjuə'rou], *s.* der Schreibtisch; das Büro.
bureaucracy [bjuə'rɔkrəsi], *s.* die Bürokratie.
burgess ['bə:dʒis], *s.* der Bürger.
burglar ['bə:glə], *s.* der Einbrecher.
burglary ['bə:gləri], *s.* der Einbruch, der Diebstahl.
burgomaster ['bə:gomɑ:stə], *s.* der Bürgermeister.
Burgundian [bə:'gʌndiən], *adj.* burgundisch. —*s.* der Burgunder.
Burgundy (1) ['bə:gəndi], *s.* das Burgund.
Burgundy (2) ['bə:gəndi], *s.* der Burgunder(-wein).

burial ['beriəl], *das* Begräbnis; — *ground,* der Kirchhof, Friedhof; — *service,* die Totenfeier, Trauerfeier.
burlesque [bə:'lesk], *s.* die Burleske, Posse.
burly ['bə:li], *adj.* dick, stark.
Burmese [bə:'mi:z], *adj.* birmesisch. — *s.* der Birmese.
burn [bə:n], *v.a., v.n. irr.* brennen, verbrennen. — *s.* das Brandmal.
burner ['bə:nə], *s.* der Brenner.
burnish ['bə:niʃ], *v.a.* polieren.
burred [bə:d], *adj.* überliegend; (*Metall.*) ausgehämmert; — *over,* (*Metall.*) breitgeschmiedet.
burrow ['bʌrou], *s.* der Bau, (*rabbits etc.*). —*v.n.* sich eingraben; wühlen.
burst [bə:st], *v.a., v.n. irr.* bersten, platzen, explodieren (*explode*); — *out laughing,* laut auflachen; — *into tears,* in Tränen ausbrechen; — *into flames,* aufflammen; sprengen (*blow up*). — *s.* der Ausbruch; die Explosion.
bury ['beri], *v.a.* begraben; beerdigen.
bus [bʌs], *s.* der Autobus, Omnibus.
busby ['bʌzbi], *s.* (*Mil.*) die Bärenmütze.
bush [buʃ], *s.* der Busch.
bushel ['buʃl], *s.* der Scheffel.
bushy ['buʃi], *adj.* buschig.
business ['biznis], *s.* das Geschäft; die Beschäftigung, die Tätigkeit (*activity*); Aufgabe, Obliegenheit; der Handel (*trade*); *on* —, geschäftlich.
businesslike ['biznislaik], *adj.* geschäftsmäßig, nüchtern, praktisch.
businessman ['biznismæn], *s.* der Geschäftsmann.
bust (1) [bʌst], *s.* die Büste.
bust (2) [bʌst], *v.a., v.n.* (*coll.*) sprengen; *go* —, bankrott machen.
bustard ['bʌstəd], *s.* (*Orn.*) die Trappe.
bustle [bʌsl], *s.* der Lärm, die Aufregung. — *v.n.* aufgeregt umherlaufen; rührig sein (*be active*).
busy ['bizi], *adj.* geschäftig (*active*); beschäftigt (*engaged,* mit, *in*); *be* —, zu tun haben.
but [bʌt], *conj.* aber, jedoch; sondern. — *adv.* nur, bloß; — *yesterday,* erst gestern. — *prep.* außer; *all* — *two,* alle außer zwei.
butcher ['butʃə], *s.* der Metzger, Fleischer; —'s knife, das Fleischmesser.
butchery ['butʃəri], *s.* die Schlächterei; das Blutbad, das Gemetzel.
butler ['bʌtlə], *s.* der oberste Diener; Kellermeister.
butt [bʌt], *s.* das dicke Ende; der Kolben (*rifle*); der Stoß (*blow*); die Zielscheibe (*target*). — *v.a.* stoßen, spießen.
butter ['bʌtə], *s.* die Butter. — *v.a.* mit Butter bestreichen; — *up,* schmeicheln (*Dat.*).
butterfly ['bʌtəflai], *s.* (*Ent.*) der Schmetterling.
buttery ['bʌtəri], *s.* die Speisekammer.

329

buttock(s)

buttock(s) ['bʌtək(s)], *s.* der Hintere,
das Gesäß (*usually pl.*) (*vulg.*).
button [bʌtn], *s.* der Knopf. — *v.a.* —
up, knöpfen, zumachen.
buttress ['bʌtris], *s.* der Strebepfeiler.
buxom ['bʌksəm], *adj.* drall, gesund.
buy [bai], *v.a. irr.* kaufen.
buzz [bʌz], *s.* das Summen. — *v.n.*
summen.
buzzard ['bʌzəd], *s.* (*Orn.*) der Bussard.
by [bai], *prep.* (*beside*) neben, an;
(*near*) nahe; (*before*) gegen, um, bei;
(*about*) bei; (*from, with*) durch, von,
mit; — *the way*, nebenbei bemerkt;
— *way of*, mittels. — *adv.* (*nearby*)
nahe; nebenan.
by-election ['baiilekʃən], *s.* die Nachwahl; Ersatzwahl.
bygone ['baigɔn], *adj.* vergangen.
bylaw, byelaw ['bailɔ:], *s.* die Bestimmung.
Byzantine [bai'zæntain], *adj.* byzan-
tinisch.

C

C [si:]. das C (*also Mus.*).
cab [kæb], *s.* (*horse-drawn*) die Droschke,
der Wagen; das Taxi; —*stand*, der
Droschkenhalteplatz; (*Motor.*) der
Taxiplatz, Taxistand.
cabaret ['kæbərei], *s.* das Kabarett, die
Kleinbühne.
cabbage ['kæbidʒ], *s.* (*Bot.*) der Kohl.
cabin ['kæbin], *s.* die Kabine (*boat*);
die Hütte (*hut*); — *-boy*, der Schiffs-
junge.
cabinet ['kæbinet], *s.* das Kabinett
(*government*); der Schrank (*cupboard*);
das kleine Zimmer *or* Nebenzimmer
(*mainly Austr.*); (*Rad.*) das Gehäuse;
— *maker*, der Kunsttischler.
cable [keibl], *s.* das Kabel (*of metal*),
das Seil (*metal or rope*); das Telegramm. — *v.a.* kabeln, telegraphieren.
cablegram ['keiblgræm], *s.* die (Kabel-)
Depesche.
cabman ['kæbmən], *s.* der Taxichauf-
feur.
caboose [kə'bu:s], *s.* die Schiffsküche.
cabriolet [kæbrio'lei], *s.* das Kabriolett.
cackle [kækl], *v.n.* gackern (*hens*);
schnattern (*geese*); (*fig.*) schwatzen.
cacophony [kə'kɔfəni], *s.* der Mißklang.
cad [kæd], *s.* der gemeine Kerl, Schuft.
cadaverous [kə'dævərəs], *adj.* leichenhaft.
caddie ['kædi], *s.* der Golfjunge.
caddy ['kædi], *s.* *tea* —, die Teebüchse,
Teedose.
cadence ['keidəns], *s.* (*Phonet.*) der
Tonfall; (*Mus.*) die Kadenz.
cadet [kə'det], *s.* (*Mil.*) der Kadett.
cadge [kædʒ], *v.a.* erbetteln.

Caesar ['si:zə]. Cäsar, *m.*
Caesarean [si'zɛəriən], *adj.* cäsarisch; —
operation or *section*, (*Med.*) der
Kaiserschnitt.
cafeteria [kæfə'tiəriə], *s.* das Selbst-
bedienungsrestaurant.
cage [keidʒ], *s.* (*Zool.*) der Käfig;
(*Orn.*) das Vogelbauer. — *v.a.*
einfangen, einsperren.
cagey ['keidʒi], *adj.* (*coll.*) argwöhnisch,
zurückhaltend; schlau.
cairn [kɛən], *s.* (*Archaeol.*) der Stein-
haufen, der Grabhügel.
caitiff ['keitif], *adj.* niederträchtig. — *s.*
der Schuft.
cajole [kə'dʒoul], *v.a.* schmeicheln (*Dat.*).
cake [keik], *s.* der Kuchen; — *of soap*,
das Stück Seife; *have o.'s* — *and eat
it*, alles haben. — *v.a., v.n.* zusammen-
backen; —*d with dirt*, mit Schmutz
beschmiert.
calamity [kə'læmiti], *s.* das Unheil,
Unglück; Elend.
calcareous [kæl'kɛəriəs], *adj.* (*Geol.*)
kalkartig.
calculate ['kælkjuleit], *v.a.* berechnen.
calculation [kælkju'leiʃən], *s.* die
Berechnung.
calendar ['kæləndə], *s.* der Kalender.
calf [kɑ:f], *s.* (*Zool.*) das Kalb; (*Anat.*)
die Wade; — *love*, die Jugendliebe.
calibre ['kælibə], *s.* das Kaliber.
calico ['kælikou], *s.* der Kaliko, Kattun.
Caliph ['keilif], *s.* der Kalif.
calk (1) [kɔ:k], *v.a.* beschlagen (*horse*).
calk (2), **caulk** [kɔ:k], *v.a.* (*Naut.*) ab-
dichten.
call [kɔ:l], *v.a., v.n.* rufen, herbeirufen;
(*Am.*) antelefonieren, anrufen (*ring
up*); (*name*) nennen; — *to account*, zur
Rechenschaft ziehen; (*summon*) kommen lassen; — *for*, abholen; *this* —*s
for*, das berechtigt zu. — *s.* der Ruf,
Anruf; die (innere) Berufung, der
Beruf.
callbox ['kɔ:lbɔks] *see* **phone box**.
calling ['kɔ:liŋ], *s.* der Beruf, das
Gewerbe (*occupation*).
callous ['kæləs], *adj.* schwielig (*hands*);
(*fig.*) unempfindlich, hart, gemein.
callow ['kælou], *adj.* ungefiedert (*bird*);
(*fig.*) unerfahren.
calm [kɑ:m], *adj.* ruhig, still; gelassen.
— *s.* die Ruhe; (*Naut.*) Windstille.
— *v.a.* beruhigen. — *v.n.* — *down*,
sich beruhigen, sich legen (*storm etc.*).
caloric [kə'lɔrik], *adj.* Wärme-,
warm; (*Chem.*) kalorisch.
calorie, calory ['kæləri], *s.* die Kalorie.
calumny ['kæləmni], *s.* die Verleumdung.
calve [kɑ:v], *v.n.* kalben, Kälber
kriegen.
cambric ['kæmbrik], *s.* der Batist (*textile*).
camel ['kæməl], *s.* (*Zool.*) das Kamel.
cameo ['kæmiou], *s.* die Kamee.
camera ['kæmərə], *s.* (*Phot.*) die
Kamera.
camomile ['kæməmail], *s.* (*Bot.*) die
Kamille.

captain

camp [kæmp], *s.* das Lager; Zeltlager.
— *v.n.* sich lagern, ein Lager aufschlagen, zelten.
campaign [kæm'pein], *s.* der Feldzug.
— *v.n.* einen Feldzug mitmachen;
(*fig.*) Propaganda machen.
camphor ['kæmfə], *s.* der Kampfer.
camping ['kæmpiŋ], *s.* die Lagerausrüstung (*equipment*); das Lagern
(*activity*), das Zelten.
can (1) [kæn], *s.* die Kanne; die Büchse;
watering —, die Gießkanne. — *v.a.*
(*Am.*) einmachen, einkochen (*fruit*).
can (2) [kæn], *v. aux. irr.* können,
imstande sein, vermögen.
Canadian [kə'neidiən], *adj.* kanadisch.
— *s.* der Kanadier.
canal [kə'næl], *s.* der Kanal; — *lock,*
die Kanalschleuse.
canalize ['kænəlaiz], *v.a.* kanalisieren,
leiten.
cancel ['kænsəl], *v.a.* widerrufen, absagen
(*show*); aufheben, ungültig machen.
cancellation [kænsə'leiʃən], *s.* die
Aufhebung, Absage, Widerrufung.
cancer ['kænsə], *s.* (*Med., Astron.*) der
Krebs.
cancerous ['kænsərəs], *adj.* (*Med.*)
krebsartig.
candelabra [kændi'lɑ:brə], *s.* der
Kandelaber, Leuchter.
candid ['kændid], *adj.* offen, aufrichtig.
candidate ['kændideit], *s.* der Kandidat, Bewerber.
candidature ['kændiditʃə], *s.* die
Kandidatur, die Bewerbung.
candied ['kændid], *adj.* gezuckert,
kandiert (*fruit*).
candle [kændl], *s.* die Kerze, das Licht.
Candlemas ['kændlməs], (*Eccl.*)
Lichtmeß.
candlestick ['kændlstik], *s.* der Kerzenleuchter.
candlewick ['kændlwik], *s.* der Kerzendocht (*textile*).
candour ['kændə], *s.* die Offenheit,
Aufrichtigkeit.
candy ['kændi], *s.* (*Am.*) das Zuckerwerk, (*pl.*) Süßigkeiten. — *v.a.*
verzuckern.
cane [kein], *s.* (*Bot.*) das Rohr, der
Rohrstock; Spazierstock. — *v.a.* (mit
dem Stock) schlagen.
canine ['kænain], *adj.* Hunde-, hündisch; — *tooth,* der Eckzahn.
canister ['kænistə], *s.* die Blechbüchse,
der Kanister.
canker ['kæŋkə], *s.* (*Bot.*) der Brand;
(*Bot.*) der Pflanzenrost; (*fig.*) eine
zerfressende Krankheit.
cannibal ['kænibəl], *s.* der Kannibale,
Menschenfresser.
cannon ['kænən], *s.* die Kanone, das
Geschütz.
canoe [kə'nu], *s.* das Kanu.
canon ['kænən], *s.* (*Mus., Eccl.*) der
Kanon; die Regel; (*Eccl.*) der Domherr; — *law,* das kanonische Recht.
canonize ['kænənaiz], *v.a.* (*Eccl.*)
kanonisieren, heiligsprechen.

canopy ['kænəpi], *s.* der Baldachin.
cant [kænt], *s.* die Heuchelei.
can't, cannot [kɑ:nt,'kænɔt] see **can** (2).
cantankerous [kæn'tæŋkərəs], *adj.*
zänkisch, mürrisch.
cantata [kæn'tɑ:tə], *s.* (*Mus.*) die
Kantate.
canteen [kæn'ti:n], *s.* die Kantine (*restaurant*); die Besteckgarnitur (*set of
cutlery*).
canter ['kæntə], *s.* der Galopp, der
Kurzgalopp.
canticle ['kæntikl], *s.* (*Eccl.*) der
Lobgesang, das Loblied.
canto ['kæntou], *s.* (*Lit.*) der Gesang.
canton ['kæntən], *s.* (*Pol.*) der Kanton,
der Bezirk.
canvas ['kænvəs], *s.* das Segeltuch;
(*Art*) die Malerleinwand; die Zeltplane (*tent*).
canvass ['kænvəs], *v.a., v.n.* (*Pol.*)
um Stimmen werben.
canvasser ['kænvəsə], *s.* (*Pol.*) der
Werber, Stimmensammler.
cap [kæp], *s.* die Kappe, Mütze; die
Haube; der Deckel. — *v.a.* übertreffen.
capability [keipə'biliti], *s.* die Fähigkeit.
capable ['keipəbl], *adj.* fähig (*Genit.*),
imstande (*of,* zu); tüchtig.
capacious [kə'peiʃəs], *adj.* geräumig.
capacity [kə'pæsiti], *s.* der Inhalt, die
Geräumigkeit; die Fassungskraft
(*intellect*); die Leistungsfähigkeit
(*ability*); der Fassungsraum (*space*).
cape (1) [keip], *s.* (*Tail.*) der Kragenmantel.
cape (2) [keip], *s.* (*Geog.*) das Kap, das
Vorgebirge.
caper ['keipə], *s.* der Sprung, Luftsprung. — *v.n.* in die Luft springen.
capillary [kə'piləri], *adj.* haarfein; —
tubing, die Haarröhre, die Kapillarröhre.
capital ['kæpitl], *s.* (*Comm.*) das
Kapital; die Hauptstadt (*capital city*);
— *punishment,* die Todesstrafe; —
letter, der Großbuchstabe. — *adj.*
(*coll.*) ausgezeichnet, vorzüglich.
capitalize ['kæpitəlaiz], *v.a.* (*Comm.*)
kapitalisieren; ausnutzen.
capitation [kæpi'teiʃən], *s.* die Kopfsteuer.
capitulate [kə'pitjuleit], *v.n.* kapitulieren.
capon ['keipən], *s.* (*Zool.*) der Kapaun.
caprice [kə'pri:s], *s.* die Kaprize, Laune.
capricious [kə'priʃəs], *adj.* launenhaft,
eigensinnig.
Capricorn ['kæprikɔ:n], (*Astron.*) der
Steinbock; *tropic of* —, der Wendekreis des Steinbocks.
capriole ['kæprioul], *s.* der Luftsprung.
capsize [kæp'saiz], *v.n.* umkippen,
kentern (*boat*).
capstan ['kæpstən], *s.* (*Engin.*) die
Ankerwinde; (*Mech.*) die Erdwinde;
(*Naut.*) das Gangspill.
capsular ['kæpsjulə], *adj.* kapselförmig.
capsule ['kæpsju:l], *s.* die Kapsel.
captain ['kæptin], *s.* (*Naut.*) der
Kapitän; (*Mil.*) der Hauptmann.

captious ['kæpʃəs], *adj.* zänkisch, streitsüchtig; verfänglich.

captivate ['kæptiveit], *v.a.* einnehmen, gewinnen.

captive ['kæptiv], *s.* der Gefangene. — *adj.* gefangen.

capture ['kæptʃə], *s.* die Gefangennahme (*men*); Erbeutung (*booty*).

Capuchin ['kæputʃin], *s.* (*Eccl.*) der Kapuziner.

car [ka:], *s.* (*Motor.*) der Wagen; das Auto; (*Am.*) der Eisenbahnwagen.

carafe [kæ'ræf], *s.* die Karaffe, Wasserflasche.

caravan ['kærəvæn], *s.* die Karawane; der Wohnwagen.

caraway ['kærəwei],*s.*(*Bot.*)der Kümmel.

carbine ['ka:bain], *s.* der Karabiner.

carbolic [ka:'bɔlik], *adj.* — *acid*, (*Chem.*) die Karbolsäure.

carbon ['ka:bən], *s.* (*Chem.*) der Kohlenstoff.

carbonate ['ka:bəneit], *s.* (*Chem.*) das kohlensaure Salz, Karbonat.

carbonize ['ka:bənaiz], *v.a.* verkohlen. — *v.n.* (*Chem., Geol.*) zu Kohle werden.

carbuncle ['ka:bʌnkl], *s.* (*Min.*) der Karfunkel; (*Med.*) der Karbunkel.

carburettor [ka:bju'retə], *s.* (*Motor.*) der Vergaser.

carcase, carcass ['ka:kəs], *s.* der Kadaver.

card (1) [ka:d], *s.* die Karte, Postkarte; *playing* —, die Spielkarte; *put your* —*s on the table*, rück mit der Wahrheit heraus!

card (2) [ka:d], *v.a.* krempeln (*wool*); kardätschen (*cotton*).

cardboard ['ka:dbɔ:d], *s.* die Pappe, der Pappendeckel.

cardiac ['ka:diæk], *adj.* (*Med.*) Herz–.

cardinal ['ka:dinl], *s.* (*Eccl.*) der Kardinal. — *adj.* Kardinal–, grundlegend.

cardiogram ['ka:diogræm], *s.* (*Med.*) das Kardiogramm.

cardsharper ['ka:dʃa:pə], *s.* der Falschspieler.

care [kɛə], *s.* die Sorge (*anxiety*, um, *for*); *with* —, mit Sorgfalt, genau; *care of* (*abbr. c/o on letters*) bei; *take* —, sich in acht nehmen. — *v.n.* — *for*, sich interessieren, gern haben.

careen [kə'ri:n], *v.a.* (*Naut.*) kielholen, umlegen.

career [kə'riə], *s.* die Karriere, Laufbahn.

careful ['kɛəful], *adj.* sorgfältig, vorsichtig, umsichtig.

carefulness ['kɛəfulnis], *s.* die Vorsicht, Sorgfalt, Umsicht.

careless ['kɛəlis], *adj.* unachtsam, nachlässig.

carelessness ['kɛəlisnis], *s.* die Nachlässigkeit, Unachtsamkeit.

caress [kə'res], *v.a.* liebkosen, herzen. — *s.* die Liebkosung, die Zärtlichkeit.

caretaker ['kɛəteikə], *s.* der Hausmeister.

careworn ['kɛəwɔ:n], *adj.* abgehärmt, von Sorgen gebeugt.

cargo ['ka:gou], *s.* die Fracht, die Ladung.

caricature [kærikə'tjuə *or* 'kærikətʃə], *s.* die Karikatur. — *v.a.* karikieren, verzerren.

Carinthian [kə'rinθjən], *adj.* kärntnerisch.

carmine ['ka:main], *s.* der Karmin.

carnage ['ka:nidʒ], *s.* das Blutbad.

carnal [ka:nl], *adj.* fleischlich, sinnlich.

carnation [ka:'neiʃən], *s.* (*Bot.*) die Nelke.

carnival ['ka:nivl], *s.* der Karneval.

carnivorous [ka:'nivərəs], *adj.* fleischfressend.

carol ['kærəl], *s.* *Christmas* —, das Weihnachtslied.

carotid [kə'rɔtid], *s.* (*Anat.*) die Halspulsader.

carousal [kə'rauzəl], *s.* das Gelage, das Gezeche.

carouse [kə'rauz], *v.n.* zechen, schmausen.

carp (1) [ka:p], *s.* (*Zool.*) der Karpfen.

carp (2) [ka:p], *v.n.* bekritteln, tadeln.

Carpathian Mountains [ka:'peiθjən 'mauntinz]. die Karpathen, *f. pl.*

carpenter ['ka:pəntə], *s.* der Zimmermann; Tischler.

carpentry ['ka:pəntri], *s.* die Tischlerei, das Zimmerhandwerk.

carpet ['ka:pit], *s.* der Teppich; — *bag*, die Reisetasche.

carriage ['kæridʒ], *s.* der Wagen, Waggon; das Verhalten, die Haltung (*bearing*); (*Comm.*) — *paid*, einschließlich Zustellung; — *way*, der Straßendamm.

carrier ['kæriə], *s.* der Fuhrmann, Fuhrunternehmer.

carrion ['kæriən], *s.* das Aas.

carrot ['kærət], *s.* (*Bot.*) die Mohrrübe; die Karotte.

carry ['kæri], *v.a.* tragen; bringen; führen (*on vehicle*), fahren (*convey*); — *interest*, Zinsen tragen; (*Comm.*) — *forward*, übertragen; — *two* (*in adding up*), zwei weiter; — *on*, weitermachen, fortfahren; — *through*, durchführen, durchhalten. — *v.n.* vernehmbar sein (*of sound*); — *on*, weiterarbeiten, weiterexistieren.

cart [ka:t], *s.* der Karren, Frachtwagen.

cartel [ka:'tel], *s.* (*Comm.*) das Kartell.

Carthage ['ka:θidʒ]. Karthago, *n.*

carthorse ['ka:θɔ:s], *s.* das Zugpferd.

cartilage ['ka:tilidʒ], *s.* der Knorpel.

carton ['ka:tən], *s.* (*cardboard box*) der Karton, die Schachtel.

cartoon [ka:'tu:n], *s.* die Karikatur; — *film*, der Trickfilm.

cartridge ['ka:tridʒ], *s.* die Patrone.

cartwright ['ka:trait], *s.* der Stellmacher, Wagenbauer.

carve [ka:v], *v.a.* schneiden (*cut*); schnitzen (*wood*), meißeln (*stone*), tranchieren (*meat*).

carver ['kɑːvə], s. der Schnitzer (wood); das Tranchiermesser (carving knife).

cascade [kæs'keid], s. der Wasserfall.

case (1) [keis], s. der Kasten, Behälter; das Futteral, Etui (spectacles); das Gehäuse (watch); die Kiste (wooden box); (Typ.) der Schriftkasten.

case (2) [keis], s. der Fall (event); (Law) der Rechtsfall, der Umstand (circumstance); in —, falls.

casement ['keismənt], s. der Fensterflügel, das Fenster (frame).

caseous ['keisjəs], adj. käsig.

cash [kæʃ], s. bares Geld; die Barzahlung; — box, die Kasse. — v.a. einlösen (cheque).

cashier [kæ'ʃiə], s. der Kassierer. — v.a. (Mil.) entlassen.

cashmere ['kæʃmiə], s. die Kaschmirwolle (wool).

casing ['keisiŋ], s. die Hülle; das Gehäuse (case); die Haut (sausage skin).

cask ['kɑːsk], s. das Faß.

casket ['kɑːskit], s. das Kästchen; (Am.) der Sarg.

Caspian (Sea) ['kæspiən (siː)]. das kaspische Meer.

cassock ['kæsək], s. die Soutane.

cast [kɑːst], v.a. irr. werfen (throw); (Metall.) gießen; (Theat.) besetzen; (plaster) formen; — off, abwerfen; — anchor, ankern; — o.'s skin, sich häuten; — down, niederschlagen; — a vote, die Stimme abgeben. — s. der Wurf; (Metall.) der Guß; (Theat.) die Besetzung; der Abguß (plaster). — adj. — iron, das Gusseisen; — steel, der Gußstahl.

castanets [kæstə'nets], s. pl. (Mus.) die Kastagnetten, f. pl.

castaway ['kɑːstəwei], adj. weggeworfen; (Naut.) schiffbrüchig.

caste [kɑːst], s. die Kaste.

caster ['kɑːstə], s. der Streuer, die Streubüchse; — sugar, Streuzucker.

casting ['kɑːstiŋ], s. (Metall.) das Gießen, der Guß.

castle [kɑːsl], s. die Burg, das Schloß; (Chess) der Turm.

castor (1) ['kɑːstə], s. (Zool.) der Biber.

castor (2) ['kɑːstə] see caster.

castor (3) **oil** ['kɑːstər 'oil], s. das Rizinusöl.

castrate [kæs'treit], v.a. kastrieren.

castration [kæs'treiʃən], s. die Kastration.

casual ['kæʒjuəl], adj. zufällig; gelassen (manner); gelegentlich; flüchtig.

casualty ['kæʒjualti], s. der Unglücksfall; — ward, die Unfallstation; (pl.) die Verluste, m. pl.

cat [kæt], s. die Katze; tom —, der Kater; — burglar, der Fassadenkletterer; —'s eye, das Katzenauge, der Rückstrahler, der Reflektor.

cataclysm ['kætəklizm], s. die Sintflut, die Überschwemmung.

catacomb ['kætəkuːm], s. die Katakombe.

catalogue ['kætələg], s. der Katalog, das Verzeichnis. — v.a. im Katalog verzeichnen, katalogisieren.

catapult ['kætəpult], s. die Schleuder (hand); (Mil.) die Wurfmaschine. — v.a. schleudern.

cataract ['kætərækt], s. der Wasserfall (water); (Med.) der Star.

catarrh [kə'tɑː], s. (Med.) der Katarrh.

catastrophe [kə'tæstrəfi], s. die Katastrophe, das Unglück.

catastrophic [kætəs'trɔfik], adj. katastrophal, unheilvoll.

catch [kætʃ], v.a. irr. fangen, auffangen, fassen; überfallen (— unawares, ambush); — a cold, sich einen Schnupfen zuziehen, sich erkälten; erreichen (train, etc.); — redhanded, bei frischer Tat ertappen. — s. der Fang (fish); die Beute (prey, booty); der Haken (hook, also fig.).

catchpenny ['kætʃpeni], s. der Flitterkram, Lockartikel. — adj. marktschreierisch.

catchphrase, catchword ['kætʃfreiz, 'kætʃwəːd], s. das (billige) Schlagwort.

catechism ['kætikizm], s. der Katechismus.

categorical [kæti'gɔrikəl], adj. kategorisch, entschieden.

category ['kætigəri], s. die Kategorie, Klasse, Gruppe, Gattung.

cater ['keitə], v.n. Lebensmittel einkaufen; verpflegen; (fig.) sorgen (for, für).

caterer ['keitərə], s. der Lebensmittellieferant.

catering ['keitəriŋ], s. die Verpflegung.

caterpillar ['kætəpilə], s. (Ent.) die Raupe; (Mech.) der Raupenschlepper.

caterwaul ['kætəwɔːl], v.n. miauen.

cathedral [kə'θiːdrəl], s. der Dom, die Kathedrale.

Catholic ['kæθəlik], adj. katholisch. — s. der Katholik.

catholic ['kæθəlik], adj. allumfassend.

Catholicism [kə'θɔlisizm], s. der Katholizismus.

catkin ['kætkin], s. (Bot.) das Kätzchen; pussy-willow —, das Palmkätzchen.

cattle [kætl], s. pl. das Vieh; — plague, die Rinderpest; — show, die Viehausstellung.

caucus ['kɔːkəs], s. die Wahlversammlung; der Wahlausschuß; (Anat.) die Eihaut.

caul [kɔːl], s. die Haarnetz; (Anat.) die Eihaut.

cauldron ['kɔːldrən], s. der Kessel.

cauliflower ['kɔliflauə], s. (Bot.) der Blumenkohl.

caulk [kɔːk], v.a. kalfatern (see under **calk** (2)).

causal ['kɔːzəl], adj. ursächlich.

causality [kɔ'zæliti], s. der ursächliche Zusammenhang; die Kausalität.

cause [kɔːz], s. die Ursache. — v.a. verursachen.

causeway ['kɔːzwei], s. der Damm.

caustic ['kɔːstik], adj. ätzend; beißend.

cauterize

cauterize [ˈkɔːtəraiz], v.a. (Med.) ätzen, ausbrennen.

caution [ˈkɔːʃən], s. die Vorsicht (care); die Warnung (warning). — v.a. (Law) ermahnen; warnen.

cautionary [ˈkɔːʃənəri], adj. warnend.

cautious [ˈkɔːʃəs], adj. vorsichtig, behutsam.

cautiousness [ˈkɔːʃəsnis], s. die Vorsicht, Behutsamkeit.

cavalcade [kævəlˈkeid], s. die Kavalkade; (Mil.) der Reiterzug.

cavalry [ˈkævəlri], s. die Kavallerie, die Reiterei.

cave [keiv], s. die Höhle. — v.a. aushöhlen. — v.n. — in, einstürzen, einfallen.

caveat [ˈkeiviæt], s. (Law) die Warnung; der Vorbehalt.

cavern [ˈkævən], s. die Höhle.

cavernous [ˈkævənəs], adj. (Geog., Geol.) voll Höhlen.

caviare [kæviˈɑː], s. der Kaviar.

cavil [ˈkævil], v.n. nörgeln (at, über), tadeln (Acc.).

cavity [ˈkæviti], s. die Höhlung.

caw [kɔː], v.n. (Orn.) krächzen.

cease [siːs], v.a. einstellen. — v.n. aufhören.

ceaseless [ˈsiːslis], adj. unaufhörlich.

cedar [ˈsiːdə], s. (Bot.) die Zeder.

cede [siːd], v.a. überlassen. — v.n. nachgeben.

ceiling [ˈsiːliŋ], s. die Decke (room); (Comm.) die Preisgrenze.

celebrate [ˈselibreit], v.a. feiern; zelebrieren.

celebrated [ˈselibreitid], adj. berühmt.

celebration [seliˈbreiʃən], s. die Feier.

celebrity [siˈlebriti], s. die Berühmtheit; der „Star".

celerity [siˈleriti], s. die Behendigkeit, Schnelligkeit.

celery [ˈseləri], s. (Bot.) der Sellerie.

celestial [siˈlestjəl], adj. himmlisch.

celibacy [ˈselibəsi], s. die Ehelosigkeit; (Eccl.) das Zölibat.

celibate [ˈselibit], adj. unverheiratet.

cell [sel], s. die Zelle.

cellar [ˈselə], s. der Keller; salt —, das Salzfaß.

cellarage [ˈseləridʒ], s. die Kellerei; die Einkellerung (storage).

cellarer [ˈselərə], s. der Kellermeister.

cellular [ˈseljulə], adj. zellartig, Zell-.

Celt [kelt, selt], s. der Kelte.

Celtic [ˈkeltik, ˈseltik], adj. keltisch.

cement [siˈment], s. der Zement, Mörtel. — v.a. auszementieren, verkitten.

cemetery [ˈsemətri], s. der Kirchhof, der Friedhof.

cenotaph [ˈsenotæf or -taːf], s. das Ehrengrabmal, Ehrendenkmal.

censer [ˈsensə], s. (Eccl.) das Weihrauchfaß.

censor [ˈsensə], s. der Zensor.

censorious [senˈsɔːriəs], adj. kritisch, tadelsüchtig.

censure [ˈsenʃə], s. der Tadel, Verweis. — v.a. tadeln.

census [ˈsensəs], s. die Volkszählung.

cent [sent], s. (Am.) der Cent (coin); (Comm.) per —, das Prozent.

centenarian [sentiˈnɛəriən], adj. hundertjährig. — s. der Hundertjährige.

centenary [senˈtiːnəri], s. die Hundertjahrfeier.

centennial [senˈtenjəl], adj. alle hundert Jahre, hundertjährig.

centipede [ˈsentipiːd], s. (Zool.) der Tausendfüßler.

central [ˈsentrəl], adj. zentral.

centralize [ˈsentrəlaiz], v.a. zentralisieren.

centre [ˈsentə], s. das Zentrum, der Mittelpunkt; die Mitte.

centric(al) [ˈsentrik(əl)], adj. (Engin., Maths.) zentral.

centrifugal [senˈtrifjugəl], adj. zentrifugal.

centrifuge [senˈtrifjuːdʒ], s. die Zentrifuge.

centripetal [senˈtripitl], adj. zentripetal, zum Mittelpunkt hinstrebend.

century [ˈsentʃuri], s. das Jahrhundert.

cereal [ˈsiəriəl], adj. vom Getreide, Getreide—. — s. die Kornmehlspeise.

cerebral [ˈseribrəl], adj. Gehirn-.

ceremonial [seriˈmounjəl], adj. feierlich, förmlich (formal). — s. das Zeremoniell.

ceremonious [seriˈmounjəs], adj. feierlich, zeremoniell.

ceremony [ˈseriməni], s. die Zeremonie, die Feier.

certain [ˈsɔːtin], adj. sicher, gewiß.

certainty [ˈsɔːtinti], s. die Gewißheit.

certificate [sɔːˈtifikit], s. das Zeugnis, die Bescheinigung.

certification [sɔːtifiˈkeiʃən], s. die Bescheinigung, Bezeugung.

certify [ˈsɔːtifai], v.a. bescheinigen, bezeugen, beglaubigen.

certitude [ˈsɔːtitjuːd], s. die Gewißheit.

cerulean [siˈruːljən], adj. himmelblau.

cesspool [ˈsespuːl], s. die Senkgrube.

cessation [seˈseiʃən], s. das Aufhören; (of hostilities) der Waffenstillstand.

cession [ˈseʃən], s. die Abtretung, der Verzicht (of, auf).

chafe [tʃeif], v.a. wärmen, warmreiben; erzürnen (annoy); wundreiben (skin). — v.n. toben, wüten.

chafer [ˈtʃeifə], s. (Ent.) der Käfer.

chaff [tʃɑːf], s. die Spreu; die Neckerei (teasing). — v.a. necken.

chaffer [ˈtʃæfə], v.n. handeln, schachern (haggle).

chaffinch [ˈtʃæfintʃ], s. (Orn.) der Buchfink.

chagrin [ʃæˈgriːn], s. der Verdruß, der Ärger.

chain [tʃein], s. die Kette. — v.a. anketten.

chair [tʃɛə], s. der Stuhl; (Univ.) Lehrstuhl. — v.a. vorsitzen (Dat.).

chairman [ˈtʃɛəmən], s. der Vorsitzende.

chalice [ˈtʃælis], s. (Eccl.) der Kelch.

chalk [tʃɔːk], s. die Kreide. — v.a. —
up, ankreiden, anschreiben.
chalky [ˈtʃɔːki], adj. (Geol.) kreidig,
kreideartig.
challenge [ˈtʃælindʒ], v.a. herausfordern; in Frage stellen (question);
anhalten (of a sentry). — s. die Herausforderung; das Anhalten (by a
sentry); die Einwendung.
chalybeate [kəˈlibiət], adj. (Med.)
eisenhaltig.
chamber [ˈtʃeimbə], s. das Zimmer, die
Kammer.
chamberlain [ˈtʃeimbəlin], s. der
Kammerherr.
chambermaid [ˈtʃeimbəmeid], s. das
Zimmermädchen, Kammermädchen.
chameleon [kəˈmiːljən], s. (Zool.) das
Chamäleon.
chamois [ˈʃæmwaː], s. (Zool.) die Gemse.
champagne [ʃæmˈpein], s. der Champagner, der Sekt.
champion [ˈtʃæmpjən], s. der Meister,
Verteidiger. — v.a. vertreten (cause);
beschützen (person).
chance [tʃaːns], s. der Zufall; die
Gelegenheit (opportunity); die
Möglichkeit (possibility); take a —,
es darauf ankommen lassen; by —,
zufällig. — v.a. zufällig tun, geraten;
riskieren (risk).
chancel [ˈtʃaːnsəl], s. (Eccl.) der Chor,
der Altarplatz.
chancellor [ˈtʃaːnsələ], s. der Kanzler.
chancery [ˈtʃaːnsəri], s. das Kanz-
leigericht.
chandelier [ʃændəˈliə], s. der Arm-
leuchter, Kronleuchter.
chandler [ˈtʃaːndlə], s. der Lichtzieher;
Krämer; (corn merchant) der Korn-
händler.
change [tʃeindʒ], s. die Änderung; das
Umsteigen (trains); small —, das
Kleingeld; die Veränderung; Abwechs-
lung. — v.a. ändern (alter); wechseln
(money); umsteigen (trains); eintauschen, umtauschen (exchange); sich
umziehen (clothes). — v.n. sich (ver)-
ändern, anders werden, umschlagen;
(Railw.) — for, umsteigen nach.
changeable [ˈtʃeindʒəbl], adj. veränderlich.
changeling [ˈtʃeindʒliŋ], s. der Wechselbalg.
changeover [ˈtʃeindʒouvə], s. der
Wechsel; der Umschalter; die Umstellung.
channel [ˈtʃænəl], s. der Kanal. — v.a.
leiten, kanalisieren.
chant [tʃaːnt], v.a., v.n. (Eccl.) singen.
— s. (Mus.) der Kantus, der litur-
gische Gesang.
chaos [ˈkeiɔs], s. das Chaos.
chaotic [keiˈɔtik], adj. chaotisch.
chap (1) [tʃæp], s. der Riss (skin etc.).
— v.n. Risse bekommen.
chap (2) [tʃæp], s. (usually in pl.) der
Kinnbacken.
chap (3) [tʃæp], s. (coll.) der Kerl, der
Bursche.

chapel [ˈtʃæpəl], s. (Eccl.) die Kapelle.
chaperon [ˈʃæpəroun], s. die Anstands-
dame. — v.a. begleiten, bemuttern.
chaplain [ˈtʃæplin], s. der Kaplan.
chapter [ˈtʃæptə], s. das Kapitel.
char [tʃaː], v.a. verkohlen. — v.n.
(coll.) putzen, Hausarbeit verrichten
(do housework). — s. (coll.) die Haus-
hilfe, die Hausgehilfin, Putzfrau.
character [ˈkærəktə], s. der Charakter
(personality); das Zeichen (sign, symbol); (Maths.) die Ziffer; das Zeugnis
(testimonial).
characteristic [kærəktəˈristik], adj.
charakteristisch, typisch.
characterize [ˈkærəktəraiz], v.a. charakterisieren, kennzeichnen.
charade [ʃəˈraːd], s. die Scharade, das
Silbenrätsel.
charcoal [ˈtʃaːkoul], s. die Holzkohle;
— burner, der Köhler.
charge [tʃaːdʒ], v.a. laden, aufladen;
(Law) beschuldigen; (Mil.) angreifen;
belasten (with a bill); — up to s.o.,
jemandem etwas anrechnen; verlangen
(price). — s. die Ladung, der Auftrag
(order); die Aufsicht; to be in —, die
Aufsicht haben; (Law) der Beschuldi-
gung, Anklage; das Mündel (of a
guardian); (pl.) die Kosten, Spesen.
chargeable [ˈtʃaːdʒəbl], adj. anzurech-
nend; steuerbar (of objects).
charger [ˈtʃaːdʒə], s. das Schlachtroß.
chariness [ˈtʃeərinis], s. die Behutsamkeit.
chariot [ˈtʃæriət], s. der Kriegswagen.
charioteer [tʃæriəˈtiə], s. der Wagen-
lenker.
charitable [ˈtʃæritəbl], adj. wohltätig,
mild, mildtätig.
charitableness [ˈtʃæritəblnis], s. die
Wohltätigkeit, Milde.
charity [ˈtʃæriti], s. die Güte; Nächs-
tenliebe; Mildtätigkeit (alms); die
Barmherzigkeit (charitableness); der
wohltätige Zweck (cause); sister of —,
barmherzige Schwester.
charlatan [ˈʃaːlətən], s. der Scharlatan,
Pfuscher.
charm [tʃaːm], s. der Zauber (magic);
der Reiz. — v.a. bezaubern.
chart [tʃaːt], s. (Geog.) die Karte. — v.a.
auf der Karte einzeichnen.
charter [ˈtʃaːtə], s. die Urkunde;
(Naut.) die Schiffsmiete. — v.a.
mieten, chartern, heuern (ship, plane);
ein Privileg geben, bevorrechtigen.
charwoman [ˈtʃaːwumən], s. die
Putzfrau, Reinemacherin.
chary [ˈtʃeəri], adj. behutsam; vorsichtig (cautious); sparsam (thrifty).
chase [tʃeis], v.a. jagen, verfolgen. — s.
die Jagd (hunt); das Gehege (game
preserve).
chaser [ˈtʃeisə], s. der Verfolger (pursuer); die Schiffskanone (gun).
chasm [kæzm], s. die Kluft; der
Abgrund.
chassis [ˈʃæsi], s. (Motor.) das Fahr-
gestell.

335

chaste

chaste [tʃeist], *adj.* keusch, züchtig.

chasten [tʃeisn], *v.a.* züchtigen; reinigen.

chastize [tʃæs'taiz], *v.a.* züchtigen.

chastity [tʃæstiti], *s.* die Keuschheit, Züchtigkeit.

chasuble [tʃæzjubl], *s. (Eccl.)* das Meßgewand.

chat [tʃæt], *v.n.* plaudern. — *s.* das Geplauder.

chattel [tʃætl], *s. (usually in pl.)* die Habe; *goods and —s,* Hab und Gut.

chatter [tʃætə], *v.n.* schwätzen; schnattern. — *s.* das Geschwätz *(talk).*

chatterbox [tʃætəbɔks], *s.* die Plaudertasche.

chatty [tʃæti], *adj.* geschwätzig.

chauffeur [ʃoufə, ʃou'fə:], *s. (Motor.)* der Fahrer.

chauffeuse [ʃou'fə:z], *s.* die Fahrerin.

chauvinism [ʃouvinizm], *s.* der Chauvinismus.

cheap [tʃi:p], *adj.* billig.

cheapen [tʃi:pən], *v.a.* herabsetzen, erniedrigen *(value).*

cheapness [tʃi:pnis], *s.* die Billigkeit *(price).*

cheat [tʃi:t], *v.a., v.n.* betrügen. — *s.* der Betrüger.

cheating [tʃi:tiŋ], *s.* das Betrügen; der Betrug.

check [tʃek], *s.* der Einhalt, der Halt; die Kontrolle; das Hindernis *(obstacle).* *(Chess)* Schach; *(Am.) see* **cheque.** — *v.a.* zurückhalten, aufhalten *(stop);* überprüfen. — *v.n.* Schach bieten *(Dat.).*

checker *see under* **chequer.**

checkmate [tʃekmeit], *s.* das Schachmatt.

cheek [tʃi:k], *s.* die Wange, die Backe; die Unverschämtheit *(impertinence).* — *v.a.* unverschämt sein *or* handeln *(s.o.,* an jemandem).

cheeky [tʃi:ki], *adj.* frech, unverschämt.

cheer [tʃiə], *v.a.* anfeuern, anspornen; zujubeln; — *up,* aufmuntern. — *v.n.* — *up,* Mut fassen. — *s.* der Zuruf; der Beifallsruf *(acclaim); three —s,* ein dreifaches Hoch *(for,* auf).

cheerful [tʃiəful], *adj.* fröhlich, froh.

cheerless [tʃiəlis], *adj.* unfreundlich, freudlos.

cheese [tʃi:z], *s.* der Käse; — *straw,* die Käsestange.

cheesecloth [tʃi:zklɔθ], *s. (Am.)* das Nesseltuch.

cheeseparing [tʃi:zpɛəriŋ], *adj.* knauserig.

cheesy [tʃi:zi], *adj.* käsig; *(sl.)* schlecht aussehend.

cheetah [tʃi:tə], *s. (Zool.)* der Jagdleopard.

chemical [kemikəl], *adj.* chemisch. — *s.* die Chemikalie, das chemische Element; das chemische Produkt.

chemise [ʃi'mi:z], *s.* das Frauenhemd.

chemist [kemist], *s.* der Chemiker; Drogist; Apotheker *(dispenser).*

chemistry [kemistri], *s.* die Chemie.

cheque, *(Am.)* **check** [tʃek], *s. (Fin.)* der Scheck.

chequer, checker [tʃekə], *s.* das scheckige Muster, Würfelmuster. — *v.a.* würfelig machen, bunt machen.

cherish [tʃeriʃ], *v.a.* hegen, wertschätzen, lieben.

cherry [tʃeri], *s. (Bot.)* die Kirsche; — *brandy,* das Kirschwasser.

chess [tʃes], *s.* das Schachspiel; —*man,* die Schachfigur; —*board,* das Schachbrett.

chest [tʃest], *s.* die Truhe *(box);* die Kiste; *(Anat.)* Brust; — *of drawers,* die Kommode.

chestnut [tʃestnʌt], *s. (Bot.)* die Kastanie; *(horse)* der Braune. — *adj.* kastanienbraun.

chew [tʃu:], *v.a.* kauen; —*ing gum,* der Kaugummi.

chic [ʃi:k], *adj.* elegant, schick.

chicanery [ʃi'keinəri], *s.* die Schikane, Haarspalterei, Kleinlichkeit.

chicken [tʃikin], *s.* das Huhn, Kücken; — *soup,* die Hühnersuppe.

chickenpox [tʃikinpɔks], *s. (Med.)* die Windpocken.

chicory [tʃikəri], *s. (Bot.)* die Zichorie.

chide [tʃaid], *v.a. irr.* schelten.

chief [tʃi:f], *s.* der Häuptling *(of tribe); (Am. coll.)* der Chef *(boss).* — *adj.* hauptsächlich, Haupt-, oberst.

chieftain [tʃi:ftin], *s.* der Häuptling *(of tribe);* Anführer *(leader).*

chilblain [tʃilblein], *s.* die Frostbeule.

child [tʃaild], *s.* das Kind.

childbirth [tʃaildbə:θ], *s.* die Niederkunft.

childhood [tʃaildhud], *s.* die Kindheit.

childish [tʃaildiʃ], *adj.* kindisch.

childlike [tʃaildlaik], *adj.* kindlich, wie ein Kind.

Chilean [tʃiliən], *adj.* chilenisch. — *s.* der Chilene.

chill [tʃil], *s.* die Kälte, der Frost; die Erkältung. — *v.a.* kalt machen *(freeze);* erstarren lassen *(make rigid);* entmutigen *(discourage).*

chilly [tʃili], *adj.* frostig, eisig, eiskalt.

chime [tʃaim], *s.* das Glockengeläute. — *v.n.* klingen, läuten.

chimera [ki'miərə], *s.* das Hirngespinst, das Trugbild.

chimney [tʃimni], *s.* der Kamin, der Schornstein; —*pot,* —*stack,* der Schornstein; —*sweep,* der Kaminfeger, Schornsteinfeger.

chimpanzee [tʃimpæn'zi:], *s. (Zool.)* der Schimpanse.

chin [tʃin], *s. (Anat.)* das Kinn.

china [tʃainə], *s.* das Porzellan; — *ware,* das Küchengeschirr.

chine (1) [tʃain], *s.* das Rückgrat.

chine (2) [tʃain], *s. (Geog.)* der Kamm.

Chinaman [tʃainəmən], *s. (obs.)* der Chinese.

Chinese [tʃai'ni:z], *adj.* chinesisch. — *s.* der Chinese.

chink [tʃink], *s.* die Ritze, der Spalt.

chip [tʃip], *v.a.* schnitzeln (*wood*); ausbrechen (*stone*); in kleine Stücke schneiden. — *v.n.* — *off*, abbröckeln; — *in*, (*coll.*) sich hineinmischen. —*s.* der Span (*wood*); der Splitter (*glass, stone*); (*pl.*) Pommes frites (*pl.*) (*potatoes*).

chiromancy ['kaiərɔmænsi], *s.* das Handlesen.

chiropodist [ki'rɔpədist], *s.* der Fußpfleger.

chirp [tʃəːp], *v.n.* zwitschern (*birds*), zirpen (*crickets*).

chirping ['tʃəːpiŋ], *s.* das Gezwitscher (*birds*), das Gezirpe (*crickets*).

chisel [tʃizl], *s.* der Meißel. — *v.a.* meißeln.

chit [tʃit], *s.* das Stück Papier; (*coll.*) junges Ding; —*chat*, das Geplauder.

chivalrous ['ʃivəlrəs], *adj.* ritterlich; tapfer (*brave*).

chivalry ['ʃivlri], *s.* die Ritterlichkeit (*courtesy*); Tapferkeit (*bravery*).

chive [tʃaiv], *s.* (*Bot.*) der Schnittlauch.

chlorate ['klɔːreit], *s.* (*Chem.*) das Chlorsalz.

chlorine ['klɔːriːn], *s.* (*Chem.*) das Chlor, Chlorgas.

chloroform ['klɔrəfɔːm], *s.* das Chloroform. — *v.a.* chloroformieren.

chocolate ['tʃɔkəlit], *s.* die Schokolade. — *adj.* schokoladenfarben.

choice [tʃɔis], *s.* die Wahl; Auswahl (*selection*). — *adj.* auserlesen.

choir ['kwaiə], *s.* der Chor.

choke [tʃouk], *v.a.*, *v.n.* ersticken; verstopfen (*block*). — *s.* (*Elec.*) die Drosselspule; (*Motor.*) die Starterklappe.

choler ['kɔlə], *s.* die Galle; (*fig.*) der Zorn (*anger*).

cholera ['kɔlərə], *s.* (*Med.*) die Cholera.

choleric ['kɔlərik], *adj.* jähzornig, cholerisch.

choose [tʃuːz], *v.a. irr.* wählen, auswählen (*select*).

choosy ['tʃuːzi], *adj.* wählerisch.

chop [tʃɔp], *v.a.* abhacken (*cut off*), hacken (*meat*). — *s.* das Kotelett (*meat*).

chopper ['tʃɔpə], *s.* das Hackbeil (*axe*); das Hackmesser (*knife*).

choppy ['tʃɔpi], *adj.* bewegt (*sea*), stürmisch.

chopstick ['tʃɔpstik], *s.* das Eßstäbchen.

choral ['kɔːrəl], *adj.* Chor-; — *society*, der Gesangverein.

chorale [kɔːrɑːl], *s.* (*Eccl.*, *Mus.*) der Choral.

chord [kɔːd], *s.* die Saite; (*Geom.*) die Sehne; (*Mus.*) der Akkord.

chorister ['kɔristə], *s.* der Chorknabe (*boy*), Chorsänger.

chorus ['kɔːrəs], *s.* der Chor (*opera*); der Refrain (*song*).

Christ [kraist], Christus, *m.*

christen [krisn], *v.a.* taufen (*baptize*), nennen (*name*).

Christendom ['krisndəm], *s.* die Christenheit.

christening ['krisniŋ], *s.* die Taufe.

Christian ['kristjən], *s.* der Christ (*believer in Christ*). — *adj.* christlich; — *name*, der Vorname.

Christianity [kristi'æniti], *s.* die christliche Religion, das Christentum.

Christmas ['krisməs], *s.* (die) Weihnachten; das Weihnachtsfest; — *Eve*, der heilige Abend.

chromatic [krɔ'mætik], *adj.* (*Mus.*) chromatisch.

chrome [kroum], *s.* das Chrom.

chronic ['krɔnik], *adj.* chronisch.

chronicle ['krɔnikl], *s.* die Chronik. — *v.a.* (in einer Chronik) verzeichnen.

chronological [krɔnə'lɔdʒikəl], *adj.* chronologisch.

chronology [krɔ'nɔlədʒi], *s.* die Chronologie.

chronometer [krɔ'nɔmitə], *s.* das Chronometer.

chrysalis ['krisəlis], *s.* (*Ent.*) die Puppe.

chrysanthemum [kri'zænθəməm], *s.* (*Bot.*) die Chrysantheme.

chub [tʃʌb], *s.* (*Zool.*) der Döbel.

chubby ['tʃʌbi], *adj.* pausbäckig, plump.

chuck [tʃʌk], *v.a.* (*coll.*) — *out*, hinauswerfen. — *v.n.* glucken (*chicken*).

chuckle [tʃʌkl], *v.n.* kichern. — *s.* das Kichern.

chum [tʃʌm], *s.* (*coll.*) der Freund, Kamerad. — *v.n.* (*coll.*) — *up*, sich befreunden (*with*, mit).

chump [tʃʌmp], *s.* der Klotz (*wood*).

chunk [tʃʌŋk], *s.* das große Stück (*meat etc.*).

church [tʃəːtʃ], *s.* die Kirche.

churchwarden [tʃəːtʃ'wɔːdn], *s.* der Kirchenvorsteher.

churchyard ['tʃəːtʃjɑːd], *s.* der Friedhof.

churl [tʃəːl], *s.* der Grobian, der grobe Kerl.

churlish ['tʃəːliʃ], *adj.* grob, unfein.

churn [tʃəːn], *s.* das Butterfaß. — *v.a.* mischen, schütteln (*butter etc.*); — *up*, aufwühlen (*stir up*).

chute [ʃuːt], *s.* die Gleitbahn.

cider ['saidə], *s.* der Apfelmost.

cigar [si'gɑː], *s.* die Zigarre; — *case*, das Zigarrenetui.

cigarette [sigə'ret], *s.* die Zigarette; — *holder*, die Zigarettenspitze; — *lighter*, das Feuerzeug.

cinder ['sində], *s.* (*usually in pl.*) die Asche (*fire*); die Schlacke (*furnace*).

Cinderella [sində'relə], das Aschenbrödel, Aschenputtel.

cinema ['sinimə], *s.* das Kino.

cinematography [sinimə'tɔgrəfi], *s.* die Filmkunst.

Cingalese *see* **Singhalese**.

cinnamon ['sinəmən], *s.* der Zimt.

cipher ['saifə], *s.* die Ziffer; die Geheimschrift (*code*). — *v.n.* rechnen. — *v.a.* chiffrieren (*code*).

Circassian [səː'kæsiən], *adj.* tscherkessisch. — *s.* der Tscherkesse.

circle

circle [sə:kl], s. der Zirkel, Kreis; (social) Gesellschaftskreis; (Theat.) der Rang. — v.a. umringen. — v.n. umkreisen; sich drehen (revolve).

circuit [ˈsə:kit], s. der Kreislauf; (Elec.) der Stromkreis.

circuitous [sə:ˈkju:itəs], adj. weitschweifig, weitläufig.

circular [ˈsə:kjulə], adj. rund, kreisförmig, Rund-; — tour, die Rundreise. — s. das Rundschreiben (letter); der Werbebrief (advertising).

circulate [ˈsə:kjuleit], v.a. in Umlauf setzen. — v.n. umlaufen, kreisen, zirkulieren.

circulation [sə:kjuˈleiʃən], s. die Zirkulation, der Kreislauf (blood); die Verbreitung, Auflage (newspaper); der Umlauf (banknotes).

circumcise [ˈsə:kəmsaiz], v.a. beschneiden.

circumference [sə:ˈkʌmfərəns], s. der Umfang.

circumscribe [ˈsə:kəmskraib], v.a. beschränken, einengen (narrow down); umschreiben (paraphrase).

circumspect [ˈsə:kəmspekt], adj. umsichtig, vorsorglich.

circumspection [sə:kəmˈspekʃən], s. die Umsicht, Vorsicht.

circumstance [ˈsə:kəmstæns, -stɑ:ns], s. der Umstand; pomp and —, großer Aufmarsch.

circumstantial [sə:kəmˈstænʃəl], adj. umständlich; zu einem Umstand gehörig; eingehend; — evidence, der Indizienbeweis.

circumvent [sə:kəmˈvent], v.a. überlisten, hintergehen.

circus [ˈsə:kəs], s. der Zirkus; der Platz.

cirrhus [ˈsirəs], s. die Federwolke.

Cistercian [sisˈtə:ʃən], s. der Zisterzienser (monk).

cistern [ˈsistən], s. die Zisterne, der Wasserbehälter.

citadel [ˈsitədəl], s. die Zitadelle, die Burg.

citation [saiˈteiʃən], s. das Zitat; (Law) die Zitierung, Vorladung; (Mil.) die rühmliche Erwähnung.

cite [sait], v.a. zitieren (quote); (Law) vorladen.

citizen [ˈsitizən], s. der Bürger, Staatsbürger (national); fellow —, der Mitbürger.

citizenship [ˈsitizənʃip], s. das Bürgerrecht, die Staatsangehörigkeit.

citrate [ˈsitreit], s. (Chem.) das Zitrat.

citric [ˈsitrik], adj. (Chem.) Zitronen-.

citron [ˈsitrən], s. die Zitrone. — adj. zitronenfarben.

city [ˈsiti], s. die Stadt; die Großstadt; die City. — adj. städtisch.

civic [ˈsivik], adj. Stadt-, städtisch (ceremonial); bürgerlich.

civil [ˈsivil], adj. zivil; höflich (polite); — engineer, der Zivilingenieur; — service, der Beamtendienst, die Beamtenlaufbahn, der Staatsdienst; — war, der Bürgerkrieg.

civilian [siˈviljən], s. der Zivilist.

civility [siˈviliti], s. die Höflichkeit.

civilization [sivilaiˈzeiʃən], s. die Zivilisation.

civilize [ˈsivilaiz], v.a. zivilisieren, verfeinern (refine).

clack [klæk], v.n. klappern (wood etc.); plaudern, plappern.

clad [klæd], adj. gekleidet.

claim [kleim], v.a. Anspruch erheben (to, auf); fordern (demand); behaupten (assert). — s. der Anspruch; die Forderung (demand); das Recht.

claimant [ˈkleimənt], s. der Beanspruchende, Ansprucherheber.

clairvoyance [klɛəˈvɔiəns], s. das Hellsehen.

clairvoyant [klɛəˈvɔiənt], s. der Hellseher.

clam [klæm], s. (Zool.) die Venusmuschel; shut up like a —, verschwiegen sein.

clamber [ˈklæmbə], v.n. klettern.

clamminess [ˈklæminis], s. die Feuchtigkeit, Klebrigkeit.

clammy [ˈklæmi], adj. feucht, klebrig.

clamorous [ˈklæmərəs], adj. lärmend, laut, ungestüm.

clamour [ˈklæmə], s. das Geschrei, der Lärm. — v.n. laut schreien (for, nach, Dat.).

clamp [klæmp], s. die Klammer, die Klampe. — v.a. festklammern.

clan [klæn], s. die Sippe, die Familie.

clandestine [klænˈdestin], adj. heimlich, verstohlen.

clang [klæŋ], s. der Schall, das Geklirr. — v.n. erschallen. — v.a. erschallen lassen.

clangour [ˈklæŋə], s. das Getöse, der Lärm.

clank [klæŋk], s. das Geklirre, das Gerassel (metal).

clannish [ˈklæniʃ], adj. stammesbewußt; engherzig (narrow).

clap [klæp], v.a. schlagen, zusammenschlagen (hands). — v.n. Beifall klatschen (Dat.).

clapperboard [ˈklæpəbɔ:d], s. (Film) das Klappbrett, die Klapptafel; der Klöppel (beater, in lacemaking).

claptrap [ˈklæptræp], s. der billige Effekt, das eitle Geschwätz (gossip).

claret [ˈklærit], s. der Rotwein.

clarification [klærifiˈkeiʃən], s. die Klarstellung, Aufklärung.

clarify [ˈklærifai], v.a. klarstellen.

clari(o)net [klæri(ə)ˈnet], s. (Mus.) die Klarinette.

clarion [ˈklæriən], s. (Mus.) die Zinke, Trompete; — call, der laute Ruf.

clash [klæʃ], v.a. zusammenschlagen. — v.n. aufeinanderprallen, zusammenfallen (dates); widerstreiten (views). — s. (fig.) der Zusammenstoß, der Widerstreit.

clasp [klɑ:sp], v.a. ergreifen, festhalten. — s. der Haken (hook); die Schnalle, die Spange (buckle, brooch); — knife, das Taschenmesser.

cloisters

class [klɑːs], *s.* die Klasse.
classic(al) ['klæsik(əl)], *adj.* klassisch.
classics ['klæsiks], *s. pl.* die Klassiker, *m. pl.*; die klassische Philologie (*subject of study*).
classification [klæsifi'keiʃən], *s.* die Klassifizierung.
classify ['klæsifai], *v.a.* klassifizieren.
clatter ['klætə], *s.* das Getöse, Geklirr. — *v.a., v.n.* klappern, klirren.
Claus [klɔːz]. Claus, Nicholas, *m.*; *Santa* —, der heilige Nikolaus, Knecht Ruprecht, Weihnachtsmann.
clause [klɔːz], *s.* (*Gram.*) der Nebensatz; die Klausel (*contract*); (*Law*) der Vertragspunkt.
claw [klɔː], *s.* die Klaue, die Kralle. — *v.a.* kratzen.
clay [klei], *s.* der Ton, Lehm.
clayey ['kleii], *adj.* lehmig, tonig.
clean [kliːn], *adj.* rein, reinlich (*habits*); sauber; — *shaven*, glattrasiert. — *v.a.* reinigen, putzen.
cleaner ['kliːnə], *s.* die Reinemacherin, die Putzfrau.
cleanliness ['klenlinis], *s.* die Reinlichkeit, Sauberkeit.
cleanse [klenz], *v.a.* reinigen.
clear [kliə], *adj.* klar, hell; deutlich (*meaning*); schuldlos (*not guilty*). — *s. in the* —, nicht betroffen, schuldlos. — *v.a.* (*Chem.*) klären; (*Law*) für unschuldig erklären; verzollen (*pass through customs*); springen (über, *Acc.*). — *v.n.* (— *up*), sich aufklären, aufhellen (*weather*).
clearance ['kliərəns], *s.* die Räumung; — *sale*, der Ausverkauf; die Verzollung (*customs*).
clearing ['kliəriŋ], *s.* die Lichtung (*in wood*); (*Comm.*) die Verrechnung.
clearness ['kliənis], *s.* die Deutlichkeit, die Klarheit, Helle.
cleave [kliːv], *v.a. irr.* spalten (*wood*). — *v.n.* sich spalten.
cleaver ['kliːvə], *s.* das Hackmesser.
cleek [kliːk], *s.* der Golfschläger.
clef [klef], *s.* (*Mus.*) der Schlüssel.
cleft [kleft], *s.* der Spalt. — *adj.* — *palate*, die Gaumenspalte.
clemency ['klemənsi], *s.* die Milde, Gnade (*mercy*).
clement ['klemənt], *adj.* mild (*climate*); gnädig (*merciful*).
clench [klentʃ], *v.a.* zusammenpressen; ballen (*fist*).
clergy ['kləːdʒi], *s.* (*Eccl.*) die Geistlichkeit.
clergyman ['kləːdʒimən], *s.* (*Eccl.*) der Geistliche.
clerical ['klerikl], *adj.* (*Eccl.*) geistlich; beamtlich, Beamten-, Büro- (*office*); — *work*, die Büroarbeit.
clerk [klɑːk], *s.* der Schreiber, der Bürogehilfe (*junior*), der Bürobeamte, Büroangestellte (*senior*); *bank* —, der Bankbeamte.
clever ['klevə], *adj.* klug; intelligent; geschickt (*deft*); gewandt, listig (*cunning*).

cleverness ['klevənis], *s.* die Klugheit (*intelligence*); die Schlauheit (*cunning*); die Begabung (*talent*); die Geschicklichkeit (*skill*).
clew [kluː] *see* **clue.**
click [klik], *v.a., v.n.* einschnappen (*lock*); zusammenschlagen (*o.'s heels*, die Hacken); schnalzen (*o.'s tongue*); (*sl.*) zusammenpassen (*of two people*). — *s.* das Einschnappen (*lock*); das Zusammenschlagen (*heels*); das Schnalzen (*tongue*).
client ['klaiənt], *s.* (*Law*) der Klient; (*Comm.*) der Kunde.
clientele [kliːən'tel], *s.* die Klientel, die Kundschaft.
cliff [klif], *s.* die Klippe.
climate ['klaimit], *s.* das Klima.
climatic [klai'mætik], *adj.* klimatisch.
climax ['klaimæks], *s.* der Höhepunkt.
climb [klaim], *v.a.* erklettern, erklimmen. — *v.n.* klettern, bergsteigen; (*Aviat.*) steigen. — *s.* der Aufstieg, die Ersteigung.
climber ['klaimə], *s.* der Bergsteiger (*mountaineer*); (*Bot.*) die Schlingpflanze.
clinch [klintʃ], *v.a.* vernieten, befestigen; — *a deal*, einen Handel abschließen. — *s.* der feste Griff; die Umklammerung (*boxing*).
cling [kliŋ], *v.n. irr.* sich anklammern, festhalten (*to*, an).
clinic ['klinik], *s.* die Klinik.
clinical ['klinikl], *adj.* klinisch.
clink [kliŋk], *s.* das Geklirre; (*coll.*) das Gefängnis. — *v.a.* klingen — *glasses*, mit den Gläsern anstoßen.
clinker ['kliŋkə], *s.* der Backstein; die Schlacke.
clip (1) [klip], *v.a.* stutzen, beschneiden; lochen (*ticket*).
clip (2) [klip], *v.a.* befestigen. — *s. paper* —, die Büroklammer.
clippings ['klipiŋz], *s. pl.* die Abschnitte; die Schnitzel (*waste*); Zeitungsausschnitte, *m. pl.*
cloak [klouk], *s.* der Mantel, der Deckmantel (*cover*). — *v.a.* verbergen.
cloakroom ['kloukruːm], *s.* die Garderobe; — *free*, keine Garderobegebühr; (*Railw.*) die Gepäckaufbewahrung.
clock [klɔk], *s.* die (große) Uhr, Wanduhr; — *face*, das Zifferblatt. — *v.n.* — *in*, die Zeitkarte (Kontrollkarte) stempeln lassen, eintreffen (*arrive*).
clockwise ['klɔkwaiz], *adv.* im Uhrzeigersinne.
clod [klɔd], *s.* die Erdscholle, der Erdklumpen; (*sl.*) der Lümmel (*lout*).
clog [klɔg], *v.a.* belasten, hemmen, verstopfen. — *v.n.* sich verstopfen. — *s.* der Holzschuh.
cloisters ['klɔistəz], *s. pl.* (*Eccl., Archit.*) der Kreuzgang.

close

close [klouz], *v.a.* schließen, verschließen; beenden (*meeting etc.*). —
v.n. — *in on*, über einen hereinbrechen,
umzingeln. — *s.* das Ende, der Schluß;
[klous] der Domplatz. — [klous], *adj.*
nahe (*near*); knapp (*narrow*); nahe-
stehend, vertraut (*friend*); schwül
(*weather*); geizig (*miserly*).

closeness ['klousnis], *s.* die Nähe
(*nearness*); die Schwüle (*weather*);
die Vertrautheit (*familiarity*).

closet ['klɔzit], *s.* der Wandschrank
(*cupboard*); das kleine Zimmer; das
Klosett (*W.C.*). — *v.r.* — *o.s. with*,
sich mit jemandem zurückziehen, sich
vertraulich beraten.

closure ['klouʒə], *s.* der Schluß; der
Abschluß (einer Debatte).

clot [klɔt], *s.* das Klümpchen. — *v.n.*
sich verdicken, gerinnen; —*ted cream*,
dicke Sahne.

cloth [klɔθ], *s.* das Tuch; der Stoff; die
Leinwand (*bookbinding*); *American* —,
das Wachstuch; — *printing*, der
Zeugdruck.

clothe [klouð], *v.a.* kleiden. — *v.r.* sich
kleiden.

clothes [klouðz], *s. pl.* die Kleider, *n. pl.*;
die Kleidung; die Wäsche (*washing*);
— *basket*, der Wäschekorb; — *press*,
der Kleiderschrank.

clothier ['klouðiə], *s.* der Tuchmacher
(*manufacturer*); der Tuchhändler
(*dealer*).

clothing ['klouðiŋ], *s.* die Kleidung.

cloud [klaud], *s.* die Wolke; *under a* —, in
Ungnade; —*burst*, der Wolkenbruch.
— *v.a.* bewölken, verdunkeln. — *v.n.*
— *over*, sich umwölken.

cloudiness ['klaudinis], *s.* die Um-
wölkung, der Wolkenhimmel.

cloudy ['klaudi], *adj.* wolkig, bewölkt,
umwölkt.

clout [klaut], *s.* (*obs.*) der Lappen (*rag*);
(*coll.*) der Schlag (*hit*). — *v.a.* schlagen
(*hit*).

clove [klouv], *s.* die Gewürznelke (*spice*).

clove(n) [klouv(n)], *adj.* gespalten.

clover ['klouvə], *s.* (*Bot.*) der Klee; *to
be in* —, Glück haben, es gut haben.

clown [klaun], *s.* der Hanswurst. — *v.n.*
den Hanswurst spielen.

clownish ['klauniʃ], *adj.* tölpelhaft.

clownishness ['klauniʃnis], *s.* die
Derbheit, Tölpelhaftigkeit.

cloy [klɔi], *v.n.* übersättigen, anwidern,
anekeln.

club (1) [klʌb], *s.* die Keule (*stick*). —
v.a. (einen) mit einer Keule schlagen.

club (2) [klʌb], *s.* der Klub, der Verein. —
v.n. — *together*, zusammen beitragen,
zusammensteuern (*contribute jointly*).

club (3) [klʌb], *s.* (*cards*) das Treff, die
Eichel (*German cards*).

clubfoot ['klʌbfut], *s.* der Klumpfuß.

cluck [klʌk], *v.n.* glucken (*hen*).

clue [klu:], *s.* der Anhaltspunkt,
Leitfaden, die Richtlinie, die Angabe
(*crossword*); *no* —, keine blasse
Ahnung.

clump [klʌmp], *s.* der Klumpen; die
Gruppe.

clumsiness ['klʌmzinis], *s.* die Unbeholfenheit, Ungeschicklichkeit.

clumsy ['klʌmzi], *adj.* unbeholfen,
schwerfällig, ungeschickt.

Cluniac ['klu:njæk]. (*Eccl.*) der Klu-
niazenser.

cluster ['klʌstə], *s.* die Traube (*grapes*),
der Büschel. — *v.n.* in Büscheln
wachsen *or* stehen, dicht gruppiert
sein.

clutch [klʌtʃ], *v.a.* ergreifen, packen
(*grip*). — *s.* der Griff; (*Motor.*) die
Kupplung.

coach [koutʃ], *s.* die Kutsche; der
Wagen, der Autobus; der Privatlehrer
(*teacher*). — *v.a.* unterrichten,
vorbereiten (*for examinations etc.*).

coachman ['koutʃmən], *s.* der Kutscher.

coagulate [kou'ægjuleit], *v.a.* gerinnen
lassen. — *v.n.* gerinnen.

coagulation [kouægju'leiʃən], *s.* das
Gerinnen.

coal [koul], *s.* die Kohle; — *mine*, das
Kohlenbergwerk; die Kohlengrube; —
miner, der Bergmann.

coalesce [kouə'les], *v.n.* zusammen-
wachsen, sich vereinigen.

coalescence [kouə'lesəns], *s.* die Verschmelzung.

coalition [kouə'liʃən], *s.* (*Pol.*) die
Koalition, das Bündnis.

coarse [kɔ:s], *adj.* grob; gemein
(*manner*).

coarseness ['kɔ:snis], *s.* die Grobheit,
Unfeinheit.

coast [koust], *s.* die Küste. — *v.n.* (an
der Küste) entlangfahren; gleiten,
rodeln.

coat [kout], *s.* der Mantel, Rock; die
Jacke (*jacket*); das Fell (*animal*); —
of arms, das Wappenschild; — *of
mail*, das Panzerhemd; — *of paint*, der
Anstrich. — *v.a.* überziehen, bemalen
(*paint*).

coathanger ['kouthæŋə], *s.* der Kleiderbügel.

coating ['koutiŋ], *s.* der Überzug.

coax [kouks], *v.a.* beschwatzen; überreden (*persuade*).

cob (1) [kɔb], *s.* der Gaul.

cob (2) [kɔb], *s.* (*Orn.*) der Schwan.

cob (3) [kɔb], *s.* der (Mais)Kolben
(*corn on the* —).

cobble [kɔbl], *v.a.* flicken (*shoes*).

cobbled ['kɔbld], *adj.* mit Kopfsteinen
gepflastert.

cobbler ['kɔblə], *s.* der Schuhflicker.

cobble(stone) ['kɔbl(stoun)], *s.* das
Kopfsteinpflaster.

cobweb ['kɔbweb], *s.* das Spinngewebe.

cock [kɔk], *s.* (*Orn.*) der Hahn; (*Engin.*)
der Sperrhahn, Hahn; — *sparrow*, das
Sperlingsmännchen; — *-a-doodle-doo!*
kikeriki!

cockade [kɔ'keid], *s.* die Kokarde.

cockatoo [kɔkə'tu:], *s.* (*Orn.*) der
Kakadu.

collier

cockchafer ['kɔktʃeifə], s. (Ent.) der Maikäfer.
cockerel ['kɔkərəl], s. (Orn.) der junge Hahn.
cockswain [kɔksn] see **coxswain.**
cockle [kɔkl], s. (Zool.) die Herzmuschel.
cockney ['kɔkni], s. der geborene Londoner.
cockpit ['kɔkpit], s. (Aviat.) der Pilotensitz, die Kanzel, der Führerraum.
cockroach ['kɔkroutʃ], s. (Ent.) die Schabe.
cocksure ['kɔkʃuə], adj. zuversichtlich, allzu sicher.
cocoa ['koukou], s. der Kakao.
coconut ['koukɔnʌt], s. die Kokosnuß.
cocoon [kə'ku:n], s. der Kokon, die Puppe (of silkworm).
cod [kɔd], s. der Kabeljau, Dorsch; — liver oil, der Lebertran; dried —, der Stockfisch.
coddle [kɔdl], v.a. verhätscheln, verweichlichen.
code [koud], s. das Gesetzbuch, der Kodex; die Chiffre (cipher). — v.a. chiffrieren, schlüsseln.
codify ['koudifai], v.a. kodifizieren.
coerce [kou'ə:s], v.a. zwingen.
coercion [kou'ə:ʃən], s. der Zwang.
coercive [kou'ə:siv], adj. zwingend.
coeval [kou'i:vəl], adj. gleichaltrig, gleichzeitig.
coexist [kouig'zist], v.n. zugleich existieren, nebeneinander leben.
coffee ['kɔfi], s. der Kaffee; — grinder, die Kaffeemühle; — grounds, der Kaffeesatz; — pot, die Kaffeekanne; — set, das Kaffee service.
coffer ['kɔfə], s. der Kasten, die Truhe.
coffin ['kɔfin], s. der Sarg.
cog [kɔg], s. der Zahn (on wheel); — wheel, das Zahnrad.
cogency ['koudʒənsi], s. die zwingende Kraft, Triftigkeit.
cogent ['koudʒənt], adj. zwingend, triftig.
cogitate ['kɔdʒiteit], v.n. nachdenken.
cogitation [kɔdʒi'teiʃən], s. die Überlegung, das Nachdenken.
cognate ['kɔgneit], adj. verwandt.
cognisance ['kɔgnizəns], s. die Erkenntnis; die Kenntnisnahme; (Law) die gerichtliche Kenntnisnahme.
cognisant ['kɔgnizənt], adj. wissend, in vollem Wissen (of, Genit.).
cognition [kɔg'niʃən], s. die Kenntnis, das Erkennen.
cohabit [kou'hæbit], v.n. zusammenleben.
cohabitation [kouhæbi'teiʃən], s. das Zusammenleben.
coheir [kou'εə], s. der Miterbe.
cohere [kou'hiə], v.n. zusammenhängen.
coherence [kou'hiərəns], s. der Zusammenhang.
coherent [kou'hiərənt], adj. zusammenhängend.

cohesion [kou'hi:ʒən], s. (Phys.) die Kohäsion.
coiffure [kwæ'fjuə], s. die Frisur, die Haartracht.
coil [kɔil], s. (Elec.) die Spule (of Winding. — v.a. aufwickeln; umwickeln, (auf)spulen. — v.n. sich winden.
coin [kɔin], s. die Münze, das Geldstück. — v.a. münzen, prägen; — a phrase, eine Redewendung prägen.
coinage ['kɔinidʒ], s. die Prägung.
coincide [kouin'said], v.n. zusammenfallen, zusammentreffen.
coincidence [kou'insidəns], s. das Zusammenfallen, Zusammentreffen; der Zufall (chance).
coincident [kou'insidənt], adj. zusammentreffend.
coke [kouk], s. der Koks. — v.a. (Chem., Engin.) verkoken.
cold [kould], adj. kalt; gefühllos, kühl. — s. die Kälte (temperature); die Erkältung (indisposition).
coldish ['kouldiʃ], adj. kühl.
coldness ['kouldnis], s. die Kälte (temperature); die Kaltherzigkeit (heartlessness).
colic ['kɔlik], s. die Kolik.
collaborate [kə'læbəreit], v.n. zusammenarbeiten.
collaboration [kəlæbə'reiʃən], s. die Zusammenarbeit; die Mitwirkung, Mitarbeit (assistance).
collaborator [kə'læbəreitə], s. der Mitarbeiter.
collapse [kə'læps], s. der Zusammenbruch. — v.n. zusammenbrechen (disintegrate); zerfallen, einstürzen.
collapsible [kə'læpsibl], adj. zerlegbar, zusammenlegbar, zusammenklappbar.
collar ['kɔlə], s. der Kragen; —bone, das Schlüsselbein (Anat.); dog —, das Halsband; (coll.) der Priesterkragen; —stud, der Kragenknopf. — v.a. beim Kragen fassen, ergreifen.
collate [kɔ'leit], v.a. vergleichen (texts etc.).
collateral [kɔ'lætərəl], adj. Seiten-, von beiden Seiten. — s. (Am.) die Garantie, Bürgschaft.
collation [kɔ'leiʃən], s. die Vergleichung, der Vergleich (texts etc.); der Imbiß.
colleague ['kɔli:g], s. der Kollege, die Kollegin.
collect [kə'lekt], v.a. sammeln, zusammenbringen. — v.n. sich versammeln. — ['kɔlikt], s. (Eccl.) die Kollekte.
collection [kə'lekʃən], s. die Sammlung.
collective [kə'lektiv], adj. kollektiv, gemeinsam. — s. (Pol.) das Kollektiv.
collector [kə'lektə], s. der Sammler.
college ['kɔlidʒ], s. das Kollegium; das College; die Hochschule, Universität.
collide [kə'laid], v.n. zusammenstoßen.
collie ['kɔli], s. der Schäferhund.
collier ['kɔliə], s. der Kohlenarbeiter; das Kohlenfrachtschiff (boat).

341

collision

collision [kə'liʒən], s. der Zusammenstoß, Zusammenprall.
collocate ['kɔləkeit], v.a. ordnen.
collodion [kə'loudjən], s. (Chem.) das
Kollodium.
colloquial [kə'loukwiəl], adj. umgangssprachlich, Umgangs-.
colloquy ['kɔlekwi], s. die Unterredung,
das Gespräch (formal).
collusion [kə'lu:ʒən], s. das heimliche
Einverständnis, die unstatthafte Partnerschaft; die Verdunkelung.
collusive [kə'lu:ziv], adj. abgekartet.
Cologne [kə'loun]. Köln, n.; eau de —,
Kölnisch Wasser.
Colombian [kə'lɔmbjən], adj. kolum-
bisch. — s. der Kolumbier.
colon (1) ['koulən], s. das Kolon, der
Doppelpunkt.
colon (2) ['koulən], s. (Med.) der
Dickdarm.
colonel [kə:nl], s. (Mil.) der Oberst; —
-in-chief, der Generaloberst, der oberste Befehlshaber; lieutenant- —, der
Oberstleutnant.
colonial [kə'lounjəl], adj. kolonial, aus
den Kolonien.
colonist ['kɔlənist], s. der Siedler;
Ansiedler.
colonization [kɔlənai'zeiʃən], s. die
Kolonisierung, Besiedelung.
colonize ['kɔlənaiz], v.a. besiedeln,
kolonisieren.
colonnade [kɔlə'neid], s. die Kolonnade,
der Säulengang.
colony ['kɔləni], s. die Kolonie.
colophony [kə'lɔfəni], s. das Kolo-
phonium (resin).
coloration [kʌlə'reiʃən], s. die Färbung,
Tönung.
colossal [kə'lɔsəl], adj. kolossal, riesig,
riesenhaft.
colour ['kʌlə], s. die Farbe; (complexion) die Gesichtsfarbe; (paint)
die Farbe, der Anstrich; (dye) die
Färbung. — v.a. färben; anstreichen
(paint house etc.).
colt [koult], s. das Füllen.
columbine ['kɔləmbain], s. (Bot.) die
Akelei.
column ['kɔləm], s. die Säule; die
Spalte (press); (also Mil.) die Kolonne.
colza ['kɔlzə], s. (Bot.) der Raps.
coma ['koumə], s. (Med.) das Koma,
die Schlafsucht.
comb [koum], s. der Kamm. — v.a.
kämmen; (fig.) genau untersuchen.
combat ['kʌmbət, 'kɔmbət], s. der
Kampf, das Gefecht; in single —, im
Duell, Zweikampf. — v.a. kämpfen,
bekämpfen.
combatant ['kʌmbətənt, 'kɔmb-], s. der
Kämpfer.
comber ['koumə], s. der Wollkämmer.
combination [kɔmbi'neiʃən], s. die
Kombination, die Verbindung.
combine [kəm'bain], v.a. kombinieren,
verbinden. — v.n. sich verbinden. —
['kɔmbain], s. (Comm.) der Trust,
Ring.

combustible [kəm'bʌstibl], adj. verbrennbar; feuergefährlich.
combustion [kəm'bʌstʃən], s. die
Verbrennung.
come [kʌm], v.n. kommen; — about,
sich ereignen (event); — across,
stoßen auf (Acc.); — by (s.th.),
ergattern, erwerben; — for, abholen;
— forth, forward, hervorkommen,
hervortreten; — from, herkommen
von, — in, hereinkommen; — off, (of
object) loskommen, (succeed) glücken;
— out (appear), herauskommen;
— to o.s., zu sich kommen; — of age,
mündig werden; — to o.'s senses,
zur Besinnung or Vernunft kommen;
that is still to —, das steht uns noch
bevor.
comedian [kə'mi:djən], s. der Komödiant, Komiker (stage).
comedy ['kɔmədi], s. die Komödie, das
Lustspiel.
comeliness ['kʌmlinis], s. die Anmut,
Schönheit.
comely ['kʌmli], adj. anmutig, schön.
comestible [kə'mestibl], s. (usually pl.)
die Eßwaren, f. pl.
comet ['kɔmit], s. der Komet.
comfit ['kʌmfit], s. das Konfekt, die
Bonbons.
comfort ['kʌmfət], s. der Trost (solace);
der Komfort, die Bequemlichkeit. —
v.a. trösten.
comforter ['kʌmfətə], s. der Tröster;
(Am.) die Steppdecke.
comfortless ['kʌmfətlis], adj. trostlos,
unbehaglich.
comic ['kɔmik], adj. komisch; —
writer, humoristischer Schriftsteller.
— s. die Bilderzeitung (children's
paper).
comical ['kɔmikl], adj. lächerlich, zum
Lachen, komisch.
comma ['kɔmə], s. das Komma, der
Beistrich; inverted —s, die Anführungszeichen.
command [kə'ma:nd], v.a., v.n. (Mil.)
kommandieren; über jemanden verfügen (have s.o. at o.'s disposal). — s.
der Befehl.
commandant [kɔmən'dænt], s. der
Kommandant, Befehlshaber.
commander [kə'ma:ndə], s. der Befehlshaber.
commandment [kə'ma:ndmənt], s.
(Rel.) das Gebot.
commemorate [kə'meməreit], v.a.
feiern, gedenken (Genit.).
commemoration [kəmemə'reiʃən], s.
die Feier, die Gedächtnisfeier.
commemorative [kə'memərətiv], adj.
Gedächtnis-.
commence [kə'mens], v.a., v.n. beginnen, anfangen.
commencement [kə'mensmənt], s. der
Anfang, der Beginn.
commend [kə'mend], v.a. empfehlen,
loben (praise).
commendable [kə'mendəbl], adj. emp-
fehlenswert.

342

commendation [kɔmen'deiʃən], s. die Empfehlung.

commensurable, commensurate [kə'menʃərəbl, kə'menʃərit], adj. kommensurabel, entsprechend; angemessen.

comment ['kɔment], v.n. kommentieren (on, zu, Dat.). — s. der Kommentar; die Bemerkung (remark).

commentary ['kɔməntəri], s. der Kommentar.

commentator ['kɔmənteitə], s. der Kommentator, Berichterstatter.

commerce ['kɔmə:s], s. der Handel; college of —, die Handelsschule.

commercial [kə'mə:ʃəl], adj. kommerziell, kaufmännisch, Handels-; — traveller, der Handelsreisende, Vertreter; — manager, der geschäftliche Leiter.

commingle [kə'miŋgl], v.a. vermischengefühl.

commiserate [kə'mizəreit], v.n. bemitleiden; — with s.o., mit einem Mitgefühl haben.

commissariat [kɔmi'sɛəriət], s. (Pol.) das Kommissariat.

commissary ['kɔmisəri], s. der Kommissar. — adj. kommissarisch.

commission [kə'miʃən], s. die Kommission; (Mil.) der Offiziersrang; die Begehung (of crime); (Law) die (offizielle) Kommission; der Auftrag, die Bestellung (order).

commissionaire [kəmiʃən'ɛə], s. der Portier.

commissioned [kə'miʃənd], adj. bevollmächtigt.

commissioner [kə'miʃənə], s. (Pol.) der Kommissar, der Bevollmächtigte.

commit [kə'mit], v.a. begehen (do); übergeben (consign); anvertrauen (entrust). — v.r. sich verpflichten.

committal [kə'mitl], s. das Übergeben; die Überantwortung.

committee [kə'miti], s. das Kommitee, der Ausschuß.

commodious [kə'moudiəs], adj. bequem, geräumig.

commodity [kə'mɔditi], s. (Comm.) die Ware, der Artikel.

commodore ['kɔmədɔ:], s. (Naut.) der Kommodore, der Kommandant eines Geschwaders.

common ['kɔmən], adj. gewöhnlich (usual); gemein (vulgar); allgemein (general); in —, gemeinschaftlich; — sense, der gesunde Menschenverstand; the — man, der kleine Mann. — n. pl. House of Commons, das Unterhaus.

commoner ['kɔmənə], s. der Bürger; (Parl.) Mitglied des Unterhauses.

commonness ['kɔmənnis], s. die Gemeinheit (vulgarity); das häufige Vorkommen (frequency).

commonplace ['kɔmənpleis], adj. alltäglich. — s. der Gemeinplatz.

commonwealth ['kɔmənwelθ], s. die Staatengemeinschaft, der Staatenbund; das Commonwealth.

commotion [kə'mouʃən], s. die Erschütterung; der Aufruhr; der Lärm.

communal ['kɔmjunəl], adj. gemeinschaftlich, allgemein; (Pol.) Kommunal-.

commune ['kɔmju:n], s. (Pol.) die Kommune. — [kə'mju:n], v.n. sich unterhalten.

communicable [kə'mju:nikəbl], adj. mitteilbar; übertragbar.

communicate [kə'mju:nikeit], v.a. mitteilen; verkünden (proclaim); benachrichtigen. — v.n. in Verbindung stehen.

communication [kəmju:ni'keiʃən], s. die Mitteilung; Verlautbarung; die Verkündigung (proclamation); die Information; (Elec.) die Verbindung; (pl.), die Verbindungslinie; —s engineering, Fernmeldetechnik.

communion [kə'mju:njən], s. (Eccl.) die Kommunion; das heilige Abendmahl; die Gemeinschaft (fellowship).

Communism ['kɔmjunizm], s. (Pol.) der Kommunismus.

Communist ['kɔmjunist], s. der Kommunist. — adj. kommunistisch.

community [kə'mju:niti], s. die Gemeinschaft.

commutable [kə'mju:təbl], adj. umtauschbar, auswechselbar.

commutation [kɔmju'teiʃən], s. der Austausch; (Law) die Herabsetzung (of sentence).

commutator ['kɔmjuteitə], s. (Elec.) der Umschalter.

commute [kə'mju:t], v.n. hin und her fahren, pendeln, mit Zeitkarte fahren (travel). — v.a. herabsetzen (sentence).

compact ['kɔmpækt], adj. kompakt, fest; gedrängt (succinct); kurz, bündig (short).

companion [kəm'pænjən], s. der Gefährte, die Gefährtin.

companionable [kəm'pænjənəbl], adj. gesellig, freundlich.

companionship [kəm'pænjənʃip], s. die Geselligkeit; die Gesellschaft.

company ['kʌmpəni], s. die Gesellschaft; (Mil.) die Kompanie; der Freundeskreis (circle of friends); (Comm.) die Handelsgesellschaft; limited (liability) —, Gesellschaft mit beschränkter Haftung; public (private) —, Gesellschaft des öffentlichen (privaten) Rechtes.

comparative [kəm'pærətiv], adj. vergleichend, relativ. — s. (Gram.) der Komparativ.

compare [kəm'pɛə], v.a. vergleichen. — v.n. sich vergleichen lassen.

comparison [kəm'pærisən], s. der Vergleich; die Gleichnis (simile).

compartment [kəm'pa:tmənt], s. (Railw.) das Abteil; die Abteilung.

compass ['kʌmpəs], s. der Umkreis, Umfang (scope); (Naut.) der Kompaß; point of the —, der Kompaßstrich; (Engin.) der Zirkel.

compassion

compassion [kəm'pæʃən], *s.* die Barmherzigkeit, das Mitleid, das Erbarmen.
compassionate [kəm'pæʃənit], *adj.* mitleidig; (*Mil.*) — *leave,* der Sonderurlaub.
compatibility [kəmpæti'biliti], *s.* die Verträglichkeit, Vereinbarkeit.
compatible [kəm'pætibl], *adj.* verträglich, vereinbar.
compatriot [kəm'peitriət], *s.* der Landsmann.
compel [kəm'pel], *v.a.* zwingen, nötigen.
compendium [kəm'pendjəm], *s.* das Kompendium, die kurze Schrift, die kurze Darstellung.
compensate ['kɔmpənseit], *v.a.* kompensieren, einem Ersatz leisten.
compensation [kɔmpən'seiʃən], *s.* der Ersatz, die Wiedergutmachung.
compensatory [kɔmpən'seitəri], *adj.* ausgleichend, Ersatz-.
compete [kəm'pi:t], *v.n.* wetteifern, konkurrieren.
competence, competency ['kɔmpitəns, -nsi], *s.* die Kompetenz; Zuständigkeit; Befähigung (*capability*); Tüchtigkeit (*ability*).
competent ['kɔmpitənt], *adj.* kompetent; zuständig; fähig (*capable*); tüchtig (*able*).
competition [kɔmpi'tiʃən], *s.* die Konkurrenz; die Mitbewerbung (*for job*).
competitive [kəm'petitiv], *adj.* Konkurrenz-, konkurrierend.
competitor [kəm'petitə], *s.* (*Comm.*) der Konkurrent; der Mitbewerber (*fellow applicant*), Teilnehmer (*sport*).
complacent [kəm'pleisənt], *adj.* selbstzufrieden, selbstgefällig.
complain [kəm'plein], *v.n.* sich beklagen (*of,* über, *Acc.*).
complaint [kəm'pleint], *s.* die Klage; Beschwerde (*grievance*); das Leiden (*illness*).
complement ['kɔmplimənt], *s.* die Ergänzung, Gesamtzahl. — [-'ment], *v.a.* ergänzen.
complementary [kɔmpli'mentəri], *adj.* Ergänzungs-, ergänzend.
complete [kəm'pli:t], *adj.* komplett; voll (*full up*); vollkommen (*perfect*). — *v.a.* vollenden (*end*); ergänzen (*make whole*).
completeness [kəm'pli:tnis], *s.* die Vollendung (*condition*); Ganzheit (*wholeness*).
completion [kəm'pli:ʃən], *s.* die Vollendung (*fulfilment*); die Beendigung (*ending*); der Abschluß.
complex ['kɔmpleks], *adj.* (*Maths.*) komplex; kompliziert (*complicated*). — *s.* der Komplex (*Archit., Psych.*).
complexion [kəm'plekʃən], *s.* die Gesichtsfarbe; (*fig.*) das Aussehen.
complexity [kəm'pleksiti], *s.* die Kompliziertheit; die Schwierigkeit.
compliance [kəm'plaiəns], *s.* die Willfährigkeit, Einwilligung.
compliant [kəm'plaiənt], *adj.* willig, willfährig.

complicate ['kɔmplikeit], *v.a.* komplizieren, erschweren.
complication [kɔmpli'keiʃən], *s.* die Komplikation, die Erschwerung.
complicity [kəm'plisiti], *s.* (*Law*) die Mitschuld.
compliment ['kɔmplimənt], *s.* das Kompliment. — [-'ment], *v.n.* Komplimente machen.
complimentary [kɔmpli'mentəri], *adj.* lobend; — *ticket,* die Freikarte.
comply [kəm'plai], *v.n.* einwilligen (*with,* in, *Acc.*); sich halten (*an, Acc.*).
compose [kəm'pouz], *v.a., v.n.* (*Mus.*) komponieren; beruhigen (*the mind*); (*Lit.*) verfassen; (*Typ.*) setzen.
composed [kəm'pouzd], *adj.* ruhig, gefaßt.
composer [kəm'pouzə], *s.* (*Mus.*) der Komponist.
composite ['kɔmpəzit], *adj.* zusammengesetzt.
composition [kɔmpə'ziʃən], *s.* (*Mus. etc.*) die Komposition; Beschaffenheit Zusammensetzung.
compositor [kəm'pɔzitə], *s.* (*Typ.*) der Schriftsetzer.
compost [kəm'pɔst], *s.* (*Agr.*) der Dünger, Kompost.
composure [kəm'pouʒə], *s.* die Gelassenheit, die Gemütsruhe, die Fassung.
compound ['kɔmpaund], *s.* (*Chem.*) die Verbindung; die Zusammensetzung. — *adj.* zusammengesetzt; kompliziert; (*Comm.*) — *interest,* die Zinseszinsen. — [kəm'paund], *v.a.* (*Chem.*) mischen, zusammensetzen.
comprehend [kɔmpri'hend], *v.a.* verstehen (*understand*); einschließen (*include*).
comprehensible [kɔmpri'hensibl], *adj.* verständlich, begreiflich.
comprehension [kɔmpri'henʃən], *s.* das Verstehen, das Erfassen; (*Psych.*) — *tests,* die Verständnisprüfung.
comprehensive [kɔmpri'hensiv], *adj.* umfassend.
compress [kəm'pres], *v.a.* komprimieren; zusammendrücken (*press together*). — ['kɔmpres], *s.* (*Med.*) die Kompresse, der Umschlag (*poultice*).
compression [kəm'preʃən], *s.* der Druck; das Zusammendrücken (*pressing together*); die Kürzung (*abridgment*).
comprise [kəm'praiz], *v.a.* umfassen, einschließen.
compromise ['kɔmprəmaiz], *v.a.* kompromittieren. — *v.n.* einen Kompromiß schließen. — *s.* der *or* das Kompromiß.
compulsion [kəm'pʌlʃən], *s.* der Zwang.
compulsory [kəm'pʌlsəri], *adj.* zwingend; Zwangs-; — *subject,* das obligatorische Fach.
compunction [kəm'pʌŋkʃən], *s.* die Gewissensbisse, *m. pl.*
computation [kɔmpju'teiʃən], *s.* die Berechnung.

condition

compute [kəmˈpjuːt], *v.a.*, *v.n.* berechnen.

computer [kəmˈpjuːtə], *s.* die automatische Rechenmaschine.

comrade [ˈkɔmrid], *s.* der Kamerad.

comradeship [ˈkɔmridʃip], *s.* die Kameradschaft.

con [kɔn], *v.a.* genau betrachten, studieren; (*ship*) steuern.

concave [ˈkɔnkeiv], *adj.* (*Phys.*) konkav.

conceal [kənˈsiːl], *v.a.* verbergen, verstecken.

concealment [kənˈsiːlmənt], *s.* die Verhehlung, die Verheimlichung (*act of concealing*); *place of* —, das Versteck.

concede [kənˈsiːd], *v.a.* zugestehen, einräumen.

conceit [kənˈsiːt], *s.* die Einbildung, der Eigendünkel (*presumption*); (*obs.*) die Idee; (*Lit.*) die (gedankliche) Spielerei.

conceited [kənˈsiːtid], *adj.* eingebildet, eitel.

conceivable [kənˈsiːvəbl], *adj.* denkbar; begreiflich (*understandable*).

conceive [kənˈsiːv], *v.a.*, *v.n.* empfangen (*become pregnant*); begreifen (*understand*).

concentrate [ˈkɔnsəntreit], *v.a.* konzentrieren. — *v.n.* sich konzentrieren (*on*, auf, *Acc.*). — *s.* (*Chem.*) das Konzentrat.

concentrated [ˈkɔnsəntreitid], *adj.* konzentriert.

concentration [kɔnsənˈtreiʃən], *s.* die Konzentration.

concentric [kɔnˈsentrik], *adj.* (*Geom.*) konzentrisch.

conception [kənˈsepʃən], *s.* die Vorstellung, der Begriff (*idea*); die Empfängnis (*of a child*).

concern [kənˈsəːn], *v.a.* (*affect*) betreffen, angehen; *be concerned with*, zu tun haben (mit, *Dat.*). — *s.* die Angelegenheit (*affair*); die Sorge (*care, business*); das Geschäft, das Unternehmen; *cause grave* —, tiefe Besorgnis erregen.

concerned [kənˈsəːnd], *adj.* (*worried*) besorgt; (*involved*) interessiert (*in*, an, *Dat.*).

concerning [kənˈsəːniŋ], *prep.* betreffend (*Acc.*), hinsichtlich (*Genit.*).

concert [ˈkɔnsət], *s.* (*Mus.*) das Konzert; Einverständnis.

concerted [kənˈsəːtid], *adj.* gemeinsam, gemeinschaftlich.

concertina [kɔnsəˈtiːnə], *s.* (*Mus.*) die Ziehharmonika.

concerto [kənˈtʃəːtou], *s.* (*Mus.*) das Konzert.

concession [kənˈseʃən], *s.* die Konzession (*licence*); das Zugeständnis.

conch [kɔŋk], *s.* die (große) Muschel.

conciliate [kənˈsilieit], *v.a.* versöhnen.

conciliation [kənsiliˈeiʃən], *s.* die Versöhnung.

conciliatory [kənˈsiliətəri], *adj.* versöhnlich.

concise [kənˈsais], *adj.* kurz, knapp.

conciseness [kənˈsaisnis], *s.* die Kürze, Knappheit.

conclave [ˈkɔnkleiv], *s.* (*Eccl.*) das Konklave.

conclude [kənˈkluːd], *v.a.*, *v.n.* schließen, beenden (*speech etc.*); (*infer*) folgern (*from*, aus, *Dat.*); abschließen (*treaty*).

conclusion [kənˈkluːʒən], *s.* der Abschluß (*treaty*); die Folgerung (*inference*); der Beschluß (*decision*).

conclusive [kənˈkluːsiv], *adj.* entscheidend, überzeugend.

concoct [kənˈkɔkt], *v.a.* zusammenbrauen, aushecken.

concoction [kənˈkɔkʃən], *s.* das Gebräu, die Mischung.

concomitant [kənˈkɔmitənt], *adj.* begleitend; Begleit-, Neben-. — *s.* der Begleitumstand.

concord [ˈkɔnkɔːd], *s.* die Eintracht, die Harmonie.

concordance [kənˈkɔːdəns], *s.* die Übereinstimmung; die Konkordanz (*of Bible etc.*).

concordant [kənˈkɔːdənt], *adj.* in Eintracht (mit), übereinstimmend (mit) (*Dat.*).

concordat [kənˈkɔːdæt], *s.* (*Eccl., Pol.*) das Konkordat.

concourse [ˈkɔnkɔːs], *s.* das Gedränge (*crowd*).

concrete [ˈkɔnkriːt], *s.* (*Build.*) der Beton; (*Log.*) das Konkrete. — *adj.* konkret, wirklich.

concur [kənˈkəː], *v.n.* übereinstimmen (*with*, mit, *Dat.*).

concurrence [kənˈkʌrəns], *s.* die Übereinstimmung.

concurrent [kənˈkʌrənt], *adj.* gleichzeitig (*simultaneous*); mitwirkend (*accompanying*).

concussion [kənˈkʌʃən], *s.* (*Med.*) die (Gehirn)Erschütterung.

condemn [kənˈdem], *v.a.* verurteilen, verdammen.

condemnable [kənˈdemnəbl], *adj.* verwerflich, verdammenswert.

condemnation [kɔndemˈneiʃən], *s.* die Verurteilung, die Verdammung.

condensate [ˈkɔndenseit], *s.* (*Chem.*) das Kondensat, das Ergebnis der Kondensation.

condensation [kɔndenˈseiʃən], *s.* die Kondensation; Verdichtung.

condensed [kənˈdensd], *adj.* (*Chem.*) kondensiert; (*Chem., Engin.*) verdichtet; gekürzt (*abridged*).

condenser [kənˈdensə], *s.* (*Chem., Engin.*) der Kondensator; (*Elec.*) der Verstärker.

condescend [kɔndiˈsend], *v.n.* sich herablassen.

condescending [kɔndiˈsendiŋ], *adj.* herablassend.

condescension [kɔndiˈsenʃən], *s.* die Herablassung.

condiment [ˈkɔndimənt], *s.* die Würze.

condition [kənˈdiʃən], *s.* der Zustand; Umstand; die Bedingung (*proviso*); der Gesundheitszustand (*physical state*).

conditional [kən'diʃənəl], *adj.* bedingt; unter der Bedingung; konditionell.

conditioned [kən'diʃənd], *adj.* vorbereitet (*for action*); geartet.

condole [kən'doul], *v.n.* Beileid ausdrücken (*with, Dat.*), kondolieren (*with, Dat.*).

condolence [kən'douləns], *s.* das Beileid.

condone [kən'doun], *v.a.* verzeihen.

conducive [kən'dju:siv], *adj.* förderlich, dienlich, nützlich (*to, Dat.*).

conduct [kən'dʌkt], *v.a.* leiten, führen; (*Phys.*) ein Leiter sein; (*Mus.*) dirigieren. — *v.r.* sich aufführen, sich benehmen. — ['kɔndʌkt], *s.* das Benehmen (*behaviour*); — *of a war*, die Kriegsführung.

conductive [kən'dʌktiv], *adj.* (*Elec.*) leitend.

conductor [kən'dʌktə], *s.* der Leiter, Führer (*leader*); (*Phys., Elec.*) der Leiter; (*Am.*) der Schaffner (*train*); (*Mus.*) der Dirigent.

conduit ['kʌn-, 'kɔndit], *s.* die Leitung, die Röhre.

cone [koun], *s.* (*Geom.*) der Kegel; (*Bot.*) der Zapfen.

coney ['kouni], *s.* (*Zool.*) das Kaninchen.

confection [kən'fekʃən], *s.* das Konfekt.

confectioner [kən'fekʃənə], *s.* der Zuckerbäcker, Konditor.

confectionery [kən'fekʃənəri], *s.* die Zuckerwaren, *f.pl.* (*sweets*); Konditoreiwaren, *f.pl.* (*cakes*); die Zuckerbäckerei (*sweet shop*); die Konditorei.

confederacy [kən'fedərəsi], *s.* der Bund (*of states*); das Bündnis (*treaty*).

confederate [kən'fedərit], *s.* der Bundesgenosse, der Verbündete. — *adj.* verbündet; — *state*, der Bundesstaat. — [-reit], *v.n.* sich verbünden (*with*, mit, *Dat.*).

confederation [kɔnfedə'reiʃən], *s.* das Bündnis (*treaty*); der Bund (*state*).

confer [kən'fə:], *v.a.* verleihen (*degree, title*). — *v.n.* beraten (*with*, mit, *Dat.*), unterhandeln (*negotiate*).

conference ['kɔnfərəns], *s.* die Konferenz, die Besprechung, die Beratung, Tagung.

confess [kən'fes], *v.a.* bekennen; beichten (*sin*); zugestehen (*acknowledge*).

confession [kən'feʃən], *s.* das Bekenntnis; die Beichte (*sin*); das Glaubensbekenntnis (*creed*).

confessor [kən'fesə], *s.* der Bekenner; *father* —, der Beichtvater.

confidant [kɔnfi'dænt], *s.* der Vertraute.

confide [kən'faid], *v.a.* anvertrauen. — *v.n.* vertrauen (*in, Dat.*).

confidence ['kɔnfidəns], *s.* das Vertrauen; die Zuversicht; — *trick*, die Bauernfängerei, der Schwindel.

confident ['kɔnfidənt], *adj.* zuversichtlich; dreist (*bold*).

confidential [kɔnfi'denʃəl], *adj.* vertraulich, privat.

confine [kən'fain], *v.a.* einschränken (*hem in*); einsperren; *be* —*d to bed*, bettlägerig sein.

confinement [kən'fainmənt], *s.* die Einschränkung (*limitation*); das Wochenbett, die Niederkunft (*childbirth*).

confines ['kɔnfainz], *s. pl.* die Grenzen, *f. pl.* (*physical*); die Einschränkungen, *f. pl.* (*limitations*).

confirm [kən'fə:m], *v.a.* bestätigen, bekräftigen (*corroborate*); (*Eccl.*) firmen, konfirmieren.

confirmation [kɔnfə'meiʃən], *s.* die Bestätigung (*corroboration*); (*Eccl.*) die Firmung, Konfirmation.

confirmed [kən'fə:md], *adj.* eingefleischt; unverbesserlich.

confiscate ['kɔnfiskeit], *v.a.* konfiszieren, einziehen, beschlagnahmen.

confiscation [kɔnfis'keiʃən], *s.* die Konfiszierung, die Einziehung, die Beschlagnahme (*customs etc.*).

conflagration [kɔnflə'greiʃən], *s.* der (große) Brand.

conflict ['kɔnflikt], *s.* der Konflikt, der Zusammenstoß. — [kən'flikt], *v.n.* in Konflikt geraten; in Widerspruch stehen.

confluence ['kɔnfluəns], *s.* (*Geog.*) der Zusammenfluß.

confluent ['kɔnfluənt], *adj.* zusammenfließend. — *s.* der Nebenfluß (*tributary*).

conform [kən'fɔ:m], *v.n.* sich anpassen.

conformation [kɔnfɔ:'meiʃən], *s.* die Anpassung.

conformist [kən'fɔ:mist], *adj.* fügsam. — *s.* das Mitglied der Staatskirche.

conformity [kən'fɔ:miti], *s.* die Gleichförmigkeit; *in* — *with*, gerade so; gemäß (*Dat.*); die Gleichheit (*equality*.)

confound [kən'faund], *v.a.* verwirren (*confuse*); vernichten (*overthrow*).

confounded [kən'faundid], *adj.* verdammt, verwünscht.

confront [kən'frʌnt], *v.a.* (*Law*) — *s.o. with*, gegenüberstellen (*put in front of*); gegenüberstehen (*stand in front of*).

confrontation [kɔnfrʌn'teiʃən], *s.* die Gegenüberstellung.

confuse [kən'fju:z], *v.a.* verwirren (*muddle*); bestürzen (*perplex*); verwechseln (*mix up*).

confusion [kən'fju:ʒən], *s.* die Verwirrung, das Durcheinander (*muddle*); die Bestürzung (*astonishment*); die Verlegenheit (*dilemma*).

confutation [kɔnfju:'teiʃən], *s.* die Widerlegung.

confute [kən'fju:t], *v.a.* widerlegen.

congeal [kən'dʒi:l], *v.n.* gefrieren (*freeze*); gerinnen.

congenial [kən'dʒi:niəl], *adj.* geistesverwandt, geistig ebenbürtig, sympathisch.

congeniality [kəndʒi:ni'æliti], *s.* die Geistesverwandtschaft.

conger ['kɔngə], *s.* (*Zool.*) der Meeraal.

congest [kən'dʒest], *v.a.* anhäufen, überfüllen.

congestion [kən'dʒestʃən], *s.* die Überfüllung; Stauung; die Übervölkerung (*overpopulation*); (*Med.*) der Blutandrang.

conglomerate [kən'glɔməreit], *v.n.* sich zusammenballen. — [–rit], *s.* das Konglomerat, die Ballung.

conglomeration [kənglɔmə'reiʃən], *s.* die Zusammenhäufung, Zusammenballung.

Congolese [kɔŋgo'li:z], *adj.* kongolesisch. — *s.* der Kongolese.

congratulate [kən'grætjuleit], *v.n.* gratulieren (*on*, zu, *Dat.*).

congratulation [kəngrætju'leiʃən], *s.* (*usually pl.*) die Glückwünsche.

congratulatory [kən'grætjuleitəri], *adj.* Glückwunsch-.

congregate [kɔŋgrigeit], *v.a.* versammeln. — *v.n.* sich versammeln, sich scharen (*round*, um, *Acc.*).

congregation [kɔŋgri'geiʃən], *s.* die Versammlung, die Schar; (*Eccl.*) die Gemeinde.

congregational [kɔŋgri'geiʃənəl], *adj.* (*Eccl.*) Gemeinde-; *Congregational Church*, unabhängige Gemeindekirche.

congress ['kɔŋgres], *s.* der Kongreß.

congruence ['kɔŋgruəns], *s.* (*Geom.*) die Kongruenz.

congruent ['kɔŋgruənt], *adj.* (*Geom.*) kongruent.

congruity [kɔŋ'gru:iti], *s.* (*Geom.*) die Übereinstimmung; die Kongruenz.

congruous ['kɔŋgruəs], *adj.* übereinstimmend, angemessen.

conic(al) ['kɔnik(əl)], *adj.* konisch, kegelförmig; (*Geom.*) — *section*, der Kegelschnitt.

conifer ['kɔnifə], *s.* (*Bot.*) der Nadelbaum.

conjecture [kən'dʒektʃə], *s.* die Mutmaßung, die Annahme. — *v.a.* mutmaßen, annehmen.

conjoin [kən'dʒɔin], *v.a.* (*Law*) verbinden.

conjugal ['kɔndʒugəl], *adj.* ehelich.

conjugate ['kɔndʒugeit], *v.a.* (*Gram.*) konjugieren.

conjugation [kɔndʒu'geiʃən], *s.* (*Gram.*) die Konjugation.

conjunction [kən'dʒʌŋkʃən], *s.* (*Gram.*) das Bindewort.

conjunctive [kən'dʒʌŋktiv], *adj.* verbindend; (*Gram.*) — *mood*, der Konjunktiv.

conjunctivitis [kən'dʒʌŋktivaitis], *s.* (*Med.*) die Bindehautentzündung.

conjuncture [kən'dʒʌŋktʃə], *s.* der Wendepunkt; die Krise (*of events*).

conjure ['kʌndʒə], *v.a.* beschwören; — *up*, heraufbeschwören. — *v.n.* zaubern.

conjurer ['kʌndʒərə], *s.* der Zauberer.

connect [kə'nekt], *v.a.* verbinden, in Zusammenhang bringen.

connection, connexion [kə'nekʃən], *s.* die Verbindung, der Zusammenhang.

connivance [kə'naivəns], *s.* die Nachsicht, das Gewährenlassen.

connive [kə'naiv], *v.n.* nachsichtig sein (*at*, bei, *Dat.*); gewähren lassen.

connoisseur [kɔne'sə:], *s.* der Kenner.

connubial [kə'nju:biəl], *adj.* ehelich.

conquer ['kɔŋkə], *v.a.* besiegen (*foe*); erobern (*place*).

conqueror ['kɔŋkərə], *s.* der Eroberer, der Sieger.

conquest ['kɔŋkwest], *s.* der Sieg, die Eroberung.

consanguinity [kɔnsæŋ'gwiniti], *s.* die Blutsverwandtschaft.

conscience ['kɔnʃəns], *s.* das Gewissen; *in all* — wahrhaftig.

conscientious [kɔnʃi'enʃəs], *adj.* gewissenhaft.

conscientiousness [kɔnʃi'enʃəsnis], *s.* die Gewissenhaftigkeit.

conscious ['kɔnʃəs], *adj.* bewußt (*Genit.*).

consciousness ['kɔnʃəsnis], *s.* das Bewußtsein.

conscript [kən'skript], *v.a.* (*Mil.*) einziehen, einberufen. — ['kɔnskript], *s.* (*Mil.*) der Rekrut, der Dienstpflichtige.

conscription [kən'skripʃən], *s.* die allgemeine Wehrpflicht.

consecrate ['kɔnsikreit], *v.a.* weihen, widmen.

consecrated ['kɔnsikreitid], *adj.* geweiht (*Dat.*).

consecration [kɔnsi'kreiʃən], *s.* die Weihe, Einweihung (*of church*); die Weihung.

consecutive [kən'sekjutiv], *adj.* aufeinanderfolgend, fortlaufend.

consecutiveness [kən'sekjutivnis], *s.* die Aufeinanderfolge.

consent [kən'sent], *v.n.* zustimmen, beistimmen (*to*, *Dat.*). — *s.* die Zustimmung, die Einwilligung.

consequence ['kɔnsikwəns], *s.* die Konsequenz; (*Log.*) Folgerung; die Folge; die Wichtigkeit (*importance*).

consequent ['kɔnsikwənt], *adj.* folgend, nachfolgend.

consequential [kɔnsi'kwenʃəl], *adj.* wichtigtuend, anmaßend; (*Log.*) folgerichtig.

consequently ['kɔnsikwəntli], *adv.* folglich, infolgedessen.

conservatism [kən'sə:vətizm], *s.* (*Pol.*) der Konservatismus; die konservative Denkweise.

conservative [kən'sə:vətiv], *adj.* (*Pol.*) konservativ.

conservatoire [kən'sə:vətwɑ:], *s.* (*Mus.*) das Konservatorium, die Musikhochschule.

conservatory [kən'sə:vətəri], *s.* (*Bot.*) das Gewächshaus.

conserve [kən'sə:v], *v.a.* konservieren, erhalten, einmachen. — *s.* (*fruit*) das Eingemachte.

consider [kən'sidə], *v.a.* in Betracht ziehen (*think over, look at*); berücksichtigen (*have regard to*); nachdenken über (*Acc.*) (*ponder*).

considerable [kən'sidərəbl], *adj.* beträchtlich, ansehnlich.

considerate [kən'sidərit], *adj.* rücksichtsvoll (*thoughtful*).

consideration [kənsidə'reiʃən], *s.* die Betrachtung (*contemplation*); die Rücksicht (*regard*) (*for*, auf, *Acc.*); die Entschädigung (*compensation*); die Belohnung (*reward*).

considering [kən'sidəriŋ], *prep.* in Anbetracht (*Genit.*).

consign [kən'sain], *v.a.* überliefern (*hand over*); übersenden (*remit*).

consignee [kənsai'ni:], *s.* (*Comm.*) der Empfänger, der Adressat (*recipient*).

consigner [kən'sainə], *s.* der Absender (*of goods*).

consignment [kən'sainmənt], *s.* die Sendung (*of goods*).

consist [kən'sist], *v.n.* bestehen (*of*, aus, *Dat.*).

consistency [kən'sistənsi], *s.* die Festigkeit, Dichtigkeit; (*Chem.*) die Konsistenz.

consistent [kən'sistənt], *adj.* konsequent; — *with,* übereinstimmend, gemäß (*Dat.*); (*Chem.*) dicht, fest.

consistory [kən'sistəri], *s.* (*Eccl.*) das Konsistorium.

consolable [kən'souləbl], *adj.* tröstlich, zu trösten.

consolation [kənso'leiʃən], *s.* der Trost; *draw —,* Trost schöpfen.

console (1) [kən'soul], *v.a.* trösten.

console (2) ['kɔnsoul], *s.* (*Archit.*) die Konsole.

consolidate [kən'sɔlideit], *v.a.* befestigen, konsolidieren. — *v.n.* fest werden.

consolidation [kənsɔli'deiʃən], *s.* die Befestigung; Festigung, Bestärkung (*confirmation*).

consonance ['kɔnsənəns], *s.* (*Phonet.*) die Konsonanz; der Einklang, die Harmonie.

consonant ['kɔnsənənt], *adj.* in Einklang (*with,* mit, *Dat.*). — *s.* der Konsonant.

consort ['kɔnsɔ:t], *s.* der Gemahl, Gatte; die Gemahlin, die Gattin. — [kən'sɔ:t], *v.n.* verkehren (*with,* mit, *Dat.*).

conspicuous [kən'spikjuəs], *adj.* auffallend, deutlich sichtbar, hervorragend.

conspiracy [kən'spirəsi], *s.* die Verschwörung.

conspirator [kən'spirətə], *s.* der Verschwörer.

conspire [kən'spaiə], *v.n.* sich verschwören.

constable ['kʌnstəbl], *s.* der Polizist, der Schutzmann.

Constance ['kɔnstəns]. Konstanze *f.* (*name*); Konstanz (*town*); *Lake —,* der Bodensee.

constancy ['kɔnstənsi], *s.* die Beständigkeit, Treue.

constant ['kɔnstənt], *adj.* (*Chem.*) konstant; treu, beständig.

constellation [kɔnste'leiʃən], *s.* die Konstellation; das Sternbild.

consternation [kɔnstə'neiʃən], *s.* die Bestürzung.

constipation [kɔnsti'peiʃən], *s.* die Verstopfung.

constituency [kən'stitjuənsi], *s.* der Wahlkreis (*electoral district*); die Wählerschaft (*voters*).

constituent [kən'stitjuənt], *adj.* wesentlich. — *s.* der Bestandteil (*component*); (*Pol.*) der Wähler.

constitute ['kɔnstitju:t], *v.a.* ausmachen (*make up*); bilden (*form*); festsetzen (*establish*); (*Pol.*) errichten (*set up*).

constitution [kɔnsti'tju:ʃən], *s.* die Konstitution (*physique*); die Errichtung (*establishment*); die Beschaffenheit, Natur (*nature*); (*Pol.*) die Verfassung.

constitutional [kɔnsti'tju:ʃənəl], *adj.* körperlich bedingt; (*Pol.*) verfassungsmäßig.

constrain [kən'strein], *v.a.* nötigen, zwingen.

constraint [kən'streint], *s.* der Zwang.

constrict [kən'strikt], *v.a.* zusammenziehen.

constriction [kən'strikʃən], *s.* die Zusammenziehung, Beengtheit.

construct [kən'strʌkt], *v.a.* errichten, bauen, konstruieren.

construction [kən'strʌkʃən], *s.* die Errichtung, der Bau, die Konstruktion.

constructive [kən'strʌktiv], *adj.* (*Engin.*) konstruktiv; behilflich (*positive*).

constructor [kən'strʌktə], *s.* der Konstrukteur, der Erbauer (*builder*).

construe [kən'stru:], *v.a.* konstruieren, deuten (*interpret*).

consul ['kɔnsəl], *s.* der Konsul; — *general,* der Generalkonsul.

consular ['kɔnsjulə], *adj.* konsularisch.

consulate ['kɔnsjulit], *s.* das Konsulat; — *-general,* das Generalkonsulat.

consult [kən'sʌlt], *v.a.* konsultieren, zu Rate ziehen; nachschlagen (*a book*). — *v.n.* sich beraten (*with,* mit, *Dat.*); (*Comm.*) als Berater hinzuziehen.

consultant [kən'sʌltənt], *s.* (*Med.*) der Facharzt; der Berater.

consultation [kɔnsəl'teiʃən], *s.* die Beratung (*advice*); die Besprechung (*discussion*); (*Med., Engin.*) die Konsultation.

consume [kən'sju:m], *v.a.* verzehren (*eat up*); verbrauchen (*use up*).

consumer [kən'sju:mə], *s.* der Verbraucher; (*Comm.*) der Konsument.

consummate [kən'sʌmit], *adj.* vollendet. — ['kɔnsəmeit], *v.a.* vollenden, vollziehen.

consummation [kɔnsə'meiʃən], *s.* die Vollziehung, Vollendung.

consumption [kən'sʌmpʃən], *s.* (*Comm.*) der Verbrauch; (*Med.*) die Schwindsucht.

consumptive [kən'sʌmptiv], *adj.* (*Med.*) schwindsüchtig.

contact ['kɔntækt], *v.a.* berühren (*touch*); in Verbindung treten (mit) (*get into touch* (*with*)). — *s.* (*Elec.*) der Kontakt; die Berührung (*touch*); die Verbindung (*connexion*).

contagion [kən'teidʒən], *s.* (*Med.*) die Ansteckung.

contagious[kən'teidʒəs],*adj.*ansteckend.

contain [kən'tein], *v.a.* enthalten (*hold*); zurückhalten (*restrain*).

container [kən'teinə], *s.* der Behälter.

contaminate [kən'tæmineit], *v.a.* verunreinigen; vergiften.

contemplate ['kɔntəmpleit], *v.a.* betrachten (*consider*). — *v.n.* nachdenken (*ponder*).

contemplation [kɔntəm'pleiʃən], *s.* die Betrachtung (*consideration*); das Sinnen (*pondering*).

contemplative [kən'templətiv], *adj.* nachdenklich, kontemplativ.

contemporaneous [kəntempə'reiniəs], *adj.* gleichzeitig.

contemporary [kən'tempərəri], *adj.* zeitgenössisch. — *s.* der Zeitgenosse.

contempt [kən'tempt], *s.* die Verachtung; — *of court*, die Gerichtsbeleidigung.

contemptible [kən'temptibl], *adj.* verächtlich, verachtungswert.

contemptibleness [kən'temptiblnis], *s.* die Verächtlichkeit.

contemptuous [kən'temptjuəs], *adj.* höhnisch, verachtungsvoll.

contemptuousness [kən'temptjuəsnis], *s.* der Hohn, der verachtungsvolle Ton, der Hochmut.

contend [kən'tend], *v.n.* streiten; bestreiten, behaupten.

content [kən'tent], *adj.* zufrieden. — *v.a.* zufriedenstellen. — ['kɔntent], *s.* (*often pl.*) der Inhalt.

contented [kən'tentid], *adj.* zufrieden.

contentedness, contentment [kən'tentidnis, kən'tentmənt], *s.* die Zufriedenheit.

contention [kən'tenʃən], *s.* der Streit, die Behauptung.

contentious [kən'tenʃəs], *adj.* streitsüchtig (*person*); strittig (*question*).

contest ['kɔntest], *s.* der Streit, Wettstreit, Wettkampf. — [kən'test], *v.a.* um etwas streiten, bestreiten.

context ['kɔntekst], *s.* der Zusammenhang.

contexture [kən'tekstʃə], *s.* (*Engin.*) der Bau, die Zusammensetzung; das Gewebe (*textile*).

contiguity [kɔnti'gju:iti], *s.* die Berührung; die Nachbarschaft.

contiguous [kən'tigjuəs], *adj.* anstossend, anliegend.

continence ['kɔntinəns], *s.* die Mäßigung (*moderation*); die Enthaltsamkeit (*abstemiousness*).

continent (1) ['kɔntinənt], *adj.* enthaltsam, mässig.

continent (2) ['kɔntinənt], *s.* das Festland, der Kontinent.

contingency [kən'tindʒənsi], *s.* der Zufall; die Möglichkeit (*possibility*).

contingent [kən'tindʒənt], *s.* der Beitrag, das Kontingent (*share*). — *adj.* möglich.

continual [kən'tinjuəl], *adj.* fortwährend, beständig.

continuance [kən'tinjuəns], *s.* die Fortdauer.

continuation [kəntinju'eiʃən], *s.* die Fortsetzung.

continue [kən'tinju:], *v.a.* fortsetzen (*go on with*); verlängern (*prolong*). — *v.n.* weitergehen, weiterführen (*of story*).

continuity [kɔnti'nju:iti], *s.* der Zusammenhang, die ununterbrochene Folge, Kontinuität (*Film*); — *girl*, die Drehbuchsekretärin.

continuous [kən'tinjuəs], *adj.* zusammenhängend, ununterbrochen, andauernd.

contort [kən'tɔ:t], *v.a.* verdrehen.

contortion [kən'tɔ:ʃən], *s.* die Verdrehung, Verkrümmung, Verzerrung.

contortionist [kən'tɔ:ʃənist], *s.* der Schlangenmensch.

contour ['kɔntuə], *s.* die Kontur, der Umriß.

contraband ['kɔntrəbænd], *adj.* Schmuggel-, geschmuggelt. — *s.* die Bannware, Schmuggelware.

contract [kən'trækt], *v.a.* zusammenziehen (*pull together*); verengen (*narrow down*); verkürzen (*shorten*); sich eine Krankheit zuziehen (— *a disease*); Schulden machen (— *debts*). — *v.n.* sich zusammenziehen, kürzer werden; einen Kontrakt abschließen (*come to terms*). — ['kɔntrækt], *s.* der Vertrag (*pact*); (*Comm.*) der Kontrakt.

contraction [kən'trækʃən], *s.* die Zusammenziehung; (*Phonet.*) die Kürzung.

contractor [kən'træktə], *s.* (*Comm.*) der Kontrahent; der Lieferant (*supplier*); *building* —, der Bauunternehmer.

contradict [kɔntrə'dikt], *v.n.* widersprechen (*Dat.*).

contradiction [kɔntrə'dikʃən], *s.* der Widerspruch.

contradictory [kɔntrə'diktəri], *adj.* in Widerspruch stehend, widersprechend.

contrarily ['kɔntrərili], *adv.* im Gegensatz dazu, hingegen, dagegen.

contrary ['kɔntrəri], *adj.* entgegengesetzt, *on the* —, im Gegenteil; [kən'treəri], widersprechend.

contrast [kən'trɑ:st], *v.a.* einander entgegenstellen, gegenüberstellen. — *v.n.* einen Gegensatz darstellen *or* bilden. — ['kɔntrɑ:st], *s.* der Kontrast (*colours*); der Gegensatz.

contravene [kɔntrə'vi:n], *v.a.* übertreten, zuwiderhandeln (*Dat.*).

contribute [kən'tribju:t], *v.a.* beitragen; beisteuern (*money, energy*).

contribution [kɔntri'bju:ʃən], *s.* der Beitrag.

contributive

contributive, contributory [kən'tri-bjutiv, kən'tribjutəri], *adj.* beitragend, Beitrags-.

contributor [kən'tribjutə], *s.* der Beitragende, der Spender (*of money*); der Mitarbeiter (*journalist etc.*).

contrite ['kɔntrait], *adj.* zerknirscht, reuevoll.

contrition [kən'triʃən], *s.* die Zerknirschung, die Reue.

contrivance [kən'traivəns], *s.* die Vorrichtung, die Erfindung.

contrive [kən'traiv], *v.a.* ausdenken, erfinden; fertigbringen (*accomplish*).

control [kən'troul], *v.a.* kontrollieren (*check*); die Leitung haben (*have command of*); die Aufsicht führen (*supervise*). — *s.* die Kontrolle; die Aufsicht; die Leitung; (*pl.*) (*Motor.*) die Steuerung; (*Aviat.*) das Leitwerk.

controller [kən'troulə], *s.* der Aufseher (*supervisor*); der Direktor (*of corporation*); der Revisor (*examiner, auditor*).

controversial [kɔntro'vəːʃəl], *adj.* umstritten, strittig.

controversy ['kɔntrovəːsi], *s.* die Kontroverse, die Streitfrage.

controvert ['kɔntrovəːt], *v.a.* bestreiten, widersprechen (*Dat.*).

contumacious [kɔntju'meiʃəs], *adj.* widerspenstig, halsstarrig.

contumacy ['kɔntjuməsi], *s.* die Widerspenstigkeit (*obstreperousness*); der Ungehorsam (*disobedience*).

contumelious [kɔntju'miːliəs], *adj.* frech, unverschämt (*insolent*).

contuse [kən'tjuːz], *v.a.* quetschen.

conundrum [kə'nʌndrəm], *s.* das Scherzrätsel.

convalescence [kɔnvə'lesəns], *s.* die Gesundung, die Genesung.

convalescent [kɔnvə'lesənt], *adj.* genesend. — *s.* der Genesende, der Rekonvaleszent.

convene [kən'viːn], *v.a.* zusammenrufen, versammeln. — *v.n.* zusammentreten, sich versammeln.

convenience [kən'viːniəns], *s.* die Bequemlichkeit; *at your early* —, umgehend; *public* —, öffentliche Bedürfnisanstalt.

convenient [kən'viːniənt], *adj.* bequem, gelegen (*meaning*) (*time*).

convent ['kɔnvənt], *s.* das (Nonnen)-Kloster.

convention [kən'venʃən], *s.* die Konvention, der Kongress (*meeting*); der Vertrag (*treaty*); die Sitte (*tradition, custom*).

conventional [kən'venʃənəl], *adj.* herkömmlich, traditionell.

conventual [kən'ventjuəl], *adj.* klösterlich.

conversation [kɔnvə'seiʃən], *s.* die Konversation, Unterhaltung; das Gespräch.

conversational [kɔnvə'seiʃənəl], *adj.* gesprächig, umgangssprachlich.

converse (1) [kən'vəːs], *v.n.* sich unterhalten (*with*, mit, *Dat.*).

converse (2) ['kɔnvəːs], *adj.* umgekehrt.

conversely ['kɔnvəːsli], *adv.* hingegen, dagegen.

conversion [kən'vəːʃən], *s.* die Umkehrung (*reversal*); (*Rel.*) die Bekehrung; (*Comm.*) die Umwechslung.

convert ['kɔnvəːt], *s.* (*Rel.*) der Bekehrte, die Bekehrte; der Konvertit. — [kən'vəːt], *v.a.* (*Rel.*) bekehren; (*Comm.*) umwechseln.

converter [kən'vəːtə], *s.* (*Rel.*) der Bekehrer; (*Metall., Elec.*) der Umformer.

convertible [kən'vəːtibl], *adj.* umwandelbar. — *s.* (*Motor.*) der or das Konvertible.

convex ['kɔnveks], *adj.* (*Phys.*) konvex.

convey [kən'vei], *v.a.* transportieren; führen (*bear, carry*); mitteilen (*impart*).

conveyance [kən'veiəns], *s.* die Beförderung (*transport*); das Fuhrwerk (*vehicle*); die Übertragung (*Law*) das Übertragungsdokument.

conveyancing [kən'veiənsiŋ], *s.* (*Law*) die legale or rechtliche Übertragung.

convict ['kɔnvikt], *s.* der Sträfling. — [kən'vikt], *v.a.* für schuldig erklären.

conviction [kən'vikʃən], *s.* die Überzeugung; (*Law*) die Überführung, die Schuldbesprechung.

convince [kən'vins], *v.a.* überzeugen.

convivial [kən'viviəl], *adj.* gesellig (*sociable*).

conviviality [kənvivi'æliti], *s.* die Geselligkeit.

convocation [kɔnvə'keiʃən], *s.* die Zusammenberufung, Festversammlung; (*Eccl.*) die Synode.

convoke [kən'vouk], *v.a.* zusammenberufen.

convolvulus [kən'vɔlvjuləs], *s.* (*Bot.*) die Winde.

convoy ['kɔnvɔi], *s.* das Geleit, die Bedeckung; (*Mil.*) der Begleitzug. — [kɔn'vɔi], *v.a.* geleiten; (*Mil.*) im Geleitzug mitführen.

convulse [kən'vʌls], *v.a.* erschüttern.

convulsion [kən'vʌlʃən], *s.* der Krampf, die Zuckung.

convulsive [kən'vʌlsiv], *adj.* krampfhaft, zuckend.

coo [kuː], *v.n.* girren (*of birds*); bill and —, schnäbeln.

cook [kuk], *v.a., v.n.* kochen; (*coll.*) — *the books*, die Bücher(Bilanz)fälschen or frisieren. — *s.* der Koch, die Köchin; *too many cooks* (*spoil the broth*), zu viele Köche (verderben den Brei).

cookery ['kukəri], *s.* die Kochkunst; — *school*, die Kochschule.

cool [kuːl], *adj.* kühl (*climate*); kaltblütig (*coldblooded*); unverschämt (*brazen*). — *s.* die Kühle. — *v.a.* abkühlen; (*fig.*) besänftigen. — *v.n.* sich abkühlen.

cooler ['kuːlə], *s.* (*Chem.*) das Kühlfaß; (*coll.*) das Gefängnis; (*sl.*) das Kittchen.

corpuscle

coop [ku:p], *s.* die Kufe; das Faß; hen —, der Hühnerkorb. — *v.a.* — up, einsperren.

cooper ['ku:pə], *s.* der Böttcher, der Faßbinder.

cooperate [kou'ɔpəreit], *v.n.* zusammenarbeiten; mitarbeiten, mitwirken.

cooperation [kouɔpə'reiʃən], *s.* die Zusammenarbeit, die Mitarbeit.

cooperative [kou'ɔpərətiv], *adj.* willig; mitwirkend. — *s.* die Konsumgenossenschaft, der Konsum.

coordinate [kou'ɔ:dineit], *v.a.* koordinieren, beiordnen. — [-nit], *adj.* (*Gram.*) koordiniert.

coordination [kouɔ:di'neiʃən], *s.* die Koordinierung.

coot [ku:t], *s.* (*Orn.*) das Wasserhuhn.

copartnership [kou'pɑ:tnəʃip], *s.* die Teilhaberschaft; die Partnerschaft in der Industrie.

cope (1) [koup], *s.* (*Eccl.*) das Pluviale, der Priesterrock; (*Build.*) die Decke.

cope (2) [koup], *v.n.* — with *s.th.*, mit etwas fertig werden, es schaffen.

coping ['koupiŋ], *s.* (*Build.*) die Kappe; — -stone or copestone, der Firststein, Schlußstein, Kappstein.

copious ['koupiəs], *adj.* reichlich; wortreich (*style*).

copiousness ['koupiəsnis], *s.* die Reichhaltigkeit, Fülle.

copper ['kɔpə], *s.* (*Metall.*) das Kupfer; (*sl.*) der Polizist; (*coll.*) der Penny, das Pennystück. — *adj.* kupfern.

copperplate ['kɔpəpleit], *s.* der Kupferstich (*etching*); (*Typ.*) die Kupferplatte.

coppery ['kɔpəri], *adj.* Kupfer-, kupfern (*colour*).

coppice, copse ['kɔpis, kɔps], *s.* das Unterholz, das Dickicht.

copulate ['kɔpjuleit], *v.n.* sich paaren, begatten.

copulation [kɔpju'leiʃən], *s.* die Paarung; der Beischlaf (*human*).

copy ['kɔpi], *v.a.* kopieren, abschreiben (*write*); imitieren, nachahmen (*imitate*). — *s.* die Kopie; carbon —, die Durchschrift; Abschrift; die Nachahmung (*imitation*); die Fälschung (*forgery*).

copybook ['kɔpibuk], *s.* das Heft.

copyist ['kɔpiist], *s.* der Kopist.

coquet, coquette [kɔ'ket], *v.n.* kokettieren.

coquette (2) [kɔ'ket], *s.* die Kokette.

coquettish [kɔ'ketiʃ], *adj.* kokett.

coral ['kɔrəl], *s.* die Koralle. — *adj.* Korallen-.

cord [kɔ:d], *s.* die Schnur, der Strick (*rope*); (*Am.*) der Bindfaden (*string*); die Klafter (*wood measure*); der Kordstoff (*textile*); vocal —, das Stimmband.

cordage ['kɔ:didʒ], *s.* (*Naut.*) das Tauwerk.

cordial (1) ['kɔ:diəl], *adj.* herzlich.

cordial (2) ['kɔ:diəl], *s.* der Fruchtsaft (konzentriert), Magenlikör.

cordiality [kɔ:di'æliti], *s.* die Herzlichkeit.

corduroy ['kɔ:djurɔi], *s.* der Kordsamt.

core [kɔ:], *s.* der Kern; das Innere (*innermost part*).

cork [kɔ:k], *s.* der Kork, der Korken. — *v.a.* verkorken.

corkscrew ['kɔ:kskru:], *s.* der Korkzieher.

cormorant ['kɔ:mərənt], *s.* (*Orn.*) der Kormoran, die Scharbe.

corn (1) [kɔ:n], *s.* das Korn, das Getreide (*wheat etc.*); (*Am.*) sweet —, der Mais.

corn (2) [kɔ:n], *s.* das Hühnerauge (*on foot*).

corned [kɔ:nd], *adj.* eingesalzt; — beef, das Pökelrindfleisch.

cornea ['kɔ:niə], *s.* (*Anat.*) die Hornhaut.

cornel-tree [kɔ:'nəltri:], *s.* (*Bot.*) der Kornelkirschbaum.

cornelian [kɔ:'ni:liən], *s.* (*Geol.*) der Karneol.

corner ['kɔ:nə], *s.* die Ecke; (*Footb.*) der Eckstoß. — *v.a.* in eine Ecke treiben; in die Enge treiben (*force*).

cornered ['kɔ:nəd], *adj.* eckig (*angular*); in die Enge getrieben, gefangen (*caught*).

cornet ['kɔ:nit], *s.* (*Mus.*) die Zinke, das Flügelhorn; (*Mil.*) der Kornett, der Fähnrich.

cornflower ['kɔ:nflauə], *s.* (*Bot.*) die Kornblume.

cornice ['kɔ:nis], *s.* (*Archit.*) das Gesims.

cornucopia [kɔ:nju'koupjə], *s.* das Füllhorn.

corollary [kə'rɔləri], *s.* (*Log.*) der Folgesatz; die Folgeerscheinung (*consequence*).

corona [kə'rounə], *s.* (*Astron.*) der Hof, Lichtkranz.

coronation [kɔrə'neiʃən], *s.* die Krönung.

coroner ['kɔrənə], *s.* der Leichenbeschauer.

coronet ['kɔrənet], *s.* die Adelskrone.

corporal (1) ['kɔ:pərəl], *s.* (*Mil.*) der Korporal, der Unteroffizier, Obergefreite.

corporal (2) ['kɔ:pərəl], *adj.* körperlich; — punishment, die Züchtigung.

corporate ['kɔ:pərit], *adj.* (*Law, Comm.*) als Körperschaft; gemeinschaftlich, einheitlich (*as a group or unit.*)

corporation [kɔ:pə'reiʃən], *s.* (*Law, Comm.*) die Körperschaft; die Korporation; die Gemeinde (*municipal*); (*sl.*) der Schmerbauch (*stoutness*).

corps [kɔ:], *s.* das Korps.

corpse [kɔ:ps], *s.* der Leichnam.

corpulence ['kɔ:pjuləns], *s.* die Korpulenz, die Beleibtheit.

corpulent ['kɔ:pjulənt], *adj.* korpulent, dick.

Corpus Christi ['kɔ:pəs 'kristi], (der) Fronleichnam, das Fronleichnamsfest.

corpuscle ['kɔ:pʌsl], *s.* (*Anat.*) das Körperchen.

correct

correct [kəˈrekt], *v.a.* korrigieren (*remove mistakes*); verbessern; tadeln (*reprove*); berichtigen (*rectify*). — *adj.* korrekt, tadellos, richtig.

correction [kəˈrekʃən], *s.* die Korrektur (*of mistakes*); die Verbesserung (*improvement*); die Richtigstellung (*restoration*); der Verweis (*censure*).

corrective [kəˈrektiv], *adj.* zur Besserung. — *s.* das Korrektiv.

correctness [kəˈrektnis], *s.* die Korrektheit (*of manner, action etc.*).

corrector [kəˈrektə], *s.* der Korrektor (*proof reader etc.*).

correlate [ˈkɔrileit], *v.a.* in Beziehung setzen, aufeinander beziehen. — [-lit], *s.* (*Log.*) das Korrelat.

correlative [kɔˈrelativ], *adj.* in Wechselbeziehung stehend.

correspond [kɔrisˈpɔnd], *v.n.* korrespondieren (*exchange letters*); entsprechen (*to, Dat.*).

correspondence [kɔrisˈpɔndəns], *s.* die Korrespondenz; der Briefwechsel (*letters*); die Übereinstimmung (*harmony*).

correspondent [kɔrisˈpɔndənt], *s.* der Korrespondent (*letter-writer*); der Journalist, Berichterstatter (*newspaper*).

corridor [ˈkɔridɔː], *s.* der Korridor; der Gang.

corrigible [ˈkɔridʒibl], *adj.* verbesserlich.

corroborate [kəˈrɔbəreit], *v.a.* bestätigen (*confirm*); bestärken (*strengthen*).

corroboration [kərɔbəˈreiʃən], *s.* die Bestätigung, die Bekräftigung.

corroborative [kəˈrɔbərativ], *adj.* bekräftigend.

corrode [kəˈroud], *v.a.* zerfressen, zersetzen, ätzen (*acid*).

corrosion [kəˈrouʒən], *s.* die Anfressung, Ätzung.

corrosive [kəˈrouziv], *adj.* ätzend.

corrugated [ˈkɔrugeitid], *adj.* gewellt, Well-; — *iron*, das Wellblech; — *paper*, die Wellpappe.

corrupt [kəˈrʌpt], *v.a.* verderben (*spoil*); bestechen (*bribe*). — *adj.* korrupt (*morals*); verdorben (*spoilt*).

corruptible [kəˈrʌptibl], *adj.* verderblich; bestechlich.

corruption [kəˈrʌpʃən], *s.* die Korruption; die Bestechung (*bribery*).

corruptness [kəˈrʌptnis], *s.* die Verdorbenheit, der Verfall.

corsair [ˈkɔːsɛə], *s.* der Korsar, der Seeräuber.

corset [ˈkɔːsit], *s.* das Korsett.

coruscate [ˈkɔrəskeit], *v.n.* schimmern, leuchten.

corvette [kɔːˈvet], *s.* (*Naut.*) die Korvette.

cosine [ˈkousain], *s.* (*Maths.*) der Kosinus.

cosiness [ˈkouzinis], *s.* die Bequemlichkeit, die Behaglichkeit (*comfort*).

cosmetic [kɔzˈmetik], *adj.* kosmetisch. — *s.* (*pl.*) das *or* die (*pl.*) Schönheitsmittel.

cosmic [ˈkɔzmik], *adj.* kosmisch.

cosmopolitan [kɔzmoˈpɔlitən], *adj.* kosmopolitisch, weltbürgerlich. — *s.* der Kosmopolit, der Weltbürger.

Cossack [ˈkɔsæk], *s.* der Kosak.

cost [kɔst], *v.a. irr.* kosten. — *v.n. irr.* zu stehen kommen. — *s.* die Kosten, *f. pl.* (*expenses*); *at all* —*s*, um jeden Preis.

costermonger [ˈkɔstəmʌŋgə], *s.* der Straßenhändler.

costly [ˈkɔstli], *adj.* kostspielig.

costume [ˈkɔstjuːm], *s.* das Kostüm; — *play*, das Zeitstück.

cosy [ˈkouzi], *adj.* behaglich, bequem.

cot (1) [kɔt], *s.* das Bettchen, Kinderbett.

cot (2) [kɔt], *s.* (*obs.*) die Hütte (*hut*).

cottage [ˈkɔtidʒ], *s.* die Hütte, das Häuschen.

cottager [ˈkɔtidʒə], *s.* der Kleinhäusler.

cotton [ˈkɔtn], *s.* die Baumwolle. — *v.n.* — *on to*, (*coll.*) sich anhängen, sich anschließen (*Dat.*); — *on*, folgen können (*understand*).

couch [kautʃ], *s.* die Chaiselongue; der Diwan. — *v.a.* (*express*) in Worte fassen.

cough [kɔf], *v.n.* husten. — *s.* der Husten; *whooping* —, der Keuchhusten.

council [ˈkaunsil], *s.* der Rat (*body*); die Ratsversammlung.

councillor [ˈkaunsilə], *s.* der Rat, das Ratsmitglied; der Stadtrat.

counsel [ˈkaunsəl], *s.* der Rat (*advice*); der Berater (*adviser*); der Anwalt (*lawyer*). — *v.a.* einen Rat geben, beraten (*Acc.*).

counsellor [ˈkaunsələ], *s.* der Ratgeber; der Ratsherr; (*Am.*) der Anwalt (*lawyer*).

count (1) [kaunt], *v.a.,v.n.* zählen; — *on s.o.*, sich auf jemanden verlassen. — *s.* die Zählung.

count (2) [kaunt], *s.* der Graf.

countenance [ˈkauntənəns], *s.* das Gesicht, die Miene. — *v.a.* begünstigen, unterstützen, zulassen.

counter (1) [ˈkauntə], *s.* der Rechner, der Zähler (*chip*); die Spielmarke; der Zahltisch (*desk*); Ladentisch (*in shop*); Schalter (*in office*).

counter (2) [ˈkauntə], *adv.* entgegen.

counteract [kauntəˈrækt], *v.a.* entgegenwirken (*Dat.*).

counteraction [kauntəˈrækʃən], *s.* die Gegenwirkung; der Widerstand (*resistance*).

counterbalance [ˈkauntəbæləns], *s.* das Gegengewicht. — [-ˈbæləns], *v.a.* ausbalancieren, ausgleichen.

countercharge [ˈkauntətʃɑːdʒ], *s.* die Gegenklage.

counterfeit [ˈkauntəfiːt, -fit], *s.* die Fälschung (*forgery*); die Nachahmung (*imitation*). — *adj.* gefälscht, falsch.

craft

counterfoil ['kauntəfɔil], *s.* das Kontrollblatt; der Kupon.

counter-intelligence ['kauntərintelidʒəns], *s.* die Spionageabwehr.

countermand [kauntə'mɑ:nd], *v.a.* widerrufen.

counterpane ['kauntəpein], *s.* die Steppdecke.

counterpart ['kauntəpɑ:t], *s.* das Gegenbild, das Gegenstück.

counterplot ['kauntəplɔt], *s.* der Gegenplan. — *v.n.* einen Gegenplan machen.

counterpoint ['kauntəpɔint], *s.* (*Mus.*) der Kontrapunkt.

counterpoise ['kauntəpɔiz], *s.* das Gegengewicht. — *v.a.* das Gleichgewicht halten.

countersign ['kauntəsain], *v.a.* gegenzeichnen, mitunterschreiben. — *s.* das Gegenzeichen.

countess ['kauntes], *s.* die Gräfin.

counting-house ['kauntiŋhaus], *s.* das Kontor.

countless ['kauntlis], *adj.* zahllos.

country ['kʌntri], *s.* das Land. — *adj.* Land-, ländlich, Bauern-.

county ['kaunti], *s.* die Grafschaft (*British*); der Landbezirk (*U.S.A.*).

couple [kʌpl], *s.* das Paar. — *v.a.* paaren, verbinden. — *v.n.* sich paaren (*pair*); sich verbinden.

couplet ['kʌplit], *s.* das Verspaar.

coupling ['kʌpliŋ], *s.* (*Mech.*) die Kupplung.

courage ['kʌridʒ], *s.* der Mut.

courageous [kə'reidʒəs], *adj.* mutig, tapfer.

courier ['kuriə], *s.* der Eilbote (*messenger*); der Reisebegleiter (*tour leader*).

course [kɔ:s], *s.* der Kurs; der Lauf (*time*); der Ablauf (*lapse of a period etc.*); die Bahn (*racing track*); *in due* —, zu gegebener Zeit; *of* —, natürlich.

courser ['kɔ:sə], *s.* das schnelle Pferd.

court [kɔ:t], *s.* der Hof (*royal etc.*); (*Law*) der Gerichtshof. — *v.a.* (*a lady*) den Hof machen (*Dat.*); — *disaster*, das Unglück herausfordern.

courteous ['kə:tiəs], *adj.* höflich.

courtesan ['kɔ:tizən *or* kɔ:ti'zæn], *s.* die Kurtisane, die Buhlerin.

courtesy ['kə:təsi], *s.* die Höflichkeit; *by* — *of*, mit freundlicher Erlaubnis von.

courtier ['kɔ:tiə], *s.* der Höfling.

courtly ['kɔ:tli], *adj.* höfisch, Hof-.

court-martial [kɔ:t'mɑ:ʃəl], *s.* das Kriegsgericht.

courtship ['kɔ:tʃip], *s.* das Werben, die Werbung, das Freien.

courtyard ['kɔ:tjɑ:d], *s.* der Hof, der Hofraum.

cousin [kʌzn], *s.* der Vetter (*male*); die Kusine (*female*).

cove [kouv], *s.* die (kleine) Bucht.

covenant ['kʌvənənt], *s.* (*Bibl.*) der Bund; (*Comm.*) der Vertrag.

cover ['kʌvə], *v.a.* decken, bedecken (*table etc.*); schützen (*protect*); — *up*, bemänteln. — *s.* die Decke (*blanket*); der Deckel (*lid*); der Einband (*book*); das Gedeck (*table*); (*Comm.*) die Deckung; — *point*, (*Cricket*) die Deckstellung; *under* —, (*Mil.*) verdeckt, unter Deckung; — *girl*, das Mädchen auf dem Titelblatt (einer Illustrierten.)

covering ['kʌvəriŋ], *s.* die Bedeckung, die Bekleidung (*clothing*).

coverlet, coverlid ['kʌvəlit, 'kʌvəlid], *s.* die Bettdecke.

covert ['kʌvə:t], *s.* der Schlupfwinkel (*hideout*); das Dickicht (*thicket*). — *adj.* verborgen, bedeckt (*covered*); heimlich (*secret*).

covet ['kʌvit], *v.a.*, *v.n.* begehren (*Acc.*), gelüsten (nach (*Dat.*)).

covetous ['kʌvitəs], *adj.* begierig, habsüchtig.

covetousness ['kʌvitəsnis], *s.* die Begierde, die Habsucht.

covey ['kʌvi], *s.* der Flug *or* die Kette (Rebhühner, *partridges*).

cow (1) [kau], *s.* die Kuh; — *-shed*, der Kuhstall.

cow (2) [kau], *v.a.* einschüchtern.

coward ['kauəd], *s.* der Feigling.

cowardice ['kauədis], *s.* die Feigheit.

cower ['kauə], *v.n.* sich kauern.

cowherd ['kauhə:d], *s.* der Kuhhirt.

cowl [kaul], *s.* die Kappe (*of monk*), die Kapuze (*hood*).

cowslip ['kauslip], *s.* (*Bot.*) die Primel, die Schlüsselblume.

coxswain [kɔksn], *s.* (*Naut.*) der Steuermann.

coy [kɔi], *adj.* scheu, spröde, zurückhaltend.

coyness ['kɔinis], *s.* die Sprödigkeit.

crab [kræb], *s.* (*Zool.*) die Krabbe; — *apple*, (*Bot.*) der Holzapfel.

crabbed [kræbd], *adj.* mürrisch (*temper*); unleserlich (*handwriting*).

crack [kræk], *s.* der Riß (*fissure*); der Krach, Schlag; der Sprung; die komische Bemerkung (*remark*). — *adj.* (*coll.*) erstklassig; — *shot*, der Meisterschütze. — *v.a.* aufbrechen; aufknacken (*nut, safe*); — *a joke*, eine witzige Bemerkung machen. — *v.n.* — *under strain*, unter einer Anstrengung zusammenbrechen; bersten (*break*).

cracked, crackers [krækd, 'krækəz], *adj.* (*coll.*) verrückt.

cracker ['krækə], *s.* der Keks; der Frosch (*firework*).

crackle [krækl], *v.n.* knistern, prasseln (*fire*); knallen, platzen (*rocket*).

cracknel ['kræknəl], *s.* die Brezel.

crackpot ['krækpɔt], *s.* (*coll.*) der verrückte Kerl.

cradle [kreidl], *s.* die Wiege. — *v.a.* einwiegen.

craft [krɑ:ft], *s.* die Fertigkeit (*skill*); das Handwerk (*trade*); die List (*cunning*); *arts and* —*s*, die Handwerkskünste.

craftsman ['krɑːftsmən], s. der (gelernte) Handwerker.

crafty ['krɑːfti], adj. listig, schlau.

crag [kræg], s. die Klippe.

cragged, craggy [krægd, 'krægi], adj. felsig, schroff.

cram [kræm], v.a. vollstopfen (stuff full); (coll.) pauken (coach). — v.n. büffeln.

crammer ['kræmə], s. (coll.) der Einpauker, Privatlehrer (tutor).

cramp [kræmp], s. (Med.) der Krampf; die Klammer (tool). — v.a. einengen (narrow); verkrampfen.

cramped [kræmpd], adj. krampfhaft; eingeengt; beengt (enclosed).

cranberry ['krænbəri], s. (Bot.) die Preiselbeere.

crane [krein], s. (Orn.) der Kranich; (Engin.) der Kran. — v.a. — o.'s neck, den Hals ausrecken.

crank (1) [kræŋk], s. (Motor.) die Kurbel; — -handle, die Andrehwelle; (Motor., Engin.) —shaft, die Kurbelwelle, die Kurbel.

crank (2) [kræŋk], s. der Sonderling, der sonderbare Kauz (eccentric).

cranky ['kræŋki], adj. sonderbar.

cranny ['kræni], s. der Spalt, der Riß; nook and —, Eck und Spalt.

crape [kreip], s. der Krepp, Flor.

crash [kræʃ], s. der Krach; (Motor.) Zusammenstoß; (Aviat.) Absturz. — v.n. krachen (noise); stürzen, abstürzen (fall).

crass [kræs], adj. derb, grob, kraß.

crate [kreit], s. der Packkorb (basket); die Kiste (wood).

crater ['kreitə], s. (Geol.) der Krater.

cravat [krə'væt], s. die breite Halsbinde, das Halstuch (scarf); die Krawatte.

crave [kreiv], v.a. (dringend) verlangen (for, nach, Dat.).

craven ['kreivn], adj. feig, mutlos. — s. der Feigling.

craving ['kreiviŋ], s. das starke Verlangen.

craw [krɔː], s. (Zool.) der Vogelkropf.

crawl [krɔːl], v.n. kriechen; kraulen (swim).

crawling ['krɔːliŋ], s. das Kriechen; das Kraulschwimmen.

crayon ['kreiən], s. der Farbstift, der Pastellstift.

craze [kreiz], s. die Manie; die verrückte Mode (fashion).

craziness ['kreizinis], s. die Verrücktheit.

crazy ['kreizi], adj. verrückt.

creak [kriːk], v.n. knarren.

cream [kriːm], s. der Rahm, die Sahne; whipped —, die Schlagsahne, (Austr.) der Schlagobers. — v.a. — off, (die Sahne) abschöpfen; (fig.) das Beste abziehen.

creamery ['kriːməri], s. die Molkerei.

creamy ['kriːmi], adj. sahnig.

crease [kriːs], s. die Falte (trousers etc.); — -resistant, knitterfrei. — v.a. falten (fold). — v.n. knittern.

create [kri'eit], v.a. erschaffen, schaffen.

creation [kri'eiʃən], s. die Schöpfung.

creative [kri'eitiv], adj. schöpferisch.

creator [kri'eitə], s. der Schöpfer.

creature ['kriːtʃə], s. das Geschöpf.

credence ['kriːdəns], s. der Glaube.

credentials [kri'denʃəlz], s. pl. das Zeugnis, das Beglaubigungsschreiben; die Legitimation (proof of identity).

credibility [kredi'biliti], s. die Glaubwürdigkeit.

credible ['kredibl], adj. glaubwürdig, glaublich.

credit ['kredit], s. (Comm.) der Kredit; der gute Ruf (reputation); das Guthaben (assets). — v.a. — s.o. with s.th., jemandem etwas gutschreiben; glauben (believe).

creditable ['kreditəbl], adj. ehrenwert, lobenswert.

creditor ['kreditə], s. (Comm.) der Gläubiger.

credulity [kre'djuːliti], s. die Leichtgläubigkeit.

credulous ['kredjuləs], adj. leichtgläubig.

creed [kriːd], s. das Glaubensbekenntnis.

creek [kriːk], s. die kleine Bucht; das Flüßchen (small river).

creel [kriːl], s. der Fischkorb.

creep [kriːp], s. (Geol.) der Rutsch; (pl., coll.) the —s, die Gänsehaut, das Gruseln.— v.n.irr.kriechen; (furtively) sich einschleichen.

creeper ['kriːpə], s. die Schlingpflanze, das Rankengewächs; (Sch.) der Kriecher; Virginia —, der wilde Wein.

creepy ['kriːpi], adj. kriechend; gruselig (frightening).

cremate [kri'meit], v.a. einäschern.

cremation [kri'meiʃən], s. die Verbrennung, Einäscherung.

crematorium, (Am.) crematory [kremə'tɔːriəm, 'kremətəri], s. das Krematorium.

Creole ['kriːoul], s. der Kreole.

crepuscular [kri'pʌskjulə], adj. dämmerig.

crescent ['kresənt], adj. wachsend, zunehmend. — s. der (zunehmende) Mond, die Mondsichel; das Hörnchen.

cress [kres], s. (Bot.) die Kresse; mustard and —, die Gartenkresse.

crest [krest], s. der Kamm (cock); der Gipfel (hill); der Kamm (wave); der Busch (helmet); das Wappenschild (Heraldry).

crestfallen ['krestfɔːlən], adj. entmutigt, mutlos, niedergeschlagen.

Cretan ['kriːtən], adj. kretisch. — s. der Kreter, die Kreterin.

cretonne ['kretɔn], s. die Kretonne.

crevasse [krə'væs], s. die Gletscherspalte.

crevice ['krevis], s. der Riß.

crew (1) [kruː], s. (Naut., Aviat.) die Besatzung; (Naut.) die Schiffsmannschaft; die Mannschaft (team); (Am.) — -cut, die Bürstenfrisur.

crew (2) [kru:] *see* **crow**.

crib [krib], *s.* die Krippe (*Christmas*); die Wiege (*cradle*); (*Sch.*) die Eselsbrücke. — *v.a.* (*Sch.*) abschreiben (*copy*).

crick [krik], *s.* (*in neck*) der steife Hals.

cricket ['krikit], *s.* (*Ent.*) das Heimchen, die Grille; (*Sport*) das Cricket(spiel).

crime [kraim], *s.* das Verbrechen; — *fiction*, die Detektivromane, *m. pl.*

criminal ['kriminəl], *s.* der Verbrecher. — *adj.* — *case*, der Kriminalfall; verbrecherisch (*act*); — *investigation*, die Fahndung.

crimp [krimp], *v.a.* kräuseln (*hair*).

crimson ['krimzən], *adj.* karmesinrot.

cringe [krindʒ], *v.n.* kriechen.

crinkle ['kriŋkl], *v.a., v.n.* kräuseln. — *s.* die Falte.

crinoline ['krinəlin], *s.* der Reifrock.

cripple [kripl], *s.* der Krüppel. — *v.a.* verkrüppeln; lahmlegen (*immobilize*).

crisis ['kraisis], *s.* die Krise, der Wendepunkt; die Notlage.

crisp [krisp], *adj.* kraus (*hair*); knusperig (*bread*); frisch.

criss-cross ['kriskrɔs], *adv.* kreuz und quer.

criterion [krai'tiəriən], *s.* das Kennzeichen, das Kriterium.

critic ['kritik], *s.* der Kritiker; Rezensent (*reviewer*).

critical ['kritikəl], *adj.* kritisch.

criticism ['kritisizm], *s.* die Kritik (*of, an, Dat.*); Rezension, Besprechung (*review*).

criticize ['kritisaiz], *v.a.* kritisieren.

croak [krouk], *v.n.* krächzen (*raven*); quaken (*frog*).

croaking ['kroukiŋ], *s.* das Krächzen, das Gekrächze (*raven*); das Quaken (*frog*).

Croat ['krouæt], *s.* der Kroate.

Croatian [krou'eifən], *adj.* kroatisch.

crochet ['kroufei], *s.* die Häkelei; — *hook*, die Häkelnadel. — *v.a., v.n.* häkeln.

crock [krɔk], *s.* der Topf, der irdene Krug; der alte Topf; (*coll.*) old —, der Invalide, Krüppel.

crockery ['krɔkəri], *s.* (*Comm.*) die Töpferware; das Geschirr (*household*).

crocodile ['krɔkədail], *s.* das Krokodil.

crocus ['kroukəs], *s.* (*Bot.*) der Krokus, die Safranblume.

croft [krɔft], *s.* das Kleinbauerngut.

crofter ['krɔftə], *s.* der Kleinbauer.

crone [kroun], *s.* das alte Weib; die Hexe (*witch*).

crony ['krouni], *s.* (*coll.*) old —, der alte Freund.

crook [kruk], *s.* der Krummstab (*staff*); der Schwindler (*cheat*). — *v.a.* krümmen, biegen.

crooked ['krukid], *adj.* krumm; (*fig.*) schwindlerisch, verbrecherisch.

crookedness ['krukidnis], *s.* die Krummheit; die Durchtriebenheit (*slyness*).

croon [kru:n], *v.n.* leise singen; (*Am.*) im modernen Stil singen.

crooner ['kru:nə], *s.* der Jazzsänger.

crop [krɔp], *s.* der Kropf (*bird*); die Ernte (*harvest*); der (kurze) Haarschnitt; *riding* —, die Reitpeitsche. — *v.a.* stutzen (*cut short*). — *v.n.* — *up*, auftauchen.

crosier ['krouziə], *s.* (*Eccl.*) der Bischofsstab.

cross [krɔs], *s.* das Kreuz. — *v.a.* (*Zool., Bot.*) kreuzen; überqueren (*road, on foot*); *s.o.'s path*, einem in die Quere kommen. — *v.n.* überfahren (*übers Wasser*); hinübergehen; — *over*, übersetzen (*on boat or ferry*). — *v.r.* sich bekreuzigen. — *adj.* mürrisch (*grumpy*), verstimmt; *at* — *purposes*, ohne einander zu verstehen; *make* —, verstimmen. — *adv.* kreuzweise; — *-eyed*, schielend; — *-grained*, wider den Strich, schlecht aufgelegt.

crossbow ['krɔsbou], *s.* die Armbrust.

crossbreed ['krɔsbri:d], *s.* die Mischrasse, der Mischling.

cross-examine [krɔsig'zæmin], *v.a., v.n.* (*Law*) ins (Kreuz-)Verhör nehmen.

crossing ['krɔsiŋ], *s.* die Straßenkreuzung; (*Naut.*) die Überfahrt; der Straßenübergang; Kreuzweg.

crossroads ['krɔsroudz], *s.* der Kreuzweg, die Kreuzung.

crossword ['krɔswə:d], *s.* das Kreuzworträtsel.

crotch [krɔtʃ], *s.* der Haken.

crotchet ['krɔtʃit], *s.* (*Mus.*) die Viertelnote; die Grille (*mood*).

crotchety ['krɔtʃiti], *adj.* grillenhaft, verschroben.

crouch [krautʃ], *v.n.* sich ducken (*squat*); sich demütigen (*cringe*).

croup (1) [kru:p], *s.* (*Med.*) der Krupp.

croup (2) [kru:p], *s.* die Kruppe.

crow [krou], *s.* (*Orn.*) die Krähe; das Krähen (*of cock*). — *v.n. irr.* krähen (*cock*).

crowbar ['krouba:], *s.* das Brecheisen.

crowd [kraud], *s.* die Menge (*multitude*); das Gedränge (*throng*). — *v.n.* — *in*, sich hineindrängen, dazudrängen; — *around*, sich herumscharen um (*Acc.*).

crown [kraun], *s.* die Krone (*diadem or coin*); der Gipfel (*mountain*); (*Anat.*) der Scheitel; — *lands*, Krongüter (*n. pl.*), Landeigentum der Krone, *n.*; — *prince*, der Kronprinz; — *of thorns*, die Dornenkrone. — *v.a.* krönen.

crucial ['kru:fəl], *adj.* entscheidend, kritisch.

crucifix ['kru:sifiks], *s.* das Kruzifix.

crucify ['kru:sifai], *v.a.* kreuzigen.

crude [kru:d], *adj.* roh, ungekocht, unreif; grob (*manners*); ungeschliffen.

crudity ['kru:diti], *s.* die Rohheit; Grobheit (*manners*).

cruel ['kru:əl], *adj.* grausam.

cruelty ['kru:əlti], *s.* die Grausamkeit.

cruet ['kru:it], *s.* das Salz- *oder* Pfefferfäßchen; das Fläschchen.

355

cruise [kru:z], *v.n.* (*Naut.*) kreuzen. — *s.* die Seefahrt, die Seereise; *pleasure* —, die Vergnügungsreise (zu Wasser).

cruiser [ʹkru:zə], *s.* (*Naut.*) der Kreuzer; *battle* —, der Panzerkreuzer.

crumb [krʌm], *s.* die Krume. — *v.a.* zerbröckeln, zerkrümeln.

crumble [krʌmbl], *v.n.* zerfallen, zerbröckeln.

crumpet [ʹkrʌmpit], *s.* das Teebrötchen, das Teeküchlein.

crumple [krʌmpl], *v.a.* zerknittern (*material*). — *v.n.* — *up*, zusammenbrechen.

crunch [krʌntʃ], *v.a.* zerstoßen, zermalmen. — *v.n.* knirschen.

crusade [kru:ʹseid], *s.* der Kreuzzug.

crusader [kru:ʹseidə], *s.* der Kreuzfahrer.

crush [krʌʃ], *v.a.* zerdrücken; zerstoßen (*pulverize*); drängen (*crowd*); zertreten (*tread down*); (*fig.*) vernichten. — *s.* das Gedränge (*throng*); (*coll.*) have a — *on*, verknallt sein, in einen verliebt sein.

crust [krʌst], *s.* die Kruste, die Rinde (*bread*). — *v.a.* mit einer Kruste bedecken. — *v.n.* verkrusten.

crustaceous [krʌsʹteiʃəs], *adj.* (*Zool.*) krustenartig, Krustentier-.

crusty [ʹkrʌsti], *adj.* krustig, knusperig (*pastry, bread*); mürrisch (*grumpy*).

crutch [krʌtʃ], *s.* die Krücke.

crux [krʌks], *s.* der entscheidende Punkt, der springende Punkt, die Schwierigkeit.

cry [krai], *v.n.* schreien, rufen; weinen (*weep*). — *v.a.* — *down*, niederschreien. — *s.* der Schrei; der Zuruf (*call*).

crypt [kript], *s.* (*Eccl.*) die Krypta, die Gruft.

crystal [ʹkristəl], *s.* der Kristall.

crystallize [ʹkristəlaiz], *v.n.* sich kristallisieren, Kristalle bilden.

cub [kʌb], *s.* (*Zool.*) das Junge. — *v.n.* Junge haben, Junge werfen.

Cuban [ʹkju:bən], *adj.* kubanisch. — *s.* der Kubaner.

cube [kju:b], *s.* der Würfel; (*Maths.*) — *root*, die Kubikwurzel. — *v.a.* zur Dritten (Potenz) erheben; kubieren.

cubic(al) [ʹkju:bik(əl)], *adj.* kubisch, zur dritten Potenz.

cubit [ʹkju:bit], *s.* die Elle.

cuckoo [ʹkuku:], *s.* (*Orn.*) der Kuckuck.

cucumber [ʹkju:kʌmbə], *s.* (*Bot.*) die Gurke; *cool as a* —, ruhig und gelassen.

cud [kʌd], *s.* das wiedergekäute Futter; *chew the* —, wiederkauen (*also fig.*).

cuddle [kʌdl], *v.a.* liebkosen, an sich drücken. — *v.n.* sich anschmiegen.

cudgel [ʹkʌdʒəl], *s.* der Knüttel; *take up the* — *s for*, sich für etwas einsetzen.

cue (1) [kju:], *s.* (*Theat.*) das Stichwort. — *v.a.* einem (*Theat.*) das Stichwort or (*Mus.*) den Einsatz geben.

cue (2) [kju:], *s.* der Billardstock. — *v.a.* (*Billiards*) abschießen.

cuff (1) [kʌf], *s.* die Manschette, der Aufschlag (*shirt*); —*links*, die Manschettenknöpfe.

cuff (2) [kʌf], *s.* der Schlag. — *v.a.* schlagen, puffen.

culinary [ʹkju:linəri], *adj.* kulinarisch; Küchen-, Eß-, Speisen-.

cull [kʌl], *v.a.* auswählen, auslesen (*from books*).

culminate [ʹkʌlmineit], *v.n.* kulminieren, den Höhepunkt erreichen.

culpable [ʹkʌlpəbl], *adj.* schuldig; strafbar.

culprit [ʹkʌlprit], *s.* der Schuldige, Verbrecher.

cult [kʌlt], *s.* der Kult, die Verehrung; der Kultus.

cultivate [ʹkʌltiveit], *v.a.* kultivieren; (*Agr.*) anbauen; pflegen (*acquaintance*); bilden (*mind*).

cultivation [kʌltiʹveiʃən], *s.* (*Agr.*) der Anbau; die Bildung (*mind*).

culture [ʹkʌltʃə], *s.* die Kultur, die Bildung.

cumbersome [ʹkʌmbəsəm], *adj.* beschwerlich, lästig.

cunning [ʹkʌniŋ], *s.* die List, die Schlauheit. — *adj.* listig, schlau.

cup [kʌp], *s.* die Tasse (*tea*—); der Becher (*handleless*); (*Eccl.*) der Kelch; der Pokal (*sports*); — *final*, das Endspiel. — *v.a.* (*Med.*) schröpfen.

cupboard [ʹkʌbəd], *s.* der Schrank.

cupola [ʹkju:polə], *s.* (*Archit., Metall.*) die Kuppel.

cur [kə:], *s.* der Köter; (*fig.*) der Schurke.

curable [ʹkjuərəbl], *adj.* heilbar.

curate [ʹkjuərit], *s.* der Hilfsgeistliche.

curative [ʹkjuərətiv], *adj.* heilsam, heilend.

curator [kjuəʹreitə], *s.* der Kurator, Verwalter, Direktor.

curb [kə:b], *v.a.* zügeln, bändigen. — *s.* der Zaum (*bridle*).

curd [kə:d], *s.* der Rahmkäse, der Milchkäse; (*pl.*) der Quark.

curdle [kə:dl], *v.a.* gerinnen lassen. — *v.n.* gerinnen; erstarren.

cure [kjuə], *s.* die Kur, die Heilung. — *v.a.* kurieren, wieder gesundmachen; einpökeln (*foodstuffs*).

curfew [ʹkə:fju:], *s.* die Abendglocke (*bells*); das Ausgehverbot, die Polizeistunde (*police*).

curio [ʹkjuəriou], *s.* die Kuriosität, das Sammlerstück; die Rarität.

curiosity [kjuəriʹositi], *s.* die Neugier; Merkwürdigkeit.

curious [ʹkjuəriəs], *adj.* neugierig (*inquisitive*); seltsam, sonderbar (*strange*).

curl [kə:l], *v.a.* kräuseln, (in Locken) wickeln. — *v.n.* sich kräuseln. — *s.* die Haarlocke.

curler [ʹkə:lə], *s.* der Lockenwickler.

curlew [ʹkə:lju:], *s.* (*Orn.*) der Brachvogel.

curly [ʹkə:li], *adj.* lockig.

currant [ʹkʌrənt], *s.* (*Bot.*) die Korinthe, die Johannisbeere.

dais

currency ['kʌrənsi], s. die Währung (*money*); der Umlauf (*circulation*).
current ['kʌrənt], adj. im Umlauf; allgemein gültig, eben gültig; jetzig (*modern*). — s. (*Elect.*) der Strom; die Strömung (*river*); der Zug (*air*).
curry (1) ['kʌri], v.a. gerben (*tan*); — comb, der Pferdestriegel; — favour, sich einschmeicheln.
curry (2) ['kʌri], s. das indische Ragout. — v.a. würzen.
curse [kə:s], v.a., v.n. verfluchen; verwünschen. — s. der Fluch; die Verwünschung.
cursive ['kə:siv], adj. kursiv, Kursiv-.
cursory ['kə:səri], adj. kursorisch, oberflächlich.
curt [kə:t], adj. kurz angebunden (*speech, manner*).
curtail [kə:'teil], v.a. stutzen, beschränken (*scope*); verkürzen (*time*).
curtain ['kə:tin], s. die Gardine; der Vorhang; (*Mil.*) — fire, das Sperrfeuer; — lecture, die Gardinenpredigt; — speech, die Ansprache vor dem Vorhang. — v.a. verhüllen (*hide*); mit Vorhängen versehen (*hang curtains*).
curtness ['kə:tnis], s. die Kürze; die Barschheit.
curts(e)y ['kə:tsi], s. der Knicks. — v.n. knicksen, einen Knicks machen.
curve [kə:v], s. die Krümmung; (*Geom.*) die Kurve. — v.a. krümmen, biegen. — v.n. sich biegen.
curved [kə:vd], adj. krumm, gebogen.
cushion ['kuʃən], s. das Kissen. — v.a. polstern.
custody ['kʌstədi], s. die Obhut; Bewachung, Haft.
custom ['kʌstəm], s. die Sitte, die Tradition; der Gebrauch, Brauch (*usage*); die Kundschaft (*trade*); (*pl.*) der Zoll (*duty*).
customary ['kʌstəməri], adj. gewohnt, althergebracht, gebräuchlich.
customer ['kʌstəmə], s. der Kunde, die Kundin.
cut [kʌt], v.a. irr. schneiden; — (*s.o.*), ignorieren; — o.'s teeth, zahnen; this won't — any ice, das wird nicht viel nützen; — both ways, das ist ein zweischneidiges Schwert; — a lecture, eine Vorlesung schwänzen; — short, unterbrechen. — adj. — out for, wie gerufen zu or für; — to the quick, aufs tiefste verletzt; — glass, das geschliffene Glas; — price, verbilligt. — s. der Schnitt (*section*); der Hieb (*gash*); (*Art*) der Stich; — in salary, eine Gehaltskürzung; die Abkürzung, die Kürzung (*abridgment*).
cute [kju:t], adj. klug, aufgeweckt; (*Am.*) süß, niedlich.
cutler ['kʌtlə], s. der Messerschmied.
cutlery ['kʌtləri], s. das Besteck (*tableware*); (*Comm.*) die Messerschmiedwaren, f. pl.
cutlet ['kʌtlit], s. das Kotelett, das Rippchen.

cut-throat ['kʌtθrout], s. der Halsabschneider; — competition, Konkurrenz auf Leben und Tod.
cuttle [kʌtl], s. (*Zool.*) der Tintenfisch.
cyanide ['saiənaid], s. (*Chem.*) zyanidsaures Salz; das Zyanid, die Blausäure.
cyclamen ['sikləmən], s. (*Bot.*) das Alpenveilchen.
cycle [saikl], s. (*Geom.*) der Kreis; (*Mus., Zool.*) der Zyklus; (*coll.*) das Fahrrad. — v.n. (*coll.*) radfahren; zirkulieren (*round*, um, *Acc.*).
cyclone ['saikloun], s. der Wirbelwind, der Wirbelsturm.
cyclopaedia [saiklo'pi:djə] see **encyclopaedia**.
cylinder ['silində], s. der Zylinder; die Walze.
cymbal ['simbəl], s. (*Mus.*) die Zimbel, das Becken.
cynic ['sinik], s. der Zyniker.
cynical ['sinikəl], adj. zynisch.
cypress ['saiprəs], s. (*Bot.*) die Zypresse.
Cypriot ['sipriət], adj. zyprisch. — s. der Zypriote.
czar [za:], s. der Zar.
Czech [tʃek], **Czechoslovak(ian)** [tʃeko'slouvæk, tʃekoslo'vækjən], adj. tschechisch. —s. der Tscheche.

D

D [di:], das D (*also Mus.*).
dab [dæb], v.a. leicht berühren. — s. der leichte Schlag (*blow*).
dabble [dæbl], v.n. sich in etwas versuchen, pfuschen (*in*, in, *Dat.*).
dabbler ['dæblə], s. der Pfuscher, Stümper.
dace [deis], s. (*Zool.*) der Weißfisch.
dad, daddy [dæd, 'dædi], s. der Papa; Vati; daddy longlegs, die Bachmücke, die langbeinige Mücke.
dado ['deidou], s. die Täfelung.
daffodil ['dæfədil], s. (*Bot.*) die Narzisse.
dagger ['dægə], s. der Dolch; at —s drawn, spinnefeind; look —s, mit Blicken durchbohren.
dahlia ['deiljə], s. (*Bot.*) die Dahlie, die Georgine.
daily ['deili], adj. täglich; Tages-. — s. (*newspaper*) die Tageszeitung; (*woman*) die Putzfrau.
dainties ['deintiz], s. pl. das Backwerk, das kleine Gebäck, das Teegebäck.
daintiness ['deintinis], s. die Feinheit; die Kleinheit; die Leckerhaftigkeit.
dainty ['deinti], adj. fein, klein, zierlich; lecker (*food*).
dairy ['dɛəri], s. die Molkerei, die Meierei.
dairyman ['dɛərimən], s. der Milchmann; der Senne (*in Alps*).
dais [deis, 'deiis], s. das Podium.

357

daisy

daisy ['deizi], s. (Bot.) das Gänseblümchen, das Marienblümchen.

dale [deil], s. das Tal.

dalliance ['dæliəns], s. die Tändelei, Liebelei; Verzögerung.

dally ['dæli], v.n. die Zeit vertrödeln.

dam (1) [dæm], s. der Damm. — v.a. eindämmen, abdämmen.

dam (2) [dæm], s. (Zool.) die Tiermutter.

damage ['dæmidʒ], s. der Schaden; der Verlust (loss); (pl.) (Law) der Schadenersatz. — v.a. beschädigen.

damageable ['dæmidʒəbl], adj. leicht zu beschädigen.

damask ['dæməsk], s. der Damast (textile). — adj. damasten, aus Damast.

dame [deim], s. die Dame (title); (Am.) (coll.) die junge Dame, das Fräulein.

damn [dæm], v.a. verdammen.

damnable ['dæmnəbl], adj. verdammenswert, verdammt.

damnation [dæm'neiʃən], s. die Verdammung, Verdammnis.

damn(ed) [dæm(d)], adj. & adv. verwünscht, verdammt.

damp [dæmp], adj. feucht, dumpfig. — s. die Feuchtigkeit; (Build.) — course, die Schutzschicht. — v.a. dämpfen, befeuchten; — the spirits, die gute Laune verderben.

damsel ['dæmzəl], s. die Jungfer; das Mädchen.

damson ['dæmzən], s. (Bot.) die Damaszenerpflaume.

dance [da:ns], v.a., v.n. tanzen. — s. der Tanz; lead s.o. a —, einem viel Mühe machen.

dandelion ['dændilaiən], s. (Bot.) der Löwenzahn.

dandle [dændl], v.a. hätscheln; schaukeln.

dandy ['dændi], s. der Geck, der Stutzer.

Dane [dein], s. der Däne.

dane [dein], s. great —, die Dogge.

Danish ['deiniʃ], adj. dänisch.

danger ['deindʒə], s. die Gefahr.

dangerous ['deindʒərəs], adj. gefährlich.

dangle [dæŋgl], v.a. baumeln lassen. — v.n. baumeln, hängen.

dank [dæŋk], adj. feucht, naßkalt.

Danube ['dænju:b]. die Donau.

dapper ['dæpə], adj. schmuck; niedlich; elegant.

dappled [dæpld], adj. scheckig, bunt.

Dardanelles, The [da:də'nelz]. die Dardanellen, pl.

dare [dɛə], v.n. irr. wagen; I — say, das meine ich wohl, ich gebe zu.

daredevil ['dɛədevl], s. der Wagehals, der Draufgänger.

daring ['dɛəriŋ], s. die Kühnheit.

dark [da:k], adj. dunkel, finster. — s. die Dunkelheit; shot in the —, ein Schuß aufs Geratewohl, ins Blaue.

darken ['da:kən], v.a. verdunkeln, verfinstern. — v.n. dunkel werden.

darkish ['da:kiʃ], adj. nahezu dunkel.

darkness ['da:knis], s. die Dunkelheit, Finsternis.

darkroom ['da:kru:m], s. die Dunkelkammer.

darling ['da:liŋ], s. der Liebling. — adj. lieb, teuer.

darn (1) [da:n], v.a. stopfen.

darn (2) [da:n], v.a. verdammen.

darn(ed) [da:n(d)], (excl.) verdammt.

darning ['da:niŋ], s. das Stopfen; — needle, die Stopfnadel.

dart [da:t], s. der Pfeil; der Spieß (spear); (pl.) das Pfeilwurfspiel. — v.n. losstürmen, sich stürzen.

dash [dæʃ], v.a. zerschmettern, zerstören (hopes). — v.n. stürzen. — s. der Schlag (blow); die Eleganz; (Typ.) der Gedankenstrich; (Motor.) — -board, das Schaltbrett, Armaturenbrett.

dashing ['dæʃiŋ], adj. schneidig.

dastard ['dæstəd], s. der Feigling, die Memme.

dastardly ['dæstədli], adj., adv. feige.

data ['deitə], s. pl. (Science) die Angaben, die Daten.

date (1) [deit], s. das Datum; (Am.) die Verabredung; out of —, veraltet (antiquated), altmodisch (out of fashion). — v.a. datieren; (Am.) ausführen. — v.n. das Datum tragen.

date (2) [deit], s. (Bot.) die Dattel.

dative ['deitiv], s. (Gram.) der Dativ.

daub [dɔ:b], v.a. bekleksen; (coll.) bemalen. — s. die Klekserei; (coll.) die Malerei.

daughter ['dɔ:tə], s. die Tochter; — -in-law, die Schwiegertochter.

daunt [dɔ:nt], v.a. einschüchtern.

dauphin ['dɔ:fin], s. der Dauphin.

daw [dɔ:], s. (Orn.) die Dohle.

dawdle ['dɔ:dl], v.n. trödeln, die Zeit vertrödeln.

dawdler ['dɔ:dlə], s. der Trödler, Tagedieb, die Schlafmütze.

dawn [dɔ:n], s. das Morgengrauen, die Morgendämmerung. — v.n. dämmern, tagen.

day [dei], s. der Tag; the other —, neulich; every —, täglich; one —, eines Tages; by —, bei or am Tage.

daybreak ['deibreik], s. der Tagesanbruch.

daytime ['deitaim], s. in the —, bei Tage.

daze [deiz], v.a. blenden (dazzle); betäuben (stupefy).

dazzle [dæzl], v.a. blenden.

deacon ['di:kən], s. (Eccl.) der Diakon.

deaconess ['di:kənes], s. (Eccl.) die Diakonisse.

dead [ded], adj. tot; stop —, plötzlich anhalten; as — as mutton, mausetot; — from the neck up, (coll.) dumm wie die Nacht. — adv. — beat, erschöpft; (Am.) —sure, ganz sicher. — s. in the — of night, in tiefster Nacht; (pl.) die Toten.

deaden [dedn], *v.a.* abschwächen (*weaken*); abtöten (*anæsthetise*).
deadly ['dedli], *adj.* tödlich.
deadness ['dednis], *s.* die Leblosigkeit; Mattheit (*tiredness*).
deaf [def], *adj.* taub; — *and dumb*, taubstumm.
deafen [defn], *v.a.* betäuben.
deafmute ['defmju:t], *s.* der Taubstumme.
deal (1) [di:l], *s.* das Geschäft; die Anzahl; *a fair or square* —, eine anständige Behandlung; *a good* —, beträchtlich; *a great* — *of*, sehr viel; *make a* —, ein Geschäft abschliessen; *it's a* —! abgemacht! — *v.a. irr.* austeilen; Karten geben (*cards*); — *a blow*, einen Schlag erteilen. — *v.n. irr.* — *with s.th.*, etwas behandeln.
deal (2) [di:l], *s.* (*Bot.*) das Kiefernholz, die Kiefer; — *board*, das Kiefernholzbrett.
dealer ['di:lə], *s.* der Händler.
dean [di:n], *s.* der Dekan.
dear [diə], *adj.* teuer, lieb (*beloved*); teuer, kostspielig (*expensive*); — *me!* ach, Du lieber Himmel! —, —! du liebe Zeit! — *John!* Lieber Hans!
dearness ['diənis], *s.* die Teuerung, das Teuersein.
dearth [də:θ], *s.* der Mangel (*of*, an, *Dat.*).
death [deθ], *s.* der Tod; der Todesfall; — *penalty*, die Todesstrafe; — *warrant*, das Todesurteil.
deathbed ['deθbed], *s.* das Totenbett, Sterbebett.
deathblow ['deθblou], *s.* der Todesstoß.
deathless ['deθlis], *adj.* unsterblich.
debar [di'ba:], *v.a.* ausschließen (*from*, von, *Dat.*).
debase [di'beis], *v.a.* erniedrigen, verschlechtern.
debatable [di'beitəbl], *adj.* strittig.
debate [di'beit], *s.* die Debatte. — *v.a., v.n.* debattieren.
debauch [di'bɔ:tʃ], *v.a., v.n.* verführen; verderben.
debauchee [di'bɔ:tʃi:], *s.* der Schwelger, der Wüstling.
debenture [di'bentʃə], *s.* der Schuldschein.
debilitate [di'biliteit], *v.a.* schwächen.
debit ['debit], *s.* die Schuldseite, das Soll (*in account*). — *v.a.* belasten.
debt [det], *s.* die Schuld; *run into* — *or incur* —*s*, Schulden machen.
debtor ['detə], *s.* der Schuldner.
decade ['dekəd, 'dekeid], *s.* das Jahrzehnt; die Dekade.
decadence ['dekədəns], *s.* die Dekadenz, der Verfall.
decalogue ['dekələg], *s.* (*Bibl.*) die zehn Gebote.
decamp [di'kæmp], *v.n.* aufbrechen, ausreißen.
decant [di'kænt], *v.a.* abfüllen, abgießen.
decanter [di'kæntə], *s.* die Karaffe.

decapitate [di:'kæpiteit], *v.a.* enthaupten köpfen.
decapitation [di:kæpi'teiʃən], *s.* die Enthauptung.
decay [di'kei], *v.n.* in Verfall geraten. — *s.* der Verfall, die Verwesung.
decease [di'si:s], *s.* das Hinscheiden, der Tod. — *v.n.* sterben, dahinscheiden, verscheiden.
deceit [di'si:t], *s.* der Betrug; die List (*cunning*).
deceive [di'si:v], *v.a.* betrügen.
deceiver [di'si:və], *s.* der Betrüger.
December [di'sembə], *s.* der Dezember.
decency ['di:sənsi], *s.* der Anstand; die Anständigkeit, Ehrlichkeit; die Schicklichkeit.
decent ['di:sənt], *adj.* anständig.
decentralize [di:'sentrəlaiz], *v.a.* dezentralisieren.
deception [di'sepʃən], *s.* der Betrug.
deceptive [di'septiv], *adj.* trügerisch.
decide [di'said], *v.a., v.n.* entscheiden; bestimmen (*determine*).
decimal ['desiməl], *adj.* dezimal.
decimate ['desimeit], *v.a.* dezimieren, herabsetzen (*reduce*).
decipher [di'saifə], *v.a.* entziffern (*read*); dechiffrieren (*decode*).
decision [di'siʒən], *s.* die Entscheidung, der Beschluß (*resolution*); die Entschlossenheit (*decisiveness*).
decisive [di'saisiv], *adj.* entscheidend.
decisiveness [di'saisivnis], *s.* die Entschiedenheit.
deck [dek], *s.* (*Naut.*) das Deck; — *chair*, der Liegestuhl. — *v.a.* — (*out*), ausschmücken.
declaim [di'kleim], *v.a.* deklamieren.
declamation [deklə'meiʃən], *s.* die Deklamation.
declamatory [di'klæmətəri], *adj.* Deklamations-, deklamatorisch, Vortrags-.
declaration [deklə'reiʃən], *s.* die Erklärung; die Deklaration.
declare [di'kleə], *v.a.* erklären. — *v.n.* sich erklären.
declared [di'kleəd], *adj.* erklärt, offen.
declension [di'klenʃən], *s.* (*Gram.*) die Deklination, die Abwandlung.
declinable [di'klainəbl], *adj.* (*Gram.*) deklinierbar.
declination [dekli'neiʃən], *s.* (*Phys.*) die Abweichung, Deklination.
decline [di'klain], *v.n.* abweichen (*deflect*); abnehmen (*decrease*); sich weigern (*refuse*); fallen (*price*). — *v.a.* (*Gram.*) deklinieren; ablehnen (*turn down*). — *s.* die Abnahme (*decrease*); der Verfall (*decadence*); der Abhang (*slope*).
declivity [di'kliviti], *s.* der Abhang.
decode [di:'koud], *v.a.* entziffern, dechiffrieren.
decompose [di:kəm'pouz], *v.n.* verwesen; zerfallen, sich zersetzen. — *v.a.* auflösen.

decorate

decorate ['dekəreit], *v.a.* dekorieren (*honour*); ausschmücken (*beautify*); ausmalen (*paint*).

decoration [dekə'reiʃən], *s.* die Dekoration, der Orden (*medal*); die Ausschmückung (*ornamentation*); die Ausmalung (*décor*).

decorator ['dekəreitə], *s.* der Zimmermaler.

decorous ['dekərəs or di'kɔːrəs], *adj.* anständig, sittsam.

decorum [di'kɔːrəm], *s.* das Dekorum, das anständige Benehmen.

decoy [di'kɔi], *s.* der Köder (*bait*). — *v.a.* locken, anlocken.

decrease [di'kriːs], *v.a.* vermindern, verringern. — *v.n.* abnehmen. — ['diːkriːs], *s.* die Abnahme, die Verringerung.

decree [di'kriː], *s.* der Beschluß (*resolution*); (*Law*) das Urteil; — *nisi*, das provisorische Scheidungsurteil. — *v.a., v.n.* eine Verordnung erlassen; beschließen (*decide*).

decrepit [di'krepit], *adj.* abgelebt; gebrechlich (*frail*).

decry [di'krai], *v.a.* verrufen; in Verruf bringen.

dedicate ['dedikeit], *v.a.* widmen, weihen, zueignen (*to, Dat.*).

dedication [dedi'keiʃən], *s.* die Widmung, Weihung; die Zueignung.

dedicatory ['dedikeitəri], *adj.* zueignend.

deduce [di'djuːs], *v.a.* schließen (*conclude*); ableiten (*derive*).

deduct [di'dʌkt], *v.a.* abziehen (*subtract*); abrechnen (*take off*).

deduction [di'dʌkʃən], *s.* der Abzug (*subtraction*); die Folgerung (*inference*); der Rabatt (*in price*).

deductive [di'dʌktiv], *adj.* (*Log.*) deduktiv.

deed [diːd], *s.* die Tat, die Handlung (*action*); (*Law*) die Urkunde, das Dokument.

deem [diːm], *v.a.* erachten, halten für.

deep [diːp], *adj.* tief; — *freeze*, die Tiefkühlung; (*fig.*) dunkel. — *s.* die Tiefe (*des Meeres*).

deepen [diːpn], *v.a.* vertiefen. — *v.n.* tiefer werden; sich vertiefen.

deer [diə], *s.* (*Zool.*) das Rotwild, der Hirsch; — *stalking*, die Pirsch.

deface [di'feis], *v.a.* entstellen, verunstalten.

defalcate [di'fælkeit], *v.n.* Gelder unterschlagen.

defamation [defə'meiʃən], *s.* die Verleumdung.

defamatory [di'fæmətəri], *adj.* verleumderisch.

defame [di'feim], *v.a.* verleumden.

default [di'fɔːlt], *v.n.* (vor Gericht) ausbleiben. — *s.* der Fehler (*error*); die Unterlassung (*omission*).

defaulter [di'fɔːltə], *s.* der Pflichtvergessene; (*Law*) der Schuldige.

defeat [di'fiːt], *v.a.* schlagen, besiegen. — *s.* die Niederlage.

defect [di'fekt], *s.* der Fehler, Makel. — *v.n.* abfallen (*desert, from,* von, *Dat.*).

defection [di'fekʃən], *s.* der Abfall.

defective [di'fektiv], *adj.* fehlerhaft, mangelhaft.

defectiveness [di'fektivnis], *s.* die Mangelhaftigkeit, die Fehlerhaftigkeit.

defence [di'fens], *s.* die Verteidigung.

defenceless [di'fenslis], *adj.* wehrlos.

defencelessness [di'fenslisnis], *s.* die Wehrlosigkeit.

defend [di'fend], *v.a.* verteidigen.

defendant [di'fendənt], *s.* (*Law*) der Angeklagte.

defensive [di'fensiv], *adj.* verteidigend. — *s.* die Defensive; *be on the —*, sich verteidigen.

defer [di'fəː], *v.a.* aufschieben (*postpone*). — *v.n.* sich unterordnen, sich fügen (*to, Dat.*).

deference ['defərəns], *s.* der Respekt, die Achtung (*to,* vor, *Dat.*).

deferential [defə'renʃəl], *adj.* ehrerbietig, respektvoll.

defiance [di'faiəns], *s.* der Trotz, die Herausforderung.

defiant [di'faiənt], *adj.* trotzig, herausfordernd.

deficiency [di'fiʃənsi], *s.* die Unzulänglichkeit, der Mangel (*quantity*); die Fehlerhaftigkeit (*quality*).

deficient [di'fiʃənt], *adj.* unzulänglich (*quantity*); fehlerhaft (*quality*).

deficit ['defisit], *s.* das Defizit, der Fehlbetrag.

defile (1) [di'fail], *v.a.* schänden, beflecken.

defile (2) ['diːfail], *v.n.* vorbeimarschieren (*march past*) (an, *Dat.*). — *s.* der Engpaß.

defilement [di'failmənt], *s.* die Schändung.

define [di'fain], *v.a.* definieren, begrenzen; bestimmen (*determine*).

definite ['definit], *adj.* bestimmt (*certain*); klar, deutlich (*clear*); endgültig (*final*).

definition [defi'niʃən], *s.* die Definition, die Klarheit; (*Maths.*) die Bestimmung.

definitive [di'finitiv], *adj.* definitiv, endgültig (*final*); bestimmt (*certain*).

deflect [di'flekt], *v.a.* ablenken (*divert*). — *v.n.* abweichen (von, *Dat.*).

defoliation [di:fouli'eiʃən], *s.* der Blätterfall.

deform [di'fɔːm], *v.a.* verunstalten, entstellen. — *v.n.* (*Metall.*) sich verformen.

deformity [di'fɔːmiti], *s.* die Entstellung; die Häßlichkeit (*ugliness*).

defraud [di'frɔːd], *v.a.* betrügen.

defray [di'frei], *v.a.* bestreiten, bezahlen (*costs*).

deft [deft], *adj.* geschickt, gewandt.

deftness ['deftnis], *s.* die Gewandtheit, die Geschicktheit.

defunct [di'fʌŋkt], *adj.* verstorben. — *s.* der Verstorbene.

defy [di'fai], *v.a.* trotzen (*Dat.*).
degenerate [di'dʒenəreit], *v.n.* entarten; herabsinken (*sink low*). —[-rit], *adj.* degeneriert, entartet.
degradation [degri'deiʃən], *s.* die Absetzung, Entsetzung, Degradierung.
degrade [di'greid], *v.a.* (*Mil.*) degradieren; entwürdigen; vermindern.
degraded [di'greidid], *adj.* heruntergekommen.
degrading [di'greidiŋ], *adj.* entehrend.
degree [di'gri:], *s.* (*Meas., Univ.*) der Grad; (*Univ.*) die akademische Würde; die Stufe (*step, stage*); die Ordnung, die Klasse (*order, class*); *by* —*s*, nach und nach, allmählich.
deify [di:ifai], *v.a.* vergöttern.
deign [dein], *v.n.* geruhen, belieben.
deity [di:iti], *s.* die Gottheit.
dejected [di'dʒektid], *adj.* niedergeschlagen.
dejection [di'dʒekʃən], *s.* die Niedergeschlagenheit.
delay [di'lei], *v.a., v.n.* aufschieben (*put off*); verzögern (*retard*). — *s.* der Aufschub; die Verzögerung.
delectable [di'lektəbl], *adj.* erfreulich, köstlich.
delectation [delek'teiʃən], *s.* die Freude, das Ergötzen (*in, an, Dat.*).
delegate ['deligit], *s.* der Delegierte, Abgeordnete; der Vertreter. — ['deligeit], *v.a.* delegieren, entsenden.
delegation [deli'geiʃən], *s.* die Delegation, die Abordnung.
delete [di'li:t], *v.a.* tilgen, (aus-)streichen, auslöschen (*writing*).
deletion [di'li:ʃən], *s.* die Tilgung, die Auslöschung.
deleterious [deli'tiəriəs], *adj.* schädlich.
delf [delf], *s.* das Delfter Porzellan.
deliberate [di'libərit], *adj.* absichtlich (*intentional*); vorsichtig (*careful*); bedächtig (*thoughtful*). — [-reit], *v.n.* beratschlagen, Rat halten. — *v.a.* überlegen, bedenken.
deliberateness [di'libəritnis], *s.* die Bedächtigkeit (*thoughtfulness*); die Absichtlichkeit (*intention*).
deliberation [dilibə'reiʃən], *s.* die Überlegung, die Beratung.
delicacy ['delikəsi], *s.* die Feinheit, Zartheit (*manner*); der Leckerbissen (*luxury food*); die Schwächlichkeit (*health*).
delicate ['delikit], *adj.* fein (*manner*); schwächlich (*sickly*); kitzlig, heikel (*difficult*).
delicious [di'liʃəs], *adj.* köstlich (*food*).
deliciousness [di'liʃənis], *s.* die Köstlichkeit.
delight [di'lait], *s.* das Entzücken, das Vergnügen; *Turkish* —, türkisches Konfekt; *take* — *in*, an etwas Gefallen finden, sich freuen (*an, über*). — *v.a., v.n.* entzücken, erfreuen (*in, an, Dat.*).
delightful [di'laitful], *adj.* entzückend, bezaubernd.

delimit [di:'limit], *v.a.* abgrenzen, begrenzen.
delimitation [di:limi'teiʃən], *s.* die Begrenzung, Abgrenzung.
delineate [di'linieit], *v.a.* umreißen, entwerfen, skizzieren (*draft, sketch*); schildern, beschreiben (*describe*).
delineation [dilini'eiʃən], *s.* die Skizze, der Entwurf (*sketch, draft*); die Schilderung (*description*).
delinquency [di'liŋkwənsi], *s.* das Verbrechen.
delinquent [di'liŋkwənt], *adj.* verbrecherisch. — *s.* der Verbrecher, Missetäter (*criminal*).
deliquesce [deli'kwes], *v.n.* (*Chem.*) zergehen, zerschmelzen.
deliquescence [deli'kwesəns], *s.* das Zerschmelzen, die Schmelzbarkeit.
deliquescent [deli'kwesənt], *adj.* leicht schmelzbar (*melting*); leicht zerfliessend (*butter etc.*).
delirious [di'liriəs], *adj.* (*Med.*) phantasierend, wahnsinnig.
delirium [di'liriəm], *s.* (*Med.*) das Delirium; der Wahnsinn (*madness*); das Phantasieren (*raving*); — *tremens*, der Säuferwahnsinn.
deliver [di'livə], *v.a.* abliefern, überreichen (*hand over*); liefern (*goods*); befreien (*free*); erlösen (*redeem*); zustellen (*letters etc.*); entbinden (*woman of child*).
deliverance [di'livərəns], *s.* die Erlösung (*redemption*); die Befreiung (*liberation*); die Übergabe.
delivery [di'livəri], *s.* die Befreiung (*liberation*); (*Med.*) die Niederkunft, Entbindung; der Vortrag (*speech*); die Lieferung, die Zustellung (*goods*); — *man*, der Zustellbote; — *van*, der Lieferwagen.
dell [del], *s.* das enge Tal.
delude [di'lu:d], *v.a.* betrügen, täuschen.
deluge ['delju:dʒ], *s.* die Überschwemmung. — *v.a.* überschwemmen.
delusion [di'lu:ʒən], *s.* die Täuschung, das Blendwerk.
delusive, delusory [di'lu:ziv, di'lu:zəri], *adj.* täuschend, trügerisch.
delve [delv], *v.n.* graben.
demagogic(al) [demə'gɔdʒik(əl)], *adj.* demagogisch.
demagogue ['demagɔg], *s.* der Demagoge, der Aufrührer.
demand [di'ma:nd], *v.a.* verlangen, fordern. — *s.* die Forderung, das Begehren (*desire*); *on* —, auf Verlangen; *in great* —, viel gefragt; *supply and* —, Angebot und Nachfrage.
demarcate [di:'ma:keit], *v.a.* abgrenzen; abstecken (*field*).
demarcation [di:ma:'keiʃən], *s.* die Abgrenzung; — *line*, die Grenzlinie.
demeanour [di'mi:nə], *s.* das Benehmen.
demented [di'mentid], *adj.* wahnsinnig, von Sinnen, toll.
demerit [di:'merit], *s.* der Fehler.

demesne

demesne [di'mi:n *or* -'mein], *s.* das Erbgut; die Domäne.

demi- ['demi], *prefix.* halb-.

demigod ['demigɔd], *s.* der Halbgott.

demijohn ['demidʒɔn], *s.* der Glasballon.

demise [di'maiz], *s.* der Tod, das Hinscheiden. — *v.a.* (*Law*) vermachen.

demisemiquaver ['demisemikweivə], *s.* (*Mus.*) die Zweiunddreißigstelnote.

demobilize [di:'moubilaiz], *v.a.* demobilisieren.

democracy [di'mɔkrəsi], *s.* die Demokratie.

democratic [demo'krætik], *adj.* demokratisch.

demolish [di'mɔliʃ], *v.a.* demolieren, zerstören, niederreißen.

demon ['di:mən], *s.* der Dämon, der Teufel; *a — for work,* ein unersättlicher Arbeiter.

demoniac [di'mouniæk], **demoniacal** [di:mə'naiəkl], *adj.* besessen, teuflisch.

demonstrable [di'mɔnstrəbl], *adj.* beweisbar, nachweislich (*verifiable*).

demonstrate ['demənstreit], *v.a., v.n.* beweisen (*prove*); demonstrieren.

demonstration [demən'streiʃən], *s.* der Beweis (*theoretical*); die Demonstration (*practical*); (*Pol.*) Kundgebung.

demonstrative [di'mɔnstrətiv], *adj.* (*Gram.*) demonstrativ; überschwenglich (*emotional*).

demoralize [di:'mɔrəlaiz], *v.a.* demoralisieren.

demote [di:'mout], *v.a.* (*Mil., official*) degradieren.

demotion [di:'mouʃən], *s.* (*Mil., official*) die Degradierung.

demur [di'mə:], *v.n.* Anstand nehmen; Einwendungen machen (*raise objections*); zögern, zaudern (*hesitate*). — *s.* der Zweifel, der Skrupel.

demure [di'mjuə], *adj.* sittsam, zimperlich; spröde (*prim*).

demureness [di'mjuənis], *s.* die Sittsamkeit; die Sprödigkeit (*primness*).

den [den], *s.* die Höhle, Grube; *lion's —,* die Löwengrube.

denial [di'naiəl], *s.* die Verneinung, das Dementi (*negation*); das Ableugnen (*disclaimer*); die Absage (*refusal*).

denizen ['denizən], *s.* der Bürger, der Alteingesessene.

denominate [di'nɔmineit], *v.a.* nennen, benennen (*name*).

denomination [dinɔmi'neiʃən], *s.* die Bezeichnung; der Nennwert (*currency*); (*Rel.*) das Bekenntnis.

denominational [dinɔmi'neiʃənəl], *adj.* konfessionell.

denominator [di'nɔmineitə], *s.* (*Maths.*) der Nenner.

denote [di'nout], *v.a.* bezeichnen, kennzeichnen.

dénouement [dei'nu:mã], *s.* die Entwicklung, die Darlegung, die Lösung.

denounce [di'nauns], *v.a.* denunzieren, angeben, (*Law*) anzeigen.

dense [dens], *adj.* dicht; (*coll.*) beschränkt (*stupid*).

density ['densiti], *s.* die Dichte; — *of population,* die Bevölkerungsdichte.

dent (1) [dent], *s.* die Beule.

dent (2) [dent], *s.* die Kerbe (*in wood*); der Einschnitt (*cut*).

dental [dentl], *adj.* Zahn-; — *studies,* zahnärztliche Studien; — *treatment,* die Zahnbehandlung. — *s.* (*Phonet.*) der Zahnlaut.

dentist ['dentist], *s.* der Zahnarzt.

dentistry ['dentistri], *s.* die Zahnheilkunde.

denude [di'nju:d], *v.a.* entblößen; berauben (*of, Genit.*).

denunciation [dinʌnsi'eiʃən], *s.* die Denunzierung, die Anzeige.

deny [di'nai], *v.a.* verneinen (*negate*); abschlagen (*refuse*); verleugnen (*refuse to admit*).

deodorant, deodorizer [di:'oudərənt, di:'oudəraizə], *s.* der Geruchsentzieher (*apparatus*); der Deodorant.

deodorize [di:'oudəraiz], *v.a.* geruchlos machen.

depart [di'pa:t], *v.n.* abreisen, abfahren (*for,* nach, *Dat.*); scheiden.

department [di'pa:tmənt], *s.* die Abteilung; — *store,* das Kaufhaus.

departmental [di:pa:t'mentl], *adj.* Abteilungs-.

departure [di'pa:tʃə], *s.* die Abreise, die Abfahrt.

depend [di'pend], *v.n.* abhängen, abhängig sein (*upon,* von, *Dat.*); sich verlassen (*upon,* auf, *Acc.*); *that —s,* das kommt darauf an.

dependable [di'pendəbl], *adj.* verläßlich, zuverlässig.

dependant [di'pendənt], *s.* das abhängige Familienmitglied (*member of family*); der Angehörige, Abhängige.

dependence [di'pendəns], *s.* die Abhängigkeit (*need*); das Vertrauen, der Verlaß (*reliance*).

dependency [di'pendənsi], *s.* (*Pol.*) die abhängige Kolonie.

dependent [di'pendənt], *adj.* abhängig (*upon,* von, *Dat.*).

depict [di'pikt], *v.a.* schildern, beschreiben.

deplete [di'pli:t], *v.a.* entleeren (*make empty*); erschöpfen (*exhaust*).

depletion [di'pli:ʃən], *s.* die Entleerung.

deplorable [di'plɔ:rəbl], *adj.* bedauernswert, bedauerlich.

deplore [di'plɔ:], *v.a.* beklagen.

deploy [di'plɔi], *v.a.* entfalten. — *v.n.* sich entfalten; (*Mil.*) aufmarschieren.

deployment [di'plɔimənt], *s.* (*Mil.*) das Deployieren; die Entfaltung.

deponent [di'pounənt], *s.* (*Law*) der vereidigte Zeuge. — *adj.* (*Gram.*) (*verb*) das Deponens.

depopulate [di:'pɔpjuleit], *v.a.* entvölkern.

deport [di'pɔ:t], *v.a.* deportieren.

deportation [di:pɔ:'teiʃən], *s.* die Deportation.

design

deportment [di'pɔːtmənt], s. die körperliche Haltung (physical); das Benehmen (social).

depose [di'pouz], v.a. absetzen (remove from office); (Law) zu Papier bringen (write down); schriftlich erklären (declare in writing).

deposit [di'pɔzit], s. (Comm.) die Anzahlung; (Geol., Chem.) der Niederschlag; (Geol.) die Ablagerung; (Comm.) — account, das Depositenkonto. — v.a. (Geol., Chem.) absetzen; (Comm.) anzahlen, einzahlen.

deposition [di:pə'ziʃən], s. die Niederschrift, die schriftliche Erklärung; die Absetzung (removal from office).

depositor [di'pɔzitə], s. (Comm.) der Einzahler.

depository [di'pɔzitəri], s. das Lagerhaus.

depot ['depou], s. das Depot, das Lagerhaus (store); (Am.) der Bahnhof.

deprave [di'preiv], v.a. verderben.

depraved [di'preivd], adj. (moralisch) verdorben.

depravity [di'præviti], s. die Verdorbenheit, die Verworfenheit.

deprecate ['deprikeit], v.a. mißbilligen (disapprove of; Acc.); sich verbitten.

deprecation [depri'keiʃən], s. die Abbitte; die Mißbilligung (disapproval).

depreciate [di'priːʃieit], v.a. abwerten, herabwürdigen. — v.n. an Wert verlieren, im Wert sinken.

depreciation [dipriːʃi'eiʃən], s. die Abwertung; der Verlust (loss); (Pol., Comm.) die Entwertung.

depredation [depri'deiʃən], s. das Plündern, der Raub.

depress [di'pres], v.a. niederdrücken (press down); deprimieren (morale).

depressed [di'prest], adj. niedergeschlagen.

depression [di'preʃən], s. das Niederdrücken (action); (Pol.) die Depression; die Niedergeschlagenheit (despondency); das Tief (weather).

deprivation [depri'veiʃən], s. der Verlust (lack); die Beraubung (robbery).

deprive [di'praiv], v.a. berauben (of, Genit.); wegnehmen (of, Acc.).

depth [depθ], s. die Tiefe; — charge, die Unterwasserbombe; in the —s of night, in tiefster Nacht; (Phys.) — of focus, die Tiefenschärfe; be out of o.'s —, den Grund unter seinen Füßen verloren haben, ratlos sein (be helpless); — sounder, das Echolot.

deputation [depju'teiʃən], s. die Deputation, die Abordnung.

depute [di'pjuːt], v.a. abordnen, entsenden.

deputize ['depjutaiz], v.n. vertreten (for, Acc.).

deputy ['depjuti], s. der Abgeordnete, der Deputierte (delegate); der Vertreter (replacement).

derail [di:'reil], v.a. zum Entgleisen bringen. — v.n. entgleisen.

derailment [di:'reilmənt], s. die Entgleisung.

derange [di'reindʒ], v.a. verwirren, stören.

derangement [di'reindʒmənt], s. die Verwirrung; die Geistesstörung (madness).

derelict ['derilikt], adj. verlassen.

dereliction [deri'likʃən], s. das Verlassen; — of duty, die Pflichtvergessenheit.

deride [di'raid], v.a. verlachen, verhöhnen.

derision [di'riʒən], s. die Verhöhnung.

derisive [di'raisiv], adj. höhnisch, spöttisch.

derivable [di'raivəbl], adj. ableitbar.

derivation [deri'veiʃən], s. die Ableitung.

derivative [di'rivətiv], adj. abgeleitet. — s. das abgeleitete Wort.

derive [di'raiv], v.a., v.n. ableiten, herleiten.

derogation [dero'geiʃən], s. die Herabsetzung.

derrick ['derik], s. der Ladebaum.

dervish ['dəːviʃ], s. der Derwisch.

descant ['deskænt], s. (Mus.) der Diskant or die Sopran. — [dis'kænt], v.n. sich verbreiten (on, über, Acc.).

descend [di'send], v.n. hinab- or herabsteigen (go down); abstammen (stem from).

descendant [di'sendənt], s. der Nachkomme.

descent [di'sent], s. der Abstieg (going down); der Fall (decline); die Abstammung (forebears); der Abhang (slope); (Aviat.) die Landung.

describable [dis'kraibəbl], adj. zu beschreiben, beschreibbar.

describe [dis'kraib], v.a. beschreiben, schildern.

description [dis'kripʃən], s. die Beschreibung; of any —, jeder Art.

descriptive [dis'kriptiv], adj. schildernd, beschreibend.

desecrate ['desikreit], v.a. entweihen, entheiligen.

desecration [desi'kreiʃən], s. die Entweihung, die Schändung.

desert (1) ['dezət], s. die Wüste.

desert (2) [di'zəːt], v.a. verlassen, im Stiche lassen. — v.n. desertieren.

desert (3) [di'zəːt], s. (usually pl.) das Verdienst.

desertion [di'zəːʃən], s. (Mil.) die Fahnenflucht.

deserve [di'zəːv], v.a. verdienen.

deserving [di'zəːviŋ], adj. verdienstvoll.

design [di'zain], v.a. entwerfen (plan); vorhaben (intend); bestimmen (determine). — s. der Entwurf (sketch); der Plan (draft); die Absicht, das Vorhaben (intention); das Muster (pattern).

designate

designate ['dezigneit], *v.a.* bezeichnen (*mark*); ernennen (*appoint*). — [-nit], *adj.* ernannt; *chairman —*, der künftige Vorsitzende.

designation [dezig'neiʃən], *s.* die Bestimmung, Ernennung (*appointment*); die Bezeichnung (*mark*).

designer [di'zainə], *s.* der Zeichner, der Graphiker (*artist*); der Ränkeschmied (*schemer*).

designing [di'zainiŋ], *adj.* hinterlistig, schlau.

desirable [di'zaiərəbl], *adj.* erwünscht, wünschenswert.

desire [di'zaiə], *s.* der Wunsch, die Begierde; das Verlangen, die Sehnsucht (*longing*). — *v.a.* verlangen, begehren.

desirous [di'zaiərəs], *adj.* begierig (*of, inf.*).

desist [di'zist], *v.n.* ablassen, aufhören.

desk [desk], *s.* der Schreibtisch; das Pult; — *lamp*, die Tischlampe *or* Bürolampe.

desolate ['desəlit], *adj.* verlassen, öde; trostlos (*sad*). — [-leit], *v.a.* verwüsten (*lay waste*).

desolation [desə'leiʃən], *s.* die Verwüstung (*of land*); die Trostlosigkeit (*sadness*).

despair [dis'pɛə], *v.n.* verzweifeln (*of, an, Dat.*). — *s.* die Verzweiflung.

despatch, dispatch [dis'pætʃ], *v.a.* absenden, befördern (*post*); abfertigen (*send*); erledigen (*deal with*); töten (*kill*). — *s.* die Abfertigung (*clearance*); die Eile (*speed*); die Depesche (*message*).

desperado [despə'reidou, -'rɑ:dou], *s.* der Wagehals, der Draufgänger.

desperate ['despərit], *adj.* verzweifelt.

desperation [despə'reiʃən], *s.* die Verzweiflung.

despicable ['despikəbl], *adj.* verächtlich.

despise [dis'paiz], *v.a.* verachten.

despite [dis'pait], *prep.* trotz (*Genit., Dat.*).

despoil [dis'pɔil], *v.a.* plündern, ausrauben.

despondency [dis'pɔndənsi], *s.* die Verzweiflung, Verzagtheit.

despondent [dis'pɔndənt], *adj.* verzagend, verzweifelnd, mutlos.

despot ['despɔt], *s.* der Despot, der Tyrann.

despotic [des'pɔtik], *adj.* despotisch.

despotism ['despətizm], *s.* (*Pol.*) der Despotismus.

dessert [di'zə:t], *s.* das Dessert, der Nachtisch.

destination [desti'neiʃən], *s.* die Bestimmung, das Ziel; der Bestimmungsort (*address*); das Reiseziel (*journey*).

destine ['destin], *v.a.* bestimmen.

destiny ['destini], *s.* das Geschick; das Schicksal, das Verhängnis (*fate*).

destitute ['destitju:t], *adj.* verlassen (*deserted*); hilflos, mittellos (*poor*); in bitterer Not (*in great distress*).

destitution [desti'tju:ʃən], *s.* die Notlage, die bittere Not.

destroy [dis'trɔi], *v.a.* zerstören (*buildings*); verwüsten; vernichten (*lives*).

destroyer [dis'trɔiə], *s.* der Zerstörer.

destructible [dis'trʌktibl], *adj.* zerstörbar.

destruction [dis'trʌkʃən], *s.* die Zerstörung (*of buildings*), die Verwüstung; die Vernichtung.

destructive [dis'trʌktiv], *adj.* zerstörend, verderblich.

destructiveness [dis'trʌktivnis], *s.* die Zerstörungswut, der Zerstörungssinn.

desultory ['dezəltəri], *adj.* unmethodisch, sprunghaft; oberflächlich (*superficial*).

detach [di'tætʃ], *v.a.* absondern, trennen.

detachment [di'tætʃmənt], *s.* die Absonderung (*separation*); (*Mil.*) das Kommando.

detail [di'teil], *v.a.* im einzelnen beschreiben (*describe minutely*); (*Mil.*) abkommandieren. — ['di:teil], *s.* die Einzelheit.

detailed ['di:teild], *adj.* ausführlich; detailliert, ins Einzelne gehend (*report etc.*); [di'teild], (*Mil.*) abkommandiert.

detain [di'tein], *v.a.* aufhalten, zurückhalten; festhalten (*in prison*).

detect [di'tekt], *v.a.* entdecken, aufdecken.

detection [di'tekʃən], *s.* die Entdeckung, die Aufdeckung.

detective [di'tektiv], *s.* der Detektiv.

detention [di'tenʃən], *s.* (*Law*) die Haft; die Vorenthaltung (*of articles*).

deter [di'tə:], *v.a.* abschrecken.

detergent [di'tə:dʒənt], *s.* das Reinigungsmittel.

deteriorate [di'tiəriəreit], *v.n.* sich verschlimmern, verschlechtern.

deterioration [ditiəriə'reiʃən], *s.* die Verschlimmerung.

determinable [di'tə:minəbl], *adj.* bestimmbar.

determinate [ditə'minit], *adj.* festgesetzt, bestimmt.

determination [di'tə:mi'neiʃən], *s.* die Entschlossenheit (*resoluteness*); die Bestimmung (*identification*); der Entschluß (*resolve*).

determine [di'tə:min], *v.a.* bestimmen (*ascertain*); beschließen (*resolve*).

deterrent [di'terənt], *s.* das Abschreckungsmittel.

detest [di'test], *v.a.* verabscheuen.

detestable [di'testəbl], *adj.* abscheulich.

detestation [detes'teiʃən], *s.* der Abscheu (*of, vor, Dat.*).

dethrone [di:'θroun], *v.a.* entthronen, vom Thron verdrängen.

detonate ['di:- *or* 'detoneit], *v.n.* detonieren, explodieren. — *v.a.* explodieren, detonieren lassen, zum Detonieren bringen.

detonation [deto'neiʃən], s. die Detonation, die Explosion.

detonator ['detoneitə], s. der Zünder, die Zündpatrone; (*Railw.*) der Knallpatrone.

detour ['deituə *or* di'tuə], s. der Umweg; (*Civil Engin.*) die Umleitung. — v.n. (*Am.*) einen Umweg machen. — v.a. (*Am.*) umleiten (*re-route*).

detract [di'trækt], v.a., v.n. abziehen; schmälern.

detraction [di'trækʃən], s. die Schmälerung, die Verleumdung (*slander*).

detractive [di'træktiv], adj. verleumderisch.

detractor [di'træktə], s. der Verleumder.

detriment ['detrimənt], s. der Nachteil, der Schaden.

detrimental [detri'mentl], adj. nachteilig; abträglich; schädlich (*harmful*).

deuce (1) [dju:s], s. die Zwei (*game*); (*Tennis*) der Einstand.

deuce (2) [dju:s], s. (*coll.*) der Teufel.

devastate ['devəsteit], v.a. verwüsten, verheeren.

devastating ['devəsteitiŋ], adj. schrecklich, verheerend.

devastation [devəs'teiʃən], s. die Verheerung, die Verwüstung.

develop [di'veləp], v.a. entwickeln. — v.n. sich entwickeln; sich entfalten (*prove, turn out*).

developer [di'veləpə], s. (*Phot.*) das Entwicklungsmittel.

development [di'veləpmənt], s. die Entwicklung.

developmental [divеləp'mentl], adj. Entwicklungs-.

deviate ['di:vieit], v.n. abweichen.

deviation [di:vi'eiʃən], s. die Abweichung.

device [di'vais], s. die Vorrichtung (*equipment*); der Kunstgriff (*trick*).

devil [devl], s. der Teufel; der Lehrling, Laufbursche (*printer's, lawyer's*); *the — take the hindmost!* — v.n. in der Lehre sein (*for*, bei, *Dat.*).

devilish ['devəliʃ], adj. teuflisch.

devilment, devilry ['devəlmənt, 'devəlri], s. die Teufelei, die Teufelslaune.

devious ['di:viəs], adj. abweichend; abgelegen; abwegig.

deviousness ['di:viəsnis], s. die Abschweifung, Verirrung.

devise [di'vaiz], v.a. erfinden (*invent*); ersinnen (*think out*).

deviser, devisor [di'vaizə], s. der Erfinder (*inventor*); der Erblasser (*testator*).

devoid [di'void], adj. frei (*of*, von, *Dat.*); ohne (*Acc.*).

devolve [di'vɔlv], v.a. übertragen (*transfer*); abwälzen (*pass on burden*) (*to*, auf, *Acc.*). — v.n. zufallen (*Dat.*).

devote [di'vout], v.a. widmen; aufopfern (*sacrifice*).

devoted [di'voutid], adj. ergeben (*affectionate*); geweiht (*consecrated*).

devotee [devo'ti:], s. der Anhänger; der Verehrer (*fan*).

devotion [di'vouʃən], s. die Hingabe; die Aufopferung (*sacrifice*); die Andacht (*prayer*).

devotional [di'vouʃənəl], adj. Andachts-.

devour [di'vauə], v.a. verschlingen.

devout [di'vaut], adj. andächtig, fromm.

devoutness [di'vautnis], s. die Frömmigkeit.

dew [dju:], s. der Tau.

dewy [dju:i], adj. betaut, taufeucht.

dexterity [deks'teriti], s. die Gewandtheit, die Fertigkeit.

dexterous ['dekstərəs], adj. gewandt, geschickt.

diabetes [daiə'bi:ti:z], s. (*Med.*) die Zuckerkrankheit.

diabetic [daiə'betik], s. (*Med.*) der Zuckerkranke. — adj. zuckerkrank.

diabolic(al) [daiə'bɔlik(əl)], adj. teuflisch.

diadem ['daiədem], s. das Diadem, das Stirnband.

diæresis [dai'iərəsis], s. die Diärese.

diagnose [daiəg'nouz], v.a. diagnostizieren, als Diagnose finden, befinden.

diagnosis [daiəg'nousis], s. die Diagnose, der Befund.

diagonal [dai'ægənəl], adj. diagonal, schräg. — s. (*Geom.*) die Diagonale.

diagram ['daiəgræm], s. das Diagramm.

dial ['daiəl], s. das Zifferblatt; (*Teleph.*) die Wählerscheibe. — v.a., v.n. (*Teleph.*) wählen.

dialect ['daiəlekt], s. der Dialekt, die Mundart.

dialectic [daiə'lektik], s. (*Phil.*) die Dialektik.

dialektical [daiə'lektikəl], adj. dialektisch, logisch.

dialogue ['daiəlɔg], s. der Dialog, das Zwiegespräch.

diameter [dai'æmitə], s. der Durchmesser.

diametrical [daiə'metrikəl], adj. diametral; gerade entgegengesetzt.

diamond ['daiəmənd], s. der Diamant; (*Cards*) das Karo.

diaper ['daiəpə], s. (*Am.*) die Windel.

diaphragm ['daiəfræm], s. (*Anat.*) das Zwerchfell; (*Phys.*) die Membran.

diarrhœa [daiə'ria], s. (*Med.*) der Durchfall.

diary ['daiəri], s. das Tagebuch, der Kalender.

diatribe ['daiətraib], s. der Tadel, der Angriff (*verbal*), die Schmähschrift (*written*).

dibble [dibl], s. der Pflanzstock. — v.n. Pflanzen stecken, anpflanzen.

dice [dais], s. pl. die Würfel (*sing.* **die**). — v.a. würfeln, werfen.

dicker

dicker ['dikə], v.n. (Am.) feilschen, handeln.

dicky ['diki], s. das Vorhemd.

dictate [dik'teit], v.a., v.n. diktieren, vorschreiben.

dictation [dik'teiʃən], s. (Sch.) das Diktat.

dictator [dik'teitə], s. der Diktator.

dictatorship [dik'teitəʃip], s. die Diktatur.

diction ['dikʃən], s. die Ausdrucksweise (speech).

dictionary ['dikʃənri], s. das Wörterbuch.

didactic [di'dæktik], adj. lehrhaft, Lehr-.

die (1) [dai], v.n. sterben (of, an, Dat.); — away, verebben.

die (2) [dai], s. der Würfel (cube); die Gießform (mould); der Stempel (punch); (Metall.) das Gesenk (swage); — casting, der Spritzguß; — castings, die Spritzgußteile, Gußteile; — forging, das Gesenkschmiedestück.

die (3) [dai] see under dice.

dielectric [daii'lektrik], adj. dielektrisch.

diet (1) ['daiət], s. (Pol.) der Landtag, Reichstag.

diet (2) ['daiət], s. (Med.) die Diät. — v.n. (Med.) eine Diät halten. — v.a. (Med.) eine Diät vorschreiben.

dietary, dietetic ['daiətəri, daiə'tetik], adj. diätetisch.

differ ['difə], v.n. sich unterscheiden (be different from, von, Dat.); anderer Meinung sein (be of different opinion).

difference ['difərəns], s. (Maths.) die Differenz; der Unterschied (discrepancy); die Meinungsverschiedenheit (divergence of opinion).

different ['difərənt], adj. verschieden, verschiedenartig.

differentiate [difə'renʃieit], v.n. (Maths.) differenzieren; einen Unterschied machen (between, zwischen, Dat.).

difficult ['difikəlt], adj. schwierig, schwer.

difficulty ['difikəlti], s. die Schwierigkeit.

diffidence ['difidəns], s. die Schüchternheit.

diffident ['difidənt], adj. schüchtern.

diffraction [di'frækʃən], s. die Ablenkung, (Phys., Optics) die Brechung.

diffuse [di'fju:z], v.a. ausgießen (pour); verbreiten (spread). — [di'fju:s], adj. verbreitet, weitschweifig (style); zerstreut.

diffuseness [di'fju:snis], s. die Weitläufigkeit (style).

diffusion [di'fju:ʒən], s. (Phys.) die Diffusion, die Zerstreuung, die Verbreitung.

dig (1) [dig], v.a. irr. graben; — in the ribs, in die Rippen stoßen. — v.n. (coll.) wohnen (live in lodgings).

dig (2) [dig], v.a. (coll.) verstehen.

digger ['digə], s. der Gräber; (coll.) der Australier.

digest [di'dʒest], v.a. (Anat.) verdauen. — ['daidʒest], s. die Sammlung von Auszügen; (pl.) Pandekten.

digestibility [didʒesti'biliti], s. die Verdaulichkeit.

digestible [di'dʒestibl], adj. verdaulich.

digestion [di'dʒestʃən], s. die Verdauung.

digestive [di'dʒestiv], adj. Verdauungs-; — biscuit, das Kornmehlkeks; — organs, die Verdauungsorgane.

digit ['didʒit], s. (Maths.) die (einstellige) Zahl; der Zahlenwert.

digitalis [didʒi'teilis], s. (Bot.) der Fingerhut.

dignified ['dignifaid], adj. würdig, würdevoll.

dignify ['dignifai], v.a. ehren (honour); zieren (decorate).

dignitary ['dignitəri], s. der Würdenträger.

dignity ['digniti], s. die Würde.

digress [dai'gres], v.n. abweichen, abschweifen.

digression [dai'greʃən], s. die Abweichung, die Abschweifung.

digressive [dai'gresiv], adj. abschweifend (style).

digs [digz], s. pl. (coll.) das (möblierte) Zimmer, die Wohnung.

dike [daik], s. der Graben, der Deich. — v.a. eindeichen, eindämmen.

dilapidated [di'læpideitid], adj. baufällig.

dilapidation [dilæpi'deiʃən], s. die Baufälligkeit, der Verfall.

dilate [d(a)i'leit], v.a. erweitern, ausdehnen. — v.n. sich ausdehnen; sich auslassen (speak) (on, über, Acc.).

dilation [d(a)i'leiʃən], s. die Erweiterung (expansion); die Auslassung (speaking).

dilatoriness ['dilətərinis], s. die Saumseligkeit.

dilatory ['dilətəri], adj. zögernd, aufschiebend, saumselig.

dilemma [d(a)i'lemə], s. das Dilemma, die Klemme.

diligence ['dilidʒəns], s. der Fleiß, die Emsigkeit.

diligent ['dilidʒənt], adj. fleißig, arbeitsam.

dilly-dally ['dili'dæli], v.n. tändeln, zaudern, Zeit vertrödeln.

dilute [d(a)i'lju:t], v.a. (Chem.) verdünnen; schwächen (weaken).

dilution [d(a)i'lju:ʃən], s. die Verdünnung.

diluvial, diluvian [d(a)i'lju:viəl, -iən], adj. Diluvial-, des Diluviums; sintflutlich.

dim [dim], adj. trübe, unklar; (Phys.) abgeblendet. — v.a. abdunkeln, abblenden.

dimension [d(a)i'menʃən], s. die Dimension, das Maß.

dimensional [d(a)i'menʃənəl], adj. dimensional.

366

discernment

diminish [di'miniʃ], v.a. vermindern. — v.n. sich vermindern.

diminution [dimi'nju:ʃən], s. die Verringerung, die Verminderung.

diminutive [di'minjutiv], adj. verkleinernd, klein. — s. (Gram.) das Verkleinerungswort.

dimness ['dimnis], s. die Trübheit; die Düsterkeit (dark).

dimple [dimpl], s. das Grübchen.

dimpled [dimpld], adj. mit einem Grübchen.

din [din], s. das Getöse, der Lärm.

dine [dain], v.n. speisen, essen.

dinginess ['dindʒinis], s. die Dunkelheit, die Schäbigkeit.

dingy ['dindʒi], adj. dunkel, schäbig.

dinner ['dinə], s. das Essen; das Festessen (formal); — jacket, der Smoking.

dint [dint], s. der Nachdruck, der Schlag; by — of, mittels (Genit.).

diocesan [dai'ɔsisən], adj. (Eccl.) einer Diözese angehörig, Diözesan-.

diocese ['daiəsis], s. (Eccl.) die Diözese.

dip [dip], v.a. eintauchen, eintunken; abblenden (lights). — v.n. (unter)tauchen; sinken; sich flüchtig einlassen (into, in). — s. die Senke; der Abhang (slope).

diphtheria [dif'θiəriə], s. (Med.) die Diphtherie.

diphthong ['difθɔŋ], s. (Phonet.) der Diphthong.

diploma [di'ploumə], s. das Diplom; teaching —, das Lehrerdiplom.

diplomacy [di'plouməsi], s. die Diplomatie.

diplomatic [diplo'mætik], adj. diplomatisch, taktvoll; urkundlich (documents). — s. (pl.) das Studium der Urkunden.

diplomat(ist) ['diplomæt, di'ploumətist], s. (Pol.) der Diplomat.

dipper ['dipə], s. der Taucher.

dire [daiə], adj. fürchterlich, schrecklich; — necessity, bittere Not.

direct [d(a)i'rekt], adj. direkt, unmittelbar. — v.a. leiten (be in charge of); hinweisen, hinlenken; den Weg zeigen (tell the way to); anordnen (arrange for).

direction [d(a)i'rekʃən], s. die Leitung (management); (Geog.) die Richtung, Himmelsrichtung; die Anordnung (arrangement, order); —s for use, die Gebrauchsanweisung.

director [d(a)i'rektə], s. der Direktor; der Leiter.

directory [d(a)i'rektəri], s. das Adreßbuch; das Telephonbuch.

dirge [də:dʒ], s. der Trauergesang.

dirigible ['diridʒibl], adj. lenkbar, leitbar.

dirt [də:t], s. der Schmutz, der Kot, Dreck. — adj. — cheap, spottbillig.

dirty ['də:ti], adj. schmutzig; gemein (joke).

disability [disə'biliti], s. die Unfähigkeit, das Unvermögen (inability); die Schädigung (impairment of health).

disable [dis'eibl], v.a. unfähig or untauglich machen.

disablement [dis'eiblmənt], s. die Versehrung, die Verkrüppelung.

disabuse [disə'bju:z], v.a. aufklären, eines Besseren belehren.

disaccustom [disə'kastəm], v.a. entwöhnen, abgewöhnen.

disadvantage [disəd'va:ntidʒ], s. der Nachteil.

disaffection [disə'fekʃən], s. die Abneigung; der Widerwille.

disagree [disə'gri:], v.n. nicht übereinstimmen, nicht einer Meinung sein.

disagreeable [disə'griəbl], adj. unangenehm, verdrießlich; unfreundlich.

disagreement [disə'gri:mənt], s. die Uneinigkeit (disunity); die Meinungsverschiedenheit (difference of opinion).

disallow [disə'lau], v.a. nicht gestatten; in Abrede stellen.

disappear [disə'piə], v.n. verschwinden.

disappearance [disə'piərəns], s. das Verschwinden.

disappoint [disə'pɔint], v.a. enttäuschen.

disappointment [disə'pɔintmənt], s. die Enttäuschung.

disapprobation [disæpro'beiʃən], s. die Mißbilligung.

disapproval [disə'pru:vəl], s. die Mißbilligung.

disapprove [disə'pru:v], v.a. mißbilligen (of, Acc.).

disarm [dis'a:m], v.a. entwaffnen. — v.n. abrüsten.

disarmament [dis'a:məmənt], s. die Abrüstung.

disarray [disə'rei], v.a. in Unordnung bringen. — s. die Unordnung (disorder); die Verwirrung (confusion).

disaster [di'za:stə], s. das Unglück; das Unheil, die Katastrophe.

disastrous [di'za:strəs], adj. unheilvoll, schrecklich.

disavow [disə'vau], v.a. ableugnen.

disavowal [disə'vauəl], s. das Ableugnen.

disband [dis'bænd], v.a. entlassen (dismiss); auflösen (dissolve).

disbar [dis'ba:], v.a. (Law) von der Rechtspraxis ausschließen.

disbelief [disbi'li:f], s. der Unglaube (incredulity); der Zweifel (doubt).

disbelieve [disbi'li:v], v.a. nicht glauben; bezweifeln.

disburse [dis'bə:s], v.a. auszahlen, ausgeben.

disbursement [dis'bə:smənt], s. die Auszahlung, die Ausgabe.

disc [disk], s. (also Med.) die Scheibe; die Platte (record).

discard [dis'ka:d], v.a. ablegen, beiseite legen, aufgeben.

discern [di'zə:n or di'sə:n], v.a. unterscheiden; wahrnehmen, bemerken.

discernment [di'sə:nmənt], s. die Urteilskraft (powers of judgment); die Einsicht.

discharge

discharge [dis'tʃɑːdʒ], *v.a.* entlassen
(*dismiss*); abfeuern (*pistol*); abladen,
ausladen (*cargo*); bezahlen (*debt*);
tun, erfüllen (*duty*). — *s.* die Entladung (*gun*); die Entlassung (*dismissal*); die Bezahlung (*debt*); die
Erfüllung (*duty*).

disciple [di'saipl], *s.* (*Bibl.*) der Jünger;
der Schüler.

disciplinarian [disipli'nɛəriən], *s.* der
Zuchtmeister.

disciplinary ['disiplinəri], *adj.* disziplinarisch.

discipline ['disiplin], *s.* die Disziplin,
die Zucht. — *v.a.* disziplinieren,
züchtigen.

disclaim [dis'kleim], *v.a.* verleugnen
(*deny*); nicht anerkennen (*refuse to
acknowledge*); verzichten (*renounce*).

disclaimer [dis'kleimə], *s.* der Widerruf.

disclose [dis'klouz], *v.a.* eröffnen,
enthüllen.

disclosure [dis'klouʒə], *s.* die Eröffnung, die Enthüllung.

discoloration [diskʌlə'reiʃən], *s.* die
Entfärbung, Verfärbung.

discomfiture [dis'kʌmfitʃə], *s.* die
Verwirrung.

discomfort [dis'kʌmfət], *s.* das Unbehagen; die Beschwerde.

disconcert [diskən'səːt], *v.a.* außer
Fassung bringen (*upset*); vereiteln
(*frustrate*).

disconnect [diskə'nekt], *v.a.* trennen
(*separate*); abstellen.

disconsolate [dis'kɔnsəlit], *adj.* trostlos, untröstlich.

discontent [diskən'tent], *s.* die Unzufriedenheit, das Mißvergnügen. —
v.a. mißvergnügt stimmen.

discontinuance [diskən'tinjuəns], *s.* die
Beendigung (*finish*); das Aufhören
(*suspension*); die Unterbrechung (*interruption*).

discontinue [diskən'tinju:], *v.a.* nicht
fortsetzen; unterbrechen (*interrupt*);
einstellen.

discord ['diskɔːd], *s.* die Zwietracht
(*disagreement*); (*Mus.*) der Mißklang.

discordance [dis'kɔːdəns], *s.* die Uneinigkeit.

discordant [dis'kɔːdənt], *adj.* uneinig,
widersprechend.

discount ['diskaunt], *s.* (*Comm.*) der
Abzug, der Rabatt; *allow a —*, einen
Rabatt gewähren; *be at a —*, unbeliebt sein, nicht geschätzt sein; *sell
at a —*, unter dem Preis verkaufen.
— [dis'kaunt], *v.a.* (*Comm.*) diskontieren, einen Rabatt gewähren; nur
mit Vorsicht aufnehmen (*accept with
doubt*).

discountable [dis'kauntəbl], *adj.* diskontierbar, in Abzug zu bringen.

discountenance [dis'kauntinəns], *v.a.*
mißbilligen.

discourage [dis'kʌridʒ], *v.a.* entmutigen; abraten (*from*, von, *Dat.*).

discouragement [dis'kʌridʒmənt], *s.*
die Entmutigung.

discourse [dis'kɔːs], *v.n.* einen Vortrag
halten (*on*, über, *Acc.*); sprechen. —
['diskɔːs], *s.* der Vortrag; das Gespräch, die Rede.

discourteous [dis'kəːtiəs], *adj.* unhöflich.

discourtesy [dis'kəːtəsi], *s.* die Unhöflichkeit.

discover [dis'kʌvə], *v.a.* entdecken.

discovery [dis'kʌvəri], *s.* die Entdeckung.

discredit [dis'kredit], *s.* der üble Ruf;
die Schande. — *v.a.* in schlechten
Ruf bringen; diskreditieren.

discreditable [dis'kreditəbl], *adj.*
schimpflich.

discreet [dis'kriːt], *adj.* diskret, verschwiegen; vorsichtig (*cautious*).

discrepancy [dis'krepənsi], *s.* die Diskrepanz, der Widerspruch; der Unterschied (*difference*).

discretion [dis'kreʃən], *s.* die Diskretion; die Klugheit; der Takt (*tact*);
die Verschwiegenheit (*silence*); *at
your —*, nach Ihrem Belieben; *use
your —*, handle nach deinem Ermessen; handeln Sie nach Ihrem Ermessen.

discretionary [dis'kreʃənəri], *adj.* willkürlich, uneingeschränkt.

discriminate [dis'krimineit], *v.a., v.n.*
unterscheiden (*distinguish*); absondern
(*separate*).

discriminating [dis'krimineitin], *adj.*
scharfsinnig; einsichtig.

discriminatory [dis'krimineitəri], *adj.*
einen Unterschied machend; —
legislation, das Ausnahmegesetz.

discursive [dis'kəːsiv], *adj.* diskursiv,
ohne Zusammenhang.

discuss [dis'kʌs], *v.a.* besprechen,
erörtern.

discussion [dis'kʌʃən], *s.* die Diskussion, das Gespräch.

disdain [dis'dein], *s.* die Verachtung.
— *v.a.* verachten, verschmähen;
herabsetzen (*belittle*).

disdainful [dis'deinful], *adj.* geringschätzig, verächtlich.

disease [di'ziːz], *s.* die Krankheit.

diseased [di'ziːzd], *adj.* krank.

disembark [disim'bɑːk], *v.n.* aussteigen, landen. — *v.a.* aussteigen
lassen, ausschiffen.

disembarkation [disembɑː'keiʃən], *s.*
die Ausschiffung; die Landung.

disenchant [disin'tʃɑːnt], *v.a.* ernüchtern.

disenchantment [disin'tʃɑːntmənt], *s.*
die Ernüchterung.

disengage [disin'geidʒ], *v.a.* losmachen,
befreien (*release*); freigeben. — *v.n.*
(*Mil.*) sich absetzen.

disengaged [disin'geidʒd], *adj.* frei
(*unoccupied*).

disentangle [disin'tængl], *v.a.* entwirren; befreien (*free*).

disentanglement [disin'tænglmənt], *s.*
die Entwirrung, die Befreiung.

disfavour [dis'feivə], s. die Ungunst, die Ungnade.
disfigure [dis'figə], v.a. entstellen, verunstalten.
disfiguration [disfigjuə'reiʃən], s. die Entstellung, die Verunstaltung.
disfranchise [dis'fræntʃaiz], v.a. das Wahlrecht entziehen (Dat.).
disgorge [dis'gɔːdʒ], v.a. ausspeien.
disgrace [dis'greis], v.a. entehren, Schande bringen. — s. die Ungnade, Schande (shame); die Entehrung (putting to shame).
disgraceful [dis'greisful], adj. schändlich, entehrend.
disgruntled [dis'grʌntld], adj. verstimmt, unzufrieden.
disguise [dis'gaiz], v.a. verkleiden (dress); (fig.) verstellen. — s. die Verkleidung; die Verstellung.
disgust [dis'gʌst], s. der Ekel, der Widerwille. — v.a. anekeln; be —ed, sehr ärgerlich sein; be —ed with s. th., etwas verabscheuen.
dish [diʃ], s. die Schüssel (bowl); das Gericht (food). — v.a. (coll.) abtun (frustrate); — up, auftragen (food).
dishcloth ['diʃklɔθ], s. das Wischtuch; der Abwaschlappen.
dishearten [dis'hɑːtn], v.a. entmutigen, verzagt machen.
dishevelled [di'ʃevəld], adj. aufgelöst (hair); zerzaust (hair, clothes).
dishonest [dis'ɔnist], adj. unehrlich.
dishonesty [dis'ɔnisti], s. die Unehrlichkeit.
dishonour [dis'ɔnə], s. die Schande. — v.a. schänden, Schande bringen (über, Acc.).
dishonourable [dis'ɔnərəbl], adj. ehrlos, schimpflich.
dishwater ['diʃwɔːtə], s. das Spülwasser.
disillusion [disi'luːʒən], s. die Enttäuschung, die Ernüchterung. — v.a. enttäuschen, ernüchtern.
disinclination [disinkli'neiʃən], s. die Abneigung.
disincline [disin'klain], v.a. abgeneigt machen (Dat.).
disinfect [disin'fekt], v.a. desinfizieren.
disinfectant [disin'fektənt], s. das Desinfektionsmittel.
disinfection [disin'fekʃən], s. die Desinfektion.
disingenuous [disin'dʒenjuəs], adj. unaufrichtig, unredlich.
disinherit [disin'herit], v.a. enterben.
disinter [disin'təː], v.a. exhumieren, ausgraben.
disinterested [dis'intrəstid], adj. uneigennützig.
disinterestedness [dis'intrəstidnis], s. die Selbstlosigkeit, die Uneigennützigkeit.
disjoin [dis'dʒɔin], v.a. trennen.
disjoint [dis'dʒɔint], v.a. zerlegen, zerstückeln.
disjointedness [dis'dʒɔintidnis], s. die Zerstücktheit, die Zusammenhangslosigkeit (style of writing etc.).

disjunction [dis'dʒʌŋkʃən], s. die Trennung, die Abtrennung.
disjunctive [dis'dʒʌŋktiv], adj. (Gram.) trennend, disjunktiv.
disk [disk] see disc.
dislike [dis'laik], v.a. nicht leiden mögen, nicht gerne haben. — s. die Abneigung (of, gegen, Acc.).
dislocate ['dislokeit], v.a. verrenken (bone); (fig.) in Unordnung bringen.
dislocation [dislo'keiʃən], s. (Med.) die Verrenkung; die Verwirrung (traffic etc.).
dislodge [dis'lɔdʒ], v.a. vertreiben (drive out); entfernen (remove).
disloyal [dis'lɔiəl], adj. ungetreu; verräterisch.
disloyalty [dis'lɔiəlti], s. die Untreue (sentiment); der Verrat (act).
dismal ['dizməl], adj. trostlos, traurig (mood); düster, trüb (weather).
dismantle [dis'mæntl], v.a. niederreißen, zerlegen; abbauen.
dismay [dis'mei], v.a. erschrecken, entmutigen. — s. die Furcht, der Schrecken, die Bangigkeit.
dismember [dis'membə], v.a. zerstückeln.
dismemberment [dis'membəmənt], s. die Zerstückelung, die Aufteilung.
dismiss [dis'mis], v.a. entlassen (person); aufgeben (idea).
dismissal [dis'misəl], s. die Entlassung; (Law) die Abweisung.
dismount [dis'maunt], v.n. vom Pferd absteigen. — v.a. (die Truppen) absteigen lassen.
disobedience [diso'biːdjəns], s. der Ungehorsam.
disobedient [diso'biːdjənt], adj. ungehorsam.
disobey [diso'bei], v.a., v.n. nicht gehorchen.
disoblige [diso'blaidʒ], v.a. verletzen, unhöflich behandeln.
disorder [dis'ɔːdə], s. die Unordnung; der Aufruhr (riot). — v.a. verwirren, in Unordnung bringen.
disorderliness [dis'ɔːdəlinis], s. die Unordentlichkeit.
disorderly [dis'ɔːdəli], adj. unordentlich (unsystematic); aufrührerisch, liederlich.
disorganization [disɔːgəni'zeiʃən or -nai'zeiʃən], s. die Zerrüttung, die Auflösung (dissolution).
disorganize [dis'ɔːgənaiz], v.a. auflösen.
disown [dis'oun], v.a. verleugnen.
disparage [dis'pæridʒ], v.a. verunglimpfen (slight); herabsetzen (minimize).
disparagement [dis'pæridʒmənt], s. die Herabsetzung.
disparity [dis'pæriti], s. die Ungleichheit.
dispatch [dis'pætʃ] see despatch.
dispel [dis'pel], v.a. vertreiben, verscheuchen.

369

dispensable

dispensable [dis'pensəbl], *adj.* erläßlich, entbehrlich.

dispensation [dispen'seiʃən], *s.* die Austeilung; (*Eccl.*) die Dispensation.

dispensary [dis'pensəri], *s.* die Apotheke.

dispense [dis'pens], *v.a.* ausgeben, austeilen (*distribute*); — *with*, entbehren können, verzichten (auf, *Acc.*).

dispenser [dis'pensə], *s.* der Apotheker, der Pharmazeut.

dispersal [dis'pə:səl], *s.* das Zerstreuen, die Verteilung.

disperse [dis'pə:s], *v.a.* zerstreuen. — *v.n.* sich zerstreuen, sich verteilen.

dispirit [dis'pirit], *v.a.* mutlos machen, entmutigen.

displace [dis'pleis], *v.a.* verlegen, versetzen; (*Phys.*) verdrängen; —*d person*, der Heimatlose, der Verschleppte, der Flüchtling.

displacement [dis'pleismənt], *s.* die Versetzung (*from one place to another*); die Entwurzelung (*uprooting*); (*Phys.*) die Verdrängung; (*Naut.*) das Deplacement.

display [dis'plei], *v.a.* entfalten, ausstellen, zur Schau stellen (*show*). — *s.* die Entfaltung (*showing*), die Schaustellung, Ausstellung (*exhibition*).

displease [dis'pli:z], *v.a.* mißfallen (*Dat.*).

displeased [dis'pli:zd], *adj.* ungehalten (*at*, über, *Acc.*).

displeasure [dis'pleʒə], *s.* das Mißvergnügen, das Mißfallen (— *at*, an, *Dat.*).

disposable [dis'pouzəbl], *adj.* (*Comm.*) disponibel; zur Verfügung stehend.

disposal [dis'pouzl], *s.* die Verfügung (*ordering*); die Übergabe (*handing over*); *at o.'s* —, zur Verfügung; *bomb* —, die Unschädlichmachung der Bomben.

dispose [dis'pouz], *v.a.* einrichten (*thing*); geneigt machen (*person*); — *of*, etwas loswerden (*Acc.*). — *v.n.* anordnen (*ordain*).

disposed [dis'pouzd], *adj.* geneigt; *be well — towards s.o.*, jemandem zugeneigt sein or wohlwollend gegenüberstehen; *well —*, (in) guter Laune.

disposition [dispə'ziʃən], *s.* (*Psych.*) die Anlage; die Gemütsart (*temperament*); die Anordnung (*sequence*); der Plan, die Anlage (*of book etc.*); die Verfügung (*arrangement*).

dispossess [dispə'zes], *v.a.* enteignen, (des Besitzes) berauben (*Genit.*).

disproof [dis'pru:f], *s.* die Widerlegung.

disproportion [disprə'pɔ:ʃən], *s.* das Mißverhältnis.

disproportionate [disprə'pɔ:sənit], *adj.* unverhältnismäßig.

disprove [dis'pru:v], *v.a.* widerlegen.

disputable [dis'pju:təbl], *adj.* bestreitbar.

disputant ['dispjutənt], *s.* der Opponent, der Disputant.

disputation [dispju'teiʃən], *s.* der gelehrte Streit, die Disputation.

dispute [dis'pju:t], *s.* der Disput, die Meinungsverschiedenheit. — *v.a.*, *v.n.* streiten, verschiedener Ansicht sein; disputieren (*debate*); mit Worten streiten (*argue*).

disqualification [diskwɔlifi'keiʃən], *s.* die Disqualifizierung.

disqualify [dis'kwɔlifai], *v.a.* disqualifizieren, ausschließen.

disquiet [dis'kwaiət], *v.a.* beunruhigen, stören. — *s.* die Unruhe, die Störung.

disquisition [diskwi'ziʃən], *s.* die (lange) Abhandlung *or* Rede.

disregard [disri'gɑ:d], *v.a.* mißachten, nicht beachten. — *s.* die Außerachtlassung, die Mißachtung.

disreputable [dis'repjutəbl], *adj.* verrufen, in üblem Rufe stehend.

disrepute [disri'pju:t], *s.* der schlechte Name, der üble Ruf.

disrespect [disris'pekt], *s.* die Geringschätzung, der Mangel an Respekt. — *v.a.* (*obs.*) mißachten, geringschätzen, respektlos behandeln.

disrespectful [disris'pektful], *adj.* respektlos, unhöflich.

disrobe [dis'roub], *v.a.* entkleiden. — *v.n.* sich entkleiden.

disrupt [dis'rʌpt], *v.a.* abreißen, unterbrechen, stören (*disturb*).

disruption [dis'rʌpʃən], *s.* die Störung, die Unterbrechung (*interruption*); der Bruch.

dissatisfaction [dissætis'fækʃən], *s.* die Unzufriedenheit.

dissatisfied [dis'sætisfaid], *adj.* unzufrieden, unbefriedigt.

dissatisfy [dis'sætisfai], *v.a.* unzufrieden lassen.

dissect [di'sekt], *v.a.* zergliedern, zerlegen; (*Anat.*) sezieren.

dissection [di'sekʃən], *s.* die Zergliederung; (*Anat.*) die Sektion.

dissemble [di'sembl], *v.a.*, *v.n.* heucheln; sich verstellen.

disseminate [di'semineit], *v.a.* verbreiten.

dissemination [disemi'neiʃən], *s.* die Verbreitung.

dissension [di'senʃən], *s.* die Uneinigkeit, der Zwist (*conflict*).

dissent [di'sent], *v.n.* anderer Meinung sein; abweichen (*from*, von, *Dat.*). — *s.* die Abweichung, die abweichende Meinung.

dissenter [di'sentə], *s.* der Dissenter, das Mitglied der Freikirche.

dissertation [disə'teiʃən], *s.* die Dissertation, die Abhandlung.

dissever [di'sevə], *v.a.* trennen (*separate*); zerteilen (*divide*).

dissidence ['disidəns], *s.* die Uneinigkeit.

dissident ['disidənt], *adj.* uneinig, anders denkend.

dissimilar [di'similə], *adj.* unähnlich, ungleichartig.

dissimilarity [disimi'læriti], *s.* die Unähnlichkeit, die Ungleichartigkeit.

dissimulate [di'simjuleit], *v.a.* verhehlen (*conceal*). — *v.n.* sich verstellen, heucheln.

dissimulation [disimju'leifən], *s.* die Verstellung, Heuchelei, das Vorgeben (*pretence*).

dissipate ['disipeit], *v.a.* zerstreuen (*spread*); verschwenden (*waste*).

dissipation [disi'peifən], *s.* die Zerstreuung, die Verschwendung; die Ausschweifung.

dissociate [di'soufieit], *v.a.* trennen, lösen. — *v.r.* abrücken (von).

dissociation [disoufi'eifən], *s.* die Trennung; die Dissoziation.

dissolubility [disɔlju'biliti], *s.* die Auflösbarkeit.

dissoluble [di'sɔljubl], *adj.* auflösbar.

dissolute ['disəlju:t], *adj.* ausschweifend, lose, liederlich.

dissolution [disə'lju:fən], *s.* die Auflösung; der Tod (*death*).

dissolvable [di'zɔlvəbl], *adj.* auflösbar, löslich.

dissolve [di'zɔlv], *v.a.* auflösen; lösen. — *v.n.* sich auflösen, zergehen (*melt*).

dissonance ['disənəns], *s.* die Dissonanz, der Mißklang.

dissonant ['disənənt], *adj.* (*Mus.*) dissonant; mißhellig (*discordant*).

dissuade [di'sweid], *v.a.* abraten (*from*, von, *Dat.*).

dissuasion [di'sweiʒən], *s.* das Abraten.

dissuasive [di'sweisiv], *adj.* abratend.

distaff ['dista:f], *s.* der Spinnrocken (*spinning*); *on the — side*, auf der weiblichen Linie.

distance ['distəns], *s.* die Entfernung; die Ferne (*remoteness*). — *v.a.* hinter sich lassen, distanzieren(von,*Dat.*).

distant ['distənt], *adj.* entfernt, fern (*space*); kühl (*manner*).

distaste [dis'teist], *s.* die Abneigung (vor, *Dat.*); der Widerwille (gegen, *Acc.*).

distasteful [dis'teistful], *adj.* widerwärtig, zuwider.

distastefulness [dis'teistfulnis], *s.* die Widerwärtigkeit.

distemper (1) [dis'tempə], *s.* die Krankheit; die Staupe (*dogs*).

distemper (2) [dis'tempə], *s.* die Wasserfarbe (*paint*). — *v.a.* mit Wasserfarbe streichen.

distend [dis'tend], *v.a.* (*Med.*) ausdehnen, strecken. — *v.n.* sich ausdehnen.

distension, distention [dis'tenfən], *s.* das Dehnen; (*Med.*) die Ausdehnung, die Streckung.

distich ['distik], *s.* (*Poet.*) das Distichon.

distil [dis'til], *v.a.* destillieren. — *v.n.* (*Chem.*) destillieren, herausströpfeln.

distillation [disti'leifən], *s.* die Destillierung, (*Chem.*) der Destilliervorgang.

distiller [dis'tilə], *s.* der Branntweinbrenner.

distillery [dis'tiləri], *s.* die (Branntwein)brennerei.

distinct [dis'tiŋkt], *adj.* deutlich, klar; — *from*, verschieden von (*Dat.*).

distinction [dis'tiŋkfən], *s.* der Unterschied, die Unterscheidung (*differentiation*); die Auszeichnung (*eminence*).

distinctive [dis'tiŋktiv], *adj.* unterscheidend (*differentiating*); deutlich (*clear*); leicht zu unterscheiden (*easy to distinguish*).

distinctiveness [dis'tiŋktivnis], *s.* die Deutlichkeit (*of voice etc.*); die Eigenart, Eigentümlichkeit (*peculiarity*).

distinguish [dis'tiŋgwif], *v.a.* unterscheiden. — *v.r.* ~ *o.s.*, sich auszeichnen.

distinguishable [dis'tiŋgwifəbl], *adj.* unterscheidbar.

distinguished [dis'tiŋgwifd], *adj.* berühmt, vornehm.

distort [dis'tɔ:t], *v.a.* verdrehen, verzerren, verrenken.

distortion [dis'tɔ:fən], *s.* die Verdrehung, Verzerrung, (*fig.*) die Entstellung (*of truth etc.*).

distract [dis'trækt], *v.a.* abziehen, ablenken (*divert*); stören (*disturb*).

distracted [dis'træktid], *adj.* zerstreut; verrückt (*mentally deranged*).

distraction [dis'trækfən], *s.* die Ablenkung; die Störung (*disturbance*); *to* —, bis zur Raserei.

distrain [dis'trein], *v.a.* beschlagnahmen, in Beschlag nehmen.

distraint [dis'treint], *s.* die Beschlagnahme.

distress [dis'tres], *s.* die Not, die Trübsal. — *v.a.* betrüben (*sadden*), quälen (*torture*).

distribute [dis'tribju:t], *v.a.* verteilen, austeilen (*among*, unter, *Acc.*).

distribution [distri'bju:fən], *s.* die Verteilung; die Austeilung (*giving out*); (*Comm.*) der Vertrieb.

distributive [dis'tribjutiv], *adj.* (*Gram.*) distributiv; — *trades*, die Vertriebsgewerbe.

district ['distrikt], *s.* (*Geog., Pol.*) der Bezirk; die Gegend (*region*); der Kreis (*administrative*); — *commissioner*, der Kreisbeamte, Kreisvorsteher.

distrust [dis'trast], *v.a.* mißtrauen (*Dat.*). — *s.* das Mißtrauen (*of*, gegen, *Acc.*).

distrustful [dis'trastful], *adj.* mißtrauisch (*of*, gegen, *Acc.*).

disturb [dis'tə:b], *v.a.* stören (*trouble*); in Unordnung bringen (*disorder*).

disturbance [dis'tə:bəns], *s.* die Störung (*interruption etc.*); der Aufruhr (*riot*).

disunion [dis'ju:njən], *s.* die Entzweiung, die Zwietracht.

disunite [disju'nait], *v.a.* entzweien, Zwietracht säen zwischen. — *v.n.* sich trennen.

disuse

disuse [dis'ju:z], *v.a.* außer Gebrauch
setzen. — [-'ju:s], *s.* der Nichtge-
brauch (*abeyance*); die Entwöhnung
(*cessation of practice*).

ditch [ditʃ], *s.* der Graben; *dull as
—water,* uninteressant, langweilig.
— *v.a.* mit einem Graben umgeben
(*dig around*); graben.

ditto ['ditou], *adv.* desgleichen, dito.

ditty ['diti], *s.* das Liedchen.

diurnal [dai'ə:nəl], *adj.* täglich.

divan [di'væn], *s.* der Diwan.

dive [daiv], *v.n.* tauchen, springen (ins
Wasser); (*Aviat.*) sturzfliegen, einen
Sturzflug machen. — *s.* der Hecht-
sprung (ins Wasser); der Wasser-
sprung; der Kopfsprung; (*Aviat.*) der
Sturzflug.

diver ['daivə], *s.* (*Sport, Orn.*) der
Taucher.

diverge [dai'və:dʒ], *v.n.* abweichen,
auseinandergehen.

divergence [dai'və:dʒəns], *s.* die Abweichung, die Divergenz, Meinungsverschiedenheit.

divergent [dai'və:dʒənt], *adj.* auseinan-
dergehend, abweichend.

divers ['daivəz], *adj. pl.* etliche,
verschiedene.

diverse [dai'və:s], *adj.* verschieden,
mannigfaltig.

diversify [dai'və:sifai], *v.a.* verschieden
machen.

diversion [dai'və:ʃən], *s.* die Zerstreuung; (*Traffic*) die Umleitung.

diversity [dai'və:siti], *s.* die Verschiedenheit; die Ungleichheit (*dispa-
rity*).

divert [dai'və:t], *v.a.* ablenken, zerstreuen.

divest [di'vest *or* dai'-], *v.a.* entkleiden,
berauben (*of office,* eines Amtes).
— *v.r.* — *o.s. of,* auf etwas verzichten
(*give up*).

divide [di'vaid], *v.a.* (*Maths.*) dividieren; teilen (*share*); aufteilen (*proportion*); sondern, trennen (*separate*). —
v.n. sich teilen; (*Maths.*) sich dividieren lassen.

dividend ['dividənd], *s.* (*Comm.*) die
Dividende; (*Maths.*) der Dividend.

dividers [di'vaidəz], *s.pl.* der Stech-
zirkel.

divination [divi'neiʃən], *s.* die Wahr-
sagung (*prophecy*); die Ahnung.

divine [di'vain], *v.a.* weissagen (*prophesy*); erraten (*guess*). — *adj.* göttlich;
(*coll.*) herrlich. —*s.* (*obs.*) der Geistliche (*clergyman*).

divinity [di'viniti], *s.* die Göttlichkeit;
die Gottheit (*deity*); die Theologie.

divisibility [divizi'biliti], *s.* (*Maths.*) die
Teilbarkeit.

divisible [di'vizibl], *adj.* teilbar.

division [di'viʒən], *s.* (*Maths., Mil.*) die
Division; die Teilung (*partition*); die
Abteilung (*department*); (*Parl.*) die
Abstimmung.

divisor [di'vaizə], *s.* (*Maths.*) der
Divisor, der Teiler.

divorce [di'vɔ:s], *s.* (*Law*) die Scheidung; die Trennung (*separation*). —
v.a. sich von einem scheiden
lassen.

divulge [dai'vʌldʒ], *v.a.* ausplaudern;
verraten (*betray*); verbreiten (*spread*).

dizziness ['dizinis], *s.* der Schwindel.

dizzy ['dizi], *adj.* schwindlig.

do [du:], *v.a. irr.* tun, machen; — *o.'s
duty,* seine Pflicht erfüllen; — *o.'s
bit,* das Seinige leisten; — *o.'s homework,* seine Aufgaben machen; — *a
favour,* einen Gefallen erweisen; vollbringen (*accomplish*); — *away with,*
abschaffen (*Acc.*); einpacken. — *v.n.
this will* —, das genügt; *this won't*
—, so geht's nicht; — *without,* ohne
etwas auskommen; *how* — *you* — ?
sehr angenehm (*on introduction to
people*).

docile ['dousail], *adj.* gelehrig, lenksam,
fügsam.

docility [do'siliti], *s.* die Gelehrigkeit,
die Fügsamkeit.

dock (1) [dɔk], *s.* (*Bot.*) das Ampfer-
kraut; — *leaf,* das Ampferblatt.

dock (2) [dɔk], *s.* (*Naut.*) das Dock;
—*yard,* die Schiffswerft; (*Law*) die
Anklagebank. — *v.a.* (*Naut.*) ein
Schiff ins Dock bringen.

dock (3) [dɔk], *v.a.* stutzen (*clip*);
kürzen (*wages*).

docket ['dɔkit], *s.* der Zettel (*chit*); der
Lieferschein.

doctor ['dɔktə], *s.* (*Med.*) der Arzt, der
Doktor. — *v.a.* operieren, kastrieren
(*a cat etc.*).

doctorate ['dɔktərit], *s.* das Doktorat,
die Doktorwürde.

doctrinaire [dɔktri'nɛə], *s.* der Doktrinär. — *adj.* doktrinär.

doctrinal [dɔk'trainəl], *adj.* Lehr-.

doctrine ['dɔktrin], *s.* die Lehre, die
Doktrin.

document ['dɔkjumənt], *s.* das Dokument, die Urkunde.

documentary [dɔkju'mentəri], *adj.*
Dokumentar- (*film*); dokumentarisch
(*evidence*).

documentation [dɔkjumen'teiʃən], *s.*
die Dokumentation, Heranziehung
von Dokumenten.

dodge [dɔdʒ], *v.a.* ausweichen (*Dat.*).
— *s.* der Kniff.

dodger ['dɔdʒə], *s.* der Schwindler.

doe [dou], *s.* (*Zool.*) das Reh.

doeskin ['douskin], *s.* das Rehleder.

doff [dɔf], *v.a.* abnehmen, ablegen
(*clothes*).

dog [dɔg], *s.* der Hund; —*'s ear,* das
Eselsohr (*in book*). — *v.a.* verfolgen,
auf Schritt und Tritt folgen (*Dat.*)
(*follow closely*).

dogfish ['dɔgfiʃ], *s.* (*Zool.*) der Dornhai.

dogged ['dɔgid], *adj.* unverdrossen,
zäh.

doggedness ['dɔgidnis], *s.* die Zähigkeit.

doggerel ['dɔgərəl], *s.* der Knüttelvers.

dogma ['dɔgmə], *s.* das Dogma, der
Glaubenssatz.

dogmatic [dɔg'mætik], *adj.* dogmatisch.
dogmatism ['dɔgmətizm], *s.* der Dogmatismus.
dogmatize ['dɔgmətaiz], *v.n.* dogmatisieren.
doldrums ['douldrəmz], *s. pl.* die Schwermut, die Depression; (*Naut.*) die Windstillen, *f.pl.*
dole [doul], *s.* das Almosen; die Arbeitslosenunterstützung (*unemployment benefit*); *be on the —,* stempeln gehen, Arbeitslosenunterstützung beziehen. — *v.a. — out,* austeilen, verteilen.
doleful ['doulful], *adj.* traurig, bekümmert.
doll [dɔl], *s.* die Puppe.
dollar ['dɔlə], *s.* der Dollar.
dolman ['dɔlmən], *s.* der Dolman.
dolorous ['dɔlərəs], *adj.* (*Lit.*) schmerzlich, schmerzhaft.
dolphin ['dɔlfin], *s.* (*Zool.*) der Delphin.
dolt [doult], *s.* der Tölpel.
doltish ['doultiʃ], *adj.* tölpelhaft.
doltishness ['doultiʃnis], *s.* die Tölpelhaftigkeit.
domain [do'mein], *s.* das Gebiet, der Bereich.
dome [doum], *s.* (*Archit.*) die Kuppel, die Wölbung; der Dom.
domed [doumd], *adj.* gewölbt.
domestic [do'mestik], *adj.* Haus-, häuslich; — *animal,* das Haustier.
domesticate [do'mestikeit], *v.a.* zähmen (*tame*), zivilisieren.
domesticity [dɔmes'tisiti], *s.* die Häuslichkeit.
domicile ['dɔmisail], *s.* das Domizil; der Wohnort.
domiciled ['dɔmisaild], *adj.* wohnhaft (*at,* in, *Dat.*).
dominant ['dɔminənt], *adj.* vorherrschend. — *s.* (*Mus.*) die Dominante.
dominate ['dɔmineit], *v.a.* beherrschen. — *v.n.* herrschen.
domination [dɔmi'neiʃən], *s.* die Herrschaft.
domineer [dɔmi'niə], *v.n.* tyrannisieren.
domineering [dɔmi'niəriŋ], *adj.* überheblich, gebieterisch.
Dominican [do'minikən], *s.* der Dominikaner (*friar*).
dominion [do'minjən], *s.* die Herrschaft (*rule*); das Dominion (*Br. Commonwealth*).
domino ['dɔminou], *s.* (*pl.* **—noes**) der Domino (*mask*); (*pl.*) das Domino (*game*).
don (1) [dɔn], *s.* der Universitätsgelehrte, Universitätsdozent (*scholar*); Don (*Spanish nobleman*).
don (2) [dɔn], *v.a.* anziehen.
donate [do'neit], *v.a.* schenken, stiften.
donation [do'neiʃən], *s.* die Schenkung, die Stiftung; die Gabe (*gift*).
donkey ['dɔŋki], *s.* (*Zool.*) der Esel; — *engine,* die Hilfsmaschine.
donor ['dounə], *s.* der Spender, der Stifter; *blood —,* der Blutspender.

doom [du:m], *s.* die Verurteilung (*judgment*); der Untergang; das jüngste Gericht.
doomed [du:md], *adj.* verurteilt, verdammt (*to,* zu, *Dat.*).
Doomsday ['du:msdei], der jüngste Tag, der Tag der jüngsten Gerichtes.
door [dɔ:], *s.* die Tür(e); *next —,* nebenan; *out of —s,* draußen, im Freien; *—bell,* die Türklingel; *— latch,* die Klinke.
doorman ['dɔ:mæn], *s.* der Türsteher, der Pförtner.
dormant ['dɔ:mənt], *adj.* schlafend; unbenutzt.
dormer window ['dɔ:mə 'windou], *s.* das Dachfenster.
dormitory ['dɔ:mitri], *s.* der Schlafsaal.
dormouse ['dɔ:maus], *s.* (*Zool.*) die Haselmaus.
dose [dous], *s.* (*Med.*) die Dosis. — *v.a.* dosieren.
dot [dɔt], *s.* der Punkt, das Tüpfel. — *v.a.* punktieren; *sign on the —ted line,* unterschreiben; — *the i's and cross the t's,* äußerst genau sein.
dotage ['doutidʒ], *s.* die Altersschwäche, das Greisenalter.
dotard ['doutəd], *s.* der alte Dummkopf.
dote [dout], *v.n.* vernarrt sein (*on,* in, *Acc.*).
double [dʌbl], *adj.* (*Maths.*) doppelt; zweideutig (*meaning*); falsch (*false*); — *entry book-keeping,* doppelte Buchführung. — *s.* der Doppelgänger, die Doppelgängerin; *at the —,* im Sturmschritt. — *v.a.* (*Maths.*) verdoppeln; zusammenlegen (*fold in two*). — *v.n. — up with pain,* sich vor Schmerzen winden c krümmen.
doublet ['dʌblit], *s.* der Wams; — *and hose,* Wams und Hosen; der Pasch (*dice*); (*Ling.*) die Dublette, Doppelform.
doubt [daut], *s.* der Zweifel. — *v.a.* zweifeln (an, *Dat.*); bezweifeln.
doubtful ['dautful], *adj.* zweifelhaft, fraglich (*uncertain*).
doubtless ['dautlis], *adj.* zweifellos, ohne Zweifel.
douche [du:ʃ], *s.* die Dusche.
dough [dou], *s.* der Teig.
doughnut ['dounʌt], *s.* der Krapfen, Pfannkuchen.
doughy ['doui], *adj.* weich, teigig.
douse [daus], *v.a.* begießen, mit Wasser beschütten.
dove [dʌv], *s.* (*Orn.*) die Taube.
dovecote ['dʌvkɔt], *s.* der Taubenschlag.
dovetail ['dʌvteil], *v.a., v.n.* einpassen; fügen; *—ing,* die Einpassung, die Verzinkung.
dowager ['dauədʒə], *s.* die Witwe (*of noble family,* von Stande).
dowdy ['daudi], *adj.* schlampig, unordentlich, unelegant.
dower ['dauə], *s.* die Mitgift, die Ausstattung.

down

down (1) [daun], s. der Flaum, die Daune.

down (2) [daun], s. das Hügelland.

down (3) [daun], adv. hinunter, herunter; nieder; unter; hinab. — prep. herab; hinunter. — adj. the — train, der Zug aus London. — v.a. niederzwingen, hinunterstürzen.

downcast ['daunkɑːst], adj. niedergeschlagen.

downfall ['daunfɔːl], s. der Sturz.

downhill [daun'hil], adv. bergab. — ['daunhill], adj. abschüssig.

downpour ['daunpɔː], s. der Platzregen.

downright ['daunrait], adj. völlig. — adv. geradezu.

downward ['daunwəd], adj. abschüssig. — adv. (also **downwards**) see down.

dowry ['dauri] see dower.

doze [douz], v.n. dösen, schlummern.

dozen [dazn], s. das Dutzend.

drab [dræb], adj. eintönig; langweilig (boring).

draft [drɑːft], s. (Comm.) die Tratte; der Entwurf (sketch); (Mil.) das Detachement. — v.a. entwerfen (sketch); (Mil.) abordnen. (Am.) einziehen.

drag [dræg], v.a. schleppen. — s. (Engin.) die Schleppbremse, der Dregghaken; der Hemmschuh (wedge); —net, das Schleppnetz; —wheel, das Schlepprad.

dragoman ['drægəmən], s. der Dolmetscher.

dragon ['drægən], s. der Drache.

dragonfly ['drægənflai], s. (Ent.) die Libelle.

dragoon [drə'guːn], v.a. unterdrücken. — s. (Mil.) der Dragoner.

drain [drein], v.a. entwässern, austrocknen; trockenlegen. — v.n. ablaufen, abfließen, auslaufen. — s. der Abguß, Abzug, die Gosse (in street); (Engin.) die Dränage; —ing board, das Ablauf- or Abwaschbrett; (Phot.) —ing rack, der Trockenständer; a — on o.'s income, eine Belastung des Einkommens.

drainage ['dreinidʒ], s. die Trockenlegung, die Kanalisation.

drainpipe ['dreinpaip], s. das Abflußrohr; — trousers, die Röhrenhosen, f. pl.

drake [dreik], s. (Orn.) der Enterich.

dram [dræm], s. der Trunk; Schluck (spirits).

drama ['drɑːmə], s. das Drama, das Schauspiel.

dramatic [drə'mætik], adj. dramatisch.

dramatist ['drɑːm- or 'dræmətist], s. der Dramatiker.

dramatize ['dræmətaiz], v.a. dramatisieren.

drape [dreip], v.a. drapieren, bedecken; einhüllen (wrap). — s. (Am.) der Vorhang.

draper ['dreipə], s. der Stoffhändler, der Tuchhändler.

drapery ['dreipəri], s. — department, die Stoff- or Tuchabteilung; die Tuchhandlung (shop).

drastic ['drɑːstik or 'dræstik], adj. drastisch, radikal.

draught [drɑːft], s. der Zug (air); der Tiefgang (— of ship); der Schluck (drink); der Schlaftrunk (sleeping —); — horse, das Zugpferd; — beer, das Faßbier; —board, das Damespielbrett; (pl.) das Damespiel.

draw [drɔː], v.a. irr. ziehen (pull); zeichnen (sketch); anlocken (attract); ausschreiben (cheque); —well, der Ziehbrunnen. — s. das Los, die Verlosung (lottery); (Sport) das Unentschieden.

drawback ['drɔːbæk], s. der Nachteil, die Schattenseite.

drawbridge ['drɔːbridʒ], s. die Zugbrücke.

drawer ['drɔːə], s. die Schublade; chest of —s, die Kommode; (pl.) die Unterhosen, f. pl.

drawing ['drɔːin], s. (Art) die Zeichnung; —board, das Reißbrett; —office, das Zeichenbüro, der Zeichensaal.

drawing room ['drɔːin rum], s. das Wohnzimmer, der Salon.

drawl [drɔːl], v.n. gedehnt sprechen. — s. die gedehnte Sprechweise.

drawn [drɔːn], adj. (Sport) unentschieden.

dray [drei], s. der Rollwagen, der Karren; —man, der Kutscher, der Fuhrmann.

dread [dred], s. der Schrecken. — adj. schrecklich. — v.a. fürchten. — v.n. sich fürchten (vor, Dat.).

dreadful ['dredful], adj. schrecklich, furchtbar.

dreadnought ['drednɔːt], s. (Naut.) das große Schlachtschiff.

dream [driːm], s. der Traum. — v.n. irr. träumen; I would not — of it, es würde mir nicht im Traum einfallen, ich denke nicht im Traum daran.

dreamt [dremt] see dream.

dreamy ['driːmi], adj. verträumt, träumerisch.

dreariness ['driərinis], s. die Öde.

dreary ['driəri], adj. traurig, öde.

dredge [dredʒ], s. die Schleppnetz. — v.a. (Engin.) ausbaggern; (Naut.) dreggen.

dredger ['dredʒə], s. der Bagger, das Baggerschiff; (Cul.) die Streubüchse.

dregs [dregz], s. pl. der Bodensatz (in cup etc.); die Hefe (yeast).

drench [drentʃ], v.a. durchnässen, tränken.

Dresden ['drezdən], (china) das Meißner Porzellan.

dress [dres], s. das Kleid; die Kleidung; evening —, die Abendkleidung; full —, die Gala(kleidung); — circle, erster Rang; —maker, die Schneiderin; — rehearsal, die Generalprobe; — shirt, das Frackhemd; — suit, der Frackanzug. — v.a., v.n. (sich) anziehen.

dresser ['dresə], *s.* der Ankleider (*valet*); der Anrichtetisch (*table*).

dressing ['dresiŋ], *s.* (*Build.*) die Verkleidung; der Verband (*bandage*); der Verputz (*interior decoration*); — *gown*, der Schlafrock, Bademantel; (*Theat.*) — *room*, das Künstlerzimmer; Ankleidezimmer; — *table*, der Toilettentisch.

dressy ['dresi], *adj.* elegant; modesüchtig.

dribble [dribl], *v.n.* tröpfeln (*trickle*); geifern (*slaver*); (*Footb.*) dribbeln.

driblet ['driblit], *s.* die Kleinigkeit, die Lappalie.

drift [drift], *s.* die Richtung (*direction*); die Strömung (*stream*); das Treiben; Gestöber (*snow*). — *v.a.* treiben. — *v.n.* dahintreiben.

drill (1) [dril], *v.a.* drillen, bohren (*bore*); (*Mil.*) exerzieren; (*Agr.*) eine Furche ziehen; einstudieren (*coach*). — *s.* (*Mil.*) das Exerzieren; (*Agr.*) die Furche; der Bohrer (*tool*); — *hall*, die Übungs- or Exerzierhalle.

drill (2) [dril], *s.* der Drillich (*textile*).

drily ['draili], *adv.* trocken.

drink [driŋk], *v.a., v.n. irr.* trinken. — *s.* das Getränk, der Trank (*potion*); etwas zum Trinken (*a —*); *come, have a —*, trinken wir ein Glas (zusammen); *strong —*, geistiges Getränk.

drinkable ['driŋkəbl], *adj.* trinkbar; zum Trinken.

drinker ['driŋkə], *s.* der Trinker, Säufer; der Zecher; der Trunkenbold (*drunkard*).

drip [drip], *v.n.* tröpfeln. — *s.* das Tröpfeln.

dripping ['dripiŋ], *s.* (*Cul.*) das Bratenfett, das Schmalz.

drive [draiv], *v.a. irr.* treiben (*sheep etc.*); fahren (*a car*). — *v.n.* fahren; dahinfahren (*— along*). — *s.* die Ausfahrt, Fahrt (*trip*); die Einfahrt (*approach to house*).

driving ['draiviŋ], *s.* das Fahren; — *licence*, der Führerschein; — *school*, die Fahrschule; — *test*, die Fahrprüfung.

drivel [drivl], *s.* der Geifer; der Unsinn (*nonsense*). — *v.n.* Unsinn reden.

driver ['draivə], *s.* der Fahrer, der Chauffeur; (*Railw.*) Führer; (*Hunt.*) der Treiber.

drizzle [drizl], *v.n.* rieseln; leicht regnen. — *s.* das Rieseln, der feine Regen, der Sprühregen.

droll [droul], *adj.* drollig, possierlich.

drollery ['drouləri], *s.* die Possierlichkeit; die Schnurre.

dromedary ['drʌmədəri *or* 'drɔm-], *s.* (*Zool.*) das Dromedar.

drone (1) [droun], *s.* das Gedröhn, das Gesumme (*noise*). — *v.n.* dröhnen, summen (*hum loudly*).

drone (2) [droun], *s.* (*Ent.*) die Drohne; der Faulpelz (*lazybones*).

droop [dru:p], *v.a.* hängen lassen. — *v.n.* herabhängen; verwelken (*flowers*); ermatten (*tire*).

drop [drɔp], *s.* der Tropfen (*liquid*); das Fallen (*fall*). — *v.a.* fallen lassen; — *a brick*, eine taktlose Bemerkung machen; — *a hint*, andeuten, auf etwas hindeuten. — *v.n.* fallen.

droppings ['drɔpiŋz], *s. pl.* der Mist, Dünger (*of animals*).

dropsical ['drɔpsikəl], *adj.* (*Med.*) wassersüchtig.

dropsy ['drɔpsi], *s.* (*Med.*) die Wassersucht.

dross [drɔs], *s.* (*Metall.*) die Schlacke; der Unrat, das wertlose Zeug.

drought [draut], *s.* die Dürre, die Trockenheit.

drove [drouv], *s.* die Herde, die Trift (*cattle*).

drover ['drouvə], *s.* der Viehtreiber.

drown [draun], *v.a.* ertränken; überschwemmen (*flood*); übertönen (*noise*). — *v.n.* ertrinken.

drowse [drauz], *v.n.* schlummern, schläfrig sein.

drowsy ['drauzi], *adj.* schläfrig.

drub [drʌb], *v.a.* prügeln.

drudge [drʌdʒ], *s.* das Packtier; der Sklave, der Knecht.

drudgery ['drʌdʒəri], *s.* die Plackerei, die Plagerei (*hard toil*).

drug [drʌg], *s.* die Droge; die Medizin; das Rauschgift. — *v.a.* betäuben.

drugget ['drʌgit], *s.* der (grobe) Wollstoff.

drum [drʌm], *s.* die Trommel. — *v.n.* trommeln, austrommeln.

drunk [drʌŋk], *adj.* betrunken.

drunkard ['drʌŋkəd], *s.* der Trunkenbold.

drunkenness ['drʌŋkənnis], *s.* die Trunkenheit.

dry [drai], *adj.* trocken, dürr; ausgetrocknet, durstig (*thirsty*). — *v.a.* austrocknen, trocken machen, dörren. — *v.n.* trocken werden, trocknen.

dryad ['draiæd], *s.* die Baumnymphe Dryade.

dryness ['drainis], *s.* die Trockenheit, die Dürre.

dual ['dju:əl], *adj.* doppelt; Zwei-.

dub (1) [dʌb], *v.a.* zum Ritter schlagen; nennen (*name*).

dub (2) [dʌb], *v.a.* (*Films*) synchronisieren.

dubious ['dju:bjəs], *adj.* zweifelhaft.

ducal ['dju:kəl], *adj.* herzoglich.

duchess ['dʌtʃis], *s.* die Herzogin.

duchy ['dʌtʃi], *s.* das Herzogtum.

duck (1) [dʌk], *s.* (*Orn.*) die Ente.

duck (2) [dʌk], *v.n.* sich ducken, sich bücken; untertauchen (*in water*). — *v.a.* untertauchen, ins Wasser tauchen.

duckling ['dʌkliŋ], *s.* (*Orn.*) das Entchen.

duct [dʌkt], *s.* (*Anat.*) der Kanal; die Röhre.

ductile ['dʌktail], *adj.* dehnbar; fügsam.

dud

dud [dʌd], *s.* (*Mil.*) der Blindgänger; der Fehlschlag.

dude [dju:d], *s.* (*Am.*) der Geck.

dudgeon ['dʌdʒən], *s.* der Groll, der Unwille; *in high* —, sehr aufgebracht.

due [dju:], *adj.* gebührend, fällig, schuldig (*to, Dat.*); angemessen, recht; *this is — to carelessness*, das ist auf Nachlässigkeit zurückzuführen. — *adv.* direkt, gerade. — *s.* (*pl.*) die Gebühren.

duel ['dju:əl], *s.* das Duell. — *v.n.* sich duellieren (mit, *Dat.*).

duet [dju:'et], *s.* (*Mus.*) das Duett.

duffer ['dʌfə], *s.* der Tölpel; (*obs.*) der Hausierer.

duffle, duffel [dʌfl], *s.* der Düffel, das Düffeltuch.

dug [dʌg], *s.* die Zitze.

dug-out ['dʌg-aut], *s.* der Unterstand, der Bunker.

duke [dju:k], *s.* der Herzog; *Grand Duke*, der Großherzog.

dukedom ['dju:kdəm], *s.* das Herzogtum.

dull [dʌl], *adj.* fade, langweilig (*boring*); träge, schwerfällig (*slow to grasp*); stumpfsinnig (*obtuse*); schal, abgeschmackt (*tasteless*); schwach (*perception*); dumpf (*thud, noise*); matt (*colour*); trüb, überwölkt (*weather*); flau (*trade*). — *v.a.* abstumpfen (*senses*).

dullness ['dʌlnis], *s.* die Stumpfheit (*senses*); die Langeweile (*boredom*); die Schwerfälligkeit (*stolidity*); die Schwäche (*vision etc.*); die Stumpfsinnigkeit (*stupidity*).

dumb [dʌm], *adj.* stumm; (*sl.*) dumm; —*founded*, verblüfft; — *show*, die Pantomime; —*bell* (*Gymn.*) die Hantel.

dumbness ['dʌmnis], *s.* die Stummheit.

dummy ['dʌmi], *s.* der Strohmann (*cards*); die Kleiderpuppe (*wax figure*); der Blindgänger (*dud shell*); der Schnuller (*baby's*).

dump [dʌmp], *v.a.* kippen, abladen; —*ing ground*, der Abladeplatz. — *s.* (*Am. coll.*) das Bumslokal.

dumpling ['dʌmpliŋ], *s.* der Kloß, (*Austr.*) der Knödel.

dumps [dʌmps], *s. pl.* der Unmut, der Mißmut, die Depression.

dumpy ['dʌmpi], *adj.* untersetzt, kurz und dick.

dun (1) [dʌn], *adj.* schwarzbraun.

dun (2) [dʌn], *s.* der Gläubiger. — *v.a.* energisch mahnen.

dunce [dʌns], *s.* der Dummkopf.

dune [dju:n], *s.* die Düne.

dung [dʌŋ], *s.* der Dünger. — *v.n.* düngen.

dungeon ['dʌndʒən], *s.* der Kerker.

dupe [dju:p], *s.* der Betrogene. — *v.a.* betrügen.

duplicate ['dju:plikeit], *v.a.* verdoppeln; doppelt schreiben *or* ausfüllen (*write twice*); vervielfältigen (*stencil*). — [-kit], *s.* das Duplikat.

duplicity [dju:'plisiti], *s.* die Falschheit, die Doppelzüngigkeit.

durability [djuərə'biliti], *s.* die Dauerhaftigkeit.

durable ['djuərəbl], *adj.* dauerhaft.

duration [djuə'reiʃən], *s.* die Dauer, die Länge (*time*).

duress [djuə'res], *s.* der Zwang; *under* —, zwangsweise.

during ['djuəriŋ], *prep.* während.

dusk [dʌsk], *s.* die Dämmerung.

dusky ['dʌski], *adj.* dunkel, trüb; düster.

dust [dʌst], *s.* der Staub. — *v.a.* abstauben (*clean*); bestäuben (*pollinate*); bestreuen.

dustbin ['dʌstbin], *s.* der Mülleimer.

dusty ['dʌsti], *adj.* staubig; *not so* —, (*coll.*) nicht so übel.

Dutch [dʌtʃ], *adj.* holländisch; niederländisch; — *treat*, auf getrennte Kosten; *double* —, Kauderwelsch, Unsinn.

Dutchman ['dʌtʃmən], *s.* der Holländer, der Niederländer.

dutiful ['dju:tiful], *adj.* gehorsam, pflichttreu, pflichtbewußt.

duty ['dju:ti], *s.* die Pflicht; die Abgabe (*tax*); *customs* —, der Zoll; *be on* —, Dienst haben; (*being*) *on* —, diensthabend; *off* —, dienstfrei; —*free*, zollfrei; *in* — *bound*, von Rechts wegen, pflichtgemäß.

dwarf [dwɔ:f], *s.* der Zwerg. — *v.a.* am Wachstum hindern (*stunt*); klein erscheinen lassen (*overshadow*).

dwell [dwel], *v.n. irr.* wohnen (*be domiciled*); verweilen (*remain*).

dwelling ['dweliŋ], *s.* die Wohnung; — *place*, der Wohnort.

dwindle [dwindl], *v.n.* abnehmen, kleiner werden.

dye [dai], *v.a.* färben. — *s.* die Farbe; (*Chem.*) der Farbstoff.

dyeing ['daiiŋ], *s.* das Färben; Färbereigewerbe.

dyer ['daiə], *s.* der Färber.

dying ['daiiŋ], *s.* das Sterben; *the* —, (*pl.*) die Sterbenden, *pl.* — *adj.* sterbend.

dynamic [dai'næmik], *adj.* dynamisch.

dynamics [dai'næmiks], *s. pl.* die Dynamik.

dynamite ['dainəmait], *s.* das Dynamit.

dynamo ['dainəmou], *s.* der Dynamo, die Dynamomaschine.

dynasty ['dinəsti], *s.* die Dynastie.

dysentery ['disəntri], *s.* (*Med.*) die Ruhr.

dyspepsia [dis'pepsiə], *s.* (*Med.*) die Magenverstimmung.

dyspeptic [dis'peptik], *adj.* mit verstimmtem Magen; schlecht aufgelegt (*grumpy*).

E

E [i:]. das E (*also Mus.*); *E flat*, Es; *E sharp*, Eis; *E minor*, E-moll.

edible

each [i:tʃ], *adj., pron.* jeder, jede, jedes; — *other,* einander; — *one,* jeder einzelne.

eager ['i:gə], *adj.* eifrig, begierig.

eagerness ['i:gənis], *s.* der Eifer, die Begierde.

eagle [i:gl], *s.* (*Orn.*) der Adler; (*Am.*) das Zehndollarstück.

ear [iə], *s.* das Ohr; —*lap,* das Ohrläppchen; —*phones,* der Kopfhörer; — -*piece,* die Hörmuschel; —*drum,* das Trommelfell; — *of corn,* die Ähre.

earl [ə:l], *s.* der Graf.

earldom ['ə:ldəm], *s.* die (englische) Grafschaft.

early ['ə:li], *adj.* früh, frühzeitig.

earmark ['iəma:k], *v.a.* kennzeichnen, bezeichnen.

earn [ə:n], *v.a.* verdienen; erwerben.

earnest ['ə:nist], *s.* der Ernst; der ernste Beweis, das Handgeld; (*Comm.*) die Anzahlung; (*fig.*) der Vorgeschmack. — *adj.* ernst, ernsthaft.

earnings ['ə:niŋz], *s.* das Einkommen.

earshot ['iəʃɔt], *s.* die Hörweite.

earth [ə:θ], *s.* die Erde; der Erdboden (*soil*); der Fuchsbau (*of fox*); *down to* —, praktisch denkend; *move heaven and* —, alles daransetzen; *where on* —, wo in aller Welt.

earthen ['ə:θən], *adj.* irden, aus Erde; —*ware,* das Steingut.

earthquake ['ə:θkweik], *s.* das Erdbeben.

earthly ['ə:θli], *adj.* irdisch.

earthworm ['ə:θwə:m], *s.* (*Zool.*) der Regenwurm.

earthy ['ə:θi], *adj.* erdig; irdisch.

earwig ['iəwig], *s.* (*Ent.*) der Ohrwurm.

ease [i:z], *s.* die Leichtigkeit (*facility*); die Bequemlichkeit (*comfort*); *feel at* —, sich wie zu Hause fühlen; (*Mil.*) *stand at* —! rührt euch! *ill at* —, unbehaglich. — *v.a.* erleichtern, leichter machen; lindern (*pain*). — *v.n.* — *off,* (*Mil.*) sich auflockern.

easel [i:zl], *s.* das Gestell; die Staffelei.

easiness ['i:zinis], *s.* die Leichtigkeit, die Ungezwungenheit.

east [i:st], *adj., adv.* Ost-, ostwärts (*direction*). — *s.* der Osten, der Orient.

Easter ['i:stə]. das *or* (*n. or f. pl.*) der Ostern.

eastern ['i:stən], *adj.* östlich; morgenländisch, orientalisch (*oriental*).

easy ['i:zi], *adj.* leicht, frei; — *chair,* der Lehnstuhl, Sessel; *stand* —! rührt Euch! *take it* —, nimm's nicht so ernst; *es sich* (*Dat.*) bequem machen (*make o.s. comfortable*); (*Comm.*) — *terms,* Zahlungserleichterungen; — -*going,* gemütlich.

eat [i:t], *v.a., v.n.* irr. essen, speisen (*dine*); fressen (*of animals*); — *humble pie,* sich demütigen; — *o.'s hat,* einen Besen fressen; — *o.'s words* seine Worte bereuen.

eatable ['i:təbl], *adj.* genießbar, eßbar.

eaves [i:vz], *s. pl.* die Dachrinne, die Traufe.

eavesdrop ['i:vzdrɔp], *v.n.* belauschen (*on s.o., Acc.*).

eavesdropper ['i:vzdrɔpə], *s.* der Lauscher.

ebb [eb], *s.* die Ebbe. — *v.n.* nachlassen, abebben, abfließen.

ebonize ['ebənaiz], *v.a.* wie Ebenholz *or* schwarz beizen.

ebony ['ebəni], *s.* das Ebenholz.

ebullient [i'bʌljənt], *adj.* aufwallend.

eccentric [ik'sentrik], *adj.* exzentrisch, überspannt, wunderlich.

eccentricity [eksen'trisiti], *s.* die Exzentrizität, die Überspanntheit.

ecclesiastic [ikli:zi'æstik], *s.* der Geistliche. — *adj.* (*also* -ical) geistlich, kirchlich.

echo ['ekou], *s.* das Echo, der Widerhall. — *v.a., v.n.* widerhallen (*resound*); wiederholen (*repeat*).

eclectic [i'klektik], *adj.* eklektisch. — *s.* der Eklektiker.

eclecticism [i'klektisizm], *s.* (*Phil.*) der Eklektizismus.

eclipse [i'klips], *s.* die Verfinsterung, Finsternis (*darkness*); die Verdunklung (*darkening*). — *v.a.* verdunkeln.

ecliptic [i'kliptik], *s.* die Ekliptik, die Sonnenbahn.

economic [i:kə'nɔmik],*adj.*ökonomisch, wirtschaftlich.

economical [i:kə'nɔmikl], *adj.* (*frugal*) sparsam, wirtschaftlich.

economics [i:kə'nɔmiks], *s.* (*pl.*) die Wirtschaftslehre, die Ökonomie.

economist [i'kɔnəmist], *s.* der Ökonom der Wirtschaftsfachmann.

economize [i'kɔnəmaiz], *v.n.* sparen (*on,* mit, *Dat.*); sparsam sein mit (*Dat.*).

economy [i'kɔnəmi], *s.* die Wirtschaft; *political* —, die Nationalökonomie, Staatswirtschaftslehre.

ecstasy ['ekstəsi], *s.* die Ekstase, die Entzückung, die Verzückung.

ecstatic [iks'tætik], *adj.* ekstatisch, verzückt; entzückt (*delighted*).

Ecuadorean [ekwə'dɔ:riən], *adj.* ekuadorianisch. — *n.* der Ekuadorianer.

ecumenical [i:kju'menikəl], *adj.* ökumenisch.

eddy ['edi], *s.* der Wirbel, Strudel. — *v.n.* wirbeln.

edge [edʒ], *s.* die Schärfe, die Schneide (*blade*); die Kante (*ledge*); der Rand (*brink*); der Saum (*border*); die Ecke (*corner*); der Schnitt (*book*); die Schärfe (*wit, keenness*); *put an* — *on,* schärfen; *be on* —, nervös sein. — *v.a.* besetzen (*decorate*); umgeben; *double-* —*d,* zweischneidig; *two-* —*d,* zweischneidig, zweikantig; — *d with lace,* mit Spitze eingefaßt. — *v.n.* sich bewegen; — *forward,* langsam vorrücken; — *off,* sich abseits halten; — *away from,* abrücken.

edgy ['edʒi], *adj.* kantig, eckig; (*fig.*) nervös, reizbar.

edible['edibl], *adj.* eßbar.

377

edict ['i:dikt], s. die Verordnung.
edification [edifi'keiʃən], s. die Erbauung.
edifice ['edifis], s. der Bau, das Gebäude.
edify ['edifai], v.a. erbauen.
edit ['edit], v.a. herausgeben (book etc.).
edition [i'diʃən], s. die Ausgabe.
editor ['editə], s. der Herausgeber, der Schriftleiter; (newspaper) der Redakteur.
editorial [edi'tɔ:riəl], adj. Redaktions-. — s. der Leitartikel.
editorship ['editəʃip], s. die Redaktion; die Schriftleitung.
educate ['edjukeit], v.a. erziehen, (heran)bilden.
education [edju'keiʃən], s. die Erziehung (upbringing); die Bildung (general culture); das Bildungswesen, das Schulwesen (educational system); primary —, die Grundschulung, das Volksschulwesen; secondary —, das Mittelschulwesen, das höhere Schulwesen; university —, das Hochschulwesen (system), die Universitätsbildung (of individual); local — authority, das Schulamt, die Schulbehörde; Professor of Education, Professor der Pädagogik; further —, adult —, weitere Ausbildung, Erwachsenenbildung.
educational [edju'keiʃənəl], adj. erzieherisch (educative); Bildungs-, Unterrichts- (for education); — attainment, der Bildungsgrad, die Schulstufe (grade); — facilities, die Lehrmittel, Bildungs- or Schulungsmöglichkeiten, f. pl.
education(al)ist [edju'keiʃən(əl)ist], s. der Erzieher, der Pädagoge; der Erziehungsfachmann (theorist).
eel [i:l], s. (Zool.) der Aal.
eerie ['iəri], adj. gespenstisch, unheimlich.
efface [i'feis], v.a. auslöschen, austilgen.
effacement [i'feismənt], s. die Austilgung; self- —, die Selbstaufopferung.
effect [i'fekt], s. die Wirkung; die Folge, das Ergebnis (consequence); der Eindruck (impression); of no —, ohne jede Wirkung; carry into —, ausführen; take — from, vom . . . in Kraft treten. — v.a. bewirken (bring about).
effective [i'fektiv], adj. wirksam (having an effect); gültig (in force); dienstfähig (usable); wirklich (actual).
effectual [i'fektjuəl], adj. wirksam (effective); kräftig, energisch (strong).
effectuate [i'fektjueit], v.a. bewerkstelligen (get done); bewirken (bring about).
effeminacy [i'feminəsi], s. die Verweichlichung.
effeminate [i'feminit], adj. weichlich, verweichlicht.
effervescence [efə'vesəns], s. das Aufbrausen, Schäumen.
effervescent [efə'vesənt], adj. aufbrausend, aufschäumend.

effete [i'fi:t], adj. abgenutzt, erschöpft.
efficacious [efi'keiʃəs], adj. wirksam. energisch.
efficacy ['efikəsi], s. die Wirksamkeit, die Energie.
efficiency [i'fiʃənsi], s. die Tüchtigkeit (of person); die Wirksamkeit; die Leistung.
efficient [i'fiʃənt], adj. tüchtig; leistungsfähig; wirksam (drug etc.).
effigy ['efidʒi], s. das Bild, das Abbild.
efflorescent [eflɔ:'resənt], adj. aufblühend.
effluent ['efluənt], adj. ausfließend.
effluvium [i'flu:viəm], s. die Ausdünstung.
effort ['efət], s. die Anstrengung, die Bemühung; make an —, sich bemühen, sich anstrengen; make every —, alle Kräfte anspannen.
effrontery [i'frʌntəri], s. die Frechheit (cheek); die Unverschämtheit (impertinence).
effortless ['efətlis], adj. mühelos.
effulgence [i'fʌldʒəns], s. der Glanz, das Strahlen.
effulgent [i'fʌldʒənt], adj. schimmernd, strahlend.
effusion [i'fju:ʒən], s. die Ausgießung; der Erguß (verse etc.); der Überschwang.
effusive [i'fju:ziv], adj. überschwenglich.
egg [eg], s. das Ei; fried —, das Spiegelei; scrambled —, das Rührei; — flip, der Eierpunsch; —shell, die Eierschale. — v.a. — on, anspornen, anreizen.
eglantine ['egləntain], s. (Bot.) die wilde Rose.
egoism ['egouizm], s. der Egoismus.
ego(t)ist ['ego(t)ist], s. der Egoist.
egregious [i'gri:dʒəs], adj. ungeheuer(lich).
egress ['i:gres], s. der Ausgang, der Ausfluß (water etc.).
Egyptian [i'dʒipʃən], adj. ägyptisch. — s. der Ägypter.
eiderdown ['aidədaun], s. die Daunendecke, Steppdecke.
eiderduck ['aidədʌk], s. (Orn.) die Eidergans.
eight [eit], num. adj. acht.
eighteen [ei'ti:n], num. adj. achtzehn.
eighty ['eiti], num. adj. achtzig.
either ['aiðə], adj., pron. einer von beiden. — conj. entweder (or, oder).
ejaculate [i'dʒækjuleit], v.a., v.n. ausstoßen.
eject [i'dʒekt], v.a. hinauswerfen; ausstoßen.
ejection [i'dʒekʃən], s. die Ausstoßung.
eke [i:k], v.a. — out, verlängern, ergänzen; — out an existence, ein spärliches Auskommen finden.
elaborate [i'læbəreit], v.a. ausarbeiten, im einzelnen ausarbeiten. — [-rit], adj. detailliert, ausgearbeitet; kunstvoll (intricate); umständlich (involved).

elaboration [ilæbə'reiʃən], s. die Ausarbeitung (im einzelnen); die Detailarbeit.

elapse [i'læps], v.n. verstreichen, verfließen (time).

elastic [i'læstik], adj. elastisch. — s. das Gummiband.

elasticity [elæs'tisiti], s. (Phys.) die Elastizität.

elate [i'leit], v.a. stolz machen; ermutigen.

elated [i'leitid], adj. in gehobener Stimmung.

elation [i'leiʃən], s. der Stolz; die Begeisterung.

elbow ['elbou], s. (Anat.) der Ellenbogen; at o.'s —, bei der Hand; — room, der Spielraum. — v.a. — o.'s way through, sich durchdrängen.

elder (1) ['eldə], comp. adj. älter. — s. der Alte, der Älteste; Kirchenälteste.

elder (2) ['eldə], s. (Bot.) der Holunder.

elderly ['eldəli], adj. älter; alt; ältlich.

elect [i'lekt], v.a. erwählen (to, zu, Dat.); auswählen (choose). — adj. erwählt, auserwählt; chairman —, der gewählte Vorsitzende.

election [i'lekʃən], s. die Auswahl (selection); (Pol.) die Wahlen, f.pl.; die Wahl (choice); by(e) — —, die Bezirkswahl, die Neuwahl; — broadcast, eine Radiowahlrede.

electioneering [ilekʃən'iəriŋ], s. das Wahlmanöver, die Wahlpropaganda, der Wahlkampf.

elective [i'lektiv], adj. durch Wahl bestimmt; Wahl-.

elector [i'lektə], s. (Pol.) der Wähler; das Mitglied eines Wahlausschusses (academic etc.); der Kurfürst (prince).

electorate [i'lektərit], s. die Wählerschaft.

electress [i'lektrəs], s. die Kurfürstin (princess).

electric(al) [i'lektrik(əl)], adj. elektrisch; electrical engineer, adj. der Elektrotechniker; der Student der Elektrotechnik (trainee); electric switch, der elektrische Schalter; — razor, der elektrische Rasierapparat.

electrician [elek'triʃən], s. der Elektriker.

electricity [ilek- or elek'trisiti], s. die Elektrizität.

electrocution [ilektro'kju:ʃən], s. die Hinrichtung or der Unfall (accidental) durch Elektrizität.

electron [i'lektron], s. das Elektron.

electroplate [i'lektropleit], v.a. galvanisch versilbern.

electrotype [i'lektrotaip], s. der galvanische Abdruck, die Galvanographie.

elegance ['eligəns], s. die Eleganz.

elegant ['eligənt], adj. elegant, fein.

elegy ['elidʒi], s. (Lit.) die Elegie.

element ['elimənt], s. das Element; der Bestandteil (component).

elemental [eli'mentl], adj. elementar.

elementary [eli'mentri], adj. einfach (simple); elementar (for beginners).

elephant ['elifənt], s. (Zool.) der Elefant.

elevate ['eliveit], v.a. erheben, erhöhen.

elevation [eli'veiʃən], s. die Erhebung (lifting); (Geom.) die Elevation; die Erhöhung (rise); der Aufriß (Engin. drawing).

elevator ['eliveitə], s. (Am.) der Lift, der Aufzug, der Fahrstuhl; (Agr.) der Getreideheber.

eleven [i'levn], num. adj. elf.

elf [elf], s. der Elf, der Kobold.

elfin ['elfin], adj. Elfen-, elfenhaft.

elicit [i'lisit], v.a. herauslocken, entlocken.

eligibility [elidʒi'biliti], s. die Wählbarkeit.

eligible ['elidʒibl], adj. wählbar, passend.

eliminate [i'limineit], v.a. ausschalten, ausscheiden, eliminieren.

elimination [ilimi'neiʃən], s. die Ausschaltung, die Ausscheidung.

elision [i'liʒən], s. (Phonet.) die Auslassung, die Weglassung.

elixir [i'liksə], s. das Elixier.

elk [elk], s. (Zool.) der Elch.

ell [el], s. die Elle.

ellipse [i'lips], s. (Geom.) die Ellipse.

ellipsis [i'lipsis], s. (Gram.) die Ellipse.

elliptic(al) [i'liptik(əl)], adj. (Gram., Geom.) elliptisch.

elm [elm], s. (Bot.) die Ulme.

elocution [elə'kju:ʃən], s. der Vortrag (delivery); die Vortragskunst.

elocutionist [elə'kju:ʃənist], s. der Vortragskünstler.

elongate ['i:loŋgeit], v.a. verlängern.

elongation [i:loŋ'geiʃən], s. die Verlängerung.

elope [i'loup], v.n. entlaufen, von zu Hause fliehen.

elopement [i'loupmənt], s. das Entlaufen, die Flucht von zu Hause.

eloquence ['eləkwəns], s. die Beredsamkeit.

eloquent ['eləkwənt], adj. beredt, redegewandt.

else [els], adv. sonst, außerdem, anders; or —, sonst . . .; how — ? wie denn sonst? nobody —, sonst niemand; anyone — ? sonst noch jemand? — conj. sonst.

elsewhere [els'wɛə], adv. anderswo; anderswohin.

Elsinore ['elsinɔ:]. Helsingör, n.

elucidate [i'lju:sideit], v.a. erläutern, erklären (to s.o., Dat.).

elucidation [ilju:si'deiʃən], s. die Erläuterung, die Erklärung.

elude [i'lju:d], v.a. ausweichen, entgehen (Dat.).

elusive [i'lju:siv], adj. schwer faßbar, täuschend.

Elysian [i'li:ʒən], adj. elysisch.

emaciate [i'meiʃieit], v.a. abmagern, dünn werden.

emaciation [imeiʃi'eiʃən], s. die Abmagerung.

379

emanate ['emǝneit], v.n. ausgehen, herrühren (*derive*); ausstrahlen (*radiate*).

emancipate [i'mænsipeit], v.a. befreien, emanzipieren.

emancipation [imænsi'peiʃǝn], s. die Emanzipation.

embalm [im'ba:m], v.a. einbalsamieren.

embankment [im'bæŋkmǝnt], s. der Flußdamm, der Eisenbahndamm; die Eindämmung.

embarcation *see* embarkation.

embargo [im'ba:gou], s. die Handelssperre.

embark [im'ba:k], v.a. einschiffen. — v.n. sich einschiffen; — *upon s.th.*, an etwas herangehen, unternehmen.

embarkation [emba:'keiʃǝn], s. die Einschiffung.

embarrass [im'bærǝs], v.a. verlegen machen, in Verlegenheit bringen.

embarrassment [im'bærǝsmǝnt], s. die Verlegenheit.

embassy ['embǝsi], s. (*Pol.*) die Botschaft, die Gesandtschaft.

embed [im'bed], v.a. einbetten.

embellish [im'beliʃ], v.a. verschönern, ausschmücken; ausmalen (*story*).

embers ['embǝz], s. pl. die glühende Asche; die Kohlen, f. pl.; *Ember Days*, (*Eccl.*) die Quatembertage, m. pl.

embezzle [im'bezl], v.a. veruntreuen, unterschlagen.

embitter [im'bitǝ], v.a. verbittern.

emblazon [im'bleizn], v.a. ausmalen, auf ein Schild setzen.

emblem ['emblǝm], s. das Emblem, das Abzeichen.

emblematic(al) [emblǝ'mætik(ǝl)], adj. sinnbildlich, symbolisch.

embodiment [im'bɔdimǝnt], s. die Verkörperung.

embody [im'bɔdi], v.a. verkörpern.

embolden [im'bouldn], v.a. erkühnen, anfeuern, anspornen; *be emboldened*, sich erkühnen.

emboss [im'bɔs], v.a. in getriebener Arbeit verfertigen, prägen.

embossed [im'bɔst], adj. getrieben, in erhabener Arbeit; gestanzt.

embrace [im'breis], v.a. (*fig.*) umarmen, umfassen. — s. die Umarmung.

embrasure [im'breiʒǝ], s. die Schießscharte.

embrocation [embro'keiʃǝn], s. die Einreibung (*act*); (*Pharm.*) die Einreibsalbe.

embroider [im'brɔidǝ], v.a. sticken; verzieren, ausschmücken (*adorn*).

embroidery [im'brɔidǝri], s. die Stickerei; die Verzierung, Ausschmückung (*of story etc.*).

embroil [im'brɔil], v.a. verwickeln.

embryo ['embriou], s. der Keim; Embryo.

embryonic [embri'ɔnik], adj. im Embryostadium, im Werden.

emend [i'mend], v.a. verbessern (*text*), berichtigen.

emendation [i:men'deiʃǝn], s. die Textverbesserung.

emendator ['i:mendeitǝ], s. der Berichtiger.

emerald ['emǝrǝld], s. der Smaragd.

emerge [i'mǝ:dʒ], v.n. auftauchen, hervortreten, an den Tag kommen.

emergence [i'mǝ:dʒǝns], s. das Auftauchen, das Hervortreten.

emergency [i'mǝ:dʒǝnsi], s. der Notfall; die kritische Lage; *in case of* —, im Notfalle; — *exit*, der Notausgang; — *landing*, die Notlandung; — *measures*, Notmaßnahmen; — *brake*, die Notbremse.

emery ['emǝri], s. — *paper*, das Schmirgelpapier.

emetic [i'metik], s. das Brechmittel.

emigrant ['emigrǝnt], s. der Auswanderer.

emigrate ['emigreit], v.n. auswandern.

emigration [emi'greiʃǝn], s. die Auswanderung.

eminence ['eminǝns], s. die Anhöhe; die Eminenz, der hohe Ruf (*fame*); die eminente Stellung, die Autorität (*authority*); *Your Eminence*, Eure Eminenz.

eminent ['eminǝnt], adj. eminent, hervorragend.

emissary ['emisǝri], s. der Abgesandte, der Sendbote.

emission [i'miʃǝn], s. die Aussendung (*sending out*); die Ausstrahlung (*radiation*).

emit [i'mit], v.a. aussenden; ausstrahlen; ausströmen.

emolument [i'mɔljumǝnt], s. das (Neben)einkommen, das Zusatzgehalt, das Honorar (*fee*).

emotion [i'mouʃǝn], s. die Rührung, die Bewegung, das Gefühl, die Gemütsbewegung.

emotional [i'mouʃǝnǝl], adj. gefühlvoll.

emperor ['empǝrǝ], s. der Kaiser.

emphasis ['emfǝsis], s. der Nachdruck.

emphasize ['emfǝsaiz], v.a. betonen.

empire ['empaiǝ], s. das Reich, das Kaiserreich.

empiric(al) [emp'irik(ǝl)], adj. (*Phil.*) empirisch.

empiricism [em'pirisizm], s. (*Phil.*) der Empirizismus.

employ [im'plɔi], v.a. benutzen (*thing*); beschäftigen, anstellen (*person*).

employee [im'plɔii:], s. der Angestellte.

employer [im'plɔiǝ], s. der Arbeitgeber.

employment [im'plɔimǝnt], s. die Beschäftigung, die Arbeit.

emporium [em'pɔ:riǝm], s. der Handelsplatz; (*Naut.*) der Stapelplatz; das Warenhaus (*stores*).

empower [em'pauǝ], v.a. bevollmächtigen.

empress ['empres], s. die Kaiserin.

emptiness ['emptinis], s. die Leere, die Öde.

empty ['empti], adj. leer; — -*headed*, geistlos.

emulate ['emjuleit], *v.a.* nacheifern (*Dat.*).

emulation [emju'leiʃən], *s.* der Wetteifer, das Nacheifern.

emulous ['emjuləs], *adj.* nacheifernd, wetteifernd; eifersüchtig (*jealous*).

emulsion [i'mʌlʃən], *s.* (*Pharm.*) die Emulsion.

enable [i'neibl], *v.a.* befähigen; ermächtigen (*empower*).

enact [i'nækt], *v.a.* (*Pol.*) verordnen; verfügen (*order*); darstellen, aufführen (*on stage*).

enactment [i'næktmənt], *s.* die Verordnung.

enamel [i'næml], *v.a.* emaillieren. — *s.* die Emaille; (*Med.*) der Schmelz.

enamour [i'næmə], *v.a.* verliebt machen.

encamp [in'kæmp], *v.n.* (sich) lagern, das Lager aufschlagen.

encampment [in'kæmpmənt], *s.* das Lager.

encase [in'keis], *v.a.* einschließen, in ein Gehäuse schließen.

encashment [in'kæʃmənt], *s.* (*Comm.*) das Inkasso, die Einkassierung.

enchain [in'tʃein], *v.a.* in Ketten legen, anketten.

enchant [in'tʃɑ:nt], *v.a.* bezaubern.

enchantment [in'tʃɑ:ntmənt], *s.* die Bezauberung; der Zauber (*spell*).

encircle [in'sə:kl], *v.a.* umringen, umkreisen; (*Mil.*) einkreisen.

encirclement [in'sə:klmənt], *s.* die Einkreisung.

enclose [in'klouz], *v.a.* einschließen; einlegen (*in letter*).

enclosure [in'klouʒə], *s.* die Einfriedigung; die Beilage, Einlage (*in letter*).

encompass [in'kʌmpəs], *v.a.* umfassen, umspannen (*comprise*).

encore [ɔŋkɔ:, ɔn'kɔ:], *int.* noch einmal! —*s.* die Wiederholung, Zugabe.

encounter [in'kauntə], *v.a.* treffen; begegnen (*Dat.*). — *s.* das Zusammentreffen.

encourage [in'kʌridʒ], *v.a.* ermutigen; anspornen.

encouragement [in'kʌridʒmənt], *s.* die Ermutigung; die Förderung (*promotion*).

encroach [in'kroutʃ], *v.n.* eingreifen (*interfere*); übergreifen.

encroachment [in'kroutʃmənt], *s.* der Eingriff, der Übergriff.

encrust [in'krʌst], *v.a.* inkrustieren; verkrusten.

encumber [in'kʌmbə], *v.a.* belasten.

encumbrance [in'kʌmbrəns], *s.* die Belastung, das Hindernis.

encyclical [en'siklikl], *s.* das (päpstliche) Rundschreiben, die Enzyklika.

encylopaedia [insaiklo'pi:djə], *s.* das Lexikon, die Enzyklopädie.

encyclopaedic [insaiklo'pi:dik], *adj.* enzyklopädisch.

end [end], *s.* das Ende; der Schluß; das Ziel (*aim*); die Absicht (*intention*); in the —, am Ende, letzten Endes; to

that —, zu dem Zweck; put an — to, einer Sache ein Ende machen; make —s meet, sein Auskommen finden; burn the candle at both —s, seine Kräfte verschwenden. — *v.a.* beenden. — *v.n.* enden, Schluß machen.

ending ['endiŋ], *s.* das Ende (*of play etc.*); (*Gram.*) die Endung.

endanger [in'deindʒə], *v.a.* gefährden, in Gefahr bringen.

endear [in'diə], *v.a.* beliebt machen. — *v.r.* — o.s. to, sich lieb Kind machen bei.

endearment [in'diəmənt], *s.* term of —, ein Kosewort.

endeavour [in'devə], *v.n.* sich bemühen, sich bestreben. — *s.* das Streben, die Bestrebung, die Bemühung.

endemic(al) [en'demik(əl)], *adj.* einheimisch; endemisch.

endive ['endiv], *s.* (*Bot.*) die Endivie.

endless ['endlis], *adj.* unendlich, endlos.

endorse [in'dɔ:s], *v.a.* bestätigen (*confirm*); beipflichten; (*Fin.*) indossieren (*cheque*).

endorsement [in'dɔ:smənt], *s.* die Bestätigung (*confirmation*); (*Fin.*) das Indossament (*cheque*).

endow [en'dau], *v.a.* begaben (*talents*); ausstatten (*equip*); stiften.

endowment [en'daumənt], *s.* die Begabung (*talents*); die Stiftung; — policy, die abgekürzte Lebensversicherung.

endurable [in'djuərəbl], *adj.* erträglich.

endurance [in'djuərəns], *s.* die Ausdauer (*toughness*); die Dauer, Fortdauer (*time*); das Ertragen (*suffering*); — test, die Dauerprüfung; (*fig.*) die Geduldsprobe (*patience*).

endure [in'djuə], *v.a.* aushalten, ertragen; leiden (*suffer*).

endways, endwise ['endweiz, -waiz], *adv.* mit dem Ende nach vorne; aufrecht (*vertical*).

enemy ['enəmi], *s.* der Feind, der Gegner.

energetic [enə'dʒetik], *adj.* energisch, tatkräftig.

energy ['enədʒi], *s.* die Energie, die Tatkraft; der Nachdruck (*vehemence*).

enervate ['enə:veit], *v.a.* entkräften, schwächen.

enervation [enə:'veiʃən], *s.* die Entkräftigung, die Schwächung.

enfeeble [in'fi:bl], *v.a.* entkräften, schwächen.

enfold [in'fould], *v.a.* umschließen, umfassen; einhüllen (*veil*).

enforce [in'fɔ:s], *v.a.* erzwingen, durchsetzen.

enforcement [in'fɔ:smənt], *s.* die Erzwingung, die Durchsetzung.

enfranchise [in'fræntʃaiz], *v.a.* freilassen, befreien (*emancipate*); (*Pol.*) das Stimmrecht geben.

enfranchisement [in'fræntʃizmənt], *s.* die Befreiung, die Gewährung des Stimmrechts.

engage

engage [in'geidʒ], *v.a.* verpflichten, engagieren (*pledge*, *bind*); anstellen (*employ*); verwickeln (*in conversation*); *become* —*d*, sich verloben. — *v.n.* — *in*, sich einlassen in (*Acc.*), sich befassen mit (*Dat.*).

engagement [in'geidʒmənt], *s.* die Verpflichtung (*pledge*); die Verlobung (*betrothal*); die Verabredung (*appointment*); das Gefecht (*with enemy*).

engaging [in'geidʒiŋ], *adj.* freundlich, verbindlich (*smile etc.*); einnehmend.

engender [in'dʒendə], *v.a.* erzeugen, hervorrufen (*cause*).

engine ['endʒin], *s.* die Maschine; der Motor; (*Railw.*) die Lokomotive; *fire* —, die Feuerspritze; — *driver*, (*Railw.*) der Lokomotivführer.

engineer [endʒi'niə], *s.* der Ingenieur (*professional*); der Techniker (*technician*); (*Am.*) der Lokomotivführer (*engine driver*).

engineering [endʒi'niəriŋ], *s.* das Ingenieurwesen; der Maschinenbau; *chemical* —, die chemische Technik or Technologie; *civil* —, das Zivilingenieurwesen; *electrical* —, die Elektrotechnik or die Elektrotechnologie; *mechanical* —, der Maschinenbau, die Strukturtechnik; — *laboratory*, das technische Labor; — *workshop*, die technische Werkstatt.

English ['iŋgliʃ], *adj.* englisch; britisch. — *s.* die englische Sprache, das Englisch; (*pl.*) *the* —, die Engländer, *m.pl.*

Englishman ['iŋgliʃmən], *s.* der Engländer.

Englishwoman ['iŋgliʃwumən], *s.* die Engländerin.

engrain [in'grein], *v.a.* tief einprägen.

engrave [in'greiv], *v.a.* gravieren, eingravieren (*art*); einprägen (*impress*).

engraver [in'greivə], *s.* der Graveur, der Kupferstecher.

engraving [in'greiviŋ], *s.* der Kupferstich.

engross [in'grous], *v.a.* ganz in Anspruch nehmen, gefangen halten(*mind*).

engulf [in'gʌlf], *v.a.* verschlingen.

enhance [in'hɑːns], *v.a.* erhöhen (*raise*), steigern (*increase*).

enhancement [in'hɑːnsmənt], *s.* die Erhöhung (*pleasure*); die Steigerung (*growth*).

enigma [i'nigmə], *s.* das Rätsel.

enigmatic(al) [enig'mætik(əl)], *adj.* rätselhaft (*puzzling*); dunkel (*obscure*).

enjoin [in'dʒɔin], *v.a.* (an)befehlen (*s.o.*, *Dat.*), einschärfen (*s.o.*, *Dat.*).

enjoy [in'dʒɔi], *v.a.* genießen (*Acc.*); sich freuen (über, *Acc.*). — *v.r.* —*o.s.*, sich amüsieren.

enjoyable [in'dʒɔiəbl], *adj.* erfreulich, angenehm, genießbar.

enjoyment [in'dʒɔimənt], *s.* der Genuß, die Freude (*of*, an, *Dat.*).

enlarge [in'lɑːdʒ], *v.a.* vergrößern (*premises etc.*); erweitern (*expand*). —

v.n. sich verbreiten (*on* or *upon*, über, *Acc.*).

enlargement [in'lɑːdʒmənt], *s.* die Vergrößerung (*also Phot.*).

enlighten [in'laitn], *v.a.* erleuchten, aufklären (*explain to*).

enlightenment [in'laitnmənt], *s.* (*Eccl.*) die Erleuchtung;(*Phil.*)die Aufklärung.

enlist [in'list], *v.a.* anwerben (*Mil.*); gewinnen (*cooperation*). — *v.n.* (*Mil.*) sich anwerben lassen.

enliven [in'laivn], *v.a.* beleben, aufmuntern.

enmity ['enmiti], *s.* die Feindschaft.

ennoble [i'noubl], *v.a.* adeln; veredeln.

enormity [i'nɔːmiti], *s.* die Ungeheuerlichkeit.

enormous [i'nɔːməs], *adj.* ungeheuer; ungeheuerlich.

enough [i'nʌf], *adj.*, *adv.* genug; ausreichend; *sure* —, gewiß!; *well* —, ziemlich gut.

enquire *see under* **inquire.**

enquiry *see under* **inquiry.**

enrage [in'reidʒ], *v.a.* wütend machen.

enraged [in'reidʒd], *adj.* wütend, entrüstet.

enrapture [in'ræptʃə], *v.a.* in Entzückung versetzen, entzücken (*delight*).

enrich [in'ritʃ], *v.a.* bereichern; (*Chem.*) verbessern.

enrol [in'roul], *v.a.* einschreiben (*inscribe*); (*Mil.*) anwerben. — *v.n.* sich einschreiben; beitreten (*Dat.*).

enrolment [in'roulmənt], *s.* die Einschreibung; — *form*, das Einschreibeformular.

ensconce [in'skɔns], *v.r.* — *o.s.*, sich niederlassen.

enshrine [in'ʃrain], *v.a.* umhüllen, einschließen (*preserve*); in einem Schrein aufbewahren.

enshroud [in'ʃraud], *v.a.* einhüllen.

ensign ['ensin or 'enzən, 'ensain], *s.* (*Naut.*) die Fahne, die Flagge; (*Mil. rank*) der Fähnrich.

enslave [in'sleiv], *v.a.* unterjochen, versklaven.

ensnare [in'snɛə], *v.a.* umgarnen, verführen (*seduce*).

ensue [in'sjuː], *v.n.* folgen.

ensure [in'ʃuə], *v.a.* versichern (*assure*); sicherstellen (*make sure*).

entail [in'teil], *v.a.* zur Folge haben, mit sich bringen.

entangle [in'tæŋgl], *v.a.* verwickeln, verwirren (*confuse*).

entanglement [in'tæŋglmənt], *s.* die Verwicklung; die Verwirrung (*confusion*).

enter ['entə], *v.a.* betreten; eintreten; — *o.s name*, seinen Namen einschreiben. — *v.n.* eintreten (*in*, in, *Acc.*); — *into agreement*, einen Vertrag eingehen; — *on*, sich einlassen in (*Acc.*); — *upon a career*, eine Laufbahn antreten.

enterprise ['entəpraiz], *s.* das Unternehmen; das Wagnis (*daring*); *private* —, das Privatunternehmen; (*Econ.*)

equal

die freie Wirtschaft; *public* —, das staatliche *or* Staatsunternehmen.

enterprising ['entəpraiziŋ], *adj.* unternehmungslustig.

entertain [entə'tein], *v.a.* unterhalten (*amuse*); zu Tisch haben (*person*); hegen (*opinion*).

entertaining [entə'teiniŋ], *adj.* amüsant, unterhaltend.

entertainment [entə'teinmənt], *s.* die Unterhaltung, Vergnügung.

enthral [in'θrɔːl], *v.a.* fesseln, bannen.

enthrone [in'θroun], *v.a.* auf den Thron bringen *or* setzen.

enthusiasm [in'θjuːziæzm], *s.* die Begeisterung; die Schwärmerei.

enthusiast [in'θjuːziæst], *s.* der Enthusiast, der Schwärmer.

enthusiastic [inθjuːzi'æstik], *adj.* enthusiastisch, begeistert, schwärmerisch.

entice [in'tais], *v.a.* locken, anlocken, verlocken (*lure*).

enticement [in'taismənt], *s.* die Lockung.

entire [in'taiə], *adj.* gesamt, ganz; völlig; vollständig (*complete*).

entirety [in'taiəriti], *s.* die Gesamtheit (*totality*); das Ganze (*total*).

entitle [in'taitl], *v.a.* berechtigen; betiteln (*title*).

entitlement [in'taitlmənt], *s.* die Berechtigung.

entity ['entiti], *s.* das Wesen.

entomb [in'tuːm], *v.a.* begraben.

entomologist [entə'mɔlədʒist], *s.* der Entomologe.

entomology [entə'mɔlədʒi], *s.* die Entomologie.

entrails ['entreilz], *s. pl.* die Eingeweide, *n.pl.*

entrain [in'trein], *v.a.* (*Railw.*, *Mil.*) einsteigen lassen. — *v.n.* (*Railw.*) (in den Zug) einsteigen.

entrance (1) ['entrəns], *s.* der Eingang (*door*); — *fee*, der Eintritt; — *hall*, der Hausflur, die Vorhalle; *university* —, Zulassung zur Universität.

entrance (2) [in'trɑːns], *v.a.* entzücken, hinreißen.

entrant ['entrənt], *s.* (*to school, university etc.*) der (neu) Zugelassene; Teilnehmer.

entrap [in'træp], *v.a.* fangen, verstricken.

entreat [in'triːt], *v.a.* anflehen, ersuchen.

entreaty [in'triːti], *s.* die flehentliche *or* dringende Bitte, (*obs.*) das Ansuchen.

entrench [in'trentʃ], *v.a.* verschanzen, festsetzen.

entrenchment [in'trentʃmənt], *s.* (*Mil.*) die Verschanzung.

entrust [in'trʌst], *v.a.* anvertrauen (*s. th.*); betreuen (*s.o. with*, mit, *Dat.*).

entry ['entri], *s.* das Eintreten, der Eintritt; der Eingang (*house*); (*Comm.*) die Eintragung (*book-keeping*); *double* —, doppelte Buchführung; die Einfuhr (*import*); — *permit*, die

Einreisebewilligung; *no* —, Eintritt verboten!

entwine [in'twain], *v.a.* verflechten, herumwickeln.

enumerate [i'njuːməreit], *v.a.* aufzählen.

enumeration [injuːmə'reiʃən], *s.* die Aufzählung.

enunciate [i'nʌnsieit], *v.a.* aussprechen.

enunciation [inʌnsi'eiʃən], *s.* (*Phonet.*) die Aussprache; die Kundgebung (*declaration*).

envelop [in'veləp], *v.a.* einhüllen, umhüllen.

envelope ['enviloup, 'ɔnvəloup], *s.* die Hülle; der Umschlag, Briefumschlag (*letter*).

enviable ['enviəbl], *adj.* beneidenswert.

envious ['enviəs], *adj.* neidisch (*of s.o.*, auf, *Acc.*).

environment [in'vaiərənmənt], *s.* die Umgebung; (*Geog.*, *Zool.*) die Umwelt.

environs [in'vairənz], *s. pl.* die Umgebung, die Umgegend.

envisage [in'vizidʒ], *v.a.* sich vorstellen.

envoy ['envɔi], *s.* (*Pol.*) der Gesandte, der Bote.

envy ['envi], *s.* der Neid. — *v.a.* beneiden.

epaulette [epɔ'let], *s.* (*Mil.*) das Achselstück, die Epaulette.

ephemeral [i'femərəl], *adj.* Eintags-, Tages-; eintägig, vergänglich (*transient*).

epic ['epik], *adj.* episch. — *s.* das Epos.

epicure ['epikjuə], *s.* der Epikureer, der Feinschmecker, der Genießer.

epidemic [epi'demik], *s.* die Epidemie.

epigram ['epigræm], *s.* das Epigramm.

epigrammatic [epigrə'mætik], *adj.* epigrammatisch, kurz; treffend (*apt*).

epilepsy ['epilepsi], *s.* (*Med.*) die Epilepsie, die Fallsucht.

epileptik [epi'leptik], *s.* (*Med.*) der Epileptiker.

epilogue ['epilɔg], *s.* der Epilog.

Epiphany [i'pifəni], *s.* (*Eccl.*) das Fest der heiligen drei Könige, Epiphanias.

episcopal [i'piskəpəl], *adj.* bischöflich.

episcopate [i'piskəpit], *s.* die Bischofswürde, das Episkopat (*collective*).

episode ['episoud], *s.* die Episode.

epistle [i'pisl], *s.* die Epistel, das Sendschreiben.

epistolary [i'pistələri], *adj.* brieflich, Brief-.

epitaph ['epitɑːf], *s.* die Grabschrift.

epithet ['epiθet], *s.* das Beiwort, die Benennung.

epitome [i'pitəmi], *s.* die Epitome, der Auszug; der Abriß (*summary*).

epitomize [i'pitəmaiz], *v.a.* kürzen; einen Auszug machen von (*Dat.*).

epoch ['iːpɔk], *s.* die Epoche; — *making*, bahnbrechend.

equable ['ekwəbl], *adj.* gleich, gleichmäßig; gleichmütig (*tranquil*).

equal ['iːkwəl], *adj.* gleich, ebenbürtig (*to*, *Dat.*).

383

equality [i'kwɔliti], *s.* die Gleichheit, Ebenbürtigkeit.

equalization [i:kwəlai'zeiʃən], *s.* der Ausgleich; — *of burdens*, der Lastenausgleich.

equalize [i:'kwəlaiz], *v.a.* gleichmachen. — *v.n.* (*Footb.*) ausgleichen.

equanimity [i:kwə'nimiti], *s.* der Gleichmut.

equate [i'kweit], *v.a.* (*Maths.*) gleichsetzen.

equation [i'kweiʃən], *s.* die Gleichung.

equator [i'kweitə], *s.* (*Geog.*)der Äquator.

equatorial [ekwə'tɔ:riəl], *adj.* (*Geog.*) äquatorial.

equerry ['ekwəri], *s.* der Stallmeister; dienstuender Kammerherr (*of King*).

equestrian [i'kwestriən], *adj.* beritten; Reit-; — *art*, die Reitkunst.

equidistant [i:kwi'distənt], *adj.* gleich weit entfernt.

equilateral [i:kwi'lætərəl], *adj.* gleichseitig.

equilibrium [i:kwi'libriəm], *s.* das Gleichgewicht.

equine ['i:kwain], *adj.* Pferd-, pferdeartig.

equinoctial [i:kwi'nɔkʃəl], *adj.* äquinoktial.

equinox ['i:kwinɔks], *s.* die Tag- und Nachtgleiche.

equip [i'kwip], *v.a.* (*Mil.*) ausrüsten; ausstatten (*furnish*).

equipment [i'kwipmənt], *s.* die Ausrüstung, die Ausstattung; das Zeug.

equitable ['ekwitəbl], *adj.* unparteiisch, gerecht, billig.

equity ['ekwiti], *s.* die Billigkeit, die Unparteilichkeit.

equivalence [i'kwivələns], *s.* die Gleichwertigkeit, die Gleichheit.

equivalent [i'kwivələnt], *adj.* gleichwertig. — *s.* das Äquivalent, der gleiche Wert, der Gegenwert.

equivocal [i'kwivəkəl], *adj.* zweideutig, doppelsinnig, zweifelhaft.

era ['iərə], *s.* die Ära, die Zeitrechnung.

eradicate [i'rædikeit], *v.a.* ausrotten, austilgen, vertilgen.

eradication [irædi'keiʃən], *s.* die Ausrottung, die Vertilgung.

erase [i'reiz], *v.a.* ausradieren.

eraser [i'reizə], *s.* der Radiergummi (*India rubber*).

erasure [i'reiʒə], *s.* die Ausradierung; die Auskratzung (*scratching*).

ere [eə], *prep.* (*obs.*) vor. — *conj.* (*obs.*) ehe, bevor.

erect [i'rekt], *adj.* aufrecht, gerade. — *v.a.* aufrichten; errichten (*build*).

erection [i'rekʃən], *s.* die Errichtung (*structure*); die Aufrichtung (*putting up*).

ermine ['ə:min], *s.* der *or* das Hermelin.

erode [i'roud], *v.a.* (*Geog.*, *Geol.*) ausfressen.

erosion [i'rouʒən], *s.* die Erosion.

erotic [i'rɔtik], *adj.* erotisch.

err [ə:], *v.n.* irren.

errand ['erənd], *s.* der Auftrag, Gang;

der Botengang; — *boy*, der Laufbursche.

errant ['erənt], *adj.* herumstreifend; *knight* —, fahrender Ritter.

errata *see under* **erratum**.

erratic [i'rætik], *adj.* regellos, unberechenbar, ohne Verlaß.

erratum [e'reitəm, e'rɑ:təm], *s.* (*pl.* **errata** [e'reitə, e'rɑ:tə]) der Druckfehler.

erroneous [i'rouniəs], *adj.* irrig, irrtümlich.

error ['erə], *s.* der Irrtum, der Fehler.

erudite ['erudait], *adj.* gelehrt.

erudition [eru'diʃən], *s.* die Gelehrsamkeit.

erupt [i'rʌpt], *v.n.* ausbrechen.

eruption [i'rʌpʃən], *s.* der Ausbruch.

eruptive [i'rʌptiv], *adj.* Ausbruchs-, ausbrechend.

escalator ['eskəleitə], *s.* die Rolltreppe.

escapade [eskə'peid], *s.* der Streich (*prank*).

escape [is'keip], *v.a.*, *v.n.* entkommen, entgehen, entfliehen.

escapism [is'keipizm], *s.* die Philosophie der Weltflucht.

escapist [is'keipist], *s.* der Weltflüchtling.

escarpment [is'kɑ:pmənt], *s.* die Böschung.

eschew [is'tʃu:], *v.a.* vermeiden.

escort [is'kɔ:t], *v.a.* geleiten; decken (*cover*). — ['eskɔ:t], *s.* (*Mil.*) die Garde, die Deckung; Begleitung (*persons*); (*Mil.*) das Geleit (*conduct*).

escutcheon [is'kʌtʃən], *s.* das Wappenschild.

esoteric [eso'terik], *adj.* (*Phil.*) esoterisch, geheim, dunkel.

espalier [es'pæljə], *s.* (*Mil.*) das Spalier.

especial [is'peʃəl], *adj.* besonder, außergewöhnlich.

espionage ['espiənɑ:ʒ *or* -nidʒ], *s.* die Spionage, das Spionieren.

espouse [is'pauz], *v.a.* (ver-)heiraten; (*fig.*) eintreten (für, *Acc.*).

espy [is'pai], *v.a.* ausspähen, erspähen.

essay [e'sei], *v.a.* versuchen, probieren. — ['esei], *s.* der Versuch; der Aufsatz, Essay (*composition*).

essayist ['eseiist], *s.* der Essayist.

essence ['esəns], *s.* (*Phil.*, *Chem.*) die Essenz.

essential [i'senʃəl], *adj.* wesentlich; wichtig (*important*).

establish [is'tæbliʃ], *v.a.* feststellen, (*ascertain*); gründen (*found*); —*ed Church*, die englische Staatskirche.

establishment [is'tæbliʃmənt], *s.* die Feststellung (*ascertainment*); die Gründung (*foundation*); die Unternehmung, das Geschäft (*business*); (*Mil.*) die Aufstellung, der Bestand; (*Eccl.*) die Staatskirche.

estate [is'teit], *s.* (*Pol.*) der Stand; das Vermögen, das Gut; (*property*) — *duty*, die Vermögenssteuer; — *manager*, der Gutsverwalter; — *agent*, der

Grundstückmakler; *real —*, der Grundbesitz; (*pl.*) Immobilien, *pl.*

esteem [is'ti:m], *v.a.* schätzen (*value*); achten (*respect*). — *s.* die Wertschätzung, die Achtung.

estimable ['estiməbl], *adj.* schätzenswert.

estimate ['estimeit], *v.a.* schätzen (*evaluate*); berechnen (*calculate*). — ['estimit], *s.* die Schätzung, der Voranschlag.

estimation [esti'meiʃən], *s.* die Wertschätzung; die Achtung (*respect*).

Estonian [es'touniən], *adj.* estnisch, estländisch. — *s.* der Este, Estländer.

estrange [is'treindʒ], *v.a.* entfremden.

estrangement [is'treindʒmənt], *s.* die Entfremdung.

estuary ['estjuəri], *s.* die Mündung (*river*); der Meeresarm (*bay*).

etch [etʃ], *v.a.* (*Metall.*) ätzen; (*Art*) radieren.

etching ['etʃiŋ], *s.* (*Art*) die Radierung.

eternal [i'tə:nl], *adj.* ewig; immerwährend.

eternity [i'tə:niti], *s.* die Ewigkeit.

ether ['i:θə], *s.* der Äther.

ethereal [i'θiəriəl], *adj.* ätherisch, luftig.

ethical ['eθikl], *adj.* ethisch, sittlich.

ethics ['eθiks], *s. pl.* die Ethik, die Sittenlehre; *professional —*, das Berufsethos.

Ethiopian [i:θi'oupiən], *adj.* äthiopisch. — *s.* der Äthiopier.

ethnography [eθ'nɔgrəfi], *s.* die Ethnographie, die Völkerkunde.

etymology [eti'mɔlədʒi], *s.* die Etymologie, die Wortableitung.

eucharist ['ju:kərist], *s.* (*Eccl.*) die Eucharistie; das heilige Abendmahl.

eulogize ['ju:lədʒaiz], *v.a.* loben, preisen.

euphonium [ju'founiəm], *s.* (*Mus.*) das Bombardon, Baritonhorn.

euphony ['ju:fəni], *s.* der Wohlklang.

European [juərə'piən], *adj.* europäisch. — *s.* der Europäer.

euphemism ['ju:fimizm], *s.* der Euphemismus.

euphuism ['ju:fjuizm], *s.* (*Lit.*) die gezierte Stilart.

evacuate [i'vækjueit], *v.a.* evakuieren, räumen.

evacuation [ivækju'eiʃən], *s.* die Evakuierung, die Räumung.

evade [i'veid], *v.a.* ausweichen (*Dat.*); entgehen (*escape, Dat.*).

evanescent [evæ'nesənt], *adj.* verschwindend.

evangelical [i:væn'dʒelikəl], *adj.* evangelisch.

evangelist [i'vændʒəlist], *s.* der Evangelist.

evangelize [i'vændʒəlaiz], *v.a., v.n.* das Evangelium lehren *or* predigen.

evaporate [i'væpəreit], *v.a.* verdunsten lassen, verdampfen lassen. — *v.n.* (*Chem.*) verdunsten.

evaporation [ivæpə'reiʃən], *s.* die Verdampfung, die Verdunstung.

evasion [i'veiʒən], *s.* die Flucht (*escape*) (*from*, von, *Dat.*); die Ausflucht, das Ausweichen.

evasive [i'veiziv], *adj.* ausweichend.

eve, even (1) [i:v,i:vn], *s.* (*Poet.*) der Vorabend; Abend.

even (2) [i:vn], *adj.* eben, glatt (*smooth*); gerade (*number*); quitt (*quits*); gelassen (*temper*); gleich (*equal*). — *v.a. — out*, gleichmachen, ebnen.

even (3) [i:vn], *adv.* gerade, selbst, sogar (*emphatic*); *not —*, nicht einmal; — *though*, obwohl.

evening ['i:vniŋ], *s.* der Abend; — *gown*, das Abendkleid; — *dress*, der Abendanzug; der Smoking (*dinner jacket*); der Frack (*tails*).

evenness ['i:vənnis], *s.* die Ebenheit (*of surface*); die Gelassenheit (*of temper*).

event [i'vent], *s.* die Begebenheit, der Vorfall (*happening*); das (große) Ereignis (*state occasion*); *at all —s*, auf alle Fälle; *in the —*, im Falle, daß.

eventful [i'ventful], *adj.* ereignisreich.

eventual [i'ventjuəl], *adj.* schließlich, endlich.

ever ['evə], *adv.* je; immer, stets; nur, überhaupt; *for —*, für immer; — *so*, so sehr, sehr; — *since*, seitdem.

evergreen ['evəgri:n], *adj.* immergrün. — *s.* (*Bot.*) das Immergrün.

everlasting [evə'la:stiŋ], *adj.* ewig; dauernd; fortwährend (*continual*).

every ['evri], *adj.* jeder, jeder einzelne (*pl.* alle); — *one*, jeder einzelne; — *now and then*, dann und wann; — *other day*, jeden zweiten Tag; — *day*, alle Tage.

everybody, everyone ['evribɔdi, 'evriwʌn], *s.* jedermann, ein jeder.

everyday ['evridei], *adj.* alltäglich.

everyone *see under* **everybody**.

everything ['evriθiŋ], *s.* alles.

everywhere ['evrihweə], *adv.* überall.

evict [i'vikt], *v.a.* vertreiben (*eject*); (*Law*) (gerichtlich) kündigen (*Dat.*).

eviction [i'vikʃən], *s.* die Kündigung, die Vertreibung.

evidence ['evidəns], *s.* der Beweis (*proof*); (*Law*) das Zeugnis; *documentary —*, (*Law*) das Beweisstück; (*Law*) *give —*, eine Zeugenaussage machen.

evident ['evidənt], *adj.* klar, deutlich (*obvious*); augenscheinlich (*visible*); *self-*, selbstverständlich.

evil ['i:vil], *s.* das Übel, das Böse. — *adj.* übel, böse; — *speaking*, die üble Nachrede.

evildoer ['i:vildu:ə], *s.* der Übeltäter.

evince [i'vins], *v.a.* zeigen, dartun, an den Tag legen.

evocation [i:vo'keiʃən], *s.* die Beschwörung (*magic*); das Hervorrufen.

evocative [i'vɔkətiv], *adj.* hervorrufend, voll Erinnerungen (*of, Genit.*).

evoke [i'vouk], *v.a.* hervorrufen (*call forth*); beschwören (*conjure up*).

evolution [i:və'lju:ʃən, ev-], *s.* die Entwicklung, Evolution.

evolutionary

evolutionary [i:və'lju:fənri], adj. Evolutions-, Entwicklungs-.

evolve [i'vɔlv], v.a. entwickeln. — v.n. sich entwickeln.

ewe [ju:], s. (Zool.) das Mutterschaf.

ewer ['juə], s. die Wasserkanne.

exact [ig'zækt], adj. genau, gewissenhalf, exakt. — v.a. fordern; erpressen; eintreiben (dept.).

exacting [ig'zæktiŋ], adj. genau, anspruchsvoll.

exactitude [ig'zæktitju:d], s. die Genauigkeit.

exactly [ig'zæktli], adv. (coll.) ganz richtig!

exactness [ig'zæktnis], s. die Genauigkeit.

exaggerate [ig'zædʒəreit], v.a. übertreiben.

exaggeration [igzædʒə'reifən], s. die Übertreibung.

exalt [ig'zɔ:lt], v.a. erhöhen, erheben.

exaltation [egzɔ:l'teifən], s. die Erhöhung, die Erhebung.

exalted [ig'zɔ:ltid], adj. erhaben, hoch.

examination [igzæmi'neifən], s. die Prüfung; (Med.) die Untersuchung; (Law) das Verhör, das Untersuchungsverhör; die Ausfragung (scrutiny); — board, die Prüfungskommission.

examine [ig'zæmin], v.a. prüfen; (Med.) untersuchen; (Law) verhören; ausfragen.

examiner [ig'zæminə], s. der Examinator.

example [ig'zɑ:mpl], s. das Beispiel; for —, zum Beispiel; set an —, ein Beispiel geben.

exasperate [ig'zæspəreit], v.a. aufreizen; ärgern, aufbringen.

exasperation [igzæspə'reifən], s. die Entrüstung, die Erbitterung.

excavate ['ekskəveit], v.a. ausgraben.

excavation [ekskə'veifən], s. die Ausgrabung.

exceed [ik'si:d], v.a. überschreiten (go beyond); übertreffen (surpass). — v.n. zu weit gehen.

exceeding [ik'si:diŋ], adj. (obs.) übermäßig, übertrieben.

exceedingly [ik'si:diŋli], adv. außerordentlich; äußerst.

excel [ik'sel], v.a. übertreffen. — v.n. sich auszeichnen (in, in, Dat.).

excellence ['eksələns], s. die Vortrefflichkeit.

excellent ['eksələnt], adj. ausgezeichnet, hervorragend.

except [ik'sept], v.a. ausnehmen, ausschließen. — conj. außer (es sei denn) daß. — prep. ausgenommen, mit Ausnahme von (Dat.).

exception [ik'sepfən], s. die Ausnahme (exemption); der Einwand, Einwurf (objection).

exceptionable [ik'sepfənəbl], adj. anfechtbar (disputable); anstößig.

exceptional [ik'sepfənəl], adj. außergewöhnlich.

exceptionally [ik'sepfənəli], adv. ausnahmsweise.

excerpt [ik'sə:pt], v.a. ausziehen, exzerpieren. — ['eksə:pt], s. der Auszug, das Exzerpt.

excess [ik'ses], s. das Übermaß; carry to —, übertreiben; — fare, der Zuschlag; — luggage, das Übergewicht.

excessive [ik'sesiv], adj. übermäßig, allzuviel.

exchange [iks'tfeindʒ], s. der Austausch; stock —, die Börse; rate of —, der Kurs; bill of —, der Wechsel; der Tausch (barter). — v.a. wechseln; tauschen (barter) (against, für, Acc.); austauschen (messages etc.).

exchangeable [iks'tfeindʒəbl], adj. (Comm.) austauschbar.

exchequer [iks'tfekə], s. die Staatskasse; das Finanzamt (office); Chancellor of the Exchequer, der Schatzkanzler.

excise (1) ['eksaiz], s. die Aksize; customs and —, das Zollamt, der Zoll; — officer, der Zollbeamte, Steuerbeamte.

excise (2) [ek'saiz], v.a. (her)ausschneiden.

excision [ek'siʒən], s. das Ausschneiden, die Entfernung.

excitable [ik'saitəbl], adj. erregbar, reizbar.

excitation [eksi'teifən], s. (Phys., Chem.) die Erregung.

excitement [ik'saitmənt], s. die Erregung, Aufregung (mood).

exciting [ik'saitiŋ], adj. erregend, aufregend, packend (thrilling).

exclaim [iks'kleim], v.a. ausrufen.

exclamation [eksklə'meifən], s. der Ausruf (interjection); das Geschrei (shouting).

exclude [iks'klu:d], v.a. ausschließen.

exclusion [iks'klu:ʒən], s. der Ausschluß.

exclusive [iks'klu:siv], adj. ausschließlich (sole); exklusiv (select).

exclusiveness [iks'klu:sivnis], s. der exklusive Charakter, die Exklusivität.

excommunicate [ekskə'mju:nikeit], v.a. (Eccl.) von der Kirchengemeinde ausschließen, bannen, exkommunizieren.

excommunication [ekskəmju:ni'keifən], s. (Eccl.) die Exkommunikation, der Bann.

excoriate [eks'kɔ:rieit], v.a. häuten; abschälen (peel).

excrement ['ekskrimənt], s. das Exkrement, der Kot.

excrescence [iks'kresəns], s. der Auswuchs.

excretion [eks'kri:fən], s. die Ausscheidung, der Auswurf.

excruciate [iks'kru:fieit], v.a. martern, peinigen; excruciatingly funny, furchtbar komisch.

exculpate ['ekskʌlpeit], v.a. rechtfertigen, entschuldigen.

expenditure

exculpation [ekskʌl'peiʃən], *s.* die Entschuldigung, die Rechtfertigung.
excursion [iks'kə:ʃən], *s.* der Ausflug, die Exkursion (*outing*); die Digression (*irrelevance*); der Abstecher (*deviation*).
excusable [iks'kju:zəbl], *adj.* entschuldbar, verzeihlich.
excuse [iks'kju:s], *s.* die Entschuldigung. — [–'kju:z], *v.a.* entschuldigen (*Acc.*), verzeihen (*Dat.*).
execrable ['eksikrəbl], *adj.* abscheulich.
execrate ['eksikreit], *v.a.* verfluchen, verwünschen.
execute ['eksikju:t], *v.a.* ausführen (*carry out*); (*Law*) hinrichten (*kill*).
execution [eksi'kju:ʃən], *s.* die Ausführung (*of an order*); (*Law*) die Hinrichtung; die Pfändung (*official forfeit*).
executioner [eksi'kju:ʃənə], *s.* der Henker, der Scharfrichter.
executive [ik'sekjutiv], *adj.* ausübend, vollziehend (*of power etc.*). — *s.* (*Pol.*) die Exekutive; (*Comm.*) das Direktionsmitglied.
executor [ik'sekjutə], *s.* der Testamentsvollstrecker (*of a will*).
exemplar [ig'zemplɑ], *s.* das Muster, das Beispiel.
exemplary [ig'zempləri], *adj.* musterhaft, vorbildlich.
exemplify [ig'zemplifai], *v.a.* durch Beispiel(e) erläutern.
exempt [ig'zempt], *v.a.* ausnehmen, befreien, verschonen (*spare*).
exemption [ig'zempʃən], *s.* die Ausnahme.
exequies ['eksikwiz], *s. pl.* das Leichenbegängnis, die Totenfeier.
exercise ['eksəsaiz], *s.* die Übung (*practice*); die körperliche Betätigung (*exertion*). — *v.a.* üben; — *o.'s rights*, von seinen Rechten Gebrauch machen; — *discretion*, Diskretion walten lassen; (*Mil.*) — *troops*, exerzieren.
exert [ig'zə:t], *v.a.* ausüben; — *pressure*, Druck ausüben (*upon*, auf, *Acc.*). — *v.r.* — *o.s.*, sich anstrengen.
exertion [ig'zə:ʃən], *s.* die Anstrengung, die Bemühung.
exhale [eks'heil], *v.a.* ausatmen; aushauchen; ausdünsten.
exhalation [eksha'leiʃən], *s.* die Ausatmung, die Ausdünstung.
exhaust [ig'zə:st], *v.a.* erschöpfen. — *s.* (*Motor.*) der Auspuff.
exhaustible [ig'zə:stibl], *adj.* erschöpflich.
exhaustion [ig'zə:stʃən], *s.* die Erschöpfung.
exhibit [ig'zibit], *v.a.* ausstellen (*display*); zeigen (*demonstrate*). — ['eksibit], *s.* das Ausstellungsobjekt; (*Law*) das Beweisstück.
exhibition [eksi'biʃən], *s.* die Ausstellung (*display*); (*Films*) die Vorführung (*showing*); das Stipendium (*scholarship*).

exhibitioner [eksi'biʃənə], *s.* der Stipendiat.
exhilarate [ig'ziləreit], *v.a.* aufheitern.
exhilaration [igzilə'reiʃən], *s.* die Aufheiterung.
exhort [ig'zə:t], *v.a.* ermahnen.
exhortation [egzə:'teiʃən], *s.* die Ermahnung.
exigence, exigency ['eksidʒəns, -si], *s.* das Bedürfnis, Erfordernis (*necessity*); der dringende Notfall (*emergency*).
exigent ['eksidʒənt], *adj.* dringend.
exile ['eksail], *s.* der Verbannte (*person*); das Exil, die Verbannung (*state*). — *v.a.* verbannen; des Landes verweisen.
exist [ig'zist], *v.n.* existieren.
existence [ig'zistəns], *s.* das Dasein, die Existenz.
existent [ig'zistənt], *adj.* seiend, wirklich, existierend.
existentialism [egzis'tenʃəlizm], *s.* der Existentialismus.
exit ['eksit], *s.* der Ausgang; (*Theat.*) der Abgang.
exonerate [ig'zonəreit], *v.a.* entlasten.
exorbitant [ig'zə:bitənt], *adj.* übertrieben, übermäßig.
exorcise ['eksə:saiz], *v.a.* bannen, beschwören.
exorcism ['eksə:sizm], *s.* die Geisterbeschwörung.
exotic [ig'zotik], *adj.* exotisch.
expand [iks'pænd], *v.a.* erweitern, ausbreiten, ausdehnen. — *v.n.* sich erweitern (*broaden*); sich ausdehnen (*stretch*).
expansion [iks'pænʃən], *s.* die Ausdehnung, die Ausbreitung.
expansive [iks'pænsiv], *adj.* ausgedehnt; Ausdehnungs- (*forces*); (*fig.*) mitteilsam.
expatiate [iks'peiʃieit], *v.n.* sich verbreiten (*on*, über, *Acc.*).
expatriate [eks'peitrieit], *v.a.* verbannen.
expect [iks'pekt], *v.a.* erwarten (*wait for*); glauben (*believe*); hoffen (*hope for*); — *a baby*, ein Kind erwarten.
expectant [iks'pektənt], *adj.* schwanger (*with child*); voll Erwartung.
expectation [ekspek'teiʃən], *s.* die Erwartung, die Hoffnung.
expedience, expediency [iks'pi:diəns, -si], *s.* die Zweckmäßigkeit, die Schicklichkeit.
expedient [iks'pi:diənt], *adj.* zweckmäßig, schicklich, ratsam. — *s.* das Mittel; der Ausweg.
expedite ['ekspidait], *v.a.* beschleunigen.
expedition [ekspi'diʃən], *s.* (*Mil. etc.*) die Expedition; die schnelle Abfertigung.
expeditious [ekspi'diʃəs], *adj.* schleunig, schnell.
expel [iks'pel], *v.a.* vertreiben, austreiben; (*Sch.*) verweisen (*from*, von, aus).
expend [iks'pend], *v.a.* ausgeben.
expenditure [iks'penditʃə], *s.* (*Comm.*) die Ausgabe; der Aufwand (*of energy*).

expense [iks'pens], *s.* die Ausgabe; *(pl.)* die Kosten, Auslagen, Spesen, *f. pl.*

expensive [iks'pensiv], *adj.* teuer, kostspielig.

experience [iks'piəriəns], *s.* die Erfahrung, das Erlebnis. — *v.a.* erfahren.

experienced [iks'piəriənsd], *adj.* erfahren.

experiment [iks'perimənt], *s.* das Experiment, der Versuch. — *v.n.* experimentieren, Versuche machen.

experimental [iksperi'mentl], *adj.* Probe-, probeweise, experimentell.

expert ['ekspə:t], *s.* der Fachmann; der Sachverständige.

expertise [ekspə'ti:z], *s.* die Expertise, die Fachkenntnis.

expertness [iks'pə:tnis], *s.* die Gewandtheit.

expiable ['ekspiəbl], *adj.* sühnbar.

expiation [ekspi'eiʃən], *s.* die Sühnung, die Sühne.

expiration [ekspi'reiʃən], *s.* das Ausatmen; *(fig.)* der Tod; der Ablauf *(time)*; die Verfallszeit *(lapse of validity)*.

expire [iks'paiə], *v.n.* aushauchen *(breathe)*; ablaufen *(run out)*; sterben *(die)*.

expiry [iks'pairi], *s.* die Ablaufsfrist *(of papers)*.

explain [iks'plein], *v.a.* erklären, erläutern.

explanation [eksplə'neiʃən], *s.* die Erklärung, Erläuterung.

expletive [iks'pli:tiv], *s.* das Fluchwort, der Kraftausdruck.

explicable ['eksplikəbl], *adj.* erklärlich, erklärbar.

explication [ekspli'keiʃən], *s.* die Erklärung.

explicit [iks'plisit], *adj.* ausdrücklich, deutlich.

explicitness [iks'plisitnis], *s.* die Deutlichkeit, die Bestimmtheit.

explode [iks'ploud], *v.n.* explodieren; *(Mil.)* platzen *(of a shell)*. — *v.a.* explodieren lassen.

exploit [iks'plɔit], *v.a.* ausbeuten; ausnützen *(utilize)*. — ['eksplɔit], *s.* die Heldentat, die Großtat.

exploitation [eksplɔi'teiʃən], *s.* die Ausbeutung, die Ausnützung.

exploration [eksplɔ:'reiʃən], *s.* die Erforschung.

explore [iks'plɔ:], *v.a.* erforschen, untersuchen *(investigate)*.

explosion [iks'plouʒən], *s.* die Explosion.

explosive [iks'plousiv], *adj.* explosiv. — *s.* der Sprengstoff.

exponent [iks'pounənt], *s.* *(Maths.)* der Exponent; der Vertreter *(of a theory)*.

export [eks'pɔ:t], *v.a.* ausführen, exportieren. — ['ekspɔ:t], *s.* der Export, die Ausfuhr.

exporter [eks'pɔ:tə], *s.* der Exporteur, der Ausfuhrhändler, der Exportkaufmann.

expose [iks'pouz], *v.a.* entblößen; aussetzen *(to cold etc.)*; bloßstellen *(display)*; *(Phot.)* belichten; darlegen *(set forth)*; ausstellen *(exhibit)*.

exposition [ekspo'ziʃən], *s.* die Aussetzung; die Auslegung *(interpretation)*; die Darlegung *(deposition, declaration)*; die Ausstellung *(exhibition)*.

exposure [iks'pouʒə], *s.* die Aussetzung *(to cold etc.)*; die Bloßstellung; *(Phot.)* die Belichtung.

expostulate [iks'pɔstjuleit], *v.n.* zur Rede stellen.

expound [iks'paund], *v.a.* auslegen, darlegen.

express [iks'pres], *v.a.* ausdrücken; zum Ausdruck bringen. — *adj.* ausdrücklich, eilig, Eil-; besonder; — *letter,* der Eilbrief; — *train,* der Schnellzug. — *s.* der Eilzug.

expression [iks'preʃən], *s.* der Ausdruck.

expressive [iks'presiv], *adj.* ausdrucksvoll.

expressly [iks'presli], *adv.* ausdrücklich, besonders.

expropriate [eks'prouprieit], *v.a.* enteignen.

expropriation [eksproupri'eiʃən], *s.* die Enteignung.

expulsion [iks'pʌlʃən], *s.* die Ausstoßung; der Ausschluß; die Vertreibung *(of a large number)*.

expunge [iks'pʌndʒ], *v.a.* austilgen, auslöschen.

expurgate ['ekspə:geit], *v.a.* reinigen.

exquisite ['ekskwizit], *adj.* auserlesen, vortrefflich.

extant ['ekstənt, ek'stænt], *adj.* noch vorhanden, existierend.

extempore [eks'tempəri], *adv.* aus dem Stegreif, extemporiert.

extemporize [eks'tempəraiz], *v.a.* extemporieren, improvisieren.

extend [iks'tend], *v.a.* ausdehnen *(boundaries etc.)*; ausstrecken *(a helping hand)*; verlängern *(time)*; bieten *(a welcome)*; erweitern *(enlarge)*. — *v.n.* sich erstrecken; dauern *(time)*.

extensible [iks'tensibl], *adj.* ausdehnbar.

extension [iks'tenʃən], *s.* die Ausdehnung; die Verlängerung *(time)*; *university* — *classes,* Abendkurse, *m.pl.* (der Erwachsenenbildung); *(Telephone)* der Apparat.

extensive [iks'tensiv], *adj.* ausgedehnt, umfassend.

extent [iks'tent], *s.* die Ausdehnung, die Weite; die Größe *(size)*; *to a certain* —, bis zu einem gewissen Grade; *to the* — *of £x,* bis zu einem Betrage von x Pfund.

extenuate [iks'tenjueit], *v.a.* beschönigen; mildern; *extenuating circumstances,* *(Law)* mildernde Umstände, *m. pl.*

extenuation [ikstenju'eiʃən], *s.* die Beschönigung, die Abschwächung.

factor

exterior [eks'tiəriə], *adj.* äußerlich. —
s. das Äußere.
exterminate [iks'tə:mineit], *v.a.* ausrotten, vertilgen.
extermination [iksto:mi'neiʃən], *s.* die
Ausrottung, die Vertilgung.
external [eks'tə:nl], *adj.* äußerlich;
auswärtig.
extinct [eks'tiŋkt], *adj.* ausgestorben.
extinction [iks'tiŋkʃən], *s.* das Erlöschen
(*dying*); die Vernichtung (*annihilation*); das Aussterben.
extinguish [iks'tiŋgwiʃ]. *v.a.* auslöschen; vernichten (*annihilate*). — *v.n.*
auslöschen, ausgehen (*of fire or life*).
extirpate ['eksto:peit], *v.a.* ausrotten.
extol [iks'toul], *v.a.* preisen, erheben.
extort [iks'to:t], *v.a.* erpressen.
extortion [iks'to:ʃən], *s.* die Erpressung.
extortionate [iks'to:ʃənit], *adj.* erpres-
serisch.
extra ['ekstrə], *adj.* zusätzlich. — *s.*
(*pl.*) die Nebenausgaben, *f. pl.*
extract [iks'trækt], *v.a.* (aus)ziehen
(*pull out*). — ['ekstrækt], *s.* (*Chem.*)
der Extrakt; der Auszug (*book*).
extraction [iks'trækʃən], *s.* das Ausziehen (*pulling out*); das Zahnziehen
(*tooth*); das Verfertigen eines Aus-
zuges (*book*); die Herkunft (*origin*).
extradite ['ekstrədait], *v.a.* (*Pol.*)
ausliefern.
extradition [ekstrə'diʃən], *s.* (*Pol.*) die
Auslieferung.
extraneous [eks'treiniəs], *adj.* nicht zur
Sache gehörig, unwesentlich.
extraordinary [iks'tro:dnəri], *adj.*
außerordentlich.
extravagance [iks'trævəgəns], *s.* die
Extravaganz; die Verschwendung
(*waste*).
extravagant [iks'trævəgənt], *adj.* extravagant; verschwenderisch.
extravaganza [ikstrævə'gænzə], *s.* fan-
tastisches Werk, die Burleske, Posse.
extreme [iks'tri:m], *adj.* äußerst (*utter-
most*); höchst (*highest*); extrem (*stringent*); letzt (*last*); — *unction* (*Eccl.*)
die Letzte Ölung; *in the* —, äußerst.
extremity [iks'tremiti], *s.* die äußerste
Grenze (*limit*); die Notlage (*straits,
emergency*); (*pl.*) die Extremitäten,
f. pl.
extricate ['ekstrikeit],*v.a.*herauswinden,
herauswickeln (*disentangle*), befreien.
extrude [eks'tru:d], *v.a.* ausstoßen,
(*Metall.*) auspreßen.
extrusion [eks'tru:ʒən], *s.* die Ausstoßung; die Ausziehung (*of steel etc.*).
exuberant [ig'zju:bərənt], *adj.* überschwenglich, überschäumend.
exude [ik'sju:d], *v.a.* ausschwitzen;
von sich geben (*give out*).
exult [ig'zʌlt], *v.n.* frohlocken.
exultant [ig'zʌltənt],*adj.*triumphierend.
exultation [egzʌl'teiʃən], *s.* das Frohlocken, der Jubel.
eye [ai], *v.a.* ansehen, betrachten. — *s.*
das Auge; — *of a needle*, das Nadelöhr; *an — for an —*, Aug' um Auge;
— *witness*, der Augenzeuge.

eyeball ['aibɔ:l], *s.* der Augapfel.
eyebrow ['aibrau], *s.* die Augenbraue.
eyeglass ['aiglɑ:s], *s.* der Zwicker,
Klemmer.
eyelash ['ailæʃ], *s.* die Augenwimper.
eyelid ['ailid], *s.* das Augenlid.
eyesight ['aisait], *s.* die Sehkraft, das
Augenlicht.
eyrie ['ɛəri, 'iəri], *s.* der Adlerhorst.

F

F [ef].das F (*also Mus.*).
fable [feibl], *s.* die Fabel; das Märchen.
fabric['fæbrik], *s.*das Gewebe, der Stoff.
fabricate ['fæbrikeit], *v.a.* herstellen;
(*fig.*) fabrizieren; erfinden.
fabrication [fæbri'keiʃən], *s.* (*fig.*) die
Erdichtung, die Erfindung.
fabulous ['fæbjuləs], *adj.* fabelhaft;
wunderbar.
façade [fə'sɑ:d], *s.* die Fassade.
face [feis], *v.a.* jemandem ins Gesicht
sehen (*s.o.*); gegenüberstehen, gegen-
überliegen (*lie opposite, Dat.*); —
west, nach Westen gehen (*of house,
window*). — *v.n.* — *about*, sich umdrehen; — *the* — (*Poet.*) das
Angesicht; — *to* — *with*, gegenüber
(*Dat.*); *on the* — *of it*, auf den ersten
Blick; *lose* —, sich blamieren; *have
the* — *to*, die Frechheit haben etwas
zu tun.
facet ['fæsit], *s.* die Facette; der Zug
(*feature*).
facetious [fə'si:ʃəs], *adj.* scherzhaft.
facetiousness [fə'si:ʃəsnis], *s.* die
Scherzhaftigkeit, die Witzigkeit.
facile ['fæsail], *adj.* leicht.
facilitate [fə'siliteit], *v.a.* erleichtern,
leicht machen.
facility [fə'siliti], *s.* die Leichtigkeit
(*ease*); die Gewandtheit (*deftness*); die
Möglichkeit (*possibility*); (*pl.*) die
Einrichtungen, die Möglichkeiten, *f.
pl.* (*amenities*).
facing ['feisiŋ], *s.* (*Tail.*) der Besatz, der
Aufschlag; (*Build.*) die Verkleidung;
(*Mil.*) die Schwenkung, die Wendung.
facsimile [fæk'simili], *s.* das Faksimile.
fact [fækt], *s.* die Tatsache; *as a matter
of* —, tatsächlich, in Wirklichkeit; —*s
and figures*, der Bericht mit Tatsachen
und Zahlen; *in* —, tatsächlich; *in
point of* —, in der Tat, in Wirklichkeit.
faction ['fækʃən], *s.* (*Pol.*) die Partei,
die Faktion.
factitious [fæk'tiʃəs], *adj.* nachgemacht,
künstlich.
factor ['fæktə], *s.* der Faktor; (*Comm.*)
der Agent; der Umstand (*fact*).

389

factory ['fæktəri], s. die Fabrik; — **hand**, der Fabrikarbeiter.

factual ['fæktjuəl], adj. Tatsachen-, tatsächlich.

faculty ['fækəlti], s. (Univ.) die Fakultät; die Fähigkeit (sense); (pl.) die Talente, n. pl., die Begabung; Kräfte f. pl.

fad [fæd], s. die Grille, die Laune; die Marotte.

faddy ['fædi], adj. schrullig.

fade [feid], v.n. verschießen (colour); verwelken (flower); vergehen.

fag [fæg], v.a. ermüden. — v.n. (Sch.) Dienste tun, Diener sein (for, für). — s. die Plackerei; (coll.) die Zigarette; (Sch.) der Fuchs, der neue Schüler; — **end**, der Zigarettenstummel; (Naut.) das offene Tauende; der letzte Rest (remnant).

faggot ['fægət], s. das Reisigbündel.

fail [feil], v.a. im Stiche lassen (let down); (Sch.) durchfallen (an examination, in einer Prüfung. — v.n. — to do, etwas nicht tun, fehlgehen, scheitern; versagen.

failing ['feiliŋ], adj. schwach, versagend. — s. der Mangel, Fehler.

failure ['feiljə], s. der Fehlschlag; das Versagen (weakness); das Nichteinhalten (non-compliance); das Durchfallen (in examinations); der Versager (person).

fain [fein], adv. (obs.) gern, gerne.

faint [feint], v.n. in Ohnmacht fallen, ohnmächtig werden. — adj. leise, schwach (noise etc.); — **hearted**, kleinmütig.

fair (1) [fɛə], adj. hübsch, schön (beautiful); unparteiisch, fair (impartial); anständig, angemessen (equitable); blond.

fair (2) [fɛə], s. der Jahrmarkt (market); (Comm.) die Messe, die Handelsmesse.

fairness ['fɛənis], s. die Schönheit (beauty); die Unparteilichkeit, Fairneß (objectivity); die Sportlichkeit (sportsmanship); die Anständigkeit (equity).

fairy ['fɛəri], s. die Fee.

faith [feiθ], s. der Glaube; die Treue (loyalty); das Vertrauen (trust).

faithful ['feiθful], adj. (Rel.) gläubig; treu (loyal); ergeben (devoted).

faithless ['feiθlis], adj. (Rel.) ungläubig; treulos, untreu (disloyal).

fake [feik], s. der Schwindel.

falcon ['fɔ:(l)kən], s. (Orn.) der Falke.

falconer ['fɔ:(l)knə], s. der Falkner.

falconry ['fɔ:(l)kənri], s. die Falknerei.

fall [fɔ:l], v.n. irr. fallen, abfallen (leaves); einbrechen (night); sich legen (wind); heruntergehen, sinken (price); geboren werden (pigs, lambs); — **through**, mißlingen, zunichte werden. — s. der Fall; (Am.) der Herbst (autumn); der Abhang (precipice); der Verfall (decay); der Untergang (decline).

fallacious [fə'leiʃəs], adj. trügerisch, trüglich, falsch (assumption etc.).

fallacy ['fæləsi], s. die Täuschung, der Irrtum, Trugschluß.

fallible ['fælibl], adj. fehlbar.

falling ['fɔ:liŋ], s. das Fallen; — sickness, die Fallsucht; — off, das Abnehmen (decrease); — out, der Zwist, der Streit (disunity). — adj. — star, die Sternschnuppe.

fallow ['fælou], adj. brach, fahl.

false [fɔ:ls], adj. falsch, unrichtig (untrue); — alarm, der blinde Alarm; — bottom, der Doppelboden; — start, der Fehlstart; — step, der Fehltritt; — verdict, das Fehlurteil; — pretences, die Vorspiegelung falscher Tatsachen.

falsehood ['fɔ:lshud], s. die Lüge, die Unwahrheit.

falseness ['fɔ:lsnis], s. die Falschheit; die Unaufrichtigkeit (insincerity).

falsify ['fɔ:lsifai], v.a. fälschen, verfälschen.

falsity ['fɔ:lsiti] see falseness.

falter ['fɔ:ltə], v.n. straucheln (stumble); stammeln (stammer).

fame [feim], s. der Ruhm; der Ruf; ill —, der üble Ruf.

familiar [fə'miljə], adj. vertraut, wohlbekannt, intim; gewohnt (habitual); be on — terms, auf vertrautem Fuß stehen.

familiarity [fəmili'æriti], s. die Vertrautheit, die Vertraulichkeit (intimacy).

familiarize [fə'miljəraiz], v.a. vertraut machen, bekannt machen.

family ['fæmili], s. die Familie; — doctor, der Hausarzt; (Chem.) die Gruppe; be in the — way, in anderen Umständen sein, guter Hoffnung sein, schwanger sein; — tree, der Stammbaum.

famine ['fæmin], s. die Hungersnot; — relief, Hilfe für die Hungernden.

famish ['fæmiʃ], v.n. verhungern, hungern; verschmachten.

famous ['feiməs], adj. berühmt, wohlbekannt (for, wegen).

fan [fæn], s. der Fächer (lady's); der Ventilator; (sl.) der leidenschaftliche Anhänger, der Fan; (coll.) Fanatiker (admirer). — v.a. fächeln; anfachen (flames); entfachen (hatred). — v.n. (Mil.) — out, sich ausbreiten, ausschwärmen.

fanatic [fə'nætik], s. der Fanatiker.

fanatical [fə'nætikəl], adj. fanatisch.

fanaticism [fə'nætisizm], s. der Fanatismus, die Schwärmerei.

fancier ['fænsiə], s. pigeon —, der Taubenzüchter; bird —, der Vogelzüchter.

fanciful ['fænsiful], adj. schwärmerisch, wunderlich.

fancy ['fænsi], s. die Vorliebe (preference); die Phantasie; die Laune (whim); take a — to, liebgewinnen. — adj. — dress, das Maskenanzug, das Kostüm; — goods, Galanteriewaren; — cakes, Torten, f.pl.; das Feingebäck. — v.a. denken, gern haben; (coll.) — oneself as, sich einbilden, man sei; just —! denk doch mal; denk mal an!

fanfare ['fænfɛə], s. (Mus.) die Fanfare, der Tusch.

fang [fæŋ], s. (Zool.) der Hauzahn, der Giftzahn (of snake); (Engin.) der Zapfen. — v.a. (Engin.) vollpumpen, aufpumpen und in Tätigkeit setzen.

fanlight ['fænlait], s. die Lünette, das Lichtfenster.

fantastic(al) [fæn'tæstik(əl)], adj. fantastisch.

fantasy ['fæntəsi], s. (Poet., Mus.) die Phantasie; das Hirngespinst (chimæra).

far [fɑ:], adj. weit, fern, entfernt (distant). — adv. — and wide, weit und breit; by —, bei weitem; go too —, zu weit gehen; he will go —, er wird seinen Weg machen; — sighted, weitsichtig.

farce [fɑ:s], s. die Farce, die Posse.

fare [fɛə], s. das Fahrgeld; der Fahrpreis (of taxi etc.); der Fahrgast (one travelling in taxi); — or Teilstrecke; das Essen, die Kost (food); bill of —, die Speisekarte. — v.n. ergehen (Dat.), daran sein.

farewell [fɛə'wel], interj. lebewohl! — dinner, das Abschiedsessen; — party, die Abschiedsgesellschaft.

farinaceous [færi'neiʃəs], adj. mehlig, aus Mehl.

farm [fɑ:m], s. der Pachthof, der Bauernhof; die Farm; — hand, der Landarbeiter, der Farmarbeiter; — bailiff, der Gutsverwalter. — v.a. bebauen; — out, verpachten. — v.n. Landwirt sein.

farmer ['fɑ:mə], s. der Bauer, Landwirt; der Pächter (tenant).

farmland ['fɑ:mlænd], s. das Ackerland.

farmyard ['fɑ:mjɑ:d], s. der Bauernhof, Gutshof.

farrier ['færiə], s. der Hufschmid.

farrow ['færou], s. der Wurf (pigs). — v.n. ferkeln, Junge haben.

farther ['fɑ:ðə], comp. adj., adv. ferner, weiter.

farthest ['fɑ:ðist], superl. adj., adv. fernst, weitest.

farthing ['fɑ:ðiŋ], s. der Farthing, der Heller.

fascinate ['fæsineit], v.a. bezaubern, faszinieren.

fascination [fæsi'neiʃən], s. die Bezauberung; der Reiz, der Zauberbann (spell).

fascism ['fæʃizm], s. (Pol.) der Faschismus.

fashion ['fæʃən], s. die Mode; out of —, außer Mode; die Art und Weise (manner). — v.a. gestalten, bilden (shape); fully —ed, vollgeformt or geformt, angepaßt.

fashionable ['fæʃnəbl], adj. modisch, modern; elegant.

fast (1) [fɑ:st], adj. schnell (runner); fest (firm); my watch is —, meine Uhr geht vor; a — woman, eine leichtlebige Frau; — train, der Schnellzug; — and furious, schnell wie der Wind. — adv. fest.

fast (2) [fɑ:st], v.n. (Rel.) fasten; (Rel.) — day, der Fasttag.

fasten [fɑ:sn], v.a. festbinden, festmachen (fix). — v.n. sich festhalten (on to, an, Dat.).

fastidious [fəs'tidiəs], adj. wählerisch, anspruchsvoll.

fastidiousness [fəs'tidiəsnis], s. die anspruchsvolle Art.

fat [fæt], adj. fett; dick (person). — s. das Fett; (Cul.) das Speisefett.

fatal ['feitəl], adj. tödlich (lethal); verhängnisvoll.

fatalism ['feitəlizm], s. der Fatalismus.

fatality [fə'tæliti], s. das Verhängnis; der Todesfall; der tödliche Unfall.

fate [feit], s. das Schicksal, Geschick; das Verhängnis (doom, destiny).

fated ['feitid], adj. dem Verderben (Untergang) geweiht.

fateful ['feitful], adj. verhängnisvoll, unselig.

father ['fɑ:ðə], s. der Vater; (Eccl.) Pater; — -in-law, der Schwiegervater. — v.a. Vater sein or werden von (Dat.); zeugen (procreate).

fatherland ['fɑ:ðəlænd], s. das Vaterland.

fatherly ['fɑ:ðəli], adj. väterlich; wie ein Vater.

fathom ['fæðəm], s. die Klafter. — v.a. ergründen, erforschen.

fatigue [fə'ti:g], s. die Ermüdung, die Erschöpfung; (Mil.) der Arbeitsdienst. — v.a. ermüden, erschöpfen.

fatling ['fætliŋ], s. (Agr.) das Mastvieh.

fatness ['fætnis], s. die Beleibtheit (person); die Fettheit (animals).

fatten [fætn], v.a. — up, mästen (animals); fett werden lassen. — v.n. fett werden, sich mästen (an, Dat.).

fatty ['fæti], adj. (Chem.) fett, fettig. — s. (coll.) der Dickwanst.

fatuity [fə'tju:iti], s. die Albernheit, die Dummheit.

fatuous ['fætjuəs], adj. albern, dumm, nichtssagend.

faucet ['fɔ:sit], s. der Zapfen, der Hahn.

fault [fɔ:lt], s. der Fehler; die Schuld; find— with, etwas kritisieren; tadeln; it is my —, es ist meine Schuld; at —, im Irrtum.

faultless ['fɔ:ltlis], adj. fehlerlos, fehlerfrei.

faultlessness ['fɔ:ltlisnis], s. die Fehlerlosigkeit, die fehlerlose Ausführung.

faulty ['fɔ:lti], adj. fehlerhaft, mangelhaft.

faun [fɔ:n], s. (Myth.) der Faun.

fauna ['fɔ:nə], s. die Fauna, die Tierwelt.

favour ['feivə], s. die Gunst, das Wohlwollen; (Comm.) in — of, zugunsten; do a —, einen Gefallen tun or erweisen; be in —, sehr begehrt sein, in hoher Gunst stehen. — v.a. bevorzugen, begünstigen, wohlwollend gegenüberstehen (Dat.).

favourable ['feivərəbl], adj. günstig, vorteilhaft.

favourite ['feivərit], *s.* der Favorit, der Liebling; der Günstling (*of kings*). — *adj.* Lieblings-, bevorzugt.

fawn (1) [fɔ:n], *s.* (*Zool.*) das junge Reh, das Rehkalb; — *coloured*, rehfarben. — *adj.* rehfarben, hellbraun.

fawn (2) [fɔ:n], *v.n.* schmeicheln, kriecherisch sein ((*up*)*on, Dat.*).

fawning ['fɔ:niŋ], *adj.* kriecherisch, kriechend.

fear [fiə], *s.* die Furcht, die Angst; *stand in — of s.o.*, sich vor jemandem fürchten; *for — of*, aus Angst vor (*Dat.*). — *v.a.* fürchten, befürchten.

fearful ['fiəful], *adj.* furchtsam (*full of fear*); furchtbar (*causing fear*).

fearless ['fiəlis], *adj.* furchtlos (*of, vor, Dat.*).

fearlessness ['fiəlisnis], *s.* die Furchtlosigkeit.

feasibility [fi:zi'biliti], *s.* die Tunlichkeit, die Möglichkeit.

feasible ['fi:zibl], *adj.* tunlich, möglich.

feast [fi:st], *s.* das Fest, der Festtag; der Schmaus (*good meal*). — *v.n.* schmausen (*upon*, von, *Dat.*). — *v.a.* festlich bewirten.

feat [fi:t], *s.* die Tat, die Heldentat; das Kunststück.

feather ['feðə], *s.* die Feder; *show the white —*, Feigheit an den Tag legen; — *bed*, das Federbett. — *v.a.* federn; — *o.'s nest*, sein Schäfchen ins Trockene bringen.

feature ['fi:tʃə], *s.* der Zug (*characteristic*); der Gesichtszug (*facial*). — *v.a.* charakterisieren; (*Film*) in der Hauptrolle zeigen.

February ['februəri], *s.* der Februar.

feckless ['feklis], *adj.* hilflos, unfähig.

feculence ['fekjuləns], *s.* (*Chem.*) der Bodensatz, der Hefesatz.

fecund ['fekənd], *adj.* fruchtbar.

fecundate ['fekəndeit], *v.a.* fruchtbar machen, befruchten.

fecundity [fi'kʌnditi], *s.* die Fruchtbarkeit.

federacy ['fedərəsi], *s.* der Bund, die Föderation.

federal ['fedərəl], *adj.* Bundes-, föderativ.

federalism ['fedərəlizm], *s.* der Föderalismus.

federalize ['fedərəlaiz], *v.a.* verbünden.

federation [fedə'reiʃən], *s.* die Föderation, die Verbündung; (*Pol.*) der Bund.

fee [fi:], *s.* die Gebühr (*official dues*); das Honorar (*of doctor etc.*); (*pl.*) (*Sch.*) das Schulgeld.

feeble [fi:bl], *adj.* schwach, matt; — *minded*, schwachsinnig.

feed [fi:d], *v.a. irr.* füttern; verköstigen (*humans*); unterhalten (*maintain*); zuführen (*into machine, Dat.*); *be fed up with*, etwas satt haben; — *pipe*, die Speiseröhre. — *v.n.* sich nähren (*on*, von, *Dat.*); weiden (*graze*).

feeder ['fi:də], *s.* der Kinderlatz (*bib*); (*Tech.*) der Zubringer.

feel [fi:l], *v.n. irr.* sich fühlen (*sense*); meinen (*think*). — *v.a.* berühren, betasten (*touch*); empfinden (*be aware of*).

feeler ['fi:lə], *s.* der Fühler; *put out a —*, einen Fühler ausstrecken.

feeling ['fi:liŋ], *s.* das Gefühl; *with —*, bewegt, gerührt (*moved*); grimmig (*in anger*).

feign [fein], *v.a.* vortäuschen, heucheln.

feint [feint], *s.* die Verstellung (*disguise*); die Finte (*fencing*).

felicitate [fi'lisiteit], *v.a.* Glück wünschen (*upon*, zu, *Dat.*), beglückwünschen (*Acc.*).

felicitation [filisi'teiʃən], *s.* die Beglückwünschung, der Glückwunsch.

felicitous [fi'lisitəs], *adj.* glücklich ausgedrückt, gut gesagt (*in speaking*).

felicity [fi'lisiti], *s.* die Glückseligkeit; die glückliche Ausdrucksweise (*style*).

feline ['fi:lain], *adj.* Katzen-, katzenartig.

fell (1) [fel], *adj.* grausam; *at one — swoop*, mit einem wilden Schwung.

fell (2) [fel], *v.a.* fällen (*timber*); töten (*kill*).

fell (3) [fel], *s.* das Gebirge, das Felsengelände.

fell (4) [fel], *s.* das Fell, die Haut (*skin*).

fellow ['felou], *s.* der Gefährte, Genosse (*companion*); das Mitglied eines College or einer Universität; (*coll.*) der Kerl; *queer —*, seltsamer Kauz; *— feeling*, das Mitgefühl; — *traveller*, der Weggenosse; (*Pol.*) der Mitläufer.

fellowship ['felouʃip], *s.* die Mitgliedschaft (einer Hochschule etc.) (*membership*); die Freundschaft (*friendship*); *good —*, die Geselligkeit.

felly, felloe ['feli, 'felou], *s.* die Radfelge.

felon ['felən], *s.* der Verbrecher.

felonious [fi'louniəs], *adj.* verbrecherisch.

felt [felt], *s.* der Filz.

female ['fi:meil], *adj.* weiblich. — *s.* (*Zool.*) das Weibchen.

feminine ['feminin], *adj.* weiblich. — *s.* (*Gram.*) das weibliche Geschlecht; das Weibliche.

fen [fen], *s.* das Moor, das Marschland.

fence [fens], *s.* der Zaun, das Staket. — *v.a.* umzäunen, einzäunen (*enclose*). — *v.n.* fechten (*fight with rapiers*).

fencing ['fensiŋ], *s.* die Einzäunung (*fence*); das Fechten (*with rapiers*); — *master*, der Fechtmeister.

fend [fend], *v.a. — off*, abwehren, parieren. — *v.n. — for oneself*, sich allein behelfen.

fennel [fenl], *s.* (*Bot.*) der Fenchel.

ferment [fə:'ment], *v.a.* zur Gärung bringen. — *v.n.* gären, fermentieren. — ['fə:ment], *s.* das Gärmittel (*also fig.*); (*Chem.*) das Gärungsprodukt.

fermentation [fə:men'teiʃən], *s.* die Gärung.

fern [fə:n], *s.* (*Bot.*) das Farnkraut.

ferocious [fə'rouʃəs], *adj.* wild, grimmig.

ferocity [fə'rɔsiti], *s.* die Wildheit.
ferret ['ferit], *s.* (*Zool.*) das Frett, das Frettchen. — *v.a.* — *out*, ausspüren.
ferry ['feri], *s.* die Fähre. — *v.a.* — *across*, hinüberrudern, hinüberfahren, übersetzen.
fertile ['fə:tail], *adj.* fruchtbar.
fertility [fə'tiliti], *s.* die Fruchtbarkeit.
fertilize ['fə:tilaiz], *v.a.* befruchten.
fertilizer ['fə:tilaizə], *s.* das Düngemittel, der Dünger.
fervent ['fə:vənt], *adj.* inbrünstig (*prayer*); heiß (*wish*).
fervid ['fə:vid], *adj.* glühend, heiß (*with zeal*).
fervour ['fə:və], *s.* die Inbrunst (*prayer*); die Sehnsucht (*wish*).
fester ['festə], *v.n.* schwären, eitern.
festival ['festivəl], *s.* das Fest, die Festspiele, *n. pl.*
festive ['festiv], *adj.* festlich, Fest-.
festivity [fes'tiviti], *s.* die Festlichkeit.
festoon [fes'tu:n], *s.* die Girlande. — *v.a.* behängen, mit Girlanden verzieren, schmücken.
fetch [fetʃ], *v.a.* holen, bringen.
fetching ['fetʃiŋ], *adj.* einnehmend.
fetter ['fetə], *v.a.* fesseln, binden. — *s.* (*pl.*) die Fesseln, *f. pl.*
feud [fju:d], *s.* die Fehde.
feudal ['fju:dl], *adj.* feudal, Lehns-.
fever ['fi:və], *s.* das Fieber.
few [fju:], *adj.* einige; wenige; *a* —, ein paar.
fiancé [fi'ɔ:nsei], *s.* der Verlobte, Bräutigam.
fiancée [fi'ɔ:nsei], *s.* die Verlobte, Braut.
fib [fib], *s.* (*coll.*) die Lüge. — *v.n.* (*coll.*) lügen.
fibre ['faibə], *s.* die Fiber, Faser.
fibrous ['faibrəs], *adj.* faserartig.
fickle [fikl], *adj.* unbeständig, wankelmütig.
fiction ['fikʃən], *s.* die Erdichtung (*figment*); (*Lit.*) die Romanliteratur.
fictitious [fik'tiʃəs], *adj.* erdichtet, in der Phantasie.
fiddle [fidl], *s.* (*coll.*) die Geige, Fiedel, Violine. — *v.n.* (*coll., Mus.*) geigen; schwindeln (*cheat*).
fiddlesticks! ['fidlstiks], *int.* Unsinn!
fidelity [fi'deliti], *s.* die Treue (*loyalty*); Genauigkeit; (*Engin.*) high —, Präzision, High Fidelity.
fidget ['fidʒit], *v.n.* unruhig sein.
fidgety ['fidʒiti], *adj.* nervös.
fie! [fai], *int.* pfui!
field [fi:ld], *s.* das Feld; (*fig.*) das Gebiet; — *glass*, der Feldstecher; (*Hunt.*) — *sports*, die Feldübungen, der Jagdsport. — *v.a., v.n.* abfangen, abpassen (*cricket*).
fiend [fi:nd], *s.* der Unhold, böse Geist; *fresh air* —, ein Freund der frischen Luft.
fiendish ['fi:ndiʃ], *adj.* teuflisch, boshaft.
fierce [fiəs], *adj.* wild, wütend (*beast*); — *weather*, — *cold*, die grimmige Kälte, der grimmige Winter.

fiery ['faiəri], *adj.* feurig; hitzig.
fife [faif], *s.* (*Mus.*) die Querpfeife.
fifteen [fif'ti:n], *num. adj.* fünfzehn.
fifth [fifθ], *num. adj.* der fünfte.
fifty ['fifti], *num. adj.* fünfzig.
fig [fig], *s.* (*Bot.*) die Feige.
fight [fait], *v.a., v.n. irr.* kämpfen, bekämpfen (*in battle*); raufen (*of boys*). — *s.* der Kampf; die Rauferei.
figment ['figmənt], *s.* die Erdichtung.
figurative ['figjuərətiv], *adj.* bildlich (*style*).
figure ['figə], *s.* die Figur (*body*); die Gestalt, Form (*shape*); (*Maths.*) die Zahl, die Ziffer; *cut a* —, einen Eindruck machen; *a fine* — *of a man!* ein fabelhafter Kerl! — *v.a.* — *out*, ausdenken, ausrechnen. — *v.n.* eine Rolle spielen, rangieren.
figured ['figəd], *adj.* figuriert.
figurehead ['figəhed], *s.* der scheinbare Leiter, die Representationsfigur.
filament ['filəmənt], *s.* der Faden, der Glühfaden (*bulb*).
filbert ['filbə:t], *s.* (*Bot.*) die Haselnuß.
filch [filtʃ], *v.a.* stehlen, klauen.
file [fail], *s.* (*Engin.*) die Feile; (*Mil.*) die Reihe; (*Comm.*) der Aktenstoß, das Aktenbündel, der Ordner; (*pl.*) die Akten, *f. pl.; single* —, im Gänsemarsch; *rank and* —, die große Masse; *on the* —, in den Akten. — *v.a.* feilen (*metal*); zu den Akten legen (*papers*); einreichen (*petition*).
filial ['filial], *adj.* kindlich.
filibuster ['filibʌstə], *s.* der Freibeuter; (*Am.*) (*Pol.*) die Obstruktion.
filigree ['filigri:], *s.* die Filigranarbeit.
filing ['failiŋ], *s.* (*pl.*) die Feilspäne; das Einheften (*of papers*); — *cabinet*, die Kartei.
fill [fil], *v.a.* füllen; ausfüllen (*place, job*); plombieren (*tooth*). — *up*, tanken (*with petrol*). — *s.* das volle Maß; *eat o.'s* —, sich satt essen.
fillet ['filit], *s.* das Filet (*meat*); das Band, die Binde (*band*).
filling ['filiŋ], *s.* die Plombe (*in tooth*); — *station*, die Tankstelle.
filly ['fili], *s.* das Füllen.
film [film], *s.* der Film (*cinema, Phot.*); die Haut, das Häutchen (*skin*); der Belag (*coating*). — *v.a.* aufnehmen, verfilmen, filmen (*photograph*).
filter ['filtə], *v.a.* filtrieren, filtern. — *v.n.* durchfiltern. — *s.* das Filter.
filth [filθ], *s.* der Schmutz.
filthy ['filθi], *adj.* schmutzig.
filtration [fil'treiʃən], *s.* das Filtrieren, das Durchsickern.
fin [fin], *s.* (*Zool.*) die Finne, die Flosse.
final [fainl], *adj.* letzt, endlich; endgültig. — *s.* (*Sport*) die Endrunde, das Endspiel.
finale [fi'nɑ:li], *s.* (*Mus.*) das Finale.
finality [fai'næliti], *s.* die Endgültigkeit.
finance [fi'næns *or* 'fai-], *s.* die Finanz, das Finanzwesen. — *v.a.* finanzieren.

financial [fi'nænʃəl], *adj.* finanziell, Geld-, Finanz-.

finch [fintʃ], *s.* (Orn.) der Fink.

find [faind], *v.a. irr.* finden; — *fault with,* jemanden kritisieren; *all found,* volle Verpflegung (inbegriffen). — *s.* der Fund.

finding ['faindiŋ], *s.* das Finden, der Befund; (*Law*) der Wahrspruch.

fine (1) [fain], *adj.* fein (*delicate*); dünn (*thin*); schön (*beautiful*); scharf (*distinct*); großartig (*splendid*).

fine (2) [fain], *v.a.* zu einer Geldstrafe verurteilen. — *s.* die Geldstrafe.

finery ['fainəri], *s.* der Putz; (*Engin.*) der Frischofen.

finger ['fiŋgə], *s.* der Finger; *have a — in the pie,* die Hand im Spiel haben. — *v.a.* berühren, antasten.

finish ['finiʃ], *v.a.* beenden, fertig machen, vollenden; —*ing touch,* die letzte Hand. — *v.n.* aufhören, enden. — *s.* das Ende (*end*); der letzte Schliff; die Appretur, die Fertigung.

finite ['fainait], *adj.* endlich.

Finn [fin], *s.* der Finne.

Finnish ['finiʃ], *adj.* finnisch.

fir [fə:], *s.* (*Bot.*) die Föhre, die Tanne; — *cone,* der Tannenzapfen.

fire [faiə], *s.* das Feuer; — *brigade,* die Feuerwehr; — *damp,* (*Min.*) schlagende Wetter, *n.pl.*; — *engine,* die Feuerspritze; — *extinguisher,* der Löschapparat, Feuerlöscher; — *escape,* die Rettungsleiter. — *v.a.* brennen (*clay*); anzünden, in Gang setzen (*furnace*); anspornen (*enthuse*); (*coll.*) entlassen (*dismiss*). — *v.n.* feuern (*at,* auf, *Acc.*).

firebrand ['faiəbrænd], *s.* der Aufwiegler.

fireman ['faiəmən], *s.* der Heizer.

fireplace ['faiəpleis], *s.* der Kamin.

fireproof ['faiəpru:f], *adj.* feuerfest.

fireside ['faiəsaid], *s.* der (häusliche) Herd, der Kamin.

firewood ['faiəwud], *s.* das Brennholz.

firework ['faiəwə:k], *s.* (*usually pl.*) das Feuerwerk.

firm [fə:m], *adj.* fest, hart (*solid*); entschlossen (*decided*). — *s.* die Firma.

firmament ['fə:məmənt], *s.* das Firmament, Himmelsgewölbe; der Sternenhimmel.

firmness ['fə:mnis], *s.* die Festigkeit, Entschlossenheit.

first [fə:st], *num. adj., adv.* erst; zuerst; — *of all,* zuallererst; — *born,* erstgeboren; — *rate,* erstklassig. — *s. from the —,* von Anfang an.

fiscal ['fiskəl], *adj.* fiskalisch, von der Staatskasse, Finanz-.

fish [fiʃ], *s.* der Fisch; *like a — out of water,* nicht in seinem Element; *a queer —,* ein seltsamer Kauz; —*bone,* die Gräte. — *v.n.* fischen; — *for compliments,* nach Lob haschen, nach Komplimenten fischen.

fisherman ['fiʃəmən], *s.* der Fischer.

fishery ['fiʃəri], *s.* der Fischfang.

fishing ['fiʃiŋ], *s.* das Fischen, der Fischfang; — *fly,* die Angelfliege; — *line,* die Angelschnur; — *rod,* die Angelrute; — *tackle,* das Angelgerät.

fishy ['fiʃi], *adj.* (*coll.*) anrüchig, verdächtig.

fissile ['fisail], *adj.* (*Phys.*) spaltbar.

fission ['fiʃ(ə)n], *s.* (*Phys.*) die Spaltung.

fist [fist], *s.* die Faust; *hand over —,* im Überfluß; *tight* —*ed,* geizig.

fisticuffs ['fistikʌfs], *s.* die Schlägerei, das Raufen.

fistula ['fistjulə], *s.* (*Anat.*) die Fistel.

fit (1) [fit], *v.a.* passen, anpassen (*Dat.*); einfügen (— *into s.th.*); — *in,* hineinpassen; — *on a suit,* einen Anzug anprobieren (*Dat.*); — *for a career,* zu einer Laufbahn vorbereiten; — *out,* ausrüsten. — *v.n.* passen, sich fügen (— *into*); — *in,* passen (*in, zu, Dat.*). — *adj.* geeignet, fähig (*suitable*); — *to drop,* todmüde; gesund, stark (*healthy*); schicklich (*proper*); (*Sport*) in guter Form.

fit (2) [fit], *s.* der Anfall; *by* —*s and starts,* ruckweise.

fitful ['fitful], *adj.* launenhaft; unbeständig.

fitness ['fitnis], *s.* die Tauglichkeit (*health*); die Schicklichkeit (*propriety*); die Fähigkeit (*ability*); (*Sport*) die gute Form.

fitter ['fitə], *s.* der Monteur.

fitting, fitment ['fitiŋ, 'fitmənt], *s.* die Armatur; die Montage. — *adj.* passend (*suitable*); geeignet (*appropriate*).

five [faiv], *num. adj.* fünf.

fiver ['faivə], *s.* (*coll.*) die Fünfpfundnote.

fix [fiks], *v.a.* festmachen, befestigen (*make firm*); festsetzen (*a time*); (*Am.*) herrichten, anrichten (*a meal*); — *with a glare* or *stare,* mit den Augen fixieren, scharf ansehen; — *up* (*coll.*), etwas erledigen (*something*); bedienen (*serve s.o.*). — *s.* (*coll.*) die Klemme, die Schwierigkeit, das Dilemma.

fixture ['fikstʃə], *s.* (*Sport*) die Veranstaltung; das Inventarstück (*furniture*).

fizz [fiz], *v.n.* brausen (*drink*).

fizzle ['fizl], *v.n.* zischen (*flame*); — *out,* verebben, ausgehen, zunichte werden; (*Am., coll.*) durchfallen (*fail in school*).

fizzy ['fizi], *adj.* mit Kohlensäure, sprudelnd.

flabbergast ['flæbəga:st], *v.a.* (*coll.*) verblüffen.

flabby ['flæbi], *adj.* schlaff.

flaccid ['flæksid], *adj.* schlapp, schlaff.

flag (1) [flæg], *s.* (*Mil.*) die Flagge; die Fahne; — *officer,* der Flaggoffizier; —*staff,* die Fahnenstange.

flag (2) [flæg], *v.n.* ermatten, erschlaffen.

flag (3) [flæg], *s.* (—*stone*) der Fliesstein, die Fliese. — *v.a.* mit Fliesen auslegen, mit Fliessteinen pflastern.

flop

flagon ['flægən], *s.* die Doppelflasche.

flagrant ['fleigrənt], *adj.* entsetzlich (*shocking*); schamlos (*impudent*).

flail [fleil], *s.* der Dreschflegel.

flair [flɛə], *s.* der Instinkt; (*coll.*) die Nase (*for*, für, *Acc.*).

flake [fleik], *s.* die Flocke. — *v.n. — off*, abblättern.

flame [fleim], *s.* die Flamme; (*coll.*) *old —*, die (alte) Liebe, Geliebte(r), die Flamme. — *v.n.* flammen, lodern.

flamingo [flə'miŋgou], *s.* (*Orn.*) der Flamingo.

flange [flændʒ], *s.* (*Engin.*) der Flan(t)sch.

flank [flæŋk], *s.* die Flanke, die Seite; die Weiche (*of animal*). — *v.a.* flankieren.

flannel [flænl], *s.* der Flanell.

flap [flæp], *s.* die Klappe; das Ohrläppchen (*earlobe*); der Flügelschlag (*— of wings*).

flare [flɛə], *v.n.* flammen, flackern; *— up*, aufbrausen (*in temper*). — *s.* das Aufflammen, das Aufflackern; die Leuchtkugel.

flash [flæʃ], *s.* der Blitz (*of lightning*); das Aufflammen; (*Phot.*) *—light*, das Blitzlicht. — *v.a.* aufflammen lassen, aufblitzen lassen. — *v.n.* aufflammen, aufblitzen.

flashy ['flæʃi], *adj.* großtuend, angeberisch (*bragging*); buntfarbig (*gaudy*).

flask [flɑːsk], *s.* die kleine Flasche, das Fläschchen.

flat [flæt], *adj.* flach, eben; abgestanden, schal (*drink*); *— footed*, plattfüßig; (*Mus.*) zu tief, vermindert; platt; albern (*conversation*); *— tyre*, die Panne. — *adv. — out*, ausgepumpt, erschöpft. — *s.* die Mietwohnung, Wohnung (*lodgings*); (*Mus.*) das B; (*pl.*) das Flachland; (*Theat.*) (*pl.*) die Bühnenbilder.

flatness ['flætnis], *s.* die Flachheit, die Plattheit (*of conversation etc.*).

flatten [flætn], *v.a.* flach machen; glätten (*smooth*).

flatter ['flætə], *v.a.* schmeicheln (*Dat.*).

flattery ['flætəri], *s.* die Schmeichelei.

flaunt [flɔːnt], *v.a.* prahlen, prunken (*s.th.*, mit, *Dat.*).

flavour ['fleivə], *s.* der Geschmack, die Würze; das Aroma; die Blume (*bouquet of wine*). — *v.a.* würzen.

flaw [flɔː], *s.* der Riß (*chink*); der Fehler (*fault*).

flawless ['flɔːlis], *adj.* fehlerlos.

flax [flæks], *s.* (*Bot.*) der Flachs.

flay [flei], *v.a.* schinden, die Haut abziehen (*Dat.*).

flea [fliː], *s.* (*Ent.*) der Floh.

fleck [flek], *v.a.* sprenkeln.

fledge [fledʒ], *v.a.* befiedern; *fully —d*, flügge; selbständig.

fledgling ['fledʒliŋ], *s.* der Grünschnabel, der Novize.

flee [fliː], *v.a.*, *v.n. irr.* fliehen, entfliehen (*from*, von, *Dat.*); flüchten (*vor*, *Dat.*).

fleece [fliːs], *s.* das Vlies. — *v.a.* scheren (*sheep*); ausnützen (*exploit*); berauben.

fleet [fliːt], *s.* die Flotte. — *adj.* (*Poet.*) schnellfüßig.

Fleming ['flemiŋ], *s.* der Flame.

Flemish ['flemiʃ], *adj.* flämisch.

flesh [fleʃ], *s.* das (lebende) Fleisch; die Frucht (*of fruit*).

flex [fleks], *s.* (*Elec.*) die Kontaktschnur.

flexible ['fleksibl], *adj.* biegsam; (*fig.*) anpassungsfähig.

flexion ['flekʃən], *s.* (*Gram.*) die Flexion, die Biegung.

flick [flik], *s.* der leichte Schlag. — *v.a.* leicht schlagen, berühren.

flicker ['flikə], *s.* das Flackern, das Flimmern. — *v.n.* flackern, flimmern.

flight [flait], *s.* (*Aviat.*) der Flug; die Flucht (*escape*); *— of stairs*, die Treppe, Treppenflucht.

flimsy ['flimzi], *adj.* hauchdünn (*material*); schwach (*argument*).

flinch [flintʃ], *v.n.* zurückweichen, zurückzucken (*from*, vor, *Dat.*).

fling [fliŋ], *v.a. irr.* schleudern, werfen. — *s.* der Wurf; *highland —*, schottischer Tanz; *have a last —*, sich zum letzten Mal austoben.

flint [flint], *s.* der Feuerstein.

flippancy ['flipənsi], *s.* die Leichtfertigkeit.

flippant ['flipənt], *adj.* leichtfertig, leichtsinnig, schnippisch.

flirt [fləːt], *v.n.* flirten, liebeln, (*with*, *Dat.*).

flirtation [fləː'teiʃən], *s.* die Liebelei.

flit [flit], *v.n.* hin und her flitzen; huschen.

flitch [flitʃ], *s.* die Speckseite.

flitter ['flitə], *v.n.* flattern.

float [flout], *v.n.* obenauf schwimmen, dahingleiten; *—ing ice*, das Treibeis. — *v.a.* schwimmen lassen; (*Naut.*) flott machen; (*Comm.*) gründen (a *company*); ausgeben (*a loan*). — *s.* das Floß (*raft*); der ausgeschmückte Wagen (*decorated vehicle*).

flock [flɔk], *s.* die Herde (*sheep*). — *v.n.* zusammenlaufen, sich scharen.

floe [flou], *s.* die Eisscholle.

flog [flɔg], *v.a.* peitschen (*whip*); antreiben; *— a dead horse*, sich umsonst bemühen; (*coll.*) verkaufen.

flood [flʌd], *s.* die Flut; das Hochwasser, die Überschwemmung (*flooding*); (*fig.*) die Fülle; *— gate*, die Schleuse. — *v.a.* überfluten, überschütten (*with requests*). — *v.n.* überschwemmen (*of river*).

floodlight ['flʌdlait], *s.* das Flutlicht, Scheinwerferlicht.

floor [flɔː], *s.* der Boden, der Fußboden; das Stockwerk, der Stock (*storey*); *from the —*, aus dem Plenum; *— walker*, die Aufsicht (*in stores*). — *v.a.* zu Boden strecken, überrumpeln (*surprise*).

flop [flɔp], *v.n.* (*coll.*) hinsinken, hinplumpsen; versagen (*fail*). — *s.* das Hinfallen; der Versager (*play, film etc.*).

Florentine

Florentine [ˈflɔrəntain], *adj.* florentinisch. — *s.* der Florentiner.

florid [ˈflɔrid], *adj.* blühend; überladen.

florin [ˈflɔrin], *s.* das Zweischillingstück.

florist [ˈflɔrist], *s.* der Blumenhändler.

flotsam [ˈflɔtsəm], *s.* das Strandgut, Wrackgut.

flounce (1) [flauns], *v.n.* hastig bewegen.

flounce (2) [flauns], *v.a.* mit Falbeln besetzen (*dress*). — *s.* die Falbel (*on dress*).

flounder (1) [ˈflaundə], *v.n.* umhertappen, unsicher sein.

flounder (2) [ˈflaundə], *s.* (*Zool.*) die Flunder.

flour [ˈflauə], *s.* das Mehl.

flourish [ˈflʌriʃ], *v.n.* blühen; wirken; gedeihen (*thrive*); schnörkeln, verzieren (*in writing*); Fanfaren blasen, schmettern (*trumpets*). — *s.* der Schnörkel; der Trompetenstoß, Tusch (*of trumpets*).

flout [flaut], *v.a.* verhöhnen, verspotten. — *s.* der Hohn, der Spott.

flow [flou], *v.n. irr.* fließen, strömen. — *s.* der Fluß (*of water, goods etc.*); — *of words,* der Redeschwall.

flower [ˈflauə], *s.* die Blume; die Blüte (*blossom*). — *v.n.* blühen, in Blüte stehen.

flowery [ˈflauəri], *adj.* gewählt, umständlich, geziert (*style*).

fluctuate [ˈflʌktjueit], *v.n.* schwanken.

fluctuation [flʌktjuˈeiʃən], *s.* das Schwanken.

flue [fluː], *s.* der Rauchfang (*of chimney*).

fluency [ˈfluːənsi], *s.* das fließende Sprechen, die Geläufigkeit.

fluent [ˈfluːənt], *adj.* geläufig, fließend.

fluid [ˈfluːid], *adj.* fließend, flüssig (*liquid*). — *s.* die Flüssigkeit.

fluke [fluːk], *s.* der glückliche Zufall (*chance*).

flunkey [ˈflʌŋki], *s.* der Diener, der Bediente.

flurry [ˈflʌri], *s.* die Unruhe; die Aufregung (*excitement*).

flush (1) [flʌʃ], *s.* das Erröten (*blushing*); die Aufwallung (*of anger*). — *v.a.* nachspülen (*basin*); erröten machen (*make blush*). — *v.n.* erröten.

flush (2) [flʌʃ], *adj.* in gleicher Ebene, eben.

flush (3) [flʌʃ], *v.a.* (*Hunt.*) aufscheuchen.

fluster [ˈflʌstə], *v.a.* verwirren (*muddle*); aufregen (*excite*).

flute [fluːt], *s.* (*Mus.*) die Flöte; (*Carp.*) die Hohlkehle. — *v.a.* (*Carp., Archit.*) aushöhlen. — *v.n.* (*Mus.*) flöten, Flöte spielen.

flutter [ˈflʌtə], *v.n.* flattern, unruhig sein. — *s.* die Unruhe.

flux [flʌks], *s.* das Fließen; *be in —,* in der Schwebe sein.

fly [flai], *v.a. irr.* wehen lassen, hissen (*flag*). — *v.n. irr.* (*Aviat.*) fliegen;

fliehen (*escape*); eilen (*hurry*). — *s.* (*Ent.*) die Fliege.

flyleaf [ˈflailiːf], *s.* das Vorsatzblatt.

flying [ˈflaiiŋ], *adj.* fliegend, Flug-; — *squad,* das Überfallkommando.

flyover [ˈflaiouvə], *s.* die Brückenkreuzung, Überführung.

flywheel [ˈflaiwiːl], *s.* das Schwungrad.

foal [foul], *s.* (*Zool.*) das Füllen. — *v.n.* fohlen.

foam [foum], *s.* der Schaum; — *rubber,* das Schaumgummi. — *v.n.* schäumen.

fob [fɔb], *v.a.* — *off,* abfertigen, abspeisen.

focus [ˈfoukəs], *s.* der Brennpunkt; der Mittelpunkt (*of interest*). — *v.a.* (*Phot.*) einstellen. — *v.n.* — *upon,* sich konzentrieren auf (*Acc.*).

fodder [ˈfɔdə], *s.* das Futter.

foe [fou], *s.* der Feind.

fog [fɔg], *s.* der Nebel.

fogey [ˈfougi], *s.* der Kerl, Kauz.

foible [ˈfɔibl], *s.* die Schwäche, die schwache Seite.

foil (1) [fɔil], *v.a.* vereiteln. — *s.* das Florett (*fencing rapier*).

foil (2) [fɔil], *s.* die Folie; der Hintergrund (*background*).

foist [fɔist], *v.a.* aufschwatzen (*upon, Dat.*).

fold (1) [fould], *v.a.* falten (*clothes etc.*); umarmen (*in o.'s arms*). — *v.n.* schließen, sich falten. — *s.* die Falte; (*Geol.*) die Vertiefung.

fold (2) [fould], *s.* die Herde (*sheep*); *return to the —,* zu den Seinen zurückkehren.

folder [ˈfouldə], *s.* die Mappe (*papers*); das Falzbein.

folding [ˈfouldiŋ], *adj.* Klapp-; — *chair,* der Klappstuhl; — *door,* die Flügeltür.

foliage [ˈfouljidʒ], *s.* (*Bot.*) das Laub.

folio [ˈfouliou], *s.* das Folio, der Foliant.

folk [fouk], *s.* (*also pl.*) die Leute; (*pl.*) (*Am.*) Freunde (*mode of address*).

folklore [ˈfouklɔː], *s.* die Volkskunde.

folksong [ˈfouksɔŋ], *s.* das Volkslied.

follow [ˈfɔlou], *v.a., v.n.* folgen (*Dat.*). — *suit,* dasselbe tun, Farbe bekennen.

follower [ˈfɔlouə], *s.* der Anhänger (*supporter*); der Nachfolger (*successor*); *camp —,* der Mitläufer.

folly [ˈfɔli], *s.* die Narrheit; die törichte Handlung (*action*).

foment [foˈment], *v.a.* anregen (*stimulate*); pflegen (*cultivate*); warm baden.

fond [fɔnd], *adj.* zärtlich, lieb; *be — of,* gern haben.

fondle [ˈfɔndl], *v.a.* liebkosen.

fondness [ˈfɔndnis], *s.* die Zärtlichkeit, die (Vor-)liebe.

font [fɔnt], *s.* der Taufstein (*baptismal*).

food [fuːd], *s.* die Nahrung, Speise (*nourishment*); Lebensmittel (*n.pl.*); das Futter (*for animals*); *some —,* etwas zum Essen; — *store,* das Lebensmittelgeschäft.

fool [fuːl], *s.* der Narr, Tor. — *v.a.* zum Narren halten, übertölpeln.

foolish ['fu:liʃ], *adj.* töricht, albern, närrisch (*person*); unsinnig (*act*).

foolscap ['fu:lskæp], *s.* das Kanzleipapier.

foot [fut], *s.* der Fuß; *on* —, zu Fuß; — *board*, das Trittbrett; *put o.'s* — *in it*, eine taktlose Bemerkung fallen lassen, ins Fettnäpfchen treten. — *v.a.* — *the bill*, bezahlen.

footage ['futidʒ], *s.* die Länge in Fuß.

football ['futbɔ:l], *s.* der Fußball.

footbridge ['futbridʒ], *s.* der Steg.

footing ['futiŋ], *s.* die Grundlage, Basis.

footlight ['futlait], *s.* (*usually pl.*) die Rampenlichter, *n. pl.*

footman ['futmən], *s.* der Bediente.

footprint ['futprint], *s.* die Fußstapfe.

footstool ['futstu:l], *s.* der Schemel.

fop [fɔp], *s.* der Geck.

for [fɔ:], *prep.* für (*Acc.*); anstatt (*Genit.*) (*instead of*); *in exchange* —, für, um; — *example*, zum Beispiel; — *heaven's sake*, um Himmels willen; — *two days*, zwei Tage lang; auf zwei Tage; seit zwei Tagen; *now you are* — *it!* jetzt has du's! *as* — *me*, meinetwegen, was mich anbelangt; — *all that*, trotz alledem. — *conj.* denn, weil.

forage ['fɔridʒ], *s.* das Futter. — *v.n.* furagieren.

forasmuch [fɔrəz'mʌtʃ], *conj.* (*obs.*) — *as*, insofern als.

foray ['fɔrei], *s.* der Raubzug.

forbear [fɔ:'bɛə], *v.a. irr.* vermeiden, unterlassen (*avoid*); sich enthalten (*abstain*). — *v.n.* (geduldig) hinnehmen, ertragen.

forbid [fɔ:'bid], *v.a. irr.* verbieten; *God* — *!* Gott behüte!

forbidding [fə'bidiŋ], *adj.* abschreckend.

force [fɔ:s], *s.* (*Phys.*) die Kraft; die Macht (*might*); die Gewalt (*brute* —); (*pl.*) die Streitkräfte, *f. pl.*; (*Phys.*) die Kräfte. — *v.a.* zwingen, nötigen.

forceful ['fɔ:sful], *adj.* kräftig, energisch, kraftvoll.

forceps ['fɔ:seps], *s.* (*Med.*) die Zange; die Pinzette.

forcible ['fɔ:sibl], *adj.* heftig, stark (*strong*); gewaltsam (*violent*).

ford [fɔ:d], *s.* die Furt.

fore- [fɔ:], *pref.* Vorder-, vorder.

forebear ['fɔ:bɛə], *s.* der Vorfahre.

forebode [fɔ:'boud], *v.a.* voraussagen, vorbedeuten.

forecast [fɔ:'ka:st], *v.a.* vorhersagen, voraussagen. — ['fɔ:ka:st], *s.* die Vorhersage.

foreclose [fɔ:'klouz], *v.a.* ausschließen.

forefather ['fɔ:fa:ðə], *s.* der Ahne, der Vorvater.

forefinger ['fɔ:fiŋgə], *s.* (*Anat.*) der Zeigefinger.

forego [fɔ:'gou], *v.a. irr.* vorhergehen.

foreground ['fɔ:graund], *s.* der Vordergrund.

forehead ['fɔrid], *s.* die Stirne.

foreign ['fɔrin], *adj.* fremd; ausländisch.

foreigner ['fɔrinə], *s.* der Fremde, der Ausländer.

foreland ['fɔ:lənd], *s.* das Vorgebirge.

foreman ['fɔ:mən], *s.* der Werkführer, Vorarbeiter.

foremast ['fɔ:ma:st], *s.* (*Naut.*) der Fockmast.

foremost ['fɔ:moust], *adj.* vorderst, vornehmlichst, führend. — *adv.* zuerst; *first and* —, zuallererst.

forenoon ['fɔ:nu:n], *s.* der Vormittag.

forensic [fɔ'rensik], *adj.* forensisch, gerichtsmedizinisch.

forerunner ['fɔ:rʌnə], *s.* der Vorläufer.

foresail ['fɔ:seil, 'fɔ:səl], *s.* (*Naut.*) das Focksegel.

foresee [fɔ:'si:], *v.a. irr.* vorhersehen.

foreshadow [fɔ:'ʃædou], *v.a.* vorher andeuten.

foreshorten [fɔ:'ʃɔ:tn], *v.a.* verkürzen.

foresight ['fɔ:sait], *s.* die Vorsorge, der Vorbedacht.

forest ['fɔrist], *s.* der Wald; der Urwald (*jungle*).

forestall [fɔ:'stɔ:l], *v.a.* vorwegnehmen, zuvorkommen (*Dat.*).

forester ['fɔristə], *s.* der Förster.

forestry ['fɔristri], *s.* die Forstwissenschaft (*science*); das Forstwesen (*management*).

foretaste ['fɔ:teist], *s.* der Vorgeschmack.

foretell [fɔ:'tel], *v.a. irr.* voraussagen.

forethought ['fɔ:θɔ:t], *s.* der Vorbedacht.

forewarn [fɔ:'wɔ:n], *v.a.* warnen.

forfeit ['fɔ:fit], *s.* das Pfand (*pledge*); die Einbuße (*fine*); (*pl.*) das Pfänderspiel. — *v.a.* verlieren, verwirken.

forfeiture ['fɔ:fitʃə], *s.* die Verwirkung, die Einbuße, der Verlust.

forge [fɔ:dʒ], *v.a.* schmieden (*iron*); fälschen (*falsify*). — *v.n.* — *ahead*, sich vorwärtsarbeiten. — *s.* die Schmiede (*iron*); der Eisenhammer (*hammer*).

forget [fə'get], *v.a., v.n. irr.* vergessen; — *-me-not*, das Vergißmeinnicht.

forgetful [fə'getful], *adj.* vergeßlich.

forgive [fə'giv], *v.a., v.n. irr.* vergeben, verzeihen.

forgo [fɔ:'gou], *v.a. irr.* verzichten; aufgeben.

fork [fɔ:k], *s.* die Gabel; die Abzweigung (*road*). — *v.n.* sich gabeln, sich spalten.

forlorn [fɔ:'lɔ:n], *adj.* verlassen, verloren, elend.

form [fɔ:m], *s.* die Form, die Gestalt (*shape*); die Formalität (*formality*); das Formular (*document*); *in good* —, (*Sport*) in guter Form; *bad* —, gegen den guten Ton; *a matter of* —, eine Formsache. — *v.a.* formen, gestalten (*shape*); bilden (*an association etc. of*, über, *Acc.*).

formal ['fɔ:məl], *adj.* formal, äußerlich; formell.

formality [fɔ:'mæliti], *s.* die Formalität.

397

formation

formation [fɔ:'meiʃən], s. (Mil.) die Formation; (Geol.) die Bildung; die Formung; die Aufstellung (sports team).

former ['fɔ:mə], adj. früher, vorig.

formidable ['fɔ:midəbl], adj. schrecklich, furchtbar.

formula ['fɔ:mjulə], s. die Formel.

formulate ['fɔ:mjuleit], v.a. formulieren.

forsake [fɔ:'seik], v.a. irr. verlassen, im Stich lassen.

forsooth [fɔ:'su:θ], adv. (Poet.) wahrlich, wirklich!

forswear [fɔ:'swɛə], v.a. irr. abschwören; — oneself, einen Meineid schwören.

fort, fortress [fɔ:t, 'fɔ:tris], s. das Fort, die Festung.

forth [fɔ:θ], adv. vorwärts; weiter (further); and so —, und so weiter (u.s.w.); fort (away).

forthcoming ['fɔ:θ'kʌmiŋ], adj. bevorstehend.

forthwith [fɔ:θ'wiθ], adv. sogleich.

fortieth ['fɔ:tiəθ], num. adj. vierzigst. — s. der Vierzigste.

fortification [fɔ:tifi'keiʃən], s. die Befestigung.

fortify ['fɔ:tifai], v.a. befestigen; bestärken.

fortitude ['fɔ:titju:d], s. die Tapferkeit.

fortnight ['fɔ:tnait], s. vierzehn Tage, m. pl.

fortuitous [fɔ:'tju:itəs], adj. zufällig.

fortunate ['fɔ:tʃənit], adj. glücklich, günstig.

fortune ['fɔ:tju:n], s. das Glück, das Schicksal; das Vermögen (wealth); — teller, die Wahrsagerin.

forty ['fɔ:ti], num. adj. vierzig.

forward ['fɔ:wəd], adj. vorder (in front); voreilig, vorlaut (rash); früh (early). — adv. vorne; — march! vorwärts! carry —, (Comm.) übertragen. — s. (Footb.) der Stürmer; — line, der Angriff. — v.a. weiterleiten, expedieren; (letter) please —, bitte nachsenden.

forwardness ['fɔ:wədnis], s. die Frühreife; die Voreiligkeit, Dreistigkeit.

fossil ['fɔsil], s. das Fossil.

foster ['fɔstə], v.a. nähren (feed); aufziehen (bring up); — a thought, einen Gedanken hegen; — mother, die Pflegemutter; — brother, der Pflegebruder.

foul [faul], adj. schmutzig; faul (rotten). — v.a. beschmutzen. — v.n. (Footb.) einen Verstoß begehen. — s. (Footb.) der Verstoß.

found (1) [faund], v.a. gründen, begründen.

found (2) [faund], v.a. (Metall.) gießen (cast).

foundation [faun'deiʃən], s. das Fundament; die Unterlage; die Gründung (initiation); die Stiftung (establishment); — stone, der Grundstein.

founder (1) ['faundə], s. der Gründer, Stifter.

founder (2) ['faundə], v.n. scheitern, Schiffbruch erleiden (on, an, Dat.).

foundling ['faundliŋ], s. das Findelkind, der Findling.

foundry ['faundri], s. (Metall.) die Gießerei.

fount (1) [faunt], s. (Typ.) der Schriftguss.

fount (2) [faunt] (Poet.) see fountain.

fountain ['fauntin], s. die Quelle, der Brunnen; der Springbrunnen; — pen, die Füllfeder; — head, der Urquell.

four [fɔ:], num. adj. vier; — -in-hand, das Viergespann.

fowl [faul], s. (Orn.) das Huhn, das Geflügel.

fowler ['faulə], s. der Vogelsteller, Vogelfänger.

fox [fɔks], s. (Zool.) der Fuchs; (fig.) der listige Kauz, Schlauberger (cunning fellow). — v.a. (coll.) überlisten, täuschen.

fraction ['frækʃən], s. (Maths.) der Bruch; (Mech.) der Bruchteil.

fractional ['frækʃənəl], adj. (Maths.) Bruch-, gebrochen.

fractionate ['frækʃəneit], v.a. (Chem.) fraktionieren (oil).

fractious ['frækʃəs], adj. zänkisch, streitsüchtig.

fracture ['fræktʃə], s. (Med.) der Bruch. — v.a. brechen; — o.'s leg, sich das Bein brechen.

fragile ['frædʒail], adj. zerbrechlich, gebrechlich (feeble).

fragment ['frægmənt], s. das Bruchstück, das Fragment.

fragrance ['freigrəns], s. der Wohlgeruch, Duft.

fragrant ['freigrənt], adj. wohlriechend, duftend.

frail [freil], adj. gebrechlich, schwach (feeble).

frailty ['freilti], s. die Schwäche.

frame [freim], s. der Rahmen (of picture); das Gerüst (scaffold); die Form (shape). — v.a. einrahmen (a picture); (Am.) in die Enge treiben, reinlegen (get s.o. wrongly blamed); (Comm.) entwerfen (a letter).

framework ['freimwə:k], s. der Rahmen (outline); das Fachwerk (construction).

franchise ['fræntʃaiz], s. das Wahlrecht.

Franciscan [fræn'siskən], s. der Franziskaner (friar).

frank [fræŋk], adj. offen, aufrichtig. — v.a. frankieren (letter). — s. der Frankovermerk.

frankincense ['fræŋkinsens], s. der Weihrauch.

frantic ['fræntik], adj. wahnsinnig, außer sich.

fraternal [frə'tə:nəl], adj. brüderlich.

fraternity [frə'tə:niti], s. die Bruderschaft; (Am.) der Studentenbund, -klub.

froth

fraternize ['frætənaiz], *v.n.* sich verbrüdern, fraternisieren.

fraud [frɔːd], *s.* der Betrug.

fraudulent ['frɔːdjulənt], *adj.* betrügerisch.

fraught [frɔːt], *adj.* voll (*with*, von, *Dat.*).

fray (1) [frei], *v.a.* abnutzen; — *the nerves*, auf die Nerven gehen (*Dat.*).

fray (2) [frei], *s.* der Kampf, die Schlägerei.

freak [friːk], *s.* das Monstrum, die Mißgeburt.

freakish ['friːkiʃ], *adj.* seltsam; grotesk.

freckle [frekl], *s.* die Sommersprosse.

freckled [frekld], *adj.* sommersprossig.

free [friː], *adj.* frei; offen (*frank*); — *trade area*, die Freihandelszone; *of my own* — *will*, aus freien Stücken. — *v.a.* befreien.

freebooter ['friːbuːtə], *s.* der Freibeuter.

freedom ['friːdəm], *s.* die Freiheit; — *of a city*, das Ehrenbürgerrecht.

freehold ['friːhould], *s.* der freie Grundbesitz, der Freigrundbesitz.

freeholder ['friːhouldə], *s.* der (freie) Grundbesitzer.

freeman ['friːmən], *s.* der Freibürger, Ehrenbürger.

freemason ['friːmeisn], *s.* der Freimaurer.

freewheel ['friː'wiːl], *s.* der Freilauf, das Freilaufrad. — *v.n.* mit Freilauf fahren.

freeze [friːz], *v.a. irr.* gefrieren lassen. — *v.n.* frieren, gefrieren; — *up*, zufrieren.

freight [freit], *s.* die Fracht. — *v.a.* verfrachten.

freighter ['freitə], *s.* (*Naut.*) der Frachtdampfer.

French [frentʃ], *adj.* französisch; — *bean*, die Schnittbohne; — *horn*, (*Mus.*) das Horn.

Frenchman ['frentʃmən], *s.* der Franzose.

Frenchwoman ['frentʃwumən], *s.* die Französin.

frenzied ['frenzid], *adj.* wahnsinnig, außer sich.

frequency ['friːkwənsi], *s.* (*Phys.*) die Frequenz; die Häufigkeit (*of occurrence*).

frequent ['friːkwənt], *adj.* häufig. — [fri'kwent], *v.a.* (häufig) besuchen.

fresh [freʃ], *adj.* frisch, neu; ungesalzen (*water*); (*sl.*) frech; — *water*, das Süßwasser.

fresher, freshman ['freʃə, 'freʃmən], *s.* der Neuankömmling; (*Univ.*) der Fuchs, Anfänger.

fret (1) [fret], *s.* (*Carp.*) das Gitterwerk, Laubsägewerk. — *v.a.* (*Carp.*) durchbrochen verzieren.

fret (2) [fret], *s.* der Verdruß, Ärger. — *v.n.* sich Sorgen machen.

fretful ['fretful], *adj.* verdrießlich, ärgerlich, mißmutig.

fretsaw ['fretsɔː], *s.* (*Carp.*) die Laubsäge.

friar ['fraiə], *s.* (*Eccl.*) der Mönch, Bettelmönch.

friction ['frikʃən], *s.* die Reibung; (*fig.*) die Unstimmigkeit.

Friday ['fraid(e)i], *s.* der Freitag; *Good* —, der Karfreitag.

friend [frend], *s.* der (die) Freund(in).

friendly ['frendli], *adj.* freundlich.

friendship ['frendʃip], *s.* die Freundschaft.

frigate ['frigit], *s.* (*Naut.*) die Fregatte.

fright [frait], *s.* die Furcht, der Schreck, das Entsetzen.

frighten [fraitn], *v.a.* erschrecken (*s.o.*).

frightful ['fraitful], *adj.* schrecklich.

frigid ['fridʒid], *adj.* kalt, frostig; kühl.

frill [fril], *s.* die Krause; die Ausschmückung (*style*).

frilly ['frili], *adj.* gekräuselt, geziert.

fringe [frindʒ], *s.* die Franse (*fringed edge*); der Rand (*edge*, *brink*). — *v.a.* mit Fransen besetzen, einsäumen. — *v.n.* — *on*, grenzen an (*Acc.*).

Frisian ['friːʒən], *adj.* friesisch.

frisk [frisk], *v.a.* (*sl.*) durchsuchen (*search*). — *v.n.* hüpfen (*of animals*). — *s.* der Sprung (*of animals*).

frisky ['friski], *adj.* lebhaft, munter.

fritter ['fritə], *s.* der Pfannkuchen; *apple* —, Äpfel im Schlafrock. — *v.a.* zerstückeln (*cut up*); vertrödeln (*waste*), vergeuden.

frivolity [fri'vɔliti], *s.* der Leichtsinn, die Leichtfertigkeit.

frivolous ['frivələs], *adj.* leichtsinnig, leichtfertig.

fro [frou], *adv.* *to and* —, auf und ab, hin und her.

frock [frɔk], *s.* der Kittel, das Kleid; (*Eccl.*) die Soutane, Kutte.

frog [frɔg], *s.* (*Zool.*) der Frosch.

frogman ['frɔgmən], *s.* der Tauchschwimmer, Froschmann.

frolic ['frɔlik], *s.* der Scherz; der Spaß. — *v.n.* scherzen, ausgelassen sein.

from [frɔm], *prep.* von; von ... her (*hence*); aus ... heraus (*out of*); von ... an (*starting* —); vor (*in the face of*).

front [frʌnt], *s.* die Stirn; die Vorderseite; (*Mil.*) die Front; *in* — *of*, vor (*Dat.*); — *door*, die Haustür.

frontage ['frʌntidʒ], *s.* die Front, Vorderfront (*of building*).

frontal ['frʌntl], *adj.* Stirn-, Vorder-; (*Mil.*) *attack*, der Frontalangriff. — *s.* (*Eccl.*) die Altardecke.

frontier ['frʌntjə], *s.* die Grenze; — *police*, die Grenzpolizei.

frontispiece ['frʌntispiːs], *s.* das Titelbild.

frost [frɔst], *s.* der Frost, der Reif.

frostbite ['frɔstbait], *s.* die Frostbeule.

frosted ['frɔstid], *adj.* bereift.

froth [frɔθ], *s.* der Schaum. — *v.n.* schäumen.

399

frown [fraun], *v.n.* die Stirn runzeln, finster dreinschauen. — *s.* das Stirnrunzeln.

frugal ['fru:gəl], *adj.* frugal, sparsam, einfach.

fruit [fru:t], *s.* die Frucht (*singular*); das Obst (*plural or collective*). — *v.n.* (*Bot.*) Früchte tragen.

frustrate [fras'treit], *v.a.* verhindern; vereiteln (*bring to nought*).

fry (1) [frai], *v.a.* braten; *fried potatoes,* Bratkartoffeln, *f. pl.*

fry (2) [frai], *s.* der Rogen (*of fish*); (*fig.*) die Brut, Menge.

frying pan ['fraiiŋpæn], *s.* die Bratpfanne; *out of the — into the fire,* vom Regen in die Traufe.

fuchsia ['fju:ʃə], *s.* (*Bot.*) die Fuchsie.

fudge [fʌdʒ], *s.* weiches Zuckerwerk; (*coll.*) Unsinn!

fuel ['fjuəl], *s.* der Brennstoff, Treibstoff; das Heizmaterial. — *v.a., v.n.* tanken.

fugitive ['fju:dʒitiv], *adj.* flüchtig, auf der Flucht. — *s.* der Flüchtling.

fugue [fju:g], *s.* (*Mus.*) die Fuge.

fulcrum ['fʌlkrəm], *s.* der Stützpunkt, Hebelpunkt.

fulfil [ful'fil], *v.a.* erfüllen; *— a requirement,* einem Gesetz genüge tun.

full [ful], *adj.* voll; vollständig (*complete*); *—time,* hauptberuflich.

fuller ['fulə], *s.* der Walker.

fullness ['fulnis], *s.* die Fülle.

fulsome ['fulsəm], *adj.* widerlich, ekelhaft; übermäßig.

fumble [fʌmbl], *v.n.* tappen (*for,* nach, *Dat.*).

fume [fju:m], *s.* der Rauch, Dunst; der Zorn (*anger*). — *v.n.* zornig sein, wüten (*be angered*).

fun [fʌn], *s.* der Spaß, Scherz; *have —,* sich gut unterhalten, sich amüsieren; *make — of,* zum besten haben.

function ['fʌŋkʃən], *s.* (*also Maths.*) die Funktion; das Amt (*office*); die Feier(lichkeit) (*formal occasion*). — *v.n.* funktionieren (*be in working order*); fungieren (*officiate*).

fund [fʌnd], *s.* der Fonds (*financial*); (*fig.*) die Fülle (*of,* an); *public —s,* die Staatsgelder.

fundamental [fʌndə'mentl], *adj.* grundsätzlich, wesentlich. — *s.* (*pl.*) die Grundlagen, *f.pl.*

funeral ['fju:nərəl], *s.* die Bestattung, Beerdigung.

funereal [fju:'niəriəl], *adj.* wie bei einem Begräbnis, betrübt, traurig.

fungus ['fʌŋgəs], *s.* (*Bot.*) der Pilz; der Schwamm (*mushroom*).

funk [fʌŋk], *s.* (*sl.*) die Angst, Panik. — *v.a.* fürchten.

funnel [fʌnl], *s.* der Trichter.

funny ['fʌni], *adj.* spaßhaft, komisch.

fur [fə:], *s.* der Pelz, das Fell (*coat of animal*); (*Med.*) der Belag (*on tongue*).

furbelow ['fə:bilou], *s.* die Falbel.

furbish ['fə:biʃ], *v.a.* aufputzen.

furious ['fjuəriəs], *adj.* wild, rasend, wütend.

furl [fə:l], *v.a.* (zusammen-)rollen; (*Naut.*) aufrollen.

furlong ['fə:lɔŋ], *s.* ein Achtel einer englischen Meile.

furlough ['fə:lou], *s.* der Urlaub.

furnace ['fə:nis], *s.* der Ofen, Hochofen (*steel*); (*Metall.*) der Schmelzofen.

furnish ['fə:niʃ], *v.a.* ausstatten, versehen (*equip*); möblieren (*a room etc.*).

furnisher ['fə:niʃə], *s.* der Möbelhändler; der Lieferant.

furniture ['fə:nitʃə], *s.* die Möbel, *n. pl.*; die Einrichtung.

furrier ['fariə], *s.* der Kürschner.

furrow ['farou], *s.* die Furche (*field*); die Runzel (*brow*). — *v.a.* runzeln (*brow*); Furchen ziehen (*plough up*).

further ['fə:ðə], *comp. adj., adv. see* **farther**. — *v.a.* fördern (*advance*).

furtherance ['fə:ðərəns], *s.* die Förderung (*advancement*).

furthermore ['fə:ðəmɔ:], *adv.* ferner.

furthest ['fə:ðist], *superl. adj., adv. see* **farthest**.

furtive ['fə:tiv], *adj.* verstohlen, heimlich.

fury ['fjuəri], *s.* die Wut; (*Myth.*) die Furie.

furze [fə:z], *s.* (*Bot.*) der Stechginster.

fuse [fju:z], *v.a., v.n.* schmelzen (*melt*); vereinigen (*unite*). — *s.* (*Elec.*) die Sicherung; *blow a —,* eine Sicherung durchbrennen; *— box,* der Sicherungskasten; *— wire,* der Schmelzdraht.

fuselage ['fju:zila:ʒ *or* -lidʒ], *s.* (*Aviat.*) der (Flugzeug-)rumpf.

fusible ['fju:zibl], *adj.* schmelzbar.

fusilier [fju:zi'liə], *s.* (*Mil.*) der Füsilier.

fusion ['fju:ʒən], *s.* die Verschmelzung; die Vereinigung.

fuss [fʌs], *s.* das Getue, die Umständlichkeit; *make a — about,* viel Aufhebens machen.

fussy ['fʌsi], *adj.* übertrieben genau; umständlich; geschäftig (*busy*); *— about,* genau in (*Dat.*).

fusty ['fʌsti], *adj.* moderig, muffig.

futile ['fju:tail], *adj.* nutzlos, vergeblich.

futility [fju:'tiliti], *s.* die Nutzlosigkeit.

future ['fju:tʃə], *s.* die Zukunft. — *adj.* (zu-)künftig.

fuzzy ['fʌzi], *adj.* kraus.

G

G [dʒi:]. das G (*also Mus.*); *— sharp,* das Gis; *— flat,* das Ges; *key of —,* der G Schlüssel, Violinschlüssel.

gavotte

gab [gæb], *s.* das Geschwätz; *the gift of the —*, ein gutes Mundwerk.
gabble [gæbl], *v.n.* schwatzen.
gable [geibl], *s.* der Giebel.
gad [gæd], *v.n. — about*, umherstreifen.
gadfly [gædflai], *s.* (*Ent.*) die Bremse.
gag [gæg], *s.* der Knebel; (*sl.*) der Witz. *— v.a.* knebeln.
gaiety [geiəti], *s.* die Fröhlichkeit.
gain [gein], *v.a.* gewinnen, erwerben (*earn*); *— possession*, Besitz ergreifen. *— s.* der Gewinn, Vorteil.
gainful [geinful], *adj. — employment*, die einträgliche Beschäftigung.
gainsay [geinsei *or* geinsei], *v.a.* widersprechen (*pers., Dat.*).
gait [geit], *s.* das Schreiten, der Schritt, Gang.
gaiter [geitə], *s.* die Gamasche.
galaxy [gæləksi], *s.* (*Astron.*) die Milchstraße; (*fig.*) die glänzende Versammlung.
gale [geil], *s.* der Sturm.
gall [gɔːl], *s.* die Galle. *— v.a.* verbittern, ärgern.
gallant [gælənt], *adj.* tapfer (*of soldier*); gallant, höflich (*polite*).
gallantry [gæləntri], *s.* die Tapferkeit; die Höflichkeit, Galanterie.
gallery [gæləri], *s.* die Gallerie.
galley [gæli], *s.* (*Naut.*) die Galeere; (*Typ.*) *— proof*, der Fahnenabzug.
gallon [gælən], *s.* die Gallone.
gallop [gæləp], *v.n.* galoppieren. *— s.* der Galopp.
gallows [gælouz], *s.* der Galgen.
galosh [gəlɔʃ], *s.* die Galosche.
galvanic [gælvænik], *adj.* galvanisch.
galvanize [gælvənaiz], *v.a.* galvanisieren.
gamble [gæmbl], *v.n.* um Geld spielen; *— away*, verspielen. *— s.* das Risiko.
gambol [gæmbl], *v.n.* herumspringen.
game [geim], *s.* das Spiel (*play*); das Wild, Wildbret (*pheasants etc.*); *fair —*, Freiwild, *n.*, offene Beute, *f.*
gamecock [geimkɔk], *s.* (*Orn.*) der Kampfhahn.
gamekeeper [geimkiːpə], *s.* der Wildhüter.
gammon [gæmən], *s.* der (geräucherte) Schinken (*bacon*).
gamut [gæmət], *s.* die Tonleiter.
gander [gændə], *s.* (*Orn.*) der Gänserich.
gang [gæŋ], *s.* die Bande; die Mannschaft (*workmen*). *— v.n. — up*, eine Bande bilden; *— up on s.o.*, sich gegen jemanden verbünden.
gangrene [gæŋgriːn], *s.* (*Med.*) der Brand; die Fäulnis.
gangway [gæŋwei], *s.* die Planke, der Laufgang (*on boat*); der Durchgang.
gaol, jail [dʒeil], *s.* das Gefängnis. *— v.a.* einsperren.
gaoler, jailer [dʒeilə], *s.* der Kerkermeister.
gap [gæp], *s.* die Lücke; die Bresche (*breach*).
gape [geip], *v.n.* gähnen, (*fig.*) klaffen.

garage [gærɑːʒ *or* gærɪdʒ], *s.* die Garage, die Tankstelle.
garb [gɑːb], *s.* die Tracht, Kleidung.
garbage [gɑːbidʒ], *s.* der Abfall; (*Am.*) *— can*, der Mülleimer.
garble [gɑːbl], *v.a.* verstümmeln.
garden [gɑːdn], *s.* der Garten. *— v.n.* im Garten arbeiten.
gardener [gɑːdnə], *s.* der Gärtner.
gargle [gɑːgl], *v.n.* gurgeln, spülen.
gargoyle [gɑːgɔil], *s.* (*Archit.*) der Wasserspeier.
garish [gɛəriʃ], *adj.* grell, auffallend.
garland [gɑːlənd], *s.* der Blumenkranz, die Girlande.
garlic [gɑːlik], *s.* (*Bot.*) der Knoblauch.
garment [gɑːmənt], *s.* das Gewand.
garner [gɑːnə], *v.a.* aufspeichern (*store*).
garnet [gɑːnit], *s.* der Granat.
garnish [gɑːniʃ], *v.a.* ausschmücken, verzieren.
garret [gærət], *s.* die Dachkammer.
garrison [gærisən], *s.* (*Mil.*) die Garnison. *— v.a.* stationieren.
garrulity [gærʊliti], *s.* die Schwatzhaftigkeit.
garter [gɑːtə], *s.* das Strumpfband, das Hosenband; *Order of the Garter*, der Hosenbandorden.
gas [gæs], *s.* das Gas; (*Am.*) see **gasoline**.
gaseous [geisiəs], *adj.* gasförmig, gasartig.
Gascon [gæskən], *s.* der Gaskogner.
gasoline [gæsoliːn], *s.* (*Am.*) das Benzin.
gash [gæʃ], *s.* die Schnittwunde.
gasp [gɑːsp], *v.n.* keuchen; nach Luft schnappen. *— s.* das Keuchen, das Luftschnappen.
gastric [gæstrik], *adj.* (*Anat.*) gastrisch; *— ulcer*, das Magengeschwür.
gate [geit], *s.* das Tor, der Eingang. *— v.a.* einsperren, Hausarrest geben (*Dat.*).
gateway [geitwei], *s.* die Einfahrt.
gather [gæðə], *v.a.* sammeln, einsammeln (*collect*); versammeln (*assemble*). *— v.n.* entnehmen, schließen (*infer*); sich versammeln (*come together*); aufziehen (*storm*).
gathering [gæðəriŋ], *s.* die Versammlung (*meeting*).
gauche [gouʃ], *adj.* linkisch, ungeschickt.
gaudy [gɔːdi], *adj.* übertrieben, grell, prunkhaft.
gauge [geidʒ], *v.a.* (*Engin.*) ausmessen, kalibrieren, eichen (*officially*). *— s.* der Maßstab (*scale*); (*Railw.*) die Spurweite.
gauger [geidʒə], *s.* der Eichmeister.
Gaul [gɔːl], *s.* der Gallier.
gaunt [gɔːnt], *adj.* mager; hager.
gauntlet [gɔːntlit], *s.* der (Panzer)handschuh.
gauze [gɔːz], *s.* die Gaze.
gavotte [gəvɔt], *s.* (*Mus.*) die Gavotte.

401

gay [gei], *adj.* fröhlich, heiter; bunt (*colour*).

gaze [geiz], *v.n.* starren.

gazelle [gə'zel], *s.* (*Zool.*) die Gazelle.

gazette [gə'zet], *s.* die (amtliche) Zeitung; das Amtsblatt.

gear [giə], *s.* das Gerät; (*Mech.*) das Triebwerk; (*Naut.*) das Geschirr; *switch*—, das Schaltgerät; (*Motor.*) der Gang; — *ratio*, die Übersetzung; *differential* —, der Achsenantrieb; *steering* —, die Lenkung (*of car*); — *box*, das Schaltgetriebe, die Gangschaltung; *out of* —, in Unordnung; *in top* —, mit Höchstgeschwindigkeit; *change to bottom* —, auf erste Geschwindigkeit (*or*, auf langsam) einschalten. — *v.a.* — *down*, herabsetzen; (*Engin.*) — *up*, übersetzen; — *to*, anpassen.

gelatine ['dʒeləti:n], *s.* die Gallerte, die Geleemasse.

gem [dʒem], *s.* die Gemme, der Edelstein.

gender ['dʒendə], *s.* (*Gram.*) das Geschlecht.

gene [dʒi:n], *s.* (*Biol.*) das Gen.

geneaology [dʒi:ni'ælədʒi], *s.* die Genealogie; der Stammbaum (*family tree*).

general ['dʒenərəl], *s.* (*Mil.*) der General; *lieutenant*- —, der Generalleutnant. — *adj.* allgemein, General-; — *-purpose*, für alle Zwecke; Allzweck-.

generalization [dʒenərəlai'zeiʃən], *s.* die Verallgemeinerung.

generalize ['dʒenərəlaiz], *v.a.* verallgemeinern.

generate ['dʒenəreit], *v.a.* erzeugen; (*Elec.*) Strom erzeugen.

generation [dʒenə'reiʃən], *s.* die Generation (*contemporaries*); das Zeugen (*production*); (*Elec.*) die Stromerzeugung.

generosity [dʒenə'rɔsiti], *s.* die Großmut (*magnanimity*); die Freigebigkeit (*liberality*).

generous ['dʒenərəs], *adj.* großmütig; freigebig (*with gifts*).

Genevan [dʒi'ni:vən], *adj.* genferisch. — *s.* der Genfer.

genitive ['dʒenitiv], *s.* (*Gram.*) der Wesfall, Genitiv.

genial ['dʒi:niəl], *adj.* freundlich, mild.

geniality [dʒi:ni'æliti], *s.* die Freundlichkeit, Leutseligkeit.

genital ['dʒenitəl], *adj.* Zeugungs-. — *s.* (*pl.*) die Geschlechtsteile, Genitalien, *pl.*

genius ['dʒi:niəs], *s.* das Genie; der Genius.

Genoese [dʒenou'i:z], *adj.* genuesisch. — *s.* der Genuese.

Gentile ['dʒentail], *s.* heidnisch; nicht jüdisch.

gentility [dʒen'tiliti], *s.* die Herkunft aus vornehmem Haus, Vornehmheit.

gentle ['dʒentl], *adj.* sanft, mild; gelind (*breeze*).

gentlefolk ['dʒentlfouk], *s.* bessere *or* vornehme Leute, *pl.*

gentleman ['dʒentlmən], *s.* der Gentleman, Herr; feiner Herr.

gentleness ['dʒentlnis], *s.* die Milde, Sanftheit.

gentry ['dʒentri], *s.* der niedere Adel.

genuine ['dʒenjuin], *adj.* echt.

genus ['dʒenəs], *s.* (*Biol.*) die Gattung.

geographer [dʒi'ɔgrəfə], *s.* der Geograph.

geographical [dʒi:o'græfikəl], *adj.* geographisch.

geography [dʒi'ɔgrəfi], die Geographie, Erdkunde.

geological [dʒi:o'lɔdʒikəl], *adj.* geologisch.

geologist [dʒi'ɔlədʒist], *s.* der Geologe.

geology [dʒi'ɔlədʒi], *s.* die Geologie.

geometric(al) [dʒi:o'metrik(əl)], *adj.* geometrisch.

geometrist [dʒi'ɔmətrist], *s.* der Geometer.

geometry [dʒi'ɔmətri], *s.* die Geometrie.

geranium [dʒə'reiniəm], *s.* (*Bot.*) die Geranie, das Germaniu.

germ [dʒə:m], *s.* der Keim; (*pl.*) die Bakterien, *f. pl.*

German ['dʒə:mən], *adj.* deutsch. — *s.* der, die Deutsche.

germane [dʒə:'mein], *adj.* zur Sache gehörig, zugehörig.

germinate ['dʒə:mineit], *v.n.* keimen.

Germanic [dʒə:'mænik], *adj.* germanisch.

gerund ['dʒerənd], *s.* (*Gram.*) das Gerundium.

gerundive [dʒe'rʌndiv], *s.* (*Gram.*) das Gerundiv(um).

gesticulate [dʒes'tikjuleit], *v.n.* Gebärden machen, gestikulieren.

gesture ['dʒestʃə], *s.* die Geste; der Gebärde.

get [get], *v.a.* irr. bekommen, (*coll.*) kriegen; erhalten (*receive*); erwischen (*catch up with*); einholen (*fetch*); — *over* or *across*, klar machen. — *v.n.* gelangen (*arrive*); werden (*become*); — *along*, weiterkommen; — *on* or (*Am.*) *along with s.o.*, mit jemandem auskommen; — *on in the world*, Karriere machen; — *away*, entkommen; — *down to it*, zur Sache kommen; — *in*, hineinkommen; — *off*, aussteigen; *show s.o. where he* —*s off*, jemandem seine Meinung sagen; (*Sch.*) — *through*, durchkommen (*in examination*); — *up*, aufstehen.

get-up ['getʌp], *s.* das Kostüm; die Ausstattung (*attire*).

Ghanaian [gɑ:'neiən], *adj.* ghanaisch. — *s.* der Ghanaer.

ghastly ['gɑ:stli], *adj.* furchtbar, schrecklich.

gherkin ['gə:kin], *s.* (*Bot.*) die Essiggurke.

ghost [goust], *s.* der Geist, das Gespenst.

giant ['dʒaiənt], *s.* der Riese.

gibberish ['dʒibəriʃ], *s.* das Kauderwelsch.

gibbet ['dʒibit], *s.* der Galgen.

gibe [dʒaib], *v.n.* spotten, höhnen (*at, über, Acc.*). — *s.* der Spott, Hohn; die spöttische Bemerkung (*remark*).

giblets [ˈdʒiblits], *s. pl.* das Gänseklein.

giddiness [ˈgidinis], *s.* das Schwindelgefühl.

giddy [ˈgidi], *adj.* schwindelig.

gift [gift], *s.* die Gabe, das Geschenk.

gifted [ˈgiftid], *adj.* begabt.

gig [gig], *s.* der leichte Wagen; (*Naut.*) der Nachen, das Gig.

gigantic [dʒaiˈgæntik], *adj.* riesig, riesengroß.

giggle [gigl], *v.n.* kichern. — *s.* das Kichern, Gekicher.

gild [gild], *v.a.* vergolden; verschönern; —*ing the pill*, etwas Unangenehmes (die Pille) versüßen.

gill (1) [gil], *s.* (*Biol.*) die Kieme.

gill (2) [dʒil], *s.* das Viertel einer Pinte (0.14 *l.*).

gilt [gilt], *s.* die Vergoldung; — *edged*, mit Goldschnitt; (*Comm.*) hochwertige *or* mündelsichere Staatspapiere.

gimlet [ˈgimlit], *s.* (*Carp.*) der Handbohrer.

gin [dʒin], *s.* der Gin, der Wachholderbranntwein; — *and tonic*, Gin und Tonic.

ginger [ˈdʒindʒə], *s.* der Ingwer; — -*haired*, rothaarig; — *nut*, das Ingweror Pfeffernüßchen, Ingwerkeks; — *beer*, Ingwerbier. — *v.a.* — *up*, aufstacheln, anreizen.

gingerbread [ˈdʒindʒəbred], *s.* der Lebkuchen, Pfefferkuchen.

gipsy [ˈdʒipsi], *s.* der Zigeuner.

giraffe [dʒiˈraːf], *s.* (*Zool.*) die Giraffe.

gird [gəːd], *v.a.* reg. & irr. (*Poet.*) gürten.

girder [ˈgəːdə], *s.* der Balken, Träger.

girdle [gəːdl], *v.a.* gürten, umgürten; — *the earth*, die Erde umkreisen.

girl [gəːl], *s.* das Mädchen.

girlhood [ˈgəːlhud], *s.* die Mädchenzeit, die Mädchenjahre, *n. pl.*

girlish [ˈgəːliʃ], *adj.* mädchenhaft, wie ein Mädchen.

gist [dʒist], *s.* das Wesentliche.

give [giv], *v.a. irr.* geben; — *out*, bekanntgeben, bekanntmachen; — *up*, aufgeben; — *way to*, Platz machen. — *v.n.* sich dehnen, sich strecken (*of wood, metal etc.*); — *in*, nachgeben (*to, Dat.*).

glacial [ˈgleisəl], *adj.* eisig, Gletscher-.

glacier [ˈglæsiə], *s.* der Gletscher.

glad [glæd], *adj.* froh, erfreut (*at, über, Acc.*).

gladden [glædn], *v.a.* erheitern, erfreuen.

glade [gleid], *s.* die Lichtung.

glamorous [ˈglæmərəs], *adj.* bezaubernd, blendend glanzvoll.

glamour [ˈglæmə], *s.* der Zauber; der Glanz.

glance [glaːns], *s.* der Blick; *at a* —, auf den ersten Blick. — *v.n.* flüchtig blicken.

gland [glænd], *s.* (*Anat.*) die Drüse.

glandular [ˈglændjulə], *adj.* Drüsen-, drüsig.

glare [glɛə], *s.* der blendende Glanz, das Schimmern; der (scharf) durchbohrende Blick (*stare*).

glaring [ˈglɛəriŋ], *adj.* schreiend (*of colour*); auffallend (*obvious*).

glass [glaːs], *s.* das Glas; der Spiegel (*mirror*); das Wetterglas (*barometer*); (*pl.*) die Brille (*spectacles*).

glassblower [ˈglaːsblouə], *s.* der Glasbläser.

glassworks [ˈglaːswəːks], *s.* die Glashütte.

glassy [ˈglaːsi], *adj.* gläsern.

glaze [gleiz], *s.* die Glasur. — *v.a.* glasieren; verglasen.

glazier [ˈgleiziə], *s.* der Glaser.

gleam [gliːm], *v.n.* strahlen, glänzen (*with*, vor, *Dat.*). — *s.* der Glanz, das Strahlen.

glean [gliːn], *v.a.* auflesen; erfahren (*learn*).

glebe [gliːb], *s.* das Pfarrgut.

glee (1) [gliː], *s.* die Freude, Heiterkeit.

glee (2) [gliː], *s.* (*Mus.*) der Rundgesang; — *club*, die Liedertafel.

glen [glen], *s.* das enge Tal.

glib [glib], *adj.* glatt, geläufig, zungenfertig.

glide [glaid], *v.n.* gleiten. — *s.* das Gleiten.

glider [ˈglaidə], *s.* (*Aviat.*) das Segelflugzeug.

glimmer [ˈglimə], *s.* der Schimmer, Glimmer. — *v.n.* schimmern, glimmen.

glimpse [glimps], *s.* der (flüchtige) Blick; *catch a* —, einen Blick erhaschen. — *v.a.* flüchtig blicken (*auf, Acc.*).

glisten [glisn], *v.n.* glitzern, glänzen.

glitter [ˈglitə], *v.n.* glänzen, schimmern.

gloaming [ˈgloumiŋ], *s.* die Dämmerung.

globe [gloub], *s.* der Globus, der Erdball; die Kugel.

globular [ˈglɔbjulə], *adj.* kugelförmig.

gloom [gluːm], *s.* das Dunkel; der Trübsinn, die Traurigkeit.

gloomy [ˈgluːmi], *adj.* deprimiert, trübsinnig, düster.

glorify [ˈglɔːrifai], *v.a.* verherrlichen.

glorious [ˈglɔːriəs], *adj.* herrlich; (*Mil.*) glorreich.

glory [ˈglɔːri], *s.* die Herrlichkeit, der Ruhm. — *v.n.* frohlocken (*in*, über, *Acc.*).

gloss [glɔs], *s.* der Glanz; (*Lit.*) die Glosse, Anmerkung. — *v.a.* — *over*, beschönigen; (*Lit.*) glossieren, mit Anmerkungen versehen.

glossary [ˈglɔsəri], *s.* das Glossar, die Spezialwörterliste; das Wörterbuch.

glossy [ˈglɔsi], *adj.* glänzend.

glove [glʌv], *s.* der Handschuh.

glow [glou], *v.n.* glühen. — *s.* die Glut, das Glühen; Wohlbehagen.

glower [ˈglauə], *v.n.* — *at*, feindselig ansehen, anstarren.

glue

glue [glu:], *s.* der Leim. — *v.a.* leimen, zusammenleimen.

glum [glʌm], *adj.* mürrisch, finster.

glut [glʌt], *s.* die Überfülle. — *v.a.* überladen, überfüllen.

glutinous ['glu:tinəs], *adj.* zähe, klebrig.

glutton [glʌtn], *s.* der Vielfraß.

gluttony ['glʌtəni], *s.* die Schwelgerei, Gefräßigkeit.

glycerine ['glisəri:n], *s.* das Glyzerin.

gnarled [nɑ:ld], *adj.* knorrig.

gnash [næʃ], *v.a.* knirschen (*teeth*).

gnat [næt], *s.* (*Ent.*) die Mücke.

gnaw [nɔ:], *v.a.*, *v.n.* nagen (an, *Dat.*), zernagen, zerfressen (at, *Acc.*).

gnome [noum], *s.* der Erdgeist, der Zwerg, Gnom.

go [gou], *v.n. irr.* gehen, fahren, laufen; arbeiten (*engine*); verlaufen (*event*); sich erstrecken (*distance*); — *down in the general esteem*, in der Achtung sinken; — *on*, fortfahren; — *mad*, verrückt werden; — *bald*, die Haare verlieren; — *without*, leer ausgehen, entbehren; *let* —, loslassen; — *for*, auf jemanden losgehen; — *in for*, sich interessieren für (*Acc.*); — *all out for*, energisch unternehmen; *a* —*ing concern*, ein gutgehendes Unternehmen; —*ing on for 20*, fast 20 Jahre. — *s.* der Versuch; (*coll.*) *plenty of* —, recht lebhaft, voller Schwung.

goad [goud], *v.a.* anstacheln.

goal [goul], *s.* das Ziel; (*Footb.*) das Tor.

goalkeeper ['goulki:pə], *s.* der Torwart.

goalpost ['goulpoust], *s.* der Torpfosten.

goat [gout], *s.* (*Zool.*) die Geiß, Ziege; *billy* —, der Ziegenbock; *nanny* —, die Geiß.

gobble [gɔbl], *v.a.* verschlingen, gierig essen.

goblet ['gɔblit], *s.* der Becher.

goblin ['gɔblin], *s.* der Kobold, der Gnom; der Schelm.

go-cart ['goukɑ:t], *s.* der Kinderwagen, Gängelwagen.

God [gɔd]. Gott.

god [gɔd], *s.* der Gott.

godchild ['gɔdtʃaild], *s.* das Patenkind.

goddess ['gɔdes], *s.* die Göttin.

godfather ['gɔdfɑ:ðə], *s.* der Pate.

godhead ['gɔdhed], *s.* die Gottheit.

godless ['gɔdlis], *adj.* gottlos, ungläubig.

godmother ['gɔdmʌðə], *s.* die Patin.

goggle [gɔgl], *v.n.* glotzen, starren (*stare*). — *s.* (*pl.*) die Schutzbrille.

going ['gouiŋ], *s.* das Gehen, das Funktionieren (*of machinery*); *while the* — *is good*, zur rechten Zeit.

gold [gould], *s.* das Gold; (*Fin.*) — *standard*, die Goldwährung.

goldfinch ['gouldfintʃ], *s.* (*Orn.*) der Stieglitz.

goldsmith ['gouldsmiθ], *s.* der Goldschmied.

gondola ['gɔndələ], *s.* die Gondel.

good [gud], *adj.* gut; artig, brav; *for* —, auf immer; *in* — *time*, rechtzeitig; — *and proper*, (*coll.*) wie es sich gehört, anständig; *as* — *as*, so gut wie; — *looking*, hübsch; — *natured*, gutmütig. — *s. for your own* —, in Ihrem eigenen Interesse; *that's no* —, das taugt nichts; (*pl.*) die Güter, *n.pl.*, Waren, *f.pl.*; *goods station*, der Frachbahnhof; *goods train*, der Güterzug; *goods yard*, der Güterstapelplatz.

goodbye [gud'bai], *interj.*, *s.*—! leb wohl! auf Wiedersehen!

goodness ['gudnis], *s.* die Güte.

goodwill [gud'wil], *s.* das Wohlwollen; (*Comm.*) die Kundschaft.

goose [gu:s], *s.* (*Orn.*) die Gans.

gooseberry ['guzbəri], *s.* (*Bot.*) die Stachelbeere.

gore [gɔ:], *s.* das geronnene Blut. — *v.a.* durchbohren (*pierce*, *stab*).

gorge [gɔ:dʒ], *s.* die Felsenschlucht (*ravine*); (*Anat.*) die Kehle. — *v.a.* gierig verschlingen.

gorgeous ['gɔ:dʒəs], *adj.* prachtvoll, prächtig.

gorse [gɔ:s], *s.* (*Bot.*) der Stechginster.

gory ['gɔ:ri], *adj.* blutig.

goshawk ['gɔshɔ:k], *s.* (*Orn.*) der Hühnerhabicht.

gosling ['gɔzliŋ], *s.* (*Orn.*) das Gänschen.

gospel ['gɔspəl], *s.* das Evangelium; *the* — *according to*, das Evangelium des . . .

gossamer ['gɔsəmə], *s.* das feine Gewebe; die Sommerfäden.

gossip ['gɔsip], *v.n.* klatschen; schwatzen, plaudern. — *s.* der Klatsch; der Schwätzer; die Klatschbase.

Gothic ['gɔθik], *adj.* gotisch.

gouge [gaudʒ], *s.* der Hohlmeißel. — *v.a.* aushöhlen, ausstechen.

gourd ['guəd], *s.* der Kürbis.

gout [gaut], *s.* (*Med.*) die Gicht.

govern ['gʌvən], *v.a.*, *v.n.* (*Pol.*) regieren; beherrschen; (*fig.*) leiten, herrschen.

governable ['gʌvənəbl], *adj.* lenkbar, lenksam.

governess ['gʌvənis], *s.* die Erzieherin, die Gouvernante.

government ['gʌvənmənt], *s.* die Regierung; (*Pol.*) — *benches*, die Regierungssitze; — *loan*, die Staatsanleihe.

governor ['gʌvənə], *s.* der Gouverneur, Statthalter.

gown [gaun], *s.* das Kleid (*lady's*); (*Univ.*) der Talar; (*official robe*) die Amtstracht.

grab [græb], *v.a.* packen, ergreifen. — *s.* der Zugriff.

grace [greis], *s.* die Gnade; Gunst (*favour*); die Anmut (*gracefulness*); *Your Grace*, Euer Gnaden; das Tischgebet (*prayer at table*); (*Mus.*) — *note*, die Fermate; *ten minutes'* —, zehn Minuten Aufschub. — *v.a.* schmücken, zieren, ehren.

graceful ['greisful], *adj.* anmutig, reizend; graziös (*movement*).

great

graceless ['greislis], *adj.* ungraziös.
gracious['greiʃəs],*adj.*gnädig,huldreich.
gradation [grə'deiʃən], *s.* die Abstufung, die Stufenleiter.
grade [greid], *s.* der Grad, Rang (*rank*); (*Am.*) (*Sch.*) die Klasse. — *v.a.* sortieren, ordnen.
gradient ['greidiənt], *s.* (*Geog.*) die Steigung; der Steigungswinkel (*angle*).
gradual ['grædjuəl], *adj.* allmählich.
graduate ['grædjueit], *v.n.* promovieren (*receive degree*); — *as a doctor*, als Doktor promovieren, den Doktor machen. —[-djuit], *s.* der Akademiker, Graduierte.
graft (1) [grɑːft], *s.* (*Hort., Med.*) die (Haut)übertragung. — *v.a.* (*Hort., Med.*) übertragen, anheften (*on to*, auf, *Acc.*).
graft (2) [grɑːft], *s.* (*Am.*) der unerlaubte Gewinn; das Schmiergeld; der Betrug (*swindle*).
grain [grein], *s.* das Korn, Samenkorn; das Getreide; das Gran (= 0·065 *gramme*); die Maserung (*in wood*); *against the* —, gegen den Strich.
grammar ['græmə], *s.* die Grammatik; — *school*, das Gymnasium.
grammatical [grə'mætikəl], *adj.* grammatisch.
gramme [græm], *s.* das Gramm.
gramophone ['græməfoun], *s.* das Grammophon.
granary ['grænəri], *s.* der (Korn)speicher, die Kornkammer.
grand [grænd], *adj.* groß, großartig; wunderbar; *Grand Duke*, der Großherzog. — *s.* (*Am.*) (*sl.*) 1000 Dollar; (*piano*) der Flügel; *baby* —, der Stutzflügel.
grandchild ['græntʃaild], *s.* der Enkel, die Enkelin.
grandee [græn'diː], *s.* der spanische Grande.
grandeur ['grændjə], *s.* die Größe, Pracht.
grandfather ['grændfɑːðə], *s.* der Großvater.
grandiloquent [græn'dilokwənt], *adj.* großsprecherisch.
grandmother ['grændmʌðə], *s.* die Großmutter.
grange [greindʒ], *s.* der Meierhof, das Landhaus.
granite ['grænit], *s.* der Granit.
grannie, granny ['græni], *s.* (*coll.*) die Oma.
grant [grɑːnt], *s.* die Gewährung (*of permission etc.*); die Zuwendung (*subsidy*); (*Sch.*) das Stipendium. — *v.a.* geben, gewähren; *take for* —*ed*, als selbstverständlich hinnehmen.
granular ['grænjulə], *adj.* körnig.
granulated ['grænjuleitid], *adj.* feinkörnig, Kristall- (*sugar*).
grape [greip], *s.* (*Bot.*) die Weinbeere; die Traube; — *sugar*, der Traubenzucker;*bunch of* —*s*,Weintrauben,*f. pl.*
grapefruit ['greipfruːt], *s.* die Pampelmuse.

graphic ['græfik], *adj.* (*Art*) graphisch; deutlich, bildhaft, anschaulich.
grapnel ['græpnəl], *s.* (*Naut.*) der Dreganker.
grapple ['græpl], *v.n.* — *with*, raufen, (miteinander) ringen.
grasp [grɑːsp], *v.a.* (mit der Hand) ergreifen, erfassen. — *s.* das Fassungsvermögen, die Auffassung; der Griff (*hand*).
grasping ['grɑːspiŋ], *adj.* habgierig, gewinnsüchtig.
grass [grɑːs], *s.* (*Bot.*) das Gras; der Rasen (*lawn*); — *widow*, die Strohwitwe.
grasshopper ['grɑːshɔpə], *s.* (*Ent.*) die Heuschrecke.
grate (1) [greit], *s.* der Feuerrost, der Kamin.
grate (2) [greit], *v.a.* reiben (*cheese*); schaben, kratzen. — *v.n.* knirschen; auf die Nerven gehen.
grateful ['greitful], *adj.* dankbar.
grater ['greitə], *s.* das Reibeisen; die Reibe (*electrical*).
gratification [grætifi'keiʃən], *s.* die Genugtuung, Befriedigung.
gratify ['grætifai], *v.a.* befriedigen, erfreuen.
grating ['greitiŋ], *s.* das Gitter.
gratis ['greitis], *adv.* gratis, umsonst, frei, unentgeltlich.
gratitude ['grætitjuːd], *s.* die Dankbarkeit.
gratuitous [grə'tjuːitəs], *adj.* frei, freiwillig (*voluntary*); unentgeltlich (*free of charge*); grundlos (*baseless*).
gratuity [grə'tjuːiti], *s.* das Trinkgeld (*tip*); die Gratifikation.
grave (1) [greiv], *adj.* schwer, ernst (*serious*); feierlich (*solemn*). —*s.* (*Mus.*) das Grave.
grave (2) [greiv], *s.* das Grab (*tomb*).
gravel [grævl], *s.* der Kies.
graveyard ['greivjɑːd], *s.* der Friedhof.
gravitate ['græviteit], *v.n.* gravitieren, hinstreben.
gravitation [grævi'teiʃən],*s.*die Schwerkraft.
gravitational [grævi'teiʃənəl], *adj.* (*Phys.*) Schwerkrafts-.
gravity ['græviti], *s.* der Ernst (*seriousness*); (*Phys.*) die Schwere, Schwerkraft.
gravy ['greivi], *s.* die Sauce, Soße; der Saft des Fleisches, des Bratens; — *boat*, die Sauciere.
gray, grey [grei], *adj.* grau.
graze (1) [greiz], *v.n.* weiden.
graze (2) [greiz], *v.a.* streifen (*pass closely*), abschürfen.
grazier ['greiziə], *s.* der Viehzüchter.
grease [griːs], *s.* das Fett; das Schmieröl (*machine*). — *v.a.* einfetten (*pans*); schmieren, einschmieren (*machinery*).
greasy ['griːsi], *adj.* fett, schmierig, ölig.
great [greit], *adj.* groß, bedeutend, wichtig; (*Am.*) wundervoll, wunderbar.

greatcoat

greatcoat ['greitkout], *s.* der Winter-mantel.

great-grandfather [greit'grændfɑːðə], *s.* der Urgroßvater.

greatly ['greitli], *adv.* stark, sehr.

greatness ['greitnis], *s.* die Größe, Bedeutung.

greedy ['griːdi], *adj.* gierig; gefräßig (*eater*).

Greek [griːk], *adj.* griechisch. — *s.* der Grieche.

green [griːn], *adj.* grün; neu (*new*), frisch (*fresh*).

greengage ['griːngeidʒ], *s.* (*Bot.*) die Reineclaude.

greengrocer ['griːngrousə], *s.* der Grünwarenhändler, Gemüsehändler.

greenhorn ['griːnhɔːn], *s.* der Grünschnabel.

greenhouse ['griːnhaus], *s.* das Gewächshaus, Treibhaus.

Greenlander ['griːnləndə], *s.* der Grönländer.

greet [griːt], *v.a.* grüßen, begrüßen.

greeting ['griːtiŋ], *s.* die Begrüßung; (*pl.*) Grüße, *m. pl.*

gregarious [gri'geəriəs], *adj.* gesellig.

grenade [gri'neid], *s.* die Granate.

grey *see under* gray.

greyhound ['greihaund], *s.* (*Zool.*) das Windspiel, der Windhund.

grid [grid], *s.* (*Elec.*) das Stromnetz; (*Phys.*) das Gitter.

gridiron ['gridaiən], *s.* der Bratrost, das Bratrostgitter.

grief [griːf], *s.* der Kummer, die Trauer.

grievance ['griːvəns], *s.* die Klage, Beschwerde.

grieve [griːv], *v.a.* kränken. — *v.n.* sich grämen, sich kränken (*over*, über, *Acc.*, wegen, *Genit.*).

grievous ['griːvəs], *adj.* schmerzlich.

grill [gril], *s.* der Rostbraten, Bratrost. — *v.a.* grillieren, rösten (*meat*); verhören (*question closely*).

grilling ['griliŋ], *s.* das Verhör.

grim [grim], *adj.* grimmig, finster.

grimace [gri'meis], *s.* die Grimasse, die Fratze.

grime [graim], *s.* der Schmutz, der Ruß.

grimy ['graimi], *adj.* schmutzig, rußig.

grin [grin], *v.n.* grinsen; (*coll.*) — *and bear it*, mach gute Miene zum bösen Spiel. — *s.* das Grinsen.

grind [graind], *v.a. irr.* zerreiben (*rub*); schleifen (*sharpen*); mahlen (*pulverize*); — *o.'s teeth*, mit den Zähnen knirschen. — *s.* (*coll.*) die ungeheure Anstrengung, die Plackerei.

grinder ['graində], *s.* coffee —, die Kaffeemühle; *knife* —, der Schleifer, Wetzer; der Backzahn (*molar*).

grindstone ['graindstoun], *s.* der Schleifstein; *keep o.'s nose to the* —, fest bei der Arbeit bleiben.

grip [grip], *s.* der Griff; *lose o.'s* —, nicht mehr bewältigen können (wie bisher); (*Tech.*) der Handgriff (*handle*). — *v.a.* ergreifen, festhalten.

gripe [graip], *v.n.* (*sl.*) meckern.

gripes [graips], *s. pl.* (*Med.*) das Bauchgrimmen, die Kolik.

gripping ['gripiŋ], *adj.* fesselnd (*story*).

grisly ['grizli], *adj.* scheußlich, gräßlich.

grist [grist], *s.* das Mahlgut, Gemahlene; — *to o.'s mill*, Wasser auf seine Mühle.

gristle [grisl], *s.* der Knorpel.

grit [grit], *s.* das Schrot, der Kies; der Mut (*courage*).

gritty ['griti], *adj.* körnig, kiesig, sandig.

grizzled [grizld], *adj.* grau, graumeliert.

groan [groun], *v.n.* stöhnen.

groats [grouts], *s. pl.* die Hafergrütze.

grocer ['grousə], *s.* der Kolonialwarenhändler, Feinkosthändler.

groin [groin], *s.* (*Anat.*) die Leiste; (*Archit.*) die Gewölbekante, Rippe.

groom [gruːm], *s.* der Stallknecht (*stables*); (*obs.*) der Junge (*inn*). — *v.a.* schniegeln, bürsten; schön machen.

groove [gruːv], *s.* die Rinne; die Rille (*of gramophone record*). — *v.a.* rillen; furchen (*dig a furrow*).

grope [group], *v.n.* tappen, tasten (*around*, umher).

gross [grous], *adj.* dick (*fat*); plump (*heavy-handed*); grob (*ill-mannered*); — *weight*, das Bruttogewicht; ungeheuer (*error*).

grotto ['grɔtou], *s.* die Grotte.

ground [graund], *s.* der Grund, Boden (*also pl.*); die Ursache (*cause*); — *floor*, das Erdgeschoß. — *v.n.* stranden (*of ship*).

groundwork ['graundwəːk], *s.* die Grundlagen, *f. pl.*

group [gruːp], *s.* die Gruppe. — *v.a.* gruppieren, anordnen.

grouse (1) [graus], *v.n.* (*coll.*) meckern, sich beklagen. — *s.* der Grund zur Klage, die Beschwerde.

grouse (2) [graus], *s.* (*Orn.*) das Birkhuhn, Moorhuhn.

grove [grouv], *s.* der Hain, das Wäldchen.

grovel [grɔvl], *v.n.* kriechen, schöntun (*Dat.*).

grow [grou], *v.n. irr.* wachsen, mehren (*increase*); werden (*become*). — *v.a.* anbauen, anpflanzen.

growl [graul], *v.n.* brummen, knurren. — *s.* das Gebrumme, Geknurre.

grown-up [groun'ʌp], *s.* der Erwachsene. — *adj.* erwachsen.

growth [grouθ], *s.* das Anwachsen (*increase*); das Wachstum (*growing*).

grub [grʌb], *s.* (*Zool.*) die Larve; (*coll.*) das Essen. — *v.n.* — *about*, wühlen.

grudge [grʌdʒ], *s.* der Groll; Neid (*jealousy*). — *v.a.* mißgönnen (*envy*). — *v.n.* — *doing s.th.*, etwas ungerne tun.

gruel ['gruːəl], *s.* der Haferschleim.

gruesome ['gruːsəm], *adj.* schauerlich, schrecklich.

gruff [grʌf], *adj.* mürrisch.

grumble [grʌmbl], *v.n.* murren, klagen.

grumbler ['grʌmblə], s. der Unzu-
friedene, Nörgler.

grunt [grʌnt], v.n. grunzen. — s. das
Grunzen.

guarantee [gærən'tiː], v.a. bürgen,
garantieren. — s. die Bürgschaft;
(Comm.) die Garantie.

guarantor ['gærəntɔː], s. der Bürge;
(Comm.) der Garant.

guard [gaːd], s. die Wache (watch or
watchman); (Railw.) der Schaffner; die
Schutzvorrichtung (protective device);
(fire), das Kamingitter; (for
sword) das Stichblatt. — v.a. bewachen; behüten (protect). — v.n. auf
der Hut sein; — against, sich hüten
(vor, Dat.); vorbeugen.

guarded ['gaːdid], adj. behutsam,
vorsichtig.

guardian ['gaːdjən], s. der Vormund
(of child); der Wächter.

guardianship ['gaːdjənʃip], s. (Law)
die Vormundschaft.

Guatemalan [gwæti'maːlən], adj.
guatemaltekisch. — s. der Guatemal-
teke.

Guelph [gwelf], s. der Welfe.

guess [ges], v.a. raten (a riddle). —
v.n. (Am.) glauben, meinen. — s. die
Vermutung; have a —, rate mal!

guest [gest], s. der Gast; paying —,
der Pensionär.

guffaw [gʌ'fɔː], s. das (laute) Gelächter.

guidance ['gaidəns], s. die Führung,
Anleitung.

guide [gaid], s. der Führer, Wegweiser,
Reiseführer; (Phot.) die Führung. —
v.a. führen, anleiten.

guided ['gaidid], adj. gelenkt; —
missile, das Ferngeschoß, die Rakete.

guild [gild], s. die Gilde, Zunft, Innung.

guildhall ['gildhɔːl], s. das Rathaus.

guile [gail], s. der Betrug, die Arglist.

guileless ['gaillis], adj. arglos.

guilt [gilt], s. die Schuld.

guilty ['gilti], adj. schuldig.

guinea ['gini], s. die Guinee (21 shillings); — fowl, das Perlhuhn; — pig,
das Meerschweinchen.

guise [gaiz], s. die Verkleidung (costume); die Erscheinung (appearance).

guitar [gi'taː], s. (Mus.) die Gitarre.

gulf [gʌlf], s. der Meerbusen, Golf;
der Abgrund (abyss).

gull [gʌl], s. (Orn.) die Möwe.

gullet ['gʌlit], s. (Anat.) der Schlund,
die Gurgel.

gullible ['gʌlibl], adj. leichtgläubig.

gully ['gʌli], s. die Schlucht (abyss).

gulp [gʌlp], v.a. schlucken. — s. der
Schluck, Zug.

gum (1) [gʌm], s. (Bot.) das Gummi.
— v.a. gummieren; (coll.) — up,
verderben (spoil).

gum (2) [gʌm], s. (Anat.) das Zahnfleisch.

gun [gʌn], s. das Gewehr (rifle); die
Kanone (cannon); — carriage, die
Lafette.

gunpowder ['gʌnpaudə], s. das Schieß-
pulver.

gunsmith ['gʌnsmiθ], s. der Büchsen-
macher.

gurgle [gəːgl], v.n. glucksen.

gush [gʌʃ], v.n. sich ergießen; schwärmen.

gusset ['gʌsit], s. (Tail.) der Zwickel.

gust [gʌst], s. der Windstoß.

gut [gʌt], s. (Anat.) der Darm; (pl.) die
Eingeweide, n. pl.; (coll.) der Mut.
— v.a. ausnehmen; ausleeren.

gutter ['gʌtə], s. die Rinne, Gosse.

guttersnipe ['gʌtəsnaip], s. der
Lausbube.

guttural ['gʌtərəl],adj.Kehl-.—s.(Phon.)
der Kehllaut.

guy [gai], s. die Vogelscheuche, die
verkleidete Puppe; (Am.) der Kerl.

guzzle [gʌzl], v.n. schlemmen.

gymnasium [dʒim'neiziəm], s. die
Turnhalle.

gymnastics [dʒim'næstiks], s. pl. das
Turnen; die Gymnastik.

gypsum ['dʒipsəm], s. der Gips; der
schwefelsaure Kalk.

gyrate [dʒaiə'reit], v.n. sich im Kreise
bewegen, sich drehen, kreisen.

H

H [eitʃ]. das H.

haberdasher ['hæbədæʃə], s. der Kurz-
warenhändler.

haberdashery ['hæbədæʃəri], s. die
Kurzwarenhandlung.

habit ['hæbit], s. die Gewohnheit
(custom); force of —, aus Gewohnheit,
die Macht der Gewohnheit; die
Kleidung (costume); riding —, das
Reitkostüm.

habitable ['hæbitəbl], adj. bewohnbar.

habitation [hæbi'teiʃən], s. die Wohnung.

habitual [hə'bitjuəl], adj. gewohnheitsmäßig.

habituate [hə'bitjueit], v.a. gewöhnen.

hack (1) [hæk], v.a. hacken (wood);
treten.

hack (2) [hæk], s. der Lohnschreiber;
der (alte) Gaul, das Mietpferd (horse).

hackle [hækl], v.a. hecheln.

hackney ['hækni], s. — carriage, die
Mietkutsche; das Taxi.

haddock ['hædək], s. (Zool.) der Schellfisch.

haemorrhage ['heməridʒ], s. (Med.)
die Blutung, der Blutsturz.

haemorrhoids ['heməroidz], s.pl.(Med.)
die Hämorrhoiden, f. pl.

hag [hæg], s. das alte Weib; die Hexe
(witch).

haggard ['hægəd], *adj.* hager (*lean*); häßlich, abgehärmt.

haggle [hægl], *v.n.* feilschen.

haggler ['hæglə], *s.* der Feilscher.

hail (1) [heil], *s.* der Hagel. — *v.n.* hageln.

hail (2) [heil], *v.a.* (mit einem Ruf) begrüßen; rufen. — *interj.* Heil, willkommen! — *s.* der Zuruf, Gruß.

hair [hɛə], *s.* das Haar; *split* —s, Haarspalterei treiben.

haircut ['hɛəkʌt], *s.* der Haarschnitt.

hairdresser ['hɛədresə], *s.* der Friseur.

hale [heil], *adj.* — *and hearty*, frisch und gesund, rüstig.

half [hɑːf], *adj.* halb. — *adv.* — *baked*, unreif; unterentwickelt (*stupid*) (*coll.*) *not* —, und wie! sehr gern. — *s.* die Hälfte; *too clever by* —, allzu gescheit.

halfcaste ['hɑːfkɑːst], *s.* der Mischling.

halfpenny ['heipni], *s.* der halbe Penny.

halfwit ['hɑːfwit], *s.* der Dummkopf.

halibut ['hælibət], *s.* (Zool.) der Heilbutt.

hall [hɔːl], *s.* der Saal; die Halle; der Hausflur (*entrance* —); (*Univ.*) — (*of residence*), das Studentenheim; — *porter*, der Portier.

hallmark ['hɔːlmɑːk], *s.* das Kennzeichen.

hallow ['hælou], *v.a.* weihen, heiligen.

Halloween [hælou'iːn]. der Allerheiligenabend.

halo ['heilou], *s.* der Heiligenschein (*of saint*); der Hof (*round the moon*).

hallucination [həluːsi'neiʃən], *s.* die Halluzination.

halt [hɔːlt], *v.n.* halten, haltmachen; — *! Halt!* zögern (*tarry*); —*ing speech*, die Sprechhemmung. — *v.a.* anhalten, zum Halten bringen. — *s.* (Railw.) die (kleine) Haltestelle.

halve [hɑːv], *v.a.* halbieren.

ham [hæm], *s.* (Cul.) der Schinken; (Anat.) der Schenkel; — *acting*, das Schmierentheater.

hammer ['hæmə], *s.* der Hammer. — *v.a., v.n.* hämmern; — *away at*, an etwas emsig arbeiten; — *out a problem*, ein Problem zur Lösung bringen.

hammock ['hæmək], *s.* die Hängematte.

hamper (1) ['hæmpə], *s.* der Packkorb.

hamper (2) ['hæmpə], *v.a.* behindern.

hand [hænd], *s.* die Hand; *a fair* —, eine gute Handschrift; der Uhrzeiger (*on watch, clock*); die Seite (*right, left* —); die Karten, *f. pl.* (*card game*); *play a strong* —, starke Karten halten *or* spielen; *on* —, vorrätig, auf Lager; *get out of* —, unkontrollierbar werden. — *v.a.* — *in*, einhändigen, einreichen; — *out*, austeilen; — *over*, übergeben, einhändigen.

handbag ['hændbæg], *s.* die Handtasche.

handbill ['hændbil], *s.* der Zettel, Reklamezettel (*advertising*).

handful ['hændful], *s.* die Handvoll; *to be quite a* —, genug zu schaffen geben; das Sorgenkind.

handicap ['hændikæp], *s.* das Hindernis. — *v.a.* hindern, behindern.

handicraft ['hændikrɑːft], *s.* das Handwerk; Kunsthandwerk.

handkerchief ['hæŋkətʃif], *s.* das Taschentuch.

handle [hændl], *s.* der Griff; der Henkel (*pot, vase*). — *v.a.* handhaben (*machine*); behandeln (*person*); anpacken (*problem*).

handlebar ['hændlbɑː], *s.* die Lenkstange (*bicycle*).

handmaid(en) ['hændmeid(n)], *s.* (*obs.*) die Magd.

handrail ['hændreil], *s.* das Geländer.

handshake ['hændʃeik], *s.* der Händedruck.

handsome ['hænsəm], *adj.* hübsch, schön, stattlich.

handy ['hændi], *adj.* geschickt; — *man*, der Gelegenheitsarbeiter, Mann für alles.

hang [hæŋ], *v.a. reg. & irr.* hängen; aufhängen (*suspend*); — *it!* zum Henker; — *paper*, ein Zimmer austapezieren; — *dog expression*, den Kopf hängen lassen, die betrübte Miene. — *v.n.* hängen; (*coll.*) — *on!* warte einen Moment! — *about*, herumstehen; herumlungern (*loiter*).

hanger-on [hæŋər'ɔn], *s.* der Anhänger, Mitläufer.

hangman ['hæŋmən], *s.* der Henker.

hanker ['hæŋkə], *v.n.* sich sehnen.

Hanoverian [hæno'viəriən], *adj.* hannöversch. — *s.* der Hannoveraner.

hansom ['hænsəm], *s.* die zweirädrige Droschke.

haphazard [hæp'hæzəd], *s.* der Zufall, das Geratewohl.

hapless ['hæplis], *adj.* unglücklich.

happen [hæpn], *v.n.* sich ereignen, passieren; — *to . . .*, zufällig . . .

happiness ['hæpinis], *s.* das Glück; die Glückseligkeit.

happy ['hæpi], *adj.* glücklich, glückselig.

harangue [hə'ræŋ], *s.* die Ansprache. — *v.a.* einsprechen (auf, *Acc.*); anreden.

harass ['hærəs], *v.a.* plagen, quälen.

harbinger ['hɑːbindʒə], *s.* der Vorbote, Bote.

harbour ['hɑːbə], *s.* der Hafen. — *v.a.* beherbergen (*shelter*); hegen (*cherish*).

hard [hɑːd], *adj.* schwer (*difficult*); hart (*tough*); hartherzig (*miserly*); — *up*, in Not, in Geldverlegenheit; — *of hearing*, schwerhörig.

harden ['hɑːdn], *v.a.* härten. — *v.n.* hart werden.

hardiness ['hɑːdinis], *s.* die Kraft, Stärke; die Rüstigkeit.

hardly ['hɑːdli], *adv.* kaum.

hardship ['hɑːdʃip], *s.* die Not, Bedrängnis (*need*); die Beschwerde (*complaint*).

hardware ['haːdwɛə], s. die Eisenware(n).

hardy ['haːdi], adj. abgehärtet, stark; (Bot.) — annual, ein widerstandsfähiges Jahresgewächs.

hare [hɛə], s. (Zool.) der Hase; — brained, unbedacht, gedankenlos; — lip, die Hasenscharte.

harebell ['hɛəbel], s. (Bot.) die Glockenblume.

haricot ['hærikou], s. (Bot.) — bean, die welsche Bohne.

hark [haːk], v.n. horchen.

harlequin ['haːlikwin], s. der Harlekin.

harlot ['haːlət], s. die Hure.

harm [haːm], s. das Leid, Unrecht; do — to, Schaden zufügen (Dat.). — v.a. verletzen (hurt); schaden (damage, Dat.).

harmful ['haːmful], adj. schädlich.

harmless ['haːmlis], adj. harmlos.

harmonious [haː'mouniəs], adj. harmonisch; einmütig (of one mind).

harmonize ['haːmənaiz], v.a. in Einklang bringen. — v.n. harmonieren, in Einklang stehen.

harmony ['haːməni], s. (Mus.) die Harmonie; (fig.) der Einklang, die Einmütigkeit.

harness ['haːnis], s. der Harnisch. — v.a. anschirren, anspannen (horse); (fig.) nutzbar machen.

harp [haːp], s. (Mus.) die Harfe. — v.n. (coll.) — upon, herumreiten auf (Dat.).

harpoon [haː'puːn], s. die Harpune. — v.a. harpunieren.

harrow ['hærou], s. die Egge, Harke. — v.a. harken, eggen; quälen.

harry ['hæri], v.a. verheeren, quälen.

harsh [haːʃ], adj. herb, rauh (rough); streng (severe).

hart [haːt], s. (Zool.) der Hirsch.

harvest ['haːvist], s. die Ernte; — home, das Erntefest.

hash [hæʃ], v.a. zerhacken; vermischen (mix up). — s. das Hackfleisch; make a — of things, verpfuschen, alles verderben.

hasp [hæsp or haːsp], s. der Haken, die Spange.

haste [heist], s. die Hast, Eile (hurry); die Voreiligkeit (rashness).

hasten [heisn], v.n. eilen, sich beeilen.

hasty ['heisti], adj. voreilig.

hat [hæt], s. der Hut; (coll.) talk through o.'s —, Unsinn reden.

hatch (1) [hætʃ], s. die Brut (chickens). — v.a., v.n. (aus-)brüten; aushecken (cunning).

hatch (2) [hætʃ], s. das Servierfenster (for serving food); (Naut.) die Luke.

hatch (3) [hætʃ], v.a. (Art) schraffieren.

hatchet ['hætʃit], s. das Beil, die Axt; bury the —, das Kriegsbeil begraben.

hate [heit], v.a., v.n. hassen; — to ..., nicht ... wollen. — s. der Haß, Widerwille, die Abneigung.

hateful ['heitful], adj. verhaßt (hated); gehässig (hating).

hatred ['heitrid], s. der Haß.

hatter ['hætə], s. der Hutmacher.

haughty ['hɔːti], adj. übermütig (supercilious); hochmütig, stolz (proud); hochnäsig (giving o.s. airs).

haul [hɔːl], v.a. schleppen, ziehen. — s. das Schleppen; (coll.) die Beute.

haulage ['hɔːlidʒ], s. der Schleppdienst, die Spedition.

haunch [hɔːntʃ], s. (Anat.) die Hüfte; der Schenkel (horse); die Keule (venison).

haunt [hɔːnt], v.a. heimsuchen, spuken (in, Dat.); it is —ed, hier spuktes.

have [hæv], v.a. irr. haben, besitzen (possess); erhalten; lassen; — to, müssen; — s.th. made, done, etwas machen lassen.

haven [heivn], s. der Zufluchtsort.

haversack ['hævəsæk], s. der Brotbeutel.

havoc ['hævək], s. die Verwüstung, Verheerung.

hawk (1) [hɔːk], s. (Orn.) der Habicht; der Falke (falcon).

hawk (2) [hɔːk], v.a. hausieren.

hawker ['hɔːkə], s. der Hausierer.

hawthorn ['hɔːθɔːn], s. (Bot.) der Hagedorn.

hay [hei], s. das Heu; — fever, der Heuschnupfen; — loft, der Heuboden; — rick, der Heuschober.

hazard ['hæzəd], s. der Zufall (chance); die Gefahr (danger); das Risiko (risk). — v.a. aufs Spiel setzen, riskieren.

hazardous ['hæzədəs], adj. gefährlich, gewagt.

haze [heiz], s. der Dunst, Nebeldunst.

hazel [heizl], s. (Bot.) die Haselstaude; — nut, die Haselnuß.

hazy ['heizi], adj. dunstig, nebelig.

he [hiː] pers. pron. er; — who, derjenige, welcher, wer.

head [hed], s. der Kopf; die Spitze (of arrow); der Leiter (of firm); (Sch.) der Direktor; die Überschrift (heading); die Krisis (climax); (Pol.) der Führer, das (Staats-)Oberhaupt. — v.a. anführen, führen; (Mil.) befehligen; — v.n. (Naut.) — for, Kurs nehmen auf (Acc.).

headache ['hedeik], s. (Med.) die Kopfschmerzen, m. pl.

headlamp ['hedlæmp], s. der Scheinwerfer.

headphone ['hedfoun], s. (usually pl.) der Kopfhörer.

headstrong ['hedstrɔŋ], adj. halsstarrig.

heady ['hedi], adj. hastig, ungestüm; berauschend (liquor).

heal [hiːl], v.a. heilen. — v.n. (zu)heilen, verheilen.

health [helθ], s. die Gesundheit; — resort, der Kurort; your (good) —! Gesundheit! auf Ihr Wohl! Prosit! (drinking toast).

healthy ['helθi], adj. gesund.

heap [hiːp], s. der Haufen, die Menge. — v.a. häufen, aufhäufen.

hear [hiə], v.a., v.n. irr. hören; erfahren (learn); (Law) verhören (evidence).

hearing ['hiəriŋ], s. das Gehör (auditory perception); within —, in Hörweite; (Law) das Verhör.

hearsay ['hiəsei], s. das Hörensagen.

hearse [hə:s], s. der Leichenwagen.

heart [hɑ:t], s. das Herz; der Mut (courage); das Innerste (core); by —, auswendig; take to —, beherzigen; take — from, Mut fassen (aus, Dat.).

heartburn ['hɑ:tbə:n], s. (Med.) das Sodbrennen.

heartfelt ['hɑ:tfelt], adj. herzlich.

hearth [hɑ:θ], s. der Herd.

hearty ['hɑ:ti], adj. herzlich; aufrichtig (sincere); herzhaft.

heat [hi:t], s. die Hitze, Wärme; die Brunst (animals). — v.a. heizen (fuel); erhitzen (make hot).

heath [hi:θ], s. die Heide.

heathen [hi:ðən], s. der Heide, Ungläubige.

heather ['heðə], s. (Bot.) das Heidekraut.

heating ['hi:tiŋ], s. die Heizung.

heave [hi:v], v.a. reg. & irr. heben, hieben. — v.n. sich heben und senken.

heaven [hevn], s. der Himmel; good —s! ach, du lieber Himmel!

heaviness ['hevinis], s. die Schwere.

heavy ['hevi], adj. schwer; schwerwiegend (grave).

Hebrew ['hi:bru:], adj. hebräisch. — s. der Hebräer, der Jude.

hectic ['hektik], adj. hektisch, aufgeregt.

hector ['hektə], v.a. tyrannisieren (bully). — v.n. renommieren, prahlen.

hedge [hedʒ], s. die Hecke. — v.a. einhegen, einzäunen.

hedgehog ['hedʒhɔg], s. (Zool.) der Igel.

hedgerow ['hedʒrou], s. die Baumhecke.

heed [hi:d], s. die Hut, Aufmerksamkeit. — v.a. beachten.

heedless ['hi:dlis], adj. unachtsam.

heel [hi:l], s. die Ferse (foot); der Absatz (shoe); take to o.'s —s, die Flucht ergreifen; (Am. sl.) der Lump.

heifer ['hefə], s. (Zool.) die junge Kuh.

height [hait], s. die Höhe, Anhöhe; die Größe (tallness); der Hügel (hill).

heighten [haitn], v.a. erhöhen.

heir [ɛə], s. der Erbe (to, Genit.).

heiress ['ɛəres], s. die Erbin.

heirloom ['ɛəlu:m], s. das Erbstück.

helicopter ['helikɔptə], s. (Aviat.) der Hubschrauber.

hell [hel], s. die Hölle. — interj. zum Teufel!

hellish ['heliʃ], adj. höllisch.

helm [helm], s. das Steuer, Steuerruder.

helmet ['helmit], s. der Helm.

helmsman ['helmzmən], s. (Naut.) der Steuermann.

help [help], v.a., v.n. helfen (Dat.); I cannot — laughing, ich muß lachen; I cannot — it, ich kann nichts dafür. — v.r. — o.s., sich bedienen. — s. die Hilfe, Unterstützung.

helpful ['helpful], adj. behilflich, hilfreich.

helping ['helpiŋ], s. die Portion.

helpless ['helplis], adj. hilflos.

helpmate, helpmeet ['helpmeit, -mi:t], s. der Gehilfe, die Gehilfin.

helter-skelter ['heltə'skeltə], adv. Hals über Kopf.

hem [hem], s. der Saum. — v.a. (Tail.) einsäumen, säumen.

hemisphere ['hemisfiə], s. die Halbkugel, Hemisphäre.

hemlock ['hemlɔk], s. der Schierling.

hemp [hemp], s. der Hanf.

hemstitch ['hemstitʃ], s. der Hohlsaum.

hen [hen], s. die Henne (poultry); das Weibchen (other birds).

hence [hens], adv. von hier; von jetzt an.

henceforth ['hens'fɔ:θ], adv. fortan, von nun an.

henpecked ['henpekd], adj. unter dem Pantoffel stehend.

her [hə:], pers. pron. sie (Acc.), ihr (Dat.). — poss. adj. ihr.

herald ['herəld], s. der Herold. — v.a. ankündigen.

heraldry ['herəldri], s. die Wappenkunde.

herb [hə:b], s. (Bot.) das Kraut.

herbaceous [hə:'beiʃəs], adj. krautartig.

herbage [hə:'bidʒ], s. das Gras; (Law) das Weiderecht.

herbal [hə:'bəl], adj. krautartig, Kräuter-, Kraut-.

herd [hə:d], s. die Herde. — v.n. sich zusammenfinden.

here [hiə], adv. hier.

hereafter [hiər'ɑ:ftə], adv. hernach, künftig. — s. die Zukunft; das Jenseits.

hereby [hiə'bai], adv. hiermit.

hereditary [hi'reditəri], adj. erblich.

heredity [hi'rediti], s. (Biol.) die Erblichkeit, Vererbung.

heresy ['herisi], s. die Ketzerei.

heretic ['heritik], s. der Ketzer.

heretofore ['hiətufɔ:], adv. zuvor, vormals.

heritage ['heritidʒ], s. die Erbschaft.

hermetic [hə:'metik], adj. luftdicht.

hermit ['hə:mit], s. der Eremit, Einsiedler.

hero ['hiərou], s. der Held.

heroic [hi'rouik], adj. heldenhaft, heldenmütig.

heroine ['heroin], s. die Heldin.

heroism ['heroizm], s. der Heldenmut.

heron ['herən], s. (Orn.) der Reiher.

herring ['heriŋ], s. (Zool.) der Hering; red —, die Ablenkungsfinte, das Ablenkungsmanöver; — bone, die Gräte; pickled —, der eingemachte Hering.

hers [hə:z], poss. pron. ihr, der ihre, der ihrige.

herself [hə:'self], pers. pron. sich; sie selbst.

hesitate ['heziteit], v.n. zögern, zaudern; unschlüssig sein (be undecided).

hoist

hesitation [hezi'teiʃən], *s.* das Zögern, Zaudern; das Bedenken (*deliberation*).
Hessian [ˈheʃən], *adj.* hessisch. — *s.* der Hesse.
hessian [ˈhesiən], *s.* die Sackleinwand (*textile*).
heterodox [ˈhetərədɔks], *adj.* irrgläubig.
heterogeneous [hetərəˈdʒiːniəs], *adj.* heterogen, ungleichartig.
hew [hjuː], *v.a. irr.* hauen.
hexagonal [hekˈsægənəl], *adj.* sechseckig.
hiatus [haiˈeitəs], *s.* die Lücke.
hibernate [ˈhaibəneit], *v.n.* überwintern.
hibernation [haibəˈneiʃən], *s.* der Winterschlaf.
hiccup [ˈhikʌp], *s.* (*usually pl.*) (*Med.*) der Schlucken, Schluckauf.
hickory [ˈhikəri], *s.* (*Bot.*) das Hickoryholz.
hide (1) [haid], *v.a. irr.* verstecken, verbergen. — *v.n. irr.* sich verbergen; — *and seek,* das Versteckspiel.
hide (2) [haid], *s.* die Haut (*of animal*); das Fell, (*tanned*) das Leder.
hideous [ˈhidiəs], *adj.* häßlich, scheußlich, furchtbar.
hiding (1) [ˈhaidiŋ], *s.* das Versteck.
hiding (2) [ˈhaidiŋ], *s.* die Tracht Prügel.
hierarchy [ˈhaiərɑːki], *s.* die Hierarchie.
higgle [higl] *see* **haggle**.
higgledy-piggledy [ˈhigldiˈpigldi], *adv.* wüst durcheinander.
high [hai], *adj.* hoch; erhaben, vornehm; angegangen (*meat*); — *school,* die höhere Schule; — *time,* höchste Zeit; (*Am.*) vergnügliche Zeit; *High Church,* die Hochkirche. — *s.* (*Meteor.*) das Hoch.
Highness [ˈhainis], *s.* die Hoheit (*title*).
highroad, highway [ˈhairoud, ˈhaiwei], *s.* die Haupt- *or* Landstraße.
highwayman [ˈhaiweimən], *s.* der Straßenräuber.
hike [haik], *v.n.* wandern, einen Ausflug machen. — *s.* die Wanderung, der Ausflug.
hilarious [hiˈlɛəriəs], *adj.* fröhlich, lustig, ausgelassen.
hill [hil], *s.* der Hügel, Berg.
hilt [hilt], *s.* der Griff.
him [him], *pers. pron.* ihn, ihm.
himself [himˈself], *pers. pron.* sich; er selbst.
hind [haind], *s.* (*Zool.*) die Hirschkuh, Hindin.
hinder [ˈhində], *v.a.* hindern.
hindmost [ˈhaindmoust], *adj.* hinterst; *the devil take the* —, den letzten hol der Teufel! nach mir die Sintflut!
hindrance [ˈhindrəns], *s.* das Hindernis; (*Law*) *without let or* —, ohne Hinderung.
Hindu [hinˈduː], *s.* der Hindu.
hinge [hindʒ], *s.* die Angel, der Angelpunkt. — *v.n.* sich um etwas drehen; von etwas abhängen (on, *Dat.*).

hint [hint], *v.n.* zu verstehen geben, auf etwas hindeuten (at, auf, *Acc.*), andeuten. — *s.* die Andeutung, der Fingerzeig.
hip (1) [hip], *s.* (*Anat.*) die Hüfte.
hip (2) [hip], *s.* (*Bot.*) die Hagebutte.
hire [ˈhaiə], *v.a.* (ver-)mieten (*car etc.*); anstellen (*man etc.*). — *s.* die Miete; der Lohn (*wage*); — *purchase,* der Abzahlungskauf, die Ratenzahlung.
hireling [ˈhaiəliŋ], *s.* der Mietling.
hirsute [ˈhəːsjuːt], *adj.* behaart, haarig.
his [hiz], *poss. adj.* sein, seine. — *poss. pron.* sein, der seinige, der seine.
hiss [his], *v.n.* zischen (at, auf, *Acc.*). — *s.* das Zischen.
historian [hisˈtɔːriən], *s.* der Historiker, der Geschichtsschreiber.
historical [hisˈtɔrikəl], *adj.* historisch, geschichtlich.
history [ˈhistəri], *s.* die Geschichte, die Geschichtswissenschaft.
histrionic [histriˈɔnik], *adj.* schauspielerisch.
hit [hit], *v.a. irr.* schlagen, stoßen. — *s.* der Schlag, der Treffer (*on the target*); (*Am.*) der Schlager, Erfolg (*success*); — *parade,* die Schlagerparade.
hitch [hitʃ], *v.a.* anhaken (*hook*); anhängen; — *a lift,* — *hike,* per Anhalter fahren. — *s.* der Nachteil, der Haken.
hither [ˈhiðə], *adv.* hierher.
hitherto [ˈhiðəˈtuː], *adv.* bisher.
hive [haiv], *s.* der Bienenkorb; Bienenstock; — *of bees,* der Schwarm.
hoar [hɔː], *adj.* eisgrau, weißlich; — *frost,* der Reif.
hoard [hɔːd], *v.a.* hamstern. — *s.* der Vorrat, Schatz.
hoarding [ˈhɔːdiŋ], *s.* die Umzäunung, die Bretterwand; die Reklamewand.
hoarse [hɔːs], *adj.* heiser.
hoarseness [ˈhɔːsnis], *s.* die Heiserkeit.
hoax [houks], *s.* der Betrug, die Irreführung; der Schabernack (*in fun*). — *v.a.* betrügen; foppen (*in fun*).
hobble [hɔbl], *v.n.* humpeln. — *v.a.* an den Füßen fesseln.
hobby [ˈhɔbi], *s.* das Steckenpferd, Hobby, die Liebhaberei.
hobgoblin [hɔbˈgɔblin], *s.* der Kobold.
hobnail [ˈhɔbneil], *s.* der Hufnagel.
hobnailed [ˈhɔbneild], *adj.* — *boots,* genagelte Stiefel, *m. pl.*
hobnob [hɔbˈnɔb], *v.n.* (*coll.*) vertraulich sein.
hock (1) [hɔk], *s.* (*Anat.*) das Sprunggelenk.
hock (2) [hɔk], *s.* (*wine*) der Rheinwein.
hod [hɔd], *s.* (*Build.*) der Trog; der Eimer (*coal*).
hodge-podge *see under* **hotchpotch**.
hoe [hou], *s.* die Hacke, Harke. — *v.a., v.n.* hacken, harken.
hog [hɔg], *s.* das Schwein. — *v.a.* verschlingen (*food*); an sich reißen (*grasp*).
hogshead [ˈhɔgzhed], *s.* das Oxhoft.
hoist [hɔist], *v.a.* hissen.

411

hold

hold [hould], *v.a.*, *v.n. irr.* halten (*keep*); enthalten (*contain*); behaupten (*assert*); meinen (*think*); gelten (*be valid*); — *forth*, deklamieren; — *good*, sich bewähren; — *out*, hinhalten (*hope*); (*endure*) aushalten;—*up*, aufhalten. — *s.* (*Naut.*) der Schiffsraum; die Macht (*power*).

holder ['houldə], *s.* der Inhaber, Besitzer.

holding ['houldiŋ], *s.* das Pachtgut (*farm*); der Besitz (*property*); (*Comm.*) der Trust.

hole [houl], *s.* das Loch; die Höhle (*cavity*). — *v.a.* aushöhlen; (*Golf*) ins Loch spielen.

holiday ['hɔlidei], *s.* der Feiertag; der Urlaub (*vacation*); (*pl.*) die Ferien, *pl.*

holiness ['houlinis], *s.* die Heiligkeit.

hollow ['hɔlou], *adj.* hohl. — *s.* die Höhlung; die Höhle.

holly ['hɔli], *s.* (*Bot.*) die Stechpalme.

hollyhock ['hɔlihɔk], *s.* (*Bot.*) die Stockrose.

holocaust ['hɔlɔkɔ:st], *s.* das Brandopfer; die Katastrophe.

holster ['houlstə], *s.* die Pistolentasche, die Halfter.

holy ['houli], *adj.* heilig; *Holy Week*, die Karwoche.

homage ['hɔmidʒ], *s.* die Huldigung; *pay — to*, huldigen (*Dat.*).

home [houm], *s.* das Heim, die Wohnung; die Heimat; *at —*, zu Hause; *Home Office*, das Innenministerium; — *Rule*, (*Pol.*) die Selbstverwaltung.

homer ['houmə] (*Am.*) *see* **homing pigeon.**

homesick ['houmsik], *adj.* an Heimweh leidend.

homestead ['houmsted], *s.* der Bauernhof.

homicide ['hɔmisaid], *s.* der Mord (*crime*); der Mörder (*killer*).

homily ['hɔmili], *s.* die Predigt; Moralpredigt.

homing pigeon ['houmiŋ'pidʒən], *s.* die Brieftaube.

homogeneous [hɔmə'dʒi:niəs], *adj.* homogen; gleichartig.

hone [houn], *s.* der Wetzstein. — *v.a.* (*blade, knife*) abziehen.

honest ['ɔnist], *adj.* ehrlich, aufrichtig.

honesty ['ɔnisti], *s.* die Ehrlichkeit.

honey ['hʌni], *s.* der Honig; (*Am.*, *coll.*) Liebling!

honeycomb ['hʌnikoum], *s.* die Honigwabe.

honeymoon ['hʌnimu:n], *s.* die Flitterwochen.

honorarium [ɔnə'rɛəriəm], *s.* das Honorar.

honorary ['ɔnərəri], *adj.* Ehren-, ehrenamtlich.

honour ['ɔnə], *s.* die Ehre; *your —*, Euer Ehrwürden, Euer Gnaden (*title*). — *v.a.* ehren, auszeichnen.

honourable ['ɔnərəbl], *adj.* ehrenwert, ehrenvoll; Hochwohlgeboren (*title*).

hood [hud], *s.* die Kapuze; das akademische Gradabzeichen über dem Talar; (*Hunt.*) die Haube; —*ed falcon*, der Jagdfalke (mit Haube).

hoodwink ['hudwiŋk], *v.a.* täuschen.

hoof [hu:f *or* huf], *s.* der Huf (*horse*); die Klaue.

hook [huk], *s.* der Haken; *by — or by crook*, mit allen Mitteln. — *v.a.* angeln, fangen.

hooked [hukd], *adj.* gekrümmt, hakenförmig.

hooligan ['hu:ligən], *s.* der Rowdy.

hoop [hu:p], *s.* der Reifen. — *v.a.* (ein Faß) binden.

hooper ['hu:pə], *s.* der Böttcher.

hoopoe ['hu:pou], *s.* (*Orn.*) der Wiedehopf.

hoot [hu:t], *v.n.* schreien (*owl*); ertönen (*siren*); hupen (*car*).

hooter ['hu:tə], *s.* die Sirene (*siren*); die Hupe (*car*).

hop (1) [hɔp], *v.n.* hüpfen, tanzen; —*ping mad*, ganz verrückt.

hop (2) [hɔp], *s.* (*Bot.*) der Hopfen. — *v.a.* (*beer*) hopfen, Höpfen zusetzen (*Dat.*). — *v.n.* Hopfen ernten.

hope [houp], *s.* die Hoffnung. — *v.n.* hoffen (*for*, auf, *Acc.*).

hopeless ['houplis], *adj.* hoffnungslos.

horizon [hə'raizən], *s.* der Horizont.

horizontal [hɔri'zɔntl], *adj.* horizontal, waagrecht.

horn [hɔ:n], *s.* das Horn; (*Mus.*) *French —*, das Waldhorn, Horn; (*Motor.*) die Hupe.

hornet ['hɔ:nit], *s.* (*Ent.*) die Hornisse.

hornpipe ['hɔ:npaip], *s.* (*Mus.*) der Matrosentanz; die Hornpfeife.

horrible ['hɔribl], *adj.* schrecklich.

horrid ['hɔrid], *adj.* abscheulich.

horrific [hɔ'rifik], *adj.* schrecklich, schreckenerregend.

horror ['hɔrə], *s.* der Schrecken, das Entsetzen; (*fig.*) der Greuel.

horse [hɔ:s], *s.* das Pferd, Roß; *on —back*, zu Pferd.

horseman ['hɔ:smən], *s.* der Reiter.

horsepower ['hɔ:spauə], *s.* die Pferdestärke.

horseradish ['hɔ:srædiʃ], *s.* der Meerrettich.

horseshoe ['hɔ:sʃu:], *s.* das Hufeisen.

horticulture ['hɔ:tikʌltʃə], *s.* der Gartenbau.

hose [houz], *s.* die Strümpfe, *m. pl.* (*stockings*); der Schlauch (*water pipe*).

hosiery ['houʒəri], *s.* die Strumpfwarenindustrie; die Strumpfwaren.

hospitable [hɔs'pitəbl], *adj.* gastlich, gastfreundlich.

hospital ['hɔspitl], *s.* das Krankenhaus.

hospitality [hɔspi'tæliti], *s.* die Gastlichkeit, Gastfreundschaft.

host (1) [houst], *s.* der Gastwirt (*landlord*); der Gastgeber.

host (2) [houst], *s.* (*Rel.*) *angelic —*, die Engelschar; (*Mil.*) das Heer, der Heerschar.

host (3) [houst], *s.* (*Eccl.*) die Hostie.

hostage ['hɔstidʒ], *s.* die Geisel.
hostess ['houstis *or* –tes], *s.* die Gastgeberin; *air* —, die Stewardeß.
hostile ['hɔstail], *adj.* feindlich; feindselig (*inimical*).
hot [hɔt], *adj.* heiß; hitzig (*temperament*); scharf, gewürzt (*of spices*); (*fig.*) heftig, erbittert.
hotchpotch, hodge-podge ['hɔtʃpɔtʃ, 'hɔdʒpɔdʒ], *s.* das Mischmasch.
hotel [ho(u)'tel],*s.*das Hotel,der Gasthof.
hothouse ['hɔthaus], *s.* das Treibhaus.
hound [haund], *s.* (*Zool.*) der Jagdhund. — *v.a.* hetzen.
hour ['auə], *s.* die Stunde; — *hand*, der Stundenzeiger; *for* —*s*, studenlang; *keep early* (*late*) —*s*, früh (spät) zu Bett gehen.
hourglass ['auəglɑːs], *s.* die Sanduhr.
hourly ['auəli], *adj., adv.,* stündlich.
house [haus], *s.* das Haus; (*Comm.*) die Firma. — [hauz], *v.a.* beherbergen, unterbringen.
houseboat ['hausbout], *s.* das Wohnboot.
housebreaking ['hausbreikiŋ], *s.* der Einbruch.
household ['haushould], *s.* der Haushalt.
housekeeper ['hauski:pə], *s.* die Haushälterin.
housewife ['hauswaif], *s.* die Hausfrau.
housing ['hauziŋ], *s.* die Unterbringung; — *department*, das Wohnungsamt.
hovel [hɔvl *or* hʌvl], *s.* die Hütte.
hover ['hɔvə *or* 'hʌvə], *v.n.* schweben, schwanken.
how [hau], *adv.* wie; — *do you do?* (*in introduction*) sehr angenehm; — *are you?* wie geht es Ihnen, Dir?
however [hau'evə], *adv.* wie immer, wie auch immer, wie sehr auch. — *conj.* doch, jedoch, dennoch.
howl [haul], *v.n.* heulen. — *s.* das Geheul.
hoyden ['hɔidn], *s.* das wilde Mädchen.
hub [hʌb], *s.* die Nabe (am Rad); — *of the universe*, die Mitte der Welt.
hubbub ['hʌbʌb], *s.* der Tumult, Lärm.
huckaback ['hʌkəbæk], *s.* der Zwillich (*textile*).
huckle [hʌkl], *s.* die Hüfte.
huddle [hʌdl], *v.n.* sich drängen, sich zusammenducken. — *s.* das Gedränge.
hue [hju:], *s.* der Farbton, die Tönung.
huff [hʌf], *s.* die schlechte Laune, die Mißstimmung.
huffy ['hʌfi], *adj.* mißmutig, übel gelaunt.
hug [hʌg], *v.a.* umarmen. — *s.* die Umarmung.
huge [hju:dʒ], *adj.* riesig, groß, ungeheuer.
Huguenot ['hju:gənou *or* –nɔt], *s.* der Hugenotte. — *adj.* hugenottisch, Hugenotten-.

hulk [hʌlk], *s.* (*Naut.*) das Schiffsinnere, der Schiffsrumpf; der schwerfällige Mensch.
hull [hʌl], *s.* die Hülse, Schale; (*Naut., Aviat.*) der Rumpf. — *v.a.* (*Engin.*) hülsen.
hullo! [hə'lou], *interj.* hallo!
hum [hʌm], *v.n.* summen, brummen. — *s.* das Summen, Brummen, Gemurmel (*murmuring*).
human ['hju:mən], *adj.* menschlich. — *s.* der Mensch.
humane [hju:'mein], *adj.* menschenfreundlich.
humanity [hju:'mæniti], *s.* die Menschheit (*mankind*); die Menschlichkeit (*compassion*); (*pl.*) die klassischen Fächer, *n. pl.,* die humanistischen Wissenschaften, *f. pl.*
humanize ['hju:mənaiz], *v.a.* menschlich oder gesittet machen.
humble [hʌmbl], *adj.* demütig; bescheiden (*modest*); unterwürfig (*servile*). — *v.a.* erniedrigen (*humiliate*).
humbug ['hʌmbʌg], *s.* die Schwindelei (*swindle*); der Schwindler (*crook*); der Unsinn (*nonsense*).
humdrum ['hʌmdrʌm], *adj.* langweilig, eintönig.
humid ['hju:mid], *adj.* feucht.
humidity [hju:'miditi], *s.* die Feuchtigkeit.
humiliate [hju:'milieit], *v.a.* erniedrigen.
humility [hju:'militi], *s.* die Demut.
humming-bird ['hʌmiŋbə:d], *s.* (*Orn.*) der Kolibri.
humming-top ['hʌmiŋtɔp], *s.* der Brummkreisel.
humorous ['hju:mərəs], *adj.* humoristisch, spaßhaft, komisch.
humour ['hju:mə], *s.* der Humor, die (gute) Laune. — *v.a.* in guter Laune erhalten, gut stimmen; willfahren (*Dat.*).
hump [hʌmp], *s.* der Buckel, der Höcker.
hunch [hʌntʃ], *s.* der Buckel; *have a* —, das Gefühl haben.
hunchback ['hʌntʃbæk], *s.* der Bucklige.
hundred ['hʌndrəd], *num. adj.* a —, hundert.
hundredweight ['hʌndrədweit], *s.* der (englische) Zentner.
Hungarian [hʌŋ'gɛəriən],*adj.*ungarisch. — *s.* der Ungar.
hunger ['hʌŋgə], *s.* der Hunger.
hungry ['hʌŋgri], *adj.* hungrig.
hunt [hʌnt], *s.* die Jagd. — *v.a., v.n.* jagen.
hunter ['hʌntə], *s.* der Jäger.
hurdle [hə:dl], *s.* die Hürde.
hurdy-gurdy ['hə:digə:di], *s.* der Leierkasten.
hurl [hə:l], *v.a.* schleudern, werfen.
hurly-burly ['hə:liba:li], *s.* der Wirrwarr.
hurricane ['hʌrikin], *s.* der Orkan; — *lamp*, die Sturmlaterne.
hurried ['hʌrid], *adj.* eilig, hastig.

hurry

hurry ['hʌri], v.n. eilen, sich beeilen; — to do, eiligst tun. — v.a. beschleunigen. — s. die Eile, Hast, Beschleunigung.

hurt [hə:t], v.a. irr. verletzen; wehetun (Dat.); (verbally) kränken. — s. die Verletzung, Kränkung.

hurtful ['hə:tful], adj. schädlich, kränkend.

husband ['hʌzbənd], s. der Mann, Ehemann, Gemahl. — v.a. verwalten, sparsam verfahren mit (Dat.).

husbandman ['hʌzbəndmən], s. der Landwirt.

husbandry ['hʌzbəndri], s. die Landwirtschaft.

hush [hʌʃ], v.a. zum Schweigen bringen. — s. die Stille; — money, das Schweigegeld.

husky (1) ['hʌski], adj. heiser (voice).

husky (2) ['hʌski], s. (Zool.) der Eskimohund.

hussy ['hʌzi], s. (coll.) das Frauenzimmer.

hustings ['hʌstiŋz], s. die Wahltribüne.

hustle [hʌsl], v.a. drängen, stoßen. — s. das Gedränge.

hut [hʌt], s. die Hütte, Baracke.

hutch [hʌtʃ], s. der Trog, Kasten (chest).

hybrid ['haibrid], adj. Bastard-. — s. der Bastard.

hydraulic [hai'drɔ:lik], adj. hydraulisch.

hydrogen ['haidrədʒən], s. der Wasserstoff.

hydroelectric [haidroui'lektrik], adj. hydroelektrisch.

hyena [hai'i:nə], s. (Zool.) die Hyäne.

hygiene ['haidʒi:n], s. die Hygiene, Gesundheitslehre.

hymn [him], s. die Hymne, das Kirchenlied.

hymnal ['himnəl], s. das Gesangbuch.

hyper- ['haipə], prefix. über-.

hyperbole [hai'pə:bəli], s. die Übertreibung.

hyphen ['haifən], s. der Bindestrich.

hypnosis [hip'nousis], s. die Hypnose.

hypochondriac [haipo'kɔndriæk], adj. hypochondrisch. — s. der Hypochonder.

hypocrisy [hi'pɔkrisi], s. die Heuchelei.

hypocrite ['hipəkrit], s. der Heuchler.

hypothesis [hai'pɔθisis], s. die Hypothese.

hypothetical [haipə'θetikəl], adj. hypothetisch, angenommen.

hysteria [his'tiəriə], s. die Hysterie.

I

I [ai]. das I.

I [ai], pers. pron. ich.

ice [ais], s. das Eis; — bound, eingefroren; (Naut.) — breaker, der Eisbrecher; (Am.) — box, der Kühlschrank; — cream, das Eis; das Gefrorene. — v.a. (confectionery) verzuckern; (cake) glasieren.

Icelander ['aislændə], s. der Isländer.

Icelandic [ais'lændik], adj. isländisch.

icicle ['aisikl], s. der Eiszapfen.

icy ['aisi], adj. eisig.

idea [ai'diə], s. die Idee.

ideal [ai'diəl], adj. ideal. — s. das Ideal.

idealize [ai'diəlaiz], v.a. idealisieren.

identical [ai'dentikəl], adj. identisch, gleich.

identification [aidentifi'keiʃən], s. die Gleichsetzung, Identifizierung.

identify [ai'dentifai], v.a. identifizieren, gleichsetzen.

identity [ai'dentiti], s. die Identität, Gleichheit.

idiocy ['idiəsi], s. der Blödsinn.

idiom ['idiəm], s. das Idiom, die sprachliche Eigentümlichkeit.

idiomatic [idio'mætik], adj. idiomatisch.

idiosyncrasy [idio'siŋkrəsi], s. die Empfindlichkeit; die Abneigung (gegen, Acc.); die Idiosynkrasie.

idle [aidl], adj. unnütz (useless); müßig, faul (lazy). — v.n. träge sein.

idleness ['aidlnis], s. der Müßiggang, die Faulheit.

idiot ['idiət], s. der Idiot.

idol [aidl], s. das Götzenbild; das Idol.

idolatry [ai'dɔlətri], s. die Götzenverehrung.

idolize ['aidolaiz], v.a. vergöttern, abgöttisch lieben.

idyll ['aidil or 'idil], s. die Idylle, das Idyll.

idyllic [ai'dilik or i'dilik], adj. idyllisch.

if [if], conj. wenn, falls (in case); ob (whether).

igneous ['igniəs], adj. feurig.

ignite [ig'nait], v.a. entzünden. — v.n. zur Entzündung kommen, sich entzünden.

ignition [ig'niʃən], s. die Zündung.

ignoble [ig'noubl], adj. unedel, gemein.

ignominious [igno'miniəs],adj.schimpflich, schmählich.

ignominy ['ignomini], s. die Schande, Schmach.

ignoramus [ignə'reiməs], s. der Unwissende.

ignorance ['ignərəns], s. die Unwissenheit, Unkenntnis.

ignorant ['ignərənt], adj. unwissend.

ignore [ig'nɔ:], v.a. ignorieren, nicht beachten.

ill [il], adj. böse, schlimm (bad); krank (sick); — feeling, die Verstimmung. — adv. — at ease, unbequem, verlegen; can — afford, kann sich kaum leisten …; —timed, zu unrechter Zeit.

illbred [il'bred], adj. ungezogen.

illegal [i'li:gəl], adj. illegal, ungesetzlich.

illegibility [iledʒi'biliti], s. die Unleserlichkeit.

414

illegible [i'ledʒibl], *adj.* unleserlich.
illegitimacy [ili'dʒitiməsi], *s.* die Unehelichkeit, Illegitimität.
illegitimate [ili'dʒitimit], *adj.* illegitim, unehelich.
illicit [[i'lisit], *adj.* unerlaubt.
illiteracy [i'litərəsi], *s.* die Unkenntnis des Schreibens und Lesens, das Analphabetentum.
illiterate [i'litərit], *s.* der Analphabet.
illness [ilnis], *s.* die Krankheit.
illogical [i'lɔdʒikəl], *adj.* unlogisch.
illuminate [i'lju:mineit], *v.a.* erleuchten; (*fig.*) aufklären.
illuminating [i'lju:mineitiŋ], *adj.* aufschlußreich.
illumination [ilju:mi'neiʃən], *s.* die Erleuchtung; die Erklärung (*explanation*).
illusion [i'lju:ʒən], *s.* die Illusion, Täuschung.
illusive, illusory [i'lju:ziv, i'lju:zəri], *adj.* trügerisch, täuschend.
illustrate ['iləstreit], *v.a.* erläutern; illustrieren (*with pictures*).
illustration [iləs'treiʃən], *s.* die Illustration (*pictorial*); Erläuterung, Erklärung; das Beispiel (*instance*).
illustrious [i'lʌstriəs], *adj.* glänzend, berühmt.
image ['imidʒ], *s.* das Bild; das Ebenbild; die Erscheinung (*appearance*).
imagery ['imidʒəri], *s.* der Gebrauch von Stilbildern (*style*), die Bildersprache.
imaginable [i'mædʒinəbl], *adj.* denkbar.
imaginary [i'mædʒinəri], *adj.* eingebildet, nicht wirklich, vermeintlich.
imagination [imædʒi'neiʃən], *s.* die Einbildung; die Vorstellung; die Phantasie.
imaginative [i'mædʒinətiv], *adj.* erfinderisch, voll Phantasie.
imagine [i'mædʒin], *v.a.* sich vorstellen, sich denken.
imbecile ['imbisail *or* 'imbisi:l], *adj.* schwachsinnig. — *s.* der Idiot.
imbecility [imbi'siliti], *s.* der Schwachsinn.
imbibe [im'baib], *v.a.* trinken; (*fig.*) in sich aufnehmen.
imbroglio [im'brouliou], *s.* die Verwicklung.
imbue [im'bju:], *v.a.* erfüllen, sättigen (*fig.*).
imitate ['imiteit], *v.a.* nachahmen, imitieren.
imitation [imi'teiʃən], *s.* die Nachahmung, Imitation; — *leather,* das Kunstleder.
immaculate [i'mækjulit], *adj.* unbefleckt, makellos.
immaterial [imə'tiəriəl], *adj.* unwesentlich, unwichtig.
immature [imə'tjuə], *adj.* unreif.
immeasurable [i'meʒərəbl], *adj.* unermeßlich, unmeßbar.
immediate [i'mi:djit], *adj.* unmittelbar, direkt, sofortig.

immediately [i'mi:djətli], *adv.* sofort.
immemorial [imi'mɔ:riəl], *adj.* undenklich, ewig.
immense [i'mens], *adj.* unermeßlich, ungeheuer.
immerse [i'mə:s], *v.a.* eintauchen.
immersion [i'mə:ʃən], *s.* das Eintauchen, die Versenkung; — *heater,* der Tauchsieder.
immigrant ['imigrənt], *s.* der Einwanderer.
imminent ['iminənt], *adj.* bevorstehend.
immobile [i'moubail], *adj.* unbeweglich.
immoderate [i'mɔdərit], *adj.* unmäßig.
immodest [i'mɔdist], *adj.* unbescheiden; unsittlich, unanständig (*immoral*).
immodesty [i'mɔdisti], *s.* die Unanständigkeit (*indecency*); Unbescheidenheit (*presumption*).
immolate ['iməleit], *v.a.* opfern.
immoral [i'mɔrəl], *adj.* unsittlich, unmoralisch.
immortal [i'mɔ:tl], *adj.* unsterblich.
immortalize [i'mɔ:təlaiz], *v.a.* verewigen, unsterblich machen.
immovable [i'mu:vəbl], *adj.* unbeweglich (*fig.*).
immunity [i'mju:niti], *s.* die Freiheit, Straffreiheit; Immunität.
immutable [im'ju:təbl], *adj.* unabänderlich; unveränderlich.
imp [imp], *s.* der Knirps, Kobold, kleine Schelm.
impair [im'pɛə], *v.a.* beeinträchtigen; vermindern (*reduce*).
impale [im'peil], *v.a.* aufspießen; durchbohren.
impalpable [im'pælpəbl], *adj.* unfühlbar, unmerklich.
impart [im'pɑ:t], *v.a.* erteilen; verleihen (*confer*); mitteilen (*inform*).
impartial [im'pɑ:ʃəl], *adj.* unparteiisch.
impartiality [impɑ:ʃi'æliti], *s.* die Unparteilichkeit, Objektivität.
impassable [im'pɑ:səbl], *adj.* unwegsam, unpassierbar.
impasse [im'pæs], *s.* der völlige Stillstand.
impassioned [im'pæʃənd], *adj.* leidenschaftlich.
impassive [im'pæsiv], *adj.* unempfindlich.
impatience [im'peiʃəns], *s.* die Ungeduld.
impatient [im'peiʃənt], *adj.* ungeduldig.
impeach [im'pi:tʃ], *v.a.* anklagen.
impeachment [im'pi:tʃmənt], *s.* die Anklage.
impecunious [impi'kju:niəs], *adj.* unbemittelt, mittellos.
impede [im'pi:d], *v.a.* behindern, verhindern.
impediment [im'pedimənt], *s.* das Hindernis.
impel [im'pel], *v.a.* antreiben; zwingen (*force*).

impending

impending [im'pendiŋ], *adj.* bevorstehend, drohend.
impenetrable [im'penitrəbl], *adj.* undurchdringlich, unerforschlich.
impenitent [im'penitənt], *adj.* reuelos,
unbußfertig.
imperative [im'perətiv], *adj.* zwingend
(*cogent*); dringend notwendig. — *s.*
(*Gram.*) der Imperativ, die Befehls-
form.
imperceptible [impə'septibl], *adj.* unmerklich.
imperfect [im'pə:fikt], *adj.* unvollständig, unvollkommen; fehlerhaft
(*goods etc.*). — *s.* (*Gram.*) das Imperfekt.
imperial [im'piəriəl], *adj.* kaiserlich,
Kaiser-, Reichs-.
imperil [im'peril], *v.a.* gefährden; in
Gefahr bringen, einer Gefahr aussetzen.
imperious [im'piəriəs], *adj.* gebieterisch.
imperishable [im'perifəbl], *adj.* unverwüstlich, unvergänglich.
impermeable [im'pə:miəbl], *adj.* undurchdringlich.
impersonal [im'pə:sənəl], *adj.* unper-
sönlich.
impersonate [im'pə:səneit], *v.a.* verkörpern, darstellen; sich ausgeben als.
impertinence [im'pə:tinəns], *s.* die
Anmaßung, Frechheit, Unverschämtheit.
impertinent [im'pə:tinənt], *adj.* anmaßend, frech, unverschämt.
imperturbable [impə'tə:bəbl], *adj.*
unerschütterlich, ruhig, gelassen.
impervious [im'pə:viəs], *adj.* unwegsam, undurchdringlich.
impetuous [im'petjuəs], *adj.* ungestüm, heftig.
impetus [im'pitəs], *s.* die Triebkraft,
der Antrieb.
impinge [im'pindʒ], *v.n.* verstoßen
(*on*, gegen); übergreifen (*on*, in).
implacable [im'plækəbl], *adj.* unversöhnlich.
implement ['implimənt], *s.* das Gerät.
— [impli'ment], *v.a.* (*Law*) erfüllen,
in Wirkung setzen, in Kraft treten
lassen.
implementation [implimen'teifən], *s.*
das Inkrafttreten, die Erfüllung,
Ausführung.
implicate ['implikeit], *v.a.* verwickeln.
implicit [im'plisit], *adj.* unbedingt;
einbegriffen.
implore [im'plɔ:], *v.a.* anflehen.
imply [im'plai], *v.a.* besagen, meinen;
andeuten.
impolite [impə'lait], *adj.* unhöflich,
grob.
impolitic [im'pɔlitik], *adj.* unklug, un-
politisch, undiplomatisch.
imponderable [im'pɔndərəbl], *adj.* unwägbar. — *s. pl.* unwägbare, unvor-
hersehbare Umstände, *m.pl.*
import [im'pɔ:t], *v.a.* einführen, im-
portieren; bedeuten, besagen. —

['impɔ:t], *s.* (*Comm.*) die Einfuhr, der
Import; die Bedeutung (*importance*,
meaning), Wichtigkeit (*significance*);
(*Comm.*) — *licence*, die Einfuhrgeneh-
migung.
importance [im'pɔ:təns], *s.* die Bedeutung, Wichtigkeit.
important [im'pɔ:tənt], *adj.* bedeutend,
wichtig.
importation [impɔ:'teifən], *s.* die
Einfuhr.
importune [impɔ:'tju:n], *v.a.* belästigen, angehen, dringend bitten.
impose [im'pouz], *v.a.* aufbürden,
auferlegen. — *v.n.* — *upon s.o.*, einen
belästigen.
imposition [impə'zifən], *s.* die Belästigung; (*Sch.*) die Strafarbeit.
impossible [im'pɔsibl], *adj.* unmöglich.
impostor [im'pɔstə], *s.* der Schwindler,
Betrüger.
impotent ['impətənt], *adj.* schwach,
machtlos; impotent (*sexually*).
impound [im'paund], *v.a.* beschlagnahmen, in Beschlag nehmen.
impoverish [im'pɔvərif], *v.a.* arm
machen.
impoverished [im'pɔvərifd], *adj.* ver-
armt, armselig.
impracticability [impræktikə'biliti]
s. die Unmöglichkeit, Unausführbarkeit.
impracticable [im'præktikəbl], *adj.*
unausführbar.
imprecate ['imprikeit], *v.a.* verwünschen.
impregnable [im'pregnəbl], *adj.* uneinnehmbar, unbezwinglich.
impregnate [im'pregneit], *v.a.* impreg-
nieren; (*Chem.*) sättigen.
impress [im'pres], *v.a.* beeindrucken,
imponieren (*fig.*); einprägen, ein-
pressen (*print*). — ['impres], *s.* der
Eindruck, (*Typ.*) Abdruck.
impression [im'prefən], *s.* (*fig.*) der
Eindruck; die Auflage (*books*).
impressionable [im'prefənəbl], *adj.*
eindrucksfähig, empfänglich.
impressive [im'presiv], *adj.* ergreifend, eindrucksvoll.
imprint ['imprint], *s.* der Name des
Verlags oder Druckers. — [im'print],
v.a. drucken.
imprison [im'prizn], *v.a.* gefangen-
setzen, in Haft nehmen.
imprisonment [im'priznmənt], *s.* die
Haft; (*Law*) der Arrest.
improbability [imprɔbə'biliti], *s.* die
Unwahrscheinlichkeit.
improbable [im'prɔbəbl], *adj.* unwahrscheinlich.
improbity [im'proubiti], *s.* die Unred-
lichkeit.
impromptu [im'prɔmptju:], *adj., adv.*
aus dem Stegreif, unvorbereitet.
improper [im'prɔpə], *adj.* unpassend,
unanständig (*indecent*).
impropriety [imprɔ'praiiti], *s.* die
Unanständigkeit (*indecency*); die Un-
gehörigkeit.

include

improve [im′pru:v], *v.a.* verbessern; (*Hort.*) veredeln. — *v.n.* besser werden, sich bessern; (*Med.*) sich erholen.

improvement [im′pru:vmənt], *s.* die Verbesserung; (*Med.*) die Besserung, der Fortschritt.

improvident [im′prɔvidənt], *adj.* unvorsichtig, nicht auf die Zukunft bedacht.

improvise [′imprəvaiz], *v.a.* improvisieren.

imprudent [im′pru:dənt], *adj.* unklug, unvorsichtig.

impudent [′impjudənt], *adj.* unverschämt.

impugn [im′pju:n], *v.a.* anfechten, angreifen.

impulse [′impʌls], *s.* der Impuls; der Anstoß.

impulsive [im′pʌlsiv], *adj.* impulsiv.

impunity [im′pju:niti], *s.* die Straffreiheit.

impure [im′pjuə], *adj.* (*also Metall.*, *Chem.*) unrein, unedel; unsauber.

impute [im′pju:t], *v.a.* beimessen; zurechnen, die Schuld geben für.

in [in], *prep.* in; an; zu, auf; bei; nach, unter; über; von; mit; — *the morning*, vormittags; — *case*, falls; — *any case*, auf jeden Fall; — *German*, auf deutsch; — *my opinion*, meiner Meinung nach; — *the street*, auf der Straße; — *time*, rechtzeitig. — *adv.* drinnen, innen; herein, hinein; zu Hause.

inability [inə′biliti], *s.* die Unfähigkeit.

inaccessible [inæk′sesibl], *adj.* unzugänglich.

inaccurate [i′nækjurit], *adj.* ungenau.

inaction [i′nækʃən], *s.* die Untätigkeit.

inactive [i′næktiv], *adj.* untätig.

inadequate [i′nædikwit], *adj.* unzulänglich.

inadmissible [inəd′misibl], *adj.* unzulässig.

inadvertent [inəd′və:tənt], *adj.* unbeabsichtigt; unachtsam.

inadvertently [inəd′və:təntli], *adv.* unversehens; versehentlich.

inalienable [in′eiliənəbl], *adj.* unveräußerlich.

inane [i′nein], *adj.* hohl, leer, sinnlos.

inanimate [i′nænimit], *adj.* unbeseelt, leblos.

inanity [i′næniti], *s.* die Leere, Nichtigkeit.

inapplicable [i′næplikəbl], *adj.* unanwendbar; unzutreffend.

inappropriate [inə′proupriit], *adj.* unpassend.

inarticulate [ina:′tikjulit], *adj.* unartikuliert.

inasmuch [inəz′mʌtʃ],*adv.* insofern(als).

inattentive [inə′tentiv], *adj.* unaufmerksam.

inaudible [i′nɔ:dibl], *adj.* unhörbar.

inaugural [i′nɔ:gjurəl], *adj.* Inaugural-, Eröffnungs-, Antritts-.

inaugurate [i′nɔ:gjureit], *v.a.* einweihen, eröffnen.

inauspicious [inɔ:′spiʃəs], *adj.* ungünstig.

inborn [′inbɔ:n], *adj.* angeboren.

inbred [′inbred], *adj.* in Inzucht geboren; angeboren, ererbt.

inbreeding [′inbri:diŋ], *s.* die Inzucht.

incalculable [in′kælkjuləbl], *adj.* unberechenbar.

incandescence [inkæn′desəns], *s.* die Weißglut.

incandescent [inkæn′desənt], *adj.* weißglühend.

incantation [inkæn′teiʃən], *s.* die Beschwörung.

incapable [in′keipəbl], *adj.* unfähig (*of doing s.th.*, etwas zu tun).

incapacitate [inkə′pæsiteit], *v.a.* unfähig machen.

incapacity [inkə′pæsiti], *s.* die Unfähigkeit.

incarcerate [in′ka:səreit], *v.a.* einkerkern, einsperren.

incarnate [in′ka:nit], *adj.* eingefleischt; (*Theol.*) verkörpert.

incarnation [inka:′neiʃən], *s.* die Verkörperung; (*Theol.*) Menschwerdung.

incautious [in′kɔ:ʃəs], *adj.* unvorsichtig.

incendiary [in′sendjəri], *adj.* Brand-, brennend. — *s.* der Brandstifter.

incense [in′sens], *v.a.* aufregen, erzürnen (*make angry*); (*Eccl.*) beweihräuchern. — [′insens], *s.* (*Eccl.*) der Weihrauch.

incentive [in′sentiv], *adj.* Ansporn-, Anreiz-. — *s.* der Ansporn, Anreiz; (*Comm.*) — *scheme*, das Inzentivsystem, Akkordsystem.

incessant [in′sesənt], *adj.* unaufhörlich, ununterbrochen.

incest [′insest], *s.* die Blutschande.

incestuous [in′sestjuəs], *adj.* blutschänderisch.

inch [intʃ], *s.* der Zoll. — *v.n.* — *away*, abrücken.

incident [′insidənt], *s.* der Vorfall, Zwischenfall; das Ereignis.

incidental [insi′dentl], *adj.* zufällig. — *s.* (*pl.*) zufällige Ausgaben, *f. pl.*; das Zusätzliche, Nebenausgaben, *f. pl.*

incipient [in′sipiənt], *adj.* beginnend, anfangend.

incise [in′saiz], *v.a.* einschneiden, (*Med.*) einen Einschnitt machen.

incision [in′siʒən], *s.* der Einschnitt.

incisive [in′saisiv], *adj.* einschneidend; energisch (*person*).

incite [in′sait], *v.a.* aufreizen, anspornen.

incivility [insi′viliti], *s.* die Unhöflichkeit.

inclement [in′klemənt], *adj.* unfreundlich (*weather, climate*).

inclination [inkli′neiʃən], *s.* die Neigung (*also fig.*).

incline [in′klain], *v.n.* neigen, sich neigen. — [′inklain], *s.* der Neigungswinkel; der Abhang.

include [in′klu:d], *v.a.* einschließen (*contain*); umfassen (*enclose*).

417

including

including [in'klu:diŋ], prep. einschließlich.

inclusive [in'klu:siv], adj. einschließlich, mitgerechnet.

incoherent [inko'hiərənt], adj. unzusammenhängend.

incombustible [inkəm'bʌstibl], adj. unverbrennbar.

income ['inkʌm], s. das Einkommen.

incommensurable, incommensurate [inkə'menʃərəbl, inkə'menʃərit], adj. unvereinbar, unmeßbar.

incomparable [in'kɔmpərəbl], adj. unvergleichlich.

incompatible [inkəm'pætibl], adj. unvereinbar.

incompetence, incompetency [in-'kɔmpitəns, -tənsi], s. die Inkompetenz; Unzulänglichkeit.

incompetent [in'kɔmpitənt], adj. unzuständig, inkompetent; unzulänglich.

incomplete [inkəm'pli:t], adj. unvollständig.

incomprehensible [inkɔmpri'hensibl], adj. unverständlich.

inconceivable [inkən'si:vəbl], adj. unbegreiflich.

inconclusive [inkən'klu:siv], adj. unvollständig (incomplete); unüberzeugend; ergebnislos.

incongruity [inkɔŋ'gru:iti], s. (Maths.) die Inkongruenz; (fig.) die Unangemessenheit.

incongruous [in'kɔŋgruəs], adj. inkongruent; unangemessen.

inconsequent [in'kɔnsikwənt], adj. folgewidrig.

inconsequential [inkɔnsi'kwenʃəl], adj. inkonsequent (inconsistent); unzusammenhängend.

inconsiderate [inkən'sidərit], adj. rücksichtslos, unbedachtsam.

inconsistent [inkən'sistənt], adj. inkonsequent.

inconsolable [inkən'souləbl], adj. untröstlich.

inconstancy [in'kɔnstənsi], s. die Unbeständigkeit; Untreue (fickleness).

incontestable [inkən'testəbl], adj. unanfechtbar, unbestreitbar.

incontinent [in'kɔntinənt], adj. unenthaltsam.

incontrovertible [inkɔntro'və:tibl], adj. unstreitig, unanfechtbar.

inconvenience [inkən'vi:niəns], s. die Unbequemlichkeit, Unannehmlichkeit.

inconvenient [inkən'vi:niənt], adj. unangenehm, unpassend.

inconvertible [inkən'və:tibl], adj. unveränderlich; (Comm.) unumsetzbar.

incorporate [in'kɔ:pəreit], v.a. einverleiben (Dat.), eingliedern (Acc.).

incorporated [in'kɔ:pəreitid], adj. (Am.) eingetragene Körperschaft, eingetragener Verein.

incorrect [inkə'rekt], adj. unrichtig, fehlerhaft; unschicklich, unpassend.

incorrigible [in'kɔridʒibl], adj. unverbesserlich.

incorruptible [inkə'rʌptibl], adj. unbestechlich.

increase [in'kri:s], v.a. vermehren, vergrößern (size, volume); steigern (heat, intensity); erhöhen (price). — v.n. sich vermehren, sich erhöhen; wachsen (grow). — ['inkri:s], s. die Zunahme; der Zuwachs (family); die Erhöhung.

incredible [in'kredibl], adj. unglaublich.

incredulity [inkre'dju:liti], s. die Ungläubigkeit, der Unglaube.

incredulous [in'kredjuləs], adj. ungläubig, schwer zu überzeugen.

increment ['inkrimənt], s. (Comm.) die Zulage, Gehaltserhöhung.

incriminate [in'krimineit], v.a. beschuldigen, inkriminieren.

incubate ['inkjubeit], v.a. brüten, ausbrüten. — v.n. brüten.

incubator ['inkjubeitə], s. der Brutapparat.

inculcate ['inkʌlkeit], v.a. einprägen.

inculpate ['inkʌlpeit], v.a. beschuldigen.

incumbent [in'kʌmbənt], adj. (upon, Dat.) obliegend, nötig. — s. der Pfründner, Amtsinhaber.

incur [in'kə:], v.a. auf sich laden, sich zuziehen.

incurable [in'kjuərəbl], adj. unheilbar.

incursion [in'kə:ʃən], s. der Einfall, Streifzug.

indebted [in'detid], adj. verpflichtet, dankbar (grateful); verschuldet (in debt).

indecent [in'di:sənt], adj. unschicklich, unanständig.

indecision [indi'siʒən], s. die Unentschlossenheit.

indecisive [indi'saisiv], adj. unentschlossen.

indeclinable [indi'klainəbl], adj. (Gram.) undeklinierbar.

indecorous [indi'kɔ:rəs or in'dekərəs], adj. unrühmlich, unanständig.

indeed [in'di:d], adv. in der Tat, tatsächlich.

indefatigable [indi'fætigəbl], adj. unermüdlich.

indefensible [indi'fensibl], adj. unhaltbar; unverzeihlich (unforgivable).

indefinable [indi'fainəbl], adj. unbestimmbar, undefinierbar.

indefinite [in'definit], adj. unbestimmt.

indelible [in'delibl], adj. unauslöschlich.

indelicate [in'delikit], adj. unfein.

indemnify [in'demnifai], v.a. entschädigen.

indemnity [in'demniti], die Entschädigung.

indent [in'dent], v.a. auszacken, einschneiden.

indenture [in'dentʃə], s. der Lehrbrief (apprentice); Vertrag.

independence [indi'pendəns], s. die Unabhängigkeit, Freiheit.

independent [indi'pendənt], adj. unabhängig, frei.

indescribable [indi'skraibəbl], *adj.* unbeschreiblich.

indestructible [indi'strʌktibl], *adj.* unverwüstlich; unzerstörbar.

indeterminable [indi'tə:minəbl], *adj.* unbestimmbar.

indeterminate [indi'tə:minit], *adj.* unbestimmt.

index ['indeks], *s.* (*pl.* indexes) das Inhaltsverzeichnis; (*pl.* indices) (*Maths.*) der Exponent; — finger, der Zeigefinger; (*pl.*) die Finger, Zeiger, *m. pl.* (*pointers*).

India ['indjə], das Indien; — paper, das Dünnpapier.

Indian ['indjən], *adj.* indisch; — ink, die Tusche. — *s.* der Ind(i)er.

indiarubber ['indjə'rʌbə], *s.* der Radiergummi.

indicate ['indikeit], *v.a.* anzeigen, angeben.

indication [indi'keiʃən], *s.* das Anzeichen, Merkmal, der Hinweis.

indicative [in'dikətiv], *adj.* bezeichnend (für, *Acc.*). — *s.* (*Gram.*) der Indikativ.

indict [in'dait], *v.a.* anklagen.

indictment [in'daitmənt], *s.* die Anklage.

indifference [in'difrəns], *s.* die Gleichgültigkeit.

indifferent [in'difrənt], *adj.* gleichgültig.

indigence ['indidʒəns], *s.* die Armut.

indigenous [in'didʒinəs], *adj.* eingeboren, einheimisch.

indigent ['indidʒənt], *adj.* arm, dürftig.

indigestible [indi'dʒestibl], *adj.* unverdaulich.

indigestion [indi'dʒestʃən], *s.* die Magenbeschwerden, *f. pl.*; die Magenverstimmung.

indignant [in'dignənt], *adj.* empört, unwillig, entrüstet.

indignation [indig'neiʃən], *s.* die Entrüstung, der Unwille.

indignity [in'digniti], *s.* die Schmach, der Schimpf.

indirect [indi'rekt], *adj.* indirekt, mittelbar.

indiscreet [indis'kri:t], *adj.* indiskret, unvorsichtig; unbescheiden (*immodest*); taktlos.

indiscretion [indis'kreʃən], *s.* die Indiskretion, Taktlosigkeit.

indiscriminate [indis'kriminit], *adj.* ohne Unterschied, wahllos, kritiklos.

indispensable [indis'pensəbl], *adj.* unerläßlich, unentbehrlich.

indisposed [indis'pouzd], *adj.* unwohl (*health*); unwillig (*unwilling*).

indisposition [indispə'ziʃən], *s.* das Unwohlsein (*health*); das Abgeneigtsein (*disinclination*).

indisputable [indis'pju:təbl], *adj.* unbestreitbar.

indissoluble [indi'sɔljubl], *adj.* unauflöslich.

indistinct [indis'tiŋkt], *adj.* undeutlich.

indistinguishable [indis'tiŋgwiʃəbl], *adj.* nicht zu unterscheiden, ununterscheidbar.

individual [indi'vidjuəl], *adj.* individuell, persönlich; einzeln (*single*). — *s.* das Individuum, Einzelwesen.

individuality [individju'æliti], *s.* die Individualität.

indivisible [indi'vizibl], *adj.* unteilbar.

Indo-Chinese [indotʃai'ni:z], *adj.* hinterindisch. — *s.* der Hinterind(i)er.

indolent ['indələnt], *adj.* indolent, träge.

Indonesian [indo'ni:ʒən], *adj.* indonesisch. — *s.* der Indonesier.

indoor ['indɔ:], *adj.* im Haus; drinnen (*inside*).

indoors [in'dɔ:z], *adv.* im Hause, zu Hause.

indubitable [in'dju:bitəbl], *adj.* zweifellos, unzweifelhaft.

induce [in'dju:s], *v.a.* veranlassen, bewegen, verleiten (*incite*).

inducement [in'dju:smənt], *s.* der Beweggrund (*cause*); der Anlaß (*reason*); die Verleitung (*incitement*).

induction [in'dʌkʃən], *s.* die Einführung; (*Elec.*) die Induktion.

inductive [in'dʌktiv], *adj.* (*Log.*, *Elec.*) induktiv.

indulge [in'dʌldʒ], *v.a.* nachgeben (*Dat.*); verwöhnen. — *v.n.* — *in*, frönen (*Dat.*).

indulgence [in'dʌldʒəns], *s.* die Nachsicht; das Wohlleben; (*Eccl.*) der Ablaß.

industrial [in'dʌstriəl], *adj.* industriell, Industrie-.

industrious [in'dʌstriəs], *adj.* fleißig, arbeitsam.

industry ['indəstri], *s.* die Industrie (*production*); der Fleiß (*industriousness*).

inebriate [i'ni:brieit], *v.a.* berauschen. — [-iit], *adj.* berauscht.

ineffable [i'nefəbl], *adj.* unaussprechlich.

ineffective, ineffectual [ini'fektiv, ini'fektjuəl], *adj.* unwirksam, wirkungslos; unfähig.

inefficiency [ini'fiʃənsi], *s.* die Erfolglosigkeit, Untauglichkeit.

inefficient [ini'fiʃənt], *adj.* untauglich, untüchtig.

ineligible [in'elidʒibl], *adj.* nicht wählbar.

inept [i'nept], *adj.* untüchtig, albern, dumm.

ineptitude [i'neptitju:d], *s.* die Unfähigkeit; die Dummheit (*stupidity*).

inequality [ini'kwɔliti], *s.* die Ungleichheit.

inert [i'nə:t], *adj.* träg.

inestimable [in'estiməbl], *adj.* unschätzbar.

inevitable [in'evitəbl], *adj.* unumgänglich, unvermeidlich.

inexcusable [iniks'kju:zəbl], *adj.* unverzeihlich, unentschuldbar.

inexhaustible [inig'zɔ:stibl], *adj.* unerschöpflich.

inexpedient

inexpedient [iniks'pi:djənt], *adj.* unzweckmäßig, unpraktisch, unpassend.

inexpensive [iniks'pensiv], *adj.* billig, nicht kostspielig.

inexperience [iniks'piəriəns], *s.* die Unerfahrenheit, Naivität.

inexpert [iniks'pə:t], *adj.* ungeübt, unerfahren.

inexpiable [i'nekspiəbl], *adj.* unsühnbar, nicht wieder gut zu machen.

inexplicable [i'nekspilkəbl], *adj.* unerklärlich.

inexpressible [iniks'presibl], *adj.* unaussprechlich.

inexpressive [iniks'presiv], *adj.* ausdruckslos.

inextinguishable [iniks'tiŋgwiʃəbl], *adj.* unauslöschlich.

inextricable [i'nekstrikəbl], *adj.* unentwirrbar.

infallible [in'fælibl], *adj.* unfehlbar.

infamous ['infəməs], *adj.* verrufen, abscheulich, berüchtigt.

infamy ['infəmi], *s.* die Schande; Ehrlosigkeit (*dishonour*).

infancy ['infənsi], *s.* die Kindheit, Unmündigkeit; (*fig.*) der Anfang.

infant ['infənt], *s.* das Kind, (*Law*) der Unmündige, das Mündel.

infantry ['infəntri], *s.* die Infanterie.

infatuate [in'fætjueit], *v.a.* betören.

infect [in'fekt], *v.a.* anstecken, infizieren.

infection [in'fekʃən], *s.* (*Med.*) die Ansteckung, Infektion.

infectious [in'fekʃəs], *adj.* (*Med.*) ansteckend.

infer [in'fə:], *v.a.* schließen, herleiten, folgern.

inference ['infərəns], *s.* die Folgerung.

inferior [in'fiəriə], *comp. adj.* geringer; untergeordnet (*subordinate*); schlechter (*worse*).

inferiority [infiəri'ɔriti], *s.* die Inferiorität, Minderwertigkeit.

infernal [in'fə:nəl], *adj.* höllisch.

infest [in'fest], *v.a.* heimsuchen, plagen.

infidel ['infidəl], *adj.* ungläubig. — *s.* der Heide, Ungläubige.

infiltrate ['infiltreit], *v.n.* durchsickern, durchdringen, infiltrieren.

infinite ['infinit], *adj.* unendlich.

infinitive [in'finitiv], *s.* (*Gram.*) der Infinitiv, die Nennform.

infirm [in'fə:m], *adj.* gebrechlich, schwach; siech (*sick*).

infirmary [in'fə:məri], *s.* das Krankenhaus.

infirmity [in'fə:miti], *s.* die Schwäche, Gebrechlichkeit.

inflame [in'fleim], *v.a.* entzünden.

inflammation [inflə'meiʃən], *s.* die Entzündung.

inflate [in'fleit], *v.a.* aufblasen, aufblähen; (*Comm.*) künstlich erhöhen (*values*).

inflation [in'fleiʃən], *s.* die Aufblähung; (*Comm.*) die Inflation.

inflect [in'flekt], *v.a.* (*Gram.*) biegen, flektieren, deklinieren, konjugieren.

inflection [in'flekʃən], *s.* (*Gram.*) die Biegung; (*Phonet.*) der Tonfall.

inflexible [in'fleksibl], *adj.* unbiegsam.

inflexion *see* **inflection**.

inflict [in'flikt], *v.a.* auferlegen (*impose*); beibringen (*administer*).

infliction [in'flikʃən], *s.* die Verhängung, das Beibringen.

influence ['influəns], *v.a.* beeinflussen. — *s.* der Einfluß.

influential [influ'enʃəl], *adj.* einflußreich.

influenza [influ'enzə], *s.* (*Med.*) die Grippe.

inform [in'fɔ:m], *v.a., v.n.* informieren, benachrichtigen; — *against*, jemanden denunzieren.

informal [in'fɔ:məl], *adj.* nicht formell; ungezwungen, zwanglos.

informant [in'fɔ:mənt], *s.* der Angeber.

information [infə'meiʃən], *s.* die Information, Nachricht, Auskunft.

infrequent [in'fri:kwənt], *adj.* selten.

infringe [in'frindʒ], *v.a.* übertreten.

infuriate [in'fjuərieit], *v.a.* wütend machen.

infuse [in'fju:z], *v.a.* einflößen, aufgießen, begießen.

infusion [in'fju:ʒən], *s.* die Eingießung; der Aufguß (*tea*); (*Chem.*) die Infusion.

ingenious [in'dʒi:niəs], *adj.* geistreich, genial.

ingenuity [indʒi'nju:iti], *s.* der Scharfsinn.

ingenuous [in'dʒenjuəs], *adj.* offen, unbefangen, arglos.

ingot ['ingət], *s.* der Barren.

ingrained [in'greind], *adj.* eingefleischt.

ingratiate [in'greiʃieit], *v.r.* — *o.s.*, sich beliebt machen, sich einschmeicheln (*with*, bei).

ingratitude [in'grætitju:d], *s.* die Undankbarkeit.

ingredient [in'gri:diənt], *s.* der Bestandteil; die Zutat.

inhabit [in'hæbit], *v.a.* bewohnen.

inhabitant [in'hæbitənt], *s.* der Bewohner; Einwohner.

inhale [in'heil], *v.a.* einatmen.

inherent [in'hiərənt], *adj.* eigen, angeboren (*innate*); in der Sache selbst (*intrinsic*).

inherit [in'herit], *v.a.* erben.

inheritance [in'heritəns], *s.* die Erbschaft, das Erbgut (*patrimony*); (*fig.*) das Erbe.

inhibit [in'hibit], *v.a.* hindern; —*ing factor*, der Hemmfaktor.

inhibition [ini'biʃən], *s.* (*Psych.*) die Hemmung.

inhospitable [inhɔs'pitəbl], *adj.* ungastlich, ungastfreundlich.

inhuman [in'hju:mən], *adj.* unmenschlich.

inhume [in'hju:m], *v.a.* beerdigen.

inimical [i'nimikəl], *adj.* feindlich (gesinnt), feindselig.

inimitable [i'nimitəbl], *adj.* unnachahmlich.

iniquitous [i'nikwitəs], *adj.* ungerecht, schlecht, boshaft.

iniquity [i'nikwiti], *s.* die Ungerechtigkeit (*injustice*); die Schändlichkeit (*shame*).

initial [i'niʃəl], *adj.* anfänglich. — *s.* (*Typ.*) der Anfangsbuchstabe.

initiate [i'niʃieit], *v.a.* einweihen, anfangen.

initiative [i'niʃiətiv], *s.* die Initiative; der erste Anstoß (*impulse*).

injection [in'dʒekʃən], *s.* (*Med.*) die Einspritzung, Injektion.

injudicious [indʒu'diʃəs], *adj.* unbedacht, unbesonnen; übereilt (*rash*).

injunction [in'dʒʌŋkʃən], *s.* die Vorschrift, (*Law*) die gerichtliche Verfügung.

injure ['indʒə], *v.a.* verletzen.

injurious [in'dʒuəriəs], *adj.* verletzend; schädlich (*harmful*).

injury ['indʒəri], *s.* die Verletzung, Verwundung; der Schaden (*damage*).

injustice [in'dʒʌstis], *s.* die Ungerechtigkeit.

ink [iŋk], *s.* die Tinte.

inkling ['iŋkliŋ], *s.* die Ahnung.

inkstand ['iŋkstænd], *s.* das Schreibzeug.

inlaid [in'leid], *adj.* eingelegt.

inland ['inlənd], *adj.* inländisch, Binnen-; — *revenue office*, das Steueramt, Finanzamt.

inlet ['inlit], *s.* (*Geog.*) die kleine Bucht.

inmate ['inmeit], *s.* der Insasse, Bewohner.

inmost ['inmoust], *adj.* innerst.

inn [in], *s.* der Gasthof, das Wirtshaus; *Inns of Court*, die Londoner Rechtskammern, *f. pl.*

innate [i'neit], *adj.* angeboren.

inner ['inə], *adj.* inner; geheim (*secret*).

innings ['iniŋz], *s.* das Daransein (*in Cricket*); die Reihe.

innocence ['inəsəns], *s.* die Unschuld.

innocuous [i'nɔkjuəs], *adj.* unschädlich.

innovate ['inoveit], *v.a., v.n.* als Neuerung einführen, Neuerungen machen.

innovation [ino'veiʃən], *s.* die Neuerung.

innuendo [inju'endou], *s.* das Innuendo, die Anspielung.

innumerable [i'nju:mərəbl], *adj.* unzählig, unzählbar.

inoculate [i'nɔkjuleit], *v.a.* impfen.

inoffensive [ino'fensiv], *adj.* harmlos, unschädlich.

inopportune [in'ɔpətju:n], *adj.* ungelegen.

inordinate [i'nɔ:dinit], *adj.* unmäßig.

inorganic [inɔ:'gænik], *adj.* anorganisch.

inquest ['inkwest], *s.* die gerichtliche Untersuchung (*Law*); *coroner's* —, die Leichenschau.

inquire, enquire [in'kwaiə], *v.n.* sich erkundigen (*after*, nach, *Dat.*), nachfragen.

inquiry, enquiry [in'kwaiəri], *s.* die Nachfrage; — *office*, die Auskunftsstelle.

inquisition [inkwi'ziʃən], *s.* (*Eccl.*) die Inquisition; die gerichtliche Untersuchung.

inquisitive [in'kwizitiv], *adj.* neugierig.

inquisitiveness [in'kwizitivnis], *s.* die Neugier(de).

inroad ['inroud], *s.* der Eingriff, Überfall.

insane [in'sein], *adj.* wahnsinnig.

insanity [in'sæniti], *s.* der Wahnsinn.

insatiable [in'seiʃəbl], *adj.* unersättlich.

inscribe [in'skraib], *v.a.* einschreiben (*enrôl*); widmen (*book*).

inscription [in'skripʃən], *s.* die Inschrift.

inscrutable [in'skru:təbl], *adj.* ergründlich, unerforschlich.

insect ['insekt], *s.* das Insekt, Kerbtier.

insecure [insi'kjuə], *adj.* unsicher.

insensate [in'sensit], *adj.* unsinnig (*senseless*); gefühllos..

insensible [in'sensibl], *adj.* unempfindlich; gefühllos.

insensitive [in'sensitiv], *adj.* ohne feineres Gefühl, unempfindlich.

inseparable [in'sepərəbl], *adj.* unzertrennlich, untrennbar.

insert [in'sə:t], *v.a.* einsetzen, einschalten (*add*); inserieren (*in newspaper*).

insertion [in'sə:ʃən], *s.* die Einschaltung (*addition*); die Annonce, das Inserat (*press*).

inside [in'said], *adj.* inner. — *adv.* im Innern. — *prep.* innerhalb. — *s.* das Innere.

insidious [in'sidiəs], *adj.* heimtückisch.

insight ['insait], *s.* der Einblick.

insignia [in'signiə], *s. pl.* die Insignien.

insignificance [insig'nifikəns], *s.* die Geringfügigkeit, Bedeutungslosigkeit.

insignificant [insig'nifikənt], *adj.* unbedeutend, geringfügig.

insincere [insin'siə], *adj.* unaufrichtig.

insincerity [insin'seriti], *s.* die Unaufrichtigkeit.

insinuate [in'sinjueit], *v.a.* zu verstehen geben, andeuten, anspielen auf (*Acc.*).

insinuation [insinju'eiʃən], *s.* der Wink, die Andeutung, Anspielung.

insipid [in'sipid], *adj.* schal, geschmacklos.

insist [in'sist], *v.n.* bestehen (*upon*, auf, *Dat.*).

insistence [in'sistəns], *s.* das Bestehen, Beharren.

insolence ['insələns], *s.* die Frechheit.

insolent ['insələnt], *adj.* frech, unverschämt.

insoluble [in'sɔljubl], *adj.* unlösbar; (*Chem.*) unlöslich.

insolvent [in'sɔlvənt], *adj.* insolvent, zahlungsunfähig, bankrott.

inspect [in'spekt], *v.a.* inspizieren; besichtigen.

inspection

inspection [in'spekʃən], s. die Inspektion; Besichtigung.

inspiration [inspi'reiʃən], s. die Inspiration, Erleuchtung, Begeisterung.

inspire [in'spaiə], v.a. inspirieren, begeistern.

instability [instə'biliti], s. die Unbeständigkeit, Labilität.

install [in'stɔ:l], v.a. einsetzen (in office); einbauen.

installation [instə'leiʃən], s. die Einsetzung (inauguration); die Installation.

instalment [in'stɔ:lmənt], s. die Rate; by —s, auf Abzahlung; die Fortsetzung (serial).

instance ['instəns], s. das Beispiel (example); (Law) die Instanz; at my —, auf meine dringende Bitte; for —, zum Beispiel. — v.a. als Beispiel anführen.

instant ['instənt], s. der Augenblick. — adj. gegenwärtig; sofortig; laufend (current month).

instantaneous [instən'teiniəs], adj. augenblicklich, sofortig.

instead [in'sted], adv. dafür, stattdessen; — of, (an)statt (Genit.).

instep ['instep], s. (Anat.) der Rist.

instigate ['instigeit], v.a. aufhetzen, anreizen, anstiften.

instil [in'stil], v.a. einflößen.

instinct ['instiŋkt], s. der Instinkt, Naturtrieb.

institute ['institju:t], s. das Institut. — v.a. einrichten (install); stiften (found).

institution [insti'tju:ʃən], s. die Stiftung (foundation); die Anstalt (establishment).

instruct [in'strʌkt], v.a. unterrichten, unterweisen.

instruction [in'strʌkʃən], s. der Unterricht (in schools etc.); (pl.) die Instruktionen, f. pl.; die Direktive.

instructive [in'strʌktiv], adj. instruktiv, lehrreich.

instrument ['instrumənt], s. das Instrument; Werkzeug (tool).

insubordination [insəbɔ:di'neiʃən], s. der Ungehorsam.

insufferable [in'sʌfərəbl], adj. unerträglich.

insufficient [insə'fiʃənt], adj. ungenügend, unzulänglich.

insular ['insjulə], adj. Insel-; insular (narrow-minded).

insulate ['insjuleit], v.a. absondern (separate); (Elec.) isolieren; insulating tape, das Isolierband.

insult [in'sʌlt], v.a. beleidigen.

insuperable [in'sju:pərəbl], adj. unüberwindlich.

insupportable [insə'pɔ:təbl], adj. unhaltbar (argument); unerträglich (insufferable).

insurance [in'ʃuərəns], s. die Versicherung; — policy, die Police; — premium, die Prämie; — broker, der Versicherungsmakler.

insure [in'ʃuə], v.a. versichern.

insurgent [in'sə:dʒənt], s. der Aufständische, Aufrührer.

insurmountable [insə'mauntəbl], adj. unüberwindlich.

insurrection [insə'rekʃən], s. der Aufstand, Aufruhr; die Empörung.

intact [in'tækt], adj. unversehrt, intakt.

intangible [in'tændʒibl], adj. unberührbar (untouchable); (Log.) abstrakt. — s. pl. (Log.) die Intangibilien, pl.

integer ['intidʒə], s. (Maths.) das Ganze, die ganze Zahl.

integral ['intigrəl], adj. wesentlich; vollständig. — s. (Maths.) das Integral.

integrate ['intigreit], v.a. (Maths.) integrieren.

integration [inti'greiʃən], s. (Maths.) die Integrierung; (fig.) die Integration, das völlige Aufgehen.

integrity [in'tegriti], s. die Rechtschaffenheit, Redlichkeit (probity).

intellect ['intilekt], s. der Geist, Intellekt, Verstand.

intellectual [inti'lektjuəl], adj. intellektuell. — s. der Intellektuelle.

intelligence [in'telidʒəns], s. die Intelligenz; die Nachricht (news).

intelligent [in'telidʒənt], adj. intelligent.

intelligible [in'telidʒibl], adj. verständlich.

intemperance [in'tempərəns], s. die Unmäßigkeit.

intemperate [in'tempərit], adj. unmäßig.

intend [in'tend], v.a. beabsichtigen, vorhaben.

intendant [in'tendənt], s. der Intendant, Verwalter.

intense [in'tens], adj. intensiv, heftig.

intent [in'tent], adj. gespannt, begierig, bedacht (on, auf, Acc.). — s. die Absicht.

intention [in'tenʃən], s. die Absicht.

intentioned [in'tenʃənd], adj. well-, wohlgesinnt.

inter [in'tə:], v.a. beerdigen.

intercede [intə'si:d], v.n. vermitteln (between); sich verwenden (on behalf of, für, Acc.).

intercept [intə'sept], v.a. abfangen, auffangen, hemmen.

intercession [intə'seʃən], s. die Vermittlung, Fürsprache, Fürbitte.

interchange ['intətʃeindʒ], s. der Austausch. — [-'tʃeindʒ], v.a. austauschen.

intercourse ['intəkɔ:s], s. der Verkehr, Umgang.

interdict [intə'dikt], v.a. untersagen, verbieten.

interest ['intrəst], s. das Interesse; die Beteiligung; (Comm.) die Zinsen, m. pl.; compound —, die Zinseszinsen, m. pl. — v.a. interessieren.

interested ['intrəstid], adj. (in, an, Dat.) interessiert; be — in, sich interessieren für.

422

interesting ['intrəstiŋ], *adj.* interessant.
interfere [intə'fiə], *v.n.* sich einmischen, eingreifen (*in, in, Acc.*)
interference [intə'fiərəns], *s.* die Einmischung; (*Rad.*) die Störung.
interim ['intərim], *adj.* vorläufig, Zwischen-.
interior [in'tiəriə], *adj.* innerlich. — *s.* das Innere; das Binnenland; — *decorator*, der Innenraumgestalter, der Innenarchitekt; *Ministry of the Interior*, das Innenministerium.
interjection [intə'dʒekʃən], *s.* die Interjektion; der Ausruf.
interlace [intə'leis], *v.a.* einflechten.
interleave [intə'li:v], *v.a.* durchschießen (*a book*).
interlinear [intə'liniə], *adj.* zwischenzeilig.
interlocutor [intə'lɔkjutə], *s.* der Gesprächspartner.
interloper ['intəloupə], *s.* der Eindringling.
interlude ['intəlju:d], *s.* das Zwischenspiel.
intermarry [intə'mæri], *v.n.* untereinander heiraten.
intermediate [intə'mi:diit],*adj.* Mittel-; (*Sch.*) — *certificate*, das Mittelstufenzeugnis.
interment [in'tə:mənt], *s.* die Beerdigung.
interminable [in'tə:minəbl], *adj.* endlos, langwierig.
intermingle [intə'miŋgl], *v.n.* sich vermischen.
intermission [intə'miʃən], *s.* die Pause, Unterbrechung.
intermit [intə'mit], *v.a.* unterbrechen.
intermittent [intə'mitənt], *adj.* Wechsel-, aussetzend.
internal [in'tə:nl], *adj.* intern, innerlich.
international [intə'næʃənəl], *adj.* international; — *law*, das Völkerrecht.
interpolate [intə'poleit], *v.a.* interpolieren, einschalten.
interpose [intə'pouz], *v.a.* dazwischenstellen. — *v.n.* vermitteln (*mediate*).
interpret [in'tə:prit], *v.a.* verdolmetschen; erklären (*explain*); auslegen, interpretieren.
interpretation [intə:pri'teiʃən], *s.* die Auslegung, Interpretation.
interpreter [in'tə:pritə], *s.* der Dolmetscher.
interrogate [in'terogeit], *v.a.* ausfragen, befragen, vernehmen.
interrogation [intero'geiʃən], *s.* die Befragung; (*Law*) das Verhör, die Vernehmung.
interrogative [intə'rɔgətiv], *adj.* (*Gram.*) Frage-, Interrogativ-.
interrupt [intə'rʌpt], *v.a.* unterbrechen; stören (*disturb*).
interruption [intə'rʌpʃən], *s.* die Unterbrechung; Störung (*disturbance*).
intersect [intə'sekt], *v.a.* durchschneiden.

intersperse [intə'spə:s], *v.a.* untermengen, vermischen, einstreuen.
intertwine [intə'twain], *v.a., v.n.* (sich) durchflechten.
interval ['intəvəl], *s.* der Zwischenraum; die Pause; (*Mus.*) das Interval.
intervene [intə'vi:n], *v.n.* eingreifen; als Vermittler dienen (*act as mediator*).
intervention [intə'venʃən], *s.* die Vermittlung, Intervention.
interview ['intəvju:], *v.a.* zur Vorsprache einladen (*a candidate*); interviewen. — *s.* die Vorsprache, das Interview.
intestate [in'testit], *adj.* ohne Testament.
intestines [in'testinz], *s. pl.* (*Anat.*) die Eingeweide, *n. pl.*
intimacy ['intiməsi], *s.* die Vertraulichkeit, Intimität.
intimate ['intimit], *adj.* intim, vertraut, vertraulich. — [-meit], *v.a.* andeuten, zu verstehen geben.
intimation [inti'meiʃən], *s.* der Wink, die Andeutung.
intimidate [in'timideit], *v.a.* einschüchtern.
into ['intu], *prep.* (*Acc.*) in, in ... hinein (*towards*).
intolerable [in'tɔlərəbl], *adj.* unerträglich.
intolerance [in'tɔlərəns], *s.* die Unduldsamkeit, Intoleranz.
intonation [into'neiʃən], *s.* (*Phonet.*) die Intonation; (*Mus.*) das Anstimmen, der Tonansatz (*of instruments*).
intoxicate [in'tɔksikeit], *v.a.* berauschen.
intractable [in'træktəbl], *adj.* unbändig, unlenksam.
intransitive [in'trænsitiv *or* in'trɑ:ns-], *adj.* (*Gram.*) intransitiv.
intrepid [in'trepid], *adj.* unerschrocken, furchtlos.
intricacy ['intrikəsi], *s.* die Verwicklung (*tangle*), Schwierigkeit (*difficulty*).
intricate ['intrikit], *adj.* verwickelt, schwierig.
intrigue [in'tri:g], *s.* die Intrige. — *v.n.* intrigieren.
intrinsic [in'trinsik], *adj.* wesentlich; innerlich (*inner*).
introduce [intrə'dju:s], *v.a.* einführen, einleiten (*book etc.*); vorstellen (*person*).
introduction [intrə'dʌkʃən], *s.* die Einführung, die Bekanntmachen; die Einleitung (*preface*); die Vorstellung (*presentation to s.o., Dat.*).
introductory [intrə'dʌktəri], *adj.* einführend.
introspection [intrə'spekʃən], *s.* die Selbstbetrachtung, Introspektion.
introspective [intrə'spektiv], *adj.* nachdenklich, beschaulich.
intrude [in'tru:d], *v.n.* eindringen, sich eindrängen, stören (*be in the way*).
intrusion [in'tru:ʒən], *s.* das Eindringen.

intuition [intju'iʃən], *s.* die Intuition, Eingebung.
intuitive [in'tju:itiv], *adj.* intuitiv, gefühlsmäßig.
inundate ['inʌndeit], *v.a.* überschwemmen.
inure [i'njuə], *v.a.* gewöhnen; abhärten (*harden*).
invade [in'veid], *v.a.* angreifen, einfallen (in, *Dat.*).
invalid [in'vælid], *adj.* ungültig (*void*); ['invælid] krank (*sick*). — *s.* der Kranke, Invalide.
invalidate [in'vælideit], *v.a.* ungültig machen, für ungültig erklären.
invalidity [invə'liditi], *s.* die Ungültigkeit.
invaluable [in'væljuəbl], *adj.* von hohem Wert, wertvoll, unschätzbar.
invariable [in'vɛəriəbl], *adj.* unveränderlich. — *s.* (*Maths.*) die unveränderliche Größe; die Konstante, Unveränderliche.
invasion [in'veiʒən], *s.* die Invasion, der Einfall; Angriff (*of,* auf, *Acc.*).
invective [in'vektiv], *adj.* schmähend. — *s.* die Schmähung.
inveigh [in'vei], *v.n.* schmähen, losziehen (gegen); schimpfen (auf, *Acc.*).
inveigle [in'veigl], *v.a.* verleiten, verführen.
invent [in'vent], *v.a.* erfinden.
invention [in'venʃən], *s.* die Erfindung.
inventor [in'ventə], *s.* der Erfinder.
inventory [in'ventri], *s.* der Bestand, das Inventar; die Liste (*list*).
inverse [in'və:s,'invə:s], *adj.* umgekehrt.
inversion [in'və:ʃən], *s.* die Umkehrung; (*Gram., Maths.*) die Inversion.
invert [in'və:t], *v.a.* umstellen, umkehren. — ['invə:t], *s.* (*Chem.*) — *sugar,* der Invertzucker.
invest [in'vest], *v.a.* bekleiden; bedecken; (*Comm.*) investieren, anlegen.
investigate [in'vestigeit], *v.a.* untersuchen, erforschen.
investiture [in'vestitʃə], *s.* die Investitur; die Belehnung.
investment [in'vestmənt], *s.* die Investierung, Kapitalanlage.
inveterate [in'vetərit], *adj.* eingewurzelt, eingefleischt.
invidious [in'vidiəs], *adj.* neiderregend, verhaßt.
invigorate [in'vigəreit], *v.a.* stärken, beleben.
invincible [in'vinsibl], *adj.* unbesiegbar, unüberwindlich.
inviolable [in'vaiələbl], *adj.* unverletzlich.
invisible [in'vizibl], *adj.* unsichtbar.
invitation [invi'teiʃən], *s.* die Einladung.
invite [in'vait], *v.a.* einladen.
invocation [invo'keiʃən], *s.* die Anrufung.
invoice ['invois], *s.* die Rechnung, Faktura. — *v.a.* fakturieren.
invoke [in'vouk], *v.a.* anrufen.
involuntary [in'vɔləntri], *adj.* unfreiwillig (*unwilling*); unwillkürlich (*reflex*).

involve [in'vɔlv], *v.a.* verwickeln.
involved [in'vɔlvd], *adj.* schwierig, verwickelt, kompliziert.
invulnerable [in'vʌlnərəbl], *adj.* unverwundbar, unverletzlich.
inward ['inwəd], *adj.* inner(lich). — *adv.* (*also* inwards) einwärts, nach innen, ins Innere.
iodine ['aiədain *or* 'aiədi:n], *s.* (*Chem.*) das Jod.
Iraki, Iraqi [i'rɑːki], *adj.* irakisch. — *s.* der Iraker.
Iranian [i'reinjən], *adj.* iranisch. — *s.* der Iranier.
irascible [i'ræsibl], *adj.* jähzornig, aufbrausend.
irate [ai'reit], *adj.* erzürnt, zornig.
ire [aiə], *s.* (*Poet.*) der Zorn.
iridescent [iri'desənt], *adj.* irisierend, schillernd.
iris ['airis], *s.* (*Anat.*) die Regenbogenhaut; (*Bot.*) die Schwertlilie.
Irish ['airiʃ], *adj.* irisch, ersisch. — *s.* (*pl.*) *the —,* die Irländer, Iren, *pl.*
Irishman ['airiʃmən], *s.* der Irländer, Ire.
irk [ə:k], *v.a.* verdrießen, verärgern.
irksome ['ə:ksəm], *adj.* lästig, ärgerlich.
iron ['aiən], *s.* (*Metall.*) das Eisen; (*pl.*) die eisernen Fesseln. — *adj.* eisern, Eisen-. — *v.a.* bügeln, plätten; — *out,* schlichten, beilegen.
ironical [ai'rɔnikəl], *adj.* ironisch.
ironmonger ['aiənmʌŋgə], *s.* der Eisenhändler.
ironmould ['aiənmould], *s.* der Rostfleck.
irony ['aiərəni], *s.* die Ironie.
irradiate [i'reidieit], *v.a.* bestrahlen.
irrational [i'ræʃənəl], *adj.* (*Log.,Maths.*) irrational; unvernünftig (*without reason*).
irreconcilable [irekən'sailəbl], *adj.* unversöhnlich; unvereinbar (*incompatible*).
irregular [i'regjulə], *adj.* unregelmäßig, gegen die Regel.
irrelevant [i'reləvənt], *adj.* belanglos.
irremediable [iri'mi:diəbl], *adj.* unheilbar; nicht wieder gut zu machen.
irreparable [i'repərəbl], *adj.* unersetzlich.
irrepressible [iri'presibl], *adj.* nicht zu unterdrücken, unbezähmbar.
irreproachable [iri'proutʃəbl], *adj.* untadelhaft, tadellos.
irresistible [iri'zistibl], *adj.* unwiderstehlich.
irresolute [i'rezolju:t], *adj.* unschlüssig, unentschlossen.
irrespective [iris'pektiv], *adj.* ohne Rücksicht (*of,* auf, *Acc.*).
irresponsible [iris'pɔnsibl], *adj.* unverantwortlich.
irretrievable [iri'tri:vəbl], *adj.* unersetzlich, unwiederbringlich.
irreverent [i'revərənt], *adj.* unehrerbietig.
irrevocable [i'revəkəbl], *adj.* unwiderruflich.

irrigate ['irigeit], *v.a.* bewässern.
irritable ['iritəbl], *adj.* reizbar.
irritant ['iritənt], *s.* das Reizmittel.
irritation [iri'teiʃən], *s.* die Reizung, das Reizen; die Erzürnung.
irruption [i'rʌpʃən], *s.* der Einbruch.
island ['ailənd], *s.* die Insel.
isle [ail], *s. (Poet.)* die Insel.
isolate ['aisəleit], *v.a. (Med.)* isolieren; absondern; *(Chem.)* darstellen.
isolation [aisə'leiʃən], *s.* die Absonderung, Isolierung.
Israeli [iz'reili], *adj.* den Staat Israel betreffend. — *s.* der Israeli.
Israelite ['izreiəlait], *adj.* israelitisch. — *s.* der Israelit.
issue ['isju: *or* 'iʃu:], *s.* der Ausgang, Erfolg *(result); main* —, der Hauptpunkt; die Nachkommenschaft *(children)*; die Ausgabe *(edition)*; Herausgabe *(publication)*. — *v.a.* herausgeben; erlassen *(proclaim)*; veröffentlichen *(publish)*. — *v.n.* herrühren, stammen *(from)*.
isthmus ['isθməs], *s.* die Landenge.
it [it], *pron.* es; *with* —, damit.
Italian [i'tæljən], *adj.* italienisch. — *s.* der Italiener.
italics [i'tæliks], *s. pl. (Typ.)* der Kursivdruck, die Kursivschrift.
itch [itʃ], *s.* das Jucken. — *v.n.* jucken; — *to do s.th., (coll.)* darauf brennen, etwas zu tun.
item ['aitəm], *s.* der Posten *(in bill)*; der Programmpunkt *(agenda)*; die Einzelheit.
itemize ['aitəmaiz], *v.a. (Comm.)* aufführen; verzeichnen.
iterate ['itəreit], *v.a.* wiederholen.
itinerant [i'tinərənt], *adj.* wandernd.
its [its], *poss. adj.* sein, ihr; dessen, deren.
itself [it'self], *pron.* selber, sich; *of* —, von selbst.
ivory ['aivəri], *s.* das Elfenbein. — *adj.* aus Elfenbein, elfenbeinern.
ivy ['aivi], *s. (Bot.)* der Efeu.

J

J [dʒei], das J.
jabber ['dʒæbə], *v.n.* schnattern.
Jack [dʒæk], Hans; *Union* —, die britische Flagge; *(Cards)* der Bube.
jack [dʒæk], *s. (Motor.)* der Wagenheber. — *v.a.* — *up, (Motor.)* hochwinden.
jackal ['dʒækɔ:l], *s. (Zool.)* der Schakal.
jackass ['dʒækæs], *s. (Zool.)* der Esel.
jackdaw ['dʒækdɔ:], *s. (Orn.)* die Dohle.
jacket ['dʒækit], *s.* das Jackett, die Jacke; *dinner* —, der Smoking;

potatoes in their —s, Kartoffeln in der Schale, *f. pl.*
jade [dʒeid], *s.* der Nierenstein.
jaded ['dʒeidid], *adj.* abgeplagt, abgehärmt, ermüdet.
jag [dʒæg], *s.* die Kerbe. — *v.a.* kerben, zacken.
jagged ['dʒægid], *adj.* zackig.
jail *see under* gaol.
jailer *see under* gaoler.
jam (1) [dʒæm], *s.* die Marmelade, Konfitüre.
jam (2) [dʒæm], *s. traffic* —, die Verkehrsstauung; *(coll.) in a* —, in der Klemme. — *v.a.* zusammenpressen *(press together)*; *(Rad.)* stören.
Jamaican [dʒə'meikən], *adj.* jamaikanisch. — *s.* der Jamaikaner.
jamb [dʒæm], *s.* der Türpfosten.
jangle ['dʒæŋgl], *v.n.* klirren, rasseln. — *s.* das Geklirr, Gerassel.
janitor ['dʒænitə], *s.* der Portier.
January ['dʒænjuəri], *s.* der Januar.
japan [dʒə'pæn], *s.* lackierte Arbeit. — *v.a.* lackieren.
Japanese [dʒæpə'ni:z], *adj.* japanisch. — *s.* der Japaner.
jar (1) [dʒɑ:], *s.* der Topf, das Glas *(preserves)*.
jar (2) [dʒɑ:], *v.n.* offenstehen *(door)*; mißtönen, knarren.
jargon ['dʒɑ:gən], *s.* der Jargon.
jasmine ['dʒæzmin], *s. (Bot.)* der Jasmin.
jasper ['dʒæspə], *s.* der Jaspis.
jaundice ['dʒɔ:ndis], *s. (Med.)* die Gelbsucht; *(fig.)* der Neid *(envy)*; —*d outlook*, die Verbitterung, Mißstimmung.
jaunt [dʒɔ:nt], *s.* der Ausflug, Spaziergang. — *v.n.* herumstreifen, spazieren.
jaunty ['dʒɔ:nti], *adj.* leicht, munter, lebhaft.
jaw [dʒɔ:], *s. (Anat.)* der Kinnbacken; der Rachen *(animals)*.
jay [dʒei], *s. (Orn.)* der Häher.
jazz [dʒæz], *s.* die Jazzmusik.
jealous ['dʒeləs], *adj.* eifersüchtig.
jealousy ['dʒeləsi], *s.* die Eifersucht.
jeer ['dʒiə], *v.a., v.n.* spotten, verhöhnen.
jejune [dʒi'dʒu:n], *adj.* nüchtern, trocken.
jelly ['dʒeli], *s.* das Gelee.
jellyfish ['dʒelifiʃ], *s. (Zool.)* die Qualle.
jeopardize ['dʒepədaiz], *v.a.* gefährden.
jeopardy ['dʒepədi], *s.* die Gefahr.
jerk [dʒə:k], *v.a.* rucken, stoßen *(push)*; plötzlich bewegen *(move suddenly)*. — *v.n.* zusammenzucken. — *s. (Am. coll.)* der Kerl; der Ruck, Stoß.
jersey ['dʒə:zi], *s.* die Wolljacke.
jessamine ['dʒesəmin], *s. (Bot.)* der Jasmin.
jest [dʒest], *s.* der Spaß, Scherz. — *v.n.* scherzen.
jester ['dʒestə], *s.* der Spaßmacher, Hofnarr.

jet

jet (1) [dʒet], s. der Strahl, Wasserstrahl; (*Aviat.*) die Düse; — *engine*, der Düsenmotor; — *plane*, das Düsenflugzeug. — *v.n.* hervorspringen.

jet (2) [dʒet], s. der Gagat; — *black*, pechschwarz.

jetsam ['dʒetsəm], s. das Strandgut.

jetty ['dʒeti], s. der Hafendamm, die Landungsbrücke (*landing stage*).

Jew [dʒu:], s. der Jude.

jewel ['dʒuəl], s. das Juwel, der Edelstein.

jewel(le)ry ['dʒuəlri], s. der Schmuck; die Juwelen, *n. pl.*

Jewish ['dʒu:iʃ], *adj.* jüdisch.

Jewry ['dʒuəri], s. die Judenschaft, das Judentum.

jiffy ['dʒifi], s. (*coll.*) der Augenblick.

jig (1) [dʒig], s. die Gigue (*dance*).

jig (2) [dʒig], s. das Werkzeug (*tool*); — *saw*, die Säge; — *saw puzzle*, das Zusammenlegspiel, -setzspiel.

jilt [dʒilt], *v.a.* sitzen lassen.

jingle [dʒingl], *v.a.* klimpern, klimpern lassen (*coins etc.*). — s. das Geklimper.

job [dʒɔb], s. die Arbeit, Anstellung; die Stellung; das Geschäft; — *in hand*, die Beschäftigung.

jobber ['dʒɔbə], s. der Makler, Spekulant (*stock exchange*).

jockey ['dʒɔki], s. der Jockei, Reiter.

jocular ['dʒɔkjulə], *adj.* scherzhaft, lustig.

jocund ['dʒɔkənd], *adj.* munter, heiter.

jog [dʒɔg], *v.a.* stoßen, antreiben. — *v.n.* gemächlich traben, trotten. — s. der Trott.

join [dʒɔin], *v.a.* verbinden, zusammenfügen; (*club etc.*) beitreten (*Dat.*). — *v.n.* (*rivers*) zusammenfließen (mit, *Dat.*); (*Comm.*) sich vereinigen (mit, *Dat.*).

joiner ['dʒɔinə], s. der Tischler, Schreiner.

joint [dʒɔint], s. (*Anat.*) das Gelenk; das Stück Fleisch, der Braten (*meat*); (*sl.*) das Lokal, die Spelunke. — *adj.* vereint, gemeinsam; (*Comm.*) — *stock company*, die Aktiengesellschaft; — *heir*, der Miterbe.

joist [dʒɔist], s. (*Carp.*) der Querbalken.

joke [dʒouk], s. der Scherz, Witz.

jollity ['dʒɔliti], s. die Heiterkeit.

jolly ['dʒɔli], *adj.* fröhlich, heiter, lustig.

jolt [dʒoult], *v.a.* schütteln, erschüttern (*shake up*). — s. der Stoß.

jostle [dʒɔsl], *v.a.* stoßen, drängen. — *v.n.* drängeln.

jot [dʒɔt], s. der Punkt, das Iota. — *v.a.* — (*down*), notieren, niederschreiben.

journal ['dʒə:nəl], s. die Zeitschrift (*periodical*).

journalism ['dʒə:nəlizm], s. das Zeitungswesen, der Journalistenberuf.

journalist ['dʒə:nəlist], s. der Journalist.

journey ['dʒə:ni], s. die Reise.

joust [dʒu:st], s. das Turnier.

jovial ['dʒouviəl], *adj.* jovial, freundlich; lustig (*gay*).

joy [dʒɔi], s. die Freude.

jubilant ['dʒu:bilənt], *adj.* frohlockend.

jubilation [dʒu:bi'leiʃən], s. der Jubel.

jubilee ['dʒu:bili:], s. das Jubiläum.

Judaism [dʒu'deiizm], s. das Judentum.

judge [dʒʌdʒ], s. der Richter. — *v.a.* richten, beurteilen, entscheiden.

judgment ['dʒʌdʒmənt], s. das Urteil; das Urteilsvermögen (*discretion*), die Urteilskraft.

judicial [dʒu:'diʃəl], *adj.* richterlich, gerichtlich.

judicious [dʒu:'diʃəs], *adj.* klug, scharfsinnig.

jug [dʒʌg], s. der Krug.

juggle [dʒʌgl], *v.n.* jonglieren, gaukeln.

juggler ['dʒʌglə], s. der Jongleur.

Jugoslav see **Yugoslav**.

jugular ['dʒu:g- *or* 'dʒʌgjulə], *adj.* Kehl-, Hals-, Gurgel-. — s. (*vein*) die Halsader.

juice [dʒu:s], s. der Saft.

July [dʒu'lai]. der Juli.

jumble [dʒʌmbl], *v.a.* zusammenmischen, vermischen. — s. das gemischte Zeug; — *sale*, der Verkauf, Ausverkauf gebrauchter Dinge, Ramschverkauf.

jump [dʒʌmp], *v.n.* springen. — s. der Sprung.

junction ['dʒʌnkʃən], s. (*Railw.*) der Knotenpunkt; die Kreuzung.

juncture ['dʒʌnktʃə], s. der (kritische) Zeitpunkt.

June [dʒu:n]. der Juni.

jungle [dʒʌngl], s. der Dschungel.

junior ['dʒu:njə], *adj.* jünger; Unter-.

juniper ['dʒu:nipə], s. (*Bot.*) der Wacholder.

junk [dʒʌnk], s. (*coll.*) das alte Zeug, alte Möbelstücke, *n. pl.*

junket ['dʒʌnkit], s. der Schmaus, das Fest; (*Cul.*) dicke Milch mit Sahne. — *v.n.* schmausen, feiern (*celebrate*).

juridical [dʒuə'ridikəl], *adj.* rechtlich, gerichtlich (*in Court*).

jurisdiction [dʒuəriz'dikʃən], s. die Gerichtsbarkeit.

juror ['dʒuərə], s. der, die Geschworene.

jury ['dʒuəri], s. die Jury, das Geschworenengericht.

just [dʒʌst], *adj.* gerecht; rechtschaffen (*decent*); gehörig (*proper*). — *adv.* soeben, eben; — *as*, eben als, gerade wie.

justice ['dʒʌstis], s. die Gerechtigkeit; der Richter (*judge*).

justifiable ['dʒʌstifaiəbl], *adj.* zu rechtfertigen, berechtigt.

justify ['dʒʌstifai], *v.a.* rechtfertigen.

jut [dʒʌt], *v.n.* — (*out*), hervorragen. — s. der Vorsprung.

jute [dʒu:t], s. die Jute.

juvenile ['dʒu:vənail], *adj.* jugendlich, unreif.

juxtaposition [dʒʌkstəpə'ziʃən], s. die Nebeneinanderstellung, Gegenüberstellung.

426

K

K [kei]. das K.

kale [keil], s. (Bot.) der Krauskohl.

kaleidoscope [kə'laidəskoup], s. das Kaleidoskop.

kangaroo [kæŋgə'ru:], s. (Zool.) das Känguruh.

keel [ki:l], s. der Kiel; on an even —, bei ruhiger See; (also fig.) ruhig. — v.n. — over, umkippen.

keen [ki:n], adj. eifrig (intent); scharfsinnig (perspicacious); scharf (blade).

keenness ['ki:nnis], s. der Eifer; Scharfsinn; die Schärfe (blade).

keep [ki:p], v.a. irr. halten (hold); behalten (retain); führen (a shop); hüten (gate, dog etc.). — v.n. — doing, in etwas fortfahren; — going, weitergehen; — away, sich fernhalten; — in, indoors, zu Hause bleiben; — off, abhalten; sich fernhalten; — out, draußen bleiben; — up, aufrechterhalten. — s. das Burgverlies; der Unterhalt.

keeper ['ki:pə], s. der Hüter, Wärter; Museumsbeamte.

keeping ['ki:piŋ], s. die Verwahrung; in safe —, in guten Händen, in guter Obhut.

keepsake ['ki:pseik], s. das Andenken.

keg [keg], s. das Fäßchen.

ken [ken], s. die Kenntnis; in my —, meines Wissens. — v.a. (Scottish) kennen.

kennel [kenl], s. die Hundehütte.

kerb(stone) ['kə:b(stoun)], s. der Prellstein.

kerchief ['kə:tʃif], s. das Kopftuch, Halstuch.

kernel [kə:nl], s. der Kern.

kettle [ketl], s. der Kessel; — drum, die Kesselpauke.

key [ki:], s. der Schlüssel; (Mus.) die Tonart; die Taste (on piano etc.); — man, eine wichtige Person, Person in einer Schlüsselstellung. — v.a. — (in), einfügen, befestigen.

keyboard ['ki:bɔ:d], s. die Klaviatur, Tastatur (typewriter); — instrument, das Tasteninstrument.

keyhole ['ki:houl], s. das Schlüsselloch.

keystone ['ki:stoun], s. der Schlußstein.

kick [kik], v.a., v.n. mit dem Fuße stoßen or treten; — against s.th., sich wehren. — s. der Fußstoß, Tritt; (Footb.) — off, der Ankick; free —, der Freistoß; penalty —, der Strafstoß, der Elfmeterstoß.

kid (1) [kid], s. (Zool.) das Geißlein, Zicklein; with — gloves, mit Glacéhandschuhen; (coll.) das Kind.

kid (2) [kid], v.a. (Am. coll.) zum Narren haben, aufziehen (tease).

kidnap ['kidnæp], v.a. entführen.

kidney ['kidni], s. (Anat.) die Niere; — bean, die französische Bohne.

kill [kil], v.a. töten; schlachten (animal).

kiln [kiln], s. der Darrofen; der Ziegelofen (tiles, bricks).

kilt [kilt], s. der Schottenrock.

kin [kin], s. die Verwandtschaft; kith and —, die Verwandten, m. pl.

kind [kaind], s. die Art, Gattung, Art und Weise. — adj. freundlich, gütig, liebenswürdig.

kindle [kindl], v.a. anzünden, anfachen.

kindliness, kindness ['kaindlinis, 'kaindnis], s. die Güte, Freundlichkeit.

kindred ['kindrid], adj. verwandt.

king [kiŋ], s. der König.

kingdom ['kiŋdəm], s. das Königreich.

kink [kiŋk], s. der Knoten; (coll.) der Vogel, die Grille (obsession etc.).

kinship ['kinʃip], s. die Sippe, Verwandtschaft.

kipper ['kipə], s. der geräucherte Hering.

kiss [kis], v.a. küssen. — s. der Kuß.

kit [kit], s. (Mil.) die Ausrüstung.

kitbag ['kitbæg], s. der Tornister.

kitchen ['kitʃən], s. die Küche; — garden, der Gemüsegarten.

kite [kait], s. der Drache, Papierdrache; fly a —, einen Drachen steigen lassen; (Orn.) der Gabelweih, der (rote) Milan; (sl.) der Schwindler.

kith [kiθ], s. now only in — and kin, die Verwandten, m. pl.

kitten [kitn], s. das Kätzchen.

knack [næk], s. der Kniff, Kunstgriff.

knacker ['nækə], s. der Abdecker (horse).

knapsack ['næpsæk], s. der Rucksack, Tornister.

knave [neiv], s. der Kerl, Schurke; Bube (cards).

knead [ni:d], v.a. kneten.

knee [ni:], s. (Anat.) das Knie.

kneel [ni:l], v.n. irr. knieen, niederknieen.

knell [nel], s. die Totenglocke.

knick-knack ['niknæk], s. die Nippsache.

knife [naif], s. das Messer. — v.a. erstechen.

knight [nait], s. der Ritter; der Springer (chess).

knit [nit], v.a., v.n. reg. & irr. stricken; knitting needle, die Stricknadel.

knob [nɔb], s. der (Tür)knopf, die Türklinke; der Knorren (wood).

knock [nɔk], v.n. klopfen, schlagen. — s. der Schlag, Stoß.

knoll [noul], s. der kleine Hügel.

knot [nɔt], s. der Knoten; die Schwierigkeit (difficulty).

know [nou], v.a. irr. kennen (be acquainted with); wissen (possess knowledge (of)).

knowing ['nouiŋ], adj. wissend.

knowledge ['nɔlidʒ], s. die Kenntnis (acquaintance with); das Wissen (by

study, information etc.); die Kenntnisse (*of language etc.*).

knuckle [nʌkl], *s.* (*Anat.*) der Knöchel. — *v.n.* — *under*, sich fügen.

Kremlin ['kremlin], *s.* der Kreml.

kudos ['kju:dɔs], *s.* der Ruhm, das Ansehen.

L

L [el]. das L.

label [leibl], *s.* die Etikette, das Schildchen.

labial ['leibiəl], *adj.* (*Phonet.*) labial, Lippen-. — *s.* (*Phonet.*) der Lippenlaut.

laboratory [lə'bɔrətəri, (*Am.*) 'læbərətəri], *s.* das Laboratorium, (*coll.*) das Labor.

laborious [lə'bɔ:riəs], *adj.* mühsam.

labour ['leibə], *s.* die Arbeit, Mühe; *Labour Party*, die Arbeiterpartei; (*Med.*) die Geburtswehen, *f. pl.* — *v.n.* sich abmühen, leiden; sich anstrengen.

labourer ['leibərə], *s.* der Arbeiter, Taglöhner.

lace [leis], *s.* die Spitze, Tresse. — *v.a.* verbrämen (*trim with lace*); zuschnüren (*shoe*); stärken (*coffee with rum etc.*).

lacerate ['læsəreit], *v.a.* zerreißen.

lack [læk], *v.a.* ermangeln (*Genit.*). — *v.n.* fehlen (an, *Dat.*). — *s.* der Mangel, das Fehlen.

lackadaisical [lækə'deizikəl], *adj.* schlaff, (*coll.*) schlapp, unbekümmert.

lackey ['læki], *s.* der Lakai, Diener, Bediente.

laconic [lə'kɔnik], *adj.* lakonisch.

lacquer ['lækə], *s.* der Lack. — *v.a.* lackieren.

lad [læd], *s.* der Bursche, Junge.

ladder ['lædə], *s.* die Leiter.

lading ['leidiŋ], *s.* (*Comm.*) das Laden; die Fracht; *bill of —*, der Frachtbrief.

ladle [leidl], *s.* der Schöpflöffel, Suppenlöffel; die Kelle. — *v.a.* ausschöpfen, austeilen.

lady ['leidi], *s.* die Dame; *— -in-waiting*, die Hofdame.

ladybird ['leidibə:d], *s.* (*Ent.*) der Marienkäfer.

ladyship ['leidiʃip], *s.* (*Title*) gnädige Frau.

lag [læg], *v.n.* zurückbleiben. — *v.a.* verkleiden, isolieren (*tank*).

laggard ['lægəd], *s.* der Zauderer. — *adj.* zögernd, zaudernd.

lagoon [lə'gu:n], *s.* die Lagune.

lair [lɛə], *s.* das Lager (*of animal*).

laird [lɛəd], *s.* der schottische Gutsherr.

laity ['leiiti], *s.* die Laien, *m. pl.*

lake [leik], *s.* der See.

lamb [læm], *s.* (*Zool.*) das Lamm. — *v.n.* lammen.

lambent ['læmbənt], *adj.* brennend, lodernd, strahlend.

lame [leim], *adj.* lahm. — *v.a.* lähmen.

lament [lə'ment], *v.a., v.n.* betrauern, beweinen. — *s.* das Klagelied, die Wehklage.

lamp [læmp], *s.* die Lampe; *— -post*, der Laternenpfahl.

lampoon [læm'pu:n], *v.a.* schmähen, lächerlich machen. — *s.* die Schmähschrift.

lamprey ['læmpri], *s.* (*Zool.*) das Neunauge.

lance [lɑ:ns], *s.* (*Mil.*) die Lanze. — *v.a.* durchbohren; (*Med.*) lancieren.

lancer ['lɑ:nsə], *s.* (*Mil.*) der Ulan.

lancet ['lɑ:nsit], *s.* (*Med.*) die Lanzette.

land [lænd], *s.* das Land; das Grundstück (*plot*); *— tax*, die Grundsteuer. — *v.a.* ans Land bringen, fangen (*fish*). — *v.n.* landen.

landlord ['lændlɔ:d], *s.* der Eigentümer, der Hausherr; Wirt (*pub*).

landmark ['lændmɑ:k], *s.* der Grenzstein, das Wahrzeichen.

landscape ['lændskeip], *s.* die Landschaft.

landslide, landslip ['lændslaid, 'lændslip], *s.* der Erdrutsch.

lane [lein], *s.* der Heckenweg, Pfad; die Gasse; (*Motor.*) die Fahrbahn.

language ['læŋgwidʒ], *s.* die Sprache.

languid ['læŋgwid], *adj.* flau, matt.

languor ['læŋgə], *s.* die Mattigkeit, Flauheit.

lank [læŋk], *adj.* mager, schlank.

lantern ['læntən], *s.* die Laterne.

Laotian ['lauʃən], *adj.* laotisch. — *s.* der Laote.

lap (1) [læp], *s.* der Schoß.

lap (2) [læp], *s.* das Plätschern (*of waves*). — *v.a.* auflecken (*lick up*). — *v.n.* plätschern.

lapel [lə'pel], *s.* der Aufschlag (*of jacket*).

lapidary ['læpidəri], *adj.* lapidarisch; wuchtig.

lapse [læps], *v.n.* gleiten, fallen; verlaufen (*time*). — *s.* der Verlauf (*time*); der Fehler (*mistake*); das Verfallen (*into laziness etc.*).

lapwing ['læpwiŋ], *s.* (*Orn.*) der Kiebitz.

larceny ['lɑ:səni], *s.* der Diebstahl.

larch [lɑ:tʃ], *s.* (*Bot.*) die Lärche.

lard [lɑ:d], *s.* das Schweinefett, Schweineschmalz.

larder ['lɑ:də], *s.* die Speisekammer.

large [lɑ:dʒ], *adj.* groß; weit; dick, stark.

largesse ['lɑ:dʒes], *s.* die Freigebigkeit (*generosity*); die Schenkung (*donation*).

lark (1) [lɑ:k], *s.* (*Orn.*) die Lerche.

lark (2) [lɑ:k], *s.* (*coll.*) der Scherz. — *v.n.* scherzen.

larkspur ['lɑ:kspə:], *s.* (*Bot.*) der Rittersporn.

larva ['lɑ:və], *s.* (*Zool.*) die Larve.

leave

larynx ['læriŋks], *s.* (*Anat.*) der Kehlkopf.
lascivious [lə'siviəs], *adj.* wollüstig.
lash [læf], *s.* die Wimper (*eye*); die Peitschenschnur (*whip*), der Peitschenhieb (*stroke of whip*). — *v.a.* peitschen.
lass [læs], *s.* (*coll.*) das Mädchen.
lassitude ['læsitjuːd], *s.* die Mattigkeit.
lasso [lə'suː: *or* 'læsou], *s.* das Lasso. — *v.a.* mit einem Lasso fangen.
last (1) [laːst], *adj.* letzt, vorig, äußerst; *at long —*, endlich.
last (2) [laːst], *s.* der Leisten (*shoemaking*).
last (3) [laːst], *v.n.* dauern, anhalten; hinreichen (*be sufficient*).
lastly ['laːstli], *adv.* zuletzt.
latch [lætʃ], *v.a.* verschließen.
latchkey ['lætʃkiː], *s.* der Hausschlüssel.
late [leit], *adj.* spät; verspätet; verstorben, selig (*deceased*); neulich (*recent*); *the train is —*, der Zug hat Verspätung; *of late*, jüngst.
latent ['leitənt], *adj.* (*Med.*) latent; verborgen.
lateral ['lætərəl], *adj.* seitlich, Seiten-.
lath [laːθ], *s.* die Latte.
lathe [leið], *s.* die Drehbank.
lather ['læðə], *s.* der Seifenschaum. — *v.n., v.a.* (sich) einseifen.
Latin ['lætin], *adj.* lateinisch. — *s.* das Latein, die lateinische Sprache.
latitude ['lætitjuːd], *s.* die geographische Breite; die Weite (*width*); (*fig.*) der Spielraum (*scope*).
latter ['lætə], *adj.* letzter; später (*later*). — *s.* der Letztere.
latterly ['lætəli], *adv.* neulich, neuerdings.
lattice ['lætis], *s.* das Gitter. — *v.a.* vergittern.
Latvian ['lætviən], *adj.* lettisch. — *s.* der Lette.
laud [lɔːd], *v.a.* loben, preisen.
laudable ['lɔːdəbl], *adj.* lobenswert.
laudatory ['lɔːdətəri], *adj.* belobend.
laugh [laːf], *v.n.* lachen; *—ing stock*, der Gegenstand des Gelächters.
laughter ['laːftə], *s.* das Lachen, Gelächter.
launch [lɔːntʃ], *s.* die Barkasse. — *v.a.* vom Stapel lassen.
launching ['lɔːntʃiŋ], *s.* der Stapellauf.
laundress ['lɔːndris], *s.* die Wäscherin.
laundry ['lɔːndri], *s.* die Wäsche (*clothes*); Wäscherei (*place*).
laureate ['lɔːriit], *s.* der Hofdichter.
laurel ['lɔrəl], *s.* (*Bot.*) der Lorbeer.
lavatory ['lævətri], *s.* das W.C., der Abort, Waschraum; die Toilette; *public —*, die Bedürfnisanstalt.
lavender ['lævəndə], *s.* (*Bot.*) der Lavendel.
lavish ['læviʃ], *adj.* freigebig, verschwenderisch. — *v.a.* vergeuden.
lavishness ['læviʃnis], *s.* die Freigebigkeit, Verschwendung.
law [lɔː], *s.* das Gesetz (*statute*); das Recht (*justice*); die Jura, Jurisprudenz (*subject of study*).
lawful ['lɔːful], *adj.* gesetzlich, gesetzmäßig.
lawless ['lɔːlis], *adj.* gesetzlos; unrechtmäßig (*illegal*).
lawn (1) [lɔːn], *s.* der Rasen.
lawn (2) [lɔːn], *s.* der Batist.
lawsuit ['lɔːsuːt], *s.* der Prozeß.
lawyer ['lɔːjə], *s.* der Advokat, Rechtsanwalt, Jurist.
lax [læks], *adj.* locker, lax.
laxative ['læksətiv], *s.* das Abführmittel.
laxity ['læksiti], *s.* die Schlaffheit, Lockerheit (*of rope etc.*).
lay (1) [lei], *v.a. irr.* legen; setzen (*put*); stellen (*place*); bannen (*ghost*); *— up*, sammeln. — *v.n.* legen (*eggs*); wetten (*wager*); *— about one*, um sich schlagen.
lay (2) [lei], *s.* (*Poet.*) das Lied.
lay (3) [lei], *adj.* Laien-.
layer ['leiə], *s.* die Schicht; *— cake*, die Cremetorte.
layman ['leimən], *s.* der Laie.
laziness ['leizinis], *s.* die Faulheit.
lazy ['leizi], *adj.* faul, träge.
lea [liː], *s.* (*Poet.*) die Aue.
lead (1) [liːd], *v.a., v.n. irr.* führen, leiten; ausspielen (*cards*). — *s.* die Führung; (*Elec.*) Leitung.
lead (2) [led], *s.* das Blei; Bleilot (*plumbline*).
leader ['liːdə], *s.* der Führer; (*Mus.*) der Konzertmeister; der Leitartikel (*leading article*).
leaf [liːf], *s.* (*Bot.*) das Blatt; (*Build.*) der Türflügel. — *v.a.* (*coll.*) *— through*, durchblättern.
leafy ['liːfi], *adj.* belaubt.
league (1) [liːg], *s.* drei englische Meilen, *f.pl.*
league (2) [liːg], *s.* das Bündnis (*pact*); *be in —*, verbündet sein; *League of Nations*, der Völkerbund.
leak [liːk], *v.n.* lecken, ein Loch haben. — *s.* das Loch; (*Naut.*) das Leck.
leaky ['liːki], *adj.* leck.
lean (1) [liːn], *v.n. irr.*(sich)lehnen (an, *Acc.*), stützen (auf, *Acc.*).
lean (2) [liːn], *adj.* mager, hager.
leap [liːp], *v.n. irr.* springen. — *s.* der Sprung; *— year*, das Schaltjahr.
learn [ləːn], *v.a. irr.* lernen, erfahren.
learned ['ləːnid], *adj.* gelehrt.
learning ['ləːniŋ], *s.* die Gelehrsamkeit.
lease [liːs], *s.* die Pacht, der Mietvertrag (*of house*). — *v.a.* (ver)pachten.
leasehold ['liːshould], *s.* die Pachtung.
leash [liːʃ], *v.a.* koppeln, anbinden. — *s.* die Koppel.
least [liːst], *adj.* wenigst, geringst, mindest, kleinst. — *s.* *at* (*the*) —, wenigstens, mindestens.
leather ['leðə], *s.* das Leder. — *adj.* Leder-, ledern.
leave [liːv], *v.a. irr.* verlassen (*quit*), lassen (*let*); hinterlassen (*bequeath*). — *v.n.* Abschied nehmen, abreisen. — *s.* der Urlaub; der Abschied (*farewell*); die Erlaubnis (*permission*).

leaven

leaven [levn], s. der Sauerteig. — v.a. säuern.

Lebanese [lebəˈniːz], adj. libanesisch. — s. der Libanese.

lecture [ˈlektʃə], s. die Vorlesung; der Vortrag.

lecturer [ˈlektʃərə], s. (Univ.) der Dozent; der Vortragende (speaker).

ledge [ledʒ], s. der Sims (window).

ledger [ˈledʒə], s. (Comm.) das Hauptbuch.

lee [liː], s. die Leeseite (shelter).

leech [liːtʃ], s. (Zool.) der Blutegel.

leek [liːk], s. (Bot.) der Lauch.

leer [ˈliə], s. das Starren; der Seitenblick. — v.n. schielen (at, auf, nach); starren.

lees [liːz], s. pl. der Bodensatz, die Hefe.

left [left], adj. link. — adv. inks. — s. die linke Seite.

leg [leg], s. (Anat.) das Bein; der Schaft.

legacy [ˈlegəsi], s. das Vermächtnis, das Erbe, Erbgut.

legal [ˈliːgəl], adj. gesetzlich.

legality [liˈgæliti], s. die Gesetzlichkeit.

legatee [legəˈtiː], s. (Law) der Erbe, die Erbin.

legation [liˈgeiʃən], s. die Gesandtschaft.

legend [ˈledʒənd], s. die Legende, Sage; die Inschrift (inscription).

legendary [ˈledʒəndəri], adj. legendär, sagenhaft.

leggings [ˈlegiŋz], s. pl. die Gamaschen.

legible [ˈledʒibl], adj. leserlich.

legislation [ledʒisˈleiʃən], s. die Gesetzgebung.

legislative [ˈledʒislətiv], adj. gesetzgebend.

legislator [ˈledʒisleitə], s. der Gesetzgeber.

legitimacy [liˈdʒitiməsi], s. die Gesetzmäßigkeit; (Law) die eheliche Geburt (of birth).

legitimate [liˈdʒitimit], adj. gesetzmäßig; (Law) ehelich (child). — [-meit], v.a. für gesetzlich erklären.

legitimize [liˈdʒitimaiz], v.a. legitimieren.

leguminous [liˈgjuːminəs], adj. Hülsen–; hülsentragend.

leisure [ˈleʒə], s. die Freizeit, Muße.

leisurely [ˈleʒəli], adj., adv. gelassen, gemächlich.

lemon [ˈlemən], s. (Bot.) die Zitrone.

lemonade [leməˈneid], s. die Limonade.

lend [lend], v.a. irr. leihen; —ing library, die Leihbibliothek.

length [leŋθ], s. die Länge (extent); die Dauer (duration); at —, ausführlich.

lengthen [ˈleŋθən], v.a., v.n. (sich) verlängern.

lengthy [ˈleŋθi], adj. langwierig, lang.

lenient [ˈliːniənt], adj. nachsichtig, milde.

lens [lenz], s. die Linse (optics); das Objektiv.

Lent [lent]. die Fastenzeit.

lentil [ˈlentil], s. (Bot.) die Linse.

leprosy [ˈleprəsi], s. der Aussatz, die Leprakrankheit.

leprous [ˈleprəs], adj. aussätzig.

lesion [ˈliːʒən], s. die Verletzung.

less [les], comp. adj., adv. weniger, kleiner.

lessee [leˈsiː], s. der Pächter, Mieter.

lessen [lesn], v.a., v.n. (sich) verringern, vermindern.

lesser [ˈlesə], comp. adj. geringer; kleiner.

lesson [lesn], s. die Lehrstunde, Lektion; (pl.) der Unterricht; (Rel.) der Bibeltext.

lessor [ˈlesə], s. der Eigentümer, Vermieter.

lest [lest], conj. damit nicht; aus Furcht, daß.

let [let], v.a. irr. lassen; zulassen; vermieten; (room); — down, blamieren, enttäuschen; off, abschießen. — s. without — or hindrance, ohne Hinderung.

lethal [ˈliːθəl], adj. tödlich.

letter [ˈletə], s. der Brief; der Buchstabe (character); — box, der Briefkasten; (pl.) die Literatur.

letterpress [ˈletəpres], s. die Kopierpresse.

lettuce [ˈletis], s. (Bot.) der Salat.

level [levl], adj. eben, gleich. — s. die Ebene; das Niveau. — v.a. ebnen, ausgleichen; (Build.) planieren.

lever [ˈliːvə], s. der Hebel.

levity [ˈleviti], s. der Leichtsinn.

levy [ˈlevi], v.a. erheben (tax); auferlegen (penalty). — s. die Steuer.

lewd [ljuːd or luːd], adj. liederlich, gemein, unzüchtig.

liability [laiəˈbiliti], s. die Verantwortlichkeit; limited —, beschränkte Haftung; die Steuerpflichtigkeit (to tax), Zollpflichtigkeit (to duty).

liable [ˈlaiəbl], adj. haftbar, zahlungspflichtig.

liar [ˈlaiə], s. der Lügner.

libel [ˈlaibəl], s. die Verleumdung. — v.a. verleumden, schmähen.

libellous [ˈlaibələs], adj. verleumderisch.

liberal [ˈlibərəl], adj. (Pol.) liberal; freigebig (generous); — arts, Geisteswissenschaften, f. pl.

liberate [ˈlibəreit], v.a. befreien, freisetzen; (Law) in Freiheit setzen.

Liberian [laiˈbiːriən], adj. liberisch. — s. der Liberier.

libertine [ˈlibətiːn], s. der Wüstling.

liberty [ˈlibəti], s. die Freiheit; die Erlaubnis (permission).

librarian [laiˈbrɛəriən], s. der Bibliothekar, die Bibliothekarin.

library [ˈlaibrəri], s. die Bibliothek.

Libyan [ˈlibjən], adj. libysch. — s. der Libyer.

licence [ˈlaisəns], s. die Genehmigung, Erlaubnis (permit); driving —, der Führerschein; die Zügellosigkeit (licentiousness).

license [ˈlaisəns], v.a. genehmigen, bewilligen; licensing laws, Ausschanksgesetze, n. pl. (for alcohol).

liquidate

licentiate [lai'senʃiit], s. der Lizenziat (*degree*).

licentious [lai'senʃəs], adj. ausschweifend, liederlich, locker (*in morals*).

lichen ['laikən, 'litʃən], s. (*Bot.*) die Flechte.

lichgate ['litʃgeit], s. das Friedhofstor.

lick [lik], v.a. lecken; (*Am.*) prügeln, verhauen.

lid [lid], s. das Augenlid; der Deckel.

lie [lai], (1) v.n. lügen. — s. die Lüge (*untruth*).

lie [lai], (2) v.n. irr. liegen; — *down*, sich legen, hinlegen; sich fügen (*fig.*).

lieu [lju:], s. *in* —, an Stelle, anstatt (*Genit.*).

lieutenant [lef'tenənt], s. der Leutnant.

life [laif], s. das Leben.

lifebelt ['laifbelt], s. der Rettungsgürtel.

lifeboat ['laifbout], s. das Rettungsboot.

lifetime ['laiftaim], s. die Lebenszeit, Zeit seines Lebens.

lift [lift], s. der Aufzug, Fahrstuhl; (*coll.*) *give a* — *to*, mitnehmen (im Auto). — v.a. heben; aufheben (*abolish*); (*coll.*) klauen, stehlen.

ligament ['ligəmənt], s. das Band; (*Anat.*) die Flechse, die Sehne.

ligature ['ligətʃə], s. (*Typ.*) die Ligatur; die Verbindung.

light [lait], adj. hell, licht; blond (*hair*); leicht (*weight*). — s. das Licht; *give a* —, ein Streichholz geben, Feuer geben. — v.a. irr. beleuchten (*room*); anzünden (*fire*). — v.n. irr. — (*up*), hell werden, leuchten; (*fig.*) aufleuchten.

lighten [laitn], v.a. erhellen (*brighten*); erleichtern (*ease*).

lighter ['laitə], s. das Feuerzeug (*smoker's*); (*Naut.*) das Lichterschiff.

lighthouse ['laithaus], s. der Leuchtturm.

lightning ['laitniŋ], s. der Blitz; — *conductor*, der Blitzableiter; — *speed*, die Blitzesschnelle.

ligneous ['ligniəs], adj. holzig.

lignite ['lignait], s. die Braunkohle.

like [laik], v.a. gern haben; *I* — *to sing*, ich singe gern. — v.n. belieben, wollen; *as you* —, wie Sie wollen. — s. *his* —*s and dislikes*, seine Wünsche und Abneigungen.

like (2) [laik], adj. gleich, ähnlich. — s. *his* —, seinesgleichen. — prep. gleich, wie; *just* — *him!* das sieht ihm ähnlich! *feel* —, möchte gern; *what is it* —? wie sieht es aus?

likelihood ['laiklihud], s. die Möglichkeit; Wahrscheinlichkeit (*probability*).

likely ['laikli], adj. möglich; wahrscheinlich (*probable*).

liken ['laikən], v.a. vergleichen.

likeness ['laiknis], s. die Ähnlichkeit.

likewise ['laikwaiz], adv. ebenso, gleichfalls, auch.

liking ['laikiŋ], s. die Vorliebe (*for*, für, *Acc.*); Neigung (*for*, zu, *Dat.*); *to my*

—, nach meinem Geschmack *or* Wunsch.

lilac ['lailək], s. (*Bot.*) der Flieder.

lilt [lilt], v.a., v.n. trällern, summen. — s. die Melodie, Weise.

lily ['lili], (*Bot.*) s. die Lilie; — *of the valley*, das Maiglöckchen.

limb [lim], s. das Glied.

limber ['limbə], adj. geschmeidig.

lime (1) [laim], s. der Leim, Kalk (*chalk*).

lime (2) [laim], s. (*Bot.*) die Linde (*tree*); die Limone (*fruit*); — *juice*, der Limonensaft.

limestone ['laimstoun], s. der Kalkstein.

limit ['limit], s. die Grenze, das Ende. — v.a. begrenzen, beschränken.

limitation [limi'teiʃən], s. die Begrenzung.

limn [lim], v.a. (*Art.*) zeichnen, malen.

limp [limp], v.n. hinken. — adj. müde, schlaff.

limpid ['limpid], adj. klar, durchsichtig.

linden ['lindən], s. (*Bot.*) die Linde.

line (1) [lain], s. die Linie, Eisenbahnlinie (*Railw.*); die Zeile; der Strich; (*Mil.*) die Reihe; — *of business*, die Geschäftsbranche; (*Genealogy*) die Abstammung; *take a strong* —, entschlossen auftreten.

line (2) [lain], v.a. füttern (*a garment*).

lineage ['liniidʒ], s. die Abstammung.

lineament ['liniəmənt], s. der Gesichtszug.

linear ['liniə], adj. linear, geradlinig.

linen ['linin], s. die Leinwand; *bed* —, die Laken, Bettwäsche. — adj. leinen.

liner ['lainə], s. (*Naut.*) das Passagierschiff.

linger ['liŋgə], v.n. zögern; verweilen.

lingerie ['lɛ̃ʒəri:], s. die Damenunterwäsche.

linguist ['liŋgwist], s. der Sprachkundige, Philologe, Linguist.

liniment ['linimənt], s. (*Med.*) die Salbe.

lining ['lainiŋ], s. das Futter (*of garment*).

link [liŋk], s. das Glied (*in chain*); die Verbindung (*connexion*). — v.a. verbinden, verknüpfen.

linnet ['linit], s. (*Orn.*) der Hänfling.

linseed ['linsi:d], s. der Leinsamen; — *oil*, das Leinöl.

lint [lint], s. die Scharpie, das Verbandzeug.

lion ['laiən], s. (*Zool.*) der Löwe.

lioness ['laiənes], s. (*Zool.*) die Löwin.

lip [lip], s. (*Anat.*, *Bot.*) die Lippe (*mouth*); der Rand (*of jug*).

lipstick ['lipstik], s. der Lippenstift.

liquefy ['likwifai], v.a., v.n. flüssig machen *or* werden.

liqueur [li'kjuə], s. der Likör.

liquid ['likwid], adj. flüssig. — s. die Flüssigkeit.

liquidate ['likwideit], v.a. liquidieren; (*Comm.*) flüssig machen (*assets*); bezahlen (*pay off*).

liquor

liquor ['likə], *s.* der Alkohol.
liquorice ['likəris], *s.* die Lakritze.
lisp [lisp], *v.n.* lispeln. — *s.* der Sprachfehler, das Anstoßen, Lispeln.
list [list], *s.* die Liste, das Verzeichnis; (*Naut.*) die Schlagseite.
listen [lisn], *v.n.* horchen, zuhören.
listless ['listlis], *adj.* teilnahmslos.
litany ['litəni], *s.* (*Eccl.*) die Litanei.
literal ['litərəl], *adj.* buchstäblich.
literary ['litərəri], *adj.* literarisch, Literatur-.
literature ['litrətʃə], *s.* die Literatur.
lithe [laið], *adj.* geschmeidig.
Lithuanian [liθju'einiən], *adj.* litauisch. — *s.* der Litauer.
litigate ['litigeit], *v.n.* einen Prozeß anstrengen, litigieren, prozessieren.
litigation [liti'geiʃən], *s.* die Litigation, der Prozeß.
litter ['litə], *s.* (*Zool.*) die Jungen, *n. pl.*; die Brut; die Sänfte (*carriage*); der Abfall, die Abfälle (*waste paper etc.*). — *v.n.* (*Zool.*) Junge haben, werfen. — *v.a.* Abfälle wegwerfen, unsauber machen.
little [litl], *adj.* klein (*size, value*); gering (*value*); — *by* —, nach und nach.
liturgy ['litədʒi], *s.* (*Eccl.*) die Liturgie.
live [liv], *v.n.* leben; wohnen (*dwell*).
livelihood ['laivlihud], *s.* der Lebensunterhalt.
liveliness ['laivlinis], *s.* die Lebhaftigkeit.
lively ['laivli], *adj.* lebhaft.
liven [laivn], *v.a.* — *up*, beleben.
liver ['livə], *s.* (*Anat.*) die Leber.
livery ['livəri], *s.* die Livree (*uniform*); — *company*, die Zunftgenossenschaft.
livid ['livid], *adj.* bleich, blaß.
living ['liviŋ], *s.* das Auskommen, der Unterhalt; die Lebensweise; (*Eccl.*) die Pfründe, Pfarrstelle.
lizard ['lizəd], *s.* (*Zool.*) die Eidechse.
lo! [lou], *excl.* (*obs.*) sieh, da! siehe!
load [loud], *s.* die Last, Belastung. — *v.a.* beladen, belasten. — *v.n.* laden, aufladen.
loadstone *see* **lodestone.**
loaf [louf], *s.* der Laib (*bread*); *sugar* —, der Zuckerhut. — *v.n.* herumlungern, nichts tun.
loafer ['loufə], *s.* der Faulenzer, Drückeberger.
loam [loum], *s.* der Lehm.
loan [loun], *s.* die Anleihe. — *v.a.* leihen.
loath [louθ], *adj.* unwillig, abgeneigt.
loathe [louð], *v.a.* verabscheuen, hassen.
loathing ['louðiŋ], *s.* der Abscheu, Ekel.
loathsome ['louθsəm], *adj.* abscheulich, ekelhaft.
lobby ['lɔbi], *s.* die Vorhalle. — *v.a.* (*Pol.*) einen beeinflussen.
lobe [loub], *s.* das Läppchen.
lobster ['lɔbstə], *s.* (*Zool.*) der Hummer.
local ['loukəl], *adj.* lokal, örtlich. — *s.* (*coll.*) das Stammgasthaus (*pub*).

locality [lo'kæliti], *s.* die Lokalität, die Örtlichkeit, der Ort.
localize ['loukəlaiz], *v.a.* lokalisieren, auf einen Ort beschränken.
locate [lo'keit], *v.a.* finden (*find*); ausfindig machen.
location [lo'keiʃən], *s.* die Plazierung (*position*); die Lage; der Standort; *on* —, auf dem Gelände, auf Außenaufnahme (*film*).
loch [lɔx], *s.* (*Scot.*) der See.
lock [lɔk], *s.* das Schloß (*on door*); die Schleuse (*on waterway*); die Locke (*hair*). — *v.a.* schließen, abschließen (*door*); hemmen (*wheel*). — *v.n.* sich schließen; — *in*, ineinandergreifen (*cogs*).
locker ['lɔkə], *s.* der Schließschrank, das Schließfach.
locket ['lɔkit], *s.* das Medaillon.
locksmith ['lɔksmiθ], *s.* der Schlosser.
lock-up ['lɔkʌp], *s.* der Arrest, die Haftzelle; (*coll.*) die Garage.
locust ['loukəst], *s.* (*Ent.*) die Heuschrecke.
lodestone ['loudstoun], *s.* der Magnetstein, Magnet.
lodge [lɔdʒ], *v.n.* wohnen; logieren (*temporary*). — *v.a.* beherbergen (*accommodate*); einbringen (a *complaint, protest*). — *s.* das Haus, das Häuschen; die Loge (*Freemasons*).
lodger ['lɔdʒə], *s.* der (Unter)mieter.
lodgings ['lɔdʒiŋz], *s. pl.* das möblierte Zimmer, die Wohnung.
loft [lɔft], *s.* der Boden, Dachboden.
lofty ['lɔfti], *adj.* hoch; erhaben; stolz (*proud*).
log [lɔg], *s.* der Holzklotz, das Scheit; —*cabin*, —*house*, das Blockhaus; (*Naut.*) das Log, das Schiffstagebuch. — *v.a.* (*Naut.*) eintragen.
loggerheads ['lɔgəhedz], *s. pl. at* —, in Widerspruch, Widerstreit, im Konflikt.
logic ['lɔdʒik], *s.* die Logik.
logical ['lɔdʒikəl], *adj.* logisch.
loin [lɔin], *s.* (*Anat.*) die Lende.
loincloth ['lɔinklɔθ], *s.* der Lendenschurz.
loiter ['lɔitə], *v.n.* herumlungern; bummeln.
loiterer ['lɔitərə], *s.* der Lungerer, Faulenzer.
loitering ['lɔitəriŋ], *s.* das Herumlungern, Herumstehen, Faulenzen.
loll [lɔl], *v.n.* herumlungern.
lollipop ['lɔlipɔp], *s.* das Zuckerwerk, die Süßigkeit; (*fig.*) der Leckerbissen.
loneliness ['lounlinis], *s.* die Einsamkeit.
lonely, (*Am.*) **lonesome** ['lounli, 'lounsəm], *adj.* einsam.
long [lɔŋ], *adj.* lang. — *adv.* — *ago*, vor langer Zeit; *before* —, in kurzer Zeit. — *v.n.* sich sehnen (*for*, nach, *Dat.*).
longitude ['lɔndʒitjuːd], *s.* die Länge; (*Geog.*) der Längengrad.

longitudinal [lɔndʒi'tju:dinəl], *adj.* in der geographischen Länge, Längen-.

look [luk], *v.n.* blicken, sehen, schauen (*at*, auf, *Acc.*); — *to it*, dafür sorgen; — *out for*, Ausschau halten nach (*Dat.*); — *out!* paß auf! — *after s.o.*, sich um jemanden kümmern; — *into*, prüfen, untersuchen; — *forward to*, sich freuen (auf, *Acc.*); — *over*, durchsehen. — *s.* der Blick (*glance*); das Aussehen (*appearance*).

looking-glass ['lukiŋglɑːs], *s.* der Spiegel.

look-out ['lukaut], *s.* der Ausblick; die Ausschau.

loom [lu:m], *s.* der Webstuhl. — *v.n.* in der Ferne auftauchen (*emerge*).

loon [lu:n], *s.* (*Orn.*) der Eisvogel, Eistaucher; (*coll.*) der Narr.

loony ['lu:ni], *adj.* (*coll.*) wahnsinnig, närrisch.

loop [lu:p], *s.* die Schlinge, das Schlingband; (*Railw.*) — *line*, die Schleife.

loophole ['lu:phoul], *s.* der Ausweg, die Hintertür.

loose [lu:s], *adj.* locker, lose; liederlich (*morals*). — *v.a.* lösen.

loosen [lu:sn], *v.a.* auflockern, locker machen.

lop [lɔp], *v.a.* stutzen (*trees*).

lopsided [lɔp'saidid], *adj.* einseitig.

loquacious [lo'kweiʃəs], *adj.* geschwätzig.

loquacity [lo'kwæsiti], *s.* die Schwatzhaftigkeit.

Lord [lɔːd], *s.* (*Rel.*) the —, Gott der Herr; der Lord (*nobleman's title*); — *Mayor*, der Oberbürgermeister.

lord [lɔːd], *s.* der Herr.

lordly ['lɔːdli], *adj.* vornehm, stolz.

lore [lɔː], *s.* die Kunde.

lose [lu:z], *v.a.*, *v.n. irr.* verlieren; nachgehen (*of timepiece*).

loser ['lu:zə], *s.* der Verlierende.

loss [lɔs], *s.* der Verlust.

lot [lɔt], *s.* das Los; der Anteil (*share*); die Menge (*quantity*); die Partie (*auction*); (*Am.*) das Stück Land.

loth see **loath**.

lotion ['louʃən], *s.* das Waschmittel, das Wasser.

loud [laud], *adj.* laut; grell (*colour*).

lounge [laundʒ], *s.* der Gesellschaftsraum; (*Obs.*) die Chaiselongue; — *suit*, der Straßenanzug. — *v.n.* nichts tun, herumlungern, herumsitzen.

louse [laus], *s.* (*Zool.*) die Laus.

lout [laut], *s.* der Tölpel.

lovable ['lʌvəbl], *adj.* liebenswürdig, liebenswert.

love [lʌv], *s.* die Liebe; *for the — of God*, um Gottes Willen; *for —*, um nichts; *not for — nor money*, weder für Geld noch gute Worte, auf keinen Fall. — *v.a.*, *v.n.* lieben; —, to, gern tun.

lover ['lʌvə], *s.* der Liebhaber, der *or* die Geliebte.

low [lou], *adj.* niedrig; nieder, tief; leise; (*Mus.*) tief; (*spirits*) niedergeschlagen. — *v.n.* muhen (*of cattle*).

lowlands ['loulændz], *s. pl.* die Niederungen, *f.pl.*; die Ebene; das Unterland.

lowliness ['loulinis], *s.* die Demut, Bescheidenheit.

lowness ['lounis], *s.* die Niedrigkeit; Tiefe.

loyal ['lɔiəl], *adj.* treu, ergeben, loyal.

loyalty ['lɔiəlti], *s.* die Treue, Ergebenheit, Loyalität.

lozenge ['lɔzindʒ], *s.* die Pastille; (*Geom.*) die Raute.

lubricant ['lu:brikənt], *s.* das Schmiermittel, Schmieröl.

lubricate ['lu:brikeit], *v.a.* ölen, schmieren.

lucid ['lu:sid], *adj.* klar, deutlich.

lucidity [lu:'siditi], *s.* die Klarheit.

luck [lʌk], *s.* das Glück, der Glücksfall.

luckily ['lʌkili], *adv.* glücklicherweise.

lucky ['lʌki], *adj.* mit Glück gesegnet, glücklich.

lucrative ['lu:krətiv], *adj.* einträglich.

lucre ['lu:kə], *s.* der Gewinn.

ludicrous ['lu:dikrəs], *adj.* lächerlich, komisch.

lug [lʌg], *v.a.* schleifen, zerren; (*burden*) schleppen.

luggage ['lʌgidʒ], *s.* das Gepäck.

lugger ['lʌgə], *s.* (*Naut.*) der Logger, Lugger.

lugubrious [lu:'gju:briəs], *adj.* traurig.

lukewarm ['lu:kwɔːm], *adj.* lauwarm.

lull [lʌl], *s.* die (Wind)stille. — *v.a.* einlullen, beschwichtigen.

lullaby ['lʌləbai], *s.* das Wiegenlied.

lumbago [lʌm'beigou], *s.* (*Med.*) der Hexenschuß.

lumbar ['lʌmbə], *adj.* (*Anat.*) zu den Lenden gehörig, Lenden-.

lumber ['lʌmbə], *s.* der Kram, das alte Zeug; (*timber*) das Bauholz; — *room*, die Rumpelkammer.

luminous ['lu:minəs], *adj.* leuchtend, Leucht-.

lump [lʌmp], *s.* der Klumpen, Haufen; — *sugar*, der Würfelzucker; — *sum*, die Pauschalsumme. — *v.a.* — (*together*), zusammenwerfen.

lumpy ['lʌmpi], *adj.* klumpig.

lunacy ['lu:nəsi], *s.* der Wahnsinn.

lunatic ['lu:nətik], *adj.* wahnsinnig. — *s.* der Wahnsinnige; — *asylum*, das Irrenhaus, die Irrenanstalt.

lunch [lʌntʃ], *v.n.* zu Mittag essen. — *s.* (*also* **luncheon** ['lʌntʃən]) das Mittagessen.

lung [lʌŋ], *s.* (*Anat.*) die Lunge.

lunge [lʌndʒ], *v.n.* stoßen, stürzen. — *s.* der Stoß.

lurch [ləːtʃ], *s.* *leave in the* —, im Stiche lassen. — *v.n.* taumeln.

lure [luə], *v.a.* locken, ködern (*bait*). — *s.* der Köder (*bait*), die Lockung.

lurid ['ljuərid], *adj.* unheimlich, grell.

lurk [ləːk], *v.n.* lauern.

luscious ['lʌʃəs], *adj.* saftig, süß.

lush [lʌʃ], *adj.* üppig (*vegetation*); übermäßig.

lust

lust [lʌst], s. die Wollust, Sucht. — v.n. gelüsten (for, nach, Dat.).

lustre ['lʌstə], s. der Glanz.

lusty ['lʌsti], adj. kräftig, laut.

lute [lu:t], s. (Mus.) die Laute.

lutanist ['lu:tənist], s. (Mus.) der Lautenspieler.

Lutheran ['lu:θərən], adj. lutherisch. — s. der Lutheraner.

luxuriate [lʌg'zjuərieit], v.n. schwelgen; (Bot.) üppig wachsen.

luxurious [lʌg'zjuəriəs, lʌk'sjuə-], adj. üppig; (rich) reich ausgeschmückt, prächtig, luxuriös.

luxury ['lʌkʃəri], s. der Luxus, Aufwand.

lymph [limf], s. die Lymphe.

lynx [links], s. (Zool.) der Luchs.

lyric ['lirik], s. die Lyrik.

lyrical ['lirikəl], adj. lyrisch.

M

M [em]. das M.

macaroon [mækə'ru:n], s. die Makrone.

mace [meis], s. das Zepter.

macerate ['mæsəreit], v.a. abzehren.

machination [mæki'neiʃən], s. die Machenschaft, Ränke, m.pl.

machine [mə'ʃi:n], s. die Maschine.

mackerel ['mækərəl], s. (Zool.) die Makrele.

mackintosh ['mækintɔʃ], s. der Regenmantel.

mad [mæd], adj. verrückt, wahnsinnig.

madam ['mædəm], s. (addr.) gnädige Frau.

madden [mædn], v.a. verrückt machen.

madman ['mædmən], s. der Wahnsinnige.

madness ['mædnis], s. der Wahnsinn.

magazine [mægə'zi:n], s. die (illustrierte) Zeitschrift; (gun) der Ladestock; der Lagerraum (storeroom).

maggot ['mægət], s. (Ent.) die Made.

magic ['mædʒik], adj. zauberhaft; — lantern, die Laterna Magica. — s. der Zauber; die Magie, Zauberei.

magician [mə'dʒiʃən], s. der Zauberer.

magistracy ['mædʒistrəsi], s. die Obrigkeit (authority).

magistrate ['mædʒistr(e)it], s. der Richter.

magnanimity [mægnə'nimiti], s. der Großmut.

magnanimous [mæg'næniməs], adj. großmütig.

magnate ['mægneit], s. der Magnat, Großunternehmer.

magnet ['mægnit], s. der Magnet.

magnetic [mæg'netik], adj. magnetisch.

magnetize ['mægnitaiz], v.a. magnetisieren.

magnificence [mæg'nifisəns], s. die Herrlichkeit.

magnificent [mæg'nifisənt], adj. herrlich, großartig.

magnify ['mægnifai], v.a. vergrößern (make larger); (Rel.) verherrlichen.

magnitude ['mægnitju:d], s. die Größe; order of —, die Größenordnung.

magpie ['mægpai], s. (Orn.) die Elster.

Magyar ['mægja:], adj. madjarisch. — s. der Magyar, Madjar.

mahogany [mə'hɔgəni], s. das Mahagoni(holz).

maid [meid], s. (Poet.) das Mädchen; das Stubenmädchen (servant).

maiden [meidn], s. (Poet.) die Jungfrau, das Mädchen; — aunt, die unverheiratete Tante.

mail (1) [meil], s. die Post. — v.a. aufgeben, mit der Post senden.

mail (2) [meil], s. (Mil.) der Panzer.

maim [meim], v.a. verstümmeln, lähmen.

main (1) [mein], adj. hauptsächlich, Haupt-; (Railw.) — line, die Hauptstrecke. — s. der Hauptteil; in the —, hauptsächlich; (Poet.) das Weltmeer; (pl.) das Hauptrohr, die Hauptleitung.

main (2) [mein], s. with might and —, mit allen Kräften.

mainstay ['meinstei], s. die Hauptgrundlage, Hauptstütze.

maintain [mein'tein], v.a. erhalten, unterhalten (keep); behaupten (assert).

maintenance ['meintənəns], s. der Unterhalt, die Unterhaltskosten, pl. die Erhaltung.

maize [meiz], s. (Bot.) der Mais.

majestic [mə'dʒestik], adj. majestätisch, prunkvoll.

majesty ['mædʒəsti], s. die Majestät.

major ['meidʒə], adj. größer, älter (elder brother); wichtig (more important). — s. (Mil.) der Major; (Law) der Mündige. — v.n. (Am.) sich spezialisieren.

majority [mə'dʒɔriti], s. die Mehrheit (in numbers); (Law) die Mündigkeit; (Mil.) der Majorsrang.

make [meik], v.a. irr. machen, schaffen, herstellen (produce); (coll.) verdienen (money); he has made it! (coll.) er hat's geschafft!; — out, ausfüllen (cheque etc.); entziffern (decipher); — up, erfinden (invent); schminken (o.'s face). — v.n. what do you — of him? was halten Sie von ihm? — s. die Marke.

make-believe ['meikbəli:v], s. der Vorwand. — adj. vorgeblich.

maladjustment [mælə'dʒʌstmənt], s. die Unfähigkeit sich anzupassen; die falsche Einstellung; das Missverhältnis.

maladroit [mælə'drɔit], adj. ungeschickt, ungewandt.

malady ['mælədi], s. das Leiden, die Krankheit.

Malagasy [mælə'gæsi], adj. madagassich. — s. der Madagasse.

Malaysian [mə'leiziən], adj. malaysisch. — s. der Malaysier.

malcontent ['mælkəntent], adj. mißvergnügt.

male [meil], adj. männlich; — screw, die Schraubenspindel. — s. der Mann; (Zool.) das Männchen.

malefactor ['mælifæktə], s. der Übeltäter.

malice ['mælis], s. die Bosheit.

malicious [mə'liʃəs], adj. boshaft, böswillig.

malign [mə'lain], v.a. lästern, verleumden.

malignant [mə'lignənt], adj. bösartig.

malignity [mə'ligniti], s. die Bösartigkeit.

malinger [mə'liŋgə], v.n. sich krank stellen.

malleable ['mæliəbl], adj. (Metall.) leicht zu hämmern; (fig.) geschmeidig.

mallet ['mælit], s. der Schlegel, Holzhammer.

mallow ['mælou], s. (Bot.) die Malve.

malpractice [mæl'præktis], s. das gesetzwidrige Handeln, der Mißbrauch; die Amtsvergehung.

malt [mɔːlt], s. das Malz.

Maltese [mɔːl'tiːz], adj. maltesisch. — s. der Malteser.

maltreat [mæl'triːt], v.a. mißhandeln.

mammal ['mæməl], s. (Zool.) das Säugetier.

man [mæn], s. der Mann (adult male); der Mensch (human being); of war, das Kriegsschiff. — v.a. bemannen.

manacle ['mænəkl], s. die Handschelle. — v.a. fesseln.

manage [mænidʒ], v.a. leiten, handhaben, verwalten; how did you — it? wie haben Sie's fertiggebracht?

management ['mænidʒmənt], s. die Leitung, Führung.

manager ['mænədʒə], s. der Leiter, Geschäftsführer, Manager.

mandatary see mandatory.

mandate ['mændeit], s. das Mandat.

mandatory ['mændətəri], adj. befehlend, bevollmächtigt, beauftragt. — s. der Bevollmächtigte, Beauftragte.

mandrake ['mændreik], s. der Alraun.

mane [mein], s. die Mähne.

manganese ['mæŋgəniːz], s. (Chem.) das Mangan.

mange [meindʒ], s. die Räude.

manger ['meindʒə], s. die Krippe.

mangle (1) [mæŋgl], s. die Mangel. — v.a. rollen; mangeln (laundry).

mangle (2) [mæŋgl], v.a. verstümmeln (disfigure).

mango ['mæŋgou], s. (Bot.) die Mangofrucht.

manhood ['mænhud], s. die Mannbarkeit, das Mannesalter.

mania ['meiniə], s. der Wahnsinn, die Manie.

maniac ['meiniæk], s. der Wahnsinnige. — adj. wahnsinnig.

manifest ['mænifest], adj. deutlich, klar, offenbar.

manifestation [mænifes'teiʃən], s. die Offenbarung.

manifesto [mæni'festou], s. das Manifest.

manifold ['mænifould], adj. mannigfach.

manipulate [mə'nipjuleit], v.a. manipulieren, handhaben.

mankind [mæn'kaind], s. die Menschheit.

manly ['mænli], adj. mannhaft, männlich.

manner ['mænə], s. die Art, Sitte (custom); die Manier (bearing); das Benehmen (behaviour); (pl.) gute Sitten.

mannered ['mænəd], adj. gesittet, geartet; maniert, gekünstelt (artificial).

manor ['mænə], s. — house, das Herrenhaus, Schloß.

manorial [mə'nɔːriəl], adj. des Herrenhauses, herrschaftlich.

manservant ['mænsəvənt], s. der Bediente, Diener.

mansion ['mænʃən], s. das (herrschaftliche) Wohnhaus, Herrenhaus.

manslaughter ['mænslɔːtə], s. der Totschlag.

mantelpiece ['mæntlpiːs], s. der Kaminsims.

mantle [mæntl], s. (gas) der Glühstrumpf; (Tail.) der Mantel. — v.a. verhüllen (cloak).

manual ['mænjuəl], s. das Handbuch; (Mus.) das Handregister. — adj. Hand-.

manufacture [mænju'fæktʃə], s. die Herstellung, Erzeugung (production); (Comm.) das Fabrikat (product).

manufacturer [mænju'fæktʃərə], s. der Fabrikant, Erzeuger.

manure [mə'njuə], s. der Dünger; der Mist. — v.a. düngen.

manuscript ['mænjuskript], s. die Handschrift, das Manuskript.

many ['meni], adj. viele; as — as, ganze . . . (emphatically); — a, mancher.

map [mæp], s. die Landkarte. — v.a. —(out), nach der Karte planen.

maple [meipl], s. (Bot.) der Ahorn.

mar [mɑː], v.a. verderben.

marauder [mə'rɔːdə], s. der Plünderer.

marble [mɑːbl], s. der Marmor (rock); (pl.) die Murmel (game). — adj. marmorn.

March [mɑːtʃ], der März.

march [mɑːtʃ], s. der Marsch. — v.n. marschieren; steal a — on s.o., jemandem zuvorkommen.

marchioness [mɑːʃə'nes], s. die Marquise.

mare [meə], s. (Zool.) die Stute.

margin ['mɑːdʒin], s. der Rand.

marginal ['mɑːdʒinəl], adj. Rand-, am Rande gelegen.

marigold ['mærigould], s. (Bot.) die Dotterblume.

marine

marine [mə'riːn], *adj.* Marine-, See-. — *s.* (*Mil.*) der Seesoldat; *tell that to the Marines!* der Großmutter erzählen.

mariner ['mærinə], *s.* der Seemann.

marital ['mæritəl], *adj.* ehelich.

maritime ['mæritaim], *adj.* Meeres-, See-.

mark [maːk], *s.* das Zeichen (*sign*); (*Sch.*) die Zensur, Note; (*Comm.*) die Marke; *wide of the —*, auf dem Holzwege. — *v.a.* markieren (*make sign on*); — *my words*, merk dir das! paß auf! (*Comm.*) — *down*, den Preis heruntersetzen; *ins Auge fassen (observe closely)*; *a —ed man*, ein Gezeichneter.

market ['maːkit], *s.* der Markt. — *v.a.* auf den Markt bringen.

marksman ['maːksmən], *s.* der Schütze.

marl [maːl], *s.* der Mergel.

marmalade ['maːməleid], *s.* die Orangenmarmelade.

marmot ['maːmət], *s.* (*Zool.*) das Murmeltier.

maroon [mə'ruːn], *adj.* kastanienbraun, rotbraun.

maroon (2) [mə'ruːn], *v.a.* aussetzen.

marquee [maː'kiː], *s.* das große Zelt.

marquess, marquis ['maːkwis], *s.* der Marquis.

marriage ['mæridʒ], *s.* die Ehe, Heirat; die Hochzeit (*wedding*).

marriageable ['mæridʒəbl], *adj.* heiratsfähig.

married ['mærid], *adj.* verheiratet.

marrow ('mærou], *s.* (*Anat.*) das Mark; (*Bot.*) der Kürbis.

marry ['mæri], *v.a.* heiraten; trauen (*perform marriage ceremony*); — *off*, verheiraten (*o.'s daughter*). — *v.n.* sich verheiraten.

marsh [maːʃ], *s.* der Morast, Sumpf.

marshal ['maːʃəl], *s.* der Marschall.

marshy ['maːʃi], *adj.* morastig, sumpfig.

marten ['maːtin], *s.* (*Zool.*) der Marder.

martial ['maːʃəl], *adj.* Kriegs-, kriegerisch.

martin ['maːtin], *s.* (*Orn.*) die Mauerschwalbe.

martyr ['maːtə], *s.* der Märtyrer.

martyrdom ['maːtədəm], *s.* das Märtyrertum, der Märtyrertod.

marvel [maːvl], *v.n.* staunen (*at*, über, *Acc.*).

marvellous [maːv(ə)ləs], *adj.* wunderbar, erstaunlich.

masculine ['mæskjulin], *adj.* männlich. — *s.* (*Gram.*) das Maskulinum, das männliche Geschlecht.

mash [mæʃ], *v.a.* zerquetschen, zerdrücken. — *s.* der Brei.

mask [maːsk], *v.a.*, *v.n.* maskieren, sich vermummen. — *s.* die Maske.

mason ['meisən], *s.* der Maurer.

masonic [mə'sɔnik], *adj.* freimaurerisch.

masonry ['meisənri], *s.* das Mauerwerk.

masquerade [mæskə'reid], *s.* der Mummenschanz, die Maskerade.

Mass [mæs, maːs], *s.* (*Eccl.*) die Messe; *Low Mass*, die stille Messe; *High Mass*, das Hochamt; *Requiem Mass*, die Seelenmesse.

mass [mæs], *s.* die Masse; die Menge. — *v.a.*, *v.n.* (sich) massen, ansammeln.

massacre ['mæsəkə], *s.* das Blutbad.

massive ['mæsiv], *adj.* massiv, schwer.

mast [maːst], *s.* der Mast. — *v.a.* (*Naut.*) bemasten.

Master ['maːstə], *s.* (*Univ.*) der Magister; der junge Herr (*before boy's name*).

master ['maːstə], *s.* der Meister (*of a craft*); der Herr, Arbeitgeber (*employer*); — *key*, der Hauptschlüssel. — *v.a.* meistern, beherrschen.

masticate ['mæstikeit] *v.a.* kauen.

mastiff ['mæstif], *s.* (*Zool.*) der Kettenhund, Mastiff.

mat [mæt], *s.* die Matte.

match (1) [mætʃ], *s.* das Streichholz, Zündholz.

match (2) [mætʃ], *s.* der ebenbürtige Partner (*suitable partner*); *find o.'s —*, seinesgleichen finden; (*Sport*) das Wettspiel, der Wettkampf; Fußballkampf; (*Cricket*) das Cricketspiel. — *v.a.*, *v.n.* passen zu, anpassen; ebenbürtig sein (*be equal*).

matchless ['mætʃlis], *adj.* unvergleichlich, ohnegleichen.

mate (1) [meit], *s.* der Gefährte, Genosse; (*Naut.*) der Maat, Steuermann; (*coll.*) Freund. — *v.n.* sich paaren, sich vermehraten.

mate (2) [meit], *v.a.* (*Chess*) matt setzen.

material [mə'tiəriəl], *s.* das Material, der Stoff. — *adj.* wesentlich (*essential*); materiell (*tangible*).

materialism [mə'tiəriəlizm], *s.* der Materialismus.

maternal [mə'təːnəl], *adj.* mütterlich.

maternity [mə'təːniti], *s.* die Mutterschaft; — *ward*, die Geburtsklinik.

mathematical [mæθə'mætikəl], *adj.* mathematisch.

mathematics [mæθə'mætiks], *s.* die Mathematik.

matins ['mætinz], *s.* (*Eccl.*) die Frühmette.

matriculate [mə'trikjuleit], *v.n.* sich immatrikulieren (lassen).

matrimonial [mætri'mouniəl], *adj.* Ehe-, ehelich.

matrimony ['mætriməni], *s.* die Ehe.

matron ['meitrən], *s.* die Oberschwester, Oberin (*in hospital etc.*); die Matrone (*older woman*).

matter ['mætə], *s.* der Stoff (*substance*); die Sache, der Gegenstand (*subject*); die Angelegenheit (*case*); *printed —*, Drucksache; *what is the —?* was ist los?; *the heart of the —*, des Pudels Kern; *as a — of fact*, tatsächlich, ernst gesprochen. — *v.n.* bedeutsam sein, wichtig sein.

mattock ['mætək], *s.* die Haue.

mattress ['mætrəs], *s.* die Matratze.

mature [mə'tjuə], *adj.* reif; (*fig.*) gereift. — *v.a.*, *v.n.* reifen, zur Reife bringen; (*Comm.*) fällig werden.

matured [mə'tjuəd], *adj.* abgelagert.
maturity [mə'tjuəriti], *s.* die Reife; (*Comm.*) die Fälligkeit.
maudlin ['mɔːdlin], *adj.* rührselig, sentimental.
maul [mɔːl], *v.a.* mißhandeln.
Maundy Thursday ['mɔːndi'θəːzd(e)i]. der Gründonnerstag.
mauve [mouv], *adj.* malvenfarbig; violett.
maw [mɔː], *s.* (*Zool.*) der Magen.
mawkish ['mɔːkiʃ], *adj.* abgeschmackt, sentimental, rührselig.
maxim ['mæksim], *s.* der Grundsatz.
May [mei]. der Mai.
may (1) [mei], *v.n. aux. irr.* mögen, können; (*permissive*) dürfen.
may (2) [mei], *s.* (*Bot.*) der Weißdorn.
mayor [mɛə], *s.* der Bürgermeister.
maypole ['meipoul], *s.* der Maibaum.
maze [meiz], *s.* das Labyrinth.
me [miː], *pers. pron.* (*Acc.*) mich; (*Dat.*) mir.
mead [miːd], *s.* der Met.
meadow ['medou], *s.* die Wiese.
meagre ['miːgə], *adj.* mager, karg (*lean, poor*); dürftig.
meal (1) [miːl], *s.* das Mahl, Essen, die Mahlzeit.
meal (2) [miːl], *s.* das Mehl (*flour*).
mealy ['miːli], *adj.* mehlig; — -mouthed, frömmelnd; kleinlaut (*shy*).
mean (1) [miːn], *v.a. v.n. irr.* bedeuten (*signify*); meinen (*wish to express*); vorhaben (*intend*).
mean (2) [miːn], *adj.* mittelmäßig, Mittel- (*average*). — *s.* die Mitte.
mean (3) [miːn], *adj.* gemein, niedrig (*despicable*); geizig.
meander [mi'ændə], *s.* die Windung, das Wellenmuster. — *v.n.* sich winden, sich schlängeln.
meaning ['miːniŋ], *s.* die Bedeutung (*significance, connotation*); der Sinn.
meaningless ['miːniŋlis], *adj.* bedeutungslos.
means [miːnz], *s.* das Mittel; *by all* —, auf jeden Fall, unbedingt; *by no* —, keinesfalls; *by—of*, mittels (*Genit.*).
meantime, meanwhile ['miːntaim, 'miːnwail], *s.* die Zwischenzeit. — *adv.* in der Zwischenzeit, indessen.
measles [miːzlz], *s.* (*Med.*) die Masern, *f. pl.*; *German* —, die Röteln, *m. pl.*
measurable ['meʒərəbl], *adj.* meßbar.
measure ['meʒə], *s.* das Maß; der Maßstab (*scale*); (*Mus.*) der Takt; das Zeitmaß. — *v.a.* messen, abmessen.
meat [miːt], *s.* das Fleisch.
mechanic [mi'kænik], *s.* der Mechaniker.
mechanical [mi'kænikəl], *adj.* mechanisch, automatisch; — *engineering,* der Maschinenbau.
mechanics [mi'kæniks], *s.* die Mechanik.
medal [medl], *s.* die Medaille, der Orden.
meddle [medl], *v.n.* sich einmischen (in, *in, Acc.*).

mediæval, medieval [medi'iːvəl], *adj.* mittelalterlich.
mediate ['miːdieit], *v.n.* vermitteln, intervenieren. — *adj.* mittelbar.
mediator ['miːdieitə], *s.* der Vermittler.
medical ['medikəl], *adj.* medizinisch, ärztlich; — *orderly,* der Krankenwärter.
medicate ['medikeit], *v.a.* medizinisch behandeln.
medicine ['medsən], *s.* die Medizin, Arznei.
medieval *see* **mediæval.**
mediocre ['miːdioukə], *adj.* mittelmäßig.
mediocrity [miːdi'ɔkriti], *s.* die Mittelmäßigkeit.
meditate ['mediteit], *v.n.* nachdenken, sinnen.
meditation [medi'teiʃən], *s.* das Sinnen, Nachdenken.
Mediterranean [meditə'reiniən], *adj.* mittelländisch. — *s.* das Mittelmeer, mittelländische Meer.
medium ['miːdjəm], *s.* das Medium; das Mittel (*means*). — *adj.* mittelgroß.
medlar ['medlə], *s.* (*Bot.*) die Mispel.
medley ['medli], *s.* (*Mus.*) das Potpourri; das Gemisch (*mixture*).
meek [miːk], *adj.* sanft, mild.
meet [miːt], *v.a., v.n. irr.* treffen (*Acc.*), sich treffen (mit, *Dat.*), begegnen (*Dat.*). — *s.* (*Hunt.*) die Jagd.
meeting ['miːtiŋ], *s.* das Zusammentreffen; die Tagung, Sitzung (*conference*).
melancholy ['melənkɔli], *adj.* melancholisch, schwermütig. — *s.* die Melancholie, die Schwermut.
mellifluous [me'lifluəs], *adj.* lieblich, süß (*of sounds*).
mellow ['melou], *adj.* mild, weich, mürbe (*fruit etc.*); freundlich (*mood*). — *v.a.* milde machen, reifen lassen. — *v.n.* weich werden.
melodious [mə'loudiəs], *adj.* klangvoll, wohlklingend, melodisch.
melodrama ['melədrɑːmə], *s.* das Melodrama.
melody ['melədi], *s.* die Melodie.
melon ['melən], *s.* (*Bot.*) die Melone.
melt [melt], *v.a., v.n. reg. & irr.* schmelzen.
member ['membə], *s.* das Mitglied (*of club*); (*Parl.*) der Abgeordnete, das Glied.
membrane ['membrein], *s.* die Membran; (*Anat.*) das Häutchen.
memento [mi'mentou], *s.* das Andenken.
memoir ['memwɑː], *s.* die Denkschrift; (*pl.*) die Memoiren, *n. pl.*
memorable ['memərəbl], *adj.* denkwürdig.
memorandum [memə'rændəm], *s.* das Memorandum, die Denkschrift.
memorial [mi'mɔːriəl], *s.* das Denkmal (*monument*). — *adj.* Gedenk-, zum Gedenken, Gedächtnis-.

memory

memory ['meməri], s. die Erinnerung; das Gedächtnis (*faculty*); das Andenken (*remembrance*).

menace ['menis], s. die Drohung. — *v.a.* bedrohen.

mend [mend], *v.a.* reparieren; verbessern, ausbessern. — *v.n.* sich bessern.

mendacious [men'deiʃəs], *adj.* lügnerisch, verlogen (*lying*).

mendacity [men'dæsiti], s. die Lügenhaftigkeit, Verlogenheit.

mendicant ['mendikənt], *adj.* bettlerisch. — s. der Bettler.

mendicity [men'disiti], s. die Bettelei.

menial ['mi:niəl], *adj.* gemein, grob (*job*).

mental [mentl], *adj.* geistig; (*coll.*) geisteskrank.

mention ['menʃən], *v.a.* erwähnen; *don't — it*, gern geschehen! — s. die Erwähnung.

mentor ['mentə], s. der Ratgeber.

menu ['menju:], s. die Speisekarte.

mercantile ['mə:kəntail], *adj.* Handels-, kaufmännisch.

mercenary ['mə:sənəri], *adj.* für Geld zu haben, käuflich, feil; materiell eingestellt. — s. der Söldner.

mercer ['mə:sə], s. der Seidenhändler.

mercerised ['mə:səraizd], *adj.* (*Textile*) merzerisiert.

merchandise ['mə:tʃəndaiz], s. die Ware.

merchant ['mə:tʃənt], s. der Kaufmann.

merchantman ['mə:tʃəntmən], s. (*Naut.*) das Handelsschiff, Frachtschiff.

merciful ['mə:siful], *adj.* barmherzig, gnädig.

Mercury ['mə:kjuəri], (*Myth.*) Merkur, *m.*

mercury ['mə:kjuəri], s. (*Chem.*) das Quecksilber.

mercy ['mə:si], s. die Barmherzigkeit, Gnade.

mere (1) [miə], *adj.* bloß, allein.

mere (2) [miə], s. der Teich.

meretricious [meri'triʃəs], *adj.* falsch, täuschend.

merge [mə:dʒ], *v.n.* aufgehen lassen, verschmelzen (*combine*).

merger ['mə:dʒə], s. (*Comm.*) die Fusion, Vereinigung, Zusammenlegung.

meridian [mə'ridiən], s. der Meridian; (*fig.*) der Gipfel.

merit ['merit], s. das Verdienst, der Wert. — *v.a.* verdienen.

meritorious [meri'tɔ:riəs], *adj.* verdienstlich.

mermaid ['mə:meid], s. die Wasserjungfrau, Nixe.

merriment ['merimənt], s. die Belustigung, das Fröhlichsein, die Fröhlichkeit.

merry ['meri], *adj.* froh, fröhlich; — *go-round*, das Karussel.

mesh [meʃ], s. das Netz; die Masche (*knitting*). — *v.a.* einfangen.

mess (1) [mes], s. (*Mil.*) die Offiziersmesse.

mess (2) [mes], s. die Unordnung (*disorder*).

message ['mesidʒ], s. die Nachricht, Mitteilung, Botschaft.

messenger ['mesindʒə], s. der Bote.

Messiah [mi'saiə], s. der Messias.

metal [metl], s. das Metall.

metallurgy ['metələ:dʒi], s. die Metallurgie, Hüttenkunde.

metaphor ['metəfɔ:], s. die Metapher.

metaphorical [metə'fɔrikəl], *adj.* bildlich.

meter ['mi:tə], s. der Messer, Zähler (*gauge*); (*Am.*) see **metre** (1).

methinks [mi'θiŋks], *v. impers.* (*obs.*) mich dünkt, ich meine, mir scheint.

method ['meθəd], s. die Methode.

methodical [mi'θɔdikəl], *adj.* methodisch, systematisch.

methylate ['meθileit], *v.a.* (*Chem.*) denaturieren.

metre (1) ['mi:tə], s. der *or* das Meter (*unit of measurement*).

metre (2) ['mi:tə], s. (*Poet.*) das Versmaß.

metric ['metrik], *adj.* metrisch (*system of measurement*).

metrical ['metrikəl], *adj.* (*Poet.*) im Metrum, metrisch, Vers-.

metropolis [mi'trɔpəlis], s. die Metropole.

metropolitan [metrə'pɔlitən], *adj.* hauptstädtisch. — s. (*Eccl.*) der Erzbischof.

mettle [metl], s. der Mut (*courage*); *put s.o. on his —*, einen anspornen.

mew [mju:], s. das Miauen (*of cat*). — *v.n.* miauen.

mews [mju:z], s. *pl.* die Stallung.

Mexican ['meksikən], *adj.* mexikanisch. — s. der Mexikaner.

microphone ['maikrəfoun], s. das Mikrophon.

mid- [mid], *prefix.* mittel, Mittel-, mittler.

midday [mid'dei], s. der Mittag.

middle [midl], s. die Mitte, das Zentrum.

middling ['midliŋ], *adj.* (*coll.*) mittelmäßig.

midget ['midʒit], s. der Zwerg (*dwarf*).

midnight ['midnait], s. die Mitternacht.

midriff ['midrif], s. das Zwerchfell.

midshipman ['midʃipmən], s. (*Naut.*) der Seekadett.

midwife ['midwaif], s. die Hebamme.

mien [mi:n], s. die Miene.

might [mait], s. die Macht, Gewalt.

mighty ['maiti], *adj.* mächtig, stark.

mignonette [minjə'net], s. (*Bot.*) die Reseda.

migrate [mai'greit], *v.n.* wandern, migrieren; (*birds*) ziehen.

migratory ['maigrətəri], *adj.* Zug-, Wander-.

Milanese [milə'n:iz], *adj.* mailändisch. — *s.* der Mailänder.

mild [maild], *adj.* mild, sanft.

mildew ['mildju:], *s.* der Meltau.

mile [mail], *s.* die (englische) Meile.

mileage ['mailidʒ], *s.* die Meilenzahl.

milfoil ['milfɔil], *s.* (*Bot.*) die Schafgarbe (*yarrow*).

military ['militəri], *adj.* militärisch. — *s.* das Militär.

militia [mi'liʃə], *s.* die Miliz.

milk [milk], *v.a.* melken. — *s.* die Milch.

milksop ['milksɔp], *s.* die Memme.

milky ['milki], *adj.* milchig; *Milky Way*, die Milchstraße.

mill [mil], *s.* die Mühle; die Spinnerei (*textile*); *rolling* —, das Walzwerk; *run of the* —, gewöhnlich; *through the* —, wohl erfahren, lebenserfahren. — *v.a.* mahlen (*flour*); rollen, walzen (*steel*); rändern (*coins*); —*ed edge*, die Rändelkante. —*v.n.* — (*around*), sich drängen.

miller ['milə], *s.* der Müller.

millet ['milit], *s.* die Hirse.

milliner ['milinə], *s.* die Modistin, Putzmacherin.

millinery ['milinəri], *s.* die Putzwaren, Modewaren, *f. pl.*

million ['miljən], *s.* die Million.

milt [milt], *s.* die Fischmilch; (*Anat.*) die Milz.

mimic ['mimik], *s.* der Mimiker. — *v.a.* nachahmen.

mimicry ['mimikri], *s.* die Nachahmung; (*Zool.*) die Anpassung (*in colour*).

mince [mins], *v.a.* kleinhacken (*meat*); — *o.'s words*, affektiert sprechen; *not* — *o.'s words*, kein Blatt vor den Mund nehmen. — *s.* gehacktes Fleisch; — *pie*, die Dörrobstpastete.

mincemeat ['minsmi:t], *s.* die (gehackte) Dörrobstmischung.

mincing ['minsiŋ], *adj.* affektiert; — *steps*, trippelnde Schritte.

mind [maind], *s.* der Geist, das Gemüt; die Meinung; der Sinn; der Verstand; *what is on your* — ? was bedrückt Sie ?; *bear in* —, daran denken; *have a* —, Lust haben; *make up o.'s* —, sich entschließen; *with an open* —, unparteiisch. — *v.a.* beachten, achten (auf, *Acc.*). —*v.n. do you* — ? macht es Ihnen etwas aus ? *never* —, macht nichts; *I don't* —, mir ist's recht, meinetwegen.

minded ['maindid], *adj.* gesinnt, eingestellt.

mine (1) [main], *poss. pron.* mein, meinig.

mine (2) [main], *s.* das Bergwerk (*general*), die Grube (*coal*). — *v.a.* abbauen, graben (*Acc.*, nach, *Dat.*).

miner ['mainə], *s.* der Bergmann, Bergarbeiter; (*coll.*) der Kumpel.

mineral ['minərəl], *s.* das Mineral; (*pl.*) Mineralwasser.

mingle [miŋgl], *v.a.,v.n.* (sich) mischen.

minimize ['minimaiz], *v.a.* (möglichst) klein machen.

mining ['mainiŋ], *s.* die Hüttenkunde (*theory*); der Bergbau.

minion ['minjən], *s.* der Liebling.

minister ['ministə], *s.* (*Pol.*) der Minister; *Prime Minister*, der Ministerpräsident; (*Eccl.*) der Geistliche, Pfarrer. — *v.n.* einen Gottesdienst abhalten; dienen (*to, Dat.*).

ministration [minis'treiʃən], *s.* der Dienst, die Dienstleistung.

ministry ['ministri], *s.* das Ministerium (*department of state*); (*Eccl.*) der Beruf or das Amt des Geistlichen.

minnow ['minou], *s.* (*Zool.*) die Elritze.

minor ['mainə], *adj.* kleiner, geringer; (*Sch.*) jünger (*after boy's name*). — *s.* (*Law*) der Minderjährige, Unmündige.

minority [mai'nɔriti], *s.* die Minorität (*in numbers*); (*Law*) die Unmündigkeit.

minster ['minstə], *s.* (*Eccl.*) das Münster.

minstrel ['minstrəl], *s.* der Spielmann.

mint (1) [mint], *s.* (*Bot.*) die Minze.

mint (2) [mint], *s.* die Münzstätte. — *v.a.* münzen.

minuet [minju'et], *s.* (*Mus.*) das Menuett.

minute (1) ['minit], *s.* die Minute (*time*); (*pl.*) das Protokoll (*of meeting*). — *v.a.* zu Protokoll nehmen, protokollieren.

minute (2) [mai'nju:t], *adj.* winzig, klein.

minutiae [mai'nju:ʃii], *s.pl.* die Details, *n. pl.*, die Einzelheiten, *f. pl.*

miracle ['mirəkl], *s.* das Wunder.

miraculous [mi'rækjuləs], *adj.* wunderbar; wundertätig.

mirage [mi'rɑ:ʒ], *s.* die Luftspiegelung, die Fata Morgana.

mire [maiə], *s.* der Schlamm, Kot.

mirror ['mirə], *s.* der Spiegel. — *v.a.* reflektieren, spiegeln.

mirth [mə:θ], *s.* der Frohsinn.

misadventure [misəd'ventʃə], *s.* das Mißgeschick.

misalliance [misə'laiəns], *s.* die Mißheirat, Mesalliance.

misapply [misə'plai], *v.a.* falsch anwenden.

misapprehend [misæpri'hend], *v.a.* mißverstehen.

misapprehension [misæpri'henʃən], *s.* das Mißverständnis.

misappropriate [misə'prouprieit], *v.a.* unrechtmäßig erwerben, unterschlagen.

misbehave [misbi'heiv], *v.n.* sich schlecht benehmen.

miscalculate [mis'kælkjuleit], *v.a.,v.n.* sich verrechnen.

miscarriage [mis'kæridʒ], *s.* das Mißlingen; (*Med.*) die Fehlgeburt.

miscarry [mis'kæri], *v.n.* mißlingen; (*Med.*) fehlgebären.

miscellaneous [misə'leiniəs], *adj.* vermischt.

miscellany

miscellany [mi'seləni], *s.* der Sammelband (*of writers*); die Mischung, das Gemisch.

mischief ['mistʃif], *s.* der Unfug; *out to make* —, darauf aus, Unfug zu stiften; — *maker*, der Unheilstifter.

mischievous ['mistʃivəs], *adj.* boshaft.

misconceive [miskən'siːv], *v.a.* mißverstehen.

misconception [miskən'sepʃən], *s.* das Mißverständnis.

misconduct [mis'kɔndʌkt], *s.* das unkorrekte Verhalten; der Fehltritt.

misconstruction [miskən'strʌkʃən], *s.* die Mißdeutung.

misconstrue [miskən'struː], *v.a.* mißdeuten.

misdeed [mis'diːd], *s.* die Missetat.

misdemeanour [misdi'miːnə], *s.* (*Law.*) das Vergehen; die Missetat.

miser ['maizə], *s.* der Geizhals.

miserable ['mizərəbl], *adj.* elend, kläglich (*wretched*); nichtswürdig (*base*).

miserly ['maizəli], *adj.* geizig.

misery ['mizəri], *s.* das Elend, die Not.

misfortune [mis'fɔːtʃən], *s.* das Unglück.

misgiving [mis'giviŋ], *s.* die Befürchtung, der Zweifel (*doubt*).

misguide [mis'gaid], *v.a.* irreführen, verleiten.

mishap [mis'hæp], *s.* der Unfall.

misinform [misin'fɔːm], *v.a.* falsch informieren, falsch unterrichten.

misinterpret [misin'təːprit], *v.a.* mißdeuten.

misjudge [mis'dʒʌdʒ], *v.a.* falsch beurteilen.

mislay [mis'lei], *v.a. irr.* verlegen.

mislead [mis'liːd], *v.a. irr.* verführen, irreführen.

misnomer [mis'noumə], *s.* der falsche Name.

misogynist [mi'sɔdʒinist], *s.* der Weiberfeind.

misplace [mis'pleis], *v.a.* übel anbringen (*remark*); verlegen (*thing*).

misprint [mis'print], *v.a.* verdrucken, falsch drucken. — ['misprint], *s.* der Druckfehler.

misquote [mis'kwout], *v.a.* falsch zitieren.

misrepresent [misrepri'zent], *v.a.* falsch darstellen.

misrule [mis'ruːl], *s.* die schlechte Regierung; die Unordnung (*disorder*).

miss (1) [mis], *s.* das Fräulein.

miss (2) [mis], *v.a.* vermissen (*yearn for*); versäumen (*a train, lesson etc.*); verfehlen (*target*); — *the boat*, den Anschluß verpassen; *be missing*, fehlen.

missal [misl], *s.* (*Eccl.*) das Meßbuch.

misshapen [mis'ʃeipən], *adj.* mißgestaltet.

missile ['misail], *s.* das Geschoß; *ballistic* —, das Raketengeschoß; *guided* —, ferngesteuertes Raketengeschoss.

mission ['miʃən], *s.* die Mission; Sendung; der Auftrag (*task*).

missionary ['miʃənəri], *adj.* Missions-. — *s.* der Missionar.

missive ['misiv], *s.* das Sendschreiben.

misspell [mis'spel], *v.a.* falsch buchstabieren, falsch schreiben.

mist [mist], *s.* der Dunst; Nebel (*fog*).

mistake [mis'teik], *s.* der Fehler. — *v.a. irr.* verkennen.

mistaken [mis'teikn], *adj.* im Unrecht; irrig; *be* —, sich irren.

mistimed [mis'taimd], *adj.* zur Unzeit, unzeitig.

mistletoe ['misltou], *s.* (*Bot.*) die Mistel, der Mistelzweig.

mistress ['mistrəs], *s.* die Herrin; Hausfrau; Geliebte (*paramour*); Lehrerin (*Sch.*).

mistrust [mis'trʌst], *v.a.* mißtrauen.

misunderstand [misʌndə'stænd], *v.a. irr.* mißverstehen.

misuse [mis'juːz], *v.a.* mißbrauchen.

mite (1) [mait], *s.* (*Zool.*) die Milbe.

mite (2) [mait], *s.* das Scherflein (*coin*); (*coll.*) das Kindchen, das Kerlchen.

mitigate ['mitigeit], *v.a.* mildern.

mitre ['maitə], *s.* die Bischofsmütze, Mitra.

mitten [mitn], *s.* der Fäustling, Fausthandschuh.

mix [miks], *v.a.* mischen, vermischen. — *v.n.* verkehren.

mixed [miksd], *adj. a* — *blessing*, eine fragliche Wohltat.

mizzle [mizl], *v.n.* sprühen, rieseln.

mnemonics [ni'mɔniks], *s.* die Gedächtniskunst.

moan [moun], *v.n.* stöhnen (*wail*); klagen (*complain*). — *s.* (*coll.*) die Klage.

moat [mout], *s.* der Burggraben, Wassergraben.

mob [mɔb], *s.* der Pöbel.

mobility [mo'biliti], *s.* die Beweglichkeit.

mobilize ['moubilaiz], *v.a.* mobilisieren.

mock [mɔk], *v.a.* verspotten (*tease*); täuschen (*mislead*). — *v.n.* spotten. — *s.* der Spott, die Täuschung. — *adj.* Schein-; — *heroic*, komischheroisch.

modal [moudl], *adj.* (*Gram.*) modal, der Aussageweise nach; (*Mus.*) dem Modus nach.

mode [moud], *s.* (*Mus.*) der Modus, die Art; die Mode (*fashion*).

model [mɔdl], *s.* das Modell; das Muster (*pattern*). — *v.a., v.n.* modellieren.

moderate ['mɔdərit], *adj.* mäßig; (*climate*) gemäßigt. — [-reit], *v.a.* mäßigen; abändern.

modern ['mɔdən], *adj.* modern.

modernize ['mɔdənaiz], *v.a.* modernisieren.

modest ['mɔdist], *adj.* bescheiden.

modesty ['mɔdisti], *s.* die Bescheidenheit.

modify ['mɔdifai], *v.a.* abändern, modifizieren.

mortise

modish ['moudiʃ], *adj.* nach der neuesten Mode, modisch.
modulate ['mɔdjuleit], *v.a.* modulieren.
moil [mɔil], *v.n.* sich plagen.
moist [mɔist], *adj.* feucht.
moisten [mɔisn], *v.a.* befeuchten.
moisture ['mɔistʃə], *s.* die Feuchtigkeit.
molasses [mo'læsiz], *s.* die Melasse.
mole (1) [moul], *s.* (*Zool.*) der Maulwurf.
mole (2) [moul], *s.* das Muttermal (*skin mark*).
mole (3) [moul], *s.* der Seedamm, Hafendamm.
molecular [mo'lekjulə], *adj.* molekular.
molecule ['mɔl-, 'moulikju:l], *s.* das Molekül.
molest [mo'lest], *v.a.* belästigen.
mollify ['mɔlifai], *v.a.* besänftigen.
mollusc ['mɔləsk], *s.* (*Zool.*) die Molluske.
molt *see under* **moult**.
molten ['moultən], *adj.* geschmolzen.
moment ['moumənt], *s.* der Augenblick, Moment (*instant*); die Wichtigkeit (*importance*).
momentary ['mouməntəri], *adj.* momentan, einen Augenblick lang.
momentum [mo'mentəm], *s.* das Moment, die Triebkraft.
monarch ['mɔnək], *s.* der Monarch.
monarchy ['mɔnəki], *s.* die Monarchie.
monastery ['mɔnəstri], *s.* das (Mönchs-)kloster.
monastic [mə'næstik], *adj.* klösterlich.
Monday ['mʌndi], *s.* der Montag.
money ['mʌni], *s.* das Geld; **ready —**, bares Geld; **make —**, Geld verdienen; **— order**, die Postanweisung.
Mongolian [mɔŋ'gouliən], *adj.* mongolisch. — *s.* der Mongole.
mongrel ['mʌŋgrəl], *s.* (*Zool.*) der Mischling.
monitor ['mɔnitə], *s.* der Ermahner; (*Rad.*) der Abhörer.
monitoring ['mɔnitəriŋ], *adj.* — *service*, der Abhördienst.
monk [mʌŋk], *s.* (*Eccl.*) der Mönch.
monkey ['mʌŋki], *s.* (*Zool.*) der Affe.
monomania [mɔno'meiniə], *s.* die Monomanie, fixe Idee.
monopolize [mə'nɔpəlaiz], *v.a.* monopolisieren.
monopoly [mə'nɔpəli], *s.* das Monopol.
monosyllabic [mɔnəsi'læbik], *adj.* einsilbig.
monotonous [mə'nɔtənəs], *adj.* monoton, eintönig.
monsoon [mɔn'su:n], *s.* der Monsun.
monster ['mɔnstə], *s.* das Ungeheuer.
monstrance ['mɔnstrəns], *s.* (*Eccl.*) die Monstranz.
monstrosity [mɔns'trɔsiti], *s.* die Ungeheuerlichkeit.
monstrous ['mɔnstrəs], *adj.* ungeheuerlich.
month [mʌnθ], *s.* der Monat.
monthly ['mʌnθli], *adj.* monatlich, Monats-.

mood [mu:d], *s.* die Stimmung, Laune; (*Gram., Mus.*) der Modus.
moodiness ['mu:dinis], *s.* die Launenhaftigkeit.
moody ['mu:di], *adj.* launenhaft.
moon [mu:n], *s.* der Mond.
moonlight ['mu:nlait], *s.* das Mondlicht, der Mondschein.
moonshine ['mu:nʃain], *s.* der Mondschein; (*fig.*) Unsinn.
moonstruck ['mu:nstrʌk], *adj.* mondsüchtig; verliebt.
Moor [muə], *s.* der Mohr.
moor [muə], *s.* das Moor, Heideland.
moorage ['muəridʒ], *s.* der Ankerplatz.
moorhen ['mɔ:hen], *s.* (*Orn.*) das Moorhuhn, Wildhuhn.
moorish ['muəriʃ], *adj.* maurisch.
moot [mu:t], *v.a.* erörtern, besprechen. — *adj.* **a — point**, ein strittiger Punkt.
mop [mɔp], *s.* der Wischlappen, Mop. — *v.a.* aufwischen (*floor*), wischen (*brow*).
mope [moup], *v.n.* traurig sein.
moral ['mɔrəl], *adj.* moralisch (*high principled*); sittlich (*decent*). — *s.* die Moral (*precept*); (*pl.*) die Sitten, *f. pl.*; die Sittlichkeit.
moralize ['mɔrəlaiz], *v.n.* moralisieren, Moral predigen (*Dat.*).
morass [mo'ræs], *s.* der Morast.
morbid ['mɔ:bid], *adj.* krankhaft.
more [mɔ:], *comp. adj., adv.* mehr; **once —**, noch einmal; **all the —**, umso mehr; **the — the better**, je mehr desto besser.
moreover [mɔ:'rouvə], *adv.* zudem, überdies, weiterhin.
morning ['mɔ:niŋ], *s.* der Morgen, Vormittag; **— coat**, der Cutaway, Frack.
Moroccan [mə'rɔkən], *adj.* marokkanisch. — *s.* der Marokkaner.
Morocco [mə'rɔkou]. Marokko, *n.*
morocco [mə'rɔkou], *s.* der Saffian, das Maroquinleder.
moron ['mɔ:rɔn], *s.* der Schwachsinnige.
morose [mə'rous], *adj.* mürrisch.
morrow ['mɔrou], *s.* (*Poet.*) der Morgen.
morsel [mɔ:sl], *s.* der Bissen, das Stück.
mortal [mɔ:tl], *adj.* sterblich, tödlich; **— sin**, die Todsünde. — *s.* der Sterbliche, der Mensch.
mortality [mɔ:'tæliti], *s.* die Sterblichkeit.
mortar ['mɔ:tə], *s.* (*Build.*) der Mörtel; (*Mil.*) der Mörser.
mortgage ['mɔ:gidʒ], *s.* die Hypothek. — *v.a.* verpfänden; eine Hypothek aufnehmen (auf, *Acc.*).
mortgagee [mɔ:gi'dʒi:], *s.* der Hypothekengläubiger.
mortician [mɔ:'tiʃən], *s.* (*Am.*) *see* **undertaker**.
mortify ['mɔ:tifai], *v.a.* kasteien (*chasten*); kränken (*humiliate*).
mortise ['mɔ:tis], *s.* (*Build.*) das Zapfenloch.

441

mortuary ['mɔ:tjuəri], *s.* die Leichenhalle.

mosque [mɔsk], *s.* (*Rel.*) die Moschee.

mosquito [mɔs'ki:tou], *s.* (*Ent.*) der Moskito.

moss [mɔs], *s.* (*Bot.*) das Moos.

most [moust], *superl. adj.* meist; (*pl.*) die meisten. — *adv.* meist, meistens; höchst (*before adjectives*).

mostly ['moustli], *adv.* meistenteils.

mote [mout], *s.* das Stäubchen.

moth [mɔθ], *s.* (*Ent.*) die Motte.

mother ['mʌðə], *s.* die Mutter; — *-in-law*, die Schwiegermutter; —*of-pearl*, die Perlmutter.

motherly ['mʌðəli], *adj.* mütterlich.

motion ['mouʃən], *s.* die Bewegung, der Gang; (*Parl., Rhet.*) der Antrag. — *v.a.* bewegen — *v.n.* zuwinken (*Dat.*).

motive ['moutiv], *s.* das Motiv, der Beweggrund.

motley ['mɔtli], *adj.* scheckig, bunt.

motor ['moutə], *s.* der Motor.

motoring ['moutəriŋ], *s.* das Autofahren, der Autosport.

mottled [mɔtld], *adj.* gescheckt, gesprenkelt.

motto ['mɔtou], *s.* das Motto, der Wahlspruch.

mould (1) [mould], *s.* die Form; Gußform (*casting*); die Schablone. — *v.a.* formen, (*Metall.*) gießen, formen.

mould (2) [mould], *s.* der Schimmel (*fungus*), (*Hort.*) die Gartenerde. — *v.n.* schimmeln.

moulder (1) ['mouldə], *s.* der Bildner; (*Metall.*) der Gießer.

moulder (2) ['mouldə], *v.n.* vermodern.

mouldy ['mouldi], *adj.* moderig, schimmelig.

moult, (*Am.*) **molt** [moult], *v.n.* (*Zool.*) sich mausern.

mound [maund], *s.* der Erdhügel.

mount [maunt], *v.a.* besteigen (*horse, hill*); montieren, anbringen (*apparatus*). — *v.n.* sich belaufen (*bill*), betragen. — *s.* (*Poet.*) der Berg.

mountain ['mauntin], *s.* der Berg.

mountaineer [maunti'niə], *s.* der Bergsteiger.

mountainous ['mauntinəs], *adj.* gebirgig.

mourn [mɔ:n], *v.a., v.n.* (be)trauern.

mourner ['mɔ:nə], *s.* der Leidtragende.

mournful ['mɔ:nful], *adj.* traurig.

mourning ['mɔ:niŋ], *s.* die Trauer.

mouse [maus], *s.* (*Zool.*) die Maus.

moustache [mə'sta:ʃ], *s.* der Schnurrbart.

mouth [mauθ], *s.* (*Anat.*) der Mund; (*Geog.*) die Mündung.

movable ['mu:vəbl], *adj.* beweglich, verschiebbar.

move [mu:v], *v.a.* bewegen; (*emotionally*) rühren; den Antrag stellen (*a motion*). — *v.n.* umziehen; übersiedeln (*change residence*).

movement ['mu:vmənt], *s.* die Bewegung (*motion*); (*Mus.*) der Satz; das Gehwerk (*mechanism*).

movies ['mu:viz], *s. pl.* (*coll.*) das Kino, der Film.

mow [mou], *v.a. irr.* mähen.

much [mʌtʃ], *adj.* viel. — *adv.* sehr, bei weitem; *as — as*, ganze ...; *as — again*, noch einmal so viel.

mud [mʌd], *s.* der Schmutz, Schlamm.

muddle [mʌdl], *v.a.* verwirren. — *s.* die Verwirrung.

muff (1) [mʌf], *s.* der Muff.

muff (2) [mʌf], *v.a.* verderben (*mar*).

muffin ['mʌfin], *s.* der dünne Kuchen, der Butterkuchen.

muffle [mʌfl], *v.a.* umwickeln; dämpfen (*a sound*).

muffler ['mʌflə], *s.* das Halstuch; (*Motor.*) der Schalldämpfer.

mug [mʌg], *s.* der Krug; (*coll.*) der Tölpel.

muggy ['mʌgi], *adj.* schwül; feucht (*humid*).

mulatto [mju'lætou], *s.* der Mulatte.

mulberry ['mʌlbəri], *s.* (*Bot.*) die Maulbeere.

mule [mju:l], *s.* (*Zool.*) das Maultier, der Maulesel.

muleteer [mju:li'tiə], *s.* der Mauleseltreiber.

mulish ['mju:liʃ], *adj.* störrisch.

mull (1) [mʌl], *v.a.* würzen (*add spices to*); *mulled wine*, der Glühwein.

mull (2) [mʌl], *v.a., v.n.* — *over*, überlegen, überdenken.

multifarious [mʌlti'feəriəs], *adj.* mannigfaltig.

multiple ['mʌltipl], *s.* das Vielfache. — *adj.* vielfach.

multiply ['mʌltiplai], *v.a., v.n.* multiplizieren, (sich) vervielfachen.

multitude ['mʌltitju:d], *s.* die Menge.

multitudinous [mʌlti'tju:dinəs], *adj.* zahlreich, massenhaft.

mumble [mʌmbl], *v.a., v.n.* murmeln.

mummery ['mʌməri], *s.* der Mummenschanz.

mummy (1) ['mʌmi], *s.* die Mumie.

mummy (2) ['mʌmi], *s.* (*coll.*) die Mutti.

mumps [mʌmps], *s.* (*Med.*) der Ziegenpeter.

munch [mʌntʃ], *v.a., v.n.* kauen.

mundane ['mʌndein], *adj.* weltlich.

municipal [mju'nisipəl], *adj.* städtisch.

municipality [mjunisi'pæliti], *s.* die Stadtgemeinde.

munificence [mju'nifisəns], *s.* die Freigebigkeit.

munificent [mju'nifisənt], *adj.* freigebig.

mural ['mjuərəl], *s.* die Wandmalerei; das Wandgemälde. — *adj.* Wand-.

murder ['mə:də], *s.* der Mord. — *v.a.* ermorden, morden.

murderer ['mə:dərə], *s.* der Mörder.

murderous ['mə:dərəs], *adj.* mörderisch.

murky ['mə:ki], *adj.* trübe, unklar.

murmur ['mə:mə], *s.* das Gemurmel.

muscle [mʌsl], *s.* (*Anat.*) der Muskel.

muscular ['mʌskjulə], *adj.* (*Anat.*) muskulös, Muskel-.

muse (1) [mju:z], *v.n.* nachdenken, sinnen.

muse (2) [mju:z], *s.* (*Myth.*) die Muse.

museum [mju:'ziəm], *s.* das Museum.

mushroom ['mʌʃrum], *s.* (*Bot.*) der (eßbare) Pilz.

music ['mju:zik], *s.* die Musik; — stand, das Notenpult.

musician [mju:'ziʃən], *s.* der Musiker.

musk [mʌsk], *s.* der Moschus, Bisam.

musket ['mʌskit], *s.* die Muskete, Flinte.

muslin ['mʌzlin], *s.* der Musselin.

mussel [mʌsl], *s.* (*Zool.*) die Muschel.

must [mʌst], *v. aux. irr.* müssen; (*with neg.*) dürfen.

mustard ['mʌstəd], *s.* der Senf.

muster ['mʌstə], *v.a.* mustern. — *v.n.* sich sammeln. — *s.* die Musterung; pass —, die Prüfung bestehen.

musty ['mʌsti], *adj.* dumpf, dumpfig, muffig.

mutable ['mju:təbl], *adj.* veränderlich.

mutation [mju'teiʃən], *s.* die Veränderung; (*Maths., Genetics*) die Mutation.

mute [mju:t], *adj.* stumm. — *v.a.* (*Mus.*) dämpfen. — *s.* (*Mus.*) der Dämpfer.

mutilate ['mju:tileit], *v.a.* verstümmeln.

mutinous ['mju:tinəs], *adj.* aufrührerisch.

mutiny ['mju:tini], *s.* die Meuterei.

mutter ['mʌtə], *v.a., v.n.* murmeln.

mutton [mʌtn], *s.* das Hammelfleisch; — chop, das Hammelkotelett.

mutual ['mju:tjuəl], *adj.* gegenseitig.

muzzle [mʌzl], *s.* der Maulkorb (*of dog*); die Mündung (*of rifle*).

my [mai], *poss. adj.* mein.

myrrh [mə:], *s.* die Myrrhe.

myrtle [mə:tl], *s.* (*Bot.*) die Myrte.

myself [mai'self], *pron.* ich selbst; (*refl.*) mir, mich.

mysterious [mis'tiəriəs], *adj.* geheimnisvoll.

mystery ['mistəri], *s.* das Geheimnis.

mystic ['mistik], *s.* der Mystiker.

mystic(al) ['mistik(əl)], *adj.* mystisch, geheimnisvoll, dunkel.

mystification [mistifi'keiʃən], *s.* die Täuschung, Irreführung.

mystify ['mistifai], *v.a.* täuschen, verblüffen.

myth [miθ], *s.* der Mythos, die Mythe, Sage.

N

N [en]. das N.

nag (1) [næg], *v.a.* nörgeln.

nag (2) [næg], *s.* der Gaul.

nail [neil], *s.* der Nagel. — *v.a.* annageln.

naïve ['naii:v], *adj.* naiv.

naïveté, naïvety [nai'i:vti], *s.* die Naivität, Einfalt.

naked ['neikid], *adj.* nackt.

name [neim], *s.* der Name. — *v.a.* nennen, heißen.

nameless ['neimlis], *adj.* namenlos.

namely ['neimli], *adv.* nämlich.

namesake ['neimseik], *s.* der Namensvetter.

nap [næp], *s.* das Schläfchen. — *v.n.* schlummern, einnicken.

nape [neip], *s.* (*Anat.*) das Genick.

napkin ['næpkin], *s.* die Serviette; Windel (*baby's*).

narrate [nə'reit], *v.a.* erzählen.

narrative ['nærətiv], *s.* die Erzählung, Geschichte.

narrator [nə'reitə], *s.* der Erzähler; (*Rad.*) der Sprecher.

narrow ['nærou], *adj.* eng, schmal; — gauge, die Schmalspur; — minded, engstirnig.

nasty ['nɑ:sti], *adj.* widerlich, unangenehm.

natal [neitl], *adj.* Geburts-.

nation ['neiʃən], *s.* die Nation, das Volk.

nationality [næʃə'næliti], *s.* die Staatsangehörigkeit, Nationalität.

native ['neitiv], *adj.* einheimisch, eingeboren. — *s.* der Eingeborene.

natural ['nætʃərəl], *adj.* natürlich.

naturalist ['nætʃərəlist], *s.* der Naturforscher.

naturalization [nætʃərəlai'zeiʃən], *s.* die Naturalisierung, Einbürgerung.

naturalize ['nætʃərəlaiz], *v.a., v.n.* naturalisieren, einbürgern.

nature ['neitʃə], *s.* die Natur, das Wesen.

naught [nɔ:t], *s.* die Null.

naughty ['nɔ:ti], *adj.* unartig.

nausea ['nɔ:siə], *s.* (*Med.*) der Brechreiz, das Erbrechen.

nautical ['nɔ:tikəl], *adj.* nautisch, Schiffs-.

naval ['neivəl], *adj.* Marine-.

nave [neiv], *s.* (*Archit.*) das Schiff.

navigable ['nævigəbl], *adj.* schiffbar.

navigate ['nævigeit], *v.a., v.n.* steuern.

navigation [nævi'geiʃən], *s.* die Schiffahrt (*shipping*); das Steuern, die Navigation.

navy ['neivi], *s.* die Flotte, Marine.

Neopolitan [niə'politən], *adj.* neapolitanisch. — *s.* der Neapolitaner.

near [niə], *adj., adv.* nahe, in der Nähe. — *prep.* nahe (an *or* bei).

nearly ['niəli], *adv.* beinahe, fast.

nearness ['niənis], *s.* die Nähe.

neat [ni:t], *adj.* nett, sauber (*tidy*); rein, unvermischt, pur (*unmixed*).

neatness ['ni:tnis], *s.* die Sauberkeit.

necessary ['nesəsəri], *adj.* notwendig.

necessity [ni'sesiti], *s.* die Not, Notwendigkeit; (*pl.*) das zum Leben Nötige.

neck [nek], *s.* (*Anat.*) der Hals; stick o.'s — out, es riskieren. — *v.n.* (*Am. sl.*) knutschen.

necklace

necklace ['neklis], *s.* das Halsband, die Halskette.

necktie ['nektai], *s.* der Schlips, die Krawatte.

need [ni:d], *s.* die Not, der Bedarf. — *v.a.* brauchen, nötig haben.

needful ['ni:dful], *adj.* notwendig.

needle [ni:dl], *s.* die Nadel. — *v.a.* (*coll.*) sticheln, ärgern (*annoy*).

needy ['ni:di], *adj.* in Not befindlich, arm, bedürftig.

nefarious [ni'fɛəriəs], *adj.* nichtswürdig, schändlich.

negative ['negətiv], *adj.* negativ, verneinend. — *s.* (*Phot.*) das Negativ; die Verneinung (*denial*); *in the* —, verneinend.

neglect [ni'glekt], *v.a.* vernachlässigen, außer acht lassen. — *s.* die Vernachlässigung.

neglectful [ni'glektful], *adj.* nachlässig.

negligence ['neglidʒəns], *s.* die Nachlässigkeit.

negotiate [ni'gouʃieit], *v.a.*, *v.n.* verhandeln, unterhandeln.

negotiation [nigouʃi'eiʃən], *s.* die Unterhandlung.

Negro [ni'grou], *s.* der Neger.

neigh [nei], *v.n.* wiehern.

neighbour ['neibə], *s.* der Nachbar.

neighbourhood ['neibəhud], *s.* die Nachbarschaft, Umgebung.

neighbouring ['neibəriŋ], *adj.* Nachbar-, benachbart.

neighbourliness ['neibəlinis], *s.* das gute nachbarliche Verhältnis, die Geselligkeit.

neither ['naiðə *or* 'ni:ðə], *adj.*, *pron.* keiner (von beiden). — *conj.* auch nicht; — . . . *nor*, weder . . . noch.

Nepalese [nepə'li:z], *adj.* nepalesisch. — *s.* der Nepalese.

nephew ['nefju *or* 'nevju], *s.* der Neffe.

nerve [nə:v], *s.* der Nerv; der Mut (*courage*); die Frechheit (*impudence*); (*pl.*) die Angst, Nervosität.

nervous ['nə:vəs], *adj.* nervös; — *of*, furchtsam vor (*Dat.*), ängstlich wegen (*Genit.*).

nest [nest], *s.* das Nest; (*fig.*) — *egg*, die Ersparnisse, *f. pl.* — *v.n.* nisten.

nestle [nesl], *v.n.* sich anschmiegen.

net (1) [net], *s.* das Netz. — *v.a.* (Fische) fangen, ins Netz bekommen.

net (2) [net], *adj.* netto; ohne Verpackung; — *weight*, das Nettogewicht.

nettle [netl], *s.* (*Bot.*) die Nessel. — *v.a.* sticheln, ärgern.

neurosis [njuə'rousis], *s.* (*Med.*) die Neurose.

neutrality [nju:'træliti], *s.* die Neutralität.

never ['nevə], *adv.* nie, niemals; — *mind*, mach Dir (machen Sie sich) nichts draus!

nevertheless [nevəðə'les], *conj.* trotzdem, nichtsdestoweniger.

new [nju:], *adj.* neu; *New Year's Day*, der Neujahrstag; *New Zealander*, der Neuseeländer. — *s.* (*pl.*) die Nachrichten, *f. pl.*

newspaper ['nju:speipə], *s.* die Zeitung.

next [nekst], *adj.* nächst. — *adv.* danach.

nib [nib], *s.* die Spitze (*of pen*).

nibble [nibl], *v.a.*, *v.n.* knabbern, nagen (*at*, an, *Dat.*).

nice [nais], *adj.* fein (*scrupulous*); nett, angenehm (*pleasant*).

nicety ['naisəti], *s.* die Feinheit (*of distinction etc.*).

nickel [nikl], *s.* das Nickel; (*Am.*) das Fünfcentstück.

nickname ['nikneim], *s.* der Spitzname.

niece [ni:s], *s.* die Nichte.

Nigerian [nai'dʒiəriən], *adj.* nigerisch. — *s.* der Nigerier.

niggardly ['nigədli], *adj.* geizig.

nigh [nai], *adj.*, *adv.* (*Poet.*) nahe.

night [nait], *s.* die Nacht; *last* —, gestern abend; *the* — *before last*, vorgestern abend; *at* —, nachts.

nightingale ['naitiŋgeil], *s.* (*Orn.*) die Nachtigall.

nightmare ['naitmɛə], *s.* der Alpdruck.

nimble [nimbl], *adj.* flink; geschickt (*deft*).

nine [nain], *num. adj.* neun.

nineteen [nain'ti:n], *num. adj.* neunzehn.

ninety ['nainti], *num. adj.* neunzig.

ninth [nainθ], *num. adj.* neunte.

nip [nip], *v.a.* zwicken.

nipple [nipl], *s.* (*Anat.*) die Brustwarze.

nitrogen ['naitrədʒən], *s.* (*Chem.*) der Stickstoff.

no [nou], *part.* nein. — *adj.* kein. — *adv.* nicht; — *one*, niemand.

nobility [no'biliti], *s.* der Adel.

noble [noubl], *adj.* edel; großmütig (*magnanimous*); adlig (*well born*).

nobody ['noubədi], *pron.* niemand.

nod [nɔd], *v.n.* nicken.

noise [nɔiz], *s.* der Lärm, das Geräusch.

noiseless ['nɔizlis], *adj.* geräuschlos.

noisy ['nɔizi], *adj.* laut, lärmend.

nominal ['nɔminəl], *adj.* nominell.

nominate ['nɔmineit], *v.a.* nennen (*name*); ernennen (*appoint*).

nomination [nɔmi'neiʃən], *s.* die Nennung, Ernennung.

none [nʌn], *pron.* keiner, niemand.

nonsense ['nɔnsəns], *s.* der Unsinn.

nook [nuk], *s.* die Ecke, der Winkel.

noon [nu:n], *s.* der Mittag.

noose [nu:s], *s.* die Schlinge.

nor [nɔ:], *conj.* auch nicht; *neither* . . . —, weder . . . noch.

normal [nɔ:məl], *adj.* normal.

normalize ['nɔ:məlaiz], *v.a.* normalisieren.

Norman ['nɔ:mən], *adj.* normannisch. — *s.* der Normanne.

north [nɔ:θ], *s.* der Norden. — *adj.* nördlich.

northerly, northern ['nɔ:ðəli, 'nɔ:ðən], *adj.* nördlich, von Norden.

Norwegian [nɔ:'wi:dʒən], *adj.* norwegisch. — *s.* der Norweger.

nose [nouz], *s.* (*Anat.*) die Nase; — *dive*, der Sturzflug.

nosey ['nouzi], adj. (coll.) neugierig.
nostalgia [nɔs'tældʒə], s. das Heimweh, die Sehnsucht.
nostril ['nɔstril], s. (Anat.) das Nasenloch.
not [nɔt], adv. nicht; — at all, keineswegs.
notable ['noutəbl], adj. berühmt, wohlbekannt; bemerkenswert.
notary ['noutəri], s. der Notar.
notch [nɔtʃ], s. die Kerbe. — v.a. kerben, einkerben.
note [nout], s. die Notiz, der Zettel; (Mus.) die Note; die Bedeutung; take —s, Notizen machen; take — of, zur Kenntnis nehmen. — v.a. notieren, aufzeichnen.
notepaper ['noutpeipə], s. das Briefpapier.
noteworthy ['noutwə:ði], adj. beachtenswert.
nothing ['nʌθiŋ], pron. s. nichts; for —, umsonst; good for —, der Taugenichts.
notice ['noutis], s. die Kenntnis (attention); die Anzeige (in press etc.); Notiz; Bekanntmachung; give —, kündigen. — v.a. bemerken.
noticeable ['noutisəbl], adj. bemerkbar.
notification [noutifi'keiʃən], s. die Benachrichtigung, Bekanntmachung.
notify ['noutifai], v.a. benachrichtigen, informieren.
notion ['nouʃən], s. der Begriff (concept); die Idee (idea); die Meinung (opinion).
notoriety [noutə'raiiti], s. der üble Ruf.
notorious [no'tɔ:riəs], adj. berüchtigt.
notwithstanding [nɔtwið'stændiŋ], prep. ungeachtet (Genit.). — adv. trotzdem, dennoch. — conj. — that, obgleich.
nought [nɔ:t], s. die Null (figure 0); nichts (nothing).
noun [naun], s. (Gram.) das Hauptwort, Substantiv.
nourish ['nʌriʃ], v.a. nähren; ernähren.
nourishment ['nʌriʃmənt], s. die Nahrung.
Nova Scotian ['nouvə'skouʃən], adj. neuschottisch. [Neuschottland]
novel [nɔvl], s. (Lit.) der Roman. — adj. neu; neuartig (modern).
novelty ['nɔvlti], s. die Neuheit.
November [no'vembə], der November.
novice ['nɔvis], s. der Neuling (greenhorn); (Eccl.) der, die Novize.
novitiate [no'viʃiit], s. die Lehrzeit; (Eccl.) das Noviziat.
now [nau], adv. nun, jetzt; — and then, dann und wann, hin und wieder. — conj. — (that), da nun.
nowadays ['nauədeiz], adv. heutzutage.
nowhere ['nouhwɛə], adv. nirgends.
noxious ['nɔkʃəs], adj. (Med., Bot.) schädlich.
nozzle [nɔzl], s. die Düse; (sl.) die Schnauze.
nuclear ['nju:kliə], adj. (Phys.) nuklear, Kern-.
nucleus ['nju:kliəs], s. der Kern.

nude [nju:d], adj. nackt, bloß.
nudge [nʌdʒ], v.a. leicht anstoßen.
nudity ['nju:diti], s. die Nacktheit.
nugget ['nʌgit], s. der Klumpen.
nuisance ['nju:səns], s. die Plage, Lästigkeit; das Ärgernis (annoyance).
null [nʌl], adj. null und nichtig; ungültig.
nullify ['nʌlifai], v.a. annullieren, ungültig machen.
nullity ['nʌliti], s. die Ungültigkeit.
numb [nʌm], adj. erstarrt, gefühllos. — v.a. erstarren lassen.
number ['nʌmbə], s. die Zahl, Nummer (telephone etc.); die Anzahl (quantity); cardinal —, die Grundzahl; ordinal —, die Ordnungszahl. — v.a. nummerieren; zählen (count).
numbness ['nʌmnis], s. die Erstarrung.
numeral ['nju:mərəl], s. (Gram.) das Zahlwort.
numerical [nju:'merikəl], adj. (Maths.) Zahlen-, numerisch.
numerous ['nju:mərəs], adj. zahlreich.
numismatics [nju:miz'mætiks], s. die Münzkunde.
numskull ['nʌmskʌl], s. der Dummkopf.
nun [nʌn], s. (Eccl.) die Nonne.
nunnery ['nʌnəri], s. (Eccl.) das Nonnenkloster.
nuptials ['nʌpʃəlz], s. pl. (Lit., Poet.) die Hochzeit, das Hochzeitsfest.
nurse [nə:s], s. die Krankenschwester, Pflegerin; die Amme (wet nurse). — v.a. pflegen.
nursery ['nə:səri], s. das Kinderzimmer; (Bot.) die Pflanzschule, Baumschule (for trees); — school, der Kindergarten.
nurture ['nə:tʃə], v.a. nähren, aufziehen.
nut [nʌt], s. (Bot.) die Nuß; (Tech.) die Schraubenmutter; (Am. coll.) nuts, verrückt.
nutcracker ['nʌtkrækə], s. (usually pl.) der Nußknacker.
nutmeg ['nʌtmeg], s. (Cul.) die Muskatnuß.
nutriment ['nju:trimənt], s. die Nahrung; (animals) das Futter.
nutrition [nju:'triʃən], s. die Ernährung.
nutritious [nju:'triʃəs], adj. nahrhaft.
nutshell ['nʌtʃel], s. die Nußschale; (fig.) put in a —, kurz ausdrücken.
nymph [nimf], s. (Myth.) die Nymphe.

O

O [ou], das O. — int. oh!
oaf [ouf], s. der Tölpel.
oak [ouk], s. (Bot.) die Eiche.
oaken ['oukən], adj. eichen, aus Eichenholz.

445

oar

oar [ɔ:], s. das Ruder; *put o.'s — in*, sich einmengen.

oasis [ou'eisis], s. die Oase.

oath [ouθ], s. der Eid; der Fluch (*curse*); *commissioner for —s*, der öffentliche Notar; *take an —*, einen Eid schwören or leisten.

oats [outs], s. pl. (Bot.) der Hafer; *sow o.'s wild —s*, sich austoben, sich die Hörner ablaufen.

obdurate ['ɔbdjurit], adj. halsstarrig.

obedience [o'bi:djəns], s. der Gehorsam.

obedient [o'bi:djənt], adj. gehorsam.

obeisance [o'beisəns], s. die Verbeugung, Ehrfurchtsbezeigung.

obese [o'bi:s], adj. fettleibig, beleibt.

obey [o'bei], v.a., v.n. gehorchen (*Dat.*).

obituary [o'bitjuəri], s. der Nachruf, der Nekrolog.

object ['ɔbdʒikt], s. der Gegenstand (*thing*); (Gram.) das Objekt; der Zweck (*objective, purpose*). — [əb'dʒekt], v.n. — *to*, einwenden (*gainsay*); vorhalten (*remonstrate*).

objection [əb'dʒekʃən], s. der Einwand.

objectionable [əb'dʒekʃənəbl], adj. anstößig.

objective [əb'dʒektiv], adj. objektiv, unparteiisch. — s. das Ziel (*aim*).

obligation [ɔbli'geiʃən], s. die Verpflichtung.

obligatory [o'bligətəri, 'ɔblig-], adj. verbindlich, obligatorisch.

oblige [o'blaidʒ], v.a. verpflichten; *much obliged*, vielen Dank; *can you — me?* können Sie mir aushelfen?

obliging [o'blaidʒiŋ], adj. gefällig, zuvorkommend.

oblique [o'bli:k], adj. schräg, schief; (fig.) indirekt.

obliterate [o'blitəreit], v.a. auslöschen (*extinguish*); vertilgen (*destroy*).

oblivion [o'bliviən], s. die Vergessenheit.

oblivious [o'bliviəs], adj. vergeßlich.

oblong ['ɔblɔŋ], adj. länglich. — s. das Rechteck.

obloquy ['ɔbləkwi], s. die Schmähung, Schande.

obnoxious [ɔb'nɔkʃəs], adj. verhaßt, scheußlich.

obscene [ɔb'si:n], adj. anstößig, obszön.

obscenity [ɔb'sen-, ɔb'si:niti], s. die Obszönität.

obscure [əb'skjuə], adj. dunkel (*dark*); unbekannt (*unknown*).

obscurity [əb'skjuəriti], s. die Dunkelheit (*darkness*); die Unbekanntheit.

obsequies ['ɔbsikwiz], s. pl. das Leichenbegängnis.

obsequious [əb'si:kwiəs], adj. unterwürfig.

observance [əb'zə:vəns], s. die Befolgung, Beobachtung, das Einhalten (*Law etc.*).

observant [əb'zə:vənt], adj. aufmerksam; achtsam.

observation [ɔbzə'veiʃən], s. die Beobachtung (*watching*); die Bemerkung (*remark*).

observatory [əb'zə:vətri], s. die Sternwarte.

observe [əb'zə:v], v.a. beobachten (*watch*); bemerken (*notice, remark on*).

obsession [əb'seʃən], s. die Besessenheit, fixe Idee.

obsolete ['ɔbsəli:t], adj. veraltet.

obstacle ['ɔbstəkl], s. das Hindernis.

obstinacy ['ɔbstinəsi], s. die Hartnäckigkeit.

obstinate ['ɔbstinit], adj. hartnäckig.

obstruct [əb'strʌkt], v.a. hemmen, hindern.

obstruction [əb'strʌkʃən], s. das Hindernis, die Hemmung, Verstopfung.

obtain [əb'tein], v.a. erhalten, erlangen; bekommen (*get*).

obtrude [ɔb'tru:d], v.n. sich aufdrängen. — v.a. aufdrängen.

obtrusive [əb'tru:siv], adj. aufdringlich.

obtuse [ɔb'tju:s], adj. stumpf; dumm (*stupid*).

obviate ['ɔbvieit], v.a. vorbeugen (*Dat.*).

obvious ['ɔbviəs], adj. klar, offenbar, selbstverständlich.

occasion [o'keiʒən], s. die Gelegenheit (*chance*); der Anlaß; die Veranlassung (*cause*). — v.a. veranlassen; verursachen (*cause*).

occasional [o'keiʒənəl], adj. gelegentlich.

occident ['ɔksidənt], s. das Abendland, der Westen.

occult [ɔ'kʌlt], adj. geheim, Okkult-.

occupancy ['ɔkjupənsi], s. der Besitz, das Innehaben (*holding*).

occupant ['ɔkjupənt], s. der Inhaber; der Bewohner (*of house*), Insasse.

occupation [ɔkju'peiʃən], s. die Besetzung; (Mil.) *army of —*, die Besatzung; der Beruf, die Beschäftigung (*job*); — *with*, das Befassen mit (*Dat.*).

occupy ['ɔkjupai], v.a. (Mil.) besetzen, in Besitz nehmen; beschäftigen (*engage*); bekleiden (*office*).

occur [ə'kə:], v.n. geschehen, sich ereignen; — *to s.o.*, jemandem einfallen.

occurrence [ə'kʌrəns], s. das Geschehen, Ereignis, der Vorfall.

ocean ['ouʃən], s. der Ozean, die See, das Meer. — adj. Meeres-.

octagon ['ɔktəgən], s. das Achteck.

octagonal [ɔk'tægənəl], adj. achteckig.

October [ɔk'toubə]. der Oktober.

octogenarian [ɔktodʒi'nɛəriən], s. der Achtzigjährige.

ocular ['ɔkjulə], adj. Augen-.

oculist ['ɔkjulist], s.(Med.)der Augenarzt.

odd [ɔd], adj. ungerade; seltsam (*queer*); einzeln (*solitary*). — s. (pl.) die Wahrscheinlichkeit.

oddity ['ɔditi], s. die Seltenheit, Sonderbarkeit.

oddment ['ɔdmənt], s. (pl.) die Reste, m. pl.

ode [oud], s. (Poet.) die Ode.

odious ['oudiəs], adj. verhaßt, widerwärtig.

446

operatic

odium ['oudiəm], *s.* der Haß.
odorous ['oudərəs], *adj.* duftend, duftig.
odour ['oudə], *s.* der Geruch, Duft.
of [ɔv], *prep.* von (*Dat.*); aus (*out of*) (*Dat.*); — *course*, natürlich.
off [ɔf, ɔːf], *adv.* fort, weg; entfernt; *make* —, sich davonmachen; *far* —, weit weg; — *and on*, ab und zu; *well* —, wohlhabend. — *prep.* von (*from*); fort von; entfernt von (*distant from*).
offal [ɔfl], *s.* der Abfall.
offence [o'fens], *s.* (*Law*) das Vergehen; die Beleidigung (*insult*).
offend [o'fend], *v.a.* (*Law*) beleidigen (*insult*). — *v.n.* (*Law*) sich vergehen (gegen, *Acc.*).
offensive [o'fensiv], *adj.* beleidigend (*insulting*); anstößig (*indecent*). — *s.* die Offensive, der Angriff (*against*, auf, *Acc.*).
offer ['ɔfə], *v.a.* bieten (*auction*); anbieten (*hold out*). — *s.* das Anerbieten; (*Comm.*) das Angebot, der Antrag.
offering ['ɔfəriŋ], *s.* das Opfer.
office ['ɔfis], *s.* das Amt; die Stellung (*position*); die Funktion (*duties*); das Büro; (*Eccl.*) der Gottesdienst; *high* —, das hohe Amt; — *bearer*, der Amtswalter.
officer ['ɔfisə], *s.* (*Mil.*) der Offizier; der Beamte (*functionary*); *honorary* —, der ehrenamtliche Beamte, der Beamte im Ehrenamt.
official [o'fiʃəl], *adj.* offiziell, amtlich. — *s.* der Beamte.
officiate [o'fiʃieit], *v.n.* amtieren; fungieren.
officious [o'fiʃəs], *adj.* zudringlich, (übertrieben) dienstfertig.
offing ['ɔfiŋ], *s.* (*Naut.*) die hohe See; *in the —*, bevorstehend.
offset [ɔf'set], *v.a.* (*Comm.*) ausgleichen; (*Typ.*) offset drucken, im Offset drucken; (*fig.*) unschädlich machen, wettmachen. — ['ɔfset], (*Comm.*) die Gegenrechnung, der Ausgleich; (*Typ.*) der Offsetdruck.
offshoot ['ɔfʃuːt], *s.* der Sprößling.
offspring ['ɔfspriŋ], *s.* die Nachkommenschaft.
often [ɔfn], (*Poet.*) *oft* [ɔfn,ɔft], *adv.*oft, häufig.
ogle [ougl], *v.a., v.n.* äugeln, beäugeln, glotzen, anglotzen.
ogre ['ougə], *s.* der Menschenfresser.
oil [ɔil], *s.* das Öl. — *v.a.* einölen, einschmieren.
oilcloth ['ɔilklɔθ], *s.* das Wachstuch.
ointment ['ɔintmənt], *s.* die Salbe.
old [ould], *adj.* alt; —*fashioned*, altmodisch.
olive ['ɔliv], *s.* (*Bot.*) die Olive; *the Mount of Olives*, der Ölberg.
Olympic [o'limpik], *adj.* olympisch; *the — Games*, die Olympischen Spiele.
omelette ['ɔmlit], *s.* (*Cul.*) das Omelett, der Eierkuchen.
omen ['oumən], *s.* das (böse) Vorzeichen, das Omen.

ominous ['ɔminəs], *adj.* von schlimmer Vorbedeutung, ominös.
omission [o'miʃən], *s.* die Unterlassung; (*Typ.*) die Auslassung.
omit [o'mit], *v.a.* unterlassen (*leave undone*); auslassen (*leave out*).
omnibus ['ɔmnibəs], *s.* der Omnibus, der Autobus.
omnipotent [ɔm'nipətənt], *adj.* allmächtig.
omniscient [ɔm'nisiənt], *adj.* allwissend.
on [ɔn], *prep.* an; auf; über; vor; bei; zu; nach; um; *call* — (*s.o.*), vorsprechen (bei, *Dat.*); — *fire*, in Flammen; — *condition*, unter der Bedingung (*Comm.*); — *account*, a Konto; — *my honour*, auf mein Ehrenwort; — *purpose*, absichtlich; — *sale*, zum Verkauf. — *adv.* weiter, fort (*forward*); gültig, zutreffend (*correct, valid*); *get* —, vorwärtskommen; *get* — *with s.th.*, weitermachen; *get* — *with s.o.*, auskommen (mit, *Dat.*).
once [wʌns], *adv.* einmal; einst (*long ago*); — *more*, nochmals, noch einmal; — *and for all*, ein für alle Mal; *at* —, sogleich; — *in a while*, ab und zu. — *conj.* sobald.
one [wʌn], *num. adj.* ein, eine, ein; — *way street*, die Einbahnstraße. — *pron.* man (*impersonal*). — *s. little* —, der Kleine; *by* —, eins nach dem anderen, einzeln.
onerous ['ɔnərəs], *adj.* beschwerlich.
onion ['ʌnjən], *s.* (*Bot.*) die Zwiebel.
onlooker ['ɔnlukə], *s.* der Zuschauer.
only ['ounli], *adj.* einzig, allein. — *adv.* nur, bloß. — *conj.* jedoch.
onset ['ɔnset], *s.* der Angriff (*attack*); der Anfang (*beginning*).
onslaught ['ɔnslɔːt], *s.* der Angriff, Überfall.
onward ['ɔnwəd], *adj.* fortschreitend. — *adv.* (*also* **onwards**) vorwärts.
ooze [uːz], *s.* der Schlamm. — *v.n.* träufeln, sickern.
opacity [o'pæsiti], *s.* (*Phys.*) die Dunkelheit, Undurchsichtigkeit.
opal [oupl], *s.* der Opal.
opaque [o'peik], *adj.* (*Phys.*) dunkel, undurchsichtig.
open [oupn], *adj.* offen; offenherzig (*frank*); — *to suggestions*, einem Vorschlag zugänglich. — *v.a.* öffnen; eröffnen (*start*); — *an account*, ein Konto eröffnen. — *v.n.* sich öffnen, sich auftun.
opening ['oupniŋ], *s.* das Öffnen; die freie Stelle; die Gelegenheit (*opportunity*). — *adj.* einleitend; — *gambit*, (*Chess*) der Eröffnungszug.
openness ['oupənnis], *s.* die Offenheit, Ehrlichkeit (*frankness*).
opera ['ɔpərə], *s.* (*Mus.*) die Oper; *comic* —, die komische Oper; — *hat*, der Zylinderhut, Klapphut.
operatic [ɔpə'rætik], *adj.* (*Mus.*) Opern-.

operate

operate ['ɔpəreit], *v.a., v.n.* (*Engin.*) bedienen; (*Med.*) operieren (*on, Acc.*).

operation [ɔpə'reiʃən], *s.* (*Med., Mil.*) die Operation; die Bedienung (*of engine etc.*).

operative ['ɔpərətiv], *adj.* wirksam (*effective*). — *s.* der Arbeiter.

opiate ['oupiit], *s.* das Schlafmittel. — *adj.* einschläfernd.

opine [o'pain], *v.n.* meinen.

opinion [o'pinjən], *s.* die Meinung; *in my* —, meiner Meinung nach.

opinionated [o'pinjəneitid], *adj.* von sich eingenommen, selbstgefällig.

opium ['oupjəm], *s.* das Opium.

opponent [ə'pounənt], *s.* der Gegner.

opportune ['ɔpətjuːn], *adj.* gelegen, günstig.

opportunity [ɔpə'tjuːniti], *s.* die Gelegenheit, Chance; die Möglichkeit.

oppose [ə'pouz], *v.a.* bekämpfen; widerstehen, entgegentreten (*Dat.*).

opposite ['ɔpəzit], *adj.* entgegengesetzt; gegenüberliegend; gegensätzlich (*contrary*). — *prep.* gegenüber (*Dat.*). — *s.* das Gegenteil.

opposition [ɔpə'ziʃən], *s.* (*Parl.*) die Opposition; der Widerstand.

oppress [ə'pres], *v.a.* unterdrücken.

oppression [ə'preʃən], *s.* die Unterdrückung.

oppressive [ə'presiv], *adj.* drückend, tyrannisch.

opprobrious [ə'proubriəs], *adj.* schändlich, schimpflich.

opprobrium [ə'proubriəm], *s.* die Schande.

optician [ɔp'tiʃən], *s.* der Optiker.

optics ['ɔptiks], *s.* die Optik.

optimism ['ɔptimizm], *s.* der Optimismus.

option ['ɔpʃən], *s.* die Wahl.

optional ['ɔpʃənəl], *adj.* Wahl-, frei, beliebig.

opulence ['ɔpjuləns], *s.* der Reichtum (*an, Dat.*), die Üppigkeit.

opulent ['ɔpjulənt], *adj.* reich, üppig.

or [ɔː], *conj.* oder; noch (*after neg.*); *either* . . . —, entweder . . . oder.

oracle ['ɔrəkl], *s.* das Orakel.

oral [ɔːl], *adj.* mündlich. — *s.* die mündliche Prüfung.

orange ['ɔrindʒ,], *s.* (*Bot.*) die Orange, Apfelsine.

oration [ɔ'reiʃən], *s.* die feierliche Rede, Ansprache.

orator ['ɔrətə], *s.* der Redner.

oratorio [ɔrə'tɔːriou], *s.* (*Mus.*) das Oratorium.

oratory ['ɔrətəri], *s.* (*Eccl.*) die Kapelle; (*Rhet.*) die Redekunst.

orb [ɔːb], *s.* die Kugel; der Reichsapfel; (*Poet.*) der Himmelskörper.

orbit ['ɔːbit], *s.* (*Astron.*) die Bahn (der Gestirne), Planetenbahn.

orchard [ɔː'tʃəd], *s.* der Obstgarten.

orchestra ['ɔːkistrə], *s.* (*Mus.*) das Orchester.

ordain [ɔː'dein], *v.a.* ordinieren, anordnen; (*Eccl.*) zum Priester weihen.

ordeal ['ɔːdiəl], *s.* die Feuerprobe; Heimsuchung.

order ['ɔːdə], *s.* die Ordnung (*system*); die Verordnung (*command etc.*); (*Mil.*) der Befehl; (*Comm.*) die Bestellung; (*Biol.*) die Ordnung; der Orden (*Eccl.; also decoration*); *take* (*holy*) —*s*, ordiniert werden, Priester werden; *in* — *to*, um zu; *in* — *that*, so daß; *by* —, auf (den) Befehl. — *v.a.* befehlen, verordnen, anordnen; (*Comm.*) bestellen.

orderly ['ɔːdəli], *adj.* ordentlich, ruhig. —*s.* (*Mil.*) die Ordonanz; (*Med.*) der Gehilfe, Krankenwärter.

ordinal ['ɔːdinl], *adj., s.* (*number*) die Ordnungszahl.

ordinance ['ɔːdinəns], *s.* die Verordnung.

ordinary ['ɔːdinəri], *adj.* gewöhnlich.

ordnance ['ɔːdnəns], *s.* das schwere Geschütz; (*Mil., Geog.*) — *survey*, die Landesvermessung.

ore [ɔː], *s.* das Erz, Metall.

organ ['ɔːgən], *s.* das Organ; (*Mus.*) die Orgel; — *grinder*, der Leierkastenmann.

organic [ɔː'gænik], *adj.* organisch.

organisation [ɔːgənai'zeiʃən], *s.* die Organisation.

organise ['ɔːgənaiz], *v.a.* organisieren.

organism ['ɔːgənizm], *s.* (*Biol.*) der Organismus.

organist ['ɔːgənist], *s.* (*Mus.*) der Organist.

orgy ['ɔːdʒi], *s.* die Orgie.

oriel ['ɔːriəl], *s.* der Erker; — *window*, das Erkerfenster.

orient ['ɔːriənt], *s.* der Orient, Osten.

oriental [ɔːri'entl], *adj.* östlich.

orifice ['ɔrifis], *s.* die Öffnung, Mündung.

origin ['ɔridʒin], *s.* der Ursprung, die Herkunft.

original [ə'ridʒinl], *adj.* Ursprungs-, ursprünglich; originell (*creative*). — *s.* das Original.

originality [əridʒi'næliti], *s.* die Originalität.

originate [ə'ridʒineit], *v.n.* entstehen, entspringen. — *v.a.* hervorbringen, entstehen lassen.

ornament ['ɔːnəmənt], *s.* das Ornament; die Verzierung (*decoration*).

ornate [ɔː'neit], *adj.* geziert, geschmückt.

orphan ['ɔːfən], *s.* der, die Waise.

orphanage ['ɔːfənidʒ], *s.* das Waisenhaus.

orthodoxy ['ɔːθədɔksi], *s.* die Orthodoxie, die Rechtgläubigkeit.

orthography [ɔː'θɔgrəfi], *s.* die Rechtschreibung.

orthopaedic [ɔːθə'piːdik], *adj.* orthopädisch.

oscillate ['ɔsileit], *v.n.* oszillieren, schwingen.

oscillatory ['ɔsileitəri], *adj.* schwingend, oszillierend.

osier ['ouʒə], *s.* (*Bot.*) die Korbweide.

osprey ['ɔsprei], *s.* (*Orn.*) der Seeadler.

ossify [ˈɔsifai], *v.a.* verknöchern lassen; versteinern lassen (*stone*). — *v.n.* verknöchern; versteinern (*stone*).

ostensible [ɔsˈtensibl], *adj.* scheinbar, anscheinend, vorgeblich.

ostentation [ɔstenˈteiʃən], *s.* die Großtuerei, der Prunk.

ostentatious [ɔstenˈteiʃəs], *adj.* großtuerisch, prahlerisch, protzig.

ostler [ˈɔslə], *s.* (*obs.*) der Stallknecht.

ostracize [ˈɔstrəsaiz], *v.a.* verbannen, ausschließen.

ostrich [ˈɔstritʃ], *s.* (*Orn.*) der Strauß.

other [ˈʌðə], *adj.* ander. — *pron.*, *s. the* —, der, die, das andere.

otherwise [ˈʌðəwaiz], *conj.* sonst. — *adv.* andernfalls.

otter [ˈɔtə], *s.* (*Zool.*) die Otter.

ought [ɔ:t], *v. aux. defect.* sollte, müßte.

ounce [auns], *s.* die Unze.

our [ˈauə], *poss. adj.* unser, uns(e)re, unser.

ours [auəz], *poss. pron.* unsrig, unser, uns(e)re, unser.

ourselves [auəˈselvz], *pers. pron.* wir, wir selbst, uns selbst; (*refl.*) uns.

ousel [u:zl], *s.* (*Orn.*) die Amsel.

out [aut], *adv.* aus; draußen (*outside*); außerhalb (*outside, externally*); heraus; hinaus (*outward, away from the speaker*). — *prep.* -*of*, aus, von (*Dat.*).

outer [ˈautə], *adj.* äußer.

outfit [ˈautfit], *s.* die Ausrüstung.

outing [ˈautin], *s.* der Ausflug.

outhouse [ˈauthaus], *s.* das Nebengebäude, der Anbau.

outlaw [ˈautlɔ:], *s.* der Verbannte, der Vogelfreie.

outlay [ˈautlei], *s.* (*Comm.*) die Auslagen, die Spesen, *f. pl.*

outlet [ˈautlit], *s.* der Ausfluß, Abfluß; (*fig.*) das Ventil.

outline [ˈautlain], *s.* der Umriß, Entwurf. — [autˈlain], *v.a.* skizzieren, umreißen, kurz beschreiben.

outlive [autˈliv], *v.a.* überleben.

outlook [ˈautluk], *s.* die Aussicht, der Ausblick; die Weltanschauung (*philosophy*).

outlying [ˈautlaiin], *adj.* außenliegend, außerhalb liegend, entlegen.

outnumber [autˈnʌmbə], *v.a.* an Zahl übertreffen.

outpatient [ˈautpeiʃənt], *s.* der ambulante Patient.

outrage [ˈautreidʒ], *s.* die Beleidigung (*insult*); die Gewalttat. — [autˈreidʒ], *v.a.* verletzen, beleidigen, schänden.

outrageous [autˈreidʒəs], *adj.* schändlich, schimpflich, unerhört; übertrieben (*exaggerated*).

outright [ˈautrait], *adj.* völlig. — [autˈrait], *adv.* gerade heraus, gänzlich.

outrun [autˈrʌn], *v.a. irr.* überholen, einholen.

outset [ˈautset], *s.* der Anfang.

outshine [autˈʃain], *v.a. irr.* übertreffen.

outside [autˈsaid], *adv.* außen, draußen. — [ˈautsaid], *prep.* außerhalb (*Genit.*).

— *adj.* äußere, außenstehend. — *s.* das Äußere, die Außenseite.

outskirts [ˈautskə:ts], *s. pl.* die Umgebung, Vorstadt.

outstanding [autˈstændin], *adj.* hervorragend (*excellent*); noch unbeglichen (*unpaid*); unerledigt (*undone*).

outstay [autˈstei], *v.a.* länger bleiben, zu lange bleiben.

outvote [autˈvout], *v.a.* überstimmen.

outward [ˈautwəd], *adj.* äußere, äußerlich, auswärtig. — *adv.* (*also* **outwards**) auswärts, nach außen.

outweigh [autˈwei], *v.a.* schwerer wiegen als, überwiegen.

outwit [autˈwit], *v.a.* überlisten.

oval [ouvl], *adj.* oval. — *s.* das Oval.

ovary [ˈouvəri], *s.* (*Anat.*) der Eierstock.

ovation [oˈveiʃən], *s.* die Huldigung, Ovation.

oven [ʌvn], *s.* der Backofen; (kleine) Schmelzofen.

over [ˈouvə], *prep.* über; oberhalb. — *adv.* über; herüber; drüben; — *there*, drüben; hinüber (*across*); vorüber (*past*).

overact [ouvərˈækt], *v.n.* übertreiben.

overawe [ouvərˈɔ:], *v.a.* einschüchtern.

overbalance [ouvəˈbæləns], *v.a.* überwiegen. — *v.n.* überkippen.

overbear [ouvəˈbɛə], *v.a. irr.* überwältigen.

overbearing [ouvəˈbɛərin], *adj.* anmaßend.

overboard [ˈouvəbɔ:d], *adv.* über Bord.

overburden [ouvəˈbə:dn], *v.a.* überlasten.

overcast [ouvəˈka:st], *adj.* bewölkt.

overcharge [ouvəˈtʃa:dʒ], *v.a.* zu viel berechnen (*pers.*, *Dat.*), übervorteilen; überladen (*overload*). — *s.* die Übervorteilung; (*Tech.*) der Überdruck.

overcoat [ˈouvəkout], *s.* der Mantel; *light* —, der Überzieher.

overcome [ouvəˈkʌm], *v.a.*, *v.n. irr.* überwinden.

overdo [ouvəˈdu:], *v.a. irr.* übertreiben.

overdone [ouvəˈdʌn], *adj.* übergar, zu lange gekocht.

overdrive [ouvəˈdraiv], *v.a. irr.* abhetzen, zu weit treiben. — [ˈouvədraiv] *s.* (*Motor.*) der Schnellgang.

overdue [ouvəˈdju:], *adj.* überfällig, verfallen.

overflow [ouvəˈflou], *v.a.*, *v.n.* überfließen; überfluten (*banks*). — [ˈouvəflou], *s.* der Überfluß (*flood*); die Überschwemmung.

overgrow [ouvəˈgrou], *v.a. irr.* überwachsen, überwuchern. — *v.n.* zu groß werden.

overhang [ouvəˈhæn], *v.a. irr.* überhängen.

overhaul [ouvəˈhɔ:l], *v.a.* überholen. — [ˈouvəhɔ:l], *s.* die Überholung.

overhead [ouvəˈhed], *adv.* droben; oben (*above*). — [ˈouvəhed], *s.* (*pl.*) (*Comm.*) laufende Unkosten, *pl.*

overhear

overhear [ouvə'hiə], *v.a. irr.* zufällig
hören.
overjoyed [ouvə'dʒɔid], *adj.* entzückt.
overlap [ouvə'læp], *v.n.* überschneiden,
zusammenfallen (*dates etc.*). — ['ouvə-
læp], *s.* die Überschneidung, das
Zusammenfallen.
overload [ouvə'loud], *v.a.* überlasten;
(*Elec.*) überladen.
overlook [ouvə'luk], *v.a.* übersehen;
verzeihen (*disregard*).
overmuch [ouvə'mʌtʃ], *adv.* allzusehr.
overpay [ouvə'pei], *v.a., v.n.* zu viel
bezahlen.
overpopulated [ouvə'pɔpjuleitid], *adj.*
übervölkert.
overpower [ouvə'pauə], *v.a.* überwältigen.
overrate [ouvə'reit], *v.a.* überschätzen.
overreach [ouvə'ri:tʃ], *v.a.* übervorteilen.
override [ouvə'raid], *v.a. irr.* über-
reiten; unterdrücken (*suppress*).
overrule [ouvə'ru:l], *v.a.* nicht gelten
lassen, verwerfen.
overseer ['ouvəsiə], *s.* der Aufseher.
oversleep [ouvə'sli:p], *v.n. irr.* sich verschlafen.
overstep [ouvə'step], *v.a.* überschreiten.
overstrain [ouvə'strein], *v.a., v.n.*
(sich) zu sehr anstrengen, überanstrengen.
overt ['ouvə:t], *adj.* offenkundig;
öffentlich (*public*).
overtake [ouvə'teik], *v.a. irr.* einholen;
(*Mot.*) überholen.
overtax [ouvə'tæks], *v.a.* zu hoch
besteuern; (*fig.*) überanstrengen
(*strain*).
overthrow [ouvə'θrou], *v.a. irr.* umstürzen; (*Pol.*) stürzen. — ['ouvəθrou],
s. der Sturz.
overtime ['ouvətaim], *s.* Überstunden,
f. pl.
overture ['ouvətjuə], *s.* die Ouvertüre.
overturn [ouvə'tə:n], *v.a.* umstürzen.
— *v.n.* überschlagen.
overweening [ouvə'wi:niŋ], *adj.* eingebildet.
overweight [ouvə'weit], *s.* das Übergewicht.
overwhelm [ouvə'welm], *v.a.* überwältigen.
overwork [ouvə'wə:k], *v.n.* sich überarbeiten.
overwrought [ouvə'rɔ:t], *adj.* übermäßig erregt, aufgeregt, überreizt.
owe [ou], *v.a.* schulden. — *v.n.* verdanken (*be in debt*).
owing ['ouiŋ], *pred. adj.* — *to*, dank
(*Dat.*), zufolge (*Dat.*).
owl [aul], *s.* (*Orn.*) die Eule.
own (1) [oun], *v.a.* besitzen (*possess*).
— *adj.* eigen.
own (2) [oun], *v.a.* anerkennen (*acknowledge*).
owner ['ounə], *s.* der Besitzer, Eigentümer.
ox [ɔks], *s.* (*Zool.*) der Ochse.
oxidate ['ɔksideit] *see* **oxidise**.

oxide ['ɔksaid], *s.* (*Chem.*) das Oxyd.
oxidise ['ɔksidaiz], *v.a., v.n.* (*Chem.*)
oxydieren.
oxtail ['ɔksteil], *s.* der Ochsenschwanz.
oxygen ['ɔksidʒən], *s.* (*Chem.*) der
Sauerstoff.
oyster ['ɔistə], *s.* (*Zool.*) die Auster.
ozone ['ouzoun], *s.* (*Chem.*) das Ozon.

P

P [pi:]. das P.
pa [pa:], *s.* (*coll.*) Papa, der Vater.
pace [peis], *s.* der Gang, Schritt (*step*);
das Tempo (*rate*). — *v.n.* — *up and
down*, auf- und abschreiten. — *v.a.*
einschulen (*horse*).
Pacific, The [pə'sifik, θə]. der Stille
Ozean.
pacific [pə'sifik], *adj.* friedlich, still.
pacify ['pæsifai], *v.a.* Frieden stiften,
beruhigen.
pack [pæk], *s.* das *or* der Pack; der
Ballen (*bale*); das Rudel (*wolves*); das
Spiel (*cards*); das Paket, die Packung.
— *v.a.* packen (*a case*); parteiisch zusammensetzen; die Karten schlecht
mischen (*cheat at cards*); *packed like
sardines*, dichtgedrängt, eingepfercht.
— *v.n.* packen; seine Sachen einpacken.
package ['pækidʒ], *s.* der Ballen (*bale*);
das Gepäckstück, Paket.
packet ['pækit], *s.* das Paket; (*Naut.*)
— *boat*, das Paketboot, Postschiff.
pact [pækt], *s.* der Pakt, Vertrag.
pad [pæd], *s.* das Polster, Kissen; der
Notizblock (*writing block*). —
v.a. auspolstern; *padded cell*, die
Gummizelle.
padding ['pædiŋ], *s.* (*Tail.*) das Futter;
(*fig.*) die (nichtssagende) Ausfüllung,
das leere Geschwätz.
paddle [pædl], *v.a., v.n.* rudern, paddeln. — *s.* das Paddel, (Doppel)ruder,
das Schaufelruder; — *steamer*, der
Raddampfer.
paddock ['pædək], *s.* der Sattelplatz;
das Gehege.
padlock ['pædlɔk], *s.* das Vorhängeschloß, Vorlegeschloß.
pagan ['peigən], *adj.* heidnisch. — *s.*
der Heide.
paganism ['peigənizm], *s.* das Heidentum.
page (1) [peidʒ], *s.* der Page (*court
attendant*); Hoteljunge (*hotel boy*). —
v.a. durch Pagen suchen lassen.
page (2) [peidʒ], die Seite (*of book*). —
v.a. paginieren (*book*).
pageant ['pædʒənt], *s.* der Aufzug, der
Prunkzug; das Schaustück (*dramatic*).
pail [peil], *s.* der Eimer.

pain [pein], *s.* der Schmerz, die Pein;
(*pl.*) die Mühe; *go to a lot of* —*s*, sich
große Mühe geben. —*v.a.* schmerzen;
bekümmern (*mentally*).
paint [peint], *s.* die Farbe (*dye*); die
Schminke (*make-up*). — *v.a.* anstreichen, malen.
painter ['peintə], *s.* der Maler.
painting ['peintiŋ], *s.* das Gemälde.
pair [peə], *s.* das Paar; *two* —*s of shoes*,
zwei Paar Schuhe; *a* — *of spectacles*,
die Brille; *a* — *of scissors*, die Schere.
— *v.a.* paaren. — *v.n.* sich paaren.
pajamas [pə'dʒɑːməz] *see under*
pyjamas.
Pakistani [pɑːki'stɑːni], *adj.* paki-
stanisch. — *s.* der Pakistaner.
palace ['pæləs], *s.* der Palast.
palatable ['pælətəbl], *adj.* schmackhaft.
palatal ['pælətl], *adj.* (*Phonet.*) palatal,
Gaumen-, Vordergaumen-. — *s.*
(*Phonet.*) der Gaumenlaut.
palate ['pælit], *s.* der Gaumen.
Palatinate, The [pə'lætinit, ðə]. die
Pfalz, Pfalzgrafschaft.
palaver [pə'lɑːvə], *s.* die Unterredung;
das Palaver.
pale (1) [peil], *adj.* blaß, bleich.
pale (2) [peil], *s.* der Pfahl; *beyond the*
—, unkultiviert.
Palestinian [pælis'tiniən], *adj.* palä-
stinisch. — *s.* der Palästiner.
palette ['pælit], *s.* die Palette (*see also*
pallet (1)).
paling ['peiliŋ], *s.* der Lattenzaun; (*pl.*)
der Pfahlbau.
pall (1) [pɔːl], *s.* das Leichentuch.
pall (2) [pɔːl], *v.n.* schal werden (*become stale*).
pallet (1) ['pælit], *s.* die Palette (*painter's*); — *knife*, das Streichmesser
(*potter's etc.*).
pallet (2) ['pælit], *s.* der Strohsack.
palliative ['pæliətiv], *s.* linderndes
Mittel; (*fig.*) die Beschönigung.
pallid ['pælid], *adj.* blaß, bleich.
pallor ['pælə], *s.* die Blässe.
palm (1) [pɑːm], *s.* die Handfläche. —
v.a. — (*off*) *on to s.o.*, an jemanden
loswerden, jemandem etwas aufbinden.
palm (2) [pɑːm], *s.* (*Bot.*) die Palme;
Palm Sunday, Palmsonntag.
palmer ['pɑːmə], *s.* (*obs.*) der Pilger
(*pilgrim*).
palmist ['pɑːmist], *s.* der Handleser,
Wahrsager.
palmistry ['pɑːmistri], *s.* die Hand-
wahrsagerei.
palmy ['pɑːmi], *adj.* glorreich.
palpable ['pælpəbl], *adj.* handgreiflich,
greifbar, klar.
palpitate ['pælpiteit], *v.n.* klopfen (*of
heart*).
palsied ['pɔːlzid], *adj.* (*Med.*) gelähmt.
palsy ['pɔːlzi], *s.* (*Med.*) die Lähmung.
paltry ['pɔːltri], *adj.* erbärmlich, armselig.
pamper ['pæmpə], *v.a.* verwöhnen.
pan (1) [pæn], *s.* die Pfanne. — *v.n.* —

out, sich ausbreiten, sich weiten.
pan (2) [pæn], *v.a.* (*Phot.*) kreisen, im
Bogen führen.
panacea [pænə'siə], *s.* das Universalmittel.
pancake ['pænkeik], *s.* der Pfannkuchen.
pander ['pændə], *v.n.* fröhnen (*Dat.*),
nachgeben.
pane [pein], *s.* die Glasscheibe.
panel ['pænl], *s.* die Holzfüllung,
Täfelung (*in room*); die Liste; die
Kommission (*of experts etc.*).
pang [pæŋ], *s.* die Angst, Pein; der
Schmerz, Stich (*stab of pain*).
panic ['pænik], *s.* die Panik, der
Schrecken.
panoply ['pænəpli], *s.* (*Poet.*) die
Rüstung.
pansy ['pænzi], *s.* (*Bot.*) das Stiefmütterchen; (*sl.*) der Weichling,
Feigling.
pant [pænt], *v.n.* keuchen, schwer
atmen.
pantaloons [pæntə'luːnz] (*usually abbr.*
pants [pænts], *s. pl.* die Unterhosen,
Hosen, *f.pl.*
panther ['pænθə], *s.* (*Zool.*) der
Panther.
pantomime ['pæntəmaim], *s.* die Pantomime, das Weihnachtsstück.
pantry ['pæntri], *s.* die Speisekammer.
pap [pæp], *s.* der Kinderbrei.
papacy ['peipəsi], *s.* das Papsttum.
papal ['peipəl], *adj.* päpstlich.
paper ['peipə], *s.* das Papier (*material*);
die Zeitung (*daily* —); die Abhand-
lung (*essay*); — *knife*, der Brieföffner.
— *v.a.* tapezieren (*a room*).
paperhanger ['peipəhæŋə], *s.* der
Tapezierer.
paperweight ['peipəweit], *s.* der Briefbeschwerer.
par [pɑː], *s.* die Gleichheit, das Pari.
parable ['pærəbl], *s.* die Parabel, das
Gleichnis.
parabola [pə'ræbələ], *s.* (*Geom.*) die
Parabel.
parabolic [pærə'bɔlik], *adj.* para-
bolisch, gleichnishaft.
parachute ['pærəʃuːt], *s.* (*Aviat.*) der
Fallschirm.
parade [pə'reid], *s.* die Parade, der Aufmarsch. — *v.a.* herausstellen; *zur
Schau tragen* (*show off*). — *v.n.*
(*Mil.*) vorbeimarschieren.
paradise ['pærədais], *s.* das Paradies.
paraffin ['pærəfin], *s.* das Paraffin.
paragon ['pærəgən], *s.* das Musterkind,
Musterbeispiel, Vorbild.
paragraph ['pærəgrɑːf], *s.* der Abschnitt, Absatz, Paragraph.
Paraguayan [pærə'gwaiən], *adj.* para-
guayisch. — *s.* der Paraguayer.
parallel ['pærəlel], *adj.* parallel. — *s.*
die Parallele.
paralyse ['pærəlaiz], *v.a.* lähmen.
paralysis [pə'rælisis], *s.* die Lähmung.
paramount ['pærəmaunt], *adj.* oberst.
paramour ['pærəmuə], *s.* der *or* die
Geliebte.

451

parapet

parapet ['pærəpit], *s.* das Geländer, die Brüstung.
paraphrase ['pærəfreiz], *s.* die Umschreibung. — *v.a.* umschreiben.
parasite ['pærəsait], *s.* der Schmarotzer, Parasit.
parasol ['pærəsɔl], *s.* der Sonnenschirm.
parboil ['pɑːbɔil], *v.a.* aufkochen lassen.
parcel [pɑːsl], *s.* das Paket; Bündel (*bundle*). — *v.a.* — *up*, einpacken.
parch [pɑːtʃ], *v.a.* austrocknen.
parchment ['pɑːtʃmənt], *s.* das Pergament.
pardon [pɑːdn], *v.a.* vergeben, verzeihen (*Dat.*); begnadigen (*Acc.*) (*give amnesty*). — *s.* der Pardon, die Verzeihung; — *!*, *I beg your* — *!* bitte um Entschuldigung; *I beg your* — *?* wie bitte?
pare [pɛə], *v.a.* beschneiden (*nails*); schälen (*fruit*).
parent ['pɛərənt], *s.* der Vater, die Mutter, (*pl.*) die Eltern, *pl.*
parentage ['pɛərəntidʒ], *s.* die Abkunft, Herkunft.
parenthesis [pə'renθisis], *s.* die Parenthese, die Klammer.
parish ['pæriʃ], *s.* das Kirchspiel, die Gemeinde, die Pfarre.
parishioner [pə'riʃənə], *s.* das Gemeindemitglied.
Parisian [pə'riziən], *adj.* parisisch. — *s.* der Pariser.
park [pɑːk], *s.* der Park; (*Motor.*) der Wagenpark, Parkplatz. — *v.a.*, *v.n.* parken.
parking ['pɑːkiŋ], *s.* (*Motor.*) das Parken; — *meter*, die Parkuhr, der Parkometer.
parley [pɑːli], *s.* die Unterredung, Verhandlung. — *v.n.* verhandeln.
parliament ['pɑːləmənt], *s.* das Parlament.
parlour ['pɑːlə], *s.* das Wohnzimmer, die gute Stube; —*maid*, das Dienstmädchen; — *trick*, das Kunststück.
parochial [pə'roukiəl], *adj.* Pfarr-, Gemeinde-; (*fig.*) engstirnig.
parody ['pærədi], *s.* die Parodie. — *v.a.* parodieren.
parole [pə'roul], *s.* das Ehrenwort; (*Mil.*) das Losungswort.
paroxysm ['pærəksizm], *s.* der heftige Anfall.
parquet ['pɑːki], *s.* das Parkett; — *floor*, der Parkettfußboden.
parrot ['pærət], *s.* (*Orn.*) der Papagei.
parry ['pæri], *v.a.* parieren, abwehren.
parse [pɑːs, pɑːz], *v.a.* (*Gram.*) analysieren.
parsimony ['pɑːsiməni], *s.* die Sparsamkeit.
parsley ['pɑːsli], *s.* (*Bot.*) die Petersilie.
parson [pɑːsn], *s.* der Pastor, Pfarrer.
parsonage ['pɑːsənidʒ], *s.* das Pfarrhaus.
part [pɑːt], *s.* der Teil; Anteil (*share*); (*Theat.*) die Rolle; (*Mus.*) die Stimme;

(*Geog.*) die Gegend; *for his* —, seinerseits. — *v.n.* — (*with*), sich trennen (von, *Dat.*); — *company*, auseinandergehen.
partake [pɑː'teik], *v.n.* teilnehmen, teilhaben (*in*, an, *Dat.*).
partial [pɑːʃl], *adj.* Teil-; parteiisch (*subjective*); — *to*, eingenommen für.
participate [pɑː'tisipeit], *v.n.* teilnehmen (*in*, an, *Dat.*).
participation [pɑːtisi'peiʃən], *s.* die Teilnahme.
participle ['pɑːtisipl], *s.* (*Gram.*) das Mittelwort, Partizip(ium).
particle ['pɑːtikl], *s.* die Partikel, das Teilchen.
particular [pə'tikjulə], *adj.* besonder (*special*); einzel (*individual*); sonderbar (*queer*); ungewöhnlich; genau. — *s.* (*pl.*) die Details, *n. pl.*, Einzelheiten, *f. pl.*
parting ['pɑːtiŋ], *s.* der Abschied (*taking leave*); der Scheitel (*hair*).
partisan [pɑːti'zæn], *s.* der Partisane, Parteigänger.
partition [pɑː'tiʃən], *s.* die Teilung (*division*); die Scheidewand (*dividing wall*). — *v.a.* teilen; aufteilen (*divide up*).
partly ['pɑːtli], *adv.* zum Teil, teils.
partner ['pɑːtnə], *s.* der Partner; Teilhaber (*in business etc.*).
partnership ['pɑːtnəʃip], *s.* die Partnerschaft.
partridge ['pɑːtridʒ], *s.* (*Orn.*) das Rebhuhn.
party ['pɑːti], *s.* (*Pol.*) die Partei; (*Law*) die Partei, Seite; die Gesellschaft, die Party (*social gathering*); *throw* or *give a* — , einen Gesellschaftsabend (or eine Party) geben; *guilty* —, der schuldige Teil; (*Build.*) — *wall*, die Brandmauer.
Paschal ['pɑːskəl], *adj.* Oster-.
pass [pɑːs], *v.a.* passieren; vorbeigehen (an, *Dat.*); durchlassen (*let through*); (*Law*) — *sentence*, das Urteil fällen. — *v.n.* fortgehen, vergehen, geschehen (*happen*); vorübergehen (*of time*); — *for*, gelten; (*Sch.*) durchkommen (*exam*); *come to* —, sich ereignen. — *s.* der Paß; (*Theat.*) die Freikarte.
passable ['pɑːsəbl], *adj.* gangbar; (*fig.*) leidlich, erträglich.
passage ['pæsidʒ], *s.* der Durchgang (*thoroughfare*); das Vergehen (*of time*); die Seereise; die Stelle (*book*).
passenger ['pæsindʒə], *s.* der Reisende, Passagier; — *train*, der Personenzug.
passer-by ['pɑːsəbai], *s.* der Passant, Vorübergehende.
passing ['pɑːsiŋ], *s.* das Vorbeigehen, das Vorübergehen; (*Parl.*) das Durchgehen; das Hinscheiden (*death*). — *adj.* vorübergehend, zeitweilig.
Passion ['pæʃən], *s.* (*Eccl.*) das Leiden; (*Mus.*) die Passion; — *Week*, die Karwoche; — *flower*, die Passionsblume.
passion ['pæʃən], *s.* die Leidenschaft;

452

fly into a —, aufbrausen.

passive ['pæsiv], *adj.* passiv. — *s.* (*Gram.*) das Passiv(um).

Passover ['pɑːsouvə], *s.* (*Rel.*) das Passahfest.

passport ['pɑːspɔːt], *s.* der Reisepaß.

past [pɑːst], *adj.* vergangen. — *adv.* vorbei. — *prep.* nach (*time*). — *s.* die Vergangenheit; (*Gram.*) das Imperfekt, Präteritum.

paste [peist], *s.* die Paste, der Brei; der Kleister (*glue*). — *v.a.* kleben, kleistern.

pasteboard ['peistbɔːd], *s.* die Pappe.

pastime ['pɑːstaim], *s.* der Zeitvertreib.

pastor ['pɑːstə], *s.* (*Rel.*) der Seelsorger, Pfarrer.

pastoral ['pɑːstərəl], *adj.* Hirten-, pastoral. — *s.* (*Poet.*) das Hirtengedicht.

pastry ['peistri], *s.* (*Cul.*) die Pastete; das Gebäck; — *cook*, der Konditor, Zuckerbäcker.

pasture ['pɑːstʃə], *s.* die Weide, das Grasland. — *v.n.* weiden, grasen.

pasty ['pɑːsti, 'pæsti], *s.* (*Cul.*) die Pastete. — ['peisti], *adj.* teigig.

pat [pæt], *s.* der Klaps; der Schlag (*slap*). — *v.a.* leicht schlagen, streicheln (*gently*).

patch [pætʃ], *v.a.* flicken, ausbessern. — *s.* der Fleck (*mending material*); der Flecken (*land*); (*coll.*) *no — on him*, kein Vergleich mit ihm; *nicht zu vergleichen mit ihm*.

patent ['peitənt *or* 'pætənt], *adj.* offen, klar, patent; — *leather*, das Glanzleder. — *s.* das Patent.

patentee [peitən'tiː], *s.* der Patentinhaber.

paternal [pə'təːnəl], *adj.* väterlich.

path [pɑːθ], *s.* der Pfad, Weg, Fußsteig.

pathetic [pə'θetik], *adj.* pathetisch, rührend; armselig.

pathology [pə'θɔlədʒi], *s.* (*Med.*) die Pathologie.

pathway ['pɑːθwei], *s.* der Fußweg, Fußsteig.

patience ['peiʃəns], *s.* die Geduld; die Patience (*card game*).

patient ['peiʃənt], *adj.* geduldig. — *s.* (*Med.*) der Patient.

patrician [pə'triʃən], *adj.* patrizisch. — *s.* der Patrizier.

patrimony ['pætriməni], *s.* das (väterliche) Erbgut.

patriot ['peitriət, 'pætriət], *s.* der Patriot.

patriotism ['peitriətizm, 'pæt-], *s.* die Vaterlandsliebe, der Patriotismus.

patrol [pə'troul], *s.* die Patrouille, Streife. — *v.n.* auf Patrouille gehen.

patron ['peitrən], *s.* der Schutzherr, der Gönner; (*Comm.*) der Kunde; — *saint*, der Schutzheilige.

patronage ['pætrənidʒ], *s.* die Gönnerschaft, Huld.

patronize ['pætrənaiz], *v.a.* besuchen (*frequent*); begünstigen (*favour*).

patronizing ['pætrənaiziŋ], *adj.* herablassend.

patten [pætn], *s.* (*Archit.*) der Sockel; der Holzschuh (*clog*).

patter (1) ['pætə], *s.* das Geplätscher (*rain etc.*). — *v.n.* plätschern.

patter (2) ['pætə], *s.* das Geplauder (*chatter*). — *v.n.* schwätzen.

pattern ['pætən], *s.* das Muster; die Schablone (*in material*).

paucity ['pɔːsiti], *s.* die geringe Anzahl, der Mangel.

paunch [pɔːntʃ], *s.* der Wanst.

pauper ['pɔːpə], *s.* der Arme.

pauperize ['pɔːpəraiz], *v.a.* arm machen, verarmen lassen.

pause [pɔːz], *s.* die Pause. — *v.n.* innehalten.

pave [peiv], *v.a.* pflastern.

pavement ['peivmənt], *s.* das Pflaster; der Bürgersteig, Gehsteig.

pavilion [pə'viljən], *s.* das Gartenhaus; der Pavillon.

paw [pɔː], *s.* die Pfote; die Tatze. — *v.a.* streicheln, betasten.

pawn (1) [pɔːn], *s.* das Pfand. — *v.a.* verpfänden.

pawn (2) [pɔːn], *s.* (*Chess*) der Bauer.

pawnbroker ['pɔːnbroukə], *s.* der Pfandleiher.

pay [pei], *v.a. irr.* zahlen; bezahlen, begleichen (*bill*); — *attention*, aufpassen, Aufmerksamkeit schenken; — *o.'s respects*, Respekt zollen. — *v.n. irr.* bezahlt machen, sich lohnen (*it —s to . . .*). — *s.* (*Mil.*) der Sold; (*Comm.*) der Lohn (*wage*), die Bezahlung (*payment*).

payable ['peiəbl], *adj.* zahlbar, zu bezahlen.

payee [pei'iː], *s.* der Empfänger, Präsentant.

payer ['peiə], *s.* der Zahler; (*Comm.*) der Trassat.

payment ['peimənt], *s.* die Bezahlung, Begleichung (*of sum*).

pea [piː], *s.* (*Bot.*) die Erbse (*see also* **peas**(e)).

peace [piːs], *s.* der Friede(n); die Ruhe (*restfulness*).

peaceable ['piːsəbl], *adj.* friedlich; friedliebend.

peaceful ['piːsful], *adj.* friedlich, ruhig (*restful*).

peach [piːtʃ], *s.* (*Bot.*) der *or* (*Austr.*) die Pfirsich.

peacock ['piːkɔk], *s.* (*Orn.*) der Pfau.

peahen ['piːhen], *s.* (*Orn.*) die Pfauhenne.

peak [piːk], *s.* der Gipfel, die Spitze; der Schirm (*of cap*); — *hour*, die Stunde des Hochbetriebs, Hauptverkehrsstunde.

peal [piːl], *v.a.* läuten. — *v.n.* erschallen. — *s.* das Läuten, Geläute.

peanut ['piːnʌt], *s.* (*Bot.*) die Erdnuß.

pear [pɛə], *s.* (*Bot.*) die Birne.

pearl [pəːl], *s.* die Perle; — *barley*, die Perlgraupen, *f. pl.*; *mother of —*, die Perlmutter.

peasant

peasant ['pezənt], *s.* der Bauer.
peasantry ['pezəntri], *s.* das Bauernvolk, die Bauernschaft.
peas(e) [pi:z], *s. pl. pease pudding*, der Erbsenbrei, das Erbsenpüree.
peat [pi:t], *s.* der Torf.
pebble [pebl], *s.* der Kiesel(stein).
peck (1) [pek], *s.* der Viertelscheffel (=9 litres.)
peck (2) [pek], *s.* das Picken (*of hen*); (*coll.*) der Kuß. — *v.a.* hacken, hauen.
pecker ['pekə], *s.* die Picke, Haue; *keep your — up!* Mut bewahren!
peckish ['pekiʃ], *adj.* hungrig.
pectoral ['pektərəl], *adj.* Brust-. — *s.* das Brustmittel.
peculiar [pi'kju:liə], *adj.* eigenartig, eigentümlich (*strange*); — *to*, eigen (*Dat.*); besonder (*special*).
peculiarity [pikju:li'æriti], *s.* die Eigentümlichkeit, die Eigenartigkeit.
pecuniary [pi'kju:niəri], *adj.* Geld-, geldlich, finanziell, pekuniär.
pedagogue ['pedəgɔg], *s.* der Pädagog(e), Erzieher.
pedal [pedl] *s.* das Pedal; (*Motor.*) der Fußhebel. — *v.n.* radfahren; (*coll.*) radeln.
pedant ['pedənt], *s.* der Pedant.
pedantic [pi'dæntik], *adj.* pedantisch.
pedantry ['pedəntri], *s.* die Pedanterie.
peddle [pedl], *v.a.* hausieren.
peddling ['pedliŋ], *adj.* kleinlich, unbedeutend.
pedestal ['pedistl], *s.* der Sockel.
pedestrian [pi'destriən], *s.* der Fußgänger. — *adj.* Fuß-, Fußgänger-.
pedigree ['pedigri:], *s.* der Stammbaum.
pediment ['pedimənt], *s.* (*Archit.*) der Ziergiebel.
pedlar ['pedlə], *s.* der Hausierer.
peel [pi:l], *s.* die Schale (*of fruit*). — *v.a.* schälen. — *v.n.* sich schälen.
peep [pi:p], *v.n.* gucken. — *s.* der (schnelle) Blick, das Gucken; — *show*, der Guckkasten.
peer (1) [piə], *s.* (*Parl.*) der Pair, Lord; der Ebenbürtige (*equal*).
peer (2) [piə], *v.n.* gucken, blicken, schauen.
peerage ['piəridʒ], *s.* der (Reichs)adel.
peeress ['piəres], *s.* die Gattin eines Pairs.
peerless ['piəlis], *adj.* unvergleichlich.
peevish ['pi:viʃ], *adj.* mürrisch.
pe(e)wit ['pi:wit], *s.* (*Orn.*) der Kiebitz.
peg ['peg], *s.* der Pflock (*stake*); der Holzstift (*in wall*); *clothes —*, die Wäscheklammer. — *v.a.* anpflocken (*to ground*).
pelican ['pelikən], *s.* (*Orn.*) der Pelikan.
pellet ['pelit], *s.* das Kügelchen.
pell-mell ['pel'mel], *adv.* durcheinander.
pelt (1) [pelt], *v.a. — with*, bewerfen mit, — *a person with*, werfen nach einem (*Acc.*). — *v.n.* strömen (*rain etc.*); rennen (*hasten*).
pelt (2) [pelt], *s.* der Pelz (*of animal*).

pen (1) [pen], *s. quill —*, die Feder; *fountain —*, die Füllfeder; *ballpoint —*, der Kugelschreiber. — *v.a.* schreiben; verfassen (*compose*).
pen (2) [pen], *s.* das Gehege. — *v.a.* einschliessen (*sheep*).
penal ['pi:nəl], *adj.* Straf-; — *servitude*, die Zuchthausstrafe.
penalize ['pi:nəlaiz], *v.a.* bestrafen.
penalty ['penəlti], *s.* die Strafe.
penance ['penəns], *s.* die Buße.
pence [pens] *see under penny.*
pencil ['pensl], *s.* der Bleistift; der Stift; (*Geom.*) der Strahl. — *v.a.* niederschreiben, notieren.
pendant ['pendənt], *s.* das Ohrgehänge; (*fig.*) das Gegenstück.
pendent ['pendənt], *adj.* hängend, schwebend.
pending ['pendiŋ], *adj.* in der Schwebe; unentschieden (*undecided*). — *prep.* während (*during*); bis (zu) (*until*).
pendulum ['pendjuləm], *s.* das Pendel.
penetrate ['penitreit], *v.a.* durchdringen.
peninsula [pi'ninsjulə], *s.* die Halbinsel.
penitent ['penitənt], *s.* der Büßer. — *adj.* bußfertig.
penitentiary [peni'tenʃəri], *s.* (*Am.*) das Zuchthaus (*prison*).
penknife ['pennaif], *s.* das Taschenmesser.
pennant ['penənt], *s.* der Wimpel, das Fähnchen.
penniless ['penilis], *adj.* mittellos, ohne einen Heller Geld, arm.
pennon ['penən] *see pennant.*
penny ['peni], *s.* (*pl.* **pence** [pens], **pennies** [peniz]) der Penny; (*Am.*) das Centstück; — *farthing*, das Hochrad; — *whistle*, die Blechpfeife; *a pretty —*, hübsches Geld.
pension ['penʃən], *s.* die Pension; der Ruhegehalt. — *v.a.* (*off*) pensionieren, in den Ruhestand versetzen.
pensive ['pensiv], *adj.* nachdenklich.
Pentecost ['pentikɔst]. *das or* (*pl.*) die Pfingsten.
penthouse ['penthaus], *s.* das Wetterdach.
penurious [pi'njuəriəs], *adj.* unbemittelt, arm (*poor*); dürftig, karg (*meagre*).
penury ['penjuəri], *s.* die Not, Armut.
peony ['piəni], *s.* (*Bot.*) die Päonie, Pfingstrose.
people [pi:pl], *s. pl.* das Volk (*nation*); die Leute, Menschen (*pl.*). — *v.a.* bevölkern.
pepper ['pepə], *s.* der Pfeffer. — *v.a.* pfeffern.
per [pə:], *prep.* pro; per; durch; *as — account*, laut Rechnung.
peradventure [pə:rəd'ventʃə], *adv.* (*obs.*) von ungefähr; vielleicht (*perhaps*).
perambulator [pə'ræmbjuleitə] (*abbr. coll.*) **pram** [præm]), *s.* der Kinderwagen.

perceive [pə'si:v], *v.a.* wahrnehmen, merken.

percentage [pə'sentidʒ], *s.* der Prozentsatz (*of interest*); Prozente, *n. pl.*

perceptible [pə'septibl], *adj.* wahrnehmbar, merklich.

perception [pə'sepʃən], *s.* die Wahrnehmung, Empfindung.

perch (1) [pə:tʃ], *v.n.* aufsitzen; sitzen (*of birds*). — *s.* die Stange.

perch (2) [pə:tʃ], *s.* (*Zool.*) der Barsch.

perchance [pə'tʃɑ:ns], *adv.* vielleicht.

percolate ['pə:kəleit], *v.n.* durchsickern, durchtröpfeln.

percolator ['pə:kəleitə], *s.* die Kaffeemaschine.

percussion [pə'kʌʃən], *s.* (*Mus.*) das Schlagzeug.

peremptory ['perəmptəri, pə'remptəri], *adj.* entschieden, bestimmt (*decided*); absprechend.

perennial [pə'reniəl], *adj.* (*Bot.*) perennierend; Dauer-.

perfect ['pə:fikt], *adj.* vollkommen, vollendet, perfekt. — *s.* (*tense*) (*Gram.*) das Perfekt(um). — [pə'fekt], *v.a.* vollenden.

perfection [pə'fekʃən], *s.* die Vollendung, Vollkommenheit; *to* —, vollkommen.

perfidious [pə'fidiəs], *adj.* treulos, untreu; tückisch.

perfidy ['pə:fidi], *s.* die Treulosigkeit.

perforate ['pə:fəreit], *v.a.* durchlöchern, perforieren (*paper*); durchbohren (*pierce*).

perforce [pə'fɔ:s], *adv.* mit Gewalt, notgedrungen.

perform [pə'fɔ:m], *v.a.* ausführen (*carry out*); (*Theat.*) aufführen. — *v.n.* spielen, auftreten (*of actor*).

performance [pə'fɔ:məns], *s.* die Ausführung; Verrichtung (*execution of duty etc.*); (*Theat.*) die Aufführung.

perfume [pə'fju:m], *s.* das Parfüm; der Duft (*scent*). — *v.a.* parfümieren.

perfunctory [pə'fʌŋktəri], *adj.* nachlässig, oberflächlich, flüchtig.

perhaps [pə'hæps], *adv.* vielleicht.

peril ['peril], *s.* die Gefahr.

period ['piəriəd], *s.* die Periode (*time*); der Zeitraum (*span*); (*Am.*) der Punkt (*full stop*).

periodical [piəri'ɔdikəl], *adj.* periodisch. — *s.* die Zeitschrift.

perish ['periʃ], *v.n.* zugrunde gehen, umkommen.

perishable ['periʃəbl], *adj.* vergänglich; (leicht) verderblich (*of food*).

periwig ['periwig], *s.* die Perücke.

periwinkle (1) ['periwiŋkl], *s.* (*Zool.*) die Uferschnecke.

periwinkle (2) ['periwiŋkl], (*Bot.*) das Immergrün.

perjure [pə:dʒə], *v.r.* meineidig werden.

perjurer ['pə:dʒərə], *s.* der Meineidige.

perjury ['pə:dʒəri], *s.* der Meineid.

permanence, permanency ['pə:mə-nəns, 'pə:mənənsi], *s.* die Dauer, Beständigkeit.

permanent ['pə:mənənt], *adj.* Dauer-, dauerhaft, beständig; — *wave*, die Dauerwelle.

permeability [pə:miə'biliti], *s.* die Durchdringbarkeit, Durchlässigkeit.

permeable ['pə:miəbl], *adj.* durchdringlich.

permeate ['pə:mieit], *v.a.* durchdringen.

permissible [pə'misibl], *adj.* zulässig, statthaft.

permission [pə'miʃən], *s.* die Erlaubnis.

permit [pə'mit], *v.a.* zulassen, erlauben. — ['pə:mit], *s.* die Erlaubnis, (*official*) die Genehmigung.

permutation [pə:mju'teiʃən], *s.* (*Maths.*) die Permutation.

pernicious [pə'niʃəs], *adj.* verderblich, schädlich, bösartig.

perorate ['perəreit], *v.n.* eine (lange) Rede beschließen.

perpendicular [pə:pən'dikjulə], *adj.* senkrecht. — *s.* die Senkrechte.

perpetrate ['pə:pitreit], *v.a.* begehen (*commit*).

perpetration [pə:pi'treiʃən], *s.* die Verübung, Begehung.

perpetrator ['pə:pitreitə], *s.* der Begeher, Täter.

perpetual [pə'petjuəl], *adj.* (an-)dauernd; ewig.

perpetuate [pə'petjueit], *v.a.* verewigen.

perpetuity [pə:pi'tju:iti], *s.* die Ewigkeit.

perplex [pə'pleks], *v.a.* bestürzen, verblüffen.

perplexity [pə'pleksiti], *s.* die Bestürzung, Verwirrung.

persecute ['pə:sikju:t], *v.a.* verfolgen.

persecution [pə:si'kju:ʃən], *s.* die Verfolgung.

perseverance [pə:si'viərəns], *s.* die Ausdauer, Beharrlichkeit.

persevere [pə:si'viə], *v.n.* beharren (*in*, bei, *Dat.*).

Persian ['pə:ʃən], *adj.* persisch. — *s.* der Perser.

persist [pə'sist], *v.n.* beharren (*in*, auf, *Dat.*).

persistence [pə'sistəns], *s.* die Beharrlichkeit.

person ['pə:sən], *s.* die Person; *in* —, persönlich.

personal ['pə:sənəl], *adj.* persönlich.

personality [pə:sə'næliti], *s.* die Persönlichkeit.

personify [pə:'sɔnifai], *v.a.* verkörpern.

personnel [pə:sə'nel], *s.* das Personal; (*Comm.*) — *manager*, der Personalchef.

perspective [pə'spektiv], *s.* die Perspektive. — *adj.* perspektivisch.

perspicacious [pə:spi'keiʃəs], *adj.* scharfsichtig, scharfsinnig.

perspicacity [pə:spi'kæsiti], *s.* der Scharfblick, Scharfsinn.

perspicuity [pə:spi'kju:iti], *s.* die Durchsichtigkeit, Klarheit.

perspicuous [pə'spikjuəs], *adj.* deutlich, klar.

perspiration [pə:spi'reiʃən], *s.* der Schweiß.

perspire [pə'spaiə], *v.n.* schwitzen.

persuade [pə'sweid], *v.a.* überreden.

persuasion [pə'sweiʒən], *s.* die Überredung.

persuasive [pə'sweiziv], *adj.* überzeugend, überredend.

pert [pə:t], *adj.* naseweis, keck.

pertain [pə'tein], *v.n.* (an)gehören (*to Dat.*).

pertinacious [pə:ti'neiʃəs], *adj.* beharrlich, halsstarrig.

pertinacity [pə:ti'næsiti], *s.* die Beharrlichkeit, Halsstarrigkeit.

pertinence, pertinency ['pə:tinəns, 'pə:tinənsi], *s.* die Angemessenheit.

pertinent ['pə:tinənt], *adj.* angemessen, passend.

pertness ['pə:tnis], *s.* die Keckheit, der Vorwitz.

perturb [pə'tə:b], *v.a.* verwirren, stören, beunruhigen.

perturbation [pə:tə'beiʃən], *s.* die Verwirrung, Störung, Beunruhigung.

peruke [pə'ru:k], *s.* die Perücke.

peruse [pə'ru:z], *v.a.* durchlesen.

Peruvian [pə'ru:viən], *adj.* peruanisch. — *s.* der Peruaner.

pervade [pə'veid], *v.a.* durchdringen.

perverse [pə'və:s], *adj.* verkehrt.

perversion [pə'və:ʃən], *s.* die Perversion.

perversity [pə'və:siti], *s.* die Verdorbenheit, Widernatürlichkeit.

pervert [pə'və:t], *v.a.* verkehren, verderben. — [pə'və:t], *s.* der Verdorbene, der perverse Mensch.

perverted [pə'və:tid], *adj.* pervers (*sexually*).

pervious ['pə:viəs], *adj.* zugänglich, passierbar; durchlässig.

pessimist ['pesimist], *s.* der Pessimist.

pest [pest], *s.* (*Med.*) die Pest; (*fig.*) die Plage.

pester ['pestə], *v.a.* quälen, auf die Nerven gehen (*Dat.*).

pestiferous [pes'tifərəs], *adj.* verpestend.

pestilence ['pestiləns], *s.* (*Med.*) die Pest, Seuche.

pestle [pesl], *s.* die Mörserkeule.

pet [pet], *s.* das Haustier; der Liebling; — *name*, der Kosename. — *v.a.* liebkosen, streicheln.

petition [pi'tiʃən], *s.* die Bittschrift. — *v.a.* mit einer Bittschrift herantreten an (*Acc.*).

petrel ['petrəl], *s.* (*Orn.*) der Sturmvogel.

petrification [petrifi'keiʃən], *s.* die Versteinerung.

petrify ['petrifai], *v.a.* versteinern; (*fig.*) starr machen, bestürzen; *petrified with fright*, starr vor Entsetzen. — *v.n.* zu Stein werden.

petrol ['petrəl], *s.* das Benzin; (*crude oil*) das Petroleum; — *station*, die Tankstelle.

petticoat ['petikout], *s.* der Unterrock.

pettifogging ['petifogiŋ], *adj.* Winkel-, kleinlich, schikanös (*petty*).

pettiness ['petinis], *s.* die Kleinlichkeit.

pettish ['petiʃ], *adj.* verdrießlich.

petty ['peti], *adj.* klein, gering, kleinlich.

petulance ['petjuləns], *s.* die Launenhaftigkeit, Gereiztheit.

petulant ['petjulənt], *adj.* launenhaft.

pew [pju:], *s.* (*Eccl.*) der Kirchensitz; (*coll.*) der Sitz, Stuhl.

pewit ['pi:wit] *see* **pe(e)wit**.

pewter ['pju:tə], *s.* das Zinn; die Zinnwaren, *f. pl.* (*wares*).

pewterer ['pju:tərə], *s.* der Zinngießer.

phantom ['fæntəm], *s.* das Phantom, Trugbild; das Gespenst (*ghost*).

Pharisee ['færisi:], *s.* der Pharisäer.

pharmaceutical [fɑ:mə'sju:tikəl], *adj.* pharmazeutisch.

pharmacy ['fɑ:məsi], *s.* die Apothekerkunst (*dispensing*); die Apotheke (*dispensary*); die Pharmazeutik (*discipline*).

phase [feiz], *s.* die Phase.

pheasant ['fezənt], *s.* (*Orn.*) der Fasan.

phenomenal [fi'nɔminəl], *adj.* außerordentlich, phänomenal.

phenomenon [fi'nɔminən], *s.* das Phänomen.

phial [faiəl], *s.* die Phiole, das Fläschchen.

philanthropist [fi'lænθrəpist], *s.* der Philanthrop.

philanthropy [fi'lænθrəpi], *s.* die Philanthropie.

philatelist [fi'lætəlist], *s.* der Philatelist, Markensammler.

philately [fi'lætəli], *s.* das Markensammeln, die Philatelie, Briefmarkenkunde.

Philippine ['filipi:n], *adj.* philippinisch.

Philistine ['filistain], *s.* der Philister; (*fig.*) der Spießbürger.

philologist [fi'lɔlədʒist], *s.* der Philologe.

philology [fi'lɔlədʒi], *s.* die Philologie.

philosopher [fi'lɔsəfə], *s.* der Philosoph.

philosophize [fi'lɔsəfaiz], *v.n.* philosophieren.

philosophy [fi'lɔsəfi], *s.* die Philosophie.

phlegm [flem], *s.* das Phlegma (*mood*); (*Med.*) der Schleim.

phlegmatic [fleg'mætik], *adj.* phlegmatisch, gelassen.

phone [foun] *see under* **telephone**.

phonetics [fə'netiks], *s.* die Phonetik.

phosphorescent [fɔsfə'resənt], *adj.* phosphoreszierend, leuchtend.

phosphorus ['fɔsfərəs], *s.* (*Chem.*) der Phosphor.

photograph ['foutəgræf *or* -grɑ:f], *s.* die Photographie, das Lichtbild (*picture*). — *v.a.* photographieren, aufnehmen, (*coll.*) knipsen.

photographer [fə'tɔgrəfə], *s.* der Photograph.

photography [fə'tɔgrəfi], *s.* die Photographie.

phrase [freiz], *s.* die Phrase. — *v.a.* phrasieren, fassen, ausdrücken.

phrenology [fre'nɔlədʒi], *s.* die Phrenologie, Schädellehre.

phthisis ['θaisis], *s.* (*Med.*) die Schwindsucht.

physic ['fizik], *s.* (*obs.*) die Medizin, Arznei.

physical ['fizikəl], *adj.* körperlich (*bodily*); physikalisch (*of physics*).

physician [fi'ziʃən], *s.* der Arzt.

physics ['fiziks], *s.* die Physik.

physiognomy [fizi'ɔnəmi *or* -'ɔgnəmi], *s.* die Physiognomie, die Gesichtsbildung.

physiologist [fizi'ɔlədʒist], *s.* der Physiolog.

physiology [fizi'ɔlədʒi], *s.* die Physiologie.

piano(forte) ['pjænou('fɔ:ti), *s.* das Klavier.

pick [pik], *v.a.* pflücken (*flowers*); hacken (*hack*); — *up*, auflesen; auswählen (*select*); gewaltsam öffnen (*a lock*); anfangen (*a quarrel*). — *v.n.* *why* — *on me?* warum gerade mich auswählen? — *s.* die Picke, Spitzhacke (*axe*); die Auswahl; — *of the bunch*, (*coll.*) das Beste von allen.

picket ['pikit], *s.* die Wache; den Streikposten (*of strikers*); der Pflock (*wood*). — *v.a.* bewachen. — *v.n.* Wache stehen.

pickle [pikl], *s.* (*Cul.*) der Pökel, das Gepökelte; (*coll.*) die unangenehme Lage (*calamity*). — *v.a.* einpökeln.

pickpocket ['pikpɔkit], *s.* der Taschendieb.

picnic ['piknik], *s.* das Picknick. — *v.n.* picknicken.

pictorial [pik'tɔ:riəl], *adj.* illustriert.

picture ['piktʃə], *s.* das Bild; — *book*, das Bilderbuch; — *postcard*, die Ansichtskarte; *pretty as a* —, bildhübsch; der Film; (*pl.*) das Kino. — *v.a.* sich vorstellen.

picturesque [piktʃə'resk], *adj.* pittoresk, malerisch.

pie [pai], *s.* (*Cul.*) die Pastete (*savoury*); das Törtchen (*sweet*).

piebald ['paibɔ:ld], *adj.* scheckig. — *s.* der Schecke (*horse*).

piece [pi:s], *s.* das Stück. — *v.a.* — *together*, zusammenflicken (*mend*), zusammensetzen (*compose*).

piecemeal ['pi:smi:l], *adv.* stückweise.

pied [paid] *see* **piebald**.

pier [piə], *s.* der Hafendamm; der Pfeiler (*column*).

pierce [piəs], *v.a.* durchstechen, durchbohren.

pierglass ['piəglɑ:s], *s.* der Pfeilerspiegel.

piety ['paiəti], *s.* die Pietät, Frömmigkeit.

pig [pig], *s.* (*Zool.*) das Schwein.

pigeon ['pidʒən], *s.* (*Orn.*) die Taube.

pigeonhole ['pidʒənhoul], *s.* das Fach.

pigheaded [pig'hedid], *adj.* starrköpfig, dickköpfig.

piglet ['piglit], *s.* (*Zool.*) das Ferkel.

pigment ['pigmənt], *s.* das Pigment, der (natürliche) Farbstoff.

pigtail ['pigteil], *s.* der Haarzopf.

pike [paik], *s.* (*Zool.*) der Hecht; die Pike (*weapon*).

pile (1) [pail], *s.* der Haufen, Stoß (*paper*). — *v.a.* aufhäufen.

pile (2) [pail], *s.* (*Archit.*) der Pfahl; Pfeiler (*stone*).

pile (3) [pail], *s.* (*Text.*) der Teppichflausch (*carpet*), die Noppe (*cloth*).

piles [pailz], *s. pl.* (*Med. coll.*) die Haemorrhoiden, *pl.*

pilfer ['pilfə], *v.a.* stehlen, mausen.

pilferer ['pilfərə], *s.* der Dieb.

pilgrim ['pilgrim], *s.* der Pilger.

pill [pil], *s.* (*Med.*) die Pille.

pillage ['pilidʒ], *s.* die Plünderung. — *v.a.* ausplündern.

pillar ['pilə], *s.* der Pfeiler, die Säule; — *box*, der Briefkasten.

pillion ['piljən], *s.* der zweite Sitz, Sozius (*motorcycle*).

pillory ['piləri], *s.* der Pranger. — *v.a.* anprangern.

pillow ['pilou], *s.* das Kopfkissen.

pilot ['pailət], *s.* der Pilot; (*Naut.*) der Lotse. — *v.a.* (*Aviat.*) steuern, (*Naut.*) lotsen.

pimento [pi'mentou], *s.* (*Bot.*) der Jamaikapfeffer.

pimp [pimp], *s.* der Kuppler.

pimple [pimpl], *s.* der Pickel; (*pl.*) der Ausschlag.

pin [pin], *s.* die Stecknadel; (*Engin.*) der Bolzen, Stift; (*skittles*) der Kegel. — *v.a.* — *down*, festlegen.

pinafore ['pinəfɔ:], *s.* die Schürze, Kinderschürze.

pincers ['pinsəz], *s. pl.* die Kneifzange, Zange.

pinch [pintʃ], *v.a.* kneifen, zwicken; (*coll.*) klauen, stehlen. — *v.n.* sparen, darben. — *s.* die Prise (*tobacco*); *at a* —, wenn es sein muß.

pine (1) [pain], *s.* (*Bot.*) die Kiefer, Föhre.

pine (2) [pain], *v.n.* — *for*, schmachten (nach, *Dat.*), sich sehnen.

pineapple ['painæpl], *s.* (*Bot.*) die Ananas.

pinion ['pinjən], *s.* der Flügel (*wing*); (*Poet.*) die Schwinge; (*Mech.*) das Zahnrad; — *shaft*, die Ritzelwelle; — *spindle*, die Zahnradwelle. — *v.a.* binden, fesseln.

pink [piŋk], *adj.* rosa. — *s.* (*Bot.*) die (rosa) Nelke; (*Hunt.*) der (rote) Jagdrock; *in the* — (*of condition*), in bester Gesundheit, in bester Form.

pinnacle ['pinəkl], *s.* die Zinne, Spitze; (*fig.*) der Gipfel.

pint [paint], *s.* die Pinte (0.57 litre); (*beer*) der Schoppen.

pioneer [paiə'niə], *s.* der Pionier. — *v.a.* bahnbrechend sein, bahnen.

pious ['paiəs], *adj.* fromm.

pip

pip [pip], *s.* der Obstkern; (*Mil. coll.*) der Leutnantsstern.

pipe [paip], *s.* die Pfeife; (*Engin.*) das Rohr; die Röhre; (*Mus.*) die Pfeife. — *v.a.* pfeifen; durch Rohre leiten.

piping ['paipiŋ], *adj.* — *hot,* kochend heiß.

pipkin ['pipkin], *s.* das Töpfchen.

piquant ['pi:kənt], *adj.* pikant; scharf (*taste*).

pique [pi:k], *s.* der Groll. — *v.a.* reizen.

piracy ['pairəsi], *s.* die Seeräuberei.

pirate ['pairit], *s.* der Pirat, Seeräuber. — [pai'reit], *v.a.* (*fig.*) plagiieren, ohne Erlaubnis drucken (*books*).

pistil ['pistil], *s.* (*Bot.*) der Stempel.

pistol ['pistəl], *s.* die Pistole.

piston ['pistən], *s.* (*Mech.*) der Kolben.

pit [pit], *s.* die Grube; (*Min.*) der Schacht, das Bergwerk; (*Theat., Mus.*) der Orchesterraum; (*Theat.*) das Parterre.

pitch (1) [pitʃ], *s.* der Grad, Gipfel (*height*); (*Mus.*) der Ton, die Tonhöhe (*level*); (*Sport*) das Spielfeld. — *v.a.* werfen; feststecken; (*Mus.*) stimmen; befestigen; (*tent*) (ein Zelt) aufschlagen; — *in,* sich ins Zeug legen.

pitch (2) [pitʃ], *s.* das Pech (*tar*); — *dark,* pechschwarz.

pitchblende ['pitʃblend], *s.* die Pechblende.

pitcher ['pitʃə], *s.* der Krug.

pitchfork ['pitʃfɔ:k], *s.* die Heugabel.

piteous ['pitiəs], *adj.* erbärmlich.

pitfall ['pitfɔ:l], *s.* die Falle.

pith [piθ], *s.* das Mark; (*fig.*) der Kern, das Wesentliche; die Kraft (*strength*).

pithy ['piθi], *adj.* markig, kräftig; prägnant.

pitiable ['pitiəbl], *adj.* erbärmlich.

pitiful ['pitiful], *adj.* erbärmlich (*pitiable*); mitleidig (*sympathetic*).

pitiless ['pitilis], *adj.* erbarmungslos, grausam.

pittance ['pitəns], *s.* der Hungerlohn, das Bißchen, die Kleinigkeit.

pity ['piti], *s.* das Mitleid. — *v.a.* bemitleiden, bedauern.

pivot ['pivət], *s.* (*Mech.*) der Drehpunkt, Zapfen; (*fig.*) der Mittelpunkt, Angelpunkt. — *v.n.* zum Mittelpunkt haben, sich drehen (um).

placard ['plæka:d], *s.* das Plakat. — *v.a.* versöhnen.

placate [plə'keit], *v.a.* versöhnen.

place [pleis], *s.* der Platz, Ort, die Stelle; — *name,* der Ortsname; (*rank*) der Rang, die Rangstufe. — *v.a.* plazieren (*in a job*); legen, setzen, stellen; — *an order,* einen Auftrag geben.

placid ['plæsid], *adj.* gelassen, sanft, gutmütig.

plagiarism ['pleidʒiərizm], *s.* das Plagiat, das Plagiieren.

plague [pleig], *s.* (*Med.*) die Pest, Seuche; (*fig.*) die Plage. — *v.a.* belästigen, plagen.

plaice [pleis], *s.* (*Zool.*) die Scholle.

plain [plein], *s.* die Ebene, Fläche. — *adj.* eben, flach (*even*); schlicht,

einfach, klar; — *dealing,* ehrliche Handlungsweise; — *speaking,* offenes Sprechen, aufrichtiges Reden; (*Mus.*) — *song,* der einstimmige Chorgesang, die gregorianische Kirchenmusik.

plaintiff ['pleintif], *s.* (*Law*) der Kläger.

plaintive ['pleintiv], *adj.* klagend.

plait [plæt], *s.* der Zopf, die Flechte. — *v.a.* flechten (*hair*); falten.

plan [plæn], *s.* der Plan, Grundriß. — *v.a.* planen, entwerfen.

plane (1) [plein], *v.a.* hobeln (*wood*). — *s.* die Fläche (*surface*); die Stufe (*level*); (*coll.*) das Flugzeug (*aeroplane*).

plane (2) *see* plane-tree.

planet ['plænit], *s.* (*Astron.*) der Planet.

plane-tree ['pleintri:], *s.* (*Bot.*) die Platane.

planish ['plæniʃ], *v.a.* (*woodwork*) polieren, glätten.

plank [plæŋk], *s.* die Planke; (*Pol.*) der Programmpunkt.

plant [pla:nt], *s.* (*Bot.*) die Pflanze; (*Ind.*) die Anlage, der Betrieb. — *v.a.* anpflanzen, anlegen; — *suspicion,* Verdacht einflößen (*of, against,* gegen, *Acc.*).

plantain ['plæntein], *s.* (*Bot.*) der Wegerich; (*fruit*) der Pisang.

plantation [plæn'teiʃən], *s.* die Pflanzung, Plantage.

plaster ['pla:stə], *s.* das Pflaster (*adhesive*); (*Build.*) der Mörtel, der Mauerbewurf; — *cast,* der Gipsabdruck; — *of Paris,* der Stuck, der feine Gipsmörtel. — *v.a.* bepflastern, verputzen; (*fig.*) dick auftragen.

plastic ['plæstik], *adj.* plastisch; (*malleable*) formbar; — *surgery,* plastische Chirurgie. — *s.* der Kunststoff.

Plate, River [pleit, 'rivə], der La Plata Strom.

plate [pleit], *s.* der Teller (*dish*), die Platte, Scheibe; (*coll.*) — *glass,* das Spiegelglas; das Geschirr (*service of crockery*); *gold* —, das Goldgeschirr. — *v.a.* überziehen, versilbern, verchromen.

platform ['plætfɔ:m], *s.* (*Railw.*) der Bahnsteig; die Bühne, das Podium.

platinum ['plætinəm], *s.* das Platin.

platitude ['plætitju:d], *s.* die Plattheit, der Gemeinplatz.

platitudinous [plæti'tju:dinəs], *adj.* nichtssagend.

platoon [plə'tu:n], *s.* (*Mil.*) der Zug.

plaudit ['plɔ:dit], *s.* der Beifall.

plausible ['plɔ:zibl], *adj.* wahrscheinlich, glaubwürdig, einleuchtend.

play [plei], *s.* das Spiel (*game*); (*Theat.*) das Stück. — *v.a., v.n.* spielen.

player ['pleiə], *s.* der Spieler; (*Theat.*) der Schauspieler.

playful ['pleiful], *adj.* spielerisch, spielend.

playground ['pleigraund], *s.* der Spielplatz.

playhouse ['pleihaus], *s.* das Schauspielhaus.

playmate ['pleimeit], s. der Spielgefährte.

playwright ['pleirait], s. der Dramatiker, Schauspieldichter.

plea [pli:], s. die Bitte; das Gesuch; der Vorwand.

plead [pli:d], v.a., v.n. plädieren, sich berufen auf; vorschützen (claim).

pleasant ['plezənt], adj. angenehm, freundlich.

pleasantry ['plezəntri], s. das freundliche Wort, der Scherz (joke).

please [pli:z], v.a., v.n. gefallen; einen Gefallen tun (do a favour); — ! bitte, haben Sie die Güte!; if you —, wenn Sie nichts dagegen haben.

pleasing ['pli:ziŋ], adj. einnehmend, angenehm.

pleasure ['pleʒə], s. das Vergnügen; at your —, nach Belieben; take — in, Vergnügen finden an (Dat.).

pleat [pli:t], v.a. plissieren. — s. die Falte, das Plissee.

pledge [pledʒ], s. das Pfand, die Bürgschaft (guarantee); das Versprechen (promise). — v.a. sich verbürgen, versprechen; zutrinken (drink to).

plenary ['pli:nəri], adj. Plenar-, vollständig.

plenipotentiary [plenipo'tenʃəri], s. der Bevollmächtigte.

plenitude ['plenitju:d], s. die Fülle.

plenteous, plentiful ['plentiəs, 'plentiful], adj. reichlich, in Fülle.

plenty ['plenti], s. die Fülle.

pleurisy ['pluərəsi], s. (Med.) die Brustfellentzündung.

pliable, pliant ['plaiəbl, 'plaiənt], adj. geschmeidig, biegsam.

pliers ['plaiəz], s. pl. die Drahtzange.

plight (1) [plait], s. die Notlage.

plight (2) [plait], v.a. feierlich versprechen.

plod [plɔd], v.n. schwerfällig gehen (walk); sich plagen (work hard).

plot (1) [plɔt], s. das Stück Land, der Bauplatz.

plot (2) [plɔt], s. das Komplott, die Verschwörung; die Handlung (book, play etc.). — v.a. aushecken (ambush etc.), planen.

plough, plow [plau], s. der Pflug. — v.a. pflügen; (coll.) be —ed, durchfallen (in, in, Dat.).

ploughshare ['plauʃeə], s. die Pflugschar.

plover ['plʌvə], s. (Orn.) der Kiebitz, Regenpfeifer.

plow see under **plough**.

pluck (1) [plʌk], v.a. pflücken (flowers); rupfen (feathers); — up courage, Mut fassen.

pluck (2) [plʌk], s. (coll.) der Mut.

plucky ['plʌki], adj. mutig.

plug [plʌg], s. (Elec.) der Stecker; der Stöpsel (stopper); sparking —, (Motor.) die Zündkerze. — v.a. stöpseln, zustopfen (block); (fig.) betonen, herausstellen (repeat for advertisement).

plum [plʌm], s. (Bot.) die Pflaume; (coll.) das Beste.

plumage ['plu:midʒ], s. (Orn.) das Gefieder.

plumb [plʌm], s. das Senkblei, Lot; — -rule, die Senkwaage. — adv. senkrecht, gerade, lotrecht.

plume [plu:m], s. die (Schmuck) feder.

plump [plʌmp], adj. dick, drall.

plunder ['plʌndə], v.a., v.n. plündern. — s. die Beute, der Raub.

plunge [plʌndʒ], v.a., v.n. untertauchen, stoßen, hinabstürzen.

plunger ['plʌndʒə], s. der Taucher; (Engin.) der Tauchkolben.

pluperfect [plu:'pə:fikt], s. (Gram.) das Plusquamperfektum.

plural ['pluərəl], s. (Gram.) der Plural, die Mehrzahl.

plurality [pluə'ræliti], s. die Mehrzahl, der Plural.

plus [plʌs], prep. plus, zuzüglich.

plush [plʌʃ], s. (Text.) der Plüsch.

ply [plai], s. die Falte (fold), Lage (layer). — v.a. ausüben (trade).

plywood ['plaiwud], s. das Sperrholz, die Sperrholzplatte.

pneumonia [nju'mouniə], s. (Med.) die Lungenentzündung.

poach (1) [poutʃ], v.n. wildern; — on, übergreifen auf.

poach (2) [poutʃ], v.a. ohne Schale kochen; poached eggs, verlorene Eier, n. pl.

poacher ['poutʃə], s. der Wilderer, Wilddieb.

pocket ['pɔkit], s. die Tasche; — book, die Brieftasche; das Taschenbuch; — money, das Taschengeld.

pod [pɔd], s. (Bot.) die Schote.

poem ['pouim], s. das Gedicht.

poet ['pouit], s. der Dichter.

poetic(al) [pou'etik(l)], adj. dichterisch.

poignancy ['pɔinjənsi], s. die Schärfe.

poignant ['pɔinjənt], adj. scharf, beißend, schmerzlich.

point [pɔint], s. der Punkt (of remark, sentence); die Sache; der Zweck; die Spitze (of pencil etc.); make a —, es sich zur Aufgabe machen; in — of fact, tatsächlich; come to the —, zur Sache kommen. — v.a., v.n. spitzen, zuspitzen (pencil); — out, zeigen, (hin)deuten; — to, hinweisen auf; — the moral, die Moral erklären.

pointblank ['pɔint'blæŋk], adj., adv. schnurgerade, direkt.

pointed ['pɔintid], adj. scharf, spitzig, deutlich (remark).

pointer ['pɔintə], s. der Zeiger; (fig.) der Fingerzeig (hint).

poise [pɔiz], s. das Gleichgewicht; (fig.) angemessenes Benehmen, die Grazie. — v.a. abwägen; im Gleichgewicht halten. — v.n. schweben; —d for action, tatbereit.

poison ['pɔizn], s. das Gift. — v.a. vergiften.

poke

poke (1) [pouk], *v.a.* schüren (*fire*); stoßen; — *fun at,* sich lustig machen über. — *s.* der Stoß; — *in the ribs,* ein Rippenstoß.

poke (2) [pouk], *s.* der Sack; *a pig in a* —, die Katze im Sack.

poker (1) ['poukə], *s.* der Schürhaken, das Schüreisen.

poker (2) ['poukə], *s.* (*Cards*) das Pokerspiel.

polar ['poulə], *adj.* (*Geog.*) Polar-; (*Phys.*) polar.

polarity [po'læriti], *s.* die Polarität.

Pole [poul], *s.* der Pole.

pole (1) [poul], *s.* (*Geog.*) der Pol.

pole (2) [poul], *s.* die Stange (*rod*); der Pfahl (*upright*).

poleaxe ['poulæks], *s.* die Streitaxt.

polecat ['poulkæt], *s.* (*Zool.*) der Iltis.

polemic [pə'lemik], *s.* die Polemik, der Streit.

police [pə'li:s], *s.* die Polizei. — *v.a.* polizeilich beaufsichtigen.

policeman [pə'li:smən], *s.* der Polizist.

policy (1) ['polisi], *s.* die Politik.

policy (2) ['polisi], *s.* (*Insurance*) die Police.

Polish ['poulish], *adj.* polnisch.

polish ['polish], *v.a.* polieren. — *s.* die Politur, der Glanz.

polished ['polishd], *adj.* glatt (*smooth*); (*fig.*) wohlerzogen, fein (*manners*).

polite [pə'lait], *adj.* höflich.

politeness [pə'laitnis], *s.* die Höflichkeit.

politic ['politik], *adj.* politisch; schlau (*cunning*).

political [pə'litikəl], *adj.* politisch; staatskundig.

politician [poli'tishən], *s.* der Politiker, Staatsmann.

politics ['politiks], *s.* (*sometimes pl.*) die Politik, politische Gesinnung.

poll [poul], *s.* die Wahl (*election*). — *v.n.* abstimmen, wählen, seine Stimme abgeben.

pollard ['poləd], *s.* (*Bot.*) der gekappte Baum; (*Zool.*) das hornlose Tier.

pollen ['polən], *s.* (*Bot.*) der Blütenstaub.

pollinate ['polineit], *v.a.* (*Bot.*) bestäuben.

polling ['poulin], *s.* die Wahl, der Wahlgang (*election*); — *station,* das Wahllokal.

pollute [pə'lju:t], *v.a.* verunreinigen.

pollution [pə'lju:shən], *s.* die Verunreinigung.

poltroon [pol'tru:n], *s.* die Memme.

poly- ['poli], *pref.* viel-.

Polynesian [poli'ni:ziən], *adj.* polynesisch. — *s.* der Polynesier.

polytechnic [poli'teknik], *s.* das Technikum; polytechnische Fachschule.

pomegranate ['pom-, 'pʌmgrænit], *s.* (*Bot.*) der Granatapfel.

Pomeranian [pomə'reiniən], *adj.* pommerisch. — *s.* der Pommer; der Spitz (*dog*).

pommel [pʌml], *s.* der Sattelknopf; der Knauf (*sword*). — *v.a.* schlagen.

pomp [pomp], *s.* der Pomp, das Gepränge.

pompous ['pompəs], *adj.* hochtrabend, prahlerisch; (*manner*) schwerfällig, wichtigtuerisch.

pond [pond], *s.* der Teich.

ponder ['pondə], *v.a., v.n.* bedenken, überlegen.

ponderous ['pondərəs], *adj.* schwer, schwerfällig.

pontiff ['pontif], *s.* der Hohepriester; der Papst.

pontifical [pon'tifikəl], *adj.* bischöflich, päpstlich. — *s. pl.* die bischöfliche Amtstracht.

pontificate [pon'tifikit], *s.* das (*or* der) Pontifikat. — [-keit], *v.n.* (*coll.*) predigen.

pontoon (1) [pon'tu:n], *s.* die Schiffsbrücke, der Brückenkahn.

pontoon (2) [pon'tu:n], *s.* (*cards*) das Einundzwanzig, Vingt-et-un.

pony ['pouni], *s.* (*Zool.*) das Pony.

poodle [pu:dl], *s.* (*Zool.*) der Pudel.

pooh-pooh [pu:'pu:], *v.a.* verspotten.

pool (1) [pu:l], *s.* die Lache, der Pfuhl.

pool (2) [pu:l], *s.* (*fig.*) der gemeinsame Einsatz (*money, forces etc.*). — *v.a.* zusammenschließen.

poop [pu:p], *s.* (*Naut.*) das Heck, Hinterteil.

poor [puə], *adj.* arm, dürftig; *in* — *health,* bei schwacher Gesundheit; (*fig.*) armselig, schlecht.

pop [pop], *v.n.* knallen, explodieren. — *v.a.* (*coll.*) schnell versetzen, verpfänden.

Pope [poup], *s.* (*Eccl.*) der Papst.

poplar ['poplə], *s.* (*Bot.*) die Pappel.

poppy ['popi], *s.* (*Bot.*) der Mohn.

populace ['popjulis], *s.* der Pöbel.

popular ['popjulə], *adj.* volkstümlich, beliebt.

popularity [popju'læriti], *s.* die Beliebtheit.

populate ['popjuleit], *v.a.* bevölkern.

population [popju'leishən], *s.* die Bevölkerung.

populous ['popjuləs], *adj.* dicht bevölkert.

porcelain ['po:slin], *s.* das Porzellan, das Geschirr.

porch [po:tsh], *s.* die Eingangshalle, Vorhalle.

porcupine ['po:kjupain], *s.* (*Zool.*) das Stachelschwein.

pore (1) [po:], *s.* die Pore.

pore (2) [po:], *v.n.* sich vertiefen (*over, in*), brüten (*über*).

pork [po:k], *s.* das Schweinefleisch.

porosity [po:'rositi], *s.* die Porosität.

porous ['po:rəs], *adj.* porös.

porpoise ['po:pəs], *s.* (*Zool.*) der Tümmler, das Meerschwein.

porridge ['poridsh], *s.* (*Cul.*) der Haferbrei.

porringer ['porindshə], *s.* (*Cul.*) der Napf.

port (1) [po:t], *s.* der Hafen.

port (2) [po:t], *s.* der Portwein (*wine*).

portable ['pɔːtəbl], *adj.* tragbar; Koffer- (*radio etc.*).

portcullis [pɔːt'kʌlis], *s.* das Fallgatter.

portend [pɔː'tend], *v.a.* vorbedeuten, ahnen lassen.

portent [pɔː'tent], *s.* die Vorbedeutung.

porter ['pɔːtə], *s.* (*Railw.*) der Gepäckträger; der Pförtner, Portier (*caretaker, janitor*); das Porterbier (*beer*).

porterage ['pɔːtəridʒ], *s.* der Trägerlohn, die Zustellkosten, *f.pl.*

portfolio [pɔːt'fouliou], *s.* die Mappe; (*Pol.*) das Ressort; das Portefeuille.

portico ['pɔːtikou], *s.* (*Archit.*) die Säulenhalle.

portion ['pɔːʃən], *s.* die Portion, der Anteil. — *v.a.* aufteilen, austeilen (*share out*).

portliness ['pɔːtlinis], *s.* die Stattlichkeit (*dignity*); Behäbigkeit (*corpulence*).

portly ['pɔːtli], *adj.* stattlich (*dignified*); behäbig (*corpulent*).

portmanteau [pɔːt'mæntou], *s.* der Handkoffer.

portrait ['pɔːtrit], *s.* (*Art*) das Bildnis, Porträt.

portray [pɔː'trei], *v.a.* im Bilde darstellen, porträtieren; (*fig.*) schildern, darstellen (*describe*).

Portuguese [pɔːtju'giːz], *adj.* portugiesisch. — *s.* der Portugiese.

pose [pouz], *s.* die Haltung, Stellung (*of model etc.*). — *v.a.* in Pose stellen; aufwerfen (*question*). — *v.n.* (*as model*) stehen, sitzen; — *as*, posieren, sich ausgeben als (*pretend to be*).

poser ['pouzə], *s.* die schwierige Frage.

position [pə'ziʃən], *s.* die Lage (*situation*); die Stellung (*job*); der Stand, Rang (*rank*); (*Astron., Mil.*) die Position.

positive ['pɔzitiv], *adj.* positiv; (*fig.*) ausdrücklich, sicher (*sure*).

possess [pə'zes], *v.a.* besitzen.

possession [pə'zeʃən], *s.* der Besitz, Besitztum.

possessive [pə'zesiv], *adj.* (*Gram.*) besitzanzeigend, possessiv; (*fig.*) besitzgierig.

possibility [pɔsi'biliti], *s.* die Möglichkeit.

possible ['pɔsibl], *adj.* möglich.

post (1) [poust], *s.* der Pfosten (*pillar*).

post (2) [poust], *s.* die Post (*mail*); der Posten (*job*). — *v.a.* zur Post geben; (*coll.*) einstecken (*letter*).

postage ['poustidʒ], *s.* das Porto; — *stamp*, die Briefmarke.

postal [poustl], *adj.* Post-.

poster ['poustə], *s.* das Plakat.

posterity [pɔs'teriti], *s.* die Nachwelt.

posthumous ['pɔstjuməs], *adj.* hinterlassen, nach dem Tode, postum.

postman ['poustmən], *s.* der Briefträger.

postmark ['poustmɑːk], *s.* der Poststempel.

post-mortem [poust'mɔːtəm], *s.* — — — (*examination*), die Obduktion, Leichenschau.

post-office ['poustɔfis], *s.* das Postamt.

postpone [poust'poun], *v.a.* verschieben, aufschieben.

postscript ['poustskript], *s.* die Nachschrift.

postulate ['pɔstjuleit], *v.a.* postulieren, voraussetzen.

posture ['pɔstʃə], *s.* die Positur, Haltung (*of body*).

pot [pɔt], *s.* der Topf; die Kanne (*beer*); (*coll.*) go to —, zugrunde gehen. — *v.a.* einkochen, einmachen; (*fig.*) kürzen.

potash ʃ'pɔtæʃ], *s.* (*Chem.*) die Pottasche.

potassium [pə'tæsiəm], *s.* (*Chem.*) das Kalium.

potato [pə'teitou], *s.* (*Bot.*) die Kartoffel.

potent ['poutənt], *adj.* kräftig, stark, wirksam.

potential [pə'tenʃəl], *s.* das Potential. — *adj.* möglich, potentiell (*possible*).

potter ['pɔtə], *s.* der Töpfer.

pottery ['pɔtəri], *s.* die Töpferei; die Töpferwaren, Tonwaren, *f. pl.* (*goods*).

pouch [pautʃ], *s.* der Beutel.

poulterer ['poultərə], *s.* der Geflügelhändler.

poultice ['poultis], *s.* der Umschlag.

poultry ['poultri], *s.* das Geflügel.

pounce (1) [pauns], *s.* die Klaue. — *v.n.* — *upon*, herfallen (über, *Acc.*).

pounce (2) [pauns], *s.* das Bimssteinpulver. — *v.a.* (mit Bimsstein) abreiben.

pound (1) [paund], *s.* das Pfund; das Pfund Sterling.

pound (2) [paund], *v.a.* zerstoßen.

poundage ['paundidʒ], *s.* das Pfundgeld, die Gebühr pro Pfund.

pour [pɔː], *v.a.* gießen, schütten, einschenken. — *v.n.* strömen.

pout [paut], *v.n.* schmollen.

poverty ['pɔvəti], *s.* die Armut.

powder ['paudə], *s.* (*Mil.*) das Pulver; der Puder (*face etc.*). — *v.a.* zu Pulver machen, stoßen; (*face*) pudern.

power [pauə], *s.* die Macht, Gewalt; Kraft; Fähigkeit; — *of attorney*, die Vollmacht; (*Maths.*) die Potenz; (*Elec.*) der Strom; — *house*, — *station*, das Elektrizitätswerk; — *cut*, die Stromstörung.

powerful ['pauəful], *adj.* kräftig, mächtig, einflußreich.

powerless ['pauəlis], *adj.* kraftlos, machtlos.

pox [pɔks], *s.* (*Med.*) die Pocken, *f. pl.*; die Syphilis.

practicable ['præktikəbl], *adj.* ausführbar, tunlich.

practical ['præktikəl], *adj.* praktisch.

practice ['præktis], *s.* die Ausübung (*doing, carrying out*); die Praxis.

practise ['præktis], *v.a.* ausführen, ausüben (*a profession etc.*); üben (*rehearse*). — *v.n.* sich üben.

practised

practised ['præktisd], *adj.* geübt, geschult (in).

practitioner [præk'tiʃənə], *s.* (*Med.*) praktischer Arzt; (*Law*) Advokat.

pragmatic [præg'mætik], *adj.* pragmatisch.

prairie ['prɛəri], *s.* die Prärie.

praise [preiz], *v.a.* preisen, loben. — *s.* das Lob.

pram *see under* perambulator.

prance [prɑ:ns], *v.n.* sich bäumen; (*fig.*) sich brüsten (*brag*).

prank [præŋk], *s.* der Streich.

prate [preit], *v.n.* plappern, schwatzen.

prattle [prætl], *v.n.* plaudern, schwatzen. — *s.* das Geschwätz.

prawn [prɔ:n], *s.* (*Zool.*) die Steingarnele.

pray [prei], *v.n.* beten. — *v.a.* bitten, ersuchen (*beseech*).

prayer [prɛə], *s.* das Gebet.

preach [pri:tʃ], *v.a., v.n.* predigen.

preacher ['pri:tʃə], *s.* der Prediger.

preamble [pri:'æmbl], *s.* die Vorrede, der Einleitungsparagraph.

precarious [pri'kɛəriəs], *adj.* unsicher, prekär.

precaution [pri'kɔ:ʃən], *s.* die Vorsichtsmaßregel.

precede [pri'si:d], *v.a., v.n.* vorausgehen, den Vortritt haben.

precedence ['presidəns *or* pri'si:dəns], *s.* der Vortritt, Vorrang.

precedent ['presidənt], *s.* der Präzedenzfall.

precept ['pri:sept], *s.* die Vorschrift, Regel.

preceptor [pri'septə], *s.* der Lehrer, Lehrmeister.

precinct ['pri:siŋkt], *s.* das Gebiet, der Bezirk; (*pl.*) die Grenzen, *f. pl.*

precious ['preʃəs], *adj.* wertvoll, kostbar; — *metal,* das Edelmetall.

precipice ['presipis], *s.* der Abgrund.

precipitous [pri'sipitəs], *adj.* jäh, abschüssig.

precise [pri'sais], *adj.* genau, bestimmt.

precision [pri'siʒən], *s.* die Präzision, Genauigkeit; (*Engin.*) — *tool,* das Präzisionswerkzeug.

preclude [pri'klu:d], *v.a.* ausschließen.

precocious [pri'kouʃəs], *adj.* frühreif.

preconceive [pri:kən'si:v], *v.a.* vorher denken.

preconceived [pri:kən'si:vd], *adj.* vorgefaßt.

preconception [pri:kən'sepʃən], *s.* das Vorurteil.

precursor [pri'kə:sə], *s.* der Vorläufer.

predatory ['predətəri], *adj.* räuberisch, Raub-.

predecessor ['pri:disesə], *s.* der Vorgänger.

predestin(at)e [pri:'destin(eit)], *v.a.* vorher bestimmen; (*Theol.*) prädestinieren.

predicament [pri'dikəmənt], *s.* die Verlegenheit.

predicate ['predikit], *s.* (*Gram.*) das Prädikat. — [-keit], *v.a.* behaupten.

predict [pri'dikt], *v.a.* voraussagen, vorhersagen.

prediction [pri'dikʃən], *s.* die Vorhersage (*weather etc.*); die Weissagung (*prophecy*).

predilection [pri:di'lekʃən], *s.* die Vorliebe.

predispose [pri:dis'pouz], *v.a.* vorbereiten; empfänglich machen.

predominant [pri'dɔminənt], *adj.* vorherrschend.

predominate [pri'dɔmineit], *v.n.* vorherrschen.

pre-eminence [pri:'eminəns], *s.* der Vorrang.

prefabricate [pri:'fæbrikeit], *v.a.* vorfabrizieren, als Fertigteil herstellen, in der Fabrik herstellen.

prefabrication [pri:fæbri'keiʃən], *s.* die Vorfabrizierung.

preface ['prefis], *s.* das Vorwort.

prefatory ['prefətəri], *adj.* einleitend.

prefect ['pri:fekt], *s.* der Präfekt.

prefer [pri'fə:], *v.a.* vorziehen.

preference ['prefərəns], *s.* der Vorzug (*Comm.*) — *share,* die Vorzugsaktie.

preferment [pri'fə:mənt], *s.* die Beförderung.

prefix ['pri:fiks], *s.* die Vorsilbe. — [pri:'fiks], *v.a.* vorsetzen.

pregnancy ['pregnənsi], *s.* die Schwangerschaft.

pregnant ['pregnənt], *adj.* schwanger.

prejudge [pri:'dʒʌdʒ], *v.a.* vorher urteilen, voreilig urteilen.

prejudice ['predʒudis], *s.* das Vorurteil. — *v.a.* beeinträchtigen.

prejudicial [predʒu'diʃəl], *adj.* schädlich.

prelate ['prelit], *s.* (*Eccl.*) der Prälat.

preliminary [pri'liminəri], *adj.* vorläufig, Präliminar-. —*s.* (*pl.*) die Vorbereitungen, *f. pl.*

prelude ['prelju:d], *s.* das Vorspiel.

premature ['premətʃə], *adj.* vorschnell, übereilt, vorzeitig.

premeditate [pri:'mediteit], *v.a.* (*Law*) vorher überlegen.

Premier ['premiə], *s.* der Premierminister.

premise (1) ['premis], *s.* (*Log.*) die Prämisse; (*pl.*) das Haus, Grundstück; die Stätte, der Ort; das Lokal (*inn etc.*).

premise (2) [pri'maiz], *v.a.* vorausschicken.

premium ['pri:miəm], *s.* die Prämie.

premonition [pri:mə'niʃən], *s.* die Vorahnung.

preoccupation [pri:ɔkju'peiʃən], *s.* die Zerstreutheit.

preoccupied [pri:'ɔkjupaid], *adj.* besorgt; zerstreut (*absent-minded*).

preparation [prepə'reiʃən], *s.* die Vorbereitung; Zubereitung (*of meals*).

preparatory [pri'pærətəri], *adj.* vorbereitend; — *school,* die Vorschule.

prepare [pri'pɛə], *v.a., v.n.* vorbereiten (*for,* auf); zubereiten (*meals*).

prepay [pri:'pei], *v.a. irr.* vorausbezahlen; (*post*) frankieren.

preponderant [pri'pɔndərənt], *adj.* überwiegend.

preponderate [pri'pɔndəreit], *v.a.*, *v.n.* überwiegen.

preposition [prepə'ziʃən], *s.* (*Gram.*) die Präposition.

prepossess [pri:pə'zes], *v.a.* einnehmen, beeindrucken.

preposterous [pri'pɔstərəs], *adj.* töricht, lächerlich, unerhört.

prerogative [pri'rɔgətiv],*s.*das Vorrecht.

presage [pri'seidʒ], *v.a.* prophezeien. — ['presidʒ], *s.* die Prophezeiung.

prescient ['preʃiənt, 'pri:–], *adj.* vorahnend, vorherwissend.

prescribe [pri'skraib], *v.a.*, *v.n.* vorschreiben; (*Med.*) verschreiben, verordnen.

prescription [pri'skripʃən], *s.* die Vorschrift(*precept*); (*Med.*) das Rezept.

presence ['prezəns], *s.* die Gegenwart, Anwesenheit (*attendance*); das Äußere (*appearance*); — *of mind*, die Geistesgegenwart.

present (1) ['prezənt], *adj.* anwesend, gegenwärtig; jetzig. — *s.* (*Gram.*) das Präsens, die Gegenwart; (*time*) die Gegenwart, heutige Zeit.

present (2) [pri'zənt], *v.a.* darstellen (*on stage*); vorstellen (*introduce*); präsentieren (*arms*); schenken, geben (*gifts*). — ['prezənt], *s.* das Geschenk (*gift*).

presentation [prezən'teiʃən], *s.* die Darstellung (*stage*, *art*); die Vorstellung (*introduction*); die Überreichung (*of gift*).

presentiment [pri'zentimənt], *s.* das Vorgefühl, die Vorahnung.

presently ['prezəntli], *adv.* bald, sogleich.

preservation [prezə'veiʃən], *s.* die Erhaltung, Bewahrung.

preservative [pri'zə:vətiv], *s.* das Konservierungsmittel.

preserve [pri'zə:v], *v.a.* bewahren, erhalten; (*fruit*) einmachen. — *s.* (*Hunt.*) das Jagdgehege, Jagdrevier, (*pl.*) die Konserven, *f. pl.*

preside [pri'zaid], *v.n.* (*over*) den Vorsitz führen.

president ['prezidənt], *s.* der Präsident.

press [pres], *v.a.*, *v.n.* drücken (*push*); bügeln, plätten (*iron*); dringend bitten (*entreat*). — *s.* die Presse (*newspapers*, *printing*); der Schrank (*cupboard*); das Gedränge (*crowd*).

pressing ['presiŋ], *adj.* dringend.

pressure ['preʃə], *s.* der Druck.

prestige [pres'ti:ʒ], *s.* das Prestige, Ansehen.

presumable [pri'zju:məbl], *adj.* mutmaßlich, vermutlich.

presume [pri'zju:m], *v.a.*, *v.n.* vermuten; — *on*, sich anmaßen.

presumption [pri'zʌmpʃən], *s.* die Annahme; die Anmaßung (*arrogance*).

presumptive [pri'zʌmptiv], *adj.* mutmaßlich.

presumptuous [pri'zʌmptjuəs], *adj.* anmaßend, dreist, vermessen.

presuppose [pri:sə'pouz], *v.a.* voraussetzen.

pretence [pri'tens], *s.* der Vorwand.

pretend [pri'tend], *v.a.*, *v.n.* vortäuschen, vorgeben.

pretension [pri'tenʃən], *s.* die Anmaßung, der Anspruch (*to*, auf).

pretentious [pri'tenʃəs], *adj.* anspruchsvoll.

preterite ['pretərit], *s.* (*Gram.*) das Präteritum.

pretext ['pri:tekst], *s.* der Vorwand.

pretty ['priti], *adj.* hübsch, nett. — *adv.* (*coll.*) ziemlich.

prevail [pri'veil], *v.n.* vorherrschen, die Oberhand gewinnen.

prevalence ['prevələns], *s.* das Vorherrschen.

prevaricate [pri'værikeit], *v.n.* Ausflüchte machen.

prevent [pri'vent], *v.a.* verhindern.

prevention [pri'venʃən], *s.* die Verhinderung.

preventive [pri'ventiv],*adj.*vorbeugend.

previous ['pri:viəs], *adj.* vorhergehend.

prey [prei], *s.* die Beute, der Raub. — *v.n.* rauben, nachstellen.

price [prais], *s.* der Preis, Wert.

priceless ['praislis], *adj.* unschätzbar, unbezahlbar.

prick [prik], *s.* der Stachel, Stich (*stab*). — *v.a.* stechen (*stab*); punktieren (*puncture*).

prickle [prikl], *s.* (*Bot.*) der Stachel.

pride [praid], *s.* der Stolz. — *v.r.* — *o.s.*, sich brüsten, stolz sein (*on*, auf, *Acc.*).

priest [pri:st], *s.* (*Eccl.*) der Priester.

prig [prig], *s.* der eingebildete Tropf; Tugendheld.

priggish ['prigiʃ], *adj.* dünkelhaft, selbstgefällig.

prim [prim], *adj.* steif, spröde.

primacy ['praiməsi], *s.* der, das Primat.

primæval [prai'mi:vəl], *adj.* Ur-, anfänglich, ursprünglich.

primary ['praiməri], *adj.* erst, ursprünglich; Haupt– (*main*). — *s.* (*pl.*) (*Am.*) die Vorwahlen, *f. pl.* (*Presidential elections*).

prime [praim], *adj.* erst, wichtigst. — *s.* die Blüte, Vollendung, Vollkraft.

primer ['praimə], *s.* das Elementarbuch, die Fibel.

primitive ['primitiv], *adj.* primitiv; ursprünglich (*original*).

primness ['primnis], *s.* die Geziertheit, Steifheit.

primrose ['primrouz], *s.* (*Bot.*) die Primel.

prince [prins], *s.* der Prinz; Fürst (*rank*).

princess [prin'ses], *s.* die Prinzessin.

principal ['prinsipl], *s.* der Direktor (*business*); Rektor (*school etc.*); (*Comm.*) das Kapital; (*Mus.*) der erste Spieler. — *adj.* erst, Haupt–.

principality [prinsi'pæliti], *s.* das Fürstentum.

principle ['prinsipl], s. das Prinzip, der Grundsatz.

print [print], v.a. drucken, abdrucken. — s. (Typ., Art) der Druck; out of —, vergriffen.

printer ['printə], s. der (Buch-)drucker.

prior [praiə], adj. früher, eher; — to, vor (Dat.). — s. (Eccl.) der Prior.

priority [prai'oriti], s. die Priorität, der Vorrang.

prise [praiz], v.a. — open, gewaltsam öffnen, aufbrechen.

prism [prizm], s. das Prisma.

prison [prizn], s. das Gefängnis.

prisoner ['prizənə], s. der Gefangene, Sträfling.

pristine ['pristain], adj. ehemalig, vormalig, ursprünglich.

privacy ['praivəsi or 'privəsi], s. die Zurückgezogenheit, Stille.

private ['praivit], adj. privat, persönlich, vertraulich (confidential). — s. (Mil.) der Gemeine, Landser.

privation [prai'veiʃən], s. der Mangel, die Entbehrung (lack); die Beraubung (deprivation).

privilege ['privilidʒ], s. das Privileg, Vorrecht. — v.a. ausnehmen, privilegieren.

privy ['privi], s. der Abtritt, Abort. — adj. — to, mitwissend; Privy Council, der Staatsrat.

prize [praiz], s. der Preis, die Belohnung; — v.a. hochschätzen.

prizewinner ['praizwinə], s. der Preisträger; Nobel —, der Nobelpreisträger.

probability [probə'biliti], s. die Wahrscheinlichkeit.

probable ['probəbl], adj. wahrscheinlich.

probate ['proubeit], s. (Law) die Testamentsbestätigung.

probation [pro'beiʃən], s. die Bewährung, Bewährungsfrist (period).

probationary [pro'beiʃənəri], adj. Bewährungs-.

probe [proub], v.a. sondieren, untersuchen. — s. die Sonde, Prüfung.

probity ['proubiti], s. die Redlichkeit, Anständigkeit.

problem ['probləm], s. das Problem.

problematic [problə'mætik], adj. zweifelhaft, problematisch.

proboscis [pra'bosis], s. (Ent.) der Rüssel.

procedure [prə'si:dʒə], s. der Vorgang, das Verfahren.

proceed [prə'si:d], v.n. vorgehen, verfahren.

proceeds ['prousi:dz], s. pl. der Ertrag.

process (1) ['prouses], s. der Vorgang, Prozeß. — v.a. verarbeiten, fertigen.

process (2) [pro'ses], v.n. in einem Zuge gehen.

procession [prə'seʃən], s. der (feierliche) Umzug, die Prozession.

proclaim [prə'kleim], v.a. (Pol.) proklamieren, ausrufen.

proclamation [proklə'meiʃən], s. (Pol.) die Ausrufung, Proklamation.

proclivity [prə'kliviti], s. der Hang, die Neigung (tendency).

procrastinate [prə'kræstineit], v.a. aufschieben, vergeuden; — v.n. zögern, zaudern.

procreate ['proukrieit], v.a. zeugen, hervorbringen.

procurable [prə'kjuərəbl], adj. zu verschaffen, erhältlich.

procure [prə'kjuə], v.a. verschaffen, besorgen.

prod [prod], v.a. stoßen.

prodigal ['prodigəl], adj. verschwenderisch, vergeudend; — son, der verlorene Sohn.

prodigious [prə'didʒəs], adj. erstaunlich, ungeheuer.

prodigy ['prodidʒi], s. das Wunderkind.

produce [prə'dju:s], v.a. erzeugen, produzieren; — ['prodju:s], s. das Produkt, Erzeugnis.

producer [prə'dju:sə], s. der Erzeuger; (Theat., Cinema) der Regisseur.

product ['prodʌkt], s. das Produkt, Erzeugnis.

production [prə'dʌkʃən], s. die Produktion; die Erzeugung (industrial); das Zeigen, Vorweisen (of documents); (Theat.) die Regie.

productive [prə'dʌktiv], adj. produktiv, schöpferisch (mind); fruchtbar (soil).

profane [prə'fein], adj. profan; ruchlos.

profanity [prə'fæniti], s. die Profanierung; das Lästern.

profess [prə'fes], v.a., v.n. bekennen, erklären, sich bekennen zu.

profession [prə'feʃən], s. der (höhere) Beruf; (Eccl.) das Bekenntnis; die Beteuerung (protestation).

professional [prə'feʃənəl], adj. beruflich, berufsmäßig.

professor [prə'fesə], s. der (Universitäts) Professor.

professorship [prə'fesəʃip], s. die Professur.

proffer ['profə], v.a. anbieten (offer).

proficiency [prə'fiʃənsi], s. die Tüchtigkeit; (skill) die Beherrschung.

proficient [prə'fiʃənt], adj. bewandert, tüchtig; (in language) fließend.

profile ['proufail], s. das Profil.

profit ['profit], s. der Profit, Gewinn, Nutzen. — v.n. Nutzen ziehen. — v.a. von Nutzen sein (Dat.).

profound [prə'faund], adj. tief; gründlich (thorough).

profuse [prə'fju:s], adj. reichlich, verschwenderisch.

profusion [prə'fju:ʒən], s. der Überfluß.

progeny ['prodʒəni], s. der Nachkomme; die Nachkommenschaft.

prognosticate [prog'nostikeit], v.a. vorhersagen.

prognostication [prognosti'keiʃən], s. die Voraussage.

programme, (Am.) **program** ['prougræm], s. das Programm.

progress ['prougres], s. der Fortschritt. — [prou'gres], v.n. fortschreiten, Fortschritte machen.

progression [proˈgreʃən], s. (Maths.) die Reihe, Progression.

progressive [proˈgresiv], adj. fortschrittlich (modern); fortschreitend (continuous); progressiv.

prohibit [prouˈhibit], v.a. verbieten.

prohibition [prouiˈbiʃən], s. das Verbot.

project [prɔˈdʒekt], v.a. projizieren; entwerfen. — [ˈprɔdʒekt], s. das Projekt, der Plan.

projectile [prɔˈdʒektail], s. das Geschoß.

projection [prɔˈdʒekʃən], s. die Projektion (film); der Entwurf (plan); der Vorsprung (jutting out).

proletarian [prouliˈtɛəriən], adj. proletarisch. — s. der Prolet(arier).

prolific [prɔˈlifik], adj. fruchtbar.

prolix [ˈprouliks], adj. weitschweifig.

prologue [ˈproulɔg], s. der Prolog.

prolong [prɔˈlɔŋ], v.a. verlängern, prolongieren.

prominent [ˈprɔminənt], adj. prominent, hervorragend.

promiscuous [prɔˈmiskjuəs], adj. unterschiedslos (indiscriminate); vermischt (mixed).

promise [ˈprɔmis], v.a. versprechen. — v.n. Erwartungen erwecken. — s. das Versprechen.

promissory [ˈprɔmisəri], adj. versprechend; (Comm.) — note, der Schuldschein.

promontory [ˈprɔməntəri], s. das Vorgebirge.

promote [prɔˈmout], v.a. befördern; fördern (foster).

promotion [prɔˈmouʃən], s. die Beförderung (advancement); Förderung (fostering); (Am.) die Reklame (publicity).

prompt [prɔmpt], adj. prompt, pünktlich. — v.a. (Theat.) soufflieren; treiben (inspire).

prompter [ˈprɔmptə], s. (Theat.) der Souffleur.

promptitude [ˈprɔmptitjuːd], s. die Promptheit, Pünktlichkeit.

promulgate [ˈprɔməlgeit], v.a. bekanntmachen, verbreiten.

prone [proun], adj. geneigt, neigend.

prong [prɔŋ], s. die Zinke, Gabel.

pronominal [proˈnɔminəl], adj. (Gram.) pronominal.

pronoun [ˈprounaun], s. das Fürwort, Pronomen.

pronounce [prɔˈnauns], v.a., v.n. aussprechen (words); feierlich erklären (proclaim).

pronunciation [prənʌnsiˈeiʃən], s. die Aussprache.

proof [pruːf], s. der Beweis, die Probe; (Typ.) der Korrekturbogen. — v.a. (Engin., Chem.) imprägnieren.

prop [prɔp], s. die Stütze, der Stützpfahl. — v.a. stützen.

propaganda [prɔpəˈgændə], s. die Propaganda, Reklame.

propagate [ˈprɔpəgeit], v.a. propagieren; (Bot.) fortpflanzen.

propel [prɔˈpel], v.a. forttreiben, vorwärtstreiben.

propeller [prɔˈpelə], s. der Propeller, die Schraube.

propensity [prɔˈpensiti], s. die Neigung, der Hang.

proper [ˈprɔpə], adj. schicklich (manners); eigentümlich, eigen (peculiar).

property [ˈprɔpəti], s. das Eigentum (possession); die Eigenschaft (quality).

prophecy [ˈprɔfisi], s. die Prophezeiung, Weissagung.

prophesy [ˈprɔfisai], v.a. prophezeien.

propitiate [prɔˈpiʃieit], v.a. versöhnen.

propitiation [prəpiʃiˈeiʃən], s. die Versöhnung.

propitious [prɔˈpiʃəs], adj. gnädig, günstig, geneigt.

proportion [prɔˈpɔːʃən], s. das Verhältnis; die Proportion; der Anteil (portion); das Ebenmaß (in art).

proportionate [prɔˈpɔːʃənit], adj. im Verhältnis, verhältnismäßig, proportioniert.

proposal [prɔˈpouzəl], s. der Vorschlag, Antrag.

propose [prɔˈpouz], v.a. antragen, beantragen, vorschlagen. — v.n. — to a lady, einen Heiratsantrag machen.

proposition [prɔpəˈziʃən], s. der Vorschlag, Antrag; die Idee.

propound [prɔˈpaund], v.a. vorlegen, vorbringen (a theory etc.).

proprietor [prɔˈpraiətə], s. der Eigentümer.

propriety [prɔˈpraiəti], s. die Schicklichkeit.

propulsion [prɔˈpʌlʃən], s. der Antrieb.

prorogue [prɔˈroug], v.a. vertagen.

prosaic [prɔˈzeiik], adj. prosaisch, nüchtern.

proscribe [proˈskraib], v.a. verbieten, ächten.

proscription [proˈskripʃən], s. die Verbannung, das Verbot.

prose [prouz], s. die Prosa.

prosecute [ˈprɔsikjuːt], v.a. verfolgen; (Law) gerichtlich verfolgen, anklagen.

prosecutor [ˈprɔsikjuːtə], s. (public) der Staatsanwalt; der Kläger.

proselyte [ˈprɔsəlait], s. der Neubekehrte, Proselyt.

prospect [ˈprɔspekt], s. die Aussicht; (pl.) die Aussichten, Chancen, f.pl. — [prɔsˈpekt], v.n. suchen (for, nach, Dat.).

prospectus [prɔˈspektəs], s. der Prospekt.

prosper [ˈprɔspə], v.n. gedeihen, blühen. — v.a. segnen.

prosperity [prɔsˈperiti], s. der Wohlstand; der Reichtum; das Gedeihen (thriving).

prosperous [ˈprɔspərəs], adj. glücklich, wohlhabend.

prostitute [ˈprɔstitjuːt], s. die Prostituierte, Dirne. — v.a. erniedrigen.

prostrate [ˈprɔstreit], adj. hingestreckt, niedergeworfen, fußfällig. — [prɔsˈtreit], v.a. niederwerfen.

prosy

prosy ['prouzi], *adj.* prosaisch, weitschweifig, langweilig.

protect [prə'tekt], *v.a.* beschützen.

protection [prə'tekʃən], *s.* der Schutz; die Protektion (*favour*).

protective [prə'tektiv], *adj.* Schutz-, schützend.

protector [prə'tektə], *s.* der Beschützer; (*Engin.*) der Schutz.

protest [prə'test], *v.a., v.n.* protestieren, einwenden. — ['proutest], *s.* der Protest, Einspruch.

Protestant ['prɔtistənt], *adj.* protestantisch. — *s.* der Protestant.

protestation [prɔtes'teiʃən], *s.* die Beteuerung, Verwahrung.

protocol ['proutəkɔl], *s.* das Protokoll.

prototype ['proutətaip], *s.* das Urbild, Modell, der Prototyp.

protract [prə'trækt], *v.a.* in die Länge ziehen; hinausziehen.

protractor [prə'træktə], *s.* der Winkelmesser, Transporteur, die Schmiege.

protrude [prə'tru:d], *v.n.* herausragen, hervorstehen, vordringen.

protuberance [prə'tju:bərəns], *s.* der Höcker, der Auswuchs, die Protuberanz.

proud [praud], *adj.* stolz (*of*, auf, *Acc.*).

prove [pru:v], *v.a.* beweisen. — *v.n.* sich erweisen (*turn out*).

provender ['prɔvində], *s.* das Viehfutter.

proverb ['prɔvə:b], *s.* das Sprichwort.

proverbial [prə'və:biəl], *adj.* sprichwörtlich.

provide [prə'vaid], *v.a., v.n.* vorsehen, versorgen, verschaffen.

provided [prə'vaidid], *conj.* vorausgesetzt.

providence ['prɔvidəns], *s.* die Vorsehung.

provident ['prɔvidənt], *adj.* vorsorglich.

providential [prɔvi'denʃəl], *adj.* von der Vorsehung bestimmt.

province ['prɔvins], *s.* die Provinz, das Gebiet (*also fig.*).

provincial [prə'vinʃəl], *adj.* ländlich, Provinz-; provinziell.

provision [prə'viʒən], *s.* die Versorgung (*supply*); der Vorrat (*stock*); (*pl.*) die Lebensmittel (*victuals*).

provisional [prə'viʒənəl], *adj.* vorläufig.

proviso [prə'vaizou], *s.* der Vorbehalt.

provocation [prɔvə'keiʃən], *s.* die Herausforderung.

provoke [prə'vouk], *v.a.* herausfordern, provozieren.

prow [prau], *s.* (*Naut.*) der Bug.

prowess ['praues], *s.* die Stärke (*physical*); die körperliche Tüchtigkeit; Tapferkeit.

prowl [praul], *v.n.* herumstreichen.

proximity [prɔk'simiti], *s.* die Nähe.

proxy ['prɔksi], *s.* der Stellvertreter.

prudence ['pru:dəns], *s.* die Klugheit, Vorsicht.

prudent ['pru:dənt], *adj.* klug, vorsichtig.

prudery ['pru:dəri], *s.* die Sprödigkeit.

prudish ['pru:diʃ], *adj.* prüde, spröde, zimperlich.

prune (1) [pru:n], *s.* (*Cul.*) die Backpflaume.

prune (2) [pru:n], *v.a.* beschneiden, stutzen.

Prussian ['prʌʃən], *adj.* preußisch; — *blue*, das Berlinerblau. — *s.* der Preuße.

prussic ['prʌsik], *adj.* blausauer; — *acid*, die Blausäure.

pry [prai], *v.n.* spähen, ausforschen.

psalm [sɑ:m], *s.* der Psalm.

psychology [sai'kɔlədʒi], *s.* die Psychologie.

pub [pʌb], *s.* das Wirtshaus, die Kneipe.

puberty ['pju:bəti], *s.* die Pubertät, Mannbarkeit.

public [prə'blik], *adj.* öffentlich. — *s.* das Publikum; die Öffentlichkeit.

publican ['pʌblikən], *s.* der Gastwirt.

publication [pʌbli'keiʃən], *s.* die Veröffentlichung, Herausgabe.

publicity [pʌb'lisiti], *s.* die Werbung, die Reklame; — *manager*, der Reklamechef, Werbeleiter.

publicize ['pʌblisaiz], *v.a.* weithin bekannt machen, publizieren.

publish ['pʌbliʃ], *v.a.* veröffentlichen; verlegen (*books*); —*ing house*, der Verlag.

publisher ['pʌbliʃə], *s.* der Verleger.

pucker ['pʌkə], *v.a.* falten; runzeln (*wrinkle*). — *s.* die Falte.

pudding ['pudiŋ], *s.* der Pudding.

puddle [pʌdl], *s.* die Pfütze. — *v.a.* puddeln (*iron*).

puerile ['pjuərail], *adj.* kindisch, knabenhaft.

puff [pʌf], *v.a., v.n.* puffen, paffen, blasen; —*ed-up*, aufgebläht, stolz. — *s.* der Windstoß; — *pastry*, der Blätterteig.

pug [pʌg], *s.* (*Zool.*) der Mops.

pugnacious [pʌg'neiʃəs], *adj.* kampfsüchtig, kampflustig.

puisne ['pju:ni], *adj.* (*Law*) jünger, Unter-.

puissant ['pwi:sənt], *adj.* mächtig, stark.

puke [pju:k], *v.n.* sich erbrechen.

pull [pul], *v.a., v.n.* ziehen, reißen; zerren. — *s.* der Zug, Ruck.

pullet ['pulit], *s.* (*Orn.*) das Hühnchen.

pulley ['puli], *s.* der Flaschenzug.

pulmonary, pulmonic ['pʌlmənəri, pʌl'mɔnik], *adj.* Lungen-.

pulp [pʌlp], *s.* der Brei; das Fleisch (*of fruit*); das Mark (*marrow*); die Pulpa (*tooth*). — *v.a.* zerstampfen, zu Brei stampfen.

pulpit ['pulpit], *s.* (*Eccl.*) die Kanzel.

pulsate [pʌl'seit], *v.n.* pulsieren, schlagen.

pulse (1) [pʌls], *s.* der Puls.

pulse (2) [pʌls], *s.* (*Bot.*) die Hülsenfrüchte, *f. pl.*

pulverize ['pʌlvəraiz], *v.a.* zu Pulver stoßen, zerstoßen.

466

quadrille

pumice ['pʌmis], *s.* der Bimsstein.
pump (1) [pʌmp], *s.* die Pumpe. — *v.a.,
v.n.* pumpen; ausfragen (*question*).
pump (2) [pʌmp], *s.* der Tanzschuh
(*dancing shoe*).
pumpkin ['pʌmpkin], *s.* (*Bot.*) der
Kürbis.
pun [pʌn], *s.* das Wortspiel. — *v.n.*
Wortspiele machen.
Punch [pʌntʃ], das Kasperle; — *and
Judy*, Hanswurst und seine Frau.
punch (1) [pʌntʃ], *v.a.* schlagen,
boxen (*box*). — *s.* der Schlag (*hit*);
der Faustschlag (*boxing*).
punch (2) [pʌntʃ], *v.a.* lochen (*card*). —
s. der Pfriem (*tool*).
punch (3) [pʌntʃ], *s.* der Punsch (*drink*).
punchy ['pʌntʃi], *adj.* kurz, dick,
untersetzt.
punctilious [pʌŋk'tiliəs], *adj.* sorgfältig, spitzfindig.
punctual ['pʌŋktjuəl], *adj.* pünktlich.
punctuate ['pʌŋktjueit], *v.a.* (*Gram.*)
interpunktieren; (*fig.*) betonen.
punctuation [pʌŋktju'eiʃən], *s.* (*Gram.*)
die Interpunktion.
puncture ['pʌŋktʃə], *s.* (*Motor.*) der
Reifendefekt, die Panne; (*Med.*) die
Punktur, der Einstich. — *v.a.* (*Med.*)
punktieren.
pungent ['pʌndʒənt], *adj.* scharf,
stechend.
punish ['pʌniʃ], *v.a.* bestrafen (*s.o.*);
strafen.
punishable ['pʌniʃəbl], *adj.* strafbar.
punishment ['pʌniʃmənt], *s.* die Strafe,
Bestrafung.
punt [pʌnt], *s.* das kleine Boot, Flachboot.
puny ['pjuni], *adj.* schwach, winzig.
pup [pʌp], *s.* der junge Hund; *be
sold a* —, einen schlechten Kauf
machen. — *v.n.* Junge werfen.
pupil (1) ['pjuːpil], *s.* der Schüler.
pupil (2) ['pjuːpil], *s.* die Pupille (*eye*).
pupil(l)age ['pjuːpilidʒ], *s.* die Minder-
jährigkeit (*of minor*).
puppet ['pʌpit], *s.* die Puppe, Marionette; der Strohmann (*human tool*).
puppy ['pʌpi] *see* **pup.**
purblind ['pəːblaind], *adj.* halbblind.
purchase ['pəːtʃis], *s.* der Kauf, Einkauf. — *v.a.* kaufen.
pure ['pjuə], *adj.* pur, rein.
purge [pəːdʒ], *v.a.* reinigen. — *s.* die
Reinigung; (*Pol.*) die Säuberung.
purify ['pjuərifai], *v.a.* läutern, reinigen.
purl (1) [pəːl], *s.* die Borte; (*knitting*)
die Häkelkante.
purl (2) [pəːl], *v.n.* sich drehen,
wirbeln; (*sl.*) umkippen.
purl (3) [pəːl], *s.* das Murmeln, Rieseln
(*of brook*). — *v.n.* murmeln, rieseln.
purloin [pəːˈlɔin], *v.a.* stehlen.
purple [pəːpl], *adj.* purpurn; — *patch*,
die Glanzstelle. — *s.* der Purpur.
purport ['pəːpɔːt], *v.a.* bedeuten, Sinn
haben. — ['pəːpət], *s.* der Sinn, die
Bedeutung.
purpose ['pəːpəs], *s.* die Absicht, der
Zweck.

purposeful ['pəːpəsful], *adj.* zweck-
bewußt, energisch, zielbewußt.
purr [pəː], *v.n.* schnurren (*of cat*).
purse [pəːs], *s.* die Börse, Geldtasche;
das Portemonnaie.
pursuance [pəˈsjuəns], *s.* (*Law*) die
Verfolgung, Ausführung.
pursuant [pəˈsjuənt], *adj.* (*Law*)
zufolge, gemäß (*to, Dat.*).
pursue [pəˈsjuː], *v.a.* verfolgen.
pursuit [pəˈsjuːt], *s.* die Verfolgung;
(*pl.*) die Geschäfte, *n. pl.*; Beschäftigung.
purvey [pəˈvei], *v.a.* versorgen, liefern.
purview ['pəːvjuː], *s.* der Spielraum;
das Blickfeld.
push [puʃ], *v.a.* stoßen, drücken,
schieben, drängen; *be* —ed *for*, in der
Klemme sein. — *s.* der Stoß, Schub,
das Drängen; *at a* —, wenn absolut
nötig.
pusillanimous [pjuːsiˈlæniməs], *adj.*
kleinmütig.
puss, pussy [pus, 'pusi], *s.* (*coll.*) die
Katze, das Kätzchen, Miezchen.
put [put], *v.a. irr.* setzen (*set*), legen (*lay*),
stellen (*stand*). — *off*, aufschieben,
aus der Fassung bringen (*deflect*); —
on, anziehen, auflegen; — *it on thickly*,
es dick auftragen. — *v.n.* (*Naut.*) —
in, anlegen.
putrefy ['pjuːtrifai], *v.a., v.n.* faul
werden (*rot*), verwesen.
putrid ['pjuːtrid], *adj.* faul (*rotten*).
puttee ['pʌtiː], *s.* (*Mil.*) die Wickel-
gamasche.
putty ['pʌti], *s.* der Kitt.
puzzle [pʌzl], *s.* das Rätsel. — *v.a.* zu
denken geben (*Dat.*).
pygmy ['pigmi], *s.* der Pygmäe.
pyjamas, (*Am.*) **pajamas** [piˈdʒɑːməz,
pə-], *s. pl.* der Schlafanzug.
pyramid ['pirəmid], *s.* die Pyramide.
pyre [paiə], *s.* der Scheiterhaufen.
pyrotechnics [paiərəˈtekniks], *s. pl.*
das Feuerwerk, die Feuerwerkskunst.
python ['paiθən], *s.* (*Zool.*) die Riesenschlange.

Q

Q [kjuː]. das Q.
qua [kwei], *conj.* als.
quack [kwæk], *v.n.* quaken; (*coll.*)
quacksalbern. — *s.* der Quacksalber.
quadrangle ['kwɔdræŋgl], *s.* (*abbr.*
quad [kwɔd]), das Viereck; der Hof
(*in college etc*).
quadrant ['kwɔdrənt], *s.* der Quadrant,
Viertelkreis; (*Engin.*) der Winkelmesser.
quadrille [kwəˈdril], *s.* die Quadrille,
der Kontertanz.

467

quadruped

quadruped ['kwɔdruped], *s.* (*Zool.*) das vierfüßige Tier.

quadruple ['kwɔdrupl], *adj.* vierfach.

quaff [kwæf], *v.a.* schlucken. — *v.n.* zechen (*drink heavily*).

quagmire ['kwægmaiə], *s.* der Sumpf.

quail (1) [kweil], *s.* (*Orn.*) die Wachtel.

quail (2) [kweil], *v.n.* verzagen.

quaint [kweint], *adj.* seltsam, wunderlich, eigenartig.

quake [kweik], *v.n.* erzittern, beben.

Quaker ['kweikə], *s.* der Quäker.

qualification [kwɔlifi'keiʃən], *s.* die Befähigung, Qualifikation (*ability*); die Einschränkung (*proviso*).

qualify ['kwɔlifai], *v.a.* befähigen (*make able*); beschränken, mäßigen, qualifizieren (*modify*). — *v.n.* sich qualifizieren, das Studium abschließen.

qualitative ['kwɔlitətiv], *adj.* qualitätsmäßig, Wert-, qualitativ.

quality ['kwɔliti], *s.* die Qualität (*high class*); der Wert (*standard*).

qualm [kwɑ:m], *s.* der Skrupel.

quantitative ['kwɔntitətiv], *adj.* quantitativ.

quantity ['kwɔntiti], *s.* die Quantität, Menge.

quantum ['kwɔntəm], *s.* die Menge; das Quantum; — *theory*, die Quantentheorie.

quarantine ['kwɔrənti:n], *s.* die Quarantäne.

quarrel ['kwɔrəl], *s.* der Streit, Zwist. — *v.n.* streiten, zanken.

quarry (1) ['kwɔri], *s.* der Steinbruch.

quarry (2) ['kwɔri], *s.* die Beute (*prey*).

quart [kwɔ:t], *s.* das Viertelmaß (*1.15 litre*).

quarter ['kwɔ:tə], *s.* das Viertel (jahr); (*Arith.*) das Viertel (*also of town*); (*pl.*) das Quartier.

quartermaster ['kwɔ:təmɑ:stə], *s.* (*Mil.*) der Feldzeugmeister.

quartet(te) [kwɔ:'tet], *s.* das Quartett.

quarto ['kwɔ:tou], *s.* das Quartformat.

quartz [kwɔ:ts], *s.* der Quarz.

quash [kwɔʃ], *v.a.* unterdrücken (*suppress*); (*Law*) annullieren.

quaver ['kweivə], *s.* (*Mus.*) die Achtelnote; der Triller (*trill*). — *v.n.* tremolieren, trillern.

quay [ki:], *s.* der Kai, Hafendamm.

queen [kwi:n], *s.* die Königin.

queer [kwiə], *adj.* seltsam, sonderlich.

quell [kwel], *v.a.* unterdrücken.

quench [kwentʃ], *v.a.* löschen; stillen (*thirst*).

querulous ['kweruləs], *adj.* mürrisch, jämmerlich; zänkisch.

query ['kwiəri], *s.* die Frage. — *v.a.* in Frage stellen.

quest [kwest], *s.* das Suchen, Streben; die Suche.

question ['kwestʃən], *s.* die Frage; — *mark*, das Fragezeichen. — *v.a.* fragen, in Frage stellen; ausfragen (*s.o.*).

questionable ['kwestʃənəbl], *adj.* zweifelhaft, fraglich, bedenklich.

queue [kju:], *s.* die Schlange, das Anstellen. — *v.n.* Schlange stehen.

quibble [kwibl], *s.* das Wortspiel, die Ausflucht. — *v.n.* um Worte streiten.

quick [kwik], *adj.* schnell (*fast*); lebendig (*live*).

quicken ['kwikən], *v.a.* beleben, anfeuern.

quicklime ['kwiklaim], *s.* der ungelöschte Kalk.

quicksand ['kwiksænd], *s.* der Flugsand.

quicksilver ['kwiksilvə], *s.* (*Chem.*) das Quecksilber.

quid (1) [kwid], *s.* (*sl.*) das Pfund Sterling.

quid (2) [kwid], *s.* (*Lat.*) etwas; — *pro quo*, Gleiches um Gleichem.

quiescence [kwi'esəns], *s.* die Ruhe.

quiet ['kwaiət], *adj.* ruhig.

quietism ['kwaiətizm], *s.* der Quietismus.

quietness ['kwaiətnis], *s.* die Ruhe, Stille.

quill [kwil], *s.* der Federkiel, die Feder. — *v.a.* falten, fälteln.

quilt [kwilt], *s.* die Steppdecke.

quince [kwins], *s.* (*Bot.*) die Quitte.

quinine [kwi'ni:n], *s.* (*Med.*) das Chinin.

quinquennial [kwin'kweniəl], *adj.* fünfjährig, fünfjährlich, alle fünf Jahre.

quinsy ['kwinzi], *s.* (*Med.*) die Bräune.

quint [kwint], *s.* (*Mus.*) die Quinte.

quintessence [kwin'tesəns], *s.* die Quintessenz, der Kern, der Inbegriff.

quintuple ['kwintjupl], *adj.* fünffach.

quip [kwip], *s.* die Stichelei; die witzige Bemerkung.

quire [kwaiə], *s.* das Buch Papier.

quirk [kwə:k], *s.* die (unerwartete) Wendung; Spitzfindigkeit.

quit [kwit], *v.a., v.n.* verlassen; weggehen; (*Am.*) aufhören. — *adj.* (*pl.*) (**quits**) quitt, bezahlt.

quite [kwait], *adv.* ganz, völlig.

quiver (1) ['kwivə], *s.* der Köcher.

quiver (2) ['kwivə], *v.n.* erzittern, schauern.

quiz [kwiz], *s.* das Fragespiel, Quizprogramm (*Radio etc.*).

quoit [kɔit], *s.* die Wurfscheibe.

quorum ['kwɔ:rəm], *s.* die beschlußfähige Anzahl.

quota ['kwoutə], *s.* die Quote.

quotation [kwo'teiʃən], *s.* das Zitat; (*Comm.*) der Kostenanschlag, die Notierung.

quote [kwout], *v.a.* zitieren; (*Comm.*) einen Preis zitieren, notieren.

R

R [ɑ:(r)]. das R.

rabbet ['ræbit], *s.* die Fuge, Nute. — *v.a.* einfugen.

rabbi ['ræbai], *s.* (*Rel.*) der Rabbiner.
rabbit ['ræbit], *s.* (*Zool.*) das Kaninchen.
rabble [ræbl], *s.* der Pöbel.
rabid ['ræbid], *adj.* wütend, rasend.
race (1) [reis], *s.* die Rasse; das Geschlecht (*stock*).
race (2) [reis], *s.* das Rennen (*horses etc.*); der Wettlauf (*run*); — *course*, die Rennbahn. — *v.a.*, *v.n.* um die Wette laufen.
racial ['reiʃəl], *adj.* rassisch.
raciness ['reisinis], *s.* das Rassige, die Urwüchsigkeit.
rack [ræk], *s.* die Folterbank; das Reck (*gymnasium*); (*Railw.*) das Gepäcknetz. — *v.a.* recken, strecken; — *o.'s brains*, sich den Kopf zerbrechen.
racket (1), **racquet** ['rækit], *s.* der Tennisschläger.
racket (2) ['rækit], *s.* der Lärm (*noise, din*).
racket (3) ['rækit], *s.* (*coll.*) der Schwindel.
racketeer [ræki'tiə], *s.* der Schwindler.
racy ['reisi], *adj.* stark; pikant.
radar ['reidɑː], *s.* das Radar.
radiance ['reidiəns], *s.* der Glanz, das Strahlen.
radiant ['reidiənt], *adj.* strahlend.
radiate ['reidieit], *v.a.*, *v.n.* strahlen, ausstrahlen.
radiator ['reidieitə], *s.* der Heizapparat, Heizkörper; (*Motor.*) der Kühler.
radical ['rædikəl], *adj.* (*Pol.*) radikal; gründlich (*thorough*). — *s.* (*Pol.*) der Radikale; (*Phonet.*) der Grundlaut, Wurzellaut.
radio ['reidiou], *s.* das Radio, der Rundfunk.
radioactive [reidiou'æktiv], *adj.* radioaktiv.
radish ['rædiʃ], *s.* (*Bot.*) der Rettich.
radius ['reidiəs], *s.* der Radius, Halbmesser; (*Phys.*, *Maths.*) der Strahl (*line*).
raffle [ræfl], *s.* die Auslosung. — *v.a.* auslosen, ausspielen.
raft [rɑːft], *s.* das Floß.
rafter ['rɑːftə], *s.* der Dachsparren.
rag (1) [ræg], *s.* der Lumpen.
rag (2) [ræg], *v.a.* necken, zum Besten haben (*tease*).
ragamuffin ['rægəmʌfin], *s.* der Lumpenkerl.
rage [reidʒ], *s.* die Wut, Raserei; die Manie, Mode (*fashion*). — *v.n.* wüten, rasen.
ragged ['rægid], *adj.* zerlumpt; zackig, rauh (*rough*).
ragout [ra'guː], *s.* (*Cul.*) das Ragout.
raid [reid], *s.* der Streifzug, die Razzia; der Angriff. — *v.a.* überfallen.
rail (1) [reil], *s.* (*Railw.*) die Schiene; *by* —, mit der Eisenbahn.
rail (2) [reil], *v.n.* schmähen; spotten (*Genit.*).
railing ['reiliŋ], *s.* das Geländer, Gitter.
raillery ['reiləri], *s.* die Spöttelei, das Schmähen.

railway, (*Am.*) **railroad** ['reilwei, 'reilroud], *s.* die Eisenbahn.
raiment ['reimənt], *s.* (*Poet.*) die Kleidung.
rain [rein], *s.* der Regen. — *v.n.* regnen.
rainbow ['reinbou], *s.* der Regenbogen.
raincoat ['reinkout], *s.* der Regenmantel.
raise [reiz], *v.a.* heben (lift); steigern (*prices*); aufbringen (*army, money*); züchten (*breed*); aufziehen (*children*). — *s.* (*Am.*) die Steigerung, Erhöhung (*salary*).
raisin ['reizin], *s.* (*Bot.*) die Rosine.
rake (1) [reik], *s.* der Rechen (*tool*). — *v.a.* zusammenrechen, harken; bestreichen (*fire at*).
rake (2) [reik], *s.* der Schlemmer (*roué*).
rakish ['reikiʃ], *adj.* liederlich.
rally ['ræli], *v.a.* sammeln, versammeln. — *v.n.* sich versammeln, sich scharen. — *s.* die Massenversammlung, Kundgebung; das Treffen.
ram [ræm], *s.* der Widder; (*Mil.*) die Ramme. — *v.a.* rammen.
ramble [ræmbl], *v.n.* (im Grünen) wandern; herumschweifen; einen Ausflug machen. — *s.* der Ausflug.
rambler ['ræmblə], *s.* der Wanderer (hiker); (*Bot.*) die Heckenrose.
ramification [ræmifi'keiʃən], *s.* die Verzweigung, Verästelung (*also fig.*); (*pl.*) Zweige, *m. pl.* (*also fig.*).
ramp [ræmp], *v.n.* sich ranken (*of plants*). — *s.* die Rampe.
rampant ['ræmpənt], *adj.* zügellos, grassierend (*wild*); (*Her.*) sich bäumend.
rampart ['ræmpɑːt], *s.* der Wall.
ramshackle ['ræmʃækl], *adj.* wackelig, baufällig.
rancid ['rænsid], *adj.* ranzig.
rancour ['ræŋkə], *s.* der Groll, die Erbitterung.
random ['rændəm], *s. at* —, aufs Geratewohl. — *adj.* zufällig, Zufalls-.
range [reindʒ], *s.* die Reihe (*row, series*); (*Geog.*) die Bergkette; der Küchenherd (*stove*); (*Mil.*) die Schießstätte (*shooting ground*); die Schußweite, Reichweite (*distance*). — *v.n.* sich reihen; sich erstrecken (*stretch*); — *v.a.* rangieren, anordnen, durchstreifen.
rangefinder ['reindʒfaində], *s.* (*Phot.*) der Entfernungsmesser.
ranger ['reindʒə], *s.* der Förster, Forstgehilfe; (*Mil.*) der leichte Reiter.
rank (1) [ræŋk], *s.* die Klasse; der Rang (*order*); — *and file*, die Mannschaft (*of members*); die Mitgliedschaft, Masse. — *v.n.* sich reihen; gelten.
rank (2) [ræŋk], *adj.* übermäßig, üppig, allzu stark; ranzig (*of fat etc.*).
rankle [ræŋkl], *v.n.* nagen.
ransack ['rænsæk], *v.a.* plündern.
ransom ['rænsəm], *s.* das Lösegeld; *hold to* —, (gegen Lösegeld) gefangen halten. — *v.a.* loskaufen.

rant

rant [rænt], v.n. wüten; großtun; groß-sprechen.

rap [ræp], v.a., v.n. schlagen, klopfen.

rapacious [rə'peiʃəs], adj. raubgierig.

rape (1) [reip], v.a. vergewaltigen. — s. die Vergewaltigung.

rape (2) [reip], s. (Bot.) der Raps.

rapid ['ræpid], adj. rasch, schnell, reißend (river). — s. (pl.) die Strom-schnelle.

rapier ['reipiə], s. der Degen; (fencing) das Rapier.

rapine ['ræpain], s. (Poet.) der Raub.

rapt [ræpt], adj. entzückt; versunken.

rapture ['ræptʃə], s. das Entzücken.

rare (1) [rɛə], adj. selten.

rare (2) [rɛə], adj. (meat) rar.

rarity ['rɛəriti], s. die Seltenheit.

rascal ['rɑ:skəl], s. der Schurke.

rash (1) [ræʃ], adj. unbesonnen.

rash (2) [ræʃ], s. der Ausschlag (skin).

rasher ['ræʃə], s. die Speckschnitte.

rasp [rɑ:sp], s. die Raspel, Feile. — v.a., v.n. raspeln; heiser sein (speech).

raspberry ['rɑ:zbəri], s. (Bot.) die Himbeere.

rat [ræt], s. (Zool.) die Ratte; (fig.) der Verräter.

ratable ['reitəbl], adj. steuerpflichtig.

rate (1) [reit], s. das Mass; der Tarif; die Geschwindigkeit (speed); Gemeinde-abgabe (tax); das Verhältnis (proportion). — v.a. schätzen (estimate); (Am.) einschätzen, halten für.

rate (2) [reit], v.a. schelten (berate).

rather ['rɑ:ðə], adv. vielmehr, eher, lieber (in comparisons); — good, ziemlich gut.

ratification [rætifi'keiʃən], s. die Bestätigung; (Pol.) die Ratifizierung.

ratify ['rætifai], v.a. bestätigen; (Pol.) ratifizieren.

ratio ['reiʃiou], s. das Verhältnis.

ration ['ræʃən], s. die Ration.

rational ['ræʃənəl], adj. Vernunfts-, rationell, vernunftgemäß.

rattle [rætl], s. das Geklapper (noise); die Klapper (toy etc.); death —, das Todesröcheln. — v.a. klappern, Lärm machen; (fig.) aus der Fassung bringen; — off, herunterleiern. — v.n. rasseln, klappern.

raucous ['rɔ:kəs], adj. heiser, rauh.

ravage ['rævidʒ], v.a. verheeren. — s. (pl.) die Verheerung, Verwüstung.

rave [reiv], v.n. vernarrt sein (about, in); schwärmen (für).

raven [reivn], s. (Orn.) der Rabe.

ravenous ['rævənəs], adj. gefräßig, gierig.

ravine [rə'vi:n], s. die Schlucht.

ravish ['ræviʃ], v.a. schänden, entehren; (delight) entzücken.

raw [rɔ:], adj. rauh (rough); roh (meat); jung, grün (novice); a — deal, die unfaire Behandlung.

ray (1) [rei], s. (Phys.) der Strahl. — v.n. strahlen.

ray (2) [rei], s. (Zool.) der Rochen.

raze [reiz], v.a. radieren (erase); zer-stören (destroy).

razor ['reizə], s. der Rasierapparat; — strop, der Streichriemen.

re* [ri:], pref. wieder —, noch einmal, zurück-.

* In the following pages, only those compounds are listed in which the meaning is different from the root word or where no simple stem exists.

reach [ri:tʃ], v.a. reichen, erlangen (attain); reichen (hand); erreichen. — s. der Bereich, (fig.) die Weite.

react [ri:'ækt], v.n. reagieren (to, auf, Acc.).

read (1) [ri:d], v.a., v.n. irr. lesen; anzeigen (meter etc.); — for a degree, studieren.

read (2) [red], adj. well—, belesen.

readable ['ri:dəbl], adj. gut zu lesen, lesenswert; leserlich (legible).

reader ['ri:də], s. der Leser; (Univ.) der außerordentliche Professor; (fig.) das Lesebuch.

readiness ['redinis], s. die Bereitschaft, Bereitwilligkeit.

ready ['redi], adj. bereit, fertig; prompt; — money, das Bargeld.

real [riəl], adj. wirklich, wahr, tatsächlich; echt; — estate, der Grundbesitz.

realistic [riə'listik], adj. realistisch.

reality [ri:'æliti], s. die Wirklichkeit.

realize ['riəlaiz], v.a. (understand) begreifen; (sell) veräußern; verwirklichen.

realm [relm], s. das Reich.

reap [ri:p], v.a. ernten.

rear (1) [riə], adj. hinter, nach-. — s. der Hintergrund; (Mil.) die Nachhut.

rear (2) [riə], v.a. aufziehen, erziehen (bring up). — v.n. sich bäumen.

reason ['ri:zən], s. die Ursache, der Grund (cause); die Vernunft (reason-ableness). — v.n. argumentieren, debattieren.

reasonable ['ri:zənəbl], adj. vernünftig; verständig.

reasonably ['ri:zənəbli], adv. ziemlich, verhältnismäßig.

rebate ['ri:beit], s. der Rabatt.

rebel [rebl], s. der Rebell. — [ri'bel], v.n. sich empören.

rebound [ri:'baund], v.n. zurückprallen. —['ri:baund], s. der Rückprall.

rebuff [ri'bʌf], s. die Abweisung. — v.a. abweisen, zurückweisen.

rebuke [ri'bju:k], v.a. zurechtweisen, tadeln. — s. der Tadel, die Kritik (an).

rebut [ri'bʌt], v.a. zurückweisen.

rebuttal [ri'bʌtl], s. die Widerlegung.

recalcitrant [ri'kælsitrənt], adj. widerspenstig, störrisch.

recall [ri'kɔ:l], v.a. zurückrufen; (remember) sich erinnern.

recant [ri'kænt], v.a., v.n. widerrufen.

recapitulate [ri:kə'pitjuleit], v.a. rekapitulieren, wiederholen.

recast [ri:'kɑ:st], v.a. neu fassen, umarbeiten.

recede [ri'si:d], v.n. zurückgehen; heruntergehen (prices etc.).

refine

receipt [ri'si:t], *s.* die Empfangsbestätigung, Quittung. — *v.a.* quittieren.

receive [ri'si:v], *v.a.* erhalten, empfangen; (*Law*) Diebesgut annehmen.

receiver [ri'si:və], *s.* der Empfänger; (*Law*) der Hehler; (*Telephone*) der Hörer; (*Rad.*) der Apparat.

recent ['ri:sənt], *adj.* jüngst, neuest.

recently ['ri:səntli], *adv.* vor kurzem.

reception [ri'sepʃən], *s.* der Empfang.

receptive [ri'septiv], *adj.* empfänglich.

recess [ri'ses], *s.* (*Parl.*) die Ferien, *pl.*; die Pause; die Nische (*nook*).

recession [ri'seʃən], *s.* (*Econ.*) die Rezession, die Baisse.

recipe ['resipi], *s.* (*Cul.*) das Rezept.

recipient [ri'sipiənt], *s.* der Empfänger (*of donation etc.*).

reciprocal [ri'siprəkəl], *adj.* gegenseitig, wechselseitig.

reciprocate [ri'siprəkeit], *v.a., v.n.* erwidern, vergelten.

recital [ri'saitl], *s.* der Vortrag; (*Mus.*) das Solokonze, Kammerkonzert.

recite [ri'sait], *v.a.* vortragen; (*story*) erzählen, aufsagen.

reckless ['reklis], *adj.* leichtsinnig.

reckon ['rekən], *v.n.* rechnen (*on*, mit, *Dat.*); dafür halten, denken (*think*).

reclamation [reklə'meiʃən], *s.* (*Agr.*) die Urbarmachung; (*fig.*) die Beschwerde, Reklamation.

recline [ri'klain], *v.n.* sich zurücklehnen.

recluse [ri'klu:s], *s.* der Einsiedler.

recognition [rekəg'niʃən], *s.* die Anerkennung.

recognize ['rekəgnaiz], *v.a.* anerkennen (als) (*acknowledge*); erkennen (*know again*).

recoil [ri'kɔil], *v.n.* zurückprallen, zurückfahren.

recollect [rekə'lekt], *v.a.* sich erinnern (an, *Acc.*).

recollection [rekə'lekʃən], *s.* die Erinnerung, das Gedächtnis.

recommend [rekə'mend], *v.a.* empfehlen.

recompense ['rekəmpens], *v.a.* vergelten, entschädigen, belohnen.

reconcile ['rekənsail], *v.a.* versöhnen.

reconciliation [rekənsili'eiʃən], *s.* die Versöhnung.

recondite ['rekəndait], *adj.* dunkel, verborgen, wenig bekannt.

reconnoitre [rekə'nɔitə], *v.a.* auskundschaften.

record [ri'kɔ:d], *v.a.* notieren, eintragen (*enter*), festhalten; aufnehmen (*tape etc.*). — ['rekɔ:d], *s.* die Aufzeichnung (*in writing*); die Schallplatte (*gramophone*); (*Sports*) der Rekord.

recorder [ri'kɔ:də], *s.* der Protokollführer; (*Law*) der Richter, Syndikus, Registrator; (*Mus.*) die Blockflöte.

recount [ri'kaunt], *v.a.* erzählen.

recourse [ri'kɔ:s], *s.* die Zuflucht.

recover [ri'kʌvə], *v.a.* wiedererlangen. — *v.n.* sich erholen.

recovery [ri'kʌvəri], *s.* die Wiedererlangung (*regaining*); (*Med.*) die Genesung, Erholung.

recreation [rekri'eiʃən], *s.* die Erholung.

recrimination [rekrimi'neiʃən], *s.* die Gegenklage.

recruit [ri'kru:t], *v.a.* rekrutieren, anwerben. — *s.* der Rekrut.

rectangle ['rektæŋgl], *s.* das Rechteck.

rectify ['rektifai], *v.a.* richtigstellen; (*Elec.*) gleichrichten, umformen.

rectilinear [rekti'liniə], *adj.* geradlinig.

rectitude ['rektitju:d], *s.* die Aufrichtigkeit.

rector ['rektə], *s.* (*Eccl.*) der Pfarrer; der Rektor, Vorstand (*institution*).

recuperate [ri'kju:pəreit], *v.n.* sich erholen.

recur [ri'kə:], *v.n.* sich wieder ereignen, sich wiederholen.

recurrence [ri'kʌrəns], *s.* die Wiederholung.

red [red], *adj.* rot; — *hot*, glühend heiß.

redbreast ['redbrest], *s.* (*Orn.*) das Rotkehlchen.

redeem [ri'di:m], *v.a.* erlösen.

redemption [ri'dempʃən], *s.* die Erlösung.

redolent ['redolənt], *adj.* duftend.

redound [ri'daund], *v.n.* gereichen, sich erweisen.

redress [ri'dres], *v.a.* abhelfen (*Dat.*); wieder herstellen. — *s.* die Abhilfe.

reduce [ri'dju:s], *v.a.* vermindern, herabsetzen; (*fig.*) degradieren; — *v.n.* (*weight*) abnehmen.

reduction [ri'dʌkʃən], *s.* die Herabsetzung (*price etc.*); die Verminderung (*decrease*); (*Chem.*) die Reduktion.

redundant [ri'dʌndənt], *adj.* überflüssig.

reduplicate [ri:'dju:plikeit], *v.a.* verdoppeln.

reed [ri:d], *s.* (*Bot.*) das Schilfrohr; (*Mus.*) die Rohrpfeife.

reef [ri:f], *s.* das Riff, Felsenriff; (*Naut.*) das Reff.

reek [ri:k], *v.n.* rauchen, dampfen, riechen. — *s.* der Rauch, Dampf, der Gestank.

reel [ri:l], *s.* die Spule, Rolle, Haspel. — *v.a.* — *off*, abrollen; (*fig.*) mechanisch hersagen. — *v.n.* taumeln.

refectory [ri'fektəri], *s.* der Speisesaal; das Refektorium (*in monastery etc.*).

refer [ri'fə:], *v.n.* — *to s.th.*, weiterleiten; überweisen; — *to*, sich beziehen (auf, *Acc.*).

referee [refə'ri:], *s.* der Referent; (*Sport*) der Schiedsrichter.

reference ['refərəns], *s.* — *with* — *to*, in or mit Bezug auf; die Referenz, Empfehlung; Verweisung (*to*, auf); — *library*, die Nachschlagebibliothek; — *index*, das (Nachschlags)verzeichnis.

refine [ri'fain], *v.a.* (*Chem.*) raffinieren; (*manners*) verfeinern; (*products*) läutern, veredeln.

471

reflect

reflect [ri'flekt], *v.a.* widerspiegeln (*mirror*); ein Licht werfen (auf, *Acc.*). — *v.n.* — on, überlegen (*think over*).

reflection, reflexion [ri'flekʃən], *s.* die Überlegung, das Nachdenken; die Spiegelung, Reflexion.

reform [ri:'fɔ:m], *s.* die Reform, Verbesserung. — *v.a.* reformieren; ['ri:'fɔ:m] (sich) neu bilden. — *v.n.* sich bessern.

refractory [ri'fræktəri], *adj.* widerspenstig.

refrain (1) [ri'frein], *v.n.* — from, sich enthalten (*Genit.*); absehen von (*Dat.*).

refrain (2) [ri'frein], *s.* (*Mus., Poet.*) der Kehrreim.

refresh [ri'freʃ], *v.a.* erfrischen.

refrigerator [ri'fridʒəreitə], *s.* der Kühlschrank.

refuge ['refju:dʒ], *s.* die Zuflucht.

refugee [refju'dʒi:], *s.* der Flüchtling. — *adj.* Flüchtlings-.

refund [ri:'fʌnd], *v.a.* ersetzen, zurückzahlen. — [ri:'fʌnd], *s.* die Rückvergütung.

refusal [ri'fju:zəl], *s.* die Verweigerung.

refuse [ri'fju:z], *v.a.* verweigern, abschlagen. — *v.n.* — to, sich weigern. — ['refju:s], *s.* der Müll.

refute [ri'fju:t], *v.a.* widerlegen.

regal ['ri:gəl], *adj.* königlich.

regale [ri'geil], *v.a.* bewirten.

regalia [ri'geiliə], *s. pl.* die Kronjuwelen, *n. pl.*; (*fig.*) die Amtstracht, der Amtsschmuck.

regard [ri'ga:d], *v.a.* ansehen (*as*, als); beachten (*heed*); *as* —*s*, was ... betrifft. — *s.* die Hochachtung, Achtung (*esteem*); (*pl.*) die Grüsse, *m. pl.*

regarding [ri'ga:diŋ], *prep.* bezüglich, mit Bezug auf.

regardless [ri'ga:dlis], *adj.* rücksichtslos, ohne Rücksicht auf.

regency ['ri:dʒənsi], *s.* die Regentschaft.

regent ['ri:dʒənt], *s.* der Regent.

regiment ['redʒimənt], *s.* (*Mil.*) das Regiment. — [-ment], *v.a.* (*fig.*) regimentieren.

region ['ri:dʒən], *s.* die Gegend.

regional ['ri:dʒənəl], *adj.* örtlich, lokal, Bezirks-.

register ['redʒistə], *s.* das Register, die Liste. — *v.n.* sich eintragen.

registrar ['redʒistra:], *s.* der Registrator; der Standesbeamte (*births etc.*); der Kanzleidirektor (*institution*).

registry ['redʒistri], *s.* die Registratur.

regret [ri'gret], *v.a.* bereuen, bedauern. — *s.* die Reue; das Bedauern (*in formal apology*); *with* —, mit Bedauern.

regular ['regjulə], *adj.* regelmäßig; (*Am.*) anständig. — *s.* (*Mil.*) der Berufssoldat.

regulate ['regjuleit], *v.a.* regulieren, regeln.

regulation [regju'leiʃən], *s.* die Regelung; die Anordnung (*order*).

rehabilitate [ri:hə'biliteit], *v.a.* rehabilitieren.

rehearsal [ri'hə:sl], *s.* (*Theat., Mus.*) die Probe.

rehearse [ri'hə:s], *v.a.* proben, wiederholen.

reign [rein], *v.n.* herrschen, regieren. — *s.* die Herrschaft, Regierung.

rein [rein], *s.* der Zügel, der Zaum.

reindeer ['reindiə], *s.* (*Zool.*) das Ren, Rentier.

reinforce [ri:in'fɔ:s], *v.a.* betonen, verstärken.

reinforced [ri:in'fɔ:sd], *adj.* verstärkt; — *concrete*, der Eisenbeton.

reject [ri'dʒekt], *v.a.* ausschlagen, verwerfen.

rejection [ri'dʒekʃən], *s.* die Ablehnung, Verwerfung.

rejoice [ri'dʒɔis], *v.n.* sich freuen.

rejoin [ri:'dʒɔin], *v.a.* wiedervereinigen. — [ri'dʒɔin], *v.n.* erwidern.

rejoinder [ri'dʒɔində], *s.* die Erwiderung.

relapse [ri'læps], *s.* der Rückfall. — *v.n.* fallen, zurückfallen.

relation [ri'leiʃən], *s.* die Beziehung (*connexion*); der Verwandte (*relative*); (*pl.*) die Verwandtschaft (*family*).

relative ['relətiv], *adj.* relativ; verhältnismäßig (*in proportion*). — *s.* der, die Verwandte.

relax [ri'læks], *v.n.* sich ausruhen; nachlassen. — *v.a.* entspannen.

relay [ri'lei], *v.a.* (*Rad.*) übertragen. — ['ri:lei], *s.* — *race*, der Staffellauf.

release [ri'li:s], *v.a.* freilassen, freisetzen (*prisoner*); freigeben (*news*). — *s.* die Freigabe (*news etc.*); die Freisetzung (*liberation*).

relegate ['religeit], *v.a.* verweisen, zurückweisen.

relent [ri'lent], *v.n.* nachgeben.

relentless [ri'lentlis], *adj.* unerbittlich, unnachgiebig.

relevance ['reləvəns], *s.* die Wichtigkeit.

relevant ['reləvənt], *adj.* wichtig, sachdienlich.

reliable [ri'laiəbl], *adj.* verläßlich, zuverlässig.

reliance [ri'laiəns], *s.* das Vertrauen.

relic ['relik], *s.* das Überbleibsel; das Andenken; (*Eccl.*) die Reliquie.

relief (1) [ri'li:f], *s.* die Erleichterung, Linderung, (*easement*); die Ablösung (*guard etc.*); die Aushilfe (*extra staff etc.*).

relief (2) [ri'li:f], *s.* (*Art*) das Relief.

relieve [ri'li:v], *v.a.* erleichtern; lindern (*pain*); ablösen (*from duty*).

religion [ri'lidʒən], *s.* die Religion.

religious [ri'lidʒəs], *adj.* religiös, gläubig, fromm.

relinquish [ri'liŋkwiʃ], *v.a.* verlassen, aufgeben.

relish ['reliʃ], *v.a.* Geschmack finden an. — *v.n.* schmecken. — *s.* der Geschmack, die Würze.

reluctance [ri'lʌktəns], *s.* der Widerwille, das Zögern.

reluctant [ri'lʌktənt], *adj.* widerwillig, widerstrebend.

rely [ri'lai], *v.n.* sich verlassen (on, auf); vertrauen (auf).

remain [ri'mein], *v.n.* bleiben, zurückbleiben, übrigbleiben.

remainder [ri'meində], *s.* der Rest.

remand [ri'mɑ:nd], *v.a.* — in custody, in die Untersuchungshaft zurückschicken. — *s.* — home, die Besserungsanstalt.

remark [ri'mɑ:k], *s.* die Bemerkung. — *v.a.* bemerken.

remarkable [ri'mɑ:kəbl], *adj.* bemerkenswert, außerordentlich.

remedial [rə'mi:diəl], *adj.* Heil-, abhelfend.

remedy ['remədi], *s.* das Heilmittel, Hilfsmittel. — *v.a.* abhelfen (Dat.).

remember [ri'membə], *v.a.* sich erinnern an; — s.o. to s.o. else, jemanden von jemandem grüßen lassen.

remembrance [ri'membrəns], *s.* die Erinnerung.

remind [ri'maind], *v.a.* erinnern (of, an), mahnen.

reminiscence [remi'nisəns], *s.* die Erinnerung.

remiss [ri'mis], *adj.* nachlässig.

remission [ri'miʃən], *s.* der Nachlaß; (Rel.) die Vergebung (of sins).

remit [ri'mit], *v.a.* (Comm.) überweisen, einsenden; erlassen (forgive).

remittance [ri'mitəns], *s.* (Comm.) die Rimesse, die Überweisung.

remnant ['remnənt], *s.* der Überrest.

remonstrate ['remənstreit], *v.n.* Vorstellungen machen.

remorse [ri'mɔ:s], *s.* die Reue.

remote [ri'mout], *adj.* fern, entlegen.

removal [ri'mu:vəl], *s.* das Wegschaffen (taking away); die Übersiedlung, der Umzug.

remove [ri'mu:v], *v.a.* entfernen. — *v.n.* umziehen. — *s.* (Sch.) die Versetzungsklasse; der Verwandtschaftsgrad (relationship).

removed [ri'mu:vd], *adj.* entfernt; cousin once —, der Vetter ersten Grades.

remuneration [rimju:nə'reiʃən], *s.* die Besoldung, Entlöhnung.

rend [rend], *v.a.* reißen, zerreißen.

render ['rendə], *v.a.* leisten (service); übersetzen (translate); wiedergeben; (Comm.) — account, Rechnung vorlegen.

rendering ['rendəriŋ], *s.* die Wiedergabe, der Vortrag (of song etc.); (Comm.) die Vorlage; die Übersetzung (translation).

renegade ['renigeid], *s.* der Abtrünnige.

renewal [ri'nju:əl], *s.* die Erneuerung; die Verlängerung (extension).

rennet ['renit], *s.* das Lab.

renounce [ri'nauns], *v.a.* entsagen (Dat.), verzichten auf (Acc.).

renown [ri'naun], *s.* der Ruhm.

rent (1) [rent], *v.a.* mieten, pachten. — *s.* die Miete, Pacht (of land, farm).

rent (2) [rent], *s.* der Riß (tear).

rental [rentl], *s.* die Miete.

renunciation [rinʌnsi'eiʃən], *s.* die Entsagung, der Verzicht.

repair [ri'pɛə], *v.a.* ausbessern, reparieren. — *s.* die Reparatur; beyond —, nicht reparierbar.

reparations [repə'reiʃənz], *s. pl.* (Pol.) die Reparationen, Wiedergutmachungskosten, f. pl.

repartee [repɑ:'ti:], *s.* die treffende Antwort.

repast [ri'pɑ:st], *s.* die Mahlzeit.

repeal [ri'pi:l], *v.a.* (Parl.) aufheben, widerrufen. — *s.* die Aufhebung.

repeat [ri'pi:t], *v.a.* wiederholen.

repent [ri'pent], *v.a.* bereuen.

repercussion [ri:pə'kʌʃən], *s.* der Rückstoß, die Rückwirkung.

repertory ['repətəri], *s.* (Theat. etc.) das Repertoire, der Spielplan.

repetition [repi'tiʃən], *s.* die Wiederholung.

replace [ri:'pleis], *v.a.* ersetzen.

replete [ri'pli:t], *adj.* voll, angefüllt.

reply [ri'plai], *v.n.* antworten, erwidern. — *s.* die Antwort.

report [ri'pɔ:t], *v.a., v.n.* berichten. — *s.* der Bericht; (Sch.) das Zeugnis; der Knall (of explosion).

repose [ri'pouz], *v.n.* ruhen. — *v.a.* setzen (in, auf). — *s.* die Ruhe, der Friede.

repository [ri'pozitəri], *s.* die Niederlage, Aufbewahrungsstätte, Fundstätte.

reprehensible [repri'hensibl], *adj.* tadelnswert.

represent [repri'zent], *v.a.* repräsentieren, vertreten.

representative [repri'zentətiv], *adj.* repräsentativ, typisch. — *s.* der Stellvertreter; (Pol.) der Repräsentant.

repress [ri'pres], *v.a.* unterdrücken.

reprieve [ri'pri:v], *v.a.* begnadigen. — *s.* die Gnadenfrist.

reprimand [repri'mɑ:nd], *v.a.* verweisen, tadeln. — *s.* der Tadel.

reprint [ri:'print], *v.a.* neu drucken. — ['ri:print], *s.* der Neudruck.

reprisal [ri'praizəl], *s.* die Vergeltungsmaßregel; (pl.) die Repressalien, f. pl.

reproach [ri'proutʃ], *v.a.* vorwerfen (Dat.), tadeln. — *s.* der Vorwurf, Tadel.

reprobate ['reprəbeit], *adj.* ruchlos, verworfen.

reproduce [ri:prə'dju:s], *v.a.* reproduzieren, erzeugen.

reproof [ri'pru:f], *s.* der Vorwurf, Tadel.

reprove [ri'pru:v], *v.a.* tadeln, rügen (a person), mißbilligen (a practice).

republic

republic [riˈpʌblik], s. die Republik.
repudiate [riˈpju:dieit], v.a. zurückweisen, verwerfen.
repugnant [riˈpʌgnənt], adj. widerwärtig, ekelhaft.
repulse [riˈpʌls], v.a. (Mil.) zurückschlagen; abweisen (s.o.). — s. (Mil.) das Zurückschlagen; (fig.) die Zurückweisung.
repulsive [riˈpʌlsiv], adj. widerwärtig.
reputation [repjuˈteiʃən], s. der (gute) Ruf.
request [riˈkwest], v.a. ersuchen. — s. das Ersuchen, Ansuchen, die Bitte.
requiem [ˈrekwiəm], s. (Eccl.) das Requiem, die Totenmesse.
require [riˈkwaiə], v.a. fordern, verlangen, brauchen.
requirement [riˈkwaiəmənt], s. die Anforderung, das Erfordernis.
requisite [ˈrekwizit], adj. erforderlich.
requisition [rekwiˈziʃən], s. (Mil.) die Requisition; die Forderung.
requite [riˈkwait], v.a. vergelten.
rescind [riˈsind], v.a. für ungültig erklären, aufheben.
rescue [ˈreskju:], v.a. retten. — s. die Rettung.
research [riˈsəːtʃ], v.n. forschen, Forschung treiben. — s. die Forschung.
resemble [riˈzembl], v.a. ähnlich sein (Dat.), gleichen (Dat.).
resent [riˈzent], v.a. übelnehmen.
resentful [riˈzentful], adj. nachträgerisch; empfindlich (over–sensitive).
resentment [riˈzentmənt], s. die Empfindlichkeit; der Groll (spite).
reservation [rezəˈveiʃən], s. die Reservierung (of seat); der Vorbehalt (doubt).
reserve [riˈzəːv], v.a. reservieren, belegen (seat); (fig.) vorbehalten (o.'s position). — s. die Reserve, die Verschlossenheit (shyness); die Einschränkung (limitation); die Reserven, f. pl. (money).
reside [riˈzaid], v.n. wohnen.
resident [ˈrezidənt], adj. wohnhaft. — s. der Ansässige.
residual [riˈzidjuəl], adj. übrig bleibend.
residue [ˈrezidju:], s. der Rückstand, Rest.
resign [riˈzain], v.a. abtreten, aufgeben; (ein Amt) niederlegen. — v.n. abdanken. — v.r. — o.s. to, sich in etwas fügen, zurücktreten.
resignation [rezigˈneiʃən], s. die Resignation, der Rücktritt (from office); die Fügung, Resignation (attitude).
resin [ˈrezin], s. das Harz.
resist [riˈzist], v.a., v.n. widerstehen, Widerstand leisten (Dat.).
resistance [riˈzistəns], s. der Widerstand.
resolute [ˈrezəlju:t], adj. entschlossen.
resolution [rezəˈlju:ʃən], s. die Entschlossenheit (determination); die Entscheidung (decision); der Vorsatz, Entschluß (vow).

resolve [riˈzɔlv], v.a. auflösen (solve); beschließen (conclude). — v.n. entscheiden (decide). — s. der Beschluß, die Entscheidung.
resonance [ˈrezənəns], s. die Resonanz.
resort [riˈzɔːt], v.n. — to, seine Zuflucht nehmen (zu). — s. seaside —, das Seebad, health —, der Kurort (spa).
resound [riˈzaund], v.n. widerhallen.
resource [riˈsɔːs], s. das Hilfsmittel; (pl.) die Mittel, n. pl.
respect [riˈspekt], v.a. respektieren, achten; berücksichtigen (have regard to). — s. der Respekt, die Achtung; with — to, mit Bezug auf; in — of, bezüglich (Genit.).
respectability [rispektəˈbiliti], s. die Anständigkeit; Achtbarkeit.
respective [risˈpektiv], adj. respektiv.
respectively [risˈpektivli], adv. beziehungsweise.
respiration [respiˈreiʃən], s. die Atmung.
respiratory [risˈpaiərətri or ˈrespireitəri], adj. Atmungs-.
respire [riˈspaiə], v.n. atmen.
respite [ˈrespit], s. die Frist, der Aufschub.
resplendent [riˈsplendənt], adj. glänzend.
respond [riˈspɔnd], v.n. antworten, eingehen (to, auf).
respondent [riˈspɔndənt], s. (Law) der Beklagte.
response [riˈspɔns], s. die Antwort, Aufnahme, Reaktion; (fig.) der Widerhall.
responsibility [risponsiˈbiliti], s. die Verantwortung, Verantwortlichkeit.
responsible [riˈsponsibl], adj. verantwortlich.
responsive [riˈsponsiv], adj. empfänglich, zugänglich.
rest (1) [rest], v.n. ruhen, rasten. — s. die Ruhe, Rast; (Mus.) die Pause.
rest (2) [rest], v.n. bleiben (stay); — assured, sei (seien Sie) versichert. — s. der Rest; die übrigen, pl.
restaurant [ˈrestərɔ], s. das Restaurant.
restful [ˈrestful], adj. ruhig.
restitution [restiˈtju:ʃən], s. die Wiedergutmachung.
restive [ˈrestiv], adj. unruhig, ruhelos.
restless [ˈrestlis], adj. rastlos, unruhig.
restoration [restɔːˈreiʃən], s. die Wiederherstellung; (Hist.) die Restauration.
restore [riˈstɔː], v.a. wiederherstellen.
restrain [riˈstrein], v.a. zurückhalten, einschränken.
restraint [riˈstreint], s. die Zurückhaltung.
restrict [riˈstrikt], v.a. beschränken.
restriction [riˈstrikʃən], s. die Einschränkung.
restrictive [riˈstriktiv], adj. einschränkend.

result [ri'zʌlt], *v.n.* folgen, sich ergeben; (*come about*) erfolgen. — *s.* das Ergebnis, Resultat; (*consequence*) die Folge.

resume [ri'zju:m], *v.a.* wiederaufnehmen; (*narrative*) fortsetzen. — *v.n.* fortfahren.

résumé ['rezjumei], *s.* das Resümee, die Zusammenfassung.

resumption [ri'zʌmpʃən], *s.* die Wiederaufnahme.

resurrection [rezə'rekʃən], *s.* (*Rel.*) die Auferstehung.

resuscitate [ri'sʌsiteit], *v.a.* wiederbeleben.

retail ['ri:teil], *s.* der Kleinhandel, Einzelhandel. — [ri'teil], *v.a.* im Detail handeln, verkaufen.

retain [ri'tein], *v.a.* behalten.

retainer [ri'teinə], *s.* der Diener; Gefolgsmann; der Vorschuß (*fee*).

retake [ri:'teik], *v.a. irr.* (*Mil.*) wieder erobern; (*Phot., Film*) noch einmal aufnehmen. — *s.* (*Am.*) die Neuaufnahme (*Phot., Film*).

retaliate [ri'tælieit], *v.n.* sich rächen, vergelten.

retard [ri'ta:d], *v.a.* verzögern, verlangsamen.

retch [retʃ], *v.n.* sich erbrechen.

retentive [ri'tentiv], *adj.* behaltend, gut (*memory*).

reticent ['retisənt], *adj.* schweigsam, einsilbig.

retina ['retinə], *s.* (*Anat.*) die Netzhaut.

retinue ['retinju:], *s.* das Gefolge.

retire [ri'taiə], *v.a.*, *v.n.* sich zurückziehen (*withdraw*); in den Ruhestand treten (*from work*). — *v.a.* pensionieren.

retirement [ri'taiəmənt], *s.* die Pension, der Ruhestand; die Zurückgezogenheit (*seclusion*).

retort [ri'tɔ:t], *s.* (*Chem.*) die Retorte; die scharfe Antwort (*debate*). — *v.n.* scharf erwidern.

retouch [ri:'tʌtʃ], *v.a.* (*Phot.*) retouchieren.

retrace [ri:'treis], *v.a.* zurückverfolgen.

retreat [ri'tri:t], *v.n.* sich zurückziehen. — *s.* der Rückzug (*Mil.*); Zufluchtsort.

retrench [ri'trentʃ], *v.a.* einschränken (*restrict*); verkürzen (*shorten*). — *v.n.* sich einschränken.

retribution [retri'bju:ʃən], *s.* die Vergeltung.

retrieve [ri'tri:v], *v.a.* wieder bekommen, wieder gewinnen.

retriever [ri'tri:və], *s.* (*Zool.*) der Apportierhund, Stöberhund.

retrograde ['retrogreid], *adj.* rückgängig, rückwärts.

retrospect ['retrospekt], *s.* der Rückblick.

retrospective [retro'spektiv], *adj.* rückblickend.

return [ri'tə:n], *v.a.* zurückgeben; erwidern (*reciprocate*); abordnen, entsenden (*to Parl.*); (*figures*) einsenden. — *v.n.* zurückkehren, zurückkommen.

— *s.* die Rückkehr; (*Fin.*) der Gewinn; (*Parl.*) die Entsendung, Mandatierung; (*pl.*) (*figures*) die Einsendung; *by* — *of post*, umgehend, postwendend; — *ticket*, die Rückfahrkarte.

reunion [ri:'ju:niən], *s.* die Wiedervereinigung.

reveal [ri'vi:l], *v.a.* enthüllen, offenbaren (*show*); verraten (*betray*).

reveille [ri'væli], *s.* (*Mil.*) das Wecken, Wecksignal.

revel [revl], *v.n.* schwelgen.

revelation [revə'leiʃən], *s.* die Offenbarung.

revelry ['revəlri], *s.* die Schwelgerei.

revenge [ri'vendʒ], *s.* die Rache, Revanche. — *v.r.* (*also be revenged*) sich rächen (*on, an, Dat.*).

revenue ['revənju:], *s.* das Einkommen; *Inland* —, die Steuereinnahmen.

reverberate [ri'və:bəreit], *v.n.* widerhallen.

revere [ri'viə], *v.a.* verehren.

reverence ['revərəns], *s.* die Ehrerbietung, der Respekt; *show* —, Ehrerbietung zollen.

Reverend ['revərənd], (*abbr.* **Rev.**) (*Eccl.*) *The* —, Seine Ehrwürden; *The Very* —, Seine Hochwürden.

reverent, reverential ['revərənt, revə-'renʃəl], *adj.* ehrerbietig.

reverie ['revəri], *s.* die Träumerei.

reversal [ri'və:səl], *s.* die Umkehrung, Umstoßung.

reverse [ri'və:s], *v.a.*, *v.n.* umkehren, umdrehen. — *s.* das Gegenteil (*contrary*); die Kehrseite (*of coin*).

revert [ri'və:t], *v.a.*, *v.n.* umkehren, zurückkehren.

review [ri'vju:], *v.a.* durchsehen, prüfen (*examine*); rezensieren (*book etc.*). — *s.* die Revision; (*Mil.*) die Parade, Truppenmusterung; die Rezension, Besprechung (*book etc.*).

revile [ri'vail], *v.a.*, *v.n.* schmähen.

revise [ri'vaiz], *v.a.* korrigieren (*correct*); wiederholen (*recapitulate*); umarbeiten (*modify*).

revision [ri'viʒən], *s.* die Revision; Korrektur; Umarbeitung; Wiederholung (*recapitulation*).

revolt [ri'voult], *v.n.* sich empören, revoltieren. — *v.a.* empören. — *s.* die Empörung.

revolting [ri'voultiŋ], *adj.* ekelhaft, empörend.

revolution [revə'lju:ʃən], *s.* (*Pol.*) die Revolution; (*Motor.*) die Umdrehung.

revolve [ri'vɔlv], *v.n.* rotieren, sich drehen.

revolver [ri'vɔlvə], *s.* der Revolver.

revue [ri'vju:], *s.* (*Theat.*) die Revue.

revulsion [ri'vʌlʃən], *s.* der Ekel; der Umschwung.

reward [ri'wɔ:d], *v.a.* belohnen (*person*); vergelten (*deed*). — *s.* die Belohnung.

rheumatic [ru:'mætik], *adj.* (*Med.*) rheumatisch.

475

rheumatism

rheumatism [ˈruːmətizm], s. (Med.) der Rheumatismus.

rhetoric [ˈretərik], s. die Redekunst.

Rhodesian [roˈdiːʃən, -ˈdiːʒən], adj. rhodesisch. — s. der Rhodesier.

rhododendron [roudoˈdendrən], s. (Bot.) die Alpenrose.

rhubarb [ˈruːbaːb], s. (Bot.) der Rhabarber.

rhyme [raim], s. der Reim; no — nor reason, sinnlos.

rhythm [riðm], s. der Rhythmus.

rib [rib], s. (Anat.) die Rippe.

ribald [ˈribəld], adj. liederlich; (joke) unanständig.

ribbon [ˈribən], s. das Band.

rice [rais], s. der Reis.

rich [ritʃ], adj. reich; fruchtbar (fertile).

rick [rik], s. der Schober.

rickets [ˈrikits], s. (Med.) die englische Krankheit, die Rachitis.

rickety [ˈrikiti], adj. gebrechlich, wackelig, baufällig.

rid [rid], v.a. irr. befreien, freimachen (of, von); — o.s., sich entledigen (of, Genit.); get — of, loswerden (Acc.); be — of, los sein (Acc.).

riddance [ˈridəns], s. die Befreiung, das Loswerden.

riddle (1) [ridl], s. das Rätsel (puzzle).

riddle (2) [ridl], s. das grobe Sieb (sieve). — v.a. sieben (sieve); durchlöchern.

ride [raid], v.a., v.n. irr. reiten (on horse), fahren (on bicycle etc.); — at anchor, vor Anker liegen. — s. der Ritt (on horse), die Fahrt (in vehicle).

rider [ˈraidə], s. der Reiter (horseman); der Fahrer (cyclist etc.); der Zusatz (addition).

ridge [ridʒ], s. der Rücken (edge); die Bergkette; die Furche (furrow). — v.a. furchen.

ridicule [ˈridikjuːl], s. der Spott. — v.a. lächerlich machen.

ridiculous [riˈdikjuləs], adj. lächerlich.

rife [raif], adj. häufig, weitverbreitet.

rifle (1) [raifl], s. die Büchse, das Gewehr.

rifle (2) [raifl], v.a. ausplündern.

rift [rift], s. der Riß, Spalt, die Spalte. — v.a. spalten.

rig [rig], s. (Naut.) die Takelung; (fig.) — out, die Ausstattung. — v.a. (Naut.) (auf)takeln; (Am.) fälschen (fake); — out, ausstatten.

right [rait], adj. recht; richtig; wahr; gesund; korrekt; — hand, rechtsseitig; you are —, Sie haben recht; that's —, das stimmt. — s. das Recht; by right(s), rechtmäßig; drive on the —, rechts fahren.

righteous [ˈraitʃəs], adj. rechtschaffen, aufrecht.

rightful [ˈraitful], adj. rechtmäßig.

rigid [ˈridʒid], adj. steif; unbeugsam; streng (severe).

rigidity [riˈdʒiditi], s. die Steifheit, Unnachgiebigkeit; die Strenge.

rigmarole [ˈrigməroul], s. die Salbaderei, das Gewäsch.

rigorous [ˈrigərəs], adj. streng; genau.

rigour [ˈrigə], s. die Strenge; die Härte.

rill [ril], s. (Poet.) das Bächlein.

rim [rim], s. der Rand, die Felge.

rime [raim], s. (Poet.) der Reif.

rind [raind], s. die Rinde.

ring (1) [riŋ], s. der Ring.

ring (2) [riŋ], s. der Schall, das Läuten (bell); der Anruf (telephone); das Geläute (bells). — v.a. irr. läuten, klingeln (bell). — v.n. läuten; ertönen, tönen (call, voice).

ringleader [ˈriŋliːdə], s. der Rädelsführer.

rink [riŋk], s. die Eisbahn; Rollschuhbahn.

rinse [rins], v.a. spülen, waschen. — s. das Abspülen.

riot [ˈraiət], s. der Aufruhr. — v.n. Aufruhr stiften; meutern.

rip [rip], v.a. reißen, aufreißen. — s. der Riß.

ripe [raip], adj. reif.

ripen [ˈraipən], v.n. reifen. — v.a. reifen lassen.

ripple [ripl], s. die Welle, Kräuselwelle (water). — v.n. kräuseln (water); (Bot.) riffeln.

rise [raiz], v.n. irr. aufstehen (get up); aufsteigen (ascend); anschwellen (swell); steigen (price). — s. die Erhöhung; (Comm.) der Anstieg; die Steigerung; Erhöhung (salary); der Ursprung (origin).

rising [ˈraiziŋ], s. der Aufstand (rebellion).

risk [risk], s. das Risiko. — v.a. wagen, riskieren.

rite [rait], s. der Ritus.

ritual [ˈritjuəl], s. das Ritual.

rival [raivl], s. der Rivale, Nebenbuhler. — adj. nebenbuhlerisch, konkurrierend. — v.a. konkurrieren, wetteifern.

river [ˈrivə], s. der Fluß.

rivet [ˈrivit], s. die Niete. — v.a. nieten.

roach [routʃ], s. (Zool.) die Plötze.

road [roud], s. die Straße; der Weg.

roam [roum], v.n. herumstreifen.

roan [roun], s. der Rotschimmel (horse).

roar [rɔː], v.n. brüllen (animals); brausen (storm). — s. das Gebrüll (animal); das Getöse, Brausen, Rauschen.

roast [roust], v.a., v.n. braten, rösten. — s. der Braten.

rob [rɔb], v.a. berauben.

robbery [ˈrɔbəri], s. der Raub, die Räuberei.

robe [roub], s. die Robe.

robin [ˈrɔbin], s. (Orn.) das Rotkehlchen.

rock [rɔk], s. der Felsen, die Klippe. — v.a. schaukeln, wiegen. — v.n. wackeln, taumeln.

rocket [ˈrɔkit], s. die Rakete; (sl.) die Rüge. — v.n. hochfliegen; hochgehen (prices).

rocky [ˈrɔki], adj. felsig.

rod [rɔd], *s.* die Rute; (*fishing*) die Angelrute; die Stange (*pole*).

rodent ['roudənt], *s.* (*Zool.*) das Nagetier.

roe (1) [rou], *s.* der Fischrogen.

roe (2) [rou], *s.* (*Zool.*) das Reh, die Hirschkuh.

rogation [ro'geiʃən], *s.* das Gebet, die Litanei; *Rogation Sunday*, der Sonntag Rogate.

rogue [roug], *s.* der Schelm.

role [roul], *s.* (*Theat.*, *fig.*) die Rolle.

roll [roul], *s.* die Liste; — *call*, der Aufruf, die Parade; die Rolle; die Semmel, das Brötchen (*bread*). — *v.a.* rollen; wälzen. — *v.n.* rollen; sich wälzen; sich drehen; schlingen (*ship*); schlenkern (*person*).

roller ['roulə], *s.* die Rolle; — *bandage*, das Wickelband; — *skates*, die Rollschuhe.

rollick ['rɔlik], *v.n.* herumtollen, lustig sein.

rolling stock ['rouliŋ stɔk], *s.* (*Railw.*) der Wagenbestand.

romance [rou'mæns], *s.* die Romanze.

romantic [rou'mæntik], *adj.* romantisch.

romp [rɔmp], *s.* der Wildfang, das Tollen. — *v.n.* toben.

roof [ru:f], *s.* das Dach. — *v.a.* decken.

rook (1) [ruk], *s.* (*Orn.*) die Saatkrähe.

rook (2) [ruk], *s.* (*Chess*) der Turm.

room [ru:m, rum], *s.* der Raum, das Zimmer. — *v.n.* (*Am.*) ein Zimmer teilen (*with*, mit).

roomy ['ru:mi], *adj.* geräumig.

roost [ru:st], *s.* der Hühnerstall. — *v.n.* aufsitzen, schlafen.

root [ru:t], *s.* die Wurzel. — *v.n.* wurzeln.

rooted ['ru:tid], *adj.* eingewurzelt.

rope [roup], *s.* das Seil. — *v.a.* anseilen (*in climbing*); (*coll.*) — *in*, verwickeln, hereinziehen.

rosary ['rouzəri], *s.* (*Rel.*) der Rosenkranz.

rose [rouz], *s.* (*Bot.*) die Rose.

Rosemary ['rouzməri]. Rosemarie.

rosemary ['rouzməri], *s.* (*Bot.*) der Rosmarin.

rosin ['rɔzin] *see* **resin**.

rosy ['rouzi], *adj.* rosig.

rot [rɔt], *v.n.* faulen, modern. — *s.* die Fäulnis, Verwesung; (*coll.*) der Unsinn.

rotate [ro'teit], *v.a.*, *v.n.* (sich) drehen, rotieren.

rote [rout], *s.* by —, mechanisch, auswendig.

rotten [rɔtn], *adj.* faul, verdorben, schlecht.

rotund [ro'tʌnd], *adj.* rundlich, rund.

rough [rʌf], *adj.* rauh, grob; flüchtig, ungefähr (*approximate*); ungehobelt (*ill-mannered*).

roughshod ['rʌfʃɔd], *adj.* rücksichtslos.

round [raund], *adj.* rund. — *s.* die Runde. — *prep.* (rund) um; um ... herum. — *adv.* (rings)herum; (*around*) ungefähr; etwa (*approximately*).

roundabout ['raundəbaut], *s.* das Karussel. — *adj.* umständlich.

Roundhead ['raundhed], *s.* (*Eng. Hist.*) der Puritaner.

rouse [rauz], *v.a.* erwecken.

rout [raut], *s.* (*Mil.*) die wilde Flucht. — *v.a.* in die Flucht jagen.

route [ru:t], *s.* der Weg; die Route.

rover ['rouvə], *s.* der Wanderer, ältere Pfadfinder (*scout*); der Seeräuber (*pirate*).

row (1) [rou], *s.* die Reihe.

row (2) [rau], *s.* der Lärm, Streit. — *v.n.* (*coll.*) lärmend streiten, zanken.

row (3) [rou], *v.n.* rudern.

rowdy ['raudi], *s.* der Raufbold. — *adj.* laut, lärmend.

royal ['rɔiəl], *adj.* königlich.

royalty ['rɔiəlti], *s.* das Mitglied des Königshauses, die königliche Hoheit; (*pl.*) (*Law*) die Tantieme.

rub [rʌb], *v.a.*, *v.n.* (sich) reiben. — *s.* die Reibung; die heikle Stelle, das Problem.

rubber (1) ['rʌbə], *s.* der Gummi; Radiergummi.

rubber (2) ['rʌbə], *s.* (*Whist*) der Robber.

rubbish ['rʌbiʃ], *s.* der Abfall, Mist; (*fig.*) der Schund (*book*), der Unsinn (*nonsense*).

ruby ['ru:bi], *s.* der Rubin.

rudder ['rʌdə], *s.* das Steuerruder.

ruddy ['rʌdi], *adj.* rötlich.

rude [ru:d], *adj.* roh; grob; ungebildet; unhöflich.

rudiment ['ru:dimənt], *s.* die Anfangsgründe, die Grundlage.

rue (1) [ru:], *s.* (*Bot.*) die Raute.

rue (2) [ru:], *v.a.* beklagen, bereuen.

ruff [rʌf], *s.* die Halskrause.

ruffian ['rʌfiən], *s.* der Raufbold.

ruffle [rʌfl], *v.a.* zerzausen (*hair*); verwirren (*muddle*). — *s.* die Krause (*on dress*); die Aufregung.

rug [rʌg], *s.* die Wolldecke, der Vorleger.

rugged ['rʌgid], *adj.* rauh; uneben.

ruin ['ru:in], *s.* die Ruine; (*fig.*) der Zusammenbruch. — *v.a.* ruinieren.

rule [ru:l], *s.* die Regel, Vorschrift; die Herrschaft; *slide* —, der Rechenschieber. — *v.a.* beherrschen; regeln; lin(i)ieren (*draw lines on*). — *v.n.* herrschen (*reign*; *be valid*); lin(i)ieren (*draw lines*); entscheiden (*decide*).

ruling ['ru:liŋ], *s.* die Regelung, Entscheidung.

rum (1) [rʌm], *s.* der Rum.

rum (2) [rʌm], *adj.* (*sl.*) seltsam.

Rumanian [ru:'meiniən], *adj.* rumänisch. — *s.* der Rumäne.

rumble [rʌmbl], *v.n.* poltern, rasseln, rumpeln; (*stomach*) knurren.

ruminate ['ru:mineit], *v.n.* wiederkäuen; nachsinnen.

rummage ['rʌmidʒ], *v.a.*, *v.n.* durchstöbern.

rumour ['ru:mə], *s.* das Gerücht.

rump [rʌmp], *s.* der Rumpf, Steiß; — *steak*, das Rumpsteak.

run

run [rʌn], *v.n. irr.* laufen, rennen;
eilen; verkehren (*bus*); fließen (*flow*);
(*Theat.*) gegeben werden; lauten (*text*).
— *s.* der Lauf, das Rennen; (*Theat.*)
die Spieldauer; *in the long* —, am
Ende, auf die Dauer.
runaway ['rʌnəwei], *adj.* entlaufen. —
s. der Ausreißer.
rung [rʌn], *s.* die Sprosse.
runway ['rʌnwei], *s.* (*Aviat.*) die Rollbahn, Startbahn, Landebahn.
rupture ['rʌptʃə], *s.* (*Med.*) der Leistenbruch.
rural ['ruərəl], *adj.* ländlich.
rush (1) [rʌʃ], *s.* (*Bot.*) die Binse.
rush (2) [rʌʃ], *s.* der Ansturm, Andrang;
die Hetze; der Hochbetrieb. — *v.n.*
stürzen, in Eile sein.
Russian ['rʌʃən], *adj.* russisch. — *s.*
der Russe.
rust [rʌst], *s.* der Rost. — *v.n.* verrosten.
rustic ['rʌstik], *adj.* ländlich.
rut (1) [rʌt], *s.* die Spur; das Geleise.
rut (2) [rʌt], *s.* (*animals*) die Brunst.
ruthless ['ruːθlis], *adj.* grausam, rücksichtslos.
rye [rai], *s.* (*Bot.*) der Roggen.

S

S [es]. das S.
sable [seibl], *s.* der Zobel. — *adj.*
schwarz.
sabotage ['sæbotɑːʒ], *s.* die Sabotage.
— *v.a.* sabotieren.
sabre ['seibə], *s.* der Säbel.
sack (1) [sæk], *s.* der Sack; (*coll.*) die
Entlassung (*get the* —). — *v.a.*
(*coll.*) entlassen.
sack (2) [sæk], *v.a.* plündern (*pillage*).
sack (3) [sæk], *s.* (*obs.*) der Weißwein.
sacrament ['sækrəmənt], *s.* das Sakra-
ment.
sacred ['seikrid], *adj.* heilig.
sacrifice ['sækrifais], *s.* das Opfer. —
v.a. opfern.
sacrilege ['sækrilidʒ], *s.* das Sakrileg,
der Frevel.
sad [sæd], *adj.* traurig.
sadden ['sædn], *v.a.* betrüben.
saddle [sædl], *s.* der Sattel. — *v.a.*
satteln; (*coll.*) — *s.o. with s.th.*, einem
etwas aufhalsen.
safe [seif], *adj.* sicher (*secure*); wohlbehalten (*arrival etc.*). — *s.* der Geldschrank, das Safe.
safeguard ['seifgɑːd], *v.a.* beschützen,
garantieren. — *s.* der Schutz, die
Sicherheit.
safety ['seifti], *s.* die Sicherheit.
saffron ['sæfrən], *s.* der Safran. — *adj.*
safrangelb.

sagacious [sə'geiʃəs], *adj.* scharfsinnig.
sagacity [sə'gæsiti], *s.* der Scharfsinn.
sage (1) [seidʒ], *s.* (*Bot.*) die Salbei.
sage (2) [seidʒ], *s.* der Weise. — *adj.*
weise, klug.
sail [seil], *s.* das Segel. — *v.n.* segeln,
(*Naut.*) fahren.
sailor ['seilə], *s.* der Matrose, Seemann.
Saint [seint, sənt]. (*abbr.* **S.** *or* **St.**)
Sankt (*before name*).
saint [seint], *s.* der *or* die Heilige.
sake [seik], *s. for my son's* —, um meines
Sohnes willen; *for the* — *of peace*, um
des Friedens willen.
salacious [sə'leiʃəs], *adj.* geil; zotig
(*joke*).
salad ['sæləd], *s.* der Salat.
salary ['sæləri], *s.* das Gehalt.
sale [seil], *s.* der Verkauf; *annual* —,
(*Comm.*) der Ausverkauf.
salesman ['seilzmən], *s.* der Verkäufer.
salient ['seiliənt], *adj.* hervorspringend,
wichtig, Haupt–.
saline ['seilain], *s.* die Salzquelle. —
adj. salzhaltig.
saliva [sə'laivə], *s.* der Speichel.
sallow ['sælou], *adj.* blaß, bleich.
sally ['sæli], *s.* der Ausfall, (*fig.*)
der komische Einfall. — *v.n.* ausfallen; — *forth*, losgehen.
salmon ['sæmən], *s.* (*Zool.*) der Lachs.
saloon [sə'luːn], *s.* der Salon; (*Am.*)
das Wirtshaus, die Kneipe.
salt [sɔːlt], *s.* das Salz; — *cellar*, das
Salzfäßchen; (*coll.*) *old* —, der alte
Matrose. — *v.a.* salzen.
saltpetre [sɔːlt'piːtə], *s.* der Salpeter.
salubrious [sə'ljuːbriəs], *adj.* gesund
(*climate, neighbourhood*).
salutary ['sæljutəri], *adj.* heilsam (*lesson,
experience*).
salute [sə'ljuːt], *v.a.* grüßen. — *s.* der
Gruß, (*Mil.*) Salut.
salvage ['sælvidʒ], *s.* die Bergung,
Rettung; die Bergegut. — *v.a.* retten,
bergen.
salvation [sæl'veiʃən], *s.* die Rettung;
(*Rel.*) die Erlösung, das Heil.
salve [sælv, sɑːv], *v.a.* einsalben; heilen.
— *s.* die Salbe.
salver ['sælvə], *s.* der Präsentierteller.
salvo ['sælvou], *s.* (*Mil.*) die Salve.
Samaritan [sə'mæritən], *s.* der Samari-
ter; (*fig.*) der Wohltäter.
same [seim], *adj.* der–, die–, dasselbe.
sample [sɑːmpl], *s.* die Probe, das
Muster (*test, pack etc.*). — *v.a.* probieren; kosten (*food*).
sampler ['sɑːmplə], *s.* das Stickmuster.
sanctify ['sæŋktifai], *v.a.* heiligen.
sanctimonious [sæŋkti'mouniəs], *adj.*
scheinheilig.
sanction ['sæŋkʃən], *s.* (*Pol.*) die
Sanktion; (*fig.*) Genehmigung. — *v.a.*
genehmigen, sanktionieren.
sanctuary ['sæŋktjuəri], *s.* das Heiligtum.
sand [sænd], *s.* der Sand. — *v.a.* san-
den, bestreuen; (*floors*) abreiben.
sandal [sændl], *s.* die Sandale.

sandwich ['sænwitʃ], *s.* das belegte (Butter)brot.

sane [sein], *adj.* gesund (*mind*); vernünftig.

sanguine ['sæŋgwin], *adj.* optimistisch.

sanitary ['sænitəri], *adj.* Gesundheits-, Sanitäts-; — *towel*, die (Damen)binde.

sanity ['sæniti], *s.* die Vernunft, der gesunde Menschenverstand; (*Law*) die Zurechnungsfähigkeit.

Santa Claus [sæntə'klɔ:z]. der heilige Nikolaus, Knecht Ruprecht.

sap (1) [sæp], *s.* der Saft; (*fig.*) die Lebenskraft.

sap (2) [sæp], *v.a.* untergraben, schwächen.

sapling ['sæpliŋ], *s.* (*Bot.*) das Bäumchen, der junge Baum.

sapper ['sæpə], *s.* (*Mil.*) der Sappeur; der Schanzgräber, Pionier.

sapphire ['sæfaiə], *s.* der Saphir.

sarcasm ['sɑ:kæzm], *s.* der Sarkasmus.

sarcastic [sɑ:'kæstik], *adj.* sarkastisch.

sash (1) [sæʃ], *s.* die Schärpe.

sash (2) [sæʃ], *s.* — *window*, das Schiebefenster; — *cord*, die Fensterschnur.

Satan ['seitən]. der Satan.

satchel ['sætʃəl], *s.* die Leder(schul)tasche.

sate [seit], *v.a.* sättigen.

satellite ['sætəlait], *s.* der Satellit, Trabant.

satin ['sætin], *s.* (*Text.*) der Atlas.

satire ['sætaiə], *s.* die Satire.

satisfaction [sætis'fækʃən], *s.* die Befriedigung, Zufriedenheit.

satisfactory [sætis'fæktri], *adj.* befriedigend, genügend; zufriedenstellend.

satisfy ['sætisfai], *v.a.* befriedigen, sättigen; (*fig.*) zufriedenstellen.

saturate ['sætʃureit], *v.a.* (*Chem.*) saturieren, sättigen.

Saturday ['sætədei]. der Samstag, Sonnabend.

sauce [sɔ:s], *s.* (*Cul.*) die Sauce, Tunke; (*coll.*) die Unverschämtheit.

saucepan ['sɔ:spæn], *s.* (*Cul.*) der Kochtopf.

saucer ['sɔ:sə], *s.* die Untertasse.

saucy ['sɔ:si], *adj.* (*coll.*) unverschämt, frech.

saunter ['sɔ:ntə], *v.n.* schlendern, spazieren.

sausage ['sɔsidʒ], *s.* die Wurst.

savage ['sævidʒ], *adj.* wild. — *s.* der Wilde.

save [seiv], *v.a.* retten (*life*); (*Theol.*) erlösen; sparen (*money*); ersparen (*trouble*, *labour*); aufheben (*keep*). — *v.n.* sparen, sparsam sein. — *prep.*, *conj.* außer, außer daß, ausgenommen.

saving ['seiviŋ], *s.* das Ersparnis; *savings bank*, die Sparkasse.

saviour ['seivjə], *s.* der Retter; (*Rel.*) der Heiland.

savour ['seivə], *s.* der Geschmack; die Würze. — *v.n.* schmecken (*of*, nach, *Dat.*).

savoury ['seivəri], *adj.* schmackhaft. — *s.* pikantes Vor- or Nachgericht.

saw (1) [sɔ:], *v.a.* sägen. — *s.* die Säge.

saw (2) [sɔ:], *s.* (*obs.*) das Sprichwort.

sawyer ['sɔ:jə], *s.* der Sägearbeiter, Säger.

Saxon ['sæksən], *adj.* sächsisch. — *s.* der Sachse.

say [sei], *v.a. irr.* sagen; (*lines*, *prayer*) hersagen. — *v.n.* (*Am. coll.*) —! sagen Sie mal! — *s.* das entscheidende Wort.

saying ['seiiŋ], *s.* das Sprichwort, der Spruch.

scab [skæb], *s.* der Schorf, die Krätze.

scabbard ['skæbəd], *s.* die Degenscheide.

scaffold ['skæfəld], *s.* (*Build.*) das Gerüst; das Schafott (*place of execution*).

scald [skɔ:ld], *v.a.* verbrühen; —*ing hot*, brühheiß.

scale (1) [skeil], *s.* die Waagschale (*balance*).

scale (2) [skeil], *s.* (*Mus.*) die Skala, Tonleiter.

scale (3) [skeil], *s.* (*Geog. etc.*) die Skala, das Ausmaß, der Maßstab; *on a large —*, im großen (Maßstabe). — *v.a.* erklettern (*climb*); — *down*, im Maßstab verringern.

scale (4) [skeil], *s.* (*fish etc.*) die Schuppe. — *v.a.* schuppen, abschälen (*remove —s*).

scallop ['skɔləp], *s.* (*Zool.*) die Kammuschel.

scalp [skælp], *s.* (*Anat.*) die Kopfhaut. — *v.a.* skalpieren, die Kopfhaut abziehen.

scamp [skæmp], *s.* (*coll.*) der Taugenichts.

scan [skæn], *v.a.* (*Poet.*) skandieren; (*Rad.*) absuchen.

scandalize ['skændəlaiz], *v.a.* empören, verärgern.

scant [skænt],*adj.*selten; knapp,sparsam.

Scandinavian [skændi'neivjən], *adj.* skandinavisch. — *s.* der Skandinavier.

scanty ['skænti], *adj.* spärlich, knapp.

scapegoat ['skeipgout], *s.* der Sündenbock.

scar [skɑ:], *s.* die Narbe.

scarce [skɛəs], *adj.* selten, spärlich.

scarcely ['skɛəsli], *adv.* kaum.

scarcity ['skɛəsiti], *s.* die Seltenheit, Knappheit.

scare [skɛə], *v.a.* erschrecken, ängstigen. — *s.* der Schreck.

scarecrow ['skɛəkrou], *s.* die Vogelscheuche.

scarf [skɑ:f], *s.* der Schal, das Halstuch.

scarlet ['skɑ:lit], *adj.* scharlachrot. — *s.* der Scharlach.

scarp [skɑ:p], *s.* die Böschung.

scatter ['skætə], *v.a.*, *v.n.* (sich) zerstreuen, (sich) verbreiten; streuen.

scavenge ['skævindʒ], *v.a.* ausreinigen, auswaschen; säubern.

scavenger ['skævindʒə], *s.* der Straßenkehrer; Aasgeier.

scene

scene [si:n], *s.* die Szene, der Schauplatz; *behind the —s*, hinter den Kulissen; *— shifter*, der Kulissenschieber.

scenery ['si:nəri], *s.* die Landschaft (*nature*); (*Theat.*) das Bühnenbild, die Kulissen, *f. pl.*

scent [sent], *s.* der Geruch, Duft, das Parfüm (*perfume*); die Witterung, Fährte (*trail of hunted animal*).

sceptic ['skeptik], *s.* der Skeptiker.

sceptre ['septə], *s.* das Zepter.

schedule ['ʃedju:l, (*Am.*) 'ske–], *s.* der Plan; die Liste; der (Fahr-, Stunden-) plan; (*Law*) der Zusatz (*in documents*). — *v.a.* (*Am.*) einteilen, zuteilen (*apportion*); aufzeichnen.

scheme [ski:m], *s.* das Schema; der Plan; *— of things*, in der Gesamtplanung. — *v.n.* aushecken; Ränke schmieden.

scholar ['skɔlə], *s.* der Gelehrte, der Wissenschaftler; der Schuljunge, Schüler; (*Univ.*) der Stipendiat.

scholarly ['skɔləli], *adj.* gelehrt.

scholarship ['skɔləʃip], *s.* die Gelehrsamkeit (*learning*); das Stipendium (*award*).

scholastic [skɔ'læstik], *adj.* scholastisch. — *s.* der Scholastiker.

school [sku:l], *s.* die Schule. — *v.a.* abrichten, schulen; erziehen.

schoolboy ['sku:lbɔi], *s.* der Schüler.

schoolgirl ['sku:lgə:l], *s.* die Schülerin.

schoolmaster ['sku:lmɑ:stə], *s.* der Lehrer.

schoolmistress ['sku:lmistrəs], *s.* die Lehrerin.

schooner ['sku:nə], *s.* (*Naut.*) der Schoner.

science ['saiəns], *s.* die Wissenschaft, Naturwissenschaft (*natural —s*).

scientific [saiən'tifik], *adj.* wissenschaftlich, naturwissenschaftlich.

scientist ['saiəntist], *s.* der Gelehrte; Naturwissenschaftler, Naturforscher.

scintillate ['sintileit], *v.n.* funkeln, glänzen.

scion ['saiən], *s.* der Sprößling.

scissors ['sizəz], *s. pl.* die Schere.

scoff [skɔf], *v.a.* verspotten, verhöhnen. — *v.n.* spotten. — *s.* der Spott, Hohn.

scold [skould], *v.a.* schelten. — *v.n.* zanken.

scoop [sku:p], *v.a.* aushöhlen (*hollow out*); ausschöpfen (*ladle out*). — *s.* die Schippe, Schöpfkelle; (*fig.*) die Sensation, Erstmeldung.

scope [skoup], *s.* der Wirkungskreis, Spielraum.

scooter ['sku:tə], *s.* der (Motor)roller.

scorch [skɔ:tʃ], *v.a.* versengen, verbrennen. — *v.n.* versengt werden; (*coll.*) dahinrasen (*speed*).

score [skɔ:], *s.* die Zwanzig; die Rechnung; (*Mus.*) die Partitur; das Spielergebnis (*in game*).

scorn [skɔ:n], *v.a.* verachten. — *s.* der Spott (*scoffing*); die Geringschätzung, Verachtung.

Scot, Scotsman [skɔt, 'skɔtsmən], *s.* der Schotte.

Scotch [skɔtʃ], *s.* der Whisky.

scotch [skɔtʃ], *v.a.* ritzen; (*fig.*) vernichten.

Scotswoman ['skɔtswumən], *s.* die Schottin.

Scottish ['skɔtiʃ], *adj.* schottisch.

scoundrel ['skaundrəl], *s.* der Schurke.

scour [skauə], *v.a.* scheuern, reinigen.

scourge [skə:dʒ], *s.* die Geißel. — *v.a.* geißeln.

scout [skaut], *s.* der Kundschafter; (*Boy Scout*) der Pfadfinder.

scowl [skaul], *v.n.* finster dreinsehen. — *s.* das finstere Gesicht.

scraggy ['skrægi], *adj.* hager, dürr.

scramble [skræmbl], *v.n.* klettern. — *v.a.* verrühren; *scrambled eggs*, das Rührei.

scrap [skræp], *s.* das Stückchen, der Brocken, Fetzen; *— merchant*, der Altwarenhändler. — *v.a.* zum alten Eisen werfen, verschrotten.

scrapbook ['skræpbuk], *s.* das Sammelbuch, Bilderbuch.

scrape [skreip], *v.a., v.n.* (sich) schaben, kratzen; (*coll.*) die Klemme (*difficulty*).

scraper ['skreipə], *s.* der Fußabstreifer.

scratch [skrætʃ], *v.a., v.n.* kratzen; sich kratzen; (*Sport*) zurückziehen. — *s.* der Kratzer; *come up to —*, seinen Mann stellen.

scrawl [skrɔ:l], *v.a., v.n.* kritzeln (*scribble*); (*coll.*) unleserlich schreiben. — *s.* das Gekritzel.

scream [skri:m], *v.n.* schreien; kreischen. — *s.* der Schrei; (*coll.*) zum Schreien, zum Lachen.

screech [skri:tʃ], *v.n.* schreien, kreischen (*hoarsely*). — *s.* das Gekreisch.

screen [skri:n], *s.* der Schirm (*protection*); (*Cinema*) die Leinwand. — *v.a.* abschirmen (*shade*); (*Film*) durchspielen, vorführen; (*question*) untersuchen; ausfragen.

screening ['skri:niŋ], *s.* (*Cinema*) die Vorführung; (*Pol.*) die Befragung, Untersuchung.

screw [skru:], *v.a.* schrauben. — *s.* die Schraube.

screwdriver ['skru:draivə], *s.* der Schraubenzieher.

scribble [skribl], *v.a., v.n.* kritzeln, (unleserlich) schreiben. — *s.* das Gekritzel.

scribe [skraib], *s.* der Schreiber.

script [skript], *s.* das Manuskript; (*Film*) das Drehbuch.

scripture ['skriptʃə], *s.* die Heilige Schrift.

scroll [skroul], *s.* die Schriftrolle; (*Typ.*) der Schnörkel; die Urkunde (*document etc.*).

scrub [skrʌb], *v.a.* schrubben, reiben, scheuern.

scruff [skrʌf], *s.* (*of the neck*) das Genick.

scruple [skru:pl], *s.* der Skrupel.

scrupulous ['skru:pjuləs], *adj.* genau, gewissenhaft; allzu bedenklich.

480

scrutinize ['skru:tinaiz], *v.a.* genau prüfen, untersuchen.

scrutiny ['skru:tini], *s.* die genaue Prüfung; die Untersuchung.

scuffle [skʌfl], *v.n.* sich raufen. — *s.* die Balgerei, Rauferei.

scull [skʌl], *s.* das kurze Ruder.

scullery ['skʌləri], *s.* die Abwaschküche.

scullion ['skʌliən], *s.* (*obs.*) der Küchenjunge.

sculptor ['skʌlptə], *s.* der Bildhauer.

sculpture ['skʌlptʃə], *s.* die Bildhauerei (*activity*); die Skulptur (*piece*).

scum [skʌm], *s.* der Abschaum.

scurf [skə:f], *s.* der Schorf, Grind.

scurrilous ['skrilas], *s.* der gemein.

scurvy ['skə:vi], *s.* (*Med.*) der Skorbut. — *adj.* niederträchtig.

scutcheon ['skʌtʃən] *see* escutcheon.

scuttle (1) [skʌtl], *s.* (*Naut.*) die Springluke. — *v.a.* (*Naut.*) ein Schiff zum Sinken bringen, versenken.

scuttle (2) [skʌtl], *s.* der Kohleneimer.

scuttle (3) [skʌtl], *v.n.* eilen (*hurry*).

scythe [saið], *s.* die Sense.

sea [si:], *s.* die See, das Meer.

seal (1) [si:l], *s.* das Siegel, Petschaft. — *v.a.* (be)siegeln.

seal (2) [si:l], *s.* (*Zool.*) der Seehund, die Robbe.

seam [si:m], *s.* der Saum; die Naht; (*Min.*) die Ader, das Flöz; (*Metall.*) die Naht. — *v.a.* einsäumen.

seamstress ['si:mstrəs], *s.* die Näherin.

sear [siə], *v.a.* sengen (*burn*); trocknen; verdorren. — *adj. see* sere.

search [sə:tʃ], *v.n.* suchen (*for,* nach, *Dat.*); forschen (*for,* nach, *Dat.*). — *v.a.* untersuchen, durchsuchen (*house, case etc.*). — *s.* die Suche (*for person*); die Untersuchung (*of house etc.*).

searchlight ['sə:tʃlait], *s.* der Scheinwerfer.

seasick ['si:sik], *adj.* seekrank.

seaside ['si:said], *s.* die Küste, der Strand.

season [si:zn], *s.* die Jahreszeit, Saison; — *ticket,* die Dauerkarte. — *v.a.* würzen (*spice*). — *v.n.* reifen (*mature*).

seasoning ['si:zniŋ], *s.* die Würze.

seat [si:t], *s.* der Sitz, Sitzplatz, Stuhl. — *v.a.* setzen; fassen (*of room capacity*); *be —ed,* Platz nehmen.

seaweed ['si:wi:d], *s.* (*Bot.*) der Seetang.

secession [si'seʃən], *s.* die Loslösung, Trennung, Spaltung.

seclude [si'klu:d], *v.a.* abschließen, absondern.

seclusion [si'klu:ʒən], *s.* die Abgeschlossenheit.

second ['sekənd], *num. adj.* zweit; (*repeat*) noch ein. — *s.* die Sekunde (*time*); (*Sport*) der Sekundant. — *v.a.* sekundieren (*Dat.*), beipflichten; [si'kɔnd] abkommandieren (zu).

secondary ['sekəndri], *adj.* zweitrangig, sekundär.

secondhand ['sekəndhænd], *adj.* antiquarisch, gebraucht.

secrecy ['si:krəsi], *s.* die Heimlichkeit; *pledge to —,* die Verschwiegenheit.

secret ['si:krit], *s.* das Geheimnis. — *adj.* geheim.

secretary ['sekrətəri], *s.* der Sekretär, die Sekretärin.

secrete [si'kri:t], *v.a.* ausscheiden, absondern.

secretion [si'kri:ʃən], *s.* die Ausscheidung; (*Med.*) das Sekret.

sect [sekt], *s.* die Sekte.

section ['sekʃən], *s.* die Sektion, Abteilung (*department*); der Teil (*part*); Abschnitt (*in book etc.*).

secular ['sekjulə], *adj.* weltlich, säkulär.

secure [sə'kjuə], *adj.* sicher, gesichert. — *v.a.* sichern (*make safe*); besorgen (*obtain*).

security [sə'kjuəriti], *s.* die Sicherheit; (*Comm.*) die Garantie, Bürgschaft; (*pl.*) die Staatspapiere, Wertpapiere, *n. pl.,* Aktien, *f. pl.*

sedate [si'deit], *adj.* gesetzt, ruhig (*placid*).

sedative ['sedətiv], *adj.* beruhigend. — *s.* das Beruhigungsmittel.

sedentary ['sedəntri], *adj.* sitzend, Sitz-.

sediment ['sedimənt], *s.* der Bodensatz; (*Geol.*) das Sediment.

sedition [si'diʃən], *s.* der Aufstand.

seditious [si'diʃəs], *adj.* aufrührerisch.

seduce [si'dju:s], *v.a.* verführen.

sedulous ['sedjuləs], *adj.* emsig, fleißig.

see (1) [si:], *s.* (*Eccl.*) das (Erz)bistum; *Holy See,* der Heilige Stuhl.

see (2) [si:], *v.a., v.n. irr.* sehen; einsehen, verstehen (*understand*).

seed [si:d], *s.* die Saat; der Same (*grain*). — *v.a.* (*Sport*) aussetzen, setzen.

seediness ['si:dinis], *s.* die Schäbigkeit; Armseligkeit, das Elend.

seedy ['si:di], *adj.* elend; schäbig.

seeing ['si:iŋ], *conj.* — *that,* da doch.

seek [si:k], *v.a. irr.* suchen (*object*). — *v.n.* trachten (*to, infin.*).

seem [si:m], *v.n.* scheinen, erscheinen.

seemly ['si:mli], *adj.* schicklich, anständig.

seer [siə], *s.* der Prophet.

seesaw ['si:sɔ:], *s.* die Schaukel.

seethe [si:ð], *v.n.* kochen, (*fig.*) sieden.

segment ['segmənt], *s.* (*Geom.*) der Abschnitt.

segregate ['segrigeit], *v.a.* absondern.

segregation [segri'geiʃən], *s. — racial —,* die Rassentrennung.

seize [si:z], *v.a.* ergreifen, packen (*arrest, grasp*); beschlagnahmen (*impound*).

seizure ['si:ʒə], *s.* die Beschlagnahme (*of goods*); (*Med.*) der Anfall.

seldom ['seldəm], *adv.* selten.

select [si'lekt], *v.a.* auswählen; auslesen. — *adj.* auserlesen.

selection [si'lekʃən], *s.* die Wahl, Auswahl.

self [self], *s.* das Selbst; — — *consciousness,* die Befangenheit; — — *denial,* die Selbstverleugnung, Selbstaufopferung.

selfish

selfish ['selfiʃ], *adj.* egoistisch, selbst-süchtig.
sell [sel], *v.a. irr.* verkaufen; (*sl.*) —
(*s.o.*) *out*, jemanden verraten.
semblance ['sembləns], *s.* der Anschein, die Ähnlichkeit.
semi- ['semi], *pref.* halb.
semibreve ['semibriːv], *s.* (*Mus.*) die ganze Note.
semicircle ['semisɔːkl], *s.* der Halb-kreis.
semicolon ['semikoulən], *s.* der Strich-punkt.
semiquaver ['semikweivə], *s.* (*Mus.*) die Sechzehntelnote.
senate ['senit], *s.* der Senat.
send [send], *v.a. irr.* senden, schicken;
— *for,* holen lassen; — *-off,* die Abschiedsfeier.
Senegalese [seniɡə'liːz], *adj.* senegal-.
— *s.* der Senegalese.
senile ['siːnail], *adj.* altersschwach.
senior ['siːnjə], *adj.* älter; dienstälter (*in position*).
seniority [siːni'ɔriti], *s.* der Rangvor-tritt, das Dienstalter.
sensation [sen'seiʃən], *s.* die Empfin-dung; Sensation.
sensational [sen'seiʃənəl], *adj.* sen-sationell.
sense [sens], *v.a.* fühlen, empfinden.
— *s.* der Sinn; das Empfinden, Gefühl; *common* —, gesunder Men-schenverstand.
senseless ['senslis], *adj.* sinnlos.
sensibility [sensi'biliti], *s.* die Empfind-lichkeit.
sensible ['sensibl], *adj.* vernünftig.
sensitive ['sensitiv], *adj.* feinfühlend, empfindlich.
sensitize ['sensitaiz], *v.a.* (*Phot. etc.*) empfindlich machen.
sensual ['sensjuəl], *adj.* sinnlich, wol-lüstig.
sensuous ['sensjuəs], *adj.* sinnlich.
sentence ['sentəns], *s.* (*Gram.*) der Satz; (*Law*) das Urteil. — *v.a.* verur-teilen.
sententious [sen'tenʃəs], *adj.* spruch-reich; affektiert.
sentiment ['sentimənt], *s.* die Emp-findung, das Gefühl; die Meinung (*opinion*).
sentimental [senti'mentl], *adj.* senti-mental, gefühlvoll; empfindsam.
sentinel ['sentinəl], *s.* (*Mil.*) die Schild-wache, Wache.
separable ['sepərəbl], *adj.* trennbar.
separate ['sepəreit], *v.a.* trennen. —
[-rit], *adj.* getrennt.
separation [sepə'reiʃən], *s.* die Tren-nung.
September [sep'tembə]. der Septem-ber.
sequel ['siːkwəl], *s.* die Folge, Fortset-zung (*serial*).
sequence ['siːkwəns], *s.* die Ordnung, Reihenfolge, Aufeinanderfolge.
sequester [si'kwestə], *v.a.* absondern, entfernen.

sere [siə], *adj.* trocken, dürr.
serene [si'riːn], *adj.* heiter; gelassen, ruhig (*quiet*).
serf [sɔːf], *s.* der Leibeigene.
sergeant ['saːdʒənt], *s.* (*Mil.*) der Feldwebel.
series ['siəriz *or* 'siəriiːz], *s.* die Reihe.
serious ['siəriəs], *adj.* ernst, seriös.
sermon ['sɔːmən], *s.* die Predigt.
serpent ['sɔːpənt], *s.* (*Zool.*) die Schlange.
serpentine ['sɔːpəntain], *adj.* schlangen-artig, sich schlängelnd.
serrated [se'reitid], *adj.* (*Bot., Engin.*) zackig, gezackt.
serried ['serid], *adj.* dichtgedrängt.
servant ['sɔːvənt], *s.* der Bediente, Diener; die Magd, das Mädchen, Dienstmädchen.
serve [sɔːv], *v.a., v.n.* dienen (*Dat.*);
(*Law*) abbüßen, absitzen (*sentence*); servieren (*food*); (*Tennis*) angeben.
service ['sɔːvis], *s.* der Dienst, die Bedienung; (*Mil.*) der Militärdienst; das Service, Geschirr, Porzellan (*china*).
serviceable ['sɔːvisəbl], *adj.* brauch-bar, dienlich, benutzbar.
servile ['sɔːvail], *adj.* knechtisch.
servility [sɔː'viliti], *s.* die Kriecherei.
servitude ['sɔːvitjuːd], *s.* die Knecht-schaft.
session ['seʃən], *s.* die Sitzung; das Studienjahr, Hochschuljahr.
set [set], *v.a. irr.* setzen; stellen (*stand*); legen (*lay*); ordnen — *out*); — *a saw,* eine Säge schärfen, wetzen; fassen (*stone*); — *fire to,* in Brand setzen; — *aside,* beiseitelegen; — *to music,* vertonen; — *about,* anfangen, sich anschicken; herfallen über (*s.o.*);
— *up,* einrichten. — *v.n.* — *forth, forward,* aufbrechen; — *out,* stre-ben, trachten; (*sun*) untergehen; fest werden (*solidify*). — *s.* der Satz (*com-plete collection*); die Garnitur (*gar-ments*); der Kreis, die Clique (*circle of people*); (*Theat.*) das Bühnenbild.
settee [se'tiː], *s.* das Sofa.
setter ['setə], *s.* (*Zool.*) der Vorsteh-hund; *red* —, der Hühnerhund.
setting ['setiŋ], *s.* das Setzen; die Szene (*of play etc.*); der Sonnenunter-gang (*of the sun*); (*Typ.*) — *up,* die Auslegung, Aufstellung.
settle (1) [setl], *v.a.* ordnen, schlichten;
(*Comm.*) begleichen, bezahlen. —
v.n. sich niederlassen, siedeln; (*wea-ther*) sich aufklären.
settle (2) [setl], *s.* der Ruhesitz.
settlement ['setlmənt], *s.* (*Comm.*) die Begleichung; die Siedlung (*habita-tion*).
seven [sevn], *num. adj.* sieben.
seventeen ['sevntiːn], *num. adj.* siebzehn.
seventh [sevnθ], *num. adj.* siebente.
seventy ['sevnti], *num. adj.* siebzig.
sever ['sevə], *v.a.* trennen.
several ['sevərəl], *adj. pl.* verschiedene, mehrere.

severance ['sevərəns], s. die Trennung.
severe [si'viə], adj. streng.
severity [si'veriti], s. die Strenge.
sew [sou], v.a., v.n. nähen.
sewage ['sju:idʒ], s. das Abfuhrwasser, Kloakenwasser, Kanalwasser.
sewer (1) ['sju:ə], s. die Kanalanlage, der Abzugskanal.
sewer (2) ['souə], s. der Näher, die Näherin.
sewing ['souiŋ], s. das Nähen; — *machine*, die Nähmaschine.
sex [seks], s. das Geschlecht.
sexagenarian [seksədʒə'nɛəriən], s. der Sechzigjährige.
sextant ['sekstənt], s. der Sextant.
sexton ['sekstən], s. (Eccl.) der Küster, Totengräber.
sexual ['seksjuəl], adj. geschlechtlich, sexuell.
shabby ['ʃæbi], adj. schäbig; (fig.) erbärmlich.
shackle [ʃækl], v.a. fesseln. — s. (usually pl.) die Fesseln, f. pl.
shade [ʃeid], s. der Schatten; (pl.) (Am.) die Jalousien, f. pl. (blinds). — v.a. beschatten; (Art) schattieren, verdunkeln.
shadow ['ʃædou], s. der Schatten. — v.a. verfolgen.
shady ['ʃeidi], adj. schattig; (fig.) verdächtig.
shaft [ʃɑ:ft], s. der Schaft (handle); (Min.) der Schacht; die Deichsel (cart); der Pfeil (arrow).
shag [ʃæg], s. der Tabak.
shaggy ['ʃægi], adj. zottig.
shake [ʃeik], v.a. irr. schütteln; rütteln; (fig.) erschüttern. — v.n. zittern (tremble); wanken (waver). — s. das Zittern, Beben; (Mus.) der Triller.
shaky ['ʃeiki], adj. zitternd, wankend; rissig, wackelig (wobbly); (fig.) unsicher (insecure).
shall [ʃæl], v. aux. sollen (be supposed to); werden (future).
shallow ['ʃælou], adj. flach, seicht. — s. die Untiefe (sea).
sham [ʃæm], adj. falsch, unecht. — v.a. vortäuschen.
shambles ['ʃæmblz], s. die Unordnung; (fig.) das Schlachtfeld.
shame [ʃeim], s. die Scham (remorse); die Schande (dishonour); what a —! wie schade! — v.a. beschämen.
shamefaced ['ʃeimfeisd],adj.verschämt.
shameful ['ʃeimful], adj. schändlich (despicable).
shampoo [ʃæm'pu:], s. das Haarwaschmittel. — v.a. das Haar waschen.
shamrock ['ʃæmrɔk], s. (Bot.) der irische Klee.
shank [ʃæŋk], s. der Unterschenkel; (coll.) on Shanks's pony, zu Fuß.
shanty (1) ['ʃænti], s. die Hütte.
shanty (2) ['ʃænti], s. sea —, das Matrosenlied.
shape [ʃeip], s. die Gestalt, Figur, Form. — v.a. gestalten, formen. — v.n. Gestalt annehmen.

shapely ['ʃeipli], adj. wohlgestaltet, schön gestaltet.
share [ʃɛə], v.a., v.n. (sich) teilen. — s. der Teil, Anteil; (Comm.) die Aktie (in company).
shareholder ['ʃɛəhouldə], s. der Aktionär.
shark [ʃɑ:k], s. (Zool.) der Haifisch, Hai; (fig.) der Wucherer (profiteer), Hochstapler.
sharp [ʃɑ:p], adj. scharf; (fig.) intelligent. — s. (Mus.) das Kreuz.
sharpen [ʃɑ:pn], v.a. schärfen; spitzen (pencil).
sharpener ['ʃɑ:pnə], s. pencil —, der Bleistiftspitzer.
shatter ['ʃætə], v.a. zerschmettern. — v.n. zerbrechen.
shave [ʃeiv], v.a., v.n. (sich) rasieren; abschaben (pare). — s. die Rasur, das Rasieren.
shavings ['ʃeiviŋz], s. pl. die Hobelspäne, m. pl.
shawl [ʃɔ:l], s. der Schal, das Umschlagetuch.
she [ʃi:], pers. pron. sie.
sheaf [ʃi:f], s. die Garbe.
shear [ʃiə], v.a. irr. scheren (sheep etc.).
shears [ʃiəz], s. pl. die Schere.
sheath [ʃi:θ], s. die Scheide.
sheathe [ʃi:ð], v.a. in die Scheide stecken.
shed (1) [ʃed], s. der Schuppen.
shed (2) [ʃed], v.a. irr. vergießen (blood, tears); ausschütten.
sheen [ʃi:n], s. der Glanz.
sheep [ʃi:p], s. (Zool.) das Schaf.
sheer (1) [ʃiə], adj. rein, lauter; senkrecht.
sheer (2) [ʃiə], v.n. (Naut.) gieren, abgieren.
sheet [ʃi:t], s. das Bettuch; das Blatt, der Bogen (paper); die Platte (metal); — metal, — iron, das Eisenblech; — lightning, das Wetterleuchten.
shelf [ʃelf], s. das Brett, Regal; der Sims (mantel); (Geog.) die Sandbank; (coll.) on the —, sitzengeblieben.
shell [ʃel], s. die Schale (case); die Muschel (mussel); (Mil.) die Bombe, Granate. — v.a. schälen (peas); bombardieren, beschiessen (town).
shelter ['ʃeltə], s. das Obdach (lodging); der Unterstand, Schuppen; der Schutz (protection). — v.a. Obdach gewähren (Dat.); beschützen (protect). — v.n. sich schützen, unterstellen.
shelve [ʃelv], v.a. auf ein Brett legen; (fig.) aufschieben (postpone).
shelving ['ʃelviŋ], s. das Regal.
shepherd ['ʃepəd], s. der Schäfer, Hirt.
sheriff ['ʃerif], s. der Sheriff.
shew [ʃou] see show.
shield [ʃi:ld], s. der Schild. — v.a. schützen.
shift [ʃift], v.a. verschieben. — v.n. die Lage ändern. — s. die Veränderung, der Wechsel; (Industry) die Schicht.
shifty ['ʃifti], adj. unstet; durchtrieben.

shin [ʃin], s. (*Anat.*) das Schienbein.
shindy [ʃindi], s. der Lärm.
shine [ʃain], v.n. irr. scheinen (sun); glänzen. — s. der Glanz.
shingle (1) [ʃingl], s. (*Build.*) die Schindel; (*Hair*) der Herrenschnitt.
shingle (2) [ʃingl], s. (*Geol.*) der Kiesel.
shingles [ʃinglz], s. pl. (*Med.*) die Gürtelrose.
ship [ʃip], s. das Schiff. — v.a. verschiffen, (*Comm.*) versenden.
shipping [ʃipin], s. die Schiffahrt; (*Comm.*) der Versand, die Verfrachtung, Verschiffung.
shire [ʃaiə], s. die Grafschaft.
shirk [ʃəːk], v.a. vermeiden, sich drücken (vor, *Dat.*).
shirt [ʃəːt], s. das Hemd.
shirting [ʃəːtin], s. der Hemdenstoff.
shiver [ʃivə], v.n. zittern, beben. — s. der Schauer, Schauder.
shoal [ʃoul], s. der Schwarm; (*Naut.*) die Untiefe.
shock (1) [ʃɔk], v.a. entsetzen; erschrecken; schockieren. — s. der Schock, das Entsetzen.
shock (2) [ʃɔk], s. — of hair, zottiges Haar.
shoddy [ʃɔdi], adj. schlecht, wertlos.
shoe [ʃuː], s. der Schuh. — v.a. beschuhen; (*horse*) beschlagen.
shoelace, shoestring [ʃuːleis, ʃuːstrin], s. der Schuhsenkel, (*Austr.*) das Schuhschnürl; on a shoestring, fast ohne Geld.
shoeshine [ʃuːʃain], s. (*Am.*) der Schuhputzer.
shoestring see under **shoelace**.
shoot [ʃuːt], v.a. irr. schießen. — v.n. sprossen, hervorschießen; (*film*) aufnehmen. — s. (*Bot.*) der Sproß.
shooting [ʃuːtin], s. das Schießen; — range, der Schießstand. — adj. — star, die Sternschnuppe.
shop [ʃɔp], s. der Laden, das Geschäft; (*work*) die Werkstatt; talk —, fachsimpeln; — window, das Schaufenster. — v.n. einkaufen.
shopkeeper [ʃɔpkiːpə], s. der Kaufmann, Krämer.
shoplifter [ʃɔpliftə], s. der Ladendieb.
shore [ʃɔː], s. das Gestade, die Küste; die Stütze. — v.a. — up, stützen.
short [ʃɔːt], adj. kurz, klein, knapp; (*curt*) kurz angebunden; — of money, in Geldnot; run —, knapp werden; — sighted, kurzsichtig; be on — time working, kurz arbeiten. — s. (*Elect.*) (coll.) der Kurzschluß (short circuit); (pl.) die Kniehose, kurze Hose.
shortcoming [ʃɔːtkʌmin], s. der Fehler, Mangel.
shorten [ʃɔːtn], v.a. verkürzen, abkürzen. — v.n. kürzer werden.
shorthand [ʃɔːthænd], s. die Stenographie; — typist, die Stenotypistin.
shot [ʃɔt], s. der Schuß; (*man*) der Schütze.

shoulder [ʃouldə], s. (*Anat.*) die Schulter. — v.a. schultern, auf sich nehmen, auf die Achsel nehmen.
shout [ʃaut], v.n. schreien, rufen. — s. der Schrei, Ruf.
shove [ʃʌv], v.a. schieben, stoßen. — s. der Schub, Stoß.
shovel [ʃʌvl], s. die Schaufel. — v.a. schaufeln.
show [ʃou], v.a. irr. zeigen; (*fig.*) dartun. — v.n. sich zeigen, zu sehen sein; — off, prahlen, protzen. — v.r. — o.s. to be, sich erweisen als. — s. (*Theat.*) die Schau, Aufführung.
shower [ʃauə], s. der Schauer (rain); (*fig.*) die Fülle, der Überfluß; — (bath), die Dusche; take a — (bath), brausen. — v.a., v.n. herabregnen; überschütten.
showing [ʃouin], s. die Vorführung, der Beweis.
showy [ʃoui], adj. protzig, angeberisch.
shred [ʃred], s. der Fetzen; (*fig.*) die Spur (of evidence). — v.a. zerreißen, zerfetzen.
shrew [ʃruː], s. die Spitzmaus; (*fig.*) das zänkische Weib.
shrewd [ʃruːd], adj. schlau, verschlagen, listig.
shriek [ʃriːk], v.n. kreischen. — s. der Schrei, das Gekreisch.
shrift [ʃrift], s. give s.o. short —, mit einem kurzen Prozeß machen.
shrill [ʃril], adj. schrill, gellend, durchdringend.
shrimp [ʃrimp], s. (*Zool.*) die Garnele.
shrine [ʃrain], s. der (Reliquien)-schrein; der Altar.
shrink [ʃrink], v.n. irr. eingehen, einschrumpfen. — v.a. eingehen lassen.
shrinkage [ʃrinkidʒ], s. das Eingehen (fabric); (*Geol.*) die Schrumpfung.
shrivel [ʃrivl], v.n. einschrumpfen, sich runzeln.
shroud [ʃraud], s. das Leichentuch. — v.a. einhüllen.
Shrove Tuesday [ʃrouv], die Fastnacht.
shrub [ʃrʌb], s. (*Bot.*) der Strauch, die Staude.
shrug [ʃrʌg], v.a. (shoulders) die Achseln zucken. — s. das Achselzucken.
shudder [ʃʌdə], s. der Schauder. — v.n. schaudern.
shuffle [ʃʌfl], v.a. (cards) mischen. — v.n. schlürfen, schleppend gehen.
shun [ʃʌn], v.a. meiden.
shunt [ʃʌnt], v.a., v.n. rangieren.
shut [ʃʌt], v.a. irr. schließen. — v.n. sich schließen, zugehen; (coll.) — up! halt's Maul!
shutter [ʃʌtə], s. der Fensterladen.
shuttle [ʃʌtl], s. (*Mech.*) das Weberschiff.
shuttlecock [ʃʌtlkɔk], s. der Federball.
shy (1) [ʃai], adj. scheu, schüchtern. — v.n. scheuen (of horses).
shy (2) [ʃai], s. der Wurf.
sick [sik], adj. krank; unwohl, übel; leidend (suffering); (*fig.*) — of, überdrüssig (Genit.).

sicken [sikn], v.n. krank werden or sein; sich ekeln (be nauseated). — v.a. anekeln.

sickle [sikl], s. die Sichel.

sickness ['siknis], s. die Krankheit.

side [said], s. die Seite. — v.n. —with, Partei ergreifen für.

sideboard ['saidbɔ:d], s. das Büffet, die Anrichte.

sidereal [sai'diəriəl], adj. (Maths., Phys.) Sternen-, Stern-.

sidewalk ['saidwɔ:k] (Am.) see **pavement**.

siding ['saidiŋ],s.(Railw.)das Nebengleis.

sidle [saidl], v.n. — up to, sich heranmachen.

siege [si:dʒ], s. die Belagerung.

sieve [siv], s. das Sieb. — v.a. sieben.

sift [sift], v.a. sieben; (fig.) prüfen.

sigh [sai], v.n. seufzen. — s. der Seufzer.

sight [sait], s. die Sicht (view); die Sehkraft (sense of); der Anblick; at —, auf den ersten Blick; out of —, out of mind, aus den Augen, aus dem Sinn; (pl.) die Sehenswürdigkeiten, f. pl.; —seeing, die Besichtigung (der Sehenswürdigkeiten). — v.a. sichten.

sign [sain], s. das Zeichen; der Wink (hint); das Aushängeschild (of pub, shop etc.). — v.a. unterschreiben, unterzeichnen. — v.n. winken.

signal ['signəl], s. das Signal.

signboard ['sainbɔ:d], s. das Aushängeschild.

signet ['signit], s. das Siegel; — ring, der Siegelring.

significance [sig'nifikəns], s. die Bedeutung, der Sinn.

significant [sig'nifikənt], adj. bedeutend, wichtig.

signify ['signifai], v.a. bedeuten (mean); anzeigen (denote).

silence ['sailəns], s. das Schweigen, die Ruhe.

silent ['sailənt], adj. still; schweigsam (taciturn).

Silesian [sai'li:ʃən], adj. schlesisch. — s. der Schlesier.

silk [silk], s. (Text.) die Seide.

silkworm ['silkwə:m], s. (Ent.) die Seidenraupe.

sill [sil], s. die Schwelle; window —, das Fensterbrett.

silly ['sili], adj. albern, dumm.

silver ['silvə], s. das Silber. — v.a. versilbern. — adj. silbern.

similar ['similə], adj. ähnlich.

simile ['simili], s. (Lit.) das Gleichnis.

simmer ['simə], v.n., v.a. langsam kochen.

simper ['simpə], v.n. lächeln, grinsen.

simple [simpl], adj. einfach; (fig.) einfältig.

simpleton ['simpltən], s. der Einfaltspinsel, Tor.

simplicity [sim'plisiti], s. die Einfachheit; (fig.) die Einfalt.

simplify ['simplifai], v.a. vereinfachen.

simulate ['simjuleit], v.a. nachahmen, heucheln, vortäuschen.

simultaneous [siməl'teinjəs], adj. gleichzeitig.

sin [sin], s. die Sünde. — v.n. sündigen.

since [sins], prep. seit (Dat.). — conj. seit (time); weil, da (cause). — adv. seither, seitdem.

sincere [sin'siə], adj. aufrichtig.

sincerely [sin'siəli], adv. yours —, Ihr ergebener (letters).

sincerity [sin'seriti], s. die Aufrichtigkeit.

sine [sain], s. (Maths.) der Sinus, die Sinuskurve.

sinecure ['sainikjuə], s. der Ruheposten, die Sinekure.

sinew ['sinju:], s. (Anat.) die Sehne, der Nerv.

sinful ['sinful], adj. sündig, sündhaft.

sing [siŋ], v.a., v.n. irr. singen; — of, besingen.

singe [sindʒ], v.a. sengen.

Singhalese [siŋgə'li:z], adj. singhalesisch. — s. der Singhalese, die Singhalesin.

single [siŋgl], adj. einzeln; ledig (unmarried); single-handed, allein. — v.a. — out, auswählen.

singlet ['siŋglit], s. die Unterjacke.

singly ['siŋgli], adv. einzeln (one by one).

singular ['siŋgjulə], adj. einzigartig, einzig. — s. (Gram.) die Einzahl.

sinister ['sinistə], adj. böse, unheimlich, finster.

sink [siŋk], v.a. irr. versenken; (fig.) (differences etc.) begraben. — v.n. versinken; (Naut.) sinken, versinken. — s. das Abwaschbecken, Ausgußbecken.

sinker ['siŋkə], s. der Schachtarbeiter (man); (Naut.) das Senkblei.

sinuous ['sinjuəs], adj. gewunden.

sinus ['sainəs], s. (Anat.) die Knochenhöhle; die Bucht.

sip [sip], v.a. schlürfen, nippen. — s. das Schlückchen.

siphon ['saifən], s. (Phys.) der Heber; die Siphonflasche. — v.a. auspumpen.

Sir (1) [sə:] (title preceding Christian name) Herr von... (baronet or knight).

sir (2) [sə:], s. Herr (respectful form of address); dear —, sehr geehrter Herr (in letters).

sire [saiə], s. der Ahnherr, Vater. — v.a. zeugen (horses etc.).

siren ['saiərən], s. die Sirene.

sirloin ['sə:lɔin], s. das Lendenstück.

siskin ['siskin], s. (Orn.) der Zeisig.

sister ['sistə], s. die Schwester; (Eccl.) Nonne; —in-law, die Schwägerin.

sit [sit], v.n. irr. sitzen. — an examination, eine Prüfung machen.

site [sait], s. die Lage, der Platz.

sitting ['sitiŋ], s. die Sitzung; — room, das Wohnzimmer.

situated ['sitjueitid], adj. gelegen.

situation [sitju'eiʃən], s. die Lage, Situation; der Posten, die Stellung (post).

six [siks], num. adj. sechs; *be at —es and sevens*, durcheinander, uneinig sein.

sixteen [siks'ti:n], num. adj. sechzehn.

sixth [siksθ], num. adj. sechste.

sixty ['siksti], num. adj. sechzig.

size [saiz], s. die Größe, das Maß; (*fig.*) der Umfang.

skate (1) [skeit], s. der Schlittschuh. — v.n. Schlittschuh laufen.

skate (2) [skeit], s. (*Zool.*) der Glattrochen.

skeleton ['skelitən], s. das Skelett, Knochengerüst; — *key*, der Dietrich.

sketch [sketʃ], s. die Skizze, der Entwurf. — v.a. skizzieren, entwerfen. — v.n. Skizzen entwerfen.

sketchy ['sketʃi], adj. flüchtig.

skew [skju:], adj. schief, schräg.

skewer [skju:ə], s. der Fleischspieß.

ski [ski:], s. der Schi.

skid [skid], v.n. gleiten, schleudern, rutschen. — v.a. hemmen, bremsen (*wheel*). — s. der Hemmschuh, die Bremse (*of wheel*).

skiff [skif], s. (*Naut.*) der Nachen, Kahn.

skilful ['skilful], adj. geschickt, gewandt; (*fig.*) erfahren.

skill [skil], s. die Geschicklichkeit, Gewandtheit; (*fig.*) die Erfahrung.

skim [skim], v.a. abschöpfen, abschäumen.

skimp [skimp], v.a. knausern, sparsam sein (mit, *Dat.*).

skimpy ['skimpi], adj. knapp.

skin [skin], s. die Haut; die Schale (*fruit*); — *deep*, oberflächlich. — v.a. häuten, schinden.

skinflint ['skinflint], s. der Geizhals.

skinner ['skinə], s. der Kürschner.

skip [skip], v.n. springen, hüpfen. — v.a. (*coll.*) auslassen, überspringen. — s. der Sprung.

skipper ['skipə], s. (*Naut.*) der Kapitän; (*coll.*) der Chef.

skipping rope ['skipiŋ roup], s. das Springseil.

skirmish ['skə:miʃ], s. das Scharmützel. — v.n. scharmützeln.

skirt [skə:t], s. der Rock, Rockschoß (*woman's garment*); der Saum (*edge*). — v.a. einsäumen (*seam, edge*); grenzen, am Rande entlang gehen.

skirting (board) ['skə:tiŋ (bɔ:d)], s. die Fußleiste.

skit [skit], s. die Stichelei, die Parodie, Satire.

skittish ['skitiʃ], adj. leichtfertig.

skulk [skʌlk], v.n. lauern, herumlungern.

skull [skʌl], s. der Schädel; — *and crossbones*, der Totenkopf.

skunk [skʌŋk], s. (*Zool.*) das Stinktier; (*coll.*) der Schuft.

sky [skai], s. der (sichtbare) Himmel.

skylark ['skailɑ:k], s. (*Orn.*) die Feldlerche.

skylarking ['skailɑ:kiŋ], s. das Possenreißen, die Streiche.

skyline ['skailain], s. der Horizont.

skyscraper ['skaiskreipə], s. der Wolkenkratzer.

slab [slæb], s. die Platte (*stone*); die Tafel, das Stück.

slack [slæk], adj. schlaff (*feeble*); locker (*loose*). — s. der Kohlengrus. — v.n. nachlassen, locker werden, faulenzen.

slacken [slækn], v.a., v.n. locker werden, nachlassen.

slackness ['slæknis], s. die Schlaffheit, Faulheit.

slag [slæg], s. die Schlacke.

slake [sleik], v.a. dämpfen, löschen, stillen.

slam (1) [slæm], v.a. zuwerfen, zuschlagen (*door*). — s. der Schlag.

slam (2) [slæm], v.a. (*Cards*) Schlemm ansagen, Schlemm machen. — s. (*Cards*) der Stich.

slander ['slɑ:ndə], v.a. verleumden. — s. die Verleumdung.

slanderer ['slɑ:ndərə], s. der Verleumder.

slang [slæŋ], s. der Slang.

slant [slɑ:nt], s. die schräge Richtung, der Winkel (*angle*).

slap [slæp], v.a. schlagen. — s. der Klaps, Schlag.

slapdash ['slæpdæʃ], adj. oberflächlich.

slash [slæʃ], v.a. schlitzen, aufschlitzen; (*coll.*) (*Comm.*) herunterbringen (*prices*). — s. der Hieb, Schlag.

slate [sleit], s. der Schiefer. — v.a. mit Schiefer decken; (*fig.*) ankreiden, ausschelten (*scold*).

slattern ['slætə:n], s. die Schlampe.

slaughter ['slɔ:tə], v.a. schlachten; niedermetzeln. — s. das Schlachten; das Gemetzel.

slave [sleiv], s. der Sklave; — *driver*, der Sklavenaufseher. — v.n. — (*away*), sich placken, sich rackern.

slavery ['sleivəri], s. die Sklaverei.

slavish ['sleiviʃ], adj. sklavisch.

slay [slei], v.a. erschlagen, töten.

sled, sledge [sled, sledʒ], s. der Schlitten.

sleek [sli:k], adj. glatt. — v.a. glätten.

sleep [sli:p], v.n. irr. schlafen. — s. der Schlaf.

sleeper ['sli:pə], s. der Schläfer; (*Railw.*) die Bahnschwelle; der Schlafwagen (*sleeping car*).

sleepwalker ['sli:pwɔ:kə], s. der Nachtwandler.

sleet [sli:t], s. der Graupelregen.

sleeve [sli:v], s. der Ärmel; der Umschlag (*of record*); *have up o.'s —*, eine Überraschung bereithalten; *laugh in o.'s —*, sich ins Fäustchen lachen.

sleigh [slei], s. der Schlitten; — *ride*, die Schlittenfahrt.

sleight [slait], s. — *of hand*, der Taschenspielerstreich; der Trick.

slender ['slendə], adj. schlank, dünn, gering.

slice [slais], s. die Schnitte, Scheibe. — v.a. in Scheiben schneiden.

slick [slik], adj. glatt.

slide [slaid], v.n. irr. gleiten, rutschen (*glide*). — v.a. einschieben. — s. die Rutschbahn; (*Phot.*) das Dia, Diapositiv; — *rule*, der Rechenschieber.

snarl

slight [slait], *adj.* leicht (*light*), gering (*small*); (*fig.*) schwach, dünn(*weak*). — *s.* die Geringschätzung, Respektlosigkeit. — *v.a.* mißachten, geringschätzig behandeln.
slim [slim], *adj.* schlank.
slime [slaim], *s.* der Schleim (*phlegm*); der Schlamm (*mud*).
sling [sliŋ], *v.a. irr.* schleudern, werfen. — *s.* die Schleuder; (*Med.*) die Binde; der Wurf (*throw*).
slink [sliŋk], *v.n. irr.* schleichen.
slip [slip], *v.n.* ausgleiten; — *away*, entschlüpfen; — *up*, einen Fehltritt begehen (*err*). — *v.a.* gleiten lassen, schieben. — *s.* das Ausgleiten; (*fig.*) der Fehltritt; der Fehler (*mistake*); der Unterrock (*petticoat*); *give s.o. the* —, einem entgehen, entschlüpfen.
slipper ['slipə], *s.* der Pantoffel, Hausschuh.
slippery ['slipəri], *adj.* schlüpfrig, glatt.
slipshod ['slipʃɔd], *adj.* nachlässig.
slit [slit], *v.a.* schlitzen, spalten. — *s.* der Schlitz, Spalt.
slither ['sliðə], *v.n.* gleiten, rutschen.
sloe [slou], *s.* (*Bot.*) die Schlehe.
slogan ['slougən], *s.* das Schlagwort.
sloop [slu:p], *s.* (*Naut.*) die Schaluppe.
slop [slɔp], *s.* das Spülicht, Spülwasser.
slope [sloup], *s.* der Abhang, die Abdachung. — *v.n.* sich neigen. — *v.a.* abschrägen.
sloppy ['slɔpi], *adj.* unordentlich, nachlässig.
slot [slɔt], *s.* der Spalt, Schlitz (*slit*); die Kerbe (*notch*); — *machine*, der Automat.
sloth [slouθ], *s.* die Trägheit; (*Zool.*) das Faultier.
slouch [slautʃ], *v.n.* umherschlendern; sich schlaff halten.
slough [slau], *s.* der Morast, Sumpf.
slovenly ['slʌvnli], *adj.* schlampig, schmutzig.
slow [slou], *adj.* langsam; (*Phot.*) — *motion*, die Zeitlupenaufnahme. — *v.n.* — *down*, langsamer fahren *or* laufen.
slow-worm ['slouwə:m], *s.* (*Zool.*) die Blindschleiche.
sludge [slʌdʒ], *s.* der Schlamm, Schmutz.
slug [slʌg], *s.* (*Zool.*) die Wegschnecke; (*Am.*) die Kugel.
sluggish ['slʌgiʃ], *adj.* träg(e).
sluice [slu:s], *s.* die Schleuse. — *v.a.* ablassen (*drain*); begießen (*water*).
slum [slʌm], *s.* das Elendsviertel; Haus im Elendsviertel.
slumber ['slʌmbə], *s.* der Schlummer. — *v.n.* schlummern.
slump [slʌmp], *s.* (*Comm.*) der Tiefstand der Konjunktur; der Preissturz. — *v.n.* stürzen.
slur [slə:], *v.a.* undeutlich sprechen. — *s.* der Schandfleck, die Beleidigung; das Bindezeichen.
slush [slʌʃ], *s.* der Matsch, Schlamm; (*Lit.*) der Kitsch, die Schundliteratur.
slut [slʌt], *s.* die Schlampe.

sly [slai], *adj.* schlau, listig.
smack [smæk], *v.n.* schmecken (*of*, nach, *Dat.*). — *v.a.* schmatzen, lecken. — *s.* der Klaps. — *adv.* (*coll.*) — *in the middle*, gerade in der Mitte.
small [smɔ:l], *adj.* klein; (*fig.*) kleinlich (*petty*); — *talk*, das Geplauder.
smallpox ['smɔ:lpɔks], *s.* (*Med.*) die Blattern, *f. pl.*
smart [sma:t], *adj.* schneidig; elegant, schick (*well-dressed*). — *v.n.* schmerzen. — *s.* der Schmerz.
smash [smæʃ], *v.a.* zertrümmern, in Stücke schlagen. — *v.n.* zerschmettern; (*fig.*) zusammenbrechen. — *s.* der Krach.
smattering ['smætəriŋ], *s.* die oberflächliche Kenntnis.
smear [smiə], *v.a.* beschmieren; (*Am. coll.*) den Charakter angreifen, verleumden. — *s.* die Beschmierung, Befleckung.
smell [smel], *v.a. irr.* riechen. — *v.n.* riechen (nach, *Dat.*). — *s.* der Geruch.
smelt (1) [smelt], *v.a.* (*Metall.*) schmelzen.
smelt (2) [smelt], *s.* (*Zool.*) der Stintfisch.
smile [smail], *v.n.* lächeln. — *s.* das Lächeln.
smirk [smə:k], *v.n.* grinsen. — *s.* das Grinsen, die Grimasse.
smite [smait], *v.a. irr.* treffen, schlagen.
smith [smiθ], *s.* der Schmied.
smitten [smitn], *adj.* verliebt.
smock [smɔk], *s.* der Arbeitskittel.
smoke [smouk], *v.a., v.n.* rauchen; räuchern (*fish etc.*). — *s.* der Rauch.
smoked [smoukd], *adj.* — *ham*, der Räucherschinken.
smooth [smu:ð], *adj.* glatt, sanft (*to touch*); (*fig.*) glatt, geschmeidig, wendig. — *v.a.* glätten, ebnen.
smother ['smʌðə], *v.a.* ersticken.
smoulder ['smouldə], *v.n.* schwelen.
smudge [smʌdʒ], *v.a.* beschmutzen. — *v.n.* schmieren, schmutzen. — *s.* der Schmutzfleck, Schmutz.
smug [smʌg], *adj.* selbstgefällig.
smuggle [smʌgl], *v.a.* schmuggeln.
smuggler ['smʌglə], *s.* der Schmuggler.
smut [smʌt], *v.a., v.n.* beschmutzen. — *s.* (*fig.*) der Schmutz.
snack [snæk], *s.* der Imbiß.
snaffle [snæfl], *s.* die Trense.
snag [snæg], *s.* die Schwierigkeit; der Haken.
snail [sneil], *s.* (*Zool.*) die Schnecke.
snake [sneik], *s.* (*Zool.*) die Schlange.
snap [snæp], *v.n.* schnappen (*at*, nach, *Dat.*); (*fig.*) einen anfahren (*shout at s.o.*). — *v.a.* (er)schnappen; (*Phot.*) knipsen. — *s.* (*abbr. for* **snapshot** ['snæpʃɔt]) (*Phot.*) das Photo.
snare [snɛə], *s.* die Schlinge. — *v.a. see* **ensnare**.
snarl [sna:l], *v.n.* knurren (*dog*); — *at s.o.*, einen anfahren, anschnauzen.

487

snatch

snatch [snætʃ], *v.a.* erschnappen, erhaschen.

sneak [sni:k], *v.n.* kriechen, schleichen. — *s.* der Kriecher.

sneer [sniə], *v.n.* höhnen, verhöhnen (*at, Acc.*). — *s.* der Spott.

sneeze [sni:z], *v.n.* niesen. — *s.* das Niesen.

sniff [snif], *v.n.* schnüffeln.

snigger ['snigə], *v.n.* kichern. — *s.* das Kichern.

snip [snip], *v.a.* schneiden, schnippeln.

snipe (1) [snaip], *s.* (*Orn.*) die Schnepfe.

snipe (2) [snaip], *v.n.* schießen.

snivel [snivl], *v.n.* schluchzen (*from weeping*); verschnupft sein (*with a cold*).

snob [snɔb], *s.* der Snob.

snobbish ['snɔbiʃ], *adj.* vornehm tuend; protzig, snobistisch.

snooze [snu:z], *s.* das Schläfchen. — *v.n.* einschlafen, ein Schläfchen machen.

snore [snɔ:], *v.n.* schnarchen. — *s.* das Schnarchen.

snort [snɔ:t], *v.n.* schnaufen; schnarchen (*snore*).

snout [snaut], *s.* die Schnauze, der Rüssel.

snow [snou], *s.* der Schnee. — *v.n.* schneien.

snowdrift ['snoudrift], *s.* das Schneegestöber.

snowdrop ['snoudrɔp], *s.* (*Bot.*) das Schneeglöckchen.

snub [snʌb], *v.a.* kurz abfertigen; (*fig.*) schneiden (*ignore*). — *adj.* — *nosed*, stumpfnasig. — *s.* die Geringschätzung, das Ignorieren.

snuff [snʌf], *s.* der Schnupftabak. — *v.a.* ausblasen (*candle*).

snug [snʌg], *adj.* behaglich; geborgen (*protected*).

so [sou], *adv.* so, also; *not* — *as*, nicht so wie. — *conj.* so.

soak [souk], *v.a.* einweichen, durchtränken. — *v.n.* weichen, durchsickern (*in(to*), in, *Acc.*). — *s.* der Regenguß.

soap [soup], *s.* die Seife. — *v.a.* einseifen.

soar [sɔ:], *v.n.* sich aufschwingen, schweben.

sob [sɔb], *v.n.* schluchzen. — *s.* das Schluchzen.

sober ['soubə], *adj.* nüchtern. — *v.a.*, *v.n.* — (*down*), (sich) ernüchtern.

sobriety [so'braiəti], *s.* die Nüchternheit.

soccer ['sɔkə], *s.* (*Sport*) das Fußballspiel.

sociable ['souʃəbl], *adj.* gesellig.

social ['souʃəl], *adj.* sozial, gesellschaftlich. — *s.* die Gesellschaft (*party*).

socialism ['souʃəlizm], *s.* (*Pol.*) der Sozialismus.

socialist ['souʃəlist], *adj.* (*Pol.*) sozialistisch, Sozial-. — *s.* der Sozialist.

society [sə'saiəti], *s.* die Gesellschaft (*human* —); der Verein (*association*); (*Comm.*) die (Handels)gesellschaft.

sock (1) [sɔk], *s.* der Strumpf.

sock (2) [sɔk], *v.a.* (*sl.*) schlagen, boxen.

socket ['sɔkit], *s.* *eye* —, die Augenhöhle; (*Elec.*) die Steckdose.

sod [sɔd], *s.* der Rasen, die Erde.

sodden [sɔdn], *adj.* durchweicht.

sofa ['soufə], *s.* das Sofa.

soft [sɔft], *adj.* weich, sanft; einfältig (*stupid*).

soften [sɔfn], *v.a.* weich machen, erweichen. — *v.n.* weich werden, erweichen.

soil [sɔil], *s.* der Boden, die Erde. — *v.a.* beschmutzen.

sojourn ['sʌdʒən *or* 'sɔdʒən], *s.* der Aufenthalt. — *v.n.* sich aufhalten.

solace ['sɔlis], *s.* der Trost.

solar ['soulə], *adj.* Sonnen-.

solder ['sɔldə *or* 'sɔ:də], *v.a.* löten. — *s.* das Lötmittel.

soldier ['souldʒə], *s.* der Soldat. — *v.n.* dienen, Soldat sein.

sole (1) [soul], *s.* (*Zool.*) die Seezunge.

sole (2) [soul], *s.* die Sohle (*foot*).

sole (3) [soul], *adj.* allein, einzig.

solecism ['sɔlisizm], *s.* der Sprachschnitzer.

solemn ['sɔləm], *adj.* feierlich.

solemnize ['sɔləmnaiz], *v.a.* feiern, feierlich begehen.

solicit [sə'lisit], *v.a.* direkt erbitten, angehen, ansuchen (*for, um*).

solicitor [sə'lisitə], *s.* (*Law*) der Anwalt, Rechtsanwalt.

solicitous [sə'lisitəs], *adj.* besorgt.

solid ['sɔlid], *adj.* fest; solide; (*fig.*) gediegen; massiv (*bulky*).

solidify [sə'lidifai], *v.a.* verdichten, fest machen. — *v.n.* sich verfestigen.

soliloquy [sə'liləkwi], *s.* das Selbstgespräch, der Monolog.

solitaire [sɔli'tɛə], *s.* der Solitär; (*Am.*) die Patience.

solitary ['sɔlitəri], *adj.* einzeln (*single*); einsam (*lonely*).

solitude ['sɔlitju:d], *s.* die Einsamkeit.

solstice ['sɔlstis], *s.* die Sonnenwende.

soluble ['sɔljubl], *adj.* (*Chem.*) löslich; lösbar.

solution [sə'lju:ʃən], *s.* die Lösung.

solvable ['sɔlvəbl], *adj.* (auf)lösbar (*problem, puzzle*).

solve [sɔlv], *v.a.* lösen (*problem, puzzle*).

solvent ['sɔlvənt], *adj.* (*Chem.*) auflösend; (*Comm.*) zahlungsfähig. — *s.* das Lösungsmittel.

sombre ['sɔmbə], *adj.* düster; schwermütig, traurig.

some [sʌm], *adj.* irgend ein, etwas; (*pl.*) einige, manche; etliche.

somebody ['sʌmbɔdi], *s.* jemand.

somersault ['sʌməsɔ:lt], *s.* der Purzelbaum.

sometimes ['sʌmtaimz], *adv.* manchmal, zuweilen.

somewhat ['sʌmwɔt], *adv.* etwas, ziemlich.

somewhere ['sʌmwɛə], *adv.* irgendwo(hin).

speculate

somnambulist [sɔm'næmbjulist], *s.* der Nachtwandler.

somnolent ['sɔmnələnt], *adj.* schläfrig, schlafsüchtig.

son [sʌn], *s.* der Sohn; — *-in-law,* der Schwiegersohn.

song [sɔŋ], *s.* (*Mus.*) das Lied; der Gesang; *for a* —, spottbillig.

sonnet ['sɔnit], *s.* (*Poet.*) das Sonett.

sonorous ['sɔnərəs], *adj.* wohlklingend.

soon [su:n], *adv.* bald.

sooner ['su:nə], *comp. adv.* lieber (*rather*); früher, eher (*earlier*), *no* — *said than done,* gesagt, getan.

soot [sut], *s.* der Ruß.

soothe [su:ð], *v.a.* besänftigen.

soothsayer ['su:θseiə], *s.* der Wahrsager.

sop [sɔp], *s.* der eingetunkte Bissen; (*fig.*) die Bestechung (*bribe*).

soporific [sɔpə'rifik], *adj.* einschläfernd.

soprano [sə'prɑ:nou], *s.* (*Mus.*) der Sopran.

sorcerer ['sɔ:sərə], *s.* der Zauberer.

sorceress ['sɔ:sərəs], *s.* die Hexe.

sorcery ['sɔ:səri], *s.* die Zauberei, Hexerei.

sordid ['sɔ:did], *adj.* schmutzig; gemein.

sore [sɔ:], *adj.* wund, schmerzhaft; empfindlich. — *s.* die wunde Stelle.

sorrel (1) ['sɔrəl], *s.* (*Bot.*) der Sauerampfer.

sorrel (2) ['sɔrəl], *s.* (*Zool.*) der Rotfuchs.

sorrow ['sɔrou], *s.* der Kummer, das Leid, der Gram.

sorry ['sɔri], *adj.* traurig; *I am* —, es tut mir leid.

sort [sɔ:t], *s.* die Art, Gattung, Sorte. — *v.a.* aussortieren.

sortie ['sɔ:ti:], *s.* (*Mil.*) der Ausfall.

sot [sɔt], *s.* der Trunkenbold.

soul [soul], *s.* die Seele; *not a* —, niemand, keine Menschenseele.

sound (1) [saund], *v.n., v.a.* tönen, klingen, erklingen lassen. — *s.* der Klang, Ton, Laut.

sound (2) [saund], *adj.* gesund; (*fig.*) vernünftig (*plan etc.*); solide.

soup [su:p], *s.* die Suppe.

sour [sauə], *adj.* sauer; (*fig.*) mürrisch.

source [sɔ:s], *s.* die Quelle; der Ursprung (*origin*).

souse [saus], *v.a.* einpökeln, einsalzen.

south [sauθ], *s.* der Süden.

South African [sauθ 'æfrikən], *adj.* südafrikanisch. — *s.* der Südafrikaner.

southern ['sʌðən], *adj.* südlich, Süd-.

sou(th)-wester [sau(θ)'westə], *s.* (*Naut.*) der Südwester.

souvenir ['su:vəniə], *s.* das Andenken.

sovereign ['sɔvrin], *s.* der Herrscher (*ruler*); das Goldstück (£1 *coin*). — *adj.* allerhöchst, souverän.

Soviet ['souviit], *adj.* sowjetisch. — *s.* der Sowjet.

sow (1) [sau], *s.* (*Zool.*) die Sau.

sow (2) [sou], *v.a. irr.* säen, ausstreuen (*cast*).

spa [spɑ:], *s.* das Bad; der Kurort.

space [speis], *s.* der Zwischenraum (*interval*); der Raum, das Weltall, der Kosmos (*interplanetary*); der Platz (*room*). — *v.a.* sperren, richtig plazieren.

spacious ['speiʃəs], *adj.* geräumig.

spade [speid], *s.* der Spaten; *call a* — *a* —, das Kind beim rechten Namen nennen; (*Cards*) das Pik.

span [spæn], *s.* die Spanne (*time*); die Spannweite. — *v.a.* überspannen (*bridge*); ausmessen.

spangle ['spæŋgl], *s.* der Flitter. — *v.a.* beflittern, schmücken.

Spaniard ['spænjəd], *s.* der Spanier.

spaniel ['spænjəl], *s.* (*Zool.*) der Wachtelhund.

Spanish ['spæniʃ], *adj.* spanisch.

spanner ['spænə], *s.* der Schraubenschlüssel.

spar (1) [spɑ:], *s.* (*Naut.*) der Sparren.

spar (2) [spɑ:], *s.* (*Geol.*) der Spat.

spar (3) [spɑ:], *v.n.* boxen.

spare [spɛə], *v.a.* schonen (*save*); sparsam sein; übrig haben. — *v.n.* sparen; sparsam sein. — *adj.* übrig (*extra*); mager, hager (*lean*); Reserve- (*tyre etc.*).

sparing ['spɛəriŋ], *adj.* sparsam, karg.

spark [spɑ:k], *s.* der Funken; (*fig.*) der helle Kopf.

sparkle ['spɑ:kl], *v.n.* glänzen, funkeln. — *s.* das Funkeln.

sparrow ['spærou], *s.* (*Orn.*) der Sperling.

sparrowhawk ['spærouhɔ:k], *s.* (*Orn.*) der Sperber.

sparse [spɑ:s], *adj.* spärlich, dünn.

spasm [spæzm], *s.* der Krampf.

spasmodic [spæz'mɔdik], *adj.* krampfhaft; (*fig.*) ab und zu auftretend.

spats [spæts], *s. pl.* die Gamaschen, *f.pl.*

spatter ['spætə], *v.a.* bespritzen, besudeln.

spatula ['spætjulə], *s.* der Spachtel.

spawn [spɔ:n], *s.* der Laich, die Brut.

speak [spi:k], *v.a., v.n. irr.* sprechen, reden; — *out,* frei heraussprechen.

speaker ['spi:kə], *s.* der Sprecher.

spear [spiə], *s.* der Spieß, Speer, die Lanze. — *v.a.* aufspießen.

special [speʃl], *adj.* besonder, speziell, Sonder-.

specific [spi'sifik], *adj.* spezifisch, eigentümlich.

specify ['spesifai], *v.a.* spezifizieren.

specimen ['spesimən], *s.* die Probe; (*Comm.*) das Muster.

specious ['spi:ʃəs], *adj.* bestechend, trügerisch.

speck [spek], *s.* der Fleck.

speckle [spekl], *s.* der Tüpfel, Sprenkel. — *v.a.* sprenkeln.

spectacle ['spektəkl], *s.* das Schauspiel, der Anblick; (*pl.*) die Brille.

spectator [spek'teitə], *s.* der Zuschauer.

spectre ['spektə], *s.* das Gespenst.

speculate ['spekjuleit], *v.n.* nachsinnen, grübeln (*ponder*); spekulieren.

speculative

speculative ['spekjulətiv], *adj.* speku-
lativ; sinnend.

speech [spiːtʃ], *s.* die Rede, Ansprache;
das Sprechen (*articulation*); *figure of*
—, die Redewendung; *make a* —,
eine Rede halten.

speechify ['spiːtʃifai], *v.n.* viele Worte
machen, unermüdlich reden.

speed [spiːd], *s.* die Eile; die Geschwindigkeit (*velocity*); (*Mus.*) das Tempo.
— *v.a.* (eilig) fortschicken. — *v.n.*
eilen, schnell fahren; — *up*, sich
beeilen.

spell (1) [spel], *s.* der Zauber (*enchantment*). — *v.a.* buchstabieren (*verbally*);
richtig schreiben (*in writing*).

spell (2) [spel], *s.* die Zeitlang, Zeit
(*period*).

spellbound ['spelbaund], *adj.* bezau-
bert, gebannt.

spend [spend], *v.a. irr.* ausgeben
(*money*); verbringen (*time*); aufwenden (*energy*); erschöpfen (*exhaust*).

spendthrift ['spendθrift], *s.* der Ver-
schwender.

spew [spjuː], *v.a.* speien; ausspeien.

sphere [sfiə], *s.* die Sphäre (*also fig.*);
(*Geom.*) die Kugel.

spice [spais], *s.* die Würze (*seasoning*);
das Gewürz (*herb*). — *v.a.* würzen.

spider ['spaidə], *s.* (*Zool.*) die Spinne.

spigot ['spigət], *s.* (*Mech.*) der Zapfen.

spike [spaik], *s.* die Spitze, der lange
Nagel; (*fig.*) der Dorn. — *v.a.* durchbohren, spießen; (*Mil.*) vernageln
(*a gun*).

spill (1) [spil], *v.a. irr.* ausschütten,
vergießen; (*Am. coll.*) — *the beans*,
mit der Sprache herausrücken, alles
verraten; *it's no good crying over spilt
milk*, was geschehen ist, ist geschehen.

spill (2) [spil], *s.* der Fidibus.

spin [spin], *v.a. irr.* spinnen, drehen,
wirbeln. — *v.n.* wirbeln, sich schnell
drehen; — *dry*, schleudern. — *s.* die
schnelle Drehung; — *drier*, die
Wäscheschleuder.

spinach ['spinidʒ], *s.* (*Bot.*) der Spinat.

spinal ['spainəl], *adj.* Rückgrats-.

spine [spain], *s.* (*Anat.*) die Wirbelsäule;
der Rücken (*of book*).

spinney ['spini], *s.* das Gestrüpp.

spinster ['spinstə], *s.* die (alte) Jungfer;
die unverheiratete Dame.

spiral ['spaiərəl], *adj.* Spiral-, gewunden. — *s.* (*Geom.*) die Spirale.

spirant ['spaiərənt], *s.* (*Phonet.*) der
Spirant.

spire [spaiə], *s.* (*Archit.*) die Turmspitze.

spirit ['spirit], *s.* der Geist; das Gespenst (*ghost*); der Mut (*courage*); die
Stimmung, Verfassung (*mood*); das
geistige Getränk (*drink*), (*pl.*) Spirituosen, *pl.*; *in high* —*s*, in guter Stimmung, Laune. — *v.a.* — *away*, entführen, verschwinden lassen.

spiritual ['spiritjuəl], *adj.* geistig (*mental*); (*Rel.*) geistlich. — *s.* (*Mus.*) das
Negerlied.

spit (1) [spit], *s.* der Spieß, Bratspieß.
— *v.a.* aufspießen.

spit (2) [spit], *v.n. irr.* ausspucken. — *s.*
die Spucke.

spite [spait], *s.* der Groll; *in — of*, trotz
(*Genit.*). — *v.a.* ärgern.

spiteful ['spaitful], *adj.* boshaft.

spittle [spitl], *s.* der Speichel.

spittoon, [spi'tuːn], *s.* der Spucknapf.

splash [splæʃ], *s.* der Spritzer; *make a*
—, Aufsehen erregen. — *v.a., v.n.*
spritzen; (*fig.*) um sich werfen
(*money etc.*).

splay [splei], *v.a.* ausrenken, verrenken.

spleen [spliːn], *s.* (*Anat.*) die Milz;
(*fig.*) der Spleen, die Laune, Marotte.

splendour ['splendə], *s.* die Pracht, der
Glanz.

splice [splais], *v.a.* splissen (*Naut.*); —
the mainbrace, das Hauptfaß öffnen!

splint [splint], *s.* (*Med.*) die Schiene.

splinter ['splintə], *s.* der Span; der
Splitter (*fragment*).

split [split], *v.a. irr.* spalten; (*fig.*)
verteilen, teilen (*divide*). — *v.n.* sich
trennen; (*coll.*) — *on s.o.*, einen
verraten. — *adj.* — *second timing*, auf
den Bruchteil einer Sekunde. — *s.*
die Spaltung.

splutter ['splatə], *v.n.* sprudeln. — *s.*
das Sprudeln.

spoil [spoil], *v.a. irr.* verderben; (*child*)
verwöhnen; (*Mil.*) plündern, berau-
ben. — *v.n.* verderben. — *s.* (*pl.*) die
Beute.

spoilsport ['spoilspoːt], *s.* der Spielverderber.

spoke [spouk], *s.* die Speiche; die
Sprosse.

spokesman ['spouksmən], *s.* der Wortführer, Sprecher.

sponge [spandʒ], *s.* der Schwamm; —
cake, die Sandtorte. — *v.a.* mit dem
Schwamm wischen. — *v.n.* (*coll.*)
schmarotzen (*on*, bei, *Dat.*).

sponger ['spandʒə], *s.* (*coll.*) der
Schmarotzer (*parasite*).

sponsor ['sponsə], *s.* der Bürge (*guarantor*); der Förderer; Pate. — *v.a.*
fördern, unterstützen.

spontaneous [spon'teiniəs], *adj.* spontan, freiwillig.

spook [spuːk], *s.* der Spuk, Geist, das
Gespenst.

spool [spuːl], *s.* die Spule. — *v.a.* auf-
spulen.

spoon [spuːn], *s.* der Löffel. — *v.a.* mit
dem Löffel essen, löffeln.

sport [spoːt], *s.* der Sport; (*fig.*) der
Scherz. — *v.a.* tragen (*wear*). — *v.n.*
scherzen.

spot [spot], *s.* die Stelle, der Ort, Platz;
(*stain*) der Fleck; (*fig.*) der Schandfleck (*on o.'s honour*); *on the* —,
sogleich; auf der Stelle; *in a* —, (*Am.
coll.*) in Verlegenheit; — *cash*, Barzahlung, *f.* — *v.a.* entdecken, finden.

spotted ['spotid], *adj.* fleckig, gefleckt;
befleckt; pickelig.

spouse [spauz], *s.* der Gatte; die Gattin.

spout [spaut], *v.a.*, *v.n.* ausspeien, sprudeln, sprudeln lassen; (*sl.*) predigen, schwatzen. — *s.* die Tülle (*teapot etc.*); die Abflußröhre.
sprain [sprein], *v.a.* (*Med.*) verrenken. — *s.* die Verrenkung.
sprat [spræt], *s.* (*Zool.*) die Sprotte.
sprawl [sprɔːl], *v.n.* sich spreizen, ausbreiten.
spray [sprei], *v.a.*, *v.n.* sprühen spritzen. — *s.* die Sprühe; der Sprühregen.
spread [spred], *v.a.*, *v.n.* *irr.* ausbreiten; verbreiten (*get abroad*); streichen (*overlay with*). — *s.* die Ausbreitung; Verbreitung.
spree [spriː], *s.* das Vergnügen, der lustige Abend, Bummel.
sprig [sprig], *s.* der Zweig, Sprößling.
sprightly ['spraitli], *adj.* munter, lebhaft.
spring [spriŋ], *s.* die Quelle (*water*); der Ursprung (*origin*); der Frühling (*season*); (*Mech.*) die Feder, Sprungfeder, Spirale. — *v.n.* *irr.* springen (*jump*); entspringen (*originate*). — *v.a.* — *a surprise*, eine Überraschung bereiten.
springe [sprindʒ], *s.* der Sprenkel.
sprinkle [spriŋkl], *v.a.* (be)sprengen; (*Hort.*) berieseln.
sprint [sprint], *s.* der Kurzstreckenlauf, Wettlauf.
sprite [sprait], *s.* der Geist, Kobold.
sprout [spraut], *s.* (*Bot.*) die Sprosse, der Sprößling; *Brussels* —*s,* der Rosenkohl.
spruce (1) [spruːs], *adj.* sauber, geputzt; schmuck.
spruce (2) [spruːs], *s.* (*Bot.*) die Fichte, Rottanne.
spume [spjuːm], *s.* der Schaum.
spur [spəː], *s.* der Sporn (*goad*); (*fig.*) der Stachel; der Ansporn, Antrieb; (*Geog.*) der Ausläufer (*of range*). — *v.a.* anspornen.
spurious ['spjuəriəs], *adj.* unecht, falsch.
spurn [spəːn], *v.a.* verschmähen, verachten.
spurt [spəːt], *v.a.* spritzen. — *v.n.* sich anstrengen. — *s.* die Anstrengung.
sputter ['spʌtə], *v.a.* herausprudeln. — *v.n.* sprühen, sprudeln.
spy [spai], *s.* der Spion. — *v.n.* spionieren (*on*, bei, *Dat.*).
squabble ['skwɔbl], *v.n.* zanken. — *s.* der Zank, Streit.
squad [skwɔd], *s.* der Trupp.
squadron ['skwɔdrən], *s.* die Schwadron, das Geschwader.
squalid ['skwɔlid], *adj.* schmutzig, elend, eklig.
squall [skwɔːl], *s.* der Windstoß.
squalor ['skwɔlə], *s.* der Schmutz.
squander ['skwɔndə], *v.a.* verschwenden, vergeuden.
square [skwɛə], *s.* das Quadrat; der Platz; (*coll.*) der Philister, Spießer. — *v.a.* ausrichten; (*coll.*) ins Reine bringen. — *adj.* viereckig; quadratisch; redlich (*honest*); quitt (*quits*).

squash (1) [skwɔʃ], *v.a.* zerquetschen, zerdrücken (*press together*). — *s.* das Gedränge (*crowd*); der Fruchtsaft (*drink*).
squash (2) [skwɔʃ], *s.* (*Sport*) eine Art Racketspiel.
squat [skwɔt], *v.n.* kauern; sich niederlassen. — *adj.* stämmig, untersetzt.
squatter ['skwɔtə], *s.* der Ansiedler.
squaw [skwɔː], *s.* die Indianerfrau.
squeak [skwiːk], *v.n.* quieken, quietschen. — *s.* das Gequiek.
squeal [skwiːl], *v.n.* quieken; (*Am. coll.*) verraten, preisgeben.
squeamish ['skwiːmiʃ], *adj.* empfindlich, zimperlich.
squeeze [skwiːz], *v.a.* drücken, quetschen. — *s.* das Gedränge.
squib [skwib], *s.* der Frosch (*firework*); (*Lit.*) das Spottgedicht.
squint [skwint], *v.n.* schielen. — *s.* das Schielen.
squire [skwaiə], *s.* der Landedelmann, Junker.
squirrel ['skwirəl], *s.* (*Zool.*) das Eichhörnchen.
squirt [skwəːt], *v.a.* spritzen. — *s.* der Spritzer, Wasserstrahl; (*sl.*) der Wicht.
stab [stæb], *v.a.* erstechen, erdolchen. — *s.* der Dolchstich, Dolchstoß.
stability [stə'biliti], *s.* die Beständigkeit, Stabilität.
stable (1) [steibl], *adj.* fest, beständig; (*Phys.*) stabil.
stable (2) [steibl], *s.* der Stall.
stack [stæk], *s.* der Stoß (*pile*); der Schornstein (*chimneys*). — *v.a.* aufschichten.
staff [stɑːf], *s.* der Stab, Stock; (*Mil.*) der Stab, Generalstab; (*Sch.*) der Lehrkörper; das Personal. — *v.a.* besetzen.
stag [stæg], *s.* (*Zool.*) der Hirsch; — *party*, die Herrengesellschaft.
stage [steidʒ], *s.* (*Theat.*) die Bühne; die Stufe, das Stadium (*phase*); (*fig.*) der Schauplatz; *fare* —, die Teilstrecke. — *v.a.* (*Theat.*) inszenieren, abhalten (*hold*).
stagecoach ['steidʒkəutʃ], *s.* die Postkutsche.
stagger ['stægə], *v.n.* schwanken, wanken, taumeln. — *v.a.* (*coll.*) verblüffen (*astonish*); staffeln (*graduate*).
stagnate [stæg'neit], *v.n.* stocken, stillstehen.
staid [steid], *adj.* gesetzt, gelassen.
stain [stein], *s.* der Fleck, Makel. — *v.a.* beflecken; beizen; färben (*dye*).
stained [steind], *adj.* — *glass window*, buntes Fenster.
stainless ['steinlis], *adj.* rostfrei.
stair [stɛə], *s.* die Stufe, Stiege.
staircase ['stɛəkeis], *s.* das Treppenhaus; die Treppe.
stake [steik], *s.* der Pfahl, Pfosten; Scheiterhaufen; (*Gambling*) der Einsatz; *at* —, auf dem Spiel. — *v.a.* aufs Spiel setzen.
stale [steil], *adj.* abgestanden, schal.

stalemate

stalemate ['steilmeit], *s.* (*Chess*) das Patt; der Stillstand.

stalk (1) [stɔːk], *s.* (*Bot.*) der Stengel, Halm.

stalk (2) [stɔːk], *v.n.* stolzieren, steif gehen. — *v.a.* pirschen (*hunt*).

stall [stɔːl], *s.* die Bude (*booth*), der Stand (*stand*); (*Eccl.*) der Chorstuhl; (*Theat.*) der Sperrsitz; Parterresitz. — *v.n.* (*Motor.*) stehenbleiben.

stallion ['stæljən], *s.* (*Zool.*) der Hengst.

stalwart ['stɔːlwət], *adj.* kräftig, stark, verläßlich.

stamina ['stæminə], *s.* die Ausdauer, Widerstandskraft.

stammer ['stæmə], *v.n.* stammeln, stottern.

stamp [stæmp], *s.* der Stempel (*rubber* —); die Marke (*postage*); die Stampfe, Stanze (*die* —). — *v.a.* stempeln; (*Mech.*) stanzen; frankieren (*letters*). — *v.n.* stampfen.

stampede [stæm'piːd], *s.* die wilde Flucht. — *v.n.* in wilder Flucht davonlaufen.

stand [stænd], *v.n. irr.* stehen. — *v.a.* aushalten, standhalten (*Dat.*). — *s.* der Ständer (*hats etc.*); der Stand (*stall*); (*fig.*) die Stellung.

standard ['stændəd], *s.* der Standard (*level*); (*Mil.*) die Standarte; der Maßstab (*yardstick*). — *adj.* normal.

standing ['stændin], *s.* der Rang, das Ansehen. — *adj.* — *orders*, die Geschäftsordnung; (*Mil.*) die Vorschriften, *f. pl.*, Dauerbefehle, *m. pl.*

standpoint ['stændpɔint], *s.* der Standpunkt (*point of view*).

standstill ['stændstil], *s.* der Stillstand.

stanza ['stænzə], *s.* (*Poet.*) die Stanze, Strophe.

staple [steipl], *s.* das Haupterzeugnis; der Stapelplatz. — *adj.* Haupt-. — *v.a.* stapeln; heften (*paper*).

stapler ['steiplə], *s.* die Heftmaschine.

star [staː], *s.* der Stern; (*Theat. etc.*) der Star. — *v.n.* (*Theat. etc.*) die Hauptrolle spielen.

starboard ['staːbəd], *s.* das Steuerbord.

starch [staːtʃ], *s.* die Stärke (*laundry*). — *v.a.* stärken.

stare [stɛə], *v.n.* starren. — *s.* der starre Blick, das Starren.

stark [staːk], *adj.* völlig, ganz.

starling ['staːlin], *s.* (*Orn.*) der Star.

start [staːt], *v.n.* anfangen; aufbrechen; auffahren, aufspringen; stutzen (*jerk*); abfahren (*depart*). — *v.a.* starten (*car etc.*), in Gang setzen. — *s.* der Anfang; (*Sport*) der Start, Anlauf; der Aufbruch (*departure*); *by fits and* —s, ruckweise.

starter ['staːtə], *s.* (*Sport*) der Starter, Teilnehmer (*participant*); das Rennpferd (*horse*); (*Motor.*) der Anlasser.

startle [staːtl], *v.a.* erschrecken.

starve [staːv], *v.n.* verhungern, hungern. — *v.a.* aushungern.

state [steit], *s.* der Zustand, die Lage; (*Pol.*) der Staat; (*personal*) der Stand (*single etc.*). — *v.a.* erklären, darlegen.

stately ['steitli], *adj.* stattlich, prachtvoll.

statement ['steitmənt], *s.* die Feststellung; *bank* —, der Kontoauszug.

statesman ['steitsmən], *s.* der Staatsmann, Politiker.

statics ['stætiks], *s.* die Statik.

station ['steiʃən], *s.* (*Railw.*) die Station; der Bahnhof; die Stellung, der Rang (*position*); (*Mil.*) die Stationierung. — *v.a.* (*Mil.*) aufstellen, stationieren; (*fig.*) hinstellen.

stationary ['steiʃənri], *adj.* stationär, stillstehend.

stationer ['steiʃənə], *s.* der Papierhändler.

stationery ['steiʃənri], *s.* das Briefpapier, Schreibpapier; die Papierwaren, *f. pl.*

statuary ['stætjuəri], *s.* die Bildhauerkunst.

statue ['stætjuː], *s.* das Standbild.

status ['steitəs], *s.* die Stellung (*rank, position*).

statute ['stætjuːt], *s.* das Statut; — *law*, das Landesrecht, Gesetzesrecht.

staunch [stɔːntʃ], *adj.* zuverlässig.

stave [steiv], *s.* die Faßdaube (*of vat*); (*Poet.*) die Strophe; (*Mus.*) die Linie. — *v.a.* — *off*, abwehren.

stay [stei], *v.n.* bleiben, verweilen, wohnen. — *v.a.* aushalten, aufhalten. — *s.* der Aufenthalt; (*pl.*) das Korsett.

stead [sted], *s.* die Stelle; *in his* —, an seiner Statt.

steadfast ['stedfaːst], *adj.* standhaft, fest.

steadiness ['stedinis], *s.* die Beständigkeit.

steady ['stedi], *adj.* fest, sicher; beständig, treu.

steak [steik], *s.* das Steak.

steal [stiːl], *v.a. irr.* stehlen. — *v.n.* sich stehlen, schleichen.

stealth [stelθ], *s.* die Heimlichkeit.

stealthy ['stelθi], *adj.* heimlich, verstohlen.

steam [stiːm], *s.* der Dampf; *get up* —, in Gang bringen *or* kommen; — *boiler*, der Dampfkessel. — *v.n.* dampfen; davondampfen. — *v.a.* dämpfen, (*Cul.*) dünsten.

steed [stiːd], *s.* das Schlachtroß.

steel [stiːl], *s.* der Stahl. — *adj.* stählern. — *v.n.* — *o.s.*, sich stählen.

steep (1) [stiːp], *adj.* steil; (*fig.*) hoch; (*coll.*) gesalzen (*price*).

steep (2) [stiːp], *v.a.* einweichen, sättigen.

steeple [stiːpl], *s.* (*Archit.*) der Kirchturm.

steeplechase ['stiːpltʃeis], *s.* das Hindernisrennen.

steeplejack ['stiːpldʒæk], *s.* der Turmdecker.

steer (1) [stiə], *s.* (*Zool.*) der junge Stier.

steer (2) [stiə], *v.a.* steuern (*guide*).

steerage ['stiəridʒ], *s.* die Steuerung; (*Naut.*) das Zwischendeck.

stellar ['stelə], *adj.* Stern-, Sternen-.

stem (1) [stem], *s.* der Stamm; (*Phonet.*) der Stamm; der Stiel, die Wurzel. — *v.n.* — *from*, kommen von, abstammen.

stem (2) [stem], *v.a.* sich entgegenstemmen (*Dat.*); (*fig.*) eindämmen.

stench [stentʃ], *s.* der Gestank.

stencil ['stensil], *s.* die Schablone, Matrize; *cut a —*, auf Matrize schreiben.

step [step], *s.* der Schritt, Tritt; (*of ladder*) die Sprosse; (*of stairs*) die Stufe. — *v.n.* treten, schreiten (*stride*). — *v.a.* (*coll.*) — *up*, beschleunigen.

step- [step], *pref.* Stief- (*brother, mother etc.*).

stereo- ['stiəriou], *pref.* Stereo-.

sterile ['sterail], *adj.* steril.

sterling ['stə:liŋ], *adj.* echt, vollwertig; *pound —*, ein Pfund Sterling.

stern (1) [stə:n], *adj.* streng.

stern (2) [stə:n], *s.* (*Naut.*) das Heck.

stevedore ['sti:vədɔ:], *s.* der Hafenarbeiter.

stew [stju:], *s.* (*Cul.*) das Schmorfleisch, das Gulasch.

steward ['stju:əd], *s.* der Verwalter; der Haushofmeister; (*Naut.*) der Steward.

stick [stik], *s.* der Stock, Stecken. — *v.a.* stecken (*insert*); kleben (*glue*). — *v.n.* stecken, haften bleiben; (*fig.*, *coll.*) — *to s.o.*, zu jemandem halten (*be loyal*).

sticky ['stiki], *adj.* klebrig; (*fig.*) prekär, schwierig (*difficult*); *come to a — end*, ein böses Ende nehmen.

stiff [stif], *adj.* steif; schwer, schwierig (*examination*); formell (*manner*).

stiffen ['stifn], *v.a.* steifen, versteifen. — *v.n.* steif werden, sich versteifen.

stifle ['staifl], *v.a.*, *v.n.* ersticken; (*fig.*) unterdrücken.

stigmatize ['stigmətaiz], *v.a.* stigmatisieren, brandmarken.

stile [stail], *s.* der Zauntritt, Übergang.

still (1) [stil], *adj.* still, ruhig. — *adv.* immer noch. — *conj.* doch, dennoch. — *v.a.* stillen, beruhigen.

still (2) [stil], *s.* die Destillierflasche, der Destillierkolben.

stilt [stilt], *s.* die Stelze.

stilted ['stiltid], *adj.* auf Stelzen; (*fig.*) hochtrabend, geschraubt.

stimulant ['stimjulənt], *s.* das Reizmittel. — *adj.* anreizend, anregend.

stimulate ['stimjuleit], *v.a.* anreizen, stimulieren, anregen.

stimulus ['stimjuləs], *s.* der Reiz, die Anregung.

sting [stiŋ], *v.a.* *irr.* stechen; (*fig.*) kränken, verwunden. — *v.n.* *irr.* stechen, brennen, schmerzen. — *s.* der Stachel (*prick*); der Stich (*stab*).

stink [stiŋk], *v.n.* *irr.* stinken. — *s.* der Gestank.

stint [stint], *s.* die Einschränkung (*limit*); das Maß, Tagespensum. — *v.a.* beschränken, einschränken.

stipend ['staipend], *s.* die Besoldung, das Gehalt.

stipendiary [stai'pendiəri], *adj.* besoldet, bezahlt.

stipulate ['stipjuleit], *v.a.* festsetzen, ausbedingen.

stir [stə:], *v.a.* rühren, bewegen. — *v.n.* sich rühren. — *s.* die Aufregung; *cause a —*, Aufsehen erregen.

stirrup ['stirəp], *s.* der Steigbügel.

stitch [stitʃ], *v.a.* sticken, nähen. — *s.* der Stich; der stechende Schmerz, der Seitenstich (*pain*).

stoat [stout], *s.* (*Zool.*) das Hermelin.

stock [stɔk], *s.* das Lager; *in —*, auf Lager; vorrätig; der Stamm, die Familie; (*Fin.*) das Kapital; — *exchange*, die Börse; (*pl.*) die Börsenpapiere, *n. pl.*, Aktien, *f.pl.* — *v.a.* halten, führen.

stockade [stɔ'keid], *s.* das Staket.

stockbroker ['stɔkbroukə], *s.* (*Fin.*) der Börsenmakler.

stockholder ['stɔkhouldə], *s.* (*Fin.*, *Am.*) der Aktionär.

stocking ['stɔkiŋ], *s.* der Strumpf.

stocktaking ['stɔkteikiŋ], *s.* die Inventuraufnahme.

stoical ['stouikəl], *adj.* stoisch.

stoke [stouk], *v.a.* schüren.

stoker ['stoukə], *s.* der Heizer.

stole [stoul], *s.* (*Eccl.*) die Stola; der Pelzkragen (*fur*).

stolid ['stɔlid], *adj.* schwerfällig, gleichgültig.

stomach ['stʌmək], *s.* der Magen; (*fig.*) der Appetit.

stone [stoun], *s.* der Stein; der Kern (*fruit*). — *v.a.* steinigen (*throw —s at*); entsteinen (*fruit*).

stony ['stouni], *adj.* steinig; (*sl.*) — *broke*, pleite.

stool [stu:l], *s.* der Schemel, Hocker; (*Med.*) der Stuhlgang.

stoop [stu:p], *v.n.* sich bücken; (*fig.*) sich herablassen.

stooping ['stu:piŋ], *adj.* gebückt.

stop [stɔp], *v.a.* halten, stoppen; aufhören; aufhalten (*halt*); — *up*, verstopfen, versperren (*block*); (*tooth*) plombieren. — *v.n.* stehen bleiben (*stand*); sich aufhalten (*stay*). — *s.* der Halt, die Haltestelle (*of bus etc.*); das Aufhalten, Innehalten (*stoppage*); das Register (*organ*); (*Gram.*) der Punkt.

stoppage ['stɔpidʒ], *s.* die Stockung, Hemmung (*hindrance*); die Arbeitseinstellung (*strike*).

stopper ['stɔpə], *s.* der Stöpsel.

storage ['stɔ:ridʒ], *s.* das Lagern.

store [stɔ:], *s.* der Vorrat, das Lagerhaus, Magazin; (*Am.*) das Kaufhaus; (*fig.*) die Menge (*of anecdotes etc.*). — *v.a.* lagern.

storey ['stɔ:ri], *s.* das Stockwerk.

stork [stɔ:k], *s.* (*Orn.*) der Storch.

storm [stɔ:m], *s.* der Sturm, das Gewitter.

story ['stɔ:ri], *s.* die Geschichte, Erzählung (*narrative*).

stout

stout [staut], *adj.* fest; stark, kräftig. — *s.* das starke Bier.

stove [stouv], *s.* der Ofen.

stow [stou], *v.a.* verstauen, packen. — *v.n. — away*, als blinder Passagier fahren.

stowaway ['stouəwei], *s.* der blinde Passagier.

straddle [strædl], *v.n.* rittlings sitzen.

straggle [strægl], *v.n.* umherschweifen, streifen; (*Bot.*) wuchern.

straight [streit], *adj.* gerade, offen. — *adv. — away*, sofort, sogleich.

straighten [streitn], *v.a.* ausrichten, gerade richten. — *v.n.* sich ausrichten.

strain [strein], *s.* die Anstrengung, Anspannung; (*Mus.*) der Ton, Stil; der Hang. — *v.a.* anstrengen, filtrieren; seihen. — *v.n.* sich anstrengen.

strainer ['streinə], *s.* der Seiher, der Filter, das Sieb.

strait [streit], *adj.* eng. — *s.* (*usually pl.*) die Enge, Meerenge.

strand (1) [strænd], *s.* der Strand.

strand (2) [strænd], *s.* die Litze (*of rope, string*).

strange [streindʒ], *adj.* fremd (*unknown*); seltsam (*queer*).

stranger ['streindʒə], *s.* der Fremdling, Fremde; der Unbekannte.

strangle [stræŋgl], *v.a.* erdrosseln, erwürgen.

strangulation [stræŋgju'leifən], *s.* die Erdrosselung, Erwürgung.

strap [stræp], *v.a.* festschnallen, anschnallen. — *s.* der Gurt, Riemen.

strapping ['stræpiŋ], *adj.* stark, stämmig.

strata *see under* **stratum.**

stratagem ['strætədʒəm], *s.* die List; (*Mil.*) der Plan.

strategy ['strætədʒi], *s.* die Strategie.

stratification [strætifi'keifən], *s.* die Schichtung; (*Geol.*) die Lagerung.

stratum ['streitəm], *s.* (*pl.* **strata** ['streitə]) die Schicht, Lage.

straw [strɔː], *s.* das Stroh; *that's the last —*, das ist die Höhe!

strawberry ['strɔːbəri], *s.* (*Bot.*) die Erdbeere.

stray [strei], *v.n.* irregehen, schweifen; sich verirren. — *adj.* irr, verirrt.

streak [striːk], *s.* der Strich; der Streifen; (*fig.*) der Anflug.

streaky ['striːki], *adj.* gestreift; (*bacon*) durchwachsen.

stream [striːm], *v.n.* strömen, wehen (*in the wind*). — *s.* die Strömung (*flow*); der Bach (*brook*), der Strom (*river*).

streamer ['striːmə], *s.* der Wimpel, das Band, die Papierschlange.

street [striːt], *s.* die Straße; *—s ahead*, weit voraus.

streetcar ['striːtkɑː], *s.* (*Am.*) *see* **tram.**

streetlamp ['striːtlæmp], *s.* die Straßenlaterne.

strength [streŋθ], *s.* die Stärke; die Kraft.

strengthen ['streŋθən], *v.a.* stärken; (*fig.*) bekräftigen (*support*).

strenuous ['strenjuəs], *adj.* anstrengend.

stress [stres], *v.a.* (*Phonet.*) betonen; (*fig.*) hervorheben. — *s.* die Betonung (*emphasis*); der Druck (*pressure*).

stretch [stretʃ], *v.a.* spannen; strecken, ausstrecken; — *a point*, eine Ausnahme machen. — *s.* die Strecke (*distance*); (*coll.*) die Zuchthausstrafe (*penal sentence*).

stretcher ['stretʃə], *s.* die Tragbahre.

strew [struː], *v.a.* streuen, ausstreuen.

strict [strikt], *adj.* streng (*severe*); genau (*exact*).

stricture ['striktʃə], *s.* der Tadel, die Kritik; (*pl.*) die kritische Rede.

stride [straid], *v.n. irr.* schreiten. — *s.* der Schritt; *take in o.'s —*, leicht bewältigen.

strident ['straidənt], *adj.* laut, lärmend; grell.

strife [straif], *s.* der Streit, Zank.

strike [straik], *v.a., v.n. irr.* schlagen; abmachen (*bargain*); (*Mus.*) — *up*, anstimmen (*song*), aufspielen (*instrument*); beginnen; — *the eye*, auffallen; streiken, in Streik treten. — *s.* der Streik, die Arbeitseinstellung.

striking ['straikiŋ], *adj.* auffallend.

string [striŋ], *s.* die Schnur; (*Mus.*) die Saite; — *quartet*, das Streichquartett; die Reihe (*series*). — *v.a.* anreihen (*beads etc.*); — *together*, verbinden. — *v.n. — along*, sich anschließen.

stringency ['strindʒənsi], *s.* die Strenge (*severity*); die Knappheit (*shortage*).

stringent ['strindʒənt], *adj.* streng (*severe*); knapp (*short*).

strip [strip], *s.* der Streifen. — *v.a., v.n.* abstreifen, (sich) entkleiden; (sich) entblößen.

stripe [straip], *s.* der (Farb)streifen; die Strieme (*mark on body*). — *v.a.* streifen, bestreifen.

strive [straiv], *v.n. irr.* sich bemühen (*for*, um, *Acc.*), streben (*for*, nach, *Dat.*).

stroke (1) [strouk], *v.a.* streicheln.

stroke (2) [strouk], *s.* der Strich (*brush*); der Streich (*sword*), der Stoß (*blow*); (*Med.*) der Schlaganfall.

stroll [stroul], *v.n.* schlendern.

strolling ['strouliŋ], *adj. — players*, die Wandertruppe.

strong [strɔŋ], *adj.* stark.

strongbox ['strɔŋbɔks], *s.* die Geldkassette.

strongroom ['strɔŋrum], *s.* der Geldtresor.

strop [strɔp], *s.* der Streichriemen.

structure ['strʌktʃə], *s.* der Bau, Aufbau; die Struktur.

struggle [strʌgl], *s.* der Kampf, das Ringen. — *v.n.* kämpfen, ringen.

strut [strʌt], *v.n.* stolzieren.

stub [stʌb], *s.* der Stumpf, Stummel (*cigarette*). — *v.a. — out*, ausmachen, auslöschen (*cigarette etc.*).

succeed

stubble [stʌbl], *s.* die Stoppel, das Stoppelfeld; die (Bart)stoppeln, *f. pl.* (*beard*).

stubborn ['stʌbən], *adj.* eigensinnig, hartnäckig.

stucco ['stʌkou], *s.* die Stuckarbeit.

stud (1) [stʌd], *s.* der Hemdenknopf, Kragenknopf (*collar* —). — *v.a.* beschlagen (*nail*); besetzen (*bejewel*).

stud (2) [stʌd], *s.* das Gestüt (*horses*).

student ['stju:dənt], *s.* der Student.

studied ['stʌdid], *adj.* geziert, absichtlich (*deliberate*); gelehrt (*learned*).

studio ['stju:diou], *s.* (*Phot.*) das Atelier; (*Film, Rad.*) das Studio.

studious ['stju:diəs], *adj.* beflissen, fleißig; lernbegierig.

study ['stʌdi], *v.a., v.n.* studieren. — *s.* das Studium; das Arbeitszimmer (*room*); (*Mus. etc.*) die Studie; (*Art*) der Entwurf; die Untersuchung (*investigation*).

stuff [stʌf], *s.* der Stoff, das Material; (*coll.*) das Zeug (*rubbish*). — *v.a.* stopfen, ausstopfen (*animals*); (*Cul.*) füllen.

stuffing ['stʌfiŋ], *s.* die Füllung, das Füllsel.

stultify ['stʌltifai], *v.a.* dumm machen.

stumble [stʌmbl], *v.n.* stolpern; — *upon*, zufällig stoßen (auf, *Acc.*).

stumbling ['stʌmbliŋ], *s.* das Stolpern; — *block*, das Hindernis, der Stein des Anstoßes.

stump [stʌmp], *s.* der Stumpf. — *v.a.* verblüffen; abstumpfen. — *v.n.* schwerfällig gehen.

stun [stʌn], *v.a.* betäuben, verdutzen.

stunning ['stʌniŋ], *adj.* betörend, fabelhaft, überwältigend.

stunt (1) [stʌnt], *v.a.* am Wachstum behindern, klein halten.

stunt (2) [stʌnt], *s.* der Trick, das Kunststück; (*Aviat.*) der Kunstflug.

stupefy ['stju:pifai], *v.a.* betäuben.

stupendous [stju:'pendəs], *adj.* erstaunlich.

stupid ['stju:pid], *adj.* dumm.

stupor ['stju:pə], *s.* die Erstarrung, Lähmung (*of mind*).

sturdy ['stə:di], *adj.* derb, stark, stämmig.

sturgeon ['stə:dʒən], *s.* (*Zool.*) der Stör.

stutter ['stʌtə], *v.n.* stottern.

sty [stai], *s.* der Schweinestall.

sty(e) [stai], *s.* (*Med.*) das Gerstenkorn (*on eyelid*).

style [stail], *s.* (*Lit.*) der Stil; der Griffel (*stylus*); die Mode (*fashion*); die Anrede (*address*). — *v.a.* anreden.

stylish ['stailiʃ], *adj.* elegant, modern.

suave [sweiv, swa:v], *adj.* höflich, gewinnend.

sub- [sʌb], *pref.* Unter-.

subaltern ['sʌbəltən], *s.* (*Mil.*) der Leutnant, Oberleutnant.

subject ['sʌbdʒikt], *s.* (*Gram.*) das Subjekt; (*Pol.*) der Untertan; der Gegenstand. — *adj.* untertan (*to,*

Dat.); — *to*, abhängig von. — [səb'dʒekt], *v.a.* unterwerfen (*to, Dat.*); aussetzen (*Dat.*).

subjunctive [səb'dʒʌŋktiv], *s.* (*Gram.*) der Konjunktiv.

sublet [sʌb'let], *v.a.* in Untermiete vermieten, untervermieten.

sublimate ['sʌblimeit], *v.a.* sublimieren (*paper*).

submarine ['sʌbməri:n], *s.* das Unterseeboot.

submission [səb'miʃən], *s.* die Unterwerfung (*subjection*); der Vorschlag (*suggestion*).

submit [səb'mit], *v.a.* unterwerfen (*subjugate*); vorlegen. — *v.n.* sich beugen (*to, Dat.*).

suborn [sʌ'bɔ:n], *v.a.* anstiften; bestechen (*corrupt*).

subpoena [sʌb'pi:nə], *s.* (*Law*) die Vorladung.

subscribe [səb'skraib], *v.a.* unterschreiben. — *v.n.* zeichnen (*to, zu*); abonnieren (*paper*).

subscription [səb'skripʃən], *s.* das Abonnement (*to, Genit.*); (*club*) der Beitrag.

subsequent ['sʌbsikwənt], *adj.* folgend.

subservient [sʌb'sə:viənt], *adj.* unterwürfig.

subside [səb'said], *v.n.* sinken; abnehmen (*decrease*).

subsidence [sʌb'saidəns, 'sʌbsidəns], *s.* das Sinken, Sichsetzen.

subsidiary [sʌb'sidjəri], *adj.* Hilfs-, Neben-.

subsidize ['sʌbsidaiz], *v.a.* unterstützen (*with money*), subventionieren.

subsidy ['sʌbsidi], *s.* die Unterstützung, Subvention.

subsist [səb'sist], *v.n.* leben, existieren.

subsistence [səb'sistəns], *s.* das Dasein, Auskommen; der Lebensunterhalt.

substance ['sʌbstəns], *s.* das Wesen, der Stoff, die Substanz.

substantial [səb'stænʃəl], *adj.* wesentlich, beträchtlich.

substantiate [səb'stænʃieit], *v.a.* dartun, nachweisen, bestätigen.

substantive ['sʌbstəntiv], *s.* (*Gram.*) das Substantiv, Hauptwort. — *adj.* (*Mil.*) effektiv, wirklich.

substitute ['sʌbstitju:t], *v.a.* ersetzen, an die Stelle setzen. — *s.* der Ersatzmann, Vertreter.

subterfuge ['sʌbtəfju:dʒ], *s.* die Ausflucht.

subtle [sʌtl], *adj.* fein, schlau, subtil.

subtract [səb'trækt], *v.a.* abziehen; (*Maths.*) subtrahieren.

suburb ['sʌbə:b], *s.* die Vorstadt, der Vorort.

subversion [səb'və:ʃən], *s.* (*Pol.*) der Umsturz.

subversive [səb'və:siv], *adj.* umstürzlerisch, umstürzend.

subway ['sʌbwei], *s.* die Unterführung; (*Am.*) die Untergrundbahn.

succeed [sək'si:d], *v.n.* erfolgreich sein, Erfolg haben. — *v.a.* nachfolgen (*Dat.*) (*follow*).

495

success [sək'ses], *s.* der Erfolg.
successful [sək'sesful], *adj.* erfolgreich.
succession [sək'seʃən], *s.* die Nachfolge.
successive [sək'sesiv], *adj.* der Reihe nach, aufeinanderfolgend.
succinct [sək'siŋkt], *adj.* bündig, kurz.
succour ['sʌkə], *v.a.* beistehen (*Dat.*), helfen (*Dat.*).
succulent ['sʌkjulənt], *adj.* saftig.
succumb [sə'kʌm], *v.n.* unterliegen (*to, Dat.*).
such [sʌtʃ], *adj.* solch, derartig. — *pron.* ein solcher; — *as*, diejenigen, alle die.
suchlike ['sʌtʃlaik], *pron.* (*coll.*) dergleichen.
suck [sʌk], *v.a., v.n.* saugen.
suckle [sʌkl], *v.a.* säugen, stillen.
suction ['sʌkʃən], *s.* das Saugen; (*Engin.*) Saug-.
Sudanese [suːdə'niːz], *adj.* sudanisch, sudanesisch. — *s.* der Sudan(es)er.
sudden [sʌdn], *adj.* plötzlich.
suds [sʌdz], *s. pl.* das Seifenwasser.
sue [sjuː], *v.a.* gerichtlich belangen, verklagen.
suède [sweid], *s.* das Wildleder.
suet ['suːit], *s.* das Nierenfett.
suffer ['sʌfə], *v.a.* ertragen, dulden. — *v.n.* leiden (*from*, an).
sufferance ['sʌfərəns], *s.* die Duldung; *on* —, nur widerwillig.
suffice [sə'fais], *v.n.* genügen, langen, (aus)reichen.
sufficient [sə'fiʃənt], *adj.* genügend, hinreichend.
suffocate ['sʌfəkeit], *v.a., v.n.* ersticken.
suffragan ['sʌfrəgən], *s.* (*Eccl.*) der Weihbischof.
suffrage ['sʌfridʒ], *s.* das Wahlrecht, Stimmrecht.
suffuse [sə'fjuːz], *v.a.* übergießen, überfließen.
sugar ['ʃugə], *s.* der Zucker; — *basin*, die Zuckerdose.
suggest [sə'dʒest], *v.a.* vorschlagen, anregen.
suggestion [sə'dʒestʃən], *s.* der Vorschlag.
suggestive [sə'dʒestiv], *adj.* zweideutig.
suicide ['sjuːisaid], *s.* der Selbstmord, Freitod.
suit [suːt], *s.* das Gesuch, die Bitte (*request*); die Farbe (*cards*); (*Law*) der Prozeß; der Anzug (*clothes*). — *v.n.* passen (*Dat.*) (*be convenient to*); passen zu (*look well with*); anpassen (*match*).
suitcase ['suːtkeis], *s.* der Handkoffer.
suitable ['suːtəbl], *adj.* passend.
suite [swiːt], *s.* das Gefolge (*following*); die Zimmerflucht (*rooms*); die Reihe (*cards*).
suitor ['suːtə], *s.* der Brautwerber, Freier.
sulk [sʌlk], *v.n.* schmollen.
sullen ['sʌlən], *adj.* düster, mürrisch.
sully ['sʌli], *v.a.* beschmutzen.
sulphur ['sʌlfə], *s.* (*Chem.*) der Schwefel.

Sultan ['sʌltən], *s.* der Sultan.
Sultana [sʌl'taːnə], *s.* die Sultanin.
sultana [sʌl'taːnə], *s.* (*Bot.*) die Sultanine.
sultry ['sʌltri], *adj.* schwül.
sum [sʌm], *s.* die Summe; (*fig.*) der Inbegriff. — *v.a., v.n.* — *up*, zusammenfassen.
summary ['sʌməri], *s.* die Zusammenfassung, der Auszug. — *adj.* summarisch.
summer ['sʌmə], *s.* der Sommer; *Indian* —, der Spätsommer, Altweibersommer, Nachsommer.
summit ['sʌmit], *s.* der Gipfel, die Spitze.
summon(s) ['sʌmən(z)], *v.a.* (*Law*) vorladen. — *s.* (**summons**) die Vorladung.
sump [sʌmp], *s.* (*Motor.*) die Ölwanne.
sumptuous ['sʌmptjuəs], *adj.* prächtig, mit Aufwand, kostbar.
sun [sʌn], *s.* die Sonne. — *v.r.* sich sonnen.
sunburn ['sʌnbəːn], *s.* der Sonnenbrand.
Sunday ['sʌnd(e)i]. der Sonntag.
sundial ['sʌndaiəl], *s.* die Sonnenuhr.
sundown ['sʌndaun] *see* **sunset**.
sundry ['sʌndri], *adj.* mehrere, verschiedene. — *s.* (*pl.*) Gemischtwaren, *f. pl.*
sunny ['sʌni], *adj.* sonnig.
sunrise ['sʌnraiz], *s.* der Sonnenaufgang.
sunset ['sʌnset], *s.* der Sonnenuntergang.
sunshade ['sʌnʃeid], *s.* das Sonnendach, der Sonnenschirm (*parasol*).
super ['suːpə], *s.* (*Theat.*) der Statist. — *adj.* (*coll.*) fein, famos.
super- ['suːpə], *pref.* über-, hinzu-.
superannuation [suːpərænju'eiʃən], *s.* die Pensionierung.
superb [su'pəːb], *adj.* hervorragend, herrlich.
supercilious [suːpə'siliəs], *adj.* hochmütig, anmaßend.
superficial [suːpə'fiʃəl], *adj.* oberflächlich.
superfluous [su'pəːfluəs], *adj.* überflüssig.
superintendent [suːpərin'tendənt], *s.* der Oberaufseher.
superior [su'piəriə], *adj.* ober, höher. — *s.* der Vorgesetzte.
superiority [suːpiəri'ɔriti], *s.* die Überlegenheit.
superlative [su'pəːlativ], *s.* (*Gram.*) der Superlativ. — *adj.* ausnehmend gut.
supermarket ['suːpəmaːkit], *s.* das Selbstbedienungsgeschäft, SB-Geschäft, der grosse Lebensmittelladen.
supersede [suːpə'siːd], *v.a.* verdrängen.
superstition [suːpə'stiʃən], *s.* der Aberglaube.
superstitious [suːpə'stiʃəs], *adj.* abergläubisch.
supervise ['suːpəvaiz], *v.a.* beaufsichtigen, überwachen.

supine [su'pain], *adj.* auf dem Rücken liegend. — ['su:pain], *s.* (*Gram.*) das Supinum.

supper ['sʌpə], *s.* das Abendessen; *Last Supper*, das Heilige Abendmahl.

supplant [sə'plɑ:nt], *v.a.* verdrängen.

supple [sʌpl], *adj.* geschmeidig, biegsam.

supplement ['sʌplimənt], *s.* die Beilage (*paper*); der Zusatz.

supplementary [sʌpli'mentri], *adj.* zusätzlich.

supplier [sə'plaiə], *s.* der Lieferant.

supply [sə'plai], *v.a.* liefern (*s. th.*); beliefern, versorgen (*s.o.*). — *s.* die Versorgung.

support [sə'pɔ:t], *v.a.* unterstützen. — *s.* die Stütze (*prop*); die Unterstützung (*financial etc.*).

suppose [sə'pouz], *v.a.* annehmen, vermuten.

supposition [sʌpə'ziʃən], *s.* die Annahme, Vermutung, Voraussetzung.

suppress [sə'pres], *v.a.* unterdrücken.

suppurate ['sʌpjureit], *v.n.* eitern.

supremacy [su'preməsi], *s.* die Überlegenheit (*pre-eminence*); Obergewalt (*power*).

supreme [su'pri:m], *adj.* höchst, oberst.

surcharge [sə:'tʃɑ:dʒ], *s.* die Sonderzahlung, der Aufschlag, Zuschlag.

sure [ʃuə], *adj.* sicher; *to be —*, sicherlich; *make —*, sich überzeugen.

surety ['ʃuəti], *s.* (*Law*) die Kaution.

surf [sə:f], *s.* die Brandung.

surface ['sə:fis], *s.* die Oberfläche.

surfeit ['sə:fit], *s.* die Übersättigung, das Übermaß. — *v.a.* übersättigen.

surge [sə:dʒ], *v.n.* wogen, rauschen. — *s.* die Woge, das Aufwallen.

surgeon ['sə:dʒən], *s.* (*Med.*) der Chirurg.

surgery ['sə:dʒəri], *s.* (*Med.*) die Chirurgie (*subject*); *— hours*, die Sprechstunde.

surgical ['sə:dʒikəl], *adj.* chirurgisch.

surly ['sə:li], *adj.* mürrisch.

surmise [sə:'maiz], *v.a.* mutmaßen, vermuten. — *s.* die Mutmaßung, Vermutung.

surmount [sə:'maunt], *v.a.* übersteigen; überwinden (*overcome*).

surname ['sə:neim], *s.* der Zuname.

surpass [sə:'pɑ:s], *v.a.* übertreffen.

surplice ['sə:plis], *s.* das Chorhemd.

surplus ['sə:pləs], *s.* der Überfluß.

surprise [sə'praiz], *s.* die Überraschung. — *v.a.* überraschen.

surrender [sə'rendə], *v.a.* übergeben, aufgeben. — *v.n.* sich ergeben. — *s.* die Waffenstreckung, Kapitulation.

surreptitious [sʌrəp'tiʃəs], *adj.* heimlich.

surround [sə'raund], *v.a.* umgeben, einschließen.

surroundings [sə'raundiŋz], *s. pl.* die Umgegend, Umgebung.

survey ['sə:vei], *s.* die Übersicht; die Vermessung. — [sə'vei], *v.a.* überblicken; vermessen.

surveyor [sə'veiə], *s.* der Vermesser, Feldmesser.

survival [sə'vaivəl], *s.* das Überleben.

survive [sə'vaiv], *v.a., v.n.* überleben, überstehen.

susceptibility [səsepti'biliti], *s.* die Empfänglichkeit.

susceptible [sə'septibl], *adj.* empfänglich, empfindlich.

suspect [səs'pekt], *v.a.* verdächtigen. — ['saspekt], *adj.* verdächtig. — *s.* die Verdachtsperson, der Verdächtigte.

suspend [səs'pend], *v.a.* aufhängen; unterbrechen (*procedure*); einstellen (*work*).

suspense [səs'pens], *s.* die Spannung (*tension*); Ungewißheit (*uncertainty*).

suspension [səs'penʃən], *s.* (*Law*) die Suspension; die Einstellung (*stoppage*); die Aufhängung, Suspension (*Motor.*) die Federung; *— bridge*, die Kettenbrücke, Hängebrücke.

suspicion [səs'piʃən], *s.* der Verdacht, Argwohn.

suspicious [səs'piʃəs], *adj.* verdächtig; argwöhnisch.

sustain [səs'tein], *v.a.* erleiden (*suffer*); ertragen (*bear*); aufrechterhalten (*maintain*).

sustenance ['sʌstinəns], *s.* der Unterhalt (*maintenance*); die Nahrung (*food*).

suture ['sju:tʃə], *s.* (*Med.*) die Naht.

suzerain ['sju:zərein], *s.* der Oberherr, Oberlehnsherr.

swab [swɔb], *s.* (*Med.*) die Laborprobe, der Abstrich; der Schrubber (*scrubber*). — *v.a.* (*Med.*) eine Probe entnehmen; schrubben (*scrub*).

swaddle [swɔdl], *s.* die Windel.

swaddling ['swɔdliŋ], *adj. — clothes*, die Windeln, *f. pl.*

swagger ['swægə], *v.n.* großtun. — *s.* das Großtun, Renommieren.

swallow (1) ['swɔlou], *s.* (*Orn.*) die Schwalbe.

swallow (2) ['swɔlou], *v.a.* schlucken; verschlingen (*devour*).

swamp [swɔmp], *s.* der Sumpf. — *v.a.* versenken (*fig.*) überschütten.

swan [swɔn], *s.* (*Orn.*) der Schwan.

swank [swæŋk], *v.n.* großtun, angeben, aufschneiden. — *s.* der Großtuer.

swap, swop [swɔp], *v.a.* eintauschen, tauschen. — *v.n.* tauschen. — *s.* der Tausch.

sward [swɔ:d], *s.* (*Poet.*) der Rasen.

swarm [swɔ:m], *v.n.* schwärmen. — *s.* der Schwarm.

swarthy ['swɔ:ði], *adj.* dunkel, dunkelbraun.

swashbuckler ['swɔʃbʌklə], *s.* der Aufschneider, Angeber, Renommist.

swastika ['swɔstikə], *s.* das Hakenkreuz.

swathe [sweið], *v.a.* einhüllen, einwickeln.

sway [swei], *v.a.* schwenken; beeinflußen. — *v.n.* schwanken, sich schwingen. — *s.* der Einfluß, die Macht.

swear

swear [swɛə], *v.a., v.n. irr.* schwören (*an oath*); fluchen (*curse*).

sweat [swet], *v.n.* schwitzen. — *s.* der Schweiß.

Swede [swi:d], *s.* der Schwede.

Swedish ['swi:diʃ], *adj.* schwedisch.

sweep [swi:p], *v.a., v.n. irr.* fegen, kehren; *a new broom —s clean*, neue Besen kehren gut. — *s.* der Schornsteinfeger (*chimney —*).

sweet [swi:t], *adj.* süß. — *s.* der Nachtisch; (*pl.*) Süßigkeiten, *f. pl.*

swell [swel], *v.a. irr.* anschwellen lassen. — *v.n.* anschwellen. — *adj., adv.* (*Am. sl.*) ausgezeichnet. — *s.* (*sl.*) der feine Kerl.

swelter ['sweltə], *v.n.* vor Hitze vergehen.

swerve [swə:v], *v.n.* abschweifen, abbiegen.

swift (1) [swift], *adj.* schnell, behende, rasch.

swift (2) [swift], *s.* (*Orn.*) die Turmschwalbe.

swill [swil], *v.a.* spülen (*rinse*); (*sl.*) saufen (*drink heavily*). — *s.* das Spülicht (*dishwater*); (*coll.*) das Gesöff.

swim [swim], *v.n. irr.* schwimmen. — *s.* das Schwimmen.

swindle [swindl], *v.a.* beschwindeln. — *s.* der Schwindel.

swine [swain], *s. pl.* die Schweine; (*sing.*) der Schweinehund, das Schwein.

swing [swiŋ], *v.a., v.n. irr.* schwingen, schaukeln. — *s.* der Schwung; die Schaukel.

swipe [swaip], *v.a.* schlagen; (*fig.*) stehlen. — *s.* der Schlag.

swirl [swə:l], *v.a., v.n.* wirbeln (*in air*). — *s.* der Wirbel.

Swiss [swis], *s.* der Schweizer. — *adj.* schweizerisch, Schweizer-.

switch [switʃ], *v.a.* (*Elec.*) — *on*, andrehen, einschalten; — *off*, abschalten; (*fig.*) wechseln, vertauschen (*change*). — *v.n.* umstellen, umschalten. — *s.* (*Elec.*) der Schalter.

switchboard ['switʃbɔ:d], *s.* die Telephonzentrale, das Schaltbrett.

switchgear ['switʃgiə], *s.* (*Elec.*) das Schaltgerät, die Schaltung.

swivel [swivl], *v.n.* drehen. — *s.* der Drehring; — *chair*, der Drehstuhl.

swoon [swu:n], *v.n.* in Ohnmacht fallen. — *s.* die Ohnmacht.

swoop [swu:p], *s.* der Stoß. — *v.n.* (herab)stoßen; stürzen; (nieder)schießen.

swop *see* swap.

sword [sɔ:d], *s.* das Schwert.

syllable ['siləbl], *s.* die Silbe.

syllabus ['siləbəs], *s.* das Verzeichnis, der Lehrplan.

symbol ['simbəl], *s.* das Symbol, Sinnbild.

sympathetic [simpə'θetik], *adj.* mitfühlend, teilnehmend; sympathisch.

sympathy ['simpəθi], *s.* die Sympathie, das Mitgefühl.

symphony ['simfəni], *s.* (*Mus.*) die Symphonie.

synchronize ['siŋkrənaiz], *v.a.* synchronisieren.

syndicate ['sindikit], *s.* die Arbeitsgruppe, das Syndikat.

synod ['sinəd], *s.* die Synode, Kirchentagung.

synonymous [si'nɔniməs], *adj.* synonym.

synopsis [si'nɔpsis], *s.* die Zusammenfassung, Übersicht.

Syrian ['siriən], *adj.* syrisch. — *s.* der Syrer.

syringe ['sirindʒ], *s.* die Spritze.

syrup ['sirəp], *s.* der Sirup.

system ['sistəm], *s.* das System.

systematize ['sistəmətaiz], *v.a.* ordnen, in ein System bringen.

T

T [ti:]. das T.

tab [tæb], *s.* das Schildchen, der Streifen.

tabard ['tæbəd], *s.* der Wappenrock, Heroldsrock.

tabby ['tæbi], *s.* (*cat*) die getigerte Katze.

table [teibl], *s.* der Tisch; (*Maths.*) die Tabelle, das Einmaleins. — *v.a.* (*Parl.*) einen Entwurf einbringen; (*Am.*) auf die lange Bank schieben.

tablecloth ['teiblklɔθ], *s.* das Tischtuch.

tablemat ['teiblmæt], *s.* der Untersatz.

tablenapkin ['teiblnæpkin], *s.* die Serviette.

tablespoon ['teiblspu:n], *s.* der Eßlöffel.

tablet ['tæblit], *s.* die Tablette (*pill*); die Schreibtafel, der Block (*writing*).

taboo [tə'bu:], *s.* das Verbot, Tabu.

tabular ['tæbjulə], *adj.* tabellarisch; wie eine Tafel.

tacit ['tæsit], *adj.* stillschweigend.

taciturn ['tæsitə:n], *adj.* schweigsam, einsilbig.

tack [tæk], *s.* der Stift; der Stich (*sewing*). — *v.a.* nageln; heften (*sew*).

tackle [tækl], *v.a.* (*Naut.*) takeln; (*Footb., fig.*) angreifen; anpacken. — *s.* (*Naut.*) das Takel; (*fig.*) das Zeug; (*Footb.*) das Angreifen.

tact [tækt], *s.* der Takt; das Zartgefühl.

tactics ['tæktiks], *s. pl.* die Taktik.

tadpole ['tædpoul], *s.* (*Zool.*) die Kaulquappe.

taffeta ['tæfitə], *s.* (*Text.*) der Taft.

tag [tæg], *s.* der Anhängezettel; das Sprichwort (*saying*). — *v.a.* anhängen. — *v.n.* — *on to*, sich anschließen.

tail [teil], *s.* der Schwanz; (*fig.*) das Ende; (*pl.*) der Frack (*tailcoat*). — *v.a.* (*Am.*) folgen (*Dat.*).

tailor ['teilə], *s.* der Schneider; —made, geschneidert, nach Maß gemacht. — *v.a.* schneidern.

taint [teint], *v.a.* beflecken; verderben (*corrupt*). — *s.* der Fleck.

take [teik], *v.a. irr.* nehmen; bringen, ergreifen (*seize*); erfordern (*require*); — *up*, aufnehmen, beginnen; ertragen (*suffer*, *tolerate*); — *breath*, Atem holen; — *care*, sich in acht nehmen; — *offence at*, Anstoß nehmen an; — *place*, stattfinden; — *for*, halten für. — *v.n.* wirken (*be effective*); — *to*, Gefallen finden (an, *Dat.*); — *to flight* or *o.'s heels*, sich aus dem Staube machen; — *after*, ähnlich sein.

takings ['teikiŋz], *s.* (*pl.*) die Einnahmen, *f. pl.*

tale [teil], *s.* das Märchen, die Geschichte.

talent ['tælənt], *s.* das Talent, die Begabung.

talented ['tæləntid], *adj.* talentiert, begabt.

talk [tɔ:k], *v.a., v.n.* reden, sprechen. — *s.* das Gespräch (*discussion*); der Vortrag (*lecture*); das Reden, Gerede (*speaking*).

talkative ['tɔ:kətiv], *adj.* geschwätzig, redselig, gesprächig.

tall [tɔ:l], *adj.* hoch (*high*); groß (*grown high*); *a — order*, eine schwierige Aufgabe; *a — story*, eine Aufschneiderei, das Seemannsgarn.

tallow ['tælou], *s.* der Talg.

tally ['tæli], *v.n.* passen (*match*); stimmen (*be correct*).

talon ['tælən], *s.* die Klaue, Kralle.

tame [teim], *adj.* zahm. — *v.a.* zähmen.

tamper ['tæmpə], *v.n.* hineinpfuschen (*with*, in, *Acc.*).

tan [tæn], *s.* die Lohe; die braune Farbe; der Sonnenbrand (*s.:.*). — *v.a.* bräunen; (*leather*) gerben; (*fig.*) verbleuen (*beat*).

tang [tæŋ], *s.* der Seetang; (*fig.*) der Beigeschmack.

tangible ['tænʤibl], *adj.* greifbar.

tangle [tæŋgl], *v.a.* verwickeln (*entangle*). — *s.* die Verwirrung, Verwicklung.

tank [tæŋk], *s.* der Tank; (*Mil.*) der Panzer; der Wasserspeicher (*cistern*). — *v.a., v.n.* tanken.

tankard ['tæŋkəd], *s.* der Maßkrug, Bierkrug.

tanner (1) ['tænə], *s.* der Gerber.

tanner (2) ['tænə], *s.* (*sl.*) das Sechspencestück.

tantalize ['tæntəlaiz], *v.a.* quälen.

tantamount ['tæntəmaunt], *adj.* gleich, gleichwertig.

tap [tæp], *v.a.* anzapfen (*barrel*); klopfen, tippen (*on shoulder etc.*); (*fig.*) anpumpen (*for money*). — *s.* der Hahn; der Zapfen (*barrel*); der leichte Schlag (*on shoulder etc.*).

tape [teip], *s.* das Band; *red —*, die Bürokratie, der Bürokratismus; — *measure*, das Bandmaß; — *recorder*, das Tonbandgerät.

taper ['teipə], *v.n.* spitz zulaufen. — *v.a.* spitzen. — *s.* die (spitze) Kerze.

tapestry ['tæpistri], *s.* die Tapete, der Wandteppich.

tapeworm ['teipwə:m], *s.* der Bandwurm.

taproot ['tæpru:t], *s.* die Pfahlwurzel, Hauptwurzel.

tar [ta:], *s.* der Teer; (*Naut. sl.*) der Matrose. — *v.a.* teeren.

tardy ['ta:di], *adj.* träge (*sluggish*), langsam.

tare (1) [tɛə], *s.* das Taragewicht, die Tara (*weight*). — *v.a.* auswägen, tarieren.

tare (2) [tɛə], *s.* (*Bot.*) die Wicke.

target ['ta:git], *s.* das Ziel; die Zielscheibe (*board*).

tariff ['tærif], *s.* der Tarif.

tarnish ['ta:niʃ], *v.a.* trüben. — *v.n.* anlaufen.

tarpaulin [ta:'pɔ:lin], *s.* die Persenning. — *v.a.* teeren.

tarry (1) ['tæri], *v.n.* zögern (*hesitate*); warten (*wait*).

tarry (2) ['ta:ri], *adj.* teerig.

tart (1) [ta:t], *s.* die Torte.

tart (2) [ta:t], *adj.* herb, sauer.

tart (3) [ta:t], *s.* (*sl.*) die Dirne.

Tartar ['ta:tə], *s.* der Tatar; (*fig.*) der Tyrann.

tartar ['ta:tə], *s.* (*Chem.*) der Weinstein.

task [ta:sk], *s.* die Aufgabe, das Tagewerk; *take to —*, zur Rechenschaft ziehen.

tassel [tæsl], *s.* die Quaste.

taste [teist], *v.a.* schmecken; versuchen, kosten. — *s.* die Probe (*tasting*); der Geschmack (*flavour*).

tasteful ['teistful], *adj.* geschmackvoll.

tasteless ['teistlis], *adj.* geschmacklos.

tasty ['teisti], *adj.* schmackhaft.

tatter ['tætə], *s.* der Lumpen. — *v.a.* in Fetzen reißen, zerfetzen.

tattle [tætl], *v.n.* schwatzen. — *s.* das Geschwätz.

tattoo (1) [tə'tu:], *s.* (*Mil.*) der Zapfenstreich, das militärische Schaustück, die Parade.

tattoo (2) [tə'tu:], *v.a.* tätowieren. — *s.* die Tätowierung.

taunt [tɔ:nt], *v.a.* höhnen, schmähen. — *s.* der Hohn, Spott.

tavern ['tævən], *s.* die Schenke.

tawdry ['tɔ:dri], *adj.* kitschig, flitterhaft.

tawny ['tɔ:ni], *adj.* braungelb, lohfarbig.

tax [tæks], *s.* die Abgabe, Steuer; Besteuerung (*taxation*). — *v.a.* besteuern; (*fig.*) anstrengen, ermüden (*strain*).

taxi ['tæksi], *s.* das Taxi.

tea [ti:], *s.* der Tee.

teach [ti:tʃ], *v.a., v.n. irr.* lehren, unterrichten.

teacher ['ti:tʃə], *s.* der Lehrer, die Lehrerin.

team [ti:m], s. (*Sport*) die Mannschaft; das Gespann (*horses*); (*fig.*) der Stab; — *spirit*, der Korpsgeist.

tear (1) [tɛə], s. der Riß (*rent*). — v.a. irr. zerreißen (*rend*).

tear (2) [tiə], s. die Träne.

tearing [′tɛəriŋ], adj. — *hurry*, rasende Eile.

tease [ti:z], v.a. necken (*mock*); aufrauhen (*roughen*).

teat [ti:t], s. die Brustwarze, Zitze.

technical [′teknikəl], adj. technisch.

technique [tek′ni:k], s. die Technik, Methode.

techy *see* **tetchy**.

tedious [′ti:diəs], adj. langweilig, lästig.

tedium [′ti:diəm], s. der Überdruß, die Langeweile.

tee [ti:], s. (*Sport*) der Golfballhalter.

teem [ti:m], v.n. wimmeln.

teenager [′ti:neidʒə], s. der, die Jugendliche; Teenager.

teeth *see under* **tooth**.

teethe [ti:ð], v.n. Zähne bekommen, zahnen.

teetotal [ti:′toutl], adj. abstinent, antialkoholisch.

teetotaller [ti:′toutlə], s. der Antialkoholiker.

telegram [′teligræm], s. das Telegramm.

telephone [′telifoun], s. (*abbr.* **phone**) das Telephon; — *booth*, die Fernsprechzelle; — *exchange*, das Fernsprechamt.

television [teli′viʒən], s. das Fernsehen; — *set*, der Fernsehapparat.

tell [tel], v.a. irr. erzählen, berichten (*relate*); verraten (*reveal*).

tell-tale [′telteil], s. der Angeber, Zuträger. — adj. sprechend; Warnungs-.

teller [′telə], s. der Zähler; der Kassier (*cashier*).

temerity [ti′meriti], s. die Verwegenheit, Tollkühnheit.

temper [′tempə], v.a. vermischen (*mix*); mäßigen (*moderate*); (*Metall.*) härten. — s. die üble Stimmung, Wut, Laune; (*Metall.*) die Härte.

temperance [′tempərəns], s. die Mäßigkeit, Enthaltsamkeit.

temperate [′tempərit], adj. gemäßigt, temperiert.

temperature [′temprətʃə], s. die Temperatur.

tempest [′tempist], s. der Sturm.

tempestuous [tem′pestjuəs], adj. stürmisch.

temple (1) [templ], s. der Tempel.

temple (2) [templ], s. (*Anat.*) die Schläfe (*side of brow*).

temporal [′tempərəl], adj. weltlich, zeitlich.

temporary [′tempərəri], adj. zeitweilig, vorläufig, provisorisch.

temporize [′tempəraiz], v.n. zögern, Zeit zu gewinnen suchen.

tempt [tempt], v.a. versuchen.

temptation [temp′teifən], s. die Versuchung.

ten [ten], num. adj. zehn.

tenth [tenθ], num. adj. zehnte. — s. der Zehnte.

tenable [′tenəbl], adj. haltbar.

tenacious [ti′neifəs], adj. zähe, festhaltend, hartnäckig.

tenacity [ti′næsiti], s. die Zähigkeit, Ausdauer.

tenancy [′tenənsi], s. das Mietverhältnis; die Mietdauer.

tenant [′tenənt], s. der Mieter, Pächter.

tench [tentʃ], s. (*Zool.*) die Schleie.

tend (1) [tend], v.a., v.n. warten, pflegen (*nurse*).

tend (2) [tend], v.n. neigen, gerichtet sein (*be inclined*).

tendency [′tendənsi], s. die Tendenz, Neigung.

tender (1) [′tendə], s. das Angebot (*offer*); *legal* —, das Zahlungsmittel. — v.a. einreichen.

tender (2) [′tendə], adj. sanft (*affectionate*); zart, zärtlich, weich (*delicate*).

tender (3) [′tendə], s. (*Railw.*) der Tender.

tendon [′tendən], s. (*Anat.*) die Sehne, Flechse.

tendril [′tendril], s. (*Bot.*) die Ranke.

tenement [′tenimənt], s. die Mietswohnung, die Mietskaserne.

tenet [′tenit], s. der Grundsatz (*principle*); die Lehre (*doctrine*).

tenfold [′tenfould], adj. zehnfach.

tennis [′tenis], s. das Tennis.

tenor [′tenə], s. (*Mus.*) der Tenor; der Sinn, Inhalt (*meaning*).

tense (1) [tens], adj. gespannt; straff (*taut*).

tense (2) [tens], s. (*Gram.*) die Zeitform.

tension [′tenʃən], s. die Spannung.

tent [tent], s. das Zelt.

tentacle [′tentəkl], s. (*Zool.*) das Fühlhorn, der Fühler.

tentative [′tentətiv], adj. versuchend, vorsichtig; (*fig.*) vorläufig.

tenterhooks [′tentəhuks], s. pl. die Spannhaken, m. pl.; *be on* —, in größter Spannung sein.

tenuous [′tenjuəs], adj. dünn, fadenscheinig, spärlich.

tenure [′tenjuə], s. der Mietbesitz, die Mietvertragslänge, das Mietrecht; — *of office*, die Amtsdauer.

tepid [′tepid], adj. lau, lauwarm.

term [tə:m], s. der Ausdruck (*expression*); die Bedingung (*condition*); der Termin, die Frist (*period*); (*Sch.*) das Semester, Trimester; *be on good* —s *with* (*s.o.*), auf gutem Fuß stehen mit. — v.a. benennen, bezeichnen.

terminate [′tə:mineit], v.a. beenden, zu Ende bringen. — v.n. zu Ende kommen.

terminus [′tə:minəs], s. die Endstation.

terrace [′teris], s. die Terrasse.

terrestrial [tə′restriəl], adj. irdisch.

terrible [′teribl], adj. schrecklich, furchtbar.

terrific [tə′rifik], adj. fürchterlich; (*coll.*) ungeheuer.

though

terrify ['terifai], *v.a.* erschrecken.
territory ['teritəri], *s.* das Gebiet.
terror ['terə], *s.* der Schrecken.
terse [tə:s], *adj.* bündig, kurz.
tertiary ['tə:ʃəri], *adj.* tertiär.
test [test], *s.* die Prüfung; (*Chem.*) die Probe; — *tube*, das Reagensglas *or* Reagenzglas. — *v.a.* prüfen.
testament ['testəmənt], *s.* das Testament.
testator [tes'teitə], *s.* der Erblasser.
testicle ['testikl], *s.* (*Anat.*) die Hode.
testify ['testifai], *v.a.* bezeugen.
testimonial [testi'mouniəl], *s.* das Zeugnis.
testimony ['testiməni], *s.* das Zeugnis, die Zeugenaussage (*oral*).
testiness ['testinis], *s.* die Verdrießlichkeit.
testy ['testi], *adj.* verdrießlich, reizbar.
tetanus ['tetənəs], *s.* (*Med.*) der Starrkrampf.
tetchy, techy ['tetʃi], *adj.* mürrisch, reizbar.
tether ['teðə], *s.* das Spannseil; (*fig.*) *at the end of o.'s —*, am Ende seiner Geduld. — *v.a.* anbinden.
text [tekst], *s.* der Text, Wortlaut.
textile ['tekstail], *s.* die Textilware, der Webstoff.
textual ['tekstjuəl], *adj.* textlich, Text-.
texture ['tekstʃə], *s.* das Gewebe, die Struktur.
Thai [tai], *adj.* Thai-, siamesisch. — *s. pl.* die Thaivölker, *pl.*
than [ðæn], *conj.* als (*after comparatives*).
thank [θæŋk], *v.a.* danken (*Dat.*). — *s.* (*pl.*) der Dank.
that [ðæt], *dem. adj.* der, die, das, jener. — *dem. pron.* der, die, das, (*absolute, no pl.*) das. — *rel. pron.* der, die, das, welcher, was. — *conj.* daß; damit (*in order —*).
thatch [θætʃ], *v.a.* decken (mit Stroh). — *s.* das Strohdach.
thaw [θɔː], *v.n.* tauen; auftauen. — *s.* das Tauwetter.
the [ðə, *before vowel* ði], *def. art.* der, die, das. — *adv.* — *bigger* — *better*, je grösser desto *or* umso besser.
theatre ['θiətə], *s.* das Theater; (*fig.*) der Schauplatz.
theatrical [θi'ætrikəl], *adj.* bühnenhaft (*of the stage*); theatralisch; Bühnen-, Theater-.
theft [θeft], *s.* der Diebstahl.
their [ðeə], *poss. adj.* ihr.
theirs [ðeəz], *poss. pron.* der, die, das ihrige, der, die, das ihre.
them [ðem], *pers. pron.* sie, ihnen.
theme [θiːm], *s.* das Thema; (*Mus.*) das Thema, Motiv.
then [ðen], *adv.* dann, damals; *by —, till —*, bis dahin. — *conj.* dann, denn. — *adj.* damalig.
thence [ðens], *adv.* von da; daher.
theology [θi'ɔlədʒi], *s.* die Theologie.
theorem ['θiərəm], *s.* (*Maths.*) der Lehrsatz, Grundsatz.
theorize ['θiəraiz], *v.n.* theoretisieren.

therapeutics [θerə'pjuːtiks], *s. pl.* die Heilkunde.
therapy ['θerəpi], *s.* die Therapie.
there [ðeə], *adv.* dort, da; dorthin, dahin (*thereto*); — *is,* — *are,* es gibt; *here and —*, hier und da.
thereabout(s) [ðeərəbaut(s)], *adv.* ungefähr, da herum.
thereafter [ðeər'aːftə], *adv.* hernach, danach.
thereby [ðeə'bai], *adv.* dadurch.
therefore ['ðeəfɔː], *adv.* darum, deshalb.
thermal, thermic ['θə:məl, 'θə:mik], *adj.* thermisch; warm; Wärme-.
thermometer [θə'mɔmitə], *s.* das Thermometer.
these [ðiːz], *dem. adj. & pron. pl.* diese.
thesis ['θiːsis], *s.* die These; die Dissertation.
they [ðei], *pers. pron. pl.* sie.
thick [θik], *adj.* dick; dicht; (*fig.*) dick befreundet; — *as thieves,* wie eine Diebsbande.
thicken ['θikən], *v.a.* verdicken. — *v.n.* dick werden.
thicket ['θikit], *s.* das Dickicht.
thickness ['θiknis], *s.* die Dicke.
thief [θiːf], *s.* der Dieb.
thieve [θiːv], *v.n.* stehlen.
thigh [θai], *s.* (*Anat.*) der Oberschenkel.
thimble [θimbl], *s.* der Fingerhut.
thin [θin], *adj.* dünn. — *v.a., v.n.* (sich) verdünnen.
thine [ðain], *poss. pron.* (*Poet.*) dein, der, die, das deinige.
thing [θiŋ], *s.* das Ding; die Sache (*matter*).
think [θiŋk], *v.a., v.n. irr.* denken; meinen, glauben.
thinker ['θiŋkə], *s.* der Denker.
third [θə:d], *num. adj.* der, die, das dritte. — *s.* das Drittel.
thirdly ['θə:dli], *adv.* drittens.
thirst [θə:st], *s.* der Durst (*for,* nach). — *v.n.* dürsten.
thirsty ['θə:sti], *adj.* durstig; *be —,* Durst haben.
thirteen [θə:'tiːn], *num. adj.* dreizehn.
thirty ['θə:ti], *num. adj.* dreißig.
this [ðis], *dem. adj.* dieser, diese, dieses. — *dem. pron.* dieser, diese; dieses; dies.
thistle [θisl], *s.* (*Bot.*) die Distel.
thither ['ðiðə], *adv.* dahin, dorthin.
tho' [ðou] *see under* **though**.
thong [θɔŋ], *s.* der Riemen (*strap*); die Peitschenschnur.
thorn [θɔːn], *s.* (*Bot.*) der Dorn.
thorough ['θʌrə], *adj.* gründlich; völlig (*complete*).
thoroughbred ['θʌrəbred], *s.* das Vollblut, der Vollblüter. — *adj.* Vollblut-.
thoroughfare ['θʌrəfeə], *s.* der Durchgang (*path*); die Durchfahrt.
those [ðouz], *dem. adj. pl.* die, jene. — *dem. pron. pl.* jene, diejenigen.
thou [ðau], *pers. pron.* (*Poet.*) du.
though [ðou], *conj.* (*abbr.* **tho'**) obgleich, obwohl, wenn auch (*even if*). — *adv.* doch, zwar.

501

thought

thought [θɔːt], s. der Gedanke; *also
past tense and participle of* think *q.v.*
thoughtful [ˈθɔːtful], *adj.* rücksichtsvoll, nachdenklich.
thoughtless [ˈθɔːtlis], *adj.* gedankenlos.
thousand [ˈθauzənd], *num. adj.* a —,
tausend. — *s.* das Tausend.
thrash [θræʃ], *v.a.* dreschen (*corn*);
prügeln (*s.o.*).
thread [θred], *s.* der Faden. — *v.a.*
einfädeln. — *v.n.* sich schlängeln,
sich winden.
threadbare [ˈθredbɛə], *adj.* fadenscheinig.
threat [θret], *s.* die Drohung.
threaten [θretn], *v.a.* drohen, androhen
(*Dat.*).
three [θriː], *num. adj.* drei.
threescore [ˈθriːskɔː], *num. adj.* sechzig.
thresh [θreʃ], *v.a.* dreschen (*corn*). —
See also thrash.
threshold [ˈθreʃould], *s.* die Schwelle
(*of door*).
thrice [θrais], *num. adv.* dreimal.
thrift [θrift], *s.* die Sparsamkeit; (*Bot.*)
die Grasnelke, Meernelke.
thrill [θril], *v.a.* packen (*grip*). — *v.n.*
erschauern, zittern (*vor*, *Dat.*). —
s. der Schauer; die Spannung.
thriller [ˈθrilə], *s.* der Thriller, der
spannende Roman *or* Film etc.
thrive [θraiv], *v.n.* gedeihen (*also fig.*);
(*fig.*) gut weiterkommen, Glück
haben.
thriving [ˈθraiviŋ], *adj.* blühend,
(*Comm.*) gut gehend.
throat [θrout], *s.* (*Anat.*) der Schlund,
die Kehle.
throb [θrɔb], *v.n.* pochen, klopfen.
throes [θrouz], *s. pl.* die Wehen, *f. pl.*;
die Schmerzen, *m. pl.*
throne [θroun], *s.* der Thron.
throng [θrɔŋ], *s.* die Menge, das
Gedränge. — *v.a.*, *v.n.* (*sich*) drängen.
throttle [θrɔtl], *s.* die Kehle, Luftröhre; (*Mech.*) das Drosselventil;
(*Motor.*) open the —, Gas geben.
through [θruː], *prep.* durch (*Acc.*);
mittels (*Genit.*) (*by means of*). — *adv.*
(*mitten*) durch.
throughout [θruːˈaut], *prep.* ganz
(*hin*)durch (*space*); während, hindurch (*time*). — *adv.* durchaus, in
jeder Beziehung.
throw [θrou], *v.a. irr.* werfen; —
open, eröffnen. — *s.* der Wurf.
thrush [θrʌʃ], *s.* (*Orn.*) die Drossel.
thrust [θrʌst], *v.a.* stoßen, drängen. —
v.n. stoßen (*at*, nach); sich drängen.
— *s.* der Stoß, Angriff; cut and —,
Hieb und Gegenhieb.
thud [θʌd], *s.* der Schlag, das Dröhnen,
der dumpfe Ton. — *v.n.* dröhnen,
aufschlagen.
thumb [θʌm], *s.* (*Anat.*) der Daumen;
rule of —, die Faustregel; (*Am.*)
tack see drawing pin. — *v.a.* durchblättern (*book*); — *a lift*, per Anhalter
fahren.
thump [θʌmp], *v.a.* schlagen, puffen. —

v.n. schlagen (*on*, auf; *against*, gegen).
— *s.* der Schlag, Stoß.
thunder [ˈθʌndə], *s.* der Donner. — *v.n.*
donnern.
thunderstruck [ˈθʌndəstrʌk], *adj.* wie
vom Donner gerührt.
Thursday [ˈθɜːzdi], *s.* der Donnerstag.
Thuringian [θuəˈrindʒiən], *adj.* thürin-
gisch. — *s.* der Thüringer.
thus [ðʌs], *adv.* so, auf diese Weise (*in
this way*).
thwart [θwɔːt], *v.a.* vereiteln, durchkreuzen.
thy [ðai], *poss. adj.* (*Poet.*) dein, deine,
dein.
thyme [taim], *s.* (*Bot.*) der Thymian.
tic [tik], *s.* (*Med.*) das Zucken.
tick (1) [tik], *s.* das Ticken (*watch*). —
v.n. ticken.
tick (2) [tik], *s.* (*coll.*) der Kredit, Borg.
ticket [ˈtikit], *s.* die Fahrkarte (*travel*);
die Eintrittskarte (*entry*); (*Am.*) der
Strafzettel (*driving*).
ticking (1) [ˈtikiŋ], *s.* das Ticken (*of
watch*).
ticking (2) [ˈtikiŋ], *s.* (*Text.*) der
Zwillich.
tickle [tikl], *v.a.*, *v.n.* kitzeln. — *s.* das
Kitzeln.
ticklish [ˈtikliʃ], *adj.* kitzlig.
tidal [taidl], *adj.* Gezeiten-, Ebbe-, Flut-.
tide [taid], *s.* die Gezeiten, *f.pl.*, die
Ebbe und Flut. — *v.a.* — *over*, hin-
weghelfen (*über*, *Acc.*).
tidiness [ˈtaidinis], *s.* die Sauberkeit,
Ordnung.
tidings [ˈtaidiŋz], *s. pl.* (*Poet.*) die
Nachricht.
tidy [ˈtaidi], *adj.* nett, sauber, ordentlich.
— *v.a.* — *up*, sauber machen.
tie [tai], *v.a.* binden, knüpfen. — *v.n.*
(*Sport*) unentschieden sein. — *s.* die
Binde, Krawatte; (*Sport*) das Unentschieden.
tier [tiə], *s.* der Rang, die Reihe, Sitz-
reihe.
tiger [ˈtaigə], *s.* (*Zool.*) der Tiger.
tight [tait], *adj.* fest, eng, dicht (*close*);
(*coll.*) betrunken (*drunk*); — fisted,
geizig (*stingy*). — *s. pl.* die Trikot-
hosen, *f.pl.*
tighten [taitn], *v.a.* festziehen.
tile [tail], *s.* der Ziegel (*roof etc.*); die
Kachel (*glazed*). — *v.a.* kacheln,
ziegeln.
till (1) [til], *prep.*, *conj.* bis.
till (2) [til], *v.a.* aufbauen, beackern
(*land*).
till (3) [til], *s.* die Ladenkasse.
tilt [tilt], *v.a.* kippen, neigen, umschlagen (*tip over*). — *v.n.* sich neigen,
kippen, kentern. — *s.* die Neigung.
timber [ˈtimbə], *s.* das Holz, Bauholz.
time [taim], *s.* die Zeit; (*Mus.*) das
Tempo, Zeitmaß; in —, zur rechten
Zeit; every —, jedesmal; what is the
—? wieviel Uhr ist es? — *v.a.* zeitlich
messen, rechtzeitig einrichten.
timely [ˈtaimli], *adj.* rechtzeitig.

toothbrush

timetable ['taimteibl], *s.* (*Railw.*) der Fahrplan; (*Sch.*) der Stundenplan.
timid ['timid], *adj.* furchtsam.
timpani ['timpəni], *s. pl.* (*Mus.*) die Kesselpauken, *f. pl.*
tin [tin], *s.* das Zinn, Weißblech; die Dose, Büchse (*preserved foods*); — *opener*, der Büchsenöffner.
tincture ['tiŋktʃə], *s.* die Tinktur, das Färbungsmittel.
tinder ['tində], *s.* der Zunder.
tinfoil ['tinfɔil], *s.* das Stanniol.
tinge [tindʒ], *v.a.* färben, anfärben. — *s.* die Färbung, leichte Farbe; (*fig.*) die Spur.
tingle [tiŋgl], *v.n.* klingen (*bells*); (*Anat.*) prickeln. — *s.* das Klingen; Prickeln.
tinker ['tiŋkə], *s.* der Kesselflicker. — *v.n.* basteln.
tinkle [tiŋkl], *v.a.* klingeln.
tinsel ['tinsəl], *s.* das Lametta, Flittergold.
tint [tint], *v.a.* färben. — *s.* die Farbe; der Farbton.
tiny ['taini], *adj.* winzig.
tip (1) [tip], *v.a.* kippen; (*coll.*) ein Trinkgeld geben (*Dat.*); (*Sport etc.*) (*coll.*) der Tip; das Trinkgeld (*gratuity*).
tip (2) [tip], *s.* die Spitze; das Mundstück (*cigarette*).
tipple [tipl], *v.n.* (viel) trinken, zechen.
tipsy ['tipsi], *adj.* beschwipst.
tiptoe ['tiptou], *s. on* —, auf Zehenspitzen.
tiptop ['tiptɔp], *adj.* (*coll.*) erstklassig.
tirade [ti'reid *or* tai'reid], *s.* der Wortschwall, die Tirade.
tire (1) [taiə], *v.a., v.n.* ermüden.
tire (2) *see under* **tyre.**
tired ['taiəd], *adj.* müde.
tiresome ['taiəsəm], *adj.* langweilig (*boring*); auf die Nerven gehend (*annoying*).
tissue ['tiʃju:], *s.* das Gewebe; — *paper,* das Seidenpapier.
titbit ['titbit], *s.* der Leckerbissen.
tithe [taið], *s.* der Zehnte.
title [taitl], *s.* der Titel, die Überschrift; (*fig.*) der Anspruch (*claim*).
titmouse ['titmaus], *s.* (*Orn.*) die Meise.
titter ['titə], *v.n.* kichern. — *s.* das Kichern.
tittle [titl], *s.* das Tüpfelchen; — *tattle,* das Geschwätz.
titular ['titjulə], *adj.* Titular-.
to [tu], *prep.* zu (*Dat.*), gegen (*Acc.*); bis (*until, as far as*), nach, an, auf; *in order* —, um zu. — [tu:], *adv.* zu; — *and fro,* hin und her.
toad [toud], *s.* (*Zool.*) die Kröte.
toadstool ['toudstu:l], *s.* (*Bot.*) der Giftpilz.
toady ['toudi], *v.n.* kriechen. — *s.* der Kriecher.
toast [toust], *s.* der Toast, das Röstbrot; der Trinkspruch. — *v.a.* toasten,

rösten; trinken auf; — *s.o.,* einen Trinkspruch ausbringen auf einen.
tobacco [tə'bækou], *s.* der Tabak.
toboggan [tə'bogən], *s.* der Rodel, der Schlitten. — *v.n.* rodeln, Schlitten fahren.
tocsin ['tɔksin], *s.* die Sturmglocke.
today [tə'dei], *adv.* heute.
toddle [tɔdl], *v.n.* watscheln; abschieben (— *off*).
toddler ['tɔdlə], *s.* (*coll.*) das kleine Kind (das gehen lernt).
toe [tou], *s.* (*Anat.*) die Zehe.
toffee ['tɔfi], *s.* der Sahnebonbon.
together [tə'geðə], *adv.* zusammen.
toil [tɔil], *v.n.* hart arbeiten. — *s.* die schwere, harte Arbeit.
toilet ['tɔilit], *s.* das Anziehen, Ankleiden; die Toilette, der Abort, das Klosett (*lavatory*).
token ['toukən], *s.* das Zeichen (*sign*); der Beweis (*proof*); das Andenken (*keepsake*).
tolerable ['tɔlərəbl], *adj.* erträglich, leidlich.
tolerance ['tɔlərəns], *s.* die Toleranz, Duldsamkeit; (*Tech.*) die Toleranz.
tolerant ['tɔlərənt], *adj.* tolerant, duldsam.
tolerate ['tɔləreit], *v.a.* ertragen, dulden.
toll [toul], *v.a., v.n.* läuten. — *s.* der Zoll; — *gate,* — *bar,* der Schlagbaum.
tomato [tə'mɑ:tou], *s.* (*Bot.*) die Tomate.
tomb [tu:m], *s.* das Grab, Grabmal.
tomboy ['tɔmbɔi], *s.* der Wildfang.
tomcat ['tɔmkæt], *s.* (*Zool.*) der Kater.
tome [toum], *s.* der große Band, (*coll.*) der Wälzer.
tomfoolery [tɔm'fu:ləri], *s.* die Narretei.
Tommy ['tɔmi], *s.* (*Mil.*) (*coll.*) der englische Soldat.
tomorrow [tə'mɔrou], *adv.* morgen; — *morning,* morgen früh; *the day after* —, übermorgen.
ton [tʌn], *s.* die Tonne.
tone [toun], *s.* der Ton, Klang; (*fig.*) die Stimmung (*mood*). — *v.a.* — *down,* abtönen, abstimmen.
tongs [tɔŋz], *s. pl.* die Zange.
tongue [tʌŋ], *s.* (*Anat.*) die Zunge.
tonic ['tɔnik], *s.* das Stärkungsmittel. — *adj.* tonisch, stärkend.
tonight [tu'nait], *adv.* heute abend, heute nacht.
tonnage ['tʌnidʒ], *s.* die Tonnage, das Tonnengeld.
tonsil ['tɔnsil], *s.* (*Anat.*) die Mandel.
tonsilitis [tɔnsi'laitis], *s.* (*Med.*) die Mandelentzündung.
tonsure ['tɔnʃə], *s.* die Tonsur.
too [tu:], *adv.* allzu, zu, allzusehr; auch (*also*).
tool [tu:l], *s.* das Werkzeug, das Gerät; *machine* —, die Werkzeugmaschine.
tooth [tu:θ], *s.* (*pl.* **teeth** [ti:θ]) der Zahn.
toothache ['tu:θeik], *s.* das Zahnweh.
toothbrush ['tu:θbrʌʃ], *s.* die Zahnbürste.

503

toothpaste

toothpaste ['tu:θpeist], *s.* die Zahnpaste.

top (1) [tɔp], *s.* die Spitze; der Gipfel (*mountain*); der Wipfel (*tree*); der Giebel (*house*); die Oberfläche (*surface*); big —, das Zirkuszeltdach; — *hat,* der Zylinder. — *v.a.* übertreffen (*surpass*); bedecken (*cover*).

top (2) [tɔp], *s.* der Kreisel (*spinning* —).

topaz ['toupæz], *s.* der Topas.

tope [toup], *v.n.* zechen, saufen.

toper ['toupə], *s.* der Zecher.

topic ['tɔpik], *s.* das Thema, der Gegenstand.

topical ['tɔpikəl], *adj.* aktuell (*up to date*).

topmost ['tɔpmoust], *adj.* höchst, oberst.

topsy-turvy ['tɔpsi 'tə:vi], *adv.* durcheinander, auf den Kopf gestellt.

torch [tɔ:tʃ], *s.* die Fackel; (*Elec.*) die Taschenlampe.

torment ['tɔ:mənt], *s.* die Qual, Marter. — [tɔ:'ment], *v.a.* quälen, martern, peinigen.

tornado [tɔ:'neidou], *s.* der Wirbelsturm.

torpid ['tɔ:pid], *adj.* starr, betäubt; (*fig.*) stumpfsinnig.

torpor ['tɔ:pə], *s.* die Starre; die Stumpfheit, Stumpfsinnigkeit.

torrent ['tɔrənt], *s.* der Gießbach, der (reißende) Strom.

torrid ['tɔrid], *adj.* brennend heiß, verbrannt.

torsion ['tɔ:ʃən], *s.* die Drehung, Windung.

tortoise ['tɔ:təs], *s.* (*Zool.*) die Schildkröte.

tortoiseshell ['tɔ:təʃel], *s.* das Schildpatt.

tortuous ['tɔ:tjuəs], *adj.* gewunden.

torture ['tɔ:tʃə], *s.* die Folter; (*fig.*) die Folterqualen, *f. pl.* —*v.a.* foltern.

Tory ['tɔ:ri], *s.* (*Pol.*) der englische Konservative.

toss [tɔs], *s.* der Wurf (*of coin, etc.*); *argue the* —, sich streiten. — *v.a.* werfen. — *v.n.* — *up,* losen.

total [toutl], *adj.* ganz, gänzlich, total. — *s.* die Gesamtsumme. — *v.a.* sich (im ganzen) belaufen auf.

totality [tou'tæliti], *s.* die Gesamtheit.

totter ['tɔtə], *v.n.* wanken, schwanken, torkeln.

touch [tʌtʃ], *v.a.* berühren; anfassen; (*coll.*) anpumpen (*for money*); — *up,* auffrischen. — *s.* die Berührung (*contact*); (*Mus.*) der Anschlag.

touching ['tʌtʃiŋ], *adj.* rührend, ergreifend.

touchline ['tʌtʃlain], *s.* (*Sport*) der Rand des Spielfeldes, die Seitenlinie.

touchy ['tʌtʃi], *adj.* empfindlich.

tough [tʌf], *adj.* zäh, widerstandsfähig (*resistant*); *get* —, grob werden; — *luck,* Pech! — *s.* (*Am. coll.*) der Grobian.

tour [tuə], *s.* die Tour, Reise; (*Theat.*) die Tournee. — *v.a., v.n.* touren, bereisen.

tourist ['tuərist], *s.* der Tourist.

tournament ['tuə-* or *'tɔ:nəmənt], *s.* der Wettkampf, das Turnier.

tout [taut], *v.n.* Kunden suchen, anlocken. — *s.* der Kundenfänger.

tow [tou], *s.* das Schlepptau. — *v.a.* ziehen, schleppen.

toward(s) [tu'wɔ:d(z), tɔ:d(z)], *prep.* gegen; gegenüber; zu . . . hin; auf . . . zu; für.

towel ['tauəl], *s.* das Handtuch.

towelling ['tauəliŋ], *s.* der Handtuchdrell; *Turkish* —, das Frottiertuch.

tower [tauə], *s.* der Turm, Zwinger. — *v.n.* emporragen, hervorragen (*über*).

towing path ['tou(iŋ) pɑ:θ] *see* **towpath.**

town [taun], *s.* die Stadt; — *crier,* der Ausrufer; — *hall,* das Rathaus (*offices*).

townsman ['taunzmən], *s.* der Städter.

towpath ['toupɑ:θ], *s.* der Treidelpfad.

toy [tɔi], *s.* das Spielzeug; (*pl.*) Spielsachen, Speilwaren, *f. pl.*; — *shop,* der Speilwarenladen. — *v.n.* spielen.

trace [treis], *s.* die Spur. — *v.a.* suchen, aufspüren; pausen (*through paper*).

track [træk], *s.* die Spur, Fährte (*path*); (*Railw.*) das Geleis(e).

tract [trækt], *s.* der Traktat (*pamphlet*); die Strecke (*stretch*).

traction ['trækʃən], *s.* das Ziehen (*pulling*); (*Tech.*) der Zug.

tractor ['træktə], *s.* der Traktor.

trade [treid], *s.* der Handel (*commerce*); das Gewerbe (*craft*); — *wind,* der Passatwind; — *union,* die Gewerkschaft. — *v.a.* — *in,* in Zahlung geben. — *v.n.* handeln, Handel treiben; — *in,* eintauschen.

trademark ['treidmɑ:k], *s.* die (Schutz)marke, das Warenzeichen.

tradesman ['treidzmən], *s.* der Lieferant.

traduce [trə'dju:s], *v.a.* verleumden.

traffic ['træfik], *s.* der Verkehr; (*Comm.*) der Handel; — *light,* die Verkehrsampel.

trafficator ['træfikeitə], *s.* (*Motor.*) der Winker.

tragedy ['trædʒədi], *s.* die Tragödie, das Trauerspiel.

tragic ['trædʒik], *adj.* tragisch.

tradition [trə'diʃən], *s.* die Tradition.

traditional [trə'diʃənəl], *adj.* traditionell.

trail [treil], *s.* die Spur, Fährte; (*Am.*) der Pfad. — *v.a.* nach sich ziehen, schleppen; (*Am.*) nachfolgen (*Dat.*).

trailer ['treilə], *s.* (*Motor.*) der Anhänger; (*Film*) die Voranzeige.

train [trein], *v.a.* ausbilden; (*Sport*) trainieren, abrichten, dressieren (*animal*). — *v.n.* (*Sport*) sich vorbereiten; sich ausbilden (*for profession*). — *s.* (*Railw.*) der Zug; (*Mil.*) der Zug, Transport; die Schleppe (*bridal gown, etc.*); — *of thought,* die Gedankenfolge.

treble

training ['treiniŋ], *s.* die Erziehung; Ausbildung; — *college*, das Lehrerseminar, die pädagogische Hochschule.

trait [trei, treit], *s.* der Zug, Wesenszug.

traitor ['treitə], *s.* der Verräter.

tram(car) ['træm(ka:)], *s.* die Straßenbahn, der Strassenbahnwagen.

trammelled [træmld], *adj.* gebunden, gefesselt.

tramp [træmp], *s.* der Landstreicher, Strolch. — *v.n.* trampeln; (zu Fuß) wandern.

trample [træmpl], *v.a.* niedertrampeln. — *v.n.* trampeln, treten.

tramway ['træmwei], *s.* die Strassenbahn.

trance [tra:ns], *s.* die Verzückung.

tranquil ['træŋkwil], *adj.* ruhig, still, friedlich.

tranquillizer ['træŋkwilaizə], *s.* (*Med.*) das Beruhigungsmittel.

transact [træn'zækt], *v.a.* abmachen; verrichten (*conclude*), erledigen.

transaction [træn'zækʃən], *s.* die Verhandlung, Abmachung, Durchführung.

transcend [træn'send], *v.a.* übersteigen.

transcendental [trænsen'dentl], *adj.* transzendental.

transcribe [træn'skraib], *v.a.* übertragen; umschreiben (*cipher etc.*); abschreiben.

transcription [træn'skripʃən], *s.* die Umschrift; die Abschrift (*copy*).

transept [trænsept], *s.* (*Archit.*) das Querschiff.

transfer [træns'fə:], *v.a.* versetzen, überführen; übertragen; überweisen (*money*). — *v.n.* verlegt werden. — ['trænsfə:], *s.* der Wechsel, Transfer; die Versetzung; Überweisung.

transfigure [træns'figə], *v.a.* verklären.

transfix [træns'fiks], *v.a.* durchbohren.

transform [træns'fɔ:m], *v.a.* verändern, umwandeln. — *v.r.* sich verwandeln.

transgress [træns'gres], *v.a.* überschreiten (*trespass on*). — *v.n.* sich vergehen.

transient ['trænsiənt], *adj.* vergänglich.

transit ['trænsit, 'trænzit], *s.* der Durchgang; die Durchfahrt, Durchfuhr (*travel*); (*Comm.*) der Transit. — *v.n.* (*Am.*) durchfahren (*of goods*).

transitive ['trænsitiv], *adj.* (*Gram.*) transitiv.

transitory ['trænsitəri], *adj.* vergänglich, flüchtig.

translate [træns'leit], *v.a.* übersetzen; versetzen (*office*).

translation [træns'leiʃən], *s.* die Übersetzung, die Übertragung.

translucent [træns'lju:sənt], *adj.* durchscheinend.

transmission [trænz'miʃən], *s.* die Übersendung, Übermittlung; (*Rad.*) die Sendung; (*Motor.*) die Transmission.

transmit [trænz'mit], *v.a.* übersenden,

übermitteln; (*Rad., T.V.*) übertragen, senden.

transmutation [trænzmju'teiʃən], *s.* die Verwandlung.

transparent [træns'pɛərənt], *adj.* durchsichtig.

transpire [træns'paiə, trænz-], *v.n.* bekannt werden.

transplant [træns'pla:nt, trænz-], *v.a.* verpflanzen; (*Med.*) übertragen.

transport [træns'pɔ:t], *v.a.* transportieren; (*fig.*) entzücken. — ['trænspɔ:t], *s.* der Transport; die Versendung (*sending*); (*fig.*) die Entzückung.

transpose [træns'pouz], *v.a.* (*Mus.*) transponieren.

transverse [trænz'və:s], *adj.* quer; schräg (*oblique*).

trap [træp], *v.a.* in eine Falle führen; ertappen (*detect*). — *s.* die Falle; der Einspänner (*gig*).

trapeze [trə'pi:z], *s.* das Trapez.

trapper ['træpə], *s.* der Fallensteller.

trappings ['træpiŋz], *s. pl.* der Schmuck; (*fig.*) die Äußerlichkeiten, *f. pl.*

trash [træʃ], *s.* (*Lit.*) der Schund; der Kitsch; das wertlose Zeug.

trashy ['træʃi], *adj.* wertlos, kitschig.

travail ['træveil], *s.* die Wehen, Sorgen, die Mühe.

travel [trævl], *v.n.* reisen. — *v.a.* bereisen. — *s.* das Reisen; — *agency*, das Reisebüro.

traveller ['trævələ], *s.* der Reisende; (*Comm.*) der Handelsreisende, Vertreter.

traverse ['trævə:s], *adj.* quer. — *s.* die Traverse, der Querbalken. — [trə'və:s], *v.a.* durchqueren; (*fig.*) durchwandern.

trawl [trɔ:l], *v.n.* (mit Schleppnetz) fischen.

trawler ['trɔ:lə], *s.* das Fischerboot, der Fischdampfer.

tray [trei], *s.* das Tablett.

treacherous ['tretʃərəs], *adj.* verräterisch; (*fig.*) gefährlich.

treachery ['tretʃəri], *s.* der Verrat.

treacle ['tri:kl], *s.* der Sirup.

tread [tred], *v.a., v.n. irr.* (be)treten, auftreten. — *s.* der Tritt, Schritt; die Lauffläche (*of a tyre*).

treason ['tri:zn], *s.* der Verrat.

treasure ['treʒə], *s.* der Schatz.

treasurer ['treʒərə], *s.* der Schatzmeister.

treasury ['treʒəri], *s.* die Schatzkammer; (*U.K.*) *the Treasury*, das Schatzamt, Finanzministerium.

treat [tri:t], *v.a.* behandeln; bewirten (*as host*). — *v.n.* (*Pol.*) unterhandeln (*negotiate*). — *s.* der Genuß (*pleasure*).

treatise ['tri:tis], *s.* die Abhandlung.

treatment ['tri:tmənt], *s.* die Behandlung.

treaty ['tri:ti], *s.* der Vertrag.

treble [trebl], *s.* (*Mus.*) die Sopranstimme, Knabenstimme, der Diskant; (*Maths.*) das Dreifache. — *v.a.* verdreifachen.

tree

tree [tri:], s. (Bot.) der Baum.
trefoil ['tri:fɔil], s. (Bot.) der drei-blätt(e)rige Klee; das Dreiblatt.
trellis ['trelis], s. das Gitter.
tremble [trembl], v.n. zittern. — s. das Zittern.
tremendous [tri'mendəs], adj. ungeheuer (groß); schrecklich.
tremor ['tremə], s. das Zittern; (Geol.) das Beben; (Med.) das Zucken.
trench [trentʃ], s. der Graben.
trenchant ['trentʃənt], adj. einschneidend, scharf.
trend [trend], s. die Tendenz; (Comm.) der Trend.
trepidation [trepi'deiʃən], s. die Angst, das Zittern.
trespass ['trespəs], v.n. sich vergehen, übertreten (law); — on, unbefugt betreten. — s. die Übertretung.
tress [tres], s. die Flechte, Haarlocke.
trestle [tresl], s. das Gestell; — table, der Klapptisch.
trial ['traiəl], s. die Probe, der Versuch; (Law) die Verhandlung, der Prozeß, das Verhör.
triangle ['traiæŋgl], s. das Dreieck; (Mus.) der Triangel.
tribe [traib], s. der Stamm.
tribulation [tribju'leiʃən], s. die Trübsal, Drangsal.
tribunal [trai'bju:nəl], s. das Tribunal, der Gerichtshof.
tributary ['tribjutəri], adj. Neben-. — s. der Nebenfluß.
tribute ['tribju:t], s. der Tribut.
trice [trais], s. in a —, im Nu.
trick [trik], s. der Kniff, Trick. — v.a. betrügen.
trickery ['trikəri], s. der Betrug.
trickle [trikl], v.n. tröpfeln, sickern. — s. das Tröpfeln.
tricky ['triki], adj. verwickelt; (fig.) bedenklich, heikel.
tricycle ['traisikl], s. das Dreirad.
tried [traid], adj. erprobt, bewährt.
triennial [trai'eniəl], adj. dreijährlich.
trifle [traifl], v.n. scherzen, spielen. — s. die Kleinigkeit; (Cul.) der süße Auflauf.
trigger ['trigə], s. der Drücker. — v.a. — off, auslösen.
trilateral [trai'lætərəl], adj. dreiseitig.
trill [tril], s. (Mus.) der Triller. — v.a., v.n. trillern.
trim [trim], adj. niedlich, schmuck; nett (dress). — v.a. beschneiden; (Naut.) — sails, einziehen. — s. die Ausrüstung; (Naut.) das Gleichgewicht.
trimmer ['trimə], s. die Putzmacherin; (fig.) der Opportunist.
trimmings ['triminz], s. pl. (fig.) der Kleinkram; (Tail.) der Besatz.
Trinity ['triniti], s. (Theol.) die Dreifaltigkeit, Dreieinigkeit.
trinket ['trinkit], s. das Geschmeide; (pl.) Schmucksachen, f. pl.
trip [trip], s. der Ausflug, die Reise. —

v.a. — up, ein Bein stellen (Dat.). — v.n. stolpern.
tripe [traip], s. die Kaldaunen, f. pl.; (fig.) der Unsinn.
triple [tripl], adj. dreifach.
triplet ['triplit], s. der Drilling; (Mus.) die Triole; (Poet.) der Dreireim.
tripod ['traipɔd], s. der Dreifuß.
tripos ['traipɔs], s. das Schlußexamen (Cambridge Univ.).
trite [trait], adj. abgedroschen.
triumph ['traiʌmf], s. der Triumph. — v.n. triumphieren.
triumphant [trai'ʌmfənt], adj. triumphierend.
trivial ['triviəl], adj. trivial, platt, alltäglich.
troll (1) [troul], v.n. trällern (hum); fischen. — s. der Rundgesang (song).
troll (2) [troul], s. der Kobold (gnome).
trolley ['trɔli], s. der Teewagen (furniture); (Tech.) die Dräsine, der Karren.
trollop ['trɔləp], s. die Schlampe.
trombone [trɔm'boun], s. (Mus.) die Posaune.
troop [tru:p], s. der Haufe; (Mil.) die Truppe, der Trupp. — v.n. sich sammeln. — v.a. Trooping the Colour, die Fahnenparade.
trophy ['troufi], s. die Trophäe, das Siegeszeichen.
tropic ['trɔpik], s. (Geog.) der Wendekreis; (pl.) die Tropen, f. pl.
tropical ['trɔpikəl], adj. tropisch.
trot [trɔt], v.n. traben. — s. der Trab, Trott.
troth [trouθ], s. (obs.) die Treue; pledge o.'s —, Treue geloben.
trouble [trʌbl], s. die Mühe, Sorge (worry); der Kummer (sadness); die Störung (disturbance). — v.a. bemühen (ask favour of); bekümmern (worry); stören (disturb).
troublesome ['trʌblsəm], adj. ärgerlich, schwierig, unangenehm.
trough [trɔf], s. der Trog; (Met.) das Tief.
trounce [trauns], v.a. verprügeln.
trouncing ['traunsiŋ], s. die Tracht Prügel.
trousers ['trauzəz], s. pl. die Hosen, f. pl.
trout [traut], s. (Zool.) die Forelle.
trowel ['trauəl], s. die Kelle.
troy(weight) ['trɔi(weit)], s. das Troygewicht.
truant ['tru:ənt], s. (Sch.) der Schulschwänzer; play —, die Schule schwänzen.
truce [tru:s], s. der Waffenstillstand.
truck (1) [trʌk], s. (Rail.) der Güterwagen; (Am.) see lorry.
truck (2) [trʌk], s. have no — with, nichts zu tun haben mit.
truculent ['trʌkjulənt], adj. streitsüchtig.
trudge [trʌdʒ], v.n. sich schleppen.
true [tru:], adj. wahr; treu (faithful); echt (genuine); richtig (correct).

truffle [trʌfl], *s.* die Trüffel.

truism ['tru:izm], *s.* der Gemeinplatz, die Binsenwahrheit.

truly ['tru:li], *adv. yours —,* Ihr ergebener.

trump [trʌmp], *s.* der Trumpf; *— card,* die Trumpfkarte. *— v.a. — up,* erfinden, erdichten.

trumpery ['trʌmpəri], *s.* der Plunder, Schund. *— adj.* wertlos, belanglos.

trumpet ['trʌmpit], *s.* (*Mus.*) die Trompete. *— v.a.* stolz austrompeten, ausposaunen. *— v.n.* trompeten.

truncate [trʌŋ'keit], *v.a.* verstümmeln, stutzen.

truncheon ['trʌnʃən], *s.* der Knüppel. *— v.a.* durchprügeln.

trundle [trʌndl], *v.n.* trudeln; sich wälzen. *— v.a. — a hoop,* Reifen schlagen.

trunk [trʌŋk], *s.* der Stamm (*tree*); der Rüssel (*of elephant*); der (große) Koffer (*chest*); *— call,* das Ferngespräch.

truss [trʌs], *s.* das Band, Bruchband. *— v.a.* zäumen, stützen; aufschürzen.

trust [trʌst], *v.a., v.n.* trauen (*Dat.*), vertrauen (*Dat.*); anvertrauen (*Dat., Acc.*). *— s.* das Vertrauen; *in —,* zu treuen Händen, als Treuhänder; (*Comm.*) der Trust.

trustworthy ['trʌstwə:ði], *adj.* zuverlässig.

truth [tru:θ], *s.* die Wahrheit.

truthful ['tru:θful], *adj.* wahrhaftig.

try [trai], *v.a. irr.* versuchen (*s. th.*); (*Law*) verhören; *— on* (*clothes*), anprobieren; *— out,* ausprobieren. *— v.n.* versuchen, sich bemühen. *— s.* der Versuch (*attempt*); (*Rugby*) der Try.

Tsar [zɑ:], *s.* der Zar.

tub [tʌb], *s.* das Faß; die Wanne (*bath*); (*Naut.*) das Übungsboot.

tube [tju:b], *s.* die Tube (*paste etc.*); die Röhre (*pipe, also Elec.*); der Schlauch (*tyre*); das Rohr (*tubing*); (*Transport*) die Londoner Untergrundbahn.

tuberous ['tju:bərəs], *adj.* knollenartig, knollig.

tubular ['tju:bjulə], *adj.* röhrenförmig.

tuck [tʌk], *s.* (*Tail.*) die Falte; (*Sch. sl.*) der Leckerbissen. *— v.a. — up,* zudecken; *— in,* einschlagen. *— v.n.* (*sl.*) *— in,* tüchtig zugreifen.

tucker ['tʌkə], *s.* (*sl.*) das Essen.

tuckshop ['tʌkʃɔp], *s.* der Schulladen.

Tuesday ['tju:zdi], *s.* der Dienstag.

tuft [tʌft], *s.* der Büschel.

tug [tʌg], *v.a.* ziehen, zerren. *— s.* (*Naut.*) der Schlepper; *— of war,* das Tauziehen.

tuition [tju:'iʃən], *s.* der Unterricht, Privatunterricht.

tulip ['tju:lip], *s.* (*Bot.*) die Tulpe.

tumble [tʌmbl], *v.n.* purzeln. *— s.* der Sturz, Fall.

tumbril ['tʌmbril], *s.* der Karren.

tumid ['tju:mid], *adj.* geschwollen.

tumour ['tju:mə], *s.* (*Med.*) die Geschwulst, der Tumor.

tumult ['tju:mʌlt], *s.* der Tumult, Auflauf; der Lärm (*noise*).

tun [tʌn], *s.* die Tonne, das Faß.

tune [tju:n], *s.* die Melodie. *— v.a.* stimmen; (*Rad.*) *— in* (*to*), einstellen (auf).

tuneful ['tju:nful], *adj.* melodisch.

tuner ['tju:nə], *s.* der (Klavier)stimmer.

tunic ['tju:nik], *s.* der Kittel.

tuning ['tju:niŋ], *s.* das Stimmen; die Abstimmung (*also Rad.*); *— fork,* die Stimmgabel.

tunnel [tʌnl], *s.* der Tunnel. *— v.n.* graben, einen Tunnel bauen.

turbid ['tə:bid], *adj.* trüb, dick.

turbot ['tə:bət], *s.* (*Zool.*) der Steinbutt.

turbulence ['tə:bjuləns], *s.* der Sturm, das Ungestüm; (*Aviat.*) die Turbulenz.

tureen [tjuə'ri:n], *s.* die Suppenterrine, Suppenschüssel.

turf [tə:f], *s.* der Rasen; (*Sport*) die Rennbahn, der Turf. *— v.a.* mit Rasen belegen; (*sl.*) *— out,* hinausschmeißen.

turgid ['tə:dʒid], *adj.* schwülstig (*style*).

Turk [tə:k], *s.* der Türke.

turkey ['tə:ki], *s.* (*Orn.*) der Truthahn.

Turkish ['tə:kiʃ], *adj.* türkisch.

turmoil ['tə:mɔil], *s.* die Unruhe, der Aufruhr.

turn [tə:n], *v.a.* wenden, drehen, kehren (*to*); *— down,* ablehnen; (*coll.*) *— in,* abgeben (*hand over*); *— on,* andrehen (*tap etc.*); *— off,* ausdrehen; *— out,* produzieren. *— v.n.* sich drehen, sich ändern; werden; *— on s.o.,* jemanden verraten; (*coll.*) *— out,* ausrücken; (*coll.*) *— up,* auftauchen. *— s.* die Drehung, Windung; der Hang; die Reihe; die Nummer (*act*); *it is my —,* ich bin an der Reihe.

turncoat ['tə:nkout], *s.* der Überläufer.

turner ['tə:nə], *s.* der Drechsler.

turnip ['tə:nip], *s.* (*Bot.*) die Rübe.

turnpike ['tə:npaik], *s.* der Schlagbaum.

turnstile ['tə:nstail], *s.* das Drehkreuz.

turntable ['tə:nteibl], *s.* die Drehscheibe.

turpentine ['tə:pəntain], *s.* der *or* das Terpentin.

turquoise ['tə:kwɔiz *or* 'tə:kɔiz], *s.* der Türkis.

turret ['tʌrit], *s.* (*Archit.*) der Turm, das Türmchen.

turtle [tə:tl], *s.* (*Zool.*) die Schildkröte; (*Orn.*) *—-dove,* die Turteltaube.

tusk [tʌsk], *s.* (*Zool.*) der Stoßzahn.

tussle [tʌsl], *s.* der Streit, die Rauferei.

tutelage ['tju:tilidʒ], *s.* die Vormundschaft.

tutor ['tju:tə], *s.* der Privatlehrer; der Tutor, Studienleiter. *— v.a.* unterrichten.

twaddle [twɔdl], *s.* das Geschwätz. *— v.n.* schwätzen.

twang [twæŋ], *s.* der scharfe Ton. *— v.n.* scharf klingen.

tweed [twi:d], *s.* (*Text.*) der Tweed.

twelfth [twelfθ], *num.adj.* zwölft; *Twelfth Night,* das Fest der Heiligen Drei Könige (*6th January*).

twelve

twelve [twelv], *num. adj.* zwölf.
twenty ['twenti], *num. adj.* zwanzig.
twice [twais], *num. adv.* zweimal, doppelt.
twig [twig], *s.* (*Bot.*) der Zweig, die Rute.
twilight ['twailait], *s.* das Zwielicht, die Dämmerung.
twill [twil], *s.* (*Text.*) der Köper. — *v.a.* köpern.
twin [twin], *s.* der Zwilling.
twine [twain], *s.* der Bindfaden, die Schnur. — *v.a.* zwirnen, drehen. — *v.n.* sich verflechten; sich winden (*plant*).
twinge [twindʒ], *s.* der Zwick, Stich.
twinkle [twiŋkl], *v.n.* blinzeln, blinken. — *s.* das Zwinkern, der Blick.
twirl [twəːl], *s.* der Wirbel. — *v.a.* schnell drehen, wirbeln.
twist [twist], *v.a.* flechten, drehen; verdrehen. — *s.* die Drehung, Krümmung; das Geflecht; (*fig.*) die Wendung (*sudden change*).
twitch [twitʃ], *v.a.* zupfen, zucken. — *v.n.* zucken. — *s.* das Zucken, der Krampf.
twitter ['twitə], *v.n.* zwitschern; (*fig.*) zittern. — *s.* das Gezwitscher; (*fig.*) die Angst.
two [tuː], *num. adj.* zwei; — *-faced*, falsch.
twofold ['tuːfould], *adj.* zweifach.
tympanum ['timpənəm], *s.* (*Med.*) das Trommelfell.
type [taip], *s.* (*Typ.*) die Type; (*Psych.*) der Typ, Typus. — *v.a., v.n.* tippen; mit der Maschine schreiben.
typewriter ['taipraitə], *s.* die Schreibmaschine.
typhoid ['taifɔid], *s.* (*Med.*) der (Unterleibs)typhus. — *adj.* typhusartig.
typist ['taipist], *s.* der (die) Maschinenschreiber(in).
typhoon [tai'fuːn], *s.* der Taifun.
typical ['tipikəl], *adj.* typisch, charakteristisch.
typography [tai'pɔgrəfi], *s.* die Typographie, Buchdruckerkunst.
tyrannical [ti'rænikəl], *adj.* tyrannisch.
tyranny ['tirəni], *s.* die Tyrannei.
tyrant ['taiərənt], *s.* der Tyrann.
tyre, (*Am.*) tire [taiə], *s.* der Reifen.
tyro ['taiərou], *s.* der Anfänger.
Tyrolese [tiro'liːz], *adj.* tirolisch, Tiroler-. — *s.* der Tiroler.

U

U [juː], *s.* das U.
ubiquitous [ju'bikwitəs], *adj.* überall da, überall zu finden.
udder ['ʌdə], *s.* (*Zool.*) das Euter.
ugly ['ʌgli], *adj.* häßlich.

Ukrainian [juː'kreiniən], *adj.* ukrainisch. — *s.* der Ukrainer.
ulcer ['ʌlsə], *s.* (*Med.*) das Geschwür.
ulcerate ['ʌlsəreit], *v.n.* (*Med.*) schwären.
ulcerous ['ʌlsərəs], *adj.* (*Med.*) geschwürig.
ulterior [ʌl'tiəriə], *adj.* weiter, ferner, weiterliegend.
ultimate ['ʌltimit], *adj.* letzt, endlich, äußerst.
ultimatum [ʌlti'meitəm], *s.* das Ultimatum.
umbrage ['ʌmbridʒ], *s.* der Schatten; *take —*, Anstoß nehmen (an, *Dat.*).
umbrella [ʌm'brelə], *s.* der Schirm, Regenschirm.
umpire ['ʌmpaiə], *s.* (*Sport*) der Schiedsrichter.
umpteen ['ʌmptiːn], *adj.* zahlreiche, verschiedene.
un- [ʌn], *negating pref.* un-, nicht-; *with verbs,* auf-, ent-, los-, ver-; *where a word is not given, see the simple form.*
unable [ʌn'eibl], *adj.* unfähig; *be —*, nicht können.
unaccustomed [ʌnə'kʌstəmd], *adj.* ungewohnt.
unaided [ʌn'eidid], *adj.* allein, ohne Hilfe.
unaware [ʌnə'wɛə], *adj.* unbewußt.
uncertain [ʌn'səːtin], *adj.* unsicher.
uncle [ʌŋkl], *s.* der Onkel.
unconscious [ʌn'kɔnʃəs], *adj.* bewußtlos; unbewusst.
uncouth [ʌn'kuːθ], *adj.* ungehobelt, roh.
unction ['ʌŋkʃən], *s.* die Salbung (*anointing*); die Salbe; *Extreme Unction,* (*Eccl.*) die Letzte Ölung.
unctuous ['ʌŋktjuəs], *adj.* salbungsvoll.
under ['ʌndə], *prep.* unter. — *adv.* darunter, unten (*underneath*); *pref.* (*compounds*) unter-.
undercarriage ['ʌndəkæridʒ],*s.*(*Aviat.*) das Fahrwerk.
underfed [ʌndə'fed], *adj.* unterernährt.
undergo [ʌndə'gou], *v.a. irr.* durchmachen, erdulden.
undergraduate [ʌndə'grædjuit], *s.* (*Univ.*) der Student.
underground ['ʌndəgraund], *adj.* unterirdisch; — *railway* die Untergrundbahn. — [ʌndə'graund], *adv.* unterirdisch.
underhand [ʌndə'hænd], *adj.* heimlich, hinterlistig.
underline [ʌndə'lain], *v.a.* unterstreichen.
undermine [ʌndə'main], *v.a.* untergraben.
underneath [ʌndə'niːθ], *adv.* unten, darunter. — ['ʌndəniːθ], *prep.* unter.
undersigned ['ʌndəsaind], *adj.* unterzeichnet. — *s.* der Unterzeichnete.
understand [ʌndə'stænd], *v.a. irr.* verstehen, begreifen.
understatement ['ʌndəsteitmənt], *s.* die zu bescheidene Festellung, Unterbewertung.

508

undertaker [ˈʌndəteikə], s. der Leichenbestatter.

undertaking [ʌndəˈteikiŋ], s. das Unternehmen (*business*); das Versprechen (*promise*).

undertone [ˈʌndətoun], s. der Unterton.

underwrite [ʌndəˈrait], v.a. irr. (*Comm.*) versichern.

underwriter [ˈʌndəraitə], s. (*Comm.*) der Assekurant, Versicherer, Mitversicherer.

undeserved [ʌndiˈzə:vd], adj. unverdient.

undeserving [ʌndiˈzə:viŋ], adj. unwürdig.

undignified [ʌnˈdignifaid], adj. würdelos.

undiscerning [ʌndiˈzə:niŋ], adj. geschmacklos.

undiscriminating [ʌndisˈkrimineitiŋ], adj. unterschiedslos, unkritisch.

undisputed [ʌndisˈpju:tid], adj. unbestritten.

undo [ʌnˈdu:], v.a. irr. zerstören (*destroy*); öffnen (*open*).

undoubted [ʌnˈdautid], adj. zweifellos.

undress [ʌnˈdres], v.a., v.n. — (sich)ausziehen. — [ˈʌndres], s. das Hauskleid.

undue [ʌnˈdju:], adj. unangemessen.

undulate [ˈʌndjuleit], v.n. wallen, Wellen schlagen.

unduly [ʌnˈdju:li], adv. ungebührlich, übermäßig.

unearth [ʌnˈə:θ], v.a. ausgraben.

unearthly [ʌnˈə:θli], adj. überirdisch.

uneasy [ʌnˈi:zi], adj. unruhig, unbehaglich.

unemployed [ʌnimˈplɔid], adj. arbeitslos.

unemployment [ʌnimˈplɔimənt], s. die Arbeitslosigkeit.

unending [ʌnˈendiŋ], adj. endlos.

uneven [ʌnˈi:vən], adj. uneben; ungerade.

unexceptionable [ʌnikˈsepʃənəbl], adj. tadellos.

unexpired [ʌniksˈpaiəd], adj. noch nicht abgelaufen, noch gültig.

unfair [ʌnˈfeə], adj. unfair; unehrlich.

unfeeling [ʌnˈfi:liŋ], adj. gefühllos.

unfit [ʌnˈfit], adj. (*Mil., Med.*) untauglich, schwach; (*food etc.*) ungenießbar.

unfold [ʌnˈfould], v.a. entfalten.

unforeseen [ʌnfɔːˈsi:n], adj. unerwartet.

unfounded [ʌnˈfaundid], adj. grundlos.

unfurnished [ʌnˈfə:niʃd], adj. unmöbliert.

ungrudging [ʌnˈɡrʌdʒiŋ], adj. bereitwillig.

unhappy [ʌnˈhæpi], adj. unglücklich.

unhinge [ʌnˈhindʒ], v.a. aus den Angeln heben.

unicorn [ˈju:nikɔ:n], s. (*Myth.*) das Einhorn.

uniform [ˈju:nifɔ:m], s. die Uniform. — adj. gleichförmig, einförmig.

union [ˈju:niən], s. die Vereinigung; trade —, die Gewerkschaft; Union Jack, die britische Nationalflagge.

unique [juːˈni:k], adj. einzigartig.

unison [ˈju:nisən], s. (*Mus.*) der Einklang, die Harmonie.

unit [ˈju:nit], s. die Einheit (*measure etc.*).

unite [ju:ˈnait], v.a. vereinen. — v.n. sich vereinen, verbünden.

unity [ˈju:niti], s. die Einigkeit.

universal [ju:niˈvə:səl], adj. allgemein.

universe [ˈju:nivə:s], s. das Weltall.

university [ju:niˈvə:siti], s. die Universität, Hochschule; — degree, der akademische Grad.

unkempt [ʌnˈkempt], adj. ungekämmt, ungepflegt.

unleavened [ʌnˈlevənd], adj. ungesäuert.

unless [ʌnˈles], conj. außer, wenn nicht, es sei denn.

unlettered [ʌnˈletəd], adj. ungebildet.

unlicensed [ʌnˈlaisənsd], adj. nicht (für Alkoholverkauf) lizenziert.

unlike [ʌnˈlaik], adj. ungleich. — [ˈʌnlaik], prep. anders als, verschieden von.

unlikely [ʌnˈlaikli], adj., adv. unwahrscheinlich.

unlock [ʌnˈlɔk], v.a. aufschließen.

unmask [ʌnˈma:sk], v.a. entlarven.

unpack [ʌnˈpæk], v.a., v.n. auspacken.

unpleasant [ʌnˈpleznt], adj. unangenehm.

unreliable [ʌnriˈlaiəbl], adj. unzuverlässig.

unremitting [ʌnriˈmitiŋ], adj. unablässig.

unrepentant [ʌnriˈpentənt], adj. reuelos.

unrest [ʌnˈrest], s. die Unruhe.

unsafe [ʌnˈseif], adj. unsicher.

unscathed [ʌnˈskeiðd], adj. unversehrt.

unscrew [ʌnˈskru:], v.a. abschrauben.

unscrupulous [ʌnˈskru:pjuləs], adj. skrupellos, gewissenlos.

unseat [ʌnˈsi:t], v.a. aus dem Sattel heben; absetzen.

unselfish [ʌnˈselfiʃ], adj. selbstlos.

unsettle [ʌnˈsetl], v.a. verwirren; (fig.) aus dem Konzept bringen.

unsew [ʌnˈsou], v.a. auftrennen.

unshrinking [ʌnˈʃriŋkiŋ], adj. unverzagt.

unsophisticated [ʌnsəˈfistikeitid], adj. naiv, natürlich.

unsparing [ʌnˈspeəriŋ], adj. schonungslos.

unstable [ʌnˈsteibl], adj. unsicher; labil.

unstitch [ʌnˈstitʃ], v.a. auftrennen.

unstop [ʌnˈstɔp], v.a. aufstöpseln, öffnen (a bottle).

unstudied [ʌnˈstʌdid], adj. ungekünstelt.

unsuccessful [ʌnsəkˈsesful], adj. erfolglos.

unsuspecting [ʌnsəˈspektiŋ], adj. arglos.

untie [ʌnˈtai], v.a. losbinden.

until [ʌnˈtil], prep., conj. bis.

untimely [ʌnˈtaimli], *adj.* vorzeitig, unzeitig.

untiring [ʌnˈtaiəriŋ], *adj.* unermüdlich.

unto [ˈʌntu], *prep.* (*Poet.*) zu.

untold [ʌnˈtould], *adj.* ungezählt, unermeßlich.

untoward [ʌnˈtɔːd *or* ʌnˈtouəd], *adj.* unangenehm; widerspenstig (*recalcitrant*).

untrustworthy [ʌnˈtrʌstwəːði], *adj.* unzuverlässig.

unveil [ʌnˈveil], *v.a.* enthüllen.

unwieldy [ʌnˈwiːldi], *adj.* sperrig, schwerfällig.

unwind [ʌnˈwaind], *v.a.* abwickeln.

unwitting [ʌnˈwitiŋ], *adj.* unwissentlich, unbewusst.

unwonted [ʌnˈwountid], *adj.* ungewohnt.

unwrap [ʌnˈræp], *v.a.* auspacken, auswickeln.

unyielding [ʌnˈjiːldiŋ], *adj.* unnachgiebig; hartnäckig.

unyoke [ʌnˈjouk], *v.a.* ausspannen.

up [ʌp], *adv.* auf, aufwärts (*upward*); aufgestanden (*out of bed*); — (*there*), oben; *what's up?* was ist los? — *to*, bis zu; *be — to s.th.*, auf etwas sein, etwas im Schilde führen; *it's — to you*, es liegt an dir. — *prep.* auf, hinauf. — *s. ups and downs*, das wechselnde Schicksal, Auf und Ab.

upbraid [ʌpˈbreid], *v.a.* tadeln.

upheaval [ʌpˈhiːvl], *s.* das Chaos, Durcheinander, die Umwälzung.

uphill [ʌpˈhil], *adv.* bergauf(wärts). — [ˈaphil], *adj.* (an)steigend; (*fig.*) mühsam.

uphold [ʌpˈhould], *v.a.* aufrechterhalten.

upholster [ʌpˈhoulstə], *v.a.* polstern.

upholstery [ʌpˈhoulstəri], *s.* die Polsterung.

upon [ʌˈpɔn] *see* **on**.

upper [ˈʌpə], *adj.* ober, höher; — *hand*, die Oberhand.

uppish [ˈʌpiʃ], *adj.* anmaßend.

upright [ˈʌprait], *adj.* aufrecht, gerade; (*fig.*) aufrichtig, rechtschaffen.

uproar [ˈʌprɔː], *s.* der Lärm, Aufruhr.

uproot [ʌpˈruːt], *v.a.* entwurzeln.

upset [ʌpˈset], *v.a.* umwerfen; (*fig.*) aus der Fassung bringen. — [ˈʌpset], *s.* das Umwerfen; (*fig.*) die Bestürzung.

upshot [ˈʌpʃɔt], *s.* der Ausgang, das Ergebnis.

upside [ˈʌpsaid], *s.* die Oberseite; — *down*, auf den Kopf gestellt.

upstairs [ʌpˈstɛəz], *adv.* oben, nach oben.

upstart [ˈʌpstaːt], *s.* der Parvenü, Emporkömmling.

upward [ˈʌpwəd], *adj.* steigend, aufwärtsgehend. — *adv.* (*also* upwards) aufwärts; — *of*, mehr als.

urban [ˈəːbən], *adj.* städtisch.

urbane [əːˈbein], *adj.* zivilisiert.

urbanity [əːˈbæniti], *s.* die Bildung, der Schliff.

urchin [ˈəːtʃin], *s.* der Schelm; (*Zool.*) *sea —*, der Seeigel.

urge [əːdʒ], *v.a.* drängen. — *s.* der Drang.

urgent [ˈəːdʒənt], *adj.* dringend, drängend, dringlich.

urine [ˈjuərin], *s.* der Urin.

urn [əːn], *s.* die Urne.

Uruguayan [juːruˈgwaiən], *adj.* uruguayisch. — *s.* der Uruguayer.

us [ʌs], *pers. pron.* uns.

usage [ˈjuːsidʒ], *s.* der (Sprach)gebrauch; die Sitte.

use [juːz], *v.a.* gebrauchen, benutzen. — [juːs], *s.* der Gebrauch, die Benutzung; der Nutzen (*usefulness*).

usher [ˈʌʃə], *s.* der Türhüter, Platzanweiser. — *v.a.* — *in*, anmelden, einführen.

usherette [ʌʃəˈret], *s.* die Platzanweiserin, Programmverkäuferin.

usual [ˈjuːʒuəl], *adj.* gewöhnlich, üblich.

usurer [ˈjuːʒərə *or* ˈjuːʒjuərə], *s.* der Wucherer.

usurp [juːˈzəːp], *v.a.* an sich reißen, usurpieren.

usury [ˈjuːʒuəri], *s.* der Wucher.

utensil [juːˈtensil], *s.* das Gerät, Werkzeug.

utility [juːˈtiliti], *s.* die Nützlichkeit (*usefulness*); der Nutzen; *public —*, (die) öffentliche Einrichtung.

utilize [ˈjuːtilaiz], *v.a.* nutzbar machen, ausbeuten, ausnützen.

utmost [ˈʌtmoust], *adj.* äußerst, weitest, höchst. — *s.* das Höchste, Äußerste.

utter [ˈʌtə], *adj.* äußerst, gänzlich. — *v.a.* äußern, aussprechen.

utterly [ˈʌtəli], *adv.* äußerst, völlig.

uvula [ˈjuːvjulə], *s.* (*Anat.*) das Zäpfchen.

V

V [viː]. das V.

vacancy [ˈveːkənsi], *s.* die freie Stelle, die Vakanz.

vacant [ˈveikənt], *adj.* frei; leer.

vacate [vəˈkeit], *v.a.* frei machen.

vacation [vəˈkeiʃən], *s.* die Niederlegung (*of a post*); die Ferien, *pl.* (*school*); der Urlaub (*holiday*).

vaccinate [ˈvæksineit], *v.a.* (*Med.*) impfen.

vaccine [ˈvæksiːn], *s.* (*Med.*) der Impfstoff.

vacillate [ˈvæsileit], *v.n.* schwanken.

vacuity [væˈkjuːiti], *s.* die Leere.

vacuous [ˈvækjuəs], *adj.* leer.

vacuum [ˈvækjuəm], *s.* das Vakuum; *— cleaner*, der Staubsauger.

vagabond [ˈvægəbɔnd], *s.* der Landstreicher.

vagary [vəˈgɛəri], *s.* die Laune, Grille.

vernal

vagrant ['veigrənt], *adj.* herumstreichend. — *s.* der Landstreicher.
vague [veig], *adj.* vage, unbestimmt, unklar.
vain [vein], *adj.* nichtig, vergeblich, eitel; *in* —, vergebens, umsonst.
vale [veil], *s.* (*Poet.*) das Tal.
valerian [və'liəriən], *s.* (*Bot.*) der Baldrian.
valet ['vælei, 'vælit], *s.* der Diener.
valiant ['væljənt], *adj.* mutig, tapfer.
valid ['vælid], *adj.* gültig, stichhaltig.
valley ['væli], *s.* das Tal.
valuable ['væljuəbl], *adj.* wertvoll, kostbar.
valuation [vælju'eifən], *s.* die Schätzung.
value ['vælju:], *s.* der Wert. — *v.a.* wertschätzen, schätzen.
valve [vælv], *s.* (*Mech.*) das Ventil; (*Rad.*) die Röhre.
vamp (1) [væmp], *s.* das Oberleder.
vamp (2) [væmp], *s.* (*Am. coll.*) der Vamp.
vampire ['væmpaiə], *s.* der Vampir.
van [væn], *s.* der Lieferwagen.
vane [vein], *s.* die Wetterfahne.
vanguard ['vænga:d], *s.* die Vorhut, der Vortrupp.
vanilla [və'nilə], *s.* die Vanille.
vanish ['vænif], *v.n.* verschwinden.
vanity ['væniti], *s.* die Nichtigkeit; die Eitelkeit (*conceit*).
vanquish ['vænkwif], *v.a.* besiegen.
vantage ['va:ntidʒ], *s.* der Vorteil; — *point*, die günstige Position.
vapid ['væpid], *adj.* leer, schal.
vapour ['veipə], *s.* der Dunst; (*Chem.*) der Dampf.
variable ['veəriəbl], *adj.* variabel, veränderlich.
variance ['veəriəns], *s.* die Uneinigkeit.
variation [veəri'eifən], *s.* die Variation; die Veränderung, Abweichung.
varicose ['værikəs], *adj.* Krampf-, krampfaderig.
variegated ['veərigeitid], *adj.* bunt, vielfarbig.
variety [və'raiəti], *s.* die Mannigfaltigkeit; (*Bot.*) die Varietät, Abart; (*Theat.*) das Varieté, das Varietétheater.
various ['veəriəs], *adj.* verschieden; mannigfaltig.
varnish ['va:nif], *s.* der Firnis, der Lack. — *v.a.* mit Firnis anstreichen, lackieren.
vary ['veəri], *v.a.* abändern. — *v.n.* sich ändern, variieren.
vase [va:z], *s.* die Vase.
vassal ['væsl], *s.* der Vasall, Lehnsmann.
vast [va:st], *adj.* ungeheuer, groß.
vat [væt], *s.* die Kufe, das große Faß.
vault [vɔ:lt], *s.* das Gewölbe; die Gruft (*grave*); (*Sport*) der Sprung, *pole* —, der Stabhochsprung. — *v.n.* springen.
vaunt [vɔ:nt], *v.a.* rühmen. — *v.n.* prahlen, sich rühmen. — *s.* die Prahlerei.
veal [vi:l], *s.* das Kalbfleisch.

veer [viə], *v.n.* sich drehen.
vegetable ['vedʒitəbl], *s.* das Gemüse.
vegetarian [vedʒi'teəriən], *adj.* vegetarisch. — *s.* der Vegetarier.
vegetate ['vedʒiteit], *v.n.* vegetieren.
vehemence ['vi:iməns], *s.* die Vehemenz, Heftigkeit.
vehicle ['vi:ikl], *s.* das Fahrzeug, Fuhrwerk; (*Motor.*) der Wagen.
veil [veil], *s.* der Schleier. — *v.a.* verschleiern.
vein [vein], *s.* die Ader.
vellum ['veləm], *s.* das feine Pergamentpapier.
velocity [vi'lɔsiti], *s.* die Geschwindigkeit, Schnelligkeit.
velvet ['velvit], *s.* (*Text.*) der Samt.
venal ['vi:nəl], *adj.* käuflich.
vend [vend], *v.a.* verkaufen; —*ing machine*, der Automat.
veneer [və'niə], *s.* das Furnier. — *v.a.* furnieren.
venerable ['venərəbl], *adj.* ehrwürdig.
venerate ['venəreit], *v.a.* verehren.
venereal [və'niəriəl], *adj.* Geschlechts-.
Venezuelan [veni'zweilən], *adj.* venezolanisch. — *s.* der Venezolaner.
vengeance ['vendʒəns], *s.* die Rache.
venison ['venizn *or* venzn], *s.* das Wildpret.
venom ['venəm], *s.* das Gift.
vent [vent], *v.a.* Luft machen (*Dat.*). — *s.* das Luftloch, die Öffnung.
ventilate ['ventileit], *v.a.* ventilieren, lüften.
ventricle ['ventrikl], *s.* (*Anat.*) die Herzkammer.
ventriloquist [ven'triləkwist], *s.* der Bauchredner.
venture ['ventʃə], *s.* das Wagnis, Unternehmen. — *v.a.* wagen, riskieren. — *v.n.* sich erlauben, (sich) wagen.
venue ['venju:], *s.* der Treffpunkt, Versammlungsort.
veracity [və'ræsiti], *s.* die Glaubwürdigkeit, Wahrhaftigkeit.
verbose [və:'bous], *adj.* wortreich, weitschweifig.
verdant ['və:dənt], *adj.* grünend, grün.
verdict ['və:dikt], *s.* das Urteil, die Entscheidung.
verdigris ['və:digri:s], *s.* der Grünspan.
verdure ['və:dʒə], *s.* das Grün.
verge [və:dʒ], *s.* der Rand, die Einfassung. — *v.n.* grenzen (*on*, an, *Acc.*).
verify ['verifai], *v.a.* bestätigen; (*Law*) beglaubigen.
verily ['verili], *adv.* (*Bibl.*) wahrlich.
veritable ['veritəbl], *adj.* wahr, echt.
vermicelli [və:mi'seli], *s.* die Nudeln, *f. pl.*
vermilion [və'miljən], *s.* das Zinnober (*paint*).
vermin ['və:min], *s. pl.* das Ungeziefer.
vermouth ['və:mu:θ, —mu:t], *s.* der Wermut.
vernacular [və'nækjulə], *s.* die Landessprache. — *adj.* einheimisch.
vernal ['və:nəl], *adj.* frühlingsartig, Frühlings-.

511

versatile

versatile ['vəːsətail], *adj.* gewandt; vielseitig.

verse [vəːs], *s.* der Vers; (*Poet.*) die Strophe.

versed [vəːsd], *adj.* bewandert.

version ['vəːʃən], *s.* die Version, Fassung, Lesart; (*fig.*) die Darstellung.

vertebrate ['vəːtibrət], *s.* (*Zool.*) das Wirbeltier. — *adj.* mit Rückenwirbeln versehen.

vertex ['vəːteks], *s.* der Zenit.

vertigo ['vəːtigou], *s.* (*Med.*) der Schwindel, das Schwindelgefühl.

verve [vəːv], *s.* der Schwung.

very ['veri], *adv.* sehr. — *adj.* echt, wirklich, wahrhaftig.

vespers ['vespəz], *s. pl.* (*Eccl.*) der Abendgottesdienst, die Vesper.

vessel [vesl], *s.* das Gefäß (*container*); (*Naut.*) das Fahrzeug, Schiff.

vest [vest], *s.* das Gewand; (*Tail.*) die Weste; das Unterhemd (*undergarment*). — *v.a.* übertragen.

vested [vestid], *adj.* — *interests,* das Eigeninteresse.

vestige ['vestidʒ], *s.* die Spur.

vestment ['vestmənt], *s.* (*Eccl.*) das Meßgewand.

vestry ['vestri], *s.* (*Eccl.*) die Sakristei.

vetch [vetʃ], *s.* (*Bot.*) die Wicke.

veterinary ['vetərinri], *adj.* tierärztlich; — *surgeon,* der Tierarzt.

veto ['viːtou], *s.* (*Pol.*) der Einspruch, das Veto.

vex [veks], *v.a.* quälen, plagen.

vexation [vek'seiʃən], *s.* die Plage, der Verdruß.

via [vaiə], *prep.* über.

vibrate [vai'breit], *v.n.* schwingen, vibrieren.

vicar ['vikə], *s.* (*Eccl.*) der Pfarrer, Vikar.

vicarious [vi'kɛəriəs], *adj.* stellvertretend.

vice (1) [vais], *s.* das Laster (*immorality*).

vice (2) [vais], *s.* (*Mech.*) der Schraubstock.

vice- [vais], *pref.* Vize-, zweiter (*chairman etc.*).

vicinity [vi'siniti], *s.* die Nachbarschaft, Nähe.

vicious ['viʃəs], *adj.* böse, bösartig.

vicissitude [vi'sisitjuːd], *s.* der Wechsel, Wandel; (*pl.*) Wechselfälle, *m. pl.*

victim ['viktim], *s.* das Opfer.

victuals [vitlz], *s. pl.* die Lebensmittel, *n. pl.*

vie [vai], *v.n.* wetteifern.

Vietnamese [vjetnəˈmiːz], *adj.* vietnamesisch. — *s.* der Vietnamese.

view [vjuː], *s.* der Anblick, die Aussicht (*panorama*); die Ansicht (*opinion*); die Absicht (*intention*). — *v.a.* betrachten; besichtigen (*inspect*).

vigil ['vidʒil], *s.* die Nachtwache.

vigilance ['vidʒiləns], *s.* die Wachsamkeit.

vigorous ['vigərəs], *adj.* kräftig, rüstig, energisch.

vigour ['vigə], *s.* die Kraft, Energie.

vile [vail], *adj.* schlecht, niedrig.

vilify ['vilifai], *v.a.* beschimpfen, erniedrigen.

villa ['vilə], *s.* das Landhaus, die Villa.

village ['vilidʒ], *s.* das Dorf.

villain ['vilən], *s.* der Schurke.

villainous ['vilənəs], *adj.* niederträchtig.

villainy ['viləni], *s.* die Niedertracht, Schändlichkeit.

vindicate ['vindikeit], *v.a.* behaupten, verteidigen; rechtfertigen (*justify*).

vindictive [vin'diktiv], *adj.* rachsüchtig.

vine [vain], *s.* (*Bot.*) der Weinstock, die Rebe.

vinegar ['vinigə], *s.* der Essig.

vintage ['vintidʒ], *s.* die Weinernte; der Jahrgang (*also fig.*).

vintner ['vintnə], *s.* der Weinbauer, Winzer.

viola [vi'oulə], *s.* (*Mus.*) die Viola, Bratsche.

violate ['vaiəleit], *v.a.* verletzen, schänden.

violence ['vaiələns], *s.* die Gewalt; die Gewalttätigkeit.

violent ['vaiələnt], *adj.* gewalttätig (*brutal*); heftig (*vehement*).

violet ['vaiəlit], *s.* (*Bot.*) das Veilchen. — *adj.* veilchenblau, violett.

violin [vaiə'lin], *s.* (*Mus.*) die Violine, Geige.

viper ['vaipə], *s.* (*Zool.*) die Viper, Natter.

virago [vi'raːgou], *s.* das Mannweib.

virgin ['vəːdʒin], *s.* die Jungfrau.

virile ['virail], *adj.* männlich, kräftig.

virtual ['vəːtjuəl], *adj.* eigentlich.

virtue ['vəːtjuː], *s.* die Tugend; *by — of,* kraft (*Genit.*).

virtuoso [vəːtju'ousou], *s.* der Virtuose.

virtuous ['vəːtjuəs], *adj.* tugendhaft.

virulent ['virulənt], *adj.* bösartig, giftig.

virus ['vaiərəs], *s.* (*Med.*) das Gift, Virus.

viscosity [vis'kɔsiti], *s.* die Zähigkeit, Zähflüssigkeit.

viscount ['vaikaunt], *s.* der Vicomte.

viscous ['viskəs], *adj.* zähflüssig, klebrig.

visibility [vizi'biliti], *s.* die Sichtbarkeit, Sicht.

visible ['vizibl], *adj.* sichtbar.

vision ['viʒən], *s.* die Sehkraft; (*fig.*) die Vision (*dream*); die Erscheinung (*apparition*).

visionary ['viʒənri], *s.* der Träumer, (*Poet.*) der Seher. — *adj.* visionär, phantastisch, seherisch.

visit ['vizit], *s.* der Besuch. — *v.a.* besuchen.

visitation [vizi'teiʃən], *s.* die Heimsuchung.

visor ['vaizə], *s.* das Visier.

vista ['vistə], *s.* (*Art*) die Aussicht, der Ausblick.

visual ['viʒuəl], *adj.* visuell, Seh-.

vital [vaitl], *adj.* lebenswichtig; (*fig.*) wesentlich.

vitality [vai'tæliti], *s.* die Lebenskraft, Vitalität.

512

vitiate ['viʃieit], *v.a.* verderben, umstoßen.

vitreous ['vitriəs], *adj.* gläsern, glasartig.

vitrify ['vitrifai], *v.a.* verglasen.

vivacious [vi'veiʃəs], *adj.* lebhaft, munter.

viva (voce) ['vaivə ('vousi)], *s.* die mündliche Prüfung.

vivacity [vi'væsiti], *s.* die Lebhaftigkeit.

vivid ['vivid], *adj.* lebhaft.

vixen ['viksən], *s.* (*Zool.*) die Füchsin; (*fig.*) das zänkische Weib.

vizier [vi'ziə], *s.* der Wesir.

vocabulary [vo'kæbjuləri], *s.* das Vokabular; der Wortschatz.

vocal ['voukəl], *adj.* laut; (*Mus.*) Stimm-, Sing-.

vocation [vo'keiʃən], *s.* die Berufung (*call*); der Beruf (*occupation*).

vociferous [vo'sifərəs], *adj.* schreiend, laut.

vogue [voug], *s.* die Mode.

voice [vɔis], *s.* die Stimme.

void [vɔid], *adj.* leer (*empty*); ungültig, (*invalid*); null and —, null und nichtig. — *s.* die Leere.

volatile ['vɔlətail], *adj.* flüchtig.

volcanic [vɔl'kænik], *adj.* vulkanisch.

volcano [vɔl'keinou], *s.* der Vulkan.

volition [və'liʃən], *s.* der Wille.

volley ['vɔli], *s.* (*Mil.*) die Salve; (*Footb.*) der Volleyschuß; (*Tennis*) der Flugball.

volt [voult], *s.* (*Elec.*) das Volt.

voltage ['voultidʒ], *s.* die Spannung.

voluble ['vɔljubl], *adj.* gesprächig, zungenfertig.

volume ['vɔlju:m], *s.* (*Phys.*) das Volumen; der Band (*book*); (*fig.*) der Umfang.

voluminous [və'lju:minəs], *adj.* umfangreich.

voluntary ['vɔləntri], *adj.* freiwillig. — *s.* (*Mus.*) das Orgelsolo.

volunteer [vɔlən'tiə], *s.* der Freiwillige. — *v.n.* sich freiwillig melden.

voluptuous [və'lʌptjuəs], *adj.* wollüstig, lüstern.

vomit ['vɔmit], *v.a., v.n.* (sich) erbrechen, übergeben.

voracious [vɔ'reiʃəs], *adj.* gierig, gefräßig.

vortex ['vɔ:teks], *s.* der Wirbel, Strudel.

vote [vout], *v.n.* (*Pol.*) wählen, abstimmen, die Stimme abgeben. — *s.* (*Pol.*) die Stimme.

voter ['voutə], *s.* der Wähler.

votive ['voutiv], *adj.* (*Eccl.*) geweiht, gelobt; Votiv-.

vouch [vautʃ], *v.a., v.n.* (sich) verbürgen, einstehen (für).

voucher ['vautʃə], *s.* der Beleg; (*Comm.*) der Gutschein.

vouchsafe [vautʃ'seif], *v.a.* bewilligen, gewähren. — *v.n.* geruhen, sich herablassen.

vow [vau], *s.* das Gelübde. — *v.a.* schwören, geloben.

vowel ['vauəl], *s.* der Vokal.

voyage ['vɔiidʒ], *s.* die Seereise. — *v.n.* zur See reisen.

vulcanize ['vʌlkənaiz], *v.a.* vulkanisieren.

vulgar ['vʌlgə], *adj.* gemein, pöbelhaft, ordinär, vulgär.

vulnerable ['vʌlnərəbl], *adj.* verwundbar, verletzbar.

vulture ['vʌltʃə], *s.* (*Orn.*) der Geier.

W

W ['dʌblju:]. das W.

wabble *see* **wobble**.

wad [wɔd], *s.* das Bündel (*notes*); der Bausch (*cotton wool*).

waddle ['wɔdl], *v.n.* watscheln.

wade [weid], *v.n.* waten, durchwaten.

wafer ['weifə], *s.* die Oblate, die Waffel; (*Eccl.*) die Hostie.

waffle ['wɔfl], *s.* (*Cul.*) die Waffel. — *v.n.* (*coll.*) schwafeln.

waft [wæft], *v.a.* wegwehen.

wag (1) [wæg], *v.a.* wedeln, schütteln.

wag (2) [wæg], *s.* der Spaßvogel.

wage (1) [weidʒ], *v.a.* unternehmen; — war, Krieg führen.

wage (2) ['weidʒ], *s.* (*often in pl.*) der Lohn.

wager ['weidʒə], *v.a.* wetten. — *s.* die Wette.

waggish ['wægiʃ], *adj.* spaßhaft, mutwillig, schelmisch.

wag(g)on ['wægən], *s.* der Wagen, Güterwagen.

wagtail ['wægteil], *s.* (*Orn.*) die Bachstelze.

waif [weif], *s.* das verwahrloste Kind; das herrenlose Gut.

wail [weil], *v.n.* wehklagen. — *s.* das Wehklagen, die Klage.

waist [weist], *s.* (*Anat.*) die Taille.

waistcoat ['weiskout, 'weskət], *s.* die Weste, das Wams.

wait [weit], *v.n.* warten; — for, warten auf; — upon, bedienen. — *v.a.* erwarten.

waiter ['weitə], *s.* der Kellner; head —, der Oberkellner; (*coll.*) der Ober.

waiting room ['weitiŋ rum], *s.* das Wartezimmer; (*Railw.*) der Wartesaal.

waive [weiv], *v.a.* aufgeben, verzichten (auf, *Acc.*).

wake (1) [weik], *v.n. irr.* wachen, aufwachen, wach sein. — *v.a.* aufwecken.

wake (2) [weik], *s.* (*Naut.*) das Kielwasser; (*fig.*) die Spur; in the — of, in den Fußstapfen (*Genit.*).

waken ['weikən], *v.a.* aufwecken. — *v.n.* aufwachen.

walk [wɔ:k], *v.n.* (zu Fuß) gehen. — *s.* der Gang (*gait*); der Spaziergang.

wall [wɔ:l], *s.* die Wand, Mauer.

wallet ['wɔlit], *s.* die Brieftasche.

wallflower ['wɔ:lflauə], *s.* (*Bot.*) der Goldlack; (*fig.*) das Mauerblümchen.

wallow ['wɔlou], *v.n.* schwelgen; sich wälzen.

walnut ['wɔ:lnʌt], *s.* (*Bot.*) die Walnuß.

walrus ['wɔ:lrəs], *s.* (*Zool.*) das Walroß.

waltz [wɔ:lts], *s.* der Walzer.

wan [wɔn], *adj.* blaß, bleich.

wand [wɔnd], *s.* der Stab.

wander ['wɔndə], *v.n.* wandern, durchwandern; (*fig.*) — *from the subject*, vom Thema abkommen.

wane [wein], *v.n.* abnehmen, verfallen.

want [wɔnt], *v.a.* brauchen, wollen, nötig haben, wünschen. — *v.n.* mangeln, fehlen. — *s.* die Not.

wanton ['wɔntən], *adj.* mutwillig, ausgelassen.

war [wɔ:], *s.* der Krieg.

warble [wɔ:bl], *v.a., v.n.* singen; (*Mus.*) trillern.

warbler ['wɔ:blə], *s.* (*Orn.*) der Singvogel.

ward [wɔ:d], *s.* die Verwahrung; das *or* der Mündel (*child in care*); (*Pol.*) der Wahlbezirk; die Station (*hospital*). — *v.a.* — *off*, abwehren.

warden [wɔ:dn], *s.* der Vorstand, Vorsteher; Rektor.

warder ['wɔ:də], *s.* der Wächter; (*in prison*) der Wärter, Gefängniswärter.

wardrobe ['wɔ:droub], *s.* der Kleiderschrank.

ware [wɛə], *s.* die Ware.

warehouse ['wɛəhaus], *s.* das Warenlager.

warfare ['wɔ:fɛə], *s.* der Krieg, die Kriegsführung.

warlike ['wɔ:laik], *adj.* kriegerisch.

warm [wɔ:m], *adj.* warm.

warn [wɔ:n], *v.a.* warnen, ermahnen.

warning ['wɔ:niŋ], *s.* die Warnung.

warp [wɔ:p], *v.a.* krümmen, verziehen (*of wood*); (*fig.*) verderben; verzerren, verdrehen. — *v.n.* sich werfen, krümmen.

warrant ['wɔrənt], *s.* (*Law*) der Haftbefehl; — *officer*, der Unteroffizier; (*Comm.*) die Vollmacht, Bürgschaft. — *v.a.* garantieren (*vouch for*); versichern (*assure*).

warranty ['wɔrənti], *s.* (*Law*) die Gewähr; Garantie.

warren ['wɔrən], *s.* das Gehege.

warrior ['wɔriə], *s.* der Krieger.

wart [wɔ:t], *s.* (*Med.*) die Warze.

wary ['wɛəri], *adj.* vorsichtig, achtsam (*careful*).

wash [wɔʃ], *v.a., v.n.* (sich) waschen; — *up*, spülen, abwaschen. — *s.* die Wäsche (*laundry*).

wasp [wɔsp], *s.* (*Ent.*) die Wespe.

waspish ['wɔspiʃ], *adj.* reizbar, zänkisch, bissig.

wassail ['wɔsl], *s.* das Trinkgelage. — *v.n.* zechen.

waste [weist], *v.a.* zerstören, verwüsten; verschwenden. — *adj.* wüst, öde. — *s.* die Verschwendung (*process*); der Abfall (*product*); — *paper*, die Makulatur; — *paper basket*, der Papierkorb.

wasteful ['weistful], *adj.* verschwenderisch.

watch [wɔtʃ], *v.a.* bewachen; beobachten (*observe*); hüten (*guard*). — *s.* die Wache (*guard*); die Uhr, Taschenuhr (*time-piece*).

watchful ['wɔtʃful], *adj.* wachsam.

watchman ['wɔtʃmən], *s.* der Nachtwächter.

water ['wɔ:tə], *s.* das Wasser; (*pl.*) die Kur; — *colour*, das Aquarell; — *gauge*, der Pegel. — *v.a.* wässern; begießen (*flowers*).

watercress ['wɔ:təkres], *s.* (*Bot.*) die Brunnenkresse.

waterproof ['wɔ:təpru:f], *adj.* wasserdicht.

watt [wɔt], *s.* (*Elec.*) das Watt.

wattle [wɔtl], *s.* (*Bot.*) die Hürde.

wave [weiv], *s.* die Welle; *permanent* —, die Dauerwelle. — *v.n.* zuwinken (*Dat.*); wehen; winken. — *v.a.* schwenken (*handkerchief*).

waver ['weivə], *v.n.* schwanken, unentschlossen sein.

wax [wæks], *s.* das Wachs, der Siegellack. — *v.a.* wachsen, bohnern.

waxen ['wæksn], *adj.* aus Wachs, wächsern.

way [wei], *s.* der Weg (*road etc.*); die Strecke; Richtung; *in no* —, keineswegs; (*pl.*) die Art und Weise; *Milky Way*, die Milchstraße.

wayward ['weiwəd], *adj.* eigensinnig.

we [wi:], *pers. pron.* wir.

weak [wi:k], *adj.* schwach, kraftlos.

weaken ['wi:kən], *v.a.* schwächen. — *v.n.* schwach werden.

weakling ['wi:kliŋ], *s.* der Schwächling.

wealth [welθ], *s.* der Wohlstand, Reichtum.

wealthy ['welθi], *adj.* wohlhabend, reich.

wean [wi:n], *v.a.* entwöhnen.

weapon ['wepən], *s.* die Waffe.

wear [wɛə], *v.a. irr.* tragen (*clothes*). — *v.n.* — *off*, sich abtragen, schäbig werden; — *out*, sich erschöpfen. — *s.* die Abnutzung.

weariness ['wiərinis], *s.* die Müdigkeit, der Überdruß.

weary ['wiəri], *adj.* müde, überdrüssig.

weasel ['wi:zl], *s.* (*Zool.*) das Wiesel.

weather ['weðə], *s.* das Wetter. — *v.a.* überstehen. — *v.n.* (*Geol.*) verwittern.

weatherbeaten ['weðəbi:tn], *adj.* abgehärtet, verwittert.

weathercock ['weðəkɔk], *s.* der Wetterhahn; (*fig.*) wetterwendischer Mensch.

weave [wi:v], *v.a. irr.* (*Text.*) weben. — *s.* das Gewebe.

web [web], *s.* das Gewebe.

wed [wed], *v.a.* heiraten; trauen (*a couple*). — *v.n.* (sich wer)heiraten.

wedding ['wediŋ], *s.* die Hochzeit; Trauung (*ceremony*).

wedge [wedʒ], *s.* der Keil. — *v.a.* keilen.

wedlock ['wedlɔk], *s.* die Ehe.

Wednesday ['wenzd(e)i]. der Mittwoch.

wee [wi:], *adj.* (*Scot.*) winzig, klein.

weed [wi:d], *s.* das Unkraut. — *v.a.* ausjäten, jäten.

week [wi:k], *s.* die Woche.

weep [wi:p], *v.n. irr.* weinen; —*ing willow,* die Trauerweide.

weigh [wei], *v.a.* wiegen, wägen; (*fig.*) abwägen, beurteilen; (*Naut.*) — *anchor,* den Anker lichten. — *v.n.* wiegen.

weighing machine ['weiiŋ mə'ʃi:n], *s.* die Waage.

weight [weit], *s.* das Gewicht; *gross* —, das Bruttogewicht; *net* —, das Nettogewicht.

weighty ['weiti], *adj.* (ge)wichtig; (*fig.*) schwer.

weir [wiə], *s.* das Wehr.

weird [wiəd], *adj.* unheimlich.

welcome ['welkəm], *adj.* willkommen. — *s.* der *or* das Willkommen. — *v.a.* willkommen heißen, begrüßen.

weld [weld], *v.a.* schweißen.

welfare ['welfeə], *s.* die Wohlfahrt, soziale Fürsorge.

well (1) [wel], *s.* der Brunnen. — *v.n.* hervorsprudeln.

well (2) [wel], *adv.* gut, wohl; *durchaus,* — *bred,* wohlerzogen. — *pred. adj.* gesund, wohl.

Welsh [welʃ], *adj.* walisisch. — *s. pl.* die Waliser, *m.pl.*

Welshman ['welʃmən], *s.* der Waliser.

welt [welt], *s.* der Rand, die Einfassung.

welter ['weltə], *s.* die Masse, das Chaos. — *v.n.* sich wälzen.

wen [wen], *s.* (*Med.*) die Schwellung.

wench [wentʃ], *s.* die Magd, das Mädchen.

west [west], *s.* der Westen. — *adj.* (*also* **westerly, western** ['westəli, 'westən]) westlich.

Westphalian [west'feiliən], *adj.* westfälisch. — *s.* der Westfale.

wet [wet], *adj.* naß, feucht; — *paint,* frisch gestrichen. — *v.a.* anfeuchten, benetzen, naß machen.

whack [hwæk], *v.a.* durchprügeln. — *s.* die Tracht Prügel, der Schlag.

whale [hweil], *s.* (*Zool.*) der Walfisch.

whalebone ['hweilboun], *s.* das Fischbein.

wharf [hwɔ:f], *s.* der Kai.

wharfinger ['hwɔ:findʒə], *s.* der Kaimeister.

what [hwɔt], *rel. & interr. pron.* was; welcher, welche, welches; was für.

what(**so**)**ever** [hwɔt(sou)'evə], *rel. pron.* was auch immer. — *adj.* einerlei welche-r, -s, -n.

wheat [hwi:t], *s.* (*Bot.*) der Weizen.

wheedle [hwi:dl], *v.a.* beschwatzen.

wheel [hwi:l], *s.* das Rad; die Umdrehung, Drehung. — *v.a., v.n.* drehen, sich drehen, schieben.

wheelbarrow ['hwi:lbærou], *s.* der Schubkarren.

wheeze [hwi:z], *v.n.* keuchen, schnaufen. — *s.* das Keuchen.

whelp [hwelp], *s.* (*Zool.*) das Junge, der junge Hund. — *v.n.* Junge werfen.

when [hwen], *adv.* (*interr.*) wann ? — *conj.* als (*in past*), wenn, während.

whence [hwens], *adv.* woher, von wo.

where [hweə], *adv.* wo, wohin; (*interr.*) wo ? wohin ?

whereabout(**s**) ['hweərəbaut(s)], *adv.* wo, wo etwa. — *s.* (**whereabouts**) der zeitweilige Aufenthalt *or* Wohnort.

whereas [hweər'æz], *conj.* wohingegen, während.

whereupon [hweərə'pɔn], *conj.* woraufhin.

wherewithal ['hweəwiðɔ:l], *s.* die gesamte Habe, das Nötige. — *adv.* (*obs.*) womit.

whet [hwet], *v.a.* wetzen, schleifen.

whether ['hweðə], *conj.* ob.

whey [hwei], *s.* die Molke.

which [hwitʃ], *rel. & interr. pron.* welcher, welche, welches; der, die, das.

whiff [hwif], *s.* der Hauch, Luftzug.

while [hwail], *s.* die Weile, Zeit. — *v.a.* — *away the time,* dahinbringen, vertreiben. — *conj.* (*also* **whilst**) während, so lange als.

whim [hwim], *s.* die Laune, Grille.

whimper ['hwimpə], *v.n.* winseln.

whimsical ['hwimzikəl], *adj.* grillenhaft.

whine [hwain], *v.n.* weinen, wimmern, klagen. — *s.* das Gewimmer, Gejammer.

whinny ['hwini], *v.n.* wiehern.

whip [hwip], *s.* die Peitsche; (*Pol.*) der Einpeitscher. — *v.a.* peitschen.

whir [hwə:], *v.n.* schwirren. — *s.* das Schwirren.

whirl [hwə:l], *s.* der Wirbel, Strudel. — *v.a., v.n.* wirbeln.

whirligig ['hwə:ligig], *s.* der Karussel.

whirlpool ['hwə:lpu:l], *s.* der Strudel.

whirr *see* **whir.**

whisk[hwisk], *v.a.* fegen ; schlagen ; —*away or off,* schnell wegtun (*a th.*), schnell fortnehmen (*a p.*). — *v.n.* — *away,* dahinhuschen. — *s.* der Schläger.

whiskers ['hwiskəz], *s.* der Backenbart, Bart.

whisky ['hwiski], *s.* der Whisky.

whisper ['hwispə], *s.* das Geflüster. *v.a., v.n.* flüstern.

whistle [hwisl], *s.* die Pfeife (*instrument*); der Pfiff (*sound*). — *v.a., v.n.* pfeifen.

whit [hwit], *s.* die Kleinigkeit; *not a* —, nicht im geringsten.

white [hwait], *adj.* weiß; — *lead,* das Bleiweiß; — *lie,* die Notlüge.

whitebait ['hwaitbeit], *s.* (*Zool.*) der Breitling.

whiten [hwaitn], *v.a.* weißen, bleichen.

whitewash ['hwaitwɔʃ], *s.* die Tünche. — *v.a.* reinwaschen.

whither ['hwiðə], *adv.* wohin; dahin wo.

whiting ['hwaitiŋ], *s.* (*Zool.*) der Weißfisch; die Schlämmkreide (*chalk*).

whitlow ['hwitlou], *s.* (*Med.*) das Nagelgeschwür.

Whitsun(tide) ['hwitsən(taid)], *s.* (das) Pfingsten; *Whit Sunday*, der Pfingstsonntag.

whittle [hwitl], *v.a.* schnitzen, abschaben.

whiz [hwiz], *v.n.* zischen; (*fig.*) vorbeiflitzen.

who [hu:], *interr. pron.* wer ?, welcher ?, welche ? — *rel. pron.* welcher, welche, welches, der, die, das.

whoever [hu:'evə], *rel. pron.* wer auch immer.

whole [houl], *adj.* ganz, völlig. — *s.* das Ganze.

wholesale ['houlseil], *adv.* im Engros. — *adj.* Engros-, Großhandels-.

wholesome ['houlsəm], *adj.* gesund.

whoop [hu:p], *s.* das Geschrei; — *v.n.* laut keuchen; —*ing cough*, der Keuchhusten.

whortleberry ['hwə:tlbəri], *s.* (*Bot.*) die Heidelbeere.

whose [hu:z], *pron.* wessen, dessen, deren.

whosoever [hu:sou'evə], *see* **whoever**.

why [hwai], *rel. & interr. adv.* warum ?

wick [wik], *s.* der Docht.

wicked ['wikid], *adj.* böse, schlecht.

wicker ['wikə], *adj.* Rohr-, geflochten.

wicket ['wikit], *s.* das Pförtchen.

wide [waid], *adj.* weit, breit; (*fig.*) umfangreich, groß, reich(*experience*).– *adv. far and —*, weit und breit; — *awake*, völlig wach.

widen [waidn], *v.a.* erweitern.

widgeon ['widʒən], *s.* die Pfeifente.

widow ['widou], *s.* die Witwe.

widower ['widouə], *s.* der Witwer.

width [widθ], *s.* die Weite, Breite.

wield [wi:ld], *v.a.* schwingen; — *power*, die Macht ausüben.

wife [waif], *s.* die Frau, Gattin.

wig [wig], *s.* die Perücke.

wild [waild], *adj.* wild.

wilderness ['wildənis], *s.* die Wildnis.

wildfire ['waildfaiə], *s.* das Lauffeuer.

wilful ['wilful], *adj.* absichtlich; vorsätzlich.

wiliness ['wailinis], *s.* die Schlauheit, Arglist.

will [wil], *s.* der Wille; (*Law*) der letzte Wille, das Testament. — *v.n.* wollen. — *v.a.* (*Law*) vermachen, hinterlassen.

willing ['wiliŋ], *adj.* bereitwillig.

will-o'-the-wisp [wiləð'wisp], *s.* das Irrlicht.

willow ['wilou], *s.* (*Bot.*) die Weide.

wily ['waili], *adj.* schlau, verschmitzt.

wimple [wimpl], *s.* der Schleier.

win [win], *v.a., v.n. irr.* gewinnen, siegen, erringen.

wince [wins], *v.n.* zucken, zusammenzucken.

winch [wintʃ], *s.* die Kurbel, Winde.

wind (1) [wind], *s.* der Wind; der Atem (*breath*); *get — of s.th.*, von etwas hören.

wind (2) [waind], *v.a. irr.* winden; wenden, drehen (*turn*); —(*up*), aufziehen (*timepiece*); — *up*, (*business, debate*) beenden. — *v.n.* sich schlängeln, winden.

windfall ['windfɔ:l], *s.* das Fallobst (*fruit*); (*fig.*) der Glücksfall.

windlass ['windləs], *s.* die Winde.

window ['windou], *s.* das Fenster; — *sill*, das Fensterbrett.

windpipe ['windpaip], *s.* (*Anat.*) die Luftröhre.

windscreen ['windskri:n], *s.* (*Motor.*) die Windschutzscheibe.

windshield ['windʃi:ld] (*Am.*) *see* **windscreen**.

windy ['windi], *adj.* windig.

wine [wain], *s.* der Wein; — *merchant*, der Weinhändler.

wing [wiŋ], *s.* der Flügel; (*Poet.*) die Schwinge.

wink [wiŋk], *s.* das Zwinkern; der Augenblick. —*v.n.* blinzeln, zwinkern.

winner ['winə], *s.* der Sieger, Gewinner.

winning ['winiŋ], *adj.* einnehmend.

winsome ['winsəm], *adj.* reizend, einnehmend.

winter ['wintə], *s.* der Winter.

wintry ['wintri], *adj.* winterlich.

wipe [waip], *v.a.* wischen, abwischen.

wire [waiə], *s.* der Draht; (*coll.*) das Telegramm; *barbed —*, der Stacheldraht. — *v.a.* verbinden; (*fig.*) telegraphieren. — *v.n.* telegraphieren.

wireless ['waiəlis], *s.* das Radio. — *adj.* drahtlos.

wirepuller ['waiəpulə], *s.* der Puppenspieler; (*fig.*) der Intrigant.

wiry ['waiəri], *adj.* zäh, stark.

wisdom ['wizdəm], *s.* die Weisheit.

wise [waiz], *adj.* weise, verständig, klug.

wiseacre ['waizeikə], *s.* der Allzuschlaue, Naseweis.

wish [wiʃ], *v.a., v.n.* wünschen. — *s.* der Wunsch.

wistful ['wistful], *adj.* nachdenklich (*pensive*); wehmütig (*sad*).

wit [wit], *s.* der Witz; Geist; Verstand; der witzige Mensch; der Witzbold.

witch [witʃ], *s.* die Hexe, Zauberin.

witchcraft ['witʃkrɑ:ft], *s.* die Zauberkunst, Hexerei.

with [wið], *prep.* mit, mitsamt, bei, durch, von.

withal [wi'ðɔ:l], *adv.* obendrein.

withdraw [wið'drɔ:], *v.a., v.n. irr.* (sich) zurückziehen; widerrufen; abheben (*money from bank*).

withdrawal [wið'drɔ:əl], *s.* der Rückzug; (*Comm. etc.*) die Widerrufung; Abhebung (*bank*).

wither ['wiðə], *v.a.* welk machen. — *v.n.* verwelken; ausdorren, verdorren (*dry up*); (*fig.*) vergehen.

withhold [wið'hould], *v.a. irr.* zurückhalten, vorenthalten.

writ

within [wi'ðin], *prep.* innerhalb; (*time*)
binnen (*Genit.*). — *adv.* darin,
drinnen.

without [wi'ðaut], *prep.* ohne; (*obs.*)
außerhalb (*outside*); *do* —; entbehren.
— *adv.* draußen, außen.

withstand [wið'stænd], *v.a. irr.* widerstehen (*Dat.*).

withy ['wiði], *s.* der Weidenzweig.

witless ['witlis], *adj.* einfältig.

witness ['witnis], *s.* der Zeuge. — *v.a.*
bezeugen, Zeuge sein von. — *v.n.*
zeugen, Zeuge sein.

witticism ['witisizm], *s.* das Bonmot,
die witzige Bemerkung.

witty ['witi], *adj.* witzig, geistreich.

wizard ['wizəd], *s.* der Zauberer.

wizened ['wizənd], *adj.* verwelkt, ver-
trocknet, runzlig.

wobble ['wɔbl], *v.n.* wackeln.

woe [wou], *s.* (*Poet.*) das Weh, Leid.

wolf [wulf], *s.* (*Zool.*) der Wolf.

woman ['wumən], *s.* die Frau, das
Weib.

womanly ['wumənli], *adj.* weiblich.

womb [wu:m], *s.* der Mutterleib,
Schoß; (*Anat.*) die Gebärmutter.

wonder ['wʌndə], *s.* das Wunder. —
v.n. sich wundern (*be amazed*); gern
wissen mögen (*like to know*); sich
fragen.

wonderful ['wʌndəful], *adj.* wunderbar.

wondrous ['wʌndrəs], *adj.* (*Poet.*)
wunderbar.

wont [wount], *s.* die Gewohnheit. —
pred. adj. gewohnt.

won't [wount] = **will not**.

woo [wu:], *v.a.* freien, werben (um).

wood [wud], *s.* das Holz (*timber*); der
Wald (*forest*).

woodbine ['wudbain], *s.* das Geißblatt.

woodcock ['wudkɔk], *s.* (*Orn.*) die
Waldschnepfe.

woodcut ['wudkʌt], *s.* (*Art*) der Holzschnitt.

wooded ['wudid], *adj.* bewaldet.

wooden [wudn], *adj.* hölzern, Holz–.

woodlark ['wudla:k], *s.* (*Orn.*) die
Heidelerche.

woodpecker ['wudpekə], *s.* (*Orn.*) der
Specht.

woodruff ['wudrʌf], *s.* (*Bot.*) der Waldmeister.

woof [wu:f], *s.* (*Text.*) der Einschlag,
das Gewebe.

wool [wul], *s.* die Wolle; — *gathering*,
zerstreut.

woollen ['wulən], *adj.* wollen, aus Wolle.

woolly ['wuli], *adj.* wollig; (*fig.*) unklar,
verschwommen.

word [wə:d], *s.* das Wort; *send* —,
Botschaft senden. — *v.a.* ausdrücken.

wording ['wə:diŋ], *s.* die Fassung, der
Stil.

work [wə:k], *s.* die Arbeit; *out of* —,
arbeitslos; das Werk (*opus*); (*pl.*) die
Fabrik. — *v.a.* arbeiten, bearbeiten; (*engine*) funktionieren.

worker ['wə:kə], *s.* der Arbeiter.

workhouse ['wə:khaus], *s.* das Armenhaus.

workshop ['wə:kʃɔp], *s.* die Werkstatt.

world [wə:ld], *s.* die Welt.

worldly ['wə:ldli], *adj.* weltlich, zeitlich.

worm [wə:m], *s.* (*Zool.*) der Wurm. —
v.a. — *o.'s way,* sich einschleichen. —
v.n. sich einschleichen.

wormeaten ['wə:mi:tn], *adj.* wurmstichig.

worry ['wʌri], *s.a., v.n.* plagen, quälen,
sorgen, ängstigen; sich beunruhigen;
don't —, bitte machen Sie sich keine
Mühe. — *s.* die Plage, Mühe, Qual,
Sorge (*about*, um, *Acc.*).

worse [wə:s], *comp. adj.,* *adv.* schlechter,
schlimmer.

worship ['wə:ʃip], *s.* die Verehrung;
der Gottesdienst (*divine* —).

worst [wə:st], *superl. adj.* schlechtest,
schlimmst. — *adv.* am schlimmsten
or schlechtesten. — *s.* das Schlimmste.

worsted ['wustid], *s.* (*Text.*) das Kammgarn.

worth [wə:θ], *adj.* wert. — *s.* der Wert.

worthy ['wə:ði], *adj.* würdig, wert,
verdient.

would [wud] *past tense of* **will**, *q.v.*

wound [wu:nd], *s.* die Wunde. —
v.a. verwunden.

wraith [reiθ], *s.* das Gespenst.

wrangle [ræŋgl], *v.n.* zanken, streiten.
— *s.* der Zank, Streit.

wrap [ræp], *v.a.* einwickeln, einhüllen.
— *s.* (*Am.*) der Mantel (*coat*), Pelz
(*fur*), Schal (*stole*).

wrapper ['ræpə], *s.* der Umschlag, die
Hülle.

wrath [rɔ:θ], *s.* der Zorn, Grimm.

wreak ,[ri:k], *v.a.* (*Lit.*) auslassen,
üben.

wreath [ri:θ], *s.* der Kranz.

wreathe [ri:ð], *v.a.* winden, bekränzen.

wreck [rek], *s.* der Schiffbruch; das
Wrack (*debris*). — *v.a.* zerstören,
zertrümmern, (*fig.*) verderben.

wren [ren], *s.* (*Orn.*) der Zaunkönig.

wrench [rentʃ], *v.a.* entreißen (*tear
from*); verdrehen. — *s.* heftiger Ruck;
(*fig.*) der (Trennungs)schmerz.

wrest [rest], *v.a.* zerren.

wrestle [resl], *v.n.* ringen, im Ringkampf kämpfen.

wrestling ['resliŋ], *s.* der Ringkampf.

wretch [retʃ], *s.* der Schuft, Lump
(*scoundrel*).

wretched ['retʃid], *adj.* elend.

wriggle [rigl], *v.n.* sich winden,
schlängeln.

wring [riŋ], *v.a. irr.* auswinden, aus-
ringen.

wrinkle [riŋkl], *s.* die Hautfalte,
Runzel. — *v.a.* runzeln (*brow*);
rümpfen (*nose*).

wrist [rist], *s.* (*Anat.*) das Handgelenk.

wristwatch ['ristwɔtʃ], *s.* die Armbanduhr.

writ [rit], *s.* die Schrift; (*Law*) die
Vorladung.

517

write

write [rait], *v.a.*, *v.n. irr.* schreiben, verfassen.
writer ['raitə], *s.* der Schreiber; (*Lit.*) der Schriftsteller.
writhe [raiθ], *v.n.* sich winden.
writing ['raitiŋ], *s.* die Schrift; der Stil (*style*).
wrong [rɔŋ], *adj.* falsch, verkehrt; *to be —*, unrecht haben. — *s.* das Unrecht. — *v.a.* Unrecht *or* Schaden tun (*Dat.*).
wrongful ['rɔŋful], *adj.* unrechtmäßig.
wrongheaded [rɔŋ'hedid], *adj.* querköpfig.
wroth [rouθ], *adj.* (*Lit.*) zornig.
wrought [rɔːt], *adj.* (*work*) gearbeitet; *— iron*, das Schmiedeeisen.
wry [rai], *adj.* verkehrt, krumm, schief, verdreht.

X

X [eks]. das X.
X-ray ['eksrei], *s.* (der) Röntgenstrahl.
xylophone ['zailəfoun], *s.* (*Mus.*) das Xylophon.

Y

Y [wai]. das Y, Ypsilon.
yacht [jɔt], *s.* (*Naut.*) die Jacht.
yachtsman ['jɔtsmən], *s.* (*Naut.*) der Segelsportler.
yap [jæp], *v.n.* kläffen.
yard (1) [jɑːd], *s.* der Hof.
yard (2) [jɑːd], *s.* die englische Elle, der Yard.
yarn [jɑːn], *s.* das Garn; (*coll.*) die Geschichte (*tale*).
yarrow ['jærou], *s.* (*Bot.*) die Schafgarbe.
yawl [jɔːl], *s.* (*Naut.*) die Yawl.
yawn [jɔːn], *v.n.* gähnen. — *s.* das Gähnen.
ye [jiː], *pron.* (*obs.*) *see* you.
year [jə: *or* jiə], *s.* das Jahr; *every other —*, alle zwei Jahre.
yearly ['jiəli], *adj.*, *adv.* jährlich.
yearn [jə:n], *v.n.* sich sehnen (nach, *Dat.*).
yeast [jiːst], *s.* die Hefe.
yell [jel], *v.n.* gellen, schreien. — *s.* der Schrei.
yellow ['jelou], *adj.* gelb; (*sl.*) feige.
yelp [jelp], *v.n.* kläffen, bellen. — *s.* das Gebelle.
yeoman ['joumən], *s.* der Freisasse; (*Mil.*) der Leibgardist (*Yeoman of the Guard*).

yes [jes], *adv.* ja; jawohl.
yesterday ['jestəd(e)i], *adv.* gestern; *the day before —*, vorgestern.
yet [jet], *conj.* doch, dennoch. — *adv.* noch, außerdem; *as —*, bisher; *not —*, noch nicht.
yew [juː], *s.* (*Bot.*) die Eibe.
yield [jiːld], *v.a.* hervorbringen, ergeben; abwerfen (*profit*). — *v.n.* nachgeben (*to, Dat.*). — *s.* der Ertrag.
yoke [jouk], *s.* das Joch (Ochsen). — *v.a.* einspannen, anspannen.
yolk [jouk], *s.* das Eidotter.
yon, yonder [jɔn, 'jɔndə], *dem. adj.* (*obs.*) jener, jene, jenes; der *or* die *or* das da drüben.
yore [jɔː], *adv.* (*obs.*) *of —*, von damals; ehedem.
you [juː], *pers. pron.* du, dich, ihr, euch; (*formal*) sie (*in letters*, Du, Dich *etc.*).
young [jʌŋ], *adj.* jung. — *s.* (*Zool.*) das Junge.
your [juə], *poss. adj.* dein, deine, dein; euer, eure, euer; (*formal*) ihr, ihre, ihr (*in letters* Dein, Euer *etc.*).
yours [jɔːz], *poss. pron.* deinig, eurig; der, die *or* das ihrige (*in letters* Deinig, der Ihrige *etc.*).
yourself [juə'self], *pers. pron.* du selbst, Sie selbst; ihr selbst; dich (selbst), euch (selbst) (*in letters* Du selbst; Dich (selbst) *etc.*).
youth [juːθ], *s.* die Jugend.
youthful ['juːθful], *adj.* jugendlich.
Yugoslav [juːgo'slɑːv], *adj.* jugoslawisch. — *s.* der Jugoslawe.
Yule, Yuletide [juːl, 'juːltaid], *s.* das Julfest, die Weihnachtszeit.

Z

Z [zed, (*Am.*) ziː]. das Z.
zany ['zeini], *s.* der Hanswurst.
zeal [ziːl], *s.* der Eifer.
zealous ['zeləs], *adj.* eifrig.
zebra ['ziːbrə], *s.* (*Zool.*) das Zebra.
zenith ['zeniθ], *s.* der Zenit, Scheitelpunkt.
zero ['ziərou], *s.* der Nullpunkt, die (Ziffer) Null; — *hour*, die festgesetzte Stunde; festgesetzter Zeitpunkt.
zest [zest], *s.* die Lust; der Genuß; die Würze.
zigzag ['zigzæg], *s.* der Zickzack. — *adj.* Zickzack-.
zinc [ziŋk], *s.* das Zink.
zip(per) ['zip(ə)], *s.* der Reißverschluß (*zip fastener*).
zone [zoun], *s.* die Zone.
zoological gardens [zouə'lɔdʒikəl gɑːdnz], *s.* (*abbr.* **zoo** [zuː]) zoologischer Garten, der Zoo, Tiergarten.

German Irregular Verbs

Note: *Where a compound irregular verb is not given, its forms are identical with those of the simple irregular verb as listed.*

Infin.	Pres. Indic. 3rd Pers. Sing.	Imperf. Indic.	Imperf. Subj.
backen	bäckt	backte (buk)	backte
befehlen	befiehlt	befahl	beföhle
beginnen	beginnt	begann	begönne
beißen	beißt	biß	bisse
bergen	birgt	barg	bürge
bersten	birst	barst	börste
bewegen	bewegt	bewog	bewöge
biegen	biegt	bog	böge
bieten	bietet	bot	böte
binden	bindet	band	bände
bitten	bittet	bat	bäte
blasen	bläst	blies	bliese
bleiben	bleibt	blieb	bliebe
braten	brät	briet	briete
brechen	bricht	brach	bräche
brennen	brennt	brannte	brennte
bringen	bringt	brachte	brächte
denken	denkt	dachte	dächte
dreschen	drischt	drosch	dräsche
dringen	dringt	drang	dränge
dürfen	darf	durfte	dürfte
empfangen	empfängt	empfing	empfinge
empfehlen	empfiehlt	empfahl	empföhle
empfinden	empfindet	empfand	empfände
erlöschen	erlischt	erlosch	erlösche

Imper.	Past Participle	English
backe	gebacken	bake
befiehl	befohlen	order, command
beginn(e)	begonnen	begin
beiß(e)	gebissen	bite
birg	geborgen	save, conceal
birst	geborsten	burst
beweg(e)	bewogen	induce
bieg(e)	gebogen	bend
biet(e)	geboten	offer
bind(e)	gebunden	tie, bind
bitte	gebeten	request
blas(e)	geblasen	blow
bleib(e)	geblieben	remain
brat(e)	gebraten	roast
brich	gebrochen	break
brenne	gebrannt	burn
bring(e)	gebracht	bring
denk(e)	gedacht	think
drisch	gedroschen	thrash
dring(e)	gedrungen	press forward
	gedurft	be permitted
empfang(e)	empfangen	receive
empfiehl	empfohlen	(re)commend
empfind(e)	empfunden	feel, perceive
erlisch	erloschen	extinguish

German Irregular Verbs

Infin.	Pres. Indic. 3rd Pers. Sing.	Imperf. Indic.	Imperf. Subj.
erschrecken (*v.n.*)	erschrickt	erschrak	erschräke
essen	ißt	aß	äße
fahren	fährt	fuhr	führe
fallen	fällt	fiel	fiele
fangen	fängt	fing	finge
fechten	ficht	focht	föchte
finden	findet	fand	fände
flechten	flicht	flocht	flöchte
fliegen	fliegt	flog	flöge
fliehen	flieht	floh	flöhe
fließen	fließt	floß	flösse
fressen	frißt	fraß	fräße
frieren	friert	fror	fröre
gebären	gebiert	gebar	gebäre
geben	gibt	gab	gäbe
gedeihen	gedeiht	gedieh	gediehe
gehen	geht	ging	ginge
gelingen (*impers.*)	(mir) gelingt	gelang	gelänge
gelten	gilt	galt	gälte
genesen	genest	genas	genäse
genießen	genießt	genoß	genösse
geschehen (*impers.*)	(mir) geschieht	geschah	geschähe
gewinnen	gewinnt	gewann	gewönne
gießen	gießt	goß	gösse
gleichen	gleicht	glich	gliche
gleiten	gleitet	glitt	glitte
graben	gräbt	grub	grübe
greifen	greift	griff	griffe

Imper.	Past Participle	English
erschrick	erschrocken	be frightened
iß	gegessen	eat
fahr(e)	gefahren	travel
fall(e)	gefallen	fall
fang(e)	gefangen	catch
ficht	gefochten	fight
find(e)	gefunden	find
flicht	geflochten	twine together
flieg(e)	geflogen	fly
flieh(e)	geflohen	flee
fließ(e)	geflossen	flow
friß	gefressen	eat (of animals)
frier(e)	gefroren	freeze
gebier	geboren	give birth to
gib	gegeben	give
gedeih(e)	gediehen	thrive
geh(e)	gegangen	go
geling(e)	gelungen	succeed
gilt	gegolten	be worth, be valid
genese	genesen	recover
genieß(e)	genossen	enjoy
	geschehen	happen
gewinn(e)	gewonnen	win
gieß(e)	gegossen	pour
gleich(e)	geglichen	equal, resemble
gleit(e)	geglitten	glide
grab(e)	gegraben	dig
greif(e)	gegriffen	grasp

German Irregular Verbs

Infin.	Pres. Indic. 3rd Pers. Sing.	Imperf. Indic.	Imperf. Subj.
haben	hat	hatte	hätte
halten	hält	hielt	hielte
hangen (*v.n.*)	hängt	hing	hinge
heben	hebt	hob	höbe
heißen	heißt	hieß	hieße
helfen	hilft	half	hülfe
kennen	kennt	kannte	kennte
klimmen	klimmt	klomm	klömme
klingen	klingt	klang	klänge
kneifen	kneift	kniff	kniffe
kommen	kommt	kam	käme
können	kann	konnte	könnte
kriechen	kriecht	kroch	kröche
laden	lädt	lud	lüde
lassen	läßt	ließ	ließe
laufen	läuft	lief	liefe
leiden	leidet	litt	litte
leihen	leiht	lieh	liehe
lesen	liest	las	läse
liegen	liegt	lag	läge
lügen	lügt	log	löge
mahlen	mahlt	mahlte	mahlte
meiden	meidet	mied	miede
messen	mißt	maß	mäße
mißlingen (*impers.*)	(mir) mißlingt	mißlang	mißlänge
mögen	mag	mochte	möchte
müssen	muß	mußte	müßte
nehmen	nimmt	nahm	nähme

Imper.	Past Participle	English
habe	gehabt	have
halt(e)	gehalten	hold
häng(e)	gehangen	hang
hebe	gehoben	lift
heiß(e)	geheißen	be called
hilf	geholfen	help
kenn(e)	gekannt	know
klimm(e)	geklommen	climb
kling(e)	geklungen	ring, sound
kneif(e)	gekniffen	pinch
komm(e)	gekommen	come
	gekonnt	be able
kriech(e)	gekrochen	creep
lad(e)	geladen	load
laß	gelassen	let
lauf(e)	gelaufen	run
leid(e)	gelitten	suffer
leih(e)	geliehen	lend
lies	gelesen	read
lieg(e)	gelegen	lie
lüg(e)	gelogen	lie, be untruthful
mahle	gemahlen	grind
meid(e)	gemieden	avoid
miß	gemessen	measure
	mißlungen	fail
	gemocht	wish, be willing
	gemußt	have to
nimm	genommen	take

German Irregular Verbs

Infin.	Pres. Indic. 3rd Pers. Sing.	Imperf. Indic.	Imperf. Subj.
nennen	nennt	nannte	nennte
pfeifen	pfeift	pfiff	pfiffe
preisen	preist	pries	priese
quellen (*v.n.*)	quillt	quoll	quölle
raten	rät	riet	riete
reiben	reibt	rieb	riebe
reißen	reißt	riß	risse
reiten	reitet	ritt	ritte
rennen	rennt	rannte	rennte
riechen	riecht	roch	röche
ringen	ringt	rang	ränge
rinnen	rinnt	rann	rönne
rufen	ruft	rief	riefe
saufen	säuft	soff	söffe
saugen	saugt	sog	söge
schaffen	schafft	schuf	schüfe
scheiden	scheidet	schied	schiede
scheinen	scheint	schien	schiene
schelten	schilt	schalt	schölte
schieben	schiebt	schob	schöbe
schießen	schießt	schoß	schösse
schinden	schindet	schund	schünde
schlafen	schläft	schlief	schliefe
schlagen	schlägt	schlug	schlüge
schleichen	schleicht	schlich	schliche
schleifen	schleift	schliff	schliffe
schließen	schließt	schloß	schlösse
schlingen	schlingt	schlang	schlänge

German Irregular Verbs

Imper.	Past Participle	English
nenne	genannt	name
pfeif(e)	gepfiffen	whistle
preis(e)	gepriesen	praise
quill	gequollen	spring
rat(e)	geraten	counsel
reib(e)	gerieben	rub
reiß(e)	gerissen	tear
reit(e)	geritten	ride
renn(e)	gerannt	run
riech(e)	gerochen	smell
ring(e)	gerungen	struggle
rinn(e)	geronnen	flow
ruf(e)	gerufen	call
sauf(e)	gesoffen	drink (to excess)
saug(e)	gesogen	suck
schaff(e)	geschaffen	create
scheid(e)	geschieden	separate
schein(e)	geschienen	appear
schilt	gescholten	scold
schieb(e)	geschoben	shove
schieß(e)	geschossen	shoot
schind(e)	geschunden	skin
schlaf(e)	geschlafen	sleep
schlag(e)	geschlagen	beat
schleich(e)	geschlichen	slink, creep
schleif(e)	geschliffen	slide, polish
schließ(e)	geschlossen	shut, close
schling(e)	geschlungen	wind, devour

German Irregular Verbs

Infin.	Pres. Indic. 3rd Pers. Sing.	Imperf. Indic.	Imperf. Subj.
schmeißen	schmeißt	schmiß	schmisse
schmelzen (v.n.)	schmilzt	schmolz	schmölze
schneiden	schneidet	schnitt	schnitte
schrecken (v.n.)	schrickt	schrak	schräke
schreiben	schreibt	schrieb	schriebe
schreien	schreit	schrie	schriee
schreiten	schreitet	schritt	schritte
schweigen	schweigt	schwieg	schwiege
schwellen	schwillt	schwoll	schwölle
schwimmen	schwimmt	schwamm	schwömme
schwinden	schwindet	schwand	schwände
schwingen	schwingt	schwang	schwänge
schwören	schwört	schwur	schwüre
sehen	sieht	sah	sähe
sein	ist	war	wäre
senden	sendet	sandte or sendete	sendete
singen	singt	sang	sänge
sinken	sinkt	sank	sänke
sinnen	sinnt	sann	sänne
sitzen	sitzt	saß	säße
sollen	soll	sollte	sollte
speien	speit	spie	spiee
spinnen	spinnt	spann	spönne
sprechen	spricht	sprach	spräche
sprießen	sprießt	sproß	sprösse
springen	springt	sprang	spränge
stechen	sticht	stach	stäche
stehen	steht	stand	stände

Imper.	Past Participle	English
schmeiß(e)	geschmissen	hurl
schmilz	geschmolzen	melt
schneid(e)	geschnitten	cut
schrick	(erschrocken)	frighten
schreib(e)	geschrieben	write
schrei(e)	geschrien	cry
schreit(e)	geschritten	stride
schweig(e)	geschwiegen	be silent
schwill	geschwollen	swell
schwimm(e)	geschwommen	swim
schwind(e)	geschwunden	vanish
schwing(e)	geschwungen	swing
schwör(e)	geschworen	swear
sieh	gesehen	see
sei	gewesen	be
send(e)	gesandt *or* gesendet	send
sing(e)	gesungen	sing
sink(e)	gesunken	sink
sinn(e)	gesonnen	meditate
sitz(e)	gesessen	sit
	gesollt	be obliged
spei(e)	gespieen	spit
spinn(e)	gesponnen	spin
sprich	gesprochen	speak
sprieß(e)	gesprossen	sprout
spring(e)	gesprungen	leap
stich	gestochen	prick
steh(e)	gestanden	stand

German Irregular Verbs

Infin.	Pres. Indic. 3rd Pers. Sing.	Imperf. Indic.	Imperf. Subj.
stehlen	stiehlt	stahl	stöhle
steigen	steigt	stieg	stiege
sterben	stirbt	starb	stürbe
stinken	stinkt	stank	stänke
stoßen	stößt	stieß	stieße
streichen	streicht	strich	striche
streiten	streitet	stritt	stritte
tragen	trägt	trug	trüge
treffen	trifft	traf	träfe
treiben	treibt	trieb	triebe
treten	tritt	trat	träte
trinken	trinkt	trank	tränke
trügen	trügt	trog	tröge
tun	tut	tat	täte
verderben	verdirbt	verdarb	verdürbe
verdrießen	verdrießt	verdroß	verdrösse
vergessen	vergißt	vergaß	vergäße
verlieren	verliert	verlor	verlöre
wachsen	wächst	wuchs	wüchse
wägen	wägt	wog	wöge
waschen	wäscht	wusch	wüsche
weichen	weicht	wich	wiche
weisen	weist	wies	wiese
werben	wirbt	warb	würbe
werden	wird	wurde	würde
werfen	wirft	warf	würfe
wiegen	wiegt	wog	wöge
winden (v.a.)	windet	wand	wände

Imper.	Past Participle	English
stiehl	gestohlen	steal
steig(e)	gestiegen	climb
stirb	gestorben	die
stink(e)	gestunken	stink
stoß(e)	gestoßen	push
streich(e)	gestrichen	stroke, touch
streit(e)	gestritten	quarrel, fight
trag(e)	getragen	carry
triff	getroffen	meet
treib(e)	getrieben	drive
tritt	getreten	step
trink(e)	getrunken	drink
trüg(e)	getrogen	deceive
tu(e)	getan	do
verdirb	verdorben (and verderbt)	spoil
verdrieß(e)	verdrossen	grieve
vergiß	vergessen	forget
verlier(e)	verloren	lose
wachs(e)	gewachsen	grow
wäg(e)	gewogen	weigh
wasch(e)	gewaschen	wash
weich(e)	gewichen	yield
weis(e)	gewiesen	show
wirb	geworben	court
werde	geworden	become
wirf	geworfen	throw
wieg(e)	gewogen	weigh
wind(e)	gewunden	wind

German Irregular Verbs

Infin.	Pres. Indic. 3rd. Pers. Sing.	Imperf. Indic.	Imperf. Subj.
wissen	weiß	wußte	wüßte
wollen	will	wollte	wollte
zeihen	zeiht	zieh	ziehe
ziehen	zieht	zog	zöge
zwingen	zwingt	zwang	zwänge

Imper.	Past Participle	English
wisse	gewußt	know
wolle	gewollt	wish, want
zeih(e)	geziehen	accuse
zieh(e)	gezogen	draw, pull
zwing(e)	gezwungen	force, compel

English Irregular Verbs

Infin.	Past Indic.	Past Participle	German
abide	abode	abode	bleiben
arise	arose	arisen	aufstehen
awake	awoke	awoke	aufwecken
be	was, were	been	sein
bear	bore	borne	tragen
beat	beat	beaten	schlagen
become	became	become	werden
beget	begot	begotten	zeugen
begin	began	begun	beginnen
bend	bent	bent	biegen
bereave	bereaved, bereft	bereaved, bereft	berauben
beseech	besought	besought	bitten
bid	bade, bid	bidden, bid	gebieten
bide	bided, bode	bided	verbleiben
bind	bound	bound	binden
bite	bit	bitten	beißen
bleed	bled	bled	bluten
blow	blew	blown	blasen
break	broke	broken	brechen
breed	bred	bred	zeugen
bring	brought	brought	bringen
build	built	built	bauen
burn	burnt, burned	burnt, burned	brennen
burst	burst	burst	bersten
buy	bought	bought	kaufen

Infin.	Past Indic.	Past Participle	German
can (*pres. indic.*)	could	—	können
cast	cast	cast	werfen
catch	caught	caught	fangen
chide	chid	chidden, chid	schelten
choose	chose	chosen	wählen
cleave	cleft, clove	cleft, cloven	spalten
cling	clung	clung	sich anklammern
clothe	clothed, clad	clothed, clad	kleiden
come	came	come	kommen
cost	cost	cost	kosten
creep	crept	crept	kriechen
crow	crowed, crew	crowed	krähen
cut	cut	cut	schneiden
dare	dared, durst	dared	wagen
deal	dealt	dealt	austeilen, handeln
dig	dug	dug	graben
do	did	done	tun
draw	drew	drawn	ziehen
dream	dreamt, dreamed	dreamt, dreamed	träumen
drink	drank	drunk	trinken
drive	drove	driven	treiben
dwell	dwelt	dwelt	wohnen
eat	ate	eaten	essen
fall	fell	fallen	fallen
feed	fed	fed	füttern
feel	felt	felt	fühlen
fight	fought	fought	kämpfen
find	found	found	finden

English Irregular Verbs

Infin.	Past Indic.	Past Participle	German
flee	fled	fled	fliehen
fling	flung	flung	schleudern
fly	flew	flown	fliegen
forbid	forbad(e)	forbidden	verbieten
forget	forgot	forgotten	vergessen
forgive	forgave	forgiven	vergeben
forsake	forsook	forsaken	verlassen
freeze	froze	frozen	frieren
get	got	got	bekommen
gird	girded, girt	girden, girt	gürten
give	gave	given	geben
go	went	gone	gehen
grind	ground	ground	mahlen
grow	grew	grown	wachsen
hang	hung	hung	hängen
have	had	had	haben
hear	heard	heard	hören
heave	heaved, hove	heaved, hove	heben
hew	hewed	hewn, hewed	hauen
hide	hid	hidden, hid	verstecken
hit	hit	hit	schlagen
hold	held	held	halten
hurt	hurt	hurt	verletzen
keep	kept	kept	halten
kneel	knelt	knelt	knien
knit	knitted, knit	knitted, knit	stricken
know	knew	known	kennen, wissen
lay	laid	laid	legen

Infin.	Past Indic.	Past Participle	German
lead	led	led	führen
lean	leant, leaned	leant, leaned	lehnen
leap	leaped, leapt	leaped, leapt	springen
learn	learned, learnt	learned, learnt	lernen
leave	left	left	lassen
lend	lent	lent	leihen
let	let	let	lassen
lie (=recline)	lay	lain	liegen
light	lit, lighted	lit, lighted	beleuchten
lost	lost	lost	verlieren
make	made	made	machen
may (*pres. indic.*)	might	—	mögen
mean	meant	meant	meinen
meet	met	met	treffen, begegnen
melt	melted	melted, molten	schmelzen
mow	mowed	mown	mähen
must (*pres. indic.*)	—	—	müssen
pay	paid	paid	zahlen
put	put	put	stellen
quit	quit(ted)	quit(ted)	verlassen
—	quoth	—	sagte
read	read	read	lesen
rend	rent	rent	reissen
rid	rid	rid	befreien
ride	rode	ridden	reiten, fahren
ring	rang	rung	klingeln
rise	rose	risen	aufstehen
run	ran	run	laufen

English Irregular Verbs

Infin.	Past Indic.	Past Participle	German
saw	sawed	sawn	sägen
say	said	said	sagen
see	saw	seen	sehen
seek	sought	sought	suchen
sell	sold	sold	verkaufen
send	sent	sent	senden
set	set	set	setzen
shake	shook	shaken	schütteln
shall (*pres. indic.*)	should	—	werden, sollen
shape	shaped	shaped, shapen	formen
shear	sheared	shorn	scheren
shed	shed	shed	vergiessen
shine	shone	shone	scheinen
shoe	shod	shod	beschuhen
shoot	shot	shot	schiessen
show	showed	shown	zeigen
shrink	shrank	shrunk	schrumpfen
shut	shut	shut	schliessen
sing	sang	sung	singen
sink	sank	sunk	sinken
sit	sat	sat	sitzen
slay	slew	slain	erschlagen
sleep	slept	slept	schlafen
slide	slid	slid	gleiten
sling	slung	slung	schleudern
slink	slunk	slunk	schleichen
slit	slit	slit	schlitzen
smell	smelt, smelled	smelt, smelled	riechen

Infin.	Past Indic.	Past Participle	German
smit	smote	smitten	schlagen
sow	sowed	sown, sowed	säen
speak	spoke	spoken	sprechen
speed	sped, speeded	sped, speeded	eilen
spell	spelt, spelled	spelt, spelled	buchstabieren
spend	spent	spent	ausgeben
spill	spilled, spilt	spilled, spilt	verschütten
spin	spun, span	spun	spinnen
spit	spat	spat	speien
split	split	split	spalten
spread	spread	spread	ausbreiten
spring	sprang	sprung	springen
stand	stood	stood	stehen
steal	stole	stolen	stehlen
stick	stuck	stuck	stecken
sting	stung	stung	stechen
stink	stank, stunk	stunk	stinken
strew	strewed	strewed, strewn	streuen
stride	strode	stridden	schreiten
strike	struck	struck, stricken	schlagen
string	strung	strung	(auf)reihen
strive	strove	striven	streben
swear	swore	sworn	schwören
sweep	swept	swept	kehren
swell	swelled	swollen, swelled	schwellen
swim	swam	swum	schwimmen
swing	swung	swung	schwingen
take	took	taken	nehmen

English Irregular Verbs

Infin.	Past Indic.	Past Participle	German
teach	taught	taught	lehren
tear	tore	torn	zerreißen
tell	told	told	erzählen
think	thought	thought	denken
thrive	thrived, throve	thrived, thriven	gedeihen
throw	threw	thrown	werfen
thrust	thrust	thrust	stoßen
tread	trod	trodden	treten
wake	woke, waked	waked, woken woke	wachen
wear	wore	worn	tragen
weave	wove	woven	weben
weep	wept	wept	weinen
will	would	—	wollen
win	won	won	gewinnen
wind	wound	wound	winden
work	worked, wrought	worked, wrought	arbeiten
wring	wrung	wrung	ringen
write	wrote	written	schreiben

Cardinal Numbers

0	nought, zero	null
1	one	eins
2	two	zwei
3	three	drei
4	four	vier
5	five	fünf
6	six	sechs
7	seven	sieben
8	eight	acht
9	nine	neun
10	ten	zehn
11	eleven	elf
12	twelve	zwölf
13	thirteen	dreizehn
14	fourteen	vierzehn
15	fifteen	fünfzehn
16	sixteen	sechzehn
17	seventeen	siebzehn
18	eighteen	achtzehn
19	nineteen	neunzehn
20	twenty	zwanzig
21	twenty-one	einundzwanzig
22	twenty-two	zweiundzwanzig
25	twenty-five	fünfundzwanzig
30	thirty	dreißig
36	thirty-six	sechsunddreißig
40	forty	vierzig
50	fifty	fünfzig
60	sixty	sechzig
70	seventy	siebzig
80	eighty	achtzig
90	ninety	neunzig
100	(one)hundred	hundert
101	(a)hundred and one	hundert(und)eins
102	(a)hundred and two	hundert(und)zwei
200	two hundred	zweihundert
300	three hundred	dreihundert
600	six hundred	sechshundert
625	six hundred and twenty-five	sechshundertfünfundzwanzig
1000	(a)thousand	tausend
1965	nineteen hundred and sixty-five	neunzehnhundertfünfundsechzig
2000	two thousand	zweitausend
1,000,000	a million	eine Million
2,000,000	two million	zwei Millionen

Various suffixes may be added to German numerals, the commonest of which are cited in the following examples:

zehnfach	tenfold
dreisilbig	trisyllabic
vierstimmig	four-part (*i.e.* for four voices)
sechsteilig	in six parts

Ordinal Numbers

1st	first	erste (abbr. 1.)
2nd	second	zweite (abbr. 2.)
3rd	third	dritte (abbr. 3.)
4th	fourth	vierte
5th	fifth	fünfte
6th	sixth	sechste
7th	seventh	siebte
8th	eighth	achte
9th	ninth	neunte
10th	tenth	zehnte
11th	eleventh	elfte
12th	twelfth	zwölfte
13th	thirteenth	dreizehnte
14th	fourteenth	vierzehnte
15th	fifteenth	fünfzehnte
16th	sixteenth	sechzehnte
17th	seventeenth	siebzehnte
18th	eighteenth	achtzehnte
19th	nineteenth	neunzehnte
20th	twentieth	zwanzigste
21st	twenty-first	einundzwanzigste
22nd	twenty-second	zweiundzwanzigste
25th	twenty-fifth	fünfundzwanzigste
30th	thirtieth	dreißigste
40th	fortieth	vierzigste
50th	fiftieth	fünfzigste
60th	sixtieth	sechzigste
70th	seventieth	siebzigste
80th	eightieth	achtzigste
90th	ninetieth	neunzigste
100th	hundredth	hundertste
102nd	hundred and second	hundert(und)zweite
200th	two hundredth	zweihundertste
300th	three hundredth	dreihundertste
625th	six hundred and twenty-fifth	sechshundertfünfundzwanzigste
1000th	thousandth	tausendste
2000th	two thousandth	zweitausendste
1,000,000th	millionth	millionste

Fractions etc.

$\frac{1}{4}$	a quarter	ein Viertel
$\frac{1}{3}$	a third	ein ·Drittel
$\frac{1}{2}$	a half	(ein)halb
$\frac{2}{3}$	two thirds	zwei Drittel
$\frac{3}{4}$	three quarters	drei Viertel
$1\frac{1}{4}$	one and a quarter	ein ein Viertel
$1\frac{1}{2}$	one and a half	anderthalb
$5\frac{1}{2}$	five and a half	fünfeinhalb
$7\frac{2}{5}$	seven and two-fifths	sieben zwei Fünftel
$\frac{15}{20}$	fifteen-twentieths	fünfzehn Zwanzigstel
.7	point seven	0,7 Null Komma sieben

541